THOMSON'S
CERTIFIED ASSOCIATE BUSINESS MANAGER

CABM Examination Preparation Guide

Mastering the Principles of Business Management

Volume 1: Theory

Australia · Canada · Mexico · Singapore · Spain · United Kingdom · United States

Certified Associate Business Manager (CABM) Examination Preparation Guide

Volume 1: Theory

VP/Editorial Director:
Jack Calhoun

VP/Editor-in-Chief:
Dave Shaut

Executive Editor:
Scott Person

Developmental Editor:
Sara Froelicher

Sr. Production Editor:
Deanna Quinn

Marketing Manager:
Mark Linton

Manufacturing Coordinator:
Charlene Taylor

Art Director:
Chris Miller

Sr. Technology Project Editor:
Matt McKinney

Production House and Compositor:
Carlisle Publisher Services

Printer:
West Group
Eagan, MN

COPYRIGHT © 2005
by South-Western, a division of Thomson Learning. Thomson Learning™ is a trademark used herein under license.

Printed in the United States of America
1 2 3 4 5 07 06 05 04

For more information
contact South-Western,
5191 Natorp Boulevard,
Mason, Ohio 45040.
Or you can visit our Internet site at:
http://www.swlearning.com

ALL RIGHTS RESERVED.
No part of this work covered by the copyright hereon may be reproduced or used in any form or by any means–graphic, electronic, or mechanical, including photocopying, recording, taping, Web distribution or information storage and retrieval systems–without the written permission of the publisher.

For permission to use material from this text or product, contact us by
Tel (800) 730-2214
Fax (800) 730-2215
http://www.thomsonrights.com

Library of Congress Control Number: 2004096951

ISBN 0-324-30452-8

Contents

Preface	ix
CABM's Common Body of Knowledge and Exam Content Specifications	xiii

General Management and Organization — Module 100

101	Corporate Strategies	2
103	Forms of Business Organizations	8
105	Management Perspectives	24
110	Functions of Management	31
140	Motivating and Communicating	57
150	Problem Solving and Decision Making	67
160	Business Policy, Culture, and Ethics	81
165	Impact of Government on Business	89
169	Business Law	121
170	Managerial Economics	158
175	Organization Design and Development	217
190	Project Management	268
195	Quantitative Techniques in Business	286
Module 100 Endnotes		310

Operations Management — Module 200

- 201 Operations Strategies — 328
- 205 Manufacturing Operations — 330
- 230 Supply Chain Management — 384
- 265 Services and Retail Operations — 409
- 295 Ethics and Operations — 459
- Module 200 Endnotes — 464

Marketing Management — Module 300

- 301 Marketing Strategies — 470
- 310 New Product Development and Product Management — 477
- 320 Advertising and Promotion — 498
- 330 Pricing Strategies — 510
- 340 Consumer Behavior and Marketing Research — 520
- 355 Marketing Channels and Distribution — 531
- 360 Electronic Commerce and Marketing — 543
- 365 Ethics and Marketing — 547
- 380 Market Segmentation and Target Markets — 553
- 385 Services and Retail Marketing — 556
- 390 Sales Administration and Management — 612
- 395 Ethics and Sales — 624
- Module 300 Endnotes — 626

Quality and Process Management — Module 400

- 401 Quality Strategies — 636
- 405 Product Quality — 638
- 410 Quality Management Practices — 639

440	Quality Control Practices	671
450	Process Management Practices	675
455	Service Quality	681
460	Business Process Analysis	688
495	Ethics and Quality	693
	Module 400 Endnotes	694

Human Resources Management — Module 500

501	Human Resources Strategies	698
510	Employee Performance and Retention Management	712
530	Staffing, Development, and Employment Practices	722
540	Workforce Diversity Management	785
570	Employee Benefits and Compensation	793
595	Ethics and Human Resources	814
	Module 500 Endnotes	815

Accounting — Module 600

601	Accounting Strategies	822
605	The Accounting Process	826
610	Assets, Liabilities, and Owners' Equity	827
620	Analysis and Use of Financial Statements	845
630	Cost Behavior, Control, and Decision Making	861
640	Product and Service Costs	875
650	Operating Budgets and Performance Evaluation	885
660	Decision Making and Accounting	915
680	Control and Accounting	937
685	Ethics and Accounting	940
	Module 600 Endnotes	942

Finance — Module 700

701	Finance Strategies	944
704	Working Capital Policy	949
705	Managing Short-Term Assets	958
710	Managing Short-Term Financing	969
715	Managing Long-Term Financing	981
720	Financial Forecasting, Planning, and Control	1015
725	Cost of Capital, Capital Structure, and Dividend Policy	1041
735	Capital Budgeting	1064
745	Financial Markets, Instruments, and Institutions	1084
755	Financial Risk Management	1095
760	Mergers, Acquisitions, and Business Valuations	1104
795	Ethics and Finance	1114
	Module 700 Appendix: Mathematical Tables	1116
	Module 700 Endnotes	1124

Information Technology — Module 800

801	Information Technology Strategies	1126
805	Information Systems Planning	1132
815	Information Technology Risk Management	1139
825	Decision Making and Information Technology	1144
845	Data and Knowledge Management	1156
850	Systems Development and Acquisition	1179
855	Managing Information Technology Resources	1205
860	Telecommunications and Networks	1216
865	Business Information Systems	1235
870	Information Technology Security and Controls	1237
875	Electronic Commerce and Information Technology	1246

880 Information Technology Contingency Plans — 1257
890 Ethics and Information Technology — 1262
Module 800 Endnotes — 1265

Corporate Control and Governance — Module 900

901 Corporate Control Strategies — 1268
910 Internal Control Framework and Control Models — 1270
930 Corporate Fraud — 1277
940 Corporate Risk Management — 1293
950 Corporate Citizenship, Accountability, and Public Policy — 1311
970 Issues Management and Crisis Management — 1326
980 Corporate Ethics and Management Assurance — 1336
990 Corporate Governance — 1347
Module 900 Endnotes — 1358

International Business — Module 1000

1001 Global Business Strategies — 1366
1010 Forms of International Business and Marketing Strategies — 1371
1020 International Risks — 1383
1030 Global Organization Structure and Control — 1386
1040 International Trade and Investment — 1403
1050 International Payments — 1414
1060 International Cultures and Protocols — 1419
1070 International Economics — 1428
1075 International Banking — 1449
1080 International Law — 1456
1090 Ethics and International Business — 1467
Module 1000 Endnotes — 1472

Glossary	1477
Subject Index	1635

Preface

Mastering the Principles of Business Management

Here is the best source to help streamline your CABM Exam preparation efforts.

The ***Certified Associate Business Manager (CABM) Examination Preparation Guide: Volume 1: Theory*** is one of a two-volume series developed solely to help you prepare for the CABM Exam. Designed with flexibility in mind, each guide can be used either in a self-study or group-study environment. Third-party review course providers such as professional associations, universities, and private organizations can also use this series to conduct review classes for CABM Exam candidates.

Developed by the best minds in the business management field, this series is a compilation of information from subject matter experts who are highly trained and experienced in the business management field. For a complete listing of these experts, see the acknowledgments section.

Based on a pre-MBA curriculum, the CABM helps you master the principles of business management, thereby enabling success on your job or preparing you for an MBA program. As a diagnostic tool, the CABM helps you determine your strengths and weaknesses in business management knowledge.

The CABM Exam consists of one part and requires two volumes to study from: Theory and Practice Guides. Theory Guide (Volume 1) covers the subject matter as defined in the Common Body of Knowledge for Business (CBKB), which is the basis for the CABM Exam. The Practice Guide (Volume 2) contains multiple-choice questions, answers, and explanations in line with the CBKB. The CBKB defines the skill and knowledge level similar to a person with a bachelor's degree from an accredited academic institution. The scope, size, and syllabus of the CABM program correspond to undergraduate studies in business. The CABM Exam contains multiple-choice questions only.

While the CABM and the Certified Business Manager (CBM) designations focus on the same 10 Learning Modules, the differences between the CABM and CBM are as follows:

Item	CABM	CBM
Scope	Pre-MBA curriculum	MBA Curriculum
Content Level	Bachelors/Undergraduate	Masters/Graduate
Focus	Basic Business Principles	Advanced Business Applications
Parts	One part	Three parts
Total Test Time	Four hours	Nine hours
Total Questions	200 multiple-choice	400 multiple-choice
Grading	Numerical Percentage	Pass/No Pass
Passing Score	75 percent	Not Applicable
Major Topics	98	168

The best way to study the Theory Guide is to review the glossary prior to reading the corresponding text. Due to the comprehensive nature of the Theory Guide, the CABM practitioner can also use it as a desk reference resource. The best way to study the Practice Guide is to self-test the questions prior to reading the study questions, answers, and explanations. When reading the Theory and Practice Guides together, read the Theory Guide first followed by the Practice Guide.

The CABM Exam focuses on 10 learning modules, which include general management and organization, operations management, marketing management, quality and process management, human resources management, accounting, finance, information technology, corporate control and governance, and international business.

Passing the CABM Exam improves analytical and technical skills, enhances the cross-functional knowledge of business, and sharpens the problem-solving and decision-making skills of a business manager (hard skills). These hard skills should be supplemented with soft skills such as verbal and nonverbal communications, listening, negotiating, and interpersonal skills.

The CABM program is sponsored and administered by the Association of Professionals in Business Management (APBM) who can be reached at the following address.

Association of Professionals in Business Management

8033 Sunset Boulevard, Suite 826, Los Angeles, California, 90046 USA

Phone: 310-657-4899 Fax: 310-657-8996

e-mail: *Info@apbm.org* Web site: www.apbm.org

Questions related to application materials, eligibility requirements, contents in the exam prep guides, examination sites and dates, fees, and other administrative matters should be directed to *info@apbm.org* or visit *www.apbm.org*.

To purchase this series, or individual guides, contact either Thomson Business and Professional Publishing, a division of Thomson, *http://certification.swlearning.com*, *www.apbm.org*. Volume purchases can be made through Thomson Business and Professional Publishing for university, corporate, government, and professional association purchases by contacting *http://certification.swlearning.com* or 1-800-842-3636.

Acknowledgments

A special thanks to the following Thomson Business and Professional Publishing authors for allowing the use of their information in developing comprehensive and high-quality study guides to prepare for the CABM Exam.

General Management and Organization, Module 100

Management by Daft, 6th edition, © 2003, ISBN 0-030-35138-3.
Essentials of Organization Theory and Design by Daft, 2nd edition, © 2001, ISBN 0-324-02097-X.
Successful Project Management by Gido/Clements, 2nd edition, © 2003, ISBN 0-324-07168-X.
Essentials of Business Law and the Legal Environment by Mann/Roberts, 7th edition, © 2001, ISBN 0-324-04052-0.
Quantitative Methods for Business by Anderson/Sweeney/Williams, 8th edition, © 2001, ISBN 0-324-04499-2.
Fundamentals of Managerial Economics by Hirschey, 7th edition, © 2002, ISBN 0-324-18331-3.

Operations Management, Module 200

Production and Inventory Management by Fogarty/Blackstone/Hoffmann, 2nd edition, © 1991, ISBN 0-538-07461-2.
Successful Service Operations Management by Metters et al., © 2003, ISBN 0-324-13556-4.
Purchasing and Supply Chain Management by Monczka et al., 2nd edition, © 2002, ISBN 0-324-02315-4.
Retailing by Dunne and Lusch, 5th edition, © 2005, ISBN 0-324-20139-7.
231 terms in Glossary from *APICS Dictionary*, 10th Edition, © 2002 by APICS—The Educational Society for Resource Management, Alexandria, Virginia, USA. Reprinted with permission.

Marketing Management, Module 300

Marketing: Best Practices by Hoffman et al., 2nd edition, © 2003, ISBN 0-030-34999-0.
Retailing by Dunne and Lusch, 5th edition, © 2005, ISBN 0-324-20139-7.

Quality and Process Management, Module 400

Management and the Control of Quality by Evans/Lindsay, 5th edition, © 2002, ISBN 0-324-06680-5.
Successful Service Operations Management by Metters et al., © 2003, ISBN 0-324-13556-4.
Glossary from the *Certified Quality Manager Handbook* by Duke Okes and Russell T. Westcott (eds.), 2nd Edition. © 2001 by ASQ Quality Press, Milwaukee, Wisconsin, USA. Reprinted with permission.

Human Resources Management, Module 500

Human Resources Management by Mathis/Jackson, 10th edition, © 2003 ISBN 0-324-07151-5.

Accounting, Module 600

Financial and Managerial Accounting by Warren/Reeve/Fess, 7th edition, © 2002, ISBN 0-324-02540-8.
International Accounting by Iqbal, 2nd edition, © 2002, ISBN 0-324-02350-2.

Finance, Module 700

Essentials of Managerial Finance by Besley/Brigham, 12th edition, © 2000, ISBN 0-030-25872-3.
Short-Term Financial Management by Maness/Zietlow, 2nd edition, © 2002, ISBN 0-030-31513-1.

Information Technology, Module 800

Management Information Systems by Oz, 3rd edition, © 2002, ISBN 0-619-06250-9.
Fundamentals of Information Systems by Ralph M. Stair and George W. Reynolds, © 2001, ISBN 0-619-03416-5.

Corporate Control and Governance, Module 900

Fraud Examination by Albrecht, 1st edition, © 2003, ISBN 0-324-16296-0.
Business and Society by Carroll/Buchholtz, 5th edition, © 2003, ISBN 0-324-11495-8.
Risk Management and Insurance by Trieschmann, 11th edition, © 2001, ISBN 0-324-01663-8.

International Business, Module 1000

International Economics by Carbaugh, 8th edition, © 2002, ISBN 0-324-05589-7.
International Business by Czinkota, 6th edition, © 2003, ISBN 0-324-17660-0.
Essentials of Business Law and the Legal Environment by Mann/Roberts, 7th edition, © 2001, ISBN 0-324-04052-0.
International Management by Rodrigues, 2nd edition, © 2001, ISBN 0-324-04150-0.
International Business Law and Its Environment by Schaffer/Earle/Agusti, 5th edition, © 2002, ISBN 0-324-06098-X.

Additional Books

The Management of Business Logistics by Coyle/Bardi/Langley, 6th edition, © 1996, ISBN 0-314-06507-5.
Operations Management by Gaither/Frazier, 9th edition, © 2002, ISBN 0-324-06685-6 (test bank only).
Corporate Finance: A Focused Approach by Ehrhardt/Brigham, © 2003, ISBN 0-324-18035-7.
Marketing Strategy by Ferrell et al., 2nd edition, © 2002, ISBN 0-030-32103-4.
Managerial Accounting by Jackson and Sawyers, © 2001, ISBN 0-030-21092-5.

About Thomson Business and Professional Publishing
(A part of The Thomson Corporation)

Thomson Business and Professional Publishing, a part of The Thomson Corporation, is the leading educational provider of business and economics materials worldwide. Thomson Business and Professional Publishing offers the most extensive selection of business education products and services on the market today for higher education, secondary education, as well as corporate and retail business environments. Integrating the latest technologies with many of its products, Thomson Business and Professional Publishing also delivers interactive learning solutions that engage learners, enhance retention, and provide results.

The Professional Portfolio

Thomson Business and Professional Publishing is pleased to add the CABM Examination Preparation Guide to its Professional Portfolio. This rapidly expanding, topic-specific collection includes corporate strategy, business and technology, finance, global business, marketing, and other significant business titles.

CABM's Common Body of Knowledge and Exam Content Specifications

The Certified Associate Business Manager (CABM) exam content specifications are based on the Common Body of Knowledge for Business (CBKB). The contents include ten Learning Modules divided into **98** sub-modules or major topics. The ten modules include the following: General Management and Organization, Operations Management, Marketing Management, Quality and Process Management, Human Resources Management, Accounting, Finance, Information Technology, Corporate Control and Governance, and International Business. Each module is given a relative weight in terms of its importance in the exam, and the number of questions in the exam will approximately correspond to that weight. The CBKB is the syllabus and curriculum for the CABM exam, basis for developing the CABM Exam Preparation Guides, and the source of input for developing the CABM Exam questions.

Common Body of Knowledge for Business

Module 100 — General Management and Organization (15%)

101	Corporate Strategies
103	Forms of Business Organizations
105	Management Perspectives
110	Functions of Management
140	Motivating and Communicating
150	Problem Solving and Decision Making
160	Business Policy, Culture, and Ethics
165	Impact of Government on Business
169	Business Law
170	Managerial Economics
175	Organization Design and Development
190	Project Management
195	Quantitative Techniques in Business

Module 200 — Operations Management (10%)

201	Operations Strategies
205	Manufacturing Operations
230	Supply Chain Management
265	Services and Retail Operations
295	Ethics and Operations

Module 300 Marketing Management (10%)

- 301 Marketing Strategies
- 310 New Product Development and Product Management
- 320 Advertising and Promotion
- 330 Pricing Strategies
- 340 Consumer Behavior and Marketing Research
- 355 Marketing Channels and Distribution
- 360 Electronic Commerce and Marketing
- 365 Ethics and Marketing
- 380 Market Segmentation and Target Markets
- 385 Services and Retail Marketing
- 390 Sales Administration and Management
- 395 Ethics and Sales

Module 400 Quality and Process Management (10%)

- 401 Quality Strategies
- 405 Product Quality
- 410 Quality Management Practices
- 440 Quality Control Practices
- 450 Process Management Practices
- 455 Service Quality
- 460 Business Process Analysis
- 495 Ethics and Quality

Module 500 Human Resources Management (10%)

- 501 Human Resources Strategies
- 510 Employee Performance and Retention Management
- 530 Staffing, Development, and Employment Practices
- 540 Workforce Diversity Management
- 570 Employee Benefits and Compensation
- 595 Ethics and Human Resources

Module 600 Accounting (10%)

- 601 Accounting Strategies
- 605 The Accounting Process
- 610 Assets, Liabilities, and Owners' Equity
- 620 Analysis and Use of Financial Statements
- 630 Cost Behavior, Control, and Decision Making
- 640 Product and Service Costs
- 650 Operating Budgets and Performance Evaluation
- 660 Decision Making and Accounting
- 680 Control and Accounting
- 685 Ethics and Accounting

Module 700 Finance (10%)

- 701 Finance Strategies
- 704 Working Capital Policy

	705	Managing Short-Term Assets
	710	Managing Short-Term Financing
	715	Managing Long-Term Financing
	720	Financial Forecasting, Planning, and Control
	725	Cost of Capital, Capital Structure, and Dividend Policy
	735	Capital Budgeting
	745	Financial Markets, Instruments, and Institutions
	755	Financial Risk Management
	760	Mergers, Acquisitions, and Business Valuations
	795	Ethics and Finance

Module 800 — Information Technology (10%)

801	Information Technology Strategies
805	Information Systems Planning
815	Information Technology Risk Management
825	Decision Making and Information Technology
845	Data and Knowledge Management
850	Systems Development and Acquisition
855	Managing Information Technology Resources
860	Telecommunications and Networks
865	Business Information Systems
870	Information Technology Security and Controls
875	Electronic Commerce and Information Technology
880	Information Technology Contingency Plans
890	Ethics and Information Technology

Module 900 — Corporate Control and Governance (10%)

901	Corporate Control Strategies
910	Internal Control Framework and Control Models
930	Corporate Fraud
940	Corporate Risk Management
950	Corporate Citizenship, Accountability, and Public Policy
970	Issues Management and Crisis Management
980	Corporate Ethics and Management Assurance
990	Corporate Governance

Module 1000 — International Business (5%)

1001	Global Business Strategies
1010	Forms of International Business and Marketing Strategies
1020	International Risks
1030	Global Organization Structure and Control
1040	International Trade and Investment
1050	International Payments
1060	International Cultures and Protocols
1070	International Economics
1075	International Banking
1080	International Law
1090	Ethics and International Business

MODULE 100

General Management and Organization

101 Corporate Strategies, 2

103 Forms of Business Organizations, 8

105 Management Perspectives, 24

110 Functions of Management, 31

140 Motivating and Communicating, 57

150 Problem Solving and Decision Making, 67

160 Business Policy, Culture, and Ethics, 81

165 Impact of Government on Business, 89

169 Business Law, 121

170 Managerial Economics, 158

175 Organization Design and Development, 217

190 Project Management, 268

195 Quantitative Techniques in Business, 286

Module 100 Endnotes, 310

Corporate Strategies

An **organizational goal** is a desired state of affairs that the organization attempts to reach.[1] A goal represents a result or end point toward which organizational efforts are directed. The choice of goals and strategy affects organization design.

Top managers give direction to organizations. They set goals and develop the strategies for their organization to attain those goals. The purpose of this section is to help you understand the types of goals organizations pursue and some of the competitive strategies managers develop to reach those goals. We will examine two significant frameworks for determining strategic action and look at how strategies affect organization design. The section also describes the most popular approaches to measuring the effectiveness of organizational efforts. To manage organizations well, managers need a clear sense of how to measure effectiveness.

Organizational Purpose

Organizations are created and continued in order to accomplish something. This purpose may be referred to as the overall goal, or mission. Different parts of the organization establish their own goals and objectives to help meet the overall goal, mission, or purpose of the organization.

Many types of goals exist in an organization, and each type performs a different function. One major distinction is between the officially stated goals, or mission, of the organization and the operative goals the organization actually pursues.

Mission

The overall goal for an organization is often called the **mission**—the organization's reason for existence. The mission describes the organization's vision, its shared values and beliefs, and its reason for being. It can have a powerful impact on an organization.[2] The mission is sometimes called the **official goals,** which are the formally stated definition of business scope and outcomes the organization is trying to achieve. Official goal statements typically define business operations and may focus on values, markets, and customers that distinguish the organization. Whether called a mission statement or official goals, the organization's general statement of its purpose and philosophy is often written down in a policy manual or the annual report.

Operative Goals

Operative goals designate the ends sought through the actual operating procedures of the organization and explain what the organization is actually trying to do.[3] Operative goals describe specific measurable outcomes and are often concerned with the short run. Operative versus official goals represent actual versus stated goals. Operative goals typically pertain to the primary tasks an organization must perform, similar to the subsystem activities.[4] These goals concern overall performance, boundary spanning, maintenance, adaptation, and production activities. Specific goals for each primary task provide direction for the day-to-day decisions and activities within departments.

OVERALL PERFORMANCE Profitability reflects the overall performance of for-profit organizations. Profitability may be expressed in terms of net income, earnings per share, or return on investment. Other overall goals are growth and output volume. Growth pertains to increases in sales or profits over time. Volume pertains to total sales or the amount of products or services delivered. Executives at Procter & Gamble have set a growth goal to double consumer-products sales to $70 billion by 2006.[5]

Not-for-profit organizations such as labor unions do not have goals of profitability, but they do have goals that attempt to specify the delivery of services to members within specified budget expense levels. Growth and volume goals also may be indicators of overall performance in not-for-profit organizations.

RESOURCES Resource goals pertain to the acquisition of needed material and financial resources from the environment. They may involve obtaining financing for the construction of new plants, finding less expensive sources for raw materials, or hiring top-quality college graduates. Many high-tech companies are having trouble hiring well-educated, computer-literate knowledge workers because of today's tight labor market. Companies such as **Sun Microsystems** are investing heavily in online recruiting programs to help them meet their resource goals in this area.

MARKET Market goals relate to the market share or market standing desired by the organization. Market goals are the responsibility of marketing, sales, and advertising departments.

EMPLOYEE DEVELOPMENT Employee development pertains to the training, promotion, safety, and growth of employees. It includes both managers and workers.

INNOVATION AND CHANGE Innovation goals pertain to internal flexibility and readiness to adapt to unexpected changes in the environment. Innovation goals are often defined with respect to the development of specific new services, products, or production processes.

PRODUCTIVITY Productivity goals concern the amount of output achieved from available resources. They typically describe the amount of resource inputs required to reach desired outputs and are thus stated in terms of "cost for a unit of production," "units produced per employee," or "resource cost per employee."

Successful organizations use a carefully balanced set of operative goals. For example, although profitability is important, some of today's best companies recognize that a single-minded focus on bottom-line profits may not be the best way to achieve high performance. In a rapidly changing environment, innovation and change goals are increasingly important, even though they may initially cause a *decrease* in profits. Employee development goals are critical for helping to maintain a motivated, committed workforce in a tight labor market.

Organizational Strategies and Design

A **strategy** is a plan for interacting with the competitive environment to achieve organizational goals. Some managers think of goals and strategies as interchangeable, but for our purposes, goals define where the organization wants to go and strategies define how it will get there. For example, a goal may be to achieve 15 percent annual sales growth; strategies to reach that goal might include aggressive advertising to attract new customers, motivating salespeople to increase the average size of customer purchases, and acquiring other businesses that produce similar products. Strategies can include any number of techniques to achieve the goal. The essence of formulating strategies is choosing whether the organization will perform different activities than its competitors or will execute similar activities more efficiently than its competitors do.[6]

One model for formulating strategies is the Porter model of competitive strategies, which provides a framework for competitive action. After describing the model, we will discuss how the choice of strategies affects organization design.

Porter's Competitive Strategies

Michael E. Porter studied a number of businesses and introduced a framework describing three competitive strategies: low-cost leadership, differentiation, and focus.[7] The focus strategy, in which the organization concentrates on a specific market or buyer group, is further divided into *focused low cost* and *focused differentiation*. This yields four basic strategies, and to use this model, managers evaluate two factors: competitive advantage and competitive scope. With respect to advantage, managers determine whether to compete through lower cost or through the ability to offer unique or distinctive products and services that can command a premium price. Managers then determine whether the organization will compete on a broad scope (competing in many customer segments) or a narrow scope (competing in a selected customer segment or group of segments). These choices determine the selection of strategies.

DIFFERENTIATION In a **differentiation** strategy, organizations attempt to distinguish their products or services from others in the industry. An organization may use advertising, distinctive product features, exceptional service, or new technology to achieve a product perceived as unique. This strategy usually targets customers who are not particularly concerned with price, so it can be quite profitable. Maytag appliances, Tommy Hilfiger clothing, and Starbucks coffee are examples of products from companies using a differentiation strategy.

A differentiation strategy can reduce rivalry with competitors and fight off the threat of substitute products because customers are loyal to the company's brand. However, companies must remember that successful differentiation strategies require a number of costly activities, such as product research and design and extensive advertising. Companies that pursue a differentiation strategy need strong marketing abilities and creative employees who are given the time and resources to seek innovations.

LOW-COST LEADERSHIP The **low-cost leadership** strategy tries to increase market share by emphasizing low cost compared to competitors. With a low-cost leadership strategy, the organization aggressively seeks efficient facilities, pursues cost reductions, and uses tight controls to produce products more efficiently than its competitors.

This strategy is concerned primarily with stability rather than taking risks or seeking new opportunities for innovation and growth. A low-cost position means the company can undercut competitors' prices and still offer comparable quality and earn a reasonable profit.

A low-cost strategy can help a company defend against current competitors because customers cannot find lower prices elsewhere. In addition, if substitute products or potential new competitors enter the picture, the low-cost producer is in a better position to prevent loss of market share.

FOCUS With Porter's third strategy, the **focus strategy,** the organization concentrates on a specific regional market or buyer group. The company will try to achieve either a low-cost advantage or a differentiation advantage within a narrowly defined market.

How Strategies Affect Organization Design

Choice of strategy affects internal organization characteristics. Organization design characteristics need to support the firm's competitive approach. For example, a company wanting to grow and invent new products looks and "feels" different from a company that is focused on maintaining market share for long-established products in a stable industry.

With a low-cost leadership strategy, managers take an efficiency approach to organization design, whereas a differentiation strategy calls for a flexible learning approach. A low-cost leadership strategy (efficiency) is associated with strong, centralized authority and tight control, standard operating procedures, and emphasis on efficient procurement and distribution systems. Employees generally perform routine tasks under close supervision and control and are not empowered to make decisions or take action on their own. A differentiation strategy, on the other hand, requires that employees be constantly experimenting and learning. Structure is fluid and flexible, with strong horizontal coordination. Empowered employees work directly with customers and are rewarded for creativity and risk-taking. The organization values research, creativity, and innovativeness over efficiency and standard procedures.

Other Factors Affecting Organization Design

Strategy is one important factor that affects organization design. Ultimately, however, organization design is a result of numerous contingencies. The emphasis given to efficiency and control versus learning and flexibility is determined by the contingencies of strategy, environment, size and life cycle, technology, and organizational culture. The organization is designed to "fit" the contingency factors.

For example, in a stable environment, the organization can have a traditional structure that emphasizes vertical control, efficiency, specialization, standard procedures, and centralized decision making. However, a rapidly changing environment may call for a more flexible structure, with strong horizontal coordination and collaboration through teams or other mechanisms. In terms of size and life cycle, young, small organizations are generally informal and have little division of labor, few rules and regulations, and ad hoc budgeting and performance systems. Large organizations such as **IBM** or **Sears,** on the other hand, have an extensive division of labor, numerous rules and regulations, and standard procedures and systems for budgeting, control, rewards, and innovation.

Design must also fit the workflow technology of the organization. For example, with mass-production technology, such as a traditional automobile assembly line, the organization functions best by emphasizing efficiency, formalization, specialization, centralized decision making, and tight control. An e-business, on the other hand, may need to be very informal and flexible. A final contingency that affects organizational design is corporate culture. An organizational culture that values teamwork, collaboration, creativity, and open communication among all employees and managers, for example, would not function well with a tight, vertical structure and strict rules and regulations.

One responsibility of managers is to design organizations that fit the contingency factors of strategy, environment, size and life cycle, technology, and culture. Finding the right "fit" leads to organizational effectiveness, whereas a poor fit can lead to decline or even the demise of the organization.

Organizational Effectiveness

Understanding organizational goals and strategies, as well as the concept of fitting design to various contingencies, is a first step toward understanding organizational effectiveness. Organizational goals represent the reason for an organization's existence and the outcomes it seeks to achieve. The next few sections explore the topic of effectiveness and how effectiveness is measured in organizations.

Goals were defined earlier as the desired future state of the organization. Organizational **effectiveness** is the degree to which an organization realizes its goals.[8] Effectiveness is a broad concept. It implicitly takes into consideration a range of variables at both the organizational and departmental levels. Effectiveness evaluates the extent to which multiple goals—whether official or operative—are attained.

Efficiency is a more limited concept that pertains to the internal workings of the organization. Organizational efficiency is the amount of resources used to produce a unit of output.[9] It can be measured as the ratio of inputs to outputs. If one organization can achieve a given production level with fewer resources than another organization it would be described as more efficient.[10]

Sometimes efficiency leads to effectiveness. In other organizations, efficiency and effectiveness are not related. An organization may be highly efficient but fail to achieve its goals because it makes a product for which there is no demand. Likewise, an organization may achieve its profit goals but be inefficient.

Overall effectiveness is difficult to measure in organizations. Organizations are large, diverse, and fragmented. They perform many activities simultaneously. They pursue multiple goals. And they generate many outcomes, some intended and some unintended.[11] Managers determine what indicators to measure in order to gauge the effectiveness of their organizations. One study found that many managers have a difficult time with the concept of evaluating effectiveness based on characteristics that are not subject to hard, quantitative measurement.[12] However, top executives at some of today's leading companies are finding new ways to measure effectiveness, using indicators such as "customer delight" and employee satisfaction. A number of approaches to measuring effectiveness look at which measurements managers choose to track. These *contingency effectiveness approaches* are based on looking at which part of the organization managers consider most important to measure.

Contingency Effectiveness Approaches

Contingency approaches to measuring effectiveness focus on different parts of the organization. Traditional approaches include the goal approach, the resource-based approach, and the internal process approach. Organizations bring resources in from the environment, and those resources are transformed into outputs delivered back into the environment, as shown in Exhibit 100.1. The **goal approach** to organizational effectiveness is concerned with the output side and whether the organization achieves its goals in terms of desired levels of output.[13] The **resource-based approach** assesses effectiveness by observing the beginning of the process and evaluating whether the organization effectively obtains resources necessary for high performance. The **internal process approach** looks at internal activities and assesses effectiveness by indicators of internal health and efficiency.

These traditional approaches all have something to offer, but each one tells only part of the story. A more recent **stakeholder approach** (also called the constituency approach) acknowledges that each organization has many constituencies that have a stake in its outcomes. The stakeholder approach focuses on the satisfaction of stakeholders as an indicator of the organization's performance.[14]

Exhibit 100.1 *Contingency Approaches to the Measurement of Organizational Effectiveness*

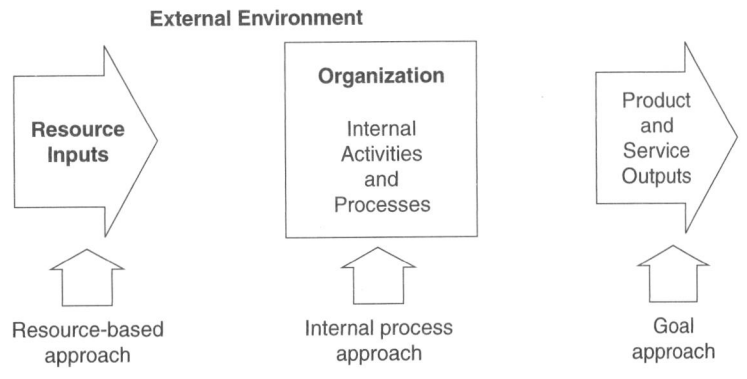

Goal Approach

The goal approach to effectiveness consists of identifying an organization's output goals and assessing how well the organization has attained those goals.[15] This is a logical approach because organizations do try to attain certain levels of output, profit, or client satisfaction. The goal approach measures progress toward attainment of those goals. For example, an important measure for the Women's National Basketball Association (WNBA) is number of tickets sold per game. During the league's first season, President Val Ackerman set a goal of 4,000 to 5,000 tickets per game. The organization actually averaged nearly 9,700 tickets per game, indicating that the WNBA was highly effective in meeting its goal for attendance.[16]

INDICATORS The important goals to consider are operative goals. Efforts to measure effectiveness have been more productive using operative goals than using official goals.[17] Official goals tend to be abstract and difficult to measure. Operative goals reflect activities the organization is actually performing.

One example of multiple goals is from a survey of U.S. business corporations.[18] Twelve goals were listed as being important to these companies. These 12 goals represent outcomes that cannot be achieved simultaneously. They illustrate the array of outcomes organizations attempt to achieve.

USEFULNESS The goal approach is used in business organizations because output goals can be readily measured. Business firms typically evaluate performance in terms of profitability, growth, market share, and return on investment. However, identifying operative goals and measuring performance of an organization are not always easy. Two problems that must be resolved are the issues of multiple goals and subjective indicators of goal attainment.

Because organizations have multiple and conflicting goals, effectiveness often cannot be assessed by a single indicator. High achievement on one goal may mean low achievement on another. Moreover, there are department goals as well as overall performance goals. The full assessment of effectiveness should take into consideration several goals simultaneously.

The other issue to resolve with the goal approach is how to identify operative goals for an organization and how to measure goal attainment. For business organizations, there are often objective indicators for certain goals, such as profit or growth. However, subjective assessment is needed for other goals, such as employee welfare or social responsibility. Someone has to go into the organization and learn what the actual goals are by talking with the top management team. Once goals are identified, subjective perceptions of goal attainment have to be used when quantitative indicators are not available. Managers rely on information from customers, competitors, suppliers, and employees, as well as their own intuition, when considering these goals. Jerre Stead, Chairman and CEO of **Ingram Micro Inc.,** the world's largest distributor of computer-technology products and services, communicates directly with hundreds of customers each week to measure the company's goal of achieving "customer delight." "These direct interactions don't provide hard numbers," he says, "but I sure do learn a lot."[19]

Although the goal approach seems to be the most logical way to assess organizational effectiveness, managers and evaluators should keep in mind that the actual measure of effectiveness is a complex process.

Resource-Based Approach

The resource-based approach looks at the input side of the transformation process. It assumes organizations must be successful in obtaining and managing valued resources in order to be effective. From a resource-based perspective, organizational effectiveness is defined as the ability of the organization, in either absolute or relative terms, to obtain scarce and valued resources and successfully integrate and manage them.[20]

INDICATORS Obtaining and successfully managing resources is the criterion by which organizational effectiveness is assessed. In a broad sense, indicators of effectiveness according to the resource-based approach encompass the following dimensions:

- Bargaining position—the ability of the organization to obtain from its environment scarce and valued resources, including financial resources, raw materials, human resources, knowledge, and technology.
- The abilities of the organization's decision makers to perceive and correctly interpret the real properties of the external environment.
- The abilities of managers to use tangible (e.g., supplies, people) and intangible (e.g., knowledge, corporate culture) resources in day-to-day organizational activities to achieve superior performance.
- The ability of the organization to respond to changes in the environment.

USEFULNESS The resource-based approach is valuable when other indicators of performance are difficult to obtain. In many not-for-profit and social welfare organizations, for example, it is hard to measure output goals or internal efficiency. Some for-profit organizations also use a resource-based approach. For example, **Mathsoft, Inc.,** which provides a broad range of technical-calculation and analytical software for business and academia, evaluates its effectiveness partly by looking at how many top-rate Ph.D.s it can recruit. CEO Charles Digate believes Mathsoft has a higher ratio of Ph.D.s to total employees than any other software company, which directly affects product quality and the company's image.[21]

Although the resource-based approach is valuable when other measures of effectiveness are not available, it does have shortcomings. For one thing, the approach only vaguely considers the organization's link to the needs of customers in the external environment. A superior ability to acquire and use resources is important only if resources and capabilities are used to achieve something that meets a need in the environment. The resource-based approach is most valuable when measures of goal attainment cannot be readily obtained.

Internal Process Approach

In the internal process approach, effectiveness is measured as internal organizational health and efficiency. An effective organization has a smooth, well-oiled internal process. Employees are happy and satisfied. Departmental activities mesh with one another to ensure high productivity. This approach does not consider the external environment. The important element in effectiveness is what the organization does with the resources it has, as reflected in internal health and efficiency.

INDICATORS One indicator of internal process effectiveness is the organization's economic efficiency. However, the best-known proponents of a process model are from the human relations approach to organizations. Such writers as Chris Argyris, Warren G. Bennis, Rensis Likert, and Richard Beckhard have all worked extensively with human resources in organizations and emphasize the connection between human resources and effectiveness.[22] Writers on corporate culture and organizational excellence have stressed the importance of internal processes. Results from a study of nearly two hundred secondary schools showed that both human resources and employee-oriented processes were important in explaining and promoting effectiveness in those organizations.[23]

These are indicators of an effective organization as seen from an internal process approach:

- Strong corporate culture and positive work climate
- Team spirit, group loyalty, and teamwork
- Confidence, trust, and communication between workers and management
- Decision making near sources of information, regardless of where those sources are on the organizational chart
- Undistorted horizontal and vertical communication; sharing of relevant facts and feelings
- Rewards to managers for performance, growth, and development of subordinates and for creating an effective working group
- Interaction between the organization and its parts, with conflict that occurs over projects resolved in the interest of the organization.[24]

USEFULNESS The internal process approach is important because the efficient use of resources and harmonious internal functioning are ways to measure effectiveness. Today, most managers believe that happy, committed, actively involved employees and a positive corporate culture are important measures of effectiveness.

The internal process approach also has shortcomings. Total output and the organization's relationship with the external environment are not evaluated. Also, evaluations of internal health and functioning are often subjective, because many aspects of inputs and internal processes are not quantifiable. Managers should be aware that this approach alone represents a limited view of organizational effectiveness.

Stakeholder Approach

The stakeholder approach integrates diverse organizational activities by focusing on organizational stakeholders. A **stakeholder** is any group within or outside an organization that has a stake in the organization's performance. Creditors, suppliers, employees, and owners are all stakeholders. Each stakeholder will have a different criterion of effectiveness because it has a different interest in the organization. Each stakeholder group has to be surveyed to learn whether the organization performs well from its viewpoint.

INDICATORS   The initial work on evaluating effectiveness on the basis of stakeholders included 97 small businesses in Texas. Seven stakeholder groups relevant to those businesses were surveyed to determine the perception of effectiveness from each viewpoint.[25] The following table shows each stakeholder and its criterion of effectiveness.

Stakeholder	Effectiveness Criteria
1. Owners	Financial return
2. Employees	Worker satisfaction, pay, supervision
3. Customers	Quality of goods and services
4. Creditors	Creditworthiness
5. Community	Contribution to community affairs
6. Suppliers	Satisfactory transactions
7. Government	Obedience to laws, regulations

The survey of stakeholders showed that a small business found it difficult to simultaneously fulfill the demands of all groups. One business may have high employee satisfaction, but the satisfaction of other groups may be lower. Nevertheless, measuring all seven stakeholders provides a more accurate view of effectiveness than any single measure. Evaluating how organizations perform across each group offers an overall assessment of effectiveness.

USEFULNESS   The strength of the stakeholder approach is that it takes a broad view of effectiveness and examines factors in the environment as well as within the organization. The stakeholder approach includes the community's notion of social responsibility, which is not formally measured in the goal, resource-based, and internal process approaches. The stakeholder approach also handles several criteria simultaneously—inputs, internal processing, outputs—and acknowledges that there is no single measure of effectiveness. The well-being of employees is just as important as attaining the owner's financial goals.

The stakeholder approach is gaining in popularity, based on the view that effectiveness is a complex, multidimensional concept that has no single measure.[26] Recent research has shown that the assessment of multiple stakeholder groups is an accurate reflection of effectiveness, especially with respect to organizational adaptability.[27] Moreover, research shows that firms really do care about their reputational status and do attempt to shape stakeholders' assessments of their performance.[28] If an organization performs poorly according to several interest groups, it is probably not meeting its effectiveness goals.

Forms of Business Organizations

There are three main forms of business organizations: (1) sole proprietorships, (2) partnerships, and (3) corporations. In terms of numbers, about 75 percent of businesses are operated as proprietorships, nearly 7 percent are partnerships, and the remaining 18 percent are corporations. Based on dollar value of sales, however, almost 90 percent of all business is conducted by corporations, while the remaining 10 percent is generated by both proprietorships and partnerships. Because most business is conducted by corporations, we will concentrate on them in this section. However, it is important to understand the differences among the three forms of business organizations.

Sole Proprietorship

Sole proprietorship   An unincorporated business consisting of one person who owns and completely controls the business.

A **sole proprietorship** is an unincorporated business consisting of one person who owns and completely controls the business. It is formed without any formality, and no documents need be filed. A sole proprietorship is not a separate taxable entity and only the sole proprietor is taxed. Sole proprietors have unlimited liability for the sole proprietorship's debts. The sole proprietor's interest in the business is freely transferable. The death of a sole proprietor dissolves the sole proprietorship.

MODULE 100. GENERAL MANAGEMENT AND ORGANIZATION

A proprietorship is an unincorporated business owned by one individual. Starting a proprietorship is fairly easy—just begin business operations. However, in most cases, even the smallest business must be licensed by the municipality (city, county, or state) in which it operates.

The proprietorship has three important *advantages*.

1. It is easily and inexpensively formed.
2. It is subject to few government regulations.
3. It is taxed like an individual, not a corporation.

The proprietorship also has four important *limitations*.

1. The proprietor has *unlimited personal liability* for business debts, which can result in losses that exceed the money he or she has invested in the company.
2. The life of a business organized as a proprietorship is limited to the life of the individual who created it.
3. Transferring ownership is somewhat difficult—disposing of the business is similar to selling a house in that the proprietor has to seek out and negotiate with a potential buyer.
4. It is difficult for a proprietorship to obtain large sums of capital, because the firm's financial strength generally is based on the financial strength of the sole owner.

For these reasons, individual proprietorships are confined primarily to small business operations. In fact, only about 1% of all proprietorships have assets that are valued at $1 million or greater, while nearly 90 percent have assets valued at $100,000 or less. However, businesses frequently are started as proprietorships and then converted to corporations when their growth causes the disadvantages of being a proprietorship to outweigh the advantages.

General Partnership

A **general partnership** is an unincorporated business association consisting of two or more persons who co-own a business for profit. It is formed without any formality and no documents need be filed. A partnership may elect not to be a separate taxable entity, in which case only the partners are taxed. Partners have unlimited liability for the partnership's debts. Each partner has an equal right to control of the partnership. Partners may assign their financial interest in the partnership, but the assignee may become a member of the partnership only if all of the members consent. The death, bankruptcy, or withdrawal of a partner dissolves a partnership.

General partnership An unincorporated business association of two or more persons to carry on as co-owners of a business for profit.

A partnership is like a proprietorship, except there are two or more owners. Partnerships can operate under different degrees of formality, ranging from informal, oral understandings to formal agreements filed with the secretary of the state in which the partnership does business. Most legal experts would recommend the partnership agreement be put in writing.

The *advantages* of a partnership are the same as for a proprietorship.

1. Formation is easy and relatively inexpensive.
2. It is subject to few government regulations.
3. It is taxed like an individual, not a corporation.

The *disadvantages* are also similar to those associated with proprietorships.

1. Unlimited liability
2. Limited life of the organization
3. Difficulty of transferring ownership
4. Difficulty of raising large amounts of capital

Regarding liability, the partners can potentially lose all of their personal assets, even those assets not invested in the business, because under partnership law each partner is liable for the business's debts. Therefore, if any partner is unable to meet his or her pro rata claim in the event the partnership goes bankrupt, the remaining partners must make good on the unsatisfied claims, drawing on their personal assets if necessary. Thus, the business-related activities of any of the firm's partners can bring ruin to the other partners, even though those partners were not a direct party to such activities. For example, the partners of the national accounting firm **Laventhol and Horwath**, a huge partnership that went bankrupt at the end of 1992 as a result of suits filed by investors who relied on faulty audit statements, learned all about the perils of doing business as a partnership—they discovered that a Texas partner who audits a savings and loan that goes under can bring ruin to a millionaire New York partner who never went near the S&L.

However, it is possible to limit the liabilities of some of the partners by establishing a *limited partnership,* wherein one (or more) partner is designated the *general partner* and the others *limited partners.* Limited partnerships are quite common in the area of real estate investment, but they do not work well with most types of businesses, including accounting firms, because one partner rarely is willing to assume all of the business's risk. Not long ago, the national accounting firms reorganized themselves as limited liability partnerships, which are partnerships in which only the assets of the partnership and the "engagement" partner (partner in charge of the situation) are at risk.

The first three disadvantages—unlimited liability, impermanence of the organization, and difficulty of transferring ownership—lead to the fourth, the difficulty partnerships have in attracting substantial amounts of funds. This is no particular problem for a slow-growing business, but if a business's products really catch on, and if it needs to raise large amounts of funds to capitalize on its opportunities, the difficulty in attracting funds becomes a real drawback. Thus, growth companies such as **Microsoft** and **Dell Computer** generally begin life as a proprietorship or partnership, but at some point they find it necessary to convert to a corporation.

Limited Partnership

Limited partnership *An unincorporated business association consisting of at least one general partner and at least one limited partner.*

A **limited partnership** is an unincorporated business association consisting of at least one general partner and at least one limited partner. It is formed by filing a certificate of limited partnership with the state. A limited partnership may elect not to be a separate taxable entity, in which case only the partners are taxed. General partners have unlimited liability for the partnership's debts; limited partners have limited liability. Each general partner has an equal right to control of the partnership; limited partners have no right to participate in control. Partners may assign their financial interest in the partnership, but the assignee may become a limited partner only if all of the members consent. The death, bankruptcy, or withdrawal of a general partner dissolves a limited partnership; the limited partners have neither the right nor the power to dissolve the limited partnership.

Limited Liability Partnership

Limited liability partnership (LLP) *A general partnership that, by making the statutorily required filing, limits the liability of its partners for some or all of the partnership's obligations.*

A registered **limited liability partnership (LLP)** is a general partnership that, by making the statutorily required filing, limits the liability of its partners for some or all of the partnership's obligations. To become an LLP, a general partnership must file with the state an application containing specified information. Nearly all of the states have enacted LLP statutes.

Limited Liability Limited Partnership

Limited liability limited partnership (LLLP) *A limited partnership in which the liability of the general partners has been limited to the same extent as in an LLP.*

A **limited liability limited partnership (LLLP)** is a limited partnership in which the liability of the general partners has been limited to the same extent as in an LLP. When authorized, the general partners in an LLLP will obtain the same degree of liability limitation that general partners can achieve in LLPs. When available, a limited partnership may register as an LLLP without having to form a new organization, as would be the case in converting to an LLC.

Joint Venture

A **joint venture** is an unincorporated business association composed of persons who combine their property, money, efforts, skill, and knowledge for the purpose of carrying out a particular business enterprise for profit. Usually, although not necessarily, it is of short duration. A joint venture, therefore, differs from a partnership, which is formed to carry on a business over a considerable or indefinite period of time. Nonetheless, except for a few differences, the law of partnerships generally governs a joint venture. An example of a joint venture is a securities underwriting syndicate or a syndicate formed to acquire a certain tract of land for subdivision and resale. Other common examples involve joint research conducted by corporations, the exploitation of mineral rights, and manufacturing operations in foreign countries.

Joint venture   An unincorporated business association of two or more persons to carry out a particular business enterprise for profit.

Corporation

A **corporation** is a legal entity separate and distinct from its owners. It is formed by filing its articles of incorporation with the state. A corporation is taxed as a separate entity, and shareholders are taxed on corporate earnings that are distributed to them. (Some corporations are eligible to elect to be taxed as Subchapter S corporations, which results in only the shareholders being taxed.) The shareholders have limited liability for the corporation's obligations. The board of directors elected by the shareholders manages the corporation. Shares in a corporation are freely transferable. The death, bankruptcy, or withdrawal of a shareholder does not dissolve the corporation. Exhibit 100.2 provides a comparison of various forms of organizations.

Corporation   A legal entity separate and distinct from its owners.

A corporation is a legal entity created by a state. It is separate and distinct from its owners and managers. This separateness gives the corporation three major *advantages*.

1. A corporation can continue after its original owners and managers are deceased; thus it is said to have *unlimited life*.
2. Ownership interests can be divided into shares of stock, which in turn can be *transferred far more easily* than can proprietorship or partnership interests.

Exhibit 100.2   *General Partnership, Limited Partnership, Corporation, and Limited Liability Company*

	General Partnership	Limited Partnership	Corporation	Limited Liability Company
Transferability	Financial interest may be assigned; membership requires consent of all partners	Financial interest may be assigned, and assignee may become limited partner if all partners consent	Freely transferable unless shareholders agree otherwise	Financial interest may be assigned; membership requires consent of all members
Liability	Partners have unlimited liability*	General partners have unlimited liability†; limited partners have limited liability	Shareholders have limited liability	All members have limited liability
Control	By all partners	By general partners, not limited partners	By board of directors elected by shareholders	By all members
Continuity	Dissolved by death, bankruptcy, or withdrawal of partner	Dissolved by death, bankruptcy, or withdrawal of general partner	Unaffected by death, bankruptcy, or withdrawal of shareholder	Dissolved by death, bankruptcy, or withdrawal of member
Taxation	May elect that only partners are taxed	May elect that only partners are taxed	Corporation taxed unless Subchapter S applies; shareholders taxed	May elect that only partners are taxed

*In an LLP, the partner's liability is limited for some or all of the partnership's obligations.
†In an LLLP, the partner's liability is limited for some or all of the partnership's obligations.

3. A corporation offers its owners *limited liability.* To illustrate the concept of limited liability, suppose you invested $10,000 to become a partner in a business that subsequently went bankrupt, owing creditors $1 million. Because the owners are liable for the debts of a partnership, you could be assessed for a share of the company's debt, and you could be held liable for the entire $1 million if your partners could not pay their shares—this is what we mean by unlimited liability. On the other hand, if you invested $10,000 in the stock of a corporation that then went bankrupt, your potential loss on the investment would be limited to your $10,000 investment.

In the case of small corporations, the limited liability feature is often a fiction, because bankers and credit managers frequently require personal guarantees from the stockholders of small, weak businesses.

These three factors—unlimited life, easy transferability of ownership interest, and limited liability—make it much easier for corporations than for proprietorships or partnerships to raise money in the financial markets.

The corporate form of business offers significant advantages over proprietorships and partnerships, but it does have two primary disadvantages.

1. Corporate *earnings are subject to double taxation*—the earnings of the corporation are taxed, and then any earnings paid out as dividends are taxed again as income to the stockholders.
2. Setting up a corporation, and filing required state and federal reports, is more complex and time consuming than for a proprietorship or a partnership.

Although a proprietorship or a partnership can commence operations without much paperwork, setting up a corporation requires that the incorporators hire a lawyer to prepare a charter and a set of bylaws. The corporate charter includes the (1) name of the proposed corporation, (2) types of activities it will pursue, (3) amount of capital stock, (4) number of directors, and (5) names and addresses of directors. The charter is filed with the secretary of the state in which the firm will be incorporated, and, when it is approved, the corporation is officially in existence. Then, after the corporation is in operation, quarterly and annual financial statements and tax reports must be filed with state and federal authorities.

A majority of major U.S. corporations are chartered in Delaware, which has, over the years, provided a favorable legal environment for corporations. It is not necessary for a firm to be headquartered, or even to conduct operations, in its state of incorporation.

The bylaws are a set of rules drawn up by the founders of the corporation to aid in governing the internal management of the company. Included are such points as (1) how directors are to be elected (all elected each year, or perhaps one-third each year for three-year terms); (2) whether the existing stockholders will have the first right to buy any new shares the firm issues (the preemptive right); and (3) procedures for changing the bylaws themselves, should conditions require it.

The value of any business other than a very small one probably will be maximized if it is organized as a corporation for these reasons.

1. Limited liability reduces the risks borne by investors, and, other things held constant, *lower risk means higher value.*
2. Corporations can attract funds more easily than can unincorporated businesses, and these funds can be invested in *growth opportunities* that help increase the firm's value.
3. Corporate ownership can be transferred more easily than ownership of either a proprietorship or a partnership. Therefore, all else equal, *investors would be willing to pay more* for a corporation than a proprietorship or partnership—this means that the corporate form of organization can enhance the value of a business.
4. Corporations are taxed differently than proprietorships and partnerships, and some of the *tax differences are beneficial* for corporations.

Most firms are managed with value maximization in mind, and this, in turn, has caused most large businesses to be organized as corporations.

Limited Liability Company

Limited liability company (LLC) An unincorporated business association that provides limited liability to all of its owners (members) and permits all of its members to participate in management of the business.

A **limited liability company (LLC)** is an unincorporated business association that provides limited liability to all of its owners (members) and permits all of its members to participate in management of the business. It may elect not to be a separate taxable entity, in which case only the members are taxed. If an LLC has only one member, it will be taxed as a sole proprietorship unless separate entity tax treatment is elected. Thus, the LLC provides many of the advantages of a general partnership plus limited liability for all its members. Its benefits outweigh those of a limited partnership in that all members of an LLC not only enjoy limited liability but also may participate in management and control of the business. Members may assign their financial interest in the LLC, but the assignee may become a member of the LLC only if all of the members consent. The death, bankruptcy, or withdrawal of a member dissolves an LLC. Every state has adopted an LLC statute.

Business Trusts

The **business trust,** sometimes called a Massachusetts trust, was devised to avoid the burdens of corporate regulation, particularly the formerly widespread prohibition denying to corporations the power to own and deal in real estate. Like an ordinary trust between natural persons, a business trust may be created by a voluntary agreement without any authorization or consent of the state. A business trust has three distinguishing characteristics: (1) the trust estate is devoted to the conduct of a business; (2) by the terms of the agreement, each beneficiary is entitled to a certificate evidencing his ownership of a beneficial interest in the trust, which he is free to sell or otherwise transfer; and (3) the trustees have the exclusive right to manage and control the business free from control of the beneficiaries. If the third condition is not met, the trust may fail, for the beneficiaries, by participating in control, would become personally liable as partners for the obligations of the business.

Business trust A trust (managed by a trustee for the benefit of a beneficiary) established to conduct a business for a profit.

The trustees are personally liable for the debts of the business unless, in entering into contractual relations with others, it is expressly stated or definitely understood between the parties that the obligation is incurred solely upon the responsibility of the trust estate. To escape personal liability on the contractual obligations of the business, the trustee must obtain the agreement or consent of the other contracting party to look solely to the assets of the trust. The personal liability of the trustees for their own torts or the torts of their agents and servants employed in the operation of the business stands on a different footing. Although this liability cannot be avoided, the risk involved may be reduced substantially or eliminated altogether by insurance. In most jurisdictions, the beneficiaries of a business trust have no liability for obligations of the business trust.

Summary of Business Organizations

Formation of General Partnerships

NATURE
Definition of Partnership an association of two or more persons to carry on as co-owners of a business for profit

Entity Theory
- *Legal Entity* an organization having a legal existence separate from that of its members; the Uniform Partnership Agreement (UPA) considers a partnership a legal entity for some purposes
- *Legal Aggregate* a group of individuals not having a legal existence separate from that of its members; the UPA considers a partnership a legal aggregate for some purposes

Types of Partners
- *General Partner* member of either a general or limited partnership with unlimited liability for its debts, full management powers, and a right to share profits
- *Limited Partner* member of a limited partnership with liability for its debts only to the extent of her capital contribution
- *Silent Partner* partner who takes no part in the partnership business
- *Secret Partner* partner whose membership in the partnership is not disclosed to the public
- *Dormant Partner* partner who is both a silent and a secret partner

FORMATION
Articles of Partnership it is preferable, although not usually required, that the partners enter into a written partnership agreement (articles of partnership)

Tests of Existence the formation of a partnership requires all of the following:
- *Association* two or more persons with legal capacity who agree to become partners
- *Business for Profit*
- *Co-ownership* includes sharing of profits, losses, and control of the business

Partnership Capital total money and property contributed by the partners for permanent use by the partnership

Partnership Property sum of all of the partnership's assets, including all property brought into the partnership or subsequently acquired by it

Tenancy in Partnership type of joint ownership that determines partners' rights in specific partnership property

Interest in Partnership partner's share in the partnership's profits and surplus
- *Assignability* a partner may sell or assign his interest in the partnership; the new owner becomes entitled to the assigning partner's share of profits and surplus but does not become a partner
- *Creditor's Rights* a partner's interest is subject to the claims of creditors, who may obtain a charging order (judicial lien) against the partner's interest

Dissolution of General Partnerships

DISSOLUTION

Definition of Dissolution the change in the relation of partners caused by any partner's ceasing to be associated with the carrying on of the business

Causes of Dissolution
- *Dissolution by Act of the Partners* a partner always has the power to dissolve a partnership, but the partnership agreement determines whether he has the right to do so
- *Dissolution by Operation of Law* a partnership is dissolved by operation of law upon (1) the death of a partner, (2) the bankruptcy of a partner or of the partnership, or (3) the subsequent illegality of the partnership
- *Dissolution by Court Order* a court will order dissolution of a partnership under certain conditions

Effects of Dissolution upon dissolution a partnership is not terminated but continues until the winding up is completed
- *Authority* a partner's actual authority to act for the partnership terminates, except so far as may be necessary to wind up partnership affairs; apparent authority continues unless notice of the dissolution is given to a third party
- *Existing Liability* dissolution does not in itself discharge the existing liability of any partner

WINDING UP

Definition of Winding Up completing unfinished business, collecting debts, and distributing assets to creditors and partners; also called liquidation

Right to Wind Up on dissolution, any partner has the right to insist on the winding up of the partnership unless the partnership agreement provides otherwise; however, a partner who has wrongfully dissolved the partnership or who has been properly expelled cannot force the liquidation of the partnership

Distribution of Assets the liabilities of a partnership are to be paid out of partnership assets in the following order: (1) amounts owing to nonpartner creditors, (2) amounts owing to partners other than for capital and profits, (3) amounts owing to partners for capital contributions, and (4) amounts owing to partners for profits

Marshaling of Assets applies only when a state court of equity administers the assets of a partnership and of its members; the process of segregating and considering separately the assets and liabilities of the partnership and the respective assets and liabilities of the individual partners
- *Partnership Creditors* are entitled to be first satisfied out of partnership assets
- *Nonpartnership Creditors* have first claim to the individually owned assets of their respective debtor-partners
- *Federal Bankruptcy* marshaling of assets is not followed if the partnership is a debtor

CONTINUATION AFTER DISSOLUTION

Right to Continue Partnership the remaining partners have the right to continue the partnership in the following situations:
- *Continuation after Wrongful Dissolution* the aggrieved partners can continue the firm by paying the withdrawing partner the value of his interest less the amount of damages they sustained as a result of the breach

- *Continuation after Expulsion* the expelled partner is entitled to be discharged from partnership liabilities and to receive cash in the net amount due him from the partnership
- *Continuation Agreement of the Partners* permits the remaining partners to keep partnership property and to carry on its business; provides a specified settlement to the departing partner

Rights of Creditors the creditors of the old partnership have claims against the continuing (new) partnership and may also proceed against all the members of the dissolved partnership

Relationship among Partners

DUTIES AMONG PARTNERS
Fiduciary Duty duty of utmost loyalty, fairness, and good faith owed by partners to each other and to the partnership

Duty of Obedience duty to act in accordance with the partnership agreement and any business decisions properly made by the partners

Duty of Care duty owed by partners to manage the partnership affairs without culpable negligence, which is greater than ordinary negligence but less than gross negligence

RIGHTS AMONG PARTNERS
Tenancy in Partnership

Interest in Partnership

Distributions transfer of partnership property from the partnership to a partner
- *Profits* each partner is entitled to an equal share of the profits unless otherwise agreed
- *Capital* after all partnership creditors have been paid, each partner is entitled to be repaid his capital contribution when the firm is terminated
- *Advances* if a partner makes an advance (loan) to the firm, he is entitled to repayment of the advance plus interest; but his repayment is subordinate to that of nonpartner creditors
- *Compensation* unless otherwise agreed, no partner is entitled to payment for acting in the partnership business

Management each partner has an equal voice in management unless otherwise agreed

Choice of Associates under the doctrine of *delectus personae,* no person can become a member of a partnership without the consent of all of the partners

Enforcement Rights
- *Information* each partner may demand full information about all partnership matters, and each partner has a duty to supply other partners with full and accurate information
- *Formal Account* complete review of all financial transactions of a partnership
- *Accounting* equitable proceeding for a complete settlement of all partnership affairs

Relationship between Partners and Third Parties

CONTRACTS
Authority to Bind Partnership a partner who has actual authority (express or implied) or apparent authority may bind the partnership
- *Actual Express Authority* authority set forth in the partnership agreement, in additional agreements among the partners, or in decisions made by a majority of the partners regarding the ordinary business of the partnership
- *Actual Implied Authority* authority that is reasonably deduced from the nature of the partnership, the terms of the partnership agreement, or the relations of the partners
- *Apparent Authority* authority that a third person may reasonably assume to exist in light of the conduct of the partners, so long as that third person has no knowledge or notice of the lack of actual authority

Partners' Liability
- *Personal Liability* if the partnership is contractually bound, each partner has joint, unlimited personal liability
- *Joint Liability* a creditor must sue all of the partners as a group

Partnership by Estoppel imposes partnership duties and liabilities on a nonpartner who has either represented himself or consented to be represented as a partner

TORTS

Respondeat Superior the partnership is liable for loss or injury caused by any wrongful act or omission of any partner while acting within the ordinary course of the business or with the authority of his copartners

Joint and Several Liability the partners are jointly and severally liable for a tort or breach of trust committed by any partner or by an employee of the firm in the course of partnership business; under such liability, the creditors may sue the partners jointly as a group or separately as individuals

OTHER POWERS

Admissions an admission by one partner within the scope of his authority may be used as evidence against the partnership

Notice a partnership is bound by notice to and knowledge of a partner

Demand a demand on one partner is a demand on the partnership

LIABILITY OF INCOMING PARTNER

Antecedent Debts the liability of an incoming partner for antecedent debts of the partnership is limited to his capital contribution

Subsequent Debts the liability of an incoming partner for subsequent debts of the partnership is unlimited

LIMITED PARTNERSHIP

Definition of a Limited Partnership a partnership formed by two or more persons under the laws of a state and having one or more general partners and one or more limited partners

Formation a limited partnership can be formed only by substantial compliance with a state limited partnership statute

- *Filing of Certificate* two or more persons must file a signed certificate of limited partnership
- *Name* inclusion of a limited partner's surname in the partnership name in most instances will result in the loss of the limited partner's limited liability
- *Contributions* may be cash, property, services, or a promise to contribute cash, property, or services
- *Defective Formation* if no certificate is filed or if the one filed does not substantially meet the statutory requirements, the formation is defective and the limited liability of the limited partners is jeopardized
- *Foreign Limited Partnerships* a limited partnership is considered "foreign" in any state other than that in which it was formed

Rights a general partner in a limited partnership has all the rights and powers of a partner in a general partnership

- *Control* the general partners have almost exclusive control and management of the limited partnership; a limited partner who participates in the control of the limited partnership may lose limited liability
- *Choice of Associates* no person may be added as a general partner or a limited partner without the consent of all partners
- *Withdrawal* a general partner may withdraw from a limited partnership at any time by giving written notice to the other partners; a limited partner may withdraw as provided in the limited partnership certificate
- *Assignment of Partnership Interest* unless otherwise provided in the partnership agreement, a partner may assign his partnership interest; an assignee may become a limited partner if all other partners consent
- *Profit and Loss Sharing* profits and losses are allocated among the partners as provided in the partnership agreement; if the partnership agreement has no such provision, then profits and losses are allocated on the basis of the contributions each partner actually made
- *Distributions* the partners share distributions of cash or other assets of a limited partnership as provided in the partnership agreement
- *Loans* both general and limited partners may be secured or unsecured creditors of the partnership
- *Information* each partner has the right to inspect and copy the partnership records
- *Derivative Actions* a limited partner may sue on behalf of a limited partnership if the general partners refuse to bring the action

Duties and Liabilities

- *Duties* general partners owe a duty of care and loyalty (fiduciary duty) to the general partners, the limited partners, and the limited partnership; limited partners do not

- *Liabilities* the general partners have unlimited liability; the limited partners have limited liability (liability for partnership obligations only to the extent of the capital that the limited partner contributed or agreed to contribute)

Dissolution
- *Causes* the limited partners have neither the right nor the power to dissolve the partnership, except by decree of the court. The following events trigger a dissolution: (1) the expiration of the time period; (2) the withdrawal of a general partner, unless all partners agree to continue the business; or (3) a decree of judicial dissolution
- *Winding Up* unless otherwise provided in the partnership agreement, the general partners who have not wrongfully dissolved the partnership may wind up its affairs
- *Distribution of Assets* the priorities for distribution are as follows: (1) creditors, including partners who are creditors; (2) partners and ex-partners in satisfaction of liabilities for unpaid distributions; (3) partners for the return of contributions, except as otherwise agreed; and (4) partners for their partnership interests in the proportions in which they share in distributions, except as otherwise agreed

LIMITED LIABILITY COMPANY

Definition a limited liability company is a noncorporate business organization that provides limited liability to *all* of its owners (members) and permits all of its members to participate in management of the business

Formation the formation of a limited liability company requires substantial compliance with a state's limited liability company statute
- *Filing* the LLC statutes generally require the central filing of articles of organization in a designated state office
- *Name* LLC statutes generally require the name of the LLC to include the words "limited liability company" or the abbreviation "LLC"
- *Contribution* the contribution of a member to a limited liability company may be cash, property, services rendered, a promissory note, or other obligation to contribute cash, property, or to perform services
- *Operating Agreement* is the basic contract governing the affairs of a limited liability company and stating the various rights and duties of the members
- *Foreign Limited Liability Companies* a limited liability company is considered "foreign" in any state other than that in which it was formed

Rights of Members a member's interest in the LLC includes the financial interest (the right to distributions) and the management interest (which consists of all other rights granted to a member by the LLC operating agreement and the LLC statute)
- *Profit and Loss Sharing* the LLC's operating agreement determines how the partners allocate the profits and losses; if the LLC's operating agreement makes no such provision, the profits and losses are typically allocated on the basis of the value of the members' contributions
- *Distributions* the members share distributions of cash or other assets of a limited liability company as provided in the operating agreement; if the LLC's operating agreement does not allocate distributions, they are typically made on the basis of the contributions each member made
- *Withdrawal* a member may withdraw and demand payment of her interest upon giving the notice specified in the statute or the LLC's operating agreement
- *Management* in the absence of a contrary agreement, each member has equal rights in the management of the LLC; but LLCs may be managed by one or more managers who may be members
- *Voting* LLC statutes often specify the voting rights of members, subject to a contrary provision in an LLC's operating agreement
- *Derivative Actions* a member has the right to bring an action on behalf of a limited liability company to recover a judgment in its favor if the managers or members with authority to bring the action have refused to do so
- *Assignment of LLC Interest* unless otherwise provided in the LLC's operating agreement, a member may assign his financial interest in the LLC; an assignee of a financial interest in an LLC may acquire the other rights by being admitted as a member of the company by all the remaining members

Duties
- *Manager-managed LLCs* the managers of manager-managed LLCs have a duty of care and loyalty; usually, members of a manager-managed LLC have no duties to the LLC or its members by reason of being a member

- *Member-managed LLCs* members of member-managed LLCs have the same duties of care and loyalty that managers have in manager-managed LLCs

Liabilities no member or manager of a limited liability company is obligated personally for any debt, obligation, or liability of the limited liability company solely by reason of being a member or acting as a manager of the limited liability company

Dissolution an LLC will automatically dissolve upon (1) the dissociation of a member, (2) the expiration of the LLC's agreed duration or the happening of any of the events specified in the articles, (3) the unanimous written consent of all the members, or (4) a decree of judicial dissolution

- *Dissociation* means that a member has ceased to be associated with the company and includes voluntary withdrawal, death, incompetence, expulsion, or bankruptcy
- *Distribution of Assets* the default rules for distributing the assets of a limited liability company are (1) to creditors, including members and managers who are creditors, except with respect to liabilities for distributions; (2) to members and former members in satisfaction of liabilities for unpaid distributions, except as otherwise agreed; (3) to members for the return of their contributions, except as otherwise agreed; and (4) to members for their limited liability company interests in the proportions in which members share in distributions, except as otherwise agreed

OTHER UNINCORPORATED BUSINESS ASSOCIATIONS

Limited Liability Partnership (LLP) is a general partnership that, by making the statutorily required filing, limits the liability of its partners for some or all of the partnership's obligations

- *Formalities* most statutes require only a majority of the partners to authorize registration as an LLP; others require unanimous approval
- *Designation* the name of the LLP must include the words "limited liability partnership" or "registered limited liability partnership," or the abbreviation "LLP"
- *Liability Limitation* some statutes limit liability only for negligent acts; others limit liability to any partnership tort or contract obligation that arose from negligence, malpractice, wrongful acts, or misconduct committed by any partner, employee, or agent of the partnership; some provide limited liability for all debts and obligations of the partnership

Limited Liability Limited Partnership is a limited partnership in which the liability of the general partners has been limited to the same extent as in an LLP

Nature of Corporations

CORPORATE ATTRIBUTES

Creature of the State a corporation may be formed only by substantial compliance with a state incorporation statute

Legal Entity a corporation is an entity apart from its shareholders, with entirely distinct rights and liabilities

Limited Liability a shareholder's liability is limited to the amount invested in the business enterprise

Free Transferability of Corporate Shares unless otherwise specified in the charter

Perpetual Existence unless the charter provides otherwise

Centralized Management shareholders of a corporation elect the board of directors to manage its business affairs; the board appoints officers to run the day-to-day operations of the business

As a Person a corporation is considered a person for some but not all purposes

As a Citizen a corporation is considered a citizen for some but not all purposes

CLASSIFICATION OF CORPORATIONS

Public or Private

- *Public Corporation* one created to administer a unit of local civil government or one created by the United States to conduct public business
- *Private Corporation* one founded by and composed of private persons for private purposes; has no governmental duties

Profit or Nonprofit

- *Profit Corporation* one founded to operate a business for profit
- *Nonprofit Corporation* one whose profits must be used exclusively for charitable, educational, or scientific purposes

Domestic or Foreign
- *Domestic Corporation* one created under the laws of a given state
- *Foreign Corporation* one created under the laws of any other state or jurisdiction; it must obtain a certificate of authority from each state in which it does intrastate business

Publicly Held or Closely Held
- *Publicly Held* corporation whose shares are owned by a large number of people and are widely traded
- *Closely Held* corporation that is owned by few shareholders and whose shares are not actively traded

Subchapter S Corporation eligible corporation electing to be taxed as a partnership under the Internal Revenue Code

Professional Corporations corporate form under which duly licensed individuals may practice their professions

Formation of a Corporation

ORGANIZING THE CORPORATION

Promoter person who takes the preliminary steps to organize a corporation
- *Promoters' Contracts* promoters remain liable on preincorporation contracts made in the name of the corporation unless the contract provides otherwise or unless a novation is effected
- *Promoters' Fiduciary Duty* promoters owe a fiduciary duty among themselves and to the corporation, its subscribers, and its initial shareholders

Subscribers persons who agree to purchase stock in a corporation
- *Preincorporation Subscription* an offer to purchase capital stock in a corporation yet to be formed which under many incorporation statutes is irrevocable for a specified time period
- *Postincorporation Subscription* a subscription agreement entered into after incorporation; an offer to enter into such a subscription is revocable any time before the corporation accepts it

FORMALITIES OF INCORPORATION

Selection of Name the name must clearly designate the entity as a corporation

Incorporators the persons who sign the articles of incorporation

Articles of Incorporation the charter or basic organizational document of a corporation

Organizational Meeting the first meeting, held to adopt the bylaws and appoint officers

Bylaws rules governing a corporation's internal management

Recognition or Disregard of Corporateness

DEFECTIVE INCORPORATION

Common Law Approach
- *Corporation de jure* one formed in substantial compliance with the incorporation statute and having all corporate attributes
- *Corporation de facto* one not formed in compliance with the statute but recognized for most purposes as a corporation
- *Corporation by Estoppel* prevents a person from raising the question of a corporation's existence
- *Defective Corporation* the associates are denied the benefits of incorporation

Statutory Approach the filing of the articles of incorporation is generally conclusive proof of proper incorporation
- *Revised Model Business Corporation Act (RMBCA)* liability is imposed only on persons who act on behalf of a defectively formed corporation knowing that there was no incorporation
- *Model Business Corporation Act (MBCA)* unlimited personal liability is imposed on all persons who act on behalf of a defectively formed corporation

PIERCING THE CORPORATE VEIL

General Rule the courts will disregard the corporate entity when it is used to defeat public convenience, commit a wrongdoing, protect fraud, or circumvent the law

Application most frequently applied to
- *Closely Held Corporations*
- *Parent-Subsidiary Corporations*

Corporate Powers

SOURCES OF CORPORATE POWERS
Statutory Powers typically include perpetual existence, right to hold property in the corporate name, and all powers necessary or convenient to effect the corporation's purposes

Express Charter Powers those stated in the articles of incorporation

Implied Powers those necessary or convenient to and consistent with the express powers

ULTRA VIRES ACTS
Definition of *Ultra Vires Acts* any action or contract that goes beyond a corporation's express and implied powers

Effect of *Ultra Vires Acts* under RMBCA, *ultra vires* acts and conveyances are not invalid

Remedies for *Ultra Vires Acts* the RMBCA provides three possible remedies

LIABILITY FOR TORTS AND CRIMES
Torts under the doctrine of *respondeat superior,* a corporation is liable for torts committed by its employees within the course of their employment

Crime a corporation may be criminally liable for violations of statutes imposing liability without fault or for an offense perpetrated by a high corporate officer or its board of directors

Debt Securities

AUTHORITY TO ISSUE DEBT SECURITIES
Definitions
- *Debt Security* source of capital creating no ownership interest and involving the corporation's promise to repay funds lent to it
- *Bond* a debt security

Rule each corporation has the power to issue debt securities as determined by the board of directors

TYPES OF DEBT SECURITIES
Unsecured Bonds called debentures, have only the obligation of the corporation behind them

Secured Bonds are claims against a corporation's general assets and a lien on specific property

Income Bonds condition to some extent the payment of interest on corporate earnings

Participating Bonds call for a stated percentage of return regardless of earnings, with additional payments dependent upon earnings

Convertible Bonds may be exchanged for other securities

Callable Bond bonds subject to redemption

Equity Securities

ISSUANCE OF SHARES
Definitions
- *Equity Security* source of capital creating an ownership interest in the corporation
- *Share* a proportionate ownership interest in a corporation
- *Treasury Stock* shares reacquired by a corporation

Authority to Issue only those shares authorized in the articles of incorporation may be issued

Preemptive Rights right to purchase a *pro rata* share of new stock offerings

Amount of Consideration for Shares shares are deemed fully paid and nonassessable when a corporation receives the consideration for which the board of directors authorized the issuance of the shares, which in the case of par value stock must be at least par

Payment for Newly Issued Shares may be cash, property, and services actually rendered, as determined by the board of directors; under the Revised Act, promises to contribute cash, property, or services are also permitted

CLASSES OF SHARES
Common Stock stock not having any special contract rights

Preferred Stock stock having contractual rights superior to those of common stock
- *Dividend Preferences* must receive full dividends before any dividend may be paid on common stock
- *Liquidation Preferences* priority over common stock in corporate assets upon liquidation

Stock Rights contractual right to purchase stock from a corporation

Dividends and Other Distributions

TYPES OF DIVIDENDS AND OTHER DISTRIBUTIONS
Distributions transfers of property by a corporation to any of its shareholders with respect to its shares; become debts of the corporation if and when declared by the board

Cash Dividends the most common type of distribution

Property Dividends distribution in form of property

Stock Dividends a ratable distribution of additional shares of stock

Stock Splits each of the outstanding shares is broken into a larger number of shares

Liquidating Dividends a distribution of capital assets to shareholders

Redemption of Shares a corporation's exercise of the right to repurchase its own shares

Acquisition of Shares a corporation's repurchase of its own shares

LEGAL RESTRICTIONS ON DIVIDENDS AND OTHER DISTRIBUTIONS
Legal Restrictions on Cash Dividends dividends may be paid only if the cash flow and applicable balance sheet tests are satisfied
- *Cash Flow Test* a corporation must not be or become insolvent (unable to pay its debts as they become due in the usual course of business)
- *Balance Sheet Test* varies among the states and includes the earned surplus test (available in all states), the surplus test, and the net assets test (used by the Model and Revised Acts)

Legal Restrictions on Liquidating Distributions states usually permit distribution in partial liquidation from capital surplus unless the company is insolvent

Legal Restrictions on Redemptions of Shares in most states, a corporation may not redeem shares when insolvent or when such redemption would render it insolvent

Legal Restrictions on Acquisition of Shares restrictions similar to those on cash dividends usually apply

DECLARATION AND PAYMENT OF DISTRIBUTIONS
Shareholders' Right to Compel a Dividend the declaration of dividends is within the discretion of the board of directors and only rarely will a court substitute its business judgment for that of the board

Effect of Declaration once properly declared, a cash dividend is considered a debt the corporation owes to the shareholders

LIABILITY FOR IMPROPER DIVIDENDS AND DISTRIBUTIONS
Directors the directors who assent to an improper dividend are liable for the unlawful amount of the dividend

Shareholder a shareholder must return illegal dividends if he knew of the illegality, if the dividend resulted from his fraud, or if the corporation is insolvent

Role of Shareholders

VOTING RIGHTS OF SHAREHOLDERS
Management Structure of Corporations structure should be defined for the statutory model of corporate governance, the typical closely held corporation, and the typical publicly held corporation

Shareholder Meetings shareholders may exercise their voting rights at both annual and special shareholder meetings

Quorum minimum number necessary to be present at a meeting in order to transact business

---

103. FORMS OF BUSINESS ORGANIZATIONS

- **Election of Directors** the shareholders elect the board at the annual meeting of the corporation
  - *Straight Voting* directors are elected by a plurality of votes
  - *Cumulative Voting* entitles shareholders to multiply the number of votes they are entitled to cast by the number of directors for whom they are entitled to vote and to cast the product for a single candidate or to distribute the product among two or more candidates
- **Removal of Directors** the shareholders may by majority vote remove directors with or without cause, subject to cumulative voting rights
- **Approval of Fundamental Changes** shareholder approval is required for charter amendments, most acquisitions, and dissolution
- **Concentrations of Voting Power**
  - *Proxy* authorization to vote another's shares at a shareholder meeting
  - *Voting Trust* transfer of corporate shares' voting rights to a trustee
  - *Shareholder Voting Agreement* used to provide shareholders with greater control over the election and removal of directors and other matters
- **Restrictions on Transfer of Shares** must be reasonable and conspicuously noted on stock certificate

ENFORCEMENT RIGHTS OF SHAREHOLDERS
- **Right to Inspect Books and Records** if the demand is made in good faith and for a proper purpose
- **Shareholder Suits**
  - *Direct Suits* brought by a shareholder or a class of shareholders against the corporation based upon the ownership of shares
  - *Derivative Suits* brought by a shareholder on behalf of the corporation to enforce a right belonging to the corporation
- **Shareholder's Right to Dissent** a shareholder has the right to dissent from certain corporate actions that require shareholder approval

Role of Directors and Officers

FUNCTION OF THE BOARD OF DIRECTORS
- **Selection and Removal of Officers**
- **Capital Structure**
- **Fundamental Changes** the directors have the power to make, amend, or repeal the bylaws, unless this power is exclusively reserved to the shareholders
- **Dividends** directors declare the amount and type of dividends
- **Management Compensation**
- **Vacancies in the Board** may be filled by the vote of a majority of the remaining directors

EXERCISE OF DIRECTORS' FUNCTIONS
- **Meeting** directors have the power to bind the corporation only when acting as a board
- **Action Taken Without a Meeting** permitted if a consent in writing is signed by all of the directors
- **Delegation of Board Powers** committees may be appointed to perform some but not all of the board's functions
- **Directors' Inspection Rights** directors have the right to inspect corporate books and records

OFFICERS
- **Role of Officers** officers are agents of the corporation
- **Authority of Officers**
  - *Actual Express Authority* arises from the incorporation statute, the charter, the bylaws, and resolutions of the directors
  - *Actual Implied Authority* authority to do what is reasonably necessary to perform actual authority
  - *Apparent Authority* acts of the principal that lead a third party to believe reasonably and in good faith that an officer has the required authority
  - *Ratification* a corporation may ratify the unauthorized acts of its officers

DUTIES OF DIRECTORS AND OFFICERS

Duty of Obedience must act within respective authority

Duty of Diligence must exercise ordinary care and prudence

Duty of Loyalty requires undeviating loyalty to the corporation

Business Judgment Rule precludes imposing liability on directors and officers for honest mistakes in judgment if they act with due care, in good faith, and in a manner reasonably believed to be in the best interests of the corporation

Indemnification a corporation may indemnify a director or officer for liability incurred if he acted in good faith and was not adjudged negligent or liable for misconduct

Liability Limitation Statutes many states now authorize corporations—with shareholder approval—to limit or eliminate the liability of directors for some breaches of duty

CHARTER AMENDMENTS

Authority to Amend statutes permit charters to be amended

Procedure the board of directors adopts a resolution, which must be approved by a majority vote of the shareholders

BUSINESS COMBINATIONS

Purchase or Lease of All or Substantially All of the Assets results in no change in the legal personality of either corporation
- *Regular Course of Business* approval by the selling corporation's board of directors is required, but shareholder authorization is not
- *Other than in Regular Course of Business* approval by the board of directors and shareholders of the selling corporation is required

Purchase of Shares a transaction by which one corporation acquires all of, or a controlling interest in, the stock of another corporation; no change occurs in the legal existence of either corporation and no formal shareholder approval of either corporation is required

Compulsory Share Exchange a transaction by which a corporation becomes the owner of all of the outstanding shares of one or more classes of stock of another corporation by an exchange that is compulsory on all owners of the acquired shares; the board of directors of each corporation and the shareholders of the corporation whose shares are being acquired must approve

Merger the combination of the assets of two or more corporations into one of the corporations
- *Procedure* requires approval by the board of directors and shareholders of each corporation
- *Short-Form Merger* a corporation that owns at least 90 percent of the outstanding shares of a subsidiary may merge the subsidiary into itself without approval by the shareholders of either corporation
- *Effect* the surviving corporation receives title to all of the assets of the merged corporation and assumes all of its liabilities; the merged corporation ceases to exist

Consolidation the combination of two or more corporations into a new corporation
- *Procedure* requires approval of the board of directors and shareholders of each corporation
- *Effect* each constituent corporation ceases to exist; the new corporation assumes all of their debts and liabilities

Going Private Transactions a combination that makes a publicly held corporation a private one; includes cash-out combinations and management buyouts

Dissenting Shareholder one who opposes a fundamental change and has the right to receive the fair value of her shares
- *Availability* dissenters' rights arise in (1) mergers, (2) consolidations, (3) sales or leases of all or substantially all of the assets of a corporation not in the regular course of business, (4) compulsory share exchanges, and (5) amendments that materially and adversely affect the rights of shares
- *Appraisal Remedy* the right of a dissenter to receive the fair value of his shares (the value of shares immediately before the corporate action to which the dissenter objects takes place, excluding any appreciation or depreciation in anticipation of such corporate action unless such exclusion would be inequitable)

DISSOLUTION

Voluntary Dissolution may be brought about by a resolution of the board of directors that is approved by the shareholders

Involuntary Dissolution may occur by administrative or judicial action taken (1) by the attorney general, (2) by shareholders under certain circumstances, and (3) by a creditor on a showing that the corporation has become unable to pay its debts and obligations as they mature in the regular course of its business

Liquidation when a corporation is dissolved, its assets are liquidated and used first to pay its liquidation expenses and its creditors according to their respective contract or lien rights; any remainder is proportionately distributed to shareholders according to their respective contract rights.

Management Perspectives

The Definition of Organization

A historical perspective on management provides a context or environment in which to interpret current opportunities and problems. However, studying history does not mean merely arranging events in chronological order; it means developing an understanding of the impact of societal forces on organizations. Studying history is a way to achieve strategic thinking, see the big picture, and improve conceptual skills. We will start by examining how social, political, and economic forces have influenced organizations and the practice of management.[29]

Social forces refer to those aspects of a culture that guide and influence relationships among people. What do people value? What do people need? What are the standards of behavior among people? These forces shape what is known as the *social contract,* which refers to the unwritten, common rules and perceptions about relationships among people and between employees and management.

Political forces refer to the influence of political and legal institutions on people and organizations. Political forces include basic assumptions underlying the political system, such as the desirability of self-government, property rights, contract rights, the definition of justice, and the determination of innocence or guilt of a crime. The spread of capitalism throughout the world has dramatically altered the business landscape. The dominance of the free-market system and growing interdependencies among the world's countries require organizations to operate differently and managers to think in new ways. At the same time, growing anti-American sentiments in many parts of the world create challenges for U.S. companies and managers. Another strong political force is the empowerment of citizens throughout the world. Power is being diffused both within and among countries as never before.[30] People are demanding empowerment, participation, and responsibility in all areas of their lives, including their work.

Economic forces pertain to the availability, production, and distribution of resources in a society. Governments, military agencies, churches, schools, and business organizations in every society require resources to achieve their goals, and economic forces influence the allocation of scarce resources. The economy of the United States and other developed countries is shifting dramatically, with the sources of wealth, the fundamentals of distribution, and the nature of economic decision making undergoing significant changes.[31] The emerging new economy is based largely on ideas, information, and knowledge rather than material resources. Supply chains and distribution of resources have been revolutionized by digital technology. Inventories, which once could trigger recessions, are declining or completely disappearing. Another economic trend is the booming importance of small and mid-sized businesses, including start-ups, which early in the 21st century grew at three times the rate of the national economy.

Classical Perspective

The early study of management as we know it today began with what is now called the *classical perspective*.

The **classical perspective** on management emerged during the 19th and early 20th centuries. The factory system that began to appear in the 1800s posed challenges that earlier organizations had not encountered. Problems arose in tooling the plants, organizing managerial structure, training employees, scheduling complex manufacturing operations, and dealing with increased labor dissatisfaction and resulting strikes.

These myriad new problems and the development of large, complex organizations demanded a new approach to coordination and control, and a "new subspecies of economic man—the salaried manager"[32]—was born. These professional managers began developing and testing solutions to the mounting challenges of organizing, coordinating, and controlling large numbers of people and increasing worker productivity. Thus began the evolution of modern management with the classical perspective.

This perspective contains three subfields, each with a slightly different emphasis: scientific management, bureaucratic organizations, and administrative principles.[33]

Scientific Management

Organizations' somewhat limited success in achieving improvements in labor productivity led a young engineer to suggest that the problem lay more in poor management practices than in labor. Frederick Winslow Taylor (1856–1915) insisted that management itself would have to change and, further, that the manner of change could be determined only by scientific study; hence, the label **scientific management** emerged. Taylor suggested that decisions based on rules of thumb and tradition be replaced with precise procedures developed after careful study of individual situations.[34]

Taylor's philosophy is encapsulated in his statement, "In the past the man has been first. In the future, the system must be first."[35] Although known as the "father of scientific management," Taylor was not alone in this area. Henry Gantt, an associate of Taylor's, developed the *Gantt Chart*—a bar graph that measures planned and completed work along each stage of production by time elapsed. Two other important pioneers in this area were the husband-and-wife team of Frank B. and Lillian M. Gilbreth. Frank B. Gilbreth (1868–1924) pioneered *time and motion study* and arrived at many of his management techniques independently of Taylor. He stressed efficiency and was known for his quest for the "one best way" to do work.

The basic ideas of scientific management are shown in Exhibit 100.3. To use this approach, managers should develop standard methods for doing each job, select workers with the appropriate abilities, train workers in the standard methods, support workers and eliminate interruptions, and provide wage incentives.

The ideas of scientific management that began with Taylor dramatically increased productivity across all industries, and they are still important today. Indeed, the concept of arranging work based on careful analysis of tasks for maximum productivity is deeply embedded in our organizations.[36] However, because scientific management ignored the social context and workers' needs, it led to increased conflict and sometimes violent clashes between managers and employees. Under this system, workers often felt exploited. This was in sharp contrast to the harmony and cooperation that Taylor and his followers had envisioned.

Exhibit 100.3 *Characteristics of Scientific Management*

General Approach
- Developed standard method for performing each job.
- Selected workers with appropriate abilities for each job.
- Trained workers in standard methods.
- Supported workers by planning their work and eliminating interruptions.
- Provided wage incentives to workers for increased output.

Contributions
- Demonstrated the importance of compensation for performance.
- Initiated the careful study of tasks and jobs.
- Demonstrated the importance of personnel selection and training.

Criticisms
- Did not appreciate the social context of work and higher needs of workers.
- Did not acknowledge variance among individuals.
- Tended to regard workers as uninformed and ignored their ideas and suggestions.

Bureaucratic Organizations

A systematic approach developed in Europe that looked at the organization as a whole is the **bureaucratic organizations** approach, a subfield within the classical perspective. Max Weber (1864–1920), a German theorist, introduced most of the concepts on bureaucratic organizations.[37]

During the late 1800s, many European organizations were managed on a personal, familylike basis. Employees were loyal to a single individual rather than to the organization or its mission. The dysfunctional consequence of this management practice was that resources were used to realize individual desires rather than organizational goals. Employees in effect owned the organization and used resources for their own gain rather than to serve customers. Weber envisioned organizations that would be managed on an impersonal, rational basis. This form of organization was called a *bureaucracy*.

Weber believed that an organization based on rational authority would be more efficient and adaptable to change because continuity is related to formal structure and positions rather than to a particular person, who may leave or die. To Weber, rationality in organizations meant employee selection and advancement based on competence rather than on "whom you know." The organization relies on rules and written records for continuity. The manager depends not on his or her personality for successfully giving orders but on the legal power invested in the managerial position.

The term *bureaucracy* has taken on a negative meaning in today's organizations and is associated with endless rules and red tape. We have all been frustrated by waiting in long lines or following seemingly silly procedures. On the other hand, rules and other bureaucratic procedures provide a standard way of dealing with employees. Everyone gets equal treatment, and everyone knows what the rules are. This has enabled many organizations to become extremely efficient.

Administrative Principles

Administrative principles A subfield of the classical management perspective that focused on the total organizaiton rather than the individual worker, delineating the managament functions of planning, organizing, commanding, coordinating, and controlling.

Another major subfield within the classical perspective is known as the **administrative principles** approach. Whereas scientific management focused on the productivity of the individual worker, the administrative principles approach focused on the total organization. The contributors to this approach included Henri Fayol, Mary Parker Follett, and Chester I. Barnard.

Henri Fayol (1841–1925) was a French mining engineer who worked his way up to become head of a major mining group known as Comambault. In his most significant work, *General and Industrial Management,* Fayol discussed 14 general principles of management, several of which are part of management philosophy today. For example:

- *Unity of Command.* Each subordinate receives orders from one—and only one—superior.
- *Division of Work.* Managerial and technical work are amenable to specialization to produce more and better work with the same amount of effort.
- *Unity of Direction.* Similar activities in an organization should be grouped together under one manager.
- *Scalar Chain.* A chain of authority extends from the top to the bottom of the organization and should include every employee.

Fayol felt that these principles could be applied in any organizational setting. He also identified five basic functions or elements of management: planning, organizing, commanding, coordinating, and controlling. These functions underlie much of the general approach to today's management theory.

Mary Parker Follett (1868–1933) wrote of the importance of common superordinate goals for reducing conflict in organizations.[38] Her work was popular with businesspeople of her day but was often overlooked by management scholars.[39] Follett's ideas served as a contrast to scientific management and are reemerging as applicable for modern managers dealing with rapid changes in today's global environment. Her approach to leadership stressed the importance of people rather than engineering techniques. Follett addressed issues that are timely today, such as ethics, power, and how to lead in a way that encourages employees to give their best. The concepts of empowerment, facilitating rather than controlling employees, and allowing employees to act depending on the authority of the situation opened new areas for theoretical study by Chester Barnard and others.[40]

One of Chester I. Barnard's (1886–1961) significant contributions was the concept of the informal organization. The *informal organization* occurs in all formal organizations and includes cliques and naturally occurring social groupings. Barnard argued that organizations are not machines and informal relationships are powerful forces that can help the organization if properly managed. Another significant contribution was the *acceptance theory of author-*

ity, which states that people have free will and can choose whether to follow management orders. People typically follow orders because they perceive positive benefit to themselves, but they do have a choice. Managers should treat employees properly because their acceptance of authority may be critical to organization success in important situations.[41]

The overall classical perspective as an approach to management was very powerful and gave companies fundamental new skills for establishing high productivity and effective treatment of employees.

Humanistic Perspective

Mary Parker Follett and Chester Barnard were early advocates of a more **humanistic perspective** on management that emphasized the importance of understanding human behaviors, needs, and attitudes in the workplace as well as social interactions and group processes.[42] We will discuss three subfields based on the humanistic perspective: the human relations movement, the human resources viewpoint, and the behavioral sciences approach.

Human resources perspective A management perspective that suggests jobs should be designed to meet higher-level needs by allowing workers to use their full potential.

The Human Relations Movement

America has always espoused the spirit of human equality. However, this spirit has not always been translated into practice when it comes to power sharing between managers and workers. The human relations school of thought considers that truly effective control comes from within the individual worker rather than from strict, authoritarian control.[43] This school of thought recognized and directly responded to social pressures for enlightened treatment of employees. The early work on industrial psychology and personnel selection received little attention because of the prominence of scientific management. Then a series of studies at a Chicago electric company, which came to be known as the **Hawthorne studies,** changed all that.

From a historical perspective, whether the studies were academically sound is of less importance than the fact that they stimulated an increased interest in looking at employees as more than extensions of production machinery. The interpretation that employees' output increased when managers treated them in a positive manner started a revolution in worker treatment for improving organizational productivity. Despite flawed methodology or inaccurate conclusions, the findings provided the impetus for the **human relations movement.** This approach shaped management theory and practice for well over a quarter-century, and the belief that human relations is the best approach for increasing productivity persists today. It also emphasized satisfaction of employees' basic needs as the key to increased worker productivity.

The Human Resources Viewpoint

The human relations movement initially espoused a "dairy farm" view of management—contented cows give more milk, so satisfied workers will give more work. Gradually, views with deeper content began to emerge. The human resources viewpoint maintained an interest in worker participation and considerate leadership but shifted the emphasis to consider the daily tasks that people perform. The **human resources viewpoint** combines prescriptions for design of job tasks with theories of motivation.[44] It says jobs should be designed so that tasks are not perceived as dehumanizing or demeaning but instead allow workers to use their full potential. Three of the best-known contributors to the human resources viewpoint were Abraham Maslow, Douglas McGregor, and William Ouchi. Other related viewpoints include Theory T and T+.

Abraham Maslow (1908–1970), a practicing psychologist, observed that his patients' problems usually stemmed from an inability to satisfy their needs. Thus, he generalized his work and suggested a hierarchy of needs. Maslow's hierarchy started with physiological needs and progressed to safety, belongingness, esteem, and, finally, self-actualization needs.

Douglas McGregor (1906–1964) had become frustrated with the early simplistic human relations notions while president of Antioch College in Ohio. He challenged both the classical perspective and the early human relations assumptions about human behavior. Based on his experiences as a manager and consultant, his training as a psychologist, and the work of Maslow, McGregor formulated his Theory X and Theory Y.[45] McGregor believed that the classical perspective was based on Theory X assumptions about workers. He also felt that a slightly modified version of Theory X fit early human relations ideas. In other words, human relations ideas did not go far enough. McGregor proposed Theory Y as a more realistic view of workers for guiding management thinking.

> **Theory X versus Theory Y** Both theories are based on contrasting assumptions about people, each of which is based on the manager's view of human nature. Theory X managers take a negative view and assume that most employees do not like work and try to avoid it. Theory Y managers take a positive view and believe that employees want to work, will seek and accept responsibility, and can offer creative solutions to organizational problems.

The point of Theory Y is that organizations can take advantage of the imagination and intellect of all their employees. Employees will exercise self-control and will contribute to organizational goals when given the opportunity. A few companies today still use Theory X management, but many are trying Theory Y techniques.

Coined by William G. Ouchi, Theory Z refers to a Japanese style of management that is characterized by long-term employment, slow promotions, considerable job rotation, consensus-style decision making, and concern for the employee as a whole.

Theory T and T+ are complementary theories based on Southeast Asian assumptions that work is a necessity but not a goal itself, people should find their rightful place in peace and harmony with their environment; absolute objectives exist only with God; in the world, persons in authority positions represent God; so their objectives should be followed; and people behave as members of a family and/or group, and those who do not are rejected by society.

The Behavioral Sciences Approach

> **Behavioral sciences approach** A subfield of the humanistic management perspective that applies social science in an organizational context, drawing from economics, psychology, sociology, and other disciplines.

The **behavioral sciences approach** develops theories about human behavior based on scientific methods and study. Behavioral science draws from sociology, psychology, anthropology, economics, and other disciplines to understand employee behavior and interaction in an organizational setting. The approach can be seen in practically every organization.

One specific set of management techniques based in the behavioral sciences approach is *organization development (OD)*. In the 1970s, organization development evolved as a separate field that applied the behavioral sciences to improve the organization's health and effectiveness through its ability to cope with change, improve internal relationships, and increase problem-solving capabilities.[46] The techniques and concepts of organization development have since been broadened and expanded to cope with the increasing complexity of organizations and the environment, and OD is still a vital approach for managers. Other concepts that grew out of the behavioral sciences approach include matrix organizations, self-managed teams, ideas about corporate culture, and management by wandering around. Indeed, the behavioral sciences approach has influenced the majority of tools, techniques, and approaches managers have applied to organizations since the 1970s. In recent years, behavioral sciences and OD techniques have been applied to help managers build learning organizations.

Management Science Perspective

> **Management science perspective** A management perspective that emerged after World War II and applied mathematics, statistics, and other quantitative techniques to managerial problems.

World War II caused many management changes. The massive and complicated problems associated with modern global warfare presented managerial decision-makers with the need for more sophisticated tools than ever before. The **management science perspective** emerged to address those problems. This view is distinguished for its application of mathematics, statistics, and other quantitative techniques to management decision making and problem solving.

Operations research consists of mathematical model building and other applications of quantitative techniques to managerial problems.

Operations management refers to the field of management that specializes in the physical production of goods or services. Operations management specialists use quantitative techniques to solve manufacturing problems. Some of the commonly used methods are forecasting, inventory modeling, linear and nonlinear programming, queuing theory, scheduling, simulation, and break-even analysis.

Information technology (IT) is the most recent subfield of the management science perspective, which is often reflected in management information systems. These systems are designed to provide relevant information to managers in a timely and cost-efficient manner. More recently, information technology within organizations has evolved to include intranets and extranets, as well as various software programs that help managers estimate costs, plan and track production, manage projects, allocate resources, or schedule employees.

Recent Historical Trends

Management is by nature complex and dynamic. Elements of each of the perspectives we have discussed are still in use today. The most prevalent is the humanistic perspective, but even it has been undergoing change in recent years. Three recent trends that grew out of the humanistic perspective are systems theory, the contingency view, and total quality management; the latter is discussed in Module 400.

Systems Theory

A **system** is a set of interrelated parts that function as a whole to achieve a common purpose.[47] A system functions by acquiring inputs from the external environment, transforming them in some way, and discharging outputs back to the environment. The basic **systems theory** of organizations includes five components: inputs, a transformation process, outputs, feedback, and the environment. *Inputs* are the material, human, financial, or information resources used to produce goods or services. The *transformation process* is management's use of production technology to change the inputs into outputs. *Outputs* include the organization's products and services. *Feedback* is knowledge of the results that influence the selection of inputs during the next cycle of the process. The *environment* surrounding the organization includes the social, political, and economic forces noted earlier in this section.

Some ideas in systems theory have had substantial impact on management thinking. These include open and closed systems, entropy, synergy, and subsystem interdependencies.[48]

Open systems must interact with the environment to survive; **closed systems** need not. In the classical and management science perspectives, organizations were frequently thought of as closed systems. In the management science perspective, closed system assumptions—the absence of external disturbances—are sometimes used to simplify problems for quantitative analysis. In reality, however, all organizations are open systems, and the cost of ignoring the environment may be failure.

> **Open system** A system that interacts with the external environment.
>
> **Closed system** A system that does not interact with the external environment.

Entropy is a universal property of systems and refers to their tendency to run down and die. If a system does not receive fresh inputs and energy from its environment, it will eventually cease to exist. Organizations must monitor their environments, adjust to changes, and continuously bring in new inputs in order to survive and prosper. Managers try to design the organization/environment interfaces to reduce entropy.

Synergy means that the whole is greater than the sum of its parts. When an organization is formed, something new comes into the world. Management, coordination, and production that did not exist before are now present. Organizational units working together can accomplish more than those same units working alone. The sales department depends on production, and vice versa.

Subsystems are parts of a system that depend on one another. Changes in one part of the organization affect other parts. The organization must be managed as a coordinated whole. Managers who understand subsystem interdependence are reluctant to make changes that do not recognize subsystem impact on the organization as a whole.

Contingency View

A second contemporary extension to management thinking is the contingency view. The classical perspective assumed a *universalist view*. Management concepts were thought to be universal; that is, whatever worked—leader style, bureaucratic structure—in one organization would work in another. In business education, however, an alternative view exists. This is the *case* view, in which each situation is believed to be unique. There are no universal principles to be found, and one learns about management by experiencing a large number of case problem situations. Managers face the task of determining what methods will work in every new situation.

To integrate these views the **contingency view** has emerged. Here neither of the other views is seen as entirely correct. Instead, certain contingencies, or variables, exist for helping management identify and understand situations. The contingency view means that a manager's response depends on identifying key contingencies in an organizational situation. For example, a consultant might mistakenly recommend the same *management-by-objectives (MBO)* system for a manufacturing firm that was successful in a school system. The contingency view

> **Contingency view** An extension of the humanistic perspective in which the successful resolution of organizational problems is thought to depend on managers' identification of key variations in the situation at hand.

tells us that what works in one setting might not work in another. Management's job is to search for important contingencies. When managers learn to identify important patterns and characteristics of their organizations, they can then fit solutions to those characteristics.

Important contingencies that managers must understand include industry, technology, the environment, and international cultures. Management practice in a rapidly changing industry, for example, will be very different from that in a stable one.

Current Directions in Management Thinking

All of the ideas and approaches discussed so far in this section go into the mix that makes up current management. However, the world has changed dramatically over the past decade or so, and organizations are experimenting with new ways of managing that more adequately respond to the demands of today's environment and customers. Two current directions in management thinking are the shift to a learning organization and managing the technology-driven workplace.

The Learning Organization

The **learning organization** can be defined as one in which everyone is engaged in identifying and solving problems, enabling the organization to continuously experiment, change, and improve, thus increasing its capacity to grow, learn, and achieve its purpose. The essential idea is problem solving, in contrast to the traditional organization designed for efficiency. In the learning organization all employees look for problems, such as understanding special customer needs. Employees also solve problems, which means putting things together in unique ways to meet a customer's needs.

To develop a learning organization, managers make changes in all the subsystems of the organization. Three important adjustments to promote continuous learning are shifting to a team-based structure, empowering employees, and sharing information.

Managing the Technology-Driven Workplace

The shift to the learning organization goes hand-in-hand with the current transition to a technology-driven workplace. Today's organizations cannot be managed and controlled in the same way organizations were managed 100 years ago—or perhaps even 20 years ago.

In addition to employees being connected electronically, organizations are becoming enmeshed in electronic networks. The world of e-business is booming as more and more business takes place by digital processes over a computer network rather than in physical space. **E-business** refers to the work an organization does by using electronic linkages (including the Internet) with customers, partners, suppliers, employees, or other key constituents. For example, organizations that use the Internet or other electronic linkages to communicate with employees or customers are engaged in e-business. A company might set up an **intranet,** an internal communications system that uses the technology and standards of the Internet but is accessible only to people within the company. The intranet looks and acts like a Web site, but it is cordoned off from the public with the use of software programs known as *firewalls.*[49] Some companies extend the communication system's function with an **extranet,** which gives access to key suppliers, partners, customers, or others outside the organization.

E-commerce is a narrower term referring specifically to business exchanges or transactions that occur electronically. E-commerce replaces or enhances the exchange of money and products with the exchange of data and information from one computer to another. Three types of e-commerce include business-to-consumer, business-to-business, and consumer-to-consumer.

New electronic technologies also shape the organization itself and how it is managed. Technology provides the architecture that supports and reinforces the new workplace. For example, one approach to information management is **enterprise resource planning** (ERP) systems, which unite all of a company's major business functions, such as order processing, product design, purchasing, inventory, manufacturing, distribution, human resources, receipt of payments, and forecasting of future demand. Because ERP weaves together all of the company's systems, managers anywhere in the organization can see the big picture and act quickly, based on up-to-the-minute information.[50] ERP prompts a new approach to management—a companywide management system in which everyone, from the CEO down to a machine operator on the factory floor, has instant access to critical information. Thus, ERP also supports management attempts to harness and leverage organizational *knowledge.*

Peter Drucker coined the term *knowledge work* more than 40 years ago,[51] but it is only in recent years that managers have genuinely recognized knowledge as an important organizational resource that should be managed just as they manage cash flow or raw materials. **Knowledge management** refers to the efforts to systematically find, organize, and make available a company's intellectual capital and to foster a culture of continuous learning and knowledge sharing so that a company's activities build on what is already known.[52] Information technology plays an important role by enabling the storage and dissemination of data and information across the organization, but technology is only one part of a larger management system.[53] A complete knowledge management system includes not only the technology for capturing and storing knowledge for easy access, but also new management values that support risk-taking, learning, and collaboration. Rather than seeing employees as factors of production and looking for ways to use human and material resources for greatest efficiency, today's most successful managers cherish people for their ability to think, create, share knowledge, and build relationships.

Functions of Management

The Definition of Management

Management is the attainment of organizational goals in an effective and efficient manner through planning, organizing, leading, and controlling organizational resources. There are two important ideas in this definition: (1) the four functions of planning, organizing, leading, and controlling and (2) the attainment of organizational goals in an effective and efficient manner. Managers use a multitude of skills to perform these functions. Management's conceptual, human, and technical skills are discussed later in the section. Exhibit 100.4 illustrates the process of how managers use resources to attain organizational goals.

Although some management theorists identify additional management functions, such as staffing, communicating, or decision making, those additional functions will be discussed as subsets of the four primary functions in Exhibit 100.4.

The Four Management Functions

Planning

Planning defines where the organization wants to be in the future and how to get there. **Planning** means defining goals for future organizational performance and deciding on the tasks and use of resources needed to attain them. A lack of planning—or poor planning—can hurt an organization's performance.

Exhibit 100.4 *The Process of Management*

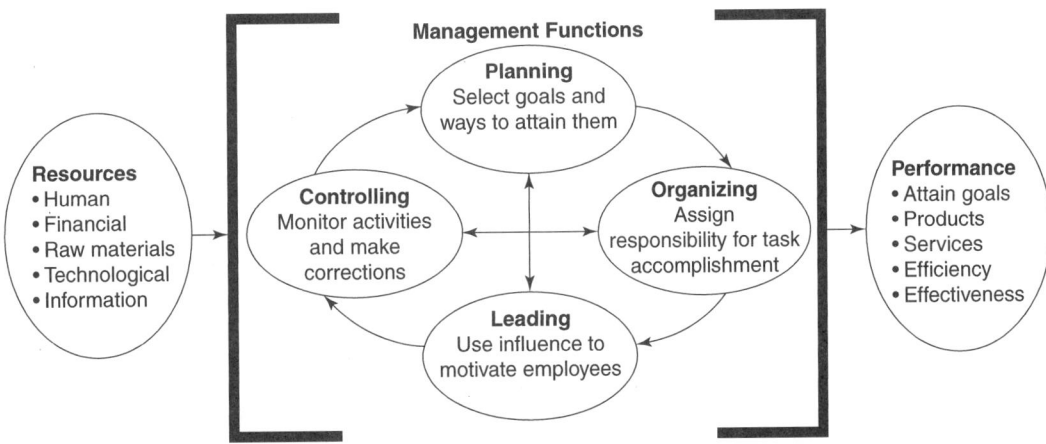

One of the primary responsibilities of managers is to decide where the organization should go in the future and how to get it there. But how do managers plan for the future in an uncertain and constantly changing environment?

In some organizations, typically small ones, planning is informal. In others, managers follow a well-defined planning framework. The company establishes a basic mission and develops formal goals and strategic plans for carrying it out. Many companies also develop *contingency plans* for unexpected circumstances and disaster recovery plans for what the organization would do in the event of a major disaster such as a hurricane, earthquake, or other crisis.

Of the four management functions—planning, organizing, leading, and controlling—planning is considered the most fundamental. Everything else stems from planning. Yet planning also is the most controversial management function. Planning cannot read an uncertain future. Planning cannot tame a turbulent environment.

In this section, we will explore the process of planning and consider how managers develop effective plans that can grow and change to meet new conditions. Special attention is given to goal setting, for that is where planning starts. Then, the various types of plans that managers use to help the organization achieve those goals are discussed, with special attention paid to crisis management planning. Finally, we will examine new approaches to planning that emphasize the involvement of employees, customers, partners, and other stakeholders in strategic thinking and execution.

Goal *A desired future state that the organization attempts to realize.*

Plan *A blueprint specifying the resource allocations, schedules, and other actions necessary for attaining goals.*

OVERVIEW OF GOALS AND PLANS Goals and plans have become general concepts in our society. A **goal** is a desired future state that the organization attempts to realize.[54] Goals are important because organizations exist for a purpose and goals define and state that purpose. A **plan** is a blueprint for goal achievement and specifies the necessary resource allocations, schedules, tasks, and other actions. Goals specify future ends; plans specify today's means. The word *planning* usually incorporates both ideas; it means determining the organization's goals and defining the means for achieving them.[55]

Exhibit 100.5 illustrates the levels of goals and plans in an organization. The planning process starts with a formal mission that defines the basic purpose of the organization, especially for external audiences. The mission is the basis for the strategic (company) level of goals and plans, which in turn shapes the tactical (divisional) level and the operational (departmental) level.[56] Top managers are typically responsible for establishing *strategic* goals and plans that reflect a commitment to both organizational efficiency and effectiveness. *Tactical* goals and plans are the responsibility of middle managers, such as the heads of major divisions or functional units. A division manager will formulate tactical plans that focus on the major actions the division must take to fulfill its part in the strategic plan set by top management. *Operational* plans identify the specific procedures or processes needed at lower levels of the organization, such as individual departments and employees. Front-line managers and supervisors develop operational plans that focus on specific tasks and processes and that help to meet tactical and strategic goals. Planning at each level supports the other levels.

Exhibit 100.5 *Levels of Goals/Plans and Their Importance*

PURPOSES OF GOALS AND PLANS The complexity of today's environment and uncertainty about the future overwhelm many managers and lead them to focus on operational issues and short-term results rather than long-term goals and plans. However, planning generally positively affects a company's performance.[57] In addition to improving financial and operational performance, developing explicit goals and plans at each level illustrated in Exhibit 100.5 is important because of the external and internal messages they send. These messages go to both external and internal audiences and provide important benefits for the organization:[58]

- *Legitimacy.* An organization's mission describes what the organization stands for and its reason for existence. It symbolizes legitimacy to external audiences such as investors, customers, and suppliers. The mission helps them and the local community look on the company in a favorable light and, hence, accept its existence. A strong mission also has an impact on employees, enabling them to become committed to the organization because they can identify with its overall purpose and reason for existence.
- *Source of Motivation and Commitment.* Goals and plans facilitate employees' identification with the organization and help motivate them by reducing uncertainty and clarifying what they should accomplish. Lack of a clear goal can damage employee motivation and commitment. With the new goal statement as a guide, employee commitment and motivation gradually improved, and the company became profitable again within three months.[59] Whereas a goal provides the "why" of an organization or subunit's existence, a plan tells the "how." A plan lets employees know what actions to undertake to achieve the goal.
- *Guides to Action.* Goals and plans provide a sense of direction. They focus attention on specific targets and direct employee efforts toward important outcomes.
- *Rationale for Decisions.* Through goal setting and planning, managers learn what the organization is trying to accomplish. They can make decisions to ensure that internal policies, roles, performance, structure, products, and expenditures will be made in accordance with desired outcomes. Decisions throughout the organization will be in alignment with the plan.
- *Standard of Performance.* Because goals define desired outcomes for the organization, they also serve as performance criteria. They provide a standard of assessment. If an organization wishes to grow by 15 percent, and actual growth is 17 percent, managers will have exceeded their prescribed standard.

The overall planning process prevents managers from thinking merely in terms of day-to-day activities. When organizations drift away from goals and plans, they typically get into trouble.

PLANNING TYPES AND PERFORMANCE The purpose of planning and goal setting is to help the organization achieve high performance. Managers use strategic, tactical, and operational goals to direct employees and resources toward achieving specific outcomes that enable the organization to perform efficiently and effectively. Overall organizational performance depends on achieving outcomes identified by the planning process. Managers use a number of planning approaches to focus the organization toward high performance. Among the most popular are management by objectives, single-use plans, standing plans, and contingency (or scenario) plans.

MANAGEMENT BY OBJECTIVES Management by objectives (MBO) is a method whereby managers and employees define goals for every department, project, and person and use them to monitor subsequent performance.[60] A model of the essential steps of the MBO process is presented in Exhibit 100.6. Four major activities must occur in order for MBO to be successful:[61]

> *Management by objectives (MBO)* A method of management whereby managers and employees define goals for every department, project, and person and use them to monitor subsequent performance.

1. *Set goals.* This is the most difficult step in MBO. Setting goals involves employees at all levels and looks beyond day-to-day activities to answer the question "What are we trying to accomplish?" A good goal should be concrete and realistic, provide a specific target and time frame, and assign responsibility. Goals may be quantitative or qualitative, depending on whether outcomes are measurable. Quantitative goals are described in numerical terms, such as "Salesperson Jones will obtain 16 new accounts in December." Qualitative goals use statements such as "Marketing will reduce complaints by improving customer service next year." Goals should be jointly derived. Mutual agreement between employee and supervisor creates the strongest commitment to achieving goals. In the case of teams, all team members may participate in setting goals.
2. *Develop action plans.* An *action plan* defines the course of action needed to achieve the stated goals. Action plans are made for both individuals and departments.

110. FUNCTIONS OF MANAGEMENT

Exhibit 100.6 *Model of the MBO Process*

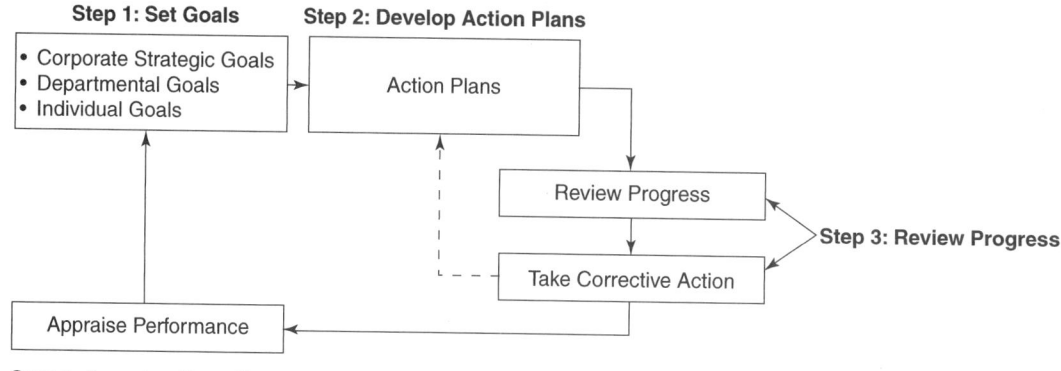

3. *Review progress.* A periodic progress review is important to ensure that action plans are working. These reviews can occur informally between managers and subordinates, where the organization may wish to conduct three-, six-, or nine-month reviews during the year. This periodic checkup allows managers and employees to see whether they are on target or whether corrective action is necessary. Managers and employees should not be locked into predefined behavior and must be willing to take whatever steps are necessary to produce meaningful results. The point of MBO is to achieve goals. The action plan can be changed whenever goals are not being met.

4. *Appraise overall performance.* The final step in MBO is to carefully evaluate whether annual goals have been achieved for both individuals and departments. Success or failure to achieve goals can become part of the performance appraisal system and the designation of salary increases and other rewards. The appraisal of departmental and overall corporate performance shapes goals for the next year. The MBO cycle repeats itself on an annual basis.

The specific application of MBO must fit the needs of each company. Many companies, such as **Intel, Tenneco, Black & Decker,** and **DuPont,** have adopted MBO, and most managers believe that MBO is an effective management tool.[62] Managers believe they are better oriented toward goal achievement when MBO is used. Like any system, MBO achieves benefits when used properly but results in problems when used improperly. Benefits and problems are summarized in Exhibit 100.7.

The benefits of the MBO process can be many. Corporate goals are more likely to be achieved when they focus on manager and employee efforts. Performance is improved because employees are committed to attaining the goal, are motivated because they help decide what is expected, and are free to be resourceful. Goals at lower levels are aligned with and enable the attainment of goals at top management levels.

Problems with MBO occur when the company faces rapid change. The environment and internal activities must have some stability for performance to be measured and compared against goals. When new goals must be set every few months, there is no time for action plans and appraisal to take effect. Also, poor employer-employee relations

Exhibit 100.7 *MBO Benefits and Problems*

Benefits of MBO	Problems with MBO
1. Manager and employee efforts are focused on activities that will lead to goal attainment.	1. Constant change prevents MBO from taking hold.
2. Performance can be improved at all company levels.	2. An environment of poor employer-employee relations reduces MBO effectiveness.
3. Employees are motivated.	3. Strategic goals may be displaced by operational goals.
4. Departmental and individual goals are aligned with company goals.	4. Mechanistic organizations and values that discourage participation can harm the MBO process.
	5. Too much paperwork saps MBO energy.

Exhibit 100.8 *Major Types of Single-Use and Standing Plans*

Single-Use Plans	Standing Plans
Program • Plans for attaining a one-time organizational goal • Major undertaking that may take several years to complete • Large in scope; may be associated with several projects Examples: Building a new headquarters 　　　　　Converting all paper files to digital	**Policy** • Broad in scope—a general guide to action • Based on organization's overall goals/strategic plan • Defines boundaries within which to make decisions Examples: Drug-free workplace policies 　　　　　Sexual harassment policies
Project • Also a set of plans for attaining a one-time goal • Smaller in scope and complexity than a program; shorter time horizon • Often one part of a larger program Examples: Renovating the office 　　　　　Setting up a company intranet	**Rule** • Narrow in scope • Describes how a specific action is to be performed • May apply to specific setting Example: No-smoking rule in areas of plant where hazardous materials are stored **Procedure** • Sometimes called a standard operating procedure • Defines a precise series of steps to attain certain goals Examples: Procedures for issuing refunds 　　　　　Procedures for handling employee grievances

reduce effectiveness because there is an element of distrust between managers and workers. Sometimes goal "displacement" occurs if employees focus exclusively on their operational goals to the detriment of other teams or departments. Overemphasis on operational goals can harm the attainment of overall goals. Another problem arises in mechanistic organizations characterized by rigidly defined tasks and rules that may not be compatible with MBO's emphasis on mutual determination of goals by employee and supervisor. In addition, when participation is discouraged, employees will lack the training and values to jointly set goals with employers. Finally, if MBO becomes a process of filling out annual paperwork rather than energizing employees to achieve goals, it becomes an empty exercise. Once the paperwork is completed, employees forget about the goals, perhaps even resenting the paperwork in the first place.

SINGLE-USE AND STANDING PLANS **Single-use plans** are developed to achieve a set of goals that are not likely to be repeated in the future. **Standing plans** are ongoing plans that are used to provide guidance for tasks performed repeatedly within the organization. Exhibit 100.8 outlines the major types of single-use and standing plans. Single-use plans typically include both programs and projects. The primary standing plans are organizational policies, rules, and procedures. Standing plans generally pertain to such matters as employee illness, absences, smoking, discipline, hiring, and dismissal. Many companies are discovering a need to develop standing plans regarding the use of e-mail.

CONTINGENCY PLANS When organizations are operating in a highly uncertain environment or dealing with long time horizons, sometimes planning can seem like a waste of time. In fact, strict plans may even hinder rather than help an organization's performance in the face of rapid technological, social, economic, or other environmental change. In these cases, managers can develop multiple future scenarios to help them form more flexible plans. **Contingency plans,** sometimes referred to as *scenarios,* define company responses to be taken in the case of emergencies, setbacks, or unexpected conditions. To develop contingency plans, managers identify uncontrollable factors, such as recession, inflation, technological developments or safety accidents. To minimize the impact of these potential factors, managers can forecast the worst-case scenarios. For example, if sales fall 20 percent and prices drop 8 percent, what will the company do? Managers can develop contingency plans that might include layoffs, emergency budgets, or new sales efforts.[63]

Contingency plans Plans that define company responses to specific situations, such as emergencies, setbacks, or unexpected conditions.

110. FUNCTIONS OF MANAGEMENT

Organizing

Organizing *The deployment of organizational resources to achieve strategic goals.*

Organizing typically follows planning and reflects how the organization tries to accomplish the plan. **Organizing** involves the assignment of tasks, the grouping of tasks into departments, and the assignment of authority and allocation of resources across the organization.

Every firm wrestles with the problem of how to organize. Reorganization often is necessary to reflect a new strategy, changing market conditions, or innovative technology. Today, many companies have found a need to make structural changes that are compatible with use of the Internet for e-business. A growing number of companies operate as network organizations, limiting themselves to a few core activities and letting outside specialists handle the rest. Others function as virtual organizations, groups of people or companies that come together for a specific purpose or project and then disband when the project is complete.

Each of these organizations is using fundamental concepts of organizing. **Organizing** is the deployment of organizational resources to achieve strategic goals. The deployment of resources is reflected in the organization's division of labor into specific departments and jobs, formal lines of authority, and mechanisms for coordinating diverse organization tasks.

Organizing is important because it follows from strategy. Strategy defines *what* to do; organizing defines *how* to do it. Organization structure is a tool that managers use to harness resources for getting things done. This section covers fundamental concepts that apply to all organizations and departments.

ORGANIZING THE VERTICAL STRUCTURE The organizing process leads to the creation of organization structure, which defines how tasks are divided and resources deployed. **Organization structure** is defined as (1) the set of formal tasks assigned to individuals and departments; (2) formal reporting relationships, including lines of authority, decision responsibility, number of hierarchical levels, and span of managers' control; and (3) the design of systems to ensure effective coordination of employees across departments.[64]

The set of formal tasks and formal reporting relationships provides a framework for vertical control of the organization. The characteristics of vertical structure are portrayed in the **organization chart,** which is the visual representation of an organization's structure.

WORK SPECIALIZATION Organizations perform a wide variety of tasks. A fundamental principle is that work can be performed more efficiently if employees are allowed to specialize.[65] **Work specialization,** sometimes called *division of labor,* is the degree to which organizational tasks are subdivided into separate jobs. Employees within each department perform only the tasks relevant to their specialized function. When work specialization is extensive, employees specialize in a single task. Jobs tend to be small, but they can be performed efficiently. Work specialization is readily visible on an automobile assembly line where each employee performs the same task over and over again. It would not be efficient to have a single employee build the entire automobile or even perform a large number of unrelated jobs.

Despite the apparent advantages of specialization, many organizations are moving away from this principle. With too much specialization, employees are isolated and do only a single, boring job. Many companies are enlarging jobs to provide greater challenges or assigning teams to tasks so that employees can rotate among the several jobs performed by the team.

Chain of command *An unbroken line of authority that links all individuals in the organization and specifies who reports to whom.*

CHAIN OF COMMAND The **chain of command** is an unbroken line of authority that links all persons in an organization and shows who reports to whom. It is associated with two underlying principles. *Unity of command* means that each employee is held accountable to only one supervisor. The *scalar principle* refers to a clearly defined line of authority in the organization that includes all employees. Authority and responsibility for different tasks should be distinct. All persons in the organization should know to whom they report as well as the successive management levels all the way to the top.

Authority, Responsibility, and Delegation The chain of command illustrates the authority structure of the organization. **Authority** is the formal and legitimate right of a manager to make decisions, issue orders, and allocate resources to achieve organizationally desired outcomes. Authority is distinguished by three characteristics:[66]

1. *Authority is vested in organizational positions, not people.* Managers have authority because of the positions they hold, and other people in the same positions would have the same authority.

2. *Authority is accepted by subordinates.* Although authority flows top down through the organization's hierarchy, subordinates comply because they believe that managers have a legitimate right to issue orders. The *acceptance theory of authority* argues that a manager has authority only if subordinates choose to accept his or her commands. If subordinates refuse to obey because the order is outside their zone of acceptance, a manager's authority disappears[67] For example, Richard Ferris, the former chairman of **United Airlines,** resigned because few people accepted his strategy of acquiring hotels, a car rental company, and other organizations to build a travel empire. When key people refused to accept his direction, his authority was lost, and he resigned.
3. *Authority flows down the vertical hierarchy.* Positions at the top of the hierarchy are vested with more formal authority than are positions at the bottom.

Responsibility is the flip side of the authority coin. **Responsibility** is the duty to perform the task or activity an employee has been assigned. Typically, managers are assigned authority commensurate with responsibility. When managers have responsibility for task outcomes but little authority, the job is possible but difficult. They rely on persuasion and luck. When managers have authority exceeding responsibility, they may become tyrants, using authority toward frivolous outcomes.[68]

Accountability is the mechanism through which authority and responsibility are brought into alignment. **Accountability** means that the people with authority and responsibility are subject to reporting and justifying task outcomes to those above them in the chain of command.[69] Subordinates must be aware that they are accountable for a task and accept the responsibility and authority for performing it. Accountability can be built into the organization structure. For example, at **Whirlpool,** incentive programs provide strict accountability. Performance of all managers is monitored, and bonus payments are tied to successful outcomes.

> **Accountability** The fact that the people with authority and responsibility are subject to reporting and justifying task outcomes to those above them in the chain of command.

Another concept related to authority is delegation.[70] **Delegation** is the process managers use to transfer authority and responsibility to positions below them in the hierarchy. Most organizations today encourage managers to delegate authority to the lowest possible level to provide maximum flexibility to meet customer needs and adapt to the environment. Managers are encouraged to delegate authority, although they often find it difficult.

Line and Staff Authority An important distinction in many organizations is between line authority and staff authority, reflecting whether managers work in line or staff departments in the organization's structure. *Line departments* perform tasks that reflect the organization's primary goal and mission. In a software company, line departments make and sell the product. In an Internet-based company, line departments would be those that develop and manage online offerings and sales. *Staff departments* include all those that provide specialized skills in support of line departments. Staff departments have an advisory relationship with line departments and typically include marketing, labor relations, research, accounting, and human resources.

Line authority means that people in management positions have formal authority to direct and control immediate subordinates. **Staff authority** is narrower and includes the right to advise, recommend, and counsel in the staff specialists' area of expertise. Staff authority is a communication relationship; staff specialists advise managers in technical areas. For example, the finance department of a manufacturing firm would have staff authority to coordinate with line departments about which accounting forms to use to facilitate equipment purchases and standardize payroll services.

SPAN OF MANAGEMENT The **span of management** is the number of employees reporting to a supervisor. Sometimes called the *span of control,* this characteristic of structure determines how closely a supervisor can monitor subordinates. Traditional views of organization design recommended a span of management of about seven subordinates per manager. However, many lean organizations today have spans of management as high as 30, 40, and even higher.

> **Span of management** The number of employees reporting to a supervisor; also called span of control.

Generally, when supervisors must be closely involved with subordinates, the span should be small, and when supervisors need little involvement with subordinates, it can be large. The following factors are associated with less supervisor involvement and thus larger spans of control:

1. Work performed by subordinates is stable and routine.
2. Subordinates perform similar work tasks.
3. Subordinates are concentrated in a single location.

110. FUNCTIONS OF MANAGEMENT

4. Subordinates are highly trained and need little direction in performing tasks.
5. Rules and procedures defining task activities are available.
6. Support systems and personnel are available for the manager.
7. Little time is required in nonsupervisory activities such as coordination with other departments or planning.
8. Managers' personal preferences and styles favor a large span.

The average span of control used in an organization determines whether the structure is tall or flat. A **tall structure** has an overall narrow span and more hierarchical levels. A **flat structure** has a wide span, is horizontally dispersed, and has fewer hierarchical levels. The trend in recent years has been toward wider spans of control as a way to facilitate delegation.[71]

Centralization *The location of decision authority near top organizational levels.*

Decentralization *The location of decision authority near lower organizational levels.*

CENTRALIZATION AND DECENTRALIZATION Centralization and decentralization pertain to the hierarchical level at which decisions are made. **Centralization** means that decision authority is located near the top of the organization. With **decentralization,** decision authority is pushed downward to lower organization levels. Organizations may have to experiment to find the correct hierarchical level at which to make decisions.

In the United States and Canada, the trend over the past 30 years has been toward greater decentralization of organizations. Decentralization is believed to relieve the burden on top managers, make greater use of workers' skills and abilities, ensure that decisions are made close to the action by well-informed people, and permit more rapid response to external changes.

However, this trend does not mean that every organization should decentralize all decisions. Managers should diagnose the organizational situation and select the decision-making level that will best meet the organization's needs. Factors that typically influence centralization versus decentralization are as follows:

1. Greater change and uncertainty in the environment are usually associated with decentralization. Today, most companies feel greater uncertainty because of intense global competition; hence, many have decentralized.
2. The amount of centralization or decentralization should fit the firm's strategy. For example, **Johnson & Johnson** gives almost complete authority to its 180 operating companies to develop and market their own products. Decentralization fits the corporate strategy of empowerment that gets each division close to customers so it can speedily adapt to their needs.[72]
3. In times of crisis or risk of company failure, authority may be centralized at the top. When Honda could not get agreement among divisions about new car models, President Nobuhiko Kawamoto made the decision himself.[73]

FORMALIZATION **Formalization** is the written documentation used to direct and control employees. Written documentation includes rulebooks, policies, procedures, job descriptions, and regulations. These documents complement the organization chart by providing descriptions of tasks, responsibilities, and decision authority. The use of rules, regulations, and written records of decisions is part of the bureaucratic model of organizations. As proposed by Max Weber, the bureaucratic model defines the basic organizational characteristics that enable the organization to operate in a logical and rational manner.

Although written documentation is intended to be rational and helpful to the organization, it often creates "red tape" that causes more problems than it solves. Some U.S. government departments are notorious for bureaucratic inefficiency.

As a practical matter, many organizations are reducing formalization and bureaucracy. Narrowly defined job descriptions, for example, tend to limit the creativity, flexibility, and rapid response needed in today's knowledge-based organizations.

Leading

Providing leadership is becoming an increasingly important management function. **Leading** is the use of influence to motivate employees to achieve organizational goals. Leading means creating a shared culture and values, communicating goals to employees throughout the organization, and infusing employees with the desire to perform at a high level. Leading involves motivating entire departments and divisions as well as those individuals working immediately with the manager. In an era of uncertainty, international competition, and a growing diversity of the workforce, the ability to shape culture, communicate goals, and motivate employees is critical to business success.

One doesn't have to be a well-known top manager to be an exceptional leader. There are many managers working quietly who also provide strong leadership within departments, teams, not-for-profit organizations, and small businesses.

THE NATURE OF LEADERSHIP There is probably no topic more important to business success today than leadership. The concept of leadership continues to evolve as the needs of organization change. Among all the ideas and writings about leadership, three aspects stand out—people, influence, and goals. Leadership occurs among people, involves the use of influence, and is used to attain goals.[74] *Influence* means that the relationship among people is not passive. Moreover, influence is designed to achieve some end or goal. Thus, **leadership** as defined here is the ability to influence people toward the attainment of goals. This definition captures the idea that leaders are involved with other people in the achievement of goals.

Leadership is reciprocal, occurring *among* people.[75] Leadership is a "people" activity, distinct from administrative paper shuffling or problem-solving activities. Leadership is dynamic and involves the use of power.

LEADERSHIP VERSUS MANAGEMENT Much has been written in recent years about the leadership role of managers. Management and leadership are both important to organizations. Effective managers have to be leaders, too, because there are distinctive qualities associated with management and leadership that provide different strengths for the organization; some of leaders qualities include visionary, inspiring, innovative, and imaginative. Some manager qualities include problem solving, analytical, authoritative, and stabilizing. Management and leadership reflect two different sets of qualities and skills that frequently overlap within a single individual. A person might have more of one set of qualities than the other, but ideally a manager develops a balance of both manager and leader qualities.

One of the major differences between manager and leader qualities relates to the source of power and the level of compliance it engenders within followers. **Power** is the potential ability to influence the behavior of others.[76] Management power comes from the individual's position in the organization. Because manager power comes from organizational structure, it promotes stability, order, and problem solving within the structure. Leadership power, on the other hand, comes from personal sources that are not as invested in the organization, such as personal interests, goals, and values. Leadership power promotes vision, creativity, and change in the organization.

Within organizations, there are typically five sources of power: legitimate, reward, coercive, expert, and referent.[77] Sometimes power comes from a person's position in the organization, while other sources of power are based on personal characteristics.

POSITION POWER The traditional manager's power comes from the organization. The manager's position gives him or her the power to reward or punish subordinates in order to influence their behavior. Legitimate power, reward power, and coercive power are all forms of position power used by managers to change employee behavior.

Legitimate Power Power coming from a formal management position in an organization and the authority granted to it is called **legitimate power.** For example, once a person has been selected as a supervisor, most workers understand that they are obligated to follow his or her direction with respect to work activities. Subordinates accept this source of power as legitimate, which is why they comply.

Reward Power Another kind of power, **reward power,** stems from the authority to bestow rewards on other people. Managers may have access to formal rewards, such as pay increases or promotions. They also have at their disposal such rewards as praise, attention, and recognition. Managers can use rewards to influence subordinates' behavior.

Coercive Power The opposite of reward power is **coercive power:** It refers to the authority to punish or recommend punishment. Managers have coercive power when they have the right to fire or demote employees, criticize, or withdraw pay increases. For example, if Paul, a salesman, does not perform as expected, his supervisor has the coercive power to criticize him, reprimand him, put a negative letter in his file, and hurt his chance for a raise.

> **Legitimate power** Power that stems from a formal management position in an organization and the authority granted to it.
>
> **Reward power** Power that results from the authority to bestow rewards on other people.
>
> **Coercive power** Power that stems from the authority to punish or recommend punishment.

Different types of position power elicit different responses in followers.[78] Legitimate power and reward power are most likely to generate follower compliance. *Compliance* means that workers will obey orders and carry out instructions, although they may personally disagree with them and may not be enthusiastic. Coercive power most often generates resistance. *Resistance* means that workers will deliberately try to avoid carrying out instructions or will attempt to disobey orders.

110. FUNCTIONS OF MANAGEMENT

PERSONAL POWER In contrast to the external sources of position power, personal power most often comes from internal sources, such as a person's special knowledge or personality characteristics. Personal power is the tool of the leader. Subordinates follow a leader because of the respect, admiration, or caring they feel for the individual and his or her ideas. Personal power is becoming increasingly important as more businesses are run by teams of workers who are less tolerant of authoritarian management.[79] Two types of personal power are expert power and referent power.

Expert power Power that stems from special knowledge of or skill in the tasks performed by subordinates.

Referent power Power that results from characteristics that command subordinates' identification with, respect and admiration for, and desire to emulate the leader.

Expert Power Power resulting from a leader's special knowledge or skill regarding the tasks performed by followers is referred to as **expert power.** When the leader is a true expert, subordinates go along with recommendations because of his or her superior knowledge. Leaders at supervisory levels often have experience in the production process that gains them promotion. At top management levels, however, leaders may lack expert power because subordinates know more about technical details than they do.

Referent Power The last kind of power, **referent power,** comes from leader personality characteristics that command subordinates' identification, respect, and admiration so they wish to emulate the leader. When workers admire a supervisor because of the way she deals with them, the influence is based on referent power. Referent power depends on the leader's personal characteristics rather than on a formal title or position and is most visible in the area of charismatic leadership, which will be discussed later in this section.

The follower reaction most often generated by expert power and referent power is commitment. *Commitment* means that workers will share the leader's point of view and enthusiastically carry out instructions. Needless to say, commitment is preferred to compliance or resistance. It is particularly important when change is the desired outcome of a leader's instructions, because change carries risk or uncertainty. Commitment assists the follower in overcoming fear of change.

EMPOWERMENT A significant recent trend in corporate America is for top executives to *empower* lower employees. Fully 74 percent of executives in a survey claimed that they are more participatory, more concerned with consensus building, and more reliant on communication than on command compared with the past. Executives no longer hoard power.

Empowering employees works because total power in the organization seems to increase. Everyone has more say and hence contributes more to organizational goals. The goal of senior executives in many corporations today is not simply to wield power but also to give it away to people who can get jobs done.[80]

LEADERSHIP TRAITS Early efforts to understand leadership success focused on the leader's personal characteristics or traits. **Traits** are the distinguishing personal characteristics of a leader, such as intelligence, values, and appearance. The early research focused on leaders who had achieved a level of greatness and hence was referred to as the *great man* approach. The idea was relatively simple: Find out what made these people great, and select future leaders who already exhibited the same traits or could be trained to develop them. Generally, research found only a weak relationship between personal traits and leader success.[81]

In addition to personality traits, physical, social, and work-related characteristics of leaders have been studied.[82]

Autocratic leader A leader who tends to centralize authority and rely on legitimate, reward, and coercive power to manage subordinates.

Democratic leader A leader who delegates authority to others, encourages participation, and relies on expert and referent power to manage subordinates.

AUTOCRATIC VERSUS DEMOCRATIC LEADERS One way to approach leader characteristics is to examine autocratic and democratic leaders. An **autocratic leader** is one who tends to centralize authority and rely on legitimate, reward, and coercive power. A **democratic leader** delegates authority to others, encourages participation, and relies on expert and referent power to influence subordinates.

The first studies on these leadership characteristics were conducted at the University of Iowa by Kurt Lewin and his associates.[83] These studies compared autocratic and democratic leaders and produced some interesting findings. The groups with autocratic leaders performed highly so long as the leader was present to supervise them. However, group members were displeased with the close, autocratic style of leadership, and feelings of hostility frequently arose. The performance of groups who were assigned democratic leaders was almost as good, and these were characterized by positive feelings rather than hostility. In addition, under the democratic style of leadership, group members performed well even when the leader was absent and left the group on its own.[84] The participative techniques and majority rule decision making used by the democratic leader trained and involved group members such that they performed well with or without the leader present. These characteristics of democratic leadership explain why the empowerment of lower employees is a popular trend in companies today.

This early work suggested that leaders were either autocratic or democratic in their approach. However, further work by Tannenbaum and Schmidt indicated that leadership could be a continuum reflecting different amounts of employee participation.[85] Thus, one leader might be autocratic (boss centered), another democratic (subordinate centered), and a third a mix of the two styles.

Most leaders have favored styles that they tend to use most often. However, while switching from autocratic to democratic or vice versa is not easy, leaders may adjust their styles depending on the situation.

BEHAVIORAL APPROACHES The autocratic and democratic styles suggest that it is the "behavior" of the leader rather than a personality trait that determines leadership effectiveness. Perhaps any leader can adopt the correct behavior with appropriate training. The focus of research has shifted from leader personality traits toward the behaviors successful leaders display. Important research programs on leadership behavior were conducted at Ohio State University, the University of Michigan, and the University of Texas.

OHIO STATE STUDIES Researchers at Ohio State University surveyed leaders to study hundreds of dimensions of leader behavior.[86] They identified two major behaviors, called *consideration* and *initiating structure.*

Consideration is the extent to which the leader is mindful of subordinates, respects their ideas and feelings, and establishes mutual trust. Considerate leaders are friendly, provide open communication, develop teamwork, and are oriented toward their subordinates' welfare.

Initiating structure is the extent to which the leader is task oriented and directs subordinate work activities toward goal attainment. Leaders with this style typically give instructions, spend time planning, emphasize deadlines, and provide explicit schedules of work activities.

Consideration and initiating structure are independent of each other, which means that a leader with a high degree of consideration may be either high or low on initiating structure. A leader may have any of four styles: high initiating structure–low consideration, high initiating structure–high consideration, low initiating structure–low consideration, or low initiating structure–high consideration. The Ohio State research found that the high consideration–high initiating structure style achieved better performance and greater satisfaction than the other leader styles. However, new research has found that effective leaders may be high on consideration and low on initiating structure or low on consideration and high on initiating structure, depending on the situation. Thus, the "high-high" style is not always the best.[87]

MICHIGAN STUDIES Studies at the University of Michigan at about the same time took a different approach by comparing the behavior of effective and ineffective supervisors.[88] The most effective supervisors were those who focused on the subordinates' human needs in order to "build effective work groups with high performance goals." The Michigan researchers used the term *employee-centered leaders* for leaders who established high performance goals and displayed supportive behavior toward subordinates. The less effective leaders were called *job-centered leaders;* these tended to be less concerned with goal achievement and human needs in favor of meeting schedules, keeping costs low, and achieving production efficiency.

TEXAS STUDIES Blake and Mouton of the University of Texas proposed a two-dimensional leadership theory called **leadership grid** that builds on the work of the Ohio State and Michigan studies.[89] Each axis on the grid is a 9-point scale, with 1 meaning low concern and 9 high concern.

Team management (9,9) often is considered the most effective style and is recommended for managers because organization members work together to accomplish tasks. *Country club management* (1,9) occurs when primary emphasis is given to people rather than to work outputs. *Authority-compliance management* (9,1) occurs when efficiency in operations is the dominant orientation. *Middle-of-the-road management* (5,5) reflects a moderate amount of concern for both people and production. *Impoverished management* (1,1) means the absence of a management philosophy; managers exert little effort toward interpersonal relationships or work accomplishment.

CONTINGENCY APPROACHES Several models of leadership that explain the relationship between leadership styles and specific situations have been developed. These are termed **contingency approaches** and include the leadership

> *Leadership grid* A two-dimensional leadership theory that measures leader's concern for people and concern for production.

> *Contingency approach* A model of leadership that describes the relationship between leadership styles and specific organizational situations.

model developed by Fiedler and his associates, the situational theory of Hersey and Blanchard, the path-goal theory presented by Evans and House, and the substitutes-for-leadership concept.

FIEDLER'S CONTINGENCY THEORY An early, extensive effort to combine leadership style and organizational situation into a comprehensive theory of leadership was made by Fiedler and his associates.[90] The basic idea is simple: Match the leader's style with the situation most favorable for his or her success. By diagnosing leadership style and the organizational situation, the correct fit can be arranged.

Leadership Style The cornerstone of Fiedler's contingency theory is the extent to which the leader's style is relationship oriented or task oriented. A *relationship-oriented leader* is concerned with people, as in the consideration style described earlier. A *task-oriented leader* is primarily motivated by task accomplishment, which is similar to the initiating structure style described earlier.

Situation Leadership situations can be analyzed in terms of three elements: the quality of leader-member relationships, task structure, and position power.[91] Each of these elements can be described as either favorable or unfavorable for the leader.

Contingency Theory When Fiedler examined the relationships among leadership style, situational favorability, and group task performance, he found the pattern as follows. Task-oriented leaders are more effective when the situation is either highly favorable or highly unfavorable. Relationship-oriented leaders are more effective in situations of moderate favorability.

The task-oriented leader excels in the favorable situation because everyone gets along, the task is clear, and the leader has power; all that is needed is for someone to take charge and provide direction. Similarly, if the situation is highly unfavorable to the leader, a great deal of structure and task direction is needed. A strong leader defines task structure and can establish authority over subordinates. Because leader-member relations are poor anyway, a strong task orientation will make no difference in the leader's popularity.

The relationship-oriented leader performs better in situations of intermediate favorability because human relations skills are important in achieving high group performance. In these situations, the leader may be moderately well liked, have some power, and supervise jobs that contain some ambiguity. A leader with good interpersonal skills can create a positive group atmosphere that will improve relationships, clarify task structure, and establish position power.

A leader, then, needs to know two things in order to use Fiedler's contingency theory. First, the leader should know whether he or she has a relationship- or task-oriented style. Second, the leader should diagnose the situation and determine whether leader-member relations, task structure, and position power are favorable or unfavorable.

Fitting leader style to the situation can yield big dividends in profits and efficiency.[92] On the other hand, using an incorrect style for the situation can cause problems.

Situational theory A contingency approach to leadership that links the leader's behavioral style with the task readiness of subordinates.

HERSEY AND BLANCHARD'S SITUATIONAL THEORY The **situational theory** of leadership is an interesting extension of the behavioral theories. More than previous theories, Hersey and Blanchard's approach focuses a great deal of attention on the characteristics of employees in determining appropriate leadership behavior. The point of Hersey and Blanchard is that subordinates vary in readiness level. People low in task readiness, because of little ability or training, or insecurity, need a different leadership style than those who are high in readiness and have good ability, skills, confidence, and willingness to work.[93]

According to the situational theory, a leader can adopt one of four leadership styles, based on a combination of relationship (concern for people) and task (concern for production) behavior. The *telling style* reflects a high concern for production and a low concern for people. This is a very directive style. It involves giving explicit directions about how tasks should be accomplished. The *selling style* is based on a high concern for both people and production. With this approach, the leader explains decisions and gives subordinates a chance to ask questions and gain clarity and understanding about work tasks. The next leader behavior style, the *participating style,* is based on a combination of high concern for people and low concern for production. The leader shares ideas with subordinates, gives them a chance to participate, and facilitates decision-making. The fourth style, the *delegating style,* reflects a low concern for both people and production. This leader style provides little direction and little support because the leader turns over responsibility for decisions and their implementation to subordinates.

The essence of Hersey and Blanchard's situational theory is to select a leader style that is appropriate for the readiness level of subordinates—their degree of education and skills, experience, self-confidence, and work attitudes. Followers may be at low, moderate, high, or very high levels of readiness.

Low Readiness Level   A telling style is appropriate when followers are at a low readiness level because of poor ability and skills, little experience, insecurity, or unwillingness to take responsibility for their own task behavior. When one or more subordinates exhibit very low levels of readiness, the leader is very specific, telling followers exactly what to do, how to do it, and when.

Moderate Readiness Level   A selling style works best for followers with moderate levels of readiness. These subordinates, for example, might lack some education and experience for the job, but they demonstrate high confidence, ability, interest, and willingness to learn. The selling style involves giving direction, but it also includes seeking input from others and clarifying tasks rather than simply instructing that they be performed.

High Readiness Level   When subordinates demonstrate a high readiness level, a participating style is effective. These subordinates might have the necessary education, experience, and skills but might be insecure in their abilities and need some guidance from the leader. The participating style enables the leader to guide followers' development and act as a resource for advice and assistance.

Very High Readiness Level   When followers have very high levels of education, experience, and readiness to accept responsibility for their own task behavior, the delegating style can effectively be used. Because of the high readiness level of followers, the leader can delegate responsibility for decisions and their implementation to subordinates, who have the skills, abilities, and positive attitudes to follow through. The leader provides a general goal and sufficient authority to do the task as followers see fit.

In summary, the telling style is best suited for subordinates who demonstrate very low levels of readiness to take responsibility for their own task behavior, the selling and participating styles work for subordinates with moderate-to-high readiness, and the delegating style is appropriate for employees with very high readiness. This contingency model is easier to understand than Fiedler's model, but it incorporates only the characteristics of followers, not those of the situation. The leader carefully diagnoses the readiness level of followers and adopts whichever style is necessary—telling, selling, participating, or delegating.

PATH-GOAL THEORY   Another contingency approach to leadership is called the path-goal theory.[94] According to the **path-goal theory,** the leader's responsibility is to increase subordinates' motivation to attain personal and organizational goals. The leader increases their motivation by either (1) clarifying the subordinates' path to the rewards that are available or (2) increasing the rewards that the subordinates value and desire. Path clarification means that the leader works with subordinates to help them identify and learn the behaviors that will lead to successful task accomplishment and organizational rewards. Increasing rewards means that the leader talks with subordinates to learn which rewards are important to them—that is, whether they desire intrinsic rewards from the work itself or extrinsic rewards such as raises or promotions. The leader's job is to increase personal payoffs to subordinates for goal attainment and to make the paths to these payoffs clear and easy to travel.[95]

> *Path-goal theory*   *A contingency approach to leadership specifying that the leader's responsibility is to increase subordinates' motivation by clarifying the behaviors necessary for task accomplishment and rewards.*

This model is called a contingency theory because it consists of three sets of contingencies—leader behavior and style, situational contingencies, and the use of rewards to meet subordinates' needs.[96] Whereas in the Fiedler theory described earlier the assumption would be to switch leaders as situations change, in the path-goal theory leaders switch their behaviors to match the situation.

Leader Behavior   The path-goal theory suggests a fourfold classification of leader behaviors.[97] These classifications are the types of leader behavior the leader can adopt and include supportive, directive, achievement-oriented, and participative styles.

Supportive leadership involves leader behavior that shows concern for subordinates' well-being and personal needs. Leadership behavior is open, friendly, and approachable, and the leader creates a team climate and treats subordinates as equals. Supportive leadership is similar to the consideration leadership described earlier.

Directive leadership occurs when the leader tells subordinates exactly what they are supposed to do. Leader behavior includes planning, making schedules, setting performance goals and behavior standards, and stressing adherence to rules and regulations. Directive leadership behavior is similar to the initiating-structure leadership style described earlier.

Participative leadership means that the leader consults with his or her subordinates about decisions. Leader behavior includes asking for opinions and suggestions, encouraging participation in decision making, and meeting with subordinates in their workplaces. The participative leader encourages group discussion and written suggestions.

110. FUNCTIONS OF MANAGEMENT

Achievement-oriented leadership occurs when the leader sets clear and challenging goals for subordinates. Leader behavior stresses high-quality performance and improvement over current performance. Achievement-oriented leaders also show confidence in subordinates and assist them in learning how to achieve high goals.

The four types of leader behavior are not considered ingrained personality traits as in the Fiedler theory; rather, they reflect types of behavior that every leader is able to adopt, depending on the situation.

Situational Contingencies The two important situational contingencies in the path-goal theory are (1) the personal characteristics of group members and (2) the work environment. Personal characteristics of subordinates include such factors as ability, skills, needs, and motivations. For example, if employees have low ability or skill, the leader may need to provide additional training or coaching in order for workers to improve performance. If subordinates are self-centered, the leader must use rewards to motivate them. Subordinates who want clear direction and authority require a directive leader who will tell them exactly what to do. Craftworkers and professionals, however, may want more freedom and autonomy and work best under a participative leadership style.

The work environment contingencies include the degree of task structure, the nature of the formal authority system, and the work group itself. The task structure is similar to the same concept described in Fiedler's contingency theory; it includes the extent to which tasks are defined and have explicit job descriptions and work procedures. The formal authority system includes the amount of legitimate power used by managers and the extent to which policies and rules constrain employees' behavior. Workgroup characteristics are the educational level of subordinates and the quality of relationships among them.

Use Of Rewards Recall that the leader's responsibility is to clarify the path to rewards for subordinates or to increase the value of rewards to enhance satisfaction and job performance. In some situations, the leader works with subordinates to help them acquire the skills and confidence needed to perform tasks and achieve rewards already available. In others, the leader may develop new rewards to meet the specific needs of a subordinate.

SUBSTITUTES FOR LEADERSHIP The contingency leadership approaches considered so far have focused on the leaders' style, the subordinates' nature, and the situation's characteristics. The final contingency approach suggests that situational variables can be so powerful that they actually substitute for or neutralize the need for leadership.[98] This approach outlines those organizational settings in which a leadership style is unimportant or unnecessary.

Substitute *A situational variable that makes a leadership style unnecessary or redundant.*

Neutralizer *A situational variable that counteracts a leadership style and prevents the leader from displaying certain behaviors.*

Exhibit 100.9 shows the situational variables that tend to substitute for or neutralize leadership characteristics. A **substitute** for leadership makes the leadership style unnecessary or redundant. For example, highly professional subordinates who know how to do their tasks do not need a leader who initiates structure for them and tells them what to do. A **neutralizer** counteracts the leadership style and prevents the leader from displaying certain behaviors. For example, if a leader has absolutely no position power or is physically removed from subordinates, the leader's ability to give directions to subordinates is greatly reduced.

Exhibit 100.9 *Substitutes and Neutralizers for Leadership*

Situational Variables		Task-Oriented Leadership	People-Oriented Leadership
Organizational characteristics:	Group cohesiveness	Substitutes for	Substitutes for
	Formalization	Substitutes for	No effect on
	Inflexibility	Neutralizes	No effect on
	Low positional power	Neutralizes	Neutralizes
	Physical separation	Neutralizes	Neutralizes
Task characteristics:	Highly structured task	Substitutes for	No effect on
	Automatic feedback	Substitutes for	No effect on
	Intrinsic satisfaction	No effect on	Substitutes for
Group characteristics:	Professionalism	Substitutes for	Substitutes for
	Training/experience	Substitutes for	No effect on

Situational variables in Exhibit 100.9 include characteristics of the group, the task, and the organization itself. For example, when subordinates are highly professional and experienced, both leadership styles are less important. The employees do not need much direction or consideration. With respect to task characteristics, highly structured tasks substitute for a task-oriented style, and a satisfying task substitutes for a people-oriented style. With respect to the organization itself, group cohesiveness substitutes for both leader styles. Formalized rules and procedures substitute for leader task orientation. Physical separation of leader and subordinate neutralizes both leadership styles.

The value of the situations described in Exhibit 100.9 is that they help leaders avoid leadership overkill. Leaders should adopt a style with which to complement the organizational situation. For example, the work situation for bank tellers provides a high level of formalization, little flexibility, and a highly structured task. The head teller should not adopt a task-oriented style, because the organization already provides structure and direction. The head teller should concentrate on a people-oriented style. In other organizations, if group cohesiveness or previous training meet employees' social needs, the leader is free to concentrate on task-oriented behaviors. The leader can adopt a style complementary to the organizational situation to ensure that both task needs and people needs of the work group will be met.

CHANGE LEADERSHIP   We defined management to include the functions of leading, planning, organizing, and controlling. But recent work on leadership has begun to distinguish leadership as something more: a quality that inspires and motivates people beyond their normal levels of performance. Leadership is particularly important in companies trying to meet the challenges of a changing environment. Leaders in many organizations have had to reconceptualize almost every aspect of how they do business to meet the needs of increasingly demanding customers, keep employees motivated and satisfied, and remain competitive in a global, information-based business environment. Some are adopting e-business solutions and becoming learning organizations poised for constant change and adaptation.

Research has found that some leadership approaches are more effective than others for bringing about change in organizations. Two types of leadership that can have a substantial impact are charismatic and transformational. These types of leadership are best understood in comparison to *transactional leadership*.[99] **Transactional leaders** clarify the role and task requirements of subordinates, initiate structure, provide appropriate rewards, and try to be considerate to and meet the social needs of subordinates. The transactional leader's ability to satisfy subordinates may improve productivity. Transactional leaders excel at management functions. They are hardworking, tolerant, and fair-minded. They take pride in keeping things running smoothly and efficiently. Transactional leaders often stress the impersonal aspects of performance, such as plans, schedules, and budgets. They have a sense of commitment to the organization and conform to organizational norms and values. Transactional leadership is important to all organizations, but leading change requires a different approach.

> *Transactional leader*   A leader who clarifies subordinates' role and task requirements, initiates structure, provides rewards, and displays consideration for subordinates.

CHARISMATIC AND VISIONARY LEADERSHIP   Charismatic leadership goes beyond transactional leadership techniques. Charisma has been referred to as "a fire that ignites followers' energy and commitment, producing results above and beyond the call of duty."[100] The **charismatic leader** has the ability to inspire and motivate people to do more than they would normally do, despite obstacles and personal sacrifice. Followers transcend their own self-interests for the sake of the department or organization. The impact of charismatic leaders is normally from (1) stating a lofty vision of an imagined future that employees identify with, (2) shaping a corporate value system for which everyone stands, and (3) trusting subordinates and earning their complete trust in return.[101] Charismatic leaders tend to be less predictable than transactional leaders. They create an atmosphere of change, and they may be obsessed by visionary ideas that excite, stimulate, and drive other people to work hard.

> *Charismatic leader*   A leader who has the ability to motivate subordinates to transcend their expected performance.

Charismatic leaders are often skilled in the art of *visionary leadership*. Visionary leaders speak to the hearts of employees, letting them be part of something bigger than them. They see beyond current realities and help followers believe in a brighter future as well. A **vision** is an attractive, ideal future that is credible yet not readily attainable.

Charismatic leaders have a strong vision for the future and can motivate others to help realize it.[102] They have an emotional impact on subordinates because they strongly believe in the vision and can communicate it to others in a way that makes the vision real, personal, and meaningful to others.

Charisma can be used for positive outcomes that benefit the group, but it can also be used for self-serving purposes that lead to deception, manipulation, and exploitation of others. When charismatic leaders respond to organizational problems in terms of the needs of the entire group rather than their own emotional needs, they can have a powerful, positive influence on organizational performance.[103]

TRANSFORMATIONAL LEADERS **Transformational leaders** are similar to charismatic leaders, but are distinguished by their special ability to bring about innovation and change by recognizing followers' needs and concerns, helping them look at old problems in new ways, and encouraging them to question the status quo. Transformational leaders create significant change in both followers and the organization.[104] They have the ability to lead changes in the organization's mission, strategy, structure, and culture, as well as to promote innovation in products and technologies. Transformational leaders do not rely solely on tangible rules and incentives to control specific transactions with followers. They focus on intangible qualities such as vision, shared values, and ideas to build relationships, give larger meaning to diverse activities, and find common ground to enlist followers in the change process.[105]

> *Transformational leader* A leader distinguished by a special ability to bring about innovation and change.

LEADING THE NEW WORKPLACE The concept of leadership is also changing because of dramatic changes in today's environment and organizations. Globalization, e-commerce, virtual organizations and telecommuting, changes in employee interests and expectations, and increasing diversity have all contributed to a shift in how we think about and practice leadership. Four areas of particular interest for leadership in the new workplace are a new concept referred to as Level 5 leadership; women's ways of leading; virtual leadership; and servant leadership.

Level 5 Leadership Level 5 leadership refers to the highest level in a hierarchy of manager capabilities. A key characteristic of Level 5 leaders is an almost complete lack of ego. In contrast to the view of great leaders as "larger-than-life" personalities with strong egos and big ambitions, Level 5 leaders often seem shy and unpretentious. Although they accept full responsibility for mistakes, poor results, or failures, Level 5 leaders give credit for successes to other people.

Women's Ways of Leading The focus on minimizing personal ambition and developing others has also been found to be common among female leaders. Recent research indicates that women's style of leadership is particularly suited to today's organizations.[106] Using data from actual performance evaluations, one study found that when rated by peers, subordinates, and bosses, female managers score significantly higher than men on abilities such as motivating others, fostering communication, and listening.[107]

This approach has been called **interactive leadership**.[108] This means that the leader favors a consensual and collaborative process, and influence derives from relationships rather than position power and formal authority.

> *Interactive leadership* A leadership style characterized by values such as inclusion, collaboration, relationship building, and caring.

Virtual Leadership The virtual workplace, in which employees work remotely from each other and from leaders, is becoming more common in today's organizations, bringing new leadership challenges. In today's workplace, many people may work from home or other remote locations, wired to the office electronically. Sometimes people come together temporarily in virtual teams to complete a project and then disband. In a virtual environment, leaders face a constant tension in trying to balance structure and accountability with flexibility.[109] They have to provide enough structure and direction so that people have a clear understanding of what is required of them, but they also have to trust that virtual workers will perform their duties responsibly without close control and supervision. Effective virtual leaders set clear goals and timelines and are very explicit about how people will communicate and coordinate their work. However, the details of day-to-day activities are left up to employees. This doesn't mean, however, that virtual workers are left on their own. Leaders take extra care to keep people informed and involved with one another and with the organization.

People who excel as virtual leaders tend to be open-minded and flexible, exhibit positive attitudes that focus on solutions rather than problems, and have superb communication, coaching, and relationship-building skills.[110] Good virtual leaders never forget that work is accomplished through *people,* not technology. Although they must understand how to select and use technology appropriately, leaders emphasize human interactions as the key to success. Building trust, maintaining open lines of communication, caring about people, and being open to subtle cues from others are essential in a virtual environment.[111]

Servant Leadership In the new workplace, the best leaders operate from the assumption that work exists for the development of the worker as much as the worker exists to do the work.[112] Servant leadership, first described by Robert Greenleaf, is leadership upside down because leaders transcend self-interest to serve others and the organization.[113] **Servant leaders** operate on two levels: for the fulfillment of their subordinates' goals and needs and for the realization of the larger purpose or mission of their organization. Servant leaders give things away—power, ideas, in-

> *Servant leader* A leader who works to fulfill subordinates' needs and goals as well as to achieve the organization's larger mission.

formation, recognition, credit for accomplishments. They truly value other people, encourage participation, share power, enhance others' self-worth, and unleash people's creativity, full commitment, and natural impulse to learn. Servant leaders bring the follower's higher motives to the work and connect them to the organizational mission and goals.

Controlling

Controlling is the fourth function in the management process. **Controlling** means monitoring employees' activities, determining whether the organization is on target toward its goals, and making corrections as necessary. Managers must ensure that the organization is moving toward its goals. New trends toward empowerment and trust of employees have led many companies to place less emphasis on top-down control and more emphasis on training employees to monitor and correct themselves.

New information technology is also helping managers provide needed organizational control without strict top-down constraints. Companies may also use information technology to put *more* constraints on employees if managers believe the situation demands it. Organization failure can result when managers are not serious about control or lack control information.

Control is a critical issue facing every manager in every organization today. At some organizations, managers need to find new ways to cut costs, build morale, and increase productivity, or the organization will not survive. Other organizations face similar challenges, such as improving customer service, minimizing the time needed to resupply merchandise in retail stores, decreasing the number of steps needed to process an online merchandise order, or improving the tracking procedures for overnight package delivery. Control, including quality control, also involves office productivity, such as elimination of bottlenecks and reduction in paperwork mistakes. In addition, every organization needs basic systems for allocating financial resources, developing human resources, analyzing financial performance, and evaluating overall profitability.

THE MEANING OF CONTROL **Organizational control** is the systematic process of regulating organizational activities to make them consistent with the expectations established in plans, targets, and standards of performance. In a classic article on the control function, Douglas S. Sherwin summarizes this concept as follows: "The essence of control is action which adjusts operations to predetermined standards, and its basis is information in the hands of managers."[114] Thus, effectively controlling an organization requires information about performance standards and actual performance, as well as actions taken to correct any deviations from the standards. Managers need to decide what information is essential, how they will obtain that information (and share it with employees), and how they can and should respond to it. Having the correct data is essential. Managers have to decide which standards, measurements, and metrics are needed to effectively monitor and control the organization and set up systems for obtaining that information.

Organizational control The systematic process through which managers regulate organizational activities to make them consistent with expectations established in plans, targets, and standards of performance.

ORGANIZATIONAL CONTROL FOCUS Control can focus on events before, during, or after a process. For example, a local automobile dealer can focus on activities before, during, or after sales of new cars. Careful inspection of new cars and cautious selection of sales employees are ways to ensure high quality or profitable sales even before those sales take place. Monitoring how salespeople act with customers would be considered control during the sales task. Counting the number of new cars sold during the month or telephoning buyers about their satisfaction with sales transactions would constitute control after sales have occurred. These three types of control are formally called *feedforward*, *concurrent*, and *feedback* and are illustrated in Exhibit 100.10.

FEEDFORWARD CONTROL Control that attempts to identify and prevent deviations before they occur is called **feedforward control**. Sometimes called *preliminary* or *preventive control*, it focuses on human, material, and financial resources that flow into the organization. Its purpose is to ensure that input quality is high enough to prevent problems when the organization performs its tasks.

Feedforward controls are evident in the selection and hiring of new employees. Organizations attempt to improve the likelihood that employees will perform up to standards by identifying the necessary skills and using tests and other screening devices to hire people who have those skills. Many organizations also conduct drug screening to ensure that job candidates or employees do not impair their ability to work safely and effectively. Another type of feedforward control is to identify and manage risks. For example, banks typically require extensive documentation before approving major loans. Large accounting firms provide value to their clients by helping identify risks they have either knowingly or unknowingly taken on, rather than just evaluating financial performance after the fact.[115]

Exhibit 100.10 *Organizational Control Focus*

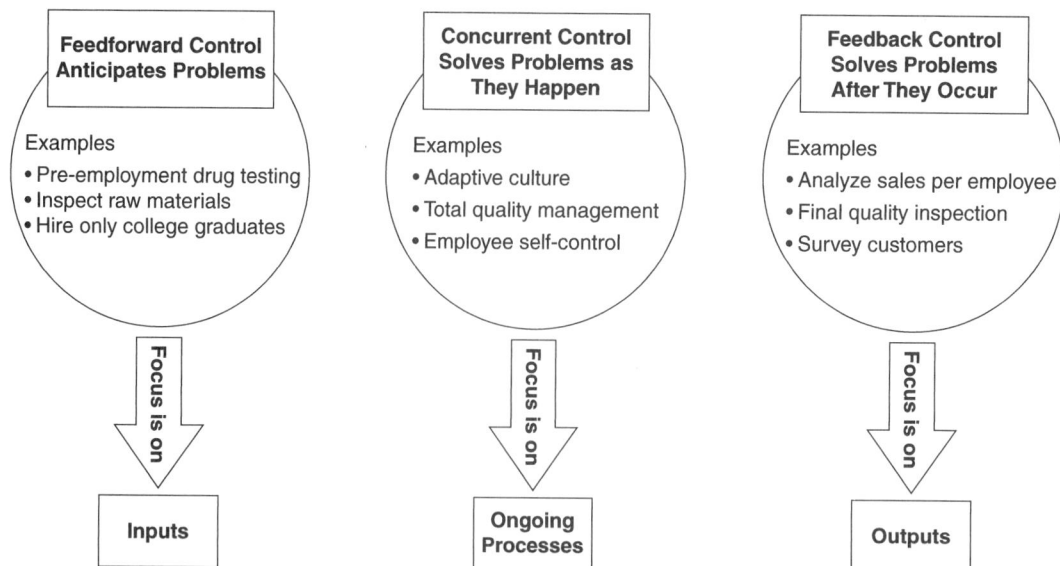

CONCURRENT CONTROL Control that monitors ongoing employee activities to ensure they are consistent with performance standards is called **concurrent control.** Concurrent control assesses current work activities, relies on performance standards, and includes rules and regulations for guiding employee tasks and behaviors.

Many manufacturing operations include devices that measure whether the items being produced meet quality standards. Employees monitor the measurements; if they see that standards are not met in some area, they make a correction themselves or signal the appropriate person that a problem is occurring. Technology advancements are adding to the possibilities for concurrent control in services as well. For example, retail stores such as **Beall's, Sunglass Hut,** and **Saks** use cash-register-management software to monitor cashiers' activities in real time and help prevent employee theft. Trucking companies like **Schneider National** and **Covenant** use computers to track the position of their trucks and monitor the status of deliveries.[116]

Other concurrent controls involve the ways in which organizations influence employees. An organization's cultural norms and values influence employee behavior, as do the norms of an employee's peers or work group. Concurrent control also includes self-control, through which individuals impose concurrent controls on their own behavior because of personal values and attitudes.

FEEDBACK CONTROL Sometimes called *postaction* or *output control,* **feedback control** focuses on the organization's outputs—in particular, the quality of an end product or service. An example of feedback control in a manufacturing department is an intensive final inspection of a refrigerator at a **General Electric** assembly plant. In Kentucky, school administrators conduct feedback control by evaluating each school's performance every other year. They review reports of students' test scores as well as the school's dropout and attendance rates. The state rewards schools with rising scores and brings in consultants to work with schools whose scores have fallen.[117]

Besides producing high-quality products and services, businesses need to earn a profit, and even nonprofit organizations need to operate efficiently to carry out their mission. Therefore, many feedback controls focus on financial measurements. Budgeting, for example, is a form of feedback control because managers monitor whether they have operated within their budget targets and make adjustments accordingly.

THE CHANGING PHILOSOPHY OF CONTROL Managers' approach to control is changing in many of today's organizations. In connection with the shift to employee participation and empowerment, many companies are adopting a *decentralized* rather than a *bureaucratic* control process. Bureaucratic control and decentralized control represent different philosophies of corporate culture. Most organizations display some aspects of both bureaucratic and decentralized control, but managers generally emphasize one or the other, depending on the organizational culture and their own beliefs about control.

Bureaucratic control involves monitoring and influencing employee behavior through extensive use of rules, policies, hierarchy of authority, written documentation, reward systems, and other formal mechanisms.[118] In contrast, **decentralized control** relies on cultural values, traditions, shared beliefs, and trust to foster compliance with organizational goals. Managers operate on the assumption that employees are trustworthy and willing to perform effectively without extensive rules and close supervision.

TOTAL QUALITY MANAGEMENT One popular approach based on a decentralized control philosophy is **total quality management (TQM),** an organizationwide effort to infuse quality into every activity in a company through continuous improvement. TQM is discussed fully in Module 400.

TRENDS IN QUALITY AND FINANCIAL CONTROL Many companies are responding to changing economic realities and global competition by reassessing organizational management and processes—including control mechanisms. Some of the major trends in quality and financial control include international quality standards, economic value-added and market value-added systems, and activity-based costing.

INTERNATIONAL QUALITY STANDARDS One impetus for total quality management in the United States is the increasing significance of the global economy. Many countries have endorsed a universal framework for quality assurance called **ISO 9000,** a set of international standards for quality management systems established by the International Organization for Standardization in 1987 and revised in late 2000.[119] Europe continues to lead in the total number of ISO 9000 certifications, but the greatest number of new certifications in recent years has been in the United States. ISO 9000 has become the recognized standard for evaluating and comparing companies on a global basis, and more U.S. companies are feeling the pressure to participate in order to remain competitive in international markets. In addition, many countries and companies require ISO 9000 certification before they will do business with an organization.

NEW FINANCIAL CONTROL SYSTEMS In addition to traditional financial tools, managers in many organizations are using systems such as economic value-added, market value-added, and activity-based costing to provide effective financial control.

Economic Value-Added (EVA) Hundreds of companies have set up **economic value-added** measurement systems as a new way to gauge financial performance. EVA can be defined as a company's net (after-tax) operating profit minus the cost of capital invested in the company's tangible assets.[120] Measuring performance in terms of EVA is intended to capture all the things a company can do to add value from its activities, such as run the business more efficiently, satisfy customers, and reward shareholders. Each job, department, or process in the organization is measured by the value added.

> **Economic value-added (EVA) system** A control system that measures performance in terms of after-tax profits minus the cost of capital invested in tangible assets.

Market Value-Added (MVA) **Market value-added** adds another dimension because it measures the stock market's estimate of the value of a company's past and projected capital investment projects. For example, when a company's market value (the value of all outstanding stock plus the company's debt) is greater than all the capital invested in it from shareholders, bondholders, and retained earnings, the company has a positive MVA, an indication that it has created wealth. A positive MVA usually goes hand-in-hand with a high EVA measurement.[121]

Activity-Based Costing (ABC) Managers measure the cost of producing goods and services so they can be sure they are selling those products for more than the cost to produce them. Traditional methods of costing assign costs to various departments or functions, such as purchasing, manufacturing, human resources, and so on. With a shift to more horizontal, flexible organizations has come a new approach called **activity-based costing,** which allocates costs across business processes. ABC attempts to identify all the various activities needed to provide a product or service and allocate costs accordingly. For example, an activity-based costing system might list the costs associated with processing orders for a particular product, scheduling production for that product, producing it, shipping it, and resolving problems with it. Because ABC allocates costs across business processes, it provides a more accurate picture of the cost of various products and services.[122] In addition, it enables managers to evaluate whether more costs go to activities that add value (meeting customer deadlines, achieving high quality) or to activities that do not add value (such as processing internal paperwork). They can then focus on reducing costs associated with non–value-added activities.

CONTROL IN THE NEW WORKPLACE Changing organizational structures and the resulting management methods that emphasize information sharing, employee participation, learning, and teamwork have led to some new approaches to control in today's workplace. Two significant aspects of control in the new workplace are open-book management and use of the balanced scorecard.

110. FUNCTIONS OF MANAGEMENT

OPEN-BOOK MANAGEMENT In an organizational environment that touts information sharing, teamwork, and the role of managers as facilitators, executives cannot hoard financial data. They must admit employees throughout the organization into the loop of financial control and responsibility to encourage active participation and commitment to organizational goals. A growing number of managers are opting for full disclosure in the form of open-book management. **Open-book management** allows employees to see for themselves—through charts, computer printouts, meetings, and so forth—the financial condition of the company. Second, open-book management shows the individual employee how his or her job fits into the big picture and affects the financial future of the organization. Finally, open-book management ties employee rewards to the company's overall success. With training in interpreting the financial data, employees can see the interdependence and importance of each function. If they are rewarded according to performance, they become motivated to take responsibility for their entire team or function, rather than merely their individual jobs.[123] Cross-functional communication and cooperation are also enhanced.

Open-book management Sharing financial information and results with all employees in the organization.

The goal of open-book management is to get every employee thinking and acting like a business owner rather than like a hired hand. To get employees to think like owners, management provides them with the same information owners have: what money is coming in and where it is going. Open-book management helps employees appreciate why efficiency is important to the organization's success. Open-book management turns traditional control on its head.

THE BALANCED SCORECARD Another recent innovation is to integrate the various dimensions of control, combining internal financial measurements and statistical reports with a concern for markets and customers as well as employees.[124] Whereas many managers once focused primarily on measuring and controlling financial performance, they are increasingly recognizing the need to evaluate other aspects of organizational performance to assess the value-creating activities of the contemporary organization.[125]

Balanced scorecard A comprehensive management control system that balances traditional financial measures with measures of customer service, internal business processes, and the organization's capacity for learning and growth.

One fresh approach is the balanced scorecard. The **balanced scorecard** is a comprehensive management control system that balances traditional financial measures with operational measures relating to a company's critical success factors.[126] A balanced scorecard contains four major perspectives: financial performance, customer service, internal business processes, and the organization's capacity for learning and growth.[127] Within these four areas, managers identify key performance metrics the organization will track. The *financial perspective* reflects a concern that the organization's activities contribute to improving short- and long-term financial performance. It includes traditional measures such as net income and return on investment. *Customer service* indicators measure such things as how customers view the organization, as well as customer retention and satisfaction. *Business process* indicators focus on production and operating statistics, such as order fulfillment or cost per order. The final component looks at the organization's *potential for learning and growth*, focusing on how well resources and human capital are being managed for the company's future. Metrics may include such things as employee retention and the introduction of new products. The components of the scorecard are designed in an integrative manner. The balanced scorecard helps managers focus on key performance measures and communicate them clearly throughout the organization. The scorecard has become the core management control system for many organizations today.

Organizational Performance

The other part of our definition of management is the attainment of organizational goals in an efficient and effective manner. Management is so important because organizations are so important. In an industrialized society where complex technologies dominate, organizations bring together knowledge, people, and raw materials to perform tasks no individual could do alone. Without organizations, how could technology be provided that enables us to share information around the world in an instant, electricity be produced from huge dams and nuclear power plants, and thousands of videos and DVDs be made available for our entertainment? Organizations pervade our society. Managers are responsible for these organizations and for seeing that resources are used wisely to attain organizational goals.

Our formal definition of an **organization** is a social entity that is goal directed and deliberately structured. *Social entity* means being made up of two or more people. *Goal directed* means designed to achieve some outcome, such as make a profit, win pay increases for members, meet spiritual needs, or provide social satisfaction. *Deliberately struc-*

tured means that tasks are divided and responsibility for their performance is assigned to organization members. This definition applies to all organizations, including both profit and not-for-profit. Small, offbeat, and not-for-profit organizations are more numerous than large, visible corporations—and just as important to society.

Based on our definition of management, the manager's responsibility is to coordinate resources in an effective and efficient manner to accomplish the organization's goals. Organizational **effectiveness** is the degree to which the organization achieves a stated goal. It means that the organization succeeds in accomplishing what it tries to do. Organizational effectiveness means providing a product or service that customers value. Organizational **efficiency** refers to the amount of resources used to achieve an organizational goal. It is based on how much raw materials, money, and people are necessary for producing a given volume of output. Efficiency can be calculated as the amount of resources used to produce a product or service.

Effectiveness The degree to which the organization achieves a stated goal.
Efficiency The use of minimal resources—raw materials, money, and people—to produce a desired volume of output.
Performance The organization's ability to attain its goals by using resources in an efficient and effective manner.

Efficiency and effectiveness can both be high in the same organization. Managers in service firms are using new technology to improve efficiency and effectiveness, too. Sometimes, however, managers' efforts to improve efficiency can hurt organizational effectiveness.

The ultimate responsibility of managers is to achieve high **performance,** which is the attainment of organizational goals by using resources in an efficient and effective manner.

Management Skills

A manager's job is complex and multidimensional and, as we shall see throughout this book, requires a range of skills. Although some management theorists propose a long list of skills, the necessary skills for managing a department or an organization can be summarized in three categories: conceptual, human, and technical.[128] The application of these skills changes as managers move up in the organization. Though the degree of each skill necessary at different levels of an organization may vary, all managers must possess skills in each of these important areas to perform effectively.

Conceptual Skills

Conceptual skill is the cognitive ability to see the organization as a whole and the relationship among its parts. Conceptual skill involves the manager's thinking, information processing, and planning abilities. It involves knowing where one's department fits into the total organization and how the organization fits into the industry, the community, and the broader business and social environment. It means the ability to *think strategically*—to take the broad, long-term view.

Conceptual skills are needed by all managers but are especially important for managers at the top. They must perceive significant elements in a situation and broad, conceptual patterns. As managers move up the hierarchy, they must develop conceptual skills or their promotability will be limited. A senior engineering manager who is mired in technical matters rather than thinking strategically will not perform well at the top of the organization. Many of the responsibilities of top managers, such as decision making, resource allocation, and innovation, require a broad view.

Human Skills

Human skill is the manager's ability to work with and through other people and to work effectively as a group member. This skill is demonstrated in the way a manager relates to other people, including the ability to motivate, facilitate, coordinate, lead, communicate, and resolve conflicts. A manager with human skills allows subordinates to express themselves without fear of ridicule and encourages participation. A manager with human skills likes other people and is liked by them.

As globalization, workforce diversity, uncertainty, and competition for highly skilled knowledge workers increase, human skills become even more crucial. Today's managers need to be genuinely concerned with the emotional needs of their employees, not just the physical needs related to their job tasks. Human skills are becoming increasingly important for managers at all levels, and particularly for those who work with employees directly on a daily basis. Organizations frequently lose good employees because of front-line bosses who fail to show respect and concern for workers.[129]

110. FUNCTIONS OF MANAGEMENT

Technical Skills

Technical skill is the understanding of and proficiency in the performance of specific tasks. Technical skill includes mastery of the methods, techniques, and equipment involved in specific functions such as engineering, manufacturing, or finance. Technical skill also includes specialized knowledge, analytical ability, and the competent use of tools and techniques to solve problems in that specific discipline. Technical skills are particularly important at lower organizational levels. Many managers get promoted to their first management job by having excellent technical skills. However, technical skills become less important than human and conceptual skills as managers move up the hierarchy.

Management Types

Managers use conceptual, human, and technical skills to perform the four management functions of planning, organizing, leading, and controlling in all organizations—large and small, manufacturing and service, profit and not-for-profit, traditional and Internet-based. But not all managers' jobs are the same. Managers are responsible for different departments, work at different levels in the hierarchy, and meet different requirements for achieving high performance.

Vertical Differences

An important determinant of the manager's job is hierarchical level. Three levels in the hierarchy include top managers, middle managers, and front-line managers. **Top managers** are at the top of the hierarchy and are responsible for the entire organization. They have such titles as president, chairperson, executive director, chief executive officer (CEO), and executive vice-president. Top managers are responsible for setting organizational goals, defining strategies for achieving them, monitoring and interpreting the external environment, and making decisions that affect the entire organization. They look to the long-term future and concern themselves with general environmental trends and the organization's overall success. Among the most important responsibilities for top managers are communicating a shared vision for the organization, shaping corporate culture, and nurturing an entrepreneurial spirit that can help the company keep pace with rapid change. Today more than ever before, top managers must engage the unique knowledge, skills, and capabilities of each employee.[130]

Middle managers work at middle levels of the organization and are responsible for business units and major departments. Examples of middle managers are department head, division head, manager of quality control, and director of the research lab. Middle managers typically have two or more management levels beneath them. They are responsible for implementing the overall strategies and policies defined by top managers. Middle managers generally are concerned with the near future and are expected to establish good relationships with peers around the organization, encourage teamwork, and resolve conflicts.

The middle manager's job has changed dramatically over the past two decades. During the 1980s and early 1990s, many organizations became lean and efficient by laying off middle managers and slashing middle management levels. Traditional pyramidal organization charts were flattened to allow information to flow quickly from top to bottom and decisions to be made with greater speed.

However, although middle management levels have been reduced, the middle manager's job in many organizations has become much more important. As more and more work is organized around teams and projects, middle managers become involved in a wider range of organizational problems and issues. Strong project managers are in white-hot demand throughout the corporate world. A **project manager** is responsible for a temporary work project that involves the participation of people from various functions and levels of the organization, and perhaps from outside the company as well. Today's middle manager might work with a variety of projects and teams at the same time, some of which cross geographical and cultural as well as functional boundaries.

Rather than managing the flow of information up and down the hierarchy, they are responsible for creating horizontal networks to help the organization quickly respond to shifting demands from the environment. Project management makes the middle manager's job much more challenging and exciting. In this new environment, middle managers need new skills: the ability to inspire and motivate a diverse group of people; negotiating skills; a willingness to listen and ability to communicate clearly; conscientiousness and integrity; and most of all, the ability to manage change and conflict.[131]

First-line managers are directly responsible for the production of goods and services. They are the first or second level of management and have such titles as supervisor, line manager, section chief, and office manager. They are responsible for groups of nonmanagement employees. Their primary concern is the application of rules and procedures to achieve efficient production, provide technical assistance, and motivate subordinates. The time horizon at this level is short, with the emphasis on accomplishing day-to-day goals.

Horizontal Differences

The other major difference in management jobs occurs horizontally across the organization. **Functional managers** are responsible for departments that perform a single functional task and have employees with similar training and skills. Functional departments include advertising, sales, finance, human resources, manufacturing, and accounting. Line managers are responsible for the manufacturing and marketing departments that make or sell the product or service. Staff managers are in charge of departments such as finance and human resources that support line departments.

General managers are responsible for several departments that perform different functions. A general manager is responsible for a self-contained division, such as a Dillard's department store, and for all of the functional departments within it. Project managers also have general management responsibility, because they coordinate people across several departments to accomplish a specific project.

Project management is a vital role in today's flatter, de-layered organizations and enables middle managers to contribute significantly to corporate success.[132]

What Is It Like to Be a Manager?

So far we have described how managers at various levels perform four basic functions that help ensure that organizational resources are used to attain high levels of performance. These tasks require conceptual, human, and technical skills. Unless someone has actually performed managerial work, it is hard to understand exactly what managers do on an hour-by-hour, day-to-day basis. The manager's job is so diverse that a number of studies have been undertaken in an attempt to describe exactly what happens. The question of what managers actually do to plan, organize, lead, and control was answered by Henry Mintzberg, who followed managers around and recorded all their activities.[133] He developed a description of managerial work that included three general characteristics and ten roles. These characteristics and roles have been supported in subsequent research.[134]

Manager Activities

One of the most interesting findings about managerial activities is how busy managers are and how hectic the average workday can be.

MANAGERIAL ACTIVITY IS CHARACTERIZED BY VARIETY, FRAGMENTATION, AND BREVITY[135] The manager's involvements are so widespread and voluminous that there is little time for quiet reflection. The average time spent on any one activity is less than nine minutes. Managers shift gears quickly. Significant crises are interspersed with trivial events in no predictable sequence.

THE MANAGER PERFORMS A GREAT DEAL OF WORK AT AN UNRELENTING PACE[136] Managers' work is fast paced and requires great energy. The managers observed by Mintzberg processed 36 pieces of mail each day, attended eight meetings, and took a tour through the building or plant. As soon as a manager's daily calendar is set, unexpected disturbances erupt. New meetings are required. During time away from the office, executives catch up on work-related reading, paperwork, and e-mail.

Manager Roles

Mintzberg's observations and subsequent research indicate that diverse manager activities can be organized into ten roles.[137] A **role** is a set of expectations for a manager's behavior. These roles are divided into three conceptual categories: informational (managing by information); interpersonal (managing through people); and decisional (managing through action). Each role represents activities that managers undertake to ultimately accomplish the functions of planning, organizing, leading, and controlling. Although it is necessary to separate the components of the manager's job to understand the different roles and activities of a manager, it is important to remember that the real job of management cannot be practiced as a set of independent parts; all the roles interact in the real world of management. As Mintzberg says, "The manager who only communicates or only conceives never gets anything done, while the manager who only 'does' ends up doing it all alone."[138]

INFORMATIONAL ROLES Informational roles describe the activities used to maintain and develop an information network. General managers spend about 75 percent of their time talking to other people. The *monitor* role involves seeking current information from many sources. The manager acquires information from others and scans written materials to stay well informed. The *disseminator* and *spokesperson* roles are just the opposite: The manager transmits current information to others, both inside and outside the organization, who can use it. With the trend toward empowerment of lower-level employees, many managers are sharing as much information as possible.

INTERPERSONAL ROLES Interpersonal roles pertain to relationships with others and are related to the human skills described earlier. The *figurehead* role involves handling ceremonial and symbolic activities for the department or organization. The manager represents the organization in his or her formal managerial capacity as the head of the unit. The presentation of employee awards by a division manager at **Taco Bell** is an example of the figurehead role. The *leader* role encompasses relationships with subordinates, including motivation, communication, and influence. The *liaison* role pertains to the development of information sources both inside and outside the organization.

DECISIONAL ROLES Decisional roles pertain to those events about which the manager must make a choice and take action. These roles often require conceptual as well as human skills. The *entrepreneur* role involves the initiation of change. Managers are constantly thinking about the future and how to get there.[139] Managers become aware of problems and search for improvement projects that will correct them. The *disturbance handler* role involves resolving conflicts among subordinates or between the manager's department and other departments. For example, the division manager for a large furniture manufacturer got involved in a personal dispute between two section heads. One section head was let go because he did not fit the team. The *resource allocator* role pertains to decisions about how to allocate people, time, equipment, budget, and other resources to attain desired outcomes. The manager must decide which projects receive budget allocations, which of several customer complaints receive priority, and even how to spend his or her own time. The *negotiator* role involves formal negotiations and bargaining to attain outcomes for the manager's unit of responsibility. For example, the manager meets and formally negotiates with others—a supplier about a late delivery, the controller about the need for additional budget resources, or the union about a worker grievance.

The relative emphasis a manager puts on these 10 roles depends on a number of factors, such as the manager's position in the hierarchy, natural skills and abilities, type of organization, or departmental goals to be achieved. Note that the importance of the leader role typically declines while the importance of the liaison role increases as a manager moves up the organizational hierarchy.

Other factors, such as changing environmental conditions, may also determine which roles are more important for a manager at any given time. For example, a top manager may regularly put more emphasis on the roles of spokesperson, figurehead, and negotiator. However, the emergence of new competitors may require more attention to the monitor role, or a severe decline in employee morale and direction may mean that the CEO has to put more emphasis on the leader role. A marketing manager may focus on interpersonal roles because of the importance of personal contacts in the marketing process, whereas a financial manager may be more likely to emphasize decisional roles such as resource allocator and negotiator. Despite these differences, all managers carry out informational, interpersonal, and decisional roles to meet the needs of the organization. Managers stay alert to needs both within and outside the organization to determine which roles are most critical at various times.

Management and the New Workplace

Characteristics

The world of organizations and management is changing. Rapid environmental shifts are causing fundamental transformations that have a dramatic impact on the manager's job. These transformations are reflected in the transition to a new workplace, as illustrated in Exhibit 100.11. The primary characteristic of the new workplace is that it is centered around bits rather than atoms—*information* and ideas rather than machines and physical assets. The shift from an industrial age to an information age has altered the nature of work, employees, and the workplace itself.[140] The old workplace was characterized by routine, specialized tasks and standardized control procedures. Employees typically performed their jobs in one specific company facility, such as an automobile factory located in Detroit or an insurance agency located in Des Moines. The organization was coordinated and controlled through the vertical hierarchy, with decision-making authority residing with upper-level managers.

In the new workplace, by contrast, work is free flowing and *flexible.* The shift is most obvious in e-commerce and Internet-based organizations, which have to respond to changing markets and competition at a second's notice. However, all organizations are facing the need for greater speed and flexibility. *Empowered employees* are expected to

Exhibit 100.11 *The Transition to a New Workplace*

	The Old Workplace	The New Workplace
Characteristics		
Resources	Atoms—physical assets	Bits—information
Work	Structured, localized	Flexible, virtual
Workers	Dependable employees	Empowered employees, free agents
Forces on Organizations		
Technology	Mechanical	Digital, e-business
Markets	Local, domestic	Global, including Internet
Workforce	Homogenous	Diverse
Values	Stability, efficiency	Change, speed
Events	Calm, predictable	Turbulent, more frequent crises
Management Competencies		
Leadership	Autocratic	Dispersed, empowering
Focus	Profits	Connection to customers, employees
Doing Work	By individuals	By teams
Relationships	Conflict, competition	Collaboration
Design	Efficient performance	Experimentation, learning organization

seize opportunities and solve problems as they emerge. The workplace is organized around networks rather than rigid hierarchies, and work is often *virtual*. Thanks to modern information and communications technology, employees can often perform their jobs from home or another remote location, at any time of the day or night. Flexible hours, telecommuting, and virtual teams are increasingly popular ways of working that require new skills from managers.

Teams in today's organizations may also include outside contractors, suppliers, customers, competitors, and *free agents* that are not affiliated with a specific organization but work on a project-by-project basis. The valued worker is one who learns quickly, shares knowledge, and is comfortable with risk, change, and ambiguity.

Forces on Organizations

The most striking change now affecting organizations and management is *technology*. There is currently a global technology explosion, and its impact on organizations and management is astonishing. Organizations are increasingly using *digital networking* technologies to tie together employees and company partners in far-flung operations. The growing use of *wireless technology* is expanding options even further, truly enabling people to work from practically anywhere, not just from a computer hooked to a company network. Wireless remote access to the Internet, for example, already enables salespeople to send and receive instant messages on hand-held devices from any location, helping them quickly close deals.[141]

One of the biggest technological advances is the *Internet*, which is transforming the way business is done. Only a few years ago, the Internet was still little more than a curiosity to many managers, but how things have changed. Companies develop *intranets* and *extranets*, communication systems that use Internet technology and tie employees, managers, free agents, customers, suppliers, partners, subcontractors, and shareholders together in a seamless information flow. Organizations are turning to *e-business* ideas and models to increase speed, cut costs, improve quality, and better serve customers.

The Internet and other new technologies are also tied closely to *globalization*, another force that is significantly affecting organizations. People around the world are connected in the flow of information, money, ideas, and products, and interdependencies are increasing. Customers today operate globally and they expect organizations to provide worldwide service.

Managers have to understand cross-cultural patterns, and they often work with virtual team members from many different countries. *Diversity* of the population and the workforce has become a fact of life for all organizations. Talented, educated knowledge workers seek opportunities all over the world, just as organizations search the world for the best minds to help them compete in a global economy. The general population of the United States, and thus of the workforce, is also growing more ethnically and racially diverse. Generational diversity is another powerful force in today's workplace, with employees of all ages working together on teams and projects in a way rarely seen in the past.

In the face of these transformations, organizations are learning to value *change* and *speed* over stability and efficiency. The fundamental paradigm during much of the 20th century was a belief that things can be stable. In contrast, the new paradigm recognizes change and chaos as the natural order of things.[142] Events in today's world are *turbulent* and *unpredictable,* with both small and large crises occurring on a more frequent basis.

In the face of these transitions, managers must rethink their approach to organizing, directing, and motivating workers. According to one consultant, many managers who have grown accustomed to the old workplace complain that employees no longer play by the rules. The consultant's response: "Why should they play by the rules? The rules are dead."[143]

New Management Competencies

Not all managers' jobs are the same. Managers rely on varied skills and perform different activities, depending on hierarchical level and job responsibilities. For all managers, however, human skills are becoming increasingly important.[144] In a survey of managers on their views of how the Internet has affected management, for example, the majority considered communicating effectively, retaining talented employees, and motivating workers to be essential management skills for the Internet world.[145] Although these abilities have always been important to managers, they take on added significance today, particularly when employees are dispersed and working in a virtual environment.

Today's best managers give up their command-and-control mindset to embrace ambiguity and create organizations that are fast, flexible, adaptable, and relationship-oriented. *Leadership* is dispersed throughout the organization, and managers empower others to gain the benefit of their ideas and creativity. The model of managers controlling workers no longer applies in a workplace where employee brainpower is more important than physical assets.[146] Moreover, managers often supervise employees who are scattered in various locations, requiring a new approach to leadership that focuses more on mentoring and providing direction and support than on giving orders and ensuring that they are followed.

Rather than a single-minded focus on profits, today's managers must recognize the critical importance of staying *connected to employees and customers.* The Internet has given increased knowledge and power to customers, so organizations have to remain flexible and adaptable to respond quickly to changing demands or competition. In some e-commerce organizations, managers have almost totally ignored profits in favor of building customer relationships. Although all organizations have to be concerned with profits sooner or later, as managers of numerous failed dot-coms learned, the emphasis these companies put on developing customers and relationships is a reflection of trends affecting all organizations.

Team-building skills are crucial for today's managers. Teams of front-line employees who work directly with customers have become the basic building block of organizations. Instead of managing a department of employees, many managers act as team leaders of ever-shifting, temporary projects, such as those that serve major customers or focus on specific markets, but many are designed to work on short-term projects or problems. Computer linkups, called *pythons,* drop from the ceiling. As people change assignments, they just unplug their pythons, move their desks and chairs to a new location, plug into a new python, and get to work on the next project.[147]

Success in the new workplace depends on the strength and quality of collaborative *relationships.* Partnerships, both within the organization and with outside customers, suppliers, and even competitors, are recognized as the key to a winning organization. New ways of working emphasize collaboration across functions and hierarchical levels as well as with other companies. E-business models that digitally link customers, suppliers, partners, and other stakeholders require managers to assess and manage relationships far beyond the confines of the traditional organization.

An important management challenge in the new workplace is to build a *learning organization* by creating an organizational climate that values experimentation and risk taking, applies current technology, tolerates mistakes and failure, and rewards nontraditional thinking and the sharing of knowledge. Everyone in the organization participates in identifying and solving problems, enabling the organization to continuously experiment, improve, and increase its capability. The role of managers is not to make decisions, but to create learning capability, where everyone is free to experiment and learn what works best.

Motivating and Communicating

The Concept of Motivation

Most of us get up in the morning, go to school or work, and behave in ways that are predictably our own. We respond to our environment and the people in it with little thought as to why we work hard, enjoy certain classes, or find some recreational activities so much fun. Yet all these behaviors are motivated by something. **Motivation** refers to the forces either within or external to a person that arouse enthusiasm and persistence to pursue a certain course of action. Employee motivation affects productivity, and part of a manager's job is to channel motivation toward the accomplishment of organizational goals.[148] The study of motivation helps managers understand what prompts people to initiate action, what influences their choice of action, and why they persist in that action over time.

A simple model of human motivation is illustrated in Exhibit 100.12. People have basic *needs*, such as for food, achievement, or monetary gain, that translate into an internal tension that motivates specific behaviors with which to fulfill the need. To the extent that the behavior is successful, the person is rewarded in the sense that the need is satisfied. The reward also informs the person that the behavior was appropriate and can be used again in the future.

Rewards are of two types: intrinsic and extrinsic. **Intrinsic rewards** are the satisfactions a person receives in the process of performing a particular action. The completion of a complex task may bestow a pleasant feeling of accomplishment, or solving a problem that benefits others may fulfill a personal mission. For example, Frances Blais sells educational materials for the intrinsic reward of helping children read well. **Extrinsic rewards** are given by another person, typically a manager, and include promotions and pay increases. They originate externally, as a result of pleasing others. Rob Michaels, who hates his sales job, nevertheless is motivated by the extrinsic reward of high pay. Although extrinsic rewards are important, good managers strive to help people achieve intrinsic rewards, as well. Today's managers are finding that the most talented and innovative employees are rarely motivated exclusively by rewards such as money and benefits, or even praise and recognition. Instead, they seek satisfaction from the work itself.[149]

Intrinsic reward The satisfaction received in the process of performing an action.
Extrinsic reward A reward given by another person.

The importance of motivation as illustrated in Exhibit 100.12 is that it can lead to behaviors that reflect high performance within organizations. One recent study found that high employee motivation goes hand-in-hand with high organizational performance and profits.[150] Managers can use motivation theory to help satisfy employees' needs and simultaneously encourage high work performance. With the recent massive layoffs in many U.S. organizations, managers are struggling to keep remaining workers focused and motivated. In addition, as the economy improves, finding and keeping talented workers may be a significant challenge because of weakened trust and commitment. Managers have to find the right combination of motivational techniques and rewards to keep workers satisfied and productive in a variety of organizational situations.

Foundations of Motivation

A manager's assumptions about employee motivation and use of rewards depend on his or her perspective on motivation. Four distinct perspectives on employee motivation have evolved: the traditional approach, the human relations approach, the human resource approach, and the contemporary approach.[151]

Exhibit 100.12 *A Simple Model of Motivation*

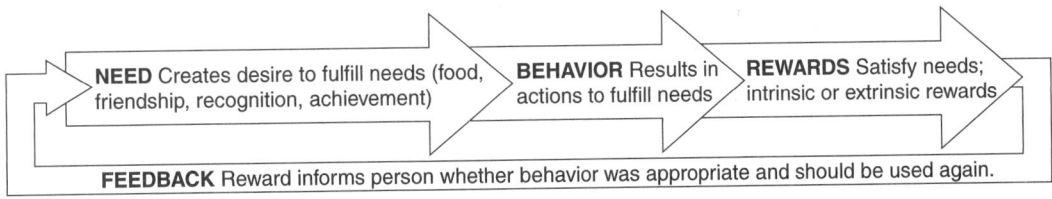

Traditional Approach

The study of employee motivation really began with the work of Frederick W. Taylor on scientific management. Recall that scientific management pertains to the systematic analysis of an employee's job for the purpose of increasing efficiency. Economic rewards are provided to employees for high performance. The emphasis on pay evolved into the notion of the *economic man*—people would work harder for higher pay. This approach led to the development of incentive pay systems, in which people were paid strictly on the quantity and quality of their work outputs.

Human Relations Approach

The economic man was gradually replaced by a more sociable employee in managers' minds. Beginning with the landmark Hawthorne studies at a Western Electric plant, noneconomic rewards, such as congenial work groups who met social needs, seemed more important than money as a motivator of work behavior.[152] For the first time, workers were studied as people, and the concept of *social man* was born.

Human Resource Approach

The human resource approach carries the concepts of economic man and social man further to introduce the concept of the *whole person*. Human resource theory suggests that employees are complex and motivated by many factors. For example, the work by McGregor on Theory X and Theory Y argued that people want to do a good job and that work is as natural and healthy as play. Proponents of the human resource approach believed that earlier approaches had tried to manipulate employees through economic or social rewards. By assuming that employees are competent and able to make major contributions, managers can enhance organizational performance. The human resource approach laid the groundwork for contemporary perspectives on employee motivation.

Contemporary Approach

The contemporary approach to employee motivation is dominated by three types of theories, each of which will be discussed in the following sections. The first are *content theories*, which stress the analysis of underlying human needs. Content theories provide insight into the needs of people in organizations and help managers understand how needs can be satisfied in the workplace. *Process theories* concern the thought processes that influence behavior. They focus on how employees seek rewards in work circumstances. *Reinforcement theories* focus on employee learning of desired work behaviors. In Exhibit 100.12, content theories focus on the concepts in the first box, process theories on those in the second, and reinforcement theories on those in the third.

Job Design for Motivation

A *job* in an organization is a unit of work that a single employee is responsible for performing. A job could include writing tickets for parking violators in New York City or doing long-range planning for the Discovery cable television channel. Jobs are important because performance of their components may provide rewards that meet employees' needs. An assembly-line worker may install the same bolt over and over, whereas an emergency room physician may provide each trauma victim with a unique treatment package. Managers need to know what aspects of a job provide motivation as well as how to compensate for routine tasks that have little inherent satisfaction. **Job design** is the application of motivational theories to the structure of work for improving productivity and satisfaction. Approaches to job design are generally classified as job simplification, job rotation, job enlargement, and job enrichment.

Job Simplification

Job simplification pursues task efficiency by reducing the number of tasks one person must do. Job simplification is based on principles drawn from scientific management and industrial engineering. Tasks are designed to be simple, repetitive, and standardized. As complexity is stripped from a job, the worker has more time to concentrate on doing more of the same routine task. Workers with low skill levels can perform the job, and the organization achieves a high level of efficiency. Indeed, workers are interchangeable, because they need little training or skill and exercise little judgment. As a motivational technique, however, job simplification has failed. People dislike routine and boring jobs and react in a number of negative ways, including sabotage, absenteeism, and unionization. Job simplification is compared with job rotation and job enlargement in Exhibit 100.13.

Exhibit 100.13 *Types of Job Design*

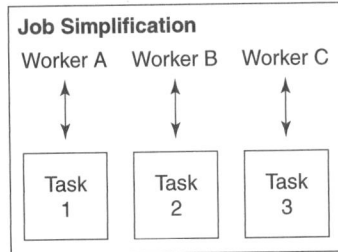
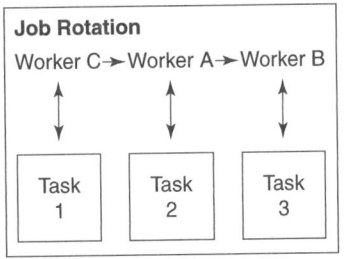
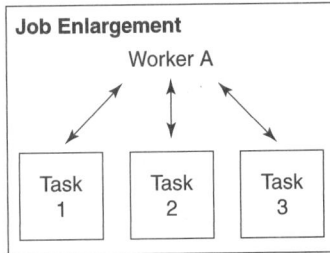

Job Rotation

Job rotation systematically moves employees from one job to another, thereby increasing the number of different tasks an employee performs without increasing the complexity of any one job. For example, an autoworker may install windshields one week and front bumpers the next. Job rotation still takes advantage of engineering efficiencies, but it provides variety and stimulation for employees. Although employees may find the new job interesting at first, the novelty soon wears off as the repetitive work is mastered.

Job Enlargement

Job enlargement combines a series of tasks into one new, broader job. This is a response to the dissatisfaction of employees with oversimplified jobs. Instead of only one job, an employee may be responsible for three or four and will have more time to do them. Job enlargement provides job variety and a greater challenge for employees.

Job Enrichment

Recall the discussion of Maslow's need hierarchy and Herzberg's two-factor theory. Rather than just changing the number and frequency of tasks a worker performs, **job enrichment** incorporates high-level motivators into the work, including job responsibility, recognition, and opportunities for growth, learning, and achievement. In an enriched job, employees have control over the resources necessary for performing it, make decisions on how to do the work, experience personal growth, and set their own work pace. Many companies have undertaken job enrichment programs to increase employees' motivation and job satisfaction.

Job Characteristics Model

One significant approach to job design is the job characteristics model developed by Richard Hackman and Greg Oldham.[153] Hackman and Oldham's research concerned **work redesign,** which is defined as altering jobs to increase both the quality of employees' work experience and their productivity. Hackman and Oldham's research into the design of hundreds of jobs yielded the **job characteristics model.** The model consists of four major parts: core job dimensions, critical psychological states, personal and work outcomes, and employee growth-need strength.

Work redesign The altering of jobs to increase both the quality of employees' work experience and their productivity.

Job characteristics model A model of job design that comprises core job dimensions, critical psychological states, and employee growth-need strength.

CORE JOB DIMENSIONS Hackman and Oldham identified five dimensions that determine a job's motivational potential: These dimensions include skill variety, task identity, task significance, autonomy, and feedback.

The job characteristics model says that the more these five core characteristics can be designed into the job, the more the employees will be motivated and the higher will be performance, quality, and satisfaction.

CRITICAL PSYCHOLOGICAL STATES The model posits that core job dimensions are more rewarding when individuals experience three psychological states in response to job design. Skill variety, task identity, and task significance tend to influence the employee's psychological state of *experienced meaningfulness of work*. The work itself is satisfying and provides intrinsic rewards for the worker. The job characteristic of autonomy influences the worker's *experienced responsibility*. The job characteristic of feedback provides the worker with *knowledge of actual results*. The employee thus knows how he or she is doing and can change work performance to increase desired outcomes.

PERSONAL AND WORK OUTCOMES The impact of the five job characteristics on the psychological states of experienced meaningfulness, responsibility, and knowledge of actual results leads to the personal and work outcomes of high work motivation, high work performance, high satisfaction, and low absenteeism and turnover.

EMPLOYEE GROWTH-NEED STRENGTH The final component of the job characteristics model is called *employee growth-need strength,* which means that people have different needs for growth and development. If a person wants to satisfy low-level needs, such as safety and belongingness, the job characteristics model has less effect. When a person has a high need for growth and development, including the desire for personal challenge, achievement, and challenging work, the model is especially effective. People with a high need to grow and expand their abilities respond favorably to the application of the model and to improvements in core job dimensions.

Motivating in the New Workplace

Despite the controversy over carrot-and-stick motivational practices, organizations are increasingly using various types of incentive compensation as a way to motivate employees to higher levels of performance. Exhibit 100.14 summarizes new motivational compensation programs. These programs can be effective if they are used appropriately and combined with motivational ideas that provide employees with intrinsic rewards and meet higher-level needs. Effective organizations do not use incentive pay plans as the sole basis of motivation.

In addition, many organizations are giving employees a voice in how pay and incentive systems are designed, which increases motivation by increasing employees' sense of involvement and control.[154] The most effective motivational programs typically involve much more than money. Two recent motivational trends are empowering employees and designing work to have greater meaning.

Empowerment

Empowerment The delegation of power or authority to subordinates.

Empowerment is the delegation of power or authority to subordinates in an organization.[155] Increasing employee power heightens motivation for task accomplishment because people improve their own effectiveness, choosing how to do a task and using their creativity.[156] Most people come into an organization with the desire to do a good job, and empowerment releases the motivation that is already there.

Empowering employees means giving them four elements that enable them to act more freely to accomplish their jobs: information, knowledge, power, and rewards.[157]

Many of today's organizations are implementing empowerment programs, but they are empowering workers to varying degrees. At some companies, empowerment means encouraging workers' ideas while managers retain final

Exhibit 100.14 *New Motivational Compensation Programs*

Program Name	Purpose
Pay for Performance	Rewards individual employees in proportion to their performance contributions. Also called merit pay.
Gain Sharing	Rewards all employees and managers within a business unit when predetermined performance targets are met. Encourages teamwork.
Employee Stock Ownership Plan (ESOP)	Gives employees part ownership of the organization, enabling them to share in improved profit performance.
Lump-Sum Bonuses	Rewards employees with a one-time cash payment based on performance.
Pay for Knowledge	Links employee salary with the number of task skills acquired. Workers are motivated to learn the skills for many jobs, thus increasing company flexibility and efficiency.
Flexible Work Schedule	Flextime allows workers to set their own hours. Job sharing allows two or more part-time workers to jointly cover one job. Telecommuting, sometimes called flex-place, allows employees to work from home or an alternate workspace.
Team-based Compensation	Rewards employees for behavior and activities that benefit the team, such as cooperation, listening, and empowering others.

authority for decisions; at others it means giving employees almost complete freedom and power to make decisions and exercise initiative and imagination.[158] Current methods of empowerment fall along a continuum, which runs from a situation in which front-line workers have almost no discretion, such as on a traditional assembly line, to full empowerment, where workers even participate in formulating organizational strategy. An example of full empowerment is when self-directed teams are given the authority to hire, discipline, and dismiss team members and to set compensation rates.

Research indicates that most people have a need for *self-efficacy,* which is the capacity to produce results or outcomes, to feel that they are effective.[159] By meeting higher-level needs, empowerment can provide powerful motivation.

Communication and the Manager's Job

How important is communication? Consider this: Managers spend at least 80 percent of every working day in direct communication with others. In other words, 48 minutes of every hour is spent in meetings, on the telephone, communicating on line, or talking informally while walking around. The other 20 percent of a typical manager's time is spent doing desk work, most of which is also communication in the form of reading and writing.[160] Managers gather important information from both inside and outside the organization and then distribute appropriate information to others who need it.

Communication permeates every management function.[161] For example, when managers perform the planning function, they gather information; write letters, memos, and reports; and then meet with other managers to explain the plan. When managers lead, they communicate to share a vision of what the organization can be and motivate employees to help achieve it. When managers organize, they gather information about the state of the organization and communicate a new structure to others. Communication skills are a fundamental part of every managerial activity.

What Is Communication?

Communication thus can be defined as the process by which information is exchanged and understood by two or more people, usually with the intent to motivate or influence behavior. Communication is not just sending information. This distinction between *sharing* and *proclaiming* is crucial for successful management. A manager who does not listen is like a used-car salesperson who claims, "I sold a car—they just did not buy it." Management communication is a two-way street that includes listening and other forms of feedback.

It is the desire to share understanding that motivates executives to visit employees on the shop floor, hold small informal meetings, or eat with employees in the company cafeteria. The things managers learn from direct communication with employees shape their understanding of the corporation.

The Communication Process

Many people think communication is simple because they communicate without conscious thought or effort. However, communication usually is complex, and the opportunities for sending or receiving the wrong messages are innumerable. No doubt, you have heard someone say, "But that's not what I meant!" Have you ever received directions you thought were clear and yet still got lost? How often have you wasted time on misunderstood instructions?

To more fully understand the complexity of the communication process, note the key elements outlined in Exhibit 100.15. Two common elements in every communication situation are the sender and the receiver. The *sender* is anyone who wishes to convey an idea or concept to others, to seek information, or to express a thought or emotion. The *receiver* is the person to whom the message is sent. The sender **encodes** the idea by selecting symbols with which to compose a message. The **message** is the tangible formulation of the idea that is sent to the receiver. The message is sent through a **channel,** which is the communication carrier. The channel can be a formal report, a telephone call or e-mail message, or a face-to-face meeting. The receiver **decodes** the symbols to interpret the meaning of the message. Encoding and decoding are potential sources for communication errors, because knowledge, attitudes, and background act as filters and create "noise" when translating from symbols to meaning. Finally, **feedback** occurs when the receiver responds to the sender's communication with a return message. Without feedback, the communication is *one-way;* with feedback, it is *two-way.* Feedback is a powerful aid to communication effectiveness, because it enables the sender to determine whether the receiver correctly interpreted the message.

Exhibit 100.15 *A Model of the Communication Process*

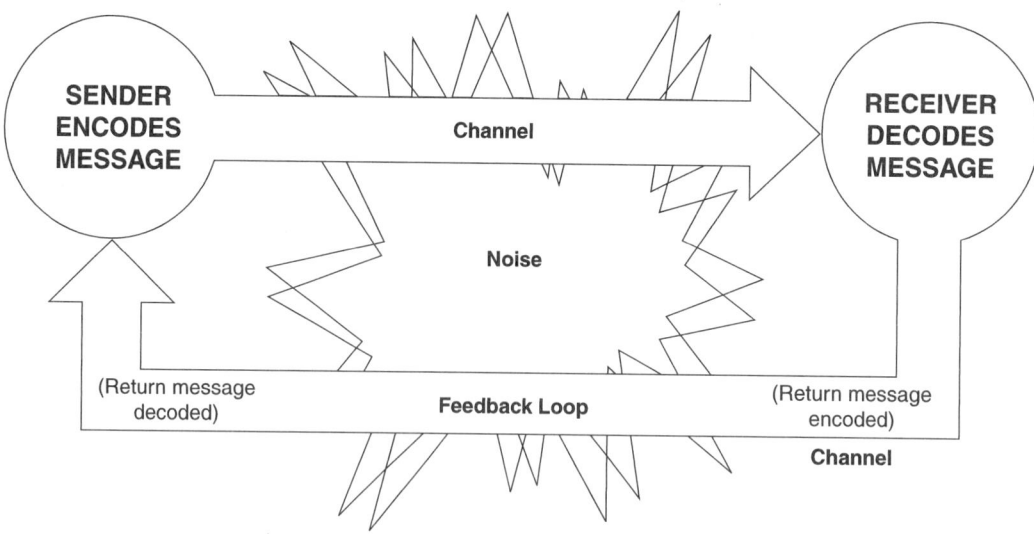

Communicating among People

The communication model in Exhibit 100.15 illustrates the components that must be mastered for effective communication. Communications can break down if sender and receiver do not encode or decode language in the same way.[162] We all know how difficult it is to communicate with someone who does not speak our language, and managers in U.S. organizations today are often trying to communicate with people who speak many different native languages and have limited English skills. However, communication breakdowns can also occur between people who speak the same language.

Many factors can lead to a breakdown in communications. For example, the selection of communication channel can determine whether the message is distorted by noise and interference. The listening skills of both parties and attention to nonverbal behavior can determine whether a message is truly shared. Thus, for managers to be effective communicators, they must understand how interpersonal factors such as communication channels, nonverbal behavior, and listening all work to enhance or detract from communication.

Organizational Communication

Another aspect of management communication concerns the organization as a whole. Organization-wide communications typically flow in three directions—downward, upward, and horizontally. Managers are responsible for establishing and maintaining formal channels of communication in these three directions. Managers also use informal channels, which means they get out of their offices and mingle with employees.

Formal Communication Channels

Formal communication channel
A communication channel that flows within the chain of command or task responsibility defined by the organization.

Formal communication channels are those that flow within the chain of command or task responsibility defined by the organization. The three formal channels include downward, upward, and horizontal communication. Downward and upward communication are the primary forms of communication used in most traditional, vertically organized companies. However, the new workplace emphasizes horizontal communication, with people constantly sharing information across departments and levels. Electronic communication such as e-mail and instant messaging have made it easier than ever for information to flow in all directions.

DOWNWARD COMMUNICATION The most familiar and obvious flow of formal communication, **downward communication,** refers to the messages and information sent from top management to subordinates in a downward direction.

Managers sometimes use creative approaches to downward communication to make sure employees get the message. Managers can communicate downward to employees in many ways. Some of the most common are through speeches, messages in company newsletters, e-mail, information leaflets tucked into pay envelopes, material on bulletin boards, and policy and procedures manuals.

Managers also have to decide what to communicate about. It is impossible for managers to communicate with employees about everything that goes on in the organization, so they have to make choices about the important information to communicate.[163] Downward communication in an organization usually encompasses these five topics:

1. *Implementation of goals and strategies*
2. *Job instructions and rationale*
3. *Procedures and practices*
4. *Performance feedback*
5. *Indoctrination*

The major problem with downward communication is *drop off*, the distortion or loss of message content. Although formal communications are a powerful way to reach all employees, much information gets lost—25 percent or so each time a message is passed from one person to the next. In addition, the message can be distorted if it travels a great distance from its originating source to the ultimate receiver.

Information drop off cannot be completely avoided, but the techniques described in the previous sections can reduce it substantially. Using the right communication channel, consistency between verbal and nonverbal messages, and active listening can maintain communication accuracy as it moves down the organization.

UPWARD COMMUNICATION Formal **upward communication** includes messages that flow from the lower to the higher levels in the organization's hierarchy. Most organizations take pains to build in healthy channels for upward communication. Employees need to air grievances, report progress, and provide feedback on management initiatives. Coupling a healthy flow of upward and downward communication ensures that the communication circuit between managers and employees is complete.[164] Five types of information communicated upward are the following:

Upward communication Messages transmitted from the lower to the higher level in the organization's hierarchy.

1. *Problems and exceptions*
2. *Suggestions for improvement*
3. *Performance reports*
4. *Grievances and disputes*
5. *Financial and accounting information*

Many organizations make a great effort to facilitate upward communication. Mechanisms include suggestion boxes, employee surveys, open-door policies, management information system reports, and face-to-face conversations between workers and executives.

Despite these efforts, however, barriers to accurate upward communication exist. Managers may resist hearing about employee problems, or employees may not trust managers sufficiently to push information upward.[165] Innovative companies search for ways to ensure that information gets to top managers without distortion.

HORIZONTAL COMMUNICATION **Horizontal communication** is the lateral or diagonal exchange of messages among peers or coworkers. It may occur within or across departments. The purpose of horizontal communication is not only to inform but also to request support and coordinate activities. Horizontal communication falls into one of three categories:

Horizontal communication The lateral or diagonal exchange of messages among peers or coworkers.

1. *Intradepartmental problem solving*. These messages take place among members of the same department and concern task accomplishment. Example: "Betty, can you help us figure out how to complete this medical expense report form?"
2. *Interdepartmental coordination*. Interdepartmental messages facilitate the accomplishment of joint projects or tasks. Example: "Bob, please contact marketing and production and arrange a meeting to discuss the specifications for the new subassembly. It looks like we might not be able to meet their requirements."
3. *Change initiatives and improvements*. These messages are designed to share information among teams and departments that can help the organization change, grow, and improve. Example: "We are streamlining the company travel procedures and would like to discuss them with your department."

Horizontal communication is particularly important in learning organizations, where teams of workers are continuously solving problems and searching for new ways of doing things. Recall that many organizations build in horizontal communications in the form of task forces, committees, or even a matrix structure to encourage coordination.

Team Communication Channels

A special type of horizontal communication is communicating in teams. In many companies today, teams are the basic building block of the organization. Team members work together to accomplish tasks, and the team's communication structure influences both team performance and employee satisfaction.

Research into team communication has focused on two characteristics: the extent to which team communications are centralized and the nature of the team's task.[166] In a **centralized network,** team members must communicate through one individual to solve problems or make decisions. In a **decentralized network,** individuals can communicate freely with other team members. Members process information equally among themselves until all agree on a decision.[167]

Informal Communication Channels

Informal communication channel A communication channel that exists outside formally authorized channels without regard for the organization's hierarchy of authority.

Informal communication channels exist outside the formally authorized channels and do not adhere to the organization's hierarchy of authority. Informal communications coexist with formal communications but may skip hierarchical levels, cutting across vertical chains of command to connect virtually anyone in the organization.

Two types of informal channels used in many organizations are *management by wandering around* and the *grapevine*.

MANAGEMENT BY WANDERING AROUND The communication technique known as **management by wandering around (MBWA)** was made famous by the books *In Search of Excellence* and *A Passion for Excellence*.[168] These books describe executives who talk directly with employees to learn what is going on. MBWA works for managers at all levels. They mingle and develop positive relationships with employees and learn directly from them about their department, division, or organization. For example, the president of ARCO had a habit of visiting a district field office. Rather than schedule a big strategic meeting with the district supervisor, he would come in unannounced and chat with the lowest-level employees. In any organization, both upward and downward communication are enhanced with MBWA. Managers have a chance to describe key ideas and values to employees and, in turn, learn about the problems and issues confronting employees.

THE GRAPEVINE The **grapevine** is an informal, person-to-person communication network of employees that is not officially sanctioned by the organization.[169] The grapevine links employees in all directions, ranging from the president through middle management, support staff, and line employees. The grapevine will always exist in an organization, but it can become a dominant force when formal channels are closed. In such cases, the grapevine is actually a service because the information it provides helps makes sense of an unclear or uncertain situation. Employees use grapevine rumors to fill in information gaps and clarify management decisions. The grapevine tends to be more active during periods of change, excitement, anxiety, and sagging economic conditions.

Communicating in the New Workplace

Managers in today's leading companies put extraordinary emphasis on open and honest communication in all directions to build trust and promote learning and problem solving. In addition to encompassing the ideas and techniques discussed so far, the new workplace also focuses on open communication, dialogue, and feedback and learning.

Open Communication

Open communication Sharing all types of information throughout the company, across functional and hierarchical levels.

A recent trend that reflects managers' increased emphasis on empowering employees, building trust and commitment, and enhancing collaboration is open communication. **Open communication** means sharing all types of information throughout the company, across functional and hierarchical levels.

Open communication runs counter to the traditional flow of selective information downward from supervisors to subordinates. By breaking down conventional hierarchical and departmental boundaries that may be barriers to communication, the organization can gain the benefit of all employees' ideas. The same ideas batted back and forth among a few managers do not lead to effective learning and change or to a network of relationships that keep companies thriving. New voices and conversations involving a broad spectrum of people revitalize and enhance organizational communication.[170]

Dialogue

Another means of fostering trust and collaboration is through dialogue. The "roots of dialogue" are *dia* and *logos*, which can be thought of as "stream of meaning." **Dialogue** is a group communication process in which people together create a stream of shared meaning that enables them to understand each other and share a view of the world.[171] People may start out at polar opposites, but by talking openly, they discover common ground, common issues, and shared goals on which they can build a better future.

A useful way to describe dialogue is to contrast it with discussion. The intent of discussion, generally, is to deliver one's point of view and persuade others to adopt it. A discussion is often resolved by logic or "beating down" opponents. Dialogue, on the other hand, asks that participants suspend their attachments to a particular viewpoint so that a deeper level of listening, synthesis, and meaning can evolve from the group. A dialogue's focus is to reveal feelings and build common ground. Both forms of communication—dialogue and discussion—can result in change. However, the result of discussion is limited to the topic being deliberated, whereas the result of dialogue is characterized by group unity, shared meaning, and transformed mindsets. As new and deeper solutions are developed, a trusting relationship is built among team members.[172]

Feedback and Learning

In the new workplace, **feedback** occurs when managers use evaluation and communication to help individuals and the organization learn and improve. Feedback enables managers to determine whether they have been successful or unsuccessful in communicating with others. It also helps them develop subordinates. At General Electric, managers are evaluated partly on their ability to give and receive effective feedback.[173] Recall from the communication model earlier in the section that feedback is an important part of the communication process. However, despite its importance, feedback is often neglected. One study found that although executives at a majority of companies agree that communication is a priority, less than half bother to tailor their messages to employees, customers, or suppliers, and even fewer seek feedback from those constituencies.[174] Using feedback can seem daunting because it potentially involves many sources. A single individual might receive feedback from supervisors, co-workers, customers, investors, suppliers, and members of partner organizations.

Successful managers focus feedback to help develop the capacities of subordinates and to teach the organization how to better reach its goals. Feedback is an important means by which individuals and organizations learn from their mistakes and improve their work. When managers enlist the whole organization in reviewing the outcomes of activities, they can quickly learn what works and what doesn't and use that information to improve the organization.

Managing Organizational Communication

Many of the ideas described in this section pertain to barriers to communication and how to overcome them. Barriers can be categorized as those that exist at the individual level and those that exist at the organizational level. First we will examine communication barriers; then we will look at techniques for overcoming them. These barriers and techniques are summarized in Exhibit 100.16.

Barriers to Communication

Barriers to communication can exist within the individual or as part of the organization.

INDIVIDUAL BARRIERS First, there are *interpersonal barriers;* these include problems with emotions and perceptions held by employees. For example, rigid perceptual labeling or categorizing of others prevents modification or alteration of opinions. If a person's mind is made up before the communication starts, communication will fail. Moreover, people with different backgrounds or knowledge may interpret a communication in different ways.

Second, *selecting the wrong channel or medium* for sending a communication can be a problem. For example, when a message is emotional, it is better to transmit it face to face rather than in writing. On the other hand, writing works best for routine messages but lacks the capacity for rapid feedback and multiple cues needed for difficult messages.

Exhibit 100.16 *Communication Barriers and Ways to Overcome Them*

Barriers	How to Overcome
Individual	
Interpersonal dynamics	Active listening
Channels and media	Selection of appropriate channel
Semantics	Knowledge of other's perspective
Inconsistent cues	MBWA
Organizational	
Status and power differences	Climate of trust, dialogue
Departmental needs and goals	Development and use of formal channels
Lack of formal channels	Encouragement of multiple channels, formal and informal
Communication network unsuited to task	Changing organization or group structure to fit communication needs
Poor coordination	Feedback and learning

> **Semantics** The meaning of words and the way they are used.

Third, *semantics* often causes communication problems. **Semantics** pertains to the meaning of words and the way they are used. A word such as *effectiveness* may mean achieving high production to a factory superintendent and employee satisfaction to a human resources staff specialist.

Fourth, sending *inconsistent cues* between verbal and nonverbal communications will confuse the receiver. If one's facial expression does not reflect one's words, the communication will contain noise and uncertainty. The tone of voice and body language should be consistent with the words, and actions should not contradict words.

ORGANIZATIONAL BARRIERS Organizational barriers pertain to factors for the organization as a whole. First is the problem of *status and power differences*. Low-power people may be reluctant to pass bad news up the hierarchy, thus giving the wrong impression to upper levels.[175] High-power people may not pay attention or may think that low-status people have little to contribute.

Second, *differences across departments in terms of needs and goals* interfere with communications. Each department perceives problems in its own terms. The production department is concerned with production efficiency whereas the marketing department's goal is to get the product to the customer in a hurry.

Third, the *absence of formal channels* reduces communication effectiveness. Organizations must provide adequate upward, downward, and horizontal communication in the form of employee surveys, open-door policies, newsletters, memos, task forces, and liaison personnel. Without these formal channels, the organization cannot communicate as a whole.

Fourth, the *communication flow* may not fit the team's or organization's task. If a centralized communication structure is used for nonroutine tasks, there will not be enough information circulated to solve problems. The organization, department, or team is most efficient when the amount of communication flowing among employees fits the task.

A final problem is *poor coordination*, so that different parts of the organization are working in isolation without knowing and understanding what other parts are doing. Top executives are out of touch with lower levels, or departments and divisions are poorly coordinated so that people do not understand how the system works together as a whole.

Overcoming Communication Barriers

Managers can design the organization so as to encourage positive, effective communication. Designing involves both individual skills and organizational actions.

INDIVIDUAL SKILLS Perhaps the most important individual skill is *active listening*. Active listening means asking questions, showing interest, and occasionally paraphrasing what the speaker has said to ensure that one is interpreting accurately. Active listening also means providing feedback to the sender to complete the communication loop.

Second, individuals should select the *appropriate channel* for the message. A complicated message should be sent through a rich channel, such as face-to-face discussion or telephone. Routine messages and data can be sent through memos, letters, or e-mail, because there is little chance of misunderstanding.

Third, senders and receivers should make a special effort to understand each other's perspective. Managers can sensitize themselves to the information receiver so that they will be better able to target the message, detect bias, and clarify missed interpretations. By communicators understanding others' perspectives, semantics can be clarified, perceptions understood, and objectivity maintained.

The fourth individual skill is *management by wandering around*. Managers must be willing to get out of the office and check communications with others. For example, John McDonnell of **McDonnell Douglas** always ate in the employee cafeteria when he visited far-flung facilities. Through direct observation and face-to-face meetings, managers develop an understanding of the organization and are able to communicate important ideas and values directly to others.

ORGANIZATIONAL ACTIONS   Perhaps the most important thing managers can do for the organization is to create a *climate of trust and openness*. Open communication and dialogue can encourage people to communicate honestly with one another. Subordinates will feel free to transmit negative as well as positive messages without fear of retribution. Efforts to develop interpersonal skills among employees can also foster openness, honesty, and trust.

Second, managers should develop and use *formal information channels* in all directions. Other techniques include direct mail, bulletin boards, and employee surveys.

Third, managers should encourage the use of *multiple channels,* including both formal and informal communications. Multiple communication channels include written directives, face-to-face discussions, MBWA, and the grapevine. Sending messages through multiple channels increases the likelihood that they will be properly received.

Fourth, the structure should *fit communication needs*. An organization can be designed to use teams, task forces, project managers, or a matrix structure as needed to facilitate the horizontal flow of information for coordination and problem solving. Structure should also reflect information needs. When team or department tasks are difficult, a decentralized structure should be implemented to encourage discussion and participation. A system of organizational *feedback and learning* can help to overcome problems of poor coordination as well.

Problem Solving and Decision Making

Every organization grows, prospers, or fails as a result of decisions by its managers. Managers often are referred to as *decision makers*. Although many of their important decisions are strategic, managers also make decisions about every other aspect of an organization, including structure, control systems, responses to the environment, and human resources. Managers scout for problems, make decisions for solving them, and monitor the consequences to see whether additional decisions are required. Good decision making is a vital part of good management, because decisions determine how the organization solves its problems, allocates resources, and accomplishes its goals.

Decision making is not easy. It must be done amid ever-changing factors, unclear information, and conflicting points of view. This section explores the decision process that underlies strategic planning. Plans and strategies are arrived at through decision making; the better the decision making, the better the strategic planning. First we will examine problem solving and decision-making characteristics. Then we will look at decision-making models and the steps executives should take when making important decisions.

Problem Solving

A problem exists when there is a gap between "what is" and "what should be." Individuals recognize a problem when they feel frustrated, frightened, angry, or anxious about a situation. Organizations recognize problems when outputs and productivity are low; when quality of products and services are poor; when people are not cooperating, sharing information, or communicating; or when there is a dysfunctional degree of conflict among people in various departments. When the gap between "what is" and "what should be" causes anxiety and inefficiency, something needs to be done to solve the problem.

```
          Point A           Gap          Point B
          "What is"   <---------------->  "What should be"
       (actual condition)              (desired condition)
```

Problem-solving tools and techniques include brainstorming, synectics (analogies), nominal group techniques, force-field analysis, story boarding, leap-frogging, and systems analysis.

A problem is the gap between where one is and where one wants to be. The process of closing the gap between the actual situation and the desired situation is problem solving. Problems do not solve themselves—people solve problems. The management principle behind problem solving is "Theory Y" in that managers will take responsibility for and interest in solving organizational problems. Effective written and oral communication skills are prerequisites to effective problem-solving skills.

Problem solving is a systematic process of bringing the actual situation or condition closer to the desired condition. Although there are many ways to handle problems, basically there are four steps to solve problems: (1) identifying the problem, (2) generating alternative solutions, (3) selecting a solution, and (4) implementing the solution. It is possible to recycle from steps 3 and 4 to steps 1 and 2.

Tools and Techniques for Problem Solving

Many tools and techniques are available for the problem solver to solve problems. They include brainstorming, synectics, nominal group technique, force-field approach, systems analysis, and others. Differences exist among the problem-solving methods, and all of them do not work equally well in differing situations. In any given situation, one or two methods might have a greater probability of leading to the desired outcomes.

Tools and Techniques for Problem Solving
- *Brainstorming* (the more ideas, the better; encourages uninhibited flow of ideas)
- *Synectics* (a highly structured approach; uses excursions, fantasies, and analogies)
- *Nominal group technique* (no real group exists; uses a very structured approach)
- *The Force-Field Analysis* (identifies inhibiting and facilitating forces)
- *Systems Analysis* (breaks down a large problem into many smaller problems)

Brainstorming

Misconceptions about brainstorming *There are two misconceptions about brainstorming: (1) there is a total lack of control and direction in a brainstorming session, and (2) brainstorming does not involve judgment or evaluation of ideas; all ideas are seen as equally effective and productive.*

The purpose of the brainstorming technique is to generate a great number of ideas—idea generation. The key is to let the members of the group feel free to express whatever ideas come to mind without fear of judgment or criticism. Uninhibited flow of ideas is permitted and negative thinking is not permitted. Recording all ideas and deferring judgment until the later phases of the analysis is the hallmark of brainstorming.

The brainstorming technique is most effective when: (1) the presence of an expert is not necessary, (2) the high level of creativity is seen as a bonus rather than an irritant, and (3) a large quantity of ideas is needed.

There are four rules for effective brainstorming sessions:

1. **Postpone evaluation of ideas**—those of others as well as one's own. This rule is the most critical, because the best way to reduce effective idea generation is to make premature evaluations and/or judgments.
2. **"Freewheeling" is welcome and invited.** Freewheeling means that any idea is permitted, no matter how outlandish or fanciful. One person's flight of fantasy may be the trigger for another's generation of a very workable idea.
3. **Many ideas are wanted.** The greater the number of ideas, the greater the possibility that quality ideas will emerge.
4. **Encourage hitchhiking.** Hitchhiking is the art of combining and improving on ideas; in other words, building on another's suggestion. Frequently, a group will develop a cue for members to use when they want to hitchhike; for example; snapping a finger. Hitchhiking is a by-product of brainstorming.

Advantages of Brainstorming	Disadvantages of Brainstorming
1. Rapid generation of ideas	1. The process focuses on idea generation, but not on specific solutions
2. Identification of many factors of a particular topic	
3. Expression of a cross-section of views from various disciplines	2. The process does not work well where problems are not open-ended

Synectics

Synectics is a technique for creating an environment that encourages creative approaches to problem solving. It is a highly structured approach for an individual who needs a group to help solve a problem. *It involves the use of nontraditional activities such as excursions and fantasies, and analogies.* Synectics is good for idea generation and team building.

Excursions and fantasies are a deliberate move to get participants away from consciously thinking about the problem. Synectics utilize the excursion for employing the subconscious mind to work on the problem and find clues to possible solutions. Excursions are productive with regard to developing possible solutions, and they also serve to energize the group members.

Analogies are an important source of ideas when searching for problem solutions. A checklist is prepared for each type of analogy including personal, direct, symbolic, fantasy, and attribute. The user works through the checklist and tries to find analogies of each type. Personal analogy is where the problem solver puts himself directly into the problem situation. Direct analogy involves searching for a setting where the same function is accomplished.

Advantages of Synectics	Disadvantages of Synectics
1. The method works exceptionally well when people feel in a rut or blocked with a problem	1. Participants may have difficulty with the excursion; some may be reluctant to fantasize
2. The process is fun—there is a lot of energy flowing	2. The process works best with small groups consisting of six to eight members
3. It generates a great number of new perspectives on the problem	3. The process works better for individual problems rather than group problems
4. In addition to structure, there is a plenty of room for flexibility	4. Although the process sounds easy, much preparation is required
5. Participants feel very involved in the process	

Symbolic analogy is associated with symbols, notations, figures, and pictures. Fantasy analogy includes magic and science fiction. In an attribute analogy system, the checklist would list attributes of an object—its name, form, function, color, and material. After listing the attributes, analogies are attached to each one by screening for useful insights. Analogies and symbols are also called free association, where unconventional thinking is encouraged.

Nominal Group Technique

The nominal group technique (NGT) is an idea-generating, consensus-building tool. *No real group exists—name only.* Strength of this process is that it permits a problem to become focused in a short period of time. It uses a very structured approach and is an excellent technique to use when the group members are drawn from various levels of the organizational hierarchy or when they are in conflict with one another. The technique gives everyone an opportunity to express ideas without being interrupted by others in the group.

Generally social psychology researchers have found that individuals working in groups generate more ideas than when they work alone. Furthermore, nominal groups, groups "in name only," where people are brought together but not allowed to communicate, have been found to be more effective for idea generation than interacting groups, where people meet to discuss, brainstorm, and exchange information. Such interacting groups tend to inhibit creative thinking. However, for purposes such as attitude change, team building, and consensus generation, interacting groups have been found superior.

The unique NGT process combines a silent time for idea generation with the social reinforcement of an interacting group setting. This structured process forces equality of participation among members in generating and sharing information about the issue. The NGT group may consist of five to eight participants.

Advantages of Nominal Group Technique	Disadvantages of Nominal Group Technique
1. The technique can be used with groups of varying backgrounds, cultures, education, or work roles who share a common problem or goal	1. The technique calls for a trained leader or group facilitator
2. NGT can be used in groups where participants do not have previous training in group process or communication skills	2. It can deal with only one question at a time
3. The highly structured process is a quick method of bringing people together to approach a common task	3. NGT is inappropriate to use in a group where interacting problem-solving and team-building skills are to be developed
4. NGT promotes the generation of many ideas surrounding an issue	
5. NGT allows for maximum and equal participation of all group members, encouraging input from many areas of expertise	
6. The process is easy to run	

The Force-Field Analysis

The force-field analysis involves the identification of a problem, the factors or forces contributing to making it a problem, and steps for generating solutions. Two main sets of forces are identified: (1) inhibiting forces—those that resist the resolution of the problem, and (2) facilitating forces—those that push the problem toward resolution. Once the forces acting upon a problem are identified, actions can be taken to decrease the major resisting forces, increase the major facilitating forces, or both. This process, then, is basically an analysis of the forces acting to keep the problem a problem.

Force field analysis calls for the definition of present conditions and desired conditions. Once a clear image of these conditions is established, effective intervention strategies can be devised to move from the present to the desired condition. As a problem-solving process, force field involves identifying and analyzing problems, developing strategies for change and clarifying specific steps to be taken to confront the problem. It is an excellent analytical tool. The outcome will be a detailed action plan outlining when, to whom, and how the problem will be addressed. The force-field approach is useful for viewing a problem that involves the entire group, and it may be combined with other problem-solving methods in order to establish a long-term plan of action.

Advantages of Force-Field Analysis	Disadvantages of Force-Field Analysis
1. The outcome of the process is a detailed action plan with evaluation criteria built in	1. The group may get lost in arguments about what the problem really is, what forces are the most important, which action steps to begin with, and so on
2. It is an excellent process for a group to use in dealing with group problems	2. Problems that are not easily and clearly defined may be difficult for this process
3. It is an effective tool to define problems, analyze problems, and develop solutions into workable action plans	3. The team leader needs to be a good listener and should be able to help the team weigh and rank alternatives
4. The group size is not a critical factor and it can be used as a team-building process	

Systems Analysis

Systems analysis breaks down a large problem into many smaller problems. It is an excellent technique if the desired outcome of the problem-solving session is a detailed understanding of a problem. The technique offers a structure for analyzing a problem and various alternative solutions. However, it does not structure the roles of the participants.

The major strengths of this process are that it offers a method of reviewing the total context of a problem. The phrase "systems analysis" does not mean analysis of computer-based information systems. The scope is broader than that—manual, automated, or both.

This method requires the problem solver to look beyond the unit of the problem to the environment for various possible solutions. It focuses on three attributes: (1) open systems, (2) multiple reasons and causes, and (3) the entire picture.

The first attribute assumes that a system is open; it interacts with its environment and can be represented by three models: hierarchical, input-output, and entities model. In the hierarchical model, systems are seen within a structure of subsystems. This framework may be useful in identifying the context in which the group finds itself. An input-output model may be useful in identifying the inputs that are needed and how they are to be transformed toward the desired outputs. The entities model may be used to form tentative hypotheses about how the group members may interact.

The second attribute of systems theory looks at multiple reasons or causes for things; it keeps the problem solver from having tunnel vision concerning the nature of the problem. The systems approach moves away from linear causation, which assumes that the effects of a situation are based on single causes. Realizing that problems often have more than one cause helps to attack the problem from several fronts.

The third attribute of the system model examines the entire picture rather than only one part or element. Remember the classic elephant story—different views of the elephant by six blind men in that they describe the elephant in different ways.

Advantages of Systems Analysis	Disadvantages of Systems Analysis
1. The problem is fully analyzed, touching upon important questions and areas of concern	1. There may be a tendency for the group to get bogged down in the process
2. Several alternatives are developed, leaving abundant options for choice	
3. Can be combined with other problem-solving methods	

Other Problem Solving Tools and Techniques

- **Imagineering**—Imagineering involves the visualization of a complex process, procedure, or operation with all waste eliminated. The imagineer assumes the role of dreamer, realist, and critic. The steps in imagineering consist of taking an action, comparing the results with the person's imagined perfect situation, and making mental correction for the next time. This approach will eventually improve the situation and bring it to the desired level. Imagineering is similar to value-analysis.
- **Value analysis**—Value analysis is a systematic study of a business process or product with a view to improving the process or product and reducing cost. Creative skills are required while doing value analysis. Its goal is to ensure that right activities are performed in the right way the first time. Industrial engineering techniques such as work measurement and simplification methods can be used to achieve the goals. A group approach that encourages free discussion and exchange of ideas is required to conduct value analysis in order to determine how the functions of particular parts, materials, or services can be performed as well or better at a lower cost. Techniques such as brainstorming, hitchhiking, and leapfrogging are used during value analysis.
- **Leapfrogging**—Leapfrogging is taking a big step forward in thinking up idealistic solutions to a problem. For example, leapfrogging can be applied to value-analyzing comparable products to identify their best features and design. These ideas are then combined into a hybrid product that, in turn, can bring new superior products to enter a new market.
- **Blasting, creating, and refining**—Blasting, creating, and refining is used when a completely new way of thinking or speculation is required or when answering a question such as "what else will do the job?" Blasting is good when the group members are free to speculate and come up with totally new ideas that were never heard of or thought about before. Creativity comes into full play.
- **Attribute listing**—Attribute listing emphasizes the detailed observation of each particular characteristic or quality of an item or situation. Attempts are then made to profitably change the characteristic or to relate it to a different item.

- **Edisonian**—Edisonian, named after Thomas Edison, involves trial-and error experimentation. This method requires a tedious and persistent search for the solution.
- **Investigative questions**—The scope includes asking six investigative (journalism) questions—what, where, why, when, who, and how—to understand the root causes of issues and problem better.
- **Cause and effect diagrams.** Cause and effect (C&E) diagrams (also called Ishikawa or fishbone diagrams) can be used to identify possible causes for a problem. The problem solver looks for the root causes by asking the "why" five or six times to move from broad (possible) causes to specific (root) causes. The idea is that by repeating the same question "why," it is believed that the true source of a problem is discovered. This process will help identify the real problem. Then, choose the most likely cause for further review. Brainstorming can be used in developing the C&E diagrams. A graph can be drawn showing the relationship between a cause (independent variable on x-axis) and effect (dependent variable on y-axis). Scatter diagrams can be used to show the root causes of a problem while the C&E diagrams can be used to show possible causes.
- **Pareto charts.** Pareto charts can be drawn to separate the "vital few" from the "trivial many." They are based on the 80/20 rule, that is, 20 percent of items contribute to 80 percent of problems.
- **Psychodramatic approaches**—It involves a role-playing and role-reversal behavior. In psychodrama the attempt is made to bring into focus all elements of an individual's problem; whereas in sociodrama the emphasis is on shared problems of group members.
- **Checklists**—Checklists focus one's attention on a logical list of diverse categories to which the problem could conceivably relate.
- **General semantics**—Approaches that help the individual to discover multiple meanings or relationships in words and expressions.
- **Morphological analysis**—A system involving the methodical interrelating of all elements of a problem in order to discover new approaches to a solution.
- **Panel consensus technique**—A way to process a large number of ideas, circumventing organizational restraints to idea-creation, using extensive participation and emphasizing methods for selecting good ideas.
- **The Delphi technique**—A method used to avoid groupthink, group members do not meet face-to-face to make decisions. Rather, each group member independently and anonymously writes down suggestions and submits comments, which are then centrally compiled. The compiled results are then distributed to the group members who, independently and anonymously, write additional comments. These comments are again centrally compiled and the process repeated until consensus is obtained. The Delphi technique is a group decision-making method.
- **Work measurement**—An industrial engineering program that applies some of the general principles of creative problem solving to the simplification of operations or procedures.
- **Storyboards**—Storyboarding is a group problem-solving technique to create a picture of relevant information. A storyboard can be created for each group that is making decisions. A positive outcome of storyboarding is that it takes less time than interviewing, and many employees can get involved in problem solving, not just the managers.
- **Humor**—In addition to being a powerful tool to relieve tension and hostility, humor is a problem-solving tool. When correctly executed, it opens the mind to seeking creative solutions to the problem. Humor can be in the form of detached jokes, quips, games, puns, and anecdotes. Humor gives perspective and solves problems. Stepping back and viewing a problem with a certain level of detachment restores perspective. A sense of humor sends messages of self-confidence, security, and control of the situation. However, humor should not be sarcastic or scornful.
- **Operations research**—Operations research is a management science discipline attempting to find optimal solutions to business problems using mathematical techniques such as simulation, linear programming, statistics, and computers.
- **Intuitive approach**—The intuitive approach is based on hunches. It does not use a scientific approach and uses subjective estimates or probabilities, which are difficult to replicate.
- **Closure** is a perceptual process that allows a person to solve a complex problem with incomplete information.
- **T-Analysis** is a tabular presentation of strengths on one side and weaknesses on the other side of the letter 'T.' The goal is to solve the weaknesses (problems).

Decision Making

Decision-Making Processes

Every organization grows, prospers, or fails as a result of decisions by its managers, and decisions can be risky and uncertain, without any guarantee of success. Decision making must be done amid constantly changing factors, unclear information, and conflicting points of view. Many organizational decisions are complete failures. Managers also make many successful decisions every day.

Definitions

Organizational decision making is formally defined as the process of identifying and solving problems. The process contains two major stages. In the **problem identification stage,** information about environmental and organizational conditions is monitored to determine if performance is satisfactory and to diagnose the cause of shortcomings. The **problem solution** stage is when alternative courses of action are considered and one alternative is selected and implemented.

Organizational decisions vary in complexity and can be categorized as programmed or nonprogrammed.[176] **Programmed decisions** are repetitive and well defined, and procedures exist for resolving the problem. They are well structured because criteria of performance are normally clear, good information is available about current performance, alternatives are easily specified, and there is relative certainty that the chosen alternative will be successful. Examples of programmed decisions include decision rules, such as when to replace an office copy machine, when to reimburse managers for travel expenses, or whether an applicant has sufficient qualifications for an assembly-line job. Many companies adopt rules based on experience with programmed decisions. For example, general pricing rules in the restaurant industry are that food is marked up three times direct cost, beer four times, and liquor six times. A rule for large hotels staffing banquets is to allow 1 server per 30 guests for a sit-down function and 1 server per 40 guests for a buffet.[177]

> **Programmed decision** A decision made in response to a situation that has occurred often enough to enable decision rules to be developed and applied in the future.

Nonprogrammed decisions are novel and poorly defined, and no procedure exists for solving the problem. They are used when an organization has not seen a problem before and may not know how to respond. Clear-cut decision criteria do not exist. Alternatives are fuzzy. There is uncertainty about whether a proposed solution will solve the problem. Typically, few alternatives can be developed for a nonprogrammed decision, so a single solution is custom-tailored to the problem.

Many nonprogrammed decisions involve strategic planning, because uncertainty is great and decisions are complex. For example, when he first began his job as CEO of **Continental Airlines,** Gordon M. Bethune decided to ground 41 planes, cut more than 4,200 jobs, and abolish cut-rate fares as part of his strategy to make the ailing airline profitable again. Bethune and other top managers had to analyze complex problems, evaluate alternatives, and make a choice about how to pull Continental out of its slump.[178] These and other decisions have proved to be right on target, as Continental has enjoyed renewed profitability and a vastly improved service record.

Particularly complex nonprogrammed decisions have been referred to as "wicked" decisions, because simply defining the problem can turn into a major task. Wicked problems are associated with manager conflicts over objectives and alternatives, rapidly changing circumstances, and unclear linkages among decision elements. Managers dealing with a wicked decision may hit on a solution that merely proves they failed to correctly define the problem to begin with.[179]

Individual Decision Making

Individual decision making by managers can be described in two ways. First is the **rational approach,** which suggests how managers should try to make decisions. Second is the **bounded rationality perspective,** which describes how decisions actually have to be made under severe time and resource constraints. The rational approach is an ideal managers may work toward but never reach.

RATIONAL APPROACH The rational approach to individual decision making stresses the need for systematic analysis of a problem followed by choice and implementation in a logical step-by-step sequence. The rational approach was developed to guide individual decision making because many managers were observed to be unsystematic and arbitrary

150. PROBLEM SOLVING AND DECISION MAKING

in their approach to organizational decisions. Although the rational model is an "ideal" not fully achievable in the real world of uncertainty, complexity, and rapid change, the model does help managers think about decisions more clearly and rationally. Managers should use systematic procedures to make decisions whenever possible. When managers have a deep understanding of the rational decision-making process, it can help them make better decisions even when there is a lack of clear information.

According to the rational approach, decision making can be broken down into eight steps.[180]

1. *Monitor the decision environment.* In the first step, a manager monitors internal and external information that will indicate deviations from planned or acceptable behavior. He or she talks to colleagues and reviews financial statements, performance evaluations, industry indices, competitors' activities, and so forth.
2. *Define the decision problem.* The manager responds to deviations by identifying essential details of the problem: where, when, who was involved, who was affected, and how current activities are influenced.
3. *Specify decision objectives.* The manager determines what performance outcomes should be achieved by a decision.
4. *Diagnose the problem.* In this step, the manager digs below the surface to analyze the cause of the problem. Additional data may be gathered to facilitate this diagnosis. Understanding the cause enables appropriate treatment.
5. *Develop alternative solutions.* Before a manager can move ahead with a decisive action plan, he or she must have a clear understanding of the various options available to achieve desired objectives. The manager may seek ideas and suggestions from other people.
6. *Evaluate alternatives.* This step may involve the use of statistical techniques or personal experience to assess the probability of success. The merits of each alternative are assessed as well as the probability that it will reach the desired objectives.
7. *Choose the best alternative.* This step is the core of the decision process. The manager uses his or her analysis of the problem, objectives, and alternatives to select a single alternative that has the best chance for success.
8. *Implement the chosen alternative.* Finally, the manager uses managerial, administrative, and persuasive abilities and gives directions to ensure that the decision is carried out. The monitoring activity (step 1) begins again as soon as the solution is implemented.

The first four steps in this sequence are the problem identification stage, and the next four steps are the problem solution stage of decision making. All eight steps normally appear in a manager's decision, although each step may not be a distinct element. Managers may know from experience exactly what to do in a situation, so one or more steps will be minimized.

The rational approach works best for programmed decisions, when problems, objectives, and alternatives are clearly defined and the decision maker has time for an orderly, thoughtful process. When decisions are nonprogrammed, ill defined, and piling on top of one another, the individual manager should still try to use the steps in the rational approach, but he or she often will have to take shortcuts by relying on intuition and experience. Deviations from the rational approach are explained by the bounded rationality perspective.

BOUNDED RATIONALITY PERSPECTIVE The point of the rational approach is that managers should try to use systematic procedures to arrive at good decisions. When organizations are facing little competition and are dealing with well-understood issues, managers generally use rational procedures to make decisions.[181] Yet research into managerial decision making shows managers often are unable to follow an ideal procedure. In today's competitive environment, decisions often must be made very quickly. Time pressure, a large number of internal and external factors affecting a decision, and the ill-defined nature of many problems make systematic analysis virtually impossible. Managers have only so much time and mental capacity and, hence, cannot evaluate every goal, problem, and alternative. The attempt to be rational is bounded (limited) by the enormous complexity of many problems. There is a limit to how rational managers can be. For example, an executive in a hurry may have a choice of fifty ties on a rack but will take the first or second one that matches his suit. The executive doesn't carefully weigh all fifty alternatives because the short amount of time and the large number of plausible alternatives would be overwhelming. The manager simply selects the first tie that solves the problem and moves on to the next task.

Large organizational decisions are not only too complex to fully comprehend, but many other constraints impinge on the decision maker. The circumstances are ambiguous, requiring social support, a shared perspective on what happens, and acceptance and agreement. In addition, personal constraints—such as decision style, work pressure, desire for prestige, or simple feelings of insecurity—may constrain either the search for alternatives or the acceptability of an alternative. All of these factors constrain a perfectly rational approach that should lead to an obviously ideal choice.[182] Even seemingly simple decisions, such as selecting a job on graduation from college, can quickly become so complex that a bounded rationality approach is used. Graduating students have been known to search for a job until they have two or three acceptable job offers, at which point their search activity rapidly diminishes. Hundreds of firms may be available for interviews, and two or three job offers are far short of the maximum number that would be possible if students made the decision based on perfect rationality.

The bounded rationality perspective is often associated with intuitive decision processes. In **intuitive decision making,** experience and judgment rather than sequential logic or explicit reasoning are used to make decisions.[183] Intuition is not arbitrary or irrational because it is based on years of practice and hands-on experience, often stored in the subconscious. When managers use their intuition based on long experience with organizational issues, they more rapidly perceive and understand problems, and they develop a gut feeling or hunch about which alternative will solve a problem, speeding the decision-making process.[184] Indeed, many universities are offering courses in creativity and intuition so business students can learn to understand and rely on these processes.

In a situation of great complexity or ambiguity, previous experience and judgment are needed to incorporate intangible elements at both the problem identification and problem solution stages.[185] A study of manager problem finding showed that 30 of 33 problems were ambiguous and ill defined.[186] Bits and scraps of unrelated information from informal sources resulted in a pattern in the manager's mind. The manager could not "prove" a problem existed but knew intuitively that a certain area needed attention. A too simple view of a complex problem is often associated with decision failure,[187] and research shows managers are more likely to respond intuitively to a perceived threat to the organization than to an opportunity.[188]

Intuitive processes are also used in the problem solution stage. A survey found that executives frequently made decisions without explicit reference to the impact on profits or to other measurable outcomes.[189] Many intangible factors—such as a person's concern about the support of other executives, fear of failure, and social attitudes—influence selection of the best alternative. These factors cannot be quantified in a systematic way, so intuition guided the choice of a solution. Managers may make a decision based on what they sense to be right rather than on what they can document with hard data.

However, managers may walk a fine line between two extremes: on the one hand, making arbitrary decisions without careful study and on the other, relying obsessively on numbers and rational analysis.[190] Remember that the bounded rationality perspective and the use of intuition applies mostly to nonprogrammed decisions. The novel, unclear, complex aspects of nonprogrammed decisions mean hard data and logical procedures are not available. A study of executive decision making found that managers simply could not use the rational approach for nonprogrammed decisions, such as when to buy a CT scanner for an osteopathic hospital or whether a city had a need for and could reasonably adopt an enterprise resource planning system.[191] In those cases, managers had limited time and resources, and some factors simply couldn't be measured and analyzed. Trying to quantify such information could cause mistakes because it may oversimplify decision criteria.

Organizational Decision Making

Organizations are composed of managers who make decisions using both rational and intuitive processes; but organization-level decisions are not usually made by a single manager. Many organizational decisions involve several managers. Problem identification and problem solution involve many departments, multiple viewpoints, and even other organizations, which are beyond the scope of an individual manager.

The processes by which decisions are made in organizations are influenced by a number of factors, particularly the organization's own internal structures as well as the degree of stability or instability of the external environment.[192] Research into organization-level decision making has identified four types of organizational decision-making processes: the management science model, the Carnegie model, the incremental decision process model, and the garbage can model.

MANAGEMENT SCIENCE MODEL The **management science model approach** to organizational decision making is the analog to the rational approach by individual managers. Management science came into being during World War II.[193] At that time, mathematical and statistical techniques were applied to urgent, large-scale military problems that were beyond the ability of individual decision makers. Mathematicians, physicists, and operations researchers used systems analysis to develop artillery trajectories, antisubmarine strategies, and bombing strategies such as salvoing (discharging multiple shells simultaneously). Consider the problem of a battleship trying to sink an enemy ship several miles away. The calculation for aiming the battleship's guns should consider distance, wind speed, shell size, speed and direction of both ships, pitch and roll of the firing ship, and curvature of the earth. Methods for performing such calculations using trial and error and intuition are not accurate, take far too long, and may never achieve success.

This is where management science came in. Analysts were able to identify the relevant variables involved in aiming a ship's guns and could model them with the use of mathematical equations. Distance, speed, pitch, roll, shell size, and so on could be calculated and entered into the equations. The answer was immediate, and the guns could begin firing. Factors such as pitch and roll were soon measured mechanically and fed directly into the targeting mechanism. Today, the human element is completely removed from the targeting process. Radar picks up the target, and the entire sequence is computed automatically.

Management science yielded astonishing success for many military problems. This approach to decision making diffused into corporations and business schools, where techniques were studied and elaborated. Today, many corporations have assigned departments to use these techniques. The computer department develops quantitative data for analysis. Operations research departments use mathematical models to quantify relevant variables and develop a quantitative representation of alternative solutions and the probability of each one solving the problem. These departments also use such devices as linear programming, Bayesian statistics, PERT charts, and computer simulations.

Management science is an excellent device for organizational decision making when problems are analyzable and when the variables can be identified and measured. Mathematical models can contain a thousand or more variables, each one relevant in some way to the ultimate outcome. Management science techniques have been used to correctly solve problems as diverse as finding the right spot for a church camp, test marketing the first of a new family of products, drilling for oil, and radically altering the distribution of telecommunications services.[194] Other problems amenable to management science techniques are the scheduling of airline employees, ambulance technicians, telephone operators, and turnpike toll collectors.[195]

Management science can accurately and quickly solve problems that have too many explicit variables for human processing. This system is at its best when applied to problems that are analyzable, are measurable, and can be structured in a logical way. Increasingly sophisticated computer technology and software programs are allowing the expansion of management science to cover a broader range of problems than ever before.

One problem with the management science approach is that quantitative data are not rich. Informal cues that indicate the existence of problems have to be sensed on a more personal basis by managers.[196] The most sophisticated mathematical analyses are of no value if the important factors cannot be quantified and included in the model. Such things as competitor reactions, consumer "tastes," and product "warmth" are qualitative dimensions. In these situations, the role of management science is to supplement manager decision making. Quantitative results can be given to managers for discussion and interpretation along with their informal opinions, judgment, and intuition. The final decision can include qualitative factors as well as quantitative calculations.

CARNEGIE MODEL The **Carnegie model** of organizational decision making is based on the work of Richard Cyert, James March, and Herbert Simon, who were all associated with Carnegie-Mellon University.[197] Their research helped formulate the bounded rationality approach to individual decision making as well as provide new insights about organization decisions. Until their work, research in economics assumed that business firms made decisions as a single entity, as if all relevant information were funneled to the top decision maker for a choice. Research by the Carnegie group indicated that organization-level decisions involved many managers and that a final choice was based on a coalition among those managers. A **coalition** is an alliance among several managers who agree about organizational goals and problem priorities.[198] It could include managers from line departments, staff specialists, and even external groups, such as powerful customers, bankers, or union representatives.

Management coalitions are needed during decision making for two reasons. First, organizational goals are often ambiguous, and operative goals of departments are often inconsistent. When goals are ambiguous and inconsistent, managers disagree about problem priorities. They must bargain about problems and build a coalition around the question of which problems to solve.

The second reason for coalitions is that individual managers intend to be rational but function with human cognitive limitations and other constraints, as described earlier. Managers do not have the time, resources, or mental capacity to identify all dimensions and to process all information relevant to a decision. These limitations lead to coalition-building behavior. Managers talk to each other and exchange points of view to gather information and reduce ambiguity. People who have relevant information or a stake in a decision outcome are consulted. Building a coalition will lead to a decision that is supported by interested parties.

The process of coalition formation has several implications for organizational decision behavior. First, decisions are made to satisfice rather than to optimize problem solutions. **Satisficing** means organizations accept a "satisfactory" rather than a maximum level of performance, enabling them to achieve several goals simultaneously. In decision making, the coalition will accept a solution that is perceived as satisfactory to all coalition members. Second, managers are concerned with immediate problems and short-run solutions. They engage in what Cyert and March called problemistic search.[199] **Problemistic search** means managers look around in the immediate environment for a

Exhibit 100.17 *Choice Processes in the Carnegie Model*

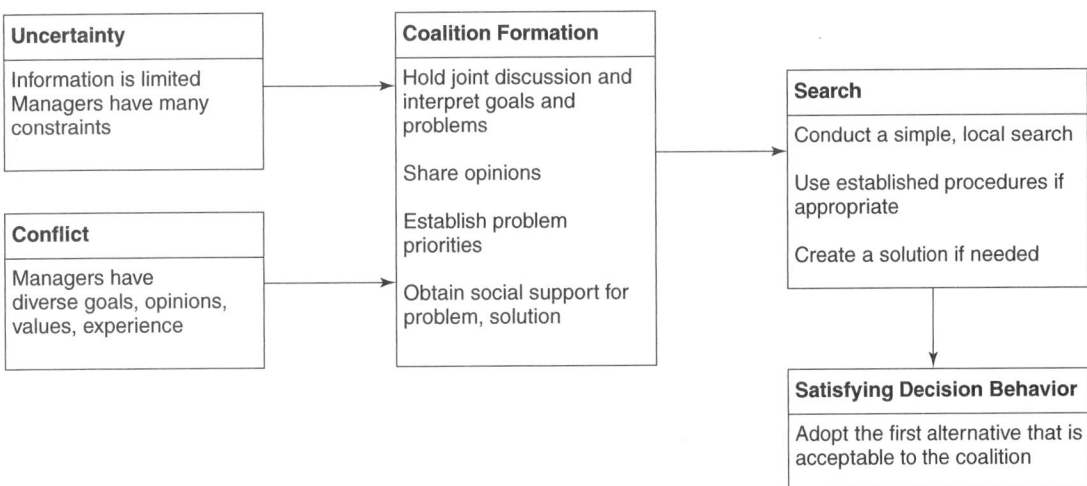

solution to quickly resolve a problem. Managers don't expect a perfect solution when the situation is ill defined and conflict-laden. This contrasts with the management science approach, which assumes that analysis can uncover every reasonable alternative. The Carnegie model says search behavior is just sufficient to produce a satisfactory solution and that managers typically adopt the first satisfactory solution that emerges. Discussion and bargaining are especially important in the problem identification stage of decision making. Unless coalition members perceive a problem, action will not be taken. The decision process described in the Carnegie model is summarized in Exhibit 100.17.

The Carnegie model points out that building agreement through a managerial coalition is a major part of organizational decision making. This is especially true at upper management levels. Discussion and bargaining are time consuming, so search procedures are usually simple and the selected alternative satisfices rather than optimizes problem solution. When problems are programmed—are clear and have been seen before—the organization will rely on previous procedures and routines. Rules and procedures prevent the need for renewed coalition formation and political bargaining. Nonprogrammed decisions, however, require bargaining and conflict resolution.

INCREMENTAL DECISION PROCESS MODEL Henry Mintzberg and his associates at McGill University in Montreal approached organizational decision making from a different perspective. They identified twenty-five decisions made in organizations and traced the events associated with these decisions from beginning to end.[200] Their research identified each step in the decision sequence. This approach to decision making, called the **incremental decision process model,** places less emphasis on the political and social factors described in the Carnegie model, but tells more about the structured sequence of activities undertaken from the discovery of a problem to its solution.[201]

Sample decisions in Mintzberg's research included choosing which jet aircraft to acquire for a regional airline, developing a new supper club, developing a new container terminal in a harbor, identifying a new market for a deodorant, installing a controversial new medical treatment in a hospital, and firing a star announcer.[202] The scope and importance of these decisions are revealed in the length of time taken to complete them. Most of these decisions took more than a year, and one-third of them took more than two years. Most of these decisions were nonprogrammed and required custom-designed solutions.

One discovery from this research is that major organization choices are usually a series of small choices that combine to produce the major decision. Thus, many organizational decisions are a series of nibbles rather than a big bite. Organizations move through several decision points and may hit barriers along the way. Mintzberg called these barriers *decision interrupts*. An interrupt may mean an organization has to cycle back through a previous decision and try something new. Decision loops or cycles are one way the organization learns which alternatives will work. The ultimate solution may be very different from what was initially anticipated.

The pattern of decision stages discovered by Mintzberg and his associates is described in three major decision phases: identification, development, and selection.

Identification Phase The identification phase begins with *recognition*. Recognition means one or more managers become aware of a problem and the need to make a decision. Recognition is usually stimulated by a problem or an opportunity. A problem exists when elements in the external environment change or when internal performance is perceived to be below standard. In the case of firing a radio announcer, comments about the announcer came from listeners, other announcers, and advertisers. Managers interpreted these cues until a pattern emerged that indicated a problem had to be dealt with.

The second step is *diagnosis,* which is where more information is gathered if needed to define the problem situation. Diagnosis may be systematic or informal, depending upon the severity of the problem. Severe problems do not have time for extensive diagnosis; the response must be immediate. Mild problems are usually diagnosed in a more systematic manner.

Development Phase The development phase is when a solution is shaped to solve the problem defined in the identification phase. The development of a solution takes one of two directions. First, *search* procedures may be used to seek out alternatives within the organization's repertoire of solutions. For example, in the case of firing a star announcer, managers asked what the radio station had done the last time an announcer had to be let go. To conduct the search, organization participants may look into their own memories, talk to other managers, or examine the formal procedures of the organization.

The second direction of development is to *design* a custom solution. This happens when the problem is novel so that previous experience has no value. Mintzberg found that in these cases, key decision makers have only a vague idea of the ideal solution. Gradually, through a trial-and-error process, a custom-designed alternative will emerge. Development of the solution is a groping, incremental procedure, building a solution brick by brick.

Selection Phase The selection phase is when the solution is chosen. This phase is not always a matter of making a clear choice among alternatives. In the case of custom-made solutions, selection is more an evaluation of the single alternative that seems feasible.

Evaluation and choice may be accomplished in three ways. The *judgment* form of selection is used when a final choice falls upon a single decision maker, and the choice involves judgment based upon experience. In analysis, alternatives are evaluated on a more systematic basis, such as with management science techniques. Mintzberg found that most decisions did not involve systematic analysis and evaluation of alternatives. *Bargaining* occurs when selection involves a group of decision makers. Each decision maker may have a different stake in the outcome, so conflict emerges. Discussion and bargaining occur until a coalition is formed, as in the Carnegie model described earlier.

When a decision is formally accepted by the organization, *authorization* takes place. The decision may be passed up the hierarchy to the responsible hierarchical level. Authorization is often routine because the expertise and knowledge rest with the lower decision makers who identified the problem and developed the solution. A few decisions are rejected because of implications not anticipated by lower-level managers.

Dynamic Factors Organizational decisions do not follow an orderly progression from recognition through authorization. Minor problems arise that force a loop back to an earlier stage. These are decision interrupts. If a custom-designed solution is perceived as unsatisfactory, the organization may have to go back to the very beginning and reconsider whether the problem is truly worth solving. Feedback loops can be caused by problems of timing, politics, disagreement among managers, inability to identify a feasible solution, turnover of managers, or the sudden appearance of a new alternative. For example, when a small Canadian airline made the decision to acquire jet aircraft, the board authorized the decision, but shortly after, a new chief executive was brought in who canceled the contract, recycling the decision back to the identification phase. He accepted the diagnosis of the problem but insisted upon a new search for alternatives. Then a foreign airline went out of business and two used aircraft became available at a bargain price. This presented an unexpected option, and the chief executive used his own judgment to authorize the purchase of the aircraft.[203]

Because most decisions take place over an extended period of time, circumstances change. Decision making is a dynamic process that may require a number of cycles before a problem is solved.

GARBAGE CAN MODEL The **garbage can model** is one of the most recent and interesting descriptions of organizational decision processes. It is not directly comparable to the earlier models, because the garbage can model deals with the pattern or flow of multiple decisions within organizations, whereas the incremental and Carnegie models focus on how a single decision is made. The garbage can model helps you think of the whole organization and the frequent decisions being made by managers throughout.

Organized Anarchy The garbage can model was developed to explain the pattern of decision making in organizations that experience extremely high uncertainty. Michael Cohen, James March, and Johan Olsen, the originators of the model, called the highly uncertain conditions an **organized anarchy,** which is an extremely organic organization.[204]

Organized anarchies do not rely on the normal vertical hierarchy of authority and bureaucratic decision rules. They are caused by three characteristics:

1. *Problematic preferences.* Goals, problems, alternatives, and solutions are ill defined. Ambiguity characterizes each step of a decision process.
2. *Unclear, poorly understood technology.* Cause-and-effect relationships within the organization are difficult to identify. An explicit database that applies to decisions is not available.
3. *Turnover.* Organizational positions experience turnover of participants. In addition, employees are busy and have only limited time to allocate to any one problem or decision. Participation in any given decision will be fluid and limited.

The organized anarchy describes organizations characterized by rapid change and a collegial, nonbureaucratic environment. No organization fits this extremely organic circumstance all the time, although contemporary learning organizations and today's Internet-based companies may experience it much of the time. Many organizations will occasionally find themselves in positions of making decisions under unclear, problematic circumstances. The garbage can model is useful for understanding the pattern of these decisions.

Streams of Events The unique characteristic of the garbage can model is that the decision process is not seen as a sequence of steps that begins with a problem and ends with a solution. Indeed, problem identification and problem solution may not be connected to each other. An idea may be proposed as a solution when no problem is specified. A problem may exist and never generate a solution. Decisions are the outcome of independent streams of events within the organization. The four streams relevant to organizational decision making are as follows:

1. *Problems.* Problems are points of dissatisfaction with current activities and performance. They represent a gap between desired performance and current activities. Problems are perceived to require attention. However, they are distinct from solutions and choices. A problem may lead to a proposed solution or it may not. Problems may not be solved when solutions are adopted.
2. *Potential solutions.* A solution is an idea somebody proposes for adoption. Such ideas form a flow of alternative solutions through the organization. Ideas may be brought into the organization by new personnel or may be invented by existing personnel. Participants may simply be attracted to certain ideas and push them as logical choices regardless of problems. Attraction to an idea may cause an employee to look for a problem to which the idea can be attached and, hence, justified. The point is that solutions exist independent of problems.
3. *Participants.* Organization participants are employees who come and go throughout the organization. People are hired, reassigned, and fired. Participants vary widely in their ideas, perception of problems, experience, values, and training. The problems and solutions recognized by one manager will differ from those recognized by another manager.
4. *Choice opportunities.* Choice opportunities are occasions when an organization usually makes a decision. They occur when contracts are signed, people are hired, or a new product is authorized. They also occur when the right mix of participants, solutions, and problems exists. Thus, a manager who happened to learn of a good idea may suddenly become aware of a problem to which it applies and, hence, can provide the organization with a choice opportunity. Match-ups of problems and solutions often result in decisions.

With the concept of four streams, the overall pattern of organizational decision making takes on a random quality. Problems, solutions, participants, and choices all flow through the organization. In one sense, the organization is a large garbage can in which these streams are being stirred. When a problem, solution, and participant happen to connect at one point, a decision may be made and the problem may be solved; but if the solution does not fit the problem, the problem may not be solved. Thus, when viewing the organization as a whole and considering its high level of uncertainty, one sees problems arise that are not solved and solutions tried that do not work. Organization decisions are disorderly and not the result of a logical, step-by-step sequence. Events may be so ill defined and complex that decisions, problems, and solutions act as independent events. When they connect, some problems are solved, but many are not.[205]

Consequences Four consequences of the garbage can decision process for organizational decision making are as follows:

1. Solutions may be proposed even when problems do not exist.
2. Choices are made without solving problems.
3. Problems may persist without being solved.
4. A few problems are solved.

Special Decision Circumstances

In a highly competitive world beset by global competition and rapid change, decision making seldom fits the traditional rational, analytical model. To cope in today's world, managers must learn to make decisions fast, especially in high-velocity environments, to learn from decision mistakes, and to avoid escalating commitment to an unsatisfactory course of action.

HIGH-VELOCITY ENVIRONMENTS In some industries today, the rate of competitive and technological change is so extreme that market data is either unavailable or obsolete, strategic windows open and shut quickly, perhaps within a few months, and the cost of a decision error is company failure. Recent research has examined how successful companies make decisions in these **high-velocity environments,** especially to understand whether organizations abandon rational approaches or have time for incremental implementation.[206]

Comparing successful with unsuccessful decisions in high-velocity environments suggests the following guidelines.

- Successful decision makers track information in real time to develop a deep and intuitive grasp of the business. Two to three intense meetings per week with all key players are usual. Decision makers track operating statistics about cash, scrap, backlog, work in process, and shipments to constantly feel the pulse of what is happening. Unsuccessful firms are more concerned with future planning and forward-looking information, with only a loose grip on immediate happenings.
- During a major decision, successful companies begin immediately to build multiple alternatives. Implementation may run in parallel before finally settling on a final choice. Slow-decision companies develop only a single alternative, moving to another only after the first one fails.
- Fast, successful decision makers seek advice from everyone and depended heavily on one or two savvy, trusted colleagues as counselors. Slow companies are unable to build trust and agreement among the best people.
- Fast companies involved everyone in the decision and try for consensus; but if consensus did not emerge, the top manager made the choice and moved ahead. Waiting for everyone to be on board created more delays than warranted. Slow companies delay decisions to achieve a uniform consensus.
- Fast, successful choices are well integrated with other decisions and the overall strategic direction of the company. Less successful choices consider the decision in isolation from other decisions; the decision is made in the abstract.[207]

When speed matters, a slow decision is as ineffective as the wrong decision. Speed is a crucial competitive weapon in a growing number of industries, and companies can learn to make decisions fast. Managers must be plugged into the pulse of the company, must seek consensus and advice, and then be ready to take the risk and move ahead.

DECISION MISTAKES AND LEARNING Organizational decisions produce many errors, especially when made under high uncertainty. Managers simply cannot determine or predict which alternative will solve a problem. In these cases, the organization must make the decision—and take the risk—often in the spirit of trial and error. If an alternative fails, the organization can learn from it and try another alternative that better fits the situation. Each failure provides new information and learning. The point for managers is to move ahead with the decision process despite the potential for mistakes. "Chaotic action is preferable to orderly inaction."[208]

In many cases, managers have been encouraged to instill a climate of experimentation, even foolishness, to facilitate creative decision making. If one idea fails, another idea should be tried. Failure often lays the groundwork for success, as when technicians at **3M** developed Post-it Notes based on a failed product—a not-very-sticky glue. Companies such as **PepsiCo** believe that if all their new products succeed, they're doing something wrong—not taking the necessary risks to develop new markets.[209]

Only by making mistakes can managers and organizations go through the process of **decision learning** and acquire sufficient experience and knowledge to perform more effectively in the future.

ESCALATING COMMITMENT A much more dangerous mistake is to persist in a course of action when it is failing. Research suggests that organizations often continue to invest time and money in a solution despite strong evidence that it is not working. Two explanations are given for why managers **escalate commitment** to a failing decision. The first is that managers block or distort negative information when they are personally responsible for a negative decision. They simply don't know when to pull the plug. In some cases, they continue to throw good money after bad even when a strategy seems incorrect and goals are not being met.[210] An example of this distortion is the reaction at **Borden** when the company began losing customers following its refusal to lower prices on dairy products. When the cost of raw milk dropped, Borden hoped to boost the profit margins of its dairy products, convinced that customers would pay a premium for the brand name. Borden's sales plummeted as low-priced competitors mopped up, but top executives stuck with their premium pricing policy for almost a year. By then, the company's dairy division was operating at a severe loss.[211]

A second explanation for escalating commitment to a failing decision is that consistency and persistence are valued in contemporary society. Consistent managers are considered better leaders than those who switch around from one course of action to another. Even though organizations learn through trial and error, organizational norms value consistency. These norms may result in a course of action being maintained, resources being squandered, and learning being inhibited.

Failure to admit a mistake and adopt a new course of action is far worse than an attitude that encourages mistakes and learning. Based on what has been said about decision making in this chapter, one can expect companies to be ultimately successful in their decision making by adopting a learning approach toward solutions. They will make mistakes along the way, but they will resolve uncertainty through the trial-and-error process.

Business Policy, Culture, and Ethics

Business Policy

Business objectives are derived from company's vision and mission (ends). Business strategy is designed to achieve those objectives (means). Business policy, along with budgets, is a part of strategy execution and implementation in that the policy supports the strategy. Business policies can be established either at high level (e.g., ethical behavior, pollution control) or low level (e.g., employee compensation and benefits, training). Similar to business strategy, business policy can be both proactive (intended and deliberate) and reactive (adaptive). Business strategy precedes business policy while business ethics succeeds business policy. Organizational culture has a powerful impact on employees' behavior and business ethics.

Organizational Culture

Organizational success or failure is often attributed to culture. In *Fortune* magazine's survey of the most admired companies, the single best predictor of overall excellence was the ability to attract, motivate, and retain talented people, and CEOs say organizational culture is their most important mechanism for enhancing this capability.[212] Southwest Airlines, Johnson & Johnson, and 3M have been praised for their innovative cultures. Culture has also been implicated in problems faced by companies such as **Kodak** and **Kellogg,** where changing the culture is considered a key to ultimate success.

The popularity of the organizational culture topic raises a number of questions. Can we identify cultures? Can culture be aligned with strategy? How can cultures be managed or changed? The best place to start is by defining culture and explaining how it can be identified in organizations.

What Is Culture?

Culture is the set of values, guiding beliefs, understandings, and ways of thinking that is shared by members of an organization and taught to new members as correct.[213] It represents the unwritten, feeling part of the organization. Everyone participates in culture, but culture generally goes unnoticed. It is only when organizations try to implement new strategies or programs that go against basic culture norms and values that they come face to face with the power of culture.

Exhibit 100.18 *Levels of Corporate Culture*

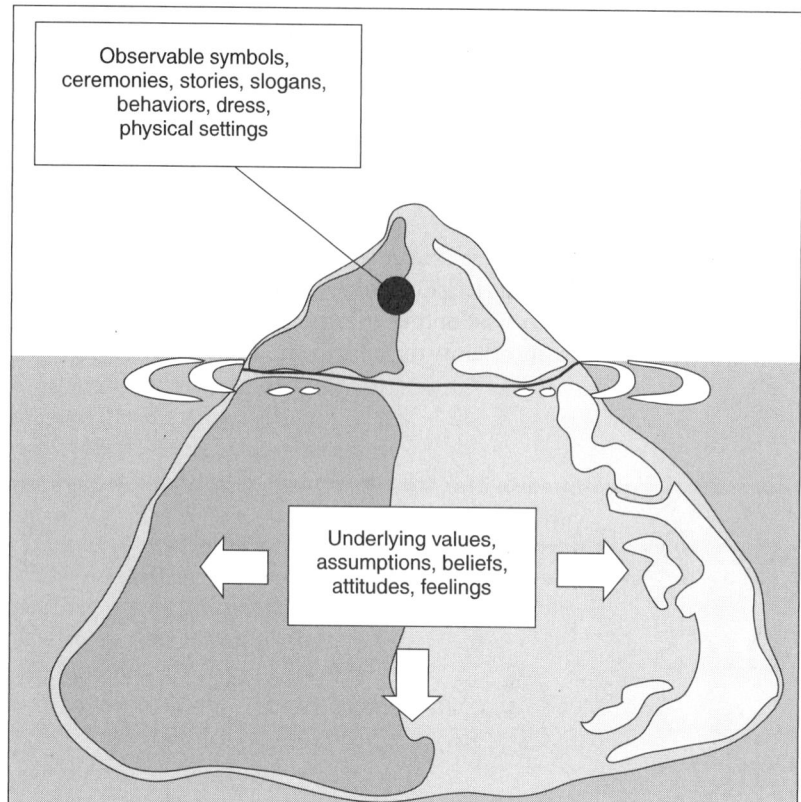

Organizational culture exists at two levels, as illustrated in Exhibit 100.18. On the surface are visible artifacts and observable behaviors—the ways people dress and act and the symbols, stories, and ceremonies organization members share. The visible elements of culture, however, reflect deeper values in the minds of organization members. These underlying values, assumptions, beliefs, and thought processes are the true culture.[214] For example, at Southwest Airlines, red "LUV" hearts emblazon the company's training manuals and other materials. The hearts are a visible symbol; the underlying value is that "we are one family of people who truly care about each other." The attributes of culture display themselves in many ways but typically evolve into a patterned set of activities carried out through social interactions.[215] Those patterns can be used to interpret culture.

Emergence and Purpose of Culture

Culture provides members with a sense of organizational identity and generates a commitment to beliefs and values that are larger than themselves. Though ideas that become part of culture can come from anywhere within the organization, an organization's culture generally begins with a founder or early leader who articulates and implements particular ideas and values as a vision, philosophy, or business strategy. When these ideas and values lead to success, they become institutionalized, and an organizational culture emerges that reflects the vision and strategy of the founder or leader.[216]

Cultures serve two critical functions in organizations: (1) to integrate members so that they know how to relate to one another, and (2) to help the organization adapt to the external environment. **Internal integration** means that members develop a collective identity and know how to work together effectively. It is culture that guides day-to-day working relationships and determines how people communicate within the organization, what behavior is acceptable or not acceptable, and how power and status are allocated. **External adaptation** refers to how the organization meets goals and deals with outsiders. Culture helps guide the daily activities of workers to meet certain goals. It can help the organization respond rapidly to customer needs or the moves of a competitor. We will discuss culture and adaptation in more detail later.

Interpreting Culture

To identify and interpret the content of culture requires that people make inferences based on observable artifacts. Artifacts can be studied but are hard to decipher accurately. An award ceremony in one company may have a different meaning than in another company. To decipher what is really going on in an organization requires detective work and probably some experience as an insider. Some of the typical and important observable aspects of culture are rites and ceremonies, stories, symbols, and language.

RITES AND CEREMONIES Important artifacts for culture are **rites and ceremonies,** the elaborate, planned activities that make up a special event and are often conducted for the benefit of an audience. Managers can hold rites and ceremonies to provide dramatic examples of what a company values. These are special occasions that reinforce specific values, create a bond among people for sharing an important understanding, and anoint and celebrate heroes and heroines who symbolize important beliefs and activities.[217]

Four types of rites that appear in organizations include passage, enhancement, renewal, and integration. *Rites of passage* facilitate the transition of employees into new social roles. *Rites of enhancement* create stronger social identities and increase the status of employees. *Rites of renewal* reflect training and development activities that improve organization functioning. *Rites of integration* create common bonds and good feelings among employees and increase commitment to the organization.

STORIES **Stories** are narratives based on true events that are frequently shared among organizational employees and told to new employees to inform them about an organization. Many stories are about company **heroes** who serve as models or ideals for serving cultural norms and values. Some stories are considered **legends** because the events are historic and may have been embellished with fictional details. Other stories are **myths,** which are consistent with the values and beliefs of the organization but are not supported by facts.[218] Stories keep alive the primary values of the organization and provide a shared understanding among all employees.

SYMBOLS Another tool for interpreting culture is the symbol. A symbol is something that represents another thing. In one sense, ceremonies, stories, slogans, and rites are all symbols. They symbolize deeper values of an organization. Another symbol is a physical artifact of the organization. Physical symbols are powerful because they focus attention on a specific item.

LANGUAGE The final technique for influencing culture is **language.** Many companies use a specific saying, slogan, metaphor, or other form of language to convey special meaning to employees. Slogans can be readily picked up and repeated by employees as well as customers of the company. **Bank One** promotes its emphasis on customer service through the slogan, "Whatever it takes." Bank One's culture encourages employees to do whatever it takes to exceed customer expectations.

Recall that culture exists at two levels—the underlying values and assumptions and the visible artifacts and observable behaviors. The slogans, symbols, and ceremonies just described are artifacts that reflect underlying company values. These visible artifacts and behaviors can be used by managers to shape company values and to strengthen organizational culture.

Organizational Design and Culture

Corporate culture should reinforce the strategy and structural design that the organization needs to be effective within its environment. For example, if the external environment requires flexibility and responsiveness, such as the environment for emerging Internet-based companies, the culture should encourage adaptability. The correct relationship among cultural values, organizational strategy and structure, and the environment can enhance organizational performance.

Studies of culture and effectiveness propose that the fit among culture, strategy and structure, and the environment is associated with four categories of culture, which are illustrated in Exhibit 100.19.[219] These categories are based on two factors: (1) the extent to which the competitive environment requires flexibility or stability, and (2) the extent to which the strategic focus and strength is internal or external. The four categories associated with these differences are adaptability/entrepreneurial, mission, clan, and bureaucratic. Each of the four cultures can be successful, depending on the needs of the external environment and the organization's strategic focus.

Exhibit 100.19 *Relationship of Environment and Strategy to Corporate Culture*

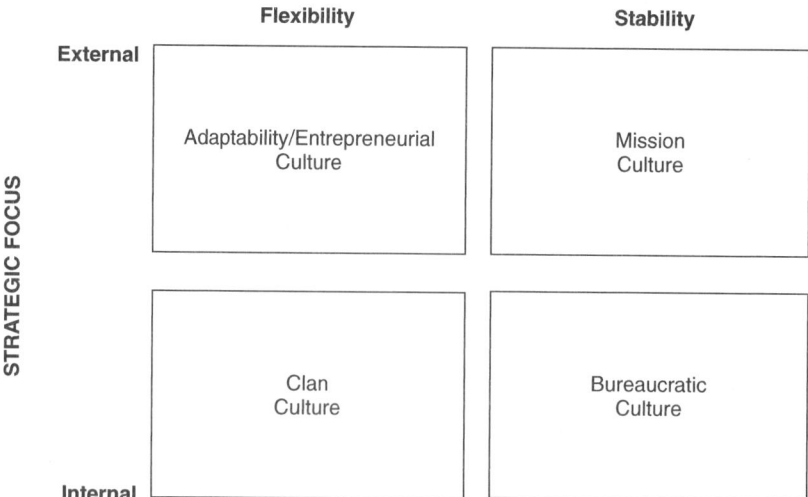

Source: Based on Daniel R. Denison and Aneil K. Mishra, "Toward a Theory of Organizational Culture and Effectiveness," *Organization Science* 6, no. 2 (March–April 1995), 204–23; R. Hooijberg and F. Petrock, "On Cultural Change: Using the Competing Values Framework to Help Leaders Execute a Transformational Strategy," *Human Resources Management* 32 (1993), 29–50; and R. E. Quinn, *Beyond Rational Management: Mastering the Paradoxes and Competing Demands of High Performance* (San Francisco: Jossey–Bass, 1988).

The Adaptability/Entrepreneurial Culture

The **adaptability/entrepreneurial culture** is characterized by strategic focus on the external environment through flexibility and change to meet customer needs. The culture encourages norms and beliefs that support the capacity of the organization to detect, interpret, and translate signals from the environment into new behavior responses. This type of company, however, doesn't just react quickly to environmental changes—it actively creates change. Innovation, creativity, and risk-taking are valued and rewarded.

Most e-commerce companies, such as **eBay, Drugstore.com** and **Buy.com,** as well as companies in the marketing, electronics, and cosmetics industries, use this type of culture because they must move quickly to satisfy customers.

The Mission Culture

An organization concerned with serving specific customers in the external environment, but without the need for rapid change, is suited to the mission culture. The **mission culture** is characterized by emphasis on a clear vision of the organization's purpose and on the achievement of goals, such as sales growth, profitability, or market share, to help achieve the purpose. Individual employees may be responsible for a specified level of performance, and the organization promises specified rewards in return. Managers shape behavior by envisioning and communicating a desired future state for the organization. Because the environment is stable, they can translate the vision into measurable goals and evaluate employee performance for meeting them. In some cases, mission cultures reflect a high level of competitiveness and a profit-making orientation.

The Clan Culture

The **clan culture** has a primary focus on the involvement and participation of the organization's members and on rapidly changing expectations from the external environment. This culture is similar to the clan form of control described in Section 175. More than any other, this culture focuses on the needs of employees as the route to high performance. Involvement and participation create a sense of responsibility and ownership and, hence, greater commitment to the organization.

Companies in the fashion and retail industries also use this culture because it releases the creativity of employees to respond to rapidly changing tastes.

The Bureaucratic Culture

The **bureaucratic culture** has an internal focus and a consistency orientation for a stable environment. This organization has a culture that supports a methodical approach to doing business. Symbols, heroes, and ceremonies support co-operation, tradition, and following established policies and practices as a way to achieve goals. Personal involvement is somewhat lower here, but that is outweighed by a high level of consistency, conformity, and collaboration among members. This organization succeeds by being highly integrated and efficient.

Culture Strength and Organizational Subcultures

A strong organizational culture can have a powerful impact on company performance. **Culture strength** refers to the degree of agreement among members of an organization about the importance of specific values. If widespread consensus exists about the importance of those values, the culture is cohesive and strong; if little agreement exists, the culture is weak.[220]

A strong culture is typically associated with the frequent use of ceremonies, symbols, stories, heroes, and slogans. These elements increase employee commitment to the desired values. In addition, managers who want to create and maintain strong corporate cultures often give emphasis to the selection and socialization of employees. For example, at Southwest Airlines, prospective employees are subjected to rigorous interviewing, sometimes even by Southwest's regular customers, so that only those who fit the culture are hired. At Trilogy Software, Inc., one of today's fastest-growing software companies, selection and socialization of new employees is a company-wide mission.

However, culture is not always uniform throughout the organization. Even in organizations that have strong cultures, there may be several sets of subcultures, particularly within large organizations. **Subcultures** develop to reflect the common problems, goals, and experiences that members of a team, department, or other unit share. An office, branch, or unit of a company that is physically separated from the company's main operations may also take on a distinctive subculture.

For example, although the dominant culture of an organization may be a mission culture, various departments may also reflect characteristics of adaptability/ entrepreneurial, clan, or bureaucratic cultures. The manufacturing department of a large organization may thrive in an environment that emphasizes order, efficiency, and obedience to rules, whereas the research and development department may be characterized by employee empowerment, flexibility, and customer focus. This is similar to the concept of differentiation, where employees in manufacturing, sales, and research departments studied by Paul Lawrence and Jay Lorsch[221] developed different values with respect to time horizon, interpersonal relationships, and formality in order to perform the job of each particular department most effectively.

Business Ethics

Of the values that make up an organization's culture, ethical values are now considered among the most important. Ethical standards are becoming part of the formal policies and informal cultures of many organizations, and courses in ethics are taught in many business schools. **Ethics** is the code of moral principles and values that governs the behaviors of a person or group with respect to what is right or wrong. Ethical values set standards as to what is good or bad in conduct and decision making.[222]

Ethics is distinct from behaviors governed by law. The **rule of law** arises from a set of codified principles and regulations that describe how people are required to act, are generally accepted in society, and are enforceable in the courts.[223]

Ethical standards for the most part apply to behavior not covered by the law, and the rule of law covers behaviors not necessarily covered by ethical standards. Current laws often reflect combined moral judgments, but not all moral judgments are codified into law. The morality of aiding a drowning person, for example, is not specified by law, and driving on the righthand side of the road has no moral basis; but in areas such as robbery or murder, rules and moral standards overlap.

Unethical conduct in organizations is surprisingly widespread. More than 54 percent of human resource professionals polled by the Society for Human Resource Management and the Ethics Resource Center reported observing employees lying to supervisors or coworkers, falsifying reports or records, or abusing drugs or alcohol while on the job.[224] Many people believe that if you are not breaking the law, then you are behaving in an ethical manner, but ethics often go far beyond the law.[225] Many behaviors have not been codified, and managers must be sensitive to emerging norms and values about those issues. **Managerial ethics** are principles that guide the decisions and behaviors of managers with regard to whether they are right or wrong in a moral sense. The notion of **social responsibility** is an extension of this idea and refers to management's obligation to make choices and take action so that the organization contributes to the welfare and interest of society as well as to itself.[226]

Examples of the need for managerial ethics are as follows:[227]

- The supervisor of a travel agency was aware that her agents and she could receive large bonuses for booking one hundred or more clients each month with an auto rental firm, although clients typically wanted the rental agency selected on the basis of lowest cost.
- The executive in charge of a parts distribution facility told employees to tell phone customers that inventory was in stock even if it was not. Replenishing the item only took one to two days, no one was hurt by the delay, and the business was kept from competitors.
- The project manager for a consulting project wondered whether some facts should be left out of a report because the marketing executives paying for the report would look bad if the facts were reported.
- A North American manufacturer operating abroad was asked to make cash payments (a bribe) to government officials and was told it was consistent with local customs, despite being illegal in North America.

These issues are exceedingly difficult to resolve and often represent dilemmas. An **ethical dilemma** arises when each alternative choice or behavior seems undesirable because of a potentially negative ethical consequence. Right or wrong cannot be clearly identified. These choices can be aided by establishing ethical values within the organization as part of corporate culture. Corporate culture can embrace the ethical values needed for business success.

Sources of Ethical Values in Organizations

The standards for ethical or socially responsible conduct are embodied within each employee as well as within the organization itself. In addition, external stakeholders can influence standards of what is ethical and socially responsible. The immediate forces that impinge on ethical decisions are summarized in Exhibit 100.20. Individual beliefs and values, a person's ethical decision framework, and moral development influence personal ethics. Organization culture, as we have already discussed, shapes the overall framework of values within the organization. Moreover, formal organization systems influence values and behaviors according to the organization's policy framework and reward systems.

Companies also respond to numerous stakeholders in determining what is right. They consider how their actions may be viewed by customers, government agencies, shareholders, and the general community, as well as the impact

Exhibit 100.20 *Forces That Shape Managerial Ethics*

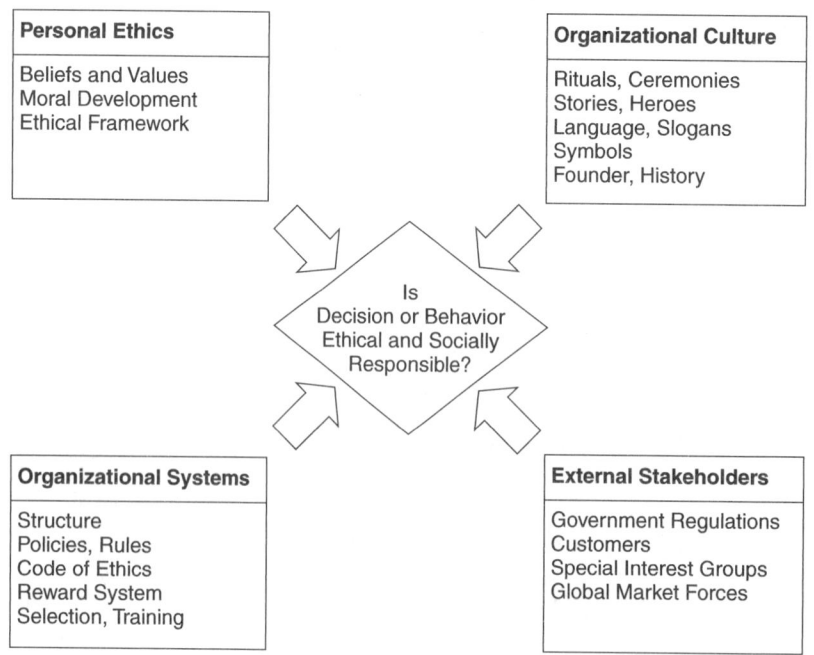

each alternative course of action may have on various stakeholders. All of these factors can be explored to understand ethical decisions in organizations.[228]

Personal Ethics

Every individual brings a set of personal beliefs and values into the workplace. Personal values and the moral reasoning that translates these values into behavior are an important aspect of ethical decision making in organizations.[229]

The family backgrounds and spiritual values of managers provide principles by which they carry out business. In addition, people go through stages of moral development that affect their ability to translate values into behavior. For example, children have a low level of moral development, making decisions and behaving to obtain rewards and avoid physical punishment. At an intermediate level of development, people learn to conform to expectations of good behavior as defined by colleagues and society. Most managers are at this level, willingly upholding the law and responding to societal expectations. At the highest level of moral development are people who develop an internal set of standards. These are self-chosen ethical principles that are more important to decisions than external expectations. Only a few people reach this high level, which can mean breaking laws if necessary to sustain higher moral principles.[230]

The other personal factor is whether managers have developed an *ethical framework* that guides their decisions. *Utilitarian theory*, for example, argues that ethical decisions should be made to generate the greatest benefits for the largest number of people. This framework is often consistent with business decisions because costs and benefits can be calculated in dollars. The *personal liberty* framework argues that decisions should be made to ensure the greatest possible freedom of choice and liberty for individuals. Liberties include freedom to act on one's conscience, free speech, due process, and the right to privacy. The *distributive justice* framework holds that moral decisions are those that promote equity, fairness, and impartiality with respect to the distribution of rewards and the administration of rules, which are essential for social cooperation.[231]

Organizational Culture

Rarely can ethical or unethical business practices be attributed entirely to the personal ethics of a single individual. Because business practices reflect the values, attitudes, and behavior patterns of an organization's culture, ethics is as much an organizational issue as a personal one. To promote ethical behavior in the workplace, companies should make ethics an integral part of the organization's culture.

Organizational Systems

The third category of influences that shape managerial ethics is formal organizational systems. This includes the basic architecture of the organization, such as whether ethical values are incorporated in policies and rules; whether an explicit code of ethics is available and issued to members; whether organizational rewards, including praise, attention, and promotions, are linked to ethical behavior; and whether ethics is a consideration in the selection and training of employees. These formal efforts can reinforce ethical values that exist in the informal culture.

External Stakeholders

Managerial ethics and social responsibility are also influenced by a variety of external stakeholders, groups outside the organization that have a stake in the organization's performance. Ethical and socially responsible decision making recognizes that the organization is part of a larger community and considers the impact of a decision or action on all stakeholders.[232] Important external stakeholders are government agencies, customers, special interest groups such as those concerned with the natural environment, and global market forces.

Companies must operate within the limits of certain government regulations, such as safety laws, environmental protection requirements, and many other laws and regulations.

Special interest groups continue to be one of the largest stakeholder concerns that companies face. Today, those concerned with corporate responsibility to the natural environment are particularly vocal. Thus, environmentalism is becoming an integral part of organizational planning and decision making for leading companies. The concept of *sustainable development*, a dual concern for economic growth and environmental sustainability, has been gaining ground among many business leaders. The public is no longer comfortable with organizations focusing solely on profit at the expense of the natural environment. Environmental sustainability—meaning that what is taken out of the environmental system for food, shelter, clothing, energy, and other human uses is restored to the system in waste that can be reused—is a part of strategy for many companies.

Another growing pressure on organizations is related to the rapidly changing global market. Companies operating globally face difficult ethical issues. Thousands of U.S. workers have lost jobs or earning power because companies can get the same work done overseas for lower costs.

Shaping Culture and Ethics through Structure and Systems

In the experience of the surveyed companies, the single most important factor in ethical decision making was the role of top management in providing commitment, leadership, and example for ethical values. The CEO and other top managers must be committed to specific values and must give constant leadership in tending and renewing those values. Values can be communicated in a number of ways—speeches, company publications, policy statements, and, especially, personal actions. Top leaders are responsible for creating and sustaining a culture that emphasizes the importance of ethical behavior for all employees every day. When the CEO engages in unethical practices or fails to take firm and decisive action in response to the unethical practices of others, this attitude filters down through the organization. Formal ethics codes and training programs are worthless if leaders do not set and live up to high standards of ethical conduct.[233]

A set of tools leaders can use to shape cultural and ethical values is the formal structure and systems of the organization. These systems have been especially effective in recent years for influencing managerial ethics.

STRUCTURE Managers can assign responsibility for ethical values to a specific position. This not only allocates organization time and energy to the problem but symbolizes to everyone the importance of ethics. One example is an **ethics committee,** which is a group of executives appointed to oversee company ethics. The committee provides rulings on questionable ethical issues and assumes responsibility for disciplining wrongdoers.

Many companies are setting up ethics offices that go beyond a "police" mentality to act more as counseling centers. Alfred C. Martinez, chairman and CEO of Sears, set up an ethics and business practices office as part of his efforts to revive the company.

Another example is an **ethics ombudsperson,** who is a single manager, perhaps with a staff, who serves as the corporate conscience. As workforces become more diverse and organizations continue to emphasize greater employee involvement, it is likely that more and more companies will assign ombudspersons to listen to grievances, investigate ethical complaints, and point out employee concerns and possible ethical abuses to top management. For the system to work, it is necessary for the person in this position to have direct access to the chairman or CEO, as does the corporate ombudsperson for **Pitney Bowes.**[234]

DISCLOSURE MECHANISMS. The ethics office, committee, or ombudsperson provides mechanisms for employees to voice concerns about ethical practices. One important function is to establish supportive policies and procedures about whistle-blowing. **Whistle-blowing** is employee disclosure of illegal, immoral, or illegitimate practices on the part of the organization.[235] One value of corporate policy is to protect whistle-blowers so they will not be transferred to lower-level positions or fired because of their ethical concerns. A policy can also encourage whistle-blowers to stay within the organization—for instance, to quietly blow the whistle to responsible managers.[236] Whistle-blowers have the option to stop organizational activities by going to newspaper or television reporters, but as a last resort.

Although whistle-blowing has become widespread in recent years, it is still risky for employees, who can lose their jobs or be ostracized by co-workers. Sometimes managers believe a whistle-blower is out of line and think they are acting correctly to fire or sabotage that employee. As ethical problems in the corporate world increase, many companies are looking for ways to protect whistle-blowers. In addition, calls are increasing for legal protection for those who report illegal or unethical business activities.[237]

When there are no protective measures, whistle-blowers suffer, and the company may continue its unethical or illegal practices.

CODE OF ETHICS A study by the Center for Business Ethics found that 90 percent of Fortune 500 companies and almost half of all other companies have developed a corporate code of ethics.[238] The code clarifies company expectations of employee conduct and makes clear that the company expects its personnel to recognize the ethical dimensions of corporate behavior.

Some companies use broader values statements within which ethics is a part. These statements define ethical values as well as corporate culture and contain language about company responsibility, quality of product, and treatment of employees. A formal statement of values can serve as a fundamental organizational document that defines what the organization stands for and legitimizes value choices for employees.[239]

A code of ethics states the values or behaviors that are expected as well as those that will not be tolerated or backed up by management's action. A code of ethics or larger values statement is an important tool in the management of organizational values.

TRAINING PROGRAMS To ensure that ethical issues are considered in daily decision making, companies can supplement a written code of ethics with employee training programs.[240]

In an important step, ethics programs also include frameworks for ethical decision making, such as the utilitarian approach described earlier in this chapter. Learning these frameworks helps managers act autonomously and still think their way through a difficult decision. In a few companies, managers are also taught about the stages of moral development, which helps to bring them to a high stage of ethical decision making. This training has been an important catalyst for establishing ethical behavior and integrity as critical components of strategic competitiveness.[241]

These formal systems and structures can be highly effective. However, they alone are not sufficient to build and sustain an ethical company. Leaders should integrate ethics into the organizational culture and support and renew ethical values through their words and actions.

Impact of Government on Business

Regulation of the Market Economy

In the new millennium, managers must be sensitive to regulatory policies both at home and abroad. This section considers the economic and social rationale for regulation, and explains the reasons behind conflicting opinions on government regulation in the market economy. Regulators must balance efficiency and equity considerations. This is a fascinating and controversial process.

Competition and the Role of Government

When considering the role of government in the market economy, it has been traditional to focus on how government influences economic activity through tax policies, law enforcement, and infrastructure investments in highways, water treatment facilities, and the like. More recently, interest has shifted to how and why the government regulates private market activity.

How Government Influences Business

Government affects what and how firms produce, influences conditions of entry and exit, dictates marketing practices, prescribes hiring and personnel policies, and imposes a host of other requirements on private enterprise. Government regulation of the market economy is a controversial topic because the power to tax or compel has direct economic consequences.

For example, local telephone service monopolies are protected by a web of local and federal regulation that gives rise to above-normal rates of return while providing access to below-market financing. Franchises that confer the right to offer cellular telephone service in a major metropolitan area are literally worth millions of dollars and can be awarded in the United States only by the Federal Communications Commission (FCC). The federal government also spends hundreds of millions of dollars per year to maintain artificially high price supports for selected agricultural products such as milk and grain, but not chicken and pork. Careful study of the motivation and methods of such regulation is essential to the study of managerial economics because of regulation's key role in shaping the managerial decision-making process.

The pervasive and expanding influence of government in the market economy can be illustrated by considering the growing role played by the FCC, a once obscure agency known only for regulation of the broadcast industry and **AT&T.** The FCC currently holds the keys to success for a number of emerging communications technologies. The FCC determines the fate of digital audio broadcasting, which does away with static on car radio channels; personal communication networks that make users reachable anywhere with a pocket phone; and interactive television, which lets customers order goods and communicate with others through a television set. The FCC has also taken on the daunting and controversial task of restricting indecent and obscene material broadcast over the Internet. As such, the FCC is the focus of debates over free speech and the government's role in shaping rapid advances in communications technology.

Although all sectors of the U.S. economy are regulated to some degree, the method and scope of regulation vary widely. Most companies escape price and profit restraint, except during periods of general wage-price control, but they are subject to operating regulations governing pollution emissions, product packaging and labeling, worker safety and health, and so on. Other firms, particularly in the financial and the public utility sectors, must comply with financial regulation in addition to such operating controls. Banks and savings and loan institutions, for example, are subject to state and federal regulation of interest rates, fees, lending policies, and capital requirements. Unlike firms in the electric power and telecommunications industries, banks and savings and loans face no explicit limit on profitability.

Regulation *Government order having the force of law.*

Economic and social considerations enter into decisions of what and how to regulate. Economic considerations relate to the cost and efficiency implications of regulatory methods. From an economic **efficiency** standpoint, a given mode of **regulation** or government control is desirable to the extent that benefits exceed costs. In terms of efficiency, the question is whether market competition by itself is sufficient, or if it needs to be supplemented with government regulation. **Equity,** or fairness, criteria must also be carefully weighed when social considerations bear on the regulatory decision-making process. Therefore, the incidence, or placement, of costs and benefits of regulatory decisions is important. If a given change in regulatory policy provides significant benefits to the poor, society may willingly bear substantial costs in terms of lost efficiency.

Economic Considerations

Economic regulation began and continues in part because of the public's perception of market imperfections. It is sometimes believed that unregulated market activity can lead to inefficiency and waste or to market failure. **Market failure** is the inability of a system of market institutions to sustain socially desirable activities or to eliminate undesirable ones.

A first cause of market failure is **failure by market structure.** For a market to realize the beneficial effects of competition, it must have many producers (sellers) and consumers (buyers), or at least the ready potential for many to enter. Some markets do not meet this condition. Consider, for example, water, power, and some telecommunications markets. If customer service in a given market area can be most efficiently provided by a single firm (a natural monopoly situation), such providers would enjoy market power and could earn economic profits by limiting output and charging high prices. As a result, utility prices and profits were placed under regulatory control, which has continued with the goal of preserving the efficiency of large-scale production while preventing the higher prices and economic profits of monopoly. When the efficiency advantages of large size are not thought to be compelling, antitrust policy limits the market power of large firms.

Externalities *Differences between private and social costs or benefits.*

A second kind of market failure is **failure by incentive.** In the production and consumption of goods and services, social values and costs often differ from the private costs and values of producers and consumers. Differences between private and social costs or benefits are called **externalities.** A negative externality is a cost of producing, marketing, or consuming a product that is not borne by the product's producers or consumers. A positive externality is a benefit of production, marketing, or consumption that is not reflected in the product pricing structure and, hence, does not accrue to the product's producers or consumers.

Environmental pollution is one well-known negative externality. Negative externalities also arise when employees are exposed to hazardous working conditions for which they are not fully compensated. Similarly, a firm that dams a river to produce energy and thereby limits the access of others to hydropower creates a negative externality. Positive externalities can result if an increase in a firm's activity reduces costs for its suppliers, who pass these cost savings on to their other customers. For example, economies of scale in semiconductor production made possible by increased computer demand have lowered input costs for all users of semiconductors. As a result, prices have fallen for computers and a wide variety of "intelligent" electronic appliances, calculators, toys, and so on. Positive externalities in production can result when a firm trains employees who later apply their knowledge in work for other firms. Positive externalities also arise when an improvement in production methods is transferred from one firm to another without compensation. The dam cited previously for its potential negative externalities might also provide positive externalities by offering flood control or recreational benefits.

In short, externalities lead to a difference between private and social costs and benefits. Firms that provide substantial positive externalities without compensation are unlikely to produce at the socially optimal level. Consumption activities that confer positive externalities may not reach the socially optimal level. In contrast, negative externalities can channel too many resources to a particular activity. Producers or consumers that generate negative externalities do not pay the full costs of production or consumption and tend to overutilize social resources.

Social Considerations

Competition promotes efficiency by giving firms incentives to produce the types and quantities of products that consumers want. Competitive pressures force each firm to use resources wisely to earn at least a normal profit. The market-based resource allocation system is efficient when it responds quickly and accurately to consumer preferences. Not only are these features of competitive markets attractive on an economic basis, but they are also consistent with basic democratic principles. Preservation of consumer choice or **consumer sovereignty** is an important feature of competitive markets. By encouraging and rewarding individual initiative, competition greatly enhances personal freedom. For this reason, less vigorous competitive pressure indicates diminishing buyer supremacy in the marketplace. Firms with market power can limit output and raise prices to earn economic profits, whereas firms in competitive markets refer to market prices to determine optimal output quantities. Regulatory policy can be a valuable tool with which to control monopolies, restoring control over price and quantity decisions to the public.

Consumer sovereignty Buyer supremacy in the marketplace.

A second social purpose of regulatory intervention is to **limit concentration** of economic and political power. It has long been recognized that economic and social relations become intertwined and that concentrated economic power is generally inconsistent with the democratic process. The laws of incorporation, first passed during the 1850s, play an important role in the U.S. economic system. These laws have allowed owners of capital (stockholders) to pool economic resources without also pooling political resources, thereby allowing big business and democracy to coexist. Of course, the large scale of modern corporations has sometimes diminished the controlling influence of individual stockholders. In these instances, regulatory and antitrust policy have limited the growth of large firms to avoid undue concentration of political power.

Important social considerations often constitute compelling justification for government intervention in the marketplace. Deciding whether a particular regulatory reform is warranted is complicated because social considerations can run counter to efficiency considerations.

Regulatory Response to Incentive Failures

To help preserve the competitive environment, government regulation addresses problems created by positive and negative externalities in production, marketing, and consumption. In granting patents and operating subsidies, government provides compensation to reward activity that provides positive externalities. Local, state, and federal governments levy taxes to limit negative externalities. Property rights, grants, taxes, and operating controls are common focal points of government/business interaction.

Who Pays the Costs of Regulation?

Regulation is expensive. The regulatory system can increase consumer prices and cut profits when dispute resolution is slow, litigation costs are high, and the outcomes of legal proceedings are risky. Socially beneficial regulatory reform involves setting rules that provide fair and efficient dispute resolution.

Regulatory Response to Structural Failures

Public utility regulation, which controls the prices and profits of established monopolies, is an attempt to enjoy the benefits of low-cost production by large firms while avoiding the social costs of unregulated monopoly. Tax and antitrust policies also address the problem of structural failures by limiting monopoly abuse.

Antitrust Policy

Antitrust policy in the United States is designed to protect competition. If competitive forces are vibrant, consumer prices are and unwarranted economic profits are low. Product quality, innovation, and economic growth also tend to be high. In a vigorously competitive economic environment, there will be corporate winners and losers. This is fine so long as the game is played fairly. When unfair methods of competition emerge, antitrust policy is brought to bear.

Problems with Regulation

The need for regulation stems from economic and social factors that stimulate market failures due to incentive or structural problems. However, despite obvious benefits, there are costs to various regulatory methods. It is therefore useful to look closely at both the problems and the unfilled promise of economic regulation.

Costs of Regulation

An obvious cost of regulation is the expense to local, state, and federal governments for supervisory agencies. In 2000, federal government estimates for administrative expenditures on business regulation totaled in excess of $18.5 billion dollars per year. Billions more are spent each year by local and state agencies. It is interesting that the largest regulatory budgets at the federal level are not those of traditional regulatory agencies, such as the Securities and Exchange Commission or Federal Trade Commission, but are those devoted to the broader regulatory activities of the Department of Labor for employment and job safety standards and the Department of Agriculture for food inspection.

Although the direct costs of regulation are immense, they may be less than the hidden or indirect costs borne by the private sector. For example, extensive reporting requirements of the Occupational Safety and Health Administration (OSHA) drive up administrative costs and product prices. Consumers also bear the cost of auto emission standards mandated by the Environmental Protection Agency (EPA). In the case of auto emissions, the National Academy of Sciences and the National Academy of Engineering estimate the annual benefits of the catalytic converter at only one-half the billions of dollars in annual costs. One might ask if the social advantages of this method of pollution control are sufficient to offset what appear to be significant economic disadvantages. Similarly, the economic and noneconomic benefits of regulation must be sufficient to offset considerable private costs for pollution control, OSHA-mandated noise reductions, health and safety equipment, FTC-mandated business reports, and so on.

Size-Efficiency Problem

Any debate concerning the problems and promise of regulation must emphasize the fact that antitrust and regulatory policy are designed to protect competition. This is not the same thing as protecting competitors. In any vigorously competitive economy there will be winners and losers. In a competitive market as large as the United States, winners tend to be enormously successful; losers quickly fade or go out of business altogether.

Capture Problem

Capture theory *Economic hypothesis suggesting that regulation is sometimes sought to limit competition and obtain government subsidies.*

It is a widely held belief that regulation is in the public interest and influences firm behavior toward socially desirable ends. However, in the early 1970s, Nobel laureate George Stigler and his colleague Sam Peltzman at the University of Chicago introduced an alternative **capture theory** of economic regulation. According to Stigler and Peltzman, the machinery and power of the state are a potential resource to every industry. With its power to prohibit or compel, to take or give money, the state can and does selectively help or hurt a vast number of industries. Because of this, regulation may be actively sought by industry. They contended that regulation is typically *acquired* by industry and is designed and operated primarily for industry's benefit.

Types of state favors commonly sought by regulated industries include direct money subsidies, control over entry by new rivals, control over substitutes and complements, and price fixing. Domestic "air mail" subsidies, Federal

Deposit Insurance Corporation (FDIC) regulation that reduces the rate of entry into commercial banking, suppression of margarine sales by butter producers, price fixing in motor carrier (trucking) regulation, and American Medical Association control of medical training and licensing can be interpreted as historical examples of control by regulated industries.

In summarizing their views on regulation, Stigler and Peltzman suggest that regulators should be criticized for pro-industry policies no more than politicians for seeking popular support. Current methods of enacting and carrying out regulations only make the pro-industry stance of regulatory bodies more likely. The only way to get different results from regulation is to change the political process of regulator selection and to provide economic rewards to regulators who serve the public interest effectively.

Capture theory is in stark contrast to more traditional **public interest theory,** which sees regulation as a government-imposed means of private-market control. Rather than viewing regulation as a "good" to be obtained, controlled, and manipulated, public interest theory views regulation as a method for improving economic performance by limiting the harmful effects of market failure. Public interest theory is silent on the need to provide regulators with economic incentives to improve regulatory performance. Unlike capture theory, a traditional view has been that the public can trust regulators to make a good-faith effort to establish regulatory policy in the public interest.

To be sure, suggestions of a capture problem are debatable. The need to provide regulators with positive economic incentives to ensure regulation in the public interest is also highly controversial. Nevertheless, growing dissatisfaction with traditional approaches to government regulation has led to a deregulation movement that continues today.

Deregulation Movement

Growing concern with the costs and problems of government regulation gave birth to a **deregulation** movement that has grown to impressive dimensions. Although it is difficult to pinpoint a single catalyst for the movement, it is hard to overlook the role played by Stigler, Peltzman, and other economists (notably, Alfred E. Kahn) who illustrated that the regulatory process can sometimes harm consumer interests.

Deregulation The reduction of government control of the free market.

Regulation Versus Deregulation Controversy

In evaluating the effects of deregulation, and in gauging the competitive implications of market exit by previously viable firms, it is important to remember that protecting competition is not the same as protecting competitors. Without regulation, it is inevitable that some competitors will fall by the wayside and that concentration will rise in some markets. Although such trends must be watched closely for anticompetitive effects, they are characteristics of a vigorously competitive environment. Although some think that there is simply a question of regulation versus deregulation, this is seldom the case. On grounds of economic and political feasibility, it is often most fruitful to consider approaches to improving existing methods of regulation.

An important problem with regulation is that regulators seldom have the information or expertise to specify, for example, the correct level of utility investment, minimum transportation costs, or the optimum method of pollution control. Because technology changes rapidly in most regulated industries, only industry personnel working at the frontier of current technology have such specialized knowledge. One method for dealing with this technical expertise problem is to have regulators focus on the preferred outcomes of regulatory processes, rather than on the technical means that industry adopts to achieve those ends. The FCC's decision to adopt downward-adjusting price caps for long-distance telephone service is an example of this developing trend toward **incentive-based regulation.** If providers of long-distance telephone service are able to reduce costs faster than the FCC-mandated decline in prices, they will enjoy an increase in profitability. By setting price caps that fall over time, the FCC ensures that consumers share in expected cost savings while companies enjoy a positive incentive to innovate. This approach to regulation focuses on the objectives of regulation while allowing industry to meet those goals in new and unique ways. Tying regulator rewards and regulated industry profits to objective, output-oriented performance criteria has the potential to create a desirable win/win situation for regulators, utilities, and the general public. For example, the public has a real interest in safe, reliable, and low-cost electric power. State and federal regulators who oversee the operations of utilities could develop objective standards for measuring utility safety, reliability, and cost efficiency. Tying firm profit rates to such performance-oriented criteria could stimulate real improvements in utility and regulator performance.

Incentive-based regulation Rules that benefit consumers through enhanced efficiency.

165. IMPACT OF GOVERNMENT ON BUSINESS

Securities Regulation

The primary purpose of federal securities regulation is to prevent fraudulent practices in the sale of securities and thereby to foster public confidence in the securities market. Federal securities law consists principally of two statutes: the Securities Act of 1933, which focuses on the issuance of securities, and the Securities Exchange Act of 1934, which deals mainly with trading in issued securities. These "secondary" transactions greatly exceed in number and dollar value the original offerings by issuers.

Both statutes are administered by the Securities and Exchange Commission (SEC), an independent, quasi-judicial agency consisting of five commissioners. In 1996 Congress enacted legislation requiring the SEC, when making rules under either of the securities statutes, to consider, in addition to the protection of investors, whether its action will promote efficiency, competition, and capital formation. The SEC has the power to seek civil injunctions in a federal district court against violation of the statutes, to recommend that the Justice Department bring criminal prosecutions, and to issue orders censuring, suspending, or expelling broker-dealers, investment advisers, and investment companies. The Securities Enforcement Remedies and Penny Stock Reform Act of 1990 granted the SEC the power to issue cease-and-desist orders and to impose administrative, civil penalties up to $550,000. Congress enacted the Private Securities Litigation Reform Act of 1995 (Reform Act) to amend both the 1933 Act and the 1934 Act. One of its provisions grants authority to the SEC to bring civil actions for specified violations of the 1934 Act against aiders and abettors (those who knowingly provide substantial assistance to a person who violates the statute).

The Reform Act sought to prevent abuses in private securities fraud lawsuits. To prevent certain state private securities class-action lawsuits alleging fraud from being used to frustrate the objectives of the Reform Act, Congress enacted The Securities Litigation Uniform Standards Act of 1998. The act sets national standards for securities class-action lawsuits involving nationally traded securities while it preserves the appropriate enforcement powers of state securities regulators but does not change the current treatment of individual lawsuits. The act amends both the 1933 Act and the 1934 Act by prohibiting any private class action suit in state or federal court by any private party based upon state statutory or common law alleging (1) an untrue statement or omission in connection with the purchase or sale of a covered security or (2) that the defendant used any manipulative or deceptive device in connection with such a transaction.

The 1933 Act has two basic objectives: (1) to provide investors with material information concerning securities offered for sale to the public and (2) to prohibit misrepresentation, deceit, and other fraudulent acts and practices in the sale of securities generally, whether they are required to be registered or not.

The 1934 Act extends protection to investors trading in securities that are already issued and outstanding. The 1934 Act also imposes disclosure requirements on publicly held corporations and regulates tender offers and proxy solicitations.

Effective October 6, 1995, the SEC provided interpretative guidance for the use of electronic media for the delivery of information required by the federal securities laws. The SEC defined *electronic media* to include audiotapes, videotapes, facsimiles, CD-ROM, electronic mail, bulletin boards, Internet Web sites, and computer networks. Basically, electronic delivery must provide notice, access, and evidence of delivery comparable to that provided by paper delivery.

The SEC has established the EDGAR (Electronic Data Gathering, Analysis, and Retrieval) computer system, which performs automated collection, validation, indexing, acceptance, and dissemination of reports required to be filed with the SEC. Its primary purpose is to increase the efficiency and fairness of the securities market for the benefit of investors, corporations, and the economy by speeding up the receipt, acceptance, dissemination, and analysis of corporate information filed with the SEC. After a phase-in period, the SEC now requires all public domestic companies to make their filings on EDGAR, except filings exempted for hardship. EDGAR filings are posted at the SEC's Web site 24 hours after the date of filing.

In addition to the federal laws regulating the sale of securities, each state has its own laws regulating such sales within its borders. Commonly called Blue Sky Laws, these statutes all have provisions prohibiting fraud in the sale of securities. In addition, most states require the registration of securities and regulate brokers and dealers.

Any person who sells securities must comply with the federal securities laws as well as with the securities laws of each state in which he intends to offer his securities. However, in 1996 Congress enacted the National Securities Markets Improvements Act, which preempted state regulation of the offerings of certain securities.

Intellectual Property

Intellectual property is an economically significant type of intangible personal property that includes trade secrets, trade symbols, copyrights, and patents. These interests are protected from **infringement,** or unauthorized use, by others. Such protection is essential to the conduct of business. For example, a company would be far less willing to invest considerable resources in research and development if resulting discoveries, inventions, and processes were not protected by patents and by regulations safeguarding trade secrets. Similarly, a company would not be secure in devoting time and money to marketing its products and services without laws to defend its trade symbols and trade names. Moreover, without copyright protection, the publishing, entertainment, and computer software industries would be vulnerable to piracy, both by competitors and by the general public.

Trade Secrets

Every business has secret information. Such information may include customer lists or contracts with suppliers and customers; it may also consist of secret formulas, processes, and production methods that are vital to the successful operation of the business. A business may disclose a trade secret in confidence to an employee with the understanding that the employee will not, in turn, reveal the information. To the extent the owner of the information obtains a patent on it, it is no longer a trade secret but is protected by patent law. Some businesses, however, choose not to obtain a patent because it provides protection for only a limited time, whereas state trade secret law protects a trade secret as long as it is kept secret. Moreover, if the courts invalidate a patent, the information will have been disclosed to competitors without the owner of the information obtaining any benefit. The Uniform Trade Secrets Act, promulgated in 1979 and amended in 1985, has been adopted by more than forty states.

Definition

Basically, a **trade secret** is commercially valuable information that is guarded from disclosure and is not general knowledge. The Uniform Trade Secrets Act defines a trade secret as

> information, including a formula, pattern, compilation, program, device, method, technique, or process that:
> (i) derives independent economic value, actual or potential, from not being generally known to, and not being readily ascertainable by proper means by, other persons who can obtain economic value from its disclosure or use, and
> (ii) is the subject of efforts that are reasonable under the circumstances to maintain its secrecy.

A famous example of a trade secret is the formula for Coca-Cola.

Misappropriation

Misappropriation of a trade secret is the wrongful use of a trade secret. A person misappropriates a trade secret of another (1) by knowingly acquiring it through improper means or (2) by disclosing or using it without consent, if his knowledge of the trade secret came under circumstances giving rise to a duty to maintain secrecy or came from a person who used improper means or who owed the owner of the trade secret a duty to maintain secrecy. Trade secrets are most frequently misappropriated in two ways: (1) an employee wrongfully uses or discloses such secrets or (2) a competitor wrongfully obtains them.

Remedies

Remedies for misappropriation of trade secrets are damages and, when appropriate, injunctive relief. Damages are awarded in the amount of either the pecuniary loss to the plaintiff caused by the misappropriation or the pecuniary gain to the defendant, whichever is greater. A court will grant an injunction to prevent a continuing or threatened misappropriation of a trade secret for as long as is necessary to protect the plaintiff from any harm attributable to the misappropriation and to deprive the defendant of any economic advantage attributable to the misappropriation.

Criminal Penalties

In 1996 Congress enacted the Economic Espionage Act of 1996 prohibiting the theft of trade secrets and providing criminal penalties for violations. (The statute does not provide any civil remedies.) The statute defines trade secrets to mean "all forms and types of financial, business, scientific, technical, economic, or engineering information, including patterns, plans, compilations, program devices, formulas, designs, prototypes, methods, techniques, processes, procedures, programs, or codes, whether tangible or intangible, and whether or how stored, compiled, or memorialized physically, electronically, graphically, photographically, or in writing if (a) the owner thereof has taken reasonable measures to keep such information secret; and (b) the information derives independent economic value, actual or potential, from not being generally known to, and not being readily ascertainable through proper means by the public."

The act broadly defines theft to include all types of conversion of trade secrets including:

1. stealing, obtaining by fraud, or concealing such information;
2. without authorization copying, duplicating, sketching, drawing, photographing, downloading, uploading, photocopying, or mailing such information; and
3. purchasing or possessing a trade secret with knowledge that it has been stolen.

The act punishes thefts of trade secrets, as well as attempts and conspiracies to steal secrets, with fines of up to $500,000, imprisonment for up to 10 years, or both. Organizations that violate the act are subject to fines of up to $5 million.

Trade Symbols

One of the earliest forms of unfair competition was the fraudulent marketing of one person's goods as those of another. Still common today, this unlawful practice is sometimes referred to as "passing off" or "palming off." Basically, "cashing in" fraudulently on the goodwill, good name, and reputation of a competitor and its products deceives the public and deprives honest businesses of trade. The Federal Trademark Act (the Lanham Act) prohibits businesses from using a false designation of origin in connection with any goods or services. This act also prohibits a business from falsely describing or representing its own goods and services. In 1988, Congress amended the act to prohibit the misrepresentation of *another* person's goods, services, or commercial activities.

The Lanham Act also established federal registration of trade symbols and protection against misuse or infringement by injunctive relief and a right of action for damages against the infringer. An infringement involves passing off one's goods or services as those of the owner of the mark in a manner that deceives the public and constitutes unfair competition.

Types of Trade Symbols

The Lanham Act recognizes four types of trade symbols or **marks**. A **trademark** is a *distinctive* mark, word, letter, number, design, picture, or combination in any arrangement that a person adopts or uses to identify the goods he manufactures or sells, as well as to distinguish them from those manufactured or sold by others. Internet domain names that are used to identify and distinguish the goods or services of one person from the goods or services of others and to indicate the source of the goods and services may be registered as a trademark. To qualify, an applicant must show that it offers services via the Internet and that it uses the Internet domain name as a source identifier.

Similar in function to the trademark, which identifies tangible goods and products, is a **service mark,** used to identify and distinguish the services of one person from those of others. For example, the titles, character names, and other distinctive elements of radio and television shows may be registered as service marks. Service marks may also consist of trade dress such as the decor or shape of buildings in which services are provided. Examples include the **Fotomart** kiosk and **Howard Johnson's** orange roof.

A **certification mark** is used on or in connection with goods or services to certify their regional or other origin, composition, mode of manufacture, quality, accuracy, or other characteristics, or that the work or labor in the goods or services was performed by members of a union or other organization. The marks "Good Housekeeping Seal of Approval" and "Underwriter's Laboratory" are examples of certification marks. The owner of the certification mark does *not* produce or provide the goods or services with which the mark is used.

A **collective mark** is a distinctive mark or symbol used to indicate either that the producer or provider belongs to a trade union, trade association, fraternal society, or other organization, or that the goods or services are produced by members of a collective group. Like the owner of a certification mark, the owner of a collective mark is not the producer or provider but rather is the group of which the producer or provider is a member. An example of a collective mark is the union mark that indicates a product's manufacture by a unionized company.

Registration

To be protected by the Lanham Act, a mark must be distinctive enough to identify clearly the origin of goods or services; it may not be immoral, deceptive, or scandalous. A trade symbol may satisfy the distinctiveness requirement in either of two ways. First, it may be *inherently distinctive* if prospective purchasers are likely to associate it with the product or service it designates because of the nature of the designation and the context in which it is used. Fanciful or arbitrary marks satisfy the distinctiveness requirement. In contrast, a descriptive or geographic designation is not inherently distinctive. Such a designation is one that is likely to be perceived by prospective purchasers as merely descriptive of the nature, qualities, or other characteristics of the goods or service with which it is used. Thus, the word *Plow* cannot be a trademark for plows, although it may be a trademark for shoes.

Descriptive or geographic designations may, however, satisfy the distinctiveness requirement through the second method: acquiring distinctiveness through a "secondary meaning." A designation acquires a **secondary meaning** when a substantial number of prospective purchasers associate the designation with the product or service it identifies.

A **generic designation** is one that is understood by prospective purchasers to denominate the general category, type, or class of goods or services with which it is used. A user cannot acquire rights in a generic designation as a trade symbol. Moreover, a trade symbol will lose its eligibility for protection if prospective purchasers come to perceive a trade symbol primarily as a generic description for the category, type, or class of goods or services with which it is used. Under the Lanham Act, the test for when this has occurred is "the primary significance of the registered mark to the relevant public rather than purchaser motivation." Examples of marks that have lost protection because they became generic include "aspirin," "thermos," "escalator," and "cellophane."

To obtain federal protection, which has a 10-year term with unlimited 10-year renewals, the mark must be registered with the Patent and Trademark Office. The registrant must either (1) have actually used the mark in commerce or (2) demonstrate a *bona fide* intent to use the mark in commerce and actually use it within six months.

Registration provides numerous advantages. It gives nationwide constructive notice of the mark to all later users. It permits the registrant to use the federal courts to enforce the mark and constitutes *prima facie* evidence of the registrant's exclusive right to use the mark. This right becomes incontestable, subject to certain specified limitations, after five years. Finally, registration provides the registrant with Customs Bureau protection against imports that threaten to infringe upon the mark.

To retain trademark protection, the owner of a mark must not abandon it by failing to make *bona fide* use of it in the ordinary course of trade. Abandonment occurs when an owner does not use a mark and no longer intends to use it. Three years of nonuse raises a presumption of abandonment, which the owner may rebut by proving her intent to resume use.

Infringement

Infringement of a mark occurs when a person without authorization uses an identical or substantially indistinguishable mark that is likely to cause confusion, to cause mistake, or to deceive. The intention to confuse purchasers is not required, nor is proof of actual confusion, although likelihood of confusion may be inferred from either. Infringement occurs if an appreciable number of ordinarily prudent purchasers are *likely* to be misled or confused as to the source of the goods or services. In deciding whether infringement has occurred, the courts consider various factors, including the strength of the mark, the intent of the unauthorized user, the degree of similarity between the two marks, the relation between the two products or services the marks identify, and the marketing channels through which the goods or services are purchased.

Remedies

The Lanham Act provides several **remedies** for infringement: (1) injunctive relief, (2) an accounting for profits, (3) damages, (4) destruction of infringing articles, (5) attorneys' fees in exceptional cases, and (6) costs. In assessing profits, the plaintiff has only to prove the gross sales made by the defendant; the defendant, in contrast, must prove any costs to be deducted in determining profits. If the court finds that the amount of recovery based on profits is either inadequate or excessive, the court may, in its discretion, award an amount it determines to be just. In assessing damages, the court *may* award up to three times the actual damages, according to the circumstances of the case. When an infringement is knowing and intentional, the court *shall* award attorneys' fees plus the greater of treble profits or treble damages, unless there are extenuating circumstances. In an action under the Federal Trademark Dilution Act of 1995, the owner of the famous mark can obtain only injunctive relief unless the person against whom the injunction is sought willfully intended to trade on the owner's reputation or to cause dilution of the famous mark. If willful intent is proven, the owner of the famous mark may also obtain the other remedies discussed.

Where a defendant has intentionally and knowingly used a counterfeit mark, the court may impose criminal sanctions; and goods bearing the counterfeit mark may be destroyed. A *counterfeit mark* means a spurious mark that is identical with, or substantially indistinguishable from, a registered mark. Criminal sanctions include a fine of up to $250,000 or imprisonment of up to five years, or both. For a repeat offense, the limits are $1 million and 15 years, respectively. For an offender who is not an individual (a corporation, for example), the fine may be up to $1 million for a first offense and up to $5 million for a repeat offense.

Trade Names

A **trade name** is any name used to identify a business, vocation, or occupation. Descriptive and generic words, and personal and generic names, although not proper trademarks, may become protected as trade names upon acquiring a special significance in the trade. A name acquires such significance, frequently referred to as a "secondary meaning," through its continuing and extended use in connection with specific goods or services, whereby the name's acquired meaning eclipses its primary meaning in the minds of many purchasers or users. Although they may not be federally registered under the Lanham Act, trade names are protected, and a person who palms off her goods or services under the trade name of another is liable in damages and also may be enjoined from doing so.

Copyrights

Copyright is a form of protection provided by the Federal Copyright Act to authors of original works, which include literary, musical, and dramatic works; pantomimes; choreographic works; pictorial, graphic, and sculptural works; motion picture and other audiovisual works; sound recordings; and architectural works. This listing is illustrative but not exhaustive; the act extends **copyright** protection to "original works of authorship in any tangible medium of expression, now known or later developed." Moreover, in 1980, the Copyright Act was amended to extend copyright protection to computer programs.

In no case does the copyright protection for an original work of authorship protect also any idea, procedure, process, system, method of operation, concept, principle, or discovery, regardless of the form in which it is described, explained, illustrated, or embodied in such work. Copyright protection extends only to an *original expression* of an idea. For example, the idea of interfamily feuding cannot be copyrighted; but a particular expression of that idea in the form of a novel, drama, movie, or opera may be thus protected.

Procedure

Although registration of the copyright is not required, because copyright protection begins as soon as the work is fixed in a tangible medium, registration is advisable nonetheless, being a condition of the remedies of statutory damages and attorneys' fees for copyright infringement. When a work is published, it is advisable, though no longer required, to place a copyright notice on all publicly distributed copies, so as to notify users about the copyright claim. If proper notice appears on the published copies to which a defendant in a copyright infringement case had access, the defendant will be unable to mitigate actual or statutory damages by asserting a defense of innocent infringement.

Rights

As amended in 1998 by the Sonny Bono Copyright Extension Act, in most instances, copyright protection lasts the duration of the author's life plus an additional seventy years. The Copyright Act gives the copyright owner the exclusive **right,** and the right to authorize others, to reproduce the copyrighted work, prepare derivative works based upon the copyrighted work, distribute copies or recordings of the copyrighted work, perform the work publicly, and display the work publicly.

Ownership

Ownership The author of the copyrighted work is usually the owner of the copyright, which may be transferred in whole or in part.

The author of a creative work owns the entire copyright. Although the actual creator of a work is usually the author, in two situations under the doctrine of **works for hire,** she is not considered the author. First, if an employee prepares a work within the scope of her employment, her employer is considered the author of the work. Second, if a work is specially ordered or commissioned for certain purposes specified in the copyright statute *and* the parties expressly agree in writing that the work shall be considered a work for hire, the person commissioning the work is deemed to be the author.

The ownership of a copyright may be transferred in whole or in part by conveyance, will, or intestate succession. However, a transfer of copyright ownership, other than by operation of law, is not valid unless a note or memorandum chronicles the transfer in writing and is signed by the owner of the rights conveyed or by the owner's duly authorized agent. An author may terminate any transfer of copyright ownership, other than that of a work for hire, during the 5-year period beginning 35 years after the transfer was granted.

Ownership of a copyright, or of any of the exclusive rights under a copyright, is distinct from the ownership of any material object that embodies the work. The transfer of ownership of any material object, including the copy or recording in which the work was first fixed, does not in itself convey any rights in the copyrighted work the object embodies; nor, in the absence of an agreement, does the transfer of copyright ownership or of any exclusive rights under a copyright convey property rights in any material object. Thus, the purchase of this textbook neither affects the publisher's copyright nor authorizes the purchaser to make and sell copies of the book, though the purchaser may rent, lend, or resell it. Were this a recorded text, however, the purchaser's latter rights would be somewhat more limited: in 1990, amendments to the Copyright Act prohibited the rental, lease, or commercial lending of sound recordings and computer programs unless authorized by the copyright owner.

Infringement and Remedies

Infringement occurs whenever somebody exercises, without authorization, the rights exclusively reserved for the copyright owner. Infringement need not be intentional. To prove infringement, the plaintiff must simply establish that he owns the copyright and that the defendant violated one or more of the plaintiff's exclusive rights under the copyright. Proof of infringement usually consists of showing that the allegedly infringing work is substantially similar to the copyrighted work and that the alleged infringer had access to the copyrighted work. The Digital Millennium Copyright Act of 1998 amended the Copyright Act to create limitations on the liability of online providers for copyright infringement when engaging in certain activities.

In order for the owner to sue for infringement, the copyright must be registered with the Copyright Office, unless the work is a Berne Convention work whose country of origin is not the United States. For an infringement occurring after registration, the following **remedies** are available: (1) injunction; (2) impoundment and possible destruction of infringing articles; (3) actual damages plus profits made by the infringer that are additional to those damages, *or* statutory damages of at least $500 but no more than $20,000 (though the ceiling may reach $100,000 if the infringement is willful), according to what the court determines to be just; (4) costs and, in the court's discretion, reasonable attorneys' fees to the prevailing party; or (5) criminal penalties of a fine of up to $10,000 or up to one year's imprisonment for willful infringement for purposes of commercial advantage or private financial gain. In 1997 Congress enacted the No Electronic Theft Act, increasing criminal penalties for certain copyright violations. Imprisonment for up to 5 years (10 years for subsequent offenses) may be imposed for willful infringement if at least 10 copies or phonorecords with a total retail value of more than $2,500 in a 180-day period are reproduced or distributed.

Patents

Through a **patent,** the federal government grants an inventor a monopolistic right to make, use, or sell an invention to the absolute exclusion of others for the period of the patent. The patent owner may also profit by licensing others to use the patent on a royalty basis. However, the patent may not be renewed: upon expiration, the invention enters the "public domain," and anyone may then use it.

Patentability

The Patent Act specifies those inventions that may be patented as **utility patents:** any new and useful process, machine, manufacture, or composition of matter or any new and useful improvement thereof. Thus, naturally occurring substances are not patentable, as the invention must be made or modified by humans. For example, the discovery of a bacterium with useful properties is not patentable, whereas the manufacture of a genetically engineered bacterium is. By the same token, laws of nature, principles, bookkeeping systems, fundamental truths, calculation methods, and ideas are not patentable. Accordingly, Einstein could not have patented his law that $E = mc^2$; nor could Newton have patented the law of gravity. Similarly, isolated computer programs are not patentable, although, as we mentioned above, they may be copyrighted.

To be patentable as a utility patent, the process, machine, manufacture, or composition of matter must meet three criteria: (1) novelty, (2) utility, and (3) non-obviousness.

In addition to utility patents, the Patent Act provides for plant patents and design patents. A **plant patent** protects a new and distinctive variety of asexually producing plant. Plant patents require (1) novelty, (2) distinctiveness, and (3) non-obviousness. A **design patent** protects a new, original, ornamental design for an article of manufacture. Design patents require (1) novelty, (2) ornamentality, and (3) non-obviousness.

Utility and plant patents have a term that begins on the date of the patent's grant and ends twenty years from the date of application. Design patents have a term of 14 years from the date of grant.

Procedure

The United States Patent and Trademark Office issues a patent upon the basis of a patent application containing a specification, which describes how the invention works, and claims, which describe the features that make the invention patentable. The applicant must be the inventor. Before granting a patent, the Patent Office carefully and thoroughly examines the prior art and determines whether the submitted invention has novelty (does not conflict with a prior pending application or a previously issued patent) and utility, and is non-obvious. A patent application is confidential, and the Patent Office will not divulge its contents. This confidentiality ends, however, upon the granting of the patent.

An applicant whose application is rejected may apply for reexamination. If the application is again rejected, the applicant may appeal to the Patent and Trademark Office's Board of Appeals, and from there to the federal courts.

Infringement

Infringement Occurs when anyone without permission makes, uses, or sells a patented invention.

Anyone who, without permission, makes, uses, or sells a patented invention is a *direct infringer*, whereas a person who actively encourages another to make, use, offer to sell, or sell a patented invention without permission is an *indirect infringer*. A *contributory infringer* is one who knowingly sells, or offers to sell, a part or component of a patented invention, unless the component is a staple or commodity or is suitable for a substantial noninfringing use. Though good faith and ignorance are defenses to contributory infringement, they are not defenses to direct infringement.

Remedies

The **remedies** for infringement under the Patent Act are (1) injunctive relief; (2) damages adequate to compensate the plaintiff but "in no event less than a reasonable royalty for the use made of the invention by the infringer"; (3) treble damages, when appropriate; (4) attorneys' fees in exceptional cases, such as those that involve knowing infringement; and (5) costs. Exhibit 100.21 summarizes issues in intellectual property.

Exhibit 100.21 *Intellectual Property Issues*

	Trade Secrets	Trade Symbols	Copyright	Patents
What Is Protected	Information	Mark	Work of authorship	Invention
Rights Protected	Use or sell	Use or sell	Reproduce, prepare derivative works, distribute, perform, or display	Make, use, or sell
Duration	Until disclosed	Until abandoned	Usually author's life plus 70 years	For utility and plant patents, 20 years from application; for design patents, 14 years from grant
Federally Protected	No	Yes	Yes	Yes
Requirements for Protection	Valuable secret	Distinctive	Original and fixed	Novel, useful, and non-obvious

Employment Law

Though the common law originally governed the relationship between employer and employee in terms of tort and contract duties (rules that are a part of the law of agency—Relationship of Principal and Agent), this common law has been supplemented—and in some instances replaced—by statutory enactments, principally at the federal level. In fact, government regulation now affects the balance and working relationship between employers and employees in three principal areas. First, the general framework in which management and labor negotiate the terms of employment is regulated by federal statutes designed to promote both labor-management harmony and the welfare of society at large. Second, federal law has been enacted to prohibit employment discrimination based upon race, sex, religion, age, disability, or national origin. Finally, Congress, in response to the changing nature of American industry and the tremendous number of industrial accidents, has intervened by mandating that employers provide their employees with a safe and healthy work environment. Moreover, all of the states have adopted workers' compensation acts to provide compensation to employees injured during the course of employment.

In this section, we will focus on these three categories of government regulation of the employment relationship: (1) labor law, (2) employment discrimination law, and (3) employee protection.

Labor Law

Traditionally, **labor law** opposed concerted activities by workers (such as strikes, picketing, and refusals to deal) to obtain higher wages and better working conditions. At various times, such activities were found to constitute criminal conspiracy, tortious conduct, and violation of antitrust law. Eventually, public pressure in response to the adverse treatment accorded labor forced Congress to intervene.

Norris–La Guardia Act

Congress enacted the **Norris–La Guardia Act** in 1932 in response to growing criticism of the use of injunctions in peaceful labor disputes. The act withdrew from the federal courts the power to issue injunctions in nonviolent **labor disputes,** broadly defined to include any controversy concerning terms or conditions of employment or union representation, regardless of whether the parties stood in an employer-employee relationship or not. More significantly, the act declared it to be U.S. policy that labor was to have full freedom to form unions, without employer interference. Accordingly, the act prohibited the so-called "yellow dog" contracts through which employers coerced their employees into promising that they would not join a union.

National Labor Relations Act

Enacted in 1935, the **National Labor Relations Act (NLRA),** or the *Wagner Act,* marked the federal government's effort to support collective bargaining and unionization. The act provides that "the right to self-organization, to form, join or assist labor organizations, to bargain collectively through representatives of their own choosing, and to engage in concerted activities for the purpose of collective bargaining or other mutual aid or protection" is, for workers, a federally protected right. Thus, the act gave employees the right to union representation when negotiating employment terms with their employers.

Moreover, the act sought to enforce the collective bargaining right by prohibiting certain employer and union activities deemed to be **unfair labor practices.** For example, the act identifies the following activities as **unfair employer practices:** (1) to interfere with employees' rights to unionize and bargain collectively; (2) to dominate the union; (3) to discriminate against union members; (4) to discriminate against an employee who has filed charges or testified under the NLRA; and (5) to refuse to bargain in good faith with duly established employee representatives.

Labor-Management Relations Act

Following the passage of the National Labor Relations Act, the country underwent a tremendous increase in union membership and labor unrest. In response to this trend, Congress passed the **Labor-Management Relations Act** (the **LMRA,** or **Taft-Hartley Act**) in 1947. The act prohibits certain **unfair union practices** and separates the prosecutorial and adjudicative functions of the National Labor Relations Board (NLRB). More specifically, the act amended the

Exhibit 100.22 *Unfair Labor Practices*

Unfair Employer Practices	Unfair Union Practices
• Interfering with right to unionize	• Coercing an employee to join the union
• Refusing to bargain in good faith	• Refusing to bargain in good faith
• Discriminating against union members	• Causing an employer to discriminate against a nonunion employee
• Dominating the union	• Featherbedding
• Discriminating against an employee	• Picketing an employer to require recognition of an uncertified union
	• Engaging in secondary activity
	• Levying excessive or discriminatory dues

NLRA by declaring the following seven union activities of the National Labor Relations Board (NLRB) to be **unfair labor practices:** (1) coercing an employee to join a union, (2) causing an employer to discharge or discriminate against a nonunion employee, (3) refusing to bargain in good faith, (4) levying excessive or discriminatory dues or fees, (5) causing an employer to pay for work not performed ("featherbedding"), (6) picketing an employer to require it to recognize an uncertified union, and (7) engaging in secondary activities. A secondary activity is a boycott, strike, or picketing of an employer with whom a union has no labor dispute in order to persuade the employer to cease doing business with the company that is the target of the labor dispute. For example, assume that a union is engaged in a labor dispute with Anderson Company. To coerce Anderson into resolving the dispute in the union's favor, the union organizes a strike against Brooking Company, with which the union has no labor dispute. The union agrees to cease striking Brooking Company if Brooking agrees to cease doing business with Anderson. The strike against Brooking is a secondary activity prohibited as an unfair labor practice. See Exhibit 100.22 for a summary of union and employer unfair labor practices.

In addition to prohibiting unfair union practices, the act also fosters employer free speech by declaring that unions or employees wishing to identify an employer labor practice as unfair cannot use as proof any employer statement of opinion or argument that contains no threat of reprisal.

The LMRA also prohibits the closed shop but permits union shops, unless a state right-to-work law prohibits the latter. A **closed shop** contract requires the employer to hire only union members. A **union shop** contract permits the employer to hire nonunion members but requires the employee to become a union member within a specified time after gaining employment and to remain a member in good standing as a condition of employment. A **right-to-work law** is a state statute that prohibits union shop contracts. However, most states permit the existence of union shops.

Finally, the act reinstates the availability of civil injunctions in labor disputes if requested of the NLRB in order to prevent an unfair labor practice. The act also empowers the president of the United States to obtain an injunction for an 80-day cooling-off period for a strike that is likely to endanger the national health or safety.

Labor-Management Reporting and Disclosure Act

The **Labor-Management Reporting and Disclosure Act,** also known as the **Landrum-Griffin Act,** is aimed at eliminating corruption in labor unions. The act attempts to eradicate corruption through an elaborate reporting system and a union "bill of rights" designed to make unions more democratic. The latter provides union members with the right to nominate candidates for union offices, to vote in elections, to attend membership meetings, to participate in union business, to express themselves freely at union meetings and conventions, and to be accorded a full and fair hearing before the union takes any disciplinary action against them.

Employment Discrimination Law

A number of federal statutes prohibit discrimination in employment on the basis of race, sex, religion, national origin, age, and disability. The cornerstone of federal employment discrimination law is Title VII of the 1964 Civil Rights Act, but other statutes and regulations are significant as well, including the **Civil Rights Act of 1991** and the **Americans with Disabilities Act of 1990.** In addition, most states have enacted similar laws prohibiting discrimination based on race, sex, religion, national origin, and disability. The Civil Rights Act of 1991 extended the coverage of both Title VII and the Americans with Disabilities Act to include United States citizens working for U.S.-owned or -controlled companies in foreign countries.

Equal Pay Act

The **Equal Pay Act** prohibits an employer from discriminating between employees on the basis of *gender* by paying unequal wages for the same work. The act forbids an employer from paying wages at a rate less than the rate at which he pays wages to employees of the opposite sex for equal work at the same establishment. Most courts define *equal work* to mean "substantially equal" rather than identical. The burden of proof is on the claimant to make a *prima facie* showing that the employer pays unequal wages for work requiring equal skill, effort, and responsibility under similar working conditions. Once the employee has demonstrated that the employer pays unequal wages for *equal* work to members of the opposite sex, the burden shifts to the employer to prove that the pay differential is based on (1) a seniority system, (2) a merit system, (3) a system that measures earnings by quantity or quality of production, or (4) any factor except gender.

Remedies include awarding back pay, awarding liquidated damages (an additional amount equal to back pay), and enjoining the employer from further unlawful conduct. Though the Department of Labor is the federal agency designated by the statute to interpret and enforce the act, in 1979 these functions were transferred to the Equal Employment Opportunity Commission.

Civil Rights Act of 1964

Title VII of the **Civil Rights Act of 1964** *prohibits* **employment discrimination** on the basis of race, color, gender, religion, or national origin in hiring, firing, compensating, promoting, training, and other employment-related processes. The definition of *"religion"* includes all aspects of religious observance and practice; the statute provides that an employer must make reasonable efforts to accommodate an employee's religious belief. The act applies to employers engaged in an industry affecting commerce and having fifteen or more employees.

When Congress passed the **Pregnancy Discrimination Act,** it extended the benefits of Title VII to pregnant women. Under the act, an employer cannot refuse to hire a pregnant woman, fire her, or force her to take maternity leave unless the employer can establish a *bona fide* occupational qualification (BFOQ) defense (discussed later in this section). The act, which protects the job reinstatement rights of women returning from maternity leave, requires employers to treat pregnancy as they would a temporary disability.

The enforcement agency for Title VII is the **Equal Employment Opportunity Commission (EEOC).** The EEOC is empowered (1) to file legal actions in its own name or to intervene in actions filed by third parties; (2) to attempt to resolve alleged violations through informal means prior to bringing suit; (3) to investigate all charges of discrimination; and (4) to issue guidelines and regulations concerning enforcement policy.

PROVING DISCRIMINATION Each of the following constitutes discriminatory conduct prohibited by the act:

1. **Disparate Treatment.** Such treatment occurs when an employer uses a prohibited criterion in making an employment decision. The Supreme Court has held that the plaintiff will have shown a *prima facie* case of discrimination if she (a) is within a protected class, (b) had applied for an open position, (c) was qualified for the position, (d) was denied the job, and (e) the employer continued to try to fill the position from a pool of applicants with the complainant's qualifications. Once the plaintiff establishes a *prima facie* case, the burden shifts to the defendant to "articulate legitimate and nondiscriminatory reasons for the plaintiff's rejection." If the defendant so rebuts, the plaintiff then has the opportunity to demonstrate that the employer's stated reason was merely a pretext.

2. **Present Effects of Past Discrimination.** Such effects result when an employer engages in conduct that on its face is "neutral"—that is, nondiscriminatory—but that actually perpetuates past discriminatory practices. For example, it has been held illegal for a union that previously had limited its membership to whites to adopt a requirement that new members be related to or recommended by existing members.

3. **Disparate Impact.** This occurs when an employer adopts "neutral" rules that adversely affect a protected class and that are not justified as being necessary to the business. Despite the employee's proof of disparate impact, the employer may prevail if it can demonstrate that the challenged practice is "job related for the position in question and consistent with business necessity." Thus, all requirements that might have a disparate impact upon women, such as height and weight requirements, must be shown to be job related. Nevertheless, under the Civil Rights Act of 1991, even if the employer can demonstrate the business necessity of the questioned practice, the complainant will still prevail if she shows that a nondiscriminatory alternative practice exists.

DEFENSES The act provides three basic defenses: (1) a *bona fide* seniority or merit system; (2) a professionally developed ability test; and (3) a *bona fide* occupational qualification. The BFOQ defense does not apply to discrimination based on race. A fourth defense, business necessity, is available in a disparate impact case.

REMEDIES Remedies for violation of the act include enjoining the employer from engaging in the unlawful behavior, taking appropriate affirmative action, and reinstating employees to their rightful place (which may include promotion) and awarding them back pay from a date not more than two years prior to the filing of the charge with the EEOC. First promulgated by executive order, as discussed next, **affirmative action** generally means the active recruitment of minority applicants, although courts also have used the remedy to impose numerical hiring ratios (quotas) and hiring goals based on race and gender. In 1985, the EEOC defined affirmative action in employment as "actions appropriate to overcome the effects of past or present practices, policies, or other barriers to equal employment opportunity."

Prior to 1991, only victims of racial discrimination could recover compensatory and punitive damages from the courts. Today, however, under the Civil Rights Act of 1991, all victims of intentional discrimination based on race, gender, religion, national origin, or disability can recover compensatory and punitive damages, except in cases involving disparate impact. In cases not involving race, the act limits the amount of recoverable damages according to the number of persons the defendant employs. Companies with 15 to 100 employees are required to pay no more than $50,000; companies with 101 to 200 employees, no more than $100,000; those with 201 to 500 employees, no more than $200,000; and those with 501 or more employees, no more than $300,000. Either party may demand a jury trial. Victims of racial discrimination are still entitled to recover unlimited compensatory and punitive damages.

Reverse discrimination Employment decisions taking into account race or gender in order to remedy past discrimination.

REVERSE DISCRIMINATION A major controversy has arisen over the use of reverse discrimination in achieving affirmative action. In this context, reverse discrimination refers to affirmative action that directs an employer to remedy the underrepresentation of a given race or gender in a traditionally segregated job by considering an individual's race or gender when hiring or promoting. An example is an employer who discriminates against white males in order to increase the proportion of females or racial minority members in a company's workforce.

Due to the absence of state action, challenges to affirmative action plans adopted by private employers—those that are not governmental units at the local, state, or federal level—are tested under Title VII of the Civil Rights Act of 1964, not under the Equal Protection Clause of the U.S. Constitution. In 1987, the U.S. Supreme Court, under a Title VII cause of action, upheld an employer's right to promote a female employee rather than a white male employee who had scored higher on a qualifying examination.

When a state or local government adopts an affirmative action plan that is challenged as constituting illegal reverse discrimination, the plan is subject to strict scrutiny under the **Equal Protection Clause** of the Fourteenth Amendment. Under the strict scrutiny test, the subject classification must (1) be justified by a compelling governmental interest and (2) be the least intrusive means available.

With regard to racial discrimination, the U.S. Supreme Court in 1989 held that the federal government has "unique remedial powers" far exceeding those of state and local governments and that federal programs enacted to address such discrimination "are subject to a different [and less burdensome] standard than such classifications prescribed by state and local governments." However, in 1995 the U.S. Supreme Court placed significant constraints upon the federal government's ability to create programs favoring minority-owned businesses over white-owned businesses and appeared to apply the same strict standard to federal programs as to those required of state and local governments. Following this decision, the EEOC issued a statement which provided that "affirmative action is lawful only when it is designed to respond to a demonstrated and serious imbalance in the workforce, is flexible, time-limited, applies only to qualified workers, and respects the rights of non-minorities and men."

SEXUAL HARASSMENT In 1980, the EEOC issued a definition of sexual harassment:

Unwelcome sexual advances, requests for sexual favors, and other verbal or physical conduct of a sexual nature constitute sexual harassment when

1. submission to such conduct is made either explicitly or implicitly a term or condition of an individual's employment,
2. submission to or rejection of such conduct by an individual is used as the basis for employment decisions affecting such individual, or
3. such conduct has the purpose or effect of reasonably interfering with an individual's work performance or creating an intimidating, hostile or offensive working environment.

The courts, including the Supreme Court, have held that sexual harassment may constitute illegal sexual discrimination in violation of Title VII. Moreover, an employer will be held liable for sexual harassment committed by one of its employees if it does not take immediate action when it knows or should have known of the harassment. When the employee engaging in sexual harassment is an agent of the employer or holds a supervisory position over the victim, the employer may be liable without knowledge or reason to know.

In 1998, the U.S. Supreme Court concluded that sex discrimination consisting of same-sex harassment is actionable under Title VII.

> **Sexual harassment** An illegal form of sexual discrimination that includes unwelcome sexual advances, requests for sexual favors, and other verbal or physical conduct of a sexual nature.

COMPARABLE WORTH Industrial statistics on salaries indicate that women earn approximately two-thirds as much as men do. Because the Equal Pay Act only requires equal pay for equal work, it does not apply to different jobs even if they are comparable. Thus, that statute provides no remedy for women who have been systematically undervalued and underpaid in "traditional" occupations, such as secretary, teacher, or nurse. As a result, women have sought redress under Title VII by arguing that the failure to pay comparable worth is discrimination on the basis of gender. The concept of **comparable worth** provides that employers should measure the relative values of different jobs through a job evaluation rating system that is free of any potential gender bias. Theoretically, the consistent application of objective criteria (including factors such as skill, effort, working conditions, responsibility, and mental demands) across job categories will ensure fair payment for all employees. For example, if evaluation under such a system found the jobs of truck driver and nurse to be at the same level, workers in both jobs would receive the same pay.

In a 1981 case, the Supreme Court held that a claim of discriminatory undercompensation based on sex could be brought under Title VII, even when female plaintiffs were performing jobs different than those of their male counterparts. As the Court noted, however, the case involved a situation in which the defendant intentionally discriminated in wages; and the defendant, not the courts, had compared the jobs in terms of value. The Court also held that the four defenses available under the Equal Pay Act would apply to a Title VII claim. Since this decision, the concept of comparable worth has met with limited success in the courts. Nonetheless, more than a dozen states have adopted legislation requiring public and private employers to pay equally for comparable work.

Executive Order

In 1965, President Johnson issued an **executive order** that prohibits discrimination by federal contractors on the basis of race, color, gender, religion, or national origin in employment on *any work* the contractor performs during the period of the federal contract. Federal contractors are also required to take affirmative action in recruiting. The Secretary of Labor, *Office of Federal Contract Compliance Programs* (OFCCP), administers enforcement of the program.

The program applies to all contractors and all of their subcontractors in excess of $10,000 who enter into a federal contract to be performed in the United States. Compliance with the affirmative action requirement differs for construction and nonconstruction contractors. All *nonconstruction* contractors with 50 or more employees or with contracts for more than $50,000 must have a written affirmative action plan in order to be in compliance. The plan must include a workforce analysis; planned corrective action, if necessary, with specific goals and timetables; and procedures for auditing and reporting. The director of the OFCCP periodically issues goals and timetables for each segment of the *construction* industry in each region of the country. As a condition precedent to bidding on a federal contract, a contractor must agree to make a good faith effort to achieve current published goals.

Age Discrimination in Employment Act of 1967

The **Age Discrimination in Employment Act (ADEA)** prohibits discrimination on the basis of age in employment areas that include hiring, firing, and compensating. The act applies to private employers having 20 or more employees and to all governmental units, regardless of size. The act also prohibits mandatory retirement for most employees, no matter what their age, unless the retirement is justified by a suitable defense.

The major statutory defenses include (1) a *bona fide* occupational qualification, (2) a *bona fide* seniority system, and (3) any other reasonable action. Remedies include back pay, injunctive relief, affirmative action, and liquidated damages equal to the amount of the award for "willful" violations.

Disability Law

The **Rehabilitation Act of 1973** attempts to assist the handicapped in obtaining rehabilitation training, access to public facilities, and employment. The act requires federal contractors and federal agencies to take affirmative action to hire qualified handicapped persons. It also prohibits discrimination on the basis of handicap in federal programs and programs receiving federal financial assistance.

A *handicapped person* is defined as an individual who (1) has a physical or mental impairment that substantially affects one or more of her major life activities, (2) has a history of major life activity impairment, *or* (3) is regarded as having such an impairment. Major life activities include functions such as caring for oneself, seeing, speaking, or walking. Alcohol and drug abuses are not considered handicapping conditions for the purposes of this statute.

Disability law Several federal acts, including the Americans with Disabilities Act, that provide assistance to the disabled in obtaining rehabilitation training, access to public facilities, and employment.

The **Americans with Disabilities Act (ADA) of 1990** forbids an employer from discriminating against any person with a disability with regard to "hiring or discharge . . . , employee compensation, advancement, job training and other terms, conditions and privileges of employment." In addition, businesses must make special accommodations, such as installing wheelchair-accessible bathrooms, for workers and customers with disabilities unless the cost is unduly burdensome. An employer may use qualification standards, tests, or selection criteria that screen out workers with disabilities if these measures are job related and consistent with business necessity and if no reasonable accommodation is possible. Remedies for violation of the ADA are those generally allowed under Title VII and include injunctive relief, reinstatement, back pay, and, for intentional discrimination, compensatory and punitive damages (capped according to company size by the Civil Rights Act of 1991).

In addition, the **Vietnam Veterans Readjustment Act of 1974** requires firms having $10,000 or more in federal contracts to engage in affirmative action for disabled veterans and Vietnam-era veterans. Exhibit 100.23 presents a summary of U.S. Federal Employment Discrimination Laws.

Exhibit 100.23 *Federal Employment Discrimination Law*

	Protected Characteristics	Prohibited Conduct	Defenses	Remedies
Equal Pay Act	Sex	Wages	Seniority Merit Quality or quantity measures Any factor other than sex	Back pay Injunction Liquidated damages Attorneys' fees
Title VII of Civil Rights Act	Race Color Sex Religion National origin	Terms, conditions, or privileges of employment	Seniority Ability test BFOQ (except for race) Business necessity (disparate impact only)	Back pay Injunction Reinstatement Compensatory and punitive damages for intentional discrimination • unlimited for race • limited for all others Attorneys' fees
Age Discrimination in Employment Act	Age	Terms, conditions, or privileges of employment	Seniority BFOQ Any other reasonable act	Back pay Injunction Reinstatement Liquidated damages for willful violation Attorneys' fees
Americans with Disabilities Act	Disability	Terms, conditions, or privileges of employment	Undue hardship Job-related criteria and business necessity Risk to public health and safety	Back pay Injunction Reinstatement Compensatory and punitive damages for damages for intentional discrimination (limited) Attorneys' fees

Employee Protection

Employees are accorded a number of job-related protections. These include a limited right not to be unfairly dismissed, a right to a safe and healthy workplace, compensation for injuries sustained in the workplace, and some financial security upon retirement or loss of employment. This section discusses (1) employee termination at will, (2) occupational safety and health, (3) employee privacy, (4) workers' compensation, (5) Social Security and unemployment insurance, (6) the Fair Labor Standards Act, (7) employee notice of termination or layoff (WARN Act), and (8) family and medical leave.

Employee Termination at Will

Under the common law, a contract of employment for other than a definite term is terminable at will by either party. Accordingly, under the common law, employers may "dismiss their employees at will for good cause, for no cause or even for cause morally wrong, without being thereby guilty of legal wrong." In recent years, however, a growing number of judicial exceptions to the rule, based on implied contract, tort, and public policy, have developed. A number of federal and state statutes enacted in the last 50 years also limit the rule, which may in addition be restricted by contractual agreement between employer and employee. In particular, most collective bargaining agreements negotiated through union representatives contain a provision prohibiting dismissal "without cause."

Employee termination at will
Under the common law, a contract of employment for other than a definite term is terminable at will by either party.

STATUTORY LIMITATIONS Federal legislation has been passed that limits the employer's right to discharge. These statutes fall into three categories: (1) those protecting certain employees from discriminatory discharge, (2) those protecting certain employees in their exercise of statutory rights, and (3) those protecting certain employees from discharge without cause.

At the state level, statutes protect workers from discriminatory discharge for filing workers' compensation claims. Also, many state statutes parallel federal legislation. Some states have adopted statutes similar to the NLRA, and many states prohibit discrimination in employment on the basis of factors such as race, creed, nationality, gender, or age. In addition, some states have statutes prohibiting discharge or other punitive actions taken for the purpose of influencing voting or, in some states, political activity.

JUDICIAL LIMITATIONS **Judicial limitations** on the employment-at-will doctrine have been based on contract law, tort law, and public policy. Cases founded in contract theory have relied on arguments maintaining, among other things, (1) that the dismissal was improper because the employee had detrimentally relied on the employer's promise of work for a reasonable time; (2) that the employment was not at will because of implied-in-fact promises of employment for a specific duration, which meant that the employer could not terminate the employee without just cause; (3) that the employment contract implied or expressly provided that the employee would not be dismissed so long as he satisfactorily performed his work; (4) that the employer had assured the employee that he would not be dismissed except for cause; or (5) that, upon entering into the employment contract, the employee gave consideration over and above the performance of services to support a promise of job security.

Courts have also created exceptions to the employment-at-will doctrine by imposing tort obligations on employers, most particularly with respect to the torts of intentional infliction of emotional distress and of interference with employment relations.

The most frequent basis for finding a discharge to be wrongful is that the discharge violates statutory or other established public policy. In general, these cases involve dismissal for (1) refusing to violate a statute, (2) exercising a statutory right, (3) performing a statutory obligation, or (4) reporting an alleged violation of a statute that is of public interest.

Occupational Safety and Health Act

In 1970, Congress enacted the **Occupational Safety and Health Act** to ensure, as far as possible, a safe and healthful working environment for every worker. The act established the **Occupational Safety and Health Administration (OSHA)** to develop standards, conduct inspections, monitor compliance, and institute enforcement actions against those who are not in compliance.

Upon each employer who is engaged in a business affecting interstate commerce, the act imposes a general duty to provide a work environment that is "free from recognized hazards that are causing or likely to cause death or serious physical harm to his employees." In addition to this general duty, the employer must comply with specific OSHA-promulgated safety rules. The act also requires employees to comply with all OSHA rules and regulations. Finally, the act prohibits any employer from discharging or discriminating against an employee who exercises her rights under the act.

Enforcing the act generally involves OSHA inspections and citations of employers, as appropriate, for (1) breach of the general duty obligation, (2) breach of specific safety and health standards, or (3) failure to keep records, make reports, or post notices required by the act.

When a violation is discovered, the offending employer receives a written citation, a proposed penalty, and a date by which the employer must remedy the breach. Citations may be contested; in such cases, the Occupational Safety and Health Review Commission assigns administrative law judges to hold hearings. The commission, at its discretion, may grant review of an administrative law judge's decision; review is not a matter of right. If no such review occurs, the judge's decision becomes the commission's final order 30 days after receipt, and the aggrieved party may then appeal the order to the appropriate U.S. Circuit Court of Appeals.

Penalties for violations are both civil and criminal. In cases involving civil penalties, serious violations require that a penalty be proposed; in contrast, for nonserious violations, penalties are discretionary and rarely proposed. The act further empowers the secretary of labor to obtain temporary restraining orders in situations where regular OSHA procedures are insufficient to halt imminently hazardous or deadly business operations.

One stated purpose of the act is to encourage state participation in regulating safety and health. The act therefore permits a state to regulate the safety and health of the work environment within its borders, provided that OSHA approves the plan. The act sets minimum acceptable standards for the states to impose, but does not require that a state plan be identical to the OSHA guidelines. More than half of the states regulate health and safety in the workplace through state-promulgated plans.

Employee Privacy

Over the last decade, employee privacy has become a major issue. The fundamental right to privacy is a product of common law protection. Thus, the tort of invasion of privacy safeguards employees from unwanted searches, electronic monitoring and other forms of surveillance, and disclosure of confidential records. The tort actually consists of four different torts: (1) unreasonable intrusion into the seclusion of another; (2) unreasonable public disclosure of private facts; (3) unreasonable publicity that places another in a false light; and (4) appropriation of a person's name or likeness. In addition, the federal government and some states have legislatively supplemented the common law in certain areas.

DRUG AND ALCOHOL TESTING Although no federal legislation deals comprehensively with **drug and alcohol tests,** legislation in a number of states either prohibits such tests altogether or prescribes certain scientific and procedural standards for conducting them. In the absence of a state statute, *private* sector employees have little or no protection from such tests. The NLRB has held, however, that drug and alcohol testing in a union setting is a mandatory subject of collective bargaining.

In 1989, the U.S. Supreme Court ruled that the employer of a *public* sector employee whose position involved public health or safety or national security could subject the employee to a drug or alcohol test without either first obtaining a search warrant or having reasonable grounds to believe the individual had engaged in any wrongdoing. Based on Supreme Court and lower court decisions, it appears that a government employer may use (1) random or universal testing when the public health or safety or national security is involved and (2) selective drug testing when there is sufficient cause to believe an employee has a drug problem.

Lie detector tests Federal statute prohibits private employers from requiring employees or prospective employees to take such tests.

LIE DETECTOR TESTS The **Federal Employee Polygraph Protection Act of 1988** prohibits private employers from requiring employees or prospective employees to undergo a **lie detector test,** inquiring about the results of such a test, or using the results of such a test or the refusal to be tested as grounds for an adverse employment decision. The act exempts government employers and, in certain situations, Energy Department contractors or persons providing consulting services for federal intelligence agencies. In addition, security firms and manufacturers of controlled substances may use a polygraph to test prospective employees. Moreover, an employer, as part of an ongoing investigation of economic loss or injury to its business, may use a polygraph test. Nevertheless, the use of the test must meet the following requirements: (1) it must be designed to investigate a specific incident or activity, not to document a chronic problem; (2) the employee to be tested must have had access to the property that is the subject of the investigation; and (3) the employer must have reason to suspect the particular employee.

Employees and prospective employees tested under any of these exemptions cannot be terminated, disciplined, or denied employment solely as a result of the test. The act further provides that those subjected to a polygraph test (1) cannot be asked intrusive or degrading questions regarding topics such as their religious beliefs, opinions as to racial matters, political views, or sexual preferences or behaviors; (2) must be given the right to review all questions before the test and to terminate the test at any time; and (3) must receive a complete copy of the test results.

Workers' Compensation

In order to provide speedier and more certain relief to injured employees, all states have adopted statutes providing for **workers' compensation.** (Several states, however, exempt specified employers from workers' compensation statutes.) These statutes create commissions or boards that determine whether an injured employee is entitled to receive compensation and, if so, how much. The basis of recovery under workers' compensation is strict liability: the employee does not have to prove that the employer was negligent. The common law defenses of contributory negligence, voluntary assumption of risk, and the fellow servant rule (which covers injury caused by the negligence of a fellow employee) are *not* available to employers in workers' compensation proceedings. Such defenses are *abolished*. The *only* requirement is that the employee be injured and that the injury arises out of and in the course of his employment. The amounts recoverable are fixed by statute for each type of injury and are lower than the amounts a court or jury would probably award in an action at common law. The courts, therefore, do not have jurisdiction over such cases, except to review decisions of the board or commission; even then, the courts may determine only whether such decisions are in accordance with the statute. If a third party, however, causes the injury, the employee may bring a tort action against that third party.

Early workers' compensation laws did not provide coverage for occupational disease, and most courts held that occupational injury did not include disease. Today, virtually all states provide general compensation coverage for occupational diseases, although the coverage varies greatly from state to state.

Social Security and Unemployment Insurance

Social Security was enacted in 1935 in an attempt to provide limited retirement and death benefits to certain employees. Since then, the benefits have greatly increased, and the federal Social Security system, which has expanded to cover almost all employees, now contains four major benefit programs: (1) Old-Age and Survivors Insurance (OASI) (providing retirement and survivor benefits), (2) Disability Insurance (DI), (3) Hospitalization Insurance (Medicare), and (4) Supplemental Security Income (SSI).

The system is financed by contributions (taxes) paid by employers, employees, and self-employed individuals. Employees and employers pay matching contributions. It is the employer's responsibility to withhold the employee's contribution and to forward the full amount of the tax to the Internal Revenue Service. Employee-made contributions are not tax deductible by the employee, whereas those made by the employer are. Self-employed persons are also required to report their taxable income and to pay the Social Security tax.

The federal *unemployment insurance* system was initially created by Title IX of the Social Security Act of 1935. Subsequently, Title IX was supplemented by the Federal Unemployment Tax Act and by numerous other federal statutes. This complex system depends upon the cooperation of state and federal programs. Federal law provides the general guidelines, standards, and requirements, while the states administer the program through their own employment laws. The system is funded by employer taxes: federal taxes generally pay the program's administrative costs, and state contributions pay for the actual benefits.

The purpose of the Federal Unemployment Tax Act is to provide **unemployment compensation** to workers who have lost their jobs, usually through no fault of their own, and cannot find other employment. Payments, generally made weekly, are based on a particular state's formula.

Fair Labor Standards Act

The **Fair Labor Standards Act (FLSA)** regulates the employment of child labor outside of agriculture. The act prohibits the employment of anyone under 14 years of age in nonfarm work, except for newspaper deliverers and child actors. Fourteen- and 15-year-olds may work for a limited number of hours outside of school hours, under specific conditions, in certain *nonhazardous* occupations. Sixteen- and 17-year-olds may work in any *nonhazardous* job, while persons 18 years old or older may work in *any* job, whether it is hazardous or not. The secretary of labor determines which occupations are considered hazardous.

In addition, the FLSA imposes wage and hour requirements upon covered employers. The act provides for a minimum hourly wage and overtime pay of time-and-a-half for hours worked in excess of forty hours per week.

However, the FLSA exempts certain workers from both its minimum wage and overtime provisions; those excluded include professionals, managers, and outside salespersons.

Worker Adjustment and Retraining Notification Act

Worker Adjustment and Retraining Notification (WARN) Act Federal statute that requires an employer to provide sixty days' advance notice of a plant closing or mass layoff.

The **Worker Adjustment and Retraining Notification Act (WARN)** requires an employer to provide 60 days' advance notice of a plant closing or mass layoff. A "plant closing" is defined as the permanent or temporary shutting down of a single site or units within a site if the shutdown results in 50 or more employees losing employment during any 30-day period. A "mass layoff" is defined as a loss of employment during a 30-day period either for 500 employees or for at least one-third of the employees at a given site, if that one-third equals or exceeds 50 employees. WARN requires that notification be given to specified state and local officials as well as to the affected employees or their union representatives. The act, which reduces the notification period with regard to failing companies and emergency situations, applies to employers with a total of 100 or more employees who in the aggregate work at least 2,000 hours per week, not including overtime.

Family and Medical Leave Act of 1993

The **Family and Medical Leave Act of 1993** requires employers with 50 or more employees and governments at the federal, state, and local levels to grant employees up to 12 weeks of leave during any 12-month period for the birth of a child; adopting or gaining foster care of a child; or the care of a spouse, child, or parent who suffers from a serious health condition. The act defines a "serious health condition" as an "illness, injury, impairment or physical or mental condition" that involves inpatient medical care at a hospital, hospice, or residential care facility or continuing medical treatment by a health-care provider. Employees are eligible for such leave if they have been employed by their present employer for at least 12 months and have worked at least 1,250 hours for their employer during the 12 months preceding the leave request. The requested leave may be paid, unpaid, or a combination of both.

Antitrust

The economic community is best served in normal times by free competition in trade and industry. It is in the public interest that quality, price, and service in an open, competitive market for goods and services be determining factors in the business rivalry for the customer's dollar. Rather than compete, however, businesses would prefer to eliminate their competition and, consequently, to enjoy a position from which they could dictate both the price of their goods and the quantity they produce. Although eliminating competition by producing a better product is the proper goal of a business, some businesses effect this elimination through illegitimate means, such as fixing prices and allocating exclusive territories to certain competitors within an industry. The law of antitrust prohibits such activities and attempts to ensure free and fair competition in the marketplace.

The common law has traditionally favored competition and has held that agreements and contracts in restraint of trade are illegal and unenforceable. In addition, although several states enacted antitrust statutes during the 1800s, the latter half of the 19th century revealed concentrations of economic power in the form of "trusts" and "combinations" that were too powerful and widespread to be curbed effectively by state action. In 1890, this awesome and uncontrollable growth of power prompted Congress to enact the Sherman Antitrust Act, the first federal statute in this field. Since then, Congress has enacted other antitrust statutes, including the Clayton Act, the Robinson-Patman Act, and the Federal Trade Commission Act. These statutes prohibit anticompetitive practices and seek to prevent unreasonable concentrations of economic power that stifle or weaken competition.

Sherman Antitrust Act

Section 1 of the Sherman Act prohibits contracts, combinations, and conspiracies that restrain trade, while Section 2 outlaws both monopolies and attempts to monopolize. Failure to comply with either section is a criminal violation and subjects the offender to fine or imprisonment or both. As amended by the 1990 Antitrust Amendments, the act subjects individual offenders to imprisonment of up to three years and fines of up to $350,000, while corporate offenders are subject to fines of up to $10,000,000 per violation. Moreover, the act empowers the federal district courts to issue injunctions restraining violations; and anyone injured by a violation is entitled to recover in a civil action **treble damages** (that is, three times the amount of the actual loss sustained). The U.S. Department of Justice and the Federal Trade Commission have the duty to institute appropriate enforcement proceedings other than treble damages actions.

In 1992, the Justice Department expanded its enforcement policy regarding the Sherman Act to cover conduct by foreign companies that harms U.S. exports. Under the new policy, the department examines conduct to determine whether it would violate the law if it occurred within borders of the United States. The department has indicated that it will focus primarily on boycotts and cartels that injure the export of U.S. products and services.

Restraint of Trade

Section 1 of the Sherman Act provides that "[e]very contract, combination in the form of trust or otherwise, or conspiracy, in restraint of trade or commerce among the several states, or with foreign nations is hereby declared to be illegal." Because the section's language is so broad, identifying the elements that constitute a violation has been largely a product of judicial interpretation.

STANDARDS As noted above, Section 1 prohibits every contract, combination, or conspiracy in restraint of trade. Taken literally, this prohibition would invalidate every unperformed contract. To avoid such an unrealistic application, the courts have interpreted this section to invalidate only *unreasonable* restraints of trade. This standard is known as the **rule of reason test,** a flexible standard under which the courts, in determining whether a challenged practice unreasonably restricts competition, consider a variety of factors, including the makeup of the relevant industry, the defendants' positions within that industry, the ability of the defendants' competitors to respond to the challenged practice, and the defendants' purpose in adopting the restraint. After reviewing the various factors, a court determines whether the challenged restraint unreasonably restricts competition.

By requiring the courts to balance the *anticompetitive* effects of every questioned restraint against its *procompetitive* effects, this standard placed a substantial burden upon the judicial system. The Supreme Court addressed this problem by declaring certain categories of restraints to be unreasonable by their very nature, that is, **illegal *per se.*** Characterizing a type of restraint as *per se* illegal significantly affects the prosecution of an antitrust suit. In such a case, the plaintiff need only show that the type of restraint occurred; she need not prove that the restraint limited competition. The defendants, in turn, may not defend on the basis that the restraint is reasonable. Furthermore, the court is not required to conduct extensive, and often difficult, economic analysis.

HORIZONTAL AND VERTICAL RESTRAINTS A trade restraint may be classified as either horizontal or vertical. A **horizontal restraint** involves collaboration among competitors at the same level in the chain of distribution. For example, an agreement among manufacturers, among wholesalers, or among retailers would be horizontal.

On the other hand, an agreement among parties who are not in direct competition at the same distribution level is a **vertical restraint.** Thus, an agreement between a manufacturer and a wholesaler is vertical. Although the distinction between horizontal and vertical restraints can become blurred, it often determines whether a restraint is illegal *per se* or should be judged by the rule of reason test. For instance, horizontal market allocations are illegal *per se,* whereas vertical market allocations are subject to the rule of reason test.

> *Horizontal restraints* Agreements among competitors.
> *Vertical restraints* Agreements among parties at different levels in the chain of distribution.

CONCERTED ACTION Section 1 does not prohibit **unilateral** conduct; rather, it forbids **concerted** action. Thus, one person or business by itself cannot violate the section. As the U.S. Supreme Court held in *Monsanto Co. v. Spray-Rite Service Corporation,* an organization has the "right to deal, or refuse to deal, with whomever it likes, as long as it does so independently." For example, if a manufacturer announces its resale prices in advance and refuses to deal with those who disagree with the pricing, there is no violation of Section 1 because the manufacturer has acted alone. On the other hand, if a manufacturer and its retailers together agree that the manufacturer will sell only to those retailers who agree to sell at a specified price, a violation of Section 1 may exist.

For purposes of the concerted action requirement, the courts view a firm and its employees as one entity. The same is also true for a corporation and its wholly owned subsidiaries; thus, the Sherman Act is not violated when a parent and its wholly owned subsidiary agree to a restraint in trade.

The concerted action requirement may be established by an express agreement. Not surprisingly, however, express agreements often are nonexistent, leaving the court to infer an interparty agreement from circumstantial evidence.

165. IMPACT OF GOVERNMENT ON BUSINESS

Conscious parallelism *Similar patterns of conduct among competitors.*

Nonetheless, similar patterns of conduct among competitors, called **conscious parallelism,** are not sufficient in themselves to imply a conspiracy in violation of Section 1. Actual conspiracy requires an *additional* factor—such as complex actions that would benefit each competitor only if all of them acted—or indications of a traditional conspiracy—such as identical sealed bids from each competitor.

Joint ventures are a form of business association organized to carry out a particular business enterprise. Competitors frequently pool their resources in order to share costs and to eliminate wasteful redundancy. The validity under antitrust law of a joint venture generally depends on the competitors' primary purpose in forming it. A joint venture that was not formed to fix prices or divide markets will be judged under the rule of reason.

However, because uncertainty about the legality of joint ventures seemed to discourage their use for joint research and development, Congress passed the National Cooperative Research Act in order to facilitate such applications. The act provides that the courts must judge joint ventures in the research and development of new technology under the rule of reason test and that treble damages do *not* apply to ventures formed in violation of Section 1 if those forming the venture have notified the Justice Department and the FTC of their intent to form the joint venture.

Price fixing *An agreement with the purpose or effect of inhibiting price competition.*

PRICE FIXING Price fixing is an agreement with the purpose or effect of inhibiting price competition; such agreements may, among other things, raise, depress, fix, peg, or stabilize prices. Price fixing is the primary and most serious example of a *per se* violation under the Sherman Act. All *horizontal* price-fixing agreements are illegal *per se*. This prohibition covers any agreement by which sellers establish *maximum* prices at which certain commodities or services are to be offered for sale, as well as those by which they set *minimum* prices. The law also prohibits sellers' agreements to change the prices of certain commodities or services simultaneously or to not advertise their prices.

The U.S. Supreme Court has condemned not only agreements among horizontal competitors that directly fix prices but also agreements that affect price indirectly. For example, in finding an agreement among beer wholesalers to eliminate interest-free short-term credit on sales to beer retailers to be illegal *per se*, the Court viewed the credit terms "as an inseparable part of price" and concluded that the agreement to eliminate interest-free short-term credit was equivalent to an agreement to eliminate discounts and, thus, was an agreement to fix prices.

Similarly, it is illegal *per se* for a seller to fix the price at which its purchasers must resell its product. This **vertical** form of price fixing—usually called *retail price maintenance*—is considered a *per se* violation of Section 1.

Despite its early and consistent condemnation of resale price maintenance agreements, the Supreme Court has found no Section 1 violation when a manufacturer who announces in advance that it will not sell to dealers who cut prices then terminates its dealers who have cut prices. Not surprisingly, courts sometimes have difficulty distinguishing between an illegal resale price maintenance agreement and a manufacturer's legal refusal to deal with a retailer who refuses to charge the manufacturer's dictated minimum price. More significantly, the U.S. Supreme Court overruled a 30-year-old precedent by holding that vertical maximum price fixing is not *per se* illegal but is to be judged by a rule of reason standard.

MARKET ALLOCATIONS Direct price fixing is not the only way to control prices. Another method is through **market allocation,** whereby competitors agree not to compete with each other in specific markets, which may be defined by geographic area, customer type, or product class. All *horizontal* agreements to divide markets have been declared illegal *per se* because they grant to the firm remaining in the market a monopolistic control over price.

Boycott *Agreement among parties not to deal with a third party.*

BOYCOTTS As noted earlier, Section 1 of the Sherman Act applies not to unilateral action but only to agreements or combinations. Accordingly, a seller's refusal to deal with any particular buyer does not violate the act; and a manufacturer can thus refuse to sell to a retailer who persists in selling below the manufacturer's suggested retail price. On the other hand, when two or more firms agree not to deal with a third party, their agreement represents a **concerted refusal to deal,** or a group **boycott,** which may violate Section 1 of the Sherman Act. Such a boycott may be clearly anticompetitive, eliminating competition or reducing market entry.

Some group boycotts are illegal *per se* while others are subject to the rule of reason. Group boycotts designed to eliminate a competitor or to force that competitor to meet a group standard are illegal *per se* if the group has market power. On the other hand, cooperative arrangements "designed to increase economic efficiency and render markets more, rather than less, competitive" are subject to the rule of reason. Finally, most courts hold that the *per se* rule of illegality for concerted refusals to deal extends only to horizontal boycotts, not to vertical refusals to deal. Most courts have held that a rule of reason test should govern all nonprice vertical restraints, including concerted refusals to deal.

Exhibit 100.24 *Restraints of Trade Under The Sherman Act*

	Standard	
Type of Restraint	Per Se Illegal	Rule of Reason
Price Fixing	Horizontal Vertical (Minimum)	Vertical (Maximum)
Market allocations	Horizontal	Vertical
Group boycotts or refusals to deal	Horizontal Vertical (Minority)	Vertical (Majority)
Tying arrangements	If seller has economic power in tying product and affects a substantial amount of interstate commerce in the tied product	If seller lacks economic power in tying product

TYING ARRANGEMENTS A **tying arrangement** occurs when the seller of a product, service, or intangible (the "tying" product) conditions its sale on the buyer's purchasing a second product, service, or intangible (the "tied" product) from the seller. For example, imagine that **Xerox,** a major manufacturer of photocopying equipment, required all purchasers of its photocopiers also to purchase from Xerox all of the paper they would use with the copiers. Xerox would thereby tie the sale of its photocopier—the *tying* product—to the sale of paper—the *tied* product.

Tying arrangement Conditioning a sale of a desired product (tying product) on the buyer's purchasing a second product (tied product).

Because tying arrangements limit buyers' freedom of choice and may exclude competitors, the law closely scrutinizes such agreements. A tying arrangement exists when a seller exploits its economic power in one market to expand its empire into another market. When the seller has considerable economic power in the tying product and more than an insubstantial amount of interstate commerce is affected in the tied product, the tying arrangement will be *per se* illegal. Economic power may be demonstrated by showing that (1) the seller occupied a dominant position in the tying market; (2) the seller's product enjoys an advantage not shared by its competitors in the tying market; or (3) a substantial number of customers have accepted the tying arrangement, and the only explanation for their willingness to comply is the seller's economic power in the tying market. If the seller lacks economic power, the tying arrangement is judged by the rule of reason test. Exhibit 100.24 presents a summary of restraints of trade under the Sherman Act.

Monopolies

Economic analysis indicates that a monopolist will use its power to limit production and increase prices. Therefore, a monopolistic market will produce fewer goods than a competitive market would and will sell these goods at higher prices. Addressing the problem of monopolization, Section 2 of the Sherman Act prohibits monopolies and any attempts or conspiracies to monopolize. Thus, Section 2 prohibits both agreements among businesses and, unlike Section 1, unilateral conduct by one firm.

MONOPOLIZATION Although the language of Section 2 ostensibly prohibits *all* monopolies, the courts have required that a firm not only must possess market power but also must have attained the monopoly power unfairly or abused that power, once attained. By itself, the possession of monopoly power is not considered a violation of Section 2 because a firm may have obtained such power through its skills in developing, marketing, and selling products—that is, through the very competitive conduct that the antitrust laws are designed to promote.

Because it is extremely rare to find an unregulated industry with only one firm, determining the presence of monopoly power involves defining the degree of market dominance that constitutes such power. **Monopoly power** is the ability to control price or to exclude competitors from the marketplace. In grappling with this question of power, the courts have developed a number of criteria; but the most common test is market share. A market share greater than 75 percent generally indicates monopoly power, while a share less than 50 percent does not. A share between 50 and 75 percent is, in itself, inconclusive.

Market share is a firm's fractional share of the total relevant product and geographic markets, but defining these relevant markets is often a difficult and subjective project for the courts. The relevant *product market,* includes products that are substitutable for the firm's product on the basis of price, quality, and adaptability for other purposes.

The relevant *geographic market* is the territory in which the firm sells its products or services. This may be at the local, regional, or national level. For instance, the relevant geographic market for the manufacture and sale of aluminum might be national, whereas that of a taxi company would be local. The scope of a geographic market depends on factors such as transportation costs, the type of product or service, and the location of competitors and customers.

If sufficient monopoly power has been proved, the law must then show that the firm has engaged in **unfair conduct.** However, the courts have yet to agree on what constitutes such conduct. One judicial approach is to place upon a firm possessing monopoly power the burden of proving that it acquired such power passively or that the power was "thrust" upon it. An alternative view is that monopoly power, combined with conduct designed to exclude competitors, violates Section 1. A third approach requires monopoly power plus some type of predatory practice, such as pricing below marginal costs.

To date, however, the U.S. Supreme Court has yet to identify the exact conduct, beyond the mere possession of monopoly power, that violates Section 2. To do so, the Court must resolve the complex and conflicting market and business policies this most basic question of monopolies involves.

ATTEMPTS TO MONOPOLIZE   Section 2 also prohibits **attempts to monopolize.** As with monopolization, the courts have had difficulty developing a standard that distinguishes undesirable conduct likely to engender a monopoly from healthy, competitive conduct. The standard test applied by the courts requires proof of a specific intent to monopolize plus a dangerous probability of success; however, among other things, this test neither defines an "intent" nor offers a standard of power by which to measure "success." Recent cases suggest that the greater the measure of market power a firm acquires, the less flagrant must its conduct be to constitute an attempt. These cases, however, do not specify any threshold level of market power.

CONSPIRACIES TO MONOPOLIZE   Section 2 also condemns conspiracies to monopolize. Few cases involve this offense alone, as any conspiracy to monopolize would also constitute, in violation of Section 1, a combination in restraint of trade.

Clayton Act

In 1914, Congress strengthened the Sherman Act by adopting the Clayton Act, which was expressly designed "to supplement existing laws against unlawful restraints and monopolies." The Clayton Act provides only for civil actions, not for criminal penalties. Private parties may bring civil actions in federal court for treble damages and attorneys' fees. In addition, the Justice Department and the Federal Trade Commission are authorized to bring civil actions, including proceedings in equity, to prevent and restrict violations of the act.

The major provisions of the Clayton Act deal with price discrimination, tying contracts, exclusive dealing, and mergers. Section 2, which deals with price discrimination, was amended and rewritten by the Robinson-Patman Act, which we will discuss next. The Clayton Act exempts labor, agricultural, and horticultural organizations from all antitrust laws.

Tying Contracts and Exclusive Dealing

Section 3 of the Clayton Act prohibits **tying arrangements** and exclusive dealing, selling, or leasing arrangements that prevent purchasers from dealing with the seller's competitors when such arrangements *may* substantially lessen competition or *tend* to create a monopoly. This section is intended to stifle fledgling anticompetitive practices before they grow into violations of Section 1 or 2 of the Sherman Act. Unlike the Sherman Act, however, Section 3 applies only to practices involving commodities, not to those that involve services, intangibles, or land.

Tying arrangement Prohibited if it tends to create a monopoly or may substantially lessen competition.

Exclusive dealing arrangement Seller or lessor conditions agreement upon the buyer's or lessee's promise not to deal in competing goods.

Tying arrangements, discussed earlier, have been labeled by the Supreme Court as serving "hardly any purpose beyond the suppression of competition." Although the Court at one time indicated that the standards applied under the Sherman Act differed from those applied under the Clayton Act, recent lower-court cases suggest that the same rules now govern both types of actions.

Exclusive dealing arrangements are agreements by which the seller or lessor of a product conditions the agreement upon the buyer's or lessee's promise not to deal in a competitor's goods. For example, a manufacturer of razors might require retailers wishing to sell its line of shaving equipment to agree not to carry competing merchandise. Such conduct, although treated more leniently than tying arrangements, violates Section 3 if it tends to create a monopoly or may substantially lessen competition. The courts treat exclusive dealing arrangements more leniently because such arrangements may bolster competition to the extent that they benefit buyers, and thus, indirectly, the ultimate consumers, by ensuring supplies, deterring price increases, and enabling long-term planning on the basis of known costs.

Mergers

In the United States, corporate mergers have helped to reshape both corporate structure and our economic system. **Mergers** are horizontal, vertical, or conglomerate, depending on the relationship between the acquirer and the company acquired. A **horizontal merger** involves a company's acquisition of all or part of the stock or assets of a competing company. For example, if IBM were to acquire **Apple,** this would be a horizontal merger. A **vertical merger** is a company's acquisition of one of its customers or suppliers. A vertical merger is a *forward* merger if the acquiring company purchases a *customer,* such as the purchase of **Revco Discount Drug Stores** by Procter & Gamble. A vertical merger is a *backward* merger if the acquiring company purchases a supplier; for example, IBM's purchase of a microchip manufacturer. The third type of merger, the **conglomerate merger,** is a catchall category that covers all acquisitions not involving a competitor, customer, or supplier.

Horizontal merger Acquisition by one company of a competing company.

Vertical merger Acquisition by one company of one of its suppliers or customers.

Conglomerate merger An acquisition by one company of another that is not a competitor, customer, or supplier.

Section 7 of the Clayton Act prohibits a corporation from merging or acquiring another corporation's stock or assets when such an action would substantially lessen competition or would tend to create a monopoly. Currently, the law regarding horizontal, vertical, and conglomerate mergers is, particularly with respect to the last two, in a state of flux.

The principal objective of the antitrust law governing mergers is to maintain competition. Accordingly, the courts scrutinize the legality of horizontal mergers most carefully. Factors that affect this review include the market share of each of the merging firms, the degree of industry concentration, the number of firms in the industry, entry barriers, market trends, the vigor and strength of other competitors in the industry, the character and history of the merging firms, market demand, and the extent of industry price competition.

Robinson-Patman Act

Originally, Section 2 of the Clayton Act prohibited sellers only from differentially pricing their products in order to injure local or regional competitors. In 1936, in an attempt to limit the power of large purchasers, Congress amended Section 2 of the Clayton Act by adopting the Robinson-Patman Act, which further prohibits **price discrimination** in interstate commerce concerning commodities of like grade and quality. More specifically, the act prohibits buyers from inducing and sellers from granting discrimination in prices. In order to constitute a violation, the price discrimination must substantially lessen competition or tend to create a monopoly.

Under this act, a seller of goods may not grant discounts to buyers, including allowances for advertisements, counter displays, and samples, unless the seller offers the same discounts to all other purchasers on proportionately equal terms. The act also prohibits other types of discounts, rebates, and allowances and makes it unlawful to sell goods at unreasonably low prices for the purpose of destroying competition or eliminating a competitor. The act also makes it unlawful for a person knowingly to "induce or receive" an illegal discrimination in price, thus imposing liability on the buyer as well as the seller. Violation of the Robinson-Patman Act, with limited exceptions, is civil, not criminal, in nature. Price differentials may be justified by proof of either a cost savings to the seller or a good faith price reduction to meet a competitor's lawful price.

Primary-Line Injury

In enacting Section 2 of the Clayton Act in 1914, Congress was concerned with sellers who sought to harm or eliminate their competitors through price discrimination. Injuries accruing to a seller's competitors are called **"primary-line" injuries.** Because the act forbids price discrimination only when such discrimination may substantially lessen competition or may tend to create a monopoly, the plaintiff in a Robinson-Patman primary-line injury case either must show that the defendant, with the intention of harming competition,

Primary-line injury Injury to a seller's competitors.

has engaged in predatory pricing or must present a detailed market analysis that demonstrates how the defendant's price discrimination actually harmed competition. To prove predatory intent, a plaintiff may rely either on direct evidence of such intent or, more commonly, on inferences drawn from the defendant's conduct, such as below-cost or unprofitable pricing for a significant period of time. A predatory pricing scheme may also be challenged under the Sherman Act.

Secondary- and Tertiary-Line Injury

Secondary-line injury *Injury to competitors of the buyers.*

In amending Section 2 of the Clayton Act through the adoption of the Robinson-Patman Act, Congress was concerned primarily with small buyers, who were harmed by the discounts that sellers granted to large buyers. Injuries that accrue to some buyers because of the lower prices granted to others are called "secondary-line" injuries. To prove the required harm to competition, a plaintiff in a **secondary-line injury** case either must show substantial and sustained intramarket price differentials or must offer a detailed market analysis that demonstrates actual harm to competition. Because courts have been willing in secondary-line injury cases to infer harm to competition from a sustained and substantial price differential, proving a secondary-line injury is generally easier than proving a primary-line injury.

Tertiary-line injury *Injury to purchasers from other secondary-line sellers.*

Tertiary-line injury occurs when the recipient of a favored price passes the benefits of the lower price on to the next level of distribution. Purchasers from other secondary-line sellers are injured in that they do not receive the benefits of the lower price; these purchasers may recover damages from the original discriminating seller.

Cost Justification

If a seller can show that it costs less to sell a product to a particular buyer, the seller may lawfully pass along the cost savings. Section 2(a) provides that the Clayton Act does not "prevent differentials which make only due allowance for differences in the cost of manufacture, sale, or delivery resulting from the differing methods or quantities in which . . . commodities are . . . sold or delivered." For example, if Retailer A orders goods from Seller X by the carload, whereas Retailer B orders in small quantities, Seller X, who delivers free-on-board (F.O.B.) buyer's warehouse, may pass along the transportation savings to Retailer A. Nonetheless, although it is possible to pass along transportation savings, passing along alleged savings in manufacturing or distribution is extremely difficult because calculating and proving such savings is a complex task. Therefore, sellers rarely rely upon the defense of cost justification.

Meeting Competition

A seller may lower its price in a good-faith attempt to meet competition. A seller may beat its competitor's price, however, if it does not know the competitor's price, cannot reasonably determine the competitor's price, and acts reasonably in setting its own price.

Federal Trade Commission Act

In 1914, through the enactment of the **Federal Trade Commission Act,** Congress created the Federal Trade Commission (FTC), charged with preventing unfair methods of competition and unfair or deceptive acts or practices in commerce. To this end, the five-member commission is empowered to conduct appropriate investigations and hearings and to issue against violators cease and desist orders that are enforceable in the federal courts. The Supreme Court has commented on the breadth of the commission's power:

> The "unfair methods of competition," which are condemned by . . . the Act, are not confined to those that were illegal at common law or that were condemned by the Sherman Act. . . . It is also clear that the Federal Trade Commission Act was designed to supplement and bolster the Sherman Act and the Clayton Act . . . *to stop in their incipiency acts and practices which, when full blown, would violate those Acts.* (Emphasis added.)

Complaints may be instituted by the FTC, which, after a hearing, "has wide latitude for judgment and the courts will not interfere except where the remedy selected has no reasonable relation to the unlawful practices found to exist." Although the FTC most frequently enters a cease and desist order having the effect of an injunction, it may order other relief, such as affirmative disclosure, corrective advertising, and the granting of patent licenses on a reasonable royalty basis. Appeals may be taken from orders of the FTC to the United States Courts of Appeals, which have exclusive jurisdiction to enforce, set aside, or modify FTC orders.

In performing its duties, the FTC investigates not only possible violations of the antitrust laws but also unfair methods of competition.

Environmental Law

As technology has advanced and people have become more urbanized, their effect on the environment has increased. Our air has become dirtier; our waters have become more polluted. While individuals and environmental groups have brought private actions against some polluters, the common law has proved unable to control environmental damage. Because of this inadequacy, the federal and state governments have enacted a variety of statutes designed to promote environmental concerns and prevent environmental harm. Although in recent years certain developed countries such as the United States have made significant progress in controlling pollutants, such is not the case worldwide. Moreover, even as we have enjoyed some success in controlling some pollutants, a new generation of environmental problems has arisen. In this section, we will discuss both common law causes of action for environmental damage and U.S. federal regulation of the environment.

Common Law Actions for Environmental Damage

Private tort actions may be used to recover for harm to the environment. For example, if Alice's land is polluted by the mill next door, Alice may sue the mill in tort for the damage to her land. In suing to recover for environmental damage, plaintiffs generally have relied on the theories of nuisance, trespass, and strict liability.

Nuisance

The term *nuisance* encompasses two distinct types of wrong: private nuisance and public nuisance. A private nuisance involves an interference with a person's use and enjoyment of his or her land; a public nuisance is an act that interferes with a public right.

PRIVATE NUISANCE To establish a **private nuisance,** a plaintiff must show that the defendant has substantially and unreasonably interfered with the use and enjoyment of the plaintiff's land. In an action for damages, the plaintiff need not prove that the defendant's conduct was unreasonable, only that the interference was unreasonable. Thus, assuming all other requirements are met, the question in a private nuisance suit for damages is whether the defendant should pay for the harm it caused the plaintiff, even if the defendant's action was not unreasonable. For example, in one case, an electric utility using a coal-burning electric generator that employed the latest scientific methods for reducing emissions was held liable for the harm it caused its neighbor's alfalfa crops, even though the utility was performing the socially useful function of creating electric power.

Although a plaintiff need not prove the defendant's conduct is unreasonable to recover in a private nuisance action for damages, such reasonableness is an issue when the plaintiff sues for an injunction. In determining whether an injunction against a nuisance is appropriate, a court will "balance the equities" by considering a number of factors, including the gravity of the harm to the plaintiff, the social value of the defendant's activity that is causing the harm, the feasibility and costs of avoiding the harm, and the public interest, if any.

The need to balance the equities has meant that courts often deny injunctions when the defendant is engaged in a socially useful activity. Additionally, injunctions are frequently denied because the defendant successfully raises an equitable defense. Consequently, private nuisance actions have been of limited value in controlling environmental damage.

PUBLIC NUISANCE To be treated as a **public nuisance,** an activity must somehow interfere with the health, safety, or comfort of the public. For example, the actions of an industrial plant in polluting a stream will be treated as a private nuisance if such actions inconvenience only the owners of land downstream but will be treated as a public nuisance if they kill the stream's marine life. Generally, only a public representative, such as the attorney general, may sue to stop a public nuisance. If, however, the nuisance inflicts upon an individual some unique harm that the general populace does not suffer, that individual may also sue to halt the nuisance. Out of concern about the economic impact of closing an industrial operation, public representatives frequently are unwilling to sue to abate a public nuisance. Consequently, because these representatives often will not, and private parties may not, sue, relatively few public nuisance actions have been brought against polluters.

165. IMPACT OF GOVERNMENT ON BUSINESS

Trespass to Land

To establish **trespass to land,** a plaintiff must show an invasion that interferes with the plaintiff's right of exclusive possession of the property and that is the direct result of an action by the defendant. For example, entering or throwing trash on someone else's land without permission constitutes a trespass. Trespass differs from private nuisance in that trespass requires an interference with the plaintiff's possession of the land. Thus, sending smoke or gas onto another's property may constitute a private nuisance but does not constitute a trespass.

Trespass often is difficult to establish in actions for environmental damage, either because the plaintiff is not in possession of the property or because the injury does not stem from an invasion of the property. Trespass actions have thus been of limited benefit in halting environmental damage.

Strict Liability for Abnormally Dangerous Activities

Strict liability Liability without fault for an individual who engages in an unduly dangerous activity in an inappropriate location.

Although they generally base tort liability on fault, the courts may hold **strictly liable,** that is, liable without fault, a person engaged in an abnormally dangerous activity. To establish such strict liability, a plaintiff must show that the defendant is carrying on an unduly dangerous activity in an inappropriate location and that the plaintiff has suffered damage because of this activity. For example, a person who operates an oil refinery in a densely populated area may be held strictly liable for any damage the refinery causes. The requirement that the activity engaged in be (1) ultrahazardous and (2) inappropriate for its locale has limited the number of strict liability actions brought against polluters.

Problems Common to Private Causes of Action

In addition to the shortcomings of each tort theory just discussed, using a private cause of action to control environmental damage presents its own problems. The costs associated with private litigation (including the payment of one's own legal fees) are high, and although overall the environmental damage may be considerable, the extent of any particular injury may not warrant pursuing a private lawsuit. Furthermore, tort actions generally do not provide relief for aesthetic, as opposed to physical, injury. Additionally, in many tort actions a significant issue of causation arises. For example, if a landowner lives near several plants, each of which emits pollution and none of which, by itself, would cause the amount of damage the landowner's property has suffered, the landowner may have difficulty recovering from any of the plant owners. Finally, even if a private plaintiff is successful, his recovery may be limited to monetary damages, leaving the defendant free to continue to pollute.

Federal Regulation of the Environment

Because private causes of action have proved inadequate to recompense and prevent environmental damage, the federal, state, and some local governments have enacted statutes designed to protect the environment. In this section, we will consider some of the more important federal environmental laws. In addition, the Environmental Protection Agency (EPA) has encouraged companies to conduct voluntary environmental audits. One of the key issues surrounding such self-audits is whether these audits are discoverable by state or federal prosecutors.

The National Environmental Policy Act

In 1969, Congress enacted the **National Environmental Policy Act (NEPA)** to establish environmental protection as a goal of federal policy. The NEPA's declaration of national environmental policy states:

> The Congress, recognizing the profound impact of man's activity on the interrelations of all components of the natural environment, particularly the profound influences of population growth, high-density urbanization, industrial expansion, resource exploitation, and new and expanding technological advances, and recognizing further the critical importance of restoring and maintaining environmental quality to the overall welfare and development of man, declares that it is the continuing policy of the Federal Government, in cooperation with State and local governments . . . to use all practicable means and measures . . . in a manner calculated to foster and promote the general welfare, to create and maintain conditions under which man and nature can exist in productive harmony, and fulfill the social, economic and other requirements of present and future generations of Americans.

The NEPA has two major substantive sections, one creating the Council on Environmental Quality (CEQ) and the other requiring that each federal agency, when recommending or reporting on proposals for legislation or other major federal action, prepare an **environmental impact statement** (EIS) if the legislation or federal action will have a significant environmental effect.

THE COUNCIL ON ENVIRONMENTAL QUALITY The **Council on Environmental Quality (CEQ),** a three-member advisory group, is not a separate administrative agency but rather is part of the Executive Office of the President; as such, it makes recommendations to the president on environmental matters and prepares annual reports on the condition of the environment. Although not expressly authorized to do so by statute, the CEQ, acting under a series of executive orders, has issued regulations regarding the content and preparation of environmental impact statements. The federal courts generally have deferred to these regulations.

ENVIRONMENTAL IMPACT STATEMENTS (EIS) Unlike most federal environmental statutes, the NEPA does not focus on a particular type of environmental damage or harmful substance but instead expresses the federal government's continuing concern with protection of the environment. The NEPA's promotion of environmental considerations is effected through the EIS requirement.

> *Environmental impact statement (EIS)* Detailed statement concerning the environmental impact of a proposed federal action.

PROCEDURE FOR PREPARING AN EIS When proposing legislation or considering a major federal action, the CEQ regulations require that a federal agency initially make an "environmental assessment," which is a short analysis of the need for an EIS. If the agency decides that no EIS is required, it must make this decision available to the public. If, on the other hand, the agency concludes that an EIS is required, the agency must engage in "scoping," which consists of consulting other relevant federal agencies and the public to determine the significant issues the EIS will address and the statement's appropriate scope. After scoping, the agency prepares a draft EIS, for which there is a comment period. After the comment period ends and revisions, if necessary, are made, a final EIS is published.

Content of an EIS The NEPA requires that an EIS describe in detail the environmental impact of a proposed action, any adverse environmental effects that could not be avoided if the proposal were implemented, alternatives to the proposed action, the relationship between local short-term uses of the environment and the maintenance and enhancement of long-term productivity, and any irreversible and irretrievable commitments of resources the proposed action would involve if it were implemented. Impact statements provide a basis for evaluating the benefits of a proposed project in light of its environmental risks and for comparing its environmental risks with those of alternatives. The Supreme Court has held that a federal agency is required to consider only all *reasonable* alternatives in its EIS.

Nature of EIS Requirement Whether the NEPA was solely procedural or whether it had a substantive component was initially unclear. The Supreme Court resolved the issue by holding that the NEPA's requirements are primarily procedural and that the NEPA does not require that the relevant federal agency attempt to mitigate the adverse effects of a proposed federal action.

The Clean Air Act

Initially, the federal government's role in controlling air pollution was quite limited. The states had primary responsibility for air pollution control, and the federal government merely supervised their efforts and offered technical and financial assistance. When state efforts proved inadequate to alleviate the problem, Congress enacted the **Clean Air Act** Amendments of 1970, greatly expanding the federal role in antipollution efforts. Major revisions to the Clean Air Act were enacted in 1977 and 1990. The act establishes two regulatory schemes, one for existing sources and one for new stationary sources. The states retain primary responsibility for regulating existing stationary sources and motor vehicles then in use (that is, in use when the act, or its subsequently enacted amendments, took effect), while the federal government regulates new sources, new vehicles, and hazardous air pollutants.

Under the act, the Environmental Protection Agency (EPA) may impose civil penalties of up to $25,000 per day of violation. Criminal penalties, which depend on the type of violation, vary greatly, providing for a maximum fine of $1 million per violation and/or 15 years' imprisonment for a knowing violation that endangers a person. For repeat convictions, the act doubles the maximum punishments.

The Clean Water Act

As with air pollution control, the primary responsibility for controlling water pollution fell initially to the states. When their efforts proved inadequate, Congress fundamentally revised the nation's water pollution laws in its 1972 amendments to the Federal Water Pollution Control Act (subsequently renamed the **Clean Water Act**). Substantially amended again in 1977, 1981, and 1987, the act attempts comprehensively to restore and maintain the chemical, physical, and biological integrity of the nation's waters.

The EPA may impose civil penalties of up to $25,000 per day for each violation. Maximum criminal penalties for knowing violations are $50,000 per day of violation and/or three years' imprisonment. For repeat convictions, the maximum punishments are doubled.

Like the Clean Air Act, the Clean Water Act establishes different schemes for existing sources and new sources. Additionally, the act provides different programs for point and nonpoint sources of pollution. A **point source** is "any discernible, confined and discrete conveyance . . . from which pollutants are or may be discharged." A **nonpoint source**, in contrast, is a land use that causes pollution, such as a pesticide runoff from farming operations.

The scope of the act is extremely broad, applying not only to all navigable waters in the United States but also to tributaries of navigable waters, interstate waters and their tributaries, the use of nonnavigable intrastate waters (if their misuse could affect interstate commerce), and freshwater wetlands.

Hazardous Substances

Technological advances have enabled human beings to produce numerous artificial substances, some of which have proven extremely hazardous to health. As the potential and actual harm from these latter substances became clear, Congress responded by enacting various substances-related statutes. Exhibit 100.25 presents a summary of major U.S. federal environmental statutes.

Exhibit 100.25 *Major Federal Environmental Statutes*

Act	Major Purpose	Maximum Civil Penalty	Maximum Criminal Penalty
National Environmental Policy Act (NEPA)	• Establish environmental protection as a major national goal • Mandate environmental impact statements be prepared prior to federal action having a significant environmental effect	None	None
Clean Air Act	• Control and reduce air pollution • Establish National Ambient Air Quality Standards	$25,000 per day of violation	$1,000,000 fine per violation and/or 15 years' imprisonment*
Clean Water Act	• Protect against water pollution • Establish effluent limitations	$25,000 per day of violation	$50,000 per day of violation and/or 3 years' imprisonment*
Federal Insecticide, Fungicide and Rodenticide Act (FIFRA)	• Regulate the sale and distribution of pesticides • Prevent pesticides having an unreasonably adverse effect on the environment	$5,000 per offense	$50,000 fine and/or 1 year imprisonment
Toxic Substances Control Act (TSCA)	• Regulate toxic substances • Prevent unreasonable risk of injury to health and the environment from hazardous wastes	$20,000 per day of violation	$25,000 fine per day of violation and/or 1 year imprisonment
Resource Conservation and Recovery Act (RCRA)	• Regulate the disposal of solid waste • Establish standards to protect human health and the environment from toxic substances	$25,000 per day of violation	$1,000,000 fine and/or 15 years' imprisonment
Comprehensive Environmental Response, Compensation and Liability Act (CERCLA, or the Superfund) and Superfund Amendments and Reauthorization Act (SARA)	• Establish a national contingency plan for responding to releases of hazardous substances • Establish a trust fund to pay for removal of hazardous waste and other remedial actions	$25,000 per day of violation; $75,000 for repeat violations	None

*Doubled for repeat convictions.

International Protection of the Ozone Layer

In 1987, the United States and 23 other countries entered into the **Montreal Protocol** on Substances that Deplete the Ozone Layer, a treaty designed to prevent pollution that harms the ozone layer. The treaty requires all signatories to reduce their production and consumption of all chemicals, in particular chlorofluorocarbons (CFCs, more commonly called freon), that deplete the ozone layer. Although having excessive ozone in the air we breathe can be hazardous, the ozone layer in the stratosphere helps to protect the earth from harmful ultraviolet radiation. By 1985, scientists believed that the release of CFCs into the atmosphere had caused a hole to develop in the ozone layer over Antarctica.

Chlorofluorocarbons, halocarbons, carbon dioxide, methane, and nitrous oxide are extremely potent "greenhouse gases," which trap heat and thereby warm the earth. Human activities, however, have increased the release of greenhouse gases, resulting in the serious threat of global warming. Scientists warn that the earth's temperature could rise by as much as 6.3 degrees over the next century due to global warming. If this occurs, the levels of the seas will rise and the climate will change over most of the earth, causing severe flooding and disruptions of agricultural production.

Business Law

Introduction to Contracts

Every business enterprise, whether large or small, must enter into contracts with its employees, its suppliers of goods and services, and its customers in order to conduct its business operations. Thus, contract law is an important subject for the business manager. Contract law is also basic to other fields of law such as agency, partnerships, corporations, sales of personal property, commercial paper, and secured transactions.

Even the most common transaction may involve many contracts. For example, in a typical contract for the sale of land, the seller promises to transfer title, or right of ownership, to the land; and the buyer promises to pay an agreed-upon purchase price. In addition, the seller may promise to pay certain taxes, and the buyer may promise to assume a mortgage on the property or to pay the purchase price to a creditor of the seller. If the parties have lawyers, they very likely have contracts with these lawyers. If the seller deposits the proceeds of the sale in a bank, he enters into a contract with the bank. If the buyer rents the property, he enters into a contract with the tenant. When one of the parties leaves his car in a parking lot to attend to any of these matters, he assumes a contractual relationship with the owner of the lot. In short, nearly every business transaction is based on contract and the expectations the agreed-upon promises create. It is therefore essential that you know the legal requirements for making binding contracts.

Development of the Law of Contracts

Contract law, like the law as a whole, is not static. It has undergone—and is still undergoing—enormous changes. In the 19th century, almost total freedom in forming contracts was the rule. However, contract formation also involved many technicalities, and the courts imposed contract liability only when the parties complied strictly with the required formalities.

During the 20th century, many of the formalities of contract formation were relaxed. Today, contractual obligations are usually recognized whenever the parties clearly intend to be bound. In addition, an increasing number of promises are now enforced in certain circumstances, even though such promises do not comply strictly with the basic requirements of a contract. In brief, the twentieth century has left its mark on contract law by limiting the absolute freedom of contract and, at the same time, by relaxing the requirements of contract formation. Accordingly, we can say that it is considerably easier now both to get into a contract and to get out of one.

Common Law

Contracts are primarily governed by state common law. An orderly presentation of this law is found in the Restatements of the Law of Contracts, a valuable authoritative reference work extensively relied on and quoted in reported judicial opinions.

Exhibit 100.26 *Law Governing Contracts*

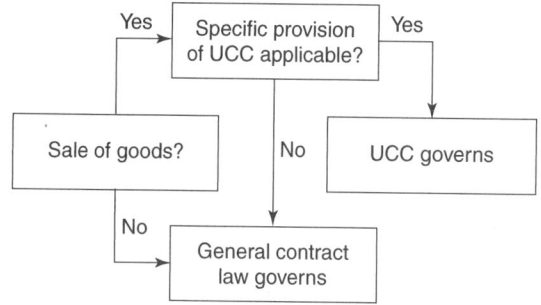

The Uniform Commercial Code

The sale of personal property is a large part of commercial activity. Article 2 of the **Uniform Commercial Code** (the Code, or UCC) governs such sales in all states except Louisiana. A **sale** consists in the passing of title to goods from seller to buyer for a price. A contract for sale includes both a present sale of goods and a contract to sell goods at a future time. The Code essentially defines **goods** as tangible personal property. **Personal property** is any property other than an interest in real property (land). For example, the purchase of a television set, an automobile, or a textbook is a sale of goods. All such transactions are governed by Article 2 of the Code, but where the Code has not specifically modified general contract law, the common law of contracts continues to apply. In other words, the law of sales is a specialized part of the general law of contracts, and the law of contracts governs unless specifically displaced by the Code.

Types of Contracts Outside the Code

General contract law (**common law**) governs all contracts outside the scope of the Code. Such contracts play a significant role in commercial activities. For example, the Code does *not* apply to employment contracts, service contracts, insurance contracts, contracts involving **real property** (land and anything attached to it, including buildings), and contracts for the sale of intangibles such as patents and copyrights. These transactions continue to be governed by general contract law. Exhibit 100.26 summarizes the types of law governing contracts.

Definition of Contract

Put simply, a **contract** is a binding agreement that the courts will enforce. The Restatement of the Law of Contracts more precisely defines a contract as "a promise or a set of promises for the breach of which the law gives a remedy, or the performance of which the law in some way recognizes a duty." A promise manifests or demonstrates the intention to act or to refrain from acting in a specified manner.

Those promises that meet *all* of the essential requirements of a binding contract are contractual and will be enforced. All other promises are *not* contractual, and usually no legal remedy is available for a **breach** of, or a failure to properly perform, these promises. (The remedies provided for breach of contract include compensatory damages, equitable remedies, reliance damages, and restitution.) Thus, a promise may be contractual (and therefore binding) or noncontractual. In other words, all contracts are promises, but not all promises are contracts (see Exhibit 100.27).

Requirements of a Contract

The four basic requirements of a contract are as follows:

1. **Mutual assent.** The parties to a contract must manifest by words or conduct that they have agreed to enter into a contract. The usual method of showing mutual assent is by offer and acceptance.
2. **Consideration.** Each party to a contract must intentionally exchange a legal benefit or incur a legal detriment as an inducement to the other party to make a return exchange.
3. **Legality of object.** The purpose of a contract must not be criminal, tortious, or otherwise against public policy.

Exhibit 100.27 *Contractual and Noncontractual Promises*

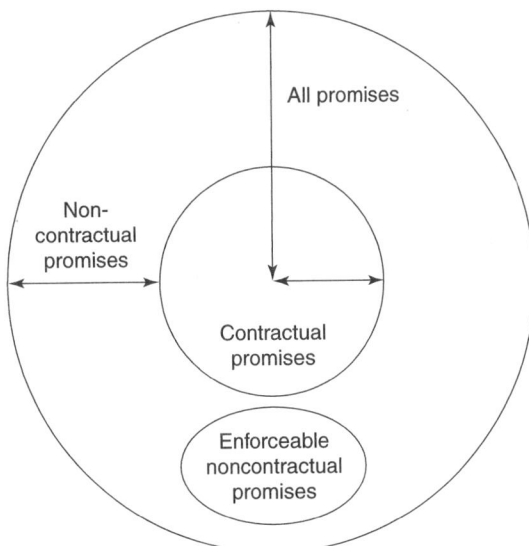

4. **Capacity.** The parties to a contract must have contractual capacity. Certain persons, such as adjudicated incompetents, have no legal capacity to contract, while others, such as minors, incompetent persons, and intoxicated persons, have limited capacity to contract. All others have full contractual capacity.

In addition, though in a limited number of instances a contract must be evidenced by a writing to be enforceable, in most cases an oral contract is binding and enforceable. Moreover, there must be an *absence* of invalidating conduct, such as duress, undue influence, misrepresentation, or mistake. (See Exhibit 100.28.) A promise meeting all of these requirements is contractual and legally binding. However, if any requirement is unmet, the promise is noncontractual.

Classification of Contracts

Contracts can be classified according to various characteristics, such as method of formation, content, and legal effect. The standard classifications are (1) express or implied contracts; (2) bilateral or unilateral contracts; (3) valid, void, voidable, or unenforceable contracts; and (4) executed or executory contracts. These classifications are not mutually exclusive. For example, a contract may be express, bilateral, valid, executory, and informal.

Express and Implied Contracts

Parties to a contract may indicate their assent either in words or by conduct implying such willingness. For instance, a regular customer known to have an account at a drugstore might pick up an item at the drugstore, show it to the clerk, and walk out. This is a perfectly valid contract. The clerk knows from the customer's conduct that she is buying the item at the specified price and wants it charged to her account. Her actions speak as effectively as words. Such a contract, formed by conduct, is an implied or, more precisely, an **implied in fact contract**; in contrast, a contract in which the parties manifest assent in words is an **express contract.** Both are contracts, equally enforceable. The difference between them is merely the manner in which the parties manifest their assent.

Bilateral and Unilateral Contracts

In the typical contractual transaction, each party makes at least one promise. For example, if Adelle says to Byron, "If you promise to mow my lawn, I will pay you $10," and Byron agrees to mow Adelle's lawn, Adelle and Byron have made mutual promises, each agreeing to do something in exchange for the promise of the other. When a contract is formed by the exchange of promises, each party is under a duty to the other. This kind of contract is called a **bilateral contract,** because each party is both a **promisor** (a person making a promise) and a **promisee** (the person to whom a promise is made).

169. BUSINESS LAW

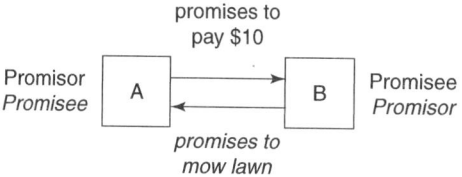

But suppose that only one of the parties makes a promise. Adelle says to Byron, "If you will mow my lawn, I will pay you $10." A contract will be formed when Byron has finished mowing the lawn and not before. At that time, Adelle becomes contractually obligated to pay $10 to Byron. Adelle's offer was in exchange for Byron's act of mowing the lawn, not for his promise to mow it. Because Byron never made a promise to mow the lawn, he was under no duty to mow it. This is a **unilateral contract** because only one of the parties has made a promise.

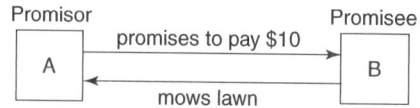

Thus, whereas a bilateral contract results from the exchange of a promise for a return promise, a unilateral contract results from the exchange of a promise either for performing an act or for refraining from doing an act. Where it is not clear whether a unilateral or bilateral contract has been formed, the courts presume that the parties intended a bilateral contract. Thus, if Adelle says to Byron, "If you will mow my lawn, I will pay you $10," and Byron replies, "OK, I will mow your lawn," a bilateral contract is formed.

Valid, Void, Voidable, and Unenforceable Contracts

By definition, a **valid contract** is one that meets all of the requirements of a binding contract. It is an enforceable promise or agreement.

A **void contract** is an agreement that does not meet all of the requirements of a binding contract. Thus, it is no contract at all; it is merely a promise or agreement that has no legal effect. An example of a void agreement is an agreement entered into by a person whom the courts have declared incompetent.

A **voidable contract,** on the other hand, though defective, is not wholly lacking in legal effect. A voidable contract is a contract; however, because of the manner in which the contract was formed or a lack of capacity of a party to it, the law permits one or more of the parties to avoid the legal duties the contract creates. If the contract is voided, both of the parties are relieved of their legal duties under the agreement. For instance, through intentional misrepresentation of a material fact (fraud), Thomas induces Regina to enter into a contract. Regina may, upon discovery of the fraud, notify Thomas that by reason of the misrepresentation, she will not perform her promise, and the law will support Regina. Although the contract induced by fraud is not void, it is voidable at the election of Regina, the defrauded party. Thomas, the fraudulent party, may make no such election. If Regina elects to avoid the contract, Thomas will be released from his promise under the agreement, although he may be liable for damages under tort law for fraud.

A contract that is neither void nor voidable may nonetheless be unenforceable. An **unenforceable contract** is one for the breach of which the law provides no remedy. For example, a contract may be unenforceable because of a failure to satisfy the requirements of the statute of frauds, which requires certain kinds of contracts to be evidenced by a writing to be enforceable. Also, the statute of limitations imposes restrictions on the time during which a party has the right to bring a lawsuit for breach of contract. After the statutory time period has passed, a contract is referred to as unenforceable, rather than void or voidable. See Exhibit 100.28 for validity of agreements.

Executed and Executory Contracts

A contract that has been fully carried out by all of the parties to it is an **executed contract.** Strictly speaking, an executed contract is no longer a contract, because all of the duties under it have been performed; but having a term for such a completed contract is useful. By comparison, the term **executory contract** applies to contracts that are still partially or entirely unperformed by one or more of the parties.

Exhibit 100.28 *Validity of Agreements*

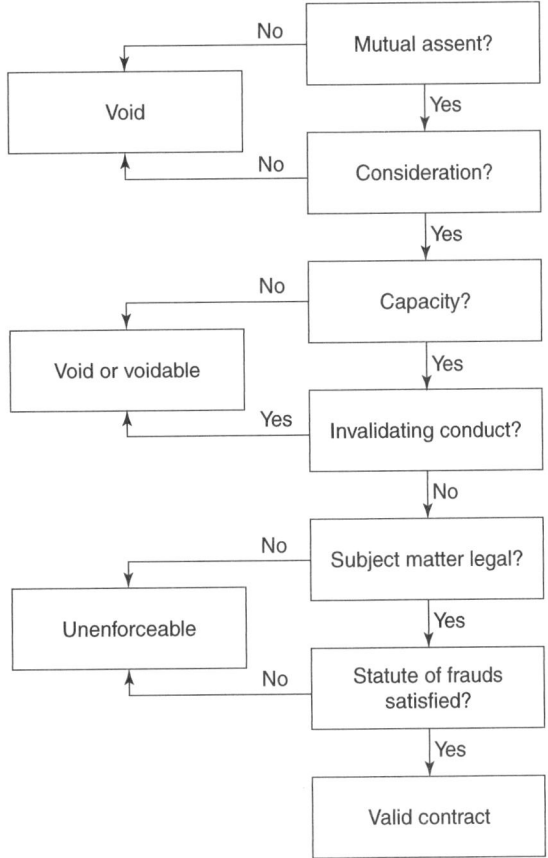

Promissory Estoppel

As a general rule, promises are not enforceable if they do not meet all the requirements of a contract. Nevertheless, in certain circumstances, the courts enforce noncontractual promises under the doctrine of **promissory estoppel** in order to avoid injustice. A noncontractual promise is enforceable when it is made under circumstances that should lead the promisor reasonably to expect that the promisee, in reliance on the promise, would be induced by it to take definite and substantial action or to forbear, and the promisee does take such action or does forbear. (See Exhibit 100.27). For example, Gordon promises Constance not to foreclose for a period of six months on a mortgage Gordon owns on Constance's land. Constance then expends $100,000 to construct a building on the land. His promise not to foreclose is binding on Gordon under the doctrine of promissory estoppel.

Quasi Contracts

In addition to express and implied in fact contracts, there are implied in law or quasi contracts, which were not included in the previous classification of contracts for the reason that a quasi (meaning "as if") contract is not a contract at all. The term *quasi contract* is used because the remedy granted for quasi contract is similar to one of the remedies available for breach of contract.

A quasi contract is not a contract because it is based neither on an express nor on an implied promise. Rather, a **contract implied in law** or **quasi contract** is an obligation imposed by law to avoid injustice. For example, Willard by mistake delivers to Roy a plain, unaddressed envelope containing $100 intended for Lucia. Roy is under no contractual obligation to return it, but Willard is permitted to

Quasi contract Obligation not based upon contract that is imposed to avoid injustice.

Exhibit 100.29 *Summary of Contracts, Promissory Estoppel, and Quasi Contracts*

	Contract	Promissory Estoppel	Quasi Contract
Type of Promise	Contractual	Noncontractual	None Void Unenforceable Invalidated
Requirements	All of the essential elements of a contract	Detrimental and justifiable reliance	Benefit conferred and knowingly accepted
Remedies	Equitable Compensatory Reliance	Promise enforced to the extent necessary to avoid injustice	Reasonable value of the benefit conferred

recover the $100 from Roy. The law imposes a quasi-contractual obligation on Roy in order to prevent his unjust enrichment at the expense of Willard. Such a recovery requires three essential elements: (1) a benefit conferred upon the defendant (Roy) by the plaintiff (Willard); (2) the defendant's (Roy's) appreciation or knowledge of the benefit; and (3) acceptance or retention of the benefit by the defendant (Roy) under circumstances making it inequitable for him to retain the benefit without compensating the plaintiff for its value.

Not infrequently, quasi contracts are used to provide a remedy when the parties enter into a void contract, an unenforceable contract, or a voidable contract that is avoided. In such a case, the law of quasi contracts will determine what recovery is permitted for any performance rendered by the parties under the invalid, unenforceable, or invalidated agreement. Exhibit 100.29 summarizes contracts, promissory estoppel, and quasi contracts.

Contract Law

Essential Elements of a Contract

Commercial law is defined as that "body of [the] law that refers to how business firms (parties) enter into contracts with each other, execute contracts, and remedy problems that arise in the process."[242] There are two major topical areas of commercial law that are of day-to-day interest to the purchasing professional: the laws regarding agency and the laws regarding contracts. We have already discussed agency law to some extent earlier in the section. Thus, we will turn our attention to the laws regarding contracts.

In its most basic form, a *contract* can be defined as an agreement between two or more parties that can be legally enforced. Note that people make agreements every day, but not every agreement can be considered a contract. A contract is an agreement between two or more people to do specified things in exchange for other specified things. For example:

> Shirley wants to go to the store to buy some potato chips but she doesn't have a car. She says to Rich, "I will pay you a dollar to take me to the store to buy some potato chips." Rich agrees and takes Shirley to the store.

The above statement can be characterized as a contract. Shirley agreed to do a specified thing *(pay Rich a dollar)* in exchange for another specified thing *(take Shirley to the store)*. In legal thinking a contract has three essential elements:

- Offer
- Acceptance
- Consideration

If any one of these elements is lacking, then an enforceable contract does not exist. Let's take a closer look at these three elements.

OFFER An *offer* is a proposal or expression by one person that he or she is willing to do something for certain terms. For example:

> Betsy goes into Mimi's wholesale video store and says to Mimi, "I want to buy 1,000 videotapes of the movie *Exterminator* from you. I will pay you $15 for each videotape."

Betsy has made a specific offer—to purchase a specific movie—in specific volumes (1,000)—at a specific price ($15,000). This constitutes a valid offer. Somewhat different is a *conditional offer,* which includes additional criteria for completion of the agreement. For example:

> Betsy goes into Mimi's wholesale video store and says to Mimi, "I want to buy 1,000 videotapes of the movie *Exterminator* from you. I will pay you $15 for each videotape IF you deliver them to my place of business on February 1, 2001."

In this case, a deadline has been added to the offer. The offer is valid if the conditions are met.

ACCEPTANCE The second important part of the contract is the *acceptance.* Legally, a contract does not exist until the offer is *formally* accepted, either verbally or in written form. The offer and acceptance have to match. If they match, there is an agreement leading up to a contract. If they don't, it's more like a negotiation: an offer, to which someone responds with a counteroffer rather than an acceptance, which continues until both sides reach an agreement or a "meeting of the minds."

It is important to note that a contract exists only when there is an agreement resulting from both an offer and an acceptance. The agreement doesn't exist until the supplier accepts the offer, and a so-called "meeting of the minds" occurs. An acceptance, as recognized by the UCC, can be in "any manner and by any medium reasonable to the circumstances." In other words, the manner and medium of acceptance by the supplier can be met either through the promise of an acceptance or by the supplier's performance of the terms and conditions of the contract—that is, the actual delivery of the requested goods or services without prior verbal advance notice.

Many customer purchase orders typically contain a written copy that outlines the procedures for acknowledgment or acceptance by suppliers. However, suppliers frequently accept or acknowledge customer orders on their own forms, which may contain different language and terms than the customers' original purchase orders. When this occurs, the supplier's terms will automatically be incorporated into the final contract unless one of the following conditions is present:

1. The supplier's terms substantially or materially alter the original intent of the offer (purchase order).
2. The buyer objects to the supplier's acceptance terms in writing.
3. The purchase order explicitly states that no alteration of terms is acceptable.

When the terms of the buyer's purchase order and the supplier's acceptance or acknowledgment conflict, and none of the conditions listed above are present, all of the terms of both the purchase order and the acceptance become part of the resulting contract *except the conflicting terms and conditions.* In effect, the conflicting terms and conditions are simply disregarded. The purchasing manager must therefore ensure that the terms and conditions of all supplier acceptance forms are carefully reviewed. If the buyer wants to avoid any dispute over the terms and conditions of the contract, the purchase order should include a statement to the effect that "Absolutely no deviation from the terms and conditions contained herein is permitted."

CONSIDERATION The third element of a contract is difficult to define. *Consideration,* which has nothing to do with being considerate or nice to people, but rather is a form of "mutual obligation"—with each party bound to perform at certain levels and agreeing to carry out their responsibilities. The law has required consideration for centuries, but it has never been able to say exactly what it is or what it is not. Consideration is something of value in the formation of the contract that gives it legal validity. In the business world, mutual promises in a contract of sale, whether express or implied, are generally sufficient consideration. For example, in the previous example, Betsy made an offer that Mimi accepted. There has also been consideration. Betsy's consideration is express: she promised to pay $15 per tape. Mimi's consideration is implied: by saying "OK," she implied that she promised to sell Betsy 1,000 tapes for $15 a piece.

Two other elements are important to consider in contract law: competent parties/mutual assent and legal subject matter.

COMPETENT PARTIES / MUTUAL ASSENT The parties to a legally enforceable contract must have full contractual capacity through being either principals or qualified agents as described earlier. In addition, both the buyer and the seller must not have engaged in any fraudulent activities when formulating the agreement. The use of force or coercion to reach an agreement is not acceptable in signing a contract because both parties must enter into the agreement on their own free will. Both parties must indicate a willingness to enter into the agreement and be bound by its terms.

LEGAL SUBJECT MATTER If an agreement has been made regarding a purpose that is illegal, then the resulting contract is null and void. The performance of a party in regard to the contract must not be an unlawful act if the agreement is to be enforceable. However, if the primary purpose of a contract is legal, but some terms contained within the agreement are not, then the contract may or may not itself be illegal depending on the seriousness of the illegal terms and the degree to which the legal and illegal terms can be separated.

Law and Purchasing

Today's global business environment has made it more important than ever for purchasing managers to understand the changing nature of law at the international, federal, state, and regional level. Purchasing's daily activities are essentially concerned with the laws regarding *contracts* and the laws regarding *agency*. The majority of purchasing law is derived primarily from the laws regarding contracts.

Contract law essentially determines the nature of agreements that are enforceable and creates legal rights between the parties. The characteristics of offer and acceptance, satisfaction, and nonperformance have all been clearly established by the law. Contracts between two or more parties allow the shifting of risk between the entities and constitute the foundation and fabric for every type of supply chain relationship. Agency law, on the other hand, deals with the role of managers as individual representatives acting on behalf of their organization. It is important that purchasing managers understand the role they play as an agent of their organization, so that they do not exceed the responsibilities bestowed upon them in this role. As agents of their organization, purchasing managers also wield a great deal of power in allocating the business of the company to their suppliers. They must also be aware of the potential for ethical abuses of this power that may be encountered.

Legal Authority and Personal Liability of the Purchasing Manager

Laws of Agency

The laws regarding agency are concerned with governing the relationship of principals and agents. An *agent* is a person or entity who has been authorized to act on behalf of some other person or entity. A *principal,* on the other hand, is the corresponding person or entity for whom agents carry out their authority. The purchasing manager/buyer is typically considered to be a general agent for the buying firm (the principal). That means that a supplier dealing with this manager/buyer has a right to rely on the individual's statements, both in written form and verbally. Conversely, the sales representative can also be considered to be an agent of the selling firm (also a principal). The sales representative may have either a broad or narrow range of powers depending on whether he or she is a general or special sales agent.

Legal Authority

Purchasing managers generally have final authority over purchasing decisions within their firms. However, this final decision may be reached through the input provided by a cross-functional sourcing team. In the end, however, someone has to sign the contract, so the purchasing manager is most often considered as the general agent. (A general agent role merely implies that the guidelines provided by the employer for this individual are quite broad and general in nature.) Since purchasing managers are responsible for a significant amount of expenditures, the employer's instructions to their purchasing managers should be expressed clearly and succinctly. The purchasing agency relationship is created between the employer and employee when the company hires an individual to perform the purchasing job. Typically, a job description provides the basis for an agreement between the employing firm and purchasing agent/manager regarding actual scope of authority.

Purchasing managers have the right to require clear and unequivocal instructions from their employers regarding the scope of their day-to-day job performance expectations. From a legal perspective, if purchasing managers carry out their duties in a faithful, ethical, and conscientious manner, then their obligations to the employers are fulfilled. However, in agreeing to perform the purchasing duties for the employer, the purchasing manager does not imply that he or she will never make mistakes. The purchasing manager's responsibilities are essentially to keep the best interests of the employer in mind when accomplishing his or her day-to-day activities.

Personal Liability

Certain individuals in many organizations have interpreted the statement "acting in the best interests of the employer" in radically different ways. There are a number of ways in which purchasing managers can be held personally liable in the conduct of their day-to-day activities, even if they were supposedly following these guidelines. Depending on the issue at hand, this personal liability can take the form of either a civil or criminal suit. The concept of apparent versus actual authority is the determining factor in such cases.

Actual authority stems from the instructions and granting of authority to the purchasing manager via the job description provided by the employer. These documents typically define the limits and parameters under which the purchasing manager is expected to operate. *Apparent authority*, on the other hand, is that level of authority perceived by the seller to be *available* to the purchasing manager. In most instances, this level of apparent authority can be defined as the scope of authority possessed by other purchasing managers of similar positions in other organizations within the same industry.

If a purchasing manager, in carrying out normal procurement responsibilities, exceeds his or her actual but not apparent authority, then the employer is still responsible for performance of the resulting contract but could seek legal action against the purchasing manager personally. Exceeding both actual and apparent authority can have dire consequences; an individual may be held directly liable by the supplier or other third party (see Exhibit 100.30).

It is in the purchasing manager's own self-interest to ensure that all suppliers or other third parties are aware that his or her actions are on behalf of the employing firm. All contracts should be signed in such a manner that demonstrate the agency relationship.

Purchasing managers can be held personally liable for their damaging and illegal activities if they perform them without the authority of their firm. This personal liability may occur even if the purchasing manager believes (incorrectly) that he or she actually possesses the authority. Any damaging acts performed outside of the manager's scope of authority (whether actual or apparent) can lead to personal liability even though such acts were intended to benefit the employer. In essence, any act that causes damage to any other person could cause a legal liability to the purchasing manager who performs such an act.

Other areas of activity for the purchasing manager that could lead to personal liability include the following:

- Deception for personal gain while behaving as an agent for the principal firm (includes taking bribes)
- Violating the lawful protection of items owned by others, such as patent infringement
- (Mis)use of proprietary information
- Violation of antitrust laws
- Unlawful transportation of hazardous materials and toxic waste

These activities are related to another important aspect of purchasing law: ethical behavior.

A good rule of thumb is to remember that purchasers must always act in the best interests of their employer. This includes maintaining loyalty, respecting confidential information, and avoiding compromising relationships that may lead to a conflict of interest.

Exhibit 100.30 *Laws of Agency*

Apparent Authority (what the seller perceives) \ Actual Authority (what the agent is authorized to buy)	Within	Exceed
Within	OK	Employer responsible for performance of contract
Exceed	Not relevant	Purchasing manager liable (dire consequences)

Sources of U.S. Purchasing Law

Before we discuss the Uniform Commercial Code (UCC), it is worthwhile to briefly review what we mean by "purchasing law." U.S. federal purchasing law is composed of three distinct sources:

- Written law, which originates in the legislative branch of government
- Administrative law, which is derived by the executive branch through the issuance of rules and regulations
- Common law, which stems from judicial branch rulings and court decisions

Written law is composed of the various acts and laws passed by elected representatives of the relevant legislative bodies. In the case of the federal government, the U.S. Congress is the source of laws and acts. In the case of individual states, the respective state legislatures are responsible for writing laws and acts governing intrastate matters. A prime example of written law is the Motor Carrier Act of 1980, which changed the ways motor carriers were able to set rates.

Administrative law is created through the issuance of rules and regulations by different governmental agencies acting within the scope of their legal authority. This source of law can originate from agencies at either the state or federal level of government. Examples of relevant U.S. agencies that have had a major impact on purchasing operations are the Internal Revenue Service within the Department of the Treasury and the Interstate Commerce Commission within the Department of Transportation.

Common law created by the judicial system plays a variety of roles because it can modify or overturn other sources of laws. In areas where written law is either indistinct or missing, the courts can actually create law through court decisions that establish a *precedence* for deciding similar cases in the future. In addition, the courts can rule that otherwise-applicable laws are unconstitutional and, subsequently, no longer applicable. Although this process may create some degree of confusion and uncertainty regarding conflicting interpretations of law between different court jurisdictions, the decisions of the judicial branch at either the state or federal level can have a significant long-term impact on buyer-seller relationships. At different times, and in different situations, there may be more than one source of law that affects different areas of purchasing practice. Although we will not go into these details, it is worthwhile noting that a great deal of confusion between conflicting sources of law has been eliminated through the passage of the Uniform Commercial Code.

Purchasing Law and the UCC

The UCC that is in use today consists of the following 10 articles:

1. General introductory provisions
2. Sales of goods and products
3. Transactions in commercial paper (bank checks, liability for endorsements)
4. Bank deposits and collections
5. Letters of credit (financial instruments issued by banks and other institutions)
6. Bank transfers
7. Warehouse receipts, bills of lading, and other documents of title to goods
8. Transfers in investment securities
9. Secured transactions
10. Technical matters

The primary portion of the Uniform Commercial Code that concerns purchasing is Article 2, which deals with sales contracts. The UCC provides benefits to the buying firm in four ways:[243]

1. If a seller makes an offer in writing, the seller has to live up to it for the period of time stated.
2. Verbal agreements, when confirmed in writing and if no objection is made, are valid.
3. The conflict between a buyer's purchase order terms and a seller's acknowledgment terms has been generally resolved in favor of the buyer.
4. As far as warranties are concerned, the purchasing manager can legally rely on the supplier to provide the item needed to do the job.

The most basic elements of Article 2 within the UCC involve the following four issues:

- Warranties
- Transportation terms and risk of loss
- Seller's rights
- Buyer's rights

Warranties

Warranties ensure that a buyer can legally rely on a supplier to provide the item needed to do a job. In its most basic form, a warranty is defined as "a promise or representation made by the seller which, if necessary, can be legally enforced."[244] In order for a warranty to be legally enforceable, it must be a formal part of the contract.

There are two major types of warranties: express and implied. An *express warranty* is one in which the manufacturer makes specific statements concerning promises, affirmations of fact, specifications, samples, and descriptions regarding the goods or services that are being sold. Express warranties may be either oral or written and it is not necessary that the words "warranty" or "guarantee" be specifically used in order to create such an express guarantee.

The other form of warranty is the *implied warranty,* which deals with the concept of *fitness for use* and *merchantability.* The implied warranty of fitness for use (particular purpose) means when the seller at the time of contracting has reason to know of any particular purpose for which the goods are required, and the buyer is relying on the seller's skill or judgment to select or furnish suitable goods, there is, unless excluded or modified, an implied warranty that the goods shall be fit for such purpose.

A warranty of merchantability means that the good being exchanged meets the standards of the trade and its quality is appropriate for ordinary use. This means that people who are in the business of selling certain products imply to their customers that the products are of "fair average quality."

The purchasing manager in day-to-day activities may occasionally encounter two other types of warranties: warranty of title and warranty of infringement. *Warranty of title* essentially indicates that the supplier warrants that it has title to the goods and that they are not stolen or subject to any security interest or liens.

The *warranty of infringement* refers to the supplier's guarantee that the goods being exchanged do not illegally infringe on another party's patent protection. The costs and penalties for patent infringement are so severe that most standard purchasing agreements contain an appropriate patent indemnification clause. If patent infringement is determined, then the damaged party can sue for an injunction to prevent further use of that item, potentially disrupting a firm's sales of products containing the item in dispute. A simple warranty of infringement in the purchaser's contracts is not enough protection. A more broad *patent indemnification clause* provides a greater level of safety for the buying organization. For example, if a firm provides design specifications that infringe on a third party's patent, the organization as well as the maker of that particular part may be subject to litigation. Patent infringement goes both ways and should be adequately protected against.

The following general suggestions can help purchasing managers to protect their organizations against warranty problems:[245]

- Write a good purchase order (and order acceptance form).
- Build a file.
- Write letters and save letters.
- Use good standard terms and conditions.
- Consider calling the seller's attention to the warranties.

Transportation Terms and Risk of Loss

Although very important, transportation documentation and delivery terms are frequently overlooked as a significant factor in many purchasing contracts. Transportation documents are used in domestic transportation to govern, direct, control, and provide information about a shipment.[246]

The *bill of lading*—perhaps the most common and singularly important shipping document—describes the origin of the shipment, provides specific directions for the carrier, delineates the transportation contract terms, and functions as a receipt for the shipment. In some circumstances, the bill of lading may also serve as a certificate of title for the shipment. The bill of lading contains the following information:

- Name and address of the consignor and consignee
- Routing instructions for the carrier
- Description of the goods being transported
- The number of items with corresponding commodity descriptions
- The freight class or rate for the commodity being shipped

The *freight bill* serves as the carrier's invoice for the freight charges involved in the movement of a particular shipment. As part of the freight bill, the Interstate Commerce Commission regulations require that credit terms be listed to avoid potential price discrimination between shippers. Freight bills may be classified as either prepaid or collect, to determine when the freight bill is to be tendered, regardless of whether the charges are paid in advance or not. On prepaid shipments, the freight bill is presented on the effective date of shipment. On collect shipments, the freight bill is presented on the effective date of delivery. Also, any adverse condition of the shipment should be noted here to facilitate any potential freight claims with the carrier.

Under the UCC, the risk of loss is with the *seller* until the title passes to the buyer. However, the following conditions can apply:

- The buyer and seller can agree in their contract as to when in the transaction the risk of loss becomes the buyer's rather than the seller's.
- If the seller is to ship goods by a third-party carrier, but the seller is *not* required to deliver the goods to a specific place (just to take the goods to the carrier), the risk of loss becomes the buyer's when the goods are delivered to the carrier.
- If the seller is required to ship goods to a specific place, the risk of loss becomes the buyer's when the goods are delivered to the specific place.
- If the goods are held by a third party who is responsible for their storage, such as a commercial warehouse, the risk of loss becomes the buyer's when the buyer receives certain documents of title or the third party acknowledges the buyer's right to take the goods.
- If the goods are defective, the risk of loss does not become the buyer's unless the defects are fixed or the buyer agrees to accept the defective goods.

Delivery terms essentially describe who is responsible for the selection of a carrier, payment of the freight bill, and the method in which the title of goods passes between the purchaser and the supplier. The term *F.O.B. (free on board)* delineates the point at which the supplier is responsible for freight charges and where the purchaser assumes title to the shipment. *F.O.B. shipping point* (or *F.O.B. origin*) indicates that the purchaser is responsible for payment of transportation costs and assumes title of the goods at the supplier's shipping dock. *F.O.B. destination* (or *F.O.B. delivered*) tells us that the supplier is responsible for transportation, and the purchaser assumes title of the goods at his or her own shipping dock. The F.O.B. term also defines which party is responsible for filing any freight damage claims. Essentially, the party who possesses title to the goods is responsible for filing the claim. The designation *C.I.F.*—similar to F.O.B. but referring to international shipments—stands for *cost, insurance, and freight,* so that essentially the contract price includes these costs in addition to the price of the goods. These costs may also include tariffs, customs duties, inspections, and so on, so buyers should be especially careful when agreeing to C.I.F. terms.

In most cases, a loss results in a freight claim being filed with the carrier to recover payment as a result of shipment loss, damage, or delay. Such documents can also be filed with the carrier to recover overcharge premiums. In order to be valid, freight claims must be filed within nine months of the date of actual or reasonable date of delivery. The carrier must respond with an acknowledgment of receipt of the claim within 30 days and then notify the claimant regarding whether or not the claim will be paid within 120 days. If the claim is not resolved within an additional 120 days, the carrier must notify the claimant of the reasons for not settling the claim each 60 days. If the carrier has refused to pay the claim, then the claimant has two years from the time the claim was disallowed to file for legal relief in the courts.

It is recommended that purchasing managers clearly specify delivery terms in the purchase contract to ensure that they receive the shipping and freight terms expected. It is important to signify these terms in as much detail as possible, even to the point of spelling out exact locations including street addresses and dock locations, if applicable. When in doubt, err on the side of increased detail. Unless otherwise specified in the purchase contract, the UCC recognizes F.O.B. origin as the default delivery term.

Sellers' and Buyers' Rights

SELLERS' RIGHTS Article 2 of the UCC is very specific about sellers' and buyers' rights. Specifically, sellers have the right to do the following:

- Sue the buyer for the purchase price of the goods if the buyer basically refuses to pay for them.
- Recover reasonable costs and expenses incurred if goods have to be resold.
- Receive compensation for additional costs and expenses incurred by reason of the buyer's wrongful conduct.

The right to sue for the purchase price of goods is basically a breach of contract lawsuit. However, if there are still goods in the seller's possession, the buyer may be required to try to resell the goods for a fair price in order to offset what the buyer owes. This becomes especially important in end-of-life strategies. The buyer should let the seller know well in advance if a product is going to be discontinued to allow the seller to deplete existing inventories.

BUYER'S RIGHTS According to the UCC, a buyer's rights include the right to do the following:

- Reject defective goods that the seller cannot repair within a reasonable time.
- Sue for breach of contract.
- Revoke acceptance of goods if the buyer discovers defects.
- Seek a court order forcing the seller to deliver the goods ("specific performance").
- Recover any extra expense incurred for having to purchase replacement goods from another seller.
- Retain the right to recover costs and expenses caused by a breach of warranty.

According to Article 2 of the UCC, a buyer cannot reject defective goods that cannot be remedied before the time required. However, the buyer has responsibilities with respect to seller goods in the buyer's possession. When a buyer accepts delivery of goods from a supplier (including a pickup from the supplier's plant), the buyer is responsible if it does not "catch" the defects. This is an excellent argument for certifying suppliers' processes and not relying on inspection as a means to ensure quality. In most cases, a supplier will want to remedy the problem to avoid conflict, but not always. If absolutely necessary, a buyer can get a court order to force the seller to deliver the goods. This might occur in a capacity problem, and is known as "specific performance." A buyer can also recover costs and expenses caused by a breach of warranty, including inspection costs, storage costs, and return shipment costs.

Cancellation of Purchase Orders and Breach of Contract

A good contract will protect the interests and rights of both buyer and seller. As a result, contractual obligations are equally binding upon both parties to the agreement. People cannot go around arbitrarily canceling or defaulting on their contracts. In some instances, however, one of the parties to a contractual arrangement may seek to cancel the agreement after it has been made. In other cases, the supplier simply fails to perform in the manner agreed to in the contract. Under these conditions, the buyer will always go back to the original contract to determine what the potential remedies are to these situations. If they are not spelled out in detail, the UCC once again provides some help.

Cancellation of Orders

Contract cancellations can generally be classified into three categories: (1) cancellation for default, (2) cancellation for convenience of the purchaser ("anticipatory breach"), or (3) cancellation by mutual consent.

Cancellation for default can be defined as failure of one of the parties to live up to the terms and conditions of the contract.

Cancellation for the convenience of the purchaser, or *anticipatory breach,* makes the purchaser liable for any resulting injury to the supplier. A general rule here is that the supplier should not be called upon to incur any loss due to the purchaser's default. Generally speaking, purchasers should stay away from this term altogether in their purchase contracts. The term is highly interpretable in court and can result in any number of negative actions.

Cancellation by mutual consent indicates that cancellation of a previously agreed-upon contract does not automatically lead to legal action. If both parties mutually agree to terminate the agreement, then they have, in effect, created another contract with the intent of nullifying the first agreement. If there is no potential loss, the supplier will often accept a purchaser's cancellation in good faith as a normal risk of doing business. Even when suppliers have purchased special components or materials in the anticipation of fulfilling their responsibilities under the agreement, the parties can usually reach a mutually agreeable resolution through the process of negotiation rather than through litigation.

Breach of Contract

Under a commercial contract, the supplier is obligated to deliver the goods according to the contract's terms and conditions, and the purchaser is likewise obligated to accept and tender payment for the goods according to the terms of the agreement. A breach of contract occurs when either party fails to perform the obligations due under the contract (without a valid or legal justification). A breach may entitle the offended party to certain remedies or damages. For example:

> Mimi's wholesale video store and Betsy now have a valid contract. Betsy has promised to buy 1,000 videotapes for $15 apiece, and Mimi has promised to deliver them to Betsy's place of business on February 1. However, Mimi never shows up with the delivery.

169. BUSINESS LAW

Mimi may indeed be liable for breach of contract. However, one of the basic rules of the UCC is that each party to a contract must give the other party the total time agreed upon to complete his or her obligations under the contract.

In major contracts, it is often apparent that a breach of contract may create major headaches for either the buyer or supplier; the level of damages in such cases is difficult to determine. To avoid this confusion, many organizations include an up-front termination or liquidated damages provision in the contract at the time of negotiation. This type of provision stipulates the mechanism to be used in determining any costs and damages to the injured party in the event of a breach of contract. Once again, spelling it out in the contract helps avoid confusion later on.

Damages

The concept of damages in the UCC is based on the remedy of a party being "made whole." In other words, a purchaser who is damaged by a breach of contract must receive damages that bring the purchaser back to the position where he or she would have been if the breach had not occurred. Damages include either actual damages (which include losses that are real, known, or can be reasonably estimated), as well as punitive damages (extra money over and above as "punishment" for the defendant's bad behavior). The UCC is quite clear on the point that punitive damages are not allowed, even if such a provision is contained in the contract. There are essentially three types of damages available to the purchaser:

- *Restitution:* Money the plaintiff actually paid to the defendant in connection with the contract.
- *Reliance:* Money the plaintiff lost because he or she was relying on the contract, depending on the defendant to live up to their obligations under the contract.
- *Expectancy:* Money the plaintiff was hoping to gain from the contract.

Back at Mimi's wholesale video store, Mimi and Betsy had a valid contract. Betsy promised to buy 1,000 videotapes for $15 apiece, and Mimi promised to deliver them to Betsy's place of business. Betsy gave Mimi $2,000 as a down payment on the delivery. Betsy also spent $5,000 building new shelves in her retail video store to hold the tapes. Finally, Betsy expected to make a profit of $20,000 after expenses from selling and/or renting the tapes to her customers. However, Mimi never delivers the tapes, and Betsy sues for breach of contract. What damages is she entitled to?

Betsy can sue for $2,000 in restitution damages for loss of the down payment, $5,000 in reliance damages for the shelves, and $20,000 in expectancy damages for the $20,000 in profits she expected to make (for a total of $27,000).

When calculating damages, there are various methods of doing so.[247] General damages are equal to the difference between the value of the purchased goods at the time of delivery against the goods' value at the time of specified delivery. Incidental damages include expenses reasonably incurred in inspection, receipt, transportation, and the care and custody of goods appropriately rejected by the purchaser. Consequential damages are those expenses incurred by the purchaser because the goods were not delivered when expected or as specified. Liquidation damages are those that result if the terms of the contract are not fulfilled and are typically defined prior to the breach under the terms of the contract.

Acceptance and Rejection of Goods

The UCC allows the purchaser to accept part of the shipment and reject the remainder for cause, or to accept or reject the entire shipment. After the point of acceptance, the supplier's rights increase and the purchaser's rights decrease. Once the purchaser accepts the goods, there is only one recourse—to make a claim against the supplier. The UCC specifies that the purchaser does not have the legal right to withhold payment from the supplier once acceptance has been made. The purchaser also does not have the right at this point to send the goods back unless the supplier consents to this action.

The legal concept of acceptance is closely related to the concept of inspection. Purchasers have a legitimate right to inspect contracted goods before accepting or rejecting them. The law is quite explicit when it states that the purchaser accept the goods within a reasonable time whether or not the goods are physically inspected. Obvious defects must be discovered and rejected within this reasonable time frame, or the purchaser has no recourse against the seller. "Latent" defects are those that could not have been easily discovered during an inspection and do not fall under this rule. In certain limited situations, the purchaser is able to revoke an acceptance of delivered goods. A purchaser may revoke a prior acceptance if a problem is discovered that substantially impairs the value of the goods.

When the goods delivered by the supplier are actually rejected by the purchaser due to nonconformance, the purchaser must provide notice to the supplier within a reasonable period of time. The purchaser should be specific in notifying the supplier that he or she is in breach of contract. General statements about the problems at hand without stating that the supplier is considered in breach of contract are not adequate notification. The exact terms "breach of contract" must be used, or the purchaser stands to lose his or her right to recourse from the supplier.

Once goods are accepted there are two obligations that the purchaser must meet in order to recover his or her rights. First, the purchaser must carry the burden of proof that the goods did not conform to the terms and conditions of the contract. Second, the purchaser must, within a reasonable time after the breach is discovered, notify the supplier of that breach or lose the chance for remedy.

Acceptance of the contracted goods by the purchaser means that ownership of the goods has been transferred. There are no rituals or formalities required to make the transfer of ownership. Any words or acts by the purchaser that provide an indication of the purchaser's intention to transfer ownership are enough to effect the transfer. Even though the goods may have been formally rejected by the purchaser, actions typifying ownership may indicate that acceptance has instead been accomplished.

In order to prevent or mitigate problems arising from the acceptance or rejection of goods, a number of steps to manage the acceptance process can be implemented by the purchaser:[248]

- The receiving department should stamp all receipts of goods with a statement something to the effect of "Received subject to inspection, count, and testing."
- A thorough set of purchase order terms and conditions should indicate that all receipts from suppliers are subject to inspection, count, and testing.
- All delivered goods should be inspected as quickly as possible, and ideally, immediately upon delivery.
- If goods are not inspected until they are used, it is a good idea to maintain a stock-rotation system to ensure that older quantities of goods are used first.
- In some cases, purchasers may want to consider putting language in their purchase order terms and conditions that defines the reasonable time for inspection and acceptance.
- An internal reporting system should be set up to ensure that defects encountered in the organization are reported to the purchasing department within a reasonable time so that remedies can be pursued.
- Contracts for such items as production equipment should contain a clause stating that acceptance will not be made until the equipment has been installed and run satisfactorily for a certain period of time.
- For hardware- and software-related contracts, the purchaser should carefully define the acceptance criteria and notify the supplier of the specific process that this equipment and software will be subjected to.

Honest Mistakes

Sometimes, in spite of the best efforts of the purchaser and the supplier, honest mistakes occur when parties draw up a purchase agreement. In such instances, careful consideration of all the circumstances are necessary to determine whether or not the resulting contract is valid or invalid. Generally, honest mistakes by a single party to the contract will *not* void the contract. If the other party was truly unaware of the mistake, then the contract is still intact. Note that mistakes made by *both* parties also do not necessarily affect the validity of the contract.

Mistakes are not covered under the UCC. The parties must rely on traditional contract law to solve any dispute resulting from a mistake. "As a general rule, a party will not be given relief against a mistake induced by his own negligence. But the rule is not inflexible and in many cases relief may be granted although the mistake involved some element of negligence, particularly when the other party has been in no way prejudiced."[249] The rules for determining whether or not a contract exists after a mistake has been made are the basic fairness rules. The judicial system will more than likely allow a supplier to be absolved from the contract due to a mistake if the supplier gave the purchaser notification of the mistake before the purchaser relied on the bid. Buyers should therefore attempt to minimize the occurrence of contractual mistakes.

Patents and Intellectual Property

As suppliers become increasingly integrated in new-product development, intellectual property agreements are becoming the norm. There are three kinds of intellectual property in the United States: (1) patents, (2) copyrights, and (3) trade secrets. Patent law has been established in several federal patent statutes including the Patent Act of 1790, 35 U.S.C. Section 1, and companion laws. Copyright law is founded in the federal statutes, particularly in the Copyright Act of 1976. Federal patent and copyright laws overrule any contradictory state statutes. By contrast, trade secret law is grounded in common law and is intended to protect unique ideas that would not otherwise have legal protection under patent and copyright law. Since common law varies by state, there is some variance in actual statutes. However, most states have created laws that are very similar.

169. BUSINESS LAW

In its most basic form, a *patent* is an agreement between the inventor and the federal government. The inventor receives the right to exclusive use of his or her invention for a period of *17 years* in exchange for a full public disclosure of that invention. Although the inventor has exclusive rights (i.e., a monopoly) to the invention during the patent period, others gain that right to the benefits of the invention following expiration of the protection period, thereby providing public benefit. A U.S. patent is applicable only to the inventor's exclusive use within the borders of the United States. Inventors wishing to expand their patent protection to other countries must file appropriate patent applications in each country in which protection is desired. Note that in some countries such as China and India, copyrights and patents may not be recognized at all.

A firm needs to protect itself from inadvertent patent infringement whenever it purchases a product from a supplier. This can best be done by including a patent indemnification clause in all purchasing documents. This clause should consist of three parts:

1. An indemnification, which seeks the supplier's assurances that the goods being contracted for do not infringe on any other party's patents
2. The right to require the supplier to defend any patent infringement suit itself
3. The right to have the purchaser's own attorneys involved in defense of any lawsuit concerning patent infringement

The UCC provides minimal protection for the purchasers in defending themselves against legal actions stemming from patent infringement. Therefore, indemnification agreements should be included in contracts with suppliers whenever possible.

A *copyright* is designed to afford protection for persons who create such original works as books, software, songs, and films. Copyright law does not require a formal application as does patent law. In addition, it is not necessary for the copyright originator to place any legend or indication on the protected material indicating that the material is copyrighted. Copyright is automatically assumed. However, most legal experts recommend that some sort of language in the form of a copyright notice be included on any works desired to be protected, along with the copyright symbol, ©. This notice provides evidence that the creator of the article in question intends to maintain copyright privileges in the event of infringement.

A *trade secret* (also known as *confidential information*) is a very broad category of intellectual property. Virtually any information believed to be confidential and important to an organization can be deemed to be a trade secret or confidential information. Resources as diverse as formulas, supplier and customer lists, procedures, and training programs could all be regarded as trade secrets. In order to receive trade secret protection under the law, the organization must take steps to minimize or preclude the distribution of its sensitive information. The information must also be deemed to possess the following three characteristics:

- It is economically valuable.
- It is not generally known.
- It is kept as a secret.

Trade secret protection becomes essentially self-serving through the actions of the organization itself. For instance, if information that could otherwise be considered trade secrets is not protected through devices such as limited access or other security precautions, then the courts have ruled that this information is not confidential and, therefore, not entitled to protection. This test of confidential information can also be applied to any information that suppliers provide to the purchasing firm through the normal course of business dealings. As before, however, the supplier must make it known that the information is proprietary and is to be kept confidential. As a precaution, any information provided to a supplier should be accompanied by notification that the information is provided in confidence and should be treated as such by the supplier. This is typically known as a *nondisclosure agreement*.

Other Laws Affecting Purchasing

Laws Affecting Global Purchasing

Many laws—U.S., foreign, and international—affect global commerce. The following discussion briefly summarizes some of the laws that can affect a purchaser's international business dealings.[250]

FOREIGN CORRUPT PRACTICES ACT   This law prohibits payments (such as bribes) that might benefit a foreign official personally. While usually pertaining to sellers, purchasers should understand this law's provisions so they can recognize situations addressed by the act.

ANTI-BOYCOTT LEGISLATION   Various laws address doing business with countries that support the boycott of one nation against another. Examples include the boycott of Israel by Arab countries and the boycott of Taiwan by mainland China. These laws require reporting of any request to participate in a boycott, which purchasers often fail to do.

EXPORT ADMINISTRATION ACT   Various laws and regulations govern, and sometimes even restrict, the export of goods, information, and services. Purchasers may not perceive that they are engaged in exporting. However, the law views certain types of drawings, specifications, and prototypes forwarded to a foreign entity as restricted exports of technology. Purchasers are urged to seek the advice of an expert when questions arise in this area.

CUSTOMS LAWS   This body of law addresses the importation of goods into the United States. Customs brokers who are familiar with customs laws can be quite valuable in understanding the rules and regulations governing importation.

FOREIGN LAWS   In addition to the U.S. laws that apply to foreign transactions, the laws and regulations of other countries involved in a business transaction may also apply. These laws will likely address contract law, export control, currency control, and criminal law. Some transactions could be illegal if structured in a certain manner.

INTERNATIONAL LAWS   Other laws may apply to a business transaction that are not part of any specific country's laws and regulations. Maritime laws are a good example of international laws that affect international commerce. Several international documents are also pertinent to international transactions. These include *The United Nations Convention on Contracts for International Sale of Goods* (CISG) and *International Contracting Terms* (INCOTERMS).

Laws Affecting Antitrust and Unfair Trade Practices

A number of federal laws deal with antitrust and competitive practices of interstate commerce. Each law seeks to promote the fair conduct of business. While most of these laws apply to the conduct of the seller, some provisions apply directly or indirectly to purchasers.

SHERMAN ANTITRUST ACT (1898)   This law prohibits actions that are "in constraint of trade" or actions that attempt to monopolize a market or create a monopoly. Legal actions under this law typically involve price fixing or other forms of collusion among sellers. However, the law also prohibits reciprocity or reciprocal purchase agreements, which was discussed in the ethics section.

FEDERAL TRADE COMMISSION ACT (1914)   This act authorizes the Federal Trade Commission to interpret trade legislation, including the provisions of the Sherman Antitrust Act that deal with restraint of trade. The FTCA also addresses unfair competition and unfair or deceptive trade practices.

CLAYTON ANTITRUST ACT (1914)   This law makes price discrimination illegal and prohibits sellers from exclusive arrangements with purchasers and/or product distributors.

ROBINSON-PATMAN ACT (1936)   This law further addresses the issue of price discrimination. It prohibits sellers from offering a discriminatory price where the effect of discrimination may limit competition or create a monopoly. There is also a provision that prohibits purchasers from inducing a discriminatory price. While a seller may legally lower price as a concession during negotiations, the purchaser should not mislead or trick the seller, thus resulting in a price that is discriminatory to other buyers in the market.

The laws governing purchasing are complex and varied. Other laws address environmental and labor issues. This overview simply points out that today's purchaser must be aware of the laws and regulations governing domestic and international purchasing. A purchaser is urged to discuss with legal counsel any questions that arise during the performance of job responsibilities. Ignorance of the law is not a valid defense.

Law and Marketing

Consumer Protection

Consumer transactions have increased enormously since World War II, and today consumer debt amounts to more than $1 trillion. Although the definition varies, a consumer transaction generally involves goods, credit, services, or land acquired for personal, household, or family purposes. Historically, consumers were subject to the rule of *caveat emptor*—let the buyer beware. The law, however, has largely abandoned this principle and now offers greater protection to consumers. Most of this protection takes the form of statutory enactments at both the state and federal levels, and a wide variety of governmental agencies are charged with enforcing these statutes. This enforcement varies enormously. In some cases, only government agencies may exercise enforcement rights, through the imposition of criminal penalties, civil penalties, injunctions, and cease and desist orders. In other cases, in addition to government's enforcement rights, consumers may privately seek the rescission of contracts and damages for harm resulting from violations of consumer protection laws. Finally, under certain consumer protection statutes such as state "lemon laws," consumers alone may exercise enforcement rights. In this section, we will examine state and federal consumer protection agencies and consumer protection statutes.

State and Federal Consumer Protection Agencies

Through the enactment of laws and regulations, legislatures and administrative bodies at the federal, state, and local levels all actively seek to shield consumers from an enormous range of harm. The most common abuses involving consumer transactions occur in the extension of credit, deceptive trade practices, unsafe products, and unfair pricing.

State and Local Consumer Protection Agencies

The many consumer protection agencies at the state and local levels typically deal with fraudulent and deceptive trade practices and fraudulent sales practices, such as false statements about a product's value or quality. In most jurisdictions, consumer protection agencies also help to resolve consumer complaints about defective goods or poor service.

Most state attorneys general facilitate consumer protection by enforcing laws against consumer fraud through judicially imposed injunctions and restitution. In recent years, as the federal government's role in consumer protection has diminished in response to the deregulatory movement, the states have correspondingly expanded their role. The National Association of Attorneys General (NAAG) has been active in coordinating lawsuits among the states. Under NAAG's guidance, several states will often simultaneously file lawsuits against a company that has been engaging in fraudulent acts involving more than one state.

In some instances, however, states have not coordinated their efforts and have, instead, acted inconsistently with respect to consumer protection, especially in health and safety matters. This lack of coordination can present serious problems to companies that sell large numbers of products in interstate commerce.

The Federal Trade Commission

At the federal level, the most significant consumer protection agency is the **Federal Trade Commission (FTC)**. Established in 1914, the FTC has two major functions: (1) under its mandate to prevent "unfair methods of competition in commerce," it is responsible for roughly half of the antitrust enforcement at the federal level and (2) under its mandate to prevent "unfair and deceptive" trade practices, it is responsible for stopping fraudulent sales techniques.

In addressing unfair and deceptive trade practices, the five-member commission (no more than three of whose members may be from the same political party) has the power to issue substantive "trade regulation rules" and to conduct appropriate investigations and hearings. Among the rules it has issued so far are those regulating used car sales, franchising and business opportunity ventures, funeral home services, and the issuance of consumer credit, as well as those requiring a "cooling-off" period for door-to-door sales.

In many instances, the agency, in considering a deceptive trade practice, may seek a **cease and desist order** rather than issue a substantive trade rule. A cease and desist order directs a party to stop a certain practice or face punishment such as a fine. In a typical situation, the FTC staff discovers a potentially deceptive practice, investigates the matter, files (if appropriate) a complaint against the alleged offender (usually referred to as the respondent), and after a hearing in front of an administrative law judge (ALJ) to determine whether a violation of the law has occurred, obtains a cease and desist order if the ALJ finds that one is necessary. The respondent may appeal to the FTC commissioners to reverse or modify the order. Appeals from orders issued by the commissioners go to the U.S. Courts of Appeals, which have exclusive jurisdiction to enforce, set aside, or modify orders of the commission.

STANDARDS Though the FTC act does not define the words *unfair* or *deceptive,* the commission has issued three policy statements addressing the meaning of **unfairness** and has provided that an injury is unfair if it is substantial, not outweighed by any benefits to consumers or competition, and is one that consumers themselves could not reasonably have avoided. The standard, therefore, applies a cost-benefit analysis to the issue of unfairness.

The second policy statement deals with the meaning of **deception**—the basis of most FTC consumer protection actions—by providing that the commission will find deception in a misrepresentation, omission, or practice that is likely to mislead a consumer acting reasonably in the circumstances, to the consumer's detriment.

Deception may occur either through false representation or material omission. Examples of deceptive practices have included advertising that a certain product would save consumers 25 percent on their automotive motor oil, when the product simply replaced a quart of oil in the engine (which normally contains four quarts of oil) and was, in fact, more expensive than the oil it replaced; placing marbles in a bowl of vegetable soup in order to displace the vegetables from the bottom of the bowl and therefore make the soup look thicker; and claiming that one drug provided greater pain relief than another named drug, when evidence actually was insufficient to prove the claim to the medical community.

Deception can also occur through a failure to *disclose* important product information if such disclosure is necessary to correct a false and material expectation created in the consumer's mind by the product or by the circumstances of sale. For example, the FTC has insisted that the failure to disclose a product's country of origin constitutes a deceptive omission, based on the agency's view that consumers assume the United States to be the country of origin of a product that bears no other country's name.

The third policy statement issued by the commission involves **ad substantiation.** This policy requires that advertisers have a reasonable basis for their claims at the time they make such claims. Moreover, in determining the reasonableness of a claim, the commission places great weight on the cost and benefits of substantiation.

Remedies

In addition to the remedies just discussed, the FTC has employed three other remedies: (1) affirmative disclosure, (2) corrective advertising, and (3) multiple product orders. **Affirmative disclosure,** a remedy frequently employed by the FTC, requires an offender to include in its advertisements certain information that will prevent the ads from being considered deceptive.

Corrective advertising goes beyond affirmative disclosure by requiring an advertiser who has made a deceptive claim to disclose in future advertisements that such prior claims were in fact untrue. The theory behind this requirement is that a previous deception's effects will continue until expressly corrected.

Multiple product orders require a deceptive advertiser to cease and desist from any future deception not only in regard to the product in question but also in regard to all products sold by the company. This remedy is particularly useful in dealing with companies that have repeatedly violated the law.

The Consumer Product Safety Commission

The **Consumer Product Safety Act (CPSA)** established an independent federal regulatory agency, the Consumer Product Safety Commission (CPSC). The purposes of the CPSA are (1) to protect the public against unreasonable risks of injury associated with consumer products, (2) to assist consumers in evaluating the comparative safety of consumer products, (3) to develop uniform safety standards for consumer products and to minimize conflicting state and local regulations, and (4) to promote research and investigation into the causes and prevention of product-related deaths, illnesses, and injuries.

Consisting of five commissioners, no more than three of whom can be from the same political party, the CPSC has authority to set safety standards for consumer products; to ban unsafe products; to issue administrative recall orders to compel repair, replacement, or refunds for products found to present substantial hazards; and to seek court orders requiring the recall of "imminently hazardous" products. In addition, Congress requires businesses under CPSC jurisdiction to notify the agency of any information indicating that their products contain defects that "could create" substantial product hazards. By triggering investigations that may lead to product recalls, these reports play a major role in the agency's regulatory activities.

169. BUSINESS LAW

The CPSC also enforces four statutes previously enforced by other agencies. These acts, commonly referred to as the "transferred acts," are the Federal Hazardous Substances Act, the Flammable Fabrics Act, the Poison Prevention Packaging Act, and the Refrigerator Safety Act. When the CPSC can regulate a product under one of these specific acts, rather than under the more general CPSA, the agency is directed to do so unless it specifically finds that regulation under the CPSA is in the public interest. Thus, a large number of CPSC regulations, such as those for toys, children's flammable sleepwear, and hazard warnings on household chemical products, arise under the transferred acts rather than under the CPSA.

When first established, the CPSC promulgated a number of **mandatory safety standards;** manufacturers either must follow these rules, which regulate product design, packaging, and warning labels, or face legal sanctions. To save time and money, the agency began to rely on industry to establish **voluntary safety standards**—rules for which noncompliance does not violate the law—reserving mandatory standards for those instances in which voluntary standards proved inadequate. In 1981, Congress enacted legislation requiring the CPSC to rely on voluntary standards "whenever compliance with such voluntary standards would eliminate or adequately reduce the risk of injury addressed and there is substantial compliance with such voluntary standards." Although the 1981 amendments do not bar the CPSC from writing mandatory standards, the CPSC has promulgated few such standards since the law was amended.

Other Federal Consumer Protection Agencies

Among the many other federal agencies that play a major consumer protection role are the **National Highway Traffic Safety Administration (NHTSA)** and the **Food and Drug Administration (FDA).**

Established in 1966 to reduce the number of deaths and injuries resulting from highway crashes, the NHTSA has the authority to set motor vehicle safety standards that promote crash prevention and crashworthiness. Manufacturers are required to report possible safety defects, and the agency may seek a recall if it determines that a particular automobile model presents a sufficiently great hazard. The NHTSA is also authorized to provide grants-in-aid for state highway safety programs and to conduct research on improving highway safety.

The Food and Drug Administration is the oldest federal consumer protection agency, dating back to 1906. The FDA enforces the Food, Drug and Cosmetic Act, enacted in 1938, which authorizes the agency to regulate "adulterated and misbranded" products. The agency uses two basic enforcement methods: it sets standards for products or requires their premarket approval. The products most often subject to premarket approval are drugs. Since 1976, the agency also has had the authority to subject medical devices such as pacemakers and intrauterine devices to premarket approval; it recently has been requiring a large and increasing number of such devices to undergo this approval process.

Although the FTC, CPSC, NHTSA, and FDA are perhaps the best-known federal consumer protection agencies, numerous others play important roles. For example, the U.S. Postal Service brings many cases every year to close down mail fraud operations and the Securities and Exchange Commission (SEC) protects consumers against fraud in the sale of securities. In addition, many other agencies assist consumers with specific types of problems that fall within an agency's scope.

Consumer Purchases

When a consumer purchases a product or obtains a service, certain rights and obligations arise. Although a number of consumer protection laws have been enacted in recent years, they still leave much of a consumer's rights and duties to state contract law. In particular, Article 2 of the Uniform Commercial Code provides the basic rules governing when a contract for the sale of goods is formed, what constitutes a breach of contract, and what rights an innocent party has against a party who commits a breach. Though many consumer protection laws add rights the UCC does not contain, they still use its tenets as building blocks. For example, many states have passed so-called "lemon laws" to provide additional contract cancellation rights to dissatisfied automobile purchasers.

Federal Warranty Protection

A **warranty** creates a duty on the seller's part to assure that the goods or services she sells will conform to certain qualities, characteristics, or conditions. A seller is not required, however, to warrant what she sells; and in general she may, by appropriate words, disclaim (exclude) or modify a particular warranty or all warranties. Because a seller's power to disclaim or modify is so flexible, consumer protection laws have been enacted to ensure that consumers understand the warranty protection provided them.

In 1974, to protect buyers and to prevent deception in selling, Congress enacted the **Magnuson-Moss Warranty Act,** which requires sellers of consumer products to provide adequate information about warranties. The FTC adminis-

Exhibit 100.31 *Magnuson-Mass Act*

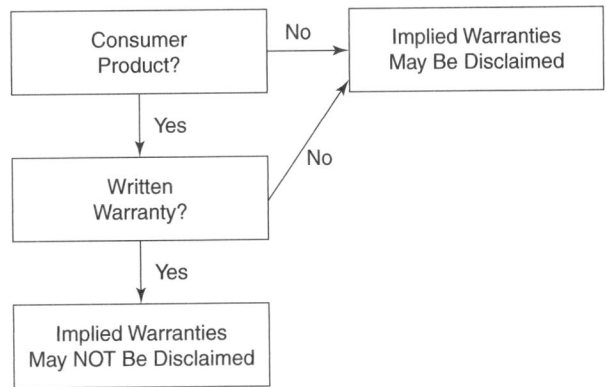

ters and enforces the act, which provides for (1) disclosure in clear and understandable language of the warranty that is to be offered, (2) a description of the warranty as either "full" or "limited," (3) a prohibition against disclaiming implied warranties if a written warranty is given, and (4) an optional informal settlement mechanism. See Exhibit 100.31 for the details of the Magnuson-Moss Warranty Act.

The act applies to consumer products with **written warranties.** A **consumer product** is any item of tangible personal property that is *normally* used for family, household, or personal use and that is distributed in commerce. The act does *not* protect commercial purchasers, partly because they are considered sufficiently knowledgeable, in terms of contracting, to protect themselves. Also, they are able to employ their own attorneys to protect themselves and, in the marketplace, can spread the cost of their injuries.

PRESALE DISCLOSURES The act contains **presale disclosure** provisions calculated to prevent confusion and deception and to enable purchasers to make educated product comparisons. A person making a warranty must, to the extent required by the rules of the Federal Trade Commission, fully and conspicuously disclose in simple and readily understood language the terms and conditions of such warranty. Separate rules apply to mail order, catalog, and door-to-door sales.

LABELING REQUIREMENTS The act further divides written warranties into two categories—limited and full—either of which, for any product costing more than $10, must be designated on the written warranty itself. The purpose of this provision is to enable the consumer to make an initial comparison of the legal rights under certain warranties. Under a **warranty** designated as **full,** the warrantor must agree to repair the product, without charge, to conform with the warranty; no limitation may be placed on the duration of any implied warranty; the consumer must be given the option of a refund or replacement if repair is unsuccessful; and consequential damages may be excluded only if the warranty conspicuously indicates their exclusion. A limited warranty is any warranty not designated as full.

LIMITATIONS ON DISCLAIMERS Most significantly, the act provides that a *written* warranty, whether full or limited, may *not disclaim any implied* warranty. Specifically, a full warranty may not disclaim, modify, or limit any implied warranty; and a limited warranty may not disclaim or modify any implied warranty but may limit its duration to that of the written warranty, provided that the limitation is reasonable, conscionable, and conspicuously displayed. Some states, however, do not allow limitations in the duration of implied warranties.

State "Lemon Laws"

A number of state legislatures have enacted **lemon laws** that attempt to provide new car purchasers with rights that are similar to full warranties under the Magnuson-Moss Warranty Act. (Some states have broadened their laws to cover used cars; some also cover motorcycles.) There are many different lemon laws, but most define a *lemon* as a car that continues to have a defect that substantially impairs its use, value, or safety, even after the manufacturer has made reasonable attempts to correct the problem. If a consumer can prove that her car is a lemon, most lemon laws require the manufacturer either to replace the car or to refund its retail price, less an allowance for the consumer's use of the car. In addition, most lemon laws provide that the consumer may recover attorneys' fees and expenses if the case goes to litigation.

169. BUSINESS LAW

Consumer Right of Rescission

In most cases, a consumer is legally obligated once he has signed a contract. Many states, however, have statutes allowing a consumer a brief period—generally two or three days—during which he may rescind an otherwise binding credit obligation if the sale was solicited in his home. Moreover, the Federal Trade Commission has also set forth a trade regulation that applies to door-to-door sales, leases, or rentals of goods and services for $25 or more, whether the sale is for cash or on credit. The regulation permits a consumer to rescind a contract within *three days* of signing.

The right of **rescission** also exists under the **Federal Consumer Credit Protection Act** (discussed more fully in the next section), which allows a consumer 3 days during which he may withdraw from any credit obligation secured by a mortgage on his home, unless the extension of credit was made to acquire the dwelling. After the consumer rescinds, the creditor has 20 days to return any money or property he has received from the consumer.

The **Interstate Land Sales Full Disclosure Act** requires a developer of unimproved land to file a detailed statement of record containing specified information about specified subdivisions with the Department of Housing and Urban Development before offering the lots for sale or lease. The developer must provide a property report (a condensed version of the statement of record) to each prospective purchaser or lessee. The act provides that a purchaser or lessee may revoke any contract or agreement for sale or lease at her option within seven days of signing the contract, and that the contract must clearly provide this right. A purchaser or lessee who does not receive a property report before signing a contract may revoke the contract within two years from the date of signing.

Consumer Credit Transactions

In the absence of special regulation, consumer credit transactions are governed by the laws that regulate commercial transactions generally. A **consumer credit transaction** is customarily defined as any credit transaction involving goods, services, or land acquired for personal, household, or family purposes. The following examples illustrate consumer credit transactions: Atkins borrows $600 from a bank to pay a dentist bill or to take a vacation; Bevins buys a refrigerator for her home from a department store and agrees to pay the purchase price in 12 equal monthly installments; Carpenter has an oil company credit card with which he purchases gasoline and tires for his family car.

Regulation of consumer credit has increased considerably because of the dramatic expansion of consumer credit and the numerous abuses in credit transactions, including misleading credit disclosures, unfair marketing practices, and oppressive collection methods. In 1968, in response to concerns about consumer credit, Congress passed the **Federal Consumer Credit Protection Act (FCCPA),** which requires creditors to disclose finance charges (including interest and other charges) and credit extension charges, and sets limits on garnishment proceedings. Since 1968, Congress has added titles to this law. Also in 1968, the National Conference of Commissioners on Uniform State Laws (the group that drafted the Uniform Commercial Code) promulgated the **Uniform Consumer Credit Code (UCCC),** which consolidated into one recommended law the regulation of all consumer credit transactions—loans and purchases on credit. Although only a few states have adopted the UCCC, its impact on the development of consumer credit has extended well beyond their borders.

Access to the Market

The **Equal Credit Opportunity Act,** enacted by Congress in 1974 and revised several times since then, prohibits all businesses that regularly extend credit from discriminating against any credit applicant on the basis of gender, marital status, race, color, religion, national origin, or age. Under the act, a creditor must notify an applicant, within 30 days of receiving an application, of the action the creditor has taken and must give specific reasons for denying credit. Although several federal agencies administer and enforce the act, the FTC has overall enforcement authority. A credit applicant aggrieved by a violation of the act may recover actual and punitive damages, plus attorneys' fees.

Disclosure Requirements

Title One of the FCCPA, also known as the **Truth-in-Lending Act,** has superseded state disclosure requirements relating to credit terms for both consumer loans and credit sales under $25,000. The act does not cover credit transactions for business, commercial, or agricultural purposes. Creditors in every state not specifically exempted by the Federal Reserve Board must comply with federal disclosure standards.

Before a consumer formally incurs a contractual obligation for credit, both state and federal statutes require the creditor to present to the consumer a written statement containing certain information about contract terms. Generally, the required disclosure concerns the cost of credit, that is, interest or sales finance charges. An important requirement in the Truth-in-Lending Act is that sales finance and interest rates must be quoted in terms of an **APR** (*annual percentage rate*) and must be calculated on a uniform basis. Congress required disclosure of this information to encourage consumers to compare credit terms, to increase competition among financial institutions, and to facilitate economic stability. Enforcement and interpretation of the Truth-in-Lending Act was assigned to the Federal Reserve Board, which issued **Regulation Z** to carry out this responsibility.

The **Fair Credit and Charge Card Disclosure Act of 1988** adds to the Truth-in-Lending Act a new section requiring all credit and charge card applications and solicitations to include extensive disclosures whose requirements depend on the type of card involved and whether the application or solicitation is by mail, telephone, or other means.

CREDIT ACCOUNTS In addition to the cost of the credit, under the Truth-in-Lending Act a creditor must inform consumers who open revolving or open-ended credit accounts about how the finance charge is computed and when it is charged, what other charges may be imposed, and whether the creditor retains or acquires a security interest. An **open-ended credit** account permits the debtor to enter into a series of credit transactions that he may pay off either in installments or in a lump sum. Examples of this type of credit include most department store credit cards, most gasoline credit cards, VISA cards, and MasterCards.

Closed-ended credit, in contrast, is credit extended for a specified time, during which the debtor generally makes periodic payments in an amount and at a time agreed upon in advance. Examples of this type of credit include most automobile financing agreements, most real estate mortgages, and numerous other major purchases. For nonrevolving or closed-ended credit accounts, the creditor must provide the consumer with information about the total amount financed; the cash price; the number, amount, and due date of installments; delinquency charges; and a description of the security, if any.

> **Open-ended credit** Account permitting debtor to enter into a series of credit transactions.
>
> **Closed-ended credit** Credit extended to debtor for a specified time.

ARMS In 1987, the Federal Reserve Board amended Regulation Z to deal with variable or adjustable rate mortgages (ARMs). The *ARM disclosure rules* apply to any loan that is (1) a closed-ended consumer transaction, (2) secured by the consumer's principal residence, (3) longer than one year in duration, and (4) subject to interest rate variation. This coverage excludes open-ended lines of credit secured by the consumer's principal dwelling. The disclosures must be made when a creditor furnishes an application to a prospective borrower or before the creditor receives payment of a nonrefundable fee, whichever occurs first. The ARM disclosure rules require that the creditor provide the consumer with a consumer handbook on ARMs and a loan program disclosure statement covering the terms of each ARM that the creditor offers.

HOME EQUITY LOANS In recent years, a popular method of consumer borrowing has been the home equity loan. In order to regulate the disclosures and advertising of these loans, in 1988 Congress enacted the **Home Equity Loan Consumer Protection Act (HELCPA).** HELCPA amends the Truth-in-Lending Act to require that lenders provide a disclosure statement and consumer pamphlet at (or, in some limited instances, within three days of) the time they provide an application to a prospective consumer borrower. HELCPA applies to all open-ended credit plans for consumer loans that are secured by the consumer's principal dwelling. Unlike other Truth-in-Lending statutes, HELCPA defines a principal dwelling to include second or vacation homes. The disclosure statement must include a statement that (1) a default on the loan may result in the consumer's loss of the dwelling; (2) some conditions must be met, such as a time by which the consumer must submit an application in order to obtain the specific terms; and (3) the creditor, under certain circumstances, may terminate the plan and accelerate the outstanding balance, prohibit further extension of credit, reduce the plan's credit limit, or impose fees upon the termination of the account. In addition, if the plan contains a fixed interest rate, the creditor must disclose each APR imposed. If the plan involves an ARM, it must include how the rate is computed, the manner in which rates will be changed, the initial rate and how it was determined, the maximum rate change that may occur in any one year, the maximum rate that can be charged under the plan, the earliest time at which the maximum interest can be reached, and an itemization of all fees the plan imposes. Regulation Z provides the consumer with the right to rescind such a plan until midnight of the third day following the opening of the plan, until delivery of a notice of the right to rescind, or until delivery of all material disclosures, whichever comes last.

BILLING ERRORS In 1975, the **Fair Credit Billing Act** went into effect to relieve some of the problems and abuses associated with credit card billing errors. The act establishes procedures for the consumer to follow in making complaints about specified billing errors and requires the creditor to explain or correct such errors. Until it responds to the complaint, the creditor may not take any action to collect the disputed amount, restrict the use of an open-ended credit account because the disputed amount is unpaid, or report the disputed amount as delinquent.

SETTLEMENT CHARGES In 1974, Congress enacted the **Real Estate Settlement Procedures Act (RESPA)** to provide consumer home purchasers with greater and more timely information on the nature and costs of the settlement process and to protect them from unnecessarily high settlement charges. The act, which applies to all federally related mortgage loans, requires advance disclosure to home buyers and sellers of all settlement costs, including attorneys' fees, credit reports, title insurance, and, if relevant, an initial escrow account statement. Nearly all first mortgage loans fall within the scope of the act. RESPA, which is administered and enforced by the Secretary of Housing and Urban Development, prohibits kickbacks and referral fees and limits the amount home buyers must place in escrow accounts to ensure payment of real estate taxes and insurance. In 1990, the National Affordable Housing Act amended RESPA to require an annual analysis of escrow accounts.

Contract Terms

Consumer credit is marketed on a mass basis. Frequently, contract documents are printed forms containing blank spaces to accommodate the contractual details the creditor will normally negotiate at the time she extends credit. Standardization and uniformity of contract terms facilitate the transfer of the creditor's rights (in most situations, those of a seller) to a third party, usually a bank or finance company.

Almost all states impose statutory ceilings on the amount that creditors may charge for the extension of consumer credit. Statutes regulating rates also specify what other charges may be made. Most statutes require a creditor to permit the debtor to pay her obligation in full at any time before the maturity date of the final installment. If the interest charge for the loan period was computed in advance and added to the principal of the loan, a debtor who prepays in full is entitled to a refund of the unearned interest already paid.

In the past, certain purchases involving consumer goods were financed in such a way that a consumer was legally obligated to make full payment of the price to a third party, even though the dealer from whom she bought the goods had committed fraud or the goods were defective. This occurred when the purchaser executed and delivered to the seller a negotiable instrument (a promissory note, draft, or check), and the seller negotiated it to a holder in due course, who purchased the note for value, in good faith, and without notice that it was overdue or that it had any defenses or claims attached to it. Though valid against the seller, the buyer's defenses—that the goods were defective or that the seller had committed fraud—were not valid against a holder in due course of the note. To preserve the claims and defenses of consumer buyers and borrowers and to make such claims and defenses available against holders in due course, the FTC adopted a rule that limits the rights of a holder in due course of an instrument evidencing a debt that arises out of a *consumer credit contract*. The rule applies to sellers and lessors of goods.

A similar rule applies to credit card issuers under the **Fair Credit Billing Act.** The act preserves a consumer's defense against the issuer (provided the consumer has made a good faith attempt to resolve the dispute with the seller), but only if (1) the seller is controlled by the card issuer or is under common control with the issuer, (2) the issuer has included the seller's promotional literature in the monthly billing statements sent to the card holder, or (3) the sale involves more than $50 and the consumer's billing address is in the same state as, or within one hundred miles of, the seller's place of business.

Consumer Credit Card Fraud

In 1984, Congress enacted the **Credit Card Fraud Act,** which closed many loopholes in prior law. The act prohibits the following practices: (1) possessing unauthorized cards, (2) counterfeiting or altering credit cards, (3) using account numbers alone, and (4) using cards obtained from a third party with his consent, even if the third party conspires to report the cards as stolen. It also imposes stiffer, criminal penalties for violation.

The FCCPA protects the *credit card holder* from loss by limiting to $50 the card holder's liability for another's unauthorized use of the holder's card. However, the card issuer may collect up to that amount for unauthorized use only if (1) the holder has accepted the card; (2) the issuer has furnished adequate notice of potential liability to the card holder; (3) the issuer has provided the card holder with a statement describing the means by which the holder may notify the card issuer of the loss or theft of the credit card; (4) the unauthorized use occurs before the card holder has notified the card issuer of the loss or theft; and (5) the card issuer has provided a method by which the person using the card can be identified as the person authorized to use the card.

Fair Reportage

Because creditors usually grant consumers credit only after investigating their creditworthiness, it is essential that the information on which creditors base such decisions is accurate and current. To this end, in 1970 Congress enacted the

Fair Credit Reporting Act, which applies to consumer reports used to secure employment, insurance, and credit. The act prohibits the inclusion of inaccurate or specified obsolete information in consumer reports and requires consumer reporting agencies to give consumers written advance notice before making an investigative report.

If the consumer does not agree that the information in the file is accurate and complete, and so notifies the agency, the agency must then reinvestigate the matter within a reasonable time, unless the complaint is frivolous or irrelevant. If reinvestigation proves that the information is inaccurate, it must promptly be deleted. If the dispute remains unresolved after reinvestigation, the consumer may submit to the agency a brief statement setting forth the nature of the dispute, and this statement must be incorporated into the report.

In 1997, Congress amended the act to restrict the use of credit reports by employers. An employer must now notify a job applicant or current employee that a report may be used and must obtain the applicant's consent prior to requesting an individual's credit report from a credit bureau. In addition, prior to taking an adverse action (refusal to hire, reassignment or termination, or denying a promotion) against the applicant or employee, the employer must provide the individual with a "pre-adverse action disclosure," which must contain the credit report and a copy of the FTC's "A Summary of Your Rights Under the Fair Credit Reporting Act."

Creditors' Remedies

A primary concern of creditors involves their rights should a debtor default or become late in payment. When the credit charge is precomputed, the creditor may impose a delinquency charge for late payments, subject to statutory limits for such charges. If, instead of being delinquent, the consumer defaults, the creditor may declare the entire balance of the debt immediately due and payable and may sue on the debt. The other courses of action that are open to the creditor depend on his security. Security provisions in consumer credit contracts may require a cosigner, an assignment of wages, a security interest in the goods sold, a security interest in other real or personal property of the debtor, and a confession of judgment clause (i.e., a clause by the defendant giving the plaintiff power to enter judgment against the defendant).

Wage Assignments and Garnishment

Wage assignments are prohibited by some states. In most states and under the FCCPA, a limitation is imposed on the amount that may be deducted from an individual's wages during any pay period. In addition, the FCCPA prohibits an employer from discharging an employee solely because of a creditor's exercise of an assignment of wages in connection with any one debt.

Even where wage assignments are prohibited, the creditor may still reach a consumer's wages through garnishment. But garnishment is available only in a court proceeding to enforce the collection of a judgment. The FCCPA and state statutes contain exemption provisions that limit the amount of wages subject to garnishment.

Security Interest

In the case of credit sales, the seller may retain a security interest in the goods sold. Many states impose restrictions on other security the creditor may obtain. Where the debt is secured by property as collateral, the creditor, on default by the debtor, may take possession of the property and, subject to the provisions of the Uniform Commercial Code, either retain it in full satisfaction of the debt or sell it and, if the proceeds are less than the outstanding debt, sue the debtor for the balance and obtain a deficiency judgment. The UCC provides that when a buyer of goods has paid 60 percent of the purchase price or 60 percent of a loan secured by consumer goods, the secured creditor may not retain the property in full satisfaction but must sell the goods and pay to the buyer that part of the sale proceeds in excess of the balance due.

In addition, federal regulation prohibits a credit seller or lender from obtaining a consumer's grant of a nonpossessory security interest in household goods. Household goods include clothing, furniture, appliances, kitchenware, personal effects, one radio, and one television; such goods specifically exclude works of art, other electronic entertainment equipment, antiques, and jewelry. This rule, which does not apply to purchased money security interests or to pledges, prevents a lender or seller from obtaining a nonpurchase money security interest covering the consumer's household goods.

Debt Collection Practices

In 1977, Congress enacted the *Fair Debt Collection Practices Act* to prevent debt collection agencies from employing abusive, deceptive, and unfair practices in the collection of consumer debts. The act, which is enforced by the Federal Trade

Commission, does not apply to creditors themselves. Rather, the act provides that any debt collector who communicates with a person other than the consumer for the purpose of acquiring information about the consumer's location may not state that the consumer owes any debt. Moreover, the act prohibits a number of abusive collection practices, including (1) communication with the consumer at unusual or inconvenient hours; (2) communication with the consumer if she is represented by an attorney; (3) harassing, oppressive, or abusive conduct, such as obscene language or threats of violence; (4) false, deceptive, or misleading representations or means of collection; and (5) unfair or unconscionable means to collect any debt.

The act requires a debt collector, within five days of the initial communication with a consumer, to provide the consumer with a written notice that includes (1) the amount of the debt; (2) the name of the current creditor; and (3) a statement informing the consumer that she can request verification of the alleged debt. The consumer may recover damages from the collection agency for violations of the act.

Product Liability: Warranties and Strict Liability

In this section, we will consider the liability of manufacturers and sellers of goods to buyers, users, consumers, and bystanders for damages caused by defective products. The rapidly expanding development of case law has established product liability as a distinct field of law that combines and enforces rules and principles of contracts, sales, negligence, strict liability, and statutory law.

One reason for the expansion of such liability has been the modern method of distributing goods. Today, retailers serve principally as a conduit of goods that are prepackaged in sealed containers and that are widely advertised by the manufacturer or distributor. This has hastened the extension of product liability coverage to include manufacturers and other parties within the chain of distribution. The extension of product liability to manufacturers, however, has not noticeably lessened the liability of a seller to his immediate purchaser. Rather, it has broadened the base of liability through the development and application of new principles of law.

Currently, the entire area of product liability has attracted a great deal of public attention. The cost of maintaining product liability insurance has skyrocketed, causing great concern in the business community. In response to the clamor over this insurance crisis, more than 40 states have revised their tort law to make successful product liability lawsuits more difficult to bring.

The liability of manufacturers and sellers of goods for a defective product, or for its failure to perform adequately, may be based on one or more of the following: (1) negligence, (2) misrepresentation, (3) violation of statutory duty, (4) warranty, and (5) strict liability in tort. In this section, we will explore the last two.

Warranties

A **warranty** creates a duty on the part of the seller to ensure that the goods he sells will conform to certain qualities, characteristics, or conditions. A seller, however, is not required to warrant the goods; and, in general, he may, by appropriate words, disclaim (exclude) or modify a particular warranty or even all warranties.

In bringing a warranty action, the buyer must prove that (1) a warranty existed, (2) the warranty has been breached, (3) the breach of the warranty proximately caused the loss suffered, and (4) notice of the breach of warranty was given to the seller. The seller has the burden of proving defenses based on the buyer's conduct. If the seller breaches his warranty, the buyer may reject or revoke acceptance of the goods. Moreover, whether the goods have been accepted or rejected, the buyer may recover a judgment against the seller for damages. Harm for which damages are recoverable includes personal injury, damage to property, and economic loss. Economic loss most commonly involves damages for loss of bargain and consequential damages for lost profits. In this section, we will examine the various types of warranties, as well as the obstacles to a cause of action for breach of warranty.

Types of Warranties

A warranty may arise out of the mere existence of a sale (a warranty of title), out of any affirmation of fact or promise made by the seller to the buyer (an express warranty), or out of the circumstances under which the sale is made (an implied warranty). In a contract for the sale of goods, it is possible to have both express and implied warranties, as well as a warranty of title. All warranties are construed as consistent with each other and cumulative, unless such construction is unreasonable.

Article 2A carries over the warranty provisions of Article 2 with relatively minor revision to reflect differences in style, leasing terminology, or leasing practices. The creation of express warranties and, except for finance leases, the imposition of the implied warranties of merchantability and fitness for a particular purpose are virtually identical to their Article 2 analogues. Article 2 and Article 2A diverge somewhat in their treatment of the warranties of title and infringement as well as in their provisions for the exclusion and modification of warranties.

Warranty of Title

Under the Code's **warranty of title,** the seller implicitly warrants (1) that the title conveyed is good and its transfer rightful and (2) that the goods are subject to no security interest or other lien (a claim on property by another for payment of debt) of which the buyer did not know at the time of contracting. In a lease, title does not transfer to the lessee. Accordingly, Article 2A's analogous provision protects the lessee's right to possession and use of the goods from the claims of other parties arising from an act or omission of the lessor.

Let us assume that Steven acquires goods from Nancy in a transaction that is void and then sells the goods to Rachel. Nancy brings an action against Rachel and recovers the goods. Steven has breached the warranty of title because he did not have good title to the goods and, therefore, his transfer of the goods to Rachel was not rightful. Accordingly, Steven is liable to Rachel for damages.

The Code does not label the warranty of title an implied warranty, even though it arises out of the sale and not out of any particular words or conduct. Instead, the Code has a separate disclaimer provision for warranty of title; thus, the Code's general disclaimer provision for implied warranties does not apply.

Express Warranties

An **express warranty** is an explicit undertaking by the seller with respect to the quality, description, condition, or performability of the goods. The undertaking may consist of an affirmation of fact or a promise that relates to the goods, a description of the goods, or a sample or model of the goods. In each of these instances, in order for an express warranty to be created, the undertaking must become or be made part of the basis of the bargain. It is not necessary, however, that the seller have a specific intention to make a warranty or use formal words such as "warrant" or "guarantee." Moreover, it is not necessary that, in order to be liable for breach of express warranty, a seller know of the falsity of a statement she makes; the seller may be acting in good faith. For example, if John mistakenly asserts to Sam that a rope will easily support 300 pounds and Sam is injured when the rope breaks while supporting only 200 pounds, John is liable for breach of an express warranty.

CREATION A seller can create an express warranty either orally or in writing. One way in which the seller may create such a warranty is by an **affirmation of fact** or a **promise** that relates to the goods (Article 2A). For example, a statement made by a seller that an automobile will get 42 miles to the gallon of gasoline or that a camera has automatic focus is an express warranty.

The Code further provides that an affirmation of the **value** of the goods or a statement purporting merely to be the seller's **opinion** or recommendation of the goods does not create a warranty (Article 2A). Such statements are not factual and do not deceive the ordinary buyer, who accepts them merely as opinions or as puffery (sales talk). A statement of value, however, may be an express warranty where the seller states the price at which the goods were purchased from a former owner, or where she gives market figures relating to sales of similar goods. These are affirmations of facts. They are statements of events, not mere opinions; and the seller is liable for breach of warranty if they are untrue. Also, although a statement of opinion by the seller is not ordinarily a warranty, the seller who is an expert and who gives an opinion as such may be liable for breach of warranty.

Practical Advice *If you are a seller, offer the buyer an opportunity to examine the goods to avoid an implied warranty for any defects that should be detected upon inspection. If you are a buyer and are offered an opportunity to examine the goods, make sure that you make a reasonable inspection of the goods.*

A seller also can create an express warranty by the use of a **description** of the goods that becomes a part of the basis of the bargain (Article 2A). Under such a warranty, the seller expressly warrants that the goods shall conform to the description. Examples include statements regarding a particular brand or type of goods, technical specifications, and blueprints.

The use of a **sample** or model is another means of creating an express warranty (Article 2A). When a sample or model is a part of the basis of the bargain, the seller expressly warrants that the entire lot of goods sold shall conform to the sample or model. A sample is a good that is actually drawn from the bulk of goods that is the subject matter of the sale. By comparison, a model is offered for inspection when the subject matter is not at hand; it is not drawn from the bulk.

The seller must deliver goods that conform to the quality and description required by the contract. In addition, the goods must possess the qualities of any sample or model used by the seller.

BASIS OF BARGAIN The Code does not require that the affirmations, promises, descriptions, samples, or models the seller makes or uses be relied on by the buyer but only that they constitute a part of the **basis of the bargain.** In other words, if they are part of the buyer's assumption underlying the sale, reliance by the buyer is presumed. Some courts merely require that the buyer know of the affirmation or promise for it to be presumed to be part of the basis of the bargain, while others require some showing of reliance.

Like statements in advertisements or catalogs, statements or promises made by the seller to the buyer prior to the sale may be express warranties, as they may form a part of the basis of the bargain. In addition, under the Code, statements or promises made by the seller subsequent to the making of the contract of sale may become express warranties even though no new consideration is given (Article 2A).

Implied Warranties

An implied warranty, unlike an express warranty, is not found in the language of the sales contract or in a specific affirmation or promise by the seller. Instead, it exists by operation of law. An **implied warranty** arises out of the circumstances under which the parties enter into their contract and depends on factors such as the type of contract or sale entered into, the seller's merchant or nonmerchant status, the conduct of the parties, and the applicability of other statutes.

Practical Advice Because the warranty of merchantability applies only to merchant sellers, when purchasing goods from a nonmerchant seller, attempt to obtain a written express warranty that the goods will be, at a minimum, of average quality and fit for ordinary purposes.

MERCHANTABILITY Under the Code, a **merchant seller** makes an implied warranty of the merchantability of goods that are of the kind in which he deals. The implied warranty of **merchantability** provides that the goods are reasonably fit for the **ordinary** purposes for which they are used, pass without objection in the trade under the contract description, and are of fair, average quality (Article 2A).

The seller must deliver goods, unless otherwise agreed, that are fit for the purposes for which goods of the same description would ordinarily be used.

FITNESS FOR PARTICULAR PURPOSE Unlike the warranty of merchantability, the implied warranty of fitness for a particular purpose applies to *any* seller, whether he is a merchant or not. The implied warranty of **fitness for a particular purpose** arises if at the time of contracting the seller had reason to know the buyer's particular purpose and to know that the buyer was relying on the seller's skill and judgment to select suitable goods (Article 2A).

The implied warranty of fitness for a particular purpose does not require any specific statement by the seller. Rather, it requires only that the seller know that the buyer, in selecting a product for her specific purpose, is relying on the seller's expertise. The buyer need not specifically inform the seller of her particular purpose; it is sufficient if the seller has reason to know it. On the other hand, the implied warranty of fitness for a particular purpose would not arise in a situation where the buyer insists on a particular product and the seller simply conveys it to her.

In contrast to the implied warranty of merchantability, the implied warranty of fitness for a particular purpose pertains to a specific purpose for, rather than the ordinary purpose of, the goods. A particular purpose may be a specific use or may relate to a special situation in which the buyer intends to use the goods. Thus, if the seller has reason to know that the buyer is purchasing a pair of shoes for mountain climbing and that the buyer is relying on the seller's judgment to furnish suitable shoes for this purpose, a sale of shoes suitable only for ordinary walking purposes would be a breach of this implied warranty. Likewise, if a buyer indicates to a seller that she needs a stamping machine to stamp 10,000 packages in an eight-hour period and that she relies upon the seller to select an appropriate machine, the seller, by selecting a machine, impliedly warrants that the machine selected will stamp 10,000 packages in an eight-hour period.

The seller must deliver goods unless otherwise agreed, that are fit for any particular purpose expressly or impliedly made known to the seller by the buyer, except when the buyer did not rely on the seller's skill and judgment when it was unreasonable for the buyer to rely on the seller.

A seller's conduct may involve both the implied warranty of merchantability *and* the implied warranty of fitness for a particular purpose.

Obstacles to Warranty Actions

A number of technical obstacles, which vary considerably from jurisdiction to jurisdiction, limit the effectiveness of warranty as a basis for recovery. These include disclaimers of warranties, limitations or modifications of warranties, privity of contract, notice of breach of warranty, and the conduct of the plaintiff.

Disclaimer of Warranties

To be effective, a **disclaimer** (negation of warranty) must be positive, explicit, unequivocal, and conspicuous. The Code calls for a reasonable construction of words or conduct to disclaim or limit warranties (Article 2A).

EXPRESS EXCLUSIONS In general, a seller cannot provide an **express warranty** and then disclaim it. A seller can, however, avoid making an express warranty by carefully refraining from making any promise or affirmation of fact relating to the goods, by refraining from making a description of the goods, or by refraining from using a sample or model in a sale (Article 2A). Oral warranties made before the execution of a written agreement containing an express disclaimer are subject to the parol evidence rule, however. Thus, if the parties intend the written contract to be the final and *complete* statement of the agreement between them, parol evidence of a warranty that *contradicts* the terms of the written contract is inadmissible.

A **warranty of title** may be excluded only by specific language or by certain circumstances, including a judicial sale or sales by sheriffs, executors, or foreclosing lienors (Article 2A). In the latter cases, the seller is clearly offering to sell only such right or title as he or a third person might have in the goods, because it is apparent that the goods are not the property of the person selling them.

To exclude or to modify an **implied warranty of merchantability,** the language of disclaimer or modification must mention *merchantability* and, in the case of a writing, must be *conspicuous.* Article 2A requires that a disclaimer of an implied warranty of merchantability mention merchantability, be in writing, and be conspicuous.

To exclude or to modify an **implied warranty of fitness for the particular purpose** of the buyer, the disclaimer must be in *writing* and *conspicuous* (Article 2A).

All implied warranties, unless the circumstances indicate otherwise, are excluded by expressions like **"as is"** or "with all faults" or by other language plainly calling the buyer's attention to the exclusion of warranties (Article 2A). Most courts require the "as is" clause to be conspicuous. Implied warranties may also be excluded by course of dealing, course of performance, or usage of trade (Article 2A).

The courts will invalidate disclaimers they consider unconscionable. The Code permits a court to limit the application of any contract or contractual provision that it finds unconscionable (Article 2A).

BUYER'S EXAMINATION OR REFUSAL TO EXAMINE If the buyer inspects the goods before entering into the contract, **implied warranties** do not apply to defects that are apparent on examination. Moreover, there is no implied warranty on defects that an examination ought to have revealed, not only when the buyer has examined the goods as fully as desired, but also when the buyer has refused to examine the goods (Article 2A).

FEDERAL LEGISLATION RELATING TO WARRANTIES OF CONSUMER GOODS To protect purchasers of consumer goods (defined as "tangible personal property normally used for personal, family or household purposes"), Congress enacted the **Magnuson-Moss Warranty Act.** The purpose of the act is to prevent deception and to make sure that consumer purchasers are adequately informed about warranties. Some courts have applied the act to leases.

The Federal Trade Commission administers and enforces the act. The commission's guidelines for the type of consumer product warranty information a seller must supply are aimed at providing the consumer with clear and useful information. More significantly, the act provides that a seller who makes a written warranty cannot disclaim any implied warranty.

Limitation or Modification of Warranties

The Code permits a seller to **limit** or **modify** the buyer's remedies for breach of warranty. One important exception to this right is the prohibition against a seller's "unconscionable" limitations or exclusions of consequential damages (Article 2A). Specifically, the "[l]imitation of consequential damages for injury to the person in the case of consumer goods is prima facie unconscionable...." In some cases, a seller may seek to impose time limits within which the warranty is effective. Except when such clauses result in unconscionability, the Code permits them; it does not, however, permit any attempt to shorten the time period for filing an action for personal injury to less than one year.

Privity of Contract

Because of the close association between warranties and contracts, a principle of law in the 19th century established that a plaintiff could not recover for breach of warranty unless he was in a contractual relationship with the defendant. This relationship is known as **privity** of contract.

Under this rule, a warranty by seller Ingrid to buyer Sylvester, who resells the goods to purchaser Lyle under a similar warranty, gives Lyle no rights against Ingrid. There is no privity of contract between Ingrid and Lyle. In the event of breach of warranty, Lyle may recover only from his seller, Sylvester, who in turn may recover from Ingrid.

Horizontal privity determines who benefits from a warranty and who may therefore sue for its breach. Horizontal privity pertains to noncontracting parties who are injured by the defective goods; this group would include users, consumers, and bystanders who are not the contracting purchaser.

The Code relaxes the requirement of horizontal privity of contract by permitting recovery on a seller's warranty, at a minimum, to members of the buyer's family or household or to a guest in his home. The Code provides three alternative sections from which the states may select. Alternative A, the least comprehensive and most widely adopted alternative, provides that a seller's warranty, whether express or implied, extends to any natural person who is in the family or household of the buyer or who is a guest in his home, if it is reasonable to expect that such person may use, consume, or be affected by the goods, and who is injured in person by breach of the warranty. Alternative B extends Alternative A to "any natural person who may reasonably be expected to use, consume or be affected by the goods." Alternative C further expands the coverage of the section to any person, not just natural persons, and to property damage as well as personal injury. (A natural person would not include artificial entities such as corporations, for example.) A seller, however, may not exclude or limit the operation of this section for injury to a person. Article 2A provides the same alternatives with slight modifications.

Nonetheless, the Code was not intended to establish outer boundaries for third-party recovery for injuries caused by defective goods. Rather, it sets a minimum standard that the states may expand through case law. Most states have judicially accepted the Code's invitation to relax the requirements of horizontal privity and, for all practical purposes, have *eliminated* horizontal privity in warranty cases.

Practical Advice If you are a seller of consumer goods and wish to disclaim the implied warranties, make sure that you do not provide any written express warranties.

Vertical privity, in determining who is liable for breach of warranty, pertains to remote sellers within the chain of distribution, such as manufacturers and wholesalers, with whom the consumer purchaser has not entered into a contract. Although the Code adopts a neutral position regarding vertical privity, the courts in most states have eliminated the requirement of vertical privity in warranty actions.

Notice of Breach of Warranty

When a buyer has accepted a tender of goods that are not as warranted by the seller, she is required to notify the seller of any breach of warranty, express or implied, as well as any other breach, within a reasonable time after she has discovered or should have discovered it. If the buyer fails to notify the seller of any breach within a reasonable time, she is barred from any remedy against the seller (Article 2A). In determining whether notice was provided in a reasonable period of time, commercial standards apply to a merchant buyer while different standards apply to a retail consumer, so as not to deprive a good faith consumer of her remedy.

Plaintiff's Conduct

Because of the development of warranty liability in the law of sales and contracts, **contributory negligence** of the buyer is no defense to an action against the seller for breach of warranty. Comparative negligence statutes do apply, however, to warranty actions in some states.

If the buyer discovers a defect in the goods that may cause injury and nevertheless proceeds to make use of them, he will not be permitted to recover damages from the seller for loss or injuries caused by such use. This is not contributory negligence but **voluntary assumption** of a known risk.

Strict Liability in Tort

The most recent and far-reaching development in the field of product liability is that of strict liability in tort. All but a very few states have now accepted the concept, which is embodied in **Section 402A** of the Restatement, Second, of Torts.

A new Restatement of the Law, Third, Torts: Products Liability, has recently been promulgated. It is far more comprehensive than the second Restatement in dealing with the liability of commercial sellers and distributors of goods for harm caused by their products.

Section 402A imposes **strict liability in tort** on merchant sellers both for personal injuries and for property damage that result from selling a product in a *defective condition, unreasonably dangerous* to the user or consumer. Section 402A applies even though "the seller has exercised all possible care in the preparation and sale of his product." Thus, negligence is not the basis of liability in strict liability cases. The essential distinction between the two doctrines is that actions in strict liability do not require the plaintiff to prove that the injury-producing defect resulted from any specific act of negligence of the seller. Strict liability actions focus on the *product*, not on the *conduct* of the manufacturer. Courts in strict liability cases are interested in the fact that a product defect arose—not in *how* it arose. Thus, even an "innocent" manufacturer—one who has not been negligent—may be liable if his product turns out to contain a defect that injures a consumer. Although liability for personal injuries caused by a defective condition that makes goods unreasonably dangerous is usually associated with sales of such goods, this type of liability also exists with respect to **leases** and **bailments** of defective goods.

> **Strict liability in tort** Merchant seller is liable for selling a product in a defective condition, unreasonably dangerous to the user.

Requirements of Strict Liability in Tort

Section 402A imposes strict liability in tort if (1) the defendant was engaged in the business of selling a product such as the defective one; (2) the defendant sold the product in a defective condition; (3) the defective condition made the product unreasonably dangerous to the user or consumer or to his property; (4) the defect in the product existed when it left the defendant's hands; (5) the plaintiff sustained physical harm or property damage by using or consuming the product; and (6) the defective condition was the proximate cause of the injury or damage.

This liability is imposed by law as a matter of public policy and does not depend on contract, either express or implied. Nor does it require reliance by the injured user or consumer on any statements made by the manufacturer or seller. It is not limited to persons in a buyer-seller relationship; thus, neither vertical nor horizontal privity is required. No notice of the defect is required to have been given by the injured user or consumer. The liability, furthermore, generally is not subject to disclaimer, exclusion, or modification by contractual agreement. Rather, it is solely in tort and arises out of the common law. It is not governed by the provisions of the Uniform Commercial Code. The majority of courts considering the question, however, have held that Section 402A imposes liability only for injury to person and damage to property, not for commercial loss (such as loss of bargain or profits), which is recoverable in an action for breach of warranty.

Merchant Sellers

Section 402A imposes liability only upon a person who is in the *business* of selling the product involved. It does not apply to an occasional seller, such as a person who trades in his used car or who sells his lawn mower to a neighbor. In this respect, the section is similar to the implied warranty of merchantability, which applies only to sales by a merchant of goods that are of the type in which he deals. A growing number of jurisdictions recognize the applicability of strict liability in tort even to merchant-sellers of *used* goods.

Defective Condition

In an action to recover damages under the rule of strict liability in tort, though the plaintiff must prove a defective condition in the product, she is not required to prove how or why or in what manner the product became defective. The plaintiff must, however, show that at the time she was injured, the condition of the product was not substantially changed from the condition in which the manufacturer or seller sold it. In general, defects may arise through faulty manufacturing, through faulty product design, or through inadequate warnings, labeling, packaging, or instructions.

MANUFACTURING DEFECT A **manufacturing defect** occurs when the product is not properly made; that is, it fails to meet its own manufacturing specifications. For instance, suppose a chair is manufactured with legs designed to be attached by four screws and glue. If the chair was produced without the appropriate screws, this would constitute a manufacturing defect.

DESIGN DEFECT A product contains a **design defect** when, despite its being produced as specified, the product is dangerous or hazardous because its design is inadequate. Design defects can result from a number of causes, including poor engineering, poor choice of materials, and poor packaging. An example of a design defect that received great notoriety was the fuel tank assembly of the Ford Pinto. A number of courts found the car to be inadequately designed because the fuel tank had been placed too close to its rear axle, causing the tank to rupture when the car was hit from behind.

Section 402A provides no guidance in determining which injury-producing designs should give rise to strict liability and which should not. Consequently, the courts have adopted widely varying approaches in applying 402A to defective design cases. Nevertheless, virtually none of the courts has upheld a judgment in a strict liability case in which the defendant demonstrated that the **"state of the art"** was such that the manufacturer (1) neither knew nor could have known of a product hazard or (2) if he knew of the product hazard, could have designed a safer product given existing technology. Thus, almost all courts evaluate the design of a product on the basis of the dangers that the manufacturer could have known at the time he produced the product.

FAILURE TO WARN A seller is under a duty to provide adequate warning of a product's possible danger, to provide appropriate directions for its safe use, and to package the product safely. Warnings do not, however, always protect sellers from liability. A seller who could have designed or manufactured a product in a safe yet cost-effective manner, but who instead chooses to produce the product cheaply and to provide a warning of the product's hazards, cannot escape liability simply by the warning. Warnings usually will avoid liability only if no cost-effective designs or manufacturing processes are available to reduce a risk of injury.

The duty to give a warning arises from a foreseeable danger of physical harm that could result from the normal or probable use of the product and from the likelihood that, unless warned, the user or consumer would not ordinarily be aware of such danger or hazard.

Unreasonably Dangerous

Section 402A liability applies only if the defective product is unreasonably dangerous to the user or consumer. An **unreasonably dangerous** product is one that contains a danger beyond that which would be contemplated by the ordinary consumer who purchases it with common knowledge of its characteristics. Thus, Comment i to Section 402A describes the difference between reasonable and unreasonable dangers: "good whiskey is not unreasonably dangerous merely because it will make some people drunk, and is especially dangerous to alcoholics; but bad whiskey, containing a dangerous amount of fuel oil, is unreasonably dangerous. Good tobacco is not unreasonably dangerous merely because the effects of smoking may be harmful; but tobacco containing something like marijuana may be unreasonably dangerous. Good butter is not unreasonably dangerous merely because, if such be the case, it deposits cholesterol in the arteries and leads to heart attacks; but bad butter, contaminated with poisonous fish oil, is unreasonably dangerous." Most courts have left the question of reasonable consumer expectations to the jury.

Obstacles to Recovery

Few of the obstacles to recovery in warranty cases present serious problems to plaintiffs in strict liability actions brought pursuant to Section 402A because this section was drafted largely to avoid such obstacles.

Disclaimers and Notice

Comment m to Section 402A provides that the basis of strict liability rests solely in tort and therefore is not subject to contractual defenses. The comment specifically states that strict product liability is not governed by the Code, that it is not affected by contractual limitations or disclaimers, and that it is not subject to any requirement that notice be given to the seller by the injured party within a reasonable time. Nevertheless, most courts have *allowed* clear and specific disclaimers of Section 402A liability in *commercial* transactions between merchants of relatively equal economic power.

Privity

With respect to horizontal privity, the strict liability in tort of manufacturers and other sellers extends not only to buyers, users, and consumers, but also to injured bystanders.

In terms of vertical privity, strict liability in tort imposes liability on any seller who is engaged in the business of selling the product, including a wholesaler or distributor as well as the manufacturer and retailer. The rule of strict liability in tort also applies to the manufacturer of a defective component that is used in a larger product if the manufacturer of the finished product has made no essential change in the component.

Plaintiff's Conduct

Many product liability defenses relate to the conduct of the plaintiff. The claim common to all of them is that the plaintiff's improper conduct so contributed to the plaintiff's injury that it would be unfair to blame the product or its seller.

CONTRIBUTORY NEGLIGENCE **Contributory negligence** is conduct on the part of the plaintiff (1) that falls below the standard to which he should conform for his own protection and (2) that is the legal cause of the plaintiff's harm. Because strict liability is designed to assess liability without fault, Section 402A rejects contributory negligence as a defense. Thus, a seller cannot defend a strict liability lawsuit on the basis of a plaintiff's negligent failure to discover a defect or to guard against its possibility. But, as discussed later, contributory negligence in the form of an assumption of the risk can bar recovery under Section 402A.

COMPARATIVE NEGLIGENCE Under **comparative negligence,** the court apportions damages between the parties in proportion to the degree of fault or negligence it finds against them. Despite Section 402A's bar of contributory negligence in strict liability cases, most courts apply comparative negligence to strict liability cases. (Some courts use the term *comparative responsibility* rather than *comparative negligence.*) There are two basic types of comparative negligence or comparative responsibility. One is pure comparative responsibility, which simply reduces the plaintiff's recovery in proportion to her fault, whatever that may be. Thus, the recovery of a plaintiff found to be 80 percent at fault in causing an accident in which she suffered a $100,000 loss would be limited to 20 percent of her damages, or $20,000. Under the other type of negligence, modified comparative responsibility, the plaintiff recovers according to the general principles of comparative responsibility *unless* she is more than 50 percent responsible for her injuries, in which case she recovers nothing. The majority of comparative negligence states follows the modified comparative responsibility approach.

VOLUNTARY ASSUMPTION OF THE RISK Assumption of risk is a defense in an action based on strict liability in tort. Basically, **assumption of the risk** is the plaintiff's express or implied consent to encounter a known danger. Thus, a person who drives an automobile after realizing that the brakes are not working and an employee who attempts to remove a foreign object from a high-speed roller press without shutting off the power have assumed the risk of their own injuries.

To establish such a defense, the defendant must show that (1) the plaintiff actually knew and appreciated the particular risk or danger the defect created; (2) the plaintiff voluntarily encountered the risk while realizing the danger; and (3) the plaintiff's decision to encounter the known risk was unreasonable.

MISUSE OR ABUSE OF THE PRODUCT Closely connected to voluntary assumption of the risk is the valid defense of misuse or abuse of the product by the injured party. **Misuse** or **abuse** occurs when the injured party knows, or should know, that he is using the product in a manner the seller did not contemplate. The major difference between misuse or abuse and assumption of the risk is that the former includes actions that the injured party does not know to be dangerous, whereas the latter does not include such conduct. Instances of such misuse or abuse include standing on a rocking chair to change a lightbulb or using a lawn mower to trim hedges. The courts, however, have significantly limited this defense by requiring that the misuse or abuse not be foreseeable by the seller. If a use is foreseeable, then the seller must take measures to guard against it.

Subsequent Alteration

Section 402A provides that liability exists only if the product reaches "the user or consumer without substantial change in the condition in which it is sold." Accordingly, most, but not all, courts would not hold a manufacturer liable for a faulty carburetor if a car dealer had removed the part and made significant changes in it before reinstalling it in an automobile.

Statute of Repose

A number of lawsuits have been brought against manufacturers many years after a product was first sold. In response, many states have adopted statutes of repose. These enactments limit the period—typically between 6 and 12 years—for which a manufacturer is liable for injury caused by a defective product. After the statutory time period has elapsed, a manufacturer ceases to be liable for such harm.

Law and Finance

Relation Between Law and Finance

Various laws impact the finance function in an effort to protect investors and creditors from misinformation and fraudulent activities. Topics such as bankruptcy, debt securities, sinking fund requirements, uniform commercial code, equity securities, stockholders' equity, and dividends are discussed in this section.

Bankruptcy

Organizations can go bankrupt when they have liquidity problems, meaning inability to meet financial obligations such as debt payments, wages, and taxes. When a business becomes insolvent (meaning having liquidity problems), it does not have enough cash to meet scheduled interest and principal payments; that is, the firm cannot service its debt obligations. A decision must be made whether to dissolve the firm through liquidation or to permit it to reorganize and thus continue. Chapter 7 of the Bankruptcy Act governs the liquidation issues while Chapter 11 of the Act addresses the reorganization issues. The final decision whether to liquidate or reorganize a firm is made by a federal bankruptcy court judge. This decision depends on whether the value of the reorganized firm is likely to be greater than the value of the firm's assets if they were sold off piecemeal.

Liquidation

Liquidation occurs if the firm is deemed to be too far gone to be saved—if it is "worth more dead than alive." If the bankruptcy court orders a liquidation, assets are distributed to secured creditors first, then wages and taxes are paid; the remaining proceeds are distributed to unsecured creditors, to preferred stockholders, and finally to common stockholders (if anything is left) in that order. The priority of claims established by federal bankruptcy statutes must be followed when distributing the proceeds from a liquidating firm.

Reorganization

In a reorganization, a committee of unsecured creditors is appointed by the court to negotiate with management on the terms of a potential reorganization. The reorganization plan might call for a restructuring of the firms' debt, in which case the interest rate might be reduced, the term to maturity lengthened, or some of the debt might be exchanged for equity. The point of the restructuring is to reduce the financial charges to a level that the firm's cash flows can support. Of course, the common stockholders also have to give up something—they normally see their position eroded as a result of additional shares of equity being given to debtholders in exchange for accepting a reduced amount of debt principal and interest. A trustee might be appointed by the court to oversee the reorganization, or the existing management might be allowed to retain control over the organization.

Debt Securities

Debt securities, which include bonds and notes, do not represent an ownership interest in the company. Rather, they create a debtor-creditor relationship between the corporation and the debtholder. The board of directors can issue bonds without the specific authorization or consent of the stockholders. A bond indenture is a form of contract between the bond issuers and the bondholders. Legal restrictions are designed to ensure that the company does nothing to cause the quality of bonds to deteriorate after they have been issued. The indenture is the legal document that spells out the rights of the bondholders and the corporation that issues the bonds.

Major funding sources of a corporation include debt securities, equity securities, and retained earnings.

Restrictive covenants cover such points as (1) early payoff of the bond, (2) maintenance of times-interest-earned ratio, (3) payment of dividends when earnings do not meet certain specifications, and (4) maintenance of current ratio and the debt ratios at specified levels. Indenture covenants not only influence a firm's financing decision, but also can force a company into bankruptcy if the covenants are violated.

Sinking Fund Requirements

Sinking fund is a required annual payment designed to amortize a bond or preferred stock issue. It is a legal provision that facilitates the orderly retirement of a bond issue. A failure to meet the sinking fund requirement causes the bond issue to become default, which might force the company into bankruptcy. In a way, the sinking fund was created to protect from possible bankruptcy.

Uniform Commercial Code

The uniform commercial code (UCC) is a system of standards that simplifies procedures for establishing short-term loan security. The heart of the UCC is the Security Agreement, a standardized document on which the specific pledged assets are listed. The assets can be items of equipment, accounts receivables, or inventory. For example, accounts receivables are either pledged or factored as security for short-term credit. Methods such as blanket liens, trust receipts, and warehouse receipts are used for inventory as security for short-term credit.

Equity Securities

Equity securities represent an ownership interest in the corporation and include both common and preferred stock. All states have statutes regulating the issuance and sale of corporate shares. **"Blue sky laws"** are statutes containing provisions prohibiting fraud in the sale of securities. In addition, a number of states require the registration of securities, and some states also regulate investment brokers, dealers, and others engaged in the selling and buying of securities. U.S. Federal statutes such as the Securities Act of 1933 and 1934 regulate the sale of securities through the use of the mails or otherwise engaged in interstate commerce.

Stockholders' Equity

A company's stockholders' equity section of the balance sheet contains three sections: contributed capital, retained earnings, and treasury stock.

- **Contributed capital** represents the investments made by the stockholders in the corporation. It includes (1) preferred stock with its par value and number of shares authorized, issued, and outstanding; (2) common stock with its par value and number of shares authorized, issued, and outstanding; and (3) paid-in capital in excess of par value. Outstanding shares that are still in circulation are equal to authorized shares minus issued shares minus treasury shares. Issued shares that are bought back and held by the firm are called *treasury shares*. Due to treasury shares, a firm can have more shares issued than are currently outstanding.

  Stockholders' equity is contributed capital plus retained earnings minus treasury stock.

- **Retained earnings** are earnings of the corporation, since its inception, less any losses and dividends, or transfers to contributed capital. They are not a pool of funds or cash to be distributed to the stockholders; instead, they represent earnings reinvested in the corporation. They represent stockholders' claims to the assets of the company resulting from profitable operations. A part of the retained earnings can be restricted or reserved for special transactions.
- **Treasury stock** is capital stock, either common or preferred, that has been issued and later reacquired by the issuing company and has not subsequently been resold or retired. A company can buy its own stock back for strategic reasons by purchasing it from the open market like any other investor.

Par value or stated value is the amount of face value per share and make up the **legal (stated) capital** of the corporation. A company cannot declare a dividend that would cause stockholders' equity to fall below the legal capital of the firm. Therefore, the par value is an arbitrary figure or a minimum cushion of capital that protects creditors and owners.

169. BUSINESS LAW

Dividends

Corporate law does not require companies to pay dividends. It is the company's board of directors' decision whether to pay a dividend or not, and if decided to pay, how much to pay and when. When decided, the dividend should be paid to outstanding stockholders of record only. Usually, factors such as working capital requirements, stockholder expectations, tax consequences, and cash availability influence the board in forming a dividend distribution policy. The ex-dividend date is controlled by law, which is two business days before the holder-of-record date. Dividends are not expenses of a corporation, hence cannot be deducted from taxes. Instead, dividends are distribution of capital to investors and stockholders.

Most states do not allow the board of directors to declare a dividend that exceeds retained earnings. When a dividend exceeds retained earnings, it is called a *liquidating dividend*, and is usually paid when a company is going out of business or reducing its operations. It is the availability of cash, not the amount of retained earnings, that decides how much dividend to pay and when. Other forms of dividends include property dividends. Neither a stock dividend nor a stock split is a distribution of assets to the stockholders.

Two types of dividend tests include the cash flow test, required by all states, and the balance sheet test, required by some states.

There are two types of legal restrictions placed on dividends. One is based on cash flow test and the other one is based on balance sheet test. The cash flow test (also called *equity insolvency test*) prohibits the payment of any dividends when the corporation either is insolvent or would become so through the payment of the dividend. Insolvency is the inability to pay debts as they become due in the usual course of business. It can be translated into difficulty of cash flows.

The balance sheet test focuses on few specific tests: (1) all states prohibit dividends paid from capital surplus or stated (legal) capital; instead, they should be paid only from earned surplus; (2) less restrictive states permit dividends to be paid out of either earned surplus or capital surplus; and (3) net asset test, which permits a company to pay dividends as long as the total assets after dividends payment is more than its total liabilities plus payments to preferential stockholders.

Surplus is the amount by which the net assets of a corporation exceeds its stated capital. Net assets is total assets minus total debts. Earned surplus is the amount of undistributed net profits, income, gains, and losses, computed from the date of incorporation. Capital surplus is the amount of surplus other than the earned surplus.

Specific Legal Rules and Restrictions Related to Finance

- A corporation may not redeem or purchase its redeemable shares when insolvent or when such redemption or purchase would render it insolvent or would reduce its net assets below a certain level.
- A corporation may purchase its own shares only out of earned surplus or, if the articles of incorporation permit or if the stockholders approve, out of capital surplus. It cannot purchase when it is insolvent or when such purchase would make it insolvent.
- When there is an exchange of stock for noncash assets, the board of directors have the right to determine the fair market value of the property.
- A share of stock that originally was issued at par value or greater and fully paid for, and that then was reacquired as treasury stock, can be reissued at less than par value without any negative financial or legal consequences.
- If a corporation decides that it will not reissue stock it has purchased (treasury stock), it can retire the stock with the approval of its stockholders.
- Preferred stockholders have a priority over common stockholders in the event of liquidation of a firm.

Law and Information Technology

Laws, directives, and regulations exist to protect consumers, industries, and the society as a whole. They do not normally provide detailed instructions for protecting computer-related assets (e.g., hardware, software, and data). Instead, they specify requirements such as restricting the availability of personal data to authorized users. Handbooks or manuals are needed to provide detailed instructions, in developing an effective, overall security approach, and in selecting cost-effective controls to meet such requirements. IT laws deal with IT security goals such as confidentiality (privacy), integrity, and availability.

Law and Quality

Product Liability Chain

Product liability is becoming a real issue to manufacturers worldwide. Generally speaking, product liability claims fall into one of three legal theories: breach of contract, negligence (fault liability), or strict liability. Breach of contract is where one party violates the terms of the contract. Negligence refers to the failure to use such care as a reasonably prudent and careful person would use under similar circumstances. Strict liability says that a seller is liable for any and all defective or hazardous products that unduly threaten a consumer's personal safety. All laws point to product sellers, distributors, post-sale duties, failure to recall, successor liability, causation, affirmative defenses, disclaimers, and apportionment of fault.

Primary Causes

The primary causes of a product liability lawsuit include design defects, engineering and production errors, and inadequate warnings and instructions. Design defects lead to inferior product quality and eventual product recalls.

Applicable Laws

The U.S. Consumer Product Safety Commission is an independent regulatory agency responsible for protecting the public from unreasonable risks of injury and death associated with consumer products. The act has jurisdiction over many consumer products used in and around the home, in schools, and in recreation. The act requires U.S. manufacturers of consumer products to report information about settled or adjudicated lawsuits and product recalls.

The Magnuson-Moss Warranty Act is the U.S. federal law that governs consumer product warranties. The act requires manufacturers and sellers of consumer products to provide consumers with detailed information about warranty coverage. In addition, it affects both the rights of consumers and the obligations of warrantors under written warranties.

Possible Actions

Actions that can be taken by manufacturers and others involved in the product liability chain include the following:

- Effective product design reviews conducted at predefined time-frames by design team. This includes introductory design reviews conducted at the new product concept stage, preliminary design reviews performed by engineering and production personnel, final design reviews conducted before actual production and final assembly of the product, and post-production design reviews to improve future efforts based on past experience. The benefit from the product design review is decreased design defects from detecting engineering and production errors and improved product quality.
- Effective product safety reviews conducted by a safety team after the product design reviews. These reviews include preliminary hazards analysis, failure mode and effects analysis, and fault tree analysis. The benefit from the product safety review is decreased design defects and overall improved product quality.
- Separate product warnings from instructions. The former call attention to danger; the latter prescribe procedures for efficient use of the product and for avoiding danger. A manufacturer is still liable for instructions that failed to alert the user to the danger they seek to avert, or where a warning alerts the user to the danger but does not enable him to avoid it. First, the manufacturer should address the instructions needed for the operation and servicing of the product. Second, the manufacturer needs to identify the critical elements the end user should be warned of in the handling and operation of the product, as well as where such warnings should be placed.
- Ensure that suppliers and subcontractors, small or large, have product liability insurance prior to being selected.
- When confronted with developing a product recall notice, do not downplay the actual hazard in the official notice. Vague, incomplete, or incorrect information communicated to product users during recall can even lead to image problems and product liability lawsuits. It is good to be honest and open-minded. Use of news releases, posters, and toll-free numbers, and mailing of personal letters to consumers, retailers, and distributors should be encouraged.

169. BUSINESS LAW

Managerial Economics

Value Maximization

Effective managerial decision making is the process of arriving at the best solution to a problem. If only one solution is possible, then no decision problem exists. When alternative courses of action are available, the best decision is the one that produces a result most consistent with managerial objectives. The process of arriving at the best managerial decision is the goal of economic optimization and the focus of managerial economics.

Optimal Decisions

Should the quality of inputs be enhanced to better meet low-cost import competition? Is a necessary reduction in labor costs efficiently achieved through an across-the-board decrease in staffing, or is it better to make targeted cutbacks? Following an increase in product demand, is it preferable to increase managerial staff, line personnel, or both? These are the types of questions facing managers on a regular basis that require a careful consideration of basic economic relations. Answers to these questions depend on the objectives and preferences of management. Just as there is no single "best" purchase decision for all customers at all times, there is no single "best" investment decision for all managers at all times. When alternative courses of action are available, the decision that produces a result most consistent with managerial objectives is the **optimal decision.**

Optimal decision Choice alternative that produces a result most consistent with managerial objectives.

A challenge that must be met in the decision-making process is characterizing the desirability of decision alternatives in terms of the objectives of the organization. Decision makers must recognize all available choices and portray them in terms of appropriate costs and benefits. The description of decision alternatives is greatly enhanced through application of the principles of managerial economics. Managerial economics also provides tools for analyzing and evaluating decision alternatives. Economic concepts and methodology are used to select the optimal course of action in light of available options and objectives.

Principles of economic analysis form the basis for describing demand, cost, and profit relations. Once basic economic relations are understood, the tools and techniques of optimization can be applied to find the best course of action. Most important, the theory and process of optimization gives practical insight concerning the value maximization theory of the firm. Optimization techniques are helpful because they offer a realistic means for dealing with the complexities of goal-oriented managerial activities.

Maximizing the Value of the Firm

In managerial economics, the primary objective of management is assumed to be maximization of the value of the firm. This *value maximization* objective is expressed in equation 1.1:

$$\text{Value} = \sum_{t=1}^{n} \frac{\text{Profit}_t}{(1=i)^t} = \sum_{t=1}^{n} \frac{\text{Total Revenue}_t - \text{Total Cost}_t}{(1+i)^t} \tag{1.1}$$

Maximizing equation 1.1 is a complex task that involves consideration of future revenues, costs, and discount rates. Total revenues are directly determined by the quantity sold and the prices received. Factors that affect prices and the quantity sold include the choice of products made available for sale, marketing strategies, pricing and distribution policies, competition, and the general state of the economy. Cost analysis includes a detailed examination of the prices and availability of various input factors, alternative production schedules, production methods, and so on. Finally, the relation between an appropriate discount rate and the company's mix of products and both operating and financial leverage must be determined. All these factors affect the value of the firm as described in equation 1.1.

To determine the optimal course of action, marketing, production, and financial decisions must be integrated within a decision analysis framework. Similarly, decisions related to personnel retention and development, organization structure, and long-term business strategy must be combined into a single integrated system that shows how managerial initiatives affect all parts of the firm. The value maximization model provides an attractive basis for such an integration. Using the principles of economic analysis, it is also possible to analyze and compare the higher costs or lower benefits of alternative, suboptimal courses of action.

The complexity of completely integrated decision analysis—or global optimization—confines its use to major planning decisions. For many day-to-day operating decisions, managers typically use less complicated, partial optimization techniques. For example, the marketing department is usually required to determine the price and advertising strategy that achieves some sales goal given the firm's current product line and marketing budget. Alternatively, a production department might minimize the cost of output at a stated quality level.

The decision process, whether it is applied to fully integrated or partial optimization problems, involves two steps. First, important economic relations must be expressed in analytical terms. Second, various optimization techniques must be applied to determine the best, or optimal, solution in the light of managerial objectives. The following material introduces a number of concepts that are useful for expressing decision problems in an economic framework.

Basic Economic Relations

Tables are the simplest and most direct form for presenting economic data. When these data are displayed electronically in the format of an accounting income statement or balance sheet, the tables are referred to as **spreadsheets**. When the underlying relation between economic data is simple, tables and spreadsheets may be sufficient for analytical purposes. In such instances, a simple **graph** or visual representation of the data can provide valuable insight. Complex economic relations require more sophisticated methods of expression. An **equation** is an expression of the functional relationship or connection among economic variables. When the underlying relation among economic variables is uncomplicated, equations offer a compact means for data description; when underlying relations are complex, equations are helpful because they permit the powerful tools of mathematical and statistical analysis to be used.

Functional Relations: Equations

The easiest way to examine basic economic concepts is to consider the functional relations incorporated in the basic valuation model. Consider the relation between output, Q, and total revenue, TR. Using functional notation, total revenue is

$$TR = f(Q) \tag{1.2}$$

Equation 1.2 is read, "Total revenue is a function of output." The value of the dependent variable (total revenue) is determined by the independent variable (output). The variable to the left of the equal sign is called the **dependent variable.** Its value depends on the size of the variable or variables to the right of the equal sign. Variables on the right-hand side of the equal sign are called **independent variables.** Their values are determined independently of the functional relation expressed by the equation.

Equation 1.2 does not indicate the specific relation between output and total revenue; it merely states that some relation exists. Equation 1.3 provides a more precise expression of this functional relation:

$$TR = P \times Q \tag{1.3}$$

where P represents the price at which each unit of Q is sold. Total revenue is equal to price times the quantity sold. If price is constant at $1.50 regardless of the quantity sold, the relation between quantity sold and total revenue is

$$TR = \$1.50 \times Q \tag{1.4}$$

Data in Exhibit 100.32 are specified by equation 1.4 and graphically illustrated in Exhibit 100.33.

Exhibit 100.32 *Relation Between Total Revenue and Output; Total Revenue = $1.50 × Output*

Total Revenue	Output
$1.50	1
3.00	2
4.50	3
6.00	4
7.50	5
9.00	6

Exhibit 100.33 *Relation Between Total Revenue and Output*

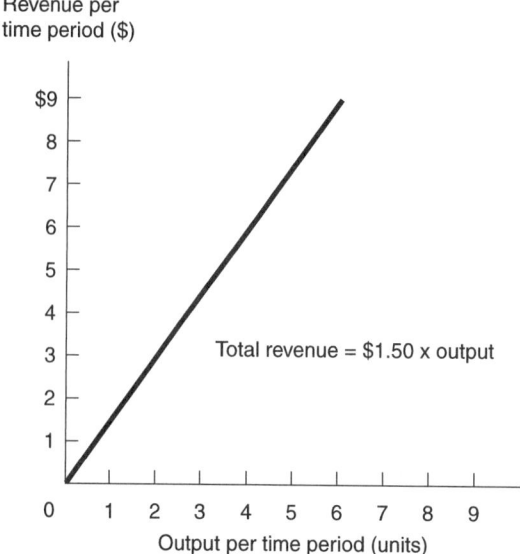

Exhibit 100.34 *Total, Marginal, and Average Relations for a Hypothetical Profit Function*

Units of Output Q (1)	Total Profits π^a (2)	Marginal Profits $\Delta\pi^b$ (3)	Average Profits $\overline{\pi}^c$ (4)
0	$ 0	$ 0	—
1	19	19	$19
2	52	33	26
3	93	41	31
4	136	43	34
5	175	39	35
6	210	35	35
7	217	7	31
8	208	−9	26

[a] The Greek letter π (pi) is frequently used in economics and business to denote profits.
[b] The symbol Δ (delta) denotes difference or change. Thus, marginal profit is expressed as $\Delta\pi = \pi_Q - \pi_{Q-1}$.
[c] Average profit ($\overline{\pi}$) equals total profit (π) divided by total output (Q): $\overline{\pi} = \pi/Q$.

Total, Average, and Marginal Relations

Total, average, and marginal relations are very useful in optimization analysis. Whereas the definitions of totals and averages are well known, the meaning of marginals needs further explanation. A **marginal** relation is the change in the dependent variable caused by a one-unit change in an independent variable. For example, **marginal revenue** is the change in total revenue associated with a one-unit change in output; **marginal cost** is the change in total cost following a one-unit change in output; and **marginal profit** is the change in total profit due to a one-unit change in output.

Exhibit 100.34 shows the relation among totals, marginals, and averages for a simple profit function. Columns 1 and 2 display output and total profits. Column 3 shows the marginal profit earned for a one-unit change in output, whereas column 4 gives the average profit per unit at each level of output. The marginal profit earned on the first unit of output is $19. This is the change from $0 profits earned when zero units of output are sold to the $19 profit earned when one unit is produced and sold. The $33 marginal profit associated with the second unit of output is the increase in total profits (= $52 − $19) that results when output is increased from one to two units. When marginal profit is positive, total profit is increasing; when marginal profit is negative, total profit is decreasing. Exhibit 100.35 illustrates this point. The marginal profit associated with each of the first seven units of output is positive, and total profits increase with output over this range. Because marginal profit of the eighth unit is negative, profits are reduced if output is raised to that level. Maximization of the profit function—or any function, for that matter—occurs at the point where the marginal switches from positive to negative.

When the marginal is greater than the average, the average must be increasing. For example, if a firm operates five retail stores with average annual sales of $350,000 per store and it opens a sixth store (the marginal store) that generates sales of $400,000, average sales per store will increase. If sales at the new (marginal) store are less than $350,000, average sales per store will decrease. Exhibit 100.35 also illustrates the relation between marginal and average values. In going from four units of output to five, the marginal profit of $39 is greater than the $34 average profit at four units; therefore, average profit increases to $35. The $35 marginal profit of the sixth unit is the same as the average profit for the first five units, so average profit remains identical between five and six units. Finally, the marginal profit of the seventh unit is below the average profit at six units, causing average profit to fall.

Marginal Analysis in Decision Making

Marginal analysis gives clear rules to follow for optimal resource allocation. As a result, geometric relations between totals and marginals offer a fruitful basis for examining the role of marginal analysis in managerial decision making.

Therefore, in determining the optimal activity level for a firm, the marginal relation tells us that so long as the increase in revenues associated with expanding output exceeds the increase in costs, continued expansion will be profitable. The optimal output level is determined when marginal revenue is equal to marginal cost, marginal profit is zero, and total profit is maximized.

Incremental Concept in Economic Analysis

The marginal concept is a key component of the economic decision-making process. It is important to recognize, however, that marginal relations measure only the effect associated with *unitary changes* in output or some other important decision variable. Many managerial decisions involve a consideration of changes that are broader in scope. For example, a manager might be interested in analyzing the potential effects on revenues, costs, and profits of a 25 percent increase in the firm's production level. Alternatively, a manager might want to analyze the profit impact of introducing an entirely new product line or assess the cost impact of changing the entire production system. In all managerial decisions, the study of *differences* or *changes* is the key element in the selection of an optimal course of action. The marginal concept, although correct for analyzing unitary changes, is too narrow to provide a general methodology for evaluating alternative courses of action.

The incremental concept is the economist's generalization of the marginal concept. Incremental analysis involves examining the impact of alternative managerial decisions or courses of action on revenues, costs, and profit. It focuses on changes or differences between the available alternatives. The **incremental change** is the change resulting from a given managerial decision. For example, the incremental revenue of a new item in a firm's product line is measured as the difference between the firm's total revenue before and after the new product is introduced.

Incremental change Total difference resulting from a decision.

Incremental Profits

Fundamental relations of incremental analysis are essentially the same as those of marginal analysis. **Incremental profit** is the profit gain or loss associated with a given managerial decision. Total profit increases so long as incremental profit is positive. When incremental profit is negative, total profit declines. Similarly, incremental profit is positive (and total profit increases) if the incremental revenue associated with a decision exceeds the incremental cost. The incremental concept is so intuitively obvious that it is easy to overlook both its significance in managerial decision making and the potential for difficulty in correctly applying it.

Incremental profit Gain or loss associated with a given managerial decision.

For this reason, the incremental concept is often violated in practice. For example, a firm may refuse to sublet excess warehouse space for $5,000 per month because it figures its cost as $7,500 per month—a price paid for a long-term lease on the facility. However, if the warehouse space represents excess capacity with no current value to the company, its historical cost of $7,500 per month is irrelevant and should be disregarded. The firm would forego $5,000 in profits by turning down the offer to sublet the excess warehouse space. Similarly, any firm that adds a standard allocated charge for fixed costs and overhead to the true incremental cost of production runs the risk of turning down profitable sales.

Care must also be exercised to ensure against incorrectly assigning overly low incremental costs to a decision. Incremental decisions involve a time dimension that simply cannot be ignored. Not only must all current revenues and costs associated with a given decision be considered, but any likely future revenues and costs must also be incorporated in the analysis. For example, assume that the excess warehouse space described earlier came about following a downturn in the overall economy. Also, assume that the excess warehouse space was sublet for one year at a price of $5,000 per month, or a total of $60,000. An incremental loss might be experienced if the firm later had to lease additional, more costly space to accommodate an unexpected increase in production. If $75,000 had to be spent to replace the sublet warehouse facility, the decision to sublet would involve an incremental loss of $15,000. To be sure, making accurate projections concerning the future pattern of revenues and costs is risky and subject to error. Nevertheless, they cannot be ignored in incremental analysis.

Another example of the incremental concept involves measurement of the incremental revenue resulting from a new product line. Incremental revenue in this case includes not only the revenue received from sale of the new product but also any change in the revenues generated by the remainder of the firm's product line. Incremental revenues include any revenue resulting from increased sales of another product, where that increase was the result of adding the new product to the firm's line. Similarly, if the new item took sales away from another of the firm's products, this loss in revenue would be accounted for in measuring the incremental revenue of the new product.

Incremental Concept Example

To further illustrate the incremental concept, consider the financing decision typically associated with business plant and equipment financing. Consider a business whose $100,000 purchase offer was accepted by the seller of a small retail facility. The firm must obtain financing to complete the transaction. The best rates it has found are at a local financial institution that offers a renewable five-year mortgage at 9 percent interest with a down payment of 20 percent, or 9.5 percent interest on a loan with only 10 percent down. In the first case, the borrower is able to finance 80 percent of the purchase price; in the second case, the borrower is able to finance 90 percent. For simplicity, assume that both loans require interest payments only during the first five years. After five years, either note would be renewable at then-current interest rates and would be restructured with monthly payments designed to amortize the loan over 20 years. An important question facing the firm is: What is the incremental cost of additional funds borrowed when 90 percent versus 80 percent of the purchase price is financed?

Because no principal payments are required, the annual financing cost under each loan alternative can be calculated easily. For the 80 percent loan, the annual financing cost in dollar terms is

$$\text{Financing Cost} = \text{Interest Rate} \times \text{Loan Percentage} \times \text{Purchase Price}$$
$$= (0.09)(0.8)(\$100,000)$$
$$= \$7,200$$

(1.5)

For a 90 percent loan, the corresponding annual financing cost is

$$\text{Financing Cost} = (0.095)(0.9)(\$100,000)$$
$$= \$8,550$$

To calculate the incremental cost of added funds borrowed under the 90 percent financing alternative, the firm must compare the additional financing costs incurred with the additional funds borrowed. In dollar terms, the incremental annual financing cost is

$$\text{Incremental Cost} = 90\% \text{ Loan Financing Cost} - 80\% \text{ Loan Financing Cost}$$
$$= \$8,550 - \$7,200$$
$$= \$1,350$$

(1.6)

In percentage terms, the incremental cost of the additional funds borrowed under the 90 percent financing alternative is

$$\text{Incremental Cost in Percentage Terms} = \frac{\text{Incremental Financing Costs}}{\text{Incremental Funds Borrowed}}$$

$$= \frac{\$8{,}550 - \$7{,}200}{\$90{,}000 - \$80{,}000}$$

$$= \frac{\$1{,}350}{\$10{,}000}$$

$$= 0.135, \text{ or } 13.5\%$$

The true incremental cost of funds for the last $10,000 borrowed under the 90 percent financing alternative is 13.5 percent, not the 9.5 percent interest rate quoted for the loan. Although this high incremental cost of funds is perhaps surprising, it is not unusual. It results because with a 90 percent loan the higher 9.5 percent interest rate is charged on the entire balance of the loan, not just on the incremental $10,000 in borrowed funds.

The incremental concept is important for managerial decision making because it focuses attention on changes or differences between available alternatives. Revenues and costs unaffected by the decision are irrelevant and should be ignored in the analysis.

Forecasting

What Is Economic Forecasting?

When companies hire new workers, they must predict the relative productivity of a wide variety of individuals with diverse skills, work histories, and personalities. How much inventory should be carried? What price should be charged during the coming holiday season? Which market is the most natural path for expansion? These and a host of everyday business decisions require that managers make informed forecasts of future economic events.

Why Is Forecasting Useful?

Managers sometimes must integrate quantitative and nonquantitative information in a way not easily modeled or characterized by numbers. In such instances, there is no substitute for the extraordinary pattern recognition capabilities of the human mind. Experienced managers sometimes "know" the correct level of inventory, or right price, despite their inability to easily explain all the factors that weigh in their decisions. Although there is no good substitute for the careful intuition of an experienced manager, some firms err in their over reliance on judgmental forecasts. In some cases, the concept of forecasting is confused with goal setting. If a company asks its staff to forecast sales for the mid-Atlantic region, for example, these "forecasts" are sometimes used as yardsticks to judge sales performance. If forecast sales are exceeded, sales performance is "good"; if forecast sales are not achieved, sales performance is "poor." This sometimes leads sales staffs to underestimate future sales in a effort to boost perceived performance. Just as a successful college football coach predicts a tough year to enhance the popular perception of a winning record, sales personnel have incentives to be overly conservative in their sales projections for new or improved products. Coaches of football teams with 8-3 records sometimes lose their jobs if fans had expected a perfect 11-0 season; brand managers of even highly successful new product introductions sometimes get fired if rosy predictions are not met.

A big advantage of the wide variety of statistical techniques commonly used in economic forecasting is that they separate the process of forecasting from the firm's goal-setting activity. When sales are forecast in an objective, systematic, and unbiased manner, the potential for accurate forecasts increases, as does the capacity for appropriate operating and planning decisions. When these forecasts involve outcomes and precipitating factors that can be quantified, it also becomes possible to access the direct ramifications of changes in controllable and uncontrollable conditions. Optimistic through pessimistic scenarios can be tested and analyzed for their performance implications and for their significance in terms of the decision-making process. Forecasting that is objective and quantitative has the potential to help almost any business; accurate business forecasting is a value-added undertaking.

Common Types of Forecasting Problems

Macroeconomic Forecast Problems

Macroeconomic forecasting
Prediction of aggregate economic activity.

Macroeconomic forecasting involves predicting aggregate measures of economic activity at the international, national, regional, or state level. Predictions of gross domestic product (GDP), unemployment, and interest rates by "blue chip" business economists capture the attention of national media, business, government, and the general public on a daily basis.[251] Other macroeconomic forecasts commonly reported in the press include predictions of consumer spending, business investment, homebuilding, exports, imports, federal purchases, state and local government spending, and so on. Macroeconomic predictions are important because they are used by businesses and individuals to make day-to-day operating decisions and long-term planning decisions. If interest rates are projected to rise, homeowners may rush to refinance fixed-rate mortgages, while businesses float new bond and stock offerings to refinance existing debt or take advantage of investment opportunities. When such predictions are accurate, significant cost savings or revenue gains become possible. When such predictions are inaccurate, higher costs and lost marketing opportunities occur.

The accuracy of any forecast is subject to the influence of controllable and uncontrollable factors. In the case of macroeconomic forecasting, uncontrollable factors loom large. Take interest rate forecasting, for example. The demand for credit and short-term interest rates rises if businesses seek to build inventories or expand plant and equipment, or if consumers wish to increase installment credit. The supply of credit rises and short-term interest rates fall if the Federal Reserve System acts to increase the money supply, or if consumers cut back on spending to increase savings. Interest rate forecasting is made difficult by the fact that business decisions to build inventories, for example, are largely based on the expected pace of overall economic activity—which itself depends on interest-rate expectations. The macroeconomic environment is interrelated in ways that are unstable and cannot be easily predicted. Even policy decisions are hard to predict. For example, Federal Reserve System policy meeting minutes are confidential until months after the fact. Is it any wonder that "Fed watching" is a favorite pastime of business economists?

Microeconomic Forecast Problems

Microeconomic forecasting Prediction of partial economic data.

In contrast with macroeconomic forecasting, **microeconomic forecasting** involves the prediction of disaggregate economic data at the industry, firm, plant, or product level. Unlike predictions of GDP growth, which are widely followed in the press, the general public often ignores microeconomic forecasts of scrap prices for aluminum, the demand for new cars, or production costs for Crest toothpaste. It is unlikely that the *CBS Evening News* will ever be interrupted to discuss an upward trend in used car prices, even though these data are an excellent predictor of new car demand. When used car prices surge, new car demand often grows rapidly; when used car prices sag, new car demand typically drops. The fact that used car prices and new car demand are closely related is not surprising given the strong substitute-good relation that exists between used cars and new cars.

Trained and experienced analysts often find it easier to accurately forecast microeconomic trends, such as the demand for new cars, than macroeconomic trends, such as GDP growth. This is because microeconomic forecasts abstract from the multitude of interrelationships that together determine the macroeconomy. With specialized knowledge about changes in new car prices, car import tariffs, car loan rates, and used cars prices, among other factors, it is possible to focus on the fairly narrow range of important factors that influence new car demand. In contrast, a similarly precise model of aggregate demand in the macroeconomy might involve thousands of economic variables and hundreds of functional relationships.

Problem of Changing Expectations

The subtle problem of changing expectations bedevils both macroeconomic and microeconomic forecasting. If business purchasing agents are optimistic about future trends in the economy and boost inventories in anticipation of surging customer demand, the resulting inventory buildup can itself contribute to economic growth. Conversely, if purchasing agents fear an economic downturn and cut back on orders and inventory growth, they themselves can be a main contributor to any resulting economic downturn. The expectations of purchasing agents and other managers can become a self-fulfilling prophecy because the macroeconomic environment represents the sum of the investment and spending decisions of business, government, and the public. In fact, the link between expectations and realizations has the potential to create an optimistic bias in government-reported statistics.

Government economists are sometimes criticized for being overly optimistic about the rate of growth in the overall economy, the future path of interest rates, or the magnitude of the federal deficit. As consumers of economic statistics, managers must realize that it can pay for government or politically motivated economists to be optimistic. If business leaders can be led to make appropriate decisions for a growing economy, their decisions can in fact help lead to a growing economy. Unlike many business economists from the private sector, government-employed and/or politically motivated economists often actively seek to manage the economic expectations of business leaders and the general public. It is vital for managers to appreciate the link between economic expectations and realizations, and to be wary of the potential for forecast bias.

Common Forecasting Techniques

Some forecasting techniques are basically quantitative; others are largely qualitative. The most commonly applied forecasting techniques can be divided into the following broad categories:

1. Qualitative techniques
2. Quantitative techniques
3. Time series analysis
4. Econometric methods

The best forecast methodology for a particular task depends on the nature of the forecasting problem. When making a choice among forecast methodologies, a number of important factors must be considered. It is always worth considering the distance into the future that one must forecast, the lead time available for making decisions, the level of accuracy required, the quality of data available for analysis, the stochastic or deterministic nature of forecast relations, and the cost and benefits associated with the forecasting problem.

Trend analysis, market experiments, consumer surveys, and the leading indicator approach to forecasting are well suited for short-term projections. Forecasting with complex econometric models and systems of simultaneous equations have proven somewhat more useful for long-run forecasting. Typically, the greater the level of sophistication, the higher the cost. If the required level of accuracy is low, less sophisticated methods can provide adequate results at minimal cost.

Qualitative Techniques

The Delphi, or panel consensus, method may be useful in technological forecasting, that is, in predicting the general state of the market, economy, or technological advances five or more years from now, based on expert opinion. (The name for this method comes from the ancient Greek oracles of Delphi who forecast future events.) The process of creating a Delphi forecast is a variation of the following: A panel of futurists is asked a question, such as, In the next 10 years which consumer products do you envision containing microprocessors as an integral part? Each specialist independently submits a list of such items to the panel coordinator. The combined lists then are sent back to each panel member for evaluation and rating of likelihood of occurrence. Panel members may see something that they hadn't thought of and rate it highly. Also, members may have second thoughts about items they themselves previously submitted. After a sufficient number of cycles (generally two or three), the result is a list with high consensus. The Delphi technique is not a suitable technique for short-range forecasting, certainly not for individual products.

When attempting to forecast demand for a new item, one faces a shortage of historical data. A useful technique is to examine the demand history for an analogous product. If the related product is very similar, quantitative techniques may be used. But if the relationship is tenuous, it may be more appropriate to relate the products only qualitatively in order to get an impression of demand patterns or aggregate demand. For example, the seasonal demand pattern for an established product such as tennis balls may be used to estimate the expected demand pattern for tennis gloves. The actual levels and trends for the latter cannot be determined in this manner with any precision, but the seasonal pattern may be expected to be similar.

Finally, we must not overlook management estimation (intuition) as a prediction method. It is widely practiced with regard to new products or unexpected changes in demand for established product lines. Not everyone has estimation talent, however. Some studies have shown that a mathematical technique, consistently followed, will lead to better results than the "expert modification" of those forecasts. Nonetheless, many mathematical techniques need significant quantities of historical data that may not be available. When substantial data are lacking, subjective management judgment may be the better alternative.

Quantitative Techniques

Intrinsic techniques use the time-sequenced history of activity for a particular item as source data to forecast future activity for that item. Such a history is commonly referred to as a time series. Some typical time-series patterns are shown in Exhibit 100.35. The characteristics of such series can be labeled in various ways, and the algebraic representation of such graphs can be accomplished by a variety of methods.

Generally, a time series can be thought of as consisting of four components or underlying factors: (1) cyclical, (2) trend, (3) seasonal, and (4) random (or irregular). The cyclical factor traditionally refers to the business cycle, to long-range trends in the overall economy. The cyclical factor can be very important in forecasting for long-range planning. However, it is of little use in forecasting demand for individual products, which rarely have sufficient data to permit a distinction between the effect of the business cycle and the effect of the product life cycle. For that reason, the time series used for short-term forecasting generally have only trend, seasonal, and random components. The trend component generally is modeled as a line, which is described by an intercept or base level, which we designate L, and a slope,

Exhibit 100.35 *Typical Time-Series Patterns*

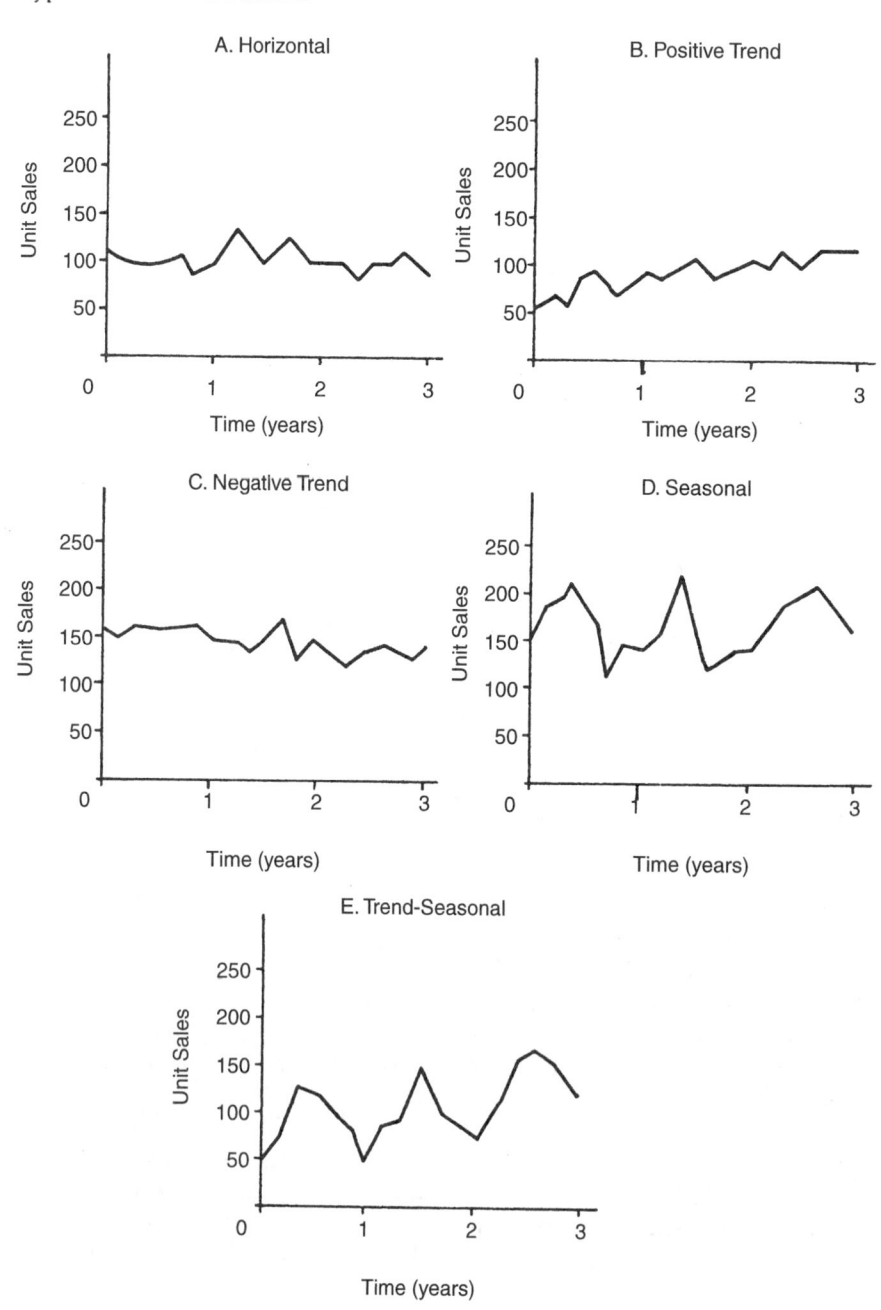

which we designate T. The trend line may be modified by a seasonal phenomenon (S). All data are somewhat muddied by a random, irregular, or otherwise unpredictable variation (R).

Mathematically this process is based on a combination multiplicative and additive model of the following sort:

$$D = (L + T) \times S + R \tag{1.7}$$

where D is demand. In this version T, trend, is expressed in the same units as L, level, and T may be positive or negative. R, random, is expressed in the same units. Its expected value is 0. S, seasonal, is a dimensionless number having an expected value of 1. For example, we may know that the demand for a certain Bruce Springsteen anthology is averaging 10,000 units per month, with a trend of minus 500 per month (the pattern is to sell 500 fewer units each month). However, the month currently being forecast is December; due to seasonal variation, December averages 40 percent higher than the typical month. Average forecast error using this model has been 800 units. In this example the demand forecast is

$$D = (10{,}000 - 500) \times 1.4 + 0 = 13{,}300 \text{ units}$$

Because the average forecast error has been 800 units, and because errors twice the average are not uncommon occurrences, we would not be surprised if December's actual sales were anywhere from $13{,}300 - 1{,}600 = 11{,}700$ units to $13{,}300 + 1{,}600 = 14{,}900$ units.

Models of the form shown in equation 1.7 are the most common, but pure multiplicative models are sometimes used. A pure multiplicative model would express both the trend and random components as percentages, so that the model could be expressed as:

$$D = L \times T \times S \times R \tag{1.8}$$

Converting the Springsteen anthology example to this notation, L is still 10,000 units, T is now $\dfrac{10{,}000 - 500}{10{,}000} = 0.95$, S is still 1.4, and R becomes 1. The forecast is then

$$D = 10{,}000 \times 0.95 \times 1.4 \times 1 = 13{,}300 \text{ units}$$

One approach to time series analysis attempts to determine the underlying components of trend and seasonal factors. The federal government uses this approach in forecasts of economic factors (unemployment, cost of living, and so on). The approach also is used by a few firms in aggregate sales forecasting.

While it may seem straightforward to determine the components of the series, sometimes referred to as *decomposition*, that is not always possible or practical. Obtaining sufficient data for time-series decomposition may not be possible, due to short product lifetimes. Four years of consistent data usually are required to make such a forecast (that is, four years of data after the item reaches the maturity stage of its product life cycle). Seasonal factors often are determined for a family of items by assuming groupings based on judgments.

Time-Series Analysis

This section discusses some of the most common techniques for forecasting from intrinsic time series without explicitly looking for seasonal or trend factors. This includes moving averages, weighted moving averages, and exponential smoothing techniques.

MOVING AVERAGES TECHNIQUES   Perhaps the simplest of all time-series forecasting techniques is a moving average. To use this method, we calculate the average of, say, three periods of actual demand and use that to forecast the next period's demand. For example,

$$D_{5,6,7} = \frac{D_5 + D_6 + D_7}{3} = F_8 \tag{1.9}$$

$$D_{6,7,8} = \frac{D_6 + D_7 + D_8}{3} = F_9 \tag{1.10}$$

where D_i = actual demand in Period i
F_i = forecast demand in Period i

Periods 5, 6, and 7 (May, June, and July) have demands of 302, 274, and 162, respectively. Adding these three numbers and dividing by 3 yields 246. If this three-period average is to be used as a forecast, it would have to forecast demand in a future period, such as Period 8. When the actual demand of Period 8 (194) is known, equation 1.10 can be used to produce a forecast for Period 9. The value for Period 5 is dropped, and the values for Periods 6 and 7 are averaged with Period 8 to obtain an average of $\frac{274 + 162 + 194}{3} = 210$.

Because each average moves ahead one period each time, dropping the oldest value and adding the most recent, this procedure is called a *moving average*.

WEIGHTED MOVING AVERAGES TECHNIQUES   More recent data are more indicative of the future than are older data. Often a weighted moving average, one that is computed to give more weight to more recent data, is more reliable than an unweighted average. A weighted moving average is computed by multiplying each period by a weighting factor and dividing the resulting product by the sum of all weighting factors. An example equation is

$$D_{5,6,7} = \frac{2D_5 + 3D_6 + 4D_7}{2 + 3 + 4} \qquad (1.11)$$

where $D_{5,6,7}$ is used to forecast demand for Period 8. The denominator of equation 2.5 is the sum of the weights. The weighted moving average is moved just as in a simple moving average system. Let's apply this formula to the data previously used for the unweighted or simple moving average. Recall that the demand for Period 5 was 302, for Period 6 was 274, and for Period 7 was 162. Then the numerator of equation 1.11 is

$$(2 \times 302) + (3 \times 274) + (4 \times 162) = 2{,}074$$

Dividing this total by the sum of the weights (9) yields 230.44, or 230 when rounded to the nearest integer.

Usually, weighted moving averages are used only when a number of periods of data are included. Weighting factors can be any values. Weights are the subjective evaluation of the forecaster of the importance of more recent data and older data in making a forecast. If a product is new and is going through the growth stage of the product life cycle, there often is not enough data to estimate the trend and seasonal components of the time series. A simple moving average is undesirable because of its tendency to lag behind a trend. The weighted moving average will alleviate this problem slightly by placing more weight on the latest data. But weighted averages still lag behind the trend and produce a forecast that is consistently low during periods of rising demand.

An impediment to the use of weighted moving averages to forecast thousands of items is that N periods of data must be retained (N being the number of demand periods used in the average). And N multiplications, $N - 1$ additions, and one division must be performed for each forecast. This amounts to a great deal of data and many calculations. Exponential smoothing, presented next, offers a method that is equivalent to a weighted moving average, but that requires fewer data and calculations.

EXPONENTIAL SMOOTHING TECHNIQUES   Probably the most popular methods used to forecast item demand are the various exponential smoothing techniques. Simple or first-order exponential smoothing can be viewed several ways. One viewpoint is that it is a forecasting technique based on the forecasting errors. If the forecast, F, for Period n is F_n and the actual demand for Period n is D_n, then one can forecast the next period as being F_n plus some fraction, α, of the current error $(D_n - F_n)$.

$$F_{n+1} = F_n + \alpha(D_n - F_n) \qquad (1.12)$$

or, rearranging the terms of equation 1.12,

$$F_{n+1} = \alpha D_n + (1 - \alpha)F_n \qquad (1.13)$$

One advantage to this method is that the data required are only the last forecast, the last actual demand, and the value of α. Computation is reduced to two multiplications and one addition for each forecast. It should also be noted that this is really a weighted moving average. Large values of α place heavier weight on the most recent actual demand data and lesser weight on historical values.

We now apply simple exponential smoothing to a small sample in order to demonstrate the technique. The only data required to provide a forecast for Period $n + 1$ are the values of α, F_n, and D_n. Let α be 0.3, F_n be 100 and D_n be 90. Then, using equation 1.13, we have

$$\begin{aligned} F_{n+1} &= (0.3)(90) + (0.7)(100) \\ &= 27 + 70 \\ &= 97 \end{aligned}$$

Now suppose the demand in Period $n + 1$ is 95. The forecast for Period $n + 2$ is then

$$F_{n+2} = (0.3)(95) + (0.7)(97)$$
$$= 28.5 + 67.9$$
$$= 96.4$$
$$= 96 \text{ because forecasts need to be integer units}$$

Finally, suppose demand in Period $n + 2$ happens to be 96. The forecast for Period $n + 3$ is then

$$F_{n+3} = (0.3)(96) + (0.7)(96)$$
$$= (0.3 + 0.7)(96)$$
$$= 96$$

The problem with simple exponential smoothing is that, as with any moving average technique, it lags behind changes in the series. Whenever the time series is increasing, the exponential forecast is biased low, and whenever the time series is decreasing, the exponential forecast is biased high. It is a fact that exponential forecasts always miss the turning point. The magnitude of the bias can be altered by changing α, but the existence of bias cannot be altered.

Econometric Methods

Econometric methods combine economic theory with statistical tools to analyze economic relations. Econometric forecasting techniques have several advantages over alternative methods.

Advantages of Econometric Methods

Econometric methods force the forecaster to make explicit assumptions about the linkages among the variables in the economic system being examined. In other words, the forecaster must deal with causal relations. This produces logical consistency in the forecast model and increases reliability.

Another advantage of econometric methods is that the forecaster can compare forecasts with actual results and use insights gained to improve the forecast model. By feeding past forecasting errors back into the model, new parameter estimates can be generated to improve future forecasting results. The type of output provided by econometric forecasts is another major advantage. Because econometric models offer estimates of actual values for forecasted variables, these models indicate both the direction and magnitude of change. Finally, perhaps the most important advantage of econometric models relates to their ability to explain economic phenomena.

Judging Forecast Reliability

In comparing forecast and actual values, how close is close enough? Is forecast reliability, or predictive consistency, transferable to other samples and time periods? These questions must be adequately addressed prior to the implementation of any successful forecasting program.

Tests of Predictive Capability

To test predictive capability, a forecast model generated over one sample or period is used to forecast data for some alternative sample or period. The reliability of a model for predicting firm sales can be tested by examining the relation between forecast and actual data for years beyond the period over which the forecast model was estimated. However, it is often desirable to test a forecast model without waiting for new data to become available. In such instances, one can divide available data into two subsamples, called a **test group** and a **forecast group.** The forecaster estimates a forecasting model using data from the test group and uses the resulting model to "forecast" the data of interest in the forecast group. A comparison of forecast and actual values can then be conducted to test the stability of the underlying cost or demand relation.

Correlation Analysis

In analyzing a model's forecast capability, the correlation between forecast and actual values is of substantial interest.

Sample Mean Forecast Error Analysis

Further evaluation of a model's predictive capability can be made through consideration of a measure called the **sample mean forecast error,** which provides a useful estimate of the average forecast error of the model. It is sometimes called the root mean squared forecast error. The smaller the sample mean forecast error, the greater the accuracy associated with the forecasting model.

Choosing the Best Forecasting Technique

To select the best technique, managers must be knowledgeable about the strengths and weaknesses of various forecast methods, the amount and quality of available data, and the human and other costs associated with generating reliable forecasts.

Data Requirements

The choice of an appropriate forecast technique often hinges on the amount of relevant historical data that is readily available and any obvious patterns in that data. For many important forecast problems, 10 years of monthly data (120 observations) are available and appropriate for forecasting future activity. In such cases, the full range of advanced forecast techniques can be considered. If only more restricted samples of data are available for analysis, then simpler forecast methods must be used.

If trend, cyclical, seasonal, or irregular patterns can be recognized, then forecast techniques that are capable of handling those patterns can be readily selected. For example, if the data are relatively stable, a simple exponential smoothing approach may be adequate. Other exponential smoothing models are appropriate for trending and seasonal data; the same model will not be applicable in all cases.

As the forecast horizon increases, the cyclical pattern of economic data may also become significant. In these cases, the need to relate the forecast variable to economic, market, and competitive factors increases, because simple trend projections may no longer be appropriate.

Time Horizon Considerations

Experience shows that sophisticated time-series models can provide accurate short-term forecasts. In the short term, the momentum of existing consumer behavior often resists dramatic change. Over a five-year period, however, customers can find new suppliers, and needs may change. For long-range forecasts, econometric models are often appropriate. In the long term, it is essential to relate the item being forecast to its "drivers," as explanatory factors are sometimes called.

The accuracy of econometric models depends on the precision with which explanatory factors can be predicted. Although these models can also be used in the short term, they are costlier and more complex than simple exponential smoothing methods. When economic conditions are stable, econometric models are seldom more accurate than more simple trend projections and exponential smoothing methods.

Simple trend, econometric models, and exponential smoothing methods are all used for problems involving three-year to five-year forecasts. Over this intermediate term, trend projection techniques are relatively inexpensive to apply, but may produce forecasts that are not as accurate as those resulting from econometric methods. When sufficient data exist and the need for accuracy is great, the use of exponential smoothing or econometric models is often recommended. Then, the generally superior short-term forecasting abilities of smoothing models emerge. Also evident over the intermediate term are the advantages of econometric models, which are superior in relating the data to be forecast to economic conditions, price changes, competitive activities, and other explanatory variables.

When both smoothing and econometric models yield similar forecasts, managers can be reasonably certain that the forecast is consistent with underlying assumptions and has a good chance of being accurate. When forecasts produced by two or more methods are significantly different, this is a warning to exercise extreme care.

Role of Judgment

The most sophisticated forecast methodology provides sufficiently accurate results at minimum cost. No one flies a jet to the grocery store. Similarly, no manager would find costly and difficult methods appropriate for solving trivial forecasting problems.

To determine a suitable level of forecast accuracy, one must compare the costs and benefits of increased accuracy. When forecast accuracy is low, the probability of significant forecasting error is high, as is the chance of making suboptimal managerial decisions. Conversely, when forecast accuracy is high, the probability of substantial forecasting error is reduced and the chance of making erroneous managerial decisions is low. It is reasonable to require a relatively high level of forecast accuracy when the costs of forecast error are high. When only minor costs result from forecast error, inexpensive and less precise methods can be justified.

It is worth emphasizing that the objective of economic forecasting is to improve on the subjective judgments made by managers. All managers forecast; the goal is to make better forecasts. Nowhere in the forecasting process is the subjective judgment of managers relied on so heavily as it is in the selection of an appropriate forecast method. When it comes to the selection of the best forecast technique, there is no substitute for seasoned business judgment.

Business Cycle

Many important economic time series are regularly influenced by cyclical and seasonal variations. It is worth considering these influences further, because the treatment of cyclical and seasonal variations plays an important role in economic forecasting.

What Is the Business Cycle?

The profit and sales performance of all companies depends to a greater or lesser extent on the vigor of the overall economy.

One of the most important economy-wide considerations for managers is the **business cycle,** or rhythmic pattern of contraction and expansion observed in the overall economy. The average duration of each cyclical contraction is 11 months, when duration is measured from the previous cyclical peak to the low point or trough of the subsequent business contraction. The average duration of each cyclical expansion is 50 months, as measured by the amount of time from the previous cyclical trough to the peak of the following business expansion. Clearly, periods of economic expansion predominate, which indicates a healthy and growing economy.

Business cycle Rhythmic pattern of contraction and expansion in the overall economy.

Economic Indicators

Whereas cyclical patterns in most economic time series are erratic and make simple projection a hazardous short-term forecasting technique, a relatively consistent relation often exists among various economic variables over time. Even though many series of economic data do not exhibit a consistent pattern over time, it is often possible to find a high degree of correlation across these series. Should the forecaster have the good fortune to discover an economic series that leads the one being forecast, the leading series can be used as a barometer for forecasting short-term change, just as a meteorologist uses changes in a mercury barometer to forecast changes in the weather.

The Conference Board, a private research group, provides extensive data on a wide variety of **economic indicators** or data series that successfully describe the pattern of projected, current, or past economic activity. Exhibit 100.36 lists 10 leading, 4 roughly coincident, and 7 lagging economic indicators of business cycle peaks that are broadly relied upon in business cycle forecasting. A **composite index** is a weighted average of leading, coincident, or lagging economic indicators.

Composite index Weighted average of leading, coincident, or lagging economic indicators.

The basis for some of these leads and lags is obvious. For example, building permits precede housing starts, and orders for plant and equipment lead production in durable goods industries. Each of these indicators directly reflects plans or commitments for the activity that follows. Other barometers are not directly related to the economic variables they forecast. An index of common stock prices is a good leading indicator of general business activity. Although the causal linkage may not be readily apparent, stock prices reflect aggregate profit expectations by investors and thus give a consensus view of the likely course of future business conditions. Thus, at any point in time, stock prices both reflect and anticipate changes in aggregate economic conditions. All of this makes macroeconomic forecasting particularly nettlesome for investors.

Economic Recessions

An **economic recession** is defined by the National Bureau of Economic Research (NBER), a private nonprofit research organization, as a significant decline in ac-

Economic recession A decline in economic activity that lasts more than a few months.

Exhibit 100.36 *Leading, Coincident, and Lagging Economic Indicators*

The Conference Board's Index of Leading Economic Indicators (LEI) is designed to signal peaks and troughs in the business cycle. The LEI is derived from 10 leading indicators, 4 coincident indicators, and 7 lagging indicators. The LEI is a useful barometer of economic activity over 3 to 6 months.

Ten Leading Indicators
- Average workweek of production workers in manufacturing
- Average initial weekly claims for state unemployment insurance
- New orders for consumer goods and materials, adjusted for inflation
- Vendor performance (companies receiving slower deliveries from suppliers)
- New orders for nonmilitary capital goods, adjusted for inflation
- New building permits issued
- Index of stock prices
- Money supply: M2 adjusted for inflation
- Spread between rates on 10-year Treasury bonds and federal funds
- Index of consumer expectations

Four Coincident Indicators
- Manufacturing and trade sales
- Employees on nonagricultural payrolls
- Industrial production
- Personal income minus transfer payments

Seven Lagging Indicators
- Average duration of unemployment
- Inventories to sales ratio, manufacturing, and trade
- Change in labor cost per unit of output, manufacturing
- Average prime rate
- Commercial and industrial loans
- Consumer installment credit to personal income ratio
- Change in consumer price index for services

Source: The Conference Board Web site at http://www.conference-board.org/economics/indicators/leading.htm.

tivity spread across the economy that lasts more than a few months. Recessions are visible in terms of falling industrial production, declining real income, and shrinking wholesale-retail trade. Recessions are also marked by rising unemployment. Although many economic recessions consist of two or more quarters of declining real GDP, it is most accurate to describe recession as a period of *diminishing* economic activity rather than a period of *diminished* economic activity. A recession begins just after the economy reaches a peak of output and employment and ends as the economy reaches its trough. The period between a month of peak economic activity and the subsequent economic low point defines the length of a recession. During recessions, economic growth is falling or the economy is actually contracting. Recessions can be caused by any serious unanticipated economic or political event.

Economic expansion A period of rising economic activity.

The period following recession is called **economic expansion.** In many cases, economic activity is below normal during both recessions and through the early part of the subsequent economic expansion. Some refer to periods of less than typical economic growth as slumps, but there is no official recognition or characterization of economic slumps. In any event, expansion is the normal state of the U.S. economy.

Finally, experienced managers realize that significant time lags are often encountered between changes in the macroeconomy and their official recognition. This means that by the time a downturn in the economy is officially recognized, the subsequent upturn has already begun! Slow reporting, hard to decipher leads and lags in the overall economy, and unpredictable ties between economic and political events combine to make accurate macroeconomic forecasting one of the toughest challenges faced in managerial economics.

Perfect Competition and Monopoly

Firms operating in perfectly competitive industries find it very difficult to sustain attractive rates of return on investment. Stark differences between buyer and seller behavior in perfectly competitive and monopoly markets are evident. These dissimilarities are characterized briefly in this section.

What Is Market Structure?

A **market** consists of all firms and individuals willing and able to buy or sell a particular product. This includes firms and individuals currently engaged in buying and selling a particular product, as well as potential entrants. **Market structure** describes the competitive environment in the market for any good or service. Market structure is typically characterized on the basis of four important industry characteristics: the number and size distribution of active buyers and sellers and potential entrants, the degree of product differentiation, the amount and cost of information about product price and quality, and conditions of entry and exit.

Market structure The competitive environment.

Effects of market structure are measured in terms of the prices paid by consumers, availability and quality of output, employment and career advancement opportunities, and the pace of product innovation, among other factors. Generally speaking, the greater the number of market participants, the more vigorous is price and product quality competition. The more even the balance of power between sellers and buyers, the more likely it is that the competitive process will yield maximum benefits. However, a close link between the numbers of market participants and the vigor of price competition does not always hold true. For example, there are literally thousands of producers in most major milk markets. Price competition is nonexistent, however, given an industry cartel that is sustained by a federal program of milk price supports. Nevertheless, there are few barriers to entry, and individual milk producers struggle to earn a normal return. In contrast, price competition can be spirited in aircraft manufacturing, newspaper, cable television, long-distance telephone service, and other markets with as few as two competitors. This is particularly true when market participants are constrained by the viable threat of potential entrants.

A **potential entrant** is an individual or firm posing a sufficiently credible threat of market entry to affect the price/output decisions of incumbent firms. Potential entrants play extremely important roles in many industries. Some industries with only a few active participants might at first appear to hold the potential for substantial economic profits. However, a number of potential entrants can have a substantial effect on the price/output decisions of incumbent firms. For example, Dell, Gateway, Hewlett-Packard, IBM, and other leading computer manufacturers are viable potential entrants into the computer component manufacturing industry. These companies use their threat of potential entry to obtain favorable prices from suppliers of microprocessors, monitors, and peripheral equipment. Despite having only a relative handful of active foreign and domestic participants, computer components manufacturing is both highly innovative and vigorously price competitive. The mere threat of entry by potential entrants is sometimes enough to keep industry prices and profits in check and to maintain a high level of productive efficiency.

Perfect Competition

Perfect competition is a market structure characterized by a large number of buyers and sellers of essentially the same product. Each market participant is too small to influence market prices. Individual buyers and sellers are **price takers**. Firms take market prices as given and devise their production strategies accordingly. Free and complete demand and supply information is available in a perfectly competitive market, and there are no meaningful barriers to entry and exit. As a result, vigorous price competition prevails. Only a normal rate of return on investment is possible in the long run. Economic profits are possible only during periods of short-run disequilibrium before rivals mount an effective competitive response.

Monopoly

Monopoly is a market structure characterized by a single seller of a product with no good substitutes. Because a monopolist is the sole provider of a desired commodity, the monopolist is the industry. Producers must compete for a share of the consumer's overall market basket of goods, but monopolists face no effective competition for specific products from either established or potential rivals. As such, monopolists are **price makers** that exercise significant control over market prices. This allows the monopolist to simultaneously determine price and output for the firm (and the industry). Substantial barriers to entry or exit deter potential entrants and offer both efficient and inefficient monopolists the opportunity for economic profits, even in the long run.

Factors that Determine the Level of Competition

Two key conditions determine the level of competition in a given market: the number and relative size of buyers and sellers, and the extent to which the product is standardized. These factors, in turn, are influenced by the nature of the product and production systems, the scope of potential entry, and buyer characteristics.

Effect of Product Characteristics on Market Structure

Good substitutes increase competition. To illustrate, rail freight and passenger service between two points is typically supplied by only one railroad. Transportation service is available from several sources, however, and railroads compete with bus lines, truck companies, barges, airlines, and private autos. The substitutability of these other modes of transportation for rail service increases the degree of competition in the transportation service market.

It is important to realize that market structures are not static. In the 1800s and early 1900s—before the introduction of trucks, buses, automobiles, and airplanes—railroads faced very little competition. Railroads could charge excessive prices and earn monopoly profits. Because of this exploitation, laws were passed giving public authorities permission to regulate railroad prices. Over the years, such regulation became superfluous given intermodal competition. Other firms were enticed by railroad profits to develop competing transportation service systems, which ultimately led to a much more competitive market structure. Today, few would argue that railroads retain significant monopoly power, and public regulation of the railroads has been greatly reduced in recognition of this fact.

Physical characteristics of a product can also influence the degree of competition. A low ratio of distribution cost to total cost, for example, tends to increase competition by widening the geographic area over which any particular producer can compete. Rapid perishability of a product yields the opposite effect. In considering the level of competition for a product, the national, regional, or local nature of the market must be considered.

Effect of Production Characteristics on Competition

When minimum efficient scale is large in relation to overall industry output, only a few firms are able to attain the output size necessary for productive efficiency. In such instances, competitive pressures may allow only a few firms to survive. On the other hand, when minimum efficient scale is small in relation to overall industry output, many firms are able to attain the size necessary for efficient operation. Holding all else equal, competition tends to be most vigorous when many efficient competitors are present in the market. This is especially true when firms of smaller-than-minimum-efficient scale face considerably higher production costs, and when the construction of minimum-efficient–scale plants involves the commitment of substantial capital, skilled labor, and material resources. When construction of minimum-efficient–scale plants requires the commitment of only modest resources or when smaller firms face no important production cost disadvantages, economies of scale have little or no effect on the competitive potential of new or entrant firms.

Effect of Entry and Exit Conditions on Competition

Maintaining above-normal profits or inefficient operations over the long run requires substantial barriers to entry, mobility, or exit. A **barrier to entry** is any factor or industry characteristic that creates an advantage for incumbents over new arrivals. Legal rights such as patents and local, state, or federal licenses can present formidable barriers to entry in pharmaceuticals, cable television, television and radio broadcasting, and other industries. A **barrier to mobility** is any factor or industry characteristic that creates an advantage for large leading firms over smaller nonleading rivals. Factors that sometimes create barriers to entry and/or mobility include substantial economies of scale, scope economies, large capital or skilled-labor requirements, and ties of customer loyalty created through advertising and other means.

It is worth keeping in mind that barriers to entry and mobility can sometimes result in compensating advantages for consumers. Even though patents can lead to monopoly profits for inventing firms, they also spur valuable new product and process development. Although efficient and innovative leading firms make life difficult for smaller rivals, they can have the favorable effect of lowering prices and increasing product quality. Therefore, a complete evaluation of the economic effects of entry barriers involves a consideration of both costs and benefits realized by suppliers and customers.

Whereas barriers to entry can impede competition by making entry or nonleading firm growth difficult, competitive forces can also be diminished through barriers to exit. A **barrier to exit** is any restriction on the ability of incumbents to redeploy assets from one industry or line of business to another. During the late 1980s, for example, several state governments initiated legal proceedings to impede plant closures by large employers in the steel, glass, automobile, and other industries. By imposing large fines or severance taxes or requiring substantial expenditures for worker retraining, they created significant barriers to exit.

By impeding the asset redeployment that is typical of any vigorous competitive environment, barriers to exit can dramatically increase both the costs and risks of doing business. Even though one can certainly sympathize with the difficult adjustments faced by both individuals and firms affected by plant closures, government actions that create barriers to exit can have the unintended effect of retarding industrial development and market competition.

Effect of Buyers on Competition

Generally speaking, if there are only a few buyers in a given market, there will be less competition than if there are many buyers. **Monopsony** exists when a single firm is the sole buyer of a desired product or input. Monopsony characterizes local labor markets with a single major employer, as well as many local agricultural markets with a single feed mill or livestock buyer. Similarly, the federal government is a monopsony buyer of military weapons and equipment. Major retailers such as **Wal-Mart, Target,** and **Sears** all enjoy monopsony power in the purchase of apparel, appliances, auto parts, and other consumer products. Such buyer power is especially strong in the purchase of "house brand" goods, where suppliers sell much if not all of their production to a single retailer. Monopsony is more common in factor input markets than in markets for final demand.

Monopsony A market with one buyer.

In terms of economic efficiency, monopsony is least harmful, and can sometimes even be beneficial, in those markets in which a monopsony buyer faces a monopoly seller. For example, consider the case of the town in which one mill is the sole employer of unskilled labor. The mill is a monopsony because it is a single buyer of labor, and it may be able to use its power to reduce wage rates below competitive levels. If workers organize a union to bargain collectively with their employer, a single monopoly seller of labor is created that could offset the employer's monopsony power and increase wages toward competitive market norms. Not only is monopsony accepted in such situations, but it is sometimes encouraged by public policy.

Effect of Product Differentiation on Competition

In addition to the number and size distribution of actual and potential competitors, market structure is also described by the degree of product differentiation. Product differentiation includes any real or perceived differences in the quality of goods and services offered to consumers. Sources of product differentiation include all of the various forms of advertising promotion, plus new products and processes made possible by effective programs of research and development.

The availability and cost of information about prices and output quality is a similarly important determinant of market structure. Competition is always most vigorous when buyers and sellers have ready access to detailed price/performance information.

Finally, market structure is broadly determined by entry and exit conditions. Low regulatory barriers, modest capital requirements, and nominal standards for skilled labor and other inputs all increase the likelihood that competition will be vigorous. Because all of these elements of market structure have important consequences for the price/output decisions made by firms, the study of market structure is an important ingredient of managerial economics.

Perfect Competition

Market characteristics described in the preceding section determine the level of competition in the market for any good or service. This section focuses on the special features of perfectly competitive markets and illustrates why perfect competition is desirable from a social perspective.

Characteristics of Perfectly Competitive Markets

Perfect competition exists when individual producers have no influence on market prices; they are price takers as opposed to price makers. This lack of influence on price typically requires

- *Large numbers of buyers and sellers.* Each firm produces a small portion of industry output, and each customer buys only a small part of the total.
- *Product homogeneity.* The output of each firm is essentially the same as the output of any other firm in the industry.
- *Free entry and exit.* Firms are not restricted from entering or leaving the industry.
- *Perfect dissemination of information.* Cost, price, and product quality information is known by all buyers and all sellers.

These basic conditions are too restrictive for perfect competition to be commonplace. Although the stock market approaches the perfectly competitive ideal, imperfections occur even there. For example, the acquisition or sale of large blocks of securities by institutional investors clearly affects prices, at least in the short run. Nevertheless, because up to 1,000 shares of any stock can be bought or sold at the current market price, the stock market approaches the ideal of a perfectly competitive market. Similarly, many industrial firms must make output decisions without any control over price, and examination of a perfectly competitive market structure provides insights into these operating decisions. A clear understanding of perfect competition also provides a reference point from which to analyze monopolistic competition and oligopoly.

Market Price Determination

Market prices in competitive industries are determined by aggregate supply and demand; individual firms have no control over price. Total industry demand reflects an aggregation of the quantities that individual firms will buy at each price. Industry supply reflects a summation of the quantities that individual firms are willing to supply at different prices. The intersection of industry demand and supply curves determines market price.

Firm Price/Output Decision

Profit maximization requires that a firm operate at the output level at which marginal revenue and marginal cost are equal. With price constant, average revenue equals marginal revenue. Therefore, maximum profits result when market price is set equal to marginal cost for firms in a perfectly competitive industry.

Firm Supply Curve

Market supply curves are the sum of supply for individual firms at various prices. The perfectly competitive firm's short-run supply curve corresponds to that portion of the marginal cost curve that lies above the average variable cost curve. Because $P = MR$ under perfect competition, the quantity supplied by the perfectly competitive firm is found at the point where $P = MC$, so long as price exceeds average variable cost.

Monopoly

Perfect monopoly lies at the opposite extreme from perfect competition on the market structure continuum. Monopoly exists when a single firm is the sole producer of a good that has no close substitutes; in other words, there is a single firm in the industry. Perfect monopoly, like perfect competition, is seldom observed.

Characteristics of Monopoly Markets

Monopoly exists when an individual producer has the ability to set market prices. Monopoly firms are price makers as opposed to price takers. Their control over price typically requires

- *A single seller.* A single firm produces all industry output. The monopoly is the industry.
- *Unique product.* Monopoly output is perceived by customers to be distinctive and preferable to its imperfect substitutes.
- *Blockaded entry and exit.* Firms are heavily restricted from entering or leaving the industry.
- *Imperfect dissemination of information.* Cost, price, and product quality information is withheld from uninformed buyers.

As in the case of perfect competition, these basic conditions are too restrictive for monopoly to be commonplace in actual markets. Few goods are produced by single producers, and fewer still are free from competition of close substitutes. Even public utilities are imperfect monopolies in most of their markets. Electric companies approach a perfect monopoly in the residential lighting market but face strong competition from gas and oil suppliers in the heating market. In all industrial and commercial power markets, electric utilities face competition from gas- and oil-powered private generators. Even though perfect monopoly rarely exists, it is still worthy of careful examination. Many of the economic relations found under monopoly can be used to estimate optimal firm behavior in the less precise, but more prevalent, partly competitive and partly monopolistic market structures that dominate the real world.

Price/Output Decision Under Monopoly

Under monopoly, the industry demand curve is identical to the firm demand curve. Because industry demand curves slope downward, monopolists also face a downward-sloping demand curve. The monopolist can set either price or quantity, but not both. Given one, the value of the other is determined along the demand curve.

A monopoly uses the same profit-maximization rule as does any other firm: It operates at the output level at which marginal revenue equals marginal cost. The monopoly demand curve is not horizontal, however, so marginal revenue does not coincide with price at any but the first unit of output. Marginal revenue is always less than price for output quantities greater than one because of the negatively sloped demand curve. Because the demand (average revenue) curve is negatively sloped and hence declining, the marginal revenue curve must lie below it. When a monopoly equates marginal revenue and marginal cost, it simultaneously determines the output level and the market price for its product.

Long-Run Equilibrium Under Monopoly

In general, any industry characterized by monopoly *sells less* output at *higher prices* than would the same industry if it were perfectly competitive. From the perspective of the firm and its stockholders, the benefits of monopoly are measured in terms of the economic profits that are possible when competition is reduced or eliminated. From a broader social perspective, these private benefits must be weighed against the costs borne by consumers in the forms of higher prices and reduced availability of desired products. Employees and suppliers also suffer from the reduced employment opportunities associated with lower production in monopoly markets.

Monopolies have an incentive to underproduce and earn economic profits. **Underproduction** results when a monopoly curtails output to a level at which the value of resources employed, as measured by the marginal cost of production, is less than the social benefit derived, where social benefit is measured by the price that customers are willing to pay for additional output. Under monopoly, marginal cost is less than price at the profit-maximizing output level. Although resulting economic profits serve the useful functions of providing incentives and helping allocate resources, it is difficult to justify above-normal profits that result from market power rather than from exceptional performance.

In this case, the firm is called a **natural monopoly,** because the market-clearing price, where $P = MC$, occurs at a point at which *long-run* average costs are still declining. In other words, market demand is insufficient to justify full utilization of even one minimum-efficient–scale plant. A single monopolist can produce the total market supply at a lower total cost than could any number of smaller firms, and competition naturally reduces the number of competitors until only a single monopoly supplier remains. Electric and local telephone utilities are classic examples of natural monopoly, because any duplication in production and distribution facilities would increase consumer costs.

Natural monopoly An industry in which the market-clearing price occurs at a point at which the monopolist's long-run average costs are still declining.

Is Monopoly Always Bad?

Natural monopoly presents something of a dilemma. On the one hand, economic efficiency could be enhanced by restricting the number of producers to a single firm. On the other hand, monopolies have an incentive to underproduce and can generate unwarranted economic profits.

Nevertheless, it is important to recognize that monopoly is not always as socially harmful as sometimes indicated. Monopoly profits are the just rewards flowing from truly important contributions of unique firms and individuals.

Countervailing Power: The Monopoly/Monopsony Confrontation

Unregulated monopoly sellers typically limit production and offer their products at high prices. The private and social costs of this behavior are often measured by above-normal profits, inefficient production methods, and lagging rates of innovation. How is this inefficiency reduced, if not eliminated, in unregulated markets? Sometimes the answer lies in the development of countervailing forces within markets.

Seller Versus Buyer Power

Countervailing power is an economic influence that creates a closer balance between previously unequal sellers and buyers. The classic example is a single employer in a small town that might take advantage of the local labor force by offering less-than-competitive wages. As the single employer, the company has a monopsony in the local labor market. Workers might decide to band together and form a union, a monopoly seller in the local labor market, to offset the monopsony power of the employer.

Compromise Solution

What is likely to occur in the case of the monopoly union/monopsony employer confrontation? Typically, wage/employment bargaining produces a compromise wage/employment outcome. Compromise achieved through countervailing power has the beneficial effect of moving the labor market away from the inefficient unchecked monopoly or monopsony solutions toward a more efficient labor market equilibrium. However, only in the unlikely event of perfectly matched monopoly/monopsony protagonists will the perfectly competitive outcome occur. Depending on the relative power of the union and the employer, either an above-market or a below-market wage outcome typically results, and employment opportunities are often below competitive employment levels. Nevertheless, monopoly/monopsony confrontations can have the beneficial effect of improving economic efficiency from that experienced under either unchecked monopoly or monopsony.

Measurement of Business Profit Rates

In long-run equilibrium, profits in perfectly competitive industries are usually just sufficient to provide a normal risk-adjusted rate of return. In monopoly markets, barriers to entry or exit can allow above-normal profits, even over the long run. Nevertheless, high profits are sometimes observed in vigorously competitive markets, while some monopolies stumble from one year to the next without realizing superior rates of return.

Link Between Market Structure and Business Profit Rates

High business profit rates are derived from some combination of high profit margins, quick total asset turnover, and a high rate of total assets to stockholders' equity. High business profits generally indicate superior efficiency, modest competition, a wise use of assets, and/or use of a risky financial structure.

Competitive Strategy in Perfectly Competitive and Monopoly Markets

In perfectly competitive markets, the ready imitation of rivals makes ongoing success a constant struggle. In monopoly markets, entry and growth by nonleading firms often eat away at proprietary advantages. In both instances, development of an effective competitive strategy is vital to long-run success.

Competitive Strategy in Perfectly Competitive Markets

Economic luck *Temporary good fortune due to unexpected changes in industry demand or cost conditions.*

Competitive strategy is the search for a favorable competitive position and durable above-normal profits in an industry or line of business.

In perfectly competitive industries, above-normal returns sometimes reflect **economic luck,** or temporary good fortune due to unexpected changes in industry demand or cost conditions. For example, during 2001 many small to mid-size oil refineries and gasoline retailers benefited greatly when oil prices unexpectedly shot up following temporary oil shortages. At the same time, many other firms experienced economic losses following the unanticipated rise in energy costs. Both sets of companies experienced a reversal of fortune when energy prices plummeted. Grain farmers also benefit mightily when export demand for agricultural products skyrockets and suffer when export demand withers.

In other instances, above-normal returns in perfectly competitive industries reflect what is known as **economic rents,** or profits due to uniquely productive inputs. An exceptionally well-trained workforce, talented management, or superior land and raw materials can all lead to above-normal profits. In parts of the country where school systems provide outstanding primary and secondary education, firms are able to hire a basic workforce with a high rate of literacy and strong basic skills. Businesses that are able to employ such workers at a typical wage are able to earn superior profits when compared with the average rate of return for all competitors in the United States and Canada. Local tax subsidies designed to attract investment and job opportunities can also lower the cost of capital and create economic rents for affected firms. In many parts of the country, government initiatives often lead to economic rents for affected firms. On the other hand, if local taxes or government regulations prove to be especially onerous, economic losses can result for affected companies.

Another important source of above-normal profits in perfectly competitive industries is **disequilibrium profits.** Disequilibrium profits are above-normal returns that can be earned in the time interval that often exists between when a favorable influence on industry demand or cost conditions first transpires and the time when competitor entry or growth finally develops.

Disequilibrium losses are below-normal returns suffered in the time interval that can arise between when an unfavorable influence on industry demand or cost conditions first transpires and the time when exit or downsizing finally occurs. When barriers to entry and exit are minimal, competitor reactions tend to be quick and disequilibrium profits are fleeting. When barriers to entry and exit are significant, competitor reactions tend to be slow and disequilibrium profits can persist for extended periods. In the quintessential perfectly competitive industry, disequilibrium profits are quickly dissipated. In real-world markets, disequilibrium profits can persist over an entire business cycle even in the most competitive industries. In retailing, for example, labor and inventory costs have been cut dramatically following the introduction of computerized price scanners. Despite the vigorously price-competitive nature of the retailing business, early innovators who first adopted the bar code technology have been able to earn above-normal profits for a number of years. Innovative grocery retailers have enjoyed dramatically lower costs and profit margins on sales of 2 percent to 3.5 percent, versus a more typical 1 percent, over a decade and more.

In equilibrium, perfectly competitive markets only offer the potential for a normal rate of return on investment. If many capable competitors offer identical products, vigorous price competition tends to eliminate disequilibrium profits. The only exception to this rule is that superior efficiency can sometimes lead to superior profits, even in perfectly competitive markets. Above-normal profits in perfectly competitive industries are usually transitory and reflect the influences of economic rents, luck, or disequilibrium conditions. If above-normal returns persist for extended periods in a given industry or line of business, then elements of uniqueness are probably at work.

Competitive Strategy in Monopoly Markets

Above-normal returns tend to be fleeting in perfectly competitive industries but can be durable for efficient firms that benefit from meaningful monopoly advantages. As in any perfectly competitive industry, above-normal profit rates can be observed if monopoly firms temporarily benefit from some unanticipated increase in demand or decrease in costs. Similarly, monopolists can benefit from temporary affluence due to unexpected changes in industry demand or cost conditions or uniquely productive inputs. What is unique about monopoly is the potential for long-lasting above-normal rates of return.

In this age of instant global communication and rapid technical advance, no monopoly is permanently secure from the threat of current or potential competitors. Product characteristics, the local or regional limits of the market, the time necessary for reactions by established or new competitors, the pace of innovation, unanticipated changes in government regulation and tax policy, and a host of additional considerations all play an important role in defining the scope and durability of monopoly power. When attempting to describe monopoly advantages, it is always helpful to consider the number and size of potential competitors, degree of product differentiation, level of information available in the marketplace, and conditions of entry.

Exhibit 100.37 summarizes major characteristics typical of perfectly competitive and monopolistic markets. To develop an effective competitive strategy, it is necessary to assess the degree to which the characteristics of an individual market embody elements of each. Although the probability of successful entry is greater in perfectly competitive markets, monopoly markets lure new and established competitors with the promise of long-lasting, above-normal returns. Because the decision to enter any new market or line of business involves a careful balancing of expected costs and expected benefits, the monopoly advantages can act as a powerful inducement to competitors. Preservation of monopoly advantages is only likely when firms maintain the distinctive and valuable characteristics sought by customers. Similarly, the search for above-normal profits is only likely to be successful when firms create products that are faster, cheaper, or better than those offered by rivals.

Exhibit 100.37 *Summary of Perfect Competition and Monopoly (Monopsony) Market-Structure Characteristics*

	Perfect Competition	Monopoly (Monopsony)
Number of actual or potential competitors	Many small buyers and sellers	A single seller (buyer) of a valued product
Product differentiation	None—each buyer and seller deals in an identical product	Very high—no close substitutes available
Information	Complete and free information on price and product quality	Highly restricted access to price and product-quality information
Conditions of entry and exit	Complete freedom of entry and exit	Very high barriers caused by economies of scale (natural monopoly), patents, copyrights, government franchises, or other factors
Profit potential	Normal profit in long run; economic profits (losses) in short run only	Potential for economic profits in both short and long run
Examples	Some agricultural markets (grain); commodity, stock, and bond markets; some nonspecialized input markets (unskilled labor)	Monopoly (sellers): Local telephone service (basic hook-up); municipal bus companies; gas, water, and electric utilities. Monopsony (buyers): state and local governments (roads); U.S. government (defense electronics)

Monopolistic Competition and Oligopoly

Contrast Between Monopolistic Competition and Oligopoly

Monopolistic competition and oligopoly provide differing perspectives on the nature of competition in imperfectly competitive markets. Attributes of the monopolistic competition and oligopoly market models are outlined in this section.

Monopolistic Competition

The economic environment faced by many firms cannot be described as perfectly competitive. Likewise, few firms enjoy clear monopoly. Real-world markets commonly embody elements of both perfect competition and monopoly. Firms often introduce valuable new products or process innovations that give rise to above-normal rates of return in the short run. In the long run, however, entry and imitation by new rivals erode the dominant market share enjoyed by early innovators, and profits eventually return to normal. Still, in sharp contrast to perfectly competitive markets, the unique product characteristics of individual firms often remain valued by consumers. Consumers often continue to prefer Campbell's Soup, Dockers, Oil of Olay, Rubbermaid, Tide, and other favorite brands long after comparable products have been introduced by rivals. The partly competitive, partly monopolistic market structure encountered by firms in the apparel, food, hotel, retailing, and consumer products industries is called monopolistic competition. Given the lack of perfect substitutes, monopolistically competitive firms exercise some discretion in setting prices—they are not price takers. However, given vigorous competition from imitators offering close but not identical substitutes, such firms enjoy only a normal risk-adjusted rate of return on investment in long-run equilibrium.

Monopolistic competition A market structure characterized by a large number of sellers of differentiated products.

Monopolistic competition is similar to perfect competition in that it entails vigorous price competition among a large number of firms. The major difference between these two market-structure models is that consumers perceive important differences among the products offered by monopolistically competitive firms, whereas the output of perfectly competitive firms is homogeneous. This gives monopolistically competitive firms at least some discretion in setting prices. However, the availability of many close substitutes limits this price-setting ability and drives profits down to a normal risk-adjusted rate of return in the long run. As in the case of perfect competition, above-normal profits are possible only in the short run, before the monopolistically competitive firm's rivals can take effective countermeasures.

Oligopoly

Oligopoly is the market structure model that describes competition among a handful of competitors sheltered by significant barriers to entry. Oligopolists might produce a homogeneous product, such as aluminum, steel, or semiconductors; or differentiated products such as Cheerios, Coca-Cola, Marlboro, MTV, and Nintendo. Innovative leading firms in the ready-to-eat cereal, beverage, cigarette, entertainment, and computer software industries, among others, have the potential for economic profits even in the long run. With few competitors, economic incentives also exist for such firms to devise illegal agreements to limit competition, fix prices, or otherwise divide markets. The history of antitrust enforcement in the United States provides numerous examples of "competitors" who illegally entered into such agreements. Yet there are also examples of markets in which vigorous competition among a small number of firms generates obvious long-term benefits for consumers. It is therefore erroneous to draw a simple link between the number of competitors and the vigor of competition.

Oligopoly A market structure characterized by few sellers and interdependent price/output decisions.

In an industry characterized by oligopoly, only a few large rivals are responsible for the bulk of industry output. As in the case of monopoly, high to very high barriers to entry are typical. Under oligopoly, the price/output decisions of firms are interrelated in the sense that direct reactions among rivals can be expected. As a result, decisions of individual firms anticipate the likely response of competitors. This competition among the few involves a wide variety of price and nonprice methods of rivalry, as determined by the institutional characteristics of each particular market. Even though limited numbers of competitors give rise to a potential for economic profits, above-normal rates of return are far from guaranteed. Competition among the few can be vigorous.

Dynamic Nature of Competition

In characterizing the descriptive relevance of the monopolistic competition and oligopoly models of seller behavior, it is important to recognize the dynamic nature of real-world markets. For example, as late as the mid 1980s it seemed appropriate to regard the automobile and personal computer manufacturing markets as oligopolistic in nature. Today, it seems fairer to regard each industry as monopolistically competitive. In the automobile industry, **GM, Ford,** and **DaimlerChrysler** have found **Toyota, Honda, Nissan,** and a host of specialized competitors to be formidable foes. Aggressive competitors like Dell, Compaq, Hewlett-Packard, and Gateway first weakened, and then obliterated, IBM's early lead in the PC business. Prices and profit margins for PCs continue to fall as improving technology continues to enhance product quality.

In many formerly oligopolistic markets, the market discipline provided by a competitive fringe of smaller domestic and foreign rivals is sufficient to limit the potential abuse of a few large competitors. In the long-distance telephone service market, for example, AT&T, **MCI WorldCom,** and **Sprint** have long dominated the industry. However, emerging competition from the so-called regional **Bell** operating companies (REBOCs), along with a host of smaller specialized providers, cause long-distance phone service price and service quality competition to be spirited. Similarly, the competitive fringe in wireless communications and cable TV promises to force dramatic change during the years ahead.

It is unfortunate, but public perceptions and government regulatory policy sometimes lag behind economic reality. It is essential that timely and accurate market structure information be available to form the basis for managerial investment decisions that relate to entry or exit from specific lines of business. Similarly, enlightened public policy requires timely information.

Monopolistic Competition

Most firms are subject to rivalry, though perhaps not as vigorous as would exist under perfect competition. Even though most firms face a large number of competitors with similar products, many still have some control over the price of their product. They cannot sell all that they want at a fixed price, nor would they lose all sales if they raised prices slightly. Most firms face downward-sloping demand curves, signifying less-than-perfect competition.

Characteristics of Monopolistically Competitive Markets

Monopolistic competition exists when individual producers have moderate influence over product prices, where each product enjoys a degree of uniqueness in the perception of customers. This market structure has some important similarities and dissimilarities with perfectly competitive markets. Monopolistic competition is characterized by

- *Large numbers of buyers and sellers.* Each firm produces a small portion of industry output, and each customer buys only a small part of the total.
- *Product heterogeneity.* The output of each firm is perceived to be essentially different from, though comparable with, the output of other firms in the industry.
- *Free entry and exit.* Firms are not restricted from entering or leaving the industry.
- *Perfect dissemination of information.* Cost, price, and product quality information is known by all buyers and all sellers.

These basic conditions are not as restrictive as those for perfect competition and are fairly commonplace in actual markets. Vigorous monopolistic competition is evident in the banking, container and packaging, discount and fashion retail, electronics, food manufacturing, office equipment, paper and forest products, and most personal and professional service industries. Although individual firms are able to maintain some control over pricing policy, their pricing discretion is severely limited by competition from firms offering close but not identical substitutes.

Monopolistic competition is a realistic description of competition in a wide variety of industries. As in perfectly competitive markets, a large number of competitors make independent decisions in monopolistically competitive markets. A price change by any one firm does not cause other firms to change prices. If price reactions did occur, then an oligopoly market structure would be present. The most distinctive characteristic of monopolistic competition is that each competitor offers a unique product that is an imperfect substitute for those offered by rivals. Each firm is able to differentiate its product from those of its adversaries. Nevertheless, each firm's demand function is significantly affected by the presence of numerous competitors producing goods that consumers view as reasonably close substitutes. Exogenous changes in demand and cost conditions also tend to have a similar effect on all firms and frequently lead to comparable pricing influences.

Product differentiation takes many forms. Quality differentials, packaging, credit terms, or superior maintenance service can all differentiate products, as can advertising that leads to brand-name identification. Because consumers evaluate products on the basis of their ability to satisfy specific wants, as well as when and where they have them, products involve not only quantity, quality, and price characteristics but time and place attributes as well. The important factor in all of these forms of product differentiation is that some consumers prefer the product of one seller to those of others.

Price/Output Decisions Under Monopolistic Competition

As its name suggests, monopolistic competition embodies elements of both monopoly and perfect competition. The monopoly aspect is most forcefully observed in the short run.

Oligopoly

The theory of monopolistic competition recognizes that firms often have some control over price but that their price flexibility is limited by a large number of close substitutes. This theory assumes that in making decisions firms do not consider competitor reactions. Such a behavioral assumption is appropriate for some industries but not others. When individual firm actions cause competitors to react, oligopoly exists.

Characteristics of Oligopoly Markets

Oligopoly is present when a handful of competitors dominate the market for a good or service and each firm makes pricing and marketing decisions in light of the expected response by rivals. Individual firms have the ability to set pricing and production strategy, and they enjoy the potential for economic profits in both the short run and the long run. Oligopoly describes markets that can be characterized as follows:

- *Few sellers.* A handful of firms produces the bulk of industry output.
- *Homogeneous or unique product.* Oligopoly output can be homogeneous (e.g., aluminum) or distinctive (e.g., ready-to-eat cereal).
- *Blockaded entry and exit.* Firms are heavily restricted from entering or leaving the industry.
- *Imperfect dissemination of information.* Cost, price, and product quality information is withheld from uninformed buyers.

In the United States, aluminum, cigarettes, electrical equipment, filmed entertainment production and distribution, glass, long-distance telecommunications, and ready-to-eat cereals are all produced and sold under conditions of oligopoly. In each of these industries, a small number of firms produces a dominant percentage of all industry output. In the ready-to-eat breakfast cereal industry, for example, Kellogg, **Kraft** (Post cereals), **General Mills, Nabisco,** and **Quaker Oats** are responsible for almost all domestic production in the United States. Durable customer loyalty gives rise to fat profit margins and rates of return on assets that are two to three times food industry norms. Corn Flakes, Sugar Frosted Flakes, Cheerios, Raisin Bran, Wheaties, and a handful of other brands continue to dominate the industry year after year and make successful entry extremely difficult. Even multinational food giant Nestlé sought and obtained a joint venture agreement with General Mills rather than enter the potentially lucrative European breakfast cereal market by itself. Long-distance telephone service is also highly concentrated, with AT&T, Sprint, and WorldCom providing almost all domestic wire-line service to residential customers.

Oligopoly also is present in a number of local markets. In many retail markets for gasoline and food, for example, only a few service stations and grocery stores compete within a small geographic area. Drycleaning services are also sometimes provided by a relative handful of firms in small- to medium-size cities and towns.

Price/Output Decisions Under Oligopoly

Demand curves relate quantity demanded to price, holding constant the effect of all other variables. One variable that is typically assumed to remain fixed is the price charged by competing firms. In oligopoly, however, if one firm changes its price, other firms react by changing their prices. The demand curve for the initial firm shifts position so that instead of moving along a single demand curve as it changes price, the firm moves to an entirely new demand curve.

Cartel Arrangements

All firms in an oligopoly market benefit if they get together and set prices to maximize industry profits. A group of competitors operating under such a formal overt agreement is called a **cartel.** If an informal covert agreement is reached, the firms are said to be operating in **collusion.** Both practices are illegal in the United States. However, cartels are legal in some parts of the world, and U.S. multinational corporations sometimes become involved with them in foreign markets. Several important domestic markets are also dominated by producer associations that operate like cartels and appear to flourish without interference from the government. Agricultural commodities such as milk are prime examples of products marketed under cartel-like arrangements. A cartel that has absolute control over all firms in an industry can operate as a monopoly.

Price Leadership

An informal but sometimes effective means for reducing oligopolistic uncertainty is through **price leadership.** Price leadership results when one firm establishes itself as the industry leader and other firms follow its pricing policy. This leadership may result from the size and strength of the leading firm, from cost efficiency, or as a result of the ability of the leader to establish prices that produce satisfactory profits throughout the industry.

Kinked Demand Curve

An often-noted characteristic of oligopoly markets is "sticky" prices. Once a general price level has been established, whether through cartel agreement or some less formal arrangement, it tends to remain fixed for an extended period. Such rigid prices are sometimes explained by what is referred to as the **kinked demand curve** theory of oligopoly prices. A kinked demand curve is a firm demand curve that has different slopes for price increases as compared with price decreases. The kinked demand curve describes a behavior pattern in which rival firms follow any decrease in price to maintain their respective market shares but refrain from following price increases, allowing their market shares to grow at the expense of the competitor increasing its price. The demand curve facing individual firms is kinked at the current price/output combination.

Nonprice Competition

"Meet it or beat it" is a pricing challenge that often results in quick competitor price reductions, and price wars always favor the deep pockets of established incumbents. As a result, many successful entrants find nonprice methods of competition an effective means for growing market share and profitability in the face of entrenched rivals.

Advantages of Nonprice Competition

Because rival firms are likely to retaliate against price cuts, oligopolists often emphasize nonprice competition to boost demand.

Effective advertising shifts the firm's demand curve to the right, thus enabling the firm to increase sales at a given price or to sell the same quantity at a higher price. Any improvement in styling or quality would have a comparable effect, as would easier credit terms, better service, and more convenient retail locations. Although competitors react to nonprice competition, their reaction is often slower and less direct than that for price changes. Nonprice changes are generally less obvious to rivals, and the design of an effective response is often time-consuming and difficult. Advertising campaigns have to be designed; media time and space must be purchased. Styling and quality changes frequently require long lead times, as do fundamental improvements in customer service. Furthermore, nonprice competition can alter customer buying habits, and regaining lost customers can prove to be difficult. Although it may take longer to establish a reputation through nonprice competition, its advantageous effects are likely to be more persistent than the fleeting benefits of a price cut.

The optimal level of nonprice competition is defined by resulting marginal benefits and marginal costs. Any form of nonprice competition should be pursued as long as marginal benefits exceed marginal costs. For example, suppose that a product has a market price of $10 per unit and a variable cost per unit of $8. If sales can be increased at an additional cost of less than $2 per unit, these additional expenditures will increase profits and should be made.

Optimal Level of Advertising

Advertising is one of the most common methods of nonprice competition. Others include personal selling, improvements in product quality, expansions in customer service, research and development, and so on. The profit-maximizing amount of nonprice competition is found by setting the marginal cost of the activity involved equal to the marginal revenue or marginal benefit derived from it. For example, the optimal level of advertising occurs at that point where the marginal revenues derived from advertising just offset the marginal cost of advertising.

The marginal revenue derived from advertising is measured by the marginal profit contribution generated. This is the difference between marginal revenue, MR, and the marginal cost of production and distribution, MC_Q, before advertising costs:

$$\text{Marginal Revenue Derived from Advertising} = \text{Marginal Revenue} - \text{Marginal Cost of Output}$$
$$MR_A = MR - MC_Q \qquad (1.14)$$

The marginal cost of advertising, again expressed in terms of the marginal cost of selling one additional unit of output, can be written:

$$\text{Marginal Cost of Advertising} = \frac{\text{Change in Advertising Expenditures}}{\text{One-Unit Change in Demand}}$$
$$MC_A = \frac{\Delta \text{Advertising Expenditures}}{\Delta \text{Demand}} = \frac{\Delta Ad}{\Delta Q} \qquad (1.15)$$

The optimal level of advertising is found where

$$\text{Marginal Revenue Derived from Advertising} = \text{Marginal Cost of Advertising}$$
$$MR - MC_Q = \frac{\Delta \text{Advertising Expenditures}}{\Delta \text{Demand}}$$
$$MR_A = MC_A$$

In general, it will pay to expand advertising expenditures so long as $MR_A > MC_A$. Because the marginal profit derived from advertising is

$$M\pi_A = MR_A - MC_A \qquad (1.16)$$

the optimal level of advertising occurs at the point where

$$M\pi_A = 0$$

As long as $MR_A > MC_A$, $M\pi_A > 0$, and it will pay to expand the level of advertising. Conversely, if $MR_A < MC_A$, then $M\pi_A < 0$, and it will pay to reduce the level of advertising expenditures. The optimal level of advertising is achieved when $MR_A = MC_A$, and $M\pi_A = 0$.

Game Theory

Game theory concepts are used to develop effective competitive strategies for setting prices, the level of product quality, research and development, advertising, and other forms of nonprice competition in oligopoly markets. Game theory concepts have also been used to set public policy for currency market intervention in emerging markets and auction strategies for broadcast spectrum in the telecommunications industry. This brief introduction shows how managers can use a simple understanding of game theory concepts to make better managerial decisions.

Game theory *General framework to help decision making when firm payoffs depend on actions taken by other firms.*

Prisoner's Dilemma

Game theory is a general framework to help decision making when firm payoffs depend on actions taken by other firms. Because decision interdependence is a prime characteristic of oligopoly markets, game theory concepts have a wide variety of applications in the study of oligopoly. In a **simultaneous-move game,** each decision maker makes choices without specific knowledge of competitor countermoves. In a **sequential-move game,** decision makers make their move after observing competitor moves. If two firms set prices without knowledge of each other's decisions, it is a simultaneous-move game. If one firm sets its price only after observing its rival's price, the firm is said to be involved in a sequential-move game. In a **one-shot game,** the underlying interaction between competitors occurs only once; in a **repeat game,** there is an ongoing interaction between competitors.

A game theory strategy is a decision rule that describes the action taken by a decision maker at any point in time. A simple introduction to game theory strategy is provided by perhaps the most famous of all simultaneous-move one-shot games: The so-called **Prisoner's Dilemma.** Suppose two suspects, Bonnie and Clyde, are jointly accused of committing a specific crime, say inside trading. Furthermore, assume that the conviction of either suspect cannot be secured without a signed confession by one or both suspects. As shown in Exhibit 100.38, if neither Bonnie nor Clyde confesses, the prosecutor will be unable to obtain a conviction, and both will be set free. If only one suspect confesses, turns state's evidence and implicates the other, then the one confessing will get the relatively light penalty of having to pay a fine and serving probation, and the implicated party will receive the harsh sentence of five years in prison. If both suspects confess, then each will receive a stiff two-year sentence. If both suspects are held in isolation, neither knows what the other will do, and a classic conflict-of-interest situation is created.

Prisoner's Dilemma *A classic conflict-of-interest situation.*

Although each suspect can control the range of sentencing outcomes, neither can control the ultimate outcome. In this situation, there is no **dominant strategy** that results in the best result for either suspect regardless of the action taken by the other. Both would be better off if they could be assured that the other would not confess, because if neither confesses both are set free. However, in failing to confess, each is exposed to the risk that the other will confess. By not confessing, they would then receive the harsh sentence of five years in prison. This uncertainty creates the Prisoner's Dilemma. To confess, or not to confess—that is the question.

Dominant strategy *Decision that gives the best result for either party regardless of the action taken by the other.*

Exhibit 100.38 *The Prisoner's Dilemma Payoff Matrix*

		Suspect #2: Clyde	
Confession Strategy		Not Confess	Confess
Suspect #1: Bonnie	Not Confess	Freedom Freedom	5-year prison term Fine and probation
	Confess	Fine and probation, 5-year prison term	2-year prison term 2-year prison term

170. MANAGERIAL ECONOMICS

Exhibit 100.39 *A Hypothetical Prisoner's Dilemma Faced by Coca-Cola and Pepsi-Cola*

		Pepsi-Cola	
		Discount Price	Regular Price
Coca-Cola	Discount Price	$4,000, $2,000	$10,000, $1,000
	Regular Price	$1,500, $6,500	$12,500, $9,000

Secure strategy Decision that guarantees the best possible outcome given the worst possible scenario.

A **secure strategy**, sometimes called the maximin strategy, guarantees the best possible outcome given the worst possible scenario. In this case, the worst possible scenario for each suspect is that the other chooses to confess. Each suspect can avoid the worst possible outcome of receiving a harsh five years in prison sentence only by choosing to confess. For each suspect, the secure strategy is to confess, thereby becoming a prisoner, because neither could solve the riddle posed by the Prisoner's Dilemma.

Though the Prisoner's Dilemma is posed within the scope of a bargaining problem between two suspects, it has obvious practical applications in business. Competitors like Coca-Cola and Pepsi-Cola confront similar bargaining problems on a regular basis. Suppose each has to decide whether or not to offer a special discount to a large grocery store retailer. Exhibit 100.40 shows that if neither offers discount pricing, a weekly profit of $12,500 will be earned by Coca-Cola, and $9,000 per week will be earned by its smaller competitor, Pepsi-Cola. This is the best possible scenario for both. However, if Coca-Cola is the only one to offer a discount, it will earn $10,000 per week, while Pepsi-Cola profits fall to $1,000 per week. If Pepsi-Cola offers a discount and Coca-Cola continues to charge the regular price, Pepsi-Cola profits will total $6,500 per week while Coca-Cola weekly profits fall to $1,500. The only secure means Coca-Cola has for avoiding the possibility of a meager $1,500 per week profit is to grant a discount price to the retailer, thereby assuring itself of a weekly profit of at least $4,000. Similarly, the only means Pepsi-Cola has of avoiding the possibility of meager profits of $1,000 per week is to also grant a discount price to the grocery retailer, thereby assuring itself of at least $2,000 in weekly profits. For both Coca-Cola and Pepsi-Cola, the only secure strategy is to offer discount prices, thereby assuring consumers of bargain prices and themselves of modest profits of $4,000 and $2,000 per week, respectively.

Nash Equilibrium

Nash equilibrium Set of decision strategies where no player can improve through a unilateral change in strategy.

In Exhibit 100.39, each firm's secure strategy is to offer a discount price regardless of the other firm's actions. The outcome is that both firms offer discount prices and earn relatively modest profits. This outcome is also called a **Nash equilibrium** because, given the strategy of its competitor, neither firm can improve its own payoff by unilaterally changing its own strategy. In the case of Coca-Cola, given that Pepsi-Cola has chosen a discount pricing strategy, it too would decide to offer discount prices. When Pepsi-Cola offers discount prices, Coca-Cola can earn profits of $4,000 rather than $1,500 per week by also offering a discount. Similarly, when Coca-Cola offers discount prices, Pepsi-Cola can earn maximum profits of $2,000 per week, versus $1,000 per week, by also offering a discount.

Clearly, profits are less than if they colluded and both charged regular prices. As seen in Exhibit 100.39, Coca-Cola would earn $12,500 per week and Pepsi-Cola would earn $9,000 per week if both charged regular prices. This is a business manifestation of the Prisoner's Dilemma because the dual discount pricing Nash equilibrium is inferior from the firms' viewpoint to a collusive outcome where both competitors agree to charge regular prices.

Of course, if firms collude and agree to charge high prices, consumers are made worse off. This is why price collusion among competitors is illegal in the United States, as discussed in Section 165.

Nash Bargaining

Nash bargaining Where two competitors haggle over some item of value.

A **Nash bargaining** game is another application of the simultaneous-move, one-shot game. In Nash bargaining, two competitors or players "bargain" over some item of value. In a simultaneous-move, one-shot game, the players have only one chance to reach an agreement.

MODULE 100. GENERAL MANAGEMENT AND ORGANIZATION

Exhibit 100.40 *Nash Bargaining Game over Profit-Pool Sharing*

	Request Strategy	Management $0	$500,000	$1,000,000
Workers	$0	$0 / $0	$0 / $500,000	$0 / $1,000,000
	$500,000	$500,000 / $0	$500,000 / $500,000	$0 / $0
	$1,000,000	$1,000,000 / $0	$0 / $0	$0 / $0

For example, suppose the board of directors specifies a $1 million profit-sharing pool provided that both management and workers can come to agreement concerning how such profits are to be distributed. For simplicity, assume that this pool can only be distributed in amounts of $0, $500,000, and $1 million. If the sum of the amounts requested by each party totals more than $1 million, neither party receives anything. If the sum of the amounts requested by each party totals no more than $1 million, each party receives the amount requested.

Exhibit 100.40 shows the nine possible outcomes from such a profit-sharing bargaining game. If the workers request $1 million, the only way that they would get any money at all is if management requests nothing. Similarly, if management requests $1 million, the only way they get money is if workers request nothing. If either party requests nothing, Nash equilibrium solutions are achieved when the other party requests the full $1 million. Thus, the ($1 million, $0) and ($0, $1 million) solutions are both Nash equilibriums. However, suppose the workers request $500,000; then the Nash equilibrium response from management would be to also request $500,000. If management requests $500,000, then the Nash equilibrium response from workers would be to also request $500,000. Thus, the ($500,000, $500,000) payoff is also a Nash equilibrium. This game involves three Nash equilibriums out of nine possible solutions. In each Nash equilibrium, the entire profit-sharing pool is paid out. In the six remaining outcomes, some of the profit-sharing pool would not be distributed. Such suboptimal outcomes can and do occur in real-life situations.

However, in contemplating the bargaining process, workers are apt to note that a request for $0 is dominated by asking for either $500,000 or $1 million. If you do not ask for anything, you are sure of getting nothing. Similarly, management will never do worse, and may do better, if it asks for something. As a result, the $0 request strategy is dominated for both parties and will tend not to be followed. In addition, a request for the entire $1 million by either party will not be successful unless the other party requests nothing. Because a $0 request by either party is not likely, neither party is likely to request the full $1 million. In this case, the logical and rational request from each party is $500,000, or an equal 50/50 sharing of the profit pool.

Repeat Games

The study of one-shot pricing and product quality games might lead one to conclude that even tacit collusion is impossible. This is not true because competitors often interact on a continuous basis. In such circumstances, firms are said to be involved in **repeat games.**

When a competitive game is repeated over and over, firms receive sequential payoffs that shape current and future strategies. For example, in Exhibit 100.39, both Coca-Cola and Pepsi-Cola might tacitly or secretly agree to charge regular prices so long as the other party continues to do so. If neither firm cheats on such a collusive agreement, discounts will never be offered, and maximum profits will be earned. Although there is an obvious risk involved with charging regular prices, there is also an obvious cost if either or both firms offer discount pricing. If each firm is convinced that the other will maintain regular prices, both will enjoy high profits. This resolve is increased if each firm is convinced that the other will quickly match any discount pricing strategy. In fact, it is rational for colluding firms to quickly and severely punish colluding competitors who "cheat" by lowering prices.

However, although it is important to recognize that the repeat nature of competitor interactions can sometimes harm consumers, it is equally important to recognize that repetitive interactions in the marketplace provide necessary incentives for firms to produce high-quality goods. In any one-shot game, it would pay firms with high-quality reputations to produce low-cost or shoddy goods. In the real world, the ongoing interaction between firms and their

> **Repeat games** A comprehensive statistical profile of the economy, from the national, to the state, to the local level.

customers provides incentives for firms to maintain product consistency. For example, both Coca-Cola and Pepsi-Cola have well-deserved reputations for providing uniformly high-quality soft drinks. They have both invested millions of dollars in product development and quality control to ensure that consumers can depend upon the taste, smell, and feel of Coca-Cola and Pepsi-Cola products. Moreover, because the value of millions of dollars spent on brand-name advertising would be lost if product quality were to deteriorate, that brand-name advertising is itself a type of quality assurance provided to customers of Coca-Cola and Pepsi-Cola. At Wal-Mart, *Satisfaction Guaranteed, or your money back,* is more than just a slogan. It is their business; it is what separates Wal-Mart from fly-by-night operators or low-quality discount stores. Similarly, customers of DaimlerChrysler depend upon that company's well-deserved reputation for producing high-quality cars, trucks, and minivans. Like any written guarantee or insurance policy, repeat transactions in the marketplace give consumers confidence that they will get what they pay for.

Market Structure Measurement

To formulate an effective competitive strategy, managers must accurately assess the current competitive environment for actual and potential products. Data gathered by the federal government, private market research firms, and trade associations are often useful for this purpose. This section shows the types of market structure data available from public sources and explains why they are important for decision-making purposes.

How Are Economic Markets Measured?

An economic market consists of all individuals and firms willing and able to buy or sell competing products during a given period. The key criterion in identifying competing products is similarity in use. Precise determination of whether a specific good is a distinct economic product involves an evaluation of cross-price elasticities for broad classes of goods. When cross-price elasticities are large and positive, goods are substitutes for each other and can be thought of as competing products in a single market. Conversely, large negative cross-price elasticities indicate complementary products. Complementary products produced by a single firm must be evaluated as a single product line serving the same market. If complementary products are produced by other companies, evaluating the potential of a given product line involves incorporating exogenous influences beyond the firm's control. When cross-price elasticities are near zero, goods are in separate economic markets and can be separately analyzed as serving distinct consumer needs. Therefore, using cross-price elasticity criteria to desegregate the firm's overall product line into its distinct economic markets is an important task confronting managers.

To identify relevant economic markets and define their characteristics, firms in the United States make extensive use of economic data collected by the Bureau of the Census of the U.S. Department of Commerce.

Competitive Strategy in Monopolistic Competition and Oligopoly Markets

Developing and implementing an effective competitive strategy in imperfectly competitive markets involves a never-ending search for uniquely attractive products. Not all industries offer the same potential for sustained profitability; not all firms are equally capable of exploiting the profit potential that is available.

Competitive Strategy in Imperfectly Competitive Markets

It is always helpful to consider the number and size distribution of competitors, degree of product differentiation, level of information available in the marketplace, and conditions of entry when attempting to define market structure. Unfortunately, these and other readily obtained data are seldom definitive. Conditions of entry and exit are subtle and dynamic, as is the role of unseen potential entrants. All of this contributes to the difficulty of correctly assessing the profit potential of current products of prospective lines of business.

Rather than consider simply what is, effective managers must contemplate what might be. This is especially true when seeking to develop an effective competitive strategy. An effective competitive strategy in imperfectly competitive

Exhibit 100.41 *Summary of Monopolistic Competition and Oligopoly (Oligopsony) Market-Structure Characteristics*

	Monopolistic Competition	Oligopoly
Number of actual or potential competitors	Many sellers	Few sellers whose decisions are directly related to those of competitors
Product differentiation	Consumers perceive differences among the products of various competitors	High or low, depending on entry and exit conditions
Information	Low-cost information on price and product quality	Restricted access to price and product-quality information; cost and other data are often proprietary
Conditions of entry and exit	Easy entry and exit	High entry or exit barriers because of economies of scale, capital requirements, advertising, research and development costs, or other factors
Profit potential	Economic (above-normal) profits in short run only; normal profit in long run	Potential for economic (above-normal) profits in both short and long run
Examples	Clothing, consumer financial services, professional services, restaurants	Automobiles, aluminum, soft drinks, investment banking, long-distance telephone service, pharmaceuticals

markets must be founded on the firm's **competitive advantage.** A competitive advantage is a unique or rare ability to create, distribute, or service products valued by customers. It is the business-world analog to what economists call **comparative advantage,** or when one nation or region of the country is better suited to the production of one product than to the production of some other product. For example, when compared with the United States and Canada, Mexico enjoys a relative abundance of raw materials and cheap labor. As such, Mexico is in a relatively good position to export agricultural products, oil, and finished goods that require unskilled labor to the U.S. and Canadian market. At the same time, the United States and Canada enjoy a relative abundance of highly educated people, capital goods, and investment resources. Therefore, the United States and Canada are in a relatively good position to export machine tools, computer equipment, education, and professional services to Mexico.

Competitive advantage A unique or rare ability to create, distribute, or service products valued by customers.

Comparative advantage When one nation or region of the country is better suited to the production of one product than to the production of some other product.

An effective competitive strategy in imperfectly competitive markets grows out of a sophisticated understanding of the rules of competition in a given line of business or industry. The ultimate aim of this strategy is to cope with or, better still, change those rules in the company's favor. To do so, managers must understand and contend with the rivalry among existing competitors, entry of new rivals, threat of substitutes, bargaining power of suppliers, and the bargaining power of buyers. Just as all industries are not alike in terms of their inherent profit potential, all firms are not alike in terms of their capacity to exploit available opportunities. In the business world, long-lasting above-normal rates of return require a sustainable competitive advantage that, by definition, cannot be easily duplicated.

This is not to suggest that advertising and other nonprice methods of competition have not been used to great advantage by many successful firms in imperfectly competitive markets. In fact, these techniques are often a primary force in developing a strong basis for product differentiation. Exhibit 100.41 summarizes major characteristics typical of the monopolistic competition and oligopoly market structures. To develop an effective competitive strategy, it is necessary to assess the degree to which an individual industry or line of business embodies elements of each of these market structures. Although the probability of successful entry is higher in monopolistically competitive markets, only difficult-to-enter oligopoly markets hold the potential for long-lasting, above-normal returns.

In sum, firms in imperfectly competitive markets have the potential to earn economic profits in the long run only to the extent that they impart a valuable degree of uniqueness to the goods or services provided. Success, measured in terms of above-normal rates of return, requires a competitive advantage in production, distribution, or marketing that cannot easily be copied. That such success is difficult to achieve and is often rather fleeting is obvious when one considers the most profitable companies in America.

170. MANAGERIAL ECONOMICS

When Large Size Is a Disadvantage

If economies of scale are substantial, larger firms are able to achieve lower costs of production or distribution than their smaller rivals. These cost advantages can translate into higher and more stable profits, and a significant competitive advantage for larger firms. Diseconomies of large-scale organizations work in the opposite direction. When diseconomies of scale are operative, larger firms suffer a cost disadvantage when compared to smaller rivals. Smaller firms are then able to translate the benefits of small size into a distinct competitive advantage. Rather than losing profits and sales opportunities to larger rivals, smaller firms can enjoy higher profit rates and gain market share over time.

Industries dominated by large firms tend to be those in which there are significant economies of scale, important advantages to vertical integration, and a prevalence of mass marketing. As a result, large organizations with sprawling plants emphasize large quantities of output at low production costs. Use of national media, especially TV advertising, is common. Industries in which "small is beautiful" tend to be characterized by diseconomies of scale, "just in time" assembly and manufacturing, and niche marketing that emphasizes the use of highly skilled individuals adept at personal selling. Small factories with flexible production schedules are common. Rather than emphasize long production runs, many smaller companies focus on product quality. Instead of the sometimes slow-to-respond hierarchical organizations of large companies, smaller companies feature "flat" organizations with quick, decentralized decision making and authority.

The villain sometimes encountered by large-scale firms is not any diseconomy of scale in the production process itself, but rather the burden that size places on effective management. Big often means complex, and complexity results in inefficiencies and bureaucratic snarls that can strangle effective communication. In the former Soviet Union, a huge, highly centralized, run-from-the-top system came crashing down as a result of its own gigantic weight. Hoping to avoid a similar fate, many large organizations are now splitting assets into smaller independent operating units that can react quickly to customer needs without the typically long delays of large organizations. IBM, for example, has split into independent operating units that compete directly with each other to provide customers with the latest in computer equipment and software. **General Motors,** seeking to become more lean and agile like Japanese competitors, established **Saturn** as an independent operating unit. **Exxon** is selling domestic exploration and production operations to smaller independents that chop overhead and earn significant profits despite low volume and depressed oil prices. These examples suggest that many large corporations are going through a metamorphosis that will favor organizations that are especially adept at reallocating capital among nimble, entrepreneurial operating units.

From electronics instrumentation to specialized steel, smaller companies have replaced larger companies in positions of industry leadership. The trend towards a higher level of efficiency for smaller companies has become so widespread that larger companies are now finding that meeting the needs of the customer sometimes requires a dramatic downsizing of the large-scale organization.

Threat of Potential Competition

The potential for above-normal rates of return is a powerful inducement to the entry of new competitors and to the rapid growth of nonleading firms. Imitation may be the sincerest form of flattery, but it is also the most effective enemy of above-normal rates of return. Regression to the mean is the rule rather than the exception for above-normal corporate profit rates over time. During recent years, after-tax rates of return on stockholders' equity have usually been in the range of 9 percent to 10 percent per year. Just as in the stock market where investors rarely earn excess returns, individual companies rarely earn in excess of 15 percent to 20 percent for more than a decade. A consistent return on equity, ROE $\geq$ 20 percent is simply unheard of for an entire industry with several competitors over a sustained period. Therefore, it seems reasonable to conclude that price and nonprice methods of competition are often vigorous, even in imperfectly competitive industries with few active or potential competitors.

Economics and Operations

Economics and Operations

Economics and operations are closely related: Operations incur costs to produce goods or to provide services. Major concepts include economies of scale, economies of scope, learning curve, and economic analysis.

Economies of Scale

For a given production plant, there is an annual volume of outputs that results in the least average unit cost. This level of output is called the **best operating level.** As the annual volume of outputs increase, average unit costs fall. These declining costs result from fixed costs and labor costs being spread over more and more units. Such savings, which are called **economies of scale,** continues to accrue as the volume of outputs increases to the best operating level for that production plant. Beyond the best operating level, additional volume of outputs results in ever-increasing average unit costs. These increasing costs arise from increasing inefficiency, difficulty in production and worker scheduling, difficulty in coordinating and communicating with more workers, reduced morale, and increased use of overtime. The impact of such factors, which are called **diseconomies of scale,** increases at an accelerating rate past the best operating level.

> *Economies of scale are obtained by spreading the costs of production over a large quantity of products. Economies of scope are obtained by spreading the costs of production over a wide variety of products. These two concepts are distinct in that scale refers to size or number whereas scope refers to functions or activities.*

Economies of Scope

Economies of scope refers to the ability to produce many product models in one plant more cheaply than in separate plants. Technological breakthroughs have contributed to this concept because changes to products can be done quickly and inexpensively, with the result that economies are created by spreading the cost of automated facilities over many product lines. This means that the cost of joint production of complementary products is less than that of producing them individually.

Another example of economies of scope is when two or more businesses operate under the same corporate facilities, thus eliminating costs for having separate services. It results from cross-business cost-saving opportunities such as common sales force, centralized management, joint research and development efforts, and sharing administrative support staff.

Learning Curve

For many manufacturing processes, average costs decline as cumulative total output increases due to improvements in the use of production equipment and procedures and reduced waste. The learning phenomenon is often characterized as a constant percentage decline in average costs as cumulative output increases. This percentage represents the proportion by which unit costs decline as the cumulative quantity of total output doubles. Learning through production experience permits the firm to produce output more efficiently at each and every output level.

The learning (experience) curve concept is different from the economies of scale concept. Scale economies relate to cost differences associated with different output levels along a single learning curve average cost. On the other hand, the learning curves relate cost differences to total cumulative output. They are measured by shifts in learning curve average cost curves over time. These shifts result from improved production efficiencies stemming from knowledge gained through production experience.

Economic Analysis

During review of automation opportunities and new product alternatives, operations management looks at economic evaluation of the prototype design. This evaluation includes estimation of production volume, costs, and profits for the new product. If satisfactory, the project will enter the production design phase. Some examples of economic analysis performed by operations management in this area include operating leverage, break-even analysis, capital budgeting techniques (e.g., payback period, net present value, internal rate of return, and profitability index), and financial ratio analysis.

170. MANAGERIAL ECONOMICS

Economics and Marketing

Demand and Supply

Around the globe, 24 hours per day, impossible-to-regulate currency markets set prices for the U.S. dollar, Japanese yen, and the European Economic and Monetary Union's euro. Much to the chagrin of sovereign governments and their official representatives, minute-by-minute variations in currency prices are wholly determined by the converging forces of supply and demand. The laws of demand and supply are so powerful that they dictate the value of money itself.

Basis for Demand

Demand is the quantity of a good or service that customers are willing and able to purchase during a specified period under a given set of economic conditions. The time frame might be an hour, a day, a month, or a year. Conditions to be considered include the price of the good in question, prices and availability of related goods, expectations of price changes, consumer incomes, consumer tastes and preferences, advertising expenditures, and so on. The amount of the product that consumers are prepared to purchase, its demand, depends on all these factors.

For managerial decision making, a prime focus is on market demand. Market demand is the aggregate of individual, or personal, demand. Insight into market demand relations requires an understanding of the nature of individual demand. Individual demand is determined by the value associated with acquiring and using any good or service and the ability to acquire it. Both are necessary for effective individual demand. Desire without purchasing power may lead to want, but not to demand.

Direct Demand

There are two basic models of individual demand. One, known as the theory of consumer behavior, relates to the **direct demand** for personal consumption products. This model is appropriate for analyzing individual demand for goods and services that directly satisfy consumer desires. The value or worth of a good or service, its **utility,** is the prime determinant of direct demand. Individuals are viewed as attempting to maximize the total utility or satisfaction provided by the goods and services they acquire and consume. This optimization process requires that consumers focus on the marginal utility (gain in satisfaction) of acquiring additional units of a given product. Product characteristics, individual preferences (tastes), and the ability to pay are all important determinants of direct demand.

Derived Demand

Derived demand Demand for inputs used in production.

Goods and services are sometimes acquired because they are important inputs in the manufacture and distribution of other products. The outputs of engineers, production workers, sales staff, managers, lawyers, consultants, office business machines, production facilities and equipment, natural resources, and commercial airplanes are all examples of goods and services demanded not for direct consumption but rather for their use in providing other goods and services. Their demand is derived from the demand for the products they are used to provide. Input demand is called **derived demand.**

The demand for mortgage money is an example. The quantity of mortgage credit demanded is not determined directly; it is derived from the more fundamental demand for housing. The demand for air transportation to resort areas is not a direct demand but is derived from the demand for recreation. Similarly, the demand for producers' goods and services used to manufacture products for final consumption is derived. Aggregate demand for consumption goods and services determines demand for the capital equipment, materials, labor, and energy used to manufacture them. For example, the demands for steel, aluminum, and plastics are all derived demands, as are the demands for machine tools and labor. None of these producers' goods are demanded because of their direct value to consumers but because of the role they play in production.

Demand for producers' goods and services is closely related to final products demand. An examination of final product demand is an important part of demand analysis for intermediate, or producers,' goods. For products whose demand is derived rather than direct, demand stems from their value in the manufacture and sale of other products. They have value because their employment has the potential to generate profits. Key components in the determination of derived demand are the marginal benefits and marginal costs associated with using a given input or factor of production. The amount of any good or service used rises when its marginal benefit, measured in terms of the value of resulting output, is greater than the marginal costs of using the input, measured in terms of wages, interest, raw material costs, or related expenses. Conversely, the amount of any input used in production falls when resulting marginal benefits are less than the marginal cost of employment. In short, derived demand is related to the profitability of using a good or service.

Regardless of whether a good or service is demanded by individuals for final consumption (direct demand) or as an input used in providing other goods and services (derived demand), the fundamentals of economic analysis offer a basis for investigating demand characteristics. For final consumption products, utility maximization as described by the theory of consumer behavior explains the basis for direct demand. For inputs used in the production of other products, profit maximization provides the underlying rationale for derived demand. Because both demand models are based on the optimization concept, fundamental direct and derived demand relations are essentially the same.

Industry Demand Versus Firm Demand

Market demand functions can be specified for an entire industry or for an individual firm, though somewhat different variables would typically be used in each case. Variables representing competitors' actions would be stressed in firm demand functions. For example, a firm's demand function would typically include competitors' prices and advertising expenditures. Demand for the firm's product line is negatively related to its own prices but positively related to the prices charged by competing firms. Demand for the firm's products would typically increase with its own advertising expenditures, but it could increase or decrease with additional advertising by other firms.

The parameters for specific variables ordinarily differ in industry versus firm demand functions. Consider the positive influence of population on the demand for Ford automobiles as opposed to automobiles in general. Although the effect is positive in each instance, the parameter value in the Ford demand function would be much smaller than that in the industry demand function. Only if Ford had 100 percent of the market—that is, if Ford were the industry—would the parameters for firm and industry demand be identical.

Because firm and industry demand functions differ, different models or equations must be estimated for analyzing these two levels of demand. However, demand concepts developed in this section apply to both firm and industry demand functions.

Basis for Supply

The term **supply** refers to the quantity of a good or service that producers are willing and able to sell during a certain period under a given set of conditions. Factors that must be specified include the price of the good in question, prices of related goods, the current state of technology, levels of input prices, weather, and so on. The amount of product that producers bring to the market—the supply of the product—depends on all these influences.

Factors That Influence Supply

The supply of a product in the market is the aggregate amount supplied by individual firms. The supply of products arises from their ability to enhance the firm's value-maximization objective. The amount of any good or service supplied will rise when the marginal benefit to producers, measured in terms of the value of output, is greater than the marginal cost of production. The amount of any good or service supplied will fall when the marginal benefit to producers is less than the marginal costs of production. Thus, individual firms will expand or reduce supply based on the expected impact on profits.

Among the factors influencing the supply of a product, the price of the product itself is often the most important. Higher prices increase the quantity of output producers want to bring to market. When marginal revenue exceeds marginal cost, firms increase supply to earn the greater profits associated with expanded output. Higher prices allow firms to pay the higher production costs that are sometimes associated with expansions in output. Conversely, lower prices typically cause producers to supply a lower quantity of output. At the margin, lower prices can have the effect of making previous levels of production unprofitable.

The prices of related goods and services can also play an important role in determining supply of a product. If a firm uses resources that can be used to produce several different products, it may switch production from one product to another depending on market conditions. For example, the supply of gasoline typically declines in autumn when the price of heating oil rises. Gasoline supply typically increases during the spring and summer months with the seasonal decline in heating oil prices. Whereas the substitution of one output for another can cause an inverse relation between the supply of one product and the price of a second, complementary production relationships result in a positive relation between supply and the price of a related product. For example, ore deposits containing lead often also contain silver. An increase in the price of lead can therefore lead to an expansion in both lead and silver production.

Technology is a key determinant of product supply. The current state of technology refers to the manner in which inputs are transformed into output. An improvement in the state of technology, including any product invention or process innovation that reduces production costs, increases the quantity and/or quality of products offered for sale at a given price.

Changes in input prices also affect supply in that an increase in input prices will raise costs and reduce the quantity that can be supplied profitably at a given market price. Alternatively, a decrease in input prices increases profitability and the quantity supplied at a given price.

For some products, especially agricultural products, weather can play an important role in determining supply. Temperature, rainfall, and wind all influence the quantity that can be supplied. Heavy rainfall in early spring, for example, can delay or prevent the planting of crops, significantly limiting supply. Abundant rain during the growing season can greatly increase the available supply at harvest time. An early freeze that prevents full maturation or heavy snow that limits harvesting activity both reduce the supply of agricultural products.

Managerial decision making requires understanding both individual firm supply and market supply conditions. Market supply is the aggregate of individual firm supply, so it is ultimately determined by factors affecting firm supply. For now, meaningful insight can be gained by understanding the nature of market supply.

Industry Supply versus Firm Supply

Just as in the case of demand, supply functions can be specified for an entire industry or an individual firm. Even though factors affecting supply are highly similar in industry versus firm supply functions, the relative importance of such influences can differ dramatically. At one extreme, if all firms used identical production methods and identical equipment, had salaried and hourly employees who were equally capable and identically paid, and had equally skilled management, then individual firm and industry supply functions would be closely related. Each firm would be similarly affected by changes in supply conditions. Each parameter in the individual firm supply functions would be smaller than in the industry supply function, however, and would reflect each firm's relative share of the market.

More typically, firms within a given industry adopt somewhat different production methods, use equipment of different vintage, and employ labor of varying skill and compensation levels. In such cases, individual firm supply levels can be affected quite differently by various factors. Korean automakers, for example, may be able to offer subcompacts profitably at average industry prices as low as, say, $15,000 per automobile. On the other hand, U.S. auto manufacturers, who have historically operated with a labor cost disadvantage, may only be able to offer a supply of subcompacts at average industry prices in excess of, say, $21,000. This means that at relatively high average prices for the industry above $21,000 per unit, both foreign and domestic auto manufacturers would be actively engaged in car production. At relatively low average prices below $21,000, only foreign producers would offer cars. This would be reflected by different parameters describing the relation between price and quantity supplied in the individual firm supply functions for Korean and U.S. automobile manufacturers.

Individual firms supply output only when doing so is profitable. When industry prices are high enough to cover the marginal costs of increased production, individual firms expand output, thereby increasing total profits and the value of the firm. To the extent that the economic capabilities of industry participants vary, so too does the scale of output supplied by individual firms at various prices.

Similarly, supply is affected by production technology. Firms operating with highly automated facilities incur large fixed costs and relatively small variable costs. The supply of product from such firms is likely to be relatively insensitive to price changes when compared to less automated firms, for which variable production costs are higher and thus more closely affected by production levels. Relatively low-cost producers can and do supply output at relatively low market prices. Of course, both relatively low-cost and high-cost producers are able to supply output profitably when market prices are high.

Market Equilibrium

Integrating the concepts of demand and supply establishes a framework for understanding how they interact to determine market prices and quantities for all goods and services. When quantity demanded and quantity supplied are in perfect balance at a given price, the product market is said to be in **equilibrium**. An equilibrium is stable when underlying demand and supply conditions are expected to remain stationary in the foreseeable future. When underlying demand and supply are dynamic rather than constant, a change in current market prices and quantities is likely. A temporary market equilibrium of this type is often referred to as an unstable equilibrium. To understand the forces that drive market prices and quantities either up or down to achieve equilibrium, the concepts of surplus and shortage must be understood.

Demand Analysis and Estimation

Nothing is more important in business than the need to identify and effectively meet customer demand. This section examines the elasticity concept as a useful means for measuring the sensitivity of demand to changes in underlying conditions.

Demand Sensitivity Analysis: Elasticity

For constructive managerial decision making, the firm must know the sensitivity or responsiveness of demand to changes in factors that make up the underlying demand function.

The Elasticity Concept

One measure of responsiveness employed not only in demand analysis but throughout managerial decision making is **elasticity,** defined as the percentage change in a dependent variable, Y, resulting from a 1 percent change in the value of an independent variable, X. The equation for calculating elasticity is

$$\text{Elasticity} = \frac{\text{Percentage Change in } Y}{\text{Percentage Change in } X} \tag{1.17}$$

The concept of elasticity simply involves the percentage change in one variable associated with a given percentage change in another variable. In addition to being used in demand analysis, the concept is used in finance, where the impact of changes in sales on earnings under different production levels (operating leverage) and different financial structures (financial leverage) are measured by an elasticity factor. Elasticities are also used in production and cost analysis to evaluate the effects of changes in input on output as well as the effects of output changes on costs.

Factors such as price and advertising that are within the control of the firm are called **endogenous variables.** It is important that management know the effects of altering these variables when making decisions. Other important factors outside the control of the firm, such as consumer incomes, competitor prices, and the weather, are called **exogenous variables.** The effects of changes in both types of influences must be understood if the firm is to respond effectively to changes in the economic environment. For example, a firm must understand the effects on demand of changes in both prices and consumer incomes to determine the price cut necessary to offset a decline in sales caused by a business recession (fall in income). Similarly, the sensitivity of demand to changes in advertising must be quantified if the firm is to respond appropriately with price or advertising changes to an increase in competitor advertising. Determining the effects of changes in both controllable and uncontrollable influences on demand is the focus of demand analysis.

Point Elasticity and Arc Elasticity

Elasticity can be measured in two different ways, point elasticity and arc elasticity. **Point elasticity** measures elasticity at a given point on a function. The point elasticity concept is used to measure the effect on a dependent variable Y of a very small or marginal change in an independent variable X. Although the point elasticity concept can often give accurate estimates of the effect on Y of very small (less than 5 percent) changes in X, it is not used to measure the effect on Y of large-scale changes, because elasticity typically varies at different points along a function. To assess the effects of large-scale changes in X, the arc elasticity concept is employed. **Arc elasticity** measures the average elasticity over a given range of a function.

Using the lowercase epsilon as the symbol for point elasticity, the point elasticity formula is written

$$\text{Point Elasticity} = \epsilon_X = \frac{\text{Percentage Change in } Y}{\text{Percentage Change in } X}$$

$$= \frac{\Delta Y/Y}{\Delta X/X} \tag{1.18}$$

$$= \frac{\Delta Y}{\Delta X} \times \frac{X}{Y}$$

170. MANAGERIAL ECONOMICS

The $\Delta Y/\Delta X$ term in the point elasticity formula is the marginal relation between Y and X, and it shows the effect on Y of a one-unit change in X. Point elasticity is determined by multiplying this marginal relation by the relative size of X to Y, or the X/Y ratio at the point being analyzed.

Point elasticity measures the percentage effect on Y of a percentage change in X at a given point on a function. If $\epsilon_X = 5$, a 1 percent increase in X will lead to a 5 percent increase in Y, and a 1 percent decrease in X will lead to a 5 percent decrease in Y. Thus, when $\epsilon_X > 0$, Y changes in the same positive or negative direction as X. Conversely, when $\epsilon_X \times 0$, Y changes in the opposite direction of changes in X. For example, if $\epsilon_X = -3$, a 1 percent increase in X will lead to a 3 percent decrease in Y, and a 1 percent decrease in X will lead to a 3 percent increase in Y.

Price Elasticity of Demand

The most widely used elasticity measure is the **price elasticity of demand,** which measures the responsiveness of the quantity demanded to changes in the price of the product, holding constant the values of all other variables in the demand function.

Price Elasticity Formula

Using the formula for point elasticity, price elasticity of demand is found as

$$\epsilon_P = \text{Point Price Elasticity} = \frac{\text{Percentage Change in Quantity (Q)}}{\text{Percentage Change in Price (P)}}$$
$$= \frac{\Delta Q/Q}{\Delta P/P} \qquad (1.19)$$
$$= \frac{\Delta Q}{\Delta P} \times \frac{P}{Q}$$

where $\Delta Q/\Delta P$ is the marginal change in quantity following a one-unit change in price, and P and Q are price and quantity, respectively, at a given point on the demand curve.

Price Elasticity and Total Revenue

One of the most important features of price elasticity is that it provides a useful summary measure of the effect of a price change on revenues. Depending on the degree of price elasticity, a reduction in price can increase, decrease, or leave total revenue unchanged. A good estimate of price elasticity makes it possible to accurately estimate the effect of price changes on total revenue.

For decision-making purposes, three specific ranges of price elasticity have been identified. Using $|\epsilon_P|$ to denote the absolute value of the price elasticity, three ranges for price elasticity are

1. $|\epsilon_P| > 1.0$, defined as elastic demand

    Example: $\epsilon_P = -3.2$ and $|\epsilon_P| = 3.2$

2. $|\epsilon_P| = 1.0$, defined as unitary elasticity

    Example: $\epsilon_P = -1.0$ and $|\epsilon_P| = 1.0$

3. $|\epsilon_P| < 1.0$, defined as inelastic demand

    Example: $\epsilon_P = -0.5$ and $|\epsilon_P| = 0.5$

With **elastic demand,** $|\epsilon_P| > 1$ and the relative change in quantity is larger than the relative change in price. A given percentage increase in price causes quantity to decrease by a larger percentage. If demand is elastic, a price increase lowers total revenue and a decrease in price raises total revenue. **Unitary elasticity** is a situation in which the percentage change in quantity divided by the percentage change in price equals -1. Because price and quantity are inversely related, a price elasticity of -1 means that the effect of a price change is exactly offset by the effect of a change in quantity demanded. The result is that total revenue, the product of price times quantity, remains constant. With **inelastic demand,** a price increase produces less than a proportionate decline in the quantity demanded, so total revenues rise. Conversely, when demand is inelastic, a price decrease generates a less than proportionate increase in quantity demanded, so total revenues falls. These relations are summarized in Exhibit 100.42.

Exhibit 100.42 *Relationship Between Price Elasticity and Total Revenue*

Elasticity	Implies	Following a Price Increase	Following a Price Decrease
Elastic demand, $|\epsilon_p| > 1$	$\%\Delta Q > \%\Delta P$	Revenue decreases	Revenue increases
Unitary elasticity, $|\epsilon_p| = 1$	$\%\Delta Q = \%\Delta P$	Revenue unchanged	Revenue unchanged
Inelastic demand $|\epsilon_p| < 1$	$\%\Delta Q < \%\Delta P$	Revenue increases	Revenue decreases

Exhibit 100.43 *Completely Inelastic Demand Curve: $\epsilon_P = 0$*
With perfectly inelastic demand, a fixed level of output is demanded irrespective of price.

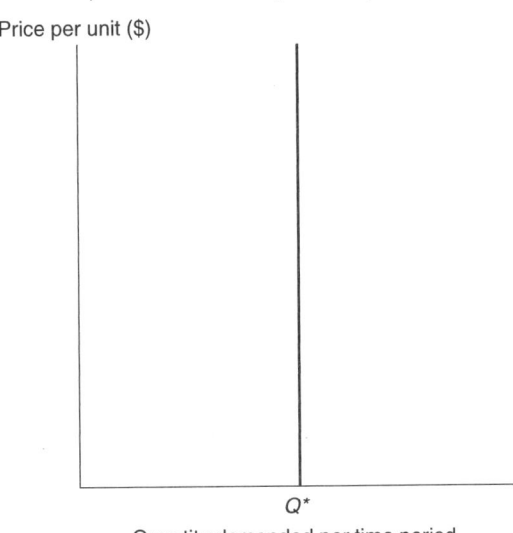

Exhibit 100.44 *Completely Elastic Demand Curve: $\epsilon_P = -\infty$*

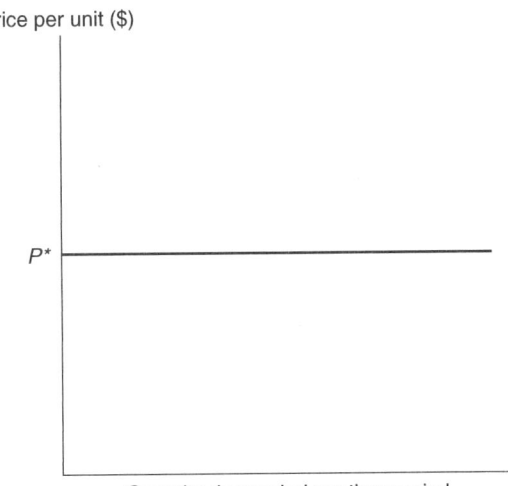

Price elasticity can range from completely inelastic, where $\epsilon_P = 0$, to perfectly elastic, where $\epsilon_P = -\infty$. To illustrate, consider first an extreme case in which the quantity demanded is independent of price so that some fixed amount, Q^*, is demanded regardless of price. When the quantity demanded of a product is completely insensitive to price, $\Delta Q/\Delta P = 0$, and price elasticity will equal zero, irrespective of the value of P/Q. The demand curve for such a good or service is perfectly vertical, as shown in Exhibit 100.43.

The other limiting case, that of infinite price elasticity, describes a product that is completely sensitive to price. The demand curve for such a good or service is perfectly horizontal, as shown in Exhibit 100.44. Here the ratio $\Delta Q/\Delta P = -\infty$ and $\epsilon_P = -\infty$, regardless of the value of P/Q.

170. MANAGERIAL ECONOMICS

The economic as well as mathematical properties of these limiting cases should be understood. A firm faced with a vertical or perfectly inelastic demand curve could charge any price and still sell Q^* units. Theoretically, such a firm could appropriate all of its customers' income or wealth. Conversely, a firm facing a horizontal or perfectly elastic demand curve could sell an unlimited quantity of output at the price P^*, but it would lose all sales if it raised prices by even a small amount. Such extreme cases are rare in the real world, but monopolies that sell necessities such as pharmaceuticals enjoy relatively inelastic demand, whereas firms in highly competitive industries such as grocery retailing face highly elastic demand curves.

Uses of Price Elasticity Information

Price elasticity information is useful for a number of purposes. Obviously, firms are required to be aware of the price elasticity of demand when they price their products. For example, a profit-maximizing firm would never choose to lower its prices in the inelastic range of the demand curve. Such a price decrease would decrease total revenue and at the same time increase costs, because the quantity demanded would rise. A dramatic decrease in profits would result. Even over the range in which demand is elastic, a firm will not necessarily find it profitable to cut price. The profitability of a price cut in the elastic range of the demand curve depends on whether the marginal revenues generated exceed the marginal cost of added production. Price elasticity information can be used to answer questions such as:

- What is the expected impact on sales of a 5 percent price increase?
- How great a price reduction is necessary to increase sales by 10 percent?
- Given marginal cost and price elasticity data, what is the profit-maximizing price?

The importance of price elasticity information was illustrated during 2000–2001 in California when electric utilities were forced to raise prices dramatically because of a rapid increase in fuel costs. The question immediately arose: How much of a cutback in quantity demanded and, hence, how much of a reduction in future capacity needs would these price increases cause? In other words, what was the price elasticity of electricity? In view of the long lead times required to build electricity-generating capacity and the major economic dislocations that arise from power outages, this was a critical question for both consumers and producers of electricity.

Price elasticity information has long played a major role in the debate over national energy policy. Some industry and government economists argue that the price elasticity of demand for energy is sufficiently large that an equilibrium of demand and supply will occur following only modest price changes. Others argue that energy price elasticities are so low that unconscionable price increases are necessary to reduce the quantity demanded to meet pending supply shortfalls. Meanwhile, bouts of falling oil prices raise fears among some that low oil prices may increase Western reliance on imported oil. These same issues have also become a focal point in controversies surrounding nuclear energy, natural gas price deregulation, and alternative renewable energy sources. In this debate on energy policy, the relation between price and quantity supplied—the price elasticity of supply—is also an important component. As with most economic issues, both demand and supply sides of the marketplace must be analyzed to arrive at a rational decision.

Another example of the importance of price elasticity information relates to the widespread discounts or reduced rates offered different customer groups. *The Wall Street Journal* offers students bargain rates; airlines, restaurants, and most hotel chains offer discounts to vacation travelers and senior citizens; large corporate customers get discounts or rebates on desktop computers, auto leases, and many other items. Many such discounts are substantial, sometimes in the range of 30 percent to 40 percent off standard list prices. The question of whether reduced prices attract sufficient additional customers to offset lower revenues per unit is directly related to the price elasticity of demand.

Price Elasticity and Marginal Revenue

There are simple, direct relations between price elasticity, marginal revenue, and total revenue. It is worth examining such relations in detail, given their importance for pricing policy.

Varying Elasticity at Different Points on a Demand Curve

All linear demand curves, except perfectly elastic or perfectly inelastic ones, are subject to varying elasticities at different points on the curve. In other words, any linear demand curve is price elastic at some output levels but inelastic at others. To see this, recall the definition of point price elasticity expressed in equation 1.20:

$$\epsilon_P = \frac{\Delta Q}{\Delta P} \times \frac{P}{Q}$$

(1.20)

The slope of a linear demand curve, $\Delta P/\Delta Q$, is constant; thus, its reciprocal, $1/(\Delta P/\Delta Q) = \Delta Q/\Delta P$, is also constant. However, the ratio P/Q varies from 0 at the point where the demand curve intersects the horizontal axis and price = 0, to $+\infty$ at the vertical price axis intercept where quantity = 0. Because the price elasticity formula for a linear curve involves multiplying a negative constant by a ratio that varies between 0 and $+\infty$, the price elasticity of a linear curve must range from 0 to $-\infty$.

Exhibit 100.45 illustrates this relation. As the demand curve approaches the vertical axis, the ratio P/Q approaches infinity and ϵ_P approaches minus infinity. As the demand curve approaches the horizontal axis, the ratio P/Q approaches 0, causing ϵ_P also to approach 0. At the midpoint of the demand curve $(\Delta Q/\Delta P) \times (P/Q) = -1$; this is the point of unitary elasticity.

Price Elasticity and Price Changes

The relation between price elasticity and total revenue can be further clarified by examining Exhibit 100.46 and Exhibit 100.47. Exhibit 100.47(a) reproduces the demand curve shown in Exhibit 100.46 along with the associated marginal revenue curve. The demand curve shown in Exhibit 100.47(a) is of the general linear form

$$P = a - bQ \qquad (1.21)$$

Exhibit 100.45 *Price Elasticity of Demand Varies Along a Linear Demand Curve*
The price elasticity of demand will vary from 0 to $-\infty$ along a linear demand curve.

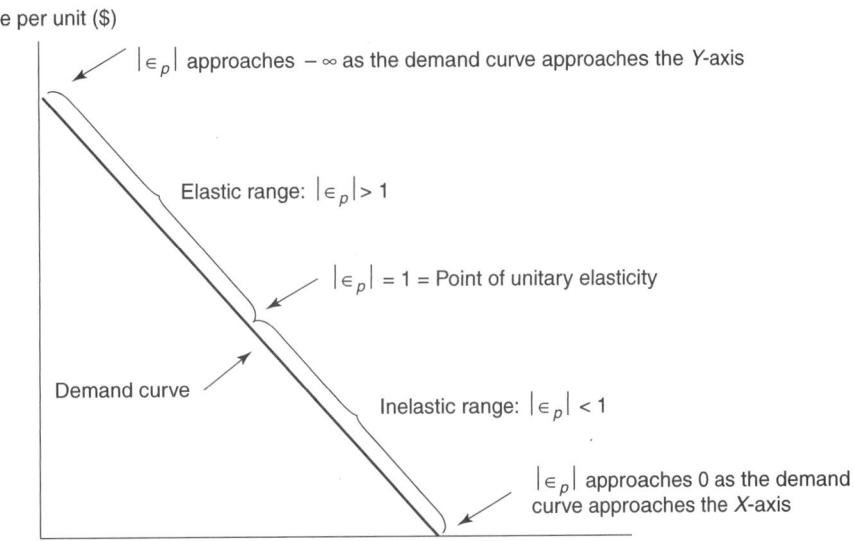

Exhibit 100.46 *Price Elasticity and Revenue Relations: A Numerical Example*

Price P	Quantity Q	Total Revenue TR = P × Q	Marginal Revenue MR = ΔTR	Arc Elasticity[a] E_P
$100	1	$100	—	—
90	2	180	$80	−6.33
80	3	240	60	−3.40
70	4	280	40	−2.14
60	5	300	20	−1.44
50	6	300	0	−1.00
40	7	280	−20	−0.69
30	8	240	−40	−0.47
20	9	180	−60	−0.29
10	10	100	−80	−0.16

[a] Because the price and quantity data in the table are discrete numbers, the price elasticities have been calculated by using the arc elasticity equation

$$E = \frac{\Delta Q}{\Delta P} \times \frac{P_2 + P_1}{Q_2 + Q_1}$$

170. MANAGERIAL ECONOMICS

Exhibit 100.47 *Relations Among Price Elasticity and Marginal, Average, and Total Revenue: (a) Demand (Average Revenue) and Marginal Revenue Curves; (b) Total Revenue*

In the range in which demand is elastic with respect to price, marginal revenue is positive and total revenue increases with a reduction in price. In the inelastic range, marginal revenue is negative and total revenue decreases with price reductions.

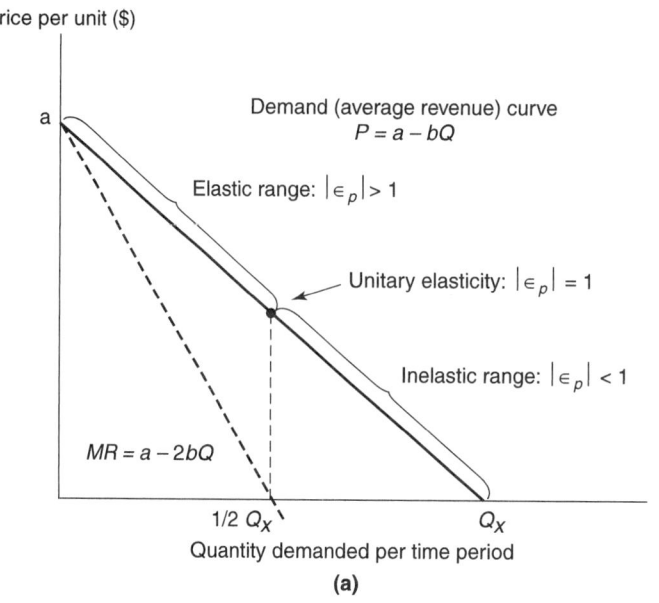

(a)

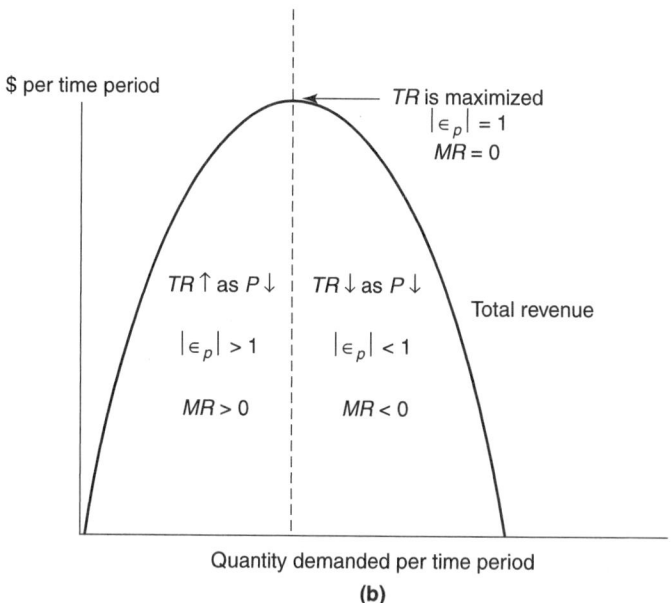

(b)

where a is the intercept and b is the slope coefficient. It follows that total revenue (TR) can be expressed as

$$TR = P \times Q$$
$$= (a - bQ) \times Q$$
$$= aQ - bQ^2$$

By definition, marginal revenue (MR) is the change in revenue following a one-unit expansion in output, $\Delta TR/\Delta Q$, and can be written

$$MR = \Delta TR/\Delta Q = a - 2bQ \qquad (1.22)$$

The relation between the demand (average revenue) and marginal revenue curves becomes clear when one compares equations 1.21 and 1.22. Each equation has the same intercept a. This means that both curves begin at the same point along the vertical price axis. However, the marginal revenue curve has twice the negative slope of the demand curve. This means that the marginal revenue curve intersects the horizontal axis at 1/2 Q_X, given that the demand curve intersects at Q_X. Exhibit 100.47(a) shows that marginal revenue is positive in the range where demand is price elastic, zero where $\epsilon_P = -1$, and negative in the inelastic range. Thus, there is an obvious relation between price elasticity and both average and marginal revenue.

As shown in Exhibit 100.47(b), price elasticity is also closely related to total revenue. Total revenue increases with price reductions in the elastic range (where $MR > 0$) because the increase in quantity demanded at the new lower price more than offsets the lower revenue per unit received at that reduced price. Total revenue peaks at the point of unitary elasticity (where $MR = 0$), because the increase in quantity associated with the price reduction exactly offsets the lower revenue received per unit. Finally, total revenue declines when price is reduced in the inelastic range (where $MR < 0$). Here the quantity demanded continues to increase with reductions in price, but the relative increase in quantity is less than the percentage decrease in price, and thus is not large enough to offset the reduction in revenue per unit sold.

The numerical example in Exhibit 100.46 illustrates these relations. It shows that from 1 to 5 units of output, demand is elastic, $|\epsilon_P| > 1$, and a reduction in price increases total revenue. For example, decreasing price from \$80 to \$70 increases the quantity demanded from 3 to 4 units. Marginal revenue is positive over this range, and total revenue increases from \$240 to \$280. For output above 6 units and prices below \$50, demand is inelastic, $|\epsilon_P| < 1$. Here price reductions result in lower total revenue, because the increase in quantity demanded is not large enough to offset the lower price per unit. With total revenue decreasing as output expands, marginal revenue must be negative. For example, reducing price from \$30 to \$20 results in revenue declining from \$240 to \$180 even though output increases from 8 to 9 units; marginal revenue in this case is $-\$60$.

Price Elasticity and Optimal Pricing Policy

Firms use price discounts, specials, coupons, and rebate programs to measure the price sensitivity of demand for their products. Armed with such knowledge, and detailed unit cost information, firms have all the tools necessary for setting optimal prices.

Optimal Price Formula

As a practical matter, firms devote enormous resources to obtain current and detailed information concerning the price elasticity of demand for their products. Price elasticity estimates represent vital information because these data, along with relevant unit cost information, are essential inputs for setting a pricing policy that is consistent with value maximization. This stems from the fact that there is a relatively simple mathematical relation between marginal revenue, price, and the point price elasticity of demand.

Given any point price elasticity estimate, relevant marginal revenues can be determined easily. When this marginal revenue information is combined with pertinent marginal cost data, the basis for an optimal pricing policy is created.

The relation between marginal revenue, price, and the point price elasticity of demand follows directly from the mathematical definition of a marginal relation. In equation form, the link between marginal revenue, price, and the point price elasticity of demand is

$$MR = P\left(1 - \frac{1}{\epsilon_P}\right) \tag{1.23}$$

Because $\epsilon_P < 0$, the number contained within brackets in equation 1.23 is always less than one. This means that $MR < P$, and the gap between MR and P will fall as the price elasticity of demand increases (in absolute value terms). For example, when $P = \$8$ and $\epsilon_P = -1.5$, $MR = \$2.67$. Thus, when price elasticity is relatively low, the optimal price is much greater than marginal revenue. Conversely, when $P = \$8$ and $\epsilon_P = -10$, $MR = \$7.20$. When the quantity demanded is highly elastic with respect to price, the optimal price is close to marginal revenue.

Exhibit 100.48 shows how profit-maximizing prices vary for a product with a \$25 marginal cost as the point price elasticity of demand varies. Note that the less elastic the demand, the greater the difference between the optimal price and marginal cost. Conversely, as the absolute value of the price elasticity of demand increases (that is, as demand becomes more price elastic), the profit-maximizing price gets closer and closer to marginal cost.

Exhibit 100.48 *Price Elasticity and Optimal Pricing Policy*

Point Price Elasticity	Marginal Cost	Profit-Maximizing Price
−1.25	$25	$125.00
−1.50	25	75.00
−2.50	25	41.67
−5.00	25	31.25
−10.00	25	27.78
−25.00	25	26.04

Determinants of Price Elasticity

There are three major influences on price elasticities: (1) the extent to which a good is considered to be a necessity; (2) the availability of substitute goods to satisfy a given need; and (3) the proportion of income spent on the product. A relatively constant quantity of a service such as electricity for residential lighting will be purchased almost irrespective of price, at least in the short run and within price ranges customarily encountered. There is no close substitute for electric service. However, goods such as men's and women's clothing face considerably more competition, and their demand depends more on price.

Similarly, the demand for "big ticket" items such as automobiles, homes, and vacation travel accounts for a large share of consumer income and will be relatively sensitive to price. Demand for less expensive products, such as soft drinks, movies, and candy, can be relatively insensitive to price. Given the low percentage of income spent on "small ticket" items, consumers often find that searching for the best deal available is not worth the time and effort. Accordingly, the elasticity of demand is typically higher for major purchases than for small ones. The price elasticity of demand for compact disc players, for example, is higher than that for compact discs.

Price elasticity for an individual firm is seldom the same as that for the entire industry. In pure monopoly, the firm demand curve is also the industry demand curve, so obviously the elasticity of demand faced by the firm at any output level is the same as that faced by the industry. Consider the other extreme—pure competition, as approximated by wheat farming. The industry demand curve for wheat is downward sloping: the lower its price, the greater the quantity of wheat that will be demanded. However, the demand curve facing any individual wheat farmer is essentially horizontal. A farmer can sell any amount of wheat at the going price, but if the farmer raises price by the smallest fraction of a cent, sales collapse to zero. The wheat farmer's demand curve—or that of any firm operating under pure competition—is perfectly elastic. Exhibit 100.45 illustrates such a demand curve.

The demand for producer goods and services is indirect, or derived from their value in use. Because the demand for all inputs is derived from their usefulness in producing other products, their demand is derived from the demand for final products. In contrast to the terms *final product* or *consumer demand,* the term *derived demand* describes the demand for all producer goods and services. Although the demand for producer goods and services is related to the demand for the final products that they are used to make, this relation is not always as close as one might suspect.

In some instances, the demand for intermediate goods is less price sensitive than demand for the resulting final product. This is because intermediate goods sometimes represent only a small portion of the cost of producing the final product. For example, suppose the total cost to build a small manufacturing plant is $1 million, and $25,000 of this cost represents the cost of electrical fixtures and wiring. Even a doubling in electrical costs from $25,000 to $50,000 would have only a modest effect on the overall costs of the plant—which would increase by only 2.5 percent from $1 million to $1,025,000. Rather than being highly price sensitive, the firm might select its electrical contractor based on the timeliness and quality of service provided. In such an instance, the firm's price elasticity of demand for electrical fixtures and wiring is quite low, even if its price elasticity of demand for the overall project is quite high.

In other situations, the reverse might hold. Continuing with our previous example, suppose that steel costs represent $250,000 of the total $1 million cost of building the plant. Because of its relative importance, a substantial increase in steel costs has a significant influence on the total costs of the overall project. As a result, the price sensitivity of the demand for steel will be close to that for the overall plant. If the firm's demand for plant construction is highly price elastic, the demand for steel is also likely to be highly price elastic.

Although the derived demand for producer goods and services is obviously related to the demand for resulting final products, this relation is not always close. When intermediate goods or services represent only a small share of overall costs, the price elasticity of demand for such inputs can be much different from that for the resulting final product. The price elasticity of demand for a given input and the resulting final product must be similar in magnitude only when the costs of that input represent a significant share of overall costs.

Cross-Price Elasticity of Demand

Demand for most products is influenced by prices for other products. Such demand interrelationships are an important consideration in demand analysis and estimation.

Substitutes and Complements

The demand for beef is related to the price of chicken. As the price of chicken increases, so does the demand for beef; consumers substitute beef for the now relatively more expensive chicken. On the other hand, a price decrease for chicken leads to a decrease in the demand for beef as consumers substitute chicken for the now relatively more expensive beef. In general, a direct relation between the price of one product and the demand for a second product holds for all substitutes. A price increase for a given product will increase demand for **substitutes;** a price decrease for a given product will decrease demand for substitutes.

Substitutes and Complements

Some goods and services—for example, cameras and film—exhibit a completely different relation. Here price increases in one product typically lead to a reduction in demand for the other. Goods that are inversely related in this manner are known as **complements;** they are used together rather than in place of each other.

The concept of **cross-price elasticity** is used to examine the responsiveness of demand for one product to changes in the price of another. Point cross-price elasticity is given by the following equation:

$$\epsilon_{PX} = \frac{\text{Percentage Change in Quantity of Y}}{\text{Percentage Change in Price of X}}$$

$$= \frac{\Delta Q_Y / Q_Y}{\Delta P_X / P_X} \tag{1.24}$$

$$= \frac{\Delta Q_Y}{\Delta P_X} \times \frac{P_X}{Q_Y}$$

where Y and X are two different products. The arc cross-price elasticity relationship is constructed in the same manner as was previously described for price elasticity:

$$\epsilon_{PX} = \frac{\text{Percentage Change in Quantity of Y}}{\text{Percentage Change in Price of X}}$$

$$= \frac{(Q_{Y2} - Q_{Y1})/[(Q_{Y2} + Q_{Y1})/2]}{(P_{X2} - P_{X1})/[(P_{X2} + P_{X1})/2]} \tag{1.25}$$

$$= \frac{\Delta Q_Y}{\Delta P_X} \times \frac{P_{X2} + P_{X1}}{Q_{Y2} + Q_{Y1}}$$

The cross-price elasticity for substitutes is always positive; the price of one good and the demand for the other always move in the same direction. Cross-price elasticity is negative for complements; price and quantity move in opposite directions for complementary goods and services. Finally, cross-price elasticity is zero, or nearly zero, for unrelated goods in which variations in the price of one good have no effect on demand for the second.

The concept of cross-price elasticity serves two main purposes. First, it is important for the firm to be aware of how demand for its products is likely to respond to changes in the prices of other goods. Such information is necessary for formulating the firm's own pricing strategy and for analyzing the risks associated with various products. This is particularly important for firms with a wide variety of products, where meaningful substitute or complementary relations exist within the firm's own product line. Second, cross-price elasticity information allows managers to measure the degree of competition in the marketplace. For example, a firm might appear to dominate a particular market or market segment, especially if it is the only supplier of a particular product. However, if the cross-price elasticity between a firm's output and products produced in related industries is large and positive, the firm is not a monopolist in the true sense and is not immune to the threat of competitor encroachment. In the banking industry, for example, individual banks clearly compete with money market mutual funds, savings and loan associations, credit unions, and commercial finance companies. The extent of competition can be measured only in terms of the cross-price elasticities of demand.

Income Elasticity of Demand

For many goods, income is another important determinant of demand. Income is frequently as important as price, advertising expenditures, credit terms, or any other variable in the demand function. This is particularly true of luxury items such as big screen televisions, country club memberships, elegant homes, and so on. In contrast, the demand for such basic commodities as salt, bread, and milk is not very responsive to income changes. These goods are bought in fairly constant amounts regardless of changes in income. Of course, income can be measured in many ways—for example, on a per capita, per household, or aggregate basis. Gross national product, national income, personal income, and disposable personal income have all served as income measures in demand studies.

Normal Versus Inferior Goods

The **income elasticity** of demand measures the responsiveness of demand to changes in income, holding constant the effect of all other variables that influence demand. Letting I represent income, income point elasticity is defined as

$$\epsilon_I = \frac{\text{Percentage Change in Quantity (Q)}}{\text{Percentage Change in Income (I)}}$$
$$= \frac{\Delta Q/Q}{\Delta I/I} \tag{1.26}$$
$$= \frac{\Delta Q}{\Delta I} \times \frac{I}{Q}$$

Income and the quantity purchased typically move in the same direction; that is, income and sales are directly rather than inversely related. Therefore, $\Delta Q/\Delta I$ and hence ϵ_I are positive. This does not hold for a limited number of products termed **inferior goods.** Individual consumer demand for such products as beans and potatoes, for example, is sometimes thought to decline as income increases, because consumers replace them with more desirable alternatives. More typical products, whose individual and aggregate demand is positively related to income, are defined as **normal goods.**

To examine income elasticity over a range of incomes rather than at a single level, the arc elasticity relation is employed:

$$\epsilon_I = \frac{\text{Percentage Change in Quantity (Q)}}{\text{Percentage Change in Income (I)}}$$
$$= \frac{(Q_2 - Q_1)/[(Q_2 + Q_1)/2]}{(I_2 - I_1)/[(I_2 + I_1)/2]} \tag{1.27}$$
$$= \frac{\Delta Q}{\Delta I} \times \frac{I_2 + I_1}{Q_2 + Q_1}$$

Arc income elasticity provides a measure of the average responsiveness of demand for a given product to a relative change in income over the range from I_1 to I_2.

In the case of inferior goods, individual demand actually rises during an economic downturn. As workers get laid off from their jobs, for example, they might tend to substitute potatoes for meat, hamburgers for steak, bus rides for automobile trips, and so on. As a result, demand for potatoes, hamburgers, bus rides, and other inferior goods can actually rise during recessions. Their demand is **countercyclical.**

Types of Normal Goods

For most products, income elasticity is positive, indicating that demand rises as the economy expands and national income increases. The actual size of the income elasticity coefficient is very important. Suppose, for example, that $\epsilon_I = 0.3$. This means that a 1 percent increase in income causes demand for the product to increase by only .3 percent. Given growing national income over time, such a product would not maintain its relative importance in the economy. Another product might have $\epsilon_I = 2.5$; its demand increases 2.5 times as fast as income. If $\epsilon_I < 1.0$ for a particular product, its producers will not share proportionately in increases in national income. However, if $\epsilon_I > 1.0$, the industry will gain more than a proportionate share of increases in income.

Goods for which $0 < \epsilon_I < 1$ are referred to as **noncyclical normal goods,** because demand is relatively unaffected by changing income. Sales of most convenience goods, such as toothpaste, candy, soda, and movie tickets, account for

Exhibit 100.49 *Relationship Between Income and Product Demand*

Inferior goods (countercyclical)	$\epsilon_I < 0$	Basic foodstuffs, generic products, bus rides
Noncyclical normal goods	$0 < \epsilon_I < 1$	Toiletries, movies, liquor, cigarettes
Cyclical normal goods	$\epsilon_I > 1$	Automobiles, housing, vacation travel, capital equipment

only a small share of the consumer's overall budget, and spending on such items tends to be relatively unaffected by changing economic conditions. For goods having $\epsilon_I > 1$, referred to as **cyclical normal goods,** demand is strongly affected by changing economic conditions. Purchase of "big ticket" items such as homes, automobiles, boats, and recreational vehicles can be postponed and tend to be put off by consumers during economic downturns. Housing demand, for example, can collapse during recessions and skyrocket during economic expansions. These relations between income and product demand are summarized in Exhibit 100.49.

Firms whose demand functions indicate high income elasticities enjoy good growth opportunities in expanding economies. Forecasts of aggregate economic activity figure importantly in their plans. Companies faced with low income elasticities are relatively unaffected by the level of overall business activity. This is desirable from the standpoint that such a business is harmed relatively little by economic downturns. Nevertheless, such a company cannot expect to share fully in a growing economy and might seek to enter industries that provide better growth opportunities.

Income elasticity figures importantly in several key national debates. Agriculture is often depressed because of the low income elasticity for most food products. This has made it difficult for farmers' incomes to keep up with those of urban workers. A somewhat similar problem arises in housing. Improving the housing stock is a primary national goal. If the income elasticity for housing is high and $\epsilon_I > 1$, an improvement in the housing stock will be a natural by-product of a prosperous economy. However, if the housing income elasticity $\epsilon_I < 1$, a relatively small percentage of additional income will be spent on houses. As a result, housing stock would not improve much over time despite a growing economy and increasing incomes. In the event that $\epsilon_I < 1$, direct government investment in public housing or rent and interest subsidies might be necessary to bring about a dramatic increase in the housing stock over time.

Pricing Practices

This section examines common pricing practices and illustrates their value as a practical means for achieving profit-maximizing prices under a wide variety of demand and cost conditions.

Markup Pricing

Markup pricing is the most commonly employed pricing method. Given the popularity of the technique, it behooves managers to fully understand the rationale for markup pricing. When this rationale is understood, markup pricing methods can be seen as the practical means for achieving optimal prices under a wide variety of demand and cost conditions.

Markup Pricing Technology

The development of pricing practices to profitably segment markets has reached a fine art with the Internet and use of high-speed computer technology. Why do *Business Week, Forbes, Fortune,* and *The Wall Street Journal* offer bargain rates to students but not to business executives? It is surely not because it costs less to deliver the *Journal* to students, and it is not out of benevolence; it is because students are not willing or able to pay the standard rate. Even at 50 percent off regular prices, student bargain rates more than cover marginal costs and make a significant profit contribution. Similarly, senior citizens who eat at **Holiday Inns** enjoy a 10 to 15 percent discount and make a meaningful contribution to profits. Conversely, relatively high prices for popcorn at movie theaters, peanuts at the ball park, and clothing at the height of the season reflect the fact that customers can be insensitive to price changes at different places and at different times of the year. Regular prices, discounts, rebates, and coupon promotions are all pricing mechanisms used to probe the breadth and depth of customer demand and to maximize profitability.

Although profit maximization requires that prices be set so that marginal revenues equal marginal cost, it is not necessary to calculate both to set optimal prices. Just using information on marginal costs and the point price elasticity of demand, the calculation of profit-maximizing prices is quick and easy. Many firms derive an optimal pricing policy using prices set to cover direct costs plus a percentage markup for profit contribution. Flexible markup pricing practices that reflect differences in marginal costs and demand elasticities constitute an efficient method for ensuring that $MR = MC$ for each line of products sold. Similarly, peak and off-peak pricing, price discrimination, and joint product pricing practices are efficient means for operating so that $MR = MC$ for each customer or customer group and product class.

Markup on Cost

In a conventional approach, firms estimate the average variable costs of producing and marketing a given product, add a charge for variable overhead, and then add a percentage markup, or profit margin. Variable overhead costs are usually allocated among all products according to average variable costs. For example, if total variable overhead costs are projected at $1.3 million per year and variable costs for planned production total $1 million, then variable overhead is allocated to individual products at the rate of 130 percent of variable cost. If the average variable cost of a product is estimated to be $1, the firm adds a charge of 130 percent of variable costs, or $1.30, for variable overhead, obtaining a fully allocated cost of $2.30. To this figure the firm might add a 30 percent markup for profits, or 69¢, to obtain a price of $2.99 per unit.

Markup on cost is the profit margin for an individual product or product line expressed as a percentage of unit cost. The markup-on-cost, or *cost-plus,* formula is given by the expression

$$\text{Markup on Cost} = \frac{\text{Price} - \text{Cost}}{\text{Cost}} \qquad (1.28)$$

The numerator of this expression, called the **profit margin,** is measured by the difference between price and cost. In the example cited previously, the 30 percent markup on cost is calculated as

$$\begin{aligned}\text{Markup on Cost} &= \frac{\text{Price} - \text{Cost}}{\text{Cost}} \\ &= \frac{\$2.99 - \$2.30}{\$2.30} \\ &= 0.30, \text{ or } 30\%\end{aligned}$$

Solving equation 1.28 for price provides the expression that determines price in a cost-plus pricing system:

$$\text{Price} = \text{Cost}\,(1 + \text{Markup on Cost}) \qquad (1.29)$$

Continuing with the previous example, the product selling price is found as

$$\begin{aligned}\text{Price} &= \text{Cost}\,(1 + \text{Markup on Cost}) \\ &= \$2.30(1.30) \\ &= \$2.99\end{aligned}$$

Markup on Price

Profit margins, or markups, are sometimes calculated as a percentage of price instead of cost. **Markup on price** is the profit margin for an individual product or product line expressed as a percentage of price, rather than unit cost as in the markup-on-cost formula. This alternative means of expressing profit margins can be illustrated by the markup-on-price formula:

$$\text{Markup on Price} = \frac{\text{Price} - \text{Cost}}{\text{Price}} \qquad (1.30)$$

Profit margin is the numerator of the markup-on-price formula, as in the markup-on-cost formula. However, unit cost has been replaced by price in the denominator.

The markup-on-cost and markup-on-price formulas are simply alternative means for expressing the relative size of profit margins. To convert from one markup formula to the other, just use the following expressions:

$$\text{Markup on Cost} = \frac{\text{Markup on Price}}{1 - \text{Markup on Price}} \qquad (1.31)$$

$$\text{Markup on Price} = \frac{\text{Markup on Cost}}{1 + \text{Markup on Cost}} \qquad (1.32)$$

Therefore, the 30 percent markup on cost described in the previous example is equivalent to a 23 percent markup on price:

$$\text{Markup on Price} = \frac{0.3}{1 + 0.3} = 0.23 \text{ or } 23\%$$

An item with a cost of $2.30, a 69¢ markup, and a price of $2.99 has a 30 percent markup on cost and a 23 percent markup on price. This illustrates the importance of being consistent in the choice of a cost or price basis when comparing markups among products or sellers.

Markup pricing is sometimes criticized as a naive pricing method based solely on cost considerations—and the wrong costs at that. Some who employ the technique may ignore demand conditions, emphasize fully allocated accounting costs rather than marginal costs, and arrive at suboptimal price decisions. However, a categorical rejection of such a popular and successful pricing practice is clearly wrong. Although inappropriate use of markup pricing formulas will lead to suboptimal managerial decisions, successful firms typically employ the method in a way that is consistent with profit maximization. Markup pricing can be viewed as an efficient rule-of-thumb approach to setting optimal prices.

Role of Cost in Markup Pricing

Although a variety of cost concepts are employed in markup pricing, most firms use a standard, or fully allocated, cost concept. Fully allocated costs are determined by first estimating direct costs per unit, then allocating the firm's expected indirect expenses, or overhead, assuming a standard or normal output level. Price is then based on standard costs per unit, irrespective of short-term variations in actual unit costs.

Unfortunately, use of the standard cost concept can create several problems. Sometimes, firms fail to adjust historical costs to reflect recent or expected price changes. Also, accounting costs may not reflect true economic costs. For example, fully allocated costs can be appropriate when a firm is operating at full capacity. During **peak** periods, when facilities are fully utilized, expansion is required to increase production. Under such conditions, an increase in production requires an increase in all plant, equipment, labor, materials, and other expenditures. However, if a firm has excess capacity, as during **off-peak** periods, only those costs that actually rise with production—the incremental costs per unit—should form a basis for setting prices.

Successful firms that employ markup pricing use fully allocated costs under normal conditions but offer price discounts or accept lower margins during off-peak periods when excess capacity is available. In some instances, output produced during off-peak periods is much cheaper than output produced during peak periods. When fixed costs represent a substantial share of total production costs, discounts of 30 percent to 50 percent for output produced during off-peak periods can often be justified on the basis of lower costs.

"Early bird" or afternoon matinee discounts at movie theaters provide an interesting example. Except for cleaning expenses, which vary according to the number of customers, most movie theater expenses are fixed. As a result, the revenue generated by adding customers during off-peak periods can significantly increase the theater's profit contribution. When off-peak customers buy regularly priced candy, popcorn, and soda, even lower afternoon ticket prices can be justified. Conversely, on Friday and Saturday nights when movie theaters operate at peak capacity, a small increase in the number of customers would require a costly expansion of facilities. Ticket prices during these peak periods reflect fully allocated costs. Similarly, **McDonald's, Burger King, Arby's,** and other fast-food outlets have increased their profitability substantially by introducing breakfast menus. If fixed restaurant expenses are covered by lunch and dinner business, even promotionally priced breakfast items can make a notable contribution to profits.

Role of Demand in Markup Pricing

Successful companies differentiate markups according to variations in product demand elasticities. Foreign and domestic automobile companies regularly offer rebates or special equipment packages for slow-selling models. Similarly, airlines promote different pricing schedules for business and vacation travelers. The airline and automobile industries are only two examples of sectors in which vigorous competition requires a careful reflection of demand and supply factors in pricing practice. In the production and distribution of many goods and services, successful firms quickly adjust prices to different market conditions.

Price Discrimination

With multiple markets or customer groups, the potential exists to enhance profits by charging different prices and markups to each relevant market segment. Market segmentation is an important fact of life for firms in the airline, entertainment, hotel, medical, legal, and professional services industries. Firms that offer goods also often segment their market between wholesale and retail buyers and between business, educational, not-for-profit, and government customers.

Requirements for Profitable Price Discrimination

Price discrimination occurs whenever different classes of customers are charged different markups for the same product. Price discrimination occurs when different customers are charged the same price despite underlying cost differences, and when price differentials fail to reflect cost discrepancies.

For price discrimination to be profitable, different price elasticities of demand must exist in the various submarkets. Unless price elasticities differ among submarkets, there is no point in segmenting the market. With identical price elasticities and identical marginal costs, profit-maximizing pricing policy calls for the same price and markup to be charged in all market segments. A **market segment** is a division or fragment of the overall market with unique demand or cost characteristics. For example, wholesale customers tend to buy in large quantities, are familiar with product costs and characteristics, and are well-informed about available alternatives. Wholesale buyers are highly price sensitive. Conversely, retail customers tend to buy in small quantities, are sometimes poorly informed about product costs and characteristics, and are often ignorant about available alternatives. As a group, retail customers are often less price sensitive than wholesale buyers. Markups charged to retail customers usually exceed those charged to wholesale buyers.

For price discrimination to be profitable, the firm must also be able to efficiently identify relevant submarkets and prevent transfers among affected customers. Detailed information must be obtained and monitored concerning customer buying habits, product preferences, and price sensitivity. Just as important, the price-discriminating firm must be able to monitor customer buying patterns to prevent reselling among customer subgroups. A highly profitable market segmentation between wholesale and retail customers can be effectively undermined if retail buyers are able to obtain discounts through willing wholesalers. Similarly, price discrimination among buyers in different parts of the country can be undermined if customers are able to resell in high-margin territories those products obtained in bargain locales.

Role Played by Consumers' Surplus

The underlying motive for price discrimination can be understood using the concept of **consumers' surplus.** Consumers' surplus is the value of purchased goods and services above and beyond the amount paid to sellers. To illustrate, consider Exhibit 100.50, in which a market equilibrium price/output combination of P^* and Q^* is shown. The total value of output to customers is given by the area under the demand curve, or area $0ABQ^*$. Because the total revenue paid to producers is price times quantity, equal to area $0P^*BQ^*$, the area P^*AB represents the value of output above the amount paid to producers—that is, the consumers' surplus. For example, if a given customer is willing to pay $200 for a certain overcoat but is able to obtain a bargain price of $150, the buyer enjoys $50 worth of consumers' surplus. If another customer places a value of only $150 on the overcoat, he or she would enjoy no consumers' surplus following a purchase for $150.

Exhibit 100.50 *Consumers' Surplus*

Consumers' surplus is shown by the area P^*AB and represents the value of output to consumers above and beyond the amount they pay to producers.

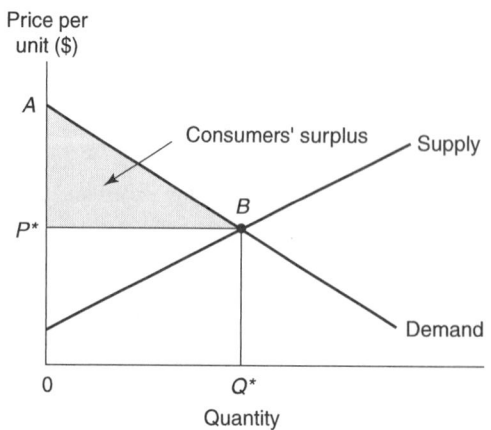

Consumers' surplus arises because individual consumers place different values on goods and services. Customers that place a relatively high value on a product will pay high prices; customers that place a relatively low value on a product are only willing to pay low prices. As one proceeds from point A downward along the market marginal curve in Exhibit 100.50, customers that place a progressively lower marginal value on the product enter the market. At low prices, both high-value and low-value customers are buyers; at high prices, only customers that place a relatively high value on a given product are buyers.

When product value differs greatly among various groups of customers, a motive for price discrimination is created. By charging higher prices to customers with a high marginal value of consumption, revenues will increase without affecting costs. Sellers with the ability to vary prices according to the value placed on their products by buyers are able to capture at least some of the value represented by consumers' surplus. Such price discrimination will always increase profits because it allows the firm to increase total revenue without affecting costs. A firm that is precise in its price discrimination always charges the maximum each market segment is willing to pay. Price discrimination is charging what the market will bear.

Finally, it is important to recognize that price discrimination does not carry any evil connotation in a moral sense. In some circumstances, price discrimination leads to lower prices for some customer groups and to a wider availability of goods and services. For example, a municipal bus company might charge lower prices for the elderly and the handicapped. In such circumstances, the bus company is price discriminating in favor of elderly and handicapped riders and against other customers. This type of price discrimination provides elderly and handicapped customers a greater opportunity to ride the bus. Because of incremental revenues provided by elderly and handicapped riders, the bus company may also be able to offer routes that could not be supported by revenues from full-fare customers alone, or it may be able to operate with a lower taxpayer subsidy.

Degrees of Price Discrimination

The extent to which a firm can engage in price discrimination is classified into three major categories. Under **first-degree price discrimination,** the firm extracts the maximum amount each customer is willing to pay for its products. Each unit is priced separately at the price indicated along each product demand curve. Such pricing precision is rare because it requires that sellers know the maximum price each buyer is willing to pay for each unit of output. Purchase decisions must also be monitored closely to prevent reselling among customers. Although first-degree price discrimination is uncommon, it has the potential to emerge in any market where discounts from posted prices are standard and effective prices are individually negotiated between buyers and sellers. When sellers possess a significant amount of market power, consumer purchases of big-ticket items such as appliances, automobiles, homes, and professional services all have the potential to involve first-degree price discrimination.

First-degree price discrimination Charging different prices to each customer.

Second-degree price discrimination, a more frequently employed type of price discrimination, involves setting prices on the basis of the quantity purchased. Bulk rates are typically set with high prices and markups charged for the first unit or block of units purchased, but progressively greater discounts are offered for greater quantities. Quantity discounts that lead to lower markups for large versus small customers are a common means of discriminating in price between retail and wholesale customers. Book publishers often charge full price for small purchases but offer 40 percent to 50 percent off list prices when 20 or more units are purchased. Public utilities, such as electric companies, gas companies, and water companies, also frequently charge block rates that are discriminatory. Consumers pay a relatively high markup for residential service, whereas commercial and industrial customers pay relatively low markups. Office equipment such as copy machines and servers (mainframe computers) are other examples of products for which second-degree price discrimination is practiced, especially when time sharing among customers is involved.

Second-degree price discrimination Charging different prices based on use rates or quantities purchased.

The most commonly observed form of price discrimination, **third-degree price discrimination,** results when a firm separates its customers into several classes and sets a different price for each customer class. Customer classifications can be based on for-profit or not-for-profit status, regional location, or customer age. *Barron's, Forbes, The Wall Street Journal,* and other publishers routinely offer educational discounts that can be in excess of 30 percent to 40 percent off list prices. These publishers are eager to penetrate the classroom on the assumption that student users will become loyal future customers. Auto companies, personal computer manufacturers, and others also prominently feature educational discounts as part of their mar-

Third-degree price discrimination Charging different prices to each customer class.

keting strategy. Many hospitals also offer price discounts to various patient groups. If unemployed and uninsured patients are routinely charged only what they can easily afford to pay for medical service, whereas employed and insured medical patients are charged maximum allowable rates, the hospital is price discriminating in favor of the unemployed and against the employed. Widespread price discounts for senior citizens represent a form of price discrimination in favor of older customers but against younger customers.

Multiple-Unit Pricing Strategies

When products have different values for different customers, profits can sometimes be enhanced by using multiple-unit pricing strategies. With multiple-unit pricing, all customers typically face the same pricing schedule, but the price paid is determined by the value to consumers of the total amount purchased. Unlike single-unit pricing, where all customers are charged a unit price that sets $MR = MC$, multiple-unit pricing can result in some combination of per-unit and "lump sum" fees. Like price discrimination, multiple-unit pricing strategies have proven an effective means for extracting consumers' surplus for the benefit of producers.

Two-Part Pricing

Two-part pricing *Per-unit fee equal to marginal cost, plus a fixed fee equal to the amount of consumers' surplus generated at that price.*

Athletic clubs, time-share vacation resorts, golf courses, and a wide variety of "membership organizations" offer goods and services using two-part pricing. A common **two-part pricing** technique is to charge all customers a fixed "membership" fee per month or per year, plus a per-unit usage charge. In general, a firm can enhance profits by charging each customer a per-unit fee equal to marginal cost, plus a fixed fee equal to the amount of consumers' surplus generated at that per-unit fee.

Bundle Pricing

Bundle pricing *Lump sum amount equal to the total area under the demand curve when $P = MC$.*

Another way firms with market power enhance profits is by a variant of two-part pricing called **bundle pricing.** If you've ever purchased a 12-pack of soft drinks, a year's supply of tax preparation services, or bought a "two-for-the-price-of-one" special, you have firsthand experience with the bundle pricing concept. When significant consumers' surplus exists, profits can be enhanced if products are purchased together as a single package or bundle of goods or services. Bundles can be of a single product, like soft drinks or legal services, or they can be comprised of closely related goods and services. For example, car manufacturers often bundle "luxury packages" comprised of new car options like power steering, power brakes, automatic transmissions, tinted glass, and so on. Similarly, car dealers often bundle services, like oil changes, transmission fluid changes, radiator flushes, and tune-ups at a "special package price."

Multiple-Product Pricing

It is difficult to think of a firm that does not produce a variety of products. Almost all companies produce multiple models, styles, or sizes of output, and each of these variations can represent a separate product for pricing purposes. Although multiple-product pricing requires the same basic analysis as for a single product, the analysis is complicated by demand and production interrelations.

Transfer Pricing

Expanding markets brought about by improvements in communication and transportation, as well as falling trade barriers, have led to the development of large, multidivision firms that cut across national boundaries. A vexing challenge for many large corporations surrounds the need to set an appropriate price for the transfer of goods and services among divisions.

Transfer Pricing Problem

The transfer pricing problem results from the difficulty of establishing profitable relationships among divisions of a single company when each separate business unit stands in **vertical relation** to the other. A vertical relation is one where the output of one division or company is the input to another. **Vertical integration** occurs when a single company controls various links in the production chain from basic inputs to final output. Media powerhouse **AOL-Time Warner, Inc.,** is vertically integrated because it owns **AOL,** an Internet service provider (ISP) and cable TV systems, plus a number of programming properties in filmed entertainment (e.g., **Warner Bros.**) and television production (e.g., HBO, CNN), commonly referred to as content providers. Vertically integrated companies in this field own and operate the distribution network and the programming that is sold over that network.

Vertical integration Single company controls various links in the production chain from basic inputs to final output.

To combat the problems of coordinating large-scale enterprises that are vertically integrated, separate profit centers are typically established for each important product or product line. Despite obvious advantages, this decentralization has the potential to create problems. The most critical of these is the problem of **transfer pricing,** or the pricing of intermediate products transferred among divisions. To maximize profits for the vertically integrated firm, it is essential that a profit margin or markup only be charged at the final stage of production. All intermediate products transferred internally must be transferred at marginal cost.

Transfer pricing The pricing of products transferred among divisions of a firm.

Transfer Pricing for Products Without External Markets

Think of the divisionalized firm as a type of internal market. Like external markets, the internal markets of divisionalized firms act according to the laws of supply and demand. Supply is offered by various upstream suppliers to meet the demand of downstream users. Goods and services must be transferred and priced each step along the way from basic raw materials to finished products.

For simplicity, consider the problem faced by a vertically integrated firm that has different divisions at distinct points along the various steps of the production process, and assume for the moment that no external market exists for transferred inputs. If each separate division is established as a profit center to provide employees with an efficiency incentive, a transfer pricing problem can occur. Suppose each selling division adds a markup over its marginal cost for inputs sold to other divisions. Each buying division would then set its marginal revenue from output equal to the division's marginal cost of input. This process would culminate in a marginal cost to the ultimate upstream user that exceeds the sum total of marginal costs for each transferring division. All of the markups charged by each transferring division drive a wedge between the firm's true marginal cost of production and the marginal cost to the last or ultimate upstream user. As a result, the ultimate upstream user buys less than the optimal amount of input and produces less than the profit-maximizing level of output.

For example, it would be inefficient if AOL, a major ISP, paid more than the marginal cost of programming produced by its own subsidiaries. If each subsidiary added a markup to the marginal cost of programming sold to the parent company, AOL would buy less than a profit-maximizing amount of its own programming. In fact, AOL would have an incentive to seek programming from other purveyors so long as the external market price was less than the internal transfer price. Such an incentive could create extreme inefficiencies, especially when the external market price is less than the transfer price but greater than the marginal cost of programming produced by AOL's own subsidiaries.

An effective transfer pricing system leads to activity levels in each division that are consistent with profit maximization for the overall enterprise. This observation leads to the most basic rule for optimal transfer pricing: *When transferred products cannot be sold in external markets, the marginal cost of the transferring division is the optimal transfer price.* One practical means for ensuring that an optimal amount of input is transferred at an optimal transfer price is to inform buying divisions that the marginal cost curve of supplying divisions is to be treated like a supply schedule. Alternatively, supplying divisions could be informed about the buying division's marginal revenue or demand curve and told to use this information in determining the quantity supplied. In either case, each division would voluntarily choose to transfer an optimal amount of input at the optimal transfer price.

Transfer Pricing with Perfectly Competitive External Markets

The transfer pricing problem is only slightly more complicated when transferred inputs can be sold in external markets. When transferred inputs can be sold in a perfectly competitive external market, the external market price represents the firm's opportunity cost of employing such inputs internally. As such, it would never pay to use inputs internally unless their value to the firm is at least as great as their value to others in the external market. This observation leads to a second key rule for optimal transfer pricing: When transferred products can be sold in perfectly competitive external markets, the external market price is the optimal transfer price. If upstream suppliers wish to supply more than downstream users desire to employ at a perfectly competitive price, excess input can be sold in the external market. If downstream users wish to employ more than upstream suppliers seek to furnish at a perfectly competitive price, excess input demand can be met through purchases in the external market. In either event, an optimal amount of input is transferred internally.

Transfer Pricing with Imperfectly Competitive External Markets

The typical case of vertical integration involves firms with inputs that can be transferred internally or sold in external markets that are not perfectly competitive. Again, it never pays to use inputs internally unless their value to the firm is at least as great as their value to others in the external market. This observation leads to a third and final fundamental rule for optimal transfer pricing: When transferred products can be sold in imperfectly competitive external markets, the optimal transfer price equates the marginal cost of the transferring division to the marginal revenue derived from the combined internal and external markets. In other words, when inputs can be sold in imperfectly competitive external markets, internal input demand must reflect the opportunity to supply input to the external market at a price in excess of marginal cost. If upstream suppliers wish to offer more input than downstream users desire to employ when input $MC = MR$ from the combined market, excess supply can be sold in the external market. If downstream users want to employ more than upstream suppliers seek to furnish when $MC = MR$, excess internal demand can be met through added purchases in the external market. In both cases, an optimal amount of input is transferred internally.

Riddles in Pricing Practice

Economic reasoning is a powerful tool that can be used to understand and improve pricing practices. For example, popular markup pricing methods can be interpreted as an efficient rule-of-thumb approach toward setting profit-maximizing prices. Similarly, multiple-unit pricing methods, like two-part pricing and bundle pricing, are efficient means for capturing additional profits when the value of goods and services varies from one consumer to another.

Still, it would be misleading to infer that there are no important remaining mysteries in pricing practice. In fact, significant riddles remain. For example, no doubt you have noticed the popularity of what is sometimes called "odd-number pricing." Prices like $6.99 are much more common than $7; 99¢ is much more commonly employed than $1.

This interpretation gains favor when one considers the fact that the popularity of odd-numbered pricing is greatest in the case of goods and services offered in vigorously price competitive environments.

In short, economic reasoning has long proved an effective means for understanding pricing practices and for designing improvements in the pricing practices of individual firms. At the same time, the relevance of input from psychology and other social and physical sciences should not be minimized. The ongoing design of effective pricing practices benefits from knowledge gained in a wide variety of areas.

Economics and Finance

The Relation Between Economics and Finance

Economics and finance are interconnected. Economics deals with interest rates (the cost of money), inflation, and trade balance. Finance deals with raising money, budgets, and business acquisition activity. The amount of money a firm can raise depends, in part, on the level of interest rates and the amount of inflation in the economy.

In this section, we will focus on interest rate levels, the determinants of market interest rates, the factors that influence interest rate levels, and how interest rates influence business decisions.

The Cost of Money

In a free economy, funds are allocated through the price system. *The interest rate is the price paid to borrow funds, whereas in the case of equity capital, investors expect to receive dividends and capital gains.* The factors that affect the supply of and demand for investment capital, and hence the cost of money, are discussed in this section.

The four most fundamental factors affecting the cost of money are (1) **production opportunities**, (2) **time preferences for consumption**, (3) **risk**, and (4) **inflation**.

Thus, we see that the interest rate paid to savers depends in a basic way on (1) the rate of return producers expect to earn on invested capital, (2) savers' time preferences for current versus future consumption, (3) the riskiness of the loan, and (4) the expected future rate of inflation. The returns borrowers expect to earn by investing the funds they borrow set an upper limit on how much they can pay for savings, while consumers' time preferences for consumption establish how much consumption they are willing to defer, hence how much they will save at different levels of interest offered by borrowers. Higher risk and higher inflation also lead to higher interest rates.

Interest Rate Levels

Funds are allocated among borrowers by interest rates. Firms with the most profitable investment opportunities are willing and able to pay the most for capital, so they tend to attract it away from less efficient firms or from those whose products are not in demand. Of course, our economy is not completely free in the sense of being influenced only by market forces—the federal government has agencies that help designated individuals or groups obtain credit on favorable terms, including small businesses, certain minorities, and firms willing to build plants in areas with high unemployment. Still, most capital in the U.S. economy is allocated through the price system.

Capital markets are interdependent and there are many capital markets in the United States. U.S. firms also invest and raise funds throughout the world, and foreigners both borrow and lend funds in the United States. There are markets in the United States for home loans, farm loans, business loans, government loans, and so forth. For each type of capital, there is a price, and these prices change over time as shifts occur in supply and demand conditions. Short-term rates are responsive to current economic conditions, whereas long-term rates primarily reflect long-run expectations for inflation. As a result, short-term rates are sometimes above and sometimes below long-term rates. The relationship between long-term and short-term rates is called the *term structure of interest rates.*

The Determinants of Market Interest Rates

In general, the quoted (or nominal) interest rate on a debt security, k, is composed of a real risk-free rate of interest, k^*, plus several premiums that reflect inflation, the riskiness of the security, and the security's marketability (or liquidity). This relationship can be expressed as follows.

$$\text{Quoted interest rate} = k = k^* + IP + DRP + LP + MRP \tag{1.33}$$

In equation 1.33 the variables are defined as follows.

- k = the quoted, or *nominal*, rate of interest on a given security. There are many different securities, hence many different quoted interest rates
- k^* = the *real risk-free rate of interest;* k^* is pronounced "k-star"
- IP = inflation premium
- DRP = default risk premium
- LP = liquidity, or marketability, premium
- MRP = maturity risk premium

We discuss the components whose sum makes up the quoted, or nominal, rate on a given security in the following sections. The term *nominal* as it is used here means the *stated* rate as opposed to the *real* rate, which is adjusted to remove the effects of inflation. If you bought a 10-year Treasury bond in March 1999, the quoted, or nominal, rate would be about 5.6 percent, but if inflation was expected to average 2.1 percent over the next 10 years, the real rate would be about $5.6\% - 2.1\% = 3.5\%$.

The Real Risk-Free Rate of Interest, k*

The **real risk-free rate of interest, k***, is defined as the interest rate that would exist on a security with a *guaranteed* pay-off (termed a riskless, or risk-free, security) if inflation was expected to be zero during the investment period. It can be thought of as the rate of interest that would exist on short-term U.S. Treasury securities in an inflation-free world. The real risk-free rate changes over time depending on economic conditions, especially (1) on the rate of return corporations and other borrowers are willing to pay to borrow funds and (2) on people's time preferences for current versus future consumption. It is difficult to measure the real risk-free rate precisely, but most experts think that k* has fluctuated in the range of 1 to 4 percent in the United States in recent years.

The Nominal, or Quoted, Risk-Free Rate of Interest, k_{RF}

The **nominal**, or **quoted, risk-free rate, k_{RF}**, is the *real risk-free rate plus a premium for expected inflation*: $k_{RF} = k^* + IP$. If we combine $k^* + IP$ and let this sum equal k_{RF}, then equation 1.34 becomes:

$$k = k_{RF} + DRP + LP + MRP \tag{1.34}$$

Inflation Premium (IP)

Inflation has a major impact on interest rates because it erodes the purchasing power of the dollar and lowers the real rate of return on investments. Investors are well aware of all this, so when they lend money, they build in an **inflation premium (IP)** equal to the *average inflation rate expected over the life of the security*. Therefore, if the real risk-free rate of interest, k^*, is 3%, and if inflation is expected to be 4% (IP = 4%) during the next year, then the quoted rate of interest on one-year T-bills would be 7%. In March of 1999, economists forecasted the one-year inflation rate to be between 1.5% and 2%, and, at the same time, the yield on one-year T-bills was about 4.7 percent. This implies that the real risk-free rate on short-term securities at that time was expected to be between 2.7 percent and 3.2 percent.

Default Risk Premium (DRP)

The risk that a borrower will *default* on a loan, which means not to pay the interest or the principal, also affects the market interest rate on a security: The greater the default risk, the higher the interest rate lenders charge (demand). Treasury securities have no default risk; thus, they generally carry the lowest interest rates on taxable securities in the United States. For corporate bonds, the better the bond's overall credit rating, the lower its default risk, and, consequently, the lower its interest rate. Note that bonds rated AAA are judged to have less default risk than bonds rated AA, AA bonds are less risky than A bonds, and so on. Ratings might also be designated AAA or Aaa, AA or Aa, and so forth, depending on the rating agency.

The difference between the quoted interest rate on a T-bond and that on a corporate bond with similar maturity, liquidity, and other features is the default risk premium (DRP).

Liquidity Premium (LP)

Liquidity generally is defined as the ability to convert an asset to cash on short notice and "reasonably" capture the amount initially invested. Of course, the most liquid asset of all is cash, and the more easily an asset can be converted to cash at a price that substantially recovers the initial amount invested, the more liquid it is considered. Consequently, financial assets are considered more liquid than real assets, such as land and equipment, and short-term financial assets generally are more liquid than long-term financial assets. Because liquidity is important, investors evaluate and include **liquidity premiums (LP)** when interest rates are established. Although it is very difficult to accurately measure liquidity premiums, a differential of at least two and probably four or five percentage points exists between the least liquid and the most liquid financial assets of similar default risk and maturity.

Maturity Risk Premium (MRP)

The prices of bonds decline whenever interest rates rise, and because interest rates can and do occasionally rise, all bonds, even Treasury bonds, have an element of risk called **interest rate risk.** As a general rule, the bonds of any organization, from the U.S. government to General Motors, have more interest rate risk the longer the maturity of the bond. Therefore, a **maturity risk premium (MRP),** which is higher the longer the years to maturity, must be included in the required interest rate. The effect of maturity risk premiums is to raise interest rates on long-term bonds relative to those on short-term bonds. This premium, like the others, is extremely difficult to measure, but (1) it seems to vary over time, rising when interest rates are more volatile and uncertain, then falling when interest rates are more stable, and (2) in recent years, the maturity risk premium on 30-year T-bonds appears to have generally been in the range of one or two percentage points.

We should mention that although long-term bonds are heavily exposed to maturity risk, short-term investments are heavily exposed to **reinvestment rate risk.** When short-term investments mature and the proceeds are reinvested, or "rolled over," a decline in interest rates would necessitate reinvestment at a lower rate and hence would lead to a decline in interest income. Thus, although "investing short" preserves one's principal, the interest income provided by short-term investments varies from year to year, depending on reinvestment rates.

Long-term bonds also have some reinvestment rate risk. To actually earn the quoted rate on a long-term bond, the interest payments must be reinvested at the quoted rate. However, if interest rates fall, the interest payments would be reinvested at a lower rate; thus, the realized return would be less than the quoted rate. Note, though, that the reinvestment rate risk is lower on a long-term bond than on a short-term bond because only the interest payments (rather than interest plus principal) on the long-term bond are exposed to reinvestment rate risk. Only zero coupon bonds are completely free of reinvestment rate risk.

The Term Structure of Interest Rates

The relationship between long- and short-term rates, which is known as the **term structure of interest rates,** is important to corporate treasurers, who must decide whether to borrow by issuing long- or short-term debt, and to investors, who must decide whether to buy long- or short-term bonds. Thus, it is important to understand (1) how long- and short-term rates are related to each other and (2) what causes shifts in their relative positions.

A **yield curve** shows the relationship between interest rates and maturities of securities. The yield curve changes both in position and in slope over time. It shows a downward slope when short-term interest rates are higher than long-term rates; an upward slope when short-term interest rates are lower than long-term rates.

Historically, long-term interest rates have been above short-term rates, so usually the yield curve has been upward sloping. For this reason, an upward-sloping curve is called a "normal" yield curve and a yield curve that slopes downward is called an inverted ("abnormal") yield curve.

Term Structure Theories (Explanations)

Several theories have been proposed to explain the shape of the yield curve. The three major ones are (1) the expectations theory, (2) the liquidity preference theory, and (3) the market segmentation theory.

EXPECTATIONS THEORY The **expectations theory** states that the yield curve depends on *expectations* concerning future inflation rates. Specifically, $k_{RF,t}$, the nominal interest rate on a U.S. Treasury bond that matures in t years, is found as follows under the expectations theory.

$$k_{RF,t} = k^* + IP_t$$

Here k* is the real risk-free interest rate, and IP_t is an inflation premium, which is equal to the *average expected rate of inflation* over the t years until the bond matures. Under the expectations theory, the maturity risk premium (MRP) is assumed to be zero, and, for Treasury securities, the default risk premium (DRP) and liquidity premium (LP) also are zero.

LIQUIDITY PREFERENCE THEORY The **liquidity preference theory** states that long-term bonds normally yield more than short-term bonds for two reasons: (1) All else equal, investors generally prefer to hold short-term securities, because such securities are more liquid in the sense that they can be converted to cash with little danger of loss of principal. Investors will, therefore, generally accept lower yields on short-term securities, and this leads to relatively low short-term rates. (2) Borrowers, on the other hand, generally prefer long-term debt, because short-term debt exposes them to the risk of having to repay the debt under adverse conditions. Accordingly, borrowers want to "lock into" long-term funds, which means they are willing to pay a higher rate, other things held constant, for long-term funds than for short-term funds—this also leads to relatively low short-term rates. Thus, lender and borrower preferences both operate to cause short-term rates to be lower than long-term rates. Taken together, these two sets of preferences—and hence the liquidity preference theory—imply that under normal conditions, a positive maturity risk premium (MRP) exists, and the MRP increases with years to maturity, causing the yield curve to be upward sloping.

MARKET SEGMENTATION THEORY Briefly, the **market segmentation theory** states that each lender and each borrower has a preferred maturity. The thrust of the market segmentation theory is that the slope of the yield curve depends on supply/demand conditions in the long- and short-term markets. Thus, according to this theory, the yield curve could at any given time be either flat, upward sloping, or downward sloping. An upward-sloping yield curve would occur when there was a large supply of short-term funds relative to demand, but a shortage of long-term funds. Similarly, a downward-sloping curve would indicate relatively strong demand for funds in the short-term market compared to that in the long-term market. A flat curve would indicate balance between the two markets.

Various tests of the theories explaining the shape of the yield curve have been conducted, and these tests indicate that all three theories have some validity. Thus, the shape of the yield curve at any given time is affected (1) by expectations about future inflation, (2) by liquidity preferences, and (3) by supply/demand conditions in long- and short-term markets. One factor might dominate at one time, another at another time, but all three affect the term structure of interest rates.

Other Factors That Influence Interest Rate Levels

Factors other than those discussed in the previous section also influence both the general level of interest rates and the shape of the yield curve. The four most important factors are (1) Federal Reserve policy, (2) the level of the federal budget deficit, (3) the foreign trade balance, and (4) the level of business activity.

Federal Reserve Policy

As you probably learned in your economics courses, (1) the money supply has a major effect on both the level of economic activity and the rate of inflation, and (2) in the United States, the Federal Reserve Board controls the money supply. If the Fed wants to control growth in the economy, it slows growth in the money supply. The initial effect of such an action is to cause interest rates to increase and inflation to stabilize. The reverse holds if the Fed loosens the money supply.

During periods when the Fed is actively intervening in the markets, the yield curve will be distorted. Short-term rates will be temporarily "too low" if the Fed is easing credit, and "too high" if it is tightening credit. Long-term rates are not affected as much by Fed intervention because they represent averages of short-term expectations. The Fed deals primarily in the short-term end of the market.

Federal Budget Deficits

If the federal government spends more than it takes in from tax revenues, it runs a deficit, and that deficit must be covered either by borrowing or by printing money. If the government borrows, this added demand for funds pushes up interest rates. If it prints money, this increases expectations for future inflation, which also drives up interest rates. Thus, the larger the federal deficit, other things held constant, the higher the level of interest rates. Whether long- or short-term rates are more affected depends on how the deficit is financed, so we cannot state, in general, how deficits will affect the slope of the yield curve.

Foreign Trade Balance

Businesses and individuals in the United States buy from and sell to people and firms in other countries. If we buy more than we sell (that is, if we import more than we export), we are said to be running a foreign trade deficit. When trade deficits occur, they must be financed, and the main source of financing is debt. The deficit could also be financed by selling assets, including gold, corporate stocks, entire companies, and real estate. The United States has financed its massive trade deficits by all of these means at various times, but the primary method has been by borrowing. Therefore, the larger our trade deficit, the more we must borrow, and as we increase our borrowing, this drives up interest rates. Also, foreigners are willing to hold U.S. debt only if the interest rate on this debt is competitive with interest rates in other countries. Therefore, if the Federal Reserve attempts to lower interest rates in the United States, causing our rates to fall below rates abroad, then foreigners will sell U.S. bonds, which will depress bond prices and cause U.S. interest rates to increase. Thus, the existence of a deficit trade balance hinders the Fed's ability to combat a recession by lowering interest rates.

Level of Business Activity

Business conditions influence interest rates. Here are the key points.

1. Because inflation increased from the late 1960s to 1981, the general tendency during this period was toward higher interest rates. However, since the 1981 peak, the trend has generally been downward.

2. Until the mid-1960s, short-term rates were almost always below long-term rates. Thus, in those years the yield curve was almost always "normal" in the sense that it was upward sloping.
3. During recessions both the demand for money and the rate of inflation tend to fall, and, at the same time, the Federal Reserve tends to increase the money supply in an effort to stimulate the economy. As a result, there is a tendency for interest rates to decline during recessions.
4. During recessions, short-term rates decline more sharply than long-term rates. This occurs because (a) the Fed operates mainly in the short-term sector, so its intervention has the strongest effect here, and (b) long-term rates reflect the average expected inflation rate over the next 20 to 30 years, and this expectation generally does not change much, even when the current rate of inflation is low (or high).

Interest Rate Levels and Stock Prices

Interest rates have two effects on corporate profits. First, because interest is a cost, the higher the rate of interest, the lower a firm's profits, other things held constant. Second, interest rates affect the level of economic activity, and economic activity affects corporate profits. Interest rates obviously affect stock prices because of their effects on profits, but, perhaps even more important, they have an effect due to competition in the marketplace between stocks and bonds. If interest rates rise sharply, investors can get higher returns in the bond market, which induces them to sell stocks and to transfer funds from the stock market to the bond market. A massive sale of stocks in response to rising interest rates obviously would depress stock prices. Of course, the reverse occurs if interest rates decline. Indeed, the bull market of December 1991, when the Dow Jones Industrial Index rose 10 percent in less than a month, was caused almost entirely by the sharp drop in long-term interest rates. On the other hand, the poor performance exhibited by the stock market in 1994—common stocks declined in average by more than three percent—resulted from sharp increase in interest rates during that year. For the past several years, as interest rates have declined and remained at historically low levels, the stock market has been the "hot" investment.

Interest Rate Levels and Business Decisions

Financing decisions would be easy if we could develop accurate forecasts of future interest rates. Unfortunately, predicting future interest rates with consistent accuracy is somewhere between difficult and impossible—people who make a living by selling interest rate forecasts say it is difficult, but many others say it is impossible. But, even if it is difficult to predict future interest rate levels, it is easy to predict that interest rates will fluctuate—they always have, and they always will. This being the case, sound financial policy calls for using a mix of long- and short-term debt, as well as equity, in such a manner that the firm can survive in most interest-rate environments. Further, the optimal financial policy depends in an important way on the nature of the firm's assets—the easier it is to sell off assets and thus to pay off debts, the more feasible it is to use large amounts of short-term debt. This makes it more feasible to finance current assets than noncurrent (fixed) assets with short-term debt.

Organization Design and Development

What Is an Organization?

Organizations as diverse as a church, a hospital, and IBM have characteristics in common. The definition to describe organizations is as follows: **organizations** are (1) social entities that (2) are goal directed, (3) are designed as deliberately structured and coordinated activity systems, and (4) are linked to the external environment.

Exhibit 100.51 *Importance of Organizations*

1. Bring together resources to achieve desired goals and outcomes
2. Produce goods and services efficiently
3. Facilitate innovation
4. Use modern manufacturing and computer-based technology
5. Adapt to and influence a changing environment
6. Create value for owners, customers, and employees
7. Accommodate ongoing challenges of diversity, ethics, and the motivation and coordination of employees

The key element of an organization is not a building or a set of policies and procedures; organizations are made up of people and their relationships with one another. An organization exists when people interact with one another to perform essential functions that help attain goals. Recent trends in management recognize the importance of human resources, with most new approaches designed to empower employees with greater opportunities to learn and contribute as they work together toward common goals. Managers deliberately structure and coordinate organizational resources to achieve the organization's purpose. However, even though work may be structured into separate departments or sets of activities, most organizations today are striving for greater horizontal coordination of work activities, often using teams of employees from different functional areas to work together on projects. Boundaries between departments as well as those between organizations are becoming more flexible and diffuse as companies face the need to respond to changes in the external environment more rapidly. An organization cannot exist without interacting with customers, suppliers, competitors, and other elements of the external environment. Today, some companies are even cooperating with their competitors, sharing information and technology to their mutual advantage.

Importance of Organizations

Organizations are all around us and shape our lives in many ways. But what contributions do organizations make? Why are they important? Exhibit 100.51 lists seven reasons organizations are important to you and to society. First, organizations bring together resources to accomplish specific goals.

Organizations also produce goods and services that customers want at competitive prices. Companies look for innovative ways to produce and distribute goods and services more efficiently. One way is through e-commerce and advanced information technology, and through the use of computer-based manufacturing technologies. Redesigning organizational structures and management practices can also contribute to increased efficiency. Organizations create a drive for innovation rather than a reliance on standard products and outmoded ways of doing things.

Organizations adapt to and influence a rapidly changing environment. Some large companies have entire departments charged with monitoring the external environment and finding ways to adapt to or influence that environment. One of the most significant changes in the external environment today is globalization.

Through all of these activities, organizations create value for their owners, customers, and employees. Managers need to understand which parts of the operation create value and which parts do not; a company can be profitable only when the value it creates is greater than the cost of resources. Finally, organizations have to cope with and accommodate today's challenges of workforce diversity and growing concerns over ethics and social responsibility, as well as find effective ways to motivate employees to work together to accomplish organizational goals.

Organizations shape our lives, and well-informed managers can shape organizations. An understanding of organization theory enables managers to design organizations to function more effectively.

Organizations as Systems

Open Systems

One significant development in the study of organizations was the distinction between closed and open systems.[252] A **closed system** would not depend on its environment; it would be autonomous, enclosed, and sealed off from the outside world. Although a true closed system cannot exist, early organization studies focused on internal systems. Early management concepts, including scientific management, leadership style, and industrial engineering, were closed-

Exhibit 100.52 *An Open System and Its Subsystems*

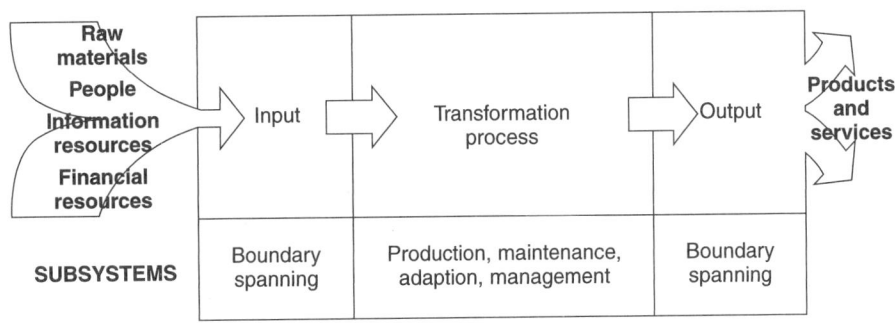

system approaches because they took the environment for granted and assumed the organization could be made more effective through internal design. The management of a closed system would be quite easy. The environment would be stable and predictable and would not intervene to cause problems. The primary management issue would be to run things efficiently.

An **open system** must interact with the environment to survive; it both consumes resources and exports resources to the environment. It cannot seal itself off. It must continuously change and adapt to the environment. Open systems can be enormously complex. Internal efficiency is just one issue—and sometimes a minor one. The organization has to find and obtain needed resources, interpret and act on environmental changes, dispose of outputs, and control and coordinate internal activities in the face of environmental disturbances and uncertainty. Every system that must interact with the environment to survive is an open system. The human being is an open system. So is the planet Earth, the city of New York, and IBM. Indeed, one problem at IBM was that top managers seemed to forget they were part of an open system. They isolated themselves within the IBM culture and failed to pay close attention to what was going on with their customers, suppliers, and competitors. The rapid changes over the past few decades, including globalization and increased competition, the explosion of the Internet and e-business, and the growing diversity of the population and workforce, have forced many managers to reorient toward an open-systems mindset and recognize their business as part of a complex, interconnected whole.

To understand the whole organization, it should be viewed as a system. A **system** is a set of interacting elements that acquires inputs from the environment, transforms them, and discharges outputs to the external environment. The need for inputs and outputs reflects dependency on the environment. Interacting elements mean that people and departments depend on one another and must work together.

Exhibit 100.53 illustrates an open system. Inputs to an organization system include employees, raw materials and other physical resources, information, and financial resources. The transformation process changes these inputs into something of value that can be exported back to the environment. Outputs include specific products and services for customers and clients. Outputs may also include employee satisfaction, pollution, and other by-products of the transformation process.

A system is made up of several **subsystems,** as illustrated at the bottom of Exhibit 100.52. These subsystems perform the specific functions required for organizational survival, such as production, boundary spanning, maintenance, adaptation, and management. The production subsystem produces the product and service outputs of the organization. Boundary subsystems are responsible for exchanges with the external environment. They include activities such as purchasing supplies or marketing products. The maintenance subsystem maintains the smooth operation and upkeep of the organization's physical and human elements. The adaptive subsystems are responsible for organizational change and adaptation. Management is a distinct subsystem, responsible for coordinating and directing the other subsystems of the organization.

Organizational Configuration

Various parts of the organization are designed to perform the key subsystem functions illustrated in Exhibit 100.60. One framework proposed by Henry Mintzberg suggests that every organization has five parts.[253] They include the technical core, top management, middle management, technical support, and administrative support. The five parts of the organization may vary in size and importance depending on the organization's environment, technology, and other factors.

TECHNICAL CORE The technical core includes people who do the basic work of the organization. It performs the production subsystem function and actually produces the product and service outputs of the organization. This is where the primary transformation from inputs to outputs takes place. The technical core is the production department in a manufacturing firm, the teachers and classes in a university, and the medical activities in a hospital. At IBM, the technical core produces hardware, software, and e-business services for clients.

TECHNICAL SUPPORT The technical support function helps the organization adapt to the environment. Technical support employees such as engineers and researchers scan the environment for problems, opportunities, and technological developments. Technical support is responsible for creating innovations in the technical core, helping the organization to change and adapt. Technical support at IBM is provided by departments such as technology, research and development, and marketing research.

ADMINISTRATIVE SUPPORT The administrative support function is responsible for the smooth operation and upkeep of the organization, including its physical and human elements. This includes human resource activities such as recruiting and hiring, establishing compensation and benefits, and employee training and development, as well as maintenance activities such as cleaning of buildings and service and repair of machines. Administrative support functions in a corporation such as IBM might include the human resources department, organizational development, the employee cafeteria, and the maintenance staff.

MANAGEMENT Management is a distinct subsystem, responsible for directing and coordinating other parts of the organization. Top management provides direction, strategy, goals, and policies for the entire organization or major divisions. Middle management is responsible for implementation and coordination at the departmental level. In traditional organizations, middle managers are responsible for mediating between top management and the technical core, such as implementing rules and passing information up and down the hierarchy.

In real-life organizations, the five parts are interrelated and often serve more than one subsystem function. For example, managers coordinate and direct other parts of the system; but they may also be involved in administrative and technical support. In addition, several of the parts serve the *boundary spanning* function mentioned in the previous section. For example, in the administrative support realm, human resources departments are responsible for working with the external environment to find quality employees. Purchasing departments acquire needed materials and supplies. In the technical support area, research and development departments work directly with the external environment to learn about new technological developments. Managers perform boundary spanning as well, such as when Lou Gerstner of IBM works directly with major customers. The important boundary spanning subsystem is embraced by several areas, rather than being confined to one part of the organization.

Dimensions of Organization Design

The systems view pertains to dynamic, ongoing activities within organizations. The next step for understanding organizations is to look at dimensions that describe specific organizational design traits. These dimensions describe organizations much the same way that personality and physical traits describe people.

Organizational dimensions fall into two types: structural and contextual. **Structural dimensions** provide labels to describe the internal characteristics of an organization. They create a basis for measuring and comparing organizations. **Contextual dimensions** characterize the whole organization, including its size, technology, environment, and goals. They describe the organizational setting that influences and shapes the structural dimensions. Contextual dimensions can be confusing because they represent both the organization and the environment. Contextual dimensions can be envisioned as a set of overlapping elements that underlie an organization's structure and work processes. To understand and evaluate organizations, one must examine both structural and contextual dimensions.[254] These dimensions of organization design interact with one another and can be adjusted to accomplish the purposes listed earlier in Exhibit 100.51.

Structural Dimensions

1. *Formalization* pertains to the amount of written documentation in the organization. Documentation includes procedures, job descriptions, regulations, and policy manuals. These written documents describe behavior and activities. Formalization is often measured by simply counting the number of pages of documentation within the organization. Large state universities, for example, tend to be high on

formalization because they have several volumes of written rules for such things as registration, dropping and adding classes, student associations, dormitory governance, and financial assistance. A small, family-owned business, in contrast, may have almost no written rules and would be considered informal.

2. *Specialization* is the degree to which organizational tasks are subdivided into separate jobs. If specialization is extensive, each employee performs only a narrow range of tasks. If specialization is low, employees perform a wide range of tasks in their jobs. Specialization is sometimes referred to as the *division of labor.*

3. *Hierarchy of authority* describes who reports to whom and the span of control for each manager. The hierarchy is depicted by the vertical lines on an organization chart, and is related to *span of control* (the number of employees reporting to a supervisor). When spans of control are narrow, the hierarchy tends to be tall. When spans of control are wide, the hierarchy of authority will be shorter.

4. *Centralization* refers to the hierarchical level that has authority to make a decision. When decision making is kept at the top level, the organization is centralized. When decisions are delegated to lower organizational levels, it is decentralized. Organizational decisions that might be centralized or decentralized include purchasing equipment, establishing goals, choosing suppliers, setting prices, hiring employees, and deciding marketing territories.

5. *Professionalism* is the level of formal education and training of employees. Professionalism is considered high when employees require long periods of training to hold jobs in the organization. Professionalism is generally measured as the average number of years of education of employees, which could be as high as 20 in a medical practice and less than 10 in a construction company.

6. *Personnel ratios* refer to the deployment of people to various functions and departments. Personnel ratios include the administrative ratio, the clerical ratio, the professional staff ratio, and the ratio of indirect to direct labor employees. A personnel ratio is measured by dividing the number of employees in a classification by the total number of organizational employees.

Contextual Dimensions

1. *Size* is the organization's magnitude as reflected in the number of people in the organization. It can be measured for the organization as a whole or for specific components, such as a plant or division. Because organizations are social systems, size is typically measured by the number of employees. Other measures such as total sales or total assets also reflect magnitude, but they do not indicate the size of the human part of the social system.

2. *Organizational technology* refers to the tools, techniques, and actions used to transform inputs into outputs. It concerns how the organization actually produces the products and services it provides for customers and includes such things as computer-aided manufacturing, advanced information systems, and the Internet. An automobile assembly line, a college classroom, and an overnight package delivery system are technologies, although they differ from one another.

3. The *environment* includes all elements outside the boundary of the organization. Key elements include the industry, government, customers, suppliers, and the financial community. Environmental elements that affect an organization the most are often other organizations.

4. The organization's *goals and strategy* define the purpose and competitive techniques that set it apart from other organizations. Goals are often written down as an enduring statement of company intent. A strategy is the plan of action that describes resource allocation and activities for dealing with the environment and for reaching the organization's goals. Goals and strategies define the scope of operations and the relationship with employees, customers, and competitors.

5. An organization's *culture* is the underlying set of key values, beliefs, understandings, and norms shared by employees. These underlying values may pertain to ethical behavior, commitment to employees, efficiency, or customer service, and they provide the glue to hold organization members together. An organization's culture is unwritten but can be observed in its stories, slogans, ceremonies, dress, and office layout.

The 11 contextual and structural dimensions discussed here are interdependent. For example, large organization size, a routine technology, and a stable environment all tend to create an organization that has greater formalization, specialization, and centralization. More detailed relationships among the dimensions are explored in later chapters of this book.

These dimensions provide a basis for the measurement and analysis of characteristics that cannot be seen by the casual observer, and they reveal significant information about an organization.

The Role of Organization Theory and Design

What topics are relevant to organization theory and design? How does a course in management or organizational behavior differ from a course in organization theory? To answer these questions, let's examine the value a person gains through the study of organization theory and consider the concept of levels of analysis.

The Value of Organization Theory

How can a study of organization theory help during this time of complexity and transition? For people who are or will be managers, organization theory provides significant insight and understanding to help them be better managers in a rapidly changing world. For example, one of the greatest threats to organizations today is the inability of management to adapt to the speed and chaos of technological change. Although companies have made massive investments in technology, they are only beginning to implement the organizational and management changes needed to make technology and the Internet competitive weapons. Understanding organization theory and design can help managers make those necessary changes by helping them see and understand how technology interacts with other elements of the organization and its environment. As in the case of IBM, many managers learn organization theory by trial and error. At IBM, managers did not initially understand the situation they were in or the contingencies to which they should respond.

In a very real sense, organization theory can make managers more competent and more influential by giving them an understanding of how organizations work. The study of organizations helps people see and understand things other people cannot see and understand. Organization theory provides ideas, concepts, and ways of thinking and interpreting that help managers effectively guide their organizations. When the old approaches are no longer working, organization theory helps managers understand why and develop new approaches to meet changing conditions.

Levels of Analysis

In systems theory, each system is composed of subsystems. Systems are nested within systems, and one **level of analysis** has to be chosen as the primary focus. Four levels of analysis normally characterize organizations, which include individual level, group level, organization level, and external environment. The individual human being is the basic building block of organizations. The human being is to the organization what a cell is to a biological system. The next higher system level is the group or department. These are collections of individuals who work together to perform group tasks. The next level of analysis is the organization itself. An organization is a collection of groups or departments that combine into the total organization. Organizations themselves can be grouped together into the next higher level of analysis, which is the interorganizational set and community. The interorganizational set is the group of organizations with which a single organization interacts. Other organizations in the community also make up an important part of an organization's environment.

Organization theory focuses on the organizational level of analysis but with concern for groups and the environment. To explain the organization, one should look not only at its characteristics but also at the characteristics of the environment and of the departments and groups that make up the organization. The focus is to help you understand organizations by examining their specific characteristics, the nature and relationships among groups and departments that make up the organization, and the collection of organizations that make up the environment.

Are individuals included in organization theory? Organization theory does consider the behavior of individuals, but in the aggregate. People are important, but they are not the primary focus of analysis. Organization theory is distinct from organizational behavior. **Organizational behavior** is the micro approach to organizations because it focuses on the individuals within organizations as the relevant units of analysis. Organizational behavior examines concepts such as motivation, leadership style, and personality and is concerned with cognitive and emotional differences among people within organizations. **Organization theory** is a macro examination of organizations because it analyzes the whole organization as a unit. Organization theory is concerned with people aggregated into departments and organizations and with the differences in structure and behavior at the organization level of analysis. Organization theory is the sociology at organizations, while organizational behavior is the psychology of organizations.

A new approach to organization studies is called meso theory. Most organizational research and many management courses specialize in either organizational behavior or organization theory. **Meso theory** (*meso* means "in between") concerns the integration of both micro and macro levels of analysis. Individuals and groups affect the organization and the organization in return influences individuals and groups. To thrive in organizations, managers and employees need to understand multiple levels simultaneously. For example, research may show that employee diversity enhances innovation. To facilitate innovation, managers need to understand how structure and context (organization theory) are related to interactions among diverse employees (organizational behavior) to foster innovation, because both macro and micro variables account for innovations.[255]

For its part, organization theory is directly relevant to top- and middle-management concerns and partly relevant to lower management. Top managers are responsible for the entire organization and must set goals, develop strategy, interpret the external environment, and decide organization structure and design. Middle management is concerned with major departments, such as marketing or research, and must decide how the department relates to the rest of the organization. Middle managers must design their departments to fit work-unit technology and deal with issues of power and politics, intergroup conflict, and information and control systems, each of which is part of organization theory. Organization theory is only partly concerned with lower management because this level of supervision is concerned with employees who operate machines, type letters, teach classes, and sell goods. Organization theory is concerned with the big picture of the organization and its major departments.

The Environmental Domain

In a broad sense the environment is infinite and includes everything outside the organization. However, the analysis presented here considers only the aspects of the environment to which the organization is sensitive and must respond to survive. Thus, **organizational environment** is defined as all elements that exist outside the boundary of the organization and have the potential to affect all or part of the organization.

The environment of an organization can be understood by analyzing its domain within external sectors. An organization's **domain** is the chosen environmental field of action. It is the territory an organization stakes out for itself with respect to products, services, and markets served. Domain defines the organization's niche and defines those external sectors with which the organization will interact to accomplish its goals. **Barnes & Noble** ignored an important part of its domain when the bookselling environment changed. The company was slow to take advantage of new technology for e-commerce, allowing the competition to gain a huge advantage.

The environment comprises several **sectors** or subdivisions of the external environment that contain similar elements. Ten sectors can be analyzed for each organization: industry, raw materials, human resources, financial resources, market, technology, economic conditions, government, sociocultural, and international. The 10 sectors and a hypothetical organizational domain are illustrated in Exhibit 100.53. For most companies, the sectors in Exhibit 100.53 can be further subdivided into the task environment and general environment.

Task Environment

The **task environment** includes sectors with which the organization interacts directly and that have a direct impact on the organization's ability to achieve its goals. The task environment typically includes the industry, raw materials, and market sectors, and perhaps the human resources and international sectors.

General Environment

The **general environment** includes those sectors that may not have a direct impact on the daily operations of a firm but will indirectly influence it. The general environment often includes the government, sociocultural, economic conditions, technology, and financial resources sectors. These sectors affect all organizations eventually.

International Context

The impact of the international sector has grown rapidly with advances in technology and communications. The distinctions between domestic and foreign companies have become increasingly irrelevant as advances in transportation and electronic technology have reduced the impact of distance and time, as well as the differences among political and monetary systems, tastes, and standards. Global trade has tripled in the past 25 years, and today it is relatively easy for a firm of any size to operate on a global scale.[256]

The increasing global interconnections have both positive and negative results for organizations. The recent economic turmoil in Asia and Eastern Europe blindsided many companies, creating great uncertainty for organizations doing business there. In addition, as the economic malaise spread to Latin America, it had an even greater impact on some U. S. companies based in Florida, since Southern Florida's economy is closely integrated with that of Latin America. **CHS Electronics,** a Miami-based firm with extensive ties to Latin America, has seen more and more of its Latin customers paying with local currency, and is finding debts harder to collect.[257]

Exhibit 100.53 *An Organizaiton's Environment and its Sectors*

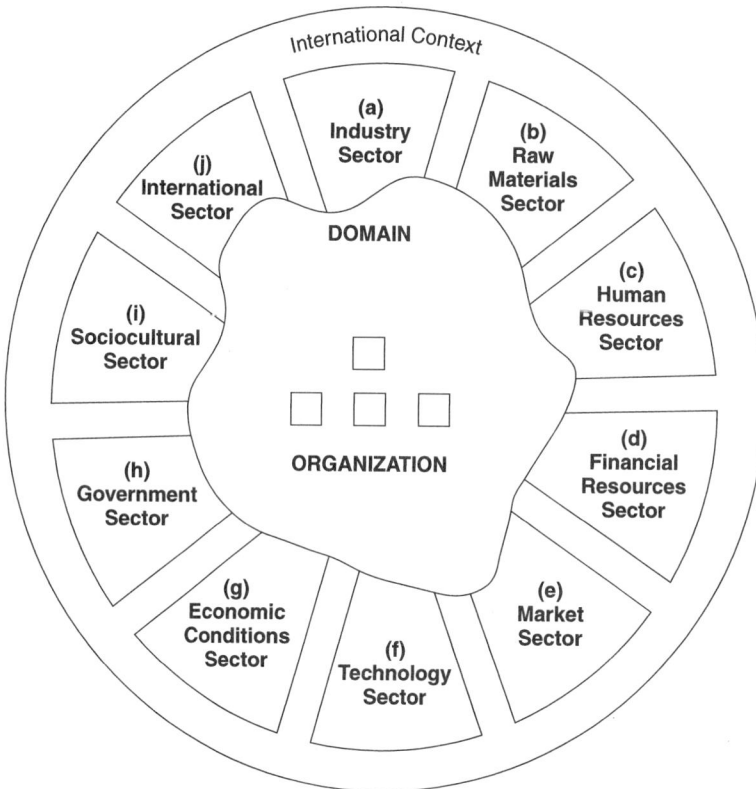

(a) Competitors, industry size and competitiveness, related industries
(b) Suppliers, manufacturers, real estate, services
(c) Labor market, employment agencies, universities, training schools, employees in other companies, unionization
(d) Stock markets, banks, savings and loans, private investors
(e) Customers, clients, potential users of products and services
(f) Techniques of production, science, computers, information technology, e-commerce
(g) Recession, unemployment rate, inflation rate, rate of investment, economics, growth
(h) City, state, federal laws and regulations, taxes, services, court system, political processes
(i) Age, values, beliefs, education, religion, work ethic, consumer and green movements
(j) Competition from and acquisition by foreign firms, entry into overseas markets, foreign customs, regulations, exchange rate

Global interconnections also mean that competitiveness has reached a new level, as companies are competing on a broader scale than ever before. Less-developed countries are challenging mature countries in a number of industries. For example, India is becoming a major player in software development, and consumer electronics manufacturing, which long ago left the United States for Japan, is now rapidly leaving Japan for other countries in Asia.

Yet there is also a positive side. Domestic markets are saturated for many companies and the primary potential for growth lies overseas. **Kimberly-Clark** and **Procter & Gamble,** which spent years slugging it out in the now-flat U.S. diaper market, are targeting new markets in China, India, Brazil, Israel, and Russia. The demand for steel in China, India, and Brazil together is expected to grow 10 percent annually in the coming years—three times the U.S. rate. **Nucor,** a U.S.-based steel company, is opening a minimill in Thailand and partnering with a Brazilian company for a $700 million steel mill in northeastern Brazil. Other steel companies, such as **LTV Corp.** and **North Star Steel,** are moving into Asia, Europe, and Australia.[258] And, despite the economic convulsions there, large Western companies such as Ford, Procter & Gamble, and Coca-Cola continue to view Southeast Asia as the big market of the future. When companies think globally, the whole world is their marketplace.

The growing importance of the international sector means that the environment for all organizations has become extremely complex and extremely competitive. However, every organization faces uncertainty domestically as well as globally. In the following sections, we will discuss in greater detail how companies cope with and respond to environmental uncertainty and instability.

Environmental Uncertainty

Organizations must cope with and manage uncertainty to be effective. **Uncertainty** means that decision makers do not have sufficient information about environmental factors, and they have a difficult time predicting external changes. Uncertainty increases the risk of failure for organizational responses and makes it difficult to compute costs and probabilities associated with decision alternatives.[259] Characteristics of the environmental domain that influence uncertainty are the extent to which the external domain is simple or complex and the extent to which events are stable or unstable.[260]

Simple–Complex Dimension

The **simple–complex dimension** concerns environmental complexity, which refers to heterogeneity, or the number and dissimilarity of external elements relevant to an organization's operations. In a complex environment, many diverse external elements interact with and influence the organization. In a simple environment, as few as three or four similar external elements influence the organization.

Simple + Stable = Low Uncertainty
Complex + Stable = Low-Moderate Uncertainty
Simple + Unstable = High-Moderate Uncertainty
Complex + Unstable = High Uncertainty

Stable–Unstable Dimension

The **stable–unstable dimension** refers to whether elements in the environment are dynamic. An environmental domain is stable if it remains the same over a period of months or years. Under unstable conditions, environmental elements shift abruptly. Instability may occur when competitors react with aggressive moves and countermoves regarding advertising and new products.

Framework

The simple–complex and stable–unstable dimensions are combined into a framework for assessing environmental uncertainty. In the *simple, stable* environment, uncertainty is low. There are only a few external elements to contend with, and they tend to remain stable. The *complex, stable* environment represents somewhat greater uncertainty. A large number of elements have to be scanned, analyzed, and acted upon for the organization to perform well. External elements do not change rapidly or unexpectedly in this environment.

Even greater uncertainty is felt in the *simple, unstable* environment.[261] Rapid change creates uncertainty for managers. Even though the organization has few external elements, those elements are hard to predict, and they react unexpectedly to organizational initiatives. The greatest uncertainty for an organization occurs in the *complex, unstable* environment. A large number of elements impinge upon the organization, and they shift frequently or react strongly to organizational initiatives. When several sectors change simultaneously, the environment becomes turbulent.[262]

A beer distributor functions in a simple, stable environment. Demand for beer changes only gradually. The distributor has an established delivery route, and supplies of beer arrive on schedule. State universities, appliance manufacturers, and insurance companies are in somewhat stable, complex environments. A large number of external elements are present, but although they change, changes are gradual and predictable.

Toy manufacturers are in simple, unstable environments. Organizations that design, make, and sell toys, as well as those that are involved in the clothing or music industry, face shifting supply and demand. Most e-commerce companies focus on a specific competitive niche and, hence, operate in simple but unstable environments. Although there may be few elements to contend with—e.g., technology, competitors—they are difficult to predict and change abruptly and unexpectedly.

The computer industry and the airline industry face complex, unstable environments. Many external sectors are changing simultaneously. In the case of airlines, in just a few years they were confronted with deregulation, the growth of regional airlines, surges in fuel costs, price cuts from competitors such as Southwest Airlines, shifting customer demand, an air-traffic controller shortage, overcrowded airports, and a reduction of scheduled flights.[263] A recent series of major air traffic disasters has further contributed to the complex, unstable environment for the industry.

Adapting to Environmental Uncertainty

Once you see how environments differ with respect to change and complexity, the next question is, "How do organizations adapt to each level of environmental uncertainty?" Environmental uncertainty represents an important contingency for organization structure and internal behaviors. Recall that organizations facing uncertainty generally encourage cross-functional communication and collaboration to help the company adapt to changes in the environment. In this section we will discuss in more detail how the environment affects organizations. An organization in a certain environment will be managed and controlled differently from an organization in an uncertain environment with respect to positions and departments, buffering and boundary spanning, organizational differentiation and integration, control processes, and future planning and forecasting. Organizations need to have the right fit between internal structure and the external environment.

Positions and Departments

As the complexity in the external environment increases, so does the number of positions and departments within the organization, which in turn increases internal complexity. This relationship is part of being an open system. Each sector in the external environment requires an employee or department to deal with it. The human resources department deals with unemployed people who want to work for the company. The marketing department finds customers. Procurement employees obtain raw materials from hundreds of suppliers. The finance group deals with bankers. The legal department works with the courts and government agencies. Today, many companies are adding e-business departments to handle electronic commerce and information technology departments to deal with the increasing complexity of computerized information and knowledge management systems.

Buffering and Boundary Spanning

The traditional approach to coping with environmental uncertainty was to establish buffer departments. The **buffering role** is to absorb uncertainty from the environment.[264] The technical core performs the primary production activity of an organization. Buffer departments surround the technical core and exchange materials, resources, and money between the environment and the organization. They help the technical core function efficiently. The purchasing department buffers the technical core by stockpiling supplies and raw materials. The human resources department buffers the technical core by handling the uncertainty associated with finding, hiring, and training production employees.

A newer approach some organizations are trying is to drop the buffers and expose the technical core to the uncertain environment. These organizations no longer create buffers because they believe being well connected to customers and suppliers is more important than internal efficiency. For example, John Deere has assembly-line workers visiting local farms to determine and respond to customer concerns. Whirlpool pays hundreds of customers to test computer-simulated products and features.[265] Opening up the organization to the environment makes it more fluid and adaptable.

Boundary-spanning roles link and coordinate an organization with key elements in the external environment. Boundary spanning is primarily concerned with the exchange of information to (1) detect and bring into the organization information about changes in the environment and (2) send information into the environment that presents the organization in a favorable light.[266]

Organizations have to keep in touch with what is going on in the environment so that managers can respond to market changes and other developments. A survey of high-tech firms found that 97 percent of competitive failures resulted from lack of attention to market changes or the failure to act on vital information.[267] To detect and bring important information into the organization, boundary personnel scan the environment. For example, a market research department scans and monitors trends in consumer tastes. Boundary spanners in engineering and research and development (R&D) departments scan new technological developments, innovations, and raw materials. Boundary spanners prevent the organization from stagnating by keeping top managers informed about environmental changes. Often, the greater the uncertainty in the environment, the greater the importance of boundary spanners.[268]

One of the fastest growing areas of boundary spanning is competitive intelligence. Companies large and small are setting up competitive intelligence departments or hiring outside specialists to gather information on competitors. Competitive intelligence gives top executives a systematic way to collect and analyze public information about rivals and use it to make better decisions.[269] Using techniques that range from Internet surfing to digging through trash cans, intelligence professionals dig up information on competitors' new products, manufacturing costs, or training methods and share it with top leaders. In today's uncertain environment, competitive intelligence is a trend that is likely to increase. In addition, companies such as **UtiliTech Inc.** of Stratford, Connecticut, and **WavePhore** Inc. of Phoenix, Arizona, regularly monitor the Internet for large corporations to see what is being said about them on the Web. This provides important information to top executives about how the company is perceived in the environment.

The boundary task of sending information into the environment to represent the organization is used to influence other people's perception of the organization. In the marketing department, advertising and sales people represent the organization to customers. Purchasers may call on suppliers and describe purchasing needs. The legal department informs lobbyists and elected officials about the organization's needs or views on political matters. Many companies set up their own Web pages to present the organization in a favorable light. To counteract hate sites that criticize their labor practices in Third World countries, **Nike** and **Unocal** both created Web sites specifically to tell their side of the story.[270]

Differentiation and Integration

Another response to environmental uncertainty is the amount of differentiation and integration among departments. Organization **differentiation** is "the differences in cognitive and emotional orientations among managers in different functional departments, and the difference in formal structure among these departments."[271] When the external environment is complex and rapidly changing, organizational departments become highly specialized to handle the uncertainty in their external sector. Success in each sector requires special expertise and behavior. Employees in a research and development department thus have unique attitudes, values, goals, and education that distinguish them from employees in manufacturing or sales departments.

One outcome of high differentiation is that coordination among departments becomes difficult. More time and resources must be devoted to achieving coordination when attitudes, goals, and work orientation differ so widely. **Integration** is the quality of collaboration among departments.[272] Formal integrators are often required to coordinate departments. When the environment is highly uncertain, frequent changes require more information processing to achieve horizontal coordination, so integrators become a necessary addition to the organization structure. Sometimes integrators are called liaison personnel, project managers, brand managers, or coordinators. Organizations with highly uncertain environments and a highly differentiated structure assign about 22 percent of management personnel to integration activities, such as serving on committees, on task forces, or in liaison roles.[273] In organizations characterized by very simple, stable environments, almost no managers are assigned to integration roles. As environmental uncertainty increases, so does differentiation among departments; hence, the organization must assign a larger percentage of managers to coordinating roles.

Lawrence and Lorsch's research concluded that organizations perform better when the levels of differentiation and integration match the level of uncertainty in the environment. Organizations that performed well in uncertain environments had high levels of both differentiation and integration, while those performing well in less uncertain environments had lower levels of differentiation and integration.

Organic versus Mechanistic Management Processes

Another response to environmental uncertainty is the amount of formal structure and control imposed on employees. Tom Burns and G. M. Stalker observed twenty industrial firms in England and discovered that external environment was related to internal management structure.[274] When the external environment was stable, the internal organization was characterized by rules, procedures, and a clear hierarchy of authority. Organizations were formalized. They were also centralized, with most decisions made at the top. Burns and Stalker called this a **mechanistic** organization system.

In rapidly changing environments, the internal organization was much looser, free-flowing, and adaptive. Rules and regulations often were not written down or, if written down, were ignored. People had to find their own way through the system to figure out what to do. The hierarchy of authority was not clear. Decision-making authority was decentralized. Burns and Stalker used the term **organic** to characterize this type of management structure.

As environmental uncertainty increases, organizations tend to become more organic, which means decentralizing authority and responsibility to lower levels, encouraging employees to take care of problems by working directly with one another, encouraging teamwork, and taking an informal approach to assigning tasks and responsibility. Thus, the organization is more fluid and is able to adapt continually to changes in the external environment.[275]

Planning and Forecasting

The final organizational response to uncertainty is to increase planning and environmental forecasting. When the environment is stable, the organization can concentrate on current operational problems and day-to-day efficiency. Long-range planning and forecasting are not needed because environmental demands in the future will be the same as they are today.

With increasing environmental uncertainty, planning and forecasting become necessary.[276] Planning can soften the adverse impact of external shifting. Organizations that have unstable environments often establish a separate planning department. In an unpredictable environment, planners scan environmental elements and analyze potential moves and countermoves by other organizations. Planning can be extensive and may forecast various scenarios for environmental contingencies. As time passes, plans are updated through replanning. However, planning does not substitute for other actions, such as boundary spanning. Indeed, under conditions of extraordinarily high uncertainty, formal planning may not be helpful because the future is so difficult to predict.

Controlling Environmental Resources

In response to the need for resources, organizations try to maintain a balance between linkages with other organizations and their own independence. Organizations maintain this balance through attempts to modify, manipulate, or control other organizations.[277] To survive, the focal organization often tries to reach out and change or control elements in the environment. Two strategies can be adopted to manage resources in the external environment: (1) establish favorable linkages with key elements in the environment and (2) shape the environmental domain.[278] Techniques to accomplish each of these strategies are summarized in Exhibit 100.54. As a general rule, when organizations sense that valued resources are scarce, they will use the strategies in Exhibit 100.54 rather than go it alone.

Establishing Interorganizational Linkages

OWNERSHIP   Companies use ownership to establish linkages when they buy a part of or a controlling interest in another company. This gives the company access to technology, products, or other resources it doesn't currently have. The communications and information technology industry has become particularly complex, and many companies have been teaming up worldwide.

A greater degree of ownership and control is obtained through acquisition or merger. An *acquisition* involves the purchase of one organization by another so that the buyer assumes control. A *merger* is the unification of two or more organizations into a single unit.[279] These forms of ownership reduce uncertainty in an area important to the acquiring company.

FORMAL STRATEGIC ALLIANCES   When there is a high level of complementarity between the business lines, geographical positions, or skills of two companies, the firms often go the route of a strategic alliance rather than ownership through merger or acquisition.[280] Such alliances are formed through contracts and joint ventures.

Contracts and joint ventures reduce uncertainty through a legal and binding relationship with another firm. Contracts come in the form of *license agreements* that involve the purchase of the right to use an asset (such as a new technology) for a specific time and *supplier arrangements* that contract for the sale of one firm's output to another. Contracts can provide long-term security by tying customers and suppliers to specific amounts and prices. *Joint ventures* result in the creation of a new organization that is formally independent of the parents, although the parents will have some control.[281] In a joint venture, organizations share the risk and cost associated with large projects or innovations. For example, Barnesandnoble.com is a joint venture between Barnes & Noble and Germany's **Bertelsmann AG.** Barnes & Noble and Bertelsmann have agreed to invest $100 million each and share the risks of the joint venture as it battles Amazon.com in the world of on-line bookselling.

COOPTATION, INTERLOCKING DIRECTORATES   Cooptation occurs when leaders from important sectors in the environment are made part of an organization. It takes place, for example, when influential customers or suppliers are

Exhibit 100.54   *Organizing Strategies for Controlling the External Environment*

Establishing Interorganizational Linkages	Controlling the Environmental Domain
1. Ownership	1. Change of domain
2. Formal strategic alliances	2. Political activity, regulation
3. Cooptation, interlocking directorates	3. Trade associations
4. Executive recruitment	4. Illegitimate activities
5. Advertising, public relations	

appointed to the board of directors, such as when the senior executive of a bank sits on the board of a manufacturing company. As a board member, the banker may become psychologically coopted into the interests of the manufacturing firm. Community leaders also can be appointed to a company's board of directors or to other organizational committees or task forces. These influential people are thus introduced to the needs of the company and are more likely to include the company's interests in their decision making.

An **interlocking directorate** is a formal linkage that occurs when a member of the board of directors of one company sits on the board of directors of another company. The individual is a communications link between companies and can influence policies and decisions. Internet startups, such as the Seattle-based companies **TechWave, AccountingNet,** and **Honkworm International,** often use this strategy to share advice and resources.[282] When one individual is the link between two companies, this is typically referred to as a **direct interlock.** An **indirect interlock** occurs when a director of company A and a director of company B are both directors of company C. They have access to one another but do not have direct influence over their respective companies.[283] Recent research shows that, as a firm's financial fortunes decline, direct interlocks with financial institutions increase. Financial uncertainty facing an industry also has been associated with greater indirect interlocks between competing companies.[284]

EXECUTIVE RECRUITMENT   Transferring or exchanging executives also offers a method of establishing favorable linkages with external organizations. For example, each year the aerospace industry hires retired generals and executives from the Department of Defense. These generals have personal friends in the department, so the aerospace companies obtain better information about technical specifications, prices, and dates for new weapon systems. They can learn the needs of the defense department and are able to present their case for defense contracts in a more effective way. Companies without personal contacts find it nearly impossible to get a defense contract. Having channels of influence and communication between organizations serves to reduce financial uncertainty and dependence for an organization.

ADVERTISING AND PUBLIC RELATIONS   A traditional way of establishing favorable relationships is through advertising. Organizations spend large amounts of money to influence the taste of consumers. Advertising is especially important in highly competitive consumer industries and in industries that experience variable demand. In the fashion industry, once-stodgy **JCPenney** turned its Arizona Jeans into one of the hottest brands around through hip advertising featuring rock music and Internet imagery. A recent ad campaign shows teens mocking ads that attempt to speak their language, ending with the tagline "Just show me the jeans."[285]

Public relations is similar to advertising, except that stories often are free and aimed at public opinion. Public relations people cast an organization in a favorable light in speeches, in press reports, and on television. Public relations attempts to shape the company's image in the minds of customers, suppliers, and government officials. For example, in an effort to survive in this antismoking era, tobacco companies have launched an aggressive public relations campaign touting smokers' rights and freedom of choice.

SUMMARY   Organizations can use a variety of techniques to establish favorable linkages that ensure the availability of scarce resources. Linkages provide control over vulnerable environmental elements. Strategic alliances, interlocking directorates, and outright ownership provide mechanisms to reduce resource dependency on the environment. U.S. companies such as IBM, Apple, AT&T, and Motorola have been quick in recent years to turn rivalry into partnership. Perhaps surprisingly, Japan's electronics companies have been slower to become involved in joint ventures and other strategic alliances.

Controlling the Environmental Domain

In addition to establishing favorable linkages to obtain resources, organizations often try to change the environment. There are four techniques for influencing or changing a firm's environmental domain.

CHANGE OF DOMAIN   The 10 sectors described earlier are not fixed. The organization decides which business it is in, the market to enter, and the suppliers, banks, employees, and location to use, and this domain can be changed.[286] An organization can seek new environmental relationships and drop old ones. An organization may try to find a domain where there is little competition, no government regulation, abundant suppliers, affluent customers, and barriers to keep competitors out. Acquisition and divestment are two techniques for altering the domain.

POLITICAL ACTIVITY, REGULATION   Political activity includes techniques to influence government legislation and regulation. In one technique, organizations pay lobbyists to express their views to members of federal and state legislatures. In the telecommunications industry, the **Baby Bells** hired powerful lobbyists to influence a sweeping new telecommunications bill giving local phone companies access to new markets.[287] Many CEOs, however, believe they should do their own lobbying. CEOs have easier access than lobbyists and can be especially effective when they do the politicking. Political activity is so important that "informal lobbyist" is an unwritten part of almost any CEO's job description.[288]

Political strategy can be used to erect regulatory barriers against new competitors or to squash unfavorable legislation. Corporations also try to influence the appointment to agencies of people who are sympathetic to their needs. The value of political activity is illustrated by the efforts of Sun Microsystems and **Netscape** to persuade the Justice Department to break up Microsoft, arguing that Microsoft had acted as a monopoly in controlling the software industry and now threatens to extend that power to Internet access. Some observers noted that if Microsoft had paid more attention to political lobbying earlier, it could have avoided Justice Department investigation.

TRADE ASSOCIATIONS Much of the work to influence the external environment is accomplished jointly with other organizations that have similar interests. Most manufacturing companies are part of the National Association of Manufacturers and also belong to associations in their specific industry. By pooling resources, these organizations can pay people to carry out activities such as lobbying legislators, influencing new regulations, developing public relations campaigns, and making campaign contributions.

ILLEGITIMATE ACTIVITIES Illegitimate activities represent the final technique companies sometimes use to control their environmental domain. Certain conditions, such as low profits, pressure from senior managers, or scarce environmental resources, may lead managers to adopt behaviors not considered legitimate.[289] Many well-known companies have been found guilty of behavior considered unlawful. Example behaviors include payoffs to foreign governments, illegal political contributions, promotional gifts, and wiretapping. Intense competition among cement producers and in the oil business during a period of decline led to thefts and illegal kickbacks.[290] In the defense industry, the intense competition for declining contracts for major weapon systems led some companies to do almost anything to get an edge, including schemes to peddle inside information and to pay off officials.[291] One study found that companies in industries with low demand, shortages, and strikes were more likely to be convicted for illegal activities, implying that illegal acts are an attempt to cope with resource scarcity.[292]

Organization-Environment Integrative Framework

Now we can summarize the two major themes about organization-environment relationships. One theme is that the amount of complexity and change in an organization's domain influences the need for information and hence the uncertainty felt within an organization. Greater information uncertainty is resolved through greater structural flexibility, and the assignment of additional departments and boundary roles. When uncertainty is low, management structures can be more mechanistic, and the number of departments and boundary roles can be fewer. The second theme pertains to the scarcity of material and financial resources. The more dependent an organization is on other organizations for those resources, the more important it is to either establish favorable linkages with those organizations or control entry into the domain. If dependence on external resources is low, the organization can maintain autonomy and does not need to establish linkages or control the external domain.

Fundamentals of Organization Structure

Every organization wrestles with the problem of how to organize, and nearly every firm undergoes reorganization at some point. Structural changes are needed to reflect new strategies or respond to changes in other contingency factors such as environment, technology, size and life cycle, and culture. For example, Xerox restructured into several horizontally aligned divisions to facilitate its differentiation strategy and speed innovative new products to market.

Organization Structure

The three key components in the definition of **organization structure** are:

1. Organization structure designates formal reporting relationships, including the number of levels in the hierarchy and the span of control of managers and supervisors.

Exhibit 100.55 *A Sample Organization Chart*

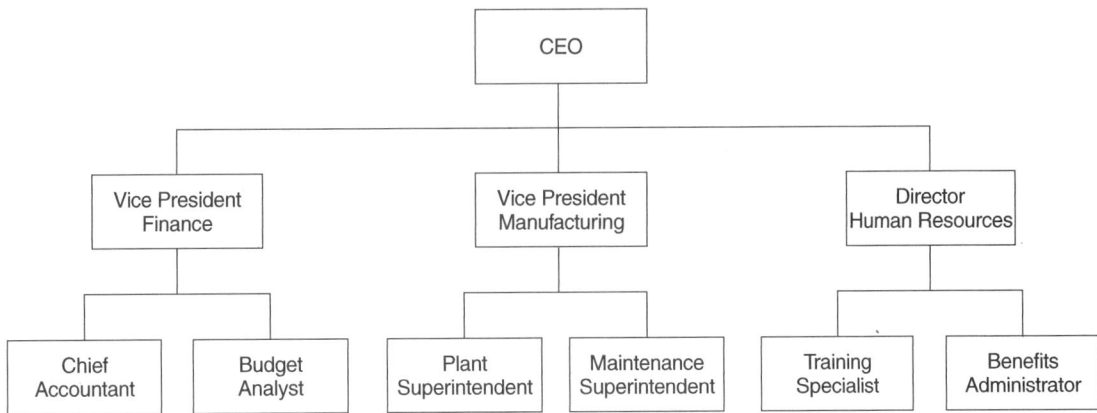

2. Organization structure identifies the grouping together of individuals into departments and of departments into the total organization.
3. Organization structure includes the design of systems to ensure effective communication, coordination, and integration of effort across departments.[293]

These three elements of structure pertain to both vertical and horizontal aspects of organizing. For example, the first two elements are the structural *framework*, which is the vertical hierarchy.[294] The third element pertains to the pattern of *interactions* among organizational employees. An ideal structure encourages employees to provide horizontal information and coordination where and when it is needed.

Organization structure is reflected in the organization chart. It isn't possible to "see" the internal structure of an organization the way we might see its manufacturing tools, offices, or products. Although we might see employees going about their duties, performing different tasks, and working in different locations, the only way to actually see the structure underlying all this activity is through the organization chart.[295] The organization chart is the visual representation of a whole set of underlying activities and processes in an organization. Exhibit 100.55 shows a sample organization chart. The organization chart can be quite useful in understanding how a company works. It shows the various parts of an organization, how they are interrelated, and how each position and department fits into the whole.

The concept of an organization chart, showing what positions exist, how they are grouped, and who reports to whom, has been around for centuries.

The type of organization structure that grew out of these efforts in the late 19th and early 20th centuries was one in which the CEO was placed at the top and everyone else was arranged in layers down below, as illustrated in Exhibit 100.55. The thinking and decision making is done by those at the top, and the physical work is performed by employees who are organized into distinct, functional departments. This structure was quite effective and became entrenched in the business world for most of the 20th century. However, this type of vertical structure is not always effective, particularly in rapidly changing environments. Over the years, organizations have developed other structural designs, many of them aimed at increasing horizontal coordination and communication and encouraging adaptation to external changes. This section will examine four basic structural designs and show how they are reflected in the organization chart.

Information-Processing Perspective on Structure

The organization should be designed to provide both vertical and horizontal information flow as necessary to accomplish the organization's overall goals. If the structure doesn't fit the information requirements of the organization, people will have either too little information or will spend time processing information that is not vital to their tasks, thus reducing effectiveness.[296] However, there is an inherent tension between vertical and horizontal mechanisms in an organization. Whereas vertical linkages are designed primarily for control, horizontal linkages are designed for coordination and collaboration, which usually means reducing control.

Organizations can choose whether to orient toward a traditional organization designed for efficiency, which emphasizes vertical communication and control, or toward a contemporary learning organization, which emphasizes

Exhibit 100.56 *The Relationship of Organization Design to Efficiency vs. Learning Outcomes*

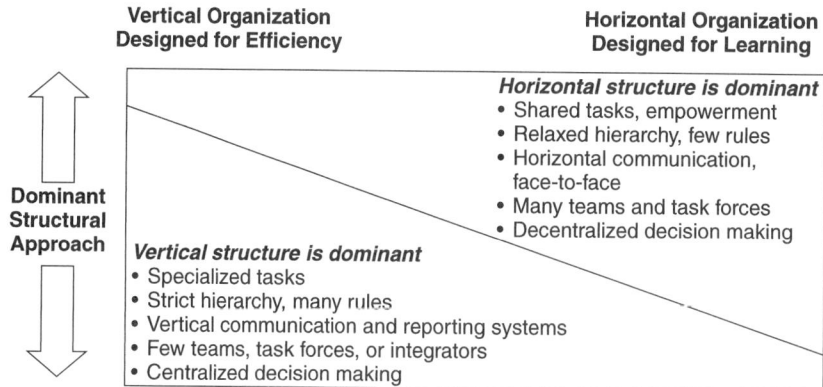

horizontal communication and coordination. Exhibit 100.56 compares organizations designed for efficiency with those designed for learning. An emphasis on efficiency and control is associated with specialized tasks, hierarchy of authority, rules and regulations, formal reporting systems, few teams or task forces, and centralized decision making. Emphasis on learning is associated with shared tasks, relaxed hierarchy and few rules, face-to-face communication, many teams and task forces, and informal, decentralized decision making. All organizations need a mix of vertical and horizontal linkages. Managers have to find the right balance to fit the organization's needs.

Vertical Linkages

Organization design should facilitate the communication among employees and departments that is necessary to accomplish the organization's overall task. *Linkage* is defined as the extent of communication and coordination among organizational elements. **Vertical linkages** are used to coordinate activities between the top and bottom of an organization and are designed primarily for control of the organization. Employees at lower levels should carry out activities consistent with top-level goals, and top executives must be informed of activities and accomplishments at the lower levels. Organizations may use any of a variety of structural devices to achieve vertical linkage, including hierarchical referral, rules, plans, and formal management information systems.[297]

HIERARCHICAL REFERRAL The first vertical device is the hierarchy, or chain of command, which is illustrated by the vertical lines in Exhibit 100.55. If a problem arises that employees don't know how to solve, it can be referred up to the next level in the hierarchy. When the problem is solved, the answer is passed back down to lower levels. The lines of the organization chart act as communication channels.

RULES AND PLANS The next linkage device is the use of rules and plans. To the extent that problems and decisions are repetitious, a rule or procedure can be established so employees know how to respond without communicating directly with their manager. Rules provide a standard information source enabling employees to be coordinated without actually communicating about every job. A plan also provides standing information for employees. The most widely used plan is the budget. With carefully designed budget plans, employees at lower levels can be left on their own to perform activities within their resource allotment.

VERTICAL INFORMATION SYSTEMS Vertical information systems are another strategy for increasing vertical information capacity. **Vertical information systems** include the periodic reports, written information, and computer-based communications distributed to managers. Information systems make communication up and down the hierarchy more efficient. Cisco Systems has turned vertical information systems into a competitive advantage by using the Internet in virtually every aspect of its operations. Larry Carter, Cisco's CFO, can call up the company's revenues, profit margins, and order information from the previous day with just a few mouse clicks. Financial data that once took weeks to gather are collected and organized automatically.[298]

Managers may use a variety of these mechanisms to provide vertical linkage and control. The other major issue in organizing is horizontal linkages for coordination and collaboration.

Horizontal Linkages

Horizontal communication overcomes barriers between departments and provides opportunities for coordination among employees to achieve unity of effort and organizational objectives. **Horizontal linkage** refers to the amount of communication and coordination horizontally across organizational departments. Its importance was discovered by Lee Iacocca when he took over Chrysler Corporation.

During his tenure at Chrysler (now DaimlerChrysler), Iacocca pushed horizontal coordination to a high level. Everyone working on a specific vehicle project—designers, engineers, and manufacturers, as well as representatives from marketing, finance, purchasing, and even outside suppliers—worked together on a single floor so they could constantly communicate. **Ford** and General Motors have also enhanced horizontal communication and coordination through mechanisms such as teams, task forces, and information systems.

Horizontal linkage mechanisms often are not drawn on the organization chart, but nevertheless are part of organization structure. The following devices are structural alternatives that can improve horizontal coordination and information flow.[299] Each device enables people to exchange information.

INFORMATION SYSTEMS A significant method of providing horizontal linkage in today's organizations is the use of cross-functional information systems. Computerized information systems can enable managers or front-line workers throughout the organization to routinely exchange information about problems, opportunities, activities, or decisions. For example, at Ford, every car and truck model has its own internal Web site to track design, production, quality control, and delivery processes. Ford's product-development system is updated hourly, enabling engineers, designers, suppliers, and other employees around the world to work from the same data, keeping the process moving and saving time and money.[300]

DIRECT CONTACT A higher level of horizontal linkage is direct contact between managers or employees affected by a problem. One way to promote direct contact is to create a special **liaison role**. A liaison person is located in one department but has the responsibility for communicating and achieving coordination with another department. Liaison roles often exist between engineering and manufacturing departments because engineering has to develop and test products to fit the limitations of manufacturing facilities. **Monsanto Co.** found another way to use direct contact. To get the R&D and commercial staffs working together, Monsanto pairs a scientist with a marketing or financial specialist as co-managers. For example, Frederick Perlak, a noted geneticist, and Kevin Holloway, with a background in marketing and human resources, oversee the global cotton team as co-directors. They work in adjoining cubicles, share a secretary, spend hours talking with one another, and together make all the key decisions about Monsanto's global cotton business. Monsanto hopes this unique mechanism, known internally as *two in the box*, will help transform the company from a chemical conglomerate into a life-sciences powerhouse.[301]

TASK FORCES Direct contact and liaison roles usually link only two departments. When linkage involves several departments, a more complex device such as a task force is required. A **task force** is a temporary committee composed of representatives from each department affected by a problem.[302] Each member represents the interest of a department and can carry information from the meeting back to that department.

Task forces are an effective horizontal linkage device for temporary issues. They solve problems by direct horizontal coordination and reduce the information load on the vertical hierarchy. Typically, they are disbanded after their tasks are accomplished.

FULL-TIME INTEGRATOR A stronger horizontal linkage device is to create a full-time position or department solely for the purpose of coordination. A **full-time integrator** frequently has a title, such as product manager, project manager, program manager, or brand manager. Unlike the liaison person described earlier, the integrator does not report to one of the functional departments being coordinated. He or she is located outside the departments and has the responsibility for coordinating several departments.

The brand manager for **Planters** Peanuts, for example, coordinates the sales, distribution, and advertising for that product. General Motors set up brand managers who are responsible for marketing and sales strategies for each of GM's new models.[303]

The integrator can also be responsible for an innovation or change project, such as developing the design, financing, and marketing of a new product. An organization chart that illustrates the location of project managers for new product development is shown in Exhibit 100.57. The project managers are drawn to the side to indicate their separation from other departments. The arrows indicate project members assigned to the new product development. New

Exhibit 100.57 *Project Manager Location in the Structure*

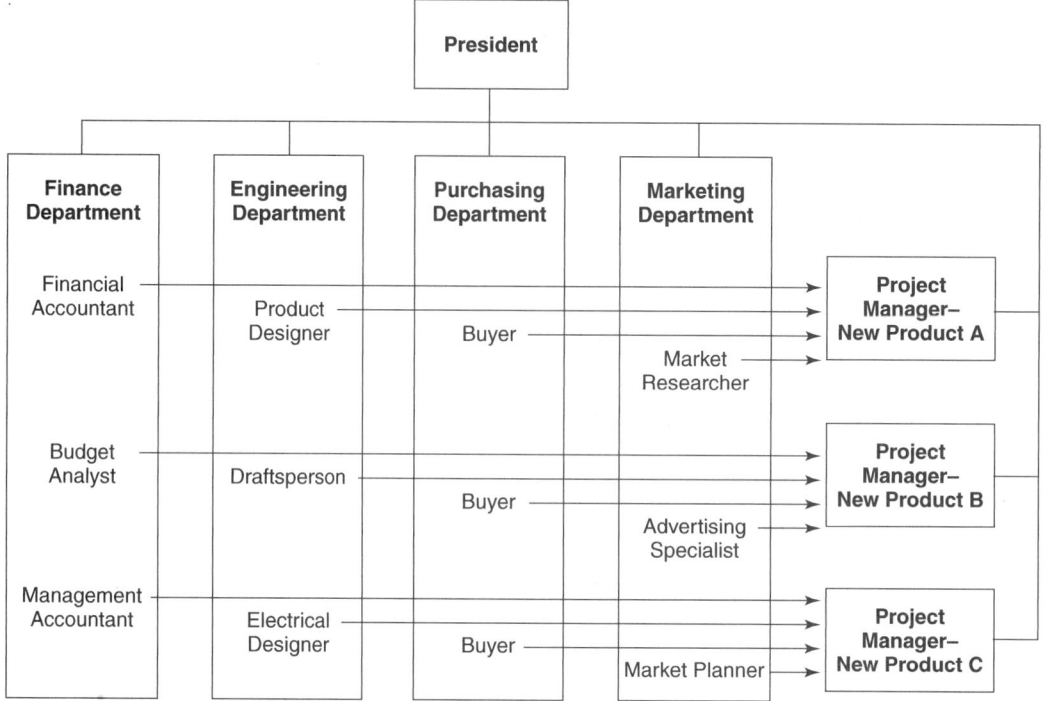

Product A, for example, has a financial accountant assigned to keep track of costs and budgets. The engineering member provides design advice, and purchasing and manufacturing members represent their areas. The project manager is responsible for the entire project. He or she sees that the new product is completed on time, is introduced to the market, and achieves other project goals. The horizontal lines in Exhibit 100.57 indicate that project managers do not have formal authority over team members with respect to giving pay raises, hiring, or firing. Formal authority rests with the managers of the functional departments, who have formal authority over subordinates.

Integrators need excellent people skills. Integrators in most companies have a lot of responsibility but little authority. The integrator has to use expertise and persuasion to achieve coordination. He or she spans the boundary between departments and must be able to get people together, maintain their trust, confront problems, and resolve conflicts and disputes in the interest of the organization.[304]

TEAMS Project teams tend to be the strongest horizontal linkage mechanism. **Teams** are permanent task forces and are often used in conjunction with a full-time integrator. When activities among departments require strong coordination over a long period of time, a cross-functional team is often the solution. Special project teams may be used when organizations have a large-scale project, a major innovation, or a new product line.

Boeing used around 250 teams to design and manufacture the 777 aircraft. Some teams were created around sections of the plane, such as the wing, cockpit, or engines, while others were developed to serve specific customers, such as **United Airlines** or **British Airways.** Boeing's teams had to be tightly integrated and coordinated to accomplish this massive project. Even the U.S. Department of the Navy has discovered the power of cross-functional teams to improve horizontal coordination and increase productivity.[305]

The **Rodney Hunt Company** develops, manufactures, and markets heavy industrial equipment and uses teams to coordinate each product line across the manufacturing, engineering, and marketing departments. Members from each team meet the first thing each day as needed to resolve problems concerning customer needs, backlogs, engineering changes, scheduling conflicts, and any other problem with the product line.

These devices represent alternatives that managers can select to increase horizontal coordination in any organization. The higher-level devices, such as full-time integrators or teams, provide more horizontal information capacity, although the cost to the organization in terms of time and human resources is greater. If horizontal communication is insufficient, departments will find themselves out of synchronization and will not contribute to the overall goals of the organization. When the amount of horizontal coordination required is high, managers should select higher-level mechanisms.

Organization Design Alternatives

The overall design of organization structure indicates three things—needed work activities, reporting relationships, and departmental groupings.

Defined Work Activities

Departments are created to perform tasks considered strategically important to the company. Defining a specific department is a way to accomplish tasks deemed valuable by the organization to accomplish its goals.

Reporting Relationships

Reporting relationships, often called the chain of command, are represented by vertical lines on an organization chart. The chain of command should be an unbroken line of authority that links all persons in an organization and shows who reports to whom. In a large organization like **EDS** or Ford Motor Company, one hundred or more charts are required to identify reporting relationships among thousands of employees. The definition of departments and the drawing of reporting relationships defines how employees are to be grouped into departments.

Departmental Grouping Options

Options for departmental grouping include functional grouping, divisional grouping, geographic grouping. **Departmental grouping** affects employees because they share a common supervisor and common resources, are jointly responsible for performance, and tend to identify and collaborate with one another.[306] For example, at **Albany Ladder Company,** the credit manager was shifted from the finance department to the marketing department. By being grouped with marketing, the credit manager started working with sales people to increase sales, thus becoming more liberal with credit than when he was located in the finance department.

Functional grouping places employees together who perform similar functions or work processes or who bring similar knowledge and skills to bear. For example, all marketing people would work together under the same supervisor, as would manufacturing and engineering people.

Divisional grouping means people are organized according to what the organization produces. All people required to produce toothpaste—including the marketing, manufacturing, and salespeople—are grouped together under one executive. In huge corporations such as EDS, some product or service lines may represent independent businesses, such as **A. T. Kearney** (management consulting), **Centrobe** (providing integrated customer care services), and **Wendover Financial Services.**

Geographic grouping means resources are organized to serve customers or clients in a particular geographical area. For example, all the activities required to serve Canada or Latin America or the eastern United States might be grouped together.

Multifocused grouping means an organization embraces two structural grouping alternatives simultaneously. This structural form is often called a *matrix* structure. The matrix will be discussed in more detail later in this chapter. An organization may need to group by function and product division simultaneously or perhaps by product division and geography.

Functional, Divisional, and Geographical Structures

Functional structure, divisional structure, and geographical structure are the three most common approaches to organization design.

Functional Structure

In a **functional structure**, activities are grouped together by common function from the bottom to the top of the organization. All engineers are located in the engineering department, and the vice president of engineering is responsible for all engineering activities. An example of the functional organization structure was shown in Exhibit 100.64 earlier in this section.

With a functional structure, all human knowledge and skills with respect to specific activities are consolidated, providing a valuable depth of knowledge for the organization. This structure is most effective when in-depth expertise is critical to meeting organizational goals, when the organization needs to be controlled and coordinated through the vertical hierarchy, and when efficiency is important. The structure can be quite effective is there is little need for horizontal coordination.

One strength of the functional structure is that it promotes economy of scale within functions. Economy of scale means all employees are located in the same place and can share facilities. Producing all products in a single plant, for example, enables the plant to acquire the latest machinery. Constructing only one facility instead of separate facilities for each product line reduces duplication and waste. The functional structure also promotes in-depth skill development of employees. Employees are exposed to a range of functional activities within their own department.[307]

The main weakness of the functional structure is a slow response to environmental changes that require coordination across departments. The vertical hierarchy becomes overloaded. Decisions pile up, and top managers do not respond fast enough. Other disadvantages of the functional structure are that innovation is slow because of poor coordination, and each employee has a restricted view of overall goals.

Today, there is a shift toward flatter, more horizontal structures. Very few of today's successful companies can maintain a strictly functional structure. Organizations compensate for the vertical functional hierarchy by installing horizontal linkages. Managers improve horizontal coordination by using information systems, direct contact between departments, full-time integrators or project managers (illustrated in Exhibit 100.66), task forces, or teams.

Divisional Structure

The term **divisional structure** is used here as the generic term for what is sometimes called a *product structure* or *strategic business units*. With this structure, divisions can be organized according to individual products, services, product groups, major projects or programs, divisions, businesses, or profit centers. The distinctive feature of a divisional structure is that grouping is based on organizational outputs.

The difference between a divisional structure and a functional structure is illustrated in Exhibit 100.58. The functional structure can be redesigned into separate product groups, and each group contains the functional departments

Exhibit 100.58 *Reorganization from Fucntional Structure to Divisional Structure at Info-Tech*

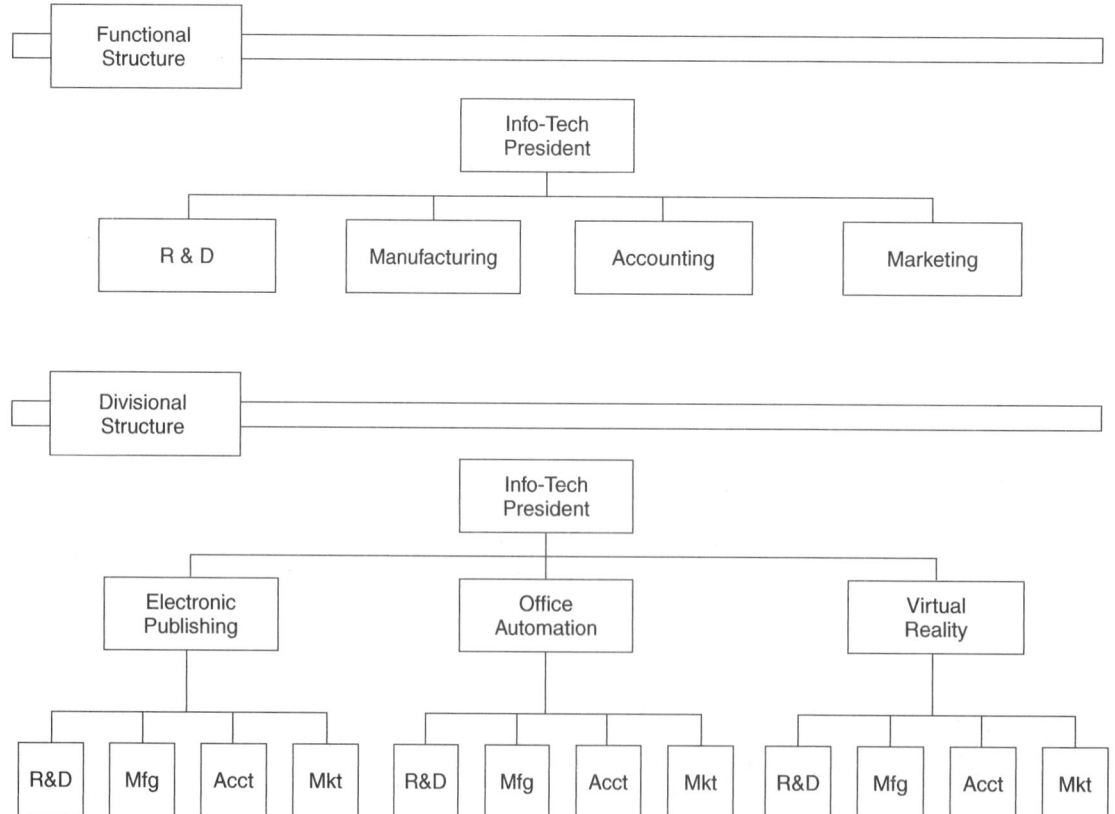

of R&D, manufacturing, accounting, and marketing. Coordination across functional departments within each product group is maximized. The divisional structure promotes flexibility and change because each unit is smaller and can adapt to the needs of its environment. Moreover, the divisional structure decentralizes decision making, because the lines of authority converge at a lower level in the hierarchy. The functional structure, by contrast, forces decisions all the way to the top before a problem affecting several functions can be resolved.

The divisional organization form of structure is excellent for achieving coordination across functional departments. It works well when organizations can no longer be adequately controlled through the traditional vertical hierarchy, and when goals are oriented toward adaptation and change. Giant, complex organizations such as General Electric, **Nestlé**, and Johnson & Johnson are subdivided into a series of smaller, self-contained organizations for better control and coordination. In these large companies, the units are sometimes called divisions, businesses, or strategic business units.

The divisional structure has several strengths.[308] This structure is suited to fast change in an unstable environment and provides high product visibility. Since each product is a separate division, clients are able to contact the correct division and achieve satisfaction. Coordination across functions is excellent. Each product can adapt to requirements of individual customers or regions. The divisional structure typically works best in organizations that have multiple products or services and enough personnel to staff separate functional units. At corporations like Johnson & Johnson, PepsiCo, and Microsoft, decision making is pushed down to the lowest levels. Each division is small enough to be quick on its feet, responding rapidly to changes in the market.

One disadvantage of using divisional structuring is that the organization loses economies of scale. Instead of fifty research engineers sharing a common facility in a functional structure, ten engineers may be assigned to each of five product divisions. The critical mass required for in-depth research is lost, and physical facilities have to be duplicated for each product line. Another problem is that product lines become separate from each other, and coordination across product lines can be difficult. As one Johnson & Johnson executive said, "We have to keep reminding ourselves that we work for the same corporation."[309]

Companies such as Hewlett-Packard and Xerox have a large number of divisions and have had real problems with horizontal coordination. The software division may produce programs that are incompatible with business computers sold by another division. Customers are frustrated when a sales representative from one division is unaware of developments in other divisions. Task forces and other linkage devices are needed to coordinate across divisions. A lack of technical specialization is also a problem in a divisional structure. Employees identify with the product line rather than with a functional specialty. R&D personnel, for example, tend to do applied research to benefit the product line rather than basic research to benefit the entire organization.

Geographical Structure

Another basis for structural grouping is the organization's users or customers. The most common structure in this category is geography. Each region of the country may have distinct tastes and needs. Each geographic unit includes all functions required to produce and market products in that region. For multinational corporations, self-contained units are created for different countries and parts of the world.

Some years ago, Apple Computer reorganized from a functional to a geographical structure to facilitate manufacture and delivery of Apple computers to customers around the world. Apple used this structure to focus managers and employees on specific geographical customers and sales targets. McDonald's divided its U.S. operations into five geographical divisions, each with its own president and staff functions such as human resources and legal.[310] The regional structure allows Apple and McDonald's to focus on the needs of customers in a geographical area.

The strengths and weaknesses of a geographic structure are similar to the divisional organization characteristics. The organization can adapt to specific needs of its own region, and employees identify with regional goals rather than with national goals. Horizontal coordination within a region is emphasized rather than linkages across regions or to the national office.

Matrix Structure

Sometimes, an organization's structure needs to be multifocused in that both product and function or product and geography are emphasized at the same time. One way to achieve this is through the **matrix structure**. The matrix can be used when both technical expertise and product innovation and change are important for meeting organizational goals. The matrix structure often is the answer when organizations find that neither the functional, divisional, nor geographical structures combined with horizontal linkage mechanisms will work.

Exhibit 100.59 *Dual-Authority Structure in a Matrix Organization*

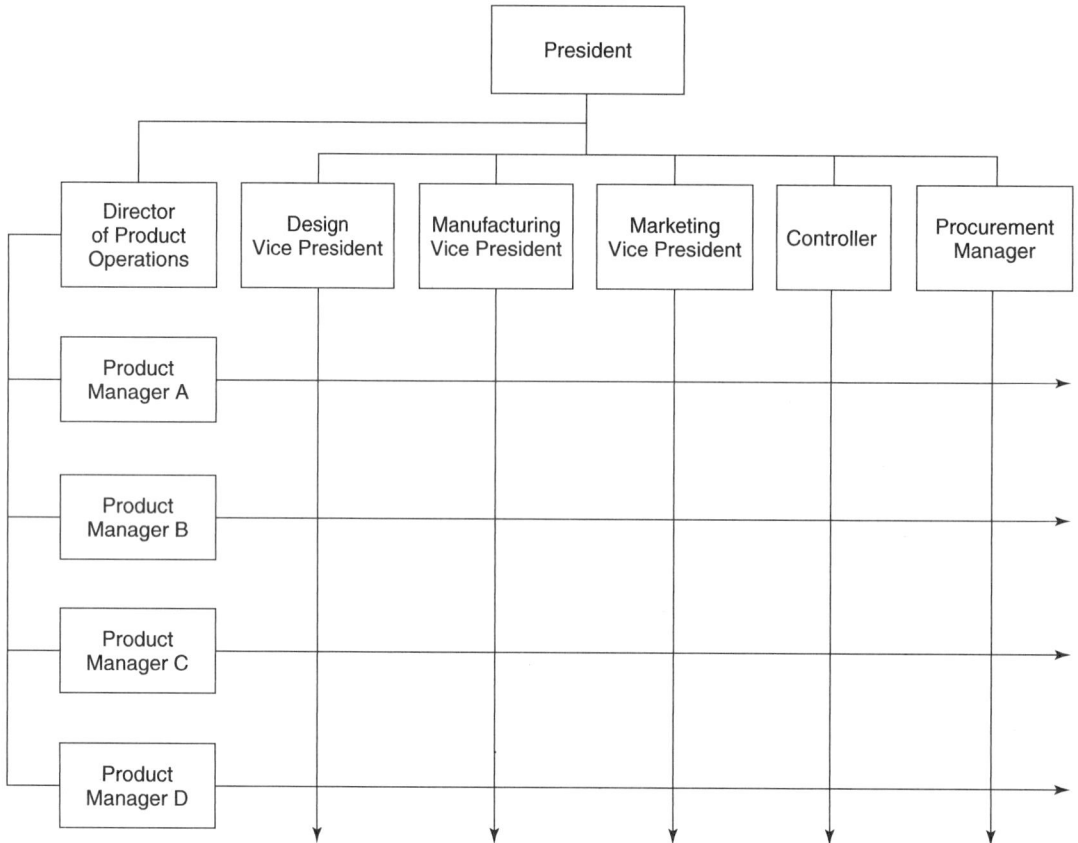

The matrix is a strong form of horizontal linkage. The unique characteristic of the matrix organization is that both product division and functional structures (horizontal and vertical) are implemented simultaneously, as shown in Exhibit 100.59. The product managers and functional managers have equal authority within the organization, and employees report to both of them. The matrix structure is similar to the use of full-time integrators or product managers described earlier in this section (Exhibit 100.57), except that in the matrix structure the product managers (horizontal) are given formal authority equal to that of the functional managers (vertical).

Conditions for the Matrix Structure

A dual hierarchy may seem an unusual way to design an organization, but the matrix is the correct structure when the following conditions are met.[311]

- *Condition 1.* Pressure exists to share scarce resources across product lines. The organization is typically medium-sized and has a moderate number of product lines. It feels pressure for the shared and flexible use of people and equipment across those products. For example, the organization is not large enough to assign engineers full-time to each product line, so engineers are assigned part-time to several products or projects.
- *Condition 2.* Environmental pressure exists for two or more critical outputs, such as for in-depth technical knowledge (functional structure) and frequent new products (divisional structure). This dual pressure means a balance of power is needed between the functional and product sides of the organization, and a dual-authority structure is needed to maintain that balance.
- *Condition 3.* The environmental domain of the organization is both complex and uncertain. Frequent external changes and high interdependence between departments require a large amount of coordination and information processing in both vertical and horizontal directions.

Under these three conditions, the vertical and horizontal lines of authority must be given equal recognition. A dual-authority structure is thereby created so the balance of power between them is equal.

Referring again to Exhibit 100.59, assume the matrix structure is for a clothing manufacturer. Product A is footwear, product B is outerwear, product C is sleepwear, and so on. Each product line serves a different market and customers. As a medium-size organization, the company must effectively use people from manufacturing, design, and marketing to work on each product line. There are not enough designers to warrant a separate design department for each product line, so the designers are shared across product lines. Moreover, by keeping the manufacturing, design, and marketing functions intact, employees can develop the in-depth expertise to serve all product lines efficiently.

The matrix formalizes horizontal teams along with the traditional vertical hierarchy and tries to give equal balance to both. However, the matrix may shift one way or the other. Many companies have found a balanced matrix hard to implement and maintain because one side of the authority structure often dominates. Recognizing this tendency, two variations of matrix structure have evolved—the **functional matrix** and the **product matrix**. In a functional matrix, the functional bosses have primary authority and the project or product managers simply coordinate product activities. In a product matrix, by contrast, the project or product managers have primary authority and functional managers simply assign technical personnel to projects and provide advisory expertise as needed. For many organizations, one of these approaches works better than the balanced matrix with dual lines of authority.[312]

All kinds of organizations have experimented with the matrix, including hospitals, consulting firms, banks, insurance companies, government agencies, and many types of industrial firms.[313] This structure has been used successfully by organizations such as IBM and Unilever, which fine-tuned the matrix to suit their own particular goals and culture.

Strengths and Weaknesses of the Matrix Structure

The matrix structure is best when environmental change is high and when goals reflect a dual requirement, such as for both product and functional goals. The dual-authority structure facilitates communication and coordination to cope with rapid environmental change and enables an equal balance between product and functional bosses. The matrix facilitates discussion and adaptation to unexpected problems. It tends to work best in organizations of moderate size with a few product lines. The matrix is not needed for only a single product line, and too many product lines make it difficult to coordinate both directions at once.

The strength of the matrix is that it enables an organization to meet dual demands from customers in the environment. Resources (people, equipment) can be flexibly allocated across different products, and the organization can adapt to changing external requirements.[314] This structure also provides an opportunity for employees to acquire either functional or general management skills, depending on their interests.

One disadvantage of the matrix is that some employees experience dual authority, which is frustrating and confusing. They need excellent interpersonal and conflict-resolution skills, which may require special training in human relations. The matrix also forces managers to spend a great deal of time in meetings.[315] If managers do not adapt to the information and power sharing required by the matrix, the system will not work. Managers must collaborate with one another rather than rely on vertical authority in decision making.

Applications of Structural Design

Each type of structure is applied in different situations and meets different needs. In describing the various structures, we touched briefly on conditions such as environmental stability or change and organizational size that are related to structure. Each form of structure—functional, divisional, geographical, matrix—represents a tool that can help managers make an organization more effective, depending on the demands of its situation.

Structural Contingencies

Managers design the organization to fit the contingency factors. Structure is influenced by environment, strategy and goals, culture, technology, and size. Of these contextual variables, the connection between competitive strategy and structure is of particular interest and has been widely studied. Structure typically reflects organizational strategy, and a change in product or market strategy frequently leads to a change in structure.[316] Once a company formulates a strategy by which it plans to achieve a competitive advantage in the marketplace, leaders design or redesign the structure to coordinate organizational activities to best achieve that advantage.

The remaining contingency factors—environment, culture, technology, and size—will be discussed in subsequent chapters. Each variable influences the appropriate structural design. Moreover, environment, culture, technology, goals, and size may also influence one another.

Symptoms of Structural Deficiency

Top executives periodically evaluate organization structure to determine whether it is appropriate to changing organization needs. Many organizations try one organization structure, then reorganize to another structure in an effort to find the right fit between internal reporting relationships and the needs of the external environment. **Compaq Computer Corporation,** for example, switched from a functional structure to a divisional structure for about a year to develop new products and then switched back to a functional structure to reduce competition among its product lines.[317]

As a general rule, when organization structure is out of alignment with organization needs, one or more of the following **symptoms of structural deficiency** appear.[318]

- *Decision making is delayed or lacking in quality.* Decision makers may be overloaded because the hierarchy funnels too many problems and decisions to them. Delegation to lower levels may be insufficient. Another cause of poor quality decisions is that information may not reach the correct people. Information linkages in either the vertical or horizontal direction may be inadequate to ensure decision quality.
- *The organization does not respond innovatively to a changing environment.* One reason for lack of innovation is that departments are not coordinated horizontally. The identification of customer needs by the marketing department and the identification of technological developments in the research department must be coordinated. Organization structure also has to specify departmental responsibilities that include environmental scanning and innovation.
- *Too much conflict is evident.* Organization structure should allow conflicting departmental goals to combine into a single set of goals for the entire organization. When departments act at cross purposes or are under pressure to achieve departmental goals at the expense of organizational goals, the structure is often at fault. Horizontal linkage mechanisms are not adequate.

Organization Size, Life Cycle, and Control

Most entrepreneurs want their organizations to grow. However, as a company grows larger and more complex, managers have to develop systems and procedures that can help them guide and control the organization. During the 20th century, large organizations became widespread, and over the past few decades, bureaucracy has been a major topic of study in organization theory.[319] Today, many organizations are trying to reduce bureaucracy to be more flexible and responsive in a rapidly changing marketplace.

However, although bureaucracy has been accused of many sins, including inefficiency, rigidity, and demeaning, routinized work that alienates both employees and customers, bureaucratic characteristics also bring many positive effects. Most large organizations have bureaucratic characteristics. These organizations provide us with abundant goods and services and surprise us with astonishing feats that are testimony to their effectiveness.

Organization Size

The question of big versus small begins with the notion of growth and the reasons so many organizations feel the need to grow large.

Pressures for Growth

Some observers believe the United States is entering a new era of "bigness," as companies strive to acquire the size and resources to compete on a global scale, to invest in new technology and to control distribution channels and guarantee access to markets. For example, more than $1.6 trillion in mergers took place worldwide in 1997 alone, with over half of that activity in the United States.[320]

There are other pressures for organizations to grow. Many executives have found that firms must grow to stay economically healthy. To stop growing is to stagnate. To be stable means that customers may not have their demands met fully or that competitors will increase market share at the expense of your company. Scale is crucial to economic health in marketing-intensive companies such as **Coca-Cola** and **Anheuser-Busch.** Greater size gives these companies power in the marketplace and thus increased revenues.[321] In addition, growing organizations are vibrant, exciting places to work, which enables these companies to attract and keep quality employees. When the number of employees is expanding, the company can offer many challenges and opportunities for advancement.

Large versus Small

Organizations feel compelled to grow, but how much and how large? What size organization is better poised to compete in a global environment?

LARGE Huge resources and economies of scale are needed for many organizations to compete globally. Only large organizations can build a massive pipeline in Alaska. Only a large corporation like **Boeing** can afford to build a 747, and only a large **American Airlines** can buy it. Only a large Johnson & Johnson can invest hundreds of millions in new products such as bifocal contact lenses and a birth control patch that delivers contraceptives through the skin.

Large companies also are standardized, often mechanistically run, and complex. The complexity offers hundreds of functional specialties within the organization to perform complex tasks and to produce complex products. Moreover, large organizations, once established, can be a presence that stabilizes a market for years. Managers can join the company and expect a career reminiscent of the "organization men" of the 1950s and 1960s. The organization can provide longevity, raises, and promotions.

SMALL The competing argument says small is beautiful because the crucial requirements for success in a global economy are responsiveness and flexibility in fast-changing markets. While the U.S. economy contains many large organizations, research shows that as global trade has accelerated, smaller organizations have become the norm. Since the mid-1960s, most of the then-existing large businesses have lost market share worldwide.[322] Today, fully 96 percent of exporters are small businesses.[323] The economic vitality of the United States, as well as most of the rest of the developed world, is tied to small and mid-sized businesses. Although many large companies have become even larger through merger, they are also less numerous as a result. Countless small businesses have sprang up to fill specialized niches and serve targeted markets.[324] The development of the Internet has provided fertile ground for the growth of small firms. In addition, the rapidly growing service sector, also contributes to a decrease in average organization size, since most service companies remain small to be more responsive to customers.[325]

Organizational Life Cycle

A useful way to think about organizational growth and change is the concept of an organizational **life cycle**,[326] which suggests that organizations are born, grow older, and eventually die. Organization structure, leadership style, and administrative systems follow a fairly predictable pattern through stages in the life cycle. Stages are sequential in nature and follow a natural progression.

Stages of Life Cycle Development

Recent work on organizational life cycle suggests that four major stages characterize organizational development.[327] These stages include entrepreneurial stage, collectivity stage, formalization stage, and elaboration stage. Growth is not easy. Each time an organization enters a new stage in the life cycle, it enters a whole new ballgame with a new set of rules for how the organization functions internally and how it relates to the external environment.[328]

1. *Entrepreneurial Stage.* When an organization is born, the emphasis is on creating a product and surviving in the marketplace. The founders are entrepreneurs, and they devote their full energies to the technical activities of production and marketing. The organization is informal and nonbureaucratic. The hours of work are long. Control is based on the owners' personal supervision. Growth is from a creative new product or service. **Apple Computer** was in the **entrepreneurial stage** when it was created by Steve Jobs and Stephen Wozniak in Wozniak's parents' garage. Small Internet-based companies such as **HomeRuns, Peapod,** and **ShopLink,** which sell groceries on-line, are currently in the entrepreneurial stage.
2. *Collectivity Stage.* If the leadership crisis is resolved, strong leadership is obtained and the organization begins to develop clear goals and direction. Departments are established along with a hierarchy of authority, job assignments, and a beginning division of labor. Employees identify with the mission of the organization and spend long hours helping the organization succeed. Members feel part of a collective, and communication and control are mostly informal although a few formal systems begin to appear. Apple Computer was in the **collectivity stage** during the rapid growth years from 1978 to 1981. Employees threw themselves into the business as the major product line was established and more than two thousand dealers signed on.
3. *Formalization Stage.* The **formalization stage** involves the installation and use of rules, procedures, and control systems. Communication is less frequent and more formal. Engineers, human resource specialists, and other

staff may be added. Top management becomes concerned with issues such as strategy and planning, and leaves the operations of the firm to middle management. Product groups or other decentralized units may be formed to improve coordination. Incentive systems based on profits may be implemented to ensure that managers work toward what is best for the overall company. When effective, the new coordination and control systems enable the organization to continue growing by establishing linkage mechanisms between top management and field units. Apple Computer was in the formalization stage in the mid-1980s.

4. *Elaboration Stage.* The solution to the red tape crisis is a new sense of collaboration and teamwork. Throughout the organization, managers develop skills for confronting problems and working together. Bureaucracy may have reached its limit. Social control and self-discipline reduce the need for additional formal controls. Managers learn to work within the bureaucracy without adding to it. Formal systems may be simplified and replaced by manager teams and task forces. To achieve collaboration, teams are often formed across functions or divisions of the company. The organization may also be split into multiple divisions to maintain a small-company philosophy. Apple Computer is currently in the **elaboration stage** of the life cycle, as are such large companies as **Caterpillar** and **Motorola**.

SUMMARY Eighty-four percent of businesses that make it past the first year still fail within five years because they can't make the transition from the entrepreneurial stage.[329] The transitions become even more difficult as organizations progress through future stages of the life cycle. Organizations that do not successfully resolve the problems associated with these transitions are restricted in their growth and may even fail.

Organizational Characteristics during the Life Cycle

As organizations evolve through the four stages of the life cycle, changes take place in structure, control systems, innovation, and goals.

ENTREPRENEURIAL Initially, the organization is small, nonbureaucratic, and a one-person show. The top manager provides the structure and control system. Organizational energy is devoted to survival and the production of a single product or service.

COLLECTIVITY This is the organization's youth. Growth is rapid, and employees are excited and committed to the organization's mission. The structure is still mostly informal, although some procedures are emerging. Strong charismatic leaders like Scott McNealy of Sun Microsystems or Steve Jobs of Apple provide direction and goals for the organization. Continued growth is a major goal.

FORMALIZATION At this point, the organization is entering midlife. Bureaucratic characteristics emerge. The organization adds staff support groups, formalizes procedures, and establishes a clear hierarchy and division of labor. Innovation may be achieved by establishing a separate research and development department. Major goals are internal stability and market expansion. Top management has to delegate, but it also implements formal control systems. At the formalization stage, organizations may also develop complementary products to offer a complete product line.

ELABORATION The mature organization is large and bureaucratic, with extensive control systems, rules, and procedures. Organization managers attempt to develop a team orientation within the bureaucracy to prevent further bureaucratization. Top managers are concerned with establishing a complete organization. Organizational stature and reputation are important. Innovation is institutionalized through an R&D department. Management may attack the bureaucracy and streamline it.

SUMMARY Growing organizations move through stages of a life cycle, and each stage is associated with specific characteristics of structure, control systems, goals, and innovation. The life cycle phenomenon is a powerful concept used for understanding problems facing organizations and how managers can respond in a positive way to move an organization to the next stage.

Organizational Bureaucracy and Control

As organizations progress through the life cycle, they usually take on bureaucratic characteristics as they grow larger and more complex. The systematic study of bureaucracy was launched by Max Weber, a sociologist who studied gov-

Exhibit 100.60 *Weber's Dimensions of Bureaucracy and Bases of Organizational Authority*

Bureaucracy	Legitimate Bases of Authority
1. Rules and procedures	1. Rational-legal
2. Specialization and division of labor	2. Traditional
3. Hierarchy of authority	3. Charismatic
4. Technically qualified personnel	
5. Separate position and incumbents	
6. Written communications and records	

ernment organizations in Europe and developed a framework of administrative characteristics that would make large organizations rational and efficient.[330] Weber wanted to understand how organizations could be designed to play a positive role in the larger society.

What Is Bureaucracy?

Although Weber perceived **bureaucracy** as a threat to basic personal liberties, he also recognized it as the most efficient possible system of organizing. He predicted the triumph of bureaucracy because of its ability to ensure more efficient functioning of organizations in both business and government settings. Weber identified a set of organizational characteristics, listed in Exhibit 100.60, that could be found in successful bureaucratic organizations.

Rules and standard procedures enabled organizational activities to be performed in a predictable, routine manner. Specialized duties meant that each employee had a clear task to perform. Hierarchy of authority provided a sensible mechanism for supervision and control. Technical competence was the basis by which people were hired rather than friendship, family ties, and favoritism that dramatically reduced work performance. The separation of the position from the position holder meant that individuals did not own or have an inherent right to the job, thus promoting efficiency. Written records provided an organizational memory and continuity over time.

Although bureaucratic characteristics carried to an extreme are widely criticized today, the rational control introduced by Weber was a significant idea and a new form of organization. Bureaucracy provided many advantages over organization forms based upon favoritism, social status, family connections, or graft, which are often unfair. For example, in Mexico, a retired American lawyer had to pay a $500 bribe to purchase a telephone, then discovered that a government official had sold his telephone number to another family. In China, the tradition of giving government posts to relatives is widespread even under communism. China's emerging class of educated people doesn't like seeing the best jobs going to children and relatives of officials.[331] By comparison, the logical and rational form of organization described by Weber allows work to be conducted efficiently and according to established rules.

Size and Structural Control

In the field of organization theory, organization size has been described as an important variable that influences structural design and methods of control. Should an organization become more bureaucratic as it grows larger? In what size organizations are bureaucratic characteristics most appropriate? More than one hundred studies have attempted to answer these questions.[332] Most of these studies indicate that large organizations are different from small organizations along several dimensions of bureaucratic structure, including formalization, centralization, and personnel ratios.

FORMALIZATION AND CENTRALIZATION **Formalization** refers to rules, procedures, and written documentation, such as policy manuals and job descriptions, that prescribe the rights and duties of employees.[333] The evidence supports the conclusion that large organizations are more formalized. The reason is that large organizations rely on rules, procedures, and paperwork to achieve standardization and control across their large numbers of employees and departments, whereas top managers can use personal observation to control a small organization.[334]

Centralization refers to the level of hierarchy with authority to make decisions. In centralized organizations, decisions tend to be made at the top. In decentralized organizations, similar decisions would be made at a lower level.

Decentralization represents a paradox because, in the perfect bureaucracy, all decisions would be made by the top administrator, who would have perfect control. However, as an organization grows larger and has more people and departments, decisions cannot be passed to the top, or senior managers would be overloaded. Thus, the research on organization size indicates that larger organizations permit greater decentrailization.[335] Hewlett-Packard decentralizes almost every aspect of its business to speed up decision making. In small startup organizations, on the other hand, the founder or top executive is often involved in every decision, large and small.

PERSONNEL RATIOS Another characteristic of bureaucracy is **personnel ratios** for administrative, clerical, and professional support staff. The most frequently studied ratio is the administrative ratio.[336] Two patterns have emerged. The first is that the ratio of top administration to total employees is actually smaller in large organizations,[337] indicating that organizations experience administrative economies as they grow larger. The second pattern concerns clerical and professional support staff ratios.[338] These groups tend to *increase* in proportion to organization size. The clerical ratio increases because of the greater communication and reporting requirements needed as organizations grow larger. The professional staff ratio increases because of the greater need for specialized skills in larger, complex organizations.

As organizations increase in size, the administrative ratio declines and the ratios for other support groups increase.[339] The net effect for direct workers is that they decline as a percentage of total employees. In summary, while top administrators do not make up a disproportionate number of employees in large organizations, the idea that proportionately greater overhead is required in large organizations is supported. Although large organizations reduced overhead during the difficult economic years of the 1980s, recent studies indicate that overhead costs for many American corporations began creeping back up again as revenues soared during the late 1990s.[340] Keeping costs for administrative, clerical, and professional support staff low represents an ongoing challenge for today's large organizations.[341]

Dynamic Control Systems

Even though many organizations are trying to decrease bureaucracy and reduce rules and procedures that constrain employees, every organization needs systems for guiding and controlling the organization. Employees may have more freedom in today's companies, but control is still a major responsibility of management.

Managers at the top and middle levels of an organization can choose among three overall approaches for control. These approaches come from a framework for organizational control proposed by William Ouchi of the University of California at Los Angeles. Ouchi suggested three control strategies that organizations could adopt—bureaucratic, market and clan.[342] Each form of control uses different types of information. However, all three types may appear simultaneously in an organization.

Bureaucratic Control

Bureaucratic control is the use of rules, policies, hierarchy of authority, written documentation, standardization, and other bureaucratic mechanisms to standardize behavior and assess performance. Bureaucratic control uses the bureaucratic characteristics defined by Weber. The primary purpose of bureaucratic rules and procedures is to standardize and control employee behavior.

Recall that as organizations progress through the life cycle and grow larger, they become more formalized and standardized. Within a large organization, thousands of work behaviors and information exchanges take place both vertically and horizontally. Rules and policies evolve through a process of trial and error to regulate these behaviors. Some degree of bureaucratic control is used in virtually every organization. Rules, regulations, and directives contain information about a range of behaviors.

BASES OF CONTROL To make bureaucratic control work, managers must have the authority to maintain control over the organization. Weber argued that legitimate, rational authority granted to managers was preferred over other types of control (for example, favoritism or payoffs) as the basis for organizational decisions and activities. Within the larger society, however, Weber identified three types of authority that could explain the creation and control of a large organization.[343]

Rational-legal authority is based on employees' belief in the legality of rules and the right of those elevated to positions of authority to issue commands. Rational-legal authority is the basis for both creation and control of most government organizations and is the most common base of control in organizations worldwide. **Traditional authority** is the belief in traditions and in the legitimacy of the status of people exercising authority through those traditions. Traditional authority is the basis for control for monarchies and churches and for some organizations in Latin America and the Persian Gulf. **Charismatic authority** is based on devotion to the exemplary character or to the heroism of an individual person and the order defined by him or her. Revolutionary military organizations are often based on the leader's charisma, as are North American organizations led by charismatic individuals such as Jack Welch or Herb Kelleher.

More than one type of authority—such as long tradition and the leader's special charisma—may exist in today's organizations, but rational–legal authority is the most widely used form to govern internal work activities and decision making, particularly in large organizations.

Management control systems are broadly defined as the formalized routines, reports, and procedures that use information to maintain or alter patterns in organizational activity.[344] Control systems include the formalized information-based activities for planning, budgeting, performance evaluation, resource allocation, and employee rewards. These systems operate as feedback systems, with the targets set in advance, outcomes compared with targets, and variance reported to managers for remedial actions.[345] These systems are valuable tools to help managers monitor and control the organization.

The four control system elements are often considered the core of management control systems. These four elements include the budget, periodic nonfinancial statistical reports, reward systems, and standard operating procedures.[346] The management control system elements enable middle and upper management to both monitor and influence major departments.

The operating budget is used to set financial targets for the year and then report costs on a monthly or quarterly basis. Periodic statistical reports are used to evaluate and monitor nonfinancial performance. These reports typically are computer-based and may be available daily, weekly, or monthly.

Reward systems offer incentives for managers and employees to improve performance and meet departmental goals. Managers and superiors may sit down and evaluate how well previous goals were met, set new goals for the year, and establish rewards for meeting the new targets. Operating procedures are traditional rules and regulations. Managers use all of these systems to correct variances and bring activities back into line.

One finding from research into management control systems is that each of the four control systems focuses on a different aspect of the production process. These four systems thus form an overall management control system that provides middle managers with control information about resource inputs, process efficiency, and output.[347] Moreover, the use of and reliance on control systems depend on the strategic targets set by top management.

The budget is used primarily to allocate resource inputs. Managers use the budget for planning the future and reducing uncertainty about the availability of human and material resources needed to perform department tasks. Computer-based statistical reports are used to control outputs. These reports contain data about output volume and quality and other indicators that provide feedback to middle management about departmental results. The reward system and the policies and procedures are directed at the production process. Operating procedures give explicit guidelines about appropriate behaviors. Reward systems provide incentives to meet goals and can help guide and correct employee activities. Managers also use direct supervision to keep departmental work activities within desired limits.

Advances in computer technology have dramatically improved the efficiency and effectiveness of management control systems. The British express delivery and logistics company **TNT UK** uses computerized management control systems to measure and control every aspect of the company's performance, helping TNT UK win the prestigious 1998 European Quality Award.[348]

Market Control

Market control occurs when price competition is used to evaluate the output and productivity of an organization. The idea of market control originated in economics.[349] A dollar price is an efficient form of control because managers can compare prices and profits to evaluate the efficiency of their corporation. Top managers nearly always use the price mechanism to evaluate performance in corporations. Corporate sales and costs are summarized in a profit-and-loss statement that can be compared against performance in previous years or with that of other corporations.

The use of market control requires that outputs be sufficiently explicit for a price to be assigned and that competition exist. Without competition, the price will not accurately reflect internal efficiency. Even some government and traditionally not-for-profit organizations are turning to market control.

Market control was once used primarily at the level of the entire organization, but it is increasingly used in product divisions. Profit centers are self-contained product divisions. Each division contains resource inputs needed to produce a product. Each division can be evaluated on the basis of profit or loss compared with other divisions. **Asea Brown Boveri (ABB)**, a multinational electrical contractor and manufacturer of electrical equipment, includes three different types of profit centers, all operating according to their own bottom line and all interacting through buying and selling with one another and with outside customers.[350]

Some firms require that individual departments interact with one another at market prices—buying and selling products or services among themselves at prices equivalent to those quoted outside the firm. To make the market control system work, internal units also have the option to buy and sell with outside companies.

Market control can only be used when the output of a company, division, or department can be assigned a dollar price and when there is competition. Companies are finding that they can apply the market control concept to internal departments such as accounting, data processing, legal departments, and information services.

Clan Control

Clan control is the use of social characteristics, such as corporate culture, shared values, commitment, traditions, and beliefs, to control behavior. Organizations that use clan control require shared values and trust among employees.[351] Clan control is important when ambiguity and uncertainty are high. High uncertainty means the organization cannot put a price on its services, and things change so fast that rules and regulations are not able to specify every correct behavior. Under clan control, people may be hired because they are committed to the organization's purpose, such as in a religious organization. New employees may be subjected to a long period of socialization to gain acceptance by colleagues. Clan control is most often used in small, informal organizations or in organizations with a strong culture, because of personal involvement in and commitment to the organization's purpose. For example, **St. Luke's Communications Ltd.,** a London advertising firm committed to equal employee ownership, is especially careful to bring in only new employees who believe in the agency's philosophy and mission. The company even turned down a $90 million contract because it would mean rapidly recruiting new employees who might not fit with St. Luke's distinctive culture. Clan control works for St. Luke's; the agency is highly respected and its revenues continue to grow.[352]

The growing use of computer networks and the Internet, which often leads to a democratic spread of information throughout the organization, may force many companies to depend less on bureaucratic control and more on shared values that guide individual actions for the corporate good.[353]

Traditional control mechanisms based on strict rules and close supervision are ineffective for controlling behavior in conditions of high uncertainty and rapid change.[354] Today's companies that are trying to become learning organizations often use clan control or *self-control* rather than relying on rules and regulations. Self-control is similar to clan control, but whereas clan control is a function of being socialized into a group, self-control stems from individual values, goals, and standards. The organization attempts to induce a change such that individual employees' own internal values and work preferences are brought in line with the organization's values and goals.[355] With self-control, employees generally set their own goals and monitor their own performance, yet companies relying on self-control need strong leaders who can clarify boundaries within which employees exercise their own knowledge and discretion.

Clan or self-control may also be used in certain departments, such as strategic planning, where uncertainty is high and performance is difficult to measure. Managers of departments that rely on these informal control mechanisms must not assume that the absence of written, bureaucratic control means no control is present. Clan control is invisible yet very powerful. One recent study found that the actions of employees were controlled even more powerfully and completely with clan control than with a bureaucratic hierarchy.[356] When clan control works, bureaucratic control is not needed.

Innovation and Change

Today, every organization must change to survive. New discoveries and inventions quickly replace standard ways of doing things. The pace of change is revealed in the fact that the parents of today's college-age students grew up without voice mail, compact discs, video games, debit cards, cellular phones, and laser checkout systems in supermarkets. The idea of communicating instantly with people around the world via the Internet was unimaginable to most people as recently as a decade ago. Managers look for ways to encourage innovation so their organizations can respond to changing circumstances. In addition, they search for techniques to help employees cope with rapid change.

The Strategic Role of Change

Every organization goes through periods of change. Sometimes, change is brought about because of forces outside the organization. At other times, managers within the company want to initiate major change or spur innovation, but they may not know how. To remain successful, organizations must embrace many types of change. Organizations that invest most of their time and resources in maintaining the status quo are unlikely to prosper in today's uncertain environment.[357] Depending on an organization's strategic needs and the demands of the external environment, managers may encourage innovation in one or more parts of the organization. They use a number of techniques to successfully implement change when and where it is needed.

Strategic Types of Change

Managers can focus on four types of change within organizations to achieve strategic advantage. These four types of change are products and services, strategy and structure, culture, and technology. Factors such as leadership, organizational strategy, and corporate culture provide an overall context within which the four types of change serve as a competitive wedge to achieve an advantage in the international environment. Each company has a unique configuration of products and services, strategy and structure, culture, and technologies that can be focused for maximum impact upon the company's chosen markets.[358]

Technology changes are changes in an organization's production process, including its knowledge and skill base, that enable distinctive competence. These changes are designed to make production more efficient or to produce greater volume. Changes in technology involve the techniques for making products or services. They include work methods, equipment, and work flow. For example, in a university, technology changes are changes in techniques for teaching courses. As another example, the British water and sewage company **Anglia Water** came up with an innovative way to use its existing technologies to devise a water efficiency recycling system called Waterwise, which allows households to use one-third less water. Anglia also adopted new information technology for disseminating technical knowledge throughout the organization.[359]

Product and service changes pertain to the product or service outputs of an organization. New products include small adaptations of existing products or entirely new product lines. New products are normally designed to increase the market share or to develop new markets, customers, or clients. When faced with intense foreign competition in the machine-tool business, **Cincinnati Milacron** transformed itself into a full-service industrial supplier, providing not only tools but all industrial plastics, fluids, and chemicals. Today, machine tools make up only about one-fourth of Milacron's total revenue base. The new products and services expanded the company's market and customer base, helping the 115-year-old organization survive while many of its counterparts in the machine-tool industry failed.[360]

Strategy and structure changes pertain to the administrative domain in an organization. The administrative domain involves the supervision and management of the organization. These changes include changes in organization structure, strategic management, policies, reward systems, labor relations, coordination devices, management information and control systems, and accounting and budgeting systems. Structure and system changes are usually top-down, that is, mandated by top management, whereas product and technology changes may often come from the bottom up. The structure was changed at Cincinnati Milacron when top executives formed "Wolfpack" teams, groups of engineers, managers, outside suppliers, and customers who work together to develop new products. A system change instituted by management in a university might be a new merit pay plan. Corporate downsizing is another example of top-down structure change.

Culture changes refer to changes in the values, attitudes, expectations, beliefs, abilities, and behavior of employees. Culture changes pertain to changes in how employees think; these are changes in mindset rather than technology, structure, or products. At **Globe Metallurgical**, a top supplier of specialty metals for the chemical and foundry industries, the old culture was marked by suspicion and distrust. Managers often dictated changes without consulting workers and sometimes shifted their approaches and policies abruptly. Globe transformed its culture to one that values employee empowerment and involvement, a new respect for management, and a new commitment to quality.[361]

The four types of changes are interdependent—a change in one often means a change in another. A new product may require changes in the production technology, or a change in structure may require new employee skills. For example, when **Shenandoah Life Insurance Company** acquired new computer technology to process claims, the technology was not fully utilized until clerks were restructured into teams of five to seven members that were compatible with the technology. The structural change was an outgrowth of the technology change. In a manufacturing company, engineers introduced robots and advanced manufacturing technologies, only to find that the technology placed greater demands on employees. Upgrading employee skills required a change in wage systems. Organizations are interdependent systems, and changing one part often has implications for other organization elements.

Elements for Successful Change

Regardless of the type or scope of change, there are identifiable stages of innovation, which generally occur as a sequence of events, though innovation stages may overlap.[362] In the research literature on innovation, **organizational change** is considered the adoption of a new idea or behavior by an organization.[363] **Organizational innovation,** in contrast, is the adoption of an idea or behavior that is new to the organization's industry, market, or general environment.[364] The first organization to introduce a new product is considered the innovator, and organizations that copy are considered to adopt changes. For purposes of managing change, however, the terms *innovation* and *change* will be used interchangeably because the **change process** within organizations tends to be identical whether a change is early or late with respect to other organizations in the environment.

Innovations typically are assimilated into an organization through a series of steps or elements. Organization members first become aware of a possible innovation, evaluate its appropriateness, and then evaluate and choose the idea.[365] The required elements of successful change are summarized in Exhibit 100.61. For a change to be successfully implemented, managers must make sure each element occurs in the organization. If one of the elements is missing, the change process will fail.

1. *Ideas.* Although creativity is a dramatic element of organizational change, creativity within organizations has not been widely and systematically studied. No company can remain competitive without new ideas; change is the outward expression of those ideas.[366] An idea is a new way of doing things. It may be a new product or service, a new management concept, or a new procedure for working together in the organization. Ideas can come from within or from outside the organization.

2. *Need.* Ideas are generally not seriously considered unless there is a perceived need for change. A perceived need for change occurs when managers see a gap between actual performance and desired performance in the organization. Managers try to establish a sense of urgency so that others will understand the need for change. Sometimes a crisis provides an undoubted sense of urgency. For example, **Midwest Contract Furnishings,** a small firm that designs and fabricates hotel interiors, faced a crisis when its largest customer, **Renaissance Hotels,** was sold to **Marriott,** which did interior designing in-house. Midwest lost 80 percent of its revenues virtually overnight.[367] In many cases, however, there is no crisis, so managers have to recognize a need and communicate it to others.[368] In addition, although many ideas are generated to meet perceived needs, innovative companies encourage the constant development of new ideas that may stimulate consideration of problems or new opportunities.

3. *Adoption.* Adoption occurs when decision makers choose to go ahead with a proposed idea. Key managers and employees need to be in agreement to support the change. For a major organizational change, the decision might require the signing of a legal document by the board of directors. For a small change, adoption might occur with informal approval by a middle manager. When Ray Kroc was CEO of McDonald's, he made the adoption decision about innovations such as the Big Mac and Egg McMuffin.

4. *Implementation.* Implementation occurs when organization members actually use a new idea, technique, or behavior. Materials and equipment may have to be acquired, and workers may have to be trained to use the new idea. Implementation is a very important step because without it, previous steps are to no avail. Implementation of change is often the most difficult part of the change process. Until people use the new idea, no change has actually taken place.

Exhibit 100.61 *Sequence of Elements for Successful Change*

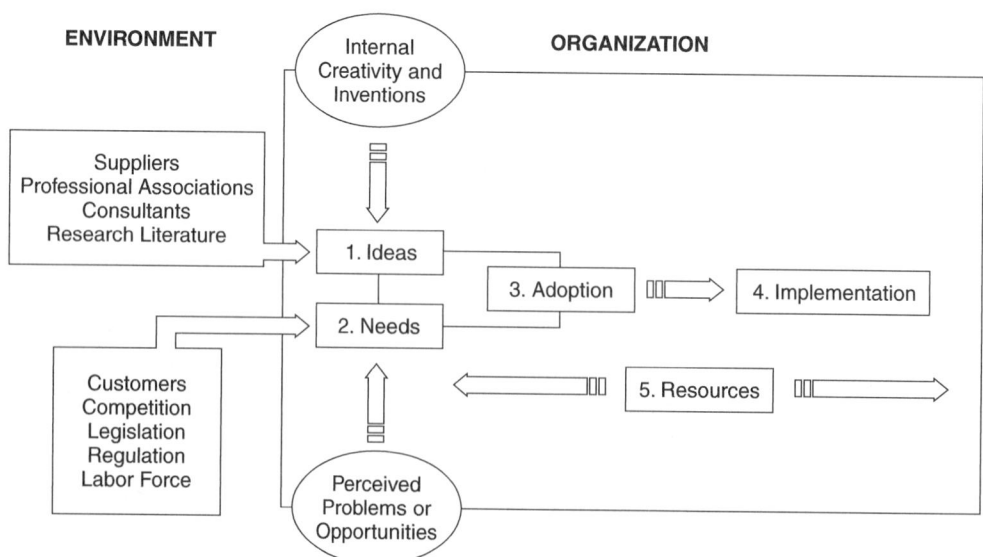

5. *Resources.* Human energy and activity are required to bring about change. Change does not happen on its own; it requires time and resources, for both creating and implementing a new idea. Employees have to provide energy to see both the need and the idea to meet that need. Someone must develop a proposal and provide the time and effort to implement it.

One point about Exhibit 100.61 is especially important. Needs and ideas are listed simultaneously at the beginning of the change sequence. Either may occur first. Many organizations adopted the computer, for example, because it seemed a promising way to improve efficiency. Today's search for a vaccine against the AIDS virus, on the other hand, was stimulated by a severe need. Whether the need or the idea occurs first, for the change to be accomplished, each of the steps in Exhibit 100.61 must be completed.

Technology Change

In today's business world, any company that isn't constantly developing, acquiring, or adapting new technology will likely be out of business in a few years. However, organizations face a contradiction when it comes to technology change, for the conditions that promote new ideas are not generally the best for implementing those ideas for routine production. An innovative organization is characterized by flexibility, empowered employees, and the absence of rigid work rules.[369] An organic, free-flowing organization is typically associated with change and is considered the best organization form for adapting to a chaotic environment.

The flexibility of an organic organization is attributed to people's freedom to create and introduce new ideas. Organic organizations encourage a bottom-up innovation process. Ideas bubble up from middle- and lower-level employees because they have the freedom to propose ideas and to experiment. A mechanistic structure, on the other hand, stifles innovation with its emphasis on rules and regulations, but it is often the best structure for efficiently producing routine products. The challenge for organizations is to create both organic and mechanistic conditions within organizations to achieve both innovation and efficiency. To achieve both aspects of technological change, many organizations use the ambidextrous approach.

The Ambidextrous Approach

Recent thinking has refined the idea of organic versus mechanistic structures with respect to innovation creation versus innovation utilization. For example, sometimes an organic structure generates innovative ideas but is not the best structure for using those ideas.[370] In other words, the initiation and the utilization of change are two distinct processes. Organic characteristics such as decentralization and employee freedom are excellent for initiating ideas; but these same conditions often make it hard to use a change because employees are less likely to comply. Employees can ignore the innovation because of decentralization and a generally loose structure.

How does an organization solve this dilemma? One approach is for the organization to be **ambidextrous**—to incorporate structures and management processes that are appropriate to both the creation and use of innovation.[371] The organization can behave in an organic way when the situation calls for the initiation of new ideas and in a mechanistic way to implement and use the ideas.

Techniques for Encouraging Technology Change

Freudenberg–NOK has created both organic and mechanistic conditions in the factory. Some of the techniques used by many companies to maintain an ambidextrous approach are switching structures, separate creative departments, venture teams, and corporate entrepreneurship.

SWITCHING STRUCTURES **Switching structures** means an organization creates an organic structure when such a structure is needed for the initiation of new ideas.[372]

CREATIVE DEPARTMENTS In many large organizations the initiation of innovation is assigned to separate **creative departments.**[373] Staff departments, such as research and development, engineering, design, and systems analysis, create changes for adoption in other departments. Departments that initiate change are organically structured to facilitate the generation of new ideas and techniques. Departments that use those innovations tend to have a mechanistic structure more suitable for efficient production. Exhibit 100.62 indicates how one department is responsible for creation and another department implements the innovation.

Exhibit 100.62 *Division of Labor Between Departments to Achieve Changes in Technology*

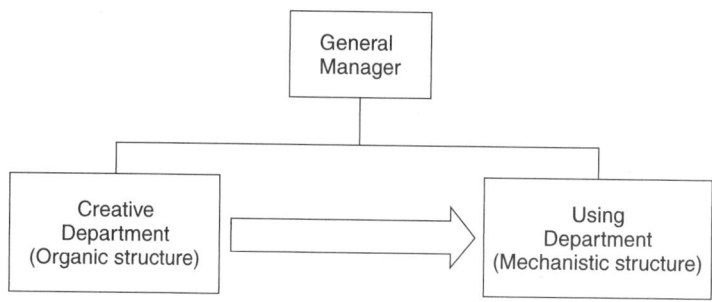

VENTURE TEAMS Venture teams are a recent technique used to give free rein to creativity within organizations. Venture teams are often given a separate location and facilities so they are not constrained by organizational procedures. Action teams and venture teams are kept small so they have autonomy and no bureaucracy emerges.

A venture team is like a small company within a large company.

A variation of the venture team concept is the **new-venture fund,** which provides financial resources for employees to develop new ideas, products, or businesses. In order to tap into its employees' entrepreneurial urges.

CORPORATE ENTREPRENEURSHIP Corporate entrepreneurship attempts to develop an internal entrepreneurial spirit, philosophy, and structure that will produce a higher than average number of innovations.[374] Corporate entrepreneurship may involve the use of creative departments and new venture teams as described above, but it also attempts to release the creative energy of all employees in the organization. The most important outcome is to facilitate **idea champions** which go by a variety of names, including advocate, intrapreneur, or change agent. Idea champions provide the time and energy to make things happen. They fight to overcome natural resistance to change and to convince others of the merit of a new idea.[375] Peter Drucker suggests that idea champions need not be within the organization, and that fostering potential idea champions among regular customers can be a highly successful approach.[376]

Companies encourage idea champions by providing freedom and slack time to creative people.

Idea champions usually come in two types. The **technical** or **product champion** is the person who generates or adopts and develops an idea for a technological innovation and is devoted to it, even to the extent of risking position or prestige. The **management champion** acts as a supporter and sponsor to shield and promote an idea within the organization.[377] The management champion sees the potential application and has the prestige and authority to get it a fair hearing and to allocate resources to it. Technical and management champions often work together because a technical idea will have a greater chance of success if a manager can be found to sponsor it. At Black & Decker, Peter Chaconas is a technical champion. He invented the Piranha circular saw blade, which is a best-selling tool accessory. Next, he invented the Bullet, which is a bit for home power drills and is the first major innovation in this product in almost one hundred years. Chaconas works full time designing products and promoting their acceptance. Randy Blevins, his boss, acts as management champion for Chaconas's ideas.[378]

Products and Services Change

Many of the concepts described for technology change are also relevant to the creation of new products and services. However, in many ways, new products and services are a special case of innovation because they are used by customers outside the organization. Since new products are designed for sale in the environment, uncertainty about the suitability and success of an innovation is very high.

Reasons for New Product Success

There is a distinct pattern of tailoring innovations to customer needs, making effective use of technology, and having influential top managers support the project. These ideas taken together indicate that the effective design for new product innovation is associated with horizontal linkage across departments.

Exhibit 100.63 *Horizontal Linkage Model for New Product Innovations*

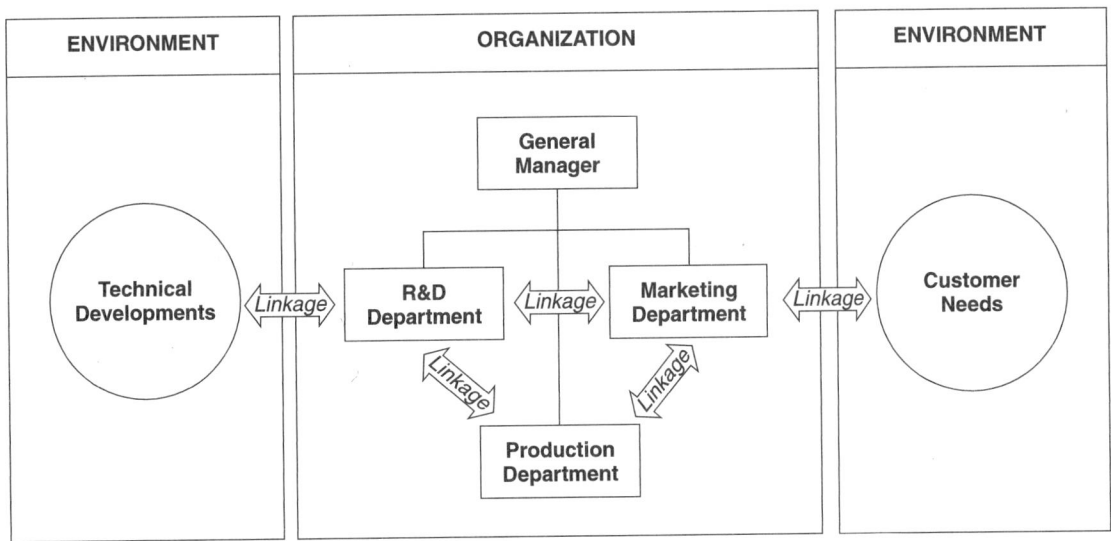

Horizontal Linkage Model

The organization design for achieving new product innovation involves three components—departmental specialization, boundary spanning, and horizontal linkages. These components are similar to the information linkage mechanisms and the differentiation and integration ideas. Exhibit 100.63 illustrates these components in the **horizontal linkage model.**

DEPARTMENTAL SPECIALIZATION   The key departments in new product development are R&D, marketing, and production. The specialization component means that the personnel in all three of these departments are highly competent at their own tasks. The three departments are differentiated from each other and have skills, goals, and attitudes appropriate for their specialized functions.

BOUNDARY SPANNING   This component means each department involved with new products has excellent linkage with relevant sectors in the external environment. R&D personnel are linked to professional associations and to colleagues in other R&D departments. They are aware of recent scientific developments. Marketing personnel are closely linked to customer needs. They listen to what customers have to say, and they analyze competitor products and suggestions by distributors.

HORIZONTAL LINKAGES   This component means that technical, marketing, and production people share ideas and information. Research people inform marketing of new technical developments to learn whether the developments are applicable to customers. Marketing people provide customer complaints and information to R&D to use in the design of new products. People from both R&D and marketing coordinate with production because new products have to fit within production capabilities so costs are not exorbitant. The decision to launch a new product is ultimately a joint decision among all three departments.

   Companies are increasingly using cross-functional teams for product development to ensure a high level of communication and coordination from the beginning. The functional diversity increases both the amount and the variety of information for new product development, enabling the design of products that meet customer needs and circumventing manufacturing and marketing problems.[379] Kellogg has revised its approach to new product development to improve horizontal collaboration. For years, product development at Kellogg was the exclusive province of marketing, which came up with new ideas and then tossed them over the wall to manufacturing. Today, however, employees work in cross-functional teams, with market researchers alongside nutritionists, food scientists, production specialists, and engineers. So far, the approach seems to be working. The company is pumping out twice as many products annually, including some decided hits, such as Raisin Bran Crunch and Rice Krispies Treats, a snack-food version of the crunchy marshmallow squares.[380]

175. ORGANIZATION DESIGN AND DEVELOPMENT

Another critical issue is designing products that can compete on a global scale and successfully marketing those products internationally. Companies such as Quaker Oats, **Häagen Dazs,** and **Levi's** are trying to improve horizontal communication and collaboration across geographical regions, recognizing that they can pick up winning product ideas from customers in other countries.

Failing to pay attention to global horizontal linkages can hurt companies trying to compete internationally. When companies enter the arena of intense international competition, horizontal coordination across countries is essential to new product development.

Strategy and Structure Change

The preceding discussion focused on new production processes and products, which are based in the technology of an organization. The expertise for such innovation lies within the technical core and professional staff groups, such as research and engineering. This section turns to an examination of structural and strategy changes.

All organizations need to make changes in their strategies and structures from time to time. In the past, when the environment was relatively stable, most organizations focused on small, incremental changes to solve immediate problems or take advantage of new opportunities. However, over the past decade, companies throughout the world have faced the need to make radical changes in strategy, structure, and management processes to adapt to new competitive demands.[381] Many organizations are cutting out layers of management and decentralizing decision making. There is a strong shift toward more horizontal structures, with teams of front-line workers empowered to make decisions and solve problems on their own. Some companies are moving their entire business into cyberspace. Many others are reorganizing and shifting their strategies as the expansion of e-commerce changes the rules. For example, online banking, credit cards, and ATMs are affecting the role of branch banks. Global competition and rapid technological change will likely lead to even greater strategy-structure realignments over the next decade.

These types of changes are the responsibility of the organization's top managers, and the overall process of change is typically different from the process for innovation in technology or new products.

The Dual-Core Approach

The dual-core approach compares administrative and technical changes. Administrative changes pertain to the design and structure of the organization itself, including restructuring, downsizing, teams, control systems, information systems, and departmental grouping. Research into administrative change suggests two things. First, administrative changes occur less frequently than do technical changes. Second, administrative changes occur in response to different environmental sectors and follow a different internal process than do technology-based changes.[382] The **dual-core approach** to organizational change identifies the unique processes associated with administrative change.[383]

Organizations—schools, hospitals, city governments, welfare agencies, government bureaucracies, and many business firms—can be conceptualized as having two cores: a technical core and an administrative core. Each core has its own employees, tasks, and environmental domain. Innovation can originate in either core.

The administrative core is above the technical core in the hierarchy. The responsibility of the administrative core includes the structure, control, and co-ordination of the organization itself and concerns the environmental sectors of government, financial resources, economic conditions, human resources, and competitors. The technical core is concerned with the transformation of raw materials into organizational products and services and involves the environmental sectors of customers and technology.[384]

The findings from research comparing administrative and technical change suggest that a mechanistic organization structure is appropriate for frequent administrative changes, including changes in goals, strategy, structure, control systems, and personnel.[385] For example, administrative changes in policy, regulations, or control systems are more critical than technical changes in many government organizations that are bureaucratically structured. Organizations that successfully adopt many administrative changes often have a larger administrative ratio, are larger in size, and are centralized and formalized compared with organizations that adopt many technical changes.[386] The reason is the top-down implementation of changes in response to changes in the government, financial, or legal sectors of the environment. In contrast, if an organization has an organic structure, lower-level employees have more freedom and autonomy and, hence, may resist top-down initiatives. An organic structure is more often used when changes in organizational technology or products are important to the organization.

The innovation approaches associated with administrative versus technical change are summarized in Exhibit 100.64. Technical change, such as changes in production techniques and innovation technology for new products, is fa-

Exhibit 100.64 *Dual-Core Approach to Organization Change*

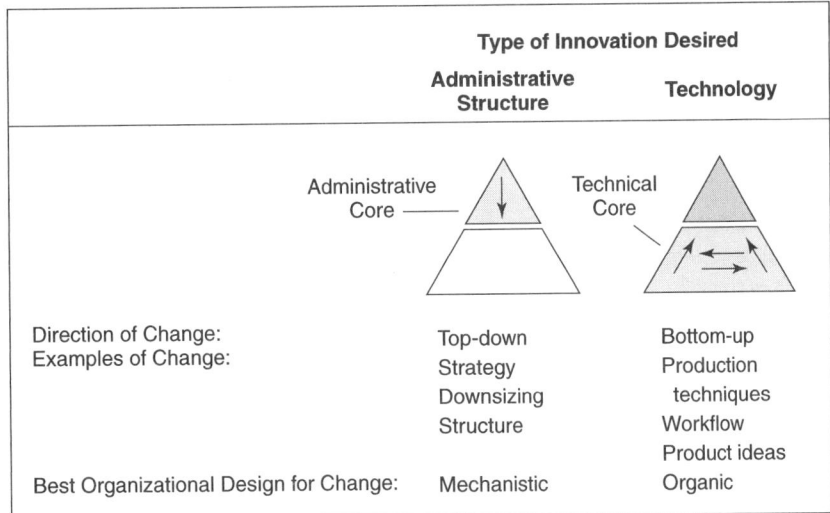

cilitated by an organic structure, which allows ideas to bubble upward from lower- and middle-level employees. Organizations that must adopt frequent administrative changes tend to use a top-down process and a mechanistic structure.

The point of the dual-core approach is that many organizations—especially not-for-profit and government organizations—must adopt frequent administrative changes, so a mechanistic structure may be appropriate. For example, research into civil service reform found that the implementation of administrative innovation was extremely difficult in organizations that had an organic technical core. The professional employees in a decentralized agency could resist civil service changes. By contrast, organizations that were considered more bureaucratic in the sense of high formalization and centralization adopted administrative changes readily.[387]

What about business organizations that are normally technologically innovative in bottom-up fashion but suddenly face a crisis and need to reorganize? Or consider a technically innovative, high-tech firm that must reorganize frequently or must suddenly cut back to accommodate changes in production technology or the environment. Technically innovative firms may suddenly have to restructure, reduce the number of employees, alter pay systems, disband teams, or form a new division.[388] The answer is to use a top-down change process. The authority for strategy and structure change lies with top management, who should initiate and implement the new strategy and structure to meet environmental circumstances. Employee input may be sought, but top managers have the responsibility to direct the change. *Downsizing, restructuring,* and *reorganizing* are common terms for what happens in times of rapid change and global competition. Often, strong top-down changes follow the installation of new top management.

Top managers should also remember that top-down change means initiation of the idea occurs at upper levels and is implemented downward. It does not mean that lower-level employees are not educated about the change or allowed to participate in it.

Culture Change

Organizations are made up of people and their relationships with one another. Changes in strategy, structure, technologies, and products do not happen on their own, and changes in any of these areas involve changes in people as well. Employees must learn how to use new technologies, or market new products, or work effectively in a team-based structure.

In a world where any organization can purchase new technology, the motivation, skill, and commitment of employees can provide the competitive edge. Human resource systems can be designed to attract, develop, and maintain an efficient force of employees.

Sometimes achieving a new way of thinking requires a focused change on the underlying corporate culture values and norms. In the last decade, numerous large corporations, including Kodak, IBM, and Ford Motor Company, have undertaken some type of culture-change initiative. Changing corporate culture fundamentally shifts how work is done in an organization and generally leads to renewed commitment and empowerment of employees and a stronger bond between the company and its customers.[389]

Two recent trends that generally lead to significant changes in corporate culture are reengineering and the implementation of total quality management programs, which require employees to think in new ways about how work is done. These trends are discussed in Module 400.

Organization development programs also focus on changing old culture values to new ways of thinking, including greater employee participation and empowerment and developing a shared companywide vision.

Organization Development

One method for bringing about significant culture change is known as **organization development (OD),** which focuses on the human and social aspects of the organization as a way to improve the organization's ability to adapt and solve problems. OD emphasizes the values of human development, fairness, openness, freedom from coercion, and individual autonomy that allows workers to perform the job as they see fit, within reasonable organizational constraints.[390] In the 1970s, OD evolved as a separate field that applied the behavioral sciences in a process of planned organizationwide change, with the goal of increasing organizational effectiveness. Organization development is not a step-by-step procedure to solve a specific problem but a process of fundamental change in the human and social systems of the organization, including organizational culture.[391]

OD uses knowledge and techniques from the behavioral sciences to improve performance through increased trust, open confrontation of problems, employee empowerment and participation, knowledge and information sharing, the design of meaningful work, cooperation and collaboration between groups, and the full use of human potential.

OD practitioners believe the best performance occurs by breaking down hierarchical and authoritarian approaches to management. However research has shown that the OD approach may not enhance performance or satisfaction in stable business environments and for routine tasks.[392] It is best for organizations that are facing environmental and technological discontinuities and rapid change.

Changing organizational culture is not easy, but organization development techniques can smooth the process. For example, OD can help managers and employees think in new ways about human relationships, making the transition to more participative management less stressful.

OD Culture Change Interventions

OD interventions involve training of specific groups or of everyone in the organization. For OD intervention to be successful, senior management in the organization must see the need for OD and provide enthusiastic support for the change. Techniques used by many organizations for improving people skills through OD include the following.

LARGE-GROUP INTERVENTION Most early OD activities involved small groups and focused on incremental change. However, in recent years, there has been growing interest in the application of OD techniques to large-group settings, which are more attuned to bringing about radical or transformational change in organizations operating in complex environments.[393] The **large-group intervention** approach[394] brings together participants from all parts of the organization—often including key stakeholders from outside the organization as well—in an off-site setting to discuss problems or opportunities and plan for change. A large-group intervention might involve fifty to five hundred people and last for several days. The off-site setting limits interference and distractions, enabling participants to focus on new ways of doing things.

TEAM BUILDING Team building promotes the idea that people who work together can work as a team. A work team can be brought together to discuss conflicts, goals, the decision-making process, communication, creativity, and leadership. The team can then plan to overcome problems and improve results. Team-building activities are also used in many companies to train task forces, committees, and new product development groups. These activities enhance communication and collaboration and strengthen the cohesiveness of organizational groups and teams.

INTERDEPARTMENTAL ACTIVITIES Representatives from different departments are brought together in a mutual location to surface conflict, diagnose its causes, and plan improvement in communication and coordination. This type of intervention has been applied to union–management conflict, headquarters–field office conflict, interdepartmental conflict, and mergers.[395]

In today's world, the workforce is becoming more and more diverse, and organizations are constantly adapting to environmental uncertainty and increasing international competition. OD interventions can respond to these new realities as organizations strive to create greater capability for change and growth.[396]

Strategies for Implementing Change

In this section, we are going to briefly discuss resistance to change at the organizational level, and some techniques managers can use to implement change.

Resistance to Change

Managers should expect to encounter resistance as they attempt to implement changes. It is natural for people to resist change, and many barriers to change exist at the individual and organizational level.[397]

1. *Excessive focus on costs.* Management may possess the mind-set that costs are all-important and may fail to appreciate the importance of a change that is not focused on costs—for example, a change to increase employee motivation or customer satisfaction.
2. *Failure to perceive benefits.* Any significant change will produce both positive and negative reactions. Education may be needed to help managers and employees perceive more positive than negative aspects of the change. In addition, if the organization's reward system discourages risk-taking, a change process may falter because employees think that the risk of making the change is too high.
3. *Lack of coordination and cooperation.* Organizational fragmentation and conflict often result from the lack of coordination for change implementation. Moreover, in the case of new technology, the old and new systems must be compatible.
4. *Uncertainty avoidance.* At the individual level, many employees fear the uncertainty associated with change. Constant communication is needed so that employees know what is going on and understand how it impacts their jobs.
5. *Fear of loss.* Managers and employees may fear the loss of power and status or even their jobs. In these cases, implementation should be careful and incremental, and all employees should be involved as closely as possible in the change process.

Implementation can typically be designed to overcome many of the organizational and individual barriers to change.

Techniques to Implement Change

Managers and employees throughout the organization are involved in the process of change. There are a number of techniques that can be used to successfully implement change.

1. *Identify a true need for change.* A careful diagnosis of the existing situation is necessary to determine the extent of the problem or opportunity. If the people affected by the change do not agree with a problem, the change process should not proceed without further analysis and communication among all employees.
2. *Find an idea that fits the need.* Finding the right idea often involves search procedures—talking with other managers, assigning a task force to investigate the problem, sending out a request to suppliers, or asking creative people within the organization to develop a solution. The creation of a new idea requires organic conditions. This is a good opportunity to encourage employee participation, because they need the freedom to think about and explore new options.[398]
3. *Get top management support.* Successful change requires the support of top management. Top managers should articulate clear innovation goals. For a single large change, such as a structural reorganization, the president and vice presidents must give their blessing and support. For smaller changes, the support of influential managers in relevant departments is required. The lack of top management support is one of the most frequent causes of implementation failure.[399]
4. *Design the change for incremental implementation.* Sometimes large changes cannot be implemented all at once or employees may feel overwhelmed and resist the change. When a large bank in South Carolina installed a complete new $6 million system to computerize processing, it was stunned that the system didn't work very well. The prospect for success of such a large change is improved if the change can be broken into subparts and each part adopted sequentially. Then designers can make adjustments to improve the innovation, and hesitant users who see success can throw support behind the rest of the change program.

5. *Develop plans to overcome resistance to change.* Many good ideas are never used because managers failed to anticipate or prepare for resistance to change by consumers, employees, or other managers. No matter how impressive the performance characteristics of an innovation, its implementation will conflict with some interests and jeopardize some alliances in the organization. To increase the chance of successful implementation, management must acknowledge the conflict, threats, and potential losses perceived by employees. Several strategies can be used by managers to overcome the resistance problem:

   - *Alignment with needs and goals of users.* The best strategy for overcoming resistance is to make sure change meets a real need. Employees in R&D often come up with great ideas that solve nonexistent problems. This happens because initiators fail to consult with the people who use a change. Resistance can be frustrating for managers, but moderate resistance to change is good for an organization. Resistance provides a barrier to frivolous changes or to change for the sake of change. The process of overcoming resistance to change normally requires that the change be good for its users.

   - *Communication and training.* Communication informs users about the need for change and about the consequences of a proposed change, preventing false rumors, misunderstanding, and resentment. In one study of change efforts, the most commonly cited reason for failure was that employees learned of the change from outsiders. Top managers concentrated on communicating with the public and with shareholders, but failed to communicate with the people who would be most intimately involved and most affected by the changes—their own employees.[400] Open communication often gives management an opportunity to explain what steps will be taken to ensure that the change will have no adverse consequences for employees. Training is also needed to help employees understand and cope with their role in the change process.

   - *Participation and involvement.* Early and extensive participation in a change should be part of implementation. Participation gives those involved a sense of control over the change activity. They understand it better, and they become committed to successful implementation. One recent study of the implementation and adoption of computer technology at two companies showed a much smoother implementation process at the company that introduced the new technology using a participatory approach.[401] The team-building and large-group intervention activities described earlier can be effective ways to involve employees in a change process.

   - *Forcing and coercion.* As a last resort, managers may overcome resistance by threatening employees with loss of jobs or promotions or by firing or transferring them. In other words, management power is used to overwhelm resistance. In most cases, this approach is not advisable because it leaves people angry at change managers, and the change may be sabotaged. However, this technique may be needed when speed is essential, such as when the organization faces a crisis. It may also be required for needed administrative changes that flow from the top down, such as downsizing the work force.[402]

6. *Create change teams.* Throughout, this section has discussed the need for resources and energy to make change happen. Separate creative departments, new venture groups, or an ad hoc team or task force are ways to focus energy on both creation and implementation. A separate department has the freedom to create a new technology that fits a genuine need. A task force can be created to see that implementation is completed. The task force can be responsible for communication, involvement of users, training, and other activities needed for change.

7. *Foster idea champions.* One of the most effective weapons in the battle for change is the idea champion. The most effective champion is a volunteer champion who is deeply committed to a new idea. The idea champion sees that all technical activities are correct and complete. An additional champion, such as a manager sponsor, may also be needed to persuade people about implementation, even using coercion if necessary.

Organizational Conflict, Power, and Politics

All organizations are a complex mix of individuals and groups pursuing various goals and interests. Conflict is a natural and inevitable outcome of the close interaction of people who may have diverse opinions and values, pursue different objectives, and have differential access to information and resources within the organization. Individuals and groups will use power and political activity to handle their differences and manage conflict.[403]

Too much conflict can be harmful to an organization. However, conflict can also be a positive force because it challenges the status quo, encourages new ideas and approaches, and leads to change.[404] Some degree of conflict occurs in all human relationships—between friends, romantic partners, and teammates as well as between parents and children, teachers and students, and bosses and employees. Conflict is not necessarily a negative force; it results from the normal interaction of varying human interests. Within organizations, individuals and groups frequently have different interests and goals they wish to achieve through the organization. Managers in all organizations regularly deal with conflict and struggle with decisions about how to get the most out of employees, enhance job satisfaction and team identification, and realize high organizational performance.

What Is Intergroup Conflict?

Intergroup conflict requires three ingredients: group identification, observable group differences, and frustration. First, employees have to perceive themselves as part of an identifiable group or department.[405] Second, there has to be an observable group difference of some form. Groups may be located on different floors of the building, members may have gone to different schools, or members may work in different departments. The ability to identify oneself as a part of one group and to observe differences in comparison with other groups is necessary for conflict.[406]

The third ingredient is frustration. Frustration means that if one group achieves its goal, the other will not; it will be blocked. Frustration need not be severe and only needs to be anticipated to set off intergroup conflict. Intergroup conflict will appear when one group tries to advance its position in relation to other groups. **Intergroup conflict** can be defined as the behavior that occurs among organizational groups when participants identify with one group and perceive that other groups may block their group's goal achievement or expectations.[407] Conflict means that groups clash directly, that they are in fundamental opposition. Conflict is similar to competition but more severe. **Competition** means rivalry among groups in the pursuit of a common prize, while conflict presumes direct interference with goal achievement.

Intergroup conflict within organizations can occur horizontally—across departments—or vertically—between different levels of the organization.[408] For example, the production department of a manufacturing company may have a dispute with quality control because new quality procedures reduce production efficiency. Teammates may argue about the best way to accomplish tasks and achieve goals. Workers may clash with bosses about new work methods, reward systems, or job assignments. Another typical source of conflict is between groups such as unions and management or franchise owners and headquarters.

Why Conflict Exists

Some specific organizational characteristics can generate conflict. These **sources of intergroup conflict** are goal incompatibility, differentiation, task interdependence, and limited resources, as illustrated in Exhibit 100.65. These characteristics of organizational relationships are determined by the contextual factors of environment, size, technology, strategy and goals, and organizational structure, which have been discussed in previous chapters. These characteristics, in turn, help shape the extent to which a rational model of behavior versus a political model of behavior is used to accomplish objectives.

Exhibit 100.65 *Sources of Conflict and Use of Rational versus Political Model*

Sources of Potential Intergroup Conflict	When Conflict Is Low, Rational Model Describes Organization		When Conflict Is High, Political Model Describes Organization
• Goal incompatibility • Differentiation • Task interdependence • Limited resources	Consistent across participants	Goals	Inconsistent, pluralistic within the organization
	Centralized	Power and control	Decentralized, shifting coalitions and interest groups
	Orderly, logical, rational	Decision process	Disorderly, result of bargaining and interplay among interests
	Norm of efficiency	Rules and norms	Free play of market forces; conflict is legitimate and expected
	Extensive, systematic, accurate	Information	Ambiguous; information used and withheld strategically

175. ORGANIZATION DESIGN AND DEVELOPMENT

GOAL INCOMPATIBILITY Goal incompatibility is probably the greatest cause of intergroup conflict in organizations.[409] The goals of each department reflect the specific objectives members are trying to achieve. The achievement of one department's goals often interferes with another department's goals. University police, for example, have a goal of providing a safe and secure campus. They can achieve their goal by locking all buildings on evenings and weekends and not distributing keys. Without easy access to buildings, however, progress toward the science department's research goals will proceed slowly. On the other hand, if scientists come and go at all hours and security is ignored, police goals for security will not be met. Goal incompatibility throws the departments into conflict with each other.

DIFFERENTIATION Differentiation was defined as "the differences in cognitive and emotional orientations among managers in different functional departments." Functional specialization requires people with specific education, skills, attitudes, and time horizons. For example, people may join a sales department because they have ability and aptitude consistent with sales work. After becoming members of the sales department, they are influenced by departmental norms and values. Departments or divisions within an organization often differ in values, attitudes, and standards of behavior, and these cultural differences lead to conflicts.[410] Cultural differences can be particularly acute in the case of mergers or acquisitions. Employees in the acquired company may have completely different work styles and attitudes, and a "we against them" attitude can develop. One reason for the failure of many mergers is that although managers can integrate financial and production technologies, they have difficulty integrating the unwritten norms and values that have an even greater impact on company success.[411]

TASK INTERDEPENDENCE Task interdependence refers to the dependence of one unit on another for materials, resources, or information. Pooled interdependence means little interaction; sequential interdependence means the output of one department goes to the next department; and reciprocal interdependence means departments mutually exchange materials and information.[412]

Generally, as interdependence increases, the potential for conflict increases.[413] In the case of pooled interdependence, units have little need to interact. Conflict is at a minimum. Sequential and reciprocal interdependence require employees to spend time coordinating and sharing information. Employees must communicate frequently, and differences in goals or attitudes will surface. Conflict is especially likely to occur when agreement is not reached about the coordination of services to each other. Greater interdependence means departments often exert pressure for a fast response because departmental work has to wait on other departments.[414]

LIMITED RESOURCES Another major source of conflict involves competition between groups for what members perceive as limited resources.[415] Organizations have limited money, physical facilities, staff resources, and human resources to share among departments. In their desire to achieve goals, groups want to increase their resources. This throws them into conflict. Managers may develop strategies, such as inflating budget requirements or working behind the scenes, to obtain a desired level of resources. Resources also symbolize power and influence within an organization. The ability to obtain resources enhances prestige. Departments typically believe they have a legitimate claim on additional resources. However, exercising that claim results in conflict. For example, in almost every organization, conflict occurs during the annual budget exercise, often creating political activity.

RATIONAL VERSUS POLITICAL MODEL The degree of goal incompatibility, differentiation, interdependence, and conflict over limited resources determines whether a rational or political model of behavior is used within the organization to accomplish goals. When goals are in alignment, there is little differentiation, departments are characterized by pooled interdependence, and resources seem abundant, managers can use a **rational model** of organization, as outlined in Exhibit 100.65. As with the rational approach to decision making, the rational model of organization is an "ideal" that is not fully achievable in the real world, though managers strive to use rational processes whenever possible. In the rational organization, behavior is not random or accidental. Goals are clear and choices are made in a logical way. When a decision is needed, the goal is defined, alternatives are identified, and the choice with the highest probability of success is selected. The rational model is also characterized by centralized power and control, extensive information systems, and an efficiency orientation.[416] The opposite view of organizational processes is the **political model**, also described in Exhibit 100.65. When differences are great, organization groups have separate interests, goals, and values. Disagreement and conflict are normal, so power and influence are needed to reach decisions. Groups will engage in the push and pull of debate to decide goals and reach decisions. Information is ambiguous and incomplete. The political model particularly describes organizations that strive for democracy and participation in decision making by empowering workers. Purely rational procedures do not work in democratic organizations, such as learning organizations.

Both rational and political processes are normally used in organizations. In most organizations, neither the rational model nor the political model characterizes things fully, but each will be used some of the time. Managers may strive to adopt rational procedures but will find that politics is needed to accomplish objectives. The political model means managers learn to acquire, develop, and use power to accomplish objectives.

Individual versus Organizational Power

In popular literature, power is often described as a personal characteristic, and a frequent topic is how one person can influence or dominate another person. You probably recall that managers have five sources of personal power.[417] *Legitimate power* is the authority granted by the organization to the formal management position a manager holds. *Reward power* stems from the ability to bestow rewards—promotion, raise, pat on the back—to other people. The authority to punish or recommend punishment is called *coercive power*. *Expert power* derives from a person's higher skill or knowledge about the tasks being performed. The last one, *referent power*, derives from personal characteristics such that people admire the manager and want to be like or identify with the manager out of respect and admiration. Each of these sources may be used by individuals within organizations.

Power in organizations, however, is often the result of structural characteristics.[418] Organizations are large, complex systems that contain hundreds, even thousands, of people. These systems have a formal hierarchy in which some tasks are more important regardless of who performs them. In addition, some positions have access to greater resources, or their contribution to the organization is more critical. Thus, the important power processes in organizations reflect larger organizational relationships, both horizontal and vertical, and organizational power usually is vested in the position, not in the person.

Power versus Authority

Power is an intangible force in organizations. It cannot be seen, but its effect can be felt. Power is often defined as the potential ability of one person (or department) to influence other persons (or departments) to carry out orders[419] or to do something they would not otherwise have done.[420] Other definitions stress that power is the ability to achieve goals or outcomes that power holders desire.[421] The achievement of desired outcomes is the basis of the definition used here: **Power** is the ability of one person or department in an organization to influence other people to bring about desired outcomes. It is the potential to influence others within the organization but with the goal of attaining desired outcomes for power holders.

Power exists only in a relationship between two or more people, and it can be exercised in either vertical or horizontal directions. The source of power often derives from an exchange relationship in which one position or department provides scarce or valued resources to other departments. When one person is dependent on another person, a power relationship emerges in which the person with the resources has greater power.[422] When power exists in a relationship, the power holders can achieve compliance with their requests. For example, the following outcomes are indicators of power in an organization:

- Obtain a larger increase in budget than other departments.
- Obtain above-average salary increases for subordinates.
- Obtain production schedules that are favorable to your department.
- Get items on the agenda at policy meetings.[423]

The concept of formal authority is related to power but is narrower in scope. **Authority** is also a force for achieving desired outcomes, but only as prescribed by the formal hierarchy and reporting relationships. Three properties identify authority:

1. *Authority is vested in organizational positions.* People have authority because of the positions they hold, not because of personal characteristics or resources.
2. *Authority is accepted by subordinates.* Subordinates comply because they believe position holders have a legitimate right to exercise authority.[424]
3. *Authority flows down the vertical hierarchy.*[425] Authority exists along the formal chain of command, and positions at the top of the hierarchy are vested with more formal authority than are positions at the bottom.

Organizational power can be exercised upward, downward, and horizontally in organizations. Formal authority is exercised downward along the hierarchy and is the same as vertical power and legitimate power. In the following sections, we will examine vertical and horizontal sources of power for employees throughout the organization.

Vertical Sources of Power

All employees along the vertical hierarchy have access to some sources of power. Although a large amount of power is typically allocated to top managers by the organization structure, employees throughout the organization often obtain power disproportionate to their formal positions and can exert influence in an upward direction. Three sources of vertical power are formal position, resources, and network centrality.[426]

FORMAL POSITION Certain rights, responsibilities, and prerogatives accrue to top positions. People throughout the organization accept the legitimate right of top managers to set goals, make decisions, and direct activities. Thus, the power from formal position is sometimes called legitimate power.[427] Senior managers often use symbols and language to perpetuate their legitimate power. Reserving the top floor for senior executives, for example, is a way to communicate legitimate authority to others in the organization.

The amount of power provided to middle managers and lower-level participants can be built into the organization's structural design. The allocation of power to middle managers and staff is important because power enables employees to be productive. When job tasks are nonroutine, and when employees participate in self-directed teams and problem-solving task forces, this encourages employees to be flexible and creative and to use their own discretion. Allowing people to make their own decisions increases their power. Power is also increased when a position encourages contact with high-level people. Access to powerful people and the development of a relationship with them provide a strong base of influence.[428] For example, in some organizations a secretary to the vice-president has more power than a department head because the secretary has access to the senior executive on a daily basis.

The logic of designing positions for more power assumes that an organization does not have a limited amount of power to be allocated among high-level and low-level employees. The total amount of power in an organization can be increased by designing tasks and interactions along the hierarchy so everyone has more influence. If the distribution of power is skewed too heavily toward the top, research suggests the organization will be less effective.[429]

RESOURCES Organizations allocate huge amounts of resources. Buildings are constructed, salaries are paid, and equipment and supplies are purchased. Each year, new resources are allocated in the form of budgets. These resources are allocated downward from top managers. Top managers often own stock, which gives them property rights over resource allocation. However, in many of today's organizations, employees throughout the organization also share in ownership, which increases their power. At St. Luke's, a London advertising agency, the company is owned entirely by its employees, from the CEO down to the janitors.

In most cases, top managers control the resources and, hence, can determine their distribution. Resources can be used as rewards and punishments, which are also sources of power. Resource allocation also creates a dependency relationship. Lower-level participants depend on top managers for the financial and physical resources needed to perform their tasks. Top management can exchange resources in the form of salaries, personnel, promotion, and physical facilities for compliance with the outcomes they desire.

NETWORK CENTRALITY **Network centrality** means being centrally located in the organization and having access to information and people that are critical to the company's success. Top executives often increase their power by surrounding themselves with a network of loyal subordinates and using the network to learn about events throughout the organization.[430] They can use their central positions to build alliances and wield substantial power in the organization.

Middle managers and lower-level employees have more power when their jobs are related to current areas of concern or opportunity. When a job pertains to pressing organizational problems, power is more easily accumulated. David Shoenfeld, who is now senior vice-president for worldwide marketing, customer service, and corporate communications at **FedEx**, increased his power by being central to solving an organizational problem. When pilots threatened to go on strike, Shoenfeld believed the best approach was to warn customers up front on the company's Web site. The strike that had crippled archrival **UPS** had warned FedEx managers about the dangers of letting customers be caught by surprise. Shoenfeld's idea of openly sharing information with customers on a regular basis through a daily "Pilot Negotiation Update" helped FedEx maintain the trust of its customers.[431] Lower-level employees may also increase their network centrality by becoming knowledgeable and expert about certain activities or by taking on difficult tasks and acquiring specialized knowledge that makes them indispensable to managers above them. People who show initiative, work beyond what is expected, take on undesirable but important projects, and show interest in learning about the company and industry often find themselves with influence. Physical location also helps because some locations are in the center of things. Central location lets a person be visible to key people and become part of important interaction networks.

Horizontal Sources of Power

Horizontal power pertains to relationships across departments. All vice-presidents are usually at the same level on the organization chart. Does this mean each department has the same amount of power? No. Horizontal power is not defined by the formal hierarchy or the organization chart. Each department makes a unique contribution to organizational success. Some departments will have greater say and will achieve their desired outcomes, whereas others will not. For example, Charles Perrow surveyed managers in several industrial firms.[432] He bluntly asked, "Which department has the most power?" among four major departments: production, sales and marketing, research and development, and finance and accounting. In most firms, sales had the greatest power. In a few firms, production was also quite powerful. On average, the sales and production departments were more powerful than R&D and finance, although substantial variation existed. Differences in the amount of horizontal power clearly occurred in those firms. Today, e-commerce departments and information services departments have growing power in many organizations.

Horizontal power is difficult to measure because power differences are not defined on the organization chart. The theoretical concept that explains relative power is called strategic contingencies.[433]

Strategic Contingencies

Strategic contingencies are events and activities both inside and outside an organization that are essential for attaining organizational goals. Departments involved with strategic contingencies for the organization tend to have greater power. Departmental activities are important when they provide strategic value by solving problems or crises for the organization. For example, if an organization faces an intense threat from lawsuits and regulations, the legal department will gain power and influence over organizational decisions because it copes with such a threat. If product innovation is the key strategic issue, the power of R&D can be expected to be high.

The strategic contingency approach to power is similar to the resource dependence model. Recall that organizations try to reduce dependency on the external environment. The strategic contingency approach to power suggests that the departments most responsible for dealing with key resource issues and dependencies in the environment will become most powerful.

Power Sources

Jeffrey Pfeffer and Gerald Salancik, among others, have been instrumental in conducting research on the strategic contingency theory.[434] Their findings indicate that a department rated as powerful may possess one or more of the characteristics illustrated in Exhibit 100.66.[435] In some organizations these five **power sources** overlap, but each provides a useful way to evaluate sources of horizontal power.

DEPENDENCY Interdepartmental dependency is a key element underlying relative power. Power is derived from having something someone else wants. The power of department A over department B is greater when department B depends on A.[436]

Many dependencies exist in organizations. Materials, information, and resources may flow between departments in one direction, such as in the case of sequential task interdependence. In such cases, the department receiving resources is in a lower power position than the department providing them. The number and strength of dependencies are also important. When seven or eight departments must come for help to the engineering department, for example, engineering is in a strong power position. In contrast, a department that depends on many other departments is in a low power position.

In a cigarette factory, one might expect that the production department would be more powerful than the maintenance department, but this was not the case in a cigarette plant near Paris.[437] The production of cigarettes was a routine process. The machinery was automated and production jobs were small in scope. Production workers were not highly skilled and were paid on a piece-rate basis to encourage high production. On the other hand, the maintenance department required skilled workers. These workers were responsible for repair of the automated machinery, which

Exhibit 100.66 *Strategic Contingencies That Influecne Horizontal Power Among Departments*

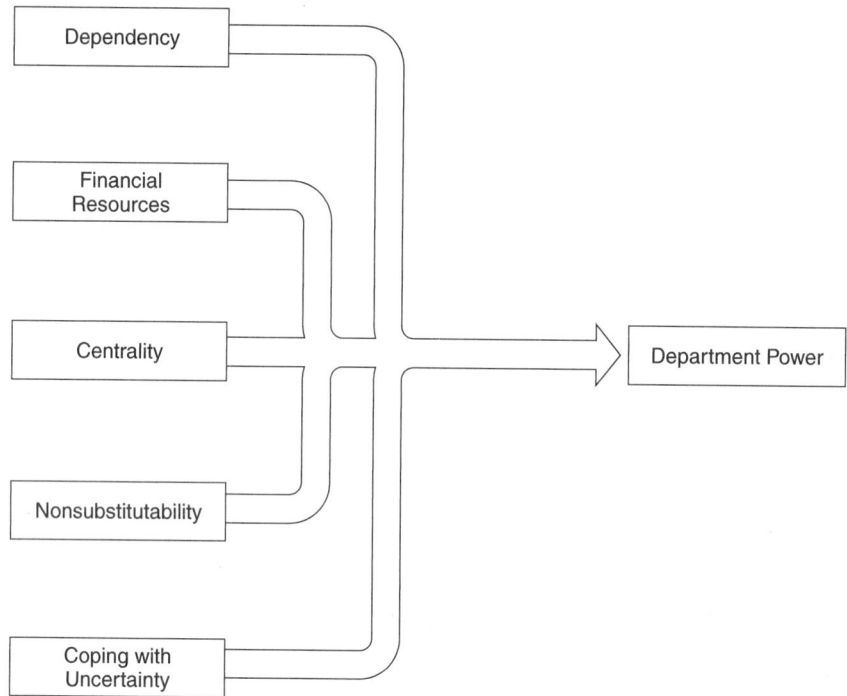

was a complex task. They had many years of experience. Maintenance was a craft because vital knowledge to fix machines was stored in the minds of maintenance personnel.

Dependency between the two groups was caused by unpredictable assembly line breakdowns. Managers could not remove the breakdown problem; consequently, maintenance was the vital cog in the production process. Maintenance workers had the knowledge and ability to fix the machines, so production managers became dependent on them. The reason for this dependence was that maintenance managers had control over a strategic contingency—they had the knowledge and ability to prevent or resolve work stoppages.

FINANCIAL RESOURCES Control over various kinds of resources, and particularly financial resources, is an important source of power in organizations. Money can be converted into other kinds of resources that are needed by other departments. Money generates dependency; departments that provide financial resources have something other departments want. Departments that generate income for an organization have greater power. The survey of industrial firms reported that sales as the most powerful unit in most of those firms. Sales had power because salespeople find customers and sell the product, thereby removing an important problem for the organization. The sales department ensures the inflow of money.

Power accrues to departments that bring in or provide resources that are highly valued by an organization. Power enables those departments to obtain more of the scarce resources allocated within the organization. "Power derived from acquiring resources is used to obtain more resources, which in turn can be employed to produce more power—the rich get richer."[438]

CENTRALITY **Centrality** reflects a department's role in the primary activity of an organization.[439] One measure of centrality is the extent to which the work of the department affects the final output of the organization. For example, the production department is more central and usually has more power than staff groups (assuming no other critical contingencies). Centrality is associated with power because it reflects the contribution made to the organization. The corporate finance department of an investment bank generally has more power than the stock research department. By contrast, in the manufacturing firms, finance tends to be low in power. When the finance department has the limited task of recording money and expenditures, it is not responsible for obtaining critical resources or for producing the products of the organization.

NONSUBSTITUTABILITY Power is also determined by **nonsubstitutability,** which means that a department's function cannot be performed by other readily available resources. Nonsubstitutability increases power. If an employee cannot be easily replaced, his or her power is greater. If an organization has no alternative sources of skill and information, a department's power will be greater. This can be the case when management uses outside consultants. Consultants might be used as substitutes for staff people to reduce the power of staff groups.

The impact of substitutability on power was studied for programmers in computer departments.[440] When computers were first introduced, programming was a rare and specialized occupation. People had to be highly qualified to enter the profession. Programmers controlled the use of organizational computers because they alone possessed the knowledge to program them. Over a period of about ten years, computer programming became a more common activity. People could be substituted easily, and the power of programming departments dropped.

COPING WITH UNCERTAINTY The sections on environment and decision making described how elements in the environment can change swiftly and can be unpredictable and complex. In the face of uncertainty, little information is available to managers on appropriate courses of action. Departments that cope with this uncertainty will increase their power.[441] Just the presence of uncertainty does not provide power; reducing the uncertainty on behalf of other departments will. When market research personnel accurately predict changes in demand for new products, they gain power and prestige because they have reduced a critical uncertainty. Forecasting is only one technique for **coping with uncertainty.** Sometimes uncertainty can be reduced by taking quick and appropriate action after an unpredictable event occurs.

Three techniques that departments can use to cope with critical uncertainties are (1) obtaining prior information, (2) prevention, and (3) absorption.[442] *Obtaining prior information* means a department can reduce an organization's uncertainty by forecasting an event. Departments increase their power through *prevention* by predicting and forestalling negative events. *Absorption* occurs when a department takes action after an event to reduce its negative consequences.

Horizontal power relationships in organizations change as strategic contingencies change. For example, in recent years, giant retailers such as Wal-Mart and **Winn-Dixie** have increased their power over magazine publishers by refusing to sell issues that contain cover photos or stories that might be objectionable to some customers. Some magazine publishers have agreed to provide advance copies so retailers can spot controversial material ahead of time and decline the issue.

Political Processes in Organizations

Politics, like power, is intangible and difficult to measure. It is hidden from view and is hard to observe in a systematic way. Two surveys uncovered the following reactions of managers toward political behavior:[443]

1. Most managers have a negative view toward politics and believe that politics will more often hurt than help an organization in achieving its goals.
2. Managers believe political behavior is common to practically all organizations.
3. Most managers think political behavior occurs more often at upper rather than lower levels in organizations.
4. Political behavior arises in certain decision domains, such as structural change, but is absent from other decisions, such as handling employee grievances.

Based on these surveys, politics seems more likely to occur at the top levels of an organization and around certain issues and decisions. Moreover, managers do not approve of political behavior. The remainder of this section explores more fully what is political behavior, when it should be used, the type of issues and decisions most likely to be associated with politics, and some political tactics that may be effective.

Definition

Power has been described as the available force or potential for achieving desired outcomes. *Politics* is the use of power to influence decisions in order to achieve those outcomes. The exercise of power and influence has led to two ways to define politics—as self-serving behavior or as a natural organizational decision process. The first definition emphasizes that politics is self-serving and involves activities that are not sanctioned by the organization.[444]

In this view, politics involves deception and dishonesty for purposes of individual self-interest and leads to conflict and disharmony within the work environment. This dark view of politics is widely held by laypeople. Recent studies have shown that workers who perceive this kind of political activity at work within their companies often have related feelings of anxiety and job dissatisfaction. Studies also support the belief that inappropriate use of politics is related to low employee morale, inferior organizational performance, and poor decision making.[445] This view of politics explains why managers in the surveys described above did not approve of political behavior.

Although politics can be used in a negative, self-serving way, the appropriate use of political behavior can serve organizational goals.[446] The second view sees politics as a natural organizational process for resolving differences among organizational interest groups.[447] Politics is the process of bargaining and negotiation that is used to overcome conflicts and differences of opinion. In this view, politics is very similar to the coalition-building decision processes.

The organization theory perspective views politics as described in the second definition—as a normal decision-making process. Politics is simply the activity through which power is exercised in the resolution of conflicts and uncertainty. Politics is neutral and is not necessarily harmful to the organization. The formal definition of organizational politics is as follows: **organizational politics** involves activities to acquire, develop, and use power and other resources to obtain the preferred outcome when there is uncertainty or disagreement about choices.[448]

Political behavior can be either a positive or a negative force. Politics is the use of power to get things accomplished—good things as well as bad. Uncertainty and conflict are natural and inevitable, and politics is the mechanism for reaching agreement. Politics includes informal discussions that enable participants to arrive at consensus and make decisions that otherwise might be stalemated or unsolvable.

When Is Political Activity Used?

Politics is a mechanism for arriving at consensus when uncertainty is high and there is disagreement over goals or problem priorities. Recall the rational versus political models described in Exhibit 100.65. The political model is associated with conflict over goals, shifting coalitions and interest groups, ambiguous information, and uncertainty. Thus, political activity tends to be most visible when managers confront nonprogrammed decisions, and is related to the Carnegie model of decision making. Because managers at the top of an organization generally deal with more nonprogrammed decisions than do managers at lower levels, more political activity will appear. Moreover, some issues are associated with inherent disagreement. Resources, for example, are critical for the survival and effectiveness of departments, so resource allocation often becomes a political issue. "Rational" methods of allocation do not satisfy participants. Three **domains of political activity** (areas in which politics plays a role) in most organizations are structural change, management succession, and resource allocation.

Structural reorganizations strike at the heart of power and authority relationships. Reorganizations change responsibilities and tasks, which also affects the underlying power base from strategic contingencies. For these reasons, a major reorganization can lead to an explosion of political activity.[449] Managers may actively bargain and negotiate to maintain the responsibilities and power bases they have.

Organizational changes such as hiring new executives, promotions, and transfers have great political significance, particularly at top organizational levels where uncertainty is high and networks of trust, cooperation, and communication among executives are important.[450] Hiring decisions can generate uncertainty, discussion, and disagreement. Managers can use hiring and promotion to strengthen network alliances and coalitions by putting their own people in prominent positions.

The third area of political activity is resource allocation. Resource allocation decisions encompass all resources required for organizational performance, including salaries, operating budgets, employees, office facilities, equipment, use of the company airplane, and so forth. Resources are so vital that disagreement about priorities exists, and political processes help resolve the dilemmas.

Using Power, Politics, and Collaboration

One theme has been that power in organizations is not primarily a phenomenon of the individual. It is related to the resources departments command, the role departments play in an organization, and the environmental contingencies with which departments cope. Position and responsibility more than personality and style determine a manager's influence on outcomes in the organization.

Power is used through individual political behavior, however. Individual managers seek agreement about a strategy to achieve their departments' desired outcomes. Individual managers negotiate decisions and adopt tactics that enable them to acquire and use power. In addition, managers develop ways to increase cooperation and collaboration within the organization to reduce damaging conflicts.

To fully understand the use of power within organizations, it is important to look at both structural components and individual behavior.[451] Although power comes from larger organizational forms and processes, the political use

Exhibit 100.67 *Power and Political Tactics in Organizations*

Tactics for Increasing the Power Base	Political Tactics for Using Power	Tactics for Enhancing Collaboration
1. Enter areas of high uncertainty	1. Build coalitions	1. Create integration devices
2. Create dependencies	2. Expand networks	2. Use confrontation and negotiation
3. Provide resources	3. Control decision premises	3. Schedule intergroup consultation
4. Satisfy strategic contingencies	4. Enhance legitimacy and expertise	4. Practice member rotation
	5. Make preferences explicit, but keep power implicit	5. Create superordinate goals

of power involves individual-level activities. This section briefly summarizes tactics that managers can use to increase the power base of their departments, political tactics they can use to achieve desired outcomes, and tactics for increasing collaboration. These tactics are summarized in Exhibit 100.67.

Tactics for Increasing the Power Base

Four **tactics for increasing power** are as follows:

1. *Enter areas of high uncertainty.* One source of departmental power is to cope with critical uncertainties.[452] If department managers can identify key uncertainties and take steps to remove those uncertainties, the department's power base will be enhanced. Uncertainties could arise from stoppages on an assembly line, from the needed quality of a new product, or from the inability to predict a demand for new services. Once an uncertainty is identified, the department can take action to cope with it. By their very nature, uncertain tasks will not be solved immediately. Trial and error will be needed, which is to the advantage of the department. The trial-and-error process provides experience and expertise that cannot easily be duplicated by other departments.

2. *Create dependencies.* Dependencies are another source of power.[453] When the organization depends on a department for information, materials, knowledge, or skills, that department will hold power over the others. This power can be increased by incurring obligations. Doing additional work that helps out other departments will obligate the other departments to respond at a future date. The power accumulated by creating a dependency can be used to resolve future disagreements in the department's favor. An equally effective and related strategy is to reduce dependency on other departments by acquiring necessary information or skills. For example, information technology departments have created dependencies in many organizations because of the rapid changes in this area. Employees in other departments depend on the information technology unit to master complex software programs, changing use of the Internet, and other advances so that they will have the information they need to perform effectively.

3. *Provide resources.* Resources are always important to organizational survival. Departments that accumulate resources and provide them to an organization in the form of money, information, or facilities will be powerful. For example, university departments with the greatest power are those that obtain external research funds for contributions to university overhead. Likewise, sales departments are powerful in industrial firms because they bring in financial resources.

4. *Satisfy strategic contingencies.* The theory of strategic contingencies says that some elements in the external environment and within the organization are especially important for organizational success. A contingency could be a critical event, a task for which there are no substitutes, or a central task that is interdependent with many others in the organization. An analysis of the organization and its changing environment will reveal strategic contingencies. To the extent that contingencies are new or are not being satisfied, there is room for a department to move into those critical areas and increase its importance and power.

In summary, the allocation of power in an organization is not random. Power is the result of organizational processes that can be understood and predicted. The abilities to reduce uncertainty, increase dependency on one's own department, obtain resources, and cope with strategic contingencies will all enhance a department's power. Once power is available, the next challenge is to use it to attain helpful outcomes.

Political Tactics for Using Power

The use of power in organizations requires both skill and willingness. Many decisions are made through political processes because rational decision processes do not fit. Uncertainty or disagreement is too high. **Political tactics for using power** to influence decision outcomes include the following:

1. *Build coalitions.* Coalition building means taking the time to talk with other managers to persuade them to your point of view.[454] Most important decisions are made outside formal meetings. Managers discuss issues with each other and reach agreements on a one-to-one basis. Effective managers are those who huddle, meeting in groups of twos and threes to resolve key issues.[455] An important aspect of coalition building is to build good relationships. Good interpersonal relationships are built on liking, trust, and respect. Reliability and the motivation to work with others rather than exploit others are part of coalition building.[456]

2. *Expand networks.* Networks can be expanded (1) by reaching out to establish contact with additional managers and (2) by co-opting dissenters. The first approach is to build new alliances through the hiring, transfer, and promotion process. Placing in key positions people who are sympathetic to the outcomes of the department can help achieve departmental goals.[457] On the other hand, the second approach, co-optation, is the act of bringing a dissenter into one's network. One example of co-optation involved a university committee whose membership was based on promotion and tenure. Several female professors who were critical of the tenure and promotion process were appointed to the committee. Once a part of the administrative process, they could see the administrative point of view and learned that administrators were not as evil as suspected. Co-optation effectively brought them into the administrative network.[458]

3. *Control decision premises.* To control decision premises means to constrain the boundaries of a decision. One technique is to choose or limit information provided to other managers. A common method is simply to put your department's best foot forward, such as selectively presenting favorable criteria. A variety of statistics can be assembled to support the departmental point of view. A university department that is growing rapidly and has a large number of students can make claims for additional resources by emphasizing its growth and large size. Such objective criteria do not always work, but they are a valuable step.

   Decision premises can be further influenced by limiting the decision process. Decisions can be influenced by the items put on an agenda for an important meeting or even by the sequence in which items are discussed.[459] Items discussed last, when time is short and people want to leave, will receive less attention than those discussed early. Calling attention to specific problems and suggesting alternatives also will affect outcomes. Stressing a specific problem to get it—rather than problems not relevant to your department—on the agenda is an example of agenda setting.

4. *Enhance legitimacy and expertise.* Managers can exert the greatest influence in areas in which they have recognized legitimacy and expertise. If a request is within the task domain of a department and is consistent with the department's vested interest, other departments will tend to comply. Members can also identify external consultants or other experts within the organization to support their cause.[460] For example, a financial vice-president in a large retail firm wanted to fire the director of human resource management. She hired a consultant to evaluate the human resource management projects undertaken to date. A negative report from the consultant provided sufficient legitimacy to fire the director, who was replaced with a director loyal to the financial vice-president.

5. *Make preferences explicit, but keep power implicit.* If managers do not ask, they seldom receive. Political activity is effective only when goals and needs are made explicit so the organization can respond. Managers should bargain aggressively and be persuasive. An assertive proposal may be accepted because other managers have no better alternatives. Moreover, an explicit proposal will often receive favorable treatment because other alternatives are ambiguous and less well defined. Effective political behavior requires sufficient forcefulness and risk taking to at least try to achieve desired outcomes.

   The use of power, however, should not be obvious.[461] If one formally draws upon his or her power base in a meeting by saying, "My department has more power, so the rest of you have to do it my way," the power will be diminished. Power works best when it is used quietly. To call attention to power is to lose it. Explicit claims for power are made by the powerless, not by the powerful. People know who has power. There is substantial agreement on which departments are more powerful. Explicit claims to power are not necessary and can even harm the department's cause.

When using any of the preceding tactics, recall that most people feel self-serving behavior hurts rather than helps an organization. If managers are perceived to be throwing their weight around or are perceived to be after things that are self-serving rather than beneficial to the organization, they will lose respect. On the other hand, managers must recognize the relational and political aspect of their work. It is not sufficient to be rational and technically competent. Politics is a way to reach agreement. When managers ignore political tactics, they may find themselves failing without understanding why.

Tactics for Enhancing Collaboration

Power and political tactics are important means for getting things done within organizations. Most organizations today have at least moderate interunit conflict. An additional approach in many organizations is to overcome conflict by stimulating cooperation and collaboration among departments to support the attainment of organizational goals. **Tactics for enhancing collaboration** include the following:

1. *Create integration devices.* Teams, task forces, and project managers who span the boundaries between departments can be used as integration devices. Bringing together representatives from conflicting departments in joint problem-solving teams is an effective way to enhance collaboration because representatives learn to understand each other's point of view.[462] Sometimes a full-time integrator is assigned to achieve cooperation and collaboration by meeting with members of the respective departments and exchanging information. The integrator has to understand each group's problems and must be able to move both groups toward a solution that is mutually acceptable.[463]

2. *Use confrontation and negotiation.* **Confrontation** occurs when parties in conflict directly engage one another and try to work out their differences. **Negotiation** is the bargaining process that often occurs during confrontation and that enables the parties to systematically reach a solution. These techniques bring appointed representatives from the departments together to work out a serious dispute.

   Confrontation and negotiation involve some risk. There is no guarantee that discussions will focus on a conflict or that emotions will not get out of hand. However, if members are able to resolve the conflict on the basis of face-to-face discussions, they will find new respect for each other, and future collaboration becomes easier. The beginnings of relatively permanent attitude change are possible through direct negotiation.

   Confrontation is successful when managers engage in a "win-win" strategy. Win-win means both departments adopt a positive attitude and strive to resolve the conflict in a way that will benefit each other.[464] If the negotiations deteriorate into a strictly win-lose strategy (each group wants to defeat the other), the confrontation will be ineffective. Top management can urge group members to work toward mutually acceptable outcomes. With a win-win strategy—which includes defining the problem as mutual, communicating openly, and avoiding threats—understanding can be changed while the dispute is resolved. With a win-lose strategy—which includes pursuing own group's outcomes, forcing the other group into submission, and using threats—understanding can be changed in favor of one party.

   One type of negotiation, used to resolve a disagreement between workers and management, is referred to as **collective bargaining.** The bargaining process is usually accomplished through a union and results in an agreement that specifies each party's responsibilities for the next two to three years.

3. *Schedule intergroup consultation.* When conflict is intense and enduring, and department members are suspicious and uncooperative, managers can bring in a third-party consultant to work with the groups. This process, sometimes called *workplace mediation,* is a strong intervention to reduce conflict because it involves bringing the disputing parties together and allowing each side to present its version of "reality." The technique has been developed by such psychologists as Robert Blake, Jane Mouton, and Richard Walton.[465]

   Department members attend a workshop, which may last for several days, away from day-to-day work problems. This approach is similar to the OD approach on innovation and change. The steps typically associated with an intergroup training session are as follows:

   a. The conflicting groups are brought into a training setting with the stated goal of exploring mutual perceptions and relationships.
   b. The conflicting groups are then separated, and each group is invited to discuss and make a list of its perceptions of itself and the other group.
   c. In the presence of both groups, group representatives publicly share the perceptions of self and other that the groups have generated, and the groups are obligated to remain silent. The objective is simply to report to the other group as accurately as possible the images that each group has developed in private.
   d. Before any exchange takes place, the groups return to private sessions to digest and analyze what they have heard; there is great likelihood that the representatives' reports have revealed to each group discrepancies between its self-image and the image the other group holds of it.

e. In public session, again working through representatives, each group shares with the other what discrepancies it has uncovered and the possible reasons for them, focusing on actual, observable behavior.

f. Following this mutual exposure, a more open exploration is permitted between the two groups on the now-shared goal of identifying further reasons for perceptual distortions.

g. A joint exploration is then conducted of how to manage future relations in such a way as to encourage cooperation among groups.[466]

Intergroup consultation can be quite demanding for everyone involved. It is fairly easy to have conflicting groups list perceptions and identify discrepancies. However, exploring their differences face-to-face and agreeing to change is more difficult. If handled correctly, these sessions can help department employees understand each other much better and lead to improved attitudes and better working relationships for years to come.

4. *Practice member rotation.* Rotation means individuals from one department can be asked to work in another department on a temporary or permanent basis. The advantage is that individuals become submerged in the values, attitudes, problems, and goals of the other department. In addition, individuals can explain the problems and goals of their original departments to their new colleagues. This enables a frank, accurate exchange of views and information.

    Rotation works slowly to reduce conflict but is very effective for changing the underlying attitudes and perceptions that promote conflict.[467]

5. *Develop shared mission and superordinate goals.* Another strategy is for top management to create a shared mission and establish superordinate goals that require cooperation among departments.[468] Organizations with strong, adaptive cultures, where employees share a larger vision for their company, are more likely to have a united, cooperative workforce. Recent studies have shown that when employees from different departments see that their goals are linked together, they will openly share resources and information.[469] To be effective, superordinate goals must be substantial, and employees must be granted the time to work cooperatively toward those goals. The reward system can also be redesigned to encourage the pursuit of the superordinate goals rather than departmental subgoals.

Project Management

Types of Project Organizations

Although there are various ways in which people can be organized to work on projects, the most common types of organization structures are functional, project, and matrix. Each type is discussed next.

Functional-Type Organization

Functional organization structures are typically used in businesses that primarily sell and produce standard products and seldom conduct external projects. For example, a company that manufactures and sells video recorders and players may have a functional organization structure. In the functional organization structure, groups consist of individuals who perform the same function, such as engineering or manufacturing, or have the same expertise or skills, such as electronics engineering or testing. Each functional group, or component, concentrates on performing its own activities in support of the company's business mission. The focus is on the technical excellence and cost competitiveness of the company's products, as well as the importance of the contribution of each functional component's expertise to the company's products.

A company with a functional structure may periodically undertake projects, but these are typically in-house projects rather than projects for external customers. Projects in a functional-type organization might involve developing new products, designing a company information system, redesigning the office floor plan, or updating the company policy and procedures manual. For such projects, a *multifunctional project team* or *task force* is formed, with members selected by company management from the appropriate subfunctions in marketing, engineering, manufacturing, and procurement. Team members may be assigned to the project either full-time or part-time, for a part of the project or for the entire project duration. In most cases, however, individuals continue to perform their regular functional jobs while they serve part-time on the project task force. One of the team members—or possibly one of the functional vice presidents—is designated as the project leader or manager.

In a functional-type organization, the project manager does not have complete authority over the project team, since administratively the members still work for their respective functional managers. Because they view their contribution to the project in terms of their technical expertise, their allegiance remains to their functional managers. If there is conflict among the team members, it usually works its way through the organization hierarchy to be resolved, slowing down the project effort. On the other hand, if the company president does give the project manager the authority to make decisions when there is disagreement among team members, decisions might reflect the interests of the project manager's own functional component rather than the best interests of the overall project. For example, take the situation in which there is disagreement about the design of a new product and the project manager, who is from the engineering function, makes a decision that reduces the engineering design cost of the product but increases the manufacturing cost. In reporting project progress to the company president, the project manager then makes some biased comments regarding the viewpoints of team members from other functional components, such as, "If manufacturing were more willing to consider other production methods, they could make the product for a lower cost. Engineering has already reduced its design costs." Such a situation could require the company president to get drawn into handling the conflict.

The functional organization structure can be appropriate for internal company projects. However, since projects are not a part of the normal routine, it's necessary to establish a clear understanding of the role and responsibilities of each person assigned to the project task force. If the project manager does not have full authority for project decisions, then she or he must rely on leadership and persuasion skills to build consensus, handle conflict, and unify the task force members to accomplish the project objective. The project manager also needs to take the time to update the other functional managers in the company regularly on the status of the project and thank them for the support of their people assigned to the task force.

There may be situations in which a task force is assigned to work on a project that is strictly within a particular functional component. For example, the manager of technical documentation may form a task force of editors and documentation specialists to develop common standards for all technical documents. In such a case, the particular functional manager has full authority over the project, and conflict can be handled more quickly than when it arises within a multifunctional project team.

Companies with functional organization structures seldom perform projects involving external customers, as such organizations do not have project managers designated to manage customer-funded projects. Rather, functional-type organizations concentrate on producing their products and selling them to various customers.

Project-Type Organization

In the project-type organization, each project is operated like a mini-company. All the resources needed to accomplish each project are assigned full-time to work on that project. A full-time project manager has complete project and administrative authority over the project team. (In the functional-type organization, the project manager may have project authority, but the functional manager retains administrative and technical authority over his or her people who are assigned to the team.) The project-type organization is well positioned to be highly responsive to the project objective and customer needs because each project team is strictly dedicated to only one project.

A project-type organization can be cost-inefficient both for individual projects and for the company. Each project must pay the salaries of its dedicated project team, even during parts of the project when they are not busy. For example, if a delay in one part of the project leaves some resources with no work to do for several weeks, project funds must cover these costs. If the amount of unapplied time becomes excessive, the project can become unprofitable and drain the profits from other projects. From a company-wide viewpoint, a project-type organization can be cost-inefficient because of the duplication of resources or tasks on several concurrent projects. Because resources are not shared, they may not be diverted to a similar concurrent project even when they are not busy on or being used for the project to which they are dedicated. Also, there is little opportunity for members of different project teams to share knowledge or technical expertise, since each project team tends to be isolated and focused strictly on its own project. However, there may be some company-wide support functions that serve all the projects such as the human resources function serves all projects.

In a project-type organization, detailed and accurate planning and an effective control system are required to assure optimum utilization of the project resources in successfully completing the project within budget.

Project organization structures are found primarily in companies that are involved in very large projects. Such projects can be of high (multimillion) dollar value and long (several years) duration. Project organization structures are prevalent in the construction and aerospace industries. They are also used in the nonbusiness environment, such as for a volunteer-managed fund-raising campaign, town centennial celebration, class reunion, or variety show.

Matrix-Type Organization

The matrix-type organization is kind of a hybrid—a mix of both the functional and project organization structures. It provides the project and customer focus of the project structure, but it retains the functional expertise of the functional structure. The project and functional components of the matrix structure each have their responsibilities in contributing jointly to the success of each project and the company. The project manager is responsible for the project results, while the functional managers are responsible for providing the resources needed to achieve the results.

The matrix-type organization provides for effective utilization of company resources. The functional components (systems engineering, testing, and so forth), home of the technical staff, provide a pool of expertise to support ongoing projects.

Project managers come under the projects component of the organization. When the company receives an order for a new system, the vice president of projects assigns a project manager to the project. A small project may be assigned to a project manager who is already managing several other small projects. A large project may be assigned a full-time project manager.

The matrix-type organization provides opportunities for people in the functional components to pursue career development through assignment to various types of projects. As they broaden their experience, individuals become more valuable for future assignments and enhance their eligibility for higher-level positions within the company. As each individual in a particular functional component develops a broad base of experience, the functional manager gains greater flexibility to assign individuals to different kinds of projects.

All of the individuals assigned to a given project comprise the project team, under the leadership of a project manager who integrates and unifies their efforts. Individuals assigned to several small projects will be members of several different project teams. Each member of a project team has a dual reporting relationship; in a sense, each member has two managers—a (temporary) project manager and a (permanent) functional manager. For a person assigned to several concurrent projects, changing work priorities can cause conflict and anxiety.

It is critical to specify to whom the team member reports and for what responsibilities or tasks. Therefore, it's important that the project management responsibilities and the functional management responsibilities be delineated in a matrix-type organization.

In the matrix organization structure, the *project manager* is the intermediary between the company and the customer. The project manager defines what has to be done (work scope), by when (schedule), and for how much money (budget) to meet the project objective and satisfy the customer. She or he is responsible for leading the development of the project plan, establishing the project schedule and budget, and allocating specific tasks and budgets to the various functional components of the company organization. Throughout the project, the project manager is responsible both for controlling the performance of the work within the project schedule and budget and for reporting project performance to the customer and to the company's upper management. A project administrator may be assigned to each project to support the project manager and project team in planning, controlling, and reporting.

Each functional manager in a matrix organization structure is responsible for how the assigned work tasks will be accomplished and who (which specific people) will do each task. The functional manager of each organization component provides technical guidance and leadership to the individuals assigned to projects. He or she is also responsible for ensuring that all tasks assigned to that functional component are completed in accordance with the project's technical requirements, within the assigned budget, and on schedule.

The matrix-type organization provides a checks-and-balances environment. The fact that potential problems can be identified through both its project and its functional structure reduces the likelihood that problems will be suppressed beyond the point where they can be corrected without jeopardizing the success of the project. The matrix organization structure allows for fast response upon problem identification because it has both a horizontal (project) and a vertical (functional) path for the flow of information.

Exhibit 100.68 *Advantages and Disadvantages of Organization Structures*

	Advantages	Disadvantages
Functional Structure	• No duplication of activities • Functional excellence	• Insularity • Slow response time • Lack of customer focus
Project Structure	• Control over resources • Responsiveness to customers	• Cost-inefficiency • Low level of knowledge transfer among projects
Matrix Structure	• Efficient utilization of resources • Functional expertise available to all projects • Increased learning and knowledge transfer • Improved communication • Customer focus	• Dual reporting relationships • Need for balance of power

Advantages and Disadvantages

The previous sections discussed the characteristics of the functional-, project-, and matrix-type organizations. Exhibit 100.68 lists some of the more significant advantages and disadvantages that are particular to each of the three organization structures.

Project Management Concepts

This section presents the definition of a project and its attributes, the life cycle of a project, the project management process, and the benefits of project management.

Attributes of a Project

A **project** is an endeavor to accomplish a specific objective through a unique set of interrelated tasks and the effective utilization of resources. The following attributes help define a project:

- A project has a well-defined **objective**—an expected result or product. The objective of a project is usually defined in terms of *scope, schedule,* and *cost.* For example, the objective of a project might be to introduce to the market—in 10 months and within a budget of $500,000—a new food-preparation appliance that meets certain predefined performance specifications. Furthermore, it is expected that the work scope will be accomplished in a *quality manner* and to the *customer's satisfaction.*
- A project is carried out through a series of *interdependent tasks*—that is, a number of nonrepetitive tasks that need to be accomplished in a certain sequence in order to achieve the project objective.
- A project utilizes various *resources* to carry out the tasks. Such resources can include different people, organizations, equipment, materials, and facilities. For example, a wedding is a project that may involve resources such as a caterer, a florist, a limousine, and a reception hall.
- A project has a *specific time frame,* or finite life span. It has a start time and a date by which the objective must be accomplished. For example, the refurbishing of an elementary school might have to be completed between June 20 and August 20.
- A project may be a *unique* or *one-time endeavor.* Some projects, like designing and building a space station, are unique because they have never before been attempted. Other projects, such as developing a new product, building a house, or planning a wedding, are unique because of the customization they require. For example, a wedding can be a simple, informal occasion, with a few friends in a chapel, or a spectacular event staged for a prince.

190. PROJECT MANAGEMENT

- A project has a customer. The **customer** is the entity that provides the funds necessary to accomplish the project. It can be a person, an organization, or a group of two or more people or organizations. When a contractor builds a customized home for a couple, the couple is the customer funding the project. When a company receives funds from the government to develop a robotic device for handling radioactive material, the customer is the government agency. When a company provides funds for a team of its employees to upgrade the firm's management information system, the term *customer* takes on a broader definition, including not only the project funder (the company's management) but also other stakeholders, such as the people who will be the end users of the information system. The person managing the project and the project team must successfully accomplish the project objective to satisfy the customer(s).
- Finally, a project involves a *degree of uncertainty*. Before a project is started, a plan is prepared based on certain assumptions and estimates. It is important to document these assumptions, since they will influence the development of the project budget, schedule, and work scope. A project is based on a unique set of tasks and estimates of how long each task should take, various resources and assumptions about the availability and capability of those resources, and estimates of the costs associated with the resources. This combination of assumptions and estimates causes a degree of uncertainty that the project objective will be completely accomplished. For example, the project scope may be accomplished by the target date, but the final cost may be much higher than anticipated because of low initial estimates for the cost of certain resources. As the project proceeds, some of the assumptions will be refined or replaced with factual information. For example, once the conceptual design of a company's annual report is finalized, the amount of time and effort needed to complete the detailed design and printing can be better estimated.

The successful accomplishment of the project objective is usually constrained by four factors: *scope, cost, schedule,* and *customer satisfaction.*

The scope of a project—also known as the **project scope** or the **work scope**—is all the work that must be done in order to satisfy the customer that the **deliverables** (the tangible product or items to be provided) *meet the requirements or acceptance criteria agreed upon at the onset of the project.* For example, the project scope might be all of the work involved in clearing the land, building a house, and landscaping to the specifications agreed upon by the contractor and the buyer. The customer expects the work scope to be accomplished in a quality manner. For example, in a house-building project, the customer expects the workmanship to be of the highest quality. Completing the work scope but leaving windows that are difficult to open and close, faucets that leak, or a landscape full of rocks will result in an unsatisfied customer.

The **cost** of a project is the amount the customer has agreed to pay for acceptable project deliverables. The project cost is based on a budget that includes an estimate of the costs associated with the various resources that will be used to accomplish the project. It might include the salaries of people who will work on the project, materials and supplies, rental of equipment or facilities, and the fees of subcontractors or consultants who will perform some of the project tasks. For example, if the project is a wedding, budgeted items might include flowers, gown, tuxedo, caterer, cake, limousine rental, photographer, and so on.

The **schedule** for a project is the timetable that specifies when each activity should start and finish. The project objective usually states the time by which the project scope must be completed in terms of a specific date agreed upon by the customer and the individual or organization performing the work. It might be the date when a town's centennial celebration will take place or the date by which you want to complete the addition of a family room to your home.

The objective of any project is to complete the scope within budget by a certain time to the customer's satisfaction. To help assure the achievement of this objective, *it is important to develop a plan before the start of the project; this plan should include all the work tasks, associated costs, and estimates of the time necessary to complete them.* The lack of such a plan increases the risk of failing to accomplish the full project scope within budget and on schedule.

Once a project is started, unforeseen circumstances may jeopardize the achievement of the project objective with respect to scope, cost, or schedule.

- The cost of some of the materials may be higher than originally estimated.
- Inclement weather may cause a delay.
- Additional redesign and modifications to a sophisticated piece of automated machinery may be required to get it to meet the performance specifications.

The challenge to the project manager is to prevent, anticipate, and/or overcome such circumstances in order to complete the project scope on schedule, within budget, and to the customer's satisfaction. *Good planning and communication* are essential to prevent problems from occurring or to minimize their impact on the achievement of the project objective when they do occur. The project manager needs to be proactive in planning and communicating and provide leadership to the project team to accomplish the project objective.

Ultimately, the responsibility of the project manager is to make sure the customer is satisfied. This goes beyond just completing the project scope within budget and on schedule or asking the customer at the end of the project if he or she is satisfied. It requires ongoing communication with the customer to keep the customer informed and to determine whether expectations have changed. Regularly scheduled meetings or progress reports, frequent phone discussions, and e-mail are examples of ways to accomplish such communications. Customer satisfaction means involving the customer as a partner in the successful outcome of the project through active participation during the project. The project manager must be aware of the degree of customer satisfaction throughout the project. By maintaining regular communication with the customer, the project manager demonstrates to the customer that he or she is genuinely concerned about the expectations of the customer; it also prevents unpleasant surprises later.

Project Life Cycle

Exhibit 100.69 shows the four phases of the **project life cycle** and the relative amount of effort and time devoted to each phase. As the project moves through its life cycle, different organizations, individuals, and resources play dominant roles.

Projects are "born" when a need is identified by the *customer*—the people or the organization willing to provide funds to have the need satisfied. For example, for a growing family, the need may be for a larger house, whereas for a company the problem may be a high scrap rate from its manufacturing process that makes its costs higher and production times longer than those of its competitors. The customer first must identify the need or problem. Sometimes the problem is identified quickly, as in the case of a disaster such as an earthquake or explosion. In other situations, it may take months for a customer to clearly identify a need, gather data on the problem, and define certain requirements that must be met by the person, project team, or contractor who will solve the problem.

This *first phase* of the project life cycle involves the identification of a need, problem, or opportunity and can result in the customer's requesting proposals from individuals, a project team, or organizations (contractors) to address the identified need or solve the problem. The need and requirements are usually written up by the customer in a document called a **request for proposal (RFP)**. Through the RFP, the customer asks individuals or contractors to submit proposals on how they might solve the problem, along with the associated cost and schedule. A couple who need a new house may spend time identifying requirements for the house—size, style, number of rooms, location, maximum amount they want to spend, and date by which they would like to move in. They may then write down these requirements and ask several contractors to provide house plans and cost estimates. A company that has identified a need to upgrade its computer system might document its requirements in an RFP and send it to several computer consulting firms.

Not all situations involve a formal RFP, however. Needs often are defined informally during a meeting or discussion among a group of individuals. Some of the individuals may then volunteer or be asked to prepare a proposal to determine whether a project should be undertaken to address the need. Such a scenario might be played out when the management of a hospital wants to establish an on-site day care center for the children of its employees. The management team or a specific manager may write down the requirements in a document and give it to an internal

Exhibit 100.69 *Project Life Cycle*

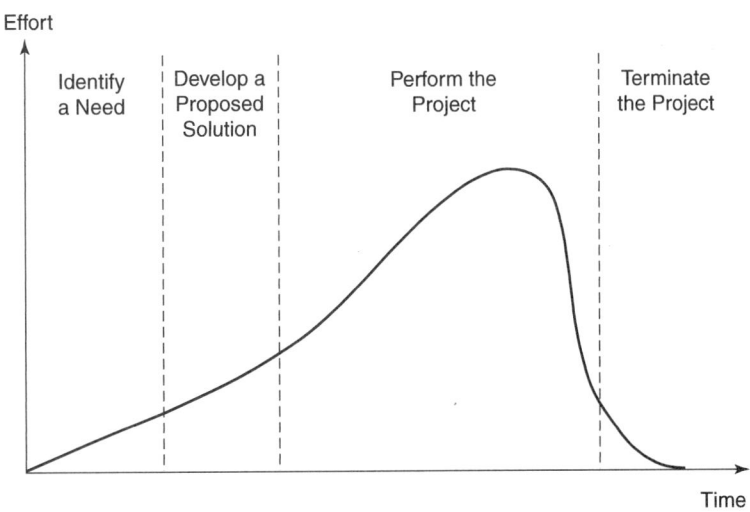

project team, which in turn will submit a proposal for how to establish the center. In this case, the contractor is the hospital's own internal project team, and the customer is the hospital's manager or, possibly, board of directors. It is important to define the right need. For example, is the need to provide an on-site day care center, or is it to provide child care for the children of the hospital's employees? Is "on-site" necessarily part of the need?

The *second phase* of the project life cycle is the development of a proposed solution to the need or problem. This phase results in the submission of a **proposal** to the customer by one or more individuals or organizations (contractors) who would like to have the customer pay them to implement the proposed solution. In this phase, the contractor effort is dominant. Contractors interested in responding to the RFP may spend several weeks developing approaches to solving the problem, estimating the types and amounts of resources that would be needed as well as the time it would take to design and implement the proposed solution. Each contractor documents this information in a written proposal. All of the contractors submit their proposals to the customer. For example, several contractors may submit proposals to a customer to develop and implement an automated invoicing and collection system. After the customer evaluates the submissions and selects the winning proposal, the customer and the winning contractor negotiate and sign a **contract** (agreement). In many situations, a request for proposal may not involve soliciting competitive proposals from external contractors. A company's own internal project team may develop a proposal in response to a management-defined need or request. In this case, the project would be performed by the company's own employees rather than by an external contractor.

The *third phase* of the project life cycle is the implementation of the proposed solution. This phase begins after the customer decides which of the proposed solutions will best fulfill the need and an agreement is reached between the customer and the individual or contractor who submitted the proposal. This phase, referred to as performing the project, involves doing the detailed planning for the project and then implementing that plan to accomplish the project objective. During the course of performing the project, different types of resources will be utilized. For example, if the project is to design and construct an office building, the project effort might first involve a few architects and engineers in developing the building plans. Then, as construction gets under way, the resources needed will substantially increase to include steelworkers, carpenters, electricians, painters, and the like. The project will wind down after the building is finished, and a smaller number of different workers will finish up the landscaping and final interior touches. This phase results in the accomplishment of the project objective, leaving the customer satisfied that the full scope of the work was completed in a quality manner, within budget, and on time. For example, the third phase is complete when a contractor has completed the design and installation of a customized automation system that satisfactorily passes performance tests and is accepted by the customer or when an internal project team within a company has completed a project, in response to a management request, which consolidated two of its facilities into one.

The *final phase* of the project life cycle is terminating the project. When a project is completed, certain close-out activities need to be performed, such as confirming that all deliverables have been provided to and accepted by the customer, that all payments have been collected, and that all invoices have been paid. An important task during this phase is evaluating performance of the project in order to learn what could be improved if a similar project were to be carried out in the future. This phase should include obtaining feedback from the customer to determine the level of the customer's satisfaction and whether the project met the customer's expectations. Also, feedback should be obtained from the project team in the form of recommendations for improving performance of projects in the future.

Project life cycles vary in length from a few weeks to several years, depending on the content, complexity, and magnitude of the project. What's more, not all projects formally go through all four phases of the project life cycle. If a group of community volunteers decide that they want to use their own time, talents, and resources to organize a food drive for the homeless, they may get right into phase three—planning the event and carrying it out. The first two phases of the life cycle would not be relevant to such a project. Likewise, if a company's general manager determines that changing the layout of equipment in the factory will increase efficiency, she might simply instruct the manufacturing manager to initiate such a project and to implement it using the company's own people. In this case, there would be no written request for proposal from external contractors.

In other situations, such as a home remodeling project for which a contractor will likely be hired, a customer may go through the first two phases of the project life cycle in a less structured, more informal manner. He may not write down all of the requirements and ask several contractors for estimates. Rather, he may call a contractor who has done satisfactory work for him or for a neighbor in the past, explain what he wants done, and ask the contractor to provide some sketches and a cost estimate.

In general, the project life cycle is followed in a more formal and structured manner when a project is conducted in a business setting. It tends to be less formal when a project is carried out by a private individual or volunteers.

The Project Management Process

Succinctly, the project management process means *planning the work and then working the plan*. A coaching staff may spend hours preparing unique plans for a game; the team then executes the plans to try to meet the objective—victory. Similarly, project management involves a process of first *establishing a plan* and then *implementing that plan* to accomplish the project objective.

The front-end effort in managing a project must be focused on establishing a baseline plan that provides a roadmap for how the project scope will be accomplished on time and within budget. This planning effort includes the following steps:

1. *Clearly define the project objective.* The definition must be agreed upon by the customer and the individual or organization who will perform the project.
2. *Divide and subdivide the project scope into major "pieces," or **work packages**.* Although major projects may seem overwhelming when viewed as a whole, one way to conquer even the most monumental endeavor is to break it down. A **work breakdown structure (WBS)** is a hierarchical tree of work elements or items accomplished or produced by the project team during the project. The work breakdown structure usually identifies the organization or individual responsible for each work package.
3. *Define the specific activities that need to be performed for each work package in order to accomplish the project objective.*
4. *Graphically portray the activities in the form of a **network diagram**.* This diagram shows the necessary sequence and interdependencies of activities to achieve the project objective.
5. *Make a **time estimate** for how long it will take to complete each activity.* It is also necessary to determine which types of resources and how many of each resource are needed for each activity to be completed within the estimated duration.
6. *Make a **cost estimate** for each activity.* The cost is based on the types and quantities of resources required for each activity.
7. *Calculate a project schedule and budget to determine whether the project can be completed within the required time, with the allotted funds, and with the available resources.* If not, adjustments must be made to the project scope, activity time estimates, or resource assignments until an achievable, realistic **baseline plan** (a roadmap for accomplishing the project scope on time and within budget) can be established.

Planning determines what needs to be done, who will do it, how long it will take, and how much it will cost. The result of this effort is a baseline plan. Taking the time to develop a well-thought-out plan is critical to the successful accomplishment of any project. Many projects have overrun their budgets, missed their completion dates, or only partially met their requirements because there was no viable baseline plan before the project was started.

The baseline plan for a project can be displayed in graphical or tabular format for each time period (week, month) from the start of the project to its completion. Information should include:

- the start and completion dates for each activity
- the amounts of the various resources that will be needed during each time period
- the budget for each time period, as well as the cumulative budget from the start of the project through each time period

Once a baseline plan has been established, it must be implemented. This involves performing the work according to the plan and controlling the work so that the project scope is achieved within the budget and schedule to the customer's satisfaction.

Once the project starts, it is necessary to monitor progress to ensure that everything is going according to plan. At this stage, the project management process involves measuring actual progress and comparing it to planned progress. To measure actual progress, it is important to keep track of which activities have actually been started and/or completed, when they were started and/or completed, and how much money has been spent or committed. If, at any time during the project, comparison of actual progress to planned progress reveals that the project is behind schedule, overrunning the budget, or not meeting the technical specifications, corrective action must be taken to get the project back on track.

Before a decision is made to implement corrective action, it may be necessary to evaluate several alternative actions to make sure the corrective action will bring the project back within the scope, time, and budget constraints of the objective. Be aware, for instance, that adding resources to make up time and get back on schedule may result in overrunning the planned budget. If a project gets too far out of control, it may be difficult to achieve the project objective without sacrificing the scope, budget, schedule, or quality.

The key to effective project control is measuring actual progress and comparing it to planned progress on a timely and regular basis and taking corrective action immediately, if necessary. Hoping that a problem will go away without corrective intervention is naive. Based on actual progress, it is possible to forecast a schedule and budget for completion of the project. If these parameters are beyond the limits of the project objective, corrective actions need to be implemented at once.

Attempting to perform a project without first establishing a baseline plan is foolhardy. It is like starting a vacation without a roadmap, itinerary, and budget. You may land up in the middle of nowhere—out of money and out of time!

Benefits of Project Management

The ultimate benefit of implementing project management techniques is having a *satisfied customer*—whether you are the customer of your own project, such as remodeling your basement, or a business (contractor) being paid by a customer to perform a project. Completing the full project scope in a quality manner, on time, and within budget provides a great feeling of satisfaction. For a contractor, it could lead to additional business from the same customer in the future or to business from new customers referred by previously satisfied customers.

"Hey! Great for the customer, but what about me? What's in it for me?" If you are the project manager, you have the satisfaction of knowing you led a successful project effort. You also have enhanced your reputation as a project manager and positioned yourself for expanded career opportunities. If you are a member of a project team that successfully accomplished a project, you feel the satisfaction of being on a winning team. You not only contributed to the project's success, but also probably expanded your knowledge and enhanced your skills along the way. If you choose to remain an individual contributor, you will be able to make a greater contribution to future, more complicated projects. If you are interested in eventually managing projects, you will be in a position to take on additional project responsibilities.

When projects are successful, everybody wins!

Cost Planning and Performance

In addition to establishing a baseline schedule for a project, it is also necessary to develop a baseline budget. Project costs are estimated when a proposal is prepared for the project. Once a decision is made to go forward with the proposed project, it is necessary to prepare a budget, or plan, for how and when funds will be spent over the duration of the project. Once the project starts, it's important to monitor actual costs and work performance to ensure that everything is within budget. At regular intervals during the project, the following cost-related parameters should be monitored:

- cumulative actual amount spent since the start of the project
- cumulative earned value of the work performed since the start of the project
- cumulative budgeted amount planned to be spent, based on the project schedule, from the start of the project

Comparisons must be made among these three parameters to evaluate whether the project is being accomplished within budget and whether the value of the work performed is in line with the actual amount expended.

If at any time during the project it is determined that the project is overrunning the budget or the value of the work performed isn't keeping up with the actual amount expended, corrective action must be taken. Once project costs get out of control, it will be very difficult to complete the project within budget. As you will see in this section, the key to effective cost control is to analyze cost performance on a timely and regular basis. Early identification of cost variances allows corrective action to be taken before the situation gets worse. In this section, you will learn how to regularly forecast, based on the actual amount spent and the value of the work performed, whether the entire project will be completed within budget.

Project Cost Estimates

Cost planning starts with the proposal for the project. It is during the development of the proposal by the contractor or project team that project costs are estimated. In some cases, the proposal will indicate only the total bottom-line cost for the proposed project. In other cases, the customer may request a detailed breakdown of various costs. The cost section of a proposal may consist of tabulations of the contractor's estimated costs for such elements as the following:

1. labor
2. materials
3. subcontractors and consultants
4. equipment and facilities rental
5. travel

In addition to the above items, the contractor or project team may include an amount for contingencies, to cover unexpected situations that may come up during the project. For example, items may have been overlooked when the project cost estimates were prepared, tasks may have to be redone because they did not work the first time, or the costs of labor (wages, salaries) or materials may escalate during a multiyear project.

Project Budgeting

The project budgeting process involves two steps. First, the project cost estimate is allocated to the various work packages in the project work breakdown structure. Second, the budget for each work package is distributed over the duration of the work package so that it's possible to determine how much of its budget should have been spent at any point in time.

Allocating the Total Budgeted Cost

Allocating total project costs for the various elements—such as labor, materials, and subcontractors—to the appropriate work packages in the work breakdown structure will establish a **total budgeted cost** (TBC) for each work package. There are two approaches to establishing the TBC for each work package. One is a top-down approach, in which total project costs (for labor, materials, and so forth) are reviewed in relation to the work scope for each work package, and a proportion of the total project cost is allocated to each work package. The other is a bottom-up approach, which is based on an estimate of the costs for the detailed activities associated with each work package. The project cost is usually estimated when the proposal for the project is prepared, but detailed plans are not usually prepared at this time. At the start of the project, however, detailed activities are defined and a network plan is developed. Once detailed activities have been defined, time, resource, and cost estimates can be made for each activity. The TBC for each work package will be the sum of the costs of all the activities that make up that work package.

Developing the Cumulative Budgeted Cost

Once a total budgeted cost has been established for each work package, the second step in the project budgeting process is to distribute each TBC over the duration of its work package. A cost is determined for each period, based on when the activities that make up the work package are scheduled to be performed. When the TBC for each work package is spread out by time period, it can be determined how much of the budget should have been spent at any point in time. This amount is calculated by adding up the budgeted costs for each time period up to that point in time. This total amount, known as the **cumulative budgeted cost** (CBC), is the amount that was budgeted to accomplish the work that was scheduled to be performed up to that point in time. The CBC is the *baseline* that will be used in analyzing the cost performance of the project.

Determining Actual Cost

Once the project starts, it is necessary to keep track of actual cost and committed cost so that they can be compared to the CBC.

Actual Cost

To keep track of **actual cost** on a project, it is necessary to set up a system to collect, on a regular and timely basis, data on funds actually expended. Such a system might include procedures and forms for gathering data. An accounting structure should be established based on the work breakdown structure numbering system so that each item of actual cost can be charged to the appropriate work package. Each work package's actual cost can then be totaled and compared to its CBC.

Committed Cost

In many projects, large dollar amounts are expended for materials or services (subcontractors, consultants) that are used over a period of time longer than one cost reporting period. These **committed costs** need to be treated in a special way so that the system periodically assigns a portion of their total cost to actual cost, rather than waiting until the materials or services are finished to charge to the total actual costs.

Committed costs are also known as *commitments* or *encumbered costs*. Costs are committed when an item (material, subcontractor) is ordered, usually by means of a purchase order, even though actual payment may take place at some later time—when the material or service has been completed, delivered, and invoiced.

Comparing Actual Cost to Budgeted Cost

As data are collected on actual cost, including portions of any committed cost, they need to be totaled by work package so that they can be compared to the cumulative budgeted cost. These are called **cumulative actual cost (CAC)**.

Determining the Value of Work Performed

Earned value (EV), the value of the work actually performed, is a key parameter that must be determined throughout the project. Comparing the cumulative actual cost to the cumulative budgeted cost tells only part of the story and can lead to wrong conclusions about the status of the project.

Just as it is important to track actual cost for a project, it is also necessary to set up a companion system to collect data on a regular and timely basis regarding the earned value of the work performed on each work package. Determining the earned value involves collecting data on the **percent complete** for each work package and then converting this percentage to a dollar amount by multiplying the TBC of the work package by the percent complete.

Cost Performance Analysis

The following four cost-related measures are used to analyze project cost performance:

- TBC   (total budgeted cost)
- CBC   (cumulative budgeted cost)
- CAC   (cumulative actual cost)
- CEV   (cumulative earned value)

They are used to determine whether the project is being performed within budget and whether the value of the work performed is in line with the actual cost.

Cost Performance Index

Another indicator of cost performance is the **cost performance index (CPI),** which is a measure of the cost efficiency with which the project is being performed. The formula for determining the CPI is

$$\text{Cost performance index} = \frac{\text{Cumulative earned value}}{\text{Cumulative actual cost}}$$

$$\text{CPI} = \frac{\text{CEV}}{\text{CAC}}$$

In the packaging machine project, the CPI as of week 8 is given by

$$\text{CPI} = \frac{\$54,000}{68,000} = 0.79$$

This ratio indicates that for every $1.00 actually expended, only $0.79 of earned value was received. Trends in the CPI should be watched carefully. When the CPI goes below 1.0 or gradually gets smaller, corrective action should be taken.

Cost Variance

Another indicator of cost performance is **cost variance (CV),** which is the difference between the cumulative earned value of the work performed and the cumulative actual cost. The formula for determining the cost variance is

$$\text{Cost variance} = \text{cumulative earned value} - \text{Cumulative actual cost}$$
$$CV = CEV - CAC$$

Like the CPI, this indicator shows the gap between the value of the work performed and the actual cost, but the CV is expressed in terms of dollars.

In the packaging machine project, the cost variance as of week 8 is given by

$$CV = \$54{,}000 - \$68{,}000 = \$14{,}000$$

This calculation indicates that the value of the work performed through week 8 is $14,000 less than the amount actually expended. It is another indication that the work performed is not keeping pace with the actual cost.

For analyzing cost performance, it is important that the data collected all be as current as possible and all be based on the same reporting period. For example, if the costs are collected as of the 30th of each month, then the percent complete estimates for the work packages should be based on work performed through the 30th of the month.

Cost Forecasting

Based on analysis of *actual* cost performance throughout the project, it is possible to forecast what the total costs will be at the completion of the project or work package. There are three different methods for determining the **forecasted cost at completion (FCAC).**

The first method assumes that the work to be performed on the remaining portion of the project or work package will be done at the same rate of efficiency as the work performed so far. The formula for calculating the FCAC using this first method is

$$\text{Forecasted cost at completion} = \frac{\text{Total budgeted cost}}{\text{Cost performance index}}$$

$$FCAC = \frac{TBC}{CPI}$$

For the packaging machine project, the forecasted cost at completion is given by

$$FCAC = \frac{\$100{,}000}{0.79} = \$126{,}582$$

As of week 8, the project has a cost efficiency, or CPI, of 0.79, and if the remainder of the project continues to be performed at this same efficiency rate, then the entire project will actually cost $126,582. If this forecast is correct, there will be an overrun of $26,582 beyond the total budgeted cost for the project of $100,000.

A second method for determining the forecasted cost at completion assumes that, regardless of the efficiency rate the project or work package has experienced in the past, the work to be performed on the remaining portion of the project or work package will be done according to budget. The formula for calculating the FCAC using this method is

$$\begin{array}{c}\text{Forcasted}\\\text{cost at}\\\text{completion}\end{array} = \begin{array}{c}\text{Cumulative}\\\text{actual}\\\text{cost}\end{array} + \left(\begin{array}{c}\text{Total}\\\text{budgeted}\\\text{cost}\end{array} - \begin{array}{c}\text{Cumulative}\\\text{earned}\\\text{value}\end{array}\right)$$

$$FCAC = CAC + (TBC - CEV)$$

For the packaging machine project, the forecasted cost at completion is given by

$$FCAC = \$68{,}000 + (\$100{,}000 - \$54{,}000)$$
$$= \$68{,}000 + \$46{,}000$$
$$= \$114{,}000$$

As of week 8, the cumulative actual cost was $68,000, but the cumulative earned value of the work performed was only $54,000. Therefore, work with an earned value of $46,000 needs to be performed to complete the project. This method assumes that the remaining work will be performed at an efficiency rate of 1.0, even though the project has been experiencing an efficiency rate of 0.79 as of the end of week 8. This method results in a forecasted cost at completion of $114,000, a forecasted overrun of $14,000 beyond the total budgeted cost for the project.

A third method for determining the forecasted cost at completion is to reestimate the costs for all the remaining work to be performed and then add this reestimate to the cumulative actual cost. The formula for determining the FCAC using this third method is

$$FCAC = CAC + \text{Reestimate of remaining work to be performed}$$

This approach can be time-consuming, but it may be necessary if the project experiences persistent deviations from the plan or if there are extensive changes.

As part of the regular cost performance analysis, the FCAC for the project should be calculated, using the first or second method described. The forecasted overrun or underrun can then be determined. When cost is forecasted to the completion of the project or work package, a small variance in a given reporting period can expand to a much greater overrun, signaling the need for corrective action.

Cost Control

The key to effective cost control is to analyze cost performance on a regular and timely basis. It is crucial that cost variances and inefficiencies be identified early so that corrective action can be taken before the situation gets worse. Once project costs get out of control, it may be very difficult to complete the project within budget.

Cost control involves the following:

1. Analyzing cost performance to determine which work packages may require corrective action
2. Deciding what specific corrective action should be taken
3. Revising the project plan, including time and cost estimates, to incorporate the planned corrective action

The cost performance analysis should include identifying those work packages that have a negative cost variance or a cost performance index of less than 1.0. Also, those work packages for which the CV or CPI has deteriorated since the prior reporting period should be identified. A concentrated effort must be applied to the work packages with negative variances, to reduce cost or improve the efficiency of the work performed. The amount of CV should determine the priority for applying these concentrated efforts; that is, the work package with the largest negative CV should be given top priority.

When evaluating work packages that have a negative cost variance, you should focus on taking corrective actions to reduce the costs of two types of activities:

1. *Activities that will be performed in the near term.* Do not plan to reduce the costs of activities that are scheduled sometime in the distant future. You'll get more timely feedback on the effects of corrective actions if they are done in the near term. If you put off corrective actions until some point in the distant future, the negative cost variance may deteriorate even further before the corrective actions are ever implemented. As the project progresses, less and less time remains in which corrective actions can be taken.
2. *Activities that have a large cost estimate.* Taking corrective measures that reduce the cost of a $20,000 activity by 10 percent will have a larger impact than totally eliminating a $300 activity. Usually, the larger the estimated cost for an activity, the greater the opportunity for a large cost reduction.

There are various ways to reduce the costs of activities. One way is to substitute less expensive materials that meet the required specifications. Maybe another supplier can be found who can supply the same material but at a lower cost. Another approach is to assign a person with greater expertise or more experience to perform or help with the activity to get it done more efficiently.

Reducing the scope or requirements for the work package or specific activities is another way to reduce costs.

In many cases, there will be a trade-off—reducing cost variances will involve a reduction in project scope or a delay in the project schedule. If the negative cost variance is very large, a substantial reduction in the work scope or quality may be required to get the project back within budget. The scope, budget, schedule, or quality of the overall project could be in jeopardy. In some cases, the customer and contractor or project team may have to acknowledge that one or more of these elements cannot be achieved. This could result in the customer's providing additional funds to cover the forecasted overrun, or it could result in a contract dispute over who caused the cost overrun and who should pay for it—the customer or the contractor.

The key to effective cost control is aggressively addressing negative cost variances and cost inefficiencies as soon as they are identified, rather than hoping that things will get better as the project goes on. Cost problems that are addressed early will have less impact on scope and schedule. Once costs get out of control, getting back within budget is likely to require reducing the project scope or extending the project schedule.

Even when projects have only positive cost variances, it is important not to let the cost variances deteriorate. If a project's cost performance is positive, a concentrated effort should be made to keep it that way. Once a project gets in trouble with cost performance, it becomes difficult to get it back on track.

The Project Manager

It is the people—not the procedures and techniques—that are critical to accomplishing the project objective. Procedures and techniques are merely tools that help people do their jobs. For example, an artist needs to have paint, canvas, and brushes to paint a portrait, but it is the skills and knowledge of the artist that allow a portrait to be created with these tools. So, too, in project management: the skills and knowledge of the people involved are vital for producing the result.

Responsibilities of the Project Manager

It is the responsibility of the project manager to make sure that the customer is satisfied, that the work scope is completed in a quality manner, within budget, and on time. The project manager has primary responsibility for providing leadership in planning, organizing, and controlling the work effort to accomplish the project objective. In other words, *the project manager provides the leadership to the project team to accomplish the project objective.* If the project team was an athletic team, the project manager would be the coach; if it was an orchestra, the project manager would be the conductor. The project manager coordinates the activities of the various team members to ensure that they perform the right tasks at the proper time as a cohesive group.

Planning

First, the project manager clearly defines the project objective and reaches agreement with the customer on this objective. The manager then communicates this objective to the project team in such a manner as to create a vision of what will constitute successful accomplishment of the objective. The project manager spearheads development of a plan to achieve the project objective. By involving the project team in developing this plan, the project manager ensures a more comprehensive plan than he or she could develop alone. Furthermore, such participation gains the commitment of the team to achieve the plan. The project manager reviews the plan with the customer to gain endorsement and then sets up a project management information system—either manual or computerized—for comparing actual progress to planned progress. It's important that this system be explained to the project team so that the team can use it properly to manage the project.

Organizing

Organizing involves securing the appropriate resources to perform the work. First, the project manager must decide which tasks should be done in house and which tasks should be done by subcontractors or consultants. For tasks that will be carried out in house, the project manager gains a commitment from the specific people who will work on the project. For tasks that will be performed by subcontractors, the project manager clearly defines the work scope and deliverables and negotiates a contract with each subcontractor. The project manager also assigns responsibility and delegates authority to specific individuals or subcontractors for the various tasks, with the understanding that they will be accountable for the accomplishment of their tasks within the assigned budget and schedule. For large projects involving many individuals, the project manager may designate leaders for specific groups of tasks. Finally, and most important, the task of organizing involves creating an environment in which the individuals are highly motivated to work together as a project team.

Controlling

To control the project, the project manager implements a project management information system designed to track actual progress and compare it with planned progress. Such a system helps the manager distinguish between busy-ness and accomplishments. Project team members monitor the progress of their assigned tasks and regularly provide data on progress, schedule, and costs. These data are supplemented by regular project review meetings. If actual progress falls behind planned progress or unexpected events occur, the project manager takes immediate action. He or she obtains input and advice from team members regarding appropriate corrective action and how to replan those parts of the project. It's important that problems, and even potential problems, be identified early and action taken. The project manager cannot take a "let's wait and see how things work out" approach—things never work out on their own. He or she must intervene and be proactive, resolving problems before they become worse.

The project manager plays the leadership role in planning, organizing, and controlling the project but does not try to do it alone. She or he involves the project team in these functions to gain their commitment to successful completion of the project.

Skills of the Project Manager

The project manager is a key ingredient in the success of a project. In addition to providing leadership in planning, organizing, and controlling the project, the manager should possess a set of skills that will both inspire the project team to succeed and win the confidence of the customer. Effective project managers have strong leadership ability, the ability to develop people, excellent communication skills, good interpersonal skills, the ability to handle stress, problem-solving skills, and time management skills.

The Project Team

A *team* is a group of individuals working interdependently to achieve a common goal. *Teamwork* is cooperative effort by members of a team to achieve that common goal. The effectiveness—or lack thereof—of the project team can make the difference between project success and project failure. Although plans and project management techniques are necessary, it is the people—the project manager and the project team— that are the key to project success; project success requires an effective project team.

Project Team Development and Effectiveness

A personal relationship between two people takes time to develop. Initially, you may be curious about each other, but apprehensive about letting your guard down and opening yourself up to the other person. As you get to know each other a little more, you may begin to notice differences in your attitudes and values, and disagreements may arise. You may be anxious about whether the relationship will or should continue. As you work through your differences, you may get to know each other better and become friends. Finally, you may develop a close relationship that helps you to be open with each other, accept each other's differences, and enjoy participating together in activities that are of mutual interest.

Likewise, teams evolve through various stages of development. In many projects, people who have never worked together are assigned to the same project team. This group of individuals must develop into an effective team to achieve the project objective successfully.

Stages of Team Development and Growth

B. W. Tuckman has defined four stages of team development: forming, storming, norming, and performing. The fifth stage is adjourning to close the project (Exhibit 100.70).

FORMING The **forming** stage of development is a period of orientation and getting acquainted. Members break the ice and test one another for friendship possibilities and task orientation. Team members find which behaviors are acceptable to others. Uncertainty is high during this stage, and members usually accept whatever power or authority is offered by either formal or informal leaders. Members are dependent on the team until they find out what the ground rules are and what is expected of them. During this initial stage, members are concerned about such things as "What is

Exhibit 100.70 *Five Stages of Team Development*

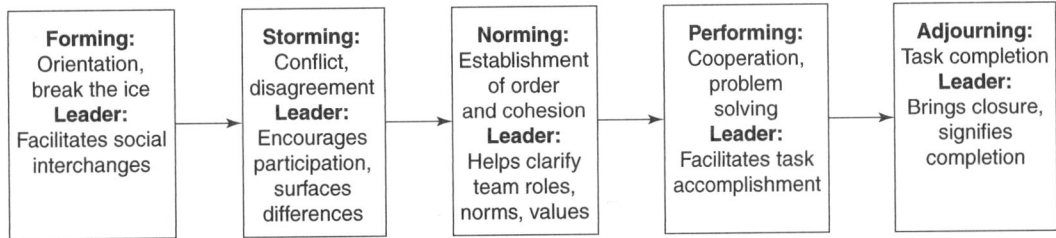

expected of me?" "What is acceptable?" "Will I fit in?" During the forming stage, the team leader should provide time for members to get acquainted with one another and encourage them to engage in informal social discussions.

STORMING During the **storming** stage, individual personalities emerge. People become more assertive in clarifying their roles and what is expected of them. This stage is marked by conflict and disagreement. People may disagree over their perceptions of the team's mission. Members may jockey for positions, and coalitions or subgroups based on common interests may form. One subgroup may disagree with another over the total team's goals or how to achieve them. The team is not yet cohesive and may be characterized by a general lack of unity. Unless teams can successfully move beyond this stage, they may get bogged down and never achieve high performance. During the storming stage, the team leader should encourage participation by each team member. Members should propose ideas, disagree with one another, and work through the uncertainties and conflicting perceptions about team tasks and goals.

NORMING During the **norming** stage, conflict is resolved, and team harmony and unity emerge. Consensus develops on who has the power, who is the leader, and members' roles. Members come to accept and understand one another. Differences are resolved, and members develop a sense of team cohesion. This stage typically is of short duration. During the norming stage, the team leader should emphasize oneness within the team and help clarify team norms and values.

PERFORMING During the **performing** stage, the major emphasis is on problem solving and accomplishing the assigned task. Members are committed to the team's mission. They are coordinated with one another and handle disagreements in a mature way. They confront and resolve problems in the interest of task accomplishment. They interact frequently and direct discussion and influence toward achieving team goals. During this stage, the leader should concentrate on managing high task performance. Both socioemotional and task specialists should contribute.

ADJOURNING The **adjourning** stage occurs in committees, task forces, and teams that have a limited task to perform and are disbanded afterward. During this stage, the emphasis is on wrapping up and gearing down. Task performance is no longer a top priority. Members may feel heightened emotionality, strong cohesiveness, and depression or even regret over the team's disbandment. They may feel happy about mission accomplishment and sad about the loss of friendship and associations. At this point, the leader may wish to signify the team's disbanding with a ritual or ceremony, perhaps giving out plaques and awards to signify closure and completeness.

The five stages of team development typically occur in sequence. In teams that are under time pressure or that will exist for only a short period of time, the stages may occur quite rapidly. The stages may also be accelerated for virtual teams. For example, bringing people together for a couple of days of team building can help virtual teams move rapidly through the forming and storming stages.

Exhibit 100.71 graphically illustrates the levels of work performance and sense of team during the four stages of team development and growth. The amount of time and effort it takes a team to move through each of the stages depends on several factors, including the number of people on the team, whether team members have worked together before, the complexity of the project, and the teamwork skills of the members.

The Effective Project Team

A project team is more than a group of individuals assigned to work on one project. A project team is a group of interdependent individuals working cooperatively to achieve the project objective. Helping these individuals develop and grow into a cohesive, effective team takes effort on the part of the project manager and each member of the project team. As noted earlier, the effectiveness—or lack thereof—of the project team can make the difference between project success and project failure. Although plans and project management techniques are necessary, it is the people—the project manager and project team—that are the key to project success; project success requires an effective project team.

Exhibit 100.71 *Level of Functioning at Various Stages of Team Development*

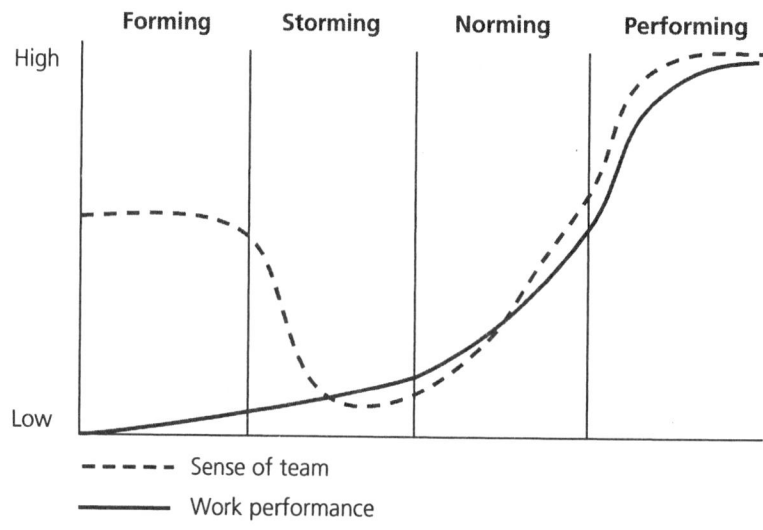

Characteristics associated with effective project teams include

- a clear understanding of the project objective
- clear expectations of each person's role and responsibilities
- a results orientation
- a high degree of cooperation and collaboration
- a high level of trust

Barriers to Team Effectiveness

Although every project team has the potential to be highly effective, there are often barriers that impede a team's achievement of the level of effectiveness of which it is capable. Following are barriers that can hinder project team effectiveness:

1. Unclear goals
2. Unclear definition of roles and responsibilities
3. Lack of project structure
4. Lack of commitment
5. Poor communication
6. Poor leadership
7. Turnover of project team members
8. Dysfunctional behavior

Being an Effective Team Member

Being a member of a project team should be an enriching and satisfying growth experience for each individual. However, growth will not just happen by itself. It requires a sense of responsibility, hard work, open-mindedness, and a desire for further self-development. Although the project manager is ultimately responsible for the success of a project, each member of the project team shares in that responsibility. Each member of the project team needs to help create and foster a positive and effective project environment.

Effective team members plan, control, and feel accountable for their individual work efforts. They have high expectations of themselves and strive to accomplish their assignments under budget and ahead of schedule. They manage their time well. They make things happen, they do not just let them happen. Effective team members do not simply work on a task until they are told to stop—they are self-directed and follow through on assignments and action items. They take pride in doing quality work instead of expecting other team members to finish, clean up, or redo any of their shabby or incomplete work. Each team member can count on all the other team members to perform their respective tasks in a quality and timely manner so as not to delay or impede the work of other team members.

Effective team members participate and communicate. They do not sit back and wait to be asked; they speak up and participate in meetings. They take the initiative, communicating with other team members and the project manager in a clear, timely, and unambiguous manner. They provide constructive feedback to each other. In particular, effective team members feel responsible for identifying problems—or potential problems—as early as possible, without pointing the finger or blaming other individuals, the customer, or the project manager for causing the problems. Effective team members are not only problem identifiers but also problem solvers. When a problem has been identified, they suggest alternative solutions and are ready and willing to collaborate with other team members to solve the problem, even if it is outside their assigned area of responsibility. Effective team members do not have a "that's not my problem" or "that's not my job" attitude; rather, they are willing to pitch in to help the team achieve the project objective.

Effective team members help to create a positive, constructive project environment in which there is no room for divisiveness. They're sensitive to the diverse composition of the project team and show respect for all members of the team. They respect others' viewpoints. They don't let pride, stubbornness, or arrogance get in the way of collaboration, cooperation, and compromise. Effective team members put the success of the project above personal gain. It has been said that there is no I in *team*—there are no individual winners or losers. When a project is successful, everybody wins!

Team Building

Socializing among team members supports team building. The better team members get to know one another, the more team building is enhanced. To ensure that individual members communicate with one another frequently, situations need to be created that foster socializing among team members. Team members can initiate some of these situations.

The team can request that team members be physically located in one office area for the duration of the project. When team members are located near one another, there is a greater chance that they will go to each other's offices or work areas to talk. Also, they will pass each other more frequently in common areas such as hallways and have a chance to stop and talk. Discussions should not always be work-related. It's important that team members get to know one another on a personal basis, without being intrusive. A certain number of personal friendships will develop during the project. Having the entire project team located in one area prevents that "us versus them" feeling that can arise when parts of the team are located in different parts of a building or plant. Such a situation can result in a project team that is really a set of several subgroups rather than a true team.

In addition to organizing social activities, the team can periodically call team meetings, as opposed to project meetings. The purpose of team meetings is to discuss openly such questions as the following: How are we working as a team? What barriers are impeding teamwork (such as procedures, resources, priorities, or communications)? What can we do to overcome these barriers? What can we do to improve teamwork? If the project manager participates in team meetings, he or she should be treated as an equal—team members should not look to the manager for the answers, and he or she should not pull rank and override the consensus of the team. It is a team meeting, not a project meeting. Only team-related issues, not project items, should be discussed. Team members should foster team building in whatever ways they can. They should not expect the project manager alone to be responsible for team building.

Conflict on Projects

Conflict on projects is inevitable. You might think that conflict is bad and should be avoided. Differences of opinion are natural, however, and must be expected. It would be a mistake to try to suppress conflict, as it can be beneficial. It provides an opportunity to gain new information, consider alternatives, develop better solutions to problems, enhance team building, and learn. As part of the team-building process, the project manager and project team need to openly acknowledge that conflict is bound to occur during the performance of the project and reach a consensus on how it should be handled. Such a discussion needs to take place at the beginning of the project, not when the first situation occurs or after there has been an emotional outburst.

Unnecessary conflict can be avoided or minimized through early involvement of the project team in planning; clear articulation of each member's role and responsibilities; open, frank, and timely communication; clear operating procedures; and sincere team-building efforts by the project manager and project team.

Personal Time Management

People involved in projects are usually very busy working on their assigned tasks, communicating, preparing documents, attending meetings, and traveling. Therefore, good time management is essential for a high-performance project team. Following are some suggestions to help you effectively manage your time:

1. At the end of each week, identify several (two to five) goals that you want to accomplish the following week.
2. At the end of each day, make a to-do list for the next day.
3. Read the daily to-do list first thing in the morning, and keep it in sight all day.
4. Control interruptions.
5. Learn to say no.
6. Make effective use of waiting time.
7. Try to handle most paperwork only once.
8. Reward yourself at the end of the week if you accomplished all your goals.

Quantitative Techniques in Business

Introduction

Quantitative Methods in Practice

In this section, we present a brief overview of the quantitative methods used in business. Over the years, practitioners have found numerous applications for the following:

LINEAR PROGRAMMING Linear programming is a problem-solving approach that has been developed for situations involving maximizing or minimizing a linear function subject to linear constraints that limit the degree to which the objective can be pursued.

INTEGER LINEAR PROGRAMMING Integer linear programming is an approach used for problems that can be set up as linear programs with the additional requirement that some or all of the decision recommendations be integer values.

PROJECT SCHEDULING: PERT/CPM In many situations, managers are responsible for planning, scheduling, and controlling projects that consist of numerous separate jobs or tasks performed by a variety of departments, individuals, and so forth. The PERT (Program Evaluation and Review Technique) and CPM (Critical Path Method) techniques help managers carry out their project scheduling responsibilities.

INVENTORY MODELS Inventory models are used by managers faced with the dual problems of maintaining sufficient inventories to meet demand for goods and, at the same time, incurring the lowest possible inventory holding costs.

WAITING-LINE OR QUEUEING MODELS Waiting-line or queueing models have been developed to help managers understand and make better decisions concerning the operation of systems involving waiting lines.

SIMULATION Simulation is a technique used to model the operation of a system. This technique employs a computer program to model the operation and perform simulation computations.

DECISION ANALYSIS Decision analysis can be used to determine optimal strategies in situations involving several decision alternatives and an uncertain or risk-filled pattern of future events.

GOAL PROGRAMMING Goal programming is a technique for solving multicriteria decision problems, usually within the framework of linear programming.

ANALYTIC HIERARCHY PROCESS This multicriteria decision-making technique permits the inclusion of subjective factors in arriving at a recommended decision.

FORECASTING Forecasting methods are techniques that can be used to predict future aspects of a business operation.

MARKOV-PROCESS MODELS Markov-process models are useful in studying the evolution of certain systems over repeated trials. For example, Markov processes have been used to describe the probability that a machine, functioning in one period, will function or break down in another period.

Quantitative Methods Used Most Frequently

The most frequently used quantitative methods are linear programming, integer programming, project scheduling, network models such as transportation and transshipment models, and simulation. Depending upon the industry, the other methods in the preceding list are used more or less frequently.

Problem Solving and Decision Making

Problem solving can be defined as the process of identifying a difference between the actual and the desired state of affairs and then taking action to resolve the difference. For problems important enough to justify the time and effort of careful analysis, the problem-solving process involves the following seven steps:

1. Identify and define the problem.
2. Determine the set of alternative solutions.
3. Determine the criterion or criteria that will be used to evaluate the alternatives.
4. Evaluate the alternatives.
5. Choose an alternative.
6. Implement the selected alternative.
7. Evaluate the results to determine whether a satisfactory solution has been obtained.

Decision making is the term generally associated with the first five steps of the problem-solving process. Thus, the first step of decision making is to identify and define the problem. Decision making ends with the choosing of an alternative, which is the act of making the decision.

Let us consider the following example of the decision-making process. For the moment assume that you are currently unemployed and that you would like a position that will lead to a satisfying career. Suppose that your job search has resulted in offers from companies in Rochester, New York; Dallas, Texas; Greensboro, North Carolina; and Pittsburgh, Pennsylvania. Thus, the alternatives for your decision problem can be stated as follows:

1. Accept the position in Rochester.
2. Accept the position in Dallas.
3. Accept the position in Greensboro.
4. Accept the position in Pittsburgh.

The next step of the problem-solving process involves determining the criteria that will be used to evaluate the four alternatives. Obviously, the starting salary is a factor of some importance. If salary were the only criterion important to you, the alternative selected as "best" would be the one with the highest starting salary. Problems in which the objective is to find the best solution with respect to one criterion are referred to as **single-criterion decision problems.**

Suppose that you have also concluded that the potential for advancement and the location of the job are two other criteria of major importance. Thus, the three criteria in your decision problem are starting salary, potential for advancement, and location. Problems that involve more than one criterion are referred to as **multicriteria decision problems.**

195. QUANTITATIVE TECHNIQUES IN BUSINESS

Exhibit 100.72 *Data for the Job Evaluation Decision-Making Problem*

Alternative	Starting Salary	Potential for Advancement	Job Location
1. Rochester	$38,500	Average	Average
2. Dallas	$36,000	Excellent	Good
3. Greensboro	$36,000	Good	Excellent
4. Pittsburgh	$37,000	Average	Good

The next step of the decision-making process is to evaluate each of the alternatives with respect to each criterion. For example, evaluating each alternative relative to the starting salary criterion is done simply by recording the starting salary for each job alternative. Evaluating each alternative with respect to the potential for advancement and the location of the job is more difficult to do, however, because these evaluations are based primarily on subjective factors that are often difficult to quantify. Suppose for now that you decide to measure potential for advancement and job location by rating each of these criteria as poor, fair, average, good, or excellent. The data you compile are shown in Exhibit 100.72.

You are now ready to make a choice from the available alternatives. What makes this choice phase so difficult is that the criteria are probably not all equally important, and no one alternative is "best" with regard to all criteria. Although we will present a method for dealing with situations like this one later, for now let us suppose that after a careful evaluation of the data in Exhibit 100.72, you have decided to select alternative 3; alternative 3 is thus referred to as the **decision.**

Models of Cost, Revenue, and Profit

Some of the most basic quantitative models arising in business and economic applications are those involving the relationship between a volume variable—such as production volume or sales volume—and cost, revenue, and profit. Through the use of these models, a manager can determine the projected cost, revenue, and/or profit associated with an established production quantity or a forecasted sales volume. Financial planning, production planning, sales quotas, and other areas of decision making can benefit from such cost, revenue, and profit models.

Cost and Volume Models

The cost of manufacturing or producing a product is a function of the volume produced. This cost can usually be defined as a sum of two costs: fixed cost and variable cost. **Fixed cost** is the portion of the total cost that does not depend on the production volume; this cost remains the same no matter how much is produced. **Variable cost,** on the other hand, is the portion of the total cost that is dependent on and varies with the production volume. To illustrate how cost and volume models can be developed, we will consider a manufacturing problem faced by Nowlin Plastics.

Nowlin Plastics produces a variety of compact disc (CD) storage cases. Nowlin's best selling product is the CD-50, a slim, plastic CD holder with a specially designed lining that protects the optical surface of the disk. Several products are produced on the same manufacturing line, and a setup cost is incurred each time a changeover is made for a new product. Suppose that the setup cost for the CD-50 is $3000. This setup cost is a fixed cost that is incurred regardless of the number of units eventually produced. In addition, suppose that variable labor and material costs are $2 for each unit produced. The cost-volume model for producing x units of the CD-50 can be written as

$$C(x) = 3000 + 2x \qquad (1.35)$$

where

x = production volume in units
$C(x)$ = total cost of producing x units

Once a production volume is established, the model in equation 1.35 can be used to compute the total production cost. For example, the decision to produce $x = 1200$ units would result in a total cost of $C(1200) = 3000 + 2(1200) = \$5400$.

Marginal cost is defined as the rate of change of the total cost with respect to production volume. That is, it is the cost increase associated with a one-unit increase in the production volume. In the cost model of equation 1.35, we see that the total cost $C(x)$ will increase by $2 for each unit increase in the production volume. Thus, the marginal cost is $2.

With more complex total cost models, marginal cost may depend on the production volume. In such cases, we could have marginal cost increasing or decreasing with the production volume x.

Revenue and Volume Models

Management of Nowlin Plastics will also want information on the projected revenue associated with selling a specified number of units. Thus, a model of the relationship between revenue and volume is also needed. Suppose that each CD-50 storage unit sells for $5. The model for total revenue can be written as

$$R(x) = 5x \qquad (1.36)$$

where

$$x = \text{sales volume in units}$$
$$R(x) = \text{total revenue associated with selling } x \text{ units}$$

Marginal revenue is defined as the rate of change of total revenue with respect to sales volume. That is, it is the increase in total revenue resulting from a one-unit increase in sales volume. In the model of equation 1.36, we see that the marginal revenue is $5. In this case, marginal revenue is constant and does not vary with the sales volume. With more complex models, we may find that marginal revenue increases or decreases as the sales volume x increases.

Profit and Volume Models

One of the most important criteria for management decision making is profit. Managers need to be able to know the profit implications of their decisions. If we assume that we will only produce what can be sold, the production volume and sales volume will be equal. We can combine equations 1.35 and 1.36 to develop a profit-volume model that will determine profit associated with a specified production-sales volume. Since total profit is total revenue minus total cost, the following model provides the profit associated with producing and selling x units:

$$\begin{aligned} P(x) &= R(x) - C(x) \\ &= 5x - (3000 + 2x) = -3000 + 3x \end{aligned} \qquad (1.37)$$

Thus, the model for profit $P(x)$ can be derived from the models of the revenue-volume and cost-volume relationships.

Breakeven Analysis

Using equation 1.37, we can now determine the profit associated with any production volume x. For example, suppose that a demand forecast indicates that 500 units of the product can be sold. The decision to produce and sell the 500 units results in a projected profit of

$$P(500) = -3000 + 3(500) = -1500$$

In other words, a loss of $1500 is predicted. If sales are expected to be 500 units, the manager may decide against producing the product. However, a demand forecast of 1800 units would show a projected profit of

$$P(1800) = -3000 + 3(1800) = 2400$$

This profit may be enough to justify proceeding with the production and sale of the product.

We see that a volume of 500 units will yield a loss, whereas a volume of 1800 provides a profit. The volume that results in total revenue equaling total cost (providing $0 profit) is called the **breakeven point.** If the breakeven point is known, a manager can quickly infer that a volume above the breakeven point will result in a profit, while a volume below the breakeven point will result in a loss. Thus, the breakeven point for a product provides valuable information for a manager who must make a yes/no decision concerning production of the product.

Let us now return to the Nowlin Plastics example and show how the profit model in equation (1.37) can be used to compute the breakeven point. The breakeven point can be found by setting the profit expression equal to zero and solving for the production volume. Using equation 1.37, we have

$$P(x) = -3000 + 3x = 0$$
$$3x = 3000$$
$$x = 1000$$

Exhibit 100.73 *Graph of the Breakeven Analysis for Nowlin Plastics*

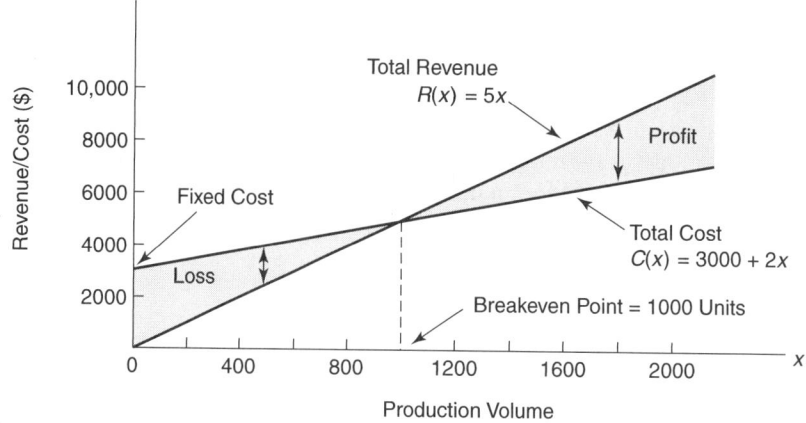

With this information, we know that production and sales of the product must be at least 1000 units before a profit can be expected. The graphs of the total cost model, the total revenue model, and the location of the breakeven point are shown in Exhibit 100.73.

Decision Analysis

Decision analysis can be used to determine an optimal strategy when a decision maker is faced with serveral decision alternatives and an uncertain or risk-filled pattern of future events. For example, a global manufacturer might be interested in determining the best location for a new plant. Suppose that the manufacturer has identified five decision alternatives corresponding to five plant locations in different countries. Making the plant lcoation decision is complicated by factors such as the world economy, demand in various regions of the world, labor availability, raw material costs, transportation costs, and so on. In such a problem, several scenarios could be developed to descrive how the varoius factors combine to form the possible uncertain future events. Then probabilities can be assigned to the events. Using profit or cost as a measure of the consequence for each decision alternative and each future event combination, the best plant location can be selected.

Even when a careful decision analysis has been conducted, the uncertain future events make the final consequence uncertain. In some cases, the selected dexision alternative may provide good or excellent results. In other cases, a relatively unlikely future event may occur causing the selected decision alternative to provide only fair or even poor results. The risk associated with any decision alternative is a direct result of the uncertainty associated with the final consequence. Through risk analysis the decision maker is provided with probability information about the favorable as well as the unfavorable consequences that may occur. Influence diagrams, payoff tables, and decision trees are used to perform decision analysis.

Risk Analysis and Sensitivity Analysis

Risk analysis is the process of predicting the outcome of a decision in the face of uncertainty. Risk analysis can be used to provide probabilities for the payoffs associated with a decision alternative. As a result, risk analysis helps the decision maker recognize the difference between the expected value of a decision alternative and the payoff that may actually occur. **Sensitivity analysis** also helps the decision maker by describing how changes in the state-of-nature probabilities and/or changes in the payoffs affect the recommended decision alternative. This is called "what-if" analysis.

Risk Analysis

A decision alternative and a state of nature combine to generate the payoff associated with a decision. The **risk profile** for a decision alternative shows the possible payoffs along with their associated probabilities.

Let us demonstrate risk analysis and the construction of a risk profile for the PDC condominium construction project. Using the expected value approach, we identified the large condominium complex (d_3) as the best decision

Exhibit 100.74 *Risk Profile for the Large Complex Decision Alternative for the PDC Condominium Project*

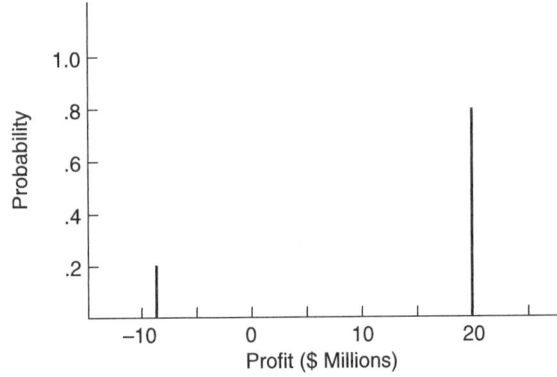

alternative. The expected value of $14.2 million for d_3 is based on a 0.8 probability of obtaining a $20 million profit and a 0.2 probability of obtaining a $9 million loss. The 0.8 probability for the $20 million payoff and the 0.2 probability for the −$9 million payoff provide the risk profile for the large complex decision alternative. This risk profile is shown graphically in Exhibit 100.74.

Sometimes a review of the risk profile associated with an optimal decision alternative may cause the decision maker to choose another decision alternative even though the expected value of the other decision alternative not as good. For example, the risk profile for the medium complex decision alternative (d_2) shows a 0.8 probability for a $14 million payoff and 0.2 probability for a $5 million payoff. Because no probability of a loss is associated with decision alternative d_2, the medium complex decision alternative would be judged less risky than the large complex decision alternative. As a result, a decision maker might prefer the less-risky medium complex decision alternative even though it has an expected value of $2 million less than the large complex decision alternative.

Sensitivity Analysis

Sensitivity analysis can be used to determine how changes in the probabilities for the states of nature and/or changes in the payoffs affect the recommended decision alternative. In many cases, the probabilities for the states of nature and the payoffs are based on subjective assessments. Sensitivity analysis helps the decision maker understand which of these inputs are critical to the choice of the best decision alternative. If a small change in the value of one of the inputs causes a change in the recommended decision alternative, the solution to the decision analysis problem is sensitive to that particular input. Extra effort and care should be taken to make sure the input value is as accurate as possible. On the other hand, if a modest to large change in the value of one of the inputs does not cause a change in the recommended decision alternative, the solution to the decision analysis problem is not sensitive to that particular input. No extra time or effort would be needed to refine the estimated input value.

One approach to sensitivity analysis is to select different values for the probabilities of the states of nature and/or the payoffs and then resolve the decision analysis problem. If the recommended decision alternative changes, we know that the solution is sensitive to the changes made. For example, suppose that in the PDC problem the probability for a strong demand is revised to 0.2 and the probability for a weak demand is revised to 0.8. Would the recommended decision alternative change? Using $P(s_1) = 0.2$, $P(s_2) = 0.8$, the revised expected values for the three decision alternatives are

$$EV(d_1) = 0.2(8) + 0.8(7) = 7.2$$
$$EV(d_2) = 0.2(14) + 0.8(5) = 6.8$$
$$EV(d_3) = 0.2(20) + 0.8(-9) = -3.2$$

With these probability assessments the recommended decision alternative is to construct a small condominium complex (d_1), with an expected value of $7.2 million. The probability of strong demand is only 0.2, so constructing the large condominium complex (d_3) is the least preferred alternative, with an expected value of −$3.2 million (a loss).

Thus, when the probability of strong demand is large, PDC should build the large complex; when the probability of strong demand is small, PDC should build the small complex. Obviously, we could continue to modify the probabilities of the states of nature and learn even more about how changes in the probabilities affect the recommended decision alternative. The drawback to this approach is the numerous calculations required to evaluate the effect of several possible changes in the state-of-nature probabilities.

195. QUANTITATIVE TECHNIQUES IN BUSINESS

Decision Analysis with Sample Information

In applying the expected value approach, we have shown how probability information about the states of nature affects the expected value calculations and thus the decision recommendation. Frequently, decision makers have preliminary or **prior probability** assessments for the states of nature that are the best probability values available at that time. However, to make the best possible decision, the decision maker may want to seek additional information about the states of nature. This new information can be used to revise or update the prior probabilities so that the final decision is based on more accurate probabilities for the states of nature. Most often, additional information is obtained through experiments designed to provide **sample information** about the states of nature. Raw material sampling, product testing, and market research studies are examples of experiments (or studies) that may enable management to revise or update the state-of-nature probabilities. These revised probabilities are called **posterior probabilities.**

Utility and Decision Making

The Meaning of Utility

Utility is a measure of the total worth of a particular outcome; it reflects the decision maker's attitude toward a collection of factors such as profit, loss, and risk. Researchers have found that as long as the monetary value of payoffs stays within a range that the decision maker considers reasonable, selecting the decision alternative with the best expected monetary value usually leads to selection of the most preferred decision. However, when the payoffs become extreme, most decision makers are not satisfied with the decision that simply provides the best expected monetary value.

As an example of a situation in which utility can help in selecting the best decision alternative, let us consider the problem faced by Swofford, Inc., a relatively small real estate investment firm located in Atlanta, Georgia. Swofford currently has two investment opportunities that require approximately the same cash outlay. The cash requirements necessary prohibit Swofford from making more than one investment at this time. Consequently, three possible decision alternatives may be considered.

The three decision alternatives, denoted d_1, d_2, and d_3, are

$$d_1 = \text{make investment } A$$
$$d_2 = \text{make investment } B$$
$$d_3 = \text{do not invest}$$

The monetary payoffs associated with the investment opportunities depend on the investment decision and on the direction of the real estate market during the next six months (the chance event). Real estate prices will go up, remain stable, or go down. Thus the Swofford states of nature, denoted by s_1, s_2, and s_3, are

$$s_1 = \text{real estate prices go up}$$
$$s_2 = \text{real estate prices remain stable}$$
$$s_3 = \text{real estate prices go down}$$

Using the best information available, Swofford has estimated the profits, or payoffs, associated with each decision alternative and state-of-nature combination. The resulting payoff table is shown in Exhibit 100.75.

Exhibit 100.75 *Payoff Table for Swofford, Inc.*

	State of Nature		
Decision Alternative	Prices Up s_1	Prices Stable s_2	Prices Down s_3
Investment A, d_1	$30,000	$20,000	−$50,000
Investment B, d_2	$50,000	−$20,000	−$30,000
Do not invest, d_3	0	0	0

Exhibit 100.76 *Diagram of a Simulation Model*

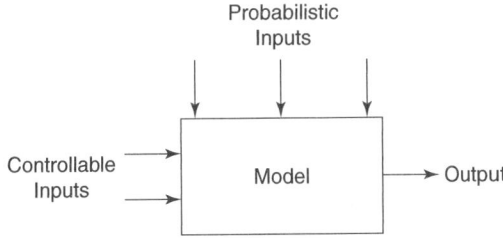

The best estimate of the probability that real estate prices will go up is 0.30; the best estimate of the probability that prices will remain stable is 0.50; and the best estimate of the probability that prices will go down is 0.20. Thus the expected values for the three decision alternatives are

$$EV(d_1) = 0.3(30,000) + 0.5(20,000) + 0.2(-50,000) = 9,000$$
$$EV(d_2) = 0.3(50,000) + 0.5(-20,000) + 0.2(-30,000) = -1,000$$
$$EV(d_3) = 0.3(0) + 0.5(0) + 0.2(0) = 0$$

Using the expected value approach, the optimal decision is to select investment A with an expected monetary value of $9000.

Simulation

Simulation is one of the most widely used quantitative approaches to decision making. It is a method for learning about a real system by experimenting with a model that represents the system. The simulation model contains the mathematical expressions and logical relationships that describe how to compute the value of the outputs given the values of the inputs. Any simulation model has two inputs: controllable inputs and probabilistic inputs. Exhibit 100.76 shows a conceptual diagram of a simulation model.

In conducting a **simulation experiment,** an analyst selects the value, or values, for the **controllable inputs.** Then values for the **probabilistic inputs** are randomly generated. The simulation model uses the values of the controllable inputs and the values of the probabilistic inputs to compute the value, or values, of the output. By conducting a series of experiments using a variety of values for the controllable inputs, the analyst learns how values of the controllable inputs affect or change the output of the simulation model. After reviewing the simulation results, the analyst is often able to make decision recommendations for the controllable inputs that will provide the desired output for the real system.

Simulation has been successfully applied in a variety of applications. The following examples are typical.

1. **New Product Development** The objective of this simulation is to determine the probability that a new product will be profitable. A model is developed relating profit (the output measure) to various probabilistic inputs such as demand, parts cost, and labor cost. The only controllable input is whether to introduce the product. A variety of possible values will be generated for the probabilistic inputs, and the resulting profit will be computed.

2. **Airline Overbooking** The objective of this simulation is to determine the number of reservations an airline should accept for a particular flight. A simulation model is developed relating profit for the flight to a probabilistic input, the number of passengers with a reservation who show up and use their reservation, and a controllable input, the number of reservations accepted for the flight. For each selected value for the controllable input, a variety of possible values will be generated for the number of passengers who show up, and the resulting profit can be computed. Similar simulation models are applicable for hotel and car rental reservation systems.

3. **Inventory Policy** The objective of this simulation is to choose an inventory policy that will provide good customer service at a reasonable cost. A model is developed relating two output measures, total inventory cost and the service level, to probabilistic inputs, such as product demand and delivery lead time from vendors, and controllable inputs, such as the order quantity and the reorder point. For each setting of the controllable inputs, a variety of possible values would be generated for the probabilistic inputs, and the resulting cost and service levels would be computed.

4. **Traffic Flow** The objective of this simulation is to determine the effect of installing a left turn signal on the flow of traffic through a busy intersection. A model is developed relating waiting time for vehicles to get through the intersection to probabilistic inputs such as the number of vehicle arrivals and the fraction that want to make a left turn, and controllable inputs such as the length of time the left turn signal is on. For each setting of the controllable inputs, values would be generated for the probabilistic inputs, and the resulting vehicle waiting times would be computed.
5. **Waiting Lines** The objective of this simulation is to determine the waiting times for customers at a bank's automated teller machine (ATM). A model is developed relating customer waiting times to probabilistic inputs such as customer arrivals and service times, and a controllable input, the number of ATM machines installed. For each value of the controllable input (the number of ATM machines), a variety of values would be generated for the probabilistic inputs and the customer waiting times would be computed.

Simulation is not an optimization technique. It is a method that can be used to describe or predict how a system will operate given certain choices for the controllable inputs and randomly generated values for the probabilistic inputs. Quantitative analysts often use simulation to determine values for the controllable inputs that are likely to lead to desirable system outputs. In this sense, simulation can be an effective tool in designing a system to provide good performance.

Other Simulation Issues

Because simulation is one of the most widely used quantitative analysis techniques, various software tools have been developed to help analysts implement a simulation model on a computer. In this section we comment on the software available and discuss some issues involved in verifying and validating a simulation model. We close the section with a discussion of some of the advantages and disadvantages of using simulation to study a real system.

Computer Implementation

The computational and record-keeping aspects of simulation models are assisted by special simulation software packages. The packages ease the tasks of developing a computer simulation model.

The use of spreadsheets for simulation has grown rapidly in recent years, and third-party software vendors have developed spreadsheet add-ins that make building simulation models on a spreadsheet much easier. These add-in packages provide an easy facility for generating random values from a variety of probability distributions and provide a rich array of statistics describing the simulation output.

To decide which software to use, an analyst will have to consider the relative merits of a spreadsheet, a special-purpose simulation package, and a general-purpose computer programming language. The goal is to select the method that is easy to use while still providing an adequate representation of the system being studied.

Verification and Validation

An important aspect of any simulation study involves confirming that the simulation model accurately describes the real system. Inaccurate simulation models cannot be expected to provide worthwhile information. Thus, before using simulation results to draw conclusions about a real system, one must take steps to verify and validate the simulation model.

Verification is the process of determining that the computer procedure that performs the simulation calculations is logically correct. Verification is largely a debugging task to make sure that no errors are in the computer procedure that implements the simulation. In some cases, an analyst may compare computer results for a limited number of events with independent hand calculations. In other cases, tests may be performed to verify that the probabilistic inputs are being generated correctly and that the output from the simulation model seems reasonable. The verification step is not complete until the user has developed a high degree of confidence that the computer procedure is error free.

Validation is the process of ensuring that the simulation model provides an accurate representation of a real system. Validation requires an agreement among analysts and managers that the logic and the assumptions used in the design of the simulation model accurately reflect how the real system operates. The first phase of the validation process is done prior to, or in conjunction with, the development of the computer procedure for the simulation process. Validation continues after the computer program has been developed with the analyst reviewing the simulation output to see whether the simulation results closely approximate the performance of the real system. If possible, the output of the simulation model is compared to the output of an existing real system to make sure that the simulation output closely approximates the performance of the real system. If this form of validation is not possible, an analyst can experiment with the simulation model and have one or more individuals experienced with the operation of the real system review the simulation output to determine whether it is a reasonable approximation of what would be obtained with the real system under similar conditions.

Verification and validation are not tasks to be taken lightly. They are key steps in any simulation study and are necessary to ensure that decisions and conclusions based on the simulation results are appropriate for the real system.

Advantages and Disadvantages of Using Simulation

The primary advantages of simulation are that it is easy to understand and that the methodology can be used to model and learn about the behavior of complex systems that would be difficult, if not impossible, to deal with analytically. Simulation models are flexible; they can be used to describe systems without requiring the assumptions that are often required by mathematical models. In general, the larger the number of probabilistic inputs a system has, the more likely that a simulation model will provide the best approach for studying the system. Another advantage of simulation is that a simulation model provides a convenient experimental laboratory for the real system. Changing assumptions or operating policies in the simulation model and rerunning it can provide results that help predict how such changes will affect the operation of the real system. Experimenting directly with a real system is often not feasible.

> *Using simulation, we can ask what-if questions and project how the real system will behave. Although simulation does not guarantee optimality, it will usually provide near-optimal solutions. In addition, simulation models often warn against poor decision strategies by projecting disastrous outcomes such as system failures, large finanical losses, and so on.*

Simulation is not without some disadvantages. For complex systems, the process of developing, verifying, and validating a simulation model can be time-consuming and expensive. In addition, each simulation run only provides a sample of how the real system will operate. As such, the summary of the simulation data only provides estimates or approximations about the real system. Consequently, simulation does not guarantee an optimal solution. Nonetheless, the danger of obtaining poor solutions is slight if the analyst exercises good judgment in developing the simulation model and if the simulation process is run long enough under a wide variety of conditions so that the analyst has sufficient data to predict how the real system will operate.

Quantitative Techniques and Operations

Operational issues and problems are big in size and scope and therefore require quantitative techniques to solve them. Most of these techniques use mathematics as the basis. Major applications of these techniques include linear programming (LP), inventory models, waiting-line models, simulation, sensitivity analysis, and operations forecasting. In this section, LP applications are highlighted, followed by operations forecasting.

Linear Programming Applications

In operations, LP techniques are commonly used to solve problems in transportation (truck) routing. Whenever a company needs to move a quantity of goods from and to multiple locations such as plants, regional warehouses, or retail stores, it faces a practical LP problem. By minimizing route mileage, operating costs can be minimized and outlays for capital investment can be kept at a minimum. Many companies can save significant amounts of money per year on shipping costs by solving LP problems of this type. Other operations-related LP applications include mixing or blending work in oil, food, paint, drug, and chemical industries.

Operations Forecasting

An essential aspect of managing any organization is planning for the future. Indeed, the long-run success of an organization is closely related to how well management is able to anticipate the future and develop appropriate strategies. Good judgment, intuition, and an awareness of the state of the economy may give a manager a rough idea or "feeling" of what is likely to happen in the future. However, converting this feeling into a number that can be used as next quarter's sales volume or next year's raw material cost per unit often is difficult. Section 170 introduces several forecasting methods used in sales and production.

Quantitative Techniques and Marketing

Linear programming can be used in media selection and marketing research. Markov process models are used in analyzing market share.

Media selection applications of linear programming are designed to help marketing managers allocate a fixed advertising budget to various advertising media. Potential media include newspapers, magazines, radio, television, and direct mail. In these applications, the objective is to maximize reach, frequency, and quality of exposure. Restrictions on the allowable allocation usually arise during consideration of company policy, contract requirements, and media availability.

An organization conducts marketing research to learn about consumers' characteristics, attitudes, and preferences. Marketing research firms that specialize in providing such information often do the actual research for client organizations. Typical services offered by a marketing research firm include designing the study, conducting market surveys, analyzing the data collected, and providing summary reports and recommendations for the client. In the research design phase, targets or quotas may be established for the number and types of respondents to be surveyed. The marketing research firm's objective is to conduct the survey so as to meet the client's needs at a minimum cost. This is a good application of linear programming technique.

Analysis of a Markov process model is not intended to optimize any particular aspect of a system. Rather, the analysis predicts or describes the future and steady-state behavior of the system. For instance, the analysis of the steady-state behavior provided a forecast or prediction of the market shares for the two competitors involved in local grocery business.

Quantitative Techniques and Finance

In this section, we will present a variety of quantitative techniques used in the finance and accounting functions. These include cash management model; depreciation, depletion, and amortization methods; the time value of money; and basic valuation of assets.

The Cash Management Model

The cash management model (Miller-Orr model) is used to monitor the cash position of a company, which is subject to fluctuations daily, weekly, or monthly. The management goal is to invest excess idle cash and to meet ongoing financial obligations. The model sets two control limits: the *lower control limit* (LCL), which is a minimum; and the *upper control limit* (UCL), which is a maximum, similar to statistical process control in a manufacturing quality control environment. As long as the target cash balance (TCB) is between LCL and UCL, no action needs to be taken. When the actual cash balance reaches the LCL (point x in Exhibit 100.78), investment securities worth of TCB-LCL are to be sold in order to return the cash balance to the target level. When the actual cash balance reaches the UCL (point y in Exhibit 100.78), investment securities worth of UCL-TCB are to be bought in order to return the cash balance to the target level. Exhibit 100.77 shows a graph for the Miller-Orr model.

Management sets the lower control limit, which acts as a safety stock or a required compensating balance. The firm needs to calculate the standard deviation of monthly net cash flows, hence its variance, in order to compute the target cash balance. The upper control limit can be calculated as $(3 \times TCB) - (2 \times LCL)$ and the average cash balance (ACB) can be calculated as $(4 \times TCB - LCL)/3$.

Other Quantitative Methods

- *Simultaneous equations are used in allocating a production department's overhead costs to service departments in a manufacturing firm.*

- *A Markov chain analysis is used to identify changes in the customer's collection experience. The analysis is related to the uncollected receivable balance percentages.*

Exhibit 100.77 *The Miller-Orr Model Graph*

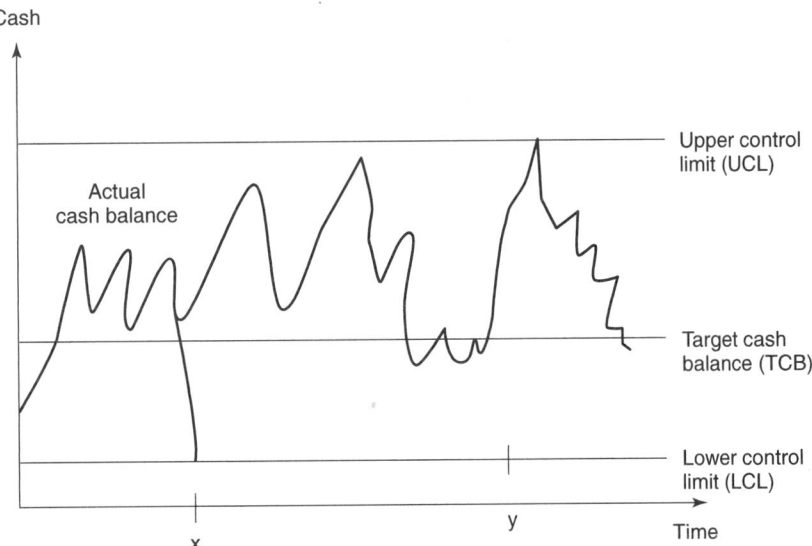

Example 1 *Firm XYZ has established a minimum cash balance requirement of $100 and a target cash balance of $400. What is the maximum cash balance for firm XYZ?*

$$UCL = (3 \times TCB) - (2 \times LCL) = (3 \times \$400) - (2 \times \$100) = \$1{,}000$$

What is the average cash balance for firm XYZ?

$$ACB = (4 \times TCB - LCL)/3 = (4 \times 400 - 100)/3 = \$500$$

How much securities can be bought if the cash balance reaches the maximum?

$$\text{Amount of securities to be bought} = UCL - TCB = \$1{,}000 - \$400 = \$600$$

Depreciation, Depletion, and Amortization Methods

Simple ratios and basic math calculations are used in allocating costs of operational, long-term, fixed assets. Cost allocation for operational assets is known as depreciation for plant and equipment, depletion for natural resources such as coal and iron ore, and amortization for intangible assets such as patents and copyrights.

Higher depreciation expense results in lower taxes and higher cash flows.

Depreciation is a process of cost allocation, not valuation of assets. The depreciation expense for an asset, which is used to manufacture a product, is part of the overhead cost and is included in the cost of goods sold and cost of inventory. Because depreciation is a non-cash expense, the amount of depreciation is added back to the accounting net income to compute cash flows for the period.

Depreciation Methods

There are two specific methods for depreciation: the straight-line method for stockholder reporting ("book") purposes, and the accelerated cost recovery method (known as Modified Accelerated Cost Recovery System, MACRS) for tax purposes. The straight line method is simple and widely used, as an equal amount of depreciable base is allocated to each year of the asset's service life. The depreciable base, which is the original cost of the equipment minus the residual value, is divided by the number of years of the asset's service life. The book value of a machine is its original cost minus the accumulated depreciation expense. The MACRS method uses asset lives and recovery allowance percentages for personal property provided by tax authorities. The yearly recovery allowance for depreciation expense is determined by multiplying each asset's depreciable basis by the applicable recovery percentages. In the MACRS method, the entire cost of an asset is expensed over its depreciable life, unlike the straight line method. This means salvage value is ignored in the MACRS method, giving businesses larger tax deductions and thereby increasing their cash flows available for reinvestment.

Example 2 *A manufacturing company purchased a machine for $200,000. The company expects the service life of the machine to be five years. It is expected that the machine will produce 100,000 units during its life. The residual value is estimated at $50,000. What is the depreciation expense per year using the straight-line method?*

Depreciable base/number of years = ($200,000 − $50,000)/5 = $150,000/5 = $30,000 per year

Depletion Methods

The activity-based units-of-production method is widely used to calculate periodic depletion of natural resources such as coal and iron ore. Depletion base is cost less any anticipated residual value. The depletion rate per unit is multiplied with actual units extracted to obtain the total depletion expense.

Example 3 *The coal deposits for a firm are estimated at 1,000,000 tons with the capitalized costs of $700,000 and residual value of $100,000. The actual coal extracted in the month of January is 400,000 tons. What is the depletion expense for the month of January?*

Depletion rate per ton = Depletion base/estimated extractable tons
0.60/ton = ($700,000 − $100,000)/1,000,000
The depletion expense for the January month = extracted tons in January × depletion rate per ton
$240,000 = 400,000 × $0.60

Amortization Methods

The capitalized cost of an intangible asset must be allocated to the periods in which the asset is expected to contribute to the company's revenue generating activities. Intangible assets such as goodwill, patents, franchises, and copyrights have no residual value, so the amortization base is simply the original cost. GAAP states that the service life of most intangible assets should not exceed 40 years. In practice, goodwill is amortized over 20 years, patents are amortized over 17 years, franchise is amortized during the life of its agreement, and copyrights are amortized over 40 years, although the actual rights exceed 40 years allowed by GAAP. The straight-line method should be used to amortize the cost of intangible assets unless the company can show that another method is more appropriate.

The Time Value of Money

Financial decision making, whether from the perspective of firms or investors, is primarily concerned with determining how value will be affected by the expected outcomes (payoffs) associated with alternative choices. For example, if you have $5,500 to invest today, you must decide what to do with the money. If you have the opportunity to purchase an investment that will return $7,020 after five years or an investment that will return $8,126 after eight years, which should you choose? To answer this question, you must determine which investment alternative has greater value to you.

All else equal, a dollar received soon is worth more than a dollar expected in the distant future because the sooner a dollar is received the quicker it can be invested to earn a positive return. So does that mean the five-year investment is more valuable than the eight-year investment? Not necessarily, because the eight-year investment promises a higher dollar payoff than the five-year investment. To determine which investment is more valuable, the dollar payoffs for the investments need to be compared at the same point in time. Thus, for these two investments, we could determine the current values of both investments by restating, or revaluing, the payoffs expected at different times in the future (for example, $7,020 in five years and $8,126 in eight years) in terms of current (today's) dollars. The concept used to revalue payoffs such as those associated with these investments is termed the *time value of money*. It is essential that both financial managers and investors have a clear understanding of the time value of money and its impact on the value of an asset. We show how the timing of cash flows affects asset values and rates of return.

The principles of time value analysis that are developed in this section have many applications, ranging from setting up schedules for paying off loans to decisions about whether to acquire new equipment. *In fact, of all the techniques used in finance, none is more important than the concept of the time value of money (TVM).*

Cash Flow Timelines

One of the most important tools in time value of money analysis is the **cash flow timeline,** which is used to help us visualize when the cash flows associated with a particular situation occur.

Cash flows are placed directly below the tick marks, and interest rates are shown directly above the cash flow time line. Unknown cash flows, which we are trying to find in the analysis, are indicated by question marks. For example, consider the following timeline:

TIME:

```
                       0   5%   1        2        3
                       |--------|--------|--------|
    Cash Flows: 2100                              ?
```

Here the interest rate for each of the three periods is 5 percent; a single amount (or lump sum) cash **outflow** is made at Time 0; and the Time 3 value is an unknown **inflow.** Because the initial $100 is an outflow (an investment), it has a minus sign. Because the Period 3 amount is an inflow, it does not have a minus sign. Note that no cash flows occur at Time 1 and Time 2.

Future Value

A dollar in hand today is worth more than a dollar to be received in the future because, if you had it now, you could invest it, earn interest, and end up with more than one dollar in the future. The process of going from today's values, which are termed present values (PV), to future values (FV) is called **compounding.** To illustrate, suppose you deposited $100 in a bank account that paid 5 percent interest each year. How much would you have at the end of one year? To begin, we define the following terms:

- PV = Present value, or beginning amount, in your account. Here PV = $100.
- i = Interest rate the bank pays on the account per year. The interest earned is based on the balance in the account at the beginning of each year, and we assume that it is paid at the end of the year. Here i = 5%, or, expressed as a decimal, i = 0.05. Throughout this chapter, we designate the interest rate as i because that symbol is used on most financial calculators. Note, though, that we use the symbol *k* to denote interest rates because *k* is used more often in the financial literature.

INT = Dollars of interest you earn during the year 5 (Beginning of year amount) × i. Here INT = $100 × 0.05 = $5 in the first year.

FV_n = Future value, or value of the account at the end of n periods (years in this case), after the interest earned has been added to the account.

n = Number of periods interest is earned. Here n = 1.

In our example, n = 1, so FV_n can be calculated as follows:

$$FV_n = FV_1 = PV + INT$$
$$= PV + (PV \times i)$$
$$= PV(1 + i)$$
$$= \$100(1 + 0.05) = \$100(1.05) = \$105.$$

Thus, the **future value (FV)** at the end of one year, FV_1, equals the present value multiplied by 1.0 plus the interest rate. So you will have $105 in one year if you invest $100 today and 5 percent interest is paid at the end of the year.

In general, the future value of an initial sum at the end of n years can be found by applying Equation 1.38.

$$FV_n = PV(1 + i)^n \tag{1.38}$$

Equation 1.38 and most other time value of money problems can be solved in three ways: numerically with a regular calculator, with interest rate tables, or with a financial calculator. We choose the first two approaches in this section.

Numerical Solution

According to Equation 1.38, to compute the future value, FV, of an amount invested today (PV) we need to determine by what multiple the amount invested will increase in the future. As you can see, the multiple by which any amount will increase is based on the total dollar interest earned, which depends on both the interest rate and the length of time interest is earned. This multiple, termed the **future value interest factor for i and n ($FVIF_{i,n}$)**, is defined as $(1 + i)^n$.

Interest Tables (Tabular Solution)

As we showed in the previous section, computing the values for $FVIF_{i,n}$ is not a very difficult task if you have a calculator handy. Exhibit 100.78 gives the future value interest factors for i values from 4 percent to 6 percent and n values from 1 to 6 periods, while Table A-3 in Module 700 Appendix contains $FVIF_{i,n}$ values for a wide range of i and n values.

Because $(1 + i)^n = FVIF_{i,n}$, equation 1.38 can be rewritten as follows.

$$FV_n = PV(1 + i)^n = PV(FVIF_{i,n}) \tag{1.39}$$

To illustrate, the FVIF for our five-year, 5 percent interest problem can be found in Exhibit 100.78 by looking down the first column to Period 5, and then looking across that row to the 5 percent column, where we see that $FVIF_{5\%,5} = 1.2763$. Then, the value of $100 after five years is found as follows:

$$FV_n = PV(FVIF_{i,n})$$
$$= \$100(FVIF_{5\%,5})$$

Exhibit 100.78 Future Value Interest Factors: $FVIF_{i,n} = (1 + i)^n$

Period (N)	4%	5%	6%
1	1.0400	1.0500	1.0600
2	1.0816	1.1025	1.1236
3	1.1249	1.1576	1.1910
4	1.1699	1.2155	1.2625
5	1.2167	**1.2763**	1.3382
6	1.2653	1.3401	1.4185

Using the interest Table A-3 in Module 700 Appendix, the future value of $1 for five years at 5 percent interest rate is 1.2763. Then the value of $100 after five years is

$$= \$100(1.2763)$$
$$= \$127.63$$

Present Value

Suppose you have some extra cash, and you have a chance to buy a low-risk security that will pay $127.63 at the end of five years. Your local bank is currently offering 5 percent interest on five-year certificates of deposit, and you regard the security as being very safe. The 5 percent rate is called your **opportunity cost rate,** or the rate of return you could earn on alternative investments of *similar risk*. How much should you be willing to pay for the security?

From the future value example presented in the previous section, we saw that an initial amount of $100 invested at 5 percent per year would be worth $127.63 at the end of five years. As we will see in a moment, you should be indifferent to the choice between $100 today and $127.63 at the end of five years, and the $100 is defined as the **present value,** or **PV,** of $127.63 due in five years when the opportunity cost rate is 5 percent. If the price of the security is anything less than $100, you should definitely buy it because it would cost you exactly $100 to produce the $127.63 in five years if you earned a 5 percent return. Therefore, if you could find another investment with the same risk that would produce the same future amount ($127.63) but it cost less than $100 (say $95), then you could earn a return higher than 5 percent by purchasing that investment. Similarly, if the price of the security is greater than $100, you should not buy it because it would cost you only $100 to produce the same future amount at the given rate of return. If the price is exactly $100, then you could either buy it or turn it down because $100 is the security's fair value if it has a 5 percent expected return.

In general, *the present value of a cash flow due n years in the future is the amount that, if it were on hand today, would grow to equal the future amount.* Because $100 would grow to $127.63 in five years at a 5 percent interest rate, $100 is the present value of $127.63 due five years in the future when the opportunity cost rate is 5 percent. Finding present values is called **discounting,** and it simply is the reverse of compounding—if you know the PV, you can compound to find the FV, while if you know the FV, you can discount to find the PV. When discounting, you would follow these steps:

CASH FLOW TIMELINE:

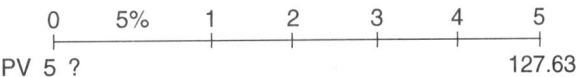

EQUATION:
To develop the present value, or discounting, equation, we begin with equation 1.40:

$$FV_n = PV(1 + i)^n = PV(FVIF_{i,n}) \qquad (1.40)$$

and then solve for PV to yield

$$PV = \frac{FV_n}{(1 + i)^n} = FV_n\left[\frac{1}{(1 + i)^n}\right] = FV_n(PVIF_{i,n}) \qquad (1.41)$$

The middle form and the last form of equation 1.41 recognizes that the interest factor $PVIF_{i,n}$ is equal to

$$PVIF_{i,n} = \frac{1}{(1 + i)^n} \qquad (1.42)$$

The term given in equation 1.42 is called the **present value interest factor for i and n ($PVIF_{i,n}$).**

Tabular Solution

Table A-1 in Module 700 Appendix contains present value interest factors for selected values of i and n, $PVIF_{i,n}$. The value of $PVIF_{i,n}$ for i = 5% and n = 5 periods is 0.7835, so the present value of $127.63 to be received after five years when the opportunity cost rate is 5 percent equals

$$PV = \$127.63 \ (PVIF_{5\%,5})$$
$$= \$127.63(0.7835)$$
$$= \$100$$

Future Value of an Annuity

An **annuity** is a series of equal payments made at fixed intervals for a specified number of periods. For example, $100 at the end of each of the next three years is a three-year annuity. The payments are given the symbol PMT, and they can occur at either the beginning or the end of each period. If the payments occur at the end of each period, as they typically do in business transactions, the annuity is called an **ordinary**, or **deferred, annuity**. If payments are made at the *beginning* of each period, the annuity is an **annuity due**. Because ordinary annuities are more common in finance, when the term *annuity* is used in this module, you should assume that the payments occur at the end of each period unless otherwise noted.

Ordinary Annuities

If you deposit $100 at the end of each year for three years in a savings account that pays 5 percent interest per year, how much will you have at the end of three years? To answer this question, we must find the future value of an ordinary annuity, FVA_n. Each payment is compounded out to the end of Period n, and the sum of the compounded payments is the future value of the annuity.

CASH FLOW TIMELINE:
Here we show the regular cash flow time line as the top portion of the diagram, but we also show how each cash flow is processed to produce the value FVA_n in the lower portion of the diagram.

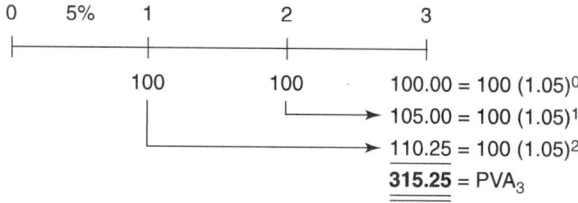

EQUATION:
The cash flow time line shows that we can compute the future value of the annuity simply by determining the future values of the individual payments and then summing the results. Thus, the equation for the future value of an ordinary annuity can be written as follows:

$$FVA_n = PMT(1 + i)^0 + PMT(1 + i)^1 + PMT(1 + i)^2$$
$$+ \ldots + PMT(1 + i)^{n-1} \quad (1.43)$$
$$= PMT \sum_{t=1}^{n} (1 + i)^{n-t} = PMT \sum_{t=0}^{n-1} (1 + i)^t$$

Note that the first line of equation 1.43 presents the annuity payments in reverse order of payment, and the superscript in each term indicates the number of periods of interest each payment receives. In other words, because the first annuity payment was made at the end of Period 1, interest would be earned in Period 2 through Period n only; thus, compounding would be for n − 1 periods rather than n periods, compounding for the second annuity payment would be for Period 3 through Period n, or n − 2 periods, and so on. The last annuity payment is made at the same time the computation is made, so there is no time for interest to be earned; thus, the superscript 0 represents the fact that no interest is earned. Simplifying the first line produces the last line of equation 1.43.

NUMERICAL SOLUTION The lower section of the cash flow time line shows the numerical solution. The future value, FV, of each cash flow is found, and those FVs are summed to find the FV of the annuity. This is a tedious process for long annuities.

The numerical solution is easier if we simplify equation 1.44 as follows:[470]

$$FVA_n = PMT \left[\sum_{t=1}^{n} (1 + i)^{n-t} \right] = PMT \left[\frac{(1 + i)^n - 1}{i} \right] \quad (1.44)$$

Using equation 1.44, the future value of $100 deposited at the end of each year for three years in a savings account that earns 5 percent interest per year is:

$$FVA_3 = \$100\left[\frac{(1.05)^3 - 1}{0.05}\right]$$
$$= \$100(3.1525)$$
$$= \$315.25$$

TABULAR SOLUTION The summation term in the brackets in equation 1.44 is called the **future value interest factor for an annuity of n payments at i interest (FVIFA$_{i,n}$):**

$$FVIFA_{i,n} = \sum_{t=1}^{n}(1+i)^{n-t} = \frac{(1+i)^n - 1}{i}$$

FVIFAs have been calculated for various combinations of i and n; Table A-4 in Module 700 Appendix contains a set of FVIFA factors. To find the answer to the three-year, $100 annuity problem, first refer to Table A-4 and look down the 5 percent column to the third period; the FVIFA is 3.1525. Thus, the future value of the $100 annuity is $315.25.

$$FVA_n = PMT(FVIFA_{i,n})$$
$$FVA_3 = \$100(FVIFA_{5\%,3})$$
$$= \$100(3.1525)$$
$$= \$315.25.$$

Annuities Due

Had the three $100 payments in the previous example been made at the *beginning* of each year, the annuity would have been an *annuity due*. In the cash flow time line, each payment would be shifted to the left one year; therefore, each payment would be *compounded for one extra year (period)*, which means each payment would earn interest for an additional year.

CASH FLOW TIMELINE:

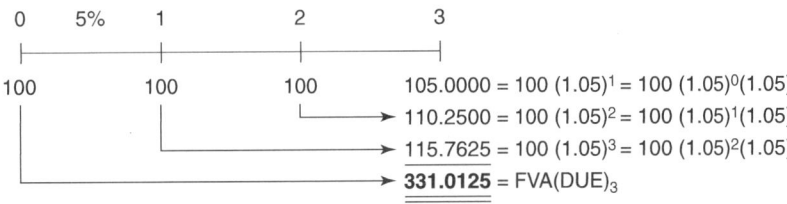

Again, the regular time line is shown at the top of the diagram, and the future value of each annuity payment at the end of Year 3 is shown in the Year 3 column, with the actual computations shown to the right.

NUMERICAL SOLUTION We can find the FV of each cash flow and then sum the results to find the FV of the annuity due, FVA(DUE)$_n$. This procedure is shown in the lower section of the cash flow time line. Note from the diagram that the difference between an ordinary annuity and an annuity due is that *each of the payments of the annuity due earns interest for one additional year*. So the numerical solution for an annuity due can also be found by adjusting equations 1.43 and 1.44 to account for the fact that each annuity payment is able to earn an additional year's interest when compared to an ordinary annuity. The solution for FVA(DUE)$_n$ is

$$FVA(DUE)_n = PMT\left[\sum_{t=1}^{n}(1+i)^t\right] = PMT\left[\left\{\sum_{t=1}^{n}(1+i)^{n-t}\right\} \times (1+i)\right] \quad (1.45)$$

$$= PMT\left[\left\{\frac{(1+i)^n - 1}{i}\right\} \times (1+i)\right]$$

The future value of the three $100 deposits made at the beginning of each year into a savings account that earns 5 percent annually is

$$FVA(DUE)_3 = \$100\left[\left\{\frac{(1.05)^3 - 1}{0.05}\right\} \times (1.05)\right]$$
$$= \$100[(3.1525) \times 1.05]$$
$$= \$331.0125$$

TABULAR SOLUTION As we have shown, for an annuity due, each payment is compounded for one additional period, so the future value interest factor for an *annuity due*, **FVIFA(DUE)$_{i,n}$**, is equal to the FVIFA$_{i,n}$ for an ordinary annuity compounded for one additional period. In other words,

$$FVIFA(DUE)_{i,n} = \left[\left\{\frac{(1+i)^n - 1}{i}\right\} \times (1+i)\right] \quad (1.46)$$
$$= [(FVIFA_{i,n})(1+i)]$$

Here is the tabular solution for FVA(DUE)$_n$:

$$FVA(DUE)_n = PMT[FVIFA(DUE)_{i,n}]$$
$$= PMT[(FVIFA_{i,n})(1+i)]$$
$$FVA(DUE)_3 = \$100[(3.1525)(1.05)]$$
$$= \$331.0125$$

The payments occur earlier than for the ordinary annuity, so more interest is earned. Therefore, the future value of the annuity due is larger—$331.01 versus $315.25 for the ordinary annuity.

Present Value of an Annuity

Suppose you were offered the following alternatives: (1) a three-year annuity with payments of $100 at the end of each year or (2) a lump-sum payment today. You have no need for the money during the next three years, so if you accept the annuity, you would simply deposit the payments in a savings account that pays 5 percent interest per year. Similarly, the lump-sum payment would be deposited into the same account. How large must the lump-sum payment today be to make it equivalent to the annuity? To answer this question, we must find the present value of an ordinary annuity, **PVA$_n$**. Each payment is discounted, and the sum of the discounted payments is the present value of the annuity.

CASH FLOW TIMELINE:

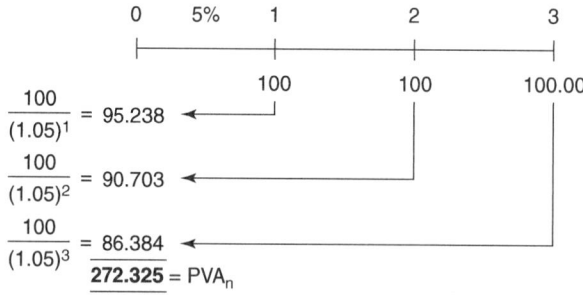

The regular cash flow time line is shown at the top of the diagram, and the numerical solution values are on the left. The PV of the annuity, PVA$_n$, is $272.325.

EQUATION:

As you can see from the cash flow time line, the present value of an annuity can be determined by computing the PV of the individual payments and summing the results. The general equation used to find the PV of an ordinary annuity is shown here:

$$PVA_n = PMT\left[\frac{1}{(1+i)^1}\right] + PMT\left[\frac{1}{(1+i)^2}\right] + \cdots + PMT\left[\frac{1}{(1+i)^n}\right]$$
$$= PMT\left[\sum_{t=1}^{n}\frac{1}{(1+i)^t}\right] \quad (1.47)$$

NUMERICAL SOLUTION One method of determining the present value of the annuity is to compute the present value of each cash flow and then sum the result. This procedure is shown in the lower left section of the cash flow time line diagram, where we see that the PV of the annuity is $272.325. This approach can be tedious if the number of annuity payments is large.

The numerical solution is easier if we simplify Equation 1.47:[471]

$$PVA_n = PMT\left[\sum_{t=1}^{n}\frac{1}{(1+i)^t}\right] = PMT\left[\frac{1-\frac{1}{(1+i)^n}}{i}\right] \quad (1.48)$$

Using Equation 1.48, the PV of the three-year annuity with end-of-year payments of $100 is

$$PVA_n = \$100\left[\frac{1-\frac{1}{(1.05)^3}}{0.05}\right]$$
$$= \$100(2.72325)$$
$$= \mathbf{\$272.325}$$

TABULAR SOLUTION The summation term in the brackets in Equation 1.47 is called the **present value interest factor for an annuity of n payments at i interest (PVIFA$_{i,n}$)**.[472]

$$PVIFA_{i,n} = \sum_{t=1}^{n}\frac{1}{(1+i)^t} = \left[\frac{1-\frac{1}{(1+i)^n}}{i}\right]$$

The values for PVIFA at different values of i and n are shown in Table A-2 of Module 700 Appendix at the back of that module.

To find the answer to the three-year, $100 annuity problem, simply refer to Table A-2 and look down the 5 percent column to the third period. The PVIFA is 2.7232, so the present value of the $100 annuity is $272.32:

$$PVA_n = PMT(PVIFA_{i,n})$$
$$PVA_3 = \$100(PVIFA_{5\%,3})$$
$$= \$100(2.7232)$$
$$= \mathbf{\$272.32}$$

Annuities Due

Had the three $100 payments in our earlier example been made at the *beginning* of each year, the annuity would have been an *annuity due*. On the cash flow time line, each payment would be shifted to the left one year, so each payment would be *discounted for one less year*. Here is the cash flow time line setup.

CASH FLOW TIMELINE:

$$\frac{100}{(1.05)^1} \times (1.05) = \frac{100}{(1.05)^0} = 100.000$$
$$\frac{100}{(1.05)^2} \times (1.05) = \frac{100}{(1.05)^1} = 95.238$$
$$\frac{100}{(1.05)^3} \times (1.05) = \frac{100}{(1.05)^2} = 90.703$$
$$\mathbf{285.941} = PVA_n$$

NUMERICAL SOLUTION Again, we can find the PV of each cash flow and then sum these PVs to find the PV of the annuity due, PVA(DUE)$_n$. This procedure is illustrated in the lower section of the time line diagram. Because the cash flows occur sooner, the PV of the annuity due exceeds that of the ordinary annuity—$285.94 versus $272.32.

The cash flow timeline shows that the difference between the PV of an annuity due and the PV of an ordinary annuity is that *each of the payments of the annuity due is discounted one less year*. So the numerical solution for an annuity due can also be found by adjusting Equations 1.47 and 1.48 to account for the fact each annuity payment will have the *opportunity* to earn an additional year's (period's) interest when compared with an ordinary annuity.

$$PVA(DUE)_n = \left[\sum_{t=0}^{n-1} \frac{1}{(1+i)^t}\right] = PMT\left[\left\{\sum_{t=1}^{n} \frac{1}{(1+i)^n}\right\} \times (1+i)\right]$$

$$= PMT\left[\left\{\frac{1 - \frac{1}{(1+i)^n}}{i}\right\} \times (1+i)\right] \tag{1.49}$$

Therefore, if the three $100 payments were made at the beginning of the year, the PV of the annuity would be:

$$= PVA(DUE)_3 = \$100\left[\left\{\frac{1 - \frac{1}{(1.05)^3}}{0.05}\right\} \times (1.05)\right]$$

$$= \$100[(2.72325)(1.05)]$$
$$= \$100(2.85941)$$
$$= \$285.941$$

TABULAR SOLUTION We can use the PVIFAs given in Table A-2 of Module 700 Appendix, which are computed for ordinary annuities, if we adjust these values to account for the fact that the payments associated with an annuity due occur one period earlier than the payments associated with an ordinary annuity. As the cash flow time line and the numerical solution indicate, the adjustment is rather simple—just multiply the PVIFA for an ordinary annuity by $(1+i)$. So, the present value interest factor for an annuity due, **PVIFA(DUE)$_{i,n}$**, is:

$$= PVIFA(DUE)_{i,n} = \left[\left\{\frac{1 - \frac{1}{(1+i)^n}}{i}\right\} \times (1+i)\right]$$
$$= [(PVIFA_{i,n})(1+i)] \tag{1.50}$$

The tabular solution for PVA(DUE)$_n$ is

$$PVA(DUE)_n = PMT[PVIFA(DUE)_{i,n}]$$
$$= PMT[(PVIFA_{i,n}) \times (1+i)]$$
$$PVA(DUE)_3 = \$100[(2.7232)(1.05)]$$
$$= \$100(2.85941)$$
$$= \$285.941$$

Amortized Loans

One of the most important applications of compound interest involves loans that are paid off in installments over time. Included are automobile loans, home mortgages, student loans, and most business debt other than very short-term loans and long-term bonds. If a loan is to be repaid in equal periodic amounts (monthly, quarterly, or annually), it is said to be an **amortized loan**. The word *amortized* comes from the Latin *mors*, meaning "death," so an amortized loan is one that is "killed off" over time.

To illustrate, suppose a firm borrows $15,000, and the loan is to be repaid in three equal payments at the end of each of the next three years. The lender is to receive 8 percnet interest on the loan balance that is outstanding at the beginning of each year. The first task is to determine the amount the firm must repay each year, or the annual payment. To find this amount, recognize that the $15,000 represents the present value of an annuity of PMT dollars per year for three years, discounted at 8 percent.

CASH FLOW TIMELINE AND EQUATION:

```
0      8%    1        2        3
|------------|--------|--------|
15,000      PMT      PMT      PMT
```

$$PVA_n = \frac{PMT}{(1+i)^1} + \frac{PMT}{(1+i)^2} + \frac{PMT}{(1+i)^3} = \sum_{t=1}^{3} \frac{PMT}{(1+i)^t}$$

$$\$15{,}000 = \sum_{t=1}^{3} \frac{PMT}{(1.08)^t}$$

Here we know everything except PMT, so we can solve the equation for PMT.

NUMERICAL SOLUTION You can solve for PMT as follows:

$$\$15{,}000 = \sum_{t=1}^{3} \frac{PMT}{(1.08)^t} = PMT\left[\sum_{t=1}^{3}\frac{1}{(1.08)^t}\right] = PMT\left[\frac{1 - \frac{1}{(1.08)^3}}{0.08}\right]$$

$$\$15{,}000 = PMT(2.2.5771)$$

$$PMT = \frac{\$15{,}000}{2.5771} = \$5{,}820.50$$

TABULAR SOLUTION Substitute in known values and look up PVIFA for I = 8% and n = 3 periods in Table A-2 of Module 700 Appendix.

$$PVA_n = PMT(PVIFA_{i,n})$$
$$\$15{,}000 = PMT(FVIFA_{8\%,3}) = PMT(2.5771)$$
$$PMT = \frac{\$15{,}000}{2.5771} = \$5{,}820.50$$

Comparison of Different Types of Interest Rates

Up to this point, we have discussed three different types of interest rates. If you will be working with relatively difficult time value problems, then it is useful to compare the three types and to know when each should be used, as we discuss next.

1. **Simple, or quoted, rate, i_{SIMPLE}.** This is the rate that is quoted by borrowers and lenders, and it is used to determine the rate earned per compounding period (periodic rate). Practitioners in the stock, bond, lending, banking, and other markets generally express financial contracts in terms of simple rates. So if you talk with a banker, broker, mortgage lender, auto finance company, or student loan officer about rates, the simple rate is the one he or she will normally quote you. However, to be meaningful, the simple rate quotation also must include the number of compounding periods per year. For example, a bank might offer 6.5 percent, compounded annually, on CDs, or a mutual fund might offer 6 percent, compounded monthly, on its money market account.

   Simple rates can be compared with one another, *but only if the instruments being compared use the same number of compounding periods per year*. Thus, to compare a 6.5 percent annual payment CD with a 6 percent monthly payment money market fund, we would need to put both instruments on an effective annual rate (EAR) basis.

   Note also that the simple rate never is shown on a time line, and it is never used as an input in a financial calculator unless compounding occurs only once a year (in which case i_{SIMPLE} = periodic rate = EAR). If more frequent compounding occurs, you must use either the periodic rate or the effective annual rate, as discussed next.

2. **Periodic rate.** This is the rate charged by a lender or paid by a borrower *each interest period*. It can be a rate per year, per six-month period, per quarter, per month, per day, or per any other time interval (usually one year or

less). For example, a bank might charge 1 percent per month on its credit card loans, or a finance company might charge 3 percent per quarter on consumer loans. We find the periodic rate as follows.

$$\text{Periodic rate} = \frac{i_{\text{SIMPLE}}}{m} \quad (1.51)$$

which implies that

$$i_{\text{SIMPLE}} = (\text{Periodic rate}) \times (m) = \text{APR} \quad (1.52)$$

Here i_{SIMPLE} is the simple annual rate and m is the number of compounding periods per year. APR, which is the **annual percentage rate,** represents the periodic rate stated on an annual basis without considering interest compounding; it is i_{SIMPLE}. *The APR never is used in actual calculations; it is simply reported to borrowers.*

If there is one payment per year, or if interest is added only once a year, then m = 1 and the periodic rate is equal to the simple rate. *But, in all cases where interest is added or payments are made more frequently than annually, the periodic rate is less than the simple rate.*

The periodic rate is used for calculations in problems where two conditions hold: (a) payments occur on a regular basis more frequently than once a year, and (b) a payment is made on each compounding (or discounting) date. Thus, if you are dealing with an auto loan that requires monthly payments, with a semiannual payment bond, or with an education loan that calls for quarterly payments, then on your cash flow time line and in your calculations you would use the Periodic rate = $i_{\text{SIMPLE}} \div m$, and the appropriate number of periods would be n × m.

3. **Effective annual rate, EAR.** This is the rate with which, under annual compounding (m = 1), we would obtain the same result as if we had used a given periodic rate with m compounding periods per year. The EAR is found as follows:

$$\text{EAR} = \left(1 + \frac{i_{\text{SIMPLE}}}{m}\right)^m - 1.0$$
$$= (1 + \text{Periodic rate})^m - 1 \quad (1.53)$$

To illustrate further, suppose you could borrow using either a credit card that charges 1 percent per month or a bank loan with a 12 percent quoted simple interest rate that is compounded quarterly. Which should you choose? To answer this question, the cost of each alternative must be expressed as an EAR.

$$\begin{aligned}
\text{Credit card loan: EAR} &= (1 + 0.01)^{12} - 1.0 \\
&= (1.01)^{12} - 1.0 \\
&= 1.126825 - 1.0 \\
&= 0.126825 = 12.6825\%. \\
\text{Bank loan: EAR} &= (1 + 0.03)^4 - 1.0 \\
&= (1.03)^4 - 1.0 \\
&= 1.125509 - 1.0 \\
&= 0.125509 = 12.5509\%.
\end{aligned}$$

Thus, the credit card loan costs a little more than the bank loan. This result should have been intuitive to you—both loans have the same 12 percent simple rate, yet you would have to make monthly payments on the credit card versus quarterly payments under the bank loan.

Summary of Time Value of Money Techniques

Financial decisions often involve situations in which someone pays money at one point in time and receives money at some other time. Dollars that are paid or received at two different points in time are different, and this difference is recognized and accounted for by time value of money (TVM) analysis. We next summarize the types of TVM analysis and the key concepts covered in this section, using the data shown in Exhibit 100.79 to illustrate the various points. Refer to the figure constantly, and try to find in it an example of the points covered as you go through this summary.

- **Compounding** is the process of determining the **future value (FV)** of a cash flow or a series of cash flows. The compounded amount, or future value, is equal to the beginning amount plus the interest earned.

$$\text{Future value (single payment): } FV_n = PV(1 + i)^n = PV(FVIF_{i,n})$$

Exhibit 100.79 *Illustration for Time Value of Money Summary*

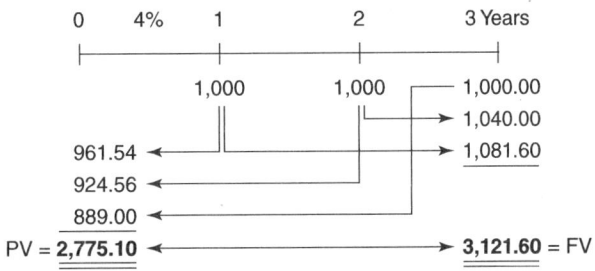

Example 4 *$924.56 compounded for two years at 4%:*
$$FV_2 = \$924.56(1.04)^2 = \$1{,}000$$

- **Discounting** is the process of finding the **present value (PV)** of a future cash flow or a series of cash flows; discounting is the reciprocal (inverse) of compounding.

Basic Valuation of Assets

The time value of money (TVM) concepts are used by managers and investors to establish the worth of any asset whose value is derived from future cash flows, including such assets as real estate, factories, machinery, oil wells, stocks, and bonds. Now, in this section, we use time value of money techniques to explain how the values of assets are determined. The material covered in the section obviously is important to investors who want to establish the values of their investments. But knowledge of valuation is equally important to financial managers because all important corporate decisions should be analyzed in terms of how they will affect the value of the firm. Remember that the goal of managerial finance is to maximize the value of the firm. Thus, it is critical that we understand the valuation process so we can determine what affects the value of the firm.

The *value* of anything, whether it is a financial asset like a stock or a bond or a real asset like a building or a piece of machinery, *is based on the present value of the cash flows the asset is expected to produce in the future.* On a cash flow timeline, value can be depicted as follows:

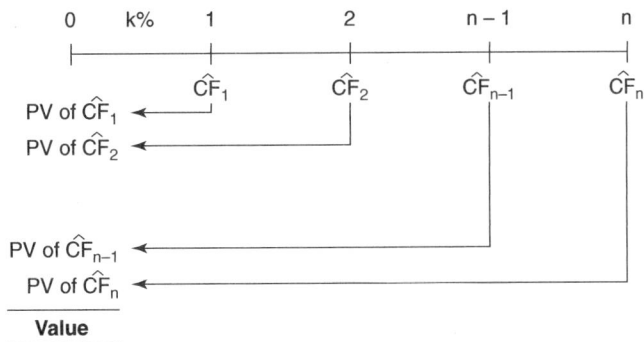

Therefore, the value of any asset can be expressed in general form as follows:

$$\text{Asset value} = V = \frac{\hat{CF}_1}{(1+k)^1} + \frac{\hat{CF}_2}{(1+k)^2} + \cdots + \frac{\hat{CF}_n}{(1+k)^n} \quad (1.54)$$

Here

$\hat{CF}_t$ = The cash flow expected to be generated by the asset in period t.

k = The return investors consider appropriate for holding such an asset. This return is usually termed the *required return,* and is based on both economic conditions and the riskiness of the asset.

According to equation 1.54, the value of an asset is affected by the cash flows it is expected to generate, $\hat{CF}$, and the return required by investors, k. As you can see, *the higher the expected cash flows, the greater the asset's value; also, the lower the required return, the greater the asset's value.*

195. QUANTITATIVE TECHNIQUES IN BUSINESS

Module 100 Endnotes

1. Amitai Etzioni, *Modern Organizations* (Englewood Cliffs, NJ: Prentice-Hall, 1964), 6.
2. David L. Calfee, "Get Your Mission Statement Working!" *Management Review* (January 1993) 54–57; John A. Pearce, II and Fred David, "Corporate Mission Statement: The Bottom Line," *Academy of Management Executive* 1 (1987), 109–16; and Christopher K. Bart, "Sex, Lies, and Mission Statements," *Business Horizons* (November–December 1997), 23–28.
3. Charles Perrow, "The Analysis of Goals in Complex Organizations," *American Sociological Review* 26 (1961), 854–66.
4. Johannes U. Stoelwinder and Martin P. Charns, "The Task Field Model of Organization Analysis and Design," *Human Relations* 34 (1981), 743–62; Anthony Raia, *Managing by Objectives* (Glenview, IL.: Scott, Foresman, 1974).
5. Peter Galuszka and Ellen Neuborne with Wendy Zellner, "P&G's Hottest New Product: P&G," *Business Week*, October 5, 1998, 92, 96.
6. Michael E. Porter, "What is Strategy?" *Harvard Business Review* (November–December 1996), 61–78.
7. Michael E. Porter, *Competitive Strategy: Techniques for Analyzing Industries and Competitors* (New York: Free Press, 1980).
8. Etzioni, *Modern Organizations*, 8.
9. Etzioni, *Modern Organizations*, 8; Gary D. Sandefur, "Efficiency in Social Service Organizations," *Administration and Society* 14 (1983), 449–68.
10. Richard M. Steers, *Organizational Effectiveness: A Behavioral View* (Santa Monica, CA: Goodyear, 1977), 51.
11. Karl E. Weick and Richard L. Daft, "The Effectiveness of Interpretation Systems," in Kim S. Cameron and David A. Whetten, eds., *Organizational Effectiveness: A Comparison of Multiple Models* (New York: Academic Press, 1982).
12. David L. Blenkhorn and Brian Gaber, "The Use of 'Warm Fuzzies' to Assess Organizational Effectiveness," *Journal of General Management*, 21, no. 2 (Winter 1995), 40–51.
13. Steven Strasser, J. D. Eveland, Gaylord Cummins, O. Lynn Deniston, and John H. Romani, "Conceptualizing the Goal and Systems Models of Organizational Effectiveness—Implications for Comparative Evaluation Research," *Journal of Management Studies* 18 (1981), 321–40.
14. Anne S. Tusi, "A Multiple-Constituency Model of Effectiveness: An Empirical Examination at the Human Resource Subunit Level," *Administrative Science Quarterly* 35 (1990), 458, 483; Charles Fombrun and Mark Shanley, "What's in a Name? Reputation Building and Corporate Strategy," *Academy of Management Journal* 33 (1990), 233–58; Terry Connolly, Edward J. Conlon, and Stuart Jay Deutsch, "Organizational Effectiveness: A Multiple-Constituency Approach," *Academy of Management Review* 5 (1980), 211–17.
15. James L. Price, "The Study of Organizational Effectiveness," *Sociological Quarterly* 13 (1972), 3–15.
16. McCauley, "Measure What Matters."
17. Richard H. Hall and John P. Clark, "An Ineffective Effectiveness Study and Some Suggestions for Future Research," *Sociological Quarterly* 21 (1980), 119–34; Price, "Study of Organizational Effectiveness;" Perrow, "Analysis of Goals."
18. Y. K. Shetty, "New Look at Corporate Goals," *California Management Review* 22, no. 2 (1979), 71–79.
19. McCauley, "Measure What Matters."
20. The discussion of the resource-based approach is based in part on Michael V. Russo and Paul A. Fouts, "A Resource-Based Perspective on Corporate Environmental Performance and Profitability," *Academy of Management Journal* 40, No. 3 (June 1997), 534–559; and Jay B. Barney, J. L. "Larry" Stempert, Loren T. Gustafson, and Yolanda Sarason, "Organizational Identity Within the Strategic Management Conversation: Contributions and Assumptions," in *Identity in Organizations: Building Theory through Conversations*," David A. Whetten and Paul C. Godfrey, eds. (Thousand Oaks, CA: Sage Publications, 1998), 83–98.
21. Lucy McCauley, "Measure What Matters."
22. Chris Argyris, *Integrating the Individual and the Organization* (New York: Wiley, 1964); Warren G. Bennis, *Changing Organizations* (New York: McGraw-Hill, 1966); Rensis Likert, *The Human Organization* (New York: McGraw-Hill, 1967); Richard Beckhard, *Organization Development Strategies and Models* (Reading, MA: Addison-Wesley, 1969).
23. Cheri Ostroff and Neal Schmitt, "Configurations of Organizational Effectiveness and Efficiency," *Academy of Management Journal* 36 (1993), 1345–61; Peter J. Frost, Larry F. Moore, Meryl Reise Louis, Craig C. Lundburg, and Joanne Martin, *Organizational Culture* (Beverly Hills, CA: Sage, 1985).
24. J. Barton Cunningham, "Approaches to the Evaluation of Organizational Effectiveness," *Academy of Management Review* 2 (1977), 463–74; Beckhard, *Organization Development*.
25. Frank Friedlander and Hal Pickle, "Components of Effectiveness in Small Organizations," *Administrative Science Quarterly* 13 (1968), 289–304.
26. Kim S. Cameron, "The Effectiveness of Ineffectiveness," in Barry M. Staw and L. L. Cummings, eds., *Research in Organizational Behavior* (Greenwich, CT: JAI Press, 1984), 235–86; Rosabeth Moss Kanter and Derick Brinkerhoff, "Organizational Performance: Recent Developments in Measurement," *Annual Review of Sociology* 7 (1981), 321–49.

27. Tusi, "A Multiple-Constituency Model of Effectiveness."
28. Fombrun and Shanley, "What's in a Name?"
29. Daniel A. Wren, *The Evolution of Management Thought,* 2nd ed. (New York: Wiley, 1979), 6–8. Much of the discussion of these forces comes from Arthur M. Schlesinger, *Political and Social History of the United States,* 1829–1925 (New York: Macmillan, 1925); and Homer C. Hockett, *Political and Social History of the United States,* 1492–1828 (New York: Macmillan, 1925).
30. Robin Wright and Doyle McManus, *Flashpoints: Promise and Peril in a New World* (New York: Alfred A. Knopf, 1991).
31. This section is based heavily on Thomas Petzinger, Jr., "So Long Supply and Demand," *The Wall Street Journal* (January 1, 2000), R31.
32. Business historian Alfred D. Chandler, Jr., quoted in Jerry Useem, "Entrepreneur of the Century," *Inc.* (20th Anniversary Issue, 1999), 159–174.
33. The following is based on Wren, *Evolution of Management Thought,* chapters 4, 5; and Claude S. George, Jr., *The History of Management Thought* (Englewood Cliffs, NJ: Prentice-Hall, 1968), chapter 4.
34. Charles D. Wrege and Ann Marie Stoka, "Cooke Creates a Classic: The Story behind F. W. Taylor's Principles of Scientific Management," *Academy of Management Review* (October 1978), 736–749; Robert Kanigel, *The One Best Way: Frederick Winslow Taylor and the Enigma of Efficiency* (New York: Viking, 1997); and Alan Farnham, "The Man Who Changed Work Forever," *Fortune*, July 21, 1997, 114.
35. Quoted in Ann Harrington, "The Big Ideas," *Fortune,* November 22, 1999, 152–154.
36. Geoffrey Colvin, "Managing in the Info Era," *Fortune,* March 6, 2000, F-5–F-9.
37. Max Weber, *General Economic History,* trans. Frank H. Knight (London: Allen & Unwin, 1927); Max Weber, *The Protestant Ethic and the Spirit of Capitalism,* trans. Talcott Parsons (New York: Scribner, 1930); and Max Weber, *The Theory of Social and Economic Organizations,* ed. and trans. A. M. Henderson and Talcott Parsons (New York: Free Press, 1947).
38. Mary Parker Follett, *The New State: Group Organization: The Solution of Popular Government* (London: Longmans, Green, 1918); and Mary Parker Follett, *Creative Experience* (London: Longmans, Green, 1924).
39. Henry C. Metcalf and Lyndall Urwick, eds., *Dynamic Administration: The Collected Papers of Mary Parker Follett* (New York: Harper & Row, 1940); Arnold, *Milestones in Management.*
40. Follett, *The New State;* Metcalf and Urwick, *Dynamic Administration* (London: Sir Isaac Pitman, 1941).
41. William B. Wolf, *How to Understand Management: An Introduction to Chester I. Barnard* (Los Angeles: Lucas Brothers, 1968); and David D. Van Fleet, "The Need-Hierarchy and Theories of Authority," *Human Relations* 9 (Spring 1982), 111–118.
42. Gregory M. Bounds, Gregory H. Dobbins, and Oscar S. Fowler, *Management: A Total Quality Perspective* (Cincinnati, OH: South-Western Publishing, 1995), 52–53.
43. Curt Tausky, *Work Organizations: Major Theoretical Perspectives* (Itasca, IL.: F. E. Peacock, 1978), 42.
44. Tausky, *Work Organizations: Major Theoretical Perspectives,* 55.
45. Douglas McGregor, *The Human Side of Enterprise* (New York: McGraw-Hill, 1960), 16–18.
46. Wendell L. French and Cecil H. Bell Jr., "A History of Organizational Development," in Wendell L. French, Cecil H. Bell Jr., and Robert A. Zawacki, *Organization Development and Transformation: Managing Effective Change* (Burr Ridge, IL: Irwin McGraw-Hill, 2000), 20–42.
47. Ludwig von Bertalanffy, Carl G. Hempel, Robert E. Bass, and Hans Jonas, "General Systems Theory: A New Approach to Unity of Science," *Human Biology* 23 (December 1951), 302–361; and Kenneth E. Boulding, "General Systems Theory—The Skeleton of Science," *Management Science* 2 (April 1956), 197–208.
48. Fremont E. Kast and James E. Rosenzweig, "General Systems Theory: Applications for Organization and Management," *Academy of Management Journal* (December 1972), 447–465.
49. Wayne Kawamoto, "Click Here for Efficiency," *BusinessWeek Enterprise,* December 7, 1998, 12–14.
50. Jeffrey Zygmont, "The Ties That Bind," *Inc. Tech* no. 3, (1998), 70–84; and Nancy Ferris, "ERP: Sizzling or Stumbling?" *Government Executive* (July 1999), 99–102.
51. Harrington, "The Big Ideas." Also see Peter Drucker, *Post-Capitalist Society,* (Oxford: Butterworth Heinemann, 1993), 5.
52. Based on Andrew Mayo, "Memory Bankers," *People Management,* January 22, 1998, 34–38; William Miller, "Building the Ultimate Resource," *Management Review* (January 1999), 42–45; and Todd Datz, "How to Speak Geek," *CIO Enterprise,* Section 2, April 15, 1999, 46–52.
53. Louisa Wah, "Behind the Buzz," *Management Review* (April 1999), 17–26.
54. Amitai Etzioni, *Modern Organizations* (Englewood Cliffs, NJ: Prentice-Hall, 1984), 6.
55. *Ibid.*
56. Max D. Richards, *Setting Strategic Goals and Objectives,* 2nd ed. (St. Paul, MN: West, 1986).
57. C. Chet Miller and Laura B. Cardinal, "Strategic Planning and Firm Performance: A Synthesis of More Than Two Decades of Research," *Academy of Management Journal* 37, no. 6 (1994), 1649–1685.

MODULE 100. ENDNOTES

58. This discussion is based on Richard L. Daft and Richard M. Steers, *Organizations: A Micro/Macro Approach* (Glenview, IL: Scott, Foresman, 1986), 319–321; Herbert A. Simon, "On the Concept of Organizational Goals," *Administrative Science Quarterly* 9 (1964), 1–22; and Charles B. Saunders and Francis D. Tuggel, "Corporate Goals," *Journal of General Management* 5 (1980), 3–13.
59. Steven L. Marks, "Say When," *Inc.* (February 1995), 19–20.
60. George S. Odiorne, "MBO: A Backward Glance," *Business Horizons* 21 (October 1978), 14–24.
61. P. Muczyk and Bernard C. Reimann, "MBO as a Complement to Effective Leadership," *The Academy of Management Executive* 3 (1989), 131–138; and W. Giegold, *Objective Setting and the MBO Process*, vol. 2 (New York: McGraw-Hill, 1978).
62. John Ivancevich, J. Timothy McMahon, J. William Streidl, and Andrew D. Szilagyi, "Goal Setting: The Tenneco Approach to Personnel Development and Management Effectiveness," *Organizational Dynamics* (Winter 1978), 48–80.
63. "Corporate Planning: Drafting a Blueprint for Success," *Small Business Report* (August 1987), 40–44.
64. John Child, *Organization: A Guide to Problems and Practice*, 2nd ed. (London: Harper & Row, 1984).
65. Adam Smith, *The Wealth of Nations* (New York: Modern Library, 1937).
66. This discussion is based on Richard L. Daft, *Organization Theory and Design*, 4th ed. (St. Paul, MN: West, 1992), 387–388.
67. C. I. Barnard, *The Functions of the Executive* (Cambridge, MN: Harvard University Press, 1938).
68. Thomas A. Stewart, "CEOs See Clout Shifting," *Fortune*, November 6, 1989, 66.
69. Michael G. O'Loughlin, "What Is Bureaucratic Accountability and How Can We Measure It?" *Administration & Society* 22, no. 3 (November 1990), 275–302.
70. Carrie R. Leana, "Predictors and Consequences of Delegation," *Academy of Management Journal* 29 (1986), 754–774.
71. Brian Dumaine, "What the Leaders of Tomorrow See," *Fortune*, July 3, 1989, 48–62.
72. Brian O'Reilly, "J&J Is on a Roll," *Fortune*, December 26, 1994, 178–191; and Joseph Weber, "A Big Company That Works," *Business Week*, May 4, 1992, 124–132.
73. Clay Chandler and Paul Ingrassia, "Just as U.S. Firms Try Japanese Management, Honda Is Centralizing," *Wall Street Journal*, April 11, 1991, A1, A10.
74. Gary Yukl, "Managerial Leadership: A Review of Theory and Research," *Journal of Management* 15 (1989), 251–289.
75. James M. Kouzes and Barry Z. Posner, "The Credibility Factor: What Followers Expect from Their Leaders," *Management Review* (January 1990), 29–33.
76. Henry Mintzberg, *Power In and Around Organizations* (Englewood Cliffs, NJ: Prentice-Hall, 1983); and Jeffrey Pfeffer, *Power in Organizations* (Marshfield, MA: Pitman, 1981).
77. J. R. P. French, Jr., and B. Raven, "The Bases of Social Power," in *Group Dynamics,* eds. D. Cartwright and Alvin F. Zander (Evanston, IL: Row, Peterson, 1960), 607–623.
78. G. A. Yukl and T. Taber, "The Effective Use of Managerial Power," *Personnel* (March–April 1983), 37–44.
79. Jay A. Conger, "The Necessary Art of Persuasion," *Harvard Business Review* (May–June 1998), 84–95.
80. Thomas A. Stewart, "New Ways to Exercise Power," *Fortune*, November 6, 1989, 52–64; and Thomas A. Stewart, "CEOs See Clout Shifting," *Fortune,* November 6, 1989, 66.
81. G. A. Yukl, *Leadership in Organizations* (Englewood Cliffs, NJ: Prentice-Hall, 1981); and S. C. Kohs and K. W. Irle, "Prophesying Army Promotion," *Journal of Applied Psychology* 4 (1920), 73–87.
82. R. Albanese and D. D. Van Fleet, *Organizational Behavior: A Managerial Viewpoint* (Hinsdale, IL: The Dryden Press, 1983).
83. K. Lewin, "Field Theory and Experiment in Social Psychology: Concepts and Methods," *American Journal of Sociology* 44 (1939), 868–896; K. Lewin and R. Lippitt, "An Experimental Approach to the Study of Autocracy and Democracy: A Preliminary Note," *Sociometry* 1 (1938), 292–300; and K. Lewin, R. Lippitt, and R. K. White, "Patterns of Aggressive Behavior in Experimentally Created Social Climates," *Journal of Social Psychology* 10 (1939), 271–301.
84. R. K. White and R. Lippitt, *Autocracy and Democracy: An Experimental Inquiry* (New York: Harper, 1960).
85. R. Tannenbaum and W. H. Schmidt, "How to Choose a Leadership Pattern," *Harvard Business Review* 36 (1958), 95–101.
86. C. A. Schriesheim and B. J. Bird, "Contributions of the Ohio State Studies to the Field of Leadership," *Journal of Management* 5 (1979), 135–145; and C. L. Shartle, "Early Years of the Ohio State University Leadership Studies," *Journal of Management* 5 (1979), 126–134.
87. P. C. Nystrom, "Managers and the High-High Leader Myth," *Academy of Management Journal* 21 (1978), 325–331; and L. L. Larson, J. G. Hunt, and Richard N. Osborn, "The Great High-High Leader Behavior Myth: A Lesson from Occam's Razor," *Academy of Management Journal* 19 (1976), 628–641.
88. R. Likert, "From Production- and Employee-Centeredness to Systems 1–4," *Journal of Management* 5 (1979), 147–156.
89. Robert R. Blake and Jane S. Mouton, *The Managerial Grid III* (Houston: Gulf, 1985).
90. Fred E. Fiedler, "Assumed Similarity Measures as Predictors of Team Effectiveness," *Journal of Abnormal and Social Psychology* 49 (1954), 381–388; F. E. Fiedler, *Leader Attitudes and Group Effectiveness* (Urbana, IL: University of Illinois Press, 1958); and F. E. Fiedler, *A Theory of Leadership Effectiveness* (New York: McGraw-Hill, 1967).

91. Fred E. Fiedler and M. M. Chemers, *Leadership and Effective Management* (Glenview, IL: Scott, Foresman, 1974).
92. Fred E. Fiedler, "Engineer the Job to Fit the Manager," *Harvard Business Review* 43 (1965), 115–122; and F. E. Fiedler, M. M. Chemers, and L. Mahar, *Improving Leadership Effectiveness: The Leader Match Concept* (New York: Wiley, 1976).
93. Paul Hersey and Kenneth H. Blanchard, *Management of Organizational Behavior: Utilizing Human Resources,* 4th ed. (Englewood Cliffs, NJ: Prentice-Hall, 1982).
94. M. G. Evans, "The Effects of Supervisory Behavior on the Path-Goal Relationship," *Organizational Behavior and Human Performance* 5 (1970), 277–298; M. G. Evans, "Leadership and Motivation: A Core Concept," *Academy of Management Journal* 13 (1970), 91–102; and B. S. Georgopoulos, G. M. Mahoney, and N. W. Jones, "A Path-Goal Approach to Productivity," *Journal of Applied Psychology* 41 (1957), 345–353.
95. Robert J. House, "A Path-Goal Theory of Leader Effectiveness," *Administrative Science Quarterly* 16 (1971), 321–338.
96. M. G. Evans, "Leadership," in *Organizational Behavior,* ed. S. Kerr (Columbus, OH: Grid, 1974), 230–233.
97. Robert J. House and Terrence R. Mitchell, "Path-Goal Theory of Leadership," *Journal of Contemporary Business* (Autumn 1974), 81–97.
98. S. Kerr and J. M. Jermier, "Substitutes for Leadership: Their Meaning and Measurement," *Organizational Behavior and Human Performance* 22 (1978), 375–403; and Jon P. Howell and Peter W. Dorfman, "Leadership and Substitutes for Leadership Among Professional and Nonprofessional Workers," *Journal of Applied Behavioral Science* 22 (1986), 29–46.
99. The terms *transactional* and *transformational* come from James M. Burns, *Leadership* (New York: Harper & Row, 1978); and Bernard M. Bass, "Leadership: Good, Better, Best," *Organizational Dynamics* 13 (Winter 1985), 26–40.
100. Katherine J. Klein and Robert J. House, "On Fire: Charismatic Leadership and Levels of Analysis," *Leadership Quarterly* 6, no. 2 (1995), 183–198.
101. Jay A. Conger and Rabindra N. Kanungo, "Toward a Behavioral Theory of Charismatic Leadership in Organizational Settings," *Academy of Management Review* 12 (1987), 637–647; Walter Kiechel III, "A Hard Look at Executive Vision," *Fortune,* October 23, 1989, 207–211; and William L. Gardner and Bruce J. Avolio, "The Charismatic Relationship: A Dramaturgical Perspective," *Academy of Management Review* 23, no. 1 (1998), 32–58.
102. Robert J. House, "Research Contrasting the Behavior and Effects of Reputed Charismatic vs. Reputed Non-Charismatic Leaders" (paper presented as part of a symposium, "Charismatic Leadership: Theory and Evidence," Academy of Management, San Diego, 1985).
103. Robert J. House and Jane M. Howell, "Personality and Charismatic Leadership," *Leadership Quarterly* 3, no. 2 (1992), 81–108; and Jennifer O'Connor, Michael D. Mumford, Timothy C. Clifton, Theodore L. Gessner, and Mary Shane Connelly, "Charismatic Leaders and Destructiveness: A Historiometric Study," *Leadership Quarterly* 6, no. 4 (1995), 529–555.
104. Bernard M. Bass, "Theory of Transformational Leadership Redux," *Leadership Quarterly* 6, no. 4 (1995), 463–478; Noel M. Tichy and Mary Anne Devanna, *The Transformational Leader* (New York: John Wiley & Sons, 1986); and Badrinarayan Shankar Pawar and Kenneth K. Eastman, "The Nature and Implications of Contextual Influences on Transformational Leadership: A Conceptual Examination," *Academy of Management Review* 22, no. 1 (1997), 80–109.
105. Richard L. Daft and Robert H. Lengel, *Fusion Leadership: Unlocking the Subtle Forces that Change People and Organizations* (San Francisco: Berrett-Koehler, 1998).
106. Judy B. Rosener, *America's Competitive Secret: Utilizing Women as a Management Strategy* (New York: Oxford University Press, 1995); Rosener, "Ways Women Lead," *Harvard Business Review* (November–December 1990), 119–125; Sally Helgesen, *The Female Advantage: Women's Ways of Leadership* (New York: Currency/Doubleday, 1990); and Bernard M. Bass and Bruce J. Avolio, "Shatter the Glass Ceiling: Women May Make Better Managers," *Human Resource Management* 33, no. 4 (Winter 1994), 549–560.
107. Rochelle Sharpe, "As Leaders, Women Rule," *BusinessWeek,* November 20, 2000, 75–84.
108. Rosener, *America's Competitive Secret,* 129–135.
109. Deborah L. Duarte and Nancy Tennant Snyder, *Mastering Virtual Teams: Strategies, Tools, and Techniques That Succeed* (San Francisco: Jossey-Bass, 1999).
110. This discussion is based on Wayne F. Cascio, "Managing a Virtual Workplace," *Academy of Management Executive* 14, no. 3 (August 2000), 81–90; and Charlene Marmer Solomon, "Managing Virtual Teams," *Workforce* (June 2001), 60–65.
111. Nancy Chase, "Learning to Lead a Virtual Team," *Quality* (August 1999), 76.
112. Daft and Lengel, *Fusion Leadership.*
113. Robert K. Greenleaf, *Servant Leadership: A Journey into the Nature of Legitimate Power and Greatness* (Mahwah, NJ: Paulist Press, 1977).
114. Douglas S. Sherwin, "The Meaning of Control," *Dunn's Business Review* (January 1956).
115. Jeannie Cameron, "Death of Traditional Accounting Will Prove to Be a Boon," *The Asian Wall Street Journal,* April 27, 1998, 16.
116. Jennifer S. Lee, "Tracking Sales and the Cashiers," *The New York Times,* July 11, 2001, C1, C6; Anna Wilde Mathews, "New Gadgets Track Truckers' Every Move," *The Wall Street Journal,* July 14, 1997, B1, B10.
117. Steve Stecklow, "Kentucky's Teachers Get Bonuses, but Some Are Caught Cheating," *The Wall Street Journal*, September 2, 1997, A1, A5.

118. William G. Ouchi, "Markets, Bureaucracies, and Clans," *Administrative Science Quarterly* 25 (1980), 129–141; and B. R. Baligia and Alfred M. Jaeger, "Multinational Corporations: Control Systems and Delegation Issues," *Journal of International Business Studies* (Fall 1984), 25–40.
119. Frank C. Barnes, "ISO 9000 Myth and Reality: A Reasonable Approach to ISO 9000," *SAM Advanced Management Journal* (Spring 1998), 23–30; and Thomas H. Stevenson and Frank C. Barnes, "Fourteen Years of ISO 9000: Impact, Criticisms, Costs, and Benefits," *Business Horizons* (May–June 2001), 45–51.
120. Don L. Bohl, Fred Luthans, John W. Slocum Jr., and Richard M. Hodgetts, "Ideas That Will Shape the Future of Management Practice," *Organizational Dynamics* (Summer 1996), 7–14.
121. K. Lehn and A. K. Makhija, "EVA and MVA as Performance Measures and Signals for Strategic Change," *Strategy & Leadership* (May–June 1996), 34–38.
122. Terence C. Pare, "A New Tool for Managing Costs," *Fortune,* June 14, 1993, 124–129; and Don L. Bohl, Fred Luthans, John W. Slocum Jr., and Richard M. Hodgetts, "Ideas that Will Shape the Future of Management Practice," *Organizational Dynamics* (Summer 1996), 7–14.
123. Perry Pascarella, "Open the Books to Unleash Your People," *Management Review* (May 1998), 58–60.
124. This discussion is based on a review of the balanced scorecard in Richard L. Daft, *Organization Theory and Design,* 7th ed. (Cincinnati, OH: South-Western College Publishing, 2001), 300–301.
125. "On Balance," a CFO Interview with Robert Kaplan and David Norton, *CFO* (February 2001), 73–78.
126. Robert Kaplan and David Norton, "The Balanced Scorecard: Measures that Drive Performance," *Harvard Business Review* (January–February 1992), 71–79; and Chee W. Chow, Kamal M. Haddad, and James E. Williamson, "Applying the Balanced Scorecard to Small Companies," *Management Accounting* 79, no. 2 (August 1997), 21–27.
127. Based on Kaplan and Norton, "The Balanced Scorecard"; Chow, Haddad, and Williamson, "Applying the Balanced Scorecard"; and Cathy Lazere, "All Together Now," *CFO* (February 1998), 28–36.
128. Robert L. Katz, "Skills of an Effective Administrator," *Harvard Business Review* 52 (September–October 1974), 90–102.
129. Sue Shellenbarger, "From Our Readers: The Bosses That Drove Me to Quit My Job," *The Wall Street Journal,* February 7, 2000, B1.
130. Christopher A. Bartlett and Sumantra Ghoshal, "Changing the Role of Top Management: Beyond Systems to People," *Harvard Business Review* (May–June 1995), 132–142; and Sumantra Ghoshal and Christopher A. Bartlett, "Changing the Role of Top Management: Beyond Structure to Processes," *Harvard Business Review* (January–February 1995), 86–96.
131. Jenny C. McCune, "Management's Brave New World," *Management Review* (October 1997), 10–14; "Middle Managers Are Back—But Now They're 'High-Impact Players,'" *The Wall Street Journal,* April 14, 1998, B1; and Geoffrey Colvin, "Revenge of the Nerds," *Fortune,* March 2, 1998, 223–224.
132. Steven W. Floyd and Bill Wooldridge, "Dinosaurs or Dynamos? Recognizing Middle Management's Strategic Role," *Academy of Management Executive* 8, no. 4 (1994), 47–57.
133. Henry Mintzberg, *The Nature of Managerial Work* (New York: Harper & Row, 1973); and Mintzberg, "Rounding Out the Manager's Job," *Sloan Management Review* (Fall 1994), 11–26.
134. Robert E. Kaplan, "Trade Routes: The Manager's Network of Relationships," *Organizational Dynamics* (Spring 1984), 37–52; Rosemary Stewart, "The Nature of Management: A Problem for Management Education," *Journal of Management Studies* 21 (1984), 323–330; John P. Kotter, "What Effective General Managers Really Do," *Harvard Business Review* (November–December 1982), 156–167; and Morgan W. McCall, Jr., Ann M. Morrison, and Robert L. Hannan, "Studies of Managerial Work: Results and Methods" (Technical Report No. 9, Center for Creative Leadership, Greensboro, NC, 1978).
135. Henry Mintzberg, "Managerial Work: Analysis from Observation," *Management Science* 18 (1971), B97–B110.
136. Mintzberg, "Managerial Work."
137. Lance B. Kurke and Howard E. Aldrich, "Mintzberg Was Right!: A Replication and Extension of *The Nature of Managerial Work,*" *Management Science* 29 (1983), 975–984; Cynthia M. Pavett and Alan W. Lau, "Managerial Work: The Influence of Hierarchical Level and Functional Specialty," *Academy of Management Journal* 26 (1983), 170–177; and Colin P. Hales, "What Do Managers Do? A Critical Review of the Evidence," *Journal of Management Studies* 23 (1986), 88–115.
138. Mintzberg, "Rounding out the Manager's Job."
139. Harry S. Jonas III, Ronald E. Fry, and Suresh Srivastva, "The Office of the CEO: Understanding the Executive Experience," *Academy of Management Executive* 4 (August 1990), 36–48.
140. Toby J. Tetenbaum, "Shifting Paradigms: From Newton to Chaos," *Organizational Dynamics* (Spring 1998), 21–32. The following section is based on Tetenbaum, "Shifting Paradigms;" John A. Byrne, "Management By Web," *BusinessWeek* (August 28, 2000), 84–96; and Mark Gimein, "CEOs Who Manage Too Much," *Fortune,* September 4, 2000, 235–242.
141. Randy Myers, "E-commerce, Unplugged," *eCFO* (Summer 2001), 53–57.
142. Tetenbaum, "Shifting Paradigms: From Newton to Chaos."
143. *Ibid.*
144. Christopher A. Bartlett and Sumantra Ghoshal, "The Myth of the Generic Manager: New Personal Competencies for New Management Roles," *California Management Review* 40, No. 1 (Fall 1997), 92–116.

145. Tom Pohlmann with Bobby Cameron, Emily Jastrzembski, and Mary Lynn Pulley, "Building e-Business Leadership," (Forrester Research 2001), from the *Wharton Leadership Digest,* Wharton Center for Leadership and Change Management, *http://leadership.wharton.upenn.edu/digest/index.shtml.*

146. Byrne, "Management By Web."

147. Scott Kirsner, "Every Day, It's a New Place," *Fast Company* (April–May 1998), 130–134; Peter Coy, "The Creative Economy," *BusinessWeek,* August 28, 2000, 76–82; and Jeremy Main, "The Shape of the New Corporation," *Working Woman* (October 1998), 60–63.

148. Richard M. Steers and Lyman W. Porter, eds., *Motivation and Work Behavior,* 3rd ed. (New York: McGraw-Hill, 1983); Don Hellriegel, John W. Slocum, Jr., and Richard W. Woodman, *Organizational Behavior,* 7th ed. (St. Paul, MN: West, 1995), 170; and Jerry L. Gray and Frederick A. Starke, *Organizational Behavior: Concepts and Applications,* 4th ed. (New York: Macmillan, 1988), 104–105.

149. Carol Hymowitz, "Readers Tell Tales of Success and Failure Using Rating Systems" (In the Lead column), *Wall Street Journal* (May 29, 2001), B1.

150. Linda Grant, "Happy Workers, High Returns," *Fortune,* January 12, 1998, 81.

151. Steers and Porter, *Motivation.*

152. J. F. Rothlisberger and W. J. Dickson, *Management and the Worker* (Cambridge, MA: Harvard University Press, 1939).

153. J. Richard Hackman and Greg R. Oldham, *Work Redesign* (Reading, MA: Addison-Wesley, 1980); and J. Richard Hackman and Greg Oldham, "Motivation through the Design of Work: Test of a Theory," *Organizational Behavior and Human Performance* 16 (1976), 250–279.

154. Ann Podolske, "Giving Employees a Voice in Pay Structures," *Business Ethics* (March–April 1998), 12.

155. Edwin P. Hollander and Lynn R. Offermann, "Power and Leadership in Organizations," *American Psychologist* 45 (February 1990), 179–189.

156. Jay A. Conger and Rabindra N. Kanungo, "The Empowerment Process: Integrating Theory and Practice," *Academy of Management Review* 13 (1988), 471–482.

157. David E. Bowen and Edward E. Lawler III, "The Empowerment of Service Workers: What, Why, How, and When," *Sloan Management Review* (Spring 1992), 31–39; and Ray W. Coye and James A. Belohav, "An Exploratory Analysis of Employee Participation," *Group and Organization Management* 20, no. 1, (March 1995), 4–17.

158. This discussion is based on Robert C. Ford and Myron D. Fottler, "Empowerment: A Matter of Degree," *Academy of Management Executive* 9, no. 3 (1995), 21–31.

159. Jay A. Conger and Rabindra N. Kanungo, "The Empowerment Process: Integrating Theory and Practice," *Academy of Management Review* 13 (1998), 471–482.

160. Henry Mintzberg, *The Nature of Managerial Work* (New York: Harper & Row, 1973).

161. Fred Luthans and Janet K. Larsen, "How Managers Really Communicate," *Human Relations* 39 (1986), 161–178; and Larry E. Penley and Brian Hawkins, "Studying Interpersonal Communication in Organizations: A Leadership Application," *Academy of Management Journal* 28 (1985), 309–326.

162. Bruce K. Blaylock, "Cognitive Style and the Usefulness of Information," *Decision Sciences* 15 (Winter 1984), 74–91.

163. Phillip G. Clampitt, Robert J. DeKoch, and Thomas Cashman, "A Strategy for Communicating about Uncertainty," *Academy of Management Executive* 14, no. 4 (2000), 41–57.

164. Michael J. Glauser, "Upward Information Flow in Organizations: Review and Conceptual Analysis," *Human Relations* 37 (1984), 613–643; and "Upward/Downward Communication: Critical Information Channels," *Small Business Report* (October 1985), 85–88.

165. Mary P. Rowe and Michael Baker, "Are You Hearing Enough Employee Concerns?" *Harvard Business Review* 62 (May–June 1984), 127–135; W. H. Read, "Upward Communication in Industrial Hierarchies," *Human Relations* 15 (February 1962), 3–15; and Daft and Steers, *Organizations.*

166. E. M. Rogers and R. A. Rogers, *Communication in Organizations* (New York: Free Press, 1976); and A. Bavelas and D. Barrett, "An Experimental Approach to Organization Communication," *Personnel* 27 (1951), 366–371.

167. This discussion is based on Daft and Steers, *Organizations.*

168. Thomas J. Peters and Robert H. Waterman Jr., *In Search of Excellence* (New York: Harper & Row, 1982); and Tom Peters and Nancy Austin, *A Passion for Excellence: The Leadership Difference* (New York: Random House, 1985).

169. Keith Davis and John W. Newstrom, *Human Behavior at Work: Organizational Behavior,* 7th ed. (New York: McGraw-Hill, 1985).

170. Gary Hamel, "Killer Strategies That Make Shareholders Rich," *Fortune,* June 23, 1997, 70–84.

171. David Bohm, *On Dialogue* (Ojai, CA: David Bohm Seminars, 1989).

172. This discussion is based on Glenna Gerard and Linda Teurfs, "Dialogue and Organizational Transformation," in *Community Building: Renewing Spirit and Learning in Business,* ed. Kazinierz Gozdz (New Leaders Press, 1995), 142–153; and Edgar H. Schein, "On Dialogue, Culture, and Organizational Learning," *Organizational Dynamics* (Autumn 1993), 40–51.

173. Carol Hymowitz, "How to Tell Employees All the Things They Don't Want to Hear" (In the Lead column), *The Wall Street Journal,* August 22, 2000, B1.

MODULE 100. ENDNOTES

174. Peter Lowry and Byron Reimus, "Ready, Aim, Communicate," *Management Review* (July 1996).
175. Janet Fulk and Sirish Mani, "Distortion of Communication in Hierarchical Relationships," in *Communication Yearbook*, vol. 9, ed. M. L. McLaughlin (Beverly Hills, CA: Sage, 1986), 483–510.
176. Herbert A. Simon, *The New Science of Management Decision* (Englewood Cliffs, NJ: Prentice-Hall, 1960), 1–8.
177. Paul J. H. Schoemaker and J. Edward Russo, "A Pyramid of Decision Approaches," *California Management Review* (Fall 1993), 9–31.
178. Wendy Zellner, "Back to Coffee, Tea, or Milk?" *Business Week*, July 3, 1995, 52–56.
179. Michael Pacanowsky, "Team Tools for Wicked Problems," *Organizational Dynamics* 23, no. 3 (Winter 1995), 36–51.
180. Earnest R. Archer, "How to Make a Business Decision: An Analysis of Theory and Practice," *Management Review* 69 (February 1980), 54–61; Boris Blai, "Eight Steps to Successful Problem Solving," *Supervisory Management* (January 1986), 7–9.
181. James W. Dean, Jr., and Mark P. Sharfman, "Procedural Rationality in the Strategic Decision-Making Process," *Journal of Management Studies* 30 (1993), 587–610.
182. Irving L. Janis, *Crucial Decisions: Leadership in Policymaking and Crisis Management* (New York: The Free Press, 1989); Paul C. Nutt, "Flexible Decision Styles and the Choices of Top Executives," *Journal of Management Studies* 30 (1993), 695–721.
183. Herbert A. Simon, "Making Management Decisions: The Role of Intuition and Emotion," *Academy of Management Executive* 1 (February 1987), 57–64; Daniel J. Eisenberg, "How Senior Managers Think," *Harvard Business Review* 62 (November–December 1984), 80–90.
184. Sefan Wally and J. Robert Baum, "Personal and Structural Determinants of the Pace of Strategic Decision Making," *Academy of Management Journal* 37, no. 4 (1994), 932–56; Orlando Behling and Norman L. Eckel, "Making Sense Out of Intuition," *Academy of Management Executive* 5, no. 1 (1991), 46–54.
185. Thomas F. Issack, "Intuition: An Ignored Dimension of Management," *Academy of Management Review* 3 (1978), 917–22.
186. Marjorie A. Lyles, "Defining Strategic Problems: Subjective Criteria of Executives," *Organizational Studies* 8 (1987), 263–80; Marjorie A. Lyles and Ian I. Mitroff, "Organizational Problem Formulation: An Empirical Study," *Administrative Science Quarterly* 25 (1980), 102–19.
187. Marjorie A. Lyles and Howard Thomas, "Strategic Problem Formulation: Biases and Assumptions Embedded in Alternative Decision-Making Models," *Journal of Management Studies* 25 (1988), 131–45.
188. Susan E. Jackson and Jane E. Dutton, "Discerning Threats and Opportunities," *Administrative Science Quarterly* 33 (1988), 370–87.
189. Ross Stagner, "Corporate Decision-Making: An Empirical Study," *Journal of Applied Psychology* 53 (1969), 1–13.
190. Ann Langley, "Between 'Paralysis by Analysis' and Extinction by Instinct,'" *Sloan Management Review* (Spring 1995), 63–76.
191. Paul C. Nutt, "Types of Organizational Decision Processes," *Administrative Science Quarterly* 29 (1984), 414–50.
192. Nandini Rajagopalan, Abdul M. A. Rasheed, and Deepak K. Datta, "Strategic Decision Processes: Critical Review and Future Decisions," *Journal of Management* 19 (1993), 349–84; Paul J. H. Schoemaker, "Strategic Decisions in Organizations: Rational and Behavioral Views," *Journal of Management Studies* 30 (1993), 107–29; Charles J. McMillan, "Qualitative Models of Organizational Decision Making," *Journal of Management Studies* 5 (1980), 22–39; Paul C. Nutt, "Models for Decision Making in Organizations and Some Contextual Variables Which Stimulate Optimal Use," *Academy of Management Review* 1 (1976), 84–98.
193. Hugh J. Miser, "Operations Analysis in the Army Air Forces in World War II: Some Reminiscences," *Interfaces* 23 (September–October 1993), 47–49; Harold J. Leavitt, William R. Dill, and Henry B. Eyring, *The Organizational World* (New York: Harcourt Brace Jovanovich, 1973), chapter 6.
194. Stephen J. Huxley, "Finding the Right Spot for a Church Camp in Spain," *Interfaces* 12 (October 1982), 108–14; James E. Hodder and Henry E. Riggs, "Pitfalls in Evaluating Risky Projects," *Harvard Business Review* (January–February 1985), 128–35.
195. Edward Baker and Michael Fisher, "Computational Results for Very Large Air Crew Scheduling Problems," *Omega* 9 (1981), 613–18; Jean Aubin, "Scheduling Ambulances," *Interfaces* 22 (March–April, 1992), 1–10.
196. Richard L. Daft and John C. Wiginton, "Language and Organization," *Academy of Management Review* (1979), 179–91.
197. Based on Richard M. Cyert and James G. March, *A Behavioral Theory of the Firm* (Englewood Cliffs, NJ: Prentice-Hall, 1963); and James G. March and Herbert A. Simon, *Organizations* (New York: Wiley, 1958).
198. William B. Stevenson, Joan L. Pearce, and Lyman W. Porter, "The Concept of 'Coalition' in Organization Theory and Research," *Academy of Management Review* 10 (1985), 256–68.
199. Cyert and March, *Behavioral Theory of the Firm*, 120–22.
200. Based on Henry Mintzberg, Duru Raisinghani, and André Théorêt, "The Structure of 'Unstructured' Decision Processes," *Administrative Science Quarterly* 21 (1976), 246–75.
201. Lawrence T. Pinfield, "A Field Evaluation of Perspectives on Organizational Decision Making," *Administrative Science Quarterly* 31 (1986), 365–88.

202. Mintzberg et al., "The Structure of 'Unstructured' Decision Processes."
203. *Ibid.*, 270.
204. Michael D. Cohen, James G. March, and Johan P. Olsen, "A Garbage Can Model of Organizational Choice," *Administrative Science Quarterly* 17 (March 1972), 1–25; Michael D. Cohen and James G. March, *Leadership and Ambiguity: The American College President* (New York: McGraw-Hill, 1974).
205. Michael Masuch and Perry LaPotin, "Beyond Garbage Cans: An AI Model of Organizational Choice," *Administrative Science Quarterly* 34 (1989), 38–67.
206. L. J. Bourgeois III and Kathleen M. Eisenhardt, "Strategic Decision Processes in High Velocity Environments: Four Cases in the Microcomputer Industry," *Management Science* 34 (1988), 816–35.
207. Kathleen M. Eisenhardt, "Speed and Strategic Course: How Managers Accelerate Decision Making," *California Management Review* (Spring 1990), 39–54.
208. Karl Weick, T*he Social Psychology of Organizing,* 2nd ed. (Reading, MA: Addison-Wesley, 1979), 243.
209. Christopher Power with Kathleen Kerwin, Ronald Grover, Keith Alexander, and Robert D. Hof, "Flops," *Business Week,* 16 August 1993, 76–82.
210. Helga Drummond, "Too Little Too Late: A Case Study of Escalation in Decision Making," *Organization Studies* 15, no. 4 (1994), 591–607; Joel Brockner, "The Escalation of Commitment to a Failing Course of Action: Toward Theoretical Progress," *Academy of Management Review* 17 (1992), 39–61; Barry M. Staw and Jerry Ross, "Knowing When to Pull the Plug," *Harvard Business Review* 65 (March–April 1987), 68–74; Barry M. Staw, "The Escalation of Commitment to a Course of Action," *Academy of Management Review* 6 (1981), 577–87.
211. Elizabeth Lesly, "Why Things Are So Sour at Borden," *Business Week,* November 22, 1993, 78–85.
212. Jeremy Kahn, "What Makes a Company Great?" *Fortune,* October 26, 1998, 218.
213. W. Jack Duncan, "Organizational Culture: 'Getting a Fix' on an Elusive Concept," *Academy of Management Executive* 3 (1989), 229–36; Linda Smircich, "Concepts of Culture and Organizational Analysis," *Administrative Science Quarterly* 28 (1983), 339–58; Andrew D. Brown and Ken Starkey, "The Effect of Organizational Culture on Communication and Information," J*ournal of Management Studies* 31, no. 6 (November 1994), 807–28.
214. Edgar H. Schein, "Organizational Culture," *American Psychologist* 45 (February 1990), 109–19.
215. Harrison M. Trice and Janice M. Beyer, "Studying Organizational Cultures through Rites and Ceremonials," *Academy of Management Review* 9 (1984), 653–69; Janice M. Beyer and Harrison M. Trice, "How an Organization's Rites Reveal Its Culture," *Organizational Dynamics* 15 (Spring 1987), 5–24; Steven P. Feldman, "Management in Context: An Essay on the Relevance of Culture to the Understanding of Organizational Change," *Journal of Management Studies* 23 (1986), 589–607; Mary Jo Hatch, "The Dynamics of Organizational Culture," *Academy of Management Review* 18 (1993), 657–93.
216. This discussion is based on Edgar H. Schein, *Organizational Culture and Leadership,* 2nd ed. (Homewood, IL: Richard D. Irwin, 1992); John P. Kotter and James L. Heskett, *Corporate Culture and Performance* (New York: Free Press, 1992).
217. Charlotte B. Sutton, "Richness Hierarchy of the Cultural Network: The Communication of Corporate Values" (unpublished manuscript, Texas A & M University, 1985); Terrence E. Deal and Allan A. Kennedy, "Culture: A New Look Through Old Lenses," *Journal of Applied Behavioral Science* 19 (1983), 498–505.
218. Trice and Beyer, "Studying Organizational Cultures through Rites and Ceremonials."
219. Based on Daniel R. Denison, *Corporate Culture and Organizational Effectiveness* (New York: Wiley, 1990), 11–15; Daniel R. Denison and Aneil K. Mishra, "Toward a Theory of Organizational Culture and Effectiveness," *Organization Science* 6, no. 2 (March-April 1995), 204–23; R. Hooijberg and F. Petrock, "On Cultural Change: Using the Competing Values Framework to Help Leaders Execute a Transformational Strategy," *Human Resource Management* 32 (1993), 29–50; R. E. Quinn, *Beyond Rational Management: Mastering the Paradoxes and Competing Demands of High Performance* (San Francisco: Jossey-Bass, 1988).
220. Bernard Arogyaswamy and Charles M. Byles, "Organizational Culture: Internal and External Fits," *Journal of Management* 13 (1987), 647–59.
221. Paul R. Lawrence and Jay W. Lorsch, *Organization and Environment* (Homewood, IL: Irwin, 1969).
222. Gordon F. Shea, *Practical Ethics* (New York: American Management Association, 1988); Linda K. Treviño, "Ethical Decision Making in Organizations: A Person–Situation Interactionist Model," *Academy of Management Review* 11 (1986), 601–17; and Linda Klebe Treviño and Katherine A. Nelson, *Managing Business Ethics: Straight Talk About How to Do It Right,* 2nd ed. (New York: John Wiley & Sons, Inc. 1999).
223. LaRue Tone Hosmer, *The Ethics of Management,* 2nd ed., (Homewood, IL: Irwin, 1991).
224. Geanne Rosenberg, "Truth and Consequences," *Working Woman* (July–August 1998), 79–80.
225. Dawn-Marie Driscoll, "Don't Confuse Legal and Ethical Standards," *Business Ethics* (July–August 1996), 44.
226. Eugene W. Szwajkowski, "The Myths and Realities of Research on Organizational Misconduct," in James E. Post, ed., *Research and Corporate Social Performance and Policy,* vol. 9 (Greenwich, CT: JAI Press, 1986), 103–22.
227. These incidents are from Hosmer, *The Ethics of Management.*

228. Linda Klebe Treviño, "A Cultural Perspective on Changing and Developing Organizational Ethics," in Richard Woodman and William Pasmore, eds., *Research and Organizational Change and Development,* vol. 4 (Greenwich, CT: JAI Press, 1990); Lynn Sharp Paine, "Managing for Organizational Integrity," *Harvard Business Review* (March/April 1994), 106–17.

229. James Weber, "Exploring the Relationship between Personal Values and Moral Reasoning," *Human Relations* 46 (1993), 435–63.

230. L. Kohlberg, "Moral Stages and Moralization: The Cognitive-Developmental Approach," in T. Likona, ed., *Moral Development and Behavior: Theory, Research, and Social Issues* (New York: Holt, Rinehart & Winston, 1976).

231. Hosmer, *The Ethics of Management.*

232. David M. Messick and Max H. Bazerman, "Ethical Leadership and the Psychology of Decision Making," *Sloan Management Review* (Winter 1996), 9–22; Dawn-Marie Driscoll, "Don't Confuse Legal and Ethical Standards," *Business Ethics,* July–August 1996, 44.

233. Andrew W. Singer, "The Ultimate Ethics Test," *Across the Board* (March 1992), 19–22; Ronald B. Morgan, "Self and Co-Worker Perceptions of Ethics and Their Relationships to Leadership and Salary," *Academy of Management Journal,* 36, no. 1 (February 1993), 200–14; Joseph L. Badaracco, Jr. and Allen P. Webb, "Business Ethics: A View From the Trenches," *California Management Review* 37, no. 2 (Winter 1995), 8–28.

234. Justin Martin, "New Tricks for an Old Trade," *Across the Board,* June 1992, 40–44.

235. Janet P. Near and Marcia P. Miceli, "Effective Whistle-Blowing," *Academy of Management Review* 20, no. 3 (1995), 679–708.

236. Richard P. Nielsen, "Changing Unethical Organizational Behavior," *Academy of Management Executive* 3 (1989), 123–30.

237. Jene G. James, "Whistle-Blowing: Its Moral Justification," in Peter Madsen and Jay M. Shafritz, eds., *Essentials of Business Ethics* (New York: Meridian Books, 1990), 160–90; Janet P. Near, Terry Morehead Dworkin, and Marcia P. Miceli, "Explaining the Whistle-Blowing Process: Suggestions from Power Theory and Justice Theory," *Organization Science* 4 (1993), 393–411.

238. Carolyn Wiley, "The ABC's of Business Ethics: Definitions, Philosophies, and Implementation," *IM* (January–February 1995), 22–27.

239. Carl Anderson, "Values-Based Management," *Academy of Management Executive* 11, no. 4 (1997), 25–46.

240. James Weber, "Institutionalizing Ethics into Business Organizations: A Model and Research Agenda," *Business Ethics Quarterly* 3 (1993), 419–36.

241. Susan J. Harrington, "What Corporate America Is Teaching about Ethics," *Academy of Management Executive* 5 (1991), 21–30.

242. Eberhard, E. Scheuing, *Purchasing Management* (Englewood Cliffs, NJ: Prentice-Hall, 1989), 55.

243. Stuart Heinritz, Paul V. Farrell, Larry C. Giunipero, and Michael G. Kolchin, *Purchasing: Principles and Applications,* 8th ed. (Englewood Cliffs, NJ: Prentice-Hall, 1991), 243.

244. Heinritz et al., *Purchasing,* 249–50.

245. Hancock, *The Law of Purchasing,* 30.09.

246. John J. Coyle, Edward J. Bardi, and C. John Langley, Jr., *The Management of Business Logistics,* 4th ed. (St. Paul, MN: West Publishing, 1988), 360.

247. Cavinato, *Purchasing and Materials Management,* 134.

248. Hancock, *The Law of Purchasing,* 10.18–23.

249. Hancock, *The Law of Purchasing,* 22.05–06.

250. Martin J., Cabarra, J. D., and Ernest Gabbard, J. D., "What's on the Books: Other Laws Affecting Purchasing and Supply," *The Purchasing and Supply Yearbook,* ed. John A. Woods (New York: McGraw-Hill, 2000), 332–39.

251. GDP measures aggregate business activity as described by the value at final point of sale of all goods and services produced in the domestic economy during a given period by both domestic and foreign-owned enterprises. Gross national product (GNP) is the value at final point of sale of all goods and services produced by *domestic* firms. As such, GNP does not reflect domestic production by foreign-owned firms (e.g., Toyota Camrys produced in Kentucky).

252. James D. Thompson, *Organizations in Action* (New York: McGraw-Hill, 1967), 4–13.

253. Henry Mintzberg, *The Structuring of Organizations* (Englewood Cliffs, NJ: Prentice-Hall, 1979), 215–297; and Henry Mintzberg, "Organization Design: Fashion or Fit?" *Harvard Business Review* 59 (January–February 1981), 103–116.

254. The following discussion was heavily influenced by Richard H. Hall, *Organizations: Structures, Processes, and Outcomes* (Englewood Cliffs, NJ: Prentice-Hall, 1991); D. S. Pugh, "The Measurement of Organization Structures: Does Context Determine Form?" *Organizational Dynamics* 1 (Spring 1973), 19–34; and D. S. Pugh, D. J. Hickson, C. R. Hinings, and C. Turner, "Dimensions of Organization Structure," *Administrative Science Quarterly* 13 (1968), 65–91.

255. Robert House, Denise M. Rousseau, and Melissa Thomas-Hunt, "The Meso Paradigm: A Framework for the Integration of Micro and Macro Organizational Behavior," *Research in Organizational Behavior* 17 (1995), 71–114.

256. Fred L. Steingraber, "How to Succeed in the Global Marketplace," *USA Today Magazine* (November 1997), 30–31.

257. Marlene Piturro, "What Are You Doing About the New Global Realities?" *Management Review* (March 1999), 17–22.

258. Raju Narisetti and Jonathan Friedland, "Diaper Wars of P&G and Kimberly-Clark Now Heat Up in Brazil," *The Wall Street Journal,* June 4, 1997; and Stephen Baker, "The Bridges That Steel Is Building," *Business Week,* June 2, 1997, 39.

259. Christine S. Koberg and Gerardo R. Ungson, "The Effects of Environmental Uncertainty and Dependence on Organizational Structure and Performance: A Comparative Study," *Journal of Management* 13 (1987), 725–37; Frances J. Milliken, "Three Types of Perceived Uncertainty About the Environment: State, Effect, and Response Uncertainty," *Academy of Management Review* 12 (1987), 133–43.

260. Robert B. Duncan, "Characteristics of Organizational Environment and Perceived Environmental Uncertainty,: *Administrative Science Quarterly* 17 (1972), 313–27; Gregory G. Dess and Donald W. Beard, "Dimensions of Organizational Task Environments," *Administrative Science Quarterly* 29 (1984), 52–73; Ray Jurkovich, "A Core Typology of Organizational Environments," *Administrative Science Quarterly* 19 (1974), 380–94.

261. Rosalie L. Tung, "Dimensions of Organizational Environments: An Exploratory Study of Their Impact on Organizational Structure," *Academy of Management Journal* 22 (1979), 672–93.

262. Joseph E. McCann and John Selsky, "Hyper-Turbulence and the Emergence of Type 5 Environments," *Academy of Management Review* 9 (1984), 460–70.

263. Judith Valente and Asra Q. Nomani, "Surge in Oil Price has Airlines Struggling, Some Just to Hang on," *The Wall Street Journal*, August 10, 1990, A1, A4.

264. James D. Thompson, *Organizations in Action* (New York: McGraw-Hill, 1967), 20–21.

265. Sally Solo, "Whirlpool: How to Listen to Consumers," *Fortune*, January 11, 1993, 77–79.

266. David B. Jemison, "The Importance of Boundary Spanning Roles in Strategic Decision-Making," *Journal of Management Studies* 21 (1984), 131–52; Mohamed Ibrahim Ahmad At-Twaijri and John R. Montanari, "The Impact of Context and Choice on the Boundary-Spanning Process: An Empirical Extension," *Human Relations* 40 (1987), 783–98.

267. Michelle Cook, "The Intelligentsia," *Business 2.0* (July 1999), 135–136.

268. Robert C. Schwab, Gerardo R. Ungson, and Warren B. Brown, "Redefining the Boundary-Spanning Environment Relationship," *Journal of Management* 11 (1985), 75–86.

269. Ken Western, "Ethical Spying," *Business Ethics* (September/October 1995), 22–23; Stan Crock, Geoffrey Smith, Joseph Weber, Richard A. Melcher, and Linda Himelstein, "They Snoop to Conquer," *Business Week*, October 28, 1996, 172–176; Kenneth A. Sawka, "Demystifying Business Intelligence," *Management Review* (October 1996), 47–51.

270. France with Muller, "A Site for Soreheads."

271. Jay W. Lorsch, "Introduction to the Structural Design of Organizations," in Gene W. Dalton, Paul R. Lawrence, and Jay W. Lorsch, eds., *Organizational Structure and Design* (Homewood, IL: Irwin and Dorsey, 1970), 5.

272. Lorsch, "Introduction to the Structural Design of Organizations," 7.

273. Jay W. Lorsch and Paul R. Lawrence, "Environmental Factors and Organizational Integration," in J. W. Lorsch and Paul R. Lawrence, eds., *Organizational Planning: Cases and Concepts* (Homewood, IL: Irwin and Dorsey, 1972), 45.

274. Tom Burns and G. M. Stalker, *The Management of Innovation* (London: Tavistock, 1961).

275. John A. Courtright, Gail T. Fairhurst, and L. Edna Rogers, "Interaction Patterns in Organic and Mechanistic Systems," *Academy of Management Journal* 32 (1989), 773–802.

276. Thomas C. Powell, "Organizational Alignment as Competitive Advantage," *Strategic Management Journal* 13 (1992), 119–34. Mansour Javidan, "The Impact of Environmental Uncertainty on Long-Range Planning Practices of the U.S. Savings and Loan Industry," *Strategic Management Journal* 5 (1984), 381–92; Tung, "Dimensions of Organizational Environments," 672–93; Thompson, *Organizations in Action*.

277. Judith A. Babcock, *Organizational Responses to Resource Scarcity and Munificence: Adaptation and Modification in Colleges within a University* (Ph.D. diss., Pennsylvania State University, 1981).

278. Peter Smith Ring and Andrew H. Van de Ven, "Developmental Processes of Corporative Interorganizational Relationships," *Academy of Management Review* 19 (1994), 90–118; Jeffrey Pfeffer, "Beyond Management and the Worker: The Institutional Function of Management," *Academy of Management Review* 1 (April 1976), 36–46; John P. Kotter, "Managing External Dependence," *Academy of Management Review* 4 (1979), 87–92.

279. Bryan Borys and David B. Jemison, "Hybrid Arrangements as Strategic Alliances: Theoretical Issues in Organizational Combinations," *Academy of Management Review* 14 (1989), 234–49.

280. Julie Cohen Mason, "Strategic Alliances: Partnering for Success," *Management Review* (May 1993), 10–15.

281. Borys and Jemison, "Hybrid Arrangements as Strategic Alliances."

282. Edward O. Welles, "Not Your Father's Industry," *Inc.* (January 1999),: 25–28.

283. Donald Palmer, "Broken Ties: Interlocking Directorates and Intercorporate Coordination," *Administrative Science Quarterly* 28 (1983), 40–55; F. David Shoorman, Max H. Bazerman, and Robert S. Atkin, "Interlocking Directorates: A Strategy for Reducing Environmental Uncertainty," *Academy of Management Review* 6 (1981), 243–51; Ronald S. Burt, *Toward a Structural Theory of Action* (New York: Academic Press, 1982).

284. James R. Lang and Daniel E. Lockhart, "Increased Environmental Uncertainty and Changes in Board Linkage Patterns," *Academy of Management Journal* 33 (1990), 106–28; Mark S. Mizruchi and Linda Brewster Stearns, "A Longitudinal Study of the Formation of Interlocking Directorates," *Administrative Science Quarterly* 33 (1988), 194–210.

285. Neuborne with Kerwin, "Generation Y."

286. Kotter, "Managing External Dependence."
287. Rick Wartzman and John Harwood, "For the Baby Bells, Government Lobbying Is Hardly Child's Play," *The Wall Street Journal,* March 15, 1994, A1.
288. David B. Yoffie, "How an Industry Builds Political Advantage," *Harvard Business Review* (May–June 1988), 82–89; Jeffrey H. Birnbaum, "Chief Executives Head to Washington to Ply the Lobbyist's Trade," *The Wall Street Journal,* March 19, 1990, A1, A16.
289. Anthony J. Daboub, Abdul M. A. Rasheed, Richard L. Priem, and David A. Gray, "Top Management Team Characteristics and Corporate Illegal Activity," *Academy of Management Review* 20, no. 1 (1995), 138–70.
290. Bryan Burrough, "Oil-Field Investigators Say Fraud Flourishes from Wells to Offices," *The Wall Street Journal,* January 15, 1985, 1, 20; Irwin Ross, "How Lawless Are Big Companies?" *Fortune,* December 1, 1980, 57–64.
291. Stewart Toy, "The Defense Scandal," *Business Week,* July 4, 1988, 28–30.
292. Barry M. Staw and Eugene Szwajkowski, "The Scarcity-Munificence Component of Organizational Environments and the Commission of Illegal Acts," *Administrative Science Quarterly* 20 (1975), 345–54.
293. John Child, *Organization* (New York: Harper & Row, 1984).
294. Stuart Ranson, Bob Hinings, and Royston Greenwood, "The Structuring of Organizational Structures," *Administrative Science Quarterly* 25 (1980), 1–17; Hugh Willmott, "The Structuring of Organizational Structure: A Note," *Administrative Science Quarterly* 26 (1981), 470–74.
295. This section is based on Frank Ostroff, *The Horizontal Organization: What the Organization of the Future Looks Like and How It Delivers Value to Customers* (New York: Oxford University Press, 1999).
296. David Nadler and Michael Tushman, *Strategic Organization Design* (Glenview, IL: Scott Foresman, 1988).
297. Based on Jay R. Galbraith, *Designing Complex Organizations* (Reading, MA: Addison-Wesley, 1973), and *Organization Design* (Reading, MA: Addison-Wesley, 1977), 81–127.
298. Eryn Brown, "9 Ways to Win on the Web," *Fortune,* May 24, 1999, 112–125.
299. Based on Galbraith, *Designing Complex Organizations*.
300. Mary J. Cronin, "Intranets Reach the Factory Floor," *Fortune,* August 18, 1997, 208; and Brown, "9 Ways to Win on the Web."
301. Timothy D. Schellhardt, "Monsanto Bets on 'Box Buddies'," *The Wall Street Journal,* February 23, 1999, B1, B10.
302. Walter Kiechel III, "The Art of the Corporate Task Force," *Fortune,* January 28, 1991, 104–5; William J. Altier, "Task Forces: An Effective Management Tool," *Management Review* (February 1987), 52–57.
303. Keith Naughton and Kathleen Kerwin, "At GM, Two Heads May Be Worse Than One," *Business Week,* August 14, 1995, 46.
304. Paul R. Lawrence and Jay W. Lorsch, "New Managerial Job: The Integrator," *Harvard Business Review* (November–December 1967), 142–51.
305. Jay R. Galbraith, *Competing with Flexible Lateral Organizations*, 2nd ed. (Reading, MA: Addison-Wesley, 1994), 17–18; Laurie P. O'Leary, "Curing the Monday Blues: A U.S. Navy Guide for Structuring Cross-Functional Teams," *National Productivity Review* (Spring 1996), 43–51.
306. Henry Mintzberg, *The Structuring of Organizations* (Englewood Cliffs, NJ: Prentice-Hall, 1979).
307. Based on Robert Duncan, "What Is the Right Organization Structure?" *Organizational Dynamics* (Winter 1979), 59–80; W. Alan Randolph and Gregory G. Dess, "The Congruence Perspective of Organization Design: A Conceptual Model and Multivariate Research Approach," *Academy of Management Review* 9 (1984), 114–27.
308. Based on Duncan, "What Is the Right Organization Structure?"
309. Weber, "A Big Company That Works."
310. John Markoff, "John Sculley's Biggest Test," *New York Times,* February 26, 1989, sec. 3,1,26; and Shelly Branch, "What's Eating McDonald's?" *Fortune,* October 13, 1997, 122–125.
311. Stanley M. Davis and Paul R. Lawrence, *Matrix* (Reading, MA: Addison-Wesley, 1977), 11–24.
312. Eric W. Larson and David H. Gobeli, "Matrix Management: Contradictions and Insight," *California Management Review* 29 (Summer 1987), 127–138.
313. Davis and Lawrence, *Matrix*, 155–180.
314. Lawton R. Burns, "Matrix Management in Hospitals: Testing Theories of Matrix Structure and Development," *Administrative Science Quarterly* 34 (1989), 349–68.
315. Christopher A. Bartlett and Sumantra Ghoshal, "Matrix Management: Not a Structure, a Frame of Mind," *Harvard Business Review* (July–August 1990), 138–45.
316. Jay R. Galbraith, *Competing with Flexible Lateral Organizations*, 2nd ed. (Reading, MA: Addison-Wesley, 1994): chapter 2; Terry L. Amburgey and Tina Dacin, "As the Left Foot Follows the Right? The Dynamics of Strategic and Structural Change," *Academy of Management Journal* 37, no. 6 (1994), 427–452; and Raymond E. Miles and W. E. Douglas Creed, "Organizational Forms and Managerial Philosophies: A Descriptive and Analytical Review," *Research in Organizational Behavior* 17 (1995), 333–372.
317. Jo Ellen Davis, "Who's Afraid of IBM?" *Business Week,* June 29, 1987, 68–74.

318. Based on Child, *Organization*, chapter 1.
319. James Q. Wilson, *Bureaucracy* (Basic Books, 1989); and Charles Perrow, *Complex Organizations: A Critical Essay* (Glenview, IL: Scott, Foresman, 1979), 4.
320. David Friedman, "Is Big Back? Or Is Small Still Beautiful?" *Inc.* (April 1998), 23–28.
321. James B. Treece, "Sometimes, You've Still Gotta Have Size," *Business Week/Enterprise* (1993), 200–01.
322. Friedman, "Is Big Back?"
323. Peter F. Drucker, "Toward the New Organization," *Executive Excellence* (February 1997), 7.
324. Thomas Petzinger, Jr., *The New Pioneers: The Men and Women Who Are Transforming the Workplace and Marketplace* (New York: Simon & Schuster, 1999), 21.
325. Glenn R. Carroll, "Organizations . . . The Smaller They Get," *California Management Review* 37, no. 1 (Fall 1994), 28–41.
326. John R. Kimberly, Robert H. Miles, and Associates, *The Organizational Life Cycle* (San Francisco: Jossey-Bass, 1980); Ichak Adices, "Organizational Passages—Diagnosing and Treating Lifecycle Problems of Organizations," *Organizational Dynamics* (Summer 1979), 3–25; Danny Miller and Peter H. Friesen, "A Longitudinal Study of the Corporate Life Cycle," *Management Science* 30 (October 1984), 1161–83; Neil C. Churchill and Virginia L. Lewis, "The Five Stages of Small Business Growth," *Harvard Business Review* 61 (May–June 1983), 30–50.
327. Larry E. Greiner, "Evolution and Revolution as Organizations Grow," *Harvard Business Review* 50 (July–August 1972), 37–46; Robert E. Quinn and Kim Cameron, "Organizational Life Cycles and Shifting Criteria of Effectiveness: Some Preliminary Evidence," *Management Science* 29 (1983), 33–51.
328. George Land and Beth Jarman, "Moving beyond Breakpoint," in Michael Ray and Alan Rinzler, eds., *The New Paradigm* (New York: Jeremy P. Tarcher/Perigee Books, 1993), 250–66; Michael L. Tushman, William H. Newman, and Elaine Romanelli, "Convergence and Upheaval: Managing the Unsteady Pace of Organizational Evolution," *California Management Review* 29 (1987), 1–16.
329. Land and Jarman, "Moving Beyond Breakpoint."
330. Max Weber, *The Theory of Social and Economic Organizations*, translated by A. M. Henderson and T. Parsons (New York: Free Press, 1947).
331. John Crewdson, "Corruption Viewed as a Way of Life," *Bryan-College Station Eagle*, November 28, 1982, 13A; Barry Kramer, "Chinese Officials Still Give Preference to Kin, Despite Peking Policies," *The Wall Street Journal*, October 29, 1985, 1, 21.
332. Allen C. Bluedorn, "Pilgrim's Progress: Trends and Convergence in Research on Organizational Size and Environment," *Journal of Management Studies* 19 (Summer 1993), 163–91; John R. Kimberly, "Organizational Size and the Structuralist Perspective: A Review, Critique, and Proposal," *Administrative Science Quarterly* (1976), 571–97; Richard L. Daft and Selwyn W. Becker, "Managerial, Institutional, and Technical Influences on Administration: A Longitudinal Analysis," *Social Forces* 59 (1980), 392–413.
333. James P. Walsh and Robert D. Dewar, "Formalization and the Organizational Life Cycle," *Journal of Management Studies* 24 (May 1987), 215–31.
334. Nancy M. Carter and Thomas L. Keon, "Specialization as a Multidimensional Construct," *Journal of Management Studies* 26 (1989), 11–28; Cheng-Kuang Hsu, Robert M. March, and Hiroshi Mannari, "An Examination of the Determinants of Organizational Structure," *American Journal of Sociology* 88 (1983), 975–96; Guy Geeraerts, "The Effect of Ownership on the Organization Structure in Small Firms," *Administrative Science Quarterly* 29 (1984), 232–37; Bernard Reimann, "On the Dimensions of Bureaucratic Structure: An Empirical Reappraisal," *Administrative Science Quarterly* 18 (1973), 462–76; Richard H. Hall, "The Concept of Bureaucracy: An Empirical Assessment," *American Journal of Sociology* 69 (1963), 32–40; William A. Rushing, "Organizational Rules and Surveillance: A Proposition in Comparative Organizational Analysis," *Administrative Science Quarterly* 10 (1966), 423–43.
335. Jerald Hage and Michael Aiken, "Relationship of Centralization to Other Structural Properties," *Administrative Science Quarterly* 12 (1967), 72–91.
336. Peter Brimelow, "How Do You Cure Injelitance?" *Forbes*, August 7, 1989, 42–44; and Jeffrey D. Ford and John W. Slocum, Jr., "Size, Technology, Environment and the Structure of Organizations," *Academy of Management Review* 2 (1977), 561–75; John D. Kasarda, "The Structural Implications of Social System Size: A Three-Level Analysis," *American Sociological Review* 39 (1974), 19–28.
337. Graham Astley, "Organizational Size and Bureaucratic Structure," *Organization Studies* 6 (1985), 201–28; Spyros K. Lioukas and Demitris A. Xerokostas, "Size and Administrative Intensity in Organizational Divisions," *Management Science* 28 (1982), 854–68; Peter M. Blau, "Interdependence and Hierarchy in Organizations," *Social Science Research* 1 (1972), 1–24; Peter M. Blau and R. A. Schoenherr, *The Structure of Organizations* (New York: Basic Books, 1971); A. Hawley, W. Boland, and M. Boland, "Population Size and Administration in Institutions of Higher Education," *American Sociological Review* 30 (1965), 252–55; Richard L. Daft, "System Influence on Organization Decision-Making: The Case of Resource Allocation," *Academy of Management Journal* 21 (1978), 6–22; B. P. Indik, "The Relationship Between Organization Size and the Supervisory Ratio," *Administrative Science Quarterly* 9 (1964), 301–12.
338. T. F. James, "The Administrative Component in Complex Organizations," *Sociological Quarterly* 13 (1972), 533–39; Daft, "System Influence on Organization Decision-Making"; E. A. Holdaway and E. A. Blowers, "Administrative Ratios and

Organization Size: A Longitudinal Examination," *American Sociological Review* 36 (1971), 278–86; John Child, "Parkinson's Progress: Accounting for the Number of Specialists in Organizations," *Administrative Science Quarterly* 18 (1973), 328–48.

339. Richard L. Daft and Selwyn Becker, "School District Size and the Development of Personnel Resources," *Alberta Journal of Educational Research* 24 (1978), 173–87.
340. Thomas A. Stewart, "Yikes! Deadwood is Creeping Back," *Fortune,* August 18, 1997, 221–222.
341. Cathy Lazere, "Resisting Temptation: The Fourth Annual SG&A Survey," *CFO* (December 1997), 64–70.
342. William G. Ouchi, "Markets, Bureaucracies, and Clans," *Administrative Science Quarterly* 25 (1980), 129–41;—idem, "A Conceptual Framework for the Design of Organizational Control Mechanisms," *Management Science* 25 (1979), 833–48.
343. Weber, *Theory of Social and Economic Organizations,* 328–340.
344. Robert Simons, "Strategic Organizations and Top Management Attention to Control Systems," *Strategic Management Journal* 12 (1991), 49–62.
345. Stephen G. Green and M. Ann Welsh, "Cybernetics and Dependents: Reframing the Control Concept," *Academy of Management Review* 13 (1988), 287–301.
346. Richard L. Daft and Norman B. Macintosh, "The Nature and Use of Formal Control Systems for Management Control and Strategy Implementation," *Journal of Management* 10 (1984), 43–66.
347. Ibid.; Scott S. Cowen and J. Kendall Middaugh II, "Matching an Organization's Planning and Control System to Its Environment," *Journal of General Management* 16 (1990), 69–84.
348. Trevor Merriden, "Measured for Success," *Management Review* (April 1999), 27–32.
349. Oliver A. Williamson, *Markets and Hierarchies: Analyses and Antitrust Implications* (New York: Free Press, 1975).
350. Raymond E. Miles, Henry J. Coleman, Jr., and W. E. Douglas Creed, "Keys to Success in Corporate Redesign," *California Management Review* 37, no. 3 (Spring 1995), 128–45.
351. Ouchi, "Markets, Bureaucracies, and Clans."
352. Anna Muoio, ed., "Growing Smart," *Fast Company* (August 1998), 73–83.
353. Stratford Sherman, "The New Computer Revolution," *Fortune,* June 14, 1993, 56–80.
354. Richard Leifer and Peter K. Mills, "An Information Processing Approach for Deciding upon Control Strategies and Reducing Control Loss in Emerging Organizations," *Journal of Management* 22, no. 1 (1996), 113–37.
355. Leifer and Mills, "An Information Processing Approach for Deciding Upon Control Strategies"; Laurie J. Kirsch, "The Management of Complex Tasks in Organizations: Controlling the Systems Development Process," *Organization Science* 7, no. 1 (January–February 1996), 1–21.
356. James R. Barker, "Tightening the Iron Cage: Concertive Control in Self-Managing Teams," *Administrative Science Quarterly* 38 (1993), 408–37.
357. Peter F. Drucker, *Management Challenges for the 21st Century* (New York: Harper Business, 1999).
358. Joseph E. McCann, "Design Principles for an Innovating Company," *Academy of Management Executive* 5 (May 1991), 76–93.
359. Stuart Crainer and Des Dearlove, "Water Works," *Management Review* (May 1999), 39–43.
360. Anita Lienert, "Jedi Masters and Paradigm Busters," *Management Review* (March, 1998), 11–14.
361. Bruce Rayner, "Trial-by-Fire Transformation: An Interview with Globe Metallurgical's Arden C. Sims," *Harvard Business Review* (May–June 1992), 117–29.
362. Richard A. Wolfe, "Organizational Innovation: Review, Critique and Suggested Research Directions," *Journal of Management Studies* 31, no. 3 (May 1994), 405–31.
363. John L. Pierce and Andre L. Delbecq, "Organization Structure, Individual Attitudes and Innovation," *Academy of Management Review* 2 (1977), 27–37; Michael Aiken and Jerald Hage, "The Organic Organization and Innovation," *Sociology* 5 (1971), 63–82.
364. Richard L. Daft, "Bureaucratic versus Nonbureaucratic Structure in the Process of Innovation and Change," in Samuel B. Bacharach, ed., *Perspectives in Organizational Sociology: Theory and Research* (Greenwich, CT: JAI Press, 1982), 129–66.
365. Alan D. Meyer and James B. Goes, "Organizational Assimilation of Innovations: A Multilevel Contextual Analysis," *Academy of Management Journal* 31 (1988), 897–923.
366. Richard W. Woodman, John E. Sawyer, and Ricky W. Griffin, "Toward a Theory of Organizational Creativity," *Academy of Management Review* 18 (1993), 293–321; Alan Farnham, "How to Nurture Creative Sparks," *Fortune,* January 10, 1994, 94–100.
367. Michael Barrier, "Managing Workers in Times of Change," *Nation's Business* (May 1998), 31–34.
368. John P. Kotter, *Leading Change* (Boston: Harvard University Press, 1996), 20–25, and "Leading Change," *Harvard Business Review* (March–April 1995), 59–67.
369. D. Bruce Merrifield, "Intrapreneurial Corporate Renewal," *Journal of Business Venturing* 8 (September 1993), 383–89; Linsu Kim, "Organizational Innovation and Structure," *Journal of Business Research* 8 (1980), 225–45; Tom Burns and G. M. Stalker, *The Management of Innovation* (London: Tavistock Publications, 1961).
370. James Q. Wilson, "Innovation in Organization: Notes toward a Theory," in James D. Thompson, ed., *Approaches to Organizational Design* (Pittsburgh: University of Pittsburgh Press, 1966), 193–218.

371. J. C. Spender and Eric H. Kessler, "Managing the Uncertainties of Innovation: Extending Thompson (1967)," *Human Relations* 48, no. 1 (1995), 35–56; Robert B. Duncan, "The Ambidextrous Organization: Designing Dual Structures for Innovation," in Ralph H. Killman, Louis R. Pondy, and Dennis Slevin, eds., *The Management of Organization*, vol. 1 (New York: North-Holland, 1976), 167–88.

372. Edward F. McDonough III and Richard Leifer, "Using Simultaneous Structures to Cope with Uncertainty," *Academy of Management Journal* 26 (1983), 727–35.

373. Judith R. Blau and William McKinley, "Ideas, Complexity, and Innovation," *Administrative Science Quarterly* 24 (1979), 200–19.

374. Daniel F. Jennings and James R. Lumpkin, "Functioning Modeling Corporate Entrepreneurship: An Empirical Integrative Analysis," *Journal of Management* 15 (1989), 485–502.

375. Jane M. Howell and Christopher A. Higgins, "Champions of Technology Innovation," *Administrative Science Quarterly* 35 (1990), 317–41; Jane M. Howell and Christopher A. Higgins, "Champions of Change: Identifying, Understanding, and Supporting Champions of Technology Innovations," *Organizational Dynamics* (Summer 1990), 40–55.

376. Peter F. Drucker, "Change Leaders," *Inc.* (June 1999), 65–72, and Peter F. Drucker, *Management Challenges for the 21st Century* (New York: Harper Business, 1999).

377. Peter J. Frost and Carolyn P. Egri, "The Political Process of Innovation," in L. L. Cummings and Barry M. Staw, eds., *Research in Organizational Behavior*, vol. 13 (New York: JAI Press, 1991), 229–95; Jay R. Galbraith, "Designing the Innovating Organization," *Organizational Dynamics* (Winter 1982), 5–25; Marsha Sinatar, "Entrepreneurs, Chaos, and Creativity—Can Creative People Really Survive Large Company Structure?" *Sloan Management Review* (Winter 1985), 57–62.

378. "Black & Decker Inventory Makes Money for Firm by Just Not 'Doing the Neat Stuff,'" *Houston Chronicle*, December 25, 1987, sec. 3, p. 2.

379. Shona L. Brown and Kathleen M. Eisenhardt, "Product Development: Past Research, Present Findings, and Future Directions," *Academy of Management Review* 20, no. 2 (1995): 343–78; Dan Dimancescu and Kemp Dwenger, "Smoothing the Product Development Path," *Management Review* (January 1996): 36–41.

380. Alex Taylor III, "Kellogg Cranks Up Its Idea Machine," *Fortune*, 5 July 1999, 181–182.

381. Raymond E. Miles, Henry J. Coleman, Jr., and W. E. Douglas Creed, "Keys to Success in Corporate Redesign," *California Management Review* 37, no. 3 (Spring 1995), 128–45.

382. Fariborz Damanpour and William M. Evan, "Organizational Innovation and Performance: The Problem of 'Organizational Lag,'" *Administrative Science Quarterly*, 29 (1984), 392–409; David J. Teece, "The Diffusion of an Administrative Innovation," *Management Science* 26 (1980), 464–70; John R. Kimberly and Michael J. Evaniski, "Organizational Innovation: The Influence of Individual, Organizational and Contextual Factors on Hospital Adoption of Technological and Administrative Innovation," *Academy of Management Journal* 24 (1981), 689–713; Michael K. Moch and Edward V. Morse, "Size, Centralization, and Organizational Adoption of Innovations," *American Sociological Review* 42 (1977), 716–25; Mary L. Fennell, "Synergy, Influence, and Information in the Adoption of Administrative Innovation," *Academy of Management Journal* 27 (1984), 113–29.

383. Richard L. Daft, "A Dual-Core Model of Organizational Innovation," *Academy of Management Journal* 21 (1978), 193–210.

384. Daft, "Bureaucratic versus Nonbureaucratic Structure"; Robert W. Zmud, "Diffusion of Modern Software Practices: Influence of Centralization and Formalization," *Management Science* 28 (1982), 1421–31.

385. Daft, "A Dual-Core Model of Organizational Innovation"; Zmud, "Diffusion of Modern Software Practices."

386. Fariborz Damanpour, "The Adoption of Technological, Administrative, and Ancillary Innovations: Impact of Organizational Factors," *Journal of Management* 13 (1987), 675–88.

387. Gregory H. Gaertner, Karen N. Gaertner, and David M. Akinnusi, "Environment, Strategy, and the Implementation of Administrative Change: The Case of Civil Service Reform," *Academy of Management Journal* 27 (1984), 525–43.

388. Claudia Bird Schoonhoven and Mariann Jelinek, "Dynamic Tension in Innovative, High Technology Firms: Managing Rapid Technology Change through Organization Structure," in Mary Ann Von Glinow and Susan Albers Mohrman, eds., *Managing Complexity in High Technology Organizations* (New York: Oxford University Press, 1990), 90–118.

389. Benson L. Porter and Warrington S. Parker, Jr., "Culture Change," *Human Resource Management* 31 (Spring–Summer 1992), 45–67.

390. W. Warner Burke, "The New Agenda for Organization Development," in Wendell L. French, Cecil H. Bell, Jr., and Robert A. Zawacki, *Organization Development and Transformation: Managing Effective Change* (Burr Ridge, IL: Irwin McGraw-Hill, 2000), 523–35.

391. W. Warner Burke, *Organization Development: A Process of Learning and Changing*, 2nd ed. (Reading, Mass.: Addison-Wesley, 1994); Wendell L. French and Cecil H. Bell, Jr., "A History of Organizational Development," in French, Bell, and Zawacki, *Organization Development and Transformation*, 20–42.

392. Michael Beer and Elisa Walton, "Developing the Competitive Organization: Interventions and Strategies," *American Psychologist* 45 (February 1990), 154–61.

393. French and Bell, "A History of Organization Development."

MODULE 100. ENDNOTES

394. The information on large-group intervention is based on Kathleen D. Dannemiller and Robert W. Jacobs, "Changing the Way Organizations Change: A Revolution of Common Sense," *The Journal of Applied Behavioral Science* 28, no. 4 (December 1992), 48–498; Barbara B. Bunker and Billie T. Alban, "Conclusion: What Makes Large Group Interventions Effective?" *The Journal of Applied Behavioral Science* 28, no. 4 (December 1992), 570–91; and Marvin R. Weisbord, "Inventing the Future: Search Strategies for Whole System Improvements," in French, Bell, and Zawacki, *Organization Development and Transformation*, 242–50.

395. Paul F. Buller, "For Successful Strategic Change: Blend OD Practices with Strategic Management," *Organizational Dynamics* (Winter 1988), 42–55.

396. Jyotsna Sanzgiri and Jonathan Z. Gottlieb, "Philosophic and Pragmatic Influences on the Practice of Organization Development, 1950–2000," *Organizational Dynamics* (Autumn 1992), 57–69.

397. Based on Carol A. Beatty and John R. M. Gordon, "Barriers to the Implementation of CAD/CAM Systems," *Sloan Management Review* (Summer 1988), 25–33.

398. Richard L. Daft and Selwyn W. Becker, *Innovation in Organizations* (New York: Elsevier, 1978); John P. Kotter and Leonard A. Schlesinger, "Choosing Strategies for Change," *Harvard Business Review* 57 (1979), 106–14.

399. Everett M. Rogers and Floyd Shoemaker, *Communication of Innovations: A Cross Cultural Approach*, 2nd ed. (New York: Free Press, 1971); Stratford P. Sherman, "Eight Big Masters of Innovation," *Fortune*, October 15, 1984, 66–84.

400. Peter Richardson and D. Keith Denton, "Communicating Change," *Human Resource Management* 35, no. 2 (Summer 1996), 203–16.

401. Philip H. Mirvis, Amy L. Sales, and Edward J. Hackett, "The Implementation and Adoption of New Technology in Organizations: The Impact on Work, People, and Culture," *Human Resource Management* 30 (Spring 1991), 113–39; Arthur E. Wallach, "System Changes Begin in the Training Department," *Personnel Journal* 58 (1979), 846–48, 872; Paul R. Lawrence, "How to Deal with Resistance to Change," *Harvard Business Review* 47 (January–February 1969), 4–12, 166–76.

402. Dexter C. Dunphy and Doug A. Stace, "Transformational and Coercive Strategies for Planned Organizational Change: Beyond the O. D. Model," *Organizational Studies* 9 (1988), 317–34; Kotter and Schlesinger, "Choosing Strategies for Change."

403. Lee G. Bolman and Terrence E. Deal, *Reframing Organizations: Artistry, Choice, and Leadership* (San Francisco: Jossey-Bass, 1991).

404. Paul M. Terry, "Conflict Management," *The Journal of Leadership Studies* 3, no. 2 (1996), 3–21; and Kathleen M. Eisenhardt, Jean L. Kahwajy, and L. J. Bourgeois III, "How Management Teams Can Have a Good Fight," *Harvard Business Review* (July–August 1997), 77–85.

405. Clayton T. Alderfer and Ken K. Smith, "Studying Intergroup Relations Imbedded in Organizations," *Administrative Science Quarterly* 27 (1982), 35–65.

406. Muzafer Sherif, "Experiments in Group Conflict," *Scientific American* 195 (1956): 54–58; Edgar H. Schein, *Organizational Psychology*, 3rd ed. (Englewood Cliffs, NJ: Prentice-Hall, 1980).

407. M. Ascalur Rahin, "A Strategy for Managing Conflict in Complex Organizations," *Human Relations* 38 (1985), 81–89; Kenneth Thomas, "Conflict and Conflict Management," in M. D. Dunnette, ed., *Handbook of Industrial and Organizational Psychology* (Chicago: Rand McNally, 1976); Stuart M. Schmidt and Thomas A. Kochan, "Conflict: Toward Conceptual Clarity," *Administrative Science Quarterly* 13 (1972), 359–70.

408. L. David Brown, "Managing Conflict among Groups," in David A. Kolb, Irwin M. Rubin, and James M. McIntyre, eds., *Organizational Psychology: A Book of Readings* (Englewood Cliffs, NJ: Prentice-Hall, 1979), 377–89; Robert W. Ruekert and Orville C. Walker, Jr., "Interactions between Marketing and R&D Departments in Implementing Different Business Strategies," *Strategic Management Journal* 8 (1987), 233–48.

409. Thomas A. Kochan, George P. Huber, and L. L. Cummings, "Determinants of Intraorganizational Conflict in Collective Bargaining in the Public Sector," *Administrative Science Quarterly* 20 (1975), 10–23.

410. Eric H. Neilsen, "Understanding and Managing Intergroup Conflict," in Jay W. Lorsch and Paul R. Lawrence, eds., *Managing Group and Intergroup Relations* (Homewood, IL: Irwin and Dorsey, 1972), 329–43; Richard E. Walton and John M. Dutton, "The Management of Interdepartmental Conflict: A Model and Review," *Administrative Science Quarterly* 14 (1969), 73–84.

411. Morty Lefkoe, "Why So Many Mergers Fail," *Fortune*, June 20, 1987, 113–14; Afsaneh Nahavandi and Ali R. Malekzadeh, "Acculturation in Mergers and Acquisitions," *Academy of Management Review* (1988), 79–90.

412. James D. Thompson, *Organizations in Action* (New York: McGraw-Hill, 1967), 54–56.

413. Walton and Dutton, "Management of Interdepartmental Conflict."

414. Joseph McCann and Jay R. Galbraith, "Interdepartmental Relationships," in Paul C. Nystrom and William H. Starbuck, eds., *Handbook of Organizational Design*, vol. 2 (New York: Oxford University Press, 1981), 60–84.

415. Roderick M. Cramer, "Intergroup Relations and Organizational Dilemmas: The Role of Categorization Processes," in L. L. Cummings and Barry M. Staw, eds., *Research in Organizational Behavior*, vol. 13 (New York: JAI Press, 1991), 191–228; Neilsen, "Understanding and Managing Intergroup Conflict"; Louis R. Pondy, "Organizational Conflict: Concepts and Models," *Administrative Science Quarterly* 12 (1968), 296–320.

416. Jeffrey Pfeffer, *Power in Organizations* (Marshfield, MA: Pitman, 1981).
417. John R. P. French, Jr., and Bertram Raven, "The Bases of Social Power," in *Group Dynamics*, D. Cartwright and A. F. Zander, eds. (Evanston, IL: Row Peterson, 1960), 607–23.
418. Ran Lachman, "Power from What? A Reexamination of Its Relationships with Structural Conditions," *Administrative Science Quarterly* 34 (1989): 231–51; Daniel J. Brass, "Being in the Right Place: A Structural Analysis of Individual Influence in an Organization," *Administrative Science Quarterly* 29 (1984), 518–39.
419. Robert A. Dahl, "The Concept of Power," *Behavioral Science* 2 (1957), 201–15.
420. W. Graham Astley and Paramijit S. Sachdeva, "Structural Sources of Intraorganizational Power: A Theoretical Synthesis," *Academy of Management Review* 9 (1984), 104–13; Abraham Kaplan, "Power in Perspective," in Robert L. Kahn and Elise Boulding, eds., *Power and Conflict in Organizations* (London: Tavistock, 1964), 11–32.
421. Gerald R. Salancik and Jeffrey Pfeffer, "The Bases and Use of Power in Organizational Decision-Making: The Case of the University," *Administrative Science Quarterly* 19 (1974), 453–73.
422. Richard M. Emerson, "Power-Dependence Relations," *American Sociological Review* 27 (1962), 31–41.
423. Rosabeth Moss Kanter, "Power Failure in Management Circuits," *Harvard Business Review* (July–August 1979), 65–75.
424. A. J. Grimes, "Authority, Power, Influence, and Social Control: A Theoretical Synthesis," *Academy of Management Review* 3 (1978), 724–35.
425. Astley and Sachdeva, "Structural Sources of Intraorganizational Power."
426. Jeffrey Pfeffer, *Managing with Power: Politics and Influence in Organizations* (Boston: Harvard Business School Press, 1992).
427. Robert L. Peabody, "Perceptions of Organizational Authority," *Administrative Science Quarterly* 6 (1962), 479.
428. Richard S. Blackburn, "Lower Participant Power: Toward a Conceptual Integration," *Academy of Management Review* 6 (1981), 127–31.
429. Kanter, "Power Failure in Management Circuits," 70.
430. Astley and Sachdeva, "Structural Sources of Intraorganizational Power"; Noel M. Tichy and Charles Fombrun, "Network Analysis in Organizational Settings," *Human Relations* 32 (1979), 923–65.
431. Eryn Brown, "9 Ways to Win on the Web," *Fortune,* May 24, 1999, 112–25.
432. Charles Perrow, "Departmental Power and Perspective in Industrial Firms," in Mayer N. Zald, ed., *Power in Organizations* (Nashville, TN: Vanderbilt University Press, 1970), 59–89.
433. D. J. Hickson, C. R. Hinings, C. A. Lee, R. E. Schneck, and J. M. Pennings, "A Strategic Contingencies Theory of Intraorganizational Power," *Administrative Science Quarterly* 16 (1971), 216–29; Gerald R. Salancik and Jeffrey Pfeffer, "Who Gets Power—and How They Hold onto It: A Strategic-Contingency Model of Power," *Organizational Dynamics* (Winter 1977), 3–21.
434. Pfeffer, *Managing with Power*; Salancik and Pfeffer, "Who Gets Power"; C. R. Hinings, D. J. Hickson, J. M. Pennings, and R. E. Schneck, "Structural Conditions of Intraorganizational Power," *Administrative Science Quarterly* 19 (1974), 22–44.
435. Carol Stoak Saunders, "The Strategic Contingencies Theory of Power: Multiple Perspectives," *Journal of Management Studies* 27 (1990), 1–18; Warren Boeker, "The Development and Institutionalization of Sub-Unit Power in Organizations," *Administrative Science Quarterly* 34 (1989), 388–510; Irit Cohen and Ran Lachman, "The Generality of the Strategic Contingencies Approach to Sub-Unit Power," *Organizational Studies* 9 (1988), 371–91.
436. Emerson, "Power-Dependence Relations."
437. Michel Crozier, *The Bureaucratic Phenomenon* (Chicago: University of Chicago Press, 1964).
438. Salancik and Pfeffer, "Bases and Use of Power in Organizational Decision Making," 470.
439. Hickson et al., "Strategic Contingencies Theory."
440. Pettigrew, *Politics of Organizational Decision Making.*
441. Hickson, et al., "Strategic Contingencies Theory."
442. *Ibid.*
443. Jeffrey Gantz and Victor V. Murray, "Experience of Workplace Politics," *Academy of Management Journal* 23 (1980), 237–51; Dan L. Madison, Robert W. Allen, Lyman W. Porter, Patricia A. Renwick, and Bronston T. Mayes, "Organizational Politics: An Exploration of Managers' Perception," *Human Relations* 33 (1980), 79–100.
444. Gerald R. Ferris and K. Michele Kacmar, "Perceptions of Organizational Politics," *Journal of Management* 18 (1992), 93–116; Parmod Kumar and Rehana Ghadially, "Organizational Politics and Its Effects on Members of Organizations," *Human Relations* 42 (1989), 305–14; Donald J. Vredenburgh and John G. Maurer, "A Process Framework of Organizational Politics," *Human Relations* 37 (1984), 47–66; Gerald R. Ferris, Dwight D. Frink, Maria Carmen Galang, Jing Zhou, Michele Kacmar, and Jack L. Howard, "Perceptions of Organizational Politics: Prediction, Stress-Related Implications, and Outcomes," *Human Relations* 49, no. 2 (1996), 233–66.
445. Ferris, et al., "Perceptions of Organizational Politics: Prediction, Stress-Related Implications, and Outcomes"; John J. Voyer, "Organizational Politics and Organizational Outcomes: An Interpretive Study," *Organization Science* 5, no. 1 (February

1994), 72–85; James W. Dean, Jr., and Mark P. Sharfman, "Does Decision Process Matter? A Study of Strategic Decision-Making Effectiveness," *Academy of Management Journal* 39, no. 2 (1996), 368–96.

446. Jeffrey Pfeffer, *Managing with Power: Politics and Influence in Organizations* (Boston, MA: Harvard Business School Press, 1992).
447. Amos Drory and Tsilia Romm, "The Definition of Organizational Politics: A Review," *Human Relations* 43 (1990), 1133–54; Vredenburgh and Maurer, "A Process Framework of Organizational Politics."
448. Pfeffer, *Power in Organizations*, 70.
449. Madison et al., "Organizational Politics"; Jay R. Galbraith, *Organizational Design* (Reading, MA: Addison-Wesley, 1977).
450. Gantz and Murray, "Experience of Workplace Politics"; Pfeffer, *Power in Organizations*.
451. Daniel J. Brass and Marlene E. Burkhardt, "Potential Power and Power Use: An Investigation of Structure and Behavior," *Academy of Management Journal* 38 (1993), 441–70.
452. Hickson et al., "A Strategic Contingencies Theory."
453. Pfeffer, *Power in Organizations*.
454. Ibid.
455. V. Dallas Merrell, *Huddling: The Informal Way to Management Success* (New York: AMACON, 1979).
456. Vredenburgh and Maurer, "A Process Framework of Organizational Politics."
457. Ibid.
458. Pfeffer, *Power in Organizations*.
459. Ibid.
460. Ibid.
461. Kanter, "Power Failure in Management Circuits"; Pfeffer, *Power in Organizations*.
462. Robert R. Blake and Jane S. Mouton, "Overcoming Group Warfare," *Harvard Business Review* (November–December 1984), 98–108.
463. Blake and Mouton, "Overcoming Group Warfare"; Paul R. Lawrence and Jay W. Lorsch, "New Management Job: The Integrator," *Harvard Business Review* 45 (November–December 1967), 142–51.
464. Robert R. Blake, Herbert A. Shepard, and Jane S. Mouton, *Managing Intergroup Conflict in Industry* (Houston: Gulf Publishing, 1964); and Doug Stewart, "'Expand the Pie Before You Divvy It Up,'" *Smithsonian* (November 1997), 78–90.
465. Robert R. Blake and Jane S. Mouton, "Overcoming Group Warfare"; Schein, *Organizational Psychology*; Blake, Shepard, and Mouton, *Managing Intergroup Conflict in Industry*; Richard E. Walton, *Interpersonal Peacemaking: Confrontation and Third-Party Consultations* (Reading, MA: Addison-Wesley, 1969).
466. Mark S. Plovnick, Ronald E. Fry, and W. Warner Burke, *Organizational Development* (Boston: Little, Brown, 1982), 89–93; Schein, *Organizational Psychology*, 177–78, reprinted by permission of Prentice-Hall, Inc.
467. Neilsen, "Understanding and Managing Intergroup Conflict"; Joseph McCann and Jay R. Galbraith, "Interdepartmental Relations."
468. Neilsen, "Understanding and Managing Intergroup Conflict"; McCann and Galbraith, "Interdepartmental Relations"; Sherif et al., *Intergroup Conflict and Cooperation*.
469. Dean Tjosvold, Valerie Dann, and Choy Wong, "Managing Conflict between Departments to Serve Customers," *Human Relations* 45 (1992), 1035–54.
470. Copeland, Koller, and Murrin, *Valuation: Measuring and Managing the Value of Companies*, 3rd ed., (John Wiley & Sons, Inc., 2000).
471. Like equation 1.62a, the simplification shown in Equation 1.63a is found by applying the algebra of geometric progressions. This equation is useful in situations in which the required values of i and n are not in the tables or when a financial calculator is not available.
472. It should be apparent from Equation 1.63 that, unlike the interest factors for the FV and PV of a lump-sum amount ($FVIF_{i,n}$ and $PVIF_{i,n}$, respectively), the interest factors for the FV and PV of an annuity ($FVIFA_{i,n}$ and $PVIFA_{i,n}$, respectively) are not reciprocals of each other. In other words, the inverse of the sum of a series of values does not equal the sum of the inverses of those same values—that is, $1/(2 + 3 + 4) = 1/9 \neq 1/2 + 1/3 + 1/4 = 13/12$.

MODULE 200

Operations Management

201 Operations Strategies, 328

205 Manufacturing Operations, 330

230 Supply Chain Management, 384

265 Services and Retail Operations, 409

295 Ethics and Operations, 459

Module 200 Endnotes, 464

Operations Strategies

The scope of the operations management module includes manufacturing, service, retail, and purchasing/supply chain management areas. A company's competitive strategy is its plan for how the company will compete in the marketplace. According to Michael Porter, three strategies of overall cost leadership, differentiation, and market focus are equally appropriate to both manufacturing and service/retail industries. Strategies for each of these areas are described next.

Manufacturing Strategy

To a manufacturer, both operational effectiveness and a good strategy are essential. Operational effectiveness is the ability to perform similar operations activities better than competitors. According to Porter, the essence of strategy means not just to improve a company's operations, but also to determine how operational effectiveness can be used to achieve a sustainable competitive advantage.

Specifically, manufacturing (production) strategies include increasing productivity, decreasing costs, and improving quality by adding value to inputs through the transformation process and producing quality outputs. It fits with the concept that consumers purchase their products from the company that offers them the most value for their money. The manufacturing strategy should fit with the overall business strategy, such as less time-to-market new products, cost minimization, improved quality, and greater market share.

Service Strategy

Service strategy focuses on customers and on satisfying their needs, which will result in a loyal customer base. Winning customers in the marketplace means competing on several dimensions. Customers base their purchase decisions on many variables, including price, convenience, reputation, and safety. The importance of a particular variable to a firm's success depends on the competitive marketplace and the preferences of individual customers.

Retail Strategy

Retail strategic planning is concerned with how a retailer responds to the environment in an effort to establish a long-term course of action. In principle, the retailer's strategic planning model should best reflect the line(s) of trade in which the retailer will operate, the market(s) it will pursue, and the retail mix it will use. Note that strategic planning requires a long-term commitment of resources by the retailer and is necessary to overcome some of the adversities of operating globally. Specifically, effective strategic planning can help protect the retailer against competitive onslaughts.

Purchasing/Supply Chain Strategy

Organizations can employ a variety of different strategies that may be unique to each commodity. While we cannot cover all of the possible variations of strategies that may emerge, we will briefly review some of the most common and important purchasing strategies. As we will see later, certain strategies are used more often than others, depending on how advanced an organization is at the purchasing strategy development process.

Supply-Base Optimization

Supply-base optimization is the process of determining the appropriate number and mix of suppliers to maintain. While this term has also been referred to as *right-sizing*, it usually relates to reducing the number of suppliers used. Moreover, suppliers who are not capable of achieving world-class performance, either currently or in the near future, may be eliminated from the supply base. This process is continuous because the needs of the business unit may always be changing. Optimization requires an analysis of the number of suppliers required currently and in the future for each purchased item.

Total Quality Management of Suppliers

Total quality management (TQM) requires suppliers to initiate statistical process control (SPC), design of experiments, process capability studies, and quality audits to focus on the elimination of process variability, improve immediate problem identification, and demonstrate corrective action capabilities. TQM also requires that suppliers develop a philosophy of zero defects while endorsing continuous improvement. Moreover, TQM emphasizes the need to meet and exceed the requirements of the customer (which in this case is the buying organization). In order to drive this change within the supply base, a purchaser must communicate to the supplier any expectations regarding quality. In particular, supplier evaluation and selection becomes crucial because of the need to select world-class suppliers. In some cases, a team from the buying company may have to work with a supplier to assess process capability, evaluate their quality philosophy, and recommend specific quality control techniques.

Global Sourcing

Global sourcing is an approach that requires purchasing to view the entire world as a potential source for parts, components, services, and finished goods. It can be used to access new markets or to gain access to the same suppliers that are helping global companies become more competitive. Although true global sourcing is somewhat limited in most industries, more and more companies are beginning to view the world as both a market and a source of supply.

The major objective of global sourcing is to provide immediate and dramatic improvements in cost and quality as determined through the commodity research process. Global sourcing is also an opportunity to gain exposure to product and process technology, increase the number of available sources, satisfy countertrade requirements, and establish a presence in foreign markets. This strategy is not contradictory to supply-base optimization since it involves locating the best-in-class suppliers in the world for a given commodity. Some buyers also source globally to introduce competition to domestic suppliers.

There are several major barriers to global sourcing that must be overcome. Inexperience with global business processes and practices, along with few personnel qualified to develop and negotiate with global suppliers or manage long material pipelines, are serious issues. In addition, more complex logistics and currency fluctuations require measuring all relevant costs before committing to a worldwide source. Finally, organizations may not be prepared to deal with the different negotiating styles practiced by different cultures, and they may have to work through a foreign host national in order to establish contacts and an agreement.

Longer-Term Supplier Relationships

Longer-term supplier relationships involve the selection of and continuous involvement with suppliers viewed as critical over an extended period of time (e.g., three years and beyond). In general, the use of longer-term supplier relationships is growing in importance, and there will probably be greater pursuit of these relationships through longer-term contracts. Some purchasers are familiar with the practice, while for others it represents a radical departure from traditional short-term approaches to supply-base management.

Longer-term relationships are sought with suppliers who have exceptional performance or unique technological expertise. Within the portfolio matrix, this would involve the few suppliers that provide items and services that are critical or of higher value. A longer-term relationship may include a joint product development relationship with shared development costs and intellectual property. In other cases, it may simply be an informal process of identifying suppliers who receive preferential treatment.

Early Supplier Design Involvement

Early supplier design involvement and selection requires key suppliers to participate at the concept or predesign phase of new product development. Supplier involvement may be informal, although the supplier may already have a purchase contract for the production of an existing item. Early involvement will increasingly take place through participation on cross-functional product development teams. This strategy recognizes that qualified suppliers have more to offer than simply the basic production of items that meet engineered specifications. Early supplier design involvement is a simultaneous engineering approach that occurs between buyer and seller, and seeks to maximize the benefits received by taking advantage of the supplier's design capabilities.

Supplier Development

In some cases, purchasers may find that suppliers' capabilities are not high enough to meet current or future expectations, yet they do not want to eliminate the supplier from the supply base. (Switching costs may be high or the supplier

Exhibit 200.1 *Stages of Supply Management Strategy Evolution*

1. Basic Beginnings	2. Moderate Development	3. Limited Integration	4. Fully Integrated Supply Chains
• Quality/cost teams • Longer-term contracts • Volume leveraging • Supply-base consolidation • Supplier quality focus	• Ad hoc supplier alliances • Cross-functional sourcing teams • Supply-base optimization • International sourcing • Cross-location sourcing teams	• Global sourcing • Strategic supplier alliances • Supplier TQM development • Total cost of ownership • Nontraditional purchase focus • Parts/service standardization • Early supplier involvement • Dock-to-stock pull systems	• Global supply chains with external customer focus • Cross-enterprise decision making • Full-service suppliers • Early sourcing • Insourcing/outsourcing to maximize core competencies of firms throughout the supply chain

has performance potential.) A solution in such cases is to work directly with a supplier to facilitate improvement in a designated functional or activity area. Buyer-seller consulting teams working jointly may accelerate overall supplier improvement at a faster rate than will actions taken independently by the supplier. The basic motivation behind this strategy is that supplier improvement and success lead to longer-term benefits to both buyer and seller. This approach supports the development of world-class suppliers in new areas of product and process technology.

Total Cost of Ownership

Total cost of ownership is the process of identifying cost considerations beyond unit price, transport, and tooling. It requires the business unit to define and measure the various cost components associated with a purchased item. In many cases, this includes costs associated with late delivery, poor quality, or other forms of supplier nonperformance. Total cost of ownership can lead to better decision making since it identifies all costs associated with a purchasing decision and the costs associated with supplier nonperformance. Cost variances from planned results can be analyzed to determine the cause of the variance. Corrective action can then prevent further problems.

Evolving Supply Management Strategies

If we compare the level of purchasing evolution to the strategies available, there is clearly an implementation sequence that emerges. Exhibit 200.1 presents the sequence of purchasing strategy execution based on research from multiple studies and interviews with many executives.[1] Organizations tend to evolve through four phases as they become mature and sophisticated in their purchasing strategy development.

Manufacturing Operations

Organizations as Production Systems

Technical core The heart of the organization's production of its product or service.

An organization is described as a system used for transforming inputs into outputs. At the center of this transformation process is the **technical core,** which is the heart of the organization's production of its product or service.[2] In an automobile company, the technical core includes the plants that manufacture automobiles. In a uni-

Exhibit 200.2 *The Organization as an Operations Management System*

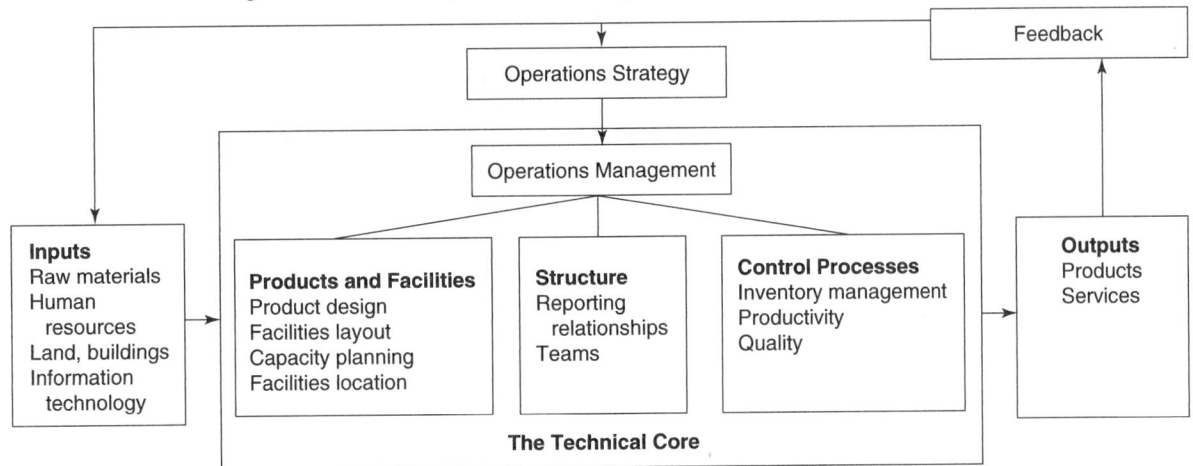

versity, the technical core includes the academic activities of teaching and research. Inputs into the technical core include human resources, land, equipment, buildings, and technology. Outputs from the technical core include the goods and services that are provided for customers and clients. Operations strategy and control feedback shape the quality of outputs and the efficiency of operations within the technical core.

The topic of operations management pertains to the day-to-day management of the technical core, as illustrated in Exhibit 200.2. **Operations management** is formally defined as the field of management that specializes in the production of goods and services and uses special tools and techniques for solving production problems. In essence, operations managers are concerned with all the activities involved in the conversion of inputs into outputs. This includes decisions about where to locate facilities and what equipment to install in them. However, as with all areas of management, operations management also requires the ability to lead people. For example, **Toyota's** operations are admired worldwide as a model of quality and efficiency, but this success is not merely a result of using the right machines or setting the right standards. U.S. automakers have had difficulty duplicating Toyota's success with lean manufacturing because they have focused primarily on the technical elements of the system and failed to implement the necessary cultural and leadership changes. "What the Big Three are doing," says Toyota's Hajime Oba, "is creating a Buddha image and forgetting to inject soul into it."[3] Toyota's system combines techniques, systems, and philosophy, such as commitment to employee empowerment and a creative culture. Besides installing the methodology for running an efficient assembly line, such as "just-in-time" shipments of supplies, managers must instill the necessary attitudes, such as concern for quality and a desire to innovate.

Operations management   The field of management that focuses on the physical production of goods or services and uses specialized techniques for solving manufacturing problems.

Manufacturing and Service Operations

Although terms such as *production* and *operations* seem to imply manufacturing organizations, operations management applies to all organizations. The service sector has increased three times as fast as the manufacturing sector in the North American economy. Today more than one-half of all businesses are service organizations and two-thirds of the U.S. workforce is employed in services, such as hospitals, hotels and resorts, financial services, or telecommunications firms. Operations management tools and techniques apply to services as well as manufacturing. Exhibit 200.3 shows differences between manufacturing and service organizations.

Manufacturing organizations are those that produce physical goods, such as cars or tennis balls. In contrast, **service organizations** produce nonphysical outputs, such as medical, educational, communication, or transportation services provided for customers. Doctors, consultants, online auction companies, and the local barber all provide services. Services also include the sale of merchandise. Although merchandise is a physical good, the service company does not manufacture it but merely sells it as a service to the customer.

Manufacturing organization   An organization that produces physical goods.

Service organization   An organization that produces nonphysical outputs that require customer involvement and cannot be stored in inventory.

205. MANUFACTURING OPERATIONS

Exhibit 200.3 *Differences between Manufacturing and Service Organizations*

Manufacturing Organizations	Service Organizations
Produce physical goods	Produce nonphysical outputs
Goods inventoried for later consumption	Simultaneous production and consumption
Quality measured directly	Quality perceived and difficult to measure
Standardized output	Customized output
Production process removed from consumer	Consumer participates in production process
Facilities site moderately important to business success	Facilities site crucial to success of firm
Capital intensive	Labor intensive
Examples:	Examples:
Automobile manufacturers	Airlines
Steel companies	Hotels
Soft-drink companies	Law firms

Sources: Based on Richard L. Daft, *Organization Theory and Design* (Cincinnati, Ohio: South-Western College Publishing, 2001), 210; and Byron J. Finch and Richard L. Luebbe, *Operations Management* (Fort Worth, Texas: The Dryden Press, 1995), 50.

Services differ from manufactured products in two ways. First, the service customer is involved in the actual production process.[4] The patient actually visits the doctor to receive the service, and it's difficult to imagine a hairstylist providing services without direct customer contact. The same is true for airlines, restaurants, and banks. Second, manufactured goods can be placed in inventory, whereas service outputs, being intangible, cannot be stored. Manufactured products such as clothes, food, cars, and DVD players all can be put in warehouses and sold at a later date. However, a hairstylist cannot wash, cut, and set hair in advance and leave it on the shelf for the customer's arrival, nor can a doctor place examinations in inventory. The service must be created and provided for the customer exactly when he or she wants it.

Despite the differences between manufacturing and service firms, they face similar operational problems. First, each kind of organization needs to be concerned with scheduling. A medical clinic must schedule appointments so that doctors' and patients' time will be used efficiently. Second, both manufacturing and service organizations must obtain materials and supplies. Third, both types of organizations should be concerned with quality and productivity. Because many operational problems are similar, operations management tools and techniques can and should be applied to service organizations as readily as they are to manufacturing operations.

Operations Strategy

Many operations managers are involved in day-to-day problem solving and lose sight of the fact that the best way to control operations is through strategic planning. The more operations managers become enmeshed in operational details, the less likely they are to see the big picture with respect to inventory buildups, parts shortages, and seasonal fluctuations. To manage operations effectively, managers must understand operations strategy.

Operations strategy The recognition of the importance of operations to the firm's success and the involvement of operations managers in the organization's strategic planning.

Operations strategy is the recognition of the important role of operations in organizational success and the involvement of operations managers in the organization's strategic planning.[5] Superior operations effectiveness can support existing strategy and contribute to new strategic directions that can be difficult for competitors to copy. When an organization's operations effectiveness is based on capabilities that are ingrained in its employees, its culture, and its operating processes, the company can be tough to beat.[6]

Exhibit 200.4 illustrates four stages in the evolution of operations strategy. Many companies are at Stage 1, in which business strategy is set without considering the capability of operations. The operations department is concerned only with labor costs and operational efficiency. For example, a major electronics instrument producer experienced a serious mismatch between strategy and the ability of operations to manufacture products. Because of fast-paced technological changes, the company was changing its products and developing new ones. The manufacturer had installed a materials-handling system in the operations department that was efficient, but it could not handle change of this magnitude. Operations managers were blamed for the company's failure to achieve strategic goals even though the operations department's capacity had never been considered during strategy formulation.

Exhibit 200.4 *Four Stages of Operations Strategy*

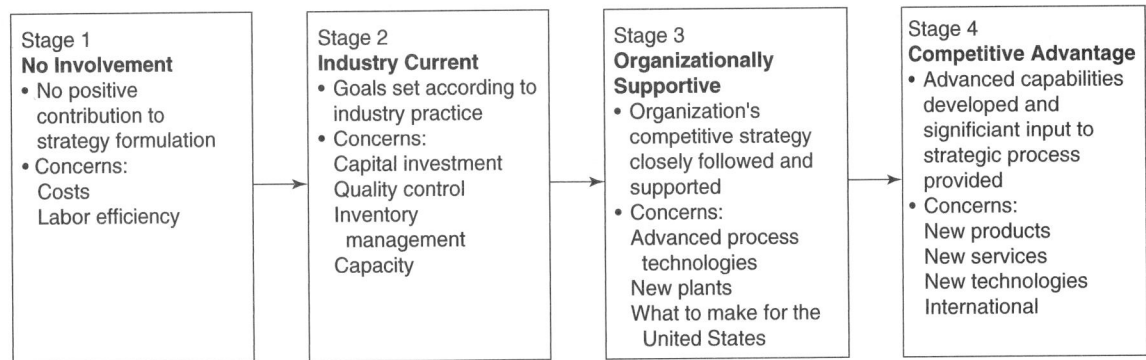

Source: Based on R. H. Haynes and S. C. Wheelright, *Restoring Our Competitive Edge: Competing through Manufacturing* (New York: Wiley, 1984).

At Stage 2, the operations department sets goals according to industry practice. The organization tries to be current with respect to operations management techniques and views capital investment in plant and equipment, quality control, or inventory management as ways to be competitive.

At Stage 3, operations managers are more strategically active. Operations strategy is in concert with company strategy, and the operations department will seek new operational techniques and technologies to enhance competitiveness. For example, computer-based business operating systems and work flow automation help employees coordinate activities across functional and geographical boundaries and pinpoint bottlenecks or outdated procedures that slow production and increase costs.

At the highest level of operations strategy, Stage 4, operations managers may pursue new technologies on their own in order to do the best possible job of delivering the product or service. At Stage 4, operations can be a genuine competitive weapon.[7] Operations departments develop new strategic concepts themselves. With the use of new technologies, operations management becomes a major force in overall company strategic planning. Operations can originate new products and processes that will add to or change company strategy.

A company that operates at Stage 3 or 4 will be more competitive than those that rely on marketing and financial strategies because customer orders are won through better price, quality, performance, delivery, or responsiveness to customer demand, and all these factors are affected by operations.

The Integrated Enterprise

As operations managers adopt a strategic approach, they appreciate that their operations are not independent of other activities. To operate efficiently and produce high-quality items that meet customers' needs, the organization must have reliable deliveries of high-quality, reasonably priced supplies and materials. It also requires an efficient and reliable system for distributing finished products, making them readily accessible to customers. Operations managers with a strategic focus therefore recognize that they need to manage the entire supply chain. **Supply chain management** is the term for managing the sequence of suppliers and purchasers, covering all stages of processing from obtaining raw materials to distributing finished goods to final consumers.[8]

Supply chain management Managing the sequence of suppliers and purchasers, covering all stages of processing from obtaining raw materials to distributing finished goods to final consumers.

The most recent advances in supply chain management involve using Internet technologies to achieve the right balance of low inventory levels and customer responsiveness. An e-supply chain creates a seamless, integrated line that stretches from customers to suppliers, as illustrated in Exhibit 200.5, by establishing electronic linkages between the organization and these external partners for the sharing and exchange of data.[9] For example, in the exhibit, as consumers purchase products in retail stores, the data are automatically fed into the retail chain's information system via an intranet. In turn, the retail chain gives access to this constantly updated data to the manufacturing company through a secure extranet link. With knowledge of this demand data, the manufacturer can produce and ship the correct products when needed. As products are made, data about raw materials used in the production process, updated inventory information, and updated forecasted demand are electronically provided to the manufacturer's suppliers via an extranet, and the suppliers automatically replenish the manufacturer's raw materials inventory as needed.

Exhibit 200.5 *The E-Supply Chain*

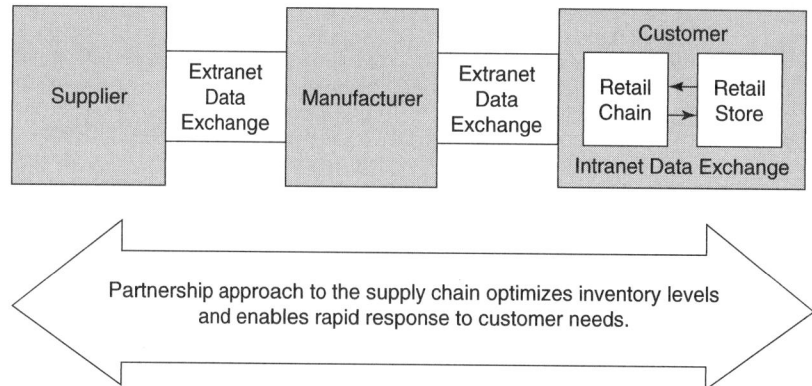

Source: Based on Jim Turcotte, Bob Silveri, and Tom Jobson, "Are You Ready for the E-Supply Chain?" *APICS—The Performance Advantage* (August 1998), 56–59.

An important aspect of supply chain management is managing relationships with suppliers.[10] Enterprise integration through the use of electronic linkages can create a level of cooperation not previously imaginable. Many supplier relationships used to be based on an *arm's length* approach, in which an organization spreads purchases among many suppliers and encourages them to compete with one another. With integration, more companies are opting for a *partnership* approach, which involves cultivating intimate relationships with a few carefully selected suppliers and collaborating closely to coordinate tasks that benefit both parties. For example, at supplier Rockwell Automation, a Greenville, South Carolina–based maker of industrial transmissions and a division of Rockwell International, electronic connections are leading to a new level of intimacy with manufacturing partners. Manufacturers have their own private Web sites on Rockwell's Internet portal, where they can view their past purchases and track their order status in real time. The extranet links directly into Rockwell's order management and warehouse management systems; when a distributor places an order for any of 85,000 parts, it is zapped to the national distribution center for almost immediate shipment.[11]

Electronic linkages also contribute to more rapid response to end consumers by reducing the time it takes to move critical data through the information pipeline. Manufacturers have immediate access to sales data and can deliver new products as needed. In addition, electronic linkages enable the rapid manufacture of customized products. Ford Motor Company is currently involved in a supply-chain makeover that will allow it to manufacture cars on a reasonable build-to-order basis, so that customers no longer have to wait months for delivery of the car of their dreams.[12]

By integrating everyone along the entire supply chain, the idea is that every organization involved can move in lock-step to meet the customer's product and time demands.

Designing Operations Management Systems

Every organization must design its production system. This process starts with the design of the product or service to be produced. A restaurant designs the food items on the menu. An automobile manufacturer designs the cars it produces. A management consulting firm designs the various types of services it will offer to clients. Other considerations in designing the production system include purchasing raw materials (procurement), facilities layout, designing production technology (automation), facilities location, and capacity planning.

Product and Service Design

The way a product or service is designed affects its appeal for customers; it also affects how easy or expensive operations will be. Some product designs are difficult to execute properly.

To prevent such problems in the first place, a growing number of businesses are using *design for manufacturability and assembly* (DFMA). Engineering designers have long fashioned products with disdain for how they would be produced. Elegant designs nearly always had too many parts. Thus, the watchword is *simplicity*, making the product easy and inexpensive to manufacture.

Using DFMA is extremely inexpensive. DFMA often requires restructuring operations, creating teams of designers, manufacturers, and assemblers to work together. They collaborate on achieving four objectives of product design:

1. *Producibility.* The degree to which a product or service can actually be produced for the customer within the firm's existing operational capacity.
2. *Cost.* The sum of the materials, labor, design, transportation, and overhead expense associated with a product or service. Striving for simplicity and few parts keeps product and service designs within reasonable costs.
3. *Quality.* The excellence of the product or service—the serviceability and value that customers gain by purchasing the product. In recent years, product design has moved toward consumer-friendly products, and companies are taking the time to ask questions such as "How do people use this product?" and "How can we make this product more user friendly?"
4. *Reliability.* The degree to which the customer can count on the product or service to fulfill its intended function. The product should function as designed for a reasonable length of time. Highly complex products often have lower reliability because more things can go wrong.

The design of services also should reflect producibility, cost, quality, and reliability. However, services have one additional design requirement: timing. *Timing* is the degree to which the provision of a service meets the customer's delivery requirements. Recall that a service cannot be stored in inventory and must be provided when the customer is present. If you take your friend or spouse to a restaurant for dinner, you expect the meal to be served in a timely manner. The powerful push for self-service reflects the need to provide service when the customer wants and needs it. Banking by machine, pumping your own gas, and trying on your own shoes are all ways that organizations provide timely service, which is important in today's time-pressured world.

Procurement

The purchasing of supplies, services, and raw materials for use in the production process, known as **procurement,** has increased in importance as an operations issue. On average, a manufacturing company spends 50 to 60 percent of its revenues to buy materials and supplies. For example, auto manufacturers spend about 60 percent of revenues on material purchases, food processors about 70 percent, and oil refineries about 80 percent, and the percentages keep going up.[13] Expenses for materials, supplies, and services also represent a huge expense for service companies. Having the right materials of the correct design and quality is essential to the smooth functioning of the production process.

Procurement Purchasing supplies, services, and raw materials for use in the production process.

The Internet and business-to-business (B2B) commerce are having a tremendous impact on procurement. Purchasing department employees can now use the Internet to search for new sources of materials, place orders, request bids via B2B marketplaces, and participate in on-line auctions. Employees have quick access to more information about availability and cost. They can often submit purchase orders on-line and track the status of orders over the Web, cutting down on operating costs and speeding up the procurement lead time.[14] For example, by eliminating purchase orders and moving procurement on-line where employees ordered from suppliers that offered the company a discount, DuPont cut procurement costs by $200 million in one recent year. In addition, the typical order is now processed in one day instead of five.[15] Verizon Wireless hopes to shave 5 to 10 percent off the $150 million it spends on procurement of temporary contract workers each year by using competitive bidding and contract management over the Internet.[16] Whether they're looking for paper clips, jet engines, or consultants, more and more companies are using the Internet to control and streamline the procurement process.

Organizations wanting to move to on-line procurement often need to look at *their direct procurement* initiatives (that is, materials and supplies that go into the company's products) separately from indirect procurement (such as paper, pens, office equipment, and conference tables) because indirect procurement needs are spread all over the organization, not just in the production area. Burlington Northern Santa Fe Railway set up an on-line procurement system for indirect supplies as a first step toward a fully Web-enabled supply chain. By starting with indirect procurement the company could avoid disrupting the day-to-day business of the company and implement a project that would act as a model for e-business skeptics in the firm.

Facilities Layout

Once a product or service has been designed and systems set up for procurement of materials, the next consideration is planning for the actual production through facilities layout. The four most common types of layout are process, product, cellular, and fixed-position.

PROCESS LAYOUT   A **process layout** is one in which all machines that perform a similar function or task are grouped together. In a machine shop, the lathes perform a similar function and are located together in one section. The

Process layout *A facilities layout in which machines that perform the same function are grouped together in one location.*

grinders are in another section of the shop. Service organizations also use process layouts. In a bank, the loan officers are in one area, the tellers in another, and the managers in a third.

The advantage of the process layout is that it has the potential for economies of scale and reduced costs. For example, having all painting done in one spray-painting area means that fewer machines and people are required to paint all products for the organization. In a bank, having all tellers located in one controlled area provides increased security. Placing all operating rooms together in a hospital makes it possible to control the environment for all rooms simultaneously.

The drawback to the process layout is that the actual path a product or service takes can be long and complicated. A product may need several different processes performed on it and thus must travel through many different areas before production is complete.

Product layout *A facilities layout in which machines and tasks are arranged according to the sequence of steps in the production of a single product.*

PRODUCT LAYOUT A **product layout** is one in which machines and tasks are arranged according to the progressive steps in producing a single product. The automobile assembly line is a classic example, because it produces a single product starting from the raw materials to the finished output. Many fast-food restaurants use the product layout, with activities arranged in sequence to produce hamburgers or fried chicken, depending on the products available.

The product layout is efficient when the organization produces huge volumes of identical products. Duplication of functions can be economical only if the volume is high enough to keep each work area busy working on specialized products.

Cellular layout *A facilities layout in which machines dedicated to sequences of production are grouped into cells in accordance with group-technology principles.*

CELLULAR LAYOUT An innovative layout, called **cellular layout,** is based on group-technology principles in which machines dedicated to sequences of operations are grouped into cells. Grouping technology into cells provides some of the efficiencies of both process and product layouts. Even more important, the U-shaped cells provide efficiencies in material and tool handling and inventory movement. One advantage is that the workers work in clusters that facilitate teamwork and joint problem solving. Staffing flexibility is enhanced because one person can operate all the machines in the cell and walking distance is small.

Fixed-position layout *A facilities layout in which the product remains in one location and the required tasks and equipment are brought to it.*

FIXED-POSITION LAYOUT The **fixed-position layout** is one in which the product remains in one location, and employees and equipment are brought to it. The fixed-position layout is used to create a product or service that is either very large or is one-of-a-kind, such as aircraft, ships, and buildings. The product cannot be moved from function to function or along an assembly line; rather, the people, materials, and machines all come to the fixed-position site for assembly and processing. This layout is not good for high volume, but it is necessary for large, bulky products and custom orders.

As the need for speed and responsiveness has increased, some organizations have been designing facilities layout to allow for a high level of flexibility.

Technology Automation

One goal of many operations managers is to implement more sophisticated technologies for producing products and services. Extremely advanced systems that can work almost unaided by employees are being designed.

SERVICE TECHNOLOGY The biggest growth in automation technologies in recent years has been in services. Restaurant kitchen managers can use computer programs to calculate the exact cost and ingredient needs for each menu item, from building a cheeseburger to putting together a seafood buffet, instead of having to perform arduous and time-consuming manual calculations. In the banking industry, automatic teller machines (ATMs) and telephone and online banking allow customers to obtain a wide range of banking services at any time. Many gas stations now have "pay-at-pump" systems where customers insert a credit or debit card to pay for their gas without having to go inside the station. In the supermarket industry, self-service checkout technology, such as that used at many **Kroger** stores, is growing in use.

Advanced technology systems are continuously being integrated into today's service organizations to improve operations efficiency. In addition, advanced production technology has long been used in manufacturing companies. Two recent approaches that are revolutionizing manufacturing are flexible manufacturing systems and CAD/CAM.

FLEXIBLE MANUFACTURING SYSTEMS The use of automated production lines that can be adapted to produce more than one kind of product is called a **flexible manufacturing system**.[17] The machinery uses computers to coordinate and integrate the machines. Automated functions include loading, unloading, storing parts, changing tools, and machining. The computer can instruct the machines to change parts, machining, and tools when a new product must be produced. This is a breakthrough compared with the product layout, in which a single line is restricted to a single product. With a flexible manufacturing system, a single production line can be readily readapted to small batches of different products based on computer instructions.

Flexible manufacturing system A small- or medium-sized automated production line that can be adopted to produce more than one product line.

Companies often adopt flexible manufacturing to support a strategy of mass customization, that is, quickly adapting products to the specific needs of individual customers. For example, at **Deere & Company**, a major manufacturer of agricultural equipment, flexible manufacturing systems enable factories to produce one-of-a-kind pieces of machinery tailored specifically to farmers' needs. The company offers 6 million possible configurations.[18]

CAD/CAM Operations management in most businesses today employs computers for the design of products, and often for their manufacture as well. **CAD** (computer-aided design) enables engineers to develop new product designs in about half the time required with traditional methods. Computers provide a visual display for the engineer and illustrate the implications of any design change.

CAM (computer-aided manufacturing) uses computers to direct manufacturing processes, as in flexible manufacturing systems. Typically, the CAM system is linked to CAD, so that the product specifications drive the manufacturing specifications. The computer system thus guides and controls the manufacturing process. For example, a sportswear manufacturer can use computers to mechanize the entire sequence of manufacturing operations—pattern scaling, layout, and printing. Computer-controlled cutting tables are installed. Once the computer has mathematically defined the geometry, it guides the cutting blade, eliminating the need for paper patterns. Computer programs also can direct fabric requisitions, production orders for cutting and sewing operations, and sewing line work.

CAD A production technology in which computers perform new-product design.

CAM A production technology in which computers help guide and control the manufacturing system.

The first applications of CAD/CAM involved computer-driven machine tools, which can cut and grind materials. However, many modern products are produced using molds, which have been machined by hand at great expense. Engineers extended the use of CAD/CAM to modernize this technology. An application called rapid prototyping (RP) uses CAD to create prototypes (models of a product) through a variety of methods, most of which involve using lasers to cut and bind slices of the object made from layers of plastic or paper. Other RP devices create prototypes by binding layers shaped from powdered steel, ceramics, or starch.

Facility Location

At some point, almost every organization must decide on the location of facilities. A bank needs to open a new branch office, **Wendy's** needs to find locations for the 100 or so restaurants opened each year, or a computer chip manufacturer needs to find a location for a new research facility or assembly and testing plant. When these decisions are made unwisely, they are expensive and troublesome for the organization.

The most common approach to selecting a site for a new location is to do a cost-benefit analysis. For example, managers at bank headquarters may identify four possible locations. The costs associated with each location are the land (purchase or lease); moving from the current facility; and construction, including zoning laws, building codes, land features, and size of the parking lot. Taxes, utilities, rents, and maintenance are other cost factors to be considered in advance. Each possible bank location also will have certain benefits. Benefits to be evaluated are accessibility of customers, location of major competitors, general quality of working conditions, and nearness to restaurants and shops, which would be desirable for both employees and customers. Once the bank managers have evaluated the worth of each benefit, they can divide total benefits by total costs for each location, then select the location with the highest ratio.

Selecting facility location is an important and complex consideration for global corporations, which must take into account cost-based variables such as transportation, exchange rates, and cost of labor. The skill levels of potential workers, the development of regional infrastructure, a good quality of life, and a favorable business climate are important considerations in selecting a location for overseas facilities. For high-tech firms, proximity to world-class research institutions and access to venture capital are also essential criteria.[19]

General Motors is locating more of its facilities near the markets where it expects sales growth, opening new factories in Argentina, Poland, China, and Thailand.[20] Low wage rates once drove such decisions at GM, but today managers are also considering the availability of local engineers, designers, and marketing experts. These people help the company design and build cars that satisfy its growing foreign markets.

Capacity Planning

Capacity planning The determination and adjustment of the organization's ability to produce products and services to match customer demand.

Capacity planning is the determination and adjustment of an organization's ability to produce products or services to match demand. For example, if a bank anticipates a customer increase of 20 percent over the next year, capacity planning is the procedure whereby it will ensure that it has sufficient capacity to service that demand.

Organizations can do several things to increase capacity. One is to create additional shifts and hire people to work on them. A second is to ask existing people to work overtime to add to capacity. A third is to outsource or subcontract extra work to other firms. A fourth is to expand a plant and add more equipment. Each of these techniques will increase the organization's ability to meet demand without risk of major excess capacity.

The biggest problem for most organizations, however, is excess capacity. When misjudgments occur, transportation companies have oil tankers sitting empty in the harbor, oil companies have refineries sitting idle, semiconductor companies have plants shuttered, developers have office buildings half full, and the service industry may have hotels or amusement parks operating at partial capacity. For example, movie theater chains have grossly overbuilt in recent years, more than doubling the number of screens in the United States between 1980 and 2000, while ticket sales increased only 43 percent.[21] The challenge is for managers to add capacity as needed without excess. For many of today's companies, the solution is contracting work out to other organizations. New organizational forms such as the network organization and the virtual organization enable companies to quickly ramp up production to increase capacity and dissolve partnerships when extra help is no longer needed.

Inventory Management

Inventory The goods that the organization keeps on hand for use in the production process up to the point of selling the final products to customers.

Finished-goods inventory Inventory consisting of items that have passed through the complete production process but have yet to be sold.

Work-in-process inventory Inventory composed of the materials that still are moving through the stages of the production process.

A large portion of the operations manager's job consists of inventory management. **Inventory** is the goods the organization keeps on hand for use in the production process. Most organizations have three types of inventory: finished goods prior to shipment, work in process, and raw materials.

Finished-goods inventory includes items that have passed through the entire production process but have not been sold. This is highly visible inventory. The new cars parked in the storage lot of an automobile factory are finished-goods inventory, as are the hamburgers and french fries stacked under the heat lamps at a **McDonald's** restaurant. Finished-goods inventory is expensive, because the organization has invested labor and other costs to make the finished product.

Work-in-process inventory includes the materials moving through the stages of the production process that are not completed products. Work-in-process inventory in an automobile plant includes engines, wheel and tire assemblies, and dashboards waiting to be installed. In a fast-food restaurant, the french fries in the fryer and hamburgers on the grill are work-in-process inventory.

Raw materials inventory includes the basic inputs to the organization's production process. This inventory is cheapest, because the organization has not yet invested labor in it. Steel, wire, glass, and paint are raw materials inventory for an auto plant. Meat patties, buns, and raw potatoes are the raw materials inventory in a fast-food restaurant.

Raw materials inventory Inventory consisting of the basic inputs to the organization's production process.

The Importance of Inventory

Inventory management is vitally important to organizations, because inventory sitting idly on the shop floor or in the warehouse costs money. Many years ago, a firm's wealth was measured by its inventory. Today inventory is recognized as an unproductive asset in cost-conscious firms. Dollars not tied up in inventory can be used in other productive ventures. Keeping inventory low is especially important for high-tech firms, because so many of their products lose value quickly, as they are replaced by more innovative and/or lower-cost models. For example, the value of a completed personal computer falls about 1 percent a week; even if shelf space for PCs were free, a company would lose money on its PC inventory.[22]

Retail giants such as **Wal-Mart, Toys 'R' Us, Home Depot,** and **Best Buy** understand that efficient inventory management is essential to competitive pricing. State-of-the-art e-business systems allow tight inventory control with the capacity to meet customer needs. The companies schedule orders to eliminate excess inventory. Their suppliers have refined their delivery systems so that the stores receive only the products needed to meet customer purchases. Another company that updated its inventory management system to enjoy these benefits is **Office Depot.**

Many companies recognize the critical role of inventory management in organizational success. The Japanese analogy of rocks and water describes the current thinking about the importance of inventory.[23] The water in the stream is the inventory in the organization. The higher the water, the less managers have to worry about the rocks, which represent problems. In operations management, these problems apply to scheduling, facilities layout, product design, and quality. When the water level goes down, managers see the rocks and must deal with them. When inventories are reduced, the problems of a poorly designed and managed production process also are revealed. The problems then must be solved. When inventory can be kept at an absolute minimum, operations management is considered excellent.

We now consider specific techniques for inventory management. Four important concepts are economic order quantity, material requirements planning, just-in-time inventory systems, and logistics and distribution management.

Economic Order Quantity

Two basic decisions that can help minimize inventory are how much raw materials to order and when to order from outside suppliers. Ordering the minimum amounts at the right time keeps the raw materials, work-in-process, and finished-goods inventories at low levels. One popular technique is **economic order quantity (EOQ)**, which is designed to minimize the total of ordering costs and holding costs for inventory items. *Ordering costs* are the costs associated with actually placing the order, such as postage, receiving, and inspection. *Holding costs* are costs associated with keeping the item on hand, such as storage space charges, finance charges, and materials-handling expenses.

The EOQ calculation indicates the order quantity size that will minimize holding and ordering costs based on the organization's use of inventory. The EOQ formula includes ordering costs (C), holding costs (H), and annual demand (D). For example, consider a hospital's need to order surgical dressings. Based on hospital records, the ordering costs for surgical dressings are $15, the annual holding cost is $6, and the annual demand for dressings is 605. The following is the formula for the economic order quantity:

$$\text{EOQ} = \sqrt{\frac{2DC}{H}} = \sqrt{\frac{2(605)(15)}{6}} = 55$$

The EOQ formula tells us that the best quantity to order is 55.

Reorder point (ROP) *The most economical level at which an inventory item should be reordered.*

The next question is when to make the order. For this decision, a different formula, called **reorder point (ROP),** is used. ROP is calculated by the following formula, which assumes that it takes three days to receive the order after the hospital has placed it:

$$\text{ROP} = \frac{D}{Time}\,(Lead\ time) = \frac{605}{365}\,(3) = 4.97,\ or\ 5$$

The reorder point tells us that because it takes three days to receive the order, at least 5 dressings should be on hand when the order is placed. As nurses use surgical dressings, operations managers will know that when the level reaches the point of 5, the new order should be placed for a quantity of 55.

This relationship is illustrated in Exhibit 200.6. Whenever the reorder point of 5 dressings is reached, the new order is initiated, and the 55 arrive just as the inventory is depleted. In a typical hospital, however, some variability in lead time and use of surgical dressings will occur. Thus, a few extra items of inventory, called *safety stock,* are used to ensure that the hospital does not run out of surgical dressings. In general, companies keep more safety stock when demand for items is highly variable. When demand is easy to predict, the safety stock may be lower. However, a careful inventory manager may take into account other criteria as well. A sizable price cut or volume discount might make a large purchase economically more attractive, especially in the case of a product the company is almost certain to need in the future.[24]

Material Requirements Planning

The EOQ formula works well when inventory items are not dependent on one another. For example, in a restaurant the demand for hamburgers is independent of the demand for milkshakes; thus, an economic order quantity is calculated for each item. A more complicated inventory problem occurs with **dependent demand inventory,** meaning that item demand is related to the demand for other inventory items. For example, if **Ford Motor Company** decides to make 100,000 cars, it will also need 400,000 tires, 400,000 rims, and 400,000 hubcaps. The demand for tires is dependent on the demand for cars.

Dependent demand inventory *Inventory in which item demand is related to the demand for other inventory items.*

The most common inventory control system used for handling dependent demand inventory is **material requirements planning (MRP).** MRP is a dependent demand inventory planning and control system that schedules the exact amount of all materials required to support the desired end product. MRP is computer based and requires sophisticated calculations to coordinate information on production scheduling, inventory location, forecasting, and ordering.

Unlike with EOQ, inventory levels are not based on past consumption; rather, they are based on precise estimates of future needs for production. MRP can dramatically reduce inventory costs. With MRP, managers can better control the quantity and timing of deliveries of raw materials, ensuring that the right

Exhibit 200.6 *Inventory Control of Surgical Dressings by EOQ*

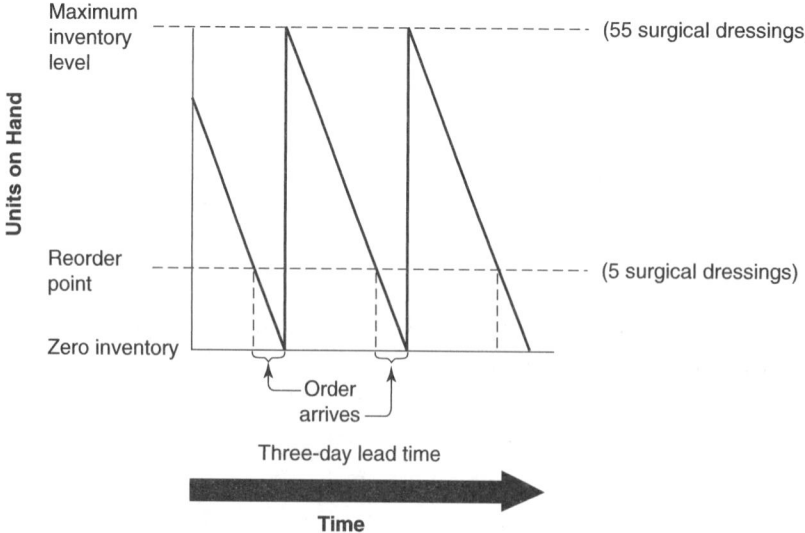

MODULE 200. OPERATIONS MANAGEMENT

materials arrive at approximately the right time they are needed in the production process. The computerized MRP system can slow or accelerate the inflow of materials in response to changes in the production schedule. These controls result in lower labor, materials, and overhead costs.[25]

Material requirements planning (MRP) A dependent demand inventory planning and control system that schedules the precise amount of all materials required to support the production of desired end products.

As competitive pressures increased, MRP gradually evolved into the broader enterprise resource planning (ERP) systems. MRP is focused only on manufacturing and inventory, while ERP incorporates computerized links to other business functions, such as human resources, finance, and sales, enabling managers to evaluate trade-offs such as the balance between workload and the human resources and manufacturing capacity.[26] ERP systems can integrate, track, and optimize functions across the entire organization. MRP systems are a valuable subset of ERP, enabling managers to have greater insight into operations so they can optimize the use of human and material resources.

Just-in-Time Inventory Systems

Just-in-time (JIT) inventory systems are designed to reduce the level of an organization's inventory and its associated costs, aiming to push to zero the amount of time that raw materials and finished products are sitting in the factory, being inspected, or in transit.[27] Sometimes these systems are referred to as *stockless systems, zero inventory systems,* or *Kanban systems*. Each system centers on the concept that suppliers deliver materials only at the exact moment needed, thereby reducing raw material inventories to zero. Moreover, work-in-process inventories are kept to a minimum because goods are produced only as needed to service the next stage of production. Finished-goods inventories are minimized by matching them exactly to sales demand. Just-in-time systems have tremendous advantages. In particular, the reduced inventory level frees productive capital for other company uses.

Just-in-time (JIT) inventory system An inventory control system that schedules materials to arrive precisely when they are needed on a production line.

Recall the analogy of the rocks and the water. To reduce inventory levels to zero means that all management and coordination problems will surface and must be resolved. Scheduling must be scrupulously precise and logistics tightly coordinated. For example, follow the movement of a shipment of odometers and speedometers from a supplier in Winchester, Virginia, to a GM Saturn plant in Spring Hill, Tennessee.

Thursday, 9 A.M.	A Ryder truck arrives at the supplier. As workers load the parts, drivers check on-board computers for destination, route, and estimated time of arrival (ETA) data.
Friday, 3 A.M.	The truck arrives at Spring Hill, Tennessee, and approaches a switching yard two miles from the Saturn plant, parking in a computer-assigned spot. The driver downloads a key-shaped floppy disk from the on-board computer into Ryder's mainframe, which relays the performance report directly to Saturn.
Friday, 12:50 P.M.	The trailer leaves the switching yard at a designated time and arrives at a predetermined receiving dock at the Saturn plant, where Saturn workers unload the parts and send them to the production line just in time.[28]

The coordination required by JIT demands that information be shared among everyone in the supply chain. Communication between only adjoining links in the supply chain is too slow. Rather, coordination requires a kind of information web in which members of the supply chain share information simultaneously with all other participants, often using Internet technologies.[29] For example, **Dell's** factory in Austin, Texas, uses on-line information exchange so effectively that it can order only the materials needed to keep production running for the next two hours. In addition, Web hook-ups to shipping companies mean that finished inventory can often be loaded onto trucks less than 15 hours after a customer submits an order.[30]

Just-in-time inventory systems also require excellent employee motivation and cooperation. Workers are expected to perform at their best because they are entrusted with the responsibility and authority to make the zero inventory system work. Employees must help one another when they fall behind and must be capable of doing different jobs. Workers experience the satisfaction of being in charge of the system and making useful improvements in the company's operations.[31]

205. MANUFACTURING OPERATIONS

Logistics and Distribution Management

Logistics *The activities required to physically move materials into the company's operations facility and to move finished products to customers.*

A critical aspect of managing inventory is efficiently moving raw materials into the facility and moving finished products out to customers. Some companies develop the necessary logistics expertise in house. **Logistics** refers to managing the movement of materials within the facility, the shipment of incoming materials from suppliers, and the shipment of outgoing products to customers. For example, Wal-Mart uses regional distribution centers, such as the one in New Braunfels, Texas, which has more than 1 million square feet of floor space, 96 dock doors for loading and unloading trailers, and 5.62 miles of conveyors for moving merchandise.[32] These regional centers receive incoming shipments from suppliers, receive orders from the retail stores, make up the orders, and load and ship merchandise orders to stores throughout the region. Distribution center employees coordinate the entire system and schedule inbound trucks from suppliers and company-owned trucks outbound to the retail stores. Using computers, the system can be so precisely coordinated that the stores don't need warehouses; orders of merchandise go directly from the trucks to the shelves, usually within 48 hours.

Other organizations outsource logistics to a growing number of contract logistics firms, such as Ryder Systems, Caliber Systems Inc., and Emery Global Logistics, which manage the movement of incoming materials and the shipment of outgoing products for the company. General Motors gained efficiencies by outsourcing logistics to Penske Logistics, which coordinates and consolidates shipments of supplies and materials for all of GM's U.S. assembly plants.[33]

Distribution *Moving finished products to customers; also called order fulfillment.*

Moving finished products out to customers is usually referred to as **distribution** or *order fulfillment*. The faster and more accurately a company can fill customer orders, the lower the costs for the organization and the greater the likelihood that the customer will return. For online companies, distribution snafus in the early days have led to greater emphasis on the nuts and bolts of order fulfillment. One approach is to rely on contract fulfillment companies such as SubmitOrder.com, which stores, packs, and ships products for companies such as **MuseumCompany.com, Kmart's BlueLight.com,** and teen fashion retailer **LimitedToo.** As soon as a customer hits the "Buy" button on MuseumCompany.com's Web page, SubmitOrder spits out the customer's mailing labels, receipt, and the shelf location for each item ordered.[34] A stock *picker* takes the paperwork and starts running to select the items and send them along a conveyor belt to a *packer* who packages the items and sends them to the appropriate dock for shipping. The whole process can take less than an hour.

SubmitOrder's computers also send hourly updates to the company so managers can replenish goods as needed. On-line catalogs can be automatically updated as soon as new merchandise arrives in the warehouse. Further automation will enable SubmitOrder pickers to remain in one part of the warehouse and assemble small portions of larger orders, allowing the company to send out as many as 5,000 orders an hour, shaving a little more off the delivery time for each package.

Traditional organizations are also finding new ways to deliver products faster and less expensively by using the Internet. In the latest advance in interorganizational collaboration, some companies share transportation information and resources with unrelated companies, even competitors, so they can share truck space and avoid hauling an empty trailer on a return trip. Subaru of America is talking with a rival automaker about the possibility of sharing rail and truck space so cars will get to dealers faster. **Nabisco** uses electronic linkages to share warehouses and trucks with companies such as **Dole** and **Lea & Perrins,** and coordinate order shipments to retailers, enabling stores to more closely match orders to consumer needs.[35] Nabisco has also joined with **General Mills** and other companies to test a new collaborative, on-line distribution network.

Managing Productivity

Productivity is significant because it influences the well-being of the entire society as well as of individual companies. The only way to increase the output of goods and services to society is to increase organizational productivity.

Measuring Productivity

What is productivity, and how is it measured? In simple terms, **productivity** is the organization's output of goods and services divided by its inputs. This means that productivity can be improved by either increasing the amount of output using the same level of inputs or reducing the number of inputs required to produce the output. Sometimes a company can even do both. **Ruggieri & Sons,** for example, invested in mapping software to help it plan deliveries of heating fuel. The software plans the most efficient routes based on the locations of customers and fuel reloading terminals, as well as the amount of fuel each customer needs. When Ruggieri switched from planning routes by hand to using the software, its drivers began driving fewer miles but making 7 percent more stops each day—in other words, burning less fuel in order to sell more fuel.[36]

The accurate measure of productivity can be complex. Two approaches for measuring productivity are total factor productivity and partial productivity. **Total factor productivity** is the ratio of total outputs to the inputs from labor, capital, materials, and energy:

$$Total\ factor\ productivity = \frac{Total\ Outputs}{Labor + Capital + Materials + Energy}$$

Total factor productivity represents the best measure of how the organization is doing. Often, however, managers need to know about productivity with respect to certain inputs. **Partial productivity** is the ratio of total outputs to a major category of inputs. For example, many organizations are interested in labor productivity, which would be measured as follows:

$$Labor\ Productivity = \frac{Total\ Outputs}{Labor\ dollars}$$

Productivity The organization's output of products and services divided by its inputs.

Total factor productivity The ratio of total outputs to the inputs from labor, capital, materials, and energy.

Partial productivity The ratio of total outputs to the inputs from a single major input category.

Calculating this formula for labor, capital, or materials provides information on whether improvements in each element are occurring. However, managers often are criticized for relying too heavily on partial productivity measures, especially direct labor.[37] Measuring direct labor misses the valuable improvements in materials, manufacturing processes, and work quality. Labor productivity is easily measured, but may show an increase as a result of capital improvements. Thus, managers will misinterpret the reason for productivity increases.

Improving Productivity

When an organization decides that improving productivity is important, there are three places to look: technological productivity, worker productivity, and managerial productivity.

Increased *technological productivity* refers to the use of more efficient machines, robots, computers, and other technologies to increase outputs. The flexible manufacturing and CAD/CAM systems described earlier in this section are technological improvements that enhance productivity. New technology can increase productivity for service firms as well. Schneider National, the largest trucking company in the United States, installed a computer terminal in each of its 26 maintenance centers and connected them to an intranet so that mechanics can access up-to-date diagrams and data for repairing trucks. Each mechanic can now fix 20 percent more tractors than before, enabling trucks to get back on the road faster.[38]

Outsourcing can also increase productivity because a specialized firm can afford to invest in the most modern technology related to the service it provides. NationsBank, for example, arranged for **Pitney Bowes Management Services** (PBMS) to handle its mail services, in part because PBMS has the computer applications to handle the task. Therefore NationsBank doesn't have to incur the cost of new technology needed to set up a modern mailing system for its 60 mail centers spread out over 16 states and the District of Columbia.[39]

Increased *worker productivity* means having workers produce more output in the same time period. Companies can improve worker productivity by establishing the means for existing employees to do more by working harder or improving work processes. Employees may simply need more knowledge, more resources, or improved task or workplace design. The company may also decide to hire employees with greater expertise or to outsource certain operations to a firm with expertise in that area, as NationsBank did to obtain the knowledge of PBMS. Improving worker productivity can be a real challenge for American companies, because too often workers have an antagonistic relationship with management. Thus, increasing employee productivity often requires improving that relationship. Many of the leadership and management approaches can enhance worker productivity by motivating and inspiring employees.

Increased *managerial productivity* simply means that managers do a better job of running the business. Leading experts in productivity and quality often have stated that the real reason for productivity problems in the United States is poor management.[40]

Management productivity improves when managers emphasize quality over quantity, break down barriers and empower their employees, and do not overmanage using numbers. Managers can learn to use reward systems, employee involvement, and teamwork. However, it is important for managers to consider the linkage between these techniques and the company's strategy—not just to blindly insert a technique into the organization's activities. For example, although many managers have encouraged their employees to share knowledge, their efforts often fail because employees see no benefits and they lose interest. In contrast, knowledge management efforts succeed when managers establish a strategy-related focus for what information is to be shared, then measure the results. At **General Electric** (GE), for example, employees focused on learning about how to improve response time. Management had determined that improvements in this area would significantly improve the company's performance. When GE instituted its knowledge management system, managers looked for—and found—improvements in such performance measures as sales per employee.[41] The difference can be attributed to better management, not to specific techniques.

Manufacturing and Service Technologies

This section explores both service and manufacturing technologies and how technology is related to organizational structure. **Technology** refers to the tools, techniques, machines, and actions used to transform organizational inputs (materials, information, ideas) into outputs (products and services).[42] Technology is an organization's production process and includes work procedures as well as machinery.

Organization technology begins with raw materials of some type (for example, unfinished steel castings in a valve manufacturing plant). Employees take action on the raw material to make a change in it (they machine steel castings), which transforms the raw material into the output of the organization (control valves ready for shipment to oil refineries). For a service organization like **Federal Express,** the production technology includes the equipment and procedures for delivering overnight mail.

Exhibit 200.7 features an example of production technology for a manufacturing plant. Note how the technology consists of raw material inputs, a transformation process that changes and adds value to these items, and the ultimate product or service output that is sold to consumers in the environment. In today's large, complex organizations, it can be hard to pinpoint technology. Technology can be partly assessed by examining the raw materials flowing into the organization,[43] the variability of work activities,[44] the degree to which the production process is mechanized,[45] the extent to which one task depends upon another in the work flow,[46] or the number of new product or service outputs.[47]

Recall that organizations have a technical core that reflects the organization's primary purpose. The technical core contains the transformation process that represents the organization's technology. As today's organizations try to become more flexible in a changing environment, new technology may influence organizational structure, but decisions about organizational structure may also shape or limit technology. Thus, the interaction between core technology and structure leads to a patterned relationship in many organizations.[48]

Organizations are made up of many departments, each of which may use a different technology to produce its outputs and meet departmental goals. Thus, research and development transforms ideas into new product proposals, and marketing transforms inventory into sales, each using a different technology. Moreover, the administrative technology used by managers to run the organization represents yet another technology. New information technology has a tremendous impact on the administrative arena.

Organization-Level Manufacturing Technology

Manufacturing technologies include traditional manufacturing processes and new computer-based manufacturing systems.

Traditional Manufacturing

WOODWARD'S STUDY The first and most influential study of manufacturing technology was conducted by Joan Woodward, a British industrial sociologist. Her research began as a field study of management principles in south Essex. The prevailing management wisdom at the time (1950s) was contained in what was known as *universal principles of management.* These principles were "one best way" prescriptions that effective organizations were expected to adopt. Woodward surveyed 100 manufacturing firms firsthand to learn how they were organized.[49] She and her

Exhibit 200.7 *Transformation Process for a Manufacturing Company*

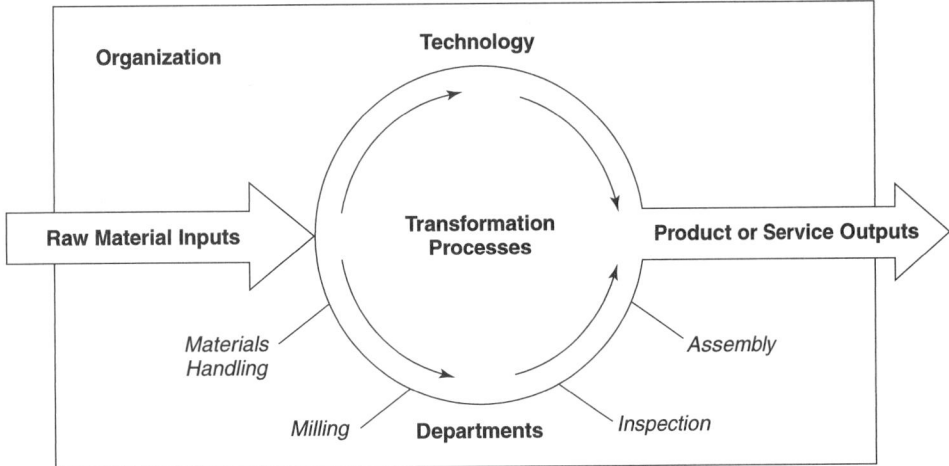

research team visited each firm, interviewed managers, examined company records, and observed the manufacturing operations. Her data included a wide range of structural characteristics (span of control, levels of management) and dimensions of management style (written versus verbal communications, use of rewards) and the type of manufacturing process. Data were also obtained that reflected commercial success of the firms.

Woodward developed a scale and organized the firms according to technical complexity of the manufacturing process. **Technical complexity** represents the extent of mechanization of the manufacturing process. High technical complexity means most of the work is performed by machines. Low technical complexity means workers play a larger role in the production process. Woodward's scale of technical complexity originally had 10 categories, and these categories were further consolidated into three basic technology groups:

- *Group I: Small-batch and unit production.* These firms tend to be job shop operations that manufacture and assemble small orders to meet specific needs of customers. Custom work is the norm. **Small-batch production** relies heavily on the human operator; it is thus not highly mechanized.
- *Group II: Large-batch and mass production.* **Large-batch production** is a manufacturing process characterized by long production runs of standardized parts. Output often goes into inventory from which orders are filled, because customers do not have special needs. Examples include most assembly lines, such as for automobiles or trailer homes.
- *Group III: Continuous process production.* In **continuous process production** the entire process is mechanized. There is no starting and stopping. This represents mechanization and standardization one step beyond those in an assembly line. Automated machines control the continuous process, and outcomes are highly predictable. Examples include chemical plants, oil refineries, liquor producers, and nuclear power plants.

Using this classification of technology, Woodward's data made sense. The number of management levels and the manager/total personnel ratio, for example, show definite increases as technical complexity increases from unit production to continuous process. This indicates that greater management intensity is needed to manage complex technology. Direct/indirect labor ratio decreases with technical complexity because more indirect workers are required to support and maintain complex machinery. Other characteristics, such as span of control, formalized procedures, and centralization, are high for mass-production technology but low for other technologies because the work is standardized. Unit production and continuous process technologies require highly skilled workers to run the machines and verbal communication to adapt to changing conditions. Mass production is standardized and routinized, so few exceptions occur, little verbal communication is needed, and employees are less skilled.

Overall, the management systems in both unit production and continuous process technology are characterized as organic. They are more free-flowing and adaptive, with fewer procedures and less standardization. Mass production, however, is mechanistic, with standardized jobs and formalized procedures. Woodward's discovery about technology thus provided substantial new insight into the causes of organization structure. In Joan Woodward's own words, "Different technologies impose different kinds of demands on individuals and organizations, and those demands had to be met through an appropriate structure."[50]

205. MANUFACTURING OPERATIONS

STRATEGY, TECHNOLOGY, AND PERFORMANCE Another portion of Woodward's study examined the success of the firms along dimensions such as profitability, market share, stock price, and reputation. As indicated, the measurement of effectiveness is not simple or precise, but Woodward was able to rank firms on a scale of commercial success according to whether they displayed above-average, average, or below-average performance on strategic objectives.

Woodward compared the structure-technology relationship against commercial success and discovered that successful firms tended to be those that had complementary structures and technologies. Many of the organizational characteristics of the successful firms were near the average of their technology category. Below-average firms tended to depart from the structural characteristics for their technology type. Another conclusion was that structural characteristics could be interpreted as clustering into organic and mechanistic management systems. Successful small-batch and continuous process organizations had organic structures, and successful mass-production organizations had mechanistic structures. Subsequent research has replicated her findings.[51]

What this illustrates for today's companies is that strategy, structure, and technology need to be aligned, especially when competitive conditions change.[52]

Failing to adopt appropriate new technologies to support strategy, or adopting a new technology and failing to realign strategy to match it, can lead to poor performance. Today's increased global competition means more volatile markets, shorter product life cycles, and more sophisticated and knowledgeable consumers; and flexibility to meet these new demands has become a strategic imperative for many companies.[53] Companies can adopt new technologies to support the strategy of flexibility. However, organization structures and management processes must also be realigned, as a highly mechanistic structure hampers flexibility and prevents the company from reaping the benefits of the new technology.[54]

Computer-Integrated Manufacturing

In the years since Woodward's research, new developments have occurred in manufacturing technology. New manufacturing technologies include robots, numerically controlled machine tools, and computerized software for product design, engineering analysis, and remote control of machinery. The ultimate technology is called **computer-integrated manufacturing** (CIM).[55] Also called *advanced manufacturing technology, agile manufacturing, the factory of the future, smart factories,* or *flexible manufacturing systems,* CIM links together manufacturing components that previously stood alone. Thus, robots, machines, product design, and engineering analysis are coordinated by a single computer.

The result has already revolutionized the shop floor, enabling large factories to deliver a wide range of custom-made products at low mass-production costs.[56] Computer-integrated manufacturing also enables small companies to go toe-to-toe with large factories and low-cost foreign competitors.

Computer-integrated manufacturing is typically the result of three subcomponents.

- *Computer-aided design (CAD).* Computers are used to assist in the drafting, design, and engineering of new parts. Designers guide their computers to draw specified configurations on the screen, including dimensions and component details. Hundreds of design alternatives can be explored, as can scaled-up or scaled-down versions of the original.[57]

- *Computer-aided manufacturing (CAM).* Computer-controlled machines in materials handling, fabrication, production, and assembly greatly increase the speed at which items can be manufactured. CAM also permits a production line to shift rapidly from producing one product to any variety of other products by changing the instruction tapes or software in the computer. CAM enables the production line to quickly honor customer requests for changes in product design and product mix.[58]

- *Integrated Information Network.* A computerized system links all aspects of the firm—including accounting, purchasing, marketing, inventory control, design, production, and so forth. This system, based on a common data and information base, enables managers to make decisions and direct the manufacturing process in a truly integrated fashion.

The combination of CAD, CAM, and integrated information network systems represents the highest level of computer-integrated manufacturing. A new product can be designed on the computer, and a prototype can be produced untouched by human hands. The ideal factory can switch quickly from one product to another, working fast and with precision, without paperwork or recordkeeping to bog down the system.[59]

A company can adopt CAD in its engineering design department and/or CAM in its production area and make substantial improvements in efficiency and quality. However, when all three components are brought together in a truly advanced plant, the results are breathtaking.

This ultra-advanced system is not achieved piecemeal. CIM reaches its ultimate level to improve quality, customer service, and cost-cutting when all parts are used interdependently. The integration of CIM and flexible work processes is changing the face of manufacturing. The wave of the manufacturing future is **mass customization,** whereby factories are able to mass-produce products designed to exact customer specification. Today, you can buy a computer assembled to your exact specifications, jeans customized for your body, glasses molded to precisely fit and flatter your face, CDs with music tracks that you select, and pills with the exact blend of vitamins and minerals you want.

PERFORMANCE The awesome advantage of CIM is that products of different sizes, types, and customer requirements freely intermingle on the assembly line. Bar codes imprinted on a part enable machines to make instantaneous changes—such as putting a larger screw in a different location—without slowing the production line. A manufacturer can turn out an infinite variety of products in unlimited batch sizes. In traditional manufacturing systems studied by Woodward, choices were limited to the diagonal. Small batches allowed for high product flexibility and custom orders, but because of the "craftsmanship" involved in custom-making products, batch size was necessarily small. Mass production could have large-batch size, but offered limited product flexibility. Continuous process could produce a single standard product in unlimited quantities. Computer-integrated manufacturing allows plants to break free of this diagonal and to increase both batch size and product flexibility at the same time. When taken to its ultimate level, CIM allows for mass customization, with each specific product tailored to customer specification. This high-level use of CIM has been referred to as *computer-aided craftsmanship* because computers tailor each product to meet a customer's exact needs.[60] The Internet plays an important role in the trend toward mass customization because it enables companies to keep in close touch with each individual customer in addition to making it easier and faster to coordinate customer orders with factory tooling and supply requirements.

Studies suggest that with CIM, machine utilization is more efficient, labor productivity increases, scrap rates decrease, and product variety and customer satisfaction increase.[61] Many U.S. manufacturing companies are reinventing the factory using CIM and associated management systems to increase productivity.

STRUCTURAL IMPLICATIONS Research into the relationship between CIM and organizational characteristics is beginning to emerge. Compared with traditional mass production technologies, CIM has a narrow span of control, few hierarchical levels, adaptive tasks, low specialization, decentralization, and the overall environment is characterized as organic and self-regulative. Employees need the skills to participate in teams, training is broad (so workers are not overly specialized) and frequent (so workers are up to date). Expertise tends to be cognitive so workers can process abstract ideas and solve problems. Interorganizational relationships in CIM firms are characterized by changing demand from customers—which is easily handled with the new technology—and close relationships with a few suppliers that provide top-quality raw materials.[62]

Technology alone cannot give organizations the benefits of flexibility, quality, increased production, and greater customer satisfaction. Research suggests that CIM can become a competitive burden rather than a competitive advantage unless organizational structures and management processes are redesigned to take advantage of the new technology.[63] However, when top managers make a commitment to implement new structures and processes that empower workers and support a learning and knowledge-creating environment, CIM can help companies be more competitive.

Organization-Level Service Technology

One of the biggest changes occurring in the technology of organizations is the growing service sector. The percentage of the workforce employed in manufacturing continues to decline not only in the United States, but in Canada, France, Germany, the United Kingdom, and Sweden as well. In the United States, services now generate 74 percent of the gross domestic product and account for 79 percent of all jobs.[64] Service technologies are different from manufacturing technologies and, in turn, require a specific organization structure.

Service Firms

DEFINITION Whereas manufacturing organizations achieve their primary purpose through the production of products, service organizations accomplish their primary purpose through the production and provision of services, such as education, health care, transportation, banking, and hospitality. Studies of service organizations have focused on the unique dimensions of service technologies.

The most obvious difference is that service technology produces an *intangible output*, rather than a tangible product, such as a refrigerator produced by a manufacturing firm. A service is abstract and often consists of knowledge and ideas rather than a physical product. Thus, whereas manufacturers' products can be inventoried for later sale, services are characterized by *simultaneous production and consumption*. A client meets with a doctor or attorney, for example, and students and teachers come together in the classroom. A service is an intangible product that does not exist until it is requested by the customer. It cannot be stored, inventoried, or viewed as a finished good. If a service is not consumed immediately upon production, it disappears.[65] This typically means that service firms are *labor and knowledge intensive*, with many employees needed to meet the needs of customers, whereas manufacturing firms tend to be capital intensive, relying on mass production, continuous process, and advanced manufacturing technologies.[66]

Direct interaction between customer and employee is generally very high with services, while there is little direct interaction between customers and employees in the technical core of a manufacturing firm. This direct interaction means that the *human element* (employees) becomes extremely important in service firms. Whereas most people never meet the workers who manufactured their cars, they interact directly with the salesperson who sold them their Subaru or Pontiac Grand Am. The treatment received from the salesperson—or by a doctor, lawyer, or hairstylist—affects the perception of the service received and the customer's level of satisfaction. The *quality of a service is perceived* and cannot be directly measured and compared in the same way that the quality of a product can. Another characteristic that affects customer satisfaction and perception of quality service is rapid response time. A service must be provided when the customer wants and needs it. When you take a friend to dinner, you want to be seated and served in a timely manner; you would not be very satisfied if the hostess or manager told you to come back tomorrow when there would be more tables or servers available to accommodate you.

The final defining characteristic of service technology is that *site selection is often much more important* than with manufacturing. Because services are intangible, they have to be located where the customer wants to be served. Services are dispersed and located geographically close to customers. For example, fast-food franchises usually disperse their facilities into local stores. Most towns of even moderate size today have two or more McDonald's restaurants rather than one huge one in order to provide service where customers want it.

In reality, it is difficult to find organizations that reflect 100 percent service or 100 percent manufacturing characteristics. Some service firms take on characteristics of manufacturers, and vice versa. Many manufacturing firms are placing a greater emphasis on customer service to differentiate themselves and be more competitive, which is one reason for the increased use of computer-integrated manufacturing. In addition, manufacturing organizations have departments such as purchasing, human resources, and marketing that are based on service technology. On the other hand, organizations such as gas stations, stockbrokers, retail stores, and fast-food restaurants may belong to the service sector, even though the provision of a product is a significant part of the transaction. The vast majority of organizations involve some combination of products and services. The important point is that all organizations can be classified along a continuum that includes both manufacturing and service characteristics.

NEW DIRECTIONS IN SERVICES Service firms have always tended toward providing *customized output*—that is, providing exactly the service each customer wants and needs. For example, when you visit a hairstylist, you don't automatically get the same cut the stylist gave the three previous clients. The stylist cuts your hair the way you request it. However, the trend toward mass customization that is revolutionizing manufacturing has had a significant impact on the service sector as well. Customer expectations of what constitutes good service are rising.[67] Service companies such as the **Ritz-Carlton Hotels, USAA,** an insurance and financial services company, and **Wells Fargo Bank** are using new technology to keep customers coming back. All Ritz-Carlton hotels are linked to a database filled with the preferences of half-a-million guests, allowing any desk clerk or bellhop to find out what your favorite wine is, whether you're allergic to feather pillows, and how many extra towels you want in your room. At Wells Fargo, customers can apply over the Internet and get a three-second decision on a loan structured specifically for them.[68]

Designing the Service Organization

The feature of service technologies with a distinct influence on organizational structure and control systems is the need for technical core employees to be close to the customer.[69] The differences between service and product organizations necessitated by customer contact are summarized in Exhibit 200.8.

The impact of customer contact on organization structure is reflected in the use of boundary roles and structural disaggregation.[70] Boundary roles are used extensively in manufacturing firms to handle customers and to reduce disruptions for the technical core. They are used less in service firms because a service is intangible and cannot be passed along by boundary spanners, so service customers must interact directly with technical employees, such as doctors or brokers.

Exhibit 200.8 *Configuration and Structural Characteristics of Service Organizations versus Product Organizations*

Structure	Service	Product
1. Separate boundary roles	Few	Many
2. Geographical dispersion	Much	Little
3. Decision making	Decentralized	Centralized
4. Formalization	Lower	Higher
Human Resources		
1. Employee skill level	Higher	Lower
2. Skill emphasis	Interpersonal	Technical

A service firm deals in information and intangible outputs and does not need to be large. Its greatest economies are achieved through disaggregation into small units that can be located close to customers. Stockbrokers, doctors' clinics, consulting firms, and banks disperse their facilities into regional and local offices. Some fast-food chains, such as **Taco Bell,** are taking this a step further, selling chicken tacos and bean burritos anywhere people gather—airports, supermarkets, college campuses, or street corners. Manufacturing firms, on the other hand, tend to aggregate operations in a single area that has raw materials and an available workforce. A large manufacturing firm can take advantage of economies derived from expensive machinery and long production runs.

Service technology also influences internal organization characteristics used to direct and control the organization. For one thing, the skills of technical core employees need to be higher. These employees need enough knowledge and awareness to handle customer problems rather than just enough to perform a single, mechanical task. Some service organizations give their employees the knowledge and freedom to make decisions and do whatever is needed to satisfy customers, whereas others, such as McDonald's, have set rules and procedures for customer service. Yet in all cases, service employees need social and interpersonal skills as well as technical skills.[71] Because of higher skills and structural dispersion, decision making often tends to be decentralized in service firms, and formalization tends to be low. Many Taco Bell outlets operate with no manager on the premises. Self-directed teams manage inventory, schedule work, order supplies, and train new employees.

Understanding the nature of service technology helps managers align strategy, structure, and management processes that may be quite different from those for a product-based or traditional manufacturing technology. In addition, as mentioned earlier, manufacturing organizations are placing greater emphasis on service, and managers can use these concepts and ideas to strengthen their company's service orientation.

Now let's turn to another perspective on technology, that of production activities within specific organizational departments. Departments often have characteristics similar to those of service technology, providing services to other departments within the organization.

Departmental Technology

This section shifts to the department level of analysis for departments not necessarily within the technical core. Each department in an organization has a production process that consists of a distinct technology. General Motors has departments for engineering, R&D, human resources, advertising, quality control, finance, and dozens of other functions. This section analyzes the nature of departmental technology and its relationship with departmental structure.

The framework that has had the greatest impact on the understanding of departmental technologies was developed by Charles Perrow.[72] Perrow's model is useful for a broad range of technologies, which makes it ideal for research into departmental activities.

Variety

Perrow specified two dimensions of departmental activities that are relevant to organization structure and process. The first is the number of exceptions in the work. This refers to task **variety,** which is the frequency of unexpected and novel events that occur in the conversion process. When individuals encounter a large number of unexpected situations, with frequent problems, variety is considered high. When there are few problems, and when day-to-day job requirements are repetitious, technology contains little variety. Variety in departments can range from repeating a single act, such as on an assembly line, to working on a series of unrelated problems or projects.

Analyzability

The second dimension of technology concerns the **analyzability** of work activities. When the conversion process is analyzable, the work can be reduced to mechanical steps and participants can follow an objective, computational procedure to solve problems. Problem solution may involve the use of standard procedures, such as instructions and manuals, or technical knowledge, such as that in a textbook or handbook. On the other hand, some work is not analyzable. When problems arise, it is difficult to identify the correct solution. There is no store of techniques or procedures to tell a person exactly what to do. The cause of or solution to a problem is not clear, so employees rely on accumulated experience, intuition, and judgment. The final solution to a problem is often the result of wisdom and experience and not the result of standard procedures. Philippos Poulos, a tone regulator at **Steinway & Sons,** has an unanalyzable technology. Tone regulators carefully check each piano's hammers to be sure they produce the proper Steinway sound.[73] These quality control tasks require years of experience and practice. Standard procedures will not tell a person how to do such tasks.

Framework

CATEGORIES OF TECHNOLOGY The dimensions of variety and analyzability form the basis for four major categories of technology: routine, craft, engineering, and nonroutine.

Routine technologies are characterized by little task variety and the use of objective, computational procedures. The tasks are formalized and standardized. Examples include an automobile assembly line and a bank teller department.

Craft technologies are characterized by a fairly stable stream of activities, but the conversion process is not analyzable or well understood. Tasks require extensive training and experience because employees respond to intangible factors on the basis of wisdom, intuition, and experience. Although advances in machine technologies seem to have reduced the number of craft technologies in organizations, a few craft technologies remain. For example, steel furnace engineers continue to mix steel based on intuition and experience, pattern makers at apparel firms still convert rough designers' sketches into salable garments, and gas and oil explorationists use their internal divining rods to determine where millions will be spent on drilling operations.

Engineering technologies tend to be complex because there is substantial variety in the tasks performed. However, the various activities are usually handled on the basis of established formulas, procedures, and techniques. Employees normally refer to a well-developed body of knowledge to handle problems. Engineering and accounting tasks usually fall in this category.

Nonroutine technologies have high task variety, and the conversion process is not analyzable or well understood. In nonroutine technology, a great deal of effort is devoted to analyzing problems and activities. Several equally acceptable options typically can be found. Experience and technical knowledge are used to solve problems and perform the work. Basic research, strategic planning, and other work that involves new projects and unexpected problems are nonroutine.

ROUTINE VERSUS NONROUTINE TECHNOLOGY Variety and analyzability can be combined into a single dimension of technology. This dimension is called routine versus nonroutine technology. The analyzability and variety dimensions are often correlated in departments, meaning that technologies high in variety tend to be low in analyzability, and technologies low in variety tend to be analyzable. Departments can be evaluated along a single dimension of routine versus nonroutine that combines both analyzability and variety, which is a useful shorthand measure for analyzing departmental technology.

The following questions show how departmental technology can be analyzed for determining its placement on Perrow's technology framework. Employees normally circle a number from one to seven in response to each question.

Variety
1. To what extent would you say your work is routine?
2. Does most everyone in this unit do about the same job in the same way most of the time?
3. Are unit members performing repetitive activities in doing their jobs?

Analyzability
1. To what extent is there a clearly known way to do the major types of work you normally encounter?
2. To what extent is there an understandable sequence of steps that can be followed in doing your work?
3. To do your work, to what extent can you actually rely on established procedures and practices?

If answers to these questions indicate high scores for analyzability and low scores for variety, the department would have a routine technology. If the opposite occurs, the technology would be nonroutine. Low variety and low analyzability indicate a craft technology, and high variety and high analyzability indicate an engineering technology. As a practical matter, most departments fit somewhere along the diagonal and can be most easily characterized as routine or nonroutine.

Department Design

Once the nature of a department's technology has been identified, then the appropriate structure can be determined. Department technology tends to be associated with a cluster of departmental characteristics, such as the skill level of employees, formalization, and pattern of communication. Definite patterns do exist in the relationship between work-unit technology and structural characteristics, which are associated with departmental performance.[74] Key relationships between technology and other dimensions of departments are described in this section and are summarized in Exhibit 200.9.

The overall structure of departments may be characterized as either organic or mechanistic. Routine technologies are associated with a mechanistic structure and processes, with formal rules and rigid management processes. Nonroutine technologies are associated with an organic structure, and department management is more flexible and free-flowing. The specific design characteristics of formalization, centralization, staff qualifications, span of control, and communication and coordination vary, depending on work-unit technology.

1. *Formalization.* Routine technology is characterized by standardization and division of labor into small tasks that are governed by formal rules and procedures. For nonroutine tasks, the structure is less formal and less standardized. When variety is high, as in a research department, fewer activities are covered by formal procedures.[75]

2. *Centralization.* In routine technologies, most decision making about task activities is centralized to management.[76] In engineering technologies, employees with technical training tend to acquire moderate decision authority because technical knowledge is important to task accomplishment. Production employees

Exhibit 200.9 *Relationship of Department Technology to Structural and Management Characteristics*

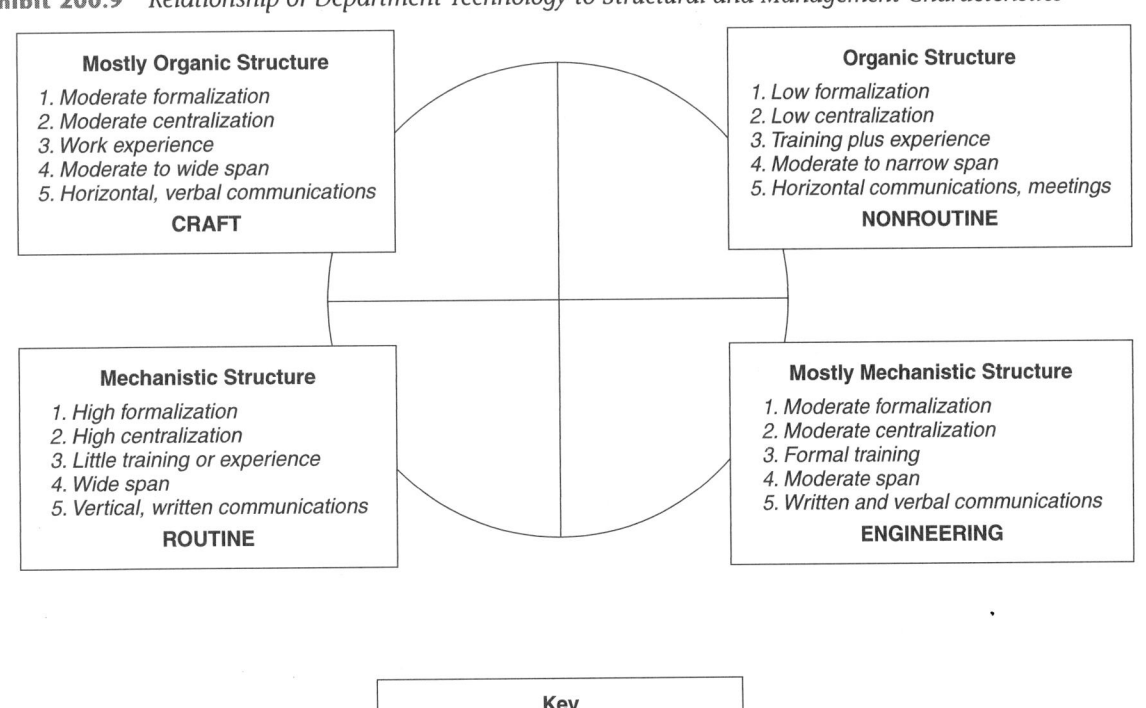

who have long experience obtain decision authority in craft technologies because they know how to respond to problems. Decentralization to employees is greatest in nonroutine settings, where many decisions are made by employees.

3. *Staff qualifications.* Work staff in routine technologies typically require little education or experience, which is congruent with repetitious work activities. In work units with greater variety, staff are more skilled and often have formal training in technical schools or universities. Training for craft activities, which are less analyzable, is more likely to be through job experience. Nonroutine activities require both formal education and job experience.[77]

4. *Span of control.* Span of control is the number of employees who report to a single manager or supervisor. This characteristic is normally influenced by departmental technology. The more complex and nonroutine the task, the more problems arise in which the supervisor becomes involved. Although the span of control may be influenced by other factors, such as skill level of employees, it typically should be smaller for complex tasks because on such tasks the supervisor and subordinate must interact frequently.[78]

5. *Communication and coordination.* Communication activity and frequency increase as task variety increases.[79] Frequent problems require more information sharing to solve problems and ensure proper completion of activities. The direction of communication is typically horizontal in nonroutine work units and vertical in routine work units.[80] The form of communication varies by task analyzability.[81] When tasks are highly analyzable, statistical and written forms of communication (memos, reports, rules, and procedures) are frequent. When tasks are less analyzable, information typically is conveyed face-to-face, over the telephone, or in group meetings.

Two important points are reflected in Exhibit 200.9. First, departments do differ from one another and can be categorized according to their workflow technology.[82] Second, structural and management processes differ based on departmental technology. Managers should design their departments so that requirements based on technology can be met. Design problems are most visible when the design is clearly inconsistent with technology. Studies have found that when structure and communication characteristics did not reflect technology, departments tended to be less effective.[83] Employees could not communicate with the frequency needed to solve problems.

Workflow Interdependence Among Department

So far, this section has explored how organization and department technologies influence structural design. The final characteristic of technology that influences structure is called interdependence. **Interdependence** means the extent to which departments depend on each other for resources or materials to accomplish their tasks. Low interdependence means that departments can do their work independently of each other and have little need for interaction, consultation, or exchange of materials. High interdependence means departments must constantly exchange resources.

Types

James Thompson defined three types of interdependence that influence organization structure.[84] These interdependencies are illustrated in Exhibit 200.10 and are discussed in the following sections.

POOLED **Pooled interdependence** is the lowest form of interdependence among departments. In this form, work does not flow between units. Each department is part of the organization and contributes to the common good of the organization, but works independently. McDonald's restaurants or branch banks are examples of pooled interdependence. An outlet in Chicago need not interact with an outlet in Urbana. Pooled interdependence may be associated with the relationships within a *divisional structure*. Divisions or branches share financial resources from a common pool, and the success of each division contributes to the success of the overall organization.

Thompson proposed that pooled interdependence would exist in firms with what he called a mediating technology. A **mediating technology** provides products or services that mediate or link clients from the external environment and, in so doing, allows each department to work independently. Banks, brokerage firms, and real estate offices all mediate between buyers and sellers, but the offices work independently within the organization.

The management implications associated with pooled interdependence are quite simple. Thompson argued that managers should use rules and procedures to standardize activities across departments. Each department should use the same procedures and financial statements so the outcomes of all departments can be measured and pooled. Very little day-to-day coordination is required among units.

Exhibit 200.10 *Thompson's Classification of Interdependence and Management Implications*

Form of Interdependence	Demands on Horizontal Communication, Decision Making	Type of Coordination Required	Priority for Locating Units Close Together
Pooled (bank) — Clients	Low communication	Standardization, rules, procedures	Low
Sequential (assembly line) — Client	Medium communication	Plans, schedules, feedback	Medium
Reciprocal (hospital) — Client	High communication	Mutual adjustment, cross-departmental meetings, teamwork	High

SEQUENTIAL When interdependence is of serial form, with parts produced in one department becoming inputs to another department, then it is called **sequential interdependence.** The first department must perform correctly for the second department to perform correctly. This is a higher level of interdependence than pooled, because departments exchange resources and depend upon others to perform well. Sequential interdependence creates a greater need for horizontal mechanisms such as integrators or task forces.

Sequential interdependence occurs in what Thompson called **long-linked technology,** which "refers to the combination in one organization of successive stages of production; each stage of production uses as its inputs the production of the preceding stage and produces inputs for the following stage."[85] Large organizations that use assembly line production, such as in the automobile industry, use long-linked technologies and are characterized by sequential interdependence between plants or departments.

The management requirements for sequential interdependence are more demanding than for pooled interdependence. Coordination among the linked plants or departments is required. Since the interdependence implies a one-way flow of materials, extensive planning and scheduling are generally needed. Plant B needs to know what to expect from Plant A so both can perform effectively. Some day-to-day communication among plants is also needed to handle unexpected problems and exceptions that arise.

RECIPROCAL The highest level of interdependence is **reciprocal interdependence.** This exists when the output of operation A is the input to operation B, and the output of operation B is the input back again to operation A. The outputs of departments influence those departments in reciprocal fashion.

Reciprocal interdependence tends to occur in organizations with what Thompson called **intensive technologies,** which provide a variety of products or services in combination to a client. Hospitals are an excellent example because they provide coordinated services to patients. A patient may move back and forth between X ray, surgery, and physical therapy as needed to be cured. A firm developing new products is another example. Intense coordination is needed between design, engineering, manufacturing, and marketing to combine all their resources to suit the customer's product need.

Management requirements are greatest in the case of reciprocal interdependence. Reciprocal interdependence requires that departments work together intimately and be closely coordinated. The structure must allow for frequent horizontal communication and adjustment, perhaps through the use of permanent teams. Extensive planning is required in hospitals, for example, but plans will not anticipate or solve all problems. Daily interaction and mutual adjustment among departments are required. Managers from several departments are jointly involved in face-to-face coordination, teamwork, and decision making. Reciprocal interdependence is the most complex interdependence for organizations to handle.

Structural Priority

As indicated in Exhibit 200.10, since decision making, communication, and coordination problems are greatest for reciprocal interdependence, reciprocal interdependence should receive first priority in organization structure. New product development is one area of reciprocal interdependence that is of growing concern to managers as companies face increasing pressure to get new products to market fast. Many firms are revamping the design-manufacturing relationship by closely integrating computer-aided design (CAD) and computer-aided manufacturing (CAM) technologies discussed earlier in this section.[86] Activities that are reciprocally interdependent should be grouped close together in the organization so managers have easy access to one another for mutual adjustment. These units should report to the same person on the organization chart and should be physically close so the time and effort for coordination can be minimized. Poor coordination will result in poor performance for the organization. If reciprocally interdependent units are not located close together, the organization should design mechanisms for coordination, such as daily meetings between departments or an intranet to facilitate communication. The next priority is given to sequential interdependencies, and finally to pooled interdependencies.

This strategy of organizing keeps the communication channels short where coordination is most critical to organizational success. For example, **Boise Cascade Corporation** experienced poor service to customers because customer service reps located in New York City were not coordinating with production planners in Oregon plants. Customers couldn't get delivery as needed. Boise was reorganized, and the two groups were consolidated under one roof, reporting to the same supervisor at division headquarters. Now customer needs are met because customer service reps work with production planning to schedule customer orders.

Structural Implications

Most organizations experience various levels of interdependence, and structure can be designed to fit these needs. In a manufacturing firm, new product development entails reciprocal interdependence among the design, engineering, purchasing, manufacturing, and sales departments. Perhaps cross-functional teams could be used to handle the back-and-forth flow of information and resources. Once a product is designed, its actual manufacture would be sequential interdependence, with a flow of goods from one department to another, such as among purchasing, inventory, production control, manufacturing, and assembly. The actual ordering and delivery of products is pooled interdependence, with warehouses working independently. Customers could place an order with the nearest facility, which would not require coordination among warehouses, except in unusual cases such as a stock outage.

When consultants analyzed NCR to learn why the development of new products was so slow, they followed the path from initial idea to implementation. The problem was that the development, production, and marketing of products took place in separate divisions, and communication across the three interdependent groups was difficult. NCR broke up its traditional organization structure and created several stand-alone units of about 500 people, each with its own development, production, and marketing people. The new structure enabled new products to be introduced in record time.

Impact of Technology on Job Design

So far, this section has described models for analyzing how manufacturing, service, and department technologies influence structure and management processes. The relationship between a new technology and organization seems to follow a pattern, beginning with immediate effects on the content of jobs, followed (after a longer period) by impact on design of the organization. The ultimate impact of technology on employees can be partially understood through the concepts of job design and sociotechnical systems.

Job Design

Job design includes the assignment of goals and tasks to be accomplished by employees. Managers may consciously change job design to improve productivity or worker motivation. For example, when workers are involved in performing boring, repetitive tasks, managers may introduce **job rotation,** which means moving employees from job to job to give them a greater variety of tasks. However, managers may also unconsciously influence job design through the introduction of new technologies, which can change how jobs are done and the very nature of jobs.[87] Managers should understand how the introduction of a new technology may affect employees' jobs. The common theme of new technologies in the workplace is that they in some way substitute machinery for human labor in transforming inputs into outputs. Automated teller machines (ATMs) have replaced thousands of human bank tellers, for example.

In addition to actually replacing human workers, technology may have several different effects on the human jobs that remain. Research has indicated that mass-production technologies tend to produce **job simplification,** which means that the variety and difficulty of tasks performed by a single person is reduced. The consequence is boring, repetitive jobs that generally provide little satisfaction. More advanced technology, on the other hand, tends to cause **job enrichment,** meaning that the job provides greater responsibility, recognition, and opportunities for growth and development. These technologies create a greater need for employee training and education because workers need higher-level skills and greater competence to master their tasks. For example, ATMs took most the routine tasks (deposits and withdrawals) away from bank tellers and left them with the more complex tasks that require higher-level skills. Studies of computer-integrated manufacturing (CIM) found that it produces three noticeable results for employees: more opportunities for intellectual mastery and enhanced cognitive skills for workers; more worker responsibility for results; and greater interdependence among workers, enabling more social interaction and the development of teamwork and coordination skills.[88] Advanced manufacturing technology may also contribute to **job enlargement,** which is an expansion of the number of different tasks performed by an employee. Because fewer workers are needed with the new technology, each employee has to be able to perform a greater number and variety of tasks.

With advanced technology, workers have to keep learning new skills because technology is changing so rapidly. Advances in *information technology* are having a significant effect on jobs in the service industry, including doctors' offices and medical clinics, law firms, financial planners, and libraries. Workers may find that their jobs change almost daily because of new software programs, increased use of the Internet, and other advances in information technology.

Advanced technology does not always have a positive effect on employees, but research findings in general are encouraging, suggesting that jobs for workers are enriched rather than simplified, engaging their higher mental capacities, offering opportunities for learning and growth, and providing greater job satisfaction.

Sociotechnical Systems

The **sociotechnical systems approach** recognizes the interaction of technical and human needs in effective job design, combining the needs of people with the organization's need for technical efficiency. The *socio* portion of the approach refers to the people and groups who work in organizations and how work is organized and coordinated. The *technical* portion refers to the materials, tools, machines, and processes used to transform organizational inputs into outputs.

The goal of the sociotechnical systems approach is to design the organization for **joint optimization,** which means that an organization functions best only when the social and technical systems are designed to fit the needs of one another. Designing the organization to meet human needs while ignoring the technical systems, or changing technology to improve efficiency while ignoring human needs, may inadvertently cause performance problems. The sociotechnical systems approach attempts to find a balance between what workers want and need and the technical requirements of the organization's production system.[89]

Although there have been failures, in many of these applications, the joint optimization of changes in technology and structure to meet the needs of people, as well as efficiency, improved performance, safety, quality, absenteeism, and turnover. In some cases, work design was not the most efficient based on technical and scientific principles, but worker involvement and commitment more than made up for the difference. Thus, once again research shows that new technologies need not have a negative impact on workers, because the technology often requires higher-level mental and social skills and can be organized to encourage the involvement and commitment of employees, thereby benefiting both the employee and the organization.

The sociotechnical systems principle that people should be viewed as resources and provided with appropriate skills, meaningful work, and suitable rewards becomes even more important in today's world of growing technological complexity.[90] One study found that organizations that put too much faith in machines and technology and pay little attention to the appropriate management of people do not achieve advances in productivity and flexibility. Today's most successful companies strive to find the right mix of machines, computer systems, and people and the most effective way to coordinate them.[91]

Manufacturing Planning and Scheduling

This section describes the manufacturing resource (facilities and equipment) planning that precedes completion of the initial production plan. However, an initial production plan is implicitly required when deciding the number and size of facilities because those decisions affect capacity, and capacity limits the options available to production planning. In addition, a numerical example is used in the description of the relationship of production planning, sales planning, and financial planning.

Although manufacturing strategies and plans may be reviewed annually, major changes in strategies and facilities do not occur that often in most organizations. However, production planning does occur on a regular basis. For example, the production plan is extended (rolled forward) by three months every quarter in some firms. Thus, production planning bridges the long- and medium-range planning horizons. By its very nature, the production plan addresses what is known as the *aggregate planning problem*.

The aggregate planning problem is, strictly speaking, a medium-range planning problem because it normally covers a 12-month period. It is included in this section because long-range plans must be based on the decision of how the aggregate planning problem will be solved. In particular, the organization needs to decide whether to follow a chase, level, or combination plan, as described later in this section.

Manufacturing Resource Planning

Long-Range Planning

The strategic plan is the basis for long-range planning that includes product and sales planning, manufacturing planning, and production planning. Its final output is an integrated business plan. These planning activities are part of strategic planning and often occur concurrently with the activities described previously. They verify the feasibility, or lack thereof, of the mission and the strategic objectives.

Product and Sales Planning

Product and sales planning includes macro-level decisions concerning the product lines the company plans to produce, the markets to be served (including the target population and geographic areas), and the levels of demand anticipated for the various product lines. Product line and market planning decisions are explicit commitments to an organizational direction. It usually is difficult in the short run to change them. Organizational growth and prosperity will be influenced substantially by the wisdom of these decisions. Product and sales planning answers the following questions:

What products does the firm plan to produce?
In what areas and to which customer groups does the company plan to sell its products?
What are the quality and pricing level targets?
What are the expected life cycles of the products and where are they now?
What are the market entry and exit strategies of the firm?

THE PRODUCT AND SALES PLANNING Product and sales planning decisions are interrelated. The defined market affects the product design, including all the attributes of quality, the production volume, and the desired unit cost. The product and the sales plan are also the dominant determinants of the resources required for marketing, engineering, manufacturing, and distribution.

Expanding sales activities into a new geographic territory, such as the decision of **Coca-Coca Bottling Company** to enter China, and the entering of a new product or service field, such as the decision of **McDonnell Douglas Corporation** to market computer software systems, are two examples of strategic decisions. Both of these decisions reveal a change in the mission of the organizations and had a substantial impact on the resources required.

The demarcation between business forecasting and product and sales planning is not easily discernible in all cases, and information flows in both directions. Using the inputs received from the business forecast and an analysis of the organization's competitive strengths, product and sales planning determines which markets and products are viable in terms of demand, capabilities, and organizational objectives. Final product line and sales planning decisions are not made until the long-range planning loop is closed by verification of manufacturing and financial feasibility as illustrated in Exhibit 200.11.

Exhibit 200.11 *Production Plans*

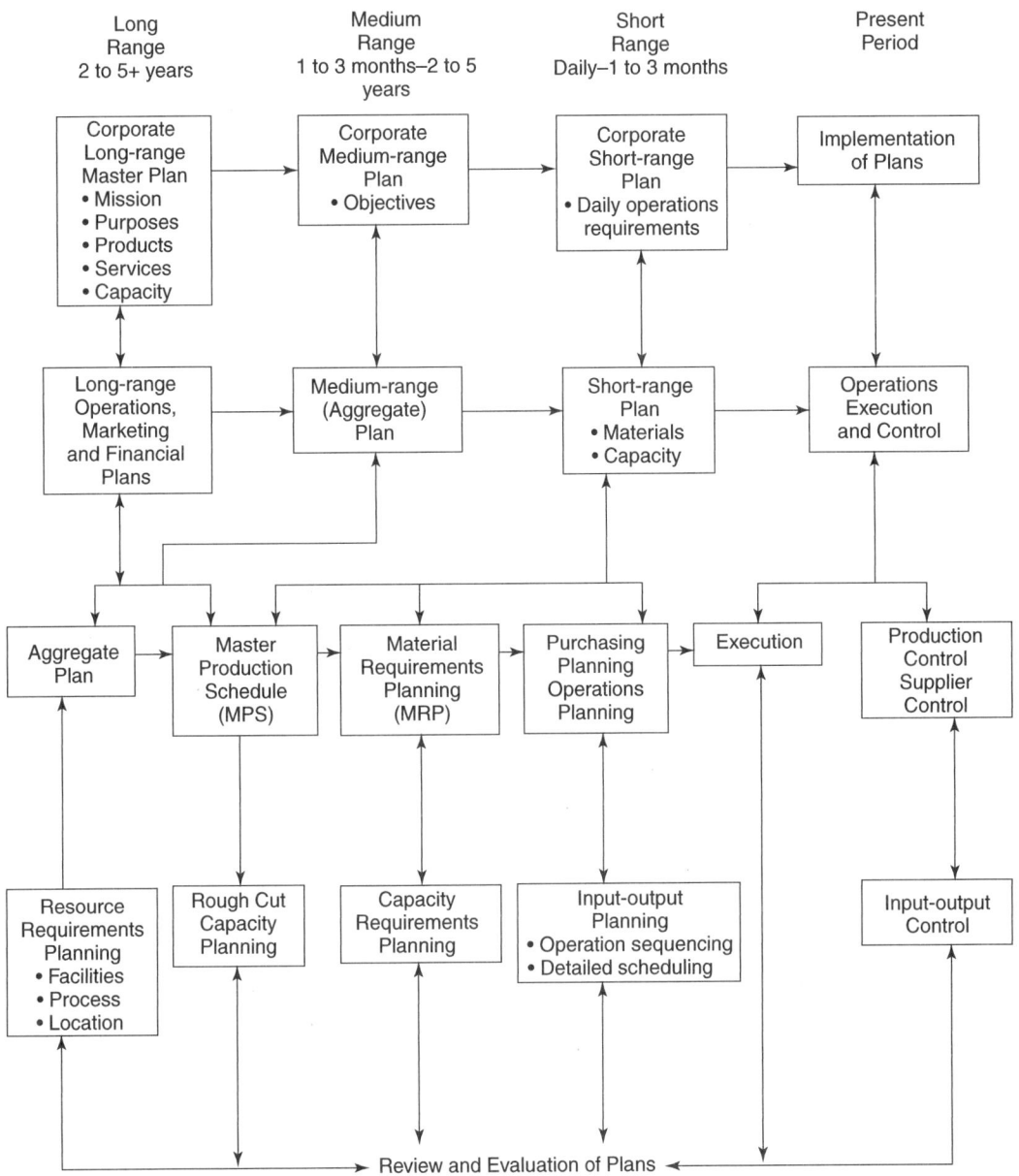

PRODUCT LIFE CYCLES AND STRATEGIES   The demand for the vast majority of products goes through the stages of growth, stability, and decay. However, the life spans of different products vary. Many toys have life spans of less than a year, whereas durable goods such as refrigerators have life spans of three or more years. The lengths of the different stages for a particular product line are determined by public acceptance, social and economic conditions, and the rate of development of competing technical and styling innovations. For example, a product in the decay stage of its life may be buoyed by healthy economic conditions and merchandising. However, unless it is redesigned, its demand is likely to decrease at an increasing rate. By the same token, the right new product at the propitious moment in a technological-social sense may experience greater demand than economic conditions alone would warrant. This type of analysis leads to recommendations concerning the development of new product lines and the phasing out of some existing products.

Market entry and exit decisions usually have a major effect on manufacturing. Most new products experience a relatively large number of engineering changes as the design develops, and demand tends to be relatively low in the early phases of a developing market. Low demand and frequent variations in design recommend different capacity

Exhibit 200.12 *Product Life Cycle*

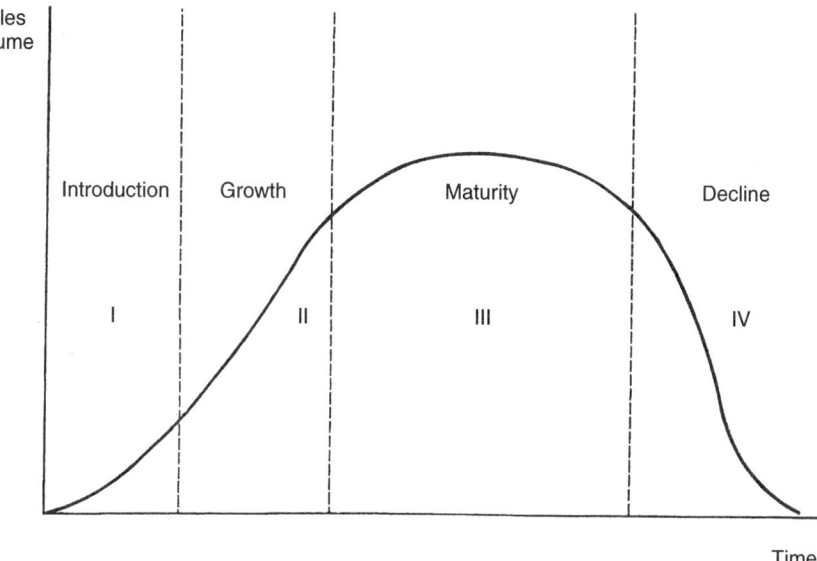

and processes than the high demand and stable design found in established products. However, successful entry early in the life of a new product usually earns better returns.

The product life cycle development is often grouped into four stages, for convenience of discussion, as shown in Exhibit 200.12. Stage I is product introduction, Stage II is growth, Stage III is maturity, Stage IV is decline. The production facilities appropriate for each stage of production are different. In Stage I the product is usually assembled from purchased parts available from other manufacturers. Parts that are manufactured in-house may be built at special prototyping facilities. Many new products die at this stage for lack of demand.

The products that enter Stage II often are manufactured in a job-shop environment or perhaps a batch-flow environment. Both environments provide plenty of volume flexibility. Products that become very successful usually are moved to a dedicated-flow environment built specifically to manufacture that product for the maturity stage. As the product declines, surplus machines may be removed from the facility, or the facility itself may be converted to a batch-flow facility.

In a just-in-time (JIT) system employing a U-shaped line, the facility often is built during the growth stage with sufficient capacity to handle the eventual demand. Because the workers all are multifunctional, changes in demand during Stages II, III, and IV are accommodated by adding or subtracting workers. In the extreme, one worker may walk a part through every stage of manufacture. For non-JIT environments, matching the volume of demand to the proper production environment is a crucial part of competitiveness. For this reason, product managers who stay with the product commonly are employed in addition to the facility managers. For the product manager, it is important to realize that the elements of competition may vary from stage to stage. In Stage I the most important determinant of success is product performance. In Stage II, as the product gains popularity, the most important determinant is price and availability. In Stage III the product often becomes a commodity, competing purely on price. In Stage IV the competition returns to price and availability, as competitors cease production and service parts are important.

Manufacturing Planning

Strategic, long-range, manufacturing planning decisions may be grouped in the following four major areas:

1. Value-added decisions
2. Facility size, location, and degree of focus decisions
3. Manufacturing management philosophy decisions, which include decisions concerning human resource management polices, production and inventory control systems, and management approaches such as just-in-time and total quality management
4. Process flow and facility layout decisions.

These decisions should be integrated to maintain consistency and to assure that they are mutually supportive.

VALUE-ADDED DECISIONS The term *value-added* refers to the additional utility provided the customer when a product is transformed by the manufacturing process or moved within the distribution system. Few, if any, major clothing manufacturers raise sheep from which to obtain wool for the clothing they manufacture. Some have woolen mills and others do not. The latter purchase material from various textile and woolen mills and manufacture the clothing. **Edison Brothers** in St. Louis purchases shoes from many different manufacturers and markets them through the hundreds of retail outlets it has throughout North America. Edison Brothers is an example of a company that adds value primarily through distribution and marketing activities. Other companies add value through final preparation, assembly, and packaging. Still others are involved in obtaining raw materials, processing the raw materials, fabricating components, and building the final product. An example of the latter is an oil company that has oil exploration activities, operates oil wells and refineries, and also runs its own distribution systems and retail outlets.

FACILITY SIZE, LOCATION, AND FOCUS DECISIONS Facility size is a function of economies and diseconomies of scale, both of which are influenced by the labor- versus capital-intensity of the manufacturing process, the manufacturing focus desired, and the desired number of employees per location. These strategic decisions affect the number of facilities and the task of production and inventory management (PIM).[92]

MANUFACTURING MANAGEMENT PHILOSOPHY DECISIONS The values, norms, and policies that are the underpinning of production procedures and systems should be consistent with the overall organization philosophy. For example, an organization philosophy of "each employee is an associate" will affect hiring, employee development opportunities, layoff policies, and employee participation in decision making. In a similar manner, a policy of "24-hour delivery" should affect production and inventory management practices.

PROCESS FLOW AND FACILITY LAYOUT DECISIONS Product, market, and production plans frequently require additional resources such as facilities and equipment that in turn require financing. Normal operations require working capital, and sales generate income. The financial capability of the organization to carry out the long-range plans should be verified. After the availability of the required resources is assured, a commitment can be made to the production plan.

Integrating Plans

Commitment to a strategic plan does not occur until the long-range planning cycle—including preparation of the business forecast, product and sales planning, production planning, resource planning, and financial planning—has been completed.

Exhibit 200.11 depicts the major long-range-level planning activities and their interaction. Although PIM personnel play a major role only in production planning and resource planning, an understanding of their role is enhanced by a discussion of all five activities.

Product, sales, and production planning should be conducted interactively with resource planning. The availability of facilities, processes, equipment, and personnel depends on the lead time for acquiring the facilities and equipment, the organization's financial strength, technological difficulty of the tasks, and the availability of the required engineering and other personnel.

New products may require additional personnel, such as design and process engineers, as well as additional manufacturing capacity. Geographic expansion of the market usually requires additional distribution facilities, and an increased aggregate volume increases manufacturing capacity requirements.

The determination of personnel requirements in areas such as engineering and marketing is the task of the management of those functional areas. Calculation of manufacturing capacity requirements is the point at which PIM usually enters long-range planning. Distribution capacity requirements may be calculated by marketing, PIM, or a joint task force of those two departments. Facilities and equipment required for manufacturing and distribution are affected by value-added, location, plant size, and process decisions.

The Business Plan

The planned aggregate sales income, the planned cost of sales, and all other planned operating expenses for all products and services per period provide a basis for calculating the planned net income of an organization. This enables the organization to calculate the planned return on investment (ROI) or return on assets (ROA) and to estimate what funds will be available for either distribution to stockholders or reinvestment in the organization.

The business plan, the sales plan, and the production plan must be consistent and mutually supportive. Exhibit 200.13 uses October data developed from the data in Exhibits 200.15, 200.16, and 200.17 through 200.20 to illustrate the relationships among the production plan, the sales plan, and the business plan. For example, the planned income is based on planned shipments, the sales prices of the products shipped, the projected cost of sales, and other allocated costs. The sales plan projects sales (shipments) of 700 units of Product Group A in October at $45 each, thus generating $31,500 revenue. The total variable and fixed costs allocated to these units is $28,000. Subtracting the total costs from revenue renders a net income of $3,500 for Product Group A in October.

During October the planned income from the sales of Product Groups A, B, and C is $5,300. The natural question is, From where do the income and cost values come? The income of each product group is based on the projected weighted average sales price for the anticipated (forecast) product sales of the items that constitute the group (the product mix). The total revenue is the sum of the revenue from all groups. The variable costs of each group are calculated and then added to the other costs allocated to the group to obtain the group's total costs. Adding the costs of all product groups renders the aggregate costs. The net total income then equals the difference between the total revenue and the total costs. (The costs are a natural derivative of the resource requirements planning system, as described in the following sections; the projected revenue is a natural derivative of the sales plan.)

Production Planning

The necessary inputs for production planning are:

1. The product and sales plan
2. The management strategy and policy concerning the aggregate planning problem
3. The manufacturing processes for the different product groups
4. The efficiency and capacity of work centers
5. The identification of bottleneck work centers
6. The allocation of manufacturing resources (plants and equipment) to producing specific products

Production planning uses the information from product and sales planning to plan the aggregate rates of production and the inventory levels by time period for groups of products. Output levels are specified in the broadest terms possible: tons, barrels, yards, dollars, and standard hours of production. The specificity of product line and product differentiation required at this level depends on the nature of the product and the equipment required to manufacture it. For example, automotive engine blocks usually are machined on a specially designed, high-speed, automated or semiautomated line. A line built for the manufacture of four-cylinder engines ordinarily cannot be used to manufacture six-cylinder engines. Thus, the long-range production plan must separate four- and six-cylinder engine requirements to obtain a valid estimate of facility and equipment requirements. This may be accomplished merely by multiplying the estimated total demand by the anticipated proportion of the various engine sizes.

Smoothing of production to compensate for varying seasonal demand rates is planned in this time frame. The important point is that it is the production plan that establishes customer service level goals, target inventory levels, size of the backlog if any, production rates, size of the workforce, levels of hiring and firing, and plans for overtime and subcontracting. The production plan is the basis for determining capacity requirements that must be consistent with capacity availability.

The objective of the production plan is to provide sufficient finished goods by period to meet the sales plan objectives while staying within financial and production capacity constraints. When demand varies from period to period, planning production to exceed demand in one period can provide inventory to fill excessive demand in a following period.

Exhibit 200.14 illustrates a production plan for the three product groups shown in Exhibit 200.13. The number of product groups used to encompass all products should be no greater than that required to determine resource requirements. Individual production plans may be required for divisions or plants within a firm. As the production period approaches, planning becomes more refined and a master production schedule (MPS) is developed. The MPS is a statement of all anticipated manufacturing of items within product groups by planning period. In some firms the production plan is developed in greater detail into what is called a medium-range plan and later is refined into an MPS. In others, the production plan is unfolded directly into the MPS at some point, nine months prior to execution, for example. In other firms the production plan and the MPS may be one and the same. The approach selected by a specific organization depends on the diversity of its product lines, the manufacturing processes, and its data-processing capabilities.

Exhibit 200.13 *Relationship Among Sales, Production, and Financial Plans*

Product Group		Production (units) Sept.	Production (units) Oct.			Financial (dollars)		
A				Cost	$ 40			
				Price	45			
	Production		720	Production costs	28,800			
	Shipments	180	700	Revenue	31,500	Cost of sales	$28,000	
	Ending inventory		200	Ending inventory	8,000	Change in inventory	800	Income $3,500
B				Cost	$ 33			
				Price	38			
	Production		240	Production costs	7,920			
	Shipments	250	250	Revenue	9,500	Cost of sales	$ 8,250	
	Ending inventory		240	Ending inventory	7,920	Change in inventory	−330	Income $1,250
C				Cost	$ 35			
				Price	40			
	Production		160	Production costs	5,600			
	Shipments	50	110	Revenue	4,400	Cost of sales	$ 3,850	
	Ending inventory		100	Ending inventory	3,500	Change in inventory	1,750	Income $ 550
							Total income	$5,300

Aggregate Financial Plan

Revenue	$45,400
Cost of Sales	40,100
Income	$ 5,300
Ending inventory	$19,420

Exhibit 200.14 Two-Year Production Plan, Product Groups A, B, and C

		Month							Quarter			
Period	Sept.	Oct.	Nov.	Dec.	Jan.	Feb.	Mar.	2	3	4	1	2	3
Weeks/Period[1]	5	4	4	5	4	4	5	13	13	13	13	13	13
Production Days/Period		20	18	22	19	19	25	64	63	60	63	64	63
Group A													
Production rate: units/day[2]		36	36	36	36	36	36	36	40	40	40	40	40
Production		720	648	792	684	684	900	2,304	2,520	2,400	2,520	2,560	2,520
Shipments		700	760	850	500	500	875	2,500	2,500	2,300	2,600	2,700	2,700
Ending inventory	180	200	88	30	214	398	423	227	247	347	267	127	−53
Group B													
Production rate: units/day[3]		12	12	12	12	4	4	4	4/12	12	12/4	4	4/12
Production		240	216	264	228	76	100	256	444	720	404	256	444
Shipments		250	300	350	250	60	180	180	370	900	370	180	370
Ending inventory	250	240	156	70	48	64	104	180	254	74	108	184	258
Group C													
Production rate: units/day[4]		8	8	8	8	20	20	20	22/9	9	9/22	22	22/9
Production		160	144	176	152	380	500	1,280	1,034	540	1,060	1,408	1,034
Shipments		110	115	120	180	400	460	1,340	1,060	500	1,100	1,450	1,000
Ending inventory	50	100	129	185	157	137	177	117	91	131	91	49	83

[1]The weeks per month in each quarter are assigned arbitrarily as 4, 4, 5. For example, April and May have 4 weeks, June has 5. The plant does not close for vacation.
[2]The production rate is 36 units per day for the first three quarters, 40 units per day thereafter. There is level production throughout the year. The rate change is due to long-term positive demand trend.
[3]The production rate is 12 units per day for September through January and 4 units per day for February through August, due to seasonal sales.
[4]The production rate is 8 units per day for September through January and 20 units per day for February through August. These rates increase to 9 and 22 units per day, respectively, due to long-term positive demand trend.

362   MODULE 200. OPERATIONS MANAGEMENT

The term *aggregate planning* denotes planning for a group in order to obtain a view of the planned total results. An aggregate plan may encompass a product line; the output of a plant, division, or entire organization; or planned sales in a geographic area. Aggregate financial plans are expressed in dollars and are based on the corresponding sales, production, employment, and inventory plans. All of the latter are expressed in both the appropriate units and dollars. In a large organization the grand aggregate is the total of the aggregate plans for all divisions, incorporating the sales of many different products in many different markets. The example developed in this section is relatively simple; there are only three product lines (Groups A, B, and C) and only one market. Aggregate plans are developed in the long range and used through the medium and short ranges as an overall control and guide for more detailed plans, such as the MPS. On occasion they may be modified in the medium or short ranges to cope with unforeseen developments, such as a plant fire or flood, an energy crisis, an abrupt shift in demand due to a strike at a competitor, or a sharp price decrease by a competitor.

Resource Requirements Planning

The resources required by the production plan in any period include labor, materials, facilities, and equipment (usually identified by work center), and the funds required to pay the employees, purchase the materials, and pay other expenses. (This analysis omits resources required for capital improvements, such as building new facilities, purchasing new equipment, or substantially modifying existing facilities and equipment.)

The resource requirements are determined in the following manner:

1. Obtain the planned production for each product group by period.
2. Determine the resource profile for each product group.
3. Determine the materials profile for each product group.
4. Using the planned production, resource profile, and materials profile, calculate the resource and material requirements.

Resource Profile

The product group *resource profile* states the resources required to produce one unit of a product group. It is based on the anticipated product mix of the group and includes the processing time required for all components and subassemblies and for the final assembly. Exhibit 200.15 illustrates how assembly labor is determined for Product Group A, which consists of three different items: 1, 2, and 3. The anticipated percentage of each item in the group is multiplied by the standard assembly time for the item. These results are then summed to obtain the standard assembly time for the average item in Product Group A. For example, Item 1 sales are forecast to be 50 percent of Product Group A total sales and to have a standard assembly time of 0.342 hours. Multiplying 0.50 by 0.342 gives 0.171 hours. Adding 0.171 hours to the values obtained in a similar computation for Items 2 and 3 gives an average assembly time of 0.301 hours for Product Group A, as shown in Exhibit 200.15.

Using the information in Exhibit 200.15 concerning the labor (time) required for assembling a typical unit of Product Group A, and similar information for all of the product groups and resource centers, the resource profiles for Product Groups A, B, and C are developed as shown in Exhibit 200.16.

Since all of the processes required to produce a complex assembly and its components must be included, and since many of the components must be manufactured a week or so in advance of the assembly activities, the timing of the requirements for various resources must be recognized. This is accomplished using lead-time offset information as

Exhibit 200.15 *Assembly Labor for Average Unit, Product Group A*

Item	Typical Percentage (1)	Standard Assembly Hours per Unit (2)	Average Assembly Time (1) × (2)
1	0.50	0.342	0.171
2	0.30	0.294	0.088
3	0.20	0.210	0.042
	1.00		0.301

Exhibit 200.16 *Resource Profiles for Product Groups A, B, and C Average Standard Hours per Unit*

Resource Center	Standard Hours A	B	C	Week
Assembly	0.301	0.285	0.256	1
Electrical subassembly	0.274	0.222	0.241	2
Mechanical subassembly	0.250	0.185	0.241	2
CNC machining	0.112	0.098	0.108	3
Other	0.205	0.182	0.198	3
Total	1.142	0.972	1.044	

Exhibit 200.17 *Lead-Time Offsets, Product 1*

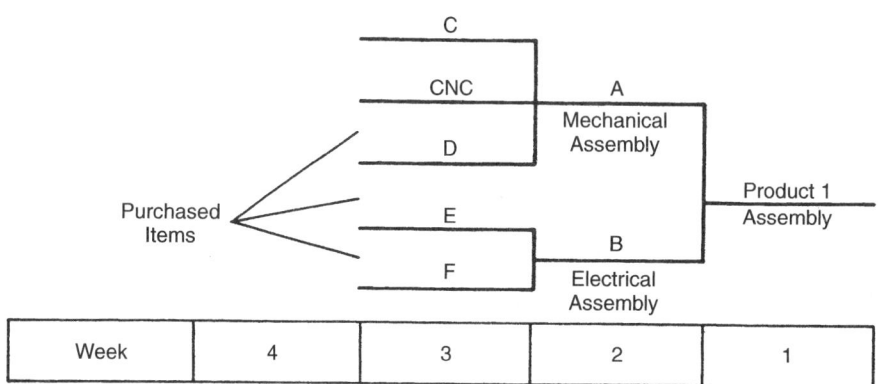

shown in Exhibit 200.17. This lead-time offset information reveals that the mechanical subassembly is usually completed one week prior to the final assembly and that the processing of components in the CNC machining department takes place two weeks prior to the final assembly. This information is especially important when planning on a weekly basis, but it will not affect less-refined plans made on a monthly basis. As an organization achieves just-in-time production, most resources will be required in the same week.

Resource Requirements

The standard labor hours required for each product group in a resource center during a period are obtained by multiplying a product group's standard time per unit in the resource center by the quantity of the group to be produced during the period. For example, multiplying the 0.301 hours required for assembling one unit of Product Group A by the 720 units planned in October renders a requirement of 216.72 standard hours for Product Group A during October in the assembly department. Performing similar calculations for Product Groups B and C and adding the requirements for all groups gives 326.08 standard hours required in the assembly department for Product Groups A, B, and C during October. To arrive at the actual hours required, the efficiency of the resource centers must be considered. Efficiency can be measured as follows:

$$\text{Efficiency} = \frac{\text{Standard Hours}}{\text{Actual Hours}}$$

which may be transformed to

$$\text{Actual Hours} = \frac{\text{Standard Hours}}{\text{Efficiency}}$$

Exhibit 200.18 Resource Requirements (Standard and Actual Hours in October)

Product Group	Assembly	Electrical Subassembly	Mechanical Subassembly	CNC Machining	Other
A	216.72	197.28	180.00	80.64	147.60
B	68.40	53.28	44.40	23.52	43.68
C	40.96	38.56	38.56	17.28	31.68
Total standard hours	326.08	289.12	262.96	121.44	222.96
Efficiency	0.95	0.95	0.95	0.95	0.95
Actual hours	343.24	304.34	276.80	127.83	234.69

Exhibit 200.19 Comparison of Required and Available Capacity by Resource Center

Resource Center	A	B	C	Total	Available (demonstrated) Capacity	Deficiencies
Assembly	216.72	68.40	40.96	326.08	300	−26.08
Electrical subassembly	197.28	53.28	38.56	289.12	320	
Mechanical subassembly	180.00	44.40	38.56	262.96	280	
CNC machining	80.64	23.52	17.28	121.44	200	

In our example, the efficiency of the assembly department is 0.95. Thus, the actual total hours required for Product Groups A, B, and C in the assembly department during October is 343.24 hours. The resource requirements for all periods and all departments are calculated in the same manner. These values are shown in Exhibit 200.18.

It is important to note that control begins in the planning process as the planned resource requirements are compared to the available capacity as shown in Exhibit 200.19. The available capacity in standard hours is based on the actual output that each department (resource center) has achieved in standard hours of output in the recent past. Exhibit 200.19 reveals that sufficient capacity exists in all departments except assembly.

Financial Resources

The financial resources required are the sum of materials, direct labor, and all other costs. The direct labor costs per unit are equal to the cost of labor per hour times the estimated actual labor hours required. The total cost of labor in our example is $20 per hour, which includes wages and fringe benefits such as insurance, holidays, and vacation. For the typical unit of Product A, 1.142 standard hours are required. Using the efficiency equation shown earlier, the actual hours equal 1.142 ÷ 0.95 = 1.202. Thus, the labor cost per unit is $24.04 (1.202 × $20). This information is recorded in Exhibit 200.20 along with the labor requirements and costs for Product Groups A, B and C.

Materials costs are available from the bill of material, which lists all purchased materials and components as well as their costs. The composite cost per unit of a product group is obtained in the same manner as the average labor cost per unit. That is, the typical materials costs of Product Group A equal the weighted average of the materials costs of the three products in the group.

Exhibit 200.20 *Total Cost per Unit*

Product Group	Total Standard Hours	Total Actual Hours	Cost of Labor	Cost of Materials	Sales and Administrative Costs	Total Cost
A	1.142	1.202	$24.04	$7.96	$8.00	$40.00
B	0.972	1.023	20.46	5.54	7.00	33.00
C	1.044	1.099	21.98	6.02	7.00	35.00

Integration of Plans

Exhibits 200.14 and 200.21 depict an example of an integrated sales, production, and financial plan for the next 24 months. Exhibit 200.14 gives the shipments (sales), production, and inventory investment in units. Exhibit 200.21 lists the same information, as well as the change in inventory and net income in dollars. Both plans are stated in monthly periods for the next 6 months and in quarterly periods for the last 18 months of the two-year plan. It is a common practice to present plans for the more proximate periods in smaller time increments. For example, master planning and rough-cut capacity planning will develop weekly plans for the first few months.

Although *aggregate planning* is a generic term covering many different plans, references to "the aggregate planning problem" are concerned with the specific decision situation described in the remainder of this section.

The Aggregate Planning Problem and Capacity Planning

The aggregate planning problem concerns the allocation of resources such as personnel, facilities, equipment, and inventory so that the planned products and services (the output) are available when needed. The aggregate plan usually covers a 12- to 24-month period, and as time passes, may be updated monthly or quarterly. Prior long-range facility decisions limit the capacity available and may limit aggregate planning options. Thus, long-range facility planning must consider the aggregate planning strategy.

Let us examine the cause of the aggregate planning problem and some approaches for meeting the challenge. Not only do snow blowers and lawn mowers have seasonal demand, but furniture, appliances, automobiles, clothing, small tools, and many other items have demand with substantial seasonal variation, year after year. Variation in the demand for consumer goods generates seasonal demand for the raw materials, components, and supplies used in their manufacture. Exhibit 200.22 shows three typical situations: (1) relatively stable demand—bread and milk, for example; (2) single-cycle demand, or one high- and one low-demand cycle annually—retail sales of many items at Christmas, for example; and (3) dual high and low cycles annually—shaving lotion sales peak at Christmas and Father's Day, for example. Other seasonal variations in demand are possible, but examination of these three patterns will provide a basis for studying the concepts and techniques useful for aggregate planning under all situations.

With relatively steady demand, there is no aggregate planning problem. Facilities, capacity, the workforce, and materials are planned for production at that steady rate. However, seasonal demand patterns present management with the following three options:

1. Modify or manage demand.
2. Manage supply (output) in the following ways:
   a. Provide ample capacity and flexibility to have the output match demand (the chase strategy).
   b. Produce at a level rate and store some of the output to meet peak demand (the level production strategy).
3. Some combination of 1 and 2.

Exhibit 200.21 Two-Year Production Plan (Units and Dollars)

			Month								Quarter			
Period	Sept.	Oct.	Nov.	Dec.	Jan.	Feb.	Mar.	2	3	4	1	2	3
Group A													
Production		720	648	792	684	684	900	2,304	2,520	2,400	2,520	2,560	2,520
Shipments		700	760	850	500	500	875	2,500	2,500	2,300	2,600	2,700	2,700
Inventory (End)	180	200	88	30	214	398	423	227	247	347	267	127	−53
Cost of Sales		$28,000	$30,400	$34,000	$20,000	$20,000	$35,000	$100,000	$100,000	$92,000	$104,000	$108,000	$108,000
Revenue		$31,500	$34,200	$38,250	$22,500	$22,500	$39,375	$112,500	$112,500	$103,500	$117,000	$121,500	$121,500
Profit		$ 3,500	$ 3,800	$ 4,250	$ 2,500	$ 2,500	$ 4,375	$ 12,500	$ 12,500	$ 13,000	$ 13,000	$ 13,500	$ 13,500
Inventory value	$7,200	$ 8,000	$ 3,520	$ 1,200	$ 8,560	$15,920	$16,920	$ 9,080	$ 9,880	$ 13,880	$ 10,680	$ 5,080	($ 2,120)
Group B													
Production		240	216	264	228	76	100	256	444	720	404	256	444
Shipments		250	300	350	250	60	60	180	370	900	370	180	370
Inventory (End)	250	240	156	70	48	64	104	180	254	74	108	184	258
Cost of Sales		$ 8,250	$ 9,900	$11,550	$ 8,250	$ 1,980	$ 1,980	$ 5,940	$ 12,210	$ 29,700	$ 12,210	$ 5,940	$ 12,210
Revenue		$ 9,500	$11,400	$13,300	$ 9,500	$ 2,280	$ 2,280	$ 6,840	$ 14,060	$ 34,200	$ 14,060	$ 6,840	$ 14,060
Profit		$ 1,250	$ 1,500	$ 1,750	$ 1,250	$ 300	$ 300	$ 900	$ 1,850	$ 4,500	$ 1,850	$ 900	$ 1,850
Inventory value	$8,250	$ 7,920	$ 5,148	$ 2,310	$ 1,584	$ 2,112	$ 3,432	$ 5,940	$ 8,382	$ 2,442	$ 3,564	$ 6,072	$ 8,514
Group C													
Production		160	144	176	152	380	500	1,280	1,034	540	1,060	1,408	1,034
Shipments		110	115	120	180	400	460	1,340	1,060	500	1,100	1,450	1,000
Inventory (End)	50	100	129	185	157	137	177	117	91	131	91	49	83
Cost of Sales		$ 3,850	$ 4,025	$ 4,200	$ 6,300	$14,000	$16,100	$ 46,900	$ 37,100	$ 17,500	$ 38,500	$ 50,750	$ 35,000
Revenue		$ 4,400	$ 4,600	$ 4,800	$ 7,200	$16,000	$18,400	$ 53,600	$ 42,400	$ 20,000	$ 44,000	$ 58,000	$ 40,000
Profit		$ 550	$ 575	$ 600	$ 900	$ 2,000	$ 2,300	$ 6,700	$ 5,300	$ 2,500	$ 5,500	$ 7,250	$ 5,000
Inventory value	$1,750	$ 3,500	$ 4,515	$ 6,475	$ 5,495	$ 4,795	$ 6,195	$ 4,095	$ 3,185	$ 4,585	$ 3,185	$ 1,715	$ 2,905

Exhibit 200.22 *Typical Monthly Aggregate Demand Patterns*

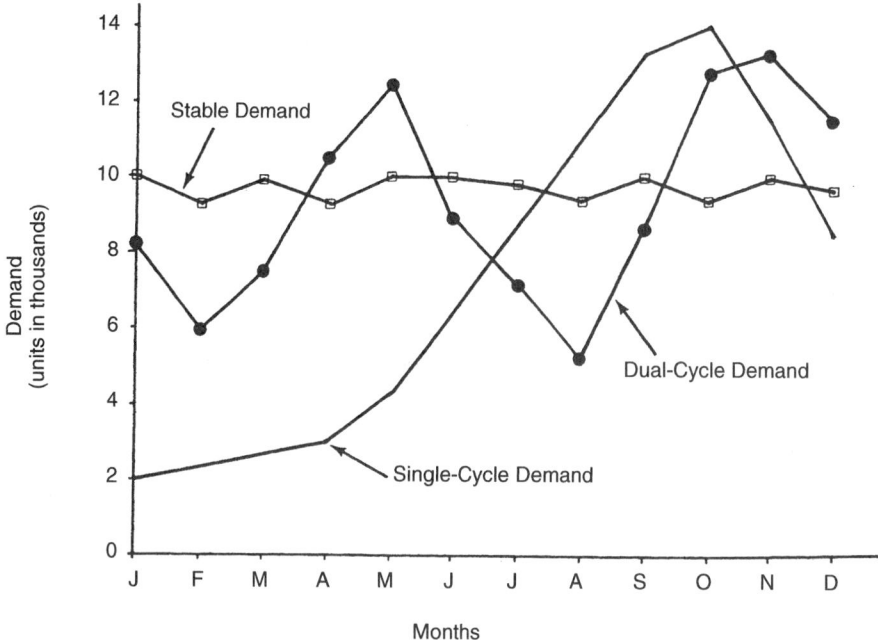

Managing Demand

Changing the demand pattern can reduce the aggregate planning problem and in some cases uncover other sources of income and profit. Possible methods of modifying demand include the following:

1. **Complementary products.** Developing and marketing new products whose primary demand is in the present off-season can reduce the demand-capacity imbalance. For example, some lawn equipment companies have been successful in manufacturing and marketing snow removal equipment, while swimsuit manufacturers have entered the ski-apparel business. Many service organizations have developed complementary services: combining heating and air conditioning repair; adding weekend courses and evening continuing education programs at educational institutions traditionally offering only weekday programs; and adding a breakfast menu at a fast-food restaurant.

2. **Promotion, advertising, and price incentives.** The right combination of a desired service or product, value for the price, and promotion can increase customer demand in normally slack periods. Major league baseball in the United States has been very successful in using attractions such as glove night and jacket night to increase attendance at games that normally have small- to medium-sized crowds.

    Reduced pricing can shift demand to periods that normally have low demand. Local transit companies offer shoppers reduced bus fares in nonrush hours. Theaters often have reduced prices for matinee and dinner-hour shows, and many restaurants have early bird specials. Other examples include reduced rates for off-season travel and time period differentials in long-distance telephone rates. Special financing arrangements may also be used to manage demand. For example, department stores offer November purchasers the option of a late January payment without interest. Similarly, some manufacturers of recreational boats offer retailers the option of later payment without interest for purchases in the preseason months. Thus, the manufacturing company reduces its storage space needs and obtains the sale, while the retailer avoids the financial cost of the inventory and has a better opportunity for early sales to the final customer.

3. **Reservations and backlogs.** Service organizations frequently ask or require that customers reserve capacity by means of an appointment. This could include a reservation for dinner where a specific time is reserved, or a specific space reservation, such as a hotel room or airline seat. This practice enables both the customer and the service provider to plan with greater certainty. In other instances, customers are willing to enter a waiting line for a service. For example, customers often must wait until a restaurant table, service technician, or emergency room physician is available. The service provider agrees to serve the customer as soon as the capacity is available.

Similar conditions exist in manufacturing, especially in a seller's market. The customer must order well in advance of the actual need date. Thus, the customer places an order for later delivery (similar to an appointment), and the manufacturer produces to a backlog of orders. For example, the **Custom Shirt Shop** of New Jersey has retail outlets throughout the United States that accept the customer's order with payment. The factory then mails the tailor-made shirts to the customer six to eight weeks later. Using a backlog as a planning approach is feasible only when the customer perceives the quality of the product worthy of the wait—and the cost.

Although modifying demand often makes an important contribution to solving the aggregate planning problem, it rarely solves it completely. Other actions are required to manage the supply so that it meets surges in demand. The primary methods of doing this are described next.

Managing Supply

Two basic strategies represent opposite ends of the spectrum of supply management approaches used in solving the aggregate planning problem. One, the *chase strategy*, is designed to allow for sufficient capacity and flexibility to enable production output to match the demand. Using this approach, the production rate may vary widely, as illustrated in Exhibit 200.23. The rationale of the chase strategy is to avoid high inventory carrying cost when demand varies substantially by varying employment levels, using overtime, subcontracting, and/or assigning production employees to maintenance or training activities during low-demand periods. In some cases, such as agriculture, this is a necessity; harvesting must take place when the crop is ready. It also is a necessity for some service organizations. For example, the hospital emergency room must be able to handle trauma cases as they arrive. However, the chase strategy is not necessary or economically practical in many situations. Examples include situations in which employees have a guaranteed annual wage and those in which equipment capacity is well below the maximum demand rate.

At the other end of the spectrum is the *level production strategy*. This strategy is designed to allow for the same production rate throughout the year and to have inventory or backorders absorb variations in demand, as illustrated in Exhibit 200.24. This makes sense when demand is relatively stable, but following this approach in some situations, such as the manufacture of artificial Christmas trees, will result in excessive inventory carrying costs.

Traditionally, the aggregate planning problem has been viewed as an analysis of the trade-off between production rate change costs and inventory carrying costs. However, more flexible manufacturing and service systems are being developed in many organizations. These systems have the ability to change output rates quickly and inexpensively.

Exhibit 200.23 *The Chase Production Strategy*

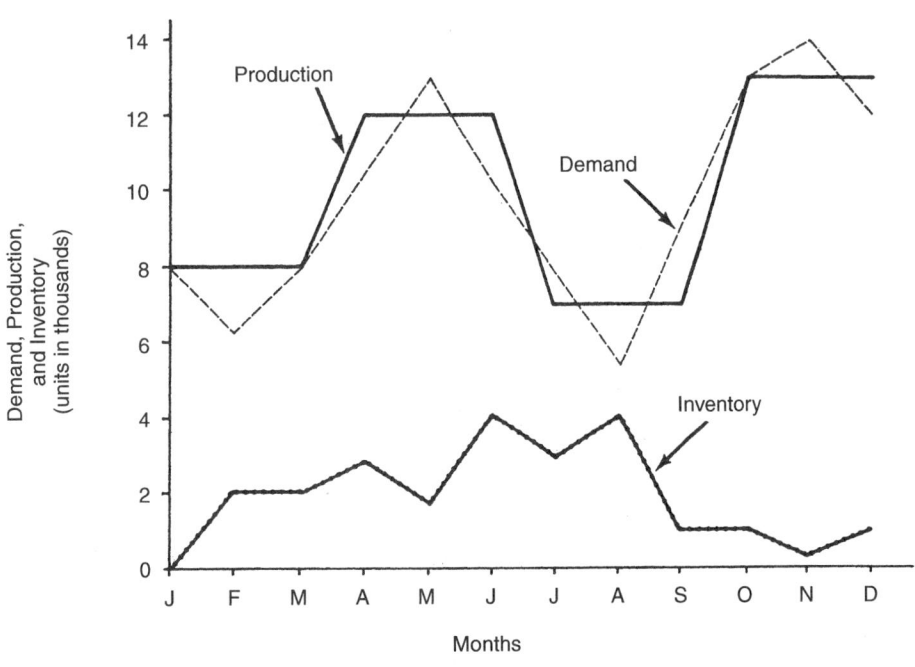

Exhibit 200.24 *The Level Production Strategy*

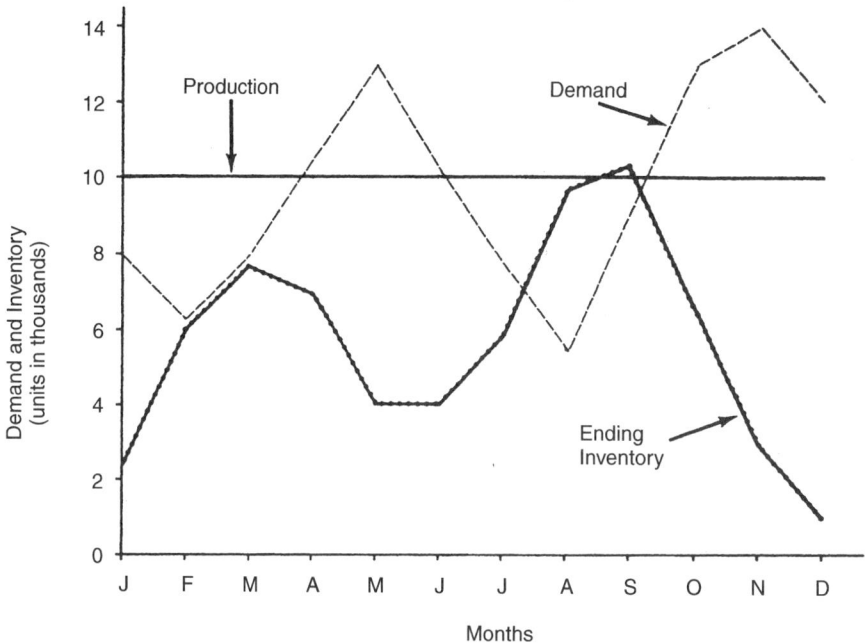

Costs Relevant to the Aggregate Planning Decision

The costs resulting from the aggregate planning decision fall into two major categories: (1) inventory costs and (2) production rate change costs.

INVENTORY COSTS Inventory costs include the following: (1) the costs of carrying inventory and (2) the capital costs of added storage facilities beyond those required for level production. Manufacturing items in one period for sale in later periods during which forecast demand exceeds planned production results in inventory carrying costs. These carrying costs include the costs of storage, capital invested, insurance, taxes for the items held in storage, as well as breakage, deterioration, and obsolescence. In addition, increasing inventory beyond certain levels requires additional storage capacity, which requires additional storage facilities, equipment, and possibly personnel. Furthermore, when working capital requires additional debt, interest rates may be increased due to the altered capital structure of the organization. This, in turn, may increase the carrying cost rate.

Management often views inventory as occupying free space—that is, space not useful for any other purpose. This is misleading. **Marion Laboratories, Inc.,** of Kansas City has reduced its inventory space requirements by more than 75,000 square feet through improved inventory management. **Miller Fluid Power** of Bensenville, Illinois, has achieved similar savings. Both companies achieved these savings through increased production flexibility and improved production planning, purchasing, and aggregate planning. Both have also converted this space to income-producing activities. Exhibit 200.25 depicts the general nature of the inventory costs that affect the aggregate planning decision. Note that carrying costs increase at a constant rate from that point at which inventory exists. Discontinuities occur when additional capacity is required (Point B). As inventory shortages (negative inventory investments) increase, backorder and stockout costs rise exponentially.

PRODUCTION RATE CHANGE COSTS Production rate change costs include the following items:

1. Facilities and equipment (greater capacity)
2. Hiring and releasing employees
3. Overtime and undertime
4. Part-time and temporary personnel
5. Subcontracting
6. Cooperative agreements

Exhibit 200.25 *Aggregate Inventory Costs versus Inventory Investment*

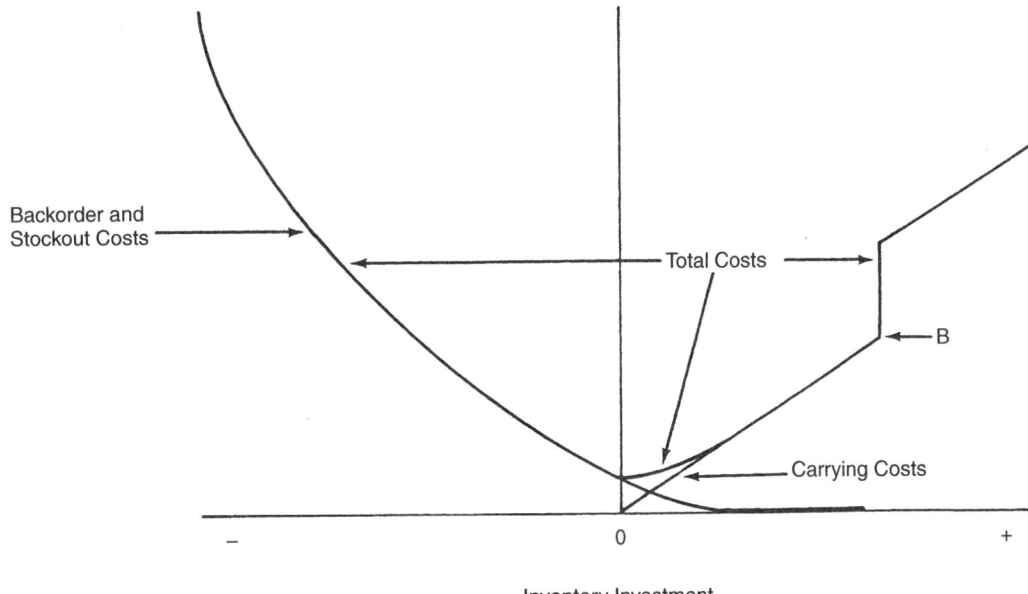

Facility and Equipment Costs The processing capacity required to match peaks in demand (a chase strategy) is greater than that required to maintain a level production rate. This often means that a larger facility and more equipment are required when initiating or changing to a chase strategy than when following a level production strategy. These decisions and costs are usually part of long-range facility planning. Thus, they provide de facto policy constraints within which aggregate capacity planning decisions must be made. For example, restaurants have a given number of tables, manufacturing plants have equipment with specific processing capabilities and speeds, and elementary schools have a limited number of classrooms and seats. Increasing the facility capacity usually takes longer than one year. The exception is when an existing facility can be purchased and readied for use in a few months. For example, beverage bottling companies occasionally are able to purchase and modify a competitor's plant in a relatively short time.

Hiring and Releasing Employees In some cases, increased capacity requires hiring and training new employees, an expensive activity. There are learning curve effects, and new employees usually require more instruction than experienced employees. In general, new employees are more susceptible to accidents, more likely to generate scrap, and generally less productive. In a tight market, new employees tend to be marginal and the situation is worsened. Even in a labor market with an abundance of skilled labor, the recruiting, selection, and training costs can be substantial.

Releasing employees increases unemployment insurance and often lowers morale and productivity. Organizations with a policy of seasonal layoffs often have difficulty obtaining the more competent employees. In addition, some labor agreements require the employer to pay furloughed employees a substantial portion of their base pay for periods of up to one year.

Overtime and Undertime Increasing labor capacity by scheduling overtime avoids the costs of hiring and training and does not increase the total fringe benefit costs for holidays, vacations, and insurance. However, direct costs usually increase due to both premium wages and decreasing productivity rates. This decrease in productivity is especially true when weekly overtime becomes excessive or lasts for more than a month or so. Undertime exists when there are more personnel on the payroll than required to produce the planned output. The costs of undertime can be reduced by having a flexible work force, flexible work rules governing personnel utilization, and appropriate planning. For example, **Sunnen Products Company,** a St. Louis manufacturer of honing equipment and hones, has avoided layoffs during slack periods for approximately a half century by (1) using production personnel for plant and equipment maintenance and factory layout changes, (2) running smaller production quantities (more setup time), and (3) providing training programs. Sunnen has operated profitably with a no-layoff policy, good wages and benefits, no strikes, and a productive workforce.

Part-Time and Temporary Personnel Part-time employment is often beneficial for both the employer and the employee. Many individuals in the workforce desire less than full-time employment and fill the organization's need for personnel to work only during peak demand periods. Relatively permanent part-time employees can be effective and efficient members of an organization. Some temporary personnel also return on a regular basis, every Christmas or summer for example, and possess much of the experience and knowledge of permanent full-time employees. Since the wages and fringe benefits of part-time employees are frequently less than those of full-time employees, there is a savings in both hours worked and rate of pay. On the other hand, since temporary and part-time employees have a minimal relationship with an organization, it is difficult to imbue them with a full understanding and appreciation of organizational goals and policies concerning critical areas, such as quality and customer service. Inconsistent quality and service from excessive use of poorly trained part-time or temporary personnel can more than counterbalance the cost savings.

Subcontracting Using other firms on a regular basis to perform manufacturing and professional services, such as engineering, marketing research, and software development, can be an effective method of balancing supply and demand. Subcontractors can be especially valuable when treated as an important link in the production chain. They should be provided with an adequate description of the product requirements (specifications, quantity, and due date) and production process as well as assistance with tooling. As trust and confidence develop, subcontractors often suggest improvements in the product design, manufacturing process, or marketing approach.

Subcontracting is a two-way street. Manufacturing companies producing a product for either an industrial market or the general public often subcontract their excess capacity. For example, the Kidder-Stacy Company of Springfield, Massachusetts, machines parts for other firms when their machine shop capacity is not being utilized fully.

Cooperative Agreements Working agreements based on the sharing of personnel and equipment to meet surges in demand or the need for expertise or equipment possessed by only one or two members of a group of organizations is common. For example, neighboring fire protection districts, hospitals, and police departments often share in providing paramedic services. Electric utilities often have cooperative agreements through power sharing. In addition, many universities offer off-campus courses and programs at community colleges, and some share faculty.

Aggregate Planning Models and Decision Techniques

Many different approaches are available for solving the aggregate planning problem. The more prominent methods include the following:

1. Trial and error or heuristic methods
2. Linear programming
3. Linear decision rules
4. Goal programming
5. Simulation

Trial and error is by far the most commonly used method. Since 1970, methods 2 through 4 have slowly gained greater acceptance as mathematical aggregate planning models. Recently, Goldratt has argued persuasively that interaction among constraints can be captured accurately only by simulation.[93]

Sensitivity Analysis

The aggregate production plan is based on a set of forecast demands and costs. They are treated as certain, but that is rarely the case. Important questions to answer include: If the actual demand is higher or lower than the forecast, what penalty will the organization pay in each case? Will the plan selected still be the most economical if the actual production rate change costs and inventory carrying costs turn out to be substantially different from the estimates?

In the latter case, the production planner can use the existing forecast demand and revised estimates, both higher and lower, of inventory carrying costs and production rate change costs to determine how sensitive the decision is to changes in these parameters. For example, if the cost of money changes rather quickly and the actual carrying cost per dollar of inventory per year is $0.40 instead of the forecasted $0.30, then the cost of the three plans change as shown in Exhibit 200.26.

The information in Exhibit 200.26 reveals that the compromise plan now costs nearly $4,000 more than the chase plan, whereas it had cost $10,525 less. Clearly, the economics of the decision are sensitive to a one-third increase in the carrying cost rate. The effect of changes of different degrees and direction, a decrease to $0.25 per dollar of inventory for example, and of changes in other costs can be examined in a similar manner.

Exhibit 200.26 *Sensitivity Analysis for Carrying Cost Rate Change*

	$0.30 Carrying Cost Rate			$0.40 Carrying Cost Rate		
Plan	Level	Chase	Compromise	Level	Chase	Compromise
Inventory	$84,125	$16,500	$59,125	$112,167	$22,000	$78,833
Hire/Fire	—	45,200	7,000	—	45,200	7,000
Overtime	—	15,050	—	—	15,050	—
Total	$84,125	$76,750	$66,125	$112,167	$82,250	$85,833

Controlling the Aggregate Plan

Once the plan is implemented and execution occurs, management must exercise control. Rarely are actual production and demand quantities equal to the planned quantities. Comparing actual cumulative demand and production with forecast demand and production enables the planner to determine if the situation is under control. Either unexpectedly high demand or actual production that is substantially below the planned level will result in insufficient inventories to fill all orders during subsequent peak demand periods. Unusually low demand or production exceeding the plan can result in excessive inventory. Tabulating and plotting actual and planned results enables the planner to determine if the spread between planned and actual requires remedial action.

Aggregate planning is a dynamic planning and control device. The aggregate plan is not static; it is reviewed monthly and revised as required.

Master Scheduling

Production planning and resource requirements planning are aggregate plans of production and capacity generally taking 1 to 10 years to complete execution. These plans combine (aggregate) similar products into product groups, combine demand into monthly totals, and often group personnel requirements across departments. The time comes when individual products and services must be scheduled at specific work centers. This is accomplished by *master scheduling*—producing a plan to manufacture specific items or provide specific services within a given time period.

Rough-cut capacity planning (RCCP) is the process of determining if the plan is feasible; it determines whether the organization has sufficient capacity to carry out the plan. Although RCCP is more refined than resource requirements planning (RRP), it is called "rough cut" because it is less refined than capacity requirements planning (CRP).

Exhibit 200.27 illustrates how master scheduling and rough-cut capacity planning relate to the corporate and operations planning.

Exhibit 200.27 *Relationship of Master Production Scheduling to Other Manufacturing Planning and Control Activities*

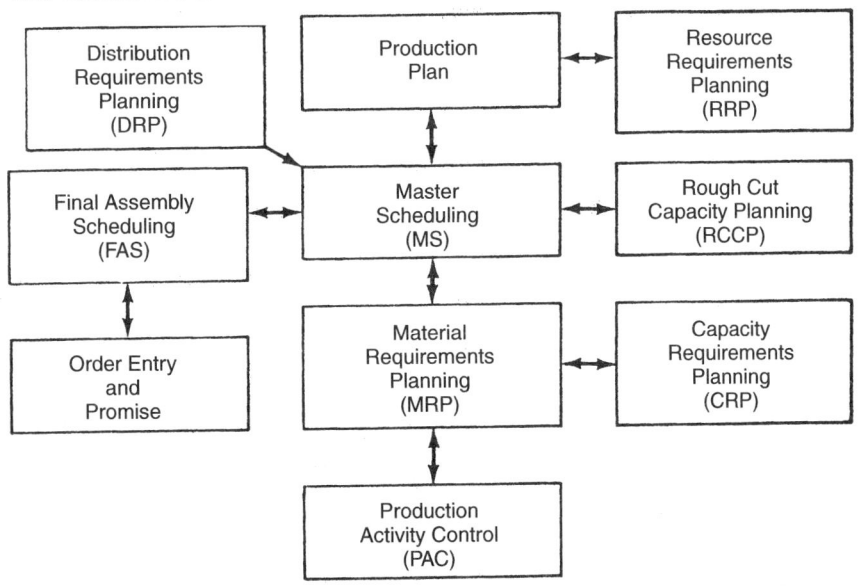

Exhibit 200.28 *Master Schedule, Product 1, Group A*

	Week			
	32	33	34	35
Forecast	150	100	50	50
MPS	169	169	22	0
Backlog (Orders booked)	110	80	5	15

Master Scheduling and the MPS

The master schedule (MS) is a presentation of the demand, including the forecast and the backlog (customer orders received), the master production schedule (the supply plan), the projected on hand (POH) inventory, and the available-to-promise (ATP) quantity. The master production schedule (MPS) is the primary output of the master scheduling process. The MPS specifies the end items the organization anticipates manufacturing each period. End items are either final products or the items from which final assemblies (products) are made. Thus, the MPS is the plan for providing the supply to meet the demand. An example of a master schedule only including the MPS and the backlog is shown in Exhibit 200.28.

The RCCP calculates the capacity, often in standard hours, required to achieve the MPS. It is based on the MPS.

Interfaces

The master schedule (MS) is a key link in the manufacturing planning and control chain. The MS interfaces with marketing, distribution planning, production planning, and capacity planning. It also drives the material requirements planning (MRP) system as shown in Exhibit 200.27.

Master scheduling calculates the quantity required to meet demand requirements from all sources. Exhibit 200.29 shows a case in which the distribution requirements are the gross requirements for the MS. Material requirements planning is used to calculate the quantity required. For example, the 15 units in inventory at the end of Week 3 are subtracted from the gross requirements, 85 units, of Week 4 to determine the net requirements of 70 units for Week 4.

The MS enables marketing to make legitimate delivery commitments to field warehouses and final customers. It enables production to evaluate capacity requirements in a more detailed manner. It also provides the necessary information for production and marketing to agree on a course of action when customer requests cannot be met by normal capacity. Finally, it provides to management the opportunity to ascertain whether the business plan and its strategic objectives will be achieved.

Exhibit 200.29 *Warehouse Requirements*

		Week							
Warehouse		1	2	3	4	5	6	7	8
Toronto		15	15	15	15	15	15	15	15
Los Angeles		30	30	30	30	30	30	35	35
St. Louis		20	10	20	20	10	20	20	20
Atlanta			20		20		20		20
Dallas		15	—	15	—	15	—	15	—
Total		80	75	80	85	70	85	85	90
Master Schedule									
Gross Requirements		80	75	80	85	70	85	85	90
POH*	250	170	95	15					
Net Requirements					70	70	85	85	90

*Beginning inventory = 250

Before describing the activities involved in creating and managing the MS, we examine the different organizational environments in which master scheduling takes place. These environments are determined in large measure by an organization's strategic response to the interests of customers and to the actions of competitors. An understanding of these environments, of the bill of material, and of the planning horizon is essential to the first stage of master planning activities—designing the master schedule.

The Production Environment

The competitive strategy of an organization may be any of the following:

1. Make finished items to stock (sell from finished goods inventory)
2. Assemble final products to order and make components, 20 subassemblies, and options to stock
3. Custom design and make-to-order

The competitive nature of the market and the strategy of the organization determine which of the MS alternates it should use. It is not unusual for an organization to have different strategies for different product lines and, thus, use different MS approaches.

Make-to-Stock

The competitive strategy of make-to-stock emphasizes immediate delivery of reasonably priced off-the-shelf standard items. In this environment the MPS is the anticipated build schedule of the items required to maintain the finished goods at the desired level. Quantities on the schedule are based on manufacturing economics and the forecast demand as well as desired safety-stock levels. An end item bill of material (BOM) (described later in the section) is used in this environment. Items may be produced either on a mass-production (continuous or repetitive) line or in batch production. Case I in Exhibit 200.30 represents this situation. Note that the MPS is the same as the final assembly schedule (FAS) in this case.

Exhibit 200.30 *Some Possible Relationships*

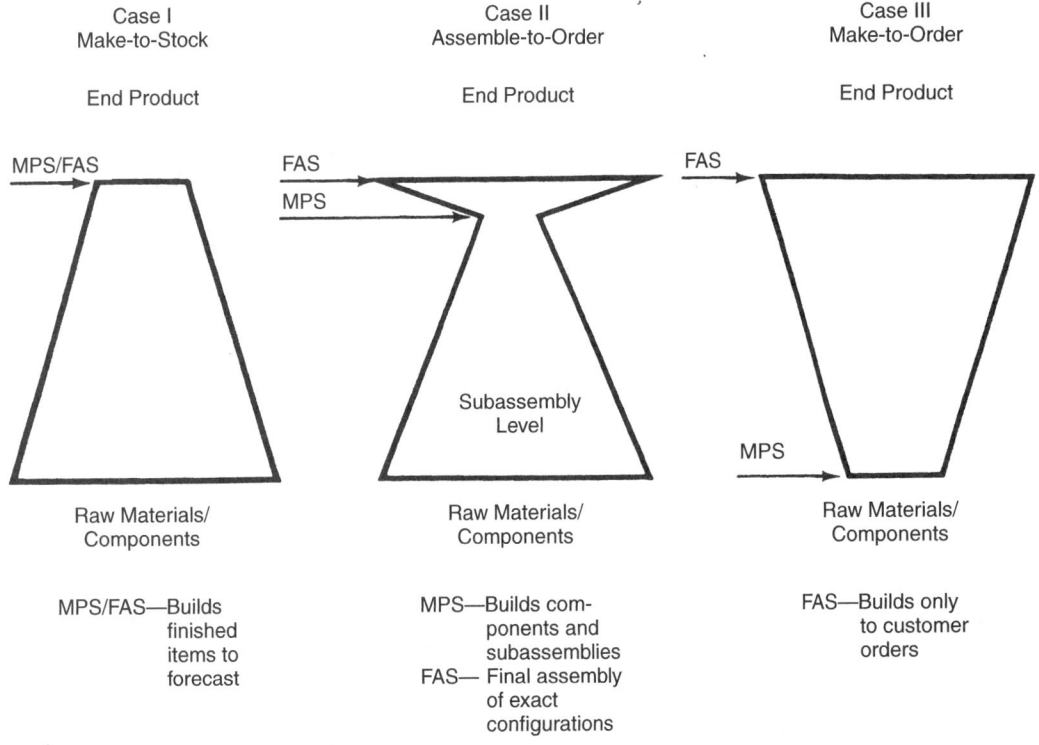

205. MANUFACTURING OPERATIONS

Exhibit 200.31 *Final Products with Subassemblies and Components*

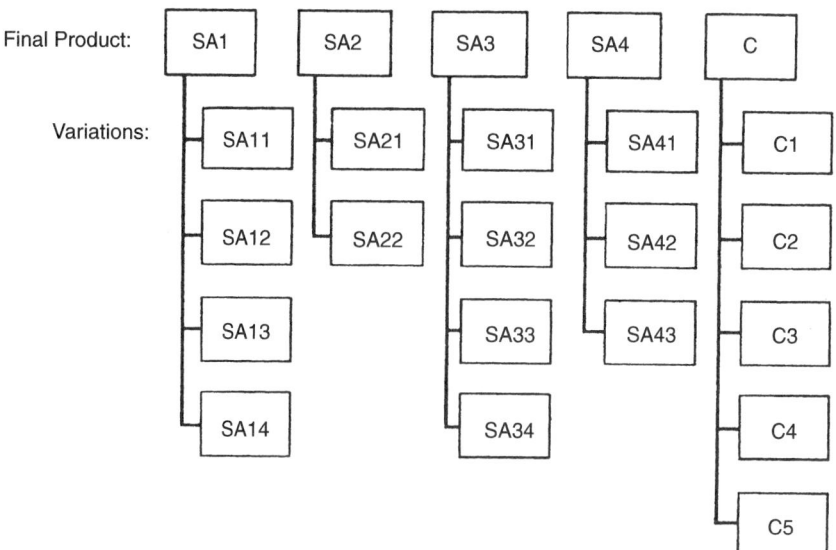

Assemble-, Finish-, or Package-to-Order

In this environment, options, subassemblies and components are either produced or purchased to stock. The competitive strategy is to be able to supply a large variety of final product configurations from standard components and subassemblies within a relatively short lead time. For example, an automobile may be ordered with or without air conditioning, an option, and a fast-food restaurant will deliver your hamburger with or without lettuce. This environment requires a forecast of options as well as of total demand. Thus, there is an MPS for the options, accessories, and common components as well as a final assembly schedule (FAS). This is Case II in Exhibit 200.30.

The advantage of this approach is that many different final products can be produced from relatively few subassemblies and components. This reduces inventory substantially. Exhibit 200.31 represents such a situation. Each final product contains four major subassemblies and a component. However, each subassembly and the component has different variations (alternates). There are four different variations of SA1, two of SA2, four of SA3, three of SA4, and five of C, which results in $4 \times 2 \times 4 \times 3 \times 5$ or 480 final product configurations. Assembling to order enables the firm to stock $4 + 2 + 4 + 3 + 5$ or 18 different items rather than 480.

Custom Design and Make-to-Order

In many situations, the final design of an item is part of what is purchased. The final product is usually a combination of standard items and items custom designed to meet the special needs of the customer. Combined material handling and manufacturing processing systems are an example, special trucks for off-the-road work on utility lines and facilities are another. Thus, there is one MPS for the raw material and the standard items that are purchased, fabricated, or built to stock and another MPS for the custom engineering, fabrication, and final assembly. Case III in Exhibit 200.30 represents this situation.

As we proceed with the discussion of the policies and procedures of master scheduling and its relationship to rough-cut capacity planning (RCCP), we will examine further the relationship of these environments to the MPS task.

The Bill of Material

An inclusive definition of a final product includes a list of the items, ingredients, or materials needed to assemble, mix, or produce that end product. This list is called a *bill of material* (BOM). The BOM can take several forms and be used in many ways. It is created as part of the design process and is used by manufacturing engineers to determine which items should be purchased and which items should be manufactured. Production control and inventory planning uses the BOM in conjunction with the master production schedule to determine the items for which purchase requisitions and production orders must be released. Accounting uses it to cost the product.

The BOM is a basic required input for many production planning and control activities, and its accuracy is crucial. In computerized systems the BOM data is contained in *BOM files,* a database organized by the *BOM processor* that also produces the BOM in the various formats required by the organization.

Single Level Bill of Material

The way in which the BOM files are organized and presented is called the structure of the bill of material. The simplest format is a *single level BOM,* as depicted in Exhibit 200.32. It consists of a list of all components needed to make the end item, including for each component (1) a unique part number, (2) a short verbal description, (3) the quantity needed for each single end item, and (4) the part's unit of measure.

Multilevel Tree Structure and Levels

While the single level BOM is sufficient when a product is assembled at one time from a set of purchased parts and raw materials, it does not adequately describe a product that has subassemblies. If we decided to make the base and socket assemblies in Exhibit 200.32, then each of those would have subitems that were purchased or manufactured. To illustrate the product structure, we can draw a "tree" having several levels, as shown in Exhibit 200.33. Note that by convention the final product is at Level 0, and the level numbers increase as one looks down the tree.

Corresponding to this tree structure is the multilevel indented BOM shown in Exhibit 200.34. Each part or assembly is given a unique number. To aid in understanding the structure, the numbers for the components of each subassembly are indented under the respective subassembly numbers. When a component is used in more than one subassembly a common parts bill may be produced for use by inventory planning. In this type of bill there is only one occurrence of the item along with its total quantity per final assembly.

Exhibit 200.32 *Single Level Bill of Material for Assembled Lamp*

ABC Lamp Company
Bill of Material Part LA01-Lamp

Part Number	Description	Quantity for Each Assembly	Unit of Measure
B100	Base assembly	1	Each
S100	14" Black shade	1	Each
A100	Socket assembly	1	Each

Exhibit 200.33 *Multilevel Tree Structure*

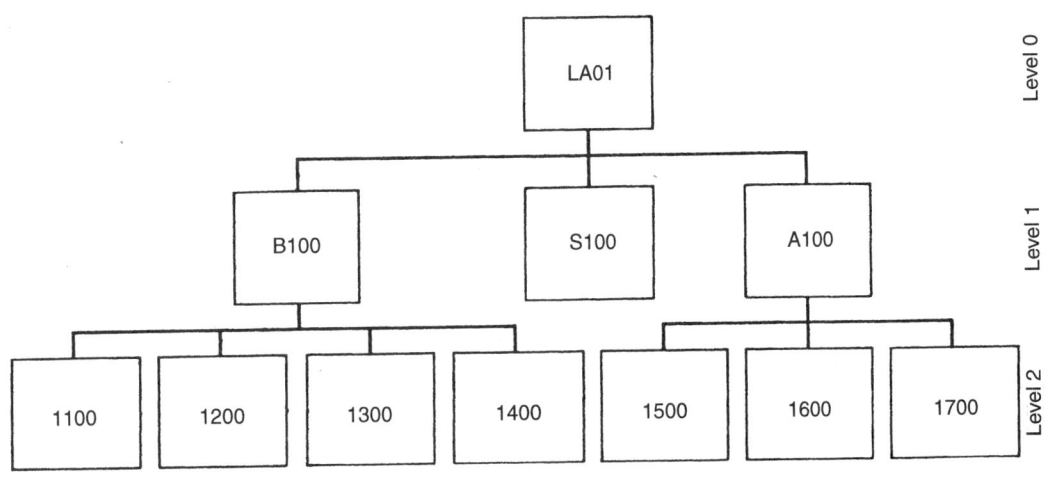

205. MANUFACTURING OPERATIONS

Exhibit 200.34 *Indented Bill of Material*

ABC Lamp Company
Bill of Material, Part LA01

Part Number	Description	Quantity for Each Assembly	Unit of Measure
B100	Base assembly	1	Each
1100	Finished shaft	1	Each
1200	7"-diameter steel plate	1	Each
1300	Hub	1	Each
1400	1/4-20 screws	4	Each
S100	14" black shade	1	Each
A100	Socket assembly	1	Each
1500	Steel holder	1	Each
1600	One-way socket	1	Each
1700	Wiring assembly	1	Each

Exhibit 200.35 *A Level Three Bill of Material*

ABC Lamp Company
Bill of Material, Part LA01

Part Number	Description	Quantity for Each Assembly	Unit of Measure
B100	Base assembly	1	Each
1100	Finished shaft	1	Each
2100	3/8" steel tubing	26	Inches
1200	7"-diameter steel plate	1	Each
1300	Hub	1	Each
1400	1/4-20 screws	4	Each
S100	14" black shade	1	Each
A100	Socket assembly	1	Each
1500	Steel holder	1	Each
1600	One-way socket	1	Each
1700	Wiring assembly	1	Each
2200	16-gauge lamp cord	12	Feet
2300	Standard plug terminal	1	Each

If the wiring assembly were itself a subassembly, then its components would be listed. On the indented BOM, the component part numbers would be further indented, as shown in Exhibit 200.35. As you see, the multilevel product structure is really made up of building blocks of single level product trees; that is, a BOM can be drawn up for each subassembly and only these single level bills need be retained. This is important when producing many different end items that have common subassemblies. We do not need to change every end item BOM when an engineering change takes place in a single common subassembly.

To illustrate this and several other real-life complexities, let us assume that we manufacture lamps with three different shades, two alternate base plates, and two types of sockets. Our original lamp was designated LA01. Working with the different components, we now can have 12 different final products. To clarify this, we can produce a common parts bill in a matrix format, as shown in Exhibit 200.36. An examination of the matrix shows that some parts are common to all models. To ease the planning task, we could group together the wiring assembly and the finished shaft with a new part number, say 4000, on the bill of material. Although these components are produced independently of one another,

Exhibit 200.36 Planning Bill of Material in Matrix Format, Part LA01 (Quantity for Each Assembly)

Part Number	Description	Unit of Measure	01	02	03	04	05	06	07	08	09	10	11	12
1100	Finished shaft	Each	1	1	1	1	1	1	1	1	1	1	1	1
2100	3/8" steel tubing	Inches	26	26	26	26	26	26	26	26	26	26	26	26
1200	7"-diameter steel plate	Each	1		1	1	1			1			1	1
1201	8"-diameter steel plate	Each						1	1		1	1		
1300	Hub	Each	1	1	1	1	1	1	1	1	1	1	1	1
1400	1/4-20 screws	Each	4	4	4	4	4	4	4	4	4	4	4	4
S100	14" black shade	Each	1	1			1	1						
S101	15" white shade	Each			1									
S102	15" cream shade	Each				1								
1500	Steel holder	Each	1	1	1	1	1	1	1	1	1	1	1	1
1600	One-way socket	Each	1	1	1	1	1	1						
1601	Three-way socket	Each							1	1	1	1	1	1
1700	Wiring assembly	Each	1	1	1	1	1	1	1	1	1	1	1	1
2200	16-gauge lamp cord	Feet	12	12	12	12	12	12	12	12	12	12	12	12
2300	Standard plug terminal	Each	1	1	1	1	1	1	1	1	1	1	1	1
B100	Base assembly—7"	Each	1	1	1		1			1		1	1	1
B101	Base assembly—8"	Each				1		1	1		1			
A100	Socket assembly—one-way	Each	1	1	1	1	1	1						
A101	Socket assembly—three-way	Each							1	1	1	1	1	1

Model

they can be grouped as common parts on the BOM for administrative purposes. This part number is never stocked and so it is called a *phantom* part. Its only purpose is to reduce the number of items on the BOM. We can go further with the concept of restructuring our BOMs and, for some products, create new numbers to represent new subassemblies (for example, subassemblies of plate, hub, and screws) in order to shorten lead times.

Another type of BOM is often useful in planning and handling engineering charges. It is referred to as a *planning bill*, a *pseudo bill*, a *phantom bill*, a *super bill*, or a *family bill*. From the matrix form of the summary bill (Exhibit 200.36), a simplified product-structure diagram (Exhibit 200.37) can be created for the family of lamps that consisted of pseudo-subassemblies—base assemblies, shades, and socket assemblies. For each of these, in place of the quantity for each unit assembled, the percentage split for each type of component is stated. Now, as we plan for a total of 10,000 lamps for each month, this planning bill can be used to derive the number of each type of component to build. Furthermore, if we decide to change to, say, a 16-inch green shade, only this single BOM, this modular bill, needs to be altered.

Option Overplanning

If the exact percentage split is uncertain, the percentage of each option can be increased to cover the uncertainty. This results in the total being more than 100 percent, as illustrated in Exhibit 200.38. The amount added can be calculated in the same manner as safety stock. Using this procedure to cover possible high side demand for each option is called *option overplanning*.

Exhibit 200.37 *Simplified Product Structure Diagram*

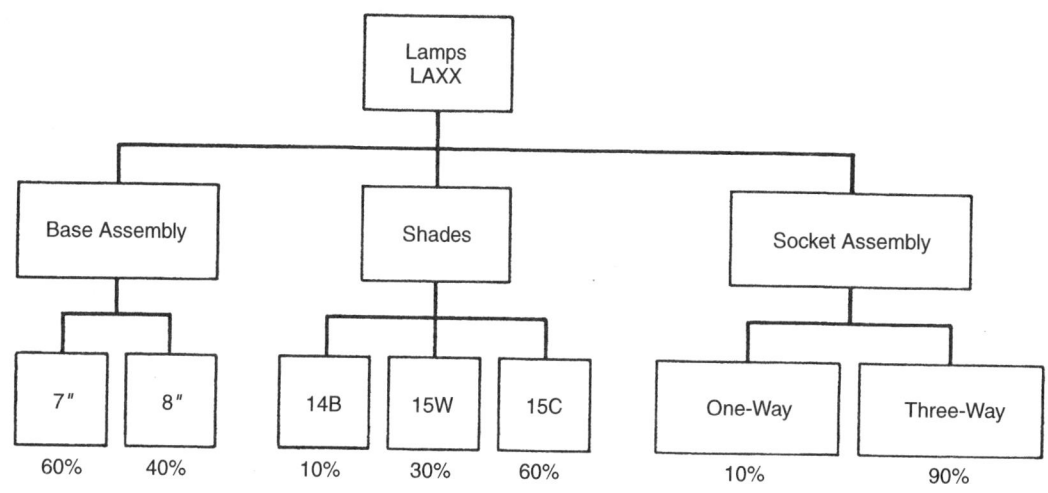

Exhibit 200.38 *Option Overplanning*

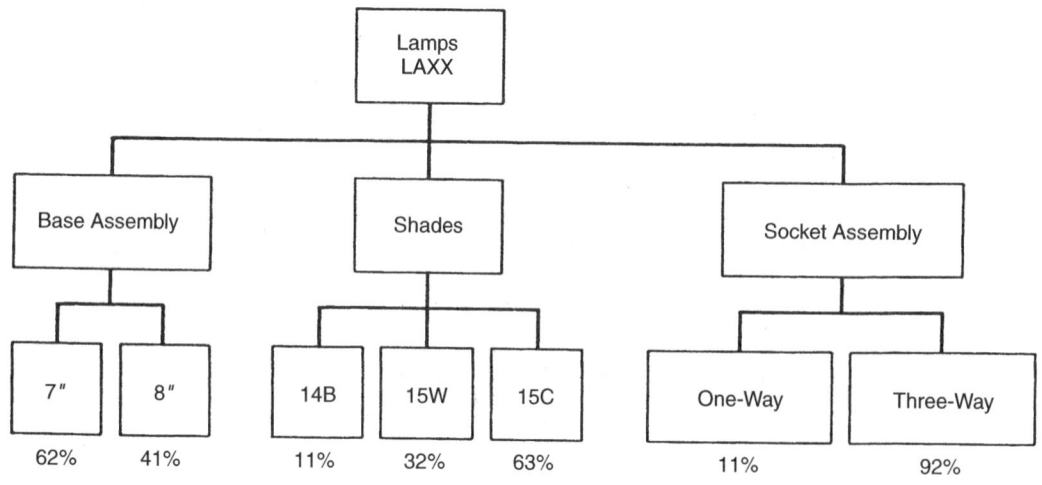

The Master Schedule Planning Horizon

A principle of planning is that a plan must cover a period at least equal to the time required to accomplish it. This means that the MS planning horizon must be at least as long as the lead time required to fabricate the MS items. This includes production and procurement time as well as engineering time in a custom-design environment. Delivery-to-customer response times (lead times) in the different production environments are illustrated in Exhibit 200.39.

Many organizations divide the planning horizon into periods with different controls on schedule changes. The closer a period is to the present, the tighter are the controls on schedule changes. For example, *time fences* (boundaries between different periods) may be established at the fourth week and the eighth week (two months), as shown in Exhibit 200.40. The location of the time fences and the nature of the approval required depend on the situation. Varying lead times, market conditions, and processing flexibility make for different time fences, sometimes at different plants within the same firm. Time fences should be tailored to specific product groups as lead time may vary widely between groups. In all cases, the MS is the vehicle for coordinating the achievement of marketing and manufacturing goals.

In Period C (a time horizon beyond two months in Exhibit 200.40) the MPS is consistent with the production plan. A good production plan will make preparation of the MS straightforward in this time frame.

In Period B (a time horizon of four to eight weeks in Exhibit 200.40) things become a bit sticky when operating at full capacity. A zero sum game exists; that is, any additions to the schedule must be counterbalanced by comparable deletions or increases in capacity. Changes in demand patterns, unusual orders, or equipment failures may warrant changes in the MPS. These changes are usually negotiated between marketing and manufacturing with the master scheduler determining their feasibility before the final decision. The product mix may change but not the production rate. In Period A (a time horizon of zero to four weeks in Exhibit 200.40) only an act of God or top management can change the MPS.

Exhibit 200.39 *Delivery-to-Customer Response Times*

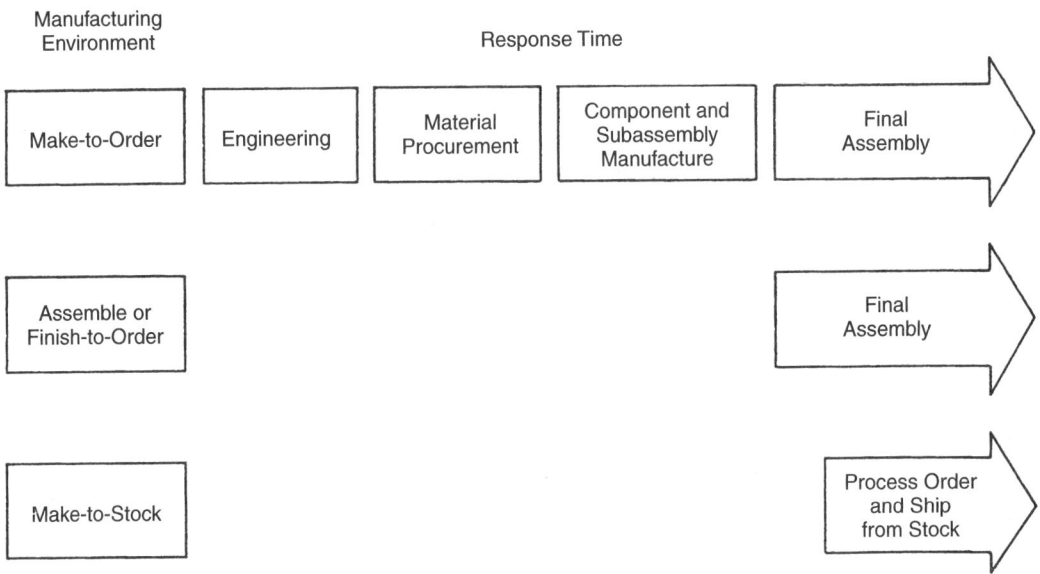

Exhibit 200.40 *MS Planning Horizons*

Period	Time Horizon	Conditions	Approval Required
A	0 to 4 weeks	Emergency	Top management
B	4 to 8 weeks	Dramatic shift in requirements	Marketing-manufacturing negotiation
C	Beyond 8 weeks	Normal	Master scheduler

As the time for order execution and manufacturing approaches, labor and material are committed. A change in the schedule can be disruptive and costly, and the costs must be compared with the benefits of the change. Following time-fence-control guidelines, which reflect realistic lead-time constraints and competitive factors, will result in an MPS that promotes manufacturing stability and productivity while providing reasonable flexibility in meeting marketing demands. However, the competitive environment may force decisions to restructure the BOM, to develop a modular BOM, to produce to stock at a higher level in the BOM, or to move time fences.

Designing, Creating, and Managing the Master Schedule

Master scheduling activities take place in three stages: (1) designing the MS, (2) creating the MS, and (3) controlling the MS.

A. Designing the MS includes the following steps:
1. Select the items; that is, select the levels in the BOM structure to be represented by the items scheduled (both components and final assemblies may be included).
2. Organize the MS by product groups.
3. Determine the planning horizon, the time fences, and the related operational guides.
4. Select the method for calculating and presenting the available-to-promise (ATP) information.

B. Creating the MS includes the following steps:
1. Obtain the necessary informational inputs, including the forecast, the backlog (customer commitments), and the inventory on hand.
2. Prepare the initial draft of the master production schedule (MPS).
3. Develop the rough-cut capacity requirements plan (RCCP).
4. If required, increase capacity or revise the initial draft of the MPS to obtain a feasible schedule.

C. Controlling the MS includes the following activities:
1. Track actual production and compare it to planned production to determine if the planned MPS quantities and delivery promises are being met.
2. Calculate the available-to-promise to determine if an incoming order can be promised in a specific period.
3. Calculate the projected on hand to determine if planned production is sufficient to fill expected future orders.
4. Use the results of the preceding activities to determine if the MPS or capacity should be revised.

Remember, the MPS lists by period the planned quantity of each MPS item to be built. The MS includes the demand, the available-to-promise, the projected on hand, and the MPS quantity by period.

The Final Assembly Schedule

The final assembly schedule (FAS) is a statement of those final products that are to be assembled from MPS items in specific time periods. In some organizations—those producing power tools, for example—MPS items and final products are identical, and one document serves as both the MPS and the FAS. In many other situations, especially when there are many more final products than there are items at the next BOM level, the two are separate and distinct.

In some cases final products differ only by the labeling or packaging of the same MPS item. In others painting or finishes may constitute the difference. In still others a vast difference may exist in the transformation of items into a variety of final products. In each of these cases an FAS that is distinct from but consistent with the MPS must be prepared. In the manufacture of automatic washers, for example, the motor, transmissions, control units, consoles, tubs, sets of assembly hardware, and various optional accessories would be MPS items, and the different models available to the customer would be final assemblies. Thus, the manufacture of motors can be authorized long before each motor is committed to the assembly of a particular model. Since the FAS is constrained by the availability of those items scheduled on the MPS plus those in inventory, the MPS and the FAS must be coordinated. This is true for both purchased and manufactured components.

Exhibit 200.41 *Coordinated FAS and MPS*

	Final Assembly Schedule				Master Production Schedule		
	Week				Week		
Item	1	2	3	Item	1	2	3
A		10	10	SA1	6	4	
				SA2	6	6	

Exhibit 200.41 is an example showing the relationship between the FAS for an assembly, A, made-to-order, and an MPS for two optional subassemblies, SA1 and SA2, which are made-to-stock with option overplanning. The assembly may be ordered with either an SA1 or an SA2 subassembly. Sales records reveal that each has an equal probability of being selected; each has received a maximum of 60 percent of the orders in any week. Thus, with an FAS for a maximum of 10 A's in Week 2, no beginning inventory for any item, and a lead time of one week for subassemblies, the MPS calls for six each of SA1 and SA2 in Week 1. Three possible demand combinations exist: five each of SA1 and SA2, four of SA1 and six of SA2, and six of SA1 and four of SA2. Two subassemblies will not be used immediately; they will be carried in stock to the next week.

Week 1 passes: Actual orders are for 10 A's, 4 with SA1 and 6 with SA2. Two SA1s are in inventory at the end of the week. This results in an MPS calling for producing four SA1's and six SA2's in Week 2 to assemble a maximum of ten A's in Week 3. The FAS and the MPS are coordinated.

In an assemble-to-order environment, the FAS frequently is stated in terms of individual customer orders and must be consistent with the shipping schedule. In a make-to-stock environment, the FAS is a commitment to produce specific quantities of catalog final products. The shipping schedule depends on available inventory and available capacity. Capacity is required for assembly and for any items that may be controlled by the FAS and not the MPS. Examples are painting, packaging, crating, and preparing shipping documents.

In any event, authorization of the final assembly schedule should be held to the last possible moment. This provides the greatest flexibility in meeting actual demand and improves customer service. Since assembly lead time and MPS item availability constrain the FAS, any planning and design that reduce this lead time and increase flexibility aid in achieving customer service objectives.

Preparation, measuring of actual output, and control of the FAS should rest with the master scheduler. This enables one individual to control all demands on resources and coordinate MPS items and the FAS, order entry items, and order-promising activities.

The Master Scheduler

Most organizations should have a master scheduler. This individual is the link between marketing, distribution, engineering, manufacturing, and planning. The tasks of the master scheduler include the following:

1. Provide delivery promise dates for incoming orders; match actual requirements with the master schedule as they materialize.
2. Evaluate the impact of top-down inputs, such as a request for the introduction of a new product in much less than the normal delivery time.
3. Evaluate the impact of bottom-up inputs, such as anticipated delay reports from the shop or purchasing indicating that particular components will not be available as scheduled or that planned production rates are not being attained.
4. Revise the master schedule when necessary because of lack of material or lack of capacity.
5. Call basic conflicts of demand and capacity to the attention of other members of management, especially marketing and manufacturing, who need to participate in resolving the problems.

Whether or not a firm has someone formally designated as the master scheduler, the tasks are essential. Combining them under the jurisdiction of one individual improves the likelihood that they will be coordinated and managed properly. Most importantly, it provides a focal point for the required coordination of marketing, manufacturing, distribution, and planning as well as a place to look for answers when things are not going as planned.

MPS Information Systems and Analysis

The complexity of most manufacturing environments requires a computerized production planning and control system with human interfaces at appropriate decision points. As noted previously, the master scheduler requires such an interface. The requirement for computer assisted planning is due to a combination of the number of items on the MPS, the large number of subassemblies and components, and the magnitude of recording and processing inventory transactions, material requirements, and capacity requirements. Today, there are literally hundreds of commercial software systems available. Some are for use with mainframe computers, others for use with minicomputers, and a growing number for use with personal computers.

The installation and availability of such a computer system often allows the organization to perform what-if analyses to answer questions such as: (1) What will be the effect of a shift in product mix on capacity requirements? (2) What will be the effect of a 10 percent increase in demand on capacity requirements? Answers to these questions, available from a computerized simulation run, will enable management to prepare plans for such contingencies.

230 Supply Chain Management

In this section, we discuss supply chain management, managing supply chain inventory, purchasing transportation services, and purchasing/supply chain performance measurement and evaluation.

Supply Chain Management

We define the terms *supply chain* and *supply chain management* as follows:[94]

The **supply chain** encompasses all activities associated with the flow and transformation of goods from the raw materials stage (extraction), through to end users, as well as the associated information flows. Material and information flows both up and down the supply chain. The supply chain includes systems management, operations and assembly, purchasing, production scheduling, order processing, inventory management, transportation, warehousing, and customer service. Supply chains are essentially a series of linked suppliers and customers; every customer is in turn a supplier to the next downstream organization until a finished product reaches the ultimate end user.

Supply chain management is the integration of these activities through improved supply chain relationships to achieve a sustainable competitive advantage.

Several factors are driving the emphasis on supply chain management today. First, the cost and availability of information resources between entities in the supply chain allow easy linkages and eliminate time delays in the network. Second, the level of competition in both domestic and international markets demands that organizations be quick, agile, and flexible. Third, customer expectations and requirements are becoming much more important. As customers become increasingly demanding, organizations and their intermediaries must be flexible and quick, or face the prospect of losing market share. A strategic, proactive approach to managing the supply chain is critical for survival.

From the focal firm's perspective (what we refer to as the purchaser), the supply chain includes (1) **internal functions,** (2) **upstream suppliers,** and (3) **downstream customers.** A firm's *internal functions* include the different processes used in transforming the inputs provided by the supplier network. This is usually referred to as *operations*. In the case of an automotive company, this includes its parts manufacturing (e.g., stamping, power train, and components), which are eventually assembled during final assembly into automobiles.

The coordination and scheduling of internal flows is challenging, particularly in a large organization. Some of the major functions include order processing, which is responsible for translating customer requirements into actual orders that are input into the system. Order processing may also involve extensive customer interaction, including quoting prices, possible delivery dates, delivery arrangements, and aftermarket service.

Another important internal function is production scheduling, which translates orders into actual plans and schedules. This may involve working with materials requirements planning and capacity-planning systems to schedule work centers, employees, and maintenance on machines.

The second major part of supply chain management involves **upstream suppliers.** In order to manage the flow of materials between all upstream organizations, firms employ an array of managers who ensure that the right materials arrive at the right time to the right internal users. Purchasing managers are responsible for ensuring that the right suppliers are selected, that they are meeting performance expectations, that appropriate contractual mechanisms are employed, and that a good relationship is maintained. They may also be responsible for driving supply-base improvement, and act as a liaison between suppliers and other internal supply chain members (engineering, accounting, etc.). Materials managers are responsible for planning, forecasting, and scheduling material flows from suppliers. They must work closely with production schedulers to ensure that suppliers are able to deliver material to the required locations, and that they have some advance warning as to future requirements so they can plan ahead.

Finally, a firm's **downstream customers** encompass downstream distribution channels, processes, and functions that the product passes through on its way to the end customer. In the case of an automotive company's suppliers, this includes finished goods and pipeline inventory, warehouses, dealer networks, and sales operations. This particular distribution channel is relatively short. Other types of supply chains may have relatively small internal supply chains but fairly long downstream distribution channels. For instance, the supply chain for a cereal manufacturer, and the extensive distribution network that is involved in getting the packaged cereal to the final customer. Within the downstream portion of the supply chain, logistics managers are responsible for the actual movement of materials between locations. One major part of logistics is transportation management, involving the selection and management of external carriers (trucking companies, airlines, railroads, shipping companies) or managing internal, private fleets of carriers. Distribution management involves the management of packaging, storing, and handling of materials at receiving docks, warehouses, and retail outlets.

There are several major flows that take place in a supply chain. Obviously, materials and services flow down the chain (from suppliers to customers), and funds flow up the chain (from customers to suppliers), but there are other flows as well. Information and knowledge also flow up and down the chain. Participants in a supply chain are willing to share such information only when there is sufficient trust between members. Thus, the management of relationships with other parties in the chain becomes paramount. Organizations are effectively forming new types of relationships (sometimes called partnerships or alliances) that require a shared resource base. For instance, organizations may provide dedicated capacity, specific information, technological capabilities, or even direct financial support for other members of their supply chain so that the entire chain can benefit as a whole.

Managing Supply Chain Inventory

Understanding Supply Chain Inventory

The best place to start our discussion of supply chain inventory is to understand the basic principles of inventory management. This section discusses the different types of inventory, the costs associated with holding inventory, and the changing view of inventory as a financial and operating liability rather than asset.

Types of Inventory

Inventory represents the largest single investment in assets for most manufacturers, wholesalers, and retailers. The five primary categories of inventory include (1) raw material and semifinished item inventory; (2) work-in-process inventory; (3) finished-goods inventory; (4) maintenance, repair, and operating (MRO) supplies inventory; and (5) pipeline in-transit/inventory.

RAW MATERIAL AND SEMIFINISHED ITEM INVENTORY This category includes the items purchased from suppliers or produced internally to directly support production requirements. Raw materials include those items purchased in a bulk or unfinished condition. Bulk quantities of chemicals, resins, or petroleum are examples of purchased raw materials. Semifinished inventory includes those items and components used as inputs during the final production process. Every producer relies on some level of raw material or semifinished inventory to support final production requirements. This type of inventory is managed primarily by purchasing, a material planning group, or supply chain managers.

230. SUPPLY CHAIN MANAGEMENT

WORK-IN-PROCESS INVENTORY At any given point in time, work-in-process (WIP) is the sum total of inventory within all processing centers. Work-in-process is incomplete—it has not yet been transformed to a saleable finished good. This includes materials that are

- Waiting to be moved to another process
- Currently being worked on at a work center
- Queuing up at a processing center due to a capacity bottleneck or machine breakdown

If WIP increases over a certain level, this may indicate production bottlenecks or delays. One study found that in most facilities, 36 percent of WIP inventory is in queue waiting to be worked on, 27 percent is waiting to be moved to another work area or center, 4 percent is in the process of being moved, and only 24 percent is actually in process.[95] If WIP builds up at a workstation, a scheduler may have to reroute the flow of material to another work center.

FINISHED-GOODS INVENTORY Finished-goods inventory includes completed items or products that are available for shipment or future customer orders. A firm that produces items in anticipation of customer orders should monitor its finished-goods inventory closely. A higher-than-anticipated level of finished goods may mean that a decrease in customer demand is occurring. A lower-than-anticipated finished-goods inventory level may indicate that customer demand is increasing. Either condition may also indicate that the forecasts of anticipated customer demand do not match current output levels.

When firms produce goods in anticipation of future customer orders, they are operating in a make-to-stock environment. They expect to hold finished inventory in anticipation of future demand. When firms produce in response to a customer order, they are operating in a make-to-order environment. Just-in-time firms usually operate in a make-to-order environment.

MAINTENANCE, REPAIR, AND OPERATING (MRO) SUPPLIES INVENTORY MRO inventory includes the items used to support production and operations. These items are not physically part of a finished product but are critical for the continuous operation of plant, equipment, and offices. Examples of MRO inventory include office supplies, spare parts, tools, and computers.

PIPELINE/IN-TRANSIT INVENTORY This inventory is in transit to a customer or is located throughout distribution channels. Most consumable goods inventory is either on trucks or on grocery store shelves. In fact, grocery stores only provide a shelf for the product but do not own any of the inventory. The supplying company or distributor owns the inventory, which receives payment when the consumer buys the product.

Inventory-Related Costs

One of the drawbacks of holding excessive inventory is the effect this has on a firm's working capital—the funds committed to operating a business, including the purchase and holding of inventory. If we hold excessive inventory, then funds are tied up unnecessarily. These funds could likely have been used more productively elsewhere. Ordering and carrying physical inventory results in a number of costs. It is critical to identify these costs so they can be better managed.

UNIT COSTS The most basic and the easiest inventory-related cost to quantify and track is unit cost. We can view the calculation of unit costs in several ways. First, each item or good purchased from a supplier or another internal facility has a related unit cost, which is the price a firm pays. Second, a finished product has a unit cost. The calculation of this cost may be more complex. Besides the direct material used to manufacture the finished product, the product also has a labor cost and allocated overhead. Cost accountants are largely responsible for identifying and assigning these costs.

ORDERING COSTS Ordering costs are a composite of the costs associated with the release of a material order. These costs may include the cost of generating and sending a material release, transportation costs, and any other cost connected with acquiring a good. If a firm produces an item or good itself, the ordering cost will also include machine setup costs.

CARRYING COSTS Carrying costs consist of three separate components: (1) cost of capital; (2) cost of storage; and (3) the costs of obsolescence, deterioration, and loss. The dollar amount invested in physical inventory has an opportunity cost associated with it. Resources committed to inventory are not available for other economic uses. Therefore, committing financial resources to holding physical inventory creates an inventory-carrying cost.

The physical storing of inventory creates costs, including any costs related to storage space, insurance costs, or the cost to maintain the inventory (such as performing cycle counts). Carrying costs vary with the level of inventory, which makes these costs variable. Fixed costs are not included as part of inventory-carrying costs because inventory levels typically have no effect on a fixed cost, at least in the short run.

Holding inventory also increases the risk of theft, damage, spoilage, and obsolescence. For example, obsolescence is a major issue in the computer industry, where inventory loses about 1.5 percent of its functionality per week due to rapidly changing technology, making the extended holding of any inventory financially risky.

For most industries, inventory costs typically range from 15 percent to 25 percent of the value of the inventory, depending on the company's cost of capital. These costs are made up of a variety of different costs that may or may not be formally measured by a company. Carrying cost is calculated as follows:

$$\text{Inventory carrying cost} = \text{Average inventory in units} \times \text{Unit price} \times \text{Carrying cost per year}$$

If a company averages 1,000 units in inventory, for which the unit price is $1.00 per unit, and the annual carrying cost is 25%, the total inventory carrying cost per year for that level of inventory is $(1{,}000 \times \$1 \times .25) = \$250$.

QUALITY COSTS Quality costs include any cost associated with nonconforming items or goods. The total cost of inventory ownership is more than simply the unit, ordering, and carrying costs. Quantifying the cost of poor quality can help identify the causes of problems. Examples of additional costs due to defective inventory include field failure costs, rework, losses due to poor product yields, inspection, lost production, and warranty costs.

OTHER COSTS The holding of inventory may create other costs. Examples include duties, tooling costs, exchange rate differentials, packaging costs, transportation and logistics costs, and administrative costs.

It is often difficult to quantify the total costs associated with ordering and carrying physical inventory. Part of this results from the historical neglect of calculating total inventory costs along with a lack of systems capable of identifying inventory-related costs. Most cost-accounting systems are not yet capable of identifying and assigning the true costs related to maintaining physical inventory. However, accounting systems based on activity-based costing (ABC) principles are increasingly able to quantify the distinct costs associated with holding inventory. The new types of enterprise resource planning (ERP) systems also aid managers to more accurately measure the actual level of inventory on hand, as opposed to "guesstimating."

Inventory Investment—Asset or Liability?

Financial managers have historically viewed inventory as a material asset with value. Inventory appears under the Current Assets column on balance sheets. Using a financial perspective, an asset is something worth maximizing—it has value to a firm.[96] Unfortunately, this perspective neglects the total cost impact of not controlling inventory investment. From a balance sheet perspective, there is no obvious disadvantage of carrying too much inventory. However, inventory costs affect financial performance directly.

Another reason for the historical neglect of inventory investment is related to traditional corporate performance measurement and evaluation systems. Profit and loss performance largely determined a manager's evaluation. Because inventory affects profit and loss indirectly (through material costs), most managers emphasized higher sales as the primary means to increase profit. Only recently have managers begun to pay more attention to inventory, as measurement systems include performance ratios such as asset turns, inventory turns, and return on investment figures. The denominator of each of these ratios includes the value of inventories. As the denominator of these ratios increases, the worse the overall performance ratio appears.

The transition from viewing inventory as a material asset to seeing it as a supply chain cost driver has been gradual. When U.S. companies competed mainly against other U.S. companies, an increase in inventory turns (a ratio of sales to average inventory) from 5 to 10 a year appeared impressive. However, the 1990s demonstrated that this level of performance was not enough to compete at world-class levels when many firms maintain minimum inventory. The efficient control of inventory investment is now a major metric that is calculated by all world-class competitors.

The Right Reasons for Carrying Inventory

Physical inventory plays an important role in all supply chains. Without inventory companies cannot build products, provide customer service, or run their operations. When deciding whether or not to maintain an investment in inventory, a single premise can be used to summarize the relative benefits of inventory: *Inventory should be held only when the benefit of holding inventory exceeds the cost of holding the inventory.* Inventory ceases to provide a benefit when it is used to disguise problems or other inefficiencies. The following section examines the proper reasons for carrying inventory, and also suggests a number of situations in which inventory is used inappropriately.

- Support production requirements
- Support operational requirements
- Support customer service requirements
- Hedge against marketplace uncertainty
- Take advantage of order quantity discounts

Each of the reasons can result in holding some level of physical inventory. Regardless of the reason for holding inventory, supply chain managers must be aware of total inventory costs. The key is to minimize inventory investment wherever possible while still meeting competitive and customer requirements.

The Wrong Reasons for Carrying Inventory

Any inventory discussion must differentiate between good and bad reasons for carrying inventory. Almost all unnecessary inventory results from a single word—uncertainty. Uncertainty results in not being able to adequately plan inventory requirements because of supply chain variability. It is also a consequence of variability in forecasting accuracy and inconsistent logistics, which usually results in greater amounts of safety stock being held as protection. The following discussion considers the sources of variability or uncertainty that, if left uncorrected, encourage an increase in inventory. These are the wrong reasons for carrying inventory.

- Poor quality and material yield
- Unreliable supplier delivery
- Extended buyer-supplier order-cycle times
- Inaccurate or uncertain demand forecasts
- Specifying custom items for standard applications
- Extended material pipelines
- Inefficient manufacturing processes

Creating the Lean Supply Chain

When inventory moves so fast that firms essentially hold zero inventory on hand, they are following a system known as the *lean supply chain*—a combination of JIT purchasing, JIT transportation, and JIT production. All three elements combine to create a supply chain that minimizes inventory investment and eliminates waste. John Shook defines *lean* as "a philosophy that seeks to shorten the time between the customer order and the shipment to the customer by eliminating waste."[97] James Womack and Daniel Jones, in their book *Lean Thinking*, argue that all activities associated with lean attempt to achieve three objectives: flow, pull, and striving for excellence.[98] *Flow* means that inventory moves through the supply chain continuously with minimal queuing or non–value-added activity being performed. *Pull* means that customer orders start the work process. An upstream work center will not create output unless a downstream work center directly requests (i.e., pulls) that output. The output is needed and consumed, leading to no inventory or waste. The third element, *striving for excellence,* means that supply chains must have perfect quality. Anything less than perfect quality leads to waste.

Exhibit 200.42 identifies the various types of supply chain waste. This exhibit explains how to eliminate the waste, and why the presence of that waste often leads to additional supply chain inventory. The elimination of supply chain waste, and the inventory that accompanies that waste, is perhaps the primary objective of a lean supply chain.

The following sections detail the three primary elements of a lean supply chain: (1) just-in-time purchasing, (2) just-in-time transportation, and (3) just-in-time production.

Exhibit 200.42 *Common Types of Supply Chain Waste*

Type of Supply Chain Waste	Effect on Inventory Investment	How to Eliminate This Waste
Overproduction	Creates excessive finished-goods inventory, excessive component, and raw material inventory at suppliers	Produce only to customer requirements
Waiting	Increases average levels of supply chain inventory as material remains in a non–value-added state longer	Coordinate flows between supply chain activities; balance the flow between work centers through coordinated production and ordering quantities
Excessive transportation and material handling	Increases possibility of damage; adds time and inventory to the material pipeline	Locate supply chain members and work centers geographically closer; use a dedicated transportation network
Unneeded production steps	Creates higher levels of work-in-process inventory as production cycles are lengthened	Process reengineer to reduce the number of steps required to produce
Excessive work-in-process inventories	Creates higher levels of supply chain inventory-carrying costs as inventory takes longer to become finished goods to the customer	Reduce setup times; better coordinate schedules between work centers; build only to customer order quantities
Unnecessary motion and effort	Creates higher levels of work-in-process inventory as production cycles lengthen	Perform industrial engineering studies to optimize movement
Defective products	Requires safety stock; rework, material, reordering, production, and transportation costs increase	Pursue zero defects throughout the supply chain, including the suppliers
Unnecessary staff	Unnecessary staff can make product lines uncompetitive, leading to reduced sales and obsolete inventory	Place decision-making authority closer to direct supply chain participants; replace staff with information
Incomplete or incorrect information	Requires safety stock or buffers across the supply chain; may result in excessive production; may result in wrong production	Develop integrated information systems; build trust among supply chain members

Just-in-Time Purchasing

Implementing a just-in-time (JIT) purchasing system is the first major element of a lean supply chain. A JIT purchasing system means receiving frequent receipts of material from suppliers to meet immediate requirements. The following features define a true JIT purchasing system:

- A commitment to zero defects by the buyer and seller
- Frequent shipment of small lot sizes according to strict quality and delivery performance standards
- Closer, even collaborative, buyer-seller relationships
- Stable production schedules sent to suppliers on a regular basis
- Extensive sharing of information between supply chain members
- Electronic data interchange capability with suppliers

Not simply a series of techniques, a JIT purchasing system is an operating philosophy that does not tolerate high inventory levels, less than perfect quality, or other inefficiency and waste between buyer and seller. JIT purchasing also requires permanent changes concerning how a firm conducts business. It is not a one-time effort or a project but rather a continuous supply chain improvement process. A true JIT purchasing system requires cultural and personnel mind-set changes of the purchaser and of suppliers. And perhaps most important, JIT purchasing does not mean pushing inventory back to the supplier. JIT purchasing requires cooperation, coordination, and information sharing to eliminate inventory throughout the supply chain.

STRUCTURAL JIT PURCHASING BARRIERS JIT purchasing between U.S. companies has been slowed or even prohibited by a variety of structural barriers that are part of the U.S. business system and culture, although industries are affected differently. Fortunately, some of these barriers are not as great as they were when JIT first became popular during the early and mid-1980s. Key factors include the following:

- *Dispersed supply base:* Most purchasers have a geographically dispersed supply base. Since JIT relies on frequent deliveries of smaller quantities from suppliers, it may be difficult to achieve a level of consistent delivery reliability from suppliers located 800 or even 8,000 miles away. The greater the distance between buyer and seller, the greater the variability around delivery times.
- *Historical buyer-seller relationships:* Buyers and sellers often lack the cooperative relationship required to pursue JIT purchasing. A true JIT system requires mutual trust and respect between parties. The historical relationship between U.S. buyers and sellers has been closer to adversarial rather than cooperative.
- *Number of suppliers:* Some supply chains still have too many suppliers to support an efficient JIT system. Like other progressive purchasing strategies, JIT requires a drastically reduced supply base to minimize the interaction and communication costs between parties. It is also impossible to develop close relationships with thousands of suppliers.
- *Supplier quality performance:* Some sellers simply have not achieved the levels of near-perfect quality required for JIT purchasing. A total commitment to product and delivery quality is a prerequisite for a successful JIT system.

These barriers are not as common with Japanese and other international competitors. The geographic size of Japan, for example, almost guarantees that buyers and suppliers are located near each other. Furthermore, Asian manufacturers historically have had closer relationships with their key suppliers—so close that buyers think of suppliers as virtual extensions of the buying company and treat them as such. This closeness allows the two firms to work together at a higher level. Nevertheless, not all has been easy for the Japanese. They face more congestion on the highways for their deliveries than encountered in the United States.

The structural barriers limiting the increased use of JIT purchasing in the United States are beginning to break down. A reduction in the number of suppliers is the most obvious change. JIT purchasing has clearly been a major factor behind the supply-base reduction effort of most U.S. companies. Another change includes buyers and sellers developing closer working relationships. The two parties are increasingly willing to share information such as production scheduling and future product development plans. Information sharing has contributed to the greater use of electronic systems linking between supply chain members.

Progressive suppliers have shown an increased willingness to locate facilities closer to key customers. For example, **DuPont** invested over $1 billion during the 1980s and early 1990s to establish facilities in southeast Michigan to support the technical and production requirements of U.S. automakers. Another trend has been the development of measurement systems to evaluate supplier quality performance, including the initial evaluation of supplier capability as well as continuous performance measurement. JIT purchasing will fail if a supplier cannot meet world-class quality levels.

Getting suppliers to cooperate in a JIT purchasing system is critical to success. One way to get that involvement and commitment is to understand the expectations that suppliers have within a JIT purchasing system. Exhibit 200.43 lists some of these expectations.

Just-in-Time Transportation

JIT transportation, another key element of a lean supply chain, refers to the efficient movement of goods between the buyer and seller. This involves frequent deliveries of smaller quantities directly to the point of use at the purchaser. A lean transportation network relies on company-owned or contracted vehicles that pick up and deliver according to a regular and repeatable schedule in a *closed loop*—a system that moves goods from supplier to purchaser and then from purchaser back to supplier with return material, such as containers. Long-term dedicated contract carriage replaces commercial carriage as the primary mode of transportation in a closed-loop transportation system.

Exhibit 200.43 *JIT Purchasing—Supplier Expectations*

• A longer-term business arrangement	• Parts designed to match the supplier's process capability
• Fair financial return	• Smoothly timed order releases
• Adequate time for planning	• Minimum number of changed orders
• Accurate forecasts	
• Correct and firm material and product specifications	

Exhibit 200.44 *JIT Transportation Delivery Systems*

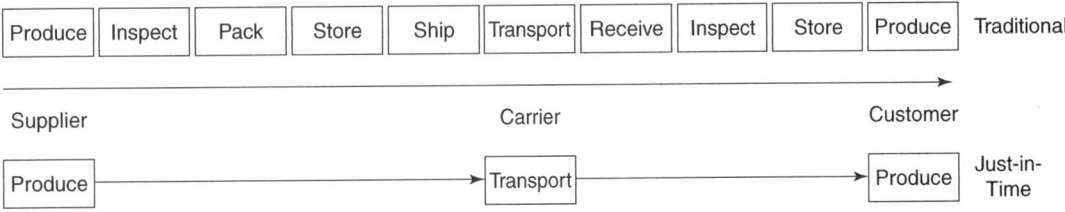

Exhibit 200.44 compares a traditional delivery system with a just-in-time delivery system. In a traditional system, the supplier and purchaser do not coordinate their material requirements or production schedules. As a result, suppliers produce material and then store that material awaiting an order from the purchaser. In a JIT system, suppliers coordinate production schedules with customer schedules. Production moves from the supplier's work center to the carrier directly to the purchaser. A JIT transportation network can eliminate up to 80 percent of the activities required in a traditional system. Designing a JIT transportation network involves certain steps:

- *Change the organizational structure:* Examples of organizational changes required to support JIT deliveries may include establishing cross-functional teams to manage the transition to JIT transportation.
- *Reduce the number of carriers:* Reduce the number of carriers, perhaps even to one per region.
- *Use longer-term contracts:* Negotiate longer-term agreements with carriers that formalize the dedicated transportation network.
- *Establish electric linkages:* Establish electronic linkages with suppliers and carriers to coordinate and control the movement of material through the network.
- *Implement a closed-loop system:* Pick up all freight from suppliers and deliver on a regular schedule. Use returnable containers to eliminate packaging waste.
- *Efficiently handle material:* Use state-of-the-art material-handling equipment and technology.

JIT transportation systems feature certain innovations that can further eliminate supply chain waste. The first includes specialized transportation vehicles that allow easy loading and unloading of smaller quantities. A common configuration resembles a beverage truck with side-loading doors. These trucks are smaller, more efficient, and more versatile. The second innovation includes the extensive use of returnable plastic or steel containers. As drivers pick up material from suppliers, they leave empty containers that were used in earlier deliveries. A third innovation involves point-of-use doors at production facilities. Since excessive material handling and travel within a facility is wasteful, delivery should be made to the door closest to where the material is needed.

Just-in-Time Production

This aspect of the lean supply chain involves taking raw and semifinished material and converting it to finished goods to satisfy customer orders. A narrow view of lean tends to focus on JIT production only while minimizing the importance of JIT purchasing and transportation. A truly lean supply chain requires all three pieces to be in place.

JIT production consists of the following elements, some of which are discussed further:

- Uniform facility loading and level scheduling
- Equipment setup reduction
- Inventory pull systems with visible signals
- Facility layout changes
- Total quality and continuous improvement
- Standardized material handling and containers
- Product and process simplification
- Total preventive maintenance
- Flexible workforce featuring teamwork
- Right performance measures

Ideally, a purchaser has suppliers that are also practicing lean supply chain production practices.

EQUIPMENT SETUP REDUCTIONS   Setup reduction involves reviewing how to minimize equipment downtime between part changeovers to facilitate small-volume production. An analogy that illustrates setup reduction is moving from a traditional tire change (longer downtime) to an Indy pit stop (downtime measured in seconds). With the Indy pit stop, the process is idle for the least amount of time possible.

Many companies start their lean production efforts by focusing on setup time reduction. There are five major approaches for improving setup times:

1. Reduce the time a piece of equipment is down for a changeover. This is achieved by planning and staging, which means knowing which part is coming next, knowing when the change will take place, and having the required tools and equipment ready before the change.
2. Study setup methods extensively. Time and motion studies will help identify wasted movement and methods.
3. Eliminate on-machine adjustments as much as possible.
4. Purchase new equipment that is easier and quicker to change.
5. Track progress toward stated time-reduction targets in order to focus the improvement efforts.

In short, setup time should become a nonevent that allows the production of small lot sizes or quantities.

INVENTORY PULL SYSTEMS WITH VISIBLE SIGNALS   Customer orders serve as a "pull" signal in a lean supply chain. Cells, work centers, and even suppliers make a component, subassembly, or product only when requested by a downstream work center. Production and movement of goods are triggered by a visible signal, such as a production card, empty container, empty designated floor space, electronic signal, or other nonverbal communication. An empty container or floor space is the trigger to produce at a work station—*empty* meaning that a downstream work center used that material (which is why it is empty) and more will be required shortly for the next customer order. Because material is produced only when requested by a work center requiring that material, no excess or unbalanced production occurs.

Pull and push systems differ dramatically. In a push system material is produced upstream and then sent, or pushed, to the next work center in the supply chain. Usually the next center is unaware that material is on its way until it arrives, which often leads to bottlenecks. This is common when producing to a forecast of anticipated demand. Eventually the material reaches the end of production and is placed in warehouse storage.

FACILITY LAYOUT CHANGES   The objective of changing the layout of a facility is to overcome the limitations of traditional layouts, which include excessive material movement, workers with narrow job classifications or specialization, and complex material-tracking requirements. The most common layout change involves moving from a process layout, where similar equipment is grouped into work centers, to a cellular layout, where dissimilar operations are grouped together to focus on a specific product line or customer. The goal is to minimize the movement of products. The cell also supports grouping employees into work teams with total accountability for a product and its quality. Exhibits 200.45 and 200.46 highlight the physical difference between a process facility and product or cellular layout.

Changing to a cellular approach is not as easy as it may sound. It can be difficult to overcome years of employee and departmental specialization, and some equipment does not lend itself to being grouped with other equipment. Also, the process of rearranging a facility is a major task that can easily disrupt production schedules and interfere with customer deliveries. Finally, equipment utilization often declines in a just-in-time system. Concern with factory utilization must shift to a concern with low inventory, balanced production, and quality assurance. This can be a problem if the performance measurement system stresses output and volume. Having equipment stand idle is better than using it to produce unneeded components, subassemblies, and finished products.

Exhibit 200.45   *Process Facility Layout Organized around Production Processes*

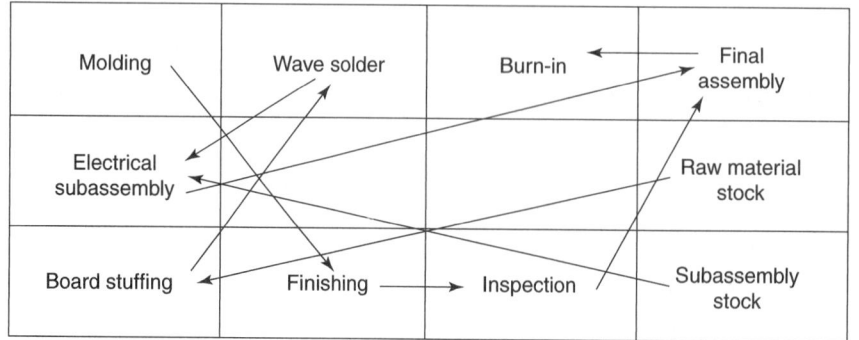

Exhibit 200.46 *Product or Cellular Layout Organized around Work Cells*

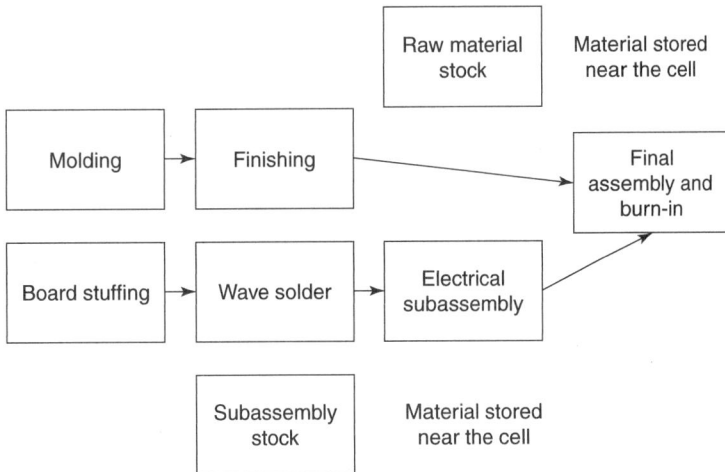

UNIFORM PLANT LOADING AND LEVEL SCHEDULING   Uniform plant loading is essential for a lean and integrated supply chain. The premise behind uniform loading is that all work centers, including work centers at the supplier, are not independent of one another. Batch sizes of component or subassembly production cannot be calculated separately from the finished-product requirements. The entire supply chain must be linked to finished-quantity requirements so there is a balanced flow of material through the supply chain with no queues or shortages.

Level scheduling means planning to build the same product mix and quantity every day during a given period. This works best for products that have a fairly consistent pattern of customer demand, such as making automobiles. Level scheduling removes the volatility that can disrupt the smooth flow of goods through the supply chain.

Approaches for Controlling Inventory Investment

Besides the activities associated with a lean supply chain, companies rely on a variety of other techniques and methods to control inventory investment throughout the supply chain. The following summarizes some of the most common, along with a brief description of each approach.

ABC Analysis

If not the first, certainly one of the first steps in gaining a handle on an inventory situation should be the performance of an ABC analysis.

Vilfredo Pareto, a 19th century Renaissance man, was the first to document the Management Principle of Materiality, which is the basis of ABC analysis. Pareto, educated as an engineer and renowned as an economist, sociologist, and political scientist, noted that many situations are dominated by a relatively few vital elements in the situation. Thus, he surmised that controlling the relatively vital few will go a long way toward controlling the situation.

Applying the ABC principle to inventory management involves:

1. Classifying inventory items on the basis of relative importance
2. Establishing different management controls for different classifications with the degree of control being commensurate with the ranked importance of each classification

The letters A, B, C represent different classifications of descending importance, but there is nothing sacred about having three classes. Criteria for classification should reflect the difficulty of controlling an item and the impact of the item on costs and profitability.

ABC analysis usually is illustrated using the annual dollar volume criteria as in Exhibit 200.47, but that is only one of many criteria that may affect the value of an item. Factors that affect the importance of an item and that may be criteria for classifying items in an ABC analysis include the following:

1. Annual dollar volume of the transactions for an item
2. Unit cost

230. SUPPLY CHAIN MANAGEMENT

3. Scarcity of material used in producing an item
4. Availability of resources, manpower, and facilities to produce an item
5. Lead time
6. Storage requirements for an item
7. Pilferage risks, shelf life, and other critical attributes
8. Cost of a stockout
9. Engineering design volatility

Whether lead time, storage requirements, possibility of pilferage, shelf life, or scarcity of resources such as raw materials, workforce personnel or facilities for production should be considered in the classification of a group of items can be determined only by examining the situation.

Criteria Other Than Dollar Volume

Exhibit 200.48 illustrates how criteria can be applied in a programmed manner with the classification of an item being determined by the yes answer that results in the highest classification.

Exhibit 200.47 *Example of ABC Analysis*

Item	Unit Cost	Annual Usage	Annual Dollar Usage	Total Annual Percentage Usage
1	0.05	50,000	$2,500	34.3
2	0.11	2,000	220	3.0
3	0.16	400	64	0.9
4	0.08	700	56	0.8
5	0.07	4,800	336	4.6
6	0.15	1,300	195	2.7
7	0.20	17,000	3,400	46.7
8	0.04	300	12	0.2
9	0.09	5,000	450	6.2
10	0.12	400	48	0.7
		81,900	$7,281	100.1

Exhibit 200.48 *Typical Decision Table for ABC Classification*

Question	Class Based on a Yes Answer*
1. Is annual usage more than $50,000?**	A
2. Is annual usage between $10,000 and $50,000?	B
3. Is annual usage less than $10,000?	C
4. Is the unit cost more than $500?	A
5. Is the unit cost between $100 and $500?	B
6. Does the physical nature of the item cause special storage problems?	B
7. Is the lead time longer than 6 months?	A
8. Is the lead time between 3 and 6 months?	B
9. Is shelf life less than 3 months?	A
10. Is shelf life greater than 3 months but less than 6 months?	B

*Final classification of an item is based on the highest classification received.
**The exact values used in annual usage, unit cost, lead time, and other criteria depend on the situation.

The Procedure

With one more caveat, that annual dollar volume alone should not be used to classify an item, the following procedure and simplified examples (Exhibits 200.47, 200.49, and 200.50) for classifying items on the basis of dollar volume are presented.

1. Determine the annual usage for each item in inventory (Exhibit 200.47).
2. Multiply the annual usage of each item by the cost of the item to obtain the total annual dollar usage of each item (Exhibit 200.47).
3. Add the total annual dollar usages of all items to determine the aggregate annual dollar inventory expenditures (Exhibit 200.47).
4. Divide the total annual dollar usage of each item by the aggregate annual expenditure for all items to obtain the percentage of total usage for each item (Exhibit 200.47).
5. List the items in rank order on the basis of the percentage of aggregate usage (Exhibit 200.49).
6. Examine annual usage distribution and group items on basis of percentage of annual usage (Exhibit 200.50).

Exhibit 200.49 and 200.50 typify real-world situations in that the classifications of some items are clearly discernible while others are debatable. Items 7 and 1 are clearly A items, while the classification of Items 2 and 6 could be either B or C.

Examples of different controls that might be used for different classifications are:

A Items

1. Frequent evaluation of forecasts and forecasting method
2. Frequent, perhaps monthly, cycle counting with tight tolerances on accuracy
3. Daily updating of records
4. Frequent review of demand requirements, order quantities, and safety stock; usually resulting in relatively small order quantities
5. Close follow-up and expediting to reduce lead time

Exhibit 200.49 *ABC Analysis—Rank by Percentage of Usage*

Item	Annual Dollar Usage	Percentage of Total	Cumulative Percentage	Item Classification
7	$3,400	46.7	46.7	A
1	2,500	34.3	81.0	A
9	450	6.2	87.2	B
5	336	4.6	91.8	B
2	220	3.0	94.8	B
6	195	2.7	97.5	B
3	64	0.9	98.4	C
4	56	0.8	99.2	C
10	48	0.6	99.8	C
8	12	0.2	100.0	C

Exhibit 200.50 *ABC Analysis—Rank by Classification*

Item Classification	Items	Percentage	Percentage Value
A	7, 1	20	81.0
B	9, 5, 2, 6	40	17.5
C	3, 4, 10, 8	40	2.5

230. SUPPLY CHAIN MANAGEMENT

B Items

　Similar to controls for A items with most control activities taking place less frequently

C Items
1. Basic rule is to *have them*
2. Simple records or no records; perhaps use a periodic review of physical inventory
3. Large order quantities and safety stock
4. Store in area readily available to production workers or order fillers
5. Count items infrequently (annually or semiannually) with scale accuracy (weighing rather than counting) acceptable

　Widespread application of electronic data processing to inventory management has had an impact on some applications of ABC analysis. Accurate and timely records now can be maintained economically on all items except very low-cost ones, such as standard rivets, washers, and other pan stock items. For record-keeping purposes, only A and C items may exist. But recordkeeping procedures are only one aspect of inventory management. Other planning and control procedures, such as evaluation of forecasts and cycle counting frequencies, still may be influenced by the result of an ABC analysis.

　Application of ABC analysis principles does not require the use of only three classifications or even that the classifications be designated A, B, and C. In an interesting presentation, Kenneth L. Campbell recommends the adoption of a descriptive classification system with five different categories each related to the functional use of the items rather than classification based only on annual dollar volume of transactions.[99]

　Before leaving ABC analysis, there are at least two or three other points that should be made. Distinct ABC analyses should be performed for different product groupings. Purchased items, manufactured items, assemblies, subassemblies, independent demand items, and dependent demand items should be analyzed separately in most situations. The analysis should not ignore trends in demand or future plans. Most items experience a product life cycle. Some are on the upswing, experiencing an increasing demand; others may have leveled off and be declining. Historical usage patterns can be misleading if followed blindly. In addition, marketing may be planning to drop a product or engineering may be planning to redesign a component. Such information must be obtained by inventory management and used in establishing planning and control procedures.

　In addition to inventory management, the principles of ABC analysis can be applied to many production and inventory control decisions. Gary Zimmerman, of **McCormick & Company, Inc.,** discusses the use of the ABC principle in establishing "trigger limits" for tracking signals in forecasting, in evaluating orders in relationship to capacity planning on the basis of the amount of critical capacity (worker or machine hours) required by the order, in scheduling by noting those primary operations that provide the bulk of the load on secondary operations, and in determining the frequency of cycle counting.[100] Rolf Norbom reports on the use of ABC principles by the **Philco-Ford Corporation** in controlling purchase part deliveries, inventory levels, and investment at a medium-sized assembly plant.[101]

Continuous Review of Excess and Obsolete Inventory

One way to control inventory investment involves evaluating inventory status on a regular basis. A reduction in problem inventory (such as obsolete inventory) creates benefits by lowering total inventory investment levels. Lower inventory levels lead to lower inventory carrying costs, increased cash flow, better utilization of storage space, and improved inventory turnover. Identification of the root causes of obsolete inventory should result in future savings by learning to better manage inventory investment. There are several basic steps to follow when reviewing inventory investment:

1. Define problem inventory.
2. Automate the inventory review system.
3. Review current inventory investment.
4. Determine courses of action.
5. Correct the underlying causes of excessive and obsolete inventory.

　Inventory may eventually become classified as problem inventory for a number of reasons. A firm may have inadequate inventory control and record-keeping procedures that result in lost inventory. When the item is eventually located, it may not be required for production or service. Marketing may be too optimistic about future sales forecasts, which results in ordering too much inventory to support lower-than-expected production schedules. Economic shifts or technological changes may bring about a sudden shift in a product mix and create excess or obsolete inventory. One particular situation occurs when a part has a short life cycle. Discussions with suppliers and supply chain managers in high-tech industries reveal that a series of smaller life cycles exists within the total product life cycle, referred to as *component life cycles*. Whatever the reason, the continuous review of excess and obsolete inventory should be a regular part of the inventory management process.

Part Simplification and Redesign

Part simplification and redesign involves the detailed analysis of a physical product to identify potential design or material changes. Successful product simplification and redesign positively affects inventory investment in three ways. First, a simplified product design usually requires fewer parts, resulting in lower inventory management costs due to a reduced number of total part numbers. Second, the elimination of unnecessary components through simplification or redesign reduces a part's total cost. A lower part cost reduces the total cost of the inventory required to support part production. Third, product redesign can result in the greater use of standardized versus customized items and/or lower-cost material substitutes. The use of standardized parts almost always results in a lower total part cost, which also reduces inventory costs and improves profit. Most product designers are trying to apply the principles of redesign and simplification during initial product design by asking certain questions:

- Can any part of the product be eliminated without impairing the operation of the complete unit?
- Can the design of the part be changed to reduce its basic cost?
- Can the design of the part be changed to permit the use of simplified and less costly production methods?
- Can less expensive but equally satisfactory materials be used in the part?
- Are standardized items available that can replace customized components?

A thorough review of these questions during product design may lead to a less costly product, which positively affects inventory investment.

Review Safety Stock Levels and Forecasting Techniques

Inaccurate forecasting techniques cause several major problems for supply chain planners. Underforecasting actual customer demand causes production and service problems (not enough is available to satisfy customer requirements). When underforecasting occurs, the supply chain must expedite additional shipments of material at a premium charge. Lost sales may also result due to a lack of finished product or inability to satisfy customer service requirements. On the other hand, an overforecasted demand requirement results in too much inventory. While a supply chain with too much inventory can meet its production schedules, it now has unnecessarily high inventory-carrying costs.

Evaluating the accuracy of the forecasting system should be a continuous activity. The starting point is a comparison of actual demand requirements to forecasted requirements over an extended period of time. The following questions should be asked when evaluating the accuracy of forecasting techniques:

- Are forecasts consistently over or under actual demand, or are forecasting errors randomly distributed?
- Do we understand why actual demand varies from forecasted demand?
- When actual demand patterns change, is the system sensitive enough to realize the change or is there an unacceptable lag?
- Are better forecasting tools or refinements available?
- Are forecasts being manually overridden by planners? If so, why?
- Is the time interval between forecasts adequate?

On-Site Supplier-Managed Inventory

Closer supplier-buyer relationships are crucial for achieving performance improvements, including improvement in the control of inventory investment. One area that features closer supplier-buyer relationships is the use of on-site suppliers to manage inventory.

Almost all organizations use distributors to provide at least some portion of their MRO requirements. A distributor may stock and sell a full range of items from different manufacturers. If the purchaser has enough volume, then the distributor may be willing to locate an employee at the purchaser's facility to manage the inventory.

Purchasers are increasingly entering into partnerships or formal agreements with distributors featuring on-site support. Besides the on-site support, these agreements stipulate that a supplier/distributor will stock a wider range of items and provide agreed-upon service levels. The buyer, in exchange for purchasing solely from the distributor, no longer stocks inventory for items under contract. The on-site representative orders on an as-needed basis, often directly into the distributor's order-processing system. This reduces the amount of paperwork required to submit an order. A buying firm avoids stocking or managing this inventory while the distributor benefits from a higher share of a purchaser's total purchase requirements. Not stocking the items relieves the purchaser of carrying inventory.

The purchase of most MRO items is a nuisance because (1) they require a disproportionate amount of a buyer's time and (2) they are usually lower-value items. A formal agreement providing on-site supplier support can reduce the MRO ordering problem. These arrangements offer an opportunity to control a category of inventory that usually does not receive enough attention. By reducing the time and effort required to obtain route inventory, purchasers and supply chain managers can focus their attention on other value-adding activities.

Material Requirement Planning Systems

When we discuss systems that forecast future demand, we are referring to independent-demand systems. This means that demand for an item is not directly dependent upon the demand for any other item. A major task of the materials manager, however, is to control the inventory of items whose demand is dependent on the production of other items. A riding lawn mower is an example of an independent-demand item. Demand for the final part is independent—expected orders determine the final amount produced. The demand for the steering wheel or tires that go on the mower, for example, are dependent on the demand for the final part number (i.e., for the lawn mower). The production and scheduling system calculates the demand for the components or subassemblies with certainty. The component part or subassembly demand is simply a function of the production schedule for the final part number.

The availability of cost-efficient computer systems has allowed firms to make great progress controlling dependent-demand inventory. A widely used system that controls dependent-demand inventory is the material requirements planning (MRP) system. This system relies on production schedules developed for final part numbers in the master production schedule (MPS) to determine the timing and quantities of materials required for components or subassemblies.

Distribution Resource Planning Systems

Distribution resource planning (DRP) systems attempt to make the most effective use of finished-goods inventories. These systems, which are concerned with inventory that has left the work-in-process status, perform many functions:

- Forecasting finished-good inventory requirements
- Establishing correct inventory levels at each stocking location
- Identifying optimal stocking locations
- Determining the timing and replenishment of finished-goods inventories
- Allocating items in short supply
- Transportation planning and vehicle-load scheduling

It is easy to see how a DRP system, combined with upstream supply chain planning systems such as MRP, can provide a total supply chain perspective.

Supply Chain Inventory Planning and Control

The establishment of a supply chain or logistical planner position responsible for coordinating and integrating material and information movement throughout the entire supply chain is gaining popularity as a way to manage inventory investment. A supply chain planner, a position often organized along product lines, manages the flow of inventory and information from suppliers through end customers. This position ties together the requirements of purchasing/materials management, production, inventory control, and product distribution.

The planner coordinates the movement and placement of inventory throughout the supply, production, and distribution channel. This person also serves as the liaison between various groups in the supply chain. Other assignments include developing production schedules, establishing production targets from marketing forecasts, determining inventory deployment at field warehouses, and continuously evaluating inventory safety stock levels. The supply chain planner also works closely with purchasing to coordinate material requirements to support production targets.

Automated Inventory-Tracking Systems

Automated inventory control systems involve computerized material and electronic data interchange (EDI) systems that track the flow of inventory throughout the entire supply chain. This approach electronically connects suppliers, production plants, field distribution centers, and even customers. A customer may be a retail outlet or an independent distributor.

An integrated systems approach relies on new forms of information technology, such as EDI and bar-code scanning, to link the entire supply chain electronically. Wal-Mart, for example, has benefited greatly from automated inventory-tracking systems, using bar-code technology to manage inventory at the point of sale to the consumer and back up the supply chain to suppliers. Tracking sales allows Wal-Mart to identify what is selling and to replenish shelves quickly. Automated tracking systems present an opportunity for controlling inventory investment throughout the entire supply chain.

Supplier-Buyer Cycle-Time Reduction

Shortening the material pipeline in terms of time between suppliers and a buyer can reduce the average amount of inventory in a system at any given time. One area of emphasis will be to support reduced order-cycle times with suppliers. A reduced (and reliable) order-cycle time positively affects inventory investment by allowing more frequent orders received in smaller quantities. Planning horizons are also shorter, which reduces the need to carry safety stock.

There are several actions that support reduced order-cycle time with suppliers:

- *Expanded EDI capability:* The electronic exchange of information in a supply chain supports paperless procurement, faster data movement, and increased information accuracy. Electronic data interchange has the potential to reduce order-cycle times by 15 percent to 40 percent from current levels.
- *Supplier development support:* Supplier development means working directly with key supply chain members to improve performance. This support may include working directly at a supplier's facilities to speed order entry, production, and delivery through the removal of waste.
- *Measure order-cycle time:* Tracking order-cycle times helps identify areas of improvement. We expect to see greater emphasis on the development of performance measures that are time oriented.
- *Focus on second- and third-tier suppliers:* Total supply chain management requires working with first-, second-, and even third-tier suppliers. The ability of a purchaser to reduce order-cycle time and inventory with its immediate suppliers is partly a function of a supplier being able to work with its suppliers. A supplier's suppliers will become an increasingly important point of interest to supply chain managers.

These are not the only actions that supply chain managers can or will emphasize to manage inventory investment. This discussion points out, however, that creative approaches exist for achieving systemwide control and management of inventory investment.

Purchasing Transportation Services

The timely and efficient movement and management of goods is critical to effective supply chain management. Many companies, like Ford, are aggressively using transportation and logistics providers to create advantages that customers benefit from directly.[102] Without effective transportation, getting the right product to the right place at the right time becomes nearly impossible. Selecting the right transportation and logistics provider is as critical as any other supplier evaluation and selection decision made within an organization.

Transportation service providers support the four major linkages throughout a typical supply chain, as shown in Exhibit 200.51: (1) inbound logistics, (2) intraorganizational movements, (3) outbound logistics, and (4) recovery and recycling. The first link includes all inbound shipments moving between a supplier and a buyer's facilities. In addition, a purchaser should theoretically also be concerned with the transportation linkages between its second-, third-, and fourth-tier suppliers. Any disruption in service or high costs at subtier supplies may eventually affect the buyer.

Exhibit 200.51 *Types of Logistics/Transportation Links*

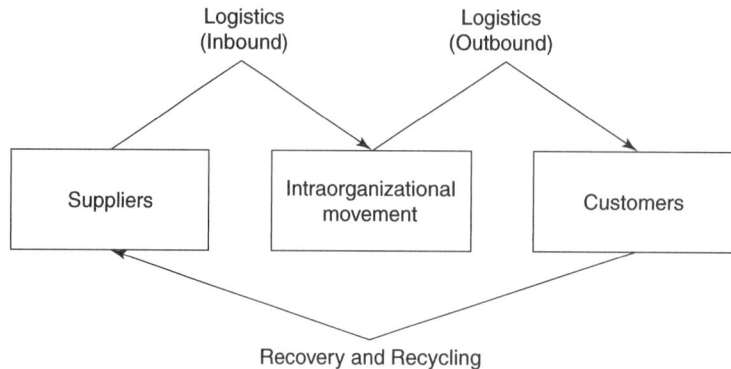

Companies with multiple production and warehouse facilities usually have a second major transportation link—intraorganizational movement. This includes movement of materials between production facilities within the same organization as well as movement to warehouse storage locations. A storage location may be in the same manufacturing complex as the production facility or at some other geographic location, which another company may control. Some companies directly control the movement of goods within this link through the use of company-owned transportation vehicles. Others are increasingly bypassing this link by producing only when they have a customer order, which allows shipment directly to the customer, and thus reduces the need for costly warehouse and distribution facilities.

The third link—outbound logistics—establishes the link between a company and its customers. Historically, the transportation department controlled the movement of outbound goods while suppliers arranged the movement of inbound freight. Since the deregulation of the transportation industry in the early 1980s, purchasing's involvement with the control of all three transportation links has increased greatly. The fourth link is one that companies are increasingly becoming concerned with—recovery and recycling of obsolete products and goods. This "reverse logistics" flow will require companies to find innovative methods of recovering and recycling products to minimize the impact on the environment.

Purchasing's Role in Buying Transportation Services

Effectively managing transportation services is important for several reasons. First, transportation is a major cost center at most manufacturing companies. Typically, transportation costs comprise 10 percent (on average) of a product's total cost structure. For many firms, logistics expenses now are second only to material costs in terms of their impact on cost of goods sold, and logistics expenditures represent one of the largest costs in international commerce.

Perhaps more important than cost savings is the direct impact transportation has on operations. Transportation affects production and scheduling systems, inventory levels, and customer order management. Companies that do not effectively manage transportation may experience increased waste and reduced competitiveness. While often taken for granted, transportation can have serious consequences if not managed properly. When managed properly, world-class transportation systems can satisfy end-customer needs faster and at a lower cost.

Deregulation has created major opportunities for purchasing to negotiate improved rates and service levels for transportation services. During the early 1980s, it became apparent that transportation offered significant cost savings if managed properly. Purchasing began to take an active role in the selection of and negotiation with transportation service providers.

When purchasing takes an active role in transportation decisions, managers often become involved with identifying and selecting inbound transportation providers, although involvement with outbound transportation providers is becoming more common. Purchasing may also negotiate freight agreements and evaluate carrier performance in a manner similar to the evaluation of suppliers of purchased items. The transportation department, if one still exists, usually involves itself with the day-today management of the transportation system or the development of transportation strategies that do not involve purchasing. This includes arranging pick-up and deliveries, processing damage claims, tracing and expediting shipments when required, coordinating intraplant and outbound movements, and auditing freight bills for accuracy. Both purchasing and transportation departments can combine their individual expertise when developing transportation strategies.

A Decision-Making Framework for Developing a Transportation Strategy

The development of a transportation strategy involves a series of decisions. Exhibit 200.52 presents a general framework outlining some of the decisions and issues a purchaser faces when formulating a transportation strategy. How a transportation network is organized will vary depending on the type of commodity or material being moved. For example, bulk raw material usually requires rail transport, while small, expensive electronic components can use quicker but more expensive modes such as airfreight. No single approach or strategy covers the entire transportation needs of a company that purchases different items and raw materials.

Determine When and Where to Control Transportation

An initial decision regarding an organization's transportation requirements involves determining when and where to control shipments. A significant amount of inbound material, for example, is still shipped *F.O.B. destination*. This designation means the seller retains title to the goods and controls the shipment until it is physically received at a purchaser's facility. Unless otherwise negotiated, this also means the seller is responsible for the cost of the physical transportation, which the buying company inevitably pays for in the unit cost of the purchased item. Controlling inbound shipment usually requires a shipping designation of *F.O.B. shipping point*.

When a seller includes transportation charges as part of the unit cost of a good, the buyer often loses the ability to track transportation expenses. This also inflates the value of the purchaser's inventory, which has tax and other financial implications. Even when a supplier assumes responsibility for transportation costs, many purchasers require the supplier to identify transportation-related costs separately from material costs. Exhibit 200.53 compares

Exhibit 200.52 *Transportation Strategy Development—A Decision-Making Process*

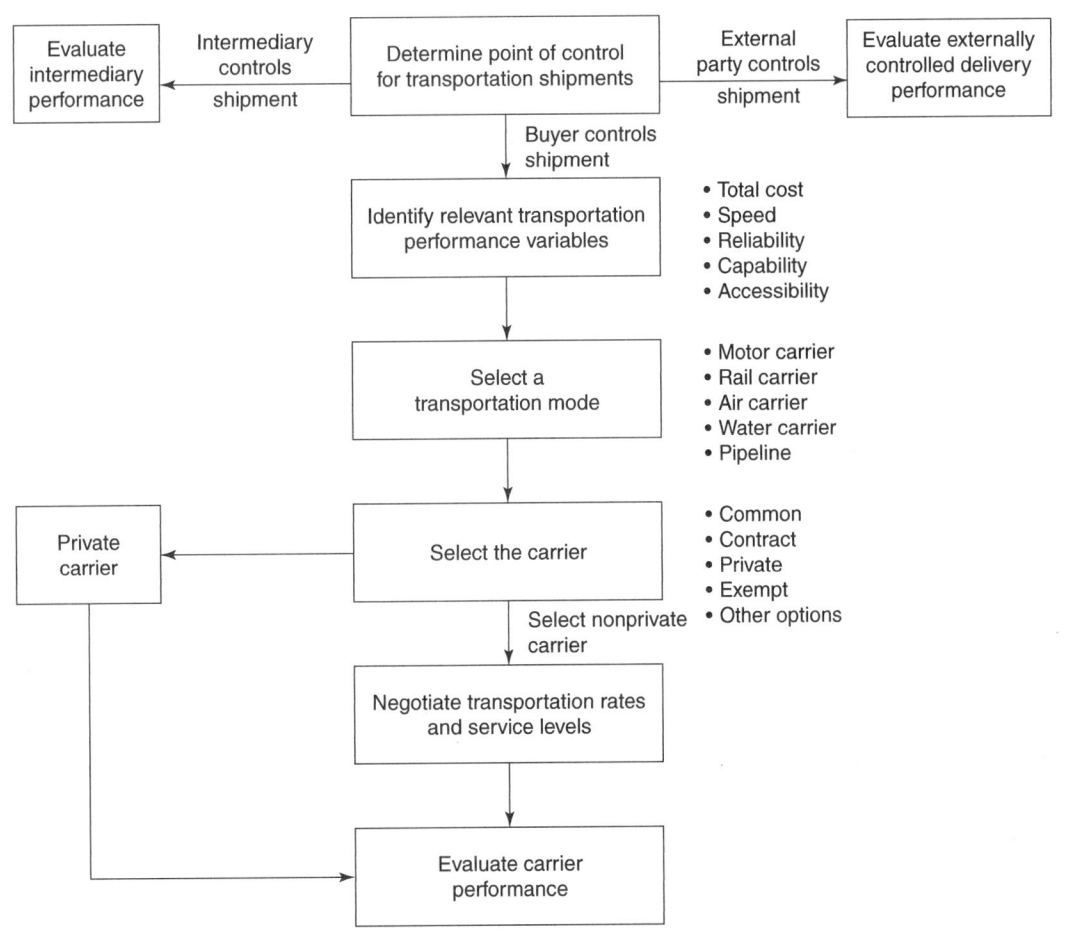

the two primary F.O.B. shipping designations and the Uniform Commercial Code (UCC) sections that apply to domestic transportation designations.

The choice of whether to insource or outsource transportation is similar to a make-or-buy decision. A purchaser who chooses to have an external party, such as a supplier or logistics service, arrange and control material movement has no further decision to make concerning transportation. For some shipments, particularly small-volume shipments, a purchaser may determine it is not worthwhile to spend the time and energy to arrange transportation. When this is the case, a possible option is to provide suppliers with a list of acceptable transportation providers. The purchaser may even have negotiated a contract with the carrier for discounted freight rates. A purchaser who relinquishes control of inbound transportation to a supplier should still evaluate the delivery performance of supplier-arranged shipments.

Another option at this phase of the decision-making process involves the use of a transportation broker or intermediary. While this option also means giving up direct control of transportation shipments, a buyer may realize some benefits. A broker or intermediary should have the buyer's best interest in mind because the buyer is a customer of the intermediary. The broker or intermediary acts as a buyer's agent when arranging transportation. The intermediary can combine shipments with other customers' shipments to achieve a lower total transportation cost. Intermediaries can also perform valuable services such as expediting shipments through customs or negotiating favorable rates directly with carriers. This option is popular for firms lacking the resources or experience to manage their transportation system. It is also an option for small shipments.

Identify Key Transportation Performance Variables

Different performance variables must be assessed carefully when developing a thorough transportation strategy. The following set of variables is assessed when comparing transportation modes as well as specific carriers within the same mode. The criteria used to measure transportation performance are shown in Exhibit 200.54.

Select a Transportation Mode

A match must exist between the key transportation performance variables identified in the previous section and the ability of the different modes or types of transportation to satisfy the requirements of these variables. For some items, it is not a difficult decision to make. For example, overseas shipments usually arrive by ocean vessel or, in a limited number of cases, by air carrier. Bulk or liquid commodities, such as raw materials or chemicals, usually arrive by rail. The most common modal decisions involve comparisons and trade-offs between rail and motor carrier; rail and inland water; and motor and air carrier. The most common modal decision for international shipments from outside of North America is between ocean vessel and air transportation.

There are five principal modes of transportation available to purchasers of transportation services: (1) motor, (2) rail, (3) air, (4) water, and (5) pipeline. A summary of the major advantages and disadvantages of each is shown in Exhibit 200.55.

Exhibit 200.53 *Defining Domestic Transportation Shipping Terms*

Shipper's Facility F.O.B. Shipping Point	Carrier	Buyer's Facility F.O.B. Destination
What does F.O.B. shipping point mean?		**What does F.O.B. destination mean?**

• Buyer controls or directs shipment
• Buyer assumes title to goods and risk of loss at seller's shipping point, unless agreed to otherwise (UCC Section 2-401)
• Seller has certain responsibilities (UCC Section 2-504):
   • To put the goods in the possession of the carrier
   • To make a proper contract for the transportation of the goods, taking into consideration the nature of the goods and other circumstances
   • To obtain and promptly deliver to the buyer any documents necessary for the buyer to take possession of the goods
   • To promptly notify the buyer of the shipment
		• Seller is required at own risk and expense to transport goods to that place and there tender delivery (UCC Section 2-319)
		• Seller assumes title to goods and risk of loss until satisfactory delivery to buyer's facility, unless agreed to otherwise (UCC Section 2-401)

Exhibit 200.54 *Criteria Used to Measure Transportation Performance*

Performance Measure	Description
Total cost	In addition to the fee charges, total cost includes the cost of extra inventory, warehousing, buffer stock, and in the case of international shipments, broker fees, customs, etc. Other cost factors such as extra managerial time may also have to be factored in.
Speed	Measured as time from when the shipment is released at the supplier's facility to the time of receipt at the buyer's receiving dock.
Reliability	Sometimes described as *fill rate*. Refers to the ability to deliver on time. Can be measured in different ways, but is typically a window of time when the delivery must be made. The measure is thus the percentage of deliveries made within the specified window.
Capability	Refers to the ability of the carrier to move the material, including special materials, hazardous materials, etc.
Accessibility	Refers to whether the carrier is capable of picking up the shipment and delivering it door-to-door.

Exhibit 200.55 *Advantages and Disadvantages of Transportation Modes*

Transportation Mode	Advantages	Disadvantages
Motor carrier	• High flexibility • Good speed • Good reliability • Good for JIT delivery • Can negotiate rates	• High cost • Limited to domestic or regional transportation • Cannot be used for large volumes
Rail carrier	• Lower cost • Can handle wide range of items • Piggyback service can increase flexibility • Direct between major cities • Greater intermodal service • Safe for hazardous materials	• Limited access to rail line or spur • Longer in-transit lead times • Less flexible—may not have rails to all locations
Air carrier	• Quick and reliable • Good for light/small, high-value shipments (e.g., electronics) • Good for expediting/emergency situations	• Very high cost • Location of large airports limits shipping points • Cannot be used for large, bulky, or hazardous shipments
Water carrier	• Good for bulk commodities (inland) and heavy, large items (international) • Can handle most types of freight • Low cost	• Limited flexibility • Seasonal availability • Very long lead times • Poor reliability (may encounter delays at ports, etc.)
Pipeline	• Good for high-volume liquids and gases • Low cost once installed	• High up-front installation costs • Limited to only certain items

Select the Carrier

Once a purchaser makes a decision about what form of transportation is best suited to transport an item, the next step involves selecting the transportation provider to transport the material. A purchaser has several options available besides simply contacting a for-hire company and arranging shipment. Firms can select a public (common) carrier, negotiate for services with a contract or exempt carrier, arrange shipments on company-owned vehicles (private carrier), or use a special type of carrier (such as FedEx or **UPS**). The most common decision is whether to use a common, contract, or exempt carrier.

COMMON CARRIERS   By law, a *common carrier* serves the general public without discrimination. Part of its operating authority comes from its obligation to serve transportation users in a fair and nondiscriminatory manner. Besides its duty not to discriminate against transportation users, a common carrier must offer reasonable rates, although rates are not published as they were during regulation. A purchaser deciding to use a common carrier, particularly a motor carrier, often has a wide choice of carriers within a geographic region. Examples of common carriers include **Roadway, Werner,** and **Schneider,** noted for its bright orange trucks.

CONTRACT CARRIERS   Companies that rely heavily on precise and frequent transportation might consider the use of a *contract carrier.* A contract carrier does not hold itself out to serve the general public as does a common carrier. The contract carrier serves a shipper (i.e., a buyer) under specific contract terms. A contract carrier, sometimes referred to as a *dedicated carrier,* serves the transportation requirements of the party with which it has a legal agreement. Contract carriers are popular with firms practicing just-in-time purchasing and delivery.

Contract carriers can offer many benefits to the transportation buyer. Besides negotiating a favorable rate, a buyer can usually receive a higher level of service than might otherwise be expected. After all, the carrier and buyer have a continuous contractual relationship.

PRIVATE CARRIERS   A private carrier includes the vehicles that a purchaser controls through direct ownership or management. Typically these vehicles move goods between company-owned facilities or from a company to its customers. At times these vehicles may be used for the inbound movement of material. Besides greater control, this offers the opportunity to increase the utilization of company-owned assets.

Probably the major drawback to using company-owned vehicles for inbound shipments is a lack of dedication to this task. It might be difficult to arrange shipments from a supplier's facility on a regular basis using company-owned vehicles. Practical experience with a number of firms indicates the use of private carriers for inbound shipments is the exception rather than the rule. When firms use a private carrier for receiving purchased items, it is usually the result of a geographically convenient arrangement between a purchaser and supplier.

EXEMPT CARRIERS   Exempt carriers are free of any regulation with respect to economic issues. They are able to gain this status because of the type of commodity they haul and the nature of their operation. These carriers usually transport agricultural products, newspapers, livestock, or fish. Exempt carriers are primarily local water carriers of bulk items.

OTHER CARRIERS   A buyer can also evaluate other shipping options, which is increasingly the case with electronic commerce (business to consumer) Internet companies. For example, FedEx and UPS fall into this category. The use of these carriers is increasingly becoming an option for smaller shipper, and shipments. They are convenient, relatively inexpensive, and extremely reliable. They also offer linked information systems that provide a substantial advantage over their competitors. For this reason, many distributors and mail order companies use FedEx and UPS as their primary provider of transportation services.

Determining the type of carrier is only part of the decision process during this phase. Purchasing must also evaluate and compare different carriers against those variables that are critical to performance. Purchasers should even evaluate their own private carrier to make sure it can meet the same performance standards required of for-hire carriers. Selecting a carrier for transportation services should be no different or less rigorous than selecting a supplier for a purchased component.

NEGOTIATE TRANSPORTATION RATES AND SERVICE LEVELS   A purchaser with fairly substantial transportation requirements across its supply chain will likely negotiate directly with a carrier for dedicated or contracted services. This does not mean that buyers negotiate only with contract carriers. Negotiation can also occur with a common carrier, particularly over transportation rates and service requirements.

A major result of transportation deregulation has been the shift of the pricing function from published tariffs and rate bureaus to the negotiating table. A purchaser can use the negotiating session to detail required service levels while the carrier can indicate what freight volumes are necessary to support a particular service level or rate. The negotiating session(s) can cover a number of topics:[103]

- Service performance guarantees with penalties and rewards based on performance
- Commitment to ship a minimum amount of volume during the life of the contract
- Handling of freight claims
- Type of equipment to be used by the carrier

- Frequency of shipments
- Establishment of information-sharing systems
- Rate discounts
- Creative and innovative joint methods to reduce total transportation costs

A purchaser does not necessarily negotiate a contract with every carrier it uses. A smart buyer, however, will take advantage of the opportunities offered in today's transportation environment by combining transportation volumes with fewer carriers to achieve shipping economies of scale.

Performance Measurement and Evaluation

Purchasing and Supply Chain Performance Measurement and Evaluation

A purchasing and supply chain performance evaluation system represents a formal, systematic approach to monitor and evaluating purchasing performance. While this sounds easy, it is often difficult to develop measures that direct behavior or activity exactly as intended. Some firms still rely on measures that harm rather than support long-term performance objectives. For example, the ability to win price concessions from a supplier is still a major objective for certain price/cost performance measures. However, if a purchaser continuously squeezes short-term price reductions from a supplier, will that supplier have the financial resources or the commitment to invest in longer-term performance improvements?

Modern purchasing and supply chain performance measurement and evaluation systems contain a variety of measures. Most of these measures fall into two broad categories: effectiveness and efficiency measures. *Effectiveness* refers to the extent to which, by choosing a certain course of action, management can meet a previously established goal or standard. *Efficiency* refers to the relationship between planned and actual sacrifices made to realize a previously agreed-upon goal.[104] Efficiency measures usually relate some input to a performance output.

Almost all measures include a standard or target against which to evaluate performance results or outcomes. It is incomplete to say, for example, that a measure will track improvement in supplier quality. We still need to compare actual improvement against a preestablished target or objective. Meeting this target, which is presumably based on world-class performance levels, will bring value to an organization. Each performance measure should include actual performance levels and a targeted performance level.

Why Measure Performance?

A number of reasons exist for measuring and evaluating purchasing and supply chain activity and performance.

SUPPORT BETTER DECISION MAKING   Measurement can lead to better decisions by making performance and results visible. It is difficult to develop performance improvement plans without understanding the areas in which performance falls short. Measurement provides a track record of purchasing performance over time and directly supports decision-making activity by management.

SUPPORT BETTER COMMUNICATION   Performance measurement can result in better communication across the supply chain, including within purchasing, between departments, with suppliers, and with executive management. For example, a purchaser must communicate clearly performance expectations to suppliers. The measures that quantify supplier performance reflect a purchaser's expectations.

PROVIDE PERFORMANCE FEEDBACK   Measurement provides the opportunity for performance feedback, which supports the prevention or correction of problems identified during the performance measurement process. Feedback also provides insight into how well a buyer, department, team, or supplier is meeting its performance objectives over time.

MOTIVATE AND DIRECT BEHAVIOR   Measurement motivates and directs behavior toward desired end results. A measurement system can accomplish this in several ways. First, the selection of performance categories and objectives indicates to purchasing personnel those activities that an organization considers critical. Second, management can motivate and influence behavior by linking the attainment of performance objectives to organizational rewards, such as pay increases.

Problems with Purchasing and Supply Chain Measurement and Evaluation

Measuring and evaluating performance, including purchasing and supply chain performance, historically has had certain problems and limitations. Mark Brown, an expert on performance measurement, argues that most managers and professionals today are like pilots trying to fly planes with only half the instruments needed and many additional instruments that measure irrelevant data.[105] He states that practically every organization has some type of problem with its measurement system.

TOO MUCH DATA AND WRONG DATA   Having too much data is the most common problem an organization has with its measurement system. A second and more serious problem is that the data that managers pay attention to are often the wrong data. The metrics are selected because of history or a feeling that the measure is related to success, which may not be the case at all. In fact, measures that managers follow may sometimes be in conflict with measures used in other units or functional areas. As a general rule, no employee should monitor more than a dozen measures, with a half of those being the most critical.

MEASURES THAT ARE SHORT-TERM FOCUSED   Many small- and medium-sized organizations have a problem of relying on measures and data that are short-term focused. Typically the only data they collect are financial and operating data. In purchasing, this would mean a short-term focus on workload and supply chain activities, while ignoring the longer-range or strategic measures.

LACK OF DETAIL   At times the data that are reported are summarized so much as to make the information meaningless. A measure that reports on a single measure of monthly supplier quality probably lacks detail. A supply manager will want to know what are the specific types of defects the supplier is experiencing, what the defects cost the buyer's company, and the supplier's quality performance over time.

An operations manager at a major automotive regional parts distribution facility receives a monthly measure of the facility's quality as measured by claims made by customers. However, he also receives reports that detail the following:

- The type of errors that are occurring (wrong part picked, damage, shortages, missed shipments, etc.)
- Which customers are making the quality claims
- Which employees are responsible for the quality errors
- The total cost of the quality claims against the facility
- The part numbers that have quality claims against them

With this information the manager can take action that will attack the root causes of the quality problems at his facility.

DRIVE THE WRONG PERFORMANCE   Unfortunately, many measures drive behavior that is not what was intended or needed. If buyers are measured on the number of purchase orders written, then they will make sure to split orders between suppliers to generate as many purchase orders as possible. Part of this is due to the fact that measuring intellectual work is difficult. However, organizations still want to look for factors that can be measured and reported. These factors may not, however, always be the right factors.

MEASURES OF BEHAVIOR VERSUS ACCOMPLISHMENTS   The problem with measuring behavior is there is no guarantee the behavior will lead to desired results. A behavioral measure that tracks the amount of purchase volume covered by corporate-wide contracts, for example, is becoming increasingly common. A better measure, however, is one that tracks the total savings due to the use of corporate-wide contracts. Another example of a behavioral measure is one that measures the number of meetings held by a commodity team each quarter. A better set of measures will track the performance results that occurred because of the team's actions. Although some set of behavioral measures will always be present, measures that capture accomplishments will be the ones that really matter.

Purchasing and Supply Chain Performance Measurement Categories

Hundreds of purchasing and supply chain measures are in existence. Perhaps the best way to summarize the vast number of separate measures is by developing performance measurement categories. Within each category, many separate measures appear that relate to each general category. Most purchasing and supply chain measures fall into one of the following categories:

1. Price performance
2. Cost effectiveness
3. Purchasing workload
4. Administration and control
5. General efficiency measures
6. Material status and control
7. Supplier performance
8. Supply chain performance
9. Strategic performance
10. Regulatory, societal, and environmental
11. Purchasing planning and research

Items 7, 8, and 9 are discussed in the following sections.

Supplier Performance Measures

Supplier performance measurement is an area in which many firms have made great progress. Purchasers generally track supplier quality, cost, and delivery along with other performance areas. Furthermore, firms are beginning to quantify the cost associated with each act of supplier nonperformance. The resulting cost figure represents the total cost of doing business with a supplier. Supplier total-cost measures allow direct comparisons between suppliers.

The supplier performance evaluation model developed by **Hewlett-Packard** represents one way to evaluate supplier performance. This model evaluates supplier performance (and the teams that manage those suppliers) in the areas of T (technology contribution), Q (quality), R (supplier responsiveness), D (delivery performance), C (cost), and E (environmental performance).

Supply Chain Performance Measures

Many measures relate to how well various aspects of the supply chain are operating.

INVENTORY It is common to have multiple measures that track different aspects of a firm's inventory investment. These measures are common with physical distribution centers. Examples include dollar value of total inventory, percentage of active to inactive part numbers, total number of part numbers, working capital savings, total inventory investment, day's supply of inventory, and inventory investment by type of purchased item (for example, production items, maintenance items, packaging materials).

It is also common to have measures that track the speed or velocity of inventory as it moves through the supply chain. This includes raw material, work-in-process, and finished-goods inventory turns. The amount of inventory maintained as safety stock is also a common measure. The accuracy of computer records that are part of the inventory location system is also closely tracked.

TRANSPORTATION Transportation measures include tracking actual transportation costs against some preestablished objective, demurrage and detention costs, transportation carrier quality and delivery performance levels, and transportation lead-time indicators.

230. SUPPLY CHAIN MANAGEMENT

CUSTOMER ORDERS These measures evaluate how well an organization is satisfying its commitment to downstream customers. Various measures include the percentage of on-time delivery, total time from customer order to customer delivery, returned orders, and warranty claims. While we have focused primarily on purchasing and upstream supply chain activities, purchasing and material planners are increasingly responsible for managing inventory from a total supply chain perspective. This may also include downstream activities.

Strategic Performance Measures

Purchasing requires measures that reflect its ability to support overall corporate and functional goals, which means a reduced emphasis on pure efficiency measures (e.g., the cost to issue a purchase order or current workload status) and greater emphasis on effectiveness measures (those that reflect purchasing's strategic contribution). Examples of the latter include tracking early supplier involvement in product design, performance gains resulting from direct supplier development efforts, or supplier-provided improvement suggestions. Within most industries, purchasing must shift from measuring itself as an administrative support function to one that provides strategic value.

Exhibit 200.56 provides examples of key strategic purchasing measures. Notice that these measures are a combination of activity and results-oriented measures. Emphasis shifts from strict indicators of personnel performance or efficiency to how well the purchasing function supports strategic supply-base management goals and objectives. To shift from an operational to a strategic perspective, the purchasing measurement and evaluation system must also shift.

The performance indicators in Exhibit 200.56 are more strategically and externally focused than traditional performance indicators. They are also specified in terms of broader purchasing goals rather than specific activity. For example, a buyer may be responsible for a performance objective stating that 75 percent of the buyer's suppliers will be quality certified by the third quarter of next year. This differs from a measure that states a buyer must process 10 requests for quotation per day on average.

Exhibit 200.56 *Examples of Strategic Purchasing Measurement Indicators*

- Percentage of purchasing's operating budget committed to on-site supplier visits
- Proportion of quality-certified suppliers to total suppliers
- Percentage of receipts free of inspection and material defects
- Total number of suppliers
- Proportion of suppliers participating in early product design or other joint value-added activities
- Revenue increase as a result of supplier-provided technology that differentiates end products to customers
- Percentage of operating budget allocated to supplier development and training
- Total cost supplier selection and evaluation measures
- Supplier lead-time indicators
- Purchasing's contribution to return on assets, return on investment, and economic value-added corporate measures
- Purchasing success with achieving cost reductions with tier 2 and tier 3 suppliers
- Percentage of purchase dollars committed to longer-term contracts
- Savings achieved from the use of companywide agreements
- Purchasing's contribution to product development cycle-time reduction
- Percentage/dollar value of items purchased from single sources
- Percentage of purchase dollars committed to highest-performing suppliers
- Percentage of purchase transactions through electronic data interchange (EDI) or Web-based systems
- Percentage of total receipts on a just-in-time basis
- Supplier quality levels, cost performance, and delivery performance compared with world-class performance targets
- Supplier development costs and benefits
- Continuous supplier performance improvement measures
- Reductions in working capital due to purchasing and supply chain efforts
- Contribution to return on investment and assets realized from strategic outsourcing efforts
- Savings achieved from part number reduction efforts
- Savings achieved from part standardization efforts

Services and Retail Operations

Service Operations

Why study service operations? Several reasons make services, and the *operations* of services in particular, worthy of study:

- Service firms constitute an overwhelmingly large percentage of the economy of every industrialized nation; the size will only increase, and it is by far the most likely economic sector for employment.
- Despite the size of the service economy, academic research has largely ignored services. The relative lack of attention given to services provides a competitive edge to those students who pursue its study.
- Many services have characteristics that are strongly different from goods. Consequently, specialized and different managerial techniques are employed in services than are employed in many manufacturing firms, and knowledge and experience gained from studying manufacturing settings does not always transfer to services.

Characteristics of Services

Focused study of the problems of service firms is useful because services, in general, have different characteristics than goods. Consequently, analogies and conceptual models formed by a study of how goods-producing industries work may not always translate to service firms. Various characteristics have been listed over the years as to how services differ from goods. Some of the ways in which services are said to differ from goods include the following:

- Services are intangible whereas goods are tangible.
- Sources are simultaneously consumed as they are produced.
- Services often require closer proximity to the customer.
- Services cannot be inventoried.

Each of these characteristics makes management more challenging and requires a different mindset from traditional managerial practices. However, a closer look at these traditionally discussed differences indicate that they are only partially true.

Intangibility of Services

The results from a service may be an emotion from hearing a song or seeing a tennis match, but frequently no *thing* is left behind. However, most services come with "facilitating goods." For example, a playbill can remind one of a good performance, or a photograph of a friend on the roller coaster at the amusement park can serve as a physical reminder of a service. Of course, the results of many service firms are quite tangible: A car that runs again or a sack full of groceries both come from service-producing businesses.

Conversely, physical goods frequently have intangible aspects. For example, the U.S. government officially defines vodka as a "colorless, odorless, tasteless" alcoholic beverage, yet consumers gladly pay four times the price of a lesser brand for a premium brand. Even though distinctions regarding the quality of vodka brands may be debatable, an intangible feeling clearly can be derived from owning a premium car, a premium antique furnishing, or an original painting by a master, which goes well beyond the physical good.

Further, just as services have "facilitating goods," nearly every good has a "facilitating service" that is tangible. At a minimum, goods often must be transported to the customer, and transportation is a service.

Simultaneous Production and Consumption

Many services are "produced" by the seller and "consumed" by the buyer at the same time. Live performances of plays or music are the quintessential examples. Simultaneity of production and consumption makes quality control and matching capacity to demand especially difficult. Some services, however, such as computer system upgrading and janitorial work, are specifically designed to be produced while the customer is *not* there. Also, many manufacturers face similar managerial difficulties with rush orders that must be done immediately and to a customer's specification.

Proximity to the Customer

Many services must be physically close to the customer. For example, placing one giant McDonald's in the middle of Nebraska isn't a good business model. For this reason, large service firms operate hundreds or thousands of units, while manufacturers operate only a few. McDonald's and Dell Computer record roughly the same revenues, yet McDonald's operates a "few" more facilities than the six Dell plants worldwide. Also, even choosing where to locate a service requires totally different criteria than a manufacturing facility, because services generally must be close to the customer.

Proximity is not always essential in services. For example, Internet-based services employ radically different strategies than services that are location-dependent. Many back-office services such as credit approval or insurance claim processing are performed halfway across the globe from the customer. Also, manufacturers of products like cement and sheetrock must be close to the customer because the cost of transportation is large relative to the cost of the product.

Services Cannot Be Inventoried

The lack of ability to build inventory or use backorders seriously influences managerial choices. Imagine approaching a store clerk for help only to be told, "I'm busy now, I'll get back to you in four to six weeks." Consumers routinely wait that long for goods delivery, but services often must be provided in a very short time or suffer a lost sale. Consequently, many services manage waiting time, rather than inventory. Of course, some exceptions are notable. Restaurant reservations are a clear example of a service that can be backordered.

For many service industries, such as retailing and wholesaling, managing physical inventory is a highly strategic endeavor. For other service firms, like hotels and airlines, effectively managing their "inventory" of hotel rooms and airline seats is essential.

On the other hand, some manufacturers must more closely manage customer waiting time than inventory. Manufacturers of custom goods suffer some of the same problems of traditional services. If all finished goods are custom-made, finished goods inventory cannot be kept, and customers may make their purchasing decision based on waiting time.

The foregoing discussion is not meant to imply that goods-producing and service-producing industries do not differ. Clear differences distinguish the management problems of the **Bolshoi Ballet** from those of **Bethlehem Steel**. However, the differences between goods and services fall on a continuum. Some service firms and manufacturers may share many similarities at the same time that firms lumped together under the "services" umbrella exhibit extreme differences. A customer of a grocery store mainly buys goods, though a grocer is a service industry, whereas the customer of a nail salon is purchasing nearly 100 percent service. Naturally, such firms face different managerial challenges.

Service Firm Classification Frameworks

A number of proposed service firm classification frameworks attempt to show where similarities among service firms may yield insights. Many service business managers seem to believe their problems are unique to their particular business, or at most their particular industry, and that they share little in common with other service industries. If this view is correct, then only individuals with vast experience within the firm or industry should be hired for management positions, and firms could at best only look at their direct competitors for help on ideas on how to improve.

The basis for academic study of the field of service operations lies in the opposite view: Commonalities can be found among the problems and challenges many businesses face. This view contends that methods, ideas, and people can span industries, and employees and ideas from other industries can bring a fresh, vital approach to a business.

To gain a perspective about which industries share certain characteristics, it is useful to classify service firms. Classification schemes provide a mental lens for viewing the commonalities between businesses that may also demonstrate vast differences.

A well-known classification scheme for service operations is called the Customer Contact Model.[106] Here, services are classified according to the amount of customer contact. High-contact services, or "pure services," include hospitals and restaurants, and a high percentage of their activity must take place in the presence of the customer. Low-contact services—called "quasi-manufacturing" firms—include distribution centers, wholesalers, and back-office facilities such as the check-processing centers of retail banks, which require virtually no face-to-face contact with customers. Services with elements of both are termed "mixed services," and include the branch offices of banks and insurance firms.

The customer as the dominant force to be considered in designing service systems represents the central guiding principle in this view. This simple, yet powerful idea can be formulated as:

$$\text{Potential Efficiency} \times f(1 - \text{Customer Contact Time/Service Creation Time})$$

This equation indicates that the "potential" efficiency of a service is limited by the amount of time the customer is involved in the system. Note, however, that it is not necessarily desirable to maximize efficiency.

Several essential insights are associated with this line of thinking. Most obviously, firms with similar levels of customer contact may encounter similar problems, and could benefit from sharing "best practices" across industry boundaries. Further, this idea states that the high-contact and low-contact areas within a company should be managed differently. For example, contact-enhancing strategies, such as specifically hiring people-oriented workers and partitioning back-office, noncontact activities away from the customer's view, should be employed in the high-contact areas. On the other hand, those pesky customers sometimes interfere with the efficiency of low contact facilities. In such cases, contact-reduction strategies, such as appointment systems or drop-off points such as automatic teller machines are appropriate. It is in the low contact facilities where traditional manufacturing techniques could be effectively borrowed to increase efficiency.

Another way to view services is provided by the Service Process Matrix proposed by Schmenner.[107] Schmenner differentiates service processes according to two major differentiating factors: the degree of interaction and customization and the degree of labor intensity.

The *Service Factory* has both low interaction and customization and low labor intensity. A quintessential example is a traditional commercial airline. Customization is quite low. If flights are scheduled for 10 A.M. and 6 P.M., they won't accommodate a customer who wants to go "around two-ish." Capital cost are enormous, with typical commercial jets costing as much as $50 to $100 million each.

Service Shops, such as hospitals, also experience high capital costs. Fortunately, hospitals can customize their services a bit more than the airlines do. *Professional Services,* such as lawyers, consultants, and accountants, combine highly customized service with a high labor intensity. Finally, *Mass Services,* like retailers and wholesalers, show higher ratios of labor to capital costs than do Service Factory firms, but do not offer highly customized services.

In theory, then, each quadrant faces managerial challenges unique to the processes within that quadrant. Both the Service Factory and Service Shop processes are capital intensive so, of course, capital purchases and technology choices are highly important. The amount of capital goods cannot easily change and usually must be highly utilized to be profitable; therefore, the challenge to managers is to smooth out demand peaks that cannot be served.

Mass Service and Professional Service firms are more labor intensive. In these areas, hiring and training of labor is of greater importance. The list of challenges is likewise different for processes with varying degrees of interaction and customization. Service Factory and Mass Service firms, with low interaction and customization, are challenged to make their services feel "warm" to the customer. Service Shop and Professional Service firms' challenges are associated with high interaction and customization issues, such as quality control.

The first decisions of a service firm take place long before staff is hired, facilities built, or even a corporate logo designed. This section provides several frameworks for considering a service organization's basic strategic decisions:

- Who will be our customers?
- What can we offer potential customers that competitors do not?
- On which customer desires will we compete?
- How will the business grow?

The answers to these basic questions both limit and guide the decisions concerning facilities, people, and procedures that an operating system will eventually possess. Basic strategy becomes the blueprint for making the managerial trade-offs discussed later in this text.

Strategic Positioning

There a number of visions of generic competitive strategies. Perhaps the most famous is Michael Porter's (1985) three strategic dimensions of cost leadership, differentiation, and focus.[108] But there are other views. Some operations textbooks view operations strategies as being based on cost, quality, speed, and flexibility. But the question can become more complex as these strategies are further segmented. For example, *quality* may be perceived as composed of as many as five or eight different dimensions, and *flexibility* as composed of a similarly different number of ways to compete, where a firm can compete on a selected subset of these dimensions. As a basic example, McDonald's is a "quality" leader in the restaurant category, if one defines quality as "conformance quality," or reliably making hamburgers and fries that taste the same from New York to California. On the other hand, **Chez Panisse** in the San Francisco area is a "quality" leader in the restaurant category for far different reasons.

Even these listed dimensions fall far short of the large number of strategic directions on which a firm may compete. For example, Porter lists only three dimensions, but "differentiation" and "focus" can take any number of specific forms within the same industry.

Strategic Service Vision

As a general way of thinking about these issues, consider the strategic service vision of Heskett, Sasser, and Schlesinger.[109] The four elements of the strategic service vision are (1) the focus on a target market, (2) the determination of a service concept, (3) the development of an operating strategy, and (4) the implementation of a service delivery system.

Target Market

Even though the focus on a target market may seem obvious, the concept is more difficult in services than it may appear. Many services, unlike most manufacturers, are forced to come in contact with potential customers who are outside their target market. For example, the target market of a high-end jewelry store may be wealthier individuals purchasing $10,000 rings, but the next person who walks in the door actually may be looking for a $10 watch—an item not even kept in inventory. While such a customer is taking up the time of salespeople and gawking loudly at the prices, the true target market customers may become impatient with the service and walk out the door. The same is true when the roles are reversed: A costume jewelry shop will never satisfy the desires of some upscale customers, so personnel must find a way around them. Unlike the workers on a manufactured item, the target market for a service firm must be known to and understood by virtually all personnel.

Focusing in on a target market means treating customers differently, which may make both employees and potential customers uncomfortable. Clearly defining a target market lets employees know which customers to go the extra mile for.

Service Concept

The service concept is stated from the point of view of the customer: What results are produced for the customer? From the customer's point of view, the service concept is the reason for choosing a particular firm. This choice can be stated in emotional as well as physical terms. The service concept can involve a feeling of security, exhilaration (especially in "experience economy" firms), or can simply be speed—a key service concept of UPS or FedEx.

Operating Strategy

The operating strategy is stated from the point of view of the firm: How should we be structured to produce the service concept? What are the most important elements to emphasize with time, money, and personnel? What instructions should be given to human resources, marketing, operations, and finance?

Service Delivery System

As the guts of the service organization, the service delivery system consists of the specific decisions made by the firm regarding personnel, procedures, equipment, capacity, facilities, and so on. The simple, guiding feature of this view links the service concept to the target market, which means that the operating strategy supports the service concept, and the service delivery system, in turn, supports the operating strategy. Although this statement sounds simple and obvious, it is less easy to implement. Differences between departments, changing service concepts over time while keeping delivery systems the same, or just well-intentioned ideas that don't match each other can get in the way.

As an example of a well-intentioned service delivery system idea that runs counter to a service concept, consider a typical airport car rental agency. Rental car agencies usually recognize that most customers want to get the car keys and get out; in other words, they want the service concept of speed from counter operations. Counter clerks, however, are often compensated on "upselling" and receive bonuses based on getting customers to upgrade from a mid-sized to a full-sized model, buy insurance, or prepay for a tank of gasoline. The company offers incentives to employees to sell these extras, because they are highly profitable to the firm. This service delivery system element emphasizes taking extra time with each customer to promote the benefits of these items, which causes lines to form and service time—the intended service concept—to deteriorate.

Managing for Service Capacity

Capacity planning for many service firms can be far more difficult than for manufacturers. Manufacturers can set capacity by looking at long-run average demand. For many service firms, however, long-run averages become somewhat meaningless when capacity must react to general seasonality, daily demand variations, and time-of-day demand fluctuations. If the average manufacturer found out that most end consumers bought their product between 2 P.M. and 3 P.M., this knowledge wouldn't change its capacity strategy at all, but it would be important information for many service firms.

Capacity decisions in service firms are not only more complex than in manufacturers, but can be more important as well. Manufacturers deal with short-term imbalances in production and demand by either carrying inventory or creating a backorder list for later shipment. In most services, the "inventory" of capacity is employee time, or a fixed asset not being used, such as a hotel room or an airplane seat, so excess inventory cannot be stored for later use. Backorders quite often cannot occur: Imagine a sales clerk at a department store stating that he will be able to speak with a customer by next Tuesday. Consequently, a temporary imbalance in supply and demand can result in either idle employees and resources if demand is smaller than supply, or lost sales to the competition if demand is larger than supply.

These factors turn simple tactical decisions into strategic ones. Consider this simple example of the basic strategic direction for service capacity. An ice cream parlor experiences the following demand for ice cream cones:

Weekdays	100–300
Saturday	500–1,500
Sunday	500–1,100

For the manufacturer supplying the cones, capacity is a simple matter: It calculates average weekly demand:

$$5(200) + 1,000 + 800 = 2,800 \text{ cones}$$

It makes 2,800/7 = 400 cones every day, and carries a small inventory of extra cones for the busier days. For the service provider who fills cones as customers walk in, however, simple arithmetic no longer applies. A strategic decision must be made. The ice cream parlor manager may use one of the four basic strategies outlined next. When considering these strategies, assume that one employee can make 100 cones per day.

1. **Provide: Ensure sufficient capacity at all times.** To carry out a provide strategy, one would want to always have enough people to handle the maximum demand, so the firm would have 15 employees working on Saturday, 11 on Sunday, and 3 the rest of the week. It is usually difficult to employ significant numbers of part-timers, so this strategy would employ enough full-time employees to meet those numbers. This strategy is associated with a high-service quality generic strategy, but it is also high cost, and would result in significant idle time for employees. Businesses with these characteristics include high-margin sales (e.g., jewelry, luxury automobiles) and those with wealthy individuals as clients (e.g., chauffeuring, private banking). Also, firms that compete on delivery speed (often called "time-based" competitors) should adopt this approach.

2. **Match: Change capacity as needed.** This strategy would use 10 employees on Saturday, 8 on Sunday, and 2 the rest of the week, with the excess Saturday and Sunday employees strictly part-timers. This approach balances service quality and costs and is representative of a large number of firms, including most mid- and low-priced restaurants and telemarketing firms.

3. **Influence: Alter demand patterns to fit firm capacity.** Here, pricing, marketing, or appointment systems flatten demand peaks to conform to capacity. It is most common in high capital-intensive services such as airlines and hotels, but highly paid professionals such as medical doctors and lawyers also commonly use it.

4. **Control: Maximize capacity utilization.** If only full-time employees could be used, five days per week, this strategy would have just two employees whose schedules overlapped on weekends. The generic strategy behind this option is to compete on cost by driving employee idle time to zero. It is often used in the public sector (e.g., driver's license bureaus) and low-margin services, as well as situations where high-priced employees want to maximize their utilization. Many physicians deliberately schedule patient appointments so tightly that a crowd is always in their waiting room. This strategy is willing to sacrifice sales at busy times to ensure the service functions efficiently all the time.

To assist in crafting these strategies, a host of specific tactics can be used to manage supply and demand. Supply management tactics include the following:

- **Workshift scheduling.** The unevenness of customer demand throughout a day means utilizing creative work schedules, such as nonuniform starting times, and workdays that have variable work hours. Work scheduling software is available to help construct flexible solutions within a match strategy.
- **Increasing customer participation.** A traditional method for a control strategy cuts total labor by encouraging customers to participate in serving themselves. For example, many fast-food restaurants use a semi-control strategy in which customers pour their own fountain drinks and procure their own condiments.
- **Adjustable (surge) capacity.** "Surge" capacity means capacity that can be available for a short period of time. By cross-training personnel for different jobs, a company can flexibly shift personnel temporarily to increase the capacity of any one position. Because cross-training is expensive to undertake, and cross-trained personnel are more expensive to retain, it is an appropriate approach within a provide strategy.
- **Sharing capacity.** Capacity can often be shared between departments or between firms for personnel or equipment that is needed only occasionally. For example, small business incubators often contract with dozens of businesses to share the same secretarial, accounting, and office management team.

Several tactics can be used to manage demand as well.

- **Partitioning demand.** It is not unusual for some components of demand to be inherently random, while some are fixed. This approach melds the more malleable demand around the tendencies of the random demand. That is, if it is known that more walk-in business generally comes in from 11 A.M. to 1 P.M., then schedule appointments either before or after that time. This approach works primarily for provide and match strategies.
- **Price incentives and promotion of off-peak demand.** This highly common method works in an influence strategy, which many of us see in our telephone bills. It is also commonly used in restaurants ("early bird" specials), hotels (both off-season and day-of-week pricing), resorts, and so on.
- **Develop complementary services.** The way to avoid the inevitable seasonality of many services is to couple countercyclical services together: Heating and air conditioning repair, ski slopes in winter and mountain bike trails in the summer. Unfortunately, this approach remains only a theoretical construct for most services.
- **Yield management.** Yield management combines three techniques: (1) overbooking, (2) assigning capacity amounts to different market segments, and (3) differential pricing in different market segments. It is used extensively by airlines, hotels, resorts, and many other industries.

Managing for Service Growth

Multisite Services Life Cycle

Like the more well-known "product life cycle" discussed in many marketing courses, it has been suggested that there is a life cycle for the service concepts involved in a multisite services firm, as well.[110] Revenues start low in the *entrepreneurial* stage as the service concept and delivery system seek to define themselves. For the small percentage of firms that continue, *multisite rationalization* involves separating the firm from the idiosyncrasies of the personality of the owner and specific first location and moving toward a "cookie-cutter" pattern that can be replicated. For firms that succeed here, they may move on to *growth*, where the service concept is replicated over many units. The *maturity* phase maintains and extends the brand, and is the most profitable phase. Finally, through competitive copying, a change in consumer tastes, or many other reasons, a firm may enter *decline*, or by rethinking its service concept, progress to *regeneration*.

These stages are worth mentioning because different strategic foci may be applicable at different developmental stages. Firm strategy will naturally change over time, which means that different operational structures, marketing plans, and different personnel may be appropriate as a firm ages.

In the *entrepreneurial* stage, the skills that matter are local marketing and public relations and a charismatic founder who can personally motivate the few personnel at an initial site. In this phase, most personnel are probably underpaid relative to peer institutions in the mature phase, and they are often in serious jeopardy of seeing very few paychecks, because most businesses in this phase fail. Yet, these people must find a way to innovate and develop the service strategy and delivery system around the service concept, or even change the service concept on the fly when trying to gain market acceptance.

In the *multisite rationalization* stage, a dominant paradigm for marketing, operations, and human resources must be selected and standardized. Motivation to go the extra mile must be replaced with procedures replicable by another employee far away who is just reading a manual. This stage requires the development of training programs, accounting systems, and procedure writing. Such development may mean taking much of the uniqueness and individual personality that characterized the entrepreneurial stage out of the various tasks.

Once in the *growth* stage, the operations and design should already be set. The skill required at this stage revolves around selling the concept to wider consumer and managerial audiences. Wider-scale advertising becomes both feasible and more important than local public relations, and investors and franchisees must be found to fund the growth.

During *maturity*, the marketing difficulties involve maintaining market position and awareness and somehow keeping a well-known concept "fresh." Operationally, maintaining standards and operational control over less-than-inspired, geographically dispersed employees becomes paramount. The lower-level employees are no longer at the hub of an exciting new idea, but instead work at a safe job in perhaps a dull, established firm. Keeping employees motivated and vigilant is difficult.

Finally, when the service concept becomes stale, revising the service concept and operationally implementing such revisions over a large network that is comfortable with the old service concept again requires the personal charisma reminiscent of an entrepreneur.

Retail Operations

Retailing consists of the final activities and steps needed to place a product in the hands of the consumer or to provide services to the consumer. In fact, retailing is actually the last step in a supply chain that may stretch from Europe or Asia to your hometown. Therefore, any firm that sells a product or provides a service to the final consumer is performing the retailing function. Regardless of whether the firm sells to the consumer in a store, through the mail, over the telephone, through the Internet, door to door, or through a vending machine, the firm is involved in retailing.

Retailing The final activities and steps needed to place merchandise made elsewhere into the hands of the consumer or to provide services to the consumer.

The Nature of Change in Retailing

Many observers of the American business scene believe that retailing is the most "staid and stable" sector of business. While this observation may have been true in the past, quite the contrary is occurring today. Retailing, which accounts for just under 20 percent of the worldwide labor force and includes every living individual as a customer, is the largest single industry in most nations and is currently undergoing changes in many exciting ways.

Currently, there are approximately 3.1 million retail establishments in the United States with total annual sales of nearly $3.3 trillion, or nearly $11,000 per capita.[111] There are 30 retail establishments for every 1,000 households. This equates to average annual sales of nearly $1 million per store.[112] Most retailers, however, are smaller, and many have annual sales of less than $500,000 annually.

These figures don't reflect the changes that have occurred behind these dollar amounts. The number of new retail enterprises that were developed in the last two decades is truly amazing. Most of these new businesses have actually been new institutional forms, such as electronic retailing, warehouse retailing, supercenters, and home delivery of both fast food and groceries. Change is truly the driving force behind retailing. Let's explore some of the trends that are affecting retailing today.

E-TAILING The great unknown for retail managers is what the ultimate role of on-line shopping will be. Most observers recognize the value of online shopping for travel, books, clothing, cosmetics, and music. But it is still unclear if on-line shopping will reach its projections for "everyday" shopping. Probably the best example of this dilemma is on-line grocery shopping. E-grocers are considered to be an important factor in the survival of the supermarket industry as it battles the inroads of the discounters' supercenters. This format first sprang up during the Internet boom in the late 1990s and promised to revolutionize the way consumers shopped for milk, toilet paper, and frozen pizzas. Instead, most went bankrupt.

One of the most dramatic changes e-tailing is creating is a shift in power between retailers and consumers. Traditionally, the retailers' control over pricing information provided them the upper hand in most transactions. The information dissemination capabilities of the Internet are making consumers better informed and thus increasing their power when transacting and negotiating

Retailers that outperform their competition in controlling costs incurred after the merchandise is acquired will be higher-profit performers.

with retailers. Clearly, e-tailing is adding a new competitive dimension to retailing. However, e-tailers must worry that many consumers will use the Internet for research, then buy the product in regular stores.

DEMOGRAPHIC SHIFTS Other significant changes in retailing over the past decade have resulted from changing demographic factors, such as the fluctuating birth rate, the growing importance of Generation Y (those born between 1978 and 1994) consumers, the fact that Generation Xers are now middle-aged and that baby boomers are nearing retirement age, and the increasing number of immigrants. Many people simply failed to realize how these factors, which had profound effects on our society, could also impact retailing.

Successful retailers must become more service-oriented, offering better value in price and quality; more promotion-oriented; and better attuned to their customers' needs. For example, one of the reasons that **Lowe's** is threatening **Home Depot's** dominance in the DIY (do-it-yourself) market is Lowe's awareness of its core customer—the female, who accounts for 60 percent of all sales and influences other sales.

Same-store sales Compares an individual store's sales to its sales for the same month in the previous year.

Market share The retailer's total sales divided by total market sales.

Also, with population growth slowing, retailers are no longer able to sustain their long-term profit projections just by building new stores and gaining additional sales, as they did in the past. Profit growth must come by either increasing same-store sales at the expense of the competition's market share or by reducing expenses without reducing services to the point of losing customers. (**Same-store sales** is a retailing term that compares an individual store's sales to its sales for the same month in the previous year. **Market share** refers to a retailer's sales as a percentage of total market sales for the product line or service category under consideration.) As a result, today's retail firms are run by professionals who are able to look at the changing environment and see opportunities, exert enormous buying power over manufacturers, and anticipate future changes before they impact the market, rather than just react to these changes after they occur. However, not even these experts always agree about what the future will bring.

STORE SIZE Further insight about the changes occurring in retailing today can be obtained by looking at the average store size for various retail categories. The largest increase in store size in recent years has been in drugstores, a reflection of the rapid growth of chains such as **Walgreens** and **Eckerd.** In addition to drugs, these stores sell a variety of general merchandise; in fact, the majority of their sales now comes from many different unrelated items, including food products, convenience goods, greeting cards, seasonal items such as gardening supplies and Christmas decorations, and even clothing. This phenomenon is referred to as **scrambled merchandising.** For example, convenience stores are said to be using a scrambled merchandising approach when they sell gasoline, bread, milk, beer, cigarettes, magazines, and fast food. The same can be said of drugstores that have a couple aisles of groceries as well as of supermarkets that sell clothing and gasoline. This scrambling of merchandise also applies to services; for instance, many supermarkets now offer banking and dry cleaning.

Scrambled merchandising Exists when a retailer handles many different and unrelated items.

There has also been an increase in the average store size by the more traditional general merchandise stores, which in many cases are combining with supermarkets to form supercenters. In contrast, some grocery stores have been shrinking in both size and the range of merchandise carried, reflecting their targeted customer's increased desire for convenience. Likewise, the average department store is now smaller; many of these retailers are closing their downtown locations, which often were their largest stores, because the downtown areas of many cities have become "ghost towns." Thus, retailers today are seeing a trend emerge: Retail stores are now either larger or smaller than their counterparts from the past. In fact, nowhere is this fact of retailing better described than with "category killers." The **category killer** got its name from its marketing strategy: Carry a large amount of merchandise in a single category at such low prices that it makes it impossible for customers to walk out without purchasing what they need, thus "killing" the competition.

Category killer A retailer that carries such a large amount of merchandise in a single category at such good prices that it makes it impossible for the customers to walk out without purchasing what they need, thus killing the competition.

However, many other category killers from the past decade have suffered financial reverses. These specialty superstore chains failed because they had a poor strategy, weak execution, or too much "me too" competition. In addition, the continued rapid growth of general merchandise discounters, such as Wal-Mart and **Target,** has contributed to their demise because these discounters can increase store space for toys during the Christmas season and decrease it during the slower toy seasons, such as summer, when they expand the space for lawn care products. Such actions enable the discounter to reduce costs and offer lower prices, whereas the "killer" must carry the full line year round.

Likewise, many other time-strapped consumers started taking their business away from the "killers" by going to the Internet or shopping at smaller, more convenient outlets closer to home, even if prices were higher.

Success in retailing depends on a retail manager's ability to properly interpret what changes are occurring and what these changes mean to the store's customers, and building a strategy to respond to those changes. Therein lies the excitement and challenge of retailing as a career.

Of course, the future can never be predicted with certainty. The answer to what the future will bring lies in the disquieting fact that retailers do not operate in a static, closed environment; they operate in a continuously changing and competitive environment. Exhibit 200.57 depicts the external environmental forces confronting retail firms. These forces include: the behavior of consumers, the behavior of competition, the behavior of supply chain members (the manufacturers and wholesalers that the retailer buys from), the legal system, the state of technology, and the socioeconomic nature of society.

A final comment about the changing face of retailing: Remember, business entrepreneurs are not obliged to conform to old legal and social standards. They are free to forge new retail approaches that capitalize on emerging market opportunities. In retailing this is all the more evident when we consider fashion trends; what in the past would have lasted for years now might last only a few months.

Categorizing Retailers

Categorizing retailers can help the reader understand competition and the changes that occur in retailing. There is no single acceptable method of classifying retail competitors, although many classification schemes have been proposed. The five most popular schemes used today are described in Exhibit 200.58.

Exhibit 200.57 *External Environmental Forces Confronting Retail Firms*

Exhibit 200.58 *Categorizing Retailers*

Census Bureau	Number of Outlets	Margin/Turnover	Location	Size
3-digit NAICS code	Single unit	Low margin/ low turns	Traditional	By sales volume
4-digit NAICS code	2–10 units	Low margin/ high turns	Central shopping districts	
5-digit NAICS code	11+ units	High margin/ low turns	Shopping centers	By number of employees
		High margin/ high turns	Free-standing nontraditional	

CENSUS BUREAU The U.S. Bureau of the Census, for purposes of conducting the Census of Retail Trade, classifies all retailers using three-digit North American Industry Classification System (NAICS) codes. The Web site for locating these codes is http://www.census.gov/epcd/www/naics.html.

As a rule, these three-digit NAICS codes are too broad to be of much use to the retail analyst. The four-digit NAICS codes provide much more information on the structure of retail competition and are easier to work with.

NUMBER OF OUTLETS Another method of classifying retailers is by the number of outlets each firm operates. Generally, retailers with several units are a stronger competitive threat because they can spread many fixed costs, such as advertising and top management salaries, over a larger number of stores and can achieve economies in purchasing. However, single-unit retailers, such as your neighborhood **IGA** grocery store, do have several advantages. They are generally owner- and family-operated and tend to have harder-working, more motivated employees. Also, they can focus all their efforts on one trade area and tailor their merchandise to that area while gaining buying efficiencies by being a member of the IGA group. In the past such stores were usually able to spot emerging customer desires sooner and respond to them faster than the larger, multiunit operations.

Any retail organization that operates more than one unit is technically a chain, but this is really not a very practical definition. The Census Bureau classifies chain stores into two size categories: 2 to 10 stores and 11 or more. We mean 11 or more units when we use the term *chain stores*.

> *Private label branding* Also often called store branding, occurs when a retailer develops its own brand name and contracts with a manufacturer to produce the merchandise with the retailer's brand on it instead of the manufacturer's name.

In recent years, chains have relied on their high level of consumer recognition to engage in **private label branding**. Private label branding, sometimes called *store branding*, is when a retailer develops its own brand name and contracts with a manufacturer to produce the product with the retailer's brand instead of buying a national brand with the manufacturer's name on it. Today, the whole concept of private label has taken on a new dimension as retailers have made these items, while not nationally advertised, nationally promoted. These private labels are advertised in the newspaper as brands and are heavily promoted in stores via displays and signage.

In the past, private labels were inexpensive knockoffs of popular items. Today, though, some of the best retailers promote their private brands near the front and center of their stores. Retailers target these private labels, which have their own distinct personality, to specific markets and advertise them in their direct mail flyers or newspaper inserts.

The major shortcoming of using the number of outlets scheme for classifying retailers is that it addresses only those retailers operating in a traditional bricks and mortar space. This scheme thus ignores many nontraditional retailers such as catalog-only and e-tailers. How many outlets does **Amazon.com** have? One could argue that each new on-line computer is a potential retail outlet for the e-tailing giant.

> *Retailers who can develop private branded merchandise that is better than their competition will experience higher profitability.*
>
> *Gross margin percentage* The gross margin divided by net sales or what percent of each sales dollar is gross margin.
>
> *Gross margin* Net sales minus the cost of goods sold.
>
> *Operating expenses* The expenses the retailer incurs in running the business other than the cost of the merchandise.
>
> *Inventory turnover* The number of times per year, on average, that a retailer sells its inventory.
>
> *High-performance retailers* Are those retailers that produce financial results substantially superior to the industry average.

MARGIN AND TURNOVER Retailers can be classified in regard to their gross margin percent and rate of inventory turnover. The **gross margin percentage** shows how much **gross margin** (net sales minus the cost of goods sold) the retailer makes as a percentage of sales; this is also referred to as the gross margin return on sales. A 40 percent gross margin indicates that on each dollar of sales the retailer generates 40 cents in gross margin dollars. This gross margin will be used to pay the retailer's **operating expenses** (the expenses the retailer incurs in running the business other than the cost of the merchandise, e.g., rent, wages, utilities, depreciation, insurance, etc.). **Inventory turnover** refers to the number of times per year, on average, that a retailer sells its inventory. Thus an inventory turnover of 12 times indicates that, on average, the retailer turns over or sells its average inventory once a month. Likewise, an average inventory of $40,000 (retail) and annual sales of $240,000 means the retailer has turned over its inventory six times in one year ($240,000 divided by $40,000), or every two months.

High-performance retailers, those who produce financial results substantially superior to the industry average, have long recognized the relationship between gross margin percent, inventory turnover, and profit. One can classify retailers into four basic types by using the concepts of margin and turnover.

Typically, the **low-margin/low-turnover retailer** will not be able to generate sufficient profits to remain competitive and survive. Thus there are no good examples of successful retailers using this approach. On the other hand, the **low-margin/high-turnover retailer** is common in the United States. Perhaps the best examples of this retailer type are the discount department stores, the warehouse clubs, and the category killers. Amazon.com is probably the best-known example of low-margin/high-turnover e-tailers. **High-margin/ low-turnover** bricks and mortar retailers are also quite common in the United States. Furniture stores, TV and appliance stores, jewelry stores, gift shops, funeral homes, and most of the mom-and-pop stores located in small towns across the country are generally good examples of high-margin/low-turnover operations. Some clicks and mortar retailers, those who sell both on-line and in physical stores, that use this approach include **Coach** and **Sharper Image.** Finally, some retailers find it possible to operate on both **high margin and high turnover.** As you might expect, this strategy can be very profitable. Probably the most popular examples are convenience food stores such as **7-Eleven, Circle K,** or **Quick Mart.** However, because in the early stages of Internet commerce most retailers are trying to achieve a high turnover rate, there are no examples of e-tailers using this strategy.

Low-margin/low-turnover retailer
A retailer that operates on a low gross margin percentage and a low rate of inventory turnover.

Low-margin/high-turnover retailer
A retailer that operates on a low gross margin percentage and a high rate of inventory turnover.

High-margin/low-turnover retailer
A retailer that operates on a high gross margin percentage and a low rate of inventory turnover.

High-margin/high-turnover retailer
A retailer that operates on a high gross margin percentage and a high rate of inventory turnover.

As indicated in the preceding paragraph, the low-margin/low-turnover retailer is the least able of the four to withstand a competitive attack because this retailer is usually unprofitable or barely profitable, and when competition increases, profits are driven even lower. On the other hand, the high-margin/high-turnover retailer is in an excellent position to withstand and counter competitive threats because profit margins enable it to finance competitive price wars.

While the margin/turnover scheme provides an encompassing classification, it fails to capture the complete array of retailers operating in today's marketplace. For example, service retailers and even some e-tailers, such as **Priceline.com,** carry no inventory. Thus, while this scheme provides a good way of analyzing merchandising retail competition, it neglects an important type of service retailing without the inventory.

LOCATION Retailers have long been classified according to their location within a metropolitan area, be it the central business district, a mall or strip shopping center, or as a freestanding unit. However, the last decade saw a major change in the locations that retailers selected. Retailers are now aware that opportunities to improve financial performance can result not only from improving the sales per square foot of traditional sites but from operating in new, nontraditional retail areas.

In the past, rather than expand into untested territories, many retailers simply renovated existing stores. This is not true today. Now retailers are reaching out for alternative retail sites. American retailers today are testing all types of nontraditional locations to expand their businesses. For example, to get more people to eat pizza when they rent videotapes, **Pizza Hut** introduced kiosks in video rental stores with direct phone lines to the local Pizza Hut. McDonald's has tested locations in service stations along interstate highways. **Loblaw,** a Canadian grocer, has a women's health club in its store near Toronto, and **E*Trade,** the on-line brokerage firm, is expanding its non-Internet presence with financial service centers in **SuperTarget** stores.

Retailers that seek out nontraditional locations to reach customers will increase their chances of being highly profitable.

Also, given the high income levels of many airline travelers and the increasing amount of layover time between flights, many retailers have opened stores in airports, an idea that originated with and has long been used by European and Asian retailers. Airport retailers have been able to succeed by offering fast service, convenience, pleasant and clean environments, product variety and quality, entertainment, and competitive prices.[113] Probably the most significant of the new, nontraditional shopping locations today is the combination of entertainment and shopping, something that was unheard of a decade ago. Today locations such as **Bass Pro** hunting and fishing superstores have proven that the edges are blurring between shopping and entertainment for the masses.

SIZE Many retail trade associations classify retailers by sales volume or number of employees. The reason for classifying by size is that the operating performance of retailers tends to vary according to size. That is, larger firms generally have lower operating costs per sales dollar than smaller firms do.

While size has been useful in the past, it is unclear whether the changes brought about by technology will make this obsolete. For example, imagine a fully automated retailer where, as a consumer places an order online, an automated stock-picking warehouse packages the selected merchandise and forwards it to the shipping area to be sent by UPS to the customer. Is Wal-Mart comparable to Amazon.com in terms of the number of employees needed?

265. SERVICES AND RETAIL OPERATIONS

The Retail Strategic Planning and Operations Management Model

Exhibit 200.59, our strategic planning and operations management model, suggests that a retailer must engage in two types of planning and management tasks: strategic planning and operations management. Each of these tasks is undertaken in order to achieve high-profit performance results. At this point, take a few moments to study this model.

Strategic Planning

Strategic planning is concerned with how the retailer responds to the environment in an effort to establish a long-term course of action. In principle, the retailer's strategic planning should best reflect the line(s) of trade in which the retailer will operate, the market(s) it will pursue, and the retail mix it will use. Remember, strategic planning requires a long-term commitment of resources by the retailer. Many retailers use the term *tactical planning* when discussing the specific details of a short-term course of action, such as getting rid of merchandise after Christmas. A long-term commitment, not a short-term one, is necessary to overcome some of the adversities of operating globally. Specifically, effective strategic planning can help protect the retailer against competitive onslaughts.

The initial steps in strategic planning are to define the firm's mission, establish goals and objectives, and perform a SWOT analysis. The next steps are to select the target market and appropriate location(s). It is important to note that most retail managers or executives have very little control over location decisions. A newly appointed manager for a chain department store could change promotional strategy, personnel, service levels, credit policies, and even prices but in all likelihood would be constrained by a long-term lease agreement. In fact, only the senior management of most chains is ever involved in location decisions. For the small retailer just starting out, however, or retailers considering expansion, location is an important decision.

After selecting the target market and location, the retailer must develop the firm's retail mix. Retailers can best perform this strategic planning only after assessing the external environment. They should be looking for an opportunity to fulfill the needs of a defined group of consumers (i.e., their target market) in a way that sets them apart from the competition. In other words, retailers should strive to seek a differential advantage over the competition. Retailers will rarely discover a means of gaining a differential advantage merely by reviewing their own internal operations or by focusing exclusively on the conventional industry structure. Strategic planning opportunities are to be found in the realities of a constantly changing environment. An effective retail strategy can result only from matching environmental forces with a retail marketing program that satisfies the customer better than anybody else. For example, **Foot Locker** has found success by concentrating on a very narrow segment of the shoe market but offering a very large selection.

Exhibit 200.59 profiles the major environmental forces that should be assessed. Briefly these are as follows:

1. *Consumer behavior.* The behavior of consumers will obviously have a significant impact on the retailer's future. Specifically, the retailer will need to understand the determinants of shopping behavior so it can identify likely changes in that behavior and develop appropriate strategies.
2. *Competitor behavior.* How competing retailers behave will have a major impact on the most appropriate strategy. Retailers must develop a competitive strategy that is not easily imitated.
3. *Supply chain behavior.* The behavior of members of the retailer's supply chain can have a significant impact on the retailer's future. For example, are certain supply chain members, such as manufacturers and/or wholesalers, always seeking to improve their position in the supply chain by establishing their own Internet sites, thus bypassing retailers? In other cases, wholesalers are requiring larger minimum orders and offering less attractive credit terms to small and medium-sized retailers. Behaviors such as these could have implications for the retailer's strategy.
4. *Socioeconomic environment.* The retailer must understand how economic and demographic trends will influence revenues and costs in the future and adapt its strategy according to these changes.
5. *Technological environment.* The technical frontiers of the retail system encompass new and better ways of performing standard retail functions. The retailer must always be aware of opportunities for lowering operating costs.
6. *Legal and ethical environment.* The retailer should be familiar with local, state, and federal regulations of the retail system. It must also understand evolving legal patterns in order to be able to design future retail strategies that are legally defensible. At the same time, the retailer must operate at the highest level of ethical behavior.

Exhibit 200.59 *Retail Strategic Planning and Operations Management Model*

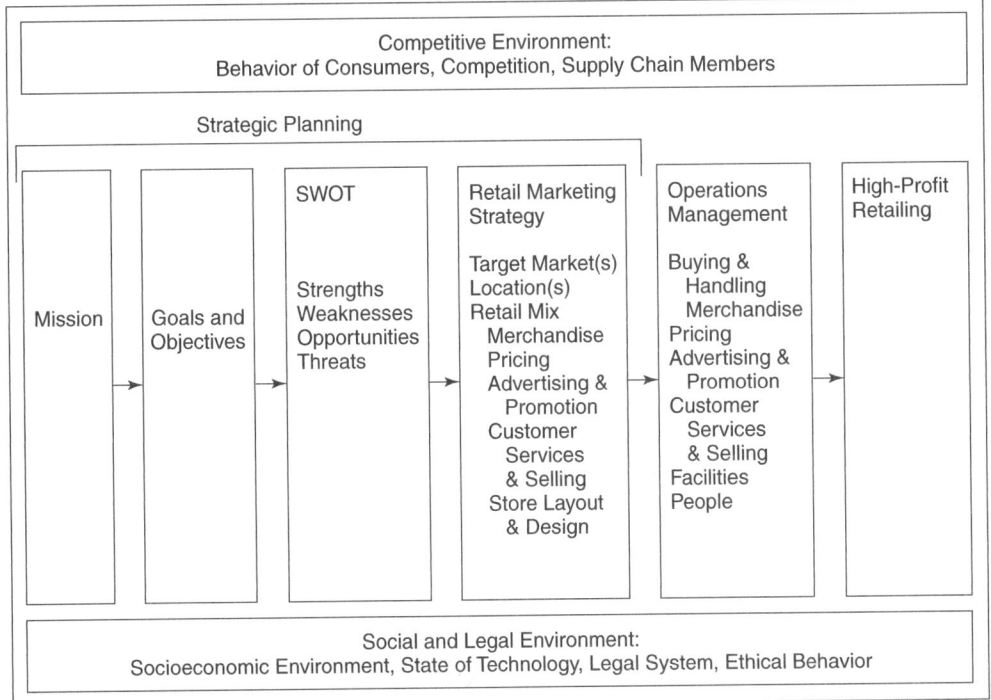

Operations Management

Operations management is concerned with maximizing the efficiency of the retailer's use of resources and with how the retailer converts these resources into sales and profits. In other words, its aim is to maximize the performance of current operations.

Operations management Deals with activities directed at maximizing the efficiency of the retailer's use of resources. It is frequently referred to as day-to-day management.

Most of the retailer's time and energy is devoted to the day-to-day activity of operations management. Our retail strategic planning and operations management model (Exhibit 200.59) shows that operations management involves managing the buying and handling of merchandise, pricing, advertising and promotion, customer services and selling, people, and facilities. All of these activities require day-to-day attention. For example, the selling floor must be maintained, customers served, merchandise bought and handled, advertisements run, and pricing decisions made each and every day. In other words, operations management is running the store.

High-Profit Retailing

The far-right box of the retail strategic planning and operations management model (Exhibit 200.59) suggests that the cumulative effect of well-designed and executed strategic and operations plans will be the achievement of high profit. Mistakes in either of these two areas will severely hamper the retailer's profit and prevent it from being among the leaders in its industry. For instance, in the early 1990s the **Gap** was hailed as the most successful innovator in the retail apparel industry. However, by 2000, the early baby boomers had already reached age 50 and had all the clothes they needed. They quit buying clothes and spent more on their homes. As a result, total home furnishing sales exceeded total apparel sales for the third year in a row, something that didn't happen in the Gap's earlier years.[114] In addition, younger adults, those in their 20s and 30s, found the merchandise at the chain's major divisions—GAP, Banana Republic, Old Navy, and GAP for Kids—less exciting and geared too much toward teenagers. After all, adults didn't want multipocketed cargo pants. Analysts also attributed the Gap's recent failure to a decision made in early 2000 to stock "new" items less frequently in order to sell clothes at full price longer. While margins improved, customers often left empty-handed in search of fresh ideas. Compounding the Gap's problems, the head of the Gap's successful on-line operations left for Wal-Mart.

To be a high-profit retailer, the retailer needs good strategic planning coupled with strong operations management.

265. SERVICES AND RETAIL OPERATIONS

The need to strive for high profit is tied to the extremely competitive nature of retailing. It is still relatively easy to start a retail business in comparison to starting a business in other industries. Thus new retail entrepreneurs are continually entering the marketplace. As competition increases and more chains use the same format, profit levels naturally deteriorate. Retailers are therefore well advised to set high profit objectives so that if their planned profits are not reached they at least have a chance of achieving average profitability. The retailer that aims only for an average profit often finds itself confronting a rather sobering financial performance.

Managing a Retailer's Finances

Merchandising The planning and control of the buying and selling of goods and services to help the retailer realize its objectives.

Many people believe that the terms *retailing* and *merchandising* are synonymous. They are not. Retailing includes all the business activities that are necessary to sell goods and services to the final consumer. **Merchandising** is only one of these activities and is concerned with the planning and control involved in the buying and selling of goods and services to help the retailer realize its objectives. Success in merchandising requires total financial planning and control. This section discusses two topics: the merchandise budget and inventory valuation.

The Merchandise Budget

Merchandise budget A plan of projected sales for an upcoming season, when and how much merchandise is to be purchased, and what markups and reductions will likely occur.

Successful retailers must have good financial planning and control of their merchandise. The retailer invests money in merchandise for profitable resale to others. A poor choice of merchandise will result in low profits, or maybe even a loss. Therefore, in order to be successful in retailing, as in any other activity, an individual must have a plan of what is to be accomplished. In retailing this plan of operation is called the merchandise budget. A **merchandise budget** is a plan of projected sales for an upcoming season, when and how much merchandise is to be purchased, and what markups and reductions will likely occur. The merchandise budget forces the retailer to develop a formal outline of merchandising objectives for the upcoming selling season.

In developing the merchandise budget, the retailer must make five major merchandising decisions:

1. What will be the anticipated sales for the department, division, or store?
2. How much stock on hand will be needed to achieve this sales plan, given the level of inventory turnover expected?
3. What reductions, if any, from the original retail price must be made in order to dispose of all the merchandise brought into the store?
4. What additional purchases must be made during the season?
5. What **gross margin** (the difference between sales and cost of goods sold) should the department, division, or store contribute to the overall profitability of the company?

Gross margin The difference between net sales and cost of goods sold.

When preparing the merchandise budget, a retailer must employ the following four rules.

First, a merchandise budget should always be prepared in advance of the selling season. The original plan is often prepared by the buyer for a particular department for approval by the divisional merchandising manager and/or the general merchandising manager. Therefore, most retail firms selling apparel and hard goods begin the process of developing the merchandise budget three to four months in advance of the budget period. This is not always the case with some specialty stores, such as music stores. A new music release is only known to the buyer about a month in advance and can be easily reordered if it goes to the top of the charts. These specialty stores also do not have to worry about markdowns since excess quantities can be returned to vendors for full credit. Generally, a firm has only two seasons a year: (1) spring/summer, usually February 1 through July 31, and (2) fall/winter, August 1 through January 31. The buyer for a particular department will usually begin to prepare merchandise budgets on or about March 1 and September 1 for the upcoming seasons.

Retailers who thoroughly analyze and project all the factors in developing a merchandise budget for an upcoming season will be more profitable.

Second, since the budget is a plan that management expects to follow in the upcoming merchandise season, the language must be easy to understand. The merchandise budget illustration has only 11 items, although the number of items contained in a budget may vary by companies due to their particular merchandise and market characteristics. Remember, the budget serves no useful purpose if it cannot be understood by all the decision makers. Also, it must contain all the information needed for that particular retailer.

Third, because the economy today is constantly changing, the merchandise budget must be planned for a relatively short period of time. Six months is the norm used by most retailers, although some retailers use a three-month, or even shorter, plan. Forecasting future sales is difficult enough without complicating the process by projecting for a time period too far into the future. The firm's general management should be concerned with long-term trends and effects on store and personnel needs. The firm's buyers are involved in the more short-term trends and effects that may influence the merchandise budget.

Fourth, the budget should be flexible enough to permit changes. All merchandise budgets are plans and estimates of predicted future events. However, it should be noted that competition and consumers are not always predictable, especially in regard to fashion preferences. Thus, any forecast is subject to error and will need revisions.

Keeping in mind this discussion of merchandising decisions and rules, review the blank six-month merchandise budget for the Housewares Department of a major department store shown in Exhibit 200.60.

Exhibit 200.60 appears to be more confusing than it really is because each element is broken into four parts: last year, plan for the upcoming season, revised plan, and actual. This is merely a means to provide the decision maker with complete information. Last year refers to last year's sales for the period; plan for the upcoming season is what the original plan projected; revised plan is the result of any revisions caused by changing market conditions after the plan was accepted; and actual is the final results.

Exhibit 200.61 presents the same material in a simpler form. Here we will only attempt to show you how and why a retailer develops a six-month merchandise plan. Exhibit 200.62 is a summary of how all the numbers in the merchandise budget are determined. Exhibit 200.61 shows the spring/summer season, February 1 to July 31, for the Two-Seasons Department Store, Department 353, with projected sales of $500,000, planned retail reductions of $50,000 or 10 percent of sales, planned initial markup of 45 percent, and a planned gross margin on purchases made of $208,750.

DETERMINING PLANNED SALES The initial step in developing a six-month merchandise budget is to estimate planned sales for the entire season and for each month. The buyer begins by examining the previous year's sales records. Adjustments are then made in the planning of sales for the upcoming merchandise budget. When comparing this year's sales to last year's sales, retailers do not always compare to the exact date (i.e., comparing February 8, 2005, sales to February 8, 2004) since the dates could fall on different days of the week. For instance, February 8 in 2004 was on a Sunday, when the retailer might be closed, and on a Tuesday in 2005. Rather, retailers use a retail reporting calendar, which divides the year into two seasons, each with six months. Thus, January 31, 2005, the first Monday of the spring season (and the first Monday of February for a retailer using the calendar) would be compared to February 2, 2004, which was the first Monday of 2004's spring season. In the year 2006, the first Monday of the spring season is January 30.

Return now to the example in Exhibit 200.61. After reviewing the data available, the buyer for Department 353 forecasted that $500,000 was a reasonable total sales figure for the future season. June, with a projected 25 percent of the total season's sales, and April, with 20 percent, are expected to be the busy months. May, with only 10 percent, is expected to be the slowest month. The remaining months will have equal sales. Since April, May, and June account for 55 percent of total sales, then February, March, and July's total must be 45 percent or 15 percent per month since they are equal. The buyer is able to determine planned monthly sales by multiplying the planned monthly sales percentage by planned total sales. Since we know February's planned monthly sales are 15 percent of the total planned sales of $500,000, February's planned sales must be $75,000 (15% × $500,000 = $75,000).

It is important to use recent trends when forecasting future sales. All too often some retailers in a no-growth market merely use last season's figures for the current season's budget. This method overlooks two major influences on projected sales volume: inflation and competition. If inflation is 10 percent and no other

Since planning future sales is the most important part of developing a merchandise budget, the retailers that do the best job of forecasting sales will be the most profitable.

changes occurred in the retail environment, then the retailer planning on selling the same physical volume as during the previous year should expect a 10 percent increase in this season's dollar sales. Similarly, if the exit of a competitor across town is expected to increase the number of customer transactions by 5 percent, this increase should be reflected in the budget. Suppose that last year's sales were $100,000, inflation is 10 percent, and the retailer expects its market share to increase by 8 percent while the total market remains stable. What should the projected sales be? A simple equation used in retail planning is

$$\text{Total sales} = \text{Average sale} \times \text{Total transactions}$$

265. SERVICES AND RETAIL OPERATIONS

Exhibit 200.60 *Sample Six-Month Merchandise Budget for Two-Seasons Department Store*

		\multicolumn{7}{c}{Six-Month Merchandise Budget Housewares Department 353}
		February	March	April	May	June	July	Total
BOM Stock	Last Year							
	Plan							
	Revised							
	Actual							
Sales	Last Year							
	Plan							
	Revised							
	Actual							
Reductions	Last Year							
	Plan							
	Revised							
	Actual							
EOM Stock	Last Year							
	Plan							
	Revised							
	Actual							
Retail Purchases	Last Year							
	Plan							
	Revised							
	Actual							
Purchases at Cost	Last Year							
	Plan							
	Revised							
	Actual							
Initial Markup	Last Year							
	Plan							
	Revised							
	Actual							
Gross Margin Dollars	Last Year							
	Plan							
	Revised							
	Actual							
BOM Stock/Sales Ratio	Last Year							
	Plan							
	Revised							
	Actual							
Sales Percentage	Last Year							
	Plan							
	Revised							
	Actual							
Retail Reduction Percentage	Last Year							
	Plan							
	Revised							
	Actual							

Stockturn: Last Year _____ Plan _____ Actual _____

On Order – Beginning of Season _____ Plan _____ Actual _____

EOM Inventory for Last Month _____ Plan _____ Actual _____

Reduction Percentage _____ Plan _____ Actual _____

Markup Percentage _____ Plan _____ Actual _____

Exhibit 200.61 *Two-Seasons Department Store, Dept. 353, Six-Month Merchandise Budget*

		February	March	April	May	June	July	Total
1.	Planned BOM Stock	$225,000	$300,000	$300,000	$250,000	$375,000	$300,000	—
2.	Planned Sales	75,000	75,000	100,000	50,000	125,000	75,000	$500,000
3.	Planned Retail Reductions	7,500	7,500	5,000	7,500	6,250	16,250	50,000
4.	Planned EOM Stock	300,000	300,000	250,000	375,000	300,000	250,000	—
5.	Planned Purchases at Retail	157,500	82,500	55,000	182,500	56,250	41,250	575,000
6.	Planned Purchases at Cost	86,625	45,375	30,250	100,375	30,937.50	22,687.50	316,250
7.	Planned Initial Markup	70,875	37,125	24,750	82,125	25,312.50	18,562.50	258,750
8.	Planned Gross Margin	63,375	29,625	19,750	74,625	19,062.50	2,312.50	208,750
9.	Planned BOM Stock-to-Sales Ratio	3	4	3	5	3	4	—
10.	Planned Sales Percentage	15%	15%	20%	10%	25%	15%	100%
11.	Planned Retail Reduction Percentage	10%	10%	5%	15%	5%	21.67%	10%

Planned Total Sales for the Period $500,000
Planned Total Retail Reduction Percentage for the Period 10%
Planned Initial Markup Percentage 45%
Planned BOM Stock for August $250,000

Exhibit 200.62 *Formulas for the Six-Month Merchandise Budget*

Determining Planned Sales for the Month

(Planned Sales Percentage for the Month) × (Planned Total Sales) = (Planned Sales for the Month)

Determining Planned BOM Stock for the Month

(Planned Sales for the Month) × (Planned BOM Stock-to-Sales Ratio for the Month)
= (Planned BOM Stock for the Month)

Determining Planned Retail Reductions for the Month

(Planned Sales for the Month) × (Planned Retail Reduction Percentage for the Month)
= (Planned Retail Reductions for the Month)

Determining Planned EOM Stock for the Month

(Planned BOM Stock for the Following Month) = (Planned EOM Stock for the Current Month)

Determining Planned Purchases at Retail for the Month

(Planned Sales for the Month) + (Planned Retail Reductions for the Month) + (Planned EOM Stock for the Month) − (Planned BOM Stock for the Month) = (Planned Purchases at Retail for the Month)

Determining Planned Purchases at Cost for the Month

(Planned Purchases at Retail for the Month) × (100% − Planned Initial Markup Percentage)
= (Planned Purchases at Cost for the Month)

Determining Planned Initial Markup for the Month

(Planned Purchases at Retail for the Month) × (Planned Initial Markup Percentage)
= (Planned Initial Markup for the Month)

or

(Planned Purchases at Retail for the Month) − (Planned Purchases at Cost for the Month)
= (Planned Initial Markup for the Month)

Determining Planned Gross Margin for the Month

(Planned Initial Markup for the Month) − (Planned Retail Reductions for the Month)
= (Planned Gross Margin for the Month)

In the preceding example, average sales would increase by the 10 percent level of inflation to 1.10 times last year's sales, and total transactions would increase by the 8 percent gain in market share to 1.08 times last year's total transactions, for an increase in total sales of 1.188 times (or 1.10 × 1.08), resulting in a total sales increase of $18,800 or budgeted total sales of $118,800.

DETERMINING PLANNED BOM AND EOM INVENTORIES Once the buyer has estimated the seasonal and monthly sales for the upcoming season, plans can be made for inventory requirements. In order to achieve projected sales figures, the merchant will generally carry stock or inventory in excess of planned sales for the period, be it a week, month, or season. The extra stock or inventory provides a merchandise assortment deep and broad enough to ensure customer sales. A common method of estimating the amount of stock to be carried is the **stock-to-sales ratio**. This ratio depicts the amount of stock to have on hand at the beginning of each month to support the forecasted sales for that month. For example, a ratio of 5:1 would suggest that the retailer have $5 in inventory (at retail price) for every $1 in forecasted sales. Planned average beginning-of-the-month (BOM) stock-to-sales ratios can also be calculated directly from a retailer's planned turnover goals. For example, a retailer wants a target turnover rate of 4.0. By dividing the annual turnover rate into 12 (the number of months in a year), the average BOM stock-to-sales ratio for the year can be computed. In this case, 12 divided by 4.0 equals 3.0. Thus the average stock-to-sales ratio for the season is 3. Generally, stock-to-sales ratios will fluctuate month to month because sales tend to fluctuate monthly. Nevertheless, it is important to always review these ratios because if they are set too high or too low, too much or too little inventory will be on hand to meet the sales target. Remember, it is just as bad to have too much inventory on hand as it is to have too little. Stocking up too much inventory could result in inventory holding costs that outweigh the gross margins to be made on sale of the merchandise.

For example, based on available data, the buyer for Department 353 in Exhibit 200.61 used a planned stock-to-sales ratio of 3.0 for February, April, and June, a ratio of 4.0 for March and July, and a ratio of 5.0 for May. The buyer was able to determine that $300,000 worth of merchandise was needed beginning March 1 due to a planned stock-to-

Stock-to-sales ratio Depicts the amount of stock to have at the beginning of each month to support the forecasted sales for that month.

sales ratio of 4.0 and planned sales of $75,000 (line 1). Two things should be noted. First, stock-to-sales ratios always express inventory levels at retail, not cost. Second, the beginning-of-the-month (BOM) inventory for one month is the end-of-the month (EOM) inventory for the previous month. This relationship can be easily seen by comparing the BOM figures (line 1) for one month with the EOM figures for the previous month (line 4).

DETERMINING PLANNED RETAIL REDUCTIONS All merchandise brought into the store for sale to consumers is not actually sold at the planned initial markup price. Therefore, when preparing the six-month budget, the buyer should make allowances for reductions in the dollar level of inventory that results from non-sale events. Generally, these planned inventory retail reductions fall into three types: markdowns, employee discounts, and stock shortages. These reductions must be planned because as the dollar value of the inventory level is reduced, the BOM stock that is planned to support next month's forecasted sales will be inadequate unless adjustments are made this month. Therefore, a buyer must remember that reductions are part of the cost of doing business.

A small number of retailers do not include planned reductions in their merchandise budgets. They simply treat them as part of the normal operation of the store and feel they should be controlled without being a separate line item in the budget. This gives management an understated, conservative planned-purchase figure, thereby having the effect of holding back some purchase reserve until the physical inventory reveals the exact amount of reductions. We have included planned reductions here for two reasons: (1) to reflect the additional purchases needed for sufficient inventory to begin the next month and (2) to point out that taking reductions is not bad. Too often, inexperienced retailers believe that taking a reduction is an admission of error and therefore they fail to mark down merchandise until it is too late in the season. A buyer must remember that reductions are part of the cost of doing business.

Retailers who recognize that reductions are part of the cost of doing business and plan appropriately will achieve higher profits.

It should be noted that the reductions in our six-month budget are listed as a percentage of planned sales. The buyer in our example has estimated monthly retail reduction percentages as shown on line 11 of Exhibit 200.61. To determine planned retail reductions for March (line 3), planned monthly sales are multiplied by the planned monthly retail reduction percentage to yield the planned monthly retail reduction of $7,500 ($75,000 × 10% = $7,500).

Reductions are one of the major items in the merchandise budget subject to constant change. One reason is that the planned reductions may prove inadequate in light of actual conditions encountered by the retailer. If retailers delay too long in taking reductions, especially those resulting from unexpected weather, they may be forced to take even larger price cuts later as the merchandise style depreciates even more in value. Alternatively, consider what happens when the department manager does such an effective merchandising job that not all the reduction money is needed for the period. The solution to both these dilemmas is found in the rules for developing a budget; namely, keeping it flexible so it can be intelligently administered.

DETERMINING PLANNED PURCHASES AT RETAIL AND COST We are now ready to determine whether additional purchases must be made during the merchandising season. The retailer will need inventory for (1) planned sales, (2) planned retail reductions, and (3) planned EOM inventory. Planned BOM inventory represents purchases that have already been made. In the six-month merchandise budget shown in Exhibit 200.61, the March planned purchases at retail for Department 353 are $82,500 (line 5). This figure was derived by (1) adding planned sales, planned retail reductions, and planned EOM inventory and (2) subtracting planned BOM inventory:

$$\$75,000 + \$7,500 + 300,000 - 300,000 = \$82,500$$

Once planned purchases at retail are determined, planned purchases at cost can be easily calculated. The retail price always represents a combination of cost plus markup. If the markup percentage is given, the portion of retail attributed to cost or the cost complement can be derived by subtracting the markup percentage from the retail percentage of 100 percent. Given that the markup percentage is 45 percent of retail for Department 353, the cost complement percentage must be 55 percent (100% − 45% = 55%). Planned purchases at cost for March (line 6) must be 55 percent of planned purchases at retail or $45,375 ($82,500 × 55% = $45,375). Planned initial markup for March (line 7) must be 45 percent of planned purchases or $37,125 ($82,500 × 45% = $37,125).

DETERMINING THE BUYER'S PLANNED GROSS MARGIN The buyer is accountable for the purchases made, the expected selling price of these purchases, the cost of these purchases, and the reductions that are involved in selling merchandise the buyer has previously purchased. Therefore, the last step in developing the merchandise budget is determining the buyer's planned gross margin for the period. As already discussed, the buyer, in making plans, recognizes

> *It is important for retailers to remember that the planned gross margin for a month in a merchandise budget, which is based on the purchases made that month, will not equal that month's gross margin on the retailer's statements, which is based on sales.*

that the initial selling price for all the products will probably not be realized and that some reductions will occur. Referring to Exhibit 200.61, the buyer's planned gross margin for February (line 8) is determined by taking planned initial markup (line 7) and subtracting planned reductions (line 3) ($70,875 − $7,500 = $63,375).

Inventory Valuation

Due to the many different merchandise lines carried, inventory valuation is quite complex. Yet the retailer must have information such as sales, additional purchases not yet received, reductions for the period, gross margin, open-to-buy, stock shortages, and inventory levels in order to operate profitably.

A retailer must make two major decisions with regard to valuing inventory: (1) the accounting inventory system and (2) the inventory pricing method to use.

ACCOUNTING INVENTORY SYSTEM Two accounting inventory systems are available for the retailer: (1) the cost method and (2) the retail method. We will describe both methods on the basis of the frequency with which inventory information is received, difficulties encountered in completing a physical inventory and maintaining records, and the extent to which stock shortages can be calculated.

> **Cost method** *An inventory valuation technique that provides a book valuation of inventory based solely on the retailer's cost of merchandise including freight.*

The Cost Method The **cost method** of inventory valuation provides a book valuation of inventory based solely on the retailer's cost, including freight. It looks only at the cost of each item as it is recorded in the accounting records when purchased. When a physical inventory is taken, all the items are counted, the cost of each item is taken from the records or the price tags, and the total inventory value at cost is calculated.

One of the easiest methods of coding the cost of merchandise on the price tag is to use the first 10 letters of the alphabet to represent the price. Here A = 1, B = 2, C = 3, D = 4, E = 5, F = 6, G = 7, H = 8, I = 9, J = 0. A product with the code HEAD has a cost of $85.14. The cost method is useful for those retailers who sell big-ticket items and allow price negotiations by customers. Sales personnel know from the code how much room there is for negotiation and still cover the cost of the merchandise plus operating expenses.

The cost method of inventory valuation does have several limitations:

1. It is difficult to do daily inventories (or even monthly inventories).
2. It is difficult to cost out each sale.
3. It is difficult to allocate freight charges to each item's cost of goods sold.

The cost method is generally used by those retailers with big-ticket items and a limited number of sales per day (e.g., an expensive jewelry store or an antique furniture store), where there are few lines or limited inventory requirements, infrequent price changes, and low turnover rates.

> **Retail method** *An inventory valuation technique that values merhcandise at current retail prices, which is then converted to cost based on a formula.*

The Retail Method The retail method of inventory values merchandise at current retail prices. It overcomes the disadvantages of the cost method by keeping detailed records of inventory based on the retail value of the merchandise. The fact that the inventory is valued in retail dollars makes it a little more difficult for the retailer to determine the cost of goods sold when computing the gross margin for a time period.

There are three basic steps in computing an ending inventory value using the retail method: calculation of the cost complement, calculation of reductions from retail value, and conversion of the adjusted retail book inventory to cost.

Step 1. Calculation of the Cost Complement Inventories, both beginning and ending, and purchases are recorded at both cost and retail levels when using the retail method. Exhibit 200.63 shows an inventory statement for Whitener's Sporting Goods for the fall season.

In Exhibit 200.63, the beginning inventory is shown at both cost and retail. Net purchases, which are the total purchases less merchandise returned to vendors, allowances, and discounts from vendors, are also valued at cost and retail. Additional markups are the total increases in the retail price of merchandise already in stock, which were caused by inflation or heavy demand and are shown at retail. Freight-in is the cost to the retailer for transportation of merchandise from the vendor and is shown in the cost column.

Using the information from Exhibit 200.63, the retailer can calculate the average relationship of cost to the retail price for all merchandise available for sale during the fall season. This calculation is called the cost complement:

$$\text{Cost complement} = \text{Total cost valuation}/\text{Total retail valuation}$$
$$= \$270,000/\$560,000 = 0.482$$

Since the cost complement is 0.482, or 48.2 percent, 48.2 cents of every retail sales dollar is composed of merchandise cost.

Step 2. Calculation of Reductions from Retail Value During the course of day-to-day business activities, the retailer must take reductions from inventory. In addition to sales, which lower the retail inventory level, retail reductions can lower retail inventory levels. These reductions include markdowns (sales; reduced prices on end-of-season, discontinued, or damaged merchandise), discounts (employee, senior citizen, student, religious, etc.), and stock shortages (employee and customer theft, breakage). Markdowns and employee discounts can be recorded throughout an accounting period, but a physical inventory is required to calculate stock shortages.

In Exhibit 200.63, it is shown that Whitener's has a retail inventory available for sale of $560,000 for the upcoming fall season. This must be reduced by actual fall season sales of $145,000, markdowns of $12,000, and discounts of $2,000. This results in an ending book value of inventory with a retail level of $401,000. This is shown in Exhibit 200.64.

Once the ending book value of inventory at retail is determined, a comparison can be made to the physical inventory to compute the actual stock shortages; if the book value is greater than the physical count, a stock shortage has occurred. If the book value is lower than the physical count, a stock overage has occurred. Shortages are due to thefts, breakages, overshipments not billed to customers, and bookkeeping errors—the most common cause. These errors result from the failure to properly record markdowns, returns, discounts, and breakages. Many retailers have greatly reduced their original shortage estimate by reviewing the season's bookkeeping entries. A stock overage, an excess of physical inventory over book inventory, is also usually the result of bookkeeping errors, either miscounting during the physical inventory or improper book entries. Exhibit 200.65 shows the results of Whitener's physical inventory and the resulting adjustment.

Because a physical inventory must be taken in order to determine shortages (overages) and retailers take a physical count only once or twice a year, shortages (overages) are often estimated in merchandise budgets, as shown in Exhibits 200.60 and 200.61. As a rule of thumb, retailers may estimate monthly shortages between 0.5 and 3 percent.

Exhibit 200.63 *Inventory Available for Whitener's Sporting Goods Sales, Fall Season*

	Cost	Retail
Beginning Inventory	$199,000	$401,000
Net Purchases	70,000	154,000
Additional Markups		5,000
Freight-in	1,000	
Total Inventory Available for Sale	$270,000	$560,000

Exhibit 200.64 *Whitener's Sporting Goods, Ending Book Value at Retail, Fall Season*

	Cost	Retail
Inventory Available for Sale at Retail		$560,000
Less Reductions:		
Sales	$145,000	
Markdowns	12,000	
Discounts	$ 2,000	
Total Reductions		159,000
Ending Book Value of Inventory at Retail		$401,000

Exhibit 200.65 *Whitener's Sporting Goods, Stock Shortage (Overage) Adjustment Entry, End of Fall Season*

	Cost	Retail
Ending Book Value of Inventory at Retail		$401,000
Physical Inventory (at retail)		398,000
Stock Shortages		$ 3,000
Adjusting Ending Book Value of Inventory at Retail		$398,000

Exhibit 200.66 *Whitener's Sporting Goods Income Statements August 1–January 31*

	Cost	Retail
Sales		$145,000
Less: Cost of Goods Sold		
Beginning Inventory (at Cost)	$200,000	
Purchases (at Cost)	70,000	
Goods Available for Sale	$270,000	
Ending Inventory (at Cost)	191,836	
Cost of Goods Sold		78,164
Gross Margin		$ 66,836
Less: Operating Expenses		
Salaries	$ 30,000	
Utilities	1,000	
Rent	19,000	
Depreciation (Fixtures + Equipment)	2,200	
Total Operating Expenses		52,200
Net Profit Before Taxes		$ 14,636

Step 3. Conversion of the Adjusted Retail Book Inventory to Cost The final step to be performed in using the retail method is to convert to cost the adjusted retail book inventory figure in order to determine the closing inventory at cost. The procedure here is to multiply the adjusted retail book inventory ($398,000 in the case of Whitener's) by the cost complement (0.482 in the Whitener's example):

$$\text{Closing inventory (at cost)} = \text{Adjusted retail} \times \text{Cost complement book inventory}$$
$$= \$398,000 \times 0.482 = \$191,836$$

Although this equation does not yield the actual closing inventory at cost, it does provide a close approximation of the cost figure. Remember that the cost complement is an average. Now that ending inventory at cost has been determined, the retailer can determine gross margin as well as net profit before taxes, if operating expenses are known. We will discuss expenses in more detail later. In the Whitener's example, let's use $30,000 for salaries, $1,000 for utilities, $19,000 for rent, and $2,200 for depreciation. These figures are shown in Exhibit 200.66.

The retail method has several advantages over the cost method of inventory valuation:

1. Accounting statements can be drawn up at any time. Inventories need not be taken for preparation of these statements.
2. Physical inventories using retail prices are less subject to error and can be completed in a shorter amount of time.
3. The retail method provides an automatic, conservative valuation of ending inventory as well as inventory levels throughout the season. This is especially useful in cases where the retailer is forced to submit insurance claims for damaged or lost merchandise.

A major complaint against the retail method is that it is a "method of averages." This refers to the fact that closing inventory is valued at the average relationship between cost and retail (the cost complement), and that large retailers offer many different classifications and lines with different relationships. This disadvantage can be overcome by computing cost complements for individual lines or departments.

Another limitation is the heavy burden placed on bookkeeping activities. The true ending book inventory value can be correctly calculated only if there are no errors in recording beginning inventory, purchases, freight-in, markups, markdowns, discounts, returns, transfers between stores, and sales. As noted earlier, many of the retailers' original shortages have later been determined to be bookkeeping errors. Most retailers today use the retail method of inventory valuation, which was created in the early 1900s.

INVENTORY PRICING METHOD Two methods of pricing inventory are FIFO and LIFO. The **FIFO** (first in, first out) method assumes that the oldest merchandise is sold before the more recently purchased merchandise. Therefore, merchandise on the shelf will reflect the most current replacement price. During inflationary periods this method allows "inventory profits" (caused by selling the less expensive earlier inventory rather than the more expensive newer inventory) to be included as income.

FIFO Stands for first in, first out and values inventory based on the assumption that the oldest merchandise is sold before the more recently purchased merchandise.

The **LIFO** (last in, first out) method is designed to cushion the impact of inflationary pressures by matching current costs against current revenues. Cost of goods sold are based on the costs of the most recently purchased inventory, while the older inventory is regarded as the unsold inventory. During inflationary periods, the LIFO method results in the application of a higher unit cost to the merchandise sold and a lower unit cost to inventory still unsold. In times of rapid inflation most retailers use the LIFO method, resulting in lower profits on the income statement, but also lower income taxes. Most retailers also prefer to use LIFO for planning purposes, since it accurately reflects replacement costs. In addition, the Internal Revenue Service permits a retailer to change its method of accounting only once.

LIFO Stands for last in, first out and values inventory based on the assumption that the most recently purchased merchandise is sold first and the oldest merchandise is sold last.

Let's study an example of the effect of the LIFO and FIFO methods of inventory valuation on the firm's financial performance. Suppose you began the year with a total inventory of 15 fax machines, which you purchased on the last day of the preceding year for $300 each. Thus, if the fax machines were the only merchandise you had in stock, your beginning inventory was $4,500 (15 × $300). Suppose also that during the year you sold 12 fax machines for $700 each, for total sales of $8,400; that in June you purchased 8 new fax machines (same make and model as your old ones) at $325; and that in November you bought 4 more at $350. Thus, your purchases were $2,600 in June and $1,400 in November for a total of $4,000, and you would still have 15 fax machines in stock at year end. Under the LIFO inventory approach, your ending inventory would be the same as it was at the beginning of the year ($4,500), since we would assume that the 12 fax machines sold were the 12 purchased during the year. However, using the FIFO approach, we would assume that we sold 12 of the original $300 fax machines and had 3 left. These three fax machines, along with June's and November's purchases, result in an ending inventory of $4,900 [(3 × $300) + (8 × $325) + (4 × $350)]. Now let's see how these approaches can affect our gross margins.

	LIFO	FIFO
Net sales	$8,400	$8,400
Less: Cost of goods sold		
Beginning inventory	$4,500	$4,500
Purchases	4,000	4,000
Goods available	$8,500	$8,500
Ending inventory	4,500	4,900
Cost of goods sold	4,000	3,600
Gross margin	$4,400	$4,800

Mechandise Buying and Handling

Dollar Merchandise Planning

According to an old retailing adage, "goods well bought are half sold." In this section, we will look at merchandise management—the merchandise buying and handling process and its effect on a store's performance.

> **Merchandise management** The analysis, planning, acquisition, handling, and control of the merchandise investments of a retail operation.

Merchandise management is the analysis, planning, acquisition, handling, and control of the merchandise investments of a retail operation. *Analysis* is used in our definition because retailers must be able to correctly identify their customers before they can determine the needs and wants of their consumers. *Planning* occurs because merchandise must be purchased 6 to 12 months in advance of the selling season. The term *acquisition* is used because, with the exception of service retailers, merchandise needs to be bought from others, either distributors or manufacturers. In addition, all retailers, even those selling only services, must acquire the equipment and fixtures needed to complete a transaction. Proper *handling* assures that the merchandise is where it is needed and in the proper shape to be sold. *Control* of the large-dollar investments in inventory is important to ensure an adequate financial return on the retailer's merchandise investment.

> **Gross margin return on inventory** Gross margin divided by average inventory at cost; alternatively it is the gross margin percentage multiplied by (net sales divided by average inventory investment).

Because inventory is the largest investment that retailers make, high-performance retailers use the gross margin return on inventory model when analyzing the performance of their inventory. **Gross margin return on inventory** (GMROI) incorporates into a single measure both inventory turnover and profit. It can be computed as follows:

$$(\text{Gross margin/Net sales}) \times (\text{Net sales/Average inventory at cost})$$
$$= (\text{Gross margin/Average inventory at cost})$$

Here the gross margin percentage (gross margin/net sales) is multiplied by net sales/dollars invested in inventory to get the retailer's gross margin dollars generated for each dollar invested in inventory. Net sales are typically computed on an annual or 12-month basis. (Note, however, that sales/dollars invested in inventory is not the same as inventory turnover. Inventory turnover measures sales/inventory at retail. In the GMROI equation, we are using inventory at cost to reflect the investment in carrying the merchandise.) Thus, if a particular item has a gross margin of 45 percent and sales per dollar of inventory investment of 4.0, its GMROI would be $1.80 ($0.45 × 4). That is, for each dollar invested in inventory, on average the retailer obtains $1.80 in gross margin annually. Gross margin dollars are used to first pay the store's operating expenses (both fixed and variable), with the remainder being the retailer's profit.

Successful merchandise management revolves around planning and control. It takes time to buy merchandise, have it delivered, record the delivery in the company records, and properly display the merchandise; therefore, it is essential to plan. Buyers need to decide today what their stock requirements will be weeks, months, a merchandising season, or even a year in advance.

> *Retailers that use the GMROI model when planning inventory and evaluating inventory decisions will be more profitable.*

As planning occurs, it is only logical that the retailer exercise control over the merchandise (dollars and units) that it plans to purchase. A good control system is vital. After all, if the retailer carries too much inventory, the costs of carrying that inventory might outweigh the gross margin to be made on the sale, especially if the retailer is forced to reduce the selling price. After concluding our discussion on the dollar amount of inventory needed for stock requirements, the remainder of this section will look at the other merchandising decisions facing the retailer: calculating the dollar amount available to be spent, planning the inventory, choosing and evaluating merchandise sources, handling vendor negotiations, and handling the merchandise in the store.

Buyers, working with upper management, are responsible for the dollar planning of merchandise requirements. Earlier, we described the various factors that must be considered in making the sales forecast, the first step in determining inventory needs. Once planned sales for the period in question have been projected, buyers are then able to use any one of four different methods for planning dollars invested in merchandise: basic stock, percentage variation, weeks' supply, and the stock-to-sales method.

> **Basic stock method (BSM)** A technique for planning dollar inventory investments that allows for a base stock level plus a variable amount of inventory that will increase or decrease at the beginning of each sales period in the same dollar amount as the period's expected sales.

BASIC STOCK METHOD The **basic stock method** (BSM) is used when retailers believe that it is necessary to have a given level of inventory available at all times. It requires that the retailer always have a base level of inventory investment regardless of the predicted sales volume. In addition to the base stock level, there will be a variable amount of inventory that will increase or decrease at the beginning of each sales period (one month in the case of our merchandise budget) in the same dollar amount as the period's sales are expected to increase or decrease. The BSM can be calculated as follows:

Average monthly sales for the season	= Total planned sales for the season/ Number of months in the season
Average stock for the season	= Total planned sales for the season/ Estimated inventory turnover rate for the season
Basic stock	= Average stock for the season − Average monthly sales for the season
Beginning-of-month (BOM) stock at retail	= Basic stock + Planned monthly sales

To illustrate the use of the basic stock method, let's look at the planned sales for Department 353 of the Two-Seasons Department Store, shown in Exhibit 200.61. Assume that the inventory turnover rate for the six months, or the number of times the average inventory is sold, for the season is 2.0.

Average monthly sales for the season	= Total planned sales/Number of months = $500,000/6 = $83,333
Average stock for the season	= Total planned sales/Inventory turnover = $500,000/2 = $250,000
Basic stock	= Average stock − Average monthly sales = $250,000 − $83,333 = $166,667
BOM @ retail (February)	= Basic stock + Planned monthly sales = $166,667 + $75,000 = $241,667
BOM @ retail (March)	= $166,667 + $75,000 = $241,667
BOM @ retail (April)	= $166,667 + $100,000 = $266,667
BOM @ retail (May)	= $166,667 + $50,000 = $216,667
BOM @ retail (June)	= $166,667 + $125,000 = $291,667
BOM @ retail (July)	= $166,667 + $75,000 = $241,667

It is obvious that $166,667 of basic stock is added to each month's planned sales to arrive at the BOM stock. In those cases where actual sales either exceed or fall short of planned sales for the month, the retailer can easily adjust the amount of overage or shortfall to bring the next month's BOM stock back in line by buying more or less stock. Therefore, the basic stock method works best if a retailer has a low turnover rate (that is, fewer than six times a year) or if sales are erratic.

PERCENTAGE VARIATION METHOD A second commonly used method for determining planned stock levels is the **percentage variation method (PVM)**. This method is used when the retailer has a high yearly turnover rate—six or more times a year. The percentage variation method assumes that the percentage fluctuations in monthly stock from average stock should be half as great as the percentage fluctuations in monthly sales from average sales.

Percent variation method (PVM) A technique for planning dollar inventory investments that assumes that the percentage fluctuations in monthly stock from average stock should be half as great as the percentage fluctuations in monthly sales from average sales.

BOM stock = Average stock for season × 1/2[1 + (Planned sales for the month/Average monthly sales)]

Since the PVM utilizes the same components as the BSM, we can use the data from the previous example.

BOM (February)	= $250,000 × 1/2[1 + ($75,000/$83,333)] = $237,500
BOM (March)	= $250,000 × 1/2[1 + ($75,000/$83,333)] = $237,500
BOM (April)	= $250,000 × 1/2[1 + ($100,000/$83,333)] = $275,000
BOM (May)	= $250,000 × 1/2[1 + ($50,000/$83,333)] = $200,000
BOM (June)	= $250,000 × 1/2[1 + ($125,000/$83,333)] = $312,500
BOM (July)	= $250,000 × 1/2[1 + ($75,000/$83,333)] = $237,500

WEEKS' SUPPLY METHOD A third method for planning inventory levels is the **weeks' supply method (WSM)**. Generally, the WSM formula is used by retailers such as grocers where inventories are planned on a weekly, not monthly, basis and where sales do not fluctuate substantially. It states that the inventory level should be set equal to a predetermined number of weeks' supply. The predetermined number of weeks' supply is directly related to the stock turnover rate desired. In the WSM, stock level in dollars varies proportionally with forecast sales. Thus, if forecast sales triple, then inventory in dollars will also triple.

> *Week's supply method (WSM)* A technique for planning dollar inventory investments that states that the inventory level should be set equal to a predetermined number of weeks' supply, which is directly related to the desired rate of stock turnover.

To illustrate the WSM, let's return to our earlier problem and use the following formulas:

Number of weeks to be stocked	= Number of weeks in the period/Stock turnover rate for the period
Average weekly sales	= Estimated total sales for the period/Number of weeks in the period
BOM stock	= Average weekly sales × Number of weeks to be stocked

Thus,

Number of weeks to be stocked	= 26/2 = 13
Average weekly sales	= $500,000/26 = $19,231
BOM stock	= $19,231 × 13 = $250,000

Having determined the number of weeks' supply to be stocked (13 weeks) and the average weekly sales ($19,231), stock levels can be replenished on a frequent or regular basis to guard against stockouts.

STOCK-TO-SALES METHOD The final method for planning inventory levels is the **stock-to-sales method (SSM)**. This method is quite easy to use but requires the retailer to have a beginning-of-the-month stock-to-sales ratio. This ratio tells the retailer how much inventory is needed at the beginning of the month to support that month's estimated sales. A ratio of 2.5, for example, would tell retailers that they should have two and one-half 2½ times that month's expected sales on hand in inventory at the beginning of the month.

> *Stock-to-sales method (SSM)* A technique for planning dollar inventory investments where the amount of inventory planned for the beginning of the month is a ratio (obtained from trade associations or the retailer's historical records) of stock-to-sales.

However, these ratios should only be used as a guide to determine how much inventory to have on hand at the beginning of each month. Successful chain store retailers have long known that even stores located near each other require not only different merchandise mixes, but also different inventory levels per sales dollars. This is a reflection of the store's trading area, layout, and competition. However, inventory turnover remains a key factor in a retailer's financial performance. Planned average beginning-of-the-month stock-to-sales goals can be easily calculated using turnover goals. If you divide the number of months in the season by the desired inventory turnover rate, an average BOM stock-to-sales ratio for the season can be computed. For example, if you desired an inventory turnover rate of 2.0 for the upcoming six-month season (4.0 annually), your average BOM stock-to-sales ratio would be 3.0 (6/2.0 = 3.0).

> *Retailers who realize that the various dollar merchandise plans are not hard and fast rules to be followed at all times for all stores will have higher profits.*

Dollar Merchandise Control

> *Open-to-buy (OTB)* Refers to the dollar amount that a buyer can currently spend on merchandise without exceeding the planned dollar stocks.

Once the buyer has planned the dollar merchandise to have on hand at the beginning of each month (or season), it becomes essential that the buyer does not make commitments for merchandise that would exceed the dollar plan. In short, the dollars planned for merchandise need to be controlled. This control is accomplished through a technique called open-to-buy. **Open-to-buy (OTB)** represents the dollar amount that a buyer can currently spend on merchandise without exceeding the planned dollar stocks discussed previously. When planning for any given month (or season), the buyer will not necessarily be able to purchase a dollar amount equal to the planned dollar stocks for that month (or season). This is because some inventory may be already on order but not yet delivered. To illustrate this point more succinctly, let's compute the open-to-buy for an upcoming month.

Assume that at the beginning of February the buyer for Department 353 of the Two-Seasons Department Store (Exhibit 200.61) has already ordered, but not yet received, $15,000 worth of merchandise at retail. Keeping planned EOM stock at $300,000 and planned reductions for February at 10 percent of planned sales, the buyer's planned purchases for February will remain $157,500. However, the open-to-buy for the month will be only $142,500 at retail since we are now accounting for that $15,000 of merchandise already ordered but not yet received. The computations would look like this:

1. Planned sales for February   +75,000
2. Plus planned reductions for February   +7,500
3. Plus end-of-month (EOM) planned retail stock   +$300,000
4. Minus beginning-of-month (BOM) stock   −225,000
5. Equals planned purchases at retail $157,500
6. Minus commitments at retail for current delivery   −15,000
7. Equals open-to-buy $142,500

The OTB figure should not be set in stone because it can be exceeded. Consumer needs are the dominant consideration. If actual sales exceed planned sales, additional quantities should be ordered above those scheduled for purchase according to the merchandise budget. This should not be a common occurrence, however. If this is the case, the sales planning process is wrong. Either the buyers are too conservative in estimating sales or they are buying the wrong merchandise. In any case, the buyer, along with management, should always determine the causes of OTB adjustments. Some common buying errors include

1. Buying merchandise that is priced either too high or too low for the store's target market.
2. Buying the wrong type of merchandise (i.e., too many tops and no skirts) or buying merchandise that is too trendy.
3. Having too much or too little basic stock on hand.
4. Buying from too many vendors.
5. Failing to identify the season's hot items early enough in the season.
6. Failing to let the vendor assist the buyer by adding new items and/or new colors to the mix. (All too often, the original order is merely repeated, resulting in a limited selection.)

Merchandise planning is a dynamic process subject to many changes. Consider the implications that could arise in planning your stock levels as a result of: (1) sales for the previous month that are lower or higher than planned, (2) reductions that are higher or lower than planned, and (3) shipments of merchandise that are delayed in transit. Understanding the consequences of each of these situations can show you the interrelationship of merchandising activities with the merchandise budget. Such occurrences serve to make retailing a challenging and exciting career choice.

Retailers who realize that their OTB, which is an important planning tool, can be adjusted in order to meet changing market conditions will achieve higher profitability.

Retail Inventory Planning

The dollar merchandise plan is only the starting point in merchandise management. Once the retailer has decided how many dollars can be invested in inventory, the dollar plan needs to be converted into an inventory plan. On the sales floor, items, not dollars, are sold. The assortment of items that will comprise the merchandise mix must then be planned.

OPTIMAL MERCHANDISE MIX Exhibit 200.67 shows the three dimensions of the optimal mix: variety, breadth, and depth. Each of these dimensions needs to be defined; however, we need first to define merchandise line or category. A **merchandise line** consists of a group of products that are closely related because they are intended for the same end use (all televisions), are sold to the same customer group (junior miss clothing), or fall

Merchandise line A group of products that are closely related because they are intended for the same end use (all televisions); are sold to the same customer group (junior miss clothing); or fall within a given price range (budget women's wear).

Exhibit 200.67 *Dimensions of and Constraints on Optimal Merchandising Mix*

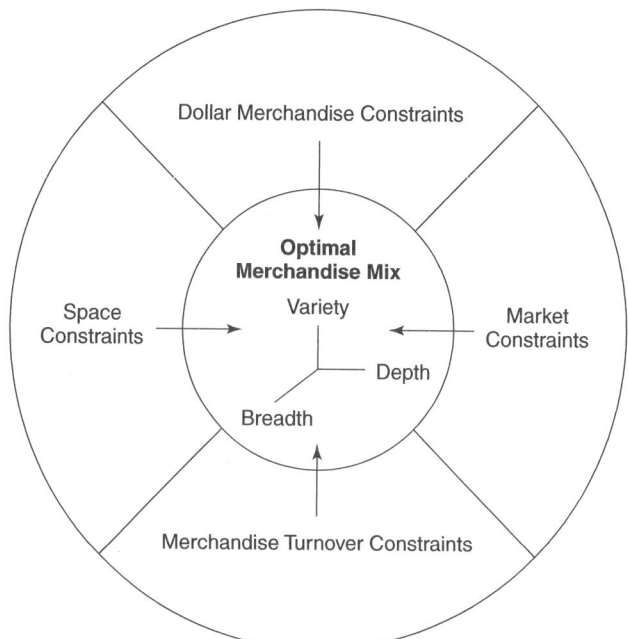

Category management Refers to the management of merchandise categories, or lines, rather than individual products, as a strategic business unit.

within a given price range (budget women's wear). Today over 90 percent of grocery retailers use the term **category management** to refer to their management of categories as a strategic business unit. That is, a supermarket buyer using category management would no longer be concerned with GMROI for just the Tide or Cheer detergent. Instead, that buyer would be concerned with the GMROI for the entire detergent line or category. For that buyer, the line or category is his or her strategic business unit.

Variety Refers to the number of different merchandise lines that the retailer stocks in the store.

Variety The **variety** of the merchandise mix refers to the number of different lines the retailer stocks in the store. For example, department stores have a large variety of merchandise lines. Some have more than one hundred departments, carrying such lines as menswear, women's wear, children's clothing, infant's wear, toys, sporting goods, appliances, cosmetics, and household goods.

On the other hand, **Office Depot**, a specialty chain, carries only one basic merchandise line: office supplies. In the middle of these two would be a retailer like **Sportsmart**, selling a complete range of sporting goods.

Breadth (or assortment) The number of merchandise brands that are found in a merchandise line.

Battle of the brands Occurs when retailers have their own products competing with the manufacturer's products for shelf space and control over display location.

Breadth **Breadth**, also called **assortment**, refers to the number of merchandise brands that are found in the merchandise line. For example, a supermarket will have a wide breadth, or assortment, in the number of different brands of mustard that it carries: six or seven national or regional brands, a private brand, and a generic brand. A 7-Eleven convenience store, however, will offer very little breadth in that it will generally carry only one or two brands in any merchandise line.

Breadth is especially a problem for retailers selling private-label brands. Retailers need to achieve a proper balance between their own private labels and the national brands. However, sometimes a powerful manufacturer may try to tie some of its merchandise lines together. That is, if the retailer carries one product, the retailer must carry the manufacturer's entire product line. But since private-label brands offer retailers a lower cost and a higher gross margin, retailers generally do not want to carry the manufacturer's complete line. Therefore, a **battle of the brands** occurs when retailers, in determining the breadth of the product assortment, have their own products competing with the manufacturer's products for shelf space and control over display location. One of the consequences of the battle of the brands is that many retailers now stock either one or both of the top brands in a product line or category as well as their own private brand. As a result, many "third-tier" brands have been left off the store's shelves.

436   MODULE 200. OPERATIONS MANAGEMENT

Depth Merchandise **depth** refers to the average number of stock-keeping units (SKUs) within each brand of the merchandise line. In the preceding example, the supermarket manager must decide which sizes and types of French's mustard to carry. The convenience store will probably carry only the regular nine-ounce jar of French's. Depth is an acute problem today because all too often retailers are constrained in the number of SKUs they can carry by the following four factors.

> **Depth** *The average number of stock-keeping units within each brand of the merchandise line.*

CONSTRAINING FACTORS Research indicates that the merchandise mix, in addition to satisfying customer wants, can actually shape those wants and impact whether and what customers purchase.[115] Exhibit 200.67 details the four constraining factors that may restrict the retailer's design of the optimal merchandise mix. Remember, just as the trading areas for each store in a chain are different, the optimal mix will be different for every store. Merchandise mix decisions are a blend of financial plans that consider the retailer's dollar and turnover constraints, the store's space constraints, as well as the constraints caused by the actions of competitors.[116]

Dollar Merchandise Contraints There seldom will be enough dollars to emphasize variety, breadth, and depth. If the decision is made to emphasize variety, it would be unrealistic to expect also to have a lot of breadth and depth.

For instance, assume for the moment that you are the owner/manager of a local gift store. You have $70,000 to invest in merchandise. If you decide that you want a lot of variety in gifts (jewelry, crystal, candles, games, cards, figurines, ashtrays, clocks, and radios), then you obviously cannot have much depth in any single item, such as crystal glassware.

Some retailers try to overcome this dollar constraint by shifting the expense of carrying inventory back on the vendor. When a retailer buys a product on **consignment,** the vendor retains the ownership of the goods, usually establishes the selling price, and is paid only when the goods are sold. Or the retailer might try to get **extra dating,** where the vendor allows the retailer some extra time before paying for the goods. For example, most textbook publishers either sell their books on consignment or give the bookstores an extra 60 days in which

> **Consignment** *When the vendor retains the ownership of the goods and usually establishes the selling price; it is paid only when the goods are sold by the retailer.*
>
> **Extra dating** *When the vendor allows the retailer extra time before payment is due for goods.*

to pay. In this way your campus bookstore orders its books in early July for an early August delivery. The bookstore then sells the books in late August or early September. However, because the books were sold on consignment, or with extra dating, the bookstore does not have to pay the publisher until October.

Space Constraints The retailer must also deal with space constraints. If depth or breadth is wanted, space is needed. If variety is to be stressed, it is also important to have enough *empty* space to separate the distinct merchandise lines. For example, consider a single counter containing cosmetics, candy, fishing tackle, women's stockings, and toys. This would obviously be an unsightly and unwise arrangement. As more variety is added, empty space becomes necessary to allow the consumer to clearly distinguish among distinct product lines.

Retailers, especially in the grocery business, have been able to turn this space constraint into an advantage by charging manufacturers slotting fees to carry their products.

Merchandise Turnover Constraints As the depth of the merchandise is increased, the retailer will be stocking more and more variations of the product to serve smaller and smaller segments. Consequently, inventory turnover will deteriorate and the chances of being out of stock will increase. One does not have to minimize variety, breadth, and depth to maximize turnover, but one must know how various merchandise mixes will affect inventory turnover.

Market Constraints Market constraints also affect decisions on variety, breadth, and depth of the merchandise mix. The three dimensions have a profound effect on how the consumer perceives the store, and consequently on the customers the store will attract. The consumer perceives a specialty store as one with limited variety and breadth of merchandise lines but considerable depth within the lines handled. An individual searching for depth in a limited set of merchandise lines such as formal menswear will thus be attracted to a menswear retailer specializing in formal wear. On the other hand, the consumer perceives the general merchandise retailer such as Target as a store with lots of variety and breadth in terms of merchandise lines, but with more constrained depth. Therefore, someone who needs to make several purchases across several merchandise lines, and who is willing to sacrifice depth of assortment, would be more attracted to the general merchandise retailer.

The constraining factors make it almost impossible for a retailer to emphasize all three dimensions. However, retailers can take some comfort in the fact that greater product selection does not necessarily mean that the consumer will get

High-profit retailers are those who realize that it is impossible to emphasize all three dimensions of the merchandise mix and therefore adjust their merchandise mix to satisfy the most profitable market segments.

more enjoyment from the shopping experience. Research has found that retailers can cut stock-keeping units (SKUs) without lowering consumer perceptions of selection. In fact, some consumers may even be more satisfied with the smaller selection.[117] This is important for retailers using the category management system to remember. After all, category management, in its effort to increase profits, typically reduces the number of SKUs as it seeks to increase inventory turnover. Nevertheless, if you are going to lose customers, you should seek to lose the less profitable ones by properly mixing your merchandise in terms of variety, breadth, and depth within the dollar, space, turnover, and market constraints.

CONFLICTS IN STOCK PLANNING Stock planning is an exercise in compromise and conflict. The conflict is multidimensional because not everything can be stocked. The conflicts are summarized as follows:

1. Maintain a strong in-stock position on genuinely new items while trying to avoid the 90 percent of new products that fail in the introductory stage. The retailer will want to carry the new products that will satisfy customers. If the consumer is sold a poor product, it hurts the retailer as much as, if not more than, the manufacturer. The problem becomes one of screening out poor products before they reach the customer. Any screening device, however, has error; the retailer might end up stocking some losers and turning down winners. Thus a basic conflict arises, but even the best of buyers will make some mistakes and be forced to use markdowns to unload slow-selling merchandise.

2. Maintain an adequate stock of the basic popular items while having sufficient inventory dollars to capitalize on unforeseen opportunities. Many times, if the retailer fills out the model stock with recommended quantities, there is little, if any, money left over for the super buy that is just around the corner. But if the retailer holds out that money and cuts back on basic stock, customers may be lost, and that super buy may never surface. For this reason, it is important that retailers realize that they should never be out of stock on staples and best-selling products.

3. Maintain high merchandise turnover goals while maintaining high margin goals. This is perhaps the most glaring conflict. Usually, items that turn over more rapidly have thinner profit margins. Therefore, developing an inventory plan that will accomplish both objectives is surely challenging.

4. Maintain adequate selection for customers while not confusing them. If customers are confronted with too many similar items, they will not be able to make up their minds and they may leave the store empty-handed and frustrated. On the other hand, if the selection is inadequate, the customer will again leave empty-handed. Thus, a delicate balance needs to be struck between too little and too much selection.

5. Maintain space productivity and utilization while not congesting the store. Take advantage of buys that will utilize the available space, but avoid buys that cause the merchandise to spill over into the aisles. Unfortunately, some of the best buys come along when space is already occupied.

As should be readily evident at this point, inventory management is no easy task. Equally challenging is the selection of vendors from whom to buy the merchandise.

Selection of Merchandising Sources

After deciding on the type and amount of inventory to be purchased, the next step is to determine where the retailer is to obtain the merchandise. All too often people have misconceptions about how retailers choose and negotiate with vendors. In reality, with proper planning and control, it can be a very rewarding experience, especially when your customers react positively to your merchandise selection. However, no matter how rewarding your buying experience is, it will also be grueling. Not only must the retail buyers determine what merchandise lines to carry, but they also must select the best possible vendor to supply them with these items and then must be able to negotiate the best deal possible with that vendor.

Unless the retailer owns a manufacturing and/or wholesale operation, the retailer must consider many criteria when selecting a merchandise source. These criteria are dependent on the retailer's type of store and merchandise sold. Generally the following criteria, which may vary across merchandise lines, should always be considered: selling history, consumers' perception of the manufacturer's reputation, reliability of delivery, trade terms, projected markup, quality of merchandise, after-sale service, transportation time, distribution center processing time, inventory carrying cost, country of origin, fashionability, and net-landed cost.[118]

Country of origin is becoming a more important issue every day, as governments use trade agreements to limit the amount of merchandise that can be imported from various countries and consumers rebel against sweatshops and the use of child labor in certain countries.

Recent research concludes that the use of private label brands (a) increases as the perceived consequences of making a buying mistake decrease, (b) increases when the different brands in the category are perceived to vary more in their quality, and (c) decreases if the category benefits are deemed to require actual trial/experience instead of being assessable through a search of package label information.[119]

> *Retailers who maintain and review both a vendor profitability analysis and a confidential vendor analysis statement before going to market will be more profitable.*

One of a retailer's greatest assets when dealing with a vendor is the retailer's past experiences with that vendor. Whether you are a small retailer doing all the buying yourself or a new buyer for a large chain, you should always approach vendors with two important pieces of information: the vendor profitability analysis statement and the confidential vendor analysis. The **vendor profitability analysis statement** provides a record of all the purchases you made last year, the discount granted you by the vendor, transportation charges paid, the original markup, markdowns, and finally, the season-ending gross margin on that vendor's merchandise. It is the positive relationship with a supplier described in the vendor profitability tables that may encourage a retail buyer to try that vendor's new product. Still, while **Mattel** is a strong player in the toy market, that relationship may not have been enough to get many toy buyers to purchase what turned out to be the most successful doll in toy market history back in 1959.

Vendor profitability analysis statement *A tool used to evaluate vendors and shows all purchases made the prior year, the discount granted, the transportation charges paid, the original markup, markdowns, and finally the season-ending gross margin on that vendor's merchandise.*

Confidential vendor analysis *Identical to the vendor profitability analysis but also provides a three-year financial summary as well as the names, titles, and negotiating points of all the vendor's sales staff.*

The **confidential vendor analysis** lists the same companies as in the profitability analysis statement but also provides a three-year financial summary as well as the names, titles, and negotiating points of the entire vendor's sales staff. This last piece of information is based on the notes taken by the buyer after the previous season's buying trip.

Based on the information obtained in the previous two reports, some retailers classify vendors into five categories.

1. **Class A Vendors** are the vendors from whom the retailer purchases large and profitable amounts of merchandise. The retailer may distinguish these vendors from others by purchasing a certain minimum quantity from them. These vendors and the retailer work together as partners. Because of the retailer's sheer size, every vendor selling to Wal-Mart is a Class A vendor.
2. **Class B Vendors** are those who generate satisfactory sales and profits for the retailer. They occasionally develop a strong product offering for the retailer.
3. **Class C Vendors** are vendors who carry outstanding lines but do not currently sell to the retailer. This is the type of vendor that the store buyer desires as a supplier.
4. **Class D Vendors** are those from whom the retailer purchases small quantities of goods on an irregular basis. Because of the expense of the small orders, it is doubtful if the purchases from these vendors produce any profits for either the retailer or the vendor.
5. **Class E Vendors** are vendors with whom the retailer has had an unfavorable experience. Only after the approval of top store officials can orders be placed with these vendors.

Class A vendors *Vendors from whom the retailer purchases large and profitable amounts of merchandise.*

Class B vendors *Vendors that generate satisfactory sales and profits for the retailer.*

Class C vendors *Vendors that carry outstanding merchandise lines but do not currently sell to the retailer.*

Class D vendors *Vendors from whom the retailer purchases small quantities of goods on an irregular basis.*

Class E vendors *Vendors with whom the retailer has had an unfavorable experience.*

Even buyers who do not go to market, but have the vendors come to them, evaluate their vendors. For years, many grocers felt that firms like **Procter & Gamble** treated retailers poorly. These grocers needed the many products that P&G manufactured, but they did not like P&G's "we win, you lose" attitude, which forced retailers to purchase the complete line of P&G products to earn merchandising money. P&G was a Class B vendor, at best. Recently, however,

P&G has developed a program in which it helps all its customers in developing their merchandise plans for the coming months and no longer requires grocers to purchase slow-moving products. This new attitude of "let's both win" has seen many supermarket managers reevaluate P&G as a Class A vendor. P&G knows that it can only be as successful as its retailers let it be.

After selecting the vendor(s), the retailer still must make a decision on the specific merchandise to be bought. Some products, such as the basic items for the particular department in question, are easy to purchase. Other products, especially new items, require more careful planning and consideration. Retailers should concern themselves with several key questions:

1. Where does this product fit into the strategic position that I have staked out for my department?
2. Will I have an exclusive with this product or will I be in competition with nearby retailers?
3. What is the estimated demand for this product in my target market?
4. What is my anticipated gross margin for this product?
5. Will I be able to obtain reliable, speedy stock replacement?
6. Can this product stand on its own, or is it merely a "me-too" item?
7. What is my expected turnover rate with this product?
8. Does this product complement the rest of my inventory?

Vendor Negotiations

Negotiation *The process of finding mutually satisfying solutions when the retail buyer and vendor have conflicting objectives.*

The climax of a successful buying plan is the active **negotiation,** which involves finding mutually satisfying solutions for parties with conflicting objectives, with those vendors that the retailer has identified as suitable supply sources. The effectiveness of this buyer-vendor relationship depends on the negotiation skills of the buyer and the economic power of the firms involved.

The retail buyer must negotiate price, delivery dates, discounts, shipping terms, and return privileges. All of these factors are significant because they affect both the firm's profitability and cash flow.

Manufacturers as well as retailers have in recent years become increasingly aware of the cost of carrying excess inventory. Likewise, both parties have also become more concerned with the time value of money and its resulting effect on each firm's cash flow. Since both parties to the negotiation process are aware of these cost factors and are trying to shift these costs to the other party, most negotiations do produce some conflict. However, successful negotiation is usually accomplished when buyers realize that the vendors are really their partners in the upcoming merchandising season. Both the buyer and the vendor are seeking to satisfy the retailer's customers better than anybody else. Therefore, buyers and vendors must resolve their conflicts and differences of opinion, remembering that negotiation is a two-way street and a long-term profitable relationship is the goal. After all, the vendor wants to develop a long-term relationship with the retailer as much as the retailer does with its customers.

The retailer who puts all the upcoming areas of negotiations and previous agreements with the vendor in writing before going to market will be more profitable.

What can be negotiated? There are many factors to be negotiated (prices, freight, delivery dates, method of shipment and shipping costs, exclusivity, guaranteed sales, markdown money, promotional allowances, return privileges, and discounts), and life is simplest when there are no surprises. Therefore, the smart buyer leaves nothing to chance and discusses everything with the vendor before purchase orders are signed. The buyer and seller together work out future plans using the buyer's merchandise budget and planned turnover. Therefore, the buyer and seller should seek to make negotiations a win-win situation where neither side feels like a loser, such as P&G and its retailers are doing today. The essence of negotiation is to trade what is cheap to you but valuable to the other party, for what is valuable to you but cheap to the other party.

The smart buyer puts all the upcoming areas of negotiations and previous agreements in letter form and sends it out before going to market. This helps to eliminate any misunderstandings afterward. Price, of course, is probably the first factor to be negotiated. Buyers should attempt to purchase the desired merchandise at the lowest possible net cost, but should not expect unreasonable discounts or price concessions. However, the buyer can try to bring about a price concession that is legal under the Robinson-Patman Act.

The buyer must be familiar with the prices and discounts allowed by each vendor. This is why past records are so important. However, the buyer must remember that his or her bargaining power is a result of his or her planned purchases from the vendor. As a result, a large retailer may be able to purchase goods from a vendor at a lower price than a small "mom-and-pop" retailer. Five different types of discounts can be negotiated.

TRADE DISCOUNT A **trade discount**, sometimes referred to as a **functional discount**, is a form of compensation that the buyer may receive for performing certain wholesaling and/or retailing services for the manufacturer. Because this discount is given for the performance of some service, the size of the discount will vary with that service. Thus, variations in trade discounts are legally justifiable on the basis of the different costs associated with doing business with various buyers.

> **Trade discount** A form of compensation that the buyer may receive for performing certain wholesaling or retailing services for the manufacturer, also referred to as a functional discount.

Trade discounts are often expressed in a chain, or series, such as "list less 40–20–10." Each figure in the chain of discounts represents a percentage reduction from the list price of an item. Assume that the list price of an item is $1,000 and that the chain of discounts is 40–20–10. The buyer who receives all these discounts would actually pay $432 for this item. The computations would look like this:

List price	$1,000
Less 40%	− 400
	600
Less 20%	− 120
	480
Less 10%	− 48
Purchase price	$ 432

To illustrate how the various chains of discount permit a vendor to compensate the members of the distribution channel for their marketing activities, let's look at the preceding example. Assume that the manufacturer sells through a channel system that includes manufacturer's agents, service wholesalers, and small retailers. The purchase price of $432 is accorded to the manufacturer's agent who negotiates a sale between the manufacturer and the service wholesaler. The manufacturers' agent then charges the service wholesaler $480 for the item, thus realizing $48 for rendering a number of marketing activities. The service wholesaler, in turn, charges a retailer $600 for the item, thus making $120. The retailer then sells the item at the suggested list price of $1,000, thus making $400 in gross margin to cover expenses and a profit.

Trade discounts are legal where they correctly reflect the costs of the intermediaries' services. Sometimes, large retailers want to buy directly from the manufacturer and pay only $432, instead of $600. This action would enable the large retailer to undercut the competition and is illegal, unless one of the three defenses of the Robinson-Patman Act can be applied.

QUANTITY DISCOUNT A **quantity discount** is a price reduction offered as an inducement to purchase large quantities of merchandise. Three types of quantity discounts are available:

1. **Noncumulative quantity discount:** a discount based on a single purchase
2. **Cumulative quantity discount:** a discount based on total amount purchased over a period of time
3. **Free merchandise:** a discount whereby merchandise is offered in lieu of price concessions

> **Quantity discount** A price reduction offered as an inducement to purchase large quantities of merchandise.
>
> **Noncumulative quantity discount** A discount based on a single purchase.
>
> **Cumulative quantity discount** A discount based on the total amount purchased over a period of time.
>
> **Free merchandise** A discount whereby merchandise is offered in lieu of price concessions.

Noncumulative quantity discounts can be legally justified by the manufacturer if costs are reduced because of the quantity involved or if the manufacturer is meeting a competitor's price in good faith. Cumulative discounts are more difficult to justify since many small orders may be involved, thereby reducing the manufacturer's savings.

265. SERVICES AND RETAIL OPERATIONS

For an example of how a quantity discount works, consider the following schedule:

Order Quantity	Discount from List Price
1 to 999	0%
1,000 to 9,999	5%
10,000 to 24,999	8%
25,000 to 49,999	10%

If a retailer that had already purchased 500 units wanted another 800 units, it would have to pay list price if the vendor uses a noncumulative policy. However, the retailer would receive a 5 percent discount on all purchases if the vendor uses a cumulative pricing policy.

Quantity discounts might not always be in the seller's best interest and should always be viewed by the buyer as an invitation for further negotiations. Consider the following price schedule published by **IBM**:[120]

Quantity	Unit Price
1–19	$5,795
20–49	$5,099
50–149	$4,636
150–249	$4,486

Let's say that as a buyer for a retail chain, you want 18 of these computers and your cost is $104,310 (18 × $5,795). But 20 would cost only $101,980 (20 × $5,099). What do you do?

You actually have four choices:

1. Tell IBM to ship 20 computers at $5,099, and you keep the extra 2.
2. Tell IBM to ship you 18 computers at $5,099 and have them keep the other 2.
3. Order 20 but tell IBM to ship you only 18 and to credit you for two computers at $5,099 each.
4. Negotiate a purchase price.

Whenever quantity discounts are offered, buyers should always check to see if by ordering more, the total purchase price may be lower.

Many times, retailers can make a quick profit from utilizing quantity discounts by selling the extra merchandise to a diverter to sell in a gray market. The diverter, which is not an authorized member of the marketing channel but still functions as an intermediary, will be able to purchase these goods cheaper from the retailer than it can from the manufacturer and sell this excess merchandise to other retailers. Also, such discounts allow the manufacturer to have its products sold in discount stores without offending all of its authorized retailers. However, many authorized retailers are upset when diverters provide discounters with such merchandise. Some retailers have dropped cosmetic lines when **Kmart**, most of whose cosmetics are diverted, started to carry the line. In addition, **Costco** has a vice president of "diverting" who purchases over $200 million worth of merchandise from unauthorized vendors.[121]

Retailers who understand how to negotiate the various discounts, especially quantity discounts, to their advantage will be more profitable.

Consider the previous retailer that needed only 18 computers and purchased 20. Here the retailer sold the two computers to a diverter for $3,500 each. As a result, the retailer was better off by $9,330 than it would have been had it bought only 18 computers at $5,795 each (18 × $5,795 = $104,310; 20 × 5,099 = $101,980 – $7,000 = $94,980). The diverter could now profit by selling these two computers to another retailer for $4,000 each.

Today diverters are important members of the retailer's channel, especially in the grocery and computer fields. Not all manufacturers or retailers feel the same way about them. Nonetheless, it was the manufacturers' pricing policies that enabled diverters to function economically.

PROMOTIONAL DISCOUNT A third type of discount is a **promotional discount,** which is given when the retailer performs an advertising or promotional service for the manufacturer. For example, a vendor might offer a retailer 50 extra jeans if (1) the retailer purchases 1,250 jeans during the season and (2) runs two newspaper advertisements featuring the jeans during the season. One of the main reasons manufacturers offer such discounts is that the rates newspapers charge local retailers are often lower than the rates charged national manufacturers. These discounts are legal as long as they are available to all competing retailers on an equal basis.

SEASONAL DISCOUNT Retailers can earn a **seasonal discount** if they purchase and take delivery of the merchandise in the off-season (e.g., buying swimwear in October). However, this does not mean that all seasonal discounts result in the purchase of merchandise out of season. Retailers in resort areas often take advantage of these discounts since swimwear is never out of season for them. As long as the same terms are available to all competing retailers, seasonal discounts are legal.

CASH DISCOUNT The final discount available to the buyer is a **cash discount** for prompt payment of bills. Cash discounts are usually stated as 2/10, net 30, which means that a 2 percent discount is given if payment is received within 10 days of the invoice date and the net amount is due within 30 days.

Although the cash discount is a common method for encouraging early payment, it can also be used as a negotiating tool by delaying the payment due date. This future-dating negotiation may take many forms. Following are several of the most common:

1. **End-of-month (EOM) dating** allows for a cash discount and the full payment period to begin on the first day of the following month instead of on the invoice date. End-of-month invoices dated after the 25th of the month are considered to be dated on the first of the following month.
2. **Middle-of-month (MOM) dating** is similar to EOM except the middle of the month is used as the starting date.
3. **Receipt of goods (ROG) dating** allows the starting date to be the date goods are received by the retailer.
4. **Extra dating (Ex)** merely allows the retailer extra or free days before the period of payment begins.
5. A final discount form to be considered, but which is not widely used today, is anticipation. **Anticipation** allows a retailer to pay the invoice in advance of the expiration of the cash discount period and earn an extra discount. However, anticipation is usually figured at an annual rate of 7 percent, which is below the current cost of money.

Many vendors have eliminated the cash discount because retailers, especially department stores, have been taking 60 to 120 days to pay and still deduct the cash discount. In fact, many vendors are requiring new accounts to pay up front, until credit is established.

DELIVERY TERMS Delivery terms are another factor to be considered in negotiations. They are important because they specify where title to the merchandise passes to the retailer, whether the vendor or buyer will pay the freight charges, and who is obligated to file any damage claims. The three most common shipping terms are

1. **Free on board (FOB) factory.** The buyer assumes title at the factory and pays all transportation costs from the vendor's factory.
2. **Free on board (FOB) shipping point.** The vendor pays the transportation to a local shipping point, but the buyer assumes title at this point and pays all further transportation costs.
3. **Free on board (FOB) destination.** The vendor pays all transportation costs and the buyer takes title upon delivery.

Promotional discount A discount provided for the retailer performing an advertising or promotional service for the manufacturer.

Seasonal discount A discount provided to retailers if they purchase and take delivery of merchandise in the off season.

Cash discount A discount offered to the retailer for the prompt payment of bills.

End-of-month (EOM) dating Allows the retailer to take a cash discount and the full payment period to begin on the first day of the following month instead of on the invoice date.

Middle-of-month (MOM) dating Allows the retailer to take a cash discount and the full payment period to begin in the middle of the month.

Receipt of goods (ROG) dating Allows the retailer to take a cash discount and the full payment period to begin when the goods are received by the retailer.

Extra dating (Ex) Allows the retailer extra or interest-free days before the period of payment begins.

Anticipation Allows the retailer to pay the invoice in advance of the end of the cash discount period and earn an extra discount.

Free on board (FOB) factory A method of charging for transportation where the buyer assumes title to the goods at the factory and pays all transportation costs from the vendor's factory.

In-Store Merchandise Handling

The retailer must have some means of handling incoming merchandise. For some types of retailers (e.g., a grocery store), this need will be significant and frequent; for others (e.g., a jeweler), it will be relatively minor and infrequent. Frequent and large deliveries entail considerable planning of merchandise receiving and handling space. For instance, consider that a full-line grocery store must have receiving docks to which 40- to 60-foot semitrailers can be backed up. Similarly, space may be needed for a small forklift to drive between the truck and the merchandise receiving area to unload the merchandise. Subsequently, the merchandise will need to be moved from the receiving area, where it will be counted and marked, to a storage area, either on the selling floor or in a separate location.

The point at which incoming merchandise is received can be a high theft point. The retail manager needs to design the receiving and handling area in order to minimize this problem. Some thefts involve the retail employees themselves; others involve outsiders. The 2002 National Retail Security Survey found that for the nation's largest retailers the average **shrinkage** rate was 1.7 percent of their annual sales. (Shrinkage is the loss of merchandise due to theft, loss, damage, or bookkeeping errors.) This translates into an industrywide net loss of $31.3 billion.[122] Therefore, several types of shrinkage caused by theft will be mentioned in the following discussion.

Vendor collusion includes the types of losses that occur when the merchandise is delivered. Typical losses involve the delivery of less merchandise than is charged for, removal of good merchandise disguised as old or stale merchandise, and stealing other merchandise from the stockroom or off the selling floor while making delivery. This type of theft often involves both the delivery people and the retail employee who signs for the delivery, with the two splitting the profit.

Employee theft occurs when employees steal merchandise where they work. Although no one knows for sure how much is stolen annually from retailers since all shrinkage statistics are based only on apprehensions, as many as 30 percent of American workers admit to stealing from their employers, even if they take only small items like a pen or pencil. Although some of the stolen goods come from the selling floor, a larger percentage is taken from the stockroom to the employee lounge and lockers, where it is kept until the employees leave with it at quitting time. Employee theft, which amounts to over $800 per apprehension, is most prevalent in food stores, department stores, and discount stores. Considering that these types of stores are usually larger in size, sales volume, and number of employees, the lack of close supervision might contribute to this problem.

Customer theft is also a problem. In fact, over a dozen shoppers are caught for every case of employee theft, although the average amount of merchandise recovered is less than $50. Stealing merchandise from the stockroom and receiving area may be easier than taking it from the selling floor for several reasons. First, much of the stockroom merchandise is not ticketed, so it is easier to get it through electronic antishoplifting devices. Second, once the thief enters the stock area, there is very little antitheft security. Most security guards watch the exits and fitting rooms. Third, there is usually an exit in the immediate area of the stockroom through which the thief can carry out the stolen goods. Some retailers have wired these exits to set off an alarm when opened without a key, helping to reduce thefts somewhat. Another innovative retailer, after determining that employees were hiding merchandise in the compressed and discarded and baled boxes that were left out as trash, started using a special spiked baler that punches holes in boxes to damage any stolen merchandise.[123]

The retailer must be aware that the opportunities for receiving, handling, and storage thefts are excellent. Therefore, steps should be taken to help cut down on these crimes. The retailer cannot watch the employees every minute to see whether or not they are honest, but some surveillance is helpful. However, the retailer must consider the employee's and customer's right to privacy versus the retailer's right to security. Legislation allows the use of electronic monitoring by video and audio systems only when advance notice is given. In effect, workers and shoppers must be informed when they are being monitored.

Free on board (FOB) shipping point A method of charging for transportation in which the vendor pays for transportation to a local shipping point where the buyer assumes title and then pays all further transportation costs.

Free on board (FOB) destination A method of charging for transportation in which the vendor pays for all transportation costs and the buyer takes title on delivery.

Shrinkage The loss of merchandise due to theft, loss, damage, or bookkeeping errors.

Vendor collusion Occurs when an employee of one of the retailer's vendors steals merchandise as it is delivered to the retailer.

Employee theft Occurs when employees of the retailer steal merchandise where they work.

Customer theft Also known as shoplifting, occurs when customers or individuals disguised as customers steal merchandise from the retailer's store.

Customer Services and Retail Selling

Customer Service

CUSTOMER MANAGEMENT **High-quality service** is defined as delivering service that meets or exceeds customers' expectations. In this definition there is no absolute level of quality service, but only service that is perceived as high quality because it meets and exceeds the expectations of customers.

In an attempt to offer the high-quality service expected and to reduce these defections, retailers are now engaging in relationship retailing programs.[124] **Relationship retailing** includes all the activities designed to attract, retain, and enhance customer relationships. No longer will retailing be driven by the expansion of large, homogeneous chains offering only low prices. Profitable retailers of the future will be those that concentrate on building long-term relations with loyal customers by promising and consistently delivering high-quality products, complemented by high-quality service, shopping aids to ease the purchase process, and by using honest prices to build and maintain a reputation for absolute trustworthiness. Loyal customers, after all, are less price conscious and less prone to shop other retailers selling the same merchandise mix.

> **High-quality service** Service that meets or exceeds customers' expectations.
>
> **Relationship retailing** Comprises all the activities designed to attract, retain, and enhance long-term relationships with customers

High-performance retailers can develop these relationships with their customers by offering two benefits:

1. *Financial benefits* that increase the customer's satisfaction, such as the frequent purchaser discounts or product upgrades already offered by some supermarkets, airlines, and hotels.
2. *Social benefits* that increase the retailer's social experience with the customer. Retailers must not forget that their stores must offer customers a combination of excitement and entertainment.

The three most basic retailing tasks include: getting consumers from your trading area into your store, converting these consumers into loyal customers, and doing so in the most efficient manner possible.

Due to significant cost cutting following the recent period of consolidation and retrenchment by retailers, this second task is even more difficult. Retailers today are so standardized in either their physical layout or Web site design, with each one carrying the same merchandise styles and colors, that customers cannot tell them apart. More important, many retailers have an indifferent and undertrained sales force. As a result, there is a complete breakdown of what is essential for a successful retailer: exciting merchandise backed up by outstanding service, and personal selling that generates loyal customers. In recent years, the intense competition from discounters caused many retailers to lower customer service levels as a means of staying price competitive. These retailers felt that reduced service levels would lower their operating costs, thus allowing increased price competitiveness. No wonder that for most customers, shopping trips do not always meet their expectations and result in an unsatisfying experience.[125]

> *High-profit retailers are those who realize that the longer a customer stays with a retailer, the more profitable that customer is to their operations.*

Retailers must differentiate themselves by meeting the needs of their customers better than the competition. Thus, retailers have again come to realize that customer service is a strength. Instead of frustrating the customer by not having the necessary stock on hand or the proper selling support on the sales floor, today's profitable retailers realize that customer service is a major demand generator for their merchandise. However, it is important that retailers also remember that when they encourage their customers to establish high expectations, the slightest disappointment in service can be a catastrophe.

Customer service consists of all those activities performed by the retailer that influence (1) the ease with which a potential customer can shop or learn about the retailer's offering, (2) the ease with which a transaction can be completed once the customer attempts to make a purchase, and (3) the customer's satisfaction with the transaction. These three elements are the pretransaction, transaction, and posttransaction components of customer service. Some common services provided by retailers include alterations, fitting rooms, delivery, gift registries, check cashing, in-home shopping, extended shopping hours, gift wrapping, charge accounts, parking, layaway, and merchandise return privileges. It must be remembered that none of these services are altruistic offerings; they are all designed to entice the customers with whom the retailer is seeking to develop a relationship.

> **Customer service** Consists of all those activities performed by the retailer that influence (1) the ease with which a potential customer can shop or learn about the store's offering, (2) the ease with which a transaction can be completed once the customer attempts to make a purchase, and (3) the customer's satisfaction with the transaction.

265. SERVICES AND RETAIL OPERATIONS

Retailers should design their customer service program around pretransaction, transaction, and posttransaction elements of the sale in order to obtain a differential competitive advantage. After all, in today's world of mass distribution, most retailers have access to the same merchandise and, therefore, retailers can seldom differentiate themselves from others solely on the basis of merchandise stocked. The same can be said regarding location and store design advantages. Retailers can, however, obtain a high degree of differentiation through their customer service programs.

A retail shopping experience is more than negotiating your way through the retailer's store, Web site, or catalog, finding the merchandise you want, interacting (or not interacting) with the staff, and paying for the merchandise. It also involves your actions before and after the transaction. Therefore, serving the customer before, during, and after the transaction can help to create new customers and strengthen the loyalty of present customers. If customer service before the transaction is poor, the probability of a transaction occurring will decline. If customer service is poor at the transaction stage, the customer may back out of the transaction. And if customer service is poor after the transaction, the probability of a repeat purchase at the same store will decline. The customer who visits a retailer and finds the service level below expectations or the product "out of stock" will become a **transient customer.** This transient, or temporary, customer will seek to find a retailer with the level of customer service he or she feels is appropriate. At any given moment, for all lines of retail trade, there are a significant number of transient customers. The retailer with a superior customer service program will have a significant advantage in making these transients loyal customers. Thus, customer service can play a significant role in building a retailer's sales volume.

Transient customer An individual who is dissatisfied with the level of customer service offered at a store or stores and is seeking an alternative store with the level of customer service that he or she thinks is appropriate.

Customer service cannot happen all by itself, but must be integrated into all aspects of retailing. That is why the profitable retailers of the future will know that the demand for their merchandise is not just price elastic, as economists would have us believe, but also *service elastic*. This means that an increase in service levels of 1 percent will result in a more than 1 percent increase in sales.

MERCHANDISE MANAGEMENT One of the best ways a retailer can serve a customer is by having in stock the merchandise that the customer wants. There are few things more disturbing to a customer than making a trip to a store for a specific item only to discover that the item is out of stock, which is why Nordstrom offers its customers a free dress shirt if it is ever out of stock on any of the basic sizes. It wants the customers to be confident of locating any style, color, or size. Basically, the better the store is at allocating inventory in proportion to customer demand patterns, the better the customer will be served.

BUILDING AND FIXTURE MANAGEMENT Retailers' decisions regarding building and fixtures can also have a significant effect on how well the customer is served. For example, consider how the following noncomprehensive list of building and fixture dimensions might influence customer service: heating and cooling levels; availability of parking space; ease of finding merchandise; layout and arrangement of fixtures; placement of restrooms and lounge areas; location of check-cashing, complaint, and returns desks; level of lighting; and width and length of aisles.

PROMOTION MANAGEMENT Promotion provides customers with information that can help them make purchase decisions. Therefore, retailers should be concerned with whether the promotion programs they develop help the consumer. The following questions can help the retailer assess whether its promotion is serving the customer:

1. Is the advertising informative and helpful?
2. Does the advertising provide all the information the customer needs?
3. Are the salespeople helpful and informative?
4. Are the salespeople friendly and courteous?
5. Are the salespeople easy to find when needed?
6. Are sufficient quantities available on sales promotion items?
7. Do salespeople know about the ad and what's being promoted and why?

This list is not comprehensive, but rather is intended only to show that customer service issues need to be considered in designing promotional programs.

PRICE MANAGEMENT Price management will also influence how well the customer is served. Are prices clearly marked and visible? Is pricing fair, honest, and straightforward? Are customers told the true price of credit? These questions suggest that the pricing decision should not be isolated from the retailer's customer service program.

CREDIT MANAGEMENT Management of credit, both in-house and bank card, should also be integrated into the customer service program. Credit, along with the retailer's layaway plans, is a significant aid in both encouraging customer loyalty and helping them purchase merchandise. Retailers' credit policies influence the customers' perception of how well they are being serviced. Some retailers, such as **Holiday Inn,** have recently begun issuing their own co-branded credit cards. They hope that these cards, in addition to increasing loyalty to the retailer and generating credit-transaction profits, will add to their database so that they can improve future promotions. For example, Holiday Inn's Visa card provides cardholders membership in its Priority Club, which translates to free food and drinks at regular Holiday Inns and credits toward free stays at any of its locations.

A RECAP Integration with the elements of the retail mix is important when retailers develop their customer service programs. Much of what has already been discussed relates either directly or indirectly, to one of the three broad categories of customer service: pretransaction, transaction, and posttransaction. Successful retailers view customer service as a way to gain an advantage over the competition. As a result, even discounters are beginning to empower all their employees, not just management, to do whatever is reasonable to take care of the customer.

> *The more profitable retailers will integrate customer service decisions with their merhcandise, building and fixtures, promotion, price, and credit management decisions.*

Common Customer Services

Much of the discussion on location, merchandise, pricing, and promotion has implications for serving the customer. However, many of the more popular types of customer services have not been mentioned or have received sparse coverage. Let us review some of them.

PRETRANSACTION SERVICES The most common **pretransaction services,** which are provided to the customer prior to entering the store, are convenient hours and information aids. Each of these makes it easier for the potential customer to shop or to learn of the retailer's offering.

> *Pretransaction services Services provided to the customer prior to entering the store.*

TRANSACTION SERVICES In the past, retailers believed that transaction services meant having salespeople who would personally take care of an individual customer. But for the profitable retailers of the future, the term **transaction services** will mean offering the conveniences customers need and then helping them get out of the store as fast as possible with their purchases. The most important transaction services are credit, layaway, gift wrapping and packaging, check cashing, personal shopping, merchandise availability, personal selling, and the sales transaction itself. These services help to facilitate transactions once customers have made a purchase decision.

> *Transaction services Services provided to customers when they are in the store shopping and transacting business.*

POSTTRANSACTION SERVICES The relationship between the retailer and the consumer has become more complex in today's service-oriented economy. Many products, such as computers, automobiles, and travel and financial services, require an extended relationship between the retailer and consumer. The longer this period of time can be extended by ensuring the customer's satisfaction with the product, the greater the chances that future sales will result. The most common **posttransaction services,** which are provided after the sale has been made, are complaint handling, merchandise returns, merchandise repair, servicing, delivery, and postsale follow-ups. Posttransaction services are especially important for on-line retailers.

> *Posttransaction services Services provided to customers after they have purchased merchandise or services.*
>
> *High-performance retailers place a very high emphasis on responsive complaint handling systems. They recognize that the cost of fixing mistakes is less than the cost of an unhappy customer.*

Determining Customer Service Levels

It is not easy to determine the optimal number and level of customer services to offer. Theoretically, however, one could argue that a retailer should add customer services until the additional revenue that is generated by higher service levels is equal to the additional cost of providing those services. In the short run, cutting back on costly customer services can usually increase profits. However, such action may present serious long-run problems as customers shop elsewhere seeking better services.

Exhibit 200.68 *Factors to Consider When Determining Customer Services to Offer*

Exhibit 200.69 *How the Retailer's Sales Force Meets the Expectations of Both Vendors and Customers*

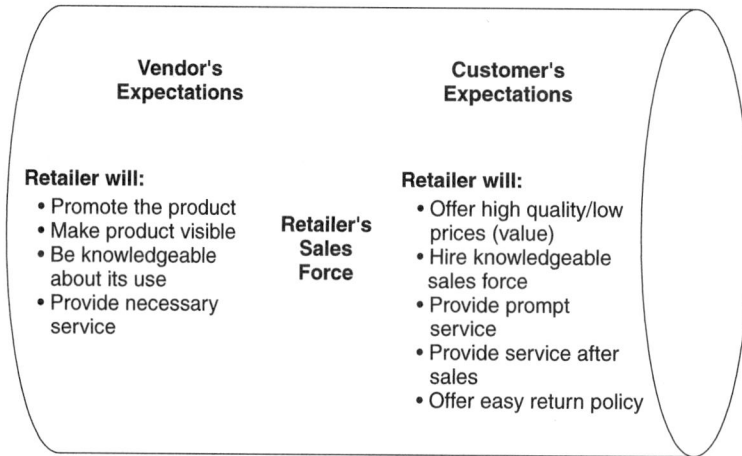

Deciding what specific customer services to offer in order to increase sales volume is a difficult question for any retailer. Exhibit 200.68 lists six factors to be considered when determining the customer services to offer: the retailer's characteristics, the services offered by the competition, the type of merchandise handled, the price image of the retailer, the income of the target market, and the cost of providing the service. It is the retailer's job to study these six areas to arrive at the service mix that will increase long-run profits by keeping present customers, enticing new customers, and projecting the right image. Above all else, retailers must remember to be realistic and not expect to satisfy the wants and needs of all customers. No strategy could be less profitable than trying to satisfy everybody. What the retailer is really trying to do is to use its sales staff as the conduit between the vendor's expectations and the customer's expectations, as shown in Exhibit 200.69.

The Retail Selling Process

Five basic steps occur during the retail selling process, including prospecting, approach, sales presentation, closing the sale, and suggestion selling. The length of time that a salesperson spends in each one of the five steps depends on the product type, the customer, and the selling situation. Variation of these steps is presented in Section 390, Sales Administration and Management, under "The Sales Process."

The Customer Service and Sales Enhancement Audit

Up to this point, we have discussed the level and type of sales personnel needed in a retail operation; the types of retail selling; the selection, training, and management of the sales force; the factors to consider when evaluating individual salespeople, and how to sell in a retail store. These are microapproaches to improving the productivity of an individual. How do we get macro answers for the performance of a whole department or a whole store? Retailers who had 49 million possible buyers walk out of their stores without any salesperson contact could partially solve the problem with an audit of the retailer's customer services and sales enhancement programs.[126]

Such an audit, which can easily be performed by the retailer's own staff or by a consultant, provides the direction that enables retailers to capture the unrealized potential of customers who walk out with no salesperson contact. It analyzes current levels of performance by selling area within each company store, revealing how customers shop the store and the extent of the service they receive. It is *not* an attempt to learn what the customers want (e.g., "friendly and competent salespeople," "low prices," "free assembly"); instead, it concentrates on the facts of their shopping experience.

The **customer service and sales enhancement audit** is usually performed by having the retailer's staff or hired researchers intercept customers as they leave the store to ask about their experience in the store. The number of customers interviewed should reflect the size and shopping patterns of each store. The objectives of the audit are to:

> *Customer service and sales enhancement audit* Provides management with a detailed analysis of current sales activity by location and by selling area.

- Identify the service, salesmanship, and sales enhancement methods that will produce more sales from the existing shopping traffic.
- Target the methods by store and selling area that will produce the most significant improvements.
- Determine the added sales that can be generated by improving the accepted service level, salesmanship, and sales enhancement programs.

Upon completion, the audit provides management with a detailed analysis of current sales activity by location and by selling area. It identifies how and where additional sales volume is available. It measures, analyzes, and reports on the specific factors.

Basic Service

1. *Customer contact.* In stores that purport to offer service, there can be no sale if the shopper has no contact with a salesperson or a cashier. Increasing the number of shoppers who are approached increases the number of shoppers who are likely to buy.
2. *Salesperson-initiated contact.* Motivated salespeople—those who do not wait for customers to approach them—can prevent walkouts and generate more sales from those shoppers who otherwise might have to spend shopping time looking for a salesperson.
3. *Customer acknowledgment.* Greeting customers within a short time frame also prevents walkouts and provides more shopping time. It keeps the shopper in a favorable buying mood.

Salesmanship

4. *Merchandise knowledge.* A salesperson with product knowledge can answer a shopper's questions, enhance the transaction, help to consummate the sales, prevent lost sales, and even add to the purchase.
5. *Needs clarification.* Asking the proper questions enables the salesperson to present and show the proper merchandise.
6. *Active selling.* Actively selling the merchandise and volunteering advice about the use and care of the goods, as well as stating the advantages of ownership, helps to consummate the sale.
7. *Suggestion selling.* Suggesting additional and/or complementary merchandise may increase the value of the sale. (The audit should also measure the number of times that suggestion selling resulted in an additional purchase.)

Sales Enhancement

8. *Impulse purchasing.* Proper selection of merchandise, packaging, location within a department, presentation, and then servicing the transaction will increase the productivity of shopping traffic.
9. *Walkouts.* Retaining sales that would otherwise be lost is one of the most direct and immediate routes to sales improvement. Offering the desired goods in easy-to-find locations is the most obvious method for reducing walkouts. However, customer contact and salesmanship can be a major deterrent of walkouts among those who come to buy.

These elements of basic service, salesmanship, and sales enhancement are measured and reported by selling area within each company store, enabling management to apply targeted training programs. It is usually not necessary to spend the money to train or retrain all personnel in each store for each of the techniques. However, when applied, the method can add significantly to the value of each transaction. For example, for a chain retailer, the incremental sales transactions for the average salesperson after the audit were:

- 10% when the salesperson initiated the contact with the shopper.
- 3%   when the salesperson acknowledged the customer's presence in a timely manner.
- 12% when the salesperson was able to answer the customer's questions.
- 14% when the salesperson asked questions to clarify the shopper's needs.
- 18% when the salesperson actively "sold" the merchandise.
- 48% when the salesperson suggested additional or complementary merchandise and the suggestion was taken.

No incremental addition for the average salesperson can be calculated for increasing contacts with shoppers, for improving the rate of impulse buying, or for reducing walkouts. The reason is obvious: when these techniques are applied and are successful, an entirely new transaction is created!

To provide management with an action program, the customer service and sales enhancement audit includes a series of exception reports showing specifically what improvement is necessary within each selling area at each company store. The dollar value is also listed, so that management can know the added volume available by applying targeted retraining programs. The report should list the causes of walkouts for each selling area at each location. Management therefore receives an analysis of current performance by selling area at each company location and the specific action necessary to capture unrealized potential. The dollar opportunity is also calculated to highlight the value of each improvement. Exception reports make it easy to implement the program.

Every day within all types of stores there are "acres of diamonds in their own backyards." Shoppers are continuing to visit stores in large numbers, many of them willing, able, and anxious to be converted into buyers. Management's task is to identify where and how that can be accomplished. That is the function of the audit.

Store Layout Management

Introduction

In fact, no other variable in the retailing mix influences the consumer's initial perception of a bricks and mortar retailer as much as the store itself. Profitable retailers today are spending a great deal of time and effort making sure the right things happen in their store and that the right customers enter the store, shop, and spend money. Simply put, for retailers the store is "where the action is," and this includes such minor details as the placement of merchandise. Although this section is concerned with the physical store, the same factors may be used to develop an e-tailer's "virtual store."

Store image *The overall perception the consumer has of the store's environment.*

Space productivity *Represents how effectively the retailer utilizes its space and is usually measured by sales per square foot of selling space or gross margin dollars per square foot of selling space.*

Although a store is composed of literally thousands of details, the two primary objectives around which all activities, functions, and goals in the store revolve are **store image** and **space productivity.** However, before discussing these two objectives, it is important to identify the elements that compose the store environment (shown in Exhibit 200.70), each of which will be discussed in detail in this section.

ELEMENTS OF THE STORE ENVIRONMENT The first decision the retailer must make in planning a store is how to allocate the scarce resource, space. The retailer creates a store layout that shows the location of all merchandise departments and the placement of circulation aisles to allow customers to move through the store. As discussed, the merchandise presentation must be exciting so as to catch and hold customers' attention, be easy to understand, and encourage shoppers to browse, evaluate, and buy. Therefore, the presentation of the merchandise is a crit-

Successful retailers, whether operating traditional or virtual stores, place a heavy emphasis on designing their physical facilities or Web site so as to enhance image and increase productivity.

Exhibit 200.70 *Elements That Compose the Store Environment*

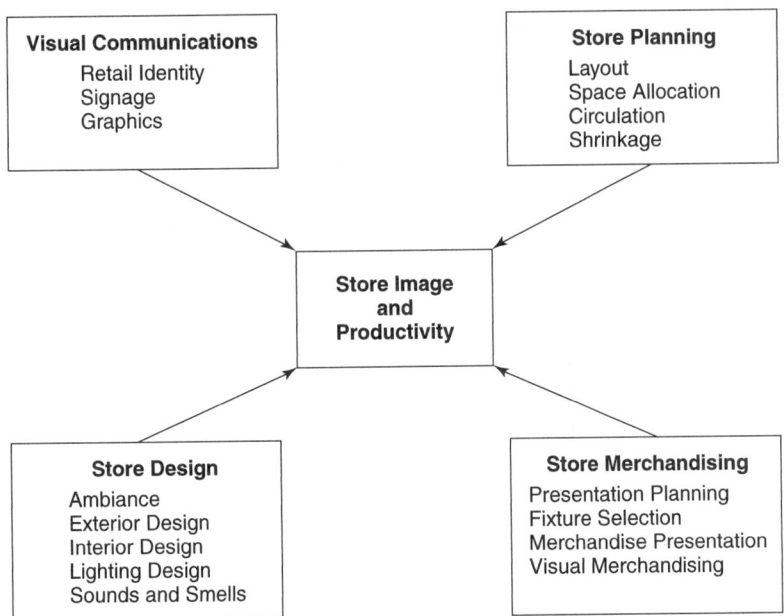

ical factor in the selling power of a store and has a significant effect on the store image. A bookstore with a high percentage of face-outs, for example, can create the image of being a specialty book boutique that carries a limited selection of exclusive titles and is, therefore, a rather pricey place to shop. A bookstore with virtually all spine-outs is often perceived as cramming in a huge selection of titles sold at low prices. Thus, merchandise presentation is a critical factor in determining both store image and productivity.

Most shoppers are accustomed to noticing the layout and design of a store, which is composed of all the elements affecting the human senses of sight, hearing, smell, and touch. An effective store layout and design, including the storefront, creates a comfortable environment that enhances the merchandise and entices shoppers to browse and buy. Lighting is an important element that should not be overlooked. Both display and in-store lighting help create the proper image and also draw customers' eyes around the store, onto merchandise, and ultimately encourage them to purchase the product.[127] Likewise, in-store graphics such as art, photography, and signs form an important visual communication link between the store and its customers by providing much-needed information on how to shop in the store.

OBJECTIVES OF THE STORE ENVIRONMENT The two primary objectives of creating the desired store image and increasing space productivity amount to a simple description of the three basic tasks of retailing.

- Get customers into the store (*store image*).
- Once they are inside the store, convert them into customers buying merchandise (*space productivity*).
- Do this in the most efficient manner possible.

The retailer must constantly balance the first two elements of the model, as they are sometimes at odds.

Developing a Store Image The starting point in creating this image is, of course, the merchandise carried in the store, along with the retailer's promotional activities, customer service, cleanliness, and sales force. That the store image serves a critical role in the store selection process is best illustrated by research in the supermarket industry showing that overall cleanliness is the most important criterion.[128] Other important criteria were clearly labeled prices, accurate and pleasant checkout clerks, and well-stocked shelves.[129]

This is why planning the store environment is so important to a retailer. Although advertising and other promotional activities are important in establishing a desired store image, the store itself makes the most significant and lasting impression on our collective consciousness and it is here that the retailer must focus great energy on creating the right image.

This effort is complicated by the knowledge that consumers are extremely fickle, able to change their feelings about retailers at any time for little substantive reason, and the fact that today there are more stores than ever vying for limited consumer dollars. It is not surprising that image engineering—the ability to create and change a store's image—becomes more important every day for a retailer's survival.

Increasing Space Productivity The store's image attracts customers. However, when customers are visiting the store or its Web site, the retailer must also convince them to make a purchase. Therefore, a store environment must increase its space productivity, a goal that is summarized in a simple but powerful truism in retailing: *The more merchandise customers are exposed to that is presented in an orderly manner, the more they tend to buy.* After all, the typical shopper in a department store goes into only two or three shopping areas per trip. By carefully planning the store environment, the retailer can encourage customers to flow through the entire store, or at least through more shopping areas, and see a wider variety of merchandise. The proper use of in-store advertising and displays will let the customer know what's happening in other departments and encourage a visit to those areas. Conversely, however, the store does not want to have merchandise pushed into every conceivable nook and cranny of the store so that customers cannot get to it.

> *High-profit retailers design their stores to expose shoppers to as much merchandise as possible, displayed in a safe and orderly manner that creates an uncongested shopping environment.*

Many retailers are focusing more attention on in-store marketing, based on the theory that marketing dollars spent inside the store, in the form of store design, merchandise presentation, visual displays, or in-store promotions, should lead to significantly greater sales and profit increases than marketing dollars spent on advertising and other out-of-store vehicles such as public relations and promotions. After all, it is easier to get a consumer who is already in your store to buy more merchandise than planned than to get a new consumer to come into your store.

One factor that detracts from space productivity is shrinkage, or the loss of merchandise through theft, loss, and damage. It is called **shrinkage** because retailers usually do not know what happened to the missing items, only that the inventory level in the store has somehow shrunk. Even stores that move customers through the entire space and effectively use in-store marketing techniques to maximize sales can fall victim to high shrinkage. Remember, when a store sells an item for $1.29, it earns only a small percentage of that sale, perhaps ranging from 15 to 60 cents. When that item is stolen, lost, or damaged, however, the store loses the cost of that $1.29 item—for example, 69 cents in the case of a $1.29 item—and this loss is deducted from the store's overall sales. Shrinkage ranges from 1 to 4 percent of retail sales. Although this may seem like a small number, consider that after-tax profit for many retailers is little more than 4 percent, so high shrinkage alone can make the difference between a profit and a loss.

> **Shrinkage** Represents merchandise that cannot be accounted for due to theft, loss, or damage.

Therefore, to enhance space productivity, retailers must incorporate planning, merchandise presentation, and design strategies that minimize shrinkage by avoiding hidden areas of the store, which shoplifters can take advantage of, and reduce the number of times merchandise must be moved, during which damage and loss can occur.

Store Planning

Planning an effective retail store resembles planning an effective piece of writing, and moving through a store as a customer is similar to reading an article or a chapter in a book. The merchandise, like words, is there for you to review, understand, and consume. But just as a book needs more than words to make sense, a store needs more than merchandise to be shopable.

The store's layout and design is like the organization of modules, sections, and subsections in this book. Grouping the words and thoughts into mental "chunks" makes the book easier to digest and understand. Unless a store specialized in only one product type, for example, candles, it would be impossible to shop if that store were not broken into departments and categories. The books would be found among the shovels, the CDs would be mixed in with the garden plants, and you would not know where to begin.

Signs and graphics are similar to the headings and punctuation, which give you cues to understanding the organization of both a book and the merchandise in a store. Without headings and subheadings, this chapter would be a stream of words, very difficult and, worse, boring to read and understand. Similarly, without signs, a store would seem like an endless sea of racks and merchandise, difficult to understand and shop.

Finally, the exhibits, charts, and boxes in this book are the retail equivalent of the visual displays and focal points, where merchandise is pulled off the shelf or racks and displayed in theatrical vignettes. Successful retailers use these settings to break up the store space, illustrate merchandise opportunities in the store, and visually demonstrate how certain merchandise goes together or can work in the consumer's life. Like photos and exhibits in a book, these visual displays elaborate on the text, or the bulk of merchandise on the racks, to make statements.

Most important, a retail store and a piece of writing are very similar in the way they affect the consumer. Many writing coaches teach aspiring writers that each time an uncommon word is used or a punctuation mark is missing,

Exhibit 200.71 *These Warning Signs May Indicate a Space Problem*

> Open spaces on the selling floor, even if the product is on hand
> Cluttered and disorganized aisles, hallways, and stockrooms
> Excessive time required to put away new receipts
> Insufficient staging space for large shipments of advertised products
> Sales associates continually required to leave the sales floor to locate additional merchandise
> Poor utilization of vertical space and excessive time required to retrieve products stored on high shelves
> Sales lag expectations for specific locations where space or fixtures are a known issue
> Off-site storage or multiple stockrooms required for a single commodity

the reader hits a "speed bump" in the writing and must mentally pause to consider what is meant. After hitting three speed bumps, the reader may conclude that the writing is too difficult to understand and quit reading.

The same is true in a retail store. All cues must work subliminally to organize the merchandise and guide shoppers effortlessly through the store. Each time shoppers become a bit confused as to where they are, where they need to go, how much an item costs, or where certain merchandise is, they become frustrated. The first or second instance may not even be consciously noticed, but shoppers may quickly become frustrated and walk out, concluding that the store is too hard to shop. Exhibit 200.71 is a list of warning signs that managers should look for, because each warning sign indicates a speed bump waiting to drive customers away from a store.

Most shoppers cannot consciously identify the elements of a good store, but certainly they know when these elements are missing. We have all experienced the feeling that a store seems to "really have it together." It's easy to shop, fun, and exciting; the merchandise is easy to understand; the associates seem friendly. You conclude that this store is a "good shop" and, with any luck, are completely oblivious to the thousands of little details that have guided you through the shopping experience.

LAYOUT In retailing, the term **floor plan** indicates where merchandise and customer service departments are located, how customers circulate through the store, and how much space is dedicated to each department. The floor plan, which is based around the predicted demands of the store's targeted customer, serves as the backbone of the store and is the fundamental structure around which every other element of the store environment takes shape. Some retailers, such as Target and Wal-Mart, analyze their cash register sales along with the demographics of the store's trading area when developing a floor plan. These retailers then structure the merchandise to the needs of each store.

Floor plan A schematic that shows where merchandise and customer service departments are located, how customers circulate through the store, and how much space is dedicated to each department.

Successful retailers place merchandise in key strategic locations. Therefore, the store's layout and design, including merchandise location, must be carefully planned to meet the retailer's merchandising goals, make the store easy to understand and shop, and allow merchandise to be effectively presented.

Almost as important as the placement of merchandise is the reduction of **stack-outs,** those pallets of merchandise set on the floor in front of the main shelves. Although stack-outs may improve the short-run sales of the featured product, their negative impact may offset these marginal sales.

Stack-outs Pallets of merchandise set out on the floor in front of the main shelves.

ALLOCATING SPACE The starting point for developing a floor plan is analyzing how the available store space, usually measured in square footage, should be allocated to various departments. This allocation can be based on mathematical calculation of the returns generated by different types of merchandise. Shoppers are most familiar with the sales floor, but this is not the only element in a retail store with which the planner must contend. There are five basic types of space needs in a store: (1) back room; (2) office and other functional spaces; (3) aisles, service areas, and other non-selling areas of the main sales floor; (4) wall merchandise space; and (5) floor merchandise space. The retailer must balance the quest for greater density of merchandise presentation with the shopability and functionality of the store. Since space is the retailer's ultimate scarce resource, rarely can the retailer fully achieve all of its desired goals. Rather, most retailers find themselves compromising on one or more dimensions, carefully weighing priorities, strategies, and special constraints.

CIRCULATION The circulation pattern not only ensures efficient movement of large numbers of shoppers through the store, exposing them to more merchandise, but also determines the character of the store. **Disney Stores,** for example, are designed to communicate the fun and excitement of the theme parks and famous characters and to entice customers to walk to the back wall. After all, chances are good that when customers get to the back, they will return using a different route. This will expose them to more merchandise and increase the chance of a sale. Four basic types of layout are used today—the free flow, grid, loop, and spine. Shoppers have been trained to associate certain circulation patterns with different types of stores to create image.

SHRINKAGE PREVENTION When planning a store's layout and design, the prevention of shrinkage due to theft, damage, and loss must be considered. Some layouts will minimize vulnerability to shoplifters. One of the most important considerations when planning the layout is visibility of the merchandise. Most shoplifting takes place in fitting rooms, blind spots, aisles crowded with extra merchandise, or behind high displays. Fitting rooms, one of the most common scenes of the shoplifting crime, should be placed in visible areas that can be monitored by associates. Historically, display fixtures have been kept no higher than eye level to allow store associates to monitor customers in other aisles. Recently, mass merchandisers have found that increased sales from the greater merchandise intensity of higher fixtures outweighs the increase in shoplifting due to reduced visibility. This depends greatly on merchandise type, however. Expensive items that are easily placed into pockets and handbags, such as compact discs, are high-theft items, and are usually kept on low fixtures to discourage shoplifting. The manager's office and other security windows can be an excellent deterrent to shoplifting if they are placed in an obvious area above the sales floor level, where managers can easily see the entire store. Electronic security systems, including sensor tags and video cameras, have become very popular, and are usually in a highly visible location to serve as a deterrent.

Store Merchandising

Retailing is theater, and in no area is that more true than in merchandise presentation. Recently retailers have been increasing their emphasis on merchandise presentation, as competition has grown and stores try to squeeze more sales out of existing square footage. There are two basic types of merchandise presentation: visual merchandising and on-shelf merchandising. In thinking of retailing as theater, visual merchandising is analogous to the stage props that set scenes and serve as backdrops.

Merchandise presentation is a complex activity best learned on the retail floor. While this section will not attempt to teach the art and science of merchandise presentation, you should be familiar with a number of basic components of merchandise presentation and their potential impact on store image and sales, including fixture type and selection and certain techniques and methods of on-shelf merchandising.

On-shelf merchandising *The display of merchandise on counters, racks, shelves, and fixtures throughout the store.*

On-shelf merchandising, which describes the merchandise that is displayed on and in counters, racks, shelves, and fixtures throughout the store, represents the stars on our theater stage. This is the merchandise that the shopper actually touches, tries on, examines, reads, understands, and hopefully buys. Therefore, on-shelf merchandising must not only present the merchandise attractively; it must also display the merchandise so it is easy to understand and accessible. Further, it must be reasonably easy to maintain, with customers themselves able to replace merchandise so it is equally appealing to the next shopper. It must not be so overwhelming that the customer is afraid to touch the merchandise. As a result of getting more than 25,000 complaints a year regarding injuries from falling merchandise, Wal-Mart has sought to reduce the height level of merchandise displays in every store. After all, despite the efforts of top management, many managers still falsely believe the best way to improve sales (and their year-end bonus) is to cram as much merchandise as possible into the store.

MERCHANDISE PRESENTATION PLANNING Retailers can choose from a large array of fixtures and hardware. This may seem to present an endless variety of ways to merchandise product, but there are essentially six methods:

1. *Shelving.* The majority of merchandise is placed on shelves that are inserted into gondolas or wall systems. Shelving is a flexible, easy-to-maintain merchandise presentation method.
2. *Hanging.* Apparel on hangers can be hung from softline fixtures, such as round racks and four-way racks, or from bars installed on gondolas or wall systems.
3. *Pegging.* Small merchandise can be hung from peghooks, which are small rods inserted into gondolas or wall systems. Used in both softlines and hardlines, pegging gives a neat, orderly appearance, but can be labor intensive to display and maintain.

4. *Folding.* Higher-margin or large, unwieldy softlines merchandise can be folded and then stacked onto shelves or placed on tables. This can create a high-fashion image, such as when bath towels are taken off peghooks and neatly folded and stacked high up the wall.
5. *Stacking.* Large hardlines merchandise can be stacked on shelves, the base decks of gondolas, or "flats," which are platforms placed directly on the floor. Stacking is easily maintained and gives an image of high volume and low price.
6. *Dumping.* Large quantities of small merchandise can be dumped in bins or baskets inserted into gondolas or wall systems. This highly effective promotional method can be used in softlines (socks, wash cloths) or hardlines (batteries, grocery products, candy), and creates a high-volume, low-cost image.

The method of merchandise presentation can have a dramatic impact on image and space productivity. Different merchandise presentation methods have been shown to strongly influence buying habits and stimulate consumers to purchase more. There is a certain "psychology of merchandise presentation," which must be carefully considered in developing merchandise presentation schemes. Fewer than 20 percent of store shoppers make an impulse (unplanned) purchase, and these purchases are made by only 60 percent of the shoppers who actually enter the store with an intent to make a specific purchase. Thus, 40 percent of the shoppers who enter a store to make a purchase are "wasted" because the store failed to use merchandise presentation to generate additional purchases.[130] This is why department store design incorporates a gauntlet of goodies to stimulate impulse buys. For example, cosmetics, usually the store's most profitable department, is always near the main entrance. Typically, the department is leased to cosmetic companies who use their own salespeople to sell the perfume, lipstick, and eye shadow. The other high-impulse items (e.g., hosiery, jewelry, handbags, and shoes) are usually nearby, while the "demand" products (e.g., furniture) are on upper floors. After all, these stores would be unprofitable if they failed to induce a significant amount of impulse buying.

SELECTING FIXTURES AND MERCHANDISE PRESENTATION METHODS Proper fixtures emphasize the key selling attributes of merchandise while not being overpowering. A good guideline for selecting fixtures—although it is not always possible to follow—is to *match the fixture to the merchandise, not the merchandise to the fixture.* This means you should only use fixtures that are sensitive to the nature of the merchandise, but all too often, retailers are forced to put merchandise on the wrong fixture.[131]

Consider intimate apparel, for instance. This is a fast-selling, high-margin merchandise category that can enhance a retailer's image in fashion merchandising. Though retailers entering this business might be tempted to place intimate apparel on existing shelves of a gondola, they would be well served to consider special fixtures to enhance the delicate qualities of intimate apparel. A large, metal, bulky gondola will overpower a small, delicate intimate apparel item, and therefore reduce sales potential. More delicate fixtures made of softer materials will enhance sales. Likewise, it would not be effective to bulk-stack fragile merchandise, because the weight of items might damage those lower in the stack. It would not make sense to peghook large, bulky items, because they take up too much room and might be too heavy for the peghook.

VISUAL MERCHANDISING The second type of merchandise presentation, **visual merchandising,** is the artistic display of merchandise and theatrical props used as scene-setting decoration in the store. While on-shelf merchandising must be tastefully displayed to encourage shopping, a store with just on-shelf merchandising would be boring. Many low-price stores contain little visual merchandising and they do appear more boring than their upscale cousins in fashion retailing, who concentrate heavily on visual merchandising displays, or "visuals," as they are often called.

Visual merchandising The artistic display of merchandise and theatrical props used as scene-setting decoration in the store.

An effective visual merchandising display has several key characteristics. Visual displays are not typically associated with a shopable fixture, but are located in a focal point, feature area, or other area remote from the on-shelf merchandising and perhaps even out of reach of the customer. Their goal is to create a feeling in the store conducive to buying merchandise.

Another characteristic of visual merchandising is its use of props and elements in addition to merchandise. In fact, visuals do not always include merchandise—they may just be interesting displays of items somehow related to the merchandise or to a mood the retailer wishes to create. A prop might be a wooden barrel, a miniature airplane, or a mock tree with autumn leaves. Visuals are like the illustrations and design elements in a book that make it interesting; they tell the customer whether this is an upscale, serious shopping experience; a frivolous, fun shopping experience; or a down and dirty, low-price shopping experience.

To be most effective, however, visuals should incorporate relevant merchandise. In apparel retailing, mannequins or figure forms are used to display merchandise as it might appear on a person, rather than hanging limply on a hanger. This helps the shopper visualize how these garments will enhance her or his appearance. Good fashion visuals include more than just one garment, to show how tops and bottoms go together and how belts, scarves, and other accessories can be combined to create an overall fashion look. This is called accessorization. When successful, visuals help the shopper translate the merchandise presentation from "garments on a rack" to "fashionable clothes that will look good on me."

The retailer should be careful in setting visuals to make sure that the displays do not create walls that make it difficult for shoppers to reach other areas of the store. In addition, the retailer should carefully consider the placement of signs. A very popular fast-food restaurant recently changed its sign placement. It originally had the signs for their specials on the way to the restrooms. Now they are visible as the customers exit the restrooms and are more relaxed.[132]

Store Design

Ambiance The overall feeling or mood projected by a store through its aesthetic appeal to human senses.

AMBIANCE Store design is the element most responsible for the first of our two goals in planning the store environment: creating a distinctive and memorable store image. Store design encompasses both the exterior and the interior of the store. On the exterior, we have the storefront, signage, and entrance, all of which are critical to attracting passing shoppers and enticing them to enter. On the inside, store design includes the architectural elements and finishes on all surfaces, such as wall coverings, floor coverings, and ceilings. There are literally hundreds of details in a store's design, and all must work together to create the desired store **ambiance,** which is the overall feeling or mood projected by a store through its aesthetic appeal to the human senses. For instance, **Warren Buffett's Nebraska Furniture Mart** uses noncomposite panels, which not only lower heating and cooling costs, but also create an upscale look.[133]

Profitable retailers employ exterior designs that pull shoppers into the store and interior designs that stimulate sales.

STOREFRONT (EXTERIOR) DESIGN If the retail store can be compared to a book, then the storefront, or store exterior, is like the book cover. It must be noticeable, easily identified by passing motorists or mall shoppers, and memorable. The storefront must clearly identify the name and general nature of the store and give some hint as to the merchandise inside. Generally, the storefront design includes all exterior signage and the architecture of the storefront itself.

In many cases, the storefront includes display windows, which serve as an advertising medium for the store. Store windows must arrest the attention of passing shoppers, enticing them inside the store. Therefore, windows should be maintained with exciting visual displays that are changed frequently, are fun and exciting, and reflect the merchandise offering inside.

INTERIOR DESIGN Unless you have ever been responsible for redecorating a house or room, you may be unaware of the dozens of design elements that go into a physical space. We can break interior design into two types of elements: the finishes applied to surfaces and the architectural shapes. Think of all the elements from the floor to the ceiling. First, we have some type of floor covering placed over a concrete or wood floor—at the least paint, but more frequently vinyl, carpet, ceramic tile, or marble. Each of these different surfaces leaves a different impression on the shopper. An unpainted concrete floor conveys a low-cost, no-frills environment. Vinyl floor covering makes another statement, which, depending on its quality, sheen, color, and design pattern, can vary from very downscale to very upscale. Carpet suggests a homelike atmosphere conducive to selling apparel. Ceramic tile and especially marble suggest an upscale, exclusive, and probably expensive shopping experience.

Retailers have even more options for covering the walls, from paint and wallpaper to hundreds of types of paneling. The ceiling must also receive a design treatment, whether it is finished drywall (a very upscale image because it is an expensive process), a suspended ceiling (very common and economical, though not distinctive), or perhaps even an open ceiling with all the pipes and wires above painted black (which suggests a low-price warehouse approach). Then, there are thousands of types of moldings that can be applied to the transitions from floor to wall to ceiling, and hundreds of architectural design elements that can be incorporated.

LIGHTING DESIGN Another important, though often overlooked, element in a successful store design is lighting. Retailers have come to understand how lighting can greatly enhance store sales. One of the keys to success for **Blockbuster Video** was its move away from the 100-watt bulbs used by its competitors to brighter lights. Brighter lighting in a wine store also influences shoppers to examine and handle more merchandise. Department stores, on the other hand, have found that raising lighting levels in fashion departments can actually discourage sales, because bright lighting suggests a discount store image.

Lighting design, however, is not limited to simple light levels. Contemporary lighting design requires an in-depth knowledge of electrical engineering and the effect of light on color and texture. Retailers have learned that different types and levels of lighting can have a significant impact on sales.[134] In addition, the types of light sources available have multiplied quickly. Today, there are literally hundreds of light fixtures and lamps (bulbs) from which to choose.

Many retailers are actually using too much outdoor lighting today, probably because of the increasing risk of accidents and/or lawsuits. Lighting is measured in foot-candles. One foot-candle is a unit of illuminant equal to one lumen per square foot.

SOUNDS AND SMELLS: TOTAL SENSORY MARKETING Effective store design appeals to the human senses of sight, hearing, smell, and touch. Obviously, the majority of design activity in a retail store is focused on affecting sight. For example, have you ever gone into a Wal-Mart store and had the greeter say "Hello" to you? Sam Walton's wife, Helen, suggested the idea of the greeter as a way to put customers in a better mood and to convey a feeling of warmth toward the retailer. However, Sam Walton soon came to realize another benefit of the greeter—they slowed customers down as they entered the store. The first 20 feet inside a store is a decompression chamber for customers as they adjust to the different lighting and climate of the store. The greeter allowed Wal-Mart not only to convey a positive message but also, as the customer slowed down to return the greeting, to attract attention to merchandise at the front of the store. Research has shown that the other senses can also be very important, and many retailers are beginning to engineer the smells and sounds in their stores.

Despite some recent academic research to the contrary,[135] smell is believed to be the most closely linked of all the senses for memory and emotions. Retailers hope that its use as a key in-store marketing tool will put consumers "in the mood."

Visual Communications

Sales associates cannot always be available to assist customers, particularly in this era of increased competitive pressure and reduced gross margins, which have caused many retailers to cut costs by reducing their sales staffs. Even department stores, which staked their reputations on high levels of personal customer service, have had to reduce their service levels and learn to rely on alternative service strategies. How, then, can retailers provide good selling communications and high customer service while controlling labor costs?

The answer is visual communications, in the form of in-store signage and graphics. Retailers can plan the store environment to incorporate signs, large photopanels, and other visual devices that serve as silent salespersons, providing shoppers with much-needed information and directions on how to shop the store, evaluate merchandise, and make purchases. Because these visual communications are inanimate objects that stay permanently in place, they require only a one-time installation cost, low maintenance, and can always be relied on to perform their function, the same way, for every shopper. Unlike sales associates, visual communications are never late for work, are never in a bad mood, and never mistreat customers. Of course, neither are they as effective as a good sales associate, who provides the personal touch that makes customers feel welcome and comfortable. But when carefully balanced with personal service, visual communications, with their reliability and low cost, can create an effective selling environment and are therefore becoming an important tool in the store designer's toolbox.

Earlier we likened a retail store to a well-written book. Visual communications are akin to the headlines, subheads, illustrations, and captions that give the reader direction and illustrate the written descriptions. Without visual communications, a store would resemble a newspaper full of words but no headlines, a jumbled, incomprehensible mess of merchandise. An effective visual communications program includes a range of messages, from large and bold directives used sparingly to provide cues to the gross organization of the space, to the smaller, more specific, and plentiful messages that describe actual merchandise. A visual communications program includes the following important elements.

RETAIL IDENTITY The first and most visible element in a comprehensive visual communications program is the retailer's identity, composed of the store name, logo, and supporting visual elements. The name and logo are seen not only on the storefront and throughout the interior, but also in advertising and all communications with the consumers, and therefore they must be catchy, memorable, and most of all, reflective of the retailer's merchandising mission. Historically, many retail companies have taken the name of their founder, as is the case with most department stores. That practice has fallen out of vogue, however, as retailing has become a game of crafty store images and catchy retail identities. A founder's name rarely captures the merchandising spirit of a company as well as names such as Bath & Body Works, Home Depot, and Toys "R" Us. Given the ever-increasing barrage of advertising messages and the waning effectiveness of each message, retailers have found it necessary to choose names that are highly distinctive as well as descriptive of their unique offerings. Today's hottest logos, reflecting "American values," include Eddie Bauer, J. Crew, L.L. Bean, Lands' End, and Old Navy.[136]

Once a name has been chosen, a logo is developed to visually portray the name in a creative and memorable manner. Again, the key is to keep the logo simple and easy to understand, while making it exciting enough to leave a lasting image in the customers' minds. The logo is often accompanied by taglines that provide more description of the store concept, such as Wal-Mart's "Always Low Prices—Always."

The logo's most prominent placement is on the outside of the store. This is critical to attracting customers and creating high store traffic. Another reason the store name and logo should be succinct and descriptive is that they often play to motorists passing by at 45 miles per hour.

INSTITUTIONAL SIGNAGE Inside the store, the first level of visual communications is known as institutional signage, or signage that describes the merchandising mission, customer service policies, and other messages on behalf of the retail institution. This signage is usually located at the store entrance, to properly greet entering customers, and at service points such as the service desk, layaway window, and cash registers. In addition, some retailers place customer service signage throughout the store, to reinforce special policies several times during the shopping trip. This signage might include messages such as "Lowest Price Guaranteed" or "All Major Credit Cards Accepted."

Directional and departmental signage Large signs that are usually placed fairly high, so they can be seen throughout the store.

Category signage Smaller than directional and departmental signage intended to be seen from a shorter distance; they are located on or close to the fixture itself where the merchandise is displayed.

Point-of-sale signage (POS) Relatively small signage that is placed very close to the merchandise and is intended to give details about specific items.

DIRECTIONAL, DEPARTMENTAL, AND CATEGORY SIGNAGE **Directional and departmental signage** serves as the highest level of organization in an overall signage program. These signs are usually large and placed fairly high, so they can be seen throughout the store. They help guide the shopper through the store and locate specific departments of interest. Not all stores use directional signage. It is not necessary in smaller stores, but in virtually all stores larger than 10,000 square feet, some type of departmental signage is used. Once a shopper locates and moves close to a particular department, category signage is used to call out and locate specific merchandise categories. **Category signage** is usually smaller, since it is intended to be seen from a shorter distance and is located on or close to the fixture itself. For instance, the departmental sign might say "Sporting Goods," be two feet high and six feet wide, and hang from the ceiling. On the other hand, the category signage might be only six inches high and two feet wide, affixed to the top of the gondola, and read "Hunting," "Tennis," or "Fitness."

POINT-OF-SALE (POS) SIGNAGE The next level of signage—even smaller, and placed closer to the merchandise—is known as **point-of-sale**, or **POS**, signage. Because POS signage is intended to give details about specific merchandise items, it usually contains more type and is affixed directly to fixtures. Always, however, the most important function of POS signage is to clearly state the price of the merchandise being signed.

POS signage includes a set of sign holders used throughout the store, along with a variety of printed signs that can be inserted into the hardware. Store associates mix and match the signage and hardware as directed by management, so that POS signage changes frequently. Special POS signs for sales, clearance, and "as advertised" are often a different color than the normal price signage to highlight these special values.

LIFESTYLE GRAPHICS Visual communications encompass more than just words. Many stores incorporate large graphics panels showing so-called lifestyle images in important departments. These photo images portray either the merchandise, often as it is being used, or simply images of related items or models that convey an image conducive to buying the product. In a high-fashion department, lifestyle photography might show a scene of movie stars arriving at a nightclub in very trendy fashions, suggesting that similar fashions are available in that department. In sporting goods, a lifestyle image might show an isolated lake surrounded by autumn-colored trees, with mist rising off the water and the sun rising in the background.

Retailers can use visual communications, such as institutional signage, directional and departmental signage, category and POS signage, and lifestyle graphics to communicate more effectively with shoppers and increase space productivity.

Retailers must be careful when choosing lifestyle photography, for as the saying goes, "beauty is in the eye of the beholder." One person's lifestyle is not necessarily another's, so lifestyle photography must be kept very general so as to be attractive to the majority and offensive to none. Increasingly, photopanels and lifestyle imagery, which can be expensive to create, are being provided free of charge to retailers by merchandise vendors, who are looking to gain an advantage for their products on the retail floor.

Ethics and Operations

Purchasing Ethics

Ethics have their basis in the field of philosophy, and identify common principles associated with appropriate versus inappropriate actions, moral duty, and obligation. Ethics are the set of moral principles or values guiding our behavior. In a business setting, ethical behavior is the use of recognized social principles involving justice and fairness throughout a business relationship. When interacting with suppliers, an ethical buyer treats them in a just, decent, fair, honest, and fitting manner. Being ethical means following a code viewed as fair by those within the profession as well as the community.[137]

Three rules are understood to be a part of ethical behavior. First, a buyer must commit his or her attention and energies for the organization's benefit rather than personal enrichment at the expense of the organization. Ethical buyers do not accept outside gifts or favors that violate their firm's ethics policy. Ethical buyers are also not tempted or influenced by the unethical practices of salespeople and do not have personal financial arrangements with suppliers. Second, a buyer must act ethically toward suppliers or potential suppliers. This means treating each supplier professionally and with respect. Finally, a buyer must uphold the ethical standards set forth by his or her profession. A code or statement of professional ethics usually formalizes the set of ethical standards.

Purchasing managers, more than any other group within a firm, experience enormous pressure to act in unethical ways. This occurs for several reasons. First, purchasing has direct control over large sums of money. A buyer responsible for a multimillion-dollar contract may find sellers using any means available to secure a favorable position. The very nature of purchasing means that a buyer must come in contact with outside, and occasionally, unethical sellers. A second reason is due to the pressure placed on many salespeople. A seller who must meet aggressive sales goals might resort to questionable sales practices.

Risks of Unethical Behavior

A buyer who performs an unethical act runs the risk that the act is also illegal. For example, a government buyer who accepts payment from a defense contractor clearly committed an unethical and illegal act. If this payment becomes known, the buyer risks legal penalty as defined by the law. The buyer's firm also risks a legal penalty. At a minimum, the buyer will probably lose his or her job.

Unethical behavior also presents a personal risk to a buyer's professional reputation. Sellers quickly become aware of buyers who are open to offers "on the side." Once a buyer earns a reputation within an industry, it is difficult to change it. A buyer also runs a risk that management will discover his or her lack of ethics and terminate employment. A professional reputation is something a buyer carries throughout an entire career. If a buyer is found guilty of accepting a bribe, companies will not only terminate the buyer, but may often pursue litigation as well. Personal financial bankruptcy or even jail sentences can result for buyers who are found guilty of accepting large bribes.

A final risk of unethical behavior is the risk to a firm's reputation. A buyer who makes purchase decisions based on factors other than legitimate business criteria risks the reputation of the entire firm. For example, quality may suffer if a buyer accepts substandard performance from a supplier who offered outside inducements. A buyer's unethical behavior can jeopardize the livelihood of others dependent on a firm's success. World-class suppliers do not have to practice unethical behavior to win contracts.

To summarize the legal perspective, accepting a supplier's outside gifts and favors in exchange for special treatment is a form of corruption. The U.S. business environment does not treat unethical behavior lightly. Buyers who practice unethical behavior subject themselves and their firms to increased risk and diminish the integrity of the purchasing profession. Firms dealing with global sourcing sometimes encounter unethical behavior, particularly in developing countries where bribery may be viewed as a routine source of extra income. However, global firms are increasingly adopting an unequivocal "zero tolerance" stance toward any form of bribery, even if it means sacrificing short-term profitability to maintain a global reputation of integrity and honesty in its dealings with suppliers.

Exhibit 200.72   *A Framework of Ethical Purchasing Behavior*

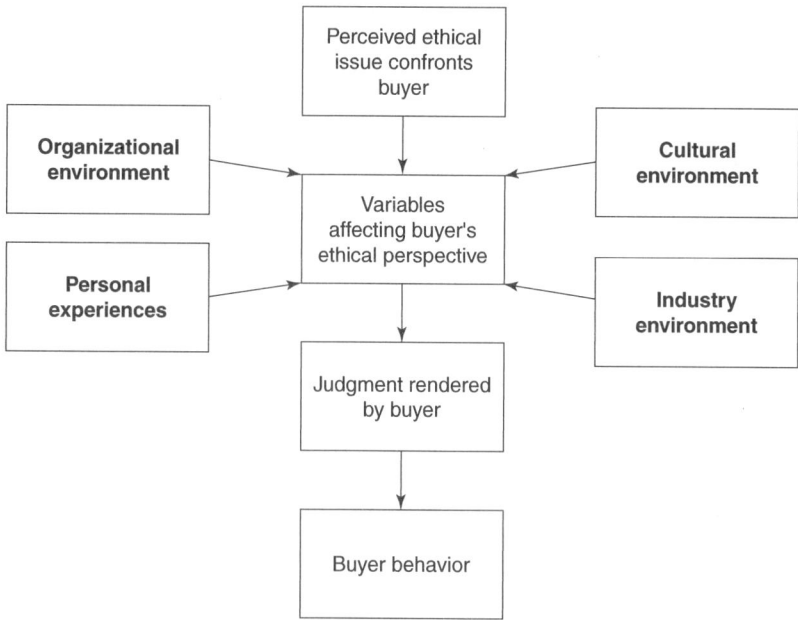

A Framework of Ethical Behavior

The manner in which a buyer responds to an ethical situation is a function of four variables: (1) organizational environment, (2) personal experiences, (3) cultural environment, and (4) industry environment. Exhibit 200.72 presents these variables within a framework of ethical purchasing behavior. Each variable presented affects a buyer's perspective when confronted with an ethical decision or issue, and includes the following:

- *Organizational environment:* Every organization has a history of accepted ethical behavior or norms. This history may be formally or informally accepted throughout the organization. Also, different managers within the same firm may have different ethical values, which can further influence a buyer's ethical perspective.
- *Personal experiences:* Each buyer's personal experiences affect his or her ethical perspective. These experiences affect a buyer's personal moral and ethical beliefs about what is right and wrong.
- *Cultural environment:* Society affects a buyer's ethical perspective by further defining the boundaries of right and wrong. Certain behaviors may be acceptable in one culture and totally unacceptable in another. Cultural environment exerts a strong influence on behavior through the passage of laws and regulations.
- *Industry environment:* Accepted or common practices within an industry can affect a buyer's perspective and behavior. These can also define acceptable boundaries of behavior.

Let us assume a buyer at Firm XYZ has the highest moral and ethical values—the buyer has strong beliefs about what is proper behavior within the purchasing profession. Conflict can occur if a manager asks the buyer to do something the buyer feels is unethical. Here, the organizational environment and personal experiences exert conflicting influences. For example, a manager may ask a buyer to award a contract because of a personal friendship with a supplier. The buyer may feel this is unethical. Does the buyer simply award the contract in compliance with the manager's instruction, and ignore his or her own personal and moral values? Or does the buyer refuse to award the contract, thereby challenging the authority of a manager and jeopardizing his or her career? While a professional buyer should know the difference between right and wrong, organizational pressures can force a buyer to behave in ways that conflict with personal values, which creates a difficult situation for most buyers.

Types of Unethical Purchasing Behavior

The definition of ethical behavior can differ from buyer to buyer or from firm to firm. Despite these possible differences, most professionals recognize certain behavior or actions as unethical.

RECIPROCITY This action involves giving preferential treatment to suppliers who are also customers of the buying organization.[138] In simple terms, it refers to a purchasing arrangement that dictates "I'll buy from you if you buy from me." The Federal Trade Commission (FTC) has taken an aggressive stance against reciprocal buying arrangements, ruling that it is illegal "to abusively use large buying power to restrict competitive market opportunities." In the early 1970s, many larger firms entered into agreements with the FTC forbidding reciprocal purchasing. These firms also eliminated their internal trade departments established to coordinate these arrangements.[139] FTC rulings have convinced most firms to prohibit reciprocal purchasing. Most firms do recognize a customer's right for consideration as a potential supplier. A buyer, however, must rely only on legitimate performance criteria to evaluate supplier capability.

PERSONAL BUYING This occurs when a purchasing department purchases material for the personal needs of its employees. Some states have outlawed such practices with statutes called *trade diversion laws*. These laws prohibit purchasing from engaging in personal buying for items not required during the normal course of business. Some exceptions to these laws do exist. For example, a firm can purchase safety shoes, hats, gloves, or even special tools required by the employee. A purchasing department can use its knowledge to purchase products conforming to specific quality standards. Personal buying is a gray area for some purchasing departments. Some firms view personal buying as a fringe benefit and service to the employee. Other firms flatly prohibit the practice. A buyer confronted with a request for personal buying should determine the legal status of the practice, and then discuss the subject with management. Personal buying can quickly get out of hand.

ACCEPTING SUPPLIER FAVORS Accepting gifts and favors from a supplier is the most common ethical infraction involving buyers. These gifts and favors can affect a buyer's judgment to evaluate and select the most capable suppliers. The policy on supplier offerings is often a confusing issue. At what point does a supplier's gift or favor depart from a friendly showing of appreciation for a firm's business to an attempt to influence a buyer's purchase decisions? Accepting free items from potential suppliers is especially questionable. Here, a supplier does not even have a purchase contract. Firms can address this issue in their ethics policy by specifying exactly what a buyer may accept from a supplier.

SHARP PRACTICES A *sharp practice* is any misrepresentation by a buyer that falls just short of actual fraud.[140] Sharp practice occurs whenever a buyer "plays games" with a supplier and operates in an underhanded manner. The practice includes many different behaviors:

- *Willful use of misinformation, when a buyer knowingly deceives a supplier to realize some advantage.* For example, requesting quotes on inflated volumes and then placing smaller orders at the reduced price is a willful use of misinformation.
- *Exaggerating problems.* A buyer who exaggerates the size of a supplier-caused problem to extract a larger penalty or concession from a supplier is using a sharp practice.
- *Requesting bids from unqualified suppliers for the sole purpose of driving a qualified supplier's price lower.* A buyer should request bids from qualified suppliers only.
- *Gaining information unfairly through deception.*
- *Sharing information on competitive quotations.* The integrity of the competitive bid process requires confidentiality. Buyers who share supplier-quoted information violate the ethics of the bid process.
- *Not compensating a supplier for design or other work.* Buyers often request design and cost-saving assistance from suppliers. A supplier who helps a buyer should receive fair compensation for their efforts.
- *Taking unfair advantage of a supplier's financial situation.* A buyer who knowingly pressures a financially troubled supplier into providing a lower than normal price places the supplier in further financial jeopardy. Taking advantage of a financially susceptible supplier is an unethical business practice.
- *Lying or misleading.* Any instance of lying or misleading a seller is a sharp practice.

FINANCIAL CONFLICTS OF INTEREST When a buyer awards business to a supplier because the buyer, the buyer's family, or relatives of the buyer have a direct financial interest in a supplier, this is considered a major unethical practice. This behavior is one reason many companies require employees to detail any investments in outside companies. Awarding a purchase contract to a company in which a buyer has a significant personal financial interest (versus owning a mutual fund that owns a small amount of stock in the company) is a serious breach of ethics. This action is similar to an executive buying or selling stock because of inside knowledge, which is an illegal act.

ISM Professional Code of Ethics

The Institute for Supply Management (ISM) (formerly the National Association of Purchasing Managers (NAPM)) is the largest organization representing the purchasing profession. In 1959, the ISM officially adopted its initial Standards of Conduct. The document serves as a guide for the ISM membership by imposing rules of conduct, particularly when a buyer's own company lacks a policy or statement of ethics. In the words of the code, "It is necessary for all of us to exercise a strict rule of personal conduct to insure that relations of a compromising nature, or even the appearance of such relations, be scrupulously avoided." The document reflects the ISM's commitment to ethical behavior and fair business dealings.

The Standards of Conduct specifies three guiding principles of purchasing practice: (1) loyalty to company, (2) justice to those with whom a buyer deals, and (3) faith in the purchasing profession. From these principles ISM derived its standards of purchasing practice or Code of Ethics:

1. Consider, first, the interest of your company in all transactions and carry out and believe in its established policies.
2. Be receptive to competent counsel from your colleagues and be guided by such counsel without impairing the dignity and responsibility of your office.
3. Buy without prejudice, seeking to obtain the maximum value for each dollar of expenditure.
4. Strive consistently for knowledge of the materials and processes of manufacture and establish practical methods for the conduct of your office.
5. Subscribe to and work for honesty and truth in buying and selling, and denounce all forms and manifestations of commercial bribery.
6. Accord a prompt and courteous reception, so far as conditions will permit, to all who call on a legitimate business mission.
7. Respect your obligations and require that obligations to you and to your concern be respected, consistent with good business practice.
8. Avoid sharp practice.
9. Counsel and assist fellow purchasing managers in the performance of their duties, whenever the occasion permits.
10. Cooperate with all organizations and individuals engaged in activities designed to enhance the development and standing of purchasing.

These standards often help guide a firm's ethical code of conduct and policy. While suggestions for modifying certain sections of the Code of Ethics have been put forth, the basic 1959 code is still intact. The ISM standards specifically state that its members should maintain standards on an even higher plane than those accepted by society—what becomes the "true test of greatness." This is stated as follows in the code:

> Nothing can undermine respect for the purchasing profession more than improper action on the part of its members with regard to gifts, gratuities, or favors. People engaged in purchasing should not accept from any supplier or prospective supplier any money, gift, or favor that might influence, or be suspected of influencing their buying decisions. We must decline to accept or must return any such gift or favor offered us or members of our immediate family. The declination of these gifts or favors must be done discreetly and courteously. Possible embarrassment resulting from refusals does not constitute a basis for exception.

The ISM Standards of Conduct is a powerful document. It holds the purchasing profession to the highest levels of ethical conduct. Companies of all sizes from many industries have used the Code of Ethics as a guide when developing their own ethical policies.

Supporting Ethical Behavior

A firm can take many actions to make sure its employees conduct business in an ethical manner. The following sections summarize the actions a firm can take to enhance the ethical behavior of its purchasing personnel.

DEVELOPING A STATEMENT OF ETHICS   Most research on purchasing ethics concludes that adopting a formal ethics policy helps define and deter potentially unethical purchasing behavior. An earlier study found that firms without formal ethical policies disclosed supplier bid prices to other suppliers at a much higher rate than firms with a formal policy prohibiting this practice.[141] Also, firms without a formal ethics policy were more likely to make discounted purchases for their employees, a questionable practice in some states. A formal ethics policy helps define the boundaries of ethical behavior.

TOP-MANAGEMENT COMMITMENT   Executive management sets the ethical code of behavior within a firm. While the highest executive may not actually write a firm's purchasing or marketing code of ethics, the ethical behavior of top executives sends a message about whether or not unethical behavior is tolerated. Lower-level managers quickly recognize top management's commitment to ethical behavior and imitate the commitment.

CLOSER BUYER-SELLER RELATIONSHIPS   Dealing with a smaller supply base or a single supplier for an item will probably do more for ethical purchasing behavior than any other recent trend or action. Firms are increasingly using buying teams to evaluate potential suppliers across different performance categories. Using a team approach to evaluate a supplier's capabilities limits the opportunity for unethical behavior. Unethical suppliers will find it tougher to influence a team of professionals. Buyers, or any other personnel within a buying firm, will also find it harder to practice unethical behavior when a team oversees the supplier selection process.

ETHICAL TRAINING   New buyers, usually at larger firms, often enter a training program before actually assuming their professional duties. One part of the training usually deals with purchasing ethics. Such a program is an opportunity to train a new buyer about a firm's ethics policy. Firms often use role playing to help buyers learn how to identify different types of unethical behavior and how to confront and deal with these situations. Ethics training reinforces a firm's commitment to the highest ethical standards.

DEVELOPING CONSISTENT BEHAVIOR   Confusion about proper ethical behavior can arise when marketing and purchasing have separate ethical standards. A firm that prohibits its purchasing personnel from accepting gifts from suppliers but allows its marketing department to distribute gifts to its customers is not acting consistently. When different standards of behavior exist within the same firm, it becomes easier for one group to rationalize or justify unethical behavior. How can it be ethical for one group (marketing) to provide gifts and favors but unethical for another group (purchasing) within the same firm to accept any items?

INTERNAL REPORTING OF UNETHICAL BEHAVIOR   Executive purchasing management should create an atmosphere that supports the reporting of unethical behavior. A buyer should be able to approach management about an ethical impropriety with confidence that management will correct the problem. A firm should also encourage suppliers to report instances of unethical behavior by anyone within the buying firm. This practice notifies suppliers that a buying firm is committed to ethical business practices. It also tells a firm's buyers that top management will not tolerate certain types of behavior. Another strategy involves preventive management to reduce the possibility of unethical purchasing behavior.

PREVENTIVE MEASURES   One common strategy is to rotate buyers among different items or commodities, which prevents a buyer from becoming too comfortable with any particular group of suppliers. While a buyer should become familiar with purchased items and suppliers, it is often a good idea to rotate personnel between buying assignments. Rotation usually occurs every several years.

Another preventive measure is to limit a buyer's purchase authority without higher-level approval. For example, a firm's policy may limit a buyer's authority for awarding purchase contracts to amounts of $10,000 or less. Contracts greater than $10,000 then require a manager's signature. A buyer must justify the selection decision based on sound purchasing criteria before obtaining the final sign-off. This provides a system of checks and balances and reduces the possibility of unethical supplier selection.

Although a fine line exists between ethical and legal behavior, we believe that ethics should always come first. However, it is also important that a qualified purchasing manager develop a fine intuition for purchasing law, as this can have a significant impact on daily and long-term actions in the profession.

Module 200 Endnotes

1. This framework for the evolution of purchasing strategy was developed by the research team of the Global Procurement and Supply Chain Benchmarking Initiative through its comprehensive benchmarking studies from 1992 to 1999. Additional support for the four-phase model can be found in the following earlier research: C. A. Watts, K. Y. Kim, and C. K. Hahn, "Linking Purchasing to Corporate Competitive Strategy," *International Journal of Purchasing and Materials Management* (Fall 1992), 2–8; J. P. Morgan, "Are You Aggressive Enough for the 1990s?" *Purchasing*, April 6, 1989, 50–57; R. Reck and B. Long, "Purchasing: A Competitive Weapon," *Journal of Purchasing and Materials Management* (Fall 1988), 2–8; V. Freeman and J. Cavinato, "Fitting Purchasing to the Strategic Organization: Frameworks, Processes, and Values," *Journal of Purchasing and Materials Management* (Winter 1990), 6–10; Robert Monczka and Robert Trent, "Evolving Sourcing Strategies for the 1990s," *International Journal of Physical Distribution and Logistics Management* 21 (1991), 4–12.
2. James D. Thompson, *Organizations in Action* (New York: McGraw-Hill, 1967).
3. Norihiko Shirouzu, "Gadget Inspector: Why Toyota Wins Such High Marks on Quality Surveys," *The Wall Street Journal*, March 15, 2001, A1, A11.
4. Gregory B. Northcraft and Richard B. Chase, "Managing Service Demand at the Point of Delivery," *Academy of Management Review* 10 (1985), 66–75; and Richard B. Chase and David A. Tanski, "The Customer Contact Model for Organization Design," Management Science 29 (1983), 1037–1050.
5. Everett E. Adam Jr. and Paul M. Swamidass, "Assessing Operations Management from a Strategic Perspective," *Journal of Management* 15 (1989), 181–203.
6. Robert H. Hayes and David M. Upton, "Operations-Based Strategy," *California Management Review* 40, no. 4 (Summer 1998), 8–25.
7. R. H. Hayes and S. C. Wheelwright, *Restoring Our Competitive Edge: Competing through Manufacturing* (New York: Wiley, 1984).
8. Definition based on Steven A. Melnyk and David R. Denzler, *Operations Management: A Value-Driven Approach* (Burr Ridge, IL.: Richard D. Irwin, 1996), 613.
9. Based on Jim Turcotte, Bob Silveri, and Tom Jobson, "Are You Ready for the E-Supply Chain?" *APICS–The Performance Advantage* (August 1998), 56–59.
10. F. Ian Stuart and David M. McCutcheon, "The Manager's Guide to Supply Chain Management," *Business Horizons* (March–April 2000), 35–44.
11. Christopher Koch, "Four Strategies," Special Section on Supply Chain Management, *CIO*, October 1, 2000, 116–128.
12. Russ Banham, "Caught in the Middle," *CFO* (May 2001), 69–74.
13. Christopher Koch, "The Big Payoff," Special Section on Supply Chain Management, *CIO*, October 1, 2000, 101–112; Norman Gaither and Greg Frazier, *Operations Management*, 9th ed. (Cincinnati, Ohio: South-Western Publishing, 2002), 428–429.
14. Gaither and Frazier, *Operations Management*, 429.
15. David Rocks, "The Net as a Lifeline," *BusinessWeek e.biz*, October 29, 2001, EB16–EB28.
16. Scott Leibs, "First Pencils, Now People," *CFO* (November 2001), 91–94.
17. Sumer C. Aggarwal, "MRP, JIT, OPT, FMS?" *Harvard Business Review* 63 (September–October 1985), 8–16; and Paul Ranky, *The Design and Operation of Flexible Manufacturing Systems* (New York: Elsevier, 1983).
18. Anita Lienert, "Plowing Ahead in Uncertain Times," *Management Review* (December 1998), 16–21.
19. Alan David MacCormack, Lawrence James Newman, III, and Donald B. Rosenfield, "The New Dynamics of Global Manufacturing Site Location," *Sloan Management Review* (Summer 1994), 69–80; and Chen May Yee, "Let's Make a Deal," *The Wall Street Journal*, September 25, 2000, R10.
20. Rebecca Blumenstein, "GM Is Building Plants in Developing Nations to Woo New Markets," *The Wall Street Journal*, August 4, 1997, A1, A5.
21. Claudia Eller and James Bates, "Not All Projections Bad for Overgrown Theater Chains," *Los Angeles Times*, September 8, 2000.
22. Evan Ramstad, "Compaq Stumbles Amid New Pressures on PCs," *Wall Street Journal*, March 9, 1998, B1, B8.
23. R. J. Schonberger, *Japanese Manufacturing Techniques: Nine Hidden Lessons in Simplicity* (New York: Free Press, 1982).
24. Cathy Lazere, "Taking Stock of Inventory: Beyond Mean and Lean," *CFO* (November 1997), 95–97.
25. Gaither and Frazier, *Operations Management*, 587.
26. Vincent A. Mabert, Ashok Soni, and M. S. Venkataramanan, "Enterprise Resource Planning: Common Myths Versus Evolving Reality," *Business Horizons* (May–June 2001), 69–76.

27. Luciana Beard and Stephen A. Butler, "Introducing JIT Manufacturing: It's Easier than You Think," *Business Horizons* (September–October 2000), 61–64.
28. Ronald Henkoff, "Delivering the Goods," *Fortune,* November 28, 1994, 64–78.
29. Noel P. Greis and John D. Kasarda, "Enterprise Logistics in the Information Era," *California Management Review* 39(4) (Summer 1997), 55–78.
30. David Rocks, "Dell's Second Web Revolution," *BusinessWeek e.biz,* September 18, 2000, EB62–EB63.
31. "Kanban: The Just-in-Time Japanese Inventory System," *Small Business Report* (February 1984), 69–71; and Richard C. Walleigh, "What's Your Excuse for Not Using JIT?" *Harvard Business Review* 64 (March–April 1986), 38–54.
32. Gaither and Frazier, *Operations Management,* 150–151.
33. Francis J. Quinn, "Logistics' New Customer Focus," *BusinessWeek* (special advertising section) March 10, 1997.
34. Carol Vinzant, "SubmitOrder Thinks Inside the Box," *eCompany* (August 2000), 58–59; and Faith Keenan, "Logistics Gets a Little Respect," *BusinessWeek e.Biz,* November 20, 2000, EB112–EB116.
35. Faith Keenan, "Logistics Gets a Little Respect," and "One Smart Cookie," *BusinessWeek e.Biz,* (November 20, 2000), EB120.
36. Emily Esterson, "First-Class Delivery," *Inc. Technology,* September 15, 1998, 89.
37. W. Bouce Chew, "No-Nonsense Guide to Measuring Productivity," *Harvard Business Review* (January–February 1988), 110–118.
38. Anna Bernasek, "Pattern for Prosperity," *Fortune* (October 2, 2000), 100–108.
39. The Outsourcing Institute, "Outsourcing: The New Midas Touch," *BusinessWeek,* (special advertising section) December 15, 1997.
40. W. E. Deming, *Quality, Productivity, and Competitive Position* (Cambridge, MA: Center for Advanced Engineering Study, MIT, 1982); and P. B. Crosby, *Quality Is Free* (New York: McGraw-Hill, 1979).
41. Charles E. Lucier and Janet D. Torsilieri, "Why Knowledge Programs Fail: A C.E.O.'s Guide to Managing Learning," *Strategy and Business* (Fourth Quarter 1997), 14–16, 21–27.
42. Charles Perrow, "A Framework for the Comparative Analysis of Organizations," *American Sociological Review* 32 (1967): 194–208; R. J. Schonberger, *World Class Manufacturing: The Next Decade,* (New York: The Free Press, 1996).
43. Linda Argote, "Input Uncertainty and Organizational Coordination in Hospital Emergency Units," *Administrative Science Quarterly* 27 (1982), 420–34; Charles Perrow, *Organizational Analysis: A Sociological Approach* (Belmont, CA.: Wadsworth, 1970); William Rushing, "Hardness of Material as Related to the Division of Labor in Manufacturing Industries," *Administrative Science Quarterly* 13 (1968), 229–45.
44. Lawrence B. Mohr, "Organizational Technology and Organization Structure," *Administrative Science Quarterly* 16 (1971), 444–59; David Hickson, Derek Pugh, and Diana Pheysey, "Operations Technology and Organization Structure: An Empirical Reappraisal," *Administrative Science Quarterly* 14 (1969), 378–97.
45. Joan Woodward, *Industrial Organization: Theory and Practice* (London: Oxford University Press, 1965); Joan Woodward, *Management and Technology* (London: Her Majesty's Stationery Office, 1958).
46. Hickson, Pugh, and Pheysey, "Operations Technology and Organization Structure"; James D. Thompson, *Organizations in Action* (New York: McGraw-Hill, 1967).
47. Edward Harvey, "Technology and the Structure of Organizations," *American Sociological Review* 33 (1968), 241–59.
48. Wanda J. Orlikowski, "The Duality of Technology: Rethinking the Concept of Technology in Organizations," *Organization Science* 3 (1992), 398–427.
49. Based on Woodward, *Industrial Organization and Management and Technology.*
50. Woodward, *Industrial Organization,* vi.
51. William L. Zwerman, *New Perspectives on Organizational Theory* (Westport, CT: Greenwood, 1970); Harvey, "Technology and the Structure of Organizations," 241–59.
52. Dean M. Schroeder, Steven W. Congden, and C. Gopinath, "Linking Competitive Strategy and Manufacturing Process Technology," *Journal of Management Studies* 32, no. 2 (March 1995),163–89.
53. Fernando F. Suarez, Michael A. Cusumano, and Charles H. Fine, "An Empirical Study of Flexibility in Manufacturing," *Sloan Management Review* (Fall 1995), 25–32.
54. Raymond F. Zammuto and Edward J. O'Connor, "Gaining Advanced Manufacturing Technologies' Benefits: The Roles of Organization Design and Culture," *Academy of Management Review* 17, no. 4 (1992), 701–28; Dean Schroeder, Steven W. Congdon, and C. Gopinath, "Linking Competitive Strategy and Manufacturing Process Technology."
55. Jack R. Meredith, "The Strategic Advantages of the Factory of the Future," *California Management Review* 29 (Spring 1987), 27–41; Jack Meredith, "The Strategic Advantages of the New Manufacturing Technologies for Small Firms," *Strategic Management Journal* 8 (1987), 249–58; Althea Jones and Terry Webb, "Introducing Computer Integrated Manufacturing," *Journal of General Management* 12 (Summer 1987), 60–74.
56. Raymond F. Zammuto and Edward J. O'Connor, "Gaining Advanced Manufacturing Technologies' Benefits: The Roles of Organization Design and Culture," *Academy of Management Review* 17 (1992), 701–28.

57. Paul S. Adler, "Managing Flexible Automation," *California Management Review* (Spring 1988), 34–56.
58. Bela Gold, "Computerization in Domestic and International Manufacturing," *California Management Review* (Winter 1989), 129–43.
59. Graham Dudley and John Hassard, "Design Issues in the Development of Computer Integrated Manufacturing (CIM)," *Journal of General Management* 16 (1990), 43–53.
60. Joel D. Goldhar and David Lei, "Variety is Free: Manufacturing In the Twenty-First Century," *Academy of Management Executive* 9, no. 4 (1995), 73–86; and Justin Martin, "Give 'Em *Exactly* What They Want," *Fortune,* October 10, 1997, 283–285.
61. Meredith, "Strategic Advantages of the Factory of the Future."
62. Patricia L. Nemetz and Louis W. Fry, "Flexible Manufacturing Organizations: Implementations for Strategy Formulation and Organization Design," *Academy of Management Review* 13 (1988): 627–38; Paul S. Adler, "Managing Flexible Automation," *California Management Review* (Spring 1988), 34–56; Jeremy Main, "Manufacturing the Right Way," *Fortune,* May 21, 1990, 54–64; Frank M. Hull and Paul D. Collins, "High-Technology Batch Production Systems: Woodward's Missing Type," *Academy of Management Journal* 30 (1987), 786–97.
63. Goldhar and Lei, "Variety Is Free: Manufacturing In The Twenty-First Century"; P. Robert Duimering, Frank Safayeni, and Lyn Purdy, "Integrated Manufacturing: Redesign the Organization before Implementing Flexible Technology," *Sloan Management Review* (Summer 1993), 47–56; Zammuto and O'Connor, "Gaining Advanced Manufacturing Technologies' Benefits."
64. "Manufacturing's Decline," *Johnson City Press,* July 17, 1999, 9; Ronald Henkoff, "Service Is Everybody's Business," *Fortune,* June 27, 1994, 48–60; Ronald Henkoff, "Finding, Training, and Keeping the Best Service Workers," *Fortune,* October 3, 1994, 110–22.
65. Byron J. Finch and Richard L. Luebbe, *Operations Management: Competing in a Changing Environment* (Fort Worth, TX: The Dryden Press, 1995), 51.
66. David E. Bowen, Caren Siehl, and Benjamin Schneider, "A Framework for Analyzing Customer Service Orientations in Manufacturing," *Academy of Management Review* 14 (1989), 79–95; Peter K. Mills and Newton Margulies, "Toward a Core Typology of Service Organizations," *Academy of Management Review* 5 (1980), 255–65; Peter K. Mills and Dennis J. Moberg, "Perspectives on the Technology of Service Operations," *Academy of Management Review* 7 (1982), 467–78; G. Lynn Shostack, "Breaking Free from Product Marketing," *Journal of Marketing* (April 1977), 73–80.
67. Ron Zemke, "The Service Revolution: Who Won?" *Management Review* (March 1997), 10–15; and Wayne Wilhelm and Bill Rossello, "The Care and Feeding of Customers," *Management Review* (March 1997), 19–23.
68. Schonfeld, "The Customized, Digitized, Have-It-Your-Way Economy."
69. Richard B. Chase and David A. Tansik, "The Customer Contact Model for Organization Design," *Management Science* 29 (1983), 1037–50.
70. *Ibid.*
71. David E. Bowen and Edward E. Lawler III, "The Empowerment of Service Workers: What, Why, How, and When," *Sloan Management Review* (Spring 1992), 31–39: Gregory B. Northcraft and Richard B. Chase, "Managing Service Demand at the Point of Delivery," *Academy of Management Review* 10 (1985), 66–75; Roger W. Schmenner, "How Can Service Businesses Survive and Prosper?" *Sloan Management Review* 27 (Spring 1986), 21–32.
72. Perrow, "Framework for Comparative Analysis" and *Organizational Analysis.*
73. Morrison, "Grand Tour."
74. Christopher Gresov, "Exploring Fit and Misfit with Multiple Contingencies," *Administrative Science Quarterly* 34 (1989), 431–53; Dale L. Goodhue and Ronald L. Thompson, "Task-Technology Fit and Individual Performance," *MIS Quarterly* (June 1995), 213–36.
75. Gresov, "Exploring Fit and Misfit with Multiple Contingencies"; Charles A. Glisson, "Dependence of Technological Routinization on Structural Variables in Human Service Organizations," *Administrative Science Quarterly* 23 (1978), 383–95; Jerald Hage and Michael Aiken, "Routine Technology, Social Structure and Organizational Goals," *Administrative Science Quarterly* 14 (1969), 368–79.
76. Gresov, "Exploring Fit and Misfit with Multiple Contingencies"; A.J. Grimes and S.M. Kline, "The Technological Imperative: The Relative Impact of Task Unit, Modal Technology, and Hierarchy on Structure," *Academy of Management Journal* 16 (1973), 583–97; Lawrence G. Hrebiniak, "Job Technologies, Supervision and Work Group Structure," *Administrative Science Quarterly* 19 (1974), 395–410; Jeffrey Pfeffer, *Organizational Design* (Arlington Heights, IL: AHM, 1978), ch. 1.
77. Patrick E. Connor, *Organizations: Theory and Design* (Chicago: Science Research Associates, 1980); Richard L. Daft and Norman B. Macintosh, "A Tentative Exploration into Amount and Equivocality of Information Processing in Organizational Work Units," *Administrative Science Quarterly* 26 (1981), 207–24.
78. Paul D. Collins and Frank Hull, "Technology and Span of Control: Woodward Revisited," *Journal of Management Studies* 23 (1986), 143–64; Gerald D. Bell, "The Influence of Technological Components of Work upon Management Control," *Academy of Management Journal* 8 (1965), 127–32; Peter M. Blau and Richard A. Schoenherr, *The Structure of Organizations* (New York: Basic Books, 1971).

79. W. Alan Randolph, "Matching Technology and the Design of Organization Units," *California Management Review* 22–23 (1980–81), 39–48; Daft and Macintosh, "Tentative Exploration into Amount and Equivocality of Information Processing"; Michael L. Tushman, "Work Characteristics and Subunit Communication Structure: A Contingency Analysis," *Administrative Science Quarterly* 24 (1979), 82–98.

80. Andrew H. Van de Ven and Diane L. Ferry, *Measuring and Assessing Organizations* (New York: Wiley, 1980); Randolph, "Matching Technology and the Design of Organization Units."

81. Richard L. Daft and Robert H. Lengel, "Information Richness: A New Approach to Managerial Behavior and Organization Design," in Barry Staw and Larry L. Cummings, eds., *Research in Organizational Behavior,* vol. 6 (Greenwich, CT: JAI Press, 1984), 191–233; Richard L. Daft and Norman B. Macintosh, "A New Approach into Design and Use of Management Information," *California Management Review* 21 (1978), 82–92; Daft and Macintosh, "Tentative Exploration in Amount and Equivocality of Information Processing"; W. Alan Randolph, "Organizational Technology and the Media and Purpose Dimensions of Organizational Communication," *Journal of Business Research* 6 (1978), 237–59; Linda Argote, "Input Uncertainty and Organizational Coordination in Hospital Emergency Units," *Administrative Science Quarterly* 27 (1982), 420–34; Andrew H. Van de Ven and Andre Delbecq, "A Task Contingent Model of Work Unit Structure," *Administrative Science Quarterly* 19 (1974), 183–97.

82. Peggy Leatt and Rodney Schneck, "Criteria for Grouping Nursing Subunits in Hospitals," *Academy of Management Journal* 27 (1984), 150–65; Robert T. Keller, "Technology-Information Processing," *Academy of Management Journal* 37, no. 1 (1994), 167–79.

83. Gresov, "Exploring Fit and Misfit with Multiple Contingencies"; Michael L. Tushman, "Technological Communication in R&D Laboratories: The Impact of Project Work Characteristics," *Academy of Management Journal* 21 (1978), 624–45; Robert T. Keller, "Technology-Information Processing Fit and the Performance of R&D Project Groups: A Test of Contingency Theory," *Academy of Management Journal* 37, no. 1 (1994), 167–79.

84. James Thompson, *Organizations in Action* (New York: McGraw-Hill, 1967).

85. Ibid., 40.

86. Paul S. Adler, "Interdepartmental Interdependence and Coordination: The Case of the Design/Manufacturing Interface," *Organization Science* 6, no. 2 (March-April 1995), 147–67.

87. Michele Liu, Héléne Denis, Harvey Kolodny, and Benjt Stymne, "Organization Design for Technological Change," *Human Relations* 43 (January 1990), 7–22.

88. Gerald I. Susman and Richard B. Chase, "A Sociotechnical Analysis of the Integrated Factory," *Journal of Applied Behavioral Science* 22 (1986), 257–70; Paul Adler, "New Technologies, New Skills," *California Management Review* 29 (Fall 1986): 9–28.

89. F. Emery, "Characteristics of Sociotechnical Systems,"Tavistock Institute of Human Relations, document 527, 1959; Passmore, Francis, and Haldeman, "Sociotechnical Systems"; and William M. Fox, "Sociotechnical System Principles and Guidelines: Past and Present," *Journal of Applied Behavioral Science* 31, no. 1 (March 1995), 91–105.

90. William A. Pasmore, "Social Science Transformed: The Socio-Technical Perspective," *Human Relations* 48, no. 1 (1995) 1–21.

91. David M. Upton, "What Really Makes Factories Flexible?" *Harvard Business Review* (July–August 1995), 74–84.

92. Robert H. Hayes, and Steven C. Wheelwright. *Restoring Our Competitive Edge: Competing Through Manufacturing* (New York: John Wiley & Sons, Inc., 1984).

93. Eliyahu M. Goldratt, *The Theory of Constraints Journal* 1, no. 5 (July–August 1989).

94. R. Handfield and E. Nichols, *Introduction to Supply Chain Management* (Upper Saddle River, NJ: Prentice Hall, 1998).

95. Robert Handfield, "Distinguishing Attributes of JIT Systems in the Make-to-Order/Assemble-to-Order Environment," *Decision Sciences Journal 24,* no. 3 (1993), 581–602.

96. Some types of inventory, such as miscellaneous office supplies, may be treated as expense items. When this is the case, wasteful inventory practices affect profit and loss directly by increasing expenses.

97. John Shook, as quoted in Jeffrey K. Liker, ed., *Becoming Lean* (Portland, OR: Productivity Press, 1998).

98. James P. Womack and Daniel T. Jones, *Lean Thinking* (New York: Simon and Schuster, 1996).

99. Campbell, Kenneth L. "Inventory Turns and ABC-Analysis-Outmoded Textbook Concepts?" *American Production and Inventory Control Conference Proceedings* (1975), 420.

100. Zimmerman, Gary. "The ABC's of Vilfredo Pareto." *Production Inventory Management* 16, no. 3 (1975), 1–9.

101. Norbom, Rolf. "The Simple ABC's (A Loose Piece Float System)." *Production and Inventory Management* 14, no. 1 (1973), 16.

102. The Council of Logistics Management defines *logistics* as "the process of planning, implementing, and controlling the efficient, effective flow and storage of goods, services, and related information from the point of origin to the point of consumption for the purpose of conforming to customer requirements." Transportation is a key element of logistics, and logistics, in turn, is a key element of supply chain management.

103. Anonymous, "Trends Facing Transportation Buyers/Carriers," *Purchasing World* (September 1998), 34.

104. Arjan J. van Wheele, "Purchasing Performance Measurement and Evaluation," *International Journal of Purchasing and Materials Management* (Fall 1984), 18–19.

105. Mark Graham Brown, *Keeping Score: Using the Right Metrics to Drive World-Class Performance* (New York: American Management Association, 1996), 15–26.

106. The Customer Contact Model was proposed by Chase (1978). The discussion of this view is summarized from Chase (1978, 1981) and Chase and Tansik (1983).
107. R. Schmenner, "How Can Service Businesses Survive and Prosper?" *Sloan Management Review,* 27 no. 3 (1986), 21–32.
108. M. E. Porter, *Competitive Strategy* (Boston: Free Press, 1985).
109. J. L. Heskett, W. E. Sasser, and L. A. Schlesinger, *The Service Profit Chain* (New York: The Free Press, 1997).
110. E. Sasser, P. Olsen, and D. Wycoff, *Management of Services Operations.* (Boston: Allyn and Bacon, Inc., 1978).
111. U.S. Bureau of the Census, *Statistical Abstract of the United States: 2001,* Tables 2, 1020, and 1024.
112. *Ibid.*
113. Matt Scallan, "Price Strategy Takes Bite of Revenue at Armstrong, But Food Sales in Line with Other Airports," *Times-Picayune,* April 5, 2003, B1.
114. "The Changing Marketplace," Barnard Retail Consulting Group, May 2000.
115. Itamar Simonson, "The Effect of Product Assortment on Buyer Preferences," *Journal of Retailing* (Fall 1999), 347–370.
116. "A Blueprint for Local Assortment Management," *Chain Store Age* (February 1997), 27–34.
117. Susan Broniarczyk, Wayne Hoyer, and Linda McAlister, "Consumers' Perceptions of Assortment Offered in a Grocery Category: The Impact of Item Reduction," *Journal of Marketing Research,* May 1998, 166–176; S. Iyengar and M. Lepper, "When Choice Is Demotivating: Can One Desire Too Much of a Good Thing?" *Journal of Personality and Social Psychology,* 6, 200, 995–1006.
118. "Finding Gold in the Supply Chain Stream," *Chain Store Age* (January 1997), 164.
119. Rajeev Batra and Indrajit Sinha, "Consumer-Level Factors Moderating the Success of Private Label Brands," *Journal of Retailing* (Summer 2000), 175–191.
120. This example is based on Roy Howell, Robert Britney, Paul Kuzdrall, and James Wilcox, "Unauthorized Channels of Distribution: Gray Markets," *Industrial Marketing Management* 15 (1986), 257–263. Used with the permission of the authors.
121. "Inside the Cult of Costco," *Fortune,* September 6, 1999, 185–190.
122. "Reducing Inventory Shrinkage Is an HR Issue," *Retail Navigator* (June 2003), 4.
123. "Anti-Theft Balers," *Chain Store Age Executive* (February 1999), 82.
124. For a detailed discussion of this topic, see Pratibha Dabholkar, David Shepherd, and Dayle Thorpe, "A Comprehensive Framework for Service Quality: An Investigation of Critical Conceptual and Measurement Issues Through a Longitudinal Study," *Journal of Retailing* (Summer 2000), 139–173.
125. University of Michigan's American Customer Satisfaction Index at http://www.bus.umich.edu/research/nqrc.
126. The following information was provided to the authors by Marvin J. Rothenberg and is used with the written permission of Marvin J. Rothenberg, Inc., Retail Marketing Consultants, Ft. Lee, NJ.
127. "Lights On: Study Shows Display Lighting Boosts Sales at GNC," *Chain Store Age,* (June 2003), 78.
128. "Store Selection Criteria," *Progressive Grocer Annual Report* (April 2003), 23 and (April 2002), 30.
129. *Ibid.*
130. The preceding material was provided for the authors' use by Marvin J. Rothenberg of Marvin J. Rothenberg, Inc., Ft. Lee, NJ.
131. For a more detailed discussion of this topic, the reader should consult the latest edition of Martin M. Pegler's *Stores of the Year* (New York: Retail Reporting Corporation, 2003).
132. Based on an example in Paco Underhill, *Why We Buy: The Science of Shopping* (New York: Simon & Schuster, 2000).
133. "Form and Function," *Chain Store Age* (June 2003), 76.
134. "Blinded by the Light," *Progressive Grocer* (August 2000), 57–58.
135. Paula Fitzgerald Bone and Pam Scholder Ellen, "Scents in the Marketplace: Explaining a Fraction of Olfaction," *Journal of Retailing* (Summer 1999), 243–262.
136. "Logos Losing Luster," *Chain Store Age* (June 2003), 23.
137. P. J. Haynes and M. M. Helms, "An Ethical Framework for Purchasing Decisions," *Management Decision* (UK) 29, no. 1 (1991), 35; H. Page, "More on Ethics—Helping Your Buyers," *Purchasing World* 30, no. 12 (December 1986), 60.
138. Haynes and Helms, "An Ethical Framework," 36.
139. R. C. Parker, G. C. Fordyce, and K. P. Graham, "Ethics in Purchasing," in L. G. Farrell and L. A. Alijian, eds., *Purchasing Handbook,* (New York: McGraw-Hill, 1982), 7–16.
140. Haynes and Helms, "An Ethical Framework," 36.
141. L. B. Forker and R. L. Janson, "Ethical Practices in Purchasing," *International Journal of Purchasing and Materials Management* 26, no. 1 (Winter 1990), 19–26.

MODULE 300

Marketing Management

301 Marketing Strategies, 470

310 New Product Development and Product Management, 477

320 Advertising and Promotion, 498

330 Pricing Strategies, 510

340 Consumer Behavior and Marketing Research, 520

355 Marketing Channels and Distribution, 531

360 Electronic Commerce and Marketing, 543

365 Ethics and Marketing, 547

380 Market Segmentation and Target Markets, 553

385 Services and Retail Marketing, 556

390 Sales Administration and Management, 612

395 Ethics and Sales, 624

Module 300 Endnotes, 626

Marketing Strategies

The Evolution of Markets via Spontaneous Economic Combustion

Spontaneous Economic Combustion

To understand why marketing is such a fascinating economic and sociological activity, we have to first understand the fundamental reason why markets developed and how marketing adds value. Markets exist because of three primary conditions—raw material scarcity, labor specialization, and consumption satiation. Simply stated, markets exist because valuable raw material resources are geographically concentrated in some locations and not in others (**raw material scarcity**); we get better at doing things the more we do them (**labor specialization**); and beyond some level of normal consumption, we tend to become less interested in consuming things the more we consume them (**consumption satiation**). Put raw material scarcity, labor specialization, and consumption satiation together in any human society and markets, marketing, and trade will be created spontaneously.

The Evolution of Marketing into a Trading Relationship Exchange Process

The Traditional View of Marketing's Evolution

The most frequently noted eras are the production era, the sales era, the marketing era, and the relationship marketing era. (See Exhibit 300.1.)

An Alternative to the Traditional View of Marketing

The primary problem with the traditional view of marketing eras is that it does not fit the facts. In reality, the idea of inventing and marketing products that customers need and want, then supplying them, has been fundamental to the development of free-market economies from prehistory on, not something that has been implemented in recent times. The history of global trade and economic development has involved bringing new, attractive products, such as flint arrowheads, bone needles, fertility figurines, chocolate, and spices, to market and creating long-term trading relationships between tribes, countries, companies, and wealthy customers.[1] Ancient economies that were very good at such relationship marketing flourished and came to dominate other economies. Eventually, these traders became targets for raiders. Military forces were subsequently formed to protect their trade, trade routes, and the fruits of their trade. Thus, there never was a production era or a sales era. In reality, what there have been are companies that become too production-oriented or too sales-oriented, at the expense of listening to the voice of the customer. Eventually, these companies are forced by the competition (with more of a marketing orientation) to become more customer-oriented, or they are driven out of the market.

What, then, has been the real history of the development of market economies and marketing? It is the history of the development of well over 10,000 product markets, each with its own unique evolutionary story.[2] Marketing schol-

Exhibit 300.1 *The Evolution of Marketing*

1. Production Era	2. Sales Era	3. Marketing Era	4. Relationship Marketing Era
Business philosophy focusing on manufacturing efficiency.	Business philosophy focusing on selling existing products.	Business philosophy focusing on customer needs and wants.	Business philosophy focusing on suppliers and keeping existing customers.

ars have attempted to draw further general conclusions about the evolution of such diverse markets and their marketing traditions and practices by focusing on the exchange process.

Marketing as an Exchange Process

According to the most widely accepted definition provided by the American Marketing Association, **marketing** is ultimately an exchange process:

> *Marketing is the process of planning and executing the conception, pricing, promotion, and distribution of ideas, goods, and services to create exchanges that satisfy individual and organizational goals.*[3]

To illustrate the fundamental concept of added value associated with the exchange process, consider the following scenario. The grower of beef would rather exchange a steak for a watermelon because he is tired of eating steak (consumption satiation) and it costs him a lot less to produce an additional steak (labor specialization) than to grow a watermelon. Similarly, the grower of watermelons also would like to exchange one of her watermelons for a steak because she is sick of eating watermelons and it costs her a lot less to produce a watermelon than a steak. Therefore, if they meet, an exchange is likely to occur between the beef farmer and the watermelon grower. When both benefit, added value has been created by the exchange. Hence, the fundamental benefit of the **exchange principle** (the law or truth underlying exchange) is added-value creation: By the simple act of exchanging goods and services for other goods and services (or for money), added value is created.

Marketing exchanges exist because they are beneficial to both parties. They are beneficial to both parties because of the principles of raw material scarcity, labor specialization, and consumption satiation. **Comparative advantage** in the cost of producing various goods has long been understood to underlay the benefits of trading. But production-based comparative advantage does not, by itself, lead to production surpluses that create trade and markets. The satiation principle is also necessary. In other words, if the more the farmer ate steak, the more he liked it and wanted more of it to eat, then he would be very happy producing more beef at an even lower cost and eating more of it than ever. In essence, the farmer would have an ever increasing interest in eating his cattle, rather than exchanging them for other products in the marketplace. Consequently, the fundamental principle of exchange is based on the principles of production-based comparative advantage (which is itself based on resource scarcity and labor specialization) and consumption satiation.

Marketing facilitates exchange by performing a variety of activities that benefit consumers, producers, and resellers alike. Marketing exchange activities include the following:

- *Buying:* Marketers, besides being skilled manufacturers, are often skilled buyers of other products from many different manufacturers that are then resold to customers under one roof. When you shop at Wal-Mart, for example, you are taking advantage of this marketer's considerable expertise in assessing quality and its volume-buying power that enables it to promise the lowest prices.
- *Selling:* By making a variety of products available under one roof, marketers sell to numerous customers in a single location, thereby alleviating the need for individual customers to deal with individual manufacturers for each and every product they desire to purchase. Selling also includes the skills of understanding, educating, and persuading customers, all much needed in a world of rapidly improving technology and increased competition.
- *Transporting:* Marketers facilitate the transportation of products by providing the products customers want, where and when they want them. Improvements in transportation, from wagon to sailboat to steamboat to jumbo jets and containerization, have made markets global, to the benefit of billions of people.
- *Storing:* Marketers store products, for example, at a grocery store, so that customers do not have to and so that manufacturers do not have to keep everything that they produce in their own inventories until each product is sold. Today, distribution logistics (sometimes called supply-chain management) combines the management of buying, transporting, and storing into a single system. Innovations in these systems have helped to reduce the cost of distribution in the U.S. economy from around 12 percent of gross domestic product (GDP) to 6 percent over the last 20 years.
- *Financing:* Marketers offer special paying (e.g., 90 days, same as cash) and leasing agreements that enable more customers access to the products they desire to purchase. Innovations in household financial services in the mid-20th-century U.S. economy led to an enormous increase in the purchase of homes and automobiles and the formation of household debt. These innovations are now taken for granted, but from the early 1930s through the early 1960s, there were many marketing departments in university business schools that taught entire courses on managing consumer credit.
- *Risk taking:* By purchasing products from manufacturers before they are sold to customers, marketers assume the risk that the products may not sell in the marketplace. This diversification of financial risk encourages manufacturer invention, innovation, and entrepreneurship that benefits everyone.

- *Standardization and grading:* Marketers play a role in standardizing and grading the quality and quantity of products made available to customers (e.g., eggs). Such standards are also often mandated by regulation but increasingly are determined by the quality of rivals' goods and services. Standards increase buyer confidence in the quality and performance of what is purchased.
- *Obtaining market information:* Marketers collect information about buyers and suppliers (1) to increase the efficiency and effectiveness of the exchange process (e.g., by suggesting changes in what is exchanged or how it is exchanged to increase the resulting satisfaction of both parties and thus the total value of the exchange) and (2) to increase the returns from a firm's deployment of assets and resources.
- *Fostering trust with trading partners:* Marketers are important boundary spanners whose goal is to build and foster trust with trading partners that ensures that the terms of trade are implemented. Trust also leads to cooperative innovations in trading processes and expansion of the relationship into new ventures, product categories, and types of services exchanged, and acts as a goodwill buffer in economic hard times or when new rivals enter the market.

Marketing as an Organizational Process

The Marketing Concept

Initially, the teaching of marketing covered two main topics: (1) how and why the unique marketing and trading institutions in different markets evolved and (2) the many and diverse ways that marketing activities (particularly undertaken in agriculture and processed foods markets) added value to the exchange process. From 50 years of such case study research and teaching emerged a consensus belief that the keys to business success were to achieve organizational goals by identifying the needs and wants of customers and delivering products that satisfy customers more effectively than competitors could. This prescription for success became known as the **marketing concept.** The marketing concept consists of three fundamental principles:[4]

1. The organization exists to identify and to satisfy the needs and wants of its potential and existing customers.
2. Satisfying customer needs is accomplished through an integrative effort throughout the organization.
3. The organizational focus should be on long-term cooperative trading relationships with customers as opposed to short-term exploitation of customers.

The marketing concept has its roots in customer orientation founded on the philosophy that production and selling efforts must be based on understanding and serving customers' needs and wants. The marketing concept puts companies and managers on notice that neither production nor sales nor customers exist in a vacuum: They exist in a competitive marketplace that is becoming increasingly more competitive. It is this competitiveness that ultimately drives the marketing concept. The problem with the marketing concept, however, is that it is too simplistic. There is a great deal more to a firm's **marketing strategy** (the planning and directing of a firm's marketing efforts) than taking the long-term perspective, focusing on the customer, and diffusing such beliefs across the organization.

The Fundamentals of Marketing Strategy

How is marketing strategy, the deployment of the resources and skills described in Exhibit 300.2, actually implemented? Markets consist of **market segments**—homogeneous groups of customers who have similar product usage wants and needs. For example, the soft drink market consists of a regular cola segment, a diet cola segment, and a caffeine-free segment, among others. As a business strategy, market segmentation allows the firm to focus its marketing efforts on narrowly defined markets. Many firms lack the resources to efficiently and effectively appeal to every segment in a market; therefore, they often choose to focus on specific segments called **target markets.** The **marketing mix,** composed of product, pricing, distribution (place), and promotion decisions, is then tailored to meet the needs and wants of specific target markets and to carve out a position in the marketplace. **Product positioning** refers to how customers perceive a product's position in the marketplace relative to the competition. Ultimately, marketing strategy directs the product positioning of the firm and directs and develops a mix of other marketing activities, processes, and practices that are specifically tailored to effectively and profitably serve the needs of a target market.

MARKETING MIX The conventional way of thinking about marketing mix is to categorize marketing decisions and activities as being related to product, pricing, distribution (place), and promotion decisions. (See Exhibit 300.3.)

Exhibit 300.2 *Marketing Strategy*

Deploying Assets and Capabilities

Marketing strategy involves deploying major financial and human capital resources, such as building an Internet presence or a sales force, to develop a superior, distinctive, and difficult to imitate competitive advantage that the company can claim as its own based on the following dimensions:

1. Superior product design and technology as measured by sales growth, performance in use (not on paper), and customer satisfaction. How does the company rate compared to its major and high-growth competition? More importantly, how is this comparison changing? Who has new product development momentum?
2. Superior distribution system alliances, technology, and sales forces as measured by sales growth, service quality effectiveness, efficiency, and distributor satisfaction. How does the company rate compared to its major and high-growth competition? More importantly, how is this comparison changing? Who has distribution system momentum?
3. Superior cost structure, which leads to lower prices and the potential for significantly lower prices as sales grow. How is the company rated compared to its major and high-growth competition? More importantly, how is this comparison changing? Who has cost reduction momentum?
4. Superior brand reputation based on a history of superior product and distribution strategy (not just a heavy advertising campaign that produces top-of-mind audience name awareness). How does the company rate compared to its major and high-growth competition? More importantly, how is this comparison changing? Who has brand reputation momentum?

Using Superior Vision

The competitive positioning advantages listed are achieved and cleverly deployed through superior vision (seeing evolutionary market trends into the future) and using the following:

1. Superior market scanning and tracking systems involving the sales force and customer and trade satisfaction tracking services. How is consumer behavior changing?
2. Superior processes that link the highest levels of company decision making (the board and executive committees) to the knowledge and market insights of the company's boundary spanners (sales force, customer service support, and market researchers).
3. Research and development that tracks trends in new emergent technology used in product and distribution system design. The company learns by imitating as well as by innovating.
4. Information technology systems that measure what is being managed and that allow real-time communication of new knowledge across cross-functional teams and sister operations in other countries.
5. Superior targeting of products and services to market segments.
6. Superior assessment of the growth potential of markets and the company's competitiveness in each market.
7. Superior marketing planning and improvisation processes that act on the above information.

Exhibit 300.3 *Elements of Marketing Mix*

Source: From John H. Lindgren, Jr. and Terence A. Shimp, *Marketing*, 1st edition. (Mason, OH: Thomson Learning, 1996).

PRODUCT DECISIONS AND ACTIVITIES Product decisions and activities encompass a wide array of processes, such as new product development, branding, packaging, labeling, and the strategic management of products throughout their technological life cycle.

Products provide **form utility**—the transformation of raw materials or labor into a finished good or service that the consumer desires. However, we would like you to think of products as more than just tangible goods. Throughout this text, unless otherwise specifically stated, the term *product* refers to *goods* (e.g., appliances, automobiles, and clothing), *services* (e.g., legal, health care, and financial), *people* (e.g., political candidates, religious leaders, and students looking for their first job), *places* (e.g., tourism destinations, shopping centers, and countries seeking economic development), and *ideas* (e.g., HIV protection, Mothers Against Drunk Driving, and antidrug campaigns). Similarly, the term *customer* includes both business customers and household consumers. No one would dispute that product markets vary greatly in large part because of differences in the types of customers who make a market. A customer can be a government, a corporation, a family business, a household, or an individual. Clearly, any firm that seeks to satisfy its customers must possess a deep understanding of how customers derive satisfaction from a purchase. In particular, it must strive to have a better understanding than its rivals. Marketing to businesses is so different from marketing to households that it is best to study them separately.

PRICING DECISIONS Pricing decisions should satisfy multiple objectives. At the very least, a firm's pricing strategy should do the following:

1. Support a product's marketing strategy
2. Achieve the financial goals of the organization
3. Fit the realities of the marketing environment

Despite decades of study by economists and market researchers, price setting is still often determined by a best-guess decision that is quickly revised when the guess turns out to be wrong.

DISTRIBUTION (PLACE) DECISIONS Distribution decisions reflect the marketer's ability to create time, place, and possession utilities for customers. *Time utility* and *place utility* reflect the marketer's ability to provide products when and where customers would like to purchase them. *Possession utility* facilitates the transfer of ownership of the product from the producer to the customer through marketing channels. A typical *marketing channel* would consist of the following channel members: the *manufacturer*, who produces the product and sells it to a wholesaler; the *wholesaler*, who resells the product to a retailer; and the *retailer*, who sells the product to the *final consumer*.

PROMOTION DECISIONS Promotion decisions communicate the firm's marketing strategy to customers and channel members who assist in the product's distribution to the market. Every firm has choices to make as to how to communicate with the market. Communication is accomplished by managing the firm's promotion mix. Elements of this mix include personal selling, advertising, publicity, and sales promotion. Each element has its advantages and disadvantages.

The Marketing Environment

Businesses do not operate in a vacuum. Environmental forces surround a firm and often change the rules of engagement. Consequently, a firm's marketing strategy must adapt to changes in the **marketing environment** if the firm is to survive and thrive. In general, a marketing environment comprises six elements. First, the firm's internal marketing environment (the *microenvironment*) consists of *objectives* and *resources*. The external marketing environment (the *macroenvironment*) consists of the *sociocultural environment, economic environment, legal/political environment, competitive environment,* and *technological environment*.

Exhibit 300.4 provides a framework that incorporates these environmental forces. The model illustrates that these forces impinge on and influence the likely successful fit of all elements of the marketing mix to the internal and external marketing environment and to the target market. Successful firms track changes in the marketing environment via environmental scanning. **Environmental scanning** identifies important trends in the micro- and macro-environments, then considers the potential impact of these changes on a firm's existing marketing strategy.

The Internal Marketing Environment

OBJECTIVES AND RESOURCES Top-level corporate executives formulate annual and long-term objectives that affect marketing decision making.[5] For example, a corporate objective to increase profits by 15 percent over the pre-

Exhibit 300.4 *Marketing Mix Fit*

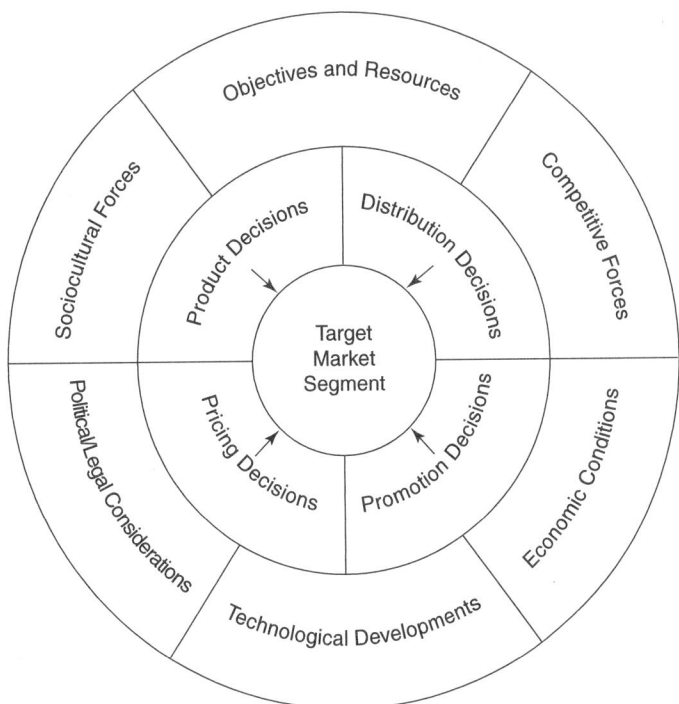

Source: From John H. Lindgren, Jr. and Terence A. Shimp, *Marketing*, 1st edition. (Mason, OH: Thomson Learning, 1996).

vious year has implications for current marketing actions. Objectives are critical to any company's success. Without objectives, a company has no direction. If no objectives are set, a company will waste a great amount of time, money, and effort in pursuing what may prove to be unprofitable or unrealistic strategies. A company must know where it is going if it is to be successful. It needs an overall set of objectives to guide its efforts. Each functional area in the company (e.g., operations, finance, and marketing) also has its own objectives, but its goals must fit into or be guided by the company's overall objectives. It is imperative that the entire company works together toward the same goals. Thus, marketing strategy is influenced by, and is to some extent constrained by, overall corporate objectives.

Marketing strategy is also constrained by available resources. A firm's resources include finances, technological and production capabilities, and managerial talent. Resource constraints prevent marketing managers from pursuing every available opportunity. For example, financial restrictions can prevent a firm from running a prime-time television campaign for a new product introduction. Instead, it may be able to afford a national radio campaign. Or a firm's current production line may not be equipped to package a trial size of an existing product. New equipment may be needed, but perhaps finances will not allow it at this time. If a firm is fully aware of its limitations, strategies can be developed and opportunities pursued that are within the company's limits.

The External Marketing Environment

Sociocultural Environment

Changes in the sociocultural environment reflect the reshaping of the world's population in terms of numbers, characteristics, behavior, and growth projections.

Customer attitudes and behavior also impact the sociocultural environment and the way marketers perceive the market. Marketers must consider the changing roles of women both in marketing their products and in reaching target markets. A traditional medium such as daytime television is no longer effective in reaching working women. Direct mail, magazines, and radio are proving to be more effective in reaching this group.

Cultural and age diversity, between and within countries, also affects the sociocultural environment. Marketers are now targeting the specific needs of ethnic markets such as African Americans, Asians, and Latinos. This change in marketing strategy reflects the growing purchasing power of ethnic groups, their increasing rate of population growth relative to the slower growth rate of Caucasian populations, and cultural differences in how different groups purchase and use products. By 2010, minorities will represent one-third of the U.S. population.

The Americanization of world culture through science, entertainment, and business has helped to reduce cultural differences, particularly among countries with highly educated populations. This opens up the possibility for global segmentation and positioning, where segmentation spreads across rather than within cultures. In short, cultures no longer follow national, political, or cultural borders as much as they did even 50 years ago.

However, many countries still have different consumer wealth, buying power, price elasticity, experience with the product category, and competitive behavior. Consequently, relatively few products can be positioned exactly the same way across the global marketplace. Those products that can be positioned usually have a strong symbolic or intangible image that transcends cultural, technological, and economic differences.

ECONOMIC ENVIRONMENT   Marketers must also monitor changes in the economic environment.[6] The economic environment includes factors such as the purchasing power of markets, per capita expenditures, employment rates, general consumer confidence, and the cost of capital that may be necessary to produce products. The mere size of markets is not enough to make a market profitable. Customers within those markets must have, in addition to the willingness to purchase products, the ability to purchase (purchasing power).

LEGAL/POLITICAL ENVIRONMENT   The legal and political environment poses another external force for the marketer. It is the job of the government to establish the rules and regulations to which businesses must conform. These rules and regulations affect each element in the marketing mix. Marketers must therefore be aware of and conform to all laws affecting their business.

As citizens, our behavior is constrained by the law and by our individual views of right and wrong. It is no different for firms that compete in domestic and international markets. Marketplaces are full of rules. Many are written into law, some are outlined in professional codes of ethics, and others are stated in company rules of good conduct. While the legal/political environment can frustrate initiative, in general it is positive for business. For example, many of the laws that affect marketing practice are in place to encourage competition and to protect consumers.

COMPETITIVE ENVIRONMENT   *Competitiveness* reflects how effective and efficient a firm is, relative to its rivals, at serving customers. *Effectiveness* pertains to the quality of products, market share, and profitability, while *efficiency* reflects response speed and low costs. Both effectiveness and efficiency ultimately depend on the strength of the firm's competitive drive and its decision-making skills.

Businesses are constantly exhorted by almost everyone—government agencies, associates monitors, and industry insiders, among others—to become more competitive. But becoming more competitive is like losing weight: It is easy to talk about, but it is not easy to do. The task is almost impossible if it is not based on a thorough competitive situation analysis. The analysis should start with a general overview of the competitive structure and dynamics of the market. This includes market share analysis, a review of the history of the market, and a search for emerging competitors that threatens to drive existing firms and their products into extinction. The analysis should then focus on major rivals and their likely behavior.

TECHNOLOGICAL ENVIRONMENT   Successful firms must also monitor changes in the technological environment. Technology is advancing at an incredible rate. Technological advances primarily influence marketing practice. They enable firms to develop new products and to compete in new markets. Technological advances also help marketers improve the way business trading is conducted on a day-to-day basis.

Clearly, monitoring the environment is critical to any firm's survival. To avoid failures, a company has to pay attention to what is going on in the marketing environment while implementing marketing strategy. It is that simple, yet many companies do not pay attention to what their sales force, sales figures, costs, and market research say is happening with regards to changes in the marketing environment. The reasons for not paying attention and acting on information are many. It may be that the firm does not conduct environmental screening analysis at all, or it collects information that is biased, or information is not passed on to the right decision makers, or the information is not timely enough. Today's senior management is often faced with numerous distractions, such as take-over attempts, lobbying efforts directed toward the government, involvement in major litigation, internal management succession battles, and labor disputes.

Reacting to changes in the marketing environment is often a challenging process. Companies often talk about valuing market research and market scanning systems, but the reality is that these activities are undertaken several layers of management away from boards of directors and executives who are making most of the marketing strategy decisions. The lesson is that a major responsibility of the marketing function in any firm is to ensure that tracking measures that monitor the marketing environment get into the hands of the most senior management of the company.

New Product Development and Product Management

Types of Products

Products[7] are the core of every organization. Whether it be a good, service, person, place, or idea, organizations need a product to offer. In general, products offer customers a bundle of attributes that address a set of needs. The attributes may include the product's **features,** its package and **brand** name, the service that supports product performance, on-time delivery, courteous and effective customer relations, an adequate warranty, and so on. Over time, customers choose products with the set of features that delivers the maximum benefit for them. Based on differences in markets, buyer attitudes and motivations, purchase patterns, and product characteristics, products can be categorized into several groups with important implications for marketing mix decisions.

In general, products can be classified as either consumer or business-to-business products, depending on *who the buyer is* and *for what purpose the product is being bought.* If a consumer purchases a product for his or her own household use, the product is called a *consumer product.* Consumer products are classified further into categories based on how the consumer views and shops for the product. Products purchased by organizations to be used in producing other products or in operating their businesses are classified as *business-to-business products.* Business-to-business products are further divided into categories based on how the products will be used.

Consumer Products

Examples and the marketing mix implications of the four kinds of consumer products are summarized in Exhibit 300.5.

- *Convenience products* are typically inexpensive items consumers purchase with little effort, which are used on a frequent basis. Consumers spend little time shopping for convenience products.
- *Shopping products* are more expensive than convenience products, so the decision to purchase them is more important. The consumer will spend more time searching for information before selecting a particular brand, and compare prices and benefits among brands offering similar features.
- *Specialty products* are high-involvement consumer purchases, where the product reflects the consumer's personality or self-image. Thus, consumers are willing to spend a great deal of time to acquire one particular brand. Substitutes are not an option.
- *Unsought products* are either unknown to the buyer or are known, but not actively being sought at this point in time. Consumers do not search for unsought products until they need or are made aware of the products.

Business-to-Business Products

The five categories of business-to-business products vary in how they are used, as well as the closeness, or strength, of the relationship between the buyer and seller.

- *Raw materials* are unprocessed products that become part of a company's finished goods. Almost all raw materials are commodities. Farm products such as milk, eggs, corn, wheat, and processed sugar are considered raw materials for the food industry, as are oil and gas for the chemical and petroleum industries. Because there is little or no differentiation between sellers, buyer-seller transactions are conducted at arm's length.
- *Supplies* are used in support of business operations but are not part of the finished product. Supplies are standardized, purchased often, and are inexpensive compared to other product categories. Examples include pens, paper, Post-It Notes, cleaning solutions, and lubricating oil. Buyer-seller interactions for supplies are arm's length, with little or no ongoing relationship between the firms.
- *Accessories* are usually standardized pieces of equipment that support the overall running of factories and businesses. They are purchased more frequently than installations, but far less frequently than supplies.

Exhibit 300.5 *Classifications and Marketing Mix Considerations for Consumer Products*

Marketing Mix Considerations	Convenience	Shopping	Specialty	Unsought
Product Examples	Soda and other soft drinks, milk, toothpaste, soap	Clothing, computers, appliances, furniture	Luxury items: Rolex watch, Jaguar cars	Insurance, medical trauma services
Consumer Attitudes	Low involvement, minimize time and decision effort, feature and price focus	Moderate to high involvement, balance between image and features/functionality	Very high involvement, image (brand) far more important than features	Unaware, possibly avoiding learning about category
Consumer Purchase Behavior	Frequent purchases, no planning, routine decisions	Less frequent purchases, planned shopping, compare along multiple dimensions	Infrequent purchases, special purchase effort, little brand comparison	Infrequent purchases, comparison shopping (features and brand) when made aware of need to purchase
Place (Distribution)	Widespread, with convenient locations	A large number of more selective outlets	Limited and exclusive, few outlets per market	More selective outlets, from few to many
Price	Inexpensive, low price	More expensive, moderate price	Very expensive, high price	Varies
Promotion	Mass communication, focus on price, availability, awareness	Mass communication and personal selling, focus on features, differentiation	Targeted communication, stress brand and status	Aggressive ads to create awareness, personal selling to close sale

Examples include printers, copiers, retail display cases, and delivery trucks. While accessories are frequently bought through arm's-length transactions, some firms have developed stronger relationships with one or two suppliers to try to reduce overall costs. For example, **USX** (formerly US Steel) has a long-term supply relationship with **Compaq** for all the firm's PCs.

- *Component parts and materials* are products that are partly assembled or already processed to be ready for assembly into the finished product. Hamburger patties, buns, ketchup, onions, and pickles are all component parts/materials for both **McDonald's** and **Burger King**. Tires, seats, and engines are components used in manufacturing new automobiles. Firms are trending toward closer buyer-seller relationships with their suppliers of components and materials, using relationship marketing to try to capture competitive advantages through differentiation and product design efficiencies.
- *Installations* are major capital goods. Usually, installations are customized, expensive, and purchased infrequently. Products such as buildings, laboratories, and major computer systems are all considered installations. The selling process is typically longer, more complex, and more challenging than for any other type of business-to-business product. The practices of relationship marketing are the norm for installations.

Without a product, there is no firm. Thus, the long-term basis for the success of a firm relies on its ability not only to market one product well, but also to continue to grow and prosper by developing new products for the marketplace. Firms have many types of products that they can choose to develop. The next section outlines issues associated with understanding and developing potentially successful products, by providing information that sets the stage for successful development.

Setting the Stage for Successful New Product Development

This section covers the three underpinnings for managing successful new product development programs: information that helps firms define and evaluate products under development, requirements for developing successful new products, and definitions of and methods for uncovering unmet needs.

Exhibit 300.6 *The Average Project Portfolio*

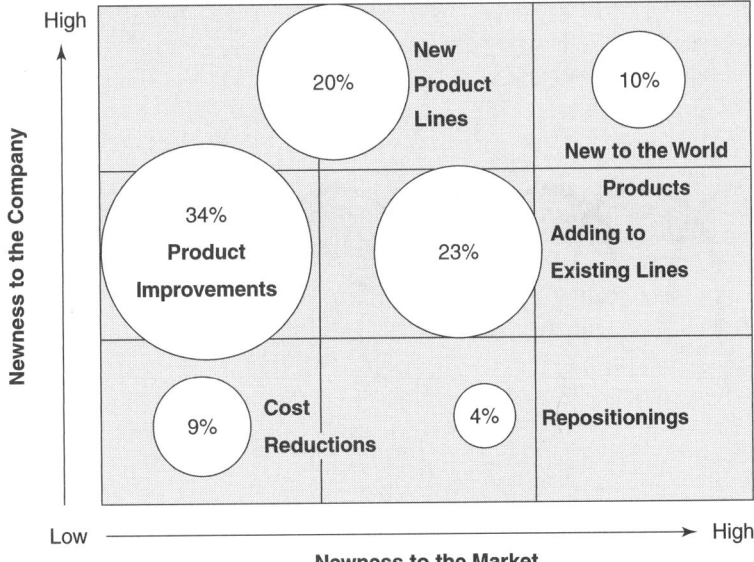

Source: From *Journal of Product Innovation Management*, Vol. 14, pp. 429–458, copyright 1997, with permission from Blackwell Publishing. www.blackwellpublishing.com

Defining Products: Newness, Success, and Failure

DEFINING WHAT WE MEAN BY *NEW* The next time you go through the grocery store, go to the cereal section and count the number of cereals that you do not recognize. Some of these products will be totally new types of cereals. Others are variants, or **line extensions,** of current products, as Honey Nut Cheerios is a line extension of Cheerios. Walk around the store and look at the packages that declare a product is "New and Improved." One dimension of newness is how new a product is in the eyes of the market. This ranges from small, incremental changes to improve one aspect of performance or to provide choice variety, to totally new types of products that solve problems never before solved for consumers.

A second dimension of newness is how new the product is to the firm. Theme parks are familiar products for consumers, but a theme park based on cars would be a very new product for **Ford Motor Company** to produce. It would require much more effort for Ford to develop a new theme park than for Disney, which has built them before, just as it would require much more effort for Disney to develop a new car than it would for Ford. While it may not make strategic sense for Ford to develop a new theme park, it might make sense for Ford to diversify beyond cars and trucks into the motorcycle market. Again, motorcycles are not new to consumers, but they would be new to Ford, and likely would require more time, effort, and risk for the company to develop than a new car.

Overall, "newness" is thus a combination of newness to the market and newness to the firm. Products that are newer on either dimension are riskier to develop and commercialize. "New-to-the-world" products—products that create an entirely new market—are the riskiest of all, but present enormous profit potential, because they represent monopoly opportunities, at least in the short term. On average, only 10 percent of the products commercialized by firms are new-to-the-world. As shown in Exhibit 300.6, most of the projects in firm portfolios are improvements to products already on the market or additions to existing lines (line extensions), and products that are new to the firm but already manufactured by competitors (new product lines).[8] Fully 70 percent of the average firm's products focus on changing or adding to current products.[9] Ultimately, however, a new product is any product a firm spends money on to change, improve, or reduce cost.

Firms do not commercialize a product, and then just reap ongoing profits. Once a product is developed and introduced to the market, competitors introduce products that improve on the initial product's performance. New technologies also become available over time that solve additional customer problems not addressed by the first-generation product. Both events require that firms manage products and product development as an ongoing spiral, as shown in Exhibit 300.7.[10] Thus, product development does not take place just once, but must be repeated over and over for a firm to stay in business in the long run. Some cycles of the spiral may only be small, incremental changes in the product. For example, in each of the two years after Ford introduced the Taurus, it made small changes in a number of components. Some changes were made to reduce costs, while others were to improve quality and performance. In other cycles, more

310. NEW PRODUCT DEVELOPMENT AND PRODUCT MANAGEMENT

Exhibit 300.7 *The New Product Development Spiral*

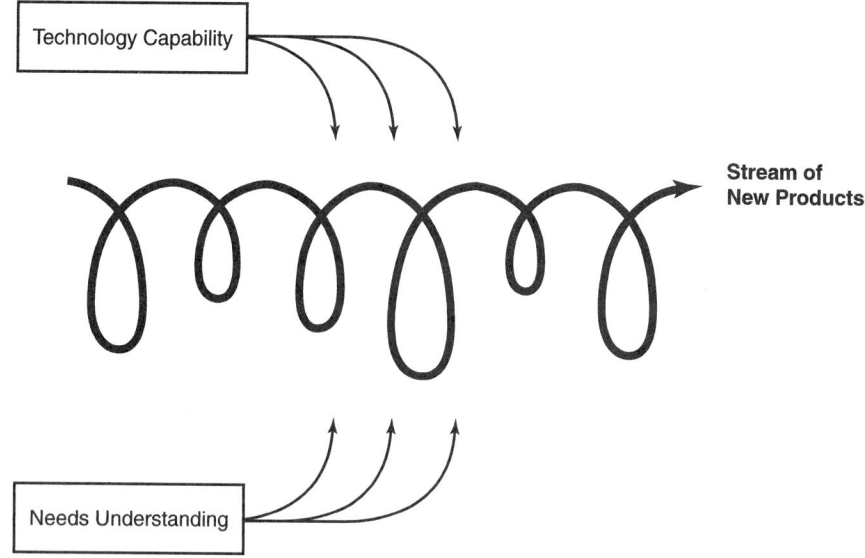

radical changes were made, as when Ford totally redesigned the Taurus for its 1996 reintroduction. The target market for the Taurus remained unchanged, as did its **core benefit proposition (CBP).** However, both the styling and many components and subsystems were updated, some with newly available technology or materials. These design changes in turn caused manufacturing changes. Just keeping pace with competitors requires repeatedly reinvigorating products to make them new in the eyes of customers.

DEFINING WHAT WE MEAN BY SUCCESS Developing new products is time- and resource-consuming, as great care must be taken to ensure the best decisions are made *before* the product reaches channel members and final consumers. Much of this section looks closely at the process and management of product development. However, before discussing methods for new product development (NPD), it is first important to consider what firms are actually attempting to achieve by introducing new products to the market. Quite frankly, new product development success is difficult to define. Whereas most firms' ultimate objective is financial success, some product development projects have goals that are more than just financial.

NPD managers recommend that *NPD project success* be measured using four items that span three dimensions.[11] One item is a measure of *financial success,* most frequently the project's profitability. A second item assesses *technical performance success,* often measuring the product's competitive advantage from a technical (performance) point of view. For example, a new **Intel** processor may be 20 percent faster than the competitor's current processor. The specific performance measure used depends on which features and specifications are important to consumers. The third dimension consists of two measurements that evaluate *success from the customer's perspective*—most frequently, *market share* and *customer satisfaction.* A new product in the ready-to-eat cereal category is considered a success if it achieves only a 1 percent share of this highly fragmented market. On the other hand, in more concentrated industries such as pickup trucks, firms look for a new truck to obtain a 20 to 25 percent share.

Achieving product success along one dimension does not necessarily mean the product will achieve success along another. For example, superior technical performance levels may not lead to a significant market share or customer satisfaction. A product can even achieve high levels of customer satisfaction without achieving profitability, if either development spending or product cost is not controlled. Unfortunately, the perfect product development project that achieves high levels of success on all three dimensions, known as the *silver bullet,* rarely exists. Firms frequently sacrifice some level of success on one dimension to achieve success on another. For instance, the objective of one project may be to increase customer satisfaction; another may be to raise the technical performance bar for the product category. Though profits need not be the primary goal of any particular project, the firm does need to generate a profit across the portfolio of products that comprise its **product mix.**

WHY PRODUCTS FAIL Achieving product success is difficult. Even though firms over the last 20 years have improved the probability that a project which starts the new product development process will succeed, it still takes almost five projects to create one market success,[12] as Exhibit 300.8 illustrates. Projects are abandoned during

Exhibit 300.8 *Project Mortality*

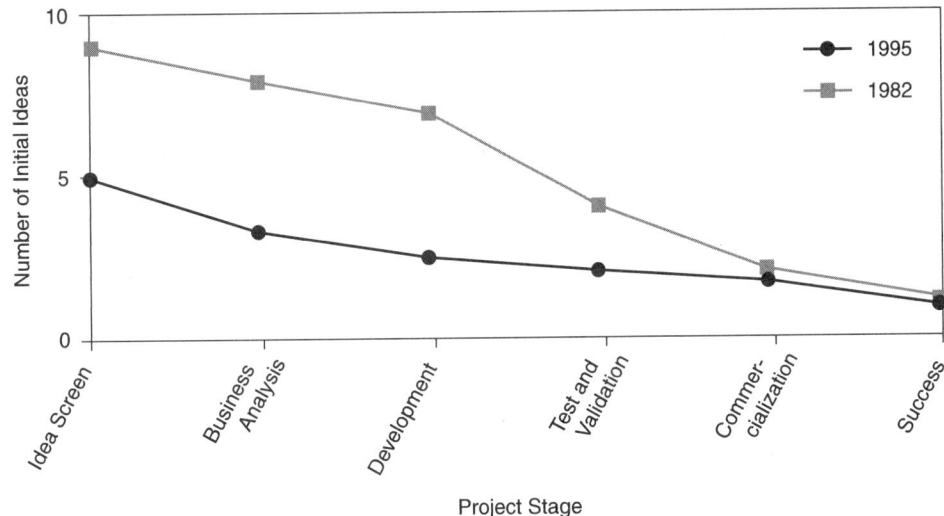

development for a number of reasons. Sometimes available technology is unable to meet desired performance specifications or a desired price point. At other times, a firm's strategy changes, rendering the product no longer interesting, or a competitor beats the firm to the market. A firm may uncover information that suggests the product as conceived would not solve customer problems, and thus they would not purchase it. Sometimes the development team is unable to interest marketing or management in commercializing the product.

Even if a product makes it to market, it can be a failure. On average, only about 55 percent of products that are launched are categorized as successes by the commercializing firms.[13] Products can fail due to either strategic or development process factors, or some combination of the two. Strategic reasons that products fail in the marketplace include:

- Failure to provide an advantage or performance improvement to customers over products already available in the market
- Lack of synergy with the technologies and manufacturing processes of the firm, requiring that the firm learn about how to design and make new technologies
- Marketing synergies lack necessary distribution channels, promotion and selling practices, or pricing policies, often because the product targets a group to whom the firm has never before marketed a product.

Additionally, products may not be successful in the marketplace because different aspects of the new product development process were not executed effectively. The most important aspects to manage effectively in the process are the predevelopment stages (idea generation and screening, preliminary investigation, and detailed investigation) and the proficiencies of both the technological and marketing-related activities within them. Failure also results when a firm fails to develop a well-thought-out **project strategy** at the outset of the process. Lack of strategy can lead to a mistargeted product, or one that lacks benefit. Finally, projects that have not garnered upper management support throughout the development process are more likely to be failures in the marketplace. Lack of management support can lead to performance that is not quite high enough to win sales, or inadequate marketing expenditures to create adequate awareness and trial when the product is launched. The next sections provide insights into how to prevent most of these failures.

Requirements for Developing Successful New Products

The objective for marketing professionals and new product development teams (NPT) is to create a series of Palm Pilots for their firm. The key is to do this not just once, but systematically and repeatedly. Actually, effective product development only requires that a firm successfully complete three activities:

1. Uncover unmet needs and problems
2. Develop a competitively advantaged product
3. Shepherd products through the firm

These three activities are simple enough in concept. Unfortunately, none of them is easy to complete. Further, if any one activity is not fully completed, the product is unlikely to succeed in the marketplace. Each activity requires that the firm master a different set of complex issues. Each issue must also be addressed across functional lines. Marketing cannot address the issues alone; neither can engineering or any other functional area. For example, developing a competitively advantaged product requires: (1) input from customers on unmet needs; (2) input from marketing as to what the competition is doing to address the need; (3) input from manufacturing about what the firm can currently build to satisfy the need; (4) input from engineering as to what additional technologies are available; (5) input from R&D about new ways of potentially addressing the need; and (6) input from finance about costs. Excelling at each NPD activity requires cooperation across multiple departments, which is still difficult to achieve in many corporations.

Another difficulty in implementing these activities arises because firms do not undertake product development solely for one purpose. Growing a business over time requires a continual process of repeatedly recommercializing old products to maintain (or grow) the firm's presence in current markets and commercializing new products to expand the firm's market presence. The activities required for sustaining current business through NPD, however, may differ from those needed for expanding market presence.

A product development team working on the next generation Palm Pilot product, for example, starts from an already available base of features, software, and manufacturing assets. All of these must be taken into account in developing a new version so that already obtained economies are not lost. Their task for the next cycle may be to gather more in-depth information, but in a narrower area of function or use, as they already have a great deal of knowledge concerning the needs of all potential customers—both existing and unrealized. *Potential customers* are the population of people or organizations who have the problem your product is trying to solve. If you are the Palm Pilot group, your potential customers are people who need to keep their complex lives organized. These people may use many different products to solve their problem. *Existing customers* are the subset of potential customers who already use your firm's products. They are already satisfied enough with your product line to purchase it. The product development team gathers further input, usually in narrow areas of function or use, from existing customers to produce refinements for the next generation of a product. But it is not until the firm understands the needs of *unrealized customers*—potential customers who are not yet using the firm's product offerings—that the firm can develop products that truly expand its market and go beyond the needs of current customers.

Fulfilling all three requirements for successful NPD results in profits, market share, and customer satisfaction.

Uncovering Unmet Needs and Problems

DEFINING CUSTOMER NEEDS Customer needs are the problems that a person or firm would like to have solved. They describe what products let you do, not how they let you do it. Customers have general problems they want solved that relate to overall product performance. These needs are readily obvious. For example, people need to "be able to communicate with others when we are not together."

Products deliver solutions to customers' problems. Telephone service solves the problem of communicating with others when we are far away, as long as the other person also has a telephone and you know the phone number (or can get it). Every competitor knows that they must develop a way to transport voices from one location to another. The traditional telephone systems' wires deliver the general function of "transporting my voice from here to there." New services may use satellites.

Customers also have very specific needs or details of the overall function that a product must solve to be truly successful. These detailed needs can be more difficult to learn, because most detailed needs are specific to particular contexts in which the product is used.

No product is perfect. Each product is a compromise, in that it only partially solves a complex set of customer problems. Ultimately, products are sets of features that deliver extremely well against some needs, adequately against others, and not at all against others. Over time, customers choose products with the set of features that delivers the maximum benefit for them. Although technologies and competitors evolve, customer needs tend to be more stable than product features.

The lessons gleaned from these examples are threefold. First, customer needs are complex. Second, developing successful products requires understanding the details of needs. Finally, while needs are rather stable, potential features and technologies change over time. Firms must repeatedly return to the drawing board to understand which new set of compromises customers prefer. Providing product development teams with a rich understanding of complex and detailed customer needs and problems prepares them to select the best technology and feature compromises to continue delivering successful products in the future.

METHODS FOR UNDERSTANDING CUSTOMER NEEDS Realistically, customers cannot tell firms exactly what products to develop. Customers are unlikely to have the technical understanding necessary to describe new features or technologies a product should have or forecast what features will best serve those needs in the future. They also cannot provide reliable information about anything with which they are not personally familiar or with which they have no experience. By definition, then, customers are not familiar with a new product a firm may be thinking of developing, and cannot provide fully reliable information when asked to react to a **concept** or **prototype.**

Does that mean that firms should not try to understand customer needs and problems? Not at all. Customers can indeed provide reliable information about products they have used and situations they have experienced. They will readily talk about problems they have had and product uses that are relevant to them. They can discuss which products and features they currently use to meet their needs—where these products fall short, where they excel, and why.

Customer needs are often ascertained initially through qualitative market research. Qualitative market research is often conducted with a small number of customers. Three methods are especially useful for gathering customer needs qualitatively: *becoming the people with the problems* the firm wants to solve, *critically observing those with the problems* of interest, and *talking to (interviewing) people in depth about their problems*. Each method produces slightly different kinds of information. No one technique is sufficient to produce a full understanding of needs. The best results are obtained when a product development team uses multiple methods to understand people's problems in great detail. Once a full set of needs has been gathered, then a number of different quantitative market research techniques can be used to predict which needs are more important.

BECOMING THE CUSTOMER: DISCOVERING PROBLEMS An enormous amount of customer knowledge and understanding can be gained by putting development team members into situations where they "become" customers and experience the problems firsthand that the firm is trying to solve. This method encourages team members to use the firm's products, and all competitors' products, in everyday as well as extraordinary situations.

Having employees become actively involved customers is the best way, sometimes the only way, to transfer **tacit knowledge** to the product development team. Becoming a routine customer for all the different products in a category may also be the most efficient way to expose development teams to the trade-offs others have made in their products and the effects these decisions have had on product function. While this technique brings rich data to the product development team, it has several inherent problems:

- The firm must learn how to transfer one person's experience and tacit knowledge to another.
- If experiences are not recorded, retaining personal knowledge becomes a critical issue if team members frequently shift jobs or leave the firm.
- Project management must take steps to ensure that team members understand that their own needs differ from needs of the "average" customer in unexpected ways.
- Being a customer takes time, money, and personal team member effort.

While personally gathering customer information is not possible in all product areas, with a little imagination it is more feasible than many firms currently realize.

ANTHROPOLOGICAL EXCURSIONS: LIVE WITH AND CRITICALLY OBSERVE CUSTOMERS Product developers who cannot become customers may be able to observe and question customers as they use products to solve problems. Developers of new medical devices for doctors cannot act as doctors and personally test devices in patient situations. However, they can observe operations, even videotape them, and then debrief doctors about what happened and why.

Sometimes observing customers in their natural settings leads directly to new products or features. Critical observation, rather than just casual viewing, is a major key to obtaining information by watching customers. Critical observation involves questioning *why* people are performing each action rather than just accepting what they are doing. The best results are achieved when team members spend significant time with enough different customers to be exposed to the full breadth of problems people encounter. They must spend enough time observing customers to uncover both normal and abnormal operating conditions. Using team members responsible for different functions is important because people with different training and expertise "see" and pay attention to different things.

Anthropological excursions identify tacit information and expose team members to customer language. It is the most effective means for gathering workflow or process-related information. These customer needs are particularly important for firms marketing products to other firms. Products they develop must fit into the workflow of those firms, which means the workflows must be fully understood. Even when questioned in detail, people frequently forget steps in a process or skip over them. Although forgotten in the course of the interviews, these steps may be crucial to product design trade-offs.

Observing and living with customers is not especially efficient. Its problems include:

- Significant team member time and expense. Events unfold slowly in real time; there are no shortcuts.
- "Natural" actions may not be captured. Videotaping or observation, no matter how well designed and intentioned, is intrusive by nature and may change behavior.
- Observations must be interpreted through the filter of team members' own experiences. It is a challenge for the team to turn observed actions into words that reliably capture customer needs.

Being customers and critically observing customers are powerful techniques for gathering rich, detailed data on customer problems. However, both activities require significant amounts of time that may not be available in every product development project. These techniques are best used in an ongoing way to continually expand a group's knowledge of customer problems. When time is short, the only means to rapidly gather customer needs is to talk to customers and get them to tell you their problems.

Voice of the customer (VOC)
One-on-one interviewing process to elicit an in-depth set of customer needs.

TALK TO CUSTOMERS TO GET NEEDS AND PROBLEMS By talking to customers, NPD teams can gather needs faster and more efficiently than by being or observing customers. A structured, in-depth, probing, one-on-one, situational interview technique called **voice of the customer** (**VOC**) can uncover both general and very detailed customer needs.[14] This method differs from standard qualitative techniques in the way questions are asked. Rather than asking customers "what do you want" directly, VOC uses indirect questions to discover wants and needs by leading customers through the ways they currently solve particular problems. VOC asks questions about functions rather than about products. Probing *why* uncovers needs.

One advantage of interviewing is that many different use situations can be investigated in a short period of time, including a range of both normal and abnormal situations. Each different use situation provides information about additional dimensions of functional performance. A good way to start an interview is to ask customers to tell about the last time they found themselves in a particular situation.

Buried in the stories customers tell about specific use instances are the nuggets of needs. Through indirect questioning, customer needs that relate to technical design aspects can be obtained, even from nontechnical customers.

While VOC is not difficult, it gathers needs differently than other qualitative market research techniques. It results in a much larger list of very detailed and context- or situation-specific customer needs. This is because the objective of VOC is to obtain a level of detail that enables teams to make engineering trade-offs during product development.

There are several keys to successfully obtaining the voice of the customer. First, it is critical to ask about functions (what customers want to do), not features (how it is done). Continually probing about why a feature is wanted or works well reveals underlying needs. Only by understanding functional needs can teams make appropriate technology and feature trade-offs in the future. A second key is that VOC only covers reality. People who have never been on one cannot accurately tell you what they would like on a romantic picnic because they really do not know. Anything they say is conjecture. The final key to success is to ask detailed questions about specific use instances. General questions ("tell me about going on picnics") elicit general needs. General needs are not as useful to the development team for designing products as are details of needs, which are obtained through using specific questions ("tell me about the last time you went on a romantic picnic"). Customers can provide tremendous levels of detail when asked to relate the story of a specific situation that occurred in the last year.

While VOC provides numerous verbal details about problems directly usable by the team, it has several drawbacks:

- The development team obtains a better understanding of a fuller set of detailed needs if the team interviews customers, but this adds to the team's development tasks.
- Interviewing customers is a nontraditional task for many team members (e.g., engineers, accountants).
- Extreme care must be taken to maintain the words of the customer and not translate individual problems into solutions before understanding the full set of customer needs.
- Tacit and process-related needs may not be complete.

No one technique easily provides all the customer needs knowledge that product development teams seek. Tacit needs are best discovered by being a customer. Process-related needs are identified most easily by critically observing customers. In-depth interviewing is the most efficient means to obtain masses of detailed needs, but may not provide tacit and process-related information. Unfortunately, few projects can afford the time and expense of fully using all these processes. Development teams need to use the most appropriate one(s), given the project's informational requirements, budget, and time frame. Once needs have been gathered, the team can turn to developing a competitively advantaged product that fully solves customers' problems.

Developing a Competitively Advantaged Product

Developing competitively advantaged products consistently over time is aided by having a strategy for what will be done and a process for how it will be accomplished. Firms with both a new product development strategy and a formal process for doing so demonstrate superior performance in terms of percentage of sales by new products, success rates, and meeting sales and profit objectives.[15]

Product Development Strategy

"If you don't know where you are going, any road will get you there." New product strategy provides the long-term destination for where the firm is going. Effective strategies for product development flow from the overall business strategy of the firm. For example, if the firm's stated strategy is to be a low-cost manufacturer, then an effective new product strategy for the business unit probably is not to develop a continuous stream of technologically leading-edge products. A more effective new product strategy might be to continually improve the cost-effectiveness of the manufacturing processes.

Effective strategies consist of a set of clear new product goals that derive directly from the overall business strategy. Areas of strategic focus can be defined in a number of ways, including:

- Markets or market segments
- Product types or categories (such as by newness categories)
- Product lines
- Technologies or technology platforms

Areas of strategic focus are then selected and prioritized, and a plan for how to attack each area is developed. A plan of attack defines the way in which the firm will compete in each strategic arena.

PROJECT STRATEGY Even after the new product development strategy for the business unit is set, a strategy for each individual product development project must be developed. A project strategy is the specific plan of how this project will proceed and why. An effective project strategy states the reasons the firm is undertaking a project and identifies specific business goals for the product. For example, it outlines whether the firm is undertaking this project to meet a previously unmet customer need, to update performance in a current product, or to counteract share losses from a newly commercialized competitive product. Each project's goals will depend, in part, on why the project is being undertaken. For example, the goal for a performance-improvement project may be increased share or customer satisfaction while maintaining profitability.

The strategy also describes the target market and core benefit proposition (CBP) for the product. It details the firms or individuals who are expected to purchase the new product. Some project teams draw pictures or create collages of people in the target market, **customer prototypes,** and hang them on the walls to remind themselves who the target market is as the project moves forward.

Finally, successful strategies require a schedule to establish key milestones, including the planned market introduction date. The schedule helps keep the team task-focused, and helps managers across the company identify key resources and activities that will be required to achieve success. Once the team and management agree on the project purposes, goals, timing, and required resources, they are ready to proceed to development.

A FRAMEWORK FOR MANAGING PRODUCT DEVELOPMENT: STAGE-GATE PROCESSES A formal **product development process,** such as that illustrated in Exhibit 300.9, outlines the normal way NPD proceeds at the firm. It defines which functions (i.e., marketing or engineering) are responsible for performing what tasks, in what order, and in conjunction with what other tasks and functions. A formalized process institutionalizes learning about what works and does not work, and how interdependent steps must be completed. Projects that follow a formalized product development process are more successful, and firms that are the best at new product development are more likely to use formalized processes for new product development.[16] Firms without formalized NPD processes depend on one or a few product development "craftsmen" who "just know how to do it." If they leave the firm, NPD knowledge leaves with them.

Most firms use a formal **Stage-Gate process** to organize the tasks for developing new products (see Exhibit 300.10). Stage-Gate processes are organized and consistent, and can be understood by and deployed across all those involved in NPD projects at a firm. Personnel responsible for each function complete tasks that are related to that function at each stage. The process acknowledges that different functions require a different expertise in each stage, all of which are nec-

Exhibit 300.9 *NPD Process Tasks and Road Map*

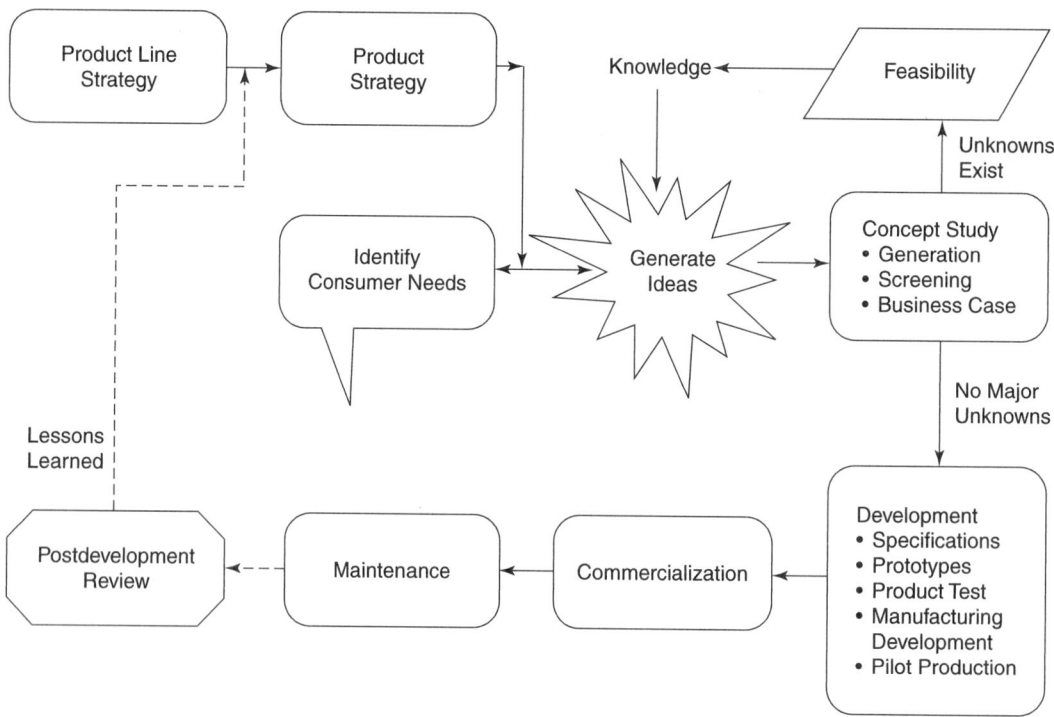

Exhibit 300.10 *A Stage-Gate Approach to NPD*

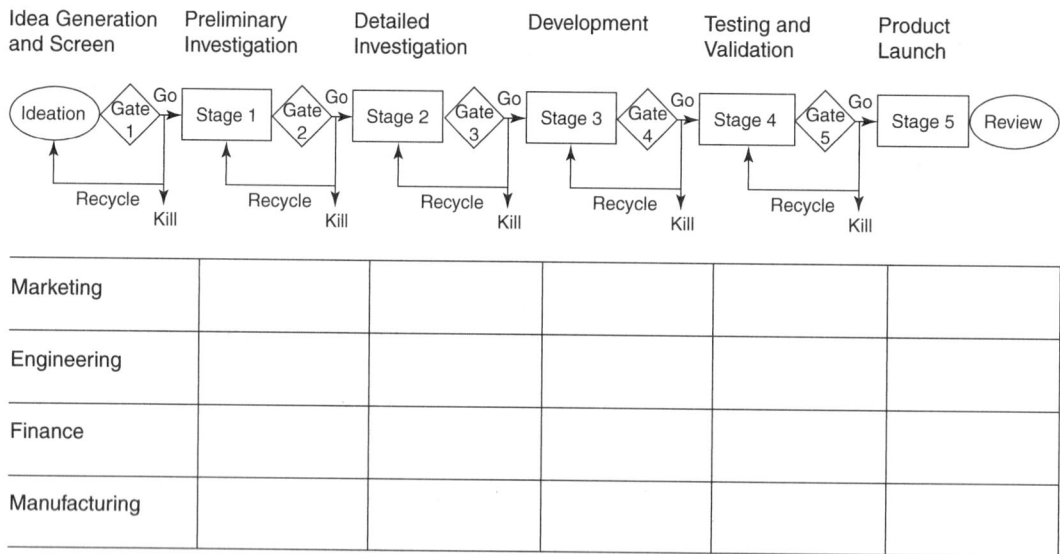

essary to successfully complete the stage. Thus, it encourages cross-functional teamwork and problem solving. As the goals for each stage are completed, management reviews progress at a gate meeting, determines whether the criteria necessary to move forward have been met, approves the tasks and resources for the next stage (go), asks for more information (recycle), or stops the project (kill). A well-designed process ensures that senior management participates in the NPD process where there is a significant jump in risk or cost.

Individual firms implement the Stage-Gate process differently, personalizing it to meet the needs of their corporation.

Generate and Screen Ideas The objective of this stage is to create one or more "interesting" new product ideas. An interesting idea solves customer problems, fits the business unit's strategy and capabilities, and presents a profit-making opportunity at reasonable risk, given the size of the profit potential. In this step, ideas are first generated and then screened against a set of criteria to determine which provide the greatest opportunity for the firm. At the end of this stage, a small number of ideas that have been screened for fit and potential reward will be ready to move forward into the next stage of development.

Ideas come from many sources. Customers may ask directly for a new product or feature. Competitors may introduce a new product that sparks an idea to counteract their effort. Employees frequently have new product ideas they are eager to suggest. Alternatively, creativity sessions can be held specifically to generate new ideas. Frequently, the problem is not generating ideas but gathering ideas from a wide variety of sources so they can be evaluated. Some firms use a database or construct a new product idea bulletin board on their intranet to collect and retain ideas over time.

The objective of idea screening is to evaluate new product ideas rationally and consistently over time, and to maintain the integrity of the process as product development team membership evolves. Initial idea screening is done based on what management already knows, rather than on information specifically developed for the project. Many firms develop a standard set of criteria that managers can use to consistently evaluate ideas. Exhibit 300.11 lists **AT&T's** idea-screening criteria. Other firms numerically rate each idea against objectives, as illustrated in Exhibit 300.12, where a larger number indicates a better rating. Ideas proceed to the next phase based either on their absolute overall rating or their rating relative to the other ideas considered.

Idea generation and screening can be completed relatively quickly, sometimes in days or hours. The resources required are usually minimal, consisting predominantly of management time, the cost of developing and maintaining an idea database, and the cost of running creativity sessions.

Preliminary Investigation   This stage develops preliminary market assessments, technical feasibility assessments, and financial assessments. This is the up-front homework necessary before detailed design work can start. Typically a small, focused, multifunctional core team of marketing and technical specialists performs this step using available resources and knowledge. At the end of the preliminary investigation, the team will know whether unknowns exist, and thus whether the project must be routed back through a research step to demonstrate feasibility, or whether the project can proceed to a detailed investigation that builds a business case based on new and more detailed information.

Exhibit 300.11   *Potential Idea Evaluation Criteria*

- **Will the market care?**
  How will consumers benefit?
  What is the total market potential?

- **Will it be important to this firm?**
  Does it fit with our strategy and goals?
  Will it create shareholder value?
  Can we obtain sufficient market share?
  Will it provide us with a comparative advantage?

- **Does it fit with our firm's capabilities?**
  Does it match our technology infrastructure?
  Does it match our marketing capabilities?
  Can we produce at a cost that will provide profits?

Exhibit 300.12   *Evaluating Ideas by Rating Them against Objectives*

	Idea 1	Idea 2	Idea 3	Idea 4
Meets customer needs	3	5	3	1
Fits manufacturing capability	1	3	5	1
Fits our strategy	5	3	1	3
Large market size	5	5	1	3
Noncyclical market	3	1	3	1
Fits distribution	5	5	1	1
Sum	22	22	14	10

The preliminary market assessment is a quick-and-dirty market study using data that can be quickly assembled to answer several questions: market attractiveness and potential, probable customer acceptance of the concept, and competitive intensity. The preliminary technical assessment identifies the key technical risks and how each might be overcome. The firm's technical staff—R&D, engineering, and manufacturing—develop rough initial technical and performance specifications and pinpoint specific technical risks in both product and manufacturing process design. Regulatory issues and competitors' patent situations also are reviewed. The preliminary financial assessment is an initial check that the project has enough revenue and profit potential to warrant continuation. At this point, potential volume, revenue and cost per item, and total development cost are extremely speculative, so these estimates are no more than ballpark figures.

Because the information used in the analyses is only that which is readily available within the firm, preliminary investigation can be completed relatively quickly, generally within a few weeks. However, completing this step requires inputs from manufacturing, technologists, marketers, and financial analysts. Thus, a lack of support by management, or from any of these functional units, can delay completion. Research has repeatedly shown that the quality of the up-front homework in preliminary investigation and business case development is strongly associated with increased new product success. A major objective, then, is to obtain functional support for each task in this stage so that high-quality answers are generated.

Detailed Investigation   Detailed investigation builds a business case for the project that provides enough solid information to upper management so that it can approve the resources necessary for product development. The business case defines and justifies the project, and details the plan for completing the project. The cross-functional team that develops the business case becomes the core of the team that will take the project through development and into the marketplace. At the end of this stage, management has all the information it needs to make a go or kill decision on the project, and the team will be poised to move rapidly into the more expensive phases of development.

Justification requires completing a *market analysis, technical assessment, concept test, competitive analysis,* and a *detailed financial analysis.* The market analysis quantifies market size and growth and analyzes market segments and buyer behavior. A competitive analysis identifies competitors and competing products, including details of product strengths and deficiencies. The team analyzes competitor strategies, position in the market, and performance. These serve as inputs for developing the marketing strategy for product commercialization. The financial analysis includes a cash flow analysis that takes into account the required timing and level of investment. This is possible because the team now has a much more detailed definition of the product specifications.

The difference between the preliminary investigation and this stage is that detailed investigation requires gathering and generating new information, rather than relying on what a firm already knows. That is, a product is defined based on the combination of a user needs study and a detailed technical assessment. A needs study may use any of the market research techniques covered earlier in this section. This information is gathered from potential customers in the target market. It cannot be developed just through internal knowledge. Additional quantitative market research may be done to understand the relative importance of different needs, preferred trade-offs between requirements, and to assess competitive product performance. The development team then translates market inputs into a technically feasible product by determining what aspects of performance deliver each customer need, developing performance specifications, and assuring feasibility of achieving those specifications. Assuring feasibility may require some laboratory work. The technologists map out the technical solutions to achieving performance and develop the route that will get them to that technical solution. Concept manufacturability is investigated simultaneously to ensure that the product can be made.

The final component of the business case is the plan of action. This includes a go/kill recommendation and a detailed plan for how physical development, testing, and manufacturing development will proceed. The plan also specifies the intended launch date for the product.

The detailed investigation stage has high levels of interdependency across tasks (see Exhibit 300.13), and is the first stage that requires a reasonable investment of time, money, and people to provide quality results. The resources required will depend on the size, complexity, and degree of uniqueness of the project. A firm can expect that even the smallest projects may require a team of three to five individuals (because each function must be represented), working at least half-time over a period of one to four months. Larger, more complex projects, however, may require four to six people working full-time for up to six months to a year. Spending enough time, money, and personnel resources during this stage in order to produce-high quality definitions, justifications, and plans saves a much larger amount of spending later to fix problems that arise because they were not dealt with in the initial phases of the project.

Development   The actual design and physical development of the product takes place during the development stage. The outputs of this stage are:

- A prototype that has been tested in-house for performance and in a limited way with customers for preliminary reaction

Exhibit 300.13 *Task Interdependencies in Building a Business Case*

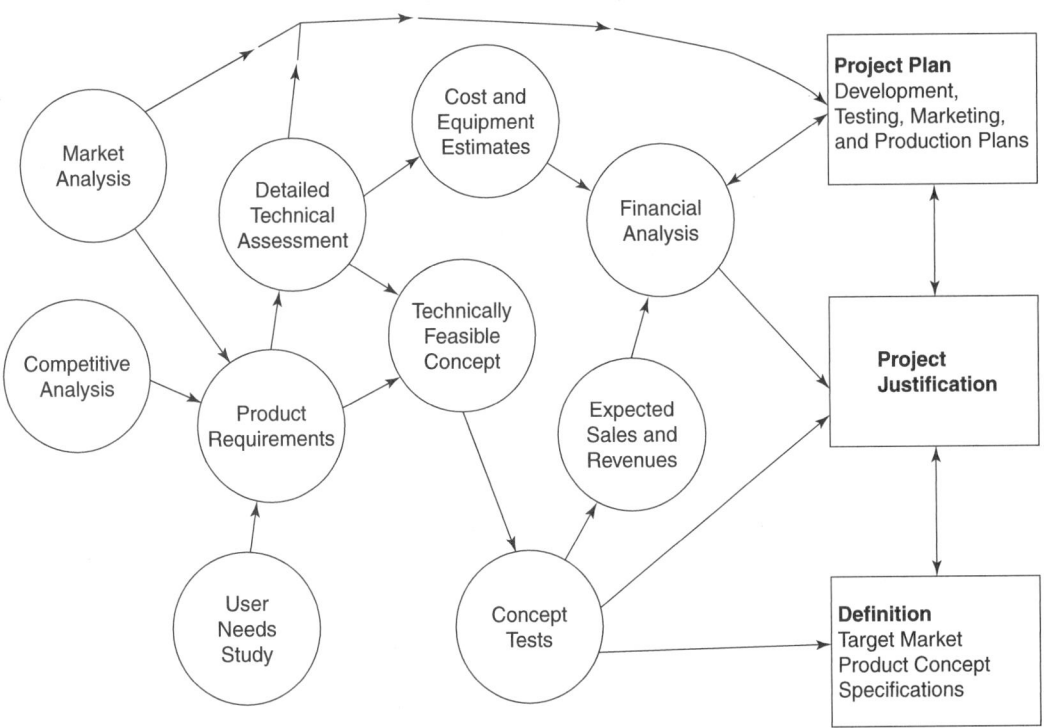

- A mapped-out manufacturing process, with critical aspects pilot tested
- A marketing launch plan
- A test and validation plan

In development, team size and resource consumption peak. Different parts of the project move forward in parallel, completed by different subgroups of the team. While some tasks can be completed by one function relatively independently, many others still require extensive interaction across functions. At the heart of a successful development stage is a plan that drives the process by organizing the efforts of all of those involved. It includes a chronological listing of tasks and the individuals responsible for completing them, with expected stop and start dates. Successful project leaders expect team members to adhere to the time lines and milestones, and proactively manage the project based on them. Project management plans can only be followed when the unknowns have been eliminated from the project prior to development.

Development time increases with the size and complexity of a project. Additionally, the relative newness of a project impacts development time. New-to-the-world projects average about 3.5 years to complete, new-to-the-firm projects take just over 2 years, major revisions of current projects require 1.5 years, line extensions 1 year, and incremental improvements take about 9 months.[17] Team size ranges from two to three people for incremental improvements to relatively simple projects such as shampoos or other customer packaged goods to hundreds, or even thousands, of people when a large and complex new-to-the-firm or new-to-the world project is undertaken. Boeing assembled an entire hierarchy of teams in developing the 777 airplane, with the total staff involved numbering in the thousands.

Testing and Validation This stage provides final project validation. The product, production process, and marketing strategy plan are all put through verification tests. The objectives are to provide management with final proof that expectations for the project in terms of performance, volume, and profit will be met, and to eliminate any final bugs in the product, process, and marketing plan. The product typically undergoes customer field trials for performance verification, and test marketing or limited rollout for testing the marketing plan. Pilot or trial production of the manufacturing process is used to produce the products tested with customers to ensure that the process operates as designed. Finally, based on the results from the field and plant trials, the expected financial outcomes are updated. Results from the field, plant, and financial analyses are presented to management for a final go/kill decision, and to obtain the investment for a full market launch.

The time and effort required in testing and validation varies greatly with the size, complexity, and newness of the project. Field-testing with customers can require as little as a week for a limited test with a few customers to as much as a year for a full test market. The expense can be as little as the cost of producing one or two products, or run as much as 5 percent of the estimated expense of going to market.

Commercialization and Launch The final activity in new product development is commercialization, the beginning of full production and commercial selling. Some of the team members on the project may change as the marketing and sales functions ramp up activities to implement the communications plan, marketing launch plan, and sales plan. Manufacturing also may add people to the team as they deploy production to one or more plants. However, to counterbalance these additions, some of the technical development team may move to a more limited role. While large amounts of money may be spent on advertising and communications at this stage, the project finally starts generating income.

Shepherding Products through the Firm

Even if a firm has uncovered a customer problem and developed a competitively advantaged product that solves the problem, it still may not be able to profit from that effort if the firm cannot bring the product to market through its own corporate infrastructure. Shepherding products through the firm is done by putting in place appropriate organizational processes, which includes developing project leaders to lead the NPD process and navigate the politics of the organization, providing appropriate organizational structures within which to manage projects, and ensuring upper management support.

LEADING NPD PROJECTS NPD project leaders fulfill a number of roles. The leader ensures that the NPD process is followed, that tasks are assigned to those who can complete them, and that those tasks are completed in a timely manner. The leader may help protect the team from external interference and may ensure that necessary resources are available to the team. Generally, the leader represents the team in formal meetings and reviews with management. Leaders can also play other roles including coaching and developing team personnel.

Project leadership can take several forms including project leaders, champions, and more recently, NPD process owners. These leadership types differ in the ways in which they fulfill leadership roles. Studies of NPD projects have found that multiple types of leadership are used during development, with no one type leading to higher performance.

Project leaders, the most frequently used leadership type in NPD, are appointed by upper management and given formal power and authority to complete the project. They guard the project's objectives, continuously communicate with team members, serve as translators across different functions, and are the primary management contact point. The project leader manages the efforts of team members from the different functions. In a "lightweight" team, the leader coordinates work through liaisons (functional representatives) but has little influence over the work. In a "heavyweight" team, the leader exerts a strong, direct, integrating influence across all functions. Shifting to heavyweight teams has been credited with reducing NPD cycle time and increasing development productivity in the automotive industry.[18]

Champions generally work outside official roles and processes to informally influence others' actions, taking an acute interest in seeing that a particular project is pursued. The role may vary from little more than stimulating awareness of the opportunity to extreme cases where the champion tries to force a project past strongly entrenched internal resistance. The champion's role in new product development has been a topic of discussion for over 30 years, with champion use reported by over 40 percent of firms. While some specific NPD successes may be due to the efforts of a particular champion, using a champion does not raise the probability that any particular project will be a success.[19]

Process owners administer the formal NPD process across business groups within the firm.[20] Process owners build and maintain expertise in the NPD process, facilitating NPD process use for all projects in the firm, and in some projects additionally serve in leadership roles. Process owners may not be responsible for the success outcome of a project, just for the implementation quality of the NPD process used. Even though this leadership type is a relatively recent development, about 12 percent of reporting firms claim that process owners lead NPD projects.

MUSTERING MANAGEMENT SUPPORT FOR NPD A consistent finding for producing successful new products is tangible and visible top management commitment to NPD. While top managers formally control the budgets and plans of NPD groups only loosely, they exert considerably tighter control over them informally in the way they allocate top management attention and contact. The NPD team's goal, then, is to obtain and retain top management commitment to the project by maintaining their attention.

Getting a project favored and approved over others requires managing more than just a rational decision-making process. It requires managing the personalities and politics of the upper managers supporting NPD at a firm to convince them that the value of a particular project warrants the necessary resources they must provide. The NPD team thus needs to continually communicate with top management about the project. Firms usually have mechanisms for formally communicating with management through gate meetings and design reviews, and during the annual budgeting process. However, communication also needs to occur informally between the team and management. Some strategies include:

- Interview specific managers for their view of project expectations or customer needs
- Send out brief (one to two paragraphs), weekly e-mail updates
- Invite managers with particular areas of expertise to participate as consultants to the project
- Request management presence in the laboratory as new prototypes are unveiled
- Use one or more managers as subjects in various phases of testing
- Create a weekly or monthly project lunch and invite managers to attend
- Invite managers to after-hours team functions, such as project picnics and parties

The objectives of some interactions are to exchange information, such as informing management about the status of the project, obstacles that are creating roadblocks, or small successes such as beating completion time to a milestone. At other times, the objectives of an interaction will be more persuasive in nature. Examples include when the team is interacting to sell the project either to a potential project sponsor, is bargaining for different or additional resources, or is defending the project from criticism by another group within the firm.

Successful product development is a multifunctional effort. Marketing has an important role to play in this effort, but by themselves marketing staff cannot ensure success. Indeed, marketing will not even lead many product development efforts. However, there are other product-related decisions over which marketing does exert control. The remainder of the section covers types of product-related decisions that are solely marketing's responsibilities.

Making Product Decisions: Branding, Packaging, and Labeling[21]

Prior to the commercialization and launch stage of new product development, marketing is responsible for making a number of decisions that will help reinforce a product's competitive position in the minds of consumers. These include decisions about branding, packaging, and labeling.

Branding Decisions

Customers handle an enormous amount of information in the course of their daily activities. Consequently, they develop efficient ways of processing information in order to make purchasing decisions. Brands are one of the most fundamental pieces of information customers use to simplify choices and reduce purchase risk. Brand names assure customers that they will receive the same quality with their next purchase as they did with their last. Consequently, buyers are willing to pay a premium for quality and assurance. For this reason, branding has become an essential element of product strategy.

Brands serve important communication functions and, in doing so, establish beliefs among customers about the attributes and general image of a product. After a brand has been established, the brand name (letters or numbers used to vocalize the brand), logo (symbols such as McDonald's golden arches and **Prudential's** rock), and trademark (brand name and/or logo that is legally protected) serve to remind and reinforce the beliefs that have been formed. To arrive at this point, the firm must have made good on its promises. The case for a new brand, however, is different. A good brand name, logo, or trademark has four important characteristics. It should:

1. Attract attention
2. Be memorable
3. Help communicate the positioning of the product
4. Distinguish the product from competing brands

BRAND EQUITY Successful brands develop **brand equity.** The financial value of brand equity is enormous. For example, **Kohlberg Kravis Roberts** purchased RJR **Nabisco** for $25 billion (double its book value); **Philip Morris** paid $12.9 billion for **Kraft** (four times book value) and $5.7 billion for **General Foods** (over four times book value). Even under the generous notion that the tangible assets of these companies were undervalued by 50 percent, this still means that the reputation and goodwill of their brand names—their brand equity—were worth billions.

Brand equity The marketplace value of a brand based on reputation and goodwill.

In addition to the financial value, brand equity also has a very important strategic value. Manufacturers have become increasingly interested in marketing new products under the umbrella of well-established brand names that are already familiar to consumers. New products marketed under well-established brand names are more likely to be accepted by channel members (e.g., wholesalers and retailers) due to the proven track record of the brand and disenchantment with the risks involved in launching new brands. Strong brand equity is not only used to roll out new products, but it also helps companies break into new markets. For example, **Kodak** used its film brand equity to break into the camera market, and Lipton tea used its brand equity to launch soup mixes. Finally, brand equity can be strategically utilized as an effective barrier to entry, making it difficult for competitors to enter or expand in the market.

BRANDING STRATEGIES: INDIVIDUAL VERSUS FAMILY BRANDING When selecting branding strategies, marketers essentially have two options. The first option is to pursue an *individual brand name strategy* where each product in a company's product mix is given a specific brand name. **Procter & Gamble** and **General Mills** are often cited as prime examples of companies that employ an individual brand name strategy. The advantage of an individual brand name strategy is that it allows a firm to develop the best brand name possible for every product. In addition, an individual brand name strategy diversifies the firm's risk by not allowing individual product failures to tarnish the reputation and image of the company's other products. The downside of an individual brand name strategy is that the firm is not taking advantage of the brand equity of existing brands that may facilitate channel and consumer acceptance of new products.

The other branding option is to use a *family brand name strategy* in which all, or a significant portion, of a company's products are associated with a family brand name. The primary advantage of a family brand name strategy is that it can be used to launch new products. Firms typically extend their family brand names in two ways:

1. The family brand is extended into product categories that are used in the same situation as the original branded product or used by the consumers of the original branded product (e.g., Coke, Diet Coke, and Caffeine-Free Coke).
2. The family brand is extended to help the company introduce products into new product categories (e.g., Fisher-Price toys introduces Fisher-Price playwear).

Over the years, variations of the family branding strategy have evolved. The three most common include:

1. Blanket family name for all products; this strategy is followed by **General Electric** and **Heinz.**
2. Separate family names for types of products; this strategy is followed by **Sears Roebuck,** which markets Kenmore appliances, Craftsman tools, and DieHard batteries.
3. Family names combined with individual brand names; this strategy is pursued by **Kellogg's** (e.g., Kellogg's Raisin Bran and Kellogg's Corn Flakes).

A strong family brand name will grab the customer's attention and may lead to product trial. It provides a foot in the door. Family branding is most effective when it is applied to a product that is complementary in usage to the original branded product.

Packaging Decisions

Each year, companies spend more on packaging than on advertising. As markets have matured and competitive differentiation has narrowed, packaging has become a very important component of marketing strategy. Sometimes a firm forgets that it is the packaged product, and not the product alone, that is sold and purchased. A product's package is often its most distinctive marketing effort. Packaging performs a number of essential functions.

- *Protection:* A package must protect the product in several different situations: in the manufacturer's warehouse, during shipment to the wholesaler and retailer, in the seller's warehouse, and in transporting the product from the seller's store to the consumer's final point of consumption.
- *Identification:* A product's package, particularly one that is distinctive, helps customers identify the product in a crowded marketplace. The classic case of an eye-catching display was the L'Eggs point-of-purchase stand with hundreds of plastic eggs in different colors.
- *Information:* The package provides another means of communicating with the customer. An informed customer gets the very best performance out of a product.
- *Packaging to enhance usage:* Several very innovative packages have added real convenience to product use. For example, when Beech-Nut apple juice switched from cans to bottles (onto which plastic nipples for babies

could be attached), sales quadrupled. Another example involved Chesebrough-Ponds who put nail polish in a special type of felt tip pen. The new packaging helped increase sales by over 20 percent.
- *Packaging to enhance disposal:* A package that is biodegradable, or made from recycled materials, will appeal to environmentally conscious market segments. Downy's (fabric softener) change to milk carton refills for fabric softener was to minimize plastic waste.
- *Packaging to enhance channel acceptance:* New shipping and warehouse technology may require standard package dimensions. *Cubic efficiency* is a term that describes how efficiently a package occupies storage, transportation, and display space. Boxes are more cubic efficient than cans, and cans are more efficient than most bottles. Packaging that suits the needs of channel members is more apt to be adopted over competitive packaging that does not.

Ultimately, effective packaging adds to the value of a product. For instance, opening and resealing, pouring, mixing, processing, and cooking may all be enhanced or made easier by creative packaging. A package also continues to communicate on the kitchen shelf, workshop bench, and, most importantly, during product use. Firms that underestimate the power of a product's packaging are making a major tactical mistake.

Labeling Decisions

A customer can tell a lot about a company by the labels it places on its products. If the label appears to be an afterthought, and contains only what is legally required, then the customer will likely conclude that the company doesn't care. On the other hand, a customer-oriented label is likely to serve the following six functions:

1. Identify the manufacturer, country of origin, and ingredients or materials comprising the product
2. Report the expiration date and the contents' grading based on a prescribed government standard (as on cartons of eggs)
3. Explain how to use the product
4. Warn about potential misuse
5. Provide easy-to-understand care instructions
6. Serve as an important communication link between the users, eventual buyers, and the company

A quality label signals a quality product. Often the label must also be designed for a particular market segment. For example, seniors need labels with large lettering. Furthermore, because many customers toss instructions and packaging away, often the only way a customer can reach a manufacturer is through the information provided on the label.

Product Management: Managing Products through Their Life Cycles

A product now has been designed, developed, and tested; brand, label, and package decisions have been made. As product development nears completion, product management is just beginning. The product must now be introduced to the market, and strategies for generating profit over the life of the *product category* (all brands that satisfy a particular need) must be developed and implemented. Exhibit 300.14 shows the general pattern of expected sales and profit over the **product life cycle.** *Innovators* and *early adopters,* customers generally willing to take more risk, buy the product shortly after introduction. During growth, product purchase begins to spread to the *early majority* of the mass market, with full penetration and adoption by the *late majority* occurring primarily in the maturity stage. Near the product's decline, only *laggards* are left purchasing the product. Marketing strategy and tactics must be adapted to meet the special opportunities and challenges presented by each stage of the life cycle, as illustrated in Exhibit 300.15.

Introduction Strategies

The introduction stage starts when a new product is presented to the market. Initial sales are slow, as potential customers must go through a learning process about the new product and its benefits before they purchase. Creating customer learning requires heavy expenditures in advertising, sampling, promotion, distribution, and personal selling, all of which contribute to profit losses at this stage. The set of marketing tactics employed must work together to make customers aware of the product and encourage them to try it.

Exhibit 300.14 *The Product Life Cycle*

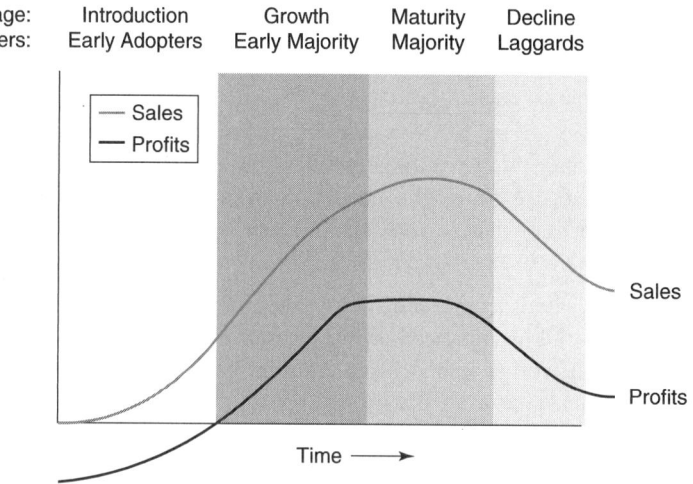

Exhibit 300.15 *Marketing Tactics and Outcomes Through the Product Life Cycle*

Outcomes	Introduction	Growth	Maturity	Decline
Sales	Low	Fast growth	Slow growth	Decline
Profits	Negligible	Positive to flat	Flat to declining	Low or zero
Cash flow	Negative	Moderate	High	Low
Customers	Innovative	Mass market	Mass market	Laggards
Competitors	Few	Growing	Many rivals	Declining number
Tactics	Introduction	Growth	Maturity	Decline
Strategic focus	Expanded market	Market penetration	Defend share	Productivity
Expenditures	High	High (declining %)	Falling	Low
Emphasis	Product awareness	Brand preference	Brand loyalty	Selective
Distribution	Patchy	Intensive	Intensive	Selective
Price	High	Lowest	Lowest	Rising
Product	Basic	Differentiated	Differentiated	Rationalized

THE INDIVIDUAL ADOPTION PROCESS Customers go through several distinct stages of learning before purchasing a new product. Ideally, a firm's marketing program helps customers move through these stages, thereby decreasing their risk in purchasing a new product. The stages customers generally go through in the *adoption process* include:

- *Awareness:* Realizing that a new product exists
- *Knowledge:* Building an understanding of what the product does, what benefits it provides, and how it works
- *Liking:* Developing positive feelings toward the product
- *Preference:* Coming to prefer this product over any other, if one were to buy
- *Purchase:* Making the decision to buy and acting upon it

To encourage adoption of a new product, firms use their marketing programs to lead potential customers through each successive stage. Before customers can develop knowledge about what a new product does, they must first have become aware that it exists. Frequently product introductions are accompanied by large initial advertising campaigns designed specifically to create awareness. Only after people develop knowledge about a product can they come to a conclusion as to whether they like it. Preference can only develop for products a person likes, which may lead to even-

Exhibit 300.16 *Factors Influencing the Rate of New Product Adoption*

- **Simplicity:** The easier it is to understand and use a new product, the faster it will be adopted by potential customers.
- **Pre-Sale:** The longer a new product is offered as a trial item, the faster it will be adopted by potential customers.
- **Visibility:** The longer a new product is known to consumers, the faster it will be adopted by potential customers.
- **Consumer Fit:** The greater the fit between a new product and a new customer in terms of price, value, and need, the faster it will be adopted by potential customers.

Source: Adapted from *Winning at New Products,* by Robert G. Cooper, p. 140. Copyright 1993 by Perseus Books, L.L.C.

Exhibit 300.17 *Customer Profiles*

- **Innovators:** Innovators, 2.5% of all potential adopters, tend to be younger, higher in social status, more cosmopolitan, and better educated than later adopter groups.
- **Early adopters:** Early adopters, 13.5% of potential adopters, enjoy the prestige and respect that comes with owning new products, but are less venturesome and more concerned with group norms and values than innovators.
- **Early majority:** The early majority, 34% of potential adopters, spends more time deciding whether to try new products and seeks the opinions of the innovators and early adopters.
- **Late majority:** The late majority, 34% of potential adopters, is less cosmopolitan and responsive to change than any of the previous groups.
- **Laggards:** 16% of all potential adopters, laggards tend to be conservative, older, low socioeconomic status, and suspicious of change.

tual purchase. The time frame required for new product acceptance varies widely from product to product. Some of the factors that influence this rate of adoption are listed in Exhibit 300.16.

The elements of the marketing program in the introduction stage of a new product's life cycle are designed to move more innovative customers (early adopters) swiftly through the learning process to purchase. Customers will be slower to adopt products that are more radically innovative, such as microwave ovens when they were first introduced in the 1970s, and products that are expensive, such as the Apple Newton. More innovative and expensive products require higher marketing effort, especially in the introduction stage.

THE DIFFUSION PROCESS Broad *product diffusion* into the mass market results from three processes. First, a firm's marketing program induces innovators and early adopters to purchase and try the product, as outlined above. Then, if the design team has developed a product that meets the needs of these customers, they will be satisfied with their purchase and tell other potential customers, generating free word-of-mouth product advertising. Finally, positive word-of-mouth endorsements work in concert with the firm's marketing program to help provide less innovative (more imitative) customers, who make up the bulk of most markets, with enough understanding of and confidence in the product to purchase it. For a more complete understanding of the profiles of the various types of customers that together create the market, see Exhibit 300.17.

Word-of-mouth approvals from customers reinforce the messages sent by the firm, giving them credibility. Hearing one's neighbors rave about their new Palm Pilot and how it changed the way they organize their life is much more powerful for many people than reading about what the product does in a print ad. Of course, if the product does not live up to expectations, negative word-of-mouth will be generated. This will almost certainly guarantee market failure, regardless of the quality of the marketing program used to launch the product. When **Apple's** Newton routinely failed to recognize the handwriting of early customers, negative word-of-mouth spread rapidly. Some small articles and cartoons poking fun at the problem were even published in the business press that further contributed to market failure.

Diffusion is only partly under the control of a firm. Diffusion is aided early in the development process by ensuring that the product solves the problems customers want solved, and by getting the details of the product right. Once launched, the firm can speed diffusion by developing a marketing program that maximizes the number of people who become early adopters. More early adopters mean that there are more users who can spread positive word-of-mouth endorsements to more potential customers early in the marketing cycle. Finally, a firm can encourage mechanisms to spread word-of-mouth endorsements throughout the target market. For example, **Amazon.com** allows readers to write and post book reviews that other Amazon.com customers can access. Whatever mechanisms the firm develops must work in concert with the rest of the marketing program surrounding the product launch.

Growth Strategies

The growth stage of the product life cycle is initially characterized by rapidly increasing product demand, new competitors entering the market in response, and rapidly increasing profits for the product varieties that customers decide best meet their needs. The firm's emphasis shifts to building and holding a set of loyal customers and distribution channel members, and sustaining sales growth as long as possible. To do this, they may invest in product improvements and expanding and strengthening distribution channels. As overall spending increases to offset competitive pressures, profits begin to level off as the product category leaves the growth stage and enters the maturity stage.

Maturity Strategies

Most product categories can be assigned to the maturity stage; therefore, marketing managers are most often dealing with mature products. During the maturity stage, sales initially increase but at a slower rate as the market becomes saturated and as competitive pressures reach their peak. Sales and profits typically decline in the latter half of the maturity stage.

Using the marketing program to maintain customer loyalty and satisfaction is important to maintaining profitability throughout the maturity stage. Airline frequent flyer programs, hotel honored guest programs, and grocery store frequent shopper programs all were developed to maintain customer loyalty and improve profits. The objective is to take the pressure off price reductions as a way to keep customers by using other tactics in the marketing mix. Several strategies can be used, even in maturity, to attempt to grow the market. For example, a firm can find new users (*market development*) or increase the usage rate per user (*market penetration*). Another mechanism for growth in the mature stage is to offer significant improvements on a routine basis (*product development*).

Decline Strategies

Even if new users are found and usage rates are increased, product sales may eventually start a long-term decline, as when a substitute product that offers a superior set of benefits displaces the "old" product. Products based on new technologies frequently lead to a current product's demise. For example, PCs and word-processing programs made typewriters obsolete.

Reduced sales do not necessarily mean that a firm should exit from the business immediately. The higher a firm's competitive strength in an industry, the longer it will want to stay in the market to reap returns from previous investments. However, the marketing tactics used at this stage will again have to be modified to maintain acceptable profitability levels. Marketing expenses, and promotion expenses in particular, will need to be reduced. IBM divested its typewriter division in the 1990s so that the business could continue operations without being burdened with the large overhead costs associated with IBM's traditional business structures. Products in decline continue to sell, but customer satisfaction (and thus loyalty) and word-of-mouth will become more important generators of sales than marketing campaigns.

Managing the Product Portfolio

Product Mix Decisions[22]

Product line The set of products a firm targets to one general market. These products are likely to share some common features and technology characteristics or be complementary products. They also are likely to share several elements of the marketing mix, such as distribution channels.

Few companies are successful by relying on a single product. Most companies manufacture and market a variety of products. All of the products a company markets can be thought of as its product mix. The mixture of products typically includes various items that are related in terms of the raw materials used to create them or the products' end-uses. A group of related items in a company's product portfolio constitutes a **product line.**

The *product mix width* is the number of different product lines a company offers. The *product mix depth* refers to the number of brands within each product line.

Any company limits its growth potential if it chooses to concentrate on a single product line. Companies that offer multiple product lines enjoy numerous benefits:

- *Protection against competition:* If a company relies on one product for success, a competitor can enter the market, undercut price, and steal market share. A company with more than one product line will not be devastated by the effects of a competitor's actions in any one particular area.
- *Increase growth and profits:* Companies offer more than one product line to boost market growth and company profits. If a product category is mature with little to no growth, a company may find it difficult to increase its share and profits unless it is willing to spend more to take market share away from a competitor.
- *Offset sales fluctuations:* Companies that offer products with seasonal variations find that multiple product lines help to offset these fluctuations in sales.
- *Achieve greater impact:* Multiple product lines allow a company to achieve greater market impact. A company with multiple lines of products often is more important to both consumers and channel members.
- *Enable economical resource usage:* Multiple product lines enable the economical use of resources. Spreading operational costs over a series of products enables a manufacturer to reduce the average production and marketing costs for all its products; this results in lower prices to customers.
- *Avoid obsolescence:* Companies offering more than one product line avoid becoming obsolete when one product line reaches the end of its life cycle.

Product Growth Opportunities[23]

Established products are the lifeblood of most companies. But a company that depends solely on its current assortment of products may be headed for trouble. Aggressive competitive activity or a major change in technology can cause a rapid decline in sales even for the most successful product. Growth is fundamental to the long-term success of any organization.

Growth opens up new sales and profit opportunities for a firm while reducing dependence on existing products for its success. Companies can pursue a number of growth options. Exhibit 300.18 presents four such options. A firm might attempt to grow its business through *market penetration* by selling more of its existing products to existing markets. The main objective of this strategy is to convince existing customers to purchase and use more of the firm's product. In other words, the firm is attempting to increase its current market share. Typical market penetration tactics include aggressive promotion campaigns and price discounts. Airlines, soft drink companies, and fast-food chains are examples of firms that actively pursue a market penetration strategy.

Firms that find new uses for existing products are pursuing *market development*. In this scenario, a firm attempts to grow its business by selling more of its existing products to new markets. Baking soda is the classic example. Although its original use was for baking, it is now marketed as a deodorizer, carpet cleaner, and toothpaste, among other uses. These new uses have attracted new markets and have increased the overall sales of the product. Other examples include Johnson & Johnson baby shampoo and Tony the Tiger Frosted Flakes, which are now being marketed to adults. In addition, the hair loss remedy Rogaine that was originally targeted to men is now being targeted to women with thinning hair.

Firms that develop new products that they feel will appeal to existing markets are pursuing a *product development strategy*. In this scenario, a firm seeks to provide its existing market with a variety of new choices.

The most risky growth option is *product diversification*. Under this option, firms pursue a growth strategy by developing new products that appeal to new markets. Product diversification enables a company to be less dependent on any one product or product line.

Exhibit 300.18 *Growth Strategies*

	Markets: Existing	Markets: New
Products: Existing	Market Penetration	Market Development
Products: New	Product Development	Product Diversification

Advertising and Promotion

Out of the thousands of brands on store shelves today, the odds are slim that a consumer will *see* any one particular item, much less buy it. Consumers are rushed for time; their lives are pressured; they are not often inclined to leisurely walk up and down every aisle, perusing every stock-keeping unit (SKU) available on the shelves. A brand may be of high quality and fairly valued, but it will fail to achieve sales and profit objectives if potential customers are unaware of it or do not perceive it favorably. Effective advertising and other forms of marketing communications are absolutely crucial to creating brand awareness, establishing positive brand identities, and moving products off store shelves.

Marketing communications also are critical to the success of business-to-business (B2B) marketers in their efforts to achieve market share and profit objectives. Many, if not most, B2B products share similarities from one supplier to the next. Product quality generally is not that different among competitors, and prices often are near equal. The real distinctions among B2B competitors frequently amount to created differences achieved through effective advertising and, more importantly, via superior service and personal selling efforts.

Regardless of the nature of the product category or type of business, marketing communications are key to a company's overall marketing mission and represent a major determinant of its success; indeed, it has been claimed that marketing and marketing communications are inseparable: "[M]arketing…is communication and communication is marketing."[24]

The Tools of Marketing Communications

The tools of marketing communications include personal selling, advertising, public relations, sales promotion, sponsorship marketing, and point-of-purchase communcations.

Personal Selling

B2B marketers rely especially heavily on **personal selling.** In the consumer market, products such as insurance, automobiles, and real estate are sold mainly through personal selling efforts. Historically, personal selling involved face-to-face interactions between salesperson and prospect, but telephone sales and other forms of electronic communications are increasingly being used.

Advertising

The purpose of **advertising** is to inform the end consumer or the B2B customer about the advertiser's products and brand benefits and ultimately to influence brand choice. Advertising is paid for by an identified sponsor, the advertiser, but is considered to be *nonpersonal* because the sponsoring firm is simultaneously communicating with multiple receivers, perhaps millions, rather than talking with a specific person or small group. Advertising attempts to keep both the brand's name and image in the customer's mind over a long period of time.

Public Relations

Publicity, which is the major PR tool, usually comes in the form of news items or editorial comments about a company's products. These items or comments receive free print space or broadcast time because media representatives consider the information pertinent and newsworthy for their reading or listening audiences. It is the job of a firm's public relations personnel to garner positive publicity for the company and its brands. These personnel also face the challenge of overcoming negative publicity when a company is faced with a product disaster (e.g., **Perrier** bottled water contaminated with benzene) or confronted with claims of unfavorable business practices (e.g., **Denny's** restaurants accused of racial discrimination).

Sales Promotion

Sales promotion is directed both at the trade (i.e., wholesalers and retailers) and at consumers. It is intended to create an immediate response (a need to acquire the product right now); by comparison, advertising and publicity are designed more to favorably influence consumer/customer expectations and attitudes over the long-term. *Trade-oriented sales pro-*

motions include the use of various types of allowances and merchandise assistance that activate wholesaler and retailer response. *Consumer-oriented sales promotions* include coupons, premiums, free samples, contests/sweepstakes, rebates, and other devices.

Sponsorship Marketing

In general, **sponsorship marketing** represents an opportunity for a company and its brands to directly target communications toward narrow, but highly desirable, audiences. This is accomplished by associating a brand with a charitable cause, a high-profile event, or a cultural affair. The use of sponsorship marketing generally is not expected to substitute for more traditional forms of marketing communications such as advertising, but rather to complement these activities. **Silk** soymilk, for example, uses traditional advertising but then supplements the gains from advertising with a brand presence at events where samples are distributed.

Point-of-Purchase Communications

Point-of-purchase communications are a final effort by the manufacturer to motivate consumers and encourage purchase of the manufacturer's brands. Research has shown that perhaps as many as three out of four buying decisions are made at the point of purchase. It is for this reason that various types of signs, mobiles, plaques, banners, shelf talkers, mechanical mannequins, lights, mirrors, plastic reproductions of products, checkout units, and various types of product displays are used extensively in retail outlets.

Advertising

There are three basic ways by which companies can add value to their offerings: by *innovating,* by *improving quality,* or by *altering consumer perceptions*. These three value-added components are completely interdependent. Advertising adds value to brands by influencing consumers' perceptions. Effective advertising causes brands to be viewed as more elegant, more stylish, more prestigious, perhaps superior to competitive offerings, and, in general, of higher perceived quality and/or value. When advertising is done effectively, brands are perceived as being higher quality or of better value, which in turn can lead to increased market share and greater profitability.

Advertising also can be considered an economic investment, an investment regarded favorably by numerous businesses throughout the United States and the world. The actual advertising process for a particular brand can be thought of as the development and implementation of an advertising strategy. *Advertising strategy* entails five major activities: *objective setting, budgeting, positioning, creating advertising messages, selecting advertising media,* and *assessing advertising effectiveness.*

Setting Advertising Objectives

Advertising objectives provide the foundation for all remaining advertising decisions. There are three major reasons for setting advertising objectives:

1. The process of setting objectives literally forces top marketing and advertising management to agree on the course advertising is to take for the following planning period, as well as the tasks it is intended to accomplish for a brand.
2. Objective setting guides the budgeting, message creation, and media selection aspects of advertising strategy.
3. Advertising objectives provide standards against which results can be measured.[25]

Advertisements are created to accomplish goals such as (1) making the target market aware of a new brand, (2) facilitating consumer understanding of a brand's attributes, (3) creating expectations about a brand's benefits, (4) enhancing attitudes toward the brand, (5) influencing purchase intentions, and (6) encouraging product trial.

Budgeting for Advertising

The advertising budgeting decision is, in many respects, the most important decision advertisers make. If too little money is spent on advertising, sales volume will not be as high as it could be, and profits will be lost. If too much money is spent, expenses will be higher than they need to be, and profits will be reduced.

Budgeting is also one of the most difficult advertising decisions. This difficulty arises because it is hard to determine precisely how effective advertising has been or might be in the future. The sales response to advertising is influenced by a multitude of factors (quality of advertising execution, intensity of competitive advertising efforts, customer taste, and other considerations), thereby making it difficult, if not impossible, to know with any certainty what amount of sales a particular advertising effort will generate.

Companies ordinarily set budgets by using judgment, applying experience with analogous situations, and using simple rules of thumb, or *heuristics*. Although criticized because they do not provide a basis for advertising budget setting that is directly related to the profitability of the advertised brand, these heuristics continue to be widely used.[26] The two most pervasive heuristics, in use by both industrial and consumer-goods advertisers, are the percentage-of-sales and objective-and-task methods.[27] The *percentage-of-sales method* involves allocating a fixed percentage of past or anticipated sales revenue to advertising. For example, a company may allocate 5 percent of the next fiscal period's anticipated sales to advertising. If sales are estimated to be $100 million for the upcoming year, the advertising budget will be $5 million. The *objective-and-task method* involves the following three-step procedure: (1) specifying the objectives that a particular advertisement or entire ad campaign is intended to accomplish; (2) identifying the specific tasks that must be accomplished in order to reach those objectives; and (3) accumulating anticipated costs to achieve the specified tasks. The outcome of this systematic, three-step process is an advertising budget that should be sufficient to achieve critical objectives.

Establishing the Brand Positioning

Brand managers work with their advertising agencies to formulate specific meaning for their brands. This meaning, or positioning, establishes how the brand is to be thought of by members of the target market and how the brand is to be perceived relative to competitive brands in the product category.

Creating Advertising Messages

Advertisers use a vast array of techniques to present their brands in the most favorable light and persuade customers to contemplate purchasing these brands. Frequently employed techniques include:

- Informational ads (such as automobile ads in the classified pages of a newspaper)
- Humorous executions (e.g., most Budweiser advertisements; **Holiday Inn's** advertising campaign with the 30-something slacker who lives at home with his parents and grandmother)
- Sex appeal (e.g., the attention-getting advertisement for **Emporio Armani's** fragrance)
- Celebrity endorsements (e.g., the McDonald's advertisement featuring Kobe Bryant)
- Various emotional appeals (nostalgia, romance, excitement, etc.)

The techniques to persuasively advertise products are limited only by advertisers' creativity and ingenuity. We pose a more straightforward question: What makes an advertisement good or effective? Although it is impractical to provide a single, all-purpose definition of what constitutes effective advertising, it is useful to talk about general characteristics.[28] At a minimum, good or effective advertising satisfies the following six considerations:

1. *It extends from sound marketing strategy.* Advertising can be effective only if it is compatible with other elements of an integrated and well-orchestrated marketing communications strategy.
2. *It takes the consumer's view.* Consumers buy product benefits, not attributes. Therefore, advertising must be stated in a way that relates to the consumer's needs, wants, and values and not strictly in terms of product characteristics.
3. *It is persuasive.* Persuasion usually occurs when there is a benefit for the consumer, and not just for the marketer.
4. *It finds a unique way to break through competitive clutter.* Advertisers continuously vie with competitors for the consumer's attention. This is no small task considering the massive number of print advertisements, broadcast commercials, and other sources of information available daily to consumers. Indeed, the situation in television advertising has been characterized as audiovisual wallpaper, which implies sarcastically that consumers pay just about as much attention to commercials as they do to the detail in their own wallpaper after it has been on the walls for awhile.[29]
5. *It never promises more than it can deliver.* This point speaks for itself, both in terms of ethics and in terms of smart business sense. Consumers learn quickly when they have been deceived and resent it.

6. *It prevents the creative idea from overwhelming the strategy.* The purpose of advertising is to persuade and influence; the purpose is not to be cute for cute's sake or humorous for humor's sake. The ineffective use of humor, for example, results in people remembering the humor but forgetting the selling message.

Effective advertising is usually *creative*. That is, it differentiates itself from the mass of mediocre advertisements; it is somehow different and out of the ordinary. Advertising that is the same as most other advertising is unable to break through the competitive clutter and fails to grab the consumer's attention. It is easier to give examples of creative advertising than to define exactly what it is. Here are three examples of what many advertising practitioners would consider effective, creative advertising:

1. The "Intel Inside" application of ingredient branding whereby this chip manufacturer convinced many computer purchasers that Intel chips substantially enhanced computer quality.
2. **Absolut** vodka's continuing magazine campaign that focuses on this brand's "hip" image by portraying the brand's unique bottle shape in trendy situations.
3. The milk-mustache campaign that associates drinking milk with a wide variety of interesting and respected celebrities.

Selecting Advertising Media

Outstanding message execution is to no avail unless messages are delivered to the right customers at the right time, and with sufficient frequency. In other words, advertising messages stand a chance of being effective only if the media strategy itself is effective. Good messages and good media go hand in hand; they are inseparable—a true marriage. Improper media selection can doom an otherwise promising advertising campaign.

Creative advertisements are more effective when placed in media whose characteristics enhance the value of the advertising message and reach the advertiser's targeted customers at the right time. A variety of decisions must be made when choosing media. In addition to determining which media to use (television, radio, magazines, etc.), the media planner must also pick *vehicles* within each medium (e.g., specific magazines or TV programs), and decide how to allocate the available budget among the various media and vehicle alternatives. Additional decisions involve determining when to advertise, choosing specific geographical locations, and deciding how to distribute the budget over time and across geographic locations.

A successful media strategy requires, first, that the target audience be clearly pinpointed. Failure to precisely define the audience results in wasted exposures; that is, some nonpurchase candidates are exposed to advertisements while some prime candidates are missed. Target audiences are usually selected based on geographic factors (e.g., ads are aimed at people residing in urban centers), demographic considerations (e.g., ads are directed to women aged 18 to 49), product-usage concerns (e.g., ads are focused on heavy product users), and lifestyle/psychographic characteristics (e.g., ads are directed to people with active, outdoor lifestyles).

A second aspect of media strategy is establishing specific objectives. Four objectives are fundamental to media planning: reach, frequency, continuity, and cost. Media planners seek answers to the following types of questions:

1. What portion of the target audience do we want to see (or read, or hear) the advertising message? (*reach*)
2. How often should the target audience be exposed to the advertisement? (*frequency*)
3. When are the best times to reach the target audience? (*continuity*)
4. What is the least expensive way to accomplish the other objectives? (*cost*)

Advertisers work with statistics such as ratings, gross rating points (GRPs), and cost per thousand (CPM) to compare different vehicles within the same medium and to make intelligent selections. For example, an advertiser might consider advertising its brand on *The West Wing*, a TV program that appeals to a wide audience and produces a rating of about 18 percentage points at a cost of approximately $400,000 per 30-second commercial. The 18 rating means that of approximately 100 million households in the United States, on average, 18 percent, or 18 million, are tuned in to this program. Theoretically, then, the advertiser would reach 18 million households every time it places a commercial on *The West Wing*. If, say, during a four-week period the advertiser placed a total of eight commercials on this program (i.e., two ads during each episode), it would accumulate a total of 144 **gross rating points (GRPs)**. GRPs simply represent the mathematical product of individual ratings times the number of times that an advertisement is aired on a TV program (or placed in a magazine). In equation form, GRPs = R × F, where R equals ratings (or reach) and F equals frequency of ad placement.

Gross rating points (GRPs) The accumulation of rating points including all vehicles in a media purchase over the span of a particular campaign.

Cost per thousand (CPM)
Calculated by dividing the cost of an ad placed in a particular ad vehicle (e.g., certain magazine) by the number of people (expressed in thousands) who are exposed to that vehicle.

Cost per thousand (CPM) (M is the Roman numeral for 1,000) is a useful statistic for comparing the cost efficiency of vehicles in the same medium. For example, in 2000 a single four-color, full-page advertisement placed in *Sports Illustrated* cost an advertiser about $180,000 and reached approximately 24 million readers. The cost of the ad per 1,000 readers is calculated as follows: CPM = Cost of ad placement divided by the size of audience expressed in thousands; therefore, $180,000 ÷ 24,000 = $7.50.

The advertiser would compare this value with the CPM to advertise in alternative vehicles. For example, in 2000 a full-page, four-color ad placed in *Sport* magazine cost approximately $50,000 and reached about 4.5 million readers. Its CPM is $11.11 (i.e., $50,000 ÷ 4,500). *Sports Illustrated* is a less expensive vehicle on a per-thousand basis than *Sport* and on a cost-basis alone is the obvious better buy. However, the choice of which magazine to select is based on considerations other than mere cost comparisons. Also crucial in the decision are considerations such as how closely a vehicle's readers/viewers match the brand's target audience and the fit between the image of the vehicle and the brand's desired image.

Advertisers have four major mass media from which to choose: television, radio, magazines, and newspapers. Each medium possesses various strengths and weaknesses. Some of the most prominent of these are summarized in Exhibit 300.19. One additional advertising medium that deserves mention is the Internet. Internet usage is growing rather dramatically throughout the world. Many advertisers have used the Internet for placing banner advertisements, for posting e-mail messages (so-called permission or opt-in emailing), and for conveying company and brand information via the creation of home pages. Internet advertisers, like advertisers in all other media, have to fight through the clutter to find ways to attract the on-line user's attention. Bigger ads, ads that pop up, and ads that offer sound and visuals are just some of the ways that have been devised to attract and hold the Internet user's attention.

Assessing Advertising Effectiveness

Assessing advertising effectiveness is a final critical aspect of advertising strategy, inasmuch as only by evaluating results is it possible to determine whether advertising objectives have been accomplished. This often requires that baseline measures be taken before an advertising campaign begins (to determine, for example, what percentage of the target audience is aware of the brand name), and then afterwards to determine whether the objective was achieved. Because, as earlier noted, billions of dollars are invested on advertising, advertisers go to great lengths to measure the effectiveness of their advertisements. There literally is an entire industry of companies that are in business to measure advertising effectiveness.

Single-source systems
Measurement of the effectiveness of advertising (whether it leads to increased sales activity). They are unique in that all the relevant data is collected by a single source, processed, and then made available in a readily usable format to retailers and manufacturers.

Perhaps the most notable development in advertising-effectiveness measurement is the advent of so-called **single-source systems.** Single-source systems became possible with the advent of two electronic-monitoring tools: television meters and optical laser scanning of universal product codes (UPC symbols) at the point of purchase. Single-source systems gather purchase data from panels of households using optical scanning equipment and merge it with household demographic characteristics. Most importantly, it is then combined with information about other marketing variables that influence household purchases (e.g., TV commercials, coupons, in-store displays, trade promotions, etc.).

Direct Advertising

In contrast to mass-media advertising, which is aimed at thousands or even millions of prospective customers, direct advertising typically is targeted to a single business or an individual consumer. The growth of direct advertising and its growing sophistication is due in large part to the advent of **database marketing.** Typical databases include purchase data and other types of relevant customer information, such as demographic details and geographic information. The information is used to profile customers and to develop effective and efficient marketing programs by communicating with individual customers and by establishing long-term communication relationships.[30]

Major advances in computer technology and database management have made it possible for companies to maintain huge databases containing millions of prospects/customers. *Niche marketing* can be fully realized by targeting promotional efforts to a company's best prospects (based on past product-category purchasing behavior), and who can be iden-

Exhibit 300.19 *Comparative Strengths and Weaknesses of Major Advertising Media*

Medium	Strengths	Weaknesses
Television	• Dramatic presentation and demonstration ability • High reach potential • Attain rapid awareness • Relatively efficient • Intrusive and impactual • Ability to integrate messages with other media such as radio	• Relatively downscale audience profile • Network audience erosion • Growing commercial clutter • High out-of-pocket cost • High production costs • Long lead time to purchase network time • Volatile cost structure
Radio	• Target selectivity • High frequency • Efficient • Able to transfer image from TV • Portable, personal medium • Low production cost • Use of local personalities • Ability to integrate messages with other media such as TV	• Commercial clutter • Some station formats relatively uninvolving for listeners • Relatively small audiences • High out-of-pocket cost to attain significant reach • Audience fractionalization
Magazines	• Efficient reach of selective audiences • Ability to match advertising with compatible editorial content • High-quality graphics • Reach light TV viewers • Opportunity to repeat ad exposure • Flexibility in target market coverage • Can deliver complex copy • Readership is not seasonal	• Not intrusive; reader controls ad exposure • Slow audience accumulation • Significant slippage from reader audience to ad-exposure audience • Clutter can be high • Long lead times to purchase magazine space • Somewhat limited geographic options • Uneven market-by-market circulation patterns
Newspapers	• Rapid audience accumulation • Timeliness • High single-day reach attainable • Short lead times to purchase newspaper space • Excellent geographic flexibility • Can convey detailed copy • Strong retail trade support • Good for merchandising and promotion • Low production cost • Excellent local market penetration	• Limited target selectivity • High out-of-pocket costs for national buys • Significant differential between national and local rates • Not intrusive • Cluttered ad environment • Generally mediocre reproduction quality

Source: © 1994 VNU Business Media, Inc.

tified in terms of specific geographic, demographic, and psychographic characteristics. Growing numbers of marketers are making heavy investments in database marketing. Database marketing offers companies four distinct "abilities":[31]

1. *Addressability*—being able to identify every customer and reach each one on an individual basis. This could also be referred to as *targetability*.
2. *Measurability*—knowing whether customers purchased something; exactly what they purchased; and how, where, and when they purchased along with their purchase history.
3. *Flexibility*—having the opportunity to appeal to different customers in different ways at different times.
4. *Accountability*—having precise figures on the gross profitability of any marketing event, and qualitative data showing the type of customers who participated in each particular event.

All types of marketers use direct mail as a strategically important advertising medium. Some automobile manufacturers, for example, are budgeting as much as 10 percent of their advertising expenditures to direct mail.

At least four factors account for the widespread use of direct-mail advertising. First, the rising expense of television advertising, along with increased audience fragmentation, has led many advertisers to reduce investments in television advertising. Second, direct mail enables unparalleled targeting of messages to desired prospects—according to one expert, it is "a lot better to talk to 20,000 prospects than 2 million suspects."[32] Third, there is increased emphasis on measurable advertising results, and direct mail is the advertising medium that best lends itself to a clear identification of how many prospects have purchased the advertised product. Finally, surveys indicate that Americans like mail advertisements.

Sales Promotion

Sales promotions are the use of any incentive by a manufacturer to induce the trade (wholesalers and retailers), and/or consumers, to buy a brand and to encourage the sales force to aggressively sell it. Retailers also use promotions to encourage greater purchasing from their customers. The incentive is in addition to the basic benefits provided by the brand and temporarily changes its perceived price or value.[33] These features require further comment. First, by definition, sales promotions involve **incentives** that are additions to, not substitutes for, the basic benefits a purchaser typically acquires when buying a particular good or service. Second, the target of the incentive may be the trade, final consumers, the sales force, or all three parties. Finally, the incentive changes a brand's perceived price/value, but only temporarily. This is to say that a sales-promotion incentive for a particular brand applies to a single purchase or perhaps several purchases during a period, but not to every purchase a consumer would make over an extended period.

The Shift from Advertising to Sales Promotion

Historically, the promotional emphasis in many consumer-goods firms was on creating promotional pull. Manufacturers advertised heavily, especially on network television, literally forcing retailers to handle their products by virtue of the fact that consumers demanded heavily advertised brands. However, over the past two decades, pull-oriented marketing has become less effective. Along with this reduced effectiveness has come an increase in the use of push-oriented sales promotion practices.[34]

The result of these developments is that advertising expenditures in mass media (television, radio, magazines, newspaper, and outdoor) have declined in most firms as a percentage of their total marketing communications expenditures. On the other hand, expenditures on sales promotions, direct marketing, sponsorships, and point-of-purchase items have steadily increased. In fact, annual studies have shown that media advertising expenditures as a proportion of companies' total marketing communications spending have declined steadily for over a decade. Whereas media advertising used to average over 40 percent of companies' marketing communications budgets, now media advertising's portion of the total budget has fallen to about 25 percent. Comparatively, consumer promotions (coupons, bonus packs, premiums, etc.) represent approximately 25 percent of the total promotional budget, and trade promotions constitute the remaining 50 percent.[35] These statistics make it clear that *the biggest shift in marketing communications expenditures has been away from media advertising toward expenditures to support the trade.* The major form of trade promotions are deals, or discounts in the form of **trade allowances,** that encourage wholesalers and retailers to purchase larger quantities of promoted brands during the period when the manufacturer places them on promotion.

Trade allowances (trade deals)
Come in a variety of forms and are offered to retailers simply for purchasing the manufacturer's brand or for performing activities in support of the manufacturer's brand.

Increased investment in sales promotions, especially trade-oriented promotions, has gone hand-in-hand with the trend toward greater push-oriented marketing. The six factors listed below account for the shift in the allocation of promotion budgets away from advertising toward sales promotion and other forms of marketing communications. These are summarized in Exhibit 300.20.

1. *Balance of Power Transfer.* Until recently, national manufacturers of consumer goods generally were more powerful and influential than the supermarkets, drug stores, and mass merchandisers that carried the manufacturers' brands. However, the balance of power began shifting when network television dipped in effectiveness as an advertising medium and, especially, with the advent of optical scanning equipment, which allowed retailers to attain as much "informational market power" as previously had been possessed only by manufacturers. The consequence for manufacturers is that for every promotional dollar used to support retailers' advertising or merchandising programs, one less dollar is available for the manufacturer's own advertising.

Exhibit 300.20 *Factors Giving Rise to the Growth of Sales Promotions*

1. Balance of power transfer
2. Increased brand parity and price sensitivity
3. Reduced brand loyalty
4. Splintering of the mass market and reduced media effectiveness
5. Short-term orientation and corporate reward structures
6. Trade and consumer responsiveness

2. *Increased Brand Parity and Price Sensitivity.* In earlier years when truly new products were being offered to the marketplace, manufacturers could effectively advertise unique advantages over competitive offerings. As product categories have matured, however, most new offerings represent slight changes from existing products, resulting in more similarities between competitive brands than differences. With fewer distinct product differences, consumers have grown more reliant on price and price incentives (coupons, cents-off deals, refunds, etc.) as a way of differentiating alternative parity brands. Because real, concrete advantages are often difficult to obtain, firms have turned increasingly to sales promotion as a means of achieving at least temporary advantages over competitors.

3. *Reduced Brand Loyalty.* Consumers have become less loyal to brands than they once were. This is partly due to the fact that brands have grown increasingly similar, thereby making it easier for consumers to switch among brands. Also, marketers have effectively trained consumers to expect that at least one brand in a product category will always be on deal with a coupon, cents-off offer, or refund; hence, many consumers rarely purchase brands other than those on deal. The upshot of all of this dealing activity is that marketers' extensive use of sales promotions has reduced brand loyalty and increased switching behavior, thereby requiring evermore dealing activity to feed consumers' insatiable desire for deals.

4. *Splintering of the Mass Market and Reduced Media Effectiveness.* Advertising efficiency is directly related to the degree of homogeneity in consumers' consumption needs and media habits. The more homogeneous are these needs and habits, the less costly it is for mass advertising to reach target audiences. However, as consumer lifestyles have become more diverse and advertising media have narrowed in their appeal, mass-media advertising is no longer as efficient as it once was. On top of this, advertising effectiveness has declined with simultaneous increases in ad clutter and escalating media costs. These combined forces have influenced many brand managers to devote proportionately larger budgets to sales promotions.

5. *Short-Term Orientation and Corporate Reward Structures.* The brand-management system and sales promotion are perfect partners. The reward structure in firms organized along brand-manager lines emphasizes short-term sales response rather than slow, long-term growth, and sales promotion is incomparable when it comes to generating quick sales response. In fact, for many brands of packaged goods, the majority of their sales are associated with some kind of promotional deal.[36]

6. *Trade and Consumer Responsiveness.* A final force that explains the shift toward sales promotion at the expense of advertising is that retailers/wholesalers (the trade) and consumers respond favorably to money-saving opportunities.

Sales Promotion: Roles and Objectives

Sales promotion is well suited for accomplishing the following 10 tasks,[37] which are summarized in Exhibit 300.21.

1. *Facilitating the Introduction of New Products to the Trade.* Sales promotions to wholesalers and retailers are often necessary to encourage the trade to handle new products. In fact, many retailers refuse to carry new products unless they receive extra compensation in the form of trade allowances, display allowances, and other forms of allowances.

2. *Obtaining Trial Purchases from Consumers.* Marketers depend on free samples, coupons, and other sales promotions to encourage trial purchases of new products. Many consumers would never try new products without these promotional inducements.

3. *Stimulating Sales Force Enthusiasm for New, Improved, or Mature Brands.* Exciting sales promotions give salespeople extra ammunition to use when interacting with buyers; they revive enthusiasm and make the salesperson's job easier and more enjoyable.

Exhibit 300.21 *Sales Promotion's Capabilities*

> 1. Facilitate the introduction of new products to the trade
> 2. Obtain trial purchases from consumers
> 3. Stimulate sales force enthusiasm
> 4. Invigorate sales of mature brand
> 5. Increase merchandise space
> 6. Neutralize competitive advertising and sales promotions
> 7. Hold current users by encouraging repeat purchasing
> 8. Increase product usage by loading consumers
> 9. Preempt competition by loading consumers
> 10. Reinforce advertising

4. *Invigorating Sales of a Mature Brand.* Sales promotion can stimulate sales of a mature brand that requires a shot in the arm.
5. *Increasing On- and Off-Shelf Merchandising Space.* Trade-oriented sales promotions enable a manufacturer to obtain extra shelf space for a temporary period. This space may be in the form of extra facing (i.e., rows of shelf space) or off-shelf space in, say, an end-aisle display.
6. *Neutralizing Competitive Advertising and Sales Promotion.* Sales promotions can be used to offset competitors' advertising and sales-promotion efforts. For example, one company's 50 cents-off coupon loses much of its appeal when a competitor simultaneously comes out with a $1 coupon.
7. *Holding Current Users by Encouraging Repeat Purchases.* Brand switching is a fact of life faced by all brand managers. The strategic use of certain forms of sales promotion can encourage at least short-run repetitive purchasing. Premium programs, refunds, and various other devices are used to encourage repeat purchasing.
8. *Increasing Brand Usage by Loading Consumers.* Consumers tend to use more of certain products (e.g., snack foods and soft drinks) when they have more of them available in their homes. Thus, sales-promotion efforts that load consumers with greater quantities than they normally would buy on a particular purchase occasion generate temporary increases in brand usage. Bonus packs and two-for-the-price-of-one deals are particularly effective loading devices.
9. *Preempting Competition by Loading Consumers.* When consumers are loaded with one company's brand, they are temporarily out of the marketplace for competitive brands. Hence, one brand's sales promotion serves to preempt sales of competitive brands.
10. *Reinforcing Advertising.* A final can-do capability of sales promotion is to reinforce advertising. An advertising campaign can be strengthened greatly by a well-coordinated sales promotion effort.

Sales promotions clearly are capable of performing important tasks. There are, however, distinct limitations that are beyond the capability of sales promotion. In particular, sales promotions cannot (1) compensate for a poorly trained sales force, (2) give the trade or consumers any compelling long-term reason to continue purchasing a brand, or (3) permanently stop an established brand's declining sales trend, or change the basic nonacceptance of an undesired brand.

Trade Promotions: Roles and Objectives

As earlier noted, manufacturers use some combination of push and pull strategies to accomplish both retail distribution and consumer purchasing. *Trade promotions,* which are directed at wholesalers, retailers, and other marketing intermediaries, represent the first step in any promotional effort. Consumer promotions are likely to fail unless trade-promotion efforts have succeeded in getting wholesalers to distribute the product, and retailers to stock adequate quantities. The special incentives offered by manufacturers to their distribution channel members are expected to be passed through to consumers in the form of price discounts offered by retailers and often stimulated by advertising support and special displays.[38] As we will see later, this does not always occur.

A manufacturer has various objectives for using trade-oriented sales promotions: (1) to introduce new or revised products, (2) to increase distribution of new packages or sizes, (3) to build retail inventories, (4) to maintain or increase the manufacturer's share of shelf space, (5) to obtain displays outside normal shelf locations, (6) to reduce excess inventories and increase turnover, (7) to achieve feature space in retailers' advertisements, (8) to counter competitive activity, and, ultimately, (9) to sell as much as possible to final consumers.[39]

Manufacturers employ a variety of trade-oriented promotional inducements, most of which are some form of trade allowance. These allowances/deals are needed to encourage retailers to stock the manufacturer's brand, discount the brand's price to consumers, feature it in advertising, or provide special display or other point-of-purchase support.[40] The most frequently used allowance is an **off-invoice allowance.** By using off-invoice allowances, manufacturers hope to increase retailers' purchasing of the manufacturer's brand and increase consumers' purchasing from retailers. This latter objective is based on the expectation that retailers will in fact pass along to consumers the discounts they receive from manufacturers, which unfortunately does not always happen.

Off-invoice trade allowances create notable problems for the manufacturers that use them. One major problem is that off-invoice allowances often induce the trade to stockpile products in order to take advantage of the temporary price reduction. This merely shifts business from the future to the present. Two prevalent practices are **forward buying** and **diverting,** both of which represent efforts on the part of wholesalers and retailers to earn money from buying on deal rather than from selling merchandise at a profit.

> **Forward buying (bridge buying)** Retailers purchase enough product during a manufacturer's off-invoice allowance period to carry the retailers over until the manufacturer's next regularly scheduled deal.

Manufacturers' off-invoice allowances typically are available every four weeks of each business quarter (which translates to about 30 percent of the year), and a number of manufacturers sell upward of 80 to 90 percent of their volume at less than full price. When a manufacturer marks down a product's price by, say, 10 percent, wholesalers and retailers commonly stock up (i.e., forward buy) with a 10- to 12-week supply. Wholesalers and retailers are rational businesspeople: they take advantage of deals!

A related buying practice, diverting, occurs when a manufacturer offers an off-invoice allowance in a particular geographical region rather than nationwide. What happens under this circumstance is that some retailers forward buy larger quantities than needed in just that region and ship out (transship) quantities to retailers in other geographical regions. The transshipping retailer earns a small profit on each item when engaging in this practice. It is estimated that the volume of merchandise involved in diverting amounts to at least $5 billion a year.[41] Interestingly, this practice of diverting in a marketing context is equivalent to what is known as *arbitrage* in finance circles, whereby financiers simultaneously buy and sell securities or foreign exchange in different markets to profit from unequal prices.

Consumer Sales Promotions: Roles and Objectives

A variety of sales promotion methods are used to encourage consumers to purchase one brand over another, to purchase a particular brand more often, and to purchase in larger quantities. *Consumer promotions* include such activities as sampling, couponing, refunding, rebating, and offering premiums, sweepstakes, and contests.

Consumers would not be responsive to sales promotions unless there was something in it for them—and, in fact, there is. All sales-promotion techniques provide consumers with incentives or inducements that encourage certain forms of behavior desired by brand marketers and/or retailers. Rewards are typically in the form of cash savings or free gifts. Sometimes rewards are immediate, while other times they are delayed. An *immediate reward* is one that delivers the savings or gift as soon as the consumer performs a marketer-specified behavior. For example, you receive cash savings at the time you redeem a coupon; pleasure is obtained immediately when you try, say, a free product while shopping in a grocery store. *Delayed rewards* are those that follow the behavior by a period of days, weeks, or even longer. For example, you may have to wait weeks before a free-in-the-mail premium object can be enjoyed. Generally speaking, consumers are more responsive to immediate rather than delayed rewards. Of course, this is in line with the natural human tendency to seek immediate rather than delayed gratification.

Manufacturers use sales promotions to accomplish three general categories of objectives: **trial impact, franchise holding/loading,** and **image reinforcement.** Exhibit 300.22 classifies a variety of sales promotion techniques by the specific objective each is primarily responsible for accomplishing, and by the type of reward, either immediate or delayed, provided consumers.[42] It is important to recognize that most forms of sales promotions perform more than a single objective. For example, refunds and rebates are classified as franchise holding/loading techniques but on some occasions they may also encourage trial purchasing. Note also that two techniques, coupons and premiums, have multiple entries. This is because these techniques achieve different objectives depending on the specific form of delivery vehicle. The choice of which sales promotion tool to use depends on the specific objectives that must be accomplished for a brand at a particular point in time, and an evaluation of the relative expense of using different tools. Coupons, for example, are widely used because types of coupons (e.g., shelf-delivered versus media-delivered) are capable of achieving different objectives, and the cost typically is not prohibitive.

Exhibit 300.22 *Major Consumer-Oriented Forms of Sales Promotions*

Consumer Reward	Marketer's Objective		
	Trial Impact	Customer Holding/Loading	Image Reinforcement
Immediate	(1) • Sampling • Instant coupons • Shelf-delivered coupons	(3) • Price-offs • Bonus packs • In-, on-, and near-pack premiums	(5)
Delayed	(2) • Media- and mail-delivered coupons • Free-in-the-mail premiums	(4) • In- and on-pack coupons • Refunds and rebates • Phone cards	(6) • Self-liquidating premiums • Contests and sweepstakes • Scanner-delivered coupons

Public Relations

Public relations, or PR, is the marketing communications tool that is uniquely suited to fostering goodwill between a company and its various publics. When effectively integrated with advertising, personal selling, and sales promotion, public relations is capable of accomplishing objectives other than goodwill. It can also increase brand awareness, build favorable attitudes toward a company and its products, and encourage purchase behavior. PR is similar to advertising because both are forms of mass communication; the difference is that the publicity generated by PR receives free news space or broadcast time in comparison to the space and time purchased in the case of advertising. The public-relations department serves as the prime source of an organization's contact with the news media.

PR efforts are aimed at various publics, primarily the following: consumers, employees, suppliers, stockholders, governments, the general public, labor groups, and citizen action groups. Our concern, however, is only with the more narrow aspect of public relations involving an organization's interactions with customers. This marketing-oriented aspect of public relations is called *marketing PR*, or *MPR* for short. Marketing PR can be further delineated as involving either proactive or reactive public relations.[43]

Proactive MPR

Proactive marketing public relations (proactive MPR)
Offensively rather than defensively oriented, and opportunity-seeking rather than problem solving. The major role of proactive MPR is in the area of product introductions or product revisions.

Proactive marketing public relations (proactive MPR) is another marketing communications tool in addition to advertising and sales promotion that can give a brand additional exposure, newsworthiness, and credibility. This last factor, credibility, largely accounts for the effectiveness of proactive MPR. Whereas sales and advertising claims are sometimes suspect—because customers question salespeople's and advertisers' motives, knowing they have a personal stake in persuading us—product announcements by a newspaper editor or television broadcaster are notably more believable. Customers are less likely to question the motivation underlying an editorial-type endorsement.

Publicity is the major tool of proactive MPR. Like advertising and personal selling, the fundamental purposes of marketing-oriented publicity are to engender brand awareness, enhance attitudes toward a company and its brands, and possibly influence purchase behavior. Companies obtain publicity using various forms of news releases, press conferences, and other types of information dissemination. News releases concerning new products, modifications in old products, and other newsworthy topics are delivered to editors of newspapers and magazines, to managers of television and radio stations, and are disseminated en masse to Internet Web sites such as Yahoo! Finance. Press conferences announce major news events of interest to the public. Photographs, tapes, and films are useful for illustrating product improvements, new products, advanced production techniques, and so forth. Of course, all forms of publicity are subject to the control and whims of the media. However, by disseminating a large volume of publicity materials and by preparing materials that fit the media's needs, a company increases its chances of obtaining beneficial publicity.

Reactive MPR

Reactive MPR is undertaken as a result of external pressures and challenges brought by competitive actions, changes in consumer attitudes, changes in government policy, or other external influences. Product defects and failures are the most dramatic factors underlying the need for reactive MPR. A number of negative publicity cases have received widespread media attention in recent years.

> *Reactive MPR* Form of defensively oriented public relations that deals with developments (such as product defects or flaws) having negative consequences for the organization. Reactive MPR attempts to repair a company's reputation, prevent market erosion, and regain lost sales.

Sponsorship Marketing

One of the fastest growing aspects of marketing and marketing communications is the practice of **corporate sponsorships.** Sponsorships range from supporting athletic events (golf and tennis tournaments, college football bowl games, etc.), to underwriting rock concerts, to throwing corporate weight behind worthy causes such as efforts to generate funds for cancer research.

At least four factors account for the growth in sponsorships.[44] First, by attaching their names to special events and causes, companies are able to avoid the clutter inherent in advertising media. Second, sponsorships help companies respond to consumers' changing media habits. For example, with the decline in network television viewing, sponsorships offer a potentially effective and cost-efficient way to reach customers. Third, sponsorships help companies gain the approval of various constituencies, including stockholders, employees, and society at large. Finally, the sponsorship of special events and causes enables marketers to target their communication and promotional efforts to specific geographic regions and/or to specific lifestyle groups. Many companies in the apparel and casual footwear business sponsor alternative sports events to appeal to younger consumers who are difficult to reach via advertising media.

Event Marketing

Thousands of companies invest in some form of **event-related marketing (ERM)** sponsorship. Event marketing is separate from advertising, sales promotion, point-of-purchase merchandising, or public relations, but it generally incorporates elements from all of these promotional tools. It is growing rapidly because these sponsorships provide companies with alternatives to the cluttered mass media, an ability to segment on a local or regional basis, and opportunities for reaching narrow lifestyle groups whose consumption behavior can be linked with the local event. Events are effective because they reach people when they are in a relaxed atmosphere and receptive to marketing messages.

> *Event-related marketing (ERM)* Form of brand promotion that ties a brand to a meaningful cultural, social, athletic, or other type of high-interest public activity.

As with every other marketing communications decision, the starting point for effective event sponsorship is to clearly specify the objectives that an event is designed to accomplish. Event marketing has no value unless it accomplishes these objectives.

Cause-Related Marketing

Cause-related marketing is a relatively narrow aspect of overall sponsorship. It involves an amalgam of public relations, sales promotion, and corporate philanthropy; however, the distinctive feature of cause-related marketing is that a company's contribution to a designated cause is linked to customers engaging in revenue-producing exchanges with the firm.[45] The contribution is contingent on the customer performing a behavior (such as buying a product or redeeming a coupon) that benefits the firm.

> *Cause-related marketing* Form of corporate philanthropy that links a company's contributions (usually monetary) to a predesignated worthy cause with the purchasing behavior of consumers.

Point-of-Purchase Communications

Marketers use a variety of items at the point of purchase to draw attention to their brands and activate consumer purchases. These include various types of signs, mobiles, plaques, banners, shelf tapes, mechanical mannequins, lights, mirrors, plastic product reproductions, checkout units, full-line merchandisers, wall posters, motion displays, and other materials. Many of these materials are temporary items, with useful life spans of only weeks or months. Others are relatively permanent fixtures that can be used for years. Whereas temporary signs and displays are particularly effective for promoting impulse purchasing, permanent point-of-purchase (P-O-P) units compartmentalize and departmentalize a store area to achieve high product visibility, facilitate customer self-service, prevent stock-outs, and help control inventory.

Brand managers recognize the value of P-O-P advertising; indeed, Point of Purchase Advertising International (POPAI), the trade association for this form of advertising, estimates that in 2000 marketers in the United States spent $17 billion on P-O-P advertising.[46] This level of expenditure can be justified by the fact that point-of-purchase materials provide a useful service for all participants in the marketing process.

- Point-of-purchase materials and displays provide value to *consumers* by delivering useful information, identifying sale items, and simplifying the shopping process by setting products apart from similar items.
- P-O-P serves *retailers* by attracting the consumers' attention, increasing their interest in shopping, and extending the amount of time spent in the store—all of which mean increased sales. P-O-P helps retailers utilize available space to the best advantage by displaying several manufacturers' products in the same unit (e.g., many varieties of vitamins and other medicinal items all in one well-organized unit). It enables retailers to better organize shelf space and to improve inventory control, volume, stock turnover, and profitability.
- For *manufacturers*, who are the marketers of branded products, P-O-P keeps the company's name and the brand name before the consumer and both reactivates and reinforces brand information the consumer has previously received through advertising. P-O-P calls attention to special offers such as sales promotions and stimulates impulse purchasing. P-O-P serves to complement the job already performed by advertising before the consumer enters a store.[47] Indeed, it represents the capstone for an integrated marketing communications program.

Because many product- and brand-choice decisions are made while the consumer is in the store, rather than before he or she arrives at the store, point-of-purchase materials play a role, perhaps the major role, in influencing unplanned purchasing.

Pricing Strategies

What Is Price? What Determines Base Price?

So what is **price?** It is not just the number on the price tag in the store (although that is clearly what most customers think of). In general terms, any exchange involves a price, and it is not always monetary. As such, price can be or incorporate rent, tuition, wages, salary, fees, fare, lease payment, interest rate, or time donated. In short, price is an exchange rate—it defines the sacrifice that one party pays another to receive something in exchange.[48] Our specific focus will be on *price as a monetary value charged by an organization for the sales of its products*. In this section, we will distinguish between two general categories of pricing decisions: (1) setting a base price for a product, and (2) making adjustments to that product's price over time (see Exhibit 300.23).

Classic economics holds some important insights about how prices should be determined. Exhibit 300.24 illustrates simple tools that help explain the interaction between buyer and seller behavior. Consider a new college student named

Exhibit 300.23 *Basic Pricing Decisions and Primary Driver: Cost*

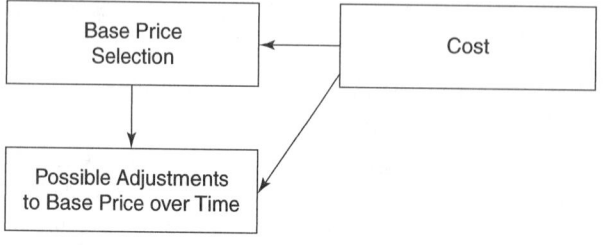

Exhibit 300.24 *Demand and Supply Curves: Jeans*

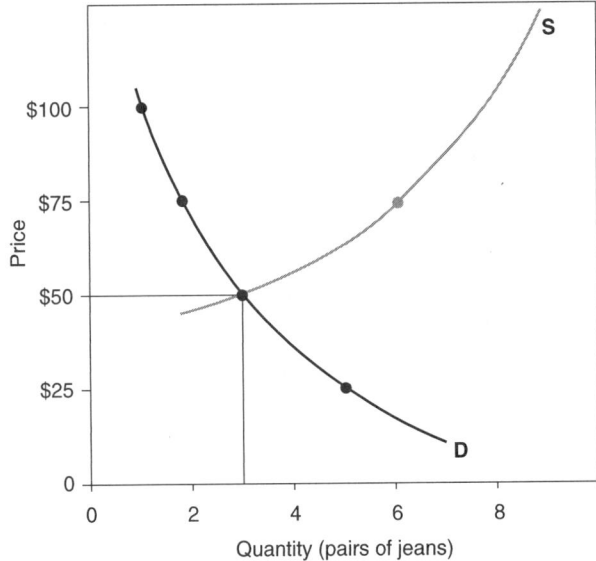

Andrew who is thinking about the purchase of one or more pairs of jeans for the coming school year. Exhibit 300.24 shows varying prices on the vertical axis and quantities on the horizontal axis. The curve labeled D illustrates the number of pairs of jeans Andrew is willing to purchase at a given price. So, at a price of $50, he would be willing to buy three pairs. If the jeans cost $75, he is only willing to buy 2 pairs. (This willingness to buy is determined by many factors, including Andrew's income and tastes, and the cost of other types of clothing.) However, market prices are determined by both the buyer's choice behavior and the seller's willingness to supply the product. The curve labeled S in Exhibit 300.24 captures this. It's called a supply curve and it indicates how many pairs of jeans a seller (say, **Levi's**) would be willing to supply at a given price. Over time, the market price would be determined by the intersection of supply and demand. In this case, demand and supply are matched up at $50.[49]

Cost-Plus Pricing: The Natural (but Sometimes Wrong) Way to Set Base Prices

There are many factors that influence pricing decisions, but the one that businesspeople most naturally think about is cost. Research conducted on pricing in large corporations concluded:

> ... the easiest way to think about a price is first to think like an accountant: price equals costs plus overhead plus a fair profit. Cost-plus pricing, furthermore, is a useful ritual, with great public-relations advantages ... a smart, prudent businessman ... admits only to wanting a "fair" return.[50]

It is no surprise that costs come into play quite significantly in setting *base prices*. Managers are generally (although not always) aware of their costs of doing business. As a result, the practice of setting prices based on costs has become firmly entrenched in the American marketplace. Both early and fairly recent studies of managerial pricing have found cost to be a dominant consideration in pricing decisions.[51] Below, we illustrate cost-plus pricing and evaluate its advantages and drawbacks. We then use the following example as a springboard to discuss other pricing methods and factors that influence pricing.

THE SYMPHONY Imagine you are a manager for a symphony orchestra.[52] The symphony season is just starting, and you have been hired as marketing director. One of your early assignments is to figure out a ticket price for a new concert series in the coming months. You have information about demand in the past (for several programs, the symphony sold about 950 of its 1,100 seats). In addition, the following costs have been identified:

Fixed Overhead	$1,500
Rehearsal Costs	$4,500
Performance Costs	$2,000
Variable Costs per Patron (programs, tickets)	$1 per patron

330. PRICING STRATEGIES

Note that some of these costs are fixed and some are variable. *Fixed costs* are costs that have no relationship to volume. They are, by definition, fixed. They do not change if more customers come to the show. The first three cost categories in our example (fixed overhead, rehearsal costs, and performance costs), totaling $8,000, are all fixed. *Variable costs,* on the other hand, are costs that are incurred for each customer. In this case, they are fairly small—only $1 per customer for tickets and programs.

To determine a price per patron using a cost-plus rule, you need to evenly spread all costs over each patron. Again, past history suggests an average attendance of 950 people. *Average total cost* can be calculated simply by adding an "average" fixed cost figure to variable cost.

$$\text{Average Total Cost} = \text{Variable Cost} + \frac{\text{Fixed Cost}}{\text{Unit Sales}}$$

In the current case, average total cost would be:

$$\$1 + \frac{(\$1{,}500 + 4{,}500 + 2{,}000)}{950} = \$9.42$$

So, for every "unit" you sell (in this case, each of the 950 seats), the orchestra incurs a cost of $9.42, accounting for both fixed and variable costs.

COST-BASED PRICING APPROACHES Many companies use one of two common approaches to setting prices based upon cost. One is to use a standard rule-of-thumb markup. The second is to build up the price by adding together both cost per unit and desired profit.

Standard Markup The orchestra has always used a rule of thumb in the past: mark up costs by 20 percent. This is effectively saying that, "for every unit we sell, we want 20 percent of the selling price to represent profit—an extra incremental profit over and above costs." The price can be easily calculated as follows:

$$\text{Selling Price} = \frac{\text{Unit Cost}}{(1 - \text{Markup \%})} = \frac{\$9.42}{(1 - .20)} = 11.775$$

So, you might charge a price of $11.75 (rounded off to the nearest quarter). Keep in mind that all this means is the profit we get from each ticket ($11.75 − $9.42 = $2.33) is 20 percent of the selling price ($2.33 ÷ $11.75). In fact, the 20 percent in this case refers to *markup on retail price* (it is simply the "markup" as a percentage of the retail price). For the sake of clarity, it is important to distinguish this from *markup on cost.* You may have heard at times that the common rule for some retailers is to determine the retail price by "doubling costs" (i.e., multiply them by 2). This reflects a simple 100 percent markup *on cost.* In the orchestra example, such a 100 percent markup rule would produce a ticket price of $18.84. Using the example we've already calculated—a retail ticket price of $11.75—we calculate the markup on cost to be 24.7 percent (i.e., $2.33 ÷ $9.42 = 24.7%).

Target Return Pricing A similar approach would be for the orchestra to add a target profit to the unit cost figure (to cover both cost and profit):

$$\text{Selling Price} = \text{Unit Cost} + \text{Desired Profit per Unit}$$

The desired profit figure could come from a couple of places. First, there may be a rule of thumb that "we'd like to earn $2 a head coming in" (which would make the price $9.42 + $2.00 = $11.42). Alternatively, the desired profit per unit may be determined based on the company's desired return on investment.[53]

Let us say you apply the standard markup (as many retailers do, for example), and you set your price at $11.75. Have you done a good job? Well, yes and no.

- You have been smart in accounting for your costs, both fixed and variable.
- The pricing method is fair—it is steeped in tradition and is a widely accepted business practice.

For these reasons, no one could argue with your approach. However, there are some drawbacks:

- The fundamental flaw of this approach to pricing is that it *ignores demand.* This approach assumes a certain demand level as given, independent of price. This, as we shall see, is at odds with one of the most fundamental relationships in all of business: quantity sold is a function of price. Generally speaking, as price goes up, demand goes down (and vice versa). Yet, you're assuming that 950 seats will be sold no matter what the price!

Note what happens if different demand levels are assumed. The average unit cost would be much higher if we assumed sales of only 850 tickets (in fact, in this case, average unit cost would be $1 + [$8,000 ÷ 850] = $10.41 rather than $9.42). This means that the $11.75 price would not be high enough to produce the 20 percent profit markup you desired. Alternatively, if ticket sales were 1,050, your unit cost would actually end up being lower ($1 + [$8,000 ÷ 1,050] = $8.62), and your price could be lower than $11.75 and still produce the desired markup return on sales. In the marketplace, because price influences customer perception of value, demand is a function of price. In other words, price determines demand, not the other way around.

- In addition, a cost-plus pricing rule *fails to account for competition*. Competitors' prices have a significant impact on sales and profit outcomes as well, because consumers make choices from competitive sets of alternatives rather than a single one. So, for example, if a new symphony was started in a nearby city, it might well compete for the dollars that patrons might normally spend on our symphony. As such, this would have implications for how high we set our price relative to competing alternatives. In fact, failing to consider these issues can have devastating consequences. Wang Laboratory developed and introduced the world's first word-processing software in 1976. The product was a great success and Wang came to dominate the market. Competition eventually increased and growth slowed, yet the company did not bring down prices to maintain the value position of its software. The reason? Their pricing was basically cost-driven. Wang managers constantly recalculated unit costs and prices to capture increasing overhead cost allocations. Prices remained high and customers made their way to less expensive alternatives.[54]

As you can see, cost-plus pricing takes into account neither price sensitivity nor competition, both of which are essential considerations in setting prices effectively. Further, as noted earlier, cost-plus pricing generally involves allocating fixed costs on a per-unit basis—that is, treating them as variable costs—even though fixed costs do not change with the number of units sold.

If calculating maximum profit is this easy, why don't more companies set prices this way? In reality, other pricing goals—like meeting competition or achieving market share goals (discussed later)—tend to be used more frequently than profit maximization. This is partly because demand curves are difficult to estimate. While managers are likely to apply their own intuitive sense of market price response in their pricing, it is rare that they will have the nice, neat information about demand. There are so many variables that affect sales in a given market that isolating the effect of price is quite difficult. However, it can be done several ways:

1. *Analytic Modeling.* The most sophisticated approach is to develop a statistical model that predicts sales based on historical observations of sales, and such variables as the firm's price, advertising, and sales force levels, competitive tactics, and other variables that may influence demand (e.g., variables capturing economic conditions). This approach allows one to isolate the effect of price on demand.

2. *Experiments.* Firms might run experiments where they change prices in certain markets but not in others, allowing them to see more precisely how such price changes influence sales.

3. *Customer Surveys.* Another approach to identifying a demand curve is to survey customers or present them with purchase scenarios in which they evaluate the product and indicate their intention to purchase at various prices. One has to be careful about interpreting these results, as customers may overstate intentions. However, such an approach can be helpful in estimating price response.[55]

4. *Managerial Judgment.* Often, managers have good insight into sales response in a market. Although there may be some error in assessment, obtaining consensus estimates of demand across several managers who are familiar with a market can provide a useful picture of the demand curve.

Let us return to our symphony pricing problem. Assume that you ask a convenience sample of target symphony customers to evaluate the likelihood that they would go to the symphony at different prices. You present the symphony as an alternative against other activities (e.g., baseball games, going out to eat, going to the art museum, going to a movie). Projecting your results to the larger population, you are able to estimate demand at each price point (see Exhibit 300.25, columns A and B).

Note that we have dropped the prices under $11 from consideration because the break-even analysis showed them to be infeasible. You ask a few local experts in the industry to look your estimates over, and everyone concurs that they are reasonable. The elasticities calculated between price points (columns C–E in Exhibit 300.25) clearly indicate that demand is inelastic (i.e., since the absolute value of all of the elasticity coefficients are less than 1). As in the wheat example earlier, this suggests that customers are not highly responsive to price. Demand does not drop off significantly when price is raised, nor does it increase substantially when price is cut. Note that total revenue only drops as you go from higher to lower prices.

Exhibit 300.25 *Elasticity and Total Revenue: Symphony Problem*

A Price	B Estimated Demand	C Percent Change in Price*	D Percent Change in Quantity	E Elasticity	F Total Revenue (A * B)
$11	1,129	−8.3%	2.6%	−0.31	$12,419
$12	1,100	−7.7%	3.2%	−0.41	$13,200
$13	1,065	−7.1%	5.0%	−0.70	$13,845
$14	1,012	−6.7%	3.9%	−0.58	$14,168
$15	973	0	0	0	$14,595

*Uses the higher price numbers as base for calculating percentage changes.

Exhibit 300.26 *Total Contribution and Total Profit: Symphony Problem*

A Price	B Estimated Demand	C Total Revenue (A * B)	D Total Variable Cost (B * $1)	E Total Contribution	F Fixed Costs	G Total Profit
$11	1,129	$12,419	$1,129	$11,290	$8,000	$3,290
$12	1,100	$13,200	$1,100	$12,100	$8,000	$4,100
$13	1,065	$13,845	$1,065	$12,780	$8,000	$4,780
$14	1,012	$14,168	$1,012	$13,156	$8,000	$5,156
$15	973	$14,595	$973	$13,622	$8,000	$5,622

Variable Cost: $1.00.

However, we are not seeking to maximize total revenue. Instead we are seeking to maximize profit. As you know, variable cost is $1.00 and fixed costs are $8,000. What price produces the maximum profit? (Don't read ahead or look at Exhibit 300.26 until you figure this out.)

The answer, perhaps not surprisingly, is the highest price ($15), which produces a total contribution of $13,622 compared to the next highest, $13,156, when price is $14 (see column E of Exhibit 300.26). The exhibit also provides fixed costs in column F and a total profit calculation in column G to confirm that the same price point ($15) is selected as profit-maximizing whether fixed costs are included or not. Incorporating fixed costs here is equivalent to subtracting a constant, which illustrates why fixed costs are not relevant to determining the profit-maximizing price in this example.

So, the profit-maximizing approach would have you setting price at $15,[56] selling approximately 973 tickets, and earning substantially more than the $2,000 profit goal.

How do you like the $15 price? Some further consideration illustrates why pricing is a little bit science and a little bit art. There actually are other considerations to be taken into account, which suggest that the short-term profit-maximizing price would not be the "right" price. In this case, the issue is auditorium capacity. The symphony board may be willing to give up some profit (as long as we've reached the $2,000 goal) in order to fill up the auditorium. Filling up the auditorium would be a public relations victory, allowing us to promote the fact that the performances are "sold out" and improving the symphony's outcomes in the longer term. Hence, other strategic considerations or objectives come into play. Exhibit 300.27 displays a larger set of factors, which may influence the selection of a base price. We examine these factors next.

Pricing Strategies: Price Drivers

Important strategic factors that play a role in setting base prices include positioning strategy, objectives, new product pricing strategies, and price-quality inferences.

Exhibit 300.27 *Determinants of Price*

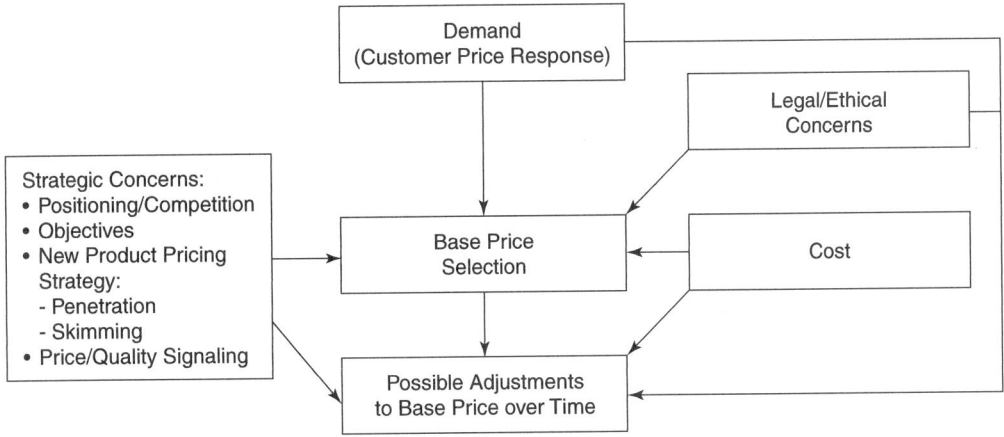

Positioning Strategy

Two strategies exist including low-cost leadership and differentiation. Returning to our symphony example, it is not likely, given the nature of the product category and the audience, that a cost leadership strategy would generally be effective. Differentiation, though, might involve positioning the symphony experience as distinct and prestigious, making it fun and unique—perhaps by offering dinner and wine with performances, an opportunity to meet with members of the orchestra or special guest stars, or rotating concert locations between very unique, attractive locations. Such efforts would merit higher prices in part because costs would be higher, but also because of the higher value being returned to patrons.

Objectives

We saw in our symphony example that $15 was the profit-maximizing price. Yet, management may have another goal in mind: Fill up the auditorium (i.e., maximize sales). *Goal-setting*, or *objective-setting*, is an important part of a firm's strategic planning process. Plans occur at both the corporate and business levels, and the objectives for a particular brand or business are in part a function of the corporation's objectives. In a classic work on pricing in large corporations conducted by the Brookings Institution, four predominant objectives in pricing were identified: to achieve a target **ROI**, to create stabilization of price and margin, to reach a market share target, and to meet or prevent competition. We address each of those individually and then consider two other commonly discussed objectives—profit maximization and survival.

PRICING TO ACHIEVE A TARGET ROI This was found to be the most common approach to pricing in the Brookings' study. Assuming a standard volume, firms add a particular margin to standard cost, which is expected to produce a target profit rate on investment. Across 20 firms, the target return figure averaged 14 percent, ranging between 8 and 20 percent.

PRICING TO CREATE STABILIZATION OF PRICE AND MARGIN Generally, this approach reflects the goal of avoiding the fluctuations in prices that are characteristic of a commodity market. Managers in the Brookings' study reflected a desire to "refrain from upping the price as high as the traffic will bear in prosperity." This motive raises questions about the fairness of frequent price changes (particularly increases), a point which has been raised more recently in an economic theory labeled *dual entitlement*.[57] The **theory of dual entitlement,** in fact, argues similarly that concerns about fairness may constrain price increases. Fairness may be an issue even when companies do not openly increase prices.

Theory of dual entitlement Holds that consumers believe there are terms in a transaction to which both consumers and sellers are "entitled" to over time. Cost-driven price increases are believed to be fair because they allow sellers to maintain their profit entitlement. Demand-driven price increases are not believed to be fair, however, since they allow sellers to increase per-unit profit, while buyers receive nothing in return.

PRICING TO REACH A MARKET SHARE TARGET Particularly when there is no patent protection on a product, firms may pursue a market share target. In most cases, firms will seek a significant share upon entry into the market. For example, 3M's Scotch Brite Never Rust soap pad was priced aggressively enough to gain a 15.4 percent market share upon introduction, taking significant share from SOS and Brillo.

PRICING TO MEET OR PREVENT COMPETITION The logic behind meeting competitors' prices is straightforward. Meeting price cuts will eliminate a competitive disadvantage, while meeting price increases (although less likely) can fatten margins. This reflects a classic tit-for-tat strategy, which has been found to be effective in promoting higher profits for all players.[58] An additional benefit is that a consistent pattern of matching competitors' price moves sends rivals the signal that "undercutting price is not a good idea because we will simply match you."

PRICING FOR PROFIT MAXIMIZATION As noted, the pursuit of this objective requires substantial cost and demand information. It has rarely been articulated as a goal by executives being interviewed about their pricing.

PRICING FOR SURVIVAL A company experiencing trouble may seek to produce an acceptable cash flow, to cover marginal costs, and simply survive. This may result when competition is especially intense, when consumer needs are changing, and/or when substantial excess capacity exists.

New Product Pricing

Two classic pricing strategies are commonly discussed for new products: skimming versus penetration.

Market (price) skimming
Strategy of pricing the new product at a relatively high level and then gradually reducing it over time.
Penetration strategy Requires that the firm enter the market at a relatively low price in an attempt to obtain market share and expand demand for its product.

PRICE SKIMMING The strategy of **market (price) skimming** requires that a large enough segment of the customer market (innovators) is willing to pay the high price for the unique value that a product provides, and that competitors cannot quickly enter with similar products at lower prices. For example, VCRs were initially priced as high as $800 to $900, but have gradually come down to around $100. Other products that followed similar price patterns are CD players, cellular phones, and multimedia computers. Intel is well known for this strategy, pricing its microprocessors for up to $1,000 per chip, but then dropping that price as new superior chips are developed. Skimming is a strategy that obviously would be more likely followed by a firm pursuing a clear differentiation strategy. In addition, a skimming strategy would tend to be pursued in the introduction phase of the product life cycle.

PRICE PENETRATION By pursuing a **penetration strategy** in the face of a retail book marketplace dominated by large chains such as **Borders** and **Barnes & Noble** (together having 13 superstores in Atlanta alone), a small bookseller called **Chapter 11** thrives with price cutting.[59] The store's slogan is "Prices So Low, You'd Think We Were Going Bankrupt" and it prices aggressively, discounting best-sellers 30 percent and all books at least 11 percent. Its new stores are small, in low-cost locations, and designed for quick shopping, all tactics quite different from the larger competitors. Such a "penetration" strategy is the opposite of a skimming strategy. Firms following such a strategy sometimes even enter a market at a loss, hoping to make up initial losses with longer term repeat purchases. This strategy makes sense when competitive imitation will occur quickly, costs are likely to drop a good deal with increases in volume, and target consumers are relatively price sensitive. Penetration pricing is the standard strategy followed by low-cost leaders.

Price-Quality Inferences

One of the downsides of penetration pricing is that customers may infer low quality from low price. This is most likely to happen under the following circumstances:

1. *Customers are uncertain about brand quality prior to purchase.* The quality of some products is difficult to judge because of their complexity (e.g., computers and cameras), while other products are difficult to assess because one cannot "try them out" prior to buying (e.g., many consumer package goods like food products).
2. *The risk to customers of a bad decision is high.* When the risk of a bad choice is high, customers often rely on price to suggest quality. Risk may vary across product categories (e.g., in general, the perceived risk associated with service purchases is higher than that for goods), perceived variance among products within the category (e.g., risk is low if all refrigerators are perceived to perform roughly the same), and consumption situations (e.g., higher risk when a disposable camera is used at a wedding or on the first day of first grade).

Although there continues to be a debate about how frequently (and when) customers use price as a signal of quality, it is fairly safe to assume that customer uncertainty about quality of a new brand is often very high, so that price-quality inference is a concern. It is also clear that firms pursuing differentiation strategies should maintain relatively high prices, for an additional reason beyond those discussed earlier: to credibly communicate their high quality to customers who may have uncertain quality assessments.

Explaining Adjustments to Base Price over Time

Most of the pricing decisions that are made for a product in its lifetime are *price change decisions*. Base price may change as a natural function of different objectives over the product life cycle, in response to specific *competitive price moves*, or as a function of special pricing tactics that may create a "schedule" of prices or even unique prices for different customers. In addition, prices may change for short periods of time as a result of the ever-popular practice of price promotion.

Variation in Objectives over the Product Life Cycle

The firm's objectives in pricing and other elements of the marketing mix will vary over the product life cycle. In the introductory phase, paying attention to costs is important, and the firm may choose to pursue a skimming or penetration strategy. In the growth phase, the firm is faced with the opposing forces of growing demand, yet increasing competition. This necessitates aggressive pricing if the firm cannot hold on to a unique product advantage. Maturity is likely to bring either stable, competitive prices or price wars if some rival attempts to get aggressive (again, this assumes no unique advantage of any rival). The firm should do its best to maintain stable prices and not rock the boat in maturity. Alternatively, some firms will attempt to innovate to break out of the commodity trap. In decline, the firm should try to keep prices up if the decision has been made to harvest the brand. Predicting when and how much to cut prices is an important task.

Competitive Price Moves

Very often, one firm's price change prompts a reaction from another. This is particularly true today as markets move quickly into maturity and face commodity status. Even brands as strong as Rubbermaid are affected by such competitive forces. Once a Wall Street darling and able to charge a price premium for its innovative new products, Rubbermaid has more recently had to lower prices in the face of growing competition and increasing retailer pressure to discount.[60] When competitors enter and improve products as an industry moves into the growth phase of its life cycle, the incumbent almost always has to respond with price and/or innovation.

It has been found that of all the marketing mix decisions, price is the one most likely to motivate a response from competitors.[61] Companies tend to keep a sharp eye on competitors' prices, especially in mature markets where overall demand is price inelastic. More recently, it has been found that management's decision to follow a competitor's price change is affected by the decision maker's perception of product price elasticity, as well as the behavior of other competitors.[62]

Price Flexing: Different Prices for Different Buyers

A naive look at pricing would lead to the assumption that once price is set, it then remains constant and is the same for all buyers. In fact, however, we have seen that prices are not static—they may change in response to changes in the firm's objectives over the product life cycle and in response to competitive price moves. Yet, even more variation in prices is introduced by both established promotion and discount practices, and innovative pricing practices related primarily to new information technology. We discuss each of these in turn.

PRICE FLEXING TO BUSINESS CUSTOMERS Although the Robinson-Patman Act places constraints on manufacturers' ability to charge business customers different prices, there is a tremendous amount of price flexing that takes place in the form of a wide variety of discounts and allowances. There are many other ways that a supplier may end up selling to different buyers for different prices. Traditional approaches that result in flexible prices include the following:

Price Shading This occurs when, during a negotiation, a salesperson reduces the base price of a product. This may occur for a variety of reasons but is most likely due to the attractiveness of obtaining the business of the particular customer being pursued (e.g., a large customer or one who promises a potentially profitable long-term relationship). It may be common for some haggling to take place and may, in fact, be a badge of honor among purchasing agents to achieve some discount off-list price. For companies attempting to pursue a strategy of differentiation, though, price shading is not desirable.

Cash or Payment Discounts These are discounts the buyer receives for either paying in cash or paying promptly. A standard payment term is "two-ten, net thirty," meaning that the buyer gets a 2 percent discount for paying in less than 10 days (otherwise, they pay the total net cost within the 30-day term). This practice effectively price discriminates between slow- and fast-paying customers.

Volume Discounting Customers who buy in larger volumes are often given more favorable terms. In fact, this is one of the key justifications for price discrimination in the eyes of the Robinson-Patman Act: total handling, shipping, and clerical expenses are lower (per unit) for larger volumes sold. Providing such discounts also encourages customers to purchase in large volumes, which has the added benefit of reducing the customer's probability of doing business with competitive firms.

> **Free on board (FOB) pricing**
> Leaves the cost and responsibility of transportation to the customer.

Geographic Pricing It is common for business customers in different regions to receive different prices since transportation costs may be accounted for in pricing. Sellers deal with freight charges in different ways. **Free on board (FOB) pricing** requires the customer to pay for all costs of transportation. This simplifies things for the seller, but also creates a disadvantage in that her products become increasingly expensive to buyers who are geographically further away. An alternative to FOB pricing is **uniform delivered pricing**, where, in effect, the seller averages the costs of transportation across all customers. A good example of this is postage stamp pricing.

Sales Promotion Allowances These are discounts that business customers (like retailers) receive for putting the manufacturer's product on sale to consumers for a particular period of time. Such allowances have become a staple in business today, particularly in consumer package goods.

Creative Alternatives to Discounting [63] Suppliers are getting very creative today with their price flexing, such that list price appears to stay fairly constant, but other tactics provide the flex. A few examples:

1. Some manufacturers provide generous financing for buyers. For example, **Lucent Technologies, Inc.** will sell equipment to startups in return for some negotiated share of the startup's (sometimes shaky) revenue.
2. Some customers are requiring long-term contracts with suppliers that guarantee no price increases for the life of the deal.
3. Suppliers may provide services (e.g., repairs) at no cost.
4. An increasing number of customers are demanding promises of quality improvement over the course of a contract at the same or lower price.

Price Customization While price shading, discounting, and the creative approaches to price flexing we've discussed clearly reflect some degree of "customizing" price for customers, new technology may make it possible for prices to be customized literally on a transaction-by-transaction basis, depending on the conditions of supply and demand at the moment. In the free market, prices are determined by the interplay of supply and demand. Prices will be higher when demand exceeds supply and they will drop as more suppliers (or more supply) enter the market. Traditionally, supply and demand adjustments have taken days, weeks, or months to occur, as information about current supply and demand slowly found its way to buyers and sellers. However, new technology has made the sharing of supply and demand information nearly instantaneous, as "the Internet, corporate networks, and wireless setups are linking people, machines, and companies around the globe—and connecting sellers and buyers as never before."[64]

Price Flexing to Consumers While there are some circumstances in which consumers negotiate pricing (e.g., new or used automobiles), you may think that retailers use a "one-price" approach almost exclusively. With a few exceptions—particularly smaller local shops, antiques, and used goods—sellers do appear to charge fixed prices for products. Even the automobile industry is seeing a trend toward *single-pricing*, both with **Saturn's** innovative sales approach and the online car vendors (e.g., **Auto-By-Tel, AutoVantage,** or **Microsoft's** CarPoint), which each sell products at no-haggle prices.[65]

Interestingly, though, there is more price flexing taking place in consumer markets than meets the eye. It takes the form of price promotion, couponing, segmented pricing, and, as we saw earlier with the business market, an increasing trend toward customization. We review each of these next.

Price Promotion **Price promotion** is a ubiquitous and effective practice in many situations, particularly early in a product's life, where the objective would be to encourage trial and to allow the seller to maintain a higher list price.

Price promotions Short-term price reductions designed to create an incentive for consumers to buy now rather than later and/or stock up on the specially priced product.

This is a version of the famous *prisoner's dilemma* from game theory, which poses the paradox of a joint decision-making situation in which the players do best by cooperating (not promoting), but each player has an individual incentive to "defect" (in our case, to do a price promotion). If both players defect, both are worse off. Once promotions get started, it may become clear to the firms that their profitability is lower, but they have a hard time raising prices back up again. Why is this so?

The reason is that consumers respond well to promotions, which encourages manufacturers to do more of them. As consumers grow accustomed to such price specials, any firm that does not price promote is likely to lose sales. So, promotions tend to increase over time, leading consumers to be more sensitive to price.[66] As this happens, retailers adapt to promotions by forward buying or diverting product. All in all, everyone's attention goes to price, when price is highlighted through increasing promotion. As a response to this vicious cycle of competitive promotions—and its related inefficiency—Procter & Gamble instituted **every day low pricing** (**EDLP**) in the early 1990s (also known as *value pricing*).

Couponing Couponing provides another means of price discrimination in that it gives some consumers—those who wish to take the time and effort to clip coupons—the capability of paying lower prices. Most coupons come from *free-standing inserts (FSIs)* in the weekend newspaper but, increasingly, coupons are available at point-of-purchase and printed on grocery register tapes.

Pricing for Different Segments Marketers very often have different marketing programs for different consumer segments.

- *Geographic Segments.* It is possible that price sensitivity varies across geographic regions. For example, some grocery retailers have different price zones and prices are likely to vary across those zones. Competition and consumer profiles may differ between geographic segments. To generate interest among potential patrons in outlying areas, the symphony (discussed earlier) might plan smaller, fun ensemble concerts at performance halls or public places in other locales priced at or below variable cost.
- *Usage Segments.* It is common for marketers to recognize high-volume users and reward them with different prices. For example, regular customers at a particular grocery store who carry the stores' frequent shopper card receive discounts at checkout that other shoppers do not receive. Where capacity is an issue for the manufacturer or service provider, the heaviest users may actually pay more. **IBM** applied this strategy to its Internet service, charging accounts that exceed a threshold level of usage an hourly fee in addition to the basic monthly rate. In contrast, symphonies and theaters often have packages that charge patrons who commit to attending a certain number of events receive a reduced price.
- *Demographic Segments.* A symphony might provide special prices for students or children to encourage attendance, or give discounts to senior citizens. This is a common strategy used by museums, athletic events, and amusement parks.
- *Time Segments.* There are many examples of how "time" provides a relevant basis for segmenting markets for pricing. Resort hotels have on- and off-season rates, reflecting differences in demand for those seasons.

Customization As discussed earlier for business markets, new technology may have a significant effect on the prices consumers pay for products and may lead to significant variation in the prices that consumers pay for the same item. For example, consumers can participate in the Internet auctions.

Consumer Behavior and Marketing Research

The Scope of Consumer Behavior

Consumer behavior is the process by which individuals or groups select, use, or dispose of goods, services, ideas, or experiences to satisfy needs and wants. This definition of consumer behavior includes a variety of activities and a number of roles that people hold as consumers. In addition to the actual purchaser (*buyer*), our definition of *consumer* includes *payers* as consumers and *users* as consumers. For example, during Christmas people frequently purchase gifts—though they are the payers and the buyers, the users are the recipients of the gifts.

Three Consumer Roles

In identifying and satisfying consumer needs and wants, it is important to recognize the significance of the various consumer roles. In each role we are concerned with a different facet of the product. As **users,** we are concerned with the product features and the uses they can be put to. As **payers,** we are concerned with the price of the product and the inherent financial considerations. It is the payer who is being targeted by ads claiming "0 down and 0% interest 'til 2005." As **buyers,** we are concerned with the logistics of procuring the product for either our own use or the use of others. For example, ads that claim consumers can order on a company's Web site as late as February 10 for products to be delivered on Valentine's Day are clearly targeted at the buyer.

To understand consumer behavior, we need to understand about consumers' *needs and wants,* their *perceptions,* how they *learn,* their *motivations and emotions,* how they form *attitudes* and how they make *purchase decisions.* In the following section we discuss the differences between consumers' needs and wants, as well as the factors that influence needs and wants.

Consumer Needs and Wants

To understand consumer behavior, we need to understand how consumers perceive, learn, and make decisions to satisfy their needs and wants. It is important to understand what the needs and wants of users, payers, and buyers are. **Needs** are unsatisfactory conditions of the consumer that prompt him or her to an action that will make the condition better. **Wants** are desires to obtain more satisfaction than is absolutely necessary to improve an unsatisfactory condition. The difference between a need and a want is that need arousal is driven by discomfort in a person's physical and psychological conditions. Wants occur when humans desire to take their physical and psychological conditions beyond the state of minimal comfort. Only when needs are satisfied do wants surface.

Psychological Bases of Consumer Behavior

Perception

The objective reality of a product matters little; what does matter is the consumer's perception of a product or a brand. **Perception** is the process by which an individual *senses, organizes,* and *interprets* the information he or she receives from the environment. Marketers seek to understand the sources of consumer perceptions and to influence them. For example, cereals are made darker in color to make them appear more masculine while mouthwashes are colored green or blue to connote a clean, fresh feeling.

Learning

Learning is a change in the content of long-term memory. Most consumer behavior is learned behavior. We learn consciously and subconsciously from a number of sources. We learn from our prior experiences, our peers, mass media, or family and friends. Learning helps us to respond better to our environment. A child who accidentally puts his hand on a hot electric bulb learns never again to touch anything resembling that object. Thus, human learning is directed at acquiring a potential for future adaptive behavior.

Motivation

Motivation is what moves people—it is the driving force for all human behavior. More formally, **motivation** is defined as the state of drive or arousal that impels behavior toward a goal-object. Thus, motivation has two components: (1) *drive or arousal,* and (2) a *goal-object.* For example, the arousal or drive is akin to stepping on the gas pedal in an automobile, whereas the goal-object is analogous to the steering of the vehicle. Having the former without the latter is dangerous and having the latter without the former is useless.

CONSUMER NEEDS The concept of needs and wants described earlier is closely aligned to the concept of motivation. Human beings have potentially infinite needs. To make sense of these various needs, psychologists have classified them. Among the most relevant classifications to marketers is Maslow's needs hierarchy.

CONSUMER EMOTIONS Needs and emotions are closely related. **Emotions** are strong, relatively uncontrolled feelings that affect our behavior.[67] Emotions are often triggered by environmental factors or events. Such emotions affect our consumption behavior. Some emotions may be internally generated. Emotions are typically accompanied by physiological changes such as dilation of the pupils of the eyes, rapid breathing, or an increase in blood pressure. We all seek positive emotional experiences and avoid negative emotional experiences. Much of the consumption or use of products is driven by and immersed in emotions.

We cuddle a baby because we feel affection and love for it. We swear at a rude driver who cuts in front of us because we feel anger and frustration. Although we have all experienced emotion, it is not easy to define. The reason is that emotion is a complex set of processes, occurring concurrently in multiple systems. Emotions have three response components: cognitive, emotional, and physiological. *Cognitive responses* are the thought processes of individuals and include beliefs, categorization, and symbolic meaning. *Emotional responses* do not involve thinking, they simply happen, often unexplainably and suddenly. Specific songs, for example, may make individuals feel happy, feel sad, or re-create other past feelings that were associated with the particular piece of music. In contrast to cognitive and emotional responses, *physiological responses* are often described in terms of physical pleasure or discomfort.

CONSUMER MOODS Do you recall the last time you really enjoyed shopping? Maybe you were in a bookstore such as Border's, and some especially mellow music was playing. You relaxed and lingered on, browsing through the books on the "new release" shelves. Maybe you ended up buying four books that day. That is the power of positive mood! This is the same reason many on-line storefronts have audio files attached, so that when you visit their Web site you hear music playing in the background.

When an emotion is less intense and transitory, it is termed a **mood.** We are in some mood all the time. We may be in a happy, sad, positive, negative, or introspective mood at any given point of time. Since we are in some mood or another at any given point of time, it is important for marketers to understand consumer moods.

Just like emotions, moods are induced both by external stimuli as well as internally by autistic thinking—that is, recalling some past incident or fantasizing about some event. The ambience of the store, demeanor of the salespeople, and the tone and manner of advertising are all marketing stimuli that can affect a person's moods.

Mood states have consequences in terms of favorable or unfavorable consumer response to marketing efforts. We generally do not buy anything from salespersons who put us in an unpleasant mood—for example, by not showing that they care about our business. Research studies indicate that consumers linger longer in positive mood environments, recall those advertisements more that had created good moods, and feel more positive toward brands based on advertising that created feelings of warmth.[68]

INVOLVEMENT **Involvement** can be defined as the degree of personal relevance of an object or product to a consumer. Involvement is a matter of degree—how relevant or how central a product is. Accordingly, we can expand the notion of involvement to refer, beyond relevance, to the degree to which a consumer finds a product of interest. While both salt and cosmetics are relevant to people, it is quite likely that consumers would be more involved in a decision about cosmetics than salt.

Involvement, defined as the degree of interest, can be viewed as having two forms: enduring involvement and situational involvement. *Enduring involvement* is the degree of interest a consumer feels about a product on an ongoing basis. In contrast, *situational involvement* is the degree of interest in a specific situation or on a specific occasion, such as when buying a product or when consuming something in the presence of an important client or friend.

Psychographics: Describing Consumer Behavior

Psychographics *Characteristics of individual that describe them in terms of their psychological and behavioral makeup.*

Another facet of motivation is **psychographics.** These are characteristics of individuals that identify them in terms of their psychological and behavioral makeup—how people occupy themselves (behavior) and what psychological factors underlie their activity pattern. Psychographics have three components: values, self-concept, and lifestyles.

Values

When you think about what is important to you in life, you are thinking about your values. **Values** are end-states of life, the goals one lives for. Psychologist Milton Rokeach has identified two groups of values: terminal and instrumental. *Terminal values* are the goals we seek in life (e.g., peace and happiness), whereas *instrumental values* are the means or behavioral standards by which we pursue our goals (e.g., honesty).

Consumer researchers felt a need to identify the values directly relevant to everyday consumer behavior. Toward this end, consumer researchers Lynn Kahle and his associates developed a list of values, consisting of nine terminal values:

1. Self-respect
2. Self-fulfillment
3. Security
4. Sense of belonging
5. Excitement
6. Sense of accomplishment
7. Fun and enjoyment
8. Being well respected
9. Warm relationships with others[69]

Consumers cluster into three groups depending on which of these values are more important to them. They are *internals* if they value self-fulfillment, excitement, a sense of accomplishment, and self-respect. These people like to be in control of their lives. In marketing terms, internals take proactive steps such as looking at nutritional labels while buying products. The second group is *externals,* who value a sense of belonging, security, and being well respected. These people like to conform and hence are more likely to buy products that they think most people buy. Externals are brand-conscious people who buy a popular brand because everybody else is buying it. Finally, *interpersonals* value warm relationships with others, as well as fun and enjoyment.

Self-Concept

Everyone has a self-image—a perception of who we are. This is called **self-concept.** Furthermore, self-concept includes an idea of what an individual currently is and what he or she would like to become. These two components of self-concept are called *actual self* and *ideal self,* respectively.

Self-concept deeply influences people's consumption, for people express their self-concept in large measure by what they consume. Individuals' self-concepts vary according to which of the three consumer roles described earlier—users, payers, and buyers—they are playing. A user might have the self-concept of a very discerning connoisseur or a very involved user. The payer might have the self-concept of being thrifty, financially prudent, or a nonchalant, money-is-no-object-to-me attitude. Finally, the buyer might have the self-concept of being a convenience seeker or service seeker or being very time conscious.

Lifestyles

To this point, we have looked at how we think of ourselves and what we value, now we will focus on the way we live—our *lifestyle.* A good way to determine the lifestyle of a person is to look at the products and brands that they consume. Lifestyle is a function of (1) a consumer's personal characteristics, namely, genetics, race, gender, age, and personality; (2) personal context, namely, culture, institutions, reference groups, and personal worth; and (3) needs and emotions. These three sets of factors together influence the pattern of our activities—how we spend time and money.

Attitude: Definition and Characteristics

Gordon Allport, the psychologist, defines **attitudes** as "learned predispositions to respond to an object or class of objects in a consistently favorable or unfavorable way."[70]

The definition has several implications:

1. Attitudes are learned. That is, they are formed on the basis of some experience with or without information about the object.
2. Attitudes are predispositions. As such they reside in the mind.
3. Attitudes cause consistent response. They precede and produce behavior.

Because attitudes precede and produce behavior, they can be used to predict behavior. Marketers use attitude measures before launching new products. Behavior also can be used to infer the underlying attitudes. In everyday life, we observe somebody's behavior toward us and use that observation to infer whether that person likes us; we then use that inferred attitude to predict how the person will behave toward us in the future. Marketers, too, often use this logic. When consumers buy a product, this purchase behavior is used to infer a favorable attitude toward the related product class, which is in turn deemed to be an indicator of the potential purchase of an item in the related product class.

Attitudes, then, are our evaluations of objects—people, places, brands, products, organizations, and so on. People evaluate objects in terms of their goodness, likability, or desirability. Consumers may hold attitudes toward salespersons in general (e.g., "Salespeople are basically all hucksters"), and about specific companies (e.g., "Company X makes good electronic appliances but not computers"). Attitudes do change with time and marketers strive to influence consumers' attitudes. Marketers try to change them if consumers have a negative attitude toward their brand and reinforce the attitude if they have a positive attitude toward their brand.

Individual Consumer Decision Making

So far we have discussed *psychological concepts* that affect consumer behavior, including consumers *needs and wants, perception, learning, motivation,* and *attitude formation.* Consumers use some or all of these processes when they make decisions to buy (or not buy) a product. Purchase decisions are sometimes made by individuals in households; at other times they are made collectively by groups of people such as spouses and children.

As discussed earlier, consumers adopt three different roles in the decision-making scenario—buyer, payer, and user. In each of these roles, consumers constantly face choices—how much to spend, what product to acquire, and where to purchase it from. These choices call for **consumer decision making.** Typically, these decisions include *whether* to purchase, *what* to purchase, *when* to purchase, from *whom* to purchase, and *how* to pay for it. Consumers have finite resources in terms of money and time, so they have to constantly weigh the possibility of either postponing or forsaking the purchase of a product. Thus we constantly make decisions about whether to purchase and what to purchase at the product level.

An important consumer behavior at this decision level is *mental budgeting*—how the budget consumers set for a product category guides their subsequent behavior as a consumer. The payer plays the most important role in mental budgeting as the user is constrained by what the payer has budgeted and whether the product is within the budget. This occurs subconsciously, even when one consumer is playing both the payer and user roles.

Following the choice at the product level, the consumer makes another what-to-purchase decision—a choice among brands. For example, if the product category–level decision is to take a vacation, the next decision is which brand to purchase—that is, which travel destination to select, how to get there, and so on. The process of consumer decision making consists of five steps, as shown in Exhibit 300.28.

Exhibit 300.28 *Customer Decision-Making Process*

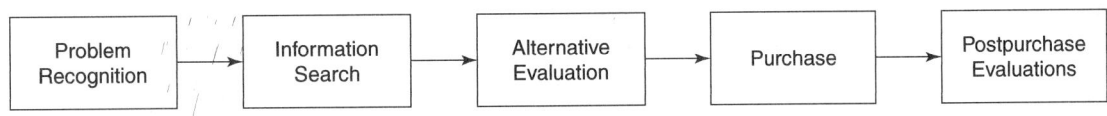

Step 1: Problem Recognition

Consumers typically make purchase decisions to satisfy a particular need or a want. Howard, for example, could realize that he is hungry and hence has to buy some food, or that the leaking faucet needs to be fixed. A consumer problem can be any state of deprivation or discomfort felt by a consumer. **Problem recognition** occurs when consumers realize that they need to do something to get back to a normal state of comfort.

Problem recognition can occur due to either an internal stimulus or an external stimulus. *Internal stimuli* are perceived states of discomfort—physical or psychological (e.g., hunger or boredom, respectively). *External stimuli* are informational cues from the marketplace that lead the consumer to realize the problem.

Step 2: Information Search

The **information search** stage of the consumer decision process could be as simple as scanning one's memory to check what product/brand was bought when the last purchase decision occurred. This can be a subconscious search for information. However, more often than not, we specifically seek information to solve the problem that has been identified. This search rarely includes every brand in existence. Consumers consider only a select subset of brands, organized as follows:

- The *awareness set* consists of brands of which a consumer is aware.
- An *evoked set* consists of the brands in a product category that the consumer remembers at the time of decision making.
- Of the brands in the evoked set, not all are deemed to fit the need. Those considered unfit are eliminated right away. The remaining brands are termed the *consideration set*—the brands a consumer will consider buying.

Initially, consumers seek information about the consideration set of brands. New information can bring additional brands into the awareness, evoked, and consideration sets. These include marketer source and nonmarketer source (e.g., consumer reports).

Step 3: Alternative Evaluation

Once consumers have the necessary information, how do they use that information as they proceed through the **alternative evaluation** stage of the consumer decision process to arrive at a specific choice? Consumers select one of the several alternatives (brands, dealers, and so on) available to them. These specific processes and steps are referred to by researchers as *choice models*. There are two broad categories of choice models: compensatory and noncompensatory.

COMPENSATORY MODEL In the *compensatory model*, the consumer arrives at a choice by considering all of the attributes of a product (or benefits of a service) and mentally trading off the alternative's perceived weakness on one or more attributes for its perceived strength on other attributes.

NONCOMPENSATORY MODELS While there are several *noncompensatory* models that have been identified, four are most common and useful. These are called conjunctive, disjunctive, lexicographic, and elimination by aspects.[71] In the *conjunctive model*, the consumer begins by setting the minimum cutoffs on all salient attributes. Each alternative is then examined on each attribute, and any alternative that meets the minimum cutoffs on all attributes can potentially be chosen.

The *disjunctive model* entails trade-offs between aspects of choice alternatives. Sometimes the consumer is willing to trade off one feature for another. For example, a homebuyer might say that the house she is willing to consider buying should have either five bedrooms or, if it has only four bedrooms, a finished basement. Although similar trade-offs are made in the compensatory model, there are differences. First, the disjunctive model considers the sheer presence or absence of attributes, rather than the degree or amount to which these attributes are present. Second, in the compensatory model, the attributes traded off need not serve the same purpose, while they tend to in the disjunctive model.

Another model consumers use to make a choice is the *lexicographic model*. In this model, attributes of alternatives are rank ordered in terms of importance. Consumers examine all alternatives on the most important criterion and identify the ones that surpass a threshold level. If more than one alternative remains in the choice set, they then consider the second most important criterion and examine the remaining alternatives with respect to that criterion's threshold level. The process continues until only one alternative remains.

The *elimination by aspects model* is similar to the lexicographic model but with one important difference: Consumers rate the attributes in order of importance and, in addition, define cutoff values. They then examine all alternatives first on the most important attribute, admitting for further consideration only those that satisfy the minimum cutoff level on this most important attribute. If more than one alternative meets the requirement, they go on to the next aspect, appraising the remaining alternatives on the second attribute.

It has been found that consumers may use any of these choice models independently or use a combination of the choice models. For some of the more important decisions, a consumer might first use a noncompensatory model and then, to further identify the choice, use a compensatory model. The noncompensatory model could be used to eliminate choices and narrow down the set of alternatives for closer comparisons.

Step 4: Purchase

Once the consumer has evaluated the alternatives, he makes a **purchase.** This appears a straightforward step, but even here consumer behavior at times becomes intriguing.

Step 5: Postpurchase Evaluations

The purchase of the product is followed by a postpurchase evaluation stage. When consumers' expectations are not met by the performance of the product, they get dissatisfied. When performance meets the expectation level, consumers are satisfied, and when consumers' expectations are surpassed by performance, they are delighted. Hence, marketers should be concerned not only with the performance of their product but also must manage consumers' expectations, knowing that whether consumers are satisfied will affect future purchase decisions.

After consumers make an important choice decision, they experience an intense need to confirm the wisdom of that decision. The flip side is that they want to avoid disconfirmation. One of the processes of this **postpurchase behavior** is *cognitive dissonance:* a postpurchase doubt the buyer experiences about the wisdom of the choice. One of the methods of reducing cognitive dissonance and confirming the soundness of one's decision is to seek further positive information about the chosen alternative and avoid negative information about the chosen alternative.

Following a satisfactory or dissatisfactory experience, consumers have three possible responses: *exit, voice,* or *loyalty.* If consumers are dissatisfied with their experience with a brand, they may decide never again to buy that brand. This places them back to the start of the decision process the next time the problem arises. Some dissatisfied consumers complain and then decide either to give the brand or marketer another chance or simply to exit. Following the complaint, negative word-of-mouth is less likely and repatronage more likely if the complaint is successfully redressed. If the complaint is not successfully redressed, the negative word-of-mouth might intensify beyond what it would have been had the consumer not made the complaint in the first place.

The third response is, of course, loyalty. Consumer loyalty means the consumer buys the same brand repeatedly. It is fair to assume that satisfied consumers are more likely to be loyal. However, the converse is not necessarily true as some researchers have found that not all satisfied consumers are loyal. Some consumers exhibit switching behavior despite being satisfied with the current brand.

Household Decision Making

Households are the basic unit of buying and consumption in a society despite the fact that what constitutes a household has changed vastly with the passage of time. A household is a consumption unit of one or more persons identified by a common location with an address. While a number of consumer decisions are no doubt made by individuals for personal consumption (e.g., buying food during office lunch hour), the more significant decisions are made by individuals jointly with other members of their household, and for joint use by the members of the household.

Household decision making is important to study as it is likely to be different from that of the individual decision-making process. The critical difference is that it is quite likely that in the individual decision-making process all three roles—buyer, user, and payer—are more likely to merge in one person, in the case of the household it is more likely that the three roles will be assumed by separate individuals. The separation of the three roles makes household buying behavior somewhat complex to track and influence. Moreover, these role allocations are dynamic. They vary from time to time, from one product to another, and from one family type to another.

The Competitive Importance of Market Research

Firms that are able to adjust their marketing strategies to reflect changes in domestic and international markets more quickly than competitors are able to sustain a competitive advantage. Often the key to this advantage lies within the firm's ability to collect, organize, and act upon information that is gathered through market research and information systems. Market research can range from executive visits to a customer's manufacturing facility through to the rather complex and very rare market testing.

From a sociological and political economy perspective, a market is made up of many diverse players, each with its own distinct interests and behavior. Successful marketing decision-making teams obviously think a lot about how consumers will react to a new product or business tactic. But they also think about how other "players" in the marketplace will react to the firm's change in business strategy. It is like a game: You have to anticipate how the different players will react to your move. Some will welcome your moves, others will be indifferent to them, and yet others will contest your moves. Then you have to think about how consumers will react to your rivals' reactions, which are called second-order effects. A market typically contains four types of players: consumers, competitors, distribution channel members, and regulators: those that monitor the marketplace. Each of these groups can be further subdivided into segments, types, and individual entities. Consequently, it is generally recommended that the study of the market be divided into four topics: consumer research, competitor research, channel research, and public policy research. The point is that market research is not just consumer research; market research into changes in competitors, channels, and public policy is given far too little attention in market research practice and teaching.

Surprisingly little is known about what market information decision makers actually use when thinking about the market, but the analysis of the content of marketing plans suggests that it sometimes may be less than adequate. It is hoped that decision makers are briefed about changes in the marketplace in other ways than solely through the content of the marketing plan, such as during informal decision-making sessions by market researchers; otherwise, a great deal of market decision making is less informed than it could be. It is highly likely that many firms might benefit from rethinking how they use market research and what they learn from such analyses.[72] In the following sections, we highlight the different techniques that are used to research consumers, competitors, and distribution channels. How firms (and their lawyers) research the regulatory and policy environment is beyond the scope of this section.

Consumer Research

For many, market research means research that focuses on final consumers and users of the good or service. Such research can take many and varied forms, with arguments for and against the cost effectiveness of different practices. If there is one rule in consumer research, though, it is that it should always include firsthand observational research by the decision makers for whom the research is being undertaken. In short, decision makers should always undertake some of the market research themselves. A firm that does not require its marketing decision makers to be involved in some form of direct observational research can hardly claim that it is customer-oriented. The excuse that executives are too busy doing other more important things simply says that the leadership is more focused on other issues than understanding its customers.

Exhibit 300.29 presents the conventional consumer research process. It indicates that in the real world consumer research often proceeds incrementally. The least costly source of answers to the perceived problem should be searched first. Major studies are undertaken only if satisfactory answers cannot be found from secondary sources, by studying other markets, or if the issue is of great importance and a precise answer is required. In the following sections we expand on the major stages presented in Exhibit 300.29. First, we search the secondary sources within and outside the firm for answers. This is often followed by fairly basic primary research, such as extensive customer visits, in-depth interviews with customers, and focus groups. This is often referred to as qualitative research because it does not generate data that can be quantitatively analyzed with much confidence. If the answer is not clear from qualitative research or if reassuring confirmation is sought, then more thorough survey research is likely to be undertaken that can provide quantitative answers using statistics and sampling techniques.

Competitor Research

The first question almost every company asks in its decision-making process is, Who are the major players in the market? That is, who has what share of market sales? *Market share* is measured as a percentage of total industry sales over a specified time period. Before determining the major players, we must define the term *market*. Clearly, problems exist

Exhibit 300.29 *The Basic Market Research Process*

1. **Problem recognition:**
   Basic questions are what happened and why?
   What is happening?
   Should we do it?

2. **Meet and define problem and determine how to solve it:**
   When is the answer needed? Limits research method that is used.
   How valuable is the answer to us? Limits research method that is used.
   How valuable is high accuracy? Limits research method that is used.

3. **Search secondary data sources and own databases:**
   Has it happened elsewhere? Check archives.
   Call outside experts for answers.
   How can syndicated research suppliers help?
   Does any published research on the problem exist? Search the Internet.
   Meet and review answers. *Stop if answers are satisfactory.*

4. **Undertake quick-and-dirty primary research:**
   Conduct an electronic voice-mail survey of the sales force.
   Call on or fax customers/distributors.
   Run focus groups. Meet and review answers. *Stop if answers are satisfactory.*

5. **Undertake thorough primary research:**
   Select sampling frame (random-sample national panel provided by market research firm).
   Choose survey technique (personal visit, mall intercept, telephone, mail). Design questionnaire.

6. **Analyze information:**
   Review descriptive statistics (such as percentages, means, standard deviations).
   Conduct relationship analyses (such as cross-tabs, chi-square, correlational analyses, structural equations modeling, logit, ANOVA, MANOVA, Conjoint).

7. **Present findings:**
   Offer progress briefings on important findings.
   Report the presentation.
   Archive findings and data under problem/topic key words.

This exhibit presents the conventional approach to research. Firms often undertake steps 1 through 4. If they require more formal primary research, they will likely hire a market research firm that will take a month or more to do the study at a cost of $10,000 to $30,000, sometimes much more.

in defining the market. A company's market share can change dramatically depending on whether the market is defined as global, a particular export market, the U.S. market, a region of the United States, a city, or a segment of users or usage. The scope of the market is normally specified by a realistic assessment of company resources and by company growth objectives. Often, the market is defined by the way market researchers are able to collect sales and market share information. This information is often supplied by government agencies, trade associations, or market research firms that survey all of the firms in a market.

The historical problem with research into competition has been too much focus on measuring the number of current competitors, the concentration of market share (the combined market share of the largest three competitors), and the current balance sheet assets of major competitors. The emphasis needs to be placed on market dynamics, such as who is introducing new manufacturing, distribution, and product development processes into the market. Competitive insight comes from explaining such drivers of success in the market, and not from knowing who has the largest market share. The acid test for such insight is whether an executive wants to know what company has the largest market share (*static thought*) or what company has experienced the largest change in market share (*dynamic thought*). Does the firm study the history of change in the industry to identify the trends in changing supply to further identify which paths the market will take in the future (i.e., production and distribution technological paths)? A dynamic analysis is thus able to identify what and who are the drivers of change in the market.[73]

The change in market share over time is a vital indicator of the competitive environment. However, market share is not the only measure of competitiveness. The following measures are often used as leading indicators of a likely change in future sales and profits:

1. *Mind share:* The percentage of customers who name the brand when asked to name the first brand that comes to mind when they think about buying a particular type of product. This indicates the consumer's top-of-mind brand awareness and preferences. How is it changing among different segments?
2. *Voice share:* The percentage of media space or time a brand has of the total media share for that industry, often measured simply as dollars spent on advertising. This is likely to lead to a change in mind share (but not always, if the messages are weak). How and why is it changing?
3. *Research and development (R&D share):* A company's expenditure as a percentage of the total industry R&D expenditure. This is a long-term predictor of new product developments, improvements in quality, cost reductions, and hence market share. It is an important measure of future competitiveness in many high-technology markets. How is it changing, and what is it being spent on?

Michael Porter's pioneering text, *Competitive Strategy,* changed the way many companies think about their competition.[74] Porter identified five forces that shape competition: *current competitors, the threat of new entrants, the threat of new substitutes, the bargaining power of distributors (or business-to-business customers),* and *the bargaining power of suppliers.* This structure can be reduced further to include simply current competitors and potential competitors and substitutes. The way distributors and suppliers behave determines the threat posed by immediate and potential competition. Distributors and suppliers are therefore not separate competitive elements but moderators or amplifiers of competition (see Exhibit 300.30). Generally, suppliers and distributors are used to gain competitive advantage and should be seen in this light. That is why distributor and channel research should be undertaken separately from competitor research. It is true that at times distributors and suppliers have to be directly considered in a competitive analysis, but only when they threaten to become a new direct competitor. A company must be on guard against new entrants and from others up and down the supply chain. This concern is best addressed in competitive research by asking and answering the questions presented in Exhibit 300.31.

Auditing Current Competitors

For most companies, it is not possible to put all current competitors under the microscope and undertake an in-depth analysis of their competitive strengths and weaknesses. However, particular competitors are always worthy of such attention, either because they are attacking with a new product or because a firm has decided, in a previous plan, to attack them. The isolation of "aggressors" or "targets" usually requires a preliminary analysis that identifies from which rivals you are gaining business and to which competitors you are losing business. This is the way you identify your immediate current competition, which may or may not be using similar technology.[75] For example, many major U.S. cities now have only one daily newspaper, yet such monopolies have not inflated profits for the publisher. The reason is simple. Although other major newspapers may have died, competition for advertising has increased from the suburban weeklies, direct marketing, and other media. Television, radio, and local magazines also have become more competitive with their news and features. The mistake the newspaper publishers made was not identifying these competitors early on when they could have taken countermeasures.[76]

The initial investment in time, effort, and expense necessary to audit competitors may be very high (amounting to several weeks or even months of an executive's or consultant's time), but it should be treated as an investment. The results will produce a report that can be built on from year to year with constantly expanding details and insights. This file then becomes part of the collective memory of your organization to be passed on to successive managers.

The competitive strategy guru Michael Porter has argued that competitive advantage in product quality and costs can come from one or more of the following stages in the added-value chain:[77]

1. Inbound logistics processes
2. Operations processes
3. Outbound logistics processes
4. Marketing and sales processes
5. Service processes

Exhibit 300.30 *Current and Potential Competition*

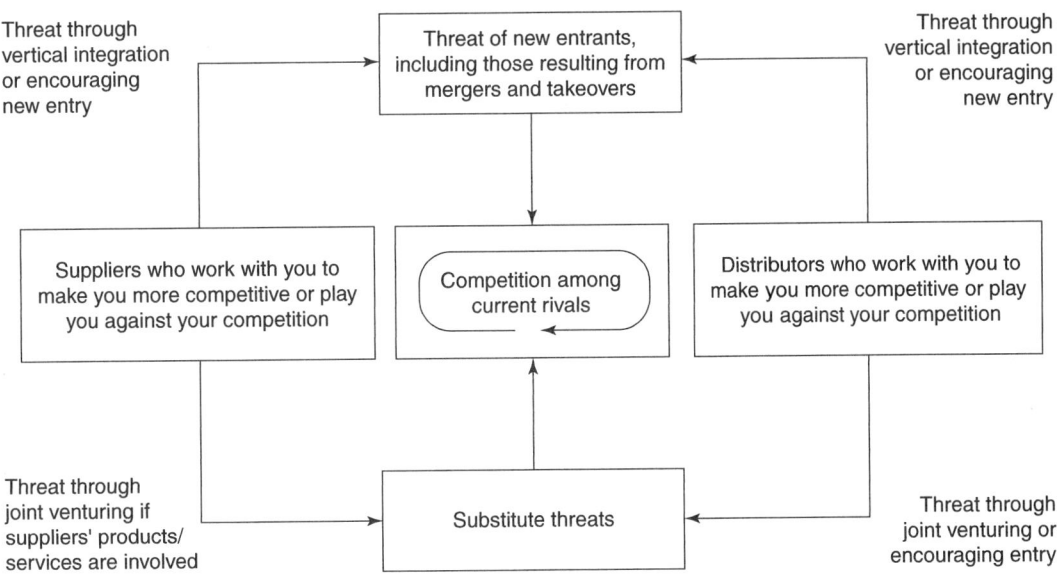

Competition occurs among current rivals. Distributors and suppliers can help or hinder a firm's efforts to become more competitive. Sometimes, they even encourage a new entrant or the development of a new substitute. They seldom, if ever, discourage such entry or the development of a new technological substitute. However, distributors and suppliers are not competitors. In fact, the trading relationship a firm has with a supplier or distributor is a cooperative effort that competes with other trading relationships in the market.

Exhibit 300.31 *New Competitive-Threats Audit*

> The skill in identifying potential new competition is to ask a series of questions that narrows in on the most likely competitor and its situation.
>
> *New Technology—Converging Markets Threat*
>
> - What price changes in other technology markets appear to influence our sales? Is this effort changing?
> - Which new technology or service is starting to be considered as a substitute for our product by consumers? Is this occurring in any particular usage situation or by any particular group of buyers? Are our existing channels encouraging such substitution?
> - What is our closest new technological or service competition?
> - Who is the major mover and shaker in this new industry?
> - What appears to be its current objective and strategy?
> - What is its growth rate?
> - What has been its effect on our sales?
> - What further threat does it pose?
> - What constraints does it face?
>
> *Channel Integration Threat*
>
> - Which supplier is most likely to become a downstream direct competitor in the near future? Why? How would it do it? Is there any evidence of this occurring?
> - Which customers are most likely to become upstream, do-it-themselves competitors in the near future? Why? How would they do it? Does any evidence of such plans exist?
>
> *Competitor Takeover—Merger Threat*
>
> - Which mergers, takeovers, or trading coalitions among competitors or from inside pose the greatest threat to our position? What evidence exists that this is likely to occur?

340. CONSUMER BEHAVIOR AND MARKETING RESEARCH

The implication is that a rival's competitive standing at all stages of the added-value chain from inbound logistics to after-sales service must be studied. This analysis should involve at least three types of information. The first type of information is a rating of the rival's performance compared or **benchmarked** against the very best in the industry. The second type of information is the direction this performance is moving (improving indicated by an up arrow and declining indicated by a down arrow beside the rating). The third type of information should be a detailed explanation as to what is unique and interesting about the rival's behavior or product, or at least the name and e-mail address of someone who can provide such detail.

Channel Research

The suggested procedure for learning about distribution channels is to first address a number of questions about what are the drivers of change in the channel (see Exhibit 300.32) and then to zero in on a detailed audit of some key resellers (sometimes called trade customers). Exhibit 300.32 lists several questions that address the impact on the distribution channel of (1) changes in technology, (2) new entrants, (3) changes in established channel relations, and (4) changes in the way existing channel members do business. The recorded music market provides an excellent example of how such changes impact product marketing.

Researching Individual Trade Customers

Once the general channel change audit has been undertaken, important trade customers will have been identified for further study. Clearly, not all of these resellers can be studied, and some good managerial judgment is needed to make sure greater attention is paid to the major players and innovators. When a manufacturer's sales force uses an account management approach for its major retail trade accounts, it should be relatively easy to complete audits of such trade customers. However, care must be taken that day-to-day operating relations do not drive the evaluations of those who are in constant contact with representatives of suppliers and resellers. The reseller audits require the auditor to stand back, to assess the changes that have occurred over the past trading year, and to explain some of the basic reasons for predicting longer-term changes.

Exhibit 300.32 *Channel Change Audit*

- **Who are the latest new entrants in the reseller market?**
  What is their competitive advantage?
  Which existing resellers are being most affected?
  How has it affected us?

- **What new trading coalitions among resellers are occurring?**
  What will be their competitive advantage?
  How will it affect us?

- **What changes in order-processing technology are now occurring?**
  What impact will they have on the way business is done?
  What competitive advantage do they provide?

- **What changes in transportation technology are now occurring?**
  What impact will they have on the way business is done?
  What competitive advantage do they provide?

- **What changes in warehousing technology are now occurring?**
  What impact will they have on the way business is done?
  What competitive advantage do they provide?

- **What changes in payment technology are now occurring?**
  What impact will they have on the way business is done?
  What competitive advantage do they provide?

Exhibit 300.33 *Individual Distributor Audit*

Company Name: _____ **Date:** _____

Summary Evaluation
- Image and reputation
- Geographical markets/customer segments served
- Major strength, unique value, and importance of this reseller
- Major weakness and failure of reseller
- Special personal relations with distributor

Detailed Evaluation
Trading Performance
- Annual sales
- Annual sales of our products
- Contribution earned from sales to this reseller
- Average stock-turn of our products
- Past average stock-turn of our products
- Profit performance

Competitive Selling Effort
- Quality of locations
- Quality of advertising
- Quality of premises
- Quality of sales staff
- Sales staff knowledge of our products
- Inventory management
- Extent we are treated as a preferred supplier
- Special marketing efforts and cooperation

Purchasing Behavior
- Recent ordering history
- Volume deals/discounts sought and given
- Other allowances and considerations sought and given:
  Freight
  Cooperative advertising
  Promotions
  Returns
  Push money and sales contests
  Special credit terms

The reseller audit in Exhibit 300.33 starts with a summary evaluation that can also be used as a short-form audit when the product team does not have the time or interest to fully evaluate particular resellers. A paragraph can be written to provide responses to the concerns listed. The evaluation can be updated on a regular basis (normally annually), so the major investment is in preparing the initial evaluation. The detailed evaluation questions have been categorized into those dealing with the reseller's trading performance, marketing position, competitive effort, and purchasing behavior. Understanding what is going right or wrong in a channel relationship almost always involves taking information and putting it together like a jigsaw puzzle. That is why it is important to add depth to the audit by answering as many questions as possible, using facts, good judgment, and best guesses. Trying to understand the reasons for a channel member's change in performance or behavior often means tracing back from its buying behavior, through trading and operating indicators, to its competitive effort and market position. Distribution market research also must forecast distributors' future competitive strengths and weaknesses.

Marketing Channels and Distribution

Marketing Channel Defined

A **marketing channel,** also referred to as a *distribution channel* or *channel of distribution*, is the network of organizations that creates time, place, and possession utilities for consumers and business users.

The creation of time, place, and possession utilities may result from marketing channels that are simple or complex. In the case of the **Volkswagen** Beetle, the channel is fairly simple. The cars are sold by the manufacturer to retail dealers, who in turn sell the cars to consumers. The cars are transported from the factory to dealer showrooms by independent railroad or truck carriers who charge a fee for their services. Thus, the participants in this marketing channel are the manufacturers, retailers, consumers, and transportation companies. Only the first three, however, are what is referred to as the *sales channel,* which is that part of the channel involved in buying, selling, and transferring title. The rail or trucking firms, which do not buy, sell, or transfer the title to the cars, are part of the *facilitating channel.* Public storage firms, insurance companies, finance companies, market research firms, and several other types of firms also frequently participate as facilitating organizations in various marketing channels.

Some marketing channels are more complex than that used for the Volkswagen Beetle. Beer, for example, which goes from manufacturers to wholesalers to retailers and then to consumers, has an extra organization (the wholesaler) in its sales channel.[78]

The simplest sales channels go directly from producers to customers, as in the case of **Dell Computer Corporation,** which sells all of its products directly from its manufacturing plants to customers. Dell's facilitating channel, however, which uses telephone, mail, and the Internet for order placement as well as **United Parcel Service (UPS), Federal Express,** and other transportation firms to deliver its computers to customers, is more complex than its sales channel.

Both the sales and facilitating channels are usually needed to create time, place, and possession utilities. But it has become a customary practice in marketing to describe and illustrate marketing channels only in terms of the sales channel, because it is the relationship involving the functions of buying, selling, and transferring of title where most of the strategic marketing issues emerge. For example, when setting up its sales channel, Volkswagen faced such marketing strategy issues as identifying and selecting the appropriate kinds of dealers to sell the new Beetles, convincing them to carry sufficient numbers of the cars, motivating the dealers to do an effective job of promoting and selling the cars, as well as making sure that they provided good servicing and warranty support. Moreover, Volkswagen also needed to make provisions for numerous other issues as part of its continuing relationship with independent dealers, such as future inventory levels expected of dealers, training of sales and service people, credit terms, evaluation of dealer performance, and numerous others. In contrast, Volkswagen's efforts to arrange for transportation, storage, insurance, and similar matters, while important, are usually not considered strategic marketing issues.

Marketing Channel Structure

The form or shape that a marketing channel takes to perform the tasks necessary to make products available to consumers is usually referred to as **channel structure.** Firms such as transportation companies, warehousing firms, insurance companies, and the like are usually referred to as *facilitating agencies,* because they are not involved in buying, selling, or transferring title and hence, as we mentioned earlier, are not considered to be part of the channel structure.

Marketing channel structure has three basic dimensions:

1. Length of the channel
2. Intensity at various levels
3. The types of intermediaries involved

Length of Channel Structure

Channel length *Number of levels in a marketing channel.*

Channel length can range from two levels, where the producer or manufacturer sells directly to consumers (direct distribution), to as many as 10 levels, where eight intermediary institutions exist between the producer and consumers. With the exception of Japan, such long channels of distribution are quite rare in industrialized countries. Much more common are channel structure lengths ranging from two levels up to five levels. Exhibit 300.34 provides an illustration of typical channel structure lengths for consumer products in developed countries.

Many customer-based factors influence the length of the channel structure, such as the size of the customer base, its geographical dispersion, and its particular behavior patterns. The nature of the product, such as its bulk and weight, perishability, value, and technical complexity, can also be very important. For example, technically complex products such as X-ray machines often require short channels because of the high degree of technical support and liaison needed by customers, which may only be available directly from the manufacturer. Moreover, length can also

Exhibit 300.34 *Examples of the Length of Dimensions of Marketing Channel Structure for Consumer Products*

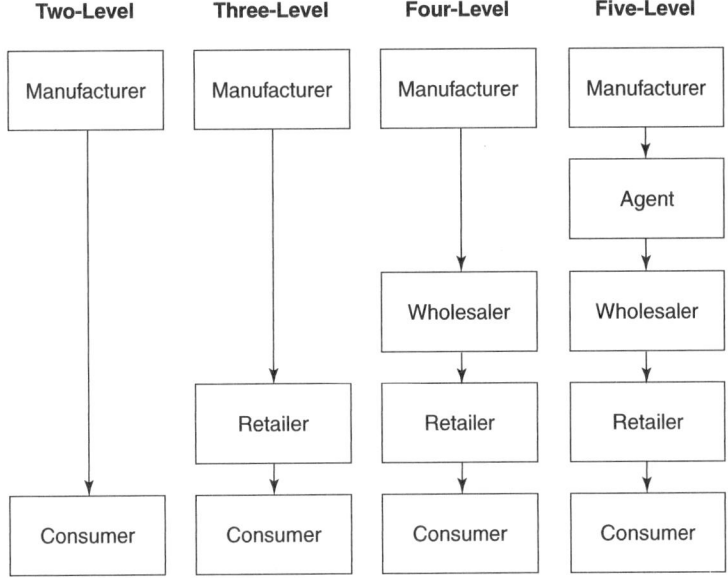

Exhibit 300.35 *Intensity of Channel Structure*

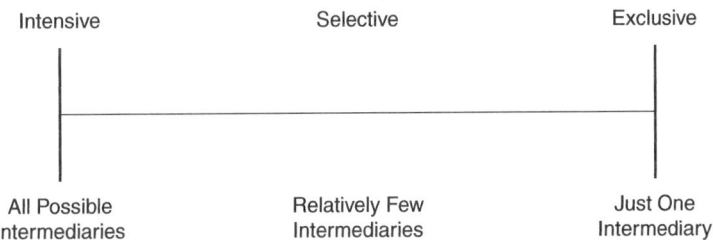

be affected by the size of the manufacturer, its financial capacity, and its desire for control. In general, larger and more well-financed manufacturers have a greater capability to bypass intermediaries and use shorter channel structures.[79] Manufacturers desiring to exercise a high degree of control over the distribution of their products are also more likely to use shorter channel structures because the shorter the channel, the higher the degree of control. Polo, by **Ralph Lauren** apparel, for example, sells only through upscale department and specialty retailers as well as its own Web site to protect the fashion image of its products.

Intensity of Channel Structure

Channel intensity is usually described in terms of intensive distribution, selective distribution, or exclusive distribution. **Intensive distribution** means that all possible intermediaries at the particular level of the channel are used. **Selective distribution** means that a smaller number of intermediaries are used, while **exclusive distribution** refers to only one intermediary used at the particular level of the channel to cover a defined territory. The intensity dimension of channel structure can be portrayed as a continuum as shown in Exhibit 300.35. Although there are many exceptions, in general, intensive distribution is associated with the distribution of convenience goods, selective distribution with shopping goods, and exclusive distribution with specialty goods. Thus, inexpensive Bic pens, Gillette razor blades, and Hallmark greeting cards (convenience goods) tend to be carried by large numbers of intermediaries, particularly at the retail level; while home appliances such as Whirlpool refrigerators and apparel such as Levi's jeans (shopping goods) are handled by relatively fewer retailers; and specialty goods such as Rolex watches or Rolls-Royce automobiles are featured by only one dealer in a specified geographical area (territory).

Types of Intermediaries in the Channel Structure

This third dimension of channel structure refers to the different kinds of intermediary institutions that can be used at the various levels of the channel. At the retail level, there may be many possibilities for some products. For example, a Snickers candy bar can be sold through many different types of retailers such as candy stores, grocery stores, drugstores, supermarkets, mass merchandisers, discount department stores, and many others. For other products, such as automobiles, the choice is more limited. We should point out, however, that in recent years with the growth of *scrambled merchandising,* where all kinds of products are sold in stores not traditionally associated with those products, the types of stores that sell various products have broadened considerably. Motor oil, for example, is now regularly available in supermarkets, while hardware items are frequently found in drugstores. Consequently, manufacturers today need to be broad-minded when considering the types of intermediaries to use in their channel structures. The conventional wisdom of particular products being distributed only through certain types of wholesalers or retailers may no longer hold. The largest U.S. seller of Dom Perignon champagne, for example, is **Costco,** a wholesale club usually known for selling bulk packs of basic groceries and general merchandise.[80]

Determinants of Channel Structure

The structure of marketing channels, in terms of their length, intensity, and types of participating intermediaries, is determined basically by three factors:

1. The distribution tasks that need to be performed
2. The economics of performing distribution tasks
3. Management's desire for control of distribution

Distribution Tasks

Distribution tasks, also often referred to as *marketing functions* or sometimes *channel functions,* have been described by various lists for many years. Such functions as buying, selling, risk taking, transportation, storage, order processing, and financing are commonly mentioned. More generalized terms can also be used to describe these tasks, such as *concentration, equalization,* and *dispersion*—whereby the main tasks of marketing channels are grouped together in familial relationships—bringing products together from many manufacturers (concentration), adjusting the quantities to balance supply and demand (equalization), and delivering them to final customers (dispersion). Others describe distribution tasks in terms of a sorting process: *accumulating* products from many producers, *sorting* them to correspond to designated target markets, and *assorting* them into conveniently associated groups to ease the shopping burden of customers. Distribution tasks have also been described in much more detailed terms where specific activities sometimes unique to the particular industry are cited.[81]

Regardless of the particular list of distribution tasks presented, the rationale is the same for all of them: Distribution functions must be performed in order to consummate transactions between buyers and sellers. The reason is that discrepancies exist between buyers and sellers that must be overcome through the performance of distribution tasks. The channel structure the firm chooses to perform these tasks reflects how the tasks are to be allocated to various marketing institutions such as wholesalers, retailers, agents, brokers, or others. The **discrepancies between production and consumption** can be separated into four basic groups:[82]

1. Discrepancies in quantity
2. Discrepancies in assortment
3. Discrepancies in time
4. Discrepancies in place

DISCREPANCIES IN QUANTITY The quantities in which products are manufactured to achieve low average costs are usually too large for any individual customer to use immediately. Wrigley's chewing gum, for example, produces literally millions of packages of gum each day. Even the most ardent gum chewer could not possibly use that much gum every day! Thus, institutions in the channel structure, such as wholesalers and retailers, provide a buffer to absorb the vast output of manufacturers and provide the smaller quantities desired by individual customers.

DISCREPANCIES IN ASSORTMENT Products are grouped for manufacturing purposes based on efficiencies of production, while customers group products based on convenience of shopping and consuming. In most cases, the production and consumption groupings are not inherently matched. For example, the thousands of items a consumer finds grouped so conveniently together in a supermarket are not, of course, produced by one manufacturer. Hundreds of relatively specialized manufacturers have made those products. The supermarket and many other intermediaries in marketing channels have performed the distribution tasks necessary to regroup this conglomeration of products, thereby overcoming the discrepancy in assortment. This enables particular manufacturers to concentrate on producing a relatively limited range of products, which when combined through marketing channels with the products of many other manufacturers, allows consumers to have wide and convenient assortments of products that greatly simplify shopping and consumption. Consumers need only stroll down the aisles, and place the chosen items in their shopping cart.

DISCREPANCIES IN TIME   Most products are not manufactured for immediate consumption or use. Hence, some mechanism must be available to hold products between the time they are produced and needed by final customers. A bottle of Snapple iced tea, a Tommy Hilfiger shirt, or a pair of Rollerblade in-line skates are not desired by consumers at the instant they roll off the production line. So intermediaries in marketing channels, particularly merchant wholesalers and retailers, who take title to and physically hold goods until they are needed by consumers, are crucial in overcoming this discrepancy in time.

DISCREPANCIES IN PLACE   The location of manufacturing facilities for products is determined by such factors as raw material availability, labor costs, expertise, historical considerations, and numerous other factors that may have little to do with where the ultimate consumers of those products are located.[83] Thus, the production and consumption of products can literally take place half a world apart from each other. In fact, today it is more likely than ever that the products we buy are made in China, Singapore, Japan, Brazil, India, or some other faraway country than in some nearby factory. Channel structures evolve or are consciously designed to connect distant manufacturers and consumers by eliminating place discrepancies.

The Economics of Performing Distribution Tasks

Given that distribution tasks must be performed to overcome the four discrepancies discussed earlier, the channel structure needs to be organized to perform tasks as efficiently as possible. The development of efficient marketing channel structures is based on two principles: specialization or division of labor and transaction efficiency.[84]

SPECIALIZATION OR DIVISION OF LABOR   The principle of **specialization or division of labor** underlies most modern production processes. Each worker in a factory focuses on performing particular manufacturing tasks and thereby develops specialized expertise and skills in performing those tasks. Such specialization results in much greater efficiency and higher output than if each worker were to perform all or most of the tasks necessary to manufacture the product him- or herself.

This 200-year-old principle shows that it applies as much to distribution as it does to production. The various intermediaries in marketing channels are analogous to production workers or stations in a factory, but instead of performing production tasks, they are performing distribution tasks. These intermediaries—whether they are wholesalers, retailers, agents, or brokers—develop expertise in distribution that manufacturers would find uneconomical to match. Moreover, many large intermediaries, such as mass merchandisers, enjoy **economies of scale and economies of scope** that would be impossible for most manufacturers to match. **Home Depot,** for instance, with over 800 giant warehouse stores enjoys great economies of scale and scope, because it is able to spread its operating costs over a vast quantity and variety of products.

Economies of scale and economies of scope Obtained by spreading the costs of distribution over a large quantity of products (scale) or over a wide variety of products (scope).

TRANSACTION EFFICIENCY   **Transaction efficiency** refers to the effort to reduce the number of transactions between producers and consumers. If many producers attempt to deal directly with large numbers of consumers, the number of transactions can be enormous. Paradoxically, by lengthening the channel structure through the addition of intermediaries, the number of transactions can actually be reduced. Consequently, transaction efficiency is increased. This is illustrated in Exhibit 300.36. As shown in the exhibit, the number of transactions has been cut in half as a result of the introduction of the retailer into the channel structure. Given that the costs of transactions can be very high, especially if personal face-to-face meetings are necessary to consummate transactions, the reduction in contacts through the use of intermediaries in the channel structure is in many cases absolutely vital for economical distribution.

Exhibit 300.36 *How the Introduction of an Intermediary Reduces the Number of Transactions*

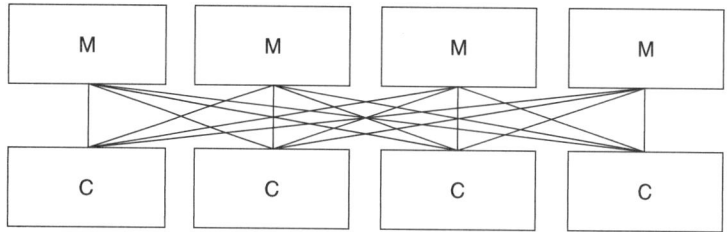

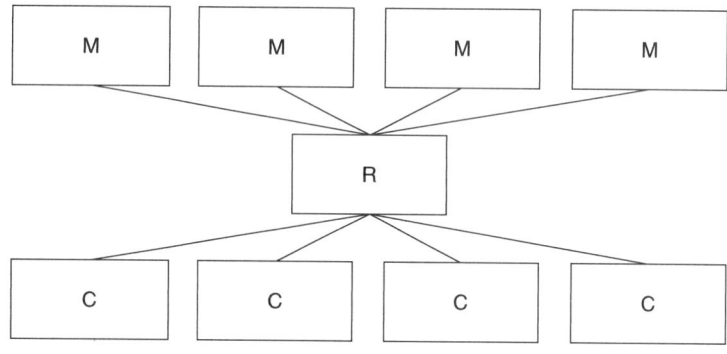

Management's Desire for Control of Distribution

Even though the economics of the performance of distribution tasks may seem to call for a particular type of marketing channel structure, a firm's desire for control of the marketing channel may outweigh the economic considerations.[85] In general, the shorter the channel structure, the higher the degree of control, and vice versa. Further, the lower the intensity of distribution, the higher the degree of control, and vice versa. For example, suppose an economic analysis, based on specialization/division of labor and transaction efficiencies, calls for a long marketing channel structure with a fairly high degree of intensity at the various levels. However, management in the manufacturing firm feels a need to protect the image of the product and also believes it is necessary to provide high levels of customer service. To do so, the manufacturer is convinced that it needs a high degree of control, and so it may opt for only one level of intermediary, with a very high degree of selectivity in appointing them as channel members, based on their willingness to take direction from the manufacturer. This is exactly the situation that **Gucci,** the Italian maker of world-famous luxury goods, found itself in. Focusing mainly on gaining distribution efficiency, Gucci ended up selling its products through several thousand retailers. This proliferation of retailers—many of whom were not of the highest stature—although providing economies of scale in the distribution of Gucci products, adversely affected the exclusive image of Gucci. Realizing the problem, Gucci restructured its marketing channels by drastically reducing the number of retailers selling its products to less than 500 worldwide. Moreover, all of these retailers were of the highest quality, and were willing to take close direction from Gucci to project a world-class quality image vital to the long-term success of Gucci. In contrast, a brand such as Fruit of the Loom underwear, which uses intensive distribution, would have far less concern about control of the channel than Gucci.

Flows in Marketing Channels

When a marketing channel is developed, a series of *channel flows* emerge. These flows provide the links that tie channel members and other agencies together in the distribution of goods and services. The most important of these flows are the (1) product flow, (2) negotiation flow, (3) ownership flow, (4) information flow, and (5) promotion flow. These flows are illustrated for Coors beer in Exhibit 300.37.

Exhibit 300.37 *Flows in the Marketing Channels for Coors Beer*

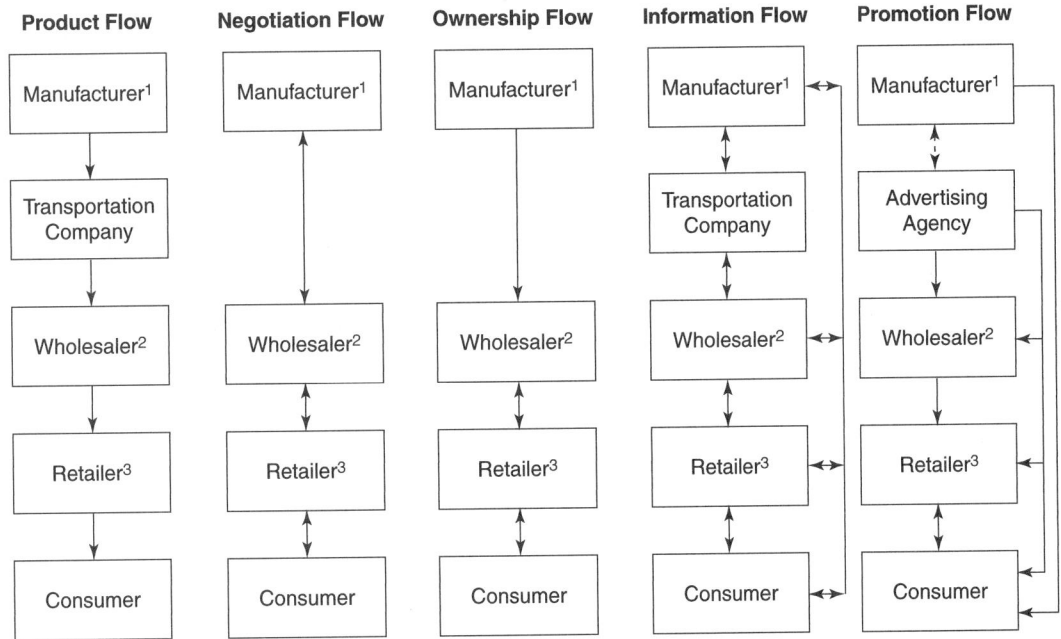

The *product flow* refers to the actual physical movement of the product from the manufacturer (Coors) through all of the parties who take physical possession of the product, from its point of production to consumers. In the case of Coors beer, the product comes from breweries and packaging plants in Colorado, Tennessee, and Virginia by way of company trucks or common carriers (transportation companies) to beer distributors (wholesalers), who in turn ship the product (usually in their own trucks) to liquor stores, supermarkets, convenience stores, restaurants, and bars (retailers), where it is finally purchased by consumers.

The *negotiation flow* represents the interplay of the buying and selling tasks associated with the transfer of title to Coors products. Notice in Exhibit 300.37 that the transportation firm is not included in this flow because it does not participate in the negotiation tasks of buying, selling, and transferring title. Notice also that the arrows flow in *both* directions, indicating that negotiations involve a mutual exchange between buyers and sellers at all levels of the channel.

The *ownership flow* shows the movement of the title to the product as it is passed along from the manufacturer to final consumers. Here again, the transportation firm is not involved because it does not take title to the product, nor is it actively involved in facilitating its transfer. It is only engaged in the transportation of the physical product itself.

Turning now to the *information flow,* we see that the transportation firm has reappeared, since all parties participate in the exchange of information. We also see that all of the arrows showing the flow from the manufacturer to consumers are two-directional, as the flow of information can be either up or down.

Finally, the *promotion flow* refers to the flow of persuasive communication in the form of advertising, personal selling, sales promotion, and public relations. Here, a new party, the advertising agency, is included in the flow because the agency is actively involved in providing and maintaining the promotion flow, especially the advertising component of promotion. The two-directional arrow connected by a broken line between the manufacturer and advertising agency is meant to show that the manufacturer and advertising agency work together closely to develop promotional strategies. All other arrows are one-directional from the advertising agency, or directly from the manufacturer to the other parties in the marketing channel.

The concept of channel flows help us to understand the scope and complexity of marketing channels. By thinking in terms of the five flows, it becomes obvious that marketing channels involve much more than just the physical flow of the product through the channel. The other flows (negotiation, ownership, information, and promotion) must also be coordinated to make products conveniently available to customers. Moreover, the concept of **flows in marketing channels** captures the dynamic nature of marketing channels. The word *flow* suggests movement or a fluid state, and in fact this is the nature of marketing channels. New forms of distribution emerge, different types of intermediaries appear in the channel while others drop out, and unusual competitive structures close

Flows in marketing channels
Movement of products, negotiation, ownership, information, and promotion through each participant in the marketing channel.

355. MARKETING CHANNELS AND DISTRIBUTION

off some avenues of distribution and open up others. Changing patterns of buyer behavior and new forms of technology such as the Internet add yet another dimension of change. Channel flows need to be adapted and managed to meet such changes.[86]

Marketing Channel Management

Marketing channel management, frequently shortened to the term *channel management,* refers to the analysis, planning, organizing, and controlling of a firm's marketing channels.[87] Channel management can be a challenging and complex process, not only because many aspects are involved, but also because of the difficulties arising from the **interorganizational context** of the channel structure. That is, marketing channels are made up of independent business organizations such as manufacturers, wholesalers, and retailers as well as agents and brokers who, although linked together in a relationship to form a marketing channel, are still independent businesses. As such, these firms have their own objectives, policies, strategies, and operating procedures, which may or may not be congruent with those of the other members of the channel. Indeed, sometimes they come into outright conflict. Moreover, in marketing channels, usually there are no clear superior/subordinate relationships, or lines of authority, so typical of management in single-firm intraorganizational settings. Hence, managing marketing channels is frequently more challenging than managing within the intraorganizational setting of a single firm.

Logistics in Marketing Channels

Logistics, also often referred to as **physical distribution** (PD), is commonly defined as "planning, implementing, and controlling the physical flows of materials and final products from points of origin to points of use to meet customers' needs at a profit."[88] In more recent years, the term **supply-chain management** has been used to describe logistical systems that emphasize close cooperation and comprehensive interorganizational management to integrate the logistical operations of the different firms in the channel.[89] Although a detailed discussion of the differences between what might be referred to as the "traditional" approach to logistics and the supply chain management approach is beyond the scope of this section, Exhibit 300.38 provides an overview of the key distinctions. In any case, whether one chooses to use the

Exhibit 300.38 *Comparison of Traditional and Supply Chain Approaches to the Management of Logistics*

Element	Approach: Traditional	Approach: Supply Chain
Inventory management approach	Independent efforts	Joint reduction in channel inventories
Total cost approach	Minimize firm costs	Channel-wide cost efficiencies
Time horizon	Short term	Long term
Amount of information sharing and monitoring	Limited to needs of current transaction	As required for planning and monitoring processes
Amount of coordination of multiple levels in the channel	Single contact for the transaction between channel pairs	Multiple contacts between levels in firms and levels in channels
Joint planning	Transaction-based	Ongoing
Compatibility of corporate philosophies	Not relevant	Compatible at least for key relationships
Breadth of supplier base	Large to increase competition and spread risk	Small to increase coordination
Channel leadership	Not needed	Needed for coordination focus
Amount of sharing risks and rewards	Each on its own	Risks and rewards shared over the long term
Speed of operations, information, and inventory flows	"Warehouse" orientation (storage, safety stock) interrupted by barriers to flows; localized to channel pairs	"Distribution center" orientation (inventory velocity) interconnecting flows, JIT quick response

Source: From Martha C. Cooper and Lisa M. Ellram, "Characteristics of Supply Chain Management and Implications for Purchasing and Logistics Strategy," The International Journal of Logistics Management 4, no. 2 (1993):16. www.ijlm.org

term *physical distribution, logistics,* or *supply chain management,* the underlying principle is the building of strong cooperation among channel members through effective interorganizational management.

The Role of Logistics

Even the most carefully designed and managed marketing channel must rely on logistics to actually make products available to customers. The creation of time and place utilities, essential for customer satisfaction, is therefore dependent on logistics. The movement of the right amount of the right products to the right place at the right time is a commonly heard description of what logistics is supposed to do. But achieving this goal is no simple job. On the contrary, mass markets, with their great diversity of customer segments spread over vast geographic areas, can make the task of logistics complex and expensive. Thus, logistics has become a gigantic industry that pervades virtually all firms, from the largest to the smallest.[90]

Logistics Systems, Costs, and Components

For many years, logistics was equated mainly with transportation. Hence the field was narrowly defined in terms of the activities involved in shipping and receiving products and was given relatively little management attention. But in recent decades, a broader perspective referred to as the **systems concept of logistics** has emerged. Rather than being thought of as separate and distinct from one another, logistical factors as diverse as transportation, materials handling, inventory control, warehousing, and packaging of goods are now recognized as interrelated components of a system. Decisions or actions affecting one component have implications for other components of the logistical system. For example, a faster mode of transportation for moving a quantity of iMacs from California to New York could result in a lower level of inventory needed in New York, which in turn could result in a smaller warehouse being required. Conversely, slower transportation for shipping iMacs from California to New York might well mean that a larger inventory and a larger warehouse would be needed in New York because of the slower rate of resupply.

The concept of logistics as a system has served as the foundation of modern logistics management. In essence, those in charge of managing logistics seek to find the optimum combination of logistics components (transportation, materials handling, order processing, inventory control, warehousing, and packaging) to meet customer service demands.

The logistics manager also attempts to achieve the desired level of customer service at the lowest cost by applying the **total cost approach.** This concept is a logical extension of the systems concept, because it addresses all of the costs of logistics taken together, rather than the cost of individual components taken separately, and seeks to minimize the total cost. Consequently, when designing a logistics system, a company must examine the cost of each component and how it affects other components. For instance, a faster mode of transport used to ship the iMacs mentioned earlier might increase transportation costs. But, because the inventory levels and warehouse space needed in New York would be smaller

> **Total cost approach** *Calculating the cost of a logistical system by addressing all of the costs of logistics together rather than individual costs taken separately, so as to minimize the total cost of logistics.*

(faster transportation allows for quicker resupply), the inventory carrying costs and warehouse costs will be lower. These savings in costs may be more than enough to offset the higher transportation costs. So, from the standpoint of the total cost of the logistics system, the increase in transportation costs for the faster mode of transport may well result in a *lower* total cost for logistics.

The use of the systems concept and the total cost approach to manage logistics is shown in Exhibit 300.39. This figure suggests not only that all the basic components of a system are related, but also that the systems concept and the total cost approach provide the guiding principles for blending the components. This blending helps ensure that the types and levels of services desired by customers will be provided at the lowest total cost for the logistics system as a whole.

The basic components of a logistics system are transportation, materials handling, order processing, inventory control, warehousing, and packaging.

TRANSPORTATION Transportation is the most obviously necessary component of any logistics system, because in virtually all cases products must be physically moved from one location to another if a transaction is to be completed. Transportation is also often the component accounting for the highest percentage of the total cost of logistics. The five major modes of transportation are truck, rail, water, pipeline, and air.

From a logistics management standpoint, the overriding issue facing a firm is choosing the optimum mode of transportation to meet customer service demands. This can be a complex task because there are so many considerations. A few of these are: Should the firm use its own carriers or common carriers? What are the different rates available? What specific transportation services are offered? How reliable are various common carriers? What modes of transport are competitors using? Moreover, if the systems concept and total cost approach are applied, the logistics manager must

Exhibit 300.39 View of Logistics Management Based on the Systems Concept and the Total Cost Approach

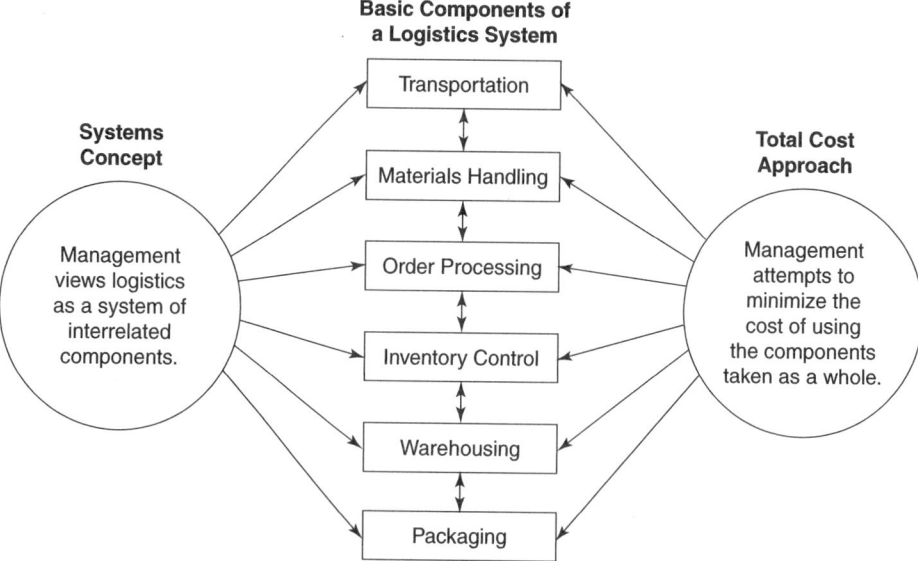

think in terms of how the transportation component interacts with and affects the total cost of logistics. Such decisions require specialized knowledge and expertise—not only of logistics systems, but also of the specialized needs of the industry involved and of the latest technologies available.[91]

MATERIALS HANDLING   Materials handling encompasses the range of activities and equipment involved in the placement and movement of products in storage areas. Questions that must be addressed when designing materials handling systems include:

- How can the distances products are moved within the warehouse during the course of receiving, storage, and shipping be minimized?
- What kinds of mechanical equipment (such as conveyor belts, cranes, and forklifts) should be used?
- How can the firm make the best use of the labor involved in receiving, handling, and shipping products?

For example, the growing use of *cross-docking* (sometimes referred to as *flow-through distribution*) has significantly enhanced materials-handling efficiency.[92] In cross-docking, products from an arriving truck are not stored in a warehouse and then resorted later to fill orders. Rather, the merchandise is simply moved across the receiving dock to other trucks for immediate delivery to stores. This eliminates the need to pick stored products at a later time. In short, products are moved directly from shipping to receiving.

ORDER PROCESSING   The importance of order processing in logistics lies in its relationships with *order cycle time*, which is the time between when an order is placed and when it is received by the customer. If order processing is cumbersome and inefficient, it can slow down the order cycle time considerably. It may even increase transportation costs if a faster mode of transportation must be used to make up for the slow order processing time. Order processing often appears to be routine but is actually the result of a great deal of planning, capital investment, and training of people.

INVENTORY CONTROL   Inventory control refers to a firm's attempt to hold the lowest level of inventory that will still enable it to meet customer demand. This is a never-ending battle that all firms face. It is a critically important one as well. Inventory carrying costs—including the costs of financing; insurance; storage; and lost, damaged, and stolen goods—on average can amount to approximately 25 percent of the value of the inventory per year. For some types of merchandise, such as perishable goods or fashion merchandise, carrying costs can be considerably higher. Yet without inventory to meet customer demand on a regular and timely basis, a firm could not stay in business for very long.

Ideally, a firm always wants to be in the position of keeping inventory at the lowest possible level while at the same time placing orders for goods in large quantities, because holding the number of its own orders to the fewest possible

Exhibit 300.40 *Economic Order Quantity (EOQ) Model*

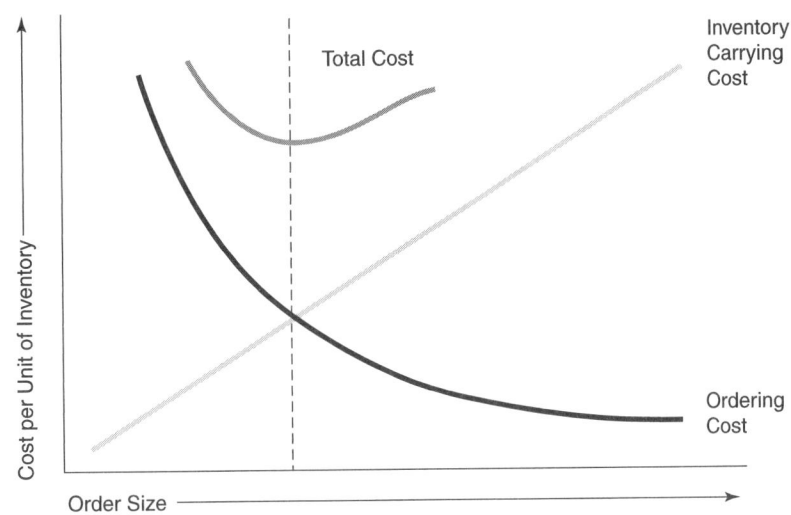

enables the firm to minimize ordering costs. Unfortunately, there is a conflict between these two objectives. Average inventory carrying costs rise in direct proportion to the level of the inventory, while average ordering costs decrease in rough proportion to the size of the order. Thus, a trade-off must be made between these two costs to find the optimum levels for both. This point, usually referred to as the *economic order quantity (EOQ),* occurs at the point at which total costs (inventory carrying cost plus ordering costs) are lowest. As Exhibit 300.40 shows, the logistics manager strives to achieve the lowest total cost by balancing inventory carrying and ordering costs.

WAREHOUSING The warehousing or storage component of a logistics system is concerned with the holding of products until they are ready to be sold. Warehousing can actually be one of the more complex components of a logistics system.[93] Quite often, when considering options for warehousing, the firm faces several key decisions, each of which can be difficult and complex. These decisions might include (1) the location of warehouse facilities, (2) the number of warehousing units, (3) the size of the units, (4) the design of the units including layout and internal systems, and (5) the question of ownership. Successful decisions in each of the areas require careful planning and may require input from experts in such fields as location analysis, real estate, operations research, and industrial engineering, in addition to logistics management.

Warehousing is closely linked to the ability of firms to provide high levels of customer service. For example, with the growth of the Internet as a mode of consumer shopping, far more shipments of *eaches*—single items as opposed to product lots—will create massive numbers of *onesie transactions* in which only a single item is purchased.[94] Moreover, consumers will expect these single items to be delivered very quickly. Experts in the warehousing industry believe such demands by Internet shoppers will increase rather than decrease the need for warehousing, because most Internet retailers will be storefronts with no inventory on hand. They will instead rely on numerous, well-located, and efficient warehouses—either their own or third parties'—to provide the level of product availability demanded by Internet shoppers.[95]

PACKAGING Packaging and the costs associated with the packaging of products are relevant as a component of the logistics system because packaging can affect the other components of the system, and vice versa. For example, the type of transport used can affect packaging and packaging costs; in the case of airfreight, for instance, packaging costs are generally reduced because risks of damage are generally lower than if rail or truck transportation are used. Materials handling and order processing procedures and costs can also be affected by packaging because well-designed packaging can help to increase efficiencies in these components of the logistics system. Effective packaging can also help control inventory carrying costs by reducing product damage. Further, warehouse space, and thus costs, can be saved if packaging is designed to be space efficient. Therefore, packaging is far more than just a promotional device for fostering product differentiation and attracting consumer attention. Packaging has an important logistical dimension that can make a significant difference in the effectiveness and efficiency of the logistics system. Indeed, a product in distinctive and attractive packaging will have even more appeal if it is also easy to handle, conveniently stackable, and shelf-space efficient.

355. MARKETING CHANNELS AND DISTRIBUTION

The Output of the Logistics System: Customer Service

Good customer service is the desired end result of virtually all business activities, and logistics is an extremely important part of these efforts. This is particularly true for those aspects of customer service that are a direct function of the logistics system, including:

1. Time from order receipt to order shipment
2. Order size and assortment constraints
3. Percentage of items out of stock
4. Percentage of orders filled accurately
5. Percentage of orders filled within a given number of days from receipt of the order
6. Percentage of orders filled
7. Percentage of customer orders that arrive in good condition
8. Order cycle time (time from order placement to order delivery)
9. Ease and flexibility of order placement

These logistics services and many others (see Exhibit 300.41) are often quantified and utilized as **logistical service standards,** against which the manufacturer's actual performance is then measured.[96] For example, the first standard shown in the list—time from order receipt to order shipment—might be set at 24 hours for 90 percent of all orders received. So, for every 100 orders received, the manufacturer must have 90 of the orders processed and shipped within 24 hours to meet the standard. The second service standard in the list—order size and assortment constraints—might be set in terms of some minimum quantity of products, and certain restrictions might be placed on mixing the various products unless specified minimum quantities of each item are ordered. A steel producer, for example, might set the minimum order for various gauges of sheet metal at two tons, and the inclusion of several gauges in a single order might require a certain combined minimum tonnage. The third standard—percentage of items out of stock, or stockouts—is almost always set in terms of a percentage of the items ordered during a given period that cannot be filled from inventory. Thus, if a manufacturer wants to fill 95 percent of the items ordered, its stockout percentage can be no higher than 5 percent to meet the standard. The other six service standards in the list can be quantified and used in a similar fashion.

In general, the higher the service standards offered, the higher the costs will be. While well-designed logistics systems and modern technology can keep these costs under control, it is usually not possible to completely escape the trade-off of higher costs for higher service standards.

A manufacturer must cover these costs either indirectly in the price it charges for products, or by passing them along to channel members in the form of service charges. In either case, there is little point in offering logistics services that channel members do not want or higher levels of service than they desire. Types and levels of logistics ser-

Exhibit 300.41 *Inventory of Logistical Aspects of Customer Service*

1. Order processing time	14. Claims response
2. Order assembly time	15. Billing procedures
3. Delivery time	16. Average order cycle time
4. Inventory reliability	17. Order cycle time variability
5. Order size constraints	18. Rush service
6. Consolidation allowed	19. Availability
7. Consistency	20. Competent technical representatives
8. Frequency of sales visits	21. Equipment demonstrations
9. Ordering convenience	22. Availability of published material
10. Order progress information	23. Accuracy in filling orders
11. Inventory backup during promotions	24. Terms of sale
12. Invoice format	25. Protective packaging
13. Physical condition of goods	26. Cooperation

Source: From John T. Mentzer, Roger Gomes, and Robert E. Knapfel, Jr. "Physical Distribution Service: A Fundamental Marketing Concept?" *Journal of the Academy of Marketing Science* (Winter 1988):55. Copyright 1988 Sage Publications. Reprinted by permission of Sage Publications.

vice that go beyond real channel member demands simply increase costs for channel members without providing them with any desired benefits. Thus the key issue in defining logistics service standards is to determine precisely the types and levels of logistics service desired by the channel members.

Electronic Commerce and Marketing

The E-Marketing Landscape

The **Internet** is a worldwide network of interconnected computers and computer networks that carry data and make information exchange possible. The **World Wide Web (Web)** is a subset of the Internet. It is a collection of hyperlinked documents or files, not computers. These documents include text, graphics, video, animation, and/or audio files. Thus, the Internet includes a number of computer networks set up by individuals, companies, and organizations, while the World Wide Web is the mechanism to link the documents available on those computers/computer networks. For purposes of this book, the terms *World Wide Web* and *Internet* will be used interchangeably.

Markets

E-marketing is the set of activities that bring customers and companies together using electronic means such as the Internet. A number of markets comprise the e-marketing landscape. The typical markets include:

1. *Business-to-Business (B2B)*—Includes all the activities of business that occur between two business entities. B2B activities include purchasing, sales, service, support, and payments systems.
2. *Business-to-Consumer (B2C)*—Includes all activities of business that occur between a business and its ultimate consumers. We think of B2C transactions as retail customers purchasing from businesses via a company Web site. The activities include sales, service, customer information, and customer support.
3. *Consumer-to-Consumer (C2C)*—Includes all activities involving interactions between consumers. C2C activities include auctions between consumers that are facilitated by firms such as eBay, personals, classified advertising, and games.
4. *Business-to-Government (B2G)*—Includes all activities involving transactions between various businesses and government entities. B2G activities include sales to the government, purchasing support, product information, and service.
5. *Government-to-Consumer (G2C)*—Includes all activities involving interactions between consumers and government entities. G2C activities include mostly information exchange.

Organizations are not limited to one model or the other. Many organizations utilize multiple models simultaneously, selling their products to other businesses (B2B), to ultimate consumers (B2C), and to the government (B2G). This section will focus on the first three types of markets: B2B, B2C, and C2C.

Types of Internet Sites

As fast as the Internet is expanding, the number and type of Internet sites are increasing. Sites can be classified into four major categories: **company/brand sites, service sites, selling sites,** and **information sites.**

E-Marketing and the Marketing Mix

E-marketing is both the same and unique in comparison to other types of marketing. All marketers attempt to deliver value to ultimate customers (final consumers, business customers, or governmental customers). Value is determined by subtracting costs from benefits. This is true in any type of marketing, electronic or otherwise. Benefits are based on consumer perceptions of the product by evaluating attributes, brands, and after-the-sale services. The costs associated with a product include the price, plus other factors such as time invested in the purchase process and psychological factors.

Ultimately, the Internet has the potential to increase benefits while lowering costs. These benefits include mass customization, digital delivery of products, and/or one-stop shopping. Lower costs can result from direct selling, segmented pricing, and/or expanded delivery services via the Web. The potential increased benefits and/or decreased costs can be explored by looking at the product, price, place (distribution), and promotion components of the marketing mix.

Product

E-marketing opens a multitude of possibilities for products. Firms in touch with their customer base have the ability to constantly evaluate customer needs and match those needs with technological developments to create new and innovative products. Product life cycles have been shortened because competitors are now able to develop products on the fly. Firms that capitalize on these phenomena and introduce new products earlier than competitors have the potential for far greater profits.

Small businesses can be big on the Web and big businesses can be small on the Web. Even the smallest firm can compete globally by using the expertise of the transportation companies today. Transportation companies such as FedEx and UPS make it easy to export products, as well as deliver them worldwide. Even the largest firm can be "small" and focus on individual needs if it can automate its systems enough. In addition, larger firms can design the self-service systems on the Web that can perform many of the customer contact functions.

Price

Standard pricing models have limited use in electronic markets. Traditional pricing theory is based on the experience curve that has declining fixed costs as volume expands. While this theory still holds for electronic markets, the shortness of the product life cycle makes volume efficiencies less likely because of constant innovation.

Many firms have created market efficiencies by lowering costs associated with the final exchange of products marketed on the Web. Self-service Web sites offer potential for lower costs and thus lower pricing on the Web. In addition to self-service, the automation of order processing and payment adds to potential savings.

Place

E-marketers have expanded the ways they sell their products. Several new channels of distribution have evolved from the use of the Internet to market goods. E-tailers represent a new distribution channel for traditional brick-and-mortar firms, as well as for firms that exist only on the Internet, such as Amazon.com.

E-marketers also have developed new ways to deliver goods and services including digital products, more efficient customer service, and new ways to sell directly to consumers. Innovative new intermediaries have emerged because of special needs associated with Internet marketing.

Promotion

In most circumstances when a company sells to consumers through traditional media, the consumer is passive in the communication process, that is, consumers typically do not interact with the company, instead they read advertisements, listen to radio ads, or view TV commercials. E-marketing is an active media where consumers must choose (click) to see something and can view it for as long or as short as they like. Additionally, even in the personal selling process, in which consumers are more active in the process, there are differences when one markets on the Web. Exhibit 300.42 shows the steps in the personal selling process and suggests different techniques that can be used when marketing on the Web.

Obviously, having consumers actively participate in the process rather than be passive bystanders affords the marketer the ability not only to save money but also to provide a higher level of service. That means that sites can be used to identify needs and wants, discover preferences, provide information and service, develop loyalty, and position the firm for future sales from the prospect.

Firms promote themselves in different ways using the medium of the Internet. Negotiating hyperlinks with related products is a critical promotional tool on the Web. Banner advertising has become very popular in recent years and provides a way to hyperlink these sites together. Mass media typically push messages to consumers, while consumers

Exhibit 300.42 *Steps in the Personal Selling Process Adapted to the Web*

	Personal Selling	Web Selling
Prospecting	Names from databases, referrals, past customers, other sources	Search engines, listserv(es), e-mail, links
Preapproach	Information gathering on needs, wants, preferences	On-line data collection, site searches, screening links
Approach	Method of contact, atmospherics, initial impressions, cold call	URL, opening Web screen, navigation
Presentation	Discussing the options, listening and replying to objections	Graphics, screen design, links to other products
Closing the Sale	Asking for the sale Filling out the order	Taking the order online, self-service
Follow-Up	Determining customer satisfaction	E-mail, other follow-up

Exhibit 300.43 *Keys to Web Design*

Things to Do:	Things to Avoid:
Provide description of the firm	Scrolling
Fast load times	Large graphic files
Consistent navigation	Reliance on one browser
Make the site interactive	Broken links
Provide ways to contact the firm	Excessive use of plug-ins
Register with search engines	
Register the domain name	
Copyright the site	
Use trademarks appropriately	
Market the site in other materials	

on the Web must actually pull advertisements by clicking. Web sites must be designed in such a way that consumers can quickly see the value of their spending time at the site. Exhibit 300.43 summarizes a number of important issues to consider when designing Web sites.

Placing a company's brochures on-line is a sure way to chase consumers from your site. **Electronic brochures,** that is, digitizing a company's print brochures and placing them on the Web as straight text, does not work! Consumers know this medium is interactive and expect to interact.

Web marketing also changes the other promotional activities of the firm. All future advertisements must contain the Web address for the company if the firm expects to grow its equity in the Web site.

Designers of Web sites need to be cognizant that their sites must do more than just sell. Web sites that offer other benefits to the ultimate consumer such as analysis of needs, assistance in product selection, information on usage with complimentary products, and meeting places for interested visitors can provide customers with reason to come back to a site over and over again.

Costs and Benefits of E-Marketing

Costs of E-Marketing

Although it is evident that there are numerous advantages for companies using e-marketing, there are two major drawbacks at this time: limited target audience and consumers' resistance to change. Both of these are likely to change as the Internet diffuses throughout our society.

LIMITED TARGET AUDIENCE   For those of us who use the Internet daily for information, e-mail, and as a mechanism to purchase products, it seems that everyone is using it. However, a very large segment of our society has yet to embrace the Internet (presently 73 million users in the United States). A majority of Internet users fit a definite profile. Although this profile is beginning to match the overall U.S. population and might match the target market of some companies, it does not match the profile of all companies.

There are still a number of underrepresented segments on the Web.[97] Most significant differences exist in higher income and higher percentages of 18- to 49-year-olds for Internet users versus the population as a whole. These numbers clearly indicate underrepresentation within certain segments of our society. Although Internet use is increasing and these numbers are changing at a rapid rate, until the demographics of Internet usage mirror society as a whole, companies must use caution in overemphasizing e-marketing in their total marketing mix.

CONSUMERS' RESISTANCE TO CHANGE   In general, people are resistant to change. This resistance was clearly demonstrated by the slow movement of people from retail stores to purchasing products via mail order catalogs. This same resistance is being demonstrated as people begin to purchase products over the Internet.

While many people think nothing of giving their credit card number to a customer service representative they don't know personally during a mail order telephone purchase, there is clear resistance among customers to typing their number into the computer and then clicking a Send button. Although someone educated in Internet security knows that decrypting a credit card number electronically is much more difficult than picking up a receipt with a number printed on it, the average user may not know this. Warranties, security measures, and other ways to augment the overall product offering to reduce the risk of consumers must be evaluated by companies to overcome consumers' resistance to change.

Benefits of E-Marketing

E-marketing can aid a company's overall marketing effort in a number of ways. First, e-marketing allows a company/brand to *increase its brand equity in the marketplace*. Company and brand sites give marketers an opportunity to communicate the overall mission of the company/brand, provide information on the attributes and/or ratings of the company/brand, and can give information on the history of the company/brand. In addition, firms can communicate information on the marketing mix offered.

Second, e-marketing allows a company to *develop prospective customers into buying customers*. Providing important information about the decision-making process can help the potential customer with external search processes. Information about a product's attributes and competitive products can aid in the decision-making process. In addition, a Web site can demonstrate a company's products in use. This kind of information can help build consumer interest in a company/brand.

E-marketing can move customers closer to purchasing a product/brand by allowing Web site visitors to match their needs with the offerings of the company. It is extremely important to remember that while traditional marketing techniques tend to be push oriented, that is, the marketer decides what consumers will see and where, e-marketing is a pull technique—consumers choose when they want to gather information and what and how much they want to know. This requires Web site designers to think differently about what should or should not be offered in the site.

Third, e-marketing can *improve customer service by allowing customers to serve themselves* when and where they choose. The self-service nature of Web sites can produce the cost savings that will ultimately pay for some sites. As more and more consumers begin to use the Internet, companies can serve these individuals without expensive distribution costs. The expansion of the number of customers served only requires that the organization have enough servers available.

The fourth benefit to marketers is that of *information transfer*. Traditionally, marketers gathered information via focus groups, mail surveys, telephone surveys, and personal interviews. These techniques can be quite expensive to implement. The Web offers a mechanism for companies to collect similar information at a fraction of the cost. It is important to recognize the potential bias that might exist in such a sample. However, as the number and demographics of Internet users begin more closely to represent a firm's target market, the collection of information on the Web might offer many benefits.

Not only can information be gathered from consumers, it also can be shared with consumers. The Web can be used to provide expensive or specialized material to consumers who request such information from the company. Annual reports are now a typical part of company Web sites. Rather than print the millions of copies that might be requested by consumers, the company now provides Web copies that consumers print out at their own expense. Other specialized material can also be provided for consumers to print out themselves. By fulfilling these types of information requests, the Web can offer substantial savings to companies.

The greatest potential for e-marketing is probably in direct marketing where catalogs can be offered online. Web-based catalogs can be changed with ease if prices and/or product offerings change. This alone can represent substantial savings for organizations that would normally print new catalogs and mail those catalogs to consumers.

Ethics and Marketing

The Social Responsibility of Marketing

The **social responsibility** of marketing has several sides. Marketing activities must be efficient and effective and not squander scarce resources. Marketing executives must be mindful of the unintended social consequences of their efforts on culture and subcultures. Marketing executives, along with all other executives in a firm, have to obey the law and participate responsibly in the making of laws. But simply abiding by the law is only a first step, and marketing executives are expected to have a strong moral compass that guides their behavior. In short, they are expected to behave according to the canons of ordinary or common decency. Finally, professional marketers are expected, as public citizens, to use their skills in promoting societal causes and in other ways that benefit humankind.

Marketing's First Social Responsibility: Be Ever More Efficient and Effective

Marketing's first responsibility to society is to advance life, liberty, and the general happiness through the creation of exchanges, markets, product innovations, and trading innovations that increase the efficiency and effectiveness of the economic process. In short, the first responsibility of marketers is to keep learning to do their job ever more efficiently and effectively. This is undertaken in the selfish pursuit of profit. But as 18th-century economist Adam Smith pointed out over 200 years ago, such self-improvement also makes markets more competitive, makes our lives as workers and customers more productive, and wastes less of the scarce resources on earth that need to be preserved for future generations. Many people believe that marketing is not fulfilling this first social responsibility very well. They believe a lot of products that are marketed are not needed and that a lot of marketing effort, particularly advertising, is wasteful and not becoming more efficient and effective.

Marketing's Second Social Responsibility: Behave Ethically

The second major social responsibility of marketing is to conduct business in an ethical manner. Most companies do live up to this responsibility. Despite the well-publicized exceptions that the media have used to help create an image that business is unethical (e.g., Enron and Arthur Andersen), many companies in the United States today are moral enterprises, led by men and women of impeccable character. The moral rudder of most enterprises is under the very solid control of senior executives, particularly the chief executive officer and senior vice presidents of sales and marketing, who lead by example and encourage a corporate culture of honesty and decency. Such enterprises often have written codes of ethics. It has been estimated that about 60 percent of U.S. companies have written codes of ethics that all employees agree to abide by. They are commonly accepted as a "given" across all employees.[98] Some larger companies have appointed an ethics officer, or ombudsperson, to further promote ethical behavior. These individuals help executives in tough decisions, and provide a safe haven (and source of support) for whistle-blowers.

United States companies are more concerned about intellectual property rights (such as not stealing patents, copyrighted material, and confidential information) and about ethical purchasing practices. Does this mean that some companies are more concerned about making sure that their buyers do not take bribes and indulge in other unethical behavior, and less concerned about the ethical behavior of their own marketing practices (such as offering bribes)? Whatever your opinion, this figure reminds us that ethical trading requires both the seller and the buyer to behave ethically. European companies seem to address purchasing and marketing ethical issues in about the same proportion. Canadian companies are somewhat more concerned about environmental issues, suggesting that concern over the environment is a more important part of the "social contract" and culture in Canada.

Exhibit 300.44 *American Marketing Association Code of Ethics*

American Marketing Association Code of Ethics

Members of the American Marketing Association are committed to ethical professional conduct. They have joined together in subscribing to this Code of Ethics embracing the following topics:

Responsibilities of the Marketer

Marketers must accept responsibility for the consequences of their activities and make every effort to ensure that their decisions, recommendations, and actions function to identify, serve, and satisfy all relevant publics: customers, organizations, and society.

Marketers' Professional Conduct must be guided by:

1. The basic rule of professional ethics: not knowingly to do harm
2. The adherence to all applicable laws and regulations
3. The accurate representation of their education, training, and experience
4. The active support, practice, and promotion of this Code of Ethics

Honesty and Fairness

Marketers shall uphold and advance the integrity, honor, and dignity of the marketing profession by:

1. Being honest in serving consumers, clients, employees, suppliers, distributors, and the public
2. Not knowingly participating in conflict of interest without prior notice to all parties involved
3. Establishing equitable fee schedules including the payment or receipt of usual, customary, and/or legal compensation for marketing exchanges

Rights and Duties of Parties in the Marketing Exchange Process

Participants in the marketing exchange process should be able to expect that

1. Products and services offered are safe and fit their intended uses
2. Communications about offered products and services are not deceptive
3. All parties intend to discharge their obligations, financial and otherwise, in good faith
4. Appropriate internal methods exist for equitable adjustment and/or redress of grievances concerning purchases

It is understood that the above would include, but is not limited to, the following responsibilities of the marketer:

In the area of product development and management:

- Disclosure of all substantial risks associated with product or service usage
- Identification of any product component substitution that might materially change the product or impact on the buyer's purchase decision
- Identification of extra cost-added features

In the area of promotions:

- Avoidance of false and misleading advertising
- Rejection of high-pressure manipulations, or misleading sales tactics
- Avoidance of sales promotions that use deception or manipulation

In the area of distribution:

- Not manipulating the availability of a product for the purpose of exploitation
- Not using coercion in the marketing channel
- Not exerting undue influence over the reseller's choice to handle a product

In the area of pricing:

- Not engaging in price fixing
- Not practicing predatory pricing
- Disclosing the full price associated with any purchase

In the area of marketing research:

- Prohibiting selling or fund-raising under the guise of conducting research
- Maintaining research integrity by avoiding misrepresentation and omission of pertinent research data
- Treating outside clients and suppliers fairly

Organizational Relationships

Marketers should be aware of how their behavior may influence or impact the behavior of others in organizational relationships. They should not demand, encourage, or apply coercion to obtain unethical behavior in their relationships with others, such as employees, suppliers, or customers.

1. Apply confidentiality and anonymity in professional relationships with regard to privileged information
2. Meet their obligations and responsibilities in contracts and mutual agreements in a timely manner
3. Avoid taking the work of others, in whole or in part, and representing this work as their own or directly benefiting from it without compensation or consent of the originator or owner
4. Avoid manipulation to take advantage of situations to maximize personal welfare in a way that unfairly deprives or damages the organization or others

Any AMA member found to be in violation of any provision of this Code of Ethics may have his or her Association membership suspended or revoked.

Source: Reprinted with permission from *The American Marketing Association Code of Ethics*, published by the American Marketing Association.

I Was Only Following Orders

A company's codes of ethics are often stated in general terms, leaving specific interpretation up to the individual salesperson or marketing executive. However, ethical dilemmas often arise during the implementation of marketing strategy. When this happens, decisions must be made without an opportunity to consult superiors. Such situations throw heavy responsibility on the marketing manager, product manager, and sales force. This ethical stress on the marketing executive can be greatly heightened by the presence of a company double standard. A company must make clear what action it will take against unethical behavior and establish credibility by following through. It must walk the walk. If actions are taken only when a company's unethical behavior is discovered and publicly challenged, then the company sends the worst signals to its marketing executives. What it says is that the company does not really mind what an executive does to achieve financial goals, as long as someone from outside does not find out. If the misconduct becomes public, the executive in question will take the fall, and the company will deny any knowledge of his or her actions. Unfortunately, many marketing decision makers face this conflict to varying degrees. It places great demand on their personal code of ethics. It also greatly undermines their respect for senior executives.

The American Marketing Association also has developed a code of ethics (see Exhibit 300.44) that marketing professionals can turn to for guidance and direction. The emphasis is on ethical trading behavior, and approximately half of the points mentioned are associated with honesty and disclosure. The code can help bolster an executive's belief that the stand that he or she is taking is ethical and socially responsible. However, the American Marketing Association, unlike some other "professional" organizations, is not in a position to provide legal support to its members who face a conflict between their personal ethics and what they are being asked to do. This places a great deal of responsibility on the individual marketing executive. Exercising this responsibility requires an understanding of what is prescribed as right and wrong. It requires an understanding of where such values and rules originate, as well as the issues and moral philosophy that underlie personal and organizational ethics.

Recognizing Ethical Issues

The set of general questions in Exhibit 300.45 can be asked by the decision maker or decision-making team seeking to develop its own ethical standards. Although most questions are self-explanatory, others need some brief justification or raise issues worth exploring.[99] It seems that the least society should require of marketing executives is that they ask such questions. Sometimes not asking a question can be as wrong as asking and giving a poor answer. For example, not considering the safety of a toy being marketed seems to be as irresponsible as considering the safety and deciding to sell the toy anyway. The effects are the same. One of the most common situations in which marketing executives suffer a lapse of ethics is when they have to make a quick decision because they are preoccupied with other concerns. The ethical sufficiency of the

Exhibit 300.45 *A Personal Ethics Checklist for Marketers*

- ☐ Am I violating the law? If yes, why?
- ☐ Are the values and ethics that I am applying in business lower than those I use to guide my personal life? If yes, why?
- ☐ Am I doing to others as I would have them do to me? If not, why not?
- ☐ Would it be wrong if everyone did what I propose to do? Why?
- ☐ Am I willfully risking the life and limb of consumers and others by my actions? If yes, why?
- ☐ Am I willfully exploiting or putting at risk children, the elderly, the illiterate, the mentally incompetent, the naive, the poor, or the environment? If yes, why?
- ☐ Am I keeping my promises? If not, why not?
- ☐ Am I telling the truth, all the truth? If not, why not?
- ☐ Am I exploiting a confidence or a trust? If yes, why?
- ☐ Am I misrepresenting my true intentions to others? If yes, why?
- ☐ Am I loyal to those who have been loyal to me? If not, why not?
- ☐ Have I set up others to take responsibility for any negative consequences of my actions? If yes, why?
- ☐ Am I prepared to redress wrongs and fairly compensate for damages? If not, why not?
- ☐ Are my values and ethics as expressed in my strategy offensive to certain groups? If yes, why?
- ☐ Am I being as efficient in my use of scarce resources as I can be? If not, why not?

This set of questions can be used as the basis for a team's or an individual's mental model to perceive and recognize an ethical issue associated with a proposed goal, strategy, program, or tactic.

> **Ethical vigilance** Paying constant attention to whether one's actions are "right" or "wrong," and if ethically "wrong," asking why one is behaving in that manner.

decision is simply not examined. **Ethical vigilance** means, in practice, asking hard questions. It is important to confront excuses and reasons for violating personal ethics. Avoiding or shelving the answers to such questions is no solution. Decision makers who ask why they do or do not behave in certain ways are more honest with themselves about their true intentions. This is the essence of executive responsibility, and it also can be the first step down the path of change. Such questions lead people to recognize that most of us have at least two codes of ethics: (1) the set we espouse and want others to apply in their behavior toward us and (2) the code of ethics that, for whatever rationalizations, we actually live up to. The more we recognize the differences between them, the closer we come to understanding how easy it is to talk about ethics in black and white, while practicing them in shades of gray.

The list of questions shown in Exhibit 300.45 is organized in approximate order of importance and by the nature of the ethical or moral principles involved. The first question in the table is the first and last question the ethical minimalist will ask. The second question addresses the application of a double standard and the basis for such a double standard. The third question addresses the extent to which marketers apply the Golden Rule: "Do unto others as you will have them do unto you." A prominent British chief executive officer has suggested that a better way of posing the question is to look at oneself and ask, "What would I think of someone who has my business ethics or took the action that I propose to take?"[100]

Marketing's Third Social Responsibility: Obey the Law

The legal and political environment is a reality to which the marketer must adapt. It is the job of the government to establish the rules and regulations to which businesses must conform. These rules and regulations affect each element in the marketing mix. Marketers must therefore be aware of and conform to all laws affecting their business. This often involves getting lawyers to review marketing mix plans.

While the legal/political environment can frustrate initiative, in general it is positive for business. For example, in the United States, many of the laws that affect marketing practice are in place to encourage competition and protect consumers (see Exhibit 300.46). Moreover, the current plague of lobbyists, who buy the influence and the votes of local, state, and national politicians in many and various ways, exists because thousands of companies and industries are trying to have law passed and law interpreted to favor the competitiveness of their particular firm or industry. In other words, if it is your law that is passed, then regulation is good; if it is someone else's law, then it is bad.

The point is that marketers can be just as shortsighted about changes in the legal/political environment as they can about changing customer needs and technological innovations. A hostile attitude toward the legal/political environment that is generalized into a hostile attitude toward public policy is unreasonable, and if it encourages a marketing strategy that willfully frustrates the letter or intent of the law, it can be disastrous.

Companies also have to be farsighted in their promotion of self-interest and in their lobbying for special regulation to protect their interests. Indeed, even the original Sherman Antitrust Act, the granddaddy of all market competition law (see Exhibit 300.46), was initially supported by the "robber barons" of the day because it was deliberately vaguely worded so as to be uninterpretable and, hence, unconstitutional.[101] They did not expect a future Supreme Court to come along and interpret the vagueness as an invitation to make law from the bench designed to serve the needs of the time. They created a monster that ultimately broke up their giant monopolistic trusts. The lesson is that self-interested lawmaking often comes back to haunt the original sponsor through unintended and unanticipated consequences.

Marketing's Fourth Social Responsibility: Help Market Good Causes

The fourth important dimension of marketing's social responsibility is to encourage its use in the promotion of worthy public causes. Today's marketers have come to recognize, as has been confirmed in a recent Roper poll, that in many markets a company's media expression of social responsibility influences consumer behavior more than advertising.[102]

Some companies have started up their own nonprofit organizations, and these are not always cynical efforts to buy public relations. They are mostly initiatives suggested by their workforce and welcomed by management, who recog-

Exhibit 300.46 *Sampling of Major Laws That Affect Marketing*

Acts	Prohibitions
Major Laws That Protect Consumers	
Child Protection Act of 1966	Prohibits the sales of hazardous toys.
Fair Packaging and Labeling Act of 1967	Requires certain information be listed on all labels and packages, including product identification, manufacturer or distributor mailing address, and the quantity of contents.
Consumer Credit Protection Act of 1968	Requires the full disclosure of annual interest rates on loans and credit purchases.
National Environmental Policy Act of 1970	Established the Environmental Protection Agency to deal with organizations that create pollution.
Consumer Product Safety Act of 1972	Created the Consumer Product Safety Commission and empowered it to specify safety standards for consumer products.
Nutritional Labeling and Education Act of 1990	Prohibits exaggerated health claims and requires all processed foods to provide nutritional information.
Americans with Disabilities Act (ADA) of 1991	Protects the rights of people with disabilities; prohibits discrimination against the disabled (illegal in public accommodations, transportation, and telecommunications).
Brady Law of 1993	Imposes a five-day waiting period and a background check before a customer can take possession of a purchased gun.
Laws That Encourage Competition	
Sherman Antitrust Act of 1890	Prohibits restraint of trade and monopolization; delineates a competitive marketing system as a national policy.
Clayton Act of 1914	Strengthens the Sherman Act by restricting such practices as race discrimination, exclusive dealing, tying contracts, and interlocking boards of directors where the effect may be to substantially lessen competition or tend to create a monopoly.
Federal Trade Commission Act of 1914	Prohibits unfair methods of competition; establishes the Federal Trade Commission, an administrative agency that investigates business practices and enforces the FTC Act.
Robinson-Patman Act of 1936	Prohibits price discrimination in sales to wholesalers, retailers, or other producers. Also prohibits selling at unreasonably low prices to eliminate competition.
Miller-Tydings Resale Price Maintenance Act of 1937	Exempts interstate fair trade contracts from compliance with antitrust requirements.
Wheeler-Lea Act of 1938	Amended the FTC Act to further outlaw unfair practices and give the FTC jurisdiction over false and misleading advertising.
Celler-Kefauver Antimerger Act of 1950	Amended the Clayton Act to include major asset purchases that decrease competition in an industry.
American Automobile Labeling Act of 1992	Requires a vehicle's manufacturer to provide a label informing consumer of where the vehicle was assembled and where its components originated.
North American Free Trade Agreement (NAFTA) of 1993	International trade agreement existing between Canada, Mexico, and the United States. Encourages trade by removing tariffs and other trade barriers among these three countries.

nize that they will build company morale and are a positive expression of a company's ethics. They are a way of expressing what should be done by a socially responsible organization rather than what should not be done.

Cause-Related Marketing

Cause-related marketing includes those activities that governments, public service organizations, companies, and individuals undertake in an effort to encourage target customer participation in socially redeeming programs. These efforts are usually delivered through educational campaigns and provide free or low-priced services at convenient times and places.

Legal and Ethical Issues in Pricing

The laws of the land represent an additional set of considerations that influence the setting of base price. Prudent marketers must be attentive to legal and ethical concerns in pricing. Yet, **price-fixing** is illegal because it restricts competition and leads to higher prices for customers.

Price Fixing

Price fixing is a violation of the **Sherman Antitrust Act,** which prohibits any contract, combination, or conspiracy that restrains trade. It is one of the key reasons that **cartels** exist.

Price Discrimination

Price discrimination is *not* illegal when the buyers are consumers (who do not compete with one another). But, a manufacturer that offers different retailers different prices without economic justification is violating the Robinson-Patman Act (1936), which amended the 1914 Clayton Act. Price discrimination is legal when:

1. *It is cost-justified.* For example, there may be cost differences in selling to two different customers. Wal-Mart, for example, obtains more favorable prices than smaller retailers because of its sheer size, and the economies that manufacturers obtain in selling in such high volumes. Alternatively, if the manufacturer's costs go up, one customer may be charged a higher price than another customer who bought before the price increase.
2. *The seller is attempting to match a competitor's lower prices.* The Robinson-Patman Act has a "good-faith clause" that allows a seller to charge a lower price to Store X than to Store Y, if a competitor is already charging Store X a lower price.
3. *There is no apparent harm to competition.*

Resale Price Maintenance

The primary concern regarding *resale price maintenance* is that retail price competition not be eliminated by manufacturers and retailers agreeing upon specific minimum prices.

Predatory Pricing

Predatory pricing has been alleged recently in the airline market. This is the classic pattern of predatory pricing in which an incumbent firm apparently attempts to drive out newer, smaller rivals with aggressive pricing. The practice of aggressive pricing and capacity expansion has come under intense scrutiny recently in the airline industry[103]—although no convictions have been made. It is quite difficult to prove predatory behavior, as federal law requires demonstrating that the alleged predator priced below an appropriate measure of its average cost and that it had a reasonable expectation that it would recoup its losses.[104] **Northwest** has argued that it is competing "fairly but aggressively" and that smaller airlines often survive in spite of these aggressive tactics. Predatory pricing continues to be "rarely tried and even more rarely successful."[105]

Markup laws are a regulatory approach to prevent predatory pricing. Such laws require a certain markup above cost in particular industries.

Exaggerated Comparative Price Advertising

A very common price advertising tactic is to compare an advertised sale price to a former price; for example, "Was $49.99, Now $29.99." Adding a comparison price has been found to significantly improve consumers' perception of savings and value in an advertised offer.[106] If such a comparative price is bona fide and "was offered to the public on a regular basis for a reasonably substantial period of time," it is perfectly legal.[107] Yet, many retailers appear to stretch this guideline, using comparison prices of questionable validity. While such charges have been considered by many state attorneys-general, few cases have gone to trial.

Ethical Concerns

There are many questions raised by customers and public policy groups about pricing practices, primarily concerning what often appears to be exorbitant prices charged by firms. In the recent past, the cereal industry has been the target of such criticism, as has the pharmaceuticals industry and the banking industry (for excessive ATM fees). Consider these additional pricing scenarios:

- A hardware store raises its price for snow shovels on the morning after a big snowstorm.
- A supermarket chain charges higher prices in its inner-city stores than its suburban stores.
- A microchip manufacturer initially charges very high prices for its new generation chip and then sharply reduces prices after the less price-sensitive buyers have purchased.
- A retailer prices dresses at 400 percent above cost.
- A consultant prices her services at $5,000 per day.
- A bank charges a $1.50 fee for ATM usage to customers who do not have an account with the bank.

Are these all ethical pricing practices? Are they all unethical? People from different backgrounds are likely to apply very different frameworks and standards in making their judgment. Further, we might judge them differently depending on whether we are buyers or sellers. All of the above behaviors can be justified from a business perspective in one of two ways: (1) demand exceeds supply, so equating the two (specifically, rationing demand) requires high prices; and/or (2) the value or return that the buyer receives from each transaction merits these higher prices. These are powerful arguments, yet it should be noted that customers do not always buy into them. Higher prices—even those justified on the basis of supply and demand—may be viewed as unfair by customers and may create resentment, which will affect long-term business. For example, a majority of consumers surveyed felt that the hardware store owner in the first example behaved unfairly.[108] Two-thirds of consumers surveyed about recent ATM fees said they changed their usage in response to the fees, with 11 percent saying they stopped using ATMs altogether.[109]

Regarding ethical standards, the law defines minimally acceptable behavior. In some states, there are *gouging laws*, which attempt to prevent substantial price increases in response to special circumstances.[110]

Business common sense defines another standard: One does not want to alienate customers and lose them. There are also personal standards of ethics, which each of us needs to think about and develop:

> Firms can facilitate ethical marketing behavior from their employees by suggesting that employees apply each of the following tests when faced with an ethical predicament: (1) act in a way that you would want others to act toward you (the Golden Rule), (2) take only actions which would be viewed as proper by an objective panel of your professional colleagues (the professional ethic), and (3) always ask, would I feel comfortable explaining this action on TV to the general public? (the TV test).[111]

Market Segmentation and Target Markets

Markets and Target Marketing

A *market* is any individual, group of individuals, or organizations willing, able, and capable of purchasing a firm's product. For example, if you want to buy a new car, you are in the new car market. Before a firm can effectively market its products to you, or to any other member of the market for that matter, it must fully understand your needs and wants from that product. However, the needs and wants from a product are not the same for everyone in a market. For example, you and your mother may both want a new car, so you are both in the new car market; but chances are good that you each want a different type of car. You may want a small, fast, red sports car while your mother would like a large, safe, dependable, white car that gets good mileage.

Generally, different groups of customers have differing needs from specific products, or *heterogeneous demand*. For example, teens may want blue jeans that are stylish, construction workers want jeans that are durable, and older "gray" consumers want jeans that are comfortable. Real differences in product preferences exist. This means that a company wanting to reach these different groups of consumers must divide the market into distinct groups based on these differences, then analyze in detail each group it wants to reach, to truly understand what customers need and want from the products they buy.

Market segments Consist of groups of consumers who are alike based on some characteristic(s).

The separation of markets into distinctive groups based on homogeneous (similar) characteristics is called *market segmentation*,[112] and is critical to reaching consumers who need different things from a product. Each of the divided markets, or **market segments,** that a company selects to reach with its marketing efforts is a target market. More formally, the specific group of customers toward which a firm directs its market efforts is the firm's *target market*. This process of matching a specialized marketing mix with the needs of a specific market segment is critical to the marketing success of a product and is called *target marketing*. To illustrate, just imagine the likely success (or failure) of cases where market needs do not match the marketing mix: Cadillac and Ensure diet supplement targeting young girls in *Teen* magazine, heavy metal music playing in upscale hotel lobbies, or mascara advertised in *GQ* magazine.

A firm will not generally want to try to appeal to *all* members of a total market in the same way, but rather may concentrate on selected groups of customers. Depending on many factors, firms may target any number of market segments, and each segment targeted may be as small as one consumer or as large as the total mass market. These targeting options are explained next.

Mass Market versus the Individual

Defining specific market segments to target with customized marketing mixes can create a distinctive competitive advantage for a company. As the continuum in Exhibit 300.47 illustrates, the options for the size of a market segment range from one mass market to one individual, or anywhere in between. For mass markets, the marketing mix is standardized to reach all customers in the same way. The smaller the size of the segments targeted, the more customized or individualized the marketing efforts toward the market can be. A firm choosing the mass market end of the continuum will choose to make one product and market that product in the same way to everyone who may want it.

Niche marketing The process of targeting a relatively small market segment with a specific, specialized marketing mix.

Moving toward the middle of the continuum, firms may define a relatively small segment, or *niche*, within a large market for targeting, called **niche marketing.**

Even smaller market segments are known as **micromarkets,** and marketing efforts aimed at these segments are called *micromarketing*. Micromarketing is the process of targeting these small, narrowly defined market segments. A large, upscale retail store, for example, may identify high-income neighborhoods within a city where the store's likely customers live. The retailer can then target those neighborhoods with announcements of special sales or store events.

On the individual consumer end of the continuum, a firm may decide to target individual consumers and personalize marketing efforts toward each.

A time-poor society and the increasing popularity of in-home, interactive shopping options, such as the Internet, are leading to greater personalization or customization in markets. Consider the choices. An individual consumer sees a mass-media advertisement, wants the product, runs out to a mass merchandiser to buy that product, and returns with a mass-produced version of that product identical to everyone else's. The consumer, on the other hand, sees the product, wants it, connects to the manufacturer's home page on the Internet, requests a customized version of the product, and has that personalized version delivered to his or her home.

This interactivity, combined with innovative technological capabilities, allows firms to create a complete picture of individual customers based on their individual characteristics and preferences, then customize marketing efforts,

Exhibit 300.47 *Continuum of Market Segmentation Size*

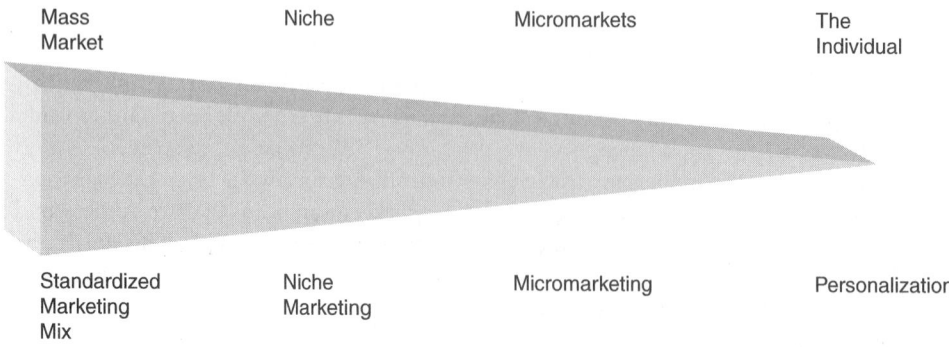

especially services and information, to fit individual customer needs. The current trend in targeting markets is clearly toward this individualization and personalization of markets. The day is coming when customers will be able to scan in their own image and "try on" clothing. In fact, Adidas is already testing a digital scanner that measures shoe size.[113] Soon, consumers may even be able to use simple computer-assisted design (CAD) programs to design their own clothes for manufacture.

Segmentation and Target Marketing

Advantages

In general, the process of segmenting markets and targeting them accordingly is a widespread practice with numerous advantages. The target market selection process is essential to marketing strategy for the following reasons:[114]

1. Identification of the market allows a company to know whom to analyze in its efforts to better understand potential and actual consumers.
2. A detailed analysis and understanding of the market allows a firm to develop and implement a marketing mix tailored to the specific needs of the market. For example, after carefully analyzing the needs of its market, Honda was able to reduce the price of its cars by reducing the number of available options, making the total product better suited to the needs of the car's "reliable" target market.
3. Identification of the market allows a company to assess potential demand for its products. For example, the total market for a principles of marketing textbook can be determined by looking at the number of college students enrolled in college business programs. The textbook publisher can then forecast the percentage of the total market it is likely to acquire, based on a specific formula and/or past experience.
4. Knowing the market allows firms to identify competing products in their specific market, and develop responsive competitive positions. Certainly, Burger King and McDonald's recognize that they are direct competitors in the burger market, and each responds to changes in the other's marketing efforts.
5. Targeting market segments with a marketing mix customized for specific market needs increases the likelihood of sales effectiveness and cost efficiencies in reaching the market. **Foot Joy,** for example, could maximize cost efficiencies by advertising its golf shoes in *Golf Digest* instead of in *Teen* or *People* magazines where most of the readers are not golfers.
6. Defining and analyzing a target market allows a firm to position its products to the market based on assessed needs and preferences. For example, **Toyota** could create a marketing mix that emphasizes an image of dependability, reliability, and good value from its cars, after understanding that these are the characteristics its market segment most desires.
7. Defining a target market allows a firm to identify opportunities. For example, the aging of the 76 million baby boomers suggests the need for products in three major areas: leisure and entertainment, pharmaceuticals and health care, and annuities.[115]

Disadvantages

A number of disadvantages to target marketing have also been identified. These disadvantages center on ethical criticisms of the practice and the possibility of missed opportunities from targeting specific segments. Firms should carefully consider these disadvantages when developing a targeted marketing plan.

1. Targeting multiple markets generally increases marketing costs.
2. Efforts toward personalization and individualization of markets can lead to proliferation of products that becomes overly burdensome and costly to manage.
3. Efforts to overly segment markets into too small niches may be viewed cynically by the targeted individual, and negatively affect consumer response to marketing efforts.
4. Narrowly segmenting a market to target may actually prevent a product from developing brand loyalty.
5. Target marketers have been widely criticized for unethical or stereotypical activities.

The most public criticism of segmenting and target marketing comes from minority and consumer groups who claim that the practice of aiming potentially harmful products to disadvantaged or vulnerable markets is highly unethical. The consumer perception of targeting potentially harmful products, such as cigarettes, alcohol, and lottery

Exhibit 300.48 *Summary of Advantages and Disadvantages of Target Marketing*

Advantages	Disadvantages
Defines the market for further analysis	Increased costs
Allows creation of a customized marketing mix	Increased number of products
Aids in assessing potential demand	Faux segmentation
Aids identification of competitors	May decrease brand loyalty
Increases sales effectiveness and efficiency	Some practices considered unethical
Aids in positioning products	Proliferates stereotyping
Aids in identifying opportunities	

tickets, toward vulnerable consumers, such as children, poor, or uneducated consumers, may have negative effects on the marketing firms. Some research evidence suggests that consumer ethical judgment of such practices can lead to behavioral reactions such as negative word-of-mouth and boycotts. In fact, plans for PowerMaster malt liquor and Uptown cigarettes aimed toward African American males and Dakota cigarettes aimed at pink-collar workers (working-class females) were canceled before the products were marketed because of public outcry.

Finally, the process of segmenting and targeting markets is akin to stereotyping and has been criticized for that reason. For decades, women were unrealistically portrayed as submissive to men, domestic, or as sex objects in advertisements, and the 50-plus market was portrayed by advertisers as doddering old people sitting on a porch and rocking all day. Images such as these further proliferate stereotyping and may actually alienate potential customers.

These criticisms and potentially negative and positive effects of segmenting and targeting markets are important for firms to consider when developing marketing strategies. A summary of these advantages and disadvantages appears in Exhibit 300.48. However, the practice of target marketing is widespread and will likely continue far into the future because firms must understand the needs of their markets and deliver an appropriate marketing mix to succeed. To do this, they must first define their market through the target market selection process.

Services and Retail Marketing

Services Marketing

Services are everywhere we turn, whether we are visiting the doctor, responding to e-mail messages, eating at a favorite restaurant, or studying at school. Simply put, the global service economy is booming. More and more, the so-called industrialized countries are discovering that their service sector is generating the majority of their gross national product. However, the growth of the service sector does not just arise within traditional service industries such as business services, the hospitality industry, health care, and other professional services. Traditional goods producers such as automotive, computer, and numerous other manufacturers are now turning to the service aspects of their operations to establish a competitive advantage in the marketplace. These previously unexplored service aspects also generate additional sources of revenue for their firms. In essence, these companies, which used to compete by marketing "boxes" (tangible goods), have now switched their competitive focus to providing unmatched, unparalleled customer services. **Hewlett-Packard** has embodied this idea through an ad saying "A Box without Service Is Just a Box."

Ample evidence documents this transition from selling boxes to service competition.[116] For example, the traditional goods-producing automotive industry now emphasizes the service aspects of its businesses: low APR financing, attractive lease arrangements, bumper-to-bumper factory warranties, low maintenance guarantees, and free shuttle services for customers. Simultaneously, automotive firms are saying less about the tangible aspects of vehicles such as gas mileage, acceleration, and leather seats in their marketing communications. Similarly, the personal computer industry promotes in-home repairs, 24-hour customer service, and leasing arrangements, and the satellite television industry now touts the benefits of digital service, pay-per-view alternatives, and security options to prevent children from viewing certain programming.

Exhibit 300.49 *Types of Services*

Government Services	Nonprofit Services	For-Profit Services	Professional Services
Police and fire protection	Community hospitals	Car rental	Legal
IRS	United Way	Movie theater	Medical
Social Security	American Red Cross	Car wash	Insurance
Social services	Credit unions	Dry cleaning	Financial
Public transportation	Civic organizations	Landscaping	Architectural
U.S. Postal Service	Humane societies	Taxi service	Accounting
Department of Motor Vehicles		Airlines	Consulting
		Salon	

The service boom looks set to continue into the near future. It seems likely that no business will succeed unless it makes service the foundation of its competitive strategy. The growing importance of services is also reflected in the changing role of the service department within organizations. In the not-so-distant past, the service department tended to be viewed as a necessary evil—it was the place that fixed the box and made good on failed production promises. As service has evolved to become a primary source of competitive advantage, the service department has grown in importance as well.

What Is a Service?

Services include a vast array of businesses ranging from profit to nonprofit services, private to government services, and unskilled to professional services (Exhibit 300.49). However, the distinction between goods and services is not always perfectly clear. In fact, providing an example of a pure good or a pure service is very difficult in today's market economies. A pure good implies that any benefits received by the consumer contain no elements supplied by service. Similarly, a pure service would contain no benefits provided by tangible elements.

In reality, many services contain at least some "goods," or tangible elements, such as the menu selections at an **Outback Steakhouse,** a MasterCard statement from **MBNA,** or the written life insurance policy that **State Farm Insurance** issues. Also, most goods at least offer "services," or intangible elements. For example, table salt is delivered to the grocery store, but a company such as **Morton Salt** that sells it to thousands of retailers may offer innovative invoicing services that further differentiate it from competitors. The distinction between goods and services is blurred even further because a number of firms conduct business on both sides of the goods/services fence. For example, **General Motors,** the goods manufacturing giant, generates 20 percent of its revenue from its financial and insurance businesses, and the car maker's biggest supplier is **Blue Cross and Blue Shield,** not a parts supplier of steel, tires, or glass as most people would have thought.[117]

Despite the confusion, the following definitions should provide a sound starting point in developing an understanding of the differences between goods and services. In general, **goods** are objects, devices, or things, whereas **services** are deeds, efforts, or performances.[118] Ultimately, the primary difference between goods and services is the property of **intangibility**—lacking physical substance. Because of intangibility, a host of marketing problems for services arise that are not always adequately solved by traditional goods-related marketing solutions. For example, how would you (1) advertise a service that no one can see; (2) price a service that has no cost of goods sold; (3) inventory a service that cannot be stored; or (4) mass-produce a service that needs to be performed by an individual (e.g., dentist, lawyer, physician)? Clearly, managing a service operation seems much more complicated than managing a firm that primarily produces and markets goods.

The Scale of Market Entities

One helpful approach to looking at the differences between goods and services is provided by the **scale of market entities**.[119] This scale displays a range of products based on their tangibility and illustrates that there is really no such thing as a pure good or a pure service. All products have some tangible and some intangible aspects. Goods are *tangible dominant*. As such, goods possess physical properties called **search attributes** that customers can feel, taste, and see prior to their purchase decisions. For example, when purchasing a car, the consumer can kick the tires, look at the engine, listen to the stereo, smell that "new-car smell," and take the car for a test drive before making the actual purchase. In contrast, services are *intangible dominant*. As such, services are primarily characterized by **experience attributes** and **credence attributes.** Experience attributes can be evaluated only during and after consumption, such as a meal at a restaurant or the quality of a haircut. Credence attributes cannot be evaluated with certainty even after consumption of the product, such as a minister's counseling or a financial advisor's retirement investment advice. Finally, businesses such as fast-food restaurants, whose products contain both a goods and services component, fall in the middle of the continuum and are characterized by a combination of search, experience, and credence attributes.

The scale of market entities affirms that companies that manufacture tangible goods and ignore, or at least forget about, the intangible service elements of their business may be overlooking a vital differential advantage in the marketplace. By defining their businesses too narrowly, these firms have developed classic cases of **marketing myopia.** For example, the typical family pizza parlor may myopically view itself as being solely in the pizza business. However, a broader view recognizes that the business provides consumers with a convenient, reasonably priced food product in a unique atmosphere that the firm has created for its customers. Interestingly, adding service aspects to a product often transforms the product from a commodity into a compelling experience, and by doing so dramatically increases the revenue-producing opportunities of the product. For example, **Build-a-Bear Workshops** offer an experience-based business model where customers and their children or grandchildren can build and accessorize their own teddy bears. Given the option of going to a store to purchase a bear for a child versus taking the child to a Build-a-Bear Workshop where they can be personally involved in producing the bear, many customers are enthusiastically opting for the latter choice.

Unique Differences between Goods and Services

Initially, the field of services marketing was slow to develop within the academic community. Many marketing educators felt the marketing of services did not differ significantly from the marketing of goods. It was still necessary to segment markets, identify target markets, and develop marketing mixes that cater to the needs of a firm's intended target market. However, since those early days, a great deal has been written regarding the specific differences between goods and services and their corresponding marketing implications. The majority of these differences are attributed to four unique characteristics—intangibility, inseparability, heterogeneity, and perishability.[120]

INTANGIBILITY Of the four unique characteristics that distinguish goods from services, *intangibility* is the primary source from which the other three characteristics emerge. As a result of their intangibility, services cannot be seen, felt, tasted, or touched in the same manner that goods can be sensed. For example, compare the differences between purchasing a movie ticket and a pair of shoes. The shoes are tangible goods, so the shoes can be objectively evaluated prior to purchase. The customer can pick up the shoes, feel the quality of materials from which they are constructed, view their specific style and color, and actually sample the shoe for comfort and fit. After purchasing the shoes, the customer takes them, claiming physical possession and ownership of a tangible product.

In comparison, the purchase of a movie ticket buys the customer an experience. Since the movie experience is intangible, the movie is subjectively evaluated. For example, the customer must rely on the judgments of others (e.g., friends, movie critics, etc.) who have previously experienced the service for *prepurchase information*. Because the information provided by others is based on their own sets of expectations and perceptions, opinions will differ regarding the value of the experience. After the movie is over, the customer returns home with a memory of the experience, retaining physical ownership of only a ticket stub. In addition, the customer's evaluation of the movie will extend beyond what was seen on the screen to include the treatment by theater employees, the behavior of other customers, and the condition of the theater's physical environment.

INSEPARABILITY One of the most intriguing characteristics of the service experience involves the concept of **inseparability.** Inseparability refers to (1) the service provider's physical connection to the service being provided; (2) the customer's involvement in the service production process; and (3) the involvement of other customers in the service production process. Unlike the manufacturer, who may seldom see an actual customer while producing goods in a factory, service providers are often in constant contact with their customers and must construct their service operations with the customer's physical presence in mind.

Service Provider Involvement For many services to occur, the provider must be physically present to deliver the service. For example, dental services require the physical presence of a dentist or hygienist, medical surgery requires a surgeon, and in-home services such as carpet cleaning require an actual individual to complete the work. Because of the intangibility of services, the service provider becomes part of the physical evidence upon which the customer's evaluation of the service experience is at least partly based.

Face-to-face interactions with customers make employee satisfaction crucial. Without a doubt, *employee satisfaction and customer satisfaction are directly related*. The interaction of dissatisfied employees with customers will lower consumers' perceptions of the firm's performance. The importance of employee satisfaction within service firms cannot be overemphasized. Customers will never be the number one priority in a company where employees are treated poorly. In fact, employees should be viewed and treated as "internal customers" of the firm.

Customer Involvement Unlike goods, which are produced, sold, and then consumed, services are first sold and then produced and consumed simultaneously. For example, a box of breakfast cereal is produced in a factory, shipped to a store where it is sold, and then consumed by customers at a place and time of the customer's choosing. In contrast, services are produced and consumed simultaneously (e.g., surgery, a haircut, an amusement park ride, etc.), so consumption takes place inside the service factory. As a result, service firms must design their operations to accommodate the customer's presence. Inseparability makes the service factory another piece of physical evidence that consumers consider when making service quality evaluations.

Interestingly, as customer contact increases, the efficiency of an operation may decrease. This happens because the customers' involvement in the production process creates uncertainties in the scheduling of production and directly impacts the type of service desired, the length of the service delivery process, and the cycle of service demand. The attempt to balance consumer needs with efficient operating procedures is a delicate art. For example, imagine attempting to staff the emergency department of a hospital with exactly the right number of personnel, who have exactly the right qualifications, on any given night.

HETEROGENEITY One of the most frequently stressed differences between goods and services is the lack of ability to control service quality before it reaches the consumer. Service encounters occur in real time, and consumers are often physically present, so if something goes wrong during the service process, it is too late to institute quality-control measures before the service reaches the customer. Indeed, the customer (and other customers who share the service experience) may be part of the quality problem. If something goes wrong during a meal in a restaurant, the service experience for a customer is bound to be affected; the manager cannot logically ask the customer to leave the restaurant, reenter, and start the meal again.

Heterogeneity, almost by definition, makes it impossible for a service operation to achieve 100 percent perfect quality on an ongoing basis. Manufacturing operations may also have problems achieving this sort of target, but they can isolate mistakes and correct them over time because mistakes tend to reoccur at the same points in the process. In contrast, many errors in service operations are one-time events; the waiter who drops a plate of food in a customer's lap creates a service failure that can be neither foreseen nor corrected ahead of time.

Another challenge heterogeneity presents is that not only does the consistency of service vary from firm to firm and among personnel within a single firm, it also varies when interacting with the same service provider on a daily basis. For example, one **Enterprise** rental car franchise can have helpful and pleasant employees, while another franchise might employ individuals who conduct their daily interactions with customers like robots. Not only can this be true among different franchises, the same can be true within a single franchise on a day-to-day basis because of the mood swings of employees.

PERISHABILITY **Perishability** also distinguishes goods from services. It refers to the fact that services cannot be inventoried in the traditional sense. Unlike goods that can be stored and sold at a later date, services that are not sold when they become available cease to exist. For example, hotel rooms that go unoccupied for the evening cannot be stored; airline seats that are not sold cannot be inventoried and added to another aircraft during the holiday season when airline seats are scarce; and service providers such as dentists, lawyers, and hairstylists cannot regain the time lost from an empty appointment book.

The inability to inventory creates profound difficulties for marketing services. In a manufacturing setting, the ability to create an inventory of goods means that their production and consumption can be separated by time and space. In other words, a good can be produced in one location and transported for sale in another, or a good can be produced in January and not released into the channels of distribution until June. Most services, however, are consumed at the point of production.

The existence of inventory also facilitates statistical quality control in goods-producing organizations. A representative sample of the inventory can be easily inspected for variations in quality. In contrast, when you spend the night at a hotel, you are likely to experience a wide range of factors that influence your good night's sleep. Finally, having inventory enables a business to separate the production and marketing departments. In service firms, however, marketing and operations constantly interact with each other and must be in synch to deliver services effectively.

Because of the effects of intangibility, inseparability, heterogeneity, and perishability, marketing plays a very different role in service-oriented organizations than it does in pure goods organizations. Clearly, the different components of the service organization are closely interwoven. The invisible and visible parts of the organization, the contact personnel and the environment in which the service is provided, the organization and its customers, and, indeed, the customers themselves are all bound together by a complex network of relationships. Consequently, the marketing department must maintain a much closer relationship with the rest of the service organization than is customary in many goods-producing businesses. The concept of operations being responsible for producing the product and marketing being responsible for selling the product cannot work in a service firm.

Understanding the Service Experience

All products, be they goods or services, deliver a bundle of benefits to the consumer.[121] The **benefit concept** is the encapsulation of these benefits in the consumer's mind. For a tangible-dominant product such as Tide laundry detergent, the benefit concept for some consumers might simply be clean clothes. However, for other consumers the benefit concept might also include attributes ascribed to the product that go beyond the mere powder or liquid, such as cleanliness, whiteness, and/or being a good parent.

In contrast to goods, services deliver a bundle of benefits through the experience that is created for the consumer. For example, most Tide customers will never see the inside of the manufacturing plant where Tide is produced; they will most likely never interact with the factory workers who produce the detergent or with the management staff who direct the workers; and they will also generally not use Tide in the presence of other customers. In comparison, **Taco Bell's** dine-in customers are physically present in the "factory" where the food is produced, and these customers *do* interact with the workers who prepare and serve the food as well as with the management staff who run the restaurant. Moreover, Taco Bell customers consume the service in the presence of other customers who may influence one another's service experience.

Exhibit 300.50 illustrates the key factors that create the service experience for the consumer. The service experience itself creates the benefit concept for the consumer. The most profound implication of the service experience is this: It demonstrates that consumers are an integral part of the service process. Their participation may be active or

Exhibit 300.50 *Factors Influencing the Service Experience*

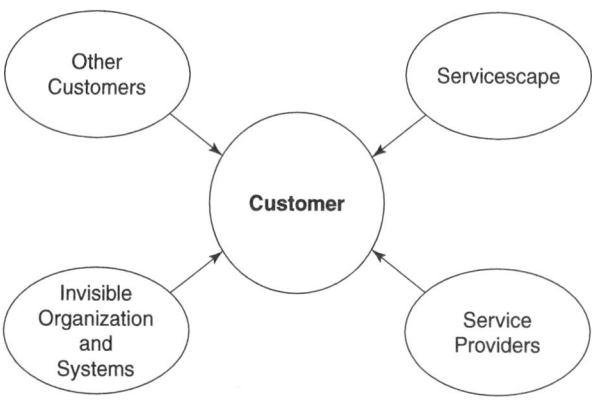

Exhibit 300.51 *Servicescape Dimensions*

Ambient Conditions	Space/Function	Signs, Symbols, and Artifacts
Temperature	Layout	Signage
Air quality	Equipment	Personal artifacts
Noise level	Furnishings	Decor
Music		Uniforms
Odors		Award plaques

Source: Reprinted with permission from *Journal of Marketing*, published by the American Marketing Association, Mary Jo Bitner, April 1992, vol. 56, no. 2, p. 60.

passive, but consumers are always involved in the service delivery process. Factors that influence the customer's service experience include dimensions that are visible and invisible to the customer:

- Servicescape (visible)
- Service providers (visible)
- Other customers (visible)
- Organizations and systems (invisible)

THE SERVICESCAPE The term **servicescape** refers to the use of physical evidence to design service environments (Exhibit 300.51).[122] Due to the intangibility of services, customers often have trouble evaluating the quality of service objectively. As a result, consumers rely on the physical evidence that surrounds the service to help them form their evaluations. Hence, the servicescape consists of *ambient conditions* such as room temperature and music; *inanimate objects* that assist the firm in completing its tasks, such as furnishings and business equipment; and *other physical evidence* such as signs, symbols, and personal artifacts such as family pictures and personal collections.

Servicescapes Use of physical evidence to design service environments.

The extensive use of physical evidence varies by the type of service firm. Service firms such as hospitals, resorts, and child-care centers often use physical evidence extensively as they design facilities and other tangibles associated with the service. In contrast, service firms such as insurance agencies and express mail drop-off locations use limited physical evidence. Regardless of the variation in usage, all service firms need to recognize the importance of managing their physical evidence because of its role in:

- packaging the service
- facilitating the service delivery process
- socializing customers and employees
- differentiating the firm from its competitors[123]

Packaging the Service A firm's physical evidence plays a major role in packaging its service. The service itself is intangible and therefore does not require a package for purely functional reasons. However, the firm's physical evidence does send quality cues to consumers and adds value to the service when it helps customers develop positive images of the service. The firm's exterior and interior elements and other tangibles create the package that surrounds the service. The firm's physical environment forms the customer's initial impression of the type and quality of the service provided. For example, Mexican and Chinese restaurants often utilize specific architectural designs that communicate to customers about their firms' offerings. Physical evidence also conveys expectations to consumers. Consumers will have one set of expectations for a restaurant with dimly lit dining rooms, soft music, and linen tablecloths and napkins; they will form quite a different set of expectations for a restaurant that has picnic tables and peanut shells covering the floor.

Facilitating the Service Process Another use of a firm's physical evidence is to facilitate the flow of activities that produce the service. Physical evidence can provide information to customers on how the service production process works. Examples include signage that specifically instructs customers; menus and brochures that explain the firm's offerings and facilitate the ordering process for consumers and providers; physical structures that direct the flow of consumers while waiting; and barriers, such as counters at a dry cleaners, that separate the technical core of the business from the customer contact areas where customers are actively involved in the production process.

Socializing Employees and Customers **Organizational socialization** is the process by which an individual adapts to and comes to appreciate the values, norms, and required behavior patterns of an organization.[124] The firm's physical evidence plays an important part in this socialization process by conveying expected roles, behaviors, and relationships among employees and between employees and customers. Physical evidence, such as the use of uniforms, helps to socialize employees toward accepting organizational goals and affects consumer perceptions of the caliber of service provided. Studies have shown that the use of uniforms:

Organizational socialization The process by which an individual adapts to and comes to appreciate the values, norms, and required behavior patterns of an organization.

- aids in identifying the firm's personnel
- presents a physical symbol that embodies the group's ideals and attributes
- implies a coherent group structure

- facilitates the perceived consistency of performance
- provides a tangible symbol of an employee's change in status (e.g., military uniforms change as personnel move through the ranks)
- assists in controlling the behavior of errant employees

One classic example of how tangible evidence affects the socialization process of employees involves women in the military. Pregnant military personnel were originally permitted to wear civilian clothing in lieu of their traditional military uniforms. However, the military soon noticed discipline and morale problems among these servicewomen as they began to lose their identification with their roles as soldiers. "Maternity uniforms are now standard issue in the Air Force, Army, and Navy, as well as at US Air, Hertz, Safeway, McDonald's, and the National Park Service."[125]

A Means of Differentiation   The effective management of the servicescape can also be a source of differentiation. For example, several airlines such as **American Airlines, United Airlines,** and **British Airways** are now expanding the amount of leg room available for passengers. British Airways differentiates itself further by featuring the first fully flat bed for passengers traveling business class.[126] In addition, the appearance of personnel and facilities often directly impact how consumers perceive the way that the firm will handle the service aspects of its business. Numerous studies have shown that well-dressed individuals are perceived as more intelligent, better workers, and more pleasant to engage in interactions.[127] Similarly, well-designed facilities are going to be perceived as better than their poorly designed counterparts.

Differentiation can also be achieved by utilizing physical evidence to reposition a service firm in the eyes of its customers. Upgrading the firm's facilities often upgrades the image of the firm in the minds of consumers and may lead to attracting more desirable market segments, which further aids in differentiating the firm from its competitors. On the other hand, note that elaborate facility upgrades may alienate some customers who believe that the firm will pass on the costs of the upgrade to consumers through higher prices. This is precisely why many offices are decorated professionally, but not lavishly.

SERVICE PROVIDERS   The second component of the service experience involves the personnel who provide the service. Simply stated, the public face of a service firm is its service providers.[128] Unlike the consumption of goods, the consumption of services often takes place where the service is produced (e.g., hair salon, dentist office, restaurant). Even when the service is provided at the consumer's residence or workplace (e.g., lawn care, housekeeping, professional massage), interactions between consumers and service providers are commonplace. As a result, service providers have a dramatic impact on the service experience. For example, when asked what irritated them most about service providers, customers have noted seven categories of complaints: apathy, brush-off, coldness, condescension, robotism, rulebook, and runaround.

Service personnel perform the dual functions of interacting with customers and reporting back to the internal organization. Strategically, service personnel are an important source of product differentiation. It is often challenging for a service organization to differentiate itself from other similar organizations in terms of the benefit bundle it offers or its delivery system. For example, many airlines offer similar bundles of benefits and fly the same types of aircraft from the same airports to the same destinations. Therefore, their only hope of a competitive advantage is from the service level—the way things are done. Hence, the factor that often distinguishes one airline from another is the poise and attitude of its service providers. **Singapore Airlines,** for example, enjoys an excellent reputation due in large part to the beauty and grace of its flight attendants. Other firms that hold a differential advantage over competitors based on personnel include the **Ritz Carlton, IBM,** and **Disney Enterprises.**[129]

OTHER CUSTOMERS   Ultimately, the success of many service encounters depends on how effectively the service firm manages its clientele. A wide range of service establishments such as restaurants, hotels, airlines, and physicians' offices serve multiple customers simultaneously. Hence, other customers can have a profound impact on an individual's service experience. Research has shown that the presence of other customers can enhance or detract from an individual's service experience.[130] The influence of other customers can be *active* or *passive*. For instance, examples of other customers actively detracting from one's service experience include unruly customers in a restaurant or a night club, children crying during a church service, or theatergoers carrying on a conversation during a play. Some passive examples include customers who show up late for appointments, thereby delaying each subsequent appointment; an exceptionally tall individual who sits directly in front of another customer at a movie theater; or the impact of being part of a crowd, which increases the waiting time for everyone in the group.

Though many customer actions that enhance or detract from the service experience are difficult to predict, service organizations can attempt to manage the behavior of customers so that they coexist peacefully. For example, firms can manage waiting times so that customers who arrive earlier than others get first priority, clearly target specific age segments to minimize potential conflicts between younger and older customers, and provide separate dining facilities for smokers and customers with children.

ORGANIZATION AND SYSTEMS The invisible component of the service experience, the organization and its systems, can also profoundly affect the consumer's service experience. A firm's organization and systems also involve a human component.

Creating Compelling Experiences

Service firms that are able to effectively mold the customer's experience via the effective management of the servicescape, service providers, other customers, and the invisible organization and system have the means to develop *compelling experiences*.[131] The development of compelling experiences is the latest competitive weapon in the war against service commodification.

The Quest for Customer Satisfaction

To market services effectively, marketing managers need to understand customers' thought processes as they assess their satisfaction with services provided (see Exhibit 300.52). Customer satisfaction is one of the most studied areas in marketing.[132]

As time went on, labor shortages also contributed to the decline in customer service. Motivated service workers were difficult to find, and who could blame them? The typical service job meant low pay, no career path, no sense of pride, and no training in customer relations. Automation also contributed to the problem. Replacing human labor with machines indeed increased the efficiency of many operating systems, but often at the expense of distancing consumers from the firm and leaving customers to fend for themselves. Finally, over the years, customers have become tougher to please. They are more informed than ever, their expectations have increased, and they are more particular about where they spend their discretionary dollars.

What Is Customer Satisfaction?

Customer satisfaction
Short-term, transaction-specific measure of whether customer perceptions meet or exceed customer expectations.

Ultimately firms achieve **customer satisfaction** through the effective management of customer *perceptions* and *expectations*. If the perceived service is better than or equal to the expected service, then customers are satisfied. Because of this, firms can increase customer satisfaction by either lowering expectations or by enhancing perceptions. Note that this entire process of comparing expectations to perceptions takes place in the minds of customers. Hence, it is the *perceived* service that matters, not the *actual* service. Companies can also manage expectations in order to produce customer satisfaction, without in any way altering the quality of the actual service delivered.

Exhibit 300.52 *Is It Always Worthwhile to Keep a Customer?*

Although saving every customer at any cost is a controversial topic and opinions are divided, some experts believe that the customer is no longer worth saving under the following conditions: • The account is no longer profitable. • Conditions specified in the sales contract are no longer being met. • Customers are abusive to the point that it lowers employee morale. • Customer demands are beyond reasonable, and fulfilling those demands would result in poor service for the remaining customer base. • The customer's reputation is so poor that associating with the customer tarnishes the image and reputation of the selling firm.

385. SERVICES AND RETAIL MARKETING

The Importance of Customer Satisfaction

The importance of customer satisfaction cannot be overstated. Without customers, the service firm has no reason to exist. Every service business needs to proactively define and measure customer satisfaction. Waiting for customers to complain in order to identify problems in the service delivery system, or gauging the firm's progress in achieving customer satisfaction based on the number of complaints received, is naive. Remember, too, that less than 5 percent of consumers with problems actually complain to companies.

The Benefits of Customer Satisfaction

Although some may argue that customers are unreasonable at times, little evidence can be found of extravagant consumer expectations.[133] Consequently, satisfying consumers is not an impossible task. In fact, meeting and exceeding customer expectations creates several valuable benefits for service firms. Positive word-of-mouth from existing customers often translates into new customers. In addition, satisfied customers purchase products more frequently and are less likely to be lost to competitors than are dissatisfied customers.

Companies who command high customer satisfaction ratings also seem to be able to insulate themselves from competitive pressures—particularly price competition. Customers are often willing to pay more and stay with a firm that meets their needs than to risk moving to a lower-priced service. Finally, firms that pride themselves on their customer satisfaction efforts generally provide better environments in which to work, and therefore have increased their chances to attract and retain the best and brightest employees. These positive work environments produce organizational cultures that challenge employees to perform and reward them for their efforts. Some companies even use their positive work environments to encourage employee applications.

In and of themselves, customer satisfaction surveys also provide several worthwhile benefits. Such surveys provide a formal means of customer feedback to the firm, which may identify existing and potential problems. Satisfaction surveys also convey the message to customers that the firm cares about their well-being and values customer input concerning its service delivery process.

Other benefits are directly derived from the results of the satisfaction surveys. Satisfaction results are often incorporated into employee performance evaluations for merit and compensation reviews. Sales managers use such results to develop sales training programs. Survey results are also useful for comparison purposes to determine how a firm stacks up against its competition. When ratings are favorable, many firms utilize the results in their corporate advertising.

Customer Satisfaction as It Relates to Customer Relationship Management

Customer relationship management Process of identifying, attracting, differentiating, and retaining customers.

One of the most recent business practices affecting customer satisfaction levels (both positively and negatively) is customer relationship management.[134] **Customer relationship management** (CRM) is the process of identifying, attracting, differentiating, and retaining customers. CRM allows a firm to focus its efforts disproportionately on its most lucrative clients. CRM is based on the adage that 80 percent of a company's profits come from 20 percent of its customers; therefore, the 20 percent should receive better service than the 80 percent. For example, when a plastics manufacturer focused on its most profitable customers, it cut the company's customer base from 800 to 90 and increased revenue by 400 percent.

The increased use of CRM practices, where high-value customers are treated superior to low-value customers, can be attributed to several trends. First, some believe that customers have created the situation themselves by opting for price, choice, and convenience over high-quality service. However, trade-offs arise with this focus on price and other factors over service concerns.

Another reason CRM is currently fashionable is that labor costs have risen, while competitive pressures have kept prices low. The end result is that gross margins have been reduced to 5 to 10 percent in many industries. With these kinds of margins, companies simply cannot afford to treat all of their customers equally. Finally, firms are expanding CRM efforts because markets are increasingly fragmented and promotional costs are on the rise.

CRM OUTCOMES Typical outcomes of CRM practices include **coding, routing, targeting,** and **sharing.** Each practice is typically associated with both positive and negative consequences for customers.

Coding Firms grade customers based on how profitable the customer's business is. Service staff are instructed to handle customers differently based on their category code.

Routing Call centers route incoming calls based on the customer's code. Customers in profitable code categories get to speak to live customer service representatives. Less profitable customers are inventoried in automated telephone queues.

Targeting Profitable customers have fees waived and are targeted for special promotions. Less profitable customers may never hear of the special deals.

Sharing Customer information is shared with other parts of the organization, and information is sold to other companies. Although the customer may be new to the organization, his or her purchase history and buying potential are well-known to insiders.

LIMITATIONS OF CRM PRACTICES Technology greatly enhances CRM processes by identifying current and potential customers, differentiating among high-value and low-value customers, and customizing offers to meet the needs of individual high-value customers. However, there are limitations. First, customers do not like hearing that some customers are valued more than others, especially where they are not the ones receiving the white glove treatment. Many companies are well aware of potential customer ill will and are fairly tight-lipped about the outcomes of their respective CRM practices. Meanwhile, in service operations where service discrimination is common such as airlines, banks, retail stores, hotels, and telecommunication companies, customer satisfaction is taking a nosedive and customer complaints are on the rise.

Another concern relating to CRM practices involves privacy issues. How much should a company really know about its customers? Ironically, in this day and age of high-tech CRM systems, experts are now suggesting that if customers want better service, they should protect their privacy. In doing so, it is recommended that customers avoid filling out surveys and be protective about credit card and Social Security information. The less companies know about customers, the less they will be able to categorize them, and the less likely customers will be treated as low-value.

CRM is also limited by its focus on past purchase patterns. In reality, what customers spend today is not necessarily a good predictor of what their behavior will be tomorrow. How many potential profitable customers are being eliminated today because their current purchasing behavior has them slotted and treated as "commoners"? Spurned by such treatment, how many of these customers defect to another provider that appreciates their potential and treats them appropriately? Life situations and spending habits do change over time.

Service discrimination also leads to some interesting ethical questions. Should only the wealthy be recipients of quality service? Is this a form of **red-lining**—the practice of identifying and avoiding unprofitable types of neighborhoods or people?

Red-lining *Practice of identifying and avoiding unprofitable types of neighborhoods or people.*

Service Quality

Service quality *Attitude formed by a long-term, overall evaluation of performance.*

Service quality researchers agree on one issue: **Service quality** is an elusive and abstract concept that is difficult to define and measure.[135] The productivity of education and government services is notoriously difficult to measure. Increases in quality, such as improving the quality of education and training governmental employees to be more pleasant throughout their daily interactions with the public, do not show up in productivity measures. In contrast, providing poor quality can ironically increase the country's gross national product (GNP).[136] If a mail-order company sends a customer the wrong product, the dollars spent on phone calls and return mailings to correct the mistake will actually add to the country's GNP. However, it is readily apparent that increases in quality can have a dramatic impact on a firm's or industry's survival. As evidence, Japan did not simply bulldoze its way into U.S. markets by offering lower prices alone—superior quality relative to the competition at that time ultimately won customers over.

What Is Service Quality?

Perhaps the best way to begin a discussion of service quality is to first attempt to distinguish service quality from customer satisfaction. Most experts agree that customer satisfaction is a short-term, transaction-specific measure, whereas service quality is an attitude formed by a long-term, comprehensive evaluation of performance. Service quality offers a way for competing services to achieve success. In particular, where a small number of firms, such as banks, offer nearly identical services competing within a small area, establishing service quality may be the only way for a firm to differentiate itself. Service quality differentiation can generate increased market share and ultimately mean the difference between financial success and failure.

Goods manufacturers have already learned this lesson and over the past decade have made producing quality goods a priority issue. Improving the quality of manufactured goods has become a major strategy for both establishing efficient, smoothly running operations and increasing consumer market share in an atmosphere of increasing customer demand for higher quality. Goods quality improvement measures have focused largely on the quality of the products themselves, and specifically on eliminating product failure. Initially, these measures were based on rigorous checking of all finished products before they came into contact with the customer. More recently, quality control has focused on the principle of ensuring quality during the manufacturing process, on "getting it right the first time," and on reducing end-of-production line failures to zero. The final evolution in goods manufacturing has been to define quality as delivering the right product to the right customer at the right time, thus extending quality beyond the good itself and using external as well as internal measures to assess overall quality.

Service quality cannot be understood in quite the same way. The service experience depends on the customer as a participant in the production process, so normal quality-control measures that depend on eliminating defects before the consumer sees the product are not applicable. Service quality is not a specific goal or program that can be achieved or completed before the final product reaches the customer. Consequently, while manufacturers of goods aim for *zero defects,* the primary goal of service firms is *zero defections.* This often entails handling problems in real time as they unfold throughout the service delivery process.

The Gap Model

The *service gap* The gap between customers' expectations of service and their perception of the service actually delivered, which is a function of the knowledge gap, the standards gap, the delivery gap, and the communications gap.

Service quality can be examined in terms of gaps that exist between expectations and perceptions on the part of management, employees, and customers.[137] The most important gap—the **service gap**—is between customers' expectations of service and their perception of the service actually delivered. Ultimately, the goal of a service firm is to close the service gap or at least narrow it as much as possible. Before the firm can close the service gap, it must close or attempt to narrow four other gaps:

The *knowledge gap*—the difference between what consumers expect of a service and what management perceives the consumers expect.

The *standards gap*—the difference between what management perceives consumers expect and the standards set for service delivery.

The *delivery gap*—the difference between the standards set for service delivery and the actual quality of service delivery. For example, do employees perform the service as they were trained?

The *communications gap*—the difference between the actual quality of service delivered and the quality of service described in the firm's external communications such as brochures and mass-media advertising.

Hence, the service gap is a function of the knowledge gap, the standards gap, the delivery gap, and the communications gap. As each of these gaps increases or decreases, the service gap responds in a similar manner.

THE KNOWLEDGE GAP The most immediate and obvious gap is usually between what customers want and what managers think customers want. Briefly, many managers think they know what their customers want but are, in fact, mistaken. Banking customers may prefer security to a good interest rate. Some restaurant customers prefer quality and taste of food over an attractive arrangement of the tables or a good view from the window. A hotel may feel that its customers prefer comfortable rooms, though the majority of them spend little time in their rooms and are more interested in on-site amenities.

When a knowledge gap occurs, a variety of other mistakes tend to follow. The wrong facilities may be provided, the wrong staff may be hired, and the wrong training may be undertaken. Services may be provided that customers have no use for, while the services they do desire are not offered. Closing this gap requires minutely detailed knowledge of what customers desire and then building responses to customer needs into the service operating system.

THE STANDARDS GAP Even if customer expectations have been accurately determined, a standards gap may open between management's perception of customer expectations and the actual standards set for service delivery, such as order processing speed, the way cloth napkins are folded, or the way customers are greeted. Simply stated, standards comprise the blueprint of the service operation—they dictate how the service delivery process is to be implemented. When developing standards, the firm should develop a flowchart of its operations to identify all points of contact with its customers. Detailed standards can then be written for (1) the way the system should operate, and (2) the behavior of contact personnel at each point in the system. For example, front-desk personnel of **Marriott** hotels may be trained to perform to specification in such areas as acknowledging the customer on arrival, establishing eye contact, smiling, completing the proper paperwork, reviewing available amenities with the customer, and providing the customer with keys to the room.

In some cases a standards gap exists because management does not believe it can or should meet customer requirements for service. Sometimes management has no commitment to the delivery of service quality. Corporate leadership may set other priorities that interfere with standards that lead to good service. For example, a company's emphasis on cost-reduction strategies that maximize short-term profits is often cited as a misguided priority that impedes the firm's progress in delivering quality services. Personal computer companies whose automated service hotlines reduce the number of customer service employees are typical examples. In some instances, customers have been forced to remain on hold for hours before they could actually speak to a real person. *Hotlines* were originally named to reflect the speed with which customers could talk with manufacturers. Now the name more appropriately reflects the customer's temper by the time he or she talks to someone who can actually help.

THE DELIVERY GAP The delivery gap is the difference between how a service is actually delivered compared to the standards set by management. The existence of a delivery gap depends on both the willingness and the ability of employees to provide the service according to specification. For example, do employees wear their name tags, do they establish eye contact, and do they thank the customer when the transaction is completed? One factor that influences the size of the delivery gap is the employees' willingness to perform the service. Obviously, willingness to provide a service can vary greatly from employee to employee and for the same employee over time. Many employees who start off working to their full potential become less willing to do so over time because of frustration and dissatisfaction with the organization. Furthermore, a considerable range exists between what employees are actually capable of accomplishing and the minimum the employees must do in order to keep their jobs. Most service managers find it difficult to keep employees working at their full potential all the time.

Other employees, no matter how willing, may simply not be able to perform the service to specification. Individuals may have been hired for jobs they are not qualified to handle or to which they are temperamentally unsuited. Some employees do not receive sufficient training for the roles expected of them. Generally, employees who are not capable of performing assigned roles are less willing to keep trying.

Finally, a delivery gap may expand due to inadequate support, such as when employees do not receive the technological and other resources necessary for them to perform their jobs in the best possible manner. Even the best employees can be discouraged if they are forced to work with out-of-date or faulty equipment, especially if the employees of competing firms have superior resources and are able to provide the same or superior levels of service with far less effort. Failure to properly support employees leads to wasted effort, poor employee productivity, unsatisfied customers, and an increase in the size of the delivery gap.

THE COMMUNICATIONS GAP The communications gap is the difference between the service the firm promises it will deliver through its external communications (e.g., brochures, advertising, etc.) and the service it actually delivers to its customers. If the firm's advertising or sales promotions promise one level of service and the consumer receives a different level of service, the communications gap widens. External communications are essentially promises the firm makes to its customers. When the communications gap is wide, the firm has broken its promises, resulting in a lack of future customer trust. A customer who orders a bottle of wine from a menu only to be told it is out of stock may feel that the offer held out on the menu has not been fulfilled. Similarly, customers who are promised delivery in three days but then wait a week to receive their order will lower their perceptions of service quality. Unfortunately, the communications gap appears to be burgeoning among firms conducting business on-line.

Customer Retention

The value of retaining existing customers is critical in these days of saturated markets and rising marketing costs. In fact, some experts believe that customer retention has a more powerful effect on profits than market share, economies of scale, and other variables commonly associated with competitive advantage. Studies have indicated that as much as 95 percent of profits come from long-term customers via profits derived from sales, referrals, and reduced operating costs.[138]

Simply stated, **customer retention** refers to focusing a firm's marketing efforts toward the existing customer base. Customer retention is the opposite of **conquest marketing,** which focuses on discounts and markdowns and developing promotional campaigns that will attract new customers from competing firms. Conquest marketing is consistent with a number of other marketing strategies that are designed to replace "disloyal" customers—termed the **leaky bucket theory.** In contrast to conquest marketing, firms engaged in customer retention efforts work to satisfy existing customers with the intent of developing long-term relationships between the firm and its current clientele. However, it should be noted that expecting 100 percent loyalty from customers is unrealistic. Previous studies have shown that only about 10 percent of buyers are truly loyal to a particular brand over a one-year period. In addition, buyers who are 100 percent loyal tend to be light purchasers. In reality, customer loyalty tends to be divided among a number of brands. **Polygamous loyalty** is apparent in a number of markets including car rentals, restaurants, and airlines. For example, 80 percent of European business travelers are members of more than one frequent flyer program.[139]

Customer Retention Tactics

Two-thirds of customers who defect to competitors do so because they feel that companies are not genuinely concerned about their well-being. Because of the lack of consistent customer service that customers often experience, firms that effectively communicate customer retention as a primary goal are noticed. Consequently, a firm's customer retention efforts should serve to successfully differentiate the firm from its competitors. Methods for retaining customers through the use of effective customer retention tactics include maintaining the proper perspective, remembering customers between sales, building trusting relationships, monitoring the service delivery process, focusing on proper installation and training, standing behind the product, providing discretionary effort, offering service guarantees, and practicing the art of service recovery.

MAINTAIN THE PROPER PERSPECTIVE Managers and employees need to remember that the company exists to meet the needs and desires of its customers. Processing customers like raw materials on an assembly line or being rude to customers is incredibly short-sighted. Companies such as **US Airways** employ slogans such as, "The U in US Airways starts with U the passenger." Credos such as this influence customer expectations and reinforce the firm's priorities to employees.

Interacting with the public is not an easy task and, unfortunately, employees occasionally fail to maintain the proper perspective. Different customers may ask the same questions of employees over and over, and not every customer is polite. Maintaining the proper perspective involves a customer-oriented frame of mind and a commitment to service. Employees need to remember that every customer has his or her own personal set of needs, and that the customer's, not the employee's, expectations define performance.

REMEMBER CUSTOMERS BETWEEN SALES Contacting customers between sales transactions is a useful approach in building relationships with the firm. The key is in making customer contact sincere and personal. Typical approaches include sending birthday, get-well, and/or anniversary cards; writing personal notes congratulating customers for their personal successes; and keeping in touch with customers concerning past services rendered and offering assistance if necessary. The goal of this tactic is to communicate to customers that the firm genuinely cares for their well-being and values the ongoing relationship.

BUILD TRUSTING RELATIONSHIPS Trust is defined as a firm belief or confidence in the honesty, integrity, and the reliability of another person. In the service environment, three major components of trust are: (1) the service provider's expertise; (2) the service provider's reliability; and (3) the service provider's concern for the customer. Strategies for building trust include:

- Protect confidential information.
- Keep promises.
- Refrain from making disparaging remarks about other customers and competitors.
- Tell the customer the truth, even when it hurts.
- Provide the customer with full information—the pros and the cons.
- Be dependable, courteous, and considerate with customers.
- Become actively involved in community affairs.

MONITOR THE SERVICE DELIVERY PROCESS After the customer has requested a specific service, monitoring the service delivery process should be a key tactic in the firm's customer retention efforts. Service providers that are able to monitor the service delivery process are able to correct service inadequacies and influence customer perceptions of service quality prior to completion. Obvious examples include the restaurant that regularly communicates with its customers throughout their meal, or the owner of the firm who contacts customers about recent purchases. Proactively seeking customer feedback throughout the process builds customer perceptions of trust and facilitates maintaining customers for life.

FOCUS ON PROPER INSTALLATION AND TRAINING Proper installation of products and training customers how to use what they have purchased saves a lot of headaches. Customers should not become frustrated over not understanding how to use something or, worse, improperly using the product, which may result in damage and further dissatisfaction. Simply dropping off a product such as a refrigerator with an automatic ice cube maker, and leaving customers to fend for themselves reinforces the idea that the company is not genuinely concerned for the customer's well-being. It leaves the impression that the company is more interested in short-term profits than in building long-term relationships.

STAND BEHIND THE PRODUCT When a customer returns a product that is in need of service or repair is no time to hide. Every firm should stand behind what it sells, and ensure that every transaction is handled to the customer's satisfaction. Most customers are realistic and understand that nothing lasts forever. Many times customers are simply looking for advice and alternative solutions to problems, and are not looking for someone to blame. Expressing a sincere concern for the customer's situation reinforces the firm's customer retention efforts.

PROVIDE DISCRETIONARY EFFORT Discretionary effort is behavior beyond the call of duty. It is the Procter & Gamble salesperson who voluntarily bags groceries at the grand opening of a new grocery store. It is the hotel that sends items misplaced by customers to their homes at no charge. It is the oil company that recognizes the special needs of its customers during weather-related disasters. Discretionary effort involves countless personal touches, little things that distinguish a one-time business transaction from an ongoing relationship.

OFFER SERVICE GUARANTEES One of the most intriguing customer retention strategies to be developed in recent years is the service guarantee.[140] Service guarantees appear to facilitate three worthwhile goals: (1) reinforce customer loyalty; (2) build market share; and (3) force the firm offering the guarantee to improve its overall service quality.

In general, successful guarantees are unrestrictive, stated in specific and clear terms, meaningful and hassle-free when invoked, and quick to be paid out. On the other hand, mistakes to avoid when constructing a guarantee include: (1) promising something that is trivial and normally expected; (2) specifying an inordinate number of conditions as part of the guarantee; and (3) making the guarantee so mild that it is never invoked.

PRACTICE THE ART OF SERVICE RECOVERY When the service is provided incorrectly, an important but often overlooked management tool is the art of **service recovery**.[141] While some companies are great at delivering service until something goes wrong, other companies thrive on recovering from service failures and impressing customers in the process. Customers of service organizations often allow the firm one mistake. Consequently, when a failure occurs, the customer generally provides the business with an opportunity to make amends. Unfortunately, many companies still drop the ball and further aggravate the customer by failing to take the opportunity to recover.

Service recovery A firm's reaction to a complaint that results in customer satisfaction and goodwill.

The customer's perception of whether the recovery strategy is just includes evaluations of the recovery process itself; the outcomes connected to the recovery strategy; and the interpersonal behaviors enacted during the recovery process. Accordingly, perceived justice consists of three components: **distributive justice, procedural justice,** and **interactional justice.**

- Distributive justice focuses on the specific outcome of a firm's recovery effort. In other words, what specifically did the offending firm offer the customer to recover from the service failure, and did this outcome (output) offset the costs (inputs) of the service failure? Typical distributive outcomes include compensation (e.g., gratis, discounts, coupons, free upgrades, and free ancillary services); offers to mend or totally replace/reperform; and apologies.
- Procedural justice examines the process that is undertaken to arrive at the final outcome. Hence, even though a customer may be satisfied with the type of recovery strategy offered, recovery evaluation may be poor due to the

process endured to obtain the recovery outcome. For example, research has indicated that when implementing identical recovery strategies, those that are implemented promptly are much more likely to be associated with higher consumer effectiveness ratings and retention rates than when restitution is delayed.

- Interactional justice refers to the manner in which the service recovery process is implemented and how recovery outcomes are presented. In other words, interactional justice involves the courtesy and politeness exhibited by personnel; empathy; effort observed in resolving the situation; and the firm's willingness to provide an explanation for why the situation occurred.

A limited amount of research exists that specifically examines the influence of perceived justice on recovery strategy effectiveness. However, the bottom line is that the three components of perceived justice should be considered when formulating effective service recovery strategies. Deploying recovery efforts that satisfy distributive justice without considering customer procedural and interactional justice needs may still result in customer defections. If service firms are truly committed to the recovery process and retaining customers for life, all three aspects of perceived justice must be integrated into the service recovery process.

Retail Marketing

Retail Customers

Retailing consists of the final activities and steps needed to place a product or service in the hands of the consumer. To be a high performer, a retailer must be able to differentiate itself from the competition. In doing so, retail managers must realize that, with the possible exception of supermarkets, their stores can't serve all possible customer types. Before developing any plans, the successful retailer must first target a specific segment(s) of the overall market to serve and study the environmental factors (competition, the behavior of the other supply chain members, and legal and ethical factors) affecting that segment(s). Only then can retailers decide on a location format and retail mix (the combination of merchandise assortment, price, promotion, customer service, and store layout) that best serves the segment(s) targeted.

Customer satisfaction *Occurs when the total shopping experience of the customer has been met or exceeded.*

The easiest way for retailers to differentiate themselves is to satisfy the customer's needs and wants better than the competition. This customer satisfaction, as we will use the term, is different from customer service. **Customer satisfaction** is determined by whether the total shopping experience has met or exceeded the customer's expectation. If it has, the customer is said to have had a rewarding shopping experience. This is important because it costs the average retailer five times as much money to get a new customer into its store as it does to retain a current customer who may be unhappy. It is important that customers are happy with their shopping experience not only for retailers, but also for the nation's economy. A relationship between customer satisfaction and consumer spending shows spending and satisfaction move together which should not be surprising since buyer satisfaction is a major demand generator. The satisfied buyer will be encouraged to engage in future spending, while the dissatisfied buyer will be more hesitant.

Customer services *Include the activities the retailer performs that influence (1) the ease with which a potential customer can shop or learn about the store's offering, (2) the ease with which a transaction can be completed once the customer attempts to make a purchase, and (3) the customer's satisfaction with the purchase.*

In addition to the tangible product or intangible service offered for sale, another part of the customer's shopping experience is the services provided by the retailer. These **customer services** are the activities performed by the retailer that influence (1) the ease with which a potential customer can shop or learn about the store's offering, (2) the ease with which a transaction can be completed once the customer attempts to make a purchase, and (3) the customer's satisfaction with the product after the purchase. These three elements are the pretransaction, transaction, and posttransaction components of customer service. Common services provided by retailers (in addition to having the product that satisfies the customer's needs and wants) include alterations, fitting rooms, delivery, gift registries, check cashing, credit, extended shopping hours, short checkout lines, gift wrapping, parking, layaway, and merchandise return privileges as well as the availability of in-home shopping options such as television, print catalogs, and Internet shopping. It must be remembered that none of these services are actually the merchandise or service offered for sale; they merely entice the customers the retailer is targeting.

If the customer is dissatisfied with either the product offered or the services provided, that customer is less likely to choose that retailer in the future, thus decreasing future sales. (In the rest of this section we will use the term *product* to designate either the physical product or service offered for sale and the term *service* to refer to the services the retailer uses to facilitate that sale. However, in the case of a service retailer, the product offered is in fact the service.) Knowing what products to carry, as well as determining which customer services to offer, is a most challenging problem for retailers as they seek ways to improve the shopping experience. Imagine listening to a radio with no tuning or volume knob. The receiver picks up many different signals, some in harmony, some in conflict, so that the result is noise coming through the speaker. You're getting something, but you can't understand it. To make sense of the confusing array of information, retailers use market segmentation techniques to tune in segments of the population, hoping to hear a series of clear messages that can then be constructed into some overall meaning.

Some retailers today claim that the declining level of satisfaction may not actually be a bad sign. They view the decline as a function of rising expectations from the customer. They claim that their merchandise or service is much better today than it was a decade ago, but that customer expectations have increased at a faster rate. They like to point out that today's consumers are fussier and demand perfection. A nearby home improvement store, for example, might have great merchandise and low prices, but the checkout lines may be too long. Likewise, understanding different customer segments and their need for convenience might stimulate the retailer to offer products through its Web site, providing a critical service component to enhance the customer's experience. As Exhibit 300.53 points out, it is important that the retailer know and understand its customer.

In Exhibit 300.53 we see the three important types of trends—population, social, and economic—that all retailers must monitor because they will affect the way customers undertake the shopping process. Retailers must perform three strategies:

1. Get as many of the targeted consumers into your store as possible.
2. Convert these consumers into customers by having them purchase merchandise.
3. Perform these first two strategies at the lowest cost possible that is consistent with the level of service that your customers expect.

If the retailer doesn't understand its customer, it won't be able to accomplish the first two strategies.

Market segmentation is a method retailers use to examine ways to segment, or break down, heterogeneous consumer populations into smaller, more homogeneous groups based on their characteristics. Market segmentation helps retailers understand who their customers are, how they think, and what they do, thus enabling the retailers to build a meaningful picture of consumer needs, desires, perceptions, and shopping behaviors and the image these consumers have of the retailer in comparison to its competitors. Only by conducting these activities can a retailer hope to satisfy the consumers' needs better than the competition. Failure to spot changes in the marketplace before the competition means the retailer will be able to react only and will be forced to adapt to what more sensitive retailers have already spotted. Thus, while the high-performance retailer will have spotted an emerging trend and made the necessary changes in its retail mix, the average

> **Market segmentation** The dividing of a heterogeneous consumer population into smaller, more homogeneous groups based on their characteristics.

Exhibit 300.53 *Current Trends Affect the Way the Consumer Behaves*

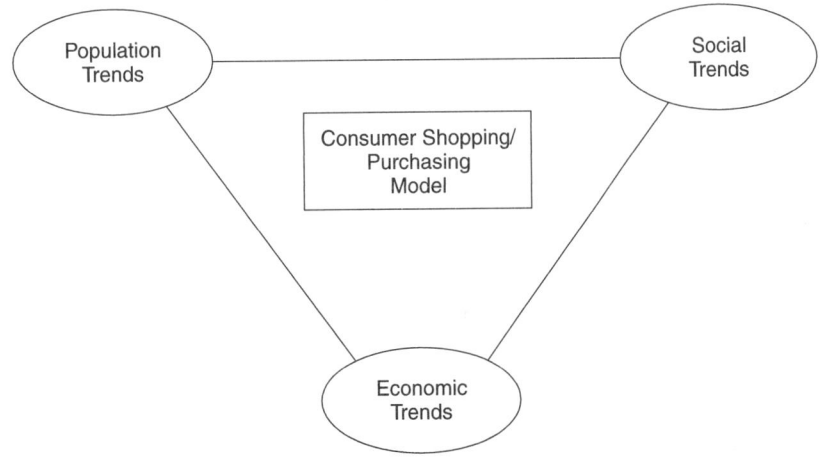

> *Retailers who focus on understanding a well-defined customer niche and serving that market with a differentiated offer will achieve high profitability.*

retailer can only be a follower or "look-alike" retailer. And what differential advantage does a "me-too" retailer offer a consumer? Copycat practices have led many retailers into financial difficulties.

Population Trends

> *Population variables Include population growth trends, age distributions, and geographic trends.*

Retailers often find it useful to group consumers according to **population variables,** such as population growth trends, age distributions, and geographic trends. This is useful for two reasons: First, such data are often linked to marketplace needs; second, the data are readily available and can easily be applied in analyzing markets.

POPULATION GROWTH Retailers have long viewed an expanding population base as synonymous with growth in retail markets.[142] Unfortunately, the nation's overall growth rate has been declining during the past three decades as families have fewer children.

Implications for Retailers An increase in population growth will mean an increased demand for goods and services domestically, but nowhere near the 80 percent increase experienced over the last half-century. Consequently, retailers will focus on taking market share from competitors, managing gross margin by controlling selling price and cost, and increasing productivity of existing stores. Another growth opportunity for retailers will be international expansion. However, later this century this may not be a solution. Demographers are predicting a major decline in worldwide fertility rates. This will lead to a global population decline, which is a radical notion in a world brought up on the idea of overpopulation. While it will take some time, worldwide retailers should be prepared for depopulation.

AGE DISTRIBUTION The age distribution of the U.S. population is changing significantly. In 1980 the median age was 30, but by 2001 it had risen to 35.6 years. The most significant change today is the bulge of early baby boomers moving into their late 50s. In the 1980s, the baby boomers with the incomes and energy to "shop till they drop" fueled the rapidly expanding retail sector, especially with regard to apparel sales. But today, as the first wave of boomers reach age 60 and older—a demographic group known as the "gray market"—they are not spending as freely they did in the past. Many are aggressively saving for retirement because of increasing concern over the long-term viability of social security and uncertainty about corporate downsizing, which has left many mature adults unemployed. It is assumed that in the future this first wave of boomers will spend less on apparel and clothing and more on medicine and recreation. They will focus more on security, good health, comfort, their homes, and safety.[143] Today's younger boomers, those between 40 and 50, are unlike the previous generations who, when they reached midlife, would pare debt and begin to save for retirement. These younger boomers instead have created a new breed of consultants—a combination of financial planner and attorney—who are equipped to advise parents and their children on how to manage what will be the largest transfer of wealth from one generation to another.

"Baby busters" or "Generation Xers"—those born between 1965 and 1977—are another interesting age group. Unlike the baby boomers, this age group is a declining percentage of the population. As of 2003 there are 46 million of these consumers.

"Generation Y," "echo boomers," or the "millennium generation" are those born between 1978 and 1994 and number over 75 million. They are emerging as a major buying and consuming force in the economy.[144] This generation is racially diverse; more than one in three is not Caucasian. Three out of four have a working mother and one out of four is in a single-parent household. There is emerging evidence that the Gen Yers' values are more traditional than those of their parents and that they have a conservative lifestyle, as evident by their tendency to live separately before marriage.

Implications for Retailers The most significant effect of an aging population is negative for retailers because, especially with regards to the boomers, their big spending years are behind them. Retailers must remember what motivates consumers to spend money. Younger adults are by their very nature acquisition-oriented. These first-time renters and home buyers need to acquire material objects and usually judge their progress by such possessions. Older adults tend to conserve what they have already acquired. Thus, as the population ages, a significant driving force for total economic growth dries up.

> *Retailers who understand the implications of the country's age distribution will be more apt to identify opportunities to improve their profitability.*

Also, because different retailers tend to serve different age groups, the changing distribution of the U.S. population poses many challenges and opportunities. Retailers should be aware of what was pointed out earlier—consumers approaching 60, the first wave of baby boomers, tend to focus more on their families and finances than those in other age groups. They also spend more on medical services and travel. Thus, the products and services that appealed to these boomers as free-spending younger consumers will not necessarily be the ones that appeal to them now as grandparents and home owners. In addition, this older market is expected to use the services of others more often. The DYI (do-it-yourself) market has begun to soften now that there are more people over 35 than under 35. As the population ages, more people are becoming "do-it-for-me's." This DIFM (do-it-for-me) trend is rapidly growing in the services arena.

For instance, two emerging do-it-for-me services are home cleaning and yard care. These services have become especially popular among dual-income households over 35, where there is little discretionary time but ample discretionary income for do-it-for-me services.

Because consumers change their spending habits as they age, the high-profit retailers of the next decade will be those that best adapt to these changes.

The "graying of America" will have enormous consequences for business in general, not just retailing, as older consumers are skeptical and uninterested in shopping. Retailers must be able to speak the older consumers' language and not talk down to or patronize them, avoid "phony friendliness," and in a tactful manner recognize that as they age, these consumers have a declining ability to deal with spatial relationships thus necessitating easy-to-navigate store layouts and clearly labeled merchandise.[145] However, it is doubtful that all the baby boomers will behave as their parents did a generation before them. Retailers who assume the baby boomers will behave as their parents will be mistaken. A 50-year-old in 2005 will not act like a 50-year-old in 1985. In fact, they may even keep some of the habits of a 30-year-old in 1985 (which is what they were), just older and wiser. Many of these "Pepsi Generation" types will probably enter the "gray market" kicking and screaming. They will demand that retailers embrace their values, such as youthfulness and invincibility, no matter what the product or service: food, insurance, entertainment, or medicine. Therefore, just as some firms seek to meet increased demand for health care services and travel, restaurants (where the over-60 category accounts for more than 30 percent of the breakfast and dinner trade) will have to consider such items as the design of their tables and seats; financial service firms will have to reconsider their product offerings to this fixed-income category of consumers; malls will offer valet parking and lounges with concierge services that not only make shopping easier but make the shopper feel pampered. Retailers in general will have to use bigger print, brighter parking lots, and fewer displays blocking store aisles, as well as rethink the way they portray and target senior citizens in their advertising.

Retailers haven't forgotten about the Gen Xers and Gen Yers. These groups are not only different in age but, according to many boomers, they are also significantly different in their buying behavior and will be difficult for retailers to reach without a well-considered effort.[146] Young consumers today don't want conspicuous consumption. In fact, they are more sophisticated than previous generations when it comes to shopping and seem to be turned off by promotions that don't take them seriously. These antifashion and antiestablishment consumers want entertainment or events when they shop.[147] That means different promotions that are relevant to them, funny, and say "we understand." Retailers dealing with this market can't fake it.

Most retailers have made a major mistake by overlooking the "tweeners," those consumers aged 8 to 12. These younger shoppers spend $10 billion annually and influence another $250 billion in purchases. Retailers of all sorts must target these shoppers as well as their parents. After all, while their parents might cite price as the number one reason for purchasing a particular item used by their children, "child request" was a close second.[148] Tweeners have trained their parents to know what to buy for them. While many companies analyze which products will appeal to the older generations, retailers seldom think about marketing specifically to children younger than teenagers. One group of retailers noticing this important segment is the hotel industry, which knows the importance of offering activities for kids, even if these programs are just glorified day-care centers that give parents a break.[149]

GEOGRAPHIC TRENDS The location of consumers in relation to the retailer often affects how they buy. In this section covering population trends, we will take a closer look at how geographic trends affect retail operations.

Shifting Geographic Centers Retailers should be concerned not only with the number of people and their ages, but also with where they reside. Consumers, especially as they get older, will not travel great distances to make retail purchases. Consumers want convenience and will therefore patronize local retail outlets.

Implications for Retailers This changing geographic shift means Northeastern and Midwestern retailers are experiencing slower growth, and national retailers are adding stores and distribution centers (warehouses) in the South and West. Furthermore, one of the biggest mistakes that retailers make is to assume that all the consumers in a certain

Retailers who develop micromarketing merchandising strategies will have higher profit.

geographic area have the same purchasing habits. While households in the Northeast tend to spend more on education, food, housing, and apparel as a percentage of consumer expenditures, they don't all spend that way. Also, Midwesterners on average spend more on entertainment and tobacco and smoking supplies; those in the South spend relatively more on transportation and health care and make more cash contributions. Finally, those in the West spend more on personal insurance and pensions, housing, and entertainment.

Micromarketing involves tailoring merchandise in each store by using the optional stock list approach, to match the preferences of its neighborhood. This is made possible by the use of computer software programs that match neighborhood demographics with product demand. Two of the biggest Sears stores in the Chicago area are nearly the same size and do about the same annual sales volume. However, the merchandise makeup of the two stores is different. The urban store, which is close to many fine bakeries, doesn't carry breadmakers, but breadmakers are popular items in the more upscale suburban store 15 miles away. Micromarketing also is important with retailers operating internationally.

Social Trends

In this section, we will continue our examination of demographic factors affecting the modern retailer by looking at several social trends: the increasing level of educational attainment, the state of marriage and divorce, the makeup of the American household, and the changing nature of work.

EDUCATION The education level of the average American is increasing. The Gen Xers, who were between the ages of 26 and 38 in 2003, are the most educated generation ever. Nearly one in three has completed four years of college. This statistic is slightly higher for men and slightly lower for women. However, this trend is rapidly changing since at many colleges and universities women outnumber men. Women are also increasingly pursuing high-paying career fields such as business, psychology, biology/life sciences, and engineering.[150]

Implications for Retailers Educational attainment is the single most reliable indicator of a person's income potential, attitudes, and spending habits. Thus, college-educated consumers differ in their buying behavior from other workers of the same age and income levels. They are more alert to price, quality, and advertised claims. However, often overlooked when using education to segment the marketplace are the 30 million Americans over the age of 25 who have some college experience but not a degree. In many ways, people with some college best define the term "average" American.[151] They have more money than high school graduates, but less than college graduates. They also fall between the groups in their propensity to shop in department stores, spend on apparel, buy new cars, travel, read books, watch TV, and invest in stocks and bonds.

Since education levels for the population, in aggregate, are expected to continue to rise, retailers can expect consumers to become increasingly sophisticated, discriminating, and independent in their search for consumer products. They will also demand a staff capable of intelligently dealing with their needs and wants.

Education is a key determinant of the use of the Internet for shopping. Today's many consumers grew up with the computer and feel comfortable with it. With their higher level of education, they are more prone to shop electronically because they don't need the assurances or hand-holding that some retailers provide. This may present problems for many traditional sellers of services. For example, travel agencies may be left out of the loop as cybershoppers "surf the net" to purchase airline tickets, hotel rooms, rental cars, and cruises.

STATE OF MARRIAGE A relatively new social phenomenon has occurred during the past quarter century. In 1970, less than 10 percent of the U.S. male population between the ages of 30 and 34 had never married and just over 6 percent of the same female population had never married. In 2000 these percentages had increased to 30 and 22 percent, respectively. Married couples are one of the slowest-growing household types not only in this country but worldwide. In 1970 males married at a median age of 23 and females at 21; today the median age for males is over 26 and for females it is 25. Not only are many people postponing marriage, some are choosing not to marry at all.

Implications for Retailers For the retailer this trend toward single-person households presents many opportunities because of the increased need for a larger number of smaller houses complete with home furnishings. This is especially true for the young adult market. The retailer may need to adjust its store hours to accommodate the needs of this market. Also, with more men living alone, supermarkets will have to direct promotions toward their needs and habits, since men tend to focus on getting specific items and then getting out of the store.

DIVORCE Since 1960, the U.S. divorce rate has increased by 250 percent. As women's wages rose, it became more profitable for them to enter the labor force. As a result, spouses became less dependent on each other and divorces increased.

Implications for Retailers When a divorce occurs, many retail purchases are required. A second household, quite similar to that of the never-married individual, is formed almost immediately. These new households need certain items such as furniture and kitchen appliances, televisions and stereos, and even linens. Divorce may impact the way people shop, once they are settled into their new homes. Retailers must make specific adjustments for divorced working women with children by adjusting store hours, providing more consumer information, and changing the product assortment.[152]

Economic Trends

In this section, we look at the effect on the modern retailer of income growth, the declining rate of personal savings, the increase in the number of working women, and the widespread use of credit in our economy.

INCOME GROWTH It appears that the rich are getting richer and the poor are getting poorer. However, this is in part misleading because income mobility in the U.S. is high. A significant proportion of the lowest-income households move up the income scale over a 10-year period and, similarly, a significant proportion of the richest households move down the income scale over a 10-year period.

Implications for Retailers The imbalance in income growth across households has created increased demand for value-oriented retailers such as discounters and manufacturers' outlets, and explains why many of the upscale retailers (such as **Macy's, Nordstrom,** and **Neiman Marcus**) have not suffered the economic pressures facing many of their lower-scale counterparts. Retailers of luxury automobiles, luxury foreign vacations, and executive-style houses in gated communities have also done well due to the growth in the number of millionaires. At the same time, the low income level and low income growth among some segments of the population explain the growth of chains such as **Dollar General.**

Economists tend to view income from two different perspectives: disposable and discretionary. **Disposable income** is simply all personal income less personal taxes. For most consumers, disposable income is their take-home pay. **Discretionary income** is disposable income minus the money needed for necessities to sustain life, such as minimal housing, minimal food, and minimal clothing. Retailers that sell necessities, such as supermarkets, like to see incomes rise and taxes decrease; they know that, while consumers won't spend all their increased disposable income on the retailer's merchandise, they will nevertheless increase spending. Retailers selling luxury goods want to see disposable income increase and the costs of necessities either decline or at least increase at a slower rate than income increases.

> **Disposable income** Personal income less personal taxes.
>
> **Discretionary income** Dsposable income minus the money needed for necessities to sustain life.

PERSONAL SAVINGS A major criticism of the U.S. economic system is that it does not reward personal savings. Savings, which are expressed as a percentage of disposable income, have dwindled since 1981. While this may seem odd, it is important to note that during the last decade, the economy and stock market experienced exceptionally strong growth until 2001. As a result, many people have quit saving and begun to invest in the stock market, which some consider a form of saving despite its additional elements of risk. (It should be pointed out that the government's numbers regarding the savings rate fail to address the treatment of capital gains. When the government measures disposable income, it counts wages, interest earned, and dividends—but not realized or unrealized capital gains.) The government's rate tends to undermeasure savings because it fails to consider the wealth effect. The wealth effect claims that for every hundred dollars of additional wealth generated in an individual's stock market holdings, the individual will spend $4 (4 percent). Such spending will lower the nation's savings rate because when the stock market goes up, spending will increase without an increase in wages and salaries. Savings will also be decreased in this example because the government will subtract the taxes on the stock market gains from disposable income.

Nevertheless, the savings rate in the U.S. is far below that of Japan, Germany, and France, which are all over 10 percent. However, given national differences in the measurements of income and savings, comparisons between countries are unclear.

Implications for Retailers Retailers have enjoyed continued sales growth over the past decade because even though median household income in fixed dollars has increased only slightly, spending and not saving has been the focus of the consumer. However, retailers must be prepared for the coming decades, when baby boomers and Gen Xers will plan for retirement by reducing their spending and increasing savings. Other economists fear that in another decade, when more boomers retire, they will start to take money out of the stock market, which could cascade into a declining market. And this could result in a reverse wealth effect because as consumers lose money in the stock market, they tend to save about four cents for every dollar lost in the market. However, if the stock market were to rise, consumers would spend more.

Types of Retail Competition

Competition in retail can be divided into intratype, intertype, and divertive.

Intratype competition Occurs when two or more retailers of the same type, as defined by NAICS codes in the Census of Retail Trade, compete directly with each other for the same households.

INTRATYPE AND INTERTYPE COMPETITION **Intratype competition** occurs when two or more retailers of the same type, as defined by SIC (Standard Industrial Classification) codes in the Census of Retail Trade, compete directly with each other for the same households. This is the most common type of retail competition: **Circuit City** competes with **Best Buy**, **Avon** competes with **Mary Kay**, **Saks Fifth Avenue** competes with **Neiman Marcus**, **Family Dollar** competes with Dollar General, and Amazon.com competes with **bn.com** (Barnes & Noble Online).

Due to the changing nature of the retailing environment, retailers are often forced to alter their strategy as their competition changes. For example, in the early 1990s Sears wanted to compete head-on with low-priced discounters such as Wal-Mart and **Kmart.** Today, after performing its own SWOT analysis and concluding that its customers do not like to push shopping carts through malls, where most of its stores are located, Sears repositioned itself against middle-of-the-road merchants **JCPenney** and **May Department Stores** by appealing to women and emphasizing apparel. To generate more up-market store traffic, Sears acquired catalog merchant **Lands' End,** whose merchandise is now found in all of its stores. Sears has also tried to capture the "nesting" trend among many consumers by developing the **Great Indoors,** large freestanding home centers that offer both deeper home furnishings and housewares selection and the convenience of at-the-door parking.

Intertype competition Occurs when two or more retailers of a different type, as defined by NAICS codes in the Census of Retail Trade, compete directly by attempting to sell the same merchandise lines to the same households.

Every time different types of retail outlets sell the same lines of merchandise and compete for the same limited consumer dollars, **intertype competition** occurs. This is increasingly seen as many retailers compete with a scrambled merchandising strategy. Scrambled merchandising is when a retailer carries many different unrelated product lines, often outside its traditional product mix, as a means of enhancing the one-stop shopping convenience for their customers. Following are some common examples:

- Discounters are handling cosmetics and fragrances that were traditionally the province of the traditional department stores.
- Supermarkets (such as **Albertson's, Kroger,** and **Safeway**) have taken market share away from fast-food restaurants with their HMRs (home meal replacements). In addition, their floral departments, greeting card sections, banks, and pharmacies have changed the competitive landscape for traditional florists, card shops, banks, and drugstores, particulary in attracting consumers who place a high priority on convenience.
- Convenience food stores (such as **7-Eleven**) sell not only motor oil and related auto care products, but have added fast food, lottery tickets, and ATMs.

In each of the preceding examples, as intertype competition expanded, gross margins on the respective merchandise lines declined. For example, combination mail-order/on-line pharmacies have gained a growing share of prescription drug sales, and the impact on locally operated or chain-operated retail drugstores has been dramatic in reducing the average gross margin return on sales of drugs. Both types of drug retailers have pressured drug manufacturers for the lowest wholesale prices since they produce virtually identical medicines for arthritis, ulcers, and other common ailments. As a result, the inflation rate for widely used prescription drugs is the lowest of any medical category.

Furthermore, new retailers are always entering the marketplace creating greater intratype and intertype competition. The Internet and eBay have made it possible for anyone to be an e-tailer.

Divertive competition Occurs when retailers intercept or divert customers from competing retailers.

DIVERTIVE COMPETITION Another concept that helps to explain the nature of competition in retailing is **divertive competition.** This occurs when retailers intercept or divert customers from competing retailers. For example, an individual may recognize that she needs to get a birthday card for a relative and will probably do this the next time she visits the local shopping mall, which has a very well stocked

Hallmark card store. However, one day while picking up a prescription at the drugstore she walks by the card stand and decides to purchase the greeting card at the drugstore. The drugstore retailer has intercepted this customer from the Hallmark store.

Another divertive tactic in use today is to have a gas station on your property to catch those customers who have already stopped at your store and do not want to make another stop to get gas. Privately held Meijer's now sells gas at 136 of its 156 supercenters in the Midwest, and Wal-Mart now operates more than 900 gas stations at its supercenters and discount stores. E-tailers use a similar ploy by displaying banners across the top of many information Web sites.

To comprehend the significance of divertive competition, which can be intertype or intratype competition, one needs to recognize that most retailers operate very close to their **break-even point** (the point where total revenues equal total expenses), but aren't really aware of this fact. For instance, supermarkets, which have extremely low gross margin return on sales, tend to have high break-even points, ranging from 94 to 96 percent of current sales. General merchandise retailers with a higher gross margin return on sales face lower break-even points of 85 to 92 percent of their current sales. In either case, a modest drop in sales volume could make these retailers unprofitable and fuel the growth of scrambled merchandising to get more of the customer's share of wallet.

> *Retailers should attempt to operate at a sales volume of 20 percent above their break-even point because this will allow them to weather major competitive assaults and thus be able to acheive a higher profit over the long term.*

> ***Break-even point*** *When total revenues equal total expenses and the retailer is making neither a profit nor a loss.*

Evolution of Retail Competition

A discussion of the evolution of retailing not only provides a better understanding of the history of retail formats, but enhances our ability to make predictions about their future. Several theories have developed to explain and describe the evolution of competition in retailing. We will review three of them briefly and describe a new concept that helps to explain why a variety of retail formats have the potential to be profitable.

THE WHEEL OF RETAILING The **wheel of retailing theory,** illustrated in Exhibit 300.54, is one of the oldest descriptions of the patterns of competitive development in retailing.[153] This theory states that new types of retailers enter the market as low-status, low-margin, and low-price operators. This entry phase allows retailers to compete effectively and take market share away from the more traditional retailers. However, as they meet with success, these new retailers gradually enter a trading-up phase and acquire more sophisticated and elaborate facilities, often becoming less efficient. This creates both a higher investment and a subsequent rise in operating costs. Predictably, these retailers will enter the vulnerability phase and must raise prices and margins, becoming vulnerable to new types of low-margin retail competitors who progress through the same pattern. This appears to be the case today with outlet malls. Once bare-bones warehouses

> ***Wheel of retailing theory*** *Describes how new types of retailers enter the market as low-status, low-margin, low-price operators; however, as they meet with success, these new retailers gradually acquire more sophisticated and elaborate facilities, and thus become vulnerable to new types of low-margin retail competitors who progress through the same pattern.*

Exhibit 300.54   *Wheel of Retailing*

for manufacturers' imperfect or excess merchandise, outlet malls have quickly evolved into fancy, almost upscale malls where retailers try to outdo each other's accent lighting, private dressing rooms, and generous return policies. As a result, the cost of operating at such locations increases and puts them in more direct comparison with increasingly competitive department stores.

While the wheel of retailing may explain the evolution of some retail forms, it is less clear about the success of some new niche retailers; retailers that successfully compete on nonprice factors, such as luxury retailers or convenience stores; and the role of cost control on improving customer satisfaction as well as competitiveness, as Wal-Mart and discount clubs have done.

Retail accordion Describes how retail institutions evolve from outlets that offer wide assortments to specialized stores and continue repeatedly through the pattern.

THE RETAIL ACCORDION Several observers of the history of retailing have noted that retail institutions evolve from outlets that offer wide merchandise assortments to specialized stores that offer narrow assortments, and then return to the wide assortment stores to continue through the pattern again and again. This contraction and expansion of merchandise assortment suggests the term **accordion**.[154]

However, the accordion theory is vague about the competitive importance of providing wide assortments for various target customer groups. For example, the customer who wants one-stop-shopping convenience has led to success for Wal-Mart's superstores and other retailers using scrambled merchandising. Simultaneously, many category killers have been successful by specializing in a deep but narrow selection of merchandise lines, and specialty stores like **Wet Seal** and high-end "hot" designers like Gucci have succeeded by offering a highly edited point of view for their customer segments. Again, a major criticism of this theory is its implication that there is one "right" direction for successful retailing, when many are possible if well executed.

Retail life cycle Describes four distinct stages that a retail institution progresses through: introduction, growth, maturity, and decline.

THE RETAIL LIFE CYCLE Another framework we will examine is the **retail life cycle.** Some experts argue that retailing institutions pass through an identifiable cycle. This cycle has four distinct stages; it starts with (1) *introduction,* (2) proceeds to *growth,* (3) then *maturity,* and ends with (4) *decline.* We discuss each stage briefly.

Introduction This stage begins with an aggressive, bold entrepreneur who is willing and able to develop a different approach to the retailing of certain products. Most often the approach is oriented to a simpler method of distribution and passing the savings on to the customer. Other times it could be centered on a distinctive product assortment, shopping ease, locational convenience, advertising, or promotion. For example, Jiffy Lube and other quick oil change service retailers offered faster "while you wait" service at more convenient locations with lower prices than conventional service stations and automobile dealers and changed the way consumers serviced their cars. During this stage profits are low, despite the increasing sales level, due to amortizing developmental costs.

Growth During the growth stage, sales, and usually profits, explode. New retailers enter the market and begin to copy the idea. For example, the rapid growth of **Starbucks** cafes encouraged other "gourmet" coffeehouses to enter the market and capture the growing interest in deeper assortments of coffee beverages and casual "lifestyle" eateries. Toward the end of the growth period, cost pressures that arise from the need for a larger staff, more complex internal systems, increased management controls, and other requirements of operating large, multiunit organizations overtake some of the favorable results. Consequently, late in this stage both market share and profitability tend to approach their maximum level.

Maturity In maturity, market share stabilizes and severe profit declines are experienced for several reasons. First, managers have become accustomed to managing a high-growth firm that was simple and small, but now they must manage a large, complex firm in a nongrowing market. Second, the industry has typically overexpanded. Third, competitive assaults will be made on these firms by new retailing formats (a bold entrepreneur starting a new retail life cycle) or more-efficient retailers consolidating the industry.

Decline Although decline is inevitable for some formats (few people get their milk delivered to the door anymore), retail managers will try to postpone it by changing the retail mix. These attempts can postpone the decline stage, but a return to earlier, attractive levels of operating performance is not likely. Sooner or later a major loss of market share will occur, profits fall, and the once promising idea is no longer needed in the marketplace. However, the retailer that can

Exhibit 300.55 *Retail Institutions in the Four Stages of the Retail Life Cycle*

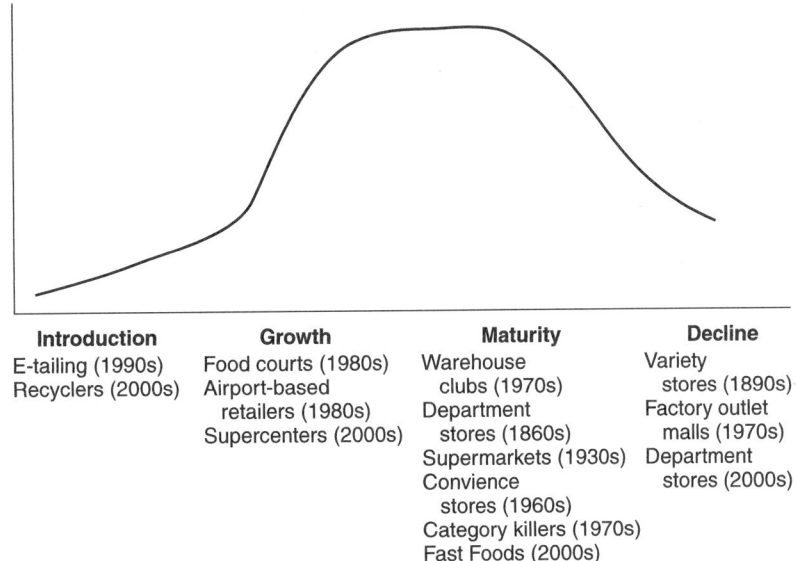

identify a small, but lucrative, customer group that insists on the traditional form (e.g., home delivery of groceries) may be able to extract a premium for its services, and extend its lifetime.

The retail life cycle is accelerating today. New and more competitive concepts now move quickly from introduction to maturity as the leading operators have aggressive growth goals and their investors demand a quick return on equity. In addition, larger retailers with capital and expertise in concept roll-out can acquire many entrepreneurs in the early stages of the retail life cycle. Exhibit 300.55 lists the various stages of the retail life cycle for many of our current retail institutions.

RESOURCE-ADVANTAGE THEORY The final theory to describe the evolution of retail competition is resource-advantage.[155] This theory is based on the idea that all firms seek superior financial performance in an ever-changing environment. Retail demand is a dynamic because consumer tastes are always changing, and supply is dynamic because, as firms search for a superior performance, they are forced to change the elements of their retail mix to match changing consumer preferences and improve firm performance.

Resource-advantage illustrates two important lessons for retailers:[156]

1. Superior performance at any point in time is the result of achieving a competitive advantage in the marketplace as a result of some tangible or intangible entity (or "resource"). The retailer is able to use this entity, such as an innovation regarding location procedures or merchandise selection, to offer greater value to the market place and/or to operate their firms at a lower cost relative to competitors.
2. All retailers cannot achieve superior results at the same time. Thus, it is important for currently high-performing retailers to maintain their vigilance over the actions of lower performing competitors, so as not to be overtaken.

Resource-advantage theory explains why retailers, realizing that they are competing in an ever-changing industry, are forced to always seek new competitive advantages and are not satisfied with maintaining the competitive status quo. The result is ongoing market turbulence in which new retail forms and offerings continually appear, and consumers continually shift their buying preferences and retail patronage. As retailers compete with each other through different combinations of merchandise selection, pricing, service, communication, positioning, distribution improvements, and relationship-building, each of these multifaceted competitive positions can meet the needs of different customer groups. The resulting fragmentation in the marketplace means that many different retail forms are viable as long as the customer group is sufficiently substantial (i.e. large enough to generate acceptable profit for the retailer), and the retailer is astute in managing its customer relationships and operations. As long as each retailer meets the needs of its target consumers better than competitors while controlling their own costs of satisfying that customer, that retailer will prosper.

This is one reason why Dollar General can survive in the same markets with large supercenters such as Wal-Mart, which offer better prices and wider assortments, and groceries. Many consumers, lacking personal transportation, rely on Dollar General as a quick, convenient place for sundries and grab-and-go foods.

The fact remains that not all customers are equally knowledgeable about retail alternatives, not all retailers are as astute about understanding their customers, not all customers have similar preferences or access to retail alternatives, and not all retailers have the resources to meet the competition for their traditional customers. As previously mentioned, Sears has attempted to drive its growth through its Great Indoors, but financial difficulties prevent it from acting on those aspirations. These marketplace discrepancies allow for less-than-optimal retail environments, but they also reveal opportunities to the retailer who is willing to study its customers and markets and do a better job in managing their operations. It is then imperative that the retailer communicate its superiority to target customers, which in turn pushes competition to a new and evolved level.

Future Changes in Retail Competition

Retailers in today's ever-changing marketplace can expect dynamic changes in retail competition. Trends shaping the retail landscape include an increase in competition from nonstore retailers, the advent of new retailing formats, heightened global competition, the integration of technology into their operations, and the increasing use of private labels.

NONSTORE RETAILING Several retail analysts predict that, as a result of several key forces at work today, nonstore sales (especially those that utilize the Internet) will experience significant growth during the next decade. With accelerated communication technology and changing consumer lifestyles, the growth potential for nonstore retailing, such as direct sellers, catalog sales, and e-tailing is staggering. Kurt Salmon Associates expects that by the year 2005, nonstore retailing will account for 55 percent of total GAF (general merchandise, apparel, and furniture) sales, up from 15 percent a decade earlier.[157] Some of the forces contributing to this growth are

- Consumers' need to save time.
- Consumers' desire to "time-shift," that is, shop when they want, not when a retailer wants to open a store.
- The erosion of enjoyment in the shopping experience.
- The lack of qualified sales help in stores to provide information.
- The explosive development of the telephone, the computer, and telecommunications that facilitates nonstore shopping.
- The consumers' preference for lower prices, which often eliminates or reduces the middleman's profit.

Therefore, traditional retailers need to continuously monitor developments in nonstore retailing.

Direct Selling Direct selling establishments engage in the sale of a consumer product or service on a person-to-person basis away from a fixed retail location, using party plans (**The Pampered Chef Ltd.**) or one-to-one selling in the home or workplace (Avon Products Inc.). Some of today's direct selling companies are incorporating additional marketing channels, such as catalogs, kiosks, and the Internet, to augment sales from traditional direct selling. The major attributes of direct selling remain the same—product quality and uniqueness, knowledge and demonstration of the product by a knowledgeable salesperson, excellent warranties and guarantees, and person-to-person interaction.[158]

Catalog Sales Mail-order retailers sell products by catalog and mail order. Catalog sales continue to be a $60 billion industry. Included are book and music clubs and retailers, jewelry firms (**Ross-Simon**), novelty retailers (**Popcorn Factory**), and specialty merchandisers such as sporting goods (**L.L. Bean**), ethnic-origin apparel (**Eziba, Sundance,** and **Peruvian Connection**), children's apparel retailers (**Right Start**), and kitchenware (**Williams-Sonoma**).

Retailers can improve their long-term profit potential if they begin today to experiment with selling in the virtual world.

E-Tailing The general belief among retail experts is that electronic, interactive, at-home shopping is definitely the place to be. Every major player in the retail industry, computer industry, telecommunications industry, and the transaction processing industry is committed to this growth. The only prerequisite needed for the Internet's success is having enough homes with PCs. Already two-thirds of American households are connected either at home or at work.

As the Internet grows to allow real-time, fully immersive three-dimensional video, Americans will spend more of their time in cyberspace. This will result in a new shopping experience. The shoppers of the next millennium will opt for the convenience, broad selection, and heightened experience of virtual shopping. Browsing will be even easier and the choices more extensive. Consumers will still want social activity outside the home; however, this won't be shopping but real entertainment—attending a sporting event or concert where, incidentally, a lot of merchandise and food will be for sale. The Internet will allow us to shop with family and friends, even if they live half the world away. However, e-tailing comes with several important considerations.

1. The Internet will not increase overall consumer demand. On-line sales will definitely cannibalize store and catalog sales. Retail Forward estimates that this cannibalization will vary across product categories. On-line shopping will be big for merchandise that is easily compared across retailers, such as books, music, video, and tickets. It will remain a minor, but growing, player for categories where customers want to experience and examine the goods before purchase, or where they dislike planning purchases in advance. For this reason, many still doubt the viability of shopping for fresh grocery items or impulse items on the Internet.

2. Clicks & mortar strategies that integrate a single message and seamless operations will be more powerful than a pure e-tailing strategy. This will be especially true once clicks and mortar retailers learn the importance of addressing the total customer experience through any contact point with the customer. For example, the customer may want to check an order that she placed in the store while she is at her home computer in her "jammies" at 11 P.M.

3. E-tailers must pay better attention to customer service. Most e-tailers do a good job during busy seasons, such as Christmas. However, in an effort to reduce operating costs, they reduce their service standards at other times. Customers are demanding such basic services as e-mail confirmation of orders and real-time confirmation of available inventory. Since customer service is a place where traditional retailers are especially vulnerable, e-tailers should seek their niche here. Even listing an e-tailer's toll-free phone number utilizing skilled call-center employees would be a plus for most e-tailers.[159] As more women join the on-line shopping world, e-tailers may find that more customers are willing to pay reasonable shipping charges for the convenience of "shop-when-I-want-to" if the merchandise selection and service are well executed.

NEW RETAILING FORMATS The practice of retailing is continually evolving. New formats are born and old ones die. Innovation in retailing is the result of constant pressure to improve efficiency and effectiveness in a continual effort to better serve the consumer. The pressure to better serve has also resulted in a shortened life cycle for retail formats. However, just as retailers find it extremely difficult to predict what will be the "hot new item" for an upcoming season, especially Christmas, they have the same trouble predicting the success of new retail formats.

HEIGHTENED GLOBAL COMPETITION The rate of change in retailing around the world appears to be directly related to the stage and speed of economic development in the countries concerned, but even the least-developed countries are experiencing dramatic changes. Retailing in other countries, however, exhibits greater diversity in its structure than it does in the United States. In some countries, such as Italy, retailing is composed largely of specialty houses carrying narrow lines. Finnish retailers generally carry a more general line of merchandise. The size of the average retailer is also diverse, from the massive **Harrod's** in London and **Mitsukoshi Ltd.** in Japan, both of which serve more than 10,000 customers a day, to the small one- or two-person stalls in developing African and Latin American nations.

New types of retailing have emerged from all countries. These changing formats can be attributed to a variety of economic and social factors that are the same worldwide: a widespread concern for health, a steady increase in the number of working women and two-income families, and the consequent upsurge in price levels, consumerism, and so forth. These factors, and their effects on consumer lifestyles, encourage high-profit retailers around the world to seek new market segments, make adjustments in the retail mix, alter location patterns, and adopt new multisegment strategies. In the process, many new retail concepts and formats have emerged and spread.

Still, it is amazing that retailers from larger countries often do not have the same success when entering a new country that retailers from smaller countries do.

Retail experts attribute this failure by large-country retailers to two factors. Some think it is a lack of understanding of the new country's culture. Wal-Mart made several major mistakes when it entered international markets. When it entered Canada, it made a classic cultural faux pas when it distributed English-language circulars in French-speaking Quebec. When entering Mexico, the chain built large parking lots at some stores only to realize that most of their customers rode the bus and then had to cross these large, empty parking lots carrying bags full of merchandise. Wal-Mart responded by creating a shuttle bus service. This was especially embarrassing for Wal-Mart since one of the key factors for their overall success was the fact that they started and stayed in small rural markets until they completely understood their customers and the channel partners.

Michael O'Connor, the former president of Super Market Institute and now a consultant, has another explanation. He feels that the failure of many retailers to succeed in international markets is because the larger countries have had successful economies and are used to success. Retailers in smaller countries do not take success for granted and thus tend to take more time and be more careful with key decisions. According to O'Connor, by being a little less sure of themselves, executives from smaller countries will seek more counsel and listen to more opinions before developing strategic plans.[160] Along the same lines, these smaller country retailers have always had to deal with international issues in order to expand. One small-country retailer who has made an impact on international retailing is Ingar Kamprad, president of IKEA, who was the first to successfully develop a warehouse retailing format that could be followed around the world. The firm's warehouse format, which is based on economies of scale in the areas of marketing, purchasing, and distribution and which utilizes customer participation in the assembly and transportation of the merchandise, generates almost 90 percent of its revenues from global operations—more than any other major worldwide retailer.[161]

INTEGRATION OF TECHNOLOGY One of the most significant trends occurring in retailing is that of technological innovation. Technology is having and will continue to have a dramatic influence on retailing. Technological innovations can be grouped under three main areas: supply chain management, customer management, and customer satisfaction.

One of the keys to success in retailing is developing the ability to monitor environmental changes, especially those pertaining to technology, and then adopting the technology that can improve the retailer's profitability.

The plethora of supply chain management techniques such as quick response (QR), just-in-time (JIT), and Efficient Consumer Response (ECR) are already being enhanced by new initiatives such as direct store delivery (DSD) and collaborative planning, forecasting, and replenishment (CPFR) systems. DSD systems have the potential to fully automate all retail inventory operations, from tracking vendor and item authorization to pricing and order taking. DSD systems provide greater accuracy and increased administrative efficiency, allowing retailers employing such systems to achieve cost advantages. Advancements in DSD systems will create more efficient operations and stronger partnerships and retailers as global competition increases. For example, U.S.-based **Giant Food, Inc.**, eliminated a tremendous amount of paperwork and dramatically increased administrative efficiency with the implementation of a DSD system. Many industry experts believe that DSD is the engine that will drive industry profits. However, gross profit numbers alone don't tell the story and, in fact, can be somewhat misleading when calculating direct and incremental costs of warehouse-delivered products. Rather, it is activity-based costing analyses that demonstrated that in categories with mixed distribution, DSD products consistently outperform those going through the warehouse. Other supply chain systems—such as CPFR, though still in its infancy—have the potential to take retailers and manufacturers far beyond continuous replenishment models in terms of reducing excess inventory levels, cutting out-of-stocks at retail, and efficiently meeting consumer demand. The bottom line is eliminating costly variations and distortions throughout the supply chain. However, technological systems such as DSD and CPFR are but the beginning of the technological revolution occurring within the supply chain. Retailers who continue to use technology in innovative ways within the supply chain will achieve greater efficiency in their operations.

Retailers on the forefront of using technology to understand their consumers will achieve higher levels of effectiveness. For example, retailers can use technology to better target their customers and provide better service to them. **Talbots** uses its catalog information to open retail outlets in locations with the greatest opportunity. Talbot's determines new store locations by examining clusters of ZIP codes that have accounted for $150,000 or more annually of classic women's and children's apparel.

Believe it or not, some of the most sophisticated users of database technology are casinos. In the past, one had to be a high roller to gain any "comps" (free products or services given to customers, such as free tickets to shows, a free night's stay, etc.). Today, when customers use the casino's gaming facilities (such as gambling at a slot machine), they can insert a card that has been assigned to them and tracks their gaming behavior. Customers then present these cards to the casino to receive individual rewards based on their use of the gaming facilities. Through the use of these cards a casino not only gains a much better understanding of their customers, enabling it to develop more effective retail strategies, but it can also reward customers at all levels, thus increasing customer satisfaction.

As technology continues to penetrate the retail marketplace, advancements in customer service and convenience will continue to be made. For example, what replacements are in store for the bar code scanners? One cause of long lines at supermarket checkouts is that each item has to be taken out of a shopper's cart, individually scanned, and then bagged. How might technology change this? Recent testing of radio frequency identifiers (RFID) on products might eliminate this process completely. In operation, the RFID reader generates a low-level radio frequency magnetic field that resonates with the tag's metal coil and capacitor, creating an electrical signal that powers the computer chip, which then transmits its stored data back to the reader. The process works well, but the tags have been expensive—as much as $200 each. However, that cost has recently fallen to less than $1 per tag. Although still too expensive for all but high-priced items, advancements in technology will soon be available, making this system affordable to implement. Imagine bagging your groceries while you shop. Once you have finished, you simply push your cart to the checkout and within a few seconds the cashier scans your entire cart, you pay, and off you go.

These technological advances are but a few of the thousands that will change the nature of retailing. What technological innovations do you see on the horizon for retailers?

INCREASING USE OF PRIVATE LABELS   As retailing continues to change, the improved use of private labels has emerged as a key business asset in developing a differential advantage for retailers. Private labels can set the retailer apart from the competition, get customers into their store (or Web site,) and bring them back. Today retailers are shifting their emphasis on the development of private label brands into high gear by using a variety of strategies to build the image of their brands, expand brand recognition, and raise their brand images in the marketplace. Further, private label brands often have lower wholesale and marketing costs, resulting in higher levels of profit compared to manufacturers' brands.

In the past, retailers believed that national brands drew customers into the store, set the standard, and lent credibility to the retailer. At the same time, retailers felt private label brands could help retailers differentiate their offerings, reach customers seeking lower prices, and boost margins due to the lower costs of private label merchandise.

Today the thinking has changed. Leading retailers, are focused on developing strong proprietary private label brands as leading brands and supporting them with major advertising and promotional programs. Private brands, such as JCPenney's "The Original Arizona Jean Company" and Wal-Mart's "George," are now effectively serving as destination draws in their own right while still providing many of the same benefits of traditional private label programs.

Following are some of the private-label branding strategies currently being used by retailers.

1. *Develop a partnership with well-known celebrities, noted experts, and institutional authorities.* Celebrity partnerships—or the use of people as private label brands—allow retailers to align with an individual whose personal reputation creates immediate brand recognition, image, or credibility. Target stores feature noted designers Mossimo Giannulli and Todd Oldham; Kmart has Martha Stewart and Joe Boxer.

2. *Develop a partnership with traditionally higher-end suppliers to bring an exclusive variation on their highly regarded brand name to market.* JCPenney is the exclusive distributor of Bisou Bisou line, a trendy line of sexy clothes; Wal-Mart now carries a new, lower-price line of jeans called Levi Strauss "Signature"; and Target has an apparel line called "Isacc Mizrahi for Target."

   These partnerships offer both parties a win-win situation. The retailer gets an exclusive private label with a great image and the opportunity to expand customer appeal, ratchet up price points, and raise margins. The manufacturer builds volume and gains access to a broad new market spectrum.

3. *Reintroduce products with strong name recognition that have fallen from the retail scene.* Old brand names do not die. They get recycled. Retailers can add cachet to their store image by resuscitating former up-market brands that have been discontinued but have not lost their image. Recycled brands can help a retailer achieve differentiation through exclusivity and attract consumers unwilling to risk buying an unknown brand name. By reviving a well-known brand with a pedigree, the retailer is able to leverage the brand's equity while still having a proprietary line.

   Wal-Mart, for example, has purchased the rights from Procter & Gamble to its discontinued White Cloud label on diapers and toilet tissues. Wal-Mart did the same with Faded Glory.

4. *Brand an entire department or business, not just a product line.* In an approach designed to differentiate its supercenter food offerings from the others, Target has taken its private-label branding strategy one step further by branding its entire supermarket section with the Archer Farms name. Not only does the Archer Farms name readily draw an association with the Target brand (the archer's target or bull's-eye) but it also enables Target to separate the two sections of the store. In fact, many consumers believe it to be a different company entirely. This may be a plus for Target with consumers who might not otherwise shop for groceries in a discount store.

   The Archer Farms market positioning strategy leads the consumer to believe that it is an upscale grocer by placing more emphasis on quality and freshness than price. Such a strategy reinforces Target's protected niche image as the "discounter for consumers who don't want to be seen in a discount store." A "fresh from the farm" tagline underscores the market positioning message. Store design features, such as green neon perimeter lighting, graphics depicting farm scenes, colorful illustrations of major food categories, and product descriptions and use suggestions all help create a differentiated grocery shopping environment. The Archer Farms name was also carried into a private-label program featuring approximately 100 SKUs (stock-keeping units).[162]

Managing the Supply Chain

The Supply Chain

Supply chains *A set of institutions that moves goods from the point of production to the point of consumption.*

Channel *Used interchangeably with supply chain.*

It is important to understand the retailer's role in the larger supply chain. A **supply chain,** which is often used interchangeably with the term **channel,** is a set of institutions that moves goods from the point of production to the point of consumption. The supply chain, or channel, might include manufacturers, wholesalers, and retailers. For example, the manufacturer could sell directly to an individual for household usage; sell to a retailer for sale to the individual; or sell to a wholesaler(s) for sale to the retailer, who then sells to the individual. Thus, supply chains consist of all the institutions and all the marketing activities (storage, financing, purchasing, transporting, etc.) that are spread over time and geographical space throughout the marketing process. If the retailer is a member of the supply chain that collectively does the best job, that retailer will have an advantage over other retailers.

Why should the retailer view itself as part of a larger channel or supply chain? Why can't it simply seek out the best assortment of goods for its customers, sell the goods, make a profit, go to the bank, and forget about the supply chain? In reality, the world of retailing is not that easy. Profits sufficient for survival and growth would be difficult, if not impossible, to achieve if the retailer ignored the supply chain. This does not mean that a channel should never be changed. Sometimes an innovative member might break out of the existing supply chain and replace it with a new one. For example, discounters changed their relationship with vendors by buying in large quantities, warehousing the merchandise in efficiently run distribution centers, and shipping to their own stores as a means of obtaining lower prices. Prior to this change, the retailers purchased smaller quantities only when the merchandise was needed.

The supply chain, or channel, is affected by five external forces: (1) consumer behavior, (2) competitor behavior, (3) the socioeconomic environment, (4) the technological environment, and (5) the legal and ethical environment. These external forces cannot be completely controlled by the retailer or any other institution in the supply chain, but they need to be taken into account when retailers make decisions. For example, a change in the minimum-wage law will usually increase the retailer's cost of doing business. The retail strategic planning and operations management model also dramatizes the importance of these external forces in retail decision making.

A supply chain or channel must perform eight marketing functions: buying, selling, storing, transporting, sorting, financing, information gathering, and risk taking. Whether the economic channel is capitalistic, socialistic, or somewhere in between, every supply chain must perform these eight marketing functions. They cannot be eliminated. They can, however, be shifted or divided among the different institutions and the consumer in the supply chain.

Retailers who understand the importance of the eight marketing functions and utilize the abilities of other supply chain members to operate the supply chain most efficiently will tend to be more profitable than those who do not understand their dependency on other supply chain members.

All forms of retailing were created by rearranging the marketing functions among institutions and consumers. For example, department stores were created specifically to build a larger and better assortment of goods. They capitalized on the opportunity to perform one or more functions better than the current competition. No longer was it necessary to travel to one store for a shirt and pants, another for shoes, and yet another for cookware; the necessary assortment was available in a single store. Supermarkets increased consumer participation by shifting more of the information gathering, buying, and transporting functions to customers. Before supermarkets, consumers could have the corner grocer select items and deliver them, but with the supermarket came self-service. Consumers had to locate the goods within the store, select them from an array of products, and transport them home. For performing more of these marketing functions, the consumer was compensated with lower prices.

A marketing function does not have to be shifted in its entirety to another institution or to the consumer but can be divided among several entities. For example, the manufacturer who does not want to perform the entire selling function could have the retailer perform part of the job through in-store promotions, local advertising, or promotions on the retailer's Web site. At the same time, the manufacturer could assume some of the tasks through national advertising and by developing its own Web site to provide product information, such as its installation, cleaning directions, and the manufacturer's warranty.

No member of the channel would want, or be able, to perform all eight marketing functions completely. For this reason, the retailer must view itself as being dependent on other supply chain members.

Exhibit 300.56 *Institutions Participating in the Supply Chain*

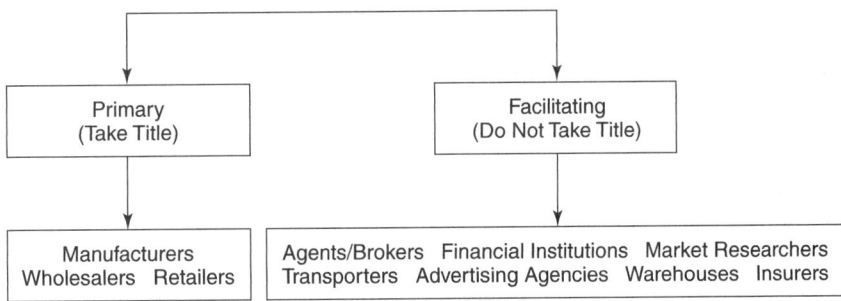

Many supply chain institutions are involved in performing the eight marketing functions. These institutions are usually broken into two categories: primary and facilitating. **Primary marketing institutions** are supply chain members that take title to the goods. **Facilitating marketing institutions** are those that do not actually take title but assist in the marketing process by specializing in the performance of certain functions. Exhibit 300.56 classifies the major institutions participating in the supply chain.

Primary marketing institutions Channel members that take title to the goods as they move through the marketing channel. They include manufacturers, wholesalers, and retailers.

Facilitating marketing institutions Those that do not actually take title but assist in the marketing process by specializing in the performance of certain marketing functions.

PRIMARY MARKETING INSTITUTIONS There are three types of primary marketing institutions: manufacturers, wholesalers, and retailers.

Because they produce goods, we don't often think of manufacturers as marketing institutions. But manufacturers cannot exist by only producing goods; they must also sell the goods produced. To produce those goods, the nation's 400,000 manufacturers must purchase many raw materials, semifinished goods, and components. In addition, manufacturers often need the assistance of other institutions in performing the eight marketing functions.

A second type of primary marketing institution is the wholesaler. Wholesalers generally buy merchandise from manufacturers and resell to retailers, other merchants, industrial institutions, and commercial users. There are 500,000 wholesalers in the United States, each performing some of the eight marketing functions. Just as it is important for retailers to continuously evaluate their own strategies, it is equally important for them to consider the strategies of the wholesalers in their channel.

The third type of primary institution is the retailer. Today there are 2.4 million retail stores or institutions and more than 1.8 million service establishments in the United States. Retailers can perform portions of all eight marketing functions.

It is possible that some firms, such as the membership warehouse clubs (**Sam's, Costco**), can act as both a wholesaler, selling to small businesses, and as a retailer, selling to households. However, for statistical purposes, the Census Bureau considers all membership warehouse clubs to be wholesalers, since the majority of their business involves wholesale transactions.

FACILITATING MARKETING INSTITUTIONS Many institutions facilitate the performance of the marketing functions. Most of these institutions specialize in one or two functions; *none of them takes title to the goods*. Institutions that facilitate buying and selling in the supply chain, or channel, include agents and brokers, who are independent businesspeople that receive a commission or fee when they are able to bring a buyer and seller together to negotiate a transaction. Seldom do agents or brokers take physical possession of the merchandise. The purchasing agents assist in buying and the others assist in selling for manufacturers.

One of the new breed of e-tailing brokers is **Priceline.com, Inc.,** which has pioneered a unique e-commerce pricing channel known as a "demand collection channel" that allows it to act without holding any inventory. Priceline's channel enables consumers to use the Internet to make bids on a wide range of products and services, while enabling sellers to generate incremental revenue. Using its "Name Your Own Price" proposition, Priceline collects consumer demand, in the form of individual customer offers guaranteed by a credit card, for a particular product or service at a price set by the customer. Priceline then either communicates that demand directly to participating sellers or accesses participating sellers' private databases to determine whether Priceline can fulfill the customer's offer and earn its brokerage commission. Priceline's unique business model can be applied to a broad range of products and services and is already being copied.

385. SERVICES AND RETAIL MARKETING

Advertising agencies also facilitate the selling process by designing effective advertisements and advising management on where and when to place these advertisements.

Institutions that facilitate the transportation function are motor, rail, and air carriers and pipeline and shipping companies. Transporters can have a significant effect on how efficiently goods move through the supply chain. These firms offer differing advantages in terms of delivery, service, and cost. Generally, the quicker the delivery, the more costly it is. However, there is usually a trade-off in that higher transportation costs enable the supply chain to have lower warehousing costs. As a result, Federal Express and UPS are often viewed by Wall Street as e-tailing stocks, because e-tailers need these two transportation companies to deliver their merchandise.

The major facilitating institution involved in storage is the **public warehouse,** which stores goods for safekeeping for any owner in return for a fee. Fees are usually based on cubic feet used per time period (month or day). Frequently, retailers take advantage of special promotional buys from manufacturers but have no space for the goods in their stores or warehouses. As a result, they find it necessary to use public warehouses.

Public warehouse Is a facility that stores goods for safekeeping for any owner in return for a fee, usually based on space occupied.

A variety of facilitating institutions also help provide information throughout the supply chain. Today many major retailers require that all their vendors be linked electronically to the retailer's computer, thereby permitting the vendors to automatically ship replacements without purchase orders and receive payment by electronic funds transfers. By saving on distribution costs, the majority of retailers have been able to hold their selling prices constant despite a slight increase in merchandise costs.

Other facilitating institutions aid in financing, such as commercial banks, merchant banks, savings and loan associations, stock exchanges, and venture capital firms. These institutions can provide, or help the retailer obtain, funds to finance marketing functions. Retailers frequently need short-term loans for working capital requirements (e.g., to handle increased inventory and accounts receivables) and long-term loans for continued growth and expansion (adding new stores or remodeling).

Finally, insurance firms can assume some of the risks in the channel. Insurance firms can insure inventories, buildings, trucks, equipment and fixtures, and other assets for the retailer and other primary marketing institutions. They can also insure against employee and customer injuries.

Control of the Supply Chain

Supply chains follow one of two basic patterns: the conventional marketing channel and the vertical marketing channel. Exhibit 300.57 provides an illustration of these major channel patterns.

Exhibit 300.57 *Marketing Channel Patterns*

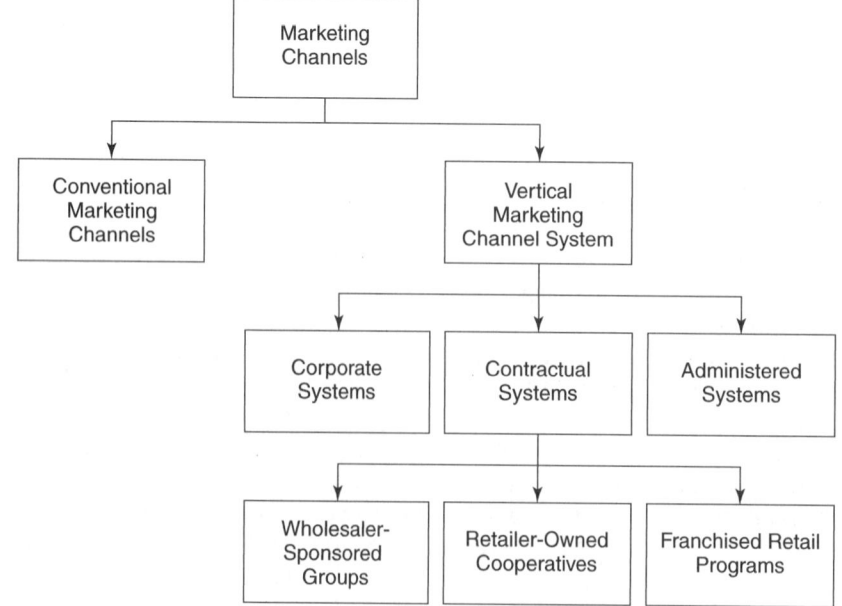

Conventional Marketing Channel A **conventional marketing channel** is one in which each member of the channel is loosely aligned with the others and takes a short-term orientation. Predictably, each member's orientation is toward the next institution in the channel and "what is happening today" as opposed to "what will happen in the future." Here the manufacturer interacts with and focuses efforts on the wholesaler, the wholesaler focuses efforts on the retailer, and the retailer focuses efforts on the final consumer. In short, all of the members focus on their immediate desire to close the sale or create a transaction. Thus the conventional marketing channel consists of a series of pairs in which the members of each pair recognize each other but not necessarily the other members of the supply chain.

The conventional marketing channel, although historically predominant in the United States, is a sloppy and inefficient method of conducting business. It fosters intense negotiations within each pair of institutions in the supply chain. In addition, members do not see the possibility of shifting or dividing the marketing functions among all the participants. Therefore, it is an unproductive method for marketing goods and has been on the decline in the United States since the early 1950s.

Vertical Marketing Channels **Vertical marketing channels** are capital-intensive networks of several levels that are professionally managed and rely on centrally programmed systems to realize the technological, managerial, and promotional economies of long-term relationships. The basic premise of working as a system is to operate as close to that elusive 100 percent efficiency level as possible. This is done by eliminating the suboptimization that exists in conventional channels and improving the channel's performance by working together.[163]

Formerly adversarial relationships between retailers and their suppliers are now giving way to new vertical channel partnerships that minimize such inefficiencies.[164] Because vertical channel members realize that it is impossible to offer consumers value without being a low-cost, high-efficiency supply chain, they have developed either **quick response (QR) systems** or **efficient consumer response (ECR) systems**. These systems, which are the same despite the different names adopted by various retail industries, are designed to obtain real-time information on consumers' actions by capturing SKU (**stock-keeping units** are the lowest level of identification of merchandise) data at point-of-purchase terminals and then transmitting this information back through the entire supply chain. This information is used to develop new or modified products, manage channelwide inventory levels, and lower total channel costs. Category management is accomplished when all the members—who in a conventional channel would have acted independently—work as team to apply the ECR concept to an entire category of merchandise.

There are three types of vertical marketing channels—corporate, contractual, and administered. Each has grown significantly in the last 50 years.

Corporate Channels **Corporate vertical marketing channels** typically consist of either a manufacturer that has integrated vertically to reach the consumer, or a retailer that has integrated vertically to create a self-supply network. The first type includes manufacturers such as **Sherwin Williams** (paint), **Hart Schaffner Marx** (men's apparel), and **Famolare** (shoes), which have created their own warehousing and retail outlets. The second type includes retailers such as **Holiday Inns**. For example, Holiday Inns has vertically integrated to control a carpet mill, furniture manufacturer, and numerous other suppliers needed to build and operate its motels.

In corporate channels it is much easier to program the channel for productivity and profit goals, since a well-established authority structure already exists.

Conventional marketing channel One in which each channel member is loosely aligned with the others and takes a short-term orientation.

Vertical marketing channels Capital-intensive networks of several levels that are professionally managed and centrally programmed to realize the technological, managerial, and promotional economies of a long-term relationship orientation.

Quick response (QR) systems Also known as **efficient consumer response (ECR) systems**, integrated information, production, and logistical systems that obtain real-time information on consumer actions by capturing sales data at point-of-purchase terminals and then transmitting this information back through the entire channel to enable efficient production and distribution scheduling.

Stock-keeping units The lowest level of identification of merchandise.

Virtually every high-profit retailer in the U.S. economy is part of a vertical purchasing channel.

Corporate vertical marketing systems Exist where one channel institution owns multiple levels of distribution and typically consists of either a manufacturer that has integrated vertically forward to reach the consumer or a retailer that has integrated vertically backward to create a self-supply network.

---

385. SERVICES AND RETAIL MARKETING

Independent retailers that have aligned themselves in a conventional marketing channel are at a significant disadvantage when competing against a corporate vertical marketing channel.

Contractual Channels **Contractual vertical marketing channels,** which include wholesaler-sponsored voluntary groups, retailer-owned cooperatives, and franchised retail programs, are supply chains that use a contract to govern the working relationship between the members. Each of these types allows for a more coordinated, systemwide perspective than conventional marketing channels. However, they are more difficult to manage than corporate vertical marketing channels because the authority and power structures are not as well defined. Channel members must give up some autonomy to gain channel economies of scale and greater market impact.

Wholesaler-Sponsored Voluntary Groups **Wholesaler-sponsored voluntary groups** are created when a wholesaler brings together a group of independently owned retailers (*independent retailers* is a term embracing anything from a single mom-and-pop store to a small local chain), grocers for example, and offers them a coordinated merchandising program (store design and layout, store site and location analysis, inventory management, accounting and bookkeeping, insurance services, pension plans, trade area studies, advertising and promotion assistance, and employee-training programs) as well as a buying program that will provide these smaller retailers with economies like those their chain store rivals are able to obtain. In return, the independent retailers agree to concentrate their purchases with that wholesaler. It is a voluntary relationship; that is, there are no membership or franchise fees. The independent retailer may terminate the relationship whenever it desires, so it is to the wholesaler's advantage to build competitive merchandise assortments and offer other services that will keep the voluntary group satisfied.

In the past, local food wholesalers got practically all of their business from independent grocers. Recently, however, as transportation costs have risen, major chains operating over a wide geographic area have also started using local or national wholesalers. While welcoming this new business, wholesalers have tried to keep their independents happy (since they still account for over 40 percent of their business) by offering them even more services.

Retailer-Owned Cooperatives Another common type of contractual vertical marketing channel is **retailer-owned cooperatives,** which are wholesale operations organized and owned by retailers. These are most common in hardware retailing. They include, for example, such familiar names as **TRU*SERV, Ace,** and **Handy Hardware.** They offer scale economies and services to member retailers, allowing their members to compete with larger chain buying organizations.

Finally, it should be pointed out that in theory, wholesale-sponsored groups should be easier to manage since they have only one owner, the wholesaler, versus the many owners of the retailer-owned group. In retailer-owned wholesale cooperatives, individual members tend to want to keep their autonomy and be less dependent on their supplier-partner for support and direction. In reality, however, just the opposite has been true. A possible explanation for this is that retailers belonging to a wholesale co-op may make greater transaction-specific investments in the form of stock ownership, vested supplier-based store identity, and end-of-year rebates on purchases that combine to erect significant exit barriers.[165]

Franchises Type of contractual vertical marketing channel is the franchise. A **franchise** is a form of licensing by which the owner of a product, service, or method (the franchisor) obtains distribution through affiliated dealers (franchisees). In many cases the franchise operation resembles a large chain with trademarks; uniform symbols, equipment, and storefronts; and standardized services, products, and practices as outlined in the franchise agreement.

Franchising is a convenient and economic means of fulfilling an individual's desire for independence with a minimum amount of risk and investment and maximum opportunities for success. This is possible through the utilization of a proven product or service and marketing method. However, the owner of a franchise gives up some freedom in business decisions that the owner of a nonfranchised business would have. In order to maintain uniformity of service and to ensure that the operations of each outlet will reflect favorably on the organization as a

---

Contractual vertical marketing systems *Use a contract to govern the working relationship between channel members and include wholesaler-sponsored voluntary groups, retailer-owned cooperatives, and franchised retail programs.*

Wholesaler-sponsored voluntary groups *Involve a wholesaler that brings together a group of independently owned retailers and offers them a coordinated merchandising and buying program that will provide them with economies like those their chain store rivals are able to obtain.*

Retailer-owned cooperatives *Wholesale institutions, organized and owned by member retailers, that offer scale economies and services to member retailers, which allows them to compete with larger chain buying organizations.*

Franchise *A form of licensing by which the owner of a product, service, or business method (the franchisor) obtains distribution through affiliated dealers (franchisees).*

Franchisors that focus their expansion efforts internationally have a higher profit potential.

Exhibit 300.58 *Advantages and Disadvantages of Franchise Ownership*

Advantages to Franchisee	Disadvantages to Franchisee
1. Franchisor provides managerial skills that are taught to franchisee.	1. Too many franchises can be located in a geographical area.
2. Franchisee can begin a business with a relatively small capital investment.	2. Too many franchisors make promises they cannot keep (e.g., overstating the income potential of a franchise).
3. Franchisee can acquire a relatively well known or established line of business.	3. Franchisors can include a buyback agreement whereby the franchisee must sell back the franchise at a given point in time or the franchise agreement is for a short duration.
4. Franchisee can acquire rights to a well-defined geographical area.	4. Under most franchise agreements, payments to the franchisor are a percentage of sales regardless of a franchisee's profitability.
5. The standardized marketing programs and operating procedures enable the franchisee to be competitive immediately.	5. Franchise systems may be too inflexible in terms of operating procedures (hours, product selection, etc.) for the franchisee. In short, the franchisee must surrender its freedom to make many decisions.
6. Because they own a piece of the action, franchisees tend to be more motivated and bottom-line oriented than managers of corporate chain stores.	

whole, the franchisor usually exercises some degree of control over the operations of franchisees, requiring them to meet stipulated standards of product and service quality and operating procedures.

Exhibit 300.58 lists some of the major advantages and disadvantages of owning a franchise.

Although only a third of U.S. franchisors are currently operating in foreign countries, another third are looking to expand internationally within the next five years. After all, why compete in overcrowded U.S. markets when many foreign markets are available? Although franchising is seen as an economic-development tool for poor countries, the most widely considered foreign markets are Canada, Japan, Mexico, Germany, the United Kingdom, and more recently Southeast Asia—the Philippines, Thailand, Taiwan, Singapore, and Indonesia.

Administered Channels The final type of vertical marketing channel is the administered channel. **Administered vertical marketing channels** are similar to conventional marketing channels, but one of the members takes the initiative to lead the channel by applying the principles of effective interorganizational management, which is the management of relationships between the various organizations in the supply chain. Administered channels, although not new in concept, have grown substantially in recent years. Frequently, administered channels are initiated by manufacturers because they have historically relied on their administrative expertise to coordinate the retailers' marketing efforts. Suppliers with dominant brands have predictably experienced the least difficulty in securing strong support from retailers and wholesalers. However, many manufacturers with "fringe" items have been able to elicit such cooperation only through the use of liberal distribution policies that take the form of attractive discounts (or discount substitutes), financial assistance, and various types of concessions that protect resellers from one or more of the risks of doing business.[166]

> **Administered vertical marketing channels** Exist when one of the channel members takes the initiative to lead the channel by applying the principles of effective interorganizational management.

Some of the concessions manufacturers offer retailers are liberal return policies, display materials for in-store use, advertising allowances, extra time for merchandise payment, employee-training programs, assistance with store layout and design, inventory maintenance, computer support, and even free merchandise.

Manufacturers that use their administrative powers to lead channels include **General Electric** (on both major and small appliances), **Sealy** (on its Posturepedic line of mattresses), **Villager** (on its dresses and sportswear lines), Scott (on its lawn-care products), **Norwalk** (on its upholstered furniture), **Keepsake** (on diamonds), and **Stanley** (on hand tools). Retailers can also dominate the channel relationship. For example, Wal-Mart, one of the earliest adopters of ECR systems, administers the relationship with almost all of its suppliers by asking that all advertising allowances, slotting fees, end display fees, and so forth be taken off the price of goods.

Managing Retailer-Supplier Relations

Retailers that are not part of a contractual channel or corporate channel will probably participate in different channels, since they will need to acquire merchandise from many suppliers. Predictably, these channels will be either conventional or administered. If retailers want to improve their performance in these channels, they must understand the principal concepts of interorganizational management. In this case, it involves a retailer managing its relations with wholesalers and manufacturers.

What are the basic concepts of interorganizational management that a retailer needs to understand? They are dependency, power, and conflict.

DEPENDENCY As we mentioned earlier, every supply chain needs to perform eight marketing functions, which can be performed by any combination of the members. None of the respective institutions can isolate itself; each depends on the others to do an effective job.

Retailer A is dependent on suppliers X, Y, and Z to make sure that goods are delivered on time and in the right quantities. Conversely, suppliers X, Y, and Z depend on retailer A to put a strong selling effort behind their goods, displaying them properly, and maybe even helping to finance consumer purchases. If retailer A does a poor job, each supplier can be adversely affected; if even one supplier does a poor job, retailer A can be adversely affected. In all these alignments, each party depends on the others to do a good job.

When each party is dependent on the others, we say that they are *interdependent*. Interdependency is at the root of the collaboration and the conflict found in channels today. To better comprehend this interdependency, an understanding of channel power is necessary.

Power The ability of one channel member to influence the decisions of the other channel members.

POWER We can use the concept of dependency to explain power, but first we must define power. **Power** is the ability of one member to influence the decisions of the other channel members. The more dependent the supplier is on the retailer, the more power the retailer has over the supplier. For example, a small manufacturer of grocery products would be very dependent on a large supermarket chain if it wanted to reach the most consumers. Therefore, that supermarket has power over the small manufacturer. Likewise many suppliers to Wal-Mart are very dependent on Wal-Mart because it is their biggest customer. For example, Wal-Mart accounts for 26 percent of Rayovac's annual sales, making Rayovac highly dependent on Wal-Mart.[167] Thus, the power one member has over another channel member is a function of how dependent the second member is on the first member to achieve its own goals.

There are six types of power:

Reward power Based on B's perception that A has the ability to provide rewards for B.

Expertise power Based on B's perception that A has some special knowledge.

Referent power Based on the identification of B with A.

Coercive power Based on B's belief that A has the capability to punish or harm B if B doesn't do what A wants.

Legitimate power Based on A's right to influence B, or B's belief that B should accept A's influence.

Informational power Based on A's ability to provide B with factual data.

1. **Reward power** is based on the ability of A to provide rewards for B. For instance, a retailer may offer a manufacturer a prominent endcap display in exchange for additional advertising monies and promotional support.
2. **Expertise power** is based on B's perception that A has some special knowledge. For example, **Midas Muffler** (a franchisor) has developed an excellent training program for store managers. Thus franchisees view the franchisor as an expert.
3. **Referent power** is based on the identification of B with A. B wants to be associated or identified with A. Examples of this are auto dealers that want to handle BMWs or Mercedes because of the cars' status or a manufacturer that wants to have its product sold in Neiman Marcus because of the image that retailer projects.
4. **Coercive power** is based on B's belief that A has the capacity to punish or harm B if B does not do what A wants. A franchisor, Burger King, for example, has the right to cancel a franchisee's contract if it fails to maintain standards concerning restaurant cleanliness, food, hours of operation, and employees.
5. **Legitimate power** is based on A's right to influence B, or B's belief that B should accept A's influence. The appearance of legitimate power is most obvious in contractual marketing channels. A manufacturer may, for example, threaten to cut off a retailer's supply if the retailer does not properly display the manufacturer's products. Also, if the retailer accepts co-op advertising dollars, the manufacturer may control the minimum retail price, since this subject is usually covered in the agreement. Otherwise the retailer is free to set the selling price. To do otherwise, without an agreement specifically covering retail price, would be a violation of certain federal antitrust laws.
6. **Informational power** is based on A's ability to provide B with factual data. Not to be confused with expertise power, informational power is when the factual data is provided independently of the relationship between A and B. An example of this power would be a small retail store sharing scanner data with a vendor.

Retailers and suppliers that use reward, expertise, referent, and informational power can foster a healthy working relationship. On the other hand, the use of coercive and legitimate power tend to elicit conflict and destroy any cooperation in the channel.

CONFLICT Conflict is inevitable in every channel relationship because retailers and suppliers are interdependent; that is, every channel member is dependent on every other member to perform some specific task. As such, interdependency has been identified as the root cause of all conflict in marketing channels. There are three major sources of conflict between retailers and their suppliers: perceptual incongruity, goal incompatibility, and domain disagreement.

Perceptual incongruity occurs when the retailer and supplier have different perceptions of reality. A retailer may perceive that the economy is entering a recession and therefore may want to cut inventory investments, while the supplier may believe that the economy will remain strong and therefore may feel that inventory investments should be maintained or possibly increased. For example, consider the following areas, which the retailer and supplier might perceive differently: the quality of the supplier's merchandise, the potential demand for the supplier's merchandise, the consumer appeal of the supplier's advertising, and the best shelf position for the supplier's merchandise. Recently, McDonald's and its franchisees have had differing views on the value of the chain's long-term tie-in with Disney's movies. Many recent Disney movies have not fared well with youngsters, and about half of the chain's 15 annual Happy Meal promotions were related to these movies and their characters.[168] Also, some retailers have refused to pay small price hikes by the manufacturers, such as a 2 percent increase in cereal prices. They don't believe that economic conditions warrant such price increases.[169]

Perceptual incongruity Occurs when the retailer and supplier have different perceptions of reality.

A second source of conflict is **goal incompatibility**, a situation in which achieving the goals of either the supplier or the retailer would hamper the performance of the other. For example, in 2003, **Nike** and **Foot Locker** were in a battle regarding the retailer's goal of gaining sales with its liberal use of "BOGOs"—industry jargon for "buy one, get one at half off" sales. Such sales encourage consumers to buy two pairs at a single outing, thereby reducing the chance the consumer would buy the second pair elsewhere.[170]

Goal incompatibility Occurs when achieving the goals of either the supplier or the retailer would hamper the performance of the other.

Another example of incompatibility between retailer and supplier goals is a situation known as dual distribution. **Dual distribution** occurs when a manufacturer that sells to independent retailers decides to also sell directly to the final consumer through its own retail outlets and/or through an Internet site. Thus the manufacturer manages a corporately owned vertical marketing channel that competes with independent retailers, which it also supplies through a conventional, administered, or contractual marketing channel. Retailers tend to become upset about dual distribution when the two channels compete at the retail level in the same geographic area.

Dual distribution Occurs when a manufacturer sells to independent retailers and also through its own retail outlets.

The problem of goal incompatibilty is not necessarily one of profit versus image goals. Even if the retailer and supplier both have a return on investment (ROI) goal, they can still be incompatible, because what is good for the retailer's ROI may not be good for the supplier's ROI. Consider the price element in the transaction between the supplier and the retailer. If the supplier obtains a higher price, its ROI will be higher, but the ROI of the retailer will be lower. Similarly, other key elements in the transaction between the retailer and supplier, such as advertising allowances, cash discounts, order quantity, and freight charges, can result in conflict.

A third source of conflict is **domain disagreements.** *Domain* refers to the decision variables that each member of the marketing channel feels it should be able to control. When the members of the marketing channel agree on who should make which decisions, domain consensus exists. When there is disagreement about who should make decisions, domain disagreement exists.

Domain disagreements Occur when there is disagreement about which member of the marketing channel should make decisions.

Consider the case of an automobile manufacturer and an automobile dealer. The dealer believes it should be able to make decisions regarding employees, local advertising, retail pricing, hours of operation, and remodeling and expansion. However, the manufacturer believes that it should be consulted on hours of operation and remodeling and expansion. As a consequence, some domain disagreement exists between manufacturer and dealer.

Another controversial domain disagreement practice in today's retail marketing channels occurs when retailers sell merchandise purchased from the vendor to discounters the manufacturer does not want selling its products. A **diverter** is an unauthorized member of a channel who buys and sells excess merchandise to and from authorized channel members. For instance, suppose a retailer could

Diverter An unauthorized member of a channel who buys and sells excess merchandise to and from authorized channel members.

buy a name-brand appliance intended to retail for $389 at $185 if it purchases 100 units. However, if the retailer orders 200 units, it can purchase the item at $158. What does the retailer do? Some retailers will purchase 200 units even though they need only 100. They in turn sell the 100 extra units at a slight loss, say $155, to a discount store that may retail the item for $219. The net result is that the retailer loses $3 a unit on 100 units or $300; however, it bought the remaining 100 units at $27 a unit less, for a savings of $2,700. As a result of this price arbitrage, the retailer is $2,400 ahead on the transaction. However, the manufacturer is upset because the appliance has been diverted into a retail channel it did not intend and over which it has no direct control.

Gray marketing When branded merchandise flows through unauthorized channels.

Similar to diverting is a practice known as **gray marketing,** where genuinely branded merchandise flows through unauthorized channels that cross national boundaries. Gray market channels develop when global conditions are conducive to profits. For example, in 2002 more than 200,000 autos were brought into the United States by importers from Canada. Cars nearly identical to U.S. models are priced $3,000 to $7,000 lower in Canada because the value of the dollar, lower wages, and a weaker economic situation force manufacturers to "price to the market." The lower prices are all the market will bear, the car manufacturers claim. Yet, under these circumstances, should American dealers be responsible for warranty work? The issue is currently before the courts.[171] Another example can be seen in the retailing of cigarettes. Since taxes have increased domestic cigarette prices 150 to 300 percent in recent years, the gray market, especially from Canada, has increased substantially. Recently, many college textbooks were being gray marketed back to the United States.

Free riding When a consumer seeks product information, usage instructions, and sometimes even warranty work from a full-service store but then, armed with the brand's model number, purchases the product from a limited-service discounter or over the Internet.

Diverting and gray marketing can lead to another problem for the channel—free-riding. **Free-riding** occurs when consumers seek product information and usage instructions about products, ranging from computers to home appliances, from a full-service specialty store. Then, armed with the brand's model number, the consumers purchase the product from a limited-service discounter or over the Internet.

Not all conflict in a channel is bad. Low levels of conflict will probably not affect any channel member's behavior and may not even be noticed. A moderate level of conflict might even cause the members to improve their efficiency, much the same as happens with some of your classmates when you are working on a team project. However, high levels of conflict will probably be dysfunctional to the channel and lead to inefficiencies and channel restructuring.

Collaboration in the Channel

Retailers who treat their fellow channel members as partners rather than enemies will tend to have a better profit performance over the long term than those who do not.

Although all channels experience some degree of conflict, the dominant behavior in successful channels is collaboration. Collaboration, where both parties seek to solve all problems with a "win-win" attitude, is necessary and beneficial because of the interdependency of retailers and suppliers. Also, retailers and suppliers must develop a partnership if they want to deal with each other on a long-term and continuing basis. As a result, many channel members have begun to follow a set of best practices as listed in Exhibit 300.59. This vendor partnership is often a critical factor for the retailer who does not want to confuse the final consumer with constant adjustments in product offerings that result from constant changes in suppliers.

FACILITATING CHANNEL COLLABORATION Collaboration in channel, or supply chain, relations is facilitated by three important types of behaviors and attitudes. These are mutual trust, two-way communication, and solidarity.

Mutual trust Occurs when both the retailer and its supplier have faith that each will be truthful and fair in their dealings with the other.

Mutual Trust **Mutual trust** occurs when the retailer trusts the supplier and the supplier trusts the retailer. In continuing relations between retailers and suppliers, mutual trust, which is built on past and present performance between the members, is critical. This trust allows short-term inequities to exist. If mutual trust is present, both parties will tolerate these inequities because they know in the long term, they will be fairly treated.[172] For example, a vendor suggests that the retailer purchase a certain product. The retailer does not believe that the product will be successful in its market. However, the

Exhibit 300.59 *Supply Chain Management Best Practices*

1. All supply chain members must remember that satisfying the retail consumer is the only way anyone can be successful.
2. Successful partners work together in good times and bad.
3. Never abandon a supply chain partner at the first sign of trouble.
4. Work together with your partners to offer products at appropriate prices. No one will win if either partner is not honest and fair with the other or with the retail customer.
5. Never abuse power in negotiations. Rather, understand your partner's needs prior to negotiations and work to satisfy those needs.
6. Share profits fairly among partners.
7. Limit the number of partners for each merchandise line. By doing so you can signal greater commitment and trust to your partners, thus building stronger relationships.
8. Set high ethical standards in your business transactions.
9. Successful partners plan together to help the supply chain operate efficiently and effectively.
10. Treat your partner as you would wish to be treated.

vendor insists that many buyers in other markets are purchasing that particular item and even agrees to "make it good" if the product does not sell. The buyer will probably buy the merchandise knowing that the supplier can be trusted to make an appropriate adjustment on the invoice amount, provide markdown money, or make up this inequity some other way in the future if the product does not sell.

Without mutual trust, retail supply chains would disintegrate. On the other hand, when trust exists, it is contagious and allows the channel to grow and prosper. This occurs because of reciprocity. If a retailer trusts a supplier to do the right thing and the supplier treats the retailer fairly, then the retailer develops more trust and the process of mutual trust continues to build.

Two-Way Communication As noted earlier, conflict is inevitable in retail channels. Consequently, two-way communication becomes the pathway for resolving disputes, which allows the channel relationship to continue. **Two-way communication** occurs when both parties openly communicate their ideas, concerns, and plans. Because of the interdependency of the retailer and supplier, two-way communication is necessary to coordinate actions. For example, when Jockey decides to run a national promotion on its underwear, it needs to coordinate this promotion with its retail channels so that when customers enter stores to shop for the items nationally advertised, they will find them displayed and in stock. Two-way communication is critical to accomplishing this coordination.

Two-way communication *Occurs when both retailer and supplier communicate openly their ideas, concerns, and plans.*

Communication is not independent of trust. Disputes can be resolved by good two-way communication, and this improves trust. Furthermore, trust facilitates open two-way communication. The process is circular and builds over time.

Solidarity Solidarity exists when a high value is placed on the relationship between a supplier and a retailer.[173] Solidarity is an attitude and thus is hard to explicitly create. Essentially, as trust and two-way communication increase, a higher degree of solidarity develops. Solidarity results in flexible dealings where adaptations are made as circumstances change. When solidarity exists, each party will come to the rescue of the other in times of trouble. For example, in the early 2000s when the economy was weak, many retailers already operating under intense competitive pressure and thin margins sought and obtained assistance, such as advertising or in-store displays, from suppliers with whom they had developed strong relationships in the past. Usually these activities are the responsibility of the retailer, but given the business climate, the vendor was able to assist. On the other hand, when solidarity does not exist, each party will abandon the other in times of trouble. This has often occurred when retailers have developed poor relationships and conflict with their suppliers. If the retailer then experiences a liquidity crisis, suppliers are likely to refuse shipment of needed merchandise. This happened with many cash-starved e-tailers in the early 2000s.

Solidarity *Exists when a high value is placed on the relationship between a supplier and retailer.*

Nowhere is this collaboration in today's channels exhibited more clearly than in the shift toward category management.

Category management (CM) A process of managing all SKUs within a product category that involves the simultaneous management of price, shelf space, merchandising strategy, promotional efforts, and other elements of the retail mix within the category based on the firm's goals, the changing environment, and consumer behavior.

Category manager An employee designated by a retailer for each category sold in its store. The category manager leverages detailed knowledge of the consumer and consumer trends, detailed point-of-sales information, and specific analysis provided by each supplier to tailor a store's offerings to the specific needs of each market. The category manager works with the suppliers to plan promotions throughout the year.

CATEGORY MANAGEMENT **Category management** involves the simultaneous management of price, shelf-space merchandising strategy, promotional efforts, and other elements of the retail mix within the category based on the firm's goals, the changing environment, and consumer behavior.[174] The task of category management is accomplished by members of a channel working as a team, not acting independently, to apply the ECR concept to an entire category of merchandise, such as all hand tools, and not just a particular brand, such as Stanley. The manager's goal is to enable the retailer to meet specific business goals such as profitability, sales volume, or inventory levels.

Retailers designate a **category manager** from among their employees for each category sold in their store. The retailer begins the process by defining specific business goals for each category. The category manager then leverages detailed knowledge of the consumer and consumer trends, detailed POS (point-of-sales) information, and specific analysis provided by each supplier to the category. With this information, the category manager creates specific modulars, which may have different facings for different stores as the retailer tailors its offerings to the specific needs of each market. In addition, category managers work with suppliers to plan promotions throughout the year to achieve the designated business goals for the category.

In cases where the solidarity of the channel partners is high, a supplier may serve as the retailer's category manager. In this case, the chosen supplier takes on the designation of category advisor. Wal-Mart, for example, uses suppliers as category advisors; the supplier works closely with the Wal-Mart buyer to ensure that the category achieves peak performance in all the stores. Normally a supplier is chosen to become a category advisor because it is the dominant provider within the specific category. However, if another supplier has better expertise in some important marketing activity, such as merchandising and/or market analysis, that supplier may also be chosen as a category advisor. Therefore, at Wal-Mart, there can potentially be multiple category advisors. The point is to take away the all-encompassing power of major suppliers such as Johnson & Johnson and P&G. Other retailers tend to rely on only one supplier to assist them. When this is the case, that advisor is called the category captain.

The category captain and/or the category advisor(s), working closely with the retail buyer, must make sure that the retailer has the best assortment for each store in order to achieve the greatest sales possible. This includes carrying the competition's merchandise. As a result, the supplier's role as the category captain or category captain has changed greatly in recent years. Whereas in the past the supplier sought to get as many of its items into the retailer's store as possible, today that supplier has to know how its products help the retailer achieve its objectives, even if this means selecting a competitor's product over its own. For retailers using a single advisor, a yearly review and possible reassignment of the supplier's status to another supplier helps to keep the category captain's recommendations objective.

To survive strong competition from other retailers, the advising supplier(s) must stay ahead of consumer trends and meet the ever-changing tastes of the consumer. To aid the supplier who serves as a category captain or advisor, the retailer provides the same POS information (except the competition's prices) that it would give to its own employee serving as the category manager.

Category managers must be ready to constantly adjust the space given to each item so that the right merchandise is in the right stores, at the right time, and in the right amount. Over the last decade, category management has enabled retailers to do a better job of staying in stock on the best-selling items and avoid being overstocked on merchandise with slower turnover. After all, the category manager is able to recognize what critical items need to remain in order to make the assortment complete. In addition, the category manager tries to create a shelf layout based on how the consumer shops.

Retailers, however, are far from passive when it comes to accepting a supplier's recommendation. They usually run the supplier's category captain's plan by a second supplier, known as the "validator." Thus **Unilever,** for example, will run a reality check for supermarkets using Procter & Gamble, as its captain proposes. Even more important, Wal-Mart insists that category captains must adhere to the retailer's strategy.

Category management is now standard practice at nearly every U.S. supermarket, convenience store, mass merchant, and drug chain. Its use is growing because the results of this collaboration benefit both retailer and supplier.

Retailers using category management report an increase in sales for both parties, a decrease in markdowns, better in-stock percentages on key items for the retailer, an increase in turnover rates and a decrease in average inventory for both retailers and wholesalers, and an increase in both members' ROI and profit.

However, when category management–oriented retailers seek to optimize each store's layout in order to maximize the gross margin dollars produced per unit of space, many times their stores tend to look just like their competitors. It was as a result of these problems that Wal-Mart replaced the "captain" with "advisors."

Supply Chain Constraints

Retailers are restricted in the relationships and agreements they may develop with supply chain, or channel, partners. These restrictions can be conveniently categorized into four areas, as shown in Exhibit 300.60.

TERRITORIAL RESTRICTIONS As related to retail trade, **territorial restrictions** can be defined as attempts by a supplier, usually a manufacturer, to limit the geographic area in which a retailer may resell its merchandise. The courts have viewed territorial restrictions as potential contracts in restraint of trade and in violation of the Sherman Antitrust Act. Thus, even though the retailer and manufacturer may both favor territorial restrictions, because of the lessening of competition between retailers selling the brand in question, the courts will often frown on such arrangements. The law does not, however, prevent manufacturers and retailers from establishing territorial limits as long as they do not exclude all other retailers or restrict the sale of the manufacturer's products. Franchise agreements have long had territorial restrictions that provide a protected zone for the franchisee. Because of these zones, the franchisee is able to develop a primary demand for the product without fear of cannibalization by another entry in the protected zone. In cases where the franchisor has permitted another franchisee to invade the "exclusive territory" of another franchisee as outlined in a contract, the original franchisee could sue the parent chain under a breach of contract claim. However, a federal appeals court ruling found that when a franchise contract expressly spells out that a franchisee does not have an exclusive territory, the franchisor has the power to place other outlets nearby.[175]

Territorial restrictions Attempts by the supplier, usually a manufacturer, to limit the geographic area in which a retailer may resell its merchandise.

DUAL DISTRIBUTION A manufacturer that sells to independent retailers and also through its own retail outlets is engaged in **dual distribution.** Thus the manufacturer manages a corporately owned vertical marketing system that competes with independent retailers, which it also supplies through a conventional, administered, or contractual marketing channel. Retailers tend to become upset about dual distribution when the two supply chains compete at the retail level in the same geographic area. For example, **Ralph Lauren** has wholly

Dual distribution Occurs when a manufacturer sells to independent retailers and also through its own retail outlets.

Exhibit 300.60 *Channel Constraints*

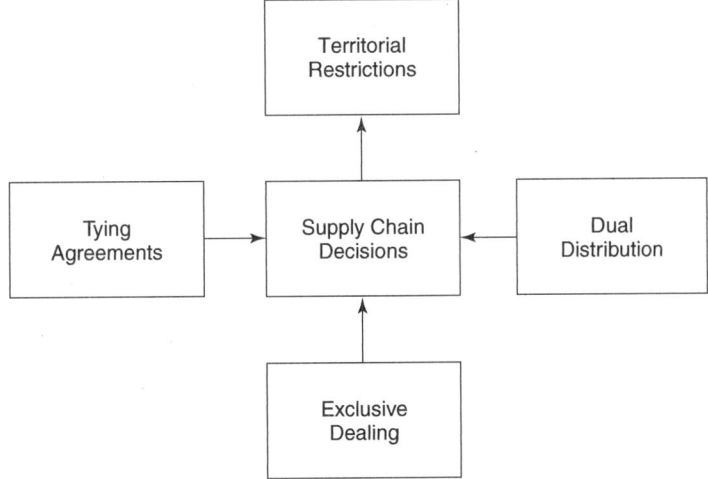

owned retail outlets and, in addition, uses major independent retailers as outlets. Such supply chain strategy can have an adverse effect on manufacturer-retailer relationships. Independent retailers will argue that dual distribution is an unfair method of competition and thus is in violation of the Sherman Act. The Internet has created new opportunities for dual distribution, which has increased the levels of channel conflict. Dual distribution also takes place when manufacturers sell similar products under different brand names for distribution through different channels, as with private labels.

Retailers who view the supply chain as a partnership and abide by the law in their relations with their partners will have higher long-term profits.

The courts have not viewed dual-distribution arrangements as antitrust violations. In fact, they have reasoned that dual distribution can actually foster competition. For example, the manufacturer may not be able to find a retailer to represent it in all trade areas, or the manufacturer may find it necessary to operate its own retail outlet to establish market share and remain competitive with other manufacturers. The courts will apply a rule-of-reason criterion. Thus the independent retailer suing a manufacturer for dual distribution will have to convince the court that it was competed against unfairly and damaged. The retailer's best bet would be to show that the manufacturer-controlled outlets were favored or subsidized (for instance, with excessive advertising allowances or lower prices) to an extent that was detrimental to the independent retailer.

One-way exclusive dealing
Occurs when the supplier agrees to give the retailer the exclusive right to merchandise the supplier's product in a particular trade area.

Two-way exclusive dealing
Occurs when the supplier offers the retailer the exclusive distribution of a merchandise line or product in a particular trade area if in return the retailer will agree to do something for the manufacturer such as heavily promote the supplier's products or not handle competing brands.

Tying agreement Exists when a seller with a strong product or service requires a buyer (the retailer) to purchase a weak product or service as a condition for buying the strong product or service.

EXCLUSIVE DEALING Retailers and their suppliers occasionally enter into exclusive dealing arrangements. In a **one-way exclusive dealing** arrangement, the supplier agrees to give the retailer the exclusive right to sell the supplier's product in a particular trade area. The retailer, however, does not agree to do anything in particular for the supplier; hence the term "one-way." For example, a weak manufacturer often has to offer one-way exclusive dealing arrangements to get shelf space at the retail level. Truly one-way arrangements are legal.

A **two-way exclusive dealing** agreement occurs when the supplier offers the retailer the exclusive distribution of a merchandise line or product if the retailer agrees to do something for the manufacturer in return. For example, the retailer might agree not to handle certain competing brands. Two-way agreements violate the Clayton Act if they substantially lessen competition or tend to create a monopoly. Specifically, the courts have generally viewed exclusive dealing as illegal when it excludes competitive products from a large share of the market and when it represents a large share of the total sales volume for a particular product type.

TYING AGREEMENTS When a seller with a strong product or service forces a buyer (the retailer) to purchase a weak product or service as a condition for buying the strong one, a **tying agreement** exists. For example, a large national manufacturer with several very highly demanded lines of merchandise may try to force the retailer to handle its entire merchandise assortment as a condition for being able to handle the more popular merchandise lines. This is called a *full-line policy.* Alternatively, a strong manufacturer may be introducing a new product and, in order to get shelf space or display space at the retail level, may require retailers to handle some of the new products before they can purchase better-established merchandise lines.

Tying arrangements have been found to be in violation of the Clayton Act, the Sherman Act, and the FTC Act. Tying is not viewed as a violation per se, but it is generally viewed as illegal if a substantial share of commerce is affected. The most serious problems involving tying arrangements are those associated with franchising. Quite often, franchise agreements contain provisions requiring the franchisee to purchase all raw materials and supplies from the franchisor. The courts generally consider tying provisions of a franchise agreement legal as long as there is sufficient proof that these arrangements are necessary to maintain quality control. Otherwise, they are viewed as unwarranted restraints of competition.[176]

In 2003 **Visa** and **MasterCard,** which are actually service retailers, paid the largest settlement to date for seeking to enforce an illegal tying agreement.

Ethics in Retailing

Ethics is a set of rules for moral human behavior. These rules or standards of moral responsibility often take the form of dos and don'ts. Some retailers have an **explicit code of ethics,** which is a written policy that states what constitutes ethical and unethical behavior. However, most often an implicit code of ethics exists. An **implicit code of ethics** is an unwritten but well understood set of rules or standards of moral responsibility. This implicit code is learned as employees become socialized into the organization and the corporate culture of the retailer.

Regardless of whether the code of ethics is explicit or implicit, it is an important guideline for making retail decisions. Shortly we will review some retail decision areas where ethical considerations are common. However, before doing so, it should be pointed out that legal behavior and ethical behavior are not necessarily the same. Unethical actions may be legal. Laws, after all, represent a formalization of behavioral standards through the political process into rules or laws. Therefore, a retailer needs to behave legally since laws represent a "formalized" set of ethical rules. In addition, retailers need to look beyond laws and engage in practices that are also ethical. One problem, though, is that "reasonable" people may disagree as to what is "right" and "wrong" behavior. For this reason retailers should develop explicit codes of ethical behavior for their employees to provide a formal indication of what is right and wrong.

> **Ethics** A set of rules for human moral behavior.
>
> **Explicit code of ethics** Consists of a written policy that states what is ethical and unethical behavior.
>
> **Implicit code of ethics** An unwritten but well understood set of rules or standards of moral responsibility.

Let's look at three retail decision areas that involve ethical considerations:

1. Buying merchandise
2. Selling merchandise
3. Retailer-employee relationships

In each of these situations the retailer faces an ethical dilemma. Note that in each of these situations, what is legal may not necessarily represent the best ethical guideline.

> *Retailers who abide by a strong set of ethical guidelines are more likely to achieve higher long-term profits.*

ETHICAL BEHAVIOR IN BUYING MERCHANDISE When buying merchandise the retailer can face at least four ethical dilemmas; these relate to product quality, sourcing, slotting fees, and bribery.

Product Quality Should a retailer inspect merchandise for product quality or leave that to the customer? Although the law does not require such inspections, most retail buyers want to ensure that their merchandise meets the expectations of the store's customers. As a result, some retailers have developed laboratory testing programs to verify quality of not only their private label products but of manufacturers' brands as well.

Sourcing Should a retailer verify the source of merchandise? A State Department document revealed that the Chinese may be exporting up to $100 million of merchandise made by prisoners, including many political prisoners, as well as counterfeiting some $800 million a year in videotapes, CDs, and books.[177] The importation of such merchandise violates American laws, yet most U.S. importers are unaware of this problem. In addition, while not against U.S. laws, some foreign merchandise sources use child labor or fail to pay a fair level of wages. The only way U.S. retailers can be sure that they are not buying illegal merchandise is to inspect all suppliers, down to the smallest subcontractors. However, some retailers are also having troubles with American suppliers. A program of careful vigilance to overcome such activities can be expensive and it is doubtful whether American consumers would be willing to bear the cost. Seeking to overcome such complaints, many retailers have begun using private investigators to check out vendors to make sure they are not buying from unsavory characters. Many other major American retailers have agreed to allow independent observers, including human rights officials, to monitor working conditions in their foreign factories. Consumers can check the U.S. Department of Labor's Web site (http://www.dol.gov) to see if a particular retailer is involved in the program. Nike, after years of being accused by many groups of using sweatshops, has agreed to release a "complete audit of the 600 plants that manufacture its shoes and apparel—gory details and all."[178]

385. SERVICES AND RETAIL MARKETING

The issue of sourcing is of particular importance to college students, as a recent study found that $2.5 billion in annual sales of college apparel (items bearing collegiate logos) had been manufactured in sweatshop factories. The University of North Carolina at Chapel Hill was the first to agree to promote humane factory working conditions from the 500 companies producing the popular sky-blue UNC T-shirts and other apparel.[179]

Slotting fees (slotting allowances)
Fees paid by a vendor for space or a slot on a retailer's shelves, as well as having its UPC number given a slot in the retailer's computer system.

Slotting Fees Should a retailer demand money, commonly called slotting fees, from a manufacturer for agreeing to add a new product to its inventory?

Bribery Should a retailer, or its employees, be allowed to accept a bribe? Bribery occurs when a retail buyer is offered an inducement (which the IRS considers to have a value greater than $25) for purchasing a vendor's products. Such inducements, it should be noted, are legal in many foreign countries. The reader may want to visit the document and publication section at the Transparency International Web site (http://www.transparency.org) to see in which countries bribes are still considered part of the normal business behavior. However, in the United States, the Foreign Corrupt Practices Act bans bribes as anticompetitive. It is, after all, hard to develop a relationship between a retailer and supplier when bribes are expected.

ETHICAL BEHAVIOR IN SELLING MERCHANDISE Ethics can also influence the selling process with regard to the products sold and the various selling practices that salespeople use.

Products Sold Should a retailer sell any product, as long as it is not illegal? For example, should a convenience store operator located near a school carry cigarette papers for those few customers who prefer to roll their own and risk selling the paper to students who might use it for smoking marijuana? Others have questioned Wal-Mart's decision not to sell magazines with front covers featuring salacious headlines and near-nude photos.[180]

Sometimes not carrying products can add to a retailer's profit. For example, **Trader Joe's,** a California-based specialty food retailer, performed a sales analysis on all its cigarettes by company and brand and found that only Marlboro merited the space allocated. Therefore, rather than carry just that one brand, the retailer dropped all cigarettes.[181]

Selling Practices Can a salesperson, while not saying anything false, be allowed to conceal certain facts from the customer? Also, should selling the "wrong" product for the customer's needs be permitted? Many retailers have ethical standards against such practices. However, as long as salespeople are paid on commission, we can expect such behavior to occur. Some highly successful retailers, such as Home Depot, have sought to overcome this dilemma by never putting their employees at odds with their own code of ethics. Bernie Marcus, the founder of Home Depot, has been quoted as saying: "The day I'm laid out dead with an apple in my mouth is the day we'll pay commissions. If you pay commissions, you imply that the small customer is not worth anything."[182] It should be pointed out, however, that paying commissions would be difficult in a self-service operation like Home Depot.

ETHICAL BEHAVIOR IN THE RETAILER-EMPLOYEE RELATIONSHIP Ethical standards can also influence the retailer-employee relationship in three ways: misuse of company assets, job switching, and employee theft.

Misuse of Company Assets Most people would agree that the stealing of merchandise is illegal, but what about other types of stealing? What about an employee who surfs the Web or trades stock on company time? Also, what about taking an extra break or using the retailer's phone for a personal long-distance call? All of these, while not subject to criminal prosecution, are forms of employee theft and should be considered when an employee develops his or her code of ethics.

Advancements in computer technology and the growth of the Internet have recently challenged one of the most treasured of American rights—the right to privacy. Most retailers have an asset that would have been unheard of a generation ago. Today's retailers have databases that contain heretofore private information about nearly every American that most consumers do not even know exists. These databases are constructed in a number of ways, including computer cookies as well as purchased information from state governments (for example, driver's license bureaus or voting records). As a result, current laws provide for consumers to opt out of such databases.

Many e-tailers, for example, know not only what purchases you made from them, but also what sections of their Web site you visited. The majority of e-tailers disclose their privacy policy on their Web site. Exhibit 300.61 shows the National Retail Federation's (NRF's) Principles on Customer Data Privacy. In general, most of the major retailers in this country adhere to the NRF's principles. However, the shakeout in e-tailing during the early part of this decade showed just how consumers' rights to privacy could be violated by retailers who had no intention of doing so.

Exhibit 300.61 *National Retail Federation Principles on Customer Data Privacy*

General Rule

The privacy of information collected by a retailer about its customers during the course of transactions with those customers should be maintained with the degree of confidentiality that the retailer reasonably anticipates would be expected of it by the typical shopper purchasing that type of merchandise from the retailer. Departures from this standard should be disclosed to customers at or before each time of occurrence, unless previously consented to by the customer or otherwise expressly permitted by law.

Practice Principles

Each retailer should adopt a customer privacy policy explaining its practices with respect to the information it collects about its customers.

Policies could either be corporate-wide or divisional depending upon the manner in which the company believes customers view its retail operations.

A retailer should make reasonable efforts to inform its customers of the existence of its customer privacy policies, and make the substance of such policies available on a regular basis.

At a minimum, a customer privacy policy should allow a customer to elect whether he or she wishes to prevent the marketing of his or her name to other unaffiliated corporations, or to "opt out" of future promotional solicitations from the company(s) to which the policy applies, or both.

Retail companies should develop procedures to reasonably ensure that customer information is not accessible to, or used by, its employees or others in contravention of its policies and customer elections, and that access to personally identifiable data for non-promotional purposes is limited to those individuals with a customer servicing need to know.

Job Switching Do employees have the right to work for whomever they want? Employees have a responsibility to their previous employer. The employer provided them with training and access to confidential information, such as vendor costs, customer lists, and future plans. When an employee leaves one retailer for another, the employee should respect the previous employer's right to retain the confidentiality of this information.

At the same time, the retailer should not seek to replace an employee, usually a manager or executive, with a lower-paid, younger person just because the employee reaches the so-called 20–40–60 plateau (20 years or more with the firm, 40 years or older, and making over $60,000 a year).

Employee Theft Just as employers have a responsibility to be fair to their employees, so do employees have a responsibility to be honest. However, many workers admit to "stealing" from their employers. Employee theft is most prevalent in food stores, department stores, and discount stores. Considering that these types of stores are usually larger in size, sales volume, and number of employees, the lack of close supervision might contribute to this problem. Some retailers, such as Wal-Mart, are trying to address this problem by offering cash bonuses just before Christmas if the store not only makes its profit goal but keeps shrinkage under a predetermined limit.

The previous discussion is not meant to be an all-inclusive list of the ethical dilemmas facing retailing today. It does, however, provide the reader with a big picture of the role of ethics in retailing.

Market Selection and Retail Location Analysis

Selecting a Target Market

Many retailing experts consider the most critical determinants of success in retailing to be, first, selecting a target market, and second, evaluating alternative ways to reach this target market.

Traditionally, for retailers desiring to reach a given target market, this has meant selecting the best location for a store. In fact, a famous retailer once said that the three major decisions in retailing are location, location, and location. There is truth in that statement because, while the other elements of the retail mix are also important, if the customer cannot reach your store conveniently, those elements become secondary. The easier it is to reach the store, the more store traffic a store will have, which will lead to higher sales.

Today, however, location is much broader than just a store's physical location because retailers are finding alternative ways to reach customers. For example, Dell sells computers and peripherals to households through the mail, over the Internet and phone; the University of Phoenix offers an MBA online via a computer in the student's home or place of business; eBay has close to 70 million registered members/users; and Tupperware continues to sell most of its kitchenware via in-home parties.

Home page The introductory or first material viewers see when they access a retailer's Internet site. It is the equivalent to a retailer's storefront in the physical world.

Virtual store The total collection of all the pages of information on the retailer's Internet site.

Ease of access Refers to the consumer's ability to easily and quickly find a retailer's Web site in cyberspace.

Retailers who select high-traffic geographic or cyberspace sites will be able to generate higher profits.

Target market The group of customers that the retailer is seeking to serve.

The Internet is becoming a major force in retailing. The equivalent of a store on the Internet is a retailer's site on the World Wide Web (www). When stopping at an e-tailer's Web site, vistors first view the firm's **home page,** which is equivalent to a storefront. From the home page a person visiting the retailer can be linked to other pages that provide more detailed information about merchandise, credit, warranties, terms of trade, and so forth. The total collection of all the pages of information on the retailer's site has become known as its **virtual store.** Whereas a traditional store is located in geographic space, a virtual store is located in cyberspace.

The counterpart to location on the Internet is the "ease of access" a consumer has to the site. **Ease of access** refers to the consumer's ability to easily and quickly find your Web site in cyberspace.

Regardless of whether retailers are planning a traditional store in geographic space or a virtual store in cyberspace, their first step is to develop a cost-effective way to reach the household and individual consumer that they have identified as their target market. It is important to realize that failure to clearly identify the target market will result in significant waste of marketing expenditures.

MARKET SEGMENTATION Market segmentation was defined as a method retailers use to examine ways to segment, or break down, heterogeneous consumer populations into smaller, more homogeneous groups based on their characteristics. Since any single retailer cannot serve all potential customers, it is important that it segment the market and select a target market(s). A **target market** is that segment of the market that the retailer decides to pursue through its marketing efforts. Retailers in the same line of retail trade often pursue different target markets. For example, **Ann Taylor** appeals to the higher-income female, **The Limited** appeals to the moderate-income female, and **Ross Dress for Less** appeals to the budget-conscious female shopper. Other women's clothiers have segmented customers based on other characteristics. For example, Charming Shoppes has been successful in targeting plus-sized women.

Sometimes it is not easy to reach every target market. For example, Generation Y types are poised to reshape the cultural landscape. However, since they have different priorities than previous generations at the same age, they will be hard to pinpoint. Canadians, on the other hand, are difficult for e-tailers to reach as they are much more reluctant than U.S. citizens to shop on-line.

The topics of target market selection and location analysis are combined here because a retailer must identify its target market(s) before it decides how to best reach that market(s). Reaching the target market can be achieved through a store-based location in which the consumer travels to the store, or through a nonstore retailing format in which products and services are offered to the consumer at a more convenient or accessible location. These are related topics because individuals of different characteristics are not randomly spread over geographic space. In fact, it has been repeatedly demonstrated that people of similar backgrounds live near each other and have similar media habits, consumption habits, activities, interests, and opinions. Because of this, retailers such as Nordstrom know where to geographically locate their stores, and merchants such as **Williams-Sonoma** (which has a very successful mail-order catalog for high-quality kitchenware) know which ZIP codes, geographic areas, or specific households to mail their catalogs.

Retailers that select markets that are measurable, accessible, and substantial will be able to generate higher profits.

IDENTIFYING A TARGET MARKET To reach a target market successfully, three criteria should be met. First, a retailer should be able to measure or describe the selected market segment using objective measures on which data is available, such as age, gender, income, education, ethnic group, religion, and so on. The most commonly available objective data is demographic, which the U.S. Census Bureau provides for businesses at little cost. Conversely, a subjective variable such as personality is more difficult to determine. For example, how can a retailer reasonably or cost-effectively measure the number of compulsive shoppers in the United States?

A second criterion is accessibility, or the degree to which the retailer can target its promotional or distribution efforts to a particular market segment. Do individuals in the target market watch certain television programs, listen to particular radio programs, frequently visit the same Web sites (i.e., cluster in cyberspace), or cluster together in neighborhoods? As we will see in this chapter, the location decision is largely determined by identifying the most effective way to reach a target market.

Finally, successful target marketing requires that the segment be substantial enough to be profitable for the retailer. Clearly, a retailer could develop a store to appeal to any market segment regardless of size, such as a store for fans of the Green Bay Packers; however, the retailer would have to ask whether enough Packer fans lived within its trade area to make the store profitable. While there are surely enough Packer fans in Wisconsin to support a store, a nonstore location such as a Web site on the Internet would be a more effective way to market to Packers fans worldwide.

Reaching Your Target Market

As noted, once a retailer identifies its target market, it must identify the most effective way to reach this market. Exhibit 300.62 illustrates the two basic retail formats that can be used to reach target markets: store-based and nonstore-based retailers. **Store-based retailers** operate from a fixed store location that requires customers travel to the store to view and select merchandise and/or services. Essentially, the retailer requires that the consumer perform part of the transportation function, which was one of the eight marketing functions. However, **nonstore-based retailers** reach the customer at home, at work, or at a place other than a store where they might be open to purchasing. As mentioned earlier, many retailers now reach customers on the Internet.

Store-based retailers Operate from a fixed store location that requires customers to travel to the store to view and select merchandise or services.

Nonstore-based retailers Intercept customers at home, at work, or at a place other than a store where they might be susceptible to purchasing.

LOCATION OF STORE-BASED RETAILERS As shown in Exhibit 300.62, there are four basic types of store-based retail locations: business districts, shopping centers/malls, freestanding units, and nontraditional locations. No one type of location is inherently better than the others. Many retailers, such as McDonald's, have been successful in all four location types. Each type of location has its own characteristics relating to the composition of competing stores, parking facilities, affinities with nonretail businesses (e.g., office buildings, hospitals, universities), and other factors.

Business Districts Historically, many retailers were located in the **central business district (CBD)**, usually an unplanned shopping area around the geographic point at which all public transportation systems converge. Many traditional department stores are located in the CBD along with a good selection of specialty shops. The makeup or the mix of retailers in a CBD is generally not the result of any advance planning, but depends on history, retail trends, and luck. Recently traditional department stores have been challenged—on one

Central business district (CBD) Usually consists of an unplanned shopping area around the geographic point at which all public transportation systems converge; it is usually in the center of the city and often where the city originated historically.

Exhibit 300.62 *Retail Formats for Accessing a Target Market*

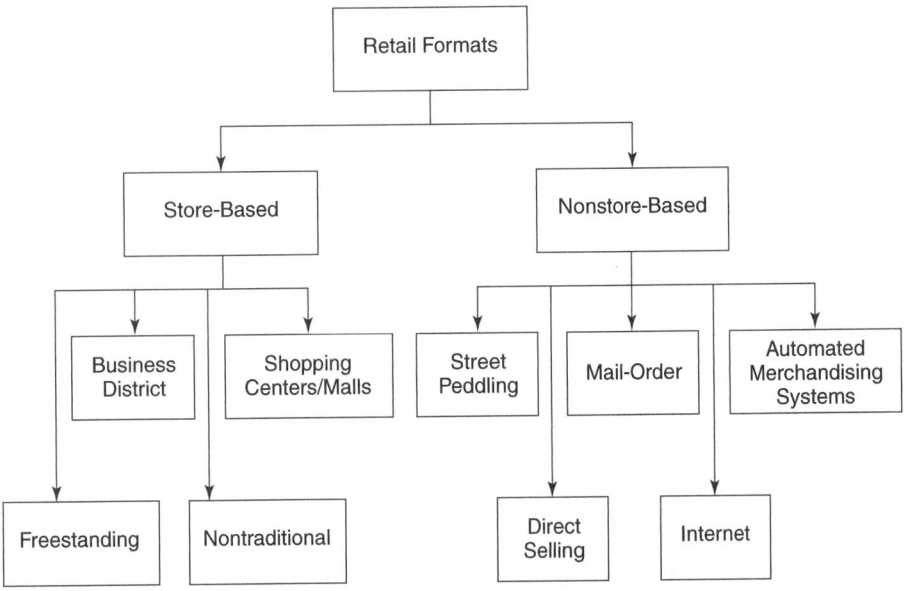

385. SERVICES AND RETAIL MARKETING

side by mass merchants, such as **Kohl's** and Wal-Mart, and category killers, and on the other side by focused specialty retailers. As a result, their market attraction has declined, which is turn has hurt the rest of the CBD. Some communities have tried to reinvigorate their city center by enhancing the shopping experience or using other nonshopping attractions. To date, however, these efforts have not been too successful.

In larger cities, secondary and neighborhood business districts have developed. A **secondary business district (SBD)** is a shopping area that is smaller than the CBD and that revolves around at least one department or variety store at a major street intersection. A **neighborhood business district (NBD)** is a shopping area that evolves to satisfy the convenience-oriented shopping needs of a neighborhood. The NBD generally contains several small stores, with the major retailer being either a supermarket or a variety store, and is located on a major artery of a residential area. An increasing number of national retail chains are finding the neighborhood business district an attractive location for new stores. These chains include retailers such as Ann Taylor, the **Body Shop, Starbucks, Crate & Barrel,** Williams-Sonoma, and **Pottery Barn.**

The single factor that distinguishes these business districts from a shopping center or mall is that they are usually unplanned. Like CBDs, the store mixture of SBDs and NBDs evolves partly by planning, partly by luck, and partly by accident. No one plans, for example, that there will be 2 department stores, 4 jewelry stores, 2 camera shops, 3 leather shops, 12 apparel shops, and 1 theater in an SBD.

Shopping Center/Mall A **shopping center**, or **mall**, is a centrally owned and/or managed shopping district that is planned, has balanced tenancy (the stores complement each other in merchandise offerings), and is surrounded by parking facilities. A shopping center has one or more **anchor stores** (a dominant large-scale store that is expected to draw customers to the center) and a variety of smaller stores. To ensure that these smaller stores complement each other, the shopping center often specifies the proportion of total space that can be occupied by each type of retailer. Similarly, the center's management places limits on the merchandise lines that each retailer may carry. A unified, cooperative advertising and promotional strategy is followed by all the retailers in the center. A shopping center location can offer a retailer several major advantages over a CBD location:

1. Heavy traffic resulting from the wide range of product offerings
2. Cooperative planning and sharing of common costs
3. Access to highways and availability of parking
4. Lower crime rate
5. Clean, neat environment

Secondary business district (SBD) Is a shopping area that is smaller than the CBD and that revolves around at least one department or variety store at a major street intersection.

Neighborhood business district (NBD) Is a shopping area that evolves to satisfy the convenience-oriented shopping needs of a neighborhood, generally contains several small stores (with the major retailer being a supermarket or a variety store), and is located on a major artery of a residential area.

Shopping center (or mall) A centrally owned or managed shopping district that is planned, has balanced tenancy (the stores complement each other in merchandise offerings), and is surrounded by parking facilities.

Anchor stores The stores in a shopping center that are the most dominant and are expected to draw customers to the shopping center.

Despite these favorable reasons for locating in a shopping center, the retailer does face several disadvantages:

1. Inflexible store hours (the retailer must stay open during mall hours and cannot be open at other times)
2. High rents
3. Restrictions as to what merchandise the retailer may sell
4. Inflexible operations and required membership in the center's merchant organization
5. Possibility of too much competition and the fact that much of the traffic is not interested in a particular product offering
6. Dominance of the smaller stores by the anchor tenant(s)

Shopping center image, preferences, and personality all attract various subsets of consumers, giving retailers located at these centers a competitive advantage over other retailers. Therefore, it is extremely important that a retailer considering a shopping center location be aware of the makeup, image, preferences, and personality of the center under question. For example, the open-air Waterford Lakes Town Center in Orlando appeals to young families by having a separate child-themed retail area called "kid*lando."

Shopping centers and their latter-day counterpart, the mall, now account for one-half of all retail sales, excluding automobile dealerships, in the United States. Seniors engage in their daily exercise, families find malls a good source of low-cost entertainment, and teens use them to seek out mates. In many cases the loyalties of shoppers toward a specific center or mall have over time become equal to or greater than their loyalties to a particular retailer. While shopping centers and malls have become a fixture of American social and economic life and are popular locations for retailers, they continue to be vastly underdeveloped in countries such as Russia.

Freestanding Location Another location option is to be freestanding. A **freestanding retailer** generally locates along major traffic arteries without any adjacent retailers selling competing products to share traffic. Freestanding retailing offers several advantages:

Freestanding retailer Generally locates along major traffic arteries and does not have any adjacent retailers to share traffic.

1. Lack of direct competition
2. Generally lower rents
3. Freedom in operations and hours
4. Facilities that can be adapted to individual needs
5. Inexpensive parking

Freestanding retailing does have some limitations:

1. Lack of drawing power of complementary stores
2. Difficulties in attracting customers for the initial visit
3. Higher advertising and promotional costs
4. Operating costs that cannot be shared with others
5. Stores that may have to be built rather than rented
6. Zoning laws that may restrict some activities

The difficulties of drawing, and then holding, customers to an isolated or freestanding store is the reason only large, well-known retailers should attempt it. Small retailers may be unable to develop a loyal customer base since customers are often unwilling to travel to a freestanding store that does not have a wide assortment of products and a local or national reputation. Wal-Mart and many convenience stores and gasoline stations have used a freestanding location strategy successfully in the past. Discount appliance stores such as Best Buy and wholesale clubs such as Costco are using them today. When these large national chains acquire land for a freestanding store, they often acquire more than they need and then "out-parcel" (i.e., sell) the remaining land to smaller retailers. Some astute local retailers and small regional chains have found it quite attractive to buy this excess land and build stores, even at a premium price, because of the traffic a large discounter like Wal-Mart generates.

Nontraditional Locations Increasingly, retailers are identifying nontraditional locations that offer greater convenience. Recognizing, for example, that a significant number of travelers spend several hours in airports and can use this time to purchase merchandise they might otherwise purchase in their local communities, retailers have stepped up their airport mall plans.

On college campuses there are increasing numbers of food courts in student unions and cosmetic counters in the campus bookstores. Truck and travel stops along interstate highways are incorporating food courts. Some franchises such as Taco Bell and **Dunkin' Donuts**

Retailers that seek to develop stores in nontraditional locations will enhance their opportunities for achieving high profits.

are putting small food service units in convenience stores and in university libraries and classroom buildings. Georgia Tech even has a supermarket on its campus.[183] Hospitals are building emergency-care clinics near where people live in the suburbs and away from the hospital, lawyers are opening storefront offices wherever there is high pedestrian traffic, and dry cleaners and copying services are locating in major office buildings. **Wells Fargo** has minimarketplaces featuring Starbucks coffee bars, dry cleaners, delis, and postal centers in its bank branches, and other banks have opened branch offices in retirement centers. Some service retailers are an exception, however, since their products are delivered to consumers at home. For example, plumbers, house painters, repair services, maid services, carpet cleaners, and lawn-care firms may not be concerned with their location. To users of financial services, location might be more important than just being a click away.

NONSTORE-BASED RETAILERS There is a great diversity and variety of nonstore-based retailers. Perhaps the oldest form is the street peddler who sells merchandise from a pushcart or temporary stall set up on a street. Street peddling is still common in some parts of the world such as Mexico, Turkey, Pakistan, India, and many parts of Africa

385. SERVICES AND RETAIL MARKETING

> *Retailers who develop multiple retail formats to reach their target market will be the star performers of the next decade.*

and South America. But it is also seen in this country in such places as New York City and San Francisco, where street-corner vendors sell T-shirts, watches, books, magazines, tobacco, candy, hot dogs, and other products. Peddlers also work in many other U.S. cities where family members operate kiosks and carts in heavily traveled areas, such as malls and the parking lots at sporting events. These small "mom-and-pop" retailers are supplied both by manufacturers and by franchisors.[184]

Retail Location Decision

The location decision for store-based retailers involves three sequential steps. First, the retailer must identify the most attractive markets in which to operate. Some retailers, such as **Toys "R" Us,** Home Depot, Wal-Mart, and **Benetton,** are international, and thus when they think of adding new locations, they consider the attractiveness of geographic expansion into foreign countries.

On the other hand, many retailers such as **County Seat Jeans,** Kmart, and **Kroger** as well as most smaller merchants concentrate only on the United States, and when considering new locations they evaluate the attractiveness of domestic markets only. Still other retailers concentrate on a small region of the United States, possibly a single state or city.

The second step in the retail location decision is to evaluate the density of demand and supply within each market and identify the most attractive sites that are available within each market. Essentially, this means identifying the sites most consistent with the retailer's target market and then identifying those for which the market is not already overstored or in which competition is not overly intense. The third step is selecting the best site (or sites) available. This stage involves estimating the revenue and expenses of a new store at various locations and then identifying the most profitable new locations. These three steps are illustrated in Exhibit 300.63.

> **Trading area** *The geographic area from which a retailer, or group of retailers, or community draws its customers.*

As stated earlier, the first step in making a good retail location decision is to identify the most attractive market or **trading area**—the geographic area from which a retailer, group of retailers, or community draws its customers—in which the retailer could locate. For instance, Dollar General, which only now is entering larger cities, has been very successful in the past by concentrating its expansion in small towns (generally those with populations under 10,000), which have less competition, easier zoning and building regulations, and lower wages and operating costs.

RETAIL LOCATION THEORIES The most attractive retail markets are not necessarily the largest. A variety of other factors need to be considered in identifying attractive markets. But to start, three methods are especially useful for identifying the best markets.

Exhibit 300.63 *Selecting a Retail Location*

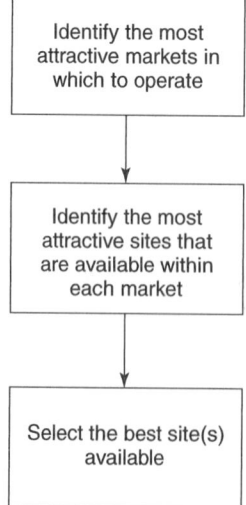

Retail Gravity Theory **Retail gravity theory** suggests that there are underlying consistencies in shopping behavior that would yield to mathematical analysis and prediction based on the notion or concept of gravity. **Reilly's law of retail gravitation**,[185] named after its developer, William Reilly, dealt with how large urbanized areas attracted customers from smaller communities serving the rural hinterland. In effect, it stated that two cities attract trade from an intermediate place approximately in direct proportion to the population of the two cities and in inverse proportion to the square of the distance from these two cities to the intermediate place. That is, people will tend to shop in the larger city if travel distance is equal, or even somewhat farther, because they believe that the larger city has a better product selection and will be worth the extra travel.

Two decades later, Reilly's original law was revised in order to determine the boundaries of a city's trading area, or to establish a point of indifference between two cities.[186] This **point of indifference** is the breaking point at which customers would be indifferent to shopping at either city.

Retail gravity theory rests on two assumptions: (1) The two competing cities are equally accessible from the major road and (2) population is a good indicator of the differences in the goods and services available in different cities. Consumers are attracted to the larger population center not because of the city's size, but because of the larger number of stores and wider product assortment available, thereby making the increased travel time worthwhile. However, in its simplicity, retail gravity theory does have several limitations. First, city population does not always reflect the available shopping facilities. For example, two neighboring cities, each with a population of 10,000 and similar demographics, would not be reflected equally if one of the cities had a shopping center with Target as the anchor store and the other did not. Second, distance is measured in miles, not the time involved for the consumer to travel that distance or the consumer's perception of that distance or time involved. Given our present highway system, this limitation is extremely important. Traveling 20 miles on an interstate highway to a mall located at an exit may be easier than the stop-and-start travel involved in going 6 miles through downtown traffic. Therefore, some retailers will substitute travel time for mileage. Finally, while the theory works reasonably well in rural areas, where distance is a major decision factor, it is not flawless.

Recent research on *outshopping*—that is, leaving your community to shop—from rural areas suggests that factors other than those considered by retail gravity theory are important. For example, in the 1990s Canada enacted such high sales taxes that millions of Canadians living near the border, which 70 percent of Canadians do, began to shop in the United States. As a result, the Canadian government was forced to repeal the tax. This is happening in reverse today, when U.S. citizens purchase cars in Canada. Purchasing merchandise online is another form of outshopping.

Some other factors that the retail gravity theory fails to consider include perceived differences between local and other trading centers, variety-seeking behavior, and other services provided, including medical services and/or entertainment facilities. Also, gravity theory is less useful in metropolitan areas where consumers typically have a number of shopping choices available within the maximum distance they are willing to travel.

Saturation Theory Another method for identifying attractive potential markets is based on retail saturation, which examines how the demand for goods and services in a potential trading area is being served by current retail establishments in comparison with other potential markets. Such analysis produces three possible outcomes:

1. Retail store saturation is a condition under which existing store facilities are utilized efficiently and meet customer needs. Retail saturation exists when a market has just enough store facilities for a given type of store to serve the population of the market satisfactorily and yield a fair profit to the owners.
2. When a market has too few stores to satisfactorily meet the needs of the customer, it is understored. In this setting average store profitability is quite high.
3. When a market has too many stores to yield a fair return on investment, it is overstored.

Saturation theory, therefore, implies a balance between the number of existing retail store facilities (supply) and their use (demand). One typically measures

---

Retail gravity theory Suggests that there are underlying consistencies in shopping behavior that yield to mathematical analysis and prediction based on the notion or concept of gravity.

Reilly's law of retail gravitation Based on Newtonian gravitational principles, explains how large urbanized areas attract customers from smaller rural communities.

Retail store saturation A condition where there are just enough store facilities for a given type of store to efficiently and satisfactorily serve the population and yield a fair profit to the owners.

Understored A condition in a community where the number of stores in relation to households is relatively low so that engaging in retailing is an attractive economic endeavor.

Overstored A condition in a community where the number of stores in relation to households is so large that engaging in retailing is usually unprofitable or marginally profitable.

saturation, overstoring, and understoring in terms of the number of stores per thousand households. The consensus among retail location experts is that the United States is currently highly saturated or overstored with retail stores, and thus retailers are taking a second look at some long-ignored markets such as older downtown areas.

Index of retail saturation (IRS)
The ratio of demand for a product (households in the geographic area multiplied by annual retail expenditures for a particular line of trade per household) divided by available supply (the square footage of retail facilities of a particular line of trade in the geographic area).

A possible indicator of understored versus overstored markets is the **index of retail saturation (IRS)**,[187] which is the ratio of demand for a product or service divided by available supply. The IRS can be measured as follows:

$$IRS = (H \times RE)/RF$$

where IRS is the index of retail saturation for an area; H is the number of households in the area; RE is the annual retail expenditures for a particular line of trade per household in the area; and RF is the square footage of retail facilities of a particular line of trade in the area (including square footage of the proposed store). If you multiply the two terms in the numerator together (households and retail expenditures per household), you obtain dollar sales. Recalling that the denominator is square footage of retail space, it is easy to see that the IRS is essentially the sales per square foot of retail space in the marketplace for a particular line of retail trade.

When the IRS takes on a high value in comparison with the line of trade in other cities, it indicates that the market is understored, and therefore a potentially attractive opportunity exists. When it takes on a low value, it indicates an overstored market, which precludes the potential of a significant opportunity. Home Depot, for example, monitors its sales per square foot for a store because it recognizes that if this ratio is too high, customers may not be well served and competition may be invited into the market. In fact, if sales per square foot are over $400, it believes it is advantageous to close a thriving store and open two smaller stores. Although this cannibalizes the existing store, it better serves customers and discourages competition from entering the market.[188]

Retailers who identify and locate in markets where the index of retail saturation is high will be able to achieve a higher profit.

As an example of how the index of retail saturation is used, consider an individual planning to open a dry cleaner in either city A or city B. This individual has the following information: Residents of both cities spend $6.28 per month on dry cleaning. The total number of households in both cities is also the same—17,000. City A, however, has 2,000 square feet of dry-cleaning facilities, and city B has 2,500 square feet; and our proposed square footage is 500 square feet. Given this information and using our formula for IRS, we can find the IRS for each city:

$$IRS \text{ (city A)} = 17,000 \times 6.28/(2,000 + 500) = 42.70$$
$$IRS \text{ (city B)} = 17,000 \times 6.28/(2,500 + 500) = 35.59$$

Thus, based solely on these two factors of demand (number of households and average expenditure for products by each household) and one factor of supply (the square footage of retail space serving this demand), the individual would choose to locate in city A, since its value of $42.70 is higher than city B's $35.59.

As nonstore-based retailing continues to grow, retailers need to recognize that the index of retail saturation may become less useful. That is because it incorporates only store-based retailing in the supply component of the index. This is not a problem in the preceding dry cleaner example, but it may be a problem for apparel retailers and computer retailers because many households use mail-order catalogs and e-tailers.

Buying Power Index *Sales & Marketing Management* magazine annually publishes the Survey of Buying Power. This survey reports on current data for metropolitan areas, cities, and states. It provides some data that are not readily available from other sources, such as the Census Bureau. These data include retail sales by specific merchandise categories, effective buying income, and total retail sales by area, population, and retail sales.

Buying power index (BPI) *An indicator of a market's overall retail potential composed of weighted measures of effective buying income (personal income, including all nontax payments such as Social Security, minus all taxes), retail sales, and population size.*

The population, retail sales, and buying income data provide the retail manager with an overview of the potential of various trading areas. By comparing one trading area to another, the retailer can develop a relative measure of each market's potential. For each area, the retailer can develop a **buying power index (BPI)**, which is a single weighted measure combining effective buying income (personal income, including all nontax payments such as social security, minus all taxes), retail sales, and population size into an overall indicator of a market's potential. Generally, business firms use a formula for BPI that was developed by *Sales & Marketing Management*. The BPI is weighted in the following manner:

$$\text{BPI} = 0.5 \text{ (the area's percentage of U.S. effective buying income)}$$
$$+ 0.3 \text{ (the area's percentage of U.S. retail sales)}$$
$$+ 0.2 \text{ (the area's percentage of U.S. population)}$$

It is obvious that effective buying income is the most important factor, followed by retail sales and population. This formula can be further refined by breaking down these general figures into more specific figures geared toward the consumers of the retailer's products.

For example, XYZ Corporation, a retail chain specializing in general merchandise goods, is considering expansion into one of two different trading areas. The proposed trading areas are the Alton–Granite City, Illinois, or Hamilton-Middletown, Ohio, markets. XYZ aims its general merchandise at the 25- to 34-year-old market with incomes over $35,000. Therefore, this age group will substitute for population, the general merchandise sales will substitute for total retail sales, and households with income over $35,000 will replace effective buying income.

Using data that can be easily obtained from *Sales & Marketing Management*, XYZ can develop the BPI for each city:

$$\text{BPI (Alton–Granite City)} = 0.5 \, (.000386) + 0.3(.00083) + 0.2(.00012) = .000466$$
$$\text{BPI (Hamilton-Middletown)} = 0.5 \, (.000717) + 0.3(.00063)$$
$$+ 0.2 \, (.000112) = .000570$$

As you can see, the BPI of Hamilton-Middletown is almost 25 percent greater than that of Alton–Granite City even though the cities are nearly equal in size. Therefore, XYZ would probably choose to expand its Ohio market rather than the Illinois market.

Remember that the BPI is broad in nature and reflects only the demand levels for the two proposed trading areas and not the supply level. Therefore, it does not reflect the saturation levels of these two markets. This can be easily remedied by dividing the BPI for each area by the area's percentage of U.S. retail selling space for general merchandise (the supply factors) to determine each area's attractiveness:

$$\text{IRS (Alton–Granite City)} = .000466/.000452 = 1.03$$
$$\text{IRS (Hamilton-Middletown)} = .000570/.000483 = 1.18$$

In this case the Ohio trading area is again chosen. This IRS formula does not reflect the availability of competing products or stores in nearby larger cities: Cincinnati, in the case of Hamilton-Middletown, and St. Louis, Missouri, in the case of Alton–Granite City.

Other Demand and Supply Factors In addition to using retail gravity theory, the index of retail saturation, and the buying power index in evaluating various potential markets, the successful retailer will also look at some other demand and supply factors for each market.

MARKET DEMAND POTENTIAL In analyzing the market potential, retailers identify certain criteria that are specific to the product line or services they are selling. The criteria chosen by one retailer might not be of use to a retailer selling a different product line. The major components of market demand potential are as follows:

1. *Population characteristics.* Population characteristics are the criteria most often used to segment markets. Although total population figures and their growth rates are of primary importance to a retailer in examining potential markets, the successful retailer can obtain a more detailed profile of a market by examining school enrollment, education, age, sex, occupation, race, and nationality. Retailers should seek to match a market's population characteristics to the population characteristics of people who desire their goods and services.
2. *Buyer behavior characteristics.* Another useful criterion for analyzing potential markets is the behavioral characteristics of buyers in the market. Such characteristics include store loyalty, consumer lifestyles, store patronage motives, geographic and climatic conditions, and product benefits sought. These data, however, are not as easily obtainable as population data.
3. *Household income.* The average household income and the distribution of household incomes can significantly influence demand for retail facilities. Further insight into the demand for retail facilities is provided by Engel's laws, which imply that spending increases for all categories of products as a result of an income increase, but that the percentage of spending in some categories increases more than for others. Thus, as average household income rises, the community will exhibit a greater demand for luxury goods and a more sophisticated demand for necessity goods.

4. *Household age profile.* The age composition of households can be an important determinant of demand for retail facilities. In communities where households tend to be young, the preferences for stores may be different from communities where the average household is relatively old. For example, older consumers spend almost four times as much at drugstores as do 30-year-olds.

5. *Household composition.* If we hold income and age constant and change the composition of the household, we will be able to identify another determinant of the demand for retail facilities. After all, households with children have different spending habits than childless households with similar incomes.

6. *Community life cycle.* Communities tend to exhibit growth patterns over time. Growth patterns of communities may be of four major types: rapid growth, continuous growth, relatively stable growth, and finally, decline. The retailer should try to identify the communities that are in a rapid or continuous growth pattern, since they will represent the best long-run opportunities.

7. *Population density.* The population density of a community equals the number of persons per square mile. Research suggests that the higher the population density, the larger the average store should be in terms of square feet and thus the fewer the number of stores that will be needed to serve a population of a given size.

8. *Mobility.* The easier it is for people to travel, the more mobile they will be.[189] When people are mobile they are willing to travel greater distances to shop. Therefore, there will be fewer but larger stores in the community. That is, in a community where mobility is high, there will be a need for fewer retailers than in a community where mobility is low.

The most attractive market areas are those in which the preceding criteria are configured in such a way that they represent maximum market potential for a particular retailer. This will vary by the type of retailer and the product lines it handles. In assessing different market areas a retailer should first establish the market demand potential criteria that characterize the target market it would like to attract.

MARKET SUPPLY FACTORS In deciding to enter a new market, the successful retailer will spend time analyzing the competition. The retailer should consider square feet per store and square feet per employee, store growth, and the quality of competition.

1. *Square feet per store.* It is helpful to obtain data on the square feet per store for the average store in the communities that are being analyzed. These data will indicate whether the community tends to have large- or small-scale retailing. And, of course, this is important in terms of assessing the extent to which the retailer's standard type of store would blend with the existing structure of retail trade in the community.

2. *Square feet per employee.* A measure that combines two major supply factors in retailing, store space and labor, is square feet of space per employee. A high number for this statistic in a community is evidence that each employee is able to handle more space. This could be due to either a high level of retail technology in the community or more self-service retailing. Since retail technology is fairly constant across communities, any difference in square feet per employee is most often due to the level of service being provided. In communities currently characterized by retailers as offering a high level of service, there may be a significant opportunity for new retailers that are oriented toward self-service.

3. *Growth in stores.* The retailer should look at the rate of growth in the number of stores for the last one to five years. When the growth is rapid, then on average the community will have better-located stores with more contemporary atmospheres. More recently located stores will coincide better with the existing demographics of the community. Their atmosphere will also better suit the tastes of the marketplace, and they will tend to incorporate the latest in retail technology. All of these factors hint that the strength of retail competition will be greater when the community has recently experienced rapid growth in the number of stores. Retailers, as well as entrepreneurs, can obtain the information needed for computing the square feet per store, square feet per employee, and growth in stores from the Urban Land Institute's *Dollars and Cents of Shopping Centers*, the National Mall Monitor's *Store Retail Tenant Directory*, and Lebhar-Friedman's *Chain Store Guide*.

4. *Quality of competition.* The three preceding supply factors reflect the quantity of competition. Retailers also need to look at the strength or quality of competition. They should attempt to identify the major retail chains and local retailers in each market and evaluate the strength of each. Answers to questions such as the following would be insightful: What is their market share or profitability? How promotional- and price-oriented are they? Are they customer-oriented? Do they tend to react to new market entrants by cutting prices, increasing advertising, or improving customer service? A retailer would think twice before competing with Wal-Mart on price, **Dillard's** on cost control, Saks Fifth Avenue on fashion, and Nordstrom's on service or shoe selection.

Quite often, when a discounter enters a small community with an extra 80,000 to 100,000 square feet of retail space, existing small-town retailers feel they cannot compete and must close down. This is undoubtedly true for the already poor-performing retailers. However, despite the discounter's enormous buying advantages, small-town retailers can compete head-on with the out-of-towners by providing better customer service, adjusting prices on products carried by the discounters, and remaining open Sundays and evenings. Customers will appreciate the increased standard of living that the discounter's prices make possible and as a result the trading area will increase. The apparel retailer, for example, should cut down on basic stock items like socks and underwear, but increase its inventory of specialty or novelty items. The sales lost on basic items will be overcome with these newer items and the larger trading area the discounter provides.

Retail Site Analysis

Once a retailer has identified the best potential market, the next task is to perform a more detailed analysis of the market. Only after careful analysis of the market can the retailer choose the best site (or sites) available. **Site analysis** consists of an evaluation of the density of demand and supply within each market. It should be augmented by an identification of the most attractive sites that are currently available within each market. The third and final step, site selection, is the selection of the best possible site.

Site analysis *An evaluation of the density of demand and supply within each market with the goal of identifying the best retail sites.*

Site analysis begins by evaluating the density of demand and supply of various areas within the chosen market by census tract, ZIP code, or some other meaningful geographic factor, and then identifying the most attractive sites, given the retailer's requirements, that are available for new stores within each market. One of the advantages of using census tract data is the availability of such data from the Census Bureau.

Census tracts are relatively small statistical subdivisions that vary in population from about 2,500 to 8,000 and are designed to include fairly homogeneous populations. They are most often found in cities and in counties of metropolitan areas—that is, the more densely populated areas of the nation.

SIZE OF TRADING AREAS Earlier we discussed the general trading area of a community. Our attention will now shift to how to determine and evaluate the trading area of specific sites within markets. In other words, we will attempt to estimate the geographic area from which a store located at a particular site will be able to attract customers.

At the same time that Reilly was developing retail gravity theory to determine the trading area for communities, William Applebaum designed a technique specifically for determining and evaluating trading areas for an individual store. Applebaum's technique was based on customer spottings. For each $100 in weekly store sales, a customer was randomly selected or spotted for an interview. These spottings usually did not require much time since the interviewer requested only demographic information, shopping habits, and some pertinent consumer attitudes toward the store and its competitors. After the home addresses of the shoppers were plotted on a map, the analyst could make some inferences about trading area size and the competition.[190]

Thus, it is relatively easy to define the trading area of an existing store. All that is necessary is to interview current customers of the store to determine where they reside. For a new store, however, the task is not so easy. There is a fair amount of conventional wisdom that has withstood the test of time about the correlation of trading area size, which can be summarized as follows:

1. Stores that sell products that the consumer wants to purchase in the most convenient manner will have a smaller trading area than so-called specialty stores.
2. As consumer mobility increases, the size of the store's trading area increases.
3. As the size of the store increases, its trading area increases because it can stock a broader and deeper assortment of merchandise, which will then attract customers from greater distances.
4. As the distance between competing stores increases, their trading areas will increase.
5. Natural and manmade obstacles such as rivers, mountains, railroads, and freeways can abruptly limit the boundaries of a trading area.

DESCRIPTION OF TRADING AREA Retailers can access, at relatively low cost, information concerning the trading area for various retail locations and the buyer behavior of the trading area. If you use your search engine to locate the Web sites of any of the firms providing geographical information services, you will see how readily available this information is to the typical retailer.

385. SERVICES AND RETAIL MARKETING

> **Demand density** *The extent to which the potential demand for the retailer's goods and services is concentrated in certain census tracts, ZIP-code areas, or parts of the community.*

DEMAND DENSITY The extent to which potential demand for the retailer's goods and services is concentrated in certain census tracts, ZIP-code areas, or parts of the community is called **demand density.** To determine the extent of demand density, retailers need to identify what they believe to be the major variables influencing their potential demand. One such method of identifying these variables is to examine the types of customers who already shop in the retailer's present stores. The variables identified should be standard demographic variables such as age, income, and education, since data will be readily available.

SUPPLY DENSITY While the demand-density map allows you to identify the area within a community that represents the highest potential demand, the location of existing retail establishments should also be mapped. This will allow you to examine the density of supply—that is, the extent to which retailers are concentrated in different areas of the market under question.

RETAIL STORE SITE AVAILABILITY Just because demand outstrips supply in certain geographic locations does not immediately imply that stores should be located in those locations. Sites must be available. Some retailers have developed a checklist of all the items they want to consider during the site analysis stage. One such list is shown in Exhibit 300.64.

Retail Store Site Selection

After completing the analysis of each segment of the desired market and identifying the best available sites within each market, retailers are now ready to make the final decision regarding location: selecting the best site (or sites) available. Retailers are well advised to use the assistance of a real estate professional at this stage. Even if the retailers or their staff have done all the analysis to this point, the assistance of a real estate professional is important. In fact, more and more large retail firms set up separate corporations just to handle their real estate transactions.

Exhibit 300.64 *Checklist for Site Evaluations*

Local Demographics	Site Characteristics
Population and/or household base	Number of parking spaces available
Population growth potential	Distance of parking areas
Lifestyles of consumers	Ease of access for delivery
Income potential	Visibility of site from street
Age makeup	History of the site
Educational makeup	Compatibility of neighboring stores
Population of nearby special markets, that is, daytime workers, students, and tourists, if applicable	Size and shape of lot
	Condition of existing building
Occupation mix	Ease of entrance and exit for traffic
Traffic Flow and Accessibility	Ease of access for handicapped customers
Number and type of vehicles passing location	Restrictions on sign usage
Access of vehicles to location	Building safety code restrictions
Number and type of pedestrians passing location	Type of zoning
Availability of mass transit, if applicable	*Cost Factors*
Accessibility of major highway artery	Terms of lease/rent agreement
Quality of access streets	Basic rent payments
Level of street congestion	Length of lease
Presence of physical barriers that affect trade area shape	Local taxes
Retail Competition	Operations and maintenance costs
Number and types of stores in area	Restrictive clauses in lease
Analysis of key players in general area	Membership in local merchants association required
Competitiveness of other merchants	Voluntary regulations by local merchants
Number and location of direct competitors in area	
Possibility of joint promotions with local merchants	

In principle, all retailers should attempt to find a **100 percent location** for their stores. A 100 percent location is one where there is no better use for the site than the retail store that is being planned. Retailers should remember that what may be a 100 percent site for one store may not be for another. The best location for a supermarket may not be the best location for a discount department store.

> **100 percent location** When there is no better use for a site than the retail store that is being planned for that site.

NATURE OF SITE Is the site currently a vacant store, a vacant parcel of land, or the site of a planned shopping center? Many of the available retail sites will be vacant stores. This is because 10 to 15 percent of stores go out of business each year. This does not mean that just because a men's apparel store failed in a location that a bookstore would do likewise. However, sometimes a piece of property becomes known as "jinxed" or "snakebit" because of the high number of business failures that have occurred there. Every town usually has one or more such areas, and restaurants, which are one of the toughest businesses to get off the ground, seem to try these locations the most.[191] Therefore, when the retail site that appears to be most suited to the retailer's needs is a vacant parcel of land, the retailer needs to investigate why it is vacant. Why have others passed up the site? Was it previously not for sale or was it priced too high? Or is there some other reason?

Finally, the site may be part of a planned shopping center. In this case, the retailer can usually be assured that it will have the proper mix of neighbors, adequate parking facilities, and good traffic. Sometimes, of course, the center has not been properly planned, and the retailer needs to be aware of these special cases. It is difficult to succeed in a shopping center in which a high percentage of space is not rented.

Traffic Characteristics The traffic that passes a site, whether it is vehicular or pedestrian, can be an important determinant of the potential sales at that site. However, more than traffic flow is important. The retailer must also determine whether the population and traffic are of the type desired. For example, a retailer of fine furs and leather coats may be considering two alternative sites: one in the central business district and the other in a group of specialty stores in a small shopping center in a very exclusive residential area. The CBD site may generate more total traffic, but the alternative site may generate more of the right type of traffic.

The retailer should evaluate two traffic-related aspects of the site. The first is the availability of sufficient parking, either at the site or nearby. One of the advantages of shopping centers is the availability of adequate parking space. If the site is not a shopping center, then the retailer will need to determine if the parking space will be adequate. It is difficult to give a precise guideline for the space that will be needed. Generally, it is a function of four factors: size of the store, frequency of customer visits, length of customer visits, and availability of public transportation. As a rule of thumb, shopping centers estimate that there should be 5 spaces for every 1,000 square feet of selling space in medium-sized centers and 10 spaces per 1,000 square feet in large centers.

A second traffic-related aspect the retailer should consider is the ease with which consumers can reach the store site. Are the roadways in good shape? Are there traffic barriers (rivers with a limited number of bridges, interstate highways with limited crossings, one-way streets, heavy street use resulting in congestion that limits exits to the site)? Remember, customers normally avoid heavily congested shopping areas and shop elsewhere in order to minimize driving time and other difficulties.

Type of Neighbors What neighboring establishments surround the site? There can be good and bad neighbors. What constitutes a good or bad neighbor depends on the type of store being considered at the site. Suppose that you plan to open a children's apparel store and are considering two alternative sites. One site already has a toy store and a gift shop; the other site has a bowling alley and an adult book store. Obviously, you know what the good and bad neighbors are.

However, determining the good and bad neighbors may not always be that easy, especially for an entrepreneur. A good neighboring business will be one that is compatible with the retailer's line of trade. When two or more businesses are compatible, they can actually help generate business for each other.[192] For example, a paint store, hardware store, and auto parts store located next to one another may increase total traffic and thus benefit them all.

Research has found that retailers experience a benefit from **store compatibility**. That is, when two compatible, or very similar, businesses (e.g., two shoe stores) locate near each other, they will show an increase in sales volume greater than what they would have achieved if they were located apart from each other. For example, when **Lowe's** opened a store near a Home Depot in Lewisville, Texas, the Home Depot store went from a category B to a category A store. This meant that the addition of a nearby competitor increased Home Depot's sales by 20 percent. This clustering doesn't always benefit competitors.

> **Store compatibility** Exists when two similar retail businesses locate next to or nearby each other and they realize a sales volume greater than what they would have achieved if they were located apart from each other.

Some retailing experts claim that this clustering of similar retailers dates back to the 1950s, when the choicest location for a gas station was believed to be an intersection that already had three other stations. Today, we see this with shoe stores in malls, auto dealerships, furniture stores, and restaurants. Clustering of stores allows customers to walk from store to store, comparing prices, products, and service. In fact, about the only situation where compatible retailers do not achieve a greater sales volume when located near each other is with membership retailers such as wholesale clubs and fitness centers. After all, consumers have already paid to use one of the retailers, so it is doubtful that they would pay to shop at the other. In such cases, one of three things would happen:

1. The retailers would fight it out to the death and both would lose.
2. The trade area would be big enough so that both could succeed.
3. One retailer would be forced to completely differentiate itself from the other, and even then they might not both survive.

TERMS OF PURCHASE OR LEASE Another consideration for the retailer at this point is the lease terms. The retailer should review the length of the lease (it could be too long or too short), the exclusivity clause (whether or not the retailer will be the only one allowed to sell a certain line of merchandise), the guaranteed traffic rate (a reduction in rent should be offered if the shopping center fails to achieve a targeted traffic level), and an anchor clause (which would also allow for a rent reduction if the anchor store in a developing center does not open on time or when you open). Lease arrangements generally call for either a fixed payment, in which the rental charge is usually based on a fixed amount per month, or a variable payment, in which rent is a specified percentage of sales with a guaranteed minimum rent. It is important for the retailer to choose the one that is best under the circumstances—perhaps a combination of the two methods.

When the retailer decides to locate in a shopping center, it usually has no other choice than to lease. However, in the case of a freestanding location, an outright purchase is often possible. Purchase and lease costs should be factored into the site's expected profitability.

EXPECTED PROFITABILITY The final step in site selection analysis is construction of a pro forma (expected) return on asset model for each possible site. The return on asset model comprises three crucial variables: net profit margin, asset turnover, and return on assets.

For purposes of evaluating sites, the potential return on equity is not relevant. This is because the financial leverage ratio (total assets divided by equity) is a top-management decision; it represents how much debt the retail enterprise is willing to assume. Most likely, the question of how to finance new store growth has already been answered or at least contemplated. The retailer should already have determined that it has or can obtain the capital to finance a new store. It is therefore reasonable and appropriate to evaluate sites on their potential return on assets and not return on equity.

If the retailer is to evaluate sites on their potential return on assets, it will need at least three estimates: total sales, total assets, and net profit. Each of these is likely to vary depending on the site. Sales estimates will be different for alternative sites because each will have unique trade area characteristics, such as the number and nature of households and the level of competition. Estimated total assets could vary because the alternative sites will likely have different prices; the cost of construction could also vary. Finally, estimated profits could vary not only due to varying sales for the different sites but different operating costs. For example, some sites may be in areas where labor expenses, taxes, or insurance rates are higher.

Sales Administration and Management

Sales and Marketing in the 21st Century

Personal selling is one of the most important elements of the promotional mix and a critical activity of marketing management; it is also the most expensive form of promotion that a firm can undertake. Recent figures indicate that the average sales call—factoring in compensation, benefits, and travel and entertainment expenses—costs the organization $169.64.[193] For firms emphasizing **consultative selling,** the average price of a sales call is even higher, $211.56.[194] Furthermore, across all industries, only one sales call in three is successful. Why then would a firm choose to utilize personal selling and incur the associated costs?

The Strategic Importance of Personal Selling

There are three primary reasons why personal selling is such an important component of a promotional strategy. First, because personal selling involves direct communication between a sales representative and a prospective customer, it is the only form of promotion that allows a firm to immediately respond to the needs of the prospect. That is, as the salesperson makes his or her presentation, the salesperson can continuously adapt the presentation to the needs of the prospect. The ability to constantly adapt to the prospective customer, in turn results in a greater number of sales. Second, personal selling allows for immediate customer feedback, so a firm has timely information regarding customer satisfaction with its offerings. Other forms of promotion, such as advertising, are company-sponsored communications directed toward the target market, but direct, *immediate* feedback from customers is not usually possible. Finally, personal selling results in an actual sale—the salesperson can leave a customer's office with an order in hand. Thus, personal selling is one of the few forms of promotion to which the sale of a specific product can be *directly* traced. Consequently, successful companies truly value their sales forces.

Due to the costs associated with personal selling, this form of promotion is not used as often for consumer markets where there are many, geographically dispersed buyers whose individual purchases will not support the average cost of a sales call. Personal selling, however, is often a must in the business-to-business market, and may be used in consumer markets where buyers tend to be fewer in number, more geographically concentrated, and more inclined to purchase in larger quantities and dollar amounts. Additionally, personal selling is usually a necessity for complex products, high-involvement buying situations, and transactions involving trade-ins.

The Evolution of Personal Selling and the Changing Face of Sales

At one time, sales companies believed customers had to be forced into making a purchase. Salespeople utilizing the **hard sell** sought to make an immediate sale without being concerned about meeting the needs of the customer; this type of selling attitude resulted in singular transactional exchanges. That is, when customers purchased from these "hard sell" representatives, and learned that the products truly did not meet the customers' needs, they recognized that the salespersons were not working to satisfy their customers. Consequently, these customers would not purchase from those salespersons again, so these representatives gained only a one-time transaction. Additionally, the hard sell sometimes bordered on the unethical or even illegal.

Today, many businesses are experimenting with approaches other than the hard sell; thus, personal selling has begun to focus on the important concept of **relationship selling.** That is, the salesperson focuses on meeting customer needs, not just selling his or her product. When the salesperson clearly identifies customer needs and seeks to provide the best product to meet those needs, the salesperson is able to develop a long-term relationship with the customer. Not only does the customer benefit from this relationship, but the salesperson also benefits by way of the many future sales that are yielded from this relationship over time. In today's business environment, the goal is to develop long-term relationships with customers. However, to assist firms in identifying the best customers on which to focus their sales efforts, companies are adopting **customer relationship management** (CRM) strategies and applications.

Similar to the way in which sales has evolved from a hard sell to a relationship selling approach, the face of the sales force has also changed such as from men to women and from nonminorities to minorities.

The Sales Professions: Rewards and Drawbacks

Several studies suggest college students are not interested in pursuing a career in the sales profession.[195] Unfortunately, the all too frequent portrayal of salespeople as fast-talking, glad-handing, slick characters with highly questionable ethics has tainted the sales profession, so that many people think of selling as an undesirable profession. They fail to realize how highly dependent large and small companies are on the revenues that salespeople generate. If you do not think this is true, try staying in business without selling something. Further, salespeople provide expertise in the field to customers seeking product information. Salespeople also spot and report potential competitive and market trends, so their companies can respond appropriately.[196] Consequently, salespeople are truly vital to the business world.

Exhibit 300.65 *Benefits of Sales Occupations*

- Flexibility in day-to-day activities
- Intrinsic reward from helping customers
- Good compensation
- Travel opportunities
- Increasing responsibilities
- High-visibility career track
- Promotion potential

Exhibit 300.66 *Desirable Salesperson Traits*

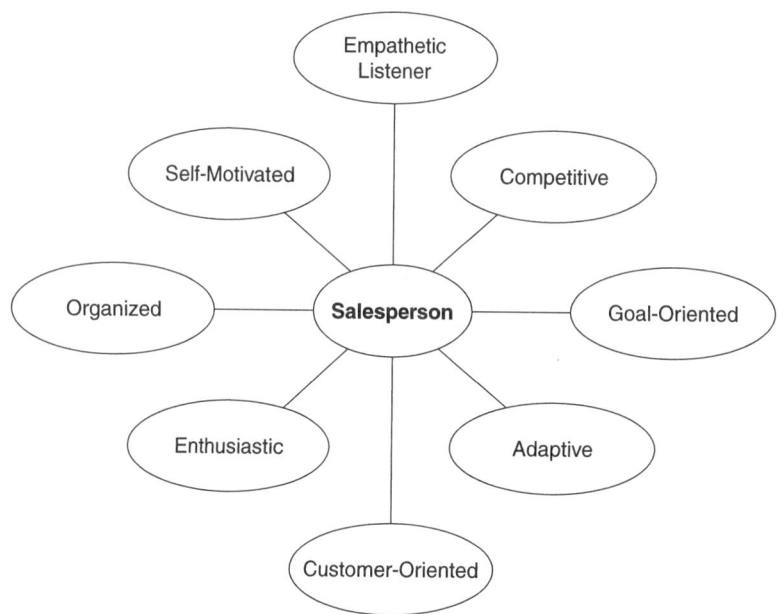

Sales positions also offer many advantages, which are summarized in Exhibit 300.65. There is great flexibility in sales activities, so no two workdays are alike. There are intrinsic rewards gained in meeting the needs of customers and feeling that you have helped someone else. There are also extrinsic rewards. First, potential compensation is quite high. Frequently, the compensation includes a company car, laptop computer, and cellular telephone to make the total compensation package even more valuable. Further, sales positions frequently offer travel opportunities, increasing responsibility, and limited supervision. Finally, it is also a great career track because of its high visibility.

Sales, like all professions, also presents a few drawbacks. The hours can be long, and it is not unusual for salespeople to experience **role conflict** (e.g., the firm demands that the salesperson obtain a high price for the firm's product, while the customer demands a low price), **role ambiguity** (e.g., many organizational departments—billing, shipping, production, marketing, public relations—may influence the salesperson's activities and create uncertainty about what is expected of the salesperson), and **job anxiety** (e.g., the salesperson must perform, often simultaneously, many tasks: meeting sales objectives, servicing old accounts and producing new accounts, developing and conducting effective sales presentations, developing product and competitor knowledge, submitting timely reports to the company, and controlling sales expenses).[197]

DESIRABLE SALESPERSON TRAITS Good salespeople must be self-motivated, organized, enthusiastic, adaptive, competitive, goal-oriented, empathetic, and most importantly, **customer-oriented,** as shown in Exhibit 300.66. This last trait has been found to be the most significant differentiating factor between successful and mediocre salespeople.

Selling Environments and Types of Salespeople

Personal selling occurs in different environments, and each environment determines which types of selling are utilized. The three environments in which personal selling may occur are telemarketing, over-the-counter selling, and field selling (see Exhibit 300.67).

Exhibit 300.67 *Selling Environments and Types of Salespeople*

Selling Environments	Selling Types
Telemarketing	Outbound telemarketers
	Inbound telemarketers
Over-the-Counter	Order takers
	Order getters
Field Selling	Professional salespeople
	National account managers
	Missionary salespeople
	Support salespeople

Telemarketing

Telemarketing utilizes the telephone for prospecting, selling, and/or following up with customers. Two types of salespeople are generally found in this environment. *Outbound telemarketers* are salespersons who use the telephone to call customers and close deals. *Inbound telemarketers,* on the other hand, are those salespeople who answer telephone calls from customers and help them place orders. Firms that employ inbound telemarketers often have toll-free phone numbers as a convenience for their customers. Of the three selling environments, telemarketing, in general, tends to rely less on relationship development with customers.

Over-the-Counter Selling

Over-the-counter selling is usually conducted in retail outlets. As a consumer, you choose to enter a store where you may be greeted by a retail salesperson. If the store you have selected is heavily oriented toward self-service, your only interaction with a salesperson may be when you have to track one down to obtain an answer to a specific question you have regarding the merchandise. In this type of store, the over-the-counter salesperson will usually act only as an **order taker,** ringing up and appropriately packaging what you wish to purchase without imparting any product-specific knowledge. On the other hand, if the store is oriented toward personal service, the salesperson is likely to try to identify what it is you are seeking and to help you with merchandise selection. The salesperson may even practice **suggestion selling.** For example, if you go into a store with the intention of purchasing a business suit, the salesperson may make suggestions regarding styles and colors. After your selection is made, the salesperson may suggest a tie or blouse that will match the suit. In these situations, the salesperson is acting as an **order getter.**

Field Selling

As in over-the-counter selling environments, salespeople involved in **field selling** may act as order takers, such as in the food industry, or as order getters, such as in the encyclopedia business. Many salespersons in the field selling environment, however, are categorized as professional salespeople, national account managers, missionary salespeople, or support salespeople.

PROFESSIONAL SALESPEOPLE *Professional salespeople* may be found in all industries, but especially in industries where products are adapted to individual customer needs, such as high-tech computers. The companies for which they work may assign professional salespeople a variety of job titles, including account executive, sales consultant, or sales representative.

NATIONAL ACCOUNT MANAGERS *National account managers* are highly skilled salespersons who call on key customers' headquarters sites, develop strategic plans for the accounts, make formal presentations to top-level executives, and assist with all the product decisions at that level.[198] Consequently, important customers associate one key person—the national account manager—with the vendor company, and the vendor company does not need to have its other salespeople call on all the local branches of a large, diverse customer.

National account managers are expected to know their customers' businesses intimately; consequently, national account managers call on very few accounts. Indeed, it is not unusual for a national account manager to be responsible for just one customer, if the customer is a very large one. Customers who are assigned national account managers have enormous sales potential and more complex buying behaviors, due to their multiple locations and various operating units. The national account manager's job is to provide these special accounts with greater attention and service to ensure that a partnership develops between the two organizations.

MISSIONARY SALESPEOPLE *Missionary salespeople* differ from other sales professionals in that they do not seek to obtain a direct order from their customers. Although they are charged with providing product information to customers, their primary goal is to persuade customers to place orders with distributors or wholesalers. For example, the goal of Kraft Foods salespeople is to convince the managers of grocery stores to place orders with food wholesalers for Kraft products. Pharmaceutical representatives are also missionary salespeople. Their job is to provide detailed information to physicians, so that the physicians will prescribe the drug to patients. These patients, in turn, will purchase the prescription from one of the pharmaceutical firm's resellers, such as a drug store.

SUPPORT SALESPEOPLE *Support salespeople* do not actually perform all the steps in the sales process; instead, their job is to support the sales force in a number of ways. Technical support salespeople serve as technical advisors to the sales force, and prospective customers, on complex products such as data networking systems. They are often teamed with a sales representative to assist with the technical aspects of sales presentations. Other support salespeople, sometimes known as merchandisers, set up product displays in the customer's business after the sales representative has obtained the customer's permission to do so. Still other types of support salespeople complete and follow up on order processing, and do other related administrative tasks in order to free the salesperson to spend more time with customers.

The Sales Process

There are eight basic steps in the sales process: prospecting, the preapproach, the approach, need identification, presentation, handling objections, gaining commitment, and follow-up (see Exhibit 300.68). In the *traditional selling method*, little time is spent on the early stages of the process—especially the approach and need identification. Consequently, the prospective buyer is not usually convinced that he or she really needs the product, so gaining commitment from the buyer is difficult, tedious, and time-consuming. In the *professional selling method*, a great deal of time is spent in the early stages—prospecting, preapproach, approach, and need identification phases, so that commitment is gained as a very nat-

Exhibit 300.68 *The Sales Process*

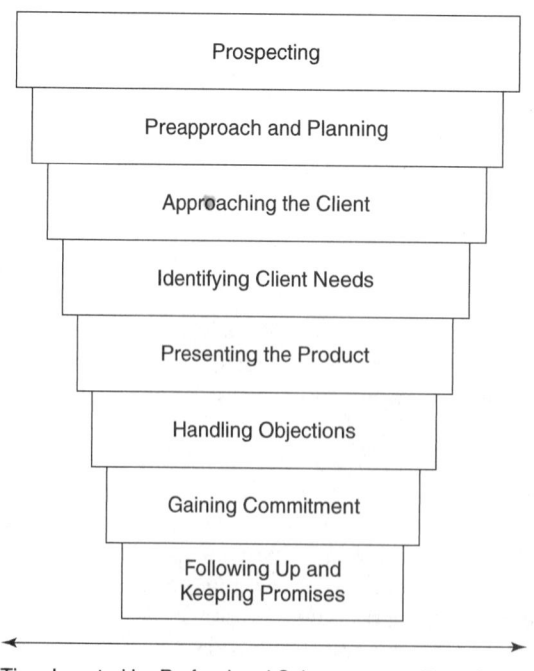

Time Invested by Professional Salesperson at Each Stage

ural, or logical, next step. Essentially, customers are convinced that the product will solve their problem, or meet their need, because early in the sales process care has been taken to establish that need and link it to the benefits of the product. In the following sections, each of the eight steps in the sales process is discussed.

Step 1: Prospecting

Prospecting involves finding **qualified sales leads.** There are many ways to find sales leads: cold calling, working trade shows, networking through industry associations or social organizations, offering educational seminars, and reading trade journals and newspaper business pages. One of the better means of finding leads, though, is through **referrals.** Generating just one referral is as effective as making 12 cold calls.[199] Prior to asking for referrals, a salesperson should ensure that the current customer is satisfied. But once a strong relationship has been established, the salesperson should not hesitate to ask for a referral. Referred leads usually mean faster closings, shorter sales cycles, and larger initial transactions.[200] Unfortunately, few salespeople ask for referrals, although over 80 percent of customers report they would gladly provide them.[201]

Although most salespeople dislike making cold calls, nearly all salespeople must conduct some **cold-calling** at some point in their careers. Some cold calling is done by phoning prospects. When utilizing the telephone for cold calls, most salespeople attempt only to secure a definite appointment with the prospect, although other salespeople will attempt to complete the sale over the phone. Cold calling may also involve stopping by the customer's business or home location without a prearranged appointment. While this face-to-face interaction can be quite effective, some customers may have strict rules concerning when salespeople are allowed to see their employees for solicitation purposes. Salespeople should familiarize themselves with the company policies before dropping in to visit.

Many salespeople have a fear of cold calling because they fear rejection. On average, a salesperson has to make 3 to 5 sales calls for every one sale; however, for some industries, this ratio may be 1 in 10 or 1 in 25 calls. Consequently, salespeople should not become discouraged. They can remain motivated by remembering that sales is a numbers game—sales representatives will likely hear many "nos" before they hear a "yes."

Once prospects have been identified, these potential buyers should be incorporated into a customer relationship management database that will help salespeople have the right information, including the most effective contact method, at the right time.[202]

Step 2: Preapproach and Planning

The preapproach is the collection of information about the potential customer and the customer's company prior to the initial visit. In very much the same way that job candidates should research any firm with whom they are going to interview, salespeople should also research any prospective client and the client's company.[203] A salesperson should seek answers to the following questions:

- Who will make the purchase decisions?
- What are that person's interests?
- What is that person's job title?
- What does the company do?
- Who are their primary competitors?
- Which direct competitors are currently doing business with the customer?
- What rules does the prospective customer have regarding salespeople?

In other words, the sales representative should want to obtain as much information as possible about the prospect and their company. One quick source for this information may be the local library or the Internet. Many firms have Web sites that provide useful company information. Researching the prospect and the prospect's company will indicate that the salesperson is serious about earning the prospect's business. This information also assists the salesperson in planning the initial presentation to the prospective customer.

Step 3: Approaching the Client

The approach is the development of rapport with the customer. Using the information the salesperson has already gathered, the salesperson begins developing a relationship with the customer. The salesperson wants to illustrate that he or she is working to understand and assist in meeting the prospective customer's needs. In this stage, it is important that the salesperson adapt to the potential customer's social style.

Exhibit 300.69 *Social Styles*

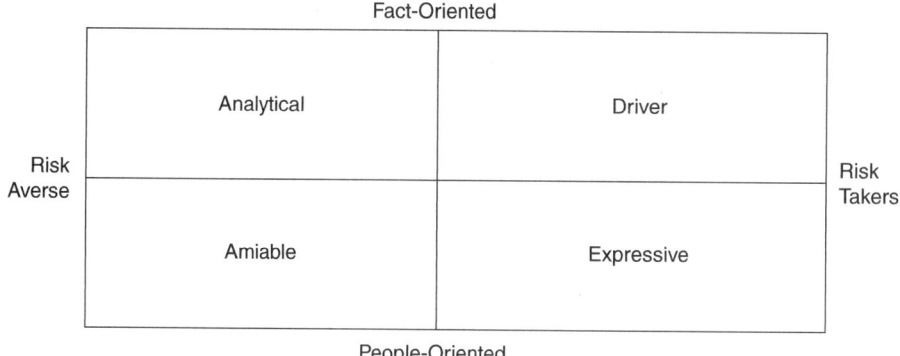

SOCIAL STYLES There are four basic social style categories,[204] which are depicted in Exhibit 300.69.

1. The *driver* is action- and goal-oriented, and makes quick decisions. To adapt to this social style, the salesperson should provide the bottom-line information first, and then work backward to fill in essential details. The driver will want only the basic facts and will not want to socialize a great deal.
2. The *analytical* is fact- and detail-oriented. This individual will require time to make decisions, while carefully weighing all the facts. To adapt to this social style, the salesperson should inundate the analytical prospect with facts and figures that can be supported with documentation. Like the driver, the analytical is not very interested in developing a personal relationship with the salesperson.
3. The *expressive* loves to socialize and will frequently base the purchase decision on the relationship with the salesperson. To adapt to this social style, the salesperson should be prepared to establish a personal relationship with the expressive prospect by telling anecdotal stories, by socializing outside the office, and by relating personal information.
4. The *amiable* tends to be a visionary with big ideas for the future, but is not a detail-oriented individual. The amiable prospect is hesitant to make quick decisions and will seek consensus from others before reaching a purchase decision. The amiable also seeks to have a personal relationship with the salesperson, as this relationship helps reduce some of the anxiety that is felt about making a decision. To adapt to this social style, the salesperson should establish a personal relationship and provide assurances that will reduce the amiable's feeling of risk. Further, the sales representative should present the product based on what it will do for the customer in the "big picture," and avoid getting into discussions of minute details.

Other factors must be considered in the approach stage. This is the salesperson's chance to make a good first impression. Consequently, the salesperson should dress neatly and professionally. Prospects should be greeted with a firm handshake and direct eye contact. Throughout the sales interview, the salesperson should maintain an open body posture to indicate interest and openness to the customer; that is, the salesperson should keep feet flat on the floor, body leaning slightly forward, direct eye contact, arms open (uncrossed), and hands open, palms slightly upward. The salesperson should also let the customer know that he or she is actively listening by rephrasing or summarizing important points the customer has made.

Step 4: Identifying Client Needs

PROBING QUESTIONS Success at the need-identification stage of the sales process requires asking probing questions of the prospective customer to determine needs. These needs may be organizational and/or personal. Organizational needs may involve finance, image, or performance issues, whereas personal needs may involve the ego or self-image. To obtain information about the prospect's needs, the salesperson should ask open-ended questions. Such questions are designed to elicit a true expression of the prospect's opinions and feelings, regardless of whether these opinions are favorable or unfavorable in the salesperson's view. The salesperson should use open-ended, or probing, questions frequently throughout the sales presentation to ensure that the customer's needs and potential concerns are addressed. The key here is to learn what prospective customers want, not just to try to sell whatever the salesperson has to offer.[205] After needs have been identified, the salesperson should gain the prospect's permission to begin the presentation.

Exhibit 300.70 *Presentation Styles*

Flexible Presentations
- Identify customer needs
- Customize presentation

Memorized Presentations
- Do not address specific needs of customer
- Scripts feature key benefits and selling points

Step 5: Presenting the Product

FEATURES VERSUS BENEFITS   Customers buy products not because of the features they offer, but because of the needs these features satisfy. Therefore, the focus of the sales presentation is the salesperson's explanation of how a product's features provide "benefits" that specifically address the prospect's previously identified needs or problems. These benefits should answer the buyer's often unvocalized question, "What's in it for me?" For example, rather than simply telling buyers that a shampoo contains special conditioners (feature), the marketer must tell the buyers that their hair will be softer and shinier (benefit) because of these special conditioners.

TYPES OF PRESENTATIONS   Presentations may be flexible or memorized (see Exhibit 300.70). *Flexible presentations* allow the salesperson to identify the customer's needs and customize the presentation specifically for the individual customer. This type of presentation is sometimes called a *need-satisfaction presentation,* and is the preferred method for professional salespeople. *Memorized presentations* require that the salesperson commit a scripted presentation to memory. This type of presentation, sometimes called a *canned presentation,* does not address the specific needs of each customer; however, the script has been built around the best key benefits and selling points of the company and the product. Salespeople who sell to consumers in their homes may employ this method of presentation. For example, book companies that sell door-to-door often have their sales representatives use memorized presentations with successful results. This approach should be used with caution since it may create a perception of unoriginality, thereby making customers feel as if they are not special or important.

To improve the effectiveness of their presentations, many salespeople now incorporate the latest technology via laptop computers. Thus, sales representatives may employ computer graphics and/or Web sites in their sales presentations to generate increased attention and interest from prospective customers.

Step 6: Handling Objections

Prospective buyers frequently raise objections as to why they should buy a particular product. However, these objections do not necessarily mean that the prospect is uninterested in the product. Instead, objections likely indicate the salesperson has failed to provide adequate information to the buyer, or has not demonstrated how the product meets the needs of the prospect. Consequently, the prospective customer is afraid that he or she may be making a mistake in purchasing the product.[206] When faced with objections, the salesperson should approach the objection as a sign of interest on the part of the prospect, and provide information that will ensure the prospect's confidence in making the purchase. As a salesperson becomes more experienced, he will recognize that certain objections occur on a regular basis. After discerning what these common objections are, the salesperson should work to provide information early in the presentation that will counter these objections. For example, if the salesperson routinely hears prospective buyers say, "The price is too high," the salesperson should strive to emphasize the higher quality or special attributes offered by the product. Consequently, the prospect will recognize that added features/higher quality compensate for the higher price; thus, good value is still offered.

PROVIDING SUPPORTING EVIDENCE   During the presentation, the salesperson should be prepared to document any statements of fact that are made. This documentation can come from a variety of sources, including letters of testimony from satisfied customers, independent reports, newspaper or magazine articles, company brochures or other literature, and product demonstrations. For example, a hotel sales manager might explain to a potential client that numerous companies have used the hotel's facilities to hold their annual meetings and have been quite satisfied. The salesperson should then produce letters of testimony from various companies that support the claim of satisfied corporate clientele.

Step 7: Gaining Commitment

Commitment is gained when the prospect agrees to take the action sought by the salesperson. Usually, this means the buyer purchases the product, or at least signs a purchase agreement. However, prospects will not usually come right out and say they want to buy what the salesperson is offering; the salesperson must ask for commitment. In other words, *the salesperson must ask for the order,* just as the interviewee should ask for the job.[207] Failure to ask for an order frequently is the cause of a salesperson's unsuccessful presentation. Indeed, salespeople do not ask customers to buy in approximately 70 percent of all sales calls! Yet, the sales profession recognizes the importance of this stage of the sales process as evidenced by the numerous books written on gaining commitment.[208]

Step 8: Following Up and Keeping Promises

The last step in the sales process, follow-up, requires that the salesperson complete any agreed upon actions. Unfortunately, while salespeople may work very hard to get a customer, they frequently fail to follow through on their promises, so they cannot keep these customers. As noted in previous sections, it is much more expensive to obtain a new customer than it is to keep an old one; consequently, it is imperative that salespeople keep any promises they make to customers.

Additionally, salespeople should stay in touch after a sale by writing thank-you notes, clipping and mailing newspaper articles of interest to the prospect, and occasionally calling on customers just to ensure that they are still happy with their purchase decisions.

Building and Managing the Sales Force

Selling is the revenue stream of the corporation. Managing this vital function requires strong skills so that the sales force will continue to generate the money to fund the rest of the organization. Sales management is the process of planning, directing, controlling, and implementing the personal selling function of the organization.

Sales managers must be good leaders who can recruit, train, motivate, and evaluate their sales representatives; manage territories; and develop sales plans and sales forecasts, while accomplishing the goals of the organization (see Exhibit 300.71).[209] They also need to be able to identify business opportunities and to create appropriate strategies. They must constantly encourage the sales team to exceed customer expectations, develop long-term relationships, and create added value for the customer.[210]

Recruiting the Sales Force

Sales managers must recruit the right individuals for any open sales positions. A sales force composed of the right people makes a big difference in how large a company can grow. The individuals the sales manager hires should possess the attributes previously discussed: empathy, competitiveness, goal orientation, customer orientation, enthusiasm, organization, and self-motivation. In addition, the sales manager should recruit individuals whose values and goals match those of the firm. This congruency will facilitate greater job satisfaction among new recruits.

To hire the best salespeople, the sales manager should not rely solely on résumés, but should pay close attention to how candidates conduct themselves throughout the interview process. For example, if the first contact is by telephone, the candidate should ask for an appointment. Candidates who do not ask are unlikely to ask for orders from prospective customers. Candidates should also demonstrate persistence by staying in touch with the sales manager, and not just waiting for the sales manager to call back. Additionally, candidates should be good listeners. Candidates

Exhibit 300.71 *Sales Manager's Tasks*

- Recruiting
- Training
- Motivating
- Compensating
- Evaluating
- Territory organization

who talk more than 50 percent of the time may not be effective at listening to prospects and customers. Finally, candidates should ask for the job. Candidates who do not ask for the job will probably be too timid to ask for commitment from prospective customers.[211]

Many sales organizations have resorted to objective tests to assist them in selecting the best sales candidates. These include personality tests, critical thinking, and role-playing.

Training the Sales Force

CORPORATE CULTURE   After hiring the best candidates, sales managers must orient recruits to the company culture. Additionally, sales managers must train new sales representatives on product and customer knowledge and selling skills. Further, training is essential to the success of the sales force. Consequently, all sales representatives, regardless of how long they have been selling, should periodically receive training to stay up-to-date and to keep their skills honed.

PRODUCT KNOWLEDGE AND SALES SKILLS   The focus of training should be on product knowledge and sales skills. Good product knowledge is essential for making presentations and handling objections; whereas the acquisition of good sales skills is necessary for moving effectively through the sales process. Sales representatives should be taught to identify the social styles of customers and alter their presentations for each customer type. In other words, sales representatives should know and practice *adaptive selling*. In addition, the sales force should learn to develop attention-getting openings and good listening skills, focus on customer needs, handle objections, and be able to close the sale. More advanced salespeople should be trained in strategic account management and the development of long-term customer relationships. They should understand the importance of identifying the organizational structure, key decision makers, and decision influencers in their customers' organizations. They must learn more about their customers' businesses and how they can help customers be more profitable. Finally, all salespeople should be trained in how to utilize the latest technology to improve their ability to serve customers.

SALES FORCE TECHNOLOGY   The use of technology among sales forces is growing. Many companies are mandating that their sales forces operate from "virtual offices" equipped with laptop computers, cell phones, and portable printer-copier-fax machines, rather than driving to corporate headquarters each day.[212] These virtual offices allow a sales force to spend more time in the field with customers. Salespeople use the laptop computers to electronically communicate with their corporate office several times a day. Indeed, sales data are now routinely processed electronically for faster service to the customer. Computers are also used to prepare sales presentations to customers, receive continuous updates on products and pricing, and as noted earlier, may be a vehicle for sales training.[213] Cell phones are also standard equipment for most sales forces, and those phones with advanced features, such as Internet capabilities, are becoming increasingly popular.

Finally, some sales managers are also suggesting their sales forces use a software program that allows sales representatives to enter their geographical location and immediately receive a listing and location of all current and potential accounts in the area. Such a program allows sales representatives to use their time more efficiently.

Frequently, sales training requires travel to a distant location and overnight stays in a hotel. For companies with large sales forces, the cost of such training can run into the millions of dollars, which precludes conducting frequent training. In today's high-tech world, though, many companies are training their sales forces with online or Web-based learning. The salespeople involved are able to use their own computers to link into a training session from their homes or hotel rooms if they are on the road visiting clients. This technology allows the sales force to come together in a virtual classroom where they can interact with classmates and the instructor.[214] Other companies are more flexible, allowing their sales forces to tap into the Internet whenever the need arises to become informed about new offerings or to refresh themselves on a particular product.[215] Consequently, firms are now able to offer their salespeople more frequent training, without requiring that the representatives leave their sales territories and their customers.

Motivating the Sales Force

Sales representatives are individuals, and what motivates one may not motivate the other.[216] Sales managers have to employ a variety of methods for keeping all of these diverse individuals motivated, or incited, to put forth maximum effort. After all, the sales profession can be a high-pressure job that involves frequent rejection. For some salespeople, working to beat the set quota and winning sales contests is a great motivator. Winning builds confidence and reinforces the notion that the individual is a great sales representative. Other salespeople are motivated by extra training sessions that challenge them and groom them for upper management positions. Sales managers may also find some top-performing individuals are motivated by acting as a mentor to newer sales representatives, or by being sought for their advice and wisdom. Some salespeople are most motivated when their strong customer service efforts are recognized throughout the company, such as printing a letter from a grateful client in the company newsletter.[217] Finally, sales forces may be driven to perform at a high level when they are having fun at work. Many companies ensure that their sales staff's morale is routinely boosted by theme days, games, and humor.[218] In summary, sales managers must identify what best motivates each of their sales representatives and then strive to motivate and reward them accordingly.

SALES FORCE QUOTAS Sales force quotas are used throughout the sales industry to further motivate salespeople and to encourage them to focus on company priorities. Basically, the sales manager provides each sales representative with a reward when the sales representative, or in some cases, the sales team, reaches a prespecified performance level called the *quota*.[219] The quota should be high enough to encourage the sales force to put forth greater effort, yet low enough to appear obtainable. Otherwise, the quotas that the sales manager sets may serve to discourage rather than motivate the sales force. Similarly, the reward offered for meeting or exceeding the quota should be of sufficient value. If it is too low, the sales force may deem that it is not worth their extra effort to achieve.

SALES COACHING Coaching involves regular praising of salespeople to let them know their efforts are appreciated. It also involves rapport-building, open communication, and modeling behavior. The goal of the sales coach is to develop a relationship of mutual trust and respect with the sales force, which in turn encourages the sales force to listen to and follow directives from the sales manager. Good sales management feedback has also been found to reduce the role conflict and role ambiguity often associated with the sales profession. Finally, the sales manager serves as a model to the sales force so they know what behavior and actions to emulate. Sales manager coaching has consistently been found to motivate salespeople to improve their performance.[220]

Sales call anxiety (SCA) Fear of negative evaluation and rejection by customers.

As part of the coaching function, sales managers should assist sales representatives in overcoming **sales call anxiety** (SCA).[221] Most often sales call anxiety surfaces during the prospecting or closing phases of the sales process, and can be quite debilitating to the success of the salesperson. Sales managers should familiarize themselves with the various strategies that exist for overcoming SCA and work with sales representatives who may be avoiding initiating customer contact or gaining customer commitment.[222]

Compensating the Sales Force

CONTINUUM: STRAIGHT SALARY TO STRAIGHT COMMISSION Sales managers may also be responsible for determining how the sales force will be compensated for their efforts. The level of compensation may be established anywhere on a continuum from straight salary on one end to straight commission on the other (see Exhibit 300.72). That is, the sales manager may choose to pay the sales force a *straight salary*, in which pay is based on units of time (year, month, week, or hour). This form of compensation provides the sales force with greater security, but may reduce their desire to put forth extra efforts, because they will not receive a direct reward for this effort. The sales manager may choose to compensate the sales force on the basis of *straight commission*, in which pay is based on units of results. In this case, the sales representatives' pay is based solely on how much they sell. For many companies this has been the traditional means of rewarding the sales force. Straight commission, however, can create a great deal of insecurity in sales representatives since some factors not in their control, like an economic recession, may cause a downturn in their sales, and hence a reduction in their salary. The third method by which the sales manager may compensate the sales force is through a combination of the previous two, *salary plus commission*. Accordingly, the sales manager pays the sales force a sufficient base salary that provides just enough money for a basic standard of living, but also pays a commission on sales that is high enough to serve as an incentive for extra sales efforts. This base salary plus high commission can allow a motivated salesperson to earn a six-figure income. A variation on this latter method of compensation is the *profit-center approach* which requires that sales revenues be used to cover the sales force's corporate expenses and contribute toward the corporation's predefined level of profitability, beyond which all remaining funds are retained by the sales

Exhibit 300.72 *The Salary Continuum*

Exhibit 300.73 *Comparison of Compensation Plans*

Straight Salary
- Provides Security
- Reduces Motivation

Straight Commission
- Increases Motivation
- Creates Insecurity

Salary Plus Commission
- Provides Job Security
- Provides Motivation

force. Supporters of this approach indicate that such a compensation plan allows the sales force to earn unlimited incomes, but also guarantees profitability for the organization (see Exhibit 300.73).[223]

In today's environment where the focus is on long-term relationships and where e-commerce is altering the sales landscape, many companies are finding it necessary to adapt their method of compensating the sales force. The use of compensation plans that incorporate high commissions on sales units encourages the sales force to make quick sales without regard to actual customer needs; it does not encourage the sales force to take the time to establish relationships with their customers. Furthermore, customers are determining the sales channel (i.e., Internet, telemarketing, face-to-face) most appropriate for their particular needs. Consequently, some companies have set up different types of compensation plans in which a portion of commission money may be tied to customer satisfaction, customer retention rates, share of customer's business, or other nonrevenue objectives, and only a small portion is linked directly to sales dollars.[224] At the same time, other incentives encourage the sales force to integrate their efforts with e-commerce and support rapid, continuous corporate change.[225] Such a compensation plan facilitates long-term relationships between the salesperson and the customer, and in the long run, will better benefit the company.

Evaluating Salespeople's Performance

Another task of the sales manager is the evaluation of the sales force's performance. Evaluation of the sales force should not be performed only once a year. In conjunction with sales coaching guidelines, sales managers should provide continual guidance and feedback.

QUALITATIVE AND QUANTITATIVE FACTORS The sales manager may choose to evaluate, or assess, the sales force on a combination of quantitative or qualitative factors. However, past studies have found that sales managers weight subjective, qualitative factors more heavily than quantitative variables when assessing salesperson performance. The most popular qualitative factors used for evaluation are communication skills, product knowledge, attitude, selling skills, initiative/aggressiveness, appearance/manner, and knowledge of the competition. The most commonly used quantitative factors are sales volume in dollars, sales volume to previous year's sales, number of new accounts, net dollar profits, and sales volume by dollar quota. Although qualitative measures of employee appraisals have value, experts suggest that sales managers should use more quantitative methods of evaluation to reduce bias in the evaluation process.[226] A promising metric that assesses a salesperson's ability to focus on both customer satisfaction and revenue maximization appears to be *RevPASH* (revenue per available salesperson hour).[227] RevPASH evaluation encourages salespeople to focus their sales efforts on customer segments that will generate the highest income, while accounting for customer expectations regarding sales force time.

Organizing and Managing Sales Territories

GEOGRAPHICAL AND PRODUCT LINE ORGANIZATION Sales managers have a number of options when it comes to organizing the sales territories of their salespeople. Sales territories organized by product line or by geographical area are the more traditional means of organizing sales forces. Under geographical and product line territory organization, salespeople are often required to sell to *all* customers within a geographic area, although their product line may be somewhat limited. In either case, though, they call on customers who represent dozens of different industries.

Today, however, more and more sales managers are organizing sales territories around customers.[228] In this case, the salesperson is asked to call on customers in one or two specific industries, regardless of where the customer is located geographically. This allows the salesperson to become an expert in the particular industry to which he or she is assigned. Consequently, the salesperson can develop a better understanding of the customer's problems, which facilitates the development of a close, long-term relationship between the sales representative and the customer.

TERRITORY ALLOCATION After deciding by which method to organize the territories, the sales manager must then divide up the territories among the company's salespeople. There are two criteria that should guide territory allocation: (1) all salespersons should feel that their territory offers as much potential as their colleagues' territory, and (2) all should feel the territory division does not require that they work harder than any other salesperson. To achieve these goals, the sales manager must determine the *revenue potential* of each account (regardless of whether the account is a current or potential customer), and how much of the sales representative's time is required to service each account.[229] Then, individual sales territories can be allocated to sales representatives in an equitable manner.

TERRITORY POTENTIAL The sales manager should also help the sales force maximize their territories' potential. The sales manager can accomplish this by encouraging sales representatives to devote their time and efforts to profitable accounts, and not waste efforts on accounts that are not potentially profitable to the company. Sales managers need to ensure that sales representatives get the maximum potential from all their accounts, and not just meet their quotas because of the large purchases of one key buyer. Finally, sales managers need to utilize market research to ensure no potential accounts are overlooked in any given territory.[230]

REVIEW OF TERRITORY ALLOCATIONS Once territories are established, the sales manager should review them on a quarterly basis. This will not only assist the sales manager with the sales budget, but may also indicate where realignment of territories needs to occur. Key areas to check are those territories where the salesperson consistently exceeds, or fails to make, his/her quota. When a salesperson regularly exceeds the set quota, the sales manager should ensure that this is not due to the territory potential being so large that the sales representative has to make virtually no effort to reach quota. If this is the case, the quota should be raised, or if the territory potential warrants it, a new representative should be added to the area. In the case of the salesperson who never makes quota, the sales manager must determine if this is a function of a person's lack of sales ability or of a territory with truly poor potential. In the latter situation, the representative's territory should be expanded to include new accounts.[231]

Analysis of a Markov process model is not intended to optimize any particular aspect of a system. Rather, the analysis predicts or describes the future and steady-state behavior of the system. For instance, the analysis of the steady-state behavior provided a forecast or prediction of the market shares for the two competitors involved in local grocery business.

Ethics and Sales

Legal and Ethical Responsibilities in Selling and Sales Management

Sales Representative's Legal Responsibilities

A sales representative has certain legal obligations to his or her employer.

- The salesperson is required to obey the instructions of the company.
- The salesperson must act with "due diligence."
- The salesperson is responsible and accountable for the company's property.
- The salesperson is expected to exhibit loyalty.
- The salesperson must relay information to the company that is relevant.[232]

Failure to meet these duties subjects the salesperson to termination, forfeiture of compensation, and liability for damages to the company.

The Firm's Legal Responsibilities

At the same time, the company has legal responsibilities to the salesperson.

- The company must comply with any agreement it makes with the salesperson.
- The company must act in good faith.
- The company must reimburse the salesperson for reasonable expenses incurred while carrying out company business.
- The company is required to warn the salesperson of any risks associated with carrying out the company's business.
- The company must protect the salesperson against legal liability for any damage, loss, or injury that occurs in the course of business.[233]

Unethical/Illegal Behaviors

Selling, like numerous other professions, offers many opportunities for unethical and illegal behaviors, and unfortunately, ethical issues are often closely tied to the type of relationships that sales representatives have with their customers and sales managers.[234] Common unethical, and sometimes illegal, practices found in the sales arena include: price discrimination and unfair pricing; gifts, gratuities, and bribes; misleading advertising; unfair competitive practices; defrauding customers; unfair credit practices; and price collusion with competitive firms.[235]

PRUDENT CLAIMS Salespersons must be especially prudent in making claims to customers about the performance, capabilities, or qualities of the salespersons' products. That is, sales representatives need to guard against overzealousness in their efforts to "make the sale." They must ensure that their presentations do not contain any false or misleading statements or promises about the products under consideration. Sales misrepresentation, which has recently come under heavy scrutiny from the courts, can result in large fines for the salesperson's company, and the salesperson's expulsion from professional organizations.[236]

CODES OF CONDUCT Sales management can reduce unethical or illegal behaviors and the ethical conflicts often experienced by sales representatives, by communicating clear, unambiguous messages concerning appropriate behaviors in various situations likely to be encountered by salespeople. These messages should be strongly supported by company codes of conduct. Sales managers can further reduce unethical behavior by appropriately reprimanding sales representatives who conduct themselves improperly.[237]

Sexual Harassment

An issue of special concern for salespeople and sales managers is sexual harassment. Because salespeople serve as boundary spanners between their own company and the companies of their customers, they can be especially vulnerable targets for sexual harassment by people outside of their own organization (e.g., customers). That is, the relationships and social interaction necessary for the sales profession may make sales representatives especially susceptible to sexual harassment. Furthermore, sexual harassment affects both males and females.[238]

Sexual harassment may take the form of sexual favors, unwanted sexual advances, or other behaviors of a sexual nature, when submission to these behaviors becomes a condition of employment, affects employment decisions such as promotions, and substantially interferes with an individual's work performance, or creates a hostile work environment.[239] Sexual harassment results in reduced job performance, and physiological and emotional health problems for the person who is harassed, which in turn affects the bottom line of the company. Consequently, sales managers should provide training on the nature and consequences of sexual harassment to prevent sexual harassment from occurring within the company or a client's company.[240]

Sales managers must take timely action if they are aware of occurrences of sexual harassment; otherwise the sales organization can be held legally responsible.[241] If the alleged harasser is a customer, the sales manager must protect the salesperson, even if such an action means losing the customer's business.[242] Such protection may necessitate reassigning the salesperson, or providing supervision for the salesperson when he or she calls on that customer. In any event, the sales manager should not make it appear the salesperson is being punished for reporting sexual harassment.[243]

395. ETHIC AND SALES

Module 300 Endnotes

1. David S. Landes, *The Wealth and Poverty of Nations* (New York: W.W. Norton & Company, 1988); Joel Mokyr, *The Lever of Riches* (Oxford: Oxford University Press, 1990).
2. A superb history of the development of the global market for clocks and watches is presented in David S. Landes, *Revolution in Time* (Cambridge, MA: Harvard University Press, 1983).
3. Peter D. Bennet, ed., *Dictionary of Marketing Terms* (Chicago: American Marketing Association, 1988), 54.
4. Adapted from William O. Bearden, Thomas N. Ingram, and Raymond W. LaForge, *Marketing*, 2nd ed. (Boston: Irwin McGraw-Hill, 1998), 8.
5. This section adopted from John H. Lindgren, Jr., and Terence A. Shimp, *Marketing: An Interactive Learning System* (Fort Worth, TX: The Dryden Press, 1996), 58.
6. This section was adapted from John Ward Anderson, "Thundering Herd," *The Louisville Courier-Journal,* January 2, 1994, A8; John E. G. Bateson and K. Douglas Hoffman, *Managing Services Marketing* (Fort Worth, TX: The Dryden Press, 1999), XI, 6.
7. *Product* refers to both physical goods such as cars and shampoos and to services such as banking, dining, and consulting, as well as to ideas and people. For example, graduates are a college "product." Developing new services frequently requires developing both a physical good as well as the intangible benefits. For example, a new hotel chain requires developing the physical building, including the room layout, the software and hardware infrastructure to handle reservations and billing, and ancillary physical spaces such as outdoor recreation and parking facilities.
8. The section "Managing the Product Portfolio," presents more on this topic.
9. Abbie Griffin, "PDMA Research on New Product Development Practices: Updating Trends and Benchmarking Best Practices," *Journal of Product Innovation Management* 14, no. 6 (1997), 429–458.
10. The section "Product Management: Managing Products through Their Life Cycles," presents more on this topic.
11. Abbie Griffin and Albert L. Page, "The PDMA Success Measurement Project: Recommended Measures for Product Development Success and Failure," *Journal of Product Innovation Management* 13 (November 1996), 478–496.
12. Abbie Griffin, "PDMA Research on New Product Development Practices," 429–458.
13. *Ibid.*
14. Abbie Griffin and John R. Hauser, "The Voice of the Customer," *Marketing Science* 12, no. 1 (1993), 1–27; Gerald Zaltman and Robin A. Higgie, "Seeing the Voice of the Customer: The Zaltman Elicitation Technique," Working Paper 9-114 (Cambridge, MA: Marketing Science Institute).
15. Griffin, "PDMA Research on New Product Development Practices," 429–458.
16. *Ibid.*
17. *Ibid.*
18. Kim B. Clark and Steven C. Wheelwright, *Managing New Product and Process Development* (New York: Free Press, 1993).
19. Stephen Markham and Abbie Griffin, "The Breakfast of Champions: Associations Between Champions and Product Development Environments, Practices and Performance," *Journal of Product Innovation Management* 14, no. 6 (1998), 436–454.
20. Michael E. McGrath, Michael T. Anthony, and Amram R. Shapiro, *Product Development: Success Through Product and Cycle-Time Excellence* (Boston: Butterworth-Heinemann, 1992).
21. This section is adapted from Peter R. Dickson, *Marketing Management* (Fort Worth, The Dryden Press, 1994), 310–322.
22. This section is adapted from John H. Lindgren, Jr. and Terry Shimp, *Marketing: An Interactive Learning System* (Fort Worth: The Dryden Press, 1996), 227–235.
23. This section is adapted from Lindgren and Shimp, *Marketing: An Interactive Learning System,* 262–264.
24. Don E. Schultz, Stanley I. Tannenbaum, and Robert F. Lauterborn, *Integrated Marketing Communications* (Lincolnwood, IL: NTC Publishing Group, 1993), 46.
25. Charles H. Patti and Charles F. Frazer, *Advertising: A Decision-Making Approach* (Hinsdale, IL: The Dryden Press, 1988), 236.
26. Fred S. Zufryden, "How Much Should Be Spent for Advertising a Brand?" *Journal of Advertising Research* (April/May 1989), 24–34.
27. Gary L. Lilien, Alvin J. Silk, Jean-Marie Choffray, and Murlidhar Rao, "Industrial Advertising Effects and Budgeting Practices," *Journal of Marketing* 40 (January 1976), 21; and Kent M. Lancaster and Judith A. Stern, "Computer-Based Advertising Budgeting Practices of Leading U.S. Consumer Advertisers," *Journal of Advertising* 12, no. 4 (1983), 6.
28. Adapted from A. Jerome Jewler, *Creative Strategy in Advertising* (Belmont, CA: Wadsworth Publishing, 1985), 7–8; and Don E. Schultz and Stanley I. Tannenbaum, *Essentials of Advertising Strategy* (Lincolnwood, IL: NTC Business Books, 1988), 9–10.

29. Stan Freberg, "Irtnog Revisited," *Advertising Age,* August 1, 1988, 32.
30. Description adapted from Don E. Schultz, "The Direct/Database Marketing Challenge to Fixed-Location Retailers," in Robert A. Peterson, ed., *The Future of U.S. Retailing: An Agenda for the 21st Century* (New York: Quorum Books, 1992), 165–184.
31. Terry G. Vavra, *Aftermarketing* (Homewood, IL: Business One Irwin, 1992), 32.
32. Don Schultz as quoted in Gary Levin, "Going Direct Route," *Advertising Age,* November 18, 1991, 37.
33. Terence A. Shimp, *Advertising, Promotion, and Supplemental Aspects of Integrated Marketing Communications,* 5th ed. (Fort Worth, TX: The Dryden Press, 2000).
34. Alvin A. Achenbaum and F. Kent Mitchel, "Pulling Away from Push Marketing," *Harvard Business Review* 65 (May–June 1987): 38–40; and Robert J. Kopp and Stephen A. Greyser, "Packaged Goods Marketing—'Pull' Companies Look to Improved 'Push'," *Journal of Consumer Marketing* 4 (Spring 1987), 13–22.
35. *Cox Direct 20th Annual Survey of Promotional Practices* (Largo, FL: Cox Direct, 1998), 40.
36. Robert C. Blattberg and Scott A. Neslin, "Sales Promotion: The Long and the Short of It," *Marketing Letters* 1, no. 1 (1989), 81–97.
37. This discussion is guided by Charles Fredericks, Jr., "What Ogilvy & Mather Has Learned About Sales Promotion," *The Tools of Promotion* (New York: Association of National Advertisers, 1975); and Don E. Schultz and William A. Robinson, *Sales Promotion Management* (Lincolnwood, IL: NTC Business Books, 1986), chap. 3.
38. Robert C. Blattberg and Alan Levin, "Modeling the Effectiveness and Profitability of Trade Promotions," *Marketing Science* 6 (Spring 1987), 125.
39. See Chakravarthi Narasimhan, "Managerial Perspectives on Trade and Consumer Promotions," *Marketing Letters* 1, no. 3 (1989), 239–251.
40. Rajiv Lal, "Manufacturer Trade Deals and Retail Price Promotions," *Journal of Marketing Research* 27 (November 1990), 428–444; and Ronald C. Curhan and Robert J. Kopp, "Obtaining Retailer Support for Trade Deals: Key Success Factors," *Journal of Advertising Research* 27 (December 1987/January 1988), 51–60.
41. Howard Schlossberg, "Exposed: Retailing's Dirty Little Secret," *Promo* (April 1994), 50–55, and Patricia Sellers, "The Dumbest Marketing Ploy," *Fortune,* October 5, 1992, 88–94.
42. For further discussion, see Shimp, *Advertising, Promotion, and Supplemental Aspects of Integrated Marketing Communications,* chap. 18.
43. Jordan Goldman, *Public Relations in the Marketing Mix* (Lincolnwood, IL: NTC Business Books, 1984).
44. Meryl Paula Gardner and Phillip Joel Shuman, "Sponsorship: An Important Component of the Promotions Mix," *Journal of Advertising* 16, no. 1 (1987), 11–17.
45. P. Rajan Varadarajan and Anil Menon, "Cause-Related Marketing: A Coalignment of Marketing Strategy and Corporate Philanthropy," *Journal of Marketing* 52 (July 1988), 58–74.
46. Cara Beardi, "POP Ups Sales Results," *Advertising Age,* July 23, 2001, 27.
47. Kevin Lane Keller, "Cue Compatibility and Framing in Advertising," *Journal of Marketing Research* 28 (February 1991), 42–57.
48. John H. Lindgren, Jr. and Terence A. Shimp, *Marketing: An Interactive Learning System* (Fort Worth, TX: The Dryden Press, 1996), 378.
49. Example used with permission from Professor Kim Sosin, UNO Center for Economic Education, College of Business Administration, University of Nebraska at Omaha, NE 68182.
50. Gilbert Burck, "The Myths and Realities of Corporate Pricing," *Fortune* (April 1972), 85. See also, Richard Thaler, "Mental Accounting and Consumer Choice," *Marketing Science* (Summer 1985), 199–214.
51. R. Hall and C. Hitch, "Price Theory and Business Behavior," *Oxford Economic Papers* (1939); and Thomas V. Bonoma, Victoria L. Crittenden, and Robert J. Dolan, "Can We Have Rigor and Relevance in Pricing Research?" in T. DeVinney, ed., *Issues in Pricing: Theory and Research,* (Lexington, MA: Lexington Books, 1988).
52. This example is adapted from Thomas T. Nagle and Reed K. Holden, *The Strategy and Tactics of Pricing,* 2nd ed. (Englewood Cliffs, NJ: Prentice Hall, 1995), 19–22.
53. For target ROI pricing, the desired profit per unit is calculated as follows:

$$\text{Desired Profit per Unit} = \frac{(\text{Target Return} + \text{Investment})}{\text{Projected Unit Sales}}$$

54. Nagle and Holden, *The Strategy and Tactics of Pricing,* 3.
55. Simulated purchase tasks have been found to provide reasonably accurate assessments of consumer response to price. See John R. Nevin, "Laboratory Experiments for Estimating Consumer Demand: A Validation Study," *Journal of Marketing Research* (August 1974), 261–268; and Raymond R. Burke, Bari A. Harlam, Barbara E. Kahn, and Leonard M. Lodish, "Comparing Dynamic Consumer Choice in Real and Computer-Simulated Environments," *Journal of Consumer Research* (June 1992), 71–82.
56. One could argue that the symphony consider an even higher price as profits show a continual upward trend as price gets higher.

57. See Daniel Kahneman, Jack L. Knetsch, and Richard H. Thaler, "Fairness as a Constraint on Profit Seeking: Entitlements in the Market," *American Economic Review* 70 (September 1986), 728–741.
58. Robert Axelrod, *The Evolution of Cooperation* (New York: Basic Books, 1984).
59. Jeffrey Tannebaum, "Small Bookseller Beats the Giants at Their Own Game," *Wall Street Journal,* November 4, 1997, B1.
60. Timothy Aeppel, "Rubbermaid Is on a Tear, Sweeping Away the Cobwebs," *Wall Street Journal,* September 8, 1998, B4.
61. Venkataraman, Chen, and MacMillan, in a study of the airline industry, find that price moves produce a competitive reaction with 75 percent probability. The probability that a competitor would match a nonprice move was 17 percent. S. Venkataraman, Ming-Jer Chen, and Ian C. MacMillan, "Anticipating Reactions: Factors That Shape Competitor Responses," in George S. Day and David J. Reibstein, eds., *Wharton on Dynamic Competitive Strategy* (New York: John Wiley and Sons, 1997).
62. Peter R. Dickson and Joel E. Urbany, "Retailer Reactions to a Competitor's Price Change," *Journal of Retailing* 70 (Spring 1994), 1–22; Joel E. Urbany and Peter R. Dickson, "Competitive Price-Cutting Momentum and Pricing Reactions," *Marketing Letters* 2, no. 4 (1991), 393–402.
63. This short section is based on the article by Howard Gleckman and Gary McWilliams, "Ask and It Shall Be Discounted," *BusinessWeek,* October 6, 1997, 116–120.
64. Amy Cortese and Marcia Stepanek, "Good-Bye to Fixed Pricing?" *Business Week,* May 4, 1998, 71.
65. Jim O'Brien, "Hot Off the Wire," *Computer Shopper* (August 1998), 474; and Mary Connelly, "Philosophy of Car Pricing Is Clear: Cut Out Games," *Advertising Age,* March 28, 1994, S28–34.
66. Carl F. Mela, Sunil Gupta, and Donald R. Lehmann, "The Long-Term Impact of Promotion and Advertising on Consumer Brand Choice," *Journal of Marketing Research* (May 1997), 248–261.
67. Richard P. Bagozzi, Mahaesh Gopinath, and Prashant U. Nyer, "The Role of Emotions in Marketing," *Journal of the Academy of Marketing Science* 27 (Spring 1999), 184–206.
68. Rajeev Batra and Douglas M. Stayman, "The Role of Mood in Advertising Effectiveness," *Journal of Consumer Research* 17, no. 2 (September 1990), 203–214.
69. Lynn R. Kahle, Sharon E. Beatty, and Pamela Homer, "Alternative Measurement Approaches to Consumer Values: The List of Values (LOV) and Values and Lifestyle (VALS)," *Journal of Consumer Research* 13 (December 1986), 405–409.
70. Gordon W. Allport, "Attitudes," in C. A. Muchinson, ed., *A Handbook of Social Psychology* (Worcester, MA: Clark University Press, 1935), 798–844.
71. Hillel J. Einhorn, "Use of Nonlinear, Noncompensatory Models in Decision Making," *Psychological Bulletin* 73 (1970), 221–230.
72. See George S. Day and Prakash Nedungadi, "Managerial Representations of Competitive Advantage," *Journal of Marketing* 58 (April 1994), 31–44; George S. Day, *Learning About Markets* (Cambridge, MA: Marketing Science Institute, 1991), 91–117; and Jeffrey Pfeffer and Gerald R. Salancik, *The External Control of Organizations: A Resource Dependence Perspective* (New York: Harper, 1978).
73. See Peter R. Dickson, Paul W. Farris, and Willem J. M. I. Verbeke, "Dynamic Strategic Thinking," *Journal of the Academy of Marketing Science* 29, 3 (2001), 216–237.
74. Michael E. Porter, *Competitive Strategy* (New York: The Free Press, 1980).
75. Thomas W. Dunfee, Louis Stern, and Frederick D. Sturdivant, "Bounding Markets in Merger Cases: Identifying Relevant Competitors," Northwestern University, *Law Review* 78 (November 1983), 733–773.
76. Subrata N. Chakravarty and Carolyn Torcellini, "Citizen Kane Meets Adam Smith," *Forbes,* February 20, 1989, 82–85.
77. Michael E. Porter, *Competitive Advantage* (New York: The Free Press, 1985).
78. Bob Ortega, "How Big Brewers Are Sidling into Retail," *Wall Street Journal,* May 18, 1998, B1, B6.
79. Gary L. Frazier and Kersi D. Antia, "Exchange Relationships and Interfirm Power in Channels of Distribution," *Journal of the Academy of Marketing Science* (Fall 1995), 21–26.
80. Ann Zimmerman, "Taking Aim at Costco, Sam's Club, Marshal's, Diamonds and Pearls," *Wall Street Journal,* August 9, 2001, A1, A4.
81. Bert Rosenbloom and Trina Larsen, "A Functional Approach to International Channel Structure and the Role of Independent Wholesalers," *Journal of Marketing Channels* (Summer 1993), 65–82.
82. Wroe Alderson, *Marketing Behavior and Executive Action* (Homewood, IL: Richard D. Irwin, 1957).
83. John W. Cebrowski, "Global Success Tied to Key Management Considerations," *Marketing News,* July 20, 1998, 14–16.
84. Rosenbloom, *Marketing Channels,* 19–22.
85. Donald V. Fites, "Make Your Dealers Your Partners," *Harvard Business Review* (March–April 1996), 84–95.
86. John O'Dell, "Land Rover's Mini-SUV Relies on Internet Marketing," *Philadelphia Inquirer,* September 9, 2001, F27.
87. Bert Rosenbloom, "Channel Management," in Michael Baker, ed., *Encyclopedia of Marketing,* (London: Routledge, 1995), 551–570.
88. Philip Kotler, *Marketing Management, Analysis, Planning, Implementation, and Control,* 9th ed. (Upper Saddle River, NJ: Prentice Hall, 1997).

89. Donald J. Bowersox and David J. Closs, *Logistics Management: An Integrated Supply Chain Process* (New York: McGraw-Hill, 1996).
90. Neil Gross, "Leapfrogging a Few Links," *BusinessWeek,* June 22, 1998, 140–142.
91. "Transportation Upgrade Boosts Productivity," *Grocery Distribution* (September/October 1997), 28–32.
92. Carol Casper, "Flow-Through: Mirage or Reality?" *Food Logistics* (October/November 1997), 44–58.
93. Ray A. Smith and Sheila Muto, "Dot-Coms' New Dilemma: Vacant Warehouses," *Wall Street Journal,* August 22, 2001, B10.
94. James Aaron Cooke, "The Retail Revolution Is Coming!" *Logistics Management* (April 1996), 48–51.
95. Steven E. Salkin, "Debunking the Myths of the Internet," *Warehousing Management* (October 1997), 29–32.
96. Carol C. Bienstock, John T. Mentzer, and Monroe Murphy Bird, "Measuring Physical Distribution Service Quality," *Journal of the Academy of Marketing Science* (Winter 1997), 31–44.
97. CyberAtlas, http://www.cyberatlas.internet.com/big_picture/demographics/article/0,,5901_959421,00.html, accessed April 2, 2002.
98. "Good Grief," *The Economist,* April 8, 1995, 57.
99. Some of the questions are based on the thinking of Gene R. Laczniak, "Framework for Analyzing Marketing Ethics," *Journal of Macromarketing* (Spring 1983), 7–18; and William David Ross, *The Right and the Good* (Oxford: Clarendon Press, 1930).
100. Sir Adrian Cadbury, "Ethical Managers Make Their Own Rules," *Harvard Business Review* 87, no. 5 (September/October 1987), 69–75.
101. Peter R. Dickson and Philippa K. Wells, "The Dubious Origins of the Sherman Antitrust Act: The Mouse That Roared," *Journal of Public Policy and Marketing: Special Issue on Competition* (Spring 2001), 1–12.
102. Claudia Gaines, "Next Step in Cause Marketing: Business Start Own Nonprofits," *Marketing News,* October 12, 1998, 4.
103. In fact, the Department of Transportation has instituted a policy that defines "unfair exclusionary tactics" and penalizes any airline engaging in such tactics. See "Department of Transportation to Major Airlines: Forewarned Is Fair Warned," *Airline Financial News,* April 13, 1998.
104. Joseph P. Guiltinan and Gregory T. Gundlach, "Aggressive and Predatory Pricing: A Framework for Analysis," *Journal of Marketing* (July 1996), 88.
105. Zellner, "How Northwest Gives Competition a Bad Name; Majors Fault DOT for Ignoring Law, History, Real-World Economics," *Aviation Daily,* July 30, 1998, 180.
106. Joel E. Urbany, William O. Bearden, and Dan C. Weilbaker, "The Effect of Plausible and Exaggerated Reference Prices on Consumer Perceptions and Price Search," *Journal of Consumer Research* (June 1988), 95–110; Kent B. Monroe, *Pricing: Making Profitable Decisions,* 2nd ed. (New York: McGraw-Hill, 1990).
107. These are the Federal Trade Commission Guides, as cited in *The State of Colorado vs. The May Department Stores Company,* Case No. 89 CV 9274, District Court, City and County of Denver, Colorado, 1990.
108. See Daniel Kahneman, Jack L. Knetsch, and Richard H. Thaler, "Fairness As a Constraint on Profit Seeking: Entitlements in the Market," *American Economic Review* 70 (September 1986), 728–741.
109. Christine Dugas, "Consumers Walking Away from ATM Charges," *USA Today,* August 16, 1996, 1B.
110. For example, the Georgia Legislature passed a price-gouging law in 1994 to prevent hotels and wholesalers from taking advantage of visitors to the Olympics in Atlanta in 1996. It is unclear how successful the law was, as many hotels were still observed to double or triple room rates. See Donna Rosato, "Some Room Rates Have Done a Triple Jump," *USA Today,* July 15, 1996, 1B.
111. Lindgren and Shimp, *Marketing: An Interactive Learning System,* 403.
112. Peter R. Dickson and James I. Ginter, "Market Segmentation, Product Differentiation, and Marketing Strategy," *Journal of Marketing* (April 1987), 1–10.
113. David Pescovitz, "The Future of Clothing," *Wired,* at http://www.wired.com/wired/archive/3.11/reality_check.html, accessed June 17, 1998.
114. Adapted from Jock Bicker, "Cohorts II: A New Approach to Market Segmentation," *Journal of Consumer Marketing* (Fall–Winter 1997), 362–380.
115. N. H. Dover, "Where There's Gray, There's Green," *Marketing News,* June 22, 1998, 2.
116. K. Douglas Hoffman and John E. G. Bateson, *Essentials of Services Marketing: Concepts, Strategies, and Cases,* 2nd ed. (Mason, OH: South-Western, 2002), 3.
117. "The Final Frontier," *The Economist,* February 20, 1993, 63.
118. G. Lyn Shostack, "Breaking Free from Product Marketing," *Journal of Marketing* 41 (April 1977), 73–80.
119. *Ibid.*
120. This section adopted from Hoffman and Bateson, *Essentials of Services Marketing,* 2nd ed., 26–51; and Valerie A. Zeithaml, A. Parasuraman, and Leonard L. Berry, "Problems and Strategies in Services Marketing," *Journal of Marketing* 49 (Spring 1985), 33–46.

121. This section adopted from Hoffman and Bateson, *Essentials of Services Marketing,* 2nd ed., 4–16; and E. Langeard, J. Bateson, C. Lovelock, and P. Eigler, *Marketing of Services: New Insights from Consumers and Managers,* Report No. 81-104 (Cambridge, MA: Marketing Science Institute, 1981).
122. Mary Jo Bitner, "Servicescapes: The Impact of Physical Surroundings on Customers and Employees," *Journal of Marketing* 56 (April 1992), 57–71.
123. Michael R. Solomon, "Packaging the Service Provider," in Christopher H. Lovelock, ed., *Managing Services Marketing, Operations, and Human Resources* (Englewood Cliffs, NJ: Prentice-Hall, 1988), 318–324.
124. Alan J. Dubinsky, Roy D. Howell, Thomas N. Ingram, and Danny N. Bellenger, "Salesforce Socialization," *Journal of Marketing* 50, no. 4 (1986), 192–207.
125. Solomon, "Packaging the Service Provider," 318–324.
126. "Plane Seats Get Bigger, Cost More: Airlines Betting Fliers Will Pay Extra for Added Legroom," *Denver Rocky Mountain News,* February 28, 2000, 2A, 31A.
127. Solomon, "Packaging the Service Provider," 318–324.
128. For more information, see Hoffman and Bateson, *Essentials of Services Marketing,* 2nd ed., 247–269.
129. John E. G. Bateson and K. Douglas Hoffman, *Managing Services Marketing,* 4th ed. (Fort Worth, TX: Harcourt College Publishers, 1999).
130. For more information, see Charles L. Martin, "Consumer-to-Consumer Relationships: Satisfaction with Other Consumers' Public Behavior," *Journal of Consumer Affairs* 30, no. 1 (1996), 146–148; and Stephen J. Grove and Raymond P. Fisk, "The Impact of Other Customers on Service Experiences: A Critical Incident Examination of Getting Along," *Journal of Retailing* 73, no. 1 (1997), 63–85.
131. Joseph B. Pine II and James H. Gilmore, *The Experience Economy* (Boston, MA: Harvard School Press, 1998).
132. This section adopted from Hoffman and Bateson, *Essentials of Services Marketing,* 2nd ed., 293–322.
133. Leonard L. Berry, A. Parasuraman, and Valerie A. Zeithaml, "Improving Service Quality in America: Lessons Learned," *Academy of Management Executive* 8, no. 2 (1994), 36.
134. This section developed from Diane Brady, "Why Service Stinks," *Business Week,* October 23, 2000, 118–128.
135. J. Joseph Cronin, Jr., and Steven A. Taylor, "Measuring Service Quality: A Reexamination and Extension," *Journal of Marketing* 56 (July 1992), 55.
136. Thomas A. Stewart, "After All You've Done for Your Customers, Why Are They Still NOT HAPPY," *Fortune,* December 11, 1995, 178–182.
137. A. Parasuraman, Valerie A. Zeithaml, and Leonard L. Berry, "A Conceptual Model of Service Quality and Its Implications for Future Research," *Journal of Marketing* 49 (Fall 1985), 41–50.
138. Frederick F. Reichheld and W. Earl Sasser, Jr., "Zero Defections: Quality Comes to Services," *Harvard Business Review* (September–October 1990), 105–111.
139. Grahame R. Dowling and Mark Uncles, "Do Customer Loyalty Programs Really Work?" *Sloan Management Review* 38, no. 4 (September 1997), 71–82.
140. Christopher W. L. Hart, Leonard A. Schlesinger, and Don Maher, "Guarantees Come to Professional Service Firms," *Sloan Management Review* (Spring 1992), 19–29.
141. Adapted from Christopher W. L. Hart, James L. Heskett, and W. Earl Sasser, "The Profitable Art of Service Recovery," *Harvard Business Review* (July–August 1990), 148–156; and K. Douglas Hoffman and Scott W. Kelley, "Perceived Justice Needs and Recovery Evaluation: A Contingency Approach," *European Journal of Marketing* 34, no. 3/4 (2000), 418–432.
142. The material in this section is taken from the most recent data and estimates available from various government publications.
143. *Vision for the New Millennium . . . ,* (Kurt Salmon Associates, 1996)
144. Carol Radice, "Targeting Tomorrow's Consumers," *Progressive Grocer* (July 1998), 55–58; "Generation Y," Business Week, February 15, 1999, 81–88; and "The Return of Grunge," *Wall Street Journal,* December 11, 2002: B1, B10.
145. "Older Consumers Don't Believe You," *Advertising Age,* August 14, 1995, 14.
146. "Generation Y," *Business Week,* February 15, 1999, 80–88.
147. "Bob's 'Get Real' with Carhart," *DSN Retailing Today,* April 7, 2003, 5, 53.
148. "Just How Deep Are Those Teen Pockets?" *Business Week,* July 30, 2001, 39 and " 'Tweeners' Latest Must Market," *Lubbock Avalanche-Journal,* April 8, 2003, 9D.
149. "Catering to Kids," *Wall Street Journal,* May 3, 2002, W1, W6.
150. "Where the Boys Aren't," *U.S. News & World Report,* February 8, 1999, 47–55.
151. Ron Feemster, "Going the Distance," *American Demographics* (September 1999), 59–64.
152. For a complete discussion of the consumer's behavior, especially differences between male and female shoppers, see Paco Underhill, *Why We Buy* (New York: Simon & Schuster, 1999).

153. Malcolm P. McNair, "Significant Trends and Developments in the Postwar Period," in A. B. Smith (ed.), *Competitive Distribution in a Free High-Level Economy and Its Implications for the University* (Pittsburgh, PA: University of Pittsburgh Press, 1958).
154. Stanley C. Hollander, "Notes on the Retail Accordion," *Journal of Retailing* (Summer 1966), 29–40, 54.
155. For a complete discussion of this theory see Shelby D. Hunt, *A General Theory of Competition* (Thousand Oaks, CA: Sage Publications: 2000).
156. Shelby D. Hunt and Robert M. Morgan, "The Resource-Advantage Theory of Competition: Dynamics, Path Dependencies, and Evolutionary Dimensions," *Journal of Marketing* (October 1996), 107–114.
157. *Vision for the New Millennium* (Atlanta: Kurt Salmon Associates, 1997).
158. The information in this section was provided by Robin Diamond of the Direct Selling Association, Washington, D.C., and "Avon Calling—Lots of New Reps," *BusinessWeek*, June 2, 2003, 53–54.
159. "Laughing All The Way to the (Phone) Bank," *U.S. News & World Report*, May 29, 2000, 46–47.
160. Michael J. O'Connor, "Global Marketing: A Retail Perspective," *International Trends in Retailing* (December 1998), 19–35.
161. For a complete discussion of the development of IKEA, see "IKEA: Create a Better Everyday Life for the Majority of People," *International Trends in Retailing* (December 1995), 45–65.
162. This information was provided in an information kit supplied by Target.
163. For a more complete discussion of this subject, see the special report, "Managing the Trading-Partner Link Is the Key to Success," *Chain Store Age* (June 2003), 1A–12A.
164. For a more complete discussion of this subject, consult Robert Buzzell and Gwen Ortmeyer, "Channel Partnerships Streamline Distribution," *Sloan Management Review* (Spring 1995), 85–96.
165. F. Robert Dwyer and Sejo Oh, "A Transaction Cost Perspective on Vertical Contractual Structure and Interchannel Competitive Strategies," *Journal of Marketing* (April 1988), 21–34.
166. Bert C. McCammon, Jr., "Perspectives for Distribution Programming," in Louis P. Bucklin, ed., *Vertical Marketing Systems* (Glenview, IL: Scott, Foresman, 1970), 45. Reprinted with permission of the author.
167. "Wal-Mart's Influence Grows," *USA Today*, January 29, 2003, 2B.
168. "Happy Meals Are No Longer Bringing Smiles at McDonald's," *Wall Street Journal*, January 31, 2003, B1, B4.
169. "Retailers Thwart Food-Price Hikes," *Advertising Age*, May 5, 2003, 3, 35.
170. "In a Clash of the Sneaker Titans, Nike Gets Leg Up on Foot Locker," *Wall Street Journal*, May 13, 2003, A1, A10.
171. "Lawsuits Filed Over Auto Prices," *USA Today*, February 20, 2003, 1B; "Same Cars Can Cost Oodles Less in Canada," *USA Today*, May 6, 2003, 1B.
172. Robert Morgan and Shelby Hunt, "The Commitment-Trust Theory of Relationship Marketing," *Journal of Marketing* (July 1994), 20–38.
173. Jan B. Heide and George John, "Do Norms Matter in Marketing Relationships?" *Journal of Marketing* (April 1992), 32–44; James C. Anderson and James A. Narus, "A Model of Distributor Firm and Manufacturer Firm Working Partnerships," *Journal of Marketing* (January 1990), 42–58.
174. The authors want to acknowledge the contributions of many of their ex-students in this section. These students are now buyers, suppliers/vendors, and category managers. In addition, we want to give special credit to Wally Switzer, president of the 4 R's of Retailing, Inc., and Kevin Blackwell, general manager of sales and marketing, Analytic Solutions, Bristol Technology Inc., for their suggestions in this section.
175. *Burger King v. Weaver;* United States Court of Appeals, Eleventh Circuit, 96–5438, 1999.
176. *Eastman Kodak Company v. Image Technical Services* (1992), 112 S. Ct. 2072.
177. "Clear Sailing for Pirates," *BusinessWeek*, July 15, 2002, 53; "China's Piracy Plague," Business Week, June 5, 2000, 44–48; "Will China Scuttle Its Pirates?" *BusinessWeek*, August 15, 1995, 40–41; "Copyright Pirates Prosper in China Despite Promises," *New York Times*, February 20, 1996, A1.
178. "Who Says Student Protests Don't Matters" *Business Week*, June 12, 2000, 94–96.
179. "NC Students End Sit-In on Sweatshop Issue," *Dallas Morning News*, April 24, 1999, 12A.
180. "Banned by Bentonville," *Advertising Age*, May 12, 2003, 16.
181. Information supplied by Bob Kahn to the authors.
182. "Companies That Serve You Best," *Fortune*, May 31, 1993, 74–88.
183. "Retailing 101," *Progressive Grocer* (January 2000), 50–56.
184. "Hot Kiosks and Carts," *Shopping Centers Today* (February 2003), 14–16.
185. William J. Reilly, *Methods for the Study of Retail Relationships*, Research Monograph, no. 4 (Austin, TX: Bureau of Business Research, University of Texas, 1929).
186. P. D. Converse, "New Laws of Retail Gravitation," *Journal of Marketing* (January 1949), 379–384.

187. Bernard LaLonde, "The Logistics of Retail Location," in William D. Stevens (ed.), *American Marketing Proceedings* (Chicago: American Marketing Association, 1961), 572.

188. "Home Depot," *Business Week,* February 13, 1995: 65.

189. Mobility can be viewed as both a household characteristic and a community characteristic. We chose to treat it as a community characteristic because the design of the community, the availability of public transportation, and the cost of operating an auto in any given area are determinants of mobility and are themselves characteristic of the community.

190. The essence of Applebaum's work, plus contributions from several of his students, can be found in William Applebaum et al., in Curt Korhblau (ed.), *Guide to Store Location Research with Emphasis on Supermarkets,* sponsored by the Supermarket Institute (Reading, MA: Addison-Wesley, 1968).

191. "Snakebit: Some Texas Properties Seem Immune to the Good Times," *Wall Street Journal,* August 27, 1997, T1, T3.

192. Richard L. Nelson, *The Selection of Retail Locations* (New York: F. W. Dodge, 1958): 66.

193. Michelle Marchetti, "What a Sales Call Costs," *Sales and Marketing Management* (September 2000), 80.

194. *Ibid.,* 80.

195. Charles Butler, "Why the Bad Rap?" *Sales & Marketing Management* (June 1996), 58–66; Andy Cohen, "Leading Edge: Sales Strikes Out on Campus," *Sales & Marketing Management* (November 1997), 13; Earl D. Honeycutt, Jr., John B. Ford, Michael J. Swenson, and William R. Swinyard, "Student Preferences for Sales Careers Around the Pacific Rim," *Industrial Marketing Management* (January 1999), 27–36; Michelle Marchetti, "Sales Reps to Go," *Sales & Marketing Management* (January 1999), 14; Erika Rasmusson, "Does Your Sales Force Need a New Look?" *Sales & Marketing Management* (May 2000), 13.

196. Butler, "Why the Bad Rap?" 58–66.

197. Many articles and books have been published regarding the effects of role conflict, role ambiguity, and job anxiety. See, for example, Douglas N. Behrman and William D. Perreault, Jr., "A Role Stress Model of the Performance and Satisfaction of Industrial Salespersons," *Journal of Marketing* 48 (Fall 1984), 9–21; Jean-Charles Chebat and Paul Kollias, "The Impact of Empowerment on Customer Contact Employees' Role in Service Organizations," *Journal of Service Research* (August), 66–81; Gilbert A. Churchill, Neil M. Ford, and Orville C. Walker, *Sales Force Management* (Homewood, IL: Richard D. Irwin, 1990); Theresa B. Flaherty, Robert Dahlstrom, and Steven J. Skinner, "Organizational Values and Role Stress As Determinants of Customer-Oriented Selling Performance," *Journal of Personal Selling & Sales Management* (Spring 1999), 1–18; Eli Jones, Donna Massey Kantak, Charles M. Futrell, and Mark W. Johnston, "Leader Behavior, Work-Attitudes, and Turnover of Salespeople: An Integrative Study," *Journal of Personal Selling & Sales Management* (Spring 1996), 13–23.

198. Thomas R. Wotruba and Stephen B. Castleberry, "Job Analysis and Hiring Practices for National Account Marketing Positions," *Journal of Personal Selling & Sales Management* 13 (Summer 1993), 49–65.

199. Sarah Lorge, "Selling 101: The Best Way to Prospect," *Sales and Marketing Management* (January 1998), 80.

200. *Ibid.*

201. *Ibid.*

202. Wendy O'Connell, "The E-vangelist: Prospective Customer Relationship Management," *Sales and Marketing Management* (March 2001), 29.

203. Brian Tracy, *Advanced Selling Strategies* (New York: Simon & Schuster, 1995).

204. David Merrill and Roger Reid, *Personal Styles and Effective Performance* (Radnor, PA: Chilton, 1981).

205. Richard Hanks, Vice President, Marriott Corporation, from presentation made at the Hospitality Sales and Marketing Association International Summit Conference, April 3, 1998, Anaheim, CA.

206. Dan Sherman, *You Can Be a Peak Performer* (San Francisco, CA: Million Dollar Press, 1996).

207. Sarah Lorge, "How to Close the Deal," *Sales & Marketing Management* 150 (April 1998), 84.

208. For example, see Thomas J. Stanley, *Selling to the Affluent: The Professional's Guide to Closing the Sales That Count* (New York: McGraw-Hill, 1997).

209. Rolph Anderson, Rajiv Mehta, and James Strong, "An Empirical Investigation of Sales Management Training Programs for Sales Managers," *Journal of Personal Selling & Sales Management* 17 (Summer 1997), 53–66.

210. Anderson, "Personal Selling and Sales Management in the New Millennium," 17–32.

211. *Entrepreneur* Small Business Square, "*Entrepreneur's* Special Report: Super Sales Tips," http://www.entrepreneur.com/Your_Business/YB_SegArticle/0,4621,299184,00.html.

212. Olivia Thetgyi, "Radical Makeovers," *Sales & Marketing Management* (April 2000), 78–88.

213. Melinda Ligos, "Point, Click, Sell," *Sales & Marketing Management* (May 1999), 50–56.

214. Melanie Berger, "Technology Update: On-the-Job Training," *Sales & Marketing Management* (February 1998), 122–125.

215. Julie Hill, "E-Briefings Change Training for a Firm in Transition," *Presentations* (February 2001), 20; Ligos, "Point, Click, Sell," 50–56.

216. Vincent Alonzo, "Motivating Matters: The Case for Trophies," *Sales & Marketing Management* (February 1998), 34–35.

217. Chad Kaydo, "Motivating Call Center Reps," *Sales & Marketing Management* 150 (April 1998), 82; Chad Kaydo, "How to Motivate Sales Stars," *Sales & Marketing Management* (May 1994), 89–92.
218. Julie Sturgeon, "Fun Sells," *Selling Power* (March 20, 2000), 56–65.
219. For a detailed discussion of sales quotas, see Rene Y. Darmon, "Selecting Appropriate Sales Quota Plan Structures and Quota-Setting Procedures," *Journal of Personal Selling & Sales Management* 17 (Winter 1997), 1–16; Charles M. Futrell, John E. Swan, and John T. Todd, "Job Performance Related to Management Control Systems for Pharmaceutical Salesmen," *Journal of Marketing Research* 13 (February 1976), 25–33; Leon Winer, "The Effect of Product Sales Quota on Sales Force Productivity," *Journal of Marketing Research* 10 (May 1973), 180–183; Thomas R. Wotruba, "The Effect of Goal Setting on the Performance of Independent Sales Agents in Direct Selling," *Journal of Personal Selling & Sales Management* 9 (Spring 1989), 22–29.
220. For a review of sales coaching, see Gregory A. Rich, "The Constructs of Sales Coaching: Supervisory Feedback, Role Modeling, and Trust," *Journal of Personal Selling & Sales Management* 18 (Winter 1998), 53–63.
221. Willem Verbeke and Richard P. Bagozzi, "Sales Call Anxiety: Exploring What It Means When Fear Rules a Sales Encounter," *Journal of Marketing* (July 2000), 88–101.
222. Pamela Yellen, "How to Blast Through Call Reluctance and Fear of Rejection," *Insurance Sales* (May/June 1998), 14–18.
223. David J. Cocks and Dennis Gould, "Sales Compensation: A New Technology-Enabled Strategy," *Compensation & Benefits Review* (January/February 2001), 27–31.
224. Geoffrey Brewer, "Brain Power," *Sales & Marketing Management* (May 1997), 38–48; Peppers and Rogers, "The Money Trap," 58–60.
225. Bill Weeks, "Setting Sales Force Compensation in the Internet Age," *Compensation & Benefits Review* (March/April 2000), 25–34.
226. For a review of evaluation factors, see Donald W. Jackson, John L. Schlacter, and William G. Wolfe, "Examining the Bases Utilized for Evaluating Salespeoples' Performance," *Journal of Personal Selling & Sales Management* 15 (Fall 1995), 57–65.
227. Judy A. Siguaw, Sheryl E. Kimes, and Jule B. Gassenheimer, "Sales Force Productivity: The Application of Revenue Management Strategies to Sales Management," Working Paper Series 2001, Cornell University, School of Hotel Administration.
228. Brewer, "Brain Power," 39–42, 46–48.
229. Michelle Marchetti, "Covering Your Turf," *Sales & Marketing Management* (May 1997), 51–57.
230. *Ibid.*
231. Erika Rasmusson, "Protecting Your Turf," *Sales & Marketing Management* (March 1998), 90.
232. Leslie M. Fine and Janice R. Franke, "Legal Aspects of Salesperson Commission Payments: Implications for the Implementation of Commission Sales Programs," *Journal of Personal Selling and Sales Management* 15 (Winter 1995), 53–68.
233. *Ibid.*
234. Edmund L. Pincoffs, *Quandaries and Virtues: Against Reductivism in Ethics* (Lawrence: University of Kansas Press, 1986).
235. Lawrence B. Chonko, John F. Tanner Jr., and William A. Weeks, "Ethics in Salesperson Decision Making: A Synthesis of Research Approaches and an Extension of the Scenario Method," *Journal of Personal Selling and Sales Management* 16 (Winter 1996), 35–52.
236. "Misrepresentation," *Supply Management* 3, January 15, 1998, 44; Amy S. Friedman, "Chubb Among Latest to Be Served with Sales Lawsuit," *National Underwriter* 100, September 2, 1996, 3, 65.
237. Chonko et al., "Ethics in Salesperson Decision Making," 35–52.
238. Cathy Owens Swift and Russell L. Kent, "Selling and Sales Management in Action—Sexual Harassment: Ramifications for Sales Managers," *Journal of Personal Selling and Sales Management* 14 (Winter 1994): 77–87.
239. Leslie M. Fine, C. David Shepherd, and Susan L. Josephs, "Sexual Harassment in the Sales Force: The Customer Is NOT Always Right," *Journal of Personal Selling and Sales Management* 14 (Fall 1994): 15–30; Swift and Kent, "Selling and Sales Management in Action—Sexual Harassment," 77–87.
240. Swift and Kent, "Selling and Sales Management in Action—Sexual Harassment," 77–87.
241. Barbara Lindemann and David Kadue, *Sexual Harassment in Employment Law* (Washington, DC: Bureau of National Affairs, 1992).
242. Fine et al., "Sexual Harassment in the Sales Force," 15–30; Swift and Kent, "Selling and Sales Management in Action—Sexual Harassment," 77–87.
243. Swift and Kent, "Selling and Sales Management in Action—Sexual Harassment," 77–87.

MODULE 400

Quality and Process Management

401 Quality Strategies, 636

405 Product Quality, 638

410 Quality Management Practices, 639

440 Quality Control Practices, 671

450 Process Management Practices, 675

455 Service Quality, 681

460 Business Process Analysis, 688

495 Ethics and Quality, 693

Module 400 Endnotes, 694

Quality Strategies

Leadership and Strategic Planning

The one thing that all quality experts agree on is that strong leadership, especially from senior managers, is absolutely necessary to develop and sustain a Total Quality (TQ) culture. **Leadership** is the ability to positively influence people and systems under one's authority to have a meaningful impact and achieve important results. Leaders may seek to motivate employees and develop enthusiasm for quality with rhetoric, but actions often speak louder than words.

Leaders create clear and visible quality values, and integrate these values into the organization's strategy. **Strategy** is the pattern of decisions that determines and reveals a company's goals, policies, and plans to meet the needs of its stakeholders. Through an effective strategy, a business creates a sustainable competitive advantage. This process of envisioning the organization's future and developing the necessary procedures and operations to achieve that future is called **strategic planning.** In today's business environment, quality is a key element of strategic planning.

Leadership for Quality

Leadership is one of the least-understood concepts in business. Even though many theories of leadership have been developed, no single approach adequately captures the essence of the concept. Most definitions of leadership reflect an assortment of behaviors; some examples follow:

- Vision that stimulates hope and mission that transforms hope into reality
- Radical servanthood that saturates the organization
- Stewardship that shepherds its resources
- Integration that drives its economy
- Courage to sacrifice personal or team goals for the greater community good
- Communication that coordinates its efforts
- Consensus that drives unity of purpose
- Empowerment that grants permission to make mistakes, encourages the honesty to admit them, and gives the opportunity to learn from them
- Conviction that provides the stamina to continually strive toward business excellence[1]

In practice, the notion of leadership can be as elusive as the notion of quality itself. This section briefly summarizes the principal concepts of leadership and prominent leadership practices in quality management.

When we think of leadership, we generally think of *executive leadership,* which focuses on the roles of senior managers in guiding an organization to fulfill its mission and meet its goals. The critical importance of senior managers' roles in business excellence is affirmed by numerous research studies and from practitioners' perspectives. In the Baldrige Criteria, as well as other frameworks such as the European Quality Award, Australian Quality Award, and Japan's Deming Prize, leadership is the first category. Among the many activities that senior executives perform are:

1. Defining and communicating business directions
2. Ensuring that goals and expectations are met
3. Reviewing business performance and taking appropriate action
4. Creating an enjoyable work environment that promotes creativity, innovation, and continual improvement
5. Soliciting input and feedback from customers
6. Ensuring that employees are effective contributors to the business
7. Motivating, inspiring, and energizing employees
8. Recognizing employee contributions
9. Providing honest feedback

As we move further into the new economy, some of the cherished views about leadership being centered at the top of the organization are being seriously challenged. Today's fluid, "de-jobbed" organizations—in which parts of the work are being done by traditional departments, parts are being done by temporary project teams, parts are being done by business partners in another organization, and parts are being done by external contract employees who are indistinguishable from the company's own workers—require a broader view of leadership:

- The formal organizational leadership that is responsible for integrating, resourcing, and orchestrating the activities of the various project teams
- The ad hoc leadership required within project teams
- Leadership in every member of every project team that incorporates the initiative, the self-management capacity, the readiness to make hard decisions, the embodiment of organizational values, and the sense of business responsibility that in the traditional organization were limited to the top people in the organization.[2]

For example, formal organizational leadership is manifested in developing clear values, creating a competitive advantage, defining customer and market focus, and encouraging continual learning. Ad hoc leadership within project teams is seen by observing the leader working to make those on the team successful, removing barriers to team performance, establishing good lines of communication, and resolving problems. Individual leadership is revealed through people maintaining the focus and discipline to consistently complete jobs, being proactive in identifying and solving problems, working for win-win agreements, and making continuous learning a personal habit.

Effective leadership requires five core leadership skills: *vision, empowerment, intuition, self-understanding,* and *value congruence.*[3] Leaders are visionaries; they manage for the future, not the past. Vision is crucial at every level during times of change. Leaders recognize the radical organizational changes taking place today as opportunities to move closer to total quality. Visionary leaders create mental and verbal pictures of desirable future states and share these visions with their organizational partners, including customers, suppliers, and employees.

Leaders empower employees to assume ownership of problems or opportunities, and to be proactive in implementing improvements and making decisions in the best interests of the organization. Empowerment threatens many managers who are accustomed to wielding their power, often coercively through fear of punishment or sanctions.[4] True power is not based upon formal position and authority, but rather aids in spreading power downward and outward and developing leadership at lower levels of the organization. It is this notion that Deming was trying to convey in one of his 14 Points: Institute Leadership.

Leaders are not afraid to follow their intuition. Even in the face of uncertainty and change, they must anticipate the future and must be prepared to make difficult decisions that will help the organization to be successful.

Self-understanding requires the ability to look at one's self and then identify relationships with employees and within the organization. It requires an examination of one's weaknesses as well as strengths. Many leaders have an insatiable appetite for knowledge and self-learning as well as a drive to develop their skills and use them effectively.

Finally, value congruence occurs when leaders integrate their values into the company's management system. Values are basic assumptions and beliefs about the nature of the business, mission, people, and relationships of an organization. Specifically, values include trust and respect for individuals, openness, teamwork, integrity, and commitment to quality. They become standards by which choices are made, and create an organizational structure in which quality is a routine part of activities and decisions. Employees quickly recognize leaders who do not apply the values they espouse or who do so inconsistently. This incongruence causes employees to constantly doubt management's message.

These core skills of vision, empowerment, intuition, self-understanding, and value congruence are reflected in the practices of quality leaders in organizations throughout the world.

Leading Practices for Leadership in Quality

In firms committed to total quality, various leadership practices share common elements. True leaders promote quality and business performance excellence in several ways.

- *They create a customer-focused strategic vision and clear quality values that serve as a basis for business decisions at all levels of the organization.* An organization's vision and values emanate from senior leaders, and often revolve around customers, both external and internal.
- *They create and sustain a leadership system and environment for empowerment, innovation, and organizational learning.* Leaders provide an environment with few bureaucratic rules and procedures. Such an environment

encourages managers to experiment and take risks, permits employees to talk openly about problems, supports teamwork, and promotes employees' understanding of their responsibilities for quality. Solectron managers, for example, foster teamwork and give workers responsibility for meeting quality goals. They encourage a strong family atmosphere, promote clear and effective communications, and recognize and reward groups for exceptional performance. Besides monetary awards, Solectron often buys lunch for an entire division or brings in ice cream for the whole corporation. At Custom Research, Inc., the four senior leaders ensure that employees have the responsibility, training, and information they need to do their jobs through empowering everyone to do whatever it takes to serve clients, working with nine other senior people to set strategy, and making middle managers the real leaders. Organizational learning requires leaders to assess organizational performance, identify opportunities for improvement and innovation, and evaluate their own leadership effectiveness.

- *They set high expectations and demonstrate substantial personal commitment and involvement in quality, often with a missionary-like enthusiasm.* A leader can inspire people to do things they do not believe they can do.
- *They integrate quality values into daily leadership and management and communicate extensively through the leadership structure and to all employees.* Successful leaders continually promote their vision throughout the organization using many forms of communication: personal interaction, talks, newsletters, seminars, e-mail, and video.
- *They integrate public responsibilities and community support into their business practices.* Leadership responsibilities include promoting ethical behavior among all employees and the protection of public health, safety, and the environment that may be affected by a company's products and services.

From all these examples, we see that leadership is the "driver" of the entire quality system. Without leadership, a total quality initiative simply becomes the "flavor of the month," which is the major reason that total quality efforts fail in many organizations. Effective leadership practice, however, is built upon a sound foundation of organization structure and theory.

Product Quality

Quality can be a confusing concept, partly because people view quality in relation to differing criteria based on their individual roles in the production-marketing chain. In addition, the meaning of quality has evolved as the quality profession has grown and matured. Neither consultants nor business professionals agree on a universal definition. A study that asked managers of 86 firms in the eastern United States to define quality produced several dozen different responses, including the following:

1. Perfection
2. Consistency
3. Eliminating waste
4. Speed of delivery
5. Compliance with policies and procedures
6. Providing a good, usable product
7. Doing it right the first time
8. Delighting or pleasing customers
9. Total customer service and satisfaction[5]

Thus, it is important to understand the various perspectives from which quality is viewed in order to fully appreciate the role it plays in the many parts of a business organization.[6]

Judgment-Based Criteria

One common notion of quality, often used by consumers, is that it is synonymous with superiority or excellence. Excellence is abstract and subjective, however, and standards of excellence may vary considerably among individuals. Hence, the transcendent definition is of little practical value to managers. It does not provide a means by which quality can be measured or assessed as a basis for decision making.

Product-Based Criteria

A second definition of quality is that it is a function of a specific, measurable variable and that differences in quality reflect differences in quantity of some product attribute, such as in the number of stitches per inch on a shirt or in the number of cylinders in an engine. This interpretation implies that higher levels or amounts of product characteristics are equivalent to higher quality. As a result, quality is often mistakenly assumed to be related to price: the higher the price, the higher the quality. However, a product need not be expensive to be considered a quality product by consumers. Also, as with the notion of excellence, the assessment of product attributes may vary considerably among individuals.

User-Based Criteria

A third definition of quality is based on the presumption that quality is determined by what a customer wants. Individuals have different wants and needs and, hence, different quality standards. This interpretation leads to a user-based definition: quality is defined as fitness *for intended use,* or how well the product performs its intended function.

> *Customer-driven quality* Many companies are using a simpler, yet powerful, definition: "quality is meeting or exceeding customer expectations."

Value-Based Criteria

A fourth approach to defining quality is based on *value;* that is, the relationship of usefulness or satisfaction to price. From this perspective, a quality product is one that is as useful as competing products and is sold at a lower price, or one that offers greater usefulness or satisfaction at a comparable price. Thus, one might purchase a generic product, rather than a brand-name one, if it performs as well as the brand-name product at a lower price.

Competition demands that businesses seek to satisfy consumers' needs at lower prices. The value approach to quality incorporates a firm's goal of balancing product characteristics (the customer side of quality) with internal efficiencies (the operations side).

Manufacturing-Based Criteria

A fifth definition of quality is a manufacturing-based definition. That is, quality is defined as the desirable outcome of engineering and manufacturing practice, or *conformance to specifications.* **Specifications** are targets and tolerances determined by designers of products and services. Targets are the ideal values for which production is to strive; tolerances are specified because designers recognize that it is impossible to meet targets all of the time in manufacturing.

Conformance to specifications is a key definition of quality, because it provides a means of measuring quality. Specifications are meaningless, however, if they do not reflect attributes that are deemed important to the consumer.

Quality Management Practices

Principles of Total Quality

Total quality is based on three fundamental principles.

1. A focus on customers and stakeholders
2. Participation and teamwork by everyone in the organization
3. A process focus supported by continuous improvement and learning

Despite their obvious simplicity, these principles are quite different from traditional management practices. Historically, companies did little to understand external customer requirements, much less those of internal customers. Managers and specialists controlled and directed production systems; workers were told what to do and how to do it, and rarely were asked for their input. Teamwork was virtually nonexistent. A certain amount of waste and error was tolerable and was controlled by post-production inspection. Improvements in quality generally resulted from technological breakthroughs instead of a relentless mindset of continuous improvement. With total quality, an organization actively seeks to identify customer needs and expectations, to build quality into work processes by tapping the knowledge and experience of its workforce, and to continually improve every facet of the organization.

CUSTOMER AND STAKEHOLDER FOCUS The customer is the principal judge of quality. Perceptions of value and satisfaction are influenced by many factors throughout the customer's overall purchase, ownership, and service experiences. To meet or exceed customer expectations, organizations must fully understand all product and service attributes that contribute to customer value and lead to satisfaction and loyalty. To accomplish this task, a company's efforts need to extend well beyond merely meeting specifications, reducing defects and errors, or resolving complaints. They must include both designing new products that truly delight the customer and responding rapidly to changing consumer and market demands. A company close to its customer knows what the customer wants, how the customer uses its products, and anticipates needs that the customer may not even be able to express. It also continually develops new ways of enhancing customer relationships.

A firm also must recognize that internal customers are as important in assuring quality as are external customers who purchase the product. Employees who view themselves as both customers of and suppliers to other employees understand how their work links to the final product. After all, the responsibility of any supplier is to understand and meet customer requirements in the most efficient and effective way possible.

Customer focus extends beyond the consumer and internal customer relationships, however. Employees and society represent important stakeholders. An organization's success depends on the knowledge, skills, creativity, and motivation of its employees and partners. Therefore, a TQ organization must demonstrate commitment to employees, provide opportunities for development and growth, provide recognition beyond normal compensation systems, share knowledge, and encourage risk-taking. Viewing society as a stakeholder is an attribute of a world-class organization. Business ethics, public health and safety, the environment, and community and professional support are necessary activities.

PARTICIPATION AND TEAMWORK Joseph Juran credited Japanese managers' full use of the knowledge and creativity of the entire workforce as one of the reasons for Japan's rapid quality achievements. When managers give employees the tools to make good decisions and the freedom and encouragement to make contributions, they virtually guarantee that better quality products and production processes will result. Employees who are allowed to participate—both individually and in teams—in decisions that affect their jobs and the customer can make substantial contributions to quality. In any organization, the person who best understands his or her job, along with how to improve both the product and the process, is the one performing it. This attitude represents a profound shift in the typical philosophy of senior management; the traditional view was that the workforce should be "managed," or to put it less formally, the workforce should leave their brains at the door. Good intentions alone are not enough to encourage employee involvement. Management's task includes formulating the systems and procedures and then putting them in place to ensure that participation becomes a part of the culture. Empowering employees to make decisions that satisfy customers without constraining them with bureaucratic rules shows the highest level of trust.

Another important element of total quality is teamwork, which focuses attention on customer-supplier relationships and encourages the involvement of the total workforce in attacking systemic problems, particularly those that cross functional boundaries. Today, the use of self-managed teams that combine teamwork and empowerment is a powerful method of employee involvement.

Traditionally, organizations were integrated vertically by linking all the levels of management in a hierarchical fashion (consider the traditional organization chart). TQ requires horizontal coordination between organizational units, such as between design and engineering, engineering and manufacturing, manufacturing and shipping, and shipping and sales. Cross-functional teams provide this focus.

Partnerships with unions, customers, suppliers, and education organizations also promote teamwork and permit the blending of an organization's core competencies and capabilities with the complementary strengths of partners, creating mutual benefits. For example, many companies seek suppliers that share their own values. They often educate them in methods of improvement. If suppliers improve, then so will the company.

PROCESS FOCUS AND CONTINUOUS IMPROVEMENT The traditional way of viewing an organization is by surveying the vertical dimension—by keeping an eye on an organization chart. However, work gets done (or fails to get done) horizontally or crossfunctionally, not hierarchically. A *process* is a sequence of activities that is intended to achieve some result. We typically think of processes in the context of production: the collection of activities and operations involved in transforming *inputs*, which are the physical facilities, materials, capital, equipment, people, and energy, into *outputs*, or the products and services. Common types of production processes include machining, mixing, assembly, filling orders, or approving loans. However, nearly every major activity within an organization involves a process that crosses traditional organizational boundaries, as illustrated in Exhibit 400.1. For example, an order fulfillment process might involve a

Exhibit 400.1 *Process Versus Function*

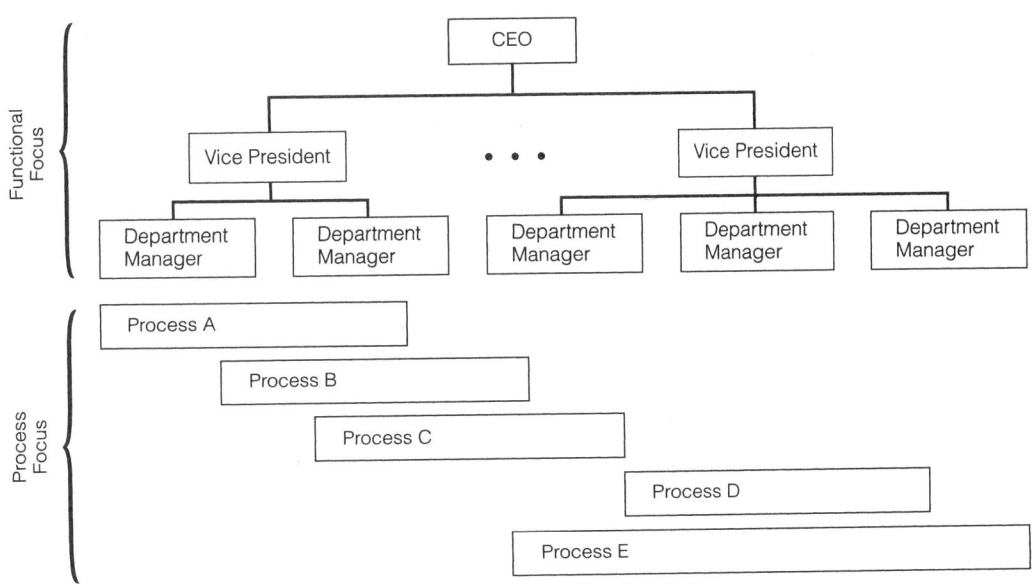

salesperson placing the order; a marketing representative entering it on the company's computer system; a credit check by finance; picking, packaging, and shipping by distribution and logistics personnel; invoicing by finance; and installation by field service engineers. A process perspective links all necessary activities together and increases one's understanding of the entire system, rather than focusing on only a small part. Many of the greatest opportunities for improving organizational performance lie in the organizational interfaces—those spaces between the boxes on an organization chart.

Continuous improvement refers to both incremental improvements that are small and gradual as well as breakthrough, or large and rapid, improvement. Improvements may take any one of several forms:

1. Enhancing value to the customer through new and improved products and services
2. Reducing errors, defects, waste, and their related costs
3. Increasing productivity and effectiveness in the use of all resources
4. Improving responsiveness and cycle-time performance for such processes as resolving customer complaints or new product introduction

Major improvements in response time may require significant simplification of work processes and often drive simultaneous improvements in quality and productivity. Thus, response time, quality, and productivity objectives should be considered together. A process focus supports continuous improvement efforts by helping to understand these synergies and to recognize the true sources of problems.

Real improvement depends on **learning,** that is, understanding why changes are successful through feedback between practices and results, which leads to new goals and approaches. A learning cycle has four stages:

1. Planning
2. Execution of plans
3. Assessment of progress
4. Revision of plans based upon assessment findings.

Infrastructure, Practices, and Tools

The three principles of total quality need to be supported by an integrated organizational infrastructure, a set of management practices, and a set of tools and techniques, which all must work together as suggested in Exhibit 400.2. **Infrastructure** refers to the basic management systems necessary to function effectively and carry out the principles of TQ. It includes the following elements:

1. Customer relationship management
2. Leadership and strategic planning

410. QUALITY MANAGEMENT PRACTICES

Exhibit 400.2 *The Scope of Total Quality*

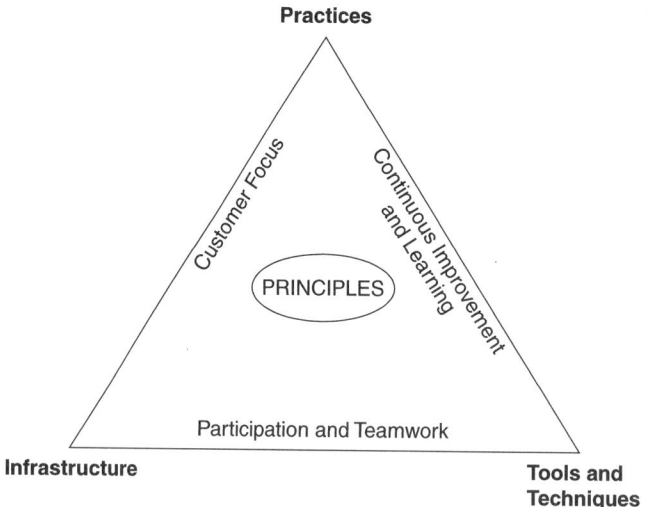

Exhibit 400.3 *Relationships Among Infrastructure, Practices, and Tools*

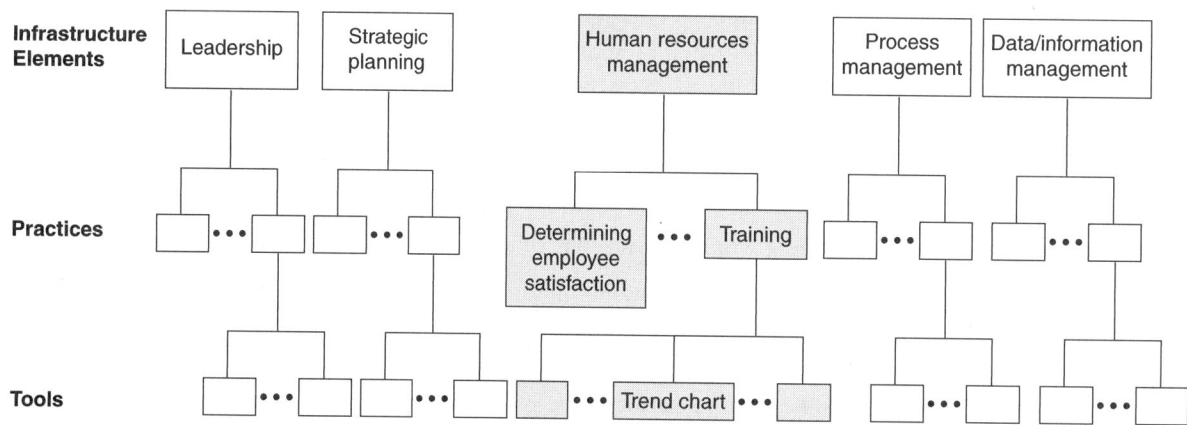

3. Human resources management
4. Process management
5. Data and information management

Practices are those activities that occur within each element of the infrastructure to achieve high performance objectives. For example, reviewing company performance is a leadership practice; training and determining employee satisfaction are human resources management practices; and coordinating design and production/delivery processes to ensure trouble-free introduction and delivery of products and services is a process management practice. **Tools** include a wide variety of graphical and statistical methods to plan work activities, collect data, analyze results, monitor progress, and solve problems. For instance, a chart showing trends in manufacturing defects as workers progress through a training program is a simple tool to monitor the effectiveness of the training; the statistical technique of experimental design is often used in product development activities. The relationships among infrastructure, practices, and tools are illustrated in Exhibit 400.3.

Three Levels of Quality

An organization that is committed to total quality must apply it at three levels: the *organizational level*, the *process level*, and the *performer/job level*. At the organizational level, quality concerns center on meeting external customer requirements. An organization must seek customer input on a regular basis. Questions such as the following help to define quality at the organizational level:

1. Which products and services meet your expectations?
2. Which do not?
3. What products or services do you need that you are not receiving?
4. Are you receiving products or services that you do not need?

Customer-driven performance standards should be used as bases for goal setting, problem solving, performance appraisal, incentive compensation, nonfinancial rewards, and resource allocation.

At the process level, organizational units are classified as functions or departments, such as marketing, design, product development, operations, finance, purchasing, billing, and so on. Because most processes are cross-functional, the danger exists that managers of particular organizational units will try to optimize the activities under their control, which can suboptimize activities for the organization as a whole. At this level, managers must ask questions such as:

1. What products or services are most important to the (external) customer?
2. What processes produce those products and services?
3. What are the key inputs to the process?
4. Which processes have the most significant effect on the organization's customer-driven performance standards?
5. Who are my internal customers and what are their needs?

At the performer level (sometimes called the job level or the task-design level), standards for output must be based on quality and customer-service requirements that originate at the organizational and process levels. These standards include requirements for such things as accuracy, completeness, innovation, timeliness, and cost. For each output of an individual's job, one must ask:

1. What is required by the customer, both internal and external?
2. How can the requirements be measured?
3. What is the specific standard for each measure?

Viewing an organization from this perspective clarifies the roles and responsibilities of all employees in pursuing quality. Top managers must focus attention at the organizational level; middle managers and supervisors at the process level; and all employees must understand quality at the performer level. Getting everyone involved is the foundation of TQ.

The Seven Management and Planning Tools

Managers may use a variety of tools and techniques, known as the *seven management and planning tools,* to implement policy deployment. These tools are particularly useful in structuring unstructured ideas, making strategic plans, and organizing and controlling large, complex projects. Thus, they can benefit all employees involved in quality planning and implementation.

Affinity Diagrams

The affinity diagram is a tool for organizing a large number of ideas, opinions, and facts relating to a broad problem or subject area. The affinity diagram, a main ingredient of the KJ method, was developed by Kawakita Jiro (KJ)—a Japanese anthropologist. In developing a vision statement, for example, senior management of MicroTech might conduct a brainstorming session to develop a list of ideas to incorporate into the vision. This list might include

Low product maintenance
Satisfied employees
Courteous order entry
Low production costs
Innovative product features
High return on investment

Seven management and planning tools include the following:
- *affinity diagrams*
- *interrelationship digraph*
- *tree diagrams*
- *matrix diagrams*
- *matrix data analysis*
- *process decision program charts*
- *arrow diagrams*

Low price
Quick delivery
Growth in shareholder value
Teamwork
Responsive technical support
Personal employee growth

Constant technology innovation
High quality
Motivated employees
Unique products
Small, lightweight designs

Once a large number of ideas have been generated, they can be grouped according to their "affinity" or relationship to each other. An affinity diagram for the preceding list is shown in Exhibit 400.4 for MicroTech.

Interrelationship Digraph

An interrelationship digraph identifies and explores causal relationships among related concepts or ideas. It shows that every idea can be logically linked with more than one other idea at a time, and allows for "lateral thinking" rather than "linear thinking." This technique is often used after the affinity diagram has clarified issues and problems. Exhibit 400.5 shows an example of how the key strategic factors for MicroTech relate to one another. The elements having the most

Exhibit 400.4 *Affinity Diagram for MicroTech*

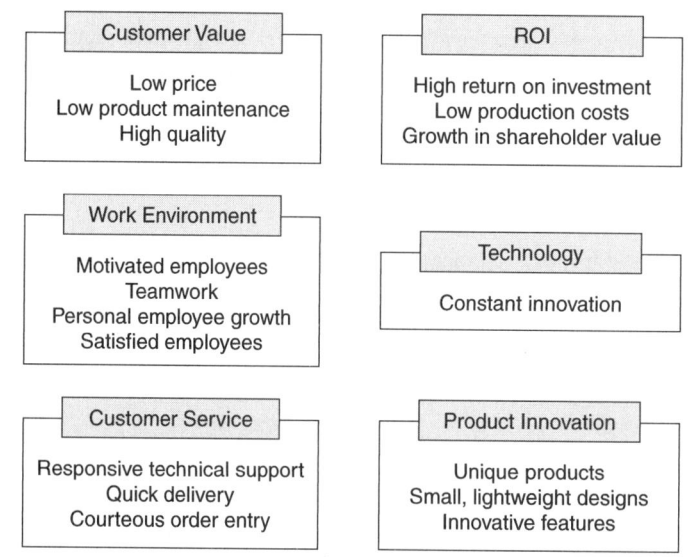

Exhibit 400.5 *Interrelationship Digraph of MicroTech's Strategic Factors*

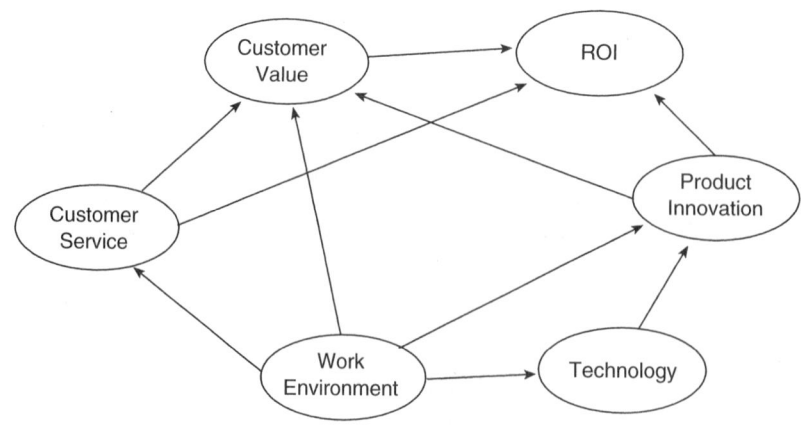

MODULE 400. QUALITY AND PROCESS MANAGEMENT

net outward-pointing arrows (number out minus number in) represent the primary drivers of the company's vision: in this case, work environment and customer service.

Tree Diagrams

A tree diagram maps out the paths and tasks necessary to complete a specific project or reach a specified goal. Thus, the planner uses this technique to seek answers to such questions as "What sequence of tasks will address the issue?" or "What factors contribute to the existence of the key problem?"

A tree diagram brings the issues and problems revealed by the affinity diagram and the interrelationship digraph down to the operational planning stage. A clear statement specifies problem or process. From this general statement, a team can be established to recommend steps to solve the problem or implement the plan. The "product" produced by this group would be a tree diagram with activities and perhaps recommendations for timing the activities. Exhibit 400.6 shows an example of how a tree diagram can be used to map out key goals and strategies for MicroTech.

Exhibit 400.6 *Tree Diagram of MicroTech Goals and Strategies*

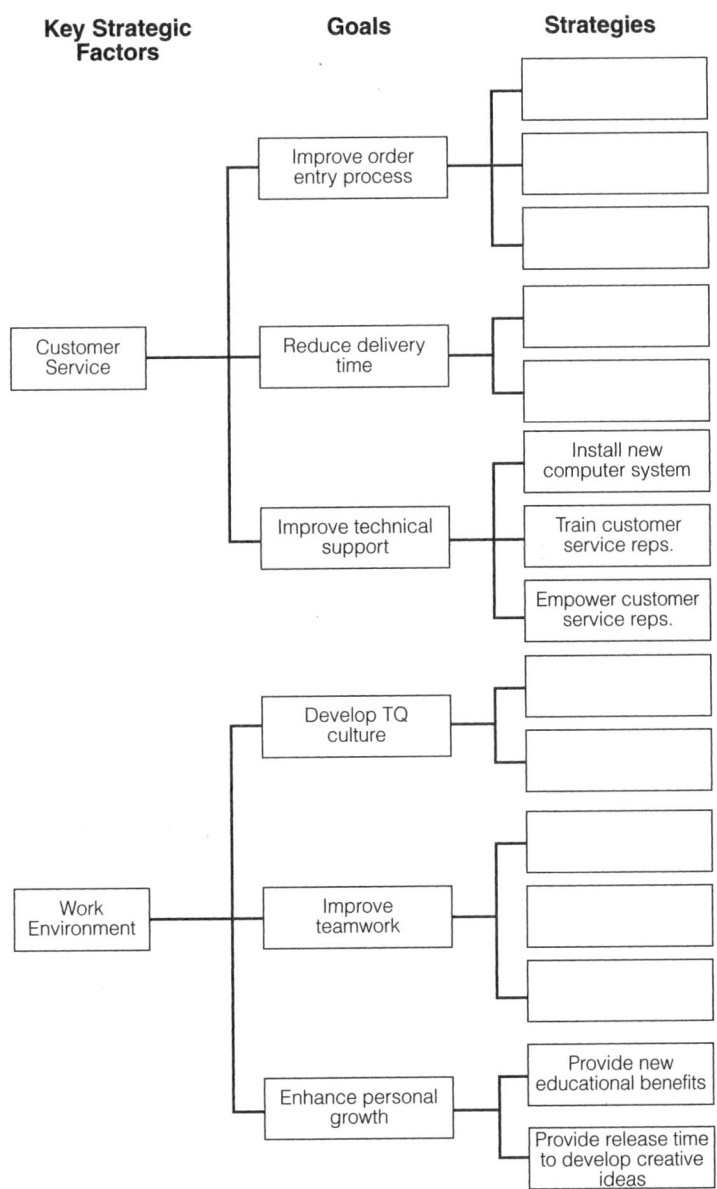

410. QUALITY MANAGEMENT PRACTICES

645

Matrix Diagrams

Matrix diagrams are "spreadsheets" that graphically display relationships between ideas, activities, or other dimensions in such a way as to provide logical connecting points between each item. A matrix diagram is one of the most versatile tools in quality planning. One example is shown in Exhibit 400.7. Here, we have listed the three principal goals articulated in MicroTech's vision statement along the rows, and the key strategies along the columns. Typically, symbols such as ●, ○, and △ are used to denote strong, medium, and weak relationships. Matrix diagrams provide a picture of how well two sets of objects or issues are related, and can identify missing pieces in the thought process. For instance, a row without many relationships might indicate that the actions proposed will not meet the company's goals. In Exhibit 400.7, we see that focused attention to these three strategies should meet MicroTech's goals. Other matrixes might relate short-term plans to medium-term objectives, or individual actions to short-term plans. These visual depictions can help managers set priorities on plans and actions.

Matrix Data Analysis

Matrix data analysis takes data and arranges them to display quantitative relationships among variables to make them more easily understood and analyzed. In its original form used in Japan, matrix data analysis is a rigorous, statistically based "factor analysis" technique. Many feel that this method, while worthwhile for many applications, is too quantitative to be used on a daily basis and have developed alternative tools that are easier to understand and implement. Some of these alternatives are similar to decision analysis matrixes that you may have studied in a quantitative methods course.

A small example of matrix data analysis is shown in Exhibit 400.8. In this example, MicroTech market researchers determined that the four most important consumer requirements are price, reliability, delivery, and technical support. Through market research, an importance weighting was developed for each. They also determined numerical ratings

Exhibit 400.7 *Matrix Diagram for MicroTech's Goals and Strategies*

Goals \ Actions	Improve Work Environment	Improve Manufacturing Technology	Develop New Products
Cost Effectiveness	●	○	
High Quality	●	●	
Shareholder Value		△	●

● = Strong relationship
○ = Medium relationship
△ = Weak relationship

Exhibit 400.8 *Matrix Data Analysis of Customer Requirements for MicroTech*

Requirement	Importance Weight	Best Competitor Evaluation	MicroTech Evaluation	Difference*
Price	.2	6	8	+2
Reliability	.4	7	8	+1
Delivery	.1	8	5	−3
Technical support	.3	7	5	−2

*MicroTech Evaluation—Best Competitor Evaluation

for the company and their best competitor. Such an analysis provides information as to which actions the company should deploy to better meet key customer requirements. For example, in Exhibit 400.8, reliability is the highest in importance, and MicroTech has a narrow lead over its best competitor; thus, it should continue to strive for improving product reliability. Also, technical support is of relatively high importance, but MicroTech is perceived to be inferior to its best competitor in this category. Thus, improving the quality of support services should be a major objective.

Process Decision Program Charts

A process decision program chart (PDPC) is a method for mapping out every conceivable event and contingency that can occur when moving from a problem statement to possible solutions. A PDPC takes each branch of a tree diagram, anticipates possible problems, and provides countermeasures that will (1) prevent the deviation from occurring, or (2) be in place if the deviation does occur.

Arrow Diagrams

For years, construction planners have used arrow diagrams in the form of CPM and PERT project-planning techniques. Arrow diagramming has also been taught extensively in quantitative methods, operations management, and other business and engineering courses in the United States for a number of years. Unfortunately, its use has generally been confined to technical experts. Adding arrow diagramming to the "quality toolbox" has made it more widely available to general managers and other nontechnical personnel.

These seven tools provide managers with improved capability to make better decisions and facilitate the implementation process. With proper planning, managers can use their time more effectively to continuously improve and innovate.

Six-Sigma

Motorola pioneered the concept of **Six-Sigma**—an approach to measuring and improving product and service quality.

Six-Sigma Metrics

Six-Sigma began by stressing a common measure for quality for products that an organization produces. In Six-Sigma terminology, a defect is any mistake or error that is passed on to the customer (many people also use the term nonconformance). A unit of work is the output of a process or an individual process step. We can measure output quality by **defects per unit (DPU)**:

$$\text{Defects per unit} = \text{Number of defects discovered}/\text{Number of units produced}$$

However, such an output measure tends to focus on the final product, not the process that produces the product. In addition, it is difficult to use for processes of varying complexity, particularly service activities. Two different processes might have significantly different numbers of opportunities for error, making appropriate comparisons difficult. The Six-Sigma concept redefines quality performance as **defects per million opportunities (dpmo)**:

$$\text{dpmo} = \text{DPU} \times 1,000,000/\text{opportunities for error}$$

For example, suppose that an airline wishes to measure the effectiveness of its baggage handling system. A DPU measure might be lost bags per customer. However, customers may have different numbers of bags; thus the number of opportunities for error is the average number of bags per customer. Thus, if the average number of bags per customer is 1.6, and the airline recorded 3 lost bags for 8,000 passengers in one month, then

$$\text{dpmo} = \frac{3}{(8,000)(1.6)} \times 1,000,000 = 234.375$$

The use of dpmo allows us to define quality broadly. In the airline case, a broad definition might mean every opportunity for a failure to meet customer expectations from initial ticketing until bags are retrieved.

Six-Sigma represents a quality level of at most *3.4 defects per million opportunities.* The theoretical basis for Six-Sigma is explained by Exhibit 400.9 in the context of manufacturing specifications. A Six-Sigma quality level corresponds to a process variation equal to half of the design tolerance (in terms of the process capability index, $C_p = 2.0$), while allowing the mean to shift as much as 1.5 standard deviations from the target.

410. QUALITY MANAGEMENT PRACTICES

Exhibit 400.9 *Six-Sigma Quality*

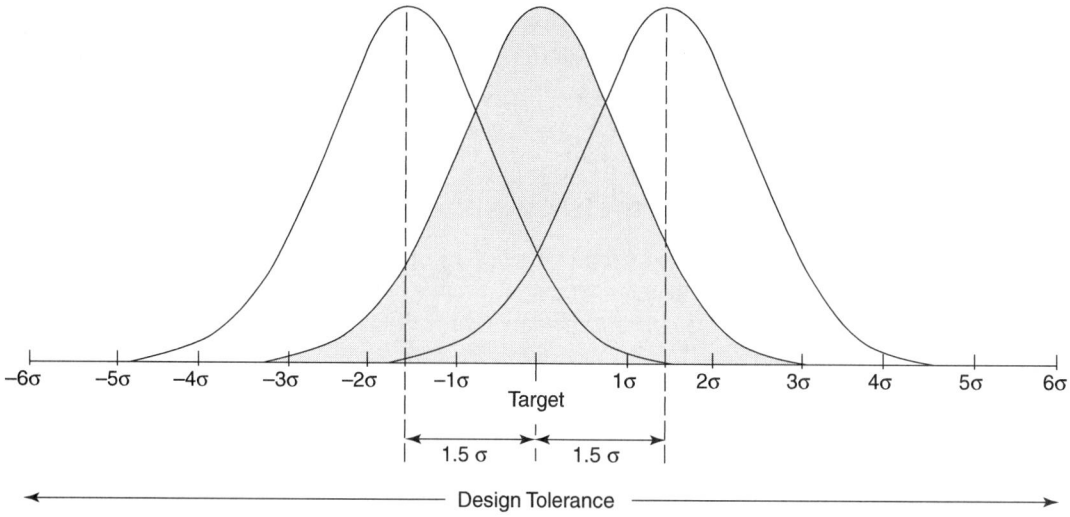

Implementing Six-Sigma

Six-Sigma has developed from simply a way of measuring quality to an overall strategy to accelerate improvements and achieve unprecedented performance levels within an organization by finding and eliminating causes of errors or defects in processes by focusing on characteristics that are critical to customers.[7] The core philosophy of Six-Sigma is based on some key concepts:

1. Emphasizing dpmo as a standard metric that can be applied to all parts of an organization: manufacturing, engineering, administrative, software, and so on
2. Providing extensive training followed by project-team deployment to improve profitability, reduce non-value-added activities, and achieve cycle-time reduction
3. Focusing on corporate sponsors responsible for supporting team activities, helping to overcome resistance to change, obtain resources, and focus the teams on overall strategic objectives
4. Creating highly qualified process improvement experts ("green belts," "black belts," and "master black belts") who can apply improvement tools and lead teams
5. Ensuring that appropriate metrics are identified early in the process and that they focus on business results
6. Setting stretch objectives for improvement

Source: Dr. Stanley A. Marash, Chairman, STAT-A-MATRIX Inc.

The recognized benchmark for Six-Sigma implementation is General Electric. GE's Six-Sigma problem-solving approach (DMAIC) employs five phases:

1. *Define (D)*
   - Identify customers and their priorities.
   - Identify a project suitable for Six-Sigma efforts based on business objectives as well as customer needs and feedback.
   - Identify CTQs (critical-to-quality characteristics) that the customer considers to have the most impact on quality.
2. *Measure (M)*
   - Determine how to measure the process and how is it performing.
   - Identify the key internal processes that influence CTQs and measure the defects currently generated relative to those processes.
3. *Analyze (A)*
   - Determine the most likely causes of defects.
   - Understand why defects are generated by identifying the key variables that are most likely to create process variation.

4. *Improve (I)*
   - Identify means to remove the causes of the defects.
   - Confirm the key variables and quantify their effects on the CTQs.
   - Identify the maximum acceptable ranges of the key variables and a system for measuring deviations of the variables.
   - Modify the process to stay within the acceptable range.
5. *Control (C)*
   - Determine how to maintain the improvements.
   - Put tools in place to ensure that the key variables remain within the maximum acceptable ranges under the modified process.

Source: Henderson, Kim M. and Evans, James R., "Successful Implementation of Six Sigma: Benchmarking General Electric Company," *Benchmarking: An International Journal* (2000), 260–281. Published with permission of Emerald Group Publishing Limited. http://www.emeraldinsight.com

Note that this approach is similar to the other quality improvement approaches we discussed and incorporates many of the same ideas. The key difference is the emphasis placed on customer requirements and the use of statistical tools and methodologies.

In many ways, Six-Sigma is the realization of many fundamental concepts of "total quality management," notably, the integration of human and process elements of improvement. Human issues include management leadership, a sense of urgency, focus on results and customers, team processes, and culture change; process issues include the use of process management techniques, analysis of variation and statistical methods, a disciplined problem-solving approach, and management by fact.

Several key principles are necessary for effective implementation of Six-Sigma:

- *Committed leadership from top management.*
- *Integration with existing initiatives, business strategy, and performance measurement.*
- *Process thinking.*
- *Disciplined customer and market intelligence gathering.*
- *A bottom-line orientation.*
- *Leadership in the trenches.* Within GE, Six-Sigma includes a diverse population of technical and nontechnical people, managers, and others from key business areas.
  - *Champions* are fully trained business leaders who promote and lead the deployment of Six-Sigma in a significant area of the business.
  - *Master black belts* are fully trained quality leaders responsible for Six-Sigma strategy, training, mentoring, deployment, and results.
  - *Black belts* are fully trained Six-Sigma experts who lead improvement teams, work projects across the business, and mentor green belts.
  - *Green belts* are full-time teachers with quantitative skills as well as teaching and leadership ability; they are fully trained quality leaders responsible for Six-Sigma strategy, training, mentoring, deployment, and results.
  - *Team members* are individuals who support specific projects in their area.
- *Training.*
- *Continuous reinforcement and rewards.*

(© 1999, American Society for Quality. Reprinted with permission from Quality Progress.)

Tools for Six-Sigma and Quality Improvement

The tools used in Six-Sigma efforts have been around for a long time. What is unique about Six-Sigma is the integration of the tools and methodology into management systems across the organization.[8] The topics covered may be categorized into seven general groups:

- *Elementary statistical tools:* basic statistics, statistical thinking, hypothesis testing, correlation, simple regression
- *Advanced statistical tools:* design of experiments, analysis of variance, multiple regression
- *Product design and reliability:* quality function deployment, failure mode and effects analysis
- *Measurement:* process capability, measurement systems analysis

- *Process control:* control plans, statistical process control
- *Process improvement:* process improvement planning, process mapping, mistake proofing
- *Implementation and teamwork:* organizational effectiveness, team assessment, facilitation tools, team development

The Original Seven Quality Control Tools

Seven simple tools—flowcharts, control charts, check sheets, histograms, Pareto diagrams, cause-and-effect diagrams, and scatter diagrams—termed the **Seven QC** (quality control) **Tools** by the Japanese, support quality improvement problem-solving efforts. Exhibit 400.10 shows the primary applications of each tool in the problem-solving process. They are designed simply so that workers at all levels can use them easily. We will briefly review each of these tools to explain their role in quality improvement, including mistake-proofing technique.

Flowcharts

To understand a process, one must first determine how it works and what it is supposed to do. Flowcharting, or **process mapping,** identifies the sequence of activities or the flow of materials and information in a process. Flowcharts help the people who are involved in the process understand it much better and more objectively. Understanding how a process works enables a team to pinpoint obvious problems, error-proof the process, streamline it by eliminating non-value-added steps, and reduce variation.

Flowcharts are best developed by having the people involved in the process—employees, supervisors, managers, and customers—construct the flowchart. A facilitator provides objectivity in resolving conflicts. The facilitator can guide the discussion through questions such as "What happens next?" "Who makes the decision at this point?" and "What operation is performed at this point?" Quite often, the group does not universally agree on the answers to these questions due to misconceptions about the process itself or a lack of awareness of the "big picture."

Flowcharts help all employees understand how they fit into a process and who are their suppliers and customers. This realization then leads to improved communication among all parties. By participating in the development of a flowchart, workers feel a sense of ownership in the process, and hence become more willing to work on improving it. If flowcharts are used in training employees, more consistency will be achieved. Flowcharts also help to pinpoint places where quality-related measurements should be taken. Once a flowchart is constructed, it can be used to identify quality problems as well as areas for productivity improvement. Questions such as "How does this operation affect the customer?" "Can we improve or even eliminate this operation?" or "Should we control a critical quality characteristic at this point?" trigger the identification of opportunities.

Control Charts

A **run chart** is a line graph in which data are plotted over time. The vertical axis represents a measurement; the horizontal axis is the time scale. The daily newspaper usually has several examples of run charts, such as the Dow Jones Industrial Average. Run charts show the performance and the variation of a process or some quality or productivity indicator over time. They can be used to track such things as production volume, costs, and customer satisfaction indexes. Run charts summarize data in a graphical fashion that is easy to understand and interpret, identify process changes and trends over time, and show the effects of corrective actions.

Exhibit 400.10 *Applications of the Seven QC Tools*

Tool	Application
Flowcharts	Understanding the mess; establishing control procedures
Control charts	Understanding the mess; holding the gains
Check sheets	Finding facts
Histograms	Identifying problems
Pareto diagrams	Understanding the mess; identifying problems
Cause-and-effect diagrams	Generating ideas
Scatter diagrams	Developing solutions

Exhibit 400.11 *The Structure of a Control Chart*

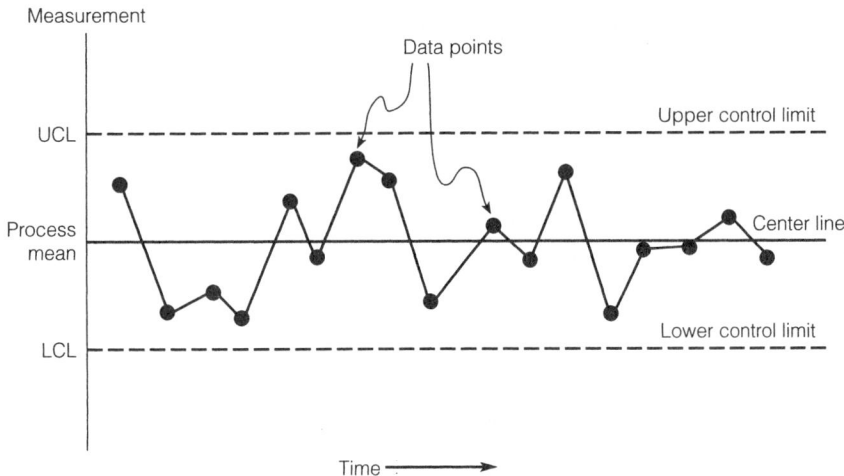

A **control chart** is simply a run chart to which two horizontal lines, called *control limits* are added: the *upper control limit (UCL)* and *lower control limit (LCL)*, as illustrated in Exhibit 400.11. Control charts were first proposed by Walter Shewhart at Bell Laboratories in the 1920s and were strongly advocated by Deming. Control limits are chosen statistically to provide a high probability (generally greater than 0.99) that points will fall between these limits if the process is in control. Control limits make it easier to interpret patterns in a run chart and draw conclusions about the state of control.

If sample values fall outside the control limits or if nonrandom patterns occur in the chart, then special causes may be affecting the process; the process is not stable. The process should be examined and corrective action taken as appropriate. If evaluation and correction are done in real time, then the chance of producing nonconforming product is minimized. Thus, as a problem-solving tool, control charts allow operators to identify quality problems as they occur. Of course, control charts alone cannot determine the source of the problem. Operators, supervisors, and engineers may have to resort to other problem-solving tools to seek the root cause.

Check Sheets

Check sheets are simple tools for data collection. Nearly any kind of form may be used to collect data. *Data sheets* are simple columnar or tabular forms used to record data. However, to generate useful information from raw data, further processing generally is necessary. Check sheets are special types of data collection forms in which the results may be interpreted on the form directly without additional processing.

Histograms

A **histogram** is a basic statistical tool that graphically shows the frequency or number of observations of a particular value or within a specified group. Histograms provide clues about the characteristics of the parent population from which a sample is taken. Patterns that would be difficult to see in an ordinary table of numbers become apparent. Histograms are extremely useful in process capability analysis to help understand variation in a process.

Some caution should be exercised when interpreting histograms. First, the data should be representative of typical process conditions. If a new employee is now operating the equipment, or the equipment, material, or method have changed, then new data should be collected. Second, the sample size should be large enough to provide good conclusions; the larger, the better. Various guidelines exist, but a suggested minimum of at least 50 observations should be drawn. Finally, any conclusions drawn should be confirmed through further study and analysis.

Pareto Diagrams

The *Pareto principle* was observed by Joseph Juran in 1950. Juran found that most effects resulted from only a few causes. Pareto analysis clearly separates the vital few from the trivial many and provides direction for selecting projects for improvement.

Pareto analysis is often used to analyze data collected in check sheets. A **Pareto distribution** is one in which the characteristics observed are ordered from largest frequency to smallest. A **Pareto diagram** is a histogram of the data from the largest frequency to the smallest. Often one also draws a cumulative frequency curve on the histogram, as shown in Exhibit 400.12. Such a visual aid clearly shows the relative magnitude of defects and can be used to identify opportunities for improvement. The most costly or significant problems stand out. Pareto diagrams can also show the results of improvement programs over time. They are less intimidating to employees who are fearful of statistics.

Pareto diagrams are used to progressively analyze specific problems. At each step, the Pareto diagram stratifies the data to more detailed levels (or it may require additional data collection), eventually isolating the most significant issues.

Cause-and-Effect Diagrams

Variation in process output and other quality problems can occur for a variety of reasons, such as materials, machines, methods, people, and measurement. The goal of problem-solving is to identify the causes of problems in order to correct them. The **cause-and-effect diagram** is an important tool in this task; it assists in the generation of ideas for problem causes and, in turn, serves as a basis for solution finding.

The cause-and-effect diagram was introduced in Japan by Kaoru Ishikawa. It is a simple, graphical method for presenting a chain of causes and effects and for sorting out causes and organizing relationships between variables. Because of its structure, it is often called a *fishbone diagram*. The general structure of a cause-and-effect diagram is shown in Exhibit 400.13. At the end of the horizontal line, a problem is listed. Each branch pointing into the main stem represents a possible cause. Branches pointing to the causes are contributors to those causes. The diagram identifies the most likely causes of a problem so that further data collection and analysis can be carried out.

Cause-and-effect diagrams are constructed in a brainstorming type of atmosphere. Everyone can get involved and feel they are an important part of the problem-solving process. Usually small groups drawn from manufacturing or management work with a trained and experienced facilitator. The facilitator guides attention to discussion of the problem and its causes, not opinions. As a group technique, the cause-and-effect method requires significant interaction between group members. The facilitator who listens carefully to the participants can capture the important ideas. A group can often be more effective by thinking of the problem broadly and considering environmental factors, political factors, employee issues, and even government policies, if appropriate.

Exhibit 400.12   *Pareto Diagram*

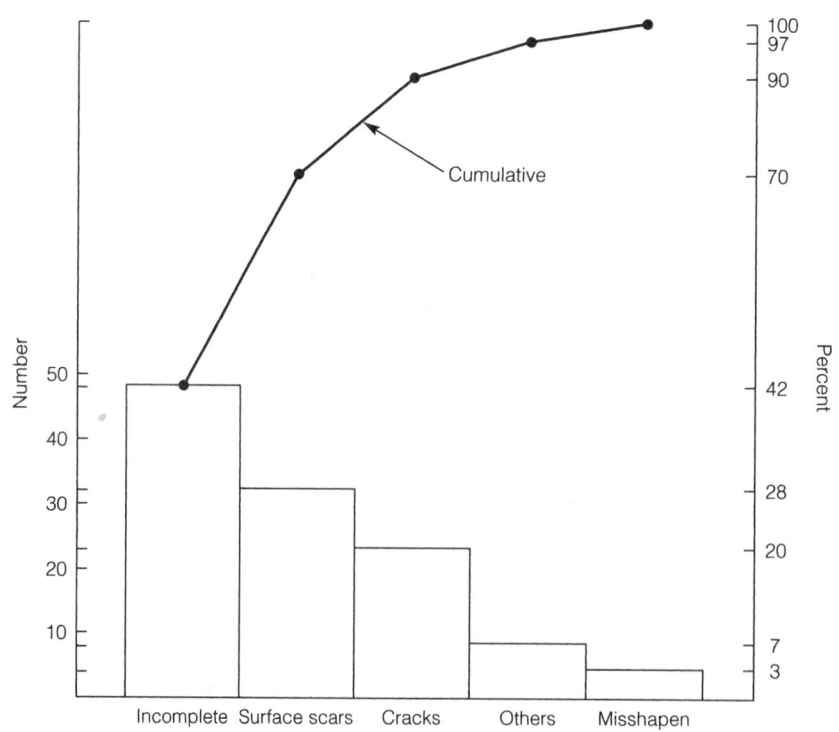

Exhibit 400.13 *General Structure of Cause-and-Effect Diagram*

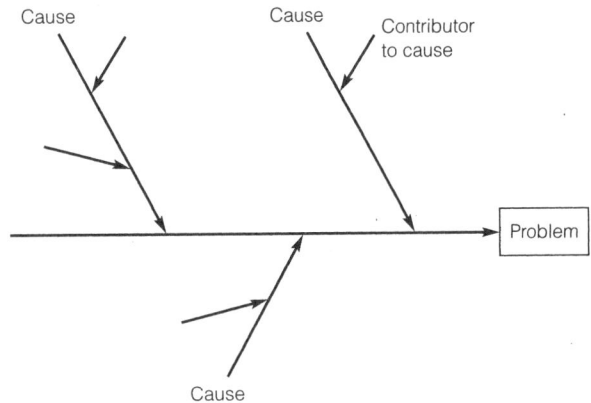

Exhibit 400.14 *Three Types of Correlation*

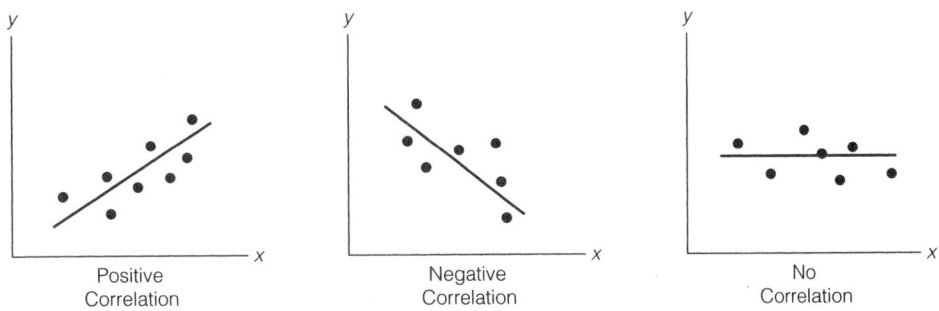

Scatter Diagrams

Scatter diagrams are the graphical component of regression analysis. Although they do not provide rigorous statistical analysis, they often point to important relationships between variables, such as the percentage of an ingredient in an alloy and the hardness of the alloy. Typically, the variables in question represent possible causes and effects obtained from Ishikawa diagrams. For example, if a manufacturer suspects that the percentage of an ingredient in an alloy is causing quality problems in meeting hardness specifications, an employee group might collect data from samples on the amount of ingredient and hardness and plot the data on a scatter diagram.

Statistical correlation analysis is used to interpret scatter diagrams. Exhibit 400.14 shows three types of correlation. If the correlation is positive, an increase in variable x is related to an increase in variable y; if the correlation is negative, an increase in x is related to a decrease in y; and if the correlation is close to zero, the variables have no linear relationship.

Poka-Yoke (Mistake-Proofing)

Human beings tend to make mistakes inadvertently. Errors can arise for a number of reasons:

- Forgetfulness due to lack of concentration
- Misunderstanding because of the lack of familiarity with a process or procedures
- Poor identification associated with lack of proper attention
- Lack of experience
- Absentmindedness
- Delays in judgment when a process is automated
- Equipment malfunctions

Typical mistakes in production are omitted processing, processing errors, setup errors, missing parts, wrong parts, and adjustment errors. Blaming workers not only discourages them and lowers morale, but does not solve the problem.

410. QUALITY MANAGEMENT PRACTICES

Poka-yoke (POH-kah YOH-kay) is an approach for mistake-proofing processes using automatic devices or methods to avoid simple human or machine error. The poka-yoke concept was developed and refined in the early 1960s by the late Shigeo Shingo, a Japanese manufacturing engineer who developed the Toyota production system (TPS).

Poka-yoke is focused on two aspects: prediction, or recognizing that a defect is about to occur and providing a warning, and detection, or recognizing that a defect has occurred and stopping the process. Many applications of poka-yoke are deceptively simple, yet creative. Usually, they are inexpensive to implement.

It has been suggested that the same concepts can be applied to services. The major differences are that service mistake-proofing must account for the customers' activities as well as those of the producer, and fail-safe methods must be set up for interactions conducted directly or by phone, mail, or other technologies, such as ATM. Chase and Stewart classify service poka-yokes by the type of error they are designed to prevent: server errors and customer errors. Server errors result from the task, treatment, or tangibles of the service. Customer errors occur during preparation, the service encounter, or during resolution.

Task errors include doing work incorrectly, work not requested, work in the wrong order, or working too slowly. Some examples of poka-yoke devices for task errors are computer prompts, color-coded cash register keys, measuring tools such as McDonald's french-fry scoop, and signaling devices. Hospitals use trays for surgical instruments that have indentations for each instrument, preventing the surgeon from leaving one of them in the patient.

Treatment errors arise in the contact between the server and the customer, such as lack of courteous behavior, and failure to acknowledge, listen, or react appropriately to the customer. A bank encourages eye contact by requiring tellers to record the customer's eye color on a checklist as they start the transaction. To promote friendliness at a fast-food restaurant, trainers provide the four specific cues for when to smile: when greeting the customer, when taking the order, when telling about the dessert special, and when giving the customer change. They encourage employees to observe whether the customer smiled back, a natural reinforcer for smiling.

Tangible errors are those in physical elements of the service, such as unclean facilities, dirty uniforms, inappropriate temperature, and document errors. Hotels wrap paper strips around towels to help the housekeeping staff identify clean linen and show which ones should be replaced. Spell-checkers in word-processing software eliminate document misspellings.

Customer errors in preparation include the failure to bring necessary materials to the encounter, the failure to understand their role in the service transaction, and the failure to engage the correct service. Digital Equipment provides a flowchart to specify how to place a service call. By guiding the customers through three yes-or-no questions, the flowchart prompts them to have the necessary information before calling.

Customer errors during an encounter can be due to inattention, misunderstanding, or simply a memory lapse, and include failure to remember steps in the process or to follow instructions. Poka-yoke examples include height bars at amusement rides that indicate rider size requirements, beepers that signal customers to remove cards from ATM machines, and locks on airplane lavatory doors that must be closed to turn on the lights. Some cashiers at restaurants fold back the top edge of credit card receipts, holding together the restaurant's copies while revealing the customer's copy.

Customer errors at the resolution stage of a service encounter include failure to signal service inadequacies, failure to learn from experience, failure to adjust expectations, and failure to execute appropriate post-encounter actions. Hotels might enclose a small gift certificate to encourage guests to provide feedback. Strategically placed tray-return stands and trash receptacles remind customers to return trays in fast-food facilities.

Mistake-proofing a service process requires identifying when and where failures generally occur. Once a failure is identified, the source must be found. The final step is to prevent the mistake from occurring through source inspection, self-inspection, or sequential checks.

The Cost of Quality

In most firms cost accounting has been an important function. All organizations measure and report costs as a basis for control and improvement. The concept of the **cost of quality** (**COQ**) emerged in the 1950s. Traditionally, the reporting of quality-related costs had been limited to inspection and testing; other costs were accumulated in overhead accounts. As managers began to define and isolate the full range of quality-related costs, a number of surprising facts emerged.[9] First, quality-related costs were much larger than previously reported, generally in the range of 20 to 40 percent of sales. Second, quality-related costs were not only related to manufacturing operations, but to ancillary services such as purchasing and customer service departments as well. Third, most of the costs resulted from poor quality and were avoidable. Finally, while the costs of poor quality were avoidable, no clear responsibility for action to reduce them was assigned, nor was any structured approach formulated to do so. As a result, many companies began to develop cost of quality programs. The "costs of quality"—or more specifically, the costs of *poor* quality—were associated with avoiding poor quality or incurred as a result of poor quality.

To establish a cost of quality approach, one must identify the activities that generate cost, measure them, report them in a way that is meaningful to managers, and analyze them to identify areas for improvement. The following sections discuss these activities in greater detail.

Quality Cost Classification

Quality costs can be organized into four major categories: prevention costs, appraisal costs, internal failure costs, and external failure costs. **Prevention costs** are investments made to keep nonconforming products from occurring and reaching the customer, including the following specific costs:

- *Quality planning costs,* such as salaries of individuals associated with quality planning and problem-solving teams, the development of new procedures, new equipment design, and reliability studies
- *Process control costs,* which include costs spent on analyzing production processes and implementing process control plans
- *Information systems costs* expended to develop data requirements and measurements
- *Training and general management costs,* including internal and external training programs, clerical staff expenses, and miscellaneous supplies.

Specific examples of prevention costs include the following: operator inspection costs, supplier ratings, supplier reviews, purchase-order technical data reviews, training, supplier certification, design reviews, pilot projects, prototype tests, vendor surveys, quality design, quality department review costs, customer surveys, product design, service design, process design, supplier reviews and rating, field trials and tests, quality planning, quality education and training, quality administration, quality system audits, design equipment, process control tools, quality tools and equipment, and supplier quality surveys.

Appraisal costs are those associated with efforts to ensure conformance to requirements, generally through measurement and analysis of data to detect nonconformances. Categories of appraisal costs include the following:

- *Test and inspection costs* associated with incoming materials, work-in-process, and finished goods, including equipment costs and salaries
- *Instrument maintenance costs,* arising from calibration and repair of measuring instruments
- *Process measurement and control costs,* which involve the time spent by workers to gather and analyze quality measurements.

Specific examples of appraisal costs include the following: purchasing appraisal costs, qualifications of supplier product, equipment calibration, receiving and shipping inspection cost, tests, product quality audits, receiving inspections, test materials, setup inspections and special tests, laboratory support and supplies, measurement equipment and supplies, maintenance labor, external appraisal costs, evaluation of inventory and parts, review of test and inspection data, outside certification costs, product quality audit, service quality audit, operations inspection and tests, purchasing appraisal costs, and source inspection costs.

Internal failure costs are incurred as a result of unsatisfactory quality found before the delivery of a product to the customer. Some examples include the following:

- *Scrap and rework costs,* including material, labor, and overhead
- *Costs of corrective action,* arising from time spent determining the causes of failure and correcting production problems
- *Downgrading costs,* such as revenue lost when selling a product at a lower price because it does not meet specifications
- *Process failures,* such as unplanned machine downtime or unplanned equipment repair.

Specific examples of internal failure costs include the following: repair, redesign, reinspection, rework, retesting, sorting, scrap, design corrective action, rework costs due to design change, scrap costs due to design change, purchasing failure cots, supplier corrective action, operations failure costs, disposition costs for nonconforming materials, operations troubleshooting costs, product liability investigation support costs, operations corrective action, reinspection and retests, cost of site visits to correct supplier quality problems, and uncontrolled labor and material costs.

External failure costs occur after poor-quality products reach the customer, specifically:

- *Costs due to customer complaints and returns,* including rework on returned items, cancelled orders, and freight premiums
- *Product recall costs* and *warranty claims,* including the cost of repair or replacement as well as associated administrative costs
- *Product liability costs,* resulting from legal actions and settlements.

Specific examples of external failure costs include the following: product warranty charges, product returns, parts recalls, liability suits, field service staff training costs, customer complaint investigations, returned goods, design retrofit costs, product recall costs, warranty claims, product liability costs, penalties and litigation costs, loss of customer goodwill, and lost sales and profits.

Experts estimate that 60 to 90 percent of total quality costs are the result of internal and external failure and are the responsibility of, but not easily controllable by, management. In the past, managers reacted to high failure costs by increasing inspection. Such actions, however, only increase appraisal costs. The overall result is little, if any, improvement in quality or profitability. In practice, an increase in prevention usually generates larger savings in all other cost categories. In a typical scenario, the cost of replacing a poor-quality component in the field might be $500; the cost of replacement after assembly might be $50; the cost of testing and replacement during assembly might be $5; and the cost of changing the design to avoid the problem might be only 50 cents.

Better prevention of poor quality clearly reduces internal failure costs, as fewer defective items are made. External failure costs also decrease. In addition, less appraisal is required, because the products are made correctly the first time. However, because production is usually viewed in the short term, many managers fail to understand or implement these ideas.

A convenient way of reporting quality costs is through a breakdown by organizational function as shown in Exhibit 400.15. This matrix serves several purposes. First, it allows all departments to recognize their contributions to

Exhibit 400.15 *Cost of Quality Matrix*

	Design Engineering	Purchasing	Production	...	Finance	...	Accounting	Totals
Prevention costs								
Quality planning								
Training								
...								
Appraisal costs								
Test and inspection								
Instruments								
...								
Internal failure costs								
Scrap								
Rework								
...								
External failure costs								
Returns								
Recall costs								
...								
Totals								

the cost of quality and participate in a cost of quality program. Second, it pinpoints areas of high quality cost and turns attention toward improvement efforts. Such a report can be implemented easily on a spreadsheet.

Quality costs are often reported as an *index,* that is, the ratio of the current value to a base period. Index numbers increase managers' understanding of the data, particularly how conditions in one period compare with those in other periods. A simple type of index is called a relative index, computed by dividing a current value by a base-period value. Sometimes the result is multiplied by 100 to express it as a percentage. As an example, consider the following direct labor costs per quarter for a manufactured product:

Quarter	Cost
1	$1,500
2	1,800
3	1,700
4	1,750

If the first quarter is the base period, the cost relative indexes expressed as percentages are computed as

Quarter	Cost Relative Index		%
1	(1,500/1,500)(100)	=	100
2	(1,800/1,500)(100)	=	120
3	(1,700/1,500)(100)	=	113.33
4	(1,750/1,500)(100)	=	116.67

Costs and prices are often sensitive to changes in the firm. For example, if the number of units produced in each quarter differs, comparisons of direct labor costs are meaningless. However, a measure such as cost per unit would provide useful information for managers.

Quality costs themselves provide little information because they may vary due to such factors as production volume or seasonality. Thus, index numbers can more effectively analyze quality cost data. Some common measurement bases are labor, manufacturing cost, sales, and units of product. Each is described here.

- *Labor-Based Index.* Quality cost per direct labor-hour represents a typical quality cost index that is easily understood by managers. Accounting departments can usually provide direct labor data, either in total labor-hours or standard labor-hours. Standard hours often provide a better measure than total labor-hours because they represent planned rather than actual production. Labor-based indexes are drastically influenced by automation and other changes in technology, however, so one must be careful in using them over long periods of time. Often quality cost per direct labor-dollar is used to eliminate the effects of inflation.
- *Cost-Based Index.* Quality cost per manufacturing cost dollar is a common index in this category. Manufacturing cost includes direct labor, material, and overhead costs that are usually available from accounting departments. Cost-based indexes are more stable than labor-based indexes because they are not affected by price fluctuations or by changes in the level of automation.
- *Sales-Based Index.* Quality cost per sales dollar is a popular index that appeals to top management. However, this measure is rather poor for short-term analysis because sales usually lag behind production and are subject to seasonal variations. In addition, a sales-based index is affected by changes in the selling price.
- *Unit-Based Index.* A common measure in this category is quality costs per unit of production. This simple index is acceptable if the output of production lines is similar; however, it is a poor measure if many different products are made. In such a case, an alternative index of quality costs per equivalent unit of output is often used. To obtain this index, different product lines are weighted to approximate a standard or "average" product that is used as a common base.

All these indexes, although used extensively in practice, have a fundamental problem. A change in the denominator can appear to be a change in the level of quality or productivity alone. For instance, if direct labor is decreased through managerial improvements, the direct labor-based index will increase even if quality does not change. Also, the common inclusion of overhead in manufacturing cost is certain to distort results. Nevertheless, use of such indexes is widespread and helpful for comparing quality costs over time. Generally, sales bases are the most popular, followed by cost, labor, and unit bases.[10]

Quality cost data can be broken down by product line, process, department, work center, time, or cost category. This categorization makes data analysis more convenient and useful to management. For example, a company might

Exhibit 400.16 *Quality Cost Categories*

| | January | | February | |
Cost Category	Product A	Product B	Product A	Product B
Prevention	$ 2,000	$ 4,000	$ 2,000	$ 4,000
Appraisal	10,000	20,000	13,000	21,000
Internal failure	19,000	106,000	16,000	107,000
External failure	54,000	146,000	52,000	156,000
Total	$85,000	$276,000	$83,000	$288,000
Standard direct labor costs	$35,000	$ 90,000	$28,000	$ 86,000

Exhibit 400.17 *Quality Cost Indexes*

| | January | | February | |
Cost Category	Product A	Product B	Product A	Product B
Prevention	0.057	0.044	0.071	0.047
Appraisal	0.286	0.222	0.464	0.244
Internal failure	0.543	1.178	0.571	1.244
External failure	1.543	1.622	1.857	1.814
Total	2.429	3.067	2.964	3.349

collect quality costs by cost category and product for each time period, say one month. An example is given in Exhibit 400.16. A total quality cost index is

$$\text{Total quality cost index} = \text{Total quality costs}/\text{Direct labor costs}$$

Alternatively, individual indexes can be computed by category, product, and time period, and are summarized in Exhibit 400.17. For example, in January, 0.057 for Product A prevention is obtained by dividing $2,000 by $35,000.

Such information can be used to identify trends or areas that require significant attention. Of course, such information can only signal areas for improvement; it cannot tell managers what the specific problems are. Teams of workers are responsible for uncovering the sources of problems and determining appropriate corrective action. For example, a steady rise in internal failure costs and decline in appraisal costs might indicate a problem in assembly, maintenance of testing equipment, or a lack of proper control of purchased parts.

In the context of quality costs, the sources of cost are rarely uniformly distributed. Pareto analysis consists of ordering cost categories from largest to smallest. For example, chances are that 70 or 80 percent of all internal failure costs are due to only one or two manufacturing problems. Identifying these "vital few," as they are called, leads to corrective action that has a high return for a low dollar input.

For most companies embarking on a quality cost program, management typically finds that the highest costs occur in the external failure category, followed by internal failure, appraisal, and prevention, in that order. Clearly, the order should be reversed; that is, the bulk of quality costs should be found in prevention, some in appraisal, perhaps a few in internal failure, and virtually none in external failure. Thus, companies should first attempt to reduce external failure costs to zero by investing in appraisal activities to discover the sources of failure and take corrective action. As quality improves, failure costs will decrease, and the amount of appraisal can be reduced with the shift of emphasis to prevention activities.

Quality Costs in Service Organizations

The nature of quality costs differs between service and manufacturing organizations. In manufacturing, quality costs are primarily product-oriented; for services, however, they are generally labor-dependent, because labor often accounts for as much as 75 percent of total costs. Traditional external failure costs such as warranty and field support are less relevant to services than to manufacturing. Process-related costs, such as customer service and complaint-handling staff and lost customers are more critical.

Internal failure costs might not be as evident in services as in manufacturing. For example, a small distributor focused a great deal of attention on minimizing inventories while trying to improve service. The company knew that backorders existed, but believed that it was simply the nature of the business. But further analysis revealed nearly one backorder for every five orders. After examining the process, the cost of backorders was determined to be $30 per transaction, for an annual cost of $200,000. The reasons were found to include suppliers not meeting delivery dates, errors in sales orders, and other non-value-added operations.[11] Internal failure costs tend to be much lower for service organizations with high customer contact, which have little opportunity to correct an error before it reaches the customer. By that time, the error becomes an external failure.

Work measurement and sampling techniques are often used extensively to gather quality costs in service organizations. For example, work measurement can be used to determine how much time an employee spends on various quality-related activities. The proportion of time spent multiplied by the individual's salary represents an estimate of the quality cost for that activity. Consumer surveys and other means of customer feedback are also used to determine quality costs for services. In general, however, the intangible nature of the output makes quality cost accounting for services difficult.

Measuring the Return on Quality (ROQ)

Total quality efforts should lead to the achievement of outstanding business results. However, a successful quality initiative does not guarantee financial success. (Many argue that without it, however, a company will eventually be doomed to failure.) Many companies fail to pay enough attention to the financial returns on quality-related investments. Financial returns not only demonstrate when the efforts are going in the right direction, but can help identify changes and improvements that need to be made before staying on the wrong path too long. For example, AT&T's chairman receives a quarterly report from each business unit that describes quality improvements and their financial impacts.

Traditionally, measuring reductions in quality-related costs through cost of quality (COQ) was the principal method of documenting the benefits of quality. However, this approach only focuses on the internal view of quality. Attention must also be paid to the external view and accounting for increases in revenues associated with improved customer satisfaction. Measuring expected revenue gains against expected costs associated with quality efforts has become known as **return on quality,** or **ROQ.** ROQ is based on four main principles:

1. Quality is an investment.
2. Quality efforts must be made financially accountable.
3. It is possible to spend too much on quality.
4. Not all quality expenditures are equally valid.

The foundation for the approach stems from the model relating quality to profitability, which proposes that quality improvement leads to financial returns through improvements in customer satisfaction and loyalty. Sophisticated statistical methods are often used to estimate these effects and the financial implications.

A prescription for implementing ROQ was described in *Business Week*:

1. *Start with an effective quality approach.* Companies that don't have the basics, such as process and inventory controls and other building blocks, will find a healthy return on quality elusive.
2. *Calculate the cost of current quality initiatives.* Cost of warranties, problem prevention, and monitoring activities all count. Measure these against the returns for delivering a product or service to the customer.
3. *Determine what key factors retain customers and what drives them away.* Conduct detailed surveys. Forecast market changes, especially quality and new-product initiatives of competitors.
4. *Focus on quality efforts most likely to improve customer satisfaction at a reasonable cost.* Figure the link between each dollar spent on quality and its effect on customer retention and market share.
5. *Roll out successful approaches after pilot-testing the most promising efforts and cutting the ones that don't have a big impact.* Closely monitor results. Build word of mouth by publicizing success stories.
6. *Improve quality efforts continually.* Measure results against anticipated gains. Beware of the competition's initiative and don't hesitate to revamp approaches accordingly. Quality never rests.[12]

The ROQ approach was applied to evaluating a training program to improve customer service skills of branch staff at Chase Manhattan Bank.[13] The intended outcomes of the program included the ability of the branch staff to identify behavior that creates a positive memorable customer experience, analyze interactions with customers, identify what customers want, and understand the nature of caring customer service. Test and control groups were used. The net present value (NPV) of the loss avoided from customers not becoming dissatisfied as a result of the training program was then estimated at $471,000 and compared to a $326,000 net present value (NPV) of training costs. The resulting return on investment, expressed in terms of ROQ, was computed to be 44.4 percent.

$$ROQ = \left(\frac{\text{NPV of benefits}}{\text{NPV of costs}}\right) - 1.00$$

$$ROQ = \frac{\$471,000}{\$326,000} - 1.00$$
$$= 1.444 - 1.00 = 0.444 = 44.4 \text{ percent}$$

This evaluation showed that a systemwide training program would likely be profitable. Results were circulated among Chase managers, and the company moved forward with expansion of the training program.

Quality and Competitive Advantage

Competitive advantage denotes a firm's ability to achieve market superiority. In the long run, a sustainable competitive advantage goes hand in hand with above-average performance. S. C. Wheelwright identified six characteristics of a strong competitive advantage:

1. It is driven by customer wants and needs. A company provides value to its customers that competitors do not.
2. It makes a significant contribution to the success of the business.
3. It matches the organization's unique resources with opportunities in the environment. No two companies have the same resources; a good strategy uses the firm's particular resources effectively.
4. It is durable and lasting, and difficult for competitors to copy. A superior research and development department, for example, can consistently develop new products or processes that enable the firm to remain ahead of competitors.
5. It provides a basis for further improvement.
6. It provides direction and motivation to the entire organization.

Each of these characteristics relates to quality, suggesting that quality is an important source of competitive advantage.

The importance of quality in achieving competitive advantage was demonstrated by several research studies during the 1980s. PIMS Associates, Inc., a subsidiary of the Strategic Planning Institute, maintains a database of 1,200 companies and studies the impact of product quality on corporate performance.[14] PIMS researchers have found that:

1. Product quality is an important determinant of business profitability.
2. Businesses that offer premium-quality products and services usually have large market shares and were early entrants into their markets.
3. Quality is positively and significantly related to a higher return on investment for almost all kinds of products and market situations. (PIMS studies have shown that firms whose products are perceived as having superior quality have more than three times the return on sales of firms whose products are perceived as having inferior quality.)
4. Instituting a strategy of quality improvement usually leads to increased market share, but at the cost of reduced short-run profitability.
5. High-quality producers can usually charge premium prices.

These findings can be summarized as in Exhibit 400.18. A product's value in the marketplace is influenced by the quality of its design. Improvements in design will differentiate the product from its competitors, improve a firm's quality reputation, and improve the perceived value of the product. This differentiation allows the company to command higher prices as well as to achieve a greater market share, which in turn leads to increased revenues, offsetting the costs of improving the design.

Improved conformance in production or service delivery leads to lower costs through savings in rework, scrap, resolution of errors, and warranty expenses. The net effect of improved quality of design and conformance is increased profits.

Exhibit 400.18 *Quality and Profitability*

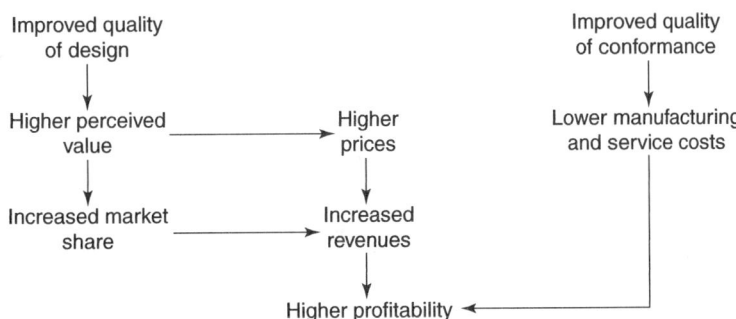

It is vital to focus quality improvement efforts on both design and conformance. Many organizations simply confine their quality efforts to defect elimination. In today's global marketplace, the absence of defects is a given, rather than a source of competitive advantage. Quality is simply the foundation for competitive advantage. Competitive success in today's market depends on such attributes as the speed of new product development, flexibility in production and delivery, and extraordinary customer service.

Quality Models

The Quality Philosophers

We will discuss several notable figures in the quality arena who developed and improved quality worldwide. These include Deming, Juran, Crosby, Conway, Feigenbaum, Ishikawa, Taguchi, Imai, Oakland, Shingo, and Shiba. We also present the Kano model from a customer classification viewpoint in understanding customer needs.

Deming Quality Model

According to Dr. W. Edwards Deming, good quality does not necessarily mean high quality. It is, rather, "a predictable degree of uniformity and dependability, at low cost, and suited to the market." He recognizes that the quality of any product or service has many scales, and may get a high mark on one scale and a low mark on another. In other words, quality is whatever the customer needs and wants. And because the customer's requirements and tastes are always changing, the solution to defining quality in terms of the customer is to constantly conduct customer research.

Deming said people are eager to do a good job and are disturbed when they cannot due to limitations imposed by management. Deming's basic philosophy on quality is that productivity improves as variability decreases. Because all things vary, he says, the statistical method of quality control is needed: "Statistical control does not imply absence of defective items. It is a state of random variation, in which the limits of variation are predictable."

There are two types of variation: chance and assignable, and, says Deming, "The difference between these is one of the most difficult things to comprehend." It is a waste of time and money to look for the cause of the chance variation, yet this is exactly what many companies do when they attempt to solve quality problems without using statistical methods. Deming advocates the use of statistics to measure performance in all areas, not just conformance to product specifications. Furthermore, it is not enough to meet specifications; one has to keep working to reduce the variation as well.

Deming is extremely critical of U.S. management and is an advocate of worker participation in decision making. He claims that management is responsible for 94 percent of quality problems, and points out that it is management's task to help people work smarter, not harder. "The first step is for management to remove the barriers that rob the hourly worker of his right to do a good job," he asserts.

Deming also criticizes motivational programs, in which he includes zero defects, and says that everyone simply doing their best is not the answer because it is also necessary that people know what to do. And he asks, "How can a man do it right the first time when the incoming material is off gauge, off color, or otherwise defective, or if his machine is not in good order?"

Deming cites the following as a typical letter from a supplier in response to an inquiry on its quality: "We are pleased to inform you that quality is our motto. We believe in quality. You will see from the enclosed pamphlet that nothing goes out of this plant until it has been thoroughly inspected. In fact, a large portion of our effort in production is spent on inspection to be sure of our quality," This, he says, "is a true confession of ignorance of what quality is, and how to achieve it."

Inspection, whether of incoming or outgoing goods, is, according to Deming, too late, ineffective, and costly. "Inspection does not improve quality, nor guarantee it," he says. Moreover, inspection is usually designed to allow a certain number of defects to enter the system. For example, a company that buys items with an acceptable quality level of 3 percent is, in effect, telling the vendor that it can send three bad items out of every 100. "The vendor will be pleased to meet these requirements," says Deming.

Deming says that judging quality requires knowledge of the "statistical evidence of quality," and that companies dealing with vendors under statistical control can eliminate inspection. "You will note from the control charts that came along with the product, far better than any inspection can tell you, what the distribution of quality is, and what it will be tomorrow." In this way, quality is predictable, and one can also safely predict that the vendor's quality will improve over time. "One of the first steps for managers of purchasing to take is to learn enough about the statistical control of quality to be able to assess the qualifications of a supplier, to be able to talk to him in statistical language," says Deming.

Deming also points out that simply checking the specifications of incoming materials may not be enough if the material encounters problems in production. "Specifications cannot tell you the whole story. The supplier must know what the material is to be used for," he says. He is critical of most producers for qualifying vendors on quality because once qualified, the vendor "has discharged his responsibility, and the purchaser accepts whatever he gets." The only effective way to qualify vendors is to see if their management abides by his 14 Points, uses statistical process control, and is willing to cooperate on the tests and use of instruments and gauges.

The best recognition one can grant a quality vendor, according to Deming, is to give that vendor more business. He points out that requiring statistical evidence of process control in selecting vendors would mean, in most companies, a drastic reduction in the number of vendors they deal with simply because not that many vendors would qualify. Nevertheless, he says, this is the only way to choose vendors, even if that means relying on a single source for critical items.

In fact, Deming advocates single sourcing. "A second source, for protection, for every item purchased is a costly practice," he says. The advantages of single sourcing include better vendor commitment, eliminating small differences between products from two suppliers, and simplifying accounting and paperwork. A disadvantage is the risk of depending on one supplier without any backup alternatives.

In response to the argument that relying on a single source can often mean paying a higher price, Deming says, "The policy of forever trying to drive down the price of anything purchased, with no regard to quality and service, can drive good vendors and good service out of business. The ways of doing business with vendors and customers that were good enough in the past must now be revised to meet new requirements of quality and productivity."

Deming's 14 Points for Management include the following.

1. Create constancy of purpose toward improvement of products and services.
2. Adopt a new philosophy. We can no longer live with commonly accepted levels of delays, mistakes, defective materials, and defective workmanship.
3. Cease dependence on mass inspection. Require, instead, statistical evidence that quality is built in.
4. End the practice of awarding business on the basis of price tag.
5. Find problems. It is management's job to work continually on the system.
6. Institute modern methods of training on the job.
7. Institute modern methods of supervision of production workers. The responsibility of forepeople must be changed from quantity to quality.
8. Drive out fear, so that everyone may work effectively for the company.
9. Break down barriers between departments through teams.
10. Eliminate numerical goals, posters, and slogans for the workforce, asking for new levels of productivity without providing methods.
11. Eliminate work standards that prescribe numerical quotas.
12. Remove barriers that stand between the hourly worker and his or her right to pride in workmanship.
13. Institute a vigorous program of education and retraining that leads to self-improvement.
14. Create a structure in top management that will push every day on the above 13 points, i.e., take action.

"A System of Profound Knowledge" is the foundation for Deming's 14 Points. This system consists of four interrelated parts: (1) appreciation for a system, (2) understanding of variation, (3) theory of knowledge, and (4) psychology.

The Deming cycle is composed of four stages: plan, do, study, and act (PDSA). The third stage—study—was formerly called "check," and the Deming cycle was known as the PDCA cycle. Deming thought "study" is more appropriate than "check": with only a "check," one might miss something. The Deming cycle is based on the premise that continuous improvement comes from the application of knowledge and its focus is on learning and implementation.

The Deming "chain reaction" theory advocates a continuous cycle of product design, manufacture, test, and sales, followed by market surveys and then redesign, and so forth. He claims that higher quality leads to lower cost and higher productivity, which, in turn, leads to more sales, greater market share, long-term competitiveness, and more jobs.

Deming identified seven "deadly diseases" that Western style of management needs to address. These include (1) lack of constancy of purpose; (2) emphasizing short-term profits and immediate dividends; (3) evaluation of performance, merit rating, or annual review; (4) mobility of top management; (5) running a company only on visible figures; (6) excessive medical costs; and (7) excessive costs of product warranty, fueled by lawyers who work on contingency fees.

Deming also identified "obstacles," which are lesser evils than his seven "deadly diseases." These obstacles include (1) neglect of long-term planning in favor of superficial immediate issues; (2) relying on technology to solve all problems; (3) relying on models set by other companies; (4) relying on business schools that teach obsolescent systems; (5) relying on quality-control departments; (6) blaming the workforce for the problems of management; (7) trying to accomplish miracles by adopting one segment (part) instead of a total system; (8) making the meeting of technical specifications an end goal; and (9) putting an inadequately tested prototype into the market.

(Source: *Federal Total Quality Management Handbook*, by the Office of Personnel Management, Appendix 1A, Washington, DC, June 1991.)

Juran Quality Model

According to Joseph M. Juran, there are two kinds of quality: "fitness for use" and "conformance to specifications." To illustrate the difference, he says a dangerous product could meet all specifications, but not be fit for use. He points out that the technical aspects of quality control have been well covered, but that firms do not know how to manage for quality. He identifies some of the problems as related to organization, communication, and coordination of functions—in other words, the human element. According to Juran, "An understanding of the human situations associated with the job will go far to solve the technical problems; in fact such understanding may be a prerequisite of a solution." For example, an inspector may incorrectly interpret specifications and thus subvert quality control efforts, or worse, he may knowingly protect favored operators or suppliers.

Juran talks about three basic steps to progress: (1) structured annual improvements combined with devotion and a sense of urgency, (2) massive training programs, and (3) upper-management leadership. In his view, less than 20 percent of quality problems are due to workers, with the remaining being caused by management. Just as all managers need some training in finance, all should have training in quality in order to oversee and participate in quality improvement projects. And top management should be included because "all major quality problems are interdepartmental." Moreover, pursuing departmental goals can sometimes undermine a company's overall quality mission, he says.

Companies should avoid "campaigns to motivate the workforce to solve the company's quality problems by doing perfect work," says Juran, because these "exhortation-only" approaches and slogans "fail to set specific goals, establish specific plans to meet these goals, or provide the needed resources." He notes, however, that upper management likes these programs because they do not detract from their time.

Juran favors the concept of quality circles because they improve communication between management and labor. He also recommends using statistical process control, but warns that it can lead to a "tool-oriented" approach. Juran does not believe that "quality is free." He explains that, because of the law of diminishing returns, there is an optimum point of quality beyond which conformance is more costly than the value of the quality obtained.

Juran recognizes purchasing's important role in quality improvement. "A company cannot produce greater precision in vacuo; it must secure greater precision for its suppliers." Juran also recognizes that purchasing's task can be much more complex than ordinarily assumed. For example, he addresses the problems of assessing the quality of contractors competing for big one-of-a-kind projects, as well as how to deal with unexpected changes in specifications.

Typical of his penchant for looking at the "big picture," Juran points out that at the same time that buyers are recognizing the need for better communication with suppliers, more and more of these suppliers are foreign firms. This puts up potential barriers to communication because of language and other cultural differences. He also points to different technological standards throughout the world and the fact that international standardization is lengthy and slow.

Juran is not in favor of single sourcing for important purchases, which he defines as product-related items such as raw materials or components. "For important purchases it is good to use multiple sources of supply. A single source can more easily neglect to sharpen its competitive edge in quality, cost, and service," he says.

Training for purchasing managers should include techniques for rating vendors, according to Juran. He adds that rating vendors is only half the process. The customer must also "make the investment of time, effort, and special skills to help poor vendors to improve."

To qualify vendors on quality, purchasing needs to conduct a formal survey to ensure that the vendor can consistently manufacture to specifications. Comparing U.S. and Japanese vendor-qualifying practices, Juran says those in the United States are not as effective. "To predict vendor adequacy, U.S. firms studied the suppliers' systems—organization structure, written procedures, manuals, audits, and so on. The Japanese firms looked at quality control training and quality of prior deliveries." He is critical of arms-length and adversarial relationships with vendors, and asserts that vendors should be part of the team.

Juran's 10 steps to quality improvement include the following:

1. Build awareness of the need and opportunity for improvement.
2. Set goals for improvement.
3. Organize to reach the goals (establish a quality council, identify problems, select projects, appoint teams, designate facilitator).
4. Provide training.
5. Carry out projects to solve problems.
6. Report progress.
7. Give recognition.
8. Communicate results.
9. Keep score.
10. Maintain momentum by making annual improvement part of the regular systems and processes of the company.

Juran's prescriptions focus on three major quality processes, called the "quality trilogy."

1. Quality planning: the process of preparing to meet quality goals
2. Quality control: the process of meeting quality goals during operations
3. Quality improvement: the process of breakthrough to unprecedented levels of performance

Juran's trilogy compares the quality processes to financial processes as follows: quality planning to operating budgets, quality control to cost control, and quality improvement to profit improvement.

Juran defines *breakthrough* as the accomplishment of any improvement that takes an organization to unprecedented levels of performance. Breakthrough attacks chronic losses or common causes of variation. The breakthrough sequence can be summarized as follows: (1) proof of the need, (2) project identification, (3) organization for improvement, (4) diagnostic journey, (5) remedial journey, and (6) holding the gain. He also believes in achieving breakthrough project by project.

(Source: *Federal Total Quality Management Handbook,* by the Office of Personnel Management, Appendix 1A, Washington, DC, June 1991.)

Crosby Quality Model

According to Philip B. Crosby's definition, *quality* is conformance to requirements, and it can only be measured by the cost of nonconformance. "Don't talk about poor quality or high quality. Talk about conformance and non-conformance," he says. This approach means that the only standard of performance is zero defects.

Crosby encourages "prevention (perfection)" as opposed to "inspection," "testing," and "checking." There is no place in his philosophy for statistically acceptable levels of quality. "People go to elaborate lengths to develop statistical levels of compliance. We have learned to believe that error is inevitable, and to plan for it." But, he says, "There is absolutely no reason for having errors or defects in any product."

Crosby talks about a quality "vaccine" that firms can use to prevent nonconformance. The three ingredients of this vaccine are determination, education, and implementation. He points out that quality improvement is a process, not a program, saying, "Nothing permanent or lasting ever comes from a program."

Crosby asserts that quality is management's responsibility, and that "We have to be as concerned about quality as we are about profit." He is doubtful, however, that this change in attitude will occur in this generation because most companies continue to compound quality problems by "hassling" their employees, which renders them de-motivated by the "thoughtless, irritating, unconcerned way they are dealt with." Crosby says a committed management can obtain a 40 percent reduction in error rates very quickly from a committed workforce; eliminating the remaining error takes a little more work.

One misconception concerning Crosby is that he primarily advocates prompting productive workers into performing better. He explains the root of this misconception: "Unfortunately, zero defects was picked up by industry as a 'motivation' program." In 1964, the Japanese adopted zero defects; Crosby says they were the only ones who correctly applied it—as a management performance standard rather than a motivation program for employees.

According to Crosby, at least half of the quality problems in purchased items are caused by not clearly stating what the requirements are. Because defects are defined as deviations from the published, announced, or agreed-upon requirements, much effort and thought should go into communicating those requirements. Crosby points to the example of Japan, where "they treat the supplier as an extension of their own business." As it is now, he says, "Half of the rejections that occur are the fault of the purchaser." For this reason, Crosby recommends rating buyers as well as vendors. "In tracking purchasing agents you find that they have a built-in defect rate," he explains.

Visiting a potential supplier to conduct a quality audit is next to useless, according to Crosby. "Unless the vendor is a complete and obvious disaster area, it is impossible to know whether their quality system will provide the proper control or not."

Crosby's 14 steps to quality improvement include the following.

1. Make it clear that management is committed to quality.
2. Form quality improvement teams with representatives from each department.
3. Determine where current and potential quality problems lie.
4. Evaluate the cost of quality and explain its use as a management tool.
5. Raise the quality awareness and personal concern of all employees.
6. Take actions to correct problems identified through previous steps.
7. Establish a committee for the zero defects program.
8. Train supervisors to actively carry out their part of the quality improvement program.
9. Hold a "zero defects day" to let all employees realize that there has been a change.
10. Encourage individuals to establish improvement goals for themselves and their groups.
11. Encourage employees to communicate to management the obstacles they face in attaining their improvement goals.
12. Recognize and appreciate those who participate.
13. Establish quality councils to communicate on a regular basis.
14. Do it all over again to emphasize that the quality improvement program never ends.

(Source: *Federal Total Quality Management Handbook,* by the Office of Personnel Management, Appendix 1A, Washington, DC, June 1991.)

Conway Quality Model

William E. Conway does not talk in terms of a specific definition of quality per se. Instead, he incorporates that into his broad definition of quality management, which he says is "development, manufacture, administration, and distribution of consistent low cost products and services that customers want and/or need." Quality management also means constant improvement in all areas of operations, including suppliers and distributors, to eliminate waste of material, capital, and time. The wasting of time is, by far, the biggest waste that occurs in most organizations, according to Conway. Excess inventory is another important form of waste because, he says, 60 percent of the space commonly used is not needed, yet a company must pay for it, pay to maintain it, and pay taxes on it.

Taking the view of the man who has been at the top of a corporation, Conway talks about the "right way to manage" rather than simply how to improve quality. He says the biggest problem is that top management is not convinced that quality increases productivity and lowers cost. Furthermore, they believe they do not have time to deal with the problem. In Conway's estimation, "The bottleneck is located at the top of the bottle."

Conway argues that what is required is the creation of a new "system of management," whose primary task is continuous improvement in all areas. This, he says, is the most important change, and means changing all the unwritten rules in a company and giving people positive reinforcement. "People work in the system, management works on the system. Workers will welcome the change," promises Conway. And while critical of U.S. management, he recognizes that "management wants and needs real help—not destructive criticism."

Conway is a strong advocate of using statistical methods to achieve quality gains, and says that one of the greatest handicaps lies in attempting to deal with productivity and quality in generalities. "The use of statistics is a common sense way of getting into specifics," he says, adding, "Statistics don't solve problems. They identify where the problems are and point managers and workers toward solutions."

Conway distinguishes between simple and sophisticated statistical techniques, which he calls "tools." The simple statistical tools are run charts, flow charts, fishbone charts, Pareto charts, histograms, and correlation charts. Surveys of customers are one of the most important tools because they tell a firm what it needs to address. According to Conway, these simple techniques can be used to solve 85 percent of a company's problems, while more complicated statistical process control methods are needed only about 15 percent of the time.

Furthermore, Conway points out that once a process is in control, the people responsible for it become more creative in eliminating variations because they know that they are personally capable of improving the system. In fact, people at the bottom make the most improvement because they learn "how to be logical all the time."

Conway says it is possible to continually improve the productivity and quality performance of everyone in a firm on a monthly basis. "In less than one year, you ought to be able to perform miracles," he predicts. He refers to this miracle as a "paradigm shift" in the way the world views quality.

Conway's call for constant improvement in all areas of operations is intended to include a company's suppliers, and here, too, the key to success is the use of statistics. "It is just as vital to achieve statistical control of quality from your vendors as it is to have it internally," he says.

Over-specification, another form of waste in Conway's view, is not solely the responsibility of engineers. Purchasing managers and anyone connected with the design of a product are also responsible. He warns that specifications—like work standards—sometimes "cap" improvements.

Conway's six tools for quality improvement include the following.

1. Human relations skills—the responsibility of management to create at every level, among all employees, the motivation and training to make the necessary improvements in the organization
2. Statistical surveys—the gathering of data about customers (internal and external), employees, technology, and equipment, to be used as a measure for future progress and to identify what needs to be done
3. Simple statistical techniques—clear charts and diagrams that help identify problems, track work flow, gauge progress, and indicate solutions
4. Statistical process control—the statistical charting of a process, whether manufacturing or non-manufacturing, to help identify and reduce variation
5. Imagineering—a key concept in problem-solving, which involves the visualization of a process, procedure, or operation with all waste eliminated
6. Industrial engineering—common techniques of pacing, work simplification, methods analysis, plant layout, and material handling to achieve improvements

(Source: *Federal Total Quality Management Handbook,* by the Office of Personnel Management, Appendix 1A, Washington, DC, June 1991.)

Feigenbaum Quality Model

A. V. Feigenbaum is best known for coining the phrase "total quality control," which he defined as ". . . an effective system for integrating the quality development, quality maintenance, and quality improvement efforts of the various groups in an organization so as to enable production and service at the most economical levels which allow full customer satisfaction." He viewed quality as a strategic business tool that requires involvement from everyone in the organization, and promoted the use of quality costs as a measurement and evaluation tool.

Feigenbaum's philosophy is summarized in his three steps to quality, which include quality leadership, modern quality technology, and organizational commitment to continuous training and motivation of the entire workforce. The Japanese latched on to his concept of total quality control as the foundation for their practice of company-wide quality control. Feigenbaum also popularized the term *hidden factory,* which described the portion of plant capacity wasted due to poor quality. Many of his ideas remain embedded in contemporary thinking, and have become important elements of the Malcolm Baldrige National Quality Award Criteria. They include the principles that the customer is the judge of quality; quality and innovation are interrelated and mutually beneficial; managing quality is the same as managing the business; quality is a continuous process of improvement; and customers and suppliers should be involved in the process.

For Feigenbaum, the word *control* represents a management tool with four steps: setting quality standards, appraising conformance to these standards, acting when the standards are exceeded, and planning for improvements in the standards.

(Source: *The Management and Control of Quality,* 5e, by Evans and Lindsay, South-Western, 2002.)

Ishikawa Quality Model

Dr. Kaoru Ishikawa influenced the development of a participative, bottom-up view of quality, which became the trademark of the Japanese approach to quality management. He was also able to get the attention of top management and persuade them that a company-wide approach to quality control was necessary for total success.

Ishikawa built on Feigenbaum's concept of total quality and promoted greater involvement by all employees, from top management to front-line staff, and reducing reliance on quality professionals and quality departments. He advocated collecting and analyzing factual data using simple visual tools, statistical techniques, and teamwork as the foundations for implementing total quality. Like others, Ishikawa believed that quality begins with the customer and therefore, understanding customers needs is the basis for improvement, and that complaints should be actively sought.

Key elements of Ishikawa's philosophy are summarized here.

1. Quality begins with education and ends with education.
2. The first step in quality is to know the requirements of customers.
3. The ideal state of quality control occurs when inspection is no longer necessary.
4. Remove the root cause, not the symptoms.
5. Quality control is the responsibility of all workers and all divisions.
6. Do not confuse the means with the objectives.
7. Put quality first and set your sights on long-term profits.
8. Marketing is the entrance and exit of quality.
9. Top management must not show anger when facts are presented by subordinates.
10. Ninety-five percent of problems in a company can be solved with simple tools for analysis and problem-solving.
11. Data without dispersion information (i.e., variability) are false data.

Ishikawa is known as the "Father of Quality Circles" and invented fishbone diagrams as problem-solving tools. The diagram is used by quality circles and quality-improvement teams worldwide to solve production and quality-related problems. The fishbone diagram is also called a *cause-and effect diagram*.

Taguchi Quality Model

Genichi Taguchi emphasizes reducing variation in the production process and in the final product as the principal way of improving quality. He believes this can be done by designing products that perform in a consistent manner, even under conditions of varying or adverse use. He also believes that one can make this happen at the design stage by appropriate statistical experimental design methods.

Taguchi views quality engineering as composed of three elements: system design, parameter design, and tolerance design. He developed a quality loss function to measure quality in monetary units that reflect both short-term and long-term losses.

Taguchi perceives quality as avoiding "loss due to functional variation." This loss will clearly be minimized when the product performs exactly as specified (performance is nominal) and will increase as the performance deviates more and more from nominal. The cost will increase more and more rapidly as the deviation increases, leading to the idea that, in many cases, a quadratic loss function may be a good approximation.

Taguchi explains the economic value of reducing product variation. He maintains that the manufacturing-based definition of quality as conformance to specification limits is inherently flawed due to built-in tolerance range. For example, if a product specification calls for 0.600 plus or minus 0.030, the 0.600 is called the *nominal specification* and the plus or minus of 0.030 is called the *tolerance range*. The nominal specification is the ideal target value for the critical quality characteristic. Taguchi's approach assumes that the smaller the variation in the nominal specification, the better the quality. In turn, products are more consistent, and total costs are less.

Taguchi also contributes to improving engineering approaches to product design. By designing a product that is insensitive to variation in manufacture, specification limits become meaningless. He advocates certain techniques of experimental design to identify the most important design variables in order to minimize the effects of uncontrollable factors on product variation. Thus, his approaches attack quality problems early in the design stage rather than react to problems that might occur later in production.

Over the years, the most widely used measure of quality has been conformance of the product to design specifications. This definition is very limited because it defines quality for a unit of product on how well manufacturing has been able to match design specifications, rather than for the product as a whole on how well the product, including its design, meets customer needs and expectations.

Taguchi's approach to quality is relatively precise. Conventional quality-control activities center on final inspection sampling or on control charts and process control. This is called *on-line quality control.* Taguchi pushed the process upstream to focus on product and process design. This is called *off-line quality control.*

Seven points to off-line quality control are proposed by Taguchi.

1. Product quality is measured by the total loss to society created by that product.
2. Continuous quality improvement and cost reduction are necessary to survive in world competition.
3. Quality improvement requires continual and repeated reduction of variation in the product or process performance around the standard nominal values.
4. Quality loss is frequently proportional to the square of the deviation of the performance from the nominal value.
5. Product and process design can have a significant impact on a product's quality and cost.
6. Performance variation can be reduced by suitable adjustment of the product's parameters and/or the process parameters.
7. The appropriate parameter settings that reduce variation can be identified with the appropriate statistically designed experiments.

(Source: *The Mangement and Control of Quality*, 5e, by Evans and Lindsay, South-Western, 2002.)

Imai Quality Model

Masaaki Imai is the author of *kaizen*, which focuses on continuous improvement in operations. The term means "gradual, unending improvement," doing little things better, and setting—and achieving—even higher standards. The message of the *kaizen* strategy is that not a single day should go by without some kind of improvement being made somewhere in the company.

Imai applies the *kaizen* to 16 management practices, including profit planning, customer satisfaction, total quality control programs, suggestion systems, small-group activities, just-in-time production, just-in-time information processing, systems improvement, cross-functional management, policy deployment or implementation, quality deployment, total productive maintenance, supplier relations, top-management commitment, corporate culture, and problem-solving in such areas as labor-management relations.

Oakland Quality Model

John S. Oakland's contribution to the quality field is to further integrate TQM into a company's strategy. He defines TQM as "a comprehensive approach to improving competitiveness, effectiveness, and flexibility through planning, organizing, and understanding each activity, and involving each individual at each level."

Oakland's quality model can be summarized in five points.

1. Identify customer-supplier relationships.
2. Set up a system to manage processes.
3. Change the company culture from what it was to a TQM culture.
4. Improve communications company-wide.
5. Demonstrate commitment to quality.

Oakland believed that understanding quality, commitment, and leadership lays a solid foundation for a company-wide TQM program. Everything else is built upon this understanding. Policies, plans, actions, systems, and measurements follow, and these require competency in the mechanics of quality management. Measurements are then put in place, followed by an analysis of the cost of quality together with a strategy for reducing it drastically. Tools and techniques required for improvement are introduced at this stage of implementation.

Capability and control are crucial to a program's start-up, as are organization for quality and a communication effort. The requisite company culture change through continuous improvement is accomplished by teamwork and ongoing training rather than a one-time event and effort. Oakland's work is full of flowcharts and diagrams, checklists and questionnaires, caveats and exhortations, and simple examples and comparisons.

(Source: *The Essences of Total Quality Management*, 2e, by John Bank, Prentice-Hall, 1992.)

Shingo Quality Model

Shigeo Shingo pioneered the zero quality control (ZQC) system, which is a mistake-proofing (poka-yoke) approach that prevents defects by monitoring process conditions at the source and correcting errors that would cause defects. ZQC will lead to achieving the goal of zero defects. Shingo found problems with the traditional approach to statistical quality control systems in terms of achieving zero defects.

He also developed a Single Minute Exchange of Die (SMED) approach, or quick changeover technique, as the single most powerful tool for JIT production that was implemented as part of the Toyota Production System. The objectives of SMED are to reduce setup and turnaround times in production assembly operations. He also implemented a non-stock production in JIT manufacturing operations as part of continuous improvement. Shingo's "seven wastes" are very popular in manufacturing.

Shiba Quality Model

S. Shiba, Graham, and Walden distinguish four hierarchical levels of quality, which they call the "four fitnesses." Shiba says one has to progress from lower levels of quality to higher levels of quality or fitness.

- **Quality Level 1: Fitness to Standard.** This is the first, lowest, step in quality. Quality is creating what the designers have specified that the product is to be and do. It focuses on statistical sampling and inspection.
- **Quality Level 2: Fitness to Needs.** This is the second step in quality. It still focuses on inspection to check whether the product meets its intended use. It basically allows a process with high statistical variation, throwing away the "tails" of the normal distribution.
- **Quality Level 3: Fitness of Costs.** This is the third level of quality. The only way to maintain the first two levels of quality and get lower costs is to move away from the high costs of "inspecting quality in" and toward "building quality in." That is, we must reduce the variability of the production process so that all units will lie within the specifications, and none will have to be discarded. The goal is 100 percent quality without inspection!
- **Quality Level 4: Fitness to Hidden Need.** This is the final, highest level of quality. It entails meeting the user's needs before the user is even aware of those needs. A company that can create a product that becomes popular before others create it, can achieve a temporary monopoly.

(Source: *Production Operations Management*, by Thomas Morton, South-Western, 1999.)

Similarities Among Quality Philosophers

Although each of the quality experts has developed his individual approach to quality improvement, the following are significant areas of agreement:

1. Producing a quality product or service costs less because there is less waste.
2. Preventing quality problems is better than detecting and correcting them.
3. Statistical data should be used to measure quality.
4. Managers need to take a leadership role in improving quality.
5. Managers and employees need training in quality improvement.
6. Companies need to develop a quality-management system.

Kano Quality Model

A Japanese professor, Noriaki Kano, suggested the following three classes of customer requirements in understanding the customer's needs in the marketplace.

1. **Dissatisfiers:** Requirements that are expected in a product or service (e.g., a radio in a car). These features are assumed by the customer to be present. If they are not present, the customer is dissatisfied.
2. **Satisfiers:** Requirements that customers say they want (e.g., a sunroof or power windows in a car). Although these requirements are generally not expected, fulfilling them creates satisfaction.
3. **Exciters/delighters:** New or innovative features that customers do not expect (e.g., collision avoidance or a navigation system in a car). Presence of such features will excite or delight customers because the features exceed their expectations.

(Source: *The Management and Control of Quality*, 5e, by Evans and Lindsay, South-Western, 2002.)

Quality Awards

The U.S. Quality Award

The Malcolm Baldrige National Quality Award is an annual award to recognize U.S. companies that excel in quality management and quality achievement. The award examination is based upon a rigorous set of criteria, called the Criteria for Performance Excellence, designed to encourage companies to enhance their competitiveness through an aligned approach to organizational performance management that results in:

1. Delivery of ever-improving value to customer, contributing to marketplace success
2. Improvement of overall organizational effectiveness and capabilities
3. Organizational and personal learning

The criteria consist of a hierarchical set of categories, items, and areas to address. The seven categories follow:

1. *Leadership:* organizational leadership and public responsibility and citizenship
2. *Strategic Planning:* strategy development and strategy deployment
3. *Customer and Market Focus:* customer and market knowledge; customer satisfaction and relationships
4. *Information and Analysis:* measurements and analysis of organizational performance; information management
5. *Human Resource Focus:* work systems; employee education, training, and development; and employee well-being and satisfaction
6. *Process Management:* product and service processes; business processes; support processes
7. *Business Results:* customer-focused results; financial and market results; human resource results; organizational effectiveness results

The Japanese Deming Prize

The Deming Prize was instituted in Japan and has several categories, including prizes for individuals, factories, and small companies, and the Deming application prize, which is an annual award presented to a company or a division of a company that has achieved distinctive performance improvements through the application of company-wide quality control.

The judging criteria consists of a checklist of 10 major categories: (1) policies; (2) the organization and its operations; (3) education and dissemination; (4) information gathering, communication and its utilization; (5) analysis; (6) standardization; (7) control/management; (8) quality assurance; (9) effects; and (10) future plans.

The Deming Prize is awarded to all companies that meet the prescribed standard. However, the small number of awards given each year is an indication of the difficulty of achieving the standard.

The European Quality Award

The European Quality Award was designed to increase awareness throughout the European Community, and businesses in particular, of the growing importance of quality to their competitiveness in the increasingly global market and to their standards of life.

The European Quality Award consists of two parts: the European Quality Prize, given to companies that demonstrate excellence in quality management practice by meeting the award criteria, and the European Quality Award, awarded to the most successful applicant.

Applicants must demonstrate that their total quality approach has contributed significantly to satisfying the expectations of customers, employees, and other constituencies. The award process is similar to the Deming Prize and Baldrige Award. The assessment is based on customer satisfaction, business results, processes, leadership, people satisfaction, resources, people management, policy and strategy, and impact on society.

The European Quality Award criteria place greater emphasis on "impact on society" than is placed on the public responsibility item in the Baldrige Award.

The Canadian Quality Award

Canada's National Quality Institute (NQI) recognizes Canada's foremost achievers of excellence through the prestigious Canada Awards for Excellence. The Canadian Awards for Business Excellence quality criteria are similar in structure to the U.S. Baldrige Award criteria, with some key differences. The major categories and items within each category follow:

1. *Leadership:* strategic direction, leadership involvement, and outcomes
2. *Customer Focus:* voice of the customer, management of customer relationships, measurements, and outcomes
3. *Planning for Improvement:* development and content of improvement plan, assessment, and outcomes
4. *People Focus:* human resource planning, participatory environment, continuous learning environment, employee satisfaction, and outcomes
5. *Process Optimization:* process definition, process control, process improvement, and outcomes
6. *Supplier Focus:* partnering and outcomes

These categories seek similar information to the Baldrige Award criteria.

The Australian Quality Award

The Australian Business Excellence Awards are administered by the Australian Quality Awards Foundation with four levels:

1. *The Business Improvement Level:* encouragement recognition for "Progress Toward Business Excellence" or "Foundation in Business Excellence"
2. *The Award Level:* representing Australian best practices; recognition as a Winner or Finalist
3. *The Award Gold Level:* open only to former Award winners; represents a revalidation and ongoing improvement
4. *The Australian Business Excellence Prize:* open only to former Award winners; represents international best practices evident throughout the organization

The assessment criteria address leadership, strategy and planning, information and knowledge, people, customer focus, processes, products and services, and business results. In this model, leadership and customer focus are the drivers of the management system and enablers of performance. Strategy, policy and planning, information and analysis, and people are the key internal components of the management system. Quality of process, product, and service is focused on how work is done to achieve the required results and obtain improvement. As with Baldrige, the model emphasizes the holistic and interconnected nature of the management process. This model has solid union support.

(Source: *The Management and Control of Quality*, 5e, by Evans and Lindsay, South-Western, 2002.)

Quality Control Practices

Statistics and Quality Control

Overview

A system should be put in place to allow the organization to determine systematically the degree to which product and services please customers, and to focus on internal process improvement. Data should be collected on features of customer satisfaction such as responsiveness, reliability, accuracy, and ease of access. The measurement systems should also focus on internal processes, especially on processes that generate variation in quality and cycle time. *Cycle time* is the time required from conception to completion of an idea or a process. When customer data indicate a problem, or when the organization wants to raise the level of customer satisfaction, the organization should focus on improving the processes that deliver the product or service.

In order to assure that processes are continuously improved, data should be collected and analyzed on a continuing basis, with particular attention to variation in processes. The causes of variation are examined to determine whether they result from special circumstances (special causes) or from recurring ("common") causes. Different strategies should be adopted to correct each occurrence. The immediate objectives of the analysis and measurement effort are to reduce rework, waste, and cycle time and to improve cost-effectiveness and accuracy. The ultimate objectives are to assure that the organization understands the extent to which customer satisfaction is being realized, where there are deficiencies and why, and to isolate causes that can be attacked systematically.

Exhibit 400.19 *Types of Variation*

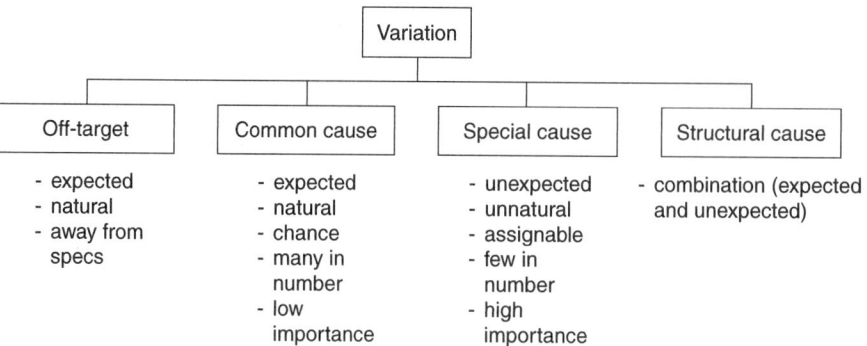

Variation

It is true in manufacturing that no two products are ever made exactly alike. Similarly, no two individuals provide the same service in exactly the same way. *Variation* means deviation from specifications, standards, or targets. The variation concept is a law of nature: no two items are the same. Variation can result in poor quality to the customer and cost to the producer. Variation must be measured and reduced for proper functioning of a process. The ability to measure variation is a requirement before it can be controlled or stabilized. When the variation is reduced, quality is improved and costs are reduced. Both input and process variation must be reduced in order to reduce the overall variation in a product.

Reduced Input Variation + Reduced Process Variation = Reduced Product Variation

Variation is present in every process as a result of a combination of four variables: (1) operator variation (due to physical and emotional conditions), (2) equipment variation (due to wear and tear), (3) materials variation (due to thickness, moisture content, and old and new materials), and (4) environmental variation (due to changes in temperature, light, and humidity). Variation is either expected or unexpected, as shown in Exhibit 400.19.

Variation affects the proper functioning of a process; that is, its output deviates from the established target (**off-target**). From a statistics point of view, off-target relates to a process average. **Common causes** affect the standard deviation of a process and they are caused by factors internal to a process. These causes are present in all processes and are called *chance* (random) *causes*. Chance causes are small in magnitude and are difficult to identify. Examples of common random causes include worker availability, number and complexity of orders, job schedules, equipment testing, work center schedules, changes in raw materials, truck schedules, and worker performance.

Special causes affect the standard deviation of a process and are factors external to a process. Special causes, also known as *assignable causes*, are large in magnitude and are not so difficult to identify. They may or may not be present in a process. Examples of special (assignable) causes include equipment breakdowns, operator changes, new raw materials, new products, new competition, or new customers.

Structural causes affect the standard deviation of a process; they are factors both internal and external to a process. They may or may not be present in a process; they are a blend of common and special causes. Examples of structural causes include sudden sales/production volume increase due to a new product or a new customer, seasonal sales, and sudden increase in profits.

Control Charts

A control chart is a statistical tool that distinguishes between natural (common) and unnatural (special) variations. The control chart method is used to measure variations in quality. The control chart is a picture of the process over time. It shows whether a process is in a stable state. It is used to improve the process quality.

Natural variation is the result of random causes. It requires management intervention to achieve quality improvement or quality system. It has been stated that 80 to 85 percent of quality problems are due to management or the quality system and that 15 to 20 percent of problems are due to operators or workers. Supervisors, operators, and technicians can correct the unnatural variation. Control charts can be drawn for variables and attributes.

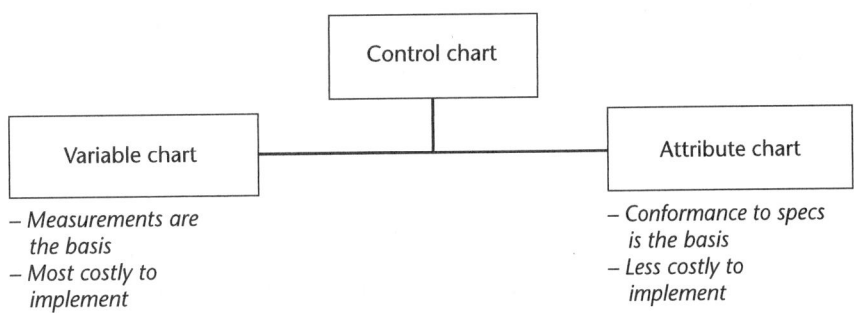

The control chart method for **variables** is a means of visualizing the variations that occur in the central tendency and dispersion of a set of observations. It measures the quality of a particular characteristic such as length, time, or temperature.

A variable chart is an excellent technique for achieving quality improvement. True process capability can be achieved only after substantial quality improvement has been made. Once true process capability is obtained, effective specifications can be determined. Here is the sequence of events taking place with the control chart:

Variable Chart → Quality Improvement → Process Capability → Specifications

The attribute chart refers to those quality characteristics that conform to specifications (specs) or do not conform to specifications. It is used where measurements are not possible, such as for color, missing parts, scratches, or damage.

Stable and Unstable Processes

When only chance causes of variation are present in a process, it is considered to be in a state of statistical control (i.e., the process is stable and predictable). When a process is in control (stable), there occurs a natural pattern of variation and only chance causes of variation are present. Small variations in operator performance, equipment performance, materials, and environmental characteristics are expected and are considered to be part of a stable process. Further improvements in the process can be achieved only by changing the input factors, that is, operator, equipment, materials, and environment. These changes require action by management through quality improvement ideas.

When an assignable cause of variation is present in a process, it is considered to be out of statistical control (i.e., the process is unstable and unpredictable). When an observed measurement falls outside its control limits, the process is said to be out-of-control (unstable). This means that an assignable cause of variation is present. The unnatural, unstable variation makes it impossible to predict future variation. The assignable causes must be found and corrected before a natural, stable process can continue.

Variable and Attribute Control Charts

VARIABLE CONTROL CHARTS Two types of variable control charts exist: the X bar chart, which is used to record the variation in the average value of samples (process average) and the R chart, which measures the range or the dispersion (process spread, standard deviation, or variability). See Exhibit 400.20.

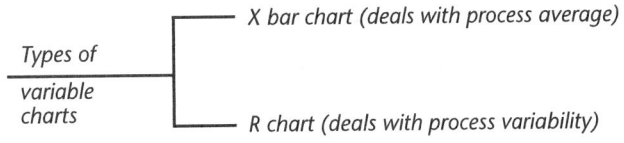

ATTRIBUTE CONTROL CHARTS Two types of attribute control charts exist: the chart for nonconforming units and the chart for nonconformities. A nonconformity is a departure of quality characteristic from its intended level that is not meeting a specification requirement. A nonconforming unit is a product or service containing at least one nonconformity.

440. QUALITY CONTROL PRACTICES

Exhibit 400.20 *Causes of Changes in Variable Charts*

Changes in X bar chart are caused by	Changes in R chart are caused by
– A different raw material – A new operator – A change in process setting – Equipment wear and tear – A change in temperature or humidity – A gradual deterioration of equipment – The seasonal effects of incoming materials – The recurring effects of temperatures and humidity (cold morning start-ups) – The periodic rotation of operators – Large differences in material quality – Large differences in test methods – Large differences in testing equipment – Two or more machines plotted on the same chart – Measuring equipment out of calibration – Errors in calculations, counting, judgment, or inspection – Taking samples from different populations instead of from the same population – Errors in using test equipment	– An inexperienced operator – An erratic machine – A gradual variation in incoming materials – Worker fatigue and inattention – A change in lubrication cycles – A gradual deterioration of worker skills – Materials from different suppliers – Different workers using the same chart in operations – Measuring equipment out of calibration – Errors in calculations, counting, judgment, or inspection – Taking samples from different populations instead of from the same population – Errors in using test equipment

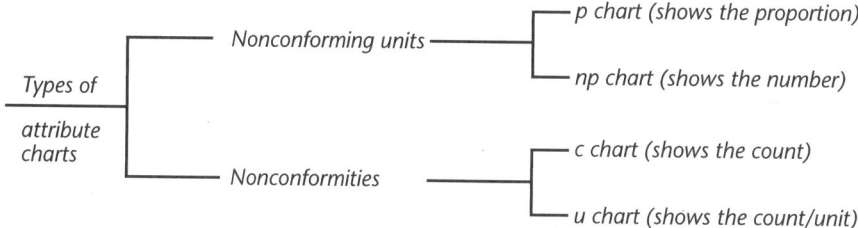

The chart for nonconforming units is based on the binomial distribution. It is shown as proportion chart (p chart) which is expressed as a fraction or a percent of nonconforming units in a sample. Another chart is number proportion chart (np chart) to represent the number of nonconforming units. The fraction nonconforming, p, is usually quite small, say 5 percent or less. Values greater than 5 percent require drastic measures other than a control chart. The p chart can be used to measure the quantity produced by a work center, by a department, by a production shift, or by an entire plant. It is also used to report the performance of an operator.

Calculation for p chart

The formula is $p = np/n$, where p is proportion of nonconformities in a sample, np is number of nonconforming units in the sample, and n is the number of units in the sample.

Example: During the second shift of production, 400 inspections are made of shipments and 4 nonconforming shipments are found. The second shift produced 10,000 units. What is the fraction of shipments nonconforming?

$$p = np/n = 4/400 = 0.01 = 1\%$$

Since 1 percent is less than 5 percent target, shipments conform to specifications or standards. Here, 10,000 production is not relevant.

The chart for nonconformities is based on the Poisson distribution. It has two charts: the c chart, which shows the count of nonconformities in an inspected unit, and the u chart, which shows the count of nonconformities per unit. The u chart is similar to the c chart except in scale and size. The scale for a u chart is continuous, but discrete for the c chart. This makes the u chart more flexible. The subgroup size is one for the c chart, and it varies for the u chart.

Long and Short Production Runs

LONG-RUN PRODUCTION PROCESSES Production runs can be long or short. X bar and R charts are used on long production runs of discrete parts. These long production runs can be discrete, continuous, or batch. Paper-making processes and oil refinery processes are examples of continuous processes. Paint, soup, and bread making are examples of batch processes. A batch chart is used in batch processing. It is a run chart, not a control chart since it does not have control limits. A product can be manufactured using a combination of continuous, batch, and discrete processes.

SHORT-RUN PRODUCTION PROCESSES A job shop with small lot size has short-run processes. The job run is completed before the central line and control limits in the control chart can be calculated. Therefore, the X bar and R charts cannot be used here. A possible solution to short-run processes is to use a specification chart, a deviation chart, a Z bar chart, or a W chart.

Information on patterns and causes can be shown on a specification chart (s chart). The control limits are established using the specifications. The deviation chart is similar to an X chart, except the plotted point is the deviation from the target. It is also called a *difference, nominal,* or *target chart.* If the variation is too great, then a z bar and z chart can be used.

The z bar and W charts are counterparts to the X bar and R charts. In X and R charts, R is the moving range of the X values, while in the z and W charts, the W is the moving range of the z values. The W chart uses the absolute value.

BOTH LONG- AND SHORT-RUN PROCESSES A precontrol chart is used for both short and long production runs. No recording, calculating, or plotting of data is involved. It is applicable to start up operations and to measure attributes. It is simple to understand. It works directly with tolerances rather than easily misunderstood control limits and control charts.

Process Management Practices

Definition of Process Management

Process management involves planning and administering the activities necessary to achieve a high level of performance in a process, and identifying opportunities for improving quality and operational performance and, ultimately, customer satisfaction. It involves the *design, control,* and *improvement* of key business processes. Design focuses on the prevention of poor quality by ensuring that products meet customer requirements and that production and delivery processes are capable of achieving high levels of performance. The distinction between control and improvement is illustrated in Exhibit 400.21. Any process performance measure naturally fluctuates around some average level. Abnormal conditions cause an unusual deviation from this pattern. Removing the causes of such abnormal conditions and maintaining level performance is the essence of control. Improvement, on the other hand, means changing the performance to a new level. Process management activities help to prevent defects and errors, eliminate waste and redundancy, and thereby lead to better quality and improved company performance through shorter cycle times, improved flexibility, and faster customer responsiveness.

Nearly every leading company has a well-defined methodology for process management. AT&T, for example, bases its methodology on the following principles:

- Process quality improvement focuses on the end-to-end process.
- The mindset of quality is one of prevention and continuous improvement.
- Everyone manages a process at some level and is simultaneously a customer and a supplier.

Exhibit 400.21 *Control Versus Improvement*

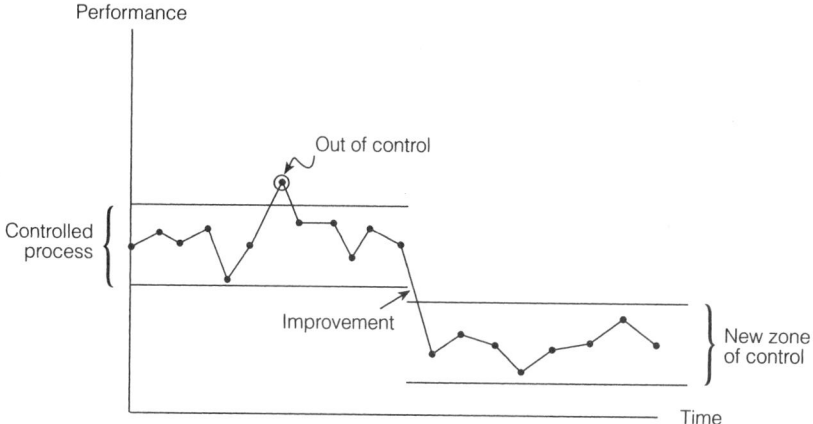

- Customer needs drive process quality improvement.
- Corrective action focuses on removing the root cause of the problem rather than on treating its symptoms.
- Process simplification reduces opportunities for errors and rework.
- Process quality improvement results from a disciplined and structured application of the quality-management principles.[15]

The Scope of Process Management

Essentially all work in an organization is performed by some process. Common business processes include acquiring customer and market knowledge, strategic planning, research and development, purchasing, developing new products or services, fulfilling customer orders, managing information, measuring and analyzing performance, and training employees, to name just a few. Individuals or groups, known as **process owners,** are accountable for process performance and have the authority to manage and improve their process. Process owners may range from high-level executives who manage cross-functional processes to workers who run machinery on the shop floor. Assigning process owners ensures that someone is responsible to manage the process and optimize its effectiveness.

Leading companies identify important business processes throughout the supply chain that affect customer satisfaction. These typically fall into four categories:

1. Product design processes
2. Production/delivery processes
3. Support processes
4. Supplier and partnering processes

Product design processes involve all activities that are performed to incorporate customer requirements, new technology, and past learning into the functional specifications of a product (i.e., a manufactured good or service), and thus define its fitness for use. **Production/delivery processes** create or deliver the actual product; examples are manufacturing, assembly, dispensing medications, teaching a class, and so on. These processes must be designed to ensure that the product will conform to specifications (the manufacturing definition of quality) and also be produced economically and efficiently. Product design greatly influences the efficiency of manufacture as well as the flexibility of service strategies, and therefore must be coordinated with production/delivery processes. The ultimate value of the product and, hence, the perceived quality to the consumer depend on both types of processes.

Design and production/delivery processes that drive the creation of products and services, are critical to customer satisfaction, and have a major impact on the strategic goals of an organization are generally considered **core processes** of a business. **Support processes** provide infrastructure for core processes, and though essential to the survival of the business, generally do not add value directly to the product or service. A process such as order entry that might be considered a core process for one company, such as a direct mail distributor, might be considered as a support process for another, for instance, a custom manufacturer. In general, core processes are driven by external customer needs while support processes are driven by internal customer needs. Because core processes do add value to products and services, they require a higher level of attention than do support processes.

For many businesses, goods and services provided by suppliers or partners account for a significant portion of the cost and value of the final product. Suppliers include not only companies that provide materials and components, but also distributors, transportation companies, and information, health care, and education providers. Key suppliers might provide unique design, integration, or marketing capabilities that are not available within the business, and therefore can be critical to achieving strategic objectives. Partners for a company might include educational institutions that collaborate on research and training. (Conversely, a company might be viewed as a partner for an educational institution.) **Supplier and partnering processes** describe how supplier and partner relationships are managed, for instance, how performance requirements are communicated and ensured, mutual assistance and training, and so on.

Major core and support processes are generally defined at the organizational level and require attention by senior managers. Each major process consists of many subprocesses that are managed by functional managers or cross-functional teams. Finally, each subprocess consists of many specific work steps performed by individuals at the performer level.

To apply the techniques of process management, processes must be (1) repeatable, and (2) measurable. Repeatability means that the process must recur over time. The cycle may be long, as with product development processes or patent applications; or it may be short, as with a manufacturing operation or an order-entry process. Measurement provides the ability to capture important quality and performance indicators to reveal patterns about process performance. Meeting these two conditions ensures that sufficient data can be collected to reveal useful information for evaluation and learning that lead to improvement and maturity.

Leading Practices in Process Management

Process management requires a disciplined effort involving all managers and workers in an organization. Companies that are recognized world leaders in quality and customer satisfaction share some common practices.

- They translate customer requirements into product and service design requirements early in the design process, taking into account linkages between product design requirements and manufacturing process requirements, supplier capabilities, and legal and environmental issues.
- They ensure that quality is built into products and services and use appropriate engineering and quantitative tools and approaches during the development process.
- They manage the product development process to enhance cross-functional communication, reduce product development time, and ensure trouble-free introduction of products and services.
- They define and document important production/delivery and support processes, and manage them as important business processes.
- They define performance requirements for suppliers, ensure that requirements are met, and develop partnering relationships with key suppliers and other organizations.
- They control the quality and operational performance of key processes and use systematic methods to identify significant variations in operational performance and output quality, determine root causes, make corrections, and verify results.
- They continuously improve processes to achieve better quality, cycle time, and overall operational performance.
- They innovate to achieve breakthrough performance using such approaches as benchmarking and reengineering.

Product Design Processes

Companies today face incredible pressures to continually improve the quality of their products while simultaneously reducing costs, to meet ever-increasing legal and environmental requirements, and to shorten product life cycles to meet changing consumer needs and remain competitive. The ability to achieve these goals depends, to a large extent, on product design. The complexity of today's products makes design a difficult activity; a single state-of-the-art integrated circuit may contain millions of transistors and involve hundreds of manufacturing steps. Nevertheless, improved designs not only reduce

Techniques used in the product design include quality engineering and quality function deployment (voice of the customer and the house of quality). Approaches such as concurrent engineering and design for manufacturability are used to increase production efficiency and quality.

costs, but increase quality. For example, a network interface card from 1990 contained about 40 chips; five years later, the entire system board of a Macintosh Performa 5200 had just 19. Fewer components typically mean fewer points of failure and less chance of assembly error.[16]

Many companies view customers as significant partners in product development, thus integrating market evaluation throughout the process. Design approaches often differ depending on the nature of products or services. For example, approaches to designing entirely new products will be unlike those that address minor changes and improvements. Design approaches might consider factors such as functional performance, cost, manufacturability, safety, and environmental impacts.

Production/Delivery and Support Processes

The design of the processes that produce and deliver goods and services can have a significant impact on cost (and hence profitability), flexibility (the ability to produce the right types and amounts of products according to customer demand or preferences), and the quality of the output. Standardized processes establish consistency of output.

Today, many companies use a strategy of **mass customization**—providing personalized, custom-designed products to meet individual preferences at prices comparable to mass-produced items. Mass customization requires significant changes to traditional manufacturing processes that focus on either customized, crafted products or mass-produced, standardized products.[17] These processes include flexible manufacturing technologies, just-in-time systems, information technology, and an emphasis on cycle time reduction.

The design of a process begins with the process owner: an individual, a team, a department, or some cross-functional group. The goal of process design is simple: to develop an efficient procedure to satisfy both internal and external customer requirements. A basic approach to process design is suggested by Motorola:

1. *Identify the product or service:* What work do I do?
2. *Identify the customer:* Who is the work for?
3. *Identify the supplier:* What do I need and from whom do I get it?
4. *Identify the process:* What steps or tasks are performed? What are the inputs and outputs for each step?
5. *Mistake-proof the process:* How can I eliminate or simplify tasks? What "poka-yoke" (i.e., mistake-proofing) devices can I use?
6. *Develop measurements and controls, and improvement goals:* How do I evaluate the process? How can I improve further?

Steps 1 through 3 address such questions as "What is the purpose of the process?" "How does the process create customer satisfaction?" and "What are the essential inputs and outputs of the process?" Step 4 focuses on the actual process design, by defining the specific tasks performed in transforming the inputs to outputs. Step 5 focuses on making the process efficient and capable of delivering high quality. Step 6 ensures that the process will be monitored and controlled to the level of required performance by gathering in-process measurements and/or customer feedback on a regular basis and using this information to control and improve the process.

The actual process design is the specification of how the process works. The first phase is to list in detail the sequence of steps—value-adding activities and specific tasks—involved in producing a product or delivering a service, usually depicted as a flowchart. Such a graphical representation provides an excellent communication device for visualizing and understanding the process. Flowcharts can become the basis for job descriptions, employee-training programs, and performance measurement. They help managers to estimate human resources, information systems, equipment, and facilities requirements. As design tools, they enable management to study and analyze processes prior to implementation in order to improve quality and operational performance.

Supplier and Partnering Processes

In business today, operations are often highly decentralized and dispersed around the world. Consequently, managing a complex network of suppliers becomes a critical interorganizational issue. Suppliers play a vital role throughout the product development process, from design through distribution. Suppliers can provide technology or production processes not internally available, early design advice, and increased capacity, which can result in lower costs, faster time-to-market, and improved quality for their customers. In turn, they are assured of stable and long-term business.

Increasingly, suppliers are viewed as partners with customers, because of the codependent relationship that develops between them. Successful suppliers have a culture in which employees and managers share in customers' goals, commitments, and risks to promote such long-term relationships. Strong customer-supplier relationships are based on three guiding principles:

1. Recognizing the strategic importance of suppliers in accomplishing business objectives, particularly minimizing the total cost of ownership
2. Developing win-win relationships through partnerships rather than as adversaries
3. Establishing trust through openness and honesty, thus leading to mutual advantages

In many companies, suppliers are treated as if they were actually a part of the organization. For example, functions such as cafeteria service, mailroom operations, and information processing are being performed by suppliers at their customers' facilities. As more and more of this type of outsourcing is done, the lines between the customer and the supplier become increasingly blurred.

To ensure that suppliers can provide high quality and reduce costs associated with incoming inspection or testing, many companies provide various types of assistance to their suppliers in developing quality assurance programs or solving quality problems. Joint conferences, training, incentives, recognition, and long-term agreements help to improve suppliers' abilities to meet key quality requirements.

Many companies segment suppliers into categories based on their importance to the business and manage them accordingly. Measurement plays an important role in supplier management. Finally, communication, feedback, and recognition or awards are important practices in supplier and partnering processes.

Feedback should provide timely and actionable information to suppliers to lead to improvement and ensure that suppliers meet the organization's performance requirements. An annual award dinner recognizes outstanding suppliers for quality and continuous improvement.

Supplier certification is used by many companies as the focal point of their supplier management system. Formal programs typically are established to rate and certify suppliers who provide quality materials in a cost-effective and timely manner. Supplier certification programs can be time-consuming and expensive to administer. Nevertheless, they are an important means of controlling incoming materials, particularly in a just-in-time environment.

Process Improvement

Prior to the total quality movement, most U.S. managers simply maintained products and processes until they could be replaced by new technology. Japanese managers, on the other hand, focused on continually improving products and processes. The MIT Commission on Industrial Productivity observed this difference and stated:

> Another area in which U.S. firms have often lagged behind their overseas competitors is in exploiting the potential for continuous improvement in the quality and reliability of their products and processes. The cumulative effect of successive incremental improvements and modifications to established products and processes can be very large and may outpace efforts to achieve technological breakthroughs.[18]

Improvement should be a proactive task of management, not simply a reaction to problems and competitive threats. Many opportunities for improvement exist, including the obvious reductions in manufacturing defects and cycle times. Organizations should also consider improving employee morale, satisfaction, and cooperation; improving managerial practices; improving the design of products with features that better meet customers' needs, and that can achieve higher performance, higher reliability, and other market-driven dimensions of quality; and improving the efficiency of manufacturing systems by reducing workers' idle time and unnecessary motions, and by eliminating unnecessary inventory, unnecessary transportation and material handling, and scrap and rework.

Traditional improvement programs such as work simplification and planned methods change focused almost exclusively on productivity and cost. A focus on quality improvement, on the other hand, is relatively recent, stimulated by the success of the Japanese.

Toyota, in particular, pioneered just-in-time (JIT). JIT showed that companies could make products with virtually zero defects, and reversed the thinking that achieving zero defects was a costly practice. In fact, JIT proved that producing extremely low defect levels typically saved money. Most importantly, JIT established a philosophy of improvement, which the Japanese call **kaizen** (pronounced ki-zen).

KAIZEN *Kaizen*, which is a Japanese word that means "gradual and orderly continuous improvement," is a philosophy that subsumes all business activities and everyone in an organization. *Kaizen* strategy has been called "the single most important concept in Japanese management—the key to Japanese competitive success." Often in the West, quality improvement is viewed simply as making improvements in product quality. In the *kaizen* philosophy, improvement in all areas of business—cost, meeting delivery schedules, employee safety and skill development, supplier relations, new product development, or productivity—serve to enhance the quality of the firm. Thus, any activity directed toward improvement falls under the *kaizen* umbrella. Activities to establish traditional quality control systems, install robotics and advanced technology, institute employee suggestion systems, maintain equipment, and implement just-in-time production systems all lead to improvement.

Kaizen focuses on small, gradual, and frequent improvements over the long term. Financial investment is minimal. Everyone participates in the process; many improvements result from the know-how and experience of workers.

The first and foremost concern of the *kaizen* philosophy is the quality of people. If the quality of people is improved, then the quality of products will follow. By instilling *kaizen* into people and training them in basic quality-improvement tools, workers can build this philosophy into their work and continually seek improvement in their jobs. This process-oriented approach to improvement encourages constant communication among workers and managers.

Three things are required for a successful *kaizen* program: operating practices, total involvement, and training. First, operating practices expose new improvement opportunities. Practices such as just-in-time reveal waste and inefficiency as well as poor quality. Second, in *kaizen*, every employee strives for improvement. Top management, for example, views improvement as an inherent component of corporate strategy and provides support to improvement activities by allocating resources effectively and providing reward structures that are conducive to improvement. Middle management can implement top-management's improvement goals by establishing, upgrading, and maintaining operating standards that reflect those goals; by improving cooperation between departments; and by making employees conscious of their responsibility for improvement and developing their problem-solving skills through training. Supervisors can direct more of their attention to improvement rather than "supervision," which, in turn, facilitates communication and offers better guidance to workers. Finally, workers can engage in improvement through suggestion systems and small-group activities as well as self-development programs that teach practical problem-solving techniques and enhanced job performance skills. All these activities require significant training, both in the philosophy and in tools and techniques.

Flexibility and Cycle-Time Reduction

Success in globally competitive markets requires a capacity for rapid change and flexibility. Electronic commerce, for instance, requires more rapid, flexible, and customized responses than traditional market outlets. **Flexibility** refers to the ability to adapt quickly and effectively to changing requirements. It might mean rapid changeover from one product to another, rapid response to changing demands, or the ability to produce a wide range of customized services. Flexibility might demand special strategies such as modular designs, sharing components, sharing manufacturing lines, and specialized training for employees. It also involves outsourcing decisions, agreements with key suppliers, and innovative partnering arrangements.

One important business metric that complements flexibility is cycle time. **Cycle time** refers to the time it takes to accomplish one cycle of a process—for instance, the time a customer orders a product to the time that it is delivered, or the time to introduce a new product. Reductions in cycle time serve two purposes. First, they speed up work processes so that customer response is improved. Second, reductions in cycle time can only be accomplished by streamlining and simplifying processes to eliminate non-value-added steps such as rework. They force improvements in quality by reducing the potential for mistakes and errors. By reducing non-value-added steps, costs are reduced as well. Thus, cycle-time reductions often drive simultaneous improvements in organization, quality, cost, and productivity. Significant reductions in cycle time cannot be achieved simply by focusing on individual subprocesses; cross-functional processes must be examined across the organization. Through this examination, the company can better understand work at the organizational level and engage in cooperative behaviors.

Agility is a term that is commonly used to characterize flexibility and short cycle times. Agility is crucial to such customer-focused strategies as mass customization, which requires rapid response and flexibility to changing consumer demand. Enablers of agility include close relationships with customers to understand their emerging needs and requirements, empowering employees as decision makers, effective manufacturing and information technology, close supplier and partner relationships, and breakthrough improvement.

Breakthrough Improvement

Breakthrough improvement refers to discontinuous change, as opposed to the gradual, continuous improvement philosophy of *kaizen*. Breakthrough improvements result from innovative and creative thinking; often these are motivated by **stretch goals,** or **breakthrough objectives.** Stretch goals force an organization to think in a radically different way, and to encourage major improvements as well as incremental ones. When a goal of 10 percent improvement is set, managers or engineers can usually meet it with some minor improvements. However, when the goal is 1,000 percent improvement, employees must be creative and think "out of the box." The seemingly impossible is often achieved, yielding dramatic improvements and boosting morale. A widely publicized example is Motorola. Motorola uses *defects per unit* as a quality measure throughout the company. A unit is any output of work, such as a line of computer code, a solder connection, or a page of a document. A **defect** is any failure to meet customer requirements. Motorola developed a concept called "Six-Sigma" quality, which refers to allowing, at most, 3.4 defects per million units. Throughout the 1990s, Motorola has continued to set challenging goals. These ambitious goals apply to all areas of the company, including order entry, sales, purchasing, manufacturing, and design. For stretch goals to be successful, they must derive unambiguously from corporate strategy. Organizations must not set goals that result in unreasonable stress to employees or punish failure. In addition, they must provide appropriate help and tools to accomplish the task. Two approaches for breakthrough improvement that help companies achieve stretch goals are *benchmarking* and *reengineering*.

Service Quality

Service Quality Concepts

Each of us consumes services every day. Eighty percent of the U.S. economy today is based on services. How much of this service is good, though? How much is great or terrific service? How much is bad service? How exactly do you measure service quality anyway?

Quality is an increasingly important element that differentiates between competing services. Unlike tangible goods, though, many services are not easily measured or tested for quality. Often, one cannot even assess their quality until after consuming them. All across the service economy, however, leading companies are obsessed with service excellence. They use service to increase productivity. They use it to be different and to earn their customers' loyalty. They seek some shelter from price competition through quality service.

In manufacturing, companies may focus on Total Quality Management (TQM) and gurus such as Deming, Juran, and Crosby. TQM involves "managing the entire organization so that it excels on all dimensions of products and services that are important to the customer" (Chase, Acquilano, and Jacobs, 2001). TQM took hold in the United States after competition from the Japanese's excellent manufacturing quality hit U.S. companies hard in the late 1970s and 1980s. Consumer confidence in U.S. goods' quality diminished and caused a quality revolution across U.S. industry. The movement affected service organizations when consumers demanded quality in everything they purchased—both goods and services.

As the U.S. economy shifts ever more to one dominated by services and consumers demand more and better quality of their service providers, managers strive to provide "customer delight" with their services by adopting parts of the quality movement so effectively utilized by manufacturers. In fact, in a recent Gallup survey, executives ranked the improvement of service and tangible product quality as the single most critical challenge facing U.S. business.

Improving the quality of services is more difficult than improving the quality of products because of the temporary nature of a service. An unsatisfactory or defective product can be replaced or repaired. However, a delivery of an unsatisfactory service is something that cannot be undone, so it is vital to deliver a satisfactory—or preferably superior—service the first time.[19]

The primary rule of total quality management is to know your customer. A good example of this axiom can be found in the travel services industry. Although this industry places its customer first in theory, in practice, customers are not always happy with the service they receive.

Gradually, the TQM movement shifted to one of return on quality (ROQ). With TQM, the drivers are too often defined internally. With ROQ, the customers set the parameters and the marketer selects those quality improvements that lead to the greatest return on investment.

Defining Service Quality

Quality is much easier to define when manufacturing tangible products. Manufacturing quality may simply involve conformance to specifications. A manufacturer can evaluate the level of a product's quality based on what was produced relative to the design specifications. A defect means a product failed to meet those specifications. The specifications come from product engineers who may be designing the product based on what market research data show that customers want or from some other type of communication that indicates customer wants and needs.

In services, evaluating the level of quality is much more elusive. Quality specifications for services come from multiple simultaneous sources, including the company and the individual customers. The company presents specifications as standard operating procedures. Customers present specifications based on their personal expectations for what their service experience will be. Misalignment between company and customer specifications for the service process leads to dissatisfaction, even when the process goes exactly as it was designed. The misalignment of specifications can be avoided through communication. However, if the service performance does not address individual customer needs, the customer will not require the service.[20]

Understanding how this process works requires understanding the difference between quality and value. Service quality is often defined as the satisfaction of expectations. The expectations, of course, are subjective and based on cognitive or formal descriptions of the service process and outcome. Service value is the satisfaction of needs. Needs are the changes that customers perceive will increase their "happiness" or decrease their "happiness." When expectations for a service provider appear to fill customer needs, customers will consider purchasing the service, otherwise they will not. For example, the same waiter who is considered witty and urbane by some diners may seem outrageous and rude to others, even though the base service is identical.

A variety of available tools can help determine customer expectations, including customer satisfaction surveys, customer perception surveys, focus groups, complaint analysis, employee research, similar industry studies, and transaction analysis.

The true key to delivering quality service comes in identifying and understanding what dimensions of quality are important to *your* customers. High quality does not have to carry a high price. Even low-cost services can be viewed as high quality when they meet the needs and expectations of the customer and the customer values the service.

Definitions of Service Quality

Many definitions attempt to describe what constitutes quality service. Some proponents of quality service state that quality can be defined only by customers and occurs when an organization supplies goods or services to a specification that satisfies the customer's needs. Others simply define quality as the satisfaction of customer expectations.

Rust, Zahorik, and Keiningham (1994) claimed that customer satisfaction and delight are both strongly influenced by customer expectations and that the term *expectations* as used by behavioral researchers is not as precise as the usage by mathematicians, which is "what is likely to happen, on average."[21] They found a bewildering array of "expectations" that reflected what might, could, will, should, or better not happen.

They define the *will expectation* as coming closest to the mathematics definition. It is the "average level of quality that is predicted based on all known information." It represents the expectation level most often meant by customers and used by researchers. When someone says that the "service exceeded my expectations," what they generally mean is that the service was better than they had predicted it would be.

The *should expectation* is what the customer feels he or she deserves from the transaction. The *ideal expectation* is what would happen under the best of circumstances and is useful as a barometer of excellence. The *minimally acceptable* level (the threshold at which mere satisfaction is achieved) is the other end of the scale along with *worst possible* (the worst outcome that can be imagined).

Most quality definitions fall short, however, of reflecting all the various perspectives of the various stakeholders. The following categories of quality definitions reflect five different perspectives:[22]

1. *Transcendent.* According to the transcendent view, quality is innate excellence and can be recognized only through experience. In other words, "You cannot define quality but you know it when you see it." It, however, provides little practical guidance to managers in the quest for quality.
2. *Product-based.* Product-based definitions rely on measurable quantities to define quality. For goods, the measures may include length of useful life, amount of a desirable ingredient (e.g., "100 percent cotton") or amount of a desirable output (e.g., "45 miles per gallon"). For services an example might be the length of time before a service is provided. Because it is based on measurable quantities, this definition allows an objective

assessment of quality. The disadvantage of a product-based definition is that it assumes all customers desire the same attributes and hence fails to account for differences in tastes and preferences of individual consumers.

3. *User-based.* This approach to defining quality begins where the product-based definition ends; it defines quality from an individual consumer's perspective. The "fitness for use" definition of quality is consistent with this approach. In other words, it is based on the premise that "quality is in the eyes of the beholder." For example, a tastefully prepared and presented meal that takes 30 minutes to deliver to a customer's table may be seen as a sign of poor quality if the meal is for lunch and the customer is in a hurry. The subjectivity of this approach leads to two problems: (1) how to decide which attributes should be included in a good or service to appeal to the largest numbers of customers, and (2) how to differentiate between attributes that provide satisfaction and those that imply quality.

4. *Manufacturing-based.* Manufacturing-based definitions view quality as an outcome of engineering and production processes. According to this approach, quality is "conformance to requirements." In other words, how well does the output match the design specifications? For example, if an airline service specifies arrival within 15 minutes of the schedule, the level of quality in terms of this specification can easily be determined by comparing actual flight arrivals with the schedule. The disadvantage of this approach is that, unless specifications are based on customers' needs and preferences, quality becomes an internal issue that helps simplify production control but fails to deliver what customers want.

5. *Value-based.* This approach incorporates value and price into the definition of quality. Quality is defined as a balance between conformance or performance and an acceptable price to the customer.

The various departments within a company each use different perspectives in their definition of quality and their subsequent measurement of the quality they produce. Marketing, for example, will be much more focused on the user-based definition.

The Customers' View of Service Quality

Increasingly, Americans say the customer service they receive ranges from rude, at best, to simply nonexistent. Businesses counter by saying an economy that fosters an instant-gratification culture and a chronic shortage of quality workers hinders efforts to cater to customers as they did before. Both sides agree on one thing: In today's service economy, service just isn't what it used to be.

Poor service plagues almost every industry that counts service as its main mission. Travelers complain of vague and uncaring airline attendants, late flights, and lost luggage. Bank account and credit card holders fume over being trapped in a voice-mail maze, never to connect to a real person. It is a trend that experts say business should work at reversing.

As the economy settles into a recession after the recent boom days, quality service will rise up as a strong competitive advantage. As the airlines and other travel services strain to adjust to heightened security needs, service issues will surely grow.

Measuring Service Quality

Clearly, quality is something customers expect and something they value when they purchase a service. But, how do we define and then measure these expectations in order to meet them? Parasuraman, Zeithaml, and Berry (1985) recognized the idea that service quality is a function of the expectations-performance gap and conducted a broad-based exploratory study in the early 1980s.[23] Their research results began to appear in 1985 and continue today with expansion into e-SQ, or electronic service quality.

Parasuraman and colleagues conducted studies in several industry sectors to develop and refine SERVQUAL, a multiple-item instrument to quantify customers' global (as opposed to transaction-specific) assessment of a company's service quality. Their model is also commonly known as the "Gaps model."

Their scale involved expectations-perceptions gap scores along five dimensions: reliability, responsiveness, assurance, empathy, and tangibles.

1. *Reliability.* Reliability involves consistency of performance and dependability. It means that the firm performs the service right the first time and that it honors its promises. Specifically, it involves accuracy in billing, keeping records correctly, and performing the service at the designated time.

2. *Responsiveness.* The willingness or readiness of employees to provide service. It involves timeliness of service including mailing a transaction slip immediately, calling the customer back quickly, and giving prompt service (e.g., setting up appointments quickly).

3. *Assurance.* This dimension relates to the knowledge, competence, and courtesy of service employees and their ability to convey trust and confidence. Competence means possession of the required skills and knowledge to perform the service. Courtesy involves politeness, respect, consideration, and friendliness of contact personnel. It also includes trustworthiness, believability, and honesty of service employees.
4. *Empathy.* The caring and individualized attention provided to customers includes the approachability and ease of contact with the service providers and their efforts to understand the customers' needs.
5. *Tangibles.* Tangibles include the physical evidence of the service, such as physical facilities, appearance of service providers, tools or equipment used to provide the service, physical presentation of the service, and other customers in the service facility.

When Zeithaml, Parasuraman, and Berry asked more than 1,900 customers of five nationally known companies to allocate 100 points across the five service quality dimensions, they averaged as follows: reliability 32 percent, responsiveness 22 percent, assurance 19 percent, empathy 16 percent, and tangibles 11 percent.[24] Though customers consistently reported that their most important quality dimension was reliability, this area seems to be where many service companies fail.

Gaps in Service Quality

The SERVQUAL model conceptualizes service quality on the basis of the differences between customers' expectations with respect to the five dimensions and their perceptions of what was actually delivered. When a difference exists, it is characterized as a "gap." This model was fashioned after remarkably consistent patterns emerged from the study's interviews. Though some perceptions about service quality were specific to the industries selected, commonalities among the industries prevailed. The commonalities suggested that a general model of service could be developed.

Parasuraman and colleagues found in their focus groups that, regardless of the type of service, consumers used basically similar criteria in evaluating service quality. These criteria fall into 10 key categories such as reliability, responsiveness, competence, access, courtesy, communication, credibility, security, understanding/knowing the customer, and tangibles such as physical facilities, tools, or equipment used to provide the service.

A consumer's view of service quality reveals that perceived service quality is the result of the consumer's comparison of expected service with perceived service. The comparison and the perceived service evaluation are not unlike that performed by consumers when evaluating goods. What differs with services is the *nature* of the characteristics upon which they are evaluated.

Service Quality Design

It is often important to design certain fail-safe[25] (mistake-proofing) techniques into a service to ensure the safety of service providers and consumers. Fail-safe constructs procedures that block mistakes from becoming service defects. Developing a service blueprint enables you to identify potential areas where service failures can occur. Similar to the design process utilized in manufacturing, a service blueprint generally consists of four stages: direction, design, testing, and introduction.[26] During the design phase, you can create fail-safe procedures or devices to signal potential mistakes and allow for their correction immediately. Mistake-proofing was discussed more in section 410.

Foolproof Service Using Poka-Yoke

The quality assurance challenge for services is to achieve zero defects in the day-to-day provision of services. The late Shigeo Shingo (known as "Mr. Improvement" in Japan), conceived of the idea of fail-safing or mistake-proofing to prevent the inevitable mistake from turning into a defect. Although widely used in manufacturing operations, poka-yoke is less well known in services. A poka-yoke (from the Japanese *yokeru*, meaning "to prevent," and *poka*, meaning "inadvertent errors") is a simple, built-in step in a process that must be performed before the next stage can be performed. In essence, it is a device or procedure that signals a mistake is about to be made. Done well, a fail-safing procedure is also usually fairly simple and inexpensive to develop.

In services, hospitals use task poka-yokes in their medical processes. Indentations on trays that hold surgical instruments mean that all the instruments needed for a given operation will be nested on the tray. It is immediately evident not only if an instrument is missing, but also *which* specific instrument is missing before the patient's incision is closed.

Encounter poka-yoke devices and procedures can be used to warn and control customer actions to prevent customer errors during the encounter. Examples of this type of poka-yoke include frames in airport check-in for passengers to gauge the allowable size of carry-on luggage, locks on airplane lavatory doors that must be turned to switch on lights (and at the same time activate the "Occupied" sign), height bars at amusement rides to assure that riders meet or do not exceed size requirements, and beepers to signal customers to remove their cards from the ATM. Another hospital innovation involves electronic order entry. Doctors enter orders for prescriptions, X-rays, and lab tests into a computer system, which instantly checks the order for possible problems such as drug interactions or allergies.

Measures of Customer Satisfaction

Good customer service and high customer satisfaction requires the commitment of management, supervisors, and front-line employees to create and maintain a strong business philosophy. These factors are influential in any business. Mastering these aspects means becoming more competitive in the marketplace today.

Excellent companies know their customers; they know their customers' needs and requirements. Although each company may approach it in different ways, they usually go to great lengths to gather this information. This information allows them to design effective and efficient services and delivery systems that satisfy customers, to position and market services effectively, and to forecast and manage demand.

L.L.Bean is often thought of as synonymous with great customer service and customer satisfaction. It displays a poster prominently all around its Freeport, Maine, facilities that defines its customer.

Rust, Zahorik, and Keiningham suggested that service operations measure their quality management success by calculating their return on quality (ROQ).[27] The steps can be broken down into four main sections: (1) exploratory research, (2) quantitative research, (3) impact of quality on satisfaction, and (4) market share and profit impact.

The central chain of events that leads from quality to profits can be summarized as follows: Service performance impacts customer satisfaction, which impacts customer retention, which changes market share, which impacts profits.

This chain of events, however, focuses on customer retention and does not include three sources of profits generated by quality improvement: (1) cost reductions due to increased efficiency, (2) the attraction of new customers resulting from positive word-of-mouth, and (3) the ability to charge higher prices.

Based on the concept that the primary purpose of every business is performing a service for customers, the service always centers on meeting customer needs. Thus, a mission of management is to identify and fulfill customer needs. To do so, companies must find out what the customer needs are, whether they are being met, and how to meet them better.

Thinking of a company as a service designed specifically to fulfill customer needs is not the natural way for most managers to view their organizations. It is essential, however, if they are to understand how customers perceive their firms. As a result, managers need to understand what is meant by "service performance," and then use that understanding to determine the actual benefits their companies offer to customers.

Common measurement tools used by market researchers to reveal service performance levels include customer satisfaction surveys, customer perception surveys, focus groups, complaint analysis, employee research, similar industry studies, and transaction analysis.

Achieving Service Quality

Costs of Service Quality

A lot of confusion surrounds the issue of whether quality costs money or saves money. In one sense, quality means the features of a service that make people willing to buy it. So it is income-oriented and affects income. To produce features, ordinarily you must invest money. In that sense, higher quality costs more. Quality also means freedom from trouble and freedom from failure, which is cost-oriented. If things fail internally, it costs the company. If they fail externally, it also costs the customer. In these cases, quality costs less.[28]

Many executives still do not agree that investments in quality pay off in terms of service improvement and profits. Indeed, many companies waste money annually in the name of quality improvement that fails to lead to increased quality or profits. The thing that actually does pay off is improving service in the eyes of the customers. Quality becomes a profit strategy when service improvements lead to perceived service improvements.[29] Studies show that, in the long run, the most important single factor affecting a business unit's performance is the quality of its products and services relative to those of competitors.

455. SERVICE QUALITY

Quality service pays off, in the final analysis, because it creates *true* customers who are glad they selected a firm after the service experience, who will use the firm's services again, and who will sing the firm's praises to others. The essence of services operations is service or, more directly, the *performance* of that service. When everything comes together to produce customer delight, profits result.

Roland Rust and colleagues (1994) summarized the facts around the costs involved with attaining and then keeping quality customers:

- It costs five times more money to acquire a new customer than to retain a current customer.
- Increasing the length of a customer relationship increases the lifetime value of the customer.
- Longer-term customers tend to purchase more.
- Familiar customers may be more efficient to deal with.[30]

Profits Tied to Quality

Quality service, in and by itself, cannot guarantee higher profits or a better bottom-line number. Failure to link a company's quality program to the bottom line through cost reductions or revenue increases could, in fact, lead to corporate failure.

Cost reductions from improving processes to do things right the first time were the basis for the initial enthusiasm for quality improvement processes in the manufacturing sector. To implement such a program, though, everybody in the organization must be convinced that things must be done right the first time. W. Edwards Deming suggested that the cost of quality is the cost to the company of doing things wrong. He insisted that management is responsible for 85 percent of a company's quality problems; workers are responsible for only 15 percent. Some estimate that product (service) design is itself responsible for 50 percent or more of a firm's quality problems.[31]

Rust and colleagues (1994) stated that the resources spent to provide quality on a consistent basis can be known collectively as the "cost of quality" and that spending usually occurs in four areas:

1. Prevention of problems
2. Inspection and appraisal to monitor ongoing quality
3. The cost to redo a defective product before it is delivered to the customer (also known as internal failures)
4. The cost to make good on a defective product after it reaches the customer (also known as external failures)[32]

They also concede that identifying and estimating these costs can be difficult, particularly in a service setting.

Implementing Quality Service

Designing Fail-Safing into Service

We already discussed one method of ensuring proper service, that of designing poka-yoke devices to help fail-safe a service. Companies often use software, procedures, or gimmicks whose purpose is to make the quality way of delivering the service the only way the service gets delivered. The good part of these devices is that they involve relatively little capital goods investment. An example is the fast-food restaurants' use of a french-fry scoop for quick action and proper portion control. Software often prompts for the next piece of data or buzzes when the wrong piece of data has been entered. Other fail-safing devices relate to the customer and affect their behavior, for example, reminder cards for appointments, special uniforms or other clues so customers know whom to ask for help, and directions mailed ahead of time.

Service Guarantees and Refunds

Many firms meet the quality challenge by offering *service guarantees* to their customers. Guarantees can be a powerful marketing tool to increase sales, but the primary objective of a guarantee should be to foster repeat business. They can even work to create and define specific service "niches" such as FedEx's guarantee of overnight delivery. Market leaders can establish the new "rules of the game" for niches they create and develop. Guarantees can take many forms. Domino Pizza's former guarantee of 30 minutes delivery or L.L.Bean's policy of "no questions asked returns" are two well-known examples.

A good service guarantee should be identified and clearly defined as part of the initial design of a service. Unfortunately, many service guarantees don't really do the job they are designed to do because they are limited in scope or are difficult to use. Often a guarantee will be offered with conditions that negate the guarantee. Airlines, for instance, guarantee on-time arrivals *except* when the delay is weather-related or air-traffic delays occur.

Christopher Hart (1988) studied service guarantees and indicated they work best when they include the following characteristics:

- *Unconditional:* Customer satisfaction without exceptions
- *Easy to understand and communicate:* Written in simple, concise language that pinpoints the promise
- *Meaningful:* Important to customers and financially significant without being overly generous
- *Easy to invoke:* No red tape or runaround to hurdle, no guilt involved
- *Easy to collect:* The procedure needs to be quick and hassle-free[33]

Hart gave five reasons why a guarantee provides a powerful tool in achieving marketing and service quality:

1. It forces the service to focus on the customers' definition of good service, rather than the expectations of management. If a company identifies the wrong things to guarantee, it will be worthless to its customers.
2. It sets up clear performance standards, which boost employee performance and morale. Employees take pride in good service and a great reputation.
3. It generates reliable data (through payouts) when performance is poor. When a payout causes financial pain, it will be easier to ensure that every necessary step will be taken to correct and prevent future such occurrences.
4. It forces an organization to examine its entire service delivery system for possible failure points. Continual review of the service goals will ensure an ongoing process improvement all through the company systems. A guarantee provides customers an easy method of giving feedback on possible failure points so that management can direct attention to remedying them as quickly as possible.
5. It builds customer loyalty, sales, and market share. A good guarantee reduces the risk of the purchase decision for customers, and it generates more sales to existing customers by enhancing loyalty.

Some service firms will not benefit from a guarantee when they already have a reputation for sterling service. These types of firms usually instill a mission of absolute customer satisfaction in all of their employees and empower them to make amends as needed. Hotels such as the Ritz-Carlton and the Four Seasons Hotels are good examples. Guests at these hotels don't need a guarantee, because it is assumed that the service will be absolutely terrific. When it is not, employees go out of their way to make it right for the guest. Nordstrom store employees enjoy a similar reputation for whatever it takes, including the famous incident when a Nordstrom shoe salesperson found the shoes the customer desired at a different store, purchased them, contacted the customer, and arranged delivery of the shoes. The "find" was transparent to the satisfied customer.

The downside of guarantees, of course, is their implication that the service may fail. A guarantee might actually make customers more aware of service defects. It might also entice some customers to cheat. Great service providers, however, live by the philosophy that only 1 percent of their customers will cheat, which should not prevent them from providing great service to the other 99 percent. Many also believe that customers only resort to cheating when they feel they are not receiving value for their money.

Service Recovery

All service providers experience moments of service failure at some point. Equipment failure, delivery delays, severe weather, or human frailties (no-shows, forgetful or careless employees) can affect a service profoundly. The most important step in service recovery is to find out as soon as possible when a service fails to meet customers' expectations. Customers who are dissatisfied but have no way of communicating their dissatisfaction to the organization may never come back. Worse yet, they will probably relate the bad experience to everyone they know. It is therefore imperative that companies facilitate customer feedback and find opportunities to correct any failure situations and create a "delighted" customer.

This feedback procedure needs to be part of the initial service design process. A key consideration focuses on empowering front-line personnel to remedy the situation immediately. These front-line emissaries need to be able to express empathy while taking concrete steps to assist the customer. All attempts to rectify the situation should occur at the time and place most critical from the *customer's* perspective.

Recovering from service failures does not happen automatically; an organization must carefully prepare for it. Hart, Heskett, and Sasser (1990) recommended the following approach:

1. *Measure the costs.* The old adage, "What gets measured gets managed," is the principle here. Service failures cost both the customer and the service organization.

2. *Break the silence and listen closely for complaints.* Many customers do not complain if they are not happy with a product or service. Consider the most frequently given reasons found by Technical Assistance Research Programs (TARP), a Washington, D.C.-based research and consulting organization:
   - It's not worth the time or effort.
   - No one would be concerned with my problem or interested in acting on it.
   - I don't know where to go or what to do.

   Clearly, if a service organization does not know about service failures, it cannot do anything about them. Using toll-free 800 numbers for complaints or suggestions; offering rewards for suggestions; and conducting regular surveys, focus groups, and interviews of lost customers all can offer new information to uncover and thus prevent service problems.

3. *Anticipate needs for recovery.* A plan and a procedure for each potential failure must be developed, and employees must be trained in these procedures. Managers who understand the service and its delivery system can anticipate where failures may occur and make plans for recovery.

4. *Act fast.* A service organization that acts quickly to correct the situation will probably impress the customer and make her or him forget the incident. Long, drawn-out processes and weeks of waiting will not help the customer forget the failure easily even if it is eventually resolved satisfactorily.

5. *Train employees.* Effective service recovery is not possible if the employees who handle complaints are not prepared for occasional service failures. Preparation involves training and empowerment. Training should include developing good communication skills, creative thinking, quick decision making, and developing an awareness of customers' concerns. One of the most effective training methods is stimulated situations and role-playing.

6. *Empower the front line.* Quick and decisive action to remedy a service failure is not possible without empowered employees. Many rules and limits on authority are established because of a fear that employees will "give away the store," which is not likely to happen with a well-trained and motivated employee. Losing customers, however, is much more likely if their problem is not solved.

7. *Close the loop.* Recovery and complaint handling must achieve closure. If the condition that led to the problem cannot be remedied, the customer must be given an explanation. If the complaint leads to a change in the service or the delivery system, the customer should be told so.[34]

Business Process Analysis

Benchmarking

The development and realization of improvement objectives, particularly stretch objectives, is often aided through a process known as benchmarking. **Benchmarking** is defined as "measuring your performance against that of best-in-class companies, determining how the best-in-class achieve those performance levels, and using the information as a basis for your own company's targets, strategies, and implementation."[35] Or more simply, it can be thought of as "the search of industry best practices that lead to superior performance."[36] The term **best practices** refers to approaches that produce exceptional results, are usually innovative in terms of the use of technology or human resources, and are recognized by customers or industry experts.

Through benchmarking, a company discovers its strengths and weaknesses and those of other industrial leaders and learns how to incorporate the best practices into its own operations. Benchmarking can provide motivation to achieve stretch goals by helping employees to see what others can accomplish. For example, to meet a stretch target of reducing the time to build new 747 and 767 airplanes at Boeing from 18 months (in 1992) to 8 months, teams studied the world's best producers of everything from computers to ships. By 1996 the time had been reduced to 10 months.[37]

Four major types of benchmarking have emerged in business. These include competitive benchmarking, process benchmarking, strategic benchmarking, and internal benchmarking.

Competitive benchmarking involves studying products, processes, or business performance of competitors in the same industry to compare pricing, quality, technical features, and other quality or performance characteristics of products and services. For example, a television cable company might compare its customer satisfaction rating or service response time to other cable companies; a manufacturer of televisions might compare its unit production costs or field failure rates against competitors. Significant gaps suggest key opportunities for improvement. Competitive benchmarking was refined into a science by Xerox during the 1970s and 1980s.

Process benchmarking emerged soon after. It centers on key work processes such as distribution, order entry, or employee training. This type of benchmarking identifies the most effective practices in companies that perform similar functions, no matter in what industry. For example, the warehousing and distribution practices of L.L.Bean were adapted by Xerox for its spare parts distribution system. Texas Instruments studied the kitting (order preparation) practices of six companies, including Mary Kay Cosmetics, and designed a process that captured the best practices of each of them, cutting kitting cycle time in half. A General Mills plant in Lodi, California, had an average machine changeover time of three hours. Then somebody said, "From three hours to 10 minutes!" Employees went to a NASCAR track and videotaped the pit crews, and studied the process to identify how the principles could be applied to the production changeover processes. Several months later, the average time fell to 17 minutes.[38] Thus, companies should not aim benchmarking solely at direct competitors; in fact, they would be mistaken to do so. If a company simply benchmarks within its own industry, it may be competitive and have an edge in those areas in which it is the industry leader. However, if benchmarks are adopted from outside the industry, a company may learn ideas and processes as well as new applications that allow it to surpass the best within its own industry and to achieve distinctive superiority.

Strategic benchmarking examines how companies compete and seeks the winning strategies that have led to competitive advantage and market success.

The typical benchmarking process can be described by the process used at AT&T.

1. *Project conception:* identify the need and decide to benchmark.
2. *Planning:* determine the scope and objectives, and develop a benchmarking plan.
3. *Preliminary data collection:* collect data on industry companies and similar processes as well as detailed data on the organization's own processes.
4. *Best-in-class selection:* select companies with best-in-class processes.
5. *Best-in-class collection:* collect detailed data from companies with best-in-class processes.
6. *Assessment:* compare the organization's and best-in-class processes and develop recommendations.
7. *Implementation planning:* develop operational improvement plans to attain superior performance.
8. *Implementation:* enact operational plans and monitor process improvements.
9. *Recalibration:* update benchmark findings and assess improvements in processes.[39]

Benchmarking has many benefits. The best practices from any industry may be creatively incorporated into a company's operations. Benchmarking is a motivating activity. It provides targets that have been achieved by others. Resistance to change may be lessened when ideas for improvement come from other industries. Technical breakthroughs from other industries that may be useful can be identified early on. Benchmarking broadens people's experience base and increases organizational learning and knowledge. To be effective, it must be applied to all facets of a business. For example, Motorola encourages everyone in the organization to ask, "Who is the best person in my own field and how might I use some of their techniques and characteristics to improve my own performance in order to be the best (executive, machine operator, chef, purchasing agent) in my 'class'?" Used in this fashion, benchmarking becomes a tool for improvement.

One of the indicators of a true learning organization is the ability to identify and transfer best practices within the organization, sometimes called **internal benchmarking.** It is an area where even the most mature organizations falter, even those that are adept at external benchmarking. The American Productivity and Quality Center (APQC) noted that executives have long been frustrated by their inability to identify or transfer outstanding practices from one location or function to another. They know that some facilities have superior practices and processes, yet operation units continue to reinvent or ignore solutions and repeat mistakes.[40] Research has shown that barriers fell into three categories: 1. lack of motivation to adopt the practice; 2. inadequate information about how to adapt the practice and make it work; and 3. lack of "absorptive capacity," the resources and skill to make and manage the change.

Business Process Reengineering

Reengineering has been defined as "the fundamental rethinking and radical redesign of business processes to achieve dramatic improvements in critical, contemporary measures of performance, such as cost, quality, service, and speed."[40] Reengineering involves asking basic questions about business processes: "Why do we do it?" and "Why is it done this way?" Such questioning often uncovers obsolete, erroneous, or inappropriate assumptions. Radical redesign involves tossing out existing procedures and reinventing the process, not just incrementally improving it. The goal is to achieve quantum leaps in performance. For example, IBM Credit Corporation cut the process of financing IBM computers, software, and services from seven days to four hours by rethinking the process. Originally, the process was designed to handle difficult applications and required four highly trained specialists and a series of handoffs. The actual work took only about 1.5 hours; the rest of the time was spent in transit or delay. By questioning the assumption that every application was unique and difficult to process, IBM Credit Corporation was able to replace the specialists by a single individual supported by a user-friendly computer system that provided access to all the data and tools that the specialists would use.

Successful reengineering requires fundamental understanding of processes, creative thinking to break away from old traditions and assumptions, and effective use of information technology. PepsiCo has embarked on a program to reengineer all of its key business processes, such as selling and delivery, equipment service and repair, procurement, and financial reporting. In the selling and delivery of its products, for example, customer reps typically experience stockouts of as much as 25 percent of product by the end of the day, resulting in late-day stops not getting full deliveries and the need to return to those accounts. Many other routes return with overstock of other products, increasing handling costs. By redesigning the system to include hand-held computers, customer reps can confirm and deliver that day's order and also take a future order for the next delivery to that customer.

Benchmarking can greatly assist reengineering efforts. Reengineering without benchmarking probably will produce 5 to 10 percent improvements; benchmarking can increase this percentage to 50 or 75 percent. When GTE reengineered eight core processes of its telephone operations, it examined the best practices of some 84 companies from diverse industries. By studying outside best practices, a company can identify and import new technology, skills, structures, training, and capabilities.

Contrary to the suggestions of many authors and consultants, reengineering is not completely different from total quality principles. The issue is not *kaizen* versus breakthrough improvement. Incremental and breakthrough improvement are complementary approaches that fall under the total quality umbrella; both are necessary to remain competitive. In fact, some suggest that reengineering requires total quality support in order to be successful.[41] Reengineering alone is often driven by upper management without the full support or understanding of the rest of the organization, and radical innovations may end up as failures. A total quality philosophy encourages participation and systematic study, measurement, and verification of results that support reengineering efforts, thus helping to ensure its success.

Business Process Improvement

Business process improvement (BPI) should be continuous, not discrete, and is an incremental change that may affect only a single task or segment of the organization. The concept of fundamental or radical change is the basis of the major difference between business process reengineering (BPR) and BPI. Quite often, BPI initiatives limit their focus to a single existing organizational unit. This in itself breaks one of the tenets of BPR, which is that BPR must focus on redesigning a fundamental business process, not on existing departments or organizational units. While BPR seeks to define what the processes should be, BPI focuses more on how to improve an existing process or service.

Through BPI, organizations can achieve significant incremental improvements in service delivery and other business factors (e.g., increase in employee's productivity). The expected outcomes of BPI are not as dramatic as those associated with BPR initiatives, but the process is also not as traumatic as in achieving the radical changes seen with BPR. In many cases, incremental changes may be achieved in situations lacking the support necessary for more radical changes. Exhibit 400.22 shows the key differences between the two concepts, BPR and BPI.

Exhibit 400.22 *Comparison Between BPR and BPI*

Element	BPR	BPI
Degree of change	Radical (e.g., 80 percent)	Incremental (e.g., 10–30 percent)
Scope	Entire process	Single area, function/unit
Time	Years	Months
Driver	Business	Technology
Focus	Redefine process	Automate/eliminate the function
Work structure	Unified	Fragmented
Orientation	Outcome	Function

Exhibit 400.23 *Comparison Between Benchmarking and Continuous Process Improvement*

Benchmarking	Continuous Process Improvement
• Develops performance measures as output. • Identifies opportunities for improvement. • Benchmarking takes a creative and novel approach to redefine objectives and focus on core issues. It could result in throwing away the existing practice and starting all over.	• The output measures or metrics from benchmarking exercise become inputs to the continuous process improvement. • Continuous improvement takes the opportunities and turns them into actions which, in turn, become values. • Continuous improvement is "tweaking" the existing process.

Continuous Process Improvement

Achieving the highest levels of quality and competitiveness requires a well-defined and well-executed approach to continuous improvement. The term *continuous improvement* refers to both incremental and breakthrough improvement. A focus on improvement needs to be part of all operations and of all work unit activities of the organization.

Improvements may be of several types: (1) enhancing value to customers through new and improved products and services; (2) reducing errors, defects, and waste; (3) improving responsiveness and cycle-time performance; (4) improving productivity and effectiveness in the use of all resources; and (5) improving the organization's performance and leadership position in fulfilling its public responsibilities and serving as a role model in corporate citizenship. Thus, improvement is driven not only by the objective to provide better products and service quality, but also by the need to be responsive and efficient—both conferring additional marketplace advantages.

To meet all of these objectives, the process of continuous improvement must include regular cycles of planning, execution, and evaluation. The correct sequence is:

Planning → Execution → Evaluation

This requires a basis—preferably a quantitative basis—for assessing progress and for deriving information for future cycles of improvement. Such information should provide direct links between desired performance and internal operations. Exhibit 400.23 presents a comparison between benchmarking and continuous process improvement because they are linked.

Types of Process Improvement

There are two types of process improvement: reactive and proactive. In a reactive situation, management looks for the next good improvement item and makes it happen with the use of seven quality control tools. These tools, mostly quantitative in nature, include check sheets, histograms, scatter diagrams, flowcharts, Pareto diagrams, cause-and-effect diagrams, and control charts.

In a proactive environment, management chooses one alternative from several alternatives it is facing and works on it. Proactive improvement is more strategic in nature and uses qualitative tools to collect data. Kawakita Jiro (KJ) has articulated five principles for collecting this type of strategic data. These principles include 360-degree view, stepping-stone approach, unexpected situations ("by chance"), intuitive capability, and real cases and personal experiences (qualitative data).

Business Process Redesign

The primary customer (internal or external) should be the driving force behind the redesign process. If managed properly, the redesigned process can increase sales, cut costs, increase profits, and improve service. The objectives of the organization determine which processes should be redesigned and in what sequence. The redesigned process must be linked to the strategic plan of the organization. Redesign means change, which must be embraced by all members of the organization. Sound business decisions, not technology, should drive the redesign process and its associated changes.

It is important to identify the problem or opportunity rather than the symptom. Solving the problem requires change which, in turn, requires change in organizational structure, policies and procedures, and organizational culture. The organizational structure should promote a risk-taking environment and facilitate the change-management process.

Once a process is redesigned, it must continually be monitored, reassessed, changed, and improved in order to meet changing demands on the organization. Reengineering is a continual process rather than a static process. It is not a one-time exercise.

Do's of Redesign

- Identify the real problem, not the symptom.
- Clearly define what the outcome of the redesigned process is.
- Determine the criteria for evaluation to determine whether the redesigned process was successful.
- Insist on leaders, not managers, to spearhead the change-management process.
- Encourage risk-taking and participative management techniques combined with employee empowerment concepts.
- Promote training and cross-training aspects of a redesigned process.
- Create constructive conflicts because they generate new ideas (no conflict, no results).
- Break down the redesign process requirements as mandatory or desirable (optional).
- Conduct feasibility analysis in economical, technical, and political areas.

Don'ts of Redesign

- Technology should not drive the change. It is an enabling force.
- Do not overanalyze a situation, as this leads to "analysis paralysis" without substantial benefit.
- New processes and procedures should not be blindly built upon old processes and procedures. Each new process and procedure should help, not hinder, the internal and external customer of the organization.

Business Process Change Management

A **process** is a set of interrelated resources and activities that transforms inputs into outputs. A product is the result of activities or processes. Two kinds of process models exist: the "as-is" process model, and the "to-be" process model. The "as-is" process model portrays how a business process is currently structured. In process improvement efforts, it is used to establish a baseline for measuring subsequent business improvement actions and progress. The "to-be" process model results from a business process redesign or reengineering action. It shows how the business process will function after the improvement action is implemented.

$$\text{"as-is" process model} \rightarrow \text{"to-be" process model} = \text{change required}$$
$$\text{(before improvement)} \quad \text{(after improvement)} \quad \text{(level of change)}$$

The difference between the "to-be" process model and the "as-is" process model indicates the amount and level of change required to achieve the desired improvement. This change needs to be managed with required resources allocated.

Business process change management focuses on the future, which requires a proactive approach in order to be effective. The change will be brought about by several factors: change in the world economic situation, competition both nationally and internationally, declines in revenues, loss of market share, reductions in budgets, or need to improve with better products and services.

Any change can be implemented successfully with resources and technology, but not easily with people. Organizational culture (employees) can be the most troubling factor in implementing organizational changes. **Organizational culture** may be defined as the underlying assumptions, beliefs, values, attitudes, and expectations shared by an organization's employees. An organization's beliefs and values affect the behavior of its employees. Many organizations are actively trying to perpetuate some cultural values and change others to increase their chances for being competitive or effective.

A cultural change is a long-term effort that takes at least 5 to 10 years to complete. The following are some techniques for perpetuating or changing organizational culture, ranked in order of importance.

1. Display top-management commitment and support for values and beliefs.
2. Train employees to convey and develop skills related to values and beliefs.
3. Develop a statement of values and beliefs.
4. Communicate values and beliefs to employees.
5. Use a management style compatible with values and beliefs.
6. Offer rewards, incentives, and promotions to encourage behavior compatible with values and beliefs.
7. Convey and support values and beliefs at organizational gatherings.
8. Make the organization's structure compatible with values and beliefs.
9. Set up systems, procedures, and processes compatible with values and beliefs.
10. Replace or change responsibilities of employees who do not support desired values and beliefs.
11. Use stories, legends, or myths to convey values and beliefs.
12. Make heroes or heroines of exemplars of values and beliefs.
13. Recruit employees who possess or will readily accept values and beliefs.
14. Use slogans to symbolize values and beliefs.
15. Assign a manager or group with primary responsibility for efforts to change or perpetuate culture.

Ethics and Quality

Ethics plays a vital role in manufacturing and service industries because of questionable business practices often employed. It has been said that quality is most effective when the organizational environment encourages openness, trust, and ethics. Ethical behavior is more than just legal behavior because laws do not cover all behavior that is considered unethical. For example, it is legal but unethical if management makes unwanted early shipment of nondefective products to customers just to meet a monthly sales target. On the other hand, it is illegal and unethical if management knows that it is shipping defective products and takes no action to stop it.

The following are some examples of unethical behavior:

- Disregarding the customer and his or her requirements in terms of product/service specification, conformance to the specification, reliability, value, and delivery. These five elements constitute quality to a customer, not just "conformance to specification."
- Questionable agreements between purchasing management and a supplier that affect quality
- Manufacturing adulterated food and drug products that are dangerous to health and life
- Use of worn manufacturing tools, jigs, molds, and templates, resulting in defective parts
- Use of improperly calibrated inspection gauges, giving misleading information
- Polluting waters with discharge of dangerous chemicals that are harmful to human and sea life
- Filling product containers with materials of less than the target weight

Poor quality often results from time pressures caused by insufficient planning and scheduling. Services are labor intensive and the quality of human interaction is a vital factor for services that involve human contact. Hence, the behavior and morale of service employees is critical in delivering a quality service experience. The quality manager has a dual role as a trustee of both the company that he or she works for and the customer that he or she serves.

Module 400 Endnotes

1. Jack Welch, Herb Kelleher, Geoffrey Colvin, and John Huey, "How to Create Great Companies and Keep Them That Way," *Fortune* 139, no. 1 (1999), 163.
2. William Bridges, "Leading the De-Jobbed Organization," in *The Leader of the Future,* Frances Hesselbein, Marshall Goldsmith, and Richard Beckhard, eds. (San Francisco: Jossey-Bass, 1996), 16–17.
3. R. E. Byrd, "Corporate Leadership Skills: A New Synthesis," *Organizational Dynamics,* Summer 1987, 34–43.
4. J. R. P. French, Jr., and B. H. Raven, "The Bases of Social Power," in *Group Dynamics: Research and Theory,* 2d ed., D. Cartwright and A. Zanders, eds., (New York: Harper & Row, 1960), 607–623.
5. Nabil Tamimi and Rose Sebastianelli, "How Firms Define and Measure Quality," *Production and Inventory Management Journal* 37, no. 3 (Third Quarter 1996), 34–39.
6. Four comprehensive reviews of the concept and definition of quality are David A. Garvin, "What Does Product Quality Really Mean?" *Sloan Management Review* 26, no. 1 (1984), 25–43; Gerald F. Smith, "The Meaning of Quality," *Total Quality Management* 4, no. 3 (1993), 235–244; Carol A. Reeves and David A. Bednar, "Defining Quality: Alternatives and Implications," *Academy of Management Review* 19, no. 3 (1994), 419–445; and Kristie W. Seawright and Scott T. Young, "A Quality Definition Continuum," *Interfaces* 26, no. 3 (May/June 1996), 107–113.
7. Ronald D. Snee, "Why Should Statisticians Pay Attention to Six Sigma?" *Quality Progress,* September 1999, 100–103.
8. A. Blanton Godfrey, "Six Sigma Quality," *Quality Digest,* May 1999, 22.
9. Frank M. Gryna, "Quality Costs," *Juran's Quality Control Handbook,* 4th ed. (New York: McGraw-Hill, 1988).
10. Edward Sullivan and Debra A. Owens, "Catching A Glimpse of Quality Costs Today," *Quality Progress* 16, no. 12 (December 1983), 21–24.
11. ASQ Quality Costs Committee, "Profiting from Quality in the Service Arena," *Quality Progress,* May 1999, 81–84.
12. "Quality: How to Make It Pay," *BusinessWeek,* August 8, 1994, 54–59.
13. Roland T. Rust, Timothy Keiningham, Stephen Clemens, and Anthony Zahorik, "Return on Quality at Chase Manhattan Bank," *Interfaces* 29, 2 (March/April 1999), 62–72.
14. *The PIMS Letter on Business Strategy,* no. 4 (Cambridge, MA: Strategic Planning Institute, 1986).
15. AT&T Quality Steering Committee, *Process Quality Management & Improvement Guidelines,* AT&T Publication Center, AT&T Bell Laboratories (1987).
16. Steven H. Wildstrom, "Price Wars Power Up Quality," *BusinessWeek,* September 18, 1995, 26.
17. Rebecca Duray and Glenn W. Milligan, "Improving Customers Satisfaction Through Mass Customization," *Quality Progress,* August 1999, 60–66.
18. M. L. Dertouzos, R. K. Lester, R. M. Solow, and the MIT Commission on Industrial Productivity, *Made in America* (Cambridge, MA: MIT Press, 1989), 74.
19. C. Pegels, *Total Quality Management* (Danvers, MA: Boyd & Fraser Publishing, 1995), 31.
20. S. E. Sampson, *Understanding Service Businesses* (Salt Lake City, UT: Brigham Young University, 1999), 330–331.
21. R. Rust, A. Zahorik, and T. Keiningham, *Return on Quality* (Chicago, Probus Publishing, 1994), 7–8.
22. C. Haksever, R. Render, R. Russell, and G. Murdick, *Service Management and Operations* (Upper Saddle River, NJ: Prentice Hall, 2000), 7; D. Garvin, *Managing Quality* (New York: The Free Press 1988), 40–46.
23. A. Parasuraman, V. Zeithaml, and L. Berry, A Conceptual Model of Service Quality and Its Implications for Future Research, *Journal of Marketing* (Fall), 41–50.
24. V. Zeithaml, A. Parasuraman, and L. Berry, *Delivering Quality Service: Balancing Customer Perceptions and Expectations* (New York: The Free Press, 1990), 46.
25. R. Chase, and D. Stewart, "Make Your Service Fail-Safe," *Sloan Management Review* Spring, 1994, 35–44.
26. E. Scheulng, and E. Johnson, "A Proposed Model for New Service Development," *The Journal of Services Marketing,* 3(2), 25–34.
27. R. Rust, A. Zahorik, and T. Keiningham. *Return on Quality* (Chicago: Probus Publishing, 1994), 7–8.
28. T. Stewart, *Fortune,* January 11,1999, 168, 170.
29. V. Zeithaml, A. Parasuraman, and L. Berry, *Delivering Quality Service: Balancing Customer Perceptions and Expectations* (New York: The Free Press, 1990), 46.
30. R. Rust, A. Zahorik, and T. Keiningham, *Return on Quality* (Chicago: Probus Publishing, 1994), 7–8.

31. R. Buzzell, and B. Gale, *The PIMS Principles* (New York: The Free Press, 1997), 107.
32. R. Rust, A. Zahorik, and T. Keiningham, *Return on Quality* (Chicago: Probus Publishing, 1994), 7–8.
33. C. Hart, "The Power of Unconditional Service Guarantees," *Harvard Business Review,* July–August, 1998, 55–60.
34. C. Hart, J. Heskett, and W. Sasser, Jr, "The Profitable Art of Service Recovery," *Harvard Business Review,* July–August, 1990, 148–156.
35. Lawrence S. Pryor, "Benchmarking: A Self-Improvement Strategy," *Journal of Business Strategy,* November/December 1989, 28–32.
36. Robert C. Camp, *Benchmarking: The Search for Industry Best Practices That Lead to Superior Performance* (Milwaukee, WI: ASQC Quality Press and UNIPUB/Quality Resources, 1989).
37. Shawn Tully, "Why to Go for Stretch Targets," *Fortune,* November 14, 1994, 45–58.
38. John Hackl, "New Beginnings: Change Is Here to Stay," editorial comment, *Quality Progress,* February 1998, 5.
39. AT&T Consumer Communication Services Summary of 1994 Application for the Malcolm Baldrige National Quality Award.
40. Carla O'Dell and C. Jackson Grayson, "Identifying and Transferring Internal Best Practices," APQC White Paper, 2000. http//www.org/free/whitepapers/cmifwp/index.htm.
41. Michael Hammer and James Champy, *Reengineering the Corporation* (New York: Harper-Business, 1993), 177–178.
42. Gerhard Plenert, "Process Re-Engineering: The Latest Fad Toward Failure," *APICS—The Performance Advantage* 4, no. 6 (June 1994), 22–24.

MODULE 500

Human Resources Management

501
Human Resources Strategies, 698

510
Employee Performance and Retention Management, 712

530
Staffing, Development, and Employment Practices, 722

540
Workforce Diversity Management, 785

570
Employee Benefits and Compensation, 793

595
Ethics and Human Resources, 814

Module 500 Endnotes, 815

Human Resources Strategies

Nature of Human Resource Management

Human resource (HR) management is the design of formal systems in an organization to ensure effective and efficient use of human talent to accomplish organizational goals.

HR Activities

HR management is composed of several groups of interlinked activities taking place within the context of the organization, including HR planning and analysis; equal employment opportunity; staffing; HR development; compensation and benefits; health, safety, and security; employee and labor management relations; and global human resources. Additionally, all managers with HR responsibilities must consider external environmental forces—legal, political, economic, social, cultural, and technological—when addressing these activities.

HR Management Challenges

The environment faced by HR management is a challenging one. Some of the most significant challenges facing HR management include (1) economic and technological changes, (2) workforce availability and quality, (3) growth in contingent workforce, (4) demographics and diversity, (5) balancing work and family, and (6) organizational restructuring and mergers and acquisitions.

HR Management Roles

Four roles exist for HR management, including strategic role, operational role, employee advocate role, and administrative role. For HR to play a strategic role, it must focus on the longer-term implications of HR issues, how changing workforce demographics and workforce shortages will affect the organization and what means will be used to address the shortages over time. The strategic role for HR will include participating in the strategic planning process, enhancing organizational performance, ensuring effective decision making on mergers acquisitions and downsizing, redesigning organizations and work processes, and ensuring financial accountability for HR results.

The operational role for HR includes identifying and implementing needed programs and policies in the organization in cooperation with operating managers. Operational activities are tactical in nature. Activities include ensuring compliance with equal employment opportunity and other laws, processing employment applications, filling current openings through interviews, training supervisors, resolving safety problems, and administering wages and salaries.

HR must be the "champion" for employees and employee issues. HR staff spends considerable time on HR "crisis management," dealing with employee problems that are both work and non-work related. Employee advocacy helps ensure fair and equitable treatment for employee regardless of personal background or circumstances. Some department or function inside the organization must monitor employee situations and respond to employee complaints about unfair treatment or inappropriate actions. Otherwise, employees would face even more lawsuits and regulatory complaints than they do now.

The administrative role includes clerical activities such as hiring employees, employee assistance programs, pension administration, background and reference checks, benefits administration, and training and development.

Exhibit 500.1 shows a summary of what is done in each of the HR roles in the organization and how all roles are important.

Strategic Human Resource Management

Many factors determine whether an organization will be successful; human resources is only one of them. Competitiveness, ability to adapt to changes in the market, and many other issues are involved too. Effective management decides where the organization needs to go, how to get there, and then regularly evaluates to see whether the organization

Exhibit 500.1 *Overview of HR Management Roles*

	Administrative Role	Operational and Advocacy Roles	Strategic Role
Focus	Administrative processing and record keeping	Operational support Representing the employees	Organizational-wide, global
Timing	Short term (less than 1 year)	Intermediate term (1–2 years)	Longer term (2–5 years)
Typical Activities	• Administering employee benefits • Conducting new employee orientations • Interpreting HR policies and procedures • Preparing equal employment reports	• Managing compensation programs • Recruiting and selecting for current openings • Conducting safety training • Resolving employee complaints • Representing employee concerns	• Assessing workforce trends and issues • Engaging in community workforce development planning • Assisting in organizational restructuring and downsizing • Advising on mergers or acquisitions • Planning compensation strategies

is on track. Strategic objectives, the external environment, internal business processes, and determining how effectiveness will be defined and measured are all issues in this process.

Human resources (HR) is (or should be) involved with all these points by identifying how it can aid in increasing organizational productivity, help deal effectively with foreign competition, or enhance innovativeness in the organization. This kind of thinking is indicative of strategic thinking.[1] **Strategic HR management** refers to organizational use of employees to gain or keep a competitive advantage against competitors. It does so through the HR department formally contributing to company-wide planning efforts, or by simply being knowledgeable about issues facing the organization.

The development of specific business strategies must be based on the areas of strength that an organization has. Referred to as *core competencies,* those strengths are the foundation for creating a competitive advantage for an organization. A **core competency** is a unique capability that creates high value and differentiates the organization from its competition. In some organizations, human resources can be a core competency.

Human Resources as a Core Competency

Certainly, many organizations have voiced the idea that their human resources differentiate them from their competitors. Organizations as widely diverse as Fed Ex, Nordstrom's Department Stores, and Dell Computers have focused on human resources as having special strategic value for the organization.

Some ways that human resources become a core competency are through attracting and retaining employees with unique professional and technical capabilities, investing in training and development of those employees, and compensating them in ways that retain and keep them competitive with their counterparts in other organizations. For example, smaller, community-oriented banks have picked up numerous small- and medium-sized commercial loan customers because they emphasize that "you can talk to the same person," rather than having to call an automated service center in another state. The focus is on their human resources as an advantage.

Organizational Strategies Based on Human Resources

Recognition has been growing that, under certain conditions, HR contributes to a competitive advantage for organizations. Exhibit 500.2 shows some possible areas where human resources may become part of a core competency.

People can be an organizational core competency when they have special capabilities to make decisions and be innovative in ways that competitors cannot easily imitate.[2] Having those capabilities requires selection, training, and retention of good employees. An employee group without those special abilities would *not* be as strong a basis for competitive advantage.

The shared values and beliefs of a workforce is called **organizational culture.** For people to be a core competency, managers must consider the culture of the organization because otherwise excellent strategies can be negated by a culture incompatible with those strategies. Further, the culture of the organization, as viewed by the people in it, affects

Exhibit 500.2 *Possible HR Areas for Core Competencies*

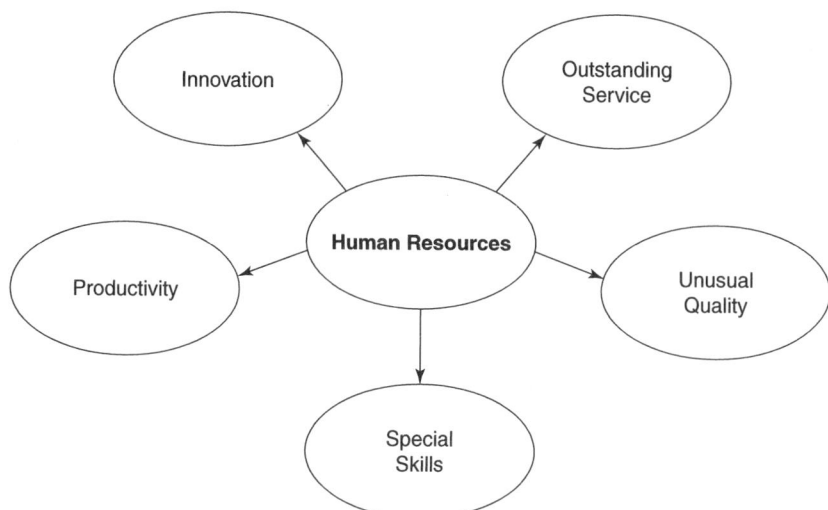

attraction and retention of competent employees. Numerous examples can be given of key technical, professional, and administrative employees leaving firms because of corporate cultures that seem to devalue people and create barriers to the use of individual capabilities.[3]

Productivity as an HR-Based Strategy

The more productive an organization, the better its competitive advantage, because the costs to produce its goods and services are lower. Better productivity does not necessarily mean more is produced; perhaps fewer people (or less money or time) were used to produce the same amount. A useful way to measure the productivity of a workforce is the total cost of people per unit of output. In its most basic sense, **productivity** is a measure of the quantity and quality of work done, considering the cost of the resources used. It is also useful to view productivity as a ratio between inputs and outputs that indicates the *value added* by an organization or in an economy.

ORGANIZATIONS AND PRODUCTIVITY Productivity at the organizational level ultimately affects profitability and competitiveness in a for-profit organization, and total costs in a not-for-profit organization. Decisions made about the value of an organization often are based on the productivity of which it is capable.[4]

Perhaps none of the resources used for productivity in organizations are so closely scrutinized as the human resources. Many of the activities undertaken in an HR system are designed to affect individual or organizational productivity. Pay, appraisal systems, training, selection, job design, and compensation are HR activities directly concerned with productivity.

A useful way to measure organizational HR productivity is by considering **unit labor cost,** which is computed by dividing the average cost of workers by their average levels of output. Using unit labor costs, one can see that a company paying relatively high wages still can be economically competitive if it can also achieve an offsetting high productivity level. Low unit labor costs can be a basis for a strategy focusing on human resources.

INCREASING PRODUCTIVITY U.S. firms have been on a decade-long crusade to improve organizational productivity. Much of the productivity improvement efforts have focused on their workforces.[5] The early stages included downsizing, reengineering jobs, increasing computer usage, and working employees harder and longer. These approaches have been useful in some firms.[6] Some ideas for the next round in productivity improvements include:

- *Outsourcing:* Contract with someone else to perform activities previously done by employees of the organization. For instance, if UPS can deliver products at a lower cost than a manufacturing company can ship them internally, then the firm could outsource shipping to UPS.
- *Making workers more efficient with capital equipment:* Typically the more spent on equipment per worker, the greater the output per worker.
- *Replacing workers with equipment:* Certain jobs are not done as well by humans. The jobs may be mindless, physically difficult, or require extreme precision. For example, a ditch usually is better dug by one person operating a backhoe than by several workers with shovels.

Exhibit 500.3 *Customer Service Dimensions*

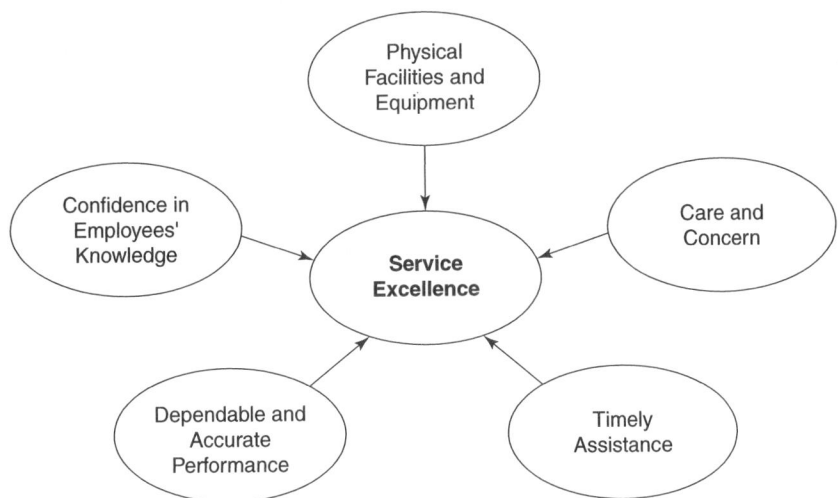

- *Helping workers work better:* Replace outmoded processes, methods, and rules. Also, find better ways of training people to work more efficiently.
- *Redesigning the work:* Some work can be redesigned to make it faster, easier, and possibly even more rewarding to employees. Such changes generally improve productivity.

Quality and Service as HR-Based Strategies

Both high-quality products and extremely good service can be strategic competitive advantages that have HR dimensions. *Quality* of production must be considered as part of productivity, because one alternative might be to produce more products and services but of lower quality. At one time, American goods suffered as a result of this trade-off. W. Edwards Deming, an American quality expert, argued that getting the job done right the *first time*—through pride in craftsmanship, excellent training, and an unwillingness to tolerate delays, defects, and mistakes—is essential to quality production.[7] However, attempts to improve quality have worked better for some firms than for others.[8]

Delivering excellent customer service is another approach to enhancing organizational competitive performance. Service begins with product design and includes interaction with customers, with the ultimate goal of meeting customers' needs. Some organizations do not produce products, only services.

Service excellence is difficult to define, but people know it when they see it. In many organizations, service quality is affected significantly by the individual employees who interact with customers. At least three of the five dimensions of service depicted in Exhibit 500.3 are HR related.

Linking HR Planning and Strategy for Competitive Advantage

Many think that organizations decide on strategies and then HR planning is done to supply the right number and kinds of employees. However, the relationship should go deeper. Exhibit 500.4 shows the relationship among the variables that determine the HR plans an organization will adopt. Business strategies affect HR plans. Consideration of human resource issues should be part of the initial input to the strategy formulation process. For example, it may be important to identify competitive advantage opportunities that fit the existing employees or assess strategic alternatives given the current capabilities of organizational human resources. HR professionals should be doing environmental scanning to know and pinpoint which skills are available and which are not. HR professionals also should be able to estimate lead times for adjusting to labor shortages or surpluses, because HR will be involved in implementing any strategies that affect people.[9]

To illustrate: A large bank wanted to become among the top 10 in size in the United States. Its strategy included developing more global business and improving customer service. HR analyses turned up a basic deficiency in the workforce—they did not have the skills and knowledge necessary to carry out the strategy. In this case a series of training and development programs was designed and implemented to close the gap.

To describe the relationship between strategy and HR, two basic strategies can be identified: *cost-leadership* and *differentiation*. An example of a company following a cost-leadership strategy might be Wal-Mart, and of the differentiation

Exhibit 500.4 *Factors That Determine HR Plans*

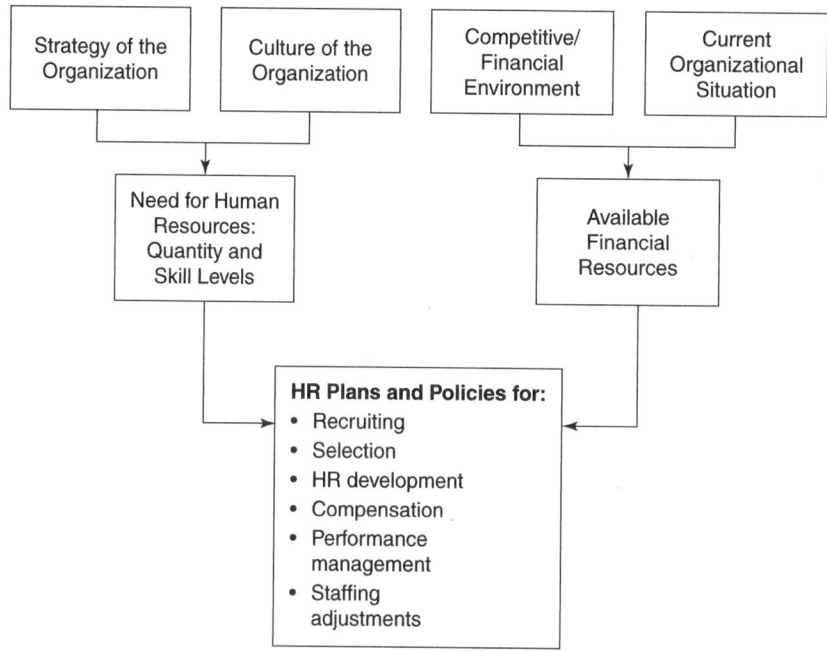

Exhibit 500.5 *Linkage of Organizational and HR Strategies*

Organizational Strategy	Strategic Focus	HR Strategy	HR Activities
Cost Leadership	• Efficiency • Stability • Cost control	• Long HR planning horizon • Build skills in existing employee • Job and employee specialization efficiency	• Promote from within • Extensive training • Hire and train for specific capabilities
Differentiation	• Growth • Innovation • Decentralization	• Shorter HR planning horizon • Hire the HR capabilities needed • Broader, more flexible jobs and employees	• External staffing • Less training • Hire and train for broad competencies

strategy Intel or Microsoft. Exhibit 500.5 compares HR needs under each strategy and suggests the HR approaches that may be most appropriate. A cost-leadership strategy may be appropriate in a relatively stable business environment because it approaches competition on the basis of low price and high quality of product or service. The differentiation strategy is more appropriate in a more dynamic environment characterized by rapid change and requires continually finding new products and new markets. The two strategies may not be mutually exclusive, because it is possible for an organization to pursue one strategy in one product or service area and another with others.

The cost-leadership strategy requires an organization to "build" its own employees to fit its specialized needs. This approach needs a longer HR planning horizon. When specific skills are necessary for a new market or product, it may be more difficult to internally develop them quickly. However, with a differentiation strategy, responsiveness means that HR planning is likely to have a shorter time frame and greater use of external sources, such as acquisition of another company with specialized employees being used to staff the organization.

Human Resource Planning

The competitive organizational strategy of the firm derived with input from HR becomes the basis for **human resource (HR) planning,** which is the process of analyzing and identifying the need for and availability of human resources so that the organization can meet its objectives. This section discusses HR planning responsibilities and the HR planning process.

Exhibit 500.6 *Typical Division of HR Responsibilities: HR Planning*

HR Unit	Managers
• Participates in strategic planning process for entire organization • Identifies HR strategies • Designs HR planning data systems • Compiles and analyzes data from managers on staffing needs • Implements HR plan as approved by top management	• Identify supply-and-demand needs for each division/department • Review/discuss HR planning information with HR specialists • Integrate HR plan with departmental plans • Monitor HR plan to identify changes needed • Review employee succession plans associated with HR plan

HR Planning Responsibilities

In most organizations that do HR planning, the top HR executive and subordinate staff specialists have most of the responsibilities for this planning. However, as Exhibit 500.6 indicates, other managers must provide information for the HR specialists to analyze. In turn, those managers need to receive data from the HR unit. Because top managers are responsible for overall strategic planning, they usually ask the HR unit to project the human resources needed to implement overall organizational goals.

HR Planning Process

The steps in the HR planning process are shown in Exhibit 500.7. Notice that the HR planning process begins with considering the organizational objectives and strategies. Then both external and internal assessments of HR needs and supply sources must be done and forecasts developed. Key to assessing internal human resources is having solid information accessible through a human resource information system (HRIS).

Once the assessments are complete, forecasts must be developed to identify the relationship between supply and demand for human resources. Management then formulates HR strategies and plans to address the imbalance, both short and long term.

HR strategies are the means used to anticipate and manage the supply of and demand for human resources. These HR strategies provide overall direction for the ways in which HR activities will be developed and managed. Finally, specific HR plans are developed to provide more specific direction for the management of HR activities.

HR strategies Means used to anticipate and manage the supply of and demand for human resources.

DEVELOPING THE HR PLAN The HR plan is guided by longer-term organizational plans. For example, in planning for human resources, an organization must consider the allocation of people to jobs over long periods of time, not just for the next month or even the next year. This level of planning requires knowledge of strategic expansions or reductions in operations and any technological changes that may affect the organization. On the basis of such analyses, plans can be made for shifting employees within the organization, laying off or otherwise cutting back the number of employees, retraining present employees, or increasing the number of employees in certain areas. Factors to consider include the current employees' knowledge, skills, and abilities in the organization and the expected vacancies resulting from retirements, promotions, transfers, or discharge.

In summary, the HR plan provides a road map for the future, identifying where employees are likely to be obtained, when employees will be needed, and what training and development of employees must occur. Through succession planning, employee career paths can be tailored to individual needs that are consistent with organizational requirements.

EVALUATING HR PLANNING The most telling evidence of successful HR planning is an organization in which the human resources are consistently aligned with the needs of the business over a period of time. If HR planning is done well, the following benefits should result:

- Upper management has a better view of the human resource dimensions of business decisions.
- HR costs may be lower because management can anticipate imbalances before they become expensive or unmanageable.

Exhibit 500.7 *HR Planning Process*

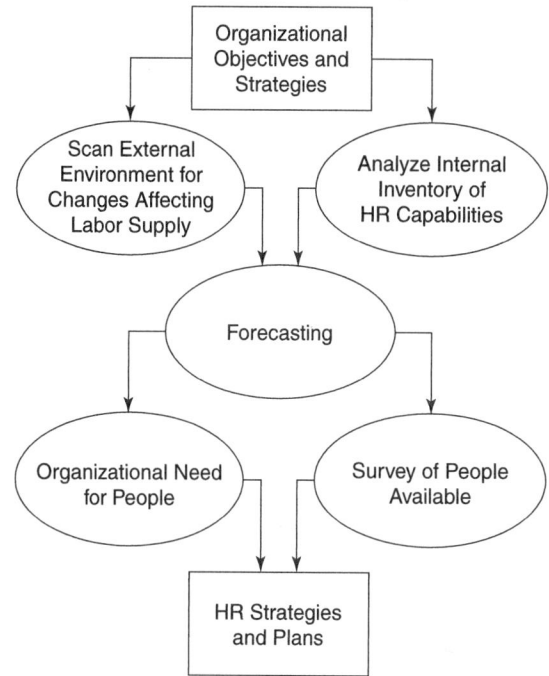

- More time is available to locate talent because needs are anticipated and identified before the actual staffing is required.
- Better opportunities exist to include members of protected groups in future growth plans to increase organizational diversity.
- Development of managers can be better planned.

Scanning the External Environment

Environmental scanning Process of studying the environment of the organization to pinpoint opportunities and threats.

At the heart of strategic planning is the knowledge gained from scanning the external environment for changes.[10] **Environmental scanning** is the process of studying the environment of the organization to pinpoint opportunities and threats. The external environment especially affects HR planning because each organization must draw from the same labor market that supplies all other employers. Indeed, one measure of organizational effectiveness is the ability of an organization to compete for a sufficient supply of human resources with the appropriate capabilities. To get a feel for the impact of environmental changes on businesses, consider the following:

- The government has deregulated major sectors of the economy.
- During the past decade an uncertainty in energy prices brought new pressures on firms having major transportation/energy expenses.
- The globalization of markets and sources of supply has increased competition in many industries
- The composition of the workforce, along with its values, age, and working approaches, has changed.[11]

Environmental factors—government, economic conditions, geographic and competition issues, and workforce changes—all must be part of environmental scanning.

Internal Assessment of the Organizational Workforce

Analyzing the jobs that will need to be done and the skills of people currently available to do them is the next part of HR planning. The needs of the organization must be compared against the labor supply available inside the organization.

Auditing Jobs and Skills

The starting point for evaluating internal strengths and weaknesses is an audit of the jobs currently being done in the organization. This comprehensive analysis of all current jobs provides a basis for forecasting what jobs will need to be done in the future. Much of the data to answer these questions should be available from existing staffing and organizational databases. The following questions are addressed during the internal assessment:

- What jobs exist now?
- How many individuals are performing each job?
- What are the reporting relationships of jobs?
- How essential is each job?
- What jobs will be needed to implement future organizational strategies?
- What are the characteristics of anticipated jobs?

Organizational Capabilities Inventory

As HR planners gain an understanding of the current and future jobs that will be necessary to carry out organizational plans, they can make a detailed audit of current employees and their capabilities. The basic source of data on employees is the HR records in the organization. By utilizing different databases in an HRIS (human resource information system), it is possible to identify the employees' knowledge, skills, and abilities (KSAs). Planners can use these inventories to determine long-range needs for recruiting, selection, and HR development. Also, that information can be the basis for determining which additional capabilities will be needed in the future workforce that may not currently exist.

Forecasting HR Supply and Demand

The information gathered from external environmental scanning and assessment of internal strengths and weaknesses is used to predict or *forecast* HR supply and demand in light of organizational objectives and strategies. **Forecasting** uses information from the past and present to identify expected future conditions. Projections for the future are, of course, subject to error.[12] Changes in the conditions on which the projections are based might even completely invalidate them, which is the chance forecasters take. Usually, though, experienced people are able to forecast with enough accuracy to benefit organizational long-range planning.

Forecasting Use of information from the past and present to identify expected future conditions.

Forecasting Methods

Methods for forecasting human resources range from a manager's best guess to a rigorous and complex computer simulation. Simple assumptions may be sufficient in certain instances, but complex models may be necessary for others. Forecasts may use either judgmental or mathematical methods, as Exhibit 500.8 indicates.

Despite the availability of sophisticated mathematical models and techniques, forecasting is still a combination of quantitative method and subjective judgment. The facts must be evaluated and weighed by knowledgeable individuals, such as managers and HR experts, who use the mathematical models as tools and make judgments to make decisions.

Exhibit 500.8 *Forcasting Methods*

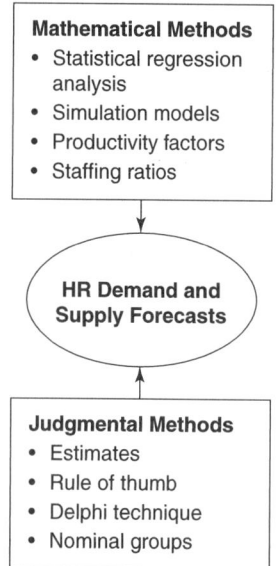

Forecasting Periods

HR forecasting should be done over three planning periods: short, intermediate, and long ranges. The most commonly used planning period is *short range*, usually a period of six months to one year. This level of planning is routine in many organizations because few assumptions about the future are necessary for such short-range plans. These short-range forecasts offer the best estimates of the immediate HR needs of an organization. Intermediate and long-range forecasting are much more difficult processes. *Intermediate* plans usually project one to five years into the future, and *long-range* plans extend beyond five years.

Forecasting the Demand for Human Resources

The demand for employees can be calculated on an organization-wide basis and/or calculated based on the needs of individual units in the organization. For example, to forecast that the firm needs 125 new employees next year might mean less than to forecast that it needs 25 new people in sales and customer service, 45 in production, 20 in accounting, 5 in HR, and 30 in the warehouse. This unit breakdown obviously allows HR planners to better pinpoint the specific skills needed than the aggregate method does.

Forecasting human resources can be done using two frameworks. One approach considers specific openings that are likely to occur and uses that as the basis for planning. The openings (or demands) are created when employees leave a position because of promotions, transfers, and terminations. The analysis always begins with the top positions in the organization, because from there no promotions to a higher level are possible.

Based on this analysis, decision rules (or "fill rates") are developed for each job or level. For example, a decision rule for a financial institution might state that 50 percent of branch supervisor openings will be filled through promotions from customer service tellers, 25 percent through promotions from personal bankers, and 25 percent from new hires. But forecasters must be aware of chain effects throughout the organization, because as people are promoted, their previous positions become available. Continuing our example, forecasts for the need for customer service tellers and personal bankers would also have to be developed. The overall purpose of this analysis is to develop a forecast of the needs for human resources by number and type for the forecasted period.

Forecasting the Supply of Human Resources

Once human resources needs have been forecasted, then their availability must be identified. Forecasting the availability of human resources considers both *external* and *internal* supplies. Although the internal supply may be easier to calculate, it is important to calculate the external supply as accurately as possible.

Exhibit 500.9 *Estimating Internal Labor Supply for a Given Unit*

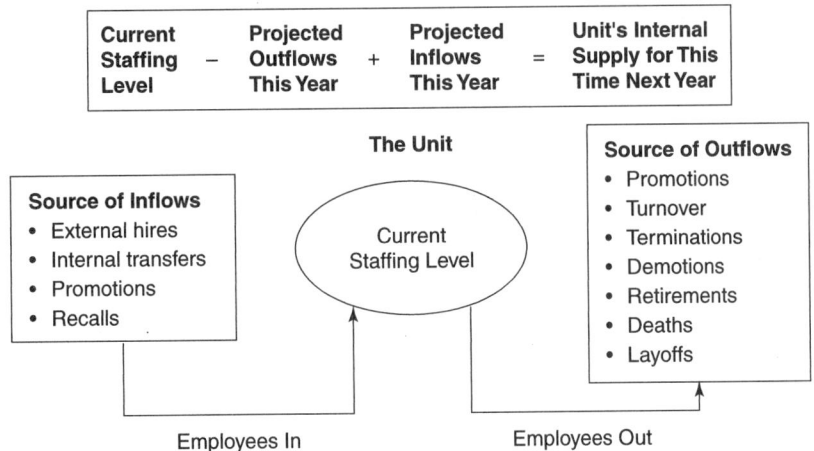

EXTERNAL SUPPLY The external supply of potential employees available to the organization needs to be estimated. Extensive use of government labor-force population estimates, trends in the industry, and many more complex and interrelated factors must be considered, including the following:[13]

- Net migration into and out of the area
- Individuals entering and leaving the workforce
- Individuals graduating from schools and colleges
- Changing workforce composition and patterns
- Economic forecasts for the next few years
- Technological developments and shifts
- Actions of competing employers
- Government regulations and pressures
- Factors affecting persons entering and leaving the workforce

INTERNAL SUPPLY Exhibit 500.9 shows in general terms how the internal supply can be calculated. Estimating internal supply considers that employees move from their current jobs into others through promotions, lateral moves, and terminations. Also, it considers that the internal supply is influenced by training and development programs, transfer and promotion policies, and retirement policies, among other factors.

Internally, *succession analysis* is one method used to forecast the supply of people for certain positions. It relies on *replacement charts*, which are succession plans developed to identify potential personnel changes, select backup candidates, promote individuals, and keep track of attribution (resignations, retirements) for each department in an organization.

A *transition matrix*, or *Markov matrix*, can be used to model the internal flow of human resources. These matrixes simply show below-average rates of historical movement from one job to another as probabilities, as the example below shows.

	Exit	Manager	Supervisor	Line Worker
Manager	.15	.85	.00	.00
Supervisor	.10	.15	.70	.05
Line Worker	.20	.00	.15	.65

Looking at the simple transition matrix table for a line worker, there is a 20 percent probability of someone being gone in 12 months, a 0 percent probability of promotion to manager, a 15 percent probability of promotion to supervisor, and a 65 percent probability of someone staying a line worker next year. Such transition matrixes form the bases for computer simulations of the internal flow of people through a large organization over time.

With all the data collected and forecasts done, an organization has the information it needs to develop an HR plan. Such a plan can be extremely sophisticated or rather rudimentary. Regardless of its degree of complexity, the ultimate purpose of the plan is to enable managers in the organization to match the available supply of labor with the forecasted demand based on the strategies of the organization. If the necessary skill levels do not exist in the present workforce, organizations can train employees in the new skills or undertake outside recruiting. Likewise, if the plan reveals that the firm employs too many people for its needs, a human resource surplus exists.

Managing Human Resource Surplus or Shortage

Planning is of little value if no subsequent action is taken. The action taken depends on the likelihood of a human resources surplus or shortage. A surplus of workers can be managed within an HR plan in a variety of ways. But regardless of the means, the actions are difficult because workforce reductions ultimately are necessary.

Workforce Reductions and the WARN Act

In this era of mergers, acquisitions, and downsizing, many workers have been laid off or had their jobs eliminated due to closing of selected offices, plants, and operations. To provide employees with sufficient notice, a federal law was passed, the Worker Adjustment and Retraining Notification (WARN) Act. This act requires employers to give a 60-day notice before a layoff or facility closing involving more than 50 people. However, part-time employees working fewer than 20 hours per week do not count toward the 50 employees. Also, seasonal employees do not have to receive WARN notification. The WARN Act also imposes stiff fines on employers who do not follow the required process and give proper notice.

Workforce Realignment

It has been called "downsizing," "rightsizing," "reduction in force" (RIF), and many other terms as well, but it almost always means cutting employees. "Layoffs" come in response to shortfall in demand for products, while "downsizing" involves job reductions based on a desire to operate more efficiently even when demand is strong.[14] Downsizing is a structural change that negates rehiring laid-off workers. However, workers who are laid off (but not as part of downsizing) may get their jobs back when demand picks up.[15]

The outcome of downsizing is a bit clearer after a decade of many examples and studies. Downsizing has worked for some firms, but it doesn't generate additional revenue. It only generates lower costs in the short term; "corporate liposuction" one observer calls it.[16] But when companies cannibalize the human resources they need to grow and innovate, disruption follows for some time.

Senior executives still see layoffs as their first-line defense against an economic downturn, but some research suggests downsizing can hurt productivity by leaving "surviving" employees overburdened and demoralized.[17] Loss of employees may mean a loss of informal knowledge of how to handle specific problems and issues or respond to specific customers or suppliers. However, focusing on trimming underperforming units or employees as part of a plan based on sound organizational strategies may make sense. Such a plan often includes cutting capital spending.[18]

Workforce realignment can occur in all forms. Some common problems include demoralized managers, lawsuits, sabotage, and a need for more security. Alternatives to layoffs should be examined first to avoid negative repercussions for organizations.

Downsizing Approaches

The need for downsizing has inspired various innovative ways of removing people from the payroll, sometimes on a massive scale. Several methods can be used when downsizing must occur: attrition, early retirement buyouts, and layoffs are the most common.

Outplacement Services

Outplacement is a group of services provided to displaced employees to give them support and assistance. It is most often used with those involuntarily removed because of performance problems or elimination of jobs. A variety of services may be available to displaced employees.[19] Outplacement services typically include personal career counseling, resume preparation and typing services, interviewing workshops, and referral assistance. Such services are generally provided by outside firms that specialize in outplacement assistance. Special severance pay arrangements also may be used. Firms commonly provide additional severance benefits and continue medical benefit coverage for a period of time at the same company-paid level as before. Other aids include retraining for different jobs, establishing on-site career centers, and contacting other employers for job placement opportunities.

In summary, a decade of experience with downsizing has led to some suggestions on how to deal with it if necessary, as follows:

- *Investigate alternatives to downsizing:* Given the potential problems of downsizing, alternatives should be seriously considered first.
- *Involve those people necessary for success in the planning for downsizing:* The downsizing process too frequently leaves out those who have to make the downsized organization operate.
- *Develop comprehensive communications plans:* Employees are entitled to advance notice so they can make plans.
- *Nurture the survivors:* Remaining employees may be confused about their future careers. These and other concerns obviously can have negative effects.
- *Outplacement pays off:* Helping separated employees find new work is good for the people and the reputation of the organization.

Assessing HR Effectiveness

A long-standing myth perpetuates the notion that one cannot really measure what the HR function does. That myth has hurt HR departments, in some cases, because it suggests that any value added by HR efforts is somehow "mystical" or "magical." That notion is, of course, untrue; HR—like marketing, legal, or finance—must be evaluated based on the value it adds to the organization. Even though defining and measuring HR effectiveness is not as straightforward as with some areas, it is part of HR planning.

Other departments, managers, and employees are the main "customers" for HR services. If those services are lacking, too expensive, or of poor quality, then the organization may have to consider outsourcing some HR activities.[20] HR can position itself as a partner in an organization, but only by demonstrating real links between what HR activities contribute and organizational results. To demonstrate to the rest of the organization that the HR unit is a partner with a positive influence on the bottom line of the business, HR professionals must be prepared to measure the results of HR activities. Then the HR unit must communicate that information to the rest of the organization. Measurement is a key to demonstrating the success of the HR activities. Exhibit 500.10 shows a general approach to evaluating the efficiency and effectiveness of HR activities.

Studies of large and medium-sized firms in the United States have found relationships between the best HR practices and reduced turnover and increased employee productivity. Further, those practices enhanced profitability and market value of the firms studied. A high-quality, highly motivated workforce is hard for competition to replicate.[21] Data to evaluate performance can come from several sources. Some of those sources are already available in most organizations, but some data may have to be collected from existing HR records, an HR audit, or HR research.

Assessing HR Effectiveness Using Records

Some diagnostic measures from records can be used to check the effectiveness of the HR function. Note how each of the following measures requires accurate records and a comprehensive human resource information system:

- HR expense per employee
- Compensation as a percent of expenses
- HR department expense as a percent of total expenses
- Cost of hires
- Turnover rate
- Absence rate
- Workers' compensation cost per employee

Assessing HR Effectiveness Using an Audit

One general means for assessing HR effectiveness is through an HR audit, similar to a financial audit. An **HR audit** is a formal research effort that evaluates the current state of HR management in an organization. These audits attempt to evaluate how well HR activities have been performed, so that management can identify areas for improvement.

HR audit *A formal research effort that evaluates the current state of HR management in an organization.*

Exhibit 500.10 *Overview of the HR Evaluation Process*

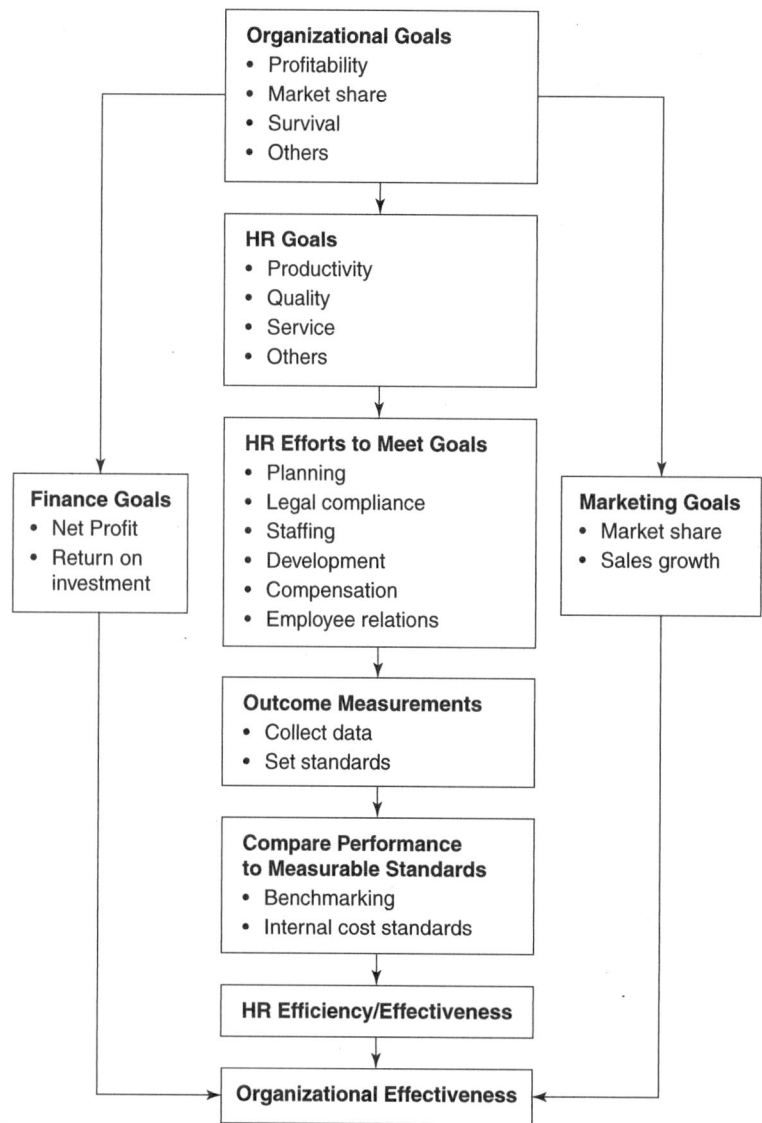

An HR audit begins with a determination by management of the objectives for the HR area. The audit then compares the actual state of HR activities with these objectives, in such areas as:

- Legal compliance (EEO, OSHA, FSLA, Privacy, ERISA, FMLA)
- Current job descriptions and specifications
- Valid recruiting and selection processes
- Wage/salary and benefits systems
- Absenteeism and turnover control measures
- Training and development effort
- Performance management system
- Employee handbook policies
- Health, safety, and security issues

Assessing HR Effectiveness Using Research

HR research is the analysis of data from HR records to determine the effectiveness of past and present HR practices. Research in general can be categorized as primary or secondary. In **primary research,** data are gathered firsthand for the specific project being conducted. Attitude surveys, questionnaires, interviews, and experiments are all primary research methods. **Secondary research** makes use of research data already gathered by others and reported in books, articles in professional journals, or other sources.

Individuals who plan to do primary research should decide first what they wish to study. Examples of primary research topics are causes of nursing employee turnover, employee attitudes about flextime, and the relationship of pre-employment physical exams to workers' compensation claims.

HR practitioners do primary research when they conduct a pay survey on information technology jobs in other companies in their geographic area, or a study of turnover costs and reasons that employees in technical jobs leave more frequently during the first 24 to 30 months of employment. Thus, primary research has specific applications to resolving actual HR problems in particular organizations.

Primary research Research method in which data are gathered firsthand for the specific project being conducted.

Secondary research Research method using data already gathered by others and reported in books, articles in professional journals, or other sources.

Secondary research includes surveys done by various professional organizations, which can provide useful perspectives. Some organizations, such as the Bureau of National Affairs and the Conference Board, sponsor surveys on HR practices in various communities, states, and regions. The results are distributed to participating organizations.

Finally, private management-consulting firms and local colleges and universities can assist in HR research. These outside researchers may be more knowledgeable and unbiased than people inside the organization. Consultants skilled in questionnaire design and data analysis can give expert advice on HR research.

HR Performance and Benchmarking

When information on HR performance has been gathered, it must be compared to a *standard,* which is a model or measure against which something is compared to determine its performance level. For example, it is meaningless to know that organizational turnover rate is 75 percent if the turnover rates at comparable organizations are unknown. One approach to assessing HR effectiveness is **benchmarking,** which compares specific measures of performance against data on those measures in other "best practices" organizations.[22] HR professionals interested in benchmarking try to locate organizations that do certain activities particularly well and thus become the "benchmarks." One means for obtaining benchmarking data is through telephone calls, which then may be followed up with questionnaires and site visits to benchmarking partners. The common benchmarked performance measures in HR management are:

- Total compensation as a percentage of net income before taxes
- Percent of management positions filled internally
- Dollar sales per employee
- Benefits as a percentage of payroll cost

Doing the Benchmarking Analysis

A useful way to analyze HR involves calculating ratios that can be compared from year to year, thus providing information about changes in HR operations. Effectiveness is best determined by comparing ratio measures with benchmarked national statistics. The comparisons should be tracked internally over time.

RETURN ON INVESTMENT (ROI) AND ECONOMIC VALUE ADDED (EVA) APPROACHES Return on investment (ROI) and economic value added (EVA) are two related approaches to measuring the contribution and cost of HR. Both calculations are a bit complex, so they are just highlighted here.

Return on investment (ROI) as a calculation shows the value of expenditures for HR activities. It can also be used to show how long it will take for the activities to pay for themselves. The following formula can be used to calculate the potential ROI for a new HR activity:

$$ROI = \frac{C}{A + B}$$

where

A = Operating costs for a new or enhanced system for the time period
B = One-time cost of acquisition and implementation
C = Value of gains from productivity improvements for the time period

Economic value added (EVA) is a firm's net operating profit after the cost of capital is deducted. Cost of capital is the minimum rate of return demanded by shareholders. When a company is making more than the cost of capital, it is creating wealth for shareholders. An EVA approach requires that all policies, procedures, measures, and methods use cost of capital as a benchmark against which their return is judged. Human resource decisions can be subjected to the same analyses. Both of these methods are useful, and specific information on them is available from other sources.

UTILITY OR COST/BENEFIT ANALYSIS   In **utility analysis,** economic or other statistical models are built to identify the costs and benefits associated with specific HR activities. These models generally contain equations that identify the relevant factors influencing the HR activity under study.

Human Resource Information Systems (HRIS)

Computers have simplified the task of analyzing vast amounts of data, and they can be invaluable aids in HR management, from payroll processing to record retention. With computer hardware, software, and databases, organizations can keep records and information better, as well as retrieve them with greater ease. A **human resource information system (HRIS)** is an integrated system providing information used in HR decision making.

Purposes of an HRIS

An HRIS serves two major purposes in organizations. One relates to administrative and operational efficiency, the other to effectiveness. The first purpose of an HRIS is to improve the efficiency with which data on employees and HR activities are compiled. Many HR activities can be performed more efficiently and with less paperwork if automated, and better information is available.

The second purpose of an HRIS is more strategic and related to HR planning. Having accessible data enables HR planning and managerial decision making to be based to a greater degree on information rather than relying on managerial perceptions and intuition.

Uses of an HRIS

An HRIS has many uses in an organization. The most basic is the automation of payroll and benefit activities. With an HRIS, employees' time records are entered into the system, and the appropriate deductions and other individual adjustments are reflected in the final paychecks. As a result of HRIS development and implementation in many organizations, several payroll functions are being transferred from accounting departments to HR departments. Another common use of HRIS is EEO/affirmative action tracking. The HRIS can be accessed via intranets and extranets.

Employee Performance and Retention Management

Just as individuals in an organization can be a competitive advantage, they can also be a liability. When few employees know how to do their jobs, when people are constantly leaving the organization, and when those employees who do remain work ineffectively, human resources becomes a competitive problem that puts the organization at a disadvantage. Individual performance, motivation, and employee retention are key for organizations to maximize the effectiveness of individual human resources.

Individual Employee Performance

Many factors affect the performance of individual employees—their abilities, efforts expended, and the organizational support they receive. The HR unit in an organization exists in part to analyze and address these areas. Exactly what the

Exhibit 500.11 *Components of Individual Performance*

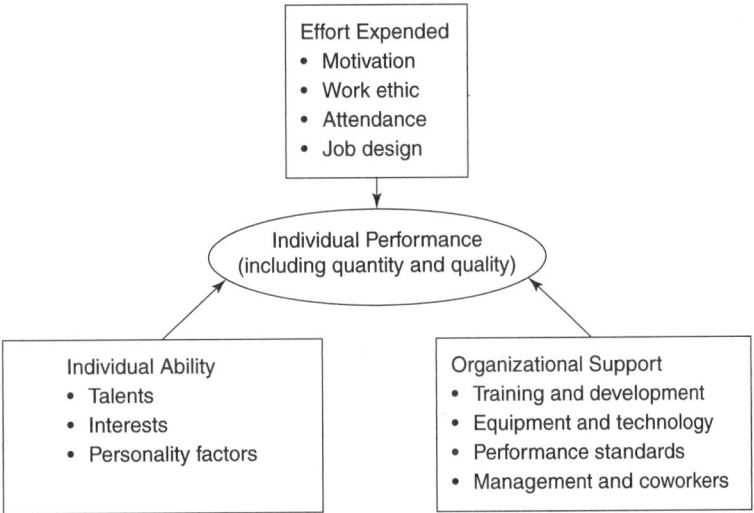

role of the HR unit in an organization "should be" depends upon what upper management expects. As with any management function, HR management activities should be developed, evaluated, and changed as necessary so that they can contribute to the competitive performance of the organization and individuals at work.

Individual Performance Factors

The three major factors that affect how a given individual performs are illustrated in Exhibit 500.11. The factors are: (1) individual ability to do the work, (2) effort level expended, and (3) organizational support. The relationship of these factors is widely acknowledged in management literature as:

$$\text{Performance } (P) = \text{Ability } (A) \times \text{Effort } (E) \times \text{Support } (S)$$

Individual performance is enhanced to the degree that all three components are present with an individual employee. However, performance is diminished if any of these factors is reduced or absent. For instance, assume that several production workers have the abilities to do their jobs and work hard, but the organization provides outmoded equipment or the management style of supervisors causes negative reactions by the workers. Or suppose a customer service representative in a call center has the abilities and an employer who provides excellent support, but the individual hates "being tied to a telephone cord" all day and is frequently absent because of the dislike of the job even though it pays well. In both cases individual performance is likely to be less than in situations where all three components are present. Individual motivation is often one of the missing variables, and an overview of motivation is presented next.

Individual Motivation

Motivation is the desire within a person causing that person to act. People usually act for one reason: to reach a goal. Thus, motivation is a goal-directed drive, and it seldom occurs in a void. The words *need, want, desire,* and *drive* are all similar to *motive,* from which the word *motivation* is derived. Understanding motivation is important because performance, reaction to compensation, and other HR concerns are affected by and influence motivation.

Approaches to understanding motivation vary because different theorists have developed their own views and models. Each approach has contributed to the understanding of human motivation and several are briefly highlighted next.

MASLOW'S HIERARCHY OF NEEDS One theory of human motivation developed by Abraham Maslow has received a great deal of exposure. In this theory, Maslow classified human needs into five categories that ascend in a definite order. Until the more basic needs are adequately fulfilled, a person will not strive to meet higher needs. Maslow's well-known hierarchy is composed of: (1) *physiological needs,* (2) *safety and security needs,* (3) *belonging and love needs,* (4) *esteem needs,* and (5) *self-actualization needs.*

An assumption often made by those using Maslow's hierarchy is that workers in modern, technologically advanced societies basically have satisfied their physiological, safety, and belonging needs. Therefore, they will be motivated by the needs for self-esteem and the esteem of others, and then self-actualization. Consequently, conditions to satisfy these needs should be present at work to enable the job itself to be meaningful and motivating.

HERZBERG'S MOTIVATION/HYGIENE THEORY Frederick Herzberg's motivation/hygiene theory assumes that one group of factors, *motivators,* accounts for high levels of job satisfaction and motivation. However, *hygiene factors* can cause dissatisfaction with work.

Motivators	**Hygiene Factors**
• Achievement	• Interpersonal relationships
• Recognition	• Company policy/administration
• Work itself	• Supervision
• Responsibility	• Salary
• Advancement	• Working conditions

The implication of Herzberg's research for management and HR practices is that even though managers carefully consider and address hygiene factors to avoid employee dissatisfaction, people may not be motivated to work harder. Herzberg suggests that only motivators cause employees to exert more effort and thereby enhance employee performance. However, subsequent research by others has questioned whether the two groups of factors are really as distinct as Herzberg outlined.

EQUITY AS A MOTIVATOR People want to be treated fairly at work, which is referred to as *equity* in management literature.[23] **Equity** is defined as the perceived fairness of what the person does compared with what the person receives. *Inputs* are what a person brings to the organization, including educational level, age, experience, productivity, and other skills or efforts. The items received by a person, or the *outcomes,* are the rewards obtained in exchange for inputs. Outcomes include pay, benefits, recognition achievement, prestige, and any other rewards received. Note that an outcome can be either tangible (such as economic benefits) or intangible (such as recognition or achievement).

The individual's view of fair value is critical to the relationship between performance and job satisfaction because one's sense of equity is an exchange and comparison process.[24] Assume an individual is an information technology (IT) specialist who exchanges talents and efforts (inputs) for the tangible and intangible rewards (outputs) the employer provides. To determine perceived equity the individual subconsciously compares talents, skills, and efforts to those of other IT specialists both internally and at other firms. That perception—correct or incorrect—significantly affects that person's valuation of the inputs and outcomes. A sense of inequity occurs when the comparison process results in an imbalance between inputs and outcomes.

One related theory by Lyman Porter and E. E. Lawler indicates that motivation is also influenced by people's expectations. If expectations are not met, people may feel that they have been unfairly treated and consequently become dissatisfied. Expectancy theory, discussed next, was developed to expand on these ideas.

EXPECTANCY THEORY This theory states that individuals base decisions about their behaviors on their expectations that one or another alternate behavior is more likely to lead to needed or desired outcomes. As Exhibit 500.12 depicts, the three crucial aspects of the behavior-outcome relationship are as follows:

- *Effort-Performance Expectations* refer to employees' beliefs that working harder will lead to performance. If people do not believe that working harder leads to performance, then their efforts may diminish.
- *Performance-Reward Linkage* considers individuals' expectations that high performance actually will lead to rewards. The performance-reward relationship indicates how instrumental or important effective performance is in producing desired results.
- *Value of Rewards* refers to how valuable the rewards are to the employee. One determinant of employees' willingness to exert effort is the degree to which they value the rewards offered by the organization.

This model of motivation suggests that individuals' levels of effort (motivation) are not simply functions of rewards. Employees must expect that they have the *ability to perform the task well*; they must feel that *high performance will result in receiving rewards;* and they must *value those rewards*. If all three conditions are met, employees will be motivated to exert greater effort.

Exhibit 500.12 *Simplified Expectancy Model of Motivation*

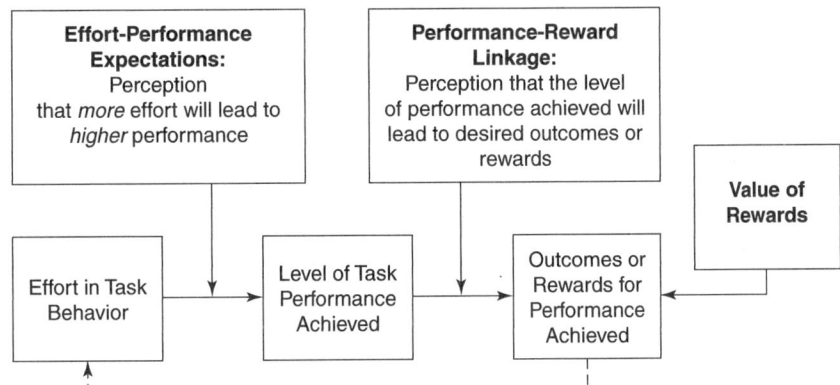

Management Implications for Motivating Individual Performance

The concepts of equity and expectancy point out that motivation is complex and individualized, but managerial strategies and tactics must be comprehensive in order to address equity and expectations of individuals. For instance, managers must determine whether inadequate individual behavior is due to low effort-performance ties (ability), low performance-reward linkages (inconsistent reward policies), or low value (low desire for the rewards).

In the case of low effort-performance ties, managers may try training to improve the relationship and thus encourage high performance. In the case of low performance-reward links, managers must look to the methods by which they appraise and reward performance.

Finally, managers must investigate the desirability of the rewards given for performance. Even if skills and rewards for performance are both high, the employee may not value the rewards. The rewards must be based on what the employees value, not what the managers value.

Many organizations spend considerable money to "motivate" their employees using a wide range of tactics. However, the effectiveness of these expenditures has been questioned, particularly given the short-term nature of many of these programs and rewards.

In summary, answering the question often asked by managers, "How do I motivate my employees?" requires managerial diagnoses of employees' efforts, abilities, and expectations. For that reason, the relationships between individuals and their organizations are an integral part of effective HR management.

Individual/Organizational Relationships

Various surveys have found that only about half of the workers in U.S. organizations are relatively satisfied with their jobs, a decline of 10 percent from five years previously. The biggest decline occurred with workers 45–54 years old. Even more concerning is that just 24 percent said they were committed to stay at least two years at their current employer. Also, about one-fifth of employees in some surveys are so dissatisfied with their jobs that they negatively affect other employees.[25] Because the long-term economic health of most organizations depends on the efforts of employees with the appropriate capabilities and motivation to perform their jobs well, organizations that are successful over time demonstrate that individual relationships do matter and should be managed effectively.

The Psychological Contract

One concept that has been useful in discussing employees' relationships with organizations is that of a **psychological contract,** which refers to the unwritten expectations employees and employers have about the nature of their work relationships. Because the psychological contract is individual and subjective in nature, it focuses on expectations about "fairness" that may not be defined clearly by employees.

Psychological contract The unwritten expectations employees and employers have about the nature of their work relationships.

Both tangible items (such as wages, benefits, employee productivity, and attendance) and intangible items (such as loyalty, fair treatment, and job security) are encompassed by psychological contracts between employers and employees. Many employers may attempt to detail their expectations through employee handbooks and policy manuals, but those materials are only part of the total "contractual" relationship.

THE CHANGING PSYCHOLOGICAL CONTRACT   At one time, employees exchanged their efforts and capabilities for a secure job that offered rising pay, good benefits, and career progression within the organization. But as organizations have downsized and cut workers who have given long and loyal service, a growing number of employees question whether they should be loyal to their employers. Closely related to the psychological contract is *psychological ownership*. When individuals feel that they have some control and perceived rights in the organization, they are more likely to be committed to the organization.[26]

Rather than just paying employees to follow orders and put in time, increasingly employers are expecting employees to utilize their knowledge, skills, and abilities to accomplish organizational results. An effective psychological contract recognizes the following components:

Employers provide:
- Competitive compensation and benefits
- Career development opportunities
- Flexibility to balance work and home life

Employees contribute:
- Continuous skill improvement and increased productivity
- Reasonable time with organization
- Extra effort when needed

Two factors affecting the relationship between individuals and organizations are economic changes and the expectations of different generations of individuals.

1. *Economic Changes*: The ebb and flow of the economy is a major factor affecting employee expectations.
2. *Generational Differences*: Much has been written about the differing expectations of individuals in different generations. These generational differences are likely to continue to create challenges and conflicts in organizations because of the differing expectations that various individuals have.[27] One of the most noticeable differences is in loyalty to organizations.

These factors affect the psychological contract in a number of ways.

Loyalty

Employees *do* believe in psychological contracts and hope their employers will honor that side of the "agreement." Many employees still want security and stability, interesting work, a supervisor they respect, and competitive pay and benefits. If these elements are not provided, employees may feel a diminished need to contribute to organizational performance. When organizations merge, lay off large numbers of employees, outsource work, and use large numbers of temporary and part-time workers, employees see fewer reasons to give their loyalty to employers in return for this loss of job security. More employers are finding that in tight labor markets, turnover of key people occurs more frequently when employee loyalty is low, which in turn emphasizes the importance of a loyal and committed workforce.

Job Satisfaction and Organizational Commitment

In its most basic sense, **job satisfaction** is a positive emotional state resulting from evaluating one's job experiences. Job *dis*satisfaction occurs when one's expectations are not met. For example, if an employee expects clean and safe working conditions on the job, then the employee is likely to be dissatisfied if the workplace is dirty and dangerous.

No simple formula can predict an individual employee's job satisfaction. Furthermore, the relationship between productivity and job satisfaction is not entirely clear. The critical factor is what employees expect from their jobs and what they receive as rewards from their jobs. Even though job satisfaction itself is important, perhaps the "bottom line" is the impact that job satisfaction has on organizational commitment, which affects employee turnover and organizational performance.[28] As Exhibit 500.13 depicts, the interaction of the individual and the job determines levels of job satisfaction/dissatisfaction and organizational commitment.

Organizational commitment is the degree to which employees believe in and accept organizational goals and desire to remain with the organization. Various research studies have revealed that people who are relatively satisfied with their jobs will be somewhat more committed to the organization.

A logical extension of organizational commitment focuses specifically on *continuance commitment* factors, which suggests that decisions to remain with or leave an organization ultimately are reflected in employee absenteeism and turnover statistics. Individuals who are not as satisfied with their jobs or who are not as committed to the organization are more likely to withdraw from the organization, either occasionally through absenteeism or permanently through turnover.

Exhibit 500.13 *Factors Affecting Job Performance and Organizational Commitment*

Absenteeism

TYPES OF ABSENTEEISM Employees can be absent from work for several reasons. Clearly, some absenteeism is inevitable. Because illness, death in the family, and other personal reasons for absences are unavoidable and understandable, many employers have sick-leave policies that allow employees a certain number of paid absent days per year for these types of *involuntary* absenteeism. However, much absenteeism is avoidable, or *voluntary* absenteeism. Often, a relatively small number of individuals in the workplace are responsible for a disproportionate share of the total absenteeism in an organization. One study found that 41 percent of employees had 0–2 days of unscheduled absences, 43 percent of employees had 3–8 days, and 13 percent of employees had 9 or more days per year.[29]

That same study and others show the close linkage between absenteeism, job satisfaction, and organizational commitment. The study results indicate that how employees feel about their jobs and their employers affects unscheduled absenteeism. Employers with lower employee morale had significantly higher absenteeism rates.

MEASURING ABSENTEEISM Controlling or reducing absenteeism must begin with continuous monitoring of the absenteeism statistics in work units. Such monitoring helps managers pinpoint employees who are frequently absent and the departments that have excessive absenteeism. Various methods of measuring or computing absenteeism exist. One formula suggested by the U.S. Department of Labor for computing absenteeism rates is as follows:

$$\text{Absenteeism rate} = \frac{\text{Number of person-days lost through job absence during period}}{(\text{Average number of employees}) \times (\text{Number of work days})} \times 100$$

This rate also can be based on number of work hours instead of number of work days.

CONTROLLING ABSENTEEISM Controlling voluntary absenteeism is easier if managers understand its causes more clearly. However, a variety of approaches can be used to reduce voluntary absenteeism. Organizational policies on absenteeism should be stated clearly in an employee handbook and stressed by supervisors and managers. The policies and rules an organization uses to govern absenteeism may provide a clue to the effectiveness of its absenteeism control efforts.[30] Absenteeism control options fall into several categories:

- *Disciplinary approach:* Many employers use a disciplinary approach. People who are absent the first time receive an oral warning, but subsequent absences bring written warnings, suspension, and finally dismissal.
- *Positive reinforcement:* Positive reinforcement includes such methods as giving employees cash, recognition, time off, or other rewards for meeting attendance standards. Offering rewards for good attendance, giving bonuses for missing fewer than a certain number of days, and "buying back" unused sick leave are all positive methods of reducing absenteeism.
- *Combination approach:* Combination approaches ideally reward desired behaviors and punish undesired behaviors. This "carrot and stick" approach uses policies and discipline to punish offenders and develops various programs and rewards for employees with outstanding attendance. One firm that has used attendance

incentives effectively is Continental Airlines. As part of its "Go Forward" Program, employees with perfect attendance receive incentives of travel and other rewards.[31]

- *"No fault" absenteeism:* Here, the reasons for absences do not matter, but the employees must manage their time rather than having managers make decisions about excused and unexcused absences. Once absenteeism exceeds normal limits, then disciplinary action up to and including termination of employment can occur.[32] The advantages of the "no fault" approach are that all employees can be covered by it, and supervisors and HR staff do not have to judge whether absences count as excused or unexcused. Therefore, employees manage their own attendance except where extreme abuses occur.

- *Paid time-off (PTO) programs:* Some employers have a *paid time-off* (PTO) program in which vacation time, holidays, and sick leave for each employee are combined into a PTO account. Employees use days from their accounts at their discretion for illness, personal time, or vacation. If employees run out of days in their accounts, then they are not paid for any additional days missed. The PTO programs generally have reduced absenteeism, particularly one-day absences, but overall time away from work often increases because employees use all of "their" time off by taking unused days as vacation days.

The disciplinary approach is the most widely used means, with most employers using policies and punitive practices. However, one survey of employers found that the PTO programs appear to be the most effective in reducing absenteeism, even though only 21 percent of the firms have such an approach.[33]

Turnover

Like absenteeism, turnover is related to job satisfaction and organizational commitment. **Turnover** occurs when employees leave an organization and have to be replaced.

TYPES OF TURNOVER Turnover is classified in a number of different ways. The following classifications can be used and are not mutually exclusive:

- **Involuntary Turnover**
  Terminations for poor performance or work rule violations

- **Voluntary Turnover**
  Employee leaves by choice

Involuntary turnover is triggered by organizational policies, work rules, and performance standards that are not met by employees. Voluntary turnover can be caused by many factors, including career opportunities, pay, supervision, geography, and personal/family reasons. Voluntary turnover also appears to increase with the size of the organization, most likely due to the larger firms having more employees who may move, the more impersonal nature of organizations, and the "organizational bureaucracy" that is present in these organizations.

- **Functional Turnover**
  Lower-performing or disruptive employees leave

- **Dysfunctional Turnover**
  Key individuals and high performers leave at critical times

Not all turnover is negative for organizations because some workforce losses are desirable, especially if those workers who leave are lower-performing, less reliable individuals, or those who are disruptive to coworkers. Unfortunately for organizations, dysfunctional turnover occurs when key individuals leave, often at crucial work times. For example, a software project leader left in the midst of a system upgrade to take a promotion at another firm in the city, causing the system upgrade timeline to slip by two months due to the difficulty of replacing the project leader.

- **Uncontrollable Turnover**
  Occurs for reasons outside the impact of the employer

- **Controllable Turnover**
  Occurs due to factors that could be influenced by the employer

Many reasons employees quit cannot be controlled by the organization and include: (1) the employee moves out of the geographic area; (2) the employee decides to stay home for family reasons; (3) the employee's spouse is transferred; or (4) a student employee graduates from college. But, it is the controllable turnover that must be addressed. Organizations are better able to retain employees if they deal with the concerns of employees that are leading to turnover. Even though some turnover is inevitable, many employers today recognize that reducing turnover is crucial. The costs of turnover, including diminished organizational productivity, have led employers to direct considerable efforts on employee retention, which is the focus of the remainder of this section.

Retention of Human Resources

Retention of employees has become a primary concern in many organizations for several reasons. As a practical matter, with lower turnover, every individual who is retained means one less person to have to recruit, select, and train. Also, organizational and individual performance is enhanced by the continuity of employees who know their jobs, coworkers, organizational services and products, and the firm's customers. One survey of supervisors and workers found that losing high performers made it more difficult for organizations to reach their business goals.[34] Additionally, continuity of employees provides better "employee image" for attracting and retaining other individuals. Another survey of chief executive officers found that they believe the greatest contribution to organizational success over the next five years will be to get and retain employee talent (26 percent).

Why People Stay or Leave

Individuals stay or leave their jobs and organizations for many different reasons. Obviously, individuals who are terminated leave at the request of the organizations. But the bigger issue in many organizations is why employees voluntarily leave. The McKinsey studies done several years apart found that the most critical factors affecting the attraction and retention of managers and executives can be classified into three areas. The areas, key items, and percentage responses are listed next:[35]

Great Company
- Value and culture (58 percent)
- Well managed (50 percent)
- Company has exciting challenges (38 percent)

Great Job
- Freedom and autonomy (56 percent)
- Job has exciting challenges (51 percent)
- Career advancement and growth (39 percent)

Compensation and Lifestyle
- Differentiated pay package (29 percent)
- High total compensation (23 percent)
- Geographic location (19 percent)
- Respect for lifestyle (12 percent)

Retention Determinants

It has been recognized by both employers and employees that some common areas affect employee retention. If certain organizational components are being provided, then other factors may affect retention. Surveys of employees consistently show that career opportunities and rewards are the two most important determinants of retention. Finally, job design/work factors and fair and supportive employee relationships with others inside the organization contribute to retention. Exhibit 500.14 shows the retention determinants.

The Retention Management Process

In addition to identifying the determinants of retention, it is important that HR professionals and their organizations have processes in place to manage retention of employees. Left to chance or infrequent attention, employee retention is not as likely to be successful. That is why using the retention management process outlined in Exhibit 500.15 is important. Each phase of the process is discussed in the following sections.

Retention Measurement and Assessment

To ensure that appropriate actions are taken to enhance retention and reduce turnover, management decisions require data and analyses rather than subjective impressions, anecdotes of selected individual situations, or panic reactions to the loss of a few key people. Therefore, having several different types of measures and analyses is important.

MEASURING TURNOVER The turnover rate for an organization can be computed in different ways. The following formula from the U.S. Department of Labor is widely used; in it *separation* means leaving the organization.

$$\text{Turnover rate} = \frac{\text{Number of employee separations during the month}}{\text{Total number of employees at midmonth}} \times 100$$

Exhibit 500.14 *Retention Determinants*

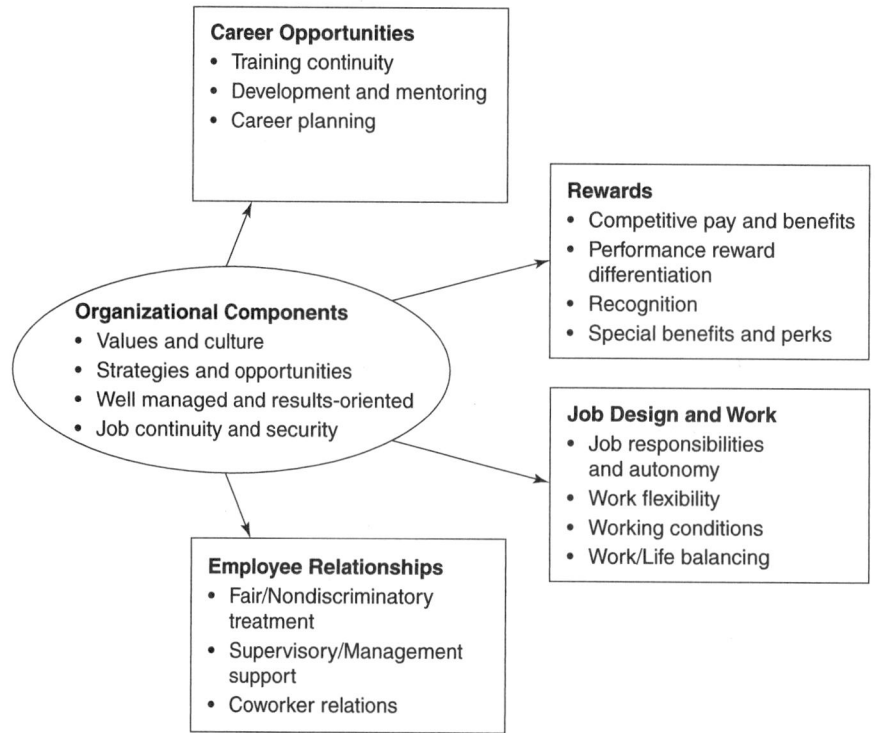

Exhibit 500.15 *The Retention Management Process*

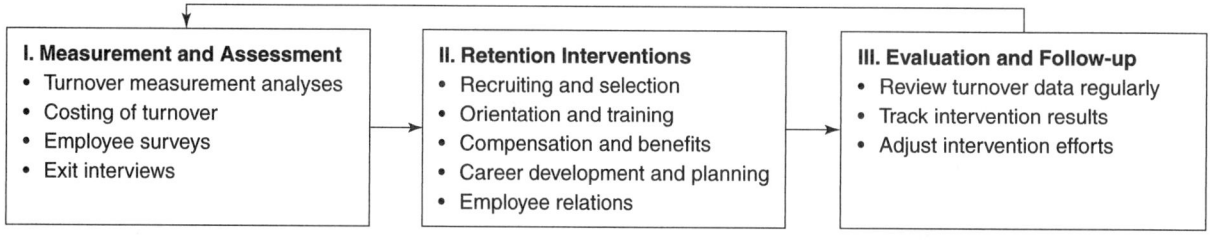

Common turnover figures range from almost zero to more than 100 percent per year, with turnover rates varying among industries. Often a part of human resource information systems, turnover data can be gathered and analyzed in a number of ways, including the following: (1) jobs and job levels; (2) departments, units, and location; (3) reason for leaving; (4) length of service; (5) demographic characteristics; (6) education and training; (7) knowledge, skills, and abilities; and (8) performance ratings/levels.

COSTS OF TURNOVER Determining turnover costs can be relatively simple or very complex, depending upon the nature of the efforts and data used. Exhibit 500.16 shows a simplified costing model. In that model if a job pays $20,000 (A) and benefits cost 40 percent (B), then the total annual cost for one employee is $28,000. Assuming 20 employees quit in the previous year (D) and that it takes three months for one employee to be fully productive, the calculation in (F) results in a per person turnover cost of $3,500. Overall, the annual turnover costs would be $70,000 for the 20 individuals who left. It should be noted that in spite of its conservative and simple nature, this model makes the point that turnover is costly. For instance, if the job is teller in a large bank where more than 150 people leave in a year, the conservative model results in turnover costs in excess of $500,000 per year.

More detailed and sophisticated turnover costing models consider a number of factors. Some of the most common areas considered include the following:[36]

- *Hiring costs:* Includes recruiting and advertising expenses, search fees, HR interviewer and staff time and salaries, employee referral fees, relocation and moving costs, supervisor and managerial time and salaries, employment testing costs, reference checking time, pre-employment medical expenses, and so on.

Exhibit 500.16 *Simplified Turnover Costing Model*

Job Title _____
- A. Typical annual pay for job
- B. Percentage of pay for benefits times (×) annual pay
- C. Total employee annual cost (add A + B)
- D. How many employees voluntarily quit in this job in the past 12 months?
- E. How long does it take for one employee to become fully productive (in months)?
- F. Per person turnover cost: (Multiply (E ÷ 12) × C × 50%*)
- G. Annual turnover cost for this job: (Multiply F × D)

*Assume 50 percent productivity throughout the learning period (E).

- *Training costs:* Includes paid orientation time, training staff time and salaries, costs of training materials, supervisors' and managers' time and salaries, coworker "coaching" time and salaries, and so on.
- *Productivity costs:* Includes lost productivity due to "break-in" time of new employees, loss of customer contacts, unfamiliarity with organizational products and services, more time to use organizational resources and systems, and so on.
- *Separation costs:* Includes HR staff and supervisor time and salaries to prevent separations, exit interview time, unemployment expenses, legal fees for separations challenged, and so on.

EMPLOYEE SURVEYS Employee surveys can be used to diagnose specific problem areas, identify employee needs or preferences, and reveal areas in which HR activities are well received or are viewed negatively. For example, questionnaires may be sent to employees to collect ideas for revising a performance appraisal system or to determine how satisfied employees are with their benefits programs. Regardless of the topic of the survey, obtaining employee input provides managers and HR professionals with data on the "retention climate" in an organization.

One specific type of survey used by many organizations is an **attitude survey** that focuses on employees' feelings and beliefs about their jobs and the organization. By serving as a means to obtain data on how employees view their jobs, their supervisors, their coworkers, and organizational policies and practices, these surveys can be starting points for reducing turnover and increasing employee retention for longer periods of time. Some employers conduct attitude surveys on a regularly scheduled basis (such as every year), while others do so intermittently. As the use of the Internet has spread, more organizations have begun conducting attitude surveys electronically.[37]

> **Attitude survey** Survey that focuses on employees' feelings and beliefs about their jobs and the organization.
>
> **Exit interview** An interview in which individuals are asked to identify reasons for leaving the organization.

EXIT INTERVIEWS One widely used type of interview is the **exit interview,** in which individuals are asked to identify reasons for leaving the organization. One survey of employers found that 87 percent of them conduct exit interviews, and more than half have used the information gathered to make changes to aid retention.[38]

Retention Interventions

Based on what the measurement and assessment data reveal, a variety of HR interventions can be undertaken to improve retention. Turnover can be controlled and reduced in several ways.[39] During the *recruiting* process, the job should be outlined and a *realistic job preview* presented, so that the reality of the job matches the expectations of the new employee. By ensuring that the expectations of potential employees match what the organization is likely to offer, voluntary turnover may be reduced.

Another way to eliminate turnover is to improve the *selection process* in order to better match applicants to jobs. By fine-tuning the selection process and hiring people who will not have disciplinary or performance problems or whose work histories suggest higher turnover potential, employers can reduce turnover. Once selected, individuals who receive effective *orientation and training* are less likely to leave.

Other HR factors are important as well. *Compensation* is important because a competitive, fair, and equitable pay system can help reduce turnover. Inadequate benefits also may lead to voluntary turnover, especially if other employers offer significantly higher compensation levels for similar jobs. *Career development and planning* can help an organization keep employees. If individuals believe they have few opportunities for career development advancement, they are more likely to leave the organization. *Employee relations,* including fair/nondiscriminatory treatment and enforcement of HR policies, can enhance retention also.

Evaluation and Follow-Up

Once retention intervention efforts have been implemented, it is important that they be evaluated and appropriate follow-up and adjustments made. Regular *review of turnover data* can identify when turnover increases or decreases among different employees classified by length of service, education, department, gender, or other factors.

Tracking intervention results also should be part of evaluation efforts. Some firms may use pilot programs to see how turnover is affected before extending the changes to the entire organization. For instance, to test the impact of flextime scheduling on employee turnover, a firm might allow flexible scheduling in one department on a pilot basis. If the turnover rate of the employees in that department drops in comparison with the turnover in other departments still working set schedules, then the experimental pilot project may indicate that flexible scheduling can reduce turnover. Next, the firm might extend the use of flexible scheduling to other departments.

Staffing, Development, and Employment Practices

Jobs

The work that needs to be done in an organization, and how it gets done, matters to both employers and employees. Important elements for *employers* are: (1) having work done properly that will lead to organization goals; (2) making sure that work is logically organized into jobs that can be compensated fairly; and (3) having work that people are willing (even eager) to do. Important factors for *employees* are: (1) having a clear understanding of what is expected in the job; (2) doing tasks they personally enjoy; (3) being rewarded appropriately for their work; and (4) having a sense that what they do is important and respected.

HR Management and Jobs

Several areas associated with jobs involve human resources professionals. The issues surrounding jobs and various approaches that can be used to address the issues are shown in Exhibit 500.17. But seldom does one design all the jobs in an organization from scratch. Jobs grow in number, evolve, and then disappear as the organization changes. So as a practical matter, the concerns with jobs are typically redesign and reengineering of existing jobs. This section addresses the issues in Exhibit 500.17 in its look at jobs in organizations.

Exhibit 500.18 shows how organizational values, strategies, and customer needs influence the work the organization has to do.[40]

Developing Jobs for Individuals and Teams

Individual responses to jobs vary because a job may be motivating to one person but not to someone else. Also, depending on how jobs are designed, they may provide more or less opportunity for employees to satisfy their job-related needs. For example, a sales job may furnish a good opportunity to satisfy social needs, whereas a training assignment may satisfy a person's need to develop expertise in a specific area. A job that gives little autonomy may not satisfy an individual's need to be creative or innovative.

Exhibit 500.17 *Job Issues and HR Approaches*

Issue	Approaches
• Dividing up organizational work into jobs • Improving existing jobs for people and productivity • Using group inputs/effort in certain jobs • Identifying what people currently are doing in specific jobs • Recording job tasks and the characteristics of the person necessary to do the job	• Work flow analysis and "reengineering" jobs • Job design/or redesign • Alternative scheduling • Teams • Job analysis • Job descriptions • Job specifications • Competency identification

Exhibit 500.18 *Influences Affecting Jobs, People, and Related HR Policies*

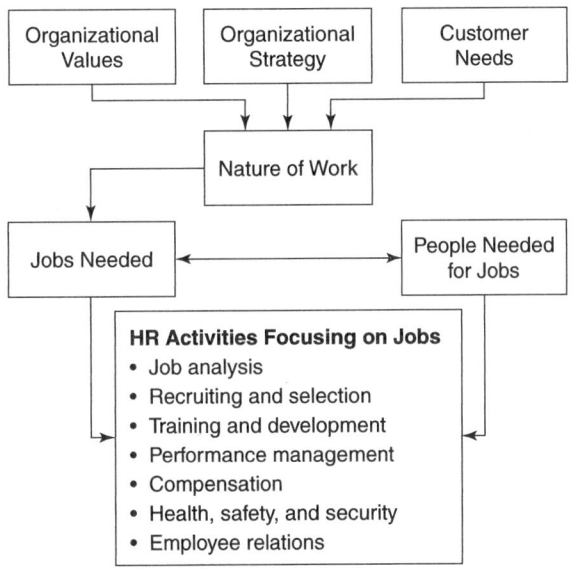

Designing or redesigning jobs encompasses many factors. **Job design** refers to organizing tasks, duties, and responsibilities into a productive unit of work. It addresses the content of jobs and the effect of jobs on employees. Identifying the components of a given job is an integral part of job design. Currently, job design is receiving greater attention for three major reasons:

Job design Organizing tasks, duties, and responsibilities into a productive unit of work.

- Job design can influence *performance* in certain jobs, especially those where employee motivation can make a substantial difference. Lower costs through reduced turnover and absenteeism also are related to good job design.
- Job design can affect *job satisfaction*. Because people are more satisfied with certain job configurations than with others, identifying what makes a "good" job becomes critical.
- Job design can affect both *physical and mental health*. Problems such as hearing loss, backache, and leg pain sometimes can be traced directly to job design, as can stress, high blood pressure, and heart disease.

Not everyone would enjoy being a physician, an engineer, or a dishwasher. But certain people like and do well at each of those jobs.[41] The person/job fit is a simple but important concept that involves matching characteristics of people with characteristics of jobs. Obviously, if a person does not fit a job, either the person can be changed or replaced, or the job can be altered. In the past, it was much more common to try to make the "round" person fit the "square" job. However, successfully reshaping people is not easy to do. By redesigning jobs, the person/job fit may be improved more easily.

530. STAFFING, DEVELOPMENT, AND EMPLOYMENT PRACTICES

Nature of Job Design

One tactic for designing or redesigning jobs is to simplify the job tasks and responsibilities. Job simplification may be appropriate when a job is to be staffed with entry-level employees. However, making a job too simple may result in a boring job that appeals to few, causing high turnover. There are several approaches useful as part of job design.

Job enlargement Broadening the scope of a job by expanding the number of different tasks to be performed.

Job enrichment Increasing the depth of a job by adding the responsibility for planning, organizing, controlling, and evaluating the job.

JOB ENLARGEMENT AND JOB ENRICHMENT Attempts to alleviate some of the problems encountered in excessive job simplification fall under the general headings of job enlargement and job enrichment. **Job enlargement** involves broadening the scope of a job by expanding the number of different tasks to be performed. **Job enrichment** is increasing the depth of a job by adding responsibility for planning, organizing, controlling, or evaluating the job. A manager might enrich a job by promoting variety, requiring more skill and responsibility, providing more autonomy, and adding opportunities for personal growth. Giving an employee more planning and controlling responsibilities over the tasks to be done also enriches. However, simply adding more similar tasks does not enrich the job. Some examples of job enrichment include:

- Giving a person an entire job rather than just a piece of the work
- Giving more freedom and authority so the employee can perform the job as he or she sees fit
- Increasing a person's accountability for work by reducing external control
- Expanding assignments so employees can learn to do new tasks and develop new areas of expertise
- Giving feedback reports directly to employees rather than to management only

Job rotation The process of shifting a person from job to job.

JOB ROTATION One technique that can break the monotony of an otherwise simple, routine job is **job rotation,** which is the process of shifting a person from job to job. For example, one week on the auto assembly line, a worker attaches doors to the rest of the body assembly. The next week, he attaches bumpers. The third week he puts in seat assemblies, then rotates back to doors again the following week. Job rotation need not be done on a weekly basis. A worker could spend one-third of a day on each job or one entire day, instead of a week, on each job. However, some argue that job rotation does little in the long run because rotating a person from one boring job to another may help somewhat initially, but the jobs are still perceived as boring. The advantage is that job rotation develops an employee's capabilities for doing several different jobs.

Characteristics of Jobs

The job characteristics model developed by Hackman and Oldham identifies five important design characteristics of jobs. Exhibit 500.19 shows that *skill variety, task identity,* and *task significance* affect the meaningfulness of work. *Autonomy* stimulates responsibility, and *feedback* provides knowledge of results. Each aspect can make a job better for the job holder to the degree that each is present.

SKILL VARIETY The extent to which the work requires several different activities for successful completion indicates its **skill variety.** For example, lower skill variety exists when an assembly-line worker performs the same two tasks repetitively. The more skills involved, the more meaningful the work is. Skill variety is not to be confused with "multitasking," which is doing several tasks at the same time with computers, telephones, personal organizers, and other gadgets. The price of multitasking may be to never get away from the job—not a "better" outcome for everyone.[42]

TASK IDENTITY The extent to which the job includes a "whole" identifiable unit of work that is carried out from start to finish and that results in a visible outcome is its **task identity.**

TASK SIGNIFICANCE The impact the job has on other people indicates its **task significance.** A job is more meaningful if it is important to other people for some reason. For instance, a soldier may experience more fulfillment when defending his or her country from a real threat than when merely training to stay ready in case such a threat arises.

Exhibit 500.19 *Job Characteristics Model*

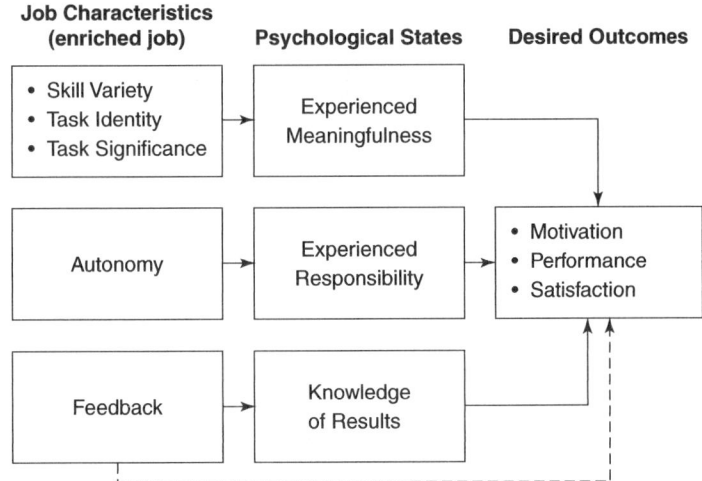

AUTONOMY The extent of individual freedom and discretion in the work and its scheduling indicates **autonomy**. More autonomy leads to a greater feeling of personal responsibility for the work.

FEEDBACK The amount of information employees receive about how well or how poorly they have performed is **feedback**. The advantage of feedback is that it helps employees to understand the effectiveness of their performance and contributes to their overall knowledge about the work. At one firm, feedback reports from customers who contact the company with problems are given directly to the employees who handle the customers' complaints, instead of being given only to the department manager.

Consequences of Job Design

Jobs designed to take advantage of these important job characteristics are more likely to be positively received by employees. Job characteristics can help distinguish between "good" and "bad" jobs. Many approaches to enhancing productivity and quality reflect efforts to expand one or more of the job characteristics.

Because of the effects of job design on performance, employee satisfaction, health, and other factors, organizations are changing or have already changed the design of some jobs.[43] Work can be designed in inefficient ways so that employees struggle to accomplish tasks and take too long to do so. In some organizations employees themselves contribute good ideas and then make the changes to succeed.

Using Teams in Jobs

Typically, a job is thought of as something done by one person. However, jobs may be designed for teams, where it is appropriate. In an attempt to make jobs more meaningful and take advantage of the increased productivity and commitment that can follow, more organizations are using teams of employees instead of individuals for jobs. Some firms have gone as far as dropping such terms as *workers* and *employees,* replacing them with *teammates, crew members, associates,* and other titles that emphasize teamwork. Teams were fully presented in Module 100, Section 180.

Other Job Design Issues: Work Schedules and Locations

Jobs consist of the tasks an employee does, the relationships required on the job, the tools one works with, and many other elements as well. Two of these important elements are when and how the work is scheduled, and where an employee is located when working. New work schedules include flextime and compressed workweek, and alternative physical work locations include telecommuting, hoteling, and virtual offices.

The Nature of Job Analysis

Job analysis Systematic way to gather and analyze information about the content, context, and the human requirements of jobs.

The most basic building block of HR management, **job analysis,** is a systematic way to gather and analyze information about the content, context, and human requirement of jobs. Exhibit 500.20 shows job analysis in perspective.

Much of the current interest in analyzing jobs stems from the importance assigned to the activity by federal and state courts. The legal defensibility of an employer's recruiting and selection procedures, performance appraisal system, employee disciplinary actions, and pay practices rests in part on the foundation of job analysis. In a number of court cases, the rulings went against employers because judges viewed their HR processes and practices as insufficiently job related. The importance of using job analysis to document HR activities must be emphasized.

It is useful to clarify the differences between job design and job analysis. Job design attempts to develop jobs that fit effectively into the flow of the organizational work that needs to be done. The more narrow focus of job analysis centers on gathering data in a formal and systematic way about what people do in their jobs.

Job analysis involves collecting information on the characteristics of a job that differentiate it from other jobs. Information that can be helpful in making the distinction includes the following:

- Work activities and behaviors
- Interactions with others
- Performance standards
- Financial and budgeting impact
- Machines and equipment used
- Working conditions
- Supervision given and received
- Knowledge, skills, and abilities needed

The information generated by job analysis may be useful in redesigning jobs, but its primary purpose is to capture a clear understanding of what is done on a job and what capabilities are needed to do it as designed. Documents that summarize the elements identified during a job analysis are job descriptions and job specifications.

Exhibit 500.20 *Job Analysis in Perspective*

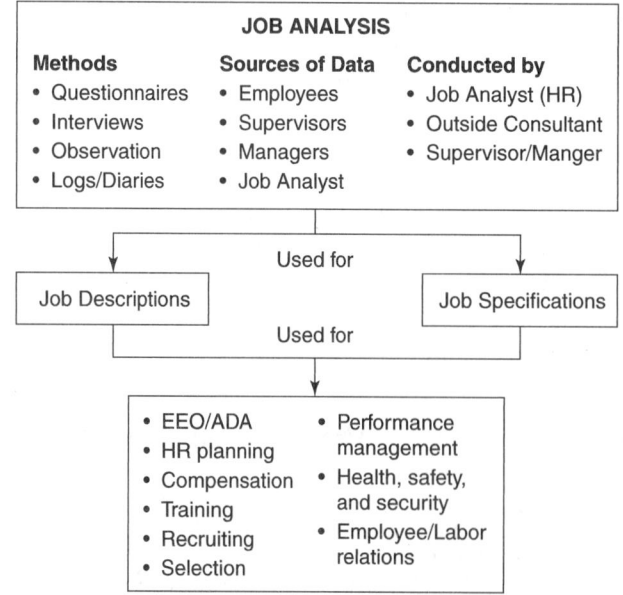

MODULE 500. HUMAN RESOURCES MANAGEMENT

Task-Based Job Analysis

Task-based job analysis is the most common form and focuses on the tasks, duties, and responsibilities performed in a job. A **task** is a distinct, identifiable work activity composed of motions, whereas a **duty** is a larger work segment composed of several tasks that are performed by an individual. Because both tasks and duties describe activities, it is not always easy or necessary to distinguish between the two. For example, if one of the employment supervisor's duties is to interview applicants, one task associated with that duty would be asking questions. **Responsibilities** are obligations to perform certain tasks and duties.

> **Task** A distinct, identifiable work activity composed of motions.
> **Duty** A larger work segment composed of several tasks that are performed by an individual.
> **Responsibilities** Obligations to perform certain tasks and duties.

The process of analyzing jobs in organizations requires planning of several factors. Some important considerations include how job analysis is to be done, who provides data, and who conducts and uses the data so that job descriptions and job specifications can be prepared and reviewed. In its most fundamental form, job analysis provides the information necessary to develop job descriptions and specifications. Once those are prepared, a wide range of HR activities follows.

Job Analysis Responsibilities

Most methods of job analysis require that a knowledgeable person describe what occurs in a job. Such information can be provided by the employee doing the job, the supervisor, and/or a trained job analyst. Each source is useful, but each has drawbacks. The supervisor seems to be the best source of information on what should be done, but employees often know more about what actually is done. However, both may lack the knowledge needed to complete a job analysis and draw the appropriate conclusions from it. Thus, job analysis requires a high degree of coordination and cooperation between the HR unit and operating managers.

The responsibility for job analysis depends on who can best perform various aspects of the process. In larger companies, the HR unit supervises the process to maintain its integrity and writes the job descriptions and specifications for uniformity. The operating managers review the efforts of the HR unit to ensure accuracy and completeness. They also may request reanalysis when jobs change significantly. In small organizations, operating managers perform all the work activities.

Stages in the Job Analysis Process

The process of job analysis must be conducted in a logical manner, following appropriate management and professional psychometric practices. Therefore, analysts usually follow a multistage process, regardless of the specific job analysis methods used. The stages for a typical job analysis, as outlined next, may vary somewhat with the number of jobs included. Exhibit 500.21 summarizes the job analysis process.

    I. Planning the Job Analysis
    II. Preparing for Job Analysis
    III. Conducting the Job Analysis
    IV. Developing Job Descriptions and Job Specifications
    V. Maintaining and Updating Job Descriptions and Job Specifications

Job Analysis Methods

Job analysis information about what people are doing in their jobs can be gathered in a variety of ways. One consideration is who is to conduct the job analysis. Most frequently, a member of the HR staff coordinates this effort. Depending on which of the methods is used, others who often participate are managers, supervisors, and employees doing the jobs. For more complex analyses, industrial engineers may conduct time and motion studies. Another consideration is the method to be used. Common methods are observations, interviews, questionnaires, and specialized methods of analysis (e.g. computerized). The use of a combination of these approaches depends on the situation and the organization. Exhibit 500.22 shows typical areas covered in a job analysis questionnaire.

Exhibit 500.21 *Stages in the Job Analysis Process*

```
I. Planning the Job Analysis
   A. Identify objectives of job analysis
   B. Obtain top management support
```
↓
```
II. Preparing for Job Analysis
    A. Identify jobs and methodology
    B. Review existing job documentation
    C. Communicate process to managers/employees
```
↓
```
III. Conducting the Job Analysis
     A. Gather job analysis data
     B. Review and compile data
```
↓
```
IV. Developing Job Descriptions and Job Specifications
    A. Draft job descriptions and specifications
    B. Review drafts with managers and employees
    C. Identify recommendations
    D. Finalize job descriptions and recommendations
```
↓
```
V. Maintaining and Updating Job Descriptions and Job Specifications
   A. Update job descriptions and specifications as organization changes
   B. Periodically review all jobs
```

Exhibit 500.22 *Typical Areas Covered in a Job Analysis Questionnaire*

Duties and Percent of Time Spent on Each • Regular duties • Special duties performed less frequently	**Contact with Other People** • Internal contacts • External contacts
Supervision • Supervision given to others • Supervision received from the boss	**Physical Dimensions** • Physical demands • Working conditions
Decisions Made • Records and reports repaired • Materials and equipment used • Financial/budget responsibilities	**Job-Holder Characteristics** • Knowledge • Skills • Abilities • Training needed

Behavioral Aspects of Job Analysis

A detailed examination of jobs, although necessary, can be a demanding and threatening experience for both managers and employees, in part because job analysis can identify the difference between what currently is being performed in a job and what *should* be done. Job analysis involves determining what the "core" job is. This determination may require discussion with managers about the design of the job. Often the content of a job may reflect the desires and skills of the incumbent employee.

Employees and managers also have some tendency to inflate the importance and significance of their jobs. Because job analysis information is used for compensation purposes, both managers and employees hope that "puffing up" their jobs will result in higher pay levels.

Legal Aspects of Job Analysis

Equal employment laws, regulations, and court cases emphasize that legal compliance must focus on the jobs that individuals perform. The 1978 Uniform Selection Guidelines make it clear that HR requirements must be tied to specific job-related factors if employers are to defend their actions as a business necessity.

Job Analysis and the Americans with Disabilities Act (ADA)

HR managers and their organizations must identify job activities and then document the steps taken to identify job responsibilities.[44] One result of the ADA is increased emphasis by employers on conducting job analysis, as well as developing and maintaining current and accurate job descriptions and job specifications.

The ADA requires that organizations identify the **essential job functions,** which are the fundamental duties of a job. The term *essential functions* does not include the marginal functions of the positions. **Marginal functions** are those duties that are part of a job but are incidental or ancillary to the purpose and nature of a job. Exhibit 500.23 shows three major considerations used in determining essential functions and marginal functions.[45] Job analysts, HR staff members, and operating managers must evaluate and make decisions when the information on the three considerations is not clear.

Essential job functions Fundamental duties of a job.
Marginal functions Duties that are part of a job but are incidental or ancillary to the purpose and nature of a job.

An important part of job analysis is to obtain information about what duties are being performed and what percentage of time is devoted to each duty. As the ADA suggests, the percentage of time spent on a duty generally indicates its relative importance. How often the duties are performed also becomes important. If duties are regularly performed daily, weekly, and/or monthly, they are more likely to be seen as essential. However, a task performed only infrequently or when helping another worker on a totally unrelated job more likely falls in the marginal category.[46]

Another consideration is the ease or difficulty involved in assigning a duty to be performed by someone else, or in a different job. For instance, assume an assembler of electronic components places the completed parts in a bin next to the work area. At the end of each day, the bin of completed parts must be carried to another room for use in final assembly of a product. Carrying the bin to the other room probably would be defined as a marginal task,

Exhibit 500.23 *Determining Essential and Marginal Functions*

Considerations	Essential Functions	Marginal Functions
Percentage of time spent	• Significant time spent: often 20% of time or more	• Generally less than 10% of time
Frequency	• Performed regularly: daily, weekly, monthly	• Performed infrequently or when substituting in part of another job
Importance	• Task has consequences to other parts of job and other jobs	• Task is unrelated to job and has little consequence if not performed

530. STAFFING, DEVELOPMENT, AND EMPLOYMENT PRACTICES

because assigning someone else to carry it would not likely create major workflow problems with other jobs and workers.

Job analysis also can identify the physical demands of jobs. An understanding of the skills and capabilities used on a job is critical. For example, a customer service representative must be able to hear well enough to take customer orders. However, hearing may be less essential for a heavy equipment operator in a quarry.

Job Analysis and Wage/Hour Regulations

Typically, job analysis identifies the percentage of time spent on each duty in a job. This information helps determine whether someone should be classified as exempt or nonexempt under the wage/hour laws.

As will be noted in the compensation section, the federal Fair Labor Standards Act (FLSA) and most state wage/hour laws indicate that the percentage of time employees spend on manual, routine, or clerical duties affects whether they must be paid overtime for hours worked in excess of 40 per week. To be exempt from overtime, the employees must perform their *primary duties* as executive, administrative, or professional employees. *Primary* has been interpreted to mean occurring at least 50 percent of the time. Additionally, the exemption regulations state that no more than 20 percent (40 percent in retail settings) of the time can be spent on manual, routine, or clerical duties.

Other legal-compliance efforts, such as those involving workplace safety and health, can also be aided through the data provided by job analysis. In summary, it is extremely difficult for an employer to have a legal staffing system without performing job analysis. Truly, job analysis is the most basic HR activity.

Job Descriptions and Job Specifications

The output from analysis of a job is used to develop a job description and its job specifications. Together, they summarize job analysis information in a readable format and provide the basis for defensible job-related actions. They also identify individual jobs for employees by providing documentation from management.

Job description *Identification of the tasks, duties, and responsibilities of a job.*

In most cases, the job description and job specifications are combined into one document that contains several different sections. A **job description** identifies the tasks, duties, and responsibilities of a job. It describes what is done, why it is done, where it is done, and briefly, how it is done. Then, **performance standards** can flow directly from a job description and indicate what the job accomplishes and how performance is measured in key areas of the job description.[47] The reason for including the performance standards is clear. If employees know what is expected and how performance is to be measured, they have a much better chance of performing satisfactorily. Exhibit 500.24 shows job description duty statements and some performance standards used for a customer response representative in a telecommunications firm.

Unfortunately, performance standards often are omitted from job descriptions. Even if performance standards have been identified and matched to job descriptions, they may not be communicated to employees if the job descriptions are not provided to employees, but used only as tools by the HR department and managers. Such an approach limits the value of job descriptions.

Job specifications *The knowledge, skills, and abilities (KSAs) an individual needs to perform a job satisfactorily.*

While the job description describes activities to be done, the **job specifications** list the knowledge, skills, and abilities an individual needs to perform a job satisfactorily. Knowledge, skills, and abilities (KSAs) include education, experience, work skill requirements, personal abilities, and mental and physical requirements. Job specifications for a data entry operator might include a required educational level, a certain number of months of experience, a typing ability of 60 words per minute, a high degree of visual concentration, and ability to work under time pressure. It is important to note that accurate job specifications identify what KSAs a person needs to do the job, not necessarily what qualifications the current employee possesses.

Job Description Components

A typical job description contains several major parts such as job identification, general summary, essential functions and duties, job specifications, and disclaimers. The job description should not be viewed as a "contract" between the employer and the employee.

Exhibit 500.24 *Sample Job Duty Statements and Performance Standards*

	Job Title: Customer Response Representative Supervisor: Customer Response Supervisor	
Duty		**Performance Standards**
Discusses nonpayment of bills with customers and notifies them of nonpayment disconnecting of service.		• Flags accounts within two days that are not to be disconnected according to discussions with Local Manager. • Mails notices to cable television customers to be received at least five days prior to disconnection date. • Determines which accounts require credit deposit, based on prior payment history. • Calmly discusses the nonpayment status of the account along with options for reconnection with customers. • Disconnects and reconnects long distance calling cards for nonpayments with 100% accuracy.
Receives and records trouble reports from customers on mechanized trouble-reporting system for telephone or proper form for cable television. Dispatches reports to appropriate personnel.		• Completes all required trouble information on the trouble-reporting system accurately with no more than five errors annually. • Dispatches trouble ticket information to voice mail with 100% accuracy. • Tests line if needed or as requested by technician for telephone troubles.

The Competency Approach to Job Analysis

More and more often, commentators and writers address the notion that the nature of jobs and work is changing so much that the concept of a "job" may be obsolete for many people. In some high-technology industries, employees work in cross-functional project teams and shift from project to project. Organizations in these industries focus less on performing specific tasks and duties and more on fulfilling responsibilities and attaining results. For example, a project team of eight employees developing software to allow various credit cards to be used with ATMs worldwide will work on many different tasks, some individually and some with other team members. When that project is finished those employees will move to other projects, possibly with other employers. Such shifts may happen several times per year. Therefore, the basis for recruiting, selecting, and compensating these individuals is their competence and capabilities, not just what they do. Writing an accurate job description for such a job would be difficult or even impossible.

In many industries traditional jobs will continue to exist. Studying these jobs and their work consequences is relatively easy because of the repetitiveness of the work and the limited number of tasks each worker performs, so the task-based approach to job analysis is appropriate.

Clearly, studying the two different types of jobs—lower-skilled ones and more varied, highly technical ones—requires different approaches. Focusing on the competencies that individuals need to perform jobs, rather than on the tasks, duties, and responsibilities composing a job emphasizes how significantly people's capabilities influence organizational performance. Instead of thinking of individuals having jobs that are relatively stable and can be written up into typical job descriptions, it may be more relevant to focus on the competencies used.

Competencies are basic characteristics that can be linked to enhanced performance by individuals or teams. Exhibit 500.25 shows examples of commonly identified competencies.

Competencies Basic characteristics that can be linked to enhanced performance by individuals or teams.

A growing number of organizations use some facets of competency analysis. The three primary reasons organizations use a competency approach are: (1) to communicate valued behaviors throughout the organization, (2) to raise the competency levels of the organization, and (3) to emphasize the capabilities of people to enhance organizational competitive advantage.

530. STAFFING, DEVELOPMENT, AND EMPLOYMENT PRACTICES

Exhibit 500.25 *Examples of Competencies*

- Customer focus
- Team orientation
- Technical expertise
- Results orientation
- Leadership
- Innovation
- Adaptability
- Decisiveness

Competency Analysis Methodology

Unlike the traditional approach to analyzing jobs, which identifies the tasks, duties, knowledge, and skills associated with a job, the competency approach considers how the knowledge and skills are used. The competency approach also attempts to identify the hidden factors that are often critical to superior performance. For instance, many supervisors talk about employees' attitudes, but they have difficulty identifying what they mean by *attitude*. The competency approach uses some methodologies to help supervisors articulate examples of what they mean by attitude and how those factors affect performance.

One method used to determine competencies is *behavioral event interviews*. This process involves the following steps:

1. A team of senior managers identifies future performance results areas critical to the business and strategic plans of the organization. These concepts may be broader than those used in the past.
2. Panel groups are assembled, composed of individuals knowledgeable about the jobs in the company. This group can include both high- and low-performing employees, supervisors, managers, trainers, and others.
3. A facilitator from HR or an outside consultant interviews the panel members to get specific examples of job behaviors and actual occurrences on the jobs. During the interview the individuals are also asked about their thoughts and feelings during each of the described events.
4. Using the behavioral events, the facilitator develops detailed descriptions of each of the competencies. Descriptive phases provide clarity and specifics so that employees, supervisors, managers, and others in the organization have a clearer understanding of the competencies associated with individual jobs.
5. The competencies are rated and levels needed to meet them are identified. Then the competencies are specified for each of the jobs.
6. Finally, standards of performance are identified and tied to the jobs. Appropriate selection screening, training, and compensation processes that focus on competencies must be developed and implemented.

Possible Legal Problems with the Competency Approach

Traditional task-based job analysis provides a rational basis for such activities as compensation, selection, and training, all of which are subject to legal action by employees if they believe they are being wronged in some way. The traditional job analysis approach has been used successfully to substantiate employment decisions. Currently, there is little legal precedent regarding competency analysis, which leaves it open to legal challenge as not being as job-related as the traditional approach.[48]

Recruiting in Labor Markets

The staffing process matches people with jobs through recruiting and selection. This section examines recruiting and the next examines selection. **Recruiting** is the process of generating a pool of qualified applicants for organizational jobs. If the number of available candidates only equals the number of people to be hired, no real selection is required—the choice has already been made. The organization must either leave some openings unfilled or take all the candidates.

Various employers have faced shortages of workers who have the appropriate knowledge, skills, and abilities (KSAs). However, because business cycles go up and down, the demand for labor changes and the number of people looking for work changes. Because staffing takes place in labor markets, learning some basics about labor markets aids understanding of recruiting.

Exhibit 500.26 *Labor Market Components*

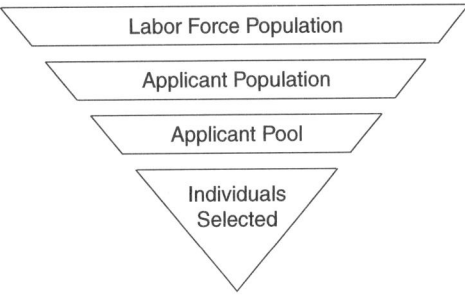

Labor Markets

Labor markets are the external supply pool from which employers attract employees. To understand where recruiting takes place, the sources of employees can be thought of as a funnel (Exhibit 500.26), in which the broad scope of markets narrow progressively to the point of selection and job offers. Of course, if the selected candidate rejects the offer, then HR staff members must move back up the funnel to the applicant pool to other candidates, and in extreme cases to reopen the recruiting process. It is important for recruiting efforts to address a number of specific issues that affect employers in today's labor markets.

Labor Market Components

The broadest labor market component is the **labor force population** made up of all individuals who are available for selection if all possible recruitment strategies are used. This large number of potential applicants may be reached using many different recruiting methods—for example, newspaper ads, Internet, colleges, word-of-mouth, etc. Each recruiting method will reach different segments of the labor force population.

The **applicant population** is a subset of the labor force population that is available for selection using a particular recruiting approach.

At least four recruiting decisions affect reaching the applicant population:

- *Recruiting method:* Advertising medium chosen, including use of employment agencies.
- *Recruiting message:* What is said about the job and how it is said.
- *Applicant qualifications required:* Education level and amount of experience necessary.
- *Administrative procedures:* When recruiting is done, applicant follow-up, and use of previous applicant files.

In tight labor markets, many employers try to expand the applicant population in a number of ways. For instance, *welfare-to-work* programs have been used to expand the applicant population for jobs requiring lower KSAs. Another way that employers expand the applicant population is to consider *ex-convicts*. Care in evaluating the individuals and ensuring appropriate placements given their backgrounds and capabilities is needed, but giving individuals second chances has paid off in some situations for both small and large employers.[49]

The **applicant pool** consists of all persons who are actually evaluated for selection. Many factors can affect the size of the applicant pool. For example, the reputation of the organization and industry as a place to work, the screening efforts of the organization, and the information available all may affect the applicant population. Assuming a suitable candidate can be found, the organization then selects the individual and makes the job offer.

Applicant pool All persons who are actually evaluated for selection.

Labor Markets and Recruiting Issues

Throughout all of the labor market components from the labor force population through the applicant pool, the supply of and demand for workers in various labor markets substantially affect the staffing strategies of organizations. An organization can use a number of different ways to identify labor markets, including by geographic area, industry and occupation, and education/technical qualifications.

Exhibit 500.27 *Strategic Recruiting Stages*

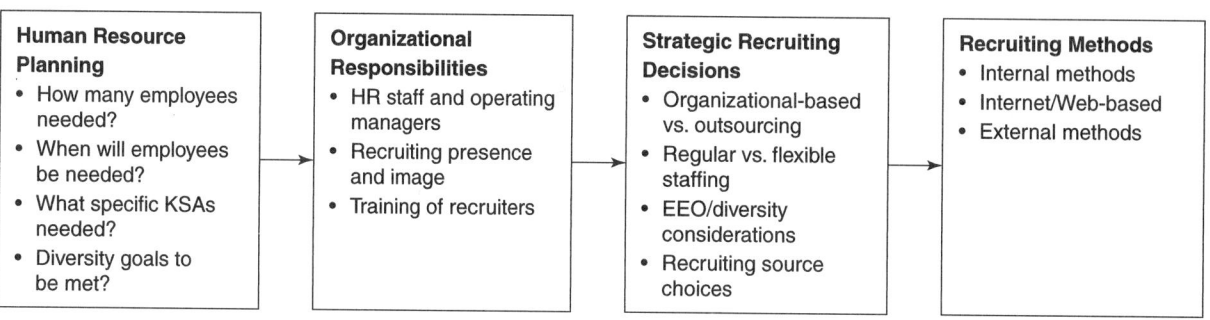

Exhibit 500.28 *Typical Division of HR Responsibilities: Recruiting*

HR Unit	Managers
• Forecasts recruiting needs.	• Anticipate needs for employees to fill vacancies.
• Prepares copy for recruiting adds and campaigns.	• Determine KSAs needed from applicants.
• Plans and conducts recruiting efforts.	• Assist in recruiting effort with information about job requirements.
• Audits and evaluates all recruiting activities.	• Review success/failure of recruiting activities.

Strategic Approach to Recruiting

A strategic approach to recruiting becomes more important as labor markets shift and become more competitive. Strategic HR planning efforts help to align HR strategies with organizational goals and plans. Therefore, it is important that recruiting be a part of strategic HR Planning. Walgreens, the drugstore chain, had to cut back its expansion plans to open new stores because of a shortage of trained pharmacists. This example illustrates how HR planning and recruiting issues affect organizational strategic plans.[50]

The decisions made about recruiting dictate not only the kinds and numbers of applicants, but also how difficult or successful recruiting efforts may be. Exhibit 500.27 shows an overview of the strategic recruiting stages.

Even during periods of reduced hiring, implementing long-range plans means keeping in contact with outside recruiting sources to maintain visibility while also maintaining employee recruiting channels in the organization. These activities allow management to match recruiting activity with organizational and human resource plans.

Organizational Recruiting Activities

In most organizations, HR staff members handle the bulk of recruiting efforts. Exhibit 500.28 shows a typical distribution of recruiting responsibilities between the HR department and operating managers in all but the smallest organizations.

Use of HR staff to recruit is common for all but hard-to-fill specialized openings and executive management jobs. For such jobs, employers frequently contact search firms specializing in specific areas, such as information technology, physician recruitment, or industry sales representatives. Because these search firms typically charge fees of 20 percent to 30 percent of the annual salary of the person recruited, many employers use their own HR staff to do as much recruiting as possible.

Strategic Recruiting Decisions

Based on the recruiting needs identified as part of HR planning, a number of recruiting decisions must be made. The most important ones include organizational-based versus outsourcing and regular versus flexible staffing. Recruiting decisions must also meet diversity considerations.

Exhibit 500.29 *Advantages and Disadvantages of Internal and External Recruiting Sources*

Recruiting Source	Advantages	Disadvantages
Internal	• Morale of promotee • Better assessment of abilities • Lower cost for some jobs • Motivator for good performance • Causes a succession of promotions • Have to hire only at entry level	• Inbreeding • Possible morale problems of those not promoted • "Political" infighting for promotions • Need for management development program
External	• New "blood" brings new perspectives • Cheaper and faster than training professionals • No group of political supporters in organization already • May bring new industry insights	• May not select someone who will "fit" the job or organization • May cause morale problems for internal candidates not selected • Longer "adjustment" or orientation time

Recruiting Source Choices: Internal versus External

Recruiting strategy and policy decisions entail identifying where to recruit, whom to recruit, and how recruiting will be done. One of the first decisions determines the extent to which internal or external sources and methods will be used. Both promoting from within the organization (internal recruitment) or hiring from outside the organization (external recruitment) to fill openings come with associated advantages and disadvantages. Exhibit 500.29 shows some of the major advantages and disadvantages of internal versus external recruiting.

Most employers combine the use of internal and external methods. Organizations that face a rapidly changing competitive environment and conditions may need to place a heavier emphasis on external sources in addition to developing internal sources. However, for those organizations existing in environments that change slowly, promotion from within may be more suitable.

Once the various recruiting policy decisions have been addressed, then the actual recruiting methods can be identified and used. These include internal and external sources, as well as Internet/Web-based approaches.

Internal Recruiting

Pursuing internal recruiting with the advantages mentioned earlier means using various sources developed and managed inside the organization. Exhibit 500.30 depicts the common internal recruiting methods.

Internal Recruiting Processes

Within the organization tapping into databases, job postings, promotions, and transfers provide the means that allow current employees to move to other jobs. The design of these processes outline ways for employees to "surface" and be considered for openings as they occur. Filling openings internally may add motivation for employees to stay and grow in the organization rather than pursuing career opportunities elsewhere.

ORGANIZATIONAL DATABASES The increased use of human resource information systems (HRIS) allows HR staff members to maintain background and KSA information on existing employees. As openings arise, HR employment specialists can access databases by entering job requirements and then receive a listing of current employees meeting the job requirement. Various types of employment software sort employee data by occupational fields, education, areas of career interests, previous work histories, and other factors.

The advantage of such databases is that they can be linked to other HR activities. Opportunities for career development and advancement are major reasons why individuals stay or leave their employers. With databases, internal opportunities for individuals can be identified. Employee profiles are continually updated to include such items

530. STAFFING, DEVELOPMENT, AND EMPLOYMENT PRACTICES

Exhibit 500.30 *Internal Recruiting Methods*

- Organizational databases
- Job posting system
- Promotion and transfers
- Current employee referrals
- Re-recruiting former employees

as additional training or education completed, special projects worked on, and career plans and desires noted during performance appraisal and career mentoring discussions.

Job posting A system in which the employer provides notices of job openings and employees respond to apply.

JOB POSTING The major means for recruiting employees for other jobs within the organization is **job posting,** a system in which the employer provides notices of job openings and employees respond by applying for specific openings. Without some sort of job posting system, it is difficult for many employees to find out what jobs are open elsewhere in the organization. The organization can notify employees of job vacancies in a number of ways, including posting notices on bulletin boards, using employee newsletters, and sending out e-mails to managers and employees. But posting job openings on company intranet and Internet Web sites has grown in use. In a unionized organization, job posting and bidding can be quite formal because the procedures often are spelled out in labor agreements. Seniority lists may be used by organizations that make promotions based strictly on seniority, so candidates are considered for promotions in the order of seniority.

Regardless of the means used, the purpose of the job posting system is to provide employees more opportunities to move within the organization. When establishing and managing a job posting system, a number of answers to many potential questions must be addressed:

- What happens if no qualified candidates respond to postings?
- Must employees inform their supervisors that they are posting for another job?
- Are there restrictions on how long an employee must stay in a job before posting for another one?
- How much notice should an employee be required to give before transferring to a new department?
- When should job notices not be posted?

Job posting systems can be ineffective if handled improperly. Jobs generally are posted before any external recruiting is done. The organization must allow a reasonable period of time for present employees to check notices of available jobs before it considers external applicants. When employees' bids are turned down, they should have discussions with their supervisors or someone in the HR area regarding the knowledge, skills, and abilities (KSAs) they need in order to improve their opportunities in the future.

PROMOTIONS AND JOB TRANSFERS Many organizations choose to fill vacancies through promotions or transfers from within whenever possible. Although most often successful, promotions and transfers from within have some drawbacks as well. The person's performance on one job may not be a good predictor of performance on another, because different skills may be required on the new job. For example, not every high-performing worker makes a successful supervisor. In most supervisory jobs, an ability to accomplish the work through others requires skills in influencing and dealing with people and those skills may not have been a factor in nonsupervisory jobs.

As employees transfer to or are promoted to other jobs, individuals must be recruited to fill their vacated jobs. Planning on how to fill those openings should occur prior to job transfers or promotions, not afterwards. It is clear that people in organizations with fewer levels may have less frequent chances for promotion. Also, in most organizations, promotions may not be an effective way to speed the movement of protected-class individuals up through the organization if that is an organizational concern.

Employee-Focused Recruiting

One reliable source of potential recruits is suggestions from current or former employees. Because current and former employees are familiar with the employer, their references often are high-potential candidates, because most employees usually do not refer individuals who are likely to be unqualified or make the employees look bad. Also, follow-up with former employees is likely to be done only with persons who were solid employees previously.

CURRENT EMPLOYEE REFERRALS A reliable source of people to fill vacancies is composed of acquaintances, friends, and family members of employees. The current employees can acquaint potential applicants with the advantages of a job with the company, furnish letters of introduction, and encourage them to apply. However, using only word-of-mouth or current employee referrals can violate equal employment regulations if protected-class individuals are underrepresented in the current organizational workforce. Therefore, some external recruiting might be necessary to avoid legal problems in this area.

Utilizing this source is usually one of the most effective methods of recruiting because many qualified people can be reached at a low cost. In an organization with numerous employees, this approach can develop quite a large pool of potential employees. Some studies have found that new workers recruited through current employee referrals have longer tenure with organizations than those from other recruiting sources.

Tight labor markets in many geographic areas and certain occupational fields prompted many employers to establish employee referral incentive programs. One study found that mid-sized and larger employers are much more likely to use employee referral bonuses.[51] Some referral programs provide different amounts for hard-to-fill jobs compared to basic referrals for common openings.

RE-RECRUITING FORMER EMPLOYEES AND APPLICANTS Former employees and former applicants represent another source for recruitment. Both cases offer a time-saving advantage, because something is already known about the potential employees.[52] Known as *re-recruiting* because the individuals previously were successfully recruited, former employees are considered an internal source in the sense that they have ties to the employer and may be called "boomerangers" because they left and came back. Individuals who left for other jobs might be willing to return because the other job and employers turned out to be less attractive than initially thought.

Key issues in the decision to re-recruit someone include the reasons why the individual left originally and if performance and capabilities were solid. Another potential source of applicants can be found in the organizational files or an applicant database. Although not entirely an internal source, those who have previously applied for jobs can be recontacted, which can be a quick and inexpensive way to fill an unexpected opening. For instance, one firm that needed two cost accountants immediately contacted qualified previous applicants and was able to hire those individuals who were disenchanted with their current jobs at other companies.

Internet Recruiting

Organizations first started using computers as a recruiting tool by advertising jobs on a bulletin board service from which prospective applicants would contact employers. Then some companies began to take e-mail applications. Today the Internet has become a primary means for employers to search for job candidates and for applicants to look for jobs. The explosive growth in Internet use is a key reason. Internet users tap the Internet to search for jobs almost as frequently as reading newspaper classified ads. Also many of these Internet users post or submit resumes on the Internet.

Advantages of Internet Recruiting

Employers have found a number of advantages in using Internet recruiting. A primary one is that many employers have realized cost savings using Internet recruiting compared to other sources such as newspaper advertising, employment agencies and search firms, and other external sources. Some employers experience savings from several hundred dollars per hire to as high as $4,000 to $6,000 for senior professional and management jobs.[53]

Internet recruiting also can save considerable *time*. Applicants can respond quickly to job postings by sending e-mails, rather than using "snail mail." Recruiters can respond to qualified candidates more quickly and establish times for interviews or request additional candidate information.

An expanded pool of applicants can be generated using Internet recruiting. In fact, a large number of candidates may see any given job listing, although exposure depends on which Internet sources are used. One side benefit of the Internet is that jobs literally are posted globally, so potential applicants in other geographic areas and countries can view job openings posted on the Web.

Disadvantages of Internet Recruiting

The positives associated with Internet recruiting come with a number of disadvantages. By getting broader exposure, employers also may get more unqualified applicants. A survey of HR recruiters found that one-third of them felt Internet recruiting created additional work for HR staff members.[54] More resumes must be reviewed, more e-mails dealt with, and specialized applicant tracking software may be needed to handle the increase in applicants caused in many Internet recruiting efforts. A related concern is that many individuals who access job sites are just browsers who may submit resumes just to see what happens, but who are not seriously looking for new jobs.

Another issue with Internet recruiting is that applicants may have limited Internet access, especially individuals from lower socioeconomic groups and certain racial/ethnic minority groups. Consequently, employers using Internet recruiting may not be reaching as diverse a recruitment pool as might be desired. Even in the face of these disadvantages, it is likely that Internet recruiting will continue to grow in usage. Employers and job seekers alike are seeing e-recruiting as a major part of external recruiting.

External Recruiting

Many different external sources are available for recruiting. In some tight labor markets multiple sources and methods may be used to attract candidates for the variety of jobs available in organizations. Some of the more prominent methods are highlighted next.

College and University Recruiting

At the college or university level, the recruitment of students is a significant source for entry-level professional and technical employees. Most colleges and universities maintain career placement offices in which employers and applicants can meet.

The major determinants affecting an employer's selection of colleges and universities at which to conduct interviews are:

- Current and anticipated job openings
- College reputation
- Experiences with placement offices and previous graduates
- Organizational budget constraints
- Cost of available talent and typical salaries
- Market competition

College recruiting can be expensive; therefore, an organization should determine if the jobs it is trying to fill really require persons with college degrees. A great many jobs do not; yet many employers insist on filling them with college graduates. The result may be employees who must be paid more and who are likely to leave if the jobs are not sufficiently challenging.

School Recruiting

High schools or vocational/technical schools may be a good source of new employees for some organizations. Many schools have a centralized guidance or placement office. Promotional brochures that acquaint students with starting jobs and career opportunities can be distributed to counselors, librarians, or others. Participating in career days and giving tours of the company to school groups are other ways of maintaining good contact with school sources. Cooperative programs in which students work part-time and receive some school credits also may be useful in generating qualified future applicants for full-time positions.

Labor Unions

Labor unions are a source of certain types of workers. In some industries, such as construction, unions have traditionally supplied workers to employers. A labor pool is generally available through a union, and workers can be dispatched to particular jobs to meet the needs of the employers.

In some instances, the union can control or influence recruiting and staffing needs. An organization with a strong union may have less flexibility than a nonunion company in deciding who will be hired and where that person will be placed. Unions also can work to an employer's advantage through apprenticeship and cooperative staffing programs, as they do in the building and printing industries.

Employment Agencies and Search Firms

Every state in the United States has its own state-sponsored employment agency. These agencies operate branch offices in many cities throughout the states and do not charge fees to applicants or employers.

Private employment agencies also operate in most cities. For a fee collected from either the employee or the employer, these agencies do some preliminary screening and put the organization in touch with applicants. Private employment agencies differ considerably in the level of service, costs, policies, and types of applicants they provide. Employers can reduce the range of possible problems from these sources by giving complete job descriptions and specifications on jobs to be filled.

Some employment agencies focus their efforts on executive, managerial, and professional positions. These executive search firms are split into two groups: (1) contingency firms that charge a fee only after a candidate has been hired by a client company, and (2) retainer firms that charge a client a set fee whether or not the contracted search is successful. Most of the larger firms work on a retainer basis.

Competitive Sources

Other sources for recruiting include professional and trade associations, trade publications, and competitors. Many professional societies and trade associations publish newsletters or magazines and have Web sites containing job ads. Such sources may be useful for recruiting specialized professionals needed in an industry.

Some employers have extended recruiting to customers. Customers at these firms can receive application blanks, apply on-line using in-store kiosks, or schedule interviews with managers or HR staff members while in the stores. Other firms have included employment announcements when sending out customer bills or newsletters.

Media Sources

Media sources such as newspapers, magazines, television, radio, and billboards are widely used. Some firms have used direct mail by purchasing lists of individuals in certain fields or industries. Whatever medium is used, it should be tied to the relevant labor market and provide sufficient information on the company and the job. Exhibit 500.31 shows information a good recruiting advertisement should include. Notice that desired qualifications, details on the job and application process, and an overview of the organization are all important.

Job Fairs and Special Events

Employers in tight labor markets or needing to fill a large number of jobs quickly have used job fairs and special recruiting events. Job fairs also have been held by economic development entities, employer associations, HR associations, and other community groups in order to assist bringing employers and potential job candidates together. One

Exhibit 500.31 *What to Include in an Effective Recruiting Ad*

EMPLOYMENT OPPORTUNITY

Information on the Job and Process of Application

- Job title and responsibilities
- Location of job
- Starting pay range
- Closing date for application
- Whether or not to submit a résumé and cover letter
- Whether calls are invited
- Where to mail application or résumé

Candidate Desired Qualifications

- Years of experience
- Three to five key characteristics of successful candidates

Information About the Organization

- That it is an EEO employer
- Its primary business

cautionary note: Some employers at this and other job fairs may see current employees "shopping" for jobs at other employers.

Some firms also establish special events such as open houses, sponsor community events at which recruiters try to obtain applications from attendees, and use other means to recruit individuals. For instance, "drive-through" job fairs at shopping malls have been used by employers in a number of communities. At one such job fair, interested persons can drive up to a tent outside the mall and pick up applications from a "menu board" of employers, then park and interview in the tent with recruiters if time allows.

Creative Recruiting Methods

In tight labor markets and industries with significant shortages of qualified applicants, employers turn to more creative recruiting methods. Regardless of the methods used, the goal is to generate a pool of qualified applicants so that the jobs in organizations are filled in a timely manner. Some methods may be more effective at recruiting for certain jobs than others. To illustrate, some examples include the following:

- Using a plane towing an advertising banner over beach areas
- Advertising jobs on local movie theater screens as part of the pre-show entertainment
- Holding raffles for employees who refer candidates, with cars and trips being prizes
- Offering free rock concert tickets to the first 20 applicants hired
- Setting up recruiting tables at bowling alleys, minor league baseball games, or stock car races
- Recruiting younger technical employees at video game parlors
- Sponsoring book fairs in order to recruit publishing company sales representatives
- As part of U.S. military recruiting, employers guarantee enlistees jobs after completing military service
- Parking motor homes—all set up for interviews, testing, and hiring—in parking lots at the malls with signs saying, "Want a job? Apply here."

Recruiting Evaluation

In order to determine how effective various recruiting sources and methods have been, it is important to evaluate recruiting efforts. The primary way to find out whether recruiting efforts are cost effective is to conduct formal analyses as part of recruiting evaluation.

Evaluating Recruiting Costs and Benefits

Because recruiting activities are important, the costs and benefits associated with them should be analyzed. When doing a cost-benefit analysis to evaluate recruiting efforts, costs may include both direct costs (advertising, recruiters' salaries, travel, agency fees, telephone) and the indirect costs (involvement of operating managers, public relations, image). Cost-benefit information on each recruiting source can be calculated. Comparing the length of time applicants from each source stay in the organization with the cost of hiring from that source offers a useful perspective also.

Evaluating Time Required to Fill Openings

The length of time it takes to fill openings is one of the most common means of evaluating recruiting efforts. If openings are not filled quickly with qualified candidates, the work and productivity of the organization likely suffer. Generally speaking, it is useful to calculate the average amount of time it takes from contact to hire for each source of applicants, because some sources may produce recruits faster than others.

Evaluating Recruiting Quantity and Quality

As additional means of evaluating recruiting, organizations can see how their recruiting efforts compare with past patterns and with the recruiting performance of other organizations. Certain measures of recruiting effectiveness are quite useful in indicating whether sufficient numbers of the targeted applicant population group are being attracted. Information on job performance, absenteeism, cost of training, and turnover by recruiting source helps to adjust future recruiting. For example, some companies find that recruiting at certain colleges or universities furnishes stable, high performers, whereas other schools provide employees who are more prone to leave the organization. General areas for evaluating recruiting include the following:

- *Quantity of applicants:* Because the goal of a good recruiting program is to generate a large pool of applicants from which to choose, quantity is a natural place to begin evaluation. Is it sufficient to fill job vacancies?
- *EEO goals met:* The recruiting program is the key activity used to meet goals for hiring protected-class individuals. It is especially relevant when a company is engaged in affirmative action to meet such goals. Does recruiting provide qualified applicants with an appropriate mix of protected-class individuals?
- *Quality of applicants:* In addition to quantity, the issue arises as to whether or not the qualifications of the applicant pool are sufficient to fill the job openings. Do the applicants meet job specifications, and do they perform the jobs well after hire?

YIELD RATIOS One means for evaluating recruiting efforts is to determine **yield ratios,** which compare the number of applicants at one stage of the recruiting process to the number at another stage. The result is a tool for approximating the necessary size of the initial applicant pool. It is useful to visualize the yield ratios as a pyramid, whereby the employer starts with a broad base of applicants that progressively narrows. As Exhibit 500.32 depicts, to end up with 5 hires for the job in question, the company must begin with 100 applicants in the pool, as long as yield ratios remain as shown.

Yield ratios A comparison of the number of applicants at one stage of the recruiting process to the number at the next stage.

A different approach to using yield ratios suggests that over time, organizations can develop ranges for crucial ratios. When a given indicator ratio falls outside that range, it may indicate problems in the recruiting process. For example, in college recruiting the following ratios might be useful:

$$\frac{\text{College seniors given second interview}}{\text{Total number of seniors interviewed}} = \text{Range of 30–50\%}$$

$$\frac{\text{Number who accept offer}}{\text{Number invited to the company to visit}} = \text{Range of 50–70\%}$$

$$\frac{\text{Number who were hired}}{\text{Number offered a job}} = \text{Range of 70–80\%}$$

$$\frac{\text{Number finally hired}}{\text{Total number interviewed on campus}} = \text{Range of 10–20\%}$$

SELECTION RATE Another useful calculation is to determine the **selection rate,** which is the percentage hired from a given group of candidates. It equals the number hired divided by the number of applicants; for example, a rate of 30 percent would indicate that 3 out of 10 applicants were hired. The percentage typically

Selection rate The percentage hired from a given group of candidates.

Exhibit 500.32 *Recruiting Evaluation Pyramid*

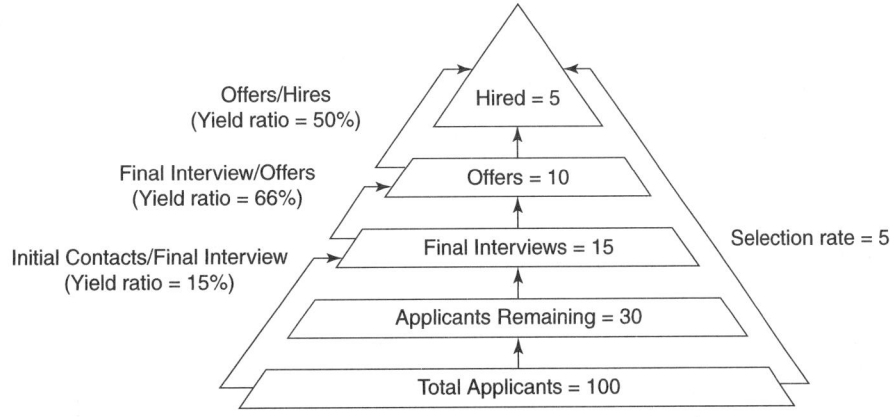

goes down as unemployment rates in the job market decrease, because fewer qualified candidates typically are available. The selection rate is also affected by the validity of the selection process. A relatively unsophisticated selection program might pick 8 out of 10 applicants for the job. Four of those might turn out to be good employees. A more valid selection process might pick 5 out of 10 applicants but all perform well.

ACCEPTANCE RATE Calculating the acceptance rate helps identify how successful the organization is at hiring the candidates that it wants to employ. After going through all the effort to screen, interview, and make job offers, hopefully most candidates accept job offers. If not, then HR might want to look at reasons why managers and HR staff cannot "close the deal." It is common for HR staff members to track the reasons candidates turn down job offers, the rejection rate, in order to learn how competitive the employer is compared with other employers and what factors are causing candidates to choose employment elsewhere.

SUCCESS BASE RATE A longer-term measure of recruiting effectiveness is to track the success rate of applicants. This rate indicates whether the quality of the employees hired results in employees who perform well and have low turnover. For example, assume that if 10 people were hired at random, one would expect four of them to be good employees. Thus, a successful recruiting program should be aimed at attracting the 4 in 10 who are capable of doing well on this particular job. Realistically, no recruiting program will attract only the 4 in 10 who will succeed. However, efforts to make the recruiting program attract the largest proportion of those in the base rate group can make recruiting efforts more effective.

The success base rate can be determined by comparing the number of past applicants who have become successful employees using historical data within the organization. Also, it can be compared to the success rates of other employers in the area or industry using benchmarking data.

Increasing Recruiting Effectiveness

The efforts to evaluate recruiting should be used to make recruiting activities more effective. Using the data to target different applicant pools, tap broader labor markets, utilize different recruiting methods, improve internal handling and interviewing of applicants, and train recruiters and managers all can increase recruiting effectiveness. Other beneficial activities include:

- *Applicant tracking systems* to collect data on applicants and provide various analyses.[55]
- *Realistic job previews* that provide job candidates with accurate details about the organization and the job.
- *Responsive recruitment process* in which applicants receive timely responses, get feedback on the process when promised, and are treated with consideration.

Another key way to increase recruiting effectiveness rests on the recruiters themselves. The reactions of candidates to those involved in the recruiting process can turn off recruits or create excitement. A number of studies on the reactions of applicants to recruiters has revealed that recruiters who are knowledgeable about the jobs and their employers and who treat applicants with respect and enthusiasm are viewed more positively.[56] This positive image is more likely to result in more applicants pursuing employment opportunities with an employer, which is vital in the labor markets faced by many organizations today.

Selecting and Placing Human Resources

Selection decisions are an important part of successful HR management. Some even would argue that these decisions are the most important part. Organizational performance improvement for an employer may come from changes in incentive pay plans, improved training, or better job design; but unless the employer begins with the necessary people with the appropriate capabilities in place, those results may not occur.

Selection and Placement

Selection is the process of choosing individuals who have needed qualifications to fill jobs in an organization. Without qualified employees, an organization is less likely to succeed. Organizations on average reject a high percentage of applicants. In some situations about five out of six applicants for jobs are rejected. Perhaps the best perspective on selection and placement comes from two HR truisms that clearly identify the importance of effective employment selection.

- *"Good training will not make up for bad selection."* When the right people with the appropriate capabilities are not selected for jobs, employers have difficulty later trying to train those individuals.
- *"Hire hard, manage easy."* The amount of time and effort spent in selecting the right people for jobs may make managing them as employees much less difficult because more problems will be eliminated.

Selection Responsibilities

Organizations vary in how they allocate selection responsibilities between HR specialists and operating managers. Until the impact of EEO regulations became widespread, selection often was carried out in an unplanned manner in many organizations. The need to meet EEO requirements has forced organizations to plan better in this regard. Still, in some organizations, each department screens and hires its own employees. Many managers insist on selecting their own people because they are sure no one else can choose employees for them as well as they can themselves. This practice is particularly prevalent in smaller firms. But the validity and fairness of such an approach may be questionable.

Other organizations have the HR unit do the initial screening of the candidates, while managers or supervisors make the final selection. As a rule, the higher the position being filled, the greater the likelihood that the ultimate hiring decisions will be made by operating managers rather than HR specialists. Typical selection responsibilities are shown in Exhibit 500.33.

Selection responsibilities are affected by the existence of a central employment office, which usually is part of an HR department. In smaller organizations, especially in those with fewer than 100 employees, a full-time employment specialist or unit may be impractical. But for larger employers, centralizing employment within one unit may be appropriate for several reasons:

- It is easier for applicants to have only one place in which to apply for jobs.
- Contact with outside applicant sources is easier because those contacts can be handled through one central location.
- Managers can concentrate on their operating responsibilities rather than on time-consuming interviewing and selection efforts.
- Selection costs may be cut by avoiding duplication of effort.
- People well-trained in EEO regulations handle a major part of the process to reduce future lawsuits and the costs associated with them.

The employment function in any organization may be concerned with some or all of the following activities: (1) receiving applications, (2) interviewing applicants, (3) administering tests to applicants, (4) conducting background investigations, (5) arranging for physical examinations, (6) placing and assigning new employees, (7) coordinating follow-up of these employees, (8) exit interviewing of departing employees, and (9) maintaining appropriate records and reports.

Exhibit 500.33 *Typical Division of HR Responsibilities: Selection*

HR Unit	Managers
• Provides initial reception for applicants	• Requisition employees with specific qualifications to fill jobs
• Conducts initial screening interview	
• Administers appropriate employment tests	• Participate in selection process as appropriate
• Obtains background and reference information and arranges for the employment physical examination, if used	• Interview final candidates
	• Make final selection decision, subject to advice of HR specialists
• Refers top candidates to managers for final selection	• Provide follow-up information on the suitability of selected individuals
• Evaluates success of selection process	

530. STAFFING, DEVELOPMENT, AND EMPLOYMENT PRACTICES

Placement

The ultimate purpose of selection is **placement,** or fitting a person to the right job. More than anything else, placement of human resources should be seen as a matching process. How well an employee is matched to a job affects the amount and quality of the employee's work. This matching also directly affects training and operating costs. Individuals who are unable to produce the expected amount and quality of work can cost an organization a great deal of money and time.

PERSON-JOB FIT Selection and placement entail much more than just choosing the best available person. Selecting the appropriate capabilities and talents—which come packaged in a human being—attempts to "fit" what the applicant can and wants to do with what the organization needs. The task is further complicated by the difficulty in discerning exactly what the applicant really can and wants to do, as well as other intangible factors that may affect the fit.

Person-job fit Matching the KSAs of people with the characteristics of jobs.

Selection and placement activities typically focus on applicants' knowledge, skills, and abilities (KSAs). The **person-job fit** is a simple but important concept that involves matching the KSAs of people with the characteristics of jobs. Obviously, without a good fit between the KSAs of the person and the demands of the job, the likelihood of lower employee performance, higher turnover and absenteeism, and other HR problems increases. Much of selection is concerned with gathering needed information on the applicants' KSAs through application forms, resumes, interviews, tests, and other means.

Having the needed KSAs is important for an employee to do a job well. Specific KSAs may be used to hire people for a given job: math skills, ability to weld, or a knowledge of spreadsheets. Job analysis can provide the basis for identifying KSAs needed in a job if it is done properly. People already in jobs can help identify the most important KSAs for success as part of job analysis. This is suitable especially in the following placement situations:

- KSAs brought to jobs are more critical than what is learned on the jobs.
- Jobs change infrequently and employees are closely monitored against well-established performance standards.
- The needed KSAs are observable, clearly identified, and closely linked to task performance on the jobs.

Person-organization fit The congruence between individuals and organizational factors.

PERSON-ORGANIZATION FIT In addition to matching individuals to jobs, employers also increasingly try to determine the congruence between individuals and organizational factors to achieve **person-organization fit,** as Exhibit 500.34 depicts.

Person-organization fit is important when general factors of job success are as important as specific KSAs. For example, if an employer hires at the entry level and promotes from within for most jobs, specific KSAs might be less important than general cognitive and problem-solving abilities and work ethic. Ability to learn allows a person to grasp new information and make good decisions based on that job knowledge. Work ethic

Exhibit 500.34 *Person-Organization Fit*

might include thoroughness, responsibility, and an organized approach to the job. Person-organization fit is used in the following placement situations:

- Organization culture is unique and teamwork is highly valued.
- Employees work independently and have considerable judgment and discretion in doing their work.
- Most KSAs can be learned on the job if the person has basic cognitive abilities, work ethic, and other capabilities.
- Jobs and the organization change often and employee adaptability and creativity are expected.

Determining person-organization fit may require use of multiple selection means and take considerable time and effort. Multiple in-depth interviews; use of extensive ability, aptitude, and psychological tests; and involvement of several levels of managers and employees are just some ways of ensuring person-organization fit.[57]

Criteria, Predictors, and Job Performance

Whether an employer uses specific KSAs or the more general approach, effective selection of employees involves using criteria and predictors of job performance. At the heart of an effective selection system is knowledge of what constitutes appropriate job performance and what employee characteristics are associated with that performance. First, an employer defines employee success (performance) and then, using that definition as a basis, determines the employee specifications required to achieve success. A **selection criterion** is a characteristic that a person must have to do the job successfully. A preexisting ability is often a selection criterion. Exhibit 500.35 shows that ability, motivation, intelligence, conscientiousness, appropriate risk, and permanence might be good selection criteria for many jobs.

> **Selection criterion** Characteristic that a person must have to do a job successfully.

To predict whether a selection criterion (such as "motivation" or "ability") is present, employers try to identify predictors as measurable indicators of selection criteria. For example, in Exhibit 500.35 three good predictors for some criteria might be individual interests, salary requirements, and tenure on previous jobs.

The information gathered about an applicant should be focused on finding predictors of the likelihood that the applicant will be able to perform the job well. Predictors can take many forms, but any selection tool used (for example, application form, test, interview, education requirements, or years of experience required) should be used only if it is a valid predictor of job performance. Using invalid predictors can result in selecting the "wrong" candidate and rejecting the "right" one. Validity and reliability of a predictor are important.

VALIDITY In selection, validity is the correlation between a predictor and job performance. Validity occurs to the extent that a predictor actually predicts what it is supposed to predict. Validity depends on the situation in which the selection device is being used. For example, a psychological test designed to predict aptitude for child-care jobs might not be valid in predicting sales aptitudes for marketing representative jobs.

Exhibit 500.35 *Job Performance, Selection Criteria, and Predictors*

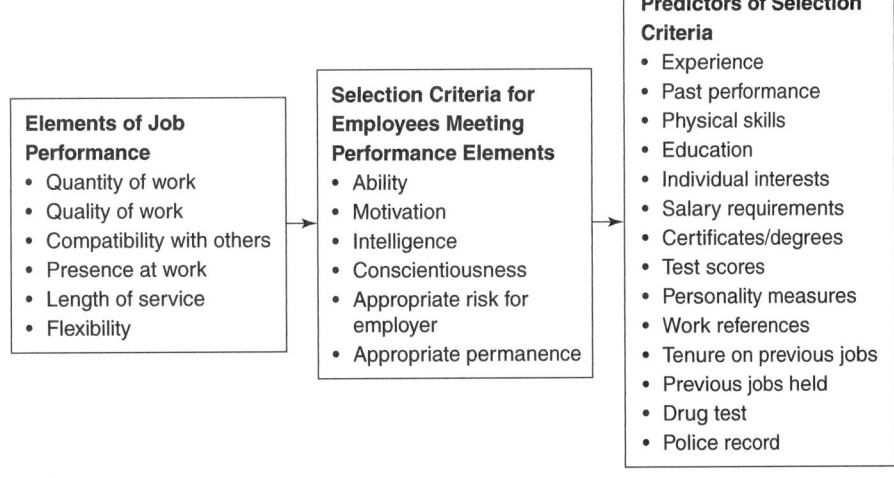

RELIABILITY   Reliability of a predictor is the extent to which it repeatedly produces the same results, over time. For example, if the same person took a test in December and scored 75, but upon taking it in March scored significantly higher, the test may not be reliable. Thus, reliability has to do with the consistency of predictors in selection.

Combining Predictors

If an employer chooses to use only one predictor (for example, a test) to select who will be hired, the decision is straightforward. If the test is valid and encompasses a major dimension of a job, and the applicant does well on the test, he or she can be hired. In this single-predictor approach, selection accuracy depends on how valid that single predictor is at predicting performance.

When using several predictors, all must be met. For example, when requiring three years of experience, having a college degree, and attaining a certain score on an aptitude test, qualified candidates are those who possess all of those criteria.

When using more than one predictor, they must be combined in some way.[58] Two different approaches for combining predictors are:

- *Multiple hurdles:* A minimum cutoff is set on each predictor, and each minimum level must be "passed." For example, in order to be hired a candidate for a sales representative job must achieve a minimum education level, a certain score on a sales aptitude test, and a minimum score on a structured interview.
- *Compensatory approach:* In this approach, scores from individual predictors are added together and combined into an overall score, thus allowing a higher score on one predictor to offset or compensate for a lower score on another. The combined index takes into consideration performance on all predictors.

The Selection Process

Most organizations take steps to process applicants for jobs. Variations on the basic process depend on organizational size, nature of jobs to be filled, number of people to be selected, the use of electronic technology, and other factors. This process can take place in a day or over a much longer period of time. If the applicant is processed in one day, the employer usually checks references after selection. One or more phases of the process may be omitted or the order changed, depending on the employer. Exhibit 500.36 represents a selection process typical in many organizations.

Legal Concerns in the Selection Process

Selection is subject to a number of legal concerns, especially all the equal employment opportunity (EEO) regulations and laws. Throughout the selection process, application forms, interviews, tests, background investigations, and any other selection activities must be conducted in a nondiscriminatory manner. Also, applicants not hired should be rejected only for job-related reasons, not based on protected-class or personal factors, which are illegal. Several means are used to narrow who is defined as an applicant, not just someone expressing interest in employment. Common ones are shown in Exhibit 500.37.

Exhibit 500.36   *Selection Process Flowchart*

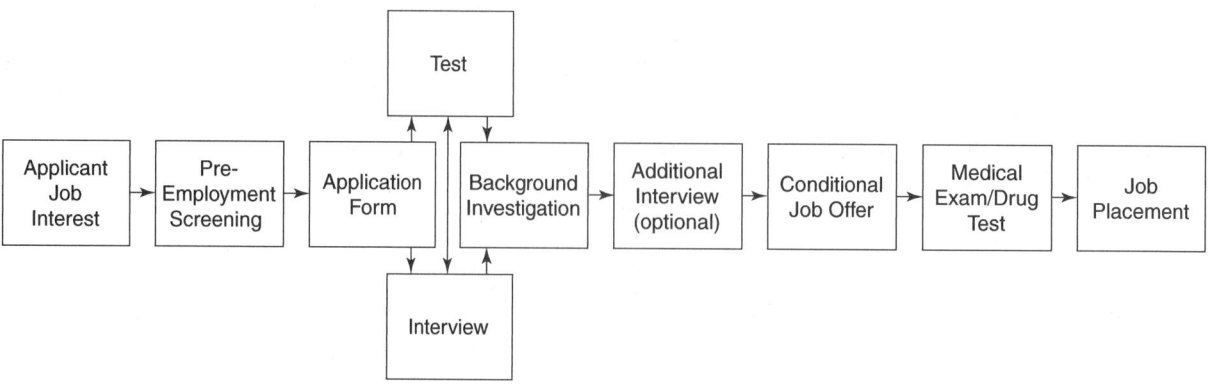

Exhibit 500.37 *Limiting Who Becomes an Applicant*

REALISTIC JOB PREVIEWS Most job seekers appear to know little about organizations prior to applying for jobs. Consequently, job seekers tend to give considerable weight to the information received from prospective employers in the recruiting/selection process when making decisions of whether or not to accept jobs. For applicants, information on pay, nature of the work, geographic location, and opportunity for promotion is useful. Unfortunately, some employers oversell their jobs in recruiting advertisements, making them appear better than they really are.

Through the process of a **realistic job preview (RJP)**, job applicants are provided with an accurate picture of a job, including the "organizational realities" of a job, so that applicants can more accurately evaluate their own job expectations. With an RJP, the organization hopes to prevent unrealistic expectations, which helps reduce employee disenchantment and ultimately employee dissatisfaction and turnover. A review of research on RJPs found that they tend to be effective in that regard.[59]

Realistic job preview (RJP) The process through which a job applicant receives an accurate picture of a job.

Pre-Employment Screening

Many employers conduct pre-employment screening in order to determine if applicants meet the minimum qualifications for open jobs. For example, one firm that hires security guards and armored-car drivers uses a prescreening interview to verify whether an applicant meets the minimum qualifications of having a valid driver's license, being free of any criminal convictions in the past seven years, and having been trained to use a pistol. Because these minimum standards are required, it would be a waste of time for any applicant who could not meet them to fill out an application form. Other areas typically covered by other employers include types of available jobs, applicants' pay expectations, job location, and travel requirements. Electronic screening can be done as well.

Regardless of the electronic pre-employment systems used, the screening analyses must be job-related, without using age, gender, or other data as screening criteria. Otherwise, potential illegal discrimination complaints could not be defended well.

Application Forms

Application forms are widely used and can take many different formats. Properly prepared, the application form serves four purposes:

- It is a record of the applicant's desire to obtain a position.
- It provides the interviewer with a profile of the applicant that can be used in the interview.
- It is a basic employee record for applicants who are hired.
- It can be used for research on the effectiveness of the selection process.

Many employers use only one application form, but others need several. For example, a hospital might need one form for nurses and medical technicians, another form for clerical and office employees, another for managers and supervisors, and another for support persons in housekeeping and food-service areas.

Application forms need disclaimers and notices so that appropriate legal protections are stated by employers. Recommended disclosures, disclaimers, and notices appearing on applications include:

- *Employment-at-will:* Indicates the right of the employer or applicant to terminate the employment relationship at any time with or without notice or cause (where applicable by state law).
- *Reference contacts:* Requests permission to contact references listed by applicants.
- *Employment testing:* Notifies applicants of required drug tests, physical exams, or other tests.

- *Application time limit:* Indicates how long applications are active (typically six months) and that individuals must reactivate applications after that period.
- *Information falsification:* Conveys to an applicant signing the form that falsification of application information is grounds for termination.

Other application information includes: immigration forms, EEO considerations, résumés that serve as applications, and biodata and weighted application forms.

A number of federal, state, and local governmental employers rate training and experience on applications and résumés. The submitted applications and résumés are examined using checklists, and candidates are ranked using the results in order to determine those to be interviewed or tested.

Selection Testing

According to the Uniform Selection Guidelines issued by the EEOC, any employment requirement is a "test." The focus in this section is on specific tests because a number of employers feel that formal tests can be of great benefit in the selection process when properly used and administered. One survey showed that 69 percent of employers use some type of pre-employment testing. Most entry-level applicants (92 percent) are tested in some way, but just one half of all executives receive some types of testing.[60]

Ability Tests

Tests that assess an individual's ability to perform in a specific manner are grouped as ability tests. Sometimes further differentiated into *aptitude* and *achievement* tests, each of the several types of ability tests is briefly examined next.

Cognitive ability tests Tests that measure an individual's thinking, memory, reasoning, and verbal and mathematical abilities.

Cognitive ability tests measure an individual's thinking, memory, reasoning, and verbal and mathematical abilities. Tests such as these can be used to test applicants' basic knowledge of terminology and concepts, word fluency, spatial orientation, comprehension and retention span, and general and conceptual reasoning. The Wonderlic Personnel Test and the General Aptitude Test Battery (GATB) are two widely used tests of this type. The important consideration when using cognitive ability tests is to ensure that the cognitive concepts tested are clearly job-related. For example, giving a sales clerk applicant a basic mathematics test may be useful to determine the individual's ability to make change and determine customers' bills when both purchases and returns are being handled.

Physical ability tests Tests that measure individual abilities such as strength, endurance, and muscular movement.

Physical ability tests measure individual abilities such as strength, endurance, and muscular movement. At an electric utility, line workers regularly must lift and carry equipment, climb ladders, and perform other physical tasks. Testing applicants' mobility, strength, and other physical attributes is job-related. A type of physical ability test, *functional capacity testing,* measures such areas as range of motion, strength and posture, cardiovascular fitness, and other facets.[61] Care should be taken to limit physical ability testing until after a conditional job offer is made in order to avoid violating the provisions of the Americans with Disabilities Act (ADA).

Psychomotor tests Tests that measure dexterity, hand-eye coordination, arm-hand steadiness, and other factors.

Work sample tests Tests that require an applicant to perform a simulated job task.

Different skill-based tests can be used, including **psychomotor tests** that measure a person's dexterity, hand-eye coordination, arm-hand steadiness, and other factors. Such tests as the MacQuarie Test for Mechanical Ability can measure manual dexterity for assembly-line workers and others regularly using psychomotor skills.

Many organizations use situational or **work sample tests,** which require an applicant to perform a simulated job task that is part of the target job. Having an applicant for a financial analyst's job prepare a computer spreadsheet is one such test. Requiring a person applying for a truck driver's job to back a truck to a loading dock is another. An "in-basket" test is a work sample test in which a job candidate is asked to respond to memos in a hypothetical in-basket that are typical of the problems faced by people holding that job. The key for any work sample test is the behavioral consistency between the criteria of the job and the requirements for the test.

Managerial Tests

An assessment center is composed of a series of evaluative exercises and tests used for selection and development. Most often used in the selection process when filling managerial openings, an assessment center uses multiple exercises and multiple raters. In one assessment center, candidates go through a comprehensive interview, pencil-and-paper test, individual and group simulations, and work exercises (work sample tests). The candidates' performances are then evaluated by a panel of trained raters. It is crucial to any assessment center that the tests and exercises reflect the job content and types of problems faced on the jobs for which individuals are being screened.

Personality Tests

Personality is a unique blend of individual characteristics that affect interaction with the environment and help define a person. Of the many different types of personality tests, one of the most widely known and used is the Minnesota Multiphasic Personality Inventory (MMPI). It was originally developed to diagnose major psychological disorders and has become widely used as a selection test. From this and many other personality tests, an extensive number of personality characteristics can be identified and used. The Myers-Briggs test is another widely used test of this type.

The multitude of different personality traits has long frustrated psychologists, who have argued that there is a relatively small number of underlying *major* traits. The most widely accepted approach to these underlying personality traits (although not the only one) is often referred to as the "Big Five" personality traits. The Big Five that can be considered generally useful predictors of training success and job performance are shown in Exhibit 500.38.

Of the Big Five, conscientiousness has been found to be related to job success across most organizations and occupations. Extroversion has been found to predict success in jobs requiring social interaction, such as many sales jobs. The usefulness of the other three varies depending on the kind of jobs and organizations. When used in selection, psychological or personality testing requires that a solid job-related link be made.

Honesty/Integrity Testing

Different types of tests are being used by employers to assess the honesty and integrity of applicants and employees. They include standardized honesty/integrity tests and polygraphs. Both are controversial.

Exhibit 500.38 *Big Five Personality Characteristics*

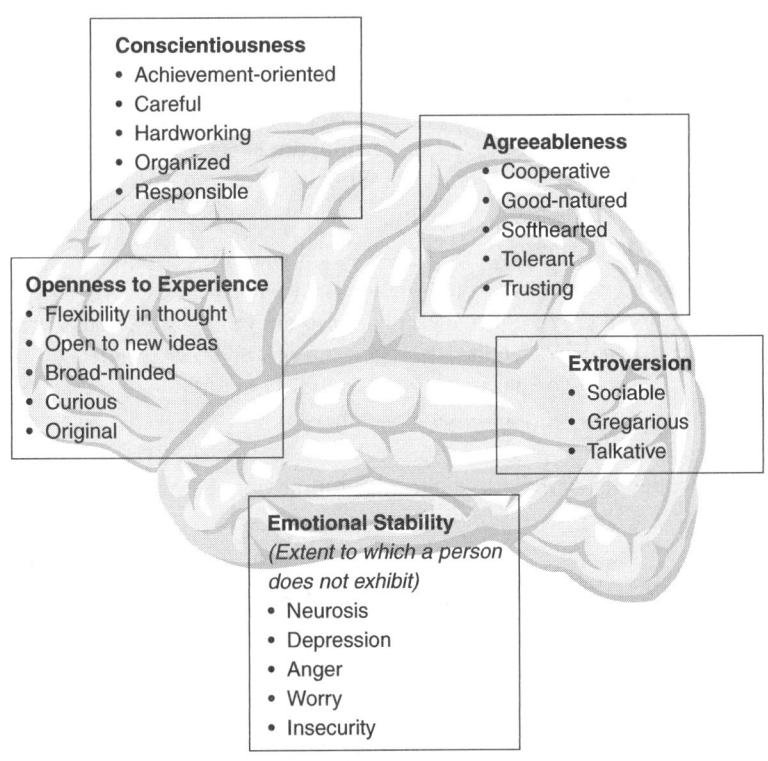

Employers use these tests for several reasons. Firms such as retailers use honesty tests to screen out potentially dishonest individuals and decrease the incidence of employee theft. These firms believe that giving honesty tests not only helps them to screen out potentially dishonest individuals, but also sends a message to applicants and employees alike that dishonesty will not be tolerated.

Two types of tests assess honesty and integrity of individuals. *Overt integrity tests* inquire specifically about individual honesty and attitudes and behavior regarding theft. Samples of such overt questions on some of these tests might include:

- Would you tell your boss if you knew another employee was stealing from the company?
- Is it okay to borrow company equipment to use at home if the property is always returned?
- Have you ever told a lie?
- Have you ever wished you were physically more attractive?

The other type, *personality-oriented integrity* tests, uses psychological concepts such as dependability, respect for authority, and others. Analyses of these dimensions are used to identify individuals whose psychological "profile" indicates greater or lesser integrity orientations.

Honesty/integrity tests may be valid as broad screening devices for organizations if used properly. However, it is important that the tests be chosen, used, and evaluated to ensure that they are and remain valid and reliable. They should be used as one piece of the selection process along with applications, interviews, and other data.[62] One documented concern about integrity tests is the "fake-ability" of the tests. Research indicates that the ability of the test takers to "fake" honesty and pass integrity tests is higher with overt tests than personality tests.[63] Also, the use of these tests can have a negative public relations impact on applicants. A final concern is that the types of questions asked may constitute invasion of individual privacy.

POLYGRAPHS AND THE EMPLOYEE POLYGRAPH PROTECTION ACT The polygraph, more generally and incorrectly referred to as the "lie detector," is a mechanical device that measures a person's galvanic skin response, heart rate, and breathing rate. The theory behind the polygraph is that if a person answers incorrectly, the body's physiological responses will "reveal" the falsification through the polygraph's recording mechanisms. As a result of concerns, Congress passed the Employee Polygraph Protection Act, which prohibits polygraph use for pre-employment screening purposes by most employers. However, federal, state, and local government agencies are exempt from the act. Also exempted are certain private-sector employers such as security companies and pharmaceutical companies. The act does allow employers to continue to use polygraphs as part of internal investigations of theft or losses. But the polygraph test should be taken voluntarily, and the employee should be allowed to end the test at any time.

Controversial and Questionable Tests

Some questionable tests sometimes are used in employee selection. But experts warn of the legal and ethical problems in using these techniques for employee selection. For instance, graphology and psychics have been used by various employers.

- *Graphology* (handwriting analysis): This type of "test" uses an "analysis" of an individual's handwriting. Such characteristics as how people dot an *i* or cross a *t*, whether they write with a left or right slant, and the size and boldness of the letters they form supposedly tell graphologists about the individuals' personalities and their suitability for employment. It is popular in France, Israel, and several other countries, but is used on a limited basis in the United States. However, formal scientific evaluations of graphology are not easily found. Its value as a personality predictor is somewhat questionable and may not be easily validated as job-related.
- *Psychics:* Similarly, some firms use psychics to help select managerial talent. The psychics are supposedly able to determine if a person is suited for a job both intellectually and emotionally. However, most businesses would not want anyone to know that they used "psychic advisers."

Testing Considerations and Concerns

Selection testing can provide useful insights on the abilities and characteristics of applicants that may not be determined through interviews or other means. Person-job fit can be enhanced through ability and other tests focusing on specific KSAs. Tests are particularly beneficial in obtaining information to determine person-organization fit, so that a good match occurs between applicants' values, expectations, and capabilities and organizational values, culture, and management issues.

However, testing must be used carefully and appropriately. Too often, tests are used for automatic disqualification or acceptance, rather than as additional information to be evaluated and compared with other sources of information such as interviews and background investigations. Also, concerns exist about the negative reactions that some applicants have to certain types of tests, such as honesty/integrity and personality tests. Depending upon the tests used, testing costs can be significant, which must be balanced with the consequences of making "bad hires." Finally, selection testing can and has raised legal concerns and liability for employers.

LEGAL CONCERNS AND SELECTION TESTING Employers must continue to emphasize that selection tests used must be job-related and nondiscriminatory to protected-class members. Several court cases have ruled that some tests used by employers, particularly psychological personality tests, are illegally discriminatory. In another case, a general knowledge test used by shipping firms and longshore unions was found to discriminate against minority applicants who applied for dock shipping jobs because the failure rates for Hispanic, Asian, and African American applicants was significantly higher.[64] In summary, the role of testing in the selection process must be kept in perspective because tests represent only one possible data source, and they must be used appropriately and legally.

Selection Interviewing

Selection interviewing of job applicants is done to both obtain additional information and to clarify information gathered throughout the selection process. Typically, interviews are conducted at two levels: first in the HR department as an initial interview, and then second as an in-depth interview often involving HR staff members and operating supervisors and managers in the departments where the individuals will work.

In both interviews, but particularly the in-depth interview, information from various sources is pulled together in order to identify conflicting information that may have emerged from tests, application forms, and references. As a result, the interviewer must obtain as much pertinent information about the applicant as possible during the limited interview time and evaluate this information against job standards.

An interviewer making a hiring recommendation must be able to identify the factors determining that decision. Lawyers recommend the following in order to minimize EEO concerns with interviewing:

- Identify objective criteria related to the job to be sought in the interview.
- Specify decision-making criteria used.
- Provide multiple levels of review for difficult or controversial decisions.
- Use structured interviews, with the same questions asked of all those interviewed for a specific job.

As Exhibit 500.39 shows, there are a number of different types of interviews. They range from the structured to unstructured and vary in terms of effectiveness. Each of the types is discussed next.

Exhibit 500.39 *Types of Selection Interviews*

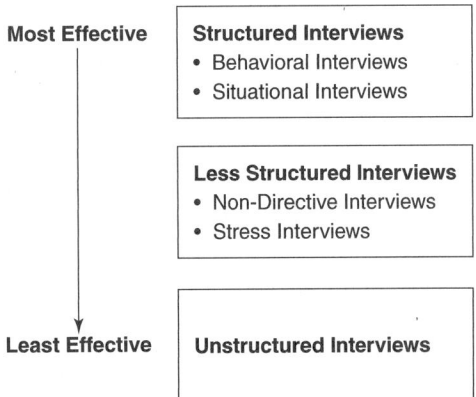

Structured Interviews

Structured interview Interview that uses a set of standardized questions asked of all job applicants.

A **structured interview** uses a set of standardized questions asked of all applicants. The interviewer asks every applicant the same basic questions, so that comparisons among applicants can more easily be made. This type of interview allows an interviewer to prepare job-related questions in advance and then complete a standardized interviewee evaluation form that provides documentation indicating why one applicant was selected over another. Sample questions that might be asked of all applicants for a retail sales clerk opening are as follows:

- I noticed on your application that you were previously employed with _____. How did you get a job there?
- Tell me about your responsibilities and duties with _____.
- Describe a time you were frustrated as a customer because of the way a store clerk treated you. What do you think should have been done?
- How many hours can you work a week without your school work and/or personal life being negatively affected?

The structured interview is especially useful in the initial screening because of the large number of applicants in this step of the selection process. Even for more in-depth interviews, the structured interview does not have to be rigid. The predetermined questions should be asked in a logical manner, but interviewers should avoid reading the questions word for word down the list. Also, the applicants should be allowed adequate opportunity to explain their answers, and each interviewer should probe until he or she fully understands applicants' responses.

Research on interviews consistently finds the structured interview to be more reliable and valid than other approaches.[65] This format for the interview ensures that a given interviewer has similar information on each candidate. Also, when several interviewers ask the same questions of applicants, there is greater consistency in the subsequent evaluation of candidates by different interviewers.

Behavioral interview Interview in which applicants give specific examples of how they have performed a certain task or handled a problem in the past.

BEHAVIORAL INTERVIEW More and more interviewers are using an experienced-based type of structured interview. In the **behavioral interview** applicants are asked to give specific examples of how they have performed a certain task or handled a problem in the past. The notion that past behaviors are good predictors of future actions provides the logic behind behavioral interviews. Learning about how candidates describe their previous behaviors helps determine which applicants may be best suited for current jobs.[66] For example, applicants might be asked the following questions:

- How did you handle a situation that had no rules or guidelines for employee discipline?
- Why did you choose that approach?
- How did your supervisor react?
- How was the situation finally resolved?

The results of behavioral interviews can be scored like any other type of structured interview using predetermined dimensions and then compared to interviewer judgments. Also, behavioral interviews generally provide better validity than general structured interviews or less structured methods.[67]

Situational interview A structured interview composed of questions about how applicants might handle specific job situations.

SITUATIONAL INTERVIEW The **situational interview** is a type of structured interview that is composed of questions about how applicants might handle specific job situations. Interview questions are based on job analysis and checked by experts in the job so they will be content valid. For some situational interviews, job experts also rate responses to the questions to facilitate ranking candidates. The interviewer can code the suitability of the answer, assign point values, and add up the total number of points an interviewee received. Some organizations also use creative interviewing tactics along with situational interviewing questions.

Less Structured and Unstructured Interviews

Unfortunately, too many interviews occur unplanned and without any structure. Often, these interviews are conducted by operating managers or supervisors who have had little training on interviewing do's and don'ts. The unstructured interview occurs when the interviewer "wings it," asking such questions as "Tell me about yourself," that have no direct purpose identified.

NONDIRECTIVE INTERVIEW The **nondirective interview** uses questions that are developed from the answers to previous questions. The interviewer asks general questions designed to prompt the applicant to discuss herself or himself. The interviewer then picks up on an idea in the applicant's response to shape the next question. For example, if the applicant says, "One aspect that I enjoyed in my last job was my supervisor," the interviewer might ask, "What type of supervisor do you most enjoy working with?"

> *Nondirective interview* Interview that uses questions that are developed from the answers to previous questions.

As with any less structured interview, difficulties with a nondirective interview include keeping it job related and obtaining comparable data on various applicants. Many nondirective interviews are only semiorganized; the result is that a combination of general and specific questions is asked in no set order, and different questions are asked of different applicants for the same job. Comparing and ranking candidates is more open to subjective judgments and legal challenges under this format.

STRESS INTERVIEW The **stress interview** is a special type of interview designed to create anxiety and put pressure on the applicant to see how the person responds. In a stress interview, the interviewer assumes an extremely aggressive and insulting posture. Those who use this approach often justify its use with individuals who will encounter high degrees of stress on the job, such as a consumer-complaint clerk in a department store or an air traffic controller.

> *Stress interview* Interview designed to create anxiety and put pressure on an applicant to see how the person responds.

However, the stress interview is a high-risk approach for an employer. The typical applicant is already somewhat anxious in any interview, and the stress interview can easily generate a poor image of the interviewer and the employer. Consequently, an applicant that the organization wishes to hire might turn down the job offer. Even so, many interviewers deliberately put applicants under stress.[68]

Who Does Interviews?

Interviews can be done individually, by several individuals in sequence, or by panels or teams of interviewers. For some jobs, such as entry-level, lesser skilled jobs, applicants are interviewed by an HR representative alone. Other jobs are filled using multiple interviews, beginning with an HR interviewer, followed by interviews conducted by appropriate supervisors and managers. Then a selection decision is made based on discussions by those who have conducted the interviews. When an interviewee must see several people, often many of the interviews are redundant and therefore unnecessarily time consuming.

In a **panel interview,** several interviewers interview the candidate at the same time. All the interviewers hear the same responses. For example, to select a new marketing manager in a distribution firm, three vice presidents interviewed the top two candidates after the vice president of sales had conducted individual interviews to identify the two finalists. On the negative side, without planning by the panel of interviewers, an unstructured interview can result. Also, applicants are frequently uncomfortable with the group interview format.

> *Panel interview* Interview in which several interviewers interview the candidate at the same time.
> *Team interview* Interview in which applicants are interviewed by the team members with whom they will work.

The prevalence of work teams has increased the use of **team interviews,** in which applicants are interviewed by the "team members" with whom they will work. To be successful, team members may be involved in selecting their co-workers. However, a good deal of training is required to make sure that teams understand the selection process, interviewing, and legal constraints. Further, a selection procedure in which the team votes for the top choice may be inappropriate; usually the decision should be made by consensus, which may take longer.

VIDEO INTERVIEWING A number of employers use video interviewing to augment or replace in-depth telephone interviews.[69] Applicants are asked to go to video conferencing facilities scheduled by the employer. At the designated time, the applicant and those conducting the interview are video linked. The greatest use of video interviewing is done by large corporations, executive recruiting firms, and colleges and university placement offices, who offer such facilities to aid both students and employers.[70]

Savings on time and travel costs are an advantage of video interviewing. Often, the video interviews are used to narrow a pool of candidates down to two or three finalists who then are interviewed in person. Video technology using the Internet and digital cameras presents additional interviewing options to employers as well.

Effective Interviewing

Many people think that the ability to interview is an innate talent, but this contention is difficult to support. Just because someone is personable and likes to talk is no guarantee that the person will be a good interviewer. Interviewing skills are developed through training. There have been a number of suggestions developed to make interviewing more effective. Several key ones commonly cited are as follows:

- *Planning the interview* is important. Interviewers should review pre-employment screening information, the application or resume, and the appropriate job description before beginning the interview and then identify specific areas for questioning during the interview.
- *Controlling the interview* includes knowing in advance what information must be collected, systematically collecting it, and stopping when that information has been collected. But, effective interviewers should talk no more than about 25 percent of the time in an in-depth interview.
- The *questioning techniques* an interviewer uses can and do significantly affect the type and quality of the information obtained.[71] Describe, who, what, when, why, tell me, how, and which are all good ways to begin questions that will produce longer and more informative answers. Exhibit 500.40 lists questions often used in selection interviews.

Certain kinds of questions should be avoided in selection interviews:

- *Yes/No questions:* Unless verifying specific information, it is best to avoid questions that can be answered "Yes" or "No." For example, "Did you have good attendance on your last job?" The answer will probably be "yes."
- *Obvious questions:* An obvious question is one for which the interviewer already has the answer and the applicant knows it.
- *Questions that rarely produce a true answer:* An example is, "How did you get along with your coworkers?" The likely answer is, "Just fine."
- *Leading questions:* A leading question is one to which the answer is obvious from the way that the question is asked. For example, "How do you like working with other people?" Answer: "I like it."
- *Illegal questions:* Questions that involve information such as race, age, gender, national origin, marital status, and number of children are illegal. They are just as inappropriate in the interview as on the application form.
- *Questions that are not job related:* All questions asked should be directly related to the job for which the interviewee has applied.

AVOID LISTENING RESPONSES Effective interviewers avoid listening responses, such as nodding, pausing, making casual remarks, echoing, and mirroring. A friendly but neutral demeanor is appropriate. Listening responses are an essential part of everyday, normal conversation, but they may unintentionally provide feedback to the applicant. Applicants may try to please interviewers and look to the interviewers' listening responses for cues. Even though the listening responses may be subtle, they do provide information to applicants.

However, by giving no response to applicants' answers, interviewers may present the appearance of boredom or inattention. Therefore, interviewers should make a neutral comment, acknowledge the response, or use a reply, such as "That is interesting and useful information."

Problems in the Interview

Operating managers and supervisors most often use poor interviewing techniques because they do not interview often or lack training. Some common problems encountered in the interview are highlighted next.

SNAP JUDGMENTS Unfortunately, many interviewers make a decision on the job suitability of applicants within the first two to four minutes of the interview and spend the balance of the interview looking for evidence to support it. This impression may be based on a review of an individual's application blank or on more subjective factors such as dress or appearance. Ideally, the interviewer should collect all the information possible on an applicant before making a judgment.

Exhibit 500.40 *Common Selection Interview Questions*

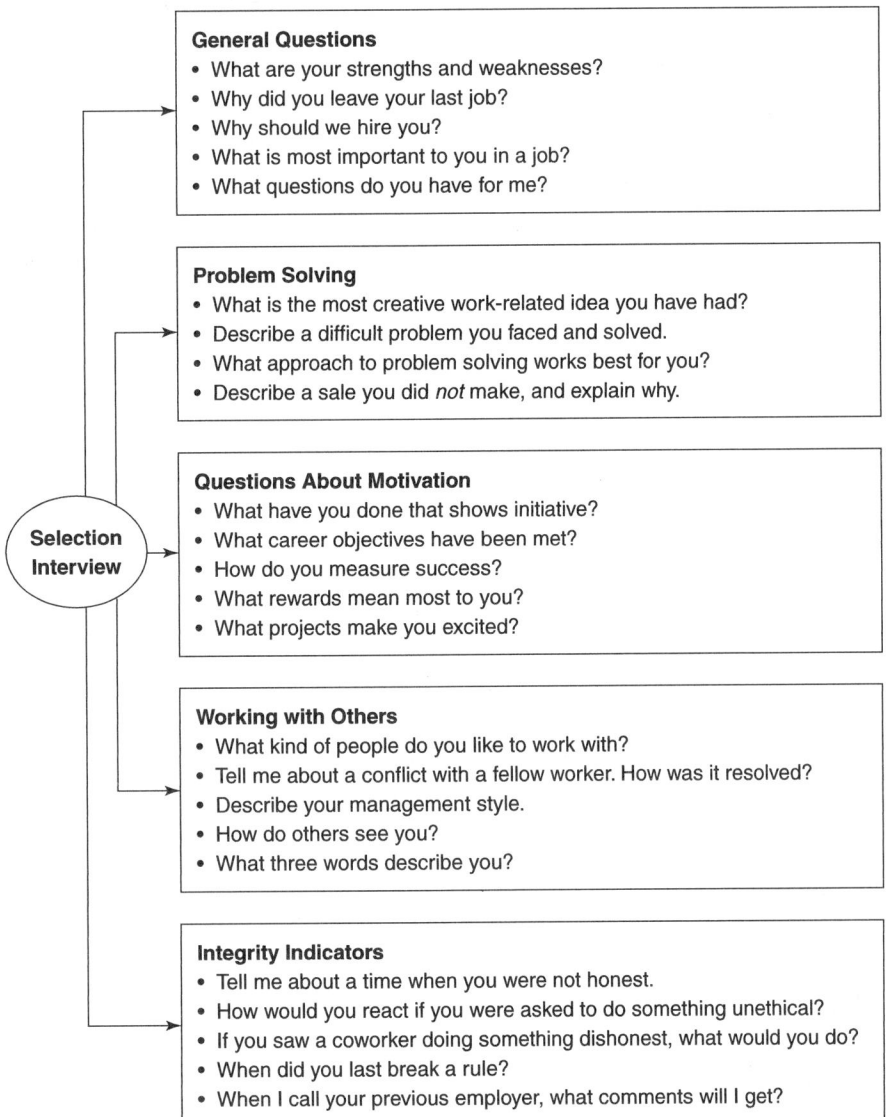

NEGATIVE EMPHASIS As might be expected, unfavorable information about an applicant is the biggest factor considered in interviewers' decisions about overall suitability. Unfavorable information is given roughly twice the weight of favorable information. Often, a single negative characteristic may bar an individual from being accepted, whereas no amount of positive characteristics will guarantee a candidate's acceptance.

HALO EFFECT Interviewers should try to avoid the halo effect, which occurs when an interviewer allows a prominent characteristic to overshadow other evidence. The *halo effect* is present if an interviewer lets a candidate's accomplishments in athletics overshadow other characteristics, which leads the interviewer to hire the applicant because "athletes make good salespeople." *Devil's horns* (a reverse halo effect), such as inappropriate dress or a low grade-point average, may affect an interviewer as well.

BIASES AND STEREOTYPING Personal biases and stereotyping of applicants should be avoided in interviews. The "similarity" bias occurs because interviewers tend to favor or select people they perceive to be similar to themselves. This similarity can be in age, race, sex, previous work experiences, personal background, or other factors. Also, as workforce demographics shift, interviewers should avoid stereotyping individuals because of demographic characteristics and differences.

530. STAFFING, DEVELOPMENT, AND EMPLOYMENT PRACTICES

CULTURAL NOISE The interviewer must learn to recognize and handle cultural noise, which comes from responses the applicant believes are socially acceptable rather than factual. An interviewer can handle cultural noise by not encouraging it. If the interviewer supports cultural noise, the applicant will take the cue and continue those kinds of answers. Instead, the applicant can be made aware that the interviewer is not being taken in and interviewer control over the interview can be reestablished. Interview problems exist with both interviewers and applicants.

Reliability and Validity of Interviews

Virtually all employers use interviews as part of the employment process. Therefore, interviews must be reliable, exhibiting a consistency in the ability of interviewers to pick the same capabilities again and again in applicants. Some interviewers may be better than others at selecting individuals who will perform well. A high *intra*rater reliability (the same interviewer) can be demonstrated, but only moderate-to-low *inter*rater reliability (different interviewers), is generally shown. Interrater reliability liability becomes important when each of several interviewers is each selecting employees from a pool of applicants, or if the employer uses team or panel interviews with multiple interviewers.

The interview is popular with employers because it has high "face validity," because it seems valid to employers and they like it. In the case of interviews the assumption often made is that if someone interviews well and the information obtained in the interview is useful, then the individual will perform well on the job.

However, research over several decades consistently confirms that the interview is not an especially valid predictor of job performance and success, particularly when using unstructured interviews. An especially problematic issue occurs when interviewers make judgments about applicants' personality characteristics based on interviewing questions.[72] But use of structured interviews can increase validity of selection interviewing.

Background Investigation

Background investigation may take place either before or after the in-depth interview. It costs the organization some time and money, but it generally proves beneficial when making selection decisions. Background references can be obtained from several sources. Some information tends to be useful and relevant, depending on the jobs for which applicants are being considered.

Personal references, such as those from relatives, clergy, or friends, often are of little value, and should not even be used. No applicant asks somebody who would give a negative response to write a recommendation. Instead, greater reliance should be placed on work-related references from previous employers and supervisors.

Medical Examinations and Inquiries

Medical information on applicants may be used to determine the individual's physical and mental capability for performing jobs. Physical standards for jobs should be realistic, justifiable, and geared to the job requirements. Workers with disabilities can perform satisfactorily in many jobs. However, in many places, they are rejected because of their disabilities, rather than being screened and placed in appropriate jobs.

Making the Job Offer

The final step of the selection process is making a job offer. Often extended over the phone, many job offers are formalized in letters and sent to applicants. It is important that the offer document be reviewed by legal counsel and that the terms and conditions of employment be clearly identified. Care should be taken to avoid vague, general statements and promises about bonuses, work schedules, or other matters that might change later. These documents also should provide for the individuals to sign an acceptance of the offer and return it to the employer, who should place it in the individual's personnel files.

Training and Human Resources

The competitive pressures facing organizations today require employees whose knowledge and ideas are current, and whose skills and abilities can deliver results. As organizations compete and change, training becomes even more critical than before. Employees who must adapt to the myriad of changes facing organizations must be trained continually in order to maintain and update their capabilities. Also, managers must have training and development to enhance their leadership skills and abilities. In a number of situations, employers have documented that effective training produces productivity gains that more than offset the cost of the training.

The Nature of Training

Training is a process whereby people acquire capabilities to aid in the achievement of organizational goals. Because this process is tied to a variety of organizational purposes, training can be viewed either narrowly or broadly. In a limited sense, training provides employees with specific, identifiable knowledge and skills for use in their present jobs. Sometimes a distinction is drawn between *training* and *development,* with development being broader in scope and focusing on individuals gaining new capabilities useful for both present and future jobs.

The Context of Training

Contemporary training in organizations has evolved significantly over the past decade. The changes have been reflected in a number of ways.[73]

- *Organizational competitiveness and training.* More employers are recognizing that training their human resources is vital.
- *Training as a revenue source.* Some organizations have identified that training can be a source of business revenues.
- *Integration of job performance, training, and learning.* Job performance, training, and employee learning must be integrated to be effective.

Training and Performance Consulting

Training must be linked to enhancing organizational performance. This occurs most effectively when a performance-consulting approach is used. **Performance consulting** is a process in which a trainer (either internal or external to the organization) and the organizational client work together to boost workplace performance in support of business goals.

As Exhibit 500.41 depicts, performance consulting compares desired and actual organizational results with desired and actual employee performance. Once these comparisons are made, then performance consulting takes a multifaceted approach to performance issues.[74] It does so by:

- Focusing on identifying and addressing *root causes* of performance problems
- Recognizing that the *interaction of individual and organizational factors* influences employee performance
- Documenting the *actions and accomplishments* of high performers and comparing them with actions of more typical performers[75]

Exhibit 500.41 *Performance Consulting*

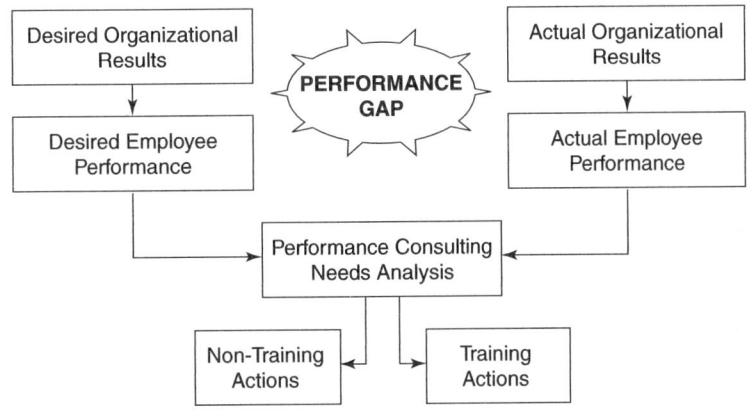

Regardless of whether the trainer is internal to the firm or an outside training consultant, a performance consulting approach sees that training cannot automatically solve every employee performance problem. Instead, training must be viewed as one piece of a larger "bundled solution." For instance, some employee performance issues might be resolved by creating a training program for employees, while other situations might call for compensation or job design changes.

The following scenario illustrates the performance consulting approach. Assume you are the HR training specialist in a large pharmaceutical firm, and the marketing manager for the Midwestern sales region contacts you about creating a training program for sales representatives. Over the last six months, the manager has noticed that new account sales are down and asks you to develop a new customized training program on assertive communications and selling skills for the sales representatives.

Instead of just developing a training program, use of performance consulting means gathering more information in order to identify: (1) the root causes of the recent new account sales slump in the Midwest region, (2) the various individual salesperson and organizational factors contributing to this slump, and (3) the primary reasons for the gap between high-performance salespeople and lower-performance salespeople in this specific region. Obtaining all of this information helps in determining whether *any training* (much less assertive communications skills training) will play a role in the integrative performance improvement solution. Perhaps recent changes in the sales incentive compensation plan has resulted in emphasis on existing accounts or maybe changes in sales territory assignments have caused problems. Whatever the causes, a tailored and comprehensive performance consulting approach is needed to get to the root of the sales decline.

Integrating Training Responsibilities

One of the most important implications resulting from the performance consulting approach is that HR staff members and trainers work as partners with operating managers to integrate training that bolsters both individual employee and organizational performance. A typical division of training responsibilities is shown in Exhibit 500.42. The HR unit serves as a source of expert training assistance and coordination. The unit often operates with a more long-range view of employee training and development for the entire organization than do individual operating managers. The difference is especially true at lower levels in the organization.

Managers are likely to be the best source of technical information used in skills training. They also are in a better position to decide when employees need training or retraining. Their close and continual interaction with employees puts managers in the most appropriate place to determine and discuss employee career possibilities and plans with individual employees. Therefore, a "training partnership" between the HR staff members and operating managers is important.

Strategic Training

Training adds value to an organization by linking training strategy to organizational objectives, goals, and business strategies. *Strategic training* focuses on efforts that develop competencies, value, and competitive advantages for the organization. This basically means that training and learning interventions must be based on organizational strategic plans and HR planning efforts. Strategic training also implies that HR and training professionals need to be involved in organizational change and strategic planning in order to develop training plans and activities that support top management's strategic decisions. Thus, effective training helps the firm create competitive advantage.

Exhibit 500.42 *Typical Division of HR Responsibilities: Training*

HR Unit	Managers
• Prepares skill-training materials	• Provide technical information
• Coordinates training efforts	• Monitor training needs
• Conducts or arranges for off-the-job training	• Conduct and monitor continuing on-the-job training
• Coordinates career plans and employee development efforts	• Continually discuss employees' growth and future potential
• Provides input and expertise for organizational development	• Participate in organizational change efforts

Training is strategic when it: (1) develops essential worker capabilities, (2) encourages adaptability to change, (3) promotes ongoing learning in the organization, (4) creates and disseminates new knowledge throughout the organization, and (5) facilitates communication and focus.[76] Consider as an example a group of managers attending a training session where the firm's hottest new products are being discussed, with the managers developing some creative ways to reach target audiences who would benefit from these new products.

Linking Training to Business Strategies

To understand how to link training and business strategies, it is useful to understand some basic business strategy concepts. A *low-cost leader business strategy* attempts to increase market share by focusing on the low cost of the firm's products or services, compared to competitors (e.g., Wal-Mart, Bic pens, Southwest Airlines). In contrast, firms with a *differentiation business strategy* try to make their products or services different from others in the industry in terms of quality, exceptional service, new technology, or perceived distinctiveness (e.g., Maytag products, Mercedes autos, Rolex watches).

The primary implications of organizational business strategies for the firm's training efforts emphasize the need for training programs and activities to support the firm's business strategy.[77] For instance, if a company is trying to distinguish itself from its competition based on customer service quality, then significant customer service training is needed to support the firm's strategic thrust. However, if another firm differentiates itself from competitors with products or services that customers perceive as distinctive and unique, then training resources should be shifted to keeping employees abreast of the latest advertising and marketing ideas. For instance, an exclusive jewelry store selling Rolex watches and expensive jewelry must ensure that its employees are trained on all of the models, features, and operations of such items. Also, training in dress, appearance, communications, and special customer relations skills also support the firm's business strategies. These scenarios are just two brief examples of how training must parallel business strategies.

Developing a Strategic Training Plan

The framework for developing a strategic training plan contains four major stages. Each is highlighted next.

1. *Strategize:* HR and training managers must first work with management to determine how training will link strategically to the strategic business plan, with an eye toward employee and organizational performance improvement.
2. *Plan:* Planning must occur in order to deliver training that will provide positive results for the organization and its employees. As part of planning, the objectives and expectations of training should be identified, and specific, measurable learning objectives created in order to track the effectiveness of the training.
3. *Organize:* Then, the training must be organized by deciding how training will occur, obtaining the resources needed, and developing the training interventions. All these activities culminate in the actual training.
4. *Justify:* Finally, measuring and evaluating the extent to which training meets the objectives set will legitimize training efforts. Past mistakes in training can be explicitly identified in this phase. Learning from these mistakes provides an effective way to improve future training.

The benefits of strategic training are numerous. First, it enables HR and training professionals to get intimately involved with the business, partner with operating managers to help solve their problems, and make significant contributions to organizational results. Strategic training also may prevent HR professionals and trainers from chasing fads or the hottest or latest type of training gimmick. Additionally, a strategic training mindset also reduces the likelihood of thinking that training can solve most employee or organizational problems. As in the earlier situation where the marketing manager was convinced his employees needed assertive communications skills training, it is not uncommon for operating managers, HR professionals, and trainers to react to problems by saying, "I need a training program on X." With a strategic training focus, the response is more likely to be an assessment of such requests to determine what training and/or non-training approaches might address the performance issues.

The Training Process

Effective implementation of strategic training requires use of a systematic training process. Exhibit 500.43 depicts the four phases of the training process: assessment, design, delivery, and evaluation. Using such a process reduces the likelihood that unplanned, uncoordinated, and haphazard training efforts will occur. A discussion of each phase of the training process follows next.

Exhibit 500.43 *Training Process*

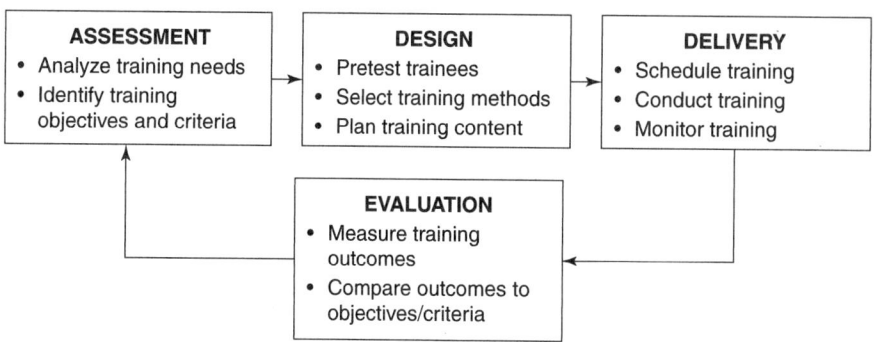

Exhibit 500.44 *Sources of Training Needs Assessment*

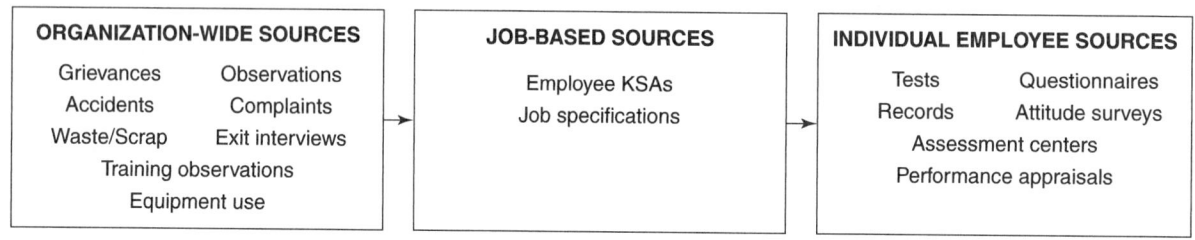

Training Needs Assessment

Training is designed to help the organization accomplish its objectives. Therefore, assessing organizational training needs represents the diagnostic phase of setting training objectives. This assessment considers employee and organizational performance issues to determine if training can help. Using the performance consulting approach mentioned earlier, it is important that non-training factors be considered also, such as compensation, organization structure, job design, and physical work settings. When training needs are identified, the assessment efforts then specify the objectives to be accomplished.[78] Exhibit 500.44 shows the three sources of training needs assessment analyses.

Once training needs have been identified using appropriate analyses, then training objectives and priorities must be established by identifying a *gap analysis,* which indicates the distance between where an organization is with its employee capabilities and where it needs to be. Training objectives and priorities are set to close the gap. Three types of training objectives can be set:

- *Knowledge:* Impart cognitive information and details to trainees.
- *Skill:* Develop behavior changes in how jobs and task requirements are performed.
- *Attitude:* Create interest in and awareness of the importance of training.

The success of training should be measured in terms of the objectives set. Useful objectives are measurable. For example, an objective for a new sales clerk might be to "demonstrate the ability to explain the function of each product in the department within two weeks." This objective serves as a check on internalization, or whether the person really learned and is able to use the training.

Because training seldom is an unlimited budget item and because organizations have multiple training needs, prioritization is necessary. Ideally, management ranks training needs based on organizational objectives. Conducting the training most needed to improve the performance of the organization will produce visible results more quickly.

Training Design

Once training objectives have been determined, training design can be done. Whether job-specific or broader in nature, training must be designed to address the assessed needs. Effective training design considers learning concepts, legal issues, and different approaches to training.

Exhibit 500.45 *Elements of Training Design*

As depicted in Exhibit 500.45, there are three primary considerations when designing training: (1) determining learner readiness, (2) understanding different learning styles, and (3) designing training for transfer. Each of these elements must be considered in order for the training design to mesh together.[79]

The three types of adult learning include **active practice**, **spaced practice**, and **massed practice**.

Training Delivery

Once training has been designed, then the actual delivery of training can begin. It is generally recommended that the training be pilot-tested or conducted on a trial basis in order to ensure that the training meets the needs identified and that the design is appropriate. Regardless of the type of training done, a number of different training approaches and methods can be used. The growth of training technology continues to expand the available choices.

Regardless of the approaches used, a variety of considerations must be balanced when selecting training methods. The common variables considered are:

- Nature of training
- Subject matter
- Number of trainees
- Individual vs. team
- Self-paced vs. guided
- Training resources
- Costs
- Geographic locations
- Time allotted
- Completion timeline

Active practice The performance of job-related tasks and duties by trainees during training.

Spaced practice Several practice sessions spaced over a period of hours or days.

Massed practice The performance of all of the practice at once.

To illustrate, a large firm with many new hires may be able to conduct employee orientation using the Internet, videotapes, and specific HR staff members. However, a small firm with few new hires may have an HR staff member meet individually for several hours with the new hires. Or, supervisory training for a medium-sized company with three locations in a geographic area may bring supervisors together for a two-day workshop once a quarter. However, a large, global firm may use Web-based courses to reach supervisors throughout the world, with content available in several languages. Frequently, training is conducted internally, but other types of training make use of external or technological training resources.

Internal Training

Training internally generally applies to specific aspects of the job. It is also popular because it saves the cost of sending employees away for training and often avoids the cost of outside trainers. Often, skills-based, technical training is conducted inside organizations. Due to rapid changes in technology, the building and updating of technical skills have become crucial training needs. Basic technical skills training is also being mandated by federal regulations in areas where the Occupational Safety and Health Administration (OSHA), the Environmental Protection Agency (EPA), and other agencies have regulations.

Exhibit 500.46 *Stages for On-the-Job Training*

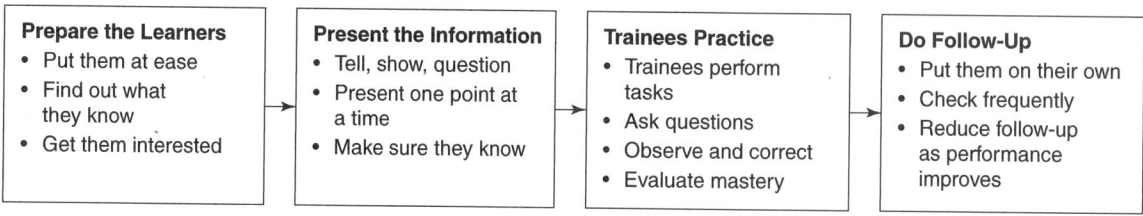

Informal training Training that occurs through interactions and feedback among employees.

INFORMAL TRAINING One internal source of training that has grown is **informal training,** which occurs through interactions and feedback among employees. Much of what employees know about their jobs they learn informally from asking questions and getting advice from other employees and their supervisors, rather than from formal training programs.

ON-THE-JOB TRAINING (OJT) The most common type of training at all levels in an organization is *on-the-job training* (OJT). Different from informal training that often occurs spontaneously, OJT should be planned. The supervisor or manager conducting the training must be able to both teach and show the employees what to do. Based on a special guided form of training known as *job instruction training,* on-the-job training is most effective if a logical progression of stages is used, as shown in Exhibit 500.46.

On-the-job training is by far the most commonly used form of training because it is flexible and relevant to what employees do. However, OJT has some problems as well. Often, those doing the training may have no experience in training, no time to do it, and no desire to participate. Under such conditions, learners essentially are on their own, and training likely will not be effective. Another problem is that OJT can disrupt regular work. Unfortunately, OJT can amount to no training at all in some circumstances, especially if the trainers simply abandon the trainees to learn the job alone. Also, bad habits or incorrect information from the supervisor or manager can be transferred to the trainees. On the other hand, well-planned and well-executed OJT can be very effective.

External Training

External training is used extensively by organizations of all sizes. Large organizations use external training in the absence of needed internal training capabilities or when many people need to be trained quickly. External training may be the best option for training in smaller firms due to limitations in the size of their HR staffs and in the number of employees who may need various types of specialized training. Whatever the size of the organization, external training occurs for several reasons:

- It may be less expensive for an employer to have an outside trainer conduct training in areas where internal training resources are limited.
- The organization may have insufficient time to develop internal training materials.
- The HR staff may not have the necessary level of expertise for the subject matter in which training is needed.
- There are advantages to having employees interact with managers and peers in other companies in training programs held externally.

OUTSOURCING OF TRAINING Many employers of all sizes outsource training to external training firms, consultants, and other entities.

A popular route for some employers is to use vendors and suppliers to train employees. Several computer software vendors offer employees technical certifications on their software. Many suppliers, including software providers, also have users' conferences where employees from a number of employers receive detailed training on using the software and new features being added. Some vendors conduct the training inside the organization as well if sufficient numbers of employees are to be trained.

GOVERNMENT-SUPPORTED JOB TRAINING Federal, state, and local governments provide a wide range of external training assistance. Government programs on both the state and federal levels provide training support to employers who hire new workers, particularly those who are long-term unemployed or have been receiving welfare

Exhibit 500.47 *Developing E-Learning*

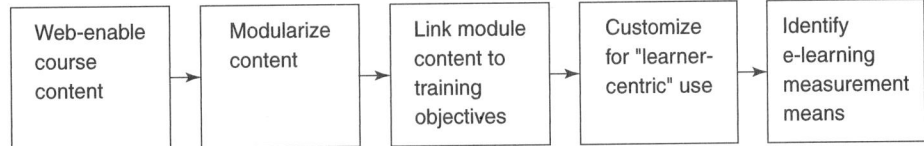

benefits. The Workforce Investment Partnership Act (WIPA) provides states block grant programs that target adult education, disadvantaged youth, and family literacy. Employers hiring and training individuals who meet the WIPA criteria receive tax credits and other assistance for six months or more, depending upon the program regulations.

E-Learning: Training On-line

E-learning is defined as the use of the Internet or an organizational intranet to conduct training on-line. Many people possess a familiarity with the Internet, which has so dramatically altered the way people do business, locate information, and communicate. An intranet is similar to the Internet, but it is a private organizational network behind "firewall" software that restricts access to authorized users, including employees participating in e-learning.

e-learning The use of the Internet or an organizational intranet to conduct training on-line.

The explosive growth in the use of the Internet changes many aspects of how training is done in organizations. As more and more employees use computers and have access to Internet portals, their employers look at the World Wide Web as a means for distributing training to employees located in widely dispersed locations and jobs. Exhibit 500.47 shows how to develop e-learning.

Training Methods

Whether delivered internally, externally, or through e-learning, appropriate training methods must be chosen. These methods include cooperative training, instructor-led classroom and conference training, and distance training/learning.

Evaluation of Training

Evaluation of training compares the posttraining results to the objectives expected by managers, trainers, and trainees. Too often, training is conducted with little thought of measuring and evaluating it later to see how well it worked. Because training is both time-consuming and costly, evaluation should be done.

Levels of Evaluation

It is best to consider how training is to be evaluated before it begins. Donald L. Kirkpatrick identified four levels at which training can be evaluated.[80] As Exhibit 500.48 shows, evaluating training becomes successively more difficult as evaluation moves from reaction to learning to behavior, and then to results measures. But the training that affects behavior and results instead of reaction and learning-level evaluations provides greater value.

REACTION Organizations evaluate the reaction level of trainees by conducting interviews or by administering questionnaires to the trainees. Assume that 30 managers attend a two-day workshop on effective interviewing skills. A reaction-level measure could be gathered by having the managers complete a survey that asked them to rate the value of the training, the style of the instructors, and the usefulness of the training to them. However, immediate reactions may measure only how much the people liked the training rather than how it benefited them or it affected how they conduct interviews.

LEARNING Learning levels can be evaluated by measuring how well trainees have learned facts, ideas, concepts, theories, and attitudes. Tests on the training material are commonly used for evaluating learning and can be given both before and after training to compare scores. If test scores indicate learning problems, then instructors get feedback and courses are redesigned so that the content can be delivered more effectively. Of course, learning enough to pass a test does not guarantee that trainees will remember the training content months later or will change job behaviors.

530. STAFFING, DEVELOPMENT, AND EMPLOYMENT PRACTICES

Exhibit 500.48 *Levels of Training Evaluation*

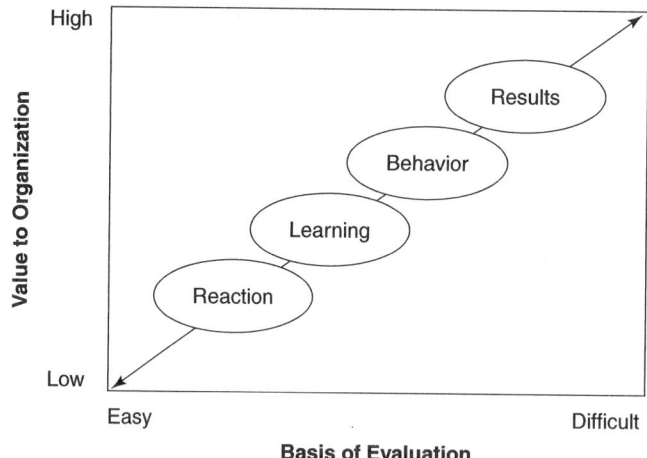

BEHAVIOR Evaluating training at the behavioral level means: (1) measuring the effect of training on job performance through interviews of trainees and their coworkers, and (2) observing job performance. For instance, a behavioral evaluation of the managers who participated in the interviewing workshop might be done by observing them conducting actual interviews of applicants for jobs in their departments. If the managers asked questions as they were trained and used appropriate follow-up questions, then behavioral indicators of the interviewing training could be obtained. However, behaviors are more difficult to measure than reaction and learning. Even if behaviors do change, the results that management desires may not be obtained.

RESULTS Employers evaluate results by measuring the effect of training on the achievement of organizational objectives. Because results such as productivity, turnover, quality, time, sales, and costs are relatively concrete, this type of evaluation can be done by comparing records before and after training. For the interviewing training, records of the number of individuals hired to the offers of employment made prior to and after the training could be gathered.

The difficulty with measuring results is pinpointing whether changes were actually the result of training or other factors of major impact. For example, managers who completed the interviewing training program can be measured on employee turnover before and after the training. But turnover is also dependent on the current economic situation, the demand for products, and many other factors.

Cost-Benefit Analyses

Training results can also be examined on the basis of costs and benefits associated with the training through a **cost-benefit analysis**. Exhibit 500.49 shows some costs and benefits that may result from training. Even though some benefits (such as attitude changes) are hard to quantify, comparison of costs and benefits associated with training remains a way to determine whether training is cost effective.[81] For example, one firm evaluated a traditional safety training program and found that the program did not lead to a reduction in accidents. Therefore, the training was redesigned and better safety practices resulted. However, careful measurement of both the costs and the benefits may be difficult.

Return on Investment (ROI)

In organizations training often is expected to produce a return on investment (ROI). Unfortunately, in too many circumstances, training is justified because someone liked it, rather than based on resource accountability.[82]

Benchmarking Training

Rather than evaluating training internally, some organizations use benchmark measures of training that are compared from one organization to others. To do benchmarking, HR professionals in an organization gather data on training and compare them to data on training at other organizations in the industry and of their size.

Exhibit 500.49 *Balancing Costs and Benefits of Training*

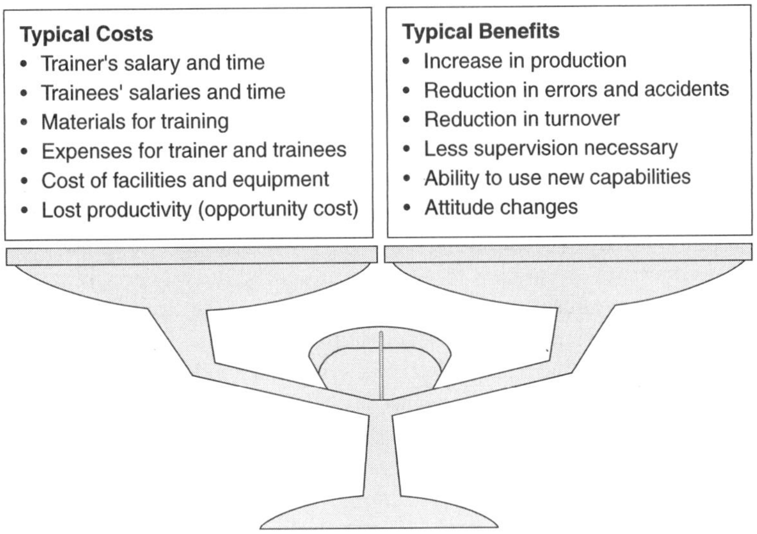

Typical Costs
- Trainer's salary and time
- Trainees' salaries and time
- Materials for training
- Expenses for trainer and trainees
- Cost of facilities and equipment
- Lost productivity (opportunity cost)

Typical Benefits
- Increase in production
- Reduction in errors and accidents
- Reduction in turnover
- Less supervision necessary
- Ability to use new capabilities
- Attitude changes

Evaluation Designs

Even if benchmarking data are not available, internal evaluation of training programs can be designed in a number of ways. The rigor of the three designs discussed next increases with each level.

POST-MEASURE The most obvious way to evaluate training effectiveness is to determine after the training whether the individuals can perform the way management wants them to perform. Assume that a customer service manager has 20 representatives who need to improve their data entry speeds. After a one-day training session, they take a test to measure their speeds. If the representatives can all type the required speed after training, was the training beneficial? It is difficult to say; perhaps most of them could have done as well before training. Test results do not always clearly indicate whether the typing speed is a result of the training or could have been achieved without training.

PRE-/POST-MEASURE By designing the evaluation differently, the issue of pre-test skill levels could have been considered. If the manager had measured the data entry speed before and after training, she could have known whether the training made any difference. However, a question remains. Was a change in speed a response to the training, or did these employees simply work faster because they knew they were being tested? People often perform better when they know their efforts are being evaluated.

PRE-/POST-MEASURE WITH CONTROL GROUP Another evaluation design can address this problem. In addition to the 20 representatives who will be trained, a manager can test another group of representatives who will not be trained to see if they do as well as those who are to be trained. This second group is called a *control group*. After training, if the trained representatives work significantly faster than those who were not trained, the manager can be reasonably sure that the training was effective.

Other designs also can be used, but these three are the most common ones. When possible, the pre-/post-measure or pre-/post-measure with control group design should be used, because each provides a much stronger evaluation than the post-measure design alone.

Careers and HR Development

When organizational strategies involve endless organizational restructurings and downsizing, it is difficult to know what a career is, much less how to develop one. Further, some employers wonder why they should worry about career "development" for employees when the future likely holds fewer internal promotion opportunities and more movement in and out of organizations by individuals. Even though these views may seem extreme, employee development has changed recently in three significant ways:

1. The middle-management "ladder" in organizations now includes more horizontal rather than upward moves.
2. Many firms target their efforts to ensure that their businesses focus on core competencies.
3. The growth of project-based work makes careers a series of projects, not just steps upward in a given organization.

Traditionally, career development efforts targeted managerial personnel to look beyond their current jobs and to prepare them for a variety of future jobs in the organization. But development for all employees, not just managers, is necessary for organizations to have the needed human resource capabilities for future growth and change.

Mergers, acquisitions, restructurings, and layoffs all have influenced the way people and organizations look at careers and development. In the "new career," the individual—not the organization—manages his or her own development. Such self-development consists of personal educational experiences, training, organizational experiences, projects, and even changes in occupational fields. Under this system, the individual defines career success, which may or may not coincide with the organizational view of success.

Organizations promote this "self-reliance" as the basis for career development by telling employees they should focus on creating employability for themselves in the uncertain future. However, employability also must be defined in such a way that gives it value for the employing organization. It is a dilemma of sorts that if employers give employees unrestricted access to development opportunities, employers may not be able to retain talent in today's highly competitive labor markets.

Indeed, in some industries, changing jobs and companies every year or two is becoming more the norm than the exception. Valuable employees, deluged with job offers, change jobs at a rate much higher than in the past. Also, some individuals exhibit more loyalty to their careers than to an employer. Even though attempts to limit employees' abilities to change jobs through use of employment agreements containing noncompetition clauses put some restrictions on job hoppers, these clauses must be enforced in court, taking time and organizational resources.[83] All of these factors and more are changing how careers are defined and viewed.

Careers

A **career** is the series of work-related positions a person occupies throughout life. People pursue careers to satisfy deeply individual needs. At one time, identifying with one employer seemed to fulfill many of those needs. Now, the distinction between the way individuals and organizations view careers is significantly different.

Employers that fail to help employees focus their careers in areas that benefit the organization experience shortages of employees who believe themselves to be ready to assume new jobs and responsibilities. From the viewpoint of individuals, failure to achieve psychological success or a feeling of pride and accomplishment in their careers may cause them to change careers, look outside work for "life success," or simply be unhappy. Effective career planning considers both organization-centered and individual-centered perspectives. Exhibit 500.50 summarizes the perspectives and interaction between the organizational and individual approaches to career planning.

Exhibit 500.50 *Organizational and Individual Career Planning Perspectives*

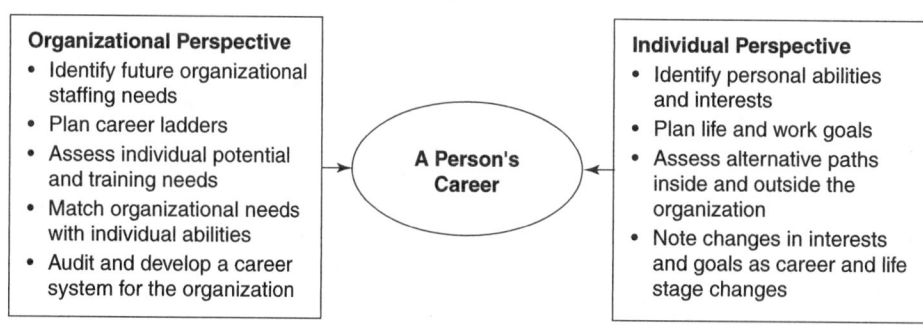

How People Choose Careers

Four general individual characteristics affect how people make career choices:

- *Interests:* People tend to pursue careers that they believe match their interests. But over time, interests change for many people, and career decisions eventually are made based on special skills, abilities, and which career paths are realistic for them.
- *Self-image:* A career is an extension of a person's self-image, as well as a molder of it. People follow careers they can "see" themselves doing and avoid those that do not fit with the perceptions of their talents, motives, and values.
- *Personality:* This factor includes an employee's personal orientation (for example, if the employee is realistic, enterprising, or artistic) and personal needs (including affiliation, power, and achievement needs). Individuals with certain personality types gravitate to different clusters of occupations.
- *Social backgrounds:* Socioeconomic status and the educational level and occupation of a person's parents are also factors included in this category. Children of a physician or a welder know from their parents what those jobs are like and may either seek or reject them based on how they view the parents' jobs.

Less is known about how and why people choose specific organizations than about why they choose specific careers. One obvious factor is timing—the availability of a job when the person is looking for work. The amount of information available about alternatives is an important factor as well. Beyond these issues, people seem to pick an organization on the basis of a "fit" between the climate of the organization as they perceive it and their own personal characteristics, interests, and needs.

General Career Progression

The typical career of many individuals today probably includes different positions, transitions, and organizations—more so than in the past, when employees were less mobile and organizations more stable as long-term employers. A typical U.S. worker holds seven jobs between ages 18 and 32, with most of those job changes occurring at earlier ages rather than later. However the median years of time spent with one employer has changed little over the last two decades. Therefore, it is useful to think about general patterns in people's lives and the effects on their careers.

Many theorists in adult development describe the first half of life as the young adult's quest for competence and a way to make a mark in the world. According to this view, a person attains happiness during this time primarily through achievement and the acquisition of capabilities. The second half of life is different. Once the adult starts to measure time from the expected end of his or her life rather than from the beginning, the need for competence and acquisition changes to the need for integrity, values, and well-being. For many people internal values take precedence over external scorecards or accomplishments such as wealth and job title status. In addition, mature adults already possess certain skills, so their focus may shift to other interests. Career-ending concerns reflect additional shifts also. Exhibit 500.51 shows a model identifying general career and life periods.

Contained within this life pattern is the idea that careers and lives are not predictably linear but cyclical.[84] Individuals experience periods of high stability, followed by transition periods with less stability, and by inevitable discoveries, disappointments, and triumphs. These cycles of structure and transition occur throughout individuals' lives and careers.

Exhibit 500.51 *General Career Periods*

Career Stage	Early Career	Mid-Career	Late Career	Career End
Age Group:	20 years	30–40 years	50 years	60–70 years
Needs:	Identifying interests, exploring several jobs	Advancing in career; lifestyle may limit options, growth, contribution	Updating skills; settled in, leader, opinions valued	Planning for retirement, examining nonwork interests
Concerns:	External rewards, acquiring more capabilities	Values, contribution, integrity, well-being	Mentoring, disengaging, organization continuance	Retirement, part-time employment

530. STAFFING, DEVELOPMENT, AND EMPLOYMENT PRACTICES

This cyclical view may be an especially useful perspective for those individuals affected by downsizing or early career plateaus in large organizations. Such a perspective argues for the importance of flexibility in an individual's career. It also emphasizes the importance of individuals continuing to acquire more and diverse knowledge, skills, and abilities.

Special Career Issues for Organizations and Employees

Although the goals and perspectives in career planning may differ for organizations and employees, three issues can be problematic for both, perhaps for different reasons. Those are career plateaus (or the lack of opportunity to move up), dealing with technical professionals who do not want to go into management, and dual-career couples.

Developing Human Resources

Development represents efforts to improve employees' ability to handle a variety of assignments and to cultivate capabilities beyond those required by the current job. Development benefits both organizations and individuals. Employees and managers with appropriate experiences and abilities may enhance organizational competitiveness and the ability to adapt to a changing environment. In the development process, individuals' careers also may evolve and gain new or different focus.[85]

Development differs from training. It is possible to train most people to run a copy machine, answer customer service questions, drive a truck, operate a computer, or assemble a radio. However, development in areas such as judgment, responsibility, decision making, and communications presents a bigger challenge. These areas may or may not develop through life experiences by individuals. A planned system of development experiences for all employees, not just managers, can help expand the overall level of capabilities in an organization. Exhibit 500.52 profiles development and compares it to training.

At the organizational level of analysis, executives craft the broader organizational strategies as well as establish a system for developing the people to manage and achieve those identified strategies. Development must be tied to this strategic planning because the firm needs to develop those talents to carry out the plans. The successful CEO plans employee and managerial succession on several levels and in several different pathways as part of that development.

Currently, more jobs take on the characteristics of *knowledge work*. Such workers combine mastery of technical expertise with the ability to work in teams, form relationships with customers, and analyze their own practices. The practice of management involves guiding and integrating increasingly autonomous, highly skilled people.

The HR Development Process

Development starts with the HR plans of an organization because these plans analyze, forecast, and identify current and future organizational needs for human resources. Also, HR planning anticipates the movement of people in the organization due to retirements, promotions, and transfers. Also, it helps identify the capabilities needed by the organization in the future and the development necessary for people to be available to meet those needs.

In Exhibit 500.53 illustrating the HR development process, HR plans first identify necessary capabilities of individuals. Such capabilities can, of course, influence planning in return. The specific abilities needed also influence decisions

Exhibit 500.52 *Development vs. Training*

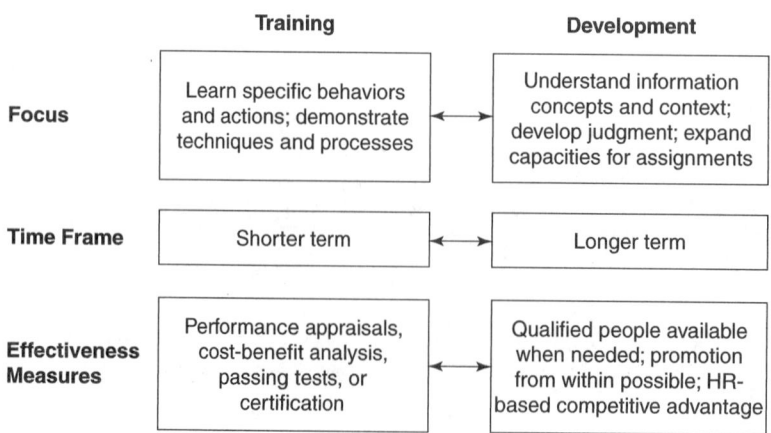

Exhibit 500.53 *The HR Development Process in an Organization*

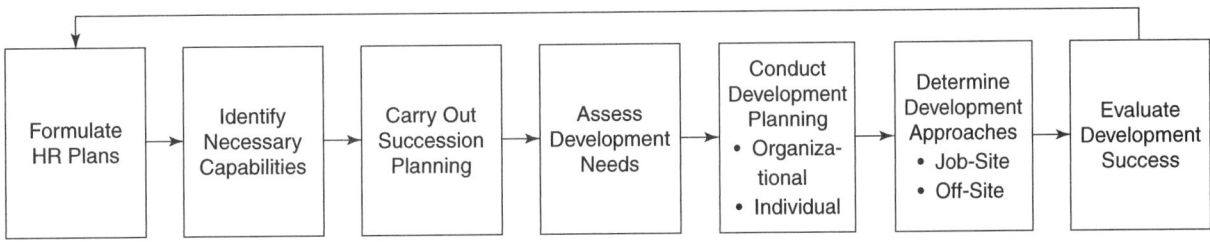

about promotions and the leadership succession process within the organization. Those decisions influence—and are influenced by—an assessment of the development needs in the organization. Two categories of development planning follow from this needs assessment: organizational and individual. Finally, the success of the developmental process must be evaluated and necessary changes made as appropriate.

Development Needs Analyses

As with training, employee development begins with analyses of the needs of both the organization and individuals. Even though evidence indicates that this analysis of an individual's development needs frequently receives insufficient attention, some industries are using innovative methods.

Either the company or the individual can analyze what a given person needs by way of development. The goal, of course, is to identify strengths and weaknesses. Methods used by organizations to assess development needs include use of assessment centers, psychological testing, and performance appraisals.

Succession Planning

Planning for the succession of key executives, managers, and other employees is an important part of HR development. **Succession planning** is a process of identifying a longer-term plan for the orderly replacement of key employees. The need to replace key employees results from promotions, transfers, retirements, deaths, disability, departures, or other reasons. Succession planning often focuses on top management, such as ensuring a CEO successor. However, limiting succession planning just to top executive jobs is one of the greatest mistakes made.[86] For instance, identifying successors for accounting managers, marketing directors, admissions supervisors, IT technicians, physical therapists, and other key jobs is just as crucial as succession planning for the top executive jobs in a health-care institution.

> **Succession planning** Process of identifying a longer-term plan for the orderly replacement of key employees.

Succession Planning Process

Whether in small or large firms, succession planning is linked to strategic HR planning.[87] Both the quantity and capabilities of potential successors must be linked to organizational strategies and HR plans. For example, a retailer whose key merchandising managers are likely to retire soon must consider the implications for future merchandising and store expansion plans, particularly if the firm plans to enter or withdraw from offering certain lines of goods. Based on these broader planning efforts, the succession planning process shown in Exhibit 500.54 is recommended.

Two coordinated activities begin the actual succession planning process. First, the development of preliminary replacement charts ensures that the right individuals with sufficient capabilities and experience to perform the targeted jobs are available at the right time. Replacement charts (similar to depth charts used by football teams) both show the backup "players" at each position and identify positions without a current qualified backup. The charts identify who could take over key jobs if someone leaves, retires, dies unexpectedly, or otherwise creates a vacancy.

In conjunction with developing replacement charts, assessing the capabilities of current employees and their career interests allows companies to create career development plans for employees. As mentioned earlier, managers may perform these assessments based on performance appraisals and other information. Organizations also use psychological tests, assessment centers, or other individual assessment means to identify individual development needs and possible career moves for employees. Then HR efforts to develop the capabilities of the individuals facilitate orderly and planned successions. Finally, as with most planning efforts, periodic review and reassessment both organization-wide and with individuals ensures that the succession plan remains current and aligned with organizational strategies and HR plans.

530. STAFFING, DEVELOPMENT, AND EMPLOYMENT PRACTICES

Exhibit 500.54 *Succession Planning Process*

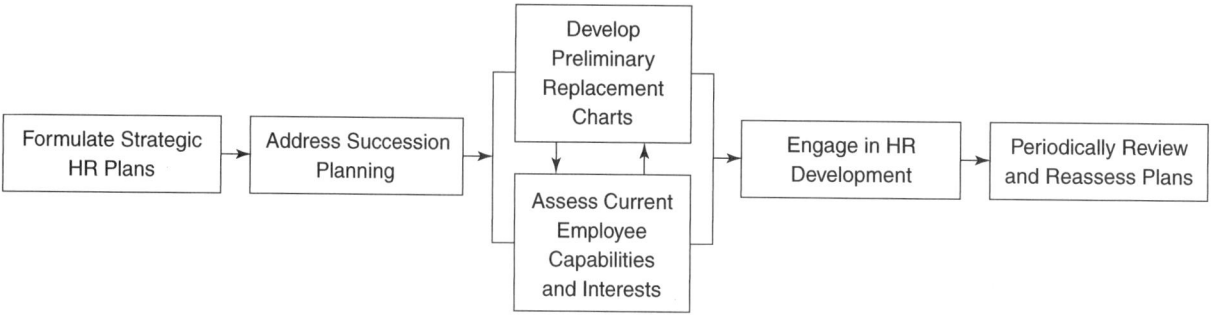

Exhibit 500.55 *Advantages and Disadvantages of Major Development Approaches*

Job-Site Methods	Advantages	Disadvantages
• Coaching	• Natural and job-related	• Difficulty in finding good coaches
• Committee Assignments/Meetings	• Involve participants in critical processes	• Can be time waster
• Job Rotation	• Gives excellent overview of the organization	• Long start-up time
• Assistant-to Positions	• Provides exposure to an excellent manager	• Possible shortage of good assignments
• On-line Development	• Flexible	• Niche not yet well defined
• Corporate Universities/ Development Centers	• Can combine academic and real world at work	• May be "university" in name only
• Learning Organization	• Perhaps the ideal mindset for development	• Essentially a theoretical, idealistic notion for most organizations
Off-Site Methods	**Advantages**	**Disadvantages**
• Classroom Courses and Degrees	• Familiar, accepted, status	• Does not always improve performance
• Human Relations Training	• Deals with important management skills	• Difficult to measure effectiveness
• Simulations	• Realism and integration	• Inappropriate "game playing"
• Sabbaticals	• Rejuvenating as well as developmental	• Expensive; employees may lose contact with job
• Outdoor Training	• Increases self-confidence and teamwork through physical challenges	• Not appropriate for all because of physical nature; dangerous

Choosing a Development Approach

Common development approaches can be categorized under two major headings—job-site development and off-site development. Both are appropriate in developing managers and other employees. Investing in human intellectual capital, whether at work or off the job, becomes imperative for organizations as "knowledge work" aspects increase for almost all employers. Yet identifying exactly the right mix and approaches for development needs remains an art rather than a science.[88]

To be effective, a development approach must mesh with HR strategies to meet organizational goals. Exhibit 500.55 summarizes the major advantages and disadvantages of the various on-site and off-site approaches to development.

Exhibit 500.56 *Managerial Lessons and Job Experience*

Job Transitions	Experiences	Obstacles
Individuals forced to deal with entirely new jobs, problems, people, responsibilities, etc.	Starting or changing some major organizational feature, decision-making responsibility, influencing others without formal authority	Bad job situation, difficult boss, demanding clients, unsupportive peers, negative economic circumstances, etc.

Necessary Lessons to Be Learned

- **Setting Agendas** — Developing technical/business knowledge, taking responsibility, setting goals
- **Handling Relationships** — Dealing successfully with people
- **Management Values** — Understanding successful management behavior
- **Personality Qualities** — Having the temperament necessary to deal with the chaos and ambiguity of executive life
- **Self-Awareness** — Understanding oneself and how one affects others

Management Development

Although development is important for all employees, it is essential for managers. Effective management development imparts the knowledge and judgment needed by managers. Without appropriate development, managers may lack the capabilities to best deploy and manage resources (including employees) throughout the organization. Necessary capabilities often a focus of management development include leadership, dealing with change, coaching and advising subordinates, controlling operations, and providing performance feedback.

Former U.S. president Dwight D. Eisenhower said leadership is the "art of getting someone else to do something you want done because he wants to do it." An effective leader creates positive change and is important for an organization. But like all development, leadership may be difficult to teach to others.[89]

Experience plays a central role in management development. Indeed, experience often contributes more to the development of senior managers than classroom training does, because much of their experience occurs in varying circumstances on the job over time. Yet, despite a need for effective managers, finding such managers for middle-level jobs is often difficult. At the middle-management level, some individuals refuse to take management jobs. "You're a backstop, caught in the middle between upper management and the workforce," a cost account manager (who quit management) noted. "I was told 50 hours a week was not enough and that I had to work my people harder.... The few dollars more were not worth the pain." Similarly, few companies seem to take the time to develop their own executive-level managers. Instead executives often are hired from the outside.

Exhibit 500.56 shows some lessons and features important in effectively developing both middle- and upper-level managers. Next, the most widely used management development methods are examined individually.

Managerial Modeling

A common adage in management development says that managers tend to manage as they were managed. In other words, managers learn by behavior modeling, or copying someone else's behavior. This tendency is not surprising, because a great deal of human behavior is learned by modeling. Children learn by modeling the behaviors of parents and older children. Management development efforts can take advantage of natural human behavior by matching young or developing managers with appropriate models and then reinforcing the desirable behaviors exhibited. Note that the modeling process involves more than straightforward imitation, or copying; it is considerably more complex. For example, one can learn what not to do by observing a model who does something wrong. Thus, exposure to both positive and negative models can benefit a new manager.

530. STAFFING, DEVELOPMENT, AND EMPLOYMENT PRACTICES

Management Coaching

Coaching combines observation with suggestions. Like modeling, it complements the natural way humans learn. A brief outline of good coaching pointers often includes the following:

- Explaining appropriate behavior
- Making clear why actions were taken
- Accurately stating observations
- Providing possible alternatives/suggestions
- Following up/reinforcing

In the context of management development, coaching involves a relationship between two managers for a period of time as they perform their jobs. Effective coaching requires patience and good communication skills.

Mentoring

Mentoring A relationship in which experienced managers aid individuals in the earlier stages of their careers.

Mentoring is a relationship in which experienced managers aid individuals in the earlier stages of their careers. Such a relationship provides an environment for conveying technical, interpersonal, and organizational skills from the more-experienced to the less-experienced person. Not only does the inexperienced employee benefit, but the mentor may enjoy the challenge of sharing his or her wisdom.

However, mentoring is not without its problems. Young minority managers frequently report difficulty finding mentors. Also, men generally show less willingness than women to be mentors. Further, mentors who are dissatisfied with their jobs and those who teach a narrow or distorted view of events may not help a young manager's development. Fortunately, many managers have a series of advisors or mentors during their careers and may find advantages in learning from the different mentors. For example, the unique qualities of individual mentors may help less-experienced managers identify key behaviors in management success and failure. Further, those being mentored may find previous mentors to be useful sources for networking.[90] Exhibit 500.57 describes the four stages in most successful mentoring relationships.

Women and Management Development

In virtually all countries in the world, the proportion of women holding management jobs is lower than the proportion of men holding such jobs. The term *glass ceiling* has been used to describe the situation in which women fail to progress into top management positions. Women are making slow but steady strides into management and the executive suite. Nationally, women hold 49 percent of managerial/professional positions and 12 percent of corporate officer positions, and those figures are higher in certain geographical regions.[91]

One approach to breaking through the glass ceiling is mentoring. For example, in some firms women with mentors move up more often than those without mentors. Most of the literature on women and mentoring, based on various narratives of successful women executives, suggests that breaking the glass ceiling requires developing political sophistication, building credibility, refining a management style, and shouldering responsibilities.[92] Research studies have found women generally to rate high in the skills needed for success where teamwork and partnering are important.[93]

Exhibit 500.57 *Stages in Mentoring Relationships*

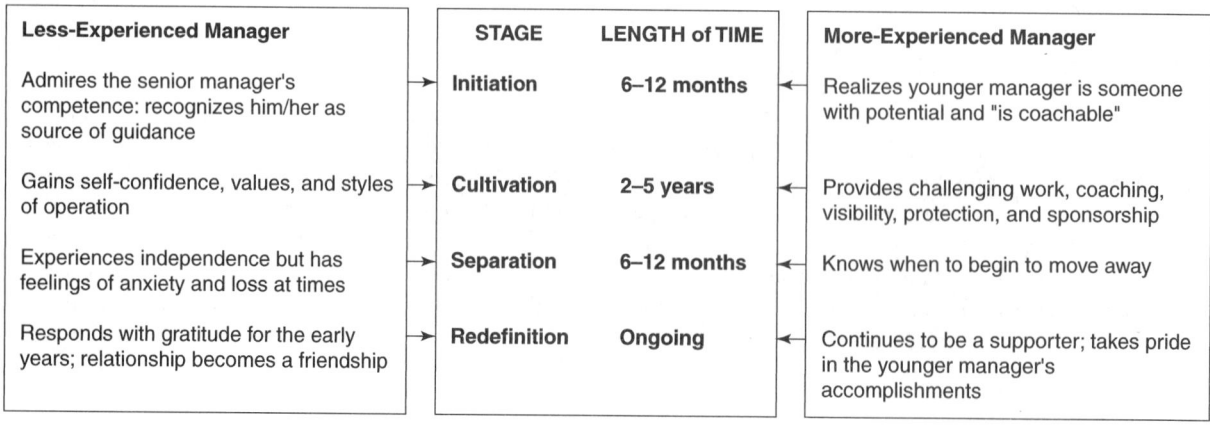

Executive Education

Executives in an organization often face difficult jobs due to changing and unknown circumstances. "Churning" at the top of organizations and the stresses of executive jobs contribute to increased turnover in these positions.[94] In an effort to decrease turnover, some organizations are experimenting with a relatively recent phenomenon: special education for executives. This type of training supplements executive education traditionally offered by university business schools and includes strategy formulation, financial models, logistics, alliances, and global issues.[95]

Problems with Management Development Efforts

Development efforts are subject to certain common mistakes and problems. Most of the management development problems in the United States have resulted from inadequate HR planning and a lack of coordination of HR development efforts. Common problems include the following:

- Inadequate needs analysis
- Trying out fad programs or training methods
- Abdicating responsibility for development to HR staff alone
- Trying to substitute training for selection
- Lack of training among those who lead the development activities
- Using only "courses" as the road to development
- Encapsulated development

The last item requires some additional explanation. **Encapsulated development** occurs when an individual learns new methods and ideas in a development course and returns to a work unit that is still bound by old attitudes and methods. Therefore, the trainee cannot apply new ways to handle certain situations because of resistance from those having an investment in the *status quo*. The development was "encapsulated" in the classroom and essentially not used on the job.

Performance Management and Appraisal

All employers want employees who perform their jobs well. However, an effective performance management system increases the likelihood that such performance will occur.[96] A **performance management system** consists of the processes used to identify, encourage, measure, evaluate, improve, and reward employee performance. As shown in Exhibit 500.58, performance management links organizational strategy to results. The figure lists common performance management practices and outcomes in the strategy-results loop. As identified by HR professionals, a performance management system should do the following:[97]

- Provide information to employees about their performance.
- Clarify what the organization expects.

Exhibit 500.58 *Linkage Between Strategy, Outcomes, and Organizational Results*

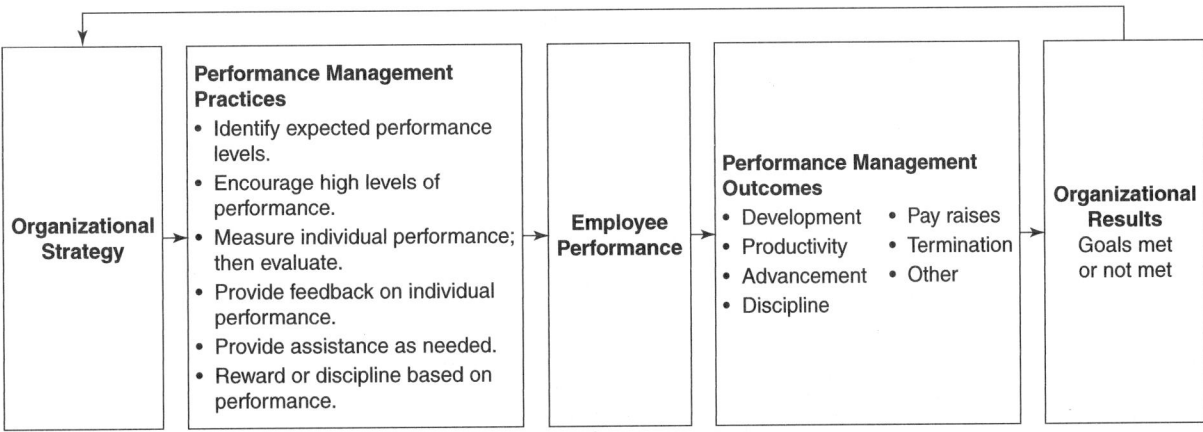

- Identify development needs.
- Document performance for personnel records.

Even well-intentioned employees do not always know what is expected or how to improve their performances, which makes some kind of performance management system necessary. Further, if dismissal of an employee becomes necessary, employers risk a negative legal outcome if they cannot show evidence that the employee has been advised of his or her performance problems.

Identifying and Measuring Employee Performance

Performance is essentially what an employee does or does not do. Employee performance common to most jobs includes the following elements:

- Quantity of output
- Quality of output
- Timeliness of output
- Presence at work
- Cooperativeness

Other dimensions of performance beyond these general ones apply to various jobs. Specific **job criteria** or dimensions of job performance identify the most important elements in a given job. For example, a college professor's job might include the job criteria of teaching, research, and service. Job criteria are the most important factors people do in their jobs because they define what the organization pays an employee to do; therefore, the performance of individuals on job criteria should be measured and compared against standards, and then the results communicated to the employee.

Most jobs have more than one job criterion or dimension. In sports and many other jobs, multiple job criteria are the rule rather than the exception. Often a given individual might demonstrate better performance on some job criteria than others. Also, some criteria might be more important than others to the organization. Weights can be used to show the relative importance of several job criteria in one job.

Types of Performance Information

Managers receive three different types of information about how employees are performing their jobs. *Trait-based* information identifies a subjective character trait of the employee—such as attitude, initiative, or creativity—and may have little to do with a specific job. Traits tend to be ambiguous, and court decisions generally have held that performance appraisals based on traits such as "adaptability" and "general demeanor" are too vague to use when making performance-based HR decisions.

Behavior-based information focuses on specific behaviors that lead to job success. For a salesperson, the behavior of "verbal persuasion" can be observed and used as information on performance. Although more difficult to identify, behavioral information clearly specifies the behaviors management wants to see. A potential problem arises when any of several behaviors can lead to successful performance in a given situation. For example, identifying successful "verbal persuasion" for a salesperson might be difficult because the approach used by one salesperson may not be successful when used by another.

Results-based information considers employee accomplishments. For jobs in which measurement is easy and obvious, a results-based approach works well. However, that which is measured tends to be emphasized. But this emphasis may leave out equally important but unmeasurable parts of the job. For example, a car sales representative who gets paid *only* for sales may be unwilling to do paperwork or other work not directly related to selling cars. Further, ethical or even legal issues may arise when only results are emphasized and not how the results were achieved.

Relevance of Performance Criteria

Measuring performance requires the use of relevant criteria that focus on the most important aspects of employees' jobs.[98] For example, measuring customer service representatives in an insurance claims center on their "attitude" may be less relevant than measuring the number of calls handled properly. This example stresses that the most important job criteria should be identified and linked to the employees' job descriptions.

Potential Performance Criteria Problems

Performance measures that leave out some important job duties are considered *deficient*. For example, when measuring the performance of an employment interviewer, if only the number of applicants hired and not the quality of those hired is evaluated, performance measurement is likely to be deficient. On the other hand, including some irrelevant criteria *contaminates* the measure. An example of a contaminated criterion might be "appearance" for a telemarketing sales representative whom customers never see. Managers need to guard against using deficient or contaminated criteria in measuring performance.[99]

Performance measures also can be thought of as objective or subjective. *Objective* measures can be directly measured or counted—for example, the number of cars sold or the number of invoices processed. *Subjective* measures require judgment on the part of the evaluator and are more difficult to measure. One example of a subjective measure is a supervisor's ratings of an employee's "attitude," which cannot be seen directly. Unlike subjective measures, objective measures tend to be more narrowly focused, which sometimes leads to them being inadequately defined. However, subjective measures may be prone to contamination or other random errors. Neither is a panacea, and both objective and subjective measures should be used carefully.[100]

Performance Standards

Performance standards define the expected levels of performance, and are "benchmarks," or "goals," or "targets"—depending on the approach taken. Realistic, measurable, clearly understood performance standards benefit both organizations and employees. In a sense, performance standards define what satisfactory job performance is. And they need to be established *before* the work is performed. Well-defined standards ensure that everyone involved knows the levels of accomplishment expected.

Both numerical and nonnumerical standards can be established. Sales quotas and production output standards are familiar numerical performance standards. A standard of performance can also be based on nonnumerical criteria. Consider the following performance standards as illustrating both types.

> *Job Criterion.* Keep current on supplier technology.
> *Performance Standards:* 1. Every four months, invite suppliers to make presentation of newest technology. 2. Visit supplier plants twice per year. 3. Attend trade shows quarterly.
>
> *Job Criterion.* Do price or cost anaylsis as appropriate.
> *Performance Standard:* Performance is acceptable when employee follows all requirements of the procedure "Price and Cost Analysis."

How well employees meet established standards is often expressed as either numerical (5, 4, 3, 2, 1) or verbal ratings, for example, "outstanding" or "unsatisfactory." If more than one person is involved in the rating, they may find it difficult to agree on the exact level of performance achieved relative to the standard. Exhibit 500.59 defines the terms one company uses in evaluating employee performance. Notice that each level specifies performance standards, rather than numbers, in order to minimize variation in interpretations of the standards.

Someone external to a given job, such as a supervisor or a quality control inspector, frequently sets the standards for the job. However, standards can be written effectively by employees as well. Experienced employees usually know

Exhibit 500.59 *Terms Defining Standards at One Company*

5	**Outstanding.** The person is so successful at this job criterion that special note should be made. Compared with the usual standards and the rest of the department, this performance ranks in the top 10%.
4	**Very Good.** Performance at this level is a better-than-average performance for the unit, given the common standards and unit results.
3	**Satisfactory.** Performance is at or above the minimum standards. This level of performance is what one would expect from most experienced, competent employees.
2	**Marginal.** Performance is somewhat below the minimum-level standard on this job dimension. However, potential to improve the rating within a reasonable time frame is evident.
1	**Unsatisfactory.** Performance on this item in the job is well below standard. Whether the person can improve to meet minimum standards is questionable.

what constitutes satisfactory performance of tasks in their job descriptions, and so do their supervisors. Therefore, these individuals often can participate in setting standards with their managers.

Uses of Performance Appraisal

Performance appraisal is the process of evaluating how well employees perform their jobs when compared to a set of standards, and then communicating that information to those employees. Performance appraisal also is called *employee rating, employee evaluation, performance review, performance evaluation,* and *results appraisal.*

Performance appraisal is widely used for administering wages and salaries, giving performance feedback, and identifying individual employee strengths and weaknesses. Most U.S. employers use performance appraisal systems for office, professional, technical, supervisory, middle management, and nonunion production workers. Globally, these systems provide benefits in a variety of work situations. However, despite their widespread use, not everyone enthusiastically endorses performance appraisals. Criticisms revolve around the way they are done and the results. Those criticisms include:

- With today's emphasis on teamwork, appraisals focus too much on the individual and do too little to develop employees to perform better.[101]
- Most employees who receive reviews and supervisors who give them generally rate the process a resounding failure.[102]
- Most appraisals are inconsistent, short-term oriented, subjective, and valuable only for identifying employees performing extremely well or poorly.[103]

Poorly done performance appraisals lead to disappointing results for all concerned. But to have no formal performance appraisal done may limit an employer's options regarding discipline and dismissal. Performance appraisals can answer questions about whether the employer acted fairly or how the employer actually knew that the employee's performance did not meet standards.[104] Even though an employer technically may not need a reason to terminate an employee, as a practical matter, appraisals can provide justification for such actions should they become necessary. Employees also benefit if appraisals help them know where they need to improve, even after a positive appraisal.[105]

Organizations generally use performance appraisals in two potentially conflicting roles. One role is to measure performance for the purpose of making pay or other administrative decisions about employees. Promotions or terminations might hinge on these ratings, often creating stress for managers doing the appraisals. The other role focuses on the development of individuals. In that role, the manager acts more as counselor than as judge, which may change the atmosphere of the relationship. The developmental type of performance appraisal emphasizes identifying potential and planning employees' growth opportunities and direction. Exhibit 500.60 shows the two potentially conflicting roles for performance appraisal.

Administrative Uses

A performance appraisal system is often the link between rewards employees hope to receive and their productivity. The linkage can be thought of as follows:

$$\text{Productivity} \rightarrow \text{Performance appraisal} \rightarrow \text{Rewards}$$

Exhibit 500.60 *Conflicting Roles for Performance Appraisal*

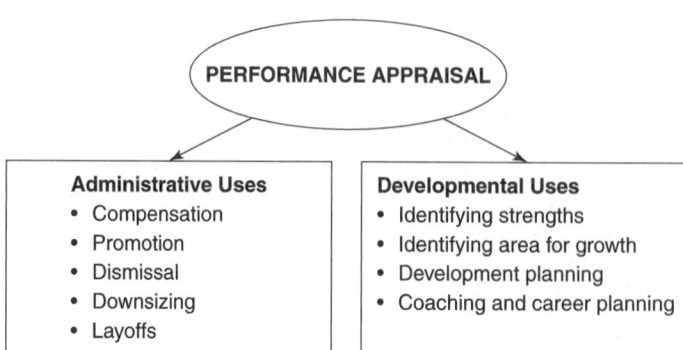

Performance-based compensation affirms the idea that pay raises should be given for performance accomplishments rather than for seniority. In this system, the manager historically has been the evaluator of a subordinate's performance and also the one who makes compensation recommendations for the employee. If any part of the appraisal process fails, the better performing employees do not receive larger pay increases, resulting in perceived inequity in compensation.

Many U.S. workers say they see little connection between their efforts and the size of their paychecks. However, the use of performance appraisal to determine pay is common. Employees are especially interested in other administrative uses of performance appraisal, such as decisions about promotion, termination, layoff, and transfer assignments. For example, the order of layoffs can be justified by performance appraisals. For this reason, if an employer claims that the decision was performance-based, the performance appraisals must document clearly the differences in employee performance. Similarly, promotion or demotion based on performance must be documented through performance appraisals. Thus, necessity probably accounts for the widespread administrative use of performance appraisals.

Development Uses

Performance appraisal can be a primary source of information and feedback for employees, which is often key to their future development. In the process of identifying employee strengths, weaknesses, potentials, and training needs through performance appraisal feedback, supervisors can inform employees about their progress, discuss what areas they need to develop, and identify development plans. The manager's role in such a situation parallels that of a coach. A coach rewards good performance with recognition, explains what improvement is necessary, and shows employees how to improve. After all, people do not always know where and how to improve, and managers should not expect improvement if they are unwilling to explain where and how improvement can occur.

The purpose of developmental feedback is to change or reinforce individual behavior, rather than to compare individuals—as in the case of administrative uses of performance appraisal. Positive reinforcement for desired behaviors contributes to both individual and organizational development.[106] The development function of performance appraisal also can identify areas in which the employee might wish to grow. For example, in a performance appraisal interview targeted exclusively to development, an employee found out that the only factor keeping her from being considered for a management job in her firm was a working knowledge of cost accounting. Her supervisor suggested that she consider taking such a course at night at the local college.

The use of teams provides a different set of circumstances for developmental appraisal. The manager may not see all of the employee's work, but team members do. Teams *can* provide developmental feedback. However, it is still an open question whether teams can handle administrative appraisals. When teams are allowed to design appraisal systems, they tend to "get rid of judgment," and avoid differential rewards. Perhaps, then, group appraisal is best suited to developmental purposes.

Informal versus Systematic Appraisal

Performance appraisal can occur in two ways: informally or systematically. A supervisor conducts *informal appraisal* whenever necessary. The day-to-day working relationship between a manager and an employee offers an opportunity for the employee's performance to be evaluated.[107] A manager communicates this evaluation through conversation on the job, over coffee, or by on-the-spot examination of a particular piece of work. Informal appraisal is especially appropriate when time is an issue, because delays in giving feedback weaken its motivational effect. Frequent informal feedback to employees also can prevent surprises during a formal evaluation. However, informal appraisal can become *too* informal.

A *systematic appraisal* is used when the contact between manager and employee is formal, and a system is in place to report managerial impressions and observations on employee performance. One survey found that almost 90 percent of employers have a formal performance management system or process.[108] Although informal appraisal is useful, and even necessary, it should not take the place of formal appraisal. Even some Chief Executive Officers receive, and indeed often want, formal appraisal of their performance by Boards of Directors.

Appraisal Responsibilities

The appraisal process can benefit both the organization and the individuals involved, if done properly. As Exhibit 500.61 shows, the HR unit typically designs a performance appraisal system. The manager then appraises employees using the appraisal system. During development of the formal appraisal system, managers usually offer input as to how the final system will work.

Exhibit 500.61 *Typical Division of HR Responsibilities: Performance Appraisal*

HR Unit	Managers
• Designs and maintains formal system	• Typically rate performance of employees
• Trains raters	• Prepare formal appraisal documents
• Tracks timely receipt of appraisals	• Review appraisals with employees
• Reviews completed appraisals for consistency	• Identify development areas

It is important for operating managers to understand appraisal as *their* responsibility. Through this process, good employees can be developed to be even better, and poor employees' performances are improved or they are removed from the organization.[109] Performance appraisal is not simply an HR requirement; it must also be a management process, because guiding employees' performance is probably the most important responsibility of managers.[110] Although HR does not drive performance management, it assists the individual operating managers who do.

TIMING OF APPRAISALS   Most companies require managers to conduct appraisals once or twice a year, most often annually. New employees commonly receive an appraisal 60–90 days after employment, again at six months, and annually thereafter. "Probationary employees" who are new and in a trial period should be informally evaluated often—perhaps weekly for the first month and monthly thereafter until the end of the introductory period. After that, annual reviews may be sufficient. Some high-technology employers promise accelerated appraisals—every six months instead of each year—so that employees receive more frequent raises. These companies report a subsequent reduction in turnover among these turnover-prone employees because more feedback has been given.

Systematic appraisals feature a regular time interval, which distinguishes them from informal appraisals. Both employees and managers know that performance will be reviewed on a regular basis, and they can plan for performance discussions. Informal appraisals can be conducted whenever a manager feels they are desirable.[111]

APPRAISALS AND PAY DISCUSSIONS   Many experts argue that performance appraisals and pay discussions should be separate. Two major reasons support this view. One is that employees often focus more on the pay amount received than on the appraisal feedback that identifies what they have done well or need to improve. Second, sometimes managers manipulate performance appraisal ratings to justify the desired pay treatment they wish to give specific individuals.

Who Conducts Appraisals?

Performance appraisal can be conducted by anyone familiar with the performance of individual employees. Possibilities include the following:

- Supervisors who rate their employees
- Employees who rate their superiors
- Team members who rate each other
- Outside sources
- Employees' self-appraisal
- Multisource (360° feedback) appraisal

The rating of employees by their supervisors or managers is the most common method. The immediate superior has the main responsibility for appraisals in most organizations, although often the supervisor's boss may review and approve the appraisals. The growing use of teams and a concern with customer input contribute to the two fast-growing sources of appraisal information: team members and sources outside the organization. Multisource appraisal (or 360° feedback) combines numerous methods and has grown in usage recently. Multisources include manager, coworkers/peers, subordinates, self-evaluation, and customers.

Supervisory Rating of Subordinates

Traditional rating of employees by supervisors is based on the assumption that the immediate supervisor is the person most qualified to evaluate the employee's performance realistically and fairly. Toward this end, some supervisors keep performance logs noting their employees' accomplishments. These logs provide specific examples to use when rating performance. Exhibit 500.62 shows the traditional review process by which supervisors conduct performance appraisals on employees.

Methods for Appraising Performance

Performance can be appraised by a number of methods. In Exhibit 500.63, the various methods are categorized into four groups. In this section, after describing each method, the discussion considers combinations of methods which may occur across different jobs in the same organization and even within the same jobs when appropriate.

The different methods raise the question of whether performance is measured against a valid standard. An employee's performance can be compared to the duties spelled out in the job description or it can be compared to the performance or results of others. Performance can also be rated against expected behaviors that should be made known in advance.

Exhibit 500.62 *Traditional Performance Appraisal: Logic and Process*

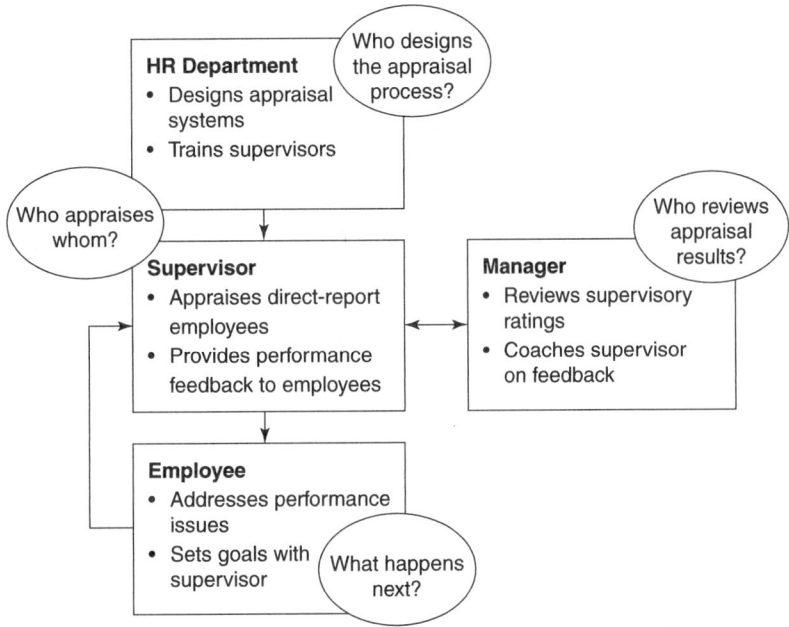

Exhibit 500.63 *Performance Appraisal Methods*

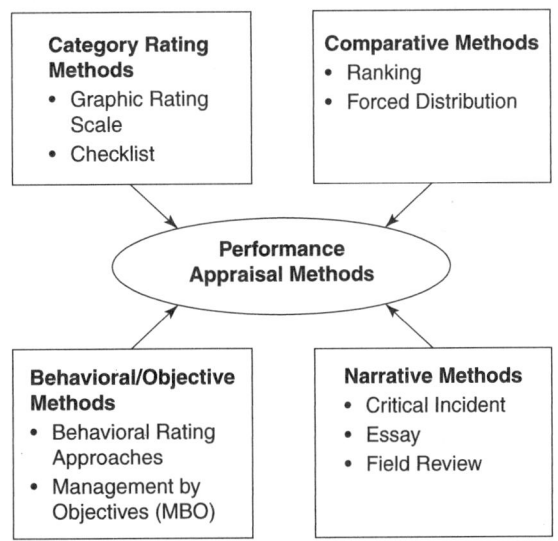

530. STAFFING, DEVELOPMENT, AND EMPLOYMENT PRACTICES

Category Rating Methods

The simplest methods for appraising performance are category rating methods, which require a manager to mark an employee's level of performance on a specific form divided into categories of performance. The graphic rating scale and checklist are common category rating methods.

Comparative Methods

Comparative methods require that managers directly compare the performance of their employees against one another. For example, a data-entry operator's performance would be compared with that of other data-entry operators by the computing supervisor. Comparative techniques include ranking and forced distribution.

Narrative Methods

Managers and HR specialists frequently are required to provide written appraisal information. Documentation and description are the essence of the critical incident, the essay, and the field review methods. These methods, which include critical incident, essay, and field review, describe an employee's actions and may indicate an actual rating as well.

Behavioral/Objectives Methods

Behavioral rating approach
Assesses an employee's behaviors instead of other characteristics.

In an attempt to overcome some of the difficulties of the methods just described, **behavioral rating approaches** attempt to assess an employee's *behaviors* instead of other characteristics. Some of the different behavioral approaches are *behaviorally anchored rating scales (BARS)*, *behavioral observation scales (BOS)*, and *behavioral expectation scales (BES)*. BARS compare what the employee does with possible behaviors that might be shown on the job. BOS count the number of times certain behaviors are exhibited. BES order behaviors on a continuum to define outstanding, average, and unacceptable performance.

Behavioral rating approaches describe specific examples of employee job behaviors. In BARS, these examples are "anchored" or measured against a scale of performance levels. Exhibit 500.64 contains a behavioral observation rating scale that rates customer service skills for individuals taking orders for a national catalog retailer. Spelling out the behaviors associated with each level of performance helps minimize some of the problems noted earlier for other approaches. An example of objective methods is management by objectives (MBO).

Combinations of Methods

No single appraisal method is best for all situations. Therefore, a performance measurement system that uses a combination of the preceding methods may be sensible in certain circumstances. Using combinations may offset some of the advantages and disadvantages of individual methods. Category rating methods are easy to develop, but they

Exhibit 500.64 *Customer Service Skills (BOS)*

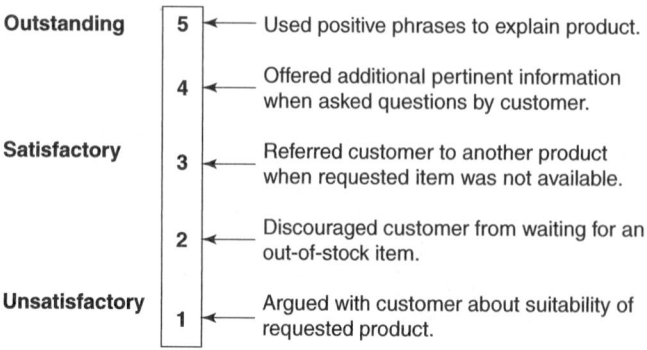

usually do little to measure strategic accomplishments. Further, they may make interrater reliability problems worse. Comparative approaches help reduce leniency, central tendency, and strictness errors, which makes them useful for administrative decisions such as pay raises. But the comparative approaches do a poor job of linking performance to organizational goals, and they do not provide feedback for improvement as well as other methods do.

Narrative methods work best for development because they potentially generate more feedback information. However, without good definitions of criteria or standards, they can be so unstructured as to be of little value. Also, these methods work poorly for administrative uses. The behavioral/objective approaches work well to link performance to organizational goals, but both can require much more effort and time to define expectations and explain the process to employees. These approaches may not work well for lower-level jobs.

When managers can articulate what they want a performance appraisal system to accomplish, they can choose and/or mix the methods just mentioned to realize the advantages they want. For example, one combination might include a graphic rating scale of performance on major job criteria, a narrative of developmental needs, and an overall ranking of employees in a department. Different categories of employees (e.g., salaried exempt, nonexempt salaried, maintenance) might require different combinations.

Rater Errors

There are many possible sources of error in the performance appraisal process. One of the major sources is mistakes made by the rater. Although completely eliminating these errors is impossible, making raters aware of them through training is helpful. Exhibit 500.65 lists some of the most common rater errors.

Varying Standards

When appraising employees, a manager should avoid applying different standards and expectations for employees performing similar jobs. Inequities in assessments, whether real or perceived, generally anger employees. Such problems often result from the use of ambiguous criteria and subjective weightings by supervisors.[112]

Recency/Primacy Effect

The **recency effect** occurs when a rater gives greater weight to recent events when appraising an individual's performance. Giving a student a course grade based only on his performance in the last week of class, or giving a drill press operator a high rating even though she made the quota only in the last two weeks of the rating period are examples. The opposite is the **primacy effect,** where information received first gets the most weight.

Exhibit 500.65 *Common Rater Errors*

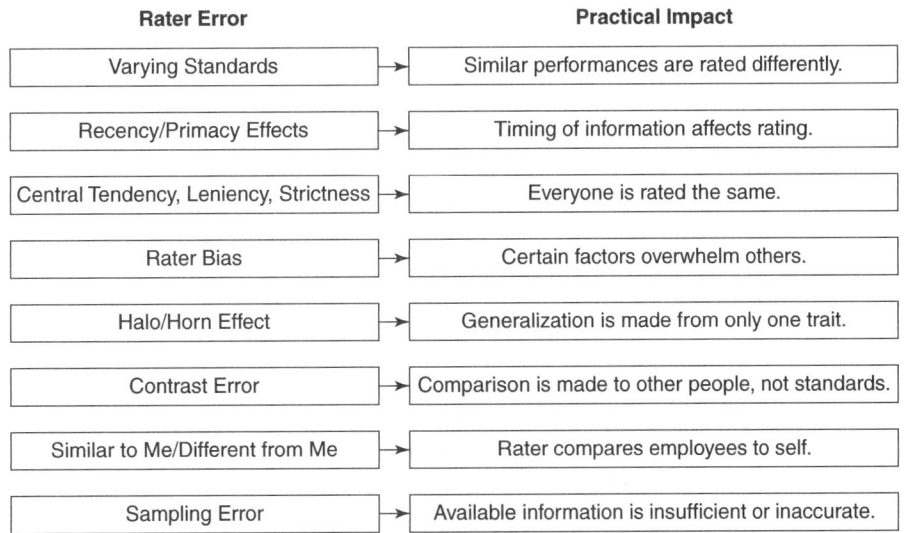

Central Tendency, Leniency, and Strictness Errors

Ask students, and they will tell you which professors tend to grade easier or harder. A manager also may develop a similar *rating pattern*. Appraisers who rate all employees within a narrow range (i.e., everyone is average) commit a **central tendency error,** where even the poor performers receive an average rating.

Rating patterns also may exhibit leniency or strictness. The *leniency error* occurs when ratings of all employees fall at the high end of the scale. The *strictness error* occurs when a manager uses only the lower part of the scale to rate employees. To avoid conflict, managers often rate employees higher than they should be rated. This "ratings boost" is especially likely when no manager or HR representative reviews the completed appraisals.

Rater Bias

Rater bias occurs when a rater's values or prejudices distort the rating. Such bias may be unconscious or quite intentional. For example, a manager's dislike of certain ethnic groups may cause distortion in appraisal information for some people. Judgments about age, religion, seniority, sex, appearance, or other arbitrary classifications also may skew appraisal ratings if the appraisal process is not properly designed. A review of appraisal ratings by higher-level managers may help correct this problem.

Halo/Horn Effect

The **halo effect** occurs when a manager rates an employee high on all job criteria because of performance in one area. For example, if a worker has few absences, her supervisor might give her a high rating in all other areas of work, including quantity and quality of output, because of her dependability. The manager may not really think about the employee's other characteristics separately, resulting in the halo effect. The "horns" effect is the opposite, where one characteristic may lead to an overall lower rating.

Contrast Error

Rating should be done using established standards. The **contrast error** is the tendency to rate people relative to others rather than against performance standards. For example, if everyone else in a group performs at a mediocre level, a person performing somewhat better may be rated as excellent because of the contrast effect. But in a group performing well, the same person might receive a lower rating. Although it may be appropriate to compare people at times, the rating usually should reflect performance against job requirements, not against other people.

Similar to/Different from Me

Sometimes raters are influenced by whether people show the same or different characteristics from the rater. Again the error comes in measuring someone against another person rather than on how well the individual fulfills the expectations of the job.

Sampling Error

If the rater has seen only a small sample of the person's work, an appraisal may be subject to sampling error. For example, assume 95 percent of the work of an employee has been satisfactory, but the boss saw only the 5 percent that had errors. If the supervisor then rates the person as poor, then a sampling error has occurred. Ideally the work being rated should be a good representative sample of all the work done.

Appraisal Feedback

After completing appraisals, managers need to communicate the results to give employees a clear understanding of how they stand in the eyes of their immediate superiors and the organization. Organizations commonly require managers to discuss appraisals with employees. The appraisal feedback interview provides an opportunity to clear up any misunderstandings on both sides. In this interview, the manager should focus on counseling and development, and not just tell the employee, "Here is how you rate and why." Emphasizing development gives both parties an opportunity to consider the employee's performance as part of appraisal feedback.

Exhibit 500.66 *Appraisal Interview Hints*

DO	DO NOT
• Prepare in advance.	• Do all the talking.
• Focus on performance and development.	• Lecture the employee.
• Be specific about reasons for ratings.	• Mix performance appraisal and salary or promotion issues.
• Decide on specific steps to be taken for improvement.	• Concentrate only on the negative.
• Consider the supervisor's role in the subordinate's performance.	• Be overly critical or "harp on" a failing.
• Reinforce desired behaviors.	• Feel it is necessary that both parties agree in all areas.
• Focus on future performance.	• Compare the employee with others.

The Appraisal Interview

The appraisal interview presents both an opportunity and a danger. It can be an emotional experience for the manager and the employee, because the manager must communicate both praise and constructive criticism. A major concern for managers is how to emphasize the positive aspects of the employee's performance, while still discussing ways to make needed improvements. If the interview is handled poorly, the employee may feel resentment that could lead to conflict, which could be reflected in future work.[113]

Employees usually approach an appraisal interview with some concern. They often feel that discussions about performance are both personal and important to their continued job success. At the same time, they want to know how their managers feel about their performance. Exhibit 500.66 summarizes hints for an effective appraisal interview for supervisors and managers.

Feedback as a System

The three commonly recognized components of a feedback system include data, evaluation of that data, and some action based on the evaluation. *Data* are factual pieces of information regarding observed actions or consequences. Most often data are facts that report what happened, such as "Charlie broke a photon," or "Mary spoke harshly to an engineer." For instance, when Mary spoke harshly to the engineer, it may have been an instance of poor communications and reflected a lack of sensitivity. However, it also may have been a proper and necessary action. Someone must *evaluate* the meaning or value of the data.

Evaluation is the way the feedback system reacts to the facts, and it requires performance standards. Management might evaluate the same factual information differently than would customers (for example, regarding merchandise exchange or credit decisions) or coworkers. Evaluation can be done by the person supplying the data, by a supervisor, or by a group.

For feedback to cause change, some decisions must be made regarding subsequent *action*. In traditional appraisal systems, the manager makes specific suggestions regarding future actions the employee might take. Employee input often is encouraged as well. In 360° feedback, those people from whom information was solicited might also suggest actions that the individual may consider. It may be necessary to involve those providing information if the subsequent actions are highly interdependent and require coordination with the information providers. Regardless of the feedback process used, all three components (data, evaluation, and action) are necessary parts of a successful feedback system.[114]

Reactions of Managers

Managers and supervisors who must complete appraisals of their employees often resist the appraisal process. Many managers feel that their role calls on them to assist, encourage, coach, and counsel employees to improve their performance. However, being a judge on the one hand and a coach and counselor on the other may cause internal conflict and confusion for many managers.[115]

The fact that appraisals may affect an employee's future career also may cause raters to alter or bias their ratings. This bias is even more likely when managers know that they will have to communicate and defend their ratings to the employees, their bosses, or HR specialists. From the manager's viewpoint, providing negative feedback to an employee in an appraisal interview can be easily avoided by making the employee's ratings positive, thus avoiding unpleasantness in an interpersonal situation. But avoidance helps no one. A manager owes an employee a well-considered appraisal.

Reactions of Appraised Employees

Employees may well see the appraisal process as a threat and feel that the only way to get a higher rating is for someone else to receive a low rating. This win/lose perception is encouraged by comparative methods of rating. However, both parties can win and no one must lose. Emphasis on the self-improvement and developmental aspects of appraisal appears to be the most effective means to reduce zero-sum reactions from those participating in the appraisal process.

Another common employee reaction resembles students' reactions to tests. A professor may prepare a test he or she feels is fair, but it does not necessarily follow that students will feel the test is fair. They simply may see it differently. Likewise, employees being appraised may not necessarily agree with the manager doing the appraising. In most cases, however, employees will view appraisals done well as what they are meant to be—constructive feedback.[116]

Legal and Effective Performance Appraisals

A number of court decisions have focused attention on performance appraisals, particularly on equal employment opportunity (EEO) concerns. The Uniform Guidelines issued by the Equal Employment Opportunity Commission (EEOC) and other federal enforcement agencies make it clear that performance appraisals must be job-related and nondiscriminatory.

Performance Appraisals and the Law

Because appraisals are supposed to measure how well employees are doing their jobs, it may seem unnecessary to emphasize that performance appraisals must be job-related. Yet courts have ruled in numerous cases that performance appraisals were discriminatory and not job-related.[117]

The elements of a performance appraisal system that can survive court tests can be determined from existing case law. Various cases have identified the elements of a legally defensible performance appraisal to include the following:

- Performance appraisal criteria based on job analysis
- Absence of disparate impact and evidence of validity
- Formal evaluation criteria that limit managerial discretion
- Formal rating instrument linked to job duties and responsibilities
- Personal knowledge of and contact with appraised individual
- Training of supervisors in conducting appraisals
- Review process that prevents one manager, acting alone, from controlling an employee's career
- Counseling to help poor performers improve

Clearly, employers should have fair and nondiscriminatory performance appraisals. To do this, employers must decide how to design their appraisal systems to satisfy the courts, enforcement agencies, and their employees.[118]

Effective Performance Management

Regardless of the approach used, managers must understand the intended outcome of performance management.[119] When performance management is used to develop employees as resources, it usually works. When management uses one key part of performance management, the performance appraisal, to punish employees, or when raters fail to understand its limitations, performance management is less effective. In its simplest form, as part of a performance management process, performance appraisal is a manager's observation: "Here are your strengths and weaknesses, and here is a way to develop for the future." Done well, performance management can lead to higher employee motivation and satisfaction. But in an era of continuous improvement, an ineffective performance management system poses a huge liability. To be effective, a performance management system will be

- Consistent with the strategic mission of the organization.
- Beneficial as a development tool.
- Useful as an administrative tool.
- Legal and job-related.

- Viewed as generally fair by employees.
- Effective in documenting employee performance.

Most systems can be improved by training supervisors in doing performance appraisals. Because conducting the appraisals is critical in a performance management system, training should center around minimizing rater errors and providing a common frame of reference on how raters observe and recall information.

Organizationally, managers exhibit a tendency to distill performance into a single number that can be used to support pay raises. Systems based on this concept reduce the complexity of each person's contribution in order to satisfy compensation system requirements. Such systems are too simplistic to provide the employees useful feedback or help managers pinpoint training and development needs. In fact, use of a single numerical rating often blocks productive performance discussions because the system attaches a label to a person's performance, which the manager must then defend.

Workforce Diversity Management

Managing Diversity

Diversity is the differences among people. Diversity is seen in demographic differences in the workforce. The U.S. workforce is more diverse racially; women are in the labor force in much greater numbers than ever before; and the average age of the workforce is now considerably older than before. The concept of diversity typically includes the dimensions depicted in Exhibit 500.67. As a result of these and other demographic shifts, HR management in organizations has had to adapt to a more diverse labor force both externally and internally. Among the problems to be addressed as part of managing diversity is to deal with a number of concerns often cited by protected-group individuals as well as others. Two common concerns are *perceived hostile organizational cultures* and *stereotyping*.

Many protected group persons perceive that they work in organizational cultures that are hostile to them. For instance, the perceptions are striking when racial/ethnic minorities are interviewed. Over a 20-year period, 75 percent to 85 percent of African American workers surveyed consistently indicated a belief that people of color had to perform better than whites to get ahead.[120] Studies of the perceptions of women workers have revealed similar beliefs.

The primary way to overcome these perceptions is to have an active diversity management program. Only by working to create a culture that is inclusive can organizational cultures be seen as less hostile by racial/ethnic minorities, women, older workers, those with disabilities, as well as those who are white, male, and younger.

Another concern often voiced by people of color is the stereotyping that occurs. Often these stereotypes are based on previous negative experiences and limited recent contacts with people in a certain group. The result of stereotyping in workplaces is to create conflicts between groups of people and to lead to less workplace interaction and cooperation, which is why managing diversity is so important.

Approaches to Managing Diversity

Organizations can approach the management of diversity from several different perspectives. The continuum can run from resistance to creation of an inclusive diversity culture. The increasing diversity of the workforce available, combined with growing shortages of workers in many occupations and industries, has forced more employers to recognize that diversity must be addressed. Further, the increasing prevalence of protected-group members filing legal complaints has increased the legal liabilities faced by employers who resist diversity and engage in discriminatory employment practices. Therefore, organizations large and small see important reasons for proactively addressing diversity issues. These employers experience significant benefits because of their diversity efforts, including those described next.

DIVERSITY AND ORGANIZATIONAL PERFORMANCE A number of organizations have found that because they serve a diverse set of customers, there are significant business reasons for having a diverse workforce.[121] The employees have greater cultural understanding of how products and services can be viewed and accepted by different

Exhibit 500.67 *Dimensions of Diversity*

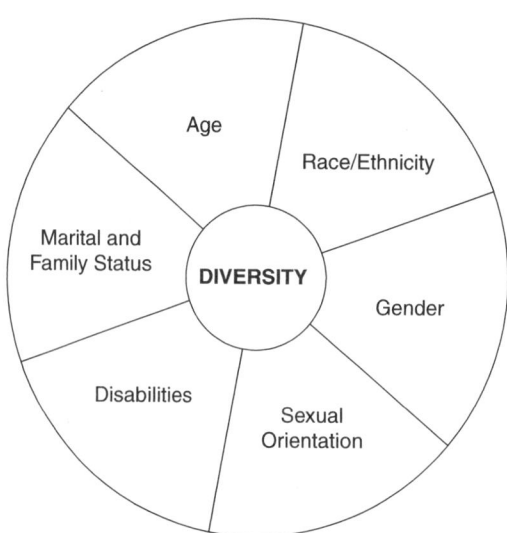

groups. The value of diversity is reinforced by a survey that found a majority of both HR professionals and job seekers believe diversity initiatives have made organizations more successful.[122] Even though many organizations have instituted diversity programs, most of them have not documented how diversity efforts affect organizational performance.

RECRUITING AND RETENTION A second reason for diversity efforts is that they aid in recruiting and retaining workers from diverse backgrounds. Not surprisingly, people of different backgrounds prefer to work in an organization where there are others "like" them. Support for the important role that diversity plays in recruiting and retention comes from a study of 750 diverse professional job holders. That study found that one-third of minority and female job candidates will rule out an employer because of perceived lack of diversity.[123]

DIVERSE THINKING AND PROBLEM SOLVING Another advantage of embracing diversity is to get more diverse thinking and problem solving. Groups containing people with widely varying backgrounds are more likely to see factors and issues differently and consider a greater range of decision alternatives. One example illustrates this point. A group of managers was planning the introduction of a new telecommunications service. By having African American and Hispanic employees who come from less affluent economic backgrounds as part of the planning, the firm developed multitier pricing and service plans that would appeal to low- and moderate- income consumers, not just the more affluent ones.

REDUCTION IN DISCRIMINATION COMPLAINTS AND COSTS Even if all the advantages of diversity are ignored, efforts that ensure compliance with EEO laws and regulations can reduce the time and legal costs associated with discrimination complaints. Legal experts and others have noticed that when employers tolerate incidents of discrimination or other inappropriate actions to individuals based on "being different," then isolated incidents spread to become bigger organizational issues.[124]

Diversity Management Programs and Activities

A wide variety of programs and activities have been used in organizations as part of diversity management efforts. Exhibit 500.68 shows common components of diversity management efforts. For diversity to succeed, the most crucial component is for diversity to be seen as a commitment throughout the organization, beginning with top management.[125] Diversity results must be measured and management accountability for achieving these results must be emphasized and rewarded. Once management accountability for diversity results has been established, then a number of different activities can be implemented as part of a diversity management program, including diversity training.

Exhibit 500.68 *Common Diversity Management Components*

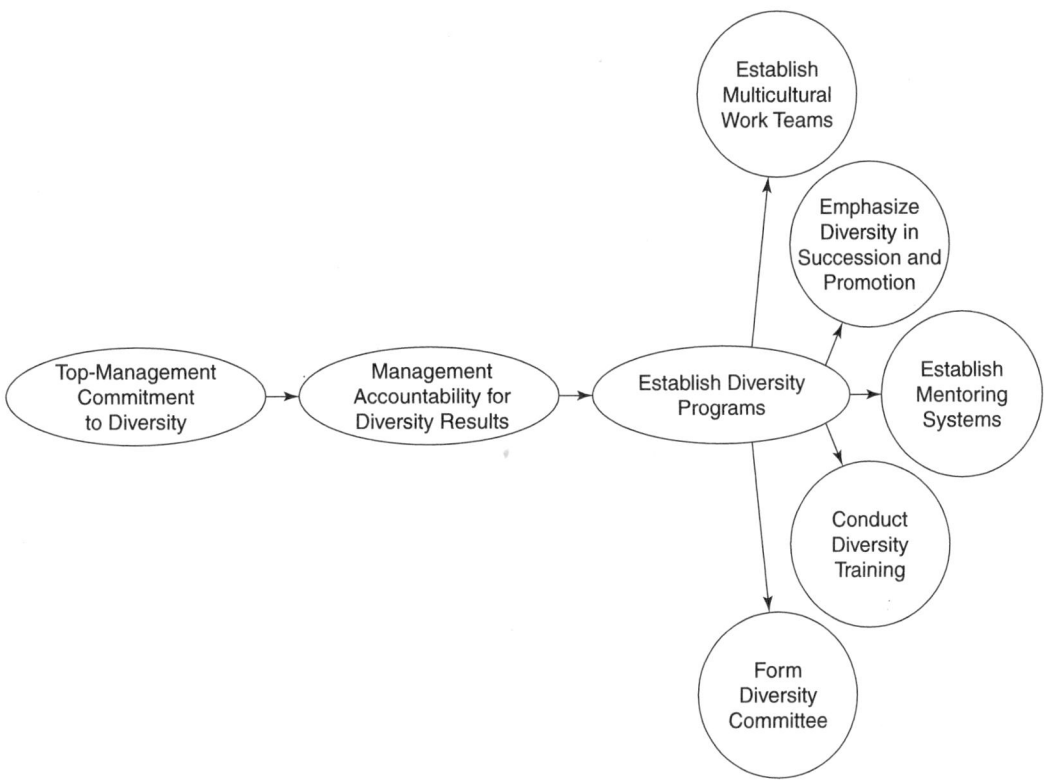

Diversity Training

There are a number of different goals for diversity training.[126] One prevalent goal is to minimize discrimination and harassment lawsuits. But other goals focus on improving acceptance and understanding of people with different backgrounds, experiences, capabilities, and lifestyles.

Components of Diversity Training

Approaches to training vary, but often include at least three components. *Legal awareness* is the first and most common component of diversity training. Here the training focuses on the legal implications of discrimination. A limited approach to diversity training stops with these legal "do's and don'ts."

By introducing *cultural awareness,* employers hope to build greater understanding of the differences among people. Cultural awareness training assists all participants to see and accept the differences in people with widely varying cultural backgrounds.

The third component of diversity training—*sensitivity training*—is more difficult. The aim here is to "sensitize" people to the differences among them and how their words and behaviors are seen by others. Some diversity training includes exercises containing examples of harassment and other behaviors.

Effects of Diversity Training

The effects of diversity training are viewed as mixed by both organizations and participants. Relatively few studies have been done on the effectiveness of diversity training expenditures, other than asking participants how they felt about the training. There is some concern that the programs may be interesting or entertaining, but may not produce longer-term changes in people's attitudes and behaviors toward others with characteristics different from their own.

Mixed reviews about the effectiveness of diversity training suggest that either the programs or how they are implemented are suspect. Two common complaints are:

1. Diversity training tends to draw attention to differences, building walls rather than breaking them down.
2. Much of the content in diversity training is viewed as "politically correct," which blames majority individuals, particularly white males, for past wrongs.

Some argue that diversity training more often than not has failed, pointing out that it does not reduce discrimination and harassment complaints. Rather than reducing conflict, in a number of situations diversity training has heightened hostility and conflicts.[127] In a number of firms it has produced divisive effects, and has not taught the behaviors needed for employees to get along in a diverse workplace.

This last point, focusing on behaviors, seems to hold the most promise for making diversity training more effective. For instance, dealing with cultural diversity as part of training efforts for sales representatives and managers has produced positive results.[128] Teaching appropriate behaviors and skills in relationships with others is more likely to produce satisfactory results than focusing just on attitudes and beliefs among diverse employees.

Backlash against Diversity Efforts

The negative consequences of diversity training manifest themselves more broadly in a backlash against diversity efforts. This backlash takes two main forms. First, and somewhat surprisingly, the individuals in protected groups, such as women and racial minorities, sometimes see the diversity efforts as inadequate and nothing but "corporate public relations." Thus, it appears that by establishing diversity programs, employers are raising the expectation levels of protected group individuals, but the programs are not meeting these expectations.[129] This failure can result in further disillusionment and more negativity toward the organization by those who would initially appear to benefit the most from such programs.

On the other side, a number of those individuals who are not in protected groups, primarily white males, believes the emphasis on diversity sets them up as scapegoats for the societal problems created by increasing diversity. Surveys of white males frequently show hostility and anger at diversity efforts. Those programs are widely perceived as only benefitting women and minorities and taking away opportunities for men and nonminorities.[130] This resentment and hostility is usually directed at affirmative action programs that employers have instituted.

Affirmative Action and Diversity Efforts

Affirmative action began as a requirement for federal government contractors to document the inclusion of women and racial minorities in the workforce. As part of those government regulations, covered employers must submit plans describing their attempts to narrow the gaps between the composition of their workforces and that of labor markets where they obtain employees. A practical concern with affirmative action efforts is how to "count" individuals with a multiracial background.

By setting *goals, targets,* and *time tables* as part of affirmative action efforts, employers specify how many of which types of individuals they hope to have in their workforce in the future. By specifying these goals the employers say they are trying to "appropriately include protected group members" or "ensure a balanced and representative workforce." These phrases and others like them commonly are used to describe the thrust of affirmative action.

However, critics of affirmative action say that regardless of the language used, subsequent actions lead to the use of *preferential selection* for protected group members over equally qualified white males and others not covered by the EEO regulations. The result is *reverse discrimination,* whereby a person is refused employment opportunities because of being the "wrong" race, sex, age, or other classification. Supporters have offered many reasons why affirmative action is necessary and important, while opponents argue against it.

AFFIRMATIVE ACTION AND COURT DECISIONS As the composition of U.S. courts has changed, judicial views of affirmative action have changed also. Many of these decisions have been close votes in the courts, especially at the U.S. Supreme Court. Obviously as judges are appointed who are either more favorable or more skeptical of affirmative action, the legal status of affirmative action might change.

Regardless of the viewpoints held about affirmative action, diversity is a reality that is a strategic HR concern to be addressed in all organizations. Also, despite the differing philosophical views of affirmative action, there are still a large number of EEO regulations and laws that exist. HR professionals must ensure that their organizations comply with EEO requirements for different protected groups.

Sex/Gender Issues in Equal Employment

The influx of women into the workforce has major social, economic, and organizational consequences. The percentage of the total U.S. civilian workforce has increased dramatically since 1950, to where women comprise almost half of today's workers.

A major reason for the increasing share of women in the workforce is that more women with children are working than in previous decades. About 76 percent of women ages 25–54 are in the workforce. Further, about half of all currently working women are single, separated, divorced, widowed, or otherwise single heads of households. Consequently, they are "primary" income earners, not co-income providers, who often must balance family and work responsibilities.

As part of managing diversity, it is important that employers take steps to have policies compatible with workers who are pregnant or are new parents. Due to the Pregnancy Discrimination Act, employers must not discriminate against pregnant women when making selection, promotion, training, or other employment-related decisions. The Family and Medical Leave Act (FMLA) requirements also affect the management of pregnant workers and new parents. This act applies to both female and male employees who are new parents, either through adoptions or natural births. Many employers have policies allowing new mothers to nurse or use breast pumps during business hours away from their worksites.[131]

Sex Discrimination in Jobs and Careers

The growth in the number of women in the workforce has led to more sex/gender issues related to jobs and careers. Additionally, the selection and promotion criteria that employers use can discriminate against women. Some cases have found that women were not allowed to enter certain jobs or job fields. Particularly problematic is the use of marital or family status as a basis for not selecting women.

NEPOTISM Many employers have policies that restrict or prohibit **nepotism**, the practice of allowing relatives to work for the same employer. Other firms require only that relatives not work directly for or with each other or be placed in a position where potential collusion or conflicts could occur. The policies most frequently cover spouses, brothers, sisters, mothers, fathers, sons, and daughters. Generally, employer antinepotism policies have been upheld by courts, in spite of the concern that they tend to discriminate against women more than men (because women tend to be denied employment or leave employers more often as a result of marriage to other employees).

Nepotism Practice of allowing relatives to work for the same employer.

JOB ASSIGNMENTS AND "NONTRADITIONAL JOBS" One result of the increasing number of women in the workforce is the movement of women into jobs traditionally held by men. The U.S. Department of Labor defines nontraditional occupations for women as those in which women comprise 25 percent or less of the total number employed.[132]

The right of employers to reassign women from hazardous jobs to ones that may be lower paying because of health-related concerns is another issue. Employers' fears about higher health insurance costs, and even possible lawsuits involving such problems as birth defects caused by damage sustained during pregnancy, have led some employers to institute reproductive and fetal protection policies. However, the U.S. Supreme Court has ruled such policies are illegal. Also, having different job conditions for men and women usually is held to be discriminatory. In a related area, a U.S. district court case found that the exclusion of prescription contraceptions from an employer's benefits plan constitutes sex discrimination.[133]

THE GLASS CEILING For years, women's groups have alleged that women in workplaces encounter a **glass ceiling**, which refers to discriminatory practices that have prevented women and other protected-class members from advancing to executive-level jobs. The extent of the problem is seen in the results of a survey of 825 large firms, in which women accounted for only 3.9 percent of the highest-paid executives, and only 1 percent of the firms had a female CEO.[134] Similar problems exist for racial/minority individuals as well.[135] In conjunction with the Civil Rights Act of 1991, a Glass Ceiling Commission conducted a study on how to shatter the glass ceiling encountered by women and other protected-class members. A number of recommendations were included in the commission's report.[136]

Glass ceiling Discriminatory practices that have prevented women and other protected-class members from advancing to executive-level jobs.

"GLASS WALLS" AND "GLASS ELEVATOR" A related problem is that women have tended to advance to senior management in a limited number of support areas, such as HR and corporate communications. Because jobs in these "supporting" areas tend to pay less than jobs in sales, marketing, operations, or finance, the overall impact is to reduce

540. WORKFORCE DIVERSITY MANAGEMENT

women's career progression and income. Limits that keep women from progressing only in certain fields have been referred to as "glass walls" or "glass elevators."

BREAKING THE GLASS A growing number of employers have recognized that "breaking the glass," whether ceilings, walls, or elevators, is good business. Some of the most common means used to "break the glass" are as follows:

- Establishing formal mentoring programs for women and racial/ethnic individuals
- Providing career rotation opportunities into operations, marketing, and sales for individuals who have shown talent in accounting, human resources, and other areas[137]
- Increasing top management and board of directors membership to include women and individuals of color
- Establishing clear goals for retention and progression of protected-class individuals and holding managers accountable for achieving these goals
- Allowing for alternative work arrangements for employees, particularly those balancing work/family responsibilities

Sexual Harassment and Workplace Relationships

As more women have entered the workforce, more men and women work together in teams and on projects. Consequently, more employers are becoming concerned about the close personal relationships that do develop at work.

Consensual Relationships and Romance at Work

When work-based friendships lead to romance and off-the-job sexual relationships, managers and employers face a dilemma: Should they "monitor" these relationships in order to protect the firm from potential legal complaints, but thereby "meddling" in employees' private, off-the-job lives? Or do they simply ignore such relationships and the potential problems they present? One study found that the way a romance relationship is viewed affects the actions that may be taken.[138] For instance, if a relationship is clearly consensual, or if it involves a supervisor-subordinate relationship, then the actions taken may be different.

The greatest concerns are romantic relationships between supervisors and subordinates, because the harassment of subordinates by supervisors is the most frequent type of sexual harassment situation. Some employers have addressed the issue of workplace romances by establishing policies permitting workplace romances, as shown by a study that over 70 percent of surveyed firms had such a policy.[139] Those policies often describe "appropriate" workplace behaviors or may require disclosure to the HR department. Employment attorneys generally recommend that the HR manager remind both parties in workplace romances of the company policy on sexual harassment and encourage either party to contact the HR department should the relationship cool and become one involving unwanted and unwelcome attentions. Also, the HR manager always should document that such conversations occurred.

Nature of Sexual Harassment

Sexual harassment is a significant concern in many organizations and can occur by men harassing women, women harassing men, or same-sex harassment. As shown by Exhibit 500.69, individuals in different roles can be sexual harassers.

Most frequently, sexual harassment occurs by a male in a supervisory or managerial position who harasses women within his "power structure." However, women managers have been found guilty of sexually harassing male employees. Also, same-sex harassment has occurred.

Third parties who are not employees also have been found to be harassers.[140] From a vending machine sales driver to a board member in a rural cooperative, employees have won sexual harassment complaints against their employers who took no action against the third party causing the harassment. Even customer service representatives and food servers have won sexual harassment complaints because their employers refused to protect the employees from regular sexual harassment by aggressive customers.

TYPES OF SEXUAL HARASSMENT Two basic types of sexual harassment have been defined by EEOC regulations and a large number of court cases. The two types are defined as follows:

1. *Quid pro quo* is harassment in which employment outcomes are linked to the individual granting sexual favors.
2. *Hostile environment* harassment exists when an individual's work performance or psychological well-being is unreasonably affected by intimidating or offensive working conditions.

Exhibit 500.69 *Potential Sexual Harassers*

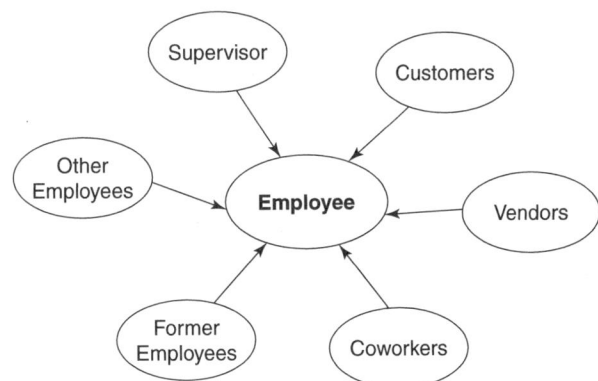

In the *quid pro quo* type, an employee may be told he or she may get promoted, receive a special raise, or be given a desirable work assignment, but only if the employee submits to granting some sexual favors to the supervisor. Unfortunately, *hostile environment* harassment is much more prevalent, partially because the standards and consequences are more varied. Actual case situations illustrate how the hostile environment standard has been used.

- The male manager at a fast-food franchise restaurant in Maryland was found guilty of sexual harassment when he repeatedly made sexual jokes and discussed sexual behavior with two younger female employees. When they complained to the manager's boss, no action was taken, and the harassment increased.[141]
- A female sales representative filed a sexual harassment charge that a male manager used offensive language, told derogatory jokes, and distributed sexually explicit materials at sales meetings. Following her complaint, the firm required the manager to take an unpaid three-month leave and have additional management training. Interestingly, the court ruled that the alleged name-calling and offensive language was not offensive because the woman used such language regularly. Ultimately the court ruled against the woman's sexual harassment complaint.[142]

Quid pro quo Sexual harassment in which employment outcomes are linked to the individual granting sexual favors.

Hostile environment Sexual harassment where an individual's work performance or psychological well-being is unreasonably affected by intimidating or offensive working conditions.

These cases and many others have revealed that commenting on dress or appearance, telling jokes that are suggestive or sexual in nature, allowing revealing photos and posters to be on display, or making continual requests to get together after work can lead to the creation of a hostile work environment. As computer and Internet technology has spread, the number of electronic sexual harassment cases has grown.

Regardless of the type of sexual harassment, it is apparent that sexual harassment has significant consequences on the organization, other employees, and especially those harassed. Follow-up interviews and research with victims of sexual harassment reveal that the harassment has both job-related and psychological effects.[143] Also, harassment even has a ripple effect on others who fear being harassed or view their employer more negatively if prompt, remedial actions do not occur. Thus, how employers respond to sexual harassment complaints is crucial for both legal reasons and employee morale.

Changing Legal Standards on Sexual Harassment

Several years ago the U.S. Supreme Court issued rulings in three different cases that significantly clarified both the legal aspects of when sexual harassment occurs and what actions employers should take to reduce their liabilities if sexual harassment claims are filed.[144] If the employee suffered any tangible employment action (such as being denied raises, being terminated, or being refused access to training) because of the sexual harassment, then the employer is liable. However, even if the employee suffered no tangible employment action, and the employer has not produced an affirmative defense, then employer liability still exists.

Only if the employer can produce evidence of an affirmative defense in which the employer took reasonable care to prohibit sexual harassment does the employer have the possibility of avoiding liability. Components of ensuring reasonable care include the following:

- Establishing a sexual harassment policy
- Communicating the policy regularly

- Training employees and managers on avoiding sexual harassment
- Investigating and taking action when complaints are voiced

Age Issues and Diversity Management

Most of the developed countries are experiencing an aging of their populations, including Australia, Japan, most European countries, and the United States. The aging of the population means many "mature workers" in organizations.

As more older workers with a lifetime of experience and skills retire, HR will face significant challenges in replacing them with workers having the capabilities and work ethic that characterize many mature workers. But, many older workers stay active in the workforce. For instance, more than half of both men and women workers over 70 are employed part-time. Also, full-time workforce participation does not drop significantly until age 65, especially for women.[145]

Employment discrimination against individuals age 40 and older is prohibited by the Age Discrimination in Employment Act (ADEA). Employers must be aware of a number of legal issues associated with managing older workers.

Individuals with Disabilities in the Workforce

Employers looking for workers with the knowledge, skills, and abilities to perform jobs often have neglected a significant source—individuals with physical or mental disabilities. At least 55 million Americans with disabilities are covered by the Americans with Disabilities Act (ADA), but only 25 percent of them are currently employed. Estimates are that as many as 10 million of these individuals could be added to the workforce if appropriate accommodations were made by employers.

The number of complaints filed under the ADA has skyrocketed in recent years. According to statistics from the EEOC, over 125,000 disability discrimination complaints were filed in the first several years the act was in effect.[146] Fortunately for employers, only 48 percent of those complaints resulted in a finding of "reasonable cause" of discrimination, leading to further compliance actions or lawsuits. Over half of all complaints had to do with discharge of employees with disabilities or employees who became disabled. Another 25 percent dealt with failure to provide reasonable accommodation.

Reasonable Accommodations

At the heart of employing individuals with disabilities is for employers to make reasonable accommodations in several areas. First, architectural barriers should not prohibit disabled individuals' access to work areas or restrooms. A second area of reasonable accommodation is the assignment of work tasks. Satisfying this requirement may mean modifying jobs, work area layouts, work schedules, or providing special equipment.[147]

Individuals with Life-Threatening Illnesses

Individuals with life-threatening illnesses have been determined by the U.S. Supreme Court to be covered by the ADA. Individuals with leukemia, cancer, or AIDS are all considered as having disabilities, and employers must respond to them appropriately or face charges of discrimination.

Religion and Spirituality in Workplaces

Diversity is also found in the religious beliefs and degrees of spirituality that employees bring to work. Title VII of the Civil Rights Act of 1964 prohibits discrimination at work on the basis of religion; also, employers are prohibited from discriminating against employees for their religious beliefs and practices.

Individuals with Differing Lifestyles and Sexual Orientations

As if demographic diversity did not place pressure enough on managers and organizations, individuals in the workforce today have widely varying lifestyles that can have work-related consequences. Legislative efforts have been made to protect individuals with differing lifestyles or sexual orientations from employment discrimination, though at present only a few cities and states have passed such laws.[148]

One specific issue that some employers have had to address is that of transgendered individuals who have had or are undergoing sex change surgery. Regarding transsexuals (individuals who have had sex-change surgery), federal court cases and the EEOC have ruled that sex discrimination under Title VII applies to a person's gender at birth. Thus, it does not apply to the new gender of those who have had gender-altering operations.

Employee Benefits and Compensation

Managing Employee Benefits

Employers provide employee benefits to their workers for being part of the organization. A **benefit** is a form of indirect compensation. Benefits often include retirement plans, vacations with pay, health insurance, educational assistance, and many more programs.

Employers in the United States often fill the role of major provider of benefits for citizens. However, in many other nations, citizens and employers are taxed to pay for government-provided benefits, such as health care and retirement programs managed through government social programs. Although federal regulations require U.S. employers to provide certain benefits, U.S. employers voluntarily provide many others.

Benefits influence employees' decisions about which particular employer to work for, whether to stay or leave employment, and when they might retire. However, the unique characteristics of benefits sometimes make them difficult to administer. For example, government involvement in benefits continues to expand. The federal and state governments *require* that certain benefits be offered (Social Security, worker's compensation, unemployment insurance, etc.), and they regulate many of the nonrequired benefits as well (retirement, family leave, flexible benefits, etc.).

Further, employees tend to take benefits for granted. For instance, so many organizations offer health insurance that employees expect it. However, benefits are also very complex and, as a result, employees may not understand them, or in many cases may not even know what benefits exist. Yet benefits are costly to the employer, averaging about 40 percent of payroll costs over the past several years (for required and voluntary benefits together). These characteristics of benefits suggest that HR managers should carefully consider the strategic role of benefits in their organizations.

Strategic Perspectives on Benefits

From the employers' perspective, employee benefits represent a double-edged sword. On one side, employers know that in order to attract and retain employees with the necessary capabilities they must offer appropriate benefits.[149] On the other side, they know the importance of controlling or even cutting costs. Benefits comprise a significant part of the total compensation package offered to employees. Total compensation includes money paid directly (such as wages and salaries) and money paid indirectly (such as benefits). Too often, both managers and employees think of only wages and salaries as compensation and fail to consider the additional costs associated with benefits expenditures.

Total compensation costs for labor amounts to more than half of total operating costs in many organizations, even more in some service operations. For example, about 80 percent of the U.S. Post Office budget is labor cost. Because of their

Exhibit 500.70 *How the Benefit Dollar Is Spent*

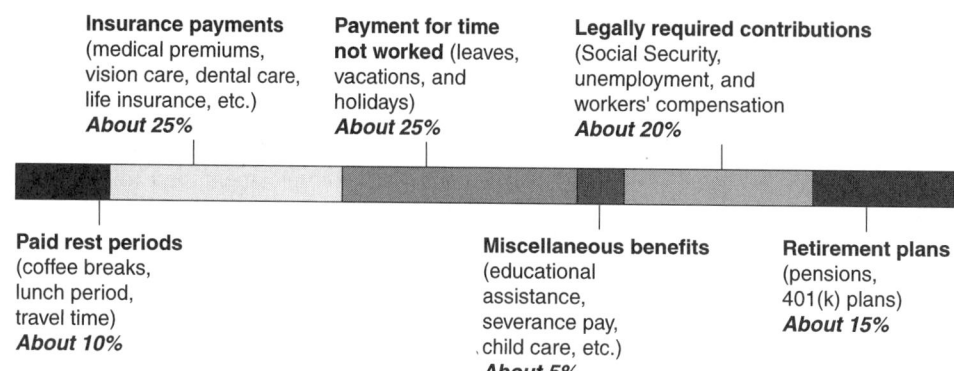

Source: Based on information in *Employee Benefits,* 2000 edition (Washington, D.C.: U.S. Chamber of Commerce, 2000).

sizable proportion of organizational costs, the compensation components of base pay, variable pay, and benefits require serious and realistic assessment and planning. Exhibit 500.70 shows where each benefit dollar typically is spent, on average, based on various, regularly-conducted surveys.

Goals for Benefits

Benefits should be looked at as part of the overall compensation strategy of the organization. For instance, an organization can choose to compete for employees by providing base compensation, variable pay, or benefits, or perhaps all three. Which approach is chosen depends on many factors, such as the competition, organizational life cycle, and corporate strategy.[150] For example, a new firm may choose to have lower base pay, and use high variable incentives to attract new employees, but keep the cost of benefits as low as possible for awhile. Or an organization that hires predominately younger female employees might choose a family-friendly set of benefits including on-site child care to attract good employees.[151]

Benefits Needs Analysis

A **benefits needs analysis** includes a comprehensive look at all aspects of benefits in a firm. Done periodically, such an analysis is more than simply deciding what benefits employees might want. A benefits needs analysis to make certain the mix of benefits is doing what it should might consider the following issues:

Benefits needs analysis A comprehensive look at all aspects of benefits.

- How much total compensation, including benefits, should be provided?
- What part should benefits comprise of the total compensation of individuals?
- What expense levels are acceptable for each benefit offered?
- Why is each type of benefit offered?
- Which employees should be given or offered which benefits?
- What is being received by the organization in return for each benefit?
- How does having a comprehensive benefits package aid in minimizing turnover or maximizing recruiting and retention of employees?
- How flexible should the package of benefits be?

Funding Benefits

Total benefits costs can be funded both by contributions made by the employer and contributions made by the employee. If the employer fully subsidizes a benefit, the cost to the employee would be zero. But if an employer chooses to pay $400 per month toward an employee's health insurance premium while the employee pays $150, then the employee contributes to covering benefits costs.

Benefit plans can be funded by purchasing insurance from an insurance provider. Premiums to be paid reflect the predicted claims and will be adjusted based on actual claims. Some large employers choose to "self-fund" and be their own insurers by setting aside moneys to cover benefits costs. Self-funding by large employers has been effective in a number of situations.

The Nature and Types of Benefits

Employers offer some benefits to aid recruiting and retention, some because they are required to do so, and some simply because doing so reinforces the company philosophy.[152] For example, insurance can be purchased at a better rate if the purchaser is a large employer that qualifies for a group rate. Further, tax laws provide beneficial tax treatment of some benefits for employees that they would not get if purchased by individuals.

Benefits generally are not taxed as income to employees. For this reason, they represent a somewhat more valuable reward to employees than an equivalent cash payment. For example, assume that employee Henry Gomez is in a 25 percent tax bracket. If Henry earns an extra $400, he must pay $100 in taxes on this amount (disregarding exemptions). But if his employer provides prescription drug coverage in a benefit plan, and he receives the $400 as payments for prescription drugs, he is not taxed on the amount; he receives the value of the entire $400. This feature makes benefits a desirable form of compensation to employees.

Types of Benefits

There are a wide range of benefits offered. Exhibit 500.71 shows the many different benefits classified by type.

GOVERNMENT-MANDATED BENEFITS There are many **mandated benefits** that employers in the United States must provide to employees by law. Social Security and unemployment insurance are funded through a tax paid by the employer based on the employee's compensation. Workers' compensation laws exist in all states. In addition, under the Family and Medical Leave Act (FMLA), employers must offer unpaid leaves to employees with certain medical or family difficulties. Other mandated benefits are available through Medicare, which provides health care for those age 65 and over. It is funded in part by an employer tax through Social Security. The Consolidated Omnibus Budget Reconciliation Act (COBRA) and the Health Insurance Portability and Accountability Act (HIPAA) mandate that an employer continue health-care coverage paid for by the employees after they leave the organization, and that most employees be able to obtain coverage if they were previously covered in a health plan.

> **Mandated benefits** Benefits that employers in the United States must provide to employees by law.

Exhibit 500.71 *Types of Benefits*

Security	Health Care	Family-Oriented
Workers' compensation (GM)	COBRA and HIPAA provisions (GM)	Family and Medical Leave Act (GM)
Unemployment compensation (GM)	Medical and dental (EV)	Dependent care (EV)
Supplemental unemployment benefits (SUB) (EV)	HMO or PPO health-care plans (EV)	Alternative work arrangements (EV)
Severance pay (EV)	Long-term care (EV)	*Time Off*
Retirement Security	Vision care (EV)	Military reserve time off (GM)
Social Security (GM)	Prescription drugs (EV)	Election and jury leaves (GM)
Early retirement options (EV)	Psychiatric counseling (EV)	Lunch and rest breaks (EV)
Pre-retirement counseling (EV)	Wellness programs (EV)	Holidays and vacations (EV)
Disability retirement benefits (EV)	*Financial, Insurance and Related*	Funeral and bereavement leaves (EV)
Health care for retirees (EV)	Life insurance (EV)	Sick leave and paid time off (EV)
Pension plans (EV)	Legal insurance (EV)	*Social and Recreational*
Individual retirement accounts (IRAs)	Disability insurance (EV)	Tennis courts (EV)
401(k) and 403(b) plans (EV)	Financial counseling (EV)	Bowling leagues (EV)
	Credit unions (EV)	Service awards (EV)
	Company-provided car and expense account (EV)	Sponsored events (athletic and social) (EV)
	Educational assistance (EV)	Cafeteria and food services (EV)
		Recreation programs (EV)

Note: Government Mandated (GM), Employer Voluntary (EV)

Additional mandated benefits have been *proposed* for many other areas, but as yet none of the proposals have been adopted. Areas in which coverage has been proposed are as follows:

- Universal health-care benefits for all workers
- Child-care assistance
- Pension plan coverage that can be transferred by workers who change jobs
- Core benefits for part-time employees working at least 500 hours per year

A major reason for these proposals is that federal and state governments want to shift many of the social costs for health care and other expenditures to employers. This shift would relieve some of the budgetary pressures facing governments who otherwise might have to raise taxes and cut spending.

VOLUNTARY BENEFITS Employers voluntarily offer other types of benefits in order to compete for and retain employees. By offering additional benefits, organizations are recognizing the need to provide greater security and benefit support to workers with widely varied personal circumstances. By offering more benefits, employers hope to strengthen the ties with their employees as valuable human resources. Also, as the workforce ages and more individuals retire, financial security in retirement becomes an issue that employees want to address. In addition, as work and jobs change to emphasize flexibility and choice, both workers and employers are realizing that choices among benefits are necessary, as evidenced by the growth in flexible benefits and cafeteria benefit plans. The following sections describe the different types of benefits that were shown in Exhibit 500.71.

Security Benefits

A number of benefits provide employee security. These benefits include some mandated by laws and others offered by employers voluntarily. The primary benefits found in most organizations include workers' compensation, unemployment compensation, and severance pay.

Retirement Security Benefits

Few people set aside sufficient financial reserves to use when they retire, so employer retirement benefits attempt to provide income for retired employees. Except for some employers with fewer than 100 employees, most employers offer some kind of retirement plan. Generally, private pensions make up a critical portion of income for people after retirement. With the baby boomer generation in the U.S. closing in on retirement, pressures on such funds are likely to grow. With more people retiring earlier, but living longer, retirement benefits are becoming a greater concern for employers, employees, and retired employees.

Health-Care Benefits

Employers provide a variety of health-care and medical benefits, usually through insurance coverage. The most common plans cover medical, dental, prescription drug, and vision care expenses for employees and their dependents. Basic health-care insurance to cover both normal and major medical expenses is also desired and expected by most employees. Dental insurance is also important to many employees. Some dental plans include orthodontic coverage, which is a major expense for some families. Some employer medical insurance plans also cover psychiatric counseling, but many do not.

The costs of health-care insurance have continued to escalate at a rate well in excess of inflation for several decades. By the 1990s, the rise in health-care costs forced many employers to make concerted efforts to control medical premium increases and other health-care costs. Estimates are that the average health-care cost per employee is over $5,500 per year.[153] Although successful for a while, the rate of increases in health-benefits costs has turned up again.

As a result of these large increases, many employers find that dealing with health-care benefits is time consuming and expensive. This is especially frustrating for employers who have found that many employees seem to take their health benefits for granted. Consequently, a growing number of firms, particularly smaller ones, have asked, "Why are we offering these benefits anyway?" and have answered the question by discontinuing health benefits altogether.[154]

Financial, Insurance, and Other Related Benefits

Employers may offer workers a wide range of special benefits: financial benefits, insurance benefits (in addition to health-related insurance), educational benefits, social benefits, and recreational benefits. From the point of view of the employer, such benefits can be useful in attracting and retaining employees. Workers like receiving special benefits, which often are not taxed as income.

Family-Oriented Benefits

The composition of families in the United States has changed significantly in the past few decades. The number of traditional families, in which the man went to work and the woman stayed home to raise children, has declined significantly, while the percentage of two-worker families has more than doubled. The growth in dual-career couples, single-parent households, and increasing work demands on many workers has increased the emphasis some employers are placing on family-oriented benefits. As mentioned before, balancing family and work demands presents a major challenge to many workers at all levels of organizations. To provide assistance, employers have established a variety of family-oriented benefits, and the federal government passed the Family and Medical Leave Act.

Time-Off Benefits

Employers give employees paid time off in a variety of circumstances. Paid lunch breaks and rest periods, holidays, and vacations are common. But leaves are given for a number of other purposes as well. Time-off benefits represent an estimated 5 percent to 13 percent of total compensation. Typical time-off benefits include holiday pay, vacation pay, and leaves of absence. Other leaves include military, election, jury duty, funeral or bereavement leave.

Social and Recreational Benefits

Some benefits and services are social and recreational in nature, such as bowling leagues, picnics, parties, employer-sponsored athletic teams, organizationally owned recreational lodges, and other sponsored activities and interest groups. As interest in employee wellness has increased, more firms provide recreational facilities and activities. But employers should retain control of all events associated with their organizations because of possible legal responsibility.

The idea behind social and recreational programs is to promote employee happiness and team spirit. Employees may appreciate this type of benefit, but managers should not necessarily expect increased job productivity or job satisfaction as a result. Other such benefits too numerous to detail are made available by various employers as well.

Benefits Administration

With the myriad of benefits and regulations, it is easy to see why many organizations must make coordinated efforts to administer benefits programs. Exhibit 500.72 shows how benefits administration responsibilities can be split between HR specialists and other managers. HR specialists play the more significant role, but managers must assume responsibility for some of the communication aspects of benefits administration.

Benefits Communication

Employees generally do not know much about the values and costs associated with the benefits they receive from employers. Yet benefits communication and benefits satisfaction are linked. Many employers have instituted special benefits communication systems to inform employees about the value of the benefits they provide.

Exhibit 500.72 *Typical Division of HR Responsibilities: Benefits Administration*

HR Unit	Managers
• Develops and administers benefit systems. • Answers employees' technical questions on benefits. • Assists employees in filing benefit claims. • Coordinates special prerequirement programs.	• Answer simple questions on benefits. • Maintain liaison with HR specialists on benefits. • Maintain good communications with employees near retirement. • Coordinate use of time-off benefits

BENEFITS STATEMENTS Some employers also give each employee an annual "personal statement of benefits" that translates benefits into dollar amounts. Federal regulations under ERISA require that employees receive an annual pension-reporting statement, which also can be included in the personal statements. By having a personalized statement, each employee can see how much his or her own benefits are worth. Employers hope that by educating employees about benefit costs, they can manage expenditures better and can give employees a better appreciation for the employers' payments.

HRIS AND BENEFITS COMMUNICATION The advent of HRIS options linked to intranets provides additional links to communicate benefits to employees. The use of employee self-service kiosks allows employees to obtain benefits information on-line. These kiosks and other information technology also allow employees to change their benefits choices, track their benefits balances, and submit questions to HR staff members and external benefits providers. HR professionals are utilizing information systems to communicate benefits information, conduct employee benefit surveys, and provide other benefits communications.

Flexible Benefits

Flexible benefits plan One that allows employees to select the benefits they prefer from groups of benefits established by the employer.

A **flexible benefits plan,** sometimes called a *flex* or *cafeteria* plan, allows employees to select the benefits they prefer from groups of benefits established by the employer. By making a variety of "dishes" or benefits available, the organization allows each employee to select an individual combination of benefits within some overall limits. As a result of the changing composition of the workforce, flexible benefits plans have grown in popularity.

Larger employers use flexible benefits plans more often than smaller ones do. Because benefits vendors require a sufficient number of employees to make providing the choices worthwhile, they generally recommend that at least 100 employees be covered to make a flexible benefits plan feasible.

Flexible benefits systems recognize that individual employee situations differ because of age, family status, and lifestyle. For instance, individuals in dual-career couples may not want the same benefits from two different employers. Under a flex plan, one of them can forego some benefits available in the partner's plan and take other benefits instead.

Flexible spending account Account that allows employees to contribute pretax dollars to buy additional benefits.

FLEXIBLE SPENDING ACCOUNTS Under current tax laws (Section 125 of the IRS Code), employees can divert some income before taxes into accounts to fund certain benefits. These **flexible spending accounts** allow employees to contribute pretax dollars to buy additional benefits. An example illustrates the advantage of these accounts to employees. Assume an employee earns $3,000 per month and has $100 per month deducted to put into a flexible spending account. That $100 does not count as gross income for tax purposes, so the employee's taxable income is reduced. The employee uses the money in the account to purchase additional benefits.

Under tax laws at the time of this writing, the funds in the account can be used only to purchase the following: (1) additional health care (including offsetting deductibles), (2) life insurance, (3) disability insurance, and (4) dependent-care benefits. Furthermore, tax regulations require that if employees do not spend all of the money in their accounts by the end of the year, they forfeit it. Therefore, it is important that employees carefully estimate the additional benefits they will use.

Flexible spending accounts have grown in popularity as more flexible benefits plans have been adopted by more employers. Of course, such plans and their tax advantages can be changed as Congress passes future health-care and tax-related legislation.

Problems with Flexible Plans

A problem with flexibility in benefit choice is that an *inappropriate benefits package* may be chosen by an employee. A young construction worker may not choose a disability benefit; however, if he or she is injured, the family may suffer financial hardship. Part of this problem can be overcome by requiring employees to select a core set of benefits (life, health, and disability insurance) and then offering options on other benefits.

Another problem can be **adverse selection,** whereby only higher-risk employees select and use certain benefits. Because many insurance plans are based on a group rate, the employer may face higher rates if insufficient numbers of employees select an insurance option.

Despite these disadvantages, it is likely that flex plans will continue to grow in popularity. The ability to match benefits to differing employee needs, while also controlling some costs, is so attractive that employers will try to find ways to overcome the disadvantages that exist in their benefits plans.

Benefits in the Future

Benefits are indeed changing and those changes and the IRS have made them increasingly complex. As a result, benefit functions are among the most outsourced in HR. Whether pension plan, health plan administration, or COBRA tracking, benefit outsourcing is a wave of the present and future. Benefits administration, service, financial reporting and accounting, and compliance and reporting can all be outsourced.

Many employees also have access to Internet-based benefits support systems. For instance, use of the Internet allows employees in a growing number of organizations to check their retirement fund balances and move funds among various financial options.

BENEFITS AND DIFFERENT GENERATIONS Individuals in generations X and Y frequently express different needs and wants from those of the baby boomer generation in many job-related areas. However, that is not so in benefits, as new college graduates often are looking for the following (in order) in their first jobs:[155]

- Medical insurance
- 401(k) plan
- Annual raises
- Life insurance
- Dental insurance

Of course, most employers already offer those benefits because their baby boomer employees want them too.

TEMPORARY AND PART-TIME EMPLOYEE BENEFITS Workers who are not regular full-time employees sometimes do not receive benefits, but that is changing. In one survey, 49 percent of employers said they offer health insurance to part-timers. The contribution is half the amount provided for full-timers.[156]

Compensation Strategies and Practices

Compensation systems in organizations must be linked to organizational objectives and strategies. Compensation also requires balancing the interests and costs of the employer with the expectations of employees. An effective compensation program in an organization addresses four objectives:

- Legal compliance with all appropriate laws and regulations
- Cost effectiveness for the organization
- Internal, external, and individual equity for employees
- Performance enhancement for the organization

Employers must balance compensation costs at a level that both ensures organizational competitiveness and provides sufficient rewards to employees for their knowledge, skills, abilities, and performance accomplishments. In order to attract, retain, and reward employees, employers provide several types of compensation.

Nature of Compensation

Compensation is an important factor affecting how and why people choose to work at one organization over others. Employers must be reasonably competitive with several types of compensation to attract and retain competent employees.

Types of Compensation

Rewards can be both intrinsic and extrinsic. *Intrinsic* rewards often include praise for completing a project or meeting performance objectives. Other psychological and social effects of compensation reflect the intrinsic type of rewards.[157] *Extrinsic* rewards are tangible and take both monetary and nonmonetary forms. Tangible components of a compensation

Exhibit 500.73 *Components of a Compensation Program (Direct and Indirect)*

Direct	Indirect
Base Pay	**Benefits**
• Wages	• Medical/life insurance
• Salaries	• Paid time off
Variable Pay	• Retirement pensions
• Bonuses	• Workers' compensation
• Incentives	• Education
• Stock options	• Others

program are of two general types (see Exhibit 500.73). With direct compensation, the employer exchanges monetary rewards for work done. Employers provide indirect compensation—like health insurance—to everyone simply based on membership in the organization. *Base pay* and *variable pay* are the most common forms of direct compensation. Indirect compensation commonly consists of employee *benefits*.

BASE PAY The basic compensation that an employee receives, usually as a wage or salary, is called **base pay.** Many organizations use two base pay categories, *hourly* and *salaried*, which are identified according to the way pay is distributed and the nature of the jobs. Hourly pay is the most common means of payment based on time, and employees paid hourly receive **wages,** which are payments directly calculated on the amount of time worked. In contrast, people paid **salaries** receive consistent payments each period regardless of the number of hours worked. Being salaried typically has carried higher status for employees than being paid wages. Some organizations maintain an all-salaried approach with their manufacturing and clerical employees in order to create a greater sense of loyalty and organizational commitment. However, they still must pay overtime to certain employees as defined by federal and state pay laws.

VARIABLE PAY Another type of direct pay is **variable pay,** which is compensation linked directly to individual, team, or organizational performance. The most common types of variable pay for most employees take the form of bonuses and incentive program payments. Executives often receive longer-term rewards such as stock options.

BENEFITS Many organizations provide numerous extrinsic rewards in an indirect manner. With indirect compensation, employees receive the tangible value of the rewards without receiving the actual cash. A **benefit** is an indirect reward—health insurance, vacation pay, or retirement pensions—given to an employee or group of employees as a part of organizational membership, regardless of performance.

Compensation Responsibilities

Compensation costs represent significant expenditures in most organizations. For instance, at one large hotel, employee payroll and benefits expenditures comprise about 60 percent of all costs. Although actual compensation costs can be easily calculated, the value derived by employers and employees proves more difficult to identify. To administer these expenditures wisely, HR specialists and other operating managers must work together.

A typical division of compensation responsibilities is illustrated in Exhibit 500.74. HR specialists guide the development and administration of an organizational compensation system and conduct job evaluations and wage surveys. Also, because of the technical complexity involved, HR specialists typically assume responsibility for developing base pay programs and salary structures and policies. HR specialists may or may not do actual payroll processing. This labor-intensive responsibility is typically among the first to be outsourced. However, today some companies are retaining in-house processing because of improvements in software and Internet processing.[158] Operating managers evaluate the performance of employees and consider their performance when deciding compensation increases within the policies and guidelines established by the HR unit and upper management.

Exhibit 500.74 *Typical Division of HR Responsibilities: Compensation*

HR Unit	Managers
• Develops and administers the compensation system. • Conducts job evaluation and wage surveys. • Develops wage/salary structures and policies.	• Attempt to match performance and rewards. • Recommend pay rates and increases based on guidelines from HR unit. • Evaluate employee performance for compensation purposes.

Compensation System Design Issues

Compensation decisions must be viewed strategically. Because so many organizational funds are spent on compensation-related activities, it is critical for top management and HR executives to match compensation practices with what the organization is trying to accomplish.

Consider the following examples. The compensation practices that typically exist in a new organization may be different from those in a mature, more bureaucratic organization. If a firm wishes to create an innovative, entrepreneurial culture, it may offer bonuses and stock equity programs so that employees can participate in the growth and success of the company, but set its base pay and benefits at relatively modest levels. However, for a large, stable organization, more structured pay and benefit programs may be more common. Or an employer that sees brand identification as a major business objective may want a stable workforce to ensure continuity, so compensation strategy should encourage retention. But for a high-tech firm that needs new ideas and a quick trip to market for new products, compensation might be designed to favor recruiting and marketing successes over retention.

Organizations must make a number of important decisions about the nature of a compensation system. Some decisions include the following: What philosophy and approach will be taken? How will the firm react to market pay levels? Is the job to be paid on the person's level of competence? Will pay be individual or team based?

Compensation Philosophies

The two basic compensation philosophies lie on opposite ends of a continuum. At one end of the continuum in Exhibit 500.75 is the *entitlement* philosophy; at the other end is the *performance-oriented* philosophy.[159] Most compensation systems fall somewhere in between.

A Range of Compensation Approaches

Companies regard pay as an important tool for recruiting, motivating, and retaining good people. Indeed, those goals change little over time, but the ways in which some companies approach them differ dramatically from previous approaches. Performance-based pay, tailored to the strategic circumstances of each organization, may consist of base pay, an annual bonus, a profit sharing plan, stock options, and a choice of various other benefits. Such a "total rewards" package would have been uncommon for a worker in 1950, but it is increasingly common today.[160]

The "human capital" within a firm that is performing well is likely to want to split the gains with the owners or shareholders. Variable pay combined with base pay can do that. Variable pay also shifts some of the risk of running a labor-intensive business from the company to the employees when the company is not doing well. Exhibit 500.76 presents some of the choices organizations must make regarding compensation approaches.

Decisions about Compensation Levels

Even though a company might wish to pay the top salaries in an industry on philosophical grounds, it may not be possible. Competition that keeps prices of products and services under control forces companies to control the cost of labor too. Especially when competing with lower-wage countries such as China or Mexico, the compensation paid to some U.S. workers has become an issue. However, in some industries competition is not as critical a factor. An organization may be able to pay employees more (or less) than other employers.

Exhibit 500.75 *Continuum of Compensation Philosophies*

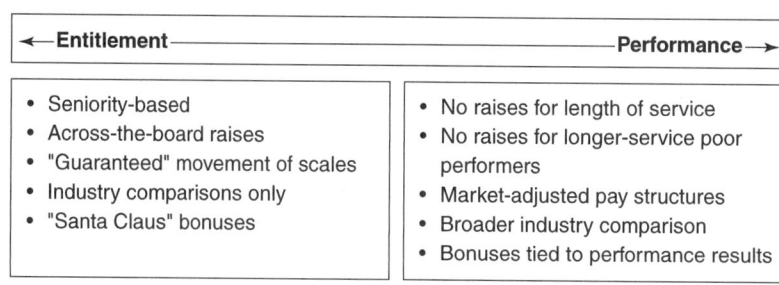

Exhibit 500.76 *Compensation Approaches*

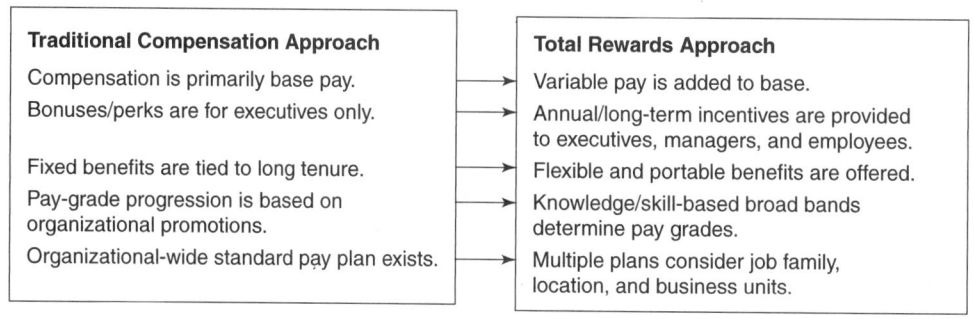

Exhibit 500.77 *Compensation Quartile Strategies*

Some organizations establish specific policies about where they wish to be positioned in the labor market. These policies use a *quartile strategy*, as illustrated in Exhibit 500.77. Data in pay surveys reveal that the actual dollar difference between quartiles is generally 15 percent to 20 percent.

Most employers choose to position themselves in the *second quartile* (median), in the middle of the market, based on pay survey data of other employers' compensation plans. Choosing this level attempts to balance employer cost pressures and the need to attract and retain employees by providing mid-level compensation levels.

An employer using a *first-quartile* approach may choose to pay below-market compensation for several reasons. The employer may be experiencing a shortage of funds, making it unable to pay more and still meet objectives. Also, when an abundance of workers is available, particularly those with lower skills, a below-market approach can be used to attract sufficient workers at a lesser cost. The downside of this strategy is that higher turnover of workers is more likely. If the labor market supply tightens, then attracting and retaining workers becomes more difficult.

A *third-quartile* approach uses an aggressive pay-above-market emphasis. This strategy generally enables a company to attract and retain sufficient workers with the required capabilities and to be more selective when hiring. However, because it is a higher-cost approach, organizations often look for ways to increase the productivity of employees receiving above-market wages.

Competency-Based Pay

The design of most compensation programs rewards employees for carrying out their tasks, duties, and responsibilities. The job requirements determine which employees have higher base rates. Employees receive more for doing jobs that require a greater variety of tasks, more knowledge and skills, greater physical effort, or more demanding working conditions.[161]

However, some organizations are emphasizing competencies rather than tasks. A number of organizations are paying employees for the competencies they demonstrate rather than just for the specific tasks performed. Paying for competencies rewards employees who exhibit more versatility and continue to develop their competencies. In knowledge-based pay (KBP) or skill-based pay (SBP) systems, employees start at a base level of pay and receive increases as they learn to do other jobs or gain other skills and therefore become more valuable to the employer. For example, a printing firm operates two-color, four-color, and six-color presses. The more colors, the more skill required of the press operators. Under a KBP or SBP system, press operators increase their pay as they learn how to operate the more complex presses, even though sometimes they may be running only two-color jobs. The success of competency plans requires managerial commitment to a philosophy different from the traditional one in organizations.[162] This approach places far more emphasis on training employees and supervisors. Also, workflow must be adapted to allow workers to move from job to job as needed.

When an organization moves to a competency-based system, considerable time must be spent identifying the required competencies for various jobs. Then each *block* of competencies must be priced using market data. Progression of employees must be possible, and they must be paid appropriately for all of their competencies. Any *limitations* on the numbers of people who can acquire more competencies should be clearly identified. *Training* in the appropriate competencies is particularly critical. Also, a competency-based system needs to acknowledge or certify employees as they acquire certain competencies, and then to verify the maintenance of those *competencies*. In summary, use of a competency-based system requires significant investment of management time and commitment.

Because competency plans focus on the growth and development of employee competencies, employees who continue to develop their competencies also benefit by receiving pay raises. With more organizations recognizing the value of competency-based systems, their usage has doubled in the last five years—16 percent of organizations now use such systems.[163] Both the organization and employees can benefit from a properly designed and implemented competency-based system. Some possible outcomes are identified in Exhibit 500.78.

Individual versus Team Rewards

As organizations have shifted to using work teams, they face the logical concern of how to develop compensation programs that build on the team concept. At issue is how to compensate the individual whose performance may also be evaluated on the basis of team achievement. Paying everyone on teams the same amount, even though they demonstrate differing competencies and levels of performance, obviously creates equity concerns for many employees.[164]

Many organizations use team rewards as variable pay above base pay. For base pay, individual compensation is based on competency- or skill-based approaches. Variable pay rewards for teams are most frequently distributed annually as a specified dollar amount, not as a percentage of base pay.

Based on experiences in the team-based environment, several factors should be considered when using team-based reward systems:

- Use skill-based pay for the base.
- Make the system simple and understandable.
- Use variable pay based on business entity performance.

Exhibit 500.78 *Competency-Based Systems Outcomes*

Organization-Related Outcomes	Employee-Related Outcomes
• Greater workforce flexibility	• Enhanced employee understanding of organizational "big picture"
• Increased effectiveness of work teams	• Greater employee self-management capabilities
• Fewer bottlenecks in workflow	• Improved employee satisfaction
• Increased worker output per hour	• Greater employee commitment
• More career-enhancement opportunities	

- Distribute variable rewards at the team level.
- Maintain a high degree of employee involvement.

But team-based pay does not always succeed easily. In summary, the most successful uses of team-based compensation have been as variable pay on top of base pay. Rather than substituting for base pay programs, team-based rewards appear to be useful in rewarding performance of a team beyond the satisfactory level.

Variable Pay and Executive Compensation

Do people work harder if pay is tied to performance? The answer appears to be: yes, under the right circumstances. People do spend more time working when offered incentives to do so, as opposed to simply receiving base pay for the hours worked.[165]

Employers apparently believe it too, because a growing number are altering their traditional compensation programs to provide some part of employee's pay in a variable fashion. Typically, an employer bases a portion of the pay on how well the individual, group/team, and/or organization performs. The percentages vary somewhat, but roughly two thirds of companies currently offer variable pay through individual incentives, around a third offer group/team incentives, and over half offer organizational performance incentives.[166] Of course, it would be possible to offer all three at once. This section examines variable pay, including executive compensation as a special kind of variable pay.

Variable Pay: Incentives for Performance

Variable pay is compensation linked to individual, team, and organizational performance. Traditionally also known as *incentives,* variable pay plans attempt to provide tangible rewards to employees for performance beyond normal expectations. The philosophical foundation of variable pay rests on several basic assumptions:

- Some jobs contribute more to organizational success than others.
- Some people perform better than others.
- Employees who perform better should receive more compensation.
- A portion of some employees' total compensation should be contingent on performance.

Contrast the assumptions with a pay system based on seniority or length of service:

- Time spent each day is the primary measure of contribution.
- Length of service with the organization is the primary differentiating factor among people.
- Contributions to the organization are recognized through different amounts of base pay.
- Giving rewards to some people but not others is divisive and hampers employees' working together.

Types of Variable Pay

Individual incentives are given to reward the effort and performance of individuals. Some of the most common means of providing individuals variable pay includes piece-rate systems, sales commissions, and bonuses. Others include special recognition rewards such as trips or merchandise. Two widely used individual incentives focus on employee safety and attendance. However, individual incentives can present drawbacks. One of the potential difficulties with individual incentives is that an employee may focus on what is best individually and may block or inhibit performance of other individuals with whom the employee is competing. Competition intensifies if only the top performer or winner receives incentives, which is why *team or group incentives* have been developed.

When an organization rewards an entire work group or *team* for its performance, cooperation among the members usually increases. However, competition among different teams for rewards can lead to decline in overall performance under certain circumstances. The most common *team* or *group incentives* are gainsharing plans, where employee teams that meet certain goals share in the gains measured against performance targets. Often, gainsharing programs focus on quality improvement, cost reduction, and other measurable results.

Organizational incentives reward people based on the performance results of the entire organization. This approach assumes that all employees working together can generate greater organizational results that lead to better financial performance. These programs often share some of the financial gains to the firm with employees through

Exhibit 500.79 *Types of Variable Pay Plans*

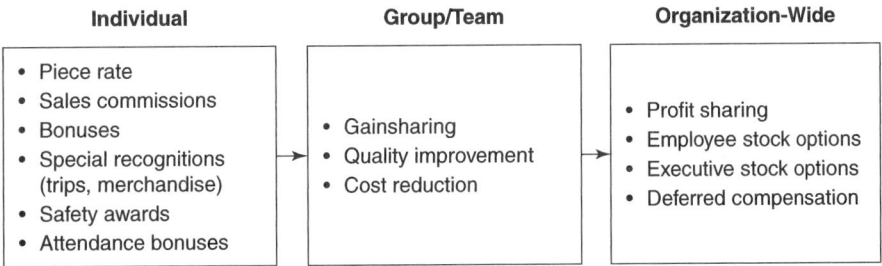

payments calculated as a percentage of each employee's base pay. Also, organizational incentives may be given as a lump-sum amount to all employees, or different amounts may be given to different levels of employees throughout the organization. The most prevalent forms of organization-wide incentives are profit-sharing plans and employee stock plans. For senior managers and executives, variable pay plans often are established to provide stock options and other forms of deferred compensation that minimize the tax liabilities of the recipients. Exhibit 500.79 shows some of the programs under each type of incentive or variable pay plan.

Successes and Failures of Variable Pay Plans

Even though variable pay has grown in popularity, some attempts to implement it have succeeded and others have not. One study suggests that about 74 percent of companies have a variable pay plan of some sort. Of those, most feel these plans have been successful in aligning pay with performance for executives (79 percent), managers (73 percent), and exempt/professionals (60 percent). However, only 48 percent felt variable pay was effective for nonexempt/administrative personnel.[167]

Most employees prefer that performance rewards increase their base pay, rather than be given as a one-time, lump-sum payment. Further, employees prefer individual rewards to group/team or organizational incentives. Incentives *do* work, but they are not a panacea. The enthusiasm that many employers have for variable pay is not shared universally by workers. The success of variable pay plans depends upon the circumstances. The next section discusses several factors that affect successful variable pay plans.

Factors Affecting Successful Variable Pay Plans

Most employers adopt variable pay incentives in order to (1) link individual performance to business goals and (2) reward superior performance.[168] Other goals might include improving productivity or increasing employee retention. Variable pay plans can be considered successful if they meet the goals the organization had for them when they were initiated. Exhibit 500.80 shows a number of different elements that can affect the success of a variable pay plan. These factors have been categorized into three areas.

- Does the plan fit the organization?
- Are the behaviors encouraged by the plan the ones desired?
- Is the plan being administered properly?

Individual Incentives

As noted earlier, individual incentive systems try to relate individual effort to pay. Conditions necessary for the use of individual incentive plans are as follows:

- *Identification of individual performance:* The performance of each individual must be measured and identified because each employee has job responsibilities and tasks that can be separated from those of other employees.
- *Independent work:* Individual contributions result from independent work and effort given by individual employers.
- *Individual competitiveness desired:* Because individuals generally pursue the individual incentives for themselves, competition among employees often occurs. Therefore, independent competition in which some individuals "win" and others do not must be desired.

570. EMPLOYEE BENEFITS AND COMPENSATION

Exhibit 500.80 *Factors for Successful Variable Pay Plans*

- *Individualism stressed in organizational culture:* The culture of the organization must be one that emphasizes individual growth, achievements, and rewards. If an organization emphasizes teamwork and cooperation, then individual incentives will be counterproductive.

Piece-Rate Systems

Straight piece-rate system *A pay system in which wages are determined by multiplying the number of units produced by the piece rate for one unit.*

Differential piece-rate system *A system in which employees are paid one piece-rate wage for units produced up to a standard output and a higher piece-rate wage for units produced over the standard.*

The most basic individual incentive system is the piece-rate system, whether of the straight or differential type. Under the **straight piece-rate system,** wages are determined by multiplying the number of units produced (such as garments sewn or customers contacted) by the piece rate for one unit. The rate per piece does not change regardless of the number of pieces produced. Because the cost is the same for each unit, the wage for each employee is easy to figure, and labor costs can be accurately predicted.

A **differential piece-rate system** pays employees one piece-rate wage for units produced up to a standard output and a higher piece-rate wage for units produced over the standard.

For example, assume that the standard quota for a worker is set at 300 units per day and the standard rate is 14 cents per unit. For all units over the standard, however, the employee receives 20 cents per unit. But the worker producing 400 units in one day will get $62 in wages (300 × 14 cents) + (100 × 20 cents). There are many possible combinations of straight and differential piece-rate systems that can be used depending on situational factors.

Despite their incentive value, piece-rate systems are difficult to use because standards for many types of jobs are difficult and costly to determine. In some instances, the cost of determining and maintaining the standards may be greater than the benefits derived. Jobs in which individuals have limited control over output or in which high standards of quality are necessary also may be unsuited to piecework.

Bonuses

Bonus *A one-time payment that does not become part of the employee's base pay.*

Individual employees may receive additional compensation payments in the form of a **bonus,** which is a one-time payment that does not become part of the employee's base pay. Generally, bonuses are less costly to the employer than other pay increases because they do not become part of employees' base wages, upon which future percentage increases are figured. Growing in popularity, individual bonuses often are used at the executive levels in organizations, but bonus usage also has spread to jobs at all levels in some firms.

Bonuses also can be used to reward employees for contributing new ideas, developing skills, or obtaining professional certifications. When the skills or certification requirements are acquired by an employee, a pay increase or a one-time bonus may follow. For example, a financial services firm provides the equivalent of two weeks' pay to employees who master job-relevant computer skills.

A bonus can recognize performance by an employee, a team, or the organization as a whole. When performance results are good, bonuses go up. When performance results are not met, bonuses go down. Most employers base part of the employee's bonus on individual performance and part on the company if appropriate.

Whatever method of determining bonuses is used, legal experts recommend that bonus plans be described in writing. A number of lawsuits have been filed by employees who leave organizations demanding payment of bonuses promised to them.

Special Incentive Programs

Numerous special incentive programs that provide awards to individuals have been used, ranging from one-time contests for meeting performance targets to rewards for performance over time. For instance, safe-driving awards are given to truck drivers with no accidents or violations on their records during a year. Although special programs also can be developed for groups and for entire organizations, these programs often focus on rewarding only high-performing individuals.

AWARDS Cash merchandise, gift certificates, and travel are the most frequently used incentive rewards. Cash is still highly valued by many employees because they have discretion on how to spend it. However, travel awards appeal to many employees. Goodyear Tire & Rubber Company conducted an experiment in which some employees received cash and another set of employees received merchandise and other noncash rewards. The employees receiving the noncash incentives outperformed those receiving only cash by 46 percent. Other similar studies have concluded that many employees like the continuing "trophy" value of merchandise.[169]

RECOGNITION AWARDS Another type of program recognizes individual employees for their performance or service. For instance, many organizations in service industries such as hotels, restaurants, and retailers have established "employee of the month" and "employee of the year" awards. In the hotel industry more than half of the hotels surveyed use favorable guest comment cards as the basis to provide recognition awards to desk clerks, housekeepers, and other hourly employees.

Recognition awards often work best when given to recognize specific efforts and activities targeted by the organization as important. Even though the criteria for selecting award winners may be subjectively determined in some situations, formally identified criteria provide greater objectivity and are more likely to be seen as rewarding performance, rather than as favoritism. When giving recognition awards, organizations should use specific examples to describe clearly how those receiving the awards were selected.[170]

SERVICE AWARDS Another common type of reward given to individual employees is the *service award*. Although these awards often may be portrayed as rewarding performance over a number of years, in reality, they are determined by length of service, and performance plays little or no role.

Sales Compensation and Incentives

The compensation paid to employees involved with sales and marketing is partly or entirely tied to individual sales performance. Better-performing salespeople receive more total compensation than those selling less. Sales incentives are perhaps the most widely used individual incentive.

Measuring Sales Performance

Successfully using variable sales compensation requires establishing clear performance criteria and measures. Generally, no more than three sales performance measures should be used in a sales compensation plan. Consultants criticize many sales commission plans as being too complex to motivate sales representatives. Other plans may be too simple, focusing only on the salesperson's pay, not on organizational objectives. Although many companies use an individual's

Exhibit 500.81 *Different Bases for Sales Incentives, in Order of Use*

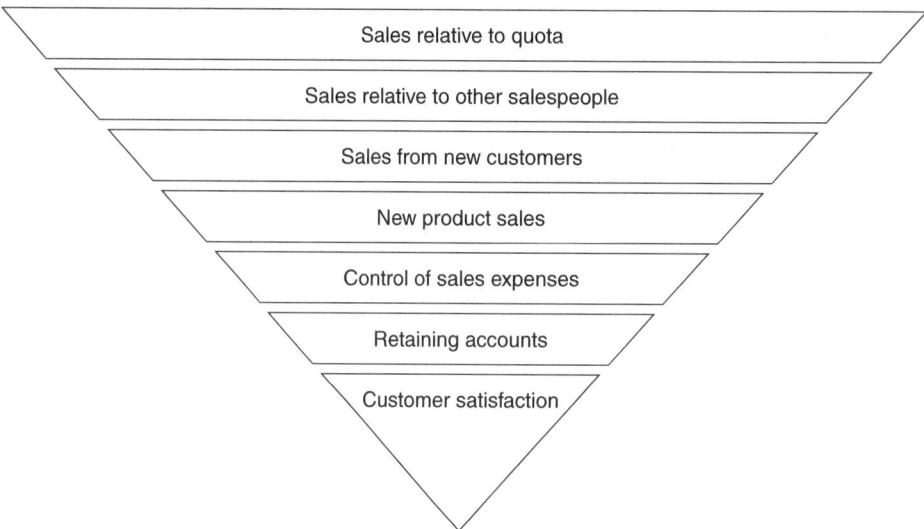

sales revenue compared to established quotas as the primary performance measure, performance could be measured better if these organizations used a variety of criteria, including obtaining new accounts and selling high-value versus low-value items that reflect marketing plans. Exhibit 500.81 shows the criteria commonly used to determine incentive payments for salespeople based on a number of different surveys and studies.

Sales Compensation Plans

Sales compensation plans are generally of several different types. The types are based on the degree to which total compensation includes some variable pay tied to sales performance. A look at each type of sales compensation follows next.

SALARY ONLY Some firms pay salespeople only a salary. The salary-only approach is useful when an organization emphasizes serving and retaining existing accounts over generating new sales and accounts. This approach is frequently used to protect the income of new sales representatives for a period of time while they are building up their sales clientele. Generally, the salary-only approach may extend no more than six months, at which point sales plus commission or bonuses are implemented. However, salespeople who want extrinsic rewards function less effectively in salary-only plans because they are less motivated to sell without additional performance-related compensation.[171]

STRAIGHT COMMISSION An individual incentive system widely used in sales jobs is the **commission,** which is compensation computed as a percentage of sales in units or dollars. Commissions are integrated into the pay given to sales workers in three common ways: straight commission, salary plus commission, and bonuses.

In the straight commission system, a sales representative receives a percentage of the value of the sales made. Consider a sales representative working for a consumer products company. She receives no compensation if no sales are made, but for all sales made in her territory, she receives a percentage of the total amount. The advantage of this system is that the sales representative must sell to earn. The disadvantage is that it offers no security for the sales staff.

Draw An amount advanced from and repaid to future commissions earned by the employee.

To offset this insecurity, some employers use a **draw** system, in which sales representatives can draw advance payments against future commissions. The amount drawn then is deducted from future commission checks. However, arrangements must be made for repayment of drawn amounts if individuals leave the organization before earning their draws in commissions.

SALARY PLUS COMMISSION OR BONUSES The most frequently used form of sales compensation is the *salary plus commission,* which combines the stability of a salary with the performance aspect of a commission. Many organizations also pay salespeople salaries and then offer bonuses as a percentage of base pay tied to meeting various levels of sales targets or other criteria. A common split is 70 percent salary to 30 percent commission, although the split varies by industry and with other factors.

Sales Compensation Challenges

Sales incentives work well or they would not be so widely used. However, they do present many challenges—from calculating total pay correctly to dealing with sales in e-business, to causing competition among salespeople.[172] Often sales compensation plans become quite complex, and complexity can lead to mistakes.

Selling over the Internet brings with it incentive compensation challenges. Sophisticated e-commerce sites are forcing companies to develop new incentive compensation approaches to avoid conflict between the traditional sales representative and the new "relationship managers" who work from the Web sites.[173]

The last few years have seen the growth of sales compensation plans that pit one salesperson against another. For example, in the "stack rank plan" the top 20 percent of sales performers get the highest bonus, the next 30 percent get the second highest, the next 30 percent get third highest, and the bottom 20 percent get nothing. Often, the best salespeople are motivated by incentive plans based on performance measures within their control.[174] But these plans tend to dramatically reduce teamwork and make the climate negative.

Some sales organizations combine both individual- and group-sales bonus programs. In these programs, a portion of the sales incentive is linked to the attainment of group sales goals. This approach encourages cooperation and teamwork for the salespeople to work together. Team incentives in situations other than sales jobs are discussed next.

Group/Team-Based Variable Pay

A group of employees is not necessarily a "team," but either one can be the basis for variable compensation. The use of work teams in organizations has implications for compensation of the teams and their members. Interestingly, although the use of teams has increased substantially in the past few years, the question of how to equitably compensate the individuals who compose the team remains a significant challenge. As Exhibit 500.82 notes, organizations establish group or team variable pay plans for a number of reasons. According to several studies about 70 percent of large firms use work groups or teams in some way. Of those, about 36 percent say they use group incentives, and 10 percent say they use team-based pay.[175]

Distributing Team Incentives

Several decisions about methods of distributing and allocating team rewards must be made. The two primary approaches for distributing team rewards are as follows:

1. *Same size reward for each team member:* In this approach, all team members receive the same payout, regardless of job levels, current pay, or seniority.
2. *Different size rewards for each team member:* Using this approach, employers vary individual rewards based upon such factors as contribution to team results, current pay, years of experience, and skill levels of jobs performed.

Generally, more organizations use the first approach as an addition to different levels of individual pay. This method is used to reward team performance by making the team incentive equal, while still recognizing that individual pay differences exist and are important to many employees.[176] The size of the team incentive can be determined either by using a percentage of base pay for the individuals or the team as a whole, or by offering a specific dollar amount. For example, one firm pays team members individual base rates that reflect years of experience and any additional training that team members have. Additionally, the team reward is distributed to all as a flat dollar amount.

Exhibit 500.82 *Why Organizations Establish Team Pay Plans*

Problems with Team-Based Incentives

The difference between rewarding team members *equally* or *equitably* triggers many of the problems associated with team-based incentives. Rewards distributed equally in amount to all team members may be perceived as "unfair" by employees who work harder, have more capabilities, or perform more difficult jobs. This problem is compounded when a poorly performing individual negatively influences the team results. Also, employees working in teams have shown a relatively low level of satisfaction with rewards that are the same for all, rather than having rewards based on performance, which often may be viewed more equitably.

Generally, managers view the concept of people working in teams as beneficial. But many employees still expect to be paid based on individual performance, to a large extent. Until this individualism is recognized and compensation programs are developed that are viewed as more equitable by more "team members," caution should be used in developing and implementing team-based incentives.

Successful Team Incentives

The unique nature of the team and its members figures prominently in the success of establishing team-based rewards. The employer must consider the history of the group and its past performance. Use of incentives generally has proven to be more successful where groups have been used in the past and where those groups have performed well. However, simultaneously introducing the teamwork concept and changing to team-based incentives has not been as successful.[177]

Another consideration for the success of team-based incentives is the size of the team. If a team becomes too large, employees may feel their individual efforts will have little or no effect on the total performance of the group and the resulting rewards. Team-based incentive plans may encourage teamwork in small groups where interdependence is high. Therefore, in those groups the use of team-based performance measures is recommended. Such plans have been used in many service-oriented industries, where a high degree of contact with customers requires teamwork. Conditions for successful team incentives are shown in Exhibit 500.83. If these conditions cannot be met, then either individual or organizational incentives may be more appropriate.

Types of Group Incentives

Group/team-based reward systems use various ways of compensating individuals. The components include individual wages and salaries in addition to team-based rewards. Most team-based organizations continue to pay individuals based either on the jobs performed or their competencies and capabilities. The two most frequently used types of group/team incentives situations are work teams and gainsharing.

Exhibit 500.83 *Conditions for Successful Team Incentives*

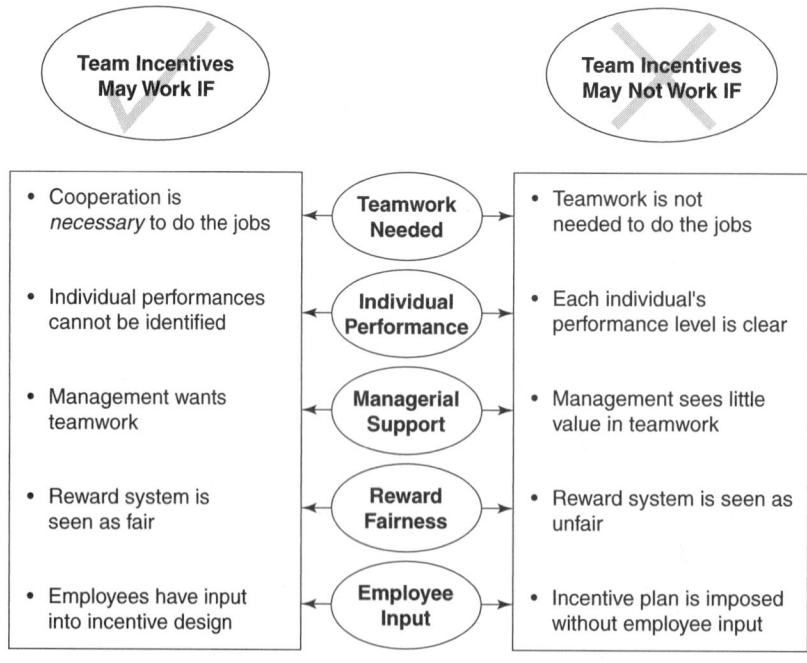

WORK TEAMS Team-based pay plans may reward all members equally on the basis of group output, cost savings, or quality improvement. For example, at Alta Distributing, each warehouse employee might receive $20 for each 1 percent improvement over baseline in the shipping group's rate of on-time delivery each month. The baseline is 90 percent on-time deliveries. A 93 percent on-time rate for August would mean each group member would receive a $60 bonus based on group performance.

The design of most group incentives is based on a "self-funding" principle, which means that the money to be used as incentive rewards is obtained through improvement of organizational results.[178] A good example is gainsharing, which can be group or plantwide in its incentive scope.

GAINSHARING **Gainsharing** is the sharing with employees of greater-than-expected gains in profits and/or productivity. Gainsharing attempts to increase "discretionary efforts," that is, the difference between the maximum amount of effort a person can exert and the minimum amount of effort necessary to keep from being fired. Workers in many organizations currently are not paid for discretionary efforts, but are paid to meet the minimum acceptable level of effort required. However, when workers demonstrate discretionary efforts, the organization can afford to pay them more than the going rate, because the extra efforts produce financial gains over and above the returns of minimal efforts. To begin a gainsharing program, management must identify the ways in which increased productivity, quality, and financial performance can occur and decide that some of the gains should be shared with employees.

Gainsharing The sharing with employees of greater-than-expected gains in profits and/or productivity.

The rewards can be distributed in four ways:

1. A flat amount for all employees
2. Same percentage of base salary for all employees
3. Percentage of the gains by category of employees
4. A percentage based on individual performance against measures

The first two methods generally are preferred because they promote and reward teamwork and cooperation more than the other two methods. Where performance measures are used, only those measures that employees actually can affect should be considered. Often, measures such as labor costs, overtime hours, and quality benchmarks are used. Both organizational measures and departmental measures may be used, with the weights for gainsharing split between the two categories. Naturally, an individual's performance must be satisfactory in order for that individual to receive the gainsharing payments.

Two older approaches similar to gainsharing exist. One, called Improshare, sets group piece-rate standards and pays weekly bonuses when the standard is exceeded. The other—the Scanlon plan—uses employee committees and passes on savings to the employees.

Organizational Incentives

An organizational incentive system compensates all employees in the organization based on how well the organization as a whole performs during the year. The basic concept behind organizational incentive plans is that overall results depend on organizational or plant-wide cooperation. The purpose of these plans is to produce better results by rewarding cooperation throughout the organization. For example, conflict between marketing and production can be overcome if management uses an incentive system that emphasizes organization-wide profit and productivity. To be effective, an organizational incentive program should include everyone from nonexempt employees to managers and executives. Common organizational incentive systems include profit sharing, employee stock options, and employee stock ownership plans (ESOPs).

Profit Sharing

As the name implies, **profit sharing** distributes some portion of organizational profits to employees. The primary objectives of profit-sharing plans include the following:

- Improve productivity
- Recruit or retain employees
- Improve product/service quality
- Improve employee morale

Exhibit 500.84 *Profit-Sharing Plan Framework Choices*

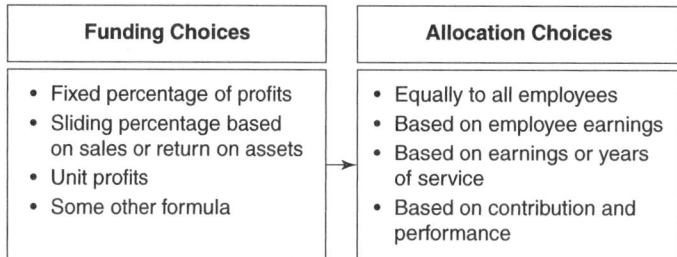

Typically, the percentage of the profits distributed to employees is agreed on by the end of the year before distribution. In some profit-sharing plans, employees receive portions of the profits at the end of the year; in others, the profits are deferred, placed in a fund, and made available to employees on retirement or on their leaving the organization. Exhibit 500.84 shows how profit-sharing plans can be set up.

Unions sometimes are skeptical of profit-sharing plans.[179] Often, the level of profits is influenced by factors not under the employees' control, such as accounting decisions, marketing efforts, competition, and elements of executive compensation. However, in recent years, some unions have supported profit-sharing plans that tie employees' pay increases to improvements against organizational performance measures, not just the "bottom-line" numbers.

DRAWBACKS OF PROFIT-SHARING PLANS When used throughout an organization, including lower-echelon workers, profit-sharing plans can have some drawbacks. First, management must be willing to disclose financial and profit information to employees. As many people know, both the definition and level of profit can depend on the accounting system used and decisions made. Therefore, to be credible, management must be willing to disclose sufficient financial and profit information to alleviate the skepticism of employees, particularly if profit-sharing levels are reduced from previous years. Second, profits may vary a great deal from year to year, resulting in windfalls and losses beyond the employees' control. Third, payoffs far removed from employees' efforts may fail to strongly link higher rewards with better performance.

Employee Stock Options

Stock options, once the exclusive domain of executive compensation, are now being used throughout some organizations. Employee stock options give employees the right to purchase a fixed number of shares of company stock at a specified price for a limited period of time. If the stock's market price exceeds the exercise price, employees can exercise the option and sell the stock at a profit. If the price falls below the exercise price, the option is worthless. Purchasing and holding company stock is thought to give employees a vested "ownership" in seeing the company do well. However, the incentive value of the stock is reduced whenever employees' stock value declines, as happened in 2000 when the stock market dropped. Obviously, stock prices do not always go up; and when stock values decline, employee anxiety increases. Nevertheless, using stock plans as a means of providing additional compensation to employees appears to help focus employee efforts on increasing organizational performance.[180] Employees tend to like stock-related benefits but do not understand many of the complexities.[181]

This discussion has highlighted plans that provide employees opportunities to receive stock options or purchase company stock. However, a more extensive approach results in employees actually owning all or significant parts of their employers.

Employee Stock Ownership Plans (ESOPs)

Employee stock ownership plan (ESOP) A plan whereby employees gain stock ownership in the organization for which they work.

An **employee stock ownership plan (ESOP)** is designed to give employees stock ownership in the organization for which they work. According to the National Center for Employee Ownership, an estimated 15,000 firms in the United States offer broad employee-ownership programs. Within these firms, approximately 10,000 have established ESOPs covering about 9 million workers.[182]

ESTABLISHING AN ESOP An organization establishes an ESOP by using its stock as collateral to borrow capital from a financial institution. Once the loan repayment begins through the use of company profits, the lender releases a certain amount of stock, which the company allocates to an employee stock ownership trust (ESOT). The company then assigns shares of stock kept in the trust to individual employees based on length of service and pay level. On retirement, death, or separation from the organization, employees or their beneficiaries can sell the stock back to the trust or on the open market, if the stock is publicly traded.

ADVANTAGES AND DISADVANTAGES OF ESOPs Establishing an ESOP creates several advantages. The major one is that the firm can receive favorable tax treatment of the earnings earmarked for use in the ESOP. Second, an ESOP gives employees a "piece of the action" so that they can share in the growth and profitability of their firm. As a result, employee ownership may be effective in motivating employees to be more productive and focused on organizational performance. In one survey of more than 1,100 ESOP companies, about 60 percent said productivity had increased, and 68 percent said financial performance was higher since converting to an ESOP.[183]

Many people approve of the concept of employee ownership as a kind of "people's capitalism." However, the sharing also can be a disadvantage because employees may feel "forced" to join, thus placing their financial future at greater risk. Both their wages/salaries and their retirement benefits depend on the performance of their employer. This concentration poses even greater risk for retirees because the value of pension fund assets also depends on how well the company does.

Another drawback is the use of ESOPs as a management tool to fend off unfriendly takeover attempts. Holders of employee-owned stock often align with management to turn down bids that would benefit outside stockholders but would replace management and restructure operations. Surely, ESOPs were not created to entrench inefficient management. Despite these disadvantages, ESOPs continue to grow in popularity.

FASB RULES Employee stock ownership plans are subject to certain tax laws. Perhaps in part because of the increase in popularity of ESOPs, companies have been required to disclose how much they would have earned if the stock options they gave employees had been charged against company income. The Financial Accounting Standards Board (FASB) now requires companies to report the value of the stock options they give employees, but some real controversy has occurred over how to value the options.

Executive Compensation

A history of executive compensation shows that a combination of events has created today's situation in the United States.[184] Strong demand for executives, the tax structure, stock market performance, and pay-for-performance notions have all contributed. Many organizations, especially large ones, administer executive compensation differently from compensation for lower-level employees.

U.S. executives—typically someone in the top two levels of an organization, such as chief executive officer (CEO), president, or senior vice-president—do rather well in compensation. Also, pay for female executives is about 45 percent less than that of men until adjusted for age and experience, then the gap shrinks to about 5 percent or less.[185]

Elements of Executive Compensation

At the heart of most executive compensation plans is the idea that executives should be rewarded if the organization grows in profitability and value over a period of years. Because of the high tax brackets they fall in, most executives want their compensation provided in ways that offer significant tax savings. Therefore, their total compensation packages are more significant than their base pay. Especially when the base salary is $1 million or more, the executive often is interested in the mix of items in the total package, including current and deferred compensation. As Exhibit 500.85 shows, the common components of executive compensation are salaries, annual bonuses, long-term incentives, supplemental benefits, and perquisites.

Exhibit 500.85 *Executive Compensation Components*

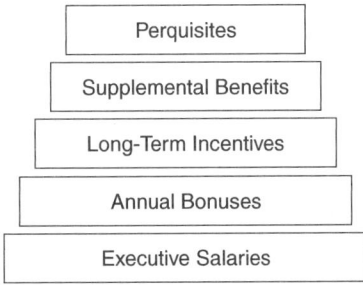

Executive Compensation and the Board of Directors

In most organizations, the board of directors is the major policy-setting entity. For publicly traded companies covered by federal regulatory agencies, such as the Securities and Exchange Commission (SEC), the board of directors must approve executive compensation packages. Even for many nonprofit organizations, Internal Revenue Service regulations require boards of directors review and approve the compensation for top-level executives. In both family-owned and privately owned firms, boards of directors may have less involvement in establishing and reviewing the compensation packages for key executives. Conpensation committees make recommendations on salaries for top officers.

Ethics and Human Resources

Ethics and HR Management

As the issues faced in HR management increase in number and complexity, so do the pressures and challenges of acting ethically. Ethical issues pose fundamental questions about fairness, justice, truthfulness, and social responsibility. Concerns arise about the ethical standards used by managers and employees, particularly those in business organizations.[186] But it appears that the concerns are well-founded. Some of the most frequent problems are cheating on expense accounts, paying or accepting bribes and kickbacks, forging signatures, and lying about sick leave.

What Is Ethical Behavior?

Ethics deals with what "ought" to be done. For the HR professional it is the way in which the manager *ought* to act relative to a given human resource issue. However, determining specific actions is not always easy. Ethical issues in management, including HR issues, have five dimensions:

- *Extended consequences:* Ethical decisions have consequences beyond the decisions themselves. Closing a plant and moving it to another location to avoid unionization of a workforce has an impact on the affected workers, their families, the community, and other businesses.
- *Multiple alternatives:* Various alternatives exist in most decision-making situations, so the issue may involve how far to "bend" rules. For example, deciding how much flexibility to offer employees with family problems, while denying other employees similar flexibility, may require considering various alternatives.
- *Mixed outcomes:* Decisions with ethical dimensions often involve weighing some beneficial outcomes against some negative ones. For example, preserving the jobs of some workers in a plant might require eliminating the jobs of others. The result would be a mix of negative and positive outcomes for the organization and the affected employees.
- *Uncertain consequences:* The consequences of decisions with ethical dimensions often are not known. Should employees' personal lifestyles or family situations eliminate them from promotion even though they clearly are the most qualified candidates?
- *Personal effects:* Ethical decisions often affect the personal lives of employees, their families, and others. Allowing foreign customers to dictate that they will not have a female or minority sales representative call on them may help with the business relationship short term, but what are the effects on the employees and future career opportunities?

Responding to Ethical Situations

To respond to situations with ethical elements, there are some guidelines to consider. Just complying with the laws does not guarantee ethical behavior. Laws and regulations cannot cover every situation HR professionals and employees will face. Instead, people must be guided by values and personal behavior "codes," including the following:

- Does the behavior or result meet all applicable *laws, regulations,* and *government codes?*
- Does the behavior or result achieved meet all *organizational standards* of ethical behavior?
- Does the behavior or result achieved meet *professional standards* of ethical behavior?

Ethical Issues in HR Management

HR professionals regularly are faced with ethical issues. To help HR professionals deal with ethical issues, the Society for Human Resource Management (SHRM) has developed a code of ethics for its members.

According to a study, most employees surveyed indicated that they had seen unethical workplace conduct in the previous year. The most common unethical incidents by employees were lying to supervisors, employee drug or alcohol abuse, and falsification of records.[187] With HR management in an international environment, other ethical pressures arise. Such practices as gift giving and hiring vary in other countries, and some of those practices would not be accepted as ethical in the United States. Consequently, all managers, including HR managers, must deal with ethical issues and be sensitive to how they interplay with HR activities. One way to address ethical issues in organizations is to conduct training of executives, managers, and employees. However, training of managers and employees in ethics compliance has not necessarily reduced employee misconduct.[188]

Module 500 Endnotes

1. Luis Gomez-Mejia, "Moving Forward," *HR News,* Spring 2000, 1–2.
2. Michael A. Hitt et. al., "Direct and Moderating Effects of Human Capital on Strategy and Performance in Professional Service Firms," *Academy of Management Journal,* 44 (2001), 13.
3. Daniel M. Cable et al., "The Source and Accuracy of Job Applicants' Beliefs About Organizational Culture," *Academy of Management Journal,* 43 (2000), 1076–1086.
4. Jennifer Reingold and Marcia Stepanek, "Why the Productivity Revolution Will Spread," *BusinessWeek,* February 14, 2000, 112–118.
5. "Facts and Figures," *Bulletin to Management,* February 17, 2000, 53.
6. George Hager, *USA Today,* March 21, 2000, 1B.
7. "An Inside Job," *The Economist,* July 15, 2000, 61; and Jeffrey Garten, "The War for Better Quality Is Far from Won," *BusinessWeek,* December 18, 2000, 32.
8. Thomas J. Douglas and William Q. Judge, Jr., "Total Quality Management Implementation and Competitive Advantage," *Academy of Management Journal,* 44 (2001), 158.
9. Charles Greer, *Strategic Human Resource Management,* 2nd ed. (Upper Saddle River, NJ: Prentice Hall, 2001).
10. Reginald M. Beal, "Competing Effectively: Environmental Scanning," *Journal of Small Business Management,* January 2000, 27.
11. Raymond Suutari, "Coping with Change," *CMA Management,* March 2000, 16.
12. Barry Gerhart et al., "Measurement Error in Research on Human Resources," *Personnel Psychology,* 53 (2000), 803.
13. John Bound and Harry Holzer, "Demand Shifts, Population Adjustments, and Labor Market Outcomes," *Journal of Labor Economics,* January 2000, 20.
14. "The Skinny on Downsizing," *BusinessWeek,* August 28, 2000, 38,
15. "The Strategic Difference Between Layoffs and Downsizing," *Bulletin to Management,* February 22, 2001, 61.
16. "Louis Lavelle, "Corporate Liposuction Can Have Nasty Side Effects," *BusinessWeek,* July 17, 2000, 74–75.
17. Jon Hilsenrath, "Many Say Layoffs Hurt Companies More Than They Help," *The Wall Street Journal,* February 21, 2001, A2.
18. Charles Whalen, "Downsizing Spending," *BusinessWeek,* September 11, 2000, 30.
19. Rachel Silverman, "Laid-Off Workers Find Job Search No Longer a Cinch," *The Wall Street Journal,* February 6, 2001, B1.
20. Brian S. Klaas, "HR Outsourcing and Its Impact: The Role of Transaction Costs," *Personnel Psychology,* 52 (1999), 113–136.

21. "HR Metric," *Bulletin to Management,* January 18, 2001, 20.
22. John Yuva, "Benchmarking for the Future," *Purchasing Today,* January 2001, 40–49.
23. For a review of research and methods used to measure equity, see Kerry S. Sauley and Arthur G. Bedeian, "Equity Sensitivity: Construction of a Measure and Examination of Its Psychometric Properties," *Journal of Management* 26 (2000), 885–910.
24. Edward L. Powers, "Employee Loyalty in the New Millennium," *S.A.M. Advanced Management Journal,* Summer 2000, 4–8.
25. Shari Caudron, "The Myth of Job Happiness," *Workforce,* April 2001, 32–36; and "Jobs a Labor of Love? Not in U.S.," *Omaha World-Herald,* September 3, 2001, 3D.
26. Jon L. Pierce, Tatiana Kostova, and Kurt T. Dirks, "Toward a Theory of Psychological Ownership in Organizations," *Academy of Management Review,* 26 (2001), 298–310.
27. James B. Lathrop, Jr., "Employers Can Expect Greater Conflict in Four-Generation Workforce," *HR News,* February 2001, 23.
28. Daniel J. Koys, "The Effects of Employee Satisfaction, Organizational Citizenship Behavior, and Turnover on Organizational Effectiveness," *Personnel Psychology,* 54 (2001), 101–114.
29. "CCH Absenteeism Survey," *CCH Human Resource Management,* November 1, 2000.
30. Paul Falcone, "Tackling Excessive Absenteeism," *HR Magazine,* April 2000, 139–144.
31. Linda Micco, "Continental Soars from Worst to First by Engaging Employees at Every Turn," *Bulletin to Management,* November 30, 2000, S1.
32. "Link Absenteeism and Benefits and Help Cut Costs," *HR Focus,* April 2000, 5–6.
33. "CCH Absenteeism Survey."
34. "Everyone Feels Loss When Top Performers Leave the Job," *Working Age,* May/June 2000, 5.
35. *War for Talent* (New York: McKinsey & Company, 1998).
36. Wayne F. Cascio, *Costing Human Resources* (Cincinnati: South-Western Publishing, 2000), 73–75.
37. Kwan Jee, "Best Practices of Web-Based Employee Opinion Surveys," *The Next Frontier,* September 2001, 13–15.
38. *SHRM Retention Practices Survey* (Alexandria VA: Society for Human Resource Management, 2000), 10.
39. D. Mitchell, "How to Reduce the High Cost of Turnover," available at *http://www.ijob.com/news,* October 30, 2000.
40. Bob Cardy, "Considering the Source," *HR News,* Spring 2000, 10–11.
41. A. E. M. Van Vianen, "Person-Organization Fit: The Match Between Newcomers' and Recruiters' Preferences for Organizational Cultures," *Personnel Psychology* 53 (2000), 113–149.
42. Maria Puente, "Multi-Tasking to the MAX?" *USA Today,* April 25, 2000, 10.
43. Eric Raimy, "Back to the Table," *Human Resource Executive,* March 2001, 1.
44. Don Caruth and Gail Handlogten, "Avoiding HR Lawsuits," *Credit Union Executive,* November–December 2001, 25.
45. Matthew Miklave and A. Jonathan Trafimow, "Expect to See Your Words on Tomorrow's Front Page," *Workforce,* June 2000, 180.
46. Stephen Sonneberg, "Mental Disabilities in the Workplace," *Workforce,* June 2000, 143.
47. Joanne Wojcik, "Focus on Performance," *Business Insurance,* July 10, 2000, 20.
48. Carla Joinson, "Refocusing Job Descriptions," *HR Magazine,* January 2001, 67–72.
49. Mark Tatge, "With Unemployment Low, a New Group Is in Demand: Ex-Cons," *The Wall Street Journal,* April 24, 2000, A1+.
50. "Walgreen's Expansion Plans Stymied by Lack of Pharmacists," *Chicago Tribune,* May 15, 2000.
51. Thomas G. Moehrle, "The Cost and Incidence of Referral, Hiring, and Retention Bonuses," *Compensation and Working Conditions,* Winter 2000, 37–42.
52. Carolyn Hirschman, "Reserve Space for Rehires," *HR Magazine,* January 2000, 58–64.
53. Skip Corsini, "Wired to Hire," *Training,* June 2001, 50–54.
54. "Online Recruiting: What Works, What Doesn't," *HR Focus,* March 2000, 1+.
55. William Dickmeyer, "Applicant Tracking Reports Make Data Meaningful," *Workforce,* February 2001, 65–67.
56. James A. Breaugh and Mary Starke, "Research on Employee Recruitment," *Journal of Management,* 26 (2000), 405–424.
57. Stephanie Armour, "Job Seekers Get Put Through the Wringer," *The USA Today,* August 17, 2001, 1B+.
58. For more details, see Herbert G. Heneman III, Timothy A. Judge, and Robert L. Heneman, *Staffing Organizations* (Middleton WI: Mendota House, Irwin McGraw-Hill, 2000), 553–558.
59. Jean M. Philips, "Effects of Realistic Job Previews on Multiple Organizational Outcomes," *Academy of Management Journal* 41 (1998), 673–690; and Peter W. Horn et al., "An Exploratory Investigation into Theoretical Mechanisms Underlying Realistic Job Previews," *Personnel Psychology* 51 (1998), 421.
60. Linda A. Jones, "Most Companies Employ Pre-Employment Testing Methods," *Human Resource Executive,* January 2001, 37.
61. Craig S. Philson, "Functional Capacity Testing," *Occupational Health and Safety,* January 2000, 78–84.
62. James E. Wanek, "Integrity and Honesty Testing," *International Journal of Selection and Assessment,* 7 (1999), 183–195.

63. George M. Alliger and Stephen A. Dwight, "A Meta-Analytical Investigation of the Susceptibility of Integrity Tests to Faking and Coaching," *Educational & Psychological Measurement,* 60 (2000), 59–73.
64. *Equal Employment Opportunity Commission v. Pacific Maritime Commission,* CD-CA, CV 00-01516 DT JWJ, February 22, 2000.
65. Timothy A. Judge, "The Employment Interview: A Review of Recent Research and Recommendations for Future Research," *Human Resource Management,* 10 (2000), 383–407.
66. "Interview Questions That Hit the Mark," *Harvard Management Update,* March 2001, 9.
67. Yoau Ganzach, et al., "Making Decisions from an Interview: Expert Measurement and Mechanical Combination," *Personnel Psychology,* 53 (2000), 1–20; and Allen Huffcutt et al. "Comparison of Situational and Behavior Description Interview Questions for Higher-Level Positions," *Personnel Psychology* 54 (2001), 619–644.
68. Based on Martha Frase-Blunt, "Games Interviewers Play," *HR Magazine,* January 2001, 106–114; and Diane E. Lewis, "Brainteasers Join Interviews in Hiring," *Omaha World-Herald,* February 2, 2000, 1G.
69. David Kelly, "Can Video Conferencing Help HR Get the Picture?" available at *www.hr-esource.com,* July 16, 2001.
70. Mike Frost, "Video Interviewing," *HR Magazine,* August 2001, 93–98.
71. Stanley M. Slowik, "Objective Pre-Employment Interviewing: Balancing Recruitment, Selection, and Retention Goals," *Public Personnel Management,* 30 (2001), 77–94.
72. Murray R. Barrick, Gregory Patton, and Shanna N. Haugland, "Accuracy of Interviewer Judgments of Job Applicant Personality Traits," *Personnel Psychology,* 53 (2000), 925–945.
73. The authors acknowledge the assistance and contribution of Lisa A. Burke, PhD, SPHR in structuring the chapter and providing content in several sections.
74. For example, see James Robinson, *The Evolving Performance Consultant Job* (Pittsburg, PA: Partners in Charge, Inc., 2000).
75. Michael Wykes, J. March-Swets, and L. Rynbrandt, "Performance Analysis: Field Operations Management," in J. Phillips, Ed., *In Action: Performance Consulting and Analysis* (Alexandria, VA: American Society of Training and Development, 2000), 135–153.
76. Joseph Wilson, "Strategic Training: Creating Advantage and Value," in Lisa A. Burke, ed., *High-Impact Training Solutions* (Westport, CT: Quorum Publishers, 2001).
77. Ramon Valle et al., "Business Strategy, Work Processes, and Human Resource Training: Are They Congruent?" *Journal of Organizational Behavior* 21 (2000), 283–297.
78. Elwood F. Holton III, Reid A. Bates, and Sharon S. Naquin, "Large-Scale Performance-Driven Training Needs Assessment: A Case Study," *Public Personnel Management* 29 (2000), 249–267.
79. Based on concepts and models suggested by Lisa A. Burke, PhD, SPHR.
80. Donald L. Kirkpatrick, *Evaluating Training Programs: The Four Levels* (New York: Barrett-Kohler, 1998).
81. Robert W. Rowden, "A Practical Guide to Assessing the Value of Training in Your Company," *National Productivity Review,* Autumn 2000, 9–13.
82. Ben Worthen, "Measuring the ROI of Training," *CIO,* February 15, 2001, 128–136.
83. Scott Thurm, "No Exit Strategies," *The Wall Street Journal,* February 6, 2001, 1A.
84. Dave Patel, "Rearranging the Life Cycle," *HR Magazine,* January 2002, 104.
85. Scott E. Seibert et al., "A Social Capital Theory of Career Success," *The Academy of Management Journal* 44 (2001), 219–237.
86. Scott T. Fleischmann, "Succession Management for the Entire Organization," *Employment Relations Today,* Summer 2000, 53–62.
87. For details on developing succession plans, see William J. Rothwell, *Effective Succession Planning* (New York: AMACOM, 2000).
88. Kevin Dobbs, "Training on the Fly," *Sales and Marketing Management,* November 2000, 92.
89. Stephanie Overman, "Lackluster Leadership Development Hurts Corporate Performance," *HR News,* December 2001, 9.
90. Monica C. Higgins and Kathy E. Fram, "Reconceptualizing Mentoring at Work: A Developmental Network Perspective," *Academy of Management Review* 26 (2001), 264.
91. "Women in Management," *Omaha World-Herald,* December 3, 2000, 1G.
92. Carol Hymowitz, "In Turbulent Climate, Pioneering Women Face Special Scrutiny," *The Wall Street Journal,* March 3, 2001, B1.
93. Pallavi Gogoi, "As Leaders, Women Rule," *BusinessWeek,* November 20, 2000, 75.
94. "Churning at the Top," *The Economist,* March 17, 2001, 67.
95. Tom Starner, "The Winds of Change," *Human Resource Executive,* December 2001, A2–A5.
96. "Performance," *Bulletin to Management,* July 13, 2000, p. 5.
97. "SHRM Performance Management Survey," *Society for Human Resource Management Research,* 2000, 7.
98. "General Motors and Whirlpool: Two Approaches for Developing Performance Benchmarks," *HR Focus,* June 2000, 7–10.
99. Carolyn Pye Sostrom, "Measure Right, Measure Now," *Purchasing Today,* January 2000, 33–40.
100. Mark A. Siders et al., "The Relationships of Internal and External Commitment Foci to Objective Job Performance Measures," *Academy of Management Journal* 44 (2001), 570.
101. Dayton Fandray, "The New Thinking in Performance Appraisals," *Workforce,* May 2001, 36–40.

102. "Some Say Evaluations Do More Harm Than Good," *Bulletin to Management,* April 20, 2000, 127.
103. Jon Segal, "86 Your Appraisal Process?" *HR Magazine,* October 2000, 199.
104. Carla Joinson, "Making Sure Employees Measure Up," *HR Magazine,* March 2001, 36–41.
105. Mark Koziel, "Giving and Receiving Performance Evaluations," *The CPA Journal,* December 2000, 22.
106. Carol Hymowitz, "Managers Tell How to Spot 'Gold Talent' in Old and New Hires," *The Wall Street Journal,* March 27, 2001, B1.
107. Don Merit, "Improving Job Performance," *American Printer,* March 2000, 82.
108. "Performance Management Practices," available at *www.ddi.com.*
109. Michael Scott, "7 Pitfalls for Managers When Handling Poor Performance and How to Overcome Them," *Manage,* February 2000, 12–13.
110. Lin Grensing-Pophal, "Motivate Managers to Review Performance," *HR Magazine,* March 2001, 45.
111. Maria Clapham, "Employee Creativity: The Role of Leadership," *The Academy of Management Executive,* August 2000, 138.
112. Yitzhak Fried, et al. "Rater Positive and Negative Mood Predispositions," *Journal of Occupational and Organizational Psychology,* September 2000, 373.
113. Winston Fletcher, "Sitting in Judgment on Others," *Management Today,* August 2000, 30.
114. Joshua Freedman, "Feedback for Performance," *Priorities* 4 (2001), 28.
115. Kathy Simmons, "Ostrich Management," *The Rotarian,* September 2000, 6.
116. Susan Scherreik, "Your Performance Review," *BusinessWeek,* December 17, 2001, 139–140.
117. "Is a Negative Job Evaluation an Adverse Employment Action?" *Bulletin to Management,* September 14, 2000, 115; "EEO Performance Reviews," *Bulletin to Management,* February 24, 2000, 62.
118. Timothy S. Bland, "Anatomy of an Employment Lawsuit," *HR Magazine,* March 2001, 145.
119. Dick Grate, "Performance Appraisal Reappraised," *Harvard Business Review,* January 2000, 21.
120. Robert L. Grossman, "Race in the Workplace," *HR Magazine,* March 2000, 41–45.
121. Pepi Sappal, "Dare to Be Different," *Global HR,* May 2001, 16–19.
122. Based on data in SHRM/Career Journal.com "Impact of Diversity, Initiatives Poll," October 2000, available at *www.shrm.org.*
123. *Diversity Recruitment Report 2001,* available at *www.wetfeet.com;* and "Change Your Perspective, Attract a More Diverse Workforce," newsletter, March 31, 2001, available at *www.hr-esource.com.*
124. "Assessing, Solving Issues of Color Reveal Gray Areas," *Bulletin to Management,* July 27, 2000, 239.
125. Jacqueline A. Gilbert and John M. Ivancevich, "Valuing Diversity: A Tale of Two Organizations," *Academy of Management Executive,* February 2000, 93–105.
126. Lorraine Gutierrez, Jan Kruzich, Teresa Jones, and Nora Coronado, "Identifying Goals and Outcome Measures for Diversity Training," *Administration in Social Work* 24 (2000), 53–71.
127. Andrew R. McIlvaine, "Hostile Environments," *Human Resource Executive,* December 2000, 71–75.
128. Victoria D. Bush and Thomas N. Ingram, "Building and Assessing Cultural Diversity Skills: Implications for Sales Training," *Industrial Marketing Management,* January 2001, 65–76.
129. *SHRM/Fortune Impact of Diversity Initiatives on Bottom Line* (Alexandria VA: Society for Human Resource Management, 2001).
130. Vidu Soni, "A Twenty-First Century Perception for Diversity in the Public Sector," *Public Administration Review,* September/October 2000, 395–408.
131. Cheryl Dore, "Room for Mom," *Human Resource Executive,* March 15, 2001, 42–47; and Diane Brady, "Give Nursing Moms a Break," *BusinessWeek,* August 6, 2001, 70.
132. "Nontraditional Occupations for Women in 2000," U.S. Department of Labor, Women's Bureau, 2001, available at *www.dol.gov/dol/wb.*
133. *Erickson v. Bartell Drug Co.* C00-1213L. (2001) WL 649651.
134. Louis Lavelle, "For Female CEOs, It's Stingy at the Top," *BusinessWeek,* April 23, 2001, 70–71.
135. Eric Raimy, "Cultural Captives," *Human Resource Executive,* June 1, 2001, 53–55.
136. Glass Ceiling Commission, *A Solid Investment: Making Use of the Nation's Human Capital* (Washington, DC: U.S. Department of Labor, 1995).
137. "Managers and Diversity," *Omaha World-Herald,* April 22, 2001, 1G.
138. Charles A. Pierce, Herman Agunis, and Susan K. R. Adams, "Effects of a Dissolved Workplace Romance and Rater Characteristics on Responses to a Sexual Harassment Accusation," *Academy of Management Journal* 43 (2000), 869–880.
139. Allison Bloom, "Love Is in the Air," *MSN Careers,* February 23, 2001.
140. Gillian Flynn, "Third-Party Sexual Harassment: Commonplace and Laden with Liability," *Workforce,* November 2000, 88–92.
141. *EEOC v. R&R Ventures,* 00-1702 (4th Circuit), April 2, 2001.
142. "Courts Consider What Constitutes a Hostile Work Environment," *Fair Employment Practices,* August 31, 2000, 108.

143. Libert J. Munson, Charles Hulin, and Fritz Drasgow, "Longitudinal Analysis of Dispositional Influences and Sexual Harassment: Effects on Job and Psychological Outcomes," *Personnel Psychology* 53 (2000), 21–46.
144. *Burlington Industries v. Ellerth*, U.S. S.Ct. No. 97-569, June 26, 1998; *Faragher v. Boca Raton*, U.S. S.Ct. No. 97-282, June 26, 1998; and *Oncale v. Sundowner Offshore Services*, U.S. S.Ct. No. 96-568, March 4, 1998.
145. Patrick J. Pursell, "Older Workers: Employment and Retirement Trends," *Monthly Labor Review,* October 2000, 22.
146. Susan J. Wells, "Is the ADA Working?" *HR Magazine,* April 2001, 38–46.
147. Kathryn Tyler, "Looking for a Few Good Workers?" *HR Magazine,* December 2000, 129–134.
148. Maureen Minehan, "Transgendered Employees Winning Protection," available at *http://hr-esource.com,* August 20, 2001.
149. Daniel Moskowitz, "Care Package," *Human Resource Executive,* May 1, 2001, 1.
150. "Baby Boomers Need Attention Too," *Bulletin to Management,* July 13, 2000, 5–6.
151. Margaret M. Clark, "Employers Cater to Changing Benefit Needs, Survey Finds," *HR-News,* May 2001, 17; and Lore Lawrence, "Companies Still Offering Perks, but HR's Taking Another Look," *HR-News,* June 2001, 4.
152. Rodney K. Platt, "Value of Benefits Remains Constant," *Workspan,* June 2000, 34–39.
153. Julie Appleby, "Health Insurance Prices to Soar," *USA Today,* August 27, 2001, 1A–2A; and Steve Jordan, "Health Insurance Costs Set to Soar," *Omaha World-Herald,* November 4, 2001, 1D.
154. Jack Bruner, "Value of Health Coverage," *ACA Journal,* First Quarter 2000, 57.
155. "New Grads, Employers See Eye to Eye," *Bulletin to Management,* March 8, 2001, 75.
156. Robert Schwab, "Employers Forced to Expand Benefits," *The Denver Post,* September 3, 2000, GL.
157. Paul W. Mulvey et al., "Rewards of Work," *WorldatWork Journal,* Third Quarter 2000, 6.
158. Bob Acosta, "Internet Payroll Processing," *Workspan,* February 2001, 16.
159. Gerald E. Ledford and Elizabeth J. Hawk, "Compensation Strategy," *ACA Journal,* First Quarter 2000, 28.
160. George T. Milkovich and Jennifer Stevens, "From Pay to Rewards: 100 Years of Change," *ACA Journal,* First Quarter 2000, 6–18.
161. E. Stewart Huckman, "Pay the Person, Not the Job," *Training and Development,* October 2000, 52–57.
162. Jörgen Sandberg, "Understanding Competence at Work," *Harvard Business Review,* March 2001, 24.
163. Dana Rahbar-Daniels et al., "Here To Stay," *WorldatWork Journal,* First Quarter 2001, 70–77.
164. B. L. Kirkman, "Understanding Why Team Members Won't Share," *Small Group Research,* 31, no. 2, n.d., 175–209.
165. G. A. Matthews and Alyce M. Dickinson, "Effects of Alternative Activities on Time Allocated to Task Performance Under Different Percentages of Incentive Pay," *Journal of Organizational Behavior Management* 20 (2000), 3.
166. "SHRM Examines Success of Incentive Pay Plans," *IOMA's Report on Hourly Compensation,* March 1, 2000, 1.
167. "Study Questions If Incentive Pay Is Really Hitting Its Mark," *IOMA Report on Salary Surveys,* February 2000, 13.
168. "Short-Term Incentives Considered Ineffective, Survey Reveals," *HR News,* January 2000, 5.
169. Marlene A. Prost, "New Worth," *Human Resource Executive,* February 2001, 78.
170. Paul A. Gilseter, "Online Incentives Sizzle—and You Shine," *Workforce,* January 2001, 44.
171. Lisa J. Riley and Arthur Anderson, "Little Things Make a Big Difference," *Workspan,* May 2001, 57.
172. Bill Weeks, "Running On Empty?" *Workspan,* January 2002, 20–24.
173. Nina McIntyre, "Rewards in the E-Business World," *Workspan,* July 2000, 31.
174. Chad Albrecht and Mike O'Hara, "Its Not All Relative," *WorldatWork Journal,* Third Quarter 2001, 59–64.
175. "Four Studies Track What Alternative Pay Plans Work Best," *IOMA's Report on Salary Surveys,* January 2000, 10.
176. Todd Manas, and M. H. L. Vuitton, "Combining Reward Elements to Create the Right Team Chemistry," *Workspan,* November 12, 2000, 46–52.
177. Jerry McAdams and Elizabeth J. Hawk, "Making Group Incentive Plans Work," *WorldatWork Journal,* Third Quarter 2000, 28–34.
178. Edilberto F. Montemayer, "Pay and Incentive Systems," in *Managing Human Resources in the 21st Century* (Cincinnati: South-Western Publishing, 2000), 17.7.
179. Jeanie Casison and Tina Benetiz, "Division of Labor," *Incentive,* September 2001, 52–57.
180. Ruth Simon, "Options Overdose," *The Wall Street Journal,* June 4, 2001, C1.
181. Barbara Estes et al., "Stock Options: Are They Still the Brass Ring?" *Workspan,* May 2001, 24.
182. Corey Rosen, NCEO, "A Brief Introduction to Employee Ownership," available at *www. NCEO.org.*
183. "More Companies See Value in Employee Stock Plans," *Omaha World-Herald,* January 26, 1997, 46R.
184. Bruce Ellig, "CEO Pay: A 20th-Century Review," *WorldatWork Journal,* Third Quarter 2000, 71–78.
185. Michael McKee, "History, Age Push at Ceiling," *The Denver Post,* October 21, 2000, C1.
186. Jim Kerstetter, "The Dark Side of the Valley," *BusinessWeek,* July 17, 2000, 42.
187. "Ethics Policies Are Big with Employees," *Bulletin to Management,* June 29, 2000, 201–202.
188. "Ethics Programs Aren't Stemming Employee Misconduct, a Study Indicates," *The Wall Street Journal,* May 11, 2000, 1.

MODULE 600

Accounting

601 Accounting Strategies, 822

605 The Accounting Process, 826

610 Assets, Liabilities, and Owner's Equity, 827

620 Analysis and Use of Financial Statements, 845

630 Cost Behavior, Control, and Decision Making, 861

640 Product and Service Costs, 875

650 Operating Budgets and Performance Evaluation, 885

660 Decision Making and Accounting, 915

680 Control and Accounting, 937

685 Ethics and Accounting, 940

Module 600 Endnotes, 942

601 Accounting Strategies

The Accounting Function

The accounting function in a firm is a service activity. Its objective is to provide quantitative information, primarily financial in nature, about economic entities that is intended to be useful in making economic decisions. The economic decision makers, whether they are external or internal to a firm, must recognize that the information they receive from the accounting function of a firm constitute only a part of the information they need to make sound decisions. Examples of external decision makers include investors, creditors, and regulators. Examples of internal decision makers are managers, owners, and employees.

The reports generated from accounting information can be thought of as the tools of the accounting trade. Those attempting to use the accounting reports must have a thorough and clear understanding of what these tools can do and what they cannot do. The decision makers should be aware of the limitations of the accounting tools and imperfections of the accounting information due to estimations and judgments involved.

Both internal and external decision makers are attempting to predict the future and timing of cash flows of the firm in terms of determining whether they will be paid, when they will be paid, and how much they will be paid. Here cash is the ultimate measuring criterion in evaluating a firm's success or failure.

The accounting function collects the raw data from business transactions and converts them into information useful to the decision maker. In this regard, the accounting information should contain two qualitative characteristics: primary and secondary qualities. See Exhibit 600.1 for qualities of accounting information.

The challenge to the accounting management, as well as to the senior management of a firm, is to develop strategies to achieve the primary and secondary qualitative characteristics of useful accounting information. When accounting information has these qualitative characteristics, the firm can provide the useful and needed quantitative information to decision makers.

Primary Qualities

The two primary qualities that distinguish useful accounting information are relevance and reliability. If either of these qualities is missing, accounting information will not be useful. Relevance means the information must have a bearing on a particular decision situation. Relevant accounting information possesses at least two characteristics: timeliness and predictive value or feedback value. Timeliness means accounting information must be provided in time to influence a particular decision. Predictive value means accounting information can be used to predict the future and timing of cash flows. Feedback value means the accounting function must provide decision makers with information that allows them to assess the progress or economic worth of an investment.

To be considered reliable, accounting information must possess three qualities: verifiability, representational faithfulness, and neutrality. Information is considered verifiable if several individuals, working independently, would arrive at similar conclusions using the same data. Representational faithfulness means accounting information must report what actually happened. Neutrality means accounting information must be free of bias or distortion.

Exhibit 600.1 *Qualities of Accounting Information*

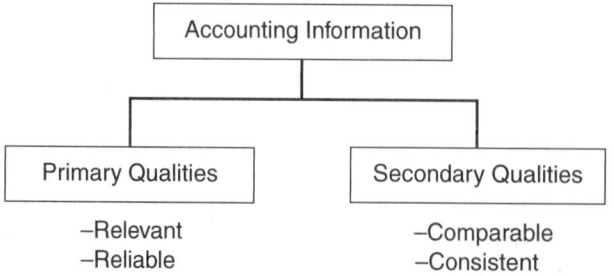

Secondary Qualities

"Secondary qualities" does not mean that these characteristics are of lesser importance than the primary qualities. If a secondary characteristic is missing, the accounting information is not necessarily useless. The secondary qualities of useful information are comparability and consistency. Comparability means accounting reports generated for one firm may be easily and usefully compared with the accounting reports generated for other firms. If the two firms use totally different accounting methods, it would be very difficult to make a useful comparison of their data and information. Consistency means that a firm systematically uses the same accounting methods and procedures from one accounting period to the next accounting period.

In addition to the primary and secondary qualities, the accounting information must be understandable to economic decision makers. "Earnings management" strategy can destroy the primary and secondary qualities of accounting information.

The Role of Accounting in Business

What is the role of accounting in business? The simplest answer to this question is that accounting provides information for managers to use in operating the business. In addition, accounting provides information to other stakeholders to use in assessing the economic performance and condition of the business.

In a general sense, accounting can be defined as an information system that provides reports to stakeholders about the economic activities and condition of a business. You may think of accounting as the "language of business." This is because accounting is the means by which business information is communicated to the stakeholders. For example, accounting reports summarizing the profitability of a new product help **Coca-Cola's** management decide whether to continue selling the product. Likewise, financial analysts use accounting reports in deciding whether to recommend the purchase of Coca-Cola's stock. Banks use accounting reports in determining the amount of credit to extend to Coca-Cola. Suppliers use accounting reports in deciding whether to offer credit for Coca-Cola's purchases of supplies and raw materials. State and federal governments use accounting reports as a basis for assessing taxes on Coca-Cola.

> Accounting is an information system that provides reports to stakeholders about the economic activities and condition of a business.

Accrual accounting, which matches revenues against expenses, provides most useful information for decision makers. The process by which accounting provides information to business stakeholders is illustrated in Exhibit 600.2. A business must first identify its stakeholders. It must then assess the various informational needs of those stakeholders and design its accounting system to meet those needs. Finally, the accounting system records the economic data about business activities and events, which the business reports to the stakeholders according to their informational needs.

Stakeholders use accounting reports as a primary source of information on which they base their decisions. They use other information as well. For example, in deciding whether to extend credit to an appliance store, a banker might

Exhibit 600.2 *Accounting Information and the Stakeholders of a Business*

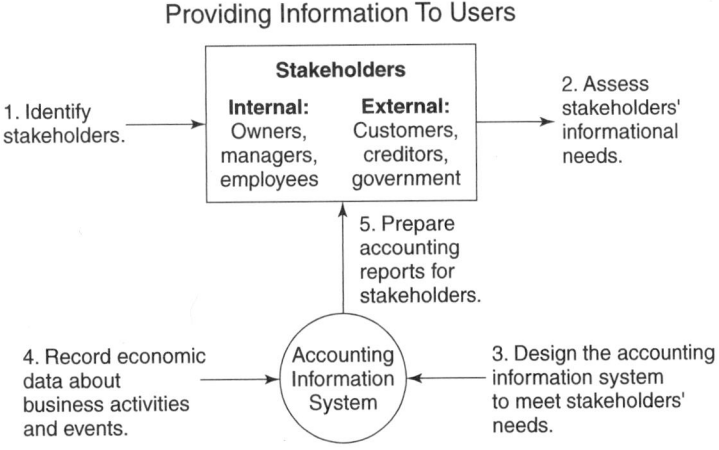

use economic forecasts to assess the future demand for the store's products. During periods of economic downturn, the demand for consumer appliances normally declines. The banker might inquire about the ability and reputation of the managers of the business. For small corporations, bankers may require major stockholders to personally guarantee the loans of the business. Finally, bankers might consult industry publications that rank similar businesses as to their quality of products, customer satisfaction, and future prospects for growth.

Generally Accepted Accounting Principles

If the management of a company could record and report financial data as it saw fit, comparisons among companies would be difficult, if not impossible. Thus, financial accountants follow **generally accepted accounting principles (GAAP)** in preparing reports. These reports allow investors and other stakeholders to compare one company to another.

Next, we emphasize accounting principles and concepts. It is through this emphasis on the "why" of accounting as well as the "how" that you will gain an understanding of the full significance of accounting. In the following paragraphs, we discuss the business entity concept, the cost concept, the matching concept, and other concepts.

The Business Entity Concept

The individual business unit is the business entity for which economic data are needed. This entity could be an automobile dealer, a department store, or a grocery store. The business entity must be identified, so that the accountant can determine which economic data should be analyzed, recorded, and summarized in reports.

The **business entity concept** is important because it limits the economic data in the accounting system to data related directly to the activities of the business. In other words, the business is viewed as an entity separate from its owners, creditors, or other stakeholders. For example, the accountant for a business with one owner (a proprietorship) would record the activities of the business only, not the personal activities, property, or debts of the owner.

The Cost Concept

If a building is bought for $150,000, that amount should be entered into the buyer's accounting records. The seller may have been asking $170,000 for the building up to the time of the sale. The buyer may have initially offered $130,000 for the building. The building may have been assessed at $125,000 for property tax purposes. The buyer may have received an offer of $175,000 for the building the day after it was acquired. These latter amounts have no effect on the accounting records because they did not result in an exchange of the building from the seller to the buyer. The **cost concept** is the basis for entering the *exchange price, or cost, of $150,000* into the accounting records for the building.

Continuing the illustration, the $175,000 offer received by the buyer the day after the building was acquired indicates that it was a bargain purchase at $150,000. To use $175,000 in the accounting records, however, would record an illusory or unrealized profit. If, after buying the building, the buyer accepts the offer and sells the building for $175,000, a profit of $25,000 is then realized and recorded. The new owner would record $175,000 as the cost of the building.

Using the cost concept involves two other important accounting concepts—objectivity and the unit of measure. The **objectivity concept** requires that the accounting records and reports be based upon objective evidence. In exchanges between a buyer and a seller, both try to get the best price. Only the final agreed-upon amount is objective enough for accounting purposes. If the amounts at which properties were recorded were constantly being revised upward and downward based on offers, appraisals, and opinions, accounting reports would soon become unstable and unreliable.

The **unit of measure concept** requires that economic data be recorded in dollars. Money is a common unit of measurement for reporting uniform financial data and reports.

The Matching Concept

The matching concept, which is based on accrual accounting, refers to the matching of expenses and revenues (hence net income) for an accounting period. Under the accrual basis, revenues are reported in the income statement in which they are earned. Similarly, expenses are reported in the same period as the revenues to which they relate. Under the cash basis of accounting, revenues and expenses are reported in the income statement in the period in which cash is received or paid.

Other Accounting Concepts

The materiality concept implies that errors, which could occur during journalizing and posting transactions, should be significant enough to affect the decision making process. All material errors should be discovered and corrected. The accounting period concept breaks the economic life of a business into time periods, and requires that accounting reports be prepared at periodic intervals. The revenue recognition concept, which is based on accrual accounting, refers to the recognition of revenues in the period in which they are earned.

The Differences Between Managerial and Financial Accounting

Although economic information can be classified in many ways, accountants often divide accounting information into two types: financial and managerial. The diagram in Exhibit 600.3 illustrates the relationship between financial accounting and managerial accounting. Understanding this relationship is useful in understanding the information needs of management.

Financial accounting information is reported in statements that are useful for persons or institutions who are "outside" or external to the organization. Examples of such users include shareholders, creditors, government agencies, and the general public. To the extent that management uses the financial statements in directing current operations and planning future operations, the two areas of accounting overlap. For example, in planning future operations, management often begins by evaluating the results of past activities as reported in the financial statements. The financial statements objectively and periodically report the results of past operations and the financial condition of the business according to GAAP.

Managerial accounting information includes both historical and estimated data used by management in conducting daily operations, planning future operations, and developing overall business strategies. The characteristics of managerial accounting are influenced by the varying needs of management. First, managerial accounting reports provide both objective measures of past operations and subjective estimates about future decisions. Using subjective estimates in managerial accounting reports assists management in responding to business opportunities. Second, managerial reports need not be prepared according to generally accepted accounting principles. Because only management uses managerial accounting information, the accountant can provide the information according to management's needs. Third, managerial accounting reports may be provided periodically, as with financial accounting, or at any time management needs information. For example, if senior management is deciding on a geographical expansion, a managerial accounting report can be developed in a format and within a time frame to assist management in the decision. Lastly, managerial accounting reports can be prepared to report information for the business entity or a segment of the entity, such as a division, product, project, or territory.

Exhibit 600.3 *Financial Accounting and Managerial Accounting*

Financial Accounting

| Financial Statements | Users: External and Management | Objective | Prepared according to GAAP | Prepared periodically | Business entity |

Characteristics

Managerial Accounting

| Management Reports | Users: Management | Objective and Subjective | Prepared according to management needs | Prepared periodically or as needed | Business entity or segment |

Characteristics

Exhibit 600.4 *Accounting Cycle*

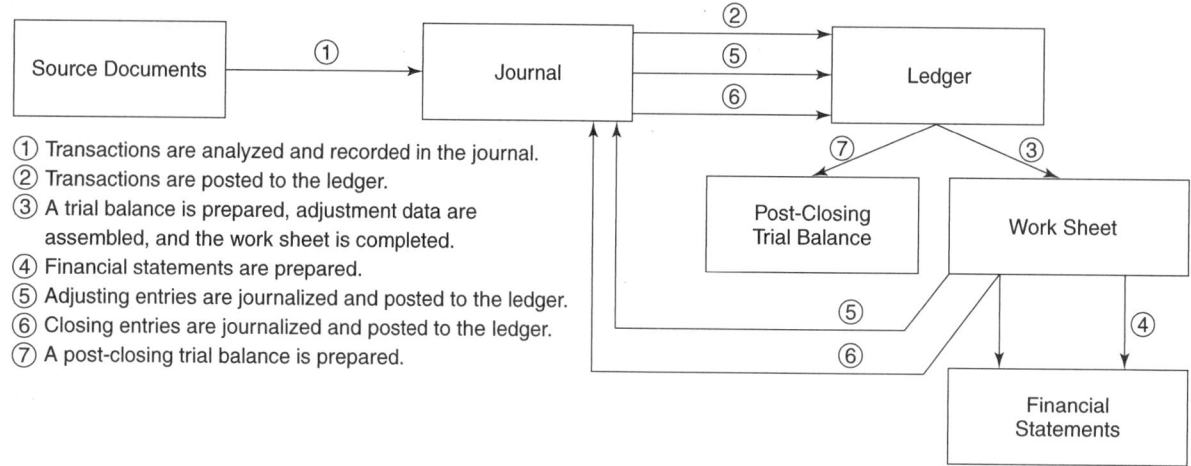

① Transactions are analyzed and recorded in the journal.
② Transactions are posted to the ledger.
③ A trial balance is prepared, adjustment data are assembled, and the work sheet is completed.
④ Financial statements are prepared.
⑤ Adjusting entries are journalized and posted to the ledger.
⑥ Closing entries are journalized and posted to the ledger.
⑦ A post-closing trial balance is prepared.

605 The Accounting Process

Accounting Cycle

The process that begins with analyzing and journalizing transactions and ends with the post-closing trial balance is called the *accounting cycle*. The most important output of the accounting cycle is the financial statements, such as income statement, balance sheet, retained earning statement, and statement of cash flows.

Understanding the steps of the accounting cycle is essential for further study of accounting. The basic steps of the cycle are shown, by number, in the flowchart in Exhibit 600.4.

The accrual accounting and its related matching concept require an analysis and updating of some accounts when financial statements are prepared. This process is achieved through adjusting entries at the end of the accounting period. All adjusting entries affect at least one income statement account (revenue or expense) and one balance sheet account (asset or liability).

Accounts are of two types: real and temporary. The real accounts are permanent accounts with positive balances that appear in the balance sheet. The temporary accounts are nominal accounts such as expenses and revenue accounts in the income statement, and will have zero balances. Closing entries are dated in the journal as of the last day of the accounting period, although they are actually journalized after the end of the accounting period. Closing entry transfer the balances of temporary accounts to the retained earnings account thus leaving them with a zero balance. This transfer is facilitated through an income summary account, which is a clearing account. Finally, the income summary account is closed to retained earnings account.

Reversing entry, which is an optional entry, may be used to simplify the analysis and recording of adjusting entries such as wages expenses and payable. It reverses an adjusting entry. Not all firms need reversing entries.

The accounts and amounts listed in the post-closing trail balance should agree exactly with the accounts and amounts listed on the balance sheet at the end of the period. This includes unearned rent, prepaid insurance, unearned fees, accounts receivable, accounts payable, wages payable, and others.

Fiscal Year

The annual accounting period adopted by a business is known as its **fiscal year.** Fiscal years begin with the first day of the month selected and end on the last day of the following 12th month. The period most commonly used is the calendar year. Other periods are not unusual, especially for businesses organized as corporations. For example, a corporation may adopt a fiscal year that ends when business activities have reached the lowest point in its annual operating cycle. Such a fiscal year is called the **natural business year.** At the low point in its operating cycle, a business has more time to analyze the results of operations and to prepare financial statements.

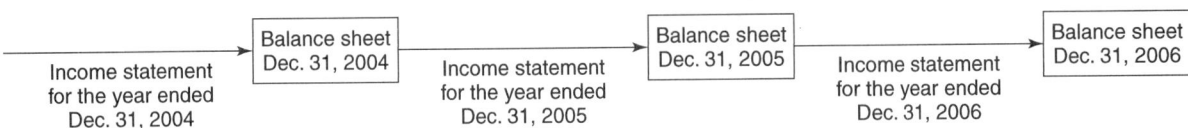

Financial History of a Business

Because companies with fiscal years often have highly seasonal operations, investors and others should be careful in interpreting partial year reports for such companies. That is, you should expect the results of operations for these companies to vary significantly throughout the fiscal year.

The financial history of a business may be shown by a series of balance sheets and income statements for several fiscal years. If the life of a business is expressed by a line moving from left to right, the series of balance sheets and income statements may be graphed as above.

Assets, Liabilities, and Owner's Equity

The Accounting Equation

The resources owned by a business are its assets. Examples of assets include cash, land, buildings, and equipment. The rights or claims to the assets are normally divided into two principal types: (1) the rights of creditors and (2) the rights of owners. The rights of creditors represent debts of the business and are called **liabilities**. The rights of the owners are called **owner's equity**. The relationship between the two may be stated in the form of an equation, as follows.

$$\text{Assets} = \text{Liability} + \text{Owner's Equity}$$

This equation is known as the **accounting equation**. It is usual to place liabilities before owner's equity in the accounting equation because creditors have first rights to the assets. The claim of the owners is sometimes given greater emphasis by transposing liabilities to the other side of the equation, which yields:

$$\text{Assets} - \text{Liabilities} = \text{Owner's Equity}$$

To illustrate, if the assets owned by a business amount to $100,000 and the liabilities amount to $30,000, the owner's equity is equal to $70,000, as shown below.

Assets	−	Liabilities	=	Owner's Equity
$100,000	−	$30,000	=	$70,000

Example 1 *If a company's assets increase by $20,000 and its liabilities decrease by $5,000, how much did the owner's equity increase or decrease?*

Change in Assets	=	Change in Liabilities	+	Change in Owner's Equity
+$20,000	=	−$5,000	+	X
+$25,000	=			X

Business Transactions and the Accounting Equation

For example, paying a monthly telephone bill of $168 affects a business's financial condition because it now has less cash on hand. Such an economic event or condition that directly changes an entity's financial condition or directly affects its results of operations is a business transaction. For example, purchasing land for $50,000 is a business transaction. In contrast, a change in a business's credit rating does not directly affect cash or any other element of its financial condition.

All business transactions can be stated in terms of changes in the elements of the accounting equation. You will see how business transactions affect the accounting equation by studying some typical transactions. As a basis for illustration, we will use a business organized by Chris Clark.

> All business transactions can be stated in terms of changes in the elements of the accounting equation.

Assume that on November 1, 2004, Chris Clark organizes a corporation that will be known as NetSolutions. The first phase of Chris's business plan is to operate NetSolutions as a service business that provides assistance to individuals and small businesses in developing Web pages and in configuring and installing application software. Chris expects this initial phase of the business to last one to two years. During this period, Chris will gather information on the software and hardware needs of customers. During the second phase of the business plan, Chris plans to expand NetSolutions into an Internet-based retailer of software and hardware for individuals and small businesses.

Each transaction or group of similar transactions during NetSolutions' first month of operations is described in the following paragraphs. The effect of each transaction on the accounting equation is then shown.

TRANSACTION a Chris Clark deposits $25,000 in a bank account in the name of NetSolutions in return for shares of stock in the corporation. Stock issued to owners (stockholders), such as Chris Clark, is referred to as **capital stock**. The effect of this transaction is to increase the asset (cash), on the left side of the equation, by $25,000. To balance the equation, the owner's equity (capital stock), on the right side of the equation, is increased by the same amount. The effect of this transaction on NetSolutions' accounting equation is shown below.

	Assets	=	Owner's Equity
	Cash		Capital Stock
a.	25,000	=	25,000 Investment by stockholder

Note that the accounting equation shown above relates only to the business, NetSolutions. Under the business entity concept, Chris Clark's personal assets, such as a home or personal bank account, and personal liabilities are excluded from the equation.

TRANSACTION b If you purchased this textbook by paying cash, you entered into a transaction in which you exchanged one asset for another. That is, you exchanged cash for the textbook. Businesses often enter into similar transactions. NetSolutions, for example, exchanged $20,000 cash for land. The land is located in a new business park with convenient access to transportation facilities. Chris Clark plans to rent office space and equipment during the first phase of the business plan. During the second phase, Chris plans to build an office and warehouse on the land.

The purchase of the land changes the makeup of the assets but does not change the total assets. The items in the equation prior to this transaction and the effect of the transaction are shown next, as well as the new amounts, or *balances*, of the items.

	Assets			=	Owner's Equity
	Cash	+	Land		Capital Stock
Bal.	25,000			=	25,000
b.	−20,000		+20,000		
Bal.	5,000		20,000		25,000

Example 2 If NetSolutions had purchased a van for $28,000, paying $8,000 cash and signing a loan agreement (note payable) for $20,000, how would the transaction be recorded using the accounting equation?

Cash	+	Van	=	Notes Payable
−8,000	+	28,000		+20,000

TRANSACTION c You have probably used a credit card at one time or another to buy clothing or other merchandise. In this type of transaction, you received clothing for a promise to pay your credit card bill in the future. That is, you received an asset and incurred a liability to pay a future bill. During the month, NetSolutions entered into a similar transaction, buying supplies for $1,350 and agreeing to pay the supplier in the near future. This type of transaction is called a purchase *on account*. The liability created is called an **account payable.** Items such as supplies that will be used in the business in the future are called **prepaid expenses,** which are assets. The effect of this transaction is to increase assets and liabilities by $1,350, as follows.

	Assets			=	Liabilities	+	Owner's Equity
	Cash	+ Supplies	+ Land		Accounts Payable	+	Capital Stock
Bal.	5,000		20,000				25,000
c.		+1,350			+1,350		
Bal.	5,000	1,350	20,000		1,350		25,000

TRANSACTION d You may have earned money by painting houses. If so, you received money for rendering services to a customer. Likewise, a business earns money by selling goods or services to its customers. This amount is called **revenue.**

During its first month of operations, NetSolutions provided services to customers, earning fees of $7,500 and receiving the amount in cash. This transaction increased cash and the owner's equity by $7,500, as shown here.

	Assets			=	Liabilities	+	Owner's Equity	
	Cash	+ Supplies	+ Land		Accounts Payable	+ Capital Stock	+	Retained Earnings
Bal.	5,000	1,350	20,000		1,350	25,000		
d.	+ 7,500							+ 7,500 Fees earned
Bal.	12,500	1,350	20,000		1,350	25,000		7,500

You should note that the increase in owner's equity from earning revenue is listed in the equation under "Retained Earnings." **Retained earnings** is the owner's equity created by the business operations (revenues less expenses). Transactions affecting earnings are kept separate from transactions related to owner's investments (capital stock). This is useful in preparing reports to owners and creditors and in satisfying legal requirements.

Special terms may be used to describe certain kinds of revenue, such as **sales** for the sale of merchandise. Revenue from providing services is called **fees earned.** For example, a physician would record fees earned for services to patients. Other examples include **rent revenue** (money received for rent) and **interest revenue** (money received for interest).

Instead of requiring the payment of cash at the time services are provided or goods are sold, a business may accept payment at a later date. Such revenues are called *fees on account* or *sales on account*. In such cases, the firm has an **account receivable,** which is a claim against the customer. An account receivable is an asset, and the revenue is earned as if cash had been received. When customers pay their accounts, there is an exchange of one asset for another. Cash increases, while accounts receivable decreases.

TRANSACTION e If you painted houses to earn money, you probably used your own ladders and brushes. NetSolutions also spent cash or used up other assets in earning revenue. The amounts used in this process of earning revenue are called **expenses.** Expenses include supplies used, wages of employees, and other assets and services used in operating the business.

For NetSolutions, the expenses paid during the month were as follows: wages, $2,125; rent, $800; utilities, $450; and miscellaneous, $275. Miscellaneous expenses include small amounts paid for such items as postage, coffee, and magazine subscriptions. The effect of this group of transactions is the opposite of the effect of revenues. These transactions reduce cash and owner's equity, as shown here.

	Assets			=	Liabilities	+	Owner's Equity	
	Cash	+ Supplies	+ Land		Accounts Payable	+ Capital Stock	+	Retained Earnings
Bal.	12,500	1,350	20,000		1,350	25,000		7,500
e.	− 3,650							− 2,125 Wages expense
								− 800 Rent expense
								− 450 Utilities expense
								− 275 Misc. expense
Bal.	8,850	1,350	20,000		1,350	25,000		3,850

610. ASSETS, LIABILITIES, AND OWNER'S EQUITY

Businesses usually record each revenue and expense transaction separately as it occurs. However, to simplify this illustration, we have summarized NetSolutions' revenues and expenses for the month in transactions (d) and (e).

TRANSACTION f When you pay your monthly credit card bill, you decrease the cash in your checking account and also decrease the amount you owe to the credit card company. Likewise, when NetSolutions pays $950 to creditors during the month, it reduces both assets and liabilities, as shown below.

	Assets					=	Liabilities	+	Owner's Equity		
	Cash	+	Supplies	+	Land		Accounts Payable		Capital Stock	+	Retained Earnings
Bal.	8,850		1,350		20,000		1,350		25,000		3,850
f.	−950						−950				
Bal.	7,900		1,350		20,000		400		25,000		3,850

You should note that paying an amount on account is different from paying an amount for an expense. The payment of an expense reduces owner's equity, as illustrated in transaction (e). Paying an amount on account reduces the amount owed on a liability.

TRANSACTION g At the end of the month, the cost of the supplies on hand (not yet used) is $550. The remainder of the supplies ($1,350 − $550) was used in the operations of the business and is treated as an expense. This decrease of $800 in supplies and owner's equity is shown as follows.

	Assets					=	Liabilities	+	Owner's Equity		
	Cash	+	Supplies	+	Land		Accounts Payable		Capital Stock	+	Retained Earnings
Bal.	7,900		1,350		20,000		400		25,000		3,850
g.			−800								−800 Supplies expense
Bal.	7,900		550		20,000		400		25,000		3,050

TRANSACTION h At the end of the month, NetSolutions pays $2,000 to stockholders (Chris Clark) as dividends. **Dividends** are distributions of earnings to stockholders. The payment of the dividends reduces both cash and owner's equity. The effect of this transaction is shown as follows.

	Assets					=	Liabilities	+	Owner's Equity		
	Cash	+	Supplies	+	Land		Accounts Payable		Capital Stock	+	Retained Earnings
Bal.	7,900		550		20,000		400		25,000		3,050
h.	−2,000										−2,000 Dividends
Bal.	5,900		550		20,000		400		25,000		1,050

You should be careful not to confuse dividends with expenses. Dividends *do not* represent assets or services used in the process of earning revenues. The owner's equity decrease from dividends is listed in the equation under Retained Earnings. This is because dividends are considered a distribution of earnings to stockholders.

Example 3 If supplies of $2,500 were purchased during the month and supplies of $350 are on hand at the end of the month, how much is the supplies expense for the month?

$2,150 ($2,500 supplies purchased − $350 on hand)

SUMMARY The transactions of NetSolutions (a through h) are summarized as follows. They are identified by letter, and the balance of each item is shown after each transaction.

	Assets					=	Liabilities	+	Owner's Equity		
	Cash	+	Supplies	+	Land	=	Accounts Payable	+	Capital Stock	+	Retained Earnings
a.	+25,000								25,000		Investment by stockholder
b.	−20,000				+20,000						
Bal.	5,000				20,000				25,000		
c.			+1,350				+1,350				
Bal.	5,000		1,350		20,000		1,350		25,000		
d.	+7,500										+7,500 Fees earned
Bal.	12,500		1,350		20,000		1,350		25,000		7,500
e.	−3,650										−2,125 Wages expense
											− 800 Rent expense
											− 450 Utilities expense
											− 275 Misc. expense
Bal.	8,850		1,350		20,000		1,350		25,000		3,850
f.	− 950						− 950				
Bal.	7,900		1,350		20,000		400				3,850
g.			− 800								− 800 Supplies expense
Bal.	7,900		550		20,000		400		25,000		3,050
h.	−2,000										−2,000 Dividends
Bal.	5,900		550		20,000		400		25,000		1,050

In reviewing the preceding summary, you should note the following, which apply to all types of businesses.

1. The effect of every transaction is *an increase or a decrease in one or more of the accounting equation elements*.
2. The two sides of the accounting equation are *always equal*.
3. The owner's equity is *increased by amounts invested by stockholders (capital stock)* and is *decreased by dividends to stockholders (retained earnings)*. In addition, the owner's equity (retained earnings) is *increased by revenues* and is *decreased by expenses*. The effects of these four types of transactions on owner's equity are illustrated in Exhibit 600.5.

Financial Statements

After transactions have been recorded and summarized, reports are prepared for users. The accounting reports that provide this information are called **financial statements.** The principal financial statements of a corporation are the income

Exhibit 600.5 *Effects of Transactions on Owner's Equity*

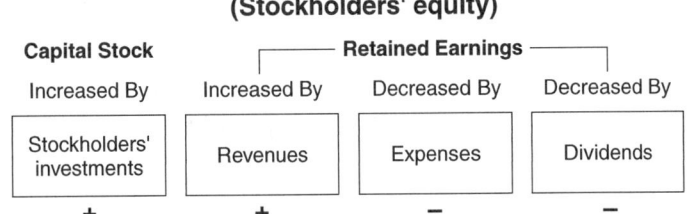

610. ASSETS, LIABILITIES, AND OWNER'S EQUITY

statement, the retained earnings statement, the balance sheet, and the statement of cash flows. The order in which the statements are normally prepared and the nature of the data presented in each statement are as follows.

- **Income statement**—A summary of the revenue and expenses *for a specific period of time,* such as a month or a year.
- **Retained earnings statement**—A summary of the changes in the earnings retained in the corporation for *a specific period of time,* such as a month or a year.
- **Balance sheet**—A list of the assets, liabilities, and owner's equity *as of a specific date,* usually at the close of the last day of a month or a year.
- **Statement of cash flows**—A summary of the cash receipts and cash payments *for a specific period of time,* such as a month or a year.

The basic features of the four statements and their interrelationships are illustrated in Exhibit 600.6. The data for the statements were taken from the summary of transactions of NetSolutions.

All financial statements should be identified by the name of the business, the title of the statement, and the *date* or *period of time*. The data presented in the income statement, the retained earnings statement, and the statement of cash flows are for a period of time. The data presented in the balance sheet are for a specific date.

Income Statement

The income statement reports the revenues and expenses for a period of time, based on the **matching concept**. This concept is applied by *matching* the expenses with the revenue generated during a period by those expenses. Revenues are recognized when the earning process is completed and an exchange has taken place. The income statement also reports the excess of the revenue over the expenses incurred. This excess of the revenue over the expenses is called **net income** or **net profit**.

Net income—the excess of revenue over expenses—increases owner's equity.

If the expenses exceed the revenue, the excess is a **net loss**.

The effects of revenue earned and expenses incurred during the month for NetSolutions were shown in the equation as increases and decreases in owner's equity (retained earnings). Net income for a period has the effect of increasing owner's equity (retained earnings) for the period, whereas a net loss has the effect of decreasing owner's equity (retained earnings) for the period.

The revenue, expenses, and the net income of $3,050 for NetSolutions are reported in the income statement in Exhibit 600.6. The order in which the expenses are listed in the income statement varies among businesses. One method is to list them in order of size, beginning with the larger items. Miscellaneous expense is usually shown as the last item, regardless of the amount. Exhibit 600.7 shows various accounts that go into the preparation of the income statement.

Retained Earnings Statement

The primary statement for analyzing changes in the owner's equity of a corporation is the retained earnings statement. The retained earnings statement is a connecting link between the income statement and the balance sheet.

Financial statements are used to evaluate the current financial condition of a business and to predict its future operating results and cash flows. For example, bank loan officers use a business's financial statements in deciding whether to grant a loan to the business. Once the loan is granted, the borrower may be required to maintain a certain level of assets in excess of liabilities. The business's financial statements are used to monitor this level.

Two types of transactions affect the retained earnings during the month: (1) the revenues and expenses that resulted in net income of $3,050 for the month and (2) dividends of $2,000 paid to stockholders. These transactions are summarized in the retained earnings statement for NetSolutions shown in Exhibit 600.6.

Because NetSolutions has been in operation for only one month, it has no retained earnings at the beginning of November. For December, however, there is a beginning balance—the balance at the end of November

Exhibit 600.6 *Financial Statements for NetSolutions*

NetSolutions
Income Statement
for the Month Ended November 30, 2004

Fees earned		$7,500.00
Operating expenses:		
Wages expense	$2,125.00	
Rent expense	800.00	
Supplies expense	800.00	
Utilities expense	450.00	
Miscellaneous expense	275.00	
Total operating expenses		4,450.00
Net income		$3,050.00

NetSolutions
Retained Earnings Statement
for the Month Ended November 30, 2004

Net income for November 2004	$3,050.00
Less dividends	2,000.00
Retained earnings, November 30, 2004	$1,050.00

NetSolutions
Balance Sheet
November 30, 2004

Assets		Liabilities		
Cash	$ 5,900.00	Accounts payable		$ 400.00
Supplies	550.00	**Stockholders' Equity**		
Land	20,000.00	Capital stock	$25,000	
		Retained earnings	1,050	26,050.00
		Total liabilities and		
Total assets	$26,450.00	stockholders' equity		$26,450.00

NetSolutions
Statement of Cash Flows
for the Month Ended November 30, 2004

Cash flows from operating activities:			
Cash received from customers	$ 7,500.00		
Deduct cash payments for expenses and			
payments to creditors	4,600.00		
Net cash flow from operating activities		$ 2,900.00	
Cash flows from investing activities:			
Cash payments for acquisition of land		(20,000.00)	
Cash flows from financing activities:			
Cash received from sale of stock	$25,000.00		
Deduct cash dividends	2,000.00		
Net cash flow from financing activities		23,000.00	
Net cash flow and November 30, 2004 cash balance		$ 5,900.00	

2004. This balance of $1,050 is reported on the retained earnings statement. To illustrate, assume that NetSolutions earned net income of $4,155 and paid dividends of $2,000 during December 2004. The retained earnings statement for NetSolutions for December 2004 is shown in Exhibit 600.8. Exhibit 600.9 shows various accounts that go into the preparation of a retained earnings statement.

610. ASSETS, LIABILITIES, AND OWNER'S EQUITY

Exhibit 600.7 *Income Statement Accounts*

Account Title	Account Classification
Advertising Expense	Operating expense
Amortization Expense	Operating expense
Cost of Merchandise (Goods) Sold	Cost of merchandise (goods sold)
Depletion Expense	Operating expense
Dividend Revenue	Other income
Exchange Gain	Other income
Exchange Loss	Other expense
Fees Earned	Revenue
Gain on Disposal of Fixed Assets	Other income
Gain on Redemption of Bonds	Extraordinary item
Gain on Sale of Investments	Other income
Income Tax Expense	Income tax
Insurance Expense	Operating expense
Interest Expense	Other expense
Interest Revenue	Other income
Loss on Disposal of Fixed Assets	Other expense
Loss on Redemption of Bonds	Extraordinary item
Loss on Sale of Investments	Other expense
Merchandise Inventory	Cost of merchandise sold
Miscellaneous Expense	Operating expense
Payroll Tax Expense	Operating expense
Pension Expense	Operating expense
Purchases	Cost of merchandise sold
Purchases Discounts	Cost of merchandise sold
Purchases Returns and Allowances	Cost of merchandise sold
Rent Expense	Operating expense
Rent Revenue	Other income
Salaries Expense	Operating expense
Sales	Revenue from sales
Sales Discounts	Revenue from sales
Sales Returns and Allowances	Revenue from sales
Supplies Expense	Operating expense
Transportation In	Cost of merchandise sold
Transportation Out	Operating expense
Uncollectible Accounts Expense	Operating expense
Utilities Expense	Operating expense
Vacation Pay Expense	Operating expense
Wages Expense	Operating expense

Exhibit 600.8 *Retained Earnings Statement for NetSolutions*

NetSolutions
Retained Earnings Statement
for the Month Ended December 30, 2004

Retained earnings, December 1, 2004		$1,050.00
Net income for the month	$4,155.00	
Less dividends	2,000.00	
Increase in retained earnings		2,155.00
Retained earnings, December 31, 2004		$3,205.00

Exhibit 600.9 *Retained Earnings Statement Accounts*

Account Title	Account Classification
Cash Dividends	Stockholders' equity
Prior Period Adjustments	Retained earnings
Property Dividends	Stockholders' equity
Reserves	Retained earnings
Restricted Earnings	Retained earnings
Retained Earnings	Stockholders' equity
Stock Dividends	Stockholders' equity
Transfers to Capital	Retained earnings
Unrestricted Earnings	Retained earnings

Balance Sheet

The balance sheet in Exhibit 600.6 reports the amounts of NetSolutions' assets, liabilities, and owner's equity at the end of November. These amounts are taken from the last line of the summary of transactions presented earlier. The form of balance sheet shown in Exhibit 600.6 is called the **account form** because it resembles the basic format of the accounting equation, with assets on the left side and the liabilities and owner's equity sections on the right side. An alternative form of balance sheet called the **report form** presents the liabilities and owner's equity sections below the assets section.

The assets section of the balance sheet normally presents assets in the order that they will be converted into cash or used in operations. Cash is presented first, followed by receivables, supplies, prepaid insurance, and other assets. The assets of a more permanent nature are shown next, such as land, buildings, and equipment.

Assets

Assets are commonly divided into classes for presentation on the balance sheet. Two of these classes are (1) current assets and (2) noncurrent assets (for example, property, plant, and equipment). Most assets are listed at historical cost.

CURRENT ASSETS Cash and other assets that are expected to be converted to cash or sold or used up usually within one year or less, through the normal operations of the business, are called **current assets**. In addition to cash, the current assets usually owned by a service business are notes receivable, accounts receivable, supplies, and other prepaid expenses.

Two common classes of assets are current assets and noncurrent or long-term assets (e.g., property, plant, and equipment).

Notes receivable are amounts customers owe. They are written promises to pay the amount of the note and possibly interest at an agreed upon rate. Accounts receivable are also amounts customers owe, but they are less formal than notes and do not provide for interest. Accounts receivable normally result from providing services or selling merchandise on account. Notes receivable and accounts receivable are current assets because they will usually be converted to cash within one year or less.

NONCURRENT ASSETS The property, plant, and equipment section may also be described as **noncurrent** or **long-term assets, fixed assets**, or **plant assets**. These assets, include equipment, machinery, buildings, and land. With the exception of land, fixed assets depreciate over a period of time. Depreciation is a noncash item. The cost, accumulated depreciation, and book value of each major type of fixed asset is normally reported on the balance sheet or in accompanying notes. The book value of a fixed asset is historical cost minus accumulated depreciation.

Liabilities

Liabilities are the amounts the business owes to creditors. The two most common classes of liabilities are (1) current liabilities and (2) long-term liabilities.

Two common classes of liabilities are current liabilities and long-term liabilities.

CURRENT LIABILITIES Liabilities that will be due within a short time (usually one year or less) and that are to be paid out of current assets are called **current liabilities**. The most common liabilities in this group are notes payable and accounts payable. Other current liability accounts commonly found in the ledger are Wages Payable, Interest Payable, Taxes Payable, and Unearned Fees.

LONG-TERM LIABILITIES Liabilities that will not be due for a long time (usually more than one year) are called **long-term liabilities.** If NetSolutions had long-term liabilities, they would be reported below the current liabilities. As long-term liabilities come due and are to be paid within one year, they are classified as current liabilities. If they are to be renewed rather than paid, they would continue to be classified as long-term. When an asset is pledged as security for a liability, the obligation may be called a *mortgage note payable* or a *mortgage payable.*

Stockholders' Equity

The stockholders' right to the assets of the business is presented on the balance sheet below the liabilities section. The stockholders' equity is added to the total liabilities, and this total must be equal to the total assets. The equity includes capital stock, additional paid-in capital, and retained earnings. Exhibit 600.10 shows various accounts that go into the preparation of a balance sheet.

Statement of Cash Flows

The **statement of cash flows** reports a firm's major cash inflows and outflows for a period. It provides useful information about a firm's ability to generate cash from operations, maintain and expand its operating capacity, meet its financial obligations, and pay dividends. *Cash* refers to cash and cash equivalents. Examples of cash equivalents include marketable securities, certificates of deposit, U.S. Treasury bills, and money market funds.

The statement of cash flows is one of the basic financial statements. It is useful to managers in evaluating past operations and in planning future investing and financing activities. It is useful to investors, creditors, and others in assessing a firm's profit potential. In addition, it is a basis for assessing the firm's ability to pay its maturing debt.

The statement of cash flows reports cash flows by three types of activities.

1. **Cash flows from operating activities** are cash flows from transactions that affect net income. It shows a summary of cash receipts and cash payments from operations. Examples of such transactions include the purchase and sale of merchandise by a retailer. The net cash flow operating activities ($2,900 in Exhibit 600.6) will normally differ from the amount of net income for the period ($3,050 in Exhibit 600.6). The difference occurs because revenues and expenses may not be recorded at the same time that cash is received from customers or paid to creditors.
2. **Cash flows from investing activities** are cash flows from transactions that affect the investments in noncurrent assets. Examples of such transactions include the sale and purchase of fixed assets, such as equipment, land, and buildings.
3. **Cash flows from financing activities** are cash flows from transactions that affect the equity and debt of the business. Examples of such transactions include issuing or retiring equity and debt securities, and cash dividends.

The statement of cash flows reports cash flows from operating, investing, and financing activities.

The cash flows from operating activities is normally presented first, followed by the cash flows from investing activities and financing activities. The total of the net cash flow from these activities is the net increase or decrease in cash for the period. The cash balance at the beginning of the period is added to the net increase or decrease in cash, resulting in the cash balance at the end of the period. The ending cash balance on the statement of cash flows equals the cash reported on the balance sheet.

Exhibit 600.11 shows common cash flow transactions reported in each of the three sections of the statement of cash flows. By reporting cash flows by operating, investing, and financing activities, significant relationships within and among the activities can be evaluated. For example, the cash receipts from issuing bonds can be related to repayments of borrowings when both are reported as financing activities. Also, the impact of each of the three activities (operating, investing, and financing) on cash flows can be identified. This allows investors and creditors to evaluate the effects of cash flows on a firm's profits and ability to pay debt.

Exhibit 600.10 *Balance Sheet Accounts*

Account Title	Account Classification
Accounts Payable	Current liability
Accounts Receivable	Current asset
Accumulated Depreciation	Fixed asset
Accumulated Depletion	Fixed asset
Allowance for Doubtful Accounts	Current asset
Bonds Payable	Long-term liability
Building	Fixed asset
Capital Stock	Stockholders' equity
Cash	Current asset
Cash Dividends Payable	Current liability
Common Stock	Stockholders' equity
Deferred Income Tax Payable	Current liability/Long-term liability
Discount on Bonds Payable	Long-term liability
Donated Capital	Stockholders' equity
Employees Federal Income Tax Payable	Current liability
Equipment	Fixed asset
Factory Overhead (Overapplied)	Deferred credit
Factory Overhead (Underapplied)	Deferred debit
Federal Income Tax Payable	Current liability
Federal Unemployment Tax Payable	Current liability
Finished Goods	Current asset
Goodwill	Intangible asset
Income Tax Payable	Current liability
Interest Receivable	Current asset
Investment in Bonds	Investment
Investment in Stocks	Investment
Investment in Subsidiary	Investment
Land	Fixed asset
Marketable Securities	Current asset
Materials	Current asset
Medicare Tax Payable	Current liability
Merchandise Inventory	Current asset
Notes Payable	Current liability/Long-term liability
Notes Receivable	Current asset/Investment
Organization Costs	Intangible asset
Patents	Intangible asset
Paid-In Capital from Sale of Treasury Stock	Stockholders' equity
Paid-In Capital in Excess of Par (Stated Value)	Stockholders' equity
Petty Cash	Current asset
Premium on Bonds Payable	Long-term liability
Prepaid Insurance	Current asset
Prepaid Rent	Current asset
Preferred Stock	Stockholders' equity
Prior Period Adjustments	Stockholders' equity
Retained Earnings	Stockholders' equity
Salaries Payable	Current liability
Sales Tax Payable	Current liability
Sinking Fund Cash	Investment
Sinking Fund Investments	Investment
Social Security Tax Payable	Current liability
State Unemployment Tax Payable	Current liability
Stock Dividends Distributable	Stockholders' equity
Supplies	Current asset
Treasury Stock	Stockholders' equity
Unearned Rent	Current liability
Vacation Pay Payable	Current liability/Long-term liability
Work in Process	Current asset

610. ASSETS, LIABILITIES, AND OWNERS' EQUITY

Exhibit 600.11 *Cash Flows*

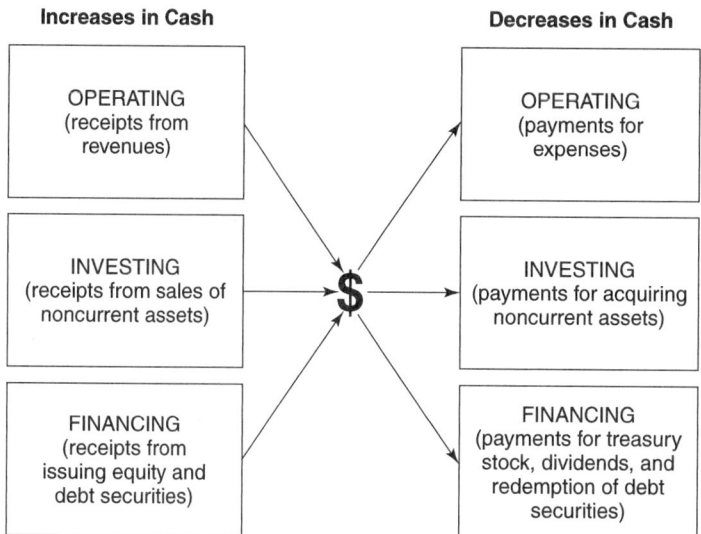

Cash Flows from Operating Activities

The most important cash flows of a business often relate to operating activities. There are two alternative methods for reporting cash flows from operating activities in the statement of cash flows. These methods are (1) the direct method and (2) the indirect method, as shown in Exhibit 600.12.

The **direct method** reports the sources of operating cash and the uses of operating cash. The major source of operating cash is cash received from customers. The major uses of operating cash include cash paid to suppliers for merchandise and services and cash paid to employees for wages. The difference between these operating cash receipts and cash payments is the net cash flow from operating activities.

The primary advantage of the direct method is that it reports the sources and uses of cash in the statement of cash flows. Its primary disadvantage is that the necessary data may not be readily available and may be costly to gather.

The **indirect method** reports the operating cash flows by beginning with net income and adjusting it for revenues and expenses that do not involve the receipt or payment of cash. In other words, accrual net income is adjusted to determine the net amount of cash flows from operating activities.

A major advantage of the indirect method is that it focuses on the differences between net income and cash flows from operations. In this sense, it shows the relationship between the income statement, the balance sheet, and the statement of cash flows. Because the data are readily available, the indirect method is normally less costly to use than the direct method. Because of these advantages, most firms use the indirect method to report cash flows from operations.

Exhibit 600.13 illustrates the cash flow from operating activities section of the statement of cash flows under the direct and indirect methods. Both statements are for NetSolutions for the month ended November 2004. Both methods show the same amount of net cash flow from operating activities, regardless of the method.

Example 4 Net income was $45,000 for the year. The accumulated depreciation balance increased by $15,000 over the year. There were no sales of fixed assets or changes in noncash current assets or liabilities. What is the cash flow from operations?

$60,000 ($45,000 + $15,000)

Example 5 Net income was $36,000 for the year. Accounts receivable increased $3,000, and accounts payable increased $5,000. What is the cash flow from operations?

$38,000 ($36,000 − $3,000 + $5,000)

Exhibit 600.12 *Methods to Report Cash Flows from Operating Activities*

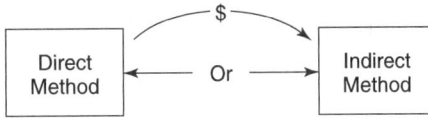

Exhibit 600.13 *Cash Flows From Operations: Direct and Indirect Methods for NetSolutions*

Direct Method		Indirect Method	
Cash flows from operating activities:		Cash flows from operating activities:	
Cash received from customers	$7,500	Net income, per income statement	$3,050
Deduct cash payments for expenses and payments to creditors	4,600	Add increase in accounts payable	400
			$3,450
		Deduct increase in supplies	550
Net cash flow from operating activities	$2,900	Net cash flow from operating activities	$2,900

Cash Flows from Investing Activities

Cash inflows from investing activities normally arise from selling fixed assets, investments, and intangible assets. Cash outflows normally include payments to acquire fixed assets, investments, and intangible assets. NetSolutions paid $20,000 to acquire land.

Cash flows from investing activities are reported on the statement of cash flows by first listing the cash inflows. The cash outflows are then presented. If the inflows are greater than the outflows, **net cash flow provided by investing activities** is reported. If the inflows are less than the outflows, **net cash flow used for investing activities** is reported.

> **Example 6** A building with a cost of $145,000 and accumulated depreciation of $35,000 was sold for a $10,000 gain. How much cash was generated from this investing activity?
> $120,000 ($145,000 − $35,000 + $10,000)

Cash Flows from Financing Activities

Cash inflows from financing activities normally arise from issuing debt or equity securities. Examples of such inflows include issuing bonds, notes payable, and preferred and common stocks. Cash outflows from financing activities include paying cash dividends, repaying debt, and acquiring treasury stock.

Cash flows from financing activities are reported on the statement of cash flows by first listing the cash inflows. The cash outflows are then presented. If the inflows are greater than the outflows, **net cash flow provided by financing activities** is reported. If the inflows are less than the outflows, **net cash flow used for financing activities** is reported.

The cash flows from financing activities section in the statement of cash flows for NetSolutions is shown below.

Cash flows from financing activities:	
Cash received from sale of stock	$25,000
Deduct cash dividends	2,000
Net cash flow from financing activities	$23,000

Example 7 *Sales reported on the income statement were $350,000. The accounts receivable balance declined $8,000 over the year. What was the amount of cash received from customers?*

$358,000 ($350,000 + $8,000)

Following is a summary of statement of cash flows for NetSolutions as of November 30, 2004:

Net cash flow from operating activities	$ 2,900
Plus net cash flow from investing activities	(20,000)
Plus net cash flow from financing activities	23,000
Equal net increase (decrease) in cash	$ 5,900
Plus cash at beginning of year	0
Equal cash at end of year	$ 5,900*

*This amount is the same as the cash account in the balance sheet as of November 30, 2004. (Exhibit 600.6)

Exhibit 600.14 shows various accounts that go into the preparation of statement of cash flows.

Noncash Investing and Financing Activities

A business may enter into investing and financing activities that do not directly involve cash. For example, it may issue common stock to retire long-term debt. Such a transaction does not have a direct effect on cash. However, the transaction does eliminate the need for future cash payments to pay interest and retire the bonds. Thus, because of their future effect on cash flows, such transactions should be reported to readers of the financial statements.

When noncash investing and financing transactions occur during a period, their effect is reported in a separate schedule. This schedule usually appears at the bottom of the statement of cash flows. For example, in such a schedule, **Amazon.com** disclosed the issuance of $217 million in common stock for Internet acquisitions. Other examples of noncash investing and financing transactions include acquiring fixed assets by issuing bonds or capital stock and issuing common stock in exchange for convertible preferred stock.

Cash Flow per Share

The term *cash flow per share* is sometimes reported in the financial press. Often, the term is used to mean "cash flow from operations per share." Such reporting may be misleading to users of the financial statements. For example, users might interpret cash flow per share as the amount available for dividends. This would not be the case if most of the cash generated by operations is required for repaying loans or for reinvesting in the business. Users might also think that cash flow per share is equivalent or perhaps superior to earnings per share. For these reasons, the financial statements, including the statement of cash flows, should not report cash flow per share.

Free Cash Flow

A valuable tool for evaluating the cash position of a business is free cash flow. **Free cash flow** is a measure of operating cash flow available for corporate purposes after providing sufficient fixed asset additions to maintain current productive capacity and dividends. Thus, free cash flow can be calculated as follows:

	Cash flow from operating activities
Less:	Cash used to purchase fixed assets to maintain productive capacity used up in producing income during the period
Less:	Cash used for dividends
	Free cash flow

Exhibit 600.14 *Statement of Cash Flow Accounts*

Account Title	Account Classification
Cash received from customers for sale of goods or services	Cash flows from operating activities
Cash received from interest on loans	Cash flows from operating activities
Cash received from dividends on investments	Cash flows from operating activities
Cash received from sale of trading securities	Cash flows from operating activities
Cash payments for operating expenses	Cash flows from operating activities
Cash payments for merchandise	Cash flows from operating activities
Cash payments for materials	Cash flows from operating activities
Cash payments for wages	Cash flows from operating activities
Cash payments for interest	Cash flows from operating activities
Cash payments for taxes	Cash flows from operating activities
Cash payments to purchase trading securities	Cash flows from operating activities
Depreciation (added to net income)	Cash flows from operating activities
Gain on sale of fixed assets (subtracted from net income)	Cash flows from operating activities
Loss on sale of fixed assets (added to net income)	Cash flows from operating activities
Net Income (starting point)	Cash flows from operating activities
Cash receipts from sale of property (e.g., land, plant, equipment, buildings)	Cash flows from investing activities
Cash receipts from collection of loans	Cash flows from investing activities
Cash receipts from sale of investments	Cash flows from investing activities
Cash payments for acquisition of property (e.g., land, plant, equipment, buildings)	Cash flows from investing activities
Cash payments to make loans	Cash flows from investing activities
Cash received from sale of stock (e.g., preferred or common)	Cash flows from financing activities
Cash received from issuing of debt	Cash flows from financing activities
Cash paid for dividends	Cash flows from financing activities
Cash paid to retire bonds payable	Cash flows from financing activities
Cash paid to repay debt	Cash flows from financing activities
Cash paid to reacquire stock (e.g., preferred or common)	Cash flows from financing activities

A company that has free cash flow is able to fund internal growth, retire debt, and enjoy financial flexibility. A company with no free cash flow is unable to maintain current productive capacity or dividend payouts to stockholders. Lack of free cash flow can be an early indicator of liquidity problems. Indeed, as stated by one analyst, "Free cash flow gives the company firepower to reduce debt and ultimately generate consistent, actual income."[2]

Example 8 Assume that O'Brien Company had cash flow from operating activities of $1,400,000. O'Brien Company invested $450,000 in fixed assets to maintain productive capacity, and another $300,000 to expand capacity. Dividends were $100,000. What is the free cash flow for O'Brien Company?

Cash flow from operating activities		$1,400,000
Less: Cash invested in fixed assets to maintain productive capacity	$450,000	
Less: Cash for dividends	100,000	550,000
Free cash flow		$ 850,000

610. ASSETS, LIABILITIES, AND OWNERS' EQUITY

A General Model for the Statement of Cash Flows

Until now, we focused on the financial data for NetSolutions. Now we present a general model of the statement of cash flows for XYZ Company that is more inclusive than that of NetSolutions.

Sources and Uses of Cash

The analysis of sources and uses of cash will help managers to see the "big picture" of cash activities regardless of their sources and uses. This analysis does not break down in a manner similar to the Statement of Cash Flows into operating, investing, and financing activities. Rather, it lists all sources of cash together in one place and all uses of cash together in one place. Cash activities of a firm could be summarized as follows.

$$\text{Cash flows from assets} = \text{Cash flows to creditors} + \text{Cash flows to owners}$$

Cash flow to creditors is computed from the interest paid minus net new borrowings. Cash flow to owners (shareholders) is computed from the dividends paid minus net new equity. Those activities that bring cash in to the firm are called *sources of cash*. Those activities that involve spending cash are called *uses* (or *applications*) of cash. Remember the accounting equation:

$$\text{Assets} = \text{Liabilities} + \text{Owner's equity}$$

An increase in the asset account or a decrease in the liability or equity account is a use of cash. Similarly, a decrease in the asset account or an increase in the liability or equity account is a source of cash. This can be represented in a table as follows:

Item	Use of Cash	Source of Cash
Asset	Increase	Decrease
Liability or Equity	Decrease	Increase

For example:

1. Buying more inventory or fixed assets increases the asset account and uses cash.
2. Paying off a loan or buying back the company stock (treasury stock) decreases the liability or equity account and uses cash.
3. Selling inventory or collecting receivables from customers decreases the asset account and provides cash.
4. Borrowing funds or selling stock increases the liability or equity account and provides cash.

Note that all "uses of cash" are deducted from net income and all "sources of cash" are added to net income when computing cash flows from operating activities.

The net addition to cash account is the difference between sources and uses of cash, and it should agree with the change in the cash account on the current balance sheet. What we need to do is trace the changes in the firm's two balance sheets (i.e., previous period and current period) to see how the firm obtained its cash and how the firm spent its cash.

Examples of sources of cash include the following.

- Decrease in accounts receivable
- Decrease in inventory
- Decrease in fixed assets
- Increase in accounts payable
- Increase in notes payable
- Increase in long-term debt
- Increase in common stock
- Increase in retained earnings

Examples of uses of cash include the following.

- Increase in accounts receivable
- Increase in inventory
- Increase in fixed assets
- Decrease in accounts payable
- Decrease in notes payable
- Decrease in long-term debt
- Decrease in common stock
- Decrease in retained earnings

Example 9 The difference between two balance sheet accounts (in thousands) for a firm is shown below.

Increase in accounts receivable	$35
Decrease in inventory	5
Increase in fixed assets	20
Increase in accounts payable	22
Decrease in long-term debt	30
Decrease in notes payable	15
Increase in common stock	50
Increase in retained earnings	40

What is the net addition to the cash account for the firm?

Sources of cash = $5 + $22 + $50 + $40 = $117
Uses of cash = $35 + $20 + $30 + $15 = $100
Net addition to cash = Sources of cash − Uses of cash = $117 − $100 = $17

Exhibit 600.15 shows the Statement of Cash Sources and Uses for the XYZ Company, where total sources ($199 million) are equal to total uses ($199 million). Exhibit 600.16 presents a Statement of Cash Flows for the XYZ Company, where it shows the cash at the end of the year 2003 as $15 million. This is the same balance in cash and marketable securities account of $15 million in the Statement of Cash Sources and Uses. The Statement of Cash Sources and Uses is an intermediate schedule to facilitate accounting of all sources and uses of cash, and is tied to the Statement of Cash Flows.

Exhibit 600.15 XYZ Company: Statement of Cash Sources and Uses During 2004 (millions of dollars)

	12/31/04	12/31/03	Change Sources	Uses
Balance Sheet Changes				
Cash and marketable securities	$ 15.0	$ 40.0	$ 25.0	
Accounts receivable	180.0	160.0		$ 20.0
Inventory	270.0	200.0		70.0
Gross plant and equipment	680.0	600.0		80.0
Accounts payable	30.0	15.0	15.0	
Accruals	60.0	55.0	5.0	
Notes payable	40.0	35.0	5.0	
Long-term bonds	300.0	255.0	45.0	
Common stock (25 million shares)	130.0	130.0		
Income Statement Information				
Net income		$ 54.0		
Add: Depreciation		50.0		
Gross cash flow from operations		$104.0	104.0	
Dividend payment		29.0	—	29.0
Totals			$199.0	$199.0

610. ASSETS, LIABILITIES, AND OWNERS' EQUITY

Exhibit 600.16 XYZ Company: Statement of Cash Flows for the Period Ending December 31, 2004 (millions of dollars)

Cash Flows from Operating Activities		
Net income		$ 54.0
Additions to net income		
Depreciation[a]	50.0	
Increase in accounts payable	15.0	
Increase in accruals	5.0	
Subtractions from net income		
Increase in accounts receivable	(20.0)	
Increase in inventory	(70.0)	
Net cash flow from operations		$ 34.0
Cash Flows from Investing Activities		
Acquisition of fixed assets		$(80.0)
Cash Flows from Financing Activities		
Increase in notes payable	$ 5.0	
Increase in bonds	45.0	
Dividend payment	(29.0)	
Net cash flow from financing		$ 21.0
Net change in cash		$(25.0)
Cash at the beginning of the year		40.0
Cash at the end of the year		$ 15.0

[a] Depreciation is a noncash expense that was deducted when calculating net income. It must be added back to show the correct cash flow from operations.

Example 10 The net income reported for Firm A for the current year on its income statement was $60,000. Depreciation on fixed assets for the year was $20,000. Balances of the current assets and current liability accounts at the end and beginning of the year are listed below.

	End	Beginning
Cash	$55,000	$60,000
Net accounts receivable	62,000	48,000
Inventories	80,000	90,000
Prepaid expense	4,000	5,000
Accounts payable	71,000	81,000
Cash dividends payable	5,000	6,000
Salaries payable	8,000	9,000

What is the cash flows from operating activities section of a statement of cash flows using the indirect method?

Cash flows from operating activities:			
Net income, per income statement			$60,000
Add:	Depreciation	$20,000	
	Decrease in inventories	10,000	
	Decrease in prepaid expense	1,000	$31,000
Deduct:	Increase in net accounts receivable	$14,000	
	Decrease in accounts payable	10,000	
	Decrease in salaries payable	1,000	$25,000
Net cash flow from operating activities			$66,000

Analysis and Use of Financial Statements

Financial Statement Analysis

How does one decide on the companies in which to invest? This section describes and illustrates common financial data that can be analyzed to assist you in making investment decisions.

Basic Analytical Procedures

The basic financial statements provide much of the information users need to make economic decisions about businesses. In this section, we illustrate how to perform a complete analysis of these statements by integrating individual analytical measures.

Analytical procedures may be used to compare items on a current statement with related items on earlier statements. For example, cash of $150,000 on the current balance sheet may be compared with cash of $100,000 on the balance sheet of a year earlier. The current year's cash may be expressed as 1.5 or 150 percent of the earlier amount, or as an increase of 50 percent or $50,000.

Analytical procedures are also widely used to examine relationships within a financial statement. To illustrate, assume that cash of $50,000 and inventories of $250,000 are included in the total assets of $1,000,000 on a balance sheet. In relative terms, the cash balance is 5 percent of the total assets, and the inventories are 25 percent of the total assets.

In this section, we will illustrate a number of common analytical measures such as horizontal analysis, vertical analysis, and common-size statement analysis. The measures are not ends in themselves. They are only guides in evaluating financial and operating data. Many other factors, such as trends in the industry and general economic conditions, should also be considered.

Horizontal Analysis

The percentage analysis of increases and decreases in related items in comparative financial statements is called **horizontal analysis.** The amount of each item on the most recent statement is compared with the related item on one or more earlier statements. The amount of increase or decrease in the item is listed, along with the percent of increase or decrease.

Horizontal analysis may compare two statements. In this case, the earlier statement is used as the base. Horizontal analysis may also compare three or more statements. In this case, the earliest date or period may be used as the base for comparing all later dates or periods. Alternatively, each statement may be compared to the immediately preceding statement. Exhibit 600.17 is a condensed comparative balance sheet for two years for Lincoln Company, with horizontal analysis.

We cannot fully evaluate the significance of the various increases and decreases in the items shown in Exhibit 600.17 without additional information. Although total assets at the end of 2004 were $91,000 (7.4 percent) less than at the beginning of the year, liabilities were reduced by $133,000 (30 percent), and stockholders' equity increased $42,000 (5.3 percent). It appears that the reduction of $100,000 in long-term liabilities was achieved mostly through the sale of long-term investments.

> **Example 11** Accounts Payable was $600,000 in the current year and $500,000 in the preceding year. What is the amount and the percentage of increase or decrease that would be shown in a balance sheet with horizontal analysis?
>
> $100,000 or 20% ($100,000/$500,000) increase

The balance sheet in Exhibit 600.17 may be expanded to include the details of the various categories of assets and liabilities. An alternative is to present the details in separate schedules. Exhibit 600.18 is a supporting schedule with horizontal analysis.

Exhibit 600.17 *Comparative Balance Sheet—Horizontal Analysis*

Lincoln Company
Comparative Balance Sheet
December 31, 2004 and 2003

	2004	2003	Increase (Decrease) Amount	Percent
Assets				
Current assets	$ 550,000	$ 533,000	$ 17,000	3.2%
Long-term investments	95,000	177,500	(82,500)	(46.5%)
Property, plant, and equipment (net)	444,500	470,000	(25,500)	(5.4%)
Intangible assets	50,000	50,000	—	—
Total assets	$1,139,500	$1,230,500	$ (91,000)	(7.4%)
Liabilities				
Current liabilities	$ 210,000	$ 243,000	$ (33,000)	(13.6%)
Long-term liabilities	100,000	200,000	(100,000)	(50.0%)
Total liabilities	$310,000	$ 443,000	$(133,000)	(30.0%)
Stockholders' Equity				
Preferred 6% stock, $100 par	$ 150,000	$ 150,000	—	—
Common stock, $10 par	500,000	500,000	—	—
Retained earnings	179,500	137,500	$ 42,000	30.5%
Total stockholders' equity	$ 829,500	$ 787,500	$ 42,000	5.3%
Total liabilities and stockholders' equity	$1,139,500	$1,230,500	$ (91,000)	(7.4%)

Exhibit 600.18 *Comparative Schedule of Current Assets—Horizontal Analysis*

Lincoln Company
Comparative Schedule of Current Assets
December 31, 2004 and 2003

	2004	2003	Increase (Decrease) Amount	Percent
Cash	$ 90,500	$ 64,700	$25,800	39.9%
Marketable securities	75,000	60,000	15,000	25.0%
Accounts receivable (net)	115,000	120,000	(5,000)	(4.2%)
Inventories	264,000	283,000	(19,000)	(6.7%)
Prepaid expenses	5,500	5,300	200	3.8%
Total current assets	$550,000	$533,000	$17,000	3.2%

The decrease in accounts receivable may be due to changes in credit terms or improved collection policies. Likewise, a decrease in inventories during a period of increased sales may indicate an improvement in the management of inventories.

The changes in the current assets in Exhibit 600.18 appear favorable. This assessment is supported by the 24.8 percent increase in net sales shown in Exhibit 600.19.

An increase in net sales may not have a favorable effect on operating performance. The percentage increase in Lincoln Company's net sales is accompanied by a greater percentage increase in the cost of goods (merchandise) sold. This has the effect of reducing gross profit. Selling expenses increased significantly, and administrative expenses increased slightly. Overall, operating expenses increased by 20.7 percent, whereas gross profit increased by only 19.7 percent.

The increase in income from operations and in net income is favorable. However, a study of the expenses and additional analyses and comparisons should be made before reaching a conclusion as to the cause.

Exhibit 600.19 *Comparative Income Statement—Horizontal Analysis*

<table>
<tr><td colspan="5" align="center">Lincoln Company
Comparative Income Statement
For the Years Ended December 31, 2004 and 2003</td></tr>
<tr><td></td><td></td><td></td><td colspan="2">Increase (Decrease)</td></tr>
<tr><td></td><td>2004</td><td>2003</td><td>Amount</td><td>Percent</td></tr>
<tr><td>Sales</td><td>$1,530,500</td><td>$1,234,000</td><td>$296,500</td><td>24.0%</td></tr>
<tr><td>Sales returns and allowances</td><td>32,500</td><td>34,000</td><td>(1,500)</td><td>(4.4%)</td></tr>
<tr><td>Net sales</td><td>$1,498,000</td><td>$1,200,000</td><td>$298,000</td><td>24.8%</td></tr>
<tr><td>Cost of goods sold</td><td>1,043,000</td><td>820,000</td><td>223,000</td><td>27.2%</td></tr>
<tr><td>Gross profit</td><td>$ 455,000</td><td>$ 380,000</td><td>$ 75,000</td><td>19.7%</td></tr>
<tr><td>Selling expenses</td><td>$ 191,000</td><td>$ 147,000</td><td>$ 44,000</td><td>29.9%</td></tr>
<tr><td>Administrative expenses</td><td>104,000</td><td>97,400</td><td>6,600</td><td>6.8%</td></tr>
<tr><td>Total operating expenses</td><td>$ 295,000</td><td>$ 244,400</td><td>$ 50,600</td><td>20.7%</td></tr>
<tr><td>Income from operations</td><td>$ 160,000</td><td>$ 135,600</td><td>$ 24,400</td><td>18.0%</td></tr>
<tr><td>Other income</td><td>8,500</td><td>11,000</td><td>(2,500)</td><td>(22.7%)</td></tr>
<tr><td></td><td>$ 168,500</td><td>$ 146,600</td><td>$ 21,900</td><td>14.9%</td></tr>
<tr><td>Other expense</td><td>6,000</td><td>12,000</td><td>(6,000)</td><td>(50.0%)</td></tr>
<tr><td>Income before income tax</td><td>$ 162,500</td><td>$ 134,600</td><td>$ 27,900</td><td>20.7%</td></tr>
<tr><td>Income tax expense</td><td>71,500</td><td>58,100</td><td>13,400</td><td>23.1%</td></tr>
<tr><td>Net income</td><td>$ 91,000</td><td>$ 76,500</td><td>$ 14,500</td><td>19.0%</td></tr>
</table>

Exhibit 600.20 *Comparative Retained Earnings Statement—Horizontal Analysis*

<table>
<tr><td colspan="5" align="center">Lincoln Company
Comparative Retained Earnings Statement
December 31, 2004 and 2003</td></tr>
<tr><td></td><td></td><td></td><td colspan="2">Increase (Decrease)</td></tr>
<tr><td></td><td>2004</td><td>2003</td><td>Amount</td><td>Percent</td></tr>
<tr><td>Retained earnings, January 1</td><td>$137,500</td><td>$100,000</td><td>$37,500</td><td>37.5%</td></tr>
<tr><td>Net income for the year</td><td>91,000</td><td>76,500</td><td>14,500</td><td>19.0%</td></tr>
<tr><td>Total</td><td>$228,500</td><td>$176,500</td><td>$52,000</td><td>29.5%</td></tr>
<tr><td>Dividends:</td><td></td><td></td><td></td><td></td></tr>
<tr><td> On preferred stock</td><td>$ 9,000</td><td>$ 9,000</td><td>—</td><td>—</td></tr>
<tr><td> On common stock</td><td>40,000</td><td>30,000</td><td>$10,000</td><td>33.3%</td></tr>
<tr><td>Total</td><td>$ 49,000</td><td>$ 39,000</td><td>$10,000</td><td>25.6%</td></tr>
<tr><td>Retained earnings, December 31</td><td>$179,500</td><td>$137,500</td><td>$42,000</td><td>30.5%</td></tr>
</table>

Exhibit 600.20 illustrates a comparative retained earnings statement with horizontal analysis. It reveals that retained earnings increased 30.5 percent for the year. The increase is due to net income of $91,000 for the year, less dividends of $49,000.

Vertical Analysis

A percentage analysis may also be used to show the relationship of each component to the total within a single statement. This type of analysis is called **vertical analysis.** Like horizontal analysis, the statements may be prepared in either detailed or condensed form. In the latter case, additional details of the changes in individual items may be presented in supporting schedules. In such schedules, the percentage analysis may be based on either the total of the schedule or the

Exhibit 600.21 *Comparative Balance Sheet—Vertical Analysis*

<table>
<tr><td colspan="5" align="center">Lincoln Company
Comparative Balance Sheet
December 31, 2004 and 2003</td></tr>
<tr><td></td><td colspan="2" align="center">2004</td><td colspan="2" align="center">2003</td></tr>
<tr><td></td><td>Amount</td><td>Percent</td><td>Amount</td><td>Percent</td></tr>
<tr><td>**Assets**</td><td></td><td></td><td></td><td></td></tr>
<tr><td>Current assets</td><td>$ 550,000</td><td>48.3%</td><td>$ 533,000</td><td>43.3%</td></tr>
<tr><td>Long-term investments</td><td>95,000</td><td>8.3</td><td>177,500</td><td>14.4</td></tr>
<tr><td>Property, plant, and equipment (net)</td><td>444,500</td><td>39.0</td><td>470,000</td><td>38.2</td></tr>
<tr><td>Intangible assets</td><td>50,000</td><td>4.4</td><td>50,000</td><td>4.1</td></tr>
<tr><td>Total assets</td><td>$1,139,500</td><td>100.0%</td><td>$1,230,500</td><td>100.0%</td></tr>
<tr><td>**Liabilities**</td><td></td><td></td><td></td><td></td></tr>
<tr><td>Current liabilities</td><td>$ 210,000</td><td>18.4%</td><td>$ 243,000</td><td>19.7%</td></tr>
<tr><td>Long-term liabilities</td><td>100,000</td><td>8.8</td><td>200,000</td><td>16.3</td></tr>
<tr><td>Total liabilities</td><td>$ 310,000</td><td>27.2%</td><td>$ 443,000</td><td>36.0%</td></tr>
<tr><td>**Stockholders' Equity**</td><td></td><td></td><td></td><td></td></tr>
<tr><td>Preferred 6% stock, $100 par</td><td>$ 150,000</td><td>13.2%</td><td>$ 150,000</td><td>12.2%</td></tr>
<tr><td>Common stock, $10 par</td><td>500,000</td><td>43.9</td><td>500,000</td><td>40.6</td></tr>
<tr><td>Retained earnings</td><td>179,500</td><td>15.7</td><td>137,500</td><td>11.2</td></tr>
<tr><td>Total stockholders' equity</td><td>$ 829,500</td><td>72.8%</td><td>$ 787,500</td><td>64.0%</td></tr>
<tr><td>Total liabilities and stockholders' equity</td><td>$1,139,500</td><td>100.0%</td><td>$1,230,500</td><td>100.0%</td></tr>
</table>

statement total. Although vertical analysis is limited to an individual statement, its significance may be improved by preparing comparative statements.

In vertical analysis of the balance sheet, each asset item is stated as a percent of the total assets. Each liability and stockholders' equity item is stated as a percent of the total liabilities and stockholders' equity. Exhibit 600.21 is a condensed comparative balance sheet with vertical analysis for Lincoln Company.

The major percentage changes in Lincoln Company's assets are in the current asset and long-term investment categories. In the Liabilities and Stockholders' Equity sections of the balance sheet, the greatest percentage changes are in long-term liabilities and retained earnings. Stockholders' equity increased from 64 percent to 72.8 percent of total liabilities and stockholders' equity in 2004. There is a comparable decrease in liabilities.

In a vertical analysis of the income statement, each item is stated as a percent of net sales. Exhibit 600.22 is a condensed comparative income statement with vertical analysis for Lincoln Company.

We must be careful when judging the significance of differences between percentages for the two years. For example, the decline of the gross profit rate from 31.7 percent in 2003 to 30.4 percent in 2004 is only 1.3 percentage points. In terms of dollars of potential gross profit, however, it represents a decline of approximately $19,500 (1.3% × $1,498,000).

> **Example 12** *At the end of the current year, Accounts Payable was $600,000 and total liabilities and stockholders' equity was $1,200,000. What percent would be shown for Accounts Payable in a balance sheet with vertical analysis?*
>
> 50% ($600,000/$1,200,000)

Common-Size Statement Analysis

Horizontal and vertical analyses with both dollar and percentage amounts are useful in assessing relationships and trends in financial conditions and operations of a business. Vertical analysis with both dollar and percentage amounts is also useful in comparing one company with another or with industry averages. Such comparisons are easier to make with the use of common-size statements. In a **common-size statement analysis,** all items are expressed in percentages.

Exhibit 600.22 *Comparative Income Statement—Vertical Analysis*

Lincoln Company
Comparative Income Statement
For the Years Ended December 31, 2004 and 2003

	2004 Amount	2004 Percent	2003 Amount	2003 Percent
Sales	$1,530,500	102.2%	$1,234,000	102.8%
Sales returns and allowances	32,500	2.2	34,000	2.8
Net sales	$1,498,000	100.0%	$1,200,000	100.0%
Cost of goods sold	1,043,000	69.6	820,000	68.3
Gross profit	$ 455,000	30.4%	$ 380,000	31.7%
Selling expenses	$ 191,000	12.8%	$ 147,000	12.3%
Administrative expenses	104,000	6.9	97,400	8.1
Total operating expenses	$ 295,000	19.7%	$ 244,400	20.4%
Income from operations	$ 160,000	10.7%	$ 135,600	11.3%
Other income	8,500	0.6	11,000	0.9
	$ 168,500	11.3%	$ 146,600	12.2%
Other expense	6,000	0.4	12,000	1.0
Income before income tax	$ 162,500	10.9%	$ 134,600	11.2%
Income tax expense	71,500	4.8	58,100	4.8
Net income	$ 91,000	6.1%	$ 76,500	6.4%

Common-size statements are useful in comparing the current period with prior periods, individual businesses, or one business with industry percentages. Industry data are often available from trade associations and financial information services. Exhibit 600.23 is a comparative common-size income statement for two businesses.

Exhibit 600.23 indicates that Lincoln Company has a slightly higher rate of gross profit than Madison Corporation. However, this advantage is more than offset by Lincoln Company's higher percentage of selling and administrative expenses. As a result, the income from operations of Lincoln Company is 10.7 percent of net sales, compared with 14.4 percent for Madison Corporation—an unfavorable difference of 3.7 percentage points.

Other Analytical Measures

In addition to the preceding analyses, other relationships may be expressed in simple ratios and percentages. Often, these items are taken from the financial statements and thus are a type of vertical analysis. Comparing these items with items from earlier periods is a type of horizontal analysis.

Example 13 *The percentages of gross profit and net income to sales for fiscal year-end 1999 for **Kmart Corp.** and **Wal-Mart Stores Inc.** are shown below.*

	Kmart Corp.	Wal-Mart Stores Inc.
Gross profit to sales	21.8%	21.0%
Net income to sales	1.5%	3.3%

Wal-Mart has a slightly lower gross profit margin than Kmart, which is likely due to lower prices. However, Wal-Mart has a much leaner operating expense structure, so it is able to earn an overall higher percentage of net income to sales.

620. ANALYSIS AND USE OF FINANCIAL STATEMENTS

Exhibit 600.23 *Common-Size Income Statement*

<table>
<tr><th colspan="3">Lincoln Company and Madison Corporation
Condensed Common-Size Income Statement
For the Year Ended December 31, 2004</th></tr>
<tr><th></th><th>Lincoln Company</th><th>Madison Corporation</th></tr>
<tr><td>Sales</td><td>102.2%</td><td>102.3%</td></tr>
<tr><td>Sales returns and allowances</td><td>2.2</td><td>2.3</td></tr>
<tr><td>Net sales</td><td>100.0%</td><td>100.0%</td></tr>
<tr><td>Cost of goods sold</td><td>69.6</td><td>70.0</td></tr>
<tr><td>Gross profit</td><td>30.4%</td><td>30.0%</td></tr>
<tr><td>Selling expenses</td><td>12.8%</td><td>11.5%</td></tr>
<tr><td>Administrative expenses</td><td>6.9</td><td>4.1</td></tr>
<tr><td>Total operating expenses</td><td>19.7%</td><td>15.6%</td></tr>
<tr><td>Income from operations</td><td>10.7%</td><td>14.4%</td></tr>
<tr><td>Other income</td><td>0.6</td><td>0.6</td></tr>
<tr><td></td><td>11.3%</td><td>15.0%</td></tr>
<tr><td>Other expense</td><td>0.4</td><td>0.5</td></tr>
<tr><td>Income before income tax</td><td>10.9%</td><td>14.5%</td></tr>
<tr><td>Income tax expense</td><td>4.8</td><td>5.5</td></tr>
<tr><td>Net income</td><td>6.1%</td><td>9.0%</td></tr>
</table>

Solvency Analysis

Some aspects of a business's financial condition and operations are of greater importance to some users than others. However, all users are interested in the ability of a business to pay its debts as they are due and to earn income. The ability of a business to meet its financial obligations (debts) is called **solvency** or **liquidity**. The ability of a business to earn income is called **profitability.**

The factors of solvency and profitability are interrelated. A business that cannot pay its debts on a timely basis may experience difficulty in obtaining credit. A lack of available credit may, in turn, lead to a decline in the business's profitability. Eventually, the business may be forced into bankruptcy. Likewise, a business that is less profitable than its competitors is likely to be at a disadvantage in obtaining credit or new capital from stockholders.

> Solvency analysis focuses on the ability of a business to pay or otherwise satisfy its current and noncurrent liabilites.

In the following paragraphs, we discuss various types of financial analyses that are useful in evaluating the solvency of a business. In the next section, we discuss various types of profitability analyses. The examples in both sections are based on Lincoln Company's financial statements presented earlier. In some cases, data from Lincoln Company's financial statements of the preceding year and from other sources are also used. These historical data are useful in assessing the past performance of a business and in forecasting its future performance. The results of financial analyses may be even more useful when they are compared with those of competing businesses and with industry averages.

Solvency analysis focuses on the ability of a business to pay or otherwise satisfy its current and noncurrent liabilities. It is normally assessed by examining balance sheet relationships, using the following major analyses:

1. Current position analysis
2. Accounts receivable analysis
3. Inventory analysis
4. The ratio of fixed assets to long-term liabilities
5. The ratio of liabilities to stockholders' equity
6. The number of times interest charges are earned

1. Current Position Analysis

To be useful in assessing solvency, a ratio or other financial measure must relate to a business's ability to pay or otherwise satisfy its liabilities. Using measures to assess a business's ability to pay its current liabilities is called **current position analysis.** Such analysis is of special interest to short-term creditors.

An analysis of a firm's current position normally includes determining the working capital, the current ratio, and the acid-test ratio. The current and acid-test ratios are most useful when analyzed together and compared to previous periods and other firms in the industry.

WORKING CAPITAL The excess of the current assets of a business over its current liabilities is called **working capital.** The working capital is often used in evaluating a company's ability to meet currently maturing debts. It is especially useful in making monthly or other period-to-period comparisons for a company. However, amounts of working capital are difficult to assess when comparing companies of different sizes or in comparing such amounts with industry figures. For example, working capital of $250,000 may be adequate for a small local hardware store, but it would be inadequate for all of **Home Depot.**

CURRENT RATIO Another means of expressing the relationship between current assets and current liabilities is the **current ratio.** This ratio is sometimes called the **working capital ratio** or **bankers' ratio.** The ratio is computed by dividing the total current assets by the total current liabilities. For Lincoln Company, working capital and the current ratio for 2004 and 2003 are as follows.

	2004	2003
Current assets	$550,000	$533,000
Current liabilities	210,000	243,000
Working capital	$340,000	$290,000
Current ratio	2.6	2.2

The current ratio is a more reliable indicator of solvency than is working capital. To illustrate, assume that as of December 31, 2004, the working capital of a competitor is much greater than $340,000, but its current ratio is only 1.3. Considering these facts alone, Lincoln Company, with its current ratio of 2.6, is in a more favorable position to obtain short-term credit than the competitor, which has the greater amount of working capital.

ACID-TEST RATIO The working capital and the current ratio do not consider the makeup of the current assets. To illustrate the importance of this consideration, the current position data for Lincoln Company and Jefferson Corporation as of December 31, 2004, are as follows.

	Lincoln Company	Jefferson Corporation
Current assets:		
Cash	$ 90,500	$ 45,500
Marketable securities	75,000	25,000
Accounts receivable (net)	115,000	90,000
Inventories	264,000	380,000
Prepaid expenses	5,500	9,500
Total current assets	$550,000	$550,000
Current liabilities	210,000	210,000
Working capital	$340,000	$340,000
Current ratio	2.6	2.6

Both companies have a working capital of $340,000 and a current ratio of 2.6. But the ability of each company to pay its current debts is significantly different. Jefferson Corporation has more of its current assets in inventories. Some of these inventories must be sold and the receivables collected before the current liabilities can be paid in full. Thus, a large amount of time may be necessary to convert these inventories into cash. Declines in market prices and a reduction in demand could also impair its ability to pay current liabilities. In contrast, Lincoln Company has cash and current assets (marketable securities and accounts receivable) that can generally be converted to cash rather quickly to meet its current liabilities.

A ratio that measures the "instant" debt-paying ability of a company is called the **acid-test ratio** or **quick ratio.** It is the ratio of the total quick assets to the total current liabilities. **Quick assets** are cash and other current assets that can be quickly converted to cash. Quick assets normally include cash, marketable securities, and receivables. The acid-test ratio data for Lincoln Company are as follows:

> The **Wm. Wrigley Company** maintains a high current ratio—3.9 for a recent year. Wrigley's stable and profitable chewing gum business has allowed it to develop a strong cash position coupled with no short-term notes payable.

	2004	2003
Quick assets:		
Cash	$ 90,500	$ 64,700
Marketable equity securities	75,000	60,000
Accounts receivable (net)	115,000	120,000
Total quick assets	$280,500	$244,700
Current liabilities	$210,000	$243,000
Acid-test ratio (Quick Ratio)	1.3	1.0

Example 14 *A balance sheet shows $300,000 of cash, marketable securities, and receivables, and $250,000 of inventories. Current liabilities are $200,000. What are (a) the current ratio and (b) the acid-test ratio?*

(a) 2.75 ($550,000/$200,000);   (b) 1.5 ($300,000/$200,000)

2. Accounts Receivable Analysis

The size and makeup of accounts receivable change constantly during business operations. Sales on account increase accounts receivable, whereas collections from customers decrease accounts receivable. Firms that grant long credit terms usually have larger accounts receivable balances than those granting short credit terms. Increases or decreases in the volume of sales also affect the balance of accounts receivable.

It is desirable to collect receivables as promptly as possible. The cash collected from receivables improves solvency. In addition, the cash generated by prompt collections from customers may be used in operations for such purposes as purchasing merchandise in large quantities at lower prices. The cash may also be used for payment of dividends to stockholders or for other investing or financing purposes. Prompt collection also lessens the risk of loss from uncollectible accounts.

ACCOUNTS RECEIVABLE TURNOVER   The relationship between credit sales and accounts receivable may be stated as the **accounts receivable turnover**. This ratio is computed by dividing net sales on account by the average net accounts receivable. It is desirable to base the average on monthly balances, which allows for seasonal changes in sales. When such data are not available, it may be necessary to use the average of the accounts receivable balance at the beginning and the end of the year. If there are trade notes receivable as well as accounts, the two may be combined. The accounts receivable turnover data for Lincoln Company are as follows. All sales were made on account.

	2004	2003
Net sales on account	$1,498,000	$1,200,000
Accounts receivable (net):		
Beginning of year	$ 120,000	$ 140,000
End of year	115,000	120,000
Total	$ 235,000	$ 260,000
Average (Total ÷ 2)	$ 117,500	$ 130,000
Accounts receivable turnover	12.7	9.2

The increase in the accounts receivable turnover for 2003 indicates that there has been an improvement in the collection of receivables. This may be due to a change in the granting of credit, in collection practices, or in both.

NUMBER OF DAYS' SALES IN RECEIVABLES Another measure of the relationship between credit sales and accounts receivable is the **number of days' sales in receivables.** This ratio is computed by dividing the net accounts receivable at the end of the year by the average daily sales on account. Average daily sales on account is determined by dividing net sales on account by 365 days. The number of days' sales in receivables is computed for Lincoln Company as follows.

	2004	2003
Accounts receivable (net), end of year	$ 115,000	$ 120,000
Net sales on account	$1,498,000	$1,200,000
Average daily sales on account (sales ÷ 365)	$ 4,104	$ 3,288
Number of days' sales in receivables	28.0*	36.5*
*Accounts receivable ÷ Average daily sales on account		

The number of days' sales in receivables is an estimate of the length of time (in days) the accounts receivable have been outstanding. Comparing this measure with the credit terms provides information on the efficiency in collecting receivables. For example, assume that the number of days' sales in receivables for Grant Inc. is 40. If Grant Inc.'s credit terms are n/45, then its collection process appears to be efficient. On the other hand, if Grant Inc.'s credit terms are n/30, its collection process does not appear to be efficient. A comparison with other firms in the same industry and with prior years also provides useful information. Such comparisons may indicate efficiency of collection procedures and trends in credit management.

> **Example 15** Sales were $1,200,000, of which 80% were on account. The accounts receivable balance at the beginning of the year was $56,000, and at the end of the year it was $40,000. What are (a) the accounts receivable turnover and (b) the number of days' sales in receivables?
>
> (a) 20 [(0.80 × $1,200,000)/($56,000 + $40,000)/2];   (b) 15.2 days [$40,000/($960,000/365)]

3. Inventory Analysis

A business should keep enough inventory on hand to meet the needs of its customers and its operations. At the same time, however, an excessive amount of inventory reduces solvency by tying up funds. Excess inventories also increase insurance expense, property taxes, storage costs, and other related expenses. These expenses further reduce funds that could be used elsewhere to improve operations. Finally, excess inventory also increases the risk of losses because of price declines or obsolescence of the inventory. Two measures that are useful for evaluating the management of inventory are the inventory turnover and the number of days' sales in inventory.

INVENTORY TURNOVER The relationship between the volume of goods (merchandise) sold and inventory may be stated as the **inventory turnover.** It is computed by dividing the cost of goods sold by the average inventory. If monthly data are not available, the average of the inventories at the beginning and the end of the year may be used. The inventory turnover for Lincoln Company is computed as follows.

	2004	2003
Cost of goods sold	$1,043,000	$820,000
Inventories:		
Beginning of year	$ 283,000	$311,000
End of year	264,000	283,000
Total	$ 547,000	$594,000
Average (Total ÷ 2)	$ 273,500	$297,000
Inventory turnover	3.8	2.8

The inventory turnover improved for Lincoln Company because of an increase in the cost of goods sold and a decrease in the average inventories. Differences across inventories, companies, and industries are too great to allow a general statement on what is a good inventory turnover. For example, a firm selling food should have a higher turnover than a firm selling furniture or jewelry. Likewise, the perishable foods department of a supermarket should have a higher turnover than the soaps and cleansers department. However, for each business or each department within a business, there is a reasonable turnover rate. A turnover lower than this rate could mean that inventory is not being managed properly.

*The inventory turnover of McDonald's Corporation for a recent year was 39, while for **Toys "R" Us Inc.**, it was 4.3. McDonald's inventory turnover is higher because it sells perishable food products, while toys can sit on the shelf longer without "spoiling."*

NUMBER OF DAYS' SALES IN INVENTORY Another measure of the relationship between the cost of goods sold and inventory is the **number of days' sales in inventory.** This measure is computed by dividing the inventory at the end of the year by the average daily cost of goods sold (cost of goods sold divided by 365). The number of days' sales in inventory for Lincoln Company is computed as follows.

	2004	2003
Inventories, end of year	$ 264,000	$283,000
Cost of goods sold	$1,043,000	$820,000
Average daily cost of goods sold (COGS ÷ 365 days)	$ 2,858	$ 2,247
Number of days' sales in inventory	92.4	125.9

The number of days' sales in inventory is a rough measure of the length of time it takes to acquire, sell, and replace the inventory. For Lincoln Company, there is a major improvement in the number of days' sales in inventory during 2003. However, a comparison with earlier years and similar firms would be useful in assessing Lincoln Company's overall inventory management.

4. Ratio of Fixed Assets to Long-Term Liabilities

Long-term notes and bonds are often secured by mortgages on fixed assets. The **ratio of fixed assets to long-term liabilities** is a solvency measure that indicates the margin of safety of the noteholders or bondholders. It also indicates the ability of the business to borrow additional funds on a long-term basis. The ratio of fixed assets to long-term liabilities for Lincoln Company is as follows.

	2004	2003
Fixed assets (net)	$444,500	$470,000
Long-term liabilities	$100,000	$200,000
Ratio of fixed assets to long-term liabilities	4.4	2.4

The major increase in this ratio at the end of 2004 is mainly due to liquidating one-half of Lincoln Company's long-term liabilities. If the company needs to borrow additional funds on a long-term basis in the future, it is in a strong position to do so.

5. Ratio of Liabilities to Stockholders' Equity

Claims against the total assets of a business are divided into two groups: (1) claims of creditors and (2) claims of owners. The relationship between the total claims of the creditors and owners—the **ratio of liabilities to stockholders' equity**—is a solvency measure that indicates the margin of safety for creditors. It also indicates the ability of the business to withstand adverse business conditions. When the claims of creditors are large in relation to the equity of the stockholders, there are usually significant interest payments. If earnings decline to the point where the company is unable to meet its interest payments, the business may be taken over by the creditors.

The relationship between creditor and stockholder equity is shown in the vertical analysis of the balance sheet. For example, the balance sheet of Lincoln Company in Exhibit 600.21 indicates that on December 31, 2004, liabilities represented

27.2 percent and stockholders' equity represented 72.8 percent of the total liabilities and stockholders' equity (100.0 percent). Instead of expressing each item as a percent of the total, this relationship may be expressed as a ratio of one to the other, as follows.

	2004	2003
Total liabilities	$310,000	$443,000
Total stockholders' equity	$829,500	$787,500
Ratio of liabilities to stockholders' equity	0.37	0.56

The ratio of liabilities to stockholders' equity varies across industries. For example, recent annual reports of some selected companies showed the following ratio of liabilities to stockholders' equity:

Continental Airlines	4.31
Procter & Gamble	1.85
Circuit City Stores	0.93

The airline industry generally uses more debt financing than the consumer product or retail industries. Thus, the airline industry is generally considered more risky.

The balance sheet of Lincoln Company shows that the major factor affecting the change in the ratio was the $100,000 decrease in long-term liabilities during 2004. The ratio at the end of both years shows a large margin of safety for the creditors.

6. Number of Times Interest Charges Are Earned

Corporations in some industries, such as airlines, normally have high ratios of debt to stockholders' equity. For such corporations, the relative risk of the debtholders is normally measured as the **number of times interest charges are earned** during the year. The higher the ratio, the lower the risk that interest payments will not be made if earnings decrease. In other words, the higher the ratio, the greater the assurance that interest payments will be made on a continuing basis. This measure also indicates the general financial strength of the business, which is of interest to stockholders and employees as well as creditors.

The amount available to meet interest charges is not affected by taxes on income. This is because interest is deductible in determining taxable income. Thus, the number of times interest charges are earned is computed as shown below.

	2004	2003
Income before income tax	$ 900,000	$ 800,000
Add interest expense	300,000	250,000
Amount available to meet interest charges	$1,200,000	$1,050,000
Number of times interest charges earned	4	4.2

Analysis such as this can also be applied to dividends on preferred stock. In such a case, net income is divided by the amount of preferred dividends to yield the **number of times preferred dividends are earned.** This measure indicates the risk that dividends to preferred stockholders may not be paid.

Example 16 *What would be the number of times interest charges are earned for a company with $1,500,000, 10% debt; net income of $120,000; and a corporate tax rate of 40%?*

$$\frac{[\$120,000/(1.0 - 0.4)] + \$150,000}{\$150,000} = 2.33$$

Profitability Analysis

The ability of a business to earn profits depends on the effectiveness and efficiency of its operations as well as the resources available to it. Profitability analysis, therefore, focuses primarily on the relationship between operating results as reported in the income statement and resources available to the business as reported in the balance sheet. Major analyses used in assessing profitability include the following:

Profitability analysis focuses on the relationship between operating results and the resources available to a business.

1. Ratio of net sales to assets
2. Rate earned on total assets
3. Rate earned on total stockholders' equity
4. Rate earned on common stockholders' equity
5. Earnings per share on common stock
6. Price-earnings ratio
7. Dividends per share of common stock
8. Dividend yield of common stock

1. Ratio of Net Sales to Assets

The **ratio of net sales to assets** is a profitability measure that shows how effectively a firm utilizes its assets. For example, two competing businesses have equal amounts of assets. If the sales of one are twice the sales of the other, the business with the higher sales is making better use of its assets.

In computing the ratio of net sales to assets, any long-term investments are excluded from total assets, because such investments are unrelated to normal operations involving the sale of goods or services. Assets may be measured as the total at the end of the year, the average at the beginning and end of the year, or the average of monthly totals. The basic data and the computation of this ratio for Lincoln Company are as follows.

	2004	2003
Net sales	$1,498,000	$1,200,000
Total assets (excluding long-term investments):		
Beginning of year	$1,053,000	$1,010,000
End of year	1,044,500	1,053,000
Total	$2,097,500	$2,063,000
Average (Total ÷ 2)	$1,048,750	$1,031,500
Ratio of net sales to assets	1.4	1.2

This ratio improved during 2004, primarily due to an increase in sales volume. A comparison with similar companies or industry averages would be helpful in assessing the effectiveness of Lincoln Company's use of its assets.

2. Rate Earned on Total Assets

The **rate earned on total assets** measures the profitability of total assets, without considering how the assets are financed. This rate is therefore not affected by whether the assets are financed primarily by creditors or stockholders.

The rate earned on total assets is computed by adding interest expense to net income and dividing this sum by the average total assets. Adding interest expense to net income eliminates the effect of whether the assets are financed by debt or equity. The rate earned by Lincoln Company on total assets is computed as follows:

	2004	2003
Net income	$ 91,000	$ 76,500
Plus interest expense	6,000	12,000
Total	$ 97,000	$ 88,500
Total assets:		
Beginning of year	$1,230,500	$1,187,500
End of year	1,139,500	1,230,500
Total	$2,370,000	$2,418,000
Average (Total ÷ 2)	$1,185,000	$1,209,000
Rate earned on total assets	8.2%	7.3%

The rate earned on total assets of Lincoln Company during 2004 improved over that of 2003. A comparison with similar companies and industry averages would be useful in evaluating Lincoln Company's profitability on total assets.

Sometimes it may be desirable to compute the **rate of income from operations to total assets.** This is especially true if significant amounts of nonoperating income and expense are reported on the income statement. In this case, any assets related to the nonoperating income and expense items should be excluded from total assets in computing the rate. In addition, using income from operations (which is before tax) has the advantage of eliminating the effects of any changes in the tax structure on the rate of earnings. When evaluating published data on rates earned on total assets, you should be careful to determine the exact nature of the measure that is reported.

3. Rate Earned on Total Stockholders' Equity

Another measure of profitability is the **rate earned on total stockholders' equity.** It is computed by dividing net income by average total stockholders' equity. In contrast to the rate earned on total assets, this measure emphasizes the rate of income earned on the amount invested by the stockholders.

The total stockholders' equity may vary throughout a period. For example, a business may issue or retire stock, pay dividends, and earn net income. If monthly amounts are not available, the average of the stockholders' equity at the beginning and the end of the year is normally used to compute this rate. For Lincoln Company, the rate earned on total stockholders' equity is computed as follows.

	2004	2003
Net income	$ 91,000	$ 76,500
Stockholders' equity:		
Beginning of year	$ 787,500	$ 750,000
End of year	829,500	787,500
Total	$1,617,000	$1,537,500
Average (Total ÷ 2)	$ 808,500	$ 768,750
Rate earned on total stockholders' equity	11.3%	10.0%

The rate earned by a business on the equity of its stockholders is usually higher than the rate earned on total assets. This occurs when the amount earned on assets acquired with creditors' funds is more than the interest paid to creditors. This difference in the rate on stockholders' equity and the rate on total assets is called **leverage.**

Lincoln Company's rate earned on stockholders' equity for 2004, 11.3 percent, is greater than the rate of 8.2 percent earned on total assets. The leverage of 3.1 percent (11.3% − 8.2%) for 2004 compares favorably with the 2.7 percent (10.0% − 7.3%) leverage for 2003. Exhibit 600.24 shows the 2004 and 2003 leverages for Lincoln Company.

4. Rate Earned on Common Stockholders' Equity

A corporation may have both preferred and common stock outstanding. In this case, the common stockholders have the residual claim on earnings. The **rate earned on common stockholders' equity** focuses only on the rate of profits earned on the amount invested by the common stockholders. It is computed by subtracting preferred dividend requirements from the net income and dividing by the average common stockholders' equity.

Lincoln Company has $150,000 of 6% nonparticipating preferred stock outstanding on December 31, 2004 and 2003. Thus, the annual preferred dividend requirement is $9,000 ($150,000 × 6%). The common stockholders' equity

Exhibit 600.24 *Leverages for Lincoln Company*

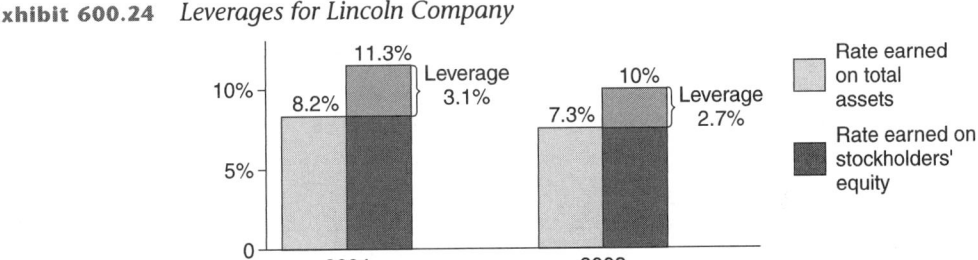

620. ANALYSIS AND USE OF FINANCIAL STATEMENTS

equals the total stockholders' equity, including retained earnings, less the par of the preferred stock ($150,000). The basic data and the rate earned on common stockholders' equity for Lincoln Company are as follows:

	2004	2003
Net income	$ 91,000	$ 76,500
Preferred dividends	9,000	9,000
Remainder—identified with common stock	$ 82,000	$ 67,500
Common stockholders' equity:		
Beginning of year	$ 637,500	$ 600,000
End of year	679,500	637,500
Total	$1,317,000	$1,237,500
Average (Total ÷ 2)	$ 658,500	$ 618,750
Rate earned on common stockholders' equity	12.5%	10.9%

The rate earned on common stockholders' equity differs from the rates earned by Lincoln Company on total assets and total stockholders' equity. This occurs if there are borrowed funds and also preferred stock outstanding, which rank ahead of the common shares in their claim on earnings. Thus, the concept of leverage, as we discussed in the preceding section, can also be applied to the use of funds from the sale of preferred stock as well as borrowing. Funds from both sources can be used in an attempt to increase the return on common stockholders' equity.

Example 17 *The approximate rates earned on assets and stockholders' equity for Adolph Coors Company and Anheuser-Busch Companies for a recent fiscal year are shown below.*

	Adolph Coors	Anheuser-Busch
Rate earned on assets	5%	13%
Rate earned on stockholders' equity	9%	30%

Anheuser-Busch has been more profitable and has benefited from a greater use of leverage than has Adolph Coors.

5. Earnings per Share on Common Stock

One of the profitability measures often quoted by the financial press is **earnings per share (EPS) on common stock.** It is also normally reported in the income statement in corporate annual reports. If a company has issued only one class of stock, the earnings per share is computed by dividing net income by the number of shares of stock outstanding. If preferred and common stock are outstanding, the net income is first reduced by the amount of preferred dividend requirements. The data on the earnings per share of common stock for Lincoln Company are as follows:

	2004	2003
Net income	$91,000	$76,500
Preferred dividends	9,000	9,000
Remainder—identified with common stock	$82,000	$67,500
Shares of common stock outstanding	50,000	50,000
Earnings per share on common stock	$ 1.64	$ 1.35

6. Price-Earnings Ratio

Another profitability measure quoted by the financial press is the **price-earnings (P/E) ratio** on common stock. The price-earnings ratio is an indicator of a firm's future earnings prospects. It is computed by dividing the market price per share of common stock at a specific date by the annual earnings per share. To illustrate, assume that the market prices per common share are 41 at the end of 2004 and 27 at the end of 2003. The price-earnings ratio on common stock of Lincoln Company is computed as follows.

Price-earnings (P/E) ratios that are much higher than the market averages are generally associated with companies with fast-growing profits. P/E ratios that are much lower than the market averages are generally associated with "out of favor" or declining profit companies.

	2004	2003
Market price per share of common stock	$41.00	$27.00
Earnings per share on common stock	÷1.64	÷1.35
Price-earnings ratio on common stock	25	20

The price-earnings ratio indicates that a share of common stock of Lincoln Company was selling for 20 times the amount of earnings per share at the end of 2002. At the end of 2003, the common stock was selling for 25 times the amount of earnings per share.

7. Dividends per Share of Common Stock

Because the primary basis for dividends is earnings, **dividends per share** and earnings per share on common stock are commonly used by investors in assessing alternative stock investments. The dividends per share for Lincoln Company were $0.80 ($40,000 ÷ 50,000 shares) for 2004 and $0.60 ($30,000 ÷ 50,000 shares) for 2003.

The dividend per share, dividend yield, and P/E ratio of a common stock are normally quoted on the daily listing of stock prices in The Wall Street Journal and other financial publications.

Dividends per share can be reported with earnings per share to indicate the relationship between dividends and earnings. Comparing these two per share amounts indicates the extent to which the corporation is retaining its earnings for use in operations. Exhibit 600.25 shows these relationships for Lincoln Company.

8. Dividend Yield of Common Stock

The **dividend yield** on common stock is a profitability measure that shows the rate of return to common stockholders in terms of cash dividends. It is of special interest to investors whose main investment objective is to receive current returns (dividends) on an investment rather than an increase in the market price of the investment. The dividend yield is computed by dividing the annual dividends paid per share of common stock by the market price per share on

Exhibit 600.25 *Dividends and Earnings per Share of Common Stock*

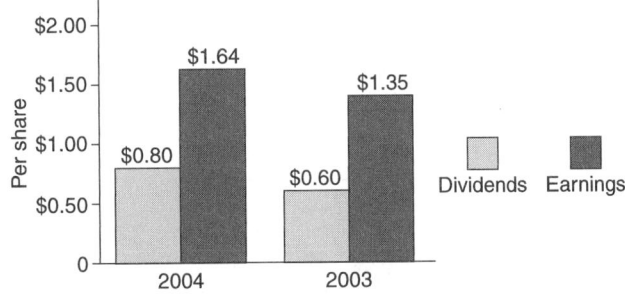

a specific date. To illustrate, assume that the market price was 41 at the end of 2004 and 27 at the end of 2003. The dividend yield on common stock of Lincoln Company is as follows.

	2004	2003
Dividends per share of common stock	$0.80	$0.60
Market price per share of common stock	÷41.00	÷27.00
Dividend yield on common stock	1.95%	2.22%

Summary of Analytical Measures

Exhibit 600.26 presents a summary of the analytical measures that we have discussed. These measures can be computed for most medium-size businesses. Depending on the specific business being analyzed, some measures might be omitted or additional measures could be developed. The type of industry, the capital structure, and the diversity of the business's operations usually affect the measures used. For example, analysis for an airline might include revenue per passenger mile and cost per available seat as measures. Likewise, analysis for a hotel might focus on occupancy rates.

Percentage analyses, ratios, turnovers, and other measures of financial position and operating results are useful analytical measures. They are helpful in assessing a business's past performance and predicting its future. They are not, however, a substitute for sound judgment. In selecting and interpreting analytical measures, conditions peculiar to a business or its industry should be considered. In addition, the influence of the general economic and business environment should be considered.

Exhibit 600.26 *Summary of Analytical Measures*

	Method of Computation	Use
Solvency measures:		
Working capital	Current assets − Current liabilities	To indicate the ability to meet currently maturing obligations
Current ratio	$\dfrac{\text{Current assets}}{\text{Current liabilities}}$	
Acid-test ratio	$\dfrac{\text{Quick assets}}{\text{Current liabilities}}$	To indicate instant debt-paying ability
Accounts receivable turnover	$\dfrac{\text{Net sales on account}}{\text{Average accounts receivable}}$	To assess the efficiency in collecting receivables and in the management of credit
Numbers of days' sales in receivables	$\dfrac{\text{Accounts receivable, end of year}}{\text{Average daily sales on account}}$	
Inventory turnover	$\dfrac{\text{Cost of goods sold}}{\text{Average inventory}}$	To assess the efficiency in the management of inventory
Number of days' sales in inventory	$\dfrac{\text{Inventory, end of year}}{\text{Average daily cost of goods sold}}$	
Ratio of fixed assets to long-term liabilities	$\dfrac{\text{Fixed assets (net)}}{\text{Long-term liabilities}}$	To indicate the margin of safety to long-term creditors
Ratio of liabilities to stockholders' equity	$\dfrac{\text{Total liabilities}}{\text{Total stockholders' equity}}$	To indicate the margin of safety to creditors
Number of times interest charges are earned	$\dfrac{\text{Income before income tax} + \text{Interest expense}}{\text{Interest expense}}$	To assess the risk to debtholders in terms of number of times interest charges were earned

Exhibit 600.26 *Continued*

	Method of Computation	Use
Profitability measures:		
Ratio of net sales to assets	$\dfrac{\text{Net sales}}{\text{Average total assets (excluding long-term investments)}}$	To assess the effectiveness in the use of assets
Rate earned on total assets	$\dfrac{\text{Net income + Interest expense}}{\text{Average total assets}}$	To assess the profitability of the assets
Rate earned on total stockholders' equity	$\dfrac{\text{Net income}}{\text{Average total stockholders' equity}}$	To assess the profitability of the investment by stockholders
Rate earned on common stockholders' equity	$\dfrac{\text{Net income} - \text{Preferred dividends}}{\text{Average common stockholders' equity}}$	To assess the profitability of the investment by common stockholders
Earnings per share on common stock	$\dfrac{\text{Net income} - \text{Preferred dividends}}{\text{Shares of common stock outstanding}}$	
Price-earnings ratio	$\dfrac{\text{Market price per share of common stock}}{\text{Earnings per share of common stock}}$	To indicate future earnings prospects, based on the relationship between market value of common stock and earnings
Dividends per share of common stock	$\dfrac{\text{Dividends}}{\text{Shares of common stock outstanding}}$	To indicate the extent to which earnings are being distributed to common stockholders
Dividend yield on common stock	$\dfrac{\text{Dividends per share of common stock}}{\text{Market price per share of common stock}}$	To indicate the rate of return to common stockholders in terms of dividends

In determining trends, the interrelationship of the measures used in assessing a business should be carefully studied. Comparable indexes of earlier periods should also be studied. Data from competing businesses may be useful in assessing the efficiency of operations for the firm under analysis. In making such comparisons, however, the effects of differences in the accounting methods used by the businesses should be considered.

Cost Behavior, Control, and Decision Making

In this section, we discuss commonly used methods for classifying costs according to how they change. We also discuss how management uses cost-volume-profit analysis as a tool in making business decisions.

Cost Behavior

Knowing how costs behave is useful to management for a variety of purposes. For example, knowing how costs behave allows managers to predict profits as sales and production volumes change. Knowing how costs behave is also useful for estimating costs. Estimated costs, in turn, affect a variety of management decisions, such as whether to use excess machine capacity to produce and sell a product at a reduced price.

Cost behavior refers to the manner in which a cost changes as a related activity changes. To understand cost behavior, two factors must be considered. First, we must identify the activities that are thought to cause the cost to be incurred. Such activities are called **activity bases** (or **activity drivers**). Second, we must specify the range of activity over which the changes in the cost are of interest. This range of activity is called the **relevant range.**

To illustrate, hospital administrators must plan and control hospital food costs. To fully understand why food costs change, the activity that causes cost to be incurred must be identified. In the case of food costs, the feeding of patients is a major cause of these costs. The number of patients *treated* by the hospital would not be a good activity base because some patients are outpatients who do not stay in the hospital. The number of patients who *stay* in the hospital, however, is a good activity base for studying food costs. Once the proper activity base is identified, food costs can then be analyzed over the range of the number of patients who normally stay in the hospital (the relevant range).

Three of the most common classifications of cost behavior are variable costs, fixed costs, and mixed costs.

Variable Costs

When the level of activity is measured in units produced, direct materials and direct labor costs are generally classified as variable costs. **Variable costs** are costs that vary in proportion to changes in the level of activity. For example, assume that Jason Inc. produces stereo sound systems under the brand name of J-Sound. The parts for the stereo systems are purchased from outside suppliers for $10 per unit and are assembled in Jason Inc.'s Waterloo plant. The direct materials costs for Model JS-12 for the relevant range of 5,000 to 30,000 units of production are shown below.

Number of Units of Model JS-12 Produced	Direct Materials Cost per Unit	Total Direct Materials Cost
5,000 units	$10	$ 50,000
10,000	10	100,000
15,000	10	150,000
20,000	10	200,000
25,000	10	250,000
30,000	10	300,000

Variable costs are the same per unit, while the total variable cost changes in proportion to changes in the activity base. For Model JS-12, for example, the direct materials cost for 10,000 units ($100,000) is twice the direct materials cost for 5,000 units ($50,000). The total direct materials cost varies in proportion to the number of units produced because the direct materials cost per unit ($10) is the same for all levels of production. Thus, producing 20,000 additional units of JS-12 will increase the direct materials cost by $200,000 (20,000 × $10), producing 25,000 additional units will increase the materials cost by $250,000, and so on.

Exhibit 600.27 illustrates how the variable costs for direct materials for Model JS-12 behave in total and on a per-unit basis as production changes.

Exhibit 600.27 Variable Cost Graphs

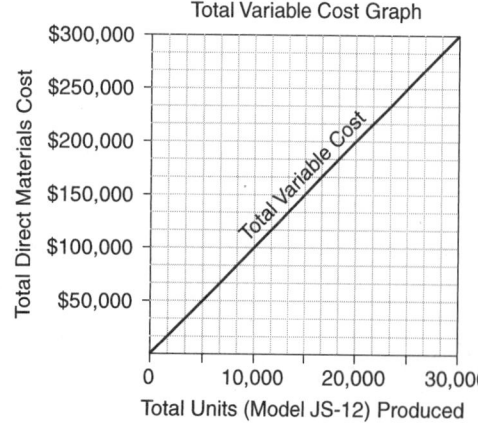
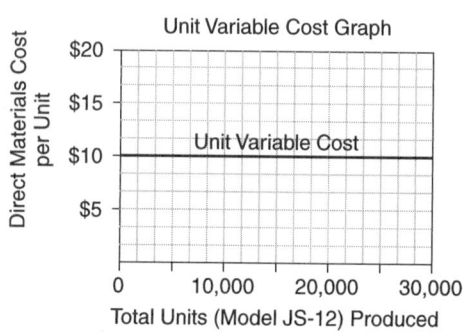

There are a variety of activity bases used by managers for evaluating cost behavior. The following list provides some examples of variable costs, along with their related activity bases for various types of businesses.

Type of Business	Cost	Activity Base
University	Instructor salaries	Number of classes
Passenger airline	Fuel	Number of miles flown
Manufacturing	Direct materials	Number of units produced
Hospital	Nurse wages	Number of patients
Hotel	Maid wages	Number of guests
Bank	Teller wages	Number of banking transactions
Insurance	Claim processing salaries	Number of claims

Fixed Costs

Fixed costs are costs that remain the same in total dollar amount as the level of activity changes. To illustrate, assume that Minton Inc. manufactures, bottles, and distributes La Fleur Perfume at its Los Angeles plant. The production supervisor at the Los Angeles plant is Jane Sovissi, who is paid a salary of $75,000 per year. The relevant range of activity for a year is 50,000 to 300,000 bottles of perfume. Sovissi's salary is a fixed cost that does not vary with the number of units produced. Regardless of the number of bottles produced within the range of 50,000 to 300,000 bottles, Sovissi receives a salary of $75,000.

Although the total fixed cost remains the same as the number of bottles produced changes, the fixed cost per bottle changes. As more bottles are produced, the total fixed costs are spread over a larger number of bottles, and thus the fixed cost per bottle decreases. This relationship is shown below for Jane Sovissi's $75,000 salary.

Number of Bottles of Perfume Produced	Total Salary for Jane Sovissi	Salary per Bottle of Perfume Produced
50,000 bottles	$75,000	$1.500
100,000	75,000	0.750
150,000	75,000	0.500
200,000	75,000	0.375
250,000	75,000	0.300
300,000	75,000	0.250

Exhibit 600.28 illustrates how the fixed cost of Jane Sovissi's salary behaves in total and on a per-unit basis as production changes. When units produced is the measure of activity, examples of fixed costs include straight-line depreciation of factory equipment, insurance on factory plant and equipment, and salaries of factory supervisors. Other examples of fixed costs and their activity bases for a variety of businesses are as follows:

Type of Business	Fixed Cost	Activity Base
University	Building depreciation	Number of students
Passenger airline	Airplane depreciation	Number of passengers
Manufacturing	Plant manager salary	Number of units produced
Hospital	Property insurance	Number of patients
Hotel	Property taxes	Number of guests
Bank	Branch manager salary	Number of customer accounts
Insurance	Computer depreciation	Number of insurance policies

Exhibit 600.28 *Fixed Cost Graphs*

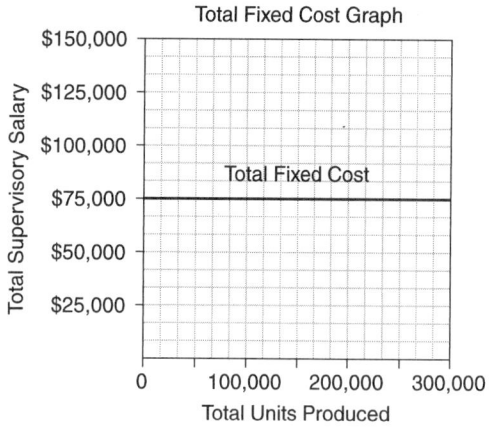
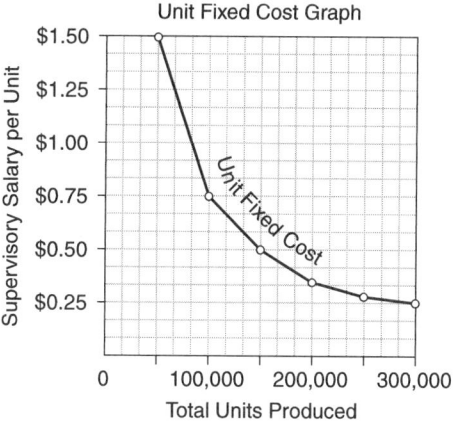

Exhibit 600.29 *Mixed Costs Graph*

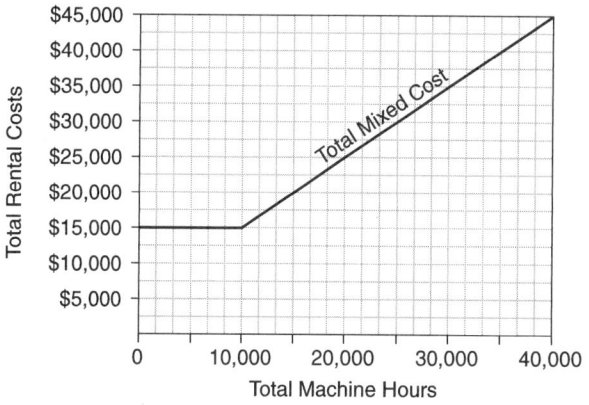

Mixed Costs

A **mixed cost** has characteristics of both a variable and a fixed cost. For example, over one range of activity, the total mixed cost may remain the same. It thus behaves as a fixed cost. Over another range of activity, the mixed cost may change in proportion to changes in the level of activity. It thus behaves as a variable cost. Mixed costs are sometimes called *semivariable* or *semifixed* costs.

To illustrate, assume that Simpson Inc. manufactures sails, using rented machinery. The rental charges are $15,000 per year, plus $1 for each machine hour used over 10,000 hours. If the machinery is used 8,000 hours, the total rental charge is $15,000. If the machinery is used 20,000 hours, the total rental charge is $25,000 [$15,000 + (10,000 hours × $1)], and so on. Thus, if the level of activity is measured in machine hours and the relevant range is 0 to 40,000 hours, the rental charges are a fixed cost up to 10,000 hours and a variable cost thereafter. This mixed cost behavior is shown graphically in Exhibit 600.29.

In analyses, mixed costs are usually separated into their fixed and variable components. The **high-low method** is a cost estimation technique that may be used for this purpose. Other methods of separating mixed costs include the scattergraph method, the least squares method, the account analysis method, and engineering methods. The high-low method uses the highest and lowest activity levels and their related costs to estimate the variable cost per unit and the fixed cost component of mixed costs.

To illustrate, assume that the Equipment Maintenance Department of Kason Inc. incurred the following costs during the past five months:

	Production	Total Cost
June	1,000 units	$45,550
July	1,500	52,000
August	2,100	61,500
September	1,800	57,500
October	750	41,250

The number of units produced is the measure of activity, and the number of units produced between June and October is the relevant range of production. For Kason Inc., the difference between the number of units produced and the difference between the total cost at the highest and lowest levels of production are as follows:

	Production	Total Cost
Highest level	2,100 units	$61,500
Lowest level	750	41,250
Difference	1,350 units	$20,250

Because the total fixed cost does not change with changes in volume of production, the $20,250 difference in the total cost is the change in the total variable cost. Hence, dividing the difference in the total cost by the difference in production provides an estimate of the variable cost per unit. For Kason Inc., this estimate is $15, as shown below.

$$\text{Variable cost per unit} = \frac{\text{Difference in total cost}}{\text{Difference in production}}$$

$$\text{Variable cost per unit} = \frac{\$20,250}{1,350 \text{ units}} = \$15$$

The fixed cost will be the same at both the highest and the lowest levels of production. Thus, the fixed cost can be estimated at either of these levels. This is done by subtracting the estimated total variable cost from the total cost, using the following total cost equation.

$$\text{Total cost} = (\text{Variable cost per unit} \times \text{Units of production}) + \text{Fixed cost}$$

Highest level:
$61,500 = (\$15 \times 2,100 \text{ units}) + \text{Fixed cost}$
$61,500 = \$31,500 + \text{Fixed cost}$
$30,000 = \text{Fixed cost}$

Lowest level:
$41,250 = (\$15 \times 750 \text{ units}) + \text{Fixed cost}$
$41,250 = \$11,250 + \text{Fixed cost}$
$30,000 = \text{Fixed cost}$

The total equipment maintenance cost for Kason Inc. can thus be analyzed as a $30,000 fixed cost and a $15 per-unit variable cost. Using these amounts in the total cost equation, the total equipment maintenance cost at other levels of production can be estimated.

Example 18 The manufacturing cost at the highest production level of 2,500 units is $125,000. The manufacturing cost at the lowest production level of 1,000 units is $80,000. Using the high-low method, what are (a) the variable cost per unit and (b) the total fixed cost?

(a) $30 per unit [($125,000 − $80,000) ÷ (2,500 − 1,000)]; (b) $50,000 [$125,000 − ($30 × 2,500)]

630. COST BEHAVIOR, CONTROL, AND DECISION MAKING

Summary of Cost Behavior Concepts

Examples of common variable, fixed, and mixed costs when the number of units produced is the activity base are:

Variable Cost	Fixed Cost	Mixed Cost
Direct materials	Depreciation expense	Quality Control Department salaries
Direct labor	Property taxes	Purchasing Department salaries
Electricity expense	Officer salaries	Maintenance expenses
Sales commissions	Insurance expense	Warehouse expenses

Mixed costs contain a fixed cost component that is incurred even if nothing is produced. For analyses, the fixed and variable cost components of mixed costs should be separated using the high-low method or other.

The following table summarizes the cost behavior attributes of variable costs and fixed costs:

	Effect of Changing Activity Level	
Cost	Total Amount	Per-Unit Amount
Variable	Increases and decreases proportionately with activity level.	Remains the same regardless of activity level.
Fixed	Remains the same regardless of activity level.	Increases and decreases inversely with activity level.

Reporting Variable and Fixed Costs for Decision Making

Separating costs into their variable and fixed components for reporting purposes can be useful for decision making. One method of reporting variable and fixed costs is called **variable costing** or **direct costing,** which is discussed in Section 660. Under variable costing, only the variable manufacturing costs (direct materials, direct labor, and variable factory overhead) are included in the product cost. The fixed factory overhead is an expense of the period in which it is incurred.

Cost-Volume-Profit Relationships

After costs have been classified as fixed and variable, their effect on revenues, volume, and profits can be studied by using cost-volume-profit analysis. **Cost-volume profit analysis** is the systematic examination of the relationships among selling prices, sales and production volume, costs, expenses, and profits.

Cost-volume-profit analysis provides management with useful information for decision making. For example, cost-volume-profit analysis may be used in setting selling prices, selecting the mix of products to sell, choosing among marketing strategies, and analyzing the effects of changes in costs on profits. In today's business environment, management must make such decisions quickly and accurately. As a result, the importance of cost-volume-profit analysis has increased in recent years.

Contribution Margin Concept

One relationship among cost, volume, and profit is the contribution margin. The **contribution margin** is the excess of sales revenues over variable costs. The contribution margin concept is especially useful in business planning because it gives insight into the profit potential of a firm. To illustrate, the income statement of Lambert Inc. in Exhibit 600.30 has been prepared in a contribution-margin format.

The contribution margin of $400,000 is available to cover the fixed costs of $300,000. Once the fixed costs are covered, any remaining amount adds directly to the income from operations of the company. Think of the fixed costs as a bucket and the contribution margin as water filling the bucket. Once the bucket is filled, the overflow represents income from operations. Up until the point of overflow, however, the contribution margin contributes to fixed costs (filling the bucket).

Exhibit 600.30 *Contribution Margin Income Statement*

Sales	$1,000,000
Variable costs	600,000
Contribution margin	$ 400,000
Fixed costs	300,000
Income from operations	$ 100,000

CONTRIBUTION MARGIN RATIO The contribution margin can also be expressed as a percentage. The **contribution margin ratio,** sometimes called the **profit-volume ratio,** indicates the percentage of each sales dollar available to cover the fixed costs and to provide income from operations. For Lambert Inc., the contribution margin ratio is 40 percent, as computed below.

$$\text{Contribution margin ratio} = \frac{\text{Sales} - \text{Variable costs}}{\text{Sales}}$$

$$\text{Contribution margin ratio} = \frac{\$1,000,000 - \$600,000}{\$1,000,000} = 40\%$$

The contribution margin ratio measures the effect on income from operations of an increase or a decrease in sales volume. For example, assume that the management of Lambert Inc. is studying the effect of adding $80,000 in sales orders. Multiplying the contribution margin ratio (40%) by the change in sales volume ($80,000) indicates that income from operations will increase $32,000 if the additional orders are obtained. The validity of this analysis is illustrated by the following contribution margin income statement of Lambert Inc.

Sales	$1,080,000
Variable costs ($1,080,000 × 60%)	648,000
Contribution margin ($1,080,000 × 40%)	$ 432,000
Fixed costs	300,000
Income from operations	$ 132,000

Variable costs as a percentage of sales are equal to 100 percent minus the contribution margin ratio. Thus, in the above income statement, the variable costs are 60 percent (100% − 40%) of sales, or $648,000 ($1,080,000 × 60%). The total contribution margin, $432,000, can also be computed directly by multiplying the sales by the contribution margin ratio ($1,080,000 × 40%).

In using the contribution margin ratio in analysis, factors other than sales volume, such as variable cost per unit and sales price, are assumed to remain constant. If such factors change, their effect must be considered.

The contribution margin ratio is also useful in setting business policy. For example, if the contribution margin ratio of a firm is large and production is at a level below 100 percent capacity, a large increase in income from operations can be expected from an increase in sales volume. A firm in such a position might decide to devote more effort to sales promotion because of the large change in income from operations that will result from changes in sales volume. In contrast, a firm with a small contribution margin ratio will probably want to give more attention to reducing costs before attempting to promote sales.

UNIT CONTRIBUTION MARGIN The unit contribution margin is also useful for analyzing the profit potential of proposed projects. The **unit contribution margin** is the dollars from each unit of sales available to cover fixed costs and provide income from operations. For example, if Lambert Inc.'s unit selling price is $20 and its unit variable cost is $12, the unit contribution margin is $8 ($20 − $12).

The *contribution margin ratio* is most useful when the increase or decrease in sales volume is measured in sales dollars. The *unit contribution margin* is most useful when the increase or decrease in sales volume is measured in sales units (quantities). To illustrate, assume that Lambert Inc. sold 50,000 units. Its income from operations is $100,000, as shown in the following contribution margin income statement:

630. COST BEHAVIOR, CONTROL, AND DECISION MAKING

Sales (50,000 units × $20)	$1,000,000
Variable costs (50,000 units × $12)	600,000
Contribution margin (50,000 units × $8)	$ 400,000
Fixed costs	300,000
Income from operations	$ 100,000

If Lambert Inc.'s sales could be increased by 15,000 units, from 50,000 units to 65,000 units, its income from operations would increase by $120,000 (15,000 units × $8), as shown below.

Sales (65,000 units × $20)	$1,300,000
Variable costs (65,000 units × $12)	780,000
Contribution margin (65,000 units × $8)	$ 520,000
Fixed costs	300,000
Income from operations	$ 220,000

Unit contribution margin analyses can provide useful information for managers. The preceding illustration indicates, for example, that Lambert could spend up to $120,000 for special advertising or other product promotions to increase sales by 15,000 units.

Example 19 *Sales are 20,000 units at $12 per unit, variable costs are $9 per unit, and fixed costs are $25,000. What are (a) the contribution margin ratio, (b) the unit contribution margin, and (c) the income from operations?*

(a) 25% [($240,000 − $180,000) ÷ $240,000];
(b) $3 per unit ($12 − $9);
(c) $35,000 ($240,000 − $180,000 − $25,000)

Mathematical Approach to Cost-Volume-Profit Analysis

Accountants use various approaches for expressing the relationship of costs, sales (volume), and income from operations (operating profit). The mathematical approach is one method that is used often in practice, while the graphic approach is another method.

The mathematical approach to cost-volume-profit analysis uses equations (1) to determine the units of sales necessary to achieve the break-even point in operations or (2) to determine the units of sales necessary to achieve a target or desired profit. We will next describe and illustrate these equations and their use by management in profit planning.

Break-Even Point

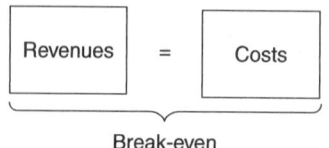

The **break-even point** is the level of operations at which a business's revenues and expired costs are exactly equal. At break-even, a business will have neither an income nor a loss from operations. The break-even point is useful in business planning, especially when expanding or decreasing operations.

To illustrate the computation of the break-even point, assume that the fixed costs for Barker Corporation are estimated to be $90,000. The unit selling price is $25, unit variable cost is $15, and unit contribution margin is $10 for Barker Corporation.

The break-even point is 9,000 units, which can be computed by using the following equation

$$\text{Break-even sales (units)} = \frac{\text{Fixed costs}}{\text{Unit contribution margin}}$$

$$\text{Break-even sales (units)} = \frac{\$90,000}{\$10} = 9,000 \text{ units}$$

The following income statement verifies the preceding computation:

Sales (9,000 units × $25)	$225,000
Variable costs (9,000 units × $15)	135,000
Contribution margin	$ 90,000
Fixed costs	90,000
Income from operations	$ 0

The break-even point is affected by changes in the fixed costs, unit variable costs, and the unit selling price. Next, we will briefly describe the effect of each of these factors on the break-even point.

EFFECT OF CHANGES IN FIXED COSTS Although fixed costs do not change in total with changes in the level of activity, they may change because of other factors. For example, changes in property tax rates or factory supervisors' salaries change fixed costs. Increases in fixed costs will raise the break-even point. Likewise, decreases in fixed costs will lower the break-even point. For example, **General Motors** closed 21 plants and eliminated 74,000 jobs to lower its break-even from approximately 7 million to 5 million automobiles through the 1990s.

To illustrate, assume that Bishop Co. is evaluating a proposal to budget an additional $100,000 for advertising. Fixed costs before the additional advertising are estimated at $600,000, and the unit contribution margin is $20. The break-even point before the additional expense is 30,000 units, computed as follows:

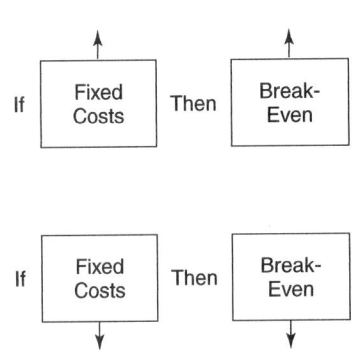

$$\text{Break-even sales (units)} = \frac{\text{Fixed costs}}{\text{Unit contribution margin}}$$

$$\text{Break-even sales (units)} = \frac{\$600,000}{\$20} = 30,000 \text{ units}$$

If the additional amount is spent, the fixed costs will increase by $100,000 and the break-even point will increase to 35,000 units, computed as follows:

$$\text{Break-even sales (units)} = \frac{\text{Fixed costs}}{\text{Unit contribution margin}}$$

$$\text{Break-even sales (units)} = \frac{\$700,000}{\$20} = 35,000 \text{ units}$$

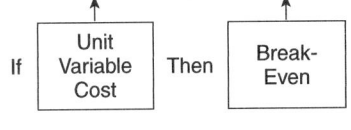

The $100,000 increase in the fixed costs requires an additional 5,000 units ($100,000 ÷ $20) of sales to break even. In other words, an increase in sales of 5,000 units is required in order to generate an additional $100,000 of total contribution margin (5,000 units × $20) to cover the increased fixed costs.

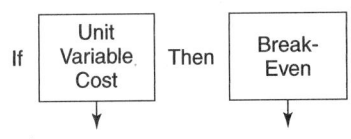

EFFECT OF CHANGES IN UNIT VARIABLE COSTS Although unit variable costs are not affected by changes in volume of activity, they may be affected by other factors. For example, changes in the price of direct materials and the wages for factory workers providing direct labor change unit variable costs. Increases in unit variable costs will raise the break-even point. Likewise, decreases in unit variable costs will lower the break-even point. For example, when fuel prices rise or decline, there is a direct impact on the break-even passenger load for **American Airlines.**

To illustrate, assume that Park Co. is evaluating a proposal to pay an additional 2% commission on sales to its salespeople as an incentive to increase sales. Fixed costs are estimated at $840,000, and the unit selling price, unit variable cost, and unit contribution margin before the additional 2% commission are as follows:

Unit selling price	$250
Unit variable cost	145
Unit contribution margin	$105

The break-even point is 8,000 units, computed as follows.

$$\text{Break-even sales (units)} = \frac{\text{Fixed costs}}{\text{Unit contribution margin}}$$

$$\text{Break-even sales (units)} = \frac{\$840,000}{\$105} = 8,000 \text{ units}$$

If the sales commission proposal is adopted, variable costs will increase by $5 per unit ($250 × 2%). This increase in the variable costs will decrease the unit contribution margin by $5 (from $105 to $100). Thus, the break-even point is raised to 8,400 units, computed as follows:

$$\text{Break-even sales (units)} = \frac{\text{Fixed costs}}{\text{Unit contribution margin}}$$

$$\text{Break-even sales (units)} = \frac{\$840,000}{\$100} = 8,400 \text{ units}$$

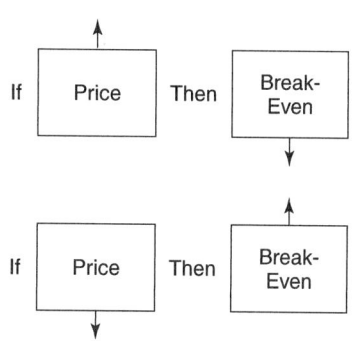

At the original break-even point of 8,000 units, the new unit contribution margin of $100 would provide only $800,000 to cover fixed costs of $840,000. Thus, an additional 400 units of sales will be required in order to provide the additional $40,000 (400 units × $100) contribution margin necessary to break even.

EFFECT OF CHANGES IN THE UNIT SELLING PRICE Increases in the unit selling price will lower the break-even point, while decreases in the unit selling price will raise the break-even point. For example, when **The Golf Channel** went from a premium cable service price of $6.95 per month to a much lower basic cable price, its break-even point increased from 6 million to 19 million subscribers.

To illustrate, assume that Graham Co. is evaluating a proposal to increase the unit selling price of its product from $50 to $60. The following data have been gathered.

	Current	Proposed
Unit selling price	$50	$60
Unit variable cost	30	30
Unit contribution margin	$20	$30
Total fixed costs	$600,000	$600,000

The break-even point based on the current selling price is 30,000 units, computed as follows:

$$\text{Break-even sales (units)} = \frac{\text{Fixed costs}}{\text{Unit contribution margin}}$$

$$\text{Break-even sales (units)} = \frac{\$600,000}{\$20} = 30,000 \text{ units}$$

If the selling price is increased by $10 per unit, the break-even point is decreased to 20,000 units, computed as follows:

$$\text{Break-even sales (units)} = \frac{\text{Fixed costs}}{\text{Unit contribution margin}}$$

$$\text{Break-even sales (units)} = \frac{\$600{,}000}{\$30} = 20{,}000 \text{ units}$$

The increase of $10 per unit in the selling price increases the unit contribution margin by $10. Thus, the break-even point decreases by 10,000 units (from 30,000 units to 20,000 units).

Example 20 *The selling price for a product is $60 per unit. The variable cost is $35 per unit, while fixed costs are $80,000. What are the following amounts: (a) the break-even point in sales units and (b) the break-even point if the selling price were increased to $67 per unit?*

(a) 3,200 units [$80,000 ÷ ($60 − $35)];
(b) 2,500 units [$80,000 ÷ ($67 − $35)]

SUMMARY OF EFFECTS OF CHANGES ON BREAK-EVEN POINT The break-even point in sales (units) moves in the same direction as changes in the variable cost per unit and fixed costs. In contrast, the break-even point in sales (units) moves in the opposite direction to changes in the sales price per unit. A summary of the impact of these changes on the break-even point in sales (units) is shown below.

Type of Change	Direction of Change	Effect of Change on Break-Even Sales (Units)
Fixed cost	Increase	Increase
	Decrease	Decrease
Variable cost per unit	Increase	Increase
	Decrease	Decrease
Unit sales price	Increase	Decrease
	Decrease	Increase

Target Profit

At the break-even point, sales and costs are exactly equal. However, the break-even point is not the goal of most businesses. Rather, managers seek to maximize profits. By modifying the break-even equation, the sales volume required to earn a target or desired amount of profit may be estimated. For this purpose, target profit is added to the break-even equation as shown below.

$$\text{Sales (units)} = \frac{\text{Fixed costs + Target profit}}{\text{Unit contribution margin}}$$

To illustrate, assume that fixed costs are estimated at $200,000, and the desired profit is $100,000. The unit selling price, unit variable cost, and unit contribution margin are as follows.

Unit selling price	$75
Unit variable cost	45
Unit contribution margin	$30

The sales volume necessary to earn the target profit of $100,000 is 10,000 units, computed as follows

$$\text{Sales (units)} = \frac{\text{Fixed costs + Target profit}}{\text{Unit contribution margin}}$$

$$\text{Sales (units)} = \frac{\$200{,}000 + \$100{,}000}{\$30} = 10{,}000 \text{ units}$$

630. COST BEHAVIOR, CONTROL, AND DECISION MAKING

The following income statement verifies this computation.

Sales (10,000 units × $75)	$750,000
Variable costs (10,000 units × $45)	450,000
Contribution margin (10,000 units × $30)	$300,000
Fixed costs	200,000
Income from operations	$100,000 ← Target profit

Example 21 *The sales price is $140 per unit, variable costs are $60 per unit, and fixed costs are $240,000. What would be (a) the break-even point in sales units and (b) the break-even point in sales units if a target profit of $50,000 is desired?*

(a) 3,000 units [$240,000 ÷ ($140 − $60)];
(b) 3,625 units [($240,000 + $50,000) ÷ ($140 − $60)]

Use of Computers in Cost-Volume-Profit Analysis

With computers, the graphic approach and the mathematical approach to cost-volume profit analysis are easy to use. Managers can vary assumptions regarding selling prices, costs, and volume and can immediately see the effects of each change on the break-even point and profit. Such an analysis is called a **"what if" analysis** or **sensitivity analysis.**

Sales Mix Considerations

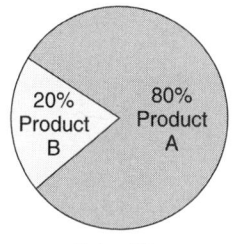

Sales Mix

In most businesses, more than one product is sold at varying selling prices. In addition, the products often have different unit variable costs, and each product makes a different contribution to profits. Thus, the sales volume necessary to break even or to earn a target profit for a business selling two or more products depends upon the sales mix. The **sales mix** is the relative distribution of sales among the various products sold by a business.

To illustrate the calculation of the break-even point for a company that sells more than one product, assume that Cascade Company sold 8,000 units of Product A and 2,000 units of Product B during the past year. The sales mix for products A and B can be expressed as percentages (80 percent and 20 percent) or as a ratio (80:20).

Cascade Company's fixed costs are $200,000. The unit selling prices, unit variable costs, and unit contribution margins for products A and B and their sales mix are as follows.

Product	Unit Selling Price	Unit Variable Cost	Unit Contribution Margin	Sales Mix
A	$ 90	$70	$20	80%
B	140	95	45	20%

In computing the break-even point, it is useful to think of the individual products as components of one overall enterprise product. For Cascade Company, this overall enterprise product is called E. We can think of the unit selling price of E as equal to the total of the unit selling prices of products A and B, multiplied by their sales mix percentages. Likewise, we can think of the unit variable cost and unit contribution margin of E as equal to the total of the unit variable costs and unit contribution margins of products A and B, multiplied by the sales mix percentages. These computations are as follows.

Unit selling price of E:	($90 × 0.8) + ($140 × 0.2) = $100
Unit variable cost of E:	($70 × 0.8) + ($ 95 × 0.2) = $ 75
Unit contribution margin of E:	($20 × 0.8) + ($ 45 × 0.2) = $ 25

The break-even point of 8,000 units of E can be determined in the normal manner as follows.

$$\text{Break-even sales (units)} = \frac{\text{Fixed costs}}{\text{Unit contribution margin}}$$

$$\text{Break-even sales (units)} = \frac{\$200,000}{\$25} = 8,000 \text{ units}$$

Since the sales mix for products A and B is 80 percent and 20 percent, the break-even quantity of A is 6,400 units (8,000 units × 80%) and B is 1,600 units (8,000 units × 20%). This analysis can be verified in the following income statement.

	Product A	Product B	Total
Sales:			
6,400 units × $90	$576,000		$576,000
1,600 units × $140		$224,000	224,000
Total sales	$576,000	$224,000	$800,000
Variable costs:			
6,400 units × $70	$448,000		$448,000
1,600 units × $95		$152,000	152,000
Total variable costs	$448,000	$152,000	$600,000
Contribution margin	$128,000	$ 72,000	$200,000
Fixed costs			200,000
Income from operations			$ 0 ← Break-even point

The effects of changes in the sales mix on the break-even point can be determined by repeating this analysis, assuming a different sales mix.

Special Cost-Volume-Profit Relationships

Some additional relationships useful to managers can be developed from cost-volume-profit data. Two of these relationships are the margin of safety and operating leverage.

Margin of Safety

The difference between the current sales revenue and the sales at the break-even point is called the **margin of safety.** It indicates the possible decrease in sales that may occur before an operating loss results. For example, if the margin of safety is low, even a small decline in sales revenue may result in an operating loss.

If sales are $250,000, the unit selling price is $25, and sales at the break-even point are $200,000, the margin of safety is 20 percent, computed as follows:

$$\text{Margin of safety} = \frac{\text{Sales} - \text{Sales at break-even point}}{\text{Sales}}$$

$$\text{Margin of safety} = \frac{\$250,000 - \$200,000}{\$250,000} = 20\%$$

The margin of safety may also be stated in terms of units. In this illustration, for example, the margin of safety of 20 percent is equivalent to $50,000 ($250,000 × 20%). In units, the margin of safety is 2,000 units ($50,000 ÷ $25). Thus, the current sales of $250,000 may decline $50,000 or 2,000 units before an operating loss occurs.

Operating Leverage

The relative mix of a business's variable costs and fixed costs is measured by the **operating leverage**. It is computed as follows:

$$\text{Operating leverage} = \frac{\text{Contribution margin}}{\text{Income from operations}}$$

Because the difference between contribution margin and income from operations is fixed costs, companies with large amounts of fixed costs will generally have a high operating leverage. Thus, companies in capital-intensive industries, such as the airline and automotive industries, will generally have a high operating leverage. A low operating leverage is normal for companies in industries that are labor-intensive, such as professional services.

Managers can use operating leverage to measure the impact of changes in sales on income from operations. A high operating leverage indicates that a small increase in sales will yield a large percentage increase in income from operations. In contrast, a low operating leverage indicates that a large increase in sales is necessary to significantly increase income from operations. To illustrate, assume the following operating data for Jones Inc. and Wilson Inc.

	Jones Inc.	Wilson Inc.
Sales	$400,000	$400,000
Variable costs	300,000	300,000
Contribution margin	$100,000	$100,000
Fixed costs	80,000	50,000
Income from operations	$ 20,000	$ 50,000

Both companies have the same sales, the same variable costs, and the same contribution margin. Jones Inc. has larger fixed costs than Wilson Inc. and, as a result, a lower income from operations and a higher operating leverage. The operating leverage for each company is computed as follows:

Jones Inc.	Wilson Inc.
$\text{Operating leverage} = \dfrac{\$100{,}000}{\$20{,}000} = 5$	$\text{Operating leverage} = \dfrac{\$100{,}000}{\$50{,}000} = 2$

Jones Inc.'s operating leverage indicates that, for each percentage point change in sales, income from operations will change five times that percentage. In contrast, for each percentage point change in sales, the income from operations of Wilson Inc. will change only two times that percentage. For example, if sales increased by 10 percent ($40,000) for each company, income from operations will increase by 50 percent (10% × 5), or $10,000 (50% × $20,000), for Jones Inc. The sales increase of $40,000 will increase income from operations by only 20 percent (10% × 2), or $10,000 (20% × $50,000), for Wilson Inc. The validity of this analysis is shown as follows.

	Jones Inc.	Wilson Inc.
Sales	$440,000	$440,000
Variable costs	330,000	330,000
Contribution margin	$110,000	$110,000
Fixed costs	80,000	50,000
Income from operations	$ 30,000	$ 60,000

For Jones Inc., even a small increase in sales will generate a large percentage increase in income from operations. Thus, Jones's managers may be motivated to think of ways to increase sales. In contrast, Wilson's managers might attempt to increase operating leverage by reducing variable costs and thereby change the cost structure.

Example 22 What is the operating leverage for a company with sales of $410,000, variable costs of $250,000, and fixed costs of $80,000?

2.0 [($410,000 − $250,000) ÷ ($410,000 − $250,000 − $80,000)]

Assumptions of Cost-Volume-Profit Analysis

The reliability of cost-volume-profit analysis depends upon the validity of several assumptions. The primary assumptions are as follows:

1. Total sales and total costs can be represented by straight lines.
2. Within the relevant range of operating activity, the efficiency of operations does not change.
3. Costs can be accurately divided into fixed and variable components.
4. The sales mix is constant.
5. There is no change in the inventory quantities during the period.

These assumptions simplify cost-volume-profit analysis. Because they are often valid for the relevant range of operations, cost-volume-profit analysis is useful to decision making.

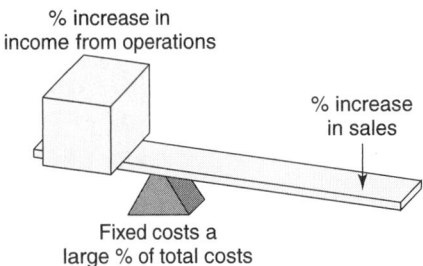

High Operating Leverage

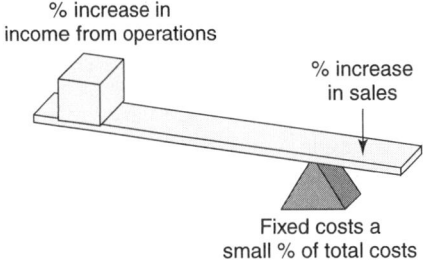

Low Operating Leverage

Product and Service Costs

Manufacturing Cost Terms

Managers rely on managerial accountants to provide useful *cost* information to support decision making. What is a cost? A **cost** is a payment of cash or its equivalent or the commitment to pay cash in the future for the purpose of generating revenues. A cost provides a benefit that is used immediately or deferred to a future period of time. If the benefit is used immediately, then the cost is an expense, such as salary expense. If the benefit is deferred, then the cost is an asset, such as equipment. As the asset is used, an expense, such as depreciation expense, is recognized.

In this section, we will illustrate manufacturing costs for Goodwell Printers, a manufacturing firm. A **manufacturing business** converts materials into a finished product through the use of machinery and labor. Goodwell Printers prints textbooks, like the one you are using now. Exhibit 600.31 provides an overview of Goodwell Printers' textbook printing operations. The Printing Department feeds large rolls of paper into printing presses. The printing presses use electricity and ink. From the Printing

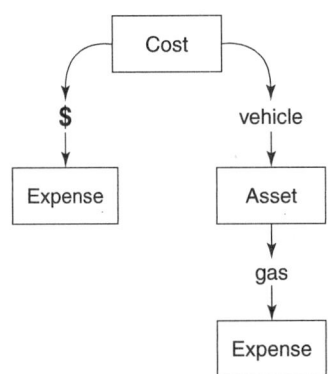

Exhibit 600.31 *Textbook Printing Operations of Goodwell Printers*

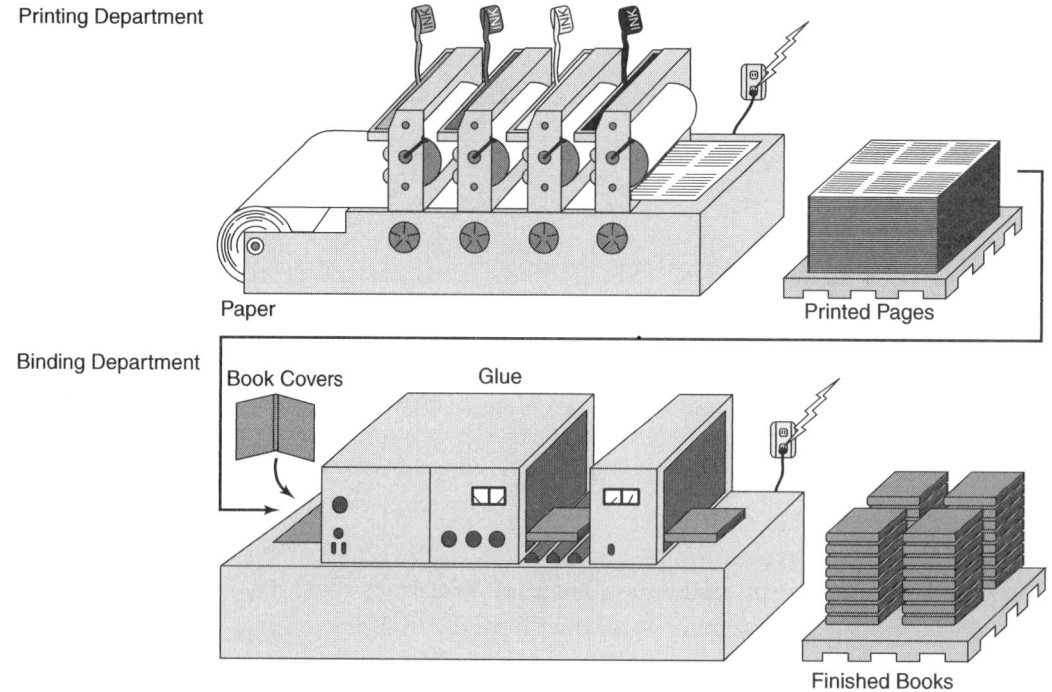

Department, the printed pages are stacked and moved to the Binding Department. In the Binding Department, the pages are cut, separated, stacked, and bound to book covers. A finished book is the final output of the Binding Department.

Materials

Some service companies also have direct materials costs. For example, fuel is a direct materials cost of a flight for an airline, while medicines are a direct materials cost to a patient in a hospital.

The cost of materials that are an integral part of the product is classified as **direct materials cost.** For example, the direct materials cost for Goodwell Printers would include paper and book covers.

As a practical matter, a direct materials cost must not only be an integral part of the finished product, but it must also be a significant portion of the total cost of the product. Other examples of direct materials costs are the cost of electronic components for a TV manufacturer and tires for an automobile manufacturer.

The costs of materials that are not a significant portion of the total product cost are termed **indirect materials.** Indirect materials are considered a part of factory overhead, which we discuss later. For Goodwell Printers, the costs of ink and binding glue are classified as indirect materials.

Factory Labor

The cost of wages of employees who are directly involved in converting materials into the manufactured product is classified as **direct labor cost.** The direct labor cost of Goodwell Printers includes the wages of the employees who operate the printing presses. Other examples of direct labor costs are carpenters' wages for a construction contractor, mechanics' wages in an automotive repair shop, machine operators' wages in a tool manufacturing plant, and assemblers' wages in a microcomputer assembly plant.

As a practical matter, a direct labor cost must not only be an integral part of the finished product, but it must also be a significant portion of the total cost of the product. For Goodwell Printers, the printing press operators' wages are a significant portion of the total cost of each book. Labor costs that do not enter directly into the manufacture of a product are termed **indirect labor** and are recorded as factory overhead. Indirect labor for Goodwell Printers might include the salaries of maintenance, plant management, and quality control personnel.

Factory Overhead Cost

Costs other than direct materials cost and direct labor cost incurred in the manufacturing process are classified as **factory overhead cost.** Factory overhead is sometimes called **manufacturing overhead** or **factory burden.** Examples of factory overhead costs, in addition to indirect materials and indirect labor, are machine depreciation, factory utilities, factory supplies, and factory insurance. In addition, payments to employees for overtime and nonproductive time (such as idle time) are considered factory overhead. For many industries, factory overhead costs are becoming a larger portion of the costs of a product as manufacturing processes become more automated.

Direct materials, direct labor, and factory overhead costs are product costs.

The direct materials, direct labor, and factory overhead costs are considered **product costs** because they are associated with making a product. The costs of converting the materials into finished products consist of direct labor and factory overhead costs, which are commonly called **conversion costs.**

Example 23 *Identify whether the following costs are direct materials, direct labor, or factory overhead for an automobile assembler: tires, quality engineering salaries, assembly wages, coil steel, painter wages, plant manager salary, cleaning fluids.*

Tires and coil steel—direct materials; assembly wages and painter wages—direct labor; quality engineering salaries, plant manager's salary, and cleaning fluids—factory overhead.

Cost Accounting System Overview

An objective of a **cost accounting system** is to accumulate product costs. Product cost information is used by managers to establish product prices, control operations, and develop financial statements. In addition, the cost accounting system improves control by supplying data on the costs incurred by each manufacturing department or process.

There are two main types of cost accounting systems for manufacturing operations: job order cost systems and process cost systems. Each of the two systems is widely used, and any one manufacturer may use more than one type.

A **job order cost system** provides a separate record for the cost of each quantity of product that passes through the factory. A particular quantity of product is termed a *job*. A job order cost system is best suited to industries that manufacture custom goods to fill special orders from customers or that produce a high variety of products for stock. Manufacturers that use a job order cost system are sometimes called **job shops.** An example of a job shop would be an apparel manufacturer, such as **Levi Strauss.**

Many service firms also use job order cost systems to accumulate the costs associated with providing client services. For example, an accounting firm will accumulate all of the costs associated with a particular client engagement, such as accountant time, copying charges, and travel costs. Recording costs in this manner helps the accounting firm control costs during a client engagement and determines client billing and profitability.

Under a **process cost system,** costs are accumulated for each of the departments or processes within the factory. A process system is best suited for manufacturers of units of product that are not distinguishable from each other during a continuous production process. An example would be an oil refinery.

Example 24 *Name two types of cost systems and a typical user of each system.*

Job order cost system: cabinet manufacturer, law practice, movie studio.
Process cost system: food processing, paper processing, metal processing, petroleum refining.

Job Order Cost Systems for Manufacturing Businesses

In this section, we will illustrate the job order cost system for a manufacturing firm, Goodwell Printers. The job order system accumulates manufacturing costs by job, as shown in Exhibit 600.32. The **materials inventory,** sometimes called **raw materials inventory,** consists of the costs of the direct and indirect materials that have not yet entered the manufacturing process. For Goodwell Printers, the materials inventory would consist of paper, ink, glue, and book covers. The **work in process inventory** consists of direct materials costs, direct labor costs, and factory overhead costs that have entered the manufacturing process but are associated with products that have not been completed. Examples are the costs of Jobs 71 and 72 that are still in the printing process shown in Exhibit 600.32. Completed jobs that have not been sold are termed **finished goods inventory.** Examples are completed printed books from Jobs 69 and 70 shown in Exhibit 600.32. Upon sale, a manufacturer will record the cost of the sale as **cost of goods sold.** An example is the case of *Physics* books sold to the bookstore in Exhibit 600.32. The *cost of goods sold* for a manufacturer is comparable to the *cost of merchandise sold* for a merchandising business.

The work in process inventory consists of direct materials, direct labor, and factory overhead costs of products not yet completed.

In a job order cost accounting system, perpetual inventory controlling accounts and subsidiary ledgers are maintained for materials, work in process, and finished goods inventories. Each inventory account is debited for all additions and is credited for all deductions. The balance of each account thus represents the balance on hand.

As with recording materials, many organizations are automating the labor-recording process. For example, in companies that build very large products, such as submarines, jet aircraft, or space vehicles, direct labor employees can be given magnetic cards, much like credit cards. These cards can be used to log in and log out of particular work assignments on particular jobs by running the card through a magnetic reader at any number of remote computer terminals.

ALLOCATING FACTORY OVERHEAD Factory overhead includes all manufacturing costs except direct materials and direct labor. Factory overhead is much different from direct labor and direct materials because it is indirectly related to the jobs. How, then, do the jobs get assigned a portion of overhead costs? The answer is through cost allocation. **Cost allocation** is the process of assigning factory overhead costs to a cost object, such as a job. The factory overhead costs are assigned to the jobs on the basis of some known measure about each job. The measure used to allocate factory overhead is frequently called an **activity base, allocation base,** or **activity driver.** The estimated activity base should be a measure that reflects the consumption or use of factory overhead cost. For example, the direct labor is recorded for each job using time tickets. Thus, direct labor could be used to allocate production-related factory overhead costs to each job. Likewise, direct materials costs are known about each job through the materials requisitions. Thus, materials-related factory overhead, such as Purchasing Department salaries, could logically be allocated to the job on the basis of direct materials cost.

PREDETERMINED FACTORY OVERHEAD RATE In order that job costs may be currently available, factory overhead may be allocated or applied to production using a **predetermined factory overhead rate.** The predetermined factory overhead rate is calculated by dividing the estimated amount of factory overhead for the forthcoming year by the estimated activity base, such as machine hours, direct materials costs, direct labor costs, or direct labor hours.

Exhibit 600.32 *Manufacturing Costs and Jobs*

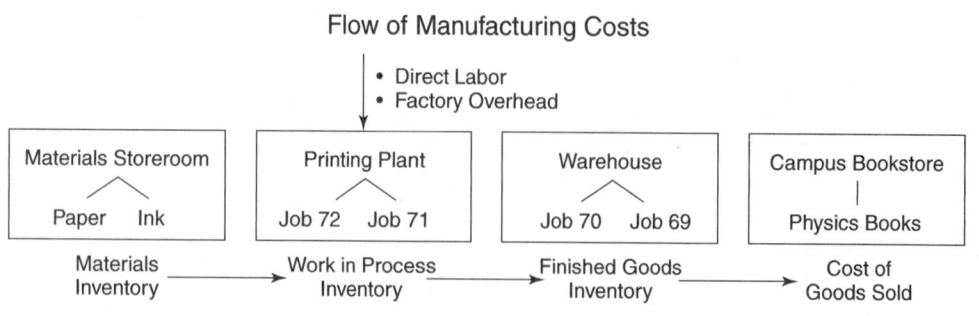

To illustrate calculating a predetermined overhead rate, assume that Goodwell Printers estimates the total factory overhead cost to be $50,000 for the year and the activity base to be 10,000 direct labor hours. The predetermined factory overhead rate would be calculated as $5 per direct labor hour, as follows.

$$\text{Predetermined factory overhead rate} = \frac{\text{Estimated total factory overhead costs}}{\text{Estimated activity base}}$$

$$\text{Predetermined factory overhead rate} = \frac{\$50,000}{10,000 \text{ direct labor hours}} = \$5 \text{ per direct labor hour}$$

Why is the predetermined overhead rate calculated from estimated numbers at the beginning of the period? The answer is *to ensure timely information.* If a company waited until the end of an accounting period when all overhead costs are known, the allocated factory overhead would be accurate but not timely. If the cost system is to have maximum usefulness, cost data should be available as each job is completed, even though there may be a small sacrifice in accuracy. Only through timely reporting can management make needed adjustments in pricing or in manufacturing methods and achieve the best possible combination of revenue and cost on future jobs.

A number of companies are using a new product-costing approach called activity-based costing. **Activity-based costing** is a method of accumulating and allocating factory overhead costs to products using many overhead rates. Each rate is related to separate factory activities, such as inspecting, moving, and machining.

Example 25 *Factory overhead costs are estimated to be $120,000. Direct labor hours are estimated to be 20,000 hours. Determine (a) the predetermined factory overhead rate and (b) the amount of factory overhead applied to a job with 30 direct labor hours.*

(a) $6 per hour ($120,000/20,000); (b) $180 ($6 × 30 hours)

APPLYING FACTORY OVERHEAD The factory overhead costs applied and the actual factory overhead costs incurred during a period will usually differ. If the amount applied exceeds the actual costs incurred, the factory overhead account will have a credit balance. This credit is described as **overapplied** or **overabsorbed factory overhead.** If the amount applied is less than the actual costs incurred, the account will have a debit balance.

If the underapplied or overapplied balance increases in only one direction and it becomes large, the balance and the overhead rate should be investigated. For example, if a large balance is caused by changes in manufacturing methods or in production goals, the factory overhead rate should be revised. On the other hand, a large underapplied balance may indicate a serious control problem caused by inefficiencies in production methods, excessive costs, or a combination of factors.

DISPOSAL OF FACTORY OVERHEAD BALANCE The balance in the factory overhead account is carried forward from month to month. It is reported on interim balance sheets as a deferred debit or credit. This balance should not be carried over to the next year, however, since it applies to the operations of the year just ended.

One approach for disposing of the balance of factory overhead at the end of the year is to transfer the entire balance to the cost of goods sold account. A more complex approach involves disposing of the balance among the work in process, finished goods, and cost of goods sold accounts.

Cost of Goods Sold

Just as there are various methods of costing materials entering into production, there are various methods of determining the cost of the finished goods sold. Examples include the first-in, first-out (FIFO) method and the last-in, first-out (LIFO) method.

Example 26 *Boxer Company completed 80,000 units at a cost of $680,000. The beginning finished goods inventory was 10,000 units at $80,000. What is the cost of goods sold for 60,000 units, assuming a FIFO cost flow?*

$505,000 [$80,000 + (50,000 × $8.50)]

Exhibit 600.33 *Income Statement of Goodwell Printers*

Goodwell Printers
Income Statement
for the Month Ended December 31, 2004

Sales		$28,000
Cost of goods sold		20,150
Gross profit		$ 7,850
Selling and administrative expenses:		
Sales salaries expense	$2,000	
Office salaries expense	1,500	
Total selling and administrative expenses		3,500
Income from operations		$ 4,350

Period Costs

In addition to product costs (direct materials, direct labor, and factory overhead), businesses also have period costs. **Period costs** are expenses that are used in generating revenue during the current period and are not involved in the manufacturing process. Period costs are generally classified into two categories: selling and administrative. **Selling expenses** are incurred in marketing the product and delivering the sold product to customers. **Administrative expenses** are incurred in the administration of the business and are not related to the manufacturing or selling functions. The income statement for Goodwell Printers would be as shown in Exhibit 600.33. Assume that Goodwell Printers sold 2,000 American history textbooks during December for $14 per unit, giving a total of $28,000 sales.

The cost of goods sold is $20,150, which includes $20,000 for direct materials, direct labor, and factory overhead cost computed at $10/unit. The cost of goods sold also includes $150 underapplied factory overhead.

Two items of period costs include $2,000 for sales salaries expense and $1,500 for office salaries expense.

Service companies, such as telecommunications, insurance, banking, broadcasting, and hospitality, typically have a large portion of their total costs as period costs. This is because most service companies do not have products that can be inventoried, and hence, they do not have product costs.

Examples of Period Costs

Selling Expenses
- Advertising expenses
- Sales salaries expenses
- Commission expenses

Administrative Expenses
- Office salaries expenses
- Office supplies expenses
- Depreciation expense–office buildings and equipment

Job Order Costing for Decision Making

The job order cost system that we developed in the previous sections can be used to evaluate an organization's cost performance. The unit costs for similar jobs can be compared over time to determine if costs are staying within expected ranges. If costs increase for some unexpected reason, the details in the job cost sheets can help discover the reasons.

To illustrate, Exhibit 600.34 shows the direct materials on the job cost sheets for Jobs 144 and 163 for a furniture company. Since both job cost sheets refer to the same type and number of chairs, the direct materials cost per unit should be about the same. However, the materials cost per chair for Job 144 is $28, while for Job 163 it is $35. For some reason, materials costs have increased since the folding chairs were produced for Job 144.

Job cost sheets can be used to investigate possible reasons for the increased cost. First, you should note that the rate for direct materials did not change. Thus, the cost increase is not related to increasing prices. What about the wood consumption? This tells us a different story. The quantity of wood used to produce 200 chairs in Job 144 is 1,600 board feet. However, Job 163 required 2,000 board feet. How can this be explained? Any one of the following explanations is possible and could be investigated further:

Exhibit 600.34 *Comparing Data from Job Cost Sheets*

Job 144
Item: 200 folding chairs

	Materials Quantity (board feet)	Materials Price	Materials Amount
Direct materials:			
Wood	1,600	$3.50	$5,600
Direct materials per chair			$28

Job 163
Item: 200 folding chairs

	Materials Quantity (board feet)	Materials Price	Materials Amount
Direct materials:			
Wood	2,000	$3.50	$7,000
Direct materials per chair			$35

1. There was a new employee who was not adequately trained for cutting the wood for chairs. As a result, the employee improperly cut and scrapped many pieces.
2. The lumber was of poor quality. As a result, the cutting operator ended up using and scrapping additional pieces of lumber.
3. The cutting tools were in need of repair. As a result, the cutting operators miscut and scrapped many pieces of wood.
4. The operator was careless. As a result of poor work, many pieces of cut wood had to be scrapped.
5. The instructions attached to the job were incorrect. The operator cut wood according to the instructions but discovered that the pieces would not fit. As a result, many pieces had to be scrapped.

You should note that many of these explanations are not necessarily related to operator error. Poor cost performance may be the result of root causes that are outside the control of the operator.

Job Order Cost Systems for Professional Service Businesses

A job order cost accounting system may be useful to the management of a professional service business in planning and controlling operations. For example, an advertising agency, an attorney, and a physician all share the common characteristic of providing services to individual customers, clients, or patients. In such cases, the customer, client, or patient can be viewed as an individual job for which costs are accumulated.

Because the "product" of a service business is service, management's focus is on direct labor and overhead costs. The cost of any materials or supplies used in rendering services for a client is usually small and is normally included as part of the overhead.

The direct labor and overhead costs of rendering services to clients are accumulated in a work-in-process account. This account is supported by a cost ledger. A job cost sheet is used to accumulate the costs for each client's job. When a job is completed and the client is billed, the costs are transferred to a cost of services account. This account is similar to the cost of merchandise sold account for a merchandising business or the cost of goods sold account for a manufacturing business. A finished goods account and related finished goods ledger are not necessary, since the revenues associated with the services are recorded after the services have been provided. The flow of costs through a service business using a job order cost accounting system is shown in Exhibit 600.35.

In practice, additional accounting considerations unique to service businesses may need to be considered. For example, a service business may bill clients on a weekly or monthly basis rather than waiting until a job is completed. In these situations, a portion of the costs related to each billing should be transferred from the work-in-process account to the cost-of-services account. A service business may also have advance billings that would be accounted for as deferred revenue until the services have been completed.

Exhibit 600.35 *Flow of Costs Through a Service Business*

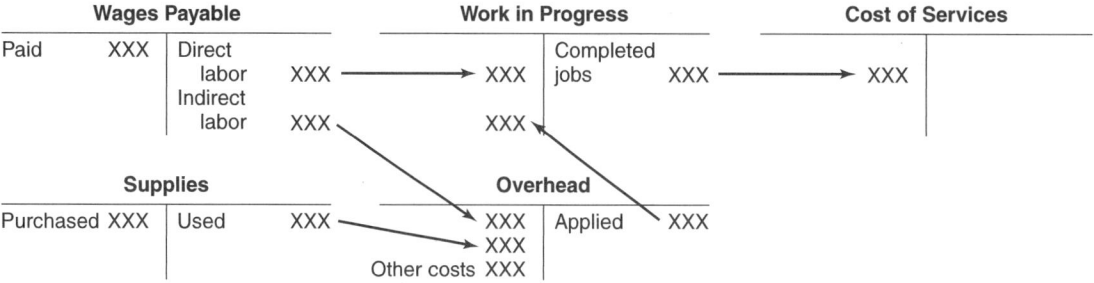

Process Cost Systems

If you bake cookies, the ingredients would include flour, sugar, and shortening. These ingredients would all be added at the beginning of the baking process by mixing them in a bowl. After mixing, do you have cookies? No. Why? Because they aren't baked (converted). But are they 100 percent complete with respect to materials? Yes, all the materials have been added to the baking process. When will they be cookies? When they are 100 percent complete with respect to materials *and* baking.

Now, assume that you ask the question, "How much cost have I incurred in baking cookies after 15 minutes (out of 30 minutes) of baking time?" The answer would require that you separate the ingredients and the electricity costs. These two costs are incurred in the baking process at different rates, and so it is convenient to identify them separately. The ingredient costs have all been incurred, since they were all introduced at the beginning of the process. The electricity costs, however, are a different story. Since the baking is only 50 percent complete, only 50 percent of the electricity costs (for the oven) have been incurred in the baking process. Therefore, the answer to the question is that all the materials costs and half the electricity costs have been incurred in the baking process after 15 minutes of baking.

In this section, we apply these concepts to manufacturers that use a process cost system. After introducing process costing, we discuss decision making with process cost system reports. We conclude the section with a brief discussion of just-in-time cost systems.

Comparing Job Order Costing and Process Costing

The job order cost system is best suited to industries that make special orders for customers or manufacture different products in groups. Industries that may use job order cost systems include special-order printing, custom-made tailoring, furniture manufacturing, shipbuilding, aircraft building, and construction. Process manufacturing is different from job-order manufacturing. **Process manufacturers** typically use large machines to process a flow of raw materials into a finished state. For example, a petrochemical business processes crude oil through numerous refining steps to produce higher grades of oil until gasoline is produced. The cost accounting system used by process manufacturers is called the **process cost system.**

In some ways, the process cost and job order cost systems are similar. Both systems accumulate product costs—direct materials, direct labor, and factory overhead—and allocate these costs to the units produced. Both systems maintain perpetual inventory accounts with subsidiary ledgers for materials, work in process, and finished goods. Both systems also provide product cost data to management for planning, directing, improving, controlling, and decision making. The main difference between the two systems is the form in which the product costs are accumulated and reported.

Exhibit 600.36 illustrates the main differences between the job order and process cost systems. In a job order cost system, product costs are accumulated by job and are summarized on job cost sheets. The job cost sheets provide unit cost information and can be used by management for product pricing, cost control, and inventory valuation. The process manufacturer does not manufacture according to "jobs." Thus, costs are accumulated by department. Each unit of product that passes through the department is similar. Thus, the production costs reported by each department provide unit cost information that can be used by management for cost control. In a job order cost system, the work-in-process inventory at the end of the accounting period is the sum of the job cost sheets for partially completed jobs. In a process cost system, the amount of work-in-process inventory is determined by allocating costs between completed and partially completed units within a department.

Process manufacturers accumulate costs by department.

Exhibit 600.36 *Job Order and Process Cost Systems Compared*

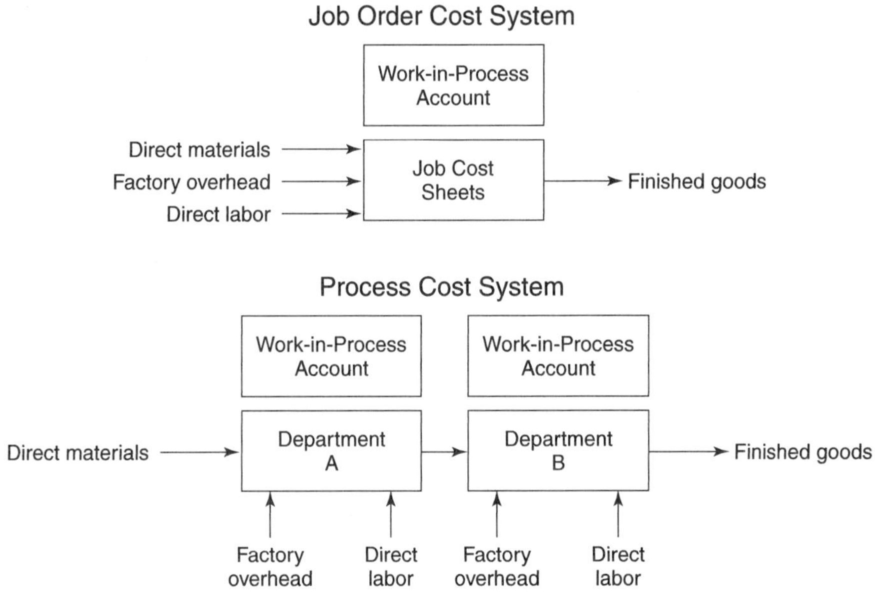

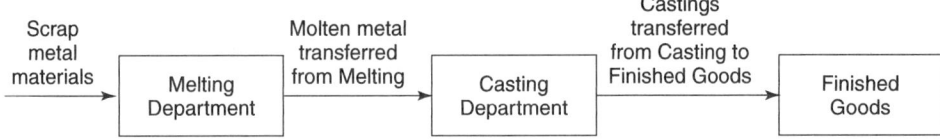

Exhibit 600.37 *Physical Flows for a Process Manufacturer*

Physical Flows and Cost Flows for a Process Manufacturer

Materials costs are a large portion of the costs for most process manufacturers. Often, the materials costs can be as high as 70 percent of the total manufacturing costs. Thus, accounting for materials costs is very important for process operations.

Exhibit 600.37 illustrates the physical flow of materials for a steel processor. Direct materials in the form of scrap metal are placed into a furnace in the Melting Department. The Melting Department uses conversion costs (direct labor and factory overhead) during the melting process. The molten metal is then transferred to the Casting Department, where it is poured into an ingot casting. The Casting Department also uses conversion costs during the casting process. The ingot castings are transferred to the finished goods inventory for shipment to customers.

The cost flows in a process cost system reflect the physical materials flows.

The First-In, First-Out (FIFO) Method

In a process cost system, the accountant determines the cost transferred out and thus the amount remaining in inventory for each department. For many manufacturing processes, materials are added at the beginning of production, and the units are moved through the production processes in a **first-in, first-out (FIFO)** flow. That is, the first units entering the production process are the first to be completed.

We assume that all materials used in the department are added at the beginning of the process, and conversion costs (direct labor and factory overhead) are incurred evenly throughout the melting process. The objective is to determine the cost of goods completed and the ending inventory valuation. We determine these amounts by using the following four steps.

1. Determine the units to be assigned costs.
2. Calculate equivalent units of production.
3. Determine the cost per equivalent unit.
4. Allocate costs to transferred and partially completed units.

Bringing It All Together: The Cost of Production Report

A **cost of production report** is normally prepared for each processing department at periodic intervals.
The report summarizes the four previous steps by providing the following production quantity and cost data:

1. The units for which the department is accountable and the disposition of those units
2. The production costs incurred by the department and the allocation of those costs between completed and partially completed units

The cost of production report is also used to control costs. Each department manager is responsible for the units entering production and the costs incurred in the department. Any failure to account for all costs and any significant differences in unit product costs from one month to another should be investigated.

Using the Cost of Production Report for Decision Making

The cost of production report is one source of information that may be used by managers to control and improve operations. This greater detail helps management isolate problems and opportunities. To illustrate, assume that the Blending Department of Holland Beverage Company prepared cost of production reports for April and May. In addition, assume that the Blending Department had no beginning or ending work-in-process inventory either month. Thus, in this simple case, there is no need to determine equivalent units of production for allocating costs between completed and partially completed units. The cost of production reports for April and May in the Blending Department are as follows:

Cost of Production Reports
Holland Beverage Company—Blending Department
for the Months Ended April 30 and May 31, 2004

	April	May
Direct materials	$ 20,000	$ 40,600
Direct labor	15,000	29,400
Energy	8,000	20,000
Repairs	4,000	8,000
Tank cleaning	3,000	8,000
Total	$ 50,000	$106,000
Units completed	÷ 100,000	÷ 200,000
Cost per unit	$ 0.50	$ 0.53

Note that the preceding reports provide more cost detail than simply reporting direct materials and conversion costs. The May results indicate that total unit costs have increased from $0.50 to $0.53, or 6 percent from the previous month. What caused this increase? To determine the possible causes for this increase, the cost of production report may be restated in per-unit terms, as shown on the next page.

Blending Department Per-Unit Expense Comparisons			
	April	May	% Change
Direct materials	$0.200	$0.203	1.50%
Direct labor	0.150	0.147	−2.00%
Energy	0.080	0.100	25.00%
Repairs	0.040	0.040	0.00%
Tank cleaning	0.030	0.040	33.33%
Total	$0.500	$0.530	6.00%

Both energy and tank cleaning per-unit costs have increased dramatically in May. Further investigation should focus on these costs. For example, an increasing trend in energy may indicate that the machines are losing fuel efficiency, thereby requiring the company to purchase an increasing amount of fuel. This unfavorable trend could motivate management to repair the machines. The tank cleaning costs could be investigated in a similar fashion.

In addition to unit production cost trends, managers of process manufacturers are also concerned about yield trends. **Yield** is the ratio of the materials output quantity to the input quantity. A yield less than one occurs when the output quantity is less than the input quantity due to materials losses during the process. For example, if 1,000 pounds of sugar entered the packing operation, and only 980 pounds of sugar were packed, the yield would be 98 percent. Two percent or 20 pounds of sugar were lost or spilled during the packing process.

Operating Budgets and Performance Evaluation

Operating Budgets

You may have financial goals for your life. To achieve these goals, it is necessary to plan for future expenses. For example, you may consider taking a part-time job to save money for school expenses for the coming school year. How much money would you need to earn and save in order to pay these expenses? One way to answer this question would be to prepare a budget. For example, a budget would show an estimate of your expenses associated with school, such as tuition, fees, and books. In addition, you would have expenses for day-to-day living, such as rent, food, and clothing. You might also have expenses for travel and entertainment. Once the school year begins, you can use the budget as a tool for guiding your spending priorities during the year.

The budget is used in businesses in much the same way as it can be used in personal life. For example, **Daimler-Chrysler** uses budgeting to determine the number of cars to be produced, number of shifts to operate, number of people to be employed, and amount of material to be purchased. The budget provides the company a "game plan" for the year. In this section, you will see how budgets can be used for financial planning and control.

Nature and Objectives of Budgeting

If you were driving across the country, you might plan your trip with the aid of a road map. The road map would lay out your route across the country, identify stopovers, and reduce your chances of getting lost. In the same way, a **budget** charts a course for a business by outlining the plans of the business in financial terms. Like the road map, the budget can help a company navigate through the year and reduce negative outcomes.

Although budgets are normally associated with profit-making businesses, they also play an important role in operating most units of government. For example, budgets are important in managing rural school districts and small villages as well as agencies of the federal government. Budgets are also important for managing the operations of churches, hospitals, and other nonprofit institutions. Individuals and families also use budgeting techniques in managing their financial affairs. In this chapter, we discuss the principles of budgeting in the context of a business organized for profit.

Objectives of Budgeting

Budgeting involves (1) establishing specific goals, (2) executing plans to achieve the goals, and (3) periodically comparing actual results with the goals. These goals include both the overall business goals as well as the specific goals for the individual units within the business. Establishing specific goals for future operations is part of the *planning* function of management, while executing actions to meet the goals is the *directing* function of management. Periodically comparing actual results with these goals and taking appropriate action is the *controlling* function of management. The relationships of these functions are illustrated in Exhibit 600.38.

PLANNING   A set of goals is often necessary to guide and focus individual and group actions. For example, students set academic goals, athletes set athletic goals, employees set career goals, and businesses set financial goals. In the same way, budgeting supports the planning process by requiring all organizational units to establish their goals for the upcoming period. These goals, in turn, motivate individuals and groups to perform at high levels. For example, **Florida Power and Light (FP&L),** an electric utility, announced plans to reduce costs by 8 percent of its total budget in order to maintain its target profitability. Using the budget to communicate these expectations throughout the organization helped FP&L to reach its target. Without the budget establishing this clear expectation, these results would have been very difficult to achieve.

Planning not only motivates employees to attain goals but also improves overall decision making. During the planning phase of the budget process, all viewpoints are considered, options identified, and cost-reduction opportunities assessed. This effort leads to better decision making for the organization. As a result, the budget process may reveal opportunities or threats that were not known prior to the budget planning process. For example, the financial planning process helped **General Motors** identify the high costs associated with its far-flung parts operations. As a result, GM decided to sell over 45 lines of businesses (radiator caps, vacuum pumps, electric motors, etc.) in order to focus on its core auto-making business.

DIRECTING   Once the budget plans are in place, they can be used to direct and coordinate operations in order to achieve the stated goals. For example, your goal to receive an "A" in a course would result in certain activities, such as reading the book, completing assignments, participating in class, and studying for exams. Such actions are fairly easy to direct and coordinate. A business, however, is much more complex and requires more formal direction and coordination. The budget is one way to direct and coordinate business activities and units to achieve stated goals. The budgetary units of an organization are called **responsibility centers.** Each responsibility center is led by a manager who has the authority over and responsibility for the unit's performance.

If there is a change in the external environment, the budget process can also be used by unit managers to readjust the operations. For example, **SKI Ltd.** uses weather information to plan expenditures at its Killington and Mt. Snow ski resorts in Vermont. When the weather is forecasted to turn cold and dry, the company increases expenditures in snow-making activities and adds to the staff in order to serve a greater number of skiers.

CONTROLLING   As time passes, the actual performance of an operation can be compared against the planned goals. This provides prompt feedback to employees about their performance. If necessary, employees can use such **feedback** to adjust their activities in the future. For example, a salesperson may be given a quota to achieve $100,000 in sales for the period. If the actual sales are only $75,000, the salesperson can use this feedback about underperformance to change sales tactics and improve future sales. Feedback is not only helpful to individuals, but it can also redirect a complete or-

Exhibit 600.38 *Planning, Directing, and Controlling*

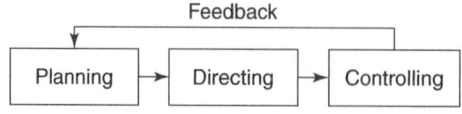

ganization. For example, the Coca-Cola Company slashed its workforce by 20 percent, or 6,000 employees, as a result of the company reporting its first quarterly earnings loss in a decade.

Comparing actual results to the plan also helps prevent unplanned expenditures. The budget encourages employees to establish their spending priorities. For example, departments in universities have budgets to support faculty travel to conferences and meetings. The travel budget communicates to the faculty the upper limit on travel. Often, desired travel exceeds the budget. Thus, the budget requires the faculty to prioritize travel-related opportunities. Later in this module, we will discuss comparing actual costs with budgeted costs in greater detail.

Human Behavior and Budgeting

In the budgeting process, business, team, and individual goals are established. Human behavior problems can arise if (1) the budget goal is unachievable (too tight), (2) the budget goal is very easy to achieve (too loose), or (3) the budget goals of the business conflict with the objectives of employees (goal conflict).

SETTING BUDGET GOALS TOO TIGHTLY People can become discouraged if performance expectations are set too high. For example, would you be inspired or discouraged by a guitar instructor expecting you to play like Eric Clapton after only a few lessons? You'd probably be discouraged. This same kind of problem can occur in businesses if employees view budget goals as unrealistic or unachievable. In such a case, the budget discourages employees from achieving the goals. On the other hand, aggressive but attainable goals are likely to inspire employees to achieve the goals. Therefore, it is important that employees (managers and nonmanagers) be involved in establishing reasonable budget estimates.

Involving all employees encourages cooperation both within and among departments. It also increases awareness of each department's importance to the overall objectives of the company. Employees view budgeting more positively when they have an opportunity to participate in the budget-setting process. This is because employees with a greater sense of control over the budget process will have a greater commitment to achieving its goals. In such cases, budgets are valuable planning tools that increase the possibility of achieving business goals.

SETTING BUDGET GOALS TOO LOOSELY Although it is desirable to establish attainable goals, it is undesirable to plan lower goals than may be possible. Such budget "padding" is termed **budgetary slack.** An example of budgetary slack is including spare employees in the plan. Managers may plan slack in the budget in order to provide a "cushion" for unexpected events or improve the appearance of operations. Budgetary slack can be avoided if lower- and mid-level managers are required to support their spending requirements with operational plans.

There is strong evidence that loose budgets may be appropriate in settings involving high uncertainty, such as research and development. The loose budget acts as a sort of "shock absorber," giving managers maneuvering room to minimize work disruptions.

Slack budgets can cause employees to develop a "spend it or lose it" mentality. This often occurs at the end of the budget period when actual spending is much less than the budget. Employees may attempt to spend the remaining budget (purchase equipment, hire consultants, purchase supplies) in order to avoid having the budget cut next period.

SETTING CONFLICTING BUDGET GOALS **Goal conflict** occurs when individual self-interest differs from business objectives. To illustrate, the manager of the Transportation Department of one company was instructed to stay within the department's budget. To meet the budget goal, the manager stopped transporting all shipments for the last two weeks of the period. Though the Transportation Department budget was met, customers were upset because they did not receive their orders. As a result, many customers stopped doing business with the company or demanded price discounts that far exceeded the additional transportation costs that should have been spent. In this example, the budget pressure caused the Transportation Department manager to make a decision that appeared correct from the department's view but was harmful to the business. Goal conflict can be avoided if budget goals are carefully designed for consistency across all areas of the organization.

Budgeting Systems

Budgeting systems vary among businesses because of such factors as organizational structure, complexity of operations, and management philosophy. Differences in budget systems are even more significant among different types of businesses,

Exhibit 600.39 *Continuous Budgeting*

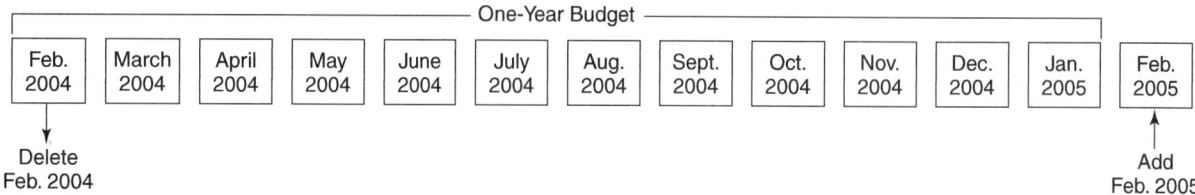

such as manufacturers and service businesses. The details of a budgeting system used by an automobile manufacturer such as **Ford** would obviously differ from a service company such as American Airlines. However, the basic budgeting concepts illustrated in the following paragraphs apply to all types of businesses and organizations.

The budgetary period for operating activities normally includes the fiscal year of a business. A year is short enough that future operations can be estimated fairly accurately, yet long enough that the future can be viewed in a broad context. However, to achieve effective control, the annual budgets are usually subdivided into shorter time periods, such as quarters of the year, months, or weeks.

A variation of fiscal-year budgeting, called **continuous budgeting,** maintains a 12-month projection into the future. The 12-month budget is continually revised by removing the data for the period just ended and adding estimated budget data for the same period next year, as shown in Exhibit 600.39.

Developing budgets for the next fiscal year usually begins several months prior to the end of the current year. This responsibility is normally assigned to a budget committee. Such a committee often consists of the budget director and such high-level executives as the controller, the treasurer, the production manager, and the sales manager. Once the budget has been approved, the budget process is monitored and summarized by the Accounting Department, which reports to the committee.

There are several methods of developing budget estimates. One method, termed **zero-based budgeting,** requires managers to estimate sales, production, and other operating data as though operations are being started for the first time. This approach has the benefit of taking a fresh view of operations each year. A more common approach is to start with last year's budget and revise it for actual results and expected changes for the coming year. Two major budgets using this approach are the static budget and the flexible budget.

Static Budget

A **static budget** shows the expected results of a responsibility center for only one activity level. Once the budget has been determined, it is not changed, even if the activity changes. Static budgeting is used by many service companies and for some administrative functions of manufacturing companies, such as purchasing, engineering, and accounting. For example, the Assembly Department manager for Colter Manufacturing Company prepared the static budget for the upcoming year, shown in Exhibit 600.40.

A disadvantage of static budgets is that they do not adjust for changes in activity levels. For example, assume that the actual amounts spent by the Assembly Department of Colter Manufacturing totaled $72,000, which is $12,000 or 20 percent ($12,000 ÷ $60,000) more than budgeted. Is this good news or bad news? At first you might think that this is a bad result. However, this conclusion may not be valid, as static budget results may be difficult to interpret. To illustrate, assume that the assembly manager constructed the budget based on plans to assemble *8,000* units during the year. However, *10,000* units were actually produced, which represents 25 percent (2,000 ÷ 8,000) more work than expected. Should the additional $12,000 in spending in excess of the budget be considered "bad news"? Maybe not. The Assembly Department provided 25 percent more output for only 20 percent additional cost.

Exhibit 600.40 *Static Budget*

Colter Manufacturing Company Assembly Department Budget for the Year Ending July 31, 2004	
Direct labor	$40,000
Electric power	5,000
Supervisor salaries	15,000
Total department costs	$60,000

Exhibit 600.41 *Flexible Budget*

Colter Manufacturing Company Assembly Department Budget for the Year Ending July 31, 2004			
Units of production	8,000	9,000	10,000
Variable cost:			
Direct labor ($5 per unit)	$40,000	$45,000	$50,000
Electric power ($0.50 per unit)	4,000	4,500	5,000
Total variable cost	$44,000	$49,500	$55,000
Fixed cost:			
Electric power	$ 1,000	$ 1,000	$ 1,000
Supervisor salaries	15,000	15,000	15,000
Total fixed cost	$16,000	$16,000	$16,000
Total department costs	$60,000	$65,500	$71,000

Exhibit 600.42 *Static and Flexible Budgets*

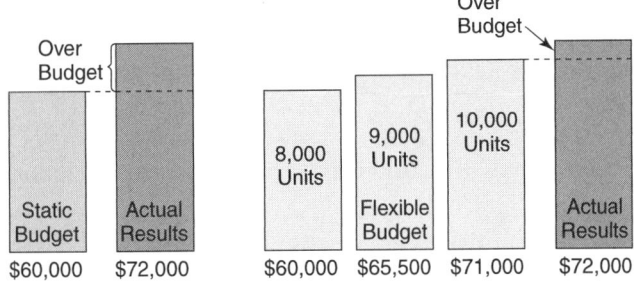

Flexible Budget

Unlike static budgets, **flexible budgets** show the expected results of a responsibility center for several activity levels. You can think of a flexible budget as a series of static budgets for different levels of activity. Such budgets are especially useful in estimating and controlling factory costs and operating expenses. Exhibit 600.41 is a flexible budget for the annual manufacturing expense in the Assembly Department of Colter Manufacturing Company.

Flexible budgets show expected results for several activity levels.

When constructing a flexible budget, we first identify the relevant activity levels. In Exhibit 600.41, there are 8,000, 9,000, and 10,000 units of production. Alternative activity bases, such as machine hours or direct labor hours, may be used in measuring the volume of activity. Second, we identify the fixed and variable cost components of the costs being budgeted. For example, in Exhibit 600.41, the electric power cost is separated into its fixed cost ($1,000 per month) and variable cost ($0.50 per unit). Lastly, we prepare the budget for each activity level by multiplying the variable cost per unit by the activity level and then adding the monthly fixed cost.

With a flexible budget, the department manager can be evaluated by comparing actual expenses to the budgeted amount for actual activity. For example, if Colter Manufacturing Company's Assembly Department actually spent $72,000 to produce 10,000 units, the manager would be considered over budget by $1,000 ($72,000 − $71,000). Under the static budget in Exhibit 600.40, the department was $12,000 over budget. This comparison is illustrated in Exhibit 600.42. The flexible budget for the Assembly Department is much more accurate than the static budget, because budget amounts adjust for changes in activity.

650. OPERATING BUDGETS AND PERFORMANCE EVALUATION

> **Example 27** At the beginning of the period, the Assembly Department budgeted direct labor of $45,000 and supervisor salaries of $30,000 for 5,000 hours of production. The department actually completed 6,000 hours of production. What is the appropriate total budget for the department, assuming that it uses flexible budgeting?
>
> $84,000 [($9 × 6,000) + $30,000]

Computerized Budgeting Systems

In developing budgets, many firms use computerized budgeting systems. Such systems speed up and reduce the cost of preparing the budget. This is especially true when large quantities of data need to be processed. Computers are also useful in continuous budgeting. Reports that compare actual results with amounts budgeted can also be prepared on a timely basis through the use of computerized systems. For example, **Fujitsu** used Enterprise Resource Planning (ERP) software to streamline its budgeting process from 6 to 8 weeks down to 10 to 15 days.

Managers often use computer spreadsheets or simulation models to represent the operating and budget relationships. By using computer simulation models, the impact of various operating alternatives on the budget can be assessed. For example, the budget can be revised to show the impact of a proposed change in indirect labor wage rates. Likewise, the budgetary effect of a proposed product line can be determined.

A common objective of using computer-based budgeting is to tie all the budgets of the organization together. In the next section, we will illustrate how a company ties its budgets together to develop a complete plan.

Master Budget

Manufacturing operations require a series of budgets that are linked together in a **master budget**. The major parts of the master budget are as follows:

Budgeted Income Statement	Budgeted Balance Sheet
Sales budget	Cash budget
Cost of goods sold budget:	Capital expenditures budget
Production budget	
Direct materials purchases budget	
Direct labor cost budget	
Factory overhead cost budget	
Selling and administrative expenses budget	

Exhibit 600.43 shows the relationship among the income statement budgets. The budget process begins by estimating sales. The sales information is then provided to the various units for estimating the production and selling and administrative expenses budgets. The production budgets are used to prepare the direct materials purchases, direct labor cost, and factory overhead cost budgets. These three budgets are used to develop the cost of goods sold budget. Once these budgets and the selling and administrative expenses budget have been completed, the budgeted income statement can be prepared.

After the budgeted income statement has been developed, the budgeted balance sheet can be prepared. Two major budgets comprising the budgeted balance sheet are the cash budget and the capital expenditures budget.

Income Statement Budgets

In the following sections, we will illustrate the major elements of the income statement budget. We will use a small manufacturing business, Elite Accessories Inc., as the basis for our illustration.

Exhibit 600.43 *Income Statement Budgets*

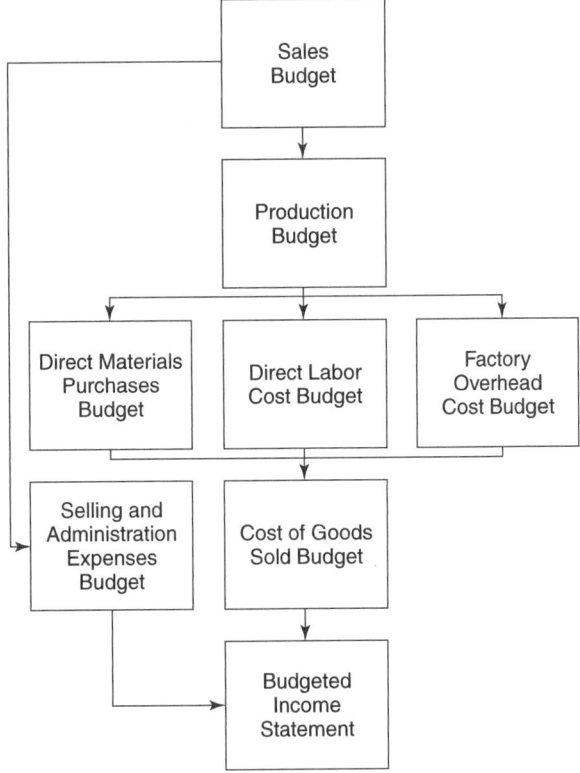

Sales Budget

The **sales budget** normally indicates for each product (1) the quantity of estimated sales and (2) the expected unit selling price. These data are often reported by region or by sales representatives.

In estimating the quantity of sales for each product, past sales volumes are often used as a starting point. These amounts are revised for factors that are expected to affect future sales, such as the factors listed below.

- backlog of unfilled sales orders
- planned advertising and promotion
- expected industry and general economic conditions
- productive capacity
- projected pricing policy
- findings of market research studies

Once an estimate of the sales volume is obtained, the expected sales revenue can be determined by multiplying the volume by the expected unit sales price. Exhibit 600.44 is the sales budget for Elite Accessories Inc.

For control purposes, management can compare actual sales and budgeted sales by product, region, or sales representative. Management would investigate any significant differences and take possible corrective actions.

Production Budget

Production should be carefully coordinated with the sales budget to ensure that production and sales are kept in balance during the period. The number of units to be manufactured to meet budgeted sales and inventory needs for each product is set forth in the **production budget.** The budgeted volume of production is determined as follows:

```
    Expected units to be sold
+   Desired units in ending inventory
−   Estimated units in beginning inventory
    ─────────────────────────────────
    Total units to be produced
```

650. OPERATING BUDGETS AND PERFORMANCE EVALUATION

Exhibit 600.44 *Sales Budget*

<table>
<tr><td colspan="4" align="center">Elite Accessories Inc.
Sales Budget
for the Year Ending December 31, 2004</td></tr>
<tr><th>Product and Region</th><th>Unit Sales Volume</th><th>Unit Selling Price</th><th>Total Sales</th></tr>
<tr><td>Wallet:</td><td></td><td></td><td></td></tr>
<tr><td>East</td><td>287,000</td><td>$12.00</td><td>$ 3,444,000</td></tr>
<tr><td>West</td><td>241,000</td><td>12.00</td><td>2,892,000</td></tr>
<tr><td>Total</td><td>528,000</td><td></td><td>$ 6,336,000</td></tr>
<tr><td>Handbag:</td><td></td><td></td><td></td></tr>
<tr><td>East</td><td>156,400</td><td>$25.00</td><td>$ 3,910,000</td></tr>
<tr><td>West</td><td>123,600</td><td>25.00</td><td>3,090,000</td></tr>
<tr><td>Total</td><td>280,000</td><td></td><td>$ 7,000,000</td></tr>
<tr><td>Total revenue from sales</td><td></td><td></td><td>$13,336,000</td></tr>
</table>

Exhibit 600.45 is the production budget for Elite Accessories Inc.

Exhibit 600.45 *Production Budget*

<table>
<tr><td colspan="3" align="center">Elite Accessories Inc.
Production Budget
for the Year Ending December 31, 2004</td></tr>
<tr><th></th><th colspan="2">Units</th></tr>
<tr><th></th><th>Wallet</th><th>Handbag</th></tr>
<tr><td>Expected units to be sold (from Exhibit 600.44)</td><td>528,000</td><td>280,000</td></tr>
<tr><td>Plus desired ending inventory, December 31, 2003</td><td>80,000</td><td>60,000</td></tr>
<tr><td>Total</td><td>608,000</td><td>340,000</td></tr>
<tr><td>Less estimated beginning inventory, January 1, 2003</td><td>88,000</td><td>48,000</td></tr>
<tr><td>Total units to be produced</td><td>520,000</td><td>292,000</td></tr>
</table>

Example 28 *Sales of 45,000 units are budgeted for the period. The estimated beginning inventory is 3,000 units, and the desired ending inventory is 5,000 units. What is the budgeted production (in units) for the period?*

47,000 units (45,000 units + 5,000 units − 3,000 units)

Direct Materials Purchases Budget

The production budget is the starting point for determining the estimated quantities of direct materials to be purchased. Multiplying these quantities by the expected unit purchase price determines the total cost of direct materials to be purchased.

  Materials required for production
+ Desired ending materials inventory
− Estimated beginning materials inventory
  Direct materials to be purchased

In Elite Accessories Inc.'s production operations, leather and lining are required for wallets and handbags. The quantity of direct materials expected to be used for each unit of product is as follows:

Wallet:	Handbag:
Leather: 0.30 square yard per unit	Leather: 1.25 square yards per unit
Lining: 0.10 square yard per unit	Lining: 0.50 square yard per unit

Based on these data and the production budget, the **direct materials purchases budget** is prepared. As shown in the budget in Exhibit 600.46, for Elite Accessories Inc. to produce 520,000 wallets, 156,000 square yards (520,000 units × 0.30 square yard per unit) of leather are needed. Likewise, to produce 292,000 handbags, 365,000 square yards (292,000 units × 1.25 square yards per unit) of leather are needed. We can compute the needs for lining in a similar manner. Then adding the desired ending inventory for each material and deducting the estimated beginning inventory determines the amount of each material to be purchased. Multiplying these amounts by the estimated cost per square yard yields the total materials purchase cost.

The direct materials purchases budget helps management maintain inventory levels within reasonable limits. For this purpose, the timing of the direct materials purchases should be coordinated between the purchasing and production departments.

Exhibit 600.46 *Direct Materials Purchases Budget*

Elite Accessories Inc.
Direct Materials Purchases Budget
for the Year Ending December 31, 2004

	Direct Materials		
	Leather	Lining	Total
Square yards required for production:			
Wallet (Note A)	156,000	52,000	
Handbag (Note B)	365,000	146,000	
Plus desired inventory, December 31, 2004	20,000	12,000	
Total	541,000	210,000	
Less estimated inventory, January 1, 2004	18,000	15,000	
Total square yards to be purchased	523,000	195,000	
Unit price (per square yard)	× $4.50	× $1.20	
Total direct materials to be purchased	$2,353,500	$234,000	$2,587,500

Note A: Leather: 520,000 units × 0.30 sq. yd. per unit = 156,000 sq. yds.
Lining: 520,000 units × 0.10 sq. yd. per unit = 52,000 sq. yds.
Note B: Leather: 292,000 units × 1.25 sq. yd. per unit = 365,000 sq. yds.
Lining: 292,000 units × 0.50 sq. yd. per unit = 146,000 sq. yds.

Direct Labor Cost Budget

The production budget also provides the starting point for preparing the direct labor cost budget. For Elite Accessories Inc., the labor requirements for each unit of product are estimated as follows:

Wallet:	Handbag:
Cutting Department: 0.10 hour per unit	Cutting Department: 0.15 hour per unit
Sewing Department: 0.25 hour per unit	Sewing Department: 0.40 hour per unit

Exhibit 600.47 *Direct Labor Cost Budget*

Elite Accessories Inc.
Direct Labor Cost Budget
for the Year Ending December 31, 2004

	Cutting	Sewing	Total
Hours required for production:			
Wallet (Note A)	52,000	130,000	
Handbag (Note B)	43,800	116,800	
Total	95,800	246,800	
Hourly rate	× $12.00	× $15.00	
Total direct labor cost	$1,149,600	$3,702,000	$4,851,600

Note A: Cutting Department: 520,000 units × 0.10 hour per unit = 52,000 hours
Sewing Department: 520,000 units × 0.25 hour per unit = 130,000 hours
Note B: Cutting Department: 292,000 units × 0.15 hour per unit = 43,800 hours
Sewing Department: 292,000 units × 0.40 hour per unit = 116,800 hours

Based on these data and the production budget, Elite Accessories Inc. prepares the direct labor budget. As shown in the budget in Exhibit 600.47, for Elite Accessories Inc. to produce 520,000 wallets, 52,000 hours (520,000 units × 0.10 hour per unit) of labor in the Cutting Department are required. Likewise, to produce 292,000 handbags, 43,800 hours (292,000 units × 0.15 hour per unit) of labor in the Cutting Department are required. In a similar manner, we can determine the direct labor hours needed in the Sewing Department to meet the budgeted production. Multiplying the direct labor hours for each department by the estimated department hourly rate yields the total direct labor cost for each department.

The direct labor needs should be coordinated between the production and personnel departments. This ensures that there will be enough labor available for production.

Example 29 Budgeted production is 22,000 units. Each unit requires 0.70 pound of steel and 0.20 direct labor hour. Steel is purchased for $45 per pound, and direct labor is $18 per hour. Steel has an estimated beginning inventory of 700 units and a desired ending inventory of 200 units. For the period, what is the budgeted (a) direct materials purchases and (b) direct labor cost?

(a) $670,500 {[(22,000 units × 0.70 lb.) + 200 lbs. − 700 lbs.] × $45};
(b) $79,200 (22,000 units × 0.20 hr. × $18)

Exhibit 600.48 *Factory Overhead Cost Budget*

Elite Accessories Inc.
Factory Overhead Cost Budget
for the Year Ending December 31, 2004

Indirect factory wages	$ 732,800
Supervisor salaries	360,000
Power and light	306,000
Depreciation of plant and equipment	288,000
Indirect materials	182,800
Maintenance	140,280
Insurance and property taxes	79,200
Total factory overhead cost	$2,089,080

Factory Overhead Cost Budget

The estimated factory overhead costs necessary for production make up the factory overhead cost budget. This budget usually includes the total estimated cost for each item of factory overhead, as shown in Exhibit 600.48.

A business may prepare supporting departmental schedules, in which the factory overhead costs are separated into their fixed and variable cost elements. Such schedules enable department managers to direct their attention to those costs for which they are responsible and to evaluate performance.

Cost of Goods Sold Budget

The direct materials purchases budget, direct labor cost budget, and factory overhead cost budget are the starting point for preparing the **cost of goods sold budget.** To illustrate, these data are combined with the desired ending inventory and the estimated beginning inventory data below to determine the budgeted cost of goods sold shown in Exhibit 600.49.

Estimated inventories on January 1, 2004:		Desired inventories on December 31, 2004:	
Finished goods	$1,095,600	Finished goods	$1,565,000
Work in process	214,400	Work in process	220,000

Exhibit 600.49 *Cost of Goods Sold Budget*

Elite Accessories Inc.
Cost of Goods Sold Budget
for the Year Ending December 31, 2004

Finished goods inventory, January 1, 2004		$ 1,095,600
Work in process inventory, January 1, 2004	$ 214,400	
Direct materials:		
Direct materials inventory, January 1, 2004 (Note A)	$ 99,000	
Direct materials purchases (from Exhibit 600.46)	2,587,500	← Direct materials purchases budget
Cost of direct materials available for use	$2,686,500	
Less direct materials inventory, December 31, 2004 (Note B)	104,400	
Cost of direct materials placed in production	$2,582,100	
Direct labor (from Exhibit 600.47)	4,851,600	← Direct labor cost budget
Factory overhead (from Exhibit 600.48)	2,089,080	← Factory overhead cost budget
Total manufacturing costs	9,522,780	
Total work in process during period	$9,737,180	
Less work in process inventory, December 31, 2004	220,000	
Cost of goods manufactured		9,517,180
Cost of finished goods available for sale		$10,612,780
Less finished goods inventory, December 31, 2004		1,565,000
Cost of goods sold		$ 9,047,780
Note A: Leather: 18,000 sq. yds. × $4.50 per sq. yd.		$ 81,000
Lining: 15,000 sq. yds. × $1.20 per sq. yd.		18,000
Direct materials inventory, January 1, 2004		$ 99,000
Note B: Leather: 20,000 sq. yds. × $4.50 per sq. yd.		$ 90,000
Lining: 12,000 sq. yds. × $1.20 per sq. yd.		14,400
Direct materials inventory, December 31, 2004		$ 104,400

650. OPERATING BUDGETS AND PERFORMANCE EVALUATION

Exhibit 600.50 *Selling and Administrative Expenses Budget*

Elite Accessories Inc.
Selling and Administrative Expenses Budget
for the Year Ending December 31, 2004

Selling expenses:		
Sales salaries expense	$715,000	
Advertising expense	360,000	
Travel expense	115,000	
Total selling expenses		$1,190,000
Administrative expenses:		
Officers' salaries expense	$360,000	
Office salaries expense	258,000	
Office rent expense	34,500	
Office supplies expense	17,500	
Miscellaneous administrative expenses	25,000	
Total administrative expenses		695,000
Total selling and administrative expenses		$1,885,000

Selling and Administrative Expenses Budget

The sales budget is often used as the starting point for estimating the selling and administrative expenses. For example, a budgeted increase in sales may require more advertising. Exhibit 600.50 is a selling and administrative expenses budget for Elite Accessories Inc.

Detailed supporting schedules are often prepared for major items in the selling and administrative expenses budget. For example, an advertising expense schedule for the Marketing Department should include the advertising media to be used (newspaper, direct mail, television), quantities (column inches, number of pieces, minutes), and the cost per unit. Attention to such details results in realistic budgets. Effective control results from assigning responsibility for achieving the budget to department supervisors.

Budgeted Income Statement

The budgets for sales, cost of goods sold, and selling and administrative expenses, combined with the data on other income, other expense, and income tax, are used to prepare the budgeted income statement. Exhibit 600.51 is a budgeted income statement for Elite Accessories Inc.

The budgeted income statement summarizes the estimates of all phases of operations. This allows management to assess the effects of the individual budgets on profits for the year. If the budgeted net income is too low, management could review and revise operating plans in an attempt to improve income.

Balance Sheet Budgets

Balance sheet budgets are used by managers to plan financing, investing, and cash objectives for the firm. The balance sheet budgets illustrated for Elite Accessories Inc. in the following sections are the cash budget and the capital expenditures budget.

Cash Budget

The cash budget presents the expected receipts and payments of cash for a period of time.

The **cash budget** is one of the most important elements of the budgeted balance sheet. The cash budget presents the expected receipts (inflows) and payments (outflows) of cash for a period of time.

Information from the various operating budgets, such as the sales budget, the direct materials purchases budget,

Exhibit 600.51 *Budgeted Income Statement*

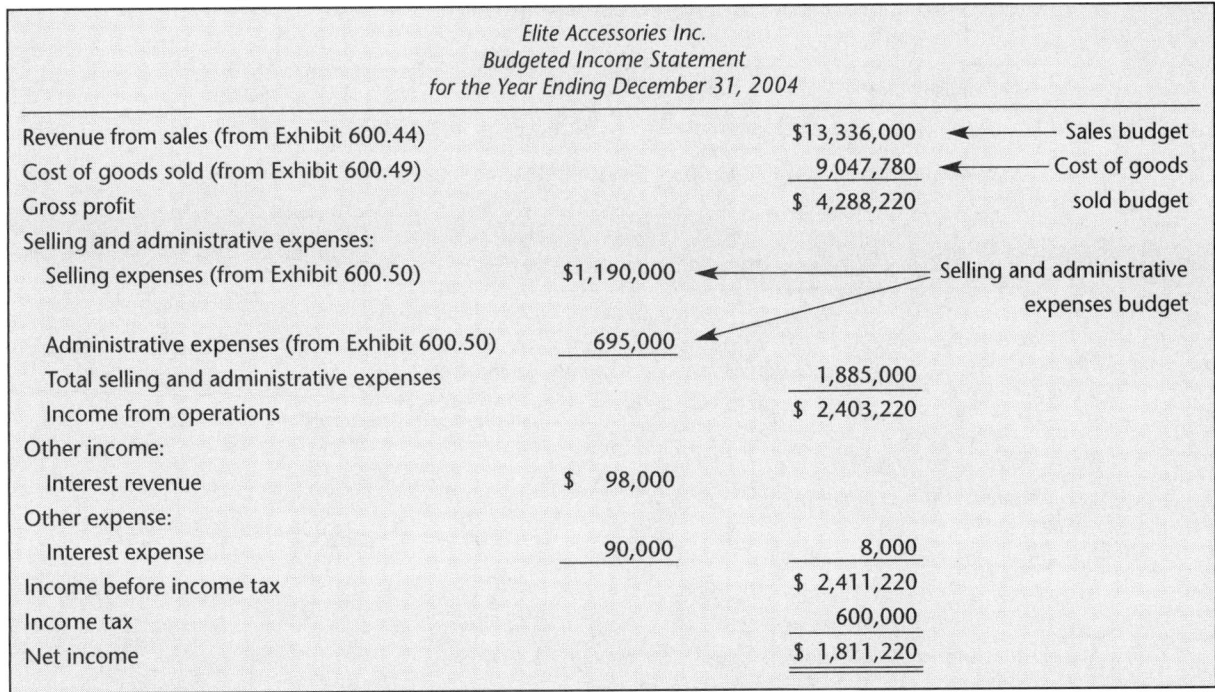

and the selling and administrative expenses budget, affects the cash budget. In addition, the capital expenditures budget, dividend policies, and plans for equity or long-term debt financing also affect the cash budget.

We illustrate the monthly cash budget for January, February, and March 2004, for Elite Accessories Inc. We begin by developing the estimated cash receipts and estimated cash payments portion of the cash budget.

ESTIMATED CASH RECEIPTS Estimated cash receipts are planned additions to cash from sales and other sources, such as issuing securities or collecting interest. A supporting schedule can be used in determining the collections from sales. To illustrate this schedule, assume the following information for Elite Accessories Inc.

Accounts receivable, January 1, 2004			$370,000
	January	February	March
Budgeted sales	$1,080,000	$1,240,000	$970,000

Elite Accessories Inc. expects to sell 10 percent of its merchandise for cash. Of the remaining 90 percent of the sales on account, 60 percent are expected to be collected in the month of the sale and the remainder in the next month.

Using this information, we prepare the schedule of collections from sales, shown in Exhibit 600.52. The cash receipts from sales on account are determined by adding the amounts collected from credit sales earned in the current period (60 percent) and the amounts accrued from sales in the previous period as accounts receivable (40 percent).

Example 30 *A company collects 25% of its sales in the month of the sale and 75% in the month following the sale. If sales are budgeted to be $750,000 for March and $900,000 for April, what are the budgeted cash receipts for April?*

$787,500 [($750,000 × 0.75) + ($900,000 × 0.25)]

ESTIMATED CASH PAYMENTS Estimated cash payments are planned reductions in cash from manufacturing costs, selling and administrative expenses, capital expenditures, and other sources, such as buying securities or paying interest or dividends. A supporting schedule can be used in estimating the cash payments for manufacturing costs. To illustrate, assume the following information for Elite Accessories Inc.

Accounts payable, January 1, 2004				$190,000
	January	February	March	
Manufacturing costs	$840,000	$780,000	$812,000	

Exhibit 600.52 *Schedule of Collections from Sales*

Elite Accessories Inc.
Schedule of Collections from Sales
for the Three Months Ending March 31, 2004

	January	February	March
Receipts from cash sales:			
Cash sales (10% × current month's sales—Note A)	$108,000	$ 124,000	$ 97,000
Receipts from sales on account:			
Collections from prior month's sales (40% of previous month's credit sales—Note B)	$370,000	$ 388,800	$446,400
Collections from current month's sales (60% of current month's credit sales—Note C)	583,200	669,600	523,800
Total receipts from sales on account	$953,200	$1,058,400	$970,200

Note A: $108,000 = $1,080,000 × 10%
$124,000 = $1,240,000 × 10%
$ 97,000 = $ 970,000 × 10%

Note B: $370,000, given as January 1, 2004 Accounts Receivable balance
$388,800 = $1,080,000 × 90% × 40%
$446,400 = $1,240,000 × 90% × 40%

Note C: $583,200 = $1,080,000 × 90% × 60%
$669,600 = $1,240,000 × 90% × 60%
$523,800 = $ 970,000 × 90% × 60%

Depreciation expense on machines is estimated to be $24,000 per month and is included in the manufacturing costs. The accounts payable were incurred for manufacturing costs. Elite Accessories Inc. expects to pay 75 percent of the manufacturing costs in the month in which they are incurred and the balance in the next month.

Using this information, we can prepare the schedule of payments for manufacturing costs, as shown in Exhibit 600.53.

In Exhibit 600.53, the cash payments are determined by adding the amounts paid from costs incurred in the current period (75 percent) and the amounts accrued as a liability from costs in the previous period (25 percent). The $24,000 of depreciation must be excluded from all calculations, since depreciation is a noncash expense that should not be included in the cash budget.

COMPLETING THE CASH BUDGET To complete the cash budget for Elite Accessories Inc., as shown in Exhibit 600.54, assume that Elite Accessories Inc. is expecting the following.

Cash balance on January 1	$280,000
Quarterly taxes paid on March 31	150,000
Quarterly interest expense paid on January 10	22,500
Quarterly interest revenue received on March 21	24,500
Sewing equipment purchased in February	274,000

Exhibit 600.53 *Schedule of Payments for Manufacturing Costs*

Elite Accessories Inc.
Schedule of Payments for Manufacturing Costs
for the Three Months Ending March 31, 2004

	January	February	March
Payments of prior month's manufacturing costs {[25% × previous month's manufacturing costs (less depreciation)]—Note A}	$190,000	$204,000	$189,000
Payments of current month's manufacturing costs {[75% × current month's manufacturing costs (less depreciation)]—Note B}	612,000	567,000	591,000
Total payments	$802,000	$771,000	$780,000

Note A: $190,000, given as January 1, 2004 Accounts Payable balance
             $204,000 = ($840,000 − $24,000) × 25%
             $189,000 = ($780,000 − $24,000) × 25%
Note B: $612,000 = ($840,000 − $24,000) × 75%
             $567,000 = ($780,000 − $24,000) × 75%
             $591,000 = ($812,000 − $24,000) × 75%

Exhibit 600.54 *Cash Budget*

Elite Accessories Inc.
Cash Budget
for the Three Months Ending March 31, 2004

	January	February	March
Estimated cash receipts from:			
Cash sales (from Exhibit 600.52)	$ 108,000	$ 124,000	$ 97,000
Collections of accounts receivable (from Exhibit 600.52)	953,200	1,058,400	970,200
Interest revenue			24,500
Total cash receipts	$1,061,200	$1,182,400	$1,091,700
Estimated cash payments for:			
Manufacturing costs (from Exhibit 600.53)	$ 802,000	$ 771,000	$ 780,000
Selling and administrative expenses	160,000	165,000	145,000
Capital additions		274,000	
Interest expense	22,500		
Income taxes			150,000
Total cash payments	$ 984,500	$1,210,000	$1,075,000
Cash increase (decrease)	$ 76,700	$ (27,600)	$ 16,700
Cash balance at beginning of month	280,000	356,700	329,100
Cash balance at end of month	$ 356,700	$ 329,100	$ 345,800
Minimum cash balance	340,000	340,000	340,000
Excess (deficiency)	$ 16,700	$ (10,900)	$ 5,800

Schedule of collections from sales ← (Cash sales / Collections of accounts receivable)
Schedule of cash payments for manufacturing costs ← (Manufacturing costs)

In addition, monthly selling and administrative expenses, which are paid in the month incurred, are estimated as follows:

	January	February	March
Selling and administrative expenses	$160,000	$165,000	$145,000

650. OPERATING BUDGETS AND PERFORMANCE EVALUATION

Exhibit 600.55 *Capital Expenditures Budget*

Elite Accessories Inc.
Capital Expenditures Budget
for the Five Years Ending December 31, 2008

Item	2004	2005	2006	2007	2008
Machinery—Cutting Department	$400,000			$280,000	$360,000
Machinery—Sewing Department	274,000	$260,000	$560,000	200,000	
Office equipment		90,000			60,000
Total	$674,000	$350,000	$560,000	$480,000	$420,000

We can compare the estimated cash balance at the end of the period with the minimum balance required by operations. Assuming that the minimum cash balance for Elite Accessories Inc. is $340,000, we can determine any expected excess or deficiency.

The minimum cash balance protects against variations in estimates and for unexpected cash emergencies. For effective cash management, much of the minimum cash balance should be deposited in income-producing securities that can be readily converted to cash. U.S. Treasury Bills or Notes are examples of such securities.

Capital Expenditures Budget

The **capital expenditures budget** summarizes plans for acquiring fixed assets. Such expenditures are necessary as machinery and other fixed assets wear out, become obsolete, or for other reasons need to be replaced. In addition, expanding plant facilities may be necessary to meet increasing demand for a company's product.

The useful life of many fixed assets extends over long periods of time. In addition, the amount of the expenditures for such assets may vary from year to year. It is normal to project the plans for a number of periods into the future in preparing the capital expenditures budget. Exhibit 600.55 is a five-year capital expenditures budget for Elite Accessories Inc.

The capital expenditures budget should be considered in preparing the other operating budgets. For example, the estimated depreciation of new equipment affects the factory overhead cost budget and the selling and administrative expenses budget. The plans for financing the capital expenditures may also affect the cash budget.

Budgeted Balance Sheet

The budgeted balance sheet estimates the financial condition at the end of a budget period. The budgeted balance sheet assumes that all operating budgets and financing plans are met. It is similar to a balance sheet based on actual data in the accounts. For this reason, we do not illustrate a budgeted balance sheet for Elite Accessories Inc. If the budgeted balance sheet indicates a weakness in financial position, revising the financing plans or other plans may be necessary. For example, a large amount of long-term debt in relation to stockholders' equity might require revising financing plans for capital expenditures. Such revisions might include issuing equity rather than debt.

Performance Evaluation

Have you ever wondered if there is an economic reason why large retail stores, such as **JCPenney Co.** and **Sears,** are divided into departments? Typically, these stores include a Men's Department, Women's Department, Appliances Department, Home Entertainment Department, and Sporting Goods Department. Each department usually has a manager who is responsible for the financial performance of the department. The store may be the responsibility of a store manager, and a group of stores within a particular geographic area may be the responsibility of a division or district manager. If you were to be hired by a department store chain, you would probably begin your career in a department. Running a department would be a valuable experience before becoming responsible for a complete store. Likewise, responsibility for a complete store provides excellent training for other management positions.

In this section, we will focus on the role of accounting in assisting managers in planning and controlling organizational units, such as divisions, stores, and departments.

Centralized and Decentralized Operations

A **centralized** business is one in which all major planning and operating decisions are made by top management. For example, a one-person, owner/manager-operated business is centralized because all plans and decisions are made by one person. In a small owner/manager-operated business, centralization may be desirable. This is because the owner/manager's close supervision ensures that the business will be operated in the way the owner/manager wishes.

Separating a business into **divisions** or operating units and delegating responsibility to unit managers is called **decentralization**. In a decentralized business, the unit managers are responsible for planning and controlling the operations of their units.

Divisions are often structured around common functions, products, customers, or regions. For example, **Delta Air Lines** is organized around *functions,* such as the Flight Operations Division. The **Procter & Gamble Company** is organized around common *products,* such as the Soap Division, which sells a wide array of cleaning products.

There is no one best amount of decentralization for all businesses. In some companies, division managers have authority over all operations, including fixed asset acquisitions and retirements. In other companies, division managers have authority over profits but not fixed asset acquisitions and retirements. The proper amount of decentralization for a company depends on its advantages and disadvantages for the company's unique circumstances.

Advantages of Decentralization

As a business grows, it becomes more difficult for top management to maintain close daily contact with all operations. In such cases, delegating authority to managers closest to the operations usually results in better decisions. These managers often anticipate and react to operating data more quickly than could top management. In addition, as a company expands into a wide range of products and services, it becomes more difficult for top management to maintain operating expertise in all product lines and services. Decentralization allows managers to focus on acquiring expertise in their areas of responsibility. For example, in a company that maintains operations in insurance, banking, and health care, managers could become "experts" in their area of operation and responsibility.

Decentralized decision making also provides excellent training for managers. This may be a factor in helping a company retain quality managers. Since the art of management is best acquired through experience, delegating responsibility allows managers to acquire and develop managerial expertise early in their careers.

Businesses that work closely with customers, such as hotels, are often decentralized. This helps managers create good customer relations by responding quickly to customers' needs. In addition, because managers of decentralized operations tend to identify with customers and with operations, they are often more creative in suggesting operating and product improvements.

Disadvantages of Decentralization

A primary disadvantage of decentralized operations is that decisions made by one manager may negatively affect the profitability of the entire company. For example, the Pizza Hut chain added chicken to its menu and ended up taking business away from KFC. Then KFC retaliated with a blistering ad campaign against Pizza Hut. This happened even though both chains are part of the same company, **Tricon Global Restaurants**!

Another potential disadvantage of decentralized operations is duplicating assets and costs in operating divisions. For example, each manager of a product line might have a separate sales force and administrative office staff. Centralizing these personnel could save money.

Responsibility Accounting

In a decentralized business, an important function of accounting is to assist unit managers in evaluating and controlling their areas of responsibility, called **responsibility centers**. **Responsibility accounting** is the process of measuring and reporting operating data by responsibility center. Three common types of responsibility centers are cost centers, profit centers, and investment centers. These three responsibility centers differ in their scope of responsibility, as shown below.

Cost Center	Profit Center	Investment Center
Cost	Revenue − Cost Profit	Revenue − Cost Profit Investment in assets

Responsibility Accounting for Cost Centers

In a **cost center,** the unit manager has responsibility and authority for controlling the costs incurred. For example, the supervisor of the Power Department has responsibility for the costs incurred in providing power. A cost center manager does not make decisions concerning sales or the amount of fixed assets invested in the center. Cost centers may vary in size from a small department to an entire manufacturing plant. In addition, cost centers may exist within other cost centers. For example, we could view an entire university as a cost center, and each college and department within the university could also be a cost center, as shown in Exhibit 600.56.

Because managers of cost centers have responsibility and authority over costs, responsibility accounting for cost centers focuses on costs. To illustrate, the budget performance reports in Exhibit 600.57 are part of a responsibility accounting system. These reports aid the managers in controlling costs.

In Exhibit 600.57, the reports prepared for the department supervisors show the budgeted and actual manufacturing costs for their departments. The supervisors can use these reports to focus on areas of significant difference, such as the difference between the budgeted and actual materials cost. The supervisor of Department 1 in Plant A may use additional information from a scrap report to determine why materials are over budget. Such a report might show that materials were scrapped as a result of machine malfunctions, improper use of machines by employees, or low-quality materials.

For higher levels of management, responsibility accounting reports are usually more summarized than for lower levels of management. In Exhibit 600.57, for example, the budget performance report for the plant manager summarizes budget and actual cost data for the departments under the manager's supervision. This report enables the plant manager to identify the department supervisors responsible for major differences. Likewise, the report for the vice-president of production summarizes the cost data for each plant. The plant managers can thus be held responsible for major differences in budgeted and actual costs in their plants.

Exhibit 600.56 *Cost Centers in a University*

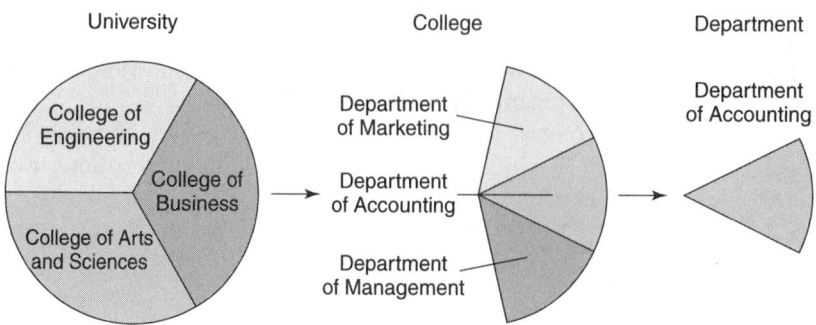

Exhibit 600.57 *Responsibility Accounting Reports for Cost Centers*

Budget Performance Report
Vice-President, Production
for the Month Ended October 31, 2004

	Budget	Actual	Over Budget	Under Budget
Administration	$ 19,500	$ 19,700	$ 200	
Plant A	467,475	470,330	2,855	
Plant B	395,225	394,300		$925
	$882,200	$884,330	$3,055	$925

Budget Performance Report
Manager, Plant A
for the Month Ended October 31, 2004

	Budget	Actual	Over Budget	Under Budget
Administration	$ 17,500	$ 17,350		$150
Department 1	109,725	111,280	$ 1,555	
Department 2	190,500	192,600	2,100	
Department 3	149,475	149,100		650
	$467,475	$470,330	$ 3,655	$800

Budget Performance Report
Supervisor, Department I—Plant A
for the Month Ended October 31, 2004

	Budget	Actual	Over Budget	Under Budget
Factory wages	$ 58,100	$ 58,000		$100
Materials	32,500	34,225	$1,725	
Supervisory salaries	6,400	6,400		
Power and light	5,750	5,690		60
Depreciation of plant and equipment	4,000	4,000		
Maintenance	2,000	1,990		
Insurance and property taxes	975	975		10
	$109,725	$111,280	$1,725	$170

Responsibility Accounting for Profit Centers

In a **profit center,** the unit manager has the responsibility and the authority to make decisions that affect both costs and revenues (and thus profits). Profit centers may be divisions, departments, or products. For example, a consumer products company might organize its brands (product lines) as divisional profit centers. The manager of each brand could have responsibility for product cost and decisions regarding revenues, such as setting sales prices. The manager of a profit center does not make decisions concerning the fixed assets invested in the center. For example, the brand manager of a consumer products company does not make the decision to expand the plant capacity for the brand.

Profit centers may be divisions, departments, or products.

Profit centers are often viewed as an excellent training assignment for new managers. For example, Lester B. Korn, Chairman and Chief Executive Officer of **Korn/Ferry International,** offered the following strategy for young executives en route to top management positions:

650. OPERATING BUDGETS AND PERFORMANCE EVALUATION

Get Profit-Center Responsibility—Obtain a position where you can prove yourself as both a specialist with particular expertise and a generalist who can exercise leadership, authority, and inspire enthusiasm among colleagues and subordinates.

Responsibility accounting reports usually show the revenues, expenses, and income from operations for the profit center. The profit center income statement should include only revenues and expenses that are controlled by the manager. **Controllable revenues** are revenues earned by the profit center. **Controllable expenses** are costs that can be influenced (controlled) by the decisions of profit center managers. For example, the manager of the Men's Department at **Nordstrom** most likely controls the salaries of department personnel but does not control the property taxes of the store.

Service Department Charges

We will illustrate profit center income reporting for the Nova Entertainment Group (NEG). Assume that NEG is a diversified entertainment company with two operating divisions organized as profit centers: the Theme Park Division and the Movie Production Division. The revenues and operating expenses for the two divisions are shown below. The operating expenses consist of the direct expenses, such as the wages and salaries of a division's employees.

	Theme Park Division	Movie Production Division
Revenues	$6,000,000	$2,500,000
Operating expenses	2,495,000	405,000

In addition to direct expenses, divisions may also have expenses for services provided by internal centralized **service departments.** These service departments are often more efficient at providing service than are outside service providers. Examples of such service departments include the following:

- Research and Development
- Government Relations
- Telecommunications
- Publications and Graphics
- Facilities Management
- Purchasing
- Information Systems
- Payroll Accounting
- Transportation
- Personnel Administration

A profit center's income from operations should reflect the cost of any internal services used by the center. To illustrate, assume that NEG established a Payroll Accounting Department. The costs of the payroll services, called **service department charges,** are charged to NEG's profit centers, as shown in Exhibit 600.58.

Service department charges are *indirect expenses* to a profit center. They are similar to the expenses that would be incurred if the profit center had purchased the services from a source outside the company. A profit center manager has control over such expenses if the manager is free to choose *how much* service is used from the service department.

Exhibit 600.58 *Payroll Accounting Department Charges to NEG's Theme Park and Movie Production Divisions*

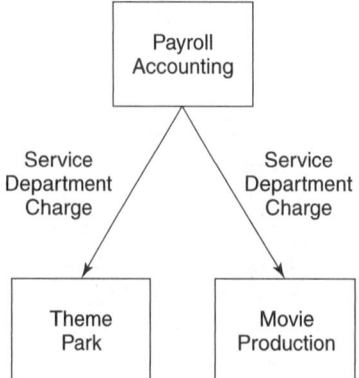

To illustrate service department charges, assume that NEG has two other service departments—Purchasing and Legal, in addition to Payroll Accounting. The expenses for the year ended December 31, 2004, for each service department are as follows:

Purchasing	$400,000
Payroll Accounting	255,000
Legal	250,000
Total	$905,000

An **activity base** for each service department is used to charge service department expenses to the Theme Park and Movie Production Divisions. The activity base for each service department is a measure of the services performed. For NEG, the service department activity bases are as follows:

Department	Activity Base
Purchasing	Number of purchase requisitions
Payroll Accounting	Number of payroll checks
Legal	Number of billed hours

The use of services by the Theme Park and Movie Production Divisions is as follows:

	Service Usage		
	Purchasing	Payroll Accounting	Legal
Theme Park Division	25,000 purchase requisitions	12,000 payroll checks	100 billed hours
Movie Production Division	15,000	3,000	900
Total	40,000 purchase requisitions	15,000 payroll checks	1,000 billed hours

The rates at which services are charged to each division are called **service department charge rates.** These rates are determined by dividing each service department's expenses by the total service usage as follows:

$$\text{Purchasing:} \frac{\$400,000}{40,000 \text{ purchase requisitions}} = \$10 \text{ per purchase requisition}$$

$$\text{Payroll Accounting:} \frac{\$255,000}{15,000 \text{ payroll checks}} = \$17 \text{ per payroll check}$$

$$\text{Legal:} \frac{\$250,000}{1,000 \text{ hours}} = \$250 \text{ per hour}$$

Example 31 *The centralized payroll department has expenses of $120,000. The department processed a total of 25,000 payroll checks for the period. If the Eastern Division has 6,000 payroll checks for the period, how much should it be charged for payroll services?*

$28,800 [($120,000/25,000) × 6,000]

The use of services by the Theme Park and Movie Production Divisions is multiplied by the service department charge rates to determine the charges to each division, as shown in Exhibit 600.59.

The Theme Park Division employs many temporary and part-time employees who are paid weekly. This is in contrast to the Movie Production Division, which has a more permanent payroll that is paid on a monthly basis. As a result,

Exhibit 600.59 *Service Department Charges to NEG Divisions*

Nova Entertainment Group
Service Department Charges to NEG Divisions
for the Year Ended December 31, 2004

Service Department	Theme Park Division	Movie Production Division
Purchasing (Note A)	$250,000	$150,000
Payroll Accounting (Note B)	204,000	51,000
Legal (Note C)	25,000	225,000
Total service department charges	$479,000	$426,000

Note A:
25,000 purchase requisitions × $10 per purchase requisition = $250,000
15,000 purchase requisitions × $10 per purchase requisition = $150,000
Note B:
12,000 payroll checks × $17 per check = $204,000
3,000 payroll checks × $17 per check = $51,000
Note C:
100 hours × $250 per hour = $25,000
900 hours × $250 per hour = $225,000

Exhibit 600.60 *Divisional Income Statements—NEG*

Nova Entertainment Group
Divisional Income Statements
for the Year Ended December 31, 2004

	Theme Park Division	Movie Production Division
Revenues*	$6,000,000	$2,500,000
Operating expenses	2,495,000	405,000
Income from operations before service department charges	$3,505,000	$2,095,000
Less service department charges:		
Purchasing	$ 250,000	$ 150,000
Payroll Accounting	204,000	51,000
Legal	25,000	225,000
Total service department charges	$ 479,000	$ 426,000
Income from operations	$3,026,000	$1,669,000

*For a profit center that sells products, the income statement would show: Net sales − Cost of goods sold = Gross profit. The operating expenses would be deducted from the gross profit to get the income from operations before service department charges.

the Theme Park Division requires 12,000 payroll checks. This results in a large service charge from Payroll Accounting to the Theme Park Division. In contrast, the Movie Production Division uses many legal services for contract negotiations. Thus, there is a large service charge from Legal to the Movie Production Division.

Profit Center Reporting

The divisional income statements for NEG are presented in Exhibit 600.60. These statements show the service department charges to the divisions.

The **income from operations** is a measure of a manager's performance. In evaluating the profit center manager, the income from operations should be compared over time to a budget. It should not be compared across profit centers, since the profit centers are usually different in terms of size, products, and customers.

Example 32 *If sales are $500,000, the cost of goods sold is $285,000, selling expenses are $85,000, and service department charges are $53,000, what is the income from operations?*

$77,000 ($500,000 − $285,000 − $85,000 − $53,000)

Responsibility Accounting for Investment Centers

In an **investment center,** the unit manager has the responsibility and the authority to make decisions that affect not only costs and revenues but also the assets invested in the center. Investment centers are widely used in highly diversified companies organized by divisions.

The manager of an investment center has more authority and responsibility than the manager of a cost center or a profit center. The manager of an investment center occupies a position similar to that of a chief operating officer or president of a company and is evaluated in much the same way.

Because investment center managers have responsibility for revenues and expenses, income from operations is an important part of investment center reporting. In addition, because the manager has responsibility for the assets invested in the center, two additional measures of performance are often used. These measures are the rate of return on investment and residual income. Top management often compares these measures across investment centers to reward performance and assess investment in the centers.

To illustrate, assume that DataLink Inc. is a cellular phone company that has three regional divisions, Northern, Central, and Southern. Condensed divisional income statements for the investment centers are shown in Exhibit 600.61.

Using only income from operations, the Central Division is the most profitable division. However, income from operations does not reflect the amount of assets invested in each center. For example, if the amount of assets invested in the Central Division is twice that of the other divisions, then the Central Division would be the least profitable in terms of the rate of return on these assets.

Rate of Return on Investment

Because investment center managers also control the amount of assets invested in their centers, they should be held accountable for the use of these assets. One measure that considers the amount of assets invested is the **rate of return on investment** (ROI) or **rate of return on assets.** It is one of the most widely used measures for investment centers and is computed as follows.

$$\text{Rate of return on investment (ROI)} = \frac{\text{Income from operations}}{\text{Invested assets}}$$

Exhibit 600.61 *Divisional Income Statements—DataLink Inc.*

DataLink Inc.
Divisional Income Statements
for the Year Ended December 31, 2004

	Northern Division	Central Division	Southern Division
Revenues	$560,000	$672,000	$750,000
Operating expenses	336,000	470,400	562,500
Income from operations before service department charges	$224,000	$201,600	$187,500
Service department charges	154,000	117,600	112,500
Income from operations	$ 70,000	$ 84,000	$ 75,000

The rate of return on investment is useful because the three factors subject to control by divisional managers (revenues, expenses, and invested assets) are used in its computation. By measuring profitability relative to the amount of assets invested in each division, the rate of return on investment can be used to compare divisions. The higher the rate of return on investment, the better the division utilizes its assets to generate income. To illustrate, the rate of return on investment for each division of DataLink Inc., based on the book value of invested assets, is as follows:

	Northern Division	Central Division	Southern Division
Income from operations	$ 70,000	$ 84,000	$ 75,000
Invested assets	$350,000	$700,000	$500,000
Rate of return on investment	20%	12%	15%

Although the Central Division generated the largest income from operations, its rate of return on investment (12 percent) is the lowest. Hence, relative to the assets invested, the Central Division is the least profitable division. In comparison, the rate of return on investment of the Northern Division is 20 percent and the Southern Division is 15 percent. These differences in the rates of return on investment can be further analyzed using an expanded formula for the rate of return on investment.

In the expanded formula, the rate of return on investment is the product of two factors. The first factor is the ratio of income from operations to sales, often called the **profit margin.** The second factor is the ratio of sales to invested assets, often called the **investment turnover.** In the illustration at the left, profits can be earned by either increasing the investment turnover (turning the crank faster), by increasing the profit margin (increasing the size of the opening), or both.

Using the expanded expression yields the same rate of return on investment for the Northern Division, 20 percent, as computed previously.

Rate of return on investment (ROI) = Profit margin × Investment turnover

$$\text{Rate of return on investment (ROI)} = \frac{\text{Income from operations}}{\text{Sales}} \times \frac{\text{Sales}}{\text{Invested assets}}$$

$$\text{ROI} = \frac{\$70,000}{\$560,000} \times \frac{\$560,000}{\$350,000}$$

$$\text{ROI} = 12.5\% \times 1.6$$

$$\text{ROI} = 20\%$$

The expanded expression for the rate of return on investment is useful in evaluating and controlling divisions. This is because the profit margin and the investment turnover focus on the underlying operating relationships of each division.

The profit margin indicates the rate of profit on each sales dollar, while the investment turnover indicates the rate of sales on each dollar of invested assets.

The profit margin component focuses on profitability by indicating the rate of profit earned on each sales dollar. If a division's profit margin increases, and all other factors remain the same, the division's rate of return on investment will increase. For example, a division might add more profitable products to its sales mix and thereby increase its overall profit margin and rate of return on investment.

The investment turnover component focuses on efficiency in using assets and indicates the rate at which sales are generated for each dollar of invested assets. The more sales per dollar invested, the greater the efficiency in using the assets. If a division's investment turnover increases, and all other factors remain the same, the division's rate of return on investment will increase. For example, a division might attempt to increase sales through special sales promotions or reduce inventory assets by using just-in-time principles, either of which would increase investment turnover.

The rate of return on investment, using the expanded expression for each division of DataLink Inc., is summarized as follows:

$$\text{Rate of return on investment (ROI)} = \frac{\text{Income from operations}}{\text{Sales}} \times \frac{\text{Sales}}{\text{Invested assets}}$$

$$\text{Northern Division (ROI)} = \frac{\$70,000}{\$560,000} \times \frac{\$560,000}{\$350,000}$$

$$\text{ROI} = 12.5\% \times 1.6$$
$$\text{ROI} = 20\%$$

$$\text{Central Division (ROI)} = \frac{\$84,000}{\$672,000} \times \frac{\$672,000}{\$700,000}$$

$$\text{ROI} = 12.5\% \times 0.96$$
$$\text{ROI} = 12\%$$

$$\text{Southern Division (ROI)} = \frac{\$75,000}{\$750,000} \times \frac{\$750,000}{\$500,000}$$

$$\text{ROI} = 10\% \times 1.5$$
$$\text{ROI} = 15\%$$

Although the Northern and Central Divisions have the same profit margins, the Northern Division investment turnover (1.6) is larger than that of the Central Division (0.96). Thus, by using its invested assets more efficiently, the Northern Division's rate of return on investment is higher than the Central Division's. The Southern Division's profit margin of 10 percent and investment turnover of 1.5 are lower than those of the Northern Division. The product of these factors results in a return on investment of 15 percent for the Southern Division, compared to 20 percent for the Northern Division.

To determine possible ways of increasing the rate of return on investment, the profit margin and investment turnover for a division may be analyzed. For example, if the Northern Division is in a highly competitive industry in which the profit margin cannot be easily increased, the division manager might focus on increasing the investment turnover. To illustrate, assume that the revenues of the Northern Division could be increased by $56,000 through increasing operating expenses, such as advertising, to $385,000. The Northern Division's income from operations will increase from $70,000 to $77,000, as shown below.

Revenues ($560,000 + $56,000)	$616,000
Operating expenses	385,000
Income from operations before service department charges	$231,000
Service department charges	154,000
Income from operations	$ 77,000

The rate of return on investment for the Northern Division, using the expanded expression, is recomputed as follows

$$\text{Rate of return on investment (ROI)} = \frac{\text{Income from operations}}{\text{Sales}} \times \frac{\text{Sales}}{\text{Invested assets}}$$

$$\text{Northern Division revised (ROI)} = \frac{\$77,000}{\$616,000} \times \frac{\$616,000}{\$350,000}$$

$$\text{ROI} = 12.5\% \times 1.76$$
$$\text{ROI} = 22\%$$

Although the Northern Division's profit margin remains the same (12.5 percent), the investment turnover has increased from 1.6 to 1.76, an increase of 10 percent (0.16 ÷ 1.6). The 10 percent increase in investment turnover also increases the rate of return on investment by 10 percent (from 20 percent to 22 percent).

In addition to using it as a performance measure, the rate of return on investment may assist management in other ways. For example, in considering a decision to expand the operations of DataLink Inc., management might consider giving priority to the Northern Division because it earns the highest rate of return on investment. If the current rates of return on investment are maintained in the future, an investment in the Northern Division will return 20 cents (20 percent) on each dollar invested. In contrast, investments in the Central Division will earn only 12 cents per dollar invested, and investments in the Southern Division will return only 15 cents per dollar.

A disadvantage of the rate of return on investment as a performance measure is that it may lead divisional managers to reject new investments that could be profitable for the company as a whole. For example, the Northern Division of DataLink Inc. has an overall rate of return on investment of 20 percent. The minimum acceptable rate of return on investment for DataLink Inc. is 10 percent. The manager of the Northern Division has the opportunity of investing in a new project that is estimated will earn a 17 percent rate of return. If the manager of the Northern Division invests in the project, however, the Northern Division's overall rate of return will decrease from 20 percent. Thus, the division manager might decide to reject the project, even though the investment would exceed DataLink's minimum acceptable rate of return on investment. The CFO of **Millennium Chemicals Inc.** referred to a similar situation by stating: "We had too many divisional executives who failed to spend money on capital projects with more than satisfactory returns because those projects would have lowered the average return on assets of their particular business."

> **Example 33** Income from operations is $35,000, invested assets are $140,000, and sales are $437,500. What is the (a) profit margin, (b) investment turnover, and (c) rate of return on investment?
>
> (a) 8% ($35,000/$437,500);
> (b) 3.125 ($437,500/$140,000);
> (c) 25% (8% × 3.125, or $35,000/$140,000)

Residual Income

An additional measure of evaluating divisional performance—residual income—is useful in overcoming some of the disadvantages associated with the rate of return on investment. **Residual income** is the excess of income from operations over a minimum acceptable income from operations, as illustrated below.

Income from Operations − Minimum Acceptable Rate of Return on Assets = Residual Income

The minimum acceptable income from operations is normally computed by multiplying a minimum rate of return by the amount of divisional assets. The minimum rate is set by top management, based on such factors as the cost of financing the business operations. To illustrate, assume that DataLink Inc. has established 10 percent as the minimum acceptable rate of return on divisional assets. The residual incomes for the three divisions are as follows:

	Northern Division	Central Division	Southern Division
Income from operations	$70,000	$84,000	$75,000
Minimum acceptable income from operations as a percent of assets:			
$350,000 × 10%	35,000		
$700,000 × 10%		70,000	
$500,000 × 10%			50,000
Residual income	$35,000	$14,000	$25,000

The Northern Division has more residual income than the other divisions, even though it has the least amount of income from operations. This is because the assets on which to earn a minimum acceptable rate of return are less for the Northern Division than for the other divisions.

The major advantage of residual income as a performance measure is that it considers both the minimum acceptable rate of return and the total amount of the income from operations earned by each division. Residual income encourages division managers to maximize income from operations in excess of the minimum. This provides an incentive to accept any project that is expected to have a rate of return in excess of the minimum. Thus, the residual income number supports both divisional and overall company objectives.

Example 34 *The International Division has income from operations of $87,000 and assets of $240,000. The minimum acceptable rate of return on assets is 12%. What is the residual income for the division?*

$58,200 [$87,000 − ($240,000 × 12%)]

The Balanced Scorecard

In addition to financial divisional performance measures, many companies also rely on nonfinancial divisional measures. One popular evaluation approach is the **balanced scorecard.** The balanced scorecard is a set of financial and nonfinancial measures that reflect multiple performance dimensions of a business. A common balanced scorecard design measures performance in the innovation and learning, customer, internal, and financial dimensions of a business. These four areas can be diagrammed as shown in Exhibit 600.62.

The innovation and learning perspective measures the amount of innovation in an organization. For example, a drug company, such as **Merck,** would measure the number of drugs in its FDA (Food and Drug Administration) approval pipeline, the amount of research and development (R&D) spending per period, and the length of time it takes to turn ideas into marketable products. Managing the performance of its R&D processes is critical to Merck's longer-term prospects and thus would be an additional performance perspective beyond the financial numbers. The customer perspective would measure customer satisfaction, loyalty, and perceptions. For example, **Amazon.com** measures the number of repeat visitors to its Web site as a measure of customer loyalty. Amazon.com needs repeat business because the costs to acquire a new customer are very high. The internal process perspective measures the effectiveness and efficiency of internal business processes. For example, **DaimlerChrysler** measures quality by the average warranty claims per automobile, measures efficiency by the average labor hours per automobile, and measures the average time to assemble each automobile. The financial perspective measures the economic performance of the responsibility center as we have illustrated in the previous sections of this chapter. All companies will use financial measures. For example, one survey found that over 70 percent of companies use income from operations as a percent of sales, 62 percent use rate of return on investment, and 13 percent use residual income as financial performance measures.

Exhibit 600.62 *The Balanced Scorecard*

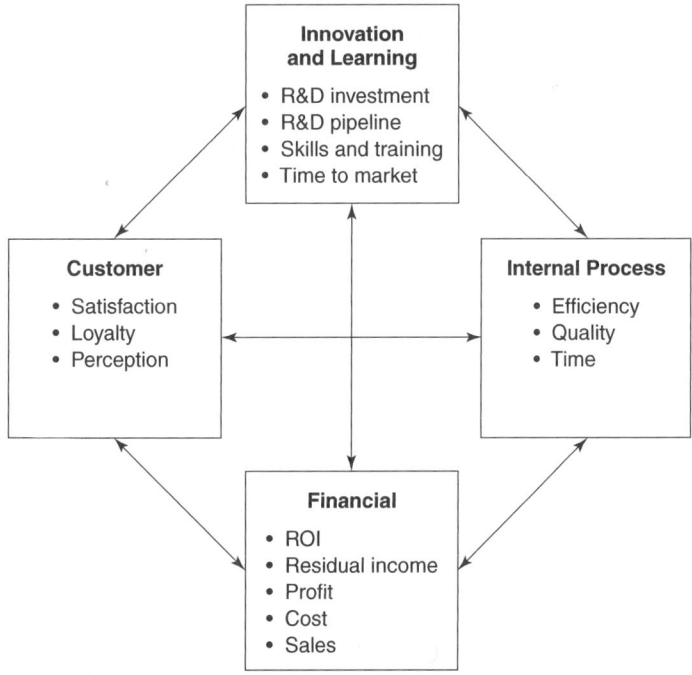

The balanced scorecard is designed to reveal the underlying nonfinancial drivers, or causes, of financial performance. For example, if a business improves customer satisfaction, this will likely lead to improved financial performance. In addition, the balanced scorecard helps managers consider trade-offs between short- and long-term performance. For example, additional investment in research and development (R&D) would penalize the short-term financial perspective, because R&D is an expense that reduces income from operations. However, the innovation perspective would measure additional R&D expenditures favorably, because current R&D expenditures will lead to future profits from new products. The balanced scorecard will motivate the manager to invest in new R&D, even though it is recognized as a current period expense. A recent survey has indicated that 40 percent of the companies use or are planning to use the balanced scorecard. Thus, the balanced scorecard is gaining acceptance because of its ability to reveal the underlying causes of financial performance, while helping managers consider the short- and long-term implications of their decisions.

Transfer Pricing

When divisions transfer products or render services to each other, a **transfer price** is used to charge for the products or services. Because transfer prices affect the goals for both divisions, setting these prices is a sensitive matter for division managers.

Transfer prices should be set so that overall company income is increased when goods are transferred between divisions. As we will illustrate, however, transfer prices may be misused in such a way that overall company income suffers.

In the following paragraphs, we discuss various approaches to setting transfer prices. Exhibit 600.63 shows the range of prices that results from common approaches to setting transfer prices. Transfer prices can be set as low as the variable cost per unit or as high as the market price. Often, transfer prices are negotiated at some point between variable cost per unit and market price.

A survey of transfer pricing practices has reported the following usage:

Cost price (variable or full)	46%
Market price	37
Negotiated price	17

Source: Roger Y. W. Tang, "Transfer Pricing in the 1990's," *Management Accounting*, February 1992, pp. 22–26.

Transfer prices may be used when decentralized units are organized as cost, profit, or investment centers. To illustrate, we will use a packaged snack food company (Wilson Company) with no service departments and two operating divisions (Eastern and Western) organized as investment centers. Condensed divisional income statements for Wilson Company, assuming no transfers between divisions, are shown in Exhibit 600.64.

Exhibit 600.63 *Commonly Used Transfer Prices*

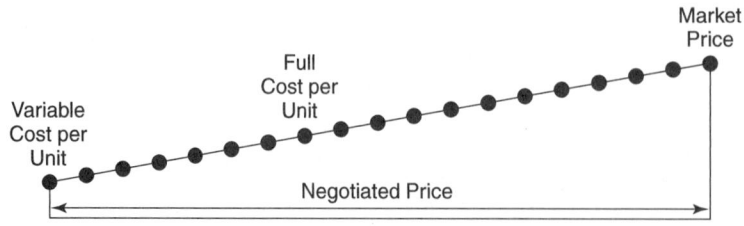

Exhibit 600.64 *Wilson Company Income Statement —No Transfers Between Divisions*

Wilson Company
Divisional Income Statements
for the Year Ended December 31, 2004

	Eastern Division	Western Division	Total
Sales:			
50,000 units × $20 per unit	$1,000,000		$1,000,000
20,000 units × $40 per unit		$800,000	800,000
			$1,800,000
Expenses:			
Variable:			
50,000 units × $10 per unit	$ 500,000		$ 500,000
20,000 units × $30* per unit		$600,000	600,000
Fixed	300,000	100,000	400,000
Total expenses	$ 800,000	$700,000	$1,500,000
Income from operations	$ 200,000	$100,000	$ 300,000

*$20 of the $30 per unit represents materials costs, and the remaining $10 per unit represents other variable conversion expenses incurred within the Western Division.

Market Price Approach

Using the **market price approach,** the transfer price is the price at which the product or service transferred could be sold to outside buyers. If an outside market exists for the product or service transferred, the current market price may be a proper transfer price.

To illustrate, assume that materials used by Wilson Company in producing snack food in the Western Division are currently purchased from an outside supplier at $20 per unit. The same materials are produced by the Eastern Division. The Eastern Division is operating at full capacity of 50,000 units and can sell all it produces to either the Western Division or to outside buyers. A transfer price of $20 per unit (the market price) has no effect on the Eastern Division's income or total company income. The Eastern Division will earn revenues of $20 per unit on all its production and sales, regardless of who buys its product. Likewise, the Western Division will pay $20 per unit for materials (the market price). Thus, the use of the market price as the transfer price has no effect on the Eastern Division's income or total company income. In this situation, the use of the market price as the transfer price is proper. The condensed divisional income statements for Wilson Company in this case are also shown in Exhibit 600.64.

Negotiated Price Approach

If unused or excess capacity exists in the supplying division (the Eastern Division), and the transfer price is equal to the market price, total company profit may not be maximized. This is because the manager of the Western Division will be indifferent toward purchasing materials from the Eastern Division or from outside suppliers. Thus, the Western Division may purchase the materials from outside suppliers. If, however, the Western Division purchases the materials from the Eastern Division, the difference between the market price of $20 and the variable costs of the Eastern Division can cover fixed costs and contribute to company profits. When the negotiated price approach is used in this situation, the manager of the Western Division is encouraged to purchase the materials from the Eastern Division.

The **negotiated price approach** allows the managers of decentralized units to agree (negotiate) among themselves as to the transfer price. The only constraint on the negotiations is that the transfer price be less than the market price but greater than the supplying division's variable costs per unit.

To illustrate the use of the negotiated price approach, assume that instead of a capacity of 50,000 units, the Eastern Division's capacity is 70,000 units. In addition, assume that the Eastern Division can continue to sell only 50,000 units to outside buyers. A transfer price less than $20 would encourage the manager of the Western Division to purchase from the Eastern Division. This is because the Western Division's materials cost per unit would decrease, and its income from operations would increase. At the same time, a transfer price above the Eastern Division's variable costs per unit of $10 (from Exhibit 600.64) would encourage the manager of the Eastern Division to use the excess capacity to supply materials to the Western Division. In doing so, the Eastern Division's income from operations would increase.

Exhibit 600.65 *Wilson Company Income Statements—Negotiated Transfer Price*

<table>
<tr><td colspan="4" align="center">Wilson Company
Divisional Income Statements
For the Year Ended December 31, 2004</td></tr>
<tr><td></td><td>Eastern Division</td><td>Western Division</td><td>Total</td></tr>
<tr><td>Sales:</td><td></td><td></td><td></td></tr>
<tr><td>50,000 units × $20 per unit</td><td>$1,000,000</td><td></td><td>$1,000,000</td></tr>
<tr><td>20,000 units × $15 per unit</td><td>300,000</td><td></td><td>300,000</td></tr>
<tr><td>20,000 units × $40 per unit</td><td></td><td>$800,000</td><td>800,000</td></tr>
<tr><td></td><td>$1,300,000</td><td>$800,000</td><td>$2,100,000</td></tr>
<tr><td>Expenses:</td><td></td><td></td><td></td></tr>
<tr><td>Variable:</td><td></td><td></td><td></td></tr>
<tr><td>70,000 units × $10 per unit</td><td>$ 700,000</td><td></td><td>$ 700,000</td></tr>
<tr><td>20,000 units × $25* per unit</td><td></td><td>$500,000</td><td>500,000</td></tr>
<tr><td>Fixed</td><td>300,000</td><td>100,000</td><td>400,000</td></tr>
<tr><td>Total expenses</td><td>$1,000,000</td><td>$600,000</td><td>$1,600,000</td></tr>
<tr><td>Income from operations</td><td>$ 300,000</td><td>$200,000</td><td>$ 500,000</td></tr>
</table>

*$10 of the $25 are variable conversion expenses incurred solely within the Western Division, and $15 per unit represents the transfer price per unit from the Eastern Division.

We continue the illustration with the aid of Exhibit 600.65, assuming that Wilson Company's division managers agree to a transfer price of $15 for the Eastern Division's product. By purchasing from the Eastern Division, the Western Division's materials cost would be $5 per unit less. At the same time, the Eastern Division would increase its sales by $300,000 (20,000 units × $15 per unit) and increase its income by $100,000 ($300,000 sales − $200,000 variable costs). The effect of reducing the Western Division's materials cost by $100,000 (20,000 units × $5 per unit) is to increase its income by $100,000. Therefore, Wilson Company's income is increased by $200,000 ($100,000 reported by the Eastern Division and $100,000 reported by the Western Division), as shown in the condensed income statements in Exhibit 600.65.

In this illustration, any transfer price less than the market price of $20 but greater than the Eastern Division's unit variable costs of $10 would increase each division's income. In addition, overall company profit would increase by $200,000. By establishing a range of $20 to $10 for the transfer price, each division manager has an incentive to negotiate the transfer of the materials.

Cost Price Approach

Under the **cost price approach**, cost is used to set transfer prices. With this approach, a variety of cost concepts may be used. For example, cost may refer to either total product cost per unit or variable product cost per unit. If total product cost per unit is used, direct materials, direct labor, and factory overhead are included in the transfer price. If variable product cost per unit is used, the fixed factory overhead component of total product cost is excluded from the transfer price.

Either actual costs or standard (budgeted) costs may be used in applying the cost price approach. If actual costs are used, inefficiencies of the producing division are transferred to the purchasing division. Thus, there is little incentive for the producing division to control costs carefully. For this reason, most companies use standard costs in the cost price approach. In this way, differences between actual and standard costs remain with the producing division for cost-control purposes.

When division managers have responsibility for cost centers, the cost price approach to transfer pricing is proper and is often used. The cost price approach may not be proper, however, for decentralized operations organized as profit or investment centers. In profit and investment centers, division managers have responsibility for both revenues and expenses. The use of cost as a transfer price ignores the supplying division manager's responsibility for revenues. When a supplying division's sales are all intracompany transfers, for example, using the cost price approach prevents the supplying division from reporting any income from operations. A cost-based transfer price may therefore not motivate the division manager to make intracompany transfers, even though they are in the best interests of the company.

Decision Making and Accounting

Decision Models in Accounting

Managers must consider the effects of alternative decisions on their businesses. In this section, we discuss differential analysis, which reports the effects of alternative decisions on total revenues and costs. We describe and illustrate practical approaches to setting product prices. We discuss how production bottlenecks influence product mix and pricing decisions. Finally, we show two income models and describe how management uses them in decision making.

Differential Analysis

Planning for future operations involves decision making. For some decisions, revenue and cost data from the accounting records may be useful. However, the revenue and cost data for use in evaluating courses of future operations or choosing among competing alternatives are often not available in the accounting records and must be estimated.

Consider:

- The decision by **General Motors** to purchase on-board communications products from **Delphi Automotive Systems** instead of making them internally.
- The decision by **Marriott** hotels to accept a special price from a bid placed on **priceline.com.**
- The decision by **TWA** to discontinue service to Rome, Madrid, and Barcelona.

In each of these decisions, the estimated revenues and costs were **relevant.** The relevant revenues and costs focus on the differences between each alternative. Costs that have been incurred in the past are not relevant to the decision. These costs are called **sunk costs.**

Differential revenue is the amount of increase or decrease in revenue expected from a course of action as compared with an alternative. To illustrate, assume that certain equipment is being used to manufacture calculators, which are expected to generate revenue of $150,000. If the equipment could be used to make digital clocks, which would generate revenue of $175,000, the differential revenue from making and selling digital clocks is $25,000.

Differential cost is the amount of increase or decrease in cost that is expected from a course of action as compared with an alternative. For example, if an increase in advertising expenditures from $100,000 to $150,000 is being considered, the differential cost of the action is $50,000.

Differential income or loss is the difference between the differential revenue and the differential costs. Differential income indicates that a particular decision is expected to be profitable, while a differential loss indicates the opposite.

Differential analysis focuses on the effect of alternative courses of action on the relevant revenues and costs. For example, if a manager must decide between two alternatives, differential analysis would involve comparing the differential revenues of the two alternatives with the differential costs.

Decision	Differential Analysis
Alternative A	
	Differential revenue
or	− Differential costs
	Differential income or loss
Alternative B	

In this section, we will discuss the use of differential analysis in analyzing the following alternatives:

1. Leasing or selling equipment
2. Discontinuing an unprofitable segment
3. Manufacturing or purchasing a needed part

4. Replacing usable fixed assets
5. Processing further or selling an intermediate product
6. Accepting additional business at a special price

1. Lease or Sell Equipment

Management may have a choice between leasing or selling a piece of equipment that is no longer needed in the business. In deciding which option is best, management may use differential analysis. To illustrate, assume that Marcus Company is considering disposing of equipment that cost $200,000 and has $120,000 of accumulated depreciation to date. Marcus Company can sell the equipment through a broker for $100,000 less a 6 percent commission. Alternatively, Potamkin Company (the lessee) has offered to lease the equipment for five years for a total of $160,000. At the end of the fifth year of the lease, the equipment is expected to have no residual value. During the period of the lease, Marcus Company (the lessor) will incur repair, insurance, and property tax expenses estimated at $35,000. Exhibit 600.66 shows Marcus Company's analysis of whether to lease or sell the equipment.

Note that in Exhibit 600.66, the $80,000 book value ($200,000 − $120,000) of the equipment is a sunk cost and is not considered in the analysis. The $80,000 is a cost that resulted from a previous decision. It is not affected by the alternatives now being considered in leasing or selling the equipment. The relevant factors to be considered are the differential revenues and differential costs associated with the lease or sell decision. This analysis is verified by the traditional analysis in Exhibit 600.67.

The alternatives presented in Exhibits 600.66 and 600.67 are relatively simple. However, regardless of the complexity, the approach to differential analysis is basically the same. Two additional factors that often need to be considered are (1) differential revenue from investing the funds generated by the alternatives and (2) any income tax

Exhibit 600.66 *Differential Analysis Report—Lease or Sell Equipment*

Proposal to Lease or Sell Equipment June 22, 2004		
Differential revenue from alternatives:		
Revenue from lease	$160,000	
Revenue from sale	100,000	
Differential revenue from lease		$60,000
Differential cost of alternatives:		
Repair, insurance, and property tax expenses	$ 35,000	
Commission expense on sale	6,000	
Differential cost of lease		29,000
Net differential income from the lease alternative		**$31,000**

Exhibit 600.67 *Traditional Analysis*

Lease or Sell			
Lease alternative:			
Revenue from lease		$160,000	
Depreciation expense for remaining five years	$80,000		
Repair, insurance, and property tax expenses	35,000	115,000	
Net gain			$45,000
Sell alternative:			
Sales price		$100,000	
Book value of equipment	$80,000		
Commission expense	6,000	86,000	
Net gain			14,000
Net differential income from the lease alternative			**$31,000**

differential. In Exhibit 600.66, there could be differential interest revenue related to investing the cash flows from the two alternatives. Any income tax differential would be related to the differences in the timing of the income from the alternatives and the differences in the amount of investment income.

2. Discontinue a Segment or Product

When a product or a department, branch, territory, or other segment of a business is generating losses, management may consider eliminating the product or segment. It is often assumed, sometimes in error, that the total income from operations of a business would be increased if the operating loss could be eliminated. Discontinuing the product or segment usually eliminates all of the product or segment's variable costs (direct materials, direct labor, sales commissions, and so on). However, if the product or segment is a relatively small part of the business, the fixed costs (depreciation, insurance, property taxes, and so on) may not be decreased by discontinuing it. It is possible in this case for the total operating income of a company to decrease rather than increase by eliminating the product or segment. To illustrate, the income statement for **Battle Creek Cereal Co.** presented in Exhibit 600.68 is for a normal year ending August 31, 2004.

Because Bran Flakes incurs annual losses, management is considering discontinuing it. Total annual operating income of $80,000 ($40,000 Toasted Oats + $40,000 Corn Flakes) might seem to be indicated by the income statement in Exhibit 600.68 if Bran Flakes is discontinued.

Discontinuing Bran Flakes, however, would actually decrease operating income by $15,000, to $54,000 ($69,000 − $15,000). This is shown by the differential analysis report in Exhibit 600.69, in which we assume that discontinuing Bran Flakes would have no effect on fixed costs and expenses.

Exhibit 600.68 *Income (Loss) by Product*

Battle Creek Cereal Co.
Condensed Income Statement
for the Year Ended August 31, 2004

	Corn Flakes	Toasted Oats	Bran Flakes	Total
Sales	$500,000	$400,000	$100,000	$1,000,000
Cost of goods sold:				
Variable costs	$220,000	$200,000	$ 60,000	$ 480,000
Fixed costs	120,000	80,000	20,000	220,000
Total cost of goods sold	$340,000	$280,000	$ 80,000	$ 700,000
Gross profit	$160,000	$120,000	$ 20,000	$ 300,000
Operating expenses:				
Variable expenses	$ 95,000	$ 60,000	$ 25,000	$ 180,000
Fixed expenses	25,000	20,000	6,000	51,000
Total operating expenses	$120,000	$ 80,000	$ 31,000	$ 231,000
Income (loss) from operations	$ 40,000	$ 40,000	$(11,000)	$ 69,000

Exhibit 600.69 *Differential Analysis Report—Discontinue an Unprofitable Segment*

Proposal to Discontinue Bran Flakes
September 29, 2004

Differential revenue from annual sales of Bran Flakes:		
Revenue from sales		$100,000
Differential cost of annual sales of Bran Flakes:		
Variable cost of goods sold	$60,000	
Variable operating expenses	25,000	85,000
Annual differential income from sales of Bran Flakes		**$ 15,000**

660. DECISION MAKING AND ACCOUNTING

Exhibit 600.70 *Traditional Analysis*

Proposal to Discontinue Bran Flakes
September 29, 2004

	Bran Flakes, Toasted Oats, and Corn Flakes	Discontinue Bran Flakes*	Toasted Oats and Corn Flakes
Sales	$1,000,000	$100,000	$900,000
Cost of goods sold:			
Variable costs	$ 480,000	$ 60,000	$420,000
Fixed costs	220,000	—	220,000
Total cost of goods sold	$ 700,000	$ 60,000	$640,000
Gross profit	$ 300,000	$ 40,000	$260,000
Operating expenses:			
Variable expenses	$ 180,000	$ 25,000	$155,000
Fixed expenses	51,000	—	51,000
Total operating expenses	$ 231,000	$ 25,000	$206,000
Income (loss) from operations	$ 69,000	$ 15,000	$ 54,000

*Fixed costs do not decline with the discontinuance of Bran Flakes.

The traditional analysis in Exhibit 600.70 verifies the preceding differential analysis. In Exhibit 600.70, only the short-term (one year) effects of discontinuing Bran Flakes are considered. When eliminating a product or segment, management may also consider the long-term effects. For example, the plant capacity made available by discontinuing Bran Flakes might be eliminated. This could reduce fixed costs. Some employees may have to be laid off, and others may have to be relocated and retrained. Further, there may be a related decrease in sales of more profitable products to those customers who were attracted by the discontinued product.

> **Example 35** Product A has a loss from operations of $18,000 and fixed costs of $25,000. Product B has a loss from operations of $12,000 and fixed costs of $8,000. All remaining products have income from operations of $75,000 and fixed costs of $30,000. (1) Which product(s) should be discontinued, and (2) what would be the estimated income from operations if the action in (1) is taken?
>
> (1) Product B; (2) $49,000 ($75,000 − $18,000 − $8,000)

3. Make or Buy a Part

The assembly of many parts is often a major element in manufacturing some products, such as automobiles. These parts may be made by the product's manufacturer, or they may be purchased. For example, some of the parts for an automobile, such as the motor, may be produced by the automobile manufacturer. Other parts, such as tires, may be purchased from other manufacturers. In addition, in manufacturing motors, such items as spark plugs and nuts and bolts may be acquired from suppliers.

Management uses differential costs to decide whether to make or buy a part. For example, if a part is purchased, management has concluded that it is less costly to buy the part than to manufacture it. Make or buy options often arise when a manufacturer has excess productive capacity in the form of unused equipment, space, and labor.

The differential analysis is similar, whether management is considering making a part that is currently being purchased or purchasing a part that is currently being made. To illustrate, assume that an automobile manufacturer has been purchasing instrument panels for $240 a unit. The factory is currently operating at 80 percent of capacity, and no major increase in production is expected in the near future. The cost per unit of manufacturing an instrument panel internally, including fixed costs, is estimated as follows:

Direct materials	$ 80
Direct labor	80
Variable factory overhead	52
Fixed factory overhead	68
Total cost per unit	$280

If the *make* price of $280 is simply compared with the *buy* price of $240, the decision is to buy the instrument panel. However, if unused capacity could be used in manufacturing the part, there would be no increase in the total amount of fixed factory overhead costs. Thus, only the variable factory overhead costs need to be considered. The relevant costs are summarized in the differential report in Exhibit 600.71.

Exhibit 600.71 *Differential Analysis Report—Make or Buy*

Proposal to Manufacture Instrument Panels February 15, 2004		
Purchase price of an instrument panel		$240.00
Differential cost to manufacture:		
Direct materials	$80.00	
Direct labor	80.00	
Variable factory overhead	52.00	212.00
Cost savings from manufacturing an instrument panel		$ 28.00

Other possible effects of a decision to manufacture the instrument panel should also be considered. For example, increasing production in the future might require using the currently idle capacity. This decision may affect employees. It may also affect future business relations with the instrument panel supplier, who may provide other essential parts. The company's decision to manufacture instrument panels might jeopardize the timely delivery of these other parts.

Example 36 *Part K can be purchased for $30 per unit. Part K can be manufactured internally using $7.50 of direct materials and 0.75 hour of direct labor at $12 per direct labor hour (dlh). Factory overhead is applied at a rate of $20 per direct labor hour. ($7 per dlh is fixed.) What is the cost savings or penalty from manufacturing the part internally?*

$3.75 cost savings {$30 − [$7.50 + (0.75 × $12) + (0.75 × $13)]}

4. Replace Equipment

The usefulness of fixed assets may be reduced long before they are considered to be worn out. For example, equipment may no longer be efficient for the purpose for which it is used. On the other hand, the equipment may not have reached the point of complete inadequacy. Decisions to replace usable fixed assets should be based on relevant costs. The relevant costs are the future costs of continuing to use the equipment versus replacement. The book values of the fixed assets being replaced are sunk costs and are irrelevant.

To illustrate, assume that a business is considering the disposal of several identical machines having a total book value of $100,000 and an estimated remaining life of five years. The old machines can be sold for $25,000. They can be replaced by a single high-speed machine at a cost of $250,000. The new machine has an estimated useful life of five years and no residual value. Analyses indicate an estimated annual reduction in variable manufacturing costs from $225,000 with the old machine to $150,000 with the new machine. No other changes in the manufacturing costs or the operating expenses are expected. The relevant costs are summarized in the differential report in Exhibit 600.72.

Exhibit 600.72 *Differential Analysis Report—Replace Equipment*

Proposal to Replace Equipment November 28, 2004		
Annual variable costs—present equipment	$225,000	
Annual variable costs—new equipment	150,000	
Annual differential decrease in cost	$ 75,000	
Number of years applicable	× 5	
Total differential decrease in cost	$375,000	
Proceeds from sale of present equipment	25,000	$400,000
Cost of new equipment		250,000
Net differential decrease in cost, 5-year total		$150,000
Annual net differential decrease in cost—new equipment		**$ 30,000**

Other factors are often important in equipment replacement decisions. For example, differences between the remaining useful life of the old equipment and the estimated life of the new equipment could exist. In addition, the new equipment might improve the overall quality of the product, resulting in an increase in sales volume. Additional factors could include the time value of money and other uses for the cash needed to purchase the new equipment.

The amount of income that is forgone from an alternative use of an asset, such as cash, is called an **opportunity cost.** For example, your opportunity cost of attending school is the income forgone from lost work hours. Although the opportunity cost does not appear as a part of historical accounting data, it is useful in analyzing alternative courses of action. To illustrate, assume that the cash outlay of $250,000 for the new equipment, less the $25,000 proceeds from the sale of the present equipment, could be invested to yield a 10 percent return. Thus, the annual opportunity cost related to the purchase of the new equipment is $22,500 (10% × $225,000).

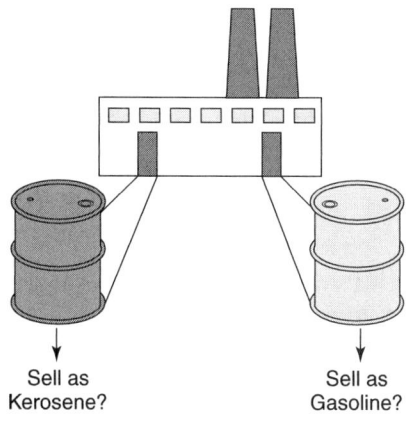

Sell as Kerosene?   Sell as Gasoline?

5. Process Further or Sell a Product

When a product is manufactured, it progresses through various stages of production. Often a product can be sold at an intermediate stage of production, or it can be processed further and then sold. In deciding whether to sell a product at an intermediate stage or to process it further, differential analysis is useful. The differential revenues from further processing are compared to the differential costs of further processing. The costs of producing the intermediate product do not change, regardless of whether the intermediate product is sold or processed further. Thus, these costs are not differential costs and are irrelevant to the decision to process further.

After initial release, film studios "process" movies further by releasing them in DVD format for the home market. Items that are relevant to making this decision are the copying and packaging costs for the disk, marketing costs associated with promoting the disk, and anticipated revenues from selling the disk. The original movie production costs are not relevant to the decision.

To illustrate, assume that a business produces kerosene in batches of 4,000 gallons. Standard quantities of 4,000 gallons of direct materials are processed, which cost $0.60 per gallon. Kerosene can be sold without further processing for $0.80 per gallon. It can be processed further to yield gasoline, which can be sold for $1.25 per gallon. Gasoline requires additional processing costs of $650 per batch, and 20 percent of the gallons of kerosene will evaporate during production. Exhibit 600.73 summarizes the differential revenues and costs in deciding whether to process kerosene to produce gasoline.

The differential income from further processing kerosene into gasoline is $150 per batch. The initial cost of producing the intermediate kerosene, $2,400 (4,000 gallons × $0.60), is not considered in deciding whether to process kerosene further. This initial cost will be incurred, regardless of whether gasoline is produced.

Exhibit 600.73 *Differential Analysis Report—Process Further or Sell*

Proposal to Process Kerosene Further October 1, 2004		
Differential revenue from further processing per batch:		
Revenue from sale of gasoline [(4,000 gallons − 800 gallons evaporation) × $1.25]	$4,000	
Revenue from sale of kerosene (4,000 gallons × $0.80)	3,200	
Differential revenue		$800
Differential cost per batch:		
Additional cost of producing gasoline		650
Differential income from further processing gasoline per batch		**$150**

Example 37 Product T is produced for $2.50 per gallon ($1.00 fixed cost) and can be sold without additional processing for $3.50 per gallon. Product T can be processed further into Product V at a cost of $1.60 per gallon ($0.90 fixed). Product V can be sold for $4.00 per gallon. What is the differential income or loss per gallon from processing Product T into Product V?

$0.20 loss [$4.00 − $3.50 − $1.60 + $0.90]

6. Accept Business at a Special Price

Differential analysis is also useful in deciding whether to accept additional business at a special price. The differential revenue that would be provided from the additional business is compared to the differential costs of producing and delivering the product to the customer. If the company is operating at full capacity, any additional production will increase both fixed and variable production costs. If, however, the normal production of the company is below full capacity, additional business may be undertaken without increasing fixed production costs. In this case, the differential costs of the additional production are the variable manufacturing costs. If operating expenses increase because of the additional business, these expenses should also be considered.

To illustrate, assume that the monthly capacity of a sporting goods business is 12,500 basketballs. Current sales and production are averaging 10,000 basketballs per month. The current manufacturing cost of $20 per unit consists of variable costs of $12.50 and fixed costs of $7.50. The normal selling price of the product in the domestic market is $30. The manufacturer receives from an exporter an offer for 5,000 basketballs at $18 each. Production can be spread over a three-month period without interfering with normal production or incurring overtime costs. Pricing policies in the domestic market will not be affected. Simply comparing the sales price of $18 with the present unit manufacturing cost of $20 indicates that the offer should be rejected. However, by focusing only on the differential cost, which in this case is the variable cost, the decision is different. Exhibit 600.74 shows the differential analysis report for this decision.

Exhibit 600.74 *Differential Analysis Report—Sell at Special Price*

Proposal to Sell Basketballs to Exporter March 10, 2004	
Differential revenue from accepting offer:	
Revenue from sale of 5,000 additional units at $18	$90,000
Differential cost of accepting offer:	
Variable costs of 5,000 additional units at $12.50	62,500
Differential income from accepting offer	**$27,500**

Proposals to sell a product in the domestic market at prices lower than the normal price may require additional considerations. For example, it may be unwise to increase sales volume in one territory by price reductions if sales volume is lost in other areas. Manufacturers must also conform to the Robinson-Patman Act, which prohibits price discrimination within the United States unless differences in prices can be justified by different costs of serving different customers.

> **Example 38** Product D is normally sold for $4.40 per unit. A special price of $3.60 is offered for the export market. The variable production cost is $3.00 per unit. An additional export tariff of 10% of revenue will be required for all export products. What is the differential income or loss per unit from selling Product D for export?
>
> $0.24 income [$3.60 − $3.00 − (0.10 × $3.60)]

Setting Normal Product-Selling Prices

Differential analysis may be useful in deciding to lower selling prices for special short-run decisions, such as whether to accept business at a price lower than the normal price. In such cases, the minimum short-run price is set high enough to cover all variable costs. Any price above this minimum price will improve profits in the short run. In the long run, however, the normal selling price must be set high enough to cover all costs and expenses (both fixed and variable) and provide a reasonable profit. Otherwise, the business may not survive.

The normal selling price can be viewed as the target selling price to be achieved in the long run. The basic approaches to setting this price are as follows:

Market Methods	Cost-Plus Methods
1. Demand-based methods	1. Total cost concept
2. Competition-based methods	2. Product cost concept
	3. Variable cost concept

Managers using the market methods refer to the external market to determine the price. Demand-based methods set the price according to the demand for the product. If there is high demand for the product, then the price may be set high, while lower demand may require the price to be set low. An example of setting different prices according to the demand for the product is found in the telecommunications industry, with low weekend rates and high business day rates for long-distance telephone calls.

Competition-based methods set the price according to the price offered by competitors. For example, if a competitor reduces the price, then management may be required to adjust the price to meet the competition. The market-based pricing approaches are discussed in greater detail in marketing courses, so we will not expand upon them here.

Managers using the cost-plus methods price the product in order to achieve a target profit. Managers add to the cost an amount called a **markup,** so that all costs plus a profit are included in the selling price. In the following paragraphs, we describe and illustrate the three cost concepts often used in applying the cost-plus approach: (1) total cost, (2) product cost, and (3) variable cost.

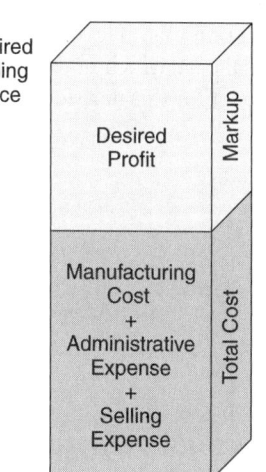

Total Cost Concept

Total Cost Concept

Using the **total cost concept,** all costs of manufacturing a product plus the selling and administrative expenses are included in the cost amount to which the markup is added. Since all costs and expenses are included in the cost amount, the dollar amount of the markup equals the desired profit.

The first step in applying the total cost concept is to determine the total cost of manufacturing the product. This cost includes the costs of direct materials, direct labor, and factory overhead and should be available from the accounting records. The next step is to add the estimated selling and administrative expenses to the total cost of manufacturing the product. The cost amount per unit is then computed by dividing the total costs by the total units expected to be produced and sold.

After the cost amount per unit has been determined, the dollar amount of the markup is determined. For this purpose, the markup is expressed as a percentage of cost. This percentage is then multiplied by the cost amount per unit. The dollar amount of the markup is then added to the cost amount per unit to arrive at the selling price.

The markup percentage for the total cost concept is determined by applying the following formula.

$$\text{Markup percentage} = \frac{\text{Desired profit}}{\text{Total costs}}$$

The numerator of the formula is only the desired profit. This is because all costs and expenses are included in the cost amount to which the markup is added. The denominator of the formula is the total costs.

To illustrate, assume that the costs for calculators of Digital Solutions Inc. are as follows.

Variable costs:	
Direct materials	$ 3.00 per unit
Direct labor	10.00
Factory overhead	1.50
Selling and administrative expenses	1.50
Total	$ 16.00 per unit
Fixed costs:	
Factory overhead	$50,000
Selling and administrative expenses	20,000

Digital Solutions Inc. desires a profit equal to a 20 percent rate of return on assets; $800,000 of assets are devoted to producing calculators; and 100,000 units are expected to be produced and sold. The calculators' total cost is $1,670,000, or $16.70 per unit, computed as follows:

Variable costs ($16.00 × 100,000 units)		$1,600,000
Fixed costs:		
Factory overhead	$50,000	
Selling and administrative expenses	20,000	70,000
Total costs		$1,670,000
Total cost per calculator ($1,670,000 ÷ 100,000 units)		$ 16.70

The desired profit is $160,000 (20% × $800,000), and the markup percentage for a calculator is 9.6 percent, computed as follows:

$$\text{Markup percentage} = \frac{\text{Desired profits}}{\text{Total costs}}$$

$$\text{Markup percentage} = \frac{\$160,000}{\$1,670,000} = 9.6\%$$

Based on the total cost per unit and the markup percentage for a calculator, Digital Solutions Inc. would price each calculator at $18.30 per unit, as shown below.

Total cost per calculator	$16.70
Markup ($16.70 × 9.6%)	1.60
Selling price	$18.30

The ability of the selling price of $18.30 to generate the desired profit of $160,000 is shown by the following income statement:

Digital Solutions Inc.
Income Statement
for the Year Ended December 31, 2004

Sales (100,000 units × $18.30)		$1,830,000
Expenses:		
Variable (100,000 units × $16.00)	$1,600,000	
Fixed ($50,000 + $20,000)	70,000	1,670,000
Income from operations		$ 160,000

The total cost concept of applying the cost-plus approach to product pricing is often used by contractors who sell products to government agencies. In many cases, government contractors are required by law to be reimbursed for their products on a total-cost-plus-profit basis.

Example 39 *The microcomputer industry is developing products that can be sold to consumers for under $1,000. By using the total cost concept, the following price can be determined:*

Motherboard	$140
Memory	50
Processor	90
Disk drive	198
Peripherals	265
Factory overhead and assembly	48
Product cost	$791
Administrative expenses	26
Total cost	$817
Manufacturer markup	91
Manufacturer's price to retailer	$908
Retailer markup	91
Retail price to final consumer	$999

Notice that there are two markups included in the final price—one for the manufacturer and one for the retailer.

Product Cost Concept

Using the **product cost concept**, only the costs of manufacturing the product, termed the *product cost*, are included in the cost amount to which the markup is added. Estimated selling expenses, administrative expenses, and profit are included in the markup. The markup percentage is determined by applying the following formula.

$$\text{Markup percentage} = \frac{\text{Desired profit} + \text{Total selling and administrative expenses}}{\text{Total manufacturing costs}}$$

The numerator of the markup percentage formula is the desired profit plus the total selling and administrative expenses. These expenses must be included in the markup, since they are not included in the cost amount to which the markup is added. The denominator of the formula includes the costs of direct materials, direct labor, and factory overhead.

To illustrate, assume the same data used in the preceding illustration. The manufacturing cost for Digital Solutions Inc.'s calculator is $1,500,000, or $15 per unit, computed as follows:

Direct materials ($3 × 100,000 units)		$ 300,000
Direct labor ($10 × 100,000 units)		1,000,000
Factory overhead:		
Variable ($1.50 × 100,000 units)	$150,000	
Fixed	50,000	200,000
Total manufacturing costs		$1,500,000
Manufacturing cost per calculator ($1,500,000 ÷ 100,000 units)		$ 15

The desired profit is $160,000 (20% × $800,000), and the total selling and administrative expenses are $170,000 [(100,000 units × $1.50 per unit) + $20,000]. The markup percentage for a calculator is 22 percent, computed as follows.

$$\text{Markup percentage} = \frac{\text{Desired profit} + \text{Total selling and administrative expenses}}{\text{Total manufacturing costs}}$$

$$\text{Markup percentage} = \frac{\$160,000 + \$170,000}{\$1,500,000}$$

$$\text{Markup percentage} = \frac{\$330,000}{\$1,500,000} = 22\%$$

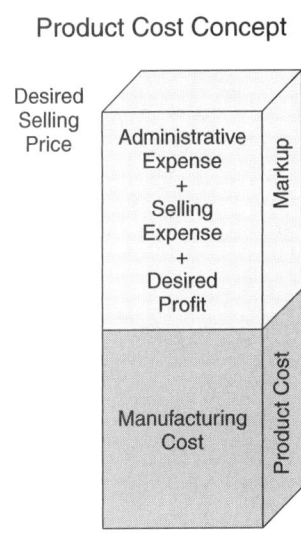

Product Cost Concept

Based on the manufacturing cost per calculator and the markup percentage, Digital Solutions Inc. would price each calculator at $18.30 per unit, as shown below.

Manufacturing cost per calculator	$15.00
Markup ($15 × 22%)	3.30
Selling price	$18.30

Variable Cost Concept

The **variable cost concept** emphasizes the distinction between variable and fixed costs in product pricing. Using the variable cost concept, only variable costs are included in the cost amount to which the markup is added. All variable manufacturing costs, as well as variable selling and administrative expenses, are included in the cost amount. Fixed manufacturing costs, fixed selling and administrative expenses, and profit are included in the markup.

The markup percentage is determined by applying the following formula:

$$\text{Markup percentage} = \frac{\text{Desired profit} + \text{Total fixed costs}}{\text{Total variable costs}}$$

The numerator of the markup percentage formula is the desired profit plus the total fixed manufacturing costs and the total fixed selling and administrative expenses. These costs and expenses must be included in the markup, since they are not included in the cost amount to which the markup is added. The denominator of the formula includes the total variable costs.

To illustrate, assume the same data as used in the two preceding illustrations. The calculator variable cost is $1,600,000, or $16.00 per unit, computed as follows.

Variable costs:	
Direct materials ($3 × 100,000 units)	$ 300,000
Direct labor ($10 × 100,000 units)	1,000,000
Factory overhead ($1.50 × 100,000 units)	150,000
Selling and administrative expenses ($1.50 × 100,000 units)	150,000
Total variable costs	$1,600,000
Variable cost per calculator ($1,600,000 ÷ 100,000 units)	$ 16

Variable Cost Concept

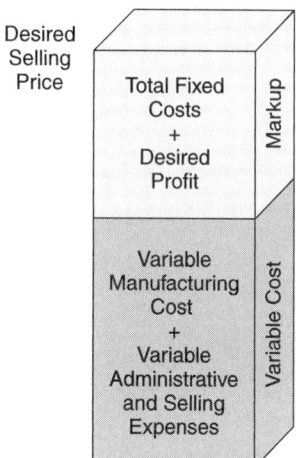

The desired profit is $160,000 (20% × $800,000), the total fixed manufacturing costs are $50,000, and the total fixed selling and administrative expenses are $20,000. The markup percentage for a calculator is 14.4 percent, computed as follows:

$$\text{Markup percentage} = \frac{\text{Desired profit} + \text{Total fixed costs}}{\text{Total variable costs}}$$

$$\text{Markup percentage} = \frac{\$160{,}000 + \$50{,}000 + \$20{,}000}{\$1{,}600{,}000}$$

$$\text{Markup percentage} = \frac{\$230{,}000}{\$1{,}600{,}000} = 14.4\%$$

Based on the variable cost per calculator and the markup percentage, Digital Solutions Inc. would price each calculator at $18.30 per unit, as shown below.

Variable cost per calculator	$16.00
Markup ($16.00 × 14.4%)	2.30
Selling price	$18.30

Example 40 *Product Z has a total cost of $30 per unit. Of this amount, $10 per unit is selling and administrative costs. The total variable cost is $18 per unit. The desired profit is $3 per unit. Determine the markup percentage on (1) total cost, (2) product cost, and (3) variable cost.*

(1) 10% ($3 ÷ $30);
(2) 65% [($10 + $3) ÷ $20];
(3) 83.3% [($12 + $3) ÷ $18]

Choosing a Cost-Plus Approach Cost Concept

All three cost concepts produced the same selling price ($18.30) for Digital Solutions Inc. In practice, however, the three cost concepts are usually not viewed as alternatives. Each cost concept requires different estimates of costs and expenses. This difficulty and the complexity of the manufacturing operations should be considered in choosing a cost concept.

To reduce the costs of gathering data, estimated (standard) costs rather than actual costs may be used with any of the three cost concepts. However, management should exercise caution when using estimated costs in applying the cost-plus approach. The estimates should be based on normal (attainable) operating levels and not theoretical (ideal) levels of performance. In product pricing, the use of estimates based on ideal- or maximum-capacity operating levels might lead to setting product prices too low. In this case, the costs of such factors as normal spoilage or normal periods of idle time might not be considered.

The decision-making needs of management are also an important factor in selecting a cost concept for product pricing. For example, managers who often make special pricing decisions are more likely to use the variable cost concept. In contrast, a government defense contractor would be more likely to use the total cost concept.

A variation of the cost concepts discussed in the preceding paragraphs is the **target cost concept.** Under this concept, which was first used by the Japanese, the selling price is assumed to be set by the marketplace. The target cost is determined by *subtracting* a desired profit from the selling price. Thus, managers must design and manufacture the product to achieve its target cost. In contrast, the three cost concepts discussed previously start with a given product cost and *add* a markup to determine the selling price. Some argue that the target cost concept may be better than the cost-plus approaches in highly competitive markets that require continual product cost reductions to remain competitive.

Activity-Based Costing

As illustrated in the preceding paragraphs, costs are an important consideration in setting product prices. To more accurately measure the costs of producing and selling products, some companies use activity-based costing. **Activity-based costing (ABC)** identifies and traces activities to specific products.

Activity-based costing may be useful in making product pricing decisions where manufacturing operations involve large amounts of factory overhead. In such cases, traditional overhead allocation using activity bases such as units produced or machine hours may yield inaccurate cost allocations. This, in turn, may result in distorted product costs and product prices. By providing more accurate product cost allocations, activity-based costing aids in setting product prices that will cover costs and expenses.

Product Profitability and Pricing Under Production Bottlenecks

An important consideration influencing production volumes and prices is production bottlenecks. A production **bottleneck (or constraint)** occurs at the point in the process where the demand for the company's product exceeds the ability to produce the product. The **theory of constraints (TOC)** is a manufacturing strategy that focuses on reducing the influence of bottlenecks on a process.

Product Profitability Under Production Bottlenecks

When a company has a bottleneck in its production process, it should attempt to maximize its profitability, subject to the influence of the bottleneck. To illustrate, assume that Snapp-Off Tool Company makes three types of wrenches: small, medium, and large. All three products are processed through a heat-treatment operation, which hardens the steel tools. Snapp-Off Tool's heat-treatment process is operating at full capacity and is a production bottleneck. The product contribution margin per unit and the number of hours of heat treatment used by each type of wrench are as follows:

	Small Wrench	Medium Wrench	Large Wrench
Sales price per unit	$130	$140	$160
Variable cost per unit	40	40	40
Contribution margin per unit	$ 90	$100	$120
Heat treatment hours per unit	1	4	8

The large wrench appears to be the most profitable product because its contribution margin per unit is the greatest. However, the contribution margin per unit can be a misleading indicator of profitability in a bottleneck operation. The correct measure of performance is the value of each bottleneck hour, or the contribution margin per bottleneck hour. Using this measure, each product has a much different profitability when compared to the contribution margin per unit information, as shown in Exhibit 600.75.

660. DECISION MAKING AND ACCOUNTING

Exhibit 600.75 *Contribution Margin per Bottleneck Hour*

	Small Wrench	Medium Wrench	Large Wrench
Sales price	$130	$140	$160
Variable cost per unit	40	40	40
Contribution margin per unit	$ 90	$100	$120
Bottleneck (heat treatment) hours per unit	÷ 1	÷ 4	÷ 8
Contribution margin per bottleneck hour	$ 90	$ 25	$ 15

The small wrench produces the most contribution margin per bottleneck (heat treatment) hour used, while the large wrench produces the smallest profit per bottleneck hour. Thus, the small wrench is the most profitable product. This information is the opposite of that implied by the unit contribution margin profit.

Example 41 *Product A has a contribution margin of $15 per unit. Product B has a contribution margin of $20 per unit. Product A requires three furnace hours, while Product B requires five furnace hours. Determine the most profitable product, assuming that the furnace is a bottleneck.*

Product A ($15 ÷ 3 hours = $5 per hour, which is greater than $20 ÷ 5 hours, or $4 per hour)

Product Pricing Under Production Bottlenecks

Each hour of a bottleneck delivers profit to the company. When a company has a production bottleneck, the contribution margin per hour of bottleneck provides a measure of the product's relative profitability. This information can also be used to adjust the product price to better reflect the value of the product's use of a bottleneck. Products that use a large number of bottleneck hours per unit require more contribution margin than products that use few bottleneck hours per unit. For example, Snapp-Off Tool Company should increase the price of the large wrench in order to deliver more contribution margin per bottleneck hour.

To determine the price of the large wrench that would equate its profitability to the small wrench, we need to solve the following equation:

$$\text{Contribution margin per bottleneck hour per small wrench} = \frac{\text{Revised price of large wrench} - \text{Variable cost per large wrench}}{\text{Bottleneck hours per large wrench}}$$

$$\$90 = \frac{\text{Revised price of large wrench} - \$40}{8}$$

$720 = Revised price of large wrench − $40
$760 = Revised price of large wrench

The large wrench's price would need to be increased to $760 in order to deliver the same contribution margin per bottleneck hour as does the small wrench, as verified below.

Revised price of large wrench	$760
Less: Variable cost per unit of large wrench	40
Contribution margin per unit of large wrench	$720
Bottleneck hours per unit of large wrench	÷ 8
Revised contribution margin per bottleneck hour	$ 90

At a price of $760, the company would be indifferent between producing and selling the small wrench or the large wrench, all else being equal. This analysis assumes that there is unlimited demand for the products. If the market were unwilling to purchase the large wrench at this price, then the company should produce the small wrench.

Income Models and Decision Making

Just as you should evaluate the relative financial impact of various choices, so must a business evaluate the financial impact of its choices. In this section we will discuss how businesses measure profitability, using absorption costing and variable costing. After illustrating and comparing these concepts, we discuss how businesses use them for controlling costs, pricing products, planning production, analyzing market segments, and analyzing contribution margins.

The Income Statement Under Variable Costing and Absorption Costing

One of the most important items affecting a business's net income is the cost of goods sold. In many cases, the cost of goods sold is larger than all of the other expenses combined. The cost of goods sold can be determined under either the absorption costing or variable costing concept.

Under **absorption costing**, all manufacturing costs are included in finished goods and remain there as an asset until the goods are sold. Absorption costing is necessary in determining historical costs for financial reporting to external users and for tax reporting.

Variable costing may be more useful to management in making decisions. In **variable costing**, which is also called **direct costing**, the cost of goods manufactured is composed only of *variable* manufacturing costs—costs that increase or decrease as the volume of production rises or falls. These costs are the direct materials, direct labor, and only those factory overhead costs that vary with the rate of production. The remaining factory overhead costs, which are fixed or nonvariable costs, are generally related to the productive capacity of the manufacturing plant and are not affected by changes in the quantity of product manufactured. Thus, the fixed factory overhead does not become a part of the cost of goods manufactured but is treated as an expense of the period in which it is incurred.

To illustrate the difference between the variable costing income statement and the absorption costing income statement, assume that Belling Co. manufactured 15,000 units at the following costs:

Absorption Costing

Inventory:
Cost of Goods Manufactured
- Direct materials
- Direct labor
- Variable factory overhead
- Fixed factory overhead

Variable Costing

Inventory:
Cost of Goods Manufactured
- Direct materials
- Direct labor
- Variable factory overhead

Period Expense → Fixed factory overhead

	Total Cost	Number of Units	Unit Cost
Manufacturing costs:			
Variable	$375,000	15,000	$25
Fixed	150,000	15,000	10
Total	$525,000		$35
Selling and administrative expenses:			
Variable ($5 per unit sold	$ 75,000		
Fixed	50,000		
Total	$125,000		

The units sell at a price of $50, as shown in the variable costing income statement for Belling Co. in Exhibit 600.76. In this income statement, variable costs are separated from fixed costs. The variable cost of goods sold, which includes the variable manufacturing costs, is deducted from sales to yield the **manufacturing margin** of $375,000. The variable selling and administrative expenses of $75,000 are deducted from the manufacturing margin to yield the contribution margin of $300,000. Thus, the **contribution margin** is sales less variable

The variable costing income statement includes only variable manufacturing costs in the cost of goods sold.

Exhibit 600.76 *Variable Costing Income Statement*

Sales (15,000 × $50)		$750,000
Variable cost of goods sold (15,000 × $25)		375,000
Manufacturing margin		$375,000
Variable selling and administrative expenses		75,000
Contribution margin		$300,000
Fixed costs:		
Fixed manufacturing costs	$150,000	
Fixed selling and administrative expenses	50,000	200,000
Income from operations		$100,000

Exhibit 600.77 *Absorption Costing Income Statement*

Sales (15,000 × $50)	$750,000
Cost of goods sold (15,000 × $35)	525,000
Gross profit	$225,000
Selling and administrative expenses ($75,000 + $50,000)	125,000
Income from operations	$100,000

costs. The income from operations of $100,000 is then determined by deducting fixed costs of $200,000 from the contribution margin.

Exhibit 600.77 shows the absorption costing income statement prepared for Belling Co. The absorption costing income statement does not distinguish between variable and fixed costs. All manufacturing costs are included in the cost of goods sold. Deducting cost of goods sold from sales yields the $225,000 gross profit. Deducting selling and administrative expenses then yields income from operations of $100,000.

> **Example 42** A company has sales of $450,000, cost of goods sold of $300,000, variable cost of goods sold of $220,000, and variable selling expenses of $50,000. What are (a) its manufacturing margin and (b) its contribution margin?
>
> (a) $230,000 ($450,000 − $220,000);   (b) $180,000 ($230,000 − $50,000)

Income Analysis Under Variable Costing and Absorption Costing

As we have illustrated, the income from operations under variable costing can differ from the income from operations under absorption costing. This difference results from change in the quantity of the finished goods inventory, which are caused by differences in the levels of sales and production. In analyzing and evaluating operations, management should be aware of the possible effects of changing inventory levels under the two concepts.

As illustrated, if absorption costing is used, management should be careful in analyzing income from operations when large changes in inventory levels occur. Managers could misinterpret increases or decreases in income from operations, due to mere changes in inventory levels, to be the result of business events, such as changes in sales volume, prices, or costs.

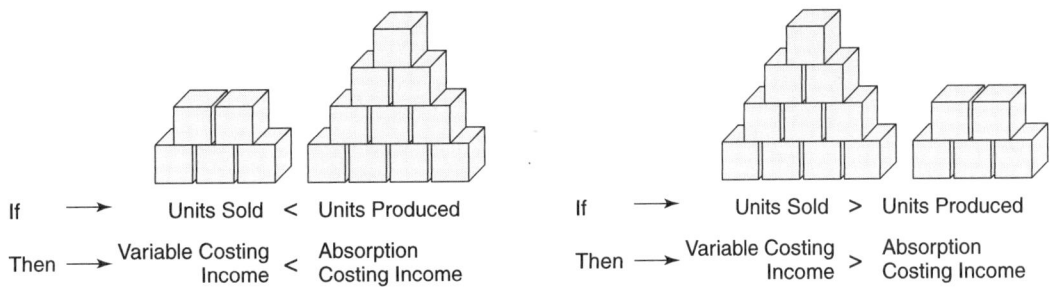

Many accountants believe that variable costing should be used for evaluating operating performance because absorption costing encourages management to produce inventory. This is because producing inventory absorbs fixed costs and causes the income from operations to appear higher, as we have illustrated above. In the long run, building inventory without the promise of future sales may lead to higher handling, storage, financing, and obsolescence costs.

Example 43 *Fixed costs are $40 per unit and variable costs are $120 per unit. Production exceeded sales by 5,000 units. What is the difference in the variable costing and absorption costing income from operations?*

Variable costing income from operations will be $200,000 ($40 per unit × 5,000) less than absorption costing income from operations.

Example 44 *The beginning inventory is 8,000 units, all of which are sold during the period. The beginning inventory fixed costs are $60 per unit, and variable costs are $300 per unit. What is the difference in the variable costing and absorption costing income from operations, assuming no ending inventory?*

Variable costing income from operations will be $480,000 ($60 per unit × 8,000) greater than absorption costing income from operations.

Example 45 *Variable costs are $100 per unit, and fixed costs are $50,000. Sales are estimated to be 4,000 units. (a) How much would absorption costing income from operations differ between a plan to produce 4,000 units and 5,000 units? (b) How much would variable costing income from operations differ between the two production plans?*

(a) $10,000 greater for 5,000 units of production
   [1,000 units × ($50,000 ÷ 5,000), or 4,000 units × ($12.50 − $10.00)];
(b) There would be no difference in income from operations.

Management's Use of Variable Costing and Absorption Costing

Managerial accountants should carefully analyze each situation in evaluating whether variable costing or absorption costing reports would be more useful to management. In many situations, preparing reports under both concepts provides useful insights. In the following paragraphs, we discuss such reports and their advantages and disadvantages to management in making decisions related to the items identified in Exhibit 600.78.

Controlling Costs

All costs are controllable in the long run by someone within a business, but they are not all controllable at the same level of management. For example, plant supervisors, as members of operating management, are responsible for controlling the use of direct materials in their departments. They have no control, however, of insurance costs related to the buildings housing their departments. For a specific level of management, **controllable costs** are costs that can be influenced by management at that level, and **noncontrollable costs** are costs that another level of management controls. This distinction is useful in fixing the responsibility for incurring costs and for reporting costs to those responsible for their control.

Exhibit 600.78 *Accounting Reports and Management Decisions*

Variable manufacturing costs are controlled at the operating level. If the product's cost includes only variable manufacturing costs, the cost can be controlled by operating management. The fixed factory overhead costs are normally the responsibility of a higher level of management. When the fixed factory overhead costs are reported as a separate item in the variable costing income statement, they are easier to identify and control than when they are spread among units of product, as they are under absorption costing.

As in the case with the fixed and variable manufacturing costs, the control of the variable and fixed operating expenses is usually the responsibility of different levels of management. Under variable costing, the variable selling and administrative expenses are reported separately from the fixed selling and administrative expenses. Because they are reported in this manner, both types of operating expenses are easier to identify and control than is the case under absorption costing.

Pricing Products

Many factors enter into determining the selling price of a product. The cost of making the product is clearly significant. Microeconomic theory states that income is maximized by expanding output to the volume where the revenue realized by the sale of an additional unit (marginal revenue) equals the cost of that unit (marginal cost). Although the degree of accuracy assumed in economic theory is rarely achieved, the concepts of marginal revenue and marginal cost are useful in setting selling prices.

In the short run, a business is committed to its existing manufacturing facilities. The pricing decision should be based upon making the best use of such capacity. The fixed costs cannot be avoided, but the variable costs can be eliminated if the company does not manufacture the product. The selling price of a product, therefore, should at least be equal to the variable costs of making and selling it. Any price above this minimum selling price contributes an amount toward covering fixed costs and providing income. Variable costing procedures yield data that emphasize these relationships.

In the long run, plant capacity can be increased or decreased. If a business is to continue operating, the selling prices of its products must cover all costs and provide a reasonable income. Hence, in establishing pricing policies for the long run, information provided by absorption costing procedures is needed.

The results of a research study indicated that the companies studied used absorption costing in making routine pricing decisions. However, these companies regularly used variable costing as a basis for setting prices in many short-run situations.

There are no simple solutions to most pricing problems. Consideration must be given to many factors of varying importance. Accounting can contribute by preparing analyses of various pricing plans for both the short run and the long run. Additional analyses useful for product pricing are further described and illustrated in a later section.

Planning Production

Planning production also has both short-run and long-run implications. In the short run, production is limited to existing capacity. Operating decisions must be made quickly before opportunities are lost. For example, a company manufacturing products with a seasonal demand may have an opportunity to obtain an off-season order that will not interfere with its production schedule nor reduce the sales of its other products. The relevant factors for such a short-run decision are the additional revenues and the additional variable costs associated with the off-season order. If the revenues from the special order will provide a contribution margin, the order should be accepted because it will increase the company's income from operations. For long-run planning, management must also consider the fixed costs.

Analyzing Market Segments

Market analysis is performed by the sales and marketing function in order to determine the profit contributed by market segments. A **market segment** is a portion of business that can be assigned to a manager for profit responsibility. Examples of market segments include sales territories, products, salespersons, and customer distribution channels. Variable costing can provide significant insight to decision making regarding such segments.

To illustrate, assume the following data for the month of March 2004 for Camelot Fragrance Company. Camelot Fragrance Company manufactures and markets the Gwenevere perfume line for women and the Lancelot cologne line for men.

	Northern Territory	Southern Territory	Total
Sales:			
Gwenevere	$60,000	$30,000	$ 90,000
Lancelot	20,000	50,000	70,000
Total territory sales	$80,000	$80,000	$160,000
Variable production costs:			
Gwenevere (12% of sales)	$ 7,200	$ 3,600	$ 10,800
Lancelot (12% of sales)	2,400	6,000	8,400
Total variable production cost by territory	$ 9,600	$ 9,600	$ 19,200
Promotion costs:			
Gwenevere (variable at 30% of sales)	$18,000	$ 9,000	$ 27,000
Lancelot (variable at 20% of sales)	4,000	10,000	14,000
Total promotion cost by territory	$22,000	$19,000	$ 41,000
Sales commissions:			
Gwenevere (variable at 20% of sales)	$12,000	$ 6,000	$ 18,000
Lancelot (variable at 10% of sales)	2,000	5,000	7,000
Total sales commissions by territory	$14,000	$11,000	$ 25,000

This information can be used by Camelot Fragrance Company to prepare a sales territory, product, and salesperson profitability analysis. Each of these is discussed on the following pages.

SALES TERRITORY PROFITABILITY ANALYSIS An income statement presenting the contribution margin by sales territories is often useful to management in evaluating past performance and in directing future sales efforts. Sales territory profitability analysis may lead management to reduce costs in lower-profit sales territories or to increase sales effort in higher-profit territories. For example, the Coca-Cola Company earns over 75 percent of its total corporate profits outside of the United States. This information motivates the Coca-Cola management to continue expanding operations and sales efforts around the world.

There are many possible explanations for profit differences between territories, including differences in pricing, sales unit volumes, media rates, selling costs, and the types of products sold. To illustrate the analysis of profit differences by sales territory, Exhibit 600.79 shows the contribution margin by sales territory for Camelot Fragrance Company.

The contribution margin for each territory consists of the sales less the variable costs associated with producing and selling products in each territory. In addition to the contribution margin, the contribution margin ratio (contribution margin divided by sales) for each territory is useful in evaluating sales territories and directing operations toward more profitable activities. For the Northern Territory, the contribution margin ratio is 43 percent ($34,400 ÷ $80,000), and for the Southern Territory the ratio is 50.5 percent ($40,400 ÷ $80,000). Although each territory had the same sales, the contribution margin ratios are different. Why is this?

660. DECISION MAKING AND ACCOUNTING

Exhibit 600.79 *Contribution Margin by Sales Territory Report*

Camelot Fragrance Company
Contribution Margin by Sales Territory
for the Month Ended March 31, 2004

	Northern Territory		Southern Territory	
Sales		$80,000		$80,000
Variable cost of goods sold		9,600		9,600
Manufacturing margin		$70,400		$70,400
Variable selling expenses:				
Promotion costs	$22,000		$19,000	
Sales commissions	14,000	36,000	11,000	30,000
Contribution margin		$34,400		$40,400
Contribution margin ratio		43%		50.5%

    In this case, the difference in territory profit performance can be explained by the difference in sales mix between the two territories. **Sales mix,** sometimes referred to as *product mix,* is defined as the relative distribution of sales among the various products sold. From the assumed information, the Southern Territory had a higher relative proportion of Lancelot sales than did the Northern Territory. If the Lancelot line is more profitable than the Gwenevere line, then we would expect the Southern Territory's overall profitability to be higher than the Northern Territory's, as shown in Exhibit 600.79. To verify the difference between the profitabilities of the two products, product profitability analysis may be performed.

    PRODUCT PROFITABILITY ANALYSIS Management should focus its sales efforts on those products that will provide the maximum total contribution margin. An income statement presenting the contribution margin by products is often used by management to guide product-related sales and promotional efforts. For example, **Ford's** *Explorer* sport utility vehicle is one of its most profitable models. Ford uses this information to motivate higher production levels and promotion effort for this brand.

    Some products are more profitable than others due to differences with respect to pricing, manufacturing costs, advertising support, or salesperson support. To illustrate the analysis of these differences, Exhibit 600.80 shows the contribution margin by product line for Camelot Fragrance Company.

    As you can see, Lancelot's contribution margin ratio is greater than Gwenevere's, even though both product lines have the same manufacturing margin as a

> *Customer, territory, product, and salesperson profit analysis is done by using a "data warehouse." A data warehouse is a relational database of revenue and cost information that can be divided into many different profit views. For example, **Johnson and Johnson's** data warehouse, called Darwin, enables managers from 50 countries around the world to see various profit views at the click of a mouse.*

Exhibit 600.80 *Contribution Margin by Product Line Report*

Camelot Fragrance Company
Contribution Margin by Product Line
for the Month Ended March 31, 2004

	Gwenevere		Lancelot	
Sales		$90,000		$70,000
Variable cost of goods sold		10,800		8,400
Manufacturing margin		$79,200		$61,600
Variable selling expenses:				
Promotion costs	$27,000		$14,000	
Sales commissions	18,000	45,000	7,000	21,000
Contribution margin		$34,200		$40,600
Contribution margin ratio		38%		58%

percent of sales. The higher contribution margin ratio is the result of Lancelot's lower promotion costs and sales commissions as a percent of sales. The sales territory profitability analysis and the product profitability analysis both indicate the superior profit performance of the Lancelot line. Thus, management should emphasize the Lancelot product line in its marketing plans, try to reduce the promotion and sales commission expenses associated with Gwenevere sales, or increase the price of Gwenevere.

SALESPERSON PROFITABILITY ANALYSIS In addition to the sales territory and product profitability analyses, sales managers may wish to evaluate the performance of salespersons. This may be done with a salesperson profitability analysis.

A report to management for use in evaluating the sales performance of each salesperson could include total sales, variable cost of goods sold, variable selling expenses, contribution margin, and contribution margin ratio. Exhibit 600.81 illustrates such a report for three salespersons in the Northern Territory of Camelot Fragrance Company.

The total sales and costs of all three salespersons agree with the sales and costs for the Northern Territory in Exhibit 600.79. Thus, this report provides the Northern Territory manager with a more detailed analysis of the territory's performance. The report indicates that Beth Williams produced the greatest contribution margin for the company but had the lowest contribution margin ratio. Beth Williams sold $40,000 of product, which is twice as much product as the other two salespersons. However, Beth Williams sold only the Gwenevere product line, which has the lowest contribution margin ratio (from Exhibit 600.80). The other two salespersons sold equal amounts of Gwenevere and Lancelot. These two salespersons had higher contribution margin ratios because of the sales of the higher-margin Lancelot line. The territory manager could use this report to encourage Rodriguez and Ginger to sell more total product, while encouraging Williams to place more selling effort on the Lancelot line.

Other factors should also be considered in evaluating the performance of salespersons. For example, sales growth rates, years of experience, customer service, size of the territory, and actual performance compared to budgeted performance may also be important.

Analyzing Contribution Margins

Another use of the contribution margin concept to assist management in planning and controlling operations focuses on differences between planned and actual contribution margins. However, mere knowledge of the differences is insufficient. Management needs information about the causes of the differences. The systematic examination of the differences between planned and actual contribution margins is termed **contribution margin analysis**.

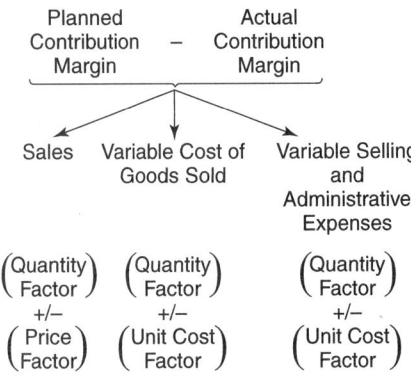

Exhibit 600.81 *Contribution Margin by Salesperson Report*

	Inez Rodriguez	Tom Ginger	Beth Williams	Northern Territory— Total
Sales	$20,000	$20,000	$40,000	$80,000
Variable cost of goods sold	2,400	2,400	4,800	9,600
Manufacturing margin	$17,600	$17,600	$35,200	$70,400
Variable selling expenses:				
Promotion costs	$ 5,000	$ 5,000	$12,000	$22,000
Sales commissions	3,000	3,000	8,000	14,000
	$ 8,000	$ 8,000	$20,000	$36,000
Contribution margin	$ 9,600	$ 9,600	$15,200	$34,400
Contribution margin ratio	48%	48%	38%	43%
Sales mix (% Lancelot sales)	50%	50%	0	25%

Camelot Fragrance Company
Contribution Margin by Salesperson—Northern Territory
for the Month Ended March 31, 2004

660. DECISION MAKING AND ACCOUNTING

Since contribution margin is the excess of sales over variable costs, a difference between the planned and actual contribution margin can be caused by (1) an increase or decrease in the amount of sales or (2) an increase or decrease in the amount of variable costs. An increase or decrease in either element may in turn be due to (1) an increase or decrease in the number of units sold or (2) an increase or decrease in the unit sales price or unit cost. The effect of these two factors on either sales or variable costs may be stated as follows:

1. **Quantity factor**—the effect of a difference in the number of units sold, assuming no change in unit sales price or unit cost. The quantity factor is the difference between the actual quantity sold and the planned quantity sold, multiplied by the planned unit sales price or unit cost.
2. **Unit price factor** or **unit cost factor**—the effect of a difference in unit sales price or unit cost on the number of units sold. The unit price or unit cost factor is the difference between the actual unit price or unit cost and the planned unit price or unit cost, multiplied by the actual quantity sold.

We will use Exhibit 600.82 for Noble Inc. for the year ended December 31, 2004, as a basis for illustrating contribution margin analysis. For the sake of simplicity, we will assume a single commodity. The analysis would be more complex if several different commodities were sold, but the basic principles would not be affected.

The analysis of these data in Exhibit 600.83 shows that the favorable increase of $25,000 in the contribution margin was due in large part to an increase in the number of units sold. This increase was partially offset by a decrease in the unit sales price and an increase in the unit cost for variable selling and administrative expenses. The decrease in the unit cost for the variable cost of goods sold was an additional favorable result of 2004 operations.

The information presented in the contribution margin analysis report is useful to management in evaluating past performance and in planning future operations. For example, the impact of the $0.50 reduction in the unit sales price on the number of units sold and on the total sales for the year is useful information that management can use in determining whether further price reductions might be desirable. The contribution margin analysis report also highlights the impact of changes in unit variable costs and expenses. For example, the $0.05 increase in the unit variable selling and administrative expenses might be a result of increased advertising expenditures. If so, the increase in the number of units sold in 2004 could be attributed to both the $0.50 price reduction and the increased advertising.

Example 46 *If the actual price was $48 per unit, the planned price was $40 per unit, and the volume sold increased by 5,000 units, to a total of 60,000 units, what would be (a) the quantity factor and (b) the unit price factor for sales?*

(a) $200,000 (5,000 units × $40 per unit); (b) $480,000 ($8 × 60,000 units)

Exhibit 600.82 *Data Table for Noble Inc.*

	Actual	Planned	Increase or (Decrease)
Sales	$937,500	$800,000	$137,500
Less: Variable cost of goods sold	$425,000	$350,000	$ 75,000
Variable selling and administrative expenses	162,500	125,000	37,500
Total	$587,500	$475,000	$112,500
Contribution margin	$350,000	$325,000	$ 25,000
Number of units sold	125,000	100,000	
Per unit:			
Sales price	$7.50	$8.00	
Variable cost of goods sold	$3.40	$3.50	
Variable selling and administrative expenses	$1.30	$1.25	

Exhibit 600.83 *Contribution Margin Analysis Report for Noble Inc.*

Noble Inc.
Contribution Margin Analysis
for the Year Ended December 31, 2004

Increase in amount of sales attributed to:			
Quantity factor:			
Increase in number of units sold in 2004	25,000		
Planned sales price in 2004	× $8.00	$200,000	
Price factor:			
Decrease in unit sales price in 2004	$(0.50)		
Number of units sold in 2004	× 125,000	(62,500)	
Net increase in amount of sales		$137,500	
Increase in amount of variable cost of goods sold attributed to:			
Quantity factor:			
Increase in number of units sold in 2004	25,000		
Planned unit cost in 2004	× $3.50	$ 87,500	
Unit cost factor:			
Decrease in unit cost in 2004	$ (0.10)		
Number of units sold in 2004	× 125,000	(12,500)	
Net increase in amount of variable cost of goods sold		$ 75,000	
Increase in amount of variable selling and administrative expenses attributed to:			
Quantity factor:			
Increase in number of units sold in 2004	25,000		
Planned unit cost in 2004	× $1.25	$ 31,250	
Unit cost factor:			
Increase in unit cost in 2004	$ 0.05		
Number of units sold in 2004	× 125,000	6,250	
Net increase in the amount of variable selling and administrative expenses		$ 37,500	
Net increase in amount of variable costs			112,500
Increase in contribution margin			$ 25,000

Control and Accounting

Control Procedures

Control procedures are established to provide reasonable assurance that business goals will be achieved, including the prevention of fraud. In the following paragraphs, we will briefly discuss control procedures that can be integrated throughout the accounting system. These procedures are listed in Exhibit 600.84.

COMPETENT PERSONNEL, ROTATING DUTIES, AND MANDATORY VACATIONS The successful operation of an accounting system requires procedures to ensure that people are able to perform the duties to which they are assigned. Hence, it is necessary that all accounting employees be adequately trained

An accounting clerk for the Grant County (Washington) Alcoholism Program was in charge of collecting money, making deposits, and keeping the records. While the clerk was away on maternity leave, the replacement clerk discovered a fraud: $17,800 in fees had been collected but had been hidden for personal gain.

Exhibit 600.84 *Internal Control Procedures*

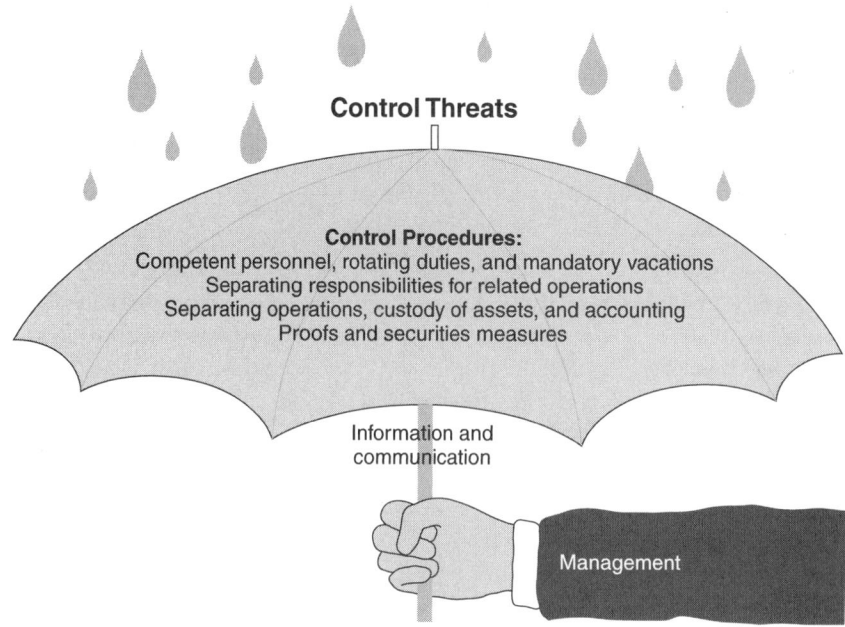

and supervised in performing their jobs. It may also be advisable to rotate duties of clerical personnel and mandate vacations for nonclerical personnel. These policies encourage employees to adhere to prescribed procedures. In addition, existing errors or fraud may be detected.

SEPARATING RESPONSIBILITIES FOR RELATED OPERATIONS To decrease the possibility of inefficiency, errors, and fraud, the responsibility for related operations should be divided among two or more persons. For example, the responsibilities for purchasing, receiving, and paying for computer supplies should be divided among three persons or departments. If the same person orders supplies, verifies the receipt of the supplies, and pays the supplier, the following abuses are possible:

1. Orders may be placed on the basis of friendship with a supplier, rather than on price, quality, and other objective factors.
2. The quantity and quality of supplies received may not be verified, thus causing payment for supplies not received or poor-quality supplies.
3. Supplies may be stolen by the employee.
4. The validity and accuracy of invoices may be verified carelessly, thus causing the payment of false or inaccurate invoices.

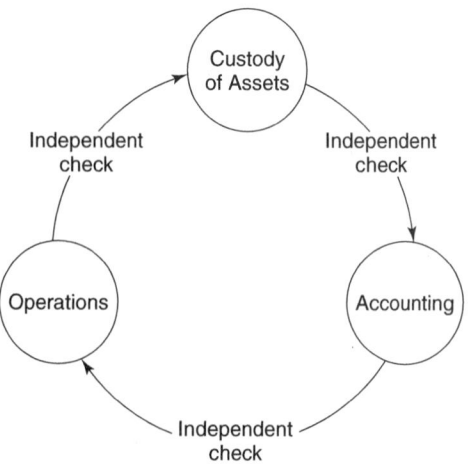

The "checks and balances" provided by dividing responsibilities among various departments requires no duplication of effort. The business documents prepared by one department are designed to coordinate with and support those prepared by other departments.

SEPARATING OPERATIONS, CUSTODY OF ASSETS, AND ACCOUNTING Control policies should establish the responsibilities for various business activities. To reduce the possibility of errors and fraud, the responsibilities for operations, custody of assets, and accounting should be separated. The accounting records then serve as an independent check on the individuals who have custody of the assets and who engage in the business operations. For example, the employees entrusted with handling cash receipts from credit customers should not record cash receipts in the accounting records. To do so would allow employees to borrow or steal cash and hide the theft in the records. Likewise, if those engaged in operating activities also record the results of operations, they could distort the accounting reports to show favorable results. For example, a store manager whose year-end bonus is based upon operating profits might be tempted to record fictitious sales in order to receive a larger bonus.

PROOFS AND SECURITY MEASURES Proofs and security measures should be used to safeguard assets and ensure reliable accounting data. This control procedure applies to many different techniques, such as authorization, approval, and reconciliation procedures. For example, employees who travel on company business may be required to obtain a department manager's approval on a travel request form.

Over $700,000 of child support money disappeared over seven years due to the alleged falsification of checks by an accountant in Indiana's Family and Social Services Administration. The fraud could have been discovered, according to the State Examiner, if the agency reconciled its books, controlled access to blank checks, and used receipts.

Other examples of control procedures include the use of bank accounts and other measures to ensure the safety of cash and valuable documents. A cash register that displays the amount recorded for each sale and provides the customer a printed receipt can be an effective part of the internal control structure. An all-night convenience store could use the following security measures to deter robberies:

1. Locate the cash register near the door, so that it is fully visible from outside the store; have two employees work late hours; employ a security guard.
2. Deposit cash in the bank daily, before 5 P.M.
3. Keep only small amounts of cash on hand after 5 P.M. by depositing excess cash in a store safe that can't be opened by employees on duty.
4. Install cameras and alarm systems.

Example 47 *Why is separation of duties considered a control procedure?*

Internal control is enhanced by separating the control of a transaction from the recordkeeping function. Fraud is more easily committed when a single individual controls both the transaction and the accounting for the transaction.

Monitoring

Monitoring the internal control system locates weaknesses and improves control effectiveness. The internal control system can be monitored through either ongoing efforts by management or by separate evaluations. Ongoing monitoring efforts may include observing both employee behavior and warning signs from the accounting system. The indicators shown in Exhibit 600.85 may be clues to internal control problems.

Separate monitoring evaluations are generally performed when there are major changes in strategy, senior management, business structure, or operations. In large businesses, internal auditors who are independent of operations normally are responsible for monitoring the internal control system. Internal auditors can report issues and concerns to an audit committee of the board of directors, who are independent of management. In addition, external auditors also evaluate internal control as a normal part of their annual financial statement audit.[3]

Information and Communication

Information and communication are essential elements of internal control. Information about the control environment, risk assessment, control procedures, and monitoring are needed by management to guide operations and ensure compliance with reporting, legal, and regulatory requirements.

In one of the largest frauds ever committed against a university, a former financial aid officer for New York University was charged with stealing $4.1 million from the state of New York. The aid officer allegedly falsified over a thousand tuition assistance checks to students who were not entitled to receive aid and who did not know about the checks. The aid officer deposited the bogus checks for personal use. The initial evidence of the fraud was the officer's spending of $785,000 on expensive jewelry.

Exhibit 600.85 *Indicators of Internal Control Problems*

Clues To Potential Problems

Warning signs with regard to people	Warning signs from the accounting system
1. Abrupt change in lifestyle (without winning the lottery). 2. Close social relationships with suppliers. 3. Refusing to take a vacation. 4. Frequent borrowing from other employees. 5. Excessive use of alcohol or drugs.	1. Missing documents or gaps in transaction numbers (could mean documents are being used for fraudulent transactions). 2. An unusual increase in customer refunds (refunds may be phony). 3. Differences between daily cash receipts and bank deposits (could mean receipts are pocketed before being deposited). 4. Sudden increase in slow payments (employee may be pocketing the payment). 5. Backlog in recording transactions (possibly an attempt to delay detection of fraud).

Management can also use external information to assess events and conditions that impact decision making and external reporting. For example, management uses information from the Financial Accounting Standards Board (FASB) to assess the impact of possible changes in reporting standards.

Ethics and Accounting

Business Ethics

The moral principles that guide the conduct of individuals are called **ethics.** Regardless of differences among individuals, proper ethical conduct implies a behavior that considers the impact of one's actions on society and others. In other words, proper ethical conduct implies that you not only consider what's in your best interest, but also what's in the best interests of others.

Ethical conduct is good business. For example, an automobile manufacturer that fails to correct a safety defect to save costs may later lose sales due to lack of consumer confidence. Likewise, a business that pollutes the environment may find itself the target of lawsuits and customer boycotts.

Businesspeople should work within an ethical framework. Although an ethical framework is based on individual experiences and training, there are a number of sound principles that form the foundation for ethical behavior:

1. *Avoid small ethical lapses.* Small ethical lapses may appear harmless in and of themselves. Unfortunately, such lapses can compromise your work. Small ethical lapses can build up and lead to larger consequences later.

2. *Focus on your long-term reputation.* One characteristic of an ethical dilemma is that it places you under severe short-term pressure. The ethical dilemma is created by the stated or unstated threat that failure to "go along" may result in undesirable consequences. You should respond to ethical dilemmas by minimizing the short-term pressures and focusing on long-term reputation instead. Your reputation is very valuable. You will lose your effectiveness if your reputation becomes tarnished.

3. *Expect to suffer adverse personal consequences for holding to an ethical position.* In some unethical organizations, managers have endured career setbacks for not budging from their ethical positions. Some managers have resigned because they were unable to support management in what they perceived as unethical behavior. Thus, in the short term, ethical behavior can sometimes adversely affect your career.

Code of Ethics

Similar to law, medicine, and engineering, accounting is a profession. Each of these fields has a code of ethics, and penalties for violating the code of ethics may include loss of the license to practice. In addition, many business organizations have developed their own ethics policies and codes of conduct for their employees to follow.

Accountants provide information about costs and benefits to management for decision making. Accountants should use professional judgment during the compilation of such costs and benefits because this information could affect sensitive areas such as health care and environment. In the last two areas, it is difficult to evaluate and assess such information objectively.

Ethics for Accountants

Next, we provide some examples of ethical and unethical scenarios for accountants.

- It is ethical when the auditor and several members of management of a company (the auditor's client) go out to lunch on the last day of the audit work and the company pays for the entire lunch. Acceptance of a free lunch would not normally be considered unethical because the auditor did not receive any special treatment.
- It is unethical when the audit partner in charge of a bank that he is auditing finances a $300,000 home mortgage loan with the bank at a lower interest rate than that offered to other customers of the bank. Acceptance of this special financing arrangement would be considered unethical because it could jeopardize the auditor's independence and objectivity required during the audit.

Of course, not all situations are as clear cut as above. Ethical dilemmas sometimes arise, and their resolution may not be easy. In some situations, the right course of action is clear even though it may have a negative effect. In other cases, the issues may be so complex and conflicting that the right course of action is not clear.

Ethics for Management

In accounting, unethical decisions may be made jointly between accountants and management of the organization. Management may be subject to the financial numbers game (1) to increase market price for their stock, (2) to improve credit quality and receive higher debt rating in order to lower borrowing cost from banks, and (3) to increase profit-based bonuses and stock options. During this game, management may resort to unethical activities such as (1) recognizing premature or fictitious revenue, (2) aggressive capitalization policies, (3) over- and/or underreported assets and liabilities, and (4) manipulating components of the income statement, balance sheet, and cash flow statements.

Authors Charles W. Mulford and Eugene E. Comiskey, in their book *The Financial Numbers Game: Detecting Creative Accounting Practices,* define the financial numbers game in several ways:[4]

- *Aggressive Accounting.* A forceful and intentional choice and application of accounting principles done in an effort to achieve desired results, typically higher current earnings, whether the practices followed are in accordance with generally accepted accounting principles (GAAP) or not.
- *Earnings Management.* The active manipulation of earnings toward a predetermined target, which may be set by management, a forecast made by stock market financial analysts, or an amount that is consistent with a smoother, more sustainable earnings stream.
- *Income Smoothing.* A form of earnings management designed to remove peaks and valleys from a normal earnings series, including steps to reduce and "store" profits during good years for use during bad (slower) years. Equity reserves can be used for income smoothing.
- *Fraudulent Financial Reporting.* Intentional misstatements or omissions of amounts or disclosures in financial statements, done to deceive financial statement users, that are determined to be fraudulent by an administrative, civil, or criminal proceeding.
- *Creative Accounting Practices.* Any and all steps used to play the financial numbers game, including the aggressive choice and application of accounting principles, fraudulent financial reporting, and any steps taken toward earnings management or income smoothing.

Module 600 Endnotes

1. Glenn Alan Cheney, "Senate Rips FASB on Stock Options," *Accounting Today,* May 23, 1994.
2. Jill Krutick, *Fortune,* March 30, 1998, p. 106.
3. Edwin C. Bliss, "Employee Theft," *Boardroom Reports,* July 15, 1994, pp. 5–6.
4. Charles W. Mulford and Eugene E. Comiskey, *The Financial Numbers Game: Detecting Creative Accounting Practices,* (John Wiley & Sons, Inc., New York, 2000).

MODULE 700

Finance

701 Finance Strategies, 944

704 Working Capital Policy, 949

705 Managing Short-Term Assets, 958

710 Managing Short-Term Financing, 969

715 Managing Long-Term Financing, 981

720 Financial Forecasting, Planning, and Control, 1015

725 Cost of Capital, Capital Structure, and Dividend Policy, 1041

735 Capital Budgeting, 1064

745 Financial Markets, Instruments, and Institutions, 1084

755 Financial Risk Management, 1095

760 Mergers, Acquisitions, and Business Valuations, 1104

795 Ethics and Finance, 1114

Module 700 Appendix, 1116

Module 700 Endnotes, 1124

Finance Strategies

The Goals of the Corporation

Business decisions are not made in a vacuum—decision makers have some objective in mind. *We operate on the assumption that management's primary goal is* **stockholder wealth maximization,** which, as we will see, translates into *maximizing the value of the firm as measured by the price of the firm's common stock.* Firms do, of course, have other objectives—in particular, managers, who make the actual decisions, are interested in their own personal satisfaction, in their employees' welfare, and in the good of the community and of society at large. Still, for the reasons set forth in the following sections, *stock price maximization is the most important goal of most corporations.*

Managerial Incentives to Maximize Shareholder Wealth

It is the stockholders who own the firm and elect the management team. Management, in turn, is supposed to operate in the best interests of the stockholders. As a stockholder of a company, you probably would want the managers to make decisions that would maximize the value of the stock you own, including dividends. We know, however, that because the stock of most large corporations is widely held, the managers of such organizations have a great deal of latitude in making business decisions. This being the case, might not managers pursue goals other than stock price maximization? For example, some have argued that the managers of a large, well-entrenched corporation could work just hard enough to keep stockholder returns at a "reasonable" level and then devote the remainder of their efforts and resources to public service activities, to employee benefits, to higher executive salaries, or to golf.

It is almost impossible to determine whether a particular management team is trying to maximize shareholder wealth or is merely attempting to keep stockholders satisfied while pursuing other goals. For example, how can we tell whether employee or community benefit programs are in the long-run best interests of the stockholders? Similarly, are relatively high executive salaries really necessary to attract and retain excellent managers, or are they just another example of managers taking advantage of stockholders?

It is impossible to give definitive answers to these questions. However, we do know that the managers of a firm operating in a competitive market will be forced to undertake actions that are reasonably consistent with shareholder wealth maximization. If they depart from this goal, they run the risk of being removed from their jobs. We will have more to say about the conflict between managers and shareholders later in the section.

Social Responsibility

Another issue that deserves consideration is **social responsibility:** Should businesses operate strictly in their stockholders' best interests, or are firms also responsible for the welfare of their employees, customers, and the communities in which they operate? Certainly firms have an ethical responsibility to provide a safe working environment, to avoid polluting the air or water, and to produce safe products. However, socially responsible actions have costs, and it is questionable whether businesses would incur these costs voluntarily. If some firms do act in a socially responsible manner while others do not, then the socially responsible firms will be at a disadvantage in attracting funds. To illustrate, suppose the firms in a given industry have **profits** and **rates of return on investment** that are close to **normal**—that is, close to the average for all firms and just sufficient to attract capital. If one company attempts to exercise social responsibility, it will have to raise prices to cover the added costs. If the other businesses in its industry do not follow suit, their costs and prices will be lower. The socially responsible firm will not be able to compete, and it will be forced to abandon its efforts. Thus, any voluntary socially responsible acts that raise costs will be difficult, if not impossible, in industries that are subject to keen competition.

What about oligopolistic firms with profits above normal levels? Cannot such firms devote resources to social projects? Undoubtedly they can, and many large, successful firms do engage in community projects, employee benefit programs, and the like, to a greater degree than would appear to be called for by pure profit- or wealth-maximization goals. Still, publicly owned firms are constrained in such actions by capital market factors. To illustrate, suppose a saver who has funds to invest is considering two alternative firms. One firm devotes a substantial part of its resources to social actions, while the other concentrates on profits and stock prices. Most investors are likely to shun the socially oriented firm, thus putting it at a disadvantage in the capital market. After all, why should the stockholders of one corporation subsidize society to a greater extent than those of other businesses? For this reason, even highly profitable firms (unless they are closely held rather than publicly owned) generally are constrained against taking unilateral cost-increasing social actions.

Does all this mean that firms should not exercise social responsibility? Not at all, but it does mean that most significant cost-increasing actions associated with social responsibility will have to be put on a *mandatory* rather than a voluntary basis, at least initially, to ensure that the burden falls uniformly on all businesses.

Stock Price Maximization and Social Welfare

If a firm attempts to maximize its stock price, is this good or bad for society? In general, it is good. Aside from such illegal actions as attempting to form monopolies, violating safety codes, and failing to meet pollution control requirements, *the same actions that maximize stock prices also benefit society*. First, note that stock price maximization requires efficient, low-cost plants that produce high-quality goods and services at the lowest possible cost. Second, stock price maximization requires the development of products that consumers want and need, so the profit motive leads to new technology, to new products, and to new jobs. Finally, stock price maximization necessitates efficient and courteous service, adequate stocks of merchandise, and well-located business establishments—these factors all are necessary to maintain a customer base that is necessary for producing sales, and thus profits. Therefore, actions that help a firm increase the price of its stock also are beneficial to society at large. This is why profit-motivated, free-enterprise economies have been so much more successful than socialistic and communistic economic systems. Because managerial finance plays a crucial role in the operation of successful firms, and because successful firms are absolutely necessary for a healthy, productive economy, it is easy to see why finance is important from a social standpoint.

Managerial Actions to Maximize Shareholder Wealth

To maximize the price of a firm's stock, what types of actions should its management take? First, consider the question of stock prices versus profits: Will **profit maximization** also result in stock price maximization? In answering this question, we must consider the matter of total corporate profits versus **earnings per share (EPS)**.

For example, suppose Xerox had 300 million shares outstanding and earned $1,200 million, or $4 per share. If you owned 100 shares of the stock, your share of the total profits would be $400. Now suppose Xerox sold another 300 million shares and invested the funds received in assets that produced $300 million of income. Total income would rise to $1,500 million, but earnings per share would decline from $4 to $2.50 = $1,500/600. Now your share of the firm's earnings would be only $250, down from $400. You (and other existing stockholders) would have suffered an earnings dilution, even though total corporate profits had risen. Therefore, other things held constant, *if management is interested in the well-being of its current stockholders, it should concentrate on earnings per share rather than on total corporate profits*.

Will maximization of expected earnings per share always maximize stockholder welfare, or should other factors be considered? Think about the *timing of the earnings*. Suppose Xerox had one project that would cause earnings per share to rise by $0.20 per year for five years, or $1 in total, while another project would have no effect on earnings for four years but would increase earnings by $1.25 in the fifth year. Which project is better—in other words, is $0.20 per year for five years better or worse than $1.25 in Year 5? The answer depends on which project adds the most to the value of the stock, which in turn depends on the time value of money to investors. Thus, timing is an important reason to concentrate on wealth as measured by the price of the stock rather than on earnings alone.

Another issue relates to *risk*. Suppose one project is expected to increase earnings per share by $1, while another is expected to raise earnings by $1.20 per share. The first project is not very risky—if it is undertaken, earnings will almost certainly rise by about $1 per share. However, the other project is quite risky, so, although our best guess is that earnings will rise by $1.20 per share, we must recognize the possibility that there might be no increase whatsoever, or even a loss. Depending on how averse stockholders are to risk, the first project might be preferable to the second.

The riskiness inherent in projected earnings per share (EPS) also depends on *how the firm is financed.* As we shall see, many firms go bankrupt every year, and the greater the use of debt, the greater the threat of bankruptcy. *Consequently, while the use of debt financing might increase projected EPS, debt also increases the riskiness of projected future earnings.*

Another issue is the matter of paying dividends to stockholders versus retaining earnings and reinvesting them in the firm, thereby causing the earnings stream to grow over time. Stockholders like cash dividends, but they also like the growth in EPS that results from plowing earnings back into the business. The financial manager must decide exactly how much of the current earnings to pay out as dividends rather than to retain and reinvest—this is called the **dividend policy decision.** The optimal dividend policy is the one that maximizes the firm's stock price.

We see, then, that the firm's stock price is dependent on the following factors:

1. Projected earnings per share
2. Timing of the earnings stream
3. Riskiness of the projected earnings
4. Use of debt
5. Dividend policy

Every significant corporate decision should be analyzed in terms of its effect on these factors and hence on the price of the firm's stock. For example, suppose Occidental Petroleum's coal division is considering opening a new mine. If this is done, can it be expected to increase EPS? Is there a chance that costs will exceed estimates, that prices and output will fall below projections, and that EPS will be reduced because the new mine was opened? How long will it take for the new mine to show a profit? How should the capital required to open the mine be raised? If debt is used, by how much will this increase Occidental's riskiness? Should Occidental reduce its current dividends and use the cash thus saved to finance the project, or should it maintain its dividends and finance the mine with external capital? Managerial finance is designed to help answer questions like these, plus many more.

Agency Relationships

An *agency relationship* exists when one or more people (the principals) hire another person (the agent) to perform a service and then delegate decision-making authority to that agent. Important agency relationships exist (1) between stockholders and managers and (2) between stockholders and creditors (debtholders).

Stockholders versus Managers

A potential **agency problem** arises whenever the manager of a firm owns less than 100 percent of the firm's common stock. If a firm is a proprietorship managed by the owner, the owner-manager will presumably operate the business in a fashion that will improve his or her own welfare, with welfare measured in the form of increased personal wealth, more leisure, or perquisites. However, if the owner-manager incorporates and sells some of the firm's stock to outsiders, a potential conflict of interests immediately arises. For example, the owner-manager might now decide not to work as hard to maximize shareholder wealth because less of this wealth will go to him or her, or decide to take a higher salary or enjoy more perquisites because part of those costs will fall on the outside stockholders. This potential conflict between two parties, the principals (outside shareholders) and the agent (manager), is an agency problem.

In general, if a conflict of interest exists, what can be done to ensure that management treats the outside stockholders fairly? Several mechanisms are used to motivate managers to act in the shareholders' best interests. These include (1) the threat of firing, (2) the threat of takeover, and (3) managerial compensation plans.

1. **The threat of firing.** It wasn't long ago that the management teams of large firms felt secure in their positions, because the chances of being ousted by stockholders were so remote that managers rarely felt their jobs were in jeopardy. This situation existed because ownership of most firms was so widely distributed, and management's control over the proxy (voting) mechanism was so strong, that it was almost impossible for dissident stockholders to gain enough votes to overthrow the managers. However, today much of the stock of an average large corporation is owned by a relatively few large institutions rather than by thousands of individual investors, and the institutional money managers have the clout to influence a firm's operations. Examples of major corporations whose managements have been ousted include **United Airlines**, **Disney**, and **IBM**.

2. **The threat of takeover. Hostile takeovers** (instances in which management does not want the firm to be taken over) are most likely to occur when a firm's stock is undervalued relative to its potential. In a hostile takeover, the managers of the acquired firm generally are fired, and any who are able to stay on lose the power they had prior to the acquisition. Thus, managers have a strong incentive to take actions that maximize stock prices. In the words of one company president, "If you want to keep control, don't let your company's stock sell at a bargain price."

   Actions to increase the firm's stock price and to keep it from being a bargain obviously are good from the standpoint of the stockholders, but other tactics that managers can use to ward off a hostile takeover might not be. Two examples of questionable tactics are *poison pills* and *greenmail*. A **poison pill** is an action a firm can take that practically kills it and thus makes it unattractive to potential suitors. Examples include Disney's plan to sell large blocks of its stock at low prices to "friendly" parties, **Scott Industries'** decision to make all of its debt immediately payable if its management changed, and **Carleton Corporation's** decision to give huge retirement bonuses, which represented a large part of the company's wealth, to its managers if the firm was taken over (such payments are called *golden parachutes*). **Greenmail,** which is like blackmail, occurs when (a) a potential acquirer (firm or individual) buys a block of stock in a company, (b) the target company's management becomes frightened that the acquirer will make a tender offer and gain control of the company, and (c) to head off a possible takeover, management offers to pay greenmail, buying the stock owned by the potential raider at a price above the existing market price without offering the same deal to other stockholders. A good example of greenmail was Disney's buyback of 11.1 percent of its stock from Saul Steinberg's Reliance Group in 1984, which gave Steinberg a quick $60 million profit (he held the stock only a few months). The day the buyback was announced, the price of Disney's stock dropped approximately 10 percent. A group of stockholders sued, and Steinberg and the Disney directors were forced to pay $45 million to Disney stockholders.

3. **Managerial compensation plans.** Increasingly, firms are tying managers' compensation to the company's performance, and this motivates managers to operate in a manner consistent with stock price maximization.

   In the 1950s and 1960s, most performance-based incentive plans involved **executive stock options,** which allowed managers to purchase stock at some future time at a given price. Because the value of the options was tied directly to the price of the stock, it was assumed that granting options would provide an incentive for managers to take actions that would maximize the stock's price. This type of managerial incentive lost favor in the 1970s, however, because the general stock market declined, and stock prices did not necessarily reflect companies' earnings growth. Incentive plans should be based on those factors over which managers have control, and because they cannot control the general stock market, stock option plans were not good incentive devices. Therefore, while 61 of the 100 largest U.S. firms used stock options as their sole incentive compensation in 1970, not even one of the largest 100 companies relied exclusively on such plans in 1999.

   An important incentive plan now is **performance shares,** which are shares of stock given to executives on the basis of performance as measured by earnings per share, return on assets, return on equity, and so on. For example, **Honeywell** uses growth in earnings per share as its primary performance measure. If the company achieves a targeted average growth in earnings per share, the managers will earn 100 percent of their shares. If the corporate performance is above the target, Honeywell's managers can earn even more shares. But if growth is below the target, they get less than 100 percent of the shares.

   All incentive compensation plans—executive stock options, performance shares, profit-based bonuses, and so forth—are designed to accomplish two things. First, these plans provide inducements to executives to act on those factors under their control in a manner that will contribute to stock price maximization. Second, the existence of such performance plans helps companies attract and retain top-level executives. Well-designed plans can accomplish both goals.

Stockholders versus Creditors

A second agency problem involves conflicts between stockholders and creditors (debtholders). Creditors lend funds to the firm at rates that are based on (1) the riskiness of the firm's existing assets, (2) expectations concerning the riskiness of future asset additions, (3) the firm's existing capital structure (that is, the amount of debt financing it uses), and (4) expectations concerning future capital structure changes. These are the factors that determine the riskiness of the firm's debt, so creditors base the interest rate they charge on expectations regarding these factors.

Now suppose the stockholders, acting through management, cause the firm to take on new ventures that have much greater risk than was anticipated by the creditors. This increased risk will cause the value of the outstanding debt to fall. If the risky ventures turn out to be successful, all of the benefits will go to the stockholders because the creditors only get a fixed return. However, if things go sour, the bondholders will have to share the losses. What this amounts to, from the stockholders' point of view, is a game of "heads I win, tails you lose," which obviously is not a good game for the bondholders.

Similarly, if the firm increases its use of debt in an effort to boost the return to stockholders, the value of the old debt will decrease, so we have another "heads I win, tails you lose" situation. To illustrate, consider what happened to **RJR Nabisco's** bondholders when, in 1988, RJR's chief executive officer announced his plan to take the company private with funds the company would borrow (termed a *leverage buyout*). Stockholders saw their shares jump in value from $56 to over $90 in just a few days, but RJR's bondholders suffered losses of approximately 20 percent. Investors immediately realized that taking RJR Nabisco private would cause the amount of its debt to rise dramatically, and thus its riskiness would soar. This, in turn, led to a huge decline in the price of RJR's outstanding bonds. Ultimately, RJR's management was not successful in its buyout attempt. But Nabisco was purchased by another company for more than $100 per share—what a gain for the stockholders!

Can and should stockholders, through their managers/agents, try to expropriate wealth from the firm's creditors? In general, the answer is no. First, because such attempts have been made in the past, creditors today protect themselves reasonably well against stockholder actions through restrictions in credit agreements. Second, if potential creditors perceive that a firm will try to take advantage of them in unethical ways, they will either refuse to deal with the firm or else will require a much higher than normal rate of interest to compensate for the risks of such "sneaky" actions. Thus, firms that try to deal unfairly with creditors either lose access to the debt markets or are saddled with higher interest rates, both of which decrease the long-run value of the stock.

In view of these constraints, it follows that the goal of maximizing shareholder wealth requires fair play with creditors: Stockholder wealth depends on continued access to capital markets, and access depends on fair play and abiding by both the letter and the spirit of credit agreements. Managers, as agents of both the creditors and the stockholders, must act in a manner that is fairly balanced between the interests of these two classes of security holders. Similarly, because of other constraints and sanctions, management actions that would expropriate wealth from any of the firm's **stakeholders** (employees, customers, suppliers, and so on) will ultimately be to the detriment of shareholders. Therefore, maximizing shareholder wealth requires the fair treatment of all stakeholders.

The External Environment

Although managerial actions affect the value of a firm's stock, external factors also influence stock prices. Included among these factors are legal constraints, the general level of economic activity, the tax laws, and conditions in the stock market. Exhibit 700.1 diagrams these general relationships. Working within the set of external constraints shown in the box at the extreme left, management makes a set of long-run strategic policy decisions that chart a future course for the firm. These policy decisions, along with the general level of economic activity and the level of corporate income taxes, influence the firm's expected profitability, the timing of its cash flows, their eventual transfer to stockholders in the form of dividends, and the degree of risk inherent in projected earnings and dividends. Profitability, timing, and risk all af-

Exhibit 700.1 *Summary of Major Factors Affecting Stock Prices*

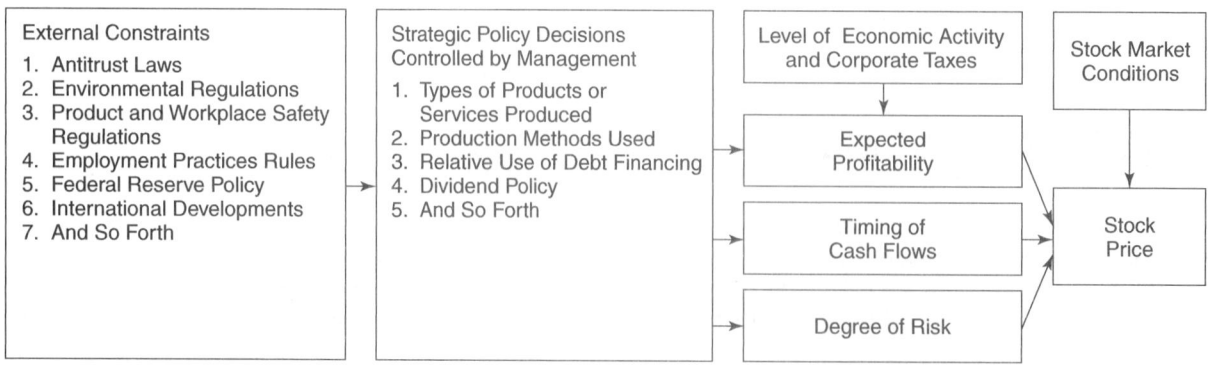

fect the price of the firm's stock, but so does another factor, conditions in the stock market as a whole, because all stock prices tend to move up and down together to some extent.

Working Capital Policy

Working Capital Management

Generally we divide financial management decisions into the management of assets (investments) and liabilities (sources of financing) in (1) the *long term* and (2) the *short term*. In this section, we discuss *short-term financial management,* also termed **working capital management,** which involves management of the current assets and the current liabilities of a firm. You will realize that a firm's value cannot be maximized in the long run unless it survives the short run. In fact, the principal reason firms fail is because they are unable to meet their working capital needs. Thus, *sound working capital management is a requisite for firm survival.* Much of a financial manager's or treasurer's time is devoted to working capital management.

Working Capital Terminology

It is useful to begin the discussion of working capital policy by reviewing some basic definitions and concepts.

1. The term **working capital,** sometimes called *gross working capital,* generally refers to current assets.
2. **Net working capital** is defined as current assets minus current liabilities.
3. The *current ratio* is calculated by dividing current assets by current liabilities, and it is intended to measure a firm's liquidity. However, a high current ratio does not insure that a firm will have the cash required to meet its needs. If inventories cannot be sold, or if receivables cannot be collected in a timely manner, then the apparent safety reflected in a high current ratio could be illusory.
4. The best and most comprehensive picture of a firm's liquidity position is obtained by examining its *cash budget.* The cash budget, which forecasts cash inflows and outflows, focuses on what really counts, the firm's ability to generate sufficient cash inflows to meet its required cash outflows. Cash budgeting will be discussed in Section 705.
5. **Working capital policy** refers to the firm's basic policies regarding (a) target levels for each category of current assets and (b) how current assets will be financed.

We must distinguish between those current liabilities that are specifically used to finance current assets and those current liabilities that represent (1) current maturities of long-term debt; (2) financing associated with a construction program that, after the project is completed, will be funded with the proceeds of a long-term security issue; or (3) the use of short-term debt to finance fixed assets.

Exhibit 700.2 contains balance sheets for Unilate Textiles constructed at three different dates. According to the definitions given, Unilate's December 31, 2004, working capital (current assets) was $465.0 million, and its net working capital was $335.0 million = $465.0 million − $130.0 million. Also, Unilate's year-end 2004 current ratio was 3.6.

What if the total current liabilities of $130 million at the end of 2004 included the current portion of long-term debt, say $10 million? This account is unaffected by changes in working capital policy because it is a function of past long-term debt financing decisions. Thus, even though we define long-term debt coming due in the next accounting period as a current liability, it is not a working capital decision variable in the current period. Similarly, if Unilate were building a new factory and initially financed the construction with a short-term loan that would be replaced later with mortgage bonds, the construction loan would not be considered part of working capital management. Although such accounts are not part of Unilate's working capital decision process, they cannot be ignored because they are *due* in the current period, and they must be taken into account when Unilate's managers construct the cash budget and assess the firm's ability to meet its current obligations (its liquidity position).

Exhibit 700.2 *Unilate Textiles: Historical and Projected Balance Sheets (millions of dollars)*

	12/31/04 (Historical)	9/30/05 (Projected)	12/31/05 (Projected)
Cash and marketable securities	$ 15.0	$ 30.0	$ 16.5
Accounts receivable	180.0	251.5	198.0
Inventories	270.0	410.0	297.0
Total current assets	$465.0	$ 691.5	$511.5
Net plant and equipment	380.0	408.5	418.0
Total assets	$845.0	$1,100.0	$929.5
Accounts payable	$30.0	$90.0	$ 33.0
Accruals	60.0	100.0	66.0
Notes payable	40.0	129.0	46.8
Total current liabilities	$130.0	$ 319.0	$145.8
Long-term bonds	300.0	309.0	309.0
Total liabilities	$430.0	$ 628.0	$454.8
Common stock	130.0	159.3	159.3
Retained earnings	285.0	312.7	315.4
Total owner's equity	$415.0	$ 472.0	$474.7
Total liabilities and equity	$845.0	$1,100.0	$929.5
Net working capital	$335.0	$ 372.5	$365.7
Current ratio	3.6	2.2	3.5

The Requirement for External Working Capital Financing

Unilate's operations and the sale of textile products are very seasonal, typically peaking in September and October. Thus, at the end of September, Unilate's inventories are significantly higher than they are at the end of the calendar year. Unilate offers significant sales incentives to wholesalers during August and September in an effort to move inventories out of its warehouses and into those of its customers; otherwise, inventories would be even higher than shown in Exhibit 700.2. Because of this sales surge, Unilate's receivables also are much higher at the end of September than at the end of December.

Consider what is expected to happen to Unilate's current assets and current liabilities from December 31, 2004, to September 30, 2005. Current assets are expected to increase from $465.0 million to $691.5 million, or by $226.5 million. Because increases on the asset side of the balance sheet must be financed by identical increases on the liabilities and equity side, the firm must raise $226.5 million to meet the expected increase in working capital over the period. However, the higher volume of purchases, plus labor expenditures associated with increased production, will cause accounts payable and accruals to increase spontaneously by only $100 million—from $90.0 million ($30.0 million in payables plus $60.0 million in accruals) to $190.0 million ($90.0 million in payables plus $100.0 million in accruals)—during the first nine months of 2005. This leaves a projected $126.5 million = $226.5 million − $100.0 million current asset financing requirement, which Unilate expects to finance primarily by an $89.0 million increase in notes payable. Therefore, for September 30, 2005, notes payable are projected to rise to $129.0 million. Notice that from December 2004 to September 2005, Unilate's net working capital is expected to increase from $335.0 million to $372.5 million, but its current ratio is expected to fall from 3.6 to 2.2. This occurs because most, but not all, of the funds invested in current assets are expected to come from current liabilities.

The fluctuations in Unilate's working capital position shown in Exhibit 700.2 result from seasonal variations. Similar fluctuations in working capital requirements, and hence in financing needs, also occur during business cycles—working capital needs typically decline during recessions but increase during booms. For some companies, such as those involved in agricultural products, seasonal fluctuations are much greater than business cycle fluctuations, but for other companies, such as appliance or automobile manufacturers, cyclical fluctuations are larger. In the following sections we look in more detail at the requirement for working capital financing, and we examine some alternative working capital policies.

The Cash Conversion Cycle

The concept of working capital management starts with borrowing money from a bank to buy inventory, selling the inventory to pay off the bank loan, and then repeating the cycle. The working capital management process that Unilate Textiles faces can be summarized as follows:

1. Unilate orders and then receives the materials it needs to produce the textile products its sells. Unilate purchases from its suppliers on credit, so an account payable is created for credit purchases. Such purchases have no immediate cash flow effect because payment is not made until some later date (perhaps 20 to 30 days after purchase).
2. Labor is used to convert the materials (cotton and wool) into finished goods (cloth products, thread, etc.). However, wages are not fully paid at the time the work is done, so accrued wages build up (maybe for a period of one or two weeks).
3. The finished products are sold, but on credit; so sales create receivables, not immediate cash inflows.
4. At some point during the cycle, Unilate must pay off its accounts payable and accrued wages. *If* these payments are made before Unilate has collected cash from its receivables, a net cash outflow occurs and this outflow must be financed.
5. The cycle is completed when Unilate's receivables are collected (perhaps in 30 to 40 days). At that time, the company is in a position to pay off the credit that was used to finance production of the product, and it can then repeat the cycle.

The preceding steps are formalized with the **cash conversion cycle** model, which focuses on the length of time between when the company makes payments, or invests in the manufacture of inventory, and when it receives cash inflows, or realizes a cash return from its investment in production.[1] The following terms are used in the model:

1. The *inventory conversion period* is the average length of time required to convert materials into finished goods and then to sell those goods; it is the amount of time the product remains in inventory in various stages of completion. The inventory conversion period is calculated by dividing inventory by the cost of goods sold per day. For example, we can compute the inventory conversion period for Unilate Textiles using the 2004 balance sheet figures shown in Exhibit 700.2. In 2004, Unilate sold $1,500 million of its product with a cost of goods sold equal to $1,230 million, so the inventory conversion period would be:

$$\text{Inventory conversion period} = \frac{\text{Inventory}}{\text{Cost of goods sold per day}} = \frac{\text{Inventory}}{\left(\dfrac{\text{Cost of goods sold}}{360}\right)} \quad (7.1)$$

$$= \frac{\$270 \text{ million}}{\left(\dfrac{\$1{,}230 \text{ million}}{360}\right)} = \frac{\$270}{\$3.417}$$

$$= 79.0 \text{ days}$$

Thus, according to its 2004 operations, it takes Unilate 79.0 days to convert materials into finished goods and then to sell those goods.

2. The *receivables collection period* is the average length of time required to convert the firm's receivables into cash—that is, to collect cash following a sale. The receivables collection period also is called the days sales outstanding (DSO), and it is calculated by dividing accounts receivable by the average credit sales per day. Because sales in 2004 equaled $1,500 million, Unilate's receivables collection period (DSO) is:

$$\text{Receivables collection period} = \text{DSO} = \frac{\text{Receivables}}{\text{Daily credit sales}} = \frac{\text{Receivable}}{\left(\dfrac{\text{Credit sales}}{360}\right)} \quad (7.2)$$

$$= \frac{\$180 \text{ million}}{\left(\dfrac{\$1{,}500 \text{ million}}{360}\right)} = \frac{\$180}{\$4.167}$$

$$= 43.2 \text{ days}$$

Thus, the cash payments associated with credit sales are not collected until 43.2 days after the sales.

Exhibit 700.3 *The Cash Conversion Cycle*

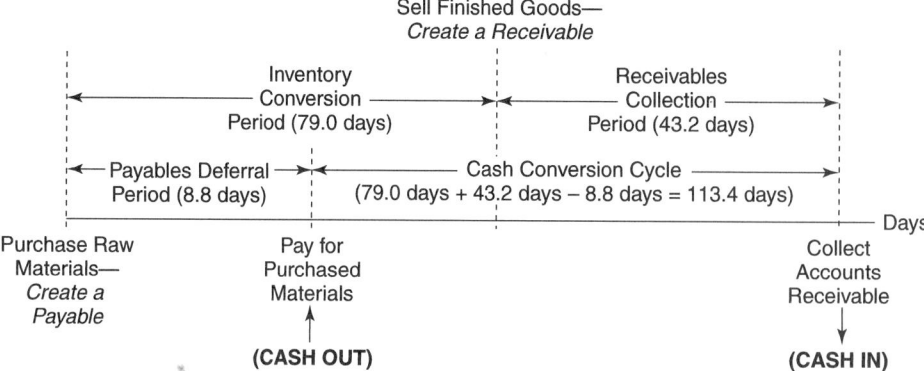

3. The *payables deferral period* is the average length of time between the purchase of raw materials and labor and the payment of cash for them. It is computed by dividing accounts payable by the daily credit purchases. Unilate's daily cost of goods sold is $3.417 million, so the payables deferral period for Unilate would be:

$$\text{Payables deferral period} = \text{DPO} = \frac{\text{Accounts payable}}{\text{Credit purchases per day}} = \frac{\text{Accounts payable}}{\left(\dfrac{\text{Cost of goods sold}}{360}\right)} \quad (7.3)$$

$$= \frac{\$30 \text{ million}}{\left(\dfrac{\$1{,}230 \text{ million}}{360}\right)} = \frac{\$30}{\$3.417}$$

$$= 8.8 \text{ days}$$

So Unilate pays its suppliers an average of 8.8 days after materials are purchased.

4. The *cash conversion cycle* computation nets out the three periods just defined, resulting in a value that equals the length of time between the firm's actual cash expenditures to pay for (invest in) productive resources (materials and labor) and its own cash receipts from the sale of products (that is, the length of time between paying for labor and materials and collecting on receivables). The cash conversion cycle thus equals the average length of time a dollar is tied up in current assets.

We can now use these definitions to analyze Unilate's cash conversion cycle. First, the concept is diagrammed in Exhibit 700.3. Thus, the cash conversion cycle can be expressed by this equation:

$$\begin{pmatrix}\text{Cash}\\ \text{conversion}\\ \text{cycle}\end{pmatrix} = \begin{pmatrix}\text{Inventory}\\ \text{conversion}\\ \text{period}\end{pmatrix} + \begin{pmatrix}\text{Receivables}\\ \text{collection}\\ \text{period}\end{pmatrix} - \begin{pmatrix}\text{Payables}\\ \text{deferral}\\ \text{period}\end{pmatrix} \quad (7.4)$$

$$= 79.0 \text{ days} + 43.2 \text{ days} - 8.8 \text{ days}$$

$$= 113.4 \text{ days}$$

To illustrate, according to Unilate's 2004 operations, it takes an average of 79.0 days to convert raw materials (cotton, wool, and so on) into finished goods (cloth, thread, and so on) and then sell them, and then it takes another 43.2 days to collect on receivables. However, 8.8 days normally elapse between receipt of raw materials and payment for them. In this case, the cash conversion cycle is 113.4 days. The *receipt* of cash from manufacturing and selling the products will be delayed by about 122 days because (1) the product will be "tied up" in inventory for 79 days, and (2) the cash from the sale will not be received until about 43 days after the selling date. But the *disbursement* of cash for the raw materials purchased will be delayed by nearly 9 days because Unilate does not pay cash for the raw materials when they are purchased. So for Unilate, the net delay in cash receipts associated with an investment (cash disbursement) in inventory is 113.4 days. What does this mean to Unilate?

Given its cash conversion cycle, Unilate knows when it starts processing its textile products that it will have to finance the manufacturing and other operating costs for a 113-day period, which is nearly one-third of a year. The firm's goal should be to shorten its cash conversion cycle as much as possible without harming operations. This would improve profits because the longer the cash conversion cycle, the greater the need for external, or nonspontaneous, financing, and such financing has a cost.

The cash conversion cycle can be shortened (1) by reducing the inventory conversion period by processing and selling goods more quickly, (2) by reducing the receivables collection period by speeding up collections, or (3) by lengthening the payables deferral period by slowing down its own payments. To the extent that these actions can be taken *without harming the return* associated with the management of these accounts, they should be carried out. So when taking actions to reduce the inventory conversion period, a firm should be careful to *avoid inventory shortages* that could cause "good" customers to buy from competitors; when taking actions to speed up the collection of receivables, a firm should be careful to *maintain good relations with its "good" credit customers;* and when taking actions to lengthen the payables deferral period, a firm should be careful *not to harm its own credit reputation*.

We can illustrate the benefits of shortening the cash conversion cycle by looking again at Unilate Textiles. Suppose Unilate must spend an average of $12.30 on materials and labor to manufacture its products, which are sold for $15.00 per unit. To generate the $1,500 million sales realized in 2004, Unilate turned out 277,778 items per day. At this rate of production, it must invest $3.417 million = $12.30 × 277,778 units each day to support the manufacturing process. This investment must be financed for 113.4 days—the length of the cash conversion cycle—so the company's working capital financing needs will be $387.5 million = 113.4 × $3.417 million. If Unilate could reduce the cash conversion cycle to 93.4 days—say, by deferring payment of its accounts payable an additional 20 days or by speeding up either the production process or the collection of its receivables—it could reduce its working capital financing requirements by $68.3 million = 20 days × $3.417 million. We see, then, that actions that affect the inventory conversion period, the receivables collection period, and the payables deferral period all affect the cash conversion cycle; hence they influence the firm's need for current assets and current asset financing.

Working Capital Investment and Financing Policies

Working capital policy involves two basic questions: (1) What is the appropriate level for current assets, both in total and by specific accounts? and (2) How should current assets be financed?

Alternative Current Asset Investment Policies

Exhibit 700.4 shows three alternative policies regarding the total amount of current assets carried. Essentially, these policies differ in that different amounts of current assets are carried to support any given level of sales. The line with the steepest slope represents a **relaxed current asset investment** (or "fat cat") **policy,** where relatively large amounts of cash, marketable securities, and inventories are carried and where sales are stimulated by the use of a credit policy that provides liberal financing to customers and a corresponding high level of receivables. Conversely, with the **restricted current asset investment** (or "lean-and-mean") **policy,** the holdings of cash, securities, inventories, and receivables are minimized. The **moderate current asset investment policy** is between the two extremes.

Under conditions of certainty—when sales, costs, lead times, payment periods, and so on, are known for sure—all firms would hold only minimal levels of current assets. Any larger amounts would increase the need for external funding without a corresponding increase in profits, while any smaller holdings would involve late payments to labor and suppliers and lost sales due to inventory shortages and an overly restrictive credit policy.

However, the picture changes when uncertainty is introduced. Here the firm requires some minimum amount of cash and inventories based on expected payments, expected sales, expected order lead times, and so on, plus additional amounts, or *safety stocks,* which enable it to deal with departures from the expected values. Similarly, accounts receivable levels are determined by credit terms, and the tougher the credit terms, the lower the receivables for any given level of sales. With a restricted current asset investment policy, the firm would hold minimal levels of safety stocks for cash and inventories, and it would have a tight credit policy even though this would mean running the risk of losing sales. A restricted, lean-and-mean current asset investment policy generally provides the highest expected return on investment, but it entails the greatest risk, while the reverse is true under a relaxed policy. The moderate policy falls in between the two extremes in terms of both expected risk and return.

In terms of the cash conversion cycle, a restricted investment policy would tend to reduce the inventory conversion and receivables collection periods, which would result in a relatively short cash conversion cycle. Conversely, a relaxed policy would create higher levels of inventories and receivables, longer inventory conversion and receivables

Exhibit 700.4 *Alternative Current Asset Investment Policies (millions of dollars)*

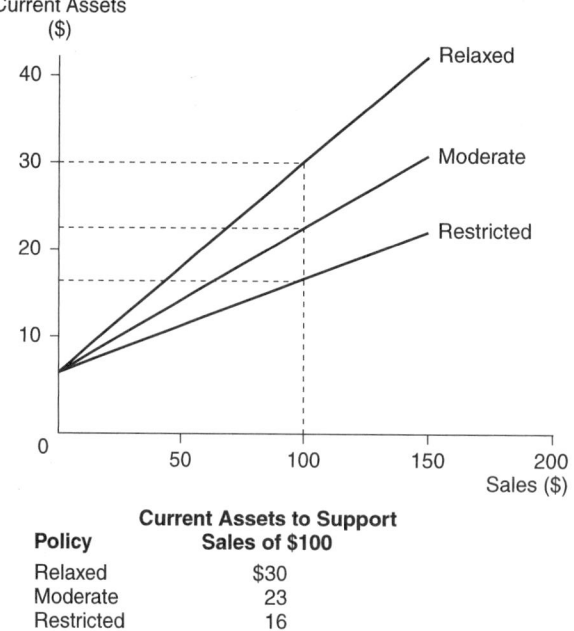

Policy	Current Assets to Support Sales of $100
Relaxed	$30
Moderate	23
Restricted	16

collection periods, and a relatively long cash conversion cycle. A moderate policy would produce a cash conversion cycle somewhere between the two extremes.

Alternative Current Asset Financing Policies

Most businesses experience seasonal fluctuations, cyclical fluctuations, or both. For example, construction firms have peaks in the spring and summer, retailers peak around Christmas, and the manufacturers who supply both construction companies and retailers follow similar patterns. Similarly, virtually all businesses must build up current assets when the economy is strong, but they then sell off inventories and have net reductions of receivables when the economy slacks off. Still, current assets rarely drop to zero, and this realization has led to the development of the idea that some current assets should be considered **permanent current assets** because their levels remain stable no matter the seasonal or economic conditions. Applying this idea to Unilate Textiles, Exhibit 700.2 (presented earlier) suggests that, at this stage in its life, Unilate's total assets are growing at a 10 percent rate, from $845.0 million at the end of 2004 to a projected $929.5 million by the end of 2005, but seasonal fluctuations are expected to push total assets up to $1,100.0 million during the firm's peak season in 2005. Assuming Unilate's permanent assets grow continuously, and at the *same rate,* throughout the year, then 9/12ths (75 percent) of the 10 percent growth in assets will accrue by the end of September and permanent assets would equal $908.4 million = $845.0 million + (9/12)($929.5 million − $845.0 million). But the actual level of assets is expected to be $1,100.0 million because this is Unilate's peak season. So at the end of September, Unilate's total assets of $1,100.0 million consist of $908.4 million of permanent assets and $191.6 million = $1,100.0 million − $908.4 million of seasonal, or **temporary, current assets.** Unilate's temporary current assets fluctuate from zero during the slow season in December to nearly $192 million during the peak season in September. Therefore, temporary current assets are those amounts of current assets that vary with respect to the seasonal or economic conditions of a firm. The manner in which the permanent and temporary current assets are financed is called the firm's *current asset financing policy.* Three approaches are described next, including the maturity matching approach, aggressive approach, and conservative approach.

Maturity Matching, or "Self-Liquidating," Approach

The **maturity matching,** or **"self-liquidating," approach** calls for matching asset and liability maturities as shown in Panel a of Exhibit 700.5. This strategy minimizes the risk that the firm will be unable to pay off its maturing obligations *if* the liquidations of the assets can be controlled to occur on or before the maturities of the obligations. To illustrate, suppose Unilate borrows on a one-year basis and uses the funds obtained to build and equip a plant. Cash flows from

Exhibit 700.5 *Alternative Current Asset Financing Policies*

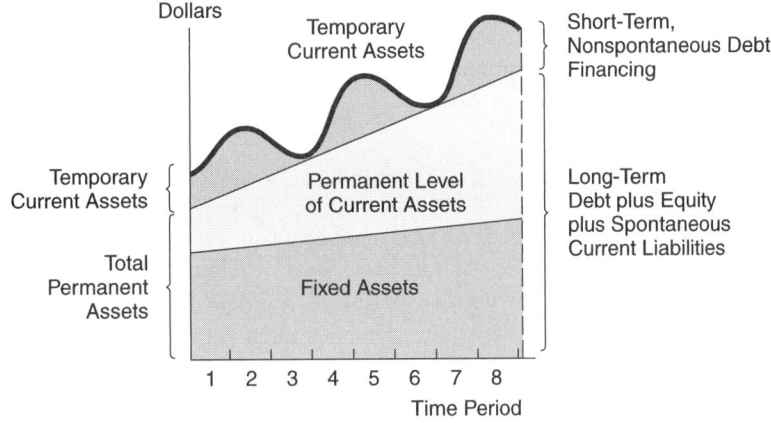

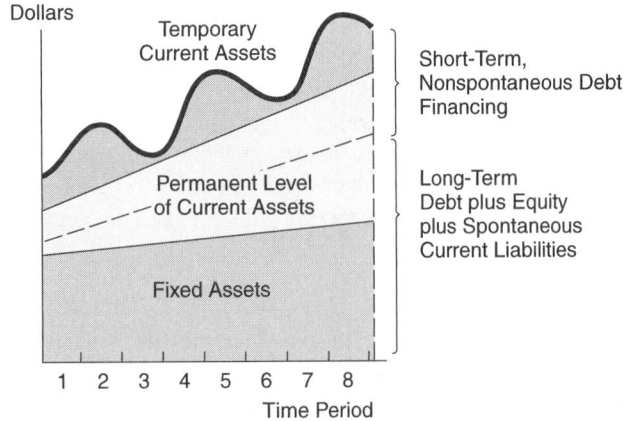

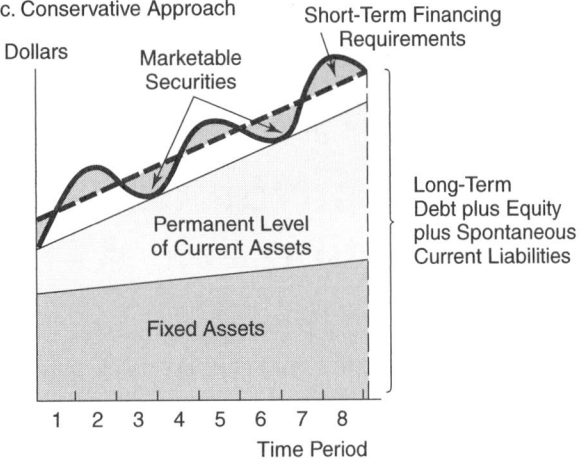

the plant (profits plus depreciation) would not be sufficient to pay off the loan at the end of only one year, so the loan would have to be renewed. If for some reason the lender refused to renew the loan, then Unilate would have problems. If the plant is financed with long-term debt, however, the required loan payments are better matched with cash flows from operations, and the problem of renewal will not arise.

At the limit, a firm could attempt to match exactly the maturity structure of its assets and liabilities. Inventory expected to be sold in 30 days could be financed with a 30-day bank loan; a machine expected to last for five years could be financed by a five-year loan; a 20-year building could be financed by a 20-year mortgage bond; and so forth.

Actually, of course, two factors prevent this exact maturity matching: (1) there is uncertainty about the lives of assets, and (2) some common equity must be used, and common equity has no maturity. To illustrate the uncertainty factor, Unilate might finance inventories with a 30-day loan, expecting to sell the inventories and to use the cash generated to retire the loan. But if sales were slow, the cash would not be forthcoming, and the use of short-term credit could end up causing a problem (for example, look at the cash conversion cycle computed for Unilate in the previous section). Still, if Unilate makes an attempt to match asset and liability maturities, we would define this as a *moderate current asset financing policy*.

Aggressive Approach

Panel b of Exhibit 700.5 illustrates the **aggressive approach,** used by a firm that (1) finances all of its temporary assets with short-term, nonspontaneous debt and (2) finances its fixed assets with long-term capital, but some of the remainder of its permanent current assets is financed with short-term, nonspontaneous credit. A look back at Exhibit 700.2 shows that Unilate actually follows this strategy. Unilate has $499.9 million in permanent current assets ($908.4 million in permanent assets less $408.5 million fixed assets) projected for September 2005, so its temporary current assets must be $191.6 million = $691.5 million − $499.9 million. However, the firm is projected to have $129.0 million in notes payable as well as temporary financing equal to about $100.0 million from peak levels of accounts payable and accruals (payables are projected to be $60.0 million higher than at the end of 2004, and accruals are projected to be $40.0 million higher). Thus, Unilate's level of temporary financing, which is $229.0 million, exceeds its level of temporary current assets, which is $191.6 million, so some part of its permanent assets is financed with temporary capital.

Returning to Exhibit 700.5, note that we used the term *relatively* in the title for Panel b because there can be different *degrees* of aggressiveness. For example, the dashed line in Panel b could have been drawn *below* the line designating fixed assets, indicating that all of the permanent current assets and part of the fixed assets were financed with short-term credit; this would be a highly aggressive, extremely nonconservative position, and the firm would be very much subject to dangers from rising interest rates as well as to loan-renewal problems. However, short-term debt often is cheaper than long-term debt, and some firms are willing to sacrifice safety for the chance of higher profits.

Conservative Approach

As shown in Panel c of Exhibit 700.5, the dashed line could also be drawn *above* the line designating permanent current assets, indicating that permanent capital is being used to finance all permanent asset requirements and also to meet some or all of the seasonal, temporary demands. In the situation depicted in our graph, the firm uses a small amount of short-term, nonspontaneous credit to meet its peak requirements, but it also meets a part of its seasonal needs by "storing liquidity" in the form of marketable securities during the off-season. The humps above the dashed line represent short-term financing; the troughs below the dashed line represent short-term security holdings. Panel c represents the **conservative approach,** which is a very safe current asset financing policy that generally is not as profitable as the other two approaches.

Advantages and Disadvantages of Short-Term Financing

The three possible financing policies or approaches described in the previous section were distinguished by the relative amounts of short-term debt used under each policy. The aggressive policy calls for the greatest use of short-term debt, while the conservative policy requires the least; maturity matching falls in between. Although using short-term credit generally is riskier than using long-term credit, short-term credit does have some significant advantages. The pros and cons of short-term financing are considered in this section.

Speed

A short-term loan can be obtained much faster than long-term credit. Lenders will insist on a more thorough financial examination before extending long-term credit, and the loan agreement will have to be spelled out in considerable detail because much can happen during the life of a 10- or 20-year loan. Therefore, if funds are needed in a hurry, the firm should look to short-term sources.

Flexibility

If the needs for funds are seasonal or cyclical, a firm might not want to commit itself to long-term debt for three reasons. First, the costs associated with issuing long-term debt are significantly greater than the costs of getting short-term credit. Second, some long-term debts carry expensive penalties for prepayments (paying prior to maturity). Accordingly, if a firm thinks its need for funds will diminish in the near future, it should choose short-term debt for the flexibility it provides. Third, long-term loan agreements always contain provisions, or covenants, that constrain the firm's future actions. Short-term credit agreements generally are much less onerous in this regard.

Cost of Long-Term versus Short-Term Debt

The yield curve normally is upward-sloping, indicating that interest rates generally are lower on short-term than on long-term debt. Thus, under normal conditions, interest costs at the time the funds are obtained will be lower if the firm borrows on a short-term rather than on a long-term basis.

Risk of Long-Term versus Short-Term Debt

Even though short-term debt is often less expensive than long-term debt, short-term credit subjects the firm to more risk than does long-term financing. This occurs for two reasons: (1) If a firm borrows on a long-term basis, its interest costs will be relatively stable, perhaps even fixed, over time, but if it uses short-term credit, its interest expense will fluctuate widely, at times reaching quite high levels. For example, the rate banks charge large corporations for short-term debt more than tripled over a two-year period in the early 1980s, rising from 6.25 percent to 21 percent. Many firms that had borrowed heavily on a short-term basis simply could not meet their rising interest costs, and as a result bankruptcies hit record levels during that period. Similarly, in 1994, because the Federal Reserve increased rates six times during the year, short-term rates increased by more than 3 percent, which created a significant burden for many firms. (2) If a firm borrows heavily on a short-term basis, it could find itself unable to repay this debt, and it might be in such a weak financial position that the lender will not extend the loan; this too could force the firm into bankruptcy. **Braniff Airlines** failed during a credit crunch in the 1980s for this very reason.

Multinational Working Capital Management

For the most part, the techniques used to manage short-term assets and liabilities in multinational corporations are the same as those used in purely domestic corporations. But multinational corporations face a far more complex task because they operate in many different business cultures, political environments, economic conditions, and so forth. Six factors complicate managerial finance in general in the international business arena: (1) different currency denominations, (2) differences in economic and legal environments, (3) language differences, (4) cultural differences, (5) governmental role, and (6) political risk. Difficulties with each of these factors are more acute when managing working capital internationally because decisions made in the short run can have significant consequences on the long-run survival of the firm and such decisions are more difficult to adjust or reverse when rules and regulations and business cultures differ significantly from one business setting to another.

The results of a recent study provide some indication of how working capital policies of U.S. firms and European firms differ.[2] First, the average cash conversion cycle of European firms (about 263 days) was more than twice the average cash conversion cycle of U.S. firms (about 116 days). A possible explanation for this disparity is that European firms had much higher growth rates than their U.S. counterparts. Second, it appears from the results of the study that U.S. firms follow much more conservative working capital policies than European firms. The average current ratio and the average quick ratio proved to be significantly greater for U.S. firms than for European firms, which suggests that corporations in the United States use significantly more long-term financing alternatives than corporations in Europe (remember that when the current ratio equals to 1.0, current assets equal current liabilities). Although a more in-depth study is needed to determine why U.S. firms seem to follow more conservative working capital policies than European firms, one possible explanation might be found in the differences that are apparent in the banking systems in Europe and in the United States. U.S. financial institutions generally are at a competitive disadvantage in the global arena because they are subject to more restrictions and regulations than banking organizations in other countries. Foreign banks generally can branch with little or no restrictions and are allowed, in many cases, to own corporations to which they also lend funds. For these reasons, European banks often have close relationships with their debtor corporations; thus, they tend to be more willing to provide short-term, risky debt than we observe in U.S. banking organizations.

Managing Short-Term Assets

Working Capital Management Policies

All else equal, the riskiness of the portfolio of assets held by a firm is based on the combination of short- and long-term investments (assets) the firm makes. The relative amount that is invested in short-term assets is a function of decisions that are made concerning the management of cash and marketable securities, accounts receivable, and inventories. Of these three assets, we generally consider cash and marketable securities to be least risky, or most *liquid*. But the degree of risk can vary for either accounts receivable or inventories, depending on the general characteristics of the firm's working capital policy. For example, we generally view receivables as relatively safe assets because they represent sales the firm expects to collect in the future. But a firm with an overly aggressive, or relaxed, credit policy might have many slow payers or bad-debt customers that make its receivables extremely risky, thus fairly *illiquid*.

In this section, we discuss working capital management policies with respect to the current (short-term) assets of the firm. Keep in mind that although short-term assets generally are safer than long-term assets, they earn a lower rate of return. Thus, all else equal, firms that hold greater amounts of short-term assets are considered less risky than firms that hold greater amounts of long-term assets; at the same time, firms with more short-term assets earn lower returns than firms with more long-term assets. Consequently, financial managers are faced with a dilemma of whether to forgo higher returns to attain lower risk or to forgo lower risk to achieve higher returns. In general, however, we will see that some amount of short-term assets is required to maintain normal operations.

Cash Management

Maximizing shareholders' value is based on cash flows. Thus, managing cash flows is an extremely important task for a financial manager. Part of this task is determining how much cash a firm should have on hand at any time to ensure normal business operations continue uninterrupted. In this section, we discuss some of the factors that affect the amount of cash firms hold, and we describe some of the cash management techniques currently used by businesses.

For the purposes of our discussion, the term *cash* refers to the funds a firm holds that can be used for immediate disbursement—this includes the amount a firm holds in its checking account as well as the amount of actual coin and currency it holds. Cash is a "nonearning, or idle, asset" that is required to pay bills. When possible, cash should be "put to work" by investing in assets that have positive expected returns. Thus, the goal of the cash manager is to minimize the amount of cash the firm must hold for use in conducting its normal business activities, yet, at the same time, to have sufficient cash to (1) pay suppliers, (2) maintain the firm's credit rating, and (3) meet unexpected cash needs.

Firms hold cash for the following reasons:

1. Cash balances are necessary in business operations because payments must be made in cash, and receipts are deposited in a cash account. Cash balances associated with routine payments and collections are known as **transactions balances.**

2. A bank often requires a firm to maintain a **compensating balance** on deposit to help offset the costs of providing services such as check clearing and cash management advice.

3. Because cash inflows and cash outflows are somewhat unpredictable, firms generally hold some cash in reserve for random, unforeseen fluctuations in cash flows. These *safety stocks* are called **precautionary balances**—the less predictable the firm's cash flows, the larger such balances should be. However, if the firm has easy access to borrowed funds—that is, if it can borrow on short notice (for example, via a line of credit at the bank)—its need for precautionary balances is reduced.

4. Sometimes cash balances are held to enable the firm to take advantage of bargain purchases that might arise. These funds are called **speculative balances.** As with precautionary balances, though, firms that have easy access

to borrowed funds are likely to rely on their ability to borrow quickly rather than to rely on cash balances for speculative purposes.

Although the cash accounts of most firms can be thought of as consisting of transactions, compensating, precautionary, and speculative balances, we cannot calculate the amount needed for each purpose, sum them, and produce a total desired cash balance because the same money often serves more than one purpose. For instance, precautionary and speculative balances can also be used to satisfy compensating balance requirements. Firms do, however, consider all four factors when establishing their target cash positions.

In addition, a firm maintains cash balances to preserve its credit rating by keeping its liquidity position in line with those of other firms in the industry. A strong credit rating enables the firm both to purchase goods from suppliers on favorable terms and to maintain an ample line of credit with its bank.

The Cash Budget

Perhaps the most critical ingredient to proper cash management is the ability to estimate the cash flows of the firm so the firm can make plans to borrow when cash is deficient or to invest when cash is in excess of what is needed. Without a doubt, financial managers will agree that the most important tool for managing cash is the cash budget (forecast). The cash budget helps management plan investment and borrowing strategies, and it also is used to provide feedback and control to improve the efficiency of cash management in the future.

The firm estimates its general needs for cash as a part of its overall budgeting, or forecasting, process. First, the firm forecasts its operating activities such as expenses and revenues for the period in question. Then, the financing and investment activities necessary to attain that level of operations must be forecasted. Such forecasts entail the construction of *pro forma* financial statements. The information provided from the *pro forma* balance sheet and income statement is combined with projections about the delay in collecting accounts receivable, the delay in paying suppliers and employees, tax payment dates, dividend and interest payment dates, and so on. All of this information is summarized in the **cash budget,** which shows the firm's projected cash inflows and cash outflows over some specified period. Generally, firms use a monthly cash budget forecasted over the next year plus a more detailed daily or weekly cash budget for the coming month. The monthly cash budgets are used for planning purposes and the daily or weekly budgets are used for actual cash control. Cash budgets were fully discussed in Module 600, Accounting, Section 650.

Cash Management Techniques

Most cash management activities are performed jointly by the firm and its primary bank, but the financial manager ultimately is responsible for the effectiveness of the cash management program. Effective cash management encompasses proper management of both the cash inflows and the cash outflows of a firm, which entails consideration of the factors discussed next.

Cash Flow Synchronization

It would be ideal if the receipt of a cash payment from a customer occurred at exactly the same time a bill needs to be paid; that portion paid out would never be idle and any excess could be invested quickly to reduce the time it is idle. Recognizing this point, companies try to arrange it so that cash inflows and cash outflows are matched as well as possible—customers are billed so their billing cycles coordinate with when the firm pays its own bills. Having **synchronized cash flows** enables a firm to reduce its cash balances, decrease its bank loans, lower interest expenses, and boost profits. The more predictable the timing of the cash flows, the greater the synchronization that can be attained—utilities and credit card companies generally have a high degree of cash flow synchronization.

Check-Clearing Process

When a customer writes and mails a check, this does *not* mean that the funds are immediately available to the receiving firm. Most of us have been told by someone that "the check is in the mail," and we also have deposited a check in an account and then been told that we cannot write checks against the deposit until the **check-clearing process** has been completed. Our bank must first make sure that the deposited check is good and then receive funds itself from the customer's bank before it will give us cash.

A check must first be delivered through the mail and then be cleared through the banking system before the money can be put to use. Checks received from customers in distant cities are especially subject to delays because of mail time and also because more parties are involved in the check-clearing process. For example, assume that you receive a check and deposit it in your bank. Your bank must send the check to the bank on which it was drawn. Only when this latter bank transfers funds to your bank are the funds available for you to use. If a check is deposited in the same bank on which it was drawn, that bank merely transfers funds by bookkeeping entries from one of its depositors to another. But most deposited checks are drawn from outside banks, so the verification, or clearing process, generally is handled by a check-clearing system, termed a *clearinghouse,* set up by the Federal Reserve or a network of banks in a particular region. The length of time required for checks to clear is a function of the distance between the payer's (check writer) bank and the payee's (depositor) bank. In the case of private clearinghouses, it can range from one to three days. The maximum time required for checks to clear through the Federal Reserve System is two days, but mail delays can slow down things on each end of the Fed's involvement in the process.

Using Float

Float is defined as the difference between the balance shown in a firm's (or individual's) checkbook and the balance on the bank's records. Suppose a firm writes, on average, checks in the amount of $5,000 each day, and it normally takes six days from the time the check is mailed until it is cleared and deducted from the firm's bank account. This will cause the firm's own checkbook to show a balance equal to $30,000 = $5,000 × 6 days smaller than the balance on the bank's records; this difference is called **disbursement float.** Now suppose the firm also receives checks in the amount of $5,000 daily, but it loses four days while they are being deposited and cleared. This will result in $20,000 of **collections float.** In total, the firm's **net float**—the difference between $30,000 positive disbursement float and the $20,000 negative collections float—will be $10,000, which means the balance the bank shows in the firm's checking account is $10,000 greater than the balance the firm shows in its own checkbook.

Delays that cause float arise because it takes time for checks (1) to travel through the mail (*mail delay*), (2) to be processed by the receiving firm (*processing delay*), and (3) to clear through the banking system (*clearing, or availability, delay*). Basically, the size of a firm's net float is a function of its ability to speed up collections on checks received and to slow down collections on checks written. Efficient firms go to great lengths to speed up the processing of incoming checks, thus putting the funds to work faster, and they try to delay their own payments as long as possible.

Acceleration of Receipts

A firm cannot use customers' payments until they are received *and* converted into a spendable form, such as cash or an increase in a checking account balance. Thus, it would benefit the firm to accelerate the collection of customers' payments and conversion of those payments into cash. Although some of the delays that cause float cannot be controlled directly, the techniques described next are used to manage collections:

LOCKBOXES A **lockbox arrangement** requires customers to send their payments to a post office box located in the area near where they live rather than directly to the firm. The firm arranges for a local bank to collect the checks from the post office box, perhaps several times a day, and to immediately deposit them into the company's checking account. By having lockboxes close to the customers, a firm can reduce float because, at the very least, (1) the mail delay is less than if the payment had to travel farther and (2) checks are cleared faster because the banks the checks are written on are in the same Federal Reserve district; thus, fewer parties are involved in the clearing process.

PREAUTHORIZED DEBITS If a firm receives regular, repetitious payments from its customers, it might want to establish a **preauthorized debit system** (sometimes called preauthorized payments). With this arrangement, the collecting firm and its customer (paying firm) enter into an agreement whereby the paying firm's bank periodically transfers funds from the paying firm's account to the collecting firm's account, even if that account is located at another bank. Preauthorized debiting accelerates the transfer of funds because mail and check-clearing delays are completely eliminated, and the processing delay is reduced substantially.

CONCENTRATION BANKING **Concentration banking** is a cash management arrangement used to mobilize funds from decentralized receiving locations, whether they are lockboxes or decentralized company locations, into one or more central cash pools. The cash manager then uses these pools for short-term investing or reallocation among the firm's various bank accounts. By pooling its cash, the firm is able to take maximum advantage of economies of scale in cash management and investment. Often commissions are less per dollar on large investments, and there are instances where investments of larger dollar amounts earn higher returns than smaller investments.

Disbursement Control

Accelerating collections represents one side of cash management, and controlling funds outflows, or disbursements, represents the other side. Three methods commonly used to control disbursements include the following:

PAYABLES CONCENTRATION Centralizing the processing of payables permits the financial manager to evaluate the payments coming due for the entire firm and to schedule the availability of funds to meet these needs on a company-wide basis, and it also permits more efficient monitoring of payables and the effects of float. A disadvantage to a centralized disbursement system is that regional offices might not be able to make prompt payment for services rendered, which can create ill will and raise the company's operating costs. But as firms become more electronically proficient, the centralization of disbursements can be coordinated more effectively and such situations should be reduced substantially.

ZERO-BALANCE ACCOUNTS A **zero-balance account (ZBA)** is a special disbursement account that has a balance equal to zero when there is no disbursement activity. Typically, a firm establishes several ZBAs in its concentration bank and funds them from a master account. As checks are presented to a ZBA for payment, funds are automatically transferred from the master account.

CONTROLLED DISBURSEMENT ACCOUNTS Whereas ZBAs typically are established at concentration banks, **controlled disbursement accounts (CDAs)** can be set up at any bank. Such accounts are not funded until the day's checks are presented against the account. The firm relies on the bank that maintains the CDA to provide information in the morning (before 11 A.M. New York time) concerning the total amount of the checks that will be presented for payment that day. This permits the financial manager (1) to transfer funds to the controlled disbursement account to cover the checks presented for payment or (2) to invest excess cash at midday, when money-market trading is at a peak.

Marketable Securities

Realistically, the management of cash and marketable securities cannot be separated—management of one implies management of the other because the amount of marketable securities held by a firm depends on its short-term cash needs.

Rationale for Holding Marketable Securities

Marketable securities, or *near-cash* assets, are extremely liquid, short-term investments that permit the firm to earn positive returns on cash that is not needed to pay bills immediately but will be needed sometime in the near term, perhaps in a few days, weeks, or months. Although such investments typically provide much lower yields than operating assets, nearly every large firm has them. The two basic reasons for owning marketable securities are as follows:

> *Near-cash assets include U.S. Treasury bills, commercial paper, negotiable CDs, money market mutual funds, and eurodollar time deposits.*

1. Marketable securities serve as a *substitute for cash balances*. Firms often hold portfolios of marketable securities, liquidating part of the portfolio to increase the cash account when cash is needed because the *marketable securities offer a place to temporarily put cash balances to work earning a positive return*. In such situations, the marketable securities could be used as a substitute for transactions balances, for precautionary balances, for speculative balances, or for all three.
2. Marketable securities are also used as a *temporary investment* (a) to finance seasonal or cyclical operations and (b) to amass funds to meet financial requirements in the near future. For example, if the firm has a conservative financing policy, then its long-term capital will exceed its permanent assets, and marketable securities will be held when inventories and receivables are low.

Characteristics of Marketable Securities

A wide variety of securities is available to firms that choose to hold marketable securities. But the characteristics generally associated with marketable securities are as follows:

1. **Maturity.** Firms hold marketable securities in order to *temporarily* invest cash that otherwise would be idle in the short run. Therefore, marketable securities are short-term investments; often they are held only for a few days or weeks. If the cash budget indicates the funds are not needed in the foreseeable future, then longer-term investments, which generally earn higher returns, should be used.
2. **Risk.** An equation for determining the nominal interest rate is:

$$k_{Nom} = k^* + IP + DRP + LP + MRP$$

   Here k^* is the real risk-free rate, IP is a premium for expected inflation, DRP is the default risk premium, LP is the liquidity (or marketability) risk premium, and MRP is the maturity (or interest rate) risk premium. Also, remember that the risk-free rate, k_{RF}, is equal to $k^* + IP$, and a U.S. Treasury bill comes closest to the risk-free rate. For other instruments considered appropriate as marketable securities, the default and liquidity risks are small, and the interest-rate risk is negligible. These risks are small because marketable securities mature in the short term, and the short run is less uncertain than the long run. Also, recall that prices of long-term investments, such as bonds, are much more sensitive to changes in interest rates than are prices of short-term investments. In general, then, the total risk associated with a portfolio of marketable securities (short term) is less than the total risk associated with a portfolio of long-term investments.
3. **Liquidity.** We generally judge an asset's *marketability* according to how quickly and easily it can be bought and sold in the financial markets. If an asset can be sold easily on short notice for close to its original purchase price, it is said to be *liquid*. Because marketable securities are held as a *substitute* for cash and as a *temporary* investment, such instruments should be very liquid.
4. **Return (Yield).** Because the marketable securities portfolio generally is composed of highly liquid, short-term securities with low risks, the returns associated with such investments are relatively low when compared to other investments. But given the purpose of the marketable securities portfolio, treasurers should not sacrifice safety for higher rates of return.

Credit Management

If you ask financial managers whether they would prefer to sell their products for cash or for credit, you would expect them to respond by saying something like this: "*If sales levels are not affected,* cash sales are preferred because payment is certain and immediate and because the costs of granting credit and maintaining accounts receivable would be eliminated." *Ideally,* then, firms would prefer to sell for cash only. So why do firms sell for credit? The primary reason most firms offer credit sales is because their competitors offer credit. Consider what you would do if you had the opportunity to purchase the same product for the same price from two different firms, but one firm required cash payment at the time of the purchase while the other firm allowed you to pay for the product one month after the purchase without any additional cost. From which firm would you purchase? Like you, firms prefer to delay their payments, especially if there are no additional costs associated with the delay.

Effective credit management is extremely important because too much credit is very costly in terms of the investment in, and maintenance of, accounts receivables, while too little credit could result in the loss of profitable sales. Carrying receivables has both direct and indirect costs, but it also has an important benefit—granting credit should increase profits. Thus, to maximize shareholders' wealth, a financial manager needs to understand how to effectively manage the firm's credit activities.

In this section, we discuss (1) the factors considered important when determining the appropriate credit policy for a firm, (2) procedures for monitoring the credit policy to ensure it is being administered properly, and (3) how to evaluate whether credit policy changes will be beneficial to the firm.

Credit Policy

The major controllable variables that affect demand for a company's products are sales prices, product quality, advertising, and the firm's **credit policy**. The firm's credit policy, in turn, includes the factors we discuss next.

1. **Credit standards** refer to the strength and creditworthiness a customer must exhibit in order to qualify for credit. The firm's credit standards are applied to determine which customers qualify for the regular credit

terms and how much credit each customer should receive. The major factors considered when setting credit standards relate to the likelihood that a given customer will pay slowly or perhaps even end up as a bad debt loss. Determining the credit quality, or creditworthiness, of a customer probably is the most difficult part of credit management. But credit evaluation is a well-established practice and a good credit manager can make reasonably accurate judgments of the probability of default exhibited by different classes of customers by examining a firm's current financial position and evaluating factors that might affect the financial position in the future.

2. **Terms of credit** are the conditions of the credit sale, especially with regard to the payment arrangements. Firms need to determine when the **credit period** begins, how long the customer has to pay for credit purchases before the account is considered delinquent, and whether a cash discount for early payment should be offered. An examination of the credit terms offered by firms in the United States would show great variety across industries—credit terms range from cash before delivery (CBD) and cash on delivery (COD) to offering **cash discounts** for early payment. For example, a firm that offers terms of 2/10 net 30 gives its customers a 2 percent discount from the purchase price if the bill is paid on or before the 10th day of the billing cycle; otherwise the entire bill (the net amount) is due by Day 30. Due to the competitive nature of trade credit, most financial managers follow the norm of the industry in which they operate when setting credit terms.

3. **Collection policy** refers to the procedures the firm follows to collect its credit accounts. The firm needs to determine when and how notification of the credit sale will be conveyed to the buyer. The quicker a customer receives an invoice, the sooner the bill *can* be paid. In today's world, firms have turned more to the use of electronics to "send" invoices to customers. One of the most important collection policy decisions is how the past-due accounts should be handled. For example, notification might be sent to customers when a bill is 10 days past due; a more severe notice, followed by a telephone call, might be used if payment is not received within 30 days; and the account might be turned over to a collection agency after 90 days.

Receivables Monitoring

Once a firm sets its credit policy, it wants to operate within the policy's limits. Thus, it is important that a firm examine its receivables periodically to determine whether customers' payment patterns have changed such that credit operations are outside the credit policy limits. For instance, if the balance in receivables increases either because the amount of "bad," or uncollectible, sales increases or because the average time it takes to collect existing credit sales increases, the firm should consider making changes in its credit policy. **Receivables monitoring** refers to the process of evaluating the credit policy to determine if a shift in the customers' payment patterns has occurred.

Traditionally, firms have monitored accounts receivables by using methods that measure the amount of time credit remains outstanding. Two such methods are the *days sales outstanding (DSO)* and the *aging schedule*.

Days Sales Outstanding (DSO)

Days sales outstanding (DSO), which is sometimes called the *average collection period,* represents the average time it takes to collect credit accounts. DSO is computed by dividing *annual* credit sales by *daily* credit sales. For example, we found the receivables collection period, or DSO, for Unilate was 43.2 days in 2004. The DSO of 43.2 days can be compared with the credit terms offered by Unilate. If Unilate's credit terms are 2/10 net 30, then we know there are customers that are delinquent when paying their accounts. In fact, if many customers are paying within 10 days to take advantage of the discount, the others would, on average, have to be taking much longer than 43.2 days. One way to check this possibility is to use an aging schedule, as described next.

Aging Schedule

An **aging schedule** is a breakdown of a firm's receivables by age of account. Exhibit 700.6 contains the December 31, 2004, aging schedule for Unilate Textiles. The standard format for aging schedules generally includes age categories broken down by month because banks and financial analysts usually want companies to report their receivables ages in this form. However, more precision, thus better monitoring information, can be attained by using narrower age categories (for example, one or two weeks).

According to Unilate's aging schedule, only 40 percent of the credit sales in December 2004 were collected within the credit period of 30 days; thus, 60 percent of the credit sales collections were delinquent. Some of the payments were delinquent by only a few days, while others were delinquent by three to four times the 30-day credit period.

Exhibit 700.6 *Unilate Textiles: Receivables Aging Schedule for 2004*

Age of Account (in days)	Net Amount Outstanding	Fraction of Total Receivables	Average Days
0–30	$ 72,000	40%	18
31–60	90,000	50	55
61–90	10,800	6	77
More than 90	7,200	4	97
	$180,000	100%	

DSO = 0.40(18 days) + 0.50(55 days) + 0.06(77 days) + 0.04(97 days)
   = 43.2 days

Management should constantly monitor the days sales outstanding and the aging schedule to detect trends, to see how the firm's collection experience compares with its credit terms, and to see how effectively the credit department is operating in comparison with other firms in the industry. If the DSO starts to lengthen or if the aging schedule begins to show an increasing percentage of past-due accounts, then the firm's credit policy might need to be tightened.

We must be careful when interpreting changes in DSO or the aging schedule, however, because if a firm experiences sharp seasonal variations, or if it is growing rapidly, then both measures could be distorted. Therefore, *a change in either the DSO or the aging schedule should be taken as a signal to investigate further, but not necessarily as a sign that the firm's credit policy has weakened.* If a firm generally experiences widely fluctuating sales patterns, some type of modified aging schedule should be used to correctly account for these fluctuations.[3] Still, days sales outstanding and the aging schedule are useful tools for reviewing the credit department's performance.

Analyzing Proposed Changes in Credit Policy

The key question when deciding on a proposed credit policy change is this: Will the firm realize a net benefit? Unless the added benefits expected from a credit policy change exceed the added costs, the policy change should *not* be made.

To illustrate how we can evaluate whether a proposed change in a firm's credit policy is appropriate, let's examine what would happen if Unilate Textiles makes changes to reduce its average collection period. Assume that Unilate's financial manager has proposed that this task be accomplished in 2005 by (1) billing customers sooner and exerting more pressure on delinquent customers to pay their bills, and (2) tightening existing credit standards slightly—the credit department will more closely examine the financial positions of credit customers and suspend the credit of customers who are considered "habitually delinquent." It is apparent that both of these actions will result in a direct increase in the costs associated with Unilate's credit policy; in fact, credit evaluation and collection costs are expected to increase from $16 million to $17 million. At the same time, even though Unilate has an extremely loyal customer base, it is expected that $2 million in annual sales will be lost to competitors because some customers will have their credit decreased or even eliminated. But because the credit policy changes will have little, if any, effect on the "good" credit customers, the financial manager does not expect there to be a change in the proportion of customers (20 percent) who currently take advantage of the cash discount. If the proposed credit policy changes are approved, the financial manager believes the average collection period, or DSO, for receivables can be reduced from 43.2 days to 35.6 days—this is more in line with the credit terms offered by Unilate (2/10 net 30), and it is closer to the industry average of 32.1 days. Also, if the average collection period is reduced, the amount "carried" in accounts receivable is reduced, which means less funds are "tied up" in receivables. Exhibit 700.7 summarizes the information about Unilate's existing credit policy and the financial manager's proposed changes.

Should Unilate adopt the financial manager's proposal? To answer this question, we need to compute the marginal costs and benefits associated with changing the existing credit policy to determine if the proposal is more advantageous than the current policy. The obvious costs to the firm include the $2 million decrease in sales and the $1 million increase in credit and collection costs, which, in combination, will decrease taxable earnings by $3 million. But the decline in sales will also reduce variable operating costs by $1.6 million = $2 million × 0.82. In addition, decreases in both credit sales and the average collection period mean less funds will be "tied up" in receivables, thus the opportunity, or carrying, cost of receivables will also be less.

Exhibit 700.7 Unilate Textiles: Existing and Proposed Credit Policies (millions of dollars)—Expected for 2005

Policy	Existing Policy	Proposed Policy
Credit terms	2/10 net 30	2/10 net 30
Gross credit sales[a]	$1,656.6	$1,654.6
Net credit sales (S)	$1,650.0	$1,648.0
Cash discount[b]	$6.6	$6.6
Variable cost ratio[c] (V)	82%	82%
Bad debts	$ 0	$ 0
Credit evaluation and collection costs	$ 16	$ 17
Days sales outstanding (DSO)	43.2 days	35.6 days

[a] We determined that Unilate's 2005 *net* forecasted sales is $1,650 million, which represents what the firm expects to collect from credit sales, net of cash discounts. The gross sales, which includes cash discounts, can be computed as follows:

Net sales = 0.80 (Gross sales) + (0.20) (1 − 0.02) (Gross sales)

= (Gross sales) [0.80 + (0.20) (0.98)] = $1,650 million

$$\text{Gross sales} = \frac{\$1{,}650 \text{ million}}{0.996} = \$1{,}656.6 \text{ million}$$

[b] Unilate offers credit terms of 2/10 net 30, and 20% of its customers take advantage of the cash discount; thus, the total cash discount is $6.6 million = (0.20) (0.02) ($1,656.6 million). This value will be the same with both credit policies.

[c] We have assumed that the variable cost of goods sold for Unilate is 82% of *net* sales. We use the same assumption here.

To compute the carrying cost, we need to determine how much Unilate has invested in receivables and the "cost" of this investment. The amount invested in receivables can be computed by determining the amount Unilate paid for the products that were sold on credit, but for which cash payment has not been received.

$$\begin{aligned}
\frac{\text{Receivables}}{\text{investment}} &= \frac{\text{Average accounts}}{\text{receivable balance}} \times \frac{\text{Variable}}{\text{cost ratio}} \\
&= \left[\text{DSO} \times (\text{Sales per day}) \right] \times \text{Variable cost ratio} \\
&= \left[\text{DSO} \times \left(\frac{S}{360} \right) \right] \times v
\end{aligned} \quad (7.5)$$

Variable cost ratio is "v". Only variable costs enter the calculation because it is this amount that represents the funds the firm has "tied up" in receivables, which is the amount that must be financed. For Unilate, the receivables investments associated with the existing and the proposed credit policies are as follows:

$$\begin{aligned}
\text{Receivables investment}_{\text{Current}} &= \left[43.2 \text{ days} \times \left(\frac{\$1{,}656.6 \text{ million}}{360} \right) \right] \times (0.82) \\
&= \$198.8 \text{ million} \times 0.82 \\
&= 163.0 \text{ million}
\end{aligned}$$

$$\begin{aligned}
\text{Receivables investment}_{\text{Proposal}} &= \left[35.6 \text{ days} \times \left(\frac{\$1{,}654.6 \text{ million}}{360} \right) \right] \times (0.82) \\
&= \$163.6 \text{ million} \times (0.82) \\
&= \$134.2 \text{ million}
\end{aligned}$$

Once the investment in receivables is computed, the receivables carrying (opportunity) cost can be computed by determining how much return these funds would have earned if they were invested elsewhere.

$$\begin{aligned}
\frac{\text{Receivables}}{\text{carrying cost}} &= \frac{\text{Receivables}}{\text{investment}} \times \frac{\text{Opportunity}}{\text{cost of funds}} \\
&= \left[\text{DSO} \times \left(\frac{S}{360} \right) \right] \times v \times k_{AR}
\end{aligned} \quad (7.6)$$

Exhibit 700.8 Unilate Textiles: Analysis of Changing Credit Policy (millions of dollars)

	Projected 2005 Revenues/Costs under Current Credit Policy	Projected 2005 Revenues/Costs under Proposed Credit Policy	Income Effect of Credit Policy Change
Gross sales[a]	$1,656.6	$1,654.6	($2.0)
Less: Cash discounts[a]	(6.6)	(6.6)	0.0
Net sales	1,650.0	1,648.0	(2.0)
Variable cost of goods sold[a]	(1,353.0)	(1,351.4)	1.6
Bad debts	(0.0)	(0.0)	0.0
Credit evaluation and collection costs	(16.0)	(17.0)	(1.0)
Receivables carrying cost	(16.3)	(13.4)	2.9
Revenues net of variable production costs and credit costs	$ 264.7	$ 266.2	$1.5
Tax impact (40%)[b]	(105.9)	(106.5)	(0.6)
After-tax revenues	$ 158.8	$ 159.7	$0.9

[a]See footnotes in Exhibit 700.7.
[b]For this example, it is not necessary to include the tax impact because the marginal tax rate will not change under the proposed credit policy changes. Therefore, if the proposal is acceptable before taxes, it is also acceptable after taxes. This might not be the case if the marginal tax rate that applies to the proposal differs from the existing rate.

where k_{AR} represents the opportunity cost associated with the funds "tied up" in accounts receivable. Therefore, if Unilate's opportunity cost for funds invested in receivables is 10 percent, the cost of carrying receivables with the existing policy and with the proposal would be as follows:

$$\text{Receivables carrying cost}_{Current} = \$163.0 \text{ million} \times 0.10 = \$16.3 \text{ million}$$
$$\text{Receivables carrying cost}_{Proposal} = \$134.2 \text{ million} \times 0.10 = \$13.4 \text{ million}$$

If the proposed credit policy changes are adopted, then the required investment in receivables will decrease by $28.8 million = $163.0 million − $134.2 million, which will decrease the cost of carrying receivables by $2.9 million, from $16.3 million to $13.4 million.

Exhibit 700.8 summarizes the results of the analysis we just described, and it illustrates the general idea behind credit policy analysis. The combined effect of all the changes in credit policy is a projected $900,000 annual increase in after-tax revenues, which suggests the credit policy changes would be beneficial for Unilate. There might, of course, be corresponding changes on the projected balance sheet—the lower sales might necessitate somewhat less cash and inventories. These changes, as well as any other changes, also would have to be considered in the analysis. For simplicity, we assume the only changes relevant to the decision to change the credit policy are those discussed here and contained in Exhibit 700.8.

The analysis in Exhibit 700.8 provides Unilate's managers with a vehicle for considering the impact of credit policy changes on the firm's income statement and balance sheet variables. However, a great deal of judgment must be applied to the decision because both customers' and competitors' responses to credit policy changes are very difficult to estimate. Nevertheless, this type of numerical analysis can provide a good starting point for credit policy decisions.

Multinational Working Capital Management

As we mentioned earlier, the methods used to manage short-term assets in multinational corporations are essentially the same as those used in purely domestic corporations. But there are some differences, which we discuss in this section.

Cash Management

Like a purely domestic company, a multinational corporation wants (1) to speed up collections and to slow down disbursements where possible, (2) to shift cash as rapidly as possible to those areas where it is needed, and (3) to try to put temporary cash balances to work earning positive returns. Multinational companies use the same general procedures for achieving these goals as domestic firms, but because of longer distances and more serious mail delays, lockbox systems and electronic funds transfers are even more important.

One potential problem a multinational company faces that a purely domestic company does not is the chance that a foreign government will restrict transfers of funds out of the country. Foreign governments sometimes limit the amount of cash that can be taken out of their countries because they want to encourage investment domestically. Even if funds can be transferred without limitation, deteriorating exchange rates might make it unattractive for a multinational firm to move funds to its operations in other countries.

Once it has been determined what funds can be transferred out of the various nations in which a multinational corporation operates, it is important to get those funds to locations where they will earn the highest returns. Whereas domestic corporations tend to think in terms of domestic securities, multinationals are more likely to be aware of investment opportunities all around the world. Most multinational corporations use one or more global concentration banks, located in money centers such as London, New York, Tokyo, Zurich, or Singapore; and their staffs in those cities, working with international bankers, are able to take advantage of the best rates available anywhere in the world.

Credit Management

Credit policy generally is more important for a multinational corporation than for a purely domestic firm for two reasons. First, much U.S. trade is with poorer, less-developed nations, and in such situations granting credit generally is a necessary condition for doing business. Second, and in large part as a result of the first point, developed nations whose economic health depends on exports often help their manufacturing firms compete internationally by granting credit to foreign countries. In Japan, for example, government agencies help firms identify potential export markets and also help potential customers arrange credit for purchases from Japanese firms. The U.S. government has programs that help domestic firms to export products, but it does not provide the degree of financial assistance that local governments offer many multinationals based in other countries.

When granting credit, the multinational firm faces a riskier situation than purely domestic firms because, in addition to the normal risks of default, (1) political and legal environments often make it more difficult to collect defaulted accounts, and (2) the multinational corporations must worry about exchange rate changes between the time a sale is made and the time a receivable is collected. We know, though, that hedging can reduce this type of risk, but at a cost.

By pointing out the risks in granting credit internationally, we are not suggesting that such credit is bad. Quite the contrary—the potential gains from international operations far outweigh the risks, at least for companies (and banks) that have the necessary expertise.

Inventory Management

Inventory management in a multinational setting is more complex than in a purely domestic setting because of logistical problems that arise with handling inventories. For example, should a firm concentrate its inventories in a few strategic centers located worldwide? Such a strategy might minimize the total amount of, thus the investment in, inventories needed to operate the global business; but it also might cause delays in getting goods from central storage locations to user locations all around the world. It is clear, however, that both working stocks and safety stocks will have to be maintained at each user location, as well as at the strategic storage centers.

Exchange rates can significantly influence inventory policy. For example, if a local currency was expected to increase in value against the dollar, a U.S. company operating in that country would want to increase stocks of local products before the rise in the currency, and vice versa. Another factor that must be considered is the possibility of import or export quotas or tariffs. Quotas restrict the quantities of products firms can bring into a country, while tariffs, like taxes, increase the prices of products that are allowed to be imported. Both quotas and tariffs are designed to restrict the ability of foreign corporations to compete with domestic companies; at the extreme, foreign products are excluded altogether.

Another danger in certain countries is the threat of expropriation, or government takeover of the firm's local operations. If the threat of expropriation is large, inventory holdings will be minimized, and goods will be brought in only as needed. Similarly, if the operation involves extraction of raw material, processing plants might be moved offshore rather than located close to the production site.

Taxes also must be considered, and they have two effects on multinational inventory management. First, countries often impose property taxes on assets, including inventories, and when this is done, the tax is based on holdings as of a specific date, say, January 1 or March 1. Such rules make it advantageous for a multinational firm (1) to schedule production so that inventories are low on the assessment date, and (2) if assessment dates vary among countries in a region, to hold safety stocks in different countries at different times during the year.

In general, then, multinational firms use techniques similar to those described in this chapter to manage current assets, but their job is more complex because business, legal, and economic environments can differ significantly from one country to another.

Short-Term Investment Strategies

There are many possible investment strategies that can be used. Generically, we divide them into passive strategies and active strategies. A **passive investment strategy** involves a minimal amount of oversight and very few transactions once the portfolio has been selected.

An **active investment strategy** involves more trading and active monitoring of the portfolio and may be motivated by a philosophy that the investor can "beat the market." In the money markets, this generally means earning higher-than-normal yield spreads and/or capital gains as a result of accurate anticipation of interest rate movements.

Passive Strategies

A popular passive strategy is the **buy-and-hold strategy.** Quite often, this is part of a "maturity matching" approach to investing that prescribes investing in a security that will mature at the end of the investment horizon. The horizon is based on how long the company can tie up the investable funds. This eliminates interest rate risk if the company does hold the security to maturity as planned, because it will receive the face value of the security at that time. The buy-and-hold strategy may be implemented by investing part or all of the portfolio in an index fund, which is a managed portfolio assembled to mirror a particular money market composite. The composite serves as an index because it is calculated by averaging the yields of a broadly based basket of securities. A **modified buy-and-hold strategy** might be used when the investor wishes to take advantage of favorable interest rate movements, should they occur. If rates come down and the portfolio report shows a paper capital gain, the investor may sell or swap for another security to capture the gain.

Active Strategies

There are numerous active strategies. One strategy is to try to spot inefficiencies in the way securities are priced at present and to buy those that are underpriced (have higher yields than warranted by their level of risk). These are then held to maturity or sold at a capital gain when the market recognizes the mispricing and corrects it by bidding up the price. One way of implementing this strategy is to study yield spreads.

Historical yield spread analysis suggests other profitable trading strategies. For temporarily underpriced securities, the yield offered will be higher than warranted by the underlying risks. Market overreactions to events such as credit rating changes (part of the event risk phenomenon) may open up some attractive yield opportunities. The historical yield spreads, computed as the difference between a given security and short-term Treasury bills on the top-quality securities for each instrument are available. The analyst compares the current yield spread for the instrument type (or given rating class) or for an individual security within that type to see if abnormally large spreads exist. An aggressive investor might research the largest spreads available, seeking to determine why they exist, and if there is no exceptional default, liquidity, or event risk associated to account for the spread, a purchase would be made.

A second, and also a very popular, active strategy is **riding the yield curve.** This involves buying securities with maturities longer than the investment horizon, fully intending to liquidate the position early. If the yield curve is stable, meaning it neither shifts nor changes slope during the holding period, the investor can generally outperform a maturity matching strategy. This occurs because the normal yield curve is upward-sloping, giving higher interest rates for longer-maturity instruments.

Aggregate Investment in Cash and Securities

The manager may select from three generic strategies when deciding what quantity of total assets to hold in the form of cash and securities: a low-liquidity, moderate-liquidity, or high-liquidity strategy. The lower the liquidity, the riskier the strategy, and the higher the strategy's expected profitability.

The **low-liquidity strategy** entails driving the investment in cash and securities to a minimum. Therefore, cash and securities are a very small proportion of total assets. Assuming that the company does not subsequently overinvest in inventories and receivables, this approach should enhance profitability while also increasing business risk. Lesser amounts invested in cash and securities implies larger amounts invested in receivables, inventories, and higher-return fixed assets. This comes at the expense of greater default and bankruptcy risk, however, because the company has a smaller liquidity cushion with which to weather unexpected and business cycle–related downturns in operating revenues. Obviously, other sources of liquidity—salability of inventories and receivables (or the ability to secure these), available credit lines, and other sources of untapped debt capacity—affect the risk (and therefore the advisability) of the low-liquidity strategy. Companies following the low-liquidity strategy justify it on the basis of untapped credit lines, which we included in the definition of the liquid reserve.

The **moderate-liquidity strategy** implies a somewhat greater investment in cash and securities, with correspondingly less risk. This strategy may be premised on a matching philosophy: the higher the level of near-term current liability obligations, the greater the proportion of assets the company should hold in cash and securities. The many defunct savings and loan associations are sober reminders of what can happen to organizations whose assets and liabilities are substantially mismatched ("duration gap").

The **high-liquidity strategy** prescribes a higher proportion of assets to be held in cash and securities. Risk of default on securities and the risk of bankruptcy are reduced because of the greater liquidity cushion, but profitability is lower as well. Companies with significant business risk or financial risk might implement this strategy. Automakers and **Microsoft** justify their high-liquidity strategies because of unknown future capital investment opportunities, such as newly-developed technologies. Again, the company's posture toward risk and the availability of other potential sources of liquidity should be analyzed before adopting a particular cash and securities strategy.

Fixed asset investments are generally property, plant, and equipment expenditures made in support of new products and market expansion, which presumably have positive net present value, thus enhancing shareholder value.

The company's present financial situation may lead it to temporarily deviate from its chosen strategy. It may invest either more or less in cash and securities than the chosen strategy indicates. The current cash-flow forecast, in connection with the amount of borrowing, the amount of untapped short-term credit lines, and the financial position of the company, might be taken into consideration. The cash and securities balance might be augmented if the cash forecast shows net cash outflows or increased uncertainty in the cash forecast and a lack of alternate sources of liquidity. The treasurer also may take other precautions, such as engaging in hedging transactions, if the cash-flow uncertainty stems from future movements in interest rates or commodity input prices. Finally, the decision maker should consider what fraction of the total will be held in cash and what fraction will be held in securities when determining the company's aggregate investment in cash and securities.

Managing Short-Term Financing

Managing Short-Term Liabilities

We discussed the decisions the financial manager must make concerning alternative current asset financing policies. We also showed how debt maturities can affect both risk and expected returns: While short-term debt generally is riskier than long-term debt, it generally is also less expensive, and it can be obtained faster and under more flexible terms. The primary purpose of this section is to examine the different types of short-term credit that are available to the financial manager. We also examine the types of issues the financial manager must consider when selecting among the various types of short-term credit—that is, short-term, or current, liabilities. We then present strategies for short-term financing.

Sources of Short-Term Financing

Statements about the flexibility, cost, and riskiness of short-term debt versus long-term debt depend, to a large extent, on the type of short-term credit that actually is used. **Short-term credit** is defined as any liability *originally* scheduled for payment within one year. There are numerous sources of short-term funds, and in the following sections we describe seven major types: (1) accruals, (2) accounts payable (trade credit), (3) short-term bank loans, (4) commercial paper, (5) letter of credit, (6) banker's acceptance, and (7) reverse repurchase agreement. The cost of bank loans is presented.

Accruals

Firms generally pay employees on a weekly, biweekly, or monthly basis, so the balance sheet typically will show some accrued wages. Similarly, the firm's own estimated income taxes, the Social Security and income taxes withheld from employee payrolls, and the sales taxes collected generally are paid on a weekly, monthly, or quarterly basis, so the balance sheet typically will show some accrued taxes along with accrued wages.

Accruals increase automatically, or spontaneously, as a firm's operations expand. Further, this type of debt generally is considered "free" in the sense that no explicit interest is paid on funds raised through accruals. However, a firm ordinarily cannot control its accruals: The timing of wage payments is set by economic forces and industry custom, while tax payment dates are established by law. Thus, firms use all the accruals they can, but they have little control over the levels of these accounts.

Accounts Payable (Trade Credit)

Firms generally make purchases from other firms on credit, recording the debt as an *account payable*. This type of financing, which is called **trade credit,** is the largest single category of short-term debt, representing about 40 percent of the current liabilities for the average nonfinancial corporation. The percentage is somewhat larger for smaller firms: Because small companies often do not qualify for financing from other sources, they rely most heavily on trade credit.

Trade credit is a *spontaneous* source of financing in the sense that it arises from ordinary business transactions. For example, suppose a firm makes average purchases of $2,000 a day on terms of net 30, meaning that it must pay for goods 30 days after the invoice date. On average, it will owe 30 times $2,000, or $60,000, to its suppliers. If its sales, and consequently its purchases, were to double, then its accounts payable also would double, to $120,000. So simply by growing, the firm would have spontaneously generated an additional $60,000 of financing. Similarly, if the terms under which it bought were extended from 30 to 40 days, its accounts payable would expand from $60,000 to $80,000. Thus, lengthening the credit period, as well as expanding sales and purchases, generates additional financing.

THE COST OF TRADE CREDIT Firms that sell on credit have a *credit policy* that includes certain *terms of credit*. For example, Microchip Electronics sells on credit with terms of 2/10, net 30, which means that Microchip gives its customers a 2 percent discount from the invoice price if payment is made within ten days of the billing date; otherwise, if the discount is not taken, the full invoice amount is due and must be paid within 30 days of the billing date.

Note that the *true* price of the products Microchip offers is the net price, which is 98 percent of the list price, because any customer can purchase an item at a 2 percent "discount" as long as payment is made within 10 days. Consider Personal Computer Company (PCC), which buys its memory chips from Microchip. One commonly used memory chip is listed at $100, so the true cost to PCC is $98. Now if PCC wants an additional 20 days of credit beyond the 10-day discount period, it will incur a finance charge of $2 per chip for that credit. Thus, the $100 list price can be thought of as follows.

$$\text{List price} = \$98 \text{ true price} + \$2 \text{ finance charge}$$

The question that PCC must ask before it takes the additional 20 days of credit from Microchip is whether the firm could obtain similar credit with better terms from some other lender, say a bank. In other words, could 20 days of credit be obtained for less than $2 per item?

PCC buys an average of 44,100 memory chips from Microchip each year (assume 360 days), which, at the net or true price, amounts to an average annual purchase equal to $4,321,800, or $12,005 per day. For simplicity, assume that Microchip is PCC's only supplier. If PCC pays on the 10th day and takes the discount, its payables will average 10 × $12,005 = $120,050. Thus, PCC will receive $120,050 of credit from its only supplier, Microchip Electronics.

Now suppose PCC decides to take the additional 20 days' credit and thus must pay the finance charge. Because PCC now will pay on the 30th day, its accounts payable will increase to 30 × $12,005 = $360,150. Under these circumstances, Microchip will be supplying PCC with an additional $240,100 = $360,150 − $120,050 of credit, which PCC could use to build up its cash account, to pay off debt, to expand inventories, or even to extend more credit to its own customers and hence to increase its own accounts receivable. So it should be apparent that a firm's policy with regard to taking or not taking cash discounts can have a significant effect on its financial statements. If PCC does not take the cash discount, its accounts payable balance will be $240,100 greater than if it does take the discount ($360,150 compared to $120,050).

The additional credit offered by Microchip has a cost—PCC must pay the finance charge by forgoing the 2 percent discount on its purchases from Microchip. By forgoing the discount, PCC actually will pay $100 rather than $98 per chip, so its annual cost for the chips will be $100 × 44,100 = $4,410,000 instead of $98 × 44,100 = $4,321,800. The additional cost should be considered a finance charge for being able to keep the funds an additional 20 days. So the annual financing cost is $4,410,000 − $4,321,800 = $88,200. Dividing the $88,200 financing cost by the $240,100 in *average* annual *additional* credit, we find the implicit cost of the additional trade credit to be 36.7 percent.

$$\text{Approximate percentage cost} = \frac{\$88,200}{\$240,100} = 36.7\%$$

Should PCC take the discount, or should it wait 20 days and pay the full invoice price? If PCC can borrow from its bank (or from other sources) at an interest rate less than 36.7 percent, it should take the discount by borrowing from its bank to obtain any additional funds it needs—PCC should *not* obtain credit in the form of accounts payable by forgoing discounts if cheaper sources, such as the bank, are available.

The following equation can be used to calculate the *approximate* percentage cost, on an annual basis, of not taking cash discounts—that is, the cost of forgoing discounts:

$$\begin{pmatrix}\text{Approximate cost}\\ \text{of forgoing a}\\ \text{cash discount (\%)}\end{pmatrix} = \frac{\text{Discount percent}}{100 - \begin{pmatrix}\text{Discount}\\ \text{percent}\end{pmatrix}} \times \frac{360 \text{ days}}{\begin{pmatrix}\text{Total days net}\\ \text{credit is available}\end{pmatrix} - \begin{pmatrix}\text{Discount}\\ \text{period}\end{pmatrix}} \quad (7.7)$$

The numerator of the first term, Discount percent, is the dollar cost per $100 invoice value of forgoing (not taking) the discount, while the denominator in this term (100 − Discount percent) represents the funds the firm has available by forgoing the discount. Thus, the first term in Equation 7.7 is the percent cost of using trade credit as a source of financing for the number of days in the credit period beyond the discount period. The denominator of the second term is the number of days of extra credit obtained by forgoing the discount; so the entire second term shows how many times each year the percent cost of the trade credit would be incurred if the firm continues this practice. To illustrate the equation, the approximate cost of not taking a discount when the terms are 2/10, net 30, is calculated as follows:

$$\begin{pmatrix}\text{Approximate cost}\\ \text{of forgoing a}\\ \text{cash discount}\end{pmatrix} = \frac{2}{100-2} \times \frac{360}{30-10} = \frac{2}{98} \times \frac{360}{20}$$

$$= 0.02041 \times 18 = 0.367 = 36.7\%$$

Notice that according to Equation 7.7, the cost of trade credit *per credit period* is always the same as long as the terms of credit do not change—in our example, the cost is 2/98 = 0.0204. Therefore, the cost of using trade credit for financing can be reduced by delaying payment of accounts payable. For example, if PCC could get away with paying in 50 days rather than in the specified 30 days, then the effective credit period would become 40 days (50 days minus 10 days), the number of times during the year the discount would be lost would fall from 18 to 360/40 = 9, and the approximate cost would drop from 36.7 percent to 18.4 percent. Similarly, the effective annual rate would drop from 43.9 percent to 19.9 percent.

The practice of paying trade credit beyond the credit period, or deliberately becoming a delinquent account, is called **stretching accounts payable.** In periods of excess capacity, firms might be able to get away with *stretching* because suppliers need the business. But there are consequences associated with credit delinquency, such as being branded a "slow payer"—the most serious is that credit might be cut off all together.

Short-Term Bank Loans

Commercial banks, whose loans generally appear on firms' balance sheets as notes payable, are second in importance to trade credit as a source of short-term financing. The influence of banks actually is greater than it appears from the dollar amounts they lend because banks provide *nonspontaneous* funds. As a firm's financing needs increase, it specifically requests additional funds from its bank. If the request is denied, the firm might be forced to abandon attractive growth opportunities. The key features of bank loans are discussed in the following paragraphs.

MATURITY   Although banks do make longer-term loans, *the bulk of their lending is on a short-term basis.* Bank loans to businesses frequently are written as 90-day notes, so the loan must be repaid or renewed at the end of 90 days. Of course, if a borrower's financial position has deteriorated, the bank might refuse to renew the loan. This can mean serious trouble for the borrower.

PROMISSORY NOTE   When a bank loan is approved, the agreement is executed by signing a **promissory note.** The note specifies (1) the amount borrowed; (2) the percentage interest rate; (3) the repayment schedule, which can call for payment either as a lump sum or as a series of installments; (4) any collateral that has to be put up as security for the loan; and (5) any other terms and conditions to which the bank and the borrower have agreed. When the note is signed, the bank credits the borrower's checking account with the amount of the loan, so on the borrower's balance sheet both cash and notes payable increase equally.

COMPENSATING BALANCES   Banks sometimes require borrowers to maintain an average demand deposit (checking account) balance equal to from 10 percent to 20 percent of the amount borrowed. This is called a **compensating balance (CB).** In effect, the bank charges borrowers for *servicing* the loans (bookkeeping, maintaining a line of credit, and so on) by requiring compensating balances, and such balances might increase the effective interest rate on the loans.

LINE OF CREDIT   A **line of credit** is an agreement between a bank and a borrower indicating the maximum credit the bank will extend to the borrower. For example, on December 31 a bank loan officer might indicate to a financial manager that the bank regards the firm as being "good" for up to $200,000 during the forthcoming year. If on January 10 the financial manager signs a 90-day promissory note for $60,000, this would be called "drawing, or taking, down" $60,000 of the total line of credit. This amount would be credited to the firm's checking account at the bank, and before repayment of the $60,000, the firm could borrow additional amounts up to a *total* of $200,000 outstanding at any one time.

When a line of credit is *guaranteed,* it is called a **revolving credit agreement.** A revolving credit agreement is similar to a regular, or general, line of credit, except the bank has a *legal obligation* to provide the funds when requested by the borrower. The bank generally charges a **commitment fee** on the unused balance (sometimes on the total credit commitment) of the credit line for guaranteeing the availability of the funds.

Note that an important feature distinguishes a revolving credit agreement from a general line of credit: The bank has a *legal obligation* to honor a revolving credit agreement, and it receives a commitment fee for guaranteeing the funds will be available when requested by the borrower. Neither the legal obligation nor the fee exists under the general line of credit.

Commercial Paper

Commercial paper is a type of unsecured promissory note issued by large, strong firms, and it is sold primarily to other businesses, to insurance companies, to pension funds, to money market mutual funds, and to banks. This form of financing has grown rapidly in recent years—in 1999, the amount of commercial paper outstanding was about the same as the amount of regular business loans.

The maximum maturity for commercial paper without SEC registration is 270 days. Also, commercial paper can only be sold to "sophisticated" investors; otherwise, SEC registration would be required even for maturities of 270 days or less.

USE OF COMMERCIAL PAPER   The use of commercial paper is restricted to a comparatively small number of firms that are *exceptionally* good credit risks. Dealers prefer to handle the "paper" of firms whose net worth is $100 million or more and whose annual borrowing exceeds $10 million. One potential problem with commercial paper is that a debtor who is in temporary financial difficulty might receive little help because commercial paper dealings generally are less personal than are bank relationships. Thus, banks generally are more able and willing to help a good customer weather a temporary storm than is a commercial paper dealer. On the other hand, using commercial paper permits a corporation to tap a wider range of credit sources, including financial institutions outside its own area and industrial corporations across the country, and this can reduce interest costs.

MATURITY AND COST Generally, commercial paper is issued in denominations of $100,000 or more, so few individuals can afford to *directly* invest in the commercial paper market. Maturities of commercial paper vary from one to nine months, with an average of about five months. The rate on commercial paper fluctuates with supply and demand conditions—it is determined in the marketplace, varying daily as conditions change. Generally, the rates on commercial paper are lower than the stated prime rate of interest. For example, in August 1999, the average rate on 90-day commercial paper was about 5.3 percent, which was about 1.7 percent less than the prime rate but nearly 0.7 percent greater than 90-day Treasury bill rates.

Commercial paper is called a discount instrument because it is sold at a price below its face, or maturity, value. So the cost of using commercial paper as a source of financing is computed the same as for a discount interest loan.

Letter of Credit

A **letter of credit** (LOC) is a promise, generally by a bank, to make payment to a party on presentation of a draft provided that the party complies with certain documentary requirements as stated in the LOC agreement. The net effect of the LOC is to trade the credit of a well-known bank for that of a perhaps lesser-known corporate borrower. LOCs are generally a required feature of international borrowing.

Banker's Acceptance

A **banker's acceptance** is a time draft drawn against a deposit in a commercial bank but with payment at maturity guaranteed by the bank. The original time draft usually is a result of international transactions between importers and exporters.

For example, a U.S. importer wishing to import goods from abroad may request its bank to issue a letter of credit on its behalf in favor of the foreign seller. If the bank finds the importer's credit standing satisfactory, it will issue such a letter, authorizing the foreign exporter to draw a time draft on it in payment for the goods delivered. Equipped with this authorization, the exporter can discount the time draft with its bank when it ships the goods, thereby receiving payment immediately; the foreign bank then forwards the time draft, along with the shipping documents, to its correspondent bank in the United States. Generally, the U.S. correspondent bank will present the time draft for "acceptance" at the importer's bank, which forwards the shipping documents to the importer, who now may claim the shipment. Once accepted by the importer's bank, the time draft becomes a negotiable money market security, referred to as a bankers acceptance that trades in the money market until the maturity date of the time draft.

Reverse Repurchase Agreement

Repurchase agreements are used as a short-term investment alternative. In essence, a **reverse repurchase agreement** (a reverse repo) is the other side of the repurchase agreement transaction. In this case, a corporate investment manager may negotiate with its bank to sell to the bank a specific dollar amount of marketable securities currently held in the firm's investment portfolio at a specified price. Thus the party currently holding the securities initiates reverse repos. In addition, the contract stipulates that the selling corporation agrees to repurchase the designated securities at the same price plus a stipulated amount of interest in an agreed-on number of days in the future. Most repos or reverse repos are overnight or 1-day contracts.

Such an agreement might be used to obtain a quick infusion of cash to offset the delay of forecasted cash receipts without actually liquidating a portion of the firm's investment portfolio. Such transactions can also be useful for end-of-year financial statement "window dressing."

The Cost of Bank Loans

The cost of bank loans varies for different types of borrowers at any given point in time and for all borrowers over time. Interest rates are higher for riskier borrowers, and rates also are higher on smaller loans because of the fixed costs involved in making and servicing loans. If a firm can qualify as a "prime credit" because of its size and financial strength, it might be able to borrow at the **prime rate,** which traditionally has been the lowest rate banks charge. Rates on other loans generally are scaled up from the prime rate.

Bank rates vary widely over time depending on economic conditions and Federal Reserve policy. When the economy is weak, then (1) loan demand usually is slack, (2) inflation is low, and (3) the Fed also makes plenty of money available to the system. As a result, rates on all types of loans are relatively low. Conversely, when the economy is booming, loan demand typically is strong and the Fed restricts the money supply; the result is high interest rates. Interest rates on other bank loans also vary, generally moving with the prime rate.

710. MANAGING SHORT-TERM FINANCING

Interest paid on a bank loan generally is calculated in one of three ways: (1) *simple interest,* (2) *discount interest,* and (3) *add-on interest.*

Use of Security in Short-Term Financing

The term asset-based financing *is often used as a synonym for* secured financing. *In recent years accounts receivable have been used as security for long-term bonds, and this permits corporations to borrow from lenders such as pension funds rather than being restricted to banks and other traditional short-term lenders.*

Thus far we have not addressed the question of whether loans should be secured. Commercial paper is never secured, but all other types of loans can be secured if this is deemed necessary or desirable. Given a choice, it ordinarily is better to borrow on an unsecured basis because the bookkeeping costs of **secured loans** often are high. However, weak firms might find that they can borrow only if they put up some type of security or that by using security they can borrow at a lower rate.

Several different kinds of security, or collateral, can be employed, including marketable securities, land or buildings, equipment, inventory, and accounts receivable. Marketable securities make excellent collateral, but few firms that need loans also hold such portfolios. Similarly, real property (land and buildings) and equipment are good forms of collateral, but they generally are used as security for long-term loans rather than for working capital loans. Therefore, most secured short-term business borrowing involves the use of accounts receivable and inventories as collateral.

To understand the use of security, consider the case of a Chicago hardware dealer who wanted to modernize and expand his store. He requested a $200,000 bank loan. After examining his business's financial statements, the bank indicated that it would lend him a maximum of $100,000 and that the interest rate would be 12 percent, discount interest, for an effective rate of 13.6 percent. The owner had a substantial personal portfolio of stocks, and he offered to put up $300,000 of high-quality stocks to support the $200,000 loan. The bank then granted the full $200,000 loan, and at a rate of only 11 percent, simple interest. The store owner also might have used his inventories or receivables as security for the loan, but processing costs would have been high.

In the past, state laws have varied greatly with regard to the use of security in financing. Today, however, nearly every secured loan is established under the **Uniform Commercial Code,** which has standardized and simplified the procedures for establishing loan security. The heart of the Uniform Commercial Code is the *Security Agreement,* a standardized document on which the specific pledged assets are listed. The assets can be items of equipment, accounts receivable, or inventories. Procedures under the Uniform Commercial Code for using accounts receivable and inventories as security for short-term credit are described in the following sections.

Accounts Receivable Financing

Accounts receivable financing involves either the pledging of receivables or the selling of receivables (called *factoring*). The **pledging** of accounts receivable is characterized by the fact that the lender not only has a claim against the receivables but also has **recourse** to the borrower: If the person or firm that bought the goods does not pay, the selling firm (borrower) rather than the lender must take the loss. Therefore, the risk of default on the pledged accounts receivable remains with the borrower. The buyer of the goods ordinarily is not notified about the pledging of the receivables, and the financial institution that lends on the security of accounts receivable generally is either a commercial bank or one of the large industrial finance companies.

Factoring, or *selling accounts receivable,* involves the purchase of accounts receivable by the lender (called a factor), generally without recourse to the borrower, which means that if the purchaser of the goods does not pay for them, the lender rather than the seller of the goods (borrower) takes the loss. Under factoring, the buyer of the goods typically is notified of the transfer and is asked to make payment directly to the lending institution. Because the factor assumes the risk of default on bad accounts, it generally carries out the credit investigation. Accordingly, factors provide not only money but also a credit department for the borrower. Incidentally, the same financial institutions that make loans against pledged receivables also serve as factors. Thus, depending on the circumstances and the wishes of the borrower, a financial institution will provide either type of receivables financing.

Procedure for Pledging Accounts Receivable

The financing of accounts receivable is initiated by a legally binding agreement between the seller of the goods and the financing institution. The agreement sets forth in detail the procedures to be followed and the legal obligations of both parties. Once the working relationship has been established, the seller periodically takes a batch of invoices to the financing institution. The lender reviews the invoices and makes credit appraisals of the buyers. Invoices of companies that do not meet the lender's credit standards are not accepted for pledging.

The financial institution seeks to protect itself at every phase of the operation. First, selection of sound invoices is one way the lender safeguards itself. Second, if the buyer of the goods does not pay the invoice, the lender still has recourse against the seller (the borrowing firm). Third, additional protection is afforded the lender because the loan generally will be less than 100 percent of the pledged receivables; for example, the lender might advance the selling firm only 75 percent of the amount of the pledged invoices. The percent advanced depends on the quality of the accounts pledged.

Procedure for Factoring Accounts Receivable

The procedures used in factoring are somewhat different from those for pledging. Again, an agreement between the seller and the factor specifies legal obligations and procedural arrangements. When the seller receives an order from a buyer, a credit approval slip is written and immediately sent to the factoring company for a credit check. If the factor approves the credit, shipment is made and the invoice is stamped to notify the buyer to make payment directly to the factoring company. If the factor does not approve the sale, the seller generally refuses to fill the order; if the sale is made anyway, the factor will not buy the account.

The factor normally performs three functions: (1) credit checking, (2) lending, and (3) risk bearing. Consider a typical factoring situation: The goods are shipped, and even though payment is not due for 30 days, the factor immediately makes funds available to the borrower (the seller of the goods). Suppose $10,000 worth of goods are shipped. Further, assume that the factoring commission for credit checking and risk bearing is 2½ percent of the invoice price, or $250, and that the interest expense is computed at a 9 percent annual rate on the invoice balance, or $75 = $10,000 × (0.09/360) × 30 days. The selling firm's accounting entry is as follows:

Cash	$ 9,175
Interest expense	75
Factoring commission	250
Reserve due from factor on collection account	500
Accounts receivable	$ 10,000

The $500 due from the factor upon collection of the account is a reserve established by the factor to cover disputes between the seller and customers over damaged goods, goods returned by customers to the seller, and the failure to make an outright sale of goods. The reserve is paid to the selling firm when the factor collects on the account.

Factoring normally is a continuous process instead of the single cycle just described. The firm that sells the goods receives an order; it transmits this order to the factor for approval; upon approval, the firm ships the goods; the factor advances the invoice amount minus withholdings to the seller; the buyer (customer) pays the factor when payment is due; and the factor periodically remits any excess in the reserve to the seller of the goods. Once a routine has been established, a continuous circular flow of goods and funds takes place between the seller, the buyers of the goods, and the factor. Thus, once the factoring agreement is in force, funds from this source are *spontaneous* in the sense that an increase in sales will automatically generate additional credit.

Visa and MasterCard represent a prime example of nonrecourse factoring. When you purchase from a retailer such as **Wal-Mart** using Visa or MasterCard, the retailer is paid only 95 to 97 percent of the invoice by these credit companies. The reason the three to 5 percent discount is charged by Visa and MasterCard is because they provide credit checking services and suffer any losses due to customer nonpayment—the retailer does not incur these costs.

Cost of Receivables Financing

Both accounts receivable pledging and factoring are convenient and advantageous, but they can be costly. The credit-checking and risk-bearing fee is 1 percent to 5 percent of the amount of invoices accepted by the factor, and it could be even more if the buyers are poor credit risks. The cost of money is reflected in the interest rate (usually two to three percentage points over the prime rate) charged on the unpaid balance of the funds advanced by the factor.

Evaluation of Receivables Financing

It cannot be said categorically that accounts receivable financing is either a good or a bad way to raise funds. Among the advantages is, first, the flexibility of this source of financing. As the firm's sales expand, more financing is needed, but a larger volume of invoices, and hence a larger amount of receivables financing, is generated automatically. Second, receivables can be used as security for loans that otherwise would not be granted. Third, factoring can provide the services of a credit department that otherwise might be available only at a higher cost.

Accounts receivable financing also has disadvantages. First, when invoices are numerous and relatively small in dollar amount, the administrative costs involved might be excessive. Second, because receivables represent the firm's most liquid noncash assets, some trade creditors might refuse to sell on credit to a firm that factors or pledges its receivables on the grounds that this practice weakens the firm's financial strength.

Future Use of Receivables Financing

It is easy to make a prediction at this point: In the future, accounts receivable financing will increase in relative importance. Computer technology is advancing rapidly toward the point where credit records of individuals and firms can be kept on electronic media. For example, one device used by retailers consists of a box which, when an individual's magnetic credit card is inserted, gives a signal that the credit is "good" and that a bank is willing to "buy" the receivable created as soon as the store completes the sale. The cost of handling invoices will be reduced greatly over present-day costs because the new systems will be so highly automated. This will make it possible to use accounts receivable financing for very small sales, and it will reduce the cost of all receivables financing. The net result will be a marked expansion of accounts receivable financing. In fact, when consumers use credit cards such as MasterCard or Visa, the seller is in effect factoring receivables. The seller receives the amount of the purchase, minus a percentage fee, the next working day. The credit card user (buyer) receives 30 days' (or so) credit, at which time he or she remits payment directly to the credit card company or sponsoring bank.

Inventory Financing

A substantial amount of credit is secured by business inventories. If a firm is a relatively good credit risk, the mere existence of the inventory might be a sufficient basis for receiving an unsecured loan. However, if the firm is a relatively poor risk, the lending institution might insist on security in the form of a *lien,* or legal claim, against the inventory. Methods for using inventories as security are discussed in this section.

Blanket Liens

The *inventory blanket lien* gives the lending institution a lien against all of the borrower's inventories. However, the borrower is free to sell inventories, and thus the value of the collateral can be reduced below the level that existed when the loan was granted. A blanket lien generally is used when the inventory put up as collateral is relatively low priced, fast moving, and difficult to identify individually. A blanket lien is also called a floating lien.

Trust Receipts

Because of the inherent weakness of the blanket lien, another procedure for inventory financing has been developed—the *trust receipt,* which is an instrument acknowledging that the goods are held in trust for the lender. Under this method, the borrowing firm, as a condition for receiving funds from the lender, signs and delivers a trust receipt for the goods. The goods can be stored in a public warehouse or held on the premises of the borrower. The trust receipt states that the goods are held in trust for the lender or are segregated on the borrower's premises on the lender's behalf and that any proceeds from the sale of the goods must be transmitted to the lender at the end of each day. Automobile dealer financing is one of the best examples of trust receipt financing.

One defect of trust receipt financing is the requirement that a trust receipt be issued for specific goods. For example, if the security is automobiles in a dealer's inventory, the trust receipts must indicate the cars by registration number. To validate its trust receipts, the lending institution must send someone to the borrower's premises periodically to see that the auto numbers are listed correctly, because auto dealers who are in financial difficulty have been known to sell cars backing trust receipts and then use the funds for other operations rather than to repay the bank. Problems are compounded if the borrower has a number of different locations, especially if they are separated geographically from the lender. To offset these inconveniences, warehouse receipt financing has come into wide use as a method of securing loans with inventory.

Warehouse Receipts

Warehouse receipt financing is another way to use inventory as security. A *public warehouse* is an independent third-party operation engaged in the business of storing goods. Items that require aging, such as tobacco and liquor, are often financed and stored in public warehouses. When the inventory products used as collateral are moved to public warehouses, the financing arrangement is termed *terminal warehousing*. Sometimes terminal warehousing is not practical because of the bulkiness of goods and the expense of transporting them to and from the borrower's premises. In such cases, a *field warehouse* might be established on the borrower's grounds. To provide inventory supervision, the lending institution employs a third party in the arrangement, the field warehousing company, which acts as its agent.

Field warehousing can be illustrated by a simple example. Suppose a firm that has iron stacked in an open yard on its premises needs a loan. A field warehousing concern can place a temporary fence around the iron, erecting a sign stating, "This is a field warehouse supervised by the Smith Field Warehousing Corporation," and then assign an employee to supervise and control the fenced-in inventory.

This example illustrates the three essential elements for the establishment of a field warehouse: (1) public notification, (2) physical control of the inventory, and (3) supervision by a custodian of the field warehousing concern. When the field warehousing operation is relatively small, the third condition is sometimes violated by hiring an employee of the borrower to supervise the inventory. This practice is viewed as undesirable by most lenders because there is no control over the collateral by a person independent of the borrowing firm.

Acceptable Products

Canned foods account for nearly 20 percent of all field warehouse loans. In addition, many other types of products provide a basis for field warehouse financing. Some of these are miscellaneous groceries, which represent nearly 15 percent; lumber products, about 10 percent; and coal and coke, about 5 percent. These products are relatively nonperishable and are sold in well-developed, organized markets. Nonperishability protects the lender if it should have to take over the security. For this reason, a bank would not make a field warehousing loan on perishables such as fresh fish; but frozen fish, which can be stored for a long time, can be field warehoused.

Cost of Financing

The fixed costs of a field warehousing arrangement are relatively high; such financing therefore is not suitable for a very small firm. If a field warehousing company sets up a field warehouse, it typically will set a minimum charge of about $25,000 per year, plus about 1 to 2 percent of the amount of credit extended to the borrower. Furthermore, the financing institution will charge an interest rate of two to three percentage points over the prime rate. An efficient field warehousing operation requires an inventory of at least $1 million.

Evaluation of Inventory Financing

The use of inventory financing, especially field warehouse financing, as a source of funds has many advantages. First, the amount of funds available is flexible because the financing is tied to the growth of inventories, which in turn is related directly to financing needs. Second, the field warehousing arrangement increases the acceptability of inventories as loan collateral; some inventories simply would not be accepted by a bank as security without such an arrangement. Third, the necessity for inventory control and safekeeping as well as the use of specialists in warehousing often results in improved warehouse practices, which in turn save handling costs, insurance charges, theft losses, and so on. Thus, field warehousing companies often save money for firms in spite of the costs of financing that we have discussed. The major disadvantages of field warehousing include the paperwork, physical separation requirements, and, for small firms, the fixed-cost element.

Short-Term Financing Strategies

Financing and the Cash Flow Timeline

At this point, we have reached a position on the company's cash flow timeline at which cash has been collected and cash has been disbursed, resulting in a daily ending cash position that may be positive or negative. If the daily cash position is positive, then the cash manager faces an investment opportunity. If the daily cash position is negative, the cash manager faces a dilemma on how to fund the cash deficit.

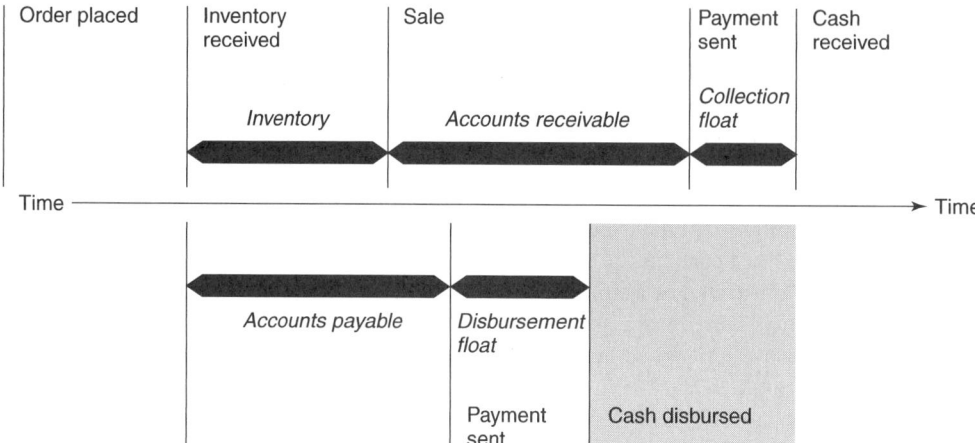

A deficit cash position may be the result of inefficient or inappropriate working capital policies. Excess accumulation of inventory, slow collections, and/or quick disbursements may lead to cash being disbursed prior to cash collection. Thus the financial manager should reevaluate the company's working capital policies to ensure the most efficient stream of cash flow resulting from operations.

Even the most efficient working capital policies, however, may result in a deficit cash position at different times during the working capital cycle. This is especially true during periods of rapid growth and during the early phase of the working capital cycle. At this point the manager must have a well-developed plan for financing short-term cash deficit positions.

Specific Financing Strategies

Over the course of its operating cycle, a firm's assets tend to fluctuate, rising as operations gear up for seasonal peak sales and then subsiding as sales fall. Exhibit 700.9 demonstrates this trend for a firm that is growing and adding to its fixed asset base. In the exhibit, assets begin to grow as time moves from the left to the right with inventory build up in anticipation of future sales. As sales pick up, inventory is maintained for a time by increased production, and receivables begin to accumulate as inventory is sold. As sales level off, production is reduced, resulting in a drop in inventory. Receivables also begin to fall as collections exceed the creation of new receivables. As receivables are collected, the cash received is used to pay off accounts payable and other short-term loans used to finance the earlier accumulation of inventory and receivables. This cycle then repeats itself as the firm approaches a new operating period.

In Exhibit 700.9, you may have noticed the decomposition of total current assets into two parts, a level of **permanent current assets** and a level of **temporary current assets.** It may seem strange to refer to current assets as permanent but a firm always has some minimum or permanent amount of inventory and receivables on its books. Although the products in inventory and the specific accounts held as receivables do turn over, there is always a minimum amount of resources invested in these accounts. This minimum level of ongoing inventory and receivables is what is referred to as permanent current assets.

The temporary component of total current assets, then, represents the accumulation of inventory in anticipation of the peak selling season and the resulting receivables generated by the increasing sales. This bulge in inventory and receivables then subsides as the firm passes through its peak-selling season.

There are three basic strategies from which the financial manager can choose as financing is sought to support the firm's asset needs over its operating cycle. The three strategies include the aggressive strategy, the conservative strategy, and the moderate strategy. These three financing strategies are illustrated in Exhibit 700.10. You may wish to refer to this exhibit as each of the strategies is discussed in the following sections.

Aggressive Strategy

The **aggressive financing strategy** is basically a maturity matching strategy. Using this strategy, the financial manager chooses to match the maturity of the source of financing with the duration of the need of cash. In the exhibit, the wavy line represents the total assets of the firm over time. Over the course of the firm's operating activities, total assets rise and fall primarily because of the fluctuations in receivables, inventory, and payables over the working capital cycle. The wavy

Exhibit 700.9 *The Firm's Fluctuating Assets over Its Operating Cycle*

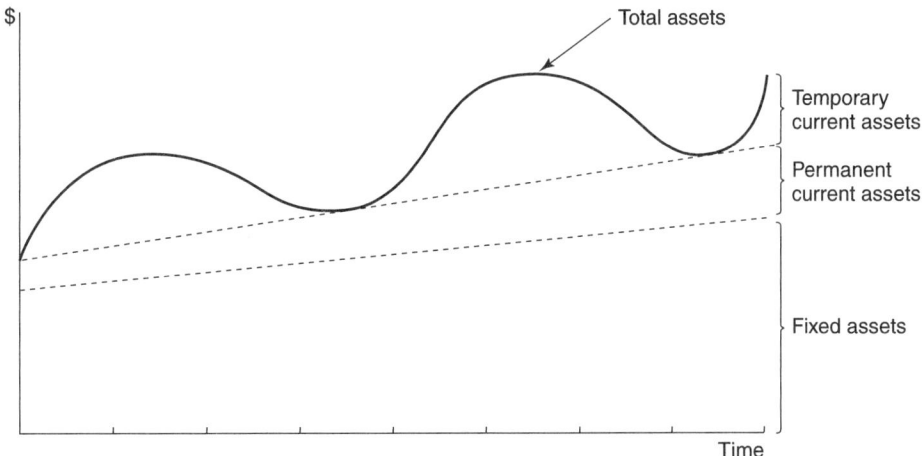

Exhibit 700.10 *Short-Term Financing Strategies*

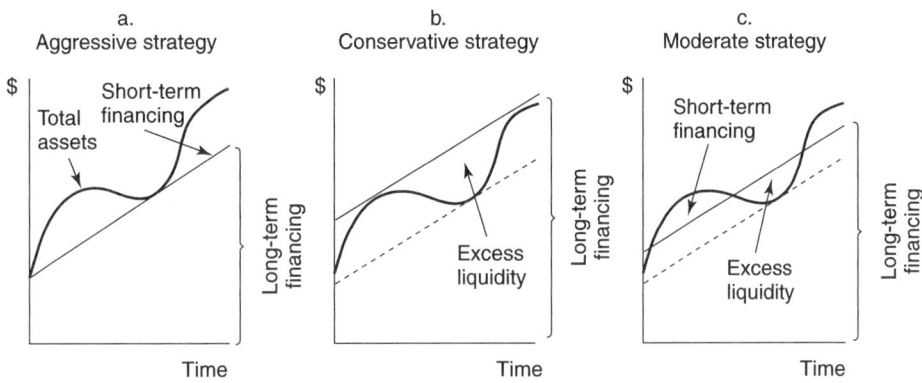

line will exhibit an upward trend if the firm is growing and adding to its fixed asset base. In Panel a of Exhibit 700.10, the firm is maximizing its reliance on short-term financing and minimizing its reliance on permanent or long-term financing. The corporation's net working capital position, as a result, is minimal because of the heavy reliance on short-term financing, and therefore the solvency position of the firm, as measured by the current ratio, will suffer. This strategy has an advantage in that during normal financial conditions, short-term sources of financing cost less than longer-term sources. For example, on April 14, 2000, 90-day Treasury bills yielded 5.67 percent while five-year Treasury notes yielded 6.18 percent. Thus there is normally a trade-off of a lower financing cost at the expense of a reduced solvency level.

Aggressive strategy versus conservative strategy versus moderate strategy

- *With aggressive financing strategy, a firm uses more short-term sources, its debt costs are low, profits are high, and solvency (liquidity) is low.*
- *With conservative financing strategy, a firm uses more long-term sources, its debt costs are high, profits are low, and solvency (liquidity) is high.*
- *With moderate financing strategy, a firm operates in between the aggressive and conservative strategies.*

There is some evidence that firms use a maturity matching strategy as reported by Beranek, Cornwell, and Choi. In their research, they found that firms do not emphasize external short-term sources in the financing of capital expenditures, nor do they use the bulk of long-term external financing in a given period to finance the acquisition of short-lived assets. Thus firms generally act as if they seek to match the maturity of their external financing with the life of their acquired assets.

Conservative Strategy

The **conservative financing strategy** uses only long-term sources to fulfill all the corporation's financing needs as demonstrated in Panel b of Exhibit 700.10. As total assets increase as a result of a build up of inventory and receivables, the firm draws down its excess liquidity stored in short-term investments. Then as inventory is sold and receivables collected, excess cash is reinvested in short-term investments. Thus over a part of its working capital cycle, the corporation has an excess solvency position, as indicated by a relatively high current ratio. Because the corporation uses no short-term financing, it will have substantial financing flexibility in acquiring new short-term sources of financing if it underestimates its actual future cash needs. Under normal financial market conditions, this strategy is relatively expensive because long-term financing sources are generally more expensive than short-term sources. However, the reliance on longer-term sources does provide a greater solvency position as measured by the current ratio.

Moderate Strategy

The **moderate financing strategy,** Panel c of Exhibit 700.10, is a blend of the extreme strategies represented by the aggressive and conservative strategies discussed previously. The exact blend of short- and long-term sources depends on the risk preferences of the corporation as well as the current financial market conditions.

The Effective Cost of Short-Term Financing

Short-term financing arrangements have several features that cause the stated interest rate on the financing to be different from the **effective interest rate.** A very general formula that forms the basis for our discussion is shown in Equation 7.8.

$$\text{Effective rate} = \frac{\text{Out-of-pocket expenses}}{\text{Usable funds}} \times \frac{365}{M} \qquad (7.8)$$

Out-of-pocket expenses include interest expense and fees. Interest expense is based on the stated interest rate and the amount borrowed over the funding period. Fees include commitment fees charged by the bank for the total amount of funds the bank stands ready to lend to the firm through a line of credit or a letter of credit facility, letter of credit fees, or commercial paper dealer fees. **Usable funds** represent the net proceeds the firm receives from the financing vehicle. If funds are received through a credit line, the amount received may be less than the amount borrowed if the bank requires the firm to leave compensating balances as a percent of the amount borrowed. If funds are received through an issue of commercial paper, then the amount received is reduced by the discounted interest paid.

The final part of Equation 7.8 annualizes the length of the borrowing period, M, assuming that it is one year or less. The effective rate thus calculated is the annualized effective simple interest rate on the financing arrangement. This equation is applied to commercial paper and a bank credit line facility in the following sections.

Effective Cost of Commercial Paper

The treasurer at Consolidated Trailways, Inc., is preparing a new issue of commercial paper through a dealer network. Commercial paper is a typical source of financing for Consolidated and the firm generally has several million dollars of paper outstanding throughout the year. In discussing the new issue with its commercial paper dealer, Consolidated has learned that new 30-day issues in the range of $1 to $5 million can be priced to sell at a 9 percent discount rate. The dealer's fee will be an annual rate of 1/8 of 1 percent and the commitment fee on a back-up line of credit will be an annual rate of .25 percent. The treasurer wants to know what the effective rate of issuing $3 million 30-day commercial paper will be.

Out-of-Pocket Costs

To apply Equation 7.8, the treasurer needs to determine the value of two variables: out-of-pocket costs and usable funds. Let's start with out-of-pocket costs. First, the major component of out-of-pocket costs is the interest that Consolidated will have to pay. The commercial paper will be issued on a discount basis; the difference between the face amount and the discounted price is the interest that the firm pays. The face amount is the $3 million stated earlier. The discounted price is the face amount minus 30 days interest, 30 days being the maturity of the paper. The discount price is $2,977,500 = $3 million − (.09 × (30/360) × $3 million). The interest paid is thus $22,500. Note that the interest computation uses a 360-day year, which is the convention with discount rates. The dealer's fee is .125 percent, which costs the firm $312.50 = $3 million × .00125 × (30/360). The commitment fee for the back-up line of credit is $625 = $3 million × (.0025 × (30/360)). The total out-of-pocket cost is the sum of the interest expense, dealer fee, and bank commitment fee, which totals $23,437.50 = $22,500 + $312.50 + $625.

Usable Funds

Next, the dollar amount of usable funds must be determined. The treasurer has determined that the discount price of the $3 million issue will result in proceeds of $2,977,500, which is equal to the face value minus the discount interest at the asked rate.

Effective Interest Rate

Plugging the values for the out-of-pocket costs and usable funds into Equation 7.8 results in the effective annualized interest rate for the 30-day commercial paper.

$$\text{Effective rate} = \frac{\$23,473.50}{\$2,977,500} \times \frac{365}{30}$$

$$\text{Effective rate} = .0958 \text{ or } 9.58\%$$

The effective cost of the paper is 58 basis points above the stated asked discount rate of 9 percent. Note the money market convention that effective rates are based on a 365-day year rather than a 360-day year.

Had Consolidated not been a regular issuer of commercial paper, using a line of credit as a back-up facility might not be appropriate. Credit lines are not generally set up for periods less than one year. Therefore the annual cost of the credit line will have to be allocated to the 30-day financing period and then annualized. This will result in an out-of-pocket cost of $30,312.50 = $22,500 + $312.50 + $7,500. The $7,500 is the annual cost of the credit line commitment fee and must now be allocated in total to the 30-day financing period. Usable funds will remain unchanged. The effective rate then becomes 12.39 percent. In this case, the use of a letter of credit rather than a line of credit as a back-up facility is more appropriate. A letter of credit can be designed to be in effect for any length of period necessary.

Managing Long-Term Financing

Traditional sources of long-term financing include common stock (equity) and bonds, term loans, and notes (debt). Alternative sources of long-term financing include preferred stocks, leases, options, warrants, and convertibles. Another possible source is treasury stock, which is company stock repurchased by the company from the open market. The treasury stock, which is taken out of circulation after its repurchase, can be resold to investors in the open market.

Common Stock

Balance Sheet Accounts and Definitions

An understanding of legal and accounting terminology is vital to both investors and financial managers if they are to avoid misinterpretations and possibly costly mistakes. Therefore, we begin our analysis of common stock with a discussion of accounting and legal issues. Consider first Exhibit 700.11 which shows the **common equity** section of Unilate Textiles' balance sheet. Unilate's owners—its stockholders—have authorized management to issue a total of 40 million shares, and management has thus far actually issued (or sold) 25 million shares. Each share has a **par value** of $1; this is the minimum amount for which new shares can be issued. A stock's par value is an arbitrary figure that originally indicated the minimum amount of money stockholders had put up. Today, firms generally are not required to establish a par value for their stock. Thus, Unilate Textiles could have elected to use *no-par* stock, in which case the common stock and additional paid-in capital accounts would have been consolidated under one account called *common stock*, which would show a 2004 balance of $130 million. During 2004, Unilate earned $54 million, paid $29 million in dividends, and retained $25 million. The $25 million was added to the $260 million accumulated **retained earnings** shown on the year-end 2003 balance sheet to produce the $285 million retained earnings at year-end 2004. Thus, since its inception, Unilate has retained, or plowed back, a total of $285 million. This is money that belongs to the stockholders that they could have received in the form of dividends. Instead, the stockholders chose to let management reinvest the $285 million in the business so growth could be achieved.

Exhibit 700.11 *Unilate Textiles Balance Sheet: Common Equity Accounts as of December 31 (millions of dollars, except per share data)*

	2004	2003
Common stock (40 million shares authorized, 25 million shares outstanding, $1 par)	$ 25.0	$ 25.0
Additional paid-in capital	105.0	105.0
Retained earnings	285.0	260.0
Total common stockholders' equity (net worth)	$415.0	$390.0
Book value per share	$16.60	$15.60

Now consider the $105 million **additional paid-in capital.** This account shows the difference between the stock's par value and what new stockholders paid when they bought newly issued shares. For example, in 1980, when Unilate was formed, 15 million shares were issued at par value; thus, the first balance sheet showed a zero for paid-in capital and $15 million for the common stock account. However, in 1983, to raise funds for expansion projects, Unilate issued 10 million shares at a market price of $11.50 per share—total value of the issue was $115 million. At that time, the common stock account was increased by $10 million ($1 par value for the 10 million shares issued), and the remainder of the $115 million issue value, $105 million, was added to additional paid-in capital. Unilate has not issued any more stock since 1983, so the only change in the common equity section since that time has been in retained earnings.

The **book value per share** shown in Exhibit 700.11 is computed by dividing the amount of total stockholders' equity, which also is called *net worth*, by the number of shares outstanding. Unilate's book value per share increased in 2004 to $16.60, from $15.60 in 2003. Whenever stock is sold at a price above book value or the change in retained earnings is positive, book value will increase, and vice versa. Because book value is a historical cost amount, investors prefer that the market value of stock be greater than its book value; a stock that is selling below its book value might suggest the company is experiencing financial difficulty.

Legal Rights and Privileges of Common Stockholders

The common stockholders are the owners of a corporation, and as such they have certain rights and privileges. The most important rights are discussed in this section. They include control of the firm and the preemptive right.

Control of the Firm

The stockholders have the right to elect the firm's directors, who in turn elect the officers who manage the business. In a small firm, the major stockholder typically assumes the positions of president and chairperson of the board of directors. In a large, publicly owned firm, the managers typically have some stock, but their personal holdings are insufficient to provide voting control. Thus, the managements of most publicly-owned firms can be removed by the stockholders if they decide a management team is not effective.

Various state and federal laws stipulate how stockholder control is to be exercised. First, corporations must hold an election of directors periodically, usually once a year, with the vote taken at the annual meeting. Frequently, one-third of the directors are elected each year for a three-year term. Each share of stock normally has one vote; thus, the owner of 1,000 shares has 1,000 votes. Stockholders can appear at the annual meeting and vote in person, but typically they transfer their right to vote to a second party by means of an instrument known as a **proxy.** Management always solicits stockholders' proxies and usually gets them. However, if earnings are poor and stockholders are dissatisfied, an outside group might solicit the proxies in an effort to overthrow management and take control of the business. This is known as a **proxy fight.**

Managers who do not have majority control (more than 50 percent of their firms' stock) are very much concerned about proxy fights and takeovers, and many attempt to get stockholder approval for changes in their corporate charters that would make takeovers more difficult. For example, a number of companies have gotten their stockholders to agree (1) to elect only one-third of the directors each year (rather than electing all directors each year); (2) to require 75 percent of the stockholders (rather than 50 percent) to approve a merger; and (3) to vote in a "poison pill" provision that would allow the stockholders of a firm that is taken over by another firm to buy shares in the second firm at a reduced price. The third provision makes the acquisition unattractive and, thus, wards off hostile takeover attempts.

Managements seeking such changes generally cite a fear that the firm will be picked up at a bargain price, but it often appears that managers' concerns about their own positions might be an even more important consideration.

The Preemptive Right

Common stockholders often have the right, called the **preemptive right,** to purchase any additional shares sold by the firm. In some states the preemptive right is automatically included in every corporate charter; in others it is necessary to insert it specifically into the charter.

The purpose of the preemptive right is twofold. First, it protects the power of control of current stockholders. If it were not for this safeguard, the management of a corporation under criticism from stockholders could prevent stockholders from removing it from office by issuing a large number of additional shares and purchasing these shares itself. Management could thereby secure control of the corporation and frustrate the will of the current stockholders.

The second, and more important, reason for the preemptive right is that it protects stockholders against a dilution of value. For example, suppose 1,000 shares of common stock, each with a price of $100, were outstanding, making the total market value of the firm $100,000. If an additional 1,000 shares were sold at $50 a share, or for $50,000, this would raise the total market value of the firm to $150,000. When the total market value is divided by the new total shares outstanding, a value of $75 a share is obtained. The old stockholders thus lose $25 per share, and the new stockholders have an instant profit of $25 per share. Thus, selling common stock at a price below the market value would dilute its price and would transfer wealth from the present stockholders to those who were allowed to purchase the new shares. The preemptive right prevents such occurrences.

Types of Common Stock

Although most firms have only one type of common stock, in some instances **classified stock** is used to meet the special needs of the company. Generally, when special classifications of stock are used, one type is designated Class A, another Class B, and so on. Small, new companies seeking to obtain funds from outside sources frequently use different types of common stock. For example, when **Genetic Concepts** went public, its Class A stock was sold to the public and paid a dividend, but this stock did not have voting rights until five years after its issue. Its Class B stock, which was retained by the organizers of the company, had full voting rights for five years, but the legal terms stated that dividends could not be paid on the Class B stock until the company had established its earning power by building up retained earnings to a designated level. The use of classified stock thus enabled the public to take a position in a conservatively financed growth company without sacrificing income, while the founders retained absolute control during the crucial, early stages of the firm's development. At the same time, outside investors were protected against excessive withdrawals of funds by the original owners. As is often the case in such situations, the Class B stock was called **founders' shares.**

> Another type of common stock is target stock, which represents a claim on a specific, usually new, part of a firm such as when starting a new business, division, branch office, warehouse, subsidiary, or a new product line.

Note that "Class A," "Class B," and so on, have no standard meanings—one firm could designate its Class B shares as founders' shares and its Class A shares as those sold to the public, while another could reverse these designations. Still other firms could use stock classifications for entirely different purposes.

Evaluation of Common Stock as a Source of Funds

Thus far the section has covered the main characteristics of common stock. Now we will appraise stock financing both from the viewpoint of the corporation and from a social perspective.

From the Corporation's Viewpoint

The advantages and disadvantages of using common stock as a financing source are listed in this section.

ADVANTAGES   Common stock offers several advantages to the corporation.

1. Common stock does not legally obligate the firm to make payments to stockholders: Only if the company generates earnings and has no pressing internal needs for them will it pay dividends.

2. Common stock carries no fixed maturity date—it never has to be "repaid" as would a debt issue.
3. Because common stock cushions creditors against losses, the sale of common stock generally increases the creditworthiness of the firm. This in turn raises its bond rating, lowers its cost of debt, and increases its future ability to use debt.
4. If a company's prospects look bright, then common stock often can be sold on better terms than debt. Stock appeals to certain groups of investors because (a) it typically carries a higher expected total return (dividends plus capital gains) than does preferred stock or debt; and (b) as a representation of the ownership of the firm, stock provides the investor with a better hedge against unanticipated inflation because common dividends tend to rise during inflationary periods.

DISADVANTAGES Disadvantages associated with issuing common stock include the following:

1. The sale of common stock gives some voting rights, and perhaps even control, to new stockholders. For this reason, additional equity financing often is avoided by managers who are concerned about maintaining control. The use of founders' shares and other classes of common stock can mitigate this problem.
2. Common stock gives new owners the right to share in the income of the firm; if profits soar, then new stockholders will share in this bonanza, whereas if debt had been used, new investors (creditors in this case) would have received only a fixed return, no matter how profitable the company had been, and existing stockholders would have received the rest. This point has given rise to an important theory: "If a firm sells a large issue of bonds, this is a signal that management expects the company to earn high profits on investments financed by the new capital and that it does not wish to share these profits with new stockholders. On the other hand, if the firm issues stock, this is a signal that its prospects are not so bright."
3. As we shall see, the costs of underwriting and distributing common stock usually are higher than those for debt or preferred stock. Flotation costs for common stock characteristically are higher because (a) the costs of investigating an equity security investment are higher than those for a comparable debt security; and (b) stocks are riskier than debt, meaning that investors must diversify their equity holdings, so a given dollar amount of new stock must be sold to a larger number of purchasers than the same amount of debt.
4. If the firm has more equity than is called for in its optimal capital structure, the average cost of capital will be higher than necessary. Therefore, a firm would not want to sell stock if the sale caused its equity ratio (1.0 minus the debt ratio) to exceed the optimal level.
5. Under current tax laws, common stock dividends are not deductible as an expense for tax purposes, but bond interest is deductible. Taxes raise the relative cost of equity as compared with debt.

From a Social Viewpoint

From a social viewpoint, common stock is a desirable form of financing because it makes businesses less vulnerable to the consequences of declines in sales and earnings. Common stock financing involves no fixed charge payments that might force a faltering firm into bankruptcy. From the standpoint of the economy as a whole, if too many firms used too much debt, business fluctuations would be amplified, and minor recessions could turn into major ones. Not long ago, when the level of leveraged mergers and buyouts was raising the aggregate debt ratio (the average debt ratio of all firms), the Federal Reserve and other authorities voiced concern over the possible dangers created by the situation, and congressional leaders debated the wisdom of social controls over corporations' use of debt. Like most important issues, this one is debatable, and the debate centers around who can better determine "appropriate" capital structures—corporate managers or government officials.

Long-Term Debt

Different groups of investors prefer different types of securities, and investors' tastes change over time. Thus, astute financial managers offer a variety of securities, and they package their new security offerings at each point in time to appeal to the greatest possible number of potential investors. In this section, we consider the various types of long-term debt available to financial managers.

Long-term debt is often called **funded debt.** When a firm "funds" its short-term debt, this means that it replaces short-term debt with securities of longer maturity. Funding does not imply that the firm places money with a trustee or other repository; and it means that the firm replaces short-term debt with long-term debt or equity. **Pacific Gas & Electric Company (PG&E)** provides a good example of funding. PG&E has a continuous construction program, and it typically uses short-term debt to finance construction expenditures. However, once short-term debt has built up to about $100 million, the company sells a stock or bond issue, uses the proceeds to pay off (or fund) its bank loans, and starts the cycle again. There is a fixed cost involved in selling stocks or bonds that makes it quite expensive to issue small amounts of these securities. Therefore, the process used by PG&E and other companies is quite logical.

Traditional Debt Instruments

There are many types of long-term debt instruments: term loans, bonds, secured and unsecured notes, marketable and nonmarketable debt, and so on. In this section, we briefly discuss the traditional long-term debt instruments, after which we examine some important features of debt contracts and some innovations in long-term debt financing.

Term Loans

A **term loan** is a contract under which a borrower agrees to make a series of interest and principal payments on specific dates to the lender. Term loans usually are negotiated directly between the borrowing firm and a financial institution—generally a bank, an insurance company, or a pension fund. Although term loans' maturities vary from 2 to 30 years, most are for periods in the 3-year to 15-year range.

Most term loans are amortized, which means they are paid off in equal installments over the life of the loan. Amortization protects the lender against the possibility that the borrower will not make adequate provisions for the loan's retirement during the life of the loan. Also, if the interest and principal payments required under a term loan agreement are not met on schedule, the borrowing firm is said to have defaulted, and it can then be forced into bankruptcy.

Term loans have three major advantages over public offerings—*speed, flexibility,* and *low issuance costs.* Because they are negotiated directly between the lender and the borrower, formal documentation is minimized. The key provisions of a term loan can be worked out much more quickly than those for a public issue, and it is not necessary for the loan to go through the Securities and Exchange Commission registration process. A further advantage of term loans has to do with future flexibility. If a bond issue is held by many different bondholders, it is virtually impossible to obtain permission to alter the terms of the agreement, even though new economic conditions might make such changes desirable. With a term loan, the borrower generally can sit down with the lender and work out mutually agreeable modifications to the contract.

The interest rate on a term loan can be either fixed for the life of the loan or variable. If a fixed rate is used, generally it will be set close to the rate on bonds of equivalent maturity and risk. If the rate is variable, it usually will be set at a certain number of percentage points over either the prime rate, the commercial paper rate, rates on Treasury securities, or the London InterBank Offered Rate (LIBOR), which is the rate of interest offered by the largest and strongest London banks on deposits of other large banks of the highest credit standing. Then, when the index rate goes up or down, so does the rate charged on the outstanding balance of the term loan. Rates might be adjusted annually, semiannually, quarterly, monthly, or on some other basis, depending on what the contract specifies. Today, most term loans made by banks have floating rates; in 1970, there were very few floating-rate term notes. With the increased volatility of interest rates in recent years, banks and other lenders have become increasingly reluctant to make long-term, fixed-rate loans.

Bonds

A **bond** is a long-term contract under which a borrower agrees to make payments of interest and principal on specific dates to the holder of the bond. Although bonds traditionally have been issued with maturities of between 20 and 30 years, in recent years shorter maturities, such as 7 to 10 years, have been used to an increasing extent. Bonds are similar to term loans, but a bond issue generally is advertised, offered to the public, and actually sold to many different investors. Indeed, thousands of individual and institutional investors might purchase bonds when a firm sells a bond issue, whereas there usually is only one lender in the case of a term loan.

However, for very large term loans, 20 or more financial institutions might form a syndicate to grant the credit. Also, it should be noted that a bond issue can be sold to one lender (or to just a few); in this case, the issue is said to be "privately placed." Companies that place bonds privately do so for the same reasons that they use term loans—speed, flexibility, and low issuance costs. With bonds the interest rate generally is fixed, although in recent years there has been an increase in the use of various types of floating rate bonds. There also are a number of different types of bonds, the more important of which are discussed next.

MORTGAGE BONDS With a **mortgage bond,** the corporation pledges certain assets as security for the bond. To illustrate, in 2000 **Scobes Corporation** needed $10 million to build a major regional distribution center. Bonds in the amount of $4 million, secured by a mortgage on the property, were issued. (The remaining $6 million was financed with equity capital.) If Scobes defaults on the bonds, the bondholders can foreclose on the property and sell it to satisfy their claims.

If Scobes chooses to, it can issue *second mortgage bonds* secured by the same $10 million plant. In the event of liquidation, the holders of these second mortgage bonds would have a claim against the property, but only after the first mortgage bondholders had been paid off in full. Thus, second mortgages are sometimes called *junior mortgages* because they are junior in priority to the claims of *senior mortgages,* or *first mortgage bonds.*

All mortgage bonds are written subject to an *indenture,* which is a legal document that spells out in detail the rights of both the bondholders and the corporation (bond issuer). Indentures generally are "open ended," meaning that new bonds might be issued from time to time under the existing indenture. However, the amount of new bonds that can be issued almost always is limited to a specified percentage of the firm's total "bondable property," which generally includes all plant and equipment. For example, **Savannah Electric Company** can issue first mortgage bonds totaling up to 60 percent of its fixed assets. If its fixed assets totaled $1 billion, and if it had $500 million of first mortgage bonds outstanding, it could, by the property test, issue another $100 million of bonds (60% of $1 billion = $600 million).

DEBENTURES A **debenture** is an unsecured bond, and as such it provides no lien against specific property as security for the obligation. Therefore, debenture holders are general creditors whose claims are protected by property not otherwise pledged. In practice, the use of debentures depends both on the nature of the firm's assets and on its general credit strength. An extremely strong company, such as **IBM,** will tend to use debentures; it simply does not need to put up property as security for its debt. Debentures also are issued by companies in industries in which it would not be practical to provide security through a mortgage on fixed assets. Examples of such industries are the large mail-order houses and commercial banks, which characteristically hold most of their assets in the form of inventory or loans, neither of which is satisfactory security for a mortgage bond.

SUBORDINATED DEBENTURES The term *subordinate* means "below," or "inferior to," and, in the event of bankruptcy, subordinated debt has claims on assets only after senior debt has been paid off. **Subordinated debentures** might be subordinated either to designated notes payable (usually bank loans) or to all other debt. In the event of liquidation or reorganization, holders of subordinated debentures cannot be paid until all senior debt, as named in the debentures' indenture, has been paid.

OTHER TYPES OF BONDS Several other types of bonds are used sufficiently often to warrant mention. First, **convertible bonds** are securities that are convertible into shares of common stock, at a fixed price, at the option of the bondholder. Convertibles have a lower coupon rate than nonconvertible debt, but they offer investors a chance for capital gains in exchange for the lower coupon rate. Bonds issued with **warrants** are similar to convertibles. Warrants are options that permit the holder to buy stock for a stated price, thereby providing a capital gain if the price of the stock rises. Bonds that are issued with warrants, like convertibles, carry lower coupon rates than straight bonds. **Income bonds** pay interest only when the firm has sufficient income to cover the interest payments. Thus, these securities cannot bankrupt a company, but from an investor's standpoint they are riskier than "regular" bonds. **Putable bonds** are bonds that can be turned in and exchanged for cash at the bondholder's option; generally, the option to turn in the bond can be exercised only if the firm takes some specified action, such as being acquired by a weaker company or increasing its outstanding debt by a large amount. With an **indexed, or purchasing power, bond,** which is popular in countries plagued by high rates of inflation, the interest rate payment is based on an inflation index such as the consumer price index; so the interest paid rises automatically when the inflation rate rises, thus protecting the bondholders against inflation.

Specific Debt-Contract Features

A firm's managers are concerned with both the effective cost of debt and any restrictions in debt contracts that might limit the firm's future actions. In this section, we discuss features that could affect either the cost of the firm's debt or the firm's future flexibility.

Bond Indentures

Earlier we discussed *agency problems,* which relate to conflicts of interest among corporate stakeholders—stockholders, bondholders, and managers. Bondholders have a legitimate fear that once they lend money to a company and are "locked in" for up to 30 years, the company will take some action that is designed to benefit stockholders but that harms bondholders. For example, **RJR Nabisco**, when it was highly rated, sold 30-year bonds with a low coupon rate, and investors bought those bonds in spite of the low yield because of their low risk. Then, after the bonds had been sold, the company announced plans to issue a great deal more debt, increasing the expected rate of return to stockholders but also increasing the riskiness of the bonds. RJR's bonds fell 20 percent the week the announcement was made. **Safeway Stores** and a number of other companies have done the same thing, and their bondholders also lost heavily as the market yield on the bonds rose and drove the prices of the bonds down.

Investors attempt to reduce agency problems by use of legal restrictions designed to ensure, insofar as possible, that the company does nothing to cause the quality of its bonds to deteriorate after they have been issued. The **indenture** is the legal document that spells out the rights of the bondholders and the corporation. A **trustee,** usually a bank, is assigned to represent the bondholders and to make sure that the terms of the indenture are carried out. The indenture might be several hundred pages in length, and it will include **restrictive covenants** that cover such points as the conditions under which the issuer can pay off the bonds prior to maturity, the level at which the issuer's times-interest-earned ratio must be maintained if the company is to sell additional bonds, and restrictions against the payment of dividends when earnings do not meet certain specifications.

> A firm will have different indentures for each major type of bond it issues, including its first mortgage bonds, its debentures, its convertibles, and so on.

The trustee is responsible both for making sure the covenants are not violated and for taking appropriate action if they are. What constitutes "appropriate action" varies with the circumstances. It might be that to insist on immediate compliance would result in bankruptcy, which in turn might lead to large losses on the bonds. In such a case, the trustee might decide that the bondholders would be better served by giving the company a chance to work out its problems rather than by forcing it into bankruptcy.

The Securities and Exchange Commission (SEC) approves indentures for publicly traded bonds and makes sure that all indenture provisions are met before allowing a company to sell new securities to the public. The indentures of many larger corporations were written back in the 1930s or 1940s, and many issues of new bonds, all covered by the same indenture, have been sold down through the years. The interest rates on the bonds, and perhaps also the maturities, will change from issue to issue, but bondholders' protection as spelled out in the indenture will be the same for all bonds of a given type.

Call Provisions

Most bonds contain a **call provision,** which gives the issuing corporation the right to call the bonds for redemption. The call provision generally states that the company must pay the bondholders an amount greater than the par value for the bonds when they are called. The additional sum, which is termed a *call premium,* typically is set equal to one year's interest if the bonds are called during the first year, and the premium declines at a constant rate of INT/N each year thereafter, where INT = annual interest and N = original maturity in years. For example, the call premium on a $1,000 par value, 10-year, 10 percent bond would generally be $100 if it were called during the first year, $90 during the second year (calculated by reducing the $100, or 10 percent, premium by one-tenth), and so on. However, bonds usually are not callable until several years (generally 5 to 10) after they are issued; bonds with these *deferred calls* are said to have *call protection.*

Suppose a company sold bonds when interest rates were relatively high. Provided the issue is callable, the company could sell a new issue of low-yielding bonds if and when interest rates drop. It could then use the proceeds to retire the high-rate issue and thus reduce its interest expense. This process is called **bond refunding.**

Sinking Funds

A **sinking fund** is a provision that facilitates the orderly retirement of a bond issue. Typically, the sinking fund provision requires the firm to retire a portion of the bond issue each year. On rare occasions the firm might be required to deposit money with a trustee, which invests the funds and then uses the accumulated sum to retire the bonds when they mature. A failure to meet the sinking fund requirement causes the bond issue to be thrown into default, which might force the company into bankruptcy. Obviously, a sinking fund can constitute a dangerous cash drain on the firm.

In most cases, the firm is given the right to handle the sinking fund in either of two ways.

1. The company can call in for redemption (at par value) a certain percentage of the bonds each year; for example, it might be able to call 2 percent of the total original amount of the issue at a price of $1,000 per bond. The bonds are numbered serially, and those called for redemption are determined by a lottery administered by the trustee.
2. The company might buy the required amount of bonds on the open market.

The firm will choose the least-cost method. If interest rates have risen, causing bond prices to fall, it will buy bonds in the open market at a discount; if interest rates have fallen, it will call the bonds. Note that a call for sinking fund purposes is quite different from a refunding call. A sinking fund call requires no call premium, but only a small percentage of the issue normally is callable in any one year.

Bond Innovations in the Past Few Decades

Zero (or very low) Coupon Bonds

Some bonds pay no interest but are offered at a substantial discount below their par values and hence provide capital appreciation rather than interest income. These securities are called **zero coupon bonds** ("*zeros*"), or *original issue discount bonds (OIDs)*. Corporations first used zeros in a major way in 1981. More recently, many large companies like **IBM** and **JCPenney** have used them to raise billions of dollars. Municipal governments also sell "zero munis," and investment bankers have in effect created zero coupon Treasury bonds by "stripping" the interest payments and selling only the right to receive principal repayment at maturity.

Not all OIDs have zero coupons. For example, a company might sell an issue of five-year bonds with a 3 percent coupon at a time when other bonds with similar ratings and maturities are yielding 9 percent. If an investor purchases these bonds at a price of $762.62, the yield to maturity would be 9 percent. The discount of $1,000 − $762.62 = $237.38 represents the capital appreciation the bondholder receives for holding the bond for five years. Thus, zero coupon bonds are just one type of original issue discount bond. Any nonconvertible bond whose coupon rate is set below the going market rate at the time of its issue will sell at a discount, and it will be classified as an OID bond.

OID bonds have lost favor with many individual investors in recent years. The primary reason is because the interest income that must be reported each year for tax purposes includes the dollar amount of interest actually received, which is $0 for zero coupons, plus the annual *prorated* capital appreciation. For example, the purchaser of the 3 percent coupon bond just mentioned actually would receive $30 interest each year. But the interest income reported for tax purposes would be $30 + ($237.38/5) = $77.48. Thus, taxes would have to be paid on prorated capital gains that would not be received for five years ($47.48 each year). For this reason, most OID bonds currently are held by institutional investors, such as insurance companies and pension funds, rather than individual investors.

Shortly after corporations began to issue zeros, investment bankers figured out a way to create zeros from U.S. Treasury bonds, which are issued only in coupon form. In 1982 **Salomon Brothers** (now **Salomon Smith Barney**) bought $1 billion of 12 percent, 30-year Treasuries. Each bond had 60 coupons worth $60 each, which represented the interest payments due every six months. Salomon then in effect clipped the coupons and placed them in 60 piles; the last pile also contained the now "stripped" bond itself, which represented a promise of $1,000 in the year 2012. These 60 piles of U.S. Treasury promises were then placed with the trust department of a bank and used as collateral for "zero coupon U.S. Treasury Trust Certificates," which are, in essence, zero coupon Treasury bonds. A pension fund that expected to need money in 2002 could have bought 20-year certificates backed by the interest the Treasury would pay in 2002. Treasury zeros are, of course, safer than corporate zeros, so they are very popular with pension fund managers.

Corporate (and municipal) zeros generally are callable at the option of the issuer, just like coupon bonds, after some stated call-protection period. The call price is set at a premium over the accrued value at the time of the call.

Stripped U.S. Treasury bonds (Treasury zeros) generally are not callable because the Treasury normally sells non-callable bonds. Thus, Treasury zeros are completely protected against reinvestment risk (the risk of having to invest cash flows from a bond at a lower rate because of a decline in interest rates).

Floating Rate Debt

In the early 1980s, inflation pushed interest rates up to unprecedented levels, causing sharp declines in the prices of long-term bonds. Even some supposedly "risk-free" U.S. Treasury bonds lost fully half their value, and a similar situation occurred with corporate bonds, mortgages, and other fixed-rate, long-term securities. As a result, many lenders became reluctant to lend money at fixed rates on a long-term basis, and they would do so only at extraordinarily high rates.

There normally is a *maturity risk premium* embodied in long-term interest rates; this premium is designed to offset the risk of declining bond prices if interest rates rise. Prior to the 1970s, the maturity risk premium on 30-year bonds was about one percentage point, meaning that under normal conditions, a firm might expect to pay about one percentage point more to borrow on a long-term than on a short-term basis. However, in the early 1980s, the maturity risk premium is estimated to have jumped to about three percentage points, which made long-term debt very expensive relative to short-term debt. Lenders were able and willing to lend on a short-term basis, but corporations were correctly reluctant to borrow on a short-term basis to finance long-term assets—such action is extremely dangerous. Therefore, there was a situation in which lenders did not want to lend on a long-term basis, but corporations needed long-term money. The problem was solved by the introduction of long-term, *floating rate debt*.

A typical **floating rate bond** works as follows. The coupon rate is set for, say, the initial six-month period, after which it is adjusted every six months based on some market rate. Some corporate issues have been tied to the Treasury bond rate, while other issues have been tied to short-term rates. Many additional provisions can be included in floating rate issues; for example, some are convertible to fixed rate debt, whereas others have upper and lower limits ("caps" and "collars") on how high or low the yield can go.

Floating rate debt is advantageous to investors because the interest rate moves up if market rates rise. This causes the market value of the debt to be stabilized, and it also provides lenders such as banks with income that is better geared to their own obligations. Moreover, floating rate debt is advantageous to corporations because by using it, firms can issue debt with a long maturity without committing themselves to paying a historically high rate of interest for the entire life of the loan. Of course, if interest rates were to move even higher after a floating rate note had been signed, the borrower would have been better off issuing conventional, fixed rate debt.

Junk Bonds

Prior to the 1980s, fixed income investors such as pension funds and insurance companies generally were unwilling to buy risky bonds, so it was almost impossible for risky companies to raise capital in the public bond markets. These companies, if they could raise debt capital at all, had to do so in the term loan market, where the loan could be tailored to satisfy the lender. Then, in the late 1970s, Michael Milken of the investment banking firm **Drexel Burnham Lambert**, relying on historical studies that showed risky bonds yielded more than enough to compensate for their risk, began to convince certain institutional investors of the merits of purchasing risky debt. Thus was born the **junk bond,** a high-risk, high-yield bond issued to finance a leveraged buyout, a merger, or a troubled company. For example, when Ted Turner attempted to buy **CBS,** he planned to finance the acquisition by issuing junk bonds to CBS's stockholders in exchange for their shares. Similarly, **Public Service of New Hampshire** financed construction of its troubled Seabrook nuclear plant with junk bonds, and junk bonds were used in the **RJR Nabisco** leveraged buyout (LBOs). In junk bond deals, the debt ratio generally is extremely high, so the bondholders must bear as much risk as stockholders normally would. The bonds' yields reflect this fact—a coupon rate of 25 percent per annum was required to sell the Public Service of New Hampshire bonds.

The phenomenal growth of the junk bond market was impressive but controversial. Significant risk, combined with unscrupulous dealings, created significant losses for investors. Recently, however, the junk bond market has begun to grow once again.

Bond Ratings

Since the early 1900s, bonds have been assigned quality ratings that reflect their probability of going into default. The two major rating agencies are **Moody's Investors Service (Moody's)** and **Standard & Poor's Corporation (S&P)**. These

Exhibit 700.12 *Moody's and S&P Bond Ratings*

	High Quality		Investment Grade		Junk Bonds — Substandard		Junk Bonds — Speculative	
Moody's	Aaa	Aa	A	Baa	Ba	B	Caa	C
S&P	AAA	AA	A	BBB	BB	B	CCC	D

NOTE: Both Moody's and S&P use "modifiers" for bonds rated below triple A. S&P uses a plus and minus system; thus, A+ designates the strongest A-rated bonds and A− the weakest. Moody's uses a 1, 2, or 3 designation, with 1 denoting the strongest and 3 the weakest; thus, within the double-A category, Aa1 is the best, Aa2 is average, and Aa3 is the weakest.

agencies' rating designations are shown in Exhibit 700.12. The triple- and double-A bonds are extremely safe. Single-A and triple-B bonds are strong enough to be called **investment grade bonds,** and they are the lowest-rated bonds that many banks and other institutional investors are permitted by law to hold. Double-B and lower bonds are speculative, or junk bonds; they have a significant probability of going into default, and many financial institutions are prohibited from buying them.

Bond Rating Criteria

Bond ratings are based on both qualitative and quantitative factors. Some of the factors considered by the bond rating agencies include the financial strength of the company as measured by various ratios, collateral provisions, seniority of the debt, restrictive covenants, provisions such as a sinking fund or a deferred call, litigation possibilities, regulation, and so on. Representatives of the rating agencies have consistently stated that no precise formula is used to set a firm's rating; all the factors listed, plus others, are taken into account, but not in a mathematically precise manner. Statistical studies have borne out this contention—researchers who have tried to predict bond ratings on the basis of quantitative data have had only limited success, indicating that the agencies use subjective judgment when establishing a firm's rating.

Importance of Bond Ratings

Bond ratings are important both to firms and to investors. First, because a bond's rating is an indicator of its default risk, the rating has a direct, measurable influence on the bond's interest rate and the firm's cost of debt. Second, most bonds are purchased by institutional investors rather than individuals, and many institutions are restricted to investment-grade securities. Thus, if a firm's bonds fall below BBB, it will have a difficult time selling new bonds because many potential purchasers will not be allowed to buy them.

Changes in Ratings

Changes in a firm's bond rating affect both its ability to borrow long-term capital and the cost of that capital. Rating agencies review outstanding bonds on a periodic basis, occasionally upgrading or downgrading a bond as a result of its issuer's changed circumstances.

Rationale for Using Different Types of Securities

Why are there so many different types of long-term securities? At least a partial answer to this question might be seen in Exhibit 700.13, which depicts the now familiar risk/return trade-off function drawn to show the risk and the expected after-personal-tax returns for the various securities of Allied Air Products. First, U.S. Treasury bills, which represent the risk-free rate, are shown for reference. The lowest-risk, long-term securities offered by Allied are its floating rate notes; these securities are free of interest rate risk, but they are exposed to some risk of default. The first mortgage bonds are somewhat riskier than the notes (because the bonds are exposed to interest rate risk), and they sell at a somewhat higher required and expected after-tax return. The second mortgage bonds are even riskier, so they have a still higher expected return. Subordinated debentures, income bonds, and preferred stocks are all increasingly risky, and their expected returns increase accordingly.

Why does Allied issue so many different classes of securities? Why not offer just one type of bond, plus common stock? The answer lies in the fact that different investors have different risk/return trade-off preferences, so to appeal

Exhibit 700.13 *Allied Air Products: Risks and Returns on Different Classes of Securities*

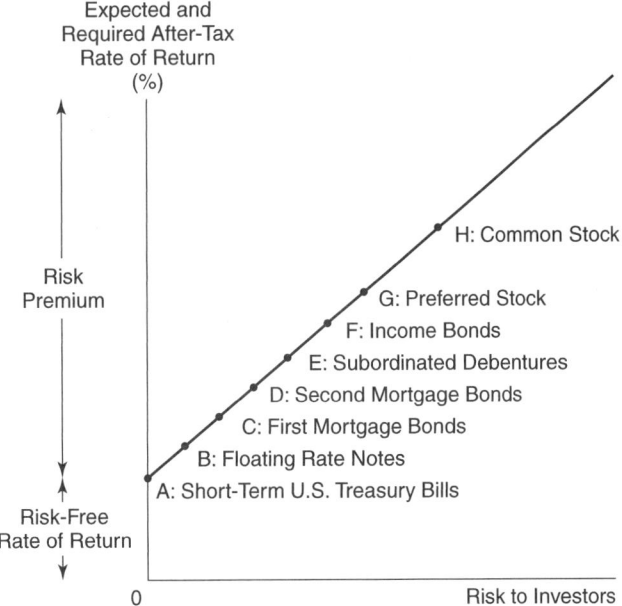

to the broadest possible market, Allied must offer securities that attract as many different types of investors as possible. Also, different securities are more popular at different points in time, and firms tend to issue whatever is popular at the time they need money. Used wisely, a policy of selling differentiated securities to take advantage of market conditions can lower a firm's overall cost of capital below what it would be if the firm used only one class of debt.

Factors Influencing Long-Term Financing Decisions

As we show in this section, many factors influence a firm's long-term financing decisions. Each factor's relative importance varies among firms at any point in time and for any given firm over time, but any company planning to raise new long-term capital should consider each of these points.

Target Capital Structure

Firms typically establish target capital structures, and one of the most important considerations in any financing decision is how the firm's actual capital structure compares to its target structure. However, few firms finance each year exactly in accordance with their target capital structures, primarily because exact adherence would increase their flotation costs. Because smaller issues of new securities have proportionally larger flotation costs, firms tend to use debt one year and stock the next.

Making fewer but larger security offerings would cause a firm's capital structure to fluctuate above and below its optimal level rather than stay right on target. However, small fluctuations near the optimal capital structure have little effect either on a firm's cost of debt and equity or on its overall cost of capital. Also, investors would recognize that its actions were prudent and that the firm would save substantial amounts of flotation costs by financing in this manner. Therefore, even though firms do tend to finance over the long haul in accordance with their target capital structures, flotation costs have a definite influence on the specific financing decisions in any given year.

Maturity Matching

Assume that Unilate Textiles decides to float a single $13.5 million nonconvertible bond issue with a sinking fund. It must next choose a maturity for the issue, taking into consideration the shape of the yield curve, management's own expectations about future interest rates, and the maturity of the assets being financed. In the case at hand, Unilate's capital projects during the next two years consist primarily of new, automated manufacturing equipment. This equipment has an expected economic life of 10 years (even though it falls into the MACRS 5-year class life). Should Unilate finance the debt portion of the capital raised for this equipment with 1-year, 10-year, 20-year, or 30-year debt, or with debt of some other maturity? *One approach is to match the maturity of the liabilities with the maturity of the assets being financed.*

Note that some of the new capital for the machinery will come from common stock, which generally is considered to be a perpetual security with an infinite maturity. Of course, common stock can always be repurchased on the open market or by other means, so its effective maturity can be reduced significantly, but generally it has no maturity.

Debt maturities, however, are specified at the time of issue. If Unilate financed its capital budgets over the next two years with 10-year sinking fund bonds, it would be matching its asset and liability maturities. The cash flows resulting from the new machinery should be sufficient to make the interest and sinking fund payments on the issue, and the bonds would be retired as the machinery wore out. If Unilate used one-year debt, it would have to pay off the loan with cash flows derived from assets other than the machinery in question. If its operations were stable, the company probably could roll over the one-year debt, but if interest rates rose, then it would have to pay a higher rate. If Unilate subsequently experienced difficulties, its lenders might be hesitant to extend the loan, and the company might be unable to obtain new short-term debt at any reasonable rate. At the other extreme, if it used 20-year or 30-year debt, Unilate would still have to service the debt long after the assets purchased with the debt had been scrapped and had ceased providing cash flows, and this would worry potential lenders.

For all these reasons, one commonly used financing strategy is to match debt maturities with asset maturities. In recognition of this fact, firms do consider maturity relationships, and this factor has a major influence on the type of debt securities used.

Interest Rate Levels

Financial managers also consider interest rate levels, both absolute and relative, when making financing decisions. For example, long-term interest rates were high by historic standards in 1981 and 1982, so many managers were reluctant to issue long-term debt and thus lock in those high costs for long periods. We already know that one solution to this problem is to use long-term debt with a call provision. Callability permits the company to refund the issue should interest rates drop, as they did in 1993. But there is a cost, because firms must pay more if they make their debt callable. Alternatively, a firm might finance with short-term debt whenever long-term rates are historically high, and then, assuming that interest rates subsequently fall, sell a long-term issue to replace the short-term debt. Of course, this strategy has its risks. If interest rates climb even higher, the firm will be forced to renew the short-term debt at higher and higher rates, or to replace the short-term debt with a long-term bond that costs more than it would have cost earlier.

Expectations about Future Interest Rates

At a time when the interest rate on AAA corporate bonds was over 12 percent, which was high by historical standards, **Exxon's** investment bankers advised the company to tap the Eurodollar bond market for relatively cheap fixed-rate financing. A *Eurodollar bond* is a bond sold outside of the United States but denominated in U.S. dollars. At the time, Exxon could have issued its bonds in London at 0.4 percentage points *below* comparable-maturity Treasury bonds. However, one Exxon officer was quoted as cautioning, "I say so what. The absolute level of rates is too high. We would rather wait." The managers of Exxon, as well as those of many other companies, were betting that the next move in interest rates would be down.

This example illustrates that firms do base their financing decisions on expectations about future interest rates. In Exxon's case, the financial staff turned out to be correct. However, the success of such a strategy requires interest rate forecasts to be right more often than they are wrong, and it is very difficult to find someone with a long-term forecasting record better than 50–50.

The Firm's Current and Forecasted Financial Conditions

If a firm's current financial condition is poor, its managers might be reluctant to issue new long-term debt because (1) a new bond issue probably would trigger a review by the rating agencies, and (2) long-term debt issued when a firm is in poor financial condition costs more and is subject to more severe restrictive covenants than debt issued from a strong position. Thus, a firm that is in a weakened condition but that is forecasting an improvement would be inclined to delay permanent financing until things improved. Conversely, a firm that is strong now but whose forecasts indicate a potentially bad time just ahead would be motivated to finance long term now rather than to wait. These scenarios imply that the capital markets are inefficient in the sense that investors do not have as much information about the firm's future as does its management. This situation undoubtedly is true at times.

The firm's earnings outlook, and the extent to which forecasted higher earnings per share are reflected in stock prices, also has an effect on the choice of securities. If a successful research and development program has just been concluded, and, consequently, management forecasts higher earnings than do most investors, the firm would not want to issue common stock. It would use debt, and then, after earnings had risen and pushed up the stock price, it would sell common stock to restore the capital structure to its target level.

Restrictions in Existing Debt Contracts

Earlier we discussed the fact that Savannah Electric Company has at times been restricted from issuing new first mortgage bonds by its indenture coverage requirements. This is just one example of how indenture covenants can influence a firm's financing decisions. Restrictions on the current ratio, the debt ratio, and so on, can also restrict a firm's ability to use different types of financing at a given time.

Availability of Collateral

Generally, for a particular firm, secured long-term debt will be less costly than unsecured debt. Thus, firms with large amounts of general-purpose (as opposed to specialized) fixed assets are likely to use a relatively large amount of debt, especially mortgage bonds. Additionally, each year's financing decision will be influenced by the amount of newly acquired assets that are available as security for new bonds.

Bond Refunding Operations

Bond refunding analysis is similar to capital budgeting analysis. Also, bond refunding can be compared to the process individuals go through to refinance a house—an existing debt (mortgage) with a high interest rate is replaced by a new debt (mortgage) with a lower interest rate.

The refunding decision actually involves two separate questions: (1) Would it be profitable to call an outstanding issue now and to replace it with a new issue? (2) Even if refunding currently is profitable, would it be better to call now or to postpone the refunding to a later date?

As we noted, refunding decisions are similar to capital budgeting decisions, and the net present value method is the primary tool. In essence, the costs of undertaking the refunding operation (the investment outlay) are compared to the present value of the interest that will be saved if the high-interest rate bond is called and replaced with a new, low-interest rate bond. If the net present value of refunding is positive, then the refunding should take place. The costs of the refunding operation consist primarily of the call premium on the old bond issue and the flotation costs associated with selling the new issue. The cash flow benefits consist primarily of the interest expenses that will be saved if the company replaces high-cost debt with low-cost debt. The discount rate used to find the present value of the interest savings is the after-tax cost of new debt—the interest saved is the difference between two relatively certain cash flow streams, so the difference essentially is riskless. Therefore, a low discount rate should be used, and that rate is today's after-tax cost of new debt in the market.

To illustrate the refunding decision, consider the Strasburg Communications Corporation, which has a $100 million, 13 percent, semiannual coupon bond outstanding with 10 years remaining to maturity. The bond has a call provision that permits the company to retire the issue by calling in the bonds at an 8 percent call premium. Investment bankers have assured Strasburg that it could issue an additional $100 million of new 10 percent coupon, 10-year bonds that pay interest semiannually. Flotation costs on the new refunding issue will amount to $4,000,000. Predictions are that long-term interest rates are unlikely to fall below 10 percent. Strasburg's marginal tax rate is 40 percent. Should the company refund the $100 million of 13 percent semiannual coupon bonds?

Strasburg's refunding analysis is presented in Exhibit 700.14. Because the marginal tax rate is 40 percent, the company's after-tax cost of new debt is equal to 6 percent, or 3 percent per six-month period. And because the bonds have semiannual coupons, there will be 20 semiannual periods in the analysis.

715. MANAGING LONG-TERM FINANCING

Exhibit 700.14 *NPV Refunding Analysis for Strasburg Communications Corporation*

```
Cost of Refunding at t = 0
Call premium on old bond (0.08 × $100 million)                    $ 8,000,000
Flotation costs on new issue                                        4,000,000
   Total initial outlay                                           $12,000,000

Semiannual Interest Savings Due to Refunding: t = 1 to 20
(10 years of payments twice a year)
Interest on old bond (0.065 × $100 million)                       $6,500,000
Interest on new bond (0.050 × $100 million)                        5,000,000
   Interest savings per period                                    $1,500,000
Increased taxes due to lower interest payment^a (0.40 × $1,500,000)  $(600,000)
   Net interest savings                                           $  900,000

Refunding Cash Flow Timeline

                                                    1               10 Year
Interest period           0      k = 3%    1        2               20
Initial outlay       (12,000,000)
Interest savings              0          900,000  900,000   ...   900,000
Net cash flow        (12,000,000)        900,000  900,000   ...   900,000

NPV of refunding at k_dT/2 = 3% is $1,389,727
```

[a] Strasburg's interest expense will decrease by $1,500,000, thus taxable income will increase by $1,500,000, if the new bond is issued. Strasburg will have to pay 0.40 × $1,500,000 = $600,000 additional taxes on this increased taxable income.

The net present value of refunding is positive, so Strasburg should refund the old bond issue—the firm's value will be increased by $1,389,727 if the old bond is retired.

Foreign Debt Instruments

Like the U.S. debt markets, the international debt markets offer a variety of instruments with many different features. In this section, we discuss a few of the more familiar types of debt that are traded internationally.

Any debt sold outside the country of the borrower is called an international debt. However, there are two important types of international debt: foreign debt and Eurodebt. **Foreign debt** is debt sold by a foreign borrower but denominated in the currency of the country in which the issue is sold. For instance, **Bell Canada** might need U.S. dollars to finance the operations of its subsidiaries in the United States. If it decides to raise the needed capital in the domestic U.S. bond market, the bond will be underwritten by a syndicate of U.S. investment bankers, denominated in U.S. dollars, and sold to U.S. investors in accordance with SEC and applicable state regulations. Except for the foreign origin of the borrower (Canada), this bond will be indistinguishable from those issued by equivalent U.S. corporations. Because Bell Canada is a foreign corporation, however, the bond will be called a *foreign bond*. Foreign bonds generally are labeled according to the country in which they are issued. For example, if foreign bonds are issued in the United States they are called *Yankee bonds*, if they are issued in Japan they are called *Samurai bonds*, and if they are issued in England they are called *Bulldog bonds*.

The term **Eurodebt** is used to designate any debt sold in a country other than the one in whose currency the debt is denominated. Examples include *Eurobonds*, such as a British firm's issue of pound bonds sold in France or a **Ford Motor Company** issue denominated in dollars and sold in Germany. The institutional arrangements by which Eurobonds are marketed are different than those for most other bond issues, with the most important distinction being a far lower level of required disclosure than normally is found for bonds issued in domestic markets, particularly in the United States. Governments tend to be less strict when regulating securities denominated in foreign currencies than they are on home-currency securities because the bonds' purchasers generally are more "sophisticated." The lower disclosure requirements result in lower total transaction costs for Eurobonds.

Eurobonds appeal to investors for several reasons. Generally, they are issued in bearer form rather than as registered bonds, so the names and nationalities of investors are not recorded. Individuals who desire anonymity, whether for privacy reasons or for tax avoidance, find Eurobonds to their liking. Similarly, most governments do not withhold taxes on interest payments associated with Eurobonds.

More than half of all Eurobonds are denominated in dollars; bonds in Japanese yen, German marks, and Dutch guilders account for most of the rest. Although centered in Europe, Eurobonds truly are international. Their underwriting syndicates include investment bankers from all parts of the world, and the bonds are sold to investors not only in Europe but also in such faraway places as Bahrain and Singapore. Until recently, Eurobonds were issued solely by multinational firms, by international financial institutions, or by national governments. Today, however, the Eurobond market also is being tapped by purely domestic U.S. firms such as electric utilities, which find that by borrowing overseas they can lower their debt costs.

Some other types of Eurodebt include the following:

1. **Eurocredits.** Eurocredits are bank loans that are denominated in the currency of a country other than where the lending bank is located. Many of these loans are very large, so the lending bank often forms a loan syndicate to help raise the needed funds and to spread out some of the risks associated with the loan.

    Interest rates on Eurocredits, as well as other short-term Eurodebt, typically are tied to a standard rate known by the acronym **LIBOR,** which stands for *London InterBank Offer Rate*. LIBOR is the rate of interest offered by the largest and strongest London banks on deposits of other large banks of the highest credit standing. In September 1999, LIBOR rates were about 1/2 percentage point above domestic U.S. bank rates on time deposits of the same maturity—5.04 percent for three-month CDs versus 5.53 percent for three-month LIBOR CDs.

2. **Euro-commercial paper (Euro-CP).** Euro-CP is similar to commercial paper issued in the United States. It is a short-term debt instrument issued by corporations, and it has typical maturities of one, three, and six months. The principal difference between Euro-CP and U.S. commercial paper is that there is not as much concern about the credit quality of Euro-CP issuers.

3. **Euronotes.** Euronotes, which represent medium-term debt, typically have maturities from 1 year to 10 years. The general features of Euronotes are much like those of longer-term debt instruments like bonds. The principal amount is repaid at maturity and interest often is paid semiannually. Most foreign companies use Euronotes like they would a line of credit, continuously issuing notes to finance medium-term needs.

Preferred Stock, Leases, Options, Warrants, and Convertibles

Alternative long-term financing arrangements include preferred stock, leases, options, warrants, and convertibles. They are alternative to traditional financing sources such as the use of common stock and various types of long-term debt.

Preferred Stock

Preferred stock is a *hybrid* security—it is similar to bonds in some respects and to common stock in others. The hybrid nature of preferred stock becomes apparent when we try to classify it in relation to bonds and common stock. Like bonds, preferred stock has a par value. Preferred dividends also are similar to interest payments in that they generally are fixed in amount and must be paid before common stock dividends can be paid. However, if the preferred dividend is not earned, the directors can omit (or "pass") it without throwing the company into bankruptcy. So although preferred stock has a fixed payment like bonds, a failure to make this payment will not lead to bankruptcy.

Accountants classify preferred stock as equity and report it in the equity portion of the balance sheet under "preferred stock" or "preferred equity." However, financial analysts sometimes treat preferred stock as debt and sometimes as equity, depending on the type of analysis being made. If the analysis is being made by a common stockholder, the key consideration is the fact that the preferred dividend is a fixed charge that reduces the amount that can be distributed to common shareholders, so from the common stockholder's point of view, preferred stock is similar to debt. Suppose, however, that the analysis is being made by a bondholder studying the firm's vulnerability to failure in the event of a decline in sales and income. If the firm's income declines, the debtholders have a prior claim to the available income ahead of preferred stockholders, and if the firm fails, debtholders have a prior claim to assets when the firm is liquidated. Thus, to a bondholder, preferred stock is similar to common equity.

From management's perspective, preferred stock lies between debt and common equity. Because failure to pay dividends on preferred stock will not force the firm into bankruptcy, preferred stock is safer to use than debt. At the same time, if the firm is highly successful, the common stockholders will not have to share that success with the preferred stockholders because preferred dividends are fixed. Remember, however, that the preferred stockholders do have a higher priority claim than the common stockholders. We see, then, that preferred stock has some of the characteristics of debt and some of the characteristics of common stock, and it is used in situations in which conditions are such that neither debt nor common stock is entirely appropriate.

Major Provisions of Preferred Stock Issues

Preferred stock has a number of features, the most important of which are discussed in the following sections. As you will see, some of the features we discuss here are also features included in debt instruments, which we discussed earlier in this section.

PRIORITY TO ASSETS AND EARNINGS Preferred stockholders have priority over common stockholders with regard to earnings and assets. Thus, dividends must be paid on preferred stock before they can be paid on the common stock, and, in the event of bankruptcy, the claims of the preferred shareholders must be satisfied before the common stockholders receive anything. To reinforce these features, most preferred stocks have coverage requirements similar to those on bonds. These restrictions limit the amount of preferred stock a company can use, and they also require a minimum level of retained earnings before common dividends can be paid.

PAR VALUE Unlike common stock, preferred stock always has a par value (or its equivalent under some other name), and this value is important. First, the par value establishes the amount due the preferred stockholders in the event of liquidation. Second, the preferred dividend frequently is stated as a percentage of the par value. For example, an issue of Duke Power's preferred stock has a par value of $100 and a stated dividend of 7.8 percent of par. The same results would, of course, be produced if this issue of Duke's preferred stock simply called for an annual dividend of $7.80.

CUMULATIVE DIVIDENDS Most preferred stock provides for **cumulative dividends;** that is, any preferred dividends not paid in previous periods must be paid before common dividends can be paid. The cumulative feature is a protective device because if the preferred stock dividends were not cumulative, a firm could avoid paying preferred and common stock dividends for, say, ten years, plowing back all its earnings, and then pay a huge common stock dividend but pay only the stipulated annual dividend to the preferred stockholders. Obviously, such an action effectively would void the preferred position the preferred stockholders are supposed to have. The cumulative feature helps prevent such abuses.

CONVERTIBILITY Approximately 40 percent of the preferred stock that has been issued in recent years is convertible into common stock. For example, on March 25, 1999, **Global Maintech** issued 1,600 shares of Series C convertible preferred that can be converted into a minimum of 400 shares of common stock at the option of the preferred shareholder.

OTHER PROVISIONS Some other provisions occasionally found in preferred stocks include the following.

1. **Voting rights.** Although preferred stock is not voting stock, preferred stockholders generally are given the right to vote for directors if the company has not paid the preferred dividend for a specified period, such as ten quarters. This feature motivates management to make every effort to pay preferred dividends.

2. **Participating.** A rare type of preferred stock is one that participates with the common stock in sharing the firm's earnings. Participating preferred stocks generally work as follows: (a) the stated preferred dividend is paid—for example, $5 a share; (b) the common stock is then entitled to a dividend in an amount up to the preferred dividend; (c) if the common dividend is raised, say to $5.50, the preferred dividend must likewise be raised to $5.50.

3. **Sinking fund.** In the past (before the mid-1970s), few preferred issues had sinking funds. Today, however, most newly issued preferred stocks have sinking funds that call for the purchase and retirement of a given percentage of the preferred stock each year. If the amount is 2 percent, which frequently is used, the preferred issue will have an average life of 25 years and a maximum life of 50 years.

4. **Call provision.** A call provision gives the issuing corporation the right to call in the preferred stock for redemption. As in the case of bonds, call provisions generally state that the company must pay an amount greater than the par value of the preferred stock, the additional sum being termed a **call premium.** For example, Ban-

gor Hydro-Electric Company has various issues of preferred stock outstanding, two of which are callable. The call prices on the two issues are $100 and $110. Before it was called in December 1997, Bangor had another callable preferred issue that included a sinking fund provision.

5. **Maturity.** Before the mid-1970s, most preferred stock was perpetual—it had no maturity and never needed to be paid off. Today, however, most new preferred stock has a sinking fund and thus an effective maturity date.

Pros and Cons of Preferred Stock

As noted here, there are both advantages and disadvantages to financing with preferred stock.

ISSUER'S (FIRM'S) VIEWPOINT By using preferred stock, a firm can fix its financial costs and thus keep more of the potential future profits for its existing set of common stockholders, yet still avoid the danger of bankruptcy if earnings are too low to meet these fixed charges. Also, by selling preferred stock rather than common stock, the firm avoids sharing control with new investors.

However, preferred stock does have a major disadvantage from the issuer's standpoint: It has a higher after-tax cost of capital than debt. The major reason for this higher cost is taxes: Preferred dividends are not deductible as a tax expense, whereas interest expense is deductible. This makes the component cost of preferred stock much greater than that of bonds—the after-tax cost of debt is approximately two-thirds of the stated coupon rate for profitable firms, whereas the cost of preferred stock is the full percentage amount of the preferred dividend. Of course, the deductibility differential is most important for issuers that are in relatively high tax brackets. If a company pays little or no taxes because it is unprofitable or because it has a great deal of accelerated depreciation, the deductibility of interest does not make much difference. Thus, the lower a company's tax bracket, the more likely it is to issue preferred stock.

BONDHOLDER'S (INVESTOR'S) VIEWPOINT In designing securities, the financial manager must consider the investor's point of view. It is sometimes asserted that preferred stock has so many disadvantages to both the issuer and the investor that it should never be issued. Nevertheless, preferred stock is being issued in substantial amounts. It provides investors with a steadier and more assured income than common stock, and it has a preference over common stock in the event of liquidation. In addition, 70 percent of the preferred dividends received by corporations are not taxable. For this reason, most preferred stock is owned by corporations.

The principal disadvantage of preferred stock from an investor's standpoint is that although preferred stockholders bear some of the ownership risks, their returns are limited. Other disadvantages are that (1) preferred stockholders have no legally enforceable right to dividends, even if a company earns a profit; and (2) *for individual as opposed to corporate investors,* after-tax bond yields generally are higher than those on preferred stock, even though the preferred is riskier.

Leases

Firms generally own fixed assets and report them on their balance sheets, but it is the *use* of buildings and equipment that is important, not their ownership per se. One way of obtaining the use of assets is to buy them, but an alternative is to lease them. Prior to the 1950s, leasing generally was associated with real estate—land and buildings. Today, however, it is possible to lease virtually any kind of fixed asset, and in 1999 more than 25 percent of all new capital equipment acquired by businesses was leased. In fact, it is estimated that 70 percent of firms listed in the *Fortune 1000* lease some equipment.

Types of Leases

Leasing takes three different forms: (1) sale-and-leaseback arrangements, (2) operating or service leases, and (3) financial or capital leases.

SALE AND LEASEBACK Under a **sale and leaseback,** a firm that owns land, buildings, or equipment sells the property and simultaneously executes an agreement to lease the property back for a particular period under specific terms. The purchaser could be an insurance company, a commercial bank, a specialized leasing company, or even an individual investor. The sale-and-leaseback plan is an alternative to taking out a mortgage loan. The firm that sells the property, or the **lessee,** immediately receives the purchase price from the buyer, or the **lessor.** At the same time, the seller-lessee firm retains the use of the property just as if it had borrowed and mortgaged the property to secure the loan. Note that under a mortgage loan arrangement, the financial institution normally would receive a series of equal payments just sufficient to amortize the loan while providing a specified rate of return to the lender on the outstanding balance. Under a sale-and-leaseback arrangement, the lease payments are set up in exactly the same way; the payments are set so the investor-lessor recoups the purchase price and earns a specified rate of return on the investment.

OPERATING, OR SERVICE, LEASES Operating leases, sometimes called *service leases*, provide for both *financing* and *maintenance*. IBM is one of the pioneers of the operating lease contract, and computers and office copying machines, together with automobiles and trucks, are the primary types of equipment involved. Ordinarily, these leases call for the lessor to maintain and service the leased equipment, and the cost of providing maintenance is built into the lease payments.

Another important characteristic of operating leases is the fact that they frequently are *not fully amortized*; in other words, the payments required under the lease contract are not sufficient to recover the full cost of the equipment. However, the lease contract is written for a period considerably shorter than the expected economic life of the leased equipment, and the lessor expects to recover all investment costs through subsequent renewal payments, through subsequent leases to other companies (lessees), or by selling the leased equipment.

A final feature of operating leases is that they frequently contain a *cancellation clause*, which gives the lessee the right to cancel the lease before the expiration of the basic agreement. This is an important consideration for the lessee, because it means that the equipment can be returned if it is rendered obsolete by technological developments or if it no longer is needed because of a decline in the lessee's business.

FINANCIAL, OR CAPITAL, LEASES Financial leases, sometimes called *capital leases*, are differentiated from operating leases in three respects: (1) they do *not* provide for maintenance services, (2) they are *not* cancelable, and (3) they are *fully amortized*—that is, the lessor receives rental payments that are equal to the full price of the leased equipment plus a return on the investment. In a typical financial lease arrangement, the firm that will use the equipment (the lessee) selects the specific items it requires and negotiates the price and delivery terms with the manufacturer. The user firm then negotiates terms with a leasing company and, once the lease terms are set, arranges to have the lessor buy the equipment from the manufacturer or the distributor. When the equipment is purchased, the user firm simultaneously executes the lease agreement.

Financial leases are similar to sale-and-leaseback arrangements, except that the leased equipment is new and the lessor buys it from a manufacturer or a distributor instead of from the user-lessee. A sale and leaseback might thus be thought of as a special type of financial lease, and both sale-and-leaseback leases and financial leases are analyzed in the same manner.

Financial-Statement Effects of Leases

Lease payments are shown as operating expenses on a firm's income statement, but under certain conditions, neither the leased assets nor the liabilities under the lease contract appear on the firm's balance sheet. For this reason, leasing is often called **off-balance-sheet financing.** This point is illustrated in Exhibit 700.15 by the balance sheets of two hypothetical firms, B (for Buy) and L (for Lease). Initially, the balance sheets of both firms are identical, and both have debt ratios of 50 percent. Each firm then decides to acquire fixed assets that cost $100. Firm B borrows $100 to make the purchase, so both an asset and a liability are recorded on its balance sheet, and its debt ratio is increased to 75 percent. Firm L leases the equipment, so its balance sheet is unchanged. The lease might call for fixed charges as high as or even higher than those on the loan, and the obligations assumed under the lease might be equally or more dangerous from the standpoint of financial safety, but the firm's debt ratio remains at 50 percent.

Exhibit 700.15 *Balance-Sheet Effects of Leasing*

Before Asset Increase				After Asset Increase							
Firms B and L				Firm B—Purchases Asset				Firm L—Leases Asset			
Current assets	$ 50	Debt	$ 50	Current assets	$ 50	Debt	$150	Current assets	$ 50	Debt	$ 50
Fixed assets	50	Equity	50	Fixed assets	150	Equity	50	Fixed assets	50	Equity	50
Total	$100		$100	Total	$200		$200	Total	$100		$100
	Debt ratio = 50%				Debt ratio = 75%				Debt ratio = 50%		

To correct this problem, the Financial Accounting Standards Board (FASB) issued **FASB #13,** which requires that for an unqualified audit report, firms that enter into financial (or capital) leases must restate their balance sheets to report leased assets as fixed assets and the present value of future lease payments as a debt. This process is called *capitalizing the lease,* and its net effect is to cause Firms B and L to have similar balance sheets, both of which will resemble the one shown for Firm B after the asset increase.

The logic behind FASB #13 is as follows: If a firm signs a lease contract, its obligation to make lease payments is just as binding as if it had signed a loan agreement. The failure to make lease payments can bankrupt a firm just as surely as can the failure to make principal and interest payments on a loan. Therefore, for all intents and purposes, a financial lease is identical to a loan. There are, however, certain legal differences between loans and leases. For example, in a bankruptcy liquidation, the lessor is entitled to take possession of the leased asset, and, if the value of the asset is less than the required payments under the lease, the lessor can enter a claim (as a general creditor) for one year's lease payments. In a bankruptcy reorganization, the lessor receives the asset plus three years' lease payments if needed to bring the value of the asset up to the remaining investment in the lease. This being the case, when a firm signs a lease agreement, it has, in effect, raised its "true" debt ratio and thereby changed its "true" capital structure. Accordingly, if the firm previously had established a target capital structure, and if there is no reason to think that the optimal capital structure has changed, then using lease financing requires additional equity backing in exactly the same manner as does the use of debt financing.

If a disclosure of the lease in the Exhibit 700.15 example were not made, then investors could be deceived into thinking that Firm L's financial position is stronger than it actually is. Even if the lease were disclosed in a footnote, investors might not fully recognize its impact and might not see that Firms B and L essentially are in the same financial position. If this were the case, Firm L would have increased its true amount of debt through a lease arrangement, but its required return on debt, k_d, its required return on equity, k_s, and consequently its weighted average cost of capital would have increased less than those of Firm B, which borrowed directly. Thus, investors would be willing to accept a lower return from Firm L because they would view it as being in a stronger financial position than Firm B. These benefits of leasing would accrue to stockholders at the expense of new investors, who were, in effect, being deceived by the fact that the firm's balance sheet did not fully reflect its true liability situation. This is why FASB #13 was issued.

A lease will be classified as a capital lease, and hence be capitalized and shown directly on the balance sheet, if any one of the following conditions exists:

1. Under the terms of the lease, ownership of the property effectively is transferred from the lessor to the lessee.
2. The lessee can purchase the property or renew the lease at less than a fair market price when the lease expires.
3. The lease runs for a period equal to or greater than 75 percent of the asset's life. Thus, if an asset has a 10-year life and if the lease is written for more than 7.5 years, the lease must be capitalized.
4. The present value of the lease payments is equal to or greater than 90 percent of the initial value of the asset.

These rules, together with strong footnote disclosures for operating leases, are sufficient to ensure that no one will be fooled by lease financing. Thus, leases are recognized to be essentially the same as debt, and they have the same effects as debt on the firm's required rate of return. Therefore, leasing generally will not permit a firm to use more financial leverage than could be obtained with conventional debt.

Options

An **option** is a contract that gives its holder the right to buy (or sell) an asset at some predetermined price within a specified period of time. "Pure options" are instruments that are created by outsiders (generally investment banking firms) rather than by the firm itself; they are bought and sold primarily by investors (or speculators). However, financial managers should understand the nature of options because this will help them structure warrant and convertible financings, both of which have similar characteristics.

Option Types and Markets

There are many types of options and option markets. To understand how options work, suppose you owned 100 shares of IBM stock that, on September 1, 1999, sold for $127.25 per share. You could sell to someone else the right to buy your 100 shares at any time during the next five months at a price of, say, $140 per share. The $140 is called the **striking,** or **exercise, price.** Such options exist, and they are traded on a number of exchanges, with the Chicago Board Options

Exchange (CBOE) being the oldest and largest. This type of option is known as a **call option** because the option holder can "call" in 100 shares of stock for purchase any time during the option period. The seller of a call option is known as an option writer. An investor who writes a call option against stock held in his or her portfolio is said to be selling *covered options;* options sold without the stock to back them up are called *naked options.*

On September 1, 1999, IBM's five-month, $140 call options sold on the CBOE for $7.50 each. Thus, for ($7.50)(100) = $750, you could buy an option contract that would give you the right to purchase 100 shares of IBM at a price of $140 per share at any time during the following five months. If the stock stayed below $140 during that period, you would lose your $750, but if the stock's price rose to $150, your $750 investment would be worth ($150 − $140)(100) = $1,000. That translates into a very healthy rate of return on your $750 investment. Incidentally, if the stock price did go up, you probably would not actually exercise your options to buy the stock; rather, you would sell the options to another option buyer, at a price greater than or equal to $10 per option—you originally paid only $7.50.

You also can buy an option that gives you the right to sell a stock at a specified price during some period in the future—this is called a **put option.** For example, suppose you expect IBM's stock price to decline from its current level sometime during the next five months. For $687.50 = $6.875 × 100 you could buy a five-month put option giving you the right to sell 100 shares (which you would not necessarily own) at a price of $120 per share ($120 is the put option striking price). If you bought a 100-share put contract for $687.50 and IBM's stock price actually fell to $110, you would make ($120 − $110)(100) = $1,000 minus the $687.50 you paid for the put option, for a net profit (before taxes and commissions) of $312.50.

Options trading is one of the hottest financial activities in the United States today. The leverage involved makes it possible for speculators with just a few dollars to make a fortune almost overnight. Also, investors with sizable portfolios can sell options against their stocks and earn the value of the options (minus brokerage commissions) even if the stocks' prices remain constant. Still, those who have profited most from the development of options trading are security firms, which earn very healthy commissions on such trades.

The corporations on whose stocks options are written, such as IBM, have nothing to do with the options market. They neither raise money in that market nor have any direct transactions in it, and option holders neither receive dividends nor vote for corporate directors (unless they exercise their options to purchase the stock, which few actually do). There have been studies by the Securities and Exchange Commission (SEC) and others as to whether options trading stabilizes or destabilizes the stock market and whether it helps or hinders corporations seeking to raise new capital. The studies have not been conclusive, but options trading is here to stay, and many regard it as the most exciting game in town.

Option Values

The value of an option is closely related to the value of the *underlying* stock, which is the stock on which the option is written, and the striking price. For example, an investor who purchases call options hopes that the value of the underlying stock goes above the striking price during the option period, because then the option could be exercised at a gross profit equal to the market value of the stock less the striking price. In this case, the investor is said to have an **in-the-money option** because he or she can exercise the call option by purchasing the stock at the striking price and then can immediately sell the stock for its market value, which is greater than the striking price. For example, if IBM's stock sells for $150 at the beginning of 2000, call options with a striking price of $140 would be in the money because the option holder could exercise the options by paying the option seller $14,000 for 100 shares of IBM stock, and then the stock could be sold on the NYSE for $15,000—the financial benefit of exercising to the option holder would be $1,000 before commissions and taxes. If the market value of IBM's stock is $130, or any other amount below the striking price, the call is said to be an **out-of-the-money option** because it would not be favorable for the option holder to exercise the call—if the investor were to exercise the call option, there would be a financial loss because the stock would be purchased at a value (the $140 striking price) greater than it could be sold (the $130 market value). The opposite relationship holds for put options because the striking price represents the price at which an investor can *sell* the stock to the put option writer (seller). To be able to sell to the put option writer, the investor first must *buy* the stock in the market (for example, on the NYSE). Thus, for a put option to be in-the-money, the striking price must be above the market value of the underlying stock.

As you can see, both the value of the underlying stock and the striking price of the option are very important in determining whether an option is in-the-money or out-of-the-money. If an option is out-of-the-money on its expiration date, it is worthless. Therefore, the stock price and the striking price are important for determining the market value of an option. In fact, options are called *derivative securities* because their values are dependent on, or derived from, the value of the underlying asset and the striking price.

In addition to the stock price and the striking price, the value of an option also depends on (1) the option's time to maturity and (2) the variability of the underlying stock's price, as explained here.

1. The longer an option has to run, the greater its value. If a call option expires at 4 P.M. today, there is not much chance that the stock price will go way up. Therefore, the option will sell at close to the difference between the stock price and the striking price (P_s − striking price), or zero if this difference is negative. On the other hand, if it has a year to go, the stock price could rise sharply, pulling the option's value up with it.

2. An option on an extremely volatile stock will be worth more than one on a very stable stock. We know that an option on a stock whose price rarely moves will not offer much chance for a large gain. On the other hand, an option on a stock that is highly volatile could provide a large gain, so such an option will be valuable. Note also that because losses on options are limited, large declines in a stock's price do not have a corresponding bad effect on call option holders. Therefore, stock price volatility can only enhance the value of an option.

If everything else were held constant, then the longer an option's life, the higher its market price would be, no matter the type of option. Also, the more volatile the price of the underlying stock, the higher the option's market price, regardless of the option type.

Suppose that for $2 you could buy a call option on a stock now selling for $20. The striking price is also $20. Now suppose the stock is highly volatile, and you think it has a 50 percent probability of selling for either $10 or $30 when the option expires in one month. What is the expected value of the option? If the stock sells for $30, the option will be worth $30 − $20 = $10. Because there is a 50–50 chance that the stock will be worth $10 or $30, the expected value of the option is $5.

$$\text{Expected value of option} = 0.5(0) + 0.5(\$10) = \$5$$

To be exactly correct, we would have to discount the $5 back for one month.

Now suppose the stock was more volatile, with a 50–50 chance of being worth zero or $20. Here the option would be worth

$$\text{Expected value of option} = 0.5(0) + 0.5(\$20) = \$10$$

This demonstrates that the greater the volatility of the stock, the greater the value of the option. The reason this result occurs is because the large loss on the stock ($20) had no more of an adverse effect on the option holder than the small loss ($10). Thus, option holders benefit greatly if a stock goes way up, but they do not lose too badly if it drops all the way to zero. These concepts have been used to develop formulas for pricing options, with the most widely used formula being the Black-Scholes model.

Warrants

A **warrant** is an option *issued by a company* that gives the holder the right to buy a stated number of shares of the company's stock at a specified price. Generally, warrants are distributed along with debt, and they are used to induce investors to buy a firm's long-term debt at a lower interest rate than otherwise would be required. For example, when **Pac-Atlantic Air (PAA)** wanted to sell $100 million of 20-year bonds in 1998, the company's investment bankers informed the financial vice president that straight bonds would be difficult to sell and that an interest rate of 11 percent would be required. However, the investment bankers suggested as an alternative that investors would be willing to buy bonds with an annual coupon rate as low as 8 percent if the company would offer 30 warrants with each $1,000 bond, each warrant entitling the holder to buy one share of common stock at a price of $12 per share. The stock was selling for $10 per share at the time, and the warrants would expire in 2005 if they had not been exercised previously.

Why would investors be willing to buy Pac-Atlantic's bonds at a yield of only 8 percent in an 11 percent market just because warrants were offered as part of the package? The answer is that warrants are long-term options, and they have a value for the reasons set forth in the previous section. In the PAA case, this value offset the low interest rate on the bonds and made the entire package of low interest bonds plus warrants attractive to investors.

Use of Warrants in Financing

Warrants generally are used by small, rapidly growing firms as "sweeteners" to help sell either debt or preferred stock. Such firms frequently are regarded as being very risky, and their bonds can be sold only if the firms are willing to pay extremely high rates of interest and to accept very restrictive indenture provisions. To avoid this, firms such as Pac-Atlantic often offer warrants along with their bonds. However, some strong firms also have used warrants. In one of the largest financings of any type ever undertaken by a business firm at the time, **AT&T** raised $1.57 billion by selling bonds with warrants. This marked the first use ever of warrants by a large, strong corporation.

Getting warrants along with bonds enables investors to share in a company's growth if that firm does in fact grow and prosper; therefore, investors are willing to accept a lower bond interest rate and less restrictive indenture provisions. A bond with warrants has some characteristics of debt and some of equity. It is a hybrid security that provides the financial manager with an opportunity to expand the firm's mix of securities and to appeal to a broader group of investors, thus lowering the firm's cost of capital. Virtually all warrants today are **detachable warrants,** meaning that after a bond with attached warrants has been sold, the warrants can be detached and traded separately from the bond. Further, when these warrants are exercised, the bonds themselves (with their low coupon rate) will remain outstanding. Thus, the warrants will bring in additional equity capital while leaving low interest rate debt on the issuer's books.

The warrants' exercise price generally is set at from 10 percent to 30 percent above the market price of the stock on the date the bond is issued. For example, if the stock sells for $10, the exercise price will probably be set in the $11 to $13 range. If the firm does grow and prosper, and if its stock price rises above the exercise price at which shares can be purchased, warrant holders will turn in their warrants, along with cash equal to the stated exercise price, in exchange for stock. Without some incentive, however, many warrants would never be exercised until just before expiration. Their value in the market would be greater than their exercise value; thus holders would sell warrants rather than exercise them.

There are three conditions that encourage holders to exercise their warrants.

1. Warrant holders surely will exercise warrants and buy stock if the warrants are about to expire with the market price of the stock above the exercise price. This means that if a firm wants its warrants exercised soon in order to raise capital, it should set a relatively short expiration date.
2. Warrant holders will tend to exercise voluntarily and buy stock if the company raises the dividend on the common stock by a sufficient amount. Because no dividend is paid on the warrant, it provides no current income. However, if the common stock pays a high dividend, it provides an attractive dividend yield. Therefore, the higher the stock's dividend, the greater the opportunity cost of holding the warrant rather than exercising it. Thus, if a firm wants its warrants exercised, it can raise the common stock's dividend.
3. Warrants sometimes have **stepped-up exercise prices,** which prod owners into exercising them. For example, the Mills Agricorp has warrants outstanding with an exercise price of $25 until December 31, 2002, at which time the exercise price will rise to $30. If the price of the common stock is over $25 just before December 31, 2002, many warrant holders will exercise their options before the stepped-up price takes effect.

Another useful feature of warrants is that they generally bring in funds only if such funds are needed. If the company grows, it probably will need new equity capital. At the same time, this growth will cause the price of the stock to rise and the warrants to be exercised, thereby allowing the firm to obtain additional cash. If the company is not successful and cannot profitably employ additional money, the price of its stock probably will not rise sufficiently to induce exercise of the options.

Convertibles

Convertible securities are bonds or preferred stocks that can be exchanged for common stock at the option of the holder. Unlike the exercise of warrants, which provides the firm with additional funds, conversion does not bring in additional capital—debt or preferred stock simply is replaced by common stock. Of course, this reduction of debt or preferred stock will strengthen the firm's balance sheet and make it easier to raise additional capital, but this is a separate action.

Conversion Ratio and Conversion Price

One of the most important provisions of a convertible security is the **conversion ratio, CR,** defined as the number of shares of stock the convertible holder receives upon conversion. Related to the conversion ratio is the conversion price, P_c, which is the effective price paid for the common stock obtained by converting a convertible security. The relationship between the conversion ratio and the conversion price can be illustrated by the convertible debentures issued at par value by Bee TV Inc. in 2000. At any time prior to maturity on July 1, 2020, a debenture holder can exchange a bond for 20 shares of common stock; therefore, CR = 20. The bond has a par value of $1,000, so the holder would be relinquishing this amount upon conversion. Dividing the $1,000 par value by the 20 shares received gives a conversion price of P_c = $50 a share:

$$\text{Conversion price} = \frac{\text{Par value of bond}}{\text{Conversion ratio}} \qquad (7.9)$$

$$= \frac{\$1,000}{20} = \$50$$

Like a warrant's exercise price, the conversion price usually is set at from 10 percent to 30 percent above the prevailing market price of the common stock at the time the convertible issue is sold. Generally, the conversion price and ratio are fixed for the life of the bond, although sometimes a stepped-up conversion price is used.

Another factor that might cause a change in the conversion price and ratio is a standard feature of almost all convertibles—the clause protecting the convertible against dilution from stock splits, stock dividends, and the sale of common stock at prices below the conversion price. The typical provision states that if common stock is sold at a price below the conversion price, the conversion price must be lowered (and the conversion ratio raised) to the price at which the new stock was issued. Also, if the stock is split (or if a stock dividend is declared), the conversion price must be lowered by the percentage of the stock split (or stock dividend). If this protection were not contained in the contract, a company could completely thwart conversion by the use of stock splits. Warrants are similarly protected against such dilution.

Use of Convertibles in Financing

Convertibles offer three important advantages from the *issuer's* standpoint. First, convertibles, like bonds with warrants, permit a company to sell debt with a lower interest rate and with less restrictive covenants than straight bonds. Second, convertibles generally are subordinated to mortgage bonds, bank loans, and other senior debt, so financing with convertibles leaves the company's access to "regular" debt unimpaired. Third, convertibles provide a way of selling common stock at prices higher than those currently prevailing. Many companies actually want to sell common stock and not debt, but they believe that the price of their stock is temporarily depressed. The financial manager might know, for example, that earnings are depressed because of start-up costs associated with a new project, but he or she might expect earnings to rise sharply during the next year or so, pulling the price of the stock along. In this case, if the company sold stock now it would be giving up too many shares to raise a given amount of money. However, if it sets the conversion price at 20 percent to 30 percent above the present market price of the stock, then 20 percent to 30 percent fewer shares will have to be given up when the bonds are converted. Notice, however, that management is counting on the stock's price rising sufficiently above the conversion price to make the bonds attractive in conversion. If earnings do not rise and pull the stock price up, and hence if conversion does not occur, the company could be saddled with debt in the face of low earnings, which could be disastrous.

How can the company be sure that conversion will occur if the price of the stock rises above the conversion price? Typically, convertibles contain a call provision that enables the issuing firm to force bondholders to convert. Suppose the conversion price is $50, the conversion ratio is 20, the market price of the common stock has risen to $60, and the call price on the convertible bond is $1,050. If the company calls the bond, bondholders could either convert into common stock with a market value of $1,200 or allow the company to redeem the bond for $1,050. Naturally, bondholders prefer $1,200 to $1,050, so conversion will occur. The call provision therefore gives the company a means of *forcing* conversion, but only if the market price of the stock is greater than the conversion price.

Convertibles are useful, but they do have three important disadvantages.

1. The use of a convertible security might, in effect, give the issuer the opportunity to sell common stock at a price higher than it could sell stock otherwise. However, if the common stock increases greatly in price, the company probably would have been better off if it had used straight debt in spite of its higher interest rate and then later sold common stock to refund the debt.

2. If the company truly wants to raise equity capital, and if the price of the stock does not rise sufficiently after the bond is issued, then the firm will be stuck with debt.

3. Convertibles typically have a low coupon interest rate, an advantage that will be lost when conversion occurs. Warrant financings, on the other hand, permit the company to continue to use the low-coupon debt for a longer period.

Reporting Earnings When Warrants or Convertibles Are Outstanding

If warrants or convertibles are outstanding, a firm theoretically can report earnings per share (EPS) in one of three ways.

1. **Simple EPS.** The earnings available to common stockholders are divided by the average number of shares *actually* outstanding during the period.
2. **Primary EPS.** The earnings available are divided by the average number of shares that would have been outstanding if warrants and convertibles *likely to be converted* in the near future had actually been exercised or converted.
3. **Fully diluted EPS.** This is similar to primary EPS except that all warrants and convertibles are *assumed to be exercised or converted,* regardless of the likelihood of either occurring.

Simple EPS is virtually never reported by firms that have warrants or convertibles likely to be exercised or converted; the SEC prohibits use of this figure, and it requires that primary and fully diluted earnings be shown on the income statement.

Valuation of Financial Assets—Bonds

Corporations raise capital in two forms—debt and equity. We will examine the valuation process for bonds (the principal type of long-term debt), and for stock (equity) and tangible assets.

A **bond** is a long-term promissory note issued by a business or governmental unit. For example, suppose on January 3, 2000, Unilate Textiles borrowed $25 million by selling 25,000 individual bonds for $1,000 each. Unilate received the $25 million, and it promised to pay the bondholders annual interest and to repay the $25 million on a specified date. The lenders were willing to give Unilate $25 million, so the value of the bond issue was $25 million. But how did the investors decide that the issue was worth $25 million? As a first step in explaining how the values of this and other bonds are determined, we need to define some terms.

1. **Principal amount, face value, maturity value, and par value.** The **principal amount** of debt generally represents the amount of money the firm borrows and promises to repay at some future date. For much debt issued by corporations, including bonds, the principal amount is repaid at maturity, so we often refer to the principal value as the **maturity value.** In addition, the principal value generally is written on the "face" of the debt instrument, or certificate, so it is also called the **face value.** Further, when the market value of debt is the same as its face value, it is said to be selling at *par*; thus the principal amount is also referred to as the **par value.** For most debt, then, *the terms principal amount, face value, maturity value, and par value refer to the same value—the amount that must be repaid by the borrower.* We use the terms interchangeably throughout the book. The face value of a corporate bond is usually set at $1,000, although multiples of $1,000 (for example, $5,000) are also used.
2. **Coupon interest rate.** The bond requires the issuer to pay a specified number of dollars of interest each year (or, more typically, each six months). When this **coupon payment,** as it is called, is divided by the par value, the result is the **coupon interest rate.** For example, Unilate's bonds have a $1,000 par value, and they pay $150 in interest each year. The bond's coupon interest is $150, so its coupon interest rate is $150/$1,000 = 15%. The $150 is the yearly "rent" on the $1,000 loan. This payment, which is fixed at the time the bond is issued, remains in force, by contract, during the life of the bond.
3. **Maturity date.** Bonds generally have a specified **maturity date** on which the par value must be repaid. Unilate's bonds, which were issued on January 3, 2000, will mature on January 2, 2015; thus, they had a 15-year maturity at the time they were issued. Most bonds have **original maturities** (the maturity at the time the bond is issued) of from 10 to 40 years, but any maturity is legally permissible. Of course, the effective maturity of a bond declines each year after it has been issued. Thus, Unilate's bonds had a 15-year original maturity, but in 2001 they had a 14-year maturity, and so on.
4. **Call provisions.** Often, bonds have a provision whereby the issuer can pay them off prior to maturity by "calling them in" from the investors. This feature is known as a **call provision.** If a bond is callable, and if interest rates in the economy decline, then the company can sell a new issue of low-interest-rate bonds and use the proceeds to retire the old, high-interest-rate issue, just as a homeowner can refinance a home mortgage.

5. **New issues versus outstanding bonds.** As we shall see, a bond's market price is determined primarily by the cash flows it generates, or the dollar interest it pays, which depends on the coupon interest rate—the higher the coupon, other things held constant, the higher the market price of the bond. At the time a bond is issued, the coupon generally is set at a level that will cause the market price of the bond to equal its par value. If a lower coupon were set, investors simply would not be willing to pay $1,000 for the bond, while if a higher coupon were set, investors would clamor for the bond and bid its price up over $1,000. Investment bankers can judge quite precisely the coupon rate that will cause a bond to sell at its $1,000 par value.

A bond that has just been issued is known as a *new issue*. (*The Wall Street Journal* classifies a bond as a new issue for about one month after it has first been issued.) Once the bond has been on the market for a while, it is classified as an *outstanding bond*, also called a *seasoned issue*. Newly issued bonds generally sell very close to par, but the prices of outstanding bonds can vary widely from par. Coupon interest payments are constant, so when economic conditions change, a bond with a $150 coupon that sold at par when it was issued can sell for more or less than $1,000 thereafter.

The Basic Bond Valuation Model

The value of any asset can be expressed in general form as follows:

$$\text{Asset value} = V = \frac{\hat{CF}_1}{(1+k)^1} + \frac{\hat{CF}_2}{(1+k)^2} + \cdots + \frac{\hat{CF}_n}{(1+k)^n} \tag{7.10}$$

Here

$\hat{CF}_t$ = The cash flow expected to be generated by the asset in period t.

k = The return investors consider appropriate for holding such an asset. This return is usually termed the *required return*, and it is based on both economic conditions and the riskiness of the asset.

According to Equation 7.10, the value of an asset is affected by the cash flows it is expected to generate, $\hat{CF}$ and the return required by investors, k. As you can see, *the higher the expected cash flows, the greater the asset's value; also, the lower the required return, the greater the asset's value.* In the remainder of this section, we discuss how this general valuation concept can be applied to determine the value of various types of assets. First, we examine the valuation process for financial assets, and then we apply the process to value real assets.

Equation 7.10 shows that the value of a financial asset is based on the cash flows expected to be generated by the asset in the future. In the case of a bond, the cash flows consist of interest payments during the life of the bond plus a return of the principal amount borrowed when the bond matures. In a cash flow timeline format, here is the situation.

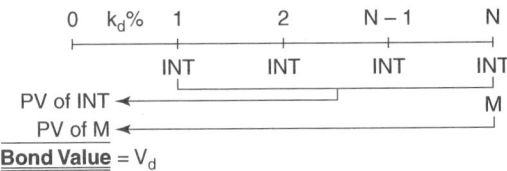

Here

k_d = The average rate of return investors require to invest in the bond. So, for the Unilate Textiles bond issue k_d = 15%.

N = The number of years before the bond matures. For the Unilate bonds, N = 15. Note that N declines each year after the bond has been issued, so a bond that had a maturity of 15 years when it was issued (original maturity = 15) will have N = 14 after one year, N = 13 after two years, and so on. Note also that at this point we assume that the bond pays interest once a year, or annually, so N is measured in years.

INT = Dollars of interest paid each period = Coupon rate × Par value. In our example, INT = 0.15 × $1,000 = $150.

M = The par, or face, value of the bond = $1,000. This amount must be paid off at maturity. In calculator terminology, FV = M = 1000.

- We can now redraw the cash flow timeline to show the numerical values for all variables except the bond's value.

```
0    15%   1          2         14        15
|_____|_____|____..____|_____|
Value      150        150        150       150
                                          1,000
                                          ─────
                                          1,150
```

Now the following general equation can be solved to find the value of any bond.

$$\text{Bond value} = V_d = \frac{\text{INT}}{(1+k_d)^1} + \frac{\text{INT}}{(1+k_d)^2} + \cdots + \frac{\text{INT}}{(1+k_d)^N} + \frac{M}{(1+k_d)^N} \quad (7.11)$$

$$= \sum_{t=1}^{n} \frac{\text{INT}}{(1+k_d)^t} + \frac{M}{(a+k_d)^N}$$

Notice the interest payments represent an annuity, and repayment of the par value at maturity represents a single, or lump-sum, payment. Thus, Equation 7.11 can be rewritten for use with the tables.

$$V_d = \text{INT}(\text{PVIFA}_{k_d,N}) + M(\text{PVIF}_{k_d,N}) \quad (7.11a)$$

Inserting values for our particular bond, we have

$$V_d = \sum_{t=1}^{15} \frac{\$150}{(1.15)^t} + \frac{\$1,000}{(1.15)}$$

$$= \$150(\hat{P}\text{VIFA}_{15\%,15}) + \$1,000(\text{PVIF}_{15\%,15})$$

The value of the bond can be computed by using three procedures: (1) numerically, (2) using the tables, and (3) with a financial calculator. We will show the first two procedures.

1. NUMERICAL SOLUTION Simply discount each cash flow back to the present and sum these PVs to find the value of the bond. This procedure is not efficient. Alternatively, we can use the following equation to find the solution.

$$V_d = \text{PV of the interest payment (an annuity)} + \text{PV of the face value (a lump-sum amount)}$$

$$= \$150 \left[\frac{1 - \frac{1}{(1.15)^{15}}}{0.15} \right] + \$1,000 \left[\frac{1}{(1.15)^{15}} \right]$$

$$= \$150(5.84737) \quad + \quad \$1,000(0.12289)$$
$$= \$877.11 \quad\quad\quad + \quad \$122.89$$
$$= \$1,000$$

2. TABULAR SOLUTION Simply look up the appropriate PVIF and PVIFA values in Tables A.1 and A.2 of Module 700 Appendix, insert them into the equation, and complete the arithmetic.

$$V_d = \$150(5.8474) \quad + \quad \$1,000(0.1229)$$
$$= \$877.11 \quad\quad\quad + \quad \$122.90$$
$$= \$1000.01 \approx \$1,000 \text{ (rounding error)}$$

Finding the Interest Rate on a Bond: Yield to Maturity

Suppose you were offered a 14-year, 15 percent coupon, $1,000 par value bond at a price of $1,368.31. What rate of interest would you earn on your investment if you bought the bond and held it to maturity? This rate is called the bond's

yield to maturity (YTM), and it is the interest rate discussed by bond traders when they talk about rates of return. To find the yield to maturity, you could solve Equation 7.11 or 7.11a for k_d:

$$V_d = \$1{,}368.31 = \frac{\$150}{(1+k_d)^1} + \cdots + \frac{\$150}{(1+k_d)^{14}} + \frac{\$1{,}000}{(1+k_d)^{14}}$$

$$= \$150(\text{PVIFA}_{k_d,14}) + \$1{,}000(\text{PVIF}_{k_d,14})$$

If you have a financial calculator, you would simply enter N = 14, PMT = 150, FV = 1000, and PV = −1368.31, and then press the I key. The calculator will blink (or perhaps go blank) for a few seconds, and then the answer, 10 percent, will appear.

If you do not have a financial calculator, you can substitute values for PVIFA and PVIF at different interest rates until you find a pair that "works" so that the present value of the interest payments combined with the present value of the repayment of the face value at maturity equals the current price of the bond. But what would be a good interest rate to use as a starting point? First, you know that the bond is selling at a premium over its par value ($1,368.31 versus $1,000), so the bond's yield to maturity must be below its 15 percent coupon rate. Therefore, you might start by trying rates below 15 percent. It could take you a while to "zero in" on the appropriate rate. It probably would be better to get an estimate of the rate by computing the *approximate* yield to maturity, which can be found with the following equation.

$$\text{Approximate yield to maturity} = \frac{\text{Annual interest} + \text{Accrued capital gains}}{\text{Average value of bond}} \quad (7.12)$$

$$= \frac{\text{INT} + \left(\dfrac{M - V_d}{N}\right)}{\left[\dfrac{2(V_d) + M}{3}\right]}$$

Equation 7.12 is based on computations of approximate yields in the past and it does not consider the time value of money, so it should be used only to approximate a bond's yield to maturity. For the bond we are examining, the approximate yield to maturity is

$$\text{Yield to maturity} = k_d \approx \frac{\$150 + \left(\dfrac{\$1{,}000 - \$1{,}368.31}{14}\right)}{\left[\dfrac{2(\$1{,}368.31) + \$1{,}000}{3}\right]}$$

$$= \frac{\$150 + (-\$26.31)}{\$1{,}245.54} = 0.0993 \approx 10\%$$

Inserting interest factors for 10 percent, you obtain a value equal to

$$V_d = \$150(7.3667) + \$1{,}000(0.2633)$$
$$= \$1{,}105.01 + \$263.30$$
$$= \$1{,}368.31$$

This calculated value is equal to the market price of the bond, so 10 percent is the bond's actual yield to maturity: k_d = YTM = 10.0 percent.

The yield to maturity (YTM) is identical to the total annual rate of return discussed in the preceding section. The YTM for a bond that sells at par consists entirely of an interest yield, but if the bond sells at a price other than its par value, the YTM consists of the interest yield plus a positive or negative capital gains yield. Note also that a bond's yield to maturity changes whenever interest rates in the economy change, and this is almost daily. One who purchases a bond and holds it until it matures will receive the YTM that existed on the purchase date, but the bond's calculated YTM will change frequently between the purchase date and the maturity date.

Valuation of Financial Assets—Equity (Stock)

Each corporation issues at least one type of stock, or equity, called *common stock*. Some corporations issue more than one type of common stock, and some issue *preferred stock* in addition to common stock. As the names imply, most equity is in the form of common stock, and preferred shareholders have preference over common shareholders when a firm distributes funds to stockholders. Dividends, as well as liquidation proceeds resulting from bankruptcy, are paid to preferred stockholders before common stockholders. But preferred stockholders generally are paid the same dividend each year, while the dividends paid to common stockholders can vary and are often dependent on current and previous earnings levels and the future growth plans of the firm. For the purposes of our discussion in this section, you need to be aware that the cash flows generated by investing in preferred stock are normally constant, while the cash flows generated by common stock can be constant, but often vary from year to year.

In this section, we examine the process to value stock, both preferred and common. We begin by introducing a general stock valuation model. Then, we apply the model to three scenarios: (1) when there is no growth in dividends so the amount paid each year remains constant (like preferred dividends), (2) when dividends increase at a constant rate each year, and (3) when dividends grow at different rates (nonconstant growth).

Definitions of Terms Used in the Stock Valuation Models

Stocks provide an expected future cash flow stream, and a stock's value is found in the same manner as the values of other assets—namely, as the present value of the expected future cash flow stream. The expected cash flows consist of two elements: (1) the dividends expected in each year and (2) the price investors expect to receive when they sell the stock, which includes the return of the original investment plus a capital gain or loss.

Before we present the general stock valuation model, we define some terms and notations we will use throughout this section.

$\hat{D}_t$ = Dividend the stockholder expects to receive at the end of Year t (pronounced "D hat t"). D_0 is the most recent dividend, which has already been paid; $\hat{D}_1$ is the next dividend expected to be paid, and it will be paid at the end of this year; $\hat{D}_2$ is the dividend expected at the end of two years; and so forth. $\hat{D}_1$ represents the first cash flow a new purchaser of the stock will receive. Note that D_0, the dividend that has just been paid, is known with certainty (thus, there is no "hat" over the D). However, all future dividends are *expected* values, so the estimate of $\hat{D}_t$ might differ among investors for some stocks.

P_0 = Actual **market price** of the stock today.

$\hat{P}_t$ = Expected price of the stock at the end of Year t. $\hat{P}_0$ is the **intrinsic,** or *theoretical,* **value** of the stock today as seen by the particular investor doing the analysis; $\hat{P}_1$ is the price *expected* at the end of one year; and so on. Note that $\hat{P}_0$ is the intrinsic value of the stock today based on a particular investor's estimate of the stock's expected dividend stream and the riskiness of that stream. Hence, whereas P_0 is fixed and is identical for all investors because it represents the price at which the stock currently can be purchased in the stock market, $\hat{P}_0$ could differ among investors depending on what they feel the firm actually is worth. The caret, or "hat", is used to indicate that $\hat{P}_t$ is an estimated value. $\hat{P}_0$, the individual investor's estimate of the intrinsic value today, could be above or below P_0, the current stock price, but an investor would buy the stock only if his or her estimate of $\hat{P}_0$ were equal to or greater than P_0.

Because there are many investors in the market, there can be many values for $\hat{P}_0$. However, we can think of a group of "average," or "marginal," investors whose actions actually determine the market price. For these marginal investors, P_0 must equal $\hat{P}_0$; otherwise, a disequilibrium would exist, and buying and selling in the market would change P_0 until $P_0 = \hat{P}_0$.

g = Expected **growth rate** in dividends as predicted by a marginal, or average, investor. (If we assume that dividends are expected to grow at a constant rate, g is also equal to the expected rate of growth in the stock's price.) Different investors might use different g's to evaluate a firm's stock, but the market price, P_0, is set on the basis of the g estimated by marginal investors.

k_s = Minimum acceptable, or **required, rate of return** on the stock, considering both its riskiness and the returns available on other investments. Again, this term generally relates to average investors.

$\dfrac{\hat{D}_1}{P_0}$ = Expected dividend yield on the stock during the coming year. If the stock is expected to pay a dividend of $1 during the next 12 months, and if its current price is $10, then the expected dividend yield is $1/$10 = 0.10 = 10%.

$\dfrac{\hat{P}_1 - P_0}{P_0}$ = Expected **capital gains yield** on the stock during the coming year. If the stock sells for $10 today, and if it is expected to rise to $10.50 at the end of one year, then the expected capital gain is $\hat{P}_1 - P_0$ = $10.50 − $10.00 = $0.50, and the expected capital gains yield is $0.50/$10 = 0.05 = 5%.

$\hat{k}_s$ = **Expected rate of return** that an investor who buys the stock anticipates, or expects to receive. $\hat{k}_s$ could be above or below k_s, but one would buy the stock only if $\hat{k}_s$ was equal to or greater than k_s. $\hat{k}_s$ = expected dividend yield plus expected capital gains yield; in other words,

$$\hat{k}_s = \frac{\hat{D}_1}{P_0} + \frac{\hat{P}_1 - P_0}{P_0}$$

In our example, the expected total return = $\hat{k}_s$ = 10% + 5% = 15%.

$\bar{k}_s$ = **Actual**, or **realized**, *after the fact* **rate of return** (pronounced "k bar s"). You might expect to obtain a return of $\hat{k}_s$ = 14% if you buy IBM stock today, but if the market goes down, you might end up next year with an actual realized return that is much lower, perhaps even negative (for example, $\bar{k}_s$ = 8%).

Expected Dividends as the Basis for Stock Values

Remember that according to Equation 7.10 the value of any asset is the present value of the cash flows expected to be generated by the asset in the future. In our discussion of bonds, we found that the value of a bond is the present value of the interest payments over the life of the bond plus the present value of the bond's maturity (or par) value. Stock prices are likewise determined as the present value of a stream of cash flows, and the basic stock valuation equation is similar to the bond valuation equation (Equation 7.11). What are the cash flows that corporations provide to their stockholders? First, think of yourself as an investor who buys a stock with the intention of holding it (in your family) forever. In this case, all that you (and your heirs) will receive is a stream of dividends, and the value of the stock today is calculated as the present value of an infinite stream of dividends, which is depicted on a cash flow timeline as follows:

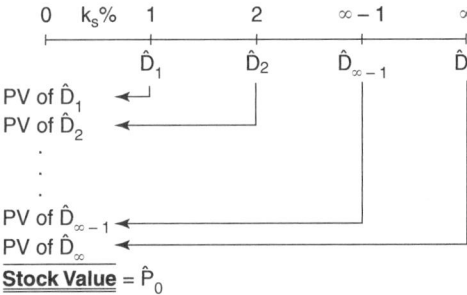

Thus, to compute the value of the stock, we must solve the following equation.

$$\text{Value of stock } V_s = \hat{P}_0 = \text{PV of expected future dividends}$$
$$= \frac{\hat{D}_1}{(1 + k_s)^1} + \frac{\hat{D}_2}{(1 + k_s)^2} + \cdots + \frac{\hat{D}_\infty}{(1 + k_s)^\infty} \qquad (7.13)$$
$$= \sum_{t=1}^{\infty} \frac{\hat{D}_t}{(1 + k_s)^t}$$

What about the more typical case, where you expect to hold the stock for a specific (finite) period and then sell it—what will be the value of $\hat{P}_0$ in this case? Unless the company is likely to be liquidated and thus to disappear, *the value of the stock is still determined by Equation 7.13*. To see this, recognize that for any individual investor, the expected cash flows consist of expected dividends plus the expected sale price of the stock. However, the sale price the current investor receives will depend on the dividends the future investor expects. Therefore, for all present and future investors in total, expected cash flows must be based on all of the expected future dividends. To put it another way, unless a firm is liquidated or sold to another concern, the cash flows it provides to its stockholders will consist only of a stream of dividends; therefore, the value of a share of its stock must be established as the present value of that expected dividend stream that will be paid throughout the life of the company.

The general validity of Equation 7.13 also can be confirmed by asking the following question: Suppose I buy a stock and expect to hold it for one year. I will receive dividends during the year plus the value $\hat{P}_1$ when I sell the stock at the end of the year. But what will determine the value of $\hat{P}_1$? The answer is that it will be determined as the present value of the dividends during Year 2 plus the stock price at the end of that year, which in turn will be determined as the present value of another set of future dividends and an even more distant stock price. This process can be continued forever, and the ultimate result is Equation 7.13.

Equation 7.13 is a generalized stock valuation model in the sense that the time pattern of $\hat{D}_t$ can be anything: $\hat{D}_t$ can be rising, falling, or constant, or it can even be fluctuating randomly, and Equation 7.13 still will hold. Often, however, the projected stream of dividends follows a systematic pattern, in which case we can develop a simplified (that is, easier to apply) version of the stock valuation model expressed in Equation 7.13. In the following sections we consider the scenarios of zero growth, constant growth, and nonconstant growth.

Scenario 1: Valuing Stocks with Zero Growth

Suppose dividends are not expected to grow at all; instead they are expected to stay the same every year. Here we have a **zero-growth stock,** for which the dividends expected in future years are equal to some constant amount—the current dividend. That is, $\hat{D}_1 = \hat{D}_2 = \cdots = \hat{D}_\infty$. Therefore, we can drop the subscripts and the "hats" on D and rewrite Equation 7.13 as follows:

$$\hat{P}_0 = \frac{D}{(1+k_s)^1} + \frac{D}{(1+k_s)^2} + \cdots + \frac{D}{(1+k_s)^\infty} \qquad (7.13a)$$

A security that is expected to pay a constant amount each year forever is called a perpetuity. Therefore, a *zero-growth stock is a perpetuity.*

Remember the value of any perpetuity is simply the payment amount divided by the discount rate, so the value of a zero-growth stock reduces to this formula:

$$\text{Value of zero-growth stock: } \hat{P}_0 = \frac{D}{k_s} \qquad (7.14)$$

For example, if we have a stock that is expected to always pay a dividend equal to $1.20, and the required rate of return associated with such an investment is 12 percent, the stock's value should be

$$\hat{P}_0 = \frac{\$1.20}{0.12} = \$10.00$$

Generally, we can find the price of a stock and the most recent dividend paid to the stockholders by looking in a financial newspaper such as *The Wall Street Journal.* Therefore, if we have a stock with constant dividends, we can solve for the expected rate of return by rearranging Equation 7.14 to produce

$$\hat{k}_s = \frac{D}{P_0} \qquad (7.14a)$$

Because we are dealing with an *expected rate of return,* we put a "hat" on the k value. Thus, if we bought a stock at a price of $10 and expected to receive a constant dividend of $1.20, our expected rate of return would be

$$\hat{k}_s = \frac{\$1.20}{\$10.00} = 0.12 = 12.0\%$$

By now, you probably have recognized that Equation 7.14 can be used to value preferred stock. Recall that preferred stocks entitle their owners to regular, or fixed, dividend payments. And, if the payments last forever, the issue is a *perpetuity* whose value is defined by Equation 7.14. To generalize, we can use Equation 7.14 to value any asset, including common stock, with expected future cash flows that exhibit the properties of a perpetuity—constant cash flows forever.

Scenario 2: Valuing Stocks with Constant Growth

In general, investors expect the earnings and common stock dividends of most companies to increase each year. Even though expected growth rates vary from company to company, it is not uncommon for investors to expect dividend growth to continue in the foreseeable future at about the same rate as that of the nominal gross national product (real GNP plus inflation). On this basis, we might expect the dividend of an average, or "normal," company to grow at a rate of 3 to 6 percent a year. Thus, if a **normal**, or **constant, growth** company's last dividend, which has already been paid, was D_0, its dividend in any future year can be forecasted as $\hat{D}_t = D_0(1 + g)^t$, where g is the constant expected rate of growth and t represents the year of the dividend forecast. For example, if a firm just paid a dividend of $1.20 (that is, $D_0 = \$1.20$), and if investors expect a 5 percent growth rate, then the estimated dividend one year hence would be $\hat{D}_1 = \$1.20(1.05) = \$1.26$; $\hat{D}_2$ would be $1.323; and the estimated dividend five years hence would be:

$$\hat{D}_5 = D_0(1 + g)^5 = \$1.20(1.05)^5 = \$1.532$$

Using this method for estimating future dividends, we can determine the current stock value, $\hat{P}_0$, using Equation 7.13 as set forth previously—in other words, we can find the expected future cash flow stream (the dividends), then calculate the present value of each dividend payment, and finally sum these present values to find the value of the stock. Thus, the intrinsic value of the stock is equal to the present value of its expected future dividends.

If g is constant, however, Equation 7.13 can be rewritten as follows:

$$\hat{P}_0 = \frac{D_0(1+g)^1}{(1+k_s)^1} + \frac{D_0(1+g)^2}{(1+k_s)^2} + \cdots + \frac{D_0(1+g)^\infty}{(1+k_s)^\infty} \quad (7.15)$$

$$= \frac{D_0(1+g)}{k_s - g} = \frac{\hat{D}_1}{k_s - g}$$

Inserting values into the last version of Equation 7.15, we find the value of our illustrative stock is $18.00.

$$\hat{P}_0 = \frac{\$1.20(1.05)}{0.12 - 0.05} = \frac{\$1.26}{0.07} = \$18.00$$

The **constant growth model** as set forth in the last term of Equation 7.15 is often called the Gordon Model, after Myron J. Gordon, who did much to develop and popularize it.

Note that Equation 7.15 is sufficiently general to encompass the zero growth case described earlier. If growth is zero, this is simply a special case of constant growth, and Equation 7.15 becomes Equation 7.14. Note also that a necessary condition for the derivation of the simplified form of Equation 7.15 is that k_s be greater than g. If the equation is used in situations where k_s is not greater than g, the results will be meaningless.

Growth in dividends occurs primarily as a result of growth in *earnings per share (EPS)*. Earnings growth, in turn, results from a number of factors, including (1) inflation, (2) the amount of earnings the company retains and reinvests, and (3) the rate of return the company earns on its equity (ROE). Regarding inflation, if output (in units) is stable and if both sales prices and input costs rise at the inflation rate, then EPS will also grow at the inflation rate. EPS also will grow as a result of the reinvestment, or plowback, of earnings. If the firm's earnings are not all paid out as dividends (that is, if some fraction of earnings is retained), the dollars of investment behind each share will rise over time, which should lead to growth in future earnings and dividends.

Expected Rate of Return on a Constant Growth Stock

We can solve Equation 7.15 for $\hat{k}_s$, again using the hat to denote that we are dealing with an expected rate of return.

$$\begin{array}{c}\text{Expected rate}\\ \text{of return}\end{array} = \begin{array}{c}\text{Expected}\\ \text{dividend yield}\end{array} + \begin{array}{c}\text{Expected growth rate,}\\ \text{or capital gains yield}\end{array} \quad (7.16)$$

$$\hat{k}_s = \frac{\hat{D}_1}{P_0} + g$$

Thus, if you buy a stock for a price $P_0 = \$18$, and if you expect the stock to pay a dividend $\hat{D}_1 = \$1.26$ one year from now and to grow at a constant rate $g = 5\%$ in the future, then your expected rate of return will be 12 percent.

$$\hat{k}_s = \frac{\$1.26}{\$18} + 0.05 = 0.07 + 0.05 = 0.12 = 12.0\%$$

In this form, we see that $\hat{k}_s$ is the *expected total return* and that it consists of an *expected dividend yield*, $\hat{D}_1/P_0 = 7\%$, plus an *expected growth rate or capital gains yield*, $g = 5\%$.

Suppose this analysis had been conducted on January 1, 2000, so $P_0 = \$18$ is the January 1, 2000 stock price and $\hat{D}_1 = \$1.26$ is the dividend expected at the end of 2000 (December 31). What is the expected stock price at the end of 2000 (or the beginning of 2001)? We would again apply Equation 7.15, but this time we would use the expected 2001 dividend, $\hat{D}_{2001} = \hat{D}_2 = \hat{D}_1(1+g) = \$1.26(1.05) = \$1.323$.

$$P_1 = \frac{\hat{D}_2}{k_s - g} = \hat{P}_{1/1/01} = \frac{\hat{D}_{12/31/01}}{k_s - g} = \frac{\$1.323}{0.12 - 0.05} = \$18.90$$

Now notice that $18.90 is 5 percent greater than P_0, the $18 price on January 1, 2000.

$$\hat{P}_{1/1/00} = \$18.00(1.05) = \$18.90$$

Thus, we would expect to make a capital gain of $18.90 − $180.00 = $0.90 during the year, which is a capital gains yield of 5 percent.

$$\text{Capital gains yield} = \frac{\text{Capital gain}}{\text{Beginning price}} = \frac{\text{Ending price} - \text{Beginning price}}{\text{Beginning price}}$$

$$= \frac{\$18.90 - \$18.00}{\$18.00} = \frac{\$0.90}{\$18.00} = 0.05 = 5.0\%$$

We could extend the analysis on out, and in each future year the expected capital gains yield would equal g = 5%, the expected dividend growth rate.

Continuing, the dividend yield in 2001 could be estimated as follows:

$$\text{Dividend yield}_{2001} = \frac{\hat{D}_{12/31/01}}{P_{1/1/01}} = \frac{\$1.323}{\$18.90} = 0.07 = 7.0\%$$

The dividend yield for 2002 could also be calculated, and again it would be 7 percent. Thus, for a constant growth stock, the following conditions must hold.

1. The dividend is expected to grow forever at a constant rate, g.
2. The stock price is expected to grow at this same rate.
3. The expected dividend yield is a constant.
4. The expected capital gains yield is also a constant, and it is equal to g.
5. The expected total rate of return, $\hat{k}_s$, is equal to the expected dividend yield plus the expected growth rate: $\hat{k}_s$ = dividend yield + g.

The term *expected* should be clarified—it means expected in a probabilistic sense, as the statistically expected outcome. Thus, if we say the growth rate is expected to remain constant at 5 percent, we mean that the best prediction for the growth rate in any future year is 5 percent, not that we literally expect the growth rate to be exactly equal to 5 percent in each future year. In this sense, the constant growth assumption is a reasonable one for many large, mature companies.

Scenario 3: Valuing Stocks with Nonconstant Growth

Firms typically go through *life cycles*. During the early part of their lives, their growth is much faster than that of the economy as a whole; then they match the economy's growth; and finally their growth is slower than that of the economy. Automobile manufacturers in the 1920s and computer software firms such as Microsoft in the 1990s are examples of firms in the early part of the cycle. Other firms, such as the those in the tobacco industry or coal industry, are currently in the waning stages of their life cycles, so their growth is not keeping pace with the general economic growth (in some cases growth is negative). Firms whose growths are not about the same as the economy's growth are called **nonconstant growth** firms.

Stock Market Equilibrium

The required return on a stock, k_s, can be found using the Security Market Line (SML) equation as it was developed in our discussion of the Capital Asset Pricing Model (CAPM).

$$k_s = k_{RF} + (k_M - k_{RF})b_s$$

If the risk-free rate of return is 8 percent, if the market risk premium is 4 percent, and if Stock X has a beta of 2, then the marginal investor will require a return of 16 percent on Stock X, calculated as follows:

$$k_x = 8\% + (12\% - 8\%)\,2.0 = 16\%$$

This 16 percent required return is shown as a point on the SML in Exhibit 700.16.

The average investor will want to buy Stock X if the expected rate of return is more than 16 percent, will want to sell it if the expected rate of return is less than 16 percent, and will be indifferent, hence will hold but not buy or sell, if the expected rate of return is exactly 16 percent. Now suppose the investor's portfolio contains Stock X, and he or she analyzes the stock's prospects and concludes that its earnings, dividends, and price can be expected to grow at a constant rate of 5 percent per year. The last dividend was $D_0 = \$2.86$, so the next expected dividend is

$$\hat{D}_1 = \$2.86(1.05) = \$3.00$$

Our average investor observes that the present price of the stock, P_0, is $30. Should he or she purchase more of Stock X, sell the present holdings, or maintain the present position?

The investor can calculate Stock X's *expected rate of return* as follows:

$$\hat{k}_x = \frac{\hat{D}_1}{P_0} + g = \frac{\$3.00}{\$30.00} + 0.05 = 0.15 = 15\%$$

This value is plotted on Exhibit 700.16 as Point X, which is below the SML. Because the expected rate of return is less than the required return, this marginal investor would want to sell the stock, as would other holders. However, few people would want to buy at the $30 price, so the present owners would be unable to find buyers unless they cut the price of the stock. Thus, the price would decline, and this decline would continue until the stock's price reached $27.27, at which point the market for this security would be in **equilibrium**, because the expected rate of return, 16 percent, would be equal to the required rate of return.

$$\hat{k}_x = \frac{\$3.00}{\$27.27} + 0.05 = 0.11 + 0.05 = 0.16 = 16\% = k_x$$

Had the stock initially sold for less than $27.27, say at $25, events would have been reversed. Investors would have wanted to buy the stock because its expected rate of return would have exceeded its required rate of return, and buy orders would have driven the stock's price up to $27.27.

Exhibit 700.16 *Expected and Required Returns on Stock X*

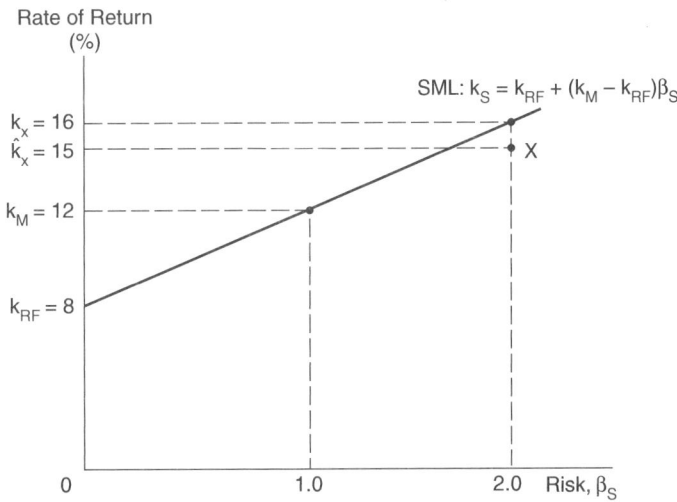

To summarize, in equilibrium these two conditions must hold:

1. The expected rate of return as seen by the marginal investor must equal the required rate of return: $\hat{k}_x = k_x$.
2. The actual market price of the stock must equal its intrinsic value as estimated by the marginal investor: $P_0 = \hat{P}_0$.

Of course, some individual investors might believe that $\hat{k}_x > k_x$ and $P_0 < \hat{P}_0$, and hence they would invest most of their funds in the stock, while other investors might have an opposite view and would sell all of their shares. However, it is the marginal investor who establishes the actual market price, and for this investor, $\hat{k}_x = k_x$ and $P_0 = \hat{P}_0$. If these conditions do not hold, trading will occur until they do hold.

The Efficient Markets Hypothesis

A body of theory called the **Efficient Markets Hypothesis (EMH)** holds (1) that stocks are always in equilibrium and (2) that it is impossible for an investor to *consistently* "beat the market." Because there are hundreds of stock market analysts, the prices of the stock adjusts almost immediately to reflect any new developments.

Financial theorists generally define three forms, or levels, of information efficiency in the market.

1. The *weak form* of the EMH states that all information contained in past price movements is fully reflected in current market prices. Therefore, information about recent, or past, trends in stock prices is of no use in selecting stocks—the fact that a stock has risen for the past three days, for example, gives us no useful clues as to what it will do today or tomorrow. People who believe that weak-form efficiency exists also believe that "tape watchers" and "chartists" are wasting their time.

2. The *semistrong form* of the EMH states that current market prices reflect all *publicly available* information. If this is true, no abnormal returns can be earned by analyzing stocks. Thus, if semistrong-form efficiency exists, it does no good to pore over annual reports or other published data because market prices will have adjusted to any good or bad news contained in such reports as soon as they came out. However, insiders (say, the presidents of companies), even under semistrong-form efficiency, can still make abnormal returns on their own companies' stocks.

3. The *strong form* of the EMH states that current market prices reflect all pertinent information, whether publicly available or privately held. If this form holds, even insiders would find it impossible to earn abnormal returns in the stock market.

Many empirical studies have been conducted to test for the three forms of market efficiency. Most of these studies suggest that the stock market is indeed highly efficient in the weak form and reasonably efficient in the semistrong form, at least for the larger and more widely followed stocks. However, the strong-form EMH does not hold, so abnormal profits can be made by those who possess inside information.

What bearing does the EMH have on financial decisions? Because stock prices do seem to reflect public information, most stocks appear to be fairly valued. This does not mean that new developments could not cause a stock's price to soar or to plummet, but it does mean that stocks, in general, are fairly priced, and the prices probably are in equilibrium—it is safe to assume $\hat{k} = k$ and $P = \hat{P}$. However, there are certainly cases in which corporate insiders have information not known to outsiders.

Valuation of Real (Tangible) Assets

In the previous sections, we found that the values of financial assets, bonds, and stocks, are based on the present value of the future cash flows expected from the assets. Valuing real assets is no different. We need to compute the present value of the expected cash flows associated with the asset. For example, suppose Unilate Textiles is considering purchasing a machine so that it can manufacture a new line of products. After five years, the machine will be worthless because it will be used up. But during the five years Unilate uses the machine, the firm will be able to increase its net cash flows by the following amounts.

Year	Expected Cash Flow, $\hat{CF}_t$
1	$120,000
2	100,000
3	150,000
4	80,000
5	50,000

If Unilate wants to earn a 14 percent return on investments like this machine, what is the value of the machine to the company? To find the answer, we need to solve for the present value of the uneven cash flow stream produced by the machine. Thus, the value of this machine can be depicted as follows:

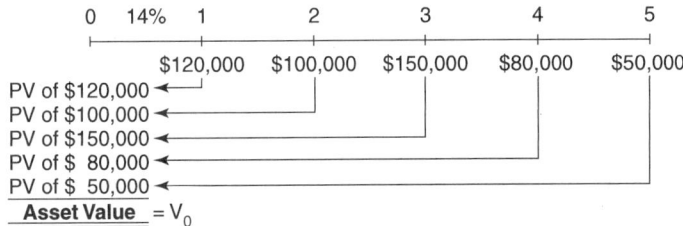

To compute the value of the machine, we simply apply Equation 7.10.

$$V_0 + \text{Present value of future CF} = \frac{\$120{,}000}{(1.14)^1} + \frac{\$100{,}000}{(1.14)^2} + \frac{\$150{,}000}{(1.14)^3} + \frac{\$80{,}000}{(1.14)^4} + \frac{\$50{,}000}{(1.14)^5}$$

The value of the machine can be computed by using three procedures: (1) numerically, (2) using the tables, and (3) with a financial calculator. We will show the first two procedures.

1. NUMERICAL SOLUTION Because the stream of cash flows is uneven (that is, it is not an annuity), we must discount each cash flow back to the present and sum these PVs to find the machine's value.

$$V_0 = \$120{,}000 \times \left[\frac{1}{(1.14)^1}\right] + \$100{,}000 \times \left[\frac{1}{(1.14)^2}\right] + \$150{,}000 \times \left[\frac{1}{(1.14)^3}\right]$$

$$+ \$80{,}000 \times \left[\frac{1}{(1.14)^4}\right] + \$50{,}000 \times \left[\frac{1}{(1.14)^5}\right]$$

$$= \$105{,}263.16 + \$76{,}946.75 + \$101{,}245.73 + \$47{,}366.42 + \$25{,}968.43$$

$$= \$356{,}790.46$$

2. TABULAR SOLUTION Simply look up the appropriate PVIF values in Table A-1 of Module 700 Appendix, insert them into the equation, and complete the arithmetic.

$$V_0 = \$120{,}000(\text{PVIF}_{14\%,1}) + \$100{,}000(\text{PVIF}_{14\%,2}) + \$150{,}000(\text{PVIF}_{14\%,3})$$
$$+ \$80{,}000(\text{PVIF}_{14\%,4}) + \$50{,}000(\text{PVIF}_{14\%,5})$$
$$= \$120{,}000(0.8772) + \$100{,}000(0.7695) + \$150{,}000(0.6750)$$
$$+ \$80{,}000(0.5921) + \$50{,}000(0.5194) = \$356{,}802 \text{ (Rounding Difference)}$$

The present value of the machine to the company is $356,802 and this is compared to the initial cash outlay to purchase the machine.

Financial Forecasting, Planning, and Control

Financial Planning and Control

In this section, we will see how a financial manager can use some of the information obtained through financial statement analysis for financial planning and control of the firm's future operations. Well-run companies generally base their operating plans on a set of forecasted financial statements. The **financial planning** process begins with a sales forecast for the next few years. Then the assets required to meet the sales targets are determined, and a decision is made concerning how to finance the required assets. At that point, income statements and balance sheets can be projected, and earnings and dividends per share, as well as the key ratios, can be forecasted.

Once the "base case" forecasted financial statements and ratios have been prepared, top managers want to know (1) how realistic the results are, (2) how to attain the results, and (3) what impact changes in operations would have on the forecasts. At this stage, which is the **financial control** phase, the firm is concerned with implementing the financial plans, or forecasts, and dealing with the feedback and adjustment process that is necessary to ensure the goals of the firm are pursued appropriately.

The first part of the section is devoted to financial planning using projected financial statements, or forecasts, and the second part of the section focuses on financial control using budgeting and the analysis of leverage to determine how changes in operations affect financial forecasts.

Financial Planning and Forecasting

Sales Forecasts

Forecasting is an essential part of the planning process, and a **sales forecast** is the most important ingredient of financial forecasting. The sales forecast generally starts with a review of sales during the past 5 to 10 years, which can be expressed in a graph.

Based on its historical sales trend, plans for new product and market introductions, and Unilate's forecast for the economy, the firm's planning committee has projected a 10 percent growth rate for sales during 2005. So 2005 sales are expected to be $1,650 million, which is 10 percent higher than 2004 sales of $1,500 million.

If the sales forecast is inaccurate, the consequences can be serious. First, if the market expands significantly *more* than Unilate has geared up for, the company probably will not be able to meet demand. Customers will buy competitors' products, and Unilate will lose market share, which will be hard to regain. On the other hand, if the projections are overly optimistic, Unilate could end up with too much plant, equipment, and inventory. This would mean low turnover ratios, high costs for depreciation and storage, and, possibly, write-offs of obsolete or unusable inventory. All of this would result in a low rate of return on equity, which in turn would depress the company's stock price. If Unilate had financed an unnecessary expansion with debt, its problems would, of course, be compounded. Remember from our analysis of its 2000 financial statements in the previous sections that Unilate's current financial position is considered poor. Thus, an accurate sales forecast is critical to the well-being of the firm.

Projected (Pro Forma) Financial Statements

Any forecast of financial requirements involves (1) determining how much money the firm will need during a given period, (2) determining how much money the firm will generate internally during the same period, and (3) subtracting the funds generated from the funds required to determine the external financial requirements. One method used to estimate external requirements is the *projected, or pro forma, balance sheet method,* which is discussed in this section.

The projected balance sheet method is straightforward—simply project the asset requirements for the coming period, then project the liabilities and equity that will be generated under normal operations, and subtract the projected liabilities and equity from the required assets to estimate the **additional funds needed (AFN)** to support the level of forecasted operations. The steps in the procedure are explained next.

STEP 1. FORECAST THE 2005 INCOME STATEMENT The **projected (pro forma) balance sheet method** begins with a forecast of sales. Next, the income statement for the coming year is forecasted to obtain an initial estimate of the amount of retained earnings the company will generate during the year. This requires assumptions about the operating cost ratio, the tax rate, interest charges, and the dividends paid. In the simplest case, the assumption is made that costs will increase at the same rate as sales; in more complicated situations, cost changes are forecasted separately. Still, the objective of this part of the analysis is to determine how much income the company will earn and then retain for reinvestment in the business during the forecasted year.

Exhibit 700.17 shows Unilate's actual 2004 income statement and the initial forecast of the 2005 income statement if the conditions just mentioned exist. To create the 2005 income forecast, we assume that sales and variable operating costs will be 10 percent greater in 2005 than in 2004. In addition, it is assumed that Unilate currently operates at full capacity, so it will need to expand its plant capacity in 2005 to handle the additional operations. Therefore, in Exhibit 700.17, the 2005 forecasts of sales, *all* operating costs, and depreciation are 10 percent greater than their 2004 levels. The result is that earnings before interest and taxes (EBIT) is forecasted to be $143 million in 2005.

Exhibit 700.17 Unilate Textiles: Actual 2004 and Projected 2005 Income Statements (millions of dollars, except per share data)

	2004 Results	2005 Forecast Basis	2005 Initial Forecast
Net sales	$1,500.0	× 1.10	$1,650.0
Cost of goods sold	(1,230.0)	× 1.10	(1,353.0)
Gross profit	$ 270.0		$ 297.0
Fixed operating costs except depreciation	(90.0)	× 1.10	(99.0)
Depreciation	(50.0)	× 1.10	(55.0)
Earnings before interest and taxes (EBIT)	$ 130.0		143.0
Less interest	(40.0)		(40.0)
Earnings before taxes (EBT)	$ 90.0		$ 103.0
Taxes (40%)	(36.0)		(41.2)
Net income	$ 54.0		$ 61.8
Common dividends	(29.0)		(29.0)
Addition to retained earnings	$ 25.0		$ 32.8
Earnings per share	$ 2.16		$ 2.47
Dividends per share	$ 1.16		$ 1.16
Number of common shares (millions)	25.00		25.00

To complete the initial forecast of 2005 income, we assume no change in the financing of the firm because, at this point, it is not known if additional financing is needed. But it is apparent that the 2005 interest expense will change if the amount of debt (borrowing) the firm needs to support the forecasted increase in operations changes. To forecast the 2005 dividends, we simply assume the dividend per share will be the same as it was in 2004, $1.16; so the total common dividends forecasted for 2005 would be $29.0 million if no additional common stock is issued. Like the interest expense amount, however, the amount of total dividends used to create this initial forecast will change if Unilate decides to sell new stock to raise any additional financing necessary to support the new operations or to raise the dividends per share paid to existing shareholders.

From the initial forecast of 2005 income contained in Exhibit 700.17, we can see that $32.8 million dollars is expected to be added to retained earnings in 2005. As it turns out, this addition to retained earnings represents the amount Unilate is expected to invest in itself (internally generated funds) to support the increase in operations in 2005. So the next step is to determine what impact this level of investment will have on the Unilate's forecasted 2005 balance sheet.

STEP 2. FORECAST THE 2005 BALANCE SHEET If we assume the 2004 end-of-year asset levels were just sufficient to support 2004 operations, then in order for Unilate's sales to increase in 2005, its assets must also grow. Because the company was operating at full capacity in 2004, *each* asset account must increase if the higher sales level is to be attained: More cash will be needed for transactions, higher sales will lead to higher receivables, additional inventory will have to be stocked, and new plant and equipment must be added for production.

Further, if Unilate's assets are to increase, its liabilities and equity must also increase—the additional assets must be financed in some manner. Some liabilities will increase *spontaneously* due to normal business relationships. For example, as sales increase, so will Unilate's purchases of raw materials, and these larger purchases will spontaneously lead to higher levels of accounts payable. Similarly, a higher level of operations will require more labor, while higher sales will result in higher taxable income. Therefore, both accrued wages and accrued taxes will increase. In general, these current liability accounts, which provide **spontaneously generated funds,** will increase at the same rate as sales.

Notes payable, long-term bonds, and common stock will not rise spontaneously with sales—rather, the projected levels of these accounts will depend on conscious financing decisions that will be made later. Therefore, for the initial forecast, it is assumed these account balances remain unchanged from their 2004 levels.

Exhibit 700.18 contains Unilate's 2004 actual balance sheet and an initial forecast of its 2005 balance sheet. The mechanics of the balance sheet forecast are similar to those used to develop the forecasted income statement. First, those balance sheet accounts that are expected to increase directly with sales are multiplied by 1.10 to obtain the initial 2005 forecasts. Thus, 2005 cash is projected to be $15.0 × 1.10 = $16.5 million, accounts receivable are projected to be $180.0 × 1.10 = $198.0 million, and so on. In our example, all assets increase with sales, so once the individual assets have been forecasted, they can be summed to complete the asset side of the forecasted balance sheet.

Exhibit 700.18 *Unilate Textiles: Actual 2004 and Projected 2005 Balance Sheets (millions of dollars)*

	2004 Balances	2005 Forecast Basis[a]	2005 Initial Forecast
Cash	$ 15.0	× 1.10	$ 16.5
Accounts receivable	180.0	× 1.10	198.0
Inventories	270.0	× 1.10	297.0
Total current assets	$465.0		$511.5
Net plant and equipment	380.0	× 1.10	418.0
Total assets	$845.0		$929.5
Accounts payable	$ 30.0	× 1.10	$ 33.0
Accruals	60.0	× 1.10	66.0
Notes payable	40.0		40.0[b]
Total current liabilities	$130.0		$139.0
Long-term bonds	300.0		300.0[b]
Total liabilities	$430.0		$439.0
Common stock	130.0		130.0[b]
Retained earnings	285.0	+$32.8[d]	317.8
Total owner's equity	$415.0		$447.8
Total liabilities and equity	$845.0		$886.8
Additional funds needed (AFN)			$ 42.7[c]

[a] × 1.10 indicates "times (1 + g)"; used for items which grow proportionally with sales.
[b] Indicates a 2004 figure carried over for the initial forecast.
[c] The "additional funds needed (AFN)" is computed by subtracting the amount of total liabilities and equity from the amount of total assets.
[d] The $32.8 million represents the "addition to retained earnings" from the 2005 Projected Income Statement given in 700.18.

Next, the spontaneously increasing liabilities (accounts payable and accruals) are forecasted. Then those liability and equity accounts whose values reflect conscious management decisions—notes payable, long-term bonds, and stock—*initially are forecasted* to remain at their 2004 levels. Thus, the amount of 2005 notes payable initially is set at $40.0 million, the long-term bond account is forecasted at $300.0 million, and so forth. The forecasted 2005 level of retained earnings will be the 2004 level plus the forecasted addition to retained earnings, which was computed as $32.8 million in the projected income statement we created in Step 1 (Exhibit 700.17).

The forecast of total assets in Exhibit 700.18 is $929.5 million, which indicates that Unilate must add $84.5 million of new assets (compared to 2004 assets) to support the higher sales level expected in 2005. However, according to the initial forecast of the 2005 balance sheet, the total liabilities and equity sum to only $886.8 million, which is an increase of only $41.8 million. So the amount of total assets exceeds the amount of total liabilities and equity by $42.7 million = $929.5 million − $886.8 million. This indicates $42.7 million of the forecasted increase in total assets will not be financed by liabilities that spontaneously increase with sales (accounts payable and accruals) or by an increase in retained earnings. Unilate can raise the additional $42.7 million, which we designate *additional funds needed (AFN)*, by borrowing from the bank as notes payable, by issuing long-term bonds, by selling new common stock, or by some combination of these actions.

The initial forecast of Unilate's financial statements has shown us that (1) higher sales must be supported by higher asset levels, (2) some of the asset increases can be financed by spontaneous increases in accounts payable and accruals and by retained earnings, and (3) any shortfall must be financed from external sources, either by borrowing or by selling new stock.

STEP 3. RAISING THE ADDITIONAL FUNDS NEEDED Unilate's financial manager will base the decision of exactly how to raise the $42.7 million additional funds needed on several factors, including its ability to handle additional debt, conditions in the financial markets, and restrictions imposed by existing debt agreements. At this point, it is important to understand that, regardless of how Unilate raises the $42.7 million AFN, the initial forecasts of both the income statement and the balance sheet will be affected. If Unilate takes on new debt, its interest expenses will rise; and if additional shares of common stock are sold, *total* dividend payments will increase if the *same dividend per share* is paid to all common stockholders. Each of these changes, which we term *financing feedbacks,* will affect the amount of additional retained earnings originally forecasted, which in turn will affect the amount of additional funds needed.

STEP 4. FINANCING FEEDBACKS As mentioned in Step 3, one complexity that arises in financial forecasting relates to **financing feedbacks.** The external funds raised to pay for new assets create additional expenses that must be reflected in the income statement and that lower the initially forecasted addition to retained earnings, which means more external funds are needed to make up for the lower amount added to retained earnings. In other words, if Unilate raised the $42.7 million AFN by issuing new debt and new common stock, it would find both the interest expense and the total dividend payments would be higher than the amounts contained in the forecasted income statement shown in Exhibit 700.17. Consequently, after adjusting for the higher interest and dividend payments, the forecasted addition to retained earnings would be lower than the initial forecast of $32.8 million. Because the retained earnings will be lower than projected, a financing shortfall will exist even after the original AFN of $42.7 million is considered. So in reality, Unilate must raise more than $42.7 million to account for the financing feedbacks that affect the amount of internal financing expected to be generated from the increase in operations. To determine the amount of external financing actually needed, we have to adjust the initial forecasts of both the income statement (Step 1) and the balance sheet (Step 2) to reflect the impact of raising the additional external financing. This process has to be repeated until AFN = 0 in Exhibit 700.18, which means Step 1 and Step 2 might have to be repeated several times to fully account for the financing feedbacks.

Exhibit 700.19 contains the adjusted 2005 preliminary forecasts for the income statement and the balance sheet of Unilate Textiles after all of the financing effects are considered. To generate the adjusted forecasts, it is assumed that of the total external funds needed, 65 percent will be raised by selling new common stock at $23 per share, 15 percent will be borrowed from the bank at an interest rate of 7 percent, and 20 percent will be raised by selling long-term bonds with a coupon interest of 10 percent. Under these conditions, it can be seen from Exhibit 700.19 that Unilate actually needs $45.0 million to support the forecasted increase in operations, not the $42.7 million contained in the initial forecast. The additional $2.3 million is needed because the added amounts of debt and common stock will cause interest and dividend payments to increase, which will decrease the contribution to retained earnings by $2.3 million.

ANALYSIS OF THE FORECAST The 2005 forecast as developed here represents a preliminary forecast, because we have completed only the first stage of the entire forecasting process. Next, the projected statements must be analyzed to determine whether the forecast meets the firm's financial targets. If the statements do not meet the targets, then elements of the forecast must be changed.

Exhibit 700.20 shows Unilate's 2004 ratios plus the projected 2005 ratios based on the preliminary forecast and the industry average ratios. The firm's financial condition at the close of 2004 was weak, with many ratios being well below the industry averages. The preliminary final forecast for 2005 (after financing feedbacks are considered), which assumes that Unilate's past practices will continue into the future, shows an improved debt position. But the overall financial position still is somewhat weak, and this condition will persist unless management takes some actions to improve things.

Unilate's management actually plans to take steps to improve its financial condition. The plans are to (1) close down certain operations, (2) modify the credit policy to reduce the collection period for receivables, and (3) better manage inventory so that products are turned over more often. These proposed operational changes will affect both the income statement and the balance sheet, so the preliminary forecast will have to be revised again to reflect the impact of such changes. When this process is complete, management will have its final forecast. To keep things simple, we do not show the final forecast here; instead, for the remaining discussions we assume the preliminary forecast is not substantially different and use it as the final forecast for Unilate's 2005 operations.

As we have shown, forecasting is an iterative process, both in the way the financial statements are generated and in the way the financial plan is developed. For planning purposes, the financial staff develops a preliminary forecast based on a continuation of past policies and trends. This provides the executives with a starting point, or "straw man" forecast. Next, the model is modified to see what effects alternative operating plans would have on the firm's earnings and financial condition. This results in a revised forecast.

Other Considerations in Forecasting

We have presented a very simple method for constructing pro forma financial statements under rather restrictive conditions. In this section, we describe some other conditions that should be considered when creating forecasts.

EXCESS CAPACITY The construction of the 2005 forecasts for Unilate was based on the assumption that the firm's 2004 operations were at full capacity, so any increase in sales would require additional assets, especially plant and equipment. If Unilate did *not* operate at full capacity in 2004, then plant and equipment would only have to be increased if

Exhibit 700.19 *Unilate Textiles: 2005 Adjusted Forecast of Financial Statements (millions of dollars)*

Income Statement

	Initial Forecast	Adjusted Forecast	Financing Adjustment
Net sales	$1,650.0	$1,650.0	
Cost of goods sold	(1,353.0)	(1,353.0)	
Gross profit	$ 297.0	$ 297.0	
Fixed operating costs except depreciation	(99.0)	(99.0)	
Depreciation	(55.0)	(55.0)	
Earnings before interest and taxes (EBIT)	$ 143.0	$ 143.0	
Less interest	(40.0)	(41.4)	(1.4)
Earnings before taxes (EBT)	$ 103.0	$ 101.6	(1.4)
Taxes (40%)	(41.2)	(40.7)	0.5
Net Income	$ 61.8	$ 61.0	(0.8)[b]
Common dividends	(29.0)	(30.5)	(1.5)
Addition to retained earnings	$ 32.8	$ 30.5	(2.3)[a]
Earnings per share	$ 2.47	$ 2.32	
Dividends per share	$ 1.16	$ 1.16	
Number of common shares (millions)	25.00	26.27	

Balance Sheet

Cash	$ 16.5	$ 16.5	
Accounts receivable	198.0	198.0	
Inventories	297.0	297.0	
Total current assets	$511.5	$511.5	
Net plant and equipment	418.0	418.0	
Total assets	$929.5	$929.5	
Accounts payable	$ 33.0	$ 33.0	
Accruals	66.0	66.0	
Notes payable	40.0	46.8	$ 6.8
Total current liabilities	$139.0	$145.8	
Long-term bonds	300.0	309.0	$ 9.0
Total liabilities	$439.0	$454.8	
Common stock	130.0	159.3	$29.3
Retained earnings	317.8	315.5	$ (2.3)[a]
Total owner's equity	$447.8	$474.8	
Total liabilities and equity $886.8	$929.5		
Additional Funds Needed (AFN)	$ 42.7	$ 0.0	$42.8 [b,c]

[a] The financing adjustment for the addition to retained earnings in the income statement is the same as the financing adjustment for retained earnings in the balance sheet.

[b] Rounding difference.

[c] The total AFN, or external funding needs, equal $42.7 million plus the $2.3 million decrease in the change in retained earnings from the initial forecast; thus, total funds needed equal $45.0 million—$6.8 million will be from new bank notes, $9.0 million will come from issuing new bonds, and $29.3 million will be raised by issuing new common stock.

Exhibit 700.20 *Unilate Textiles: Key Ratios*

	2004	Adjusted Preliminary 2005	Industry Average
Current ratio	3.6×	3.5×	4.1×
Inventory turnover	4.6×	5.6×	7.4×
Days sales outstanding	43.2 days	43.2 days	32.1 days
Total assets turnover	1.8×	1.8×	2.1×
Debt ratio	50.9%	48.9%	45.0%
Times interest earned	3.3×	3.5×	6.5×
Profit margin	3.6%	3.7%	4.7%
Return on assets	6.4%	6.6%	12.6%
Return on equity	13.0%	12.8%	17.2%

the additional sales (operations) forecasted in 2005 exceeded the unused capacity of the existing assets. For example, if Unilate actually utilized only 80 percent of its fixed assets' capacity to produce 2004 sales of $1,500 million, then

$$\$1,500.0 \text{ million} = 0.80 \times (\text{Plant capacity})$$

$$\text{Plant capacity} = \frac{\$1,500.0 \text{ million}}{0.80} = \$1,875 \text{ million}$$

In this case, then, Unilate could increase sales to $1,875 million, or by 25 percent of 2004 sales, before full capacity is reached and plant and equipment would have to be increased. In general, we can compute the sales capacity of the firm if it is known what percent of assets are utilized to produce a particular level of sales.

$$\text{Full capacity sales} = \frac{\text{Sales level}}{(\text{Percent of capacity used to generate sales level})}$$

If Unilate does not have to increase plant and equipment, fixed assets would remain at the 2004 level of $380 million, so the amount of AFN would be $4.7 million, which is $38 million (10 percent of $380 million fixed assets) less than the initial forecast reported in Exhibit 700.18.

In addition to the excess capacity of fixed assets, the firm could have excesses in other assets that can be used for increases in operations. For instance, we concluded that Unilate's inventory level at the end of 2004 probably was greater than it should have been. If true, some increase in 2005 forecasted sales can be absorbed by the above-normal inventory and production would not have to be increased until inventory levels are reduced to normal—this requires no additional financing.

In general, excess capacity means less external financing is required to support increases in operations than would be needed if the firm previously operated at full capacity.

ECONOMIES OF SCALE There are economies of scale in the use of many types of assets, and when such economies occur, a firm's variable cost of goods sold ratio is likely to change as the size of the firm changes (either increases or decreases) substantially. Currently, Unilate's variable cost ratio is 82 percent of sales; but the ratio might decrease to 80 percent of sales if operations increase significantly. If everything else is the same, changes in the variable cost ratio affect the addition to retained earnings, which in turn affects the amount of AFN.

LUMPY ASSETS In many industries, technological considerations dictate that if a firm is to be competitive, it must add fixed assets in large, discrete units; such assets often are referred to as **lumpy assets**. For example, in the paper industry, there are strong economies of scale in basic paper mill equipment, so when a paper company expands capacity, it must do so in large, lumpy increments. Lumpy assets primarily affect the turnover of fixed assets and, consequently, the financial requirements associated with expanding. For instance, if instead of $38 million Unilate needed an additional $50 million in fixed assets to increase operations 10 percent, the AFN would be much greater. With *lumpy assets,* it is possible that a small projected increase in sales would require a significant increase in plant and equipment, which would require a very large financial requirement.

Financial Control

In the previous section, we focused on financial forecasting, emphasizing how growth in sales requires additional investment in assets, which in turn generally requires the firm to raise new funds externally. In the sections that follow, we consider the planning and control systems used by financial managers when implementing the forecasts. First, we look at the relationship between sales volume and profitability under different operating conditions. These relationships provide information that is used by managers to plan for changes in the firm's level of operations, financing needs, and profitability. Later, we examine the control phase of the planning and control process, because a good control system is essential both to ensure that plans are executed properly and to facilitate a timely modification of plans if the assumptions on which the initial plans were based turn out to be different than expected.

The planning process can be enhanced by examining the effects of changing operations on the firm's profitability, both from the standpoint of profits from operations and from the standpoint of profitability after financing effects are considered.

Operating Break-even Analysis

The relationship between sales volume and operating profitability is explored in cost-volume-profit planning, or operating break-even analysis. **Operating break-even analysis** is a method of determining the point at which sales will just cover operating costs—that is, the point at which the firm's operations will break even. It also shows the magnitude of the firm's operating profits or losses if sales exceed or fall below that point. Break-even analysis is important in the planning and control process because the cost-volume-profit relationship can be influenced greatly by the proportion of the firm's investment in assets that are fixed. A sufficient volume of sales must be anticipated and achieved if fixed and variable costs are to be covered, or else the firm will incur losses from operations. In other words, if a firm is to avoid accounting losses, its sales must cover all costs—those that vary directly with production and those that remain constant even when production levels change. Costs that vary directly with the level of production generally include the labor and materials needed to produce and sell the product, while the fixed operating costs generally include costs such as depreciation, rent, and insurance expenses that are incurred regardless of the firm's production level.

Operating break-even analysis deals only with the upper portion of the income statement—the portion from sales to net operating income (NOI), which is also termed earnings before interest and taxes (EBIT). This portion generally is referred to as the *operating section*, because it contains only the revenues and expenses associated with the normal production and selling operations of the firm. Exhibit 700.21 gives the operating section of Unilate's forecasted 2005 income statement, which was shown in Exhibit 700.19. For the discussion that follows, we have assumed that all of Unilate's products sell for $15.00 each and the variable cost of goods sold per unit is $12.30, which is 82 percent of the selling price.

Exhibit 700.21 *Unilate Textiles: 2005 Forecasted Operating Income (millions of dollars)*

Sales (S)	$1,650.0
Variable cost of goods sold (VC)	(1,353.0)
Gross profit (GP)	$ 297.0
Fixed operating costs (F)	(154.0)
Net operating income (NOI) = EBIT	$ 143.0

NOTES:

Sales in units = 110 million units.

Selling price per unit = $15.00.

Variable costs per unit = $1,353/110 = $12.30

Fixed operating costs = $154 million, which includes $55 million depreciation and $99 million in other fixed costs such as rent, insurance, and general office expenses.

EBIT = Earnings Before Interest and Taxes

Break-even Chart

Exhibit 700.21 shows the net operating income for Unilate if 110 million units are produced and sold during the year. But what if Unilate doesn't sell 110 million units? Certainly, the firm's net operating income will be something other than $143 million. Exhibit 700.22 shows the total revenues and total operating costs for Unilate at various levels of sales, beginning with zero. According to the information given in Exhibit 700.21, Unilate has fixed costs, which include depreciation, rent, insurance, and so on, equal to $154 million. This amount must be paid even if the firm produces and sells nothing, so the $154 million fixed cost is represented by a horizontal line. If Unilate produces and sells nothing, its sales revenues will be zero; but *for each unit sold,* the firm's sales will increase by $15. Therefore, the total revenue line starts at the origin of the X and Y axes, and it has a slope equal to $15.00 to account for the dollar increase in sales for each additional unit sold. On the other hand, the line representing the total operating costs intersects the Y axis at $154 million, which represents the fixed costs incurred even when no products are sold, and it has a slope equal to $12.30, which is the cost directly associated with the production of each additional unit sold. The point at which the total revenue line intersects the total cost line is the **operating break-even point,** because this is where the revenues generated from sales just cover the *total operating costs* of the firm. Notice that prior to the break-even point, the total cost line is above the total revenue line, which shows Unilate will suffer operating losses because the total costs cannot be covered by the sales revenues. And, after the break-even point, the total revenue line is above the total cost line because revenues are more than sufficient to cover total operating costs, so Unilate will realize operating profits. Total costs include fixed costs and variable costs.

Break-even Computation

Exhibit 700.22 shows that Unilate must sell 57 million units to be at the operating break-even point. If Unilate sells 57 million products, it will generate $855 million in sales revenues, which will be just enough to cover the $855 million total operating costs—$154 million fixed costs and $701 million variable costs (57 million units at $12.30 per

Exhibit 700.22 *Unilate Textiles: Operating Break-even Chart*

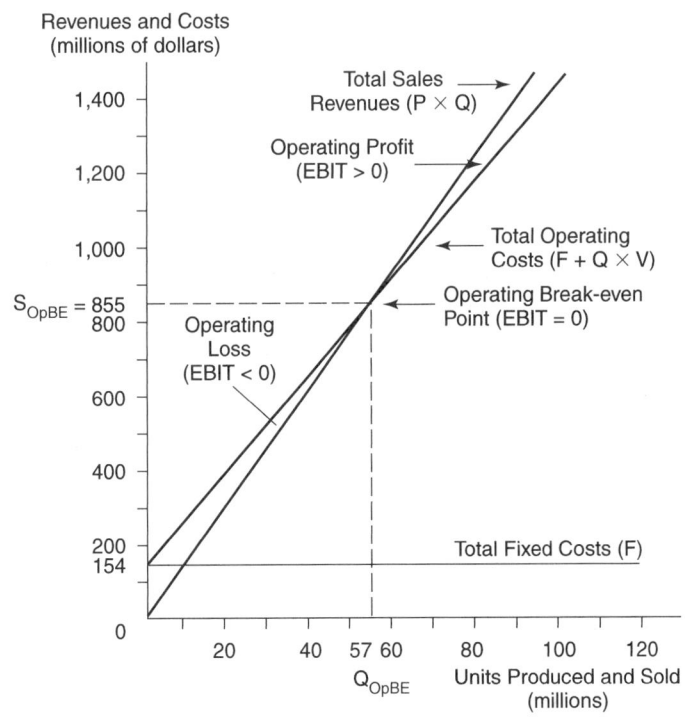

NOTES:

S_{OpBE} = operating break even in dollars
Q = sales in units: Q_{OpBE} = operating break even in units
F = fixed costs = $154 million
V = variable costs per unit = $12.30
P = price per unit = $15.00

unit). If we do not have a graph like Exhibit 700.22, how can the operating break-even point be computed? Actually, it is rather simple. Remember, the operating break-even point is where the revenues generated from sales just cover the total operating costs, which include both the costs directly attributable to producing each unit and the fixed operating costs that remain constant regardless of the production level. As long as the selling price of each unit (the slope of the total revenue line) is greater than the variable operating cost of each unit (the slope of the total operating cost line), each unit sold will generate revenues that contribute to covering the fixed operating costs. For Unilate, this contribution (termed the *contribution margin*) is $2.70, which is the difference between the $15.00 selling price and the $12.30 variable cost of each unit. To compute the operating break even for Unilate, then, we have to determine how many units need to be sold to cover the fixed operating cost of $154 million if each unit has a contribution margin equal to $2.70. Just divide the $154 million fixed cost by the $2.70 contribution margin and you will discover the break-even point is 57 million units, which equates to $855 million in sales revenues.

More formally, the operating break-even point can be found by setting the total revenues equal to the total operating costs so that net operating income (NOI) is zero. In equation form, NOI = 0 if

$$\text{Sales revenues} = \text{Total operating costs} = \text{Total variable costs} + \text{Total fixed costs}$$
$$(P \times Q) = \text{TOC} = (V \times Q) + F$$

where P is the sales price per unit, Q is the number of units produced and sold, V is the variable operating cost per unit, and F is the total fixed operating costs. Solving for the quantity that needs to be sold, Q, produces a formula that can be used to find the number of units that needs to be sold to achieve operating break even.

$$Q_{\text{OpBE}} = \frac{F}{P - V} = \frac{F}{\text{Contribution margin}} \qquad (7.17)$$

Thus, the operating break-even point for Unilate is

$$Q_{\text{OpBE}} = \frac{\$154.0 \text{ million}}{\$15.00 - \$12.30} = \frac{\$154.0 \text{ million}}{\$2.70} = 57.0 \text{ million units.}$$

In the remainder of the section, we omit the word *million* in the computations and include it only in the final answer.

From Equation 7.17, we can see that the operating break-even point is lower (higher) if the numerator is lower (higher) or if the denominator is higher (lower). Therefore, all else equal, one firm will have a lower operating break-even point than another firm if its fixed costs are lower, if selling price of its product is higher, if its variable operating cost per unit is lower, or if some combination of these exists. For instance, if Unilate could increase the sales price per unit from $15.00 to $15.80 without affecting either its fixed operating costs ($154 million) or its variable operating cost per unit ($12.30), then its operating break-even point would fall to 44 million units.

The operating break-even point also can be stated in terms of the total sales revenues needed to cover total operating costs. At this point, we just need to multiply the sales price per unit by the break-even quantity we found using Equation 7.17, which yields $855 million for Unilate. Or we can restate the contribution margin as a percent of the sales price per unit (this is called the *gross profit margin*) and then apply Equation 7.17. In other words,

$$S_{\text{OpBE}} = \frac{F}{1 - \left(\frac{V}{P}\right)} = \frac{F}{\text{Gross profit margin}} \qquad (7.18)$$

Solving Equation 7.18 for Unilate, the operating break even based on dollar sales is

$$S_{\text{OpBE}} = \frac{\$154.0}{1 - \left(\frac{\$12.30}{\$15.00}\right)} = \frac{\$154.0}{1 - 0.82} = \frac{\$154.0}{0.18} = \$855.6 \text{ million}$$

Equation 7.18 shows that 18¢ of every $1 sales revenues goes to cover the fixed operating costs, so about $855 million worth of the product must be sold to break even. (If we use Equation 7.17 to compute the operating break even rounded to two decimal places, the result is 57.04 million units; thus the dollar sales needed to break even is 57.04 × $15 = $855.6 million.)

Break-even analysis based on dollar sales rather than on units of output is useful in determining the break-even volume for a firm that sells many products at varying prices. This analysis requires only that total sales, total fixed costs, and total variable costs at a given level are known.

Using Operating Break-even Analysis

Operating break-even analysis can shed light on three important types of business decisions: (1) When making new product decisions, break-even analysis can help determine how large the sales of a new product must be for the firm to achieve profitability. (2) Break-even analysis can be used to study the effects of a general expansion in the level of the firm's operations; an expansion would cause the levels of both fixed and variable costs to rise, but it would also increase expected sales. (3) When considering modernization and automation projects, where the fixed investment in equipment is increased in order to lower variable costs, particularly the cost of labor, break-even analysis can help management analyze the consequences of purchasing these projects.

However, care must be taken when using operating break-even analysis. To apply break-even analysis as we have discussed here requires that the sales price *per unit*, the variable cost *per unit*, and the *total* fixed operating costs do not change with the level of the firm's production and sales. Within a narrow range of production and sales, this assumption probably is not a major issue. But what if the firm expects either to produce a much greater (or fewer) number of products than normal or to expand (reduce) its plant and equipment significantly? Will the numbers change? Most likely the answer is yes. Therefore, use of a single break-even chart like the one presented in Exhibit 700.22 is impractical—such a chart provides useful information, but the fact that it cannot deal with changes in the price of the product, with changing variable cost rates, and with changes in fixed cost levels suggests the need for a more flexible type of analysis. Today, such analysis is provided by computer simulation. Functions such as those expressed in Equations 7.17 and 7.18 (or more complicated versions of them) can be put into a spreadsheet or similarly modeled with other computer software, and then variables such as sales price, P, the variable cost per unit, V, and the level of fixed costs, F, can be changed. The model can instantaneously produce new versions of Exhibit 700.22, or a whole set of such graphs, to show what the operating break-even point would be under different production setups and price-cost situations.

Operating Leverage

If a high percentage of a firm's total operating costs are fixed, the firm is said to have a high degree of **operating leverage**. In physics, leverage implies the use of a lever to raise a heavy object with a small amount of force. In politics, people who have leverage can accomplish a great deal with their smallest word or action. *In business terminology, a high degree of operating leverage, other things held constant, means that a relatively small change in sales will result in a large change in operating income.*

Operating leverage arises because the firm has fixed operating costs that must be covered no matter the level of production. The impact of the leverage, however, depends on the actual operating level of the firm. For example, Unilate has $154.0 million in fixed operating costs, which are covered rather easily because the firm currently sells 110 million products; thus, it is well above its operating break-even point of 57 million units. But what would happen to the operating income if Unilate sold more or less than forecasted? To answer this question we need to determine the **degree of operating leverage (DOL)** associated with Unilate's forecasted 2005 operations.

Operating leverage can be defined more precisely in terms of the way a given change in sales volume affects operating income (NOI). To measure the effect of a change in sales volume on NOI, we calculate the degree of operating leverage, which is defined as the percentage change in NOI (or EBIT) associated with a given percentage change in sales.

$$\text{DOL} = \frac{\text{Percentage change in NOI}}{\text{Percentage change in sales}} = \frac{\left(\frac{\Delta \text{NOI}}{\text{NOI}}\right)}{\left(\frac{\Delta \text{Sales}}{\text{Sales}}\right)} = \frac{\left(\frac{\Delta \text{EBIT}}{\text{EBIT}}\right)}{\left(\frac{\Delta \text{Sales}}{\text{Sales}}\right)} = \frac{\left(\frac{\Delta \text{EBIT}}{\text{EBIT}}\right)}{\left(\frac{\Delta Q}{Q}\right)} \qquad (7.19)$$

In effect, the DOL is an index number that measures the effect of a change in sales on operating income or Earnings Before Interest and Taxes (EBIT).

Exhibit 700.21 shows that the NOI for Unilate is $143.0 million at production and sales equal to 110 million units. If the number of units produced and sold increases to 121 million, the operating income (in millions of dollars) would be

$$\text{NOI} = 121(\$15.00 - \$12.30) - \$154.0 = \$172.7$$

So the degree of operating leverage associated with this change is 2.08.

$$\text{DOL} = \frac{\left[\frac{\$172.7 - \$143.0}{\$143.0}\right]}{\left[\frac{\$15.00(121 - 110)}{\$15.00(110)}\right]} = \frac{\left(\frac{\$29.7}{\$143.0}\right)}{\left(\frac{11}{110}\right)} = \frac{0.208}{0.100} = \frac{20.8\%}{10.0\%} = 2.08\times$$

Exhibit 700.23 *Unilate Textiles: Operating Income at Sales Levels of 110 Million Units and 121 Million Units (millions of dollars)*

	2005 Forecasted Operations	Sales Increase	Unit Change	Percent Change
Sales in units (millions)	110	121	11	+10.0%
Sales revenues	$1,650.0	$1,815.0	$165.0	+10.0%
Variable cost of goods sold	(1,353.0)	(1,488.3)	(135.3)	+10.0%
Gross profit	$ 297.0	$ 326.7	$ 29.7	+10.0%
Fixed operating costs	(154.0)	(154.0)	(0.0)	0.0%
Net operating income (EBIT)	$ 143.0	$ 172.7	$ 29.7	+20.8%

To interpret the meaning of the value of the degree of operating leverage, remember we computed the percent change in operating income and then divided the result by the percent change in sales. Taken literally then, Unilate's DOL of 2.08× indicates that the percent change in operating income will be 2.08 times the percent change in sales from the current 110 million units ($1,650.0 million). So if the number of units sold increases from 110 million to 121 million, or by 10 percent, Unilate's operating income should increase by 2.08 × 10% = 20.8%—at 121 million units, *operating income* should be 20.8 percent greater than the $143.0 million generated at 110 million units of sales; the new operating income should be $172.7 million = 1.208 × $143 million. Exhibit 700.23 shows a comparison of the operating incomes generated at the two different sales levels.

The results contained in Exhibit 700.23 show that Unilate's *gross profit* would increase by $29.7 million, or by 10 percent, if sales increase 10 percent. The fixed operating costs remain constant at $154.0 million, so EBIT also increases by $29.7 million, and the total impact of a 10 percent increase in sales is a 20.8 percent increase in operating income. If the fixed operating costs were to increase in proportion to the increase in sales—that is 10 percent—then the net operating income would also increase by 10 percent because all revenues and costs would have changed by the same proportion. But in reality, fixed operating costs will not change (a 0 percent increase); thus, a 10 percent increase in Unilate's forecasted 2005 sales will result in an *additional* 10.8 percent increase in operating income. The total increase is 20.8 percent, which results because operating leverage exists.

Equation 7.19 can be simplified so that the degree of operating leverage at a particular level of operations can be calculated as follows.

$$DOL_Q = \frac{Q1P - V2}{Q1P - V2 - F} \tag{7.20}$$

Or, rearranging the terms, DOL can be stated in terms of sales revenues as follows:

$$DOL_S = \frac{(Q \times P) - (Q \times V)}{(Q \times P) - (Q \times V) - F} = \frac{S - VC}{S - VC - F} = \frac{\text{Gross profit}}{\text{EBIT}} \tag{7.20a}$$

To solve Equation 7.20 or Equation 7.20a, we only need information from Unilate's forecasted operations; we do not need information about the possible change in forecasted operations. So Q represents the forecasted 2001 level of production and sales, and S and VC are the sales and variable operating costs, respectively, at that level of operations. For Unilate, the equation solution for DOL would be

$$DOL_{54} = \frac{110(\$15.00 - \$12.30)}{110(\$15.00 - \$12.30) - \$154} = \frac{\$1,650 - \$1,353}{\$1,650 - \$1,353 - \$154}$$

$$= \frac{\$297}{\$143} = 2.08\times$$

Equation 7.20 normally is used to analyze a single product, such as **GM's** Chevrolet Cavalier, whereas Equation 7.20a is used to evaluate an entire firm with many types of products and, hence, for which "quantity in units" and "sales price" are not meaningful.

The DOL of 2.08× indicates that *each 1 percent change* in sales will result in a 2.08 percent *change* in operating income. What would happen if Unilate's sales decrease, say, by 10 percent? According to the interpretation of

Exhibit 700.24 *Unilate Textiles: Operating Income at Sales Levels of 110 Million Units and 99 Million Units (millions of dollars)*

	2005 Forecasted Operations	Sales Decrease	Unit Change	Percent Change
Sales in units (millions)	110	99	(11)	−10.0%
Sales revenues	$1,650.0	$1,485.0	$(165.0)	−10.0%
Variable cost of goods sold	(1,353.0)	(1,217.7)	135.3	−10.0%
Gross profit	$ 297.0	$ 267.3	$(29.7)	−10.0%
Fixed operating costs	(154.0)	(154.0)	(0.0)	0.0%
Net operating income (EBIT)	$ 143.0	$ 113.3	$(29.7)	−20.8%

the DOL figure, Unilate's operating income would be expected to decrease by 20.8 percent. Exhibit 700.24 shows that this actually would be the case. Therefore, the DOL value indicates the *change* (increase or decrease) in operating income resulting from a *change* (increase or decrease) in the level of operations. It should be apparent that the greater the DOL, the greater the impact of a change in operations on operating income, whether the change is an increase or a decrease.

The DOL value found by using Equation 7.20a is the degree of operating leverage only for a specific initial sales level. For Unilate, that sales level is 110 million units, or $1,650 million. The DOL value would differ if the initial (existing) level of operations differed. For example, if Unilate's operating cost structure was the same, but only 65 million units were produced and sold, the DOL would have been

$$\text{DOL}_{65} = \frac{(65)(\$15.00 - \$12.30)}{[(65)(\$15.00 - \$12.30)] - \$154.0} = \frac{\$175.5}{\$21.5} = 8.19\times$$

The DOL at 65 million units produced and sold is nearly four times greater than the DOL at 110 million units. Thus, from a base sales of 65 million units, a 10 percent increase in sales, from 65 million units to 71.5 million units, would result in a 8.16 × 10% = 81.6% increase in operating income, from $21.5 million to $39.05 million. This shows that when Unilate's operations are closer to its operating break-even point of 57 million units, its degree of operating leverage is higher.

In general, given the same operating cost structure, if a firm's level of operations is decreased, its DOL increases; or, stated differently, the closer a firm is to its operating break-even point, the greater is its degree of operating leverage. This occurs because, as Exhibit 700.22 indicates, the closer a firm is to its operating break-even point, the more likely it is to incur an operating loss due to a decrease in sales—there is not a very large buffer in operating income to absorb a decrease in sales and still be able to cover the fixed operating costs. Similarly, at the same level of production and sales, a firm's degree of operating leverage will be higher the lower the contribution margin for its products—the lower the contribution margin, the less each product sold is able to help cover the fixed operating costs, and the closer the firm is to its operating break-even point. Therefore, the higher the DOL for a particular firm, it generally can be concluded the closer the firm is to its operating break-even point, and the more sensitive its operating income is to a change in sales volume. *Greater sensitivity generally implies greater risk; thus, it can be stated that firms with higher DOLs generally are considered to have riskier operations than firms with lower DOLs.*

Operating Leverage and Operating Break-even Point

The relationship between operating leverage and the operating break-even point is illustrated in Exhibit 700.25, where various levels of operations are compared for Unilate and two other textile manufacturers. One firm has a higher contribution margin than Unilate and the other firm has lower fixed operating costs, so we know the other two firms have operating break-even points that are less than Unilate's. Allied Cloth has the lowest operating break-even point, because it has the highest contribution margin relative to its fixed costs. Unilate has the highest operating break-even point because it uses the greatest relative amount of operating leverage of the three firms. Consequently, all else equal, of the three textile manufacturers, Unilate's operating income would be magnified the most if actual sales turned out to be greater than forecasted; but it also would experience the greatest decrease in operating income if actual sales turned out to be less than expected.

Exhibit 700.25 *Relationship Between Operating Leverage and Operating Break-even Point*

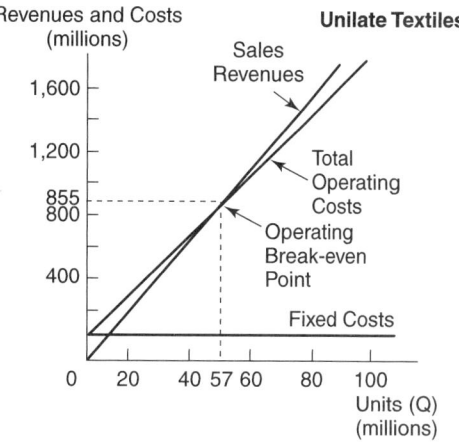

Unilate Textiles

Selling price = $15.00
Variable cost per unit = $12.30
Fixed costs = $154 million
Operating break even = 57 million units
= $855 million

Sales Level Units (Q)	Revenues ($)	Total Operating Costs	Operating Profit (EBIT)	DOL
30	$ 450	$ 523	$(73)	
60	900	892	8	20.3
110	1,650	1,507	143	2.1
150	2,250	1,999	251	1.6

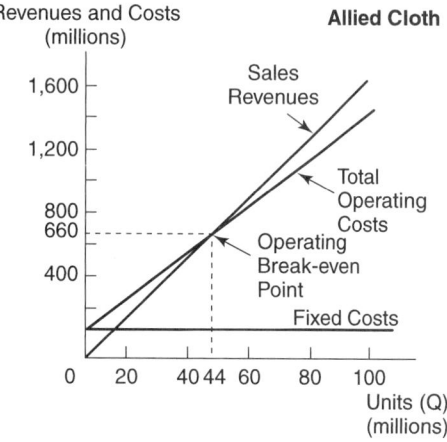

Allied Cloth

Selling price = $15.00
Variable cost per unit = $11.50
Fixed costs = $154 million
Operating break even = 44 million units
= $660 million

Sales Level Units (Q)	Revenues ($)	Total Operating Costs	Operating Profit (EBIT)	DOL
30	$ 450	$ 499	$(49)	
60	900	844	56	3.8
110	1,650	1,419	231	1.7
150	2,250	1,879	371	1.4

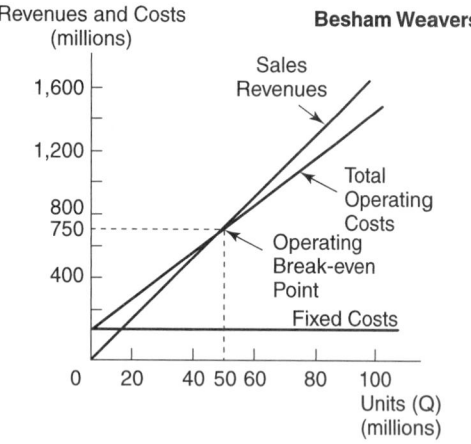

Besham Weavers

Selling price = $15.00
Variable cost per unit = $12.30
Fixed costs = $135 million
Operating break even = 50 million units
= $750 million

Sales Level Units (Q)	Revenues ($)	Total Operating Costs	Operating Profit (EBIT)	DOL
30	$ 450	$ 504	$(54)	
60	900	873	27	6.0
110	1,650	1,488	162	1.8
150	2,250	1,980	270	1.5

Financial Break-even Analysis

Operating break-even analysis deals with evaluation of production and sales to determine at what level the firm's sales revenues will just cover its operating costs; the point where the operating income is zero. **Financial break-even analysis** is a method of determining the operating income, or EBIT, the firm needs to just cover all of its *financing costs* and produce earnings per share equal to zero. Typically, the financing costs involved in financial break-even analysis consist of the interest payments to bondholders and the dividend payments to preferred stockholders. Usually these financing costs are fixed, and, in every case, they must be paid before dividends can be paid to common stockholders.

Exhibit 700.26 *Unilate Textiles: 2005 Forecasted Earnings per Share (millions of dollars)*

Earnings before interest and taxes (EBIT)	$143.0
Interest	(41.4)
Earnings before taxes (EBT)	$101.6
Taxes (40%)	(40.6)
Net income	$ 61.0
Preferred dividends	(0.0)
Earnings available to common stockholders	$ 61.0

NOTES:
$Shrs_C$ = Number of common shares outstanding = 26.3 million
EPS = Earnings per share = $61.0/26.3 = $2.32

Exhibit 700.27 *Unilate Textiles: Financial Break-even Chart*

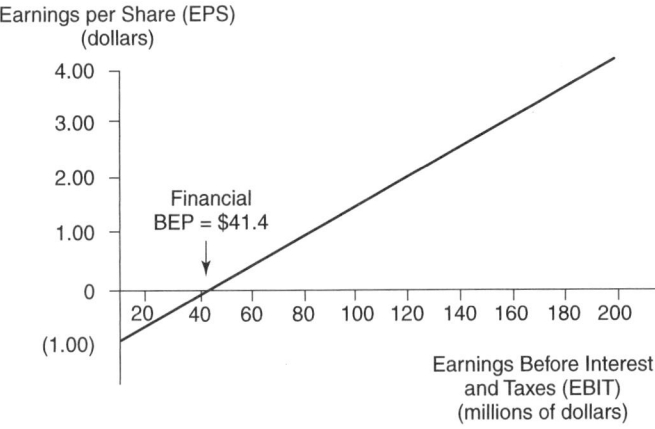

Financial break-even analysis deals with the lower portion of the income statement—the portion from operating income (EBIT) to earnings available to common stockholders. This portion of the income statement generally is referred to as the *financing section,* because it contains the expenses associated with the financing arrangements of the firm. The financing section of Unilate's forecasted 2001 income statement is contained in Exhibit 700.26.

BREAK-EVEN GRAPH Exhibit 700.27 shows the earnings per share (EPS) for Unilate at various levels of EBIT. The point at which EPS equals zero is referred to as the **financial break-even point.** As the graph indicates, the financial break-even point for Unilate is where EBIT equals $41.4 million. At this EBIT level, the income generated from operations is just sufficient to cover the financing costs, including income taxes; thus, EPS equals zero. To see this, we can compute the EPS when EBIT is $41.4 million.

Earnings before interest and taxes (EBIT)	$41.4
Interest	(41.4)
Earnings before taxes (EBT)	0.0
Taxes (40%)	(0.0)
Net income	0.0
Earnings available to common stockholders (EAC)	$ 0.0
EPS = $0/26.3 = $0	

720. FINANCIAL FORECASTING, PLANNING, AND CONTROL

BREAK-EVEN COMPUTATION The results obtained from Exhibit 700.27 can be translated algebraically to produce a relatively simple equation that can be used to compute the financial break-even point of any firm. First, remember the financial break-even point is defined as the level of EBIT that generates EPS equal to zero. Therefore, at the financial break-even point,

$$\text{EPS} = \frac{\text{Earnings available to common stockholders}}{\text{Number of common shares outstanding}} = 0 \quad (7.21)$$

$$= \frac{(\text{EBIT} - I)(1 - T) - D_{ps}}{\text{Shrs}_c} = 0$$

where EBIT is the earnings before interest and taxes, I represents the interest payments on debt, T is the marginal tax rate, D_{ps} is the amount of dividends paid to preferred stockholders, and Shrs_c is the number of common shares outstanding. Notice that EPS equals zero if the numerator in Equation 7.21, which is the earnings available to common stockholders, equals zero; so the financial break-even point also can be stated as follows.

$$(\text{EBIT} - I)(1 - T) - D_{ps} = 0$$

Rearranging this equation to solve for EBIT gives the solution for the level of EBIT needed to produce EPS equal to zero. Therefore, the computation for a firm's financial break-even point is

$$\text{EBIT}_{\text{FinBE}} = I + \frac{D_{ps}}{(1 - T)} \quad (7.22)$$

Using Equation 7.22, the financial break-even point for Unilate Textiles in 2001 is

$$\text{EBIT}_{\text{FinBE}} = \$41.4 + \frac{\$0}{1 - 0.4} = \$41.4$$

which is the same result shown in Exhibit 700.27.

According to Equation 7.22, the amount of preferred stock dividends must be stated on a before-tax basis to determine the financial break-even point. If a firm has no preferred stock though, the firm only needs to cover its interest payments, so the financial break-even point simply equals the interest expense. This is the case for Unilate, because it has no preferred stock. Because most corporations in the United States do not have preferred stock outstanding, we will not include preferred dividends in the discussions that follow.

USING FINANCIAL BREAK-EVEN ANALYSIS Financial break-even analysis can be used to help determine the impact of the firm's financing mix on the earnings available to common stockholders. When the firm uses financing alternatives that require fixed financing costs such as interest, financial leverage exists. Financial leverage affects the financing section of the income statement like operating leverage affects the operating section. This point is discussed next.

Financial Leverage

While operating leverage considers how changing sales volume affects operating income, **financial leverage** considers the impact changing operating income has on earnings per share, or earnings available to common stockholders. So operating leverage affects the operating section of the income statement, whereas financial leverage affects the financing section of the income statement. *Financial leverage takes over where operating leverage leaves off, further magnifying the effects on earnings per share of changes in the level of sales.* For this reason, operating leverage sometimes is referred to as *first-stage leverage* and financial leverage as *second-stage leverage*.

Like operating leverage, financial leverage arises because fixed costs exist; in this case, the fixed costs are associated with how the firm is financed. The **degree of financial leverage (DFL)** is defined as the percent change in earnings per share (EPS) that results from a given percent change in earnings before interest and taxes (EBIT), and it is computed as follows.

$$\text{DFL} = \frac{\text{Percent change in EPS}}{\text{Percent change in EBIT}} = \frac{\left(\dfrac{\Delta \text{EPS}}{\text{EPS}}\right)}{\left(\dfrac{\Delta \text{EBIT}}{\text{EBIT}}\right)} \quad (7.23)$$

Exhibit 700.28 shows the results of increasing Unilate's EBIT 20.8 percent. The increase in EPS is 29.2 percent, which is 1.40 times the change in EBIT; so the DFL for Unilate equals 1.40.

Exhibit 700.28 Unilate Textiles: Earnings per Share at Sales Levels of 110 Million Units and 121 Million Units (millions of dollars, except per-share data)[a]

	2005 Forecasted Operations	Sales Increase	Dollar Change	Percent Change
Sales in units (millions)	110	121		+10.0%
Earnings before interest and taxes (EBIT)	$143.0	$172.7	$29.7	+20.8%
Interest (I)	(41.4)	(41.4)	(0.0)	+ 0.0%
Earnings before taxes (EBT)	$101.6	$131.3	$29.7	+29.2%
Taxes (40%)	(40.6)	(52.5)	(11.9)	+29.2%
Net income	$ 61.0	$ 78.8	$17.8	+29.2%
Earning per share (26.3 million shares)	$ 2.32	$ 3.00	$0.68	+29.2%

The degree of financial leverage at a particular level of EBIT can be computed easily by using the following equation:

$$\text{DFL} = \frac{\text{EBIT}}{\text{EBIT} - I} = \frac{\text{EBIT}}{\text{EBIT} - [\text{Financial BEP}]} \qquad (7.24)$$

Using Equation 7.24, the DFL for Unilate Textiles at EBIT equal to $143.0 million (sales of 110 million units) is

$$\text{DFL}_{110} = \frac{\$143.0}{\$143.0 - \$41.4} = \frac{\$143.0}{\$101.6} = 1.40\times$$

The interpretation of the DFL value is the same as for the degree of operating leverage, except the starting point for evaluating financial leverage is the earnings before interest and taxes (EBIT) and the ending point is earnings per share (EPS). So because the DFL for Unilate is 1.40×, the company can expect a 1.40 percent change in EPS for every 1 percent change in EBIT; a 20.8 percent increase in EBIT results in approximately a 29.2% (20.8% × 1.40) increase in earnings available to common stockholders, thus the same percent increase in EPS (the number of common shares outstanding does not change). Unfortunately, the opposite also is true—if Unilate's 2005 EBIT is 20.8 percent below expectations, its EPS will be 29.2 percent below the forecast of $2.32, or $1.64. To prove this result is correct, construct the financing section of Unilate's income statement when EBIT equals $113.3 million = (1 − 0.208) × $143.0 million.

The value of the degree of financial leverage found using Equation 7.24 pertains to one specific initial EBIT level. If the level of sales changes, and thus the EBIT changes, so does the value computed for DFL. For example, at sales equal to 80 million units, Unilate's EBIT would be $62 million = [80 million ($15.00 − $12.30)] − $154.0 million, and the DFL value would be

$$\text{DFL}_{80} = \frac{\$62.0}{\$62.0 - \$41.4} = \frac{\$62.0}{\$20.6} = 3.01\times$$

Compared to sales equal to 110 million units, at sales equal to 80 million units Unilate would have greater difficulty covering the fixed financing costs, so its DFL is much greater. At EBIT equal to $62.0 million, Unilate is close to its financial break-even point—EBIT equal to $41.4 million—and its degree of financial leverage is high. So the more difficulty a firm has covering its fixed financing costs with operating income, the greater its degree of financial leverage. In general then, the higher the DFL for a particular firm, it generally can be concluded the closer the firm is to its financial break-even point, and the more sensitive its earnings per share is to a change in operating income. *Greater sensitivity implies greater risk; thus it can be stated that firms with higher DFLs generally are considered to have greater financial risk than firms with lower DFLs.*

Combining Operating and Financial Leverage (DTL)

Our analysis of operating leverage and financial leverage has shown that *(1) the greater the degree of operating leverage, or fixed operating costs for a particular level of operations, the more sensitive EBIT will be to changes in sales volume, and (2) the greater the degree of financial leverage, or fixed financial costs for a particular level of operations, the more sensitive*

EPS will be to changes in EBIT. Therefore, if a firm has a considerable amount of both operating and financial leverage, then even small changes in sales will lead to wide fluctuations in EPS. Look at the impact leverage has on Unilate's forecasted 2005 operations. We found that if the sales volume increases by 10 percent, Unilate's EBIT would increase by 20.8 percent; and if EBIT increases by 20.8 percent, its EPS would increase by 29.2 percent. So in combination, a 10 percent increase in sales volume would result in a 29.2 percent increase in EPS. This shows the impact of total leverage, which is the combination of both operating leverage and financial leverage, with respect to Unilate's current operations.

The degree of total leverage (DTL) is defined as the percent change in EPS resulting from a change in sales volume. This relationship can be written as follows:

$$\text{Degree of total leverage} = \text{DTL} = \frac{\left(\frac{\Delta \text{EPS}}{\text{EPS}}\right)}{\left(\frac{\Delta \text{Sales}}{\text{Sales}}\right)} = \frac{\left(\frac{\Delta \text{EBIT}}{\text{EBIT}}\right)}{\left(\frac{\Delta \text{Sales}}{\text{Sales}}\right)} \times \frac{\left(\frac{\Delta \text{EPS}}{\text{EPS}}\right)}{\left(\frac{\Delta \text{EBIT}}{\text{EBIT}}\right)} = \text{DOL} \times \text{DFL} \quad (7.25)$$

Combining the equations for DOL (Equations 7.20 and 7.20a) and for DFL (Equation 7.24), Equation 7.25 can be restated as follows:

$$\text{DTL} = \frac{\text{Gross profit}}{\text{EBIT}} \times \frac{\text{EBIT}}{\text{EBIT} - [\text{Financial BEP}]} = \frac{\text{Gross profit}}{\text{EBIT} - [\text{Financial BEP}]} \quad (7.26)$$

$$= \frac{S - VC}{\text{EBIT} - I} = \frac{Q(P - V)}{[Q(P - V) - F] - I}$$

Using Equation 7.26, the degree of total leverage (DTL) for Unilate would be

$$\text{DTL}_{110} = \frac{110(\$15.00 - \$12.30)}{[110(\$15.00 - \$12.30) - \$154.0] - \$41.4}$$

$$= \frac{\$297.0}{\$143.0 - \$41.4} = \frac{\$297.0}{\$101.6}$$

$$= 2.92\times$$

According to Equation 7.25, we could have arrived at the same result for DTL by multiplying the degree of operating leverage by the degree of financial leverage, so the DTL for Unilate would be 2.08 × 1.40 ≈ 2.92. This value indicates that for every 1 percent change in sales volume, Unilate's EPS will change by 2.92 percent; a 10 percent increase in sales will result in a 29.2 percent increase in EPS. This is exactly the impact expected.

The value of DTL can be used to compute the new earnings per share (EPS*) after a change in sales volume. We already know that Unilate's EPS will change by 2.92 percent for every 1 percent change in sales. So EPS* resulting from a 10 percent increase in sales can be computed as follows:

$$\text{EPS*} = \text{EPS}[1 + (.10)(2.92)] = \$2.32 \times (1 + 0.292) = \$3.00$$

which is the same result given in Exhibit 700.28.

The degree of combined (total) leverage concept is useful primarily for the insights it provides regarding the joint effects of operating and financial leverage on earnings per share. The concept can be used to show management, for example, that a decision to automate a plant and to finance the new equipment with debt would result in a situation in which a 10 percent decline in sales would result in a nearly 50 percent decline in earnings, whereas with a different operating and financial package, a 10 percent sales decline would cause earnings to decline only by 15 percent. Having the alternatives stated in this manner gives decision makers a better idea of the ramifications of alternative actions with respect to the firm's level of operations and how those operations are financed.

Using Leverage and Forecasting for Control

From the discussion in the previous sections, it should be clear what the impact on income would be if the 2005 sales forecast for Unilate Textiles is different than expected. If sales are greater than expected, both operating and financial leverage will magnify the "bottom line" impact on EPS (DTL = 2.92). But the opposite also holds. Consequently, if Unilate does not meet its forecasted sales level, leverage will result in a magnified loss in income compared to what is expected. This will occur because production facilities might have been expanded too greatly, inventories might be built up too quickly, and so on; the end result might be that the firm suffers a significant income loss. This loss will result in a lower than expected addition to retained earnings, which means the plans for additional external funds needed to support the firm's operations will be inadequate. Likewise, if the sales forecast is too low, then, if the firm is at full capacity, it will not be able to meet the additional demand, and sales opportunities will be lost—perhaps forever. In the previous sections, we showed only how changes in operations (2001 forecasts) affect the income generated by the firm; we did not continue the process to show the impact on the balance sheet and the financing needs of the firm. To determine the impact on the financial statements, the financial manager needs to repeat the steps discussed in the first part of this section. At this stage the financial manager needs to evaluate and act on the feedback received from the forecasting and budgeting processes. In effect, then, the forecasting (planning) and control of the firm is an ongoing activity, a vital function to the long-run survival of any firm.

The forecasting and control functions described in this section are important for several reasons. First, if the projected operating results are unsatisfactory, management can "go back to the drawing board," reformulate its plans, and develop more reasonable targets for the coming year. Second, it is possible that the funds required to meet the sales forecast simply cannot be obtained; if so, it obviously is better to know this in advance and to scale back the projected level of operations than to suddenly run out of cash and have operations grind to a halt. Third, even if the required funds can be raised, it is desirable to plan for their acquisition well in advance. Finally, any deviation from the projections needs to be dealt with to improve future forecasts and the predictability of the firm's operations to ensure the goals of the firm are being pursued appropriately.

Short-Term Financial Planning

This section demonstrates how to develop a short-term financial planning model so that the financial manager can better ascertain the overall impact that short-term financial management decisions have on the net operating cash flows of the company. With such a forecast in hand, the financial manager can better plan the firm's short-term investment and financing strategies.

A Simple Percent-of-Sales Forecasting Model

We first apply the modeling principles by developing a relatively simple financial forecasting model. The example model estimates the needed external funds required for a given sales growth estimate.

The heart of this relatively simple forecasting technique lies in the assumption that current assets and possibly noncurrent or fixed assets as well as current liabilities fluctuate proportionately with sales. For example, if total assets are currently 45 percent of sales and if it can be assumed that this relationship will remain roughly the same over the next year or two, then for every additional $1,000 of sales over the current sales level, total assets must increase by $450. This increase in assets must be financed by a source of funds, such as an increase in liabilities or an increase in equity.

One readily available financing source, often referred to as a spontaneous source, is current liabilities. Accounts payable and accrued wages vary with the level of sales. If current liabilities traditionally amount to about 25 percent of sales, then for every $1,000 of sales above the current level, current liabilities (a source of funds) will increase by $1,000 × .25, or $250.

We still have an excess of uses of funds (an increase in assets) over sources of funds (an increase in liabilities) in the amount of $200 = $450 − $250. The final source of funds considered is retained earnings. This internal source can be calculated by multiplying the firm's net profit margin m by the forecasted sales level S over the planning period multiplied by the fraction 1 minus the dividend payout ratio (dpo). This final figure represents the funds from operations that will be retained for internal investment purposes. Note that depreciation is not added back because the asset figure is net of depreciation. At this point, if uses of funds still exceed sources of funds, new external financing will be required during the planning period. This forecasting model for needed external funds (NEF) can be reduced to the relatively simple formula shown below.

$$\begin{aligned} \text{NEF} = {} & (\text{Total assets/Sales}) \times \text{Change in sales} \\ & - (\text{Current liabilities/Sales}) \times \text{Change in sales} \\ & - \text{Sales} \times \text{Net profit margin} \times [1 + (\text{Dividends/Net profit})] \\ \text{NEF} = {} & (\text{TA/S}) \times \Delta S - (\text{CL/S}) \times \Delta S - [S \times m \times (1 - \text{dpo})] \end{aligned}$$

In this equation, ΔS represents the expected change in sales over the planning period.

We now use an example to show how this forecasting model works. Assume the following data are representative of a company's financial position. Furthermore, assume that management expects sales to increase by $2.75 million during the coming year, 2005. Plugging these values into the forecasting model yields the following estimate of NEF:

Balance Sheet for 2004

Total assets	$15,580,000	Current liabilities	$4,261,000
		Long-term debt	3,638,000
		Net worth	7,681,000

Income Statement for 2004

Net sales	$12,250,000
Net profit	692,000
Dividends	429,000

Thus

$$TA/S = 1.272$$
$$CL/S = .348$$
$$m = .056$$
$$dpo = .62$$

$$NEF = (1.272 \times \$2.75) - (.348 \times \$2.75) - (\$15 \times .056 \times (1 - .62))$$
$$= \$3.498 - \$.957 - \$.319 = \$2.222$$

If sales increase by $2.75 million, then total assets will expand by $3.498 million, current liabilities will expand by $.957 million, and retained profits will expand by $.319 million. The company's 2005 balance sheet will look like the following:

2005 Total assets	= $19,078,000	= $15,580,000 + $3,498,000
2005 Current liabilities	= $5,218,000	= $4,261,000 + $957,000
2005 Long-term debt	= $3,638,000	= Assumed held constant
2005 Net worth	= $8,000,000	= $7,681,000 + $319,000

Summing up the current liabilities, long-term debt, and net worth, we arrive at a total of $16,856,000. We can see above that total assets are forecasted to be $19,078,000. Thus the financing side of the balance sheet is $2,222,000 short of the funds needed to finance the asset side of the balance sheet as predicted by the NEF equation.

The financial manager now knows that if sales grow as predicted and if the financial and operating policies are such that there should be $1.272 of assets for each dollar of sales, $.348 of current liabilities per dollar of sales, a profit margin of 5.6 percent, and 62 percent of the profits paid as dividends, then the firm must obtain $2.222 million of outside financing. This new financing may be obtained through either new debt or through new equity sources, but that level of funding must be acquired to finance the forecasted growth in assets.

Understanding the Financial Planning Model

As a company begins producing and selling a product or service, it generates revenues and expenses represented by the income statement. Our financial planning model then transforms the income statement into a cash flow statement by converting revenues into cash receipts based on collections fractions and converting expenses into cash disbursement based on payment fractions. The projected income statement and resulting cash flow statement then impact the balance sheet by changing the level of current assets (cash, receivables, and inventory), current liabilities (accounts payable), accumulated depreciation, and retained earnings. If spontaneous assets grow faster than spontaneous liabilities and equity, then additional financing is required to improve the company's financial position. The financial manager is then faced with choosing the type, amount, and maturity of financing that enhances the value of the firm. If spontaneous liabilities and equity grow faster than spontaneous assets, then excess liquidity is generated and the financial manager can either retire debt, pay a dividend, or invest in financial assets. Again, the choice made should be the one that enhances the value of the firm.

Cash Forecasting

Four factors account for corporate emphasis on short-term cash forecasts. First, cash forecasts drive the short-term investing and borrowing strategies. Selecting the maturity of a short-term investment, when to repay borrowings, or the size of a credit line to request all depend critically on the forecasted cash position. Alternating cash surpluses and shortages occur because cash receipts and disbursements are not synchronized.

Second, the forecast is an important input into short-term financial policy decisions, including disbursement policies, credit terms, and bank selection; *making decisions along the cash flow timeline requires accurate estimation of flow size and timing.* Accurate anticipation of cash balances might be less important if the company has a controlled disbursement account (particularly when funding is automated) or has sufficient balances (for example, to compensate for credit and/or noncredit services) to absorb uncertainties.

Third, cash forecasts function as a control device. Before the beginning of each year, the forecasting staff develops a cash budget, which is a forecast of cash flows and the cash balance for each month. As the year progresses, deviations of actual cash balances from cash budget projections signal the cash manager to investigate and take corrective action. Sales and marketing managers may use the cash balance variances as an early warning system when declining cash receipts are found to be the cause of the variance. Accurate forecasts can provide added value when they signal a cash shortage and the need for action before problems emerge, or corrective action as actual data become available. Sagner (2000) estimates that a $15 million portfolio will earn an added 1/5 to 1/4 of 1 percent (equal to $37,500 per year) and save an additional $5,500 in transactions costs when moving from overnight (sweep account) investing to one-month maturities.

Fourth, effective risk management is possible with forecasts of the cash-flow effects of interest rate changes, commodity price changes, and foreign exchange rate changes.

Forecasting Monthly Cash Flows

The most important cash forecast from a top management perspective is the monthly cash forecast. This forecast shows cash receipts and disbursements on a monthly basis for a minimum horizon of one year; when done before the beginning of a new fiscal year, it is called the cash budget. The cash budget is a document showing anticipated cash receipts and disbursements for a future period, usually one year. This cash budget is formulated to be consistent with the company's operating budget, which specifies planned sales and operating expenses. Many companies extend the monthly forecast out to a 5-year horizon to correspond with the company's long-range financial plan. The level of detail and anticipated accuracy diminishes with longer forecast horizons, however. The three commonly used cash forecasting approaches are the receipts and disbursements method (sometimes referred to as cash scheduling), the modified accrual method, and the pro forma balance sheet approach.

Approach 1: The Receipts and Disbursements Method

The **receipts and disbursements method** involves looking up most of the data variables in company sources and estimating cash effect timing of noncash events. The major noncash events are product sales and material purchases. Usually, receipts are listed separately on a receipts schedule and disbursements on a separate disbursements schedule. The forecaster then combines the receipts and disbursements on a projected schedule (think of it as a projected cash flow timeline) according to anticipated cash flow dates. The layout used may vary from a desk calendar to a fancy computer spreadsheet that is linked to numerous other corporate spreadsheets. Periodic and accurate intracompany communications are critical to the accuracy of the approach. Accuracy suffers when the horizon extends beyond one month, however, and earlier inaccuracies compound into large errors for longer horizons.

Format of the Receipts and Disbursements Forecast

A template that might be used for receipts and disbursements is shown in Exhibit 700.29. Note that this format takes into account beginning and ending cash (both calculated by assuming no short-term investments or borrowings), the period's cash flows, and required minimal cash levels. The ending cash for one month serves as the beginning cash for the following month. The minimum cash balance is a function of management policy that a certain emergency cash stock be held and/or a compensating balance be kept at deposit banks. The bottom line, excess cash or required total financing, is a cumulative total. It represents the account balance of the amount invested or borrowed as of the end of the period. The net cash flow indicates how much additional money is invested or paid back (on outstanding loans), if positive, or the dollar figure of investments liquidated or additional lending, if negative.

An alternative format is to use the Statement of Cash Flows format for the receipts and disbursements, thereby classifying sources and uses of cash according to whether they are operating, investing, or financing cash flows. Because businesses must include the cash flow statement as part of their reporting, monitoring forecast accuracy is simple.

Exhibit 700.29 *Template for Receipts and Disbursements Method for World Communications*

World Communications Corp.
Cash Receipts and Disbursements

	January 2005	February 2005	March 2005
BEGINNING CASH BALANCE	$ 1,500,000	$ 2,612,050	($ 1,552,238)
CASH RECEIPTS:			
Cash sales	$ 5,600,000	$ 3,500,000	$ 3,125,000
Cash collection of prior month's credit sales	$10,200,000	$ 8,400,000	$ 5,250,000
Cash collection of credit sales made 2 months ago	$ 5,750,000	$ 3,187,500	$ 2,625,000
Interest income received	$ 9,675	$ 2,535	$ 0
Cash dividends received	$ 375	$ 245	$ 165
Cash from asset sales	$ 0	$ 15	$ 0
Cash proceeds from long term borrowings	$ 4,500	$ 0	$ 0
Cash proceeds from equity issuance	$ 0	$ 0	$ 0
TOTAL CASH RECEIPTS:	$21,564,550	$15,090,295	$11,000,165
CASH DISBURSEMENTS:			
Cash purchases	$ 6,750,000	$ 2,720,000	$ 2,500,000
Cash payment for prior month credit purchases	$11,250,000	$ 4,533,333	$ 4,166,667
Cash payment for credit purchases made 2 months ago	$ 0	$ 0	$0
Interest payments	$ 250	$ 250	$ 250
Principal repayments	$ 1,000	$ 1,000	$ 1,000
Cash dividends paid	0	$12,000,000	$ 0
Tax payments	$ 1,250	$ 0	$ 0
Asset acquisitions	$ 2,450,000	$ 0	$ 1,250,000
TOTAL CASH DISBURSEMENTS:	$20,452,500	$19,254,583	$ 7,917,917
CASH FLOW (RECEIPTS − DISBURSEMENTS)	$ 1,112,050	$ 4,164,288	$ 3,082,248
ENDING CASH (BEG CASH + CASH FLOW)	$ 2,612,050	$ 1,552,238	$ 1,530,010
LESS: Minimum cash balance	$ 1,000,000	$ 1,000,000	$ 1,000,000
CASH SURPLUS (IF POSITIVE)	$ 1,612,050	0	$ 530,010
CASH SHORTFALL (IF NEGATIVE)	0	$ 2,552,238	0

Interpreting the Receipts and Disbursements Forecast

Take a closer look at Exhibit 700.29 to see how the treasury analyst can use it to make investing and borrowing decisions. The company starts the quarter with $1.5 million in cash and cash equivalents. Everything looks fine after January, with an ending cash position of $2.6 million. Even after subtracting the minimum cash balance of $1 million, there is a large cash surplus. This represents an investable balance, which usually is invested in short-term securities.

The large net cash outflow in February, mainly resulting from the dividend payment, causes the company to liquidate the short-term securities but still run short of cash. Even before considering the required minimum of $1 million, the company is unable to cover the cash outflow. The company will have to borrow more than $1 million to maintain the necessary minimum cash. March brings a net cash inflow, large enough to not only pay off the $1 million-plus credit line borrowing but also to invest in $530,010 of short-term securities.

Notice three uses for the monthly cash forecast. First, we are able to anticipate the need for credit and the amount of borrowing that should be prearranged to cover anticipated deficits. In World Communication's case, the company will likely arrange a credit line of at least $3 million because forecasts are never perfect and there might be a smaller receipt total or larger disbursement total in any given month. Or the company may allow the $1 million minimum liquidity to act as a buffer against unforeseen cash needs and only borrow $1 million. Of course, the analyst looks at least one year ahead, not merely the three months we show here. Second, we are able to project short-term investment amounts and, based on how long cash surpluses will persist, the allowable maturity of those securities. Normally, longer maturities bring higher yields, and the analyst will study the forecast for 6 or 12 months ahead to see how long projected cash surpluses will last. Third, the analyst might use such projections to help establish the company's target cash balance. The company might arrange more long-term borrowing to increase the year-beginning cash position and avoid short-term borrowing altogether. One caution when using monthly cash budgets: This forecast is giving us anticipated *end-of-month* cash balances. These could well mask larger intramonth receipt and disbursement mismatches, and the analyst will look at the historical pattern of cash flows to determine if these have occurred. This provides further motivation to arrange credit lines larger than the largest cumulative month-end cash shortage recorded in the cash forecast.

Developing the Receipts and Disbursements Forecast

The steps involved in generating the cash forecast using the receipts and disbursements method are straightforward. First, the analyst must develop or look up the company's sales forecast. Preferably, a range of sales forecasts can be developed, linked to likely scenarios for the horizon period. This enables the forecaster to incorporate the uncertainty inherent in the sales forecast through techniques such as simulation. To aid in the sales projection, the analyst may break down the sales revenue forecast into its components, unit sales and selling prices.

Second, the analyst lays out the incoming cash from cash sales, cash collections, asset sales, and other sources. But what if the company offers credit terms, and a given month's sales generates cash across several subsequent months? The historical or anticipated payment pattern for the company's customers is used to project the cash receipts from sales. Returning to the receipts and disbursement illustration (Exhibit 700.29) helps.

World Communications first projects sales for its product lines, which we show as a memo item at the top of Exhibit 700.30. Next, it studies historical collection patterns, to determine the uncollected balance fractions shown in the second column (these may already be available if the credit department is using them to monitor collection efficiency. The key is to determine when cash is received from customers—when does the customer actually make payment? A few months of actual sales will also be included in our data, because of the lag in collections. Here, the analyst is making a projection in early January, so we have actual data from October, November, and December, in case there is a three-month lag in collections. In World Communications' case, October's sales are not used, because 95 percent of sales are collected within two months, and the remaining 5 percent are uncollectible. World receives 32 percent in the month of sale, 48 percent in the next month (lag one month), and 15 percent in the second following month (lag two months). These proportions add to 100% only if World experiences negligible bad debt losses. Here, as noted, World fails to collect 5 percent of sales (100%−32%−48%−15%). To calculate January's cash receipts from sales, we take 32 percent of January's projected sales of $17.5 million, plus 48 percent of December's sales of $21.25 million, plus 15 percent of November's sales of 38.33 million. The sum is $21.55 million of cash receipts, which constitutes most of January's total cash receipts in Exhibit 700.30.

Third, cash disbursements, including payments to suppliers, employees, governments, and funds providers are arrayed. The difference in the cash receipts and disbursements gives the period's net cash flow. Many forecasters stop

Exhibit 700.30 *Cash Receipts from Sales Worksheet for World Communications*

		Projecting Cash Collections from Earlier Sales					
		Month Sales					
Item	Proportion	Oct 2004	Nov 2004	Dec 2004	Jan 2005	Feb 2005	Mar 2005
MEMO: Actual (Forecast) Sales:		$20,000,000	$38,333,333	$21,250,000	$17,500,000	$10,937,500	$9,765,625
Cash sales	32%				$ 5,600,000	$ 3,500,000	$3,125,000
Collections of credit sales:							
Lagged 1 month	48%				10,200,000	8,400,000	5,250,000
Lagged 2 months	15%				5,750,000	3,187,500	2,625,000
Lagged 3 months*	0%				0	0	0
Total cash receipts from sales					$21,550,000	$15,087,500	$11,000,000

*Bad debt loss rate is 5% (=100% − 32% − 48% − 15%).

here, but, as shown in Exhibit 700.29, it is valuable to go beyond this to add beginning cash, arriving at ending cash. Financing and investments can be handled in two different ways. They can be treated as a residual: If ending cash is negative, arrange this amount of financing; if positive, plan to invest the surplus amount. Or the financing and investing can be built into the forecast to reflect planned financing and investing. Regardless, asset sales and capital investments should be included as separate categories under receipts and disbursements. Strengths of the receipts and disbursements method include simplicity, accuracy for near-term forecasts, and attractiveness as a monitoring and control tool. Weaknesses include the inaccuracy for forecast horizons greater than three months (largely resulting from the cumulation of early errors) and the overreliance on the forecaster's judgment that typifies real-life applications of the technique.

Approach 2: The Modified Accrual Method

Modified Accrual Method

A second technique useful for monthly forecasts is the modified accrual method. Sometimes called the accrual addback technique or adjusted net income technique, the approach begins with accounting reports or the operating budget and then adjusts these numbers to reflect the timing of cash flows related to these transactions. For small businesses and nonprofit organizations doing their income statements on a cash basis, very few adjustments to the operating budget or projected income statement are necessary. The only problem encountered in that case is if the historical tracker used to develop a forecast is invalidated because of faster or slower processing of invoices, checks received, and so on. In its simplest form, the modified accrual forecast is easily determined, as shown in Equation 7.27.

$$CF_t = NI_t + NC_t - CA_t + CL_t \qquad (7.27)$$

when for period t:

CF_t = cash flow
NI_t = net income
NC_t = noncash charges
CA_t = current asset change
CL_t = current liability change

Example of the Modified Accrual Technique

AMAX Coal has assembled the following pro forma income statement and parts of its present and pro forma balance sheets, which are shown in highly condensed form.

Pro Forma Income Statement ($ mils.)

Sales	$10,000
− COGS	$ 6,000
Gross margin	$ 4,000
− operating exps.	$ 3,150*
Operating profit	$ 850
− interest exp.	$ 25
Pretax income	$ 800
− taxes	$ 300
Net income	$ 500

*Includes depreciation and other noncash charges of $145 million.

	Present Balance Sheet ($ mils.)	Pro Forma Balance Sheet ($ mils.)
Current Assets:		
Cash	$ 10	Uncertain; assume to be unchanged.
Accts. receivable	$ 970	$ 960
Inventories	$ 835	$ 820
Long-term Assets		
Property, plant, and equip.	$12,000	$11,700
Current Liabilities:		
Accounts payable	$ 745	$ 730
Notes payable	$ 500	$ 500
Long-term debt	$ 7,000	$ 8,000

Forecast Solution:
Net income and the noncash charges are taken from the projected income statement. Changes in current assets and current liabilities are calculated as (Projected Balance Sheet Amount − Present Balance Sheet Amount). If AMAX Coal, Inc., projects net income of $500 million, noncash charges of $145 million, decreases in current assets of $25 million (in this case, the change in accounts receivable plus change in inventories), and decreases in current liabilities of $15 million (here, the change in accounts payable), cash flow for the period using our simple equation is:

$$CF_t = \$500 + \$145 - (-\$25) + (-\$15) = \$655 \text{ million}$$

Current asset changes are subtracted because increases in items such as inventories drain cash flow, and current liability changes are added because they represent sources of cash flow. Typical noncash charges are depreciation, amortization of intangibles, and gains or losses on asset sales. Notice that the cash flow formula presented is an operating cash flow forecast. The change, if any, in long-term assets, long-term liabilities, and equity will not affect the forecasted cash flow. If desired, Equation 7.27 easily can be expanded to include anticipated dividends, loan interest or principal payments, acquisitions, and other episodic cash flows. At that point, however, it might be easier to simply change to a projected statement of cash flow format.

The major strength of the modified accrual technique is ease of implementation: The data are already available, in most cases, in the form of a budget or projected income statement. The adjustments to net income to arrive at cash flow are easily made, as shown above. The technique is also relatively accurate for intermediate-term forecasting, when compared with other techniques. However, it suffers from inaccuracy in the short-run horizons and may lack sufficient detail to ensure accuracy.

Approach 3: The Pro Forma Balance Sheet Method

Pro Forma Balance Sheet Method

The pro forma balance sheet approach to generating a cash forecast involves determination of the amount of cash and marketable securities by computing the difference between projected assets (excluding cash and marketable securities) and the sum of projected liabilities and owner's equity. This approach, very popular for medium-term and long-term forecasting, is illustrated in Exhibit 700.31.

In projecting the balance sheet, current liabilities and noncash assets might be predicted as a percentage of anticipated sales, and the long-term liabilities and common stock assumed to remain constant. The change in retained earnings is based on anticipated net income less planned cash dividends. If we subtract the sum of liabilities and owner's equity from noncash assets, we get a residual amount labeled "cash and marketable securities," which is our cash forecast. If this amount is negative, additional financing will have to be arranged. Then the new financing amount is plugged into the liability section; interest expense, net income, and additions to retained earnings recomputed and a new cash amount calculated. In other cases, the figure may be a large positive amount, in which case some previous borrowings may be paid down, stock repurchased, or greater expansion in fixed assets arranged. The fact that the forecast leads naturally to financial planning demonstrates the value of longer-term cash forecasts. The pro forma balance sheet approach is well suited for these longer-range cash forecasts.

Basically, the pro forma balance sheet represents a crude approximation of sources and uses of funds, with funds defined as cash and marketable securities. Liability and equity accounts represent sources of funds; asset amounts

Exhibit 700.31   *Pro Forma Balance Sheet Method*

BALANCE SHEET PROJECTION FORECASTING METHOD Cash and Marketable Securities Residual of Balance Sheet Projection			
Month			
Account	Jan	Feb	Mar
Cash and M.S.*	Plug	Plug	Plug
Accts. receivable	$ 35	$ 36	$ 36
Inventories	$ 65	$ 66	$ 68
Prepaid expenses	$ 15	$ 15	$ 16
Current assets	$115	$117	$120
Prop., plant, equipment	$210	$223	$227
TOTAL ASSETS	$325	$340	$347
Accts. payable	$ 30	$ 31	$ 31
Notes payable	$ 25	$ 26	$ 26
Accrued expenses	$ 10	$ 10	$ 10
Current liabilities	$ 65	$ 67	$ 67
Long-term liabilities	$ 45	$ 46	$ 47
TOTAL LIABILITIES	$110	$113	$114
Stockholders' equity			
Common stock	$ 5	$ 5	$ 5
Paid-in capital	$ 20	$ 20	$ 20
Retained earnings	$205	$220	$235
EQUITY	$230	$245	$260
TOTAL LIABS. and EQUITY	$340	$358	$374

*Calculation of Cash & Marketable Securities Plug Amount
Cash and M.S.
  = (Totals Liabs.
  + Stockholders' Equity)
  − Total Assets: 340 − 325 = 15   358 − 340 = 18   374 − 347 = 27

represent uses of funds. The major strength of this forecasting approach is its ease of implementation. The major weakness is the difficulty in making accurate monthly forecasts by using balance sheet projections. For annual totals, the technique is acceptable, but for monthly forecasts, the failure to adjust for differences between accrual-based net income (which drives the retained earnings projection) and cash flows arising from that income stream hurts forecast accuracy.

Cost of Capital, Capital Structure, and Dividend Policy

The Cost of Capital

It is vitally important that a firm knows how much it pays for the funds used to purchase assets. The average return required by the firm's investors determines how much must be paid to attract funds—it is the firm's average cost of funds, which more commonly is termed the *cost of capital*. The firm's cost of capital is very important because it represents the minimum rate of return that must be earned from investments, such as capital budgeting projects, to ensure the value of the firm does not decrease—the cost of capital is the firm's *required rate of return*. For example, if investors provide funds to a firm for an average cost of 15 percent, wealth will decrease if the funds are used to generate returns less than 15 percent, wealth will not change if exactly 15 percent is earned, and wealth will increase if returns greater than 15 percent can be generated.

In this section, we discuss the concept of cost of capital, how the average cost of capital is determined, and how the cost of capital is used in financial decision making. How much it costs a firm for its funds is based on the return demanded by investors—if the return offered by the firm is not high enough, then investors will not provide sufficient funds. In other words, the rate of return an investor earns on a corporate security effectively is a cost to the firm of using those funds, so the same models are used by investors and by corporate treasurers to determine required rates of return.

Our first topic in this section is the logic of the weighted average cost of capital. Next, we consider the costs of the major types of capital, after which we see how the costs of the individual components of the capital structure are brought together to form a weighted average cost of capital (WACC).

The Logic of the Weighted Average Cost of Capital

It is possible to finance a firm entirely with equity funds by issuing only stock. In that case, the cost of capital used to analyze capital budgeting decisions should be the company's required return on equity. However, most firms raise a substantial portion of their funds as long-term debt, and some also use preferred stock. For these firms, their cost of capital must reflect the average cost of the various sources of long-term funds used, not just the firms' costs of equity.

Assume that Unilate Textiles has a 10 percent cost of debt and a 13.7 percent cost of equity. Further, assume that Unilate has made the decision to finance next year's projects by selling debt only. The argument is sometimes made that the cost of capital for these projects is 10 percent because only debt will be used to finance them. However, this position is incorrect. If Unilate finances a particular set of projects with debt, the firm will be using up some of its potential for obtaining new debt in the future. As expansion occurs in subsequent years, Unilate will at some point find it necessary to raise additional equity to prevent the debt ratio from becoming too large.

To illustrate, suppose Unilate borrows heavily at 10 percent during 2005, using up its debt capacity in the process, to finance projects yielding 11.5 percent. In 2006 it has new projects available that yield 13 percent, well above the return on 2005 projects, but it cannot accept them because they would have to be financed with 13.7 percent equity money. To avoid this problem, Unilate should be viewed as an ongoing concern, and *the cost of capital used in capital budgeting should be calculated as a weighted average, or combination, of the various types of funds generally used, regardless of the specific financing used to fund a particular project.*

Basic Definitions of Cost Capital Components

The items on the right side of a firm's balance sheet—various types of debt, preferred stock, and common equity—are its **capital components.** Any increase in total assets must be financed by an increase in one or more of these capital components.

Capital is a necessary factor of production, and, like any other factor, it has a cost. The cost of each component is called the *component cost* of that particular type of capital; for example, if Unilate can borrow money at 10 percent, its component cost of debt is 10 percent. Throughout this section we concentrate on debt, preferred stock, retained earnings, and new issues of common stock, which are the four major capital structure components. We will use the following symbols to designate specific component costs of capital:

- k_d = Interest rate on the firm's debt = before-tax component cost of debt. For Unilate, k_d = 10.0%.
- k_{dT} = $k_d(1 - T)$ = After-tax component cost of debt, where T is the firm's marginal tax rate. k_{dT} is the debt cost used to calculate the weighted average cost of capital. For Unilate, T = 40%, so $k_{dT} = k_d(1 - T) = 10.0\%(1 - 0.4) = 10.0\%(0.6) = 6.0\%$.
- k_{ps} = Component cost of preferred stock. Unilate has no preferred stock at this time, but, as new funds are raised, the company plans to issue preferred stock. The cost of preferred stock, k_{ps}, will be 10.3%.
- k_s = Component cost of retained earnings (or internal equity). For Unilate, $k_s \approx 13.7\%$.
- k_e = Component cost of external equity obtained by issuing new common stock as opposed to retaining earnings. As we shall see, it is necessary to distinguish between common equity needs that can be satisfied by retained earnings and the common equity needs that are satisfied by selling new stock. This is why we distinguish between internal and external equity, k_s and k_e. Further, k_e is always greater than k_s. For Unilate, $k_e \approx 14.3\%$.
- WACC = The weighted average cost of capital. In the future, when Unilate needs *new* capital to finance asset expansion, it will raise part of the new funds as debt, part as preferred stock, and part as common equity (with common equity coming either from retained earnings or from the issuance of new common stock). We will calculate WACC for Unilate Textiles shortly.

Cost of Debt, k_{dT}

The after-tax cost of debt, k_{dT}, is the interest rate on debt, k_d, less the tax saving that results because interest is deductible. This is the same as k_d multiplied by $(1 - T)$, where T is the firm's marginal tax rate.

$$\text{After-tax component cost of debt} = k_{dT} = \text{(Bondholders' required rate of return)} - \text{(Tax savings)} \quad (7.28)$$
$$= k_d - k_d \times T$$
$$= k_d(1 - T)$$

In effect, the government pays part of the cost of debt because interest is deductible. Therefore, if Unilate can borrow at an interest rate of 10 percent, and if it has a marginal tax rate of 40 percent, then its after-tax cost of debt is 6 percent.

$$k_{dT} = k_d(1 - T) = 10.0\%(1.0 - 0.4)$$
$$= 10.0\%(0.6)$$
$$= 6.0\%$$

We use the after-tax cost of debt because the value of the firm's stock, which we want to maximize, depends on *after-tax* cash flows. Because interest is a deductible expense, it produces tax savings that reduce the net cost of debt, making the after-tax cost of debt less than the before-tax cost. We are concerned with after-tax cash flows, so after-tax rates of return are appropriate.

Cost of Preferred Stock, k_{ps}

In Section 715, we found that the dividend associated with preferred stock is constant and that preferred stock has no stated maturity. Thus, a preferred dividend, which we designate D_{ps}, represents a perpetuity, and the component **cost of preferred stock, k_{ps},** is the preferred dividend, D_{ps}, divided by the net issuing price, NP, or the price the firm receives after deducting the costs of issuing the stock, which are called *flotation costs*.

$$\text{Component cost of preferred stock} = k_{ps} = \frac{D_{ps}}{NP} = \frac{D_{ps}}{P_0 - \text{Flotation costs}} \quad (7.29)$$

For example, in the future, Unilate is going to issue preferred stock that pays a $10 dividend per share and sells for $100 per share in the market. It will cost 3 percent, or $3 per share, to issue the new preferred stock, so Unilate will net $97 per share. Therefore, Unilate's cost of preferred stock is 10.3 percent.

$$k_{ps} = \frac{\$10}{\$97}$$
$$= 0.103 = 10.3\%$$

No tax adjustments are made when calculating k_{ps} because preferred dividends, unlike interest expense on debt, are not tax deductible, so there are no tax savings associated with the use of preferred stock.

Cost of Retained Earnings, k_s

The costs of debt and preferred stock are based on the returns investors require on these securities. Similarly, the **cost of retained earnings, k_s,** is the rate of return stockholders require on equity capital the firm obtains by retaining earnings that otherwise could be distributed to common stockholders as dividends.

The reason we must assign a cost of capital to retained earnings involves the *opportunity cost principle*. The firm's after-tax earnings literally belong to its stockholders. Bondholders are compensated by interest payments, and preferred stockholders by preferred dividends, but the earnings remaining after interest and preferred dividends belong to the common stockholders, and these earnings help compensate stockholders for the use of their capital. Management can either pay out the earnings in the form of dividends or retain earnings and reinvest them in the business. If management decides to retain earnings, there is an opportunity cost involved—stockholders could have received the earnings as dividends and invested this money in other stocks, in bonds, in real estate, or in anything else. Thus, the firm should earn a return on earnings it retains that is at least as great as the return stockholders themselves could earn on alternative investments of comparable risk.

What rate of return can stockholders expect to earn on equivalent-risk investments? First, recall that stocks normally are in equilibrium, with the expected and required rates of return being equal: $\hat{k}_s = k_s$. Therefore, we can assume that Unilate's stockholders expect to earn a return of k_s on their money. *If the firm cannot invest retained earnings and earn at least k_s, it should pay these funds to its stockholders and let them invest directly in other assets that do provide this return.*

Whereas debt and preferred stocks are contractual obligations that have easily determined costs, it is not as easy to measure k_s. However, we can employ the principles applied in asset valuation to produce reasonably good cost of equity estimates. To begin, we know that if a stock is in equilibrium (which is the typical situation), then its required rate of return, k_s, is also equal to its expected rate of return, $\hat{k}_s$. Further, its required return is equal to a risk-free rate, k_{RF}, plus a risk premium, RP, whereas the expected return on a constant growth stock is equal to the stock's dividend yield, $\hat{D}_1/P_0$, plus its expected growth rate, g:

Required rate of return = Expected rate of return

$$k_s = k_{RF} + RP = \frac{\hat{D}_1}{P_0} + g = \hat{k}_s \quad (7.30)$$

Because the two must be equal, we can estimate k_s either as $k_s = k_{RF} + RP$ or as $\hat{k}_s = \hat{D}_1/P_0 + g$. Actually, three methods are commonly used for finding the cost of retained earnings: (1) the capital asset pricing model (CAPM) approach, (2) the bond-yield-plus-risk-premium approach, and (3) constant growth model using the discounted cash flow (DCF) approach. These three approaches are discussed next.

The CAPM Approach

The Capital Asset Pricing Model (CAPM) is as follows.

$$k_s = k_{RF} + (k_M - k_{RF})\beta_s \quad (7.31)$$

Equation 7.31 shows that the CAPM estimate of k_s begins with the risk-free rate, k_{RF}, to which is added a risk premium that is based on the stock's relation to the market as measured by its beta, β_s, and the magnitude of the market risk premium, which is the difference between the market return, k_M, and the risk-free rate, k_{RF}.

To illustrate the CAPM approach, assume that $k_{RF} = 7\%$, $k_M = 11\%$, and $\beta_s = 1.6$ for Unilate's common stock. Using the CAPM approach, Unilate's cost of retained earnings, k_s, is calculated as follows:

$$\begin{aligned} k_s &= 7.0\% + (11.0\% - 7.0\%)(1.6) \\ &= 7.0\% + 6.4\% \\ &= 13.4\% \end{aligned}$$

It should be noted that although the CAPM approach appears to yield an accurate, precise estimate of k_s, there actually are several problems with it. First, if a firm's stockholders are not well diversified, they might be concerned with total risk rather than with market risk only (measured by β); in this case the firm's true investment risk will not be measured by its beta, and the CAPM procedure will understate the correct value of k_s. Further, even if the CAPM method is valid, it is difficult to obtain correct estimates of the inputs required to make it operational because: (1) there is controversy about whether to use long-term or short-term Treasury yields for k_{RF}; and (2) both β_s and k_M should be estimated values, which often are difficult to obtain.

Bond-Yield-Plus-Risk-Premium Approach

Although it is a subjective procedure, analysts often estimate a firm's cost of common equity by adding a risk premium of three to five percentage points to the interest rate on the firm's own long-term debt. It is logical to think that firms with risky, low-rated, and consequently high-interest-rate debt will also have risky, high-cost equity. Using this logic to estimate the cost of common stock is relatively easy, because all we have to do is add a risk premium to a readily observable debt cost. For example, Unilate's cost of equity might be estimated as follows:

$$\begin{aligned} k_s &= \text{Bond yield} + \text{Risk premium} \\ &= 10.0\% + 4.0\% \\ &= 14.0\% \end{aligned}$$

Because the 4 percent risk premium is a judgmental estimate, the estimated value of k_s also is judgmental. Empirical work suggests that the risk premium over a firm's own bond yield generally has ranged from three to five percentage points, so this method is not likely to produce a precise cost of equity—about all it can do is get us into the right ballpark.

Constant Growth Model Using the DCF Approach

We learned that both the price and the expected rate of return on a share of common stock depend, ultimately, on the dividends expected on the stock, and the value of a share of stock can be written as follows:

$$P_0 = \frac{\hat{D}_1}{(1+k_s)^1} + \frac{\hat{D}_2}{(1+k_s)^2} + \cdots + \frac{\hat{D}_\infty}{(1+k_s)^\infty} \quad (7.32)$$

$$= \sum_{t=1}^{\infty} \frac{\hat{D}_t}{(1+k_s)^t}$$

Here P_0 is the current price of the stock; $\hat{D}_t$ is the dividend *expected* to be paid at the end of Year t; and k_s is the required rate of return. If dividends are expected to grow at a constant rate, then, Equation 7.32 reduces to

$$P_0 = \frac{\hat{D}_1}{k_s - g} \quad (7.32a)$$

We can solve Equation 7.32a for k_s to estimate the required rate of return on common equity, which for the marginal investor is also equal to the expected rate of return.

$$k_s = \hat{k}_s = \frac{\hat{D}_1}{P_0} + g \quad (7.33)$$

Thus, investors expect to receive a dividend yield, $\hat{D}_1/P_0$, plus a capital gain, g, for a total expected return of $\hat{D}/\hat{k}_s$, and in equilibrium this expected return is also equal to the required return, k_s. From this point on, we will assume that equilibrium exists, and we will use the terms k_s and $\hat{k}_s$ interchangeably, so we will drop the "hat," ^, above k_s.

To illustrate the DCF approach, suppose Unilate's stock sells for $23; the common stock dividend expected to be paid in 2001 is $1.31, which is 15¢ higher than the dividend paid in 2000; and its expected long-term growth rate is 8 percent. Unilate's expected and required rate of return, and hence its cost of retained earnings, is 13.7 percent.

$$\hat{k}_s = k_s = \frac{\$1.31}{\$23.00} + 0.08$$
$$= 0.057 + 0.08$$
$$= 0.137 = 13.7$$

This 13.7 percent is the minimum rate of return that management must expect to earn to justify retaining earnings and plowing them back into the business rather than paying them out to stockholders as dividends.

We have used three methods to estimate the cost of retained earnings, which actually is a single number. To summarize, we found the cost of common equity to be (1) 13.4 percent using the CAPM method; (2) 14.0 percent with the bond-yield-plus-risk-premium approach; and (3) 13.7 percent using the constant growth model, the DCF approach. It is not unusual to get different estimates, because each of the approaches is based on different assumptions—the CAPM assumes investors are well diversified, the bond-yield-plus-risk-premium approach assumes the cost of equity is closely related to the firm's cost of debt, and the constant growth model assumes the firm's dividends and earnings will grow at a constant rate far into the future. So which estimate should be used? Probably all of them. Many analysts use multiple approaches to estimate a single value, then average the results. For Unilate, then, the average of the estimates is 13.7% = (13.4% + 14.0% + 13.7%)/3.

People experienced in estimating equity capital costs recognize that both careful analysis and sound judgment are required. It would be nice to pretend that judgment is unnecessary and to specify an easy, precise way of determining the exact cost of equity capital. Unfortunately, this is not possible—finance is in large part a matter of judgment.

Cost of Newly Issued Common Stock, or External Equity, k_e

The **cost of new common equity, k_e,** or external equity capital, is similar to the cost of retained earnings, k_s, except it is higher because there is a cost to issuing new stock. Because the firm incurs costs when selling new securities, called **flotation costs,** the full market value of the stock cannot be used for investments—only the amount left after paying flotation costs is available. Thus, the cost of issuing new common stock (external equity), k_e, must be greater than the cost of retained earnings (internal equity), k_s, because there are no flotation costs associated with retained earnings.

In general, the cost of issuing new equity, k_e, can be found by modifying the DCF formula used to compute the cost of retained earnings, k_s, to obtain the following equation:

$$k_e = \frac{\hat{D}_1}{NP} + g = \frac{\hat{D}_1}{P_0(1 - F)} + g \qquad (7.34)$$

Here F is the percentage flotation cost (in decimal form) incurred in selling the new stock issue, so $P_0(1 - F)$ is the net price per share received by the company.

If Unilate can issue new common stock at a flotation cost of 10 percent, k_e is computed as follows:

$$k_e = \frac{\$1.31}{\$23.00(1 - 0.10)} + 0.08$$
$$= \frac{\$1.31}{\$20.70} + 0.08$$
$$= 0.143 = 14.3\%$$

Using the DCF approach to estimate the cost of retained earnings, we found that investors require a return of $k_s = 13.7\%$ on the stock. However, because of flotation costs, the company must earn more than 13.7 percent on funds obtained by selling stock if it is to provide a 13.7 percent return. Specifically, if the firm earns 14.3 percent on funds obtained from new stock, then earnings per share will not fall below previously expected earnings, the firm's expected dividend can be maintained, and, as a result, the price per share will not decline. If the firm earns less than 14.3 percent, then earnings, dividends, and growth will fall below expectations, causing the price of the stock to decline. If it earns more than 14.3 percent, the price of the stock will rise.

Weighted Average Cost of Capital, WACC

Each firm has an optimal capital structure, or mix of debt, preferred stock, and common equity, that causes its stock price to be maximized. Therefore, a rational, value-maximizing firm will establish a **target (optimal) capital structure** and then raise new capital in a manner that will keep the actual capital structure on target over time. In this section we assume that the firm has identified its optimal capital structure, it uses this optimum as the target, and it raises funds so it constantly remains on target.

The target proportions of debt, preferred stock, and common equity, along with the component costs of capital, are used to calculate the firm's **weighted average cost of capital (WACC)**. To illustrate, suppose Unilate Textiles has determined that in the future it will raise new capital according to the following proportions: 45 percent debt, 5 percent preferred stock, and 50 percent common equity (retained earnings plus common stock). In the preceding sections, we found that its before-tax cost of debt, k_d, is 10 percent, so its *after-tax* cost of debt, k_{dT}, is 6 percent; its cost of preferred stock, k_{ps}, is 10.3 percent; and its cost of common equity from retained earnings, k_s, is 13.7 percent if all of its equity financing comes from retained earnings. Now we can calculate Unilate's weighted average cost of capital (WACC) as follows.

$$\begin{aligned}
\text{WACC} &= \left[\begin{pmatrix}\text{Proportion}\\\text{of}\\\text{debt}\end{pmatrix} \times \begin{pmatrix}\text{After-tax}\\\text{cost of}\\\text{debt}\end{pmatrix}\right] + \left[\begin{pmatrix}\text{Proportion}\\\text{of preferred}\\\text{stock}\end{pmatrix} \times \begin{pmatrix}\text{Cost of}\\\text{preferred}\\\text{stock}\end{pmatrix}\right] + \left[\begin{pmatrix}\text{Proportion}\\\text{of common}\\\text{equity}\end{pmatrix} \times \begin{pmatrix}\text{Cost of}\\\text{common}\\\text{equity}\end{pmatrix}\right] \quad (7.35)\\
&= w_d k_{dT} \quad + \quad w_{ps} k_{ps} \quad + \quad w_s k_s\\
&= 0.45(6.0\%) \quad + \quad 0.05(10.3\%) \quad + \quad 0.50(13.7\%)\\
&\approx 10.1\%
\end{aligned}$$

Here w_d, w_{ps}, and w_s are the weights used for debt, preferred stock, and common equity, respectively.

Every dollar of new capital that Unilate obtains consists of 45¢ of debt with an after-tax cost of 6 percent, 5¢ of preferred stock with a cost of 10.3 percent, and 50¢ of common equity (all from additions to retained earnings) with a cost of 13.7 percent. The average cost of each whole dollar, WACC, is 10.1% as long as these conditions continue. If the component costs of capital change when new funds are raised in the future, then WACC changes. We discuss changes in the component costs of capital in the next section.

The Marginal Cost of Capital, MCC

The marginal cost of any item is the cost of another unit of that item; for example, the marginal cost of labor is the cost of adding one additional worker. The marginal cost of labor might be $25 per person if 10 workers are added but $35 per person if the firm tries to hire 100 new workers because it will be harder to find that many people willing and able to do the work. The same concept applies to capital. As the firm tries to attract more new dollars, at some point, the cost of each dollar will increase. Thus, the **marginal cost of capital (MCC)** *is defined as the cost of the last dollar of new capital that the firm raises, and the marginal cost rises as more and more capital is raised during a given period.*

In the preceding section, we computed Unilate's WACC to be 10.1 percent. As long as Unilate keeps its capital structure on target, and as long as its debt has an after-tax cost of 6 percent, its preferred stock a cost of 10.3 percent, and its common equity a cost of 13.7 percent, then its weighted average cost of capital will be 10.1 percent. Each dollar the firm raises will consist of some long-term debt, some preferred stock, and some common equity, and the cost of the whole dollar will be 10.1 percent—its marginal cost of capital (MCC) will be 10.1 percent.

The MCC Schedule

A graph that shows how the WACC changes as more and more new capital is raised by the firm is called the **marginal cost of capital schedule.** Exhibit 700.32 shows Unilate's MCC schedule if the cost of debt, cost of preferred stock, and cost of common equity *never change*. Here the dots represent dollars raised, and because each dollar of new capital will have an average cost equal to 10.1 percent, the marginal cost of capital (MCC) for Unilate is constant at 10.1 percent under the assumptions we have used to this point.

Do you think Unilate actually could raise an unlimited amount of new capital at the 10.1 percent cost? Probably not, because, as a practical matter, as a company raises larger and larger amounts of funds during a given time period, the costs of those funds begin to rise, and as this occurs, the weighted average cost of each new dollar also

Exhibit 700.32 *Marginal Cost of Capital (MCC) Schedule for Unilate Textiles*

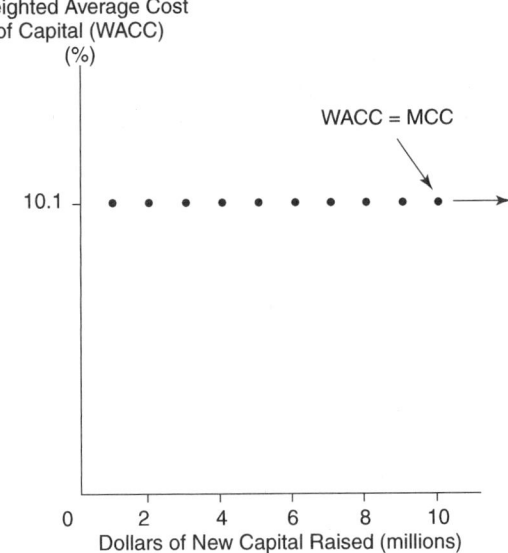

rises. Thus, companies cannot raise unlimited amounts of capital at a constant cost—at some point, the cost of each new dollar will increase, no matter what its source (debt, preferred stock, or common equity).

How much new capital can Unilate raise before it exhausts its retained earnings and is forced to sell new common stock? In other words, where will an increase in the MCC schedule occur?

We forecast that Unilate's 2001 net income would be $61 million and that $30.5 million would be paid out as dividends so that $30.5 million will be added to retained earnings (the payout ratio is 50 percent). Thus, Unilate can invest in capital projects to the point where the common equity needs equal $30.5 million before new common stock has to be issued. Remember, though, that when Unilate needs new funds, the target capital structure indicates only 50 percent of the total should be common equity; the remainder of the funds should come from issues of bonds (45 percent) and preferred stock (5 percent). Thus, we know:

$$\text{Common equity} = 0.50 \, (\text{Total new capital raised})$$

We can use this relationship to determine how much *total new capital*—debt, preferred stock, and retained earnings—can be raised before the $30.5 million of retained earnings is exhausted and Unilate is forced to sell new common stock. Just set the common equity needs equal to the retained earnings amount, and solve for the total new capital amount.

$$\text{Common equity} = \text{Retained earnings} = \$30.5 \text{ million} = 0.50 \left(\begin{array}{c} \text{Total new} \\ \text{capital raised} \end{array} \right)$$

$$\left(\begin{array}{c} \text{Total new} \\ \text{capital raised} \end{array} \right) = \frac{\$30.5 \text{ million}}{0.50} = \$61.0 \text{ million}$$

Thus, Unilate can raise a total of $61 million before it has to sell new common stock to finance its capital projects.

If Unilate needs exactly $61 million in new capital, the breakdown of the amount that would come from each source of capital and the computation for the weighted average cost of capital (WACC) would be as follows:

Capital Source	Weight	Amount in Millions	After-Tax Component Cost	WACC
Debt	0.45	$27.45	6.0%	2.7%
Preferred stock	0.05	3.05	10.3	0.5
Common equity	0.50	30.50	13.7	6.9
	1.00	$61.00		$WACC_1 = 10.1\%$

725. COST OF CAPITAL, CAPITAL STRUCTURE, AND DIVIDEND POLICY

Therefore, if Unilate needs *exactly* $61 million in new capital in 2005, retained earnings will be just enough to satisfy the common equity requirement, so the firm will not need to sell new common stock and its weighted average cost of capital (WACC) will be 10.1 percent. But what will happen if Unilate needs more than $61 million in new capital? If Unilate needs $64 million, for example, retained earnings will not be sufficient to cover the $32 million common equity requirements (50 percent of the total funds), so new common stock will have to be sold. The cost of issuing new common stock, k_e, is greater than the cost of retained earnings, k_s; hence, the WACC will be greater. If Unilate raises $64 million in new capital, the breakdown of the amount that would come from each source of capital and the computation for the weighted average cost of capital (WACC) would be as follows:

Capital Source	Weight	Amount in Millions	After-Tax Component Cost	WACC
Debt	0.45	$28.80	6.0%	2.7%
Preferred stock	0.05	3.20	10.3	0.5
Common equity	0.50	32.00	14.3	7.2
	1.00	$64.00		WACC$_2$ = 10.4%

The WACC will be greater because Unilate will have to sell new common stock, which has a higher component cost than retained earnings (14.3 percent versus 13.7 percent). Consequently, if Unilate's capital budgeting needs are greater than $61 million, new common stock will need to be sold, and its WACC will increase. The $61 million in total new capital is defined as the *retained earnings break point*, because above this amount of total capital, a break, or jump, in Unilate's MCC schedule occurs. In general, a **break point (BP)** is defined as the dollar of *new total capital* that can be raised before an increase in the firm's weighted average cost of capital occurs.

Exhibit 700.33 graphs Unilate's marginal cost of capital schedule with the retained earnings break point. Each dollar has a weighted average cost of 10.1 percent until the company has raised a total of $61 million. This $61 million will consist of $27.45 million of new debt with an after-tax cost of 6 percent, $3.05 million of preferred stock with a cost of 10.3 percent, and $30.50 million of retained earnings with a cost of 13.7 percent. However, if Unilate raises one dollar over $61 million, each new dollar will contain 50¢ of equity *obtained by selling new common equity at a cost of 14.3 percent*; therefore, WACC jumps from 10.1 percent to 10.4 percent, as calculated above and shown in Exhibit 700.34.

Note that we really don't think the MCC jumps by precisely 0.3 percent when we raise $1 over $61 million. Thus, Exhibit 700.33 should be regarded as an approximation rather than as a precise representation of reality.

Exhibit 700.33 *Marginal Cost of Capital Schedule for Unilate Textiles Using Both Retained Earnings and New Common Stock*

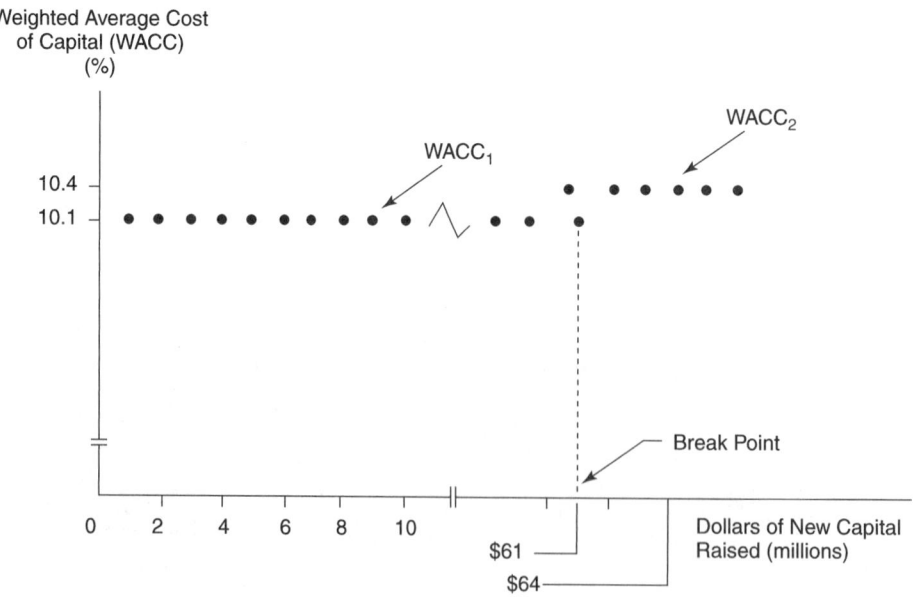

Exhibit 700.34 *WACC and Break Points for Unilate's MCC Schedule*

I. Break Points
1. $BP_{Retained\ earnings} = \$30,500,000/0.50 = \$61,000,000$
2. $BP_{Debt} = 54,000,000/0.45 = \$120,000,000$

II. Weighted Average Cost of Capital (WACC)

1. New Capital Needs: $0–$61,000,000

	Breakdown of Funds at $61,000,000	Weight ×	After-Tax Component Cost	= WACC
Debt (10%)	$ 27,450,000	0.45	6.0%	2.7%
Preferred stock	3,050,000	0.05	10.3	0.5
Common equity (Retained earnings)	30,500,000	0.50	13.7	6.9
	$ 61,000,000	1.00	WACC₁ =	10.1%

2. New Capital Needs: $61,000,001–$120,000,000

	Breakdown of Funds at $120,000,000	Weight ×	After-Tax Component Cost	= WACC
Debt (10%)	$ 54,000,000	0.45	6.0%	2.7%
Preferred stock	6,000,000	0.05	10.3	0.5
Common equity (New stock issue)	$ 60,000,000	0.50	14.3	7.2
	$120,000,000	1.00	WACC₂ =	10.4%

3. New Capital Needs: Above $120,000,000

	Breakdown of Funds at $130,000,000	Weight ×	After-Tax Component Cost	= WACC
Debt (12%)	$ 58,500,000	0.45	7.2%	3.2%
Preferred stock	6,500,000	0.05	10.3	0.5
Common equity (New stock issue)	65,000,000	0.50	14.3	7.2
	$130,000,000	1.00	WACC₃ =	10.9%

In general, a break point will occur whenever the cost of one of the capital components increases, and the break point can be determined by the following equation:

$$\text{Break point} = \frac{\text{Total amount of lower cost capital of a given type}}{\text{Proportion of this type of capital in the capital structure}} \quad (7.36)$$

We see, then, that numerous break points can occur. At the limit, we can even think of an MCC schedule with so many break points that it rises almost continuously beyond some given level of new financing.

The easiest sequence for calculating MCC schedules is as follows:

1. Use Equation 7.36 to determine each point at which a break occurs. A break will occur any time the cost of one of the capital components rises. (It is possible, however, that two capital components could both increase at the same point.) After determining the exact break points, make a list of them.
2. Determine the cost of capital for each component in the intervals between breaks.
3. Calculate the weighted averages of these component costs to obtain the WACCs in each interval, as we did in Exhibit 700.34. The WACC is constant within each interval, but it rises at each break point.

Notice that if there are n separate breaks, there will be n + 1 different WACCs. For example, two breaks means there will be three different WACCs. Also, we should note again that a different MCC schedule would result if a different capital structure is used.

725. COST OF CAPITAL, CAPITAL STRUCTURE, AND DIVIDEND POLICY

Example 1 The first break point is not necessarily the point at which retained earnings are used up; it is possible for low-cost debt to be exhausted before retained earnings have been used up. For example, if Unilate had available only $22.5 million of 10 percent debt, BP_{Debt} would occur at $50 million:

$$BP_{Debt} = \frac{\$22.5 \text{ million}}{0.45} = \$50 \text{ million}$$

Thus, the break point for debt would occur before the break point for retained earnings, which occurs at $61 million.

Capital Structure

Earlier, when we calculated the weighted average cost of capital for use in capital budgeting, we took the capital structure weights, or the mix of securities the firm uses to finance its assets, as a given. However, if the weights are changed, the calculated cost of capital, and thus the set of acceptable projects, will also change. Further, changing the capital structure will affect the riskiness inherent in the firm's common stock, and this will affect the return demanded by stockholders, k_s, and the stock's price, P_0. Therefore, the choice of a capital structure is an important decision. In this section, we discuss concepts relating to capital structure decisions.

The Target Capital Structure

Firms can choose whatever mix of debt and equity they desire to finance their assets, subject to the willingness of investors to provide such funds. And, as we shall see, many different mixes of debt and equity, or **capital structures**, exist. In some firms, such as **Chrysler Corporation**, debt accounts for more than 70 percent of the financing, while other firms, like **Microsoft**, have little or no debt. In the next few sections, we will discuss factors that affect a firm's capital structure, and we will conclude a firm should attempt to determine what its optimal, or best, mix of financing should be. But it will become apparent that determining the exact optimal capital structure is not a science, so after analyzing a number of factors, a firm establishes a **target capital structure** it believes is optimal, and which it uses as guidance for raising funds in the future. This target might change over time as conditions vary, but at any given moment the firm's management has a specific capital structure in mind, and individual financing decisions should be consistent with this target. If the actual proportion of debt is below the target level, new funds probably will be raised by issuing debt, whereas if the proportion of debt is above the target, stock probably will be sold to bring the firm back in line with the target ratio.

Capital structure policy involves a trade-off between risk and return. Using more debt raises the riskiness of the firm's earnings stream, but a higher proportion of debt generally leads to a higher expected rate of return; and, we know that the higher risk associated with greater debt tends to lower the stock's price. At the same time, however, the higher expected rate of return makes the stock more attractive to investors, which, in turn, ultimately increases the stock's price. Therefore, *the optimal capital structure is the one that strikes a balance between risk and return to achieve our ultimate goal of maximizing the price of the stock.*

Four primary factors influence capital structure decisions.

1. The first is the firm's *business risk*, or the riskiness that would be inherent in the firm's operations if it used no debt. The greater the firm's business risk, the lower the amount of debt that is optimal.
2. The second key factor is the firm's *tax position*. A major reason for using debt is that interest is tax deductible, which lowers the effective cost of debt. However, if much of a firm's income is already sheltered from taxes by accelerated depreciation or tax loss carryovers, its tax rate will be low, and debt will not be as advantageous as it would be to a firm with a higher effective tax rate.
3. The third important consideration is *financial flexibility*, or the ability to raise capital on reasonable terms under adverse conditions. Corporate treasurers know that a steady supply of capital is necessary for stable operations, which in turn are vital for long-run success. They also know that when money is tight in the economy, or when a firm is experiencing operating difficulties, a strong balance sheet is needed to obtain funds from suppliers of capital. Thus, it might be advantageous to issue equity to strengthen the firm's capital base and financial stability.

4. The fourth debt-determining factor has to do with *managerial attitude (conservatism or aggressiveness)* with regard to borrowing. Some managers are more aggressive than others; hence, some firms are more inclined to use debt in an effort to boost profits. This factor does not affect the optimal, or value-maximizing, capital structure, but it does influence the target capital structure a firm actually establishes.

These four points largely determine the target capital structure, but, as we shall see, operating conditions can cause the actual capital structure to vary from the target at any given time. For example, the debt/assets ratio of **Unisys** clearly has been much higher than its target, and the company has taken some significant corrective actions in recent years to improve its financial position.

Determining the Optimal Capital Structure

We can illustrate the effects of financial leverage using the data shown in Exhibit 700.35 for an illustrative company, which we will call OptiCap. As shown in the top section of the table, the company has no debt. Should it continue the policy of using no debt, or should it start using financial leverage? If it does decide to substitute debt for equity, how far should it go? As in all such decisions, the correct answer is that it should *choose the combination of debt and equity, or a capital structure, that will maximize the price of the firm's stock.*

EBIT/EPS Analysis of the Effects of Financial Leverage

Changes in the use of debt will cause changes in earnings per share and, consequently, in the stock price. To understand the relationship between financial leverage and earnings per share (EPS), first consider Exhibit 700.36, which shows how OptiCap's cost of debt would vary if it used different percentages of debt in its capital structure. Naturally, the higher the percentage of debt, the riskier the debt, hence the higher the interest rate lenders will charge.

Now consider Exhibit 700.37, which shows how expected EPS varies with changes in financial leverage. Section I of Exhibit 700.37 begins with a probability distribution of sales; we assume for simplicity that sales can take on only three values, $100,000, $200,000, or $300,000. In the remainder of Section I, we calculate earnings before interest and taxes (EBIT) at each of the three sales levels. Note that we assume both sales and operating costs are independent of financial leverage. Therefore, the three EBIT figures ($0, $40,000, and $80,000) will always remain the same, no matter how much debt OptiCap uses.

Exhibit 700.35 *Data on OptiCap*

I. Balance Sheet on 12/31/04

Current assets	$100,000	Debt	$ 0
Net fixed assets	100,000	Common equity (10,000 shares)	200,000
Total assets	$200,000	Total liabilities and equity	$200,000

II. Income Statement for 2004

Sales		$200,000
Fixed operating costs	$(40,000)	
Variable operating costs (60%)	(120,000)	(160,000)
Earnings before interest and taxes (EBIT)		$ 40,000
Interest		0
Taxable income		$ 40,000
Taxes (40%)		(16,000)
Net income		$ 24,000

Other Data

1. Earnings per share = EPS = $24,000/10,000 shares = $2.40.
2. Dividends per share = DPS = $24,000/10,000 shares = $2.40. Thus, OptiCap pays out all its earnings as dividends.
3. Book value per share = $200,000/10,000 shares = $20.
4. Market price per share = P_0 = $20. Thus, the stock sells at its book value, so (Market price)/(Book price) = M/B = 1.0.
5. Price/earnings ratio = P/E = $20/$2.40 = 8.33 times.

Exhibit 700.36 *Interest Rates for OptiCap with Different Debt/Asset Ratios*

Amount Borrowed[a]	Debt/Assets Ratio	Interest Rate, k_d, on All Debt
$ 20,000	10%	8.0%
40,000	20	8.3
60,000	30	9.0
80,000	40	10.0
100,000	50	12.0
120,000	60	15.0

[a]We assume that the firm must borrow in increments of $20,000. We also assume that OptiCap is unable to borrow more than $120,000, or 60% of assets, because of restrictions in its corporate charter.

Section II of Exhibit 700.37, the zero-debt case, calculates OptiCap's earnings per share at each sales level under the assumption that the company continues to use no debt. Net income is divided by the 10,000 shares outstanding to obtain EPS (remember there is no preferred stock). If sales are as low as $100,000, EPS will be zero, but it will rise to $4.80 at a sales level of $300,000. The EPS at each sales level then is multiplied by the probability of that sales level and summed to calculate the expected EPS, which is $2.40. We also calculate the standard deviation of EPS and the coefficient of variation as indicators of the firm's risk at a zero debt/assets ratio: $\sigma_{EPS} = \$1.52$, and $CV_{EPS} = 0.63$.

Section III of Exhibit 700.37 shows the financial results that could be expected if OptiCap were financed with a debt/assets ratio of 50 percent. In this situation, $100,000 of the $200,000 total capital would be debt. The interest rate on the debt, 12 percent, is taken from Exhibit 700.36. With $100,000 of 12 percent debt outstanding, the company's interest expense in Exhibit 700.37 would be $12,000 per year. This is a fixed cost—it is the same regardless of the level of sales—and it is deducted from the EBIT values as calculated in the top section. With debt = 0, there would be 10,000 shares outstanding. However, if half of the equity were replaced by debt so that debt = $100,000, there would be only 5,000 shares outstanding, and we must use this fact to determine the EPS figures that would result at each of the three possible sales levels. With a debt/assets ratio of 50 percent, the EPS figure would be −$1.44 if sales were as low as $100,000; it would rise to $3.36 if sales were $200,000; and it would soar to $8.16 if sales were as high as $300,000.

We see, then, that using leverage has both good and bad effects: higher leverage increases expected earnings per share (in this example, until the debt/assets [D/A] ratio equals 50 percent), but it also increases the firm's risk. Clearly, the debt/assets ratio should not exceed 50 percent, but where, in the range of 0 to 50 percent, should it be set? This issue is discussed in the following sections.

EPS Indifference Analysis

Another way of considering the data on OptiCap's two financing methods is through the use of **EPS indifference point**—that is, the point at which EPS is the same regardless of whether the firm uses debt or common stock. At a low level of sales, EPS is much higher if stock rather than debt is used. However, the debt line has a steeper slope, showing that earnings per share will go up faster with increases in sales if debt is used. The two lines cross at sales of $160,000. Below that level, EPS would be higher if the firm uses more common stock; above it, debt financing would produce higher earnings per share.

Degree of Leverage

In Section 720, we showed that leverage, whether operating or financial, is created when a firm has fixed costs associated either with its sales and production operations or with the types of financing it uses. We also found that the two types of leverage, operating and financial, are interrelated. Therefore, if OptiCap *reduced* its operating leverage, this probably would lead to an *increase* in its optimal use of financial leverage. On the other hand, if the firm decided to *increase* its operating leverage, its optimal capital structure probably would call for *less* debt.

Exhibit 700.37 OptiCap: EPS with Different Amounts of Financial Leverage (thousands of dollars, except per-share figures)

I. Calculation of EBIT			
Probability of indicated sales	0.2	0.6	0.2
Sales	$ 100.0	$ 200.0	$ 300.0
Fixed costs	(40.0)	(40.0)	(40.0)
Variable costs (60% of sales)	(60.0)	(120.0)	(180.0)
Total costs (except interest)	$(100.0)	$(160.0)	$(220.0)
Earnings before interest and taxes (EBIT)	$ 0.0	$ 40.0	$ 80.0
II. Situation if Debt/Assets (D/A) = 0%			
EBIT (from Section I)	$ 0.0	$ 40.0	$ 80.0
Less interest	(0.0)	(0.0)	(0.0)
Earnings before taxes (EBT)	$0.0	$ 40.0	$ 80.0
Taxes (40%)	(0.0)	(16.0)	(32.0)
Net income	$ 0.0	$ 24.0	$ 48.0
Earnings per share (EPS) on 10,000 shares[a]	$ 0.0	$ 2.40	$ 4.80
Expected EPS		$ 2.40	
Standard deviation of EPS		$ 1.52	
Coefficient of variation		0.63	
III. Situation if Debt/Assets (D/A) = 50%			
EBIT (from Section I)	$ 0.0	$ 40.0	$ 80.0
Less interest (0.12 × $100,000)	(12.0)	(12.0)	(12.0)
Earnings before taxes (EBT)	$(12.0)	$ 28.0	$ 68.0
Taxes (40%; tax credit on losses)	4.8	(11.2)	(27.2)
Net income	$(7.2)	$ 16.8	$ 40.8
Earnings per share (EPS) on 5,000 shares[a]	$ (1.44)	$ 3.36	$ 8.16
Expected EPS		$ 3.36	
Standard deviation of EPS		$ 3.04	
Coefficient of variation		0.90	

[a] The EPS figures can also be obtained using the following formula, in which the numerator amounts to an income statement at a given sales level laid out horizontally:

$$EPS = \frac{(\text{Sales} - \text{Fixed costs} - \text{Variable costs} - \text{Interest})(1 - \text{Tax rate})}{\text{Shares outstanding}} = \frac{(EBIT - I)(1 - T)}{\text{Shares outstanding}}$$

For example, with zero debt and Sales = $200,000, EPS is $2.40:

$$EPS_{D/A=0} = \frac{\$200,000 - \$40,000 - \$120,000 - 0)(0.6)}{10,000} = \$2.40$$

With 50% debt and Sales = $200,000, EPS is $3.36:

$$EPS_{D/A=0.5} = \frac{(\$200,000 - \$40,000 - \$120,000 - \$12,000)(0.6)}{5,000} = \$3.36$$

The sales level at which EPS will be equal under the two financing policies, or the indifference level of sales, S_I, can be found by setting $EPS_{D/A = 0}$ equal to $EPS_{D/A = 0.5}$ and solving for S_I:

$$EPS_{D/A=0} = \frac{S_I - \$40,000 - 0.6S_I - 0)(0.6)}{10,000} = \frac{S_I - \$400,000 - 0.6S_I - \$12,000)(0.6)}{5,000} = EPS_{D/A=0.5}$$

$$S_I = \$160,000$$

By substituting this value of sales into either equation, we can find EPS_{SI}, the earnings per share at this indifference point. In our example, $EPS_I = \$1.44$.

Degree of Operating Leverage (DOL)

The **degree of operating leverage** (DOL) is defined as the percentage change in operating income (that is, earnings before interest and taxes, or EBIT) associated with a given percentage change in sales. Thus, the degree of operating leverage is

$$\text{DOL} = \frac{\text{Percentage change in NOI}}{\text{Percentage change in sales}} = \frac{\left(\frac{\Delta \text{EBIT}}{\text{EBIT}}\right)}{\left(\frac{\Delta \text{Sales}}{\text{Sales}}\right)} = \frac{\left(\frac{\Delta \text{EBIT}}{\text{EBIT}}\right)}{\left(\frac{\Delta Q}{Q}\right)} \quad (7.37)$$

According to Equation 7.37, the DOL is an index number that measures the effect of a change in sales on operating income, or EBIT.

DOL for a particular level of production and sales, Q, can be computed using the following equation.

$$\text{DOL}_Q = \frac{Q(P - V)}{Q(P - V) - F} \quad (7.38)$$

or based on dollar sales rather than units:

$$\text{DOL}_S = \frac{S - VC}{S - VC - F} = \frac{\text{Gross profit}}{\text{EBIT}} \quad (7.38a)$$

Here, Q is the initial units of output, P is the average sales price per unit of output, V is the variable cost per unit, F is fixed operating costs, S is initial sales in dollars, and VC is total variable costs. Equation 7.38 normally is used to analyze a single product, such as IBM's PC, whereas Equation 7.38a is used to evaluate an entire firm with many types of products for which "quantity in units" and "sales price" are not meaningful.

Applying Equation 7.38a to data for OptiCap at a sales level of $200,000 as shown back in Exhibit 700.37, we find its degree of operating leverage to be 2.0.

$$\text{DOL}_{\$200,000} = \frac{\$200,000 - \$120,000}{\$200,000 - \$120,000 - \$40,000} = \frac{\$80,000}{\$40,000} = 2.0\times$$

Thus, for every 1 percent change (increase or decrease) in sales there will be a 2 percent change (increase or decrease) in EBIT. This situation is confirmed by examining Section I of Exhibit 700.37, where we see that a 50 percent increase in sales, from $200,000 to $300,000, causes EBIT to double. Note, however, that if sales decrease by 50 percent, then EBIT will decrease by 100%; according to Exhibit 700.37, EBIT decreases to $0 if sales decrease to $100,000.

Note also that the DOL is specific to the initial sales level; thus, if we evaluated OptiCap from a sales base of $300,000, there would be a different DOL.

$$\text{DOL}_{\$300,000} = \frac{\$300,000 - \$180,000}{\$300,000 - \$180,000 - \$40,000} = \frac{\$120,000}{\$80,000} = 1.5\times$$

In general, if a firm is operating at close to its breakeven level, the degree of operating leverage will be high, but DOL declines the higher the base level of sales is above breakeven sales.

Degree of Financial Leverage (DFL)

Operating leverage affects earnings before interest and taxes (EBIT), whereas financial leverage affects earnings after interest and taxes, or the earnings available to common stockholders. In terms of Exhibit 700.37, operating leverage affects the top section, whereas financial leverage affects the lower sections. *Financial leverage takes over where operating leverage leaves off, further magnifying the effects on earnings per share of changes in the level of sales.*

The **degree of financial leverage (DFL)** is defined as the percentage change in earnings per share that results from a given percentage change in earnings before interest and taxes (EBIT), and it is calculated as follows:

$$\text{DFL} = \frac{\text{Percent change in EPS}}{\text{Percentage change in EBIT}} = \frac{\left(\dfrac{\Delta \text{EPS}}{\text{EPS}}\right)}{\left(\dfrac{\Delta \text{EBIT}}{\text{EBIT}}\right)} = \frac{\text{EBIT}}{\text{EBIT} - I} \qquad (7.39)$$

At sales of $200,000 and an EBIT of $40,000, the degree of financial leverage when OptiCap has a 50 percent debt/assets ratio is

$$\text{DFL}_{S=\$200{,}000,\, \text{Debt/TA}=50\%} = \frac{\$40{,}000}{\$40{,}000 - \$12{,}000} = 1.43\times$$

Therefore, a 100 percent change (increase or decrease) in EBIT would result in a 100(1.43) = 143% change (increase or decrease) in earnings per share. This can be confirmed by referring to the lower section of Exhibit 700.37, where we see that a 100 percent increase in EBIT, from $40,000 to $80,000, produces a 143 percent increase in EPS.

$$\%\Delta\text{EPS} = \frac{\Delta \text{EPS}}{\text{EPS}_0} = \frac{\$8.16 - \$3.36}{\$3.36} = \frac{\$4.80}{\$3.36} = 1.43 = 143\%$$

If no debt were used, the degree of financial leverage would by definition be 1.0, so a 100 percent increase in EBIT would produce exactly a 100% increase in EPS. This can be confirmed from the data in Section II of Exhibit 700.37.

Degree of Total Leverage (DTL)

We have seen that (1) the greater the degree of operating leverage (or fixed operating costs), the more sensitive EBIT will be to changes in sales, and (2) the greater the degree of financial leverage (fixed financial costs), the more sensitive EPS will be to changes in EBIT. Therefore, if a firm uses a considerable amount of both operating and financial leverage, then even small changes in sales will lead to wide fluctuations in EPS.

Equation 7.38 for the degree of operating leverage can be combined with Equation 7.39 for the degree of financial leverage to produce the equation for the **degree of total leverage (DTL),** which shows how a given change in sales will affect earnings per share. Here are three equivalent equations for DTL.

$$\text{DTL} = (\text{DOL}) \times (\text{DFL})$$

$$\text{DTL} = \frac{Q(P - V)}{A(P - V) - F - I} \qquad (7.40)$$

$$\text{DTL} = \frac{S - VC}{S - VC - F - I} = \frac{\text{Gross profit}}{\text{EBIT} - I}$$

For OptiCap at sales of $200,000, we can substitute data from Exhibit 700.36 into Equation 7.40 to find the degree of total leverage if the debt ratio is 50 percent.

$$\text{DTL}_{S=\$200{,}000,\, \text{Debt/TA}=50\%} = \frac{\$200{,}000 - \$120{,}000}{\$200{,}000 - \$120{,}000 - \$40{,}000 - \$12{,}000} = \frac{\$80{,}000}{\$28{,}000}$$
$$= 2.00 \times 1.43 = 2.86\times$$

We can use the degree of total leverage (DTL) to find the new earnings per share (EPS1) for any given percentage increase in sales, proceeding as follows:

$$\begin{aligned}\text{EPS}_1 &= \text{EPS}_0 + \text{EPS}_0[(\text{DTL}) \times (\%\Delta\text{Sales})] \\ &= \text{EPS}_0[1.0 + (\text{DTL}) \times (\%\Delta\text{Sales})] \end{aligned} \qquad (7.41)$$

For example, a 50 percent (or 0.5) increase in sales, from $200,000 to $300,000, would cause EPS_0 ($3.36 as shown in Section III of Exhibit 700.37) to increase to $8.16.

$$\text{EPS}_1 = \$3.36[1.0 + (2.86)(0.5)] = \$3.36(2.43) = \$8.16.$$

This figure agrees with the one for EPS shown in Exhibit 700.37.

The degree of leverage concept is useful primarily for the insights it provides regarding the joint effects of operating and financial leverage on earnings per share. The concept can be used to show management the impact of financing the firm with debt versus common stock. For example, management might find that the current capital structure is such that a 10 percent decline in sales would produce a 50 percent decline in earnings, whereas with a different financing package, thus a different degree of total leverage, a 10 percent sales decline would cause earnings to decline by only 20 percent. Having the alternatives stated in this manner gives decision makers a better idea of the ramifications of alternative financing plans, hence different capital structures.

Liquidity and Capital Structure

There are some practical difficulties with the type of analysis described in the previous section, including the following:

1. It is virtually impossible to determine exactly how either P/E ratios or equity capitalization rates (k_s values) are affected by different degrees of financial leverage. The best we can do is make educated guesses about these relationships.
2. The managers might be more or less conservative than the average stockholder, so management might set a somewhat different target capital structure than the one that would maximize the stock price. The managers of a publicly owned firm never would admit this because, unless they owned voting control, they would be removed from office very quickly. However, in view of the uncertainties about what constitutes the value-maximizing capital structure, management could always say that the target capital structure employed is, in its judgment, the value-maximizing structure, and it would be difficult to prove otherwise. Still, if management is far off target, especially on the low side, then chances are very high that some other firm or management group will take over the company, increase its leverage, and thereby raise its value.
3. Managers of large firms, especially those that provide vital services such as electricity or telephones, have a responsibility to provide continuous service; therefore, they must refrain from using leverage to the point where the firms' long-run survivals are endangered. Long-run viability might conflict with short-run stock price maximization and capital cost minimization.

For all these reasons, managers are concerned about the effects of financial leverage on the risk of bankruptcy, and an analysis of this factor is therefore an important input in all capital structure decisions. Accordingly, managers give considerable weight to financial strength indicators such as the **times-interest-earned (TIE) ratio,** which is computed by dividing earnings before interest and taxes by interest expense. Remember that the TIE ratio provides an indication of how well the firm can cover its interest payments with operating income (EBIT)—the lower this ratio, the higher the probability that a firm will default on its debt and be forced into bankruptcy.

Particular attention should be given to the times-interest-earned (TIE) ratio because it gives a measure of how safe the debt is and how vulnerable the company is to financial distress. The TIE ratio depends on three factors: (1) the percentage of debt, (2) the interest rate on the debt, and (3) the company's profitability. Generally, the least leveraged industries, such as the drug and electronics industries, have the highest coverage ratios, whereas the utility industry, which finances heavily with debt, has a low average coverage ratio.

Capital Structure Theory

Over the years, researchers have proposed numerous theories to explain what firms' capital structures should be and why firms have different capital structures. The general theories of capital structure have been developed along two main lines: (1) tax benefit/bankruptcy cost trade-off theory and (2) signaling theory. These two theories are discussed in this section.

Tax Benefit/Bankruptcy Cost Trade-Off Theory

Modern capital structure theory began in 1958, when Professors Franco Modigliani and Merton Miller (hereafter MM) published what is considered by many to be the most influential finance article ever written.[4] MM proved—under a very restrictive set of assumptions, including that there exist no personal income taxes, no brokerage costs, and no bankruptcy—that due to the tax deductibility of interest on corporate debt, a firm's value rises continuously as more debt is used, and hence its value will be maximized by financing almost entirely with debt.

Because several of the assumptions outlined by MM obviously were, and are, unrealistic, MM's position was only the beginning of capital structure research. Subsequent researchers, and MM themselves, extended the basic theory by relaxing the assumptions. Other researchers attempted to test the various theoretical models with actual data to see exactly how stock prices and capital costs are affected by capital structure. Both the theoretical and the empirical results have added to our understanding of capital structure, but none of these studies has produced results that can be used to precisely identify a firm's optimal capital structure.

Signaling Theory

MM assumed that investors have the same information about a firm's prospects as its managers—this is called **symmetric information** because both those who are inside the firm (managers and employees) and those who are outside the firm (investors) have identical information. However, we know that in fact managers generally have better information about their firms than do outside investors. This is called **asymmetric information,** and it has an important effect on decisions to use either debt or equity to finance capital projects.

The conclusions are that firms with extremely bright prospects prefer not to finance through new stock offerings, whereas firms with poor prospects do like to finance with outside equity. How would you, as an investor, react to these conclusions? You ought to say, "If I see that a company plans to issue new stock, this should worry me because I know that management would not want to issue stock if future prospects looked good, but it would want to issue stock if things looked bad. Therefore, I should lower my estimate of the firm's value, other things held constant, if I read an announcement of a new stock offering." Of course, the negative reaction would be stronger if the stock sale was by a large, established company such as GM or IBM, which surely would have many financing options, than if it was by a small company such as **USR Industries.** For USR, a stock sale might mean truly extraordinary investment opportunities that were so large that they just could not be financed without a stock sale.

If you gave the preceding answer, your views are completely consistent with those of many sophisticated portfolio managers of institutions such as **Morgan Guaranty Trust.** *So, simply stated, the announcement of a stock offering by a mature firm that seems to have multiple financing alternatives is taken as a* **signal** *that the firm's prospects as seen by its management are not bright.* This, in turn, suggests that when a mature firm announces a new stock offering, the price of its stock should decline. Empirical studies have shown that this situation does indeed exist.

What are the implications of all this for capital structure decisions? The answer is that firms should, in normal times, maintain a **reserve borrowing capacity** that can be used in the event that some especially good investment opportunities come along. *This means that firms should generally use less debt than would be suggested by the tax benefit/bankruptcy cost trade-off.*

If you find our discussion of capital structure theory somewhat inexact, you are not alone. In truth, no one knows how to identify precisely the optimal capital structure for a firm or how to measure precisely the effect of the firm's capital structure on either its value or its cost of capital. In real life, capital structure decisions must be made more on the basis of judgment than numerical analysis. Still, an understanding of the theoretical issues as presented here is essential to making sound judgments on capital structure issues.

Dividend Policy

We refer to the cash payments, or distributions, made to stockholders from the firm's earnings, whether those earnings were generated in the current period or in previous periods, as **dividends.** Consequently, a firm's *dividend policy* involves the decision to pay out earnings or to retain them for reinvestment in the firm. Remember that, according to the constant dividend growth model, the value of common stock can be computed as $P_0 = \hat{D}_1/(k_s - g)$. This equation shows that if the firm adopts a policy of paying out more cash dividends, $\hat{D}_1$ will rise, which will tend to increase the price of the stock. However, if cash dividends are increased, then less money will be available for reinvestment and the expected future growth rate, g, will be lowered, which will depress the price of the stock. Thus, changing the dividend has two opposing effects. *The* **optimal dividend policy** *for a firm strikes that balance between current dividends and future growth that maximizes the price of the stock.*

In this section, we first examine factors that affect the optimal dividend policy and the types of dividend policies generally used by firms.

Dividend Policy and Stock Value

How do dividend policy decisions affect a firm's stock price? Academic researchers have studied this question extensively for many years, and they have yet to reach definitive conclusions. On the one hand, there are those who suggest that dividend policy is *irrelevant* because they argue that a firm's value should be determined by the basic earning power and business risk of the firm, in which case value depends only on the income (cash) produced, not on how the income is split between dividends and retained earnings (and hence growth).

Proponents of this line of reasoning, called the **dividend irrelevance theory,** would contend that investors care *only* about the *total returns* they receive, not whether they receive those returns in the form of dividends or capital gains. Thus, *if the dividend irrelevance theory is correct, there exists no optimal dividend policy because dividend policy does not affect the value of the firm.*

On the other hand, it is quite possible that investors prefer one dividend policy over another; if so, a firm's dividend policy is *relevant*. For example, it has been argued that investors prefer to receive dividends "today" because current dividend payments are more certain than the future capital gains that *might* result from investing retained earnings in growth opportunities, so k_s should decrease as the dividend payout is increased.[5]

Another factor that might cause investors to prefer a particular dividend policy is the tax effect of dividend receipts. Investors must pay taxes at the time dividends and capital gains are received. Thus, depending on his or her tax situation, an investor might prefer either a payout of current earnings as dividends, which would be taxed in the current period, or capital gains associated with growth in stock value, which would be taxed when the stock is sold, perhaps many years in the future and perhaps at different rates than dividends. Investors who prefer to delay the impact of taxes would be willing to pay more for low payout companies than for otherwise similar high-payout companies, and vice versa.

Those who believe the firm's dividend policy is relevant are proponents of the **dividend relevance theory,** which asserts dividend policy can affect the value of a firm through investors' preferences.

Investors and Dividend Policy

Although academic researchers have studied the dividend policy issue extensively, the issue remains unresolved; researchers at this time simply cannot tell corporate decision makers exactly how dividend policy affects stock prices and capital costs. But from the research, some views have been presented concerning investors' reactions to dividend policy changes and why firms have particular dividend policies. Three of these views are discussed in this section.

Information Content, or Signaling, Hypothesis

If investors expect a company's dividend to increase by 5 percent per year, and if, in fact, the dividend is increased by 5 percent, then the stock price generally will not change significantly on the day the dividend increase is announced. In Wall Street parlance, such a dividend increase would be "discounted," or *anticipated,* by the market. However, if investors expect a 5 percent increase, but the company actually increases the dividend by 25 percent—say from $2 to $2.50—this generally would be accompanied by an increase in the price of the stock. Conversely, a less-than-expected dividend increase, or a reduction, generally would result in a price decline.

It is a well-known fact that corporations are extremely reluctant to cut dividends and, therefore, *managers do not raise dividends unless they anticipate higher, or at least stable, earnings in the future to sustain the higher dividends*. This means that a larger-than-expected dividend increase is taken by investors as a *signal* that the firm's management forecasts improved future earnings, whereas a dividend reduction signals a forecast of poor earnings. Thus, it can be argued investors' reactions to changes in dividend payments do not show that investors prefer dividends to retained earnings; rather, the stock price changes simply indicate important information is contained in dividend announcements—in effect, dividend announcements provide investors with information previously known only to management. This theory is referred to as the **information content,** or **signaling, hypothesis.**

Clientele Effect

It also has been shown that it is very possible that a firm sets a particular dividend payout policy, which then attracts a *clientele* consisting of those investors who like the firm's dividend policy. For example, some stockholders, such as retired individuals, prefer current income to future capital gains, so they want the firm to pay out a higher percentage of its earnings. Other stockholders have no need for current investment income, so they favor a low payout ratio. If investors could not invest in companies with different dividend policies, it might be very expensive for them to achieve their investment goals—investors that prefer capital gains could reinvest any dividends they receive, but they first would have to pay taxes on the income. In essence, then, a **clientele effect** might exist if stockholders are attracted to companies because they have particular dividend policies. Those investors who desire current investment income can purchase shares in high-dividend-payout firms, whereas those who do not need current cash income can invest in low-payout firms. Consequently, we would expect the stock price of a firm to change if the firm changes its dividend policy, because investors will adjust their portfolios to include firms with the desired dividend policy.

Free Cash Flow Hypothesis

If it is the intent of the financial manager to maximize the value of the firm, then investors should prefer that firms pay dividends only if acceptable capital budgeting opportunities do not exist. We know that acceptable capital budgeting projects increase the value of the firm. We also know that, because flotation costs are incurred when issuing new stock, it costs a firm more to raise funds using new common equity than it does using retained earnings. So to maximize value, wherever possible a firm should use retained earnings rather than issue new common stock to finance capital budgeting projects. Thus, dividends should be paid only when *free cash flows* in excess of capital budgeting needs exist. If management does otherwise, the firm's value will not be maximized. According to the **free cash flow hypothesis,** the firm should distribute any earnings that cannot be reinvested at a rate at least as great as the investors' required rate of return, k_s (that is, the free cash flows). Everything else equal, firms that retain *free cash flows* will have lower values than firms that distribute *free cash flows* because the firms that retain free cash flows actually decrease investors' wealth by investing in projects with IRR $<$ k_s.

The free cash flow hypothesis might help to explain why investors react differently to identical dividend changes made by similar firms. For example, a firm's stock price should not change dramatically if it reduces its dividend for the purposes of investing in capital budgeting projects with positive NPVs. On the other hand, a company that reduces its dividend simply to increase free cash flows should experience a significant decline in the market value of its stock because the dividend reduction is not in the best interests of the stockholders—in this case, an agency problem exists. Thus, the free cash flow hypothesis suggests the dividend policy can provide information about the firm's behavior with respect to wealth maximization.

Dividend Policy in Practice

We have provided some insights concerning the relevance of dividend policy and how investors might view dividend payments from firms. However, no one has been able to develop a formula that can be used to tell management specifically how a given dividend policy will affect a firm's stock price. Even so, managements still must establish dividend policies. This section discusses several alternative policies and procedures that are used in practice.

Types of Dividend Payments

The dollar amounts of dividends paid by firms follow a variety of patterns. In general, though, firms pay dividends using one of the four payout policies discussed next.

RESIDUAL DIVIDEND POLICY In practice, dividend policy is very much influenced by investment opportunities and by the availability of funds with which to finance new investments. This fact has led to the development of a **residual dividend policy,** which states that a firm should follow these steps when deciding how much earnings should be paid out as dividends: (1) determine the optimal capital budget for the year, (2) determine the amount of capital needed to finance that budget, (3) use retained earnings to supply the equity component to the extent possible, and (4) pay dividends only if more earnings are available than are needed to support the optimal capital budget. The word *residual* means "left over," and the residual policy implies that dividends should be paid only out of "leftover" earnings.

The basis of the residual policy is the fact that *investors prefer to have the firm retain and reinvest earnings rather than pay them out in dividends if the rate of return the firm can earn on reinvested earnings exceeds the rate investors, on average, can themselves obtain on other investments of comparable risk.* For example, if the corporation can reinvest retained earnings at a 14 percent rate of return, whereas the best rate the average stockholder can obtain if the earnings are passed on in the form of dividends is 12 percent, then stockholders should prefer to have the firm retain the profits.

To continue, we saw that the cost of retained earnings is an *opportunity cost* that reflects rates of return available to equity investors. If a firm's stockholders can buy other stocks of equal risk and obtain a 12 percent dividend-plus-capital-gains yield, then 12 percent is the firm's cost of retained earnings. The cost of new outside equity raised by selling common stock will be higher than 12 percent because of the costs associated with the issue.

Most firms have a target capital structure that calls for at least some debt, so new financing is done partly with debt and partly with equity. As long as the firm finances with the optimal mix of debt and equity, and as long as it uses only internally generated equity (retained earnings), its marginal cost of each new dollar of capital will be minimized. Internally generated equity is available for financing a certain amount of new investment, but beyond that amount the firm must turn to more expensive new common stock. At the point where new stock must be sold, the cost of equity, and consequently the marginal cost of capital, rises.

According to the residual dividend policy, a firm that has to issue new common stock to finance capital budgeting needs does not have residual earnings, and dividends will be zero.

Because both the earnings level and the capital budgeting needs of a firm vary from year to year, strict adherence to the residual dividend policy would result in dividend variability—one year the firm might declare zero dividends because investment opportunities are good, but the next year it might pay a large dividend because investment opportunities are poor. Similarly, fluctuating earnings would also lead to variable dividends even if investment opportunities were stable over time. Thus, following the residual dividend policy would be optimal only if investors were not bothered by fluctuating dividends. However, if investors prefer stable, dependable dividends, k_s would be higher, and the stock price lower, if the firm followed the residual theory in a strict sense rather than attempting to stabilize its dividends over time.

STABLE, PREDICTABLE DIVIDENDS   In the past, many firms set a specific annual dollar dividend per share and then maintained it, increasing the annual dividend only if it seemed clear that future earnings would be sufficient to allow the new dividend to be maintained. A corollary of that policy was this rule: *Never reduce the annual dividend.*

When the economy expands quickly, inflationary pressures plus reinvested earnings generally tend to push earnings up, so many firms that would otherwise follow the stable dollar dividend payment policy switch to a "stable growth rate" policy. Here the firm sets a target growth rate for dividends (for example, 6 percent per year) and strives to increase dividends by this amount each year. Obviously, earnings must be growing at a reasonably steady rate for this policy to be feasible, but where it can be followed, such a policy provides investors with a stable real income.

There are two good reasons for paying **stable, predictable dividends** rather than following the residual dividend policy. First, given the existence of the information content, or signaling, idea, a fluctuating payment policy would lead to greater uncertainty, hence to a higher k_s and a lower stock price, than would exist under a stable policy. Second, many stockholders use dividends for current consumption, and they would be put to trouble and expense if they had to sell part of their shares to obtain cash if the company cut the dividend.

As a rule, stable, predictable dividends imply more certainty than variable dividends, thus a lower k_s and a higher firm value. So it is this dividend policy most firms favor. Even though the optimal dividend as prescribed by the residual policy might vary somewhat from year to year, a firm might delay some investment projects, depart from its target capital structure during a particular year, or even issue new common stock to avoid the problems associated with unstable dividends, and thus provide a lower k_s and a higher firm value.

CONSTANT PAYOUT RATIO   It would be possible for a firm to pay out a constant *percentage* of earnings (dividends per share divided by earnings per share), but because earnings surely will fluctuate, this policy would mean that the dollar amount of dividends would vary. For example, if **Eastman Kodak** had followed the policy of paying a constant percentage of earnings per share, say 40 percent, the dividends per share paid since 1978 would have fluctuated exactly the same as earnings per share and thus the company would have had to cut its dividend in several different years. Therefore, with the **constant payout ratio** dividend policy, if earnings fluctuate, investors would have had much greater uncertainty concerning the expected dividends each year, and chances are k_s also would be greater; hence, its stock price would be lower. Although Kodak's stock price has fluctuated somewhat, it has shown a general upward trend since the 1980s, in spite of the substantial earnings fluctuations. Had it cut the dividend to keep the payout ratio constant, Kodak's stock price would have "fallen out of bed" several times if investors interpreted the dividend reduction as a signal that management thought the earnings declines were permanent.

LOW REGULAR DIVIDEND PLUS EXTRAS   A policy of paying a low regular dividend plus a year-end extra in good years is a compromise between a stable dividend (or stable growth rate) and a constant payout rate. Such a policy gives the firm flexibility, yet investors can count on receiving at least a minimum dividend. Therefore, if a firm's earnings and cash flows are quite volatile, this policy might be its best choice. The directors can set a relatively low regular dividend—low enough so that it can be maintained even in low-profit years or in years when a considerable amount of retained earnings is needed for investments—and then supplement it with an **extra dividend** in years when excess funds are available. Ford, General Motors, and other auto companies, whose earnings fluctuate widely from year to year, formerly followed such a policy, but in recent years they have joined the crowd and now follow our first choice, a stable dividend policy.

Payment Procedures

Dividends normally are paid quarterly, and, when conditions permit, the dividend is increased. For example, on April 9, 1999, the board of directors of Eastman Kodak declared a 44¢ quarterly common stock dividend. Earlier in the year, Kodak's board indicated that it anticipated the annual dividend to be $1.76, which was the same as the dividend paid in 1998. So Kodak's stockholders were not surprised when the 44¢ quarterly dividend was announced; they would have been *shocked* if the dividend had been eliminated, because Kodak has paid a dividend for more than 40 years.

When Kodak declared the dividend, it issued the following statement (www.kodak.com):

Rochester, NY, April 9—Eastman Kodak Company's Board of Directors voted a quarterly cash dividend of 44 cents a share on the outstanding common stock of the company.

The dividend is payable July 1, 1999, to shareholders of record at the close of business, June 1, 1999.

The three dates included in this announcement are important to current stockholders. These dates, as well as the ex-dividend date, are defined as follows:

1. **Declaration date.** On the *declaration date,* April 9, 1999 in Kodak's case, the board of directors meets and declares the regular dividend. For accounting purposes, the declared dividend becomes an actual liability on the declaration date, and if a balance sheet were constructed, the amount ($0.44) × (Number of shares outstanding) would appear as a current liability, and retained earnings would be reduced by a like amount.

2. **Holder-of-record date.** At the close of business on the **holder-of-record date,** or **date of record,** the company closes its stock transfer books and produces a list of shareholders as of that date. Thus, if Kodak was notified of the sale and transfer of some stock before 5 P.M. on Tuesday, June 1, 1999, then the new owner received the dividend. However, if notification was received after June 1, the previous owner of the stock got the dividend check because his or her name appeared on the company's ownership records.

3. **Ex-dividend date.** The securities industry has set up a convention of declaring that the right to the dividend remains with the stock until two business days *prior* to the holder-of-record date. This is to ensure the company is notified of the transfer in time to record the new owner and thus pay the dividend to him or her. The date when the right to receive the next dividend payment no longer goes with the stock—new purchasers will not receive the next dividend—is called the **ex-dividend date.** In the case of Kodak, the *ex-dividend* date was Friday, May 28, 1999, which is two *business days* before the *holder-of-record* date, Tuesday, June 1, 1999. Therefore, any investor who purchased the stock on or after that date did not receive the next dividend payment associated with the stock. All else equal, then, we would expect that the price of Kodak's stock dropped on the ex-dividend date approximately by the amount of the dividend—assuming no other price fluctuations, the price at which Kodak's stock opened on Friday, May 28, should have been about 44 cents less than the close on Thursday, May 27. The price of the stock actually decreased by a little more than 44 cents due to other factors, including a general market decline on that day.

4. **Payment date.** Kodak paid the common stock dividends on July 1, 1999—this is the *payment date.* Recently, many firms have started paying dividends electronically.

Factors Influencing Dividend Policy

In addition to managements' beliefs concerning which dividend theory is most correct, a number of other factors are considered when a particular dividend policy is chosen. The factors firms take into account can be grouped into these four broad categories:

1. **Constraints on dividend payments.** The amount of dividends a firm can pay might be limited due to (1) debt contract restrictions, which often stipulate that no dividends can be paid unless certain financial measures, such as the times-interest-earned ratio, exceed stated minimums; (2) the fact that dividend payments cannot exceed the balance sheet item "retained earnings" (this is known as the *impairment of capital rule,* which is designed to protect creditors by prohibiting the company from distributing assets to stockholders before debtholders are paid); (3) cash availability, because cash dividends can be paid only with cash; and (4) restrictions imposed by the Internal Revenue Service (IRS) on improperly accumulated retained earnings. If the IRS can demonstrate that a firm's dividend payout ratio is being held down deliberately to help its stockholders avoid personal taxes, the firm is subject to heavy tax penalties. But this factor generally is relevant only to privately owned firms.

2. **Investment opportunities.** Firms that have large numbers of acceptable capital budgeting projects generally have low dividend payout ratios, and vice versa. But if a firm can accelerate or postpone projects (flexibility), then it can adhere more closely to a target dividend policy.

3. **Alternative sources of capital.** When a firm needs to finance a given level of investment and flotation costs are high, k_e will be well above k_s, making it better to set a low payout ratio and to finance through retention rather than through sale of new common stock. Also, if the firm can adjust its debt/assets ratio without raising capital costs sharply, it can maintain a stable dollar dividend, even if earnings fluctuate, by using a variable debt/assets ratio. Another factor considered by management when making financing decisions is ownership dilution—if management is concerned about maintaining control, it might be reluctant to sell new stock; hence, the company might retain more earnings than it otherwise would.
4. **Effects of dividend policy on k_s.** The effects of dividend policy on k_s might be considered in terms of four factors: (a) stockholders' desire for current versus future income, (b) the perceived riskiness of dividends versus capital gains, (c) the tax advantage of capital gains over dividends, and (d) the information content of dividends (signaling). Because we discussed each of these factors earlier, we need only note here that the importance of each factor in terms of its effect on k_s varies from firm to firm depending on the makeup of its current and possible future stockholders.

It should be apparent from our discussions that dividend policy decisions truly are exercises in informed judgment, not decisions that can be quantified precisely. Even so, to make rational dividend decisions, financial managers must consider all of the points discussed in the preceding sections.

Stock Dividends and Stock Splits

Stock dividends and stock splits are related to the firm's cash dividend policy. The rationale for stock dividends and splits can best be explained through an example. We will use Porter Electronic Controls Inc., a $700 million electronic components manufacturer, for this purpose. Since its inception, Porter's markets have been expanding, and the company has enjoyed growth in sales and earnings. Some of its earnings have been paid out in dividends, but some are also retained each year, causing earnings per share and market price per share to grow. The company began its life with only a few thousand shares outstanding, and, after some years of growth, each of Porter's shares had a very high earnings per share (EPS) and dividends per share (DPS). When a "normal" price/earnings (P/E) ratio was applied, the derived market price was so high that few people could afford to buy a "round lot" of 100 shares. This limited the demand for the stock and thus kept the total market value of the firm below what it would have been if more shares, at a lower price, had been outstanding. To correct this situation, Porter "split its stock," as described next.

Stock Splits

Although there is little empirical evidence to support the contention, there is nevertheless a widespread belief in financial circles that an *optimal,* or *psychological, price range* exists for stocks. "Optimal" means that if the price is within this range, the P/E ratio, hence the value of the firm, will be maximized. Many observers, including Porter's management, believe that the best range for most stocks is from $20 to $80 per share. Accordingly, if the price of Porter's stock rose to $80, management probably would declare a two-for-one **stock split,** thus doubling the number of shares outstanding, halving the earnings and dividends per share, and thereby lowering the price of the stock. Each stockholder would have more shares, but each share would be worth less. If the post-split price were $40, Porter's stockholders would be exactly as well off as they were before the split because they would have twice as many shares at half the price as before the split. However, if the price of the stock were to stabilize above $40, stockholders would be better off. Stock splits can be of any size—for example, the stock could be split 2-for-1, 3-for-1, $1\frac{1}{2}$-for-1, or in any other way.

Reverse splits, which reduce the shares outstanding and increase the stock price, can even be used. For instance, a company whose stock sells for $5 might employ a 1-for-5 reverse split, exchanging one new share for five old ones and raising the value of the shares to about $25, which is within the optimal range. On February 11, 1999, for example, **Galaxy Foods** initiated a 1-for-7 reverse split to avoid being delisted from the NASDAQ SmallCap Market.

Stock Dividends

Stock dividends are similar to stock splits in that they "divide the pie into smaller slices" without affecting the fundamental position of the current stockholders. On a 5 percent stock dividend, the holder of 100 shares would receive an additional five shares (without cost); on a 20 percent stock dividend, the same holder would receive 20 new shares, and so on. Again, the total number of shares is increased, so earnings, dividends, and price per share all decline.

If a firm wants to reduce the price of its stock, should it use a stock split or a stock dividend? Stock splits generally are used after a sharp price run-up to produce a large price reduction. Stock dividends typically are used on a regular annual basis to keep the stock price more or less constrained. For example, if a firm's earnings and dividends were growing at about 10 percent per year, its stock price would tend to go up at about that same rate, and it would soon be outside the desired trading range. A 10 percent annual stock dividend would maintain the stock price within the optimal trading range.

Balance Sheet Effects

Although the economic effects of stock splits and stock dividends are virtually identical, accountants treat them somewhat differently. On a 2-for-1 split, the shares outstanding are doubled, and the stock's par value is halved. This treatment is shown in Section II of Exhibit 700.38 for Porter Electronic Controls, using a pro forma 2005 balance sheet.

Section III of Exhibit 700.38 shows the effect of a 20 percent stock dividend. With a stock dividend, the par value is not reduced, but an accounting entry is made transferring capital from the retained earnings account to the common stock and paid-in capital accounts. The transfer from retained earnings is calculated as follows:

$$\text{Dollars transferred from retained earnings} = \left[\left(\begin{array}{c}\text{Number of shares}\\\text{outstanding}\end{array}\right) \times \left(\begin{array}{c}\text{Stock dividend}\\\text{as a percent}\end{array}\right)\right] \times \left(\begin{array}{c}\text{Market price}\\\text{of the stock}\end{array}\right) \quad (7.42)$$

Porter has 5 million shares outstanding, and they sell for $80 each, so a 20 percent stock dividend would require the transfer of $80 million.

$$\text{Dollars transferred} = [(5{,}000{,}000)(0.2)](\$80) = \$80{,}000{,}000$$

As shown in the exhibit, $1 million of this $80 million is added to the common stock account and $79 million is added to the additional paid-in capital account. The retained earnings account is reduced from $285 million to $205 million.

Exhibit 700.38 *Porter Electronic Controls Inc.: Stockholders' Equity Accounts, Pro Forma, December 31, 2005 (millions of dollars, except per share values)*

I. Before a Stock Split or Stock Dividend	
Common stock (5 million shares outstanding, $1 par)	$ 5.0
Additional paid-in capital	10.0
Retained earnings	285.0
Total common stockholders' equity	$300.0
Book value per share	$ 60.0
II. After a Two-for-One Stock Split	
Common stock (10 million shares outstanding, $0.50 par)	$ 5.0
Additional paid-in capital	10.0
Retained earnings	285.0
Total common stockholders' equity	$300.0
Book value per share	$ 30.0
III. After a 20% Stock Dividend	
Common stock (6 million shares outstanding, $1 par)[a]	$ 6.0
Additional paid-in capital[b]	89.0
Retained earnings[b]	205.0
Total common stockholders' equity	$300.0
Book value per share	$ 50.0

[a] Shares outstanding are increased by 20%, from 5 million to 6 million.
[b] A transfer equal to the market value of the new shares is made from the retained earnings account to the additional paid-in capital and common stock accounts:

Transfer = [(5,000,000 shares)(0.2)]($80) = $80,000,000.

Of this $80 million, ($1 par)(1,000,000 shares) = $1,000,000 goes to common stock and the remaining $79 million to paid-in capital.

Price Effects

Several empirical studies have examined the effects of stock splits and stock dividends on stock prices. These studies suggest that investors see stock splits and stock dividends for what they are—*simply additional pieces of paper*. If stock dividends and splits are accompanied by higher earnings and cash dividends, then investors will bid up the price of the stock. However, if stock dividends are not accompanied by increases in earnings and cash dividends, the dilution of earnings and dividends per share causes the price of the stock to drop by the same percentage as the stock dividend. Thus, the fundamental determinants of price are the underlying earnings and cash dividends per share, and stock splits and stock dividends merely cut the pie into thinner slices.

Dividend Policies Around the World

The dividend policies of companies around the world vary considerably. A recent study found the dividend payout ratios of companies range from 10.5 percent in the Philippines to nearly 70 percent in Taiwan.[6] As a percent of earnings, the dividends paid out in Canada, France, Italy, and the United States range from about 20 percent to 25 percent, in Spain and the United Kingdom the range is from 30 percent to 40 percent, in Germany and Mexico the rate is between 40 percent and 50 percent, and it is more than 50 percent for companies in Japan and Southeast Asian countries.

Why do international differences in dividend policies exist? It seems logical to attribute the differences to dissimilar tax structures because both dividends and capital gains are taxed differently around the world. The tax codes in most developed countries encourage personal investing and savings more than the U.S. Tax Code. For example, Germany, Italy, and many other European countries do not tax capital gains, and in most other developed countries, including Japan, France, and Canada, capital gains are not taxed unless they exceed some minimum amount. Further, in Germany and Italy, dividends are not taxed as income, and in most other countries some amount of dividends is tax-exempt. The general conclusion we can make, then, is that in countries where capital gains are not taxed, investors should show a preference for companies that retain earnings rather than pay dividends. But it has been found that differences in taxes do not explain the differences in dividend payout ratios among the countries.

A study by Rafael La Porta, Florencio Lopez-de-Silanes, Andrei Shleifer, and Robert W. Vishny offers some insight into the dividend policy differences that exist around the world. They suggest that, all else equal, companies pay out greater amounts of earnings as dividends in countries that have measures that help protect the rights of minority stockholders. In such countries, though, firms with many growth opportunities tend to pay lower dividends, which is to be expected because the funds are needed to finance the growth and shareholders are willing to forgo current income in hopes of greater future benefits. On the other hand, in countries where shareholders' rights are not well protected, investors prefer dividends because there is great uncertainty about whether management will use earnings for self-gratification rather than for the benefit of the firm. Investors in these countries accept any dividends they can get—that is, they prefer a "bird in the hand." Some countries, including Brazil, Chile, Colombia, Greece, and Venezuela, have regulations that mandate firms pay dividends. In these countries, minority shareholders have few, if any, legally protected rights.

In summary, it appears the most important factor that determines whether stockholders prefer earnings be retained or paid out as dividends is the level of risk associated with future expected dividends, which is mitigated to some degree by regulations that protect minority shareholders' rights.

Capital Budgeting

Importance of Capital Budgeting

In this section, we apply asset valuation concepts to investment decisions involving the fixed assets of a firm, or *capital budgeting*. Here the term *capital* refers to fixed assets used in production, while a *budget* is a plan that details projected inflows and outflows during some future period. Thus, the capital budget is an outlay of planned expenditures on fixed assets, and **capital budgeting** is the process of analyzing projects and deciding which are acceptable investments and which actually should be purchased.

A number of factors combine to make capital budgeting decisions perhaps the most important ones financial managers must make. First, the impact of capital budgeting is long term; thus, the firm loses some decision-making flexibility when capital projects are purchased. For example, when a firm invests in an asset with a 10-year economic life, its operations are affected for 10 years—the firm is "locked in" by the capital budgeting decision. Further, because asset expansion is fundamentally related to expected future sales, a decision to buy a fixed asset that is expected to last ten years involves an implicit 10-year sales forecast.

An error in the forecast of asset requirements can have serious consequences. If the firm invests too much in assets, it will incur unnecessarily heavy expenses. But if it does not spend enough on fixed assets, it might find that inefficient production and inadequate capacity lead to lost sales that are difficult, if not impossible, to recover. Timing is also important in capital budgeting—capital assets must be ready to come "on line" when they are needed; otherwise, opportunities might be lost.

Effective capital budgeting can improve both the timing of asset acquisitions and the quality of assets purchased. A firm that forecasts its needs for capital assets in advance will have an opportunity to purchase and install the assets before they are needed. Unfortunately, many firms do not order capital goods until they approach full capacity or are forced to replace worn-out equipment. If many firms order capital goods at the same time, backlogs result, prices increase, and firms are forced to wait for the delivery of machinery; in general, the quality of the capital goods deteriorates. If a firm foresees its needs and purchases capital assets early, it can avoid these problems.

Finally, capital budgeting is also important because the acquisition of fixed assets typically involves substantial expenditures, and before a firm can spend a large amount of money, it must have the funds available—large amounts of money are not available automatically. Therefore, a firm contemplating a major capital expenditure program must arrange its financing well in advance to be sure the funds required are available.

Generating Ideas for Capital Projects

The same general concepts that we developed for valuing financial assets are involved in capital budgeting. However, whereas a set of stocks and bonds exists in the financial markets, and investors select from this set, capital budgeting projects are created by the firm. For example, a sales representative might report that customers frequently ask for a particular product that the company does not currently produce. The sales manager then discusses the idea with the marketing research group to determine the size of the market for the proposed product. If it appears likely that a significant market does exist, cost accountants and engineers will be asked to estimate production costs. And then if it appears the product can be produced and sold at a sufficient profit, the project will be undertaken.

A firm's growth, and even its ability to remain competitive and to survive, depends on a constant flow of ideas for new products, ways to make existing products better, and ways to produce output at a lower cost. Accordingly, a well-managed firm will go to great lengths to develop good capital budgeting proposals. Some firms even provide incentives to employees to encourage suggestions that lead to beneficial investment proposals. If a firm has capable and imaginative executives and employees, and if its incentive system works properly, many ideas for capital investment will be advanced.

Because some capital investment ideas will be good and others will not, procedures must be established for evaluating the worth of such projects to the firm. Our topic in the remainder of this section is the evaluation of the acceptability of capital projects.

Project Classifications

Capital budgeting decisions generally are termed either *replacement decisions* or *expansion decisions*. **Replacement decisions** involve determining whether capital projects should be purchased to take the place of (replace) existing assets that might be worn out, damaged, or obsolete. Usually the replacement projects are necessary to maintain or improve profitable operations using the existing production levels. On the other hand, if a firm is considering whether to *increase* operations by adding capital projects to existing assets that will help produce either more of its existing products or entirely new products, **expansion decisions** are made.

Some of the capital budgeting decisions involve *independent projects,* while others will involve *mutually exclusive projects.* **Independent projects** are projects whose cash flows are not affected by one another, so the acceptance of one project does not affect the acceptance of the other project(s)—*all independent projects can be purchased if they all are acceptable.* For example, if Microsoft decided to purchase the **NBC** television network, it still could produce its computer software. On the other hand, if a capital budgeting decision involves **mutually exclusive projects,** then when one project is taken on, the others must be rejected—*only one mutually exclusive project can be purchased, even if they* *all are acceptable.* For example, **Global Sports and Entertainment, Ltd.** has a parcel of land on which it wants to build either an amusement park or a domed sports arena. The land is not large enough for both alternatives, so if Global chooses to build the amusement park, it could not build the arena, and vice versa.

In general, relatively simple calculations, and only a few supporting documents, are required for replacement decisions, especially maintenance-type investments in profitable plants. More detailed analysis is required for cost-reduction replacements, for expansion of existing product lines, and especially for investments in new products or areas. Also, within each category projects are broken down by their dollar costs: Larger investments require both more detailed analysis and approval at a higher level within the firm. Thus, although a plant manager might be authorized to approve maintenance expenditures up to $10,000 on the basis of a relatively unsophisticated analysis, the full board of directors might have to approve decisions that involve either amounts greater than $1 million or expansions into new products or markets. Statistical data generally are lacking for new product decisions, so here judgments, as opposed to detailed cost data, are especially important.

Similarities Between Capital Budgeting and Asset Valuation

Capital budgeting decisions involve valuation of assets, or projects. Therefore, capital budgeting involves exactly the same steps used in general asset valuation.

1. Determine the cost, or purchase price, of the asset.
2. Estimate the cash flows expected from the project, including the salvage value of the asset at the end of its expected life. This is similar to estimating the future dividend or interest payment stream on a stock or bond, along with the stock's expected selling price or the bond's maturity value.
3. Evaluate the riskiness of the projected cash flows to determine the appropriate rate of return to use for computing the present value of the estimated cash flows. For this assessment, management needs information about the probability distributions of the cash flows.
4. Compute the present value of the expected cash flows to obtain an estimate of the asset's value to the firm. This is equivalent to finding the present value of a stock's expected future dividends.
5. Compare the present value of the future expected cash flows with the initial investment, or cost, required to acquire the asset. Alternatively, the expected rate of return on the project can be calculated and compared with the rate of return considered appropriate for the project.

If an individual investor identifies and invests in a stock or bond whose true value is greater than its market price, the value of the investor's portfolio will increase. Similarly, if a firm identifies (or creates) an investment opportunity with a present value greater than its cost, the value of the firm will increase. Thus, there is a very direct link between capital budgeting and stock values: The more effective the firm's capital budgeting procedures, the higher the price of its stock.

Capital Budgeting Evaluation Techniques

The basic methods used by businesses to evaluate projects and to decide whether they should be accepted for inclusion in the capital budget are (1) payback (PB), (2) net present value (NPV), and (3) internal rate of return (IRR). As you will see, to determine a project's acceptability using any of these three techniques, its expected cash flows are needed. However, unlike the other two, the payback method does not consider the time value of money—so we call payback a *nondiscounting technique* and NPV and IRR *discounting techniques*. We will explain how each evaluation criterion is calculated, and then we will determine how well each performs in terms of identifying those projects that will maximize the firm's stock price.

We use the tabular and timeline cash flow data shown in Exhibit 700.39 for Project S and Project L to illustrate all the methods, and throughout this section we assume that the projects are equally risky. Note that the cash flows, $\hat{CF}_t$, are expected values and that they have been adjusted to reflect taxes, depreciation, salvage values, and any other changes in cash flows associated with the capital projects. Also, we assume that all cash flows occur at the end of the designated year. Incidentally, the S stands for *short* and the L for *long:* Project S is a short-term project in the sense that its cash inflows tend to come in sooner than Project L's.

Exhibit 700.39 *Net Cash Flows for Project S and Project L*

	Expected After-Tax Net Cash Flows, $\hat{CF}_t$	
Year (t)	Project S	Project L
0[a]	$(3,000)	$(3,000)
1	1,500	400
2	1,200	900
3	800	1,300
4	300	1,500

Project S:

0	1	2	3	4
−3,000	1,500	1,200	800	300

Project L:

0	1	2	3	4
−3,000	400	900	1,300	1,500

[a] $\hat{CF}_0$ represents the initial investment, or net cost of the project.

Exhibit 700.40 *Payback Period for Project S and Project L*

Project S:

	0	1	2	PB$_S$	3	4
Net cash flow	−3,000	1,500	1,200		800	300
Cumulative net cash flow	−3,000	−1,500	−300		500	800

Project L:

	0	1	2	3	PB$_L$	4
Net cash flow	−3,000	400	900	1,300		1,500
Cumulative net cash flow	−3,000	−2,600	−1,700	−400		1,100

Payback Period

The **payback period,** defined as the expected number of years required to recover the original investment (the cost of the asset), is the simplest and, as far as we know, the oldest *formal* method used to evaluate capital budgeting projects. To compute a project's payback period, simply add up the expected cash flows for each year until the amount initially invested in the project is recovered. The total amount of time, including the fraction of a year if appropriate, that it takes to recapture the original amount invested is the payback period. The payback calculation process for both Project S and Project L is diagrammed in Exhibit 700.40.

The exact payback period can be found using the following formula:

$$\text{Payback} = \text{PB} = \begin{pmatrix} \text{Number of years before} \\ \text{full recovery of} \\ \text{original investment} \end{pmatrix} + \begin{pmatrix} \dfrac{\text{Uncovered cost at start}}{\text{of full-recovery year}} \\ \dfrac{}{\text{Total cash flow during}} \\ \text{full-recovery year} \end{pmatrix} \quad (7.43)$$

The diagram in Exhibit 700.40 shows that the payback period for Project S is between two years and three years, so, using Equation 7.43, the exact payback period is

$$\text{PB}_S = 2 + \frac{300}{800} = 2.4 \text{ years}$$

Applying the same procedure to Project L, we find Payback$_L$ = 3.3 years.

Using payback to make capital budgeting decisions is based on the concept that it is better to recover the cost of (investment in) a project sooner rather than later. Therefore, Project S is considered better than Project L because it has a lower payback. *As a general rule, a project is considered acceptable if its payback is less than the maximum cost recovery time established by the firm.* For example, if the firm requires projects to have a payback of three years or less, Project S would be acceptable but Project L would not.

The payback method is very simple, which explains why payback traditionally has been one of the most popular capital budgeting techniques. But payback ignores the time value of money, so relying solely on this method could lead to incorrect decisions—at least if our goal is to maximize value. If a project has a payback of three years, we know how quickly the initial investment will be covered by the expected cash flows, but this information does not provide any indication of whether the return on the project is sufficient to cover the cost of the funds invested. In addition, when payback is used, the cash flows beyond the payback period are ignored. For example, even if Project L had a fifth year of cash flows equal to $50,000, its payback would remain 3.3 years, which is less desirable than the payback of 2.4 years for Project S. But, with the additional $50,000 cash flow, Project L most likely would be preferred.

Net Present Value (NPV)

To correct for the major defect of any *nondiscounting* technique—ignoring the time value of money—methods were developed to include consideration of the time value of money. One such method is the **net present value (NPV) method,** which relies on **discounted cash flow (DCF) techniques.** To implement this approach, we simply find the present value of all the future cash flows a project is expected to generate and then subtract (add a negative cash flow) its initial investment (original cost) to find the *net* benefit the firm will realize from investing in the project. *If the net benefit computed on a present value basis (that is, NPV) is positive, then the project is considered an acceptable investment.* NPV is computed using the following equation:

$$\text{NPV} = \hat{CF}_0 + \frac{\hat{CF}_1}{(1+k)^1} + \frac{\hat{CF}_2}{(1+k)^2} + \cdots + \frac{\hat{CR}_n}{(1+k)^n}$$

$$= \sum_{t=0}^{n} \frac{\hat{CF}_t}{(1+k)^t} \tag{7.44}$$

Here $\hat{CF}_t$ is the expected net cash flow at Period t, and k is the rate of return required by the firm to invest in this project. The rate of return required by the firm generally is termed the firm's cost of capital, because it is the average rate the firm must pay for the funds used to purchase capital projects. Cash outflows (expenditures on the project, such as the cost of buying equipment or building factories) are treated as negative cash flows. For Project S and Project L, only $\hat{CF}_0$ is negative, but for many large projects such as the Alaska Pipeline, an electric generating plant, or Chrysler's Neon project, outflows occur for several years before operations begin and cash flows turn positive.

At a 10 percent required rate of return, Project S's NPV is $161.33:

CASH FLOW TIMELINE FOR PROJECT S:

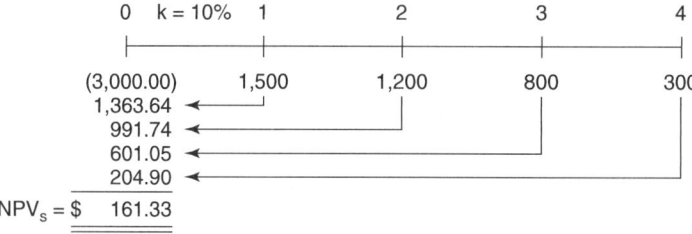

We show the regular cash flow timeline as the top portion of the diagram, and then we show the solution in the bottom left portion of the diagram.

1. NUMERICAL SOLUTION As the lower section of the cash flow timeline shows, to find the NPV, we compute the present value of each cash flow and sum the results. Using Equation 7.44, the numerical solution for the NPV for Project S is

$$PV_S = \$(3,000) + \frac{\$1,500}{(1.10)^1} + \frac{\$1,200}{(1.10)^2} + \frac{\$800}{(1.10)^3} + \frac{\$300}{(1.10)^4}$$

$$= \$(3,000) + \$1,500(0.90909) + \$1,200(0.82645) + \$800(0.75131) + \$300(0.68301)$$

$$= \$(3,000) + \$1,363.64 + \$991.74 + \$601.05 + 204.90$$

$$= \$161.33$$

Of course, if the stream of future cash flows was constant rather than nonconstant, then the future cash flow stream would represent an annuity, and our computations would be simplified.

2. **TABULAR SOLUTION** We can also write Equation 7.44 in the following form:

$$\text{NPV} = \hat{CF}_0 + \hat{CF}_1(\text{PVIF}_{k,1}) + \hat{CF}_2(\text{PVIF}_{k,2}) + \cdots + \hat{CF}_n(\text{PVIF}_{k,n})$$

$$= \hat{CF}_0 + \sum_{t=1}^{n} \hat{CF}_t(\text{PVIF}_{k,t}) \tag{7.44a}$$

Looking up the interest factors in Table A-1 of Module 700 Appendix, we compute NPV_S as follows.

```
NPV_S = $(3,000) + $1,500(0.9091) + $1,200(0.8264) + $800(0.7513) + $300(0.6830)
      = $(3,000) +     $1,363.65  +     $991.68   +   $601.04  +   $204.90
      = $161.27 (rounding difference)
```

Using the same process for Project L, we find $\text{NPV}_L = \$108.67$. On this basis, both projects should be accepted if they are independent, but Project S should be the one chosen if they are mutually exclusive.

If you look at the cash flow timeline for Project S, you can see the reason it has a positive NPV is because the initial investment of \$3,000 is recovered on a present value basis prior to the end of the project's life. In fact, if we use the payback concept developed in the previous section, we can compute how long it would take to recapture the initial outlay of \$3,000 using the discounted cash flows given in the cash flow timeline—the sum of the present values of the cash flows for the first three years is \$2,956.43, so all of the \$3,000 cost is not recovered until 3.2 years = 3 years + [(\$3,000 − \$2,956.43)/\$204.90] years. Therefore, on a present value basis, it takes 3.2 years for Project S to recover, or pay back, its original cost. This is called the **discounted payback** of Project S—it is the length of time it takes for a project's *discounted* cash flows to repay the cost of the investment. The discounted payback for Project L is 3.90 years, so Project S is more acceptable. Unlike the traditional payback computation discussed in the previous section, the discounted payback computation does consider the time value of money. *Using the discounted payback method, a project should be accepted when its discounted payback is less than its expected life* because, in such cases, the present value of the future cash flows the project is expected to generate exceeds the initial cost of the asset (initial investment)—that is, NPV > 0.

Rationale for the NPV Method

The rationale for the NPV method is straightforward. An NPV of zero signifies that the project's cash flows are just sufficient to repay the invested capital and to provide the required rate of return on that capital. If a project has a positive NPV, then it generates a return that is greater than is needed to pay for funds provided by investors, and this excess return accrues solely to the firm's stockholders. Therefore, if a firm takes on a project with a positive NPV, the position of the stockholders is improved because the firm's value is greater. In our example, shareholders' wealth would increase by \$161.33 if the firm takes on Project S but by only \$108.67 if it takes on Project L. Viewed in this manner, it is easy to see why Project S is preferred to Project L, and it also is easy to see the logic of the NPV approach.

This description of the process is somewhat oversimplified. Both analysts and investors anticipate that firms will identify and accept positive NPV projects, and current stock prices reflect these expectations. Thus, stock prices react to announcements of new capital projects only to the extent that such projects were not already expected. In this sense, we can think of a firm's value as consisting of two parts: (1) the value of its existing assets and (2) the value of its "growth opportunities," or projects with positive NPVs. AT&T is a good example of this: The company has the world's largest long-distance network plus telephone manufacturing facilities, both of which provide current earnings and cash flows, and it has **Bell Labs,** which has the *potential* for coming up with new products in the computer/telecommunications area that could be extremely profitable. Security analysts (and investors) thus analyze AT&T as a company with a set of cash-producing assets plus a set of growth opportunities that will materialize if and only if the company can come up with a number of positive NPV projects through its capital budgeting process.

Internal Rate of Return (IRR)

In Section 715, we presented procedures for finding the yield to maturity (YTM), or rate of return, on a bond—if you invest in the bond and hold it to maturity, you can expect to earn the YTM on the money you invested. Exactly the same concepts are employed in capital budgeting when the *internal rate of return method* is used. The **internal rate of return (IRR)** is the rate of return the firm expects to earn if the project is purchased; thus it is defined as the discount rate that equates the present value of a project's expected cash flows to the investment outlay, or initial cost. *As long as the project's IRR, which is its expected return, is greater than the rate of return required by the firm for such an investment, the project is acceptable.*

We can use the following equation to solve for a project's IRR:

$$\hat{CF}_0 + \frac{\hat{CF}_1}{(1+IRR)^1} + \frac{\hat{CF}_2}{(1+IRR)^2} + \cdots + \frac{\hat{CF}_n}{(1+IRR)^n} = 0$$
$$= \sum_{t=0}^{n} \frac{\hat{CF}_t}{(1+IRR)^t} = 0 \qquad (7.45)$$

For Project S, the cash flow time line for the IRR computation is as follows:

CASH FLOW TIMELINE FOR PROJECT S:
Using Equation 7.45, here is the setup for computing IRR$_S$.

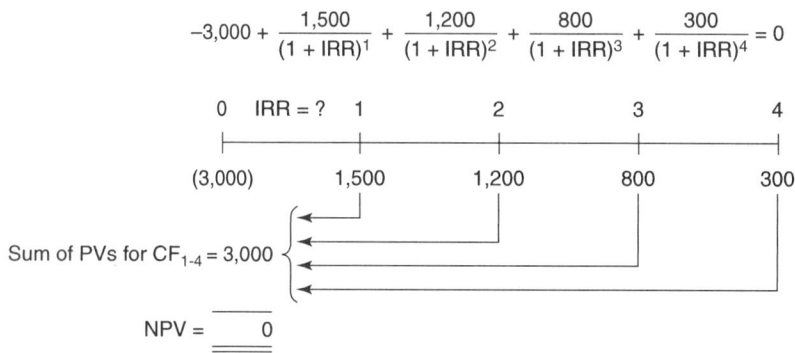

NUMERICAL AND TABULAR SOLUTION Although it is easy to find the NPV without a financial calculator, this is *not* true of the IRR. If the cash flows are constant from year to year, then we have an annuity, and we can use annuity factors presented in the Module 700 appendix to find the IRR. However, if the cash flows are not constant, as is generally the case in capital budgeting, then it is difficult to find the IRR without a financial calculator. Without a financial calculator, you basically have to solve Equation 7.45 by trial and error—try some discount rate (or corresponding PVIF factors), and see if the equation solves to zero, and if it does not, try a different discount rate until you find one that forces the equation to equal zero. The discount rate that causes the equation to equal zero is defined as the IRR. For a realistic project with a fairly long life, the trial and error approach is a tedious, time-consuming task.

Here are the IRRs for Project S and Project L.

$$IRR_S = 13.1\%$$
$$IRR_L = 11.4\%$$

Projects that have IRRs greater than their **required rates of return,** *or* **hurdle rates** *are acceptable investments.* For example, if the hurdle rate required by the firm is 10 percent, then both Project S and Project L are acceptable. If they are mutually exclusive, Project S is more acceptable than Project L because $IRR_S > IRR_L$.

Rationale for the IRR Method

Why is a project acceptable if its IRR is greater than its required rate of return? Because the IRR on a project is its expected rate of return, and if this return exceeds the cost of the funds used to finance the project, a surplus remains after paying for the funds—this surplus accrues to the firm's stockholders. Therefore, *taking on a project whose IRR exceeds its required rate of return, or cost of funds, increases shareholders' wealth.* On the other hand, if the internal rate of return is less than the cost of funds, then taking on the project imposes a cost on current stockholders. Consider what would happen if you borrowed funds at a 15 percent interest rate to invest in the stock market, and the stocks you picked earned only 13 percent. You still have to pay the 15 percent interest, so you end up losing 2 percent on the investment. On the other hand, anything you earn in excess of 15 percent is yours to keep, because only 15 percent interest has to be paid to the lender. So 15 percent is your *cost of funds,* which is what you must *require* your investments to earn to break even. It is this "breakeven" characteristic that makes the IRR useful in evaluating capital projects.

Comparison of the NPV and IRR Methods

We found the NPV for Project S is $161.33—this means that if the project is purchased, the value of the firm will increase by $161.33. The IRR for Project S is 13.1 percent—this means that if the firm purchases Project S, it will earn a 13.1 percent rate of return on its investment. We generally measure wealth in dollars, so the NPV method should be used to accomplish the goal of maximizing shareholders' wealth. In reality, using the IRR method could lead to investment decisions that increase, but do not maximize wealth. We choose to discuss the IRR method and compare it to the NPV method because many corporate executives are familiar with the meaning of IRR, it is entrenched in the corporate world, and it does have some virtues. Therefore, it is important that business managers understand the IRR method and be prepared to explain why, at times, a project with a lower IRR might be preferable to one with a higher IRR.

NPV Profiles

A graph that shows a project's NPV at various discount rates (required rates of return) is termed the project's **net present value (NPV) profile.** To construct the profiles, we calculate the projects' NPVs at various discount rates, say, 0, 5, 10, 15, and 20 percent, and plot these values on a graph.

Because the IRR is defined as the discount rate at which a project's NPV equals zero, the point where its *NPV profile crosses the X axis indicates a project's internal rate of return.* NPV profiles can be very useful in project analysis. The **crossover rate** is the discount rate at which the NPV profiles of two projects cross and, thus, at which the projects' NPVs are equal.

Independent Projects

Note that the internal rate of return formula, Equation 7.45, is simply the NPV formula, Equation 7.44, solved for the particular discount rate that forces the NPV to equal zero. Thus, the same basic equation is used for both methods, but in the NPV method the discount rate, k, is specified and the NPV is found, whereas in the IRR method the NPV is set equal to zero, and the interest rate that forces this equality (the IRR) is determined. Mathematically, therefore, the NPV and IRR methods will always lead to the same accept/reject decisions for independent projects: *If a project's NPV is positive, its IRR will exceed k, while if NPV is negative, k will exceed the IRR. In every case, if a project is acceptable using the IRR method, then the NPV method also will show it is acceptable.*

Mutually Exclusive Projects

If we assume that Project S and Project L are *mutually exclusive* rather than independent, then we can choose either Project S or Project L, or we can reject both, but we cannot invest in both. *A conflict exists* if the required rate of return is less than the crossover rate: NPV says choose Project L over Project S, while IRR says the opposite. Which answer is correct? Logic suggests that the NPV method is better because it selects the project that adds the most to shareholder wealth.

Two basic conditions can cause NPV profiles to cross and thus lead to conflicts between NPV and IRR: (1) when *project size (or scale) differences* exist, meaning that the cost of one project is larger than that of the other, or (2) when *timing differences* exist, meaning that the timing of cash flows from the two projects differs such that most of the cash flows from one project come in the early years and most of the cash flows from the other project come in the later years, as occurs with Projects L and S.

When either size or timing differences occur, the firm will have different amounts of funds to invest in the various years, depending on which of the two mutually exclusive projects it chooses. For example, if one project costs more than the other, then the firm will have more money at t = 0 to invest elsewhere if it selects the smaller project. Similarly, for projects of equal size, the one with the larger early cash inflows provides more funds for reinvestment in the early years. Given this situation, the rate of return at which differential cash flows can be invested is an important consideration.

The critical issue in resolving conflicts between mutually exclusive projects is this: How useful is it to generate cash flows earlier rather than later? The value of early cash flows depends on the rate at which we can reinvest these cash flows. *The NPV method implicitly assumes that the rate at which cash flows can be reinvested is the required rate of return, whereas the IRR method implies that the firm has the opportunity to reinvest at the project's IRR.* These assumptions are inherent in the mathematics of the discounting process. The cash flows can actually be withdrawn as dividends by the stockholders and spent on pizza, but the NPV method still assumes that cash flows can be reinvested at the required rate of return, while the IRR method assumes reinvestment at the project's IRR.

Which is the better assumption—that cash flows can be reinvested at the required rate of return or that they can be reinvested at the project's IRR? To reinvest at the IRR associated with a capital project, the firm would have to be able to reinvest the project's cash flows in another project with an identical IRR—such projects generally do not continue to exist, or it is not feasible to reinvest in such projects, because competition in the investment markets drives their prices up and their IRRs down. On the other hand, at the very least, a firm could repurchase the bonds and stock it has issued to raise capital budgeting funds and thus repay some of its investors, which would be the same as investing at its required rate of return. Thus, we conclude that the *more realistic* **reinvestment rate assumption** *is the required rate of return, which is implicit in the NPV method.* This, in turn, leads us to prefer the NPV method, at least for firms willing and able to obtain capital at a cost reasonably close to their current cost of capital.

We should reiterate that *when projects are independent, the NPV and IRR methods both provide exactly the same accept/reject decision.* However, *when evaluating mutually exclusive projects,* especially those that differ in scale or timing, *the NPV method should be used to determine which project should be purchased.*

Multiple IRRs

There is one other situation in which the IRR approach might not be usable—this is when projects have unconventional cash flow patterns. A project has a *conventional* cash flow pattern if it has cash outflows (costs) in one or more periods at the beginning of its life followed by a series of cash inflows. If, however, a project has a large cash outflow either sometime during or at the end of its life, then it has an *unconventional* cash flow pattern. Projects with unconventional cash flow patterns present unique difficulties when the IRR method is used, including the possibility of **multiple IRRs.**

There exists an IRR solution for each time the *direction* of the cash flows associated with a project is interrupted (that is, inflows change to outflows, and vice versa). For example, a conventional cash flow pattern only has one net cash outflow at the beginning of the project's life, so the direction of the cash flows changes (is interrupted) once from negative (outflow) to positive (inflow), and there is only one IRR solution. A project with a 10-year life that has cash inflows every year except that $\hat{CF}_0 < 0$ and $\hat{CF}_5 < 0$ will have two IRR solutions because the cash flow pattern has two direction changes, or interruptions—one after the initial cost is paid and another five years later.

Other Evaluation Methods Used in Capital Budgeting Analysis

There are two other methods worth mentioning here. These include accounting rate of return (ARR) method and profitability index (PI) method.

The ARR method is based on accounting data and is computed as the average annual profits after taxes divided by the initial cash outlay in the project. This accounting rate of return is then compared to the required rate of return to determine if a particular project should be accepted or rejected. Strengths of the ARR method include that it is simple and that accounting data is readily available. Drawbacks of the ARR method include that it does not consider the project's cash flows and that it ignores the time value of money.

The PI method is a benefit/cost ratio and is computed as the present value of future net cash flows divided by the initial cash outlay in the project. As long as the PI is 1.00 or greater, the project is acceptable. For any given project, the NPV method and the PI method give the same accept-reject answer. When choosing between mutually exclusive projects, the NPV method is preferred because the project's benefits are expressed in absolute terms. In contrast, the PI method expresses benefits in relative terms.

Conclusions on the Capital Budgeting Decision Methods

In the previous section, we compared the NPV and IRR methods to highlight their relative strengths and weaknesses for evaluating capital projects, and in the process we probably created the impression that "sophisticated" firms should use only one method in the decision process—NPV. However, virtually all capital budgeting decisions are analyzed by computer, so it is easy to calculate and list all the decision measures: payback, discounted payback, NPV, and IRR. In making the accept/reject decision, most large, sophisticated firms such as IBM, **General Electric**, and General Motors calculate and consider multiple measures because each provides decision makers with a somewhat different piece of relevant information.

Payback and discounted payback provide information about both the risk and the *liquidity* of a project—a long payback means (1) that the investment dollars will be locked up for many years, hence the project is relatively illiquid, and (2) that the project's cash flows must be forecast far out into the future, hence the project is probably quite risky. We generally define liquidity as the ability to convert an asset into cash quickly without loss of the original investment. Thus, in most cases, short-term assets are considered more liquid than long-term assets. A good analogy for this is the bond valuation process. An investor should never compare the yields to maturity on two bonds without considering their terms to maturity because a bond's riskiness is significantly influenced by its maturity.

NPV is important because it gives a direct measure of the dollar benefit (on a present value basis) to the firm's shareholders, so we regard NPV as the best single measure of *profitability*. IRR also measures profitability, but here it is expressed as a percentage rate of return, which many decision makers, especially nonfinancial managers, seem to prefer. Further, IRR contains information concerning a project's "safety margin," which is not inherent in NPV. To illustrate, consider the following two projects: Project T costs $10,000 at t = 0 and is expected to return $16,500 at the end of one year, while Project B costs $100,000 and has an expected payoff of $115,500 after one year. At a 10 percent required rate of return, both projects have an NPV of $5,000, so by the NPV rule we should be indifferent between the two. However, Project T actually provides a much larger margin for error. Even if its realized cash inflow were almost 40 percent below the $16,500 forecast, the firm would still recover its $10,000 investment. On the other hand, if Project B's inflows fell by only 14 percent from the forecasted $115,500, the firm would not recover its investment. Further, if no inflows were generated at all, the firm would lose only $10,000 with Project T but $100,000 if it took on Project B.

The NPV contains no information about either the "safety margin" inherent in a project's cash flow forecasts or the amount of capital at risk, but the IRR does provide "safety margin" information—Project T's IRR is a whopping 65.0 percent, while Project B's IRR is only 15.5 percent. As a result, the realized return could fall substantially for Project T, and it would still make money. Note, though, that the IRR method has a reinvestment assumption that probably is unrealistic, and it is possible for projects to have multiple IRRs.

In summary, the different methods provide different types of information to decision makers. Because it is easy to calculate them, all should be considered in the decision process. For any specific decision, more weight might be given to one method than another, but it would be foolish to ignore the information provided by any of the methods.

At this point, we should note that multinational corporations use essentially the same capital budgeting techniques that we described in this section. However, foreign governments, international regulatory environments, and financial and product markets in other countries pose certain challenges to U.S. firms that must make capital budgeting decisions for their foreign operations.

The Post-Audit

An important aspect of the capital budgeting process is the **post-audit,** which involves (1) comparing actual results with those predicted by the project's sponsors and (2) explaining why any differences occurred. For example, many firms require that the operating divisions send monthly reports for the first six months after a project goes into operation and quarterly reports thereafter, until the project's results are up to expectations. From then on, reports on the project are handled like those of other operations.

The post-audit has two main purposes.

1. **Improve forecasts.** When decision makers are forced to compare their projections to actual outcomes, there is a tendency for estimates to improve. Conscious or unconscious biases are observed and eliminated; new forecasting methods are sought as the need for them becomes apparent; and people simply tend to do everything better, including forecasting, if they know that their actions are being monitored.
2. **Improve operations.** Businesses are run by people, and people can perform at higher or lower levels of efficiency. When a divisional team has made a forecast about an investment, its members are, in a sense, putting their reputations on the line. If costs are above predicted levels, sales below expectations, and so on, executives in production, marketing, and other areas will strive to improve operations and to bring results in line with forecasts. In a discussion related to this point, an IBM executive made this statement: "You academicians worry only about making good decisions. In business, we also worry about making decisions good."

The post-audit is not a simple process—a number of factors can cause complications. First, we must recognize that each element of the cash flow forecast is subject to uncertainty, so a percentage of all projects undertaken by any reasonably venturesome firm will necessarily go awry. This fact must be considered when appraising the performances of the operating executives who submit capital expenditure requests. Second, projects sometimes fail to meet expectations for reasons beyond the control of the operating executives and for reasons that no one could realistically be expected to anticipate. For example, the 1991–1992 recession adversely affected many projects. Third, it is often difficult to separate the operating results of one investment from those of a larger system. Although some projects stand alone and permit ready identification of costs and revenues, the actual cost savings that result from a new computer system, for example, might be very hard to measure. Fourth, it is often hard to hand out blame or praise because the executives who were actually responsible for a given decision might have moved on by the time the results of a long-term investment are known.

Because of these difficulties, some firms tend to play down the importance of the post-audit. However, observations of both businesses and governmental units suggest that the best-run and most successful organizations are the ones that put the greatest emphasis on post-audits. Accordingly, we regard the post-audit as being an extremely important element in a good capital budgeting system.

Cash Flow Estimation and Risks

The most important, but also the most difficult, step in the analysis of a capital project is estimating its **cash flows**—the investment outlays and the net cash flows expected after the project is purchased. Many variables are involved in cash flow estimation, and many individuals and departments participate in the process. For example, the forecasts of unit sales and sales prices normally are made by the marketing group based on its knowledge of advertising effects, the state of the economy, competitors' reactions, and trends in consumers' tastes. Similarly, the capital outlays associated with a new product generally are determined by the engineering and product development staffs, while operating costs are estimated by cost accountants, production experts, personnel specialists, purchasing agents, and so forth. Because it is difficult to make accurate forecasts of the costs and revenues associated with a large, complex project, forecast errors can be quite large.

The financial staff's role in the forecasting process includes (1) coordinating the efforts of the other departments, such as engineering and marketing, (2) ensuring that everyone involved with the forecast uses a consistent set of economic assumptions, and (3) making sure that no biases are inherent in the forecasts. This last point is extremely important, because division managers often become emotionally involved with pet projects or develop empire-building complexes, both of which can lead to cash flow forecasting biases that make bad projects look good—on paper.

It is almost impossible to overstate the difficulties one can encounter with cash flow forecasts. Also, it is difficult to overstate the importance of these forecasts. In this section, we will give you a sense of some of the inputs that are involved in forecasting the cash flows associated with a capital project and in minimizing forecasting errors.

Relevant Cash Flows

One important element in cash flow estimation is the determination of **relevant cash flows,** which are defined as the specific set of cash flows that should be considered in the capital budgeting decision. This process can be rather difficult, but two cardinal rules can help financial analysts avoid mistakes: (1) Capital budgeting decisions must be based on *cash flows after taxes,* not accounting income, and (2) only *incremental cash flows* are relevant to the accept/reject decision. These two rules are discussed in detail in the following sections.

Cash Flow versus Accounting Income

In capital budgeting analysis, *after-tax cash flows, not accounting profits,* are used—it is cash that pays the bills and can be invested in capital projects, not profits. Cash flows and accounting profits can be very different. To illustrate, consider Exhibit 700.41, which shows how accounting profits and cash flows are related to one another. We assume that Unilate Textiles is planning to start a new division at the end of 2000; that sales and all costs, except depreciation, represent actual cash flows and are projected to be constant over time; and that the division will use accelerated depreciation, which will cause its reported depreciation charges to decline over time.

The top section of the exhibit shows the situation in the first year of operations, 2001. Accounting profits are $7 million, but the division's net cash flow—money that is available to Unilate—is $22 million. The $7 million profit is the *return on the funds* originally invested, while the $15 million of depreciation is a *return of part of the funds* originally invested, so the $22 million cash flow consists of both a return *on* and a return *of* part of the invested capital.

The bottom part of the table shows the situation projected for 2006. Here reported profits have doubled because of the decline in depreciation, but net cash flow is down sharply because taxes have doubled. The amount of money received by the firm is represented by the cash flow figure, not the net income figure. And although accounting profits are important for some purposes, it is cash flows that are relevant for the purposes of setting a value on a project

Exhibit 700.41 *Accounting Profits versus Net Cash Flow (thousands of dollars)*

	Accounting Profits	Cash Flows
I. 2001 Situation		
Sales	$50,000	$50,000
Costs except depreciation	(25,000)	(25,000)
Depreciation	(15,000)	—
Net operating income or cash flow	$10,000	$25,000
Taxes based on operating income (30%)	(3,000)	(3,000)
Net income or net cash flow	$ 7,000	$22,000
Net cash flow = Net income plus depreciation = $ 7,000 + $15,000 = $22,000		
II. 2006 Situation		
Sales	$50,000	$50,000
Costs except depreciation	(25,000)	(25,000)
Depreciation	(5,000)	—
Net operating income or cash flow	$20,000	$25,000
Taxes based on operating income (30%)	(6,000)	(6,000)
Net income or net cash flow	$14,000	$19,000
Net cash flow = Net income plus depreciation = $14,000 + $5,000 = $19,000		

using discounted cash flow (DCF) techniques—cash flows can be reinvested to create value, profits cannot. Therefore, in capital budgeting, we are interested in net cash flows, which, in most cases, we can define as

$$\text{Net cash flow} = \text{Net income} + \text{Depreciation}$$
$$= \text{Return } on \text{ capital} + \text{Return } of \text{ capital}$$

not in accounting profits per se. Actually, net cash flow should be adjusted to reflect all noncash charges, not just depreciation. However, for most projects, depreciation is by far the largest noncash charge. Also, note that Exhibit 700.41 ignores interest charges, which would be present if the firm used debt. Most firms do use debt and hence finance part of their capital budgets with debt. Therefore, the question has been raised as to whether interest charges should be reflected in capital budgeting cash flow analysis. The consensus is that interest charges should not be dealt with explicitly in capital budgeting—rather, the effects of debt financing are reflected in the cost of capital, which is used to discount the cash flows. If interest were subtracted and cash flows were then discounted, we would be double counting the cost of debt.

Incremental Cash Flows

In evaluating a capital project, we are concerned only with those cash flows that result directly from the decision to accept the project. These cash flows, called **incremental cash flows,** represent the changes in the firm's total cash flows that occur as a direct result of accepting the project. To determine if a specific cash flow is considered incremental, we need to find out whether it is affected by the purchase of the project. Cash flows that will change because the project is purchased are *incremental cash flows* that need to be included in the capital budgeting evaluation; cash flows that are not affected by the purchase of the project are not relevant to the capital budgeting decision. Unfortunately, identifying the relevant cash flows for a project is not always as simple as it seems. Some special problems in determining incremental cash flows are discussed next.

SUNK COSTS Sunk costs are not incremental costs, and they should not be included in the analysis. A **sunk cost** is an outlay that has already been committed or that has already occurred and hence is not affected by the accept/reject decision under consideration. To illustrate, in 1999 Unilate Textiles considered building a distribution center in New England in an effort to increase sales in that area of the country. To help with its evaluation, Unilate hired a consulting firm to perform a site analysis and provide a feasibility study for the project; the cost was $100,000, and this amount was expensed for tax purposes. This expenditure is *not* a relevant cost that should be included in the capital budgeting evaluation of the prospective distribution center because Unilate cannot recover this money, regardless of whether the new distribution center is built.

OPPORTUNITY COSTS   The second potential problem relates to **opportunity costs,** which are defined as the cash flows that could be generated from assets the firm already owns provided they are not used for the project in question. To illustrate, Unilate already owns a piece of land that is suitable for a distribution center. When evaluating the prospective center in New England, should the cost of the land be disregarded because no additional cash outlay would be required? The answer is no, because there is an opportunity cost inherent in the use of the property. In this case, the land could be sold to yield $150,000 after taxes. Use of the site for the distribution center would require forgoing this inflow, so the $150,000 must be charged as an opportunity cost against the project. Note that the proper land cost in this example is the $150,000 market-determined value, irrespective of whether Unilate originally paid $50,000 or $500,000 for the property. (What Unilate paid would, of course, have an effect on taxes and hence on the after-tax opportunity cost.)

EXTERNALITIES: EFFECTS ON OTHER PARTS OF THE FIRM   The third potential problem involves the effects of a project on other parts of the firm; economists call these effects **externalities.** For example, Unilate does have some existing customers in New England who would use the new distribution center because its location would be more convenient than the North Carolina distribution center they have been using. The sales, and hence profits, generated by these customers would not be new to Unilate; rather, they would represent a transfer from one distribution center to another. Thus, the net revenues produced by these customers should not be treated as incremental income in the capital budgeting decision. Although they often are difficult to quantify, externalities such as these should be considered.

SHIPPING AND INSTALLATION COSTS   When a firm acquires fixed assets, it often must incur substantial costs for shipping and installing the equipment. These charges are added to the invoice price of the equipment when the total cost of the project is being determined. Also, for depreciation purposes, the *depreciable basis* of an asset, which is the total amount that can be depreciated, includes the purchase price and any additional expenditures required to make the asset operational, including shipping and installation. Therefore, the full cost of the equipment, including shipping and installation costs, is used as the depreciable basis when depreciation charges are calculated. So if Unilate Textiles bought a computer with an invoice price of $100,000 and paid another $10,000 for shipping and installation, then the full cost of the computer, and its depreciable basis, would be $110,000.

Keep in mind that *depreciation is a noncash expense, so there is not a cash outflow associated with the recognition of depreciation expense each year.* But because depreciation is an expense, *it affects the taxable income of a firm, thus the amount of taxes paid by the firm, which is a cash flow.*

INFLATION   Inflation is a fact of life, and it should be recognized in capital budgeting decisions. If expected inflation is not built into the determination of expected cash flows, then the calculated net present value and internal rate of return will be incorrect—both will be artificially low. It is easy to avoid inflation bias—simply build inflationary expectations into the cash flows used in the capital budgeting analysis. Expected inflation should be reflected in the revenue and cost figures, thus the annual net cash flow forecasts. The required rate of return does not have to be adjusted by the firm for inflation expectations because investors include such expectations when establishing the rate at which they are willing to permit the firm to use their funds. Investors decide at what rates a firm can raise funds in the capital markets, and they include an adjustment for inflation when determining the rate that is appropriate.

Identifying Incremental Cash Flows

Generally, when we identify the incremental cash flows associated with a capital project, we separate them according to when they occur during the life of the project. In most cases, we can classify a project's incremental cash flows as (1) cash flows that occur *only at the start* of the project's life—time period 0, (2) cash flows that *continue throughout* the project's life—time periods 1 through n, and (3) cash flows that occur *only at the end,* or the termination, of the project—time period n. We discuss these three incremental cash flow classifications and identify some of the relevant cash flows next. But keep in mind, when identifying the incremental cash flows for capital budgeting, the primary question is which cash flows will be affected by purchasing the project—if a cash flow does not change, it is not relevant for the capital budgeting analysis.

Initial Investment Outlay

The **initial investment outlay** refers to the incremental cash flows that *occur only at the start of a project's life*, $\hat{CF}_0$. The initial investment includes such cash flows as the purchase price of the new project and shipping and installation costs. If the capital budgeting decision is a *replacement decision,* the initial investment must also take into account the cash flows associated with the disposal of the old, or replaced, asset, which include any cash received or paid to scrap the old asset and any tax effects associated with the disposal.

In many cases, the addition or replacement of a capital asset has an impact on the net working capital of the firm. For example, normally, additional inventories are required to support a new operation, and expanded sales also lead to additional accounts receivable.

We should note that there are instances in which the change in net working capital associated with a capital project actually results in a decrease in the firm's current funding requirements, which frees up cash flows for investment. Usually this occurs if the project being considered is much more efficient than the existing asset(s). In any event, *the change in net working capital that results from the acceptance of a project is an incremental cash flow that must be considered in the capital budgeting analysis.* And because the changes in net working capital requirements occur at the start of the project's life, this cash flow impact is an incremental cash flow that is included as a part of the initial investment outlay.

Incremental Operating Cash Flows

Most capital projects also affect the day-to-day cash flows generated by the firm. For example, Unilate has discovered that it can reduce its total operating costs by $10 million by purchasing a new weaving machine to replace a machine it has been using for 10 years. The cost reduction would result because the technological advancements of the new machine would allow Unilate to use less electricity and fewer raw materials (wool, cotton, and so on) in its manufacturing process. These cost savings, as well as any changes in depreciation expense, will affect the taxes paid by Unilate each year the new machine is in service. Thus, Unilate's normal *operating cash flows* will change if the project is accepted. We define **incremental operating cash flows** as the changes in day-to-day cash flows that result from the purchase of a capital project. The impact of incremental operating cash flows continues until the firm disposes of the asset.

In most cases, the *incremental operating cash flows* for each year can be computed directly by using the following equation:

$$\text{Incremental operating cash flow}_t = \Delta \text{Cash revenues}_t - \Delta \text{Cash expenses}_t - \Delta \text{Taxes}_t \qquad (7.46)$$

The symbols in Equation 7.46 are defined as follows:

where Δ = The Greek symbol delta, which represents the change in something.

We have emphasized that depreciation is a *noncash* expense. So why is the change in depreciation expense included in the computation of incremental operating cash flow shown in Equation 7.46? The change in depreciation expense needs to be computed because, when depreciation changes, taxable income changes and so does the amount of income taxes paid; and the amount of taxes paid is a cash flow.

Terminal Cash Flow

The **terminal cash flow** occurs at the end of the life of the project, and it is associated with the final disposal of the project and returning the firm's operations to where they were before the project was accepted. Consequently, the terminal cash flow includes the salvage value, which could be either positive (selling the asset) or negative (paying for removal), and the tax impact of the disposition of the project. In addition, we generally assume the firm returns to the operating level that existed prior to the acceptance of the project; thus, any working capital accounts changes that occurred at the beginning of the project's life will be reversed at the end of its life. For example, as an expansion project's life approaches termination, inventories will be sold off and not replaced, and receivables will also be converted to cash. As these changes occur, the firm will receive an end-of-project cash flow equal to the net working capital requirement that occurred when the project was begun. Unilate expects the life of the New England distribution center to be ten years, so the inventories at that location will be reduced to zero in the tenth year. Because inventories will not have to be replenished during the last sales period, cash flows in Year 10 will increase by $5 million.

Incorporating Risk in Capital Budgeting Analysis

To this point, we have assumed the projects being evaluated have the same risk as the projects that the firm currently possesses. However, there are three separate and distinct types of project risk that need to be examined to determine if the required rate of return used to evaluate a project should be different than the *average* required rate of the firm. The three risks are (1) the project's own **stand-alone risk,** or the risk it exhibits when evaluated alone rather than as part of a combination, or portfolio, of assets—the effect of the project on the other assets of the firm is disregarded; (2) **corporate,** or **within-firm, risk,** which is the effect a project has on the total, or overall, riskiness of the company, without considering which risk component, systematic or unsystematic, is affected—the effect the project has on the stockholders' own personal diversification is disregarded; and (3) **beta,** or **market, risk,** which is project risk assessed from the standpoint of a stockholder who holds a well-diversified portfolio. As we shall see, a particular project might have high stand-alone risk, yet taking it on might not have much effect on either the firm's risk or that of its owners because of portfolio, or diversification, effects.

As we shall see shortly, a project's stand-alone risk is measured by the variability of the project's expected returns; its corporate risk is measured by the project's impact on the firm's earnings variability; and its beta risk is measured by the project's effect on the firm's beta coefficient. Taking on a project with a high degree of either stand-alone risk or corporate risk will not necessarily affect the firm's beta to any great extent. However, if the project has highly uncertain returns, and if those returns are highly correlated with returns on the firm's other assets and also with most other assets in the economy, the project will exhibit a high degree of all three types of risk. For example, suppose General Motors decides to undertake a major expansion to build solar-powered autos. GM is not sure how its technology will work on a mass production basis, so there are great risks in the venture—its stand-alone risk is high. Management also estimates that the project will have a higher probability of success if the economy is strong, because people will have more money to spend on the new autos. This means that the project will tend to do well if GM's other divisions also do well and to do badly if other divisions do badly. This being the case, the project will also have high corporate risk. Finally, because GM's profits are highly correlated with those of most other firms, the project's beta coefficient will also be high. Thus, this project will be risky under all three definitions of risk.

Stand-Alone Risk

What about a project's stand-alone risk—is it of any importance to anyone? In theory, stand-alone risk should be of little or no concern, because we know diversification can eliminate some of this type of risk. However, it is of great importance for the following reasons:

1. It is easier to estimate a project's stand-alone risk than its corporate risk, and it is far easier to measure stand-alone risk than beta risk.
2. In the vast majority of cases, all three types of risk are highly correlated—if the general economy does well, so will the firm, and if the firm does well, so will most of its projects. Thus, stand-alone risk generally is a good proxy for hard-to-measure corporate and beta risk.
3. Because of points 1 and 2, if management wants a reasonably accurate assessment of a project's riskiness, it should spend considerable effort on determining the riskiness of the project's own cash flows—that is, its stand-alone risk.

The starting point for analyzing a project's stand-alone risk involves determining the uncertainty inherent in the project's cash flows. This analysis can be handled in a number of ways, ranging from informal judgments to complex economic and statistical analyses involving large-scale computer models. To illustrate, many of the individual cash flows in a project are subject to uncertainty. For example, sales for each year were projected at 15,000 units to be sold at a net price of $2,000 per unit, or $30 million in total. Actual unit sales almost certainly would be somewhat higher or lower than 15,000, however, and also the sales price might turn out to be different from the projected $2,000 per unit. In effect, the sales quantity and the sales price estimates are expected values taken from probability distributions. The distributions could be relatively "tight," reflecting small standard deviations and low risk, or they could be "flat," denoting a great deal of uncertainty about the final value of the variable in question and hence a high degree of stand-alone risk.

The nature of the individual cash flow distributions, and their correlations with one another, determine the nature of the NPV distribution and, thus, the project's stand-alone risk. We next discuss three techniques for assessing a project's stand-alone risk: (1) sensitivity analysis, (2) scenario analysis, and (3) Monte Carlo simulation.

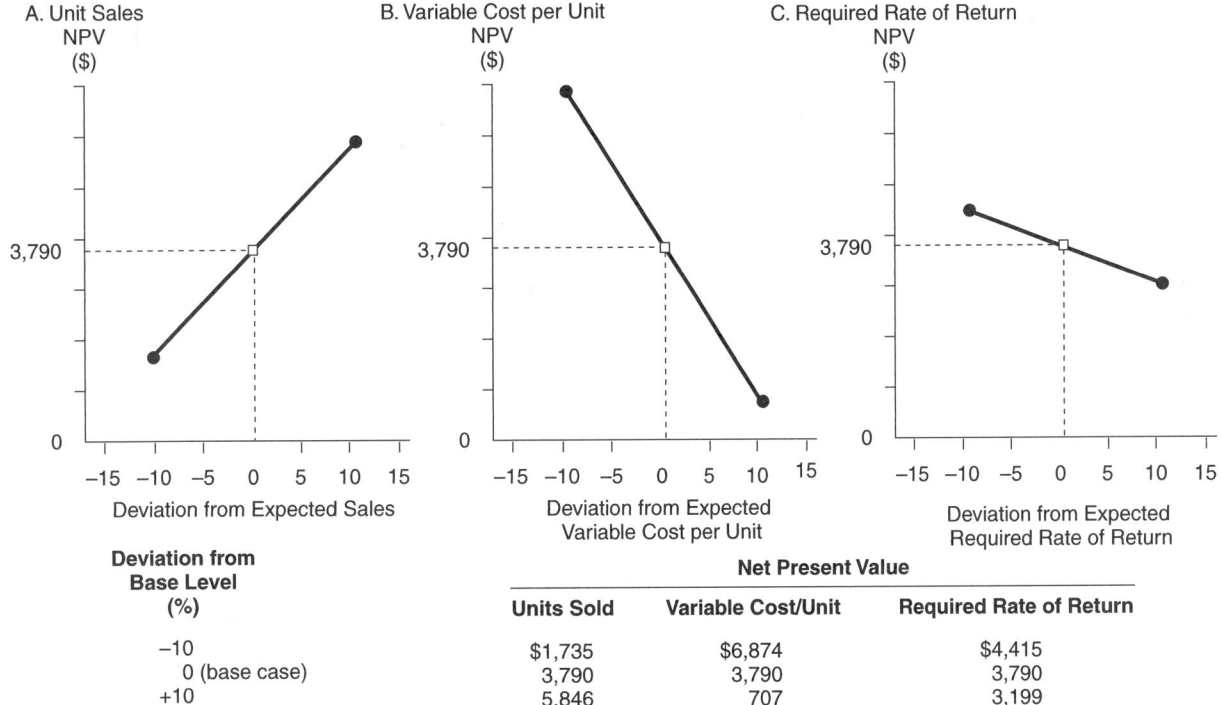

Exhibit 700.42 *Sensitivity Analysis (thousands of dollars)*

Deviation from Base Level (%)	Units Sold	Variable Cost/Unit	Required Rate of Return
−10	$1,735	$6,874	$4,415
0 (base case)	3,790	3,790	3,790
+10	5,846	707	3,199

Sensitivity Analysis

The cash flows used to determine the acceptability of a project result from forecasts of uncertain events, such as economic conditions in the future and expected demand for a product. Intuitively, then, we know the cash flow amounts used to determine the net present value of a project might be significantly different from what actually happens in the future; but those numbers represent our best, and most confident, prediction concerning the expected cash flows associated with a project. We also know that if a key input variable, such as units sold, changes, the project's NPV also will change. **Sensitivity analysis** is a technique that shows exactly how much the NPV will change in response to a given change in an input variable, other things held constant.

In a sensitivity analysis, we begin with the base case situation that was developed using the expected values for each input; next each variable is changed by specific percentage points above and below the expected value, holding other things constant; then a new NPV is calculated for each of these values; and, finally, the set of NPVs is plotted against the variable that was changed. Exhibit 700.42 shows the computer project's sensitivity graphs for three of the key input variables. The table below the graphs gives the NPVs that were used to construct the graphs. The slopes of the lines in the graphs show how sensitive NPV is to changes in each of the inputs: *the steeper the slope, the more sensitive the NPV is to a change in the variable.* In the figure we see that the project's NPV is very sensitive to changes in variable costs, less sensitive to changes in unit sales, and not very sensitive at all to changes in the required rate of return. So when estimating these variables' values, HEP should take extra care to ensure the accuracy of the forecast for variable costs per unit.

If we were comparing two projects, the one with the steeper sensitivity lines would be regarded as riskier because for that project a relatively small error in estimating a variable such as unit sales would produce a large error in the project's expected NPV. Thus, sensitivity analysis can provide useful insights into the riskiness of a project.

Scenario Analysis

Although sensitivity analysis probably is the most widely used risk analysis technique, it does have limitations. Consider, for example, a proposed coal mine project whose NPV is highly sensitive to changes in output, in variable costs, and in sales price. However, if a utility company has contracted to buy a fixed amount of coal at an inflation-adjusted price per ton, the mining venture might be quite safe in spite of its steep sensitivity lines. *In general, a project's stand-alone risk depends on both (1) the sensitivity of its NPV to changes in key variables and (2) the range of likely values of these variables as reflected in their probability distributions.* Because sensitivity analysis considers only the first factor, it is incomplete.

Exhibit 700.43 *Scenario Analysis (dollars are in thousands, except sales price)*

Scenario	Sales Volume (units)	Sales Price	NPV	Probability of Outcome (Pr_i)	$NPV \times Pr_i$
Best case	20,000	$2,500	$17,494	0.20	$3,499
Most likely case	15,000	2,000	3,790	0.60	2,274
Worst case	10,000	1,500	(6,487)	0.20	(1,297)
				1.00	Expected NPV = $4,475
					σ_{NPV} = $7,630
					CV_{NPV} = 1.7

$$\text{Expected NPV} = \sum_{i=1}^{n} PR_i(NPV_i) = 0.20(\$17,494) + 0.60(\$3,790) + 0.20(-\$6,487) = \$4,475$$

$$\sigma_{NPV} = \sqrt{\sum_{i=1}^{n} Pr_i(NPV_i - \text{Expected NPV})^2}$$

$$= \sqrt{0.20(17,494 - \$4,475)^2 + 0.60(\$3,790 - \$4,475)^2 + 0.20(-\$6,487 - \$4,475)^2} = \$7,630$$

$$CV_{NPV} = \frac{\sigma_{NPV}}{\text{Expected NPV}} = \frac{\$7,630}{\$4,475} = 1.7$$

Scenario analysis is a risk analysis technique that considers both the sensitivity of NPV to changes in key variables and the likely range of variable values. In a scenario analysis, the financial analyst asks operating managers to pick a "bad" set of circumstances (low unit sales, low sales price, high variable cost per unit, high construction cost, and so on) and a "good" set. The NPVs under the bad and good conditions are then calculated and compared to the expected, or base case, NPV.

As an example, let us return to the appliance control computer project. Assume that HEP's managers are fairly confident of their estimates of all the project's cash flow variables except price and unit sales. Further, they regard a drop in sales below 10,000 units or a rise above 20,000 units as being extremely unlikely. Similarly, they expect the sales price as set in the marketplace to fall within the range of $1,500 to $2,500. Thus, 10,000 units at a price of $1,500 defines the lower bound, or the **worst-case scenario,** whereas 20,000 units at a price of $2,500 defines the upper bound, or the **best-case scenario.** Remember that the **base case** values are 15,000 units and a price of $2,000.

To carry out the scenario analysis, we use the worst-case variable values to obtain the worst-case NPV and the best-case variable values to obtain the best-case NPV. We then use the result of the scenario analysis to determine the *expected* NPV, standard deviation of NPV, and the coefficient of variation. To complete these computations, we need an estimate of the probabilities of occurrence of the three scenarios, the Pr_i values. Suppose management estimates that there is a 20 percent probability of the worst-case scenario occurring, a 60 percent probability of the base case, and a 20 percent probability of the best case. Of course, it is *very difficult* to estimate scenario probabilities accurately. The scenario probabilities and NPVs constitute a probability distribution of returns just like those we dealt with earlier, except that the returns are measured in dollars instead of in percentages, or rates of return.

We performed the scenario analysis using a spreadsheet model, and Exhibit 700.43 summarizes the results of this analysis. We see that the base case (or most likely case) forecasts a positive NPV result; the worst case produces a negative NPV; and the best case results in a very large positive NPV. But the expected NPV for the project is $4.5 million and the project's coefficient of variation is 1.7. Now we can compare the project's coefficient of variation with the coefficient of variation of HEP's average project to get an idea of the relative riskiness of the appliance control computer project. HEP's existing projects, on average, have a coefficient of variation of about 1.0, so, on the basis of this stand-alone risk measure, HEP's managers would conclude that the appliance computer project is riskier than the firm's "average" project.

Monte Carlo Simulation

Scenario analysis provides useful information about a project's stand-alone risk. However, it is limited in that it only considers a few discrete outcomes (NPVs) for the project, even though there really are many more possibilities. **Monte Carlo simulation,** so named because this type of analysis grew out of work on the mathematics of casino gambling, ties together sensitivities and input variable probability distributions.

Simulation is more complicated than scenario analysis because the probability distribution of each uncertain cash flow variable has to be specified. Once this has been done, a value from the probability distribution for each variable is randomly chosen to compute the project's cash flows, and then these values are used to determine the project's NPV. Simulation is usually completed using a computer because the process just described is repeated again and again, say, for 500 times, which results in 500 NPVs and a probability distribution for the project's NPV values. Thus, the output produced by simulation is a probability distribution that can be used to determine the most likely range of outcomes to be expected from a project. This provides the decision maker with a better idea of the various outcomes that are possible than is available from a point estimate of the NPV. In addition, simulation software packages can be used to estimate the probability of NPV > 0, of IRR > k, and so on. This additional information can be quite helpful in assessing the riskiness of a project.

Unfortunately, Monte Carlo simulation is not easy to apply because it is often difficult to specify the relationships, or correlations, among the uncertain cash flow variables. The problem is not insurmountable, but it is important not to underestimate the difficulty of obtaining valid estimates of probability distributions and correlations among variables. Such problems have been cited as reasons Monte Carlo simulation has not been widely used in industry.

Corporate (Within-Firm) Risk

To measure corporate, or within-firm, risk, we need to determine how the capital budgeting project is related to the firm's existing assets. Remember that two assets can be combined to reduce risk if their payoffs move in opposite directions—when the payoff from one asset falls, the payoff from the other asset rises. In reality, it is not easy to find assets with payoffs that move opposite each other. As long as assets are *not* perfectly positively related (r = +1.0), some diversification, or risk reduction, can still be achieved. Many firms use this principle to reduce the risk associated with their operations—adding new projects that are not highly related to existing assets can help reduce corporate risk and reduce fluctuations associated with sales.

Corporate risk is important for three primary reasons.

1. Undiversified stockholders, including the owners of small businesses, are more concerned about corporate risk than about beta risk.
2. Empirical studies of the determinants of required rates of return (k) generally find that both beta and corporate risk affect stock prices. This suggests that investors, even those who are well diversified, consider factors other than beta risk when they establish required returns.
3. The firm's stability is important to its managers, workers, customers, suppliers, and creditors, as well as to the community in which it operates. Firms that are in serious danger of bankruptcy, or even of suffering low profits and reduced output, have difficulty attracting and retaining good managers and workers. Also, both suppliers and customers are reluctant to depend on weak firms, and such firms have difficulty borrowing money at reasonable interest rates. These factors tend to reduce risky firms' profitability and hence the prices of their stocks; thus they also make corporate risk significant.

Therefore, corporate risk is important even if a firm's stockholders are well diversified.

Beta (Market) Risk

The types of risk analysis discussed thus far in the section provide insights into a project's risk and thus help managers make better accept/reject decisions. However, these risk measures do not take account of portfolio risk, and they do not specify whether a project should be accepted or rejected. In this section, we show how the Capital Asset Pricing Model (CAPM) can be used to help overcome those shortcomings. Of course, the CAPM has shortcomings of its own, but it nevertheless offers useful insights into risk analysis in capital budgeting.

Beta (or Market) Risk and Required Rate of Return for a Project

In Section 755, we develop the concept of beta, β, as a risk measure for individual stocks. From our discussion, we concluded systematic risk is the relevant risk of a stock because unsystematic, or firm-specific, risk can be reduced significantly or eliminated through diversification. This same concept can be applied to capital budgeting projects because the firm can be thought of as a composite of all the projects it has undertaken. Thus, the relevant risk of a project can be viewed as the impact it has on the firm's systematic risk. This line of reasoning leads to the conclusion that if the beta coefficient for a project, β_{proj}, can be determined, then the **project required rate of return, k_{proj},** can be found using the following form of the CAPM equation:

$$k_{proj} = k_{RF} + (k_M - k_{RF})\beta_{proj}$$

Measuring Beta Risk for a Project

The estimation of project betas is even more difficult than for stocks and more fraught with uncertainty. One way a firm can try to measure the beta risk of a project is to find *single-product* companies in the same line of business as the project being evaluated and then use the betas of those companies to determine the required rate of return for the project being evaluated. This technique is termed the **pure play method,** and the single-product companies that are used for comparisons are called *pure play firms.* For example, if Erie could find three existing single-product firms that operate barges, it could use the average of the betas of those firms as a proxy for the barge project's beta.

The pure play approach can only be used for major assets such as whole divisions, and even then it is frequently difficult to implement because it is often impossible to find pure play proxy firms. However, when **IBM** was considering going into personal computers, it was able to obtain data on **Apple Computer** and several other essentially pure play personal computer companies. This is often the case when a firm considers a major investment outside its primary field.

Project Risk Conclusions

We have discussed the three types of risk normally considered in capital budgeting analysis—the project's stand-alone risk, within-firm (or corporate) risk, and beta (or market) risk—and we have discussed ways of assessing each. However, two important questions remain: (1) Should a firm be concerned with stand-alone and corporate risk in its capital budgeting decisions, and (2) What do we do when the stand-alone or within-firm risk assessments and the beta risk assessment lead to different conclusions?

These questions do not have easy answers. From a theoretical standpoint, well-diversified investors should be concerned only with beta risk, managers should be concerned only with stock price maximization, and these two factors should lead to the conclusion that beta risk should be given virtually all the weight in capital budgeting decisions. However, if investors are not well diversified, if the CAPM does not operate exactly as theory says it should, or if measurement problems keep managers from having confidence in the CAPM approach in capital budgeting, it might be appropriate to give stand-alone and corporate risk more weight than financial theorists suggest. Note also that the CAPM ignores bankruptcy costs, even though such costs can be substantial, and that the probability of bankruptcy depends on a firm's corporate risk, not on its beta risk. Therefore, one can easily conclude that even well-diversified investors should want a firm's management to give at least some consideration to a project's corporate risk instead of concentrating entirely on beta risk.

Although it would be desirable to reconcile these problems and to measure project risk on some absolute scale, the best we can do in practice is to determine project risk in a somewhat nebulous, relative sense. For example, we can generally say with a fair degree of confidence that a particular project has more or less stand-alone risk than the firm's average project. Then, assuming that stand-alone and corporate risk are highly correlated (which is typical), the project's stand-alone risk will be a good measure of its corporate risk. Finally, assuming that beta risk and corporate risk are highly correlated (as is true for most companies), a project with more corporate risk than average will also have more beta risk, and vice versa for projects with low corporate risk.

How Project Risk Is Considered in Capital Budgeting Decisions

Thus far, we have seen that purchasing a capital project can affect a firm's beta risk, its corporate risk, or both. We also have seen that it is extremely difficult to quantify either type of risk. In other words, although it might be possible to reach the general conclusion that one project is riskier than another, it is difficult to develop a really good *measure* of project risk. This lack of precision in measuring project risk makes it difficult to incorporate differential risk into capital budgeting decisions.

Exhibit 700.44 *Capital Budgeting Decisions Using Risk-Adjusted Discount Rates*

Project	Project Risk	Required Return	Estimated Life	Initial Investment Outlay—CF0	Incremental Operating Cash Flows— $CF_1 - CF_5$	NPV	IRR
A	Low	12%	5	$(10,000)	$2,850	$273.61	13.1%
B	Average	15	5	(11,000)	3,210	(239.58)	14.1
C	Average	15	5	(9,000)	2,750	218.43	16.0
D	High	20	5	(12,000)	3,825	(560.91)	17.9

Project Risk Classification	Required Rate of Return
Low	12%
Average	15
High	20

In reality, most firms incorporate project risk in capital budgeting decisions using the **risk-adjusted discount rate** approach. With this approach, the required rate of return, which is the rate at which the expected cash flows are discounted, is adjusted if the project's risk is substantially different from the average risk associated with the firm's existing assets. Therefore, average-risk projects would be discounted at the rate of return required of projects that are considered "average," or normal for the firm; above-average risk projects would be discounted at a higher-than-average rate; and below-average risk projects would be discounted at a rate below the firm's average rate of return. Unfortunately, because risk cannot be measured precisely, there is no accurate way of specifying exactly how much higher or lower these discount rates should be; given the present state of the art, *risk adjustments are necessarily judgmental and somewhat arbitrary.*

Although the process is not exact, many companies use a two-step procedure to develop risk-adjusted discount rates for use in capital budgeting. First, the overall required rate of return is established for the firm's existing assets. This process is completed on a division-by-division basis for very large firms, perhaps using the CAPM. Second, all projects generally are classified into three categories—high risk, average risk, and low risk. Then, the firm or division uses the average required rate of return as the discount rate for average-risk projects, reduces the average rate by one or two percentage points when evaluating low-risk projects, and raises the average rate by several percentage points for high-risk projects. For example, if a firm's basic required rate of return is estimated to be 12 percent, an 18 percent discount rate might be used for a high-risk project and a 9 percent rate for a low-risk project. Average-risk projects, which constitute about 80 percent of most capital budgets, would be evaluated at the 12 percent rate of return. Exhibit 700.44 contains an example of the application of risk-adjusted discount rates for the evaluation of four projects. Each of the four projects has a five-year life, and each is expected to generate a constant cash flow stream during its life; therefore, each project's future cash flow pattern represents an annuity. The analysis shows that only Project A and Project C are acceptable when risk is considered. Note, though, that if the average required rate of return is used to evaluate all the projects, Project C and Project D would be considered acceptable because their IRRs are greater than 12 percent. Using the average required rate of return would lead to an incorrect decision. Thus, *if project risk is not considered in capital budgeting analysis, incorrect decisions are possible.*

Although the risk-adjusted discount rate approach is far from precise, it does at least recognize that different projects have different risks, and projects with different risks should be evaluated using different required rates of return.

Capital Rationing

Independent projects are accepted if their NPVs are positive, and choices among mutually exclusive projects are made by selecting the one with the highest NPV. In this analysis, it is assumed that if in a particular year the firm has an especially large number of good projects, management simply will go into the financial markets and raise whatever funds are required to finance all of the acceptable projects. However, some firms do set limits on the amount of

> *Capital rationing is of two types: soft and hard. Soft capital rationing occurs when a business unit or project is allocated a certain amount of financing while hard capital rationing occurs when the entire company cannot raise financing due to financial distress or preexisting contractual agreement.*

funds they are willing to raise, and, if this is done, the capital budget must also be limited. This situation is known as **capital rationing.**

Elaborate and mathematically sophisticated models have been developed to help firms maximize their values when they are subject to capital rationing. However, a firm that subjects itself to capital rationing is deliberately forgoing profitable projects, and hence it is not truly maximizing its value. This point is well known, so few large, sophisticated firms ration capital today.

Financial Markets, Instruments, and Institutions

The Financial Environment

Financial managers must understand the environment and markets within which businesses operate. Therefore, in this section, we examine the markets where firms raise funds, securities are traded, and stock prices are established, as well as the institutions that operate in these markets. In the process, we will explore the principal factors that determine money costs in the economy.

The Financial Markets

Businesses, individuals, and government units often need to raise capital to fund investments. For example, suppose **Carolina Power & Light (CP&L)** forecasts an increase in the demand for electricity in North Carolina, and the company decides to build a new power plant. Because CP&L almost certainly will not have the hundreds of millions or billions of dollars needed to pay for the plant, the company will have to raise these funds in the financial markets. Or suppose you want to buy a home that costs $100,000, but you only have $20,000 in savings. How can you raise the additional $80,000? At the same time, some individuals and firms have incomes that are greater than their current expenditures, so they have funds available to invest. For example, Carol Hawk has an income of $36,000, but her expenses are only $30,000, while **Reliant Energy** agreed to invest nearly $2.5 billion over seven years to purchase power companies in Europe.

People and organizations wanting to borrow money are brought together with those having surplus funds in the *financial markets.* Unlike *physical (real) asset markets,* which are those for such products as wheat, autos, real estate, computers, and machinery, *financial asset markets* deal with stocks, bonds, mortgages, and other *claims on real assets* with respect to the distribution of future cash flows.

In a general sense, the term *financial market* refers to a conceptual "mechanism" rather than a physical location or a specific type of organization or structure. We usually describe the **financial markets** as being a system comprised of individuals and institutions, instruments, and procedures that bring together borrowers and savers, no matter the location. Note that "markets" is plural—there are a great many different financial markets, each one consisting of many institutions, in a developed economy such as the United States. Each market deals with a somewhat different type of instrument in terms of the instrument's maturity and the assets backing it. Also, different markets serve different types of customers, or operate in different parts of the country. Here are some of the major types of markets:

1. *Debt markets* are the markets where loans are traded, while *equity markets* are the markets where stocks of corporations are traded. A debt instrument is a contract that specifies the amounts, as well as the times, a borrower must repay funds provided by a lender. The borrower can be an individual, a government, or a business. On the other hand, equity represents "ownership" in a corporation and entitles stockholders to share in any cash distribution generated from income (dividends) and from liquidation of the firm.

2. *Money markets* are the markets for debt securities with maturities of one year or less, while *capital markets* are the markets for long-term debt and corporate stocks. The primary function of the money markets is to provide liquidity to businesses, governments, and individuals to meet short-term needs for cash, because, in most cases, the timings of cash inflows and cash outflows do not coincide exactly. For example, if you had funds that you do not need for tuition payments until six months from now, you can invest those funds in a money market security and earn a greater return than if the funds were left in a checking account. The primary function of the capital market is to provide the opportunity to transfer cash surpluses or deficits to future years. For example, without the availability of mortgages, most individuals could not afford to buy houses when they are young and just starting their careers.

3. *Mortgage markets* deal with loans on residential, commercial, and industrial real estate, and on farmland, while *consumer credit markets* involve loans on autos and appliances, as well as loans for education, vacations, and so forth.

4. *World, national, regional, and local markets* also exist. Thus, depending on an organization's size and scope of operations, it might be able to borrow all around the world, or it might be confined to a strictly local, even neighborhood, market.

5. *Primary markets* are the markets in which corporations (and governments) raise new capital. If General Electric (GE) were to sell a new issue of common stock to raise capital, this would be a primary market transaction. The corporation selling the newly created stock receives the proceeds from the sale in a primary market transaction. *Secondary markets* are markets in which existing, previously issued (already outstanding) securities are traded among investors. Thus, if Edgar Rice decided to buy 1,000 shares of IBM stock, the purchase would occur in the secondary market. The New York Stock Exchange is a secondary market, because it deals in outstanding, as opposed to newly issued stocks and bonds. Secondary markets also exist for mortgages, various other types of loans, and other financial assets. The corporation (or government) whose securities are being traded is not involved in a secondary market transaction and, thus, does not receive any funds from such a sale.

6. *Spot markets* and *futures markets* are terms that refer to whether the assets are being bought or sold for "on the spot" delivery (immediately or within a few days) or for delivery at some later date, such as six months or a year into the future. Futures markets have grown in importance in recent years.

A healthy economy is dependent on efficient transfers of funds from people who are net savers to firms, governments, and individuals who need funds. Without efficient transfers, the economy simply could not function: Carolina Power & Light could not raise capital, so Raleigh's citizens would have no electricity; you would not be able to buy the house you want; Carol Hawk would have no place to invest her savings; and so on. Clearly, without financial markets, the level of employment and productivity, hence our standard of living, would be much lower. Therefore, it is essential that our financial markets function efficiently—not only quickly, but also at a low cost.

Financial Institutions

Funds are transferred between those who have funds to invest (savers) and those who need the funds (borrowers) by the three different processes diagrammed in Exhibit 700.45.

1. A *direct transfer* of money and securities, as shown in the top section of Exhibit 700.45, occurs when a business sells its stocks or bonds directly to savers (investors), without going through any type of financial institution. The business delivers its securities to savers, who in turn give the firm the money it needs.

2. As shown in the middle section, a transfer also can go through an *investment banking house* such as **Morgan Stanley Dean Witter**, which serves as a middleman and facilitates the issuance of securities. The company sells its stocks or bonds to the investment bank, which in turn sells these same securities to investors. The business's securities and the savers' money merely "pass through" the investment banking house. However, the investment bank does buy and hold the securities for a period of time, so it is taking a chance—it might not be able to resell them to savers for as much as it paid. Because new securities are involved and the corporation receives money from the sale, this is a primary market transaction. It should be noted that investment banking has nothing to do with the traditional banking process as we know it—investment banking deals with the issuance of new securities, not deposits and loans.

3. Transfers can also be made through a *financial intermediary* such as a bank or a mutual fund. Here the intermediary obtains funds from savers, issuing its own securities or liabilities in exchange, and then it uses the

Exhibit 700.45 *Diagram of the Capital Formation Process*

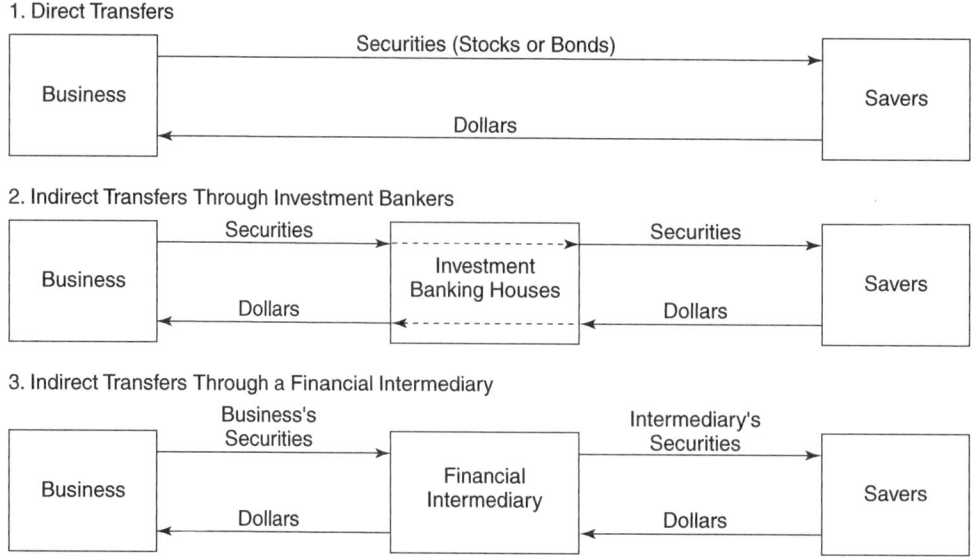

money to lend out or to purchase another business's securities. For example, a saver might give dollars to a bank, receiving from it a certificate of deposit, and then the bank might lend the money to a small business in the form of a mortgage loan. Thus, intermediaries literally create new forms of capital—in this case, certificates of deposit, which are both safer and more liquid than mortgages and thus are better securities for most savers to hold. The existence of intermediaries greatly increases the efficiency of the financial markets because, without them, savers would have to provide funds *directly* to borrowers, which would be a much costlier process.

Direct transfers of funds from savers to businesses are possible and do occur on occasion, but it is generally more efficient for a business to enlist the services of an **investment banker. Merrill Lynch,** Morgan Stanley Dean Witter, and **Goldman Sachs** are examples of financial service corporations that offer investment banking services. Such organizations (1) help corporations design securities with the features that currently are most attractive to investors, (2) buy these securities from the corporation, and (3) then resell them to savers. Although the securities are sold twice, this process really is one primary market transaction, with the investment banker acting as a middleman as funds are transferred from savers to businesses.

The **financial intermediaries** shown in the third section of Exhibit 700.45 do more than simply transfer money and securities between borrowers and savers—they literally create new financial products. Because the intermediaries generally are large, they gain economies of scale in analyzing the creditworthiness of potential borrowers, in processing and collecting loans, in pooling risks, and thus helping individual savers diversify—that is, "not put all their financial eggs in one basket." Further, a system of specialized intermediaries can enable savings to do more than just draw interest. For example, individuals can put money into banks and get both interest income and a convenient way of making payments (checking), or put money into life insurance companies and get both interest income and financial protection for their beneficiaries.

In the United States and other developed nations, a large set of specialized, highly efficient financial intermediaries has evolved. Competition and government policy have created a rapidly changing arena, however, such that different types of institutions currently perform services that formerly were reserved for others. This trend, which most certainly will continue into the future, has caused institutional distinctions to become blurred. Still, there remains a degree of institutional identity, and here are the major classes of financial intermediaries:

1. *Commercial banks,* which are the traditional "department stores of finance," serve a wide variety of customers. Historically, the commercial banks were the major institutions that handled checking accounts and through which the Federal Reserve System expanded or contracted the money supply. Today, however, other institutions also provide checking services and significantly influence the effective money supply. Conversely, commercial banking organizations provide an ever-widening range of services, including trust operations, stock brokerage services, and insurance.

   Note that commercial banking organizations are quite different from investment banks. Commercial banks lend money, whereas investment banks help companies raise capital from other parties.

Banks have different basic policies toward risk. Some banks are inclined to follow relatively conservative lending practices, while others engage in what are properly termed "creative banking practices." These policies reflect partly the personalities of officers of the bank and partly the characteristics of the bank's deposit liabilities. Thus, a bank with fluctuating deposit liabilities in a static community will tend to be a conservative lender, while a bank whose deposits are growing with little interruption might follow more liberal credit policies. Similarly, a large bank with broad diversification over geographic regions or across industries can obtain the benefit of combining and averaging risks. Thus, marginal credit risks that might be unacceptable to a small bank or a specialized bank can be pooled by a large branch banking system to reduce the overall risk of a group of marginal accounts.

Some bank loan officers are active in providing counsel and in stimulating development loans to firms in their early and formative years. Certain banks have specialized departments that make loans to firms expected to grow and thus to become more important customers. The personnel of these departments can provide valuable counseling to customers.

Banks differ in the extent to which they will support the activities of borrowers in bad times. This characteristic is referred to as the degree of *loyalty* of the bank. Some banks might put great pressure on a business to liquidate its loans when the firm's outlook becomes clouded, whereas others will stand by the firm and work diligently to help it get back on its feet.

Banks differ greatly in their degrees of loan specialization. Larger banks have separate departments that specialize in different kinds of loans—for example, real estate loans, farm loans, and commercial loans. Within these broad categories, there might be a specialization by line of business, such as steel, machinery, cattle, or textiles. The strengths of banks also are likely to reflect the nature of the business and the economic environment in which the banks operate. For example, some California banks have become specialists in lending to technology companies, while many Midwestern banks are agricultural specialists. A sound firm can obtain more creative cooperation and more active support by going to a bank that has experience and familiarity with its particular type of business. Therefore, a bank that is excellent for one firm might be unsatisfactory for another.

The size of a bank can be an important factor. Because the maximum loan a bank can make to any one customer is limited to 15 percent of the bank's capital accounts (capital stock plus retained earnings), it generally is not appropriate for large firms to develop borrowing relationships with small banks.

The term "merchant bank" originally was applied to banks that not only loaned depositors' money but also provided customers with equity capital and financial advice. Prior to 1933, U.S. commercial banks performed all types of merchant banking functions. However, about one-third of the U.S. banks failed during the Great Depression, in part because of these activities, so in 1933 the Glass-Steagall Act was passed in an effort to reduce banks' exposure to risk. In recent years, commercial banks have tried to get back into merchant banking, in part because their foreign competitors offer such services, and U.S. banks need to be able to compete with their foreign counterparts for multinational corporations' business. Currently, the larger banks, often through holding companies, do offer merchant banking, at least to a limited extent. This trend should continue, and, if it does, corporations will need to consider a bank's ability to provide a full range of commercial and merchant banking services when choosing a bank.

Some banks also provide cash management services, assist with electronic funds transfers, help firms obtain foreign exchange, and the like; and the availability of such services should be taken into account when selecting a bank. Also, if the firm is a small business whose manager owns most of its stock, the bank's willingness and ability to provide trust and estate services also should be considered.

2. *Savings and loan associations (S&Ls),* which have traditionally served individual savers and residential and commercial mortgage borrowers, take the funds of many small savers and then lend this money to home buyers and other types of borrowers. Because the savers obtain a degree of liquidity that would be absent if they bought the mortgages or other securities directly, perhaps the most significant economic function of the S&Ls is to "create liquidity" that otherwise would be lacking. Savers benefit by being able to invest their savings in more liquid, better managed, and less risky accounts (investments), whereas borrowers benefit from the economies of scale that allow them to obtain more capital at lower costs than would otherwise be possible.

3. *Credit unions* are cooperative associations whose members have a common bond, such as being employees of the same occupation or firm. Members' savings are loaned only to other members, generally for auto purchases, home improvements, and the like. Credit unions often are the cheapest source of funds available to individual borrowers.

4. *Pension funds* are retirement plans funded by corporations or government agencies for their workers and administered primarily by the trust departments of commercial banks or by life insurance companies. Pension funds invest primarily in long-term financial instruments, such as bonds, stocks, mortgages, and real estate.

5. *Life insurance companies* take savings in the form of annual premiums, then invest these funds in stocks, bonds, real estate, and mortgages, and finally make payments to the beneficiaries of the insured parties. In recent years life insurance companies have also offered a variety of tax-deferred savings plans designed to provide benefits to the participants when they retire.
6. *Mutual funds* are investment companies that accept money from savers and then use these funds to buy various types of financial assets such as stocks, long-term bonds, short-term debt instruments, and so on. These organizations pool funds and thus reduce risks through diversification. Different funds are designed to meet the objectives of different types of savers. Hence, there are income funds for those who prefer current income, growth funds for savers who are willing to accept significant risks in the hopes of higher returns, and still other funds that are used as interest-bearing checking accounts (**money market funds**). There are literally hundreds of different types of mutual funds with dozens of different goals and purposes.

Financial institutions historically have been heavily regulated in the United States, with the primary purpose of this regulation being to ensure the safety of the institutions and thus to protect depositors. However, these regulations—which have taken the form of prohibitions on nationwide branch banking, restrictions on the types of assets the institutions can buy and sell, ceilings on the interest rates they can pay, and limitations on the types of services they can provide—have tended to impede the free flow of funds from surplus to deficit areas and thus have hurt the efficiency of our financial markets. Also, for the most part, U.S. financial institutions are at a competitive disadvantage in the international financial markets because most foreign financial institutions, including banks, are not as restricted with respect to organizational structure, ability to branch, nonbanking activities, and so forth. Recognizing this fact, Congress has authorized some major changes recently, and more will be forthcoming.

The result of the ongoing regulatory changes has been a blurring of the distinctions among the different types of institutions. Indeed, the trend in the United States today is toward huge financial service organizations, which own banks, S&Ls, investment banking houses, insurance companies, pension plan operations, and mutual funds, and which have branches across the country and even around the world. In recent years, for example, **Citigroup** was formed by combining (1) **Travelers Group,** which included an insurance company (Travelers) and an investment organization (Smith Barney); (2) Salomon Brothers, which was an investment organization that included an investment banking operation; and (3) **Citicorp**, which was one of the largest banking organizations in the United States. During the same period, **BankAmerica Corporation** and **NationsBank Corporation** combined forces to form the nation's largest bank, **Bank of America,** which boasts that it serves about one-third of U.S. households and that two-thirds of large U.S. corporations use its cash management services. In general, the direction of recent mergers and acquisitions in the financial services industry is to form larger, more diversified companies that can better compete internationally.

The Stock Market

As noted earlier, secondary markets are those in which outstanding, previously issued securities are traded. By far the most active secondary market, and the most important one to financial managers, is the stock market. It is here that the prices of firms' stocks are established, and, because the primary goal of managerial finance is to maximize the firm's stock price, a knowledge of this market is essential for anyone involved in managing a business.

When we differentiate stock markets, we have traditionally divided them into two basic types: (1) *organized exchanges,* which include the New York Stock Exchange (NYSE), the American Stock Exchange (AMEX), and several regional exchanges and (2) the less formal *over-the-counter market.* But, as we shall see shortly, these lines of demarcation are much less precise today than in past years due to market mergers. Because the organized exchanges have actual physical market locations and are easier to describe and understand, we will consider them first.

The Stock Exchanges

The **organized security exchanges** are tangible physical entities. Each of the larger ones occupies its own building, has specifically designated members, and has an elected governing body—its board of governors. Members are said to have "seats" on the exchange, although everybody stands up. These seats, which are bought and sold, give the holder the right to trade on the exchange. For example, there are 1,366 seats on the New York Stock Exchange (NYSE); and, in August 1999, a seat on the NYSE sold for $2.65 million, which was an all-time high. Most of the larger investment banking houses operate *brokerage departments* that own seats on the exchanges and designate one or more of their officers as members.

Like other markets, security exchanges facilitate communication between buyers and sellers. For example, Merrill Lynch might receive an order in its Atlanta office from a customer who wants to buy 100 shares of IBM stock. Simultaneously, Morgan Stanley Dean Witter's Denver office might receive an order from a customer wishing to sell 100 shares of IBM. Each broker communicates by wire with the firm's representative on the NYSE. Other brokers throughout the country are also communicating with their own exchange members. The exchange members with *sell orders* offer the shares for sale, and they are bid for by the members with *buy orders*. Thus, the exchanges operate as *auction markets*.

The Over-the-Counter (OTC) Market

If a security is not traded on an organized exchange, it is customary to say it is traded *over the counter*. In contrast to the organized security exchanges, the **over-the-counter market** is an intangible organization that consists of a network of brokers and dealers around the country. An explanation of the term "over-the-counter" will help clarify exactly what this market is. The exchanges operate as auction markets—buy and sell orders come in more or less simultaneously, and exchange members match these orders. If a stock is traded less frequently, perhaps because it is the stock of a new or a small firm, few buy and sell orders come in, and matching them within a reasonable length of time would be difficult. To avoid this problem, some brokerage firms maintain an inventory of such stocks—they buy when individual investors want to sell and sell when investors want to buy. At one time the inventory of securities was kept in a safe, and the stocks, when bought and sold, literally were passed over the counter.

Traditionally the over-the-counter market has been defined to include all facilities that are needed to conduct security transactions not conducted on the organized exchanges. These facilities consist of (1) the relatively few *dealers* who hold inventories of over-the-counter securities and who are said to "make a market" in these securities, (2) the thousands of *brokers* who act as *agents* in bringing these dealers together with investors, and (3) the computers, terminals, and *electronic networks* that provide a communications link between dealers and brokers. Unlike the organized exchanges, the OTC does not operate as an auction market. The dealers who make a market in a particular stock continuously quote a price at which they are willing to buy the stock (the *bid price*) and a price at which they will sell shares (the *asked price*). Each dealer's prices, which are adjusted as supply and demand conditions change, can be read off computer screens all across the country. The spread between bid and asked prices represents the dealer's markup, or profit.

Most of the brokers and dealers who make up the over-the-counter market are members of a self-regulating body known as the *National Association of Security Dealers* (NASD), which licenses brokers and oversees trading practices. The computerized trading network used by NASD is known as the NASD Automated Quotation System (NASDAQ), and *The Wall Street Journal* and other newspapers contain information on NASDAQ transactions. Today, the NASDAQ is considered a sophisticated market of its own, separate from the OTC. In fact, unlike the OTC, the NASDAQ has *market makers* who continuously monitor activities in various stocks to ensure they are available to traders who want to buy or sell. And, in an effort to become more competitive with the NYSE and with international markets, the NASDAQ, the AMEX, and the Philadelphia Stock Exchange merged in 1998 to form the Nasdaq-Amex Market Group, which might best be referred to as an *organized investment network*. Increased competition among global stock markets assuredly will result in similar alliances among various exchanges/markets in the future.

In terms of numbers of issues, the majority of stocks are traded over the counter. However, because the stocks of larger companies are listed on the organized exchanges, about two-thirds of the dollar volume of stock trading takes place on those exchanges.

The Market for Common Stock

Some companies are so small that their common stocks are not actively traded; they are owned by only a few people, usually the companies' managers. Such firms are said to be *privately owned*, or **closely held, corporations,** and their stock is called *closely held stock*. In contrast, the stocks of most larger companies are owned by a large number of investors, most of whom are not active in management. Such companies are said to be **publicly owned corporations,** and their stock is called *publicly held stock*.

Institutional investors such as pension trusts, insurance companies, and mutual funds own 45 to 50 percent of all common stocks. These institutions buy and sell fairly actively, however, so they account for more than 75 percent of all transactions. Thus, the institutional investors have a heavy influence on the prices of individual stocks.

Types of Stock Market Transactions

We can classify stock market transactions into three distinct types.

1. **Trading in the outstanding shares of established, publicly owned companies: the secondary market.** Unilate Textiles has 25 million shares of stock outstanding. If the owner of 100 shares sells his or her stock, the trade is said to have occurred in the **secondary market.** Thus, the market for outstanding shares, or used shares, is the secondary market. The company receives no new money when sales occur in this market.

2. **Additional shares sold by established, publicly owned companies: the primary market.** If Unilate decides to sell (or issue) an additional one million shares to raise new equity capital, this transaction is said to occur in the **primary market.** Recall that Unilate has 40 million shares authorized but only 25 million outstanding; thus, it has 15 million authorized but unissued shares. If it had no authorized but unissued shares, management could increase the authorized shares by obtaining stockholders' approval, which would generally be granted without any arguments.

3. **New public offerings by privately held firms: the primary market.** When **Coors Brewing Company,** which was owned by the Coors family at the time, decided to sell some stock to raise capital needed for a major expansion program, it took its stock public. Whenever stock in a closely held corporation is offered to the public for the first time, the company is said to be **going public.** The market for stock that has recently gone public normally is called the **initial public offering (IPO) market.**

    Firms can go public without raising any additional capital. Or sometimes a firm goes *public* when growth opportunities no longer can be financed solely by debt and the existing stockholder base, which generally consists of the original owners and current managers of the corporation and a few investors not actively involved in the company's management. The purpose of going public is to increase the ownership base and the funding sources available to the company so that growth opportunities can be better financed and the firm's value can be increased more than otherwise would be possible. Thus, as a firm experiences greater and greater growth and its size expands significantly, there generally is pressure to go public. Unfortunately, when a firm does go public, the red tape increases, because financial reporting and disclosure guidelines and security regulations are more restrictive for public firms than for private firms.

The Decision to List the Stock

To have its stock listed, a company must apply to an exchange, pay a relatively small fee, and meet the exchange's minimum requirements. These requirements relate to the size of the company's net income as well as to the number of shares outstanding and in the hands of outsiders (as opposed to the number held by insiders, who generally do not trade their stock very actively). The company also must agree to disclose certain information to the exchange; this information is designed to help the exchange track trading patterns and thus try to prevent manipulation of the stock's price. The size qualifications increase as one moves from the regional exchanges to the AMEX and on to the NYSE.

Assuming that a company qualifies, many people believe that listing is beneficial both to the company and to its stockholders. Listed companies receive a certain amount of free advertising and publicity, and the status as a listed company enhances their prestige and reputation. This might have a beneficial effect on the sales of the firm's products, and it probably is advantageous in terms of lowering the required rate of return on its common stock. Investors respond favorably to increased information, increased liquidity, and confidence that the quoted price is not being manipulated. By providing investors with these benefits in the form of listing their companies' stock, financial managers might lower their firms' costs of capital and increase the value of their stocks.

Regulation of Securities Markets

Sales of new securities, as well as operations in the secondary markets, are regulated by the **Securities and Exchange Commission (SEC)** and, to a lesser extent, by each of the 50 states. For the most part, the SEC regulations are intended to (1) ensure investors receive fair financial disclosure from publicly traded companies and (2) discourage fraudulent and misleading behavior by firms' investors, owners, and employees to manipulate stock prices. The primary elements of SEC regulation follow.

1. The SEC has jurisdiction over all interstate offerings of new securities to the general public in amounts of $1.5 million or more. A company wishing to issue new stock must file a **registration statement** that provides financial, legal, and technical information about the company. A **prospectus** that summarizes the information

in the registration statement generally is provided to prospective investors for use in selling the securities. SEC lawyers and accountants analyze both the registration statement and the prospectus; if the information is inadequate or misleading, the SEC will delay or stop the public offering.

2. The SEC also regulates all national securities exchanges, and companies whose securities are listed on an exchange must file annual reports similar to the registration statement with both the SEC and the exchange.
3. The SEC has control over stock trades by corporate **insiders.** Officers, directors, and major stockholders must file monthly reports of changes in their holdings of the corporation's stock. Any *short-term* profits from such transactions must be handed over to the corporation.
4. The SEC has the power to prohibit manipulation by such devices as pools (aggregations of funds used to affect prices artificially) or wash sales (sales between members of the same group to record artificial transaction prices).
5. The SEC has control over the form of the proxy and the way the company uses it to solicit votes.

Control over the flow of credit into securities transactions is exercised by the Board of Governors of the Federal Reserve System. The Fed exercises this control through **margin requirements,** which represent the percentage of the purchase price that must be deposited (invested) by investors—the percentage that can be borrowed is equal to 100% less the margin requirement set by the Fed. If a great deal of margin borrowing has been going on, a decline in stock prices can result in inadequate loan coverages, which would force stock brokers to issue **margin calls,** which in turn would require investors either to put up more money or to have their margined stock sold to pay off their loans. Such forced sales would further depress the stock market and could set off a downward spiral, such as the events that took place in October 1987. The margin requirement currently is 50 percent.

States also have some control over the issuance of new securities within their boundaries. This control usually is exercised by a "corporation commissioner" or someone with a similar title. State laws relating to securities sales are called **blue sky laws** because they were put into effect to keep unscrupulous promoters from selling securities that offered the "blue sky" but that actually had little or no asset backing.

The securities industry itself realizes the importance of stable markets, sound brokerage firms, and no perception of stock manipulation. Therefore, the various exchanges work closely with the SEC to police transactions on the exchanges and to maintain the integrity and credibility of the system. Similarly, the National Association of Securities Dealers (NASD) cooperates with the SEC to police trading in the OTC market. These industry groups also cooperate with regulatory authorities to set net worth and other standards for securities firms, to develop insurance programs to protect the customers of brokerage houses, and the like.

In general, government regulation of securities trading, as well as industry self-regulation, is designed to ensure that investors receive information that is as accurate as possible, that no one artificially manipulates the market price of a given stock, and that corporate insiders do not take advantage of their position to profit in their companies' stocks at the expense of other stockholders. Neither the SEC, the state regulators, nor the industry itself can prevent investors from making foolish decisions or from having bad luck, but regulators can and do help investors obtain the best data possible for making sound investment decisions.

Financial Instruments in International Markets

For the most part, the financial securities of companies and institutions in other countries are similar to those in the United States. There are some differences, however, which we discuss in this section. Also, financial securities exist that have been created to permit investors easier access to international investments, such as *American Depository Receipts.*

American Depository Receipts

Foreign companies can be traded internationally through *depository receipts,* which represent shares of the underlying stocks of foreign companies. In the United States, most foreign stock is traded through **American Depository Receipts (ADRs).** ADRs are not foreign stocks; rather they are certificates created by such organizations as banks. The certificates represent ownership in stocks of foreign companies that are held in trust by a bank located in the country where the stock is traded. ADRs provide Americans the ability to invest in foreign companies with less complexity and difficulty than might otherwise be possible. Each ADR certificate represents a certain number of shares of stock of a foreign company, and it entitles the owner to receive any dividends paid by the company in U.S. dollars. In addition, ADRs are traded in the stock markets in the United States, which often are more liquid than foreign markets. All financial information, including values, is denominated in dollars and stated in English; thus, there are no problems with exchange rates and language translations.

In many cases, investors can purchase foreign securities directly. But such investments might be complicated by legal issues, the ability to take funds such as dividends out of the country, and interpretation into domestic terms. Thus, ADRs provide investors the ability to participate in the international financial markets without having to bear risks greater than those associated with the corporations in which the investments are made. The market values of ADRs move in tandem with the market values of the underlying stocks that are held in trust.

Foreign Equity Instruments

The equities of foreign companies are like those of U.S. corporations. The primary difference between stocks of foreign companies and those of American companies is that U.S. regulations provide greater protection of stockholders' rights than those of most other countries. In the international markets, equity generally is referred to as *Euro stock* or *Yankee stock*.

1. *Euro stock* refers to stock that is traded in countries other than the home country of the company, not including the United States. Thus, if the stock of a Japanese company is sold in Germany, it would be considered a Euro stock.
2. *Yankee stock* is stock issued by foreign companies that is traded in the United States. If a Japanese company sold its stock in the United States, it would be called Yankee stock in the international markets.

As the financial markets become more global and more sophisticated, the financial instruments offered both domestically and internationally will change. Already, foreign companies and governments have discovered that financial markets in the United States provide excellent sources of funds because a great variety of financial outlets exist. As technology improves and regulations that bar or discourage foreign investing are repealed, the financial markets of other developed countries will become more prominent and new, innovative financial products will emerge.

The Investment Banking Process

When a business (or government unit) needs to raise funds in the financial markets, it generally enlists the services of an **investment banker** (see Panel 2 in Exhibit 700.45). Merrill Lynch, Morgan Stanley Dean Witter, and Goldman Sachs are examples of companies that offer investment banking services. Such organizations (1) help corporations design securities with the features that are most attractive to investors given existing market conditions, (2) buy these securities from the corporations, and (3) then resell them to investors (savers). Although the securities are sold twice, this process really is one primary market transaction, with the investment banker acting as an intermediary (agent) as funds are transferred from savers to businesses.

We should note that investment banking has nothing to do with the traditional banking process as we know it—investment banking deals with the issuance of new securities, not deposits and loans. The major investment banking houses often are divisions of large financial service corporations engaged in a wide range of activities. For example, Merrill Lynch has a brokerage department that operates thousands of offices worldwide, as well as an investment banking department that helps companies issue securities, take over other companies, and the like. Merrill Lynch's brokers sell previously issued stocks as well as stocks that are issued through their investment banking departments. Thus, financial service organizations such as Merrill Lynch sell securities in both the secondary markets and the primary markets.

In this section we describe how securities are issued in the financial markets, and we explain the role of investment bankers in this process. Two stages are involved in raising capital where Stage I deals with the firm itself and Stage II deals with the firm and its selected investment banker.

Raising Capital: Stage I Decisions

The firm itself makes some preliminary decisions on its own, including the following:

1. **Dollars to be raised.** How much new capital do we need?
2. **Type of securities used.** Should stock, bonds, or a combination be used? Further, if stock is to be issued, should it be offered to existing stockholders or sold directly to the general public?
3. **Competitive bid versus negotiated deal.** Should the company simply offer a block of its securities for sale to the highest bidder, or should it sit down with an investment banker and negotiate a deal? These two procedures are called *competitive bids* and *negotiated deals*. Only a handful of the largest firms on the NYSE, whose securities are already well known to the investment banking community, are in a position to use the competitive bid

process. The investment banks would have to do a large amount of investigative work in order to bid on an issue unless they were already quite familiar with the firm, and the costs involved would be too high to make it worthwhile unless the investment bank was sure of getting the deal. Therefore, the vast majority of offerings of stocks or bonds are made on a negotiated basis.

4. **Selection of an investment banker.** Assuming the issue is to be negotiated, which investment banker should the firm use? Older firms that have "been to market" before will already have established a relationship with an investment banker, although it is easy enough to change investment bankers if the firm is dissatisfied. However, a firm that is just going public will have to choose an investment bank, and different investment banking houses are better suited for different companies. The older, larger "establishment houses" like Morgan Stanley Dean Witter deal mainly with large companies like AT&T, IBM, and Exxon. Other investment bankers specialize in more speculative issues like initial public offerings.

Raising Capital: Stage II Decisions

Stage II decisions, which are made jointly by the firm and its selected investment banker, include the following:

1. **Reevaluating the initial decisions.** The firm and its investment banker will reevaluate the initial decisions about the size of the issue and the type of securities to use. For example, the firm initially might have decided to raise $50 million by selling common stock, but the investment banker might convince management that it would be better off, in view of current market conditions, to limit the stock issue to $25 million and to raise the other $25 million as debt.

2. **Best efforts or underwritten issues.** The firm and its investment banker must decide whether the investment banker will work on a best efforts basis or underwrite the issue. In an **underwritten arrangement,** the investment banker generally assures the company that the entire issue will be sold, so the investment banker bears significant risks in such an offering. With this type of arrangement, the investment banking firm typically buys the securities from the issuing firm and then sells the securities in the primary markets, hoping to make a profit. In a **best efforts arrangement,** the investment banker does not guarantee that the securities will be sold or that the company will get the cash it needs. With this type of arrangement, the investment banker does not buy the securities from the issuing firm; rather the securities are handled on a contingency basis, and the investment banker is paid a commission based on the amount of the issue that is sold. The investment banker essentially promises to exert its *best efforts* when selling the securities. With a *best efforts arrangement,* the issuing firm takes the chance the entire issue will not be sold and that all the needed funds will not be raised. For example, the very day IBM signed an *underwritten* agreement to sell $1 billion of bonds in 1979, interest rates rose sharply, and bond prices fell. IBM's investment bankers lost somewhere between $10 million and $20 million. Had the offering been on a best efforts basis, IBM would have been the loser.

3. **Issuance costs.** The investment banker's fee must be negotiated, and the firm also must estimate the other expenses it will incur in connection with the issue—lawyers' fees, accountants' costs, printing and engraving, and so on. Usually, the investment banker will buy the issue from the company at a discount below the price at which the securities are to be offered to the public, and this **underwriter's spread** covers the investment banker's costs and provides a profit.

    Flotation costs as a percentage of the proceeds are higher for stocks than for bonds, and costs are also higher for small issues than for large issues. The relationship between size of issue and flotation costs is primarily due to the existence of fixed costs: certain costs must be incurred regardless of the size of the issue, so the percentage flotation cost is quite high for small issues.

4. **Setting the offering price.** If the company already is publicly owned, the **offering price** will be based on the existing market price of the stock or the yield on the bonds. For common stock, the most typical arrangement calls for the investment banker to buy the securities at a prescribed number of points below the closing price on the last day of registration. For example, on July 1, 2000, the stock of Unilate Textiles had a current price of $23, and it had traded between $20 and $25 a share during the previous three months. Unilate and its underwriter agreed that the investment banker would buy 5 million new shares at $1 below the closing price on the last day of registration, which was expected to be in early October. The stock actually closed at $20.50 on the day the SEC released the issue, so the company received $19.50 a share. The shares then were sold to the public at a price of $20.50. As is typical, Unilate's agreement had an escape clause that provided for the contract to be voided if the price of the stock had fallen below a predetermined figure. In the Unilate case, this "upset" price was set at $18.50 a share. Thus, if the closing price of the shares on the last day of registration had been $18, Unilate would have had the option of withdrawing from the agreement.

Investment bankers have an easier job if an issue is priced relatively low, but the issuer of the securities naturally wants as high a price as possible. Therefore, an inherent conflict of interest on price exists between the investment banker and the issuer. However, if the issuer is financially sophisticated and makes comparisons with similar security issues, the investment banker will be forced to price close to the market.

It is important to note that *if pressure from the new shares drives down the price of the stock, all shares outstanding, not just the new shares, will be affected.* Thus, if Unilate's stock fell from $23 to $20.50 as a result of the financing, and if the price remained at that new level, the company would incur a loss of $2.50 on each of the 25 million shares previously outstanding, or a total market value loss of $62.5 million. In a sense, that loss would be a *flotation cost* because it would be a cost associated with the new issue. However, if the company's prospects really were poorer than investors had thought, then most of the price decline eventually would have occurred anyway. On the other hand, if the company's prospects are not really all that bad (if the signal was incorrect), then over time Unilate's stock price would increase, and the company would not suffer a permanent loss of $62.5 million.

If the company is going public for the first time, it will have no established price (or demand curve), so the investment bankers will have to estimate the equilibrium price at which the stock will sell after issue. If the offering price is set below the true equilibrium price, the stock will rise sharply after issue, and the company and its original stockholders will have given away too many shares to raise the required capital. If the offering price is set above the true equilibrium price, either the issue will fail or, if the investment bankers succeed in selling the stock, their investment clients will be unhappy when the stock subsequently falls to its equilibrium level. Therefore, it is important that the equilibrium price be approximated as closely as possible.

Selling Procedures

Once the company and its investment bankers have decided how much money to raise, the type of securities to issue, and the basis for pricing the issue, they will prepare and file a registration statement and prospectus with the SEC. It generally takes about 20 days for the issue to be approved by the SEC. The final price of the stock (or the interest rate on a bond issue) is set at the close of business the day the issue clears the SEC, and the securities are then offered to the public the following day.

Investment bankers must pay the issuing firm within four days of the time the offering officially begins, so, typically, the investment bankers sell the stock within a day or two after the offering begins. But, on occasion investment bankers miscalculate, set the offering price too high, and are unable to move the issue. Similarly, the market might decline during the offering period, which again would force the investment bankers to reduce the price of the stock. In either instance, on an underwritten offering the firm would still receive the price that was agreed upon, and the investment bankers would have to absorb any losses that were incurred.

Because they are exposed to large potential losses, investment bankers typically do not handle the purchase and distribution of an issue single-handedly unless it is a very small one. If the amount of money involved is large and the risk of price fluctuations substantial, an investment banker forms an **underwriting syndicate** in an effort to minimize the amount of risk each one carries. The investment banking house that sets up the deal is called the **lead,** or **managing, underwriter.**

In addition to the underwriting syndicate, on larger offerings still more investment bankers are included in a **selling group,** which handles the distribution of securities to individual investors. The selling group includes all members of the underwriting syndicate plus additional dealers who take relatively small participations (or shares of the total issue) from the syndicate members. Members of the selling group act as selling agents and receive commissions for their efforts—they do not purchase the securities, so they do not bear the same risks the underwriting syndicate does. Thus, the underwriters act as wholesalers and bear the risks associated with the issue, whereas members of the selling group act as retailers. The number of investment banking houses in a selling group depends partly on the size of the issue; for example, the one set up when **Communications Satellite Corporation (Comsat)** went public consisted of 385 members.

Shelf Registrations

The selling procedures described previously, including the 20-day minimum waiting period between registration with the SEC and sale of the issue, apply to most security sales. However, large, well-known public companies that issue securities frequently might file a master registration statement with the SEC and then update it with a short-form statement just prior to each individual offering. In such a case, a company could decide at 10 A.M. to sell registered securities and have the sale completed before noon. This procedure is known as **shelf registration** because in effect the company puts its new securities "on the shelf" and then sells them to investors when it thinks the market is right.

Maintenance of the Secondary Market

In the case of a large, established firm like General Motors, the investment banking firm's job is finished once it has disposed of the stock and turned the net proceeds over to the company. However, when a company is going public for the first time, the investment banker is under an obligation to maintain a market for the shares after the issue has been completed. Such stocks typically are traded in the over-the-counter market, and the lead underwriter generally agrees to "make a market" in the stock and to keep it reasonably liquid. The company wants a good market to exist for its stock, as do its stockholders. Therefore, if the investment banking house wants to do business with the company in the future, to keep its own brokerage customers happy, and to have future referral business, it will hold an inventory of the shares and help to maintain an active secondary market in the stock.

Financial Risk Management

Investment Risk

In this section, we take an in-depth look at how investment risk should be measured and how it affects assets' values and rates of return. When we examined the determinants of interest rates, we defined the real risk-free rate, k^*, to be the rate of interest on a risk-free security in the absence of inflation. The actual interest rate on a particular debt security was shown to be equal to the real risk-free rate plus several premiums that reflect both inflation and the riskiness of the security in question. In this section we define more precisely what the term *risk* means as it relates to investments, we examine procedures used to measure risk, and we discuss the relationship between risk and return. It is important for both investors and financial managers to understand these concepts and use them when considering investment decisions, whether the decisions concern financial assets or real assets.

We will demonstrate in this section that each investment—each stock, bond, or physical asset—has two different types of risk: (1) diversifiable risk and (2) nondiversifiable risk. The sum of these two components is the investment's total risk. Diversifiable risk is not important to rational, informed investors because they will eliminate its effects by "diversifying" it away. The really significant risk is nondiversifiable risk—this risk is bad in the sense that it cannot be eliminated, and if you invest in anything other than riskless assets, such as short-term Treasury bills, you will be exposed to it. In the balance of the section we will explain these risk concepts and show you how risk enters into the investment decision process.

Defining and Measuring Risk

Risk is defined in *Webster's Collegiate Dictionary* as "possibility of loss or injury: *peril*." Thus, we generally use the term *risk* to refer to the chance that some unfavorable event will occur. For example, if you engage in skydiving, you are taking a chance with your life—skydiving is risky. If you bet on the horses, you are risking your money. If you invest in speculative stocks (or, really, *any* stock), you are taking a risk in the hope of making an appreciable return.

Most people view risk in the manner we just described—a chance of loss. But in reality, *risk* occurs when we cannot be certain about the outcome of a particular activity or event, so we are not sure what will occur in the future. Consequently, *risk* results from the fact that an action such as investing can produce more than one outcome in the future.

To illustrate the riskiness of financial assets, suppose you have a large amount of money to invest for one year. You could buy a Treasury security that has an expected return equal to 6 percent. The rate of return expected from this investment can be determined quite precisely because the chance of the government defaulting on Treasury securities is negligible; the outcome essentially is guaranteed, which means this is a risk-free investment. On the other hand, you could buy the common stock of a newly formed company that has developed technology that can be used to extract petroleum from the mountains in South America without defacing the landscape and without harming the ecology. The technology has yet to be proven economically feasible, so it is not known what returns the common stockholders will receive in the future. Experts who have analyzed the common stock of the company have determined that the *expected*, or average long-run, return for such an investment is 30 percent; each year the investment could yield a positive return as high as 900 percent, but there also is the possibility the company will not survive, in which case, the entire investment will be lost and the return will be –100 percent. The return investors receive each year cannot be determined precisely because more than one outcome is possible—this is a risky investment. Because there is a significant danger of actually earning considerably less than the expected return, investors probably would consider the stock to be quite risky. But there also is a very good chance the actual return will be greater than expected, which, of course, is an outcome we gladly accept. So, when we think of investment risk, along with the chance of actually receiving less than expected, we should consider the chance of actually receiving more than expected. If we consider investment risk from this perspective, we can define **risk** as the chance of receiving an actual return other than expected, which simply means there is *variability in the returns,* or outcomes, from the investment. Therefore, investment risk can be measured by the variability of the investment's returns.

Investment risk, then, is related to the possibility of actually earning a return other than expected—the greater the variability of the possible outcomes, the riskier the investment. And as we will soon discover, *the return expected from an investment is positively related to the investment's risk—a higher expected return represents an investor's compensation for taking on greater risk.* But this relationship is not quite as clear-cut as it sounds, because we generally define and evaluate risk on two different bases: (1) **stand-alone risk,** which is the risk associated with an investment when it is held by itself, not in combination with other assets, and (2) **portfolio risk,** which is the risk associated with an investment when it is held in combination with other assets, not by itself. In the remainder of the section, we define risk more precisely and differentiate between stand-alone risk and portfolio risk when determining the appropriate expected rate of return for an investment.

Measuring Stand-Alone Risk: The Standard Deviation

Because we have defined risk as the variability of returns, we can measure risk by examining the tightness of the probability distribution associated with the possible outcomes. In general, the width of a probability distribution indicates the amount of scatter, or variability, of the possible outcomes. Therefore, *the tighter the probability distribution of expected returns, the less its variability—thus the smaller the risk associated with the investment.* According to this definition, U.S. Electric is much less risky than Martin Products because the actual payoffs that are possible are closer to the expected return for U.S. Electric than for Martin Products.

To be most useful, any measure of risk should have a definite value—we need a measure of the tightness of the probability distribution. The measure we use most often is the **standard deviation,** the symbol for which is σ, pronounced "sigma." The smaller the standard deviation, the tighter the probability distribution, and, accordingly, the lower the riskiness of the investment. To calculate the standard deviation, we proceed as shown in Exhibit 700.46, taking the following steps.

1. We calculate the expected rate of return using Equation 7.47. For Martin, we previously found $\hat{k} = 15\%$.

$$\text{Expected rate of return} = \hat{k} = Pr_1 k_1 + Pr_2 k_2 + \cdots + P$$

$$= \sum_{i=1}^{n} Pr_i k_i \qquad (7.47)$$

2. Subtract the expected rate of return ($\hat{k}$) from each possible outcome (k_i) to obtain a set of deviations from $\hat{k}$.

$$\text{Deviation}_i = k_i - \hat{k}.$$

The deviations are shown in Column 3 of Exhibit 700.46.

Exhibit 700.46 *Calculating Martin Products' Standard Deviation*

Payoff k_i (1)	Expected Return $\hat{k}$ (2)		$k_i - \hat{k}$ (3)	$(k_i - \hat{k})^2$ (4)	Probability (5)	$(k_i - \hat{k})^2 Pr_i$ (4) × (5) = (6)
110%	− 15%	=	95	9,025	0.2	(9,025)(0.2) = 1,805.0
22	− 15	=	7	49	0.5	(49)(0.5) = 24.5
(60)	− 15	=	−75	5,625	0.3	(5,625)(0.3) = 1,687.5
						Variance = σ^2 = 3,517.0
						Standard deviation = $\sigma = \sqrt{\sigma^2} = \sqrt{3,517.0} = 59.3\%$

3. Square each deviation (shown in Column 4), multiply the result by the probability of occurrence for its related outcome (Column 5), and then sum these products to obtain the **variance** of the probability distribution, which is shown in Column 6. Thus, variance is defined as:

$$\text{Variance} = \sigma^2 = \sum_{i=1}^{n} (k_i - \hat{k})^2 \text{Pr}_i$$

4. Finally, we take the square root of the variance to obtain the standard deviation shown at the bottom of Column 6.

$$\text{Standard deviation} = \sigma\sqrt{\sigma^2} = \sqrt{\sum_{i=1}^{n} (k_i - \hat{k})^2 \text{Pr}_i} \qquad (7.48)$$

Thus, the standard deviation is a weighted average deviation from the expected value, and it gives an idea of how far above or below the expected value the actual value is likely to be. Martin's standard deviation is seen in Exhibit 700.46 to be 59.3 percent, and, using these same procedures, we find U.S. Electric's standard deviation to be 3.6 percent. The larger standard deviation of Martin Products indicates a greater variation of returns, thus a greater chance that the expected return will not be realized; therefore, Martin Products would be considered a riskier investment than U.S. Electric, according to this measure of risk.

Coefficient of Variation

Another useful measure to evaluate risky investments is the **coefficient of variation (CV)**, which is the standard deviation divided by the expected return:

$$\text{Coefficient of variation} = \text{CV} = \frac{\text{Risk}}{\text{Return}} = \frac{\sigma}{\hat{k}} \qquad (7.49)$$

The coefficient of variation shows the risk per unit of return, and it provides a more meaningful basis for comparison when the expected returns on two alternatives are not the same.

Measuring Portfolio Risk— Holding Combinations of Assets

In the preceding section, we considered the riskiness of investments held in isolation. Now we analyze the riskiness of investments held in portfolios. As we shall see, holding an investment, whether a stock, bond, or other asset, as part of a portfolio generally is less risky than holding the same investment all by itself. In fact, most financial assets are not held in isolation; rather, they are held as parts of portfolios. Banks, pension funds, insurance companies, mutual funds, and other financial institutions are required by law to hold diversified portfolios. Even individual investors—at least those whose security holdings constitute a significant part of their total wealth—generally hold stock portfolios, not the stock of only one firm. This being the case, from an investor's standpoint the fact that a particular stock goes up or down is not very important; what is important is the return on his or her portfolio, and the risk associated with the entire portfolio. Logically, then, *the risk and return characteristics of an investment should not be evaluated in isolation; rather, the risk and return of an individual security should be analyzed in terms of how that security affects the risk and return of the portfolio in which it is held.*

A portfolio is a collection of investment securities or assets. If you owned some General Motors stock, some Exxon stock, and some IBM stock, you would hold a three-stock portfolio.

Portfolio Returns

The **expected return on a portfolio, $\hat{k}_p$,** is simply the weighted average of the expected returns on the individual stocks in the portfolio, with the weights being the fraction of the total portfolio invested in each stock.

$$\hat{k}_p = w_1 \hat{k}_1 + w \hat{k} + \ldots + w_N \hat{k}_N$$

$$\hat{k}_P = \sum_{j=1}^{N} w_j \hat{k}_j \qquad (7.50)$$

Here the $\hat{k}_j$'s are the expected returns on the individual stocks, the w_j's are the weights, and there are N stocks in the portfolio. Note that (1) w_j is the proportion of the portfolio's dollar value invested in Stock j (that is, the value of the investment in Stock j divided by the total value of the portfolio), and (2) the w_j's must sum to 1.0.

In January 2000, a security analyst estimated that the following returns could be expected on four large companies.

	Expected Return
AT&T	10%
General Electric	13%
Microsoft	30%
Citigroup	16%

If we formed a $100,000 portfolio, investing $25,000 in each stock, the expected portfolio return would be 17.25 percent.

$$\hat{k}_P = w_1 \hat{k}_1 + w_2 \hat{k}_2 + w_3 \hat{k}_3 + w_4 \hat{k}_4$$
$$= 0.25(10\%) + 0.25(13\%) + 0.25(30\%) + 0.25(16\%)$$
$$= 17.25\%$$

Of course, after the fact and a year later, the actual **realized rates of return, $\bar{k}$,** on the individual stocks—the $\bar{k}_j$, or "k-bar," values—will almost certainly be different from their expected values, so $\bar{k}_P$ will be somewhat different from $\hat{k}_P = 17.25$ percent. For example, General Electric stock might double in price and provide a return of +100 percent, whereas Citigroup stock might have a terrible year, fall sharply, and have a return of −75 percent. Note, though, that those two events would be somewhat offsetting, so the portfolio's return might still be close to its expected return, even though the individual stocks' actual returns were far from their expected returns.

Portfolio Risk

As we just saw, the expected return of a portfolio is simply a weighted average of the expected returns of the individual stocks in the portfolio. However, unlike returns, the riskiness of a portfolio, σ_P, generally is *not* a weighted average of the standard deviations of the individual securities in the portfolio; the portfolio's risk usually is *smaller* than the weighted average of the stocks' σ's. In fact, at least theoretically, it is possible to combine two stocks that by themselves are quite risky as measured by their standard deviations and to form a portfolio that is completely riskless, or risk-free, with $\sigma_P = 0$.

What would happen if we included more than two stocks in the portfolio? *As a rule, the riskiness of a portfolio will be reduced as the number of stocks in the portfolio increases.* If we added enough stocks, could we completely eliminate risk? In general, the answer is no, but the extent to which adding stocks to a portfolio reduces its risk depends on the *degree of correlation* among the stocks: *The smaller the positive correlation coefficient, the greater the diversification effect of adding a stock to a portfolio.* If we could find a set of stocks whose correlations were negative, all risk could be eliminated. *In the typical case, where the correlations among the individual stocks are positive but less than +1.0, some, but not all, risk can be eliminated.*

Firm-Specific Risk versus Market Risk

As noted earlier, it is very difficult, if not impossible, to find stocks whose expected returns are not positively correlated—most stocks tend to do well when the economy is strong and do poorly when it is weak. Thus, even very large portfolios end up with a substantial amount of risk, but the risk generally is less than if all of the money was invested in only one stock. Some risk always remains, however, so it is virtually impossible to diversify away the effects of broad stock market movements that affect almost all stocks.

The part of a stock's risk that can be eliminated is called *diversifiable*, or *firm-specific* or *unsystematic*, *risk*; the part that cannot be eliminated is called *nondiversifiable*, or *market* or *systematic*, *risk*. The name is not especially important, but the fact that a large part of the riskiness of any individual stock can be eliminated through portfolio diversification is vitally important.

Firm-specific, or **diversifiable, risk** is caused by such things as lawsuits, strikes, successful and unsuccessful marketing programs, the winning and losing of major contracts, and other events that are unique to a particular firm. Because the actual outcomes of these events are essentially random, their effects on a portfolio can be eliminated by diversification—bad events in one firm will be offset by good events in another. **Market,** or **nondiversifiable, risk,** on the other hand, stems from factors that *systematically* affect most firms, such as war, inflation, recessions, and high interest rates. Because most stocks tend to be affected similarly (negatively) by these *market* conditions, systematic risk cannot be eliminated by portfolio diversification.

We know that investors demand a premium for bearing risk; that is, the higher the riskiness of a security, the higher the expected return required to induce investors to buy (or to hold) it. However, if investors are primarily concerned with *portfolio risk* rather than the risk of the individual securities in the portfolio, how should the riskiness of an individual stock be measured? The answer, as provided by the **Capital Asset Pricing Model (CAPM),** is this: *The relevant riskiness of an individual stock is its contribution to the riskiness of a well-diversified portfolio.* In other words, the riskiness of General Electric's stock to a doctor who has a portfolio of 40 stocks or to a trust officer managing a 150-stock portfolio is the contribution that the GE stock makes to the portfolio's riskiness. The stock might be quite risky if held by itself, but if most of this stand-alone risk can be eliminated by diversification, then its **relevant risk,** which is its *contribution to the portfolio's risk,* is much smaller than its total, or stand-alone, risk.

Are all stocks equally risky in the sense that adding them to a well-diversified portfolio would have the same effect on the portfolio's riskiness? The answer is no. Different stocks will affect the portfolio differently, so different securities have different degrees of relevant risk. How can the relevant risk of an individual stock be measured? As we have seen, all risk except that related to broad market movements can, and presumably will, be diversified away. After all, why accept risk that can be easily eliminated? *The risk that remains after diversifying is market risk, or risk that is inherent in the market, and it can be measured by evaluating the degree to which a given stock tends to move up and down with the market.*

The Concept of Beta

Remember the relevant risk associated with an individual stock is based on its systematic risk, which depends on how sensitive the firm's operations are to economic events such as interest rate changes and inflationary pressures. Because the general movements in the financial markets reflect movements in the economy, the market risk of a stock can be measured by observing its tendency to move with the market, or with an average stock that has the same characteristics as the market. The measure of a stock's sensitivity to market fluctuations is called its **beta coefficient,** and it generally is designated with the Greek symbol for beta, β. Beta is a key element of the CAPM.

Types of Risks

Earlier, we distinguished between *market risk,* which is measured by the firm's beta coefficient, and *total risk,* which includes both beta risk and a type of risk that can be eliminated by diversification (*firm-specific risk*). In Section 735 we considered how capital budgeting decisions affect the riskiness of the firm. There again we distinguished between beta risk (the effect of a project on the firm's beta) and corporate risk (the effect of the project on the firm's total risk).

Now we introduce three new dimensions of risk:

1. **Business risk** is defined as the uncertainty inherent in projections of future returns, either on assets (ROA) or on equity (ROE), if the firm uses no debt, or debt-like financing (that is, preferred stock)—it is the risk associated with the firm's operations.
2. **Financial risk** is defined as the additional risk, over and above basic business risk, placed on common stockholders that results from using financing alternatives with fixed periodic payments, such as debt and preferred stock—it is the risk associated with using debt or preferred stock.
3. **Country risk** is defined as the adverse impact of a country's environment on an MNC's cash flows.

Conceptually, the firm has a certain amount of risk inherent in its production and sales operations; this is its business risk. When it uses debt, it partitions this risk and concentrates most of it on one class of investors—the common stockholders—this is its financial risk. Use of preferred stock also adds to financial risk. Both business risk and financial risk affect the capital structure of a firm.

Business Risk

Business risk is the single most important determinant of capital structure. Smaller companies, especially single-product firms, also have a relatively high degree of business risk. Business risk varies from one industry to another and also among firms in a given industry. Further, business risk can change over time. Business risk depends on a number of factors, the more important of which include the following.

1. **Sales variability (volume and price).** The more stable the unit sales (volume) and prices of a firm's products, other things held constant, the lower its business risk.
2. **Input price variability.** A firm whose input prices (labor, product costs, and so forth) are highly uncertain is exposed to a high degree of business risk.
3. **Ability to adjust output prices for changes in input prices.** Some firms have little difficulty in raising the prices of their products when input costs rise, and the greater the ability to adjust selling prices, the lower the degree of business risk. This factor is especially important during periods of high inflation.
4. **The extent to which costs are fixed: operating leverage.** If a high percentage of a firm's operating costs are fixed and hence do not decline when demand falls off, this increases the company's business risk. This factor is called *operating leverage.*

Each of these factors is determined partly by the firm's industry characteristics, but each also is controllable to some extent by management. For example, most firms can, through their marketing policies, take actions to stabilize both unit sales and sales prices. However, this stabilization might require either large expenditures on advertising or price concessions to induce customers to commit to purchasing fixed quantities at fixed prices in the future. Similarly, firms can reduce the volatility of future input costs by negotiating long-term labor and materials supply contracts, but they might have to agree to pay prices somewhat above the current market price to obtain these contracts.

Financial Risk

Financial risk results from using **financial leverage,** which exists when a firm uses fixed income securities, such as debt and preferred stock, to raise capital. When financial leverage is created, a firm intensifies the business risk borne by the common stockholders. To illustrate, suppose 10 people decide to form a corporation to produce operating systems for personal computers. There is a certain amount of business risk in the operation. If the firm is capitalized only with common equity, and if each person buys 10 percent of the stock, then each investor will bear an equal share of the business risk. However, suppose the firm is capitalized with 50 percent debt and 50 percent equity, with five of the investors putting up their capital as debt and the other five putting up their money as equity. In this case, the cash flows received by the debtholders are based on a contractual agreement, so the investors who put up the equity will have to bear essentially all of the business risk, and their position will be twice as risky as it would have been had the firm been financed only with equity. Thus, *the use of debt intensifies the firm's business risk borne by the common stockholders.*

Country Risk

An MNC conducts country risk analysis when assessing whether to continue conducting business in a particular country. The analysis can also be used when determining whether to implement new projects in foreign countries. Country risk can be partitioned into the country's political risk and its financial risk. Financial managers must understand how to measure country risk so that they can make investment decisions that maximize their MNC's value.

Why Country Risk Analysis Is Important

Country risk is the potentially adverse impact of a country's environment on an MNC's cash flows. Country risk analysis can be used to monitor countries where the MNC is currently doing business. If the country risk level of a particular country begins to increase, the MNC may consider divesting its subsidiaries located there. Country risk analysis can also be used by MNCs as a screening device to avoid conducting business in countries with excessive risk. Events that heighten country risk tend to discourage U.S. direct foreign investment in that particular country.

Country risk analysis is not restricted to predicting major crises. It is also used by an MNC to revise its investment or financing decisions in light of recent events.

Political Risk Factors

As one might expect, many country characteristics related to the political environment can influence an MNC. An extreme form of political risk is the possibility that the host country will take over a subsidiary. In some cases of expropriation, some compensation (the amount decided by the host country government) is awarded. In other cases, the assets are confiscated and no compensation is provided. Expropriation can take place peacefully or by force. The following are some of the more common forms of political risk:

- Attitude of consumers in the host country
- Actions of host government
- Blockage of fund transfers
- Currency inconvertibility
- War
- Bureaucracy
- Corruption

Financial Risk Factors

Along with political factors, financial factors should be considered when assessing country risk. One of the most obvious financial factors is the current and potential state of the country's economy. An MNC that exports to a country or develops a subsidiary in a country is highly concerned about that country's demand for its products. This demand is, of course, strongly influenced by the country's economy. A recession in the country could severely reduce demand for the MNC's exports or products sold by the MNC's local subsidiary.

A country's economic growth is dependent on several financial factors, which are identified here.

- *Interest rates.* Higher interest rates tend to slow the growth of an economy and reduce demand for the MNC's products. Lower interest rates often stimulate the economy and increase demand for the MNC's products.
- *Exchange rates.* Exchange rates can influence the demand for the country's exports, which in turn affects the country's production and income level. A strong currency may reduce demand for the country's exports, increase the volume of products imported by the country, and therefore reduce the country's production and national income. A very weak currency can cause speculative outflows and reduce the amount of funds available to finance growth by businesses.
- *Inflation.* Inflation can affect consumers' purchasing power and therefore their demand for an MNC's goods. It also indirectly affects a country's financial condition by influencing the country's interest rates and currency value. A high level of inflation may also lead to a decline in economic growth.

Most financial factors that affect a country's economic conditions are difficult to forecast. Thus, even if an MNC considers them in its country risk assessment, it may still make poor decisions because of an improper forecast of the country's financial factors.

Some financial conditions may be caused by political risk. For example, the September 11, 2001, terrorist attack on the United States affected U.S.-based MNCs because of political risk and financial risk. Political uncertainty caused uncertainty about economic conditions, which resulted in a reduction in spending by consumers, and therefore, a reduction in cash flows of MNCs.

Types of Country Risk Assessment

Although there is no consensus as to how country risk can best be assessed, some guidelines have been developed. The first step is to recognize the difference between (1) an overall risk assessment of a country without consideration of the MNC's business and (2) the risk assessment of a country as it relates to the MNC's type of business. The first type can be referred to as **macroassessment** of country risk and the latter type as a **microassessment.** Each type is discussed in turn.

755. FINANCIAL RISK MANAGEMENT

It is important to know how an appropriate country risk assessment varies with the firm, industry, and project of concern and therefore why a macroassessment of country risk has its limitations. A microassessment is also necessary when evaluating the country risk related to a particular project proposed by a particular firm.

In addition to political variables, financial variables are also necessary for microassessment of country risk. Microfactors include the sensitivity of the firm's business to real GDP growth, inflation trends, interest rates, and other factors. Due to differences in business characteristics, some firms are more susceptible to the host country's economy than others.

In summary, the overall assessment of country risk consists of four parts:

1. Macropolitical risk
2. Macrofinancial risk
3. Micropolitical risk
4. Microfinancial risk

Although these parts can be consolidated to generate a single country risk rating, it may be useful to keep them separate so that an MNC can identify the various ways its direct foreign investment or exporting operations are exposed to country risk.

Techniques to Assess Country Risk

Once a firm identifies all the macro- and microfactors that deserve consideration in the country risk assessment, it may wish to implement a system for evaluating these factors and determining a country risk rating. Various techniques are available to achieve this objective. The following are some of the more popular techniques:

- Checklist approach
- Delphi technique
- Quantitative analysis
- Inspection visits
- Combination of techniques

Incorporating Country Risk in Capital Budgeting

If the risk rating of a country is in the tolerable range, any project related to that country deserves further consideration. Country risk can be incorporated in the capital budgeting analysis of a proposed project by adjusting the discount rate or by adjusting the estimated cash flows. Each method is discussed here.

ADJUSTMENT OF THE DISCOUNT RATE The discount rate of a proposed project is supposed to reflect the required rate of return on that project. Thus, the discount rate can be adjusted to account for the country risk. The lower the country risk rating, the higher the perceived risk and the higher the discount rate applied to the project's cash flows. This approach is convenient in that one adjustment to the capital budgeting analysis can capture country risk. However, there is no precise formula for adjusting the discount rate to incorporate country risk. The adjustment is somewhat arbitrary and may therefore cause feasible projects to be rejected or unfeasible projects to be accepted.

ADJUSTMENT OF THE ESTIMATED CASH FLOWS Perhaps the most appropriate method for incorporating forms of country risk in a capital budgeting analysis is to estimate how the cash flows would be affected by each form of risk. For example, if there is a 20 percent probability that the host government will temporarily block funds from the subsidiary to the parent, the MNC should estimate the project's net present value (NPV) under these circumstances, realizing that there is a 20 percent chance that this NPV will occur.

If there is a chance that the host government takeover will occur, the foreign project's NPV under these conditions should be estimated. Each possible form of risk has an estimated impact on the foreign project's cash flows and therefore on the project's NPV. By analyzing each possible impact, the MNC can determine the probability distribution of NPVs for the project. Its accept/reject decision on the project will be based on its assessment of the probability that the project will generate a positive NPV, as well as the size of possible NPV outcomes. Though this procedure may seem somewhat tedious, it directly incorporates forms of country risk into the cash flow estimates and explicitly illustrates the possible results from implementing the project. The more convenient method of adjusting the discount rate in accordance with the country risk rating does not indicate the probability distribution of possible outcomes.

Reducing Exposure to Host Government Takeovers

Although direct foreign investment offers several possible benefits, country risk can offset such benefits. The most severe country risk is a host government takeover. This type of takeover may result in major losses, especially when the MNC does not have any power to negotiate with the host government.

The following are the most common strategies used to reduce exposure to a host government takeover:

- Use a short-term horizon.
- Rely on unique supplies or technology.
- Hire local labor.
- Borrow local funds.
- Purchase insurance.

Use a Short-Term Horizon

An MNC may concentrate on recovering cash flow quickly so that in the event of expropriation, losses are minimized. An MNC would also exert only a minimum effort to replace worn-out equipment and machinery at the subsidiary. It may even phase out its overseas investment by selling off its assets to local investors or the government in stages over time.

Rely on Unique Supplies or Technology

If the subsidiary can bring in supplies from its headquarters (or a sister subsidiary) that cannot be duplicated locally, the host government will not be able to take over and operate the subsidiary without those supplies. Also the MNC can cut off the supplies if the subsidiary is treated unfairly.

If the subsidiary can hide the technology in its production process, a government takeover will be less likely. A takeover would be successful in this case only if the MNC would provide the necessary technology, and the MNC would do so only under conditions of a friendly takeover that would ensure that it received adequate compensation.

Hire Local Labor

If local employees of the subsidiary would be affected by the host government's takeover, they can pressure their government to avoid such action. However, the government could still keep those employees after taking over the subsidiary. Thus, this strategy has only limited effectiveness in avoiding or limiting a government takeover.

Borrow Local Funds

If the subsidiary borrows funds locally, local banks will be concerned about its future performance. If for any reason a government takeover would reduce the probability that the banks would receive their loan repayments promptly, they might attempt to prevent a takeover by the host government. However, the host government may guarantee repayment to the banks, so this strategy has only limited effectiveness. Nevertheless, it could still be preferable to a situation in which the MNC not only loses the subsidiary but also still owes home country creditors.

Purchase Insurance

Insurance can be purchased to cover the risk of expropriation. For example, the U.S. government provides insurance through the Overseas Private Investment Corporation (OPIC). The insurance premiums paid by a firm depend on the degree of insurance coverage and the risk associated with the firm. Yet, any insurance policy will typically cover only a portion of the company's total exposure to country risk.

Many home countries of MNCs have investment guarantee programs that insure to some extent the risks of expropriation, wars, or currency blockage. Some guarantee programs have a one-year waiting period or longer before compensation is paid on losses due to expropriation. Also, some insurance policies do not cover all forms of expropriation. Furthermore, to be eligible for such insurance, the subsidiary might be required by the country to concentrate on exporting rather than on local sales. Even if a subsidiary qualifies for insurance, there is a cost. Any insurance will typically cover only a portion of the assets and may specify a maximum duration of coverage, such as 15 or 20 years. A subsidiary must weigh the benefits of this insurance against the cost of the policy's premiums and potential losses in excess of coverage. The insurance can be helpful, but it does not by itself prevent losses due to expropriation.

In 1993, Russia established an insurance fund to protect MNCs against various forms of country risk. The Russian government took this action to encourage more direct foreign investment in Russia.

The World Bank has established an affiliate called the Multilateral Investment Guarantee Agency (MIGA) to provide political insurance for MNCs with direct foreign investment in less developed countries. MIGA offers insurance against expropriation, breach of contract, currency inconvertibility, war, and civil disturbances.

Impact of an MNC's Country Risk Analysis on Its Value

An MNC's country risk analysis can affect its value. The country risk analysis determines the expected cash flows derived from each foreign subsidiary in the future. A country risk analysis may also lead to a decision to divest a subsidiary, which means that the expected foreign currency cash flows generated by that subsidiary will terminate after that point. Thus, the expected foreign currency cash flows that will ultimately be remitted to the U.S. parent are influenced by the country risk analysis.

The parent's required rate of return on the funds it provides to support operations in foreign countries is also affected by its country risk analysis. During the Asian crisis, many MNCs revised their country risk assessment upward for Asian countries. Thus, the required rate of return for investment in Asian operations would have been revised upward even if no other factors changed, which reduced the value of the MNC.

Mergers, Acquisitions, and Business Valuations

Mergers and Acquisitions

The purpose of this section is to provide you with a general understanding of mergers, the motivations for mergers, and merger activity in the United States. Merger analysis, which is the evaluation of the attractiveness of a merger, should be conducted in the same manner as capital budgeting analysis. (If the present value of the cash flows expected to result from the merger exceeds the price that must be paid for the company being acquired, then the merger has a positive net present value and the acquiring firm should proceed with the acquisition.)

Rationale for Mergers

There are five principal reasons two or more firms are merged to form a single firm.

1. **Synergy.** The primary motivation for most mergers is to increase the value of the combined enterprise—the hope is that *synergy* exists so that the value of the company formed by the merger is greater than the sum of the values of the individual companies taken separately. Synergistic effects can arise from four sources: (a) *operating economies of scale* occur when cost reductions result from the combination of the companies; (b) *financial*

economies might include a higher price/earnings ratio, a lower cost of debt, or a greater debt capacity; (c) *differential management efficiency* generally results when one firm is relatively inefficient, so the merger improves the profitability of the acquired assets; and (d) *increased market power* occurs if reduced competition exists after the merger. Operating and financial economies are socially desirable, as are mergers that increase managerial efficiency; but mergers that reduce competition are both undesirable and often illegal.

In the 1880s and 1890s, many mergers occurred in the United States, and some of them clearly were directed toward gaining market power at the expense of competition rather than increasing operating efficiency. As a result, Congress passed a series of acts designed to ensure that mergers are not used as a method of reducing competition. Today, the principal acts include the Sherman Act (1890), the Clayton Act (1914), and the Celler-Kefauver Act (1950). These acts make it illegal for firms to combine in any manner if the combination will lessen competition. They are administered by the antitrust division of the Justice Department and by the Federal Trade Commission.

2. **Tax considerations.** Tax considerations have stimulated a number of mergers. For example, a firm that is highly profitable and in the highest corporate tax bracket could acquire a company with large accumulated tax losses, then use those losses to shelter its own income. Similarly, a company with large losses could acquire a profitable firm. Also, tax considerations could cause mergers to be a desirable use for excess cash. For example, if a firm has a shortage of internal investment opportunities compared to its cash flows, it will have excess cash, and its options for disposing of this excess cash are to (a) pay an extra dividend, (b) invest in marketable securities, (c) repurchase its own stock, or (d) purchase another firm. If the firm pays an extra dividend, its stockholders will have to pay taxes on the distribution. Marketable securities such as Treasury bonds provide a good temporary parking place for money, but the rate of return on such securities is less than that required by stockholders. A stock repurchase might result in a capital gain for the remaining stockholders, but it could be disadvantageous if the company has to pay a high price to acquire the stock, and, if the repurchase is designed solely to avoid paying dividends, it might be challenged by the IRS. However, using surplus cash to acquire another firm has no immediate tax consequences for either the acquiring firm or its stockholders, and this fact has motivated a number of mergers.

3. **Purchase of assets below their replacement cost.** Sometimes a firm will become an acquisition candidate because the replacement value of its assets is considerably higher than its market value. For example, in the 1980s oil companies could acquire reserves more cheaply by buying out other oil companies than by exploratory drilling. This factor was a motive in **Chevron's** acquisition of **Gulf Oil**. The acquisition of **Republic Steel** (the sixth largest steel company) by **LTV** (the fourth largest) provides another example of a firm being purchased because its purchase price was less than the replacement value of its assets. LTV found that it was less costly to purchase Republic Steel for $700 million than it would have been to construct a new steel mill. At the time, Republic's stock was selling for less than one-third of its book value. However, the merger did not help LTV's inefficient operations—ultimately, the company filed for bankruptcy.

4. **Diversification.** Managers often claim that diversification helps to stabilize the firm's earnings and thus reduces corporate risk. Therefore, diversification often is given as a reason for mergers. Stabilization of earnings certainly is beneficial to a firm's employees, suppliers, and customers, but its value to stockholders and debtholders is less clear. If an investor is worried about earnings variability, he or she probably could diversify through stock purchases (investment portfolio adjustment) more easily than the firm could through acquisitions.

5. **Maintaining control.** Some mergers and takeovers are considered *hostile* because the management of the acquired firm opposes the merger. One reason for the hostility is that the managers of the acquired companies generally lose their jobs, or at least their autonomy. Therefore, managers who own less than 50 percent plus one share of the stock in their firms look to devices that will lessen the chances of their firms' being taken over. Mergers can serve as such a device. For example, when **Enron** was under attack, it arranged to buy **Houston Natural Gas Company,** paying for Houston primarily with debt. That merger made Enron much larger and hence harder for any potential acquirer to "digest." Also, the much higher debt level resulting from the merger made it hard for any acquiring company to use debt to buy Enron. Such **defensive mergers** are difficult to defend on economic grounds. The managers involved invariably argue that synergy, not a desire to protect their own jobs, motivated the acquisition, but there can be no question that many mergers have been designed more for the benefit of managers than for stockholders.

> Mergers undertaken only to use accumulated tax losses probably would be challenged by the IRS. However, because many factors are present in any given merger, it is hard to prove that a merger was motivated only, or even primarily, by tax considerations.

Types of Mergers

Economists classify mergers into four groups: (1) horizontal, (2) vertical, (3) congeneric, and (4) conglomerate. A **horizontal merger** occurs when one firm combines with another in its same line of business. For example, the acquisition of **Chrysler** by **Daimler-Benz AG** in 1998 was a horizontal merger because both firms are automobile manufacturers. An example of a **vertical merger** is a steel producer's acquisition of one of its own suppliers, such as an iron or coal mining firm. The 1993 merger of **Merck & Co.**, a manufacturer of health care products, and **Medco Containment,** the largest mail-order pharmacy service, is an example of a vertical merger. Congeneric means "allied in nature or action"; hence, a **congeneric merger** involves related enterprises but not producers of the same product (horizontal) or firms in a producer-supplier relationship (vertical). Examples of congeneric mergers include **Viacom's** acquisitions of **Paramount Communications** and **Blockbuster Entertainment** in 1994. Viacom owns several television stations and cable systems and distributes television programming, while Paramount produces movies and other entertainment shown both on television and in theaters, and Blockbuster's principal business is the rental of movies, most of which previously have been shown in theaters. A **conglomerate merger** occurs when unrelated enterprises combine, as illustrated by **Sears, Roebuck & Company** acquisitions of **Dean Witter Reynolds Organization Inc.,** a securities broker and investment banker, and **Coldwell Banker & Company,** a real estate firm, in 1981. (Sears has since divested itself of both firms.)

> Another type of merger is beachhead merger which is used to enter a new industry to exploit perceived opportunities.

Operating economies (and also anticompetitive effects) are dependent on the type of merger involved. Vertical and horizontal mergers generally provide the greatest synergistic operating benefits, but they also are the ones most likely to be attacked by the U.S. Department of Justice. In any event, it is useful to think of these economic classifications when analyzing the feasibility of a prospective merger.

Merger Activity

Four major "merger waves" have occurred in the United States. The first was in the late 1800s, when consolidations occurred in the oil, steel, tobacco, and other basic industries. The second was in the 1920s, when the stock market boom helped financial promoters consolidate firms in a number of industries, including utilities, communications, and autos. The third was in the 1960s, when conglomerate mergers were the rage, while the fourth began in the early 1980s, and it is still going strong. Many of the recent mergers have been horizontal mergers.

The current "merger mania" has been sparked by several factors: (1) at times, the depressed level of the dollar relative to Japanese and European currencies has made U.S. companies look cheap to foreign buyers; (2) the unprecedented level of inflation that existed during the 1970s and early 1980s, which increased the replacement value of firms' assets even while a weak stock market reduced their market values; (3) the general belief among the major natural resource companies that it is cheaper to "buy reserves on Wall Street" through mergers than to explore and find them in the field; (4) attempts to ward off raiders by use of defensive mergers; (5) the development of the junk bond market, which has made it possible to use far more debt in acquisitions than had been possible earlier; and (6) the increased globalization of business, which has led to increased economies of scale and to the formation of worldwide corporations.

Many of the mergers in 1998 and 1999 resulted either because the acquired firms were considered undervalued or because it was felt economies of scale could produce less costly combined operations. Increased global competition and governmental reforms were the major reasons for merger activities in the telecommunications and financial services industries, which accounted for the nearly 50 percent of the 1998 mergers. Experts expect these industries and other industries, such as defense, consumer products, and natural resources, to become significantly reshaped as merger activity continues in the future.

Leveraged Buyouts (LBOs)

With the extraordinary merger activity that took place in the 1980s, we witnessed a huge increase in the popularity of **leveraged buyouts,** or **LBOs.** The number and size of LBOs jumped significantly during this period. This development occurred for the same reasons that mergers and divestitures occurred—the existence of potential bargains, situations in which companies were using insufficient leverage, and the development of the junk bond market, which facilitated the use of leverage in takeovers.

LBOs can be initiated in one of two ways: (1) The firm's own managers can set up a new company whose equity comes from the managers themselves, plus some equity from pension funds and other institutions. This new company then arranges to borrow a large amount of money by selling junk bonds through an investment banking firm. With the financing arranged, the management group then makes an offer to purchase all the publicly owned shares through a tender offer. (2) A specialized LBO firm, with **Kohlberg Kravis Roberts (KKR)** being the best known, will identify a potential target company, go to the management, and suggest that an LBO deal be done. KKR and other LBO firms have billions of dollars of equity, most put up by pension funds and other large investors, available for the equity portion of the deals, and they arrange junk bond financing just as would a management-led group. Generally, the newly formed company will have at least 80 percent debt, and sometimes the debt ratio is as high as 98 percent. Thus, the term *leveraged* is most appropriate.

To illustrate an LBO, consider the $25 billion leveraged buyout of **RJR Nabisco** by KKR in 1989. RJR, a leading producer of tobacco and food products with such brands as Winston, Camel, Planters, Ritz, and Oreo, was trading at about $55 a share. Then F. Ross Johnson, RJR Nabisco's president and CEO at the time, announced a $75 per share, or $17.6 billion, offer to take the firm private. The day after the announcement, RJR's stock soared to $77.25, which indicated that investors thought that the final price would be even higher than Johnson's opening bid. A few days later, KKR offered $90 per share, or $20.6 billion, for the firm. The battle between the two bidders continued until late November, when RJR's board accepted a revised KKR bid of cash and securities worth about $109 per share, for a total value of about $25.1 billion.

Was RJR worth $25 billion, or did Henry Kravis and his partners let their egos govern their judgment? At the time the LBO was initiated, analysts believed that the deal was workable, but barely. Six years after the deal, KKR had disposed of all its interest in RJR Nabisco, and many experts called the biggest LBO of its time the biggest financial flop in history.

It is not clear if LBOs are, on balance, a good or a bad idea. Some government officials and others have stated a belief that the leverage involved might destabilize the economy. On the other hand, LBOs certainly have stimulated some lethargic managements, and that is good. Good or bad, though, LBOs have helped reshape the face of corporate America.

Business Valuations

Business valuation is valuing the worth of a business entity, whether in whole or part. The value of a business is derived from its ability to generate cash flows consistently period after period over the long term. Business valuation can be performed at various milestones such as new product introduction; mergers, acquisitions, divestitures, recapitalization, and stock repurchases; capital expenditures and improvements; joint venture agreements; and ongoing review of performance of business unit operations.

The value of a firm is determined by its profitability and growth rates, which are influenced by its marketing and finance strategies.

The corporate philosophy is that shareholders are the owners of the corporation, the board of directors acts as their representatives, and the corporation's objective is to maximize the shareholder value. A company management that focuses on building and enhancing shareholder value is creating more value for its shareholders. Companies with higher labor productivity are more likely to create more value than those with lower productivity, and companies that are able to create more value will be able to create more jobs. This solid value chain is shown here.

Higher labor productivity → Higher company value → More jobs creation

Shareholder value in the stock market is the ultimate output measure of a company's performance, and is based on discounted cash flow (DCF) techniques. Financial indicators such as growth rate and return on invested capital (ROIC), which are linked to free cash flows, are useful in assessing historical performance or in setting short-term targets. DCF, which is driven by growth rate and ROIC, is valuable for strategic analysis since its focus is on long-term.[7]

ROIC is calculated as follows:

ROIC = Net operating profit after taxes divided by invested capital, where invested capital is investment in net working capital plus investment in net fixed assets plus investment in other assets.

Growth rate is calculated as follows:

Growth rate = Return on new invested capital × investment rate, where investment rate is net investment divided by operating profit.

Free cash flows are computed according to equations presented in the DCF model.

Discounted cash flow techniques combine performance across time horizons into a single result.

Managers who use DCF approaches to business valuation, focusing on increasing long-term free cash flows, ultimately will be creating higher stock prices. Attention to accounting earnings can lead to value-decreasing decisions while attention to cash flows can lead to value-increasing decisions. This is because accounting earnings are static, historical in nature, different from cash flows, and do not deal with the time value of money.

Business Valuation Models

A model is a representation of a real system. There are 11 models to help management in making sound decisions during valuation of a business opportunity. The output of these models will assist management in reaching a price to be paid or money to be invested. These models, in the order of importance and usefulness, include book value model, liquidation value model, replacement cost model, discounted abnormal earnings model, price multiples model, financial analysis model, economic-value added model, market value-added model, economic profit model, net present value model, and discounted cash flow model. In practice, a combination of models is recommended. For example, the economic-value added model should be combined with market-value added model and the net present value or DCF model. Each model will be discussed.

Book Value Model

The book value of a company's stock represents the total assets of the company less its liabilities. Other terms for book value are *net assets, shareholders' equity,* or *net worth*. The book value per share has no relation to market value per share, as book values are based on historical cost of assets, not at the current value at which they could be sold. Book values are not meaningful because they are distorted by inflation factors and different accounting assumptions used in valuing assets. One use of book value is to provide a floor value, with the true value of the company being some amount higher. The floor value is the normal minimum value that the company should command in the marketplace. Sales prices of companies are usually expressed as multiples of book values within each industry. If all firms in an industry are priced at five times the book value, and the target company involved in acquisition is only selling for two times the book value, this might be an indicator of an undervalued situation. Takeover experts look for firms that are undervalued. Industries that tend to have more liquid assets tend to have higher book values than others.

Book Value versus Market Value

- When the book value of a firm is less than its industry average, the firm is undervalued. It is an indication of inefficient utilization of the firm's assets.
- When the book value of a firm is more than its industry average, the firm is overvalued. It is an indication of efficient utilization of the firm's assets.
- Book values have no relation to market values because book values are based on historical costs while current costs are used for market values. Earnings power and cash flows also drive the market values.

Determining the book per share is relatively easier if a company has only common stock outstanding; difficult when it has both preferred and common stock. When a company has both types of stock, the equity allocated to preferred stock is subtracted, including dividends in arrears from the total stockholders' equity, to determine the equity remaining to common shareholders. In computing the common shares outstanding, treasury stock is subtracted and the common stock distributable is included.

Example 2 A firm has stockholders' equity of $1 million and treasury stock of 10,000 shares, and issued common stock of 110,000 shares. What is the book value per share of common stock?

Outstanding common stock = Issued common stock − treasury stock = 110,000 − 10,000 = 100,000 shares
Book value per share of common stock = $1,000,000/100,000 = $10 per share

Example 3 *A firm has stockholders' equity of $2,565,000 and treasury stock of 10,000 shares, issued common stock of 110,000 shares, and preferred stock of 5,000 shares issued at $100 and callable at $105 per share, with 8 percent cumulative and one year of dividends in arrears. What is the book value per share of preferred stock and common stock?*

Equity allocated to preferred stockholders = (Number of shares x callable price) + dividends in arrears = (5,000 × $105) + ($500,000 × 0.08) = $525,000 + $40,00 = $565,000.

Equity remaining to common stockholders = Total stockholders' equity − Equity allocated to preferred stockholders = $2,565,000 − $565,000 = $2,000,000

Outstanding common stock = Issued common stock − treasury stock = 110,000 − 10,000 = 100,000 shares

Book value per share of preferred stock = $565,000/5,000 = $113 per share

Book value per share of common stock = $2,000,000/100,000 = $20.00 per share

Liquidation Value Model

Liquidation value of a firm is total assets minus all liabilities and preferred stock minus all liquidation costs incurred. Liquidation value may be a more realistic measure of a firm than its book value in that liquidation price reflects the current market value of the assets and liabilities if the firm is in a growing, profitable industry. Depending on the power of negotiations of the parties involved and the asset utilization rates of a firm, liquidation prices may be set at "fire sale" prices. Note that the liquidation value is not equal to true market value because the real market value depends on the earning power of the firm's assets and how efficiently these assets are utilized by management. Sometimes, liquidation value can act as a floor value.

Replacement Cost Model

The replacement cost model is based on the estimated cost to replace a company's assets, which include both tangible and intangible assets. The concern here is that only tangible assets such as plant, equipment, and buildings are replaceable. Intangible assets such as patents, copyrights, and human and organizational capital are not replaceable. This model ignores the value of intangible assets and hence is not a complete or useful model. Because of these concerns, the replacement cost of a company's assets understate the real market value of the company. Sometimes the replacement value of a firm's assets is higher than its market value.

Discounting Abnormal Earnings Model

If a firm can earn only a normal rate of return on its book value, then investors will pay no more than the book value. The deviation of a firm's market value from its book value depends on the firm's power to generate "abnormal earnings." We define abnormal earnings as follows:

Abnormal earnings = Total earnings − Normal earnings

Abnormal earnings = Total earnings − (cost of capital × beginning book value)

The estimated value of a firm's equity is the sum of the current book value plus the discounted future abnormal earnings.

Price Multiples Model

The value of a firm is based on price multiples of "comparable" firms in the industry. This model requires calculation of the desired price multiples and then applying the multiple to the firm being valued. Examples of price multiples include: price-to-earnings (P/E) ratio, price-to-book ratio, price-to-sales ratio, price-to-cash-flow ratio, and market-to-book ratio. Next each ratio is presented briefly.

PRICE-TO-EARNINGS RATIO This ratio should vary positively with differences in abnormal earnings and negatively with differences in discount rates (risk). It assumes that a firm will be worth some multiple of its future earnings.

PRICE-TO-BOOK RATIO   This ratio should vary across firms according to differences in their future return on equity (ROE), growth in book value, and differences in discount rates.

PRICE-TO-SALES RATIO   This ratio should vary with expected profit margins. This means firms with higher expected margins are worth more in dollar sales. This ratio is the product of price-earnings ratio and earnings-to-sales ratio.

PRICE-TO-CASH-FLOW RATIO   This ratio refers to a multiple of operating earnings before depreciation and interest, or some similar measure. The numerator in this ratio should not include the value of debt (i.e., unlevered), and the denominator should use operating earnings before interest, taxes, depreciation, and amortization (EBITDA).

MARKET-TO-BOOK RATIO   This ratio is similar to the price-to-earnings ratio. It assumes that a firm will be worth some multiple of its book value.

Financial Analysis Model

The target company in the merger and acquisition analysis should have a high liquidity, a low leverage, a low price earnings (P/E) ratio, increasing cash flows, and high earnings power.

Financial analysis includes ratio analysis and cash flow analysis. The objective of ratio analysis is to evaluate the effectiveness of the firm's policies in operating, investment, and financing strategies. Effective ratio analysis involves relating the financial numbers to the underlying business factors and assumptions. While ratio analysis may not give an analyst all the answers regarding a firm's performance, it will help the analyst ask probing questions. The analyst uses income statements (net profit margin analysis) and balance sheets (asset turnover and financial leverage) for conducting the specific ratio analysis.

In ratio analysis, the analyst can (1) compare ratios for a firm over several years (a time-series comparison), (2) compare ratios for the firm and other firms in the industry (cross-sectional comparison), and (3) compare ratios to some benchmark data. Two categories of ratios include profitability and solvency ratios. Examples of profitability ratios include gross margins, ratio of net sales to assets, return on total assets, return on equity (ROE), earnings per share (EPS), price-earnings (P/E) ratio, dividends per share, dividends yield (dividend payout ratio), and sustainable growth rate. Examples of solvency ratios include current ratio, quick ratio, accounts receivable turnover, inventory turnover, debt-to-equity ratio, and number of times interest charges are earned. These ratios were discussed in Module 600, Accounting, Section 620.

While ratio analysis focuses on analyzing a firm's income statement or its balance sheet, the cash flow analysis will focus on operating, investing, and financing policies of a firm by reviewing its statement of cash flows. Cash flow analysis also provides an indication of the quality of the information in the firm's income statement and balance sheet.

Recall that accounting-based net income differs from operating cash flows because revenues and expenses are measured on an accrual basis. There are two types of accruals included in net income. First, there are current accruals, such as credit sales and unpaid expenses. Current accruals result in changes in a firm's current assets (such as accounts receivable, inventory, and prepaid expenses), and current liabilities (such as accounts payable and accrued liabilities). The second type of accruals included in the income statement is noncurrent accruals, such as depreciation, deferred taxes, and equity income from unconsolidated subsidiaries. To derive cash flow from accounting-based net income, adjustments have to be made for both these types of accruals. In addition, adjustments have to be made for nonoperating gains and losses included in net income, such as profits from sales of assets. These adjustments were fully discussed in Module 600, Accounting, Section 620.

Economic-Value-Added Model

Economic-value-added (EVA) is operating profit minus a charge for the opportunity cost of capital. An advantage of the EVA method is its integration of revenues and costs of short-term decisions into long-term capital budgeting process. A disadvantage of EVA is that it focuses only on a single period and that it does not consider risk. The EVA model can be combined with market-valued-added model, which is described next, to address this disadvantage.

The formula for calculating the EVA follows.

$$\text{EVA} = \text{Operating Profit} - (\text{Weighted Average Cost of Capital} \times \text{Capital Invested})$$

> **Example 4** *A company's financial data includes $40 million in revenues, $24 million in cost of goods sold, and $7.5 million in operating expenses. It invested $30 million in long-term capital and has a weighted-average cost of capital of 10%. What is the economic-value added for this company?*
>
> First, we need to compute the operating profit and then apply the EVA formula. Operating profit is revenues ($40 million) minus cost of goods sold ($24 million) minus operating expenses ($7.5 million), which is $8.5 million.
>
> EVA = Operating profit − (weighted average cost of capital × capital invested)
> EVA = $8,500,000 − (0.10 × $30,000,000) = $5,500,000

Market-Value-Added Model

Market-value-added (MVA) is the difference between the market value of a company's debt and equity and the amount of capital invested since its origin. The MVA measures the amount by which stock market capitalization increases in a period. Market capitalization is simply the number of shares outstanding multiplied by share price. Possible variations of the model include (1) the market-to-capital ratio which is market capitalization of a company's debt and equity divided by the amount of capital invested since its origin, (2) the market-to-book (M/B) ratio in that only the common stock is considered; that is, the market value of the common stock minus the capital invested since its origin. These are represented in terms of the equations that follow:

Market-Value-Added = Present Value of Debt + Market Value of Equity − Capital Invested

Market-to-Capital Ratio = (Present Value of Debt + Market Value of Equity)/Capital Invested

Market-Value-Added = Market Value of Common Stock − Capital Invested

> **Example 5** *A firm has 2 million common shares outstanding at a market price of $50 per share. Its debt is valued at $5 million and it employed a capital of $6 million. How much market-value is added to the firm?*
>
> Market value of equity = Number of common shares outstanding × market price per share = 2 million shares × $50 per share = $10 million
> Market-value added = Present value of debt + market value of equity − capital invested
> MVA = $5 million + $10 million − $6 million = $9 million

Economic Profit Model

According to the economic profit model, the value of a company equals the amount of capital invested plus a premium equal to the present value of the cash flows created each year.[8] Economic profit measures the value created in a company in a single period is calculated as follows:

Economic profit = Invested capital × (ROIC − WACC)

Where ROIC is return on invested capital and WACC is weighted average cost of capital. In other words, economic profit equals the difference between the return on invested capital and the weighted average cost of capital times the amount of invested capital. The economic profit is similar in concept to accounting profit, but it explicitly charges a firm for all its capital employed, not just the interest on its debt.

Two other related measures include present value of a firm's economic profit and free cash flows in perpetuity. These are calculated as follows:

Present value of a firm's economic profit in perpetuity = Economic profit per year/WACC

Present value of free cash flows in perpetuity = Free cash flows per year/WACC

Example 6 Firm A has invested a capital of $1 million, its return on invested capital is 12%, and the weighted average cost of capital is estimated at 10%. Its free cash flows per year are estimated at $100,000.

What is Firm A's economic profit per year?

Economic profit = Invested capital × (ROIC − WACC) = $1,000,000 × (0.12−0.10) = $20,000

What is Firm A's present value of economic profit in perpetuity?

Present value of economic profit = Economic profit per year/WACC = $20,000/0.10 = $200,000

What is Firm A's present value of free cash flows in perpetuity?

Present value of free cash flows = Free cash flows per year/WACC = $100,000/0.10 = $1,000,000

Net Present Value Model

Basically, the net present value (NPV) model compares the benefits of a proposed project or firm with the costs, including financing costs, and approves those projects or firms whose benefits exceed costs. The NPV model incorporates the time value of money and the riskiness of the cash flows, which are the vital elements of a valuation model. The approach is to calculate the NPV of each alternative and then select the alternative with the highest NPV. The calculation involves discounting all cash inflows (cash receipts) to the beginning of the base timeline (present), then subtracting the present value of the cash outflows (cash disbursements) from the present value of the cash inflows. The discounting is done using the cost of capital, which represents the riskiness of the cash flows. The cost of capital is called the *hurdle rate*.

Net present value (NPV) = Present value of all cash inflows − Present value of all cash outflows

If the resulting NPV is positive, the alternative is good; if negative, it is bad; if zero, it is indifferent.

Example 7 Firm A is considering the acquisition of Firm B, where the latter firm has a cash flow of $1 million per year. After acquisition, the cash flows for Firm B are expected to grow at 6% per year for 10 years. In order to achieve these cash flows, Firm A needs to invest $0.5 million annually. If the required rate of return is 12%, what is the maximum price Firm A should pay to acquire Firm B?

Year	Cash Flows	Investment	Net Cash Flows	PV Factor	PV of Net Cash Flows
1	$1,060,000	$500,000	$ 560,000	0.8929	$ 500,024
2	1,123,600	500,000	623,600	0.7972	497,134
3	1,191,016	500,000	691,016	0.7118	491,865
4	1,262,477	500,000	762,477	0.6355	484,554
5	1,338,226	500,000	838,226	0.5674	475,609
6	1,418,519	500,000	918,519	0.5066	465,322
7	1,503,630	500,000	1,003,630	0.4523	453,942
8	1,593,848	500,000	1,093,848	0.4039	441,805
9	1,689,479	500,000	1,189,479	0.3606	428,926
10	1,790,848	500,000	1,290,848	0.3220	415,653
			Total present value		$4,654,834

The present value (PV) factor is taken from Table A-1 (Module 700 Appendix) at 12% required rate of return for each of the 10 years. The maximum price that Firm A can pay to acquire Firm B is approximately $4.6 million.

Discounted Cash Flow Model

The total value of a firm is value of its debt plus value of its equity. The discounted cash flow (DCF) model goes beyond the NPV model and uses free cash flows. The economic profit model measures the value created in a company in a single period, while the DCF model measures the value over multiple periods due to its free cash flows. The DCF model focuses on discounting cash flows from operations after investment in working capital, less capital expenditures. The model does not consider interest expense and cash dividends.

The calculation involves the generation of detailed, multiple-year forecasts of cash flows available to all providers of capital (debt and equity). The forecasts are then discounted at the weighted cost of capital to arrive at an estimated present value of the firm. The value of debt is subtracted from the value of the firm to arrive at the value of equity. To accomplish this, four steps are suggested.[9]

STEP 1: Forecast free cash flows available to debt and equity holders over a finite forecast horizon (usually 5 to 10 years). The final year of the horizon is called the "terminal year." The computation of free cash flows is given below.

> Earnings before depreciation and deferred taxes
> plus depreciation (noncash charge)
> minus capital expenditures (fixed assets)
> plus deferred taxes
> minus investment in net working capital and other assets
> equals free cash flows

STEP 2: Forecast free cash flows beyond the terminal year, based on some simplifying assumption.

STEP 3: Discount free cash flows at the weighted average cost of capital, that is, the required return on the combination of debt and equity capital. The discounted amount represents the estimated present value of free cash flows available to debt and equity holders as a group.

> Present value of cash flows = Free cash flows/(cost of capital minus growth rate)
> where growth rate represents both sales and earnings growth.

STEP 4: To arrive at the estimated value of currently outstanding equity, subtract from the discounted free cash flows the estimated present value of debt. If there are nonoperating assets held by the firm that have not been included in the previous cash flow forecasts (for example, marketable securities, real estate held for sale, or investments in unrelated, unconsolidated businesses), then add their value to the equity amount. Similarly, the expected cost of unrecorded liabilities (nonoperating liabilities), and the market value of options, warrants, and convertible securities are subtracted from the equity amount. The value of currently outstanding equity is calculated as follows.

> Present value of discounted free cash flows available to debt and equity holders
> minus present value of debt
> plus value of nonoperating assets
> minus expected cost of unrecorded liabilities
> minus market value of options, warrants, and convertible securities
> equals the value of currently outstanding equity

The value of currently outstanding equity can be divided by the number of outstanding common shares to arrive at an estimated per-share value of the common stock. The estimated per-share amount can be compared with the current market price per share.

Example 8 *Firm A is planning to acquire Firm B. The forecast of financial data (in thousands) for Firm B is given below for years 2004 and 2005.*

	2004	2005
Earnings before depreciation and deferred taxes	$1,100	$1,200
Depreciation	50	75
Capital expenditures	150	200
Deferred taxes	20	25
Investment in net working capital	200	100

What is the amount of free cash flows for the year 2004?

Free cash flows for year 2004 = 1,100 + 50 − 150 + 20 − 200 = $820

What is the free cash flow growth rate for the year 2005?

Free cash flows for year 2005 = $1,200 + 75 − 200 + 25 −100 = $1,000
Free cash flow growth rate for the year 2005 = ($1,000 − $820)/$820 = 21.9%

Example 9 *Firm X is planning to acquire Firm Y. The forecast of financial data (in thousands) for Firm Y is given below for the year 2004.*

The discounted present value of free cash flows available to debt and equity holders	= $3,020
Present value of debt	= 120
Value of nonoperating assets	= 200
Market value of options	= 50

What is the value of currently outstanding equity for Firm Y?

Value of currently outstanding equity for Firm Y = $3,020 − 120 + 200 − 50 = $3,050

Ethics and Finance

Business Ethics

The word *ethics* is defined in *Webster's dictionary* as "standards of conduct or moral behavior." Business ethics can be thought of as a company's attitude and conduct toward its employees, customers, community, and stockholders. High standards of ethical behavior demand that a firm treat each party it deals with in a fair and honest manner. A firm's commitment to business ethics can be measured by the tendency of the firm and its employees to adhere to laws and regulations relating to such factors as product safety and quality, fair employment practices, fair marketing and selling practices, the use of confidential information for personal gain, community involvement, bribery, and illegal payments to foreign governments to obtain business.

There are many instances of firms engaging in unethical behavior. For example, since 1985, the employees of several prominent Wall Street investment banking houses have been sentenced to prison for illegally using insider information on proposed mergers for their own personal gain, and **E. F. Hutton,** a large brokerage firm, lost its independence through a forced merger after it was convicted of cheating its banks out of millions of dollars in a check kiting scheme. **Drexel Burnham Lambert,** one of the largest investment banking firms, went bankrupt, and its "junk bond king," Michael Milken, who had earned $550 million in just one year, was sentenced to 10 years in prison plus charged a huge fine for securities-law violations. Even more recently, Salomon Brothers Inc. was implicated in a Treasury-auction bidding scandal that resulted in the removal of key officers and a significant reorganization of the firm.

In spite of all this, the results of a recent study indicate that the executives of most major firms in the United States believe their firms should, and do, try to maintain high ethical standards in all of their business dealings. Further, most executives believe that there is a positive correlation between ethics and long-run profitability because ethical behavior (1) avoids fines and legal expenses, (2) builds public trust, (3) attracts business from customers who appreciate and support its policies, (4) attracts and keeps employees of the highest caliber, and (5) supports the economic viability of the communities in which it operates.

Most firms today have in place strong codes of ethical behavior, and they conduct training programs designed to ensure that all employees understand the correct behavior in different business situations. However, it is imperative that top management—the chairman, president, and vice presidents—be openly committed to ethical behavior and that they communicate this commitment through their own personal actions as well as through company policies, directives, and punishment/reward systems.

Specific Examples of Unethical Practices in Finance

The following is a list of specific examples of unethical practices in finance.

- Generally accepted accounting principles (GAAP) offer choices to firms in selecting accounting methods for valuing assets and liabilities. Different accounting methods can yield different asset and liability values, thus showing a different financial condition than what is in their firm's balance sheets. Similarly, revenue and expense items on income statements can be handled differently, thus showing a net income different than what it should be.
- Financial institutions and banks offer interest rates on savings and other deposits. The question is, are they offering the maximum interest rates allowed by law and at the maximum frequency of interest compounding? Improper practices can affect annual percentage rates and effective annual rates.
- Use of improper discount rate for computing a firm's unfunded pension liability to adjust earnings.
- Overstating savings and/or understating costs during preparation of capital expenditure project requests in order to obtain senior management or board of directors approvals.
- Use of "padding" techniques during operating budget preparation to increase required costs and decrease projected revenues in order to look good at the end of the year.
- The practice of allocating "hot" initial public offerings (IPOs) to the best customers and friends of the underwriter or syndicate member. Similarly, the practice of "insider trading" in leaking information to friends and relatives or for personal gain about forthcoming mergers, acquisitions, and divestitures.
- The practice of dubious actions such as paying bills late and still taking discounts, setting invoice dates well before shipping dates, and imposing large delinquency charges for late payments.
- The practice of kiting procedures to conceal cash shortages.
- The practice of lapping procedures involving customer payments.
- The practice of skimming procedures involving removal of cash.
- The practice of check-tampering schemes for an employee's personal benefit.

Module 700 Appendix

Mathematical Tables

Table A.1: *Present Value of $1 Due at the End of n Periods*

EQUATION:

$$PVIF_{i,n} = \frac{1}{(1+i)^n}$$

FINANCIAL CALCULATOR KEYS:

n, i, 0, 1.0 → N, I, PV (Table Value), PMT, FV

Period	1%	2%	3%	4%	5%	6%	7%	8%	9%	10%
1	.9901	.9804	.9709	.9615	.9524	.9434	.9346	.9259	.9174	.9091
2	.9803	.9612	.9426	.9246	.9070	.8900	.8734	.8573	.8417	.8264
3	.9706	.9423	.9151	.8890	.8638	.8396	.8163	.7938	.7722	.7513
4	.9610	.9238	.8885	.8548	.8227	.7921	.7629	.7350	.7084	.6830
5	.9515	.9057	.8626	.8219	.7835	.7473	.7130	.6806	.6499	.6209
6	.9420	.8880	.8375	.7903	.7462	.7050	.6663	.6302	.5963	.5645
7	.9327	.8706	.8131	.7599	.7107	.6651	.6227	.5835	.5470	.5132
8	.9235	.8535	.7894	.7307	.6768	.6274	.5820	.5403	.5019	.4665
9	.9143	.8368	.7664	.7026	.6446	.5919	.5439	.5002	.4604	.4241
10	.9053	.8203	.7441	.6756	.6139	.5584	.5083	.4632	.4224	.3855
11	.8963	.8043	.7224	.6496	.5847	.5268	.4751	.4289	.3875	.3505
12	.8874	.7885	.7014	.6246	.5568	.4970	.4440	.3971	.3555	.3186
13	.8787	.7730	.6810	.6006	.5303	.4688	.4150	.3677	.3262	.2897
14	.8700	.7579	.6611	.5775	.5051	.4423	.3878	.3405	.2992	.2633
15	.8613	7430	.6419	.5553	.4810	.4173	.3624	.3152	.2745	.2394
16	.8528	.7284	.6232	.5339	.4581	.3936	.3387	.2919	.2519	.2176
17	.8444	.7142	.6050	.5134	.4363	.3714	.3166	.2703	.2311	.1978
18	.8360	.7002	.5874	.4936	.4155	.3503	.2959	.2502	.2120	.1799
19	.8277	.6864	.5703	.4746	.3957	.3305	.2765	.2317	.1945	.1635
20	.8195	.6730	.5537	.4564	.3769	.3118	.2584	.2145	.1784	.1486
21	.8114	.6598	.5375	.4388	.3589	.2942	.2415	.1987	.1637	.1351
22	.8034	.6468	.5219	.4220	.3418	.2775	.2257	.1839	.1502	.1228
23	.7954	.6342	.5067	.4057	.3256	.2618	.2109	.1703	.1378	.1117
24	.7876	.6217	.4919	.3901	.3101	.2470	.1971	.1577	.1264	.1015
25	.7798	.6095	.4776	.3751	.2953	.2330	.1842	.1460	.1160	.0923
26	.7720	.5976	.4637	.3607	.2812	.2198	.1722	.1352	.1064	.0839
27	.7644	.5859	.4502	.3468	.2678	.2074	.1609	.1252	.0976	.0763
28	.7568	.5744	.4371	.3335	.2551	.1956	.1504	.1159	.0895	.0693
29	.7493	.5631	.4243	.3207	.2429	.1846	.1406	.1073	.0822	.0630
30	.7419	.5521	.4120	.3083	.2314	.1741	.1314	.0994	.0754	.0573
35	.7059	.5000	.3554	.2534	.1813	.1301	.0937	.0676	.0490	.0356
40	.6717	.4529	.3066	.2083	.1420	.0972	.0668	.0460	.0318	.0221
45	.6391	.4102	.2644	.1712	.1113	.0727	.0476	.0313	.0207	.0137
50	.6080	.3715	.2281	.1407	.0872	.0543	.0339	.0213	.0134	.0085
55	.5785	.3365	.1968	.1157	.0683	.0406	.0242	.0145	.0087	.0053

Table A.1 *Continued*

Period	12%	14%	15%	16%	18%	20%	24%	28%	32%	36%
1	.8929	.8772	.8696	.8621	.8475	.8333	.8065	.7813	.7576	.7353
2	.7972	.7695	.7561	.7432	.7182	.6944	.6504	.6104	.5739	.5407
3	.7118	.6750	.6575	.6407	.6086	.5787	.5245	.4768	.4348	.3975
4	.6355	.5921	.5718	.5523	.5158	.4823	.4230	.3725	.3294	.2923
5	.5674	.5194	.4972	.4761	.4371	.4019	.3411	.2910	.2495	.2149
6	.5066	.4556	.4323	.4104	.3704	.3349	.2751	.2274	.1890	.1580
7	.4523	.3996	.3759	.3538	.3139	.2791	.2218	.1776	.1432	.1162
8	.4039	.3506	.3269	.3050	.2660	.2326	.1789	.1388	.1085	.0854
9	.3606	.3075	.2843	.2630	.2255	.1938	.1443	.1084	.0822	.0628
10	.3220	.2697	.2472	.2267	.1911	.1615	.1164	.0847	.0623	.0462
11	.2875	.2366	.2149	.1954	.1619	.1346	.0938	.0662	.0472	.0340
12	.2567	.2076	.1869	.1685	.1372	.1122	.0757	.0517	.0357	.0250
13	.2292	.1821	.1625	.1452	.1163	.0935	.0610	.0404	.0271	.0184
14	.2046	.1597	.1413	.1252	.0985	.0779	.0492	.0316	.0205	.0135
15	.1827	.1401	.1229	.1079	.0835	.0649	.0397	.0247	.0155	.0099
16	.1631	.1229	.1069	.0930	.0708	.0541	.0320	.0193	.0118	.0073
17	.1456	.1078	.0929	.0802	.0600	.0451	.0258	.0150	.0089	.0054
18	.1300	.0946	.0808	.0691	.0508	.0376	.0208	.0118	.0068	.0039
19	.1161	.0829	.0703	.0596	.0431	.0313	.0168	.0092	.0051	.0029
20	.1037	.0728	.0611	.0514	.0365	.0261	.0135	.0072	.0039	.0021
21	.0926	.0638	.0531	.0443	.0309	.0217	.0109	.0056	.0029	.0016
22	.0826	.0560	.0462	.0382	.0262	.0181	.0088	.0044	.0022	.0012
23	.0738	.0491	.0402	.0329	.0222	.0151	.0071	.0034	.0017	.0008
24	.0659	.0431	.0349	.0284	.0188	.0126	.0057	.0027	.0013	.0006
25	.0588	.0378	.0304	.0245	.0160	.0105	.0046	.0021	.0010	.0005
26	.0525	.0331	.0264	.0211	.0135	.0087	.0037	.0016	.0007	.0003
27	.0469	.0291	.0230	.0182	.0115	.0073	.0030	.0013	.0006	.0002
28	.0419	.0255	.0200	.0157	.0097	.0061	.0024	.0010	.0004	.0002
29	.0374	.0224	.0174	.0135	.0082	.0051	.0020	.0008	.0003	.0001
30	.0334	.0196	.0151	.0116	.0070	.0042	.0016	.0006	.0002	.0001
35	.0189	.0102	.0075	.0055	.0030	.0017	.0005	.0002	.0001	*
40	.0107	.0053	.0037	.0026	.0013	.0007	.0002	.0001	*	*
45	.0061	.0027	.0019	.0013	.0006	.0003	.0001	*	*	*
50	.0035	.0014	.0009	.0006	.0003	.0001	*	*	*	*
55	.0020	.0007	.0005	.0003	.0001	*	*	*	*	*

*The factor is zero to four decimal places.

Table A.2 *Present Value of an Annuity of $1 per Period for n Periods*

EQUATION:

$$PVIFA_{i,n} = \sum_{t=1}^{N} \frac{1}{(1+i)^n} = \frac{1 - \frac{1}{(1+i)^n}}{i} = \frac{1}{i} = \frac{1}{i(1+i)^n}$$

FINANCIAL CALCULATOR KEYS:

n, i, 1.0, 0
[N] [I] [PV = Table Value] [PMT] [FV]

Number of Periods	1%	2%	3%	4%	5%	6%	7%	8%	9%
1	0.9901	0.9804	0.9709	0.9615	0.9524	0.9434	0.9346	0.9259	0.9174
2	1.9704	1.9416	1.9135	1.8861	1.8594	1.8334	1.8080	1.7833	1.7591
3	2.9410	2.8839	2.8286	2.7751	2.7232	2.6730	2.6243	2.5771	2.5313
4	3.9020	3.8077	3.7171	3.6299	3.5460	3.4651	3.3872	3.3121	3.2397
5	4.8534	4.7135	4.5797	4.4518	4.3295	4.2124	4.1002	3.9927	3.8897
6	5.7955	5.6014	5.4172	5.2421	5.0757	4.9173	4.7665	4.6229	4.4859
7	6.7282	6.4720	6.2303	6.0021	5.7864	5.5824	5.3893	5.2064	5.0330
8	7.6517	7.3255	7.0197	6.7327	6.4632	6.2098	5.9713	5.7466	5.5348
9	8.5660	8.1622	7.7861	7.4353	7.1078	6.8017	6.5152	6.2469	5.9952
10	9.4713	8.9826	8.5302	8.1109	7.7217	7.3601	7.0236	6.7101	6.4177
11	10.3676	9.7868	9.2526	8.7605	8.3064	7.8869	7.4987	7.1390	6.8052
12	11.2551	10.5753	9.9540	9.3851	8.8633	8.3838	7.9427	7.5361	7.1607
13	12.1337	11.3484	10.6350	9.9856	9.3936	8.8527	8.3577	7.9038	7.4869
14	13.0037	12.1062	11.2961	10.5631	9.8986	9.2950	8.7455	8.2442	7.7862
15	13.8651	12.8493	11.9379	11.1184	10.3797	9.7122	9.1079	8.5595	8.0607
16	14.7179	13.5777	12.5611	11.6523	10.8378	10.1059	9.4466	8.8514	8.3126
17	15.5623	14.2919	13.1661	12.1657	11.2741	10.4773	9.7632	9.1216	8.5436
18	16.3983	14.9920	13.7535	12.6593	11.6896	10.8276	10.0591	9.3719	8.7556
19	17.2260	15.6785	14.3238	13.1339	12.0853	11.1581	10.3356	9.6036	8.9501
20	18.0456	16.3514	14.8775	13.5903	12.4622	11.4699	10.5940	9.8181	9.1285
21	18.8570	17.0112	15.4150	14.0292	12.8212	11.7641	10.8355	10.0168	9.2922
22	19.6604	17.6580	15.9369	14.4511	13.1630	12.0416	11.0612	10.2007	9.4424
23	20.4558	18.2922	16.4436	14.8568	13.4886	12.3034	11.2722	10.3711	9.5802
24	21.2434	18.9139	16.9355	15.2470	13.7986	12.5504	11.4693	10.5288	9.7066
25	22.0232	19.5235	17.4131	15.6221	14.0939	12.7834	11.6536	10.6748	9.8226
26	22.7952	20.1210	17.8768	15.9828	14.3752	13.0032	11.8258	10.8100	9.9290
27	23.5596	20.7069	18.3270	16.3296	14.6430	13.2105	11.9867	10.9352	10.0266
28	24.3164	21.2813	18.7641	16.6631	14.8981	13.4062	12.1371	11.0511	10.1161
29	25.0658	21.8444	19.1885	16.9837	15.1411	13.5907	12.2777	11.1584	10.1983
30	25.8077	22.3965	19.6004	17.2920	15.3725	13.7648	12.4090	11.2578	10.2737
35	29.4086	24.9986	21.4872	18.6646	16.3742	14.4982	12.9477	11.6546	10.5668
40	32.8347	27.3555	23.1148	19.7928	17.1591	15.0463	13.3317	11.9246	10.7574
45	36.0945	29.4902	24.5187	20.7200	17.7741	15.4558	13.6055	12.1084	10.8812
50	39.1961	31.4236	25.7298	21.4822	18.2559	15.7619	13.8007	12.2335	10.9617
55	42.1472	33.1748	26.7744	22.1086	18.6335	15.9905	13.9399	12.3186	11.0140

Table A.2 *Continued*

Number of Periods	10%	12%	14%	15%	16%	18%	20%	24%	28%	32%
1	0.9091	0.8929	0.8772	0.8696	0.8621	0.8475	0.8333	0.8065	0.7813	0.7576
2	1.7355	1.6901	1.6467	1.6257	1.6052	1.5656	1.5278	1.4568	1.3916	1.3315
3	2.4869	2.4018	2.3216	2.2832	2.2459	2.1743	2.1065	1.9813	1.8684	1.7663
4	3.1699	3.0373	2.9137	2.8550	2.7982	2.6901	2.5887	2.4043	2.2410	2.0957
5	3.7908	3.6048	3.4331	3.3522	3.2743	3.1272	2.9906	2.7454	2.5320	2.3452
6	4.3553	4.1114	3.8887	3.7845	3.6847	3.4976	3.3255	3.0205	2.7594	2.5342
7	4.8684	4.5638	4.2883	4.1604	4.0386	3.8115	3.6046	3.2423	2.9370	2.6775
8	5.3349	4.9676	4.6389	4.4873	4.3436	4.0776	3.8372	3.4212	3.0758	2.7860
9	5.7590	5.3282	4.9464	4.7716	4.6065	4.3030	4.0310	3.5655	3.1842	2.8681
10	6.1446	5.6502	5.2161	5.0188	4.8332	4.4941	4.1925	3.6819	3.2689	2.9304
11	6.4951	5.9377	5.4527	5.2337	5.0286	4.6560	4.3271	3.7757	3.3351	2.9776
12	6.8137	6.1944	5.6603	5.4206	5.1971	4.7932	4.4392	3.8514	3.3868	3.0133
13	7.1034	6.4235	5.8424	5.5831	5.3423	4.9095	4.5327	3.9124	3.4272	3.0404
14	7.3667	6.6282	6.0021	5.7245	5.4675	5.0081	4.6106	3.9616	3.4587	3.0609
15	7.6061	6.8109	6.1422	5.8474	5.5755	5.0916	4.6755	4.0013	3.4834	3.0764
16	7.8237	6.9740	6.2651	5.9542	5.6685	5.1624	4.7296	4.0333	3.5026	3.0882
17	8.0216	7.1196	6.3729	6.0472	5.7487	5.2223	4.7746	4.0591	3.5177	3.0971
18	8.2014	7.2497	6.4674	6.1280	5.8178	5.2732	4.8122	4.0799	3.5294	3.1039
19	8.3649	7.3658	6.5504	6.1982	5.8775	5.3162	4.8435	4.0967	3.5386	3.1090
20	8.5136	7.4694	6.6231	6.2593	5.9288	5.3527	4.8696	4.1103	3.5458	3.1129
21	8.6487	7.5620	6.6870	6.3125	5.9731	5.3837	4.8913	4.1212	3.5514	3.1158
22	8.7715	7.6446	6.7429	6.3587	6.0113	5.4099	4.9094	4.1300	3.5558	3.1180
23	8.8832	7.7184	6.7921	6.3988	6.0442	5.4321	4.9245	4.1371	3.5592	3.1197
24	8.9847	7.7843	6.8351	6.4338	6.0726	5.4509	4.9371	4.1428	3.5619	3.1210
25	9.0770	7.8431	6.8729	6.4641	6.0971	5.4669	4.9476	4.1474	3.5640	3.1220
26	9.1609	7.8957	6.9061	6.4906	6.1182	5.4804	4.9563	4.1511	3.5656	3.1227
27	9.2372	7.9426	6.9352	6.5135	6.1364	5.4919	4.9636	4.1542	3.5669	3.1233
28	9.3066	7.9844	6.9607	6.5335	6.1520	5.5016	4.9697	4.1566	3.5679	3.1237
29	9.3696	8.0218	6.9830	6.5509	6.1656	5.5098	4.9747	4.1585	3.5687	3.1240
30	9.4269	8.0552	7.0027	6.5660	6.1772	5.5168	4.9789	4.1601	3.5693	3.1242
35	9.6442	8.1755	7.0700	6.6166	6.2153	5.5386	4.9915	4.1644	3.5708	3.1248
40	9.7791	8.2438	7.1050	6.6418	6.2335	5.5482	4.9966	4.1659	3.5712	3.1250
45	9.8628	8.2825	7.1232	6.6543	6.2421	5.5523	4.9986	4.1664	3.5714	3.1250
50	9.9148	8.3045	7.1327	6.6605	6.2463	5.5541	4.9995	4.1666	3.5714	3.1250
55	9.9471	8.3170	7.1376	6.6636	6.2482	5.5549	4.9998	4.1666	3.5714	3.1250

Table A.3 *Future Value of $1 at the End of n Periods*

EQUATION:

$FVIF_{i,n} = (1 + i)^n$

FINANCIAL CALCULATOR KEYS:

n   i   0   1.0
[N]   [I]   [PV]   [PMT]   [FV]
                                               Table Value

Period	1%	2%	3%	4%	5%	6%	7%	8%	9%	10%
1	1.0100	1.0200	1.0300	1.0400	1.0500	1.0600	1.0700	1.0800	1.0900	1.1000
2	1.0201	1.0404	1.0609	1.0816	1.1025	1.1236	1.1449	1.1664	1.1881	1.2100
3	1.0303	1.0612	1.0927	1.1249	1.1576	1.1910	1.2250	1.2597	1.2950	1.3310
4	1.0406	1.0824	1.1255	1.1699	1.2155	1.2625	1.3108	1.3605	1.4116	1.4641
5	1.0510	1.1041	1.1593	1.2167	1.2763	1.3382	1.4026	1.4693	1.5386	1.6105
6	1.0615	1.1262	1.1941	1.2653	1.3401	1.4185	1.5007	1.5869	1.6771	1.7716
7	1.0721	1.1487	1.2299	1.3159	1.4071	1.5036	1.6058	1.7138	1.8280	1.9487
8	1.0829	1.1717	1.2668	1.3686	1.4775	1.5938	1.7182	1.8509	1.9926	2.1436
9	1.0937	1.1951	1.3048	1.4233	1.5513	1.6895	1.8385	1.9990	2.1719	2.3579
10	1.1046	1.2190	1.3439	1.4802	1.6289	1.7908	1.9672	2.1589	2.3674	2.5937
11	1.1157	1.2434	1.3842	1.5395	1.7103	1.8983	2.1049	2.3316	2.5804	2.8531
12	1.1268	1.2682	1.4258	1.6010	1.7959	2.0122	2.2522	2.5182	2.8127	3.1384
13	1.1381	1.2936	1.4685	1.6651	1.8856	2.1329	2.4098	2.7196	3.0658	3.4523
14	1.1495	1.3195	1.5126	1.7317	1.9799	2.2609	2.5785	2.9372	3.3417	3.7975
15	1.1610	1.3459	1.5580	1.8009	2.0789	2.3966	2.7590	3.1722	3.6425	4.1772
16	1.1726	1.3728	1.6047	1.8730	2.1829	2.5404	2.9522	3.4259	3.9703	4.5950
17	1.1843	1.4002	1.6528	1.9479	2.2920	2.6928	3.1588	3.7000	4.3276	5.0545
18	1.1961	1.4282	1.7024	2.0258	2.4066	2.8543	3.3799	3.9960	4.7171	5.5599
19	1.2081	1.4568	1.7535	2.1068	2.5270	3.0256	3.6165	4.3157	5.1417	6.1159
20	1.2202	1.4859	1.8061	2.1911	2.6533	3.2071	3.8697	4.6610	5.6044	6.7275
21	1.2324	1.5157	1.8603	2.2788	2.7860	3.3996	4.1406	5.0338	6.1088	7.4002
22	1.2447	1.5460	1.9161	2.3699	2.9253	3.6035	4.4304	5.4365	6.6586	8.1403
23	1.2572	1.5769	1.9736	2.4647	3.0715	3.8197	4.7405	5.8715	7.2579	8.9543
24	1.2697	1.6084	2.0328	2.5633	3.2251	4.0489	5.0724	6.3412	7.9111	9.8497
25	1.2824	1.6406	2.0938	2.6658	3.3864	4.2919	5.4274	6.8485	8.6231	10.835
26	1.2953	1.6734	2.1566	2.7725	3.5557	4.5494	5.8074	7.3964	9.3992	11.918
27	1.3082	1.7069	2.2213	2.8834	3.7335	4.8223	6.2139	7.9881	10.245	13.110
28	1.3213	1.7410	2.2879	2.9987	3.9201	5.1117	6.6488	8.6271	11.167	14.421
29	1.3345	1.7758	2.3566	3.1187	4.1161	5.4184	7.1143	9.3173	12.172	15.863
30	1.3478	1.8114	2.4273	3.2434	4.3219	5.7435	7.6123	10.063	13.268	17.449
40	1.4889	2.2080	3.2620	4.8010	7.0400	10.286	14.974	21.725	31.409	45.259
50	1.6446	2.6916	4.3839	7.1067	11.467	18.420	29.457	46.902	74.358	117.39
60	1.8167	3.2810	5.8916	10.520	18.679	32.988	57.946	101.26	176.03	304.48

Table A.3 Continued

Period	12%	14%	15%	16%	18%	20%	24%	28%	32%	36%
1	1.1200	1.1400	1.1500	1.1600	1.1800	1.2000	1.2400	1.2800	1.3200	1.3600
2	1.2544	1.2996	1.3225	1.3456	1.3924	1.4400	1.5376	1.6384	1.7424	1.8496
3	1.4049	1.4815	1.5209	1.5609	1.6430	1.7280	1.9066	2.0972	2.3000	2.5155
4	1.5735	1.6890	1.7490	1.8106	1.9388	2.0736	2.3642	2.6844	3.0360	3.4210
5	1.7623	1.9254	2.0114	2.1003	2.2878	2.4883	2.9316	3.4360	4.0075	4.6526
6	1.9738	2.1950	2.3131	2.4364	2.6996	2.9860	3.6352	4.3980	5.2899	6.3275
7	2.2107	2.5023	2.6600	2.8262	3.1855	3.5832	4.5077	5.6295	6.9826	8.6054
8	2.4760	2.8526	3.0590	3.2784	3.7589	4.2998	5.5895	7.2058	9.2170	11.703
9	2.7731	3.2519	3.5179	3.8030	4.4355	5.1598	6.9310	9.2234	12.166	15.917
10	3.1058	3.7072	4.0456	4.4114	5.2338	6.1917	8.5944	11.806	16.060	21.647
11	3.4785	4.2262	4.6524	5.1173	6.1759	7.4301	10.657	15.112	21.199	29.439
12	3.8960	4.8179	5.3503	5.9360	7.2876	8.9161	13.215	19.343	27.983	40.037
13	4.3635	5.4924	6.1528	6.8858	8.5994	10.699	16.386	24.759	36.937	54.451
14	4.8871	6.2613	7.0757	7.9875	10.147	12.839	20.319	31.691	48.757	74.053
15	5.4736	7.1379	8.1371	9.2655	11.974	15.407	25.196	40.565	64.359	100.71
16	6.1304	8.1372	9.3576	10.748	14.129	18.488	31.243	51.923	84.954	136.97
17	6.8660	9.2765	10.761	12.468	16.672	22.186	38.741	66.461	112.14	186.28
18	7.6900	10.575	12.375	14.463	19.673	26.623	48.039	85.071	148.02	253.34
19	8.6128	12.056	14.232	16.777	23.214	31.948	59.568	108.89	195.39	344.54
20	9.6463	13.743	16.367	19.461	27.393	38.338	73.864	139.38	257.92	468.57
21	10.804	15.668	18.822	22.574	32.324	46.005	91.592	178.41	340.45	637.26
22	12.100	17.861	21.645	26.186	38.142	55.206	113.57	228.36	449.39	866.67
23	13.552	20.362	24.891	30.376	45.008	66.247	140.83	292.30	593.20	1178.7
24	15.179	23.212	28.625	35.236	53.109	79.497	174.63	374.14	783.02	1603.0
25	17.000	26.462	32.919	40.874	62.669	95.396	216.54	478.90	1033.6	2180.1
26	19.040	30.167	37.857	47.414	73.949	114.48	268.51	613.00	1364.3	2964.9
27	21.325	34.390	43.535	55.000	87.260	137.37	332.95	784.64	1800.9	4032.3
28	23.884	39.204	50.066	63.800	102.97	164.84	412.86	1004.3	2377.2	5483.9
29	26.750	44.693	57.575	74.009	121.50	197.81	511.95	1285.6	3137.9	7458.1
30	29.960	50.950	66.212	85.850	143.37	237.38	634.82	1645.5	4142.1	10143.
40	93.051	188.88	267.86	378.72	750.38	1469.8	5455.9	19427.	66521.	*
50	289.00	700.23	1083.7	1670.7	3927.4	9100.4	46890.	*	*	*
60	897.60	2595.9	4384.0	7370.2	20555.	56348.	*	*	*	*

*FVIF > 99,999.

Table A.4 *Future Value of an Annuity of $1 per Period for n Periods*

EQUATION:

$$FVIFA_{i,n} = \sum_{t=1}^{n} (1+i)^{n-t} = \frac{(1+i)^n - 1}{i}$$

FINANCIAL CALCULATOR KEYS:

n	i	1.0	0	
N	I	PV	PMT	FV
				Table Value

Number of Periods	1%	2%	3%	4%	5%	6%	7%	8%	9%	10%
1	1.0000	1.0000	1.0000	1.0000	1.0000	1.0000	1.0000	1.0000	1.0000	1.0000
2	2.0100	2.0200	2.0300	2.0400	2.0500	2.0600	2.0700	2.0800	2.0900	2.1000
3	3.0301	3.0604	3.0909	3.1216	3.1525	3.1836	3.2149	3.2464	3.2781	3.3100
4	4.0604	4.1216	4.1836	4.2465	4.3101	4.3746	4.4399	4.5061	4.5731	4.6410
5	5.1010	5.2040	5.3091	5.4163	5.5256	5.6371	5.7507	5.8666	5.9847	6.1051
6	6.1520	6.3081	6.4684	6.6330	6.8019	6.9753	7.1533	7.3359	7.5233	7.7156
7	7.2135	7.4343	7.6625	7.8983	8.1420	8.3938	8.6540	8.9228	9.2004	9.4872
8	8.2857	8.5830	8.8923	9.2142	9.5491	9.8975	10.260	10.637	11.028	11.436
9	9.3685	9.7546	10.159	10.583	11.027	11.491	11.978	12.488	13.021	13.579
10	10.462	10.950	11.464	12.006	12.578	13.181	13.816	14.487	15.193	15.937
11	11.567	12.169	12.808	13.486	14.207	14.972	15.784	16.645	17.560	18.531
12	12.683	13.412	14.192	15.026	15.917	16.870	17.888	18.977	20.141	21.384
13	13.809	14.680	15.618	16.627	17.713	18.882	20.141	21.495	22.953	24.523
14	14.947	15.974	17.086	18.292	19.599	21.015	22.550	24.215	26.019	27.975
15	16.097	17.293	18.599	20.024	21.579	23.276	25.129	27.152	29.361	31.772
16	17.258	18.639	20.157	21.825	23.657	25.673	27.888	30.324	33.003	35.950
17	18.430	20.012	21.762	23.698	25.840	28.213	30.840	33.750	36.974	40.545
18	19.615	21.412	23.414	25.645	28.132	30.906	33.999	37.450	41.301	45.599
19	20.811	22.841	25.117	27.671	30.539	33.760	37.379	41.446	46.018	51.159
20	22.019	24.297	26.870	29.778	33.066	36.786	40.995	45.762	51.160	57.275
21	23.239	25.783	28.676	31.969	35.719	39.993	44.865	50.423	56.765	64.002
22	24.472	27.299	30.537	34.248	38.505	43.392	49.006	55.457	62.873	71.403
23	25.716	28.845	32.453	36.618	41.430	46.996	53.436	60.893	69.532	79.543
24	26.973	30.422	34.426	39.083	44.502	50.816	58.177	66.765	76.790	88.497
25	28.243	32.030	36.459	41.646	47.727	54.865	63.249	73.106	84.701	98.347
26	29.526	33.671	38.553	44.312	51.113	59.156	68.676	79.954	93.324	109.18
27	30.821	35.344	40.710	47.084	54.669	63.706	74.484	87.351	102.72	121.10
28	32.129	37.051	42.931	49.968	58.403	68.528	80.698	95.339	112.97	134.21
29	33.450	38.792	45.219	52.966	62.323	73.640	87.347	103.97	124.14	148.63
30	34.785	40.568	47.575	56.085	66.439	79.058	94.461	113.28	136.31	164.49
40	48.886	60.402	75.401	95.026	120.80	154.76	199.64	259.06	337.88	442.59
50	64.463	84.579	112.80	152.67	209.35	290.34	406.53	573.77	815.08	1163.9
60	81.670	114.05	163.05	237.99	353.58	533.13	813.52	1253.2	1944.8	3034.8

Table A.4 *Continued*

Number of Periods	12%	14%	15%	16%	18%	20%	24%	28%	32%	36%
1	1.0000	1.0000	1.0000	1.0000	1.0000	1.0000	1.0000	1.0000	1.0000	1.0000
2	2.1200	2.1400	2.1500	2.1600	2.1800	2.2000	2.2400	2.2800	2.3200	2.3600
3	3.3744	3.4396	3.4725	3.5056	3.5724	3.6400	3.7776	3.9184	4.0624	4.2096
4	4.7793	4.9211	4.9934	5.0665	5.2154	5.3680	5.6842	6.0156	6.3624	6.7251
5	6.3528	6.6101	6.7424	6.8771	7.1542	7.4416	8.0484	8.6999	9.3983	10.146
6	8.1152	8.5355	8.7537	8.9775	9.4420	9.9299	10.980	12.136	13.406	14.799
7	10.089	10.730	11.067	11.414	12.142	12.916	14.615	16.534	18.696	21.126
8	12.300	13.233	13.727	14.240	15.327	16.499	19.123	22.163	25.678	29.732
9	14.776	16.085	16.786	17.519	19.086	20.799	24.712	29.369	34.895	41.435
10	17.549	19.337	20.304	21.321	23.521	25.959	31.643	38.593	47.062	57.352
11	20.655	23.045	24.349	25.733	28.755	32.150	40.238	50.398	63.122	78.998
12	24.133	27.271	29.002	30.850	34.931	39.581	50.895	65.510	84.320	108.44
13	28.029	32.089	34.352	36.786	42.219	48.497	64.110	84.853	112.30	148.47
14	32.393	37.581	40.505	43.672	50.818	59.196	80.496	109.61	149.24	202.93
15	37.280	43.842	47.580	51.660	60.965	72.035	100.82	141.30	198.00	276.98
16	42.753	50.980	55.717	60.925	72.939	87.442	126.01	181.87	262.36	377.69
17	48.884	59.118	65.075	71.673	87.068	105.93	157.25	233.79	347.31	514.66
18	55.750	68.394	75.836	84.141	103.74	128.12	195.99	300.25	459.45	700.94
19	63.440	78.969	88.212	98.603	123.41	154.74	244.03	385.32	607.47	954.28
20	72.052	91.025	102.44	115.38	146.63	186.69	303.60	494.21	802.86	1298.8
21	81.699	104.77	118.81	134.84	174.02	225.03	377.46	633.59	1060.8	1767.4
22	92.503	120.44	137.63	157.41	206.34	271.03	469.06	812.00	1401.2	2404.7
23	104.60	138.30	159.28	183.60	244.49	326.24	582.63	1040.4	1850.6	3271.3
24	118.16	158.66	184.17	213.98	289.49	392.48	723.46	1332.7	2443.8	4450.0
25	133.33	181.87	212.79	249.21	342.60	471.98	898.09	1706.8	3226.8	6053.0
26	150.33	208.33	245.71	290.09	405.27	567.38	1114.6	2185.7	4260.4	8233.1
27	169.37	238.50	283.57	337.50	479.22	681.85	1383.1	2798.7	5624.8	11198.0
28	190.70	272.89	327.10	392.50	566.48	819.22	1716.1	3583.3	7425.7	15230.3
29	214.58	312.09	377.17	456.30	669.45	984.07	2129.0	4587.7	9802.9	20714.2
30	241.33	356.79	434.75	530.31	790.95	1181.9	2640.9	5873.2	12941.	28172.3
40	767.09	1342.0	1779.1	2360.8	4163.2	7343.9	22729.	69377.	*	*
50	2400.0	4994.5	7217.7	10436.	21813.	45497.	*	*	*	*
60	7471.6	18535.	29220.	46058.	*	*	*	*	*	*

*FVIFA > 99,999.

Module 700 Endnotes

1. See Verlyn Richards and Eugene Laughlin, "A Cash Conversion Cycle Approach to Liquidity Analysis," *Financial Management*, Spring 1980, 32–38.
2. Chun-Hao Chang, Krishnan Dandapani, and Arun J. Prakish, "Current Assets Policies of European Corporations: A Critical Examination," *Management International Review*, Special Issue 1995/2, 105–117.
3. See Eugene F. Brigham, Louis C. Gapenski, and Phillip R. Daves, *Intermediate Financial Management*, 6th ed. (Fort Worth, Tex.: The Dryden Press, 1999), Chapter 18, for a more complete discussion of the problems with the DSO and aging schedule and how to correct for them.
4. Franco Modigliani and Merton H. Miller, "The Cost of Capital, Corporation Finance, and the Theory of Investment," *American Economic Review*, June 1958, 261–297, and "Corporate Income Taxes and the Cost of Capital," *American Economic Review*, June 1963, 433–443. Modigliani and Miller both won Nobel Prizes for their work.
5. Myron J. Gordon "Optimal Investment and Financing Policy," *Journal of Finance*, May 1963, 264–272, and John Lintner, "Dividends, Earnings, Leverage, Stock Prices, and the Supply of Capital to Corporations," *Review of Economics and Statistics*, August 1962, 243–269.
6. Rafael La Porta, Florencio Lopez-de-Silanes, Andrei Shleifer, and Robert W. Vishny, "Agency Problems and Dividend Policies Around the World," unpublished manuscript, Harvard University, November 1997.
7. Copeland, Koller, and Murrin, *Valuation: Measuring and Managing the Value of Companies*, 3rd ed. (John Wiley & Sons, Inc., 2000).
8. *Ibid.*
9. Palepu, Bernard, Healy, *Business Analysis and Valuation Using Financial Statements*, Cincinnati, OH (Southwestern Publishing Company, 1996).

MODULE 800

Information Technology*

801 Information Technology Strategies, 1126

805 Information Systems Planning, 1132

815 Information Technology Risk Management, 1139

825 Decision Making and Information Technology, 1144

845 Data and Knowledge Management, 1156

850 Systems Development and Acquisition, 1179

855 Managing Information Technology Resources, 1205

860 Telecommunications and Networks, 1216

865 Business Information Systems, 1235

870 Information Technology Security and Controls, 1237

875 Electronic Commerce and Information Technology, 1246

880 Information Technology Contingency Plans, 1257

890 Ethics and Information Technology, 1262

Module 800 Endnotes, 1265

*From *Management Information Systems,* Third Edition by Oz. ©2002. Reprinted with permission of Course Technology, a division of Thomson Learning: www.thomsonrights.com. Fax 800-730-2215.

Information Technology Strategies

Strategic Uses of Information Systems

Strategy and Strategic Moves

Although many information systems are built to solve problems, many others are built to seize opportunities. And, as anyone in business can tell you, identifying a problem is easier than creating an opportunity. Why? Because a problem already exists; it is an obstacle to a desired mode of operation and, as such, calls attention to itself. An opportunity, on the other hand, is less tangible. It takes a certain amount of vision to identify an opportunity, or to create one and seize it. Information systems that help seize opportunities are called **strategic information systems (SISs)**. They can be developed from scratch, or they can evolve from an organization's existing information systems (ISs).

The word *strategy* originates from the Greek word "*strategos*," meaning "general." In war, a strategy is a plan to gain advantage over the enemy. Other disciplines, especially business, have borrowed the term. As you know from media coverage, corporate executives often discuss actions in ways that make business competition sound like war. Businesspeople must devise decisive courses of action to win, just as generals do. In business, a strategy is a plan designed to help an organization outperform its competitors. However, business strategy, unlike battle plans, often takes the form of creating new opportunities rather than beating rivals.

In a free-market economy, it is difficult for a business to do well without some strategic planning. Although strategies vary, they tend to fall into some basic categories, such as developing a new product, identifying an unmet consumer need, changing a service to entice more customers or retain existing clients, or taking any other action that increases the organization's value through improved performance.

Many strategies do not, and cannot, involve information systems. But increasingly, corporations are able to implement certain strategies—such as maximizing sales and lowering costs—thanks to the innovative use of information systems. In other words, better information gives corporations a competitive advantage in the marketplace. A company achieves **strategic advantage** by using strategy to maximize its strengths, resulting in a **competitive advantage.** When a business uses a strategy intending to *create* a market for new products or services, it does not aim to compete with other organizations, because that market does not yet exist. Therefore, a strategic move is not always a competitive move. However, in a free-enterprise society, a market rarely remains the domain of one organization for long; thus, competition ensues almost immediately. So, we often use the terms "competitive advantage" and "strategic advantage" interchangeably.

You may have heard statements about using the World Wide Web ("the Web") strategically. Business competition is no longer limited to a particular country or even region of the world. To increase the sale of goods and services, companies must regard the entire world as their market. Because thousands of corporations and hundreds of millions of consumers have access to the Web, augmenting business via the Web has become strategic: many companies that utilized the Web early on have enjoyed greater market shares, greater experiences, and larger revenues than latecomers. Some companies developed information systems, or features of information systems, that are unique, such as "one click" purchase and reverse auctioning. Practically any Web-based system that gives a company competitive advantage is a strategic information system.

Achieving a Competitive Advantage

Let's consider competitive advantage in terms of a for-profit company whose major goal is to maximize profits by lowering costs and increasing revenue. A for-profit company achieves competitive advantage when its profits increase significantly, most commonly through increased market share. Exhibit 800.1 lists eight basic initiatives that can be used to gain competitive advantage, including offering a product or service that competitors cannot provide or providing the same product or service more attractively to customers. It is important to understand that the eight listed are the most common, but not the only, types of business strategy an organization can pursue. The essence of strategy is innovation, so competitive advantage often occurs when an organization tries a strategy that no one has tried before.

Exhibit 800.1 *Eight Basic Initiatives to Competitive Advantage*

Initiative	Benefit
1. Reduce costs	A company can gain advantage if it can sell more units at a lower price while providing quality and maintaining or increasing its profit margin.
2. Raise barriers to market entrants	A company can gain advantage if it deters potential entrants into the market, enjoying less competition and more market potential.
3. Establish high switching costs	A company can gain advantage if it creates high switching costs, making it economically infeasible for customers to buy from competitors.
4. Create new products or services	A company can gain advantage if it offers a unique product or service.
5. Differentiate products or services	A company can gain advantage if it can attract customers by convincing them its product differs from the competition's.
6. Enhance products or services	A company can gain advantage if its product or service is better than anyone else's.
7. Establish alliances	Companies from different industries can help each other gain advantage by offering combined packages of goods or services at special prices.
8. Lock in suppliers or buyers	A company can gain advantage if it can lock in either suppliers or buyers, making it economically impractical for suppliers or buyers to deal with competitors.

Exhibit 800.2 *Many Strategic Moves Can Work Together to Achieve a Competitive Advantage*

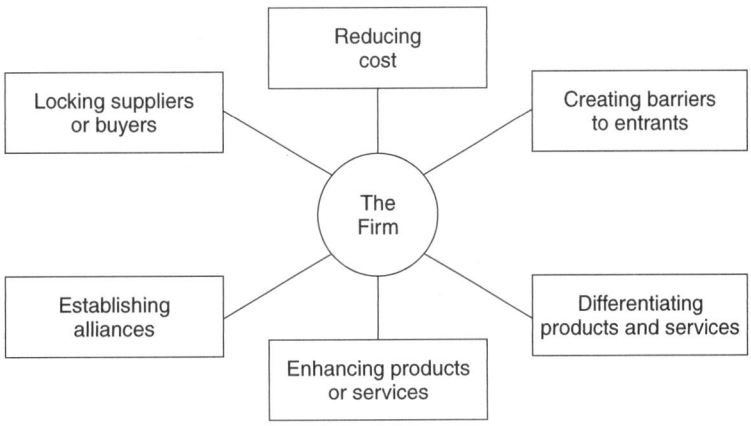

For example, **Dell** was the first PC manufacturer to use the Web to take customer orders. Competitors have long imitated the practice, but Dell, first to gain the Web-bound audience, gained more experience than other PC makers on this e-commerce vehicle and still sells more computers via the Web than its competitors. Exhibit 800.2 indicates that a company can use many strategies together to gain a competitive advantage.

Initiative 1: Reduce Costs

Customers like to pay as little as possible while still receiving the quality of service or product they need. One way to increase market share is to lower prices, and the best way to lower prices is to lower costs. For instance, if carried out successfully, massive automation of any business process gives an organization competitive advantage. The reason is simple: automation makes an organization more productive, and any cost savings can be transferred to customers through lower prices. We saw this happen in the auto industry. In the 1970s, Japanese automakers brought robots to their production and assembly lines and reduced costs—and subsequently prices—quickly and dramatically. The robots weld, paint, and assemble parts at a far lower cost than manual labor. Until their foreign competitors began to employ robots, the Japanese had a clear competitive advantage because they were able to sell high-quality cars for less than their competitors.

In the service sector, the Web has created an opportunity to automate what until recently was considered a "human-only" activity: customer service. An enormous trend toward automating on-line customer service began with companies like **FedEx**, which initially gave customers an opportunity to track their parcels' status by logging on to a dedicated, private network and database. The same approach is now implemented through the Web. Many sites today include answers to FAQs (frequently asked questions). Others have special programs that can actually respond to questions a caller poses. Other Web technologies enable customers to shop, receive information on products, select items, and pay without any need for human intervention by on-line retailers. On-line service gives businesses two major benefits: it turns service from labor-intensive to technology-intensive, which is much less expensive; and it provides customers easy access to a service seven days a week, 24 hours a day (commonly called 24/7). It cuts costs not only of expensive human labor but also of telephone and mailing charges. Companies that are first to adopt advanced systems reducing labor enjoy competitive advantage for as long as their competitors lag behind.

Initiative 2: Raise Barriers to Market Entrants

The smaller the number of companies competing within an industry, the better off each company is. Therefore, an organization may gain competitive advantage by making it difficult, or impossible, for other organizations to produce the product or service it provides. Using expertise or technology that is unavailable to competitors or prohibitively expensive is one way to bar new entrants.

Companies raise **barriers to entrants** in a number of ways. Obtaining legal protection of intellectual property such as an invention or artistic work bars competitors from freely using it. **Microsoft** and other software powerhouses have gained tremendous strategic advantages by copyrighting and patenting software. On the Web, there are numerous examples of such protection. Consider **Amazon.com**, probably the largest on-line retailer. The company secured a patent for "one click" purchases, which enables customers to enter their details, including credit information, only once. From that moment on whenever they make a purchase at the site, they can click only once to buy an item. Amazon successfully sued **BarnesandNoble.com** when B&N implemented the same technology. **Priceline.com** holds a patent for on-line reverse ("Name your price") auctioning, which prevented competitors from entering its business space.

Another barrier to potential new market entrants is the high expense of entering that market. An example is the pension fund management industry. **State Street Corporation** is one of its most successful competitors. In the 1980s, State Street committed massive amounts of money to developing ISs that helped make the company a leader in managing pension funds and international bank accounts. The huge capital allocation required to build a system to compete successfully with State Street's keeps new entrants out of the market. Instead, other pension management corporations rent State Street's technology and expertise. In fact, State Street derives about 70 percent of its revenues from selling its IS services. This company is an interesting example of an entire business refocusing around its ISs.

Initiative 3: Establish High Switching Costs

Switching costs are expenses incurred when a customer stops buying a product or service from one business and starts buying it from another. Switching costs can be explicit (such as charges the seller explicitly levies on a customer for switching) or implicit (such as the indirect costs in time and money of adjusting to a new product that does the same job as the old).

Often, explicit switching costs are fixed, nonrecurring costs, such as a penalty a buyer must pay for terminating a deal early. In the cellular telephone service industry, you can usually get an attractive deal, but if you cancel the service before a full year has passed, you have to pay a hefty penalty. So although another company's service may be more attractive, you may decide to wait the full year because the penalty outweighs the benefits of the new company's service. When you do decide to switch, you will probably discover that the telephone is not suitable for service with any other telephone company. The cost of the telephone itself, then, is another disincentive to switch.

A perfect example of indirect switching expenses are those involved in the time and money required to adjust to new software. Once a company trains its personnel to use one word-processing or spreadsheet program, a competing software company must offer a very enticing deal to make switching worthwhile. The same principle holds for many other applications, such as database management systems and Web browsers. Consider Microsoft's popular Office suite; you can download free of charge Sun Microsystems' StarOffice, a software suite that is as good as MS Office. Yet, few organizations or consumers, who are so used to MS Office, are willing to switch to StarOffice.

Initiative 4: Create New Products or Services

Clearly, creating a new and unique product or service that many organizations and individuals need gives an organization great competitive advantage. Unfortunately, the advantage lasts only until other organizations in the industry start offering an identical or similar product or service for a comparable or lower price.

Examples of this scenario abound in the software industry. For instance, **Lotus Development Corporation** became the major player in the electronic spreadsheet market after it introduced its Lotus 1-2-3 program. When two competitors tried to market similar products, Lotus sued for copyright infringement and won the court case, sustaining its market dominance for several years. However, with time, Microsoft established its Excel spreadsheet application as the world leader, not only by aggressive marketing but also by including better features in its application.

Another example of a company creating a new service is **FedEx,** which created a market in the late 1970s by providing overnight delivery service. FedEx's market share slipped when the U.S. Postal Service, **United Parcel Service**, and other companies entered the same market several years later, providing virtually the same service at the same or lower prices. However, FedEx regained market share by providing the means for clients to log on to FedEx's IS to track their own packages, a service it now offers through the Web. Clients can connect to the system and receive real-time information about any item they send or are scheduled to receive. The extra service has been credited for attracting clients back to FedEx. Competitors have emulated this initiative, too. Evidently, strategic initiatives cannot be static; they must be dynamic for a business to maintain its advantage.

We have already mentioned Amazon.com's one-click service. This unique feature, in addition to brand-name recognition and excellent overall service, has given the company a competitive advantage in the on-line retail industry. While the technologies of on-line catalogs, search engines, payment processing, wish lists, and customer feedback have been adopted by many on-line retailers and are no longer of strategic importance, the one-click feature is still a strategic technology.

One recent example of how strategic advantage can be wiped out within just a few months is in the Internet arena. **Netscape Corporation** dominated the Web browser market, which was new in 1994. By allowing individual users to download its browser free, it cornered over 80 percent of the market. The wide use of the browser by individuals moved commercial organizations to purchase the product and other software compatible with the browser. Netscape's dominance quickly diminished when Microsoft aggressively marketed its own browser, which many perceived as at least as good as Netscape's. Microsoft provided Internet Explorer free of charge to anyone and then bundled it into the operating system software distributed with almost all PCs. Even after the court-ordered unbundling, its browser still dominates. Microsoft now has over 85 percent of the browser market, while Netscape's market share has slipped to 12 percent.

Initiative 5: Differentiate Products or Services

A company can achieve a competitive advantage by persuading consumers that its product or service is better than its competitors', even if it is not. Called product differentiation, this advantage is usually achieved through advertising. Brand name success is a perfect example of product differentiation. Think of Levi's Jeans, Chanel and Lucky perfumes, and Nautica clothes. The customer buys the brand-name product, perceiving it to be superior to similar products. In fact, some products *are* the same, but units sold under a prestigious brand name sell for higher prices. You often see this phenomenon in the food, clothing, drug, and cosmetics markets.

The advent of the Internet as a business tool gives companies an opportunity to render a great number of services through the Web and e-mail, from delivering new software applications to answering frequently asked questions to presenting information about huge selections of items on the Web in vivid color and animation. All are new services. While mimicking such services is easy, companies that offered them first often manage to maintain a measure of competitive advantage because the brand name they established keeps attracting customers. For example, Amazon.com established a name for itself as the predominant seller of books, music CDs, and small appliances on the Web. Although **Barnes & Noble**, the big "brick and mortar" bookstore chain, followed suit and established its own on-line store, it found luring customers away from Amazon difficult. Clearly its brand name gives Amazon its great market share. Marketing experts have acknowledged brand-name recognition as a key to success in retail on the Web. When consumers look to purchase an item, they tend first to visit the sites that are more familiar. On-line businesses can increase brand-name recognition by inventing and implementing ISs that enhance the shopping experience and the speed at which orders are fulfilled. For example, wireless phone companies introducing the concept of "rollover" minutes is a value-adding and service differentiation initiative. This concept is facilitated by information technology.

Initiative 6: Enhance Products or Services

Instead of differentiating a product or service, an organization may actually add to it to enhance its value to the consumer, called *product* or *service enhancement*. For example, car manufacturers may entice customers by offering a longer warranty period for their cars, and real-estate agents may attract more business by providing useful financing information to potential buyers.

Since the Internet opened its doors to commercial enterprises in the early 1990s, an increasing number of companies have supplemented their products and services. Their Web sites provide up-to-date information that helps customers utilize their purchased products better or receive additional services. Companies that pioneered such Internet use reaped great rewards.

For example, **Charles Schwab** gained a huge competitive advantage over other, older brokerage companies such as **Merrill Lynch** by opening a site for on-line stock transactions. Nearly half its revenue now comes from this site, while revenue from stock trading of brick-and-mortar brokers constantly diminishes.

Initiative 7: Establish Alliances

Companies can gain competitive advantage by combining services to make them more attractive (and usually less expensive) than purchasing services separately. These alliances provide two draws for customers: combined service is cheaper and one-stop shopping is more convenient. The travel industry is very aggressive in this area. For example, airlines collaborate with hotel chains and car-rental firms to offer travel and lodging packages and with credit-card companies that offer discount ticket purchases from particular airlines or the products of particular manufacturers. Credit-card companies commonly offer frequent flier miles for every dollar spent. In all these cases, alliances create competitive advantages.

As Exhibit 800.3 indicates, by creating an alliance, organizations enjoy synergy: the combined profit for the allies from the sales of a package of goods or services exceeds the profits earned when each acts individually. Sometimes, the alliances form more than two organizations. Consider the benefits **American Express** and its business partners offer. Clients who subscribe to a corporate charge card receive a quarterly management report summarizing expenses by category and by employee, a 10 percent discount on FedEx next-business-day delivery if they pay for shipping services with the American Express card, a 10 percent discount on **Kinko's** products and copying services, a 2 percent discount on **ExxonMobil** gasoline purchases, and travel and lodging discounts from **Hertz** and **Hilton** on car rentals and lodging, respectively.

Exhibit 800.3 *Strategic Alliances Combine Services to Create Synergies*

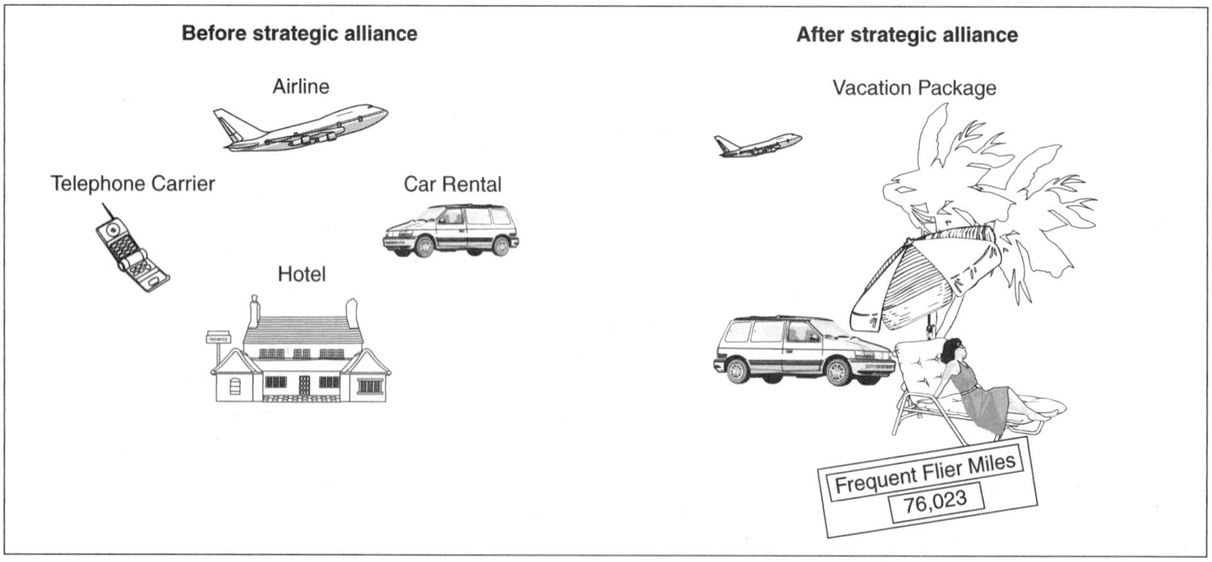

What is the common denominator of all these companies? An information system that tracks all these transactions and discounts. A package of attractive deals entices clients who need all these services (and most businesses do). Why purchase them without the discounts and other benefits? Would this offer be feasible without an IS to track transactions and discounts? Probably not.

Growing Web use for e-commerce has pushed organizations to create alliances that would be unimaginable a few years ago. Consider the alliance between **Hewlett-Packard** and FedEx. HP is a leading manufacturer of computers and computer equipment, known primarily for its excellent printers. FedEx, as we mentioned earlier, is a shipping company. HP maintains inventory of its products at FedEx facilities. When customers order items from HP via its Web site, HP routes the order, via the Web, to FedEx. FedEx packages the items and ships them to customers. This arrangement lets HP ship ordered items within hours rather than days. The alliance gives HP an advantage that other computer equipment makers do not share and gives HP a great volume of business from FedEx orders.

On the Web, the best examples of alliances are affiliate programs. Anyone who maintains a Web site can place links to commercial sites. Any purchase that results from clicking through to a commercial site rewards the first site's owner with a fee. Some on-line retailers have thousands of affiliates. The early adopters of such programs, Amazon.com, **Buy.com**, Priceline, and other large e-retailers, enjoyed a competitive advantage.

Initiative 8: Lock in Suppliers or Buyers

Organizations can achieve competitive advantage if they are powerful enough to lock either suppliers into their mode of operation or buyers to their product. Possessing bargaining power—the leverage to influence buyers and suppliers—is the key to this approach. As such, companies so large that suppliers and buyers must listen to their demands use this tactic nearly exclusively.

A firm gains bargaining power with a supplier either when the firm has few competitors or when the firm is a major competitor in its industry. In the former case, the fewer the companies that make up a supplier's customer base, the more important each company is to the supplier; in the latter case, the more important a specific company is to a supplier's success, the greater bargaining power that company has over that supplier.

The most common leverage in bargaining is purchase volume. Companies that spend millions of dollars purchasing parts and services have the power to force their suppliers to conform to their methods of operation, and even to shift some costs onto suppliers as part of the business arrangement. Consider **Wal-Mart**, the world's largest retailer. Not only does the company bring suppliers in for meetings in a warehouse where it badgers them to provide the lowest prices, but it also requires them to use information systems compatible with its own to automate processes.

One way to lock in *buyers* in a free market is to create the impression that an organization's product is significantly better than the competitors', or to enjoy a situation in which customers fear high switching costs. In the software arena, ERP (enterprise resource planning) applications are a good example. This type of software helps organizations manage a wide array of operations: purchasing, manufacturing, human resources, finance, and so forth. The software is expensive, costing hundreds of thousands or even millions of dollars. After a company purchases ERP software from a firm, it's locked to that firm's services: training, implementation, updates, and so forth. Thus, companies that sell ERP software, such as **SAP**, **Baan**, **PeopleSoft**, **J.D. Edwards**, and **Oracle**, make great efforts to improve both their software and support services to maintain leadership in this market.

Another way to lock in clients is by **creating a standard.** The software industry has pursued this strategy vigorously, especially in the Internet arena. For example, Microsoft's decision to give away its Web browser by letting both individuals and organizations download it free from its site was not altruistic. Microsoft executives knew that the greater the number of Internet Explorer users, the greater the user base. The greater the user base, the more likely organizations were to purchase Microsoft's proprietary software to help manage their Web sites. Also, once individual users committed to Internet Explorer as their main browser, they were likely to purchase Microsoft software that enhanced the browser's capabilities.

Similarly, **Adobe** gives away its Acrobat Reader software, an application that lets Web surfers open and manipulate documents created using different computers running different operating systems, such as IBM and Mac. When the Reader user base became large enough, organizations and individuals found it economically justifiable to purchase and use the writer application (the application used to create the documents) and related applications. Using this strategy put Adobe's PDF (portable data format) standard in an unrivaled position.

801. INFORMATION TECHNOLOGY STRATEGIES

Information Systems Planning

Key Steps in Information Systems Planning

Until the late 1970s, organizations planned without considering either the role IS professionals could take in the planning process or the planning that is necessary to create a productive IS department. Most companies called their IS units *data processing departments,* and data processing professionals were considered technicians who concentrated on automating processes rather than professionals who could help the organization achieve its goals. As indicated in several studies of the proliferation of IS use in corporate America in the 1970s, top management didn't realize for several years that the ISs themselves had to be planned, lest expenditures balloon uncontrollably. In the past, ISs were either not planned at all or planned bottom-up. Eventually, organizations recognized that the large amounts of time and money they spent on ISs required **IS planning**—for their deployment and for the resources needed to develop and maintain the systems. The modern approach to systems development is no longer based on reacting to emerging business needs, as it was earlier. Nowadays, ISs are often the core of business processes, and sometimes the generator of new revenue. Thus, IS managers are involved with short-range and long-range IS planning.

For example, because of their traditional focus, credit-card companies were accustomed to focusing on "processing data" and serving their existing customers well in that regard. Processing data was the main purpose of their ISs. Now, these same companies collect and use their data for many more reasons than just serving their customers' credit needs. The data are used in sophisticated data warehouses, data mining, and artificial intelligence techniques to gain more customers, create alliances with other organizations, and augment their market share by offering more services. When the focus is only to automate business processes, not much planning is required; however, when ISs are to be used for strategic purposes, planning is essential.

Not only do IS managers have to plan their activities, but now many organizations integrate their IS planning into their overall organizational strategic planning. Top management acknowledges that IT plays a role in generating business, not just in improving it in small increments. For example consider **Pep Boys**, the American auto service chain. The operations of such an organization may seem simple enough not to warrant the integration of ISs into its business planning. However, management does consider ISs in its plans, which has resulted in the development of a data warehouse of close to 2 TB (terabytes), one of the country's largest data warehouses. This warehouse is a major part of the company's long-range business plan. Among other activities, top management can use the data warehouse to find out which services are most popular with customers—information that serves a strategic purpose. The company can also use the data warehouse to continue to minimize customer returns due to car problems that were not fixed well the first time.

Reaction to needs only satisfies the needs, while planning can create opportunities. As Exhibit 800.4 indicates, IS planning has evolved over the past three decades to become fully integrated into organizations' strategic planning.

IS planning includes a few key steps that are a part of any successful planning process:

- Creating a corporate and IS mission statement
- Articulating the vision for IT within the organization

Exhibit 800.4 *Advances in Information Systems (IS) Planning Since the 1970s*

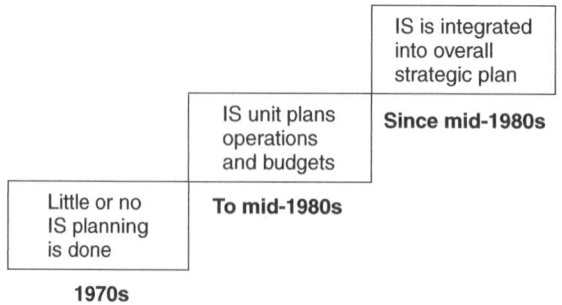

Exhibit 800.5 *The Steps of Information Systems (IS) Planning*

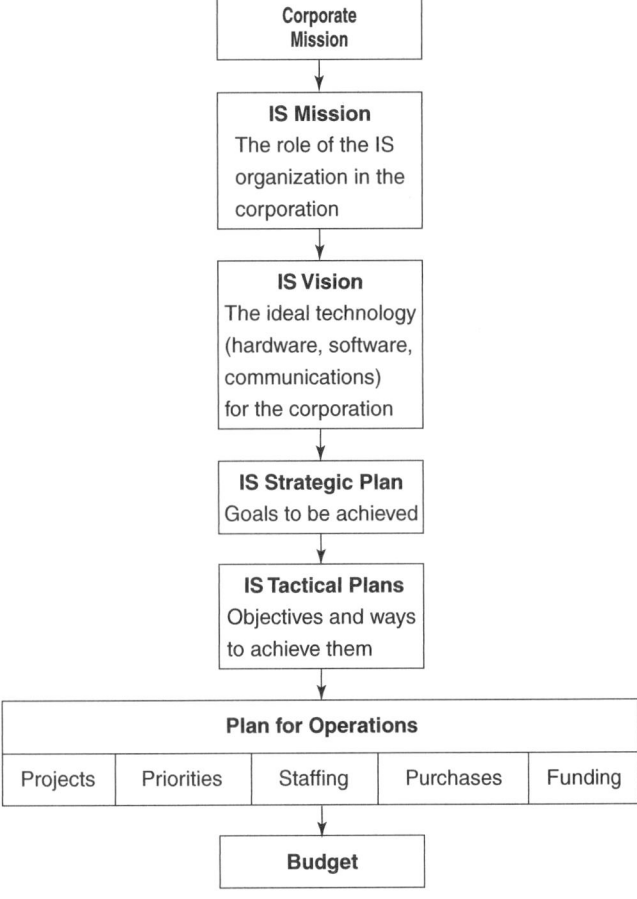

- Creating IS strategic and tactical plans
- Creating a plan for operations to achieve the mission and vision
- Creating a budget to ensure that resources are available to achieve the mission and vision (see Exhibit 800.5)

Note that the broadest, most overarching statement of an organization's purpose is sometimes referred to as its *mission* and sometimes as its *vision,* terms that are often used interchangeably. For example: a university may have a mission to provide the highest-quality education it can at affordable tuition, while attracting students from a wide range of social and economic backgrounds. Some people differentiate mission and vision by saying that the mission is a declared overall long-term purpose of the organization, and the vision is the general manner in which the mission will be accomplished.

The increasing need to collaborate both with suppliers and customers in e-commerce increases the complexity of IT planning. Now Chief Information Officers and Chief Technology Officers must not only plan their own company's ISs but also consider the ISs of their business partners. They must regard the systems of their suppliers, of their own company, and of their customers as if they were all one large system.

Prerequisites for Information Systems Planning

Several conditions must exist before effective IS planning can take place (see Exhibit 800.6), and the most important conditions relate to top management. First, top management must recognize that IT is an indispensable resource in all business activities. It must see that the impact IT has on an organization is at least as great as the impact of new manufacturing machinery and that it may significantly change the way an organization conducts its business. Without such recognition, senior managers may not agree to fund the acquisition of ISs.

Second, top management must understand that the development and use of ISs must be planned like any other complex resource. Executives must be aware that ISs are more than just computers; they are hardware, software,

Exhibit 800.6 *Prerequisites for Effective IS Planning*

> **For IS planning to be successful, top management must:**
> - Recognize IT as an indispensable resource
> - Understand that IT is a complex resource
> - Regard IT as owned by the entire organization
> - Regard ISs as a source for gaining strategic goals
> - View ISs as a tool to control power

telecommunications, people, procedures, and data. The interplay among these components must be planned to avoid waste. If the implementation is not planned well, the organization may end up with a hodgepodge of hardware and software that do not integrate well to serve the organization. While senior managers are rarely technical experts, they can always rely on internal and external advisors to explain issues such as hardware obsolescence and software incompatibility.

Third, top management must see IT as a resource owned by all members of the organization, not just the IS unit. Its development and use should be planned like human resources, manufacturing machinery, and finances.

Fourth, top management must realize that ISs are a source for achieving strategic goals, rather than merely for solving problems or supporting existing business processes. For example, top management is more likely to approve the acquisition of ISs that help augment the company's market share or sustain its position in a highly competitive market than the acquisition of computers that seemingly only make some employees happier.

Fifth, since information is power, ISs influence the distribution of power. Top management should be aware of how this power is granted or denied and should integrate that understanding into planning ISs. Top management's involvement in planning may help minimize political struggles while ensuring that employees are given appropriate access to IT resources.

When top managers recognize these realities, they ensure that ISs are planned and that IS plans become an integral part of the organizational plan.

The Corporate and IS Mission Statements

As we discussed, strategic planning starts with a corporate mission statement that details the purpose of the organization and its overall goals. These general goals provide a framework within which the organization's strategic goals will be formulated. For example, such a goal may be to become the nation's largest car-rental company. Once the corporate mission has been articulated, then each business function formulates its own mission, consistent with the organization's mission.

Although the organization's mission statement will usually not mention the IS function specifically, the IS mission statement reflects how the IS management sees its place in the organization and its responsibilities. The statement outlines the purpose of ISs in the organization. Note that the terms *IS* and *IT* are used interchangeably.

The IT Vision

As part of the mission statement, or as a separate document, the IS managers draft their vision paper. This draft is a wish list of what these professionals would like to see in terms of hardware, software, and communications, to contribute to the overall goals of the organization. For example, it may detail the following: (1) every knowledge worker who needs access to databases or business applications will have a desktop computer from which to access the resources, (2) all desktop computers will be connected by a local area network and the Internet to provide e-mail, Internet, intranet, and extranet services, (3) clients will be able to access some corporate databases through communications lines, if corporate strategy so requires, and so on. Obviously, the list may be changed as business needs change, or as new technology emerges.

Strategic and Tactical Information Systems Planning

The IS strategic plan, a part of the overall organizational strategic plan, is a more detailed extension of the IS vision paper, detailing *what* is to be achieved, with a list of specific goals. The IS tactical plan breaks down strategic goals into objectives that together describe *how* and *when* the strategic goals will be achieved. The strategic plan is established for the long run, such as three to five years, while the tactical plan usually covers one to three years. All tactical plans are subsections of the strategic plan.

Exhibit 800.7 *Rigid and Dynamic Planning*

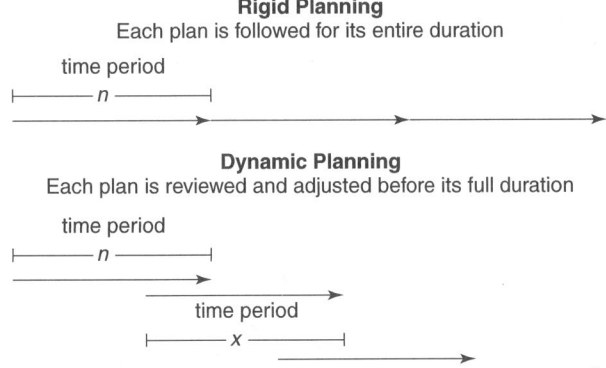

For example, a strategic *goal* may be the desire to provide end users with more flexible access to databases and tools to develop their own database applications. This goal will be translated into the tactical plan of advancing toward a client/server architecture. Of course, there are different levels of client/server architecture, and different ways to achieve this goal, which would have to be itemized in the plan for operations.

Each objective has a plan for operations, detailing the tasks involved, the department that will carry out the assignment or assignments, and the time frame within which they will be accomplished. For each objective, the plan also provides a list of resources needed to achieve the objective: personnel, hardware, software, and purchased services.

What happens after the strategic plan is in place? Although strategic plans are made for the long run, they are usually not rigid (that is, unchanged for a long period of time). Most strategic plans are dynamic—they are examined and revised relatively frequently (see Exhibit 800.7). Many organizations, especially in industries characterized by frequent change, review their plans annually or biannually and change them if necessary. Dynamic strategic IS plans are more prevalent now than several years ago because of the tremendous developments in IT: hardware and software become obsolete faster than they used to; the variety of hardware and software is much greater; and there are many more types of telecommunications lines and services. The emergence of the Web as a major vehicle for e-commerce has also made IS planning more complex. Thus, many organizations prefer to update their strategic IS plans frequently.

To translate the IS tactical objectives into action, a plan for operations is created based on the tactical plan. At this stage, projects are defined and assigned resources, including staff and funds, for execution. As the personnel and funds are allocated, the IS budget is developed. Often, management lets the new project managers select their own staff.

Large-scale projects are often lengthy and may take several years to complete. In such cases, an organization often refers to the project as an organizational unit, and the project manager is considered the head of that unit. Once the project is completed, the staff is disbanded and assigned to other projects. Realize, however, that many IS projects are not over when a new system is installed. The maintenance of a system is an ongoing effort for which dedicated professionals, sometimes working full-time, are required. It is not unusual for a project to last three or five years. Sometimes, the development team of an IS becomes a permanent organizational unit in charge of the maintenance and continual upgrading of the system. This was the case with SABRE, the pioneer airline reservation system at **American Airlines**. The project team was later spun off as a sister corporation to American Airlines, **Sabre Inc.**, and is the leading provider of technology for the travel industry.

Important Factors in IS Tactical Planning

Many IS issues are decided in the analysis and design phase of IS development, which usually follows the planning phase. However, some issues are not specific to individual systems, and they should be considered at the planning stage:

- *Flexibility.* Flexibility is the degree to which an organization can use the same hardware or software for different business functions, in different physical and logical environments, over time. Careful planning enables IS planners to designate which equipment and software may be used anywhere in an organization. Planning also allows an organization to select the best hardware and software for the long run, even if they may not be used at their optimal levels in the short run. Many companies that fail to consider flexibility of IS resources and their long-term implications find their resources are quickly obsolete. They then incur the extra costs involved in acquiring additional resources.

- *Compatibility.* Computers and peripheral equipment are not always compatible. Although different business units may prefer computers from different vendors, buying the same product for the entire enterprise may be necessary to ensure software, hardware, and telecommunications compatibility. Similarly, planners must consider how compatible software packages are, so that workers from different departments can import and share data. For example, if an organization is already committed to a certain database management system (DBMS) and is looking for a new electronic spreadsheet program, IS planners should develop a list of spreadsheet programs that are compatible with the DBMS. This way, workers will be able to import data from the database to their own spreadsheet and vice versa.
- *Connectivity.* IS planners, particularly those concerned with planning communications networks, should participate in the decision-making process for hardware and software to allow maximum connectivity among the organization's computers. Although Internet protocols and Web technologies have made it easier to link with other businesses and with consumers, some issues will need to be considered. For example, ActiveX applets run only on PCs that run Windows, and some Web pages look different when viewed with different browsers.
- *Scalability.* Scalability refers to how easy it is to augment hardware and software and their use as the business grows.

    A small organization may have one person handle all accounting data entry and report generation. As an organization grows, clerks are added to form an accounts receivable department. At that point, several people may need to use the system from their PCs at the same time. As the organization continues to grow, the accounts receivable personnel may be divided geographically or by type of customer, with separate accounts receivable departments for each. Scalability allows an organization going through change to continue providing the same features and speed of processing as when the system was used by a single employee.

    Scalability is extremely important for any organization that is engaged in e-commerce. Typically, business at a Web site starts slowly and grows in time. As the number of inquiries and transactions grows, the organization needs to add servers to handle the growing traffic. Forethought allows smooth growth of the hardware, software, and communications links by adding components instead of throwing away elements of the site and rebuilding it.

- *Standardization.* Many organizations have set standards requiring all business units to use certain hardware and software. IS managers must periodically evaluate the appropriateness of the standards and determine whether they should be maintained or updated. A grid of factors can be used to consider replacement or continuing maintenance of resources, according to the level of functional and technical quality of the resource. To assist in that type of decision, planners can map hardware pieces used by the organization in a two-dimensional diagram (see Exhibit 800.8). The two dimensions are the degree to which the hardware supports a business process (its functional quality) and the technical quality of the hardware in general. The assessment of technical quality is highly dependent on the introduction by manufacturers of similar equipment with higher quality (such as similar equipment that is more reliable, has easier-to-use features, offers faster performance, and the like). The decision may be to maintain the hardware, discard it (retire it), or upgrade or replace it.
- *Total cost of ownership.* Obviously, any planning decision must also include cost implications. In recent years, CIOs have started realizing that costs involved in the adoption of IT are not all apparent at a first glance—but they may be

Exhibit 800.8 *Hardware Planning*

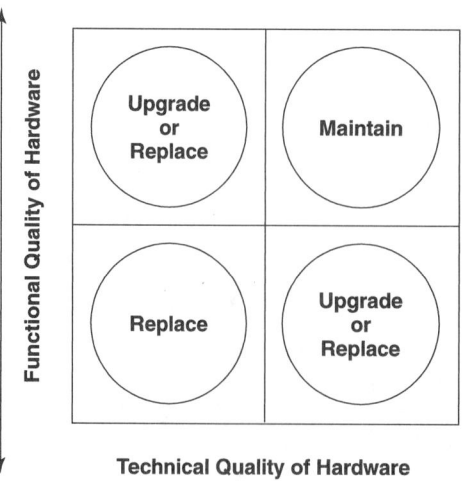

quite high. These hidden costs include time taken from employees' regular jobs for training in the use of new hardware or software, the time-prorated cost of software that cannot run on the new computers, the cost of help-desk time due to the adoption of new hardware or software, and others. Some research firms have concluded, for example, that the actual cost of a new PC purchased for an office worker may reach 10 times the cost of the computer itself.

IS Planning Initiatives

Where do IS planners get information about new IS needs, problems, and opportunities within their organizations? Four groups of people within an organization can initiate consideration of new or improved ISs, each with a different perspective: top management, line managers, users, and IS professionals (see Exhibit 800.9). Typically, top managers are concerned with strategic information systems and enterprise-wide applications because they consider the impact of such systems on the entire organization or on major parts of it. IS professionals usually draw attention to new technologies, hardware, software, and telecommunications and suggest ways to use them to improve business processes. Line managers may initiate consideration of new or improved ISs after they have talked to colleagues from other organizations or read an article in a trade journal. Users inquire how new or improved ISs can solve problems they encounter in their daily work.

Members of top management, such as a CIO, CTO, or another senior executive, typically consider new strategic ISs that can affect the entire organization. By comparison, line managers, who observe their staff daily, often recommend ISs that would improve business processes and staff performance. Users are most familiar with the strengths and weaknesses of existing systems and therefore are best qualified to recommend ways in which IS performance could be made more efficient and effective. Through discussions with their peers from competing organizations, these users also often bring ideas about better ISs to their own organizations.

Although modern IS planning and development holds that change initiatives should come from business managers, IS managers who are familiar with business processes can often see how a new technology could create a business opportunity. As a result, the initiative for IS planning and systems development may come from several sources. The results of one survey of CEOs and other executives indicates that business unit managers, IT managers, and top executives all initiate consideration of new IS development projects.

The Champion

Although a true business need usually spurs new system development, there may not be universal support from all members of an organization. For political or rational reasons, some managers may object to the development. In addition, top management is always wary of proposals that require a commitment of resources, and executives usually request substantive justification for the expense. A sound business and technical proposal for a new system is usually not enough for top management to endorse the new effort. The project needs a *champion:* a high-ranking officer who

Exhibit 800.9 *IS Planning Can Be Driven by a Variety of Sources*

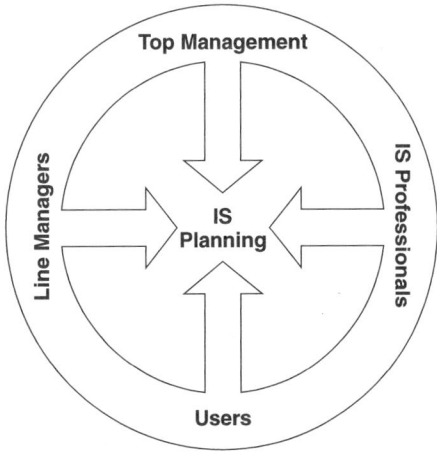

commands sufficient political clout to promote the idea that a new system is needed and—when the go-ahead is granted—to remove obstacles as the project progresses. The champion represents the top management interest in the new system. The most effective champions are executives who are not IS professionals. Their grounding in other business functions lends credence to their argument that the organization needs the system for a business operation, rather than just for the glory of the IS staff. It also conveys the impression that the champion is not influenced by narrow self-centered considerations.

A successful champion is a true leader who can do the following:

- Promote the vision of information technology in the organization
- Inspire top management and subordinates alike
- Remove barriers to realizing the vision
- Focus on both short-term and long-term objectives
- Be a torchbearer for making change happen
- Drive accountability to the lowest organizational level, so that all who are involved in the development of the new IS (1) feel responsible and therefore committed to succeeding in their roles and (2) are ready to report their progress at any time

Sometimes, the ideal champion is actually a pair of people: an IT manager as technical champion paired with a management champion. The technical manager takes responsibility for product evaluation, planning, and implementation, while the management champion helps deal with corporate culture, political issues, convincing top management of the return on investment (ROI), and the application of the new system to specific business problems.

Although champions often do not come from the ranks of IS professionals, practice shows that overall leadership skills coupled with IT knowledge create champions who drive their organizations to the forefront of business technology use. One of **Citicorp's** (now part of **Citigroup**) CEOs was the main reason the company became a leader in the use of ATMs and other advanced systems, which gave the corporation strategic advantages. The CEO of **Circuit City**, a former IS officer, championed the development and implementation of the most advanced IS in that company's market. Executives from competing electronic appliance chains admit that Circuit City's integrated inventory and customer service system is superior to theirs.

The Systems Analyst as an Agent of Change

Planning almost always deals with change: changing methods, changing the structure of business units, and changing the way workers receive, process, and communicate information. However, the physical law of inertia also applies to people. As objects will continue to move in the same direction unless their course is changed, so do people wish to continue to act in the same manner, unless they have to change. The changes created by new ISs force people to learn new procedures and use new technologies, which many people dislike, particularly if they have performed their jobs the same way for many years. Resistance to change is especially strong if the changes reward the organization but not the individual employee—the employee may perceive no tangible incentive to change.

When the change being addressed relates to developing or implementing a new IS, the systems analyst is often the agent of change who must not only explain how the system will improve business performance but also train individuals in the use of the new system (see Exhibit 800.10). To gain cooperation, the analyst must convince users that the new system will help them in their work. For instance, to clerical staff, the benefits of the new system may be a more relaxed working environment, the satisfaction of creating greater output with less effort, and, often, the satisfaction of learning how to operate a more sophisticated system and enhance work skills. The systems analyst must be a good listener. He or

Exhibit 800.10   *The Role of a System Analyst*

(Systems analysts facilitate change by motivating, educating, and training.)

she must carefully listen to employees who will use the new system and to their managers, so that the features of the system can best fit their needs.

In the past, the popular view held that the implementation of a new IS would be handled almost exclusively by the systems analyst, who would communicate almost no information until the time came to train personnel to use the system. It is now recognized that (1) the changes involved in a new IS must be communicated to employees well before the new system is delivered to them and (2) education, not just training, is a key success factor. Much of this burden is on the shoulders of the systems analyst.

Information Technology Risk Management

Risks to Information Systems

While stories about damage caused to ISs by malicious Internet attacks are popular, the truth about risks to ISs is simpler: the number-one cause of systems downtime is hardware failure. The next two contributors are fire and theft. In recent years, especially because of the growth of on-line business, corporations have considered protection of their IS resources an increasingly important issue, for good reasons. Exhibit 800.11 provides a sample of average losses in some types of businesses when ISs go down. We discuss next the most pervasive risks to IS operations.

Risks to Hardware

Risks to hardware involve physical damage to computers, peripheral equipment, and communications media. The major causes of such damage are natural disasters, blackouts and brownouts, and vandalism.

Natural Disasters

Natural disasters that pose a risk to ISs include fires, floods, earthquakes, hurricanes, tornadoes, and lightning, which can destroy hardware, software, or both, causing total or partial paralysis of systems or communications lines. Floodwater short-circuits and burns delicate components such as microchips. Lightning and voltage surges cause tiny wires to melt and destroy circuitry. Obviously, all data and programs stored in memory chips in a computer are lost when this happens. Water from floods and the heat created when circuits are shorted may also ruin the surface of storage media such as magnetic disks and tapes, thereby destroying data. In addition, wildlife and human error occasionally destroy communications lines, animals gnaw cables, and farmers occasionally cut wires inadvertently while tending their crops. The easiest way to protect against loss of data caused by natural disasters (but not only by natural disasters) is to automatically duplicate all data periodically and store the duplicate copy in a site many miles away from the office, as explained later.

Exhibit 800.11 *Cost per Hour of System Downtime*

Industry	Business Operation	Cost per Hour of Downtime
Financial	Brokerage	$6,450,000
Financial	Credit Card Authorization	$2,600,000
Financial	ATM Fees	$ 14,500
Retail	Home Catalog Sales	$ 90,000
Transportation	Airline Reservations	$ 89,500
Media	Ticket Sales	$ 69,000

Source: *Dataquest*, 2000.

Where natural damage is concerned, communications media are among the most vulnerable parts of a system because they run outside the confines of an organization's operation. Although they add significantly to the cost of communications hardware, thick protective sheaths made of special plastics protect communications cables and wires. But when lightning strikes a power line or telephone line to which a computer is connected, the computer is usually damaged. Surge protectors and similar devices that simply disconnect power to the machine rarely protect it from lightning.

Blackouts and Brownouts

Computers run on electricity. If power is disrupted, the computer and its peripheral devices cannot function, and the change in power supply can be very damaging to computer processes and storage. **Blackouts** are total losses of electrical power. In **brownouts,** the voltage of the power decreases, or there are very short interruptions in the flow of power. Power failure may not only disrupt operations but also cause irreparable damage to hardware. Occasional surges in voltage are equally harmful, because their impact on equipment is similar to that of lightning.

The popular way of handling brownouts is to connect a voltage regulator between computers and the electric network. A voltage regulator boosts or decreases voltage to smooth out drops or surges and maintains voltage within an acceptable tolerance.

To ensure against interruptions in power supply, organizations use **uninterruptible power supply (UPS) systems,** which provide an alternative power supply for a short time, as soon as a power network fails. The only practical measure against prolonged blackouts in a public electrical network is to buy and maintain a separate generator that uses gasoline or another fuel. Once the general power stops, the generator can kick in and produce the power needed for the computer system.

Vandalism

Vandalism occurs when human beings deliberately destroy computer systems. Bitter customers may damage ATMs, or disgruntled employees may destroy computer equipment out of fear that it will eliminate their jobs or simply to get even with their superiors. For instance, several years ago, postal service employees stuck paperclips in a new computer that sorted mail because they feared the new system would eliminate jobs.

It is difficult to defend computers against vandalism. ATMs and other equipment that are accessible to the public are often encased in metal boxes, but someone with persistence can still cause severe damage. In the workplace, the best measure against vandalism is to allow access only to those who have a real need for the system. Sensitive equipment, such as servers, should be locked in a special room.

Risks to Applications and Data

All computer systems are susceptible to disruption and damage. While the culprit in the destruction of hardware is often some natural disaster or power spike, the culprit in damage to software is almost always human. The major risks to software applications and data are theft of information; data alteration, destruction, and defacement; computer viruses and logic bombs; and nonmalicious mishaps.

Theft of Information

Before the advent of electronic computers, most businesses kept secret information in a safe. A thief had to physically tear a locking mechanism out or illegally obtain a key to the safe. Now even the most sensitive information is usually stored electronically somewhere on a company's information system. Today's electronic equivalent of the physical key is a code, a combination of characters that is needed to access secured data. Before the computer age, large amounts of data meant a lot of paper, which was awkward to steal and awkward to hide when stolen. These days, thousands of pages filled with information can be stored on a small magnetic disk, making information easier to steal (as the following story shows), and also easier to hide.

The leading causes of data loss are power failure/surge (45.3%), storm damage (9.4%), fire/explosion (8.2%), hardware/software error (8.2%), flood and water damage (6.7%), earthquake (5.5%), network outage (4.5%), human error/sabotage (3.2%), HVAC failure (2.3%), and miscellaneous (6.7%).

Source: Levine, D.E., "A Guide to UPS," Datamation, May 23, 2001, itmanagement.earthweb.com.

A young man worked in the research and development department of an international food company that had over 100 microcomputers in its headquarters.

In 1985 he inserted his own disk into a computer that held the formulas for flavoring products of a successful food line; he made a copy of the information and sent the disk to a former manager, who worked for a competitor. Since the manager did not know how to print out the information from the disk, he gave it to a service company to do it for him. The service person noticed that the name of the manager's company was different from the company name appearing on the printout and notified the victim company. Managers at the company had been wondering how the competitor kept introducing similar products so soon after their own new products came on the market; now they understood.

Data Alteration, Data Destruction, and Defacement

Alteration or destruction of data is often an act of mischief (in which case it is called "data diddling"). In San Francisco, **United States Leasing International** found one morning that data in its files were replaced with curses and names that should not have been there. In this case, the damage was financial: employees spent time searching for all the changed records and correcting them. In other cases, however, computer pranks such as these can put people's lives at risk.

In 1983, a group of Milwaukee teenagers accessed a computer system at Sloan-Kettering Cancer Research Institute in New York via a modem and altered patients' records just for "fun." An alert nurse noticed a double—and lethal—dose of a medication in a patient's record and called a doctor. She saved the patient's life.

In a survey conducted by the American Bar Association's Task Force on Computer Crime, respondents ranked "destruction or alteration of data" as the most significant type of computer crime. A related crime, "destruction or alteration of software," was ranked second. These two crimes are the dreaded nightmares of chief information officers and database administrators. It is not only the effort to reinstate missing or altered records that causes financial damage. Even if the actual damage is not great, IS staff must spend a lot of time scanning the data pools to ascertain the integrity of the entire resource, and they must also figure out how the perpetrator managed to circumvent security controls. This activity itself wastes the time of high-salaried employees.

Since organizations started establishing Web sites, hackers—people who access information systems without permission—have had a new target: Web pages. Each day, some organizations find their Web sites have been defaced. In the best-case scenario, Web defacement is the cyber equivalent of street graffiti—someone adds offensive text or pictures to the page. In the worst-case scenario, pages are totally replaced with offensive content. Defacement causes several types of damage: first-time visitors are not likely to stay around long enough or revisit to learn about the true nature of the site, and they may associate the offensive material with the organization; frequent visitors may never come back; and shoppers who have had a good experience with the site may leave it forever because they no longer trust its security measures.

To deface a Web site, an intruder needs to know the site's access code or codes that enable the Webmaster and other authorized people to work on the site's server and update its pages. The intruder may either obtain the codes from someone who knows them or use special software that "tries and errs" until it succeeds in accessing the pages.

Sometimes hackers do not vandalize Web pages but replace them with their own pages to send a social or political message. On July 25, 2001, hackers paid a visit to the site of the official Palestinian news agency. A title in Hebrew was placed at the top of the homepage: "Crimes committed by the Palestinian Authority and Palestinian leaders." The new page showed 137 pictures of Israelis killed in the preceding 10 months of violence. Small images of memorial candles were placed between pictures. The director of the news agency accused Israeli hackers of the deed.

Attrition (www.attrition.org), a Web site that publishes statistics on computer security breaches, reported that in the period between August 1999 and January 2001, 8,071 different Web sites were broken into and subsequently defaced. The best measure against defacement, of course, is software that protects against unauthorized access. However, since such software may fail, the public damage may be minimized by ensuring that some members of the organization monitor the home page and other essential pages frequently. When the defacement is detected shortly after it occurs, the defaced pages can be replaced with the original ones before too many visitors have seen the rogue pages.

The cure to any unauthorized entry to an IS is to find the "hole" in its security software and fix it with the appropriate software. Such software is often called a "patch." Software companies that sell server management applications often produce patches and invite clients to download and install them.

Computer Viruses and Logic Bombs

A biological virus is a microorganism that attacks the living cells of a host, either a human being or another animal. It penetrates the cells, multiplies, and then causes the cells to burst, thereby destroying them. It is rapidly transmitted from one living creature to another. Computer viruses are usually a few lines of programming code that are inserted in a legitimate program that is later copied and activated by unwary users. **Computer viruses** are so named because they act on programs and data in a fashion similar to the way viruses act on living tissue: computer viruses easily spread from computer to computer. Since so many computers are now connected to one another, and since we share many of our files with other people, we unknowingly transmit to other computers viruses that have infected our own files. Once a virus reaches a computer, it damages applications and data files. In addition to destroying legitimate applications and data files, viruses may disrupt data communications: the presence of viruses causes data communications applications to process huge numbers of messages and files for no useful purpose, which detracts from the efficiency of transmitting and receiving legitimate messages and files.

Exhibit 800.12 shows the results of a survey of 745 respondents about the frequency of security breaches they experienced. The survey was completed by *Information Security Magazine* readers, a pool of respondents that includes administrators, managers, and executives in IT, security, networking, and data management. Evidently, more companies experienced viruses than any other threat to their information systems.

Viruses are spread by way of copying infected software from someone else's disk or by receiving infected software from another computer through a communications link. A virus that spreads through networks is also called a *worm*. Because millions of people use e-mail, computer networks, especially the Internet, make it easy to spread a computer virus. The worst viruses are those that attach themselves to operating systems. As you already know, the operating system is the large program that manages and controls all basic computer resources. Since the operating system interacts with every program and data file that is used in the computer, a virus in an operating system can damage every file used.

Almost all viruses are now spread through the Internet, and almost always by e-mail. The Melissa virus of 1999, the Love Bug of 2000, and the SirCam virus of 2001 demonstrated why you should be suspicious of e-mail messages even when they seemingly come from people or organizations you know.

One way to protect against viruses is to use **antivirus software,** which is readily available on the market from companies that specialize in developing this kind of software. The problem with virus-detection software, however, is that it is usually designed to intercept only known viruses. If a new virus is designed to operate in a way not yet known, the software is unlikely to detect it. Sometimes the software can only detect a virus, but not destroy it. The user then must delete the suspect file. Most virus-detection applications allow the user to automatically, or selectively, destroy suspect programs.

Software firms that specialize in antivirus applications have also decided to fight viruses in more original ways. One method implemented by **Symantec** is the remote cure approach. A special application runs on the PCs of subscriber companies. The application periodically scans for unidentified viruses at the subscribers' sites. When a suspected virus is found, the application sends the infected file via the Internet to Symantec's labs, where the virus is tricked into believing that it is running on a desktop computer. Actually, it is running on a mainframe computer, and it is tricked into replicating (which is what viruses do). By tracking what the virus does, a special program tries to create a cure in the form of software fix. The "antidote" software is sent to the company's PC, again via the Internet.

As the Melissa, Love Bug, SirCam and similar viruses teach us, it is wise to reject e-mail messages even from known sources if the topic, timing, or circumstances are suspicious. It may also be prudent to use features such as macros judiciously. Many computer users are not aware that some documents contain macros. When you open a document that contains macros, your computer is at the mercy of the macro—that is, the person who wrote it. This sneak attack by

Exhibit 800.12 *Frequency of Security Breaches in a 12-month Period Based on a Survey of 745 Professionals*

Type of Breach	Respondents Reporting Breach	% Responding
Viruses	573	77
Employee access abuse	388	52
Unauthorized access by outsiders	175	23
Theft/destruction of computing resources	170	23
Leak of proprietary information	137	18
Theft/destruction of data	110	15
Access abuse by nonemployee	101	14
Hacking of phone/PBX/voice-mail system	86	12
Other	37	5

Source: Briney, A., "Got Security?" *Information Security Magazine*, 1999.

something appearing to be innocent is the reason why viruses such as the Love Bug (also called Love Letter) are often called "Trojan horses." In their war against Troy, the Greeks pretended they were abandoning the city's outskirts and left behind a big wooden horse as a present. The Trojans pulled the horse into the city. When night fell, Greek soldiers hidden within the horse jumped out and opened the gates for thousands of their comrades, who by then had secretly landed back on the city's shores. They conquered the city. Similarly, electronic Trojan horses are accepted innocently and then wreak havoc.

Some rogue computer programs do not spread immediately like a virus but are often significantly more damaging to the individual organization that is victimized. A **logic bomb** is software that is programmed to cause damage at a specified time to specific applications and data files. It lies dormant until a certain event takes place in the computer or until the computer's inner clock reaches the specified time; the event or time triggers the virus to start causing damage. Logic bombs are usually planted by insiders, that is, employees of the victimized organization.

Nonmalicious Mishaps

Unintentional damage to software occurs because of (1) poor training, (2) lack of adherence to simple backup procedures, or (3) simple human error. Although unintentional damage rarely occurs in robust applications, poor training may result in inappropriate use of an application so that it ruins data, unbeknownst to the user. For instance, when faced with an instruction that may change or delete data, a robust application will pose a question such as: "Are you sure you want to delete the record?" or issue a warning such as "This may destroy the file." More common damage is caused by the failure to save all work and create a backup copy. Destruction of data often happens when using a word-processing program to create text files and when updating databases.

Accidental damage to computer systems also occurs through installation of unauthorized peripheral equipment and unauthorized downloading and installation of software. The latter has been made easy thanks to the ubiquitous links to the Internet. A survey of 1,897 IS professionals from different organizations found that 48 percent of all IS security breaches were accidental. The respondents were unsure about 35 percent of the incidents and said only 17 percent could be confirmed as deliberate.

Risks to On-line Operations

The massive movement of operations to the Internet has attracted hackers who try to interrupt such operations daily. In addition to unauthorized access, data theft, and defacing of Web pages, there has been a surge in denial of service attacks. A more sophisticated but less frequent phenomenon is *spoofing*.

Denial of Service

One day in February 2000, traders at the stock brokerage firm **National Discount Brokers Group** noticed unusual activity at the firm's Web site. Customers who wanted to send buy and sell orders could not log on to the site, but the servers were experiencing heavy traffic. Many of the firm's 200,000 customers were unable to place stock orders through the firm's Web site, forcing them to relay orders on the telephone. Apparently, the site was experiencing a denial of service attack.

Denial of service (**DoS**) occurs when too many requests are received to log on to a Web site's pages. The intention of such log-in requests is to slow down legitimate traffic on the site's server, and business can slow down even to a halt. Multiple log-in requests may be perpetrated by a single person who uses specially designed software that automatically repeats requests for a long period of time. The server's or servers' frantic efforts to handle the massive amount of traffic denies legitimate visitors and business partners access to the site, and hence its name.

Such attacks can also be perpetrated from multiple computers, in which case they are called **distributed denial of service** (**DDoS**). DDoSs can be an orchestrated attack by people who have agreed to send multiple log-in requests to a site at the same time. However, most such attacks are more sophisticated; the perpetrator launches software that uses other people's computers for the attack—unbeknownst to them. Professionals call the computers used in these attacks *zombies* because of their mindless response to destructive commands. Zombie computers not only exacerbate the volume of calls but also make it impossible to track down the generator of the DDoS.

There is no apparent cure for a DoS attack, because it is impossible to stop anyone from trying to log on to a Web site. When managers realize that their site is being attacked, they usually shut it down for several hours, hoping that the attackers will get discouraged and go away. Network professionals can also try to detect the IP addresses from which a large number of requests are coming and program the server not to accept any requests from that particular server. However, blocking requests may also deny access to legitimate visitors, especially if the server is used by an ISP who provides Internet access to thousands of people and organizations. One way to mitigate DoS attacks is for an organization to use multiple servers, which is a good idea anyway to handle times of legitimate traffic increases.

No organization is immune to DDoS. Some of the most visible Web sites have been attacked, including those of **eBay**, **Amazon**, **CNN**, and the U.S. White House. All had to shut down their sites for several hours. eBay, Amazon, and other sites have lost revenue as a result. Even the Computer Emergency Response Team (CERT) was forced to shut down its site in May 2001 for 30 hours. A DDoS attack sent information into its Web site at rates several hundred times higher than normal. A 2001 report from the University of California at San Diego reveals that there are 4,000 DDoS attacks somewhere in the world each week.

Spoofing

Imagine someone hung a sign above the entrance to your store in a busy mall telling shoppers the store was closed and sending them to a competing store. For several hours you are not aware of the sign. When the equivalent happens on the Web, the act is called *spoofing*. Spoofing on the Internet may mean satirizing a Web site. But in recent years **spoofing** has also come to mean deception for the purpose of gaining access, or deception of users to make them think they are logged on to a certain Web site while they actually are logged on to another.

Most spoofing attacks are designed to embarrass organizations, but security experts worry that spoofing techniques may take a more sinister angle: a serious spoofing attack may result in massive fraud. During spoofing, the perpetrator takes advantage of certain vulnerabilities in domain name system (DNS) software. When a user types a domain name into her browser, the local DNS server sends a query through the Internet's distributed hierarchical DNS to look up the matching IP address for that domain name. Spoofers manipulate the DNS software so that the path to the IP address is redirected; visitors believe they are connected to the requested server when in fact they are connected to another. This interception and redirection is akin to someone switching your name with someone else's in a telephone directory so you receive all that person's calls.

On June 21, 2000, a group of hackers calling themselves S-11 victimized the site of **Nike**, the athletic shoe manufacturer. They redirected traffic from www.nike.com to the servers of a Scotland-based ISP. The hijacking lasted 6 to 24 hours, depending on the schedules on which different ISPs reloaded the Nike Web site. People who tried to access Nike's site were instead sent to one that criticized the company and the World Economic Forum, a pro-capitalism group that includes Nike as a member. Nike's sales through its Web site did not suffer significantly, but the spoof caused much consternation among businesses. Spoofing requires knowledge and sophistication on the perpetrator's part, and it does not occur often. Experts are working on solutions to vulnerabilities of DNS software to such acts.

Decision Making and Information Technology

Managers and Their Information Systems

Employees at different levels in an organization must make decisions that vary in scope and type. Exhibit 800.13 shows the traditional view of the types of information systems needed for an organization's different operational and managerial levels. While these relationships generally hold true, information needs vary widely in practice. With computer-based information systems making information available throughout organizational hierarchies, these traditional correlations can become blurred.

Exhibit 800.13 *Types of Information Systems Typically Used at Different Levels of an Organization's Hierarchy*

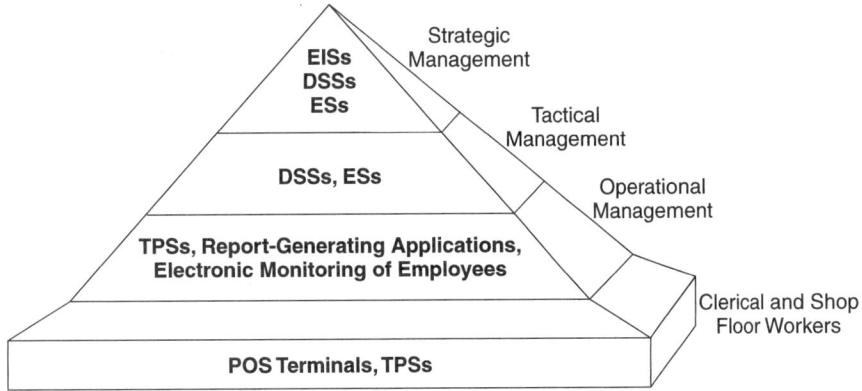

Types of Information Systems

An organization's information technology consists of the hardware, software, telecommunications, database management, and other technologies it uses to store data and make them available in the form of information for organizational decision making. Most managers today appreciate the value of making information readily available in some kind of formal, computer-based information system (CBIS). The CBIS supports organizational information and communication needs. The CBIS is a single set of hardware, software, database, telecommunications, people, and procedures that are configured to collect, manipulate, store, and process data into information. The CBIS can be operated in a batch or online mode. Payroll system is an example of batch processing where it accumulates all transactions throughout the day. At midnight, all transactions are processed and master files are updated.

A CBIS has three elements: inputs, processing, and outputs. For example, time sheets are inputs, payroll checks are outputs, and processing is payroll and deduction calculations. An example of processing is when an Internet browser transforms HTML code into a graphical display on a computer screen. Outputs can be reports, which can be classified as routine and exception. An example of routine output is giving the customer a receipt at a cash register in a department store. Trigger points are defined to produce exception reports.

One way to distinguish among the many types of information systems is to focus on the functions they perform and the people they serve in an organization. Two broad categories of information systems include operations information systems (OISs) and management information systems (MISs). OIS support information-processing needs of a business's day-to-day operations, as well as low-level operations management functions. Elements of OIS include transaction processing systems, process control systems, and office automation systems. MIS typically support the strategic decision-making needs of higher-level managers. Elements of MIS include information-reporting systems, decision support systems, executive information systems, and groupware. Other types of information systems include enterprise resource planning (ERP), customer relationship management (CRM), on-line analytical processing (OLAP) and on-line transaction processing (OLTP) systems.

Operations Information Systems

Operations information systems support daily operations and decisions that typically are made by nonmanagement employees or lower-level managers.

Transaction Processing Systems (TPSs) record and process data resulting from business operations. Workers at the bottom of the organizational hierarchy use point-of-sale terminals, order-entry systems, and other TPSs to enter data at its source at the time transactions take place. These data are the raw materials for producing useful information. One objective of any TPS is error-free data input and processing. Elements of TPS include data entry, data editing, data manipulation, data correction, data storage, and document (report) production.

TPSs are linked to applications that provide clerical workers and operational managers with up-to-date information, such as the quantity-on-hand of a certain inventory item, the latest deposit in a customer's bank account, the shipping date and contents of a customer's order, or the latest prescription filled for a customer in a drugstore. Clerical workers use the systems to perform their routine responsibilities: serving customers, placing purchase orders with suppliers, and providing information to other employees. TPSs are also used by operational managers, mainly to generate ad hoc reports, usually on-screen.

While a TPS keeps track of the size, type, and financial consequences of the organization's transactions, companies also need information about the quantity and quality of their production activities. Therefore, they may use **process control systems** (**PCSs**) to monitor and control ongoing physical processes such as temperature or pressure changes. For example, petroleum refineries, pulp and paper mills, food manufacturing plants, and electric power plants use PCS with special sensing devices that monitor and record physical phenomena such as temperature or pressure changes. The system relays the measurements or sensor-detected data to a computer for processing; employees and operations managers can check the data to look for problems requiring action.

Office automation systems (**OASs**) combine modern hardware and software such as word processors, desktop publishers, e-mail, and teleconferencing to handle the tasks of publishing and distributing information. OASs also are used to transform manual accounting procedures to electronic media.

Management Information Systems

A **management information system** (**MIS**) is a computer-based system that provides information and support for effective managerial decision making. MISs typically support strategic decision-making needs of mid-level and top management. However, as technology becomes more widely accessible, more employees are wired into networks, and organizations push decision making downward in the hierarchy, these kind of systems are seeing use at all levels of the organization.

Information reporting systems, which are the most common form of MIS, provide managers and decision-makers with reports that support day-to-day decision-making needs. These systems organize routine information in the form of pre-specified reports that managers use in day-to-day decision making. Trigger points are established to produce exception reports.

DECISION SUPPORT SYSTEMS AND EXPERT SYSTEMS Middle managers must solve problems that are typically more complex and non-routine than those faced by operational managers. Their decision-making tasks require significantly more data. Therefore, they use computer-based decision aids, including decision support systems (DSSs) and expert systems (ESs), to assist them.

Senior managers also use DSSs and ESs, although historically they have been more reluctant to use computers in their decision making. Until several years ago, it was rare to find a PC on the desk of a corporate president or vice president. This reluctance was partly because they perceived desktop computers to be more appropriate for lower-level managers and clerical staff. The sophistication and ease of use of such systems nowadays has probably contributed to the adoption of the systems by many high-ranking executives.

EXECUTIVE INFORMATION SYSTEMS In addition to the more traditional DSSs and ESs, executive information systems (EISs) provide managers with timely and concise information about the performance of their organization. EISs deliver summarized and concise information that helps managers quickly grasp business conditions. For instance, summary information (such as revenue per employee in a specific region) may attract the attention of a manager. Then, the manager can use an EIS to "drill down" and isolate the data that are related to the cause of a problem. Executives who use EISs can usually connect their computers (or have them permanently connected) to an on-line analytical processing (OLAP) server so they can view information in different combinations and receive such information fast.

Many executives also have their microcomputers connected to external commercial services that provide business and general news, including economic indices, stock and commodity prices, and summaries of information sorted by industry on a regional, national, and international basis.

While there is a general correlation between managerial level and type of IS, it is important to note that nothing prevents any member of an organization from using any type of IS. Of course, management may not put an EIS at the routine discretion of a clerk, but clerks may use DSSs, ESs, and even EISs for their work. Also, while we discuss different types of ISs, many applications are actually combinations of several types of such ISs. For example, some decision support systems are combined with expert systems techniques and OLAP capabilities to serve as sophisticated EISs.

Modern information technology systems also recognize that many organizational and managerial activities involve groups of people working together to solve problems and meet customer needs. **Groupware** is software that works on a computer network or via the Internet to link people or workgroups across a room or around the globe. The software enables managers or team members to share information and work simultaneously on the same document, chart, or diagram and see changes and comments as others make them. Sometimes called collaborative work systems, groupware systems allow people to interact with one another in an electronic meeting space and at the same time take advantage of computer-based support data. Groupware supports virtual and global teamwork by facilitating efficient and accurate sharing of ideas and simultaneous task execution. Team members in different geographical areas with varied expertise can work together almost as easily as if they were in the same room.

Other Types of Information Systems

ENTERPRISE RESOURCE PLANNING (ERP) In recent years, many corporations have opted to replace their disparate ISs with a single integrated system. Rather than using an IS, or several ISs, in each business function, all business functions are served by one system that supports different activities for different departments. Such systems are often called ERP systems. Although these systems do help in planning, their main focus is to help *run* the different functions. Therefore, their more accurate name is enterprise applications, but ERP is their more popular name. ERP systems integrate and optimize all the various business processes across the enire firm. An ERP system collects, processes, and provides information about an organization's entire business, including sales orders, product design, production, purchasing, inventory, distribution, human resources, receipt of payments, and forecasting of future demand. Because the ERP system integrates data about all aspects of operations, managers and employees at all levels can see how decisions and actions in one part of the organization affect other parts.

An ERP system helps manage an organization's data and information in multiple business functions.

Designers of ERP systems take a system approach to an enterprise. They regard all business processes, such as purchasing, manufacturing, shipping, and billing, as a chain of main and supporting activities. The chain is often called a *supply chain;* therefore, ERP systems are said to support supply chain management (SCM) systems.

When carefully implemented, ERP systems can cut costs, shorten cycle time, enhance productivity, and improve relationships with customers and suppliers. By using ERP system to integrate all aspects of its operations, **Bollinger Shipyards** cut an average of 15 percent off the time it takes to build a boat, translating into huge savings for the company.

ERP systems are quite complex. Because they are not tailored to the needs of specific clients, they often require adjustment and fine-tuning for specific businesses. Therefore, their installation and testing involve experts who are usually employees of the software vendor or professionals who are certified for such work by the vendor.

While a multimodule ERP application may cost several hundred thousand dollars, its installation and tweaking for a business's needs often costs several million dollars and takes many months to complete. Implementation of ERP systems can fail because of formidable challenges: the gap between system capabilities and business needs, lack of expertise on the consultant's part, and mismanagement of the implementation project. For example, **Hershey Foods,** the largest U.S. manufacturer of sweets, missed the great sales seasons of Halloween and Thanksgiving of 1999 because of time overruns in the implementation of a new ERP application.

CUSTOMER RELATIONSHIP MANAGEMENT Corporations regard customer service as an important part of their overall marketing and sales effort. With growing competition and so many options available to consumers, keeping customers satisfied is extremely important. Many executives will tell you that their companies do not make money (and may even lose money) on a first sale to a new customer because of the great investment in marketing. Thus, they use customer service and other techniques to ensure repeat sales and to encourage customer loyalty.

To better serve customers and learn of their changing needs, companies use customer relationship management (CRM) application systems. These applications help track past purchases and payments, update on-line answers to frequently asked questions (FAQs) about products and services, and analyze customers' contacts with the company to maintain and update an electronic customer profile.

CRM systems help collect data about customers and analyze the data into useful information to help serve customers better. They can also help managers find effective, efficient, and tailored marketing strategies. CRM systems help companies track customers' interactions with the firm and allow employees to call up a customer's past sales and service records, outstanding orders, or unresolved problems. CRM helps to coordinate sales, marketing, and customer-service departments so that all are smoothly working together to best serve customer needs. Executives can analyze CRM data to solve persistent problems and anticipate new ones. The challenge is to address the right customer, at the right time, with the right offer, instead of spending millions of dollars in mass marketing or covering numerous Web sites with ads.

Increasingly, what distinguishes an organization from its competitors are its knowledge resources, such as product ideas and the ability to identify and find solutions to customers' problems. Use of CRM systems can shorten the distance between customers and the organization, contributing to organizational success through increased customer loyalty, superior service, better information gathering and knowledge sharing, and organizational learning.

Because an increasing number of transactions are executed through the Web, managers can use data that are already in electronic form to analyze and strategize. As the Web evolved into an important vehicle for commercial activity, companies have endeavored to automate much of the relationship with customers so that they can help themselves, save company resources, still receive accurate answers to their questions, and obtain faster service.

By compiling billions of consumer clickstream data and creating behavioral models, these companies can glean individual consumers' interests from the sites they visited (what do they like?), the frequency of visits (are they loyal?), the times they surf (are they at work or at home?), and the number of times they click on ads or complete a transaction. Then, sites can display ads that match the typical interests at sites where the likely customers tend to visit. They can use software that will change the ad for each visitor by detecting the computer (IP number) from which the individual visits.

Web-based customer service provides automated customer support 24 hours per day, 365 days per year. At the same time, it saves companies the cost of labor required when humans provide the same service. Letting customers pay their bills electronically also saves (both customers and companies) the cost of postage and paper and saves the company time dealing with paper documents.

Consider the challenge that was facing a Web-based drugstore. Management wanted to reach more customers who were likely to purchase its products, but they did not have the tools to know who those people were.

ON-LINE ANALYTICAL AND TRANSACTION PROCESSING SYSTEMS Tables, even if joining data from several sources, limit the review of information to only two dimensions. Often, executives need to view information in three dimensions. For example, an executive may want to see a summary of the quantity of each product sold in each region. Then, she may want to view the total quantities of each product sold within each city of a region. And she may also want to view quantities sold of a specific product in all cities of all regions. Simple relational database processing applications (called on-line transaction processing, or OLTP, applications) cannot yield such tables. Another approach, called on-line analytical processing (OLAP), is especially designed to answer queries such as these. OLAP applications are designed to let a user virtually rotate cubes of information, whereby each side of the cube provides another two dimensions of relevant information.

Management Implications of Information Technology

Information technology (IT) and e-business can enable managers to be better connected with employees, the environment, and each other. In general, IT has positive implications for the practice of management, although it can also present problems. Some positive implications of IT for managers include improved employee effectiveness, increased efficiency, empowered employees, enhanced collaboration, and organizational learning. Some major problems with IT for managers include information overload, systems that do not meet user needs, and system projects taking a long time and more money than budget to complete.

Decision Making in Business

The success of an organization largely depends on the quality of the decisions that its managers make. When decision making involves large amounts of information and a lot of processing, computer-based systems can make the process efficient and effective. Several types of information systems support decision making: decision-support systems, executive information systems, and expert systems. In recent years applications have been developed to combine several of the features and methods; thus, the distinction between decision-support systems, executive information systems, and other types of decision-support applications is no longer discernible in many of these applications. Also, many decision-support modules are often integrated into larger enterprise applications. For example, enterprise resource planning, (ERP) systems support decision making in such areas as inventory replenishment.

Decision-Support System Components

To save time and effort in their decision making, managers use several types of decision-support applications. One such type is decision-support systems. **Decision-support systems (DSSs)** are computer-based information systems designed to help managers select one of many alternative solutions to a problem. DSSs can help corporations increase

Exhibit 800.14 *Components of a DSS and Their Interaction*

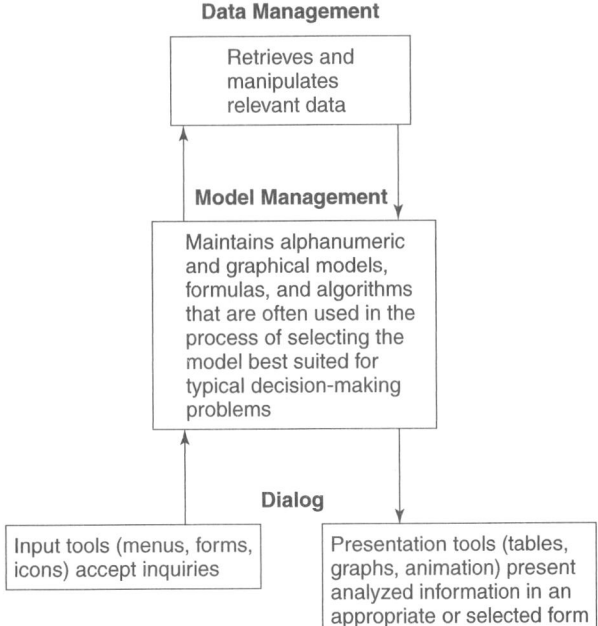

market share, reduce costs, increase profitability, and enhance product quality. By automating some of the decision-making process, the systems give managers access to analyses that were previously unavailable. Technically, certain analyses could be performed by managers, but it would be prohibitively time-consuming and would render late, and therefore bad, decisions. DSSs provide sophisticated and fast analysis of vast amounts of data and information. Although the use of DSSs typically increases with the level of management, the systems are used at all levels, and often by nonmanagerial staff.

The traditional definition of a DSS has been changing over the years. In the following sections we discuss the components of "traditional" stand-alone DSSs: either self-contained applications or applications that were designed to address a rather narrow decision-making domain. Nowadays, many companies use software such as data-mining applications, which aid in decision making but often are not called DSSs. Also, you should realize that some components of a computer-based decision aid, such as a database, may already be in place when a new DSS is developed. Therefore, you should consider the following discussion a general framework and not a rigid recipe for the development of all DSSs.

The majority of DSSs comprise three major components: a data management module, a model management module, and a dialog module (see Exhibit 800.14). Together, these modules (1) help the user enter a request in a convenient manner, (2) search vast amounts of data to focus on the relevant facts, (3) process the data through desired models, and (4) present the results in one or several manners so the output can be easily understood.

The Data Management Module

A DSS's **data management module** is a database or data warehouse that allows a decision maker to conduct the intelligence phase of decision making. For example, an investment consultant always needs access to current stock prices and those from at least the preceding few years. A data management module accesses the data and provides a means for the DSS to select data according to certain criteria: type of stock, range of years, and so on.

A DSS may use a database created specially for that system, but DSSs are usually linked to databases used for other purposes as well, such as purchasing, shipping, billing, and other daily transactions. Companies that have built data warehouses often prefer their DSSs to access the data warehouse rather than the transactional database, to minimize interference with transactions and to provide substantially more historical data than transactional databases.

Many DSSs are now closely intertwined with other organizational systems, including data warehouses, data marts, and ERP systems, from which they draw relevant data.

The Model Management Module

To turn data into useful information, the user selects a model from the **model management module,** which is a collection of models the DSS draws on to assist in decision making. A sequence of events or a pattern of behavior may become a useful model when the relationships among its inputs, outputs, and conditions can be established well enough that they can be used to analyze different parameters. Models are used to predict output on the basis of different input or different conditions or to estimate what combination of conditions and input might lead to a desired output. Models are often based on mathematical research or on experience. A model may be a widely used method to predict performance, such as "best-fit" linear analysis, or it may be built by the organization, using the experience that knowledge workers in the firm have accumulated over time. Many companies will not divulge details of the models they have programmed, because they view them as important trade secrets and as valuable assets that may give them competitive advantages. Patterns or models may be unique to a certain industry or even to an individual business. For example:

- In trying to serve customers better in a bank, operations research experts try to create a model that predicts the best positioning and scheduling of tellers.
- In the trucking business, models are developed to minimize the total mileage trucks must travel and maximize the trucks' load, while maintaining a satisfactory delivery time. Similar models are developed in the airline industry to maximize revenue.
- A model for revenue maximization in the airline industry will automatically price tickets according to the parameters the user enters: date of the flight, day of the week of the flight, departure and destination points, and the length of stay if the ticket is for a round-trip flight.
- Car rental companies use similar models to price their services by car class, rental period, and drop-off options in different countries.

Among the general statistical models, a linear regression model is the best-fit linear relationship between two variables, such as sales and the money spent on marketing. A private business may develop a linear regression model to estimate future sales based on past experience. For example, the marketing department of a shoe store chain may apply linear regression to the relationship between the dollar amount spent on television commercials and change in sales volume. This linear relationship can be translated into a program in a DSS. Then the user can enter the total amount to be spent on television commercials for the next year into the DSS, and the program will enter that figure into the model and find the estimated change in the sales volume. The relationship between the two variables can be plotted, as shown in Exhibit 800.15.

Note that the actual data points rarely lie on the regression line produced from the data. This illustrates the uncertainty involved in many models. For instance, in Exhibit 800.15, if the marketing managers tried to estimate the

Exhibit 800.15 *A Linear Regression Model for Predicting Sales Volume as a Function of Dollars Spent on Advertising*

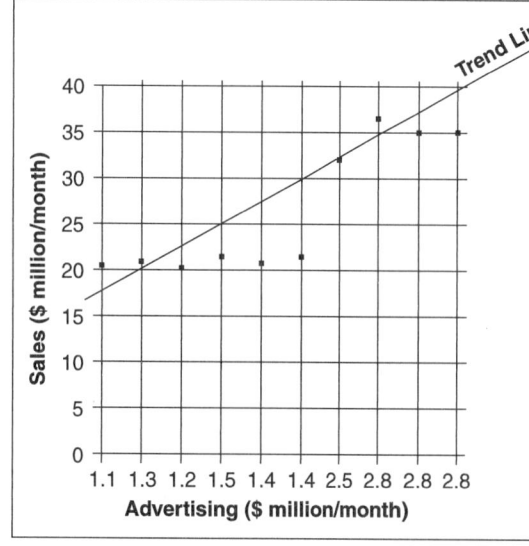

Advertising ($M/month)	Sales ($M/month)
1.1	20.3
1.3	21
1.2	20.1
1.5	22.7
1.4	21.9
1.4	22
2.5	32
2.8	36
2.8	35
2.8	34.8

sales volume resulting from spending $1.4 million per month on advertising, their estimates for both months plotted on the graph would be more than the actual sales. In spite of these discrepancies, the regression line may be adequate in general for modeling, with the understanding that results are not necessarily precise. Also note that models often describe relationships among more than two variables and that some models can be expressed as a curve, rather than a straight line.

Usually, models are not so simple. In this advertising and sales example, for instance, many more factors may play a role: the number of salespeople, the location of the stores, the types of shoes offered for sale, the television programs in which the commercials are presented, and many more parameters. Therefore, before models are programmed to become part of a DSS, the environment in which the decision will be executed must be carefully considered.

Not all DSSs are business oriented. In some areas, especially engineering, models in DSSs may simulate physical environments rather than business environments. For example, aeronautical engineers build computer models of wind tunnels to view how an aircraft with a new wing design might behave. It is significantly less expensive to construct a software model than to build a physical model. The simulation provides valuable information on vibrations, drag, metal fatigue, and other factors, in relation to various speeds and weather conditions. The output, in the form of both animated pictures and numerical tables, enables engineers to make important decisions before spending huge amounts of money to actually build aircraft—decisions such as the angle in which the aircraft wings are swept, the shape of the hull's cross section, the spreading of weight over different parts of the plane, and so forth. When using this type of model, engineers base part of their decision on visual examination of the behavior of the simulation model.

The Dialog Module

For the user to interact with the DSS, the system must provide an easy way to interact with the program. The part of the DSS that allows the user to interact with it is called the **dialog module.** It prompts the user to select a model, allowing the user to access the database and select data for the decision process or to set criteria for selecting such data. It lets the user enter parameters and change them to see how the change affects the result of the analysis. The dialog may be in the form of commands, pull-down menus, icons, dialog boxes, or any other approach. In essence, the dialog module is not different from the user interfaces of other types of applications.

The dialog module is also responsible for displaying the results of the analysis. DSSs use various textual, tabular, and graphical displays from which the decision maker can choose. In disciplines that require decisions regarding the physical construction of objects, such as aircraft or buildings, the output is often animated. For example, an architect may want to test the strength of a new structure by creating a computer model of the building and subjecting the model to increasing pressures until the construction collapses. Decisions can then be based on the sequence of events that appears on the monitor, along with the display of textual and tabular data.

Different colors and patterns may also play an important role in DSS output, by quickly drawing attention to exceptional results that do not comply with certain rules of analysis. Take the previous advertising effort scenario, for example, where the company's marketing manager is trying to decide how to spend promotional dollars (see Exhibit 800.16). The dialog component of the DSS presents a menu allowing the marketing executive to select "TV advertising" from a variety of promotional choices and to choose the amount to be spent in that channel. Now the dialog module invokes the part of the database that holds current data on advertising expenditures and sales volumes for the corresponding months. At this point, the system may either present a list of models for analyzing the data from which the user can choose or, if it is sophisticated enough, select a model automatically, based on the problem at hand. The model projects sales figures based on the data from the database, and the dialog component presents the results of the analysis. The output helps the executive make a decision by answering the question: Will the proposed amount to be spent on television commercials yield a large enough boost in sales?

Types of Decision-Support Systems

The general structure of all DSSs is similar and comprises the components detailed in Exhibit 800.16, but DSSs may differ in their degree of sophistication and the manner in which they are used. DSSs can be categorized into two basic categories: personal DSSs and group DSSs. Usually, when people refer to DSSs they mean the former type. In this discussion we add the word *personal* to distinguish DSSs used by individuals from those used by groups.

Exhibit 800.16 *A DSS Helps Marketers Make Decisions*

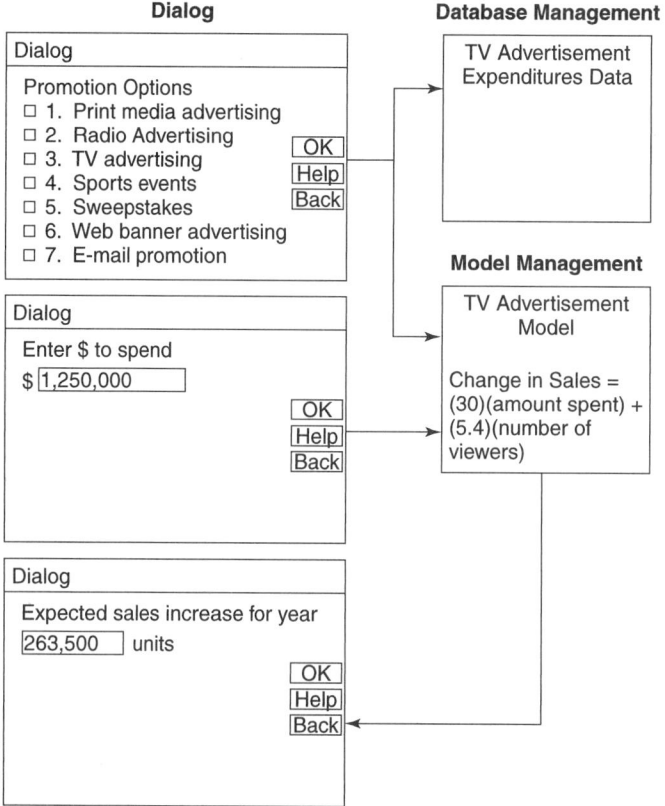

Personal Decision-Support Systems

Personal DSSs are built for the individual knowledge worker to use in his or her daily work. Usually, they run on personal computers and often contain a single model for data processing. Personal DSSs are often developed with the participation of all prospective users or of those who are most experienced. However, many software companies develop prepackaged DSSs for mass marketing based on a collaboration of specialized experts and programmers. An increasing number of personal DSSs are not tailor-made for a specific company.

With personal DSSs, raw data may be entered directly into a program by the user, or it may be drawn from a firm's database or data warehouse, from an external source, or from a combination of sources. Some companies using DSSs have policies saying that managers should act on the system's "decision." For example, **Mrs. Fields Cookies** provides store managers with DSSs that decide for the managers which types of cookies to make, what quantities of each type, and which ingredients to use, on the basis of the store's sales volumes and corporate-dictated baking instructions. In this case, the company has structured the business environment for the store managers. However, if users work in a highly unstructured environment, they must carefully examine output before acting on it or rejecting it.

The Canadian government has sponsored the development of a series of DSSs for farmers, one of which is Prairie Crop Protection Planner, a system that helps farmers plan protection of crops. When a farmer enters basic information about a particular crop and the pest problem he is experiencing—weeds, insects, or diseases—the Planner outlines options such as chemicals and ways to apply them. The farmer can describe his sprayer, the size of his field, and the current chemical prices from his local supplier, and the Prairie Crop Protection Planner calculates application rates, costs per acre, the amount of product the farmer will need to use in the sprayer's tank, and the amount of chemical he will need to spray on the entire field.

Not surprisingly, there are plenty of DSSs for investment managers, because there are many different variables to consider and complex models to use when planning portfolios for high return. Using the program, investors can create filters—that is, they can identify the criteria of the securities they are interested in by return on investment or by share price change over a particular period. Investors can also pick securities by name. Then, they can build a hypothetical portfolio, see a pie chart of the proportions of each security or type of security in the portfolio, and receive an estimated return on the investment. Investors can use the program to create multiple model portfolios and can then compare the portfolios' performances.

For several years companies have enabled employees to use a shared DSS, which is stored on a computer server and accessed through a LAN. Many companies now let employees from various sites access such DSSs using intranets. Some nonprofit organizations, such as governments and universities, provide online access to DSSs through the Web. For example, the University of Arizona placed a DSS online to help ranchers make cow-culling decisions.

Organizations can use the Internet to access data from several sites for DSS data analysis. For example, **Accrue Software** offers a DSS that uses the Internet to access data from several sources rather than just a local data warehouse. Regional managers can access information of individual stores, which was previously available only at headquarters. For example, they can access sales and inventory information for stores, by day or week for recent weeks, and compare it with data for the same period last year. The software lets them see which stores are underperforming in terms of profit. They can measure sales per square foot of selling space by stores and departments and evaluate store characteristics so the lessons learned can be applied to all the stores in the chain or region. Other applications can determine which items tend to be purchased together for better placement on shelves. Using statistical models, the DSS can provide accurate and timely sales forecasts by item and store for improved merchandise allocation and markdowns.

Group Decision-Support Systems

Often, business decisions are made by a group of managers rather than a single person. To facilitate such decision-making sessions, many organizations use group DSSs. *Group decision-support systems (GDSSs)* are usually installed in conference-room settings or through a group of networked computers. In recent years several software vendors have offered Internet-based GDSSs to accommodate users from several disparate locations. GDSSs are designed specifically to take input from multiple users interacting with the program simultaneously and converging on a decision together. Although personal DSSs can help groups make decisions, the nature of group decision making is different from that of a single individual. In individual decision making, the individual may share ideas with others, but he or she does not have to agree with any other person about the data collected, the ideas raised, or the decision made. A decision made by a group, on the other hand, can be the result of a consensus or majority vote. GDSSs are designed to provide methods such as weighing votes to overcome impasses.

Sensitivity Analysis

An outcome is almost always affected by more than one parameter; for instance, the sales volume of a product is affected by the number of salespeople, the number of regional sales representatives, the amount spent on national and local television advertising, price, competition, and so on. However, outcomes rarely respond in equal measure to changes in parameters. For instance, a small change in price per unit may result in a dramatic increase in sales, which means sales volume has a high sensitivity to product price. However, the same sales may increase only slightly in response to a huge investment in advertising dollars, which means that sales have a low sensitivity to advertising expenditure. It is important to pinpoint the parameters to which the outcome is highly sensitive, so that an organization can focus efforts where they will be most effective. Sometimes the parameters to which an outcome is most sensitive also affect other parameters, so these interactions must be carefully tracked as well.

If a company wishes to maximize profit, managers must find the optimal combination of many factors. To equip a DSS to help achieve this goal, an approximate mathematical formula that expresses the relationship between each factor and the total profit is built into the DSS. Then a **sensitivity analysis** is conducted to test the degree to which the total profit grows or shrinks if one or more of the factors is increased or decreased. The results indicate the relative sensitivity of the profit to the changes. If the outcome is affected significantly even when the parameter is changed only a little, then the sensitivity of the outcome to the parameter is said to be high. The opposite is also true: If the outcome is affected only a little even when the parameter is varied widely, the outcome is said to be insensitive to the parameter. For instance, a manager may ask, "What is the impact on total quarterly profits if television advertising is decreased by 10 percent and the number of commissioned sales representatives is increased by 5 percent?" Because questions typically are phrased in this format, sensitivity analysis is often referred to as **what if analysis**. Note that you can use a DSS to perform "what if" analyses on multiple parameters at the same time.

Executive Information Systems

Executive information systems (EISs) are decision aids specially designed for high-ranking managers, to provide them with the most essential information for running their organizations. EISs are useful in paring down information for executives, who almost always suffer from information overload. *Information overload* is a situation in which the very volume of information makes it impossible to sort through what is important. Any additional information only adds to the burden, rather than helping to solve problems and make decisions. Unlike other decision aids, EISs do not contain analytical models; rather, they consolidate and summarize data that are obtained both from within the organization and from outside sources.

You may recall that high-level managers make decisions based on highly summarized information. They review ratios such as sales per employee per quarter or per year, sales per region, return on investment, and inventory turnover for different items. EISs can display these data graphically so that exceptions can be easily spotted. Unlike regular DSSs, many EISs do not require a user to enter the values of parameters. The system is linked with the organization's databases and data warehouses and uses predetermined or selected models to respond to queries, displaying the results in the fashion requested.

The purpose of EISs is not so much to perform sophisticated analysis as it is to **drill down** in databases and data warehouses to find the most relevant information for executive decision making. Often, an executive first needs a general picture of a business situation, such as the ratio of research and development to revenue over the past three years or a ratio of inventory turnover. But more detailed (and less summarized) information may be needed to pinpoint a problem. For example, a low inventory turnover (which means that the company does not sell its inventory fast enough) may be caused by a single item that sells extremely slowly. By drilling down to more details, the executive may discover that fact, in which case the decision may be to simply stop producing the item. For this reason, many EISs are interfaced with on-line analytical processing (OLAP) applications.

Some vendors market EISs with a "what if" feature, which brings the system closer to the format and purpose of a DSS. This convergence demonstrates how meaningless the classification of computer-based decision aids is becoming.

An effective EIS has the following features:

- An easy-to-use and easy-to-learn graphical user interface
- On-request "drill down" capability that allows the executive to reach information in further detail
- On-demand financial and other ratios and indicators (such as sales per employee or ratio of divisional total actual expense to budgeted funds) that reflect organizational strengths and weaknesses
- Easy-to-use but sophisticated tools to allow navigation in databases and data warehouses
- Statistical analysis tools
- The ability to respond to ad hoc queries and sensitivity analyses
- Access to external data pools
- The ability to solve diverse business problems

Many full-blown DSSs are now sold by vendors under the label of *EIS*, probably because the term EIS is perceived as more sophisticated or more attractive to executives. The lines between DSSs and EISs have been blurred in recent years. When an organization purchases a system, management should look not at its label but at the features it offers.

Developing Decision-Support Systems

Although vendors now offer off-the-shelf DSSs, many organizations develop their own systems, especially if the systems deal with business problems that are unique to the organization. To make a wise choice, managers who consider the acquisition of a new DSS must understand what circumstances justify the investment in employee time and effort for a development project and when using an off-the-shelf DSS that serves a less specialized market is warranted, despite the compromises.

When Should a DSS Be Built?

Like investment in any information system, the investment in developing a DSS may be hundreds of thousands or even millions of dollars. Therefore, management must consider several factors before making a commitment. Following are questions that can help guide the decision.

- *What type of problem are we trying to address, and how structured is it?* Not every decision needs a DSS or EIS. In general, the less structured the problem, the more analysis it requires and the more likely it is that managers will benefit from a decision aid. But many decisions can be made with a quick look at the appropriate data. In fact, some analyses are so simple that they can be performed within seconds. Even some unstructured problems can be solved easily with common sense. But for solving highly unstructured problems, with many different models as possible analysis tools and many factors and parameters to be considered, even the most experienced managers can benefit from using a DSS.

  Highly unstructured problems are usually qualitative rather than quantitative. For instance, consider a purchasing manager for a software company deciding which supplier to use for blank recordable CDs. He or she must consider several factors, including the quality of the CDs, delivery time, price, payment terms, and warranty. If there are only two CD manufacturers, and the factors listed are similar for both, then the manager does not need a DSS to make a decision; he or she may simply negotiate a better price.

  However, if the company has many potential suppliers, the manager must consider many combinations of values, in which case a DSS could aid in the evaluation and selection of the best supplier. Similarly, if the firm tried many suppliers but found one to be more reliable in meeting delivery times and easier to work with, then the firm would most likely purchase from this supplier even if his prices were somewhat higher. Often, the business relationship is determined largely by trust: the purchasing officer simply trusts certain suppliers more than others to come through when needed. Such factors cannot be quantified and used as parameters in a DSS.

- *Are the data required for the analysis available in automated databases and data warehouses?* The accessibility of relevant data from existing internal and external databases, or from the creation of a combined new database, is an important consideration in the development of a DSS. A DSS designer may determine that an entire database needs to be maintained for the system, or that adequate interfaces can be developed for existing databases. In general, the higher the level of the managers who use decision aids, the greater the amount of external data required. Hence, DSS developers have the added challenge of effectively combining internal and external sources.

- *How often do managers encounter the problem?* The more frequently the problem occurs, the more justified the development of a DSS to solve it. If the problem is encountered rarely, the development cost will outweigh the benefits.

- *Who will use the system?* In general, the greater the number of prospective users and the higher the position of the users in the organization, the greater the positive impact a DSS will have. Depending on the level of management, if only one person, or a handful of people, will use the system, it may be more economical to have them develop their own individual systems using a fourth-generation language (4GL) or spreadsheet. However, if the sole prospective user is the company's president, and this person will use it frequently, then the investment may be justified because of the great benefit the DSS might have for the entire organization.

- *Can the prospective users spare adequate time for the development process?* The development of automated decision aids requires much time and effort of the users, so management has to be willing to let workers take time from their regular duties to help in the development effort.

The Electronic Spreadsheet: A DSS Tool

If data must be drawn from external databases and decisions require complex, special calculations, a DSS may have to be programmed from scratch. But many DSSs can be developed using inexpensive off-the-shelf software referred to as DSS tools. A DSS tool is any application that lets you build models and access the proper data. The most widely used tools are electronic spreadsheets.

Geographic Information Systems

Many business decisions concern geographic locations—either as input, as output, or both. For example, consider the process of choosing the best locations for new stores or determining how to deploy police forces optimally. For map-related decisions, *geographic information systems (GISs)* are often the best decision aids to use. GISs are systems that process location data and provide output. For instance, a GIS could be used to help a housing developer determine where to invest by tracking and displaying population changes on a map, highlighting in color increases of more than 10 percent over the past three years. With this information, a developer could easily decide where to invest on the basis of population growth trends. Other examples include the following:

- Delivery managers looking for the shortest distance a truck can travel to deliver ordered goods at the lowest cost
- School-district officials looking for the most efficient routes for busing school children to and from their homes
- City planners looking to deploy services to better serve residents, which might include police officers deciding how to deploy their forces on the basis of precinct maps indicating levels of criminal activity
- Oil companies looking to determine drilling locations on the basis of geological tests
- Hunters, fishers, hikers, and other people who look for outdoor recreation can find suitable sites and trails for their activities based on their requirements, such as local fauna and trail length

A typical GIS consists of (1) a database of quantitative and qualitative data from which information is extracted for display, (2) a database of maps, and (3) a program that displays the information on the maps. The digitized maps are produced from satellite and aerial photography. Displays may be in the form of easily understood symbols and colors or even of moving images. For instance, an oil exploration map may show different concentrations of expected crude oil deposits in different hues of red. Or, population density may be similarly displayed on a map using different hues of blue. A more sophisticated GIS may display, in colors or icons, concentrations of specific consumer groups by age, income, and other characteristics.

Web technology helps promote the use of GISs by private organizations and governments alike. Intranets allow employees to bring up thousands of maps from a central repository on their own PCs. HTML and XML, the primary languages used to compose and retrieve Web pages, support the presentation of pictures with marked areas, which makes them ideal for retrieval of marked maps. Clicking different areas of a map can bring up related information in the form of other maps or in text, utilizing the multimedia capabilities of the Web to the fullest.

For example, sales managers can bring up maps of whole continents and see how past sales have "performed" over different territories. They can zoom in and zoom out on a territory. With the click of a mouse they can receive detailed information on who serves the territory and other pertinent information.

In government work a city clerk can bring up a map of the neighborhood of a resident, zoom in on the resident's house pictured on the map, click on the picture, and receive information such as real-estate taxes owed and paid over the past several years. Further information, such as whether a neighborhood uses septic tanks or a sewage system, may be rendered by different colors. The map can also show different zoning codes, such as land designated for residential, industrial, or commercial purposes.

Data and Knowledge Management

Data Versus Information

The ability to generate more information with technology presents a serious challenge to information analysts, technicians, managers, and other users of information. They must sort through overwhelming amounts of data to identify only that information necessary for a particular purpose. **Data** are raw facts and figures that in and of themselves may not be useful. To be useful, data must be processed into finished information—that is, data that have been converted into a meaningful and useful context for specific users. **Information** is a collection of facts and figures organized in such a way that they have additional value beyond the value of the raw facts and figures themselves. An increasing challenge for managers is being able to effectively identify and access useful information. American Greetings, for example, might gather data about demographics in various parts of the country. These data are then translated into information; for example, stores in Florida require an enormous assortment of greeting cards directed at grandson, grandfather, niece, and nephew, while stores in some other parts of the country might need a larger percentage of slightly irrelevant, youth-oriented products.

The magnitude of the job of transforming data into useful information is reflected in organizations' introduction of the chief information officer (CIO) position. CIOs are responsible for managing organizational databases and implementing new information technology. As they make decisions involving the adoption and management of new technologies, CIOs integrate old and new technology to support organizational decision making, operations, and communication. Effective CIOs not only manage the technology infrastructure but also focus on information design, so that managers have high-quality information to improve decision making, solve problems, and improve performance. Ideally, the CIO combines knowledge of information technology with the ability to help managers and employees identify their information needs, as well as ways the organization can use its IT capabilities to support its strategy. An important part of the CIO's job is shaping disjointed data into clear, meaningful, and useful information.

Characteristics of Useful Information

Organizations depend on high-quality information to develop strategic plans, identify problems, and interact with other organizations. Information is of high quality if it has characteristics that make it useful for those tasks. The characteristics of useful information fall into three broad categories, such as time, content, and form.

TIME Information should be available and provided when needed, up to date, and related to be appropriate time period (past, present, or future). Major elements of time include timeliness, currency, frequency, and time period.

CONTENT Useful information is error free, suited to the user's needs, complete, concise, relevant (that is, it excludes unnecessary data), and an accurate measure of performance. Major elements of content include accuracy, relevance, completeness, conciseness, scope, and performance.

FORM The information should be provided in a form that is easy for the user to understand and that meet the user's needs for the level of detail. The presentation should be ordered and use the combination of words, numbers, and diagrams that is most helpful to the user. Also, information should be presented in a useful medium (printed documents, reports, video display, and sound). Reports should be concise, accurate, complete, and timely. Major elements of form include clarity, detail, order, presentation, and media.

Knowledge and Knowledge Management

Knowledge is an important resource similar to cash, raw materials, and energy. Knowledge is when a manager has an awareness and understanding of how to make information useful in supporting a specific task. **Knowledge management** is the process of systematically gathering knowledge, making it widely available throughout the organization, and fostering a culture of learning. Three specific technologies that facilitate knowledge management are data warehousing, data mining, and corporate Intranets or networks. Data warehousing and data mining help organizations capture and make sense of structured data. They combine related pieces of information to create knowledge. Knowledge that can be codified, written down, and contained in databases is referred to as explicit knowledge. However, much organizational knowledge is unstructured and resides in people heads (tacit knowledge). This tacit knowledge cannot be captured in a database, making it difficult to formalize and transmit. Intranets and knowledge sharing networks can support the spread of tacit knowledge. More is said about knowledge management later in this section.

Managing Digital Data

Businesses collect and dissect data for a multitude of purposes. Digital data can be stored in a variety of ways on different types of media. They can be stored in what we will call the traditional file format, in which the different pieces of information are not labeled and categorized but are stored as continuous strings of bytes. The chief advantage of this format is the efficient use of space, but the data are nonetheless difficult to locate and manipulate and are therefore of limited use. By contrast, the database format, in which each piece of data is labeled or categorized, provides a much more powerful information management tool. Data in this format can be easily accessed and manipulated in almost any way desired to create useful information and optimize productivity.

The impact of database technology on business cannot be overstated. Not only has it changed the way almost every industry conducts business, but it has also created an information industry with far-reaching effects on both our business and personal lives. Databases are behind the successful use of automated teller machines (ATMs), increased efficiency in retail stores, almost every marketing effort, and the numerous on-line search engines and electronic storefronts on the World Wide Web. Combined with interactive Web pages on the Internet, databases have made an immense contribution to e-commerce. Without them, there would be no on-line banking, no on-line consumer catalogs, no on-line stock brokerages, and no on-line chat rooms. Their impact on business has allowed fewer people to complete larger tasks, and their power has allowed organizations to learn more about us, as consumers, than we may realize. Imagine: every time you enter the URL (Web address) of a site, a special program tries to match your request with one of millions of URLs in a huge database. Every time you fill out an on-line form with details such as your address, phone number, Social Security number, or credit-card number, a program launches the data into a database, where each item is recorded for further use.

In virtually every type of business today, you must understand the power of databases. This section reviews the different approaches to organizing and manipulating data in databases and data warehouses.

The Traditional File Approach

We can roughly distinguish between two different approaches to maintaining data: traditional file organization—which has no mechanism for tagging, retrieving, and manipulating data—and the **database approach,** which does have that mechanism. To appreciate the benefits of the database approach, you must keep in mind the inconvenience involved in accessing and manipulating data in the **traditional file approach:** program/data dependency, high data redundancy, and low data integrity.

Database Approach

In the database approach, we maintain and manipulate data about entities. An **entity** is any object about which an organization chooses to collect data. It may be a student enrolled in a class, a sales transaction in a business, or a part in an inventory. In the context of data management, entity refers to all the occurrences sharing the same types of data. Therefore, it does not matter if we maintain a record of one class or many classes; the entity is "class." To understand how data are organized in a database, you must first understand the data hierarchy. The smallest piece of data is a **character** (a letter in a first or last name or address, and so on). Several characters make up data in a field (also called *data item*), such as last name, first name, and the like. A **field** is one piece of information about an entity, such as the last name or first name of a student. Several fields related to the same entity make up a **record.** A collection of related records is called a **file.** Often, several related files must be kept together. A collection of such files is referred to as a database. However, the features of a database can be enjoyed by builders and users of databases even when a database consists of a single file.

Database fields are not limited to holding text and numbers. They can hold pictures, sounds, and video clips. Fields can hold any content that can be digitized. For example, when you shop online, you can search for a product by its product name or code, and then retrieve its picture or a video clip about the product.

Database Management Systems

While a database itself is a collection of several related *files,* the program used to build databases, populate them with data, and manipulate the data is called a **database management system** (**DBMS**). The files themselves *are* the database, but DBMSs do all the work—structuring files, storing data, and linking records. If you wanted to access data from files that were stored in a traditional file approach, the records would have to be organized in a very specific way, and you would have to know exactly how many characters were designated for each type of data. A DBMS, however, does much of this work (and a lot of other work) for you.

If you are using a database, you want to be able to move rapidly from one record to another, sorting by different criteria, creating different types of reports, and analyzing the data in different ways. Because of these demands, databases

Exhibit 800.17 *Different Database Views Reveal Different Combinations of Data*

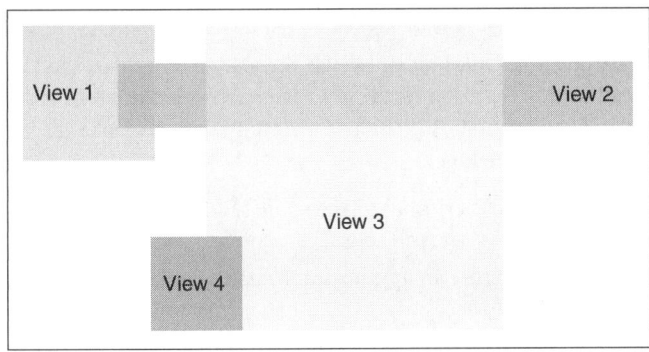

Exhibit 800.18 *Different Views of One Employee Database*

View of Human Resource Manager				
SSN	Name	D.O.B.	Hire Date	Marital Status

View of Payroll Personnel			
SSN	Hourly Rate	Benefits Code	Hours Worked

View of Project Manager	
Name	Hours Worked

are stored on direct access storage devices (DASDs), such as CDs or magnetic disks, but cannot be stored on sequential storage devices such as magnetic or optical tapes because it would take too long to access different fields.

QUERIES Data are accessed in a database by sending messages called *queries,* which request data from specific fields and direct the computer to display the results on the monitor. Queries are also entered to manipulate data. Usually, the same software that is used to construct and populate the database, that is, the DBMS, is also used to present queries. Modern DBMS programs provide fairly user-friendly means of querying a database.

SECURITY The use of databases raises security and privacy issues. The fact that data are stored only once in a database does not mean that everyone with access to that database should have access to *all* the data in it. Restricting access is easily dealt with by customizing menus for different users and requiring users to enter codes that limit access to certain fields or records. As a result, users have different views of the database, as illustrated in Exhibit 800.17. The ability to limit users' views to only specific columns or records gives the database administrator (the person who plans the database and ensures that it is up and running) another advantage: the ability to implement security measures. The measures are implemented once for the database, rather than multiple times for different files. For instance, in the database in Exhibit 800.18, while a human resource manager has access to all fields of the employee file (represented by the top, middle, and lower parts of the figure), the payroll personnel have access only to four fields of the employee file (middle part of the figure), and a project manager has access only to the Name and Hours Worked fields. Views may be limited to certain fields in a database, or certain records, or a combination thereof.

845. DATA AND KNOWLEDGE MANAGEMENT

Traditional Files Versus Databases: Pros and Cons

The advantages of storing data in database files far outweigh those of storing them in flat files. While there are some trade-offs, databases generally allow much greater flexibility, easier access by different applications, easier maintenance of data currency and integrity, and savings in both cost and time, all of which make them far superior to disparate flat files. Database advantages include the following.

1. *Reduced data redundancy.* Although there may still be some redundancy in a database, it is significantly less than in the traditional file approach. This streamlining saves storage space.
2. *Application-data independence.* Writing an application to use data from a database is much simpler than writing one to use data from flat files. To access data in a database, a program can use field names and the names of the data sets in which the data exist, such as a list of patient records in a hospital. This programming efficiency saves programming time and allows users with limited knowledge to access data through queries or even to develop simple applications.
3. *Better control.* Since all data are concentrated in one place in a database, it is easier to control access and maintain data, and it is easier to get an overall view of data about an entity.
4. *Flexibility.* Modifying a database by adding new data related to entities is much simpler than adding data to flat files.

In general, the opposite of these database advantages are the disadvantages of using traditional files to store data. The traditional file approach creates data redundancy and application-data dependence. It does not support as tight control over data currency, accuracy, and integrity as the database approach, and it provides less flexibility in data maintenance. However, the traditional file approach does have some advantages, including the following.

1. *Efficiency.* Applications written for flat files run more efficiently than those written for databases because they do not use the additional CPU time and memory space required by preprogrammed functions that are a part of the DBMS. Often, the easier a program is to use, the more CPU time and memory space it needs.
2. *Simplicity.* Constructing a database can be very complex and time-consuming. Sometimes, it may be simpler to create simple files and to develop applications for them, especially when an application accesses just one flat file.
3. *Customization.* The preprogrammed features of a DBMS allow only certain relationships among data. However, using the more flexible procedural features of a third- or fourth-generation language to build files and to access them allows a tight tailoring of applications to business needs—more so than using only the preprogrammed features of a DBMS.

The overwhelming advantages of databases raise the question: Why use flat files at all? If you were starting with a clean slate, you probably wouldn't choose to use flat files. However, businesses have accumulated a considerable amount of historical data in flat file format that they will be dealing with for many years to come. Because considerable amounts of data in businesses are still stored in flat files and accessed through applications that were written with third-generation languages such as COBOL (which by their nature are designed to access flat files), it may be too costly to switch to databases. However, almost all new data banks are developed and maintained with the aid of DBMSs.

Database Models

A **database model** is the general logical structure in which records are stored within a database. There are three different database models. They differ in the manner in which records are linked to each other. These differences, in turn, dictate the manner in which a user can navigate the database and retrieve desired records. As summarized in Exhibit 800.19, each model has advantages and disadvantages when compared with the other two.

Keys

To retrieve records from a relational database, or to sort them, you must use a key. A **key** is a field whose values identify records either for display or for processing. You may use any field as a key. A key is unique if the value (content) in that field appears only in one record. Sometimes a key is composed of several fields so that their combination provides a unique key.

Exhibit 800.19 *Advantages and Disadvantages of Database Models*

	Database Model		
	Hierarchical	Network	Relational
Conceptualization	Moderately easy	Difficult	Easy
Ease of Design	Very difficult	Moderately difficult	Difficult
Ease of Maintenance	Difficult	Very difficult	Easy
Data Redundancy	High	Low	High
Ease of Use	Moderate	Low	High

Primary Key

Depending on the software you use, you may receive the first one that meets the condition, or a list of all the records with that value in the field. The only way to be sure you are retrieving the desired record is to use a unique key (such as a Social Security number). A unique key is called a **primary key.**

Usually, a table in a relational database must have a primary key, and most relational DBMSs enforce this rule; if the designer does not designate a field as a key, the DBMS creates its own serial number field as the primary key field for the table. Once the designer of the table determines the primary key when constructing the records' format, the DBMS will not allow a user to enter two records with the same value in that column. Note that there may be situations in which more than one field may be used as a primary key. Such is the case with motor vehicles, because both the vehicle identification number (VIN) and the license plate number uniquely identify a car. Thus, a database designer may establish either field as a primary key to retrieve records.

Many DBMSs will force you to designate a primary key in each table you construct. Usually, the software requires that the primary key be the leftmost field in the record. By default, many DBMSs automatically sort the records the user enters in ascending order of the primary key.

Some relational databases use **composite keys,** a combination of two or more fields that together serve as a primary key. An example: the last name, first name, and department in a table that holds professors' records could together be considered a primary key. Unless we expect two people with the same name to lecture for the same department, the combination will be a valid primary key.

Linking

To link records from one table with records of another table, the tables must have one field in common (that is, one column in each table must contain the same type of data), and that field must be a primary key field for one of the tables. We say that this repeated field is a primary key in one table, and a **foreign key** field in the other table.

As you can see, all database design requires careful forethought. The designer must include fields for foreign keys from other tables so that joint tables can be created in the future. The inclusion of foreign keys may cause considerable data redundancy. This complexity has not diminished the popularity of relational databases, however. Since the relationships between tables are created as part of manipulating the table, the relational model supports both one-to-many (1:M) and many-to-many (M:M) relationships between records of different tables.

The Object-Oriented Structure

While the move from traditional file systems to databases was a leap forward in data management efficiency, recent years have seen a new development that may lead to even greater benefits: object-oriented databases. In object-oriented technology, an object consists of both data and the procedures that manipulate the data. So, in addition to the attributes of an entity, it also contains the relationships with other entities. The combined storage of both data and the procedures that manipulate them is referred to as "encapsulation." Thus, an object can be "planted" in different data sets. The ability in object-oriented structures to automatically create a new object by replicating all or some of the characteristics of a previously developed object (called the parent object) is called **inheritance.**

845. DATA AND KNOWLEDGE MANAGEMENT

Entity-Relationship Diagrams

Many business databases consist of multiple files with relationships among them. For example, a hospital may use a database that has a file holding the records of all its physicians, another one with all its nurses, another one with all the current patients, and so on. The administrative staff must be able to create reports that link data from multiple files. Thus, the database must be carefully planned to allow useful data manipulation and report generation. The planning task often involves the creation of a conceptual blueprint of the database. This blueprint is called an **entity-relationship** (**ER**) **diagram.** An ER diagram is a graphical representation of all entity relationships.

Components of Database Management Systems

When designers have a clear understanding of how a database should be structured to accommodate the different data sets and the relationships among them, they select a DBMS to construct the new database. While DBMSs have different interfaces, they share similar components. These components allow the user to create sets of data about entities, define fields, organize record structures, populate the database with data, and manipulate the data in the different files, records, and fields. Simple databases can often be designed by lay users, but more complex databases usually require the involvement of an experienced database designer. The components of a DBMS are the data definition language (which enables the building of schemas and data dictionaries) and the data manipulation language (which allows the user to manipulate data).

Note the difference between a record structure and a record: a *record structure* is the general structure of a record, defining the types of fields that make it up; a *record* is the actual data that pertain to a specific instance. Therefore, for a file that holds the records of professors, we need to design a record structure that describes which fields will appear in *every* actual data record (for instance, ID number, last name, first name, department name, and telephone number). A record will be the row of data describing a specific professor in the professors' file (such as, 120-33-7685, Weinrib, Janet, English, 209-8256). That is, a record contains the actual data values.

The Schema

When building a new database, users must first build a schema (from the Greek word for "plan"). The **schema** describes the structure of the database being designed: the names and types of fields in each record type and the general relationships among different sets of records or files. It includes a description of the database's structure, the names and sizes of fields, and details such as which field is a primary key. The number of records is never specified because it may change, and the maximum number of records is determined by the capacity of the storage medium.

In a hierarchical DBMS, the schema includes the relationships between parent and child record structures. Similarly, relationships must be detailed in the schema of a network database. The schema of a relational database is simpler. It describes only the record structure of each table, namely, the fields of which each record in that table will consist.

The builder of a new database must also indicate which fields will be used as primary keys. Many DBMSs also allow a builder to indicate when a field is not unique, meaning that the value in that field may be the same for more than one record.

The Data Dictionary

All the information supplied by the database developer when constructing the schema is maintained in the data dictionary, which includes the file names, record names and types, field names and types, and, if applicable, the relationships among record types. In addition, the **data dictionary** contains the notation of who is responsible for updating each part of the database and descriptions (such as titles) or names of the people who are authorized to access the different parts of the database.

Data dictionaries are often referred to as *metadata,* meaning "data about the data." They are useful when trying to understand a database designed by someone else. Many PC DBMSs do not allow the users direct access to the data dictionary. The user can view, and to a certain extent change, only the schema. But some mainframe DBMSs provide users with a facility to add to the data dictionary information such as the name of the database designer, the date the database was built, the purpose of each field and its minimum and maximum values, the people who may make changes in the schema, which people are authorized to access which data in the database, and other valuable information.

The Data Definition Language

Every DBMS must include a subprogram (in this case a language) called a **data definition language** (**DDL**) to construct the schema. This language has various commands and protocols the database designer uses to define and name the files, records, and fields in a database before beginning to populate them. In most PC DBMSs, the user interface of the DDL presents screens and prompts the designer to enter the appropriate parameters from a menu. These interfaces are intuitive and allow a database to be created by someone who may have relatively little development experience. In other DBMSs, the user must know the commands used in the DDL to construct the schema.

The Data Manipulation Language

Data manipulation language (**DML**) is the software that serves the user who is querying the database. Some DBMSs require the user to type in commands. For example, consider a database holding personnel data: ID, Last_Name, First_Name, Department, and Salary. Suppose you want a list showing the last names, department number, and salaries of employees whose department number is 4530 and whose salary is less than $25,000. It is the DML that allows such a query to be placed and executed.

Some DBMSs hide the DML from the user. Instead of statements, the user expresses a query by example (QBE). The user invokes the query module of the program, which displays the fields available, and then places check marks in the fields to be listed and conditions in the proper fields. Virtually all the popular PC relational DBMSs provide QBE dialog interfaces.

Many DBMSs are now part of fourth-generation languages (4GLs). 4GLs are flexible enough to allow programmers to use the language both to develop applications that retrieve and manipulate data from a database and also to perform tasks that have nothing to do with the database, all in the same application.

Database Architecture

Database architecture refers to both the physical and logical layouts of databases in an organization. In the past, most organizations' databases—data and programs alike—were centrally located on mainframes and accessed from remote locations throughout the company from dumb terminals. There have been significant changes in database architecture as both databases and the programs running them have moved from mainframes to PCs and from a centralized to a distributed model.

Distributed Databases

Many organizations operate through geographically remote sites. Still, much of the data used by one site is often also used by other sites. Of course, the organization can use a centrally located database and let the other sites use it through communications lines. A less expensive solution, however, is to distribute the database at different sites for all to use. This arrangement is called a *distributed database*. There are two distributed database models: replicated and fragmented.

The **database administrator** (**DBA**) can either replicate the database so there are exact copies in many locations, or fragment it, so that different parts of the database are maintained on different machines. **Replication** of the database means that a full copy of the entire database is stored at all the sites that need access to it. This approach is expensive and not conducive to data integrity, because all the updates must be performed at all the sites, and the chance of errors occurring due to delayed updates and copying errors is high.

Many organizations have opted for the other alternative: in a **fragmented** database, different parts of the database are stored in the locations where they are accessed most often, but they continue to be fully accessible to others through telecommunications. Together, all the parts make up the database. The result is just one copy of the database, distributed among the various sites by way of communications lines. Applications' use of remote fragments of the database is transparent to the users. The users do not know, and need not bother to know, which part of the database resides locally at their site and which is processed remotely. One advantage of a fragmented database is the lower communications costs. With only one copy of the database, another advantage is better data integrity. Many experts refer to fragmented databases as *distributed databases*. Note that the telecommunications lines through which data are accessed do not differ in these two approaches. Nowadays, many multisite companies enable employees and business partners to access databases through intranets and extranets using Web software.

Exhibit 800.20   *Shared Resource and Client/Server Architectures*

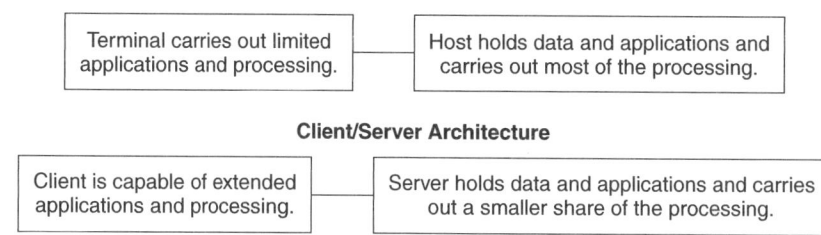

Shared Resource and Client/Server Systems

Some organizations store their databases and the applications that run them on mainframes or on minicomputers accessible remotely from dumb terminals. Others distribute their database but leave the processing of the data centralized. Some experts refer to these arrangements as *shared resource architecture*. The central resource is used by remote terminals and PCs not only for the data in its databases, but also for the applications that process the data.

However, the increasing power of microcomputers and the great progress and declining cost of data communications are driving organizations to move to what is called *client/server architecture*. IS professionals use this term loosely to describe any distribution of data and applications between a server and its clients, including allowing users to access data remotely but process it locally (see Exhibit 800.20). The server is a computer, usually a powerful PC or a minicomputer, that serves the clients—the users' PCs—by storing databases and managing remote access communications. Users can use applications on their own PCs to process data copied from the server. (Note that sometimes the *applications* that are used on the PCs are also called clients. For example, you may have heard the term "e-mail client," which simply means e-mail application.)

In a client/server network, software may run not only on a host but wherever it makes most sense. In fact, software can process "cooperatively" on various computers across the network. It seems that the computer becomes the network, and the network becomes the computer in this scenario. Often, the physical location where the processing takes place is transparent to the user; that is, the user does not know where processing physically occurs.

To use a human analogy, thoughts are processed throughout an office, not just in the mind of the boss. And thoughts are communicated as requirements of the collective process. In a client/server network, users may have much computing power at their local PC, where they can process data, produce information, and then decide what to save on the server and what to save locally in their own computers. This additional computing power is the reason that many experts say the client/server architecture empowers employees; it gives them more independence and the ability to make their own decisions regarding information.

A client/server architecture can follow any of the following four basic models:

- Applications run at a server; PCs serve as terminals, primarily formatting and validating data.
- Applications run on local PCs; the database resides at the server; no significant part of the application runs on the server.
- Applications run on both local PCs and the server; the database resides at the server.
- Applications and key elements of the database are split between the local PCs and the server. Applications call data or other procedures at other locations.

Web Databases

The Internet and its user-friendly application, the Web, would be practically useless if people could not access databases on line. The premise of the Web is that people can not only browse appealing Web pages but also search for and find information in databases. When a shopper accesses an on-line store, he or she can look for information about any of thousands or hundreds of thousands of items offered for sale. For example, when you access the site of **CDNow**, you can receive on-line information (such as an image of a CD's cover, its popularity ranking, price, and shipping time) for any of a half million music CDs. If you access **IBM's** site, you can retrieve information on each of thousands of products and services or select an article from a huge electronic library. In business-to-business e-commerce, wholesalers make their catalogs and special prices available to retailers on line. Applications at auction sites receive inquiries by type of item, color, date, and other attributes and identify records of matching items, which often include pictures and detailed descriptions. Behind each of these sites is a database. The only way for organizations to conduct these Web-based businesses is to give people outside the organizations access to their databases. In other words, the organizations must link their databases to the Internet.

Databases on the Web

Databases on the Web are used in several ways.

- *Catalogs,* in both business-to-business and business-to-consumer e-commerce. Catalog databases allow browsers to search items by key words or combinations of key words. To do so, the site provides a local search engine that scours Web pages stored in its database.
- *Libraries* of books, articles, CDs, and movie clips. These sites also often include a local search engine that allows a user to search for the key words in a title, author name, or an entire article. University faculty, staff, and students often have access to such large databases through their schools. Most of these databases are not owned by the school but are operated by organizations that specialize in library databases such as **ABI/Inform** and **UMI**.
- *Directories,* which can include names, addresses, telephone numbers, and e-mail addresses. For instance, professional associations can provide members with access to membership lists.
- *Client lists and profiles.* Usually, individual users have access to these databases only for the purpose of inserting or updating their own records. A registered user name and password are usually required to gain access to these databases. For example, **ValuPage**, a Web site that provides supermarket coupons on line, collects data on shoppers. To receive periodic e-mail messages with coupons that you can print out and use for supermarket discounts, you must first enter personal data, including your address, e-mail address, and shopping preferences. The data are sold for profit to other organizations.

From a technical point of view, on-line databases that are used with Web browsers are not different from other databases. However, an interface must be designed to work with the Web. The user must be given a form in which to enter queries or key words to obtain information from the site's database. The interface designers must provide a mechanism to figure out data that users insert in the on-line forms so that they can be placed in the proper fields in the database. The system also needs a mechanism to pass queries and key words from the user to the database. There are several such interface programs, including CGI (Common Gateway interface), API (application program interface), Java servlets, and active server pages.

Points to Consider When Linking Databases

When linking a database to the Internet, IT professionals must consider several points.

- Which application to use
- How to ensure that on-line access by Web surfers does not interfere with database updates
- How to maintain security

A CGI is an application that enables a Web surfer to fill out an on-line form with data that is then used to update a database. As just mentioned, other applications can fulfill this function, and there are some trade-offs to consider. For example, both API interfaces and Java servlets run faster than conventional CGI applications, but they are more difficult to develop and implement.

To ensure that Web surfers do not interfere with their employees' work, organizations avoid linking their transactions databases to the Internet. They are also careful when linking a data warehouse to the Internet. Usually, companies use a mirror (a copy of the original database) stored on a dedicated server to link to the Web. That server is linked directly to the Web at one end and to the server with the original database at the other end. Special software blocks access of unauthorized Web users to the original database. The mirror database is updated at regular intervals.

Organizations must understand, however, that once a computer is linked to a public network, there is a risk of unauthorized access to it and any other computer that is linked to it. Thus, security measures are critical to prevent unauthorized access. People often gain unauthorized access to deface Web pages or even destroy data in databases. To screen and block access, a special type of software called a *firewall* is used on the server.

Exhibit 800.21 *Data Are Warehoused for Analysis and Reporting*

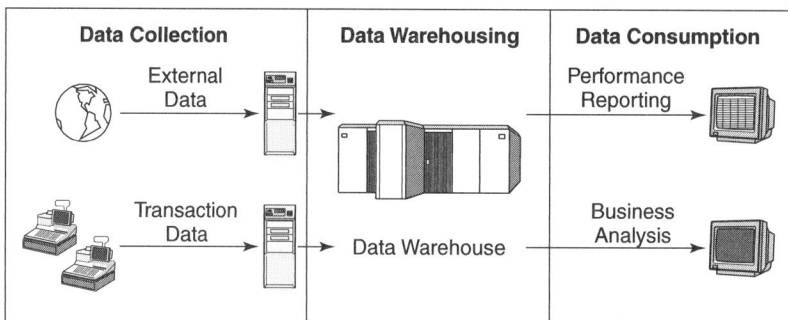

Data Warehousing

The great majority of data collections in business are used for daily transactions and operations: records of customers and their purchases and information on employees, patients, and other parties for monitoring, collection, payment, and other business or legal purposes. However, many organizations have found that if they archive transaction data, they can use them for important management decisions, such as researching market trends or tracking down fraud. The accumulated data are like a huge heap of dirt in which precious gems are hidden. If the data are organized well, and if proper tools are used to analyze the data, those gems may be found. Uncovering the gems is the purpose of data warehousing.

A **data warehouse** is a huge collection of data that supports management decision making (see Exhibit 800.21). It maintains snapshots of business conditions at predetermined points in time, such as the end of each business day or the first of every month. A data warehouse is a large—usually relational—database. The purpose of data warehouses is to let managers produce reports or analyze large amounts of archival data and make decisions. Data warehousing experts must be familiar with the types of business analyses that will be done with the data. They also have to design the data warehouse tables to be flexible enough for modifications in years to come, when business activities change or when different information must be extracted.

Data warehouses do not replace transactional databases, which are updated with daily transactions such as sales, billing, cash receipts, and returns. Instead, data warehouses are designed to record periodic "snapshots" of the transactional databases—"to provide pictures" of the different aspects of a business. This large archive contains valuable hidden information for the organization. For example, an insurance company may keep monthly tables of policy sales; it can then see trends in the types of policies customers prefer in general or by age group. Data from transactional databases are added to the data warehouse at the end of each business day, week, or month. While a transactional database contains current data, which is disposed of after some time, the data in data warehouses are accumulated and may reflect many years of business activities.

While a data warehouse combines data from databases across an entire organization, organizations also use **data marts,** smaller collections of data that focus on a particular subject or department. If a business maintains a data warehouse that consists of several data marts, they are called *dependent data marts*. If data are organized in data marts but need to be used as one large data warehouse, special software tools can unify data marts and make them appear as one large data warehouse. To uncover the valuable information contained in their data, organizations must use software that can effectively investigate data warehouses.

From Database to Data Warehouse

Unlike data warehouses, transactional databases are usually not suitable for business analysis because they contain current, not historical, data. Often, data in transactional databases are also scattered in different systems throughout an organization. The same data are often stored differently and under other names. For example, customer names may be recorded in a column called Name in one department's table and in two columns—First Name and Last Name—in another department's table. These discrepancies commonly occur when an organization uses both its own data and data it purchases from other organizations. Also, transactional systems were simply not designed for decision support. As such, they are often incompatible with computer-based decision aids such as decision support systems and executive support systems. When management decides to build a data warehouse, the IT staff must carefully consider the hardware, software, and data involved in the effort.

Hardware

The larger the data warehouse, the larger the storage capacity, the greater the memory, and the greater the processing power of the computer that is needed. Because of capacity needs, organizations often choose mainframe computers with multiple CPUs to store and manage data warehouses. The computer memory must be large enough to allow processing of huge amounts of data at once. The amount of storage space and the access speed of disks is also important. Processing millions of records may take a long time, and variations in disk speed may mean the difference between hours or minutes in processing time. And since a data warehouse is considered a highly valuable asset, all data must be automatically backed up. Keep in mind that data warehouses grow continually, because their very purpose is to hold historic records. Retail companies record millions of sales transactions daily, all of which are channeled into data warehouses. So do banks, credit-card issuers, and health-care organizations.

Data and Software

The data from which data warehouses are built usually come from within an organization, mainly from transactions, but they can also come from outside an organization. The latter may include national or regional demographic data, data from financial markets, and weather data. Data warehouse designers create metadata, that is, data about the data, including the following:

1. The source of the data, including contact information
2. Tables that are related to the data
3. Field and index information, such as the size and type of the field (whether it is text or numeric), and the ways the data are sorted
4. Programs and processes that use the data
5. Population rules: what is inserted, or updated, and how often

The designers must keep in mind scalability: the ability of the data warehouse to grow as the amount of the data and the processing needs grow. Future growth needs involve good planning in terms of both hardware and software.

Phases in Building a Data Warehouse

Once an organization has ensured that it has adequate hardware and software, it can begin building the data warehouse. Several phases are involved in building a data warehouse from transactional data: chiefly, the extraction, cleansing, and loading phases. In the **extraction phase,** the builders create the files from transactional databases and save them on the server that will hold the data warehouse.

In the **cleansing phase,** the builders modify the data into a form that allows insertion into the data warehouse. For example, they ascertain whether the data contain any spelling errors, and if there are any, they fix them. They make sure that all data are consistent. For instance, Pennsylvania may be denoted as Pa., PA, Penna, or Pennsylvania. Only one form would be used in a warehouse. Warehouse builders ensure that all addresses follow the same form, using upper- or lowercase letters consistently and defining fields uniformly (such as one field for the entire street address and a separate field for zip codes). All data that express the same type of quantities are "cleansed" to use the same measurement units.

In the **loading phase,** the builders transfer the cleansed files to the database that will serve as the data warehouse. They then compare the data in the data warehouses with the original data from the transactional database to ascertain completeness. They document the data for users, so the users know what they can find and analyze in the data warehouse.

The new data warehouse is then ready for use. It is a single source for all the data required for analysis, is accessible to more users than the transactional databases (whose access is limited only to those who record transactions), and provides a "one-stop shopping" place for data. In fact, it is not unusual for an organization to have one very large table of data with numerous fields.

Data Mining

One of the main purposes of maintaining a data warehouse is to be able to "mine" it for useful information. **Data mining** is the process of selecting, exploring, and modeling large amounts of data to discover previously unknown relationships. Data mining software searches through large amounts of data for meaningful patterns of information

Exhibit 800.22 *Potential Applications of Data Mining*

Data-Mining Application	Description
Consumer clustering	Identify the common characteristics of customers who tend to buy the same products and services from your company.
Customer churn	Identify the reason customers switch to competitors; predict which customers are likely to do so.
Fraud detection	Identify which characteristics of transactions are most likely to be fraudulent.
Direct marketing	Identify which prospective clients should be included in a mailing or e-mail list to obtain the highest response rate.
Interactive marketing	Predict what each individual accessing a Web site is most likely to be interested in seeing.
Market-based analysis	Understand what products or services are commonly purchased together, and on what days of the week.
Trend analysis	Reveal the difference between a typical customer this month and a typical customer last month.

(see Exhibit 800.22). Data mining is most often used by marketing managers, who are constantly analyzing purchasing patterns, so that potential buyers can be targeted more efficiently through special sales, product displays, or direct mail and e-mail campaigns. Data mining is an especially powerful tool in an environment in which businesses are shifting from mass-marketing a product to targeting the individual consumer with a variety of products that are likely to satisfy him or her. Some observers call this approach "marketing to one."

However, data mining is also used in banking, where it is employed to find profitable customers and patterns of fraud. For example, when **Bank of America (BofA)** looked for new approaches to retain customers, it used data-mining techniques. It merged various behavior patterns into finely tuned customer profiles. The data were clustered into smaller groups of individuals who were using banking services that didn't best support their activities. Bank employees contacted these customers and offered advice on services that would serve them better. The result was greater customer loyalty (measured in fewer accounts closed and fewer moves to other banks). The people who were contacted thought that the bank was trying to take good care of their money.

To illustrate the difference between "traditional" queries and data-mining queries, consider the following examples. A typical "traditional" query would be: "Is there a relationship between the amount of product X and the amount of product Y that we sold over the past quarter?" A typical data-mining query would be: "Discover two products most likely to sell well together on a weekend." The latter query lets the software find patterns that would otherwise not be detected through observation. While we have traditionally used data to see whether this or that pattern existed, data mining allows us to ask *what* patterns exist. Thus, some experts say that in data mining we let the computer answer questions that we do not know to ask. The combination of data warehousing techniques and data-mining software makes it easier to predict future outcomes based on patterns discovered within historical data.

To analyze the data in data warehouses, organizations can use **online analytical processing** (**OLAP**) applications, or more sophisticated software. However, while OLAP tools help find relationships by running data through statistical models, they do not answer the question that more powerful data-mining tools can answer: "What are the relationships we do not yet know?" This is because the investigator must determine which relationship the software should look for in the first place. To answer this question, other techniques are used in data mining, including artificial intelligence techniques.

Historically, banks were among the first to use data-mining techniques. **Chase Manhattan** continues to pursue the practice eagerly. The bank wanted to analyze the habits of its checking account customers for clues that might reveal how to set the minimum balance requirements. To many customers, the minimum balance requirement is a key criterion in choosing a bank. Management wanted to know whether business with these customers was profitable. If Chase was losing profitable customers because the minimum balance required was too high, that balance should be lowered; but if the bank was losing money on them, the balance should be left as is.

Management wanted answers to questions such as: How many checks do these customers write per month? Do they use ATMs or use teller service? What other accounts do they hold, and what other services do they use? Data-mining techniques provided answers. The bank found out who its profitable customers were. It lowered the minimum required balance, and the ratio of profitable customers to overall customers increased. A manager at Chase likened data mining to X-rays; a doctor can examine a patient by just looking at him or use X-rays to learn much more about the patient.

Knowledge Management

Knowledge management is the combination of activities involved in gathering, organizing, sharing, analyzing, and disseminating knowledge to improve an organization's performance.

Knowledge is usually perceived as "know-how," which is usually accumulated through experience combined with accumulating certain information or, at least, knowing where information can be found. Much knowledge is kept in people's minds, on paper notes, on discussion transcripts, and in other places that are not readily accessible to a company's employees. Therefore, knowledge management is a great challenge. Knowledge management is the attempt by organizations to put procedures and technologies in place to do the following:

- Transfer individual knowledge into databases
- Filter and separate the most relevant knowledge
- Organize that knowledge in databases that either
    1. Allow other employees to easily access the knowledge or
    2. "Push" specific knowledge to employees based on their prespecified needs

Lotus Development Corp., an **IBM** division, initiated a knowledge management project to better serve its customers. For a long time, customer support personnel logged help calls but did not record what they learned from customers about the software products the company sold. To change that, the IS department created an applet to capture this data. Now, a call to the support desk is not complete until the employee has entered the substance of the call into Lotus Notes, the software in which the applet was created. Identifying recurring problems allowed the company to enhance the training of its support desk staff in critical areas and resulted in greater customer satisfaction and more efficient response time.

KPMG, a "big five" accounting and management consulting firm, established a knowledge intranet called KWorld, available to the firm's more than 100,000 professionals in 160 different countries. In the past, consultants had to locate specialists' hard-copy documents and read through dozens of documents to find the facts and expertise they were looking for. Now, through a single corporate Web portal, the system lets any member of the consulting staff tap information detailing the experiences of other consultants with a certain type of problem, software, or client. With KWorld, expert information is available through the consultants' PCs, anywhere, anytime, and the single repository of knowledge eliminates the phenomenon of redundant searches. The knowledge base is organized around product, industry, and geographic region. A KPMG consultant assigned to a new project can log on to the KWorld system and search for all consultants with expertise in a specific industry, technology, country, or all three elements. A consultant sitting in an office in New York can use a networked PC to receive expert information on an installation of an enterprise resource planning (ERP) system in the Netherlands. Consultants are required to submit their experience with every consulting project. Fifteen full-time "knowledge editors" in New York City maintain the knowledge repository. They capture not only internal knowledge but also external information, a daily lot of some 8,000 published papers, speeches, books, and magazine articles.

Artificial Intelligence in Business

Intelligence is the ability to acquire and apply knowledge, to think, and to reason. The better equipped a person is with mental tools to learn and apply new ideas, the higher his or her intelligence. Intelligence actually includes many abilities: making associations between a previous experience and a new situation, drawing systematic conclusions, quickly adopting new ways to solve problems, being able to separate what is important from what is not in solving a problem, and determining what tools can or cannot help in handling complex situations. **Artificial intelligence (AI)** researchers and developers try to emulate the human mind in machines. Efforts by nonacademic organizations have yielded many commercial products. One of the areas in which AI has had a positive impact is business. Combined with information systems and database management systems (DBMSs), programs that use the principles of artificial intelligence can provide outstanding support for high-level decision making in business. In this section, we describe the concepts involved in artificial intelligence and the way it has enhanced business.

Although AI may still have the aura of an esoteric research area, it has actually been implemented in numerous practical applications. For example, **Charles Schwab**, the largest on-line brokerage business, has added AI functions to its Web site to handle customers' questions better. In another area, a company called **Continental Divide Robotics (CDR)** has developed a system that combines AI, signals from the GPS (global positioning system) satellites above the earth, and telecommunications in robots for monitoring parolees. A special device is attached to the parolees. If parolees leave a certain area or go near a designated house, the CDR system in the device will decide whom it should contact.

AI efforts may be classified into several categories, as illustrated in Exhibit 800.23. While the research and development in some areas, such as robotics and artificial vision, involve hardware and software, the research and development in other areas involve only software.

Robotics

Robotics engineers build machines designed to perform useful work. Contrary to popular belief, the majority of **robots** in industrial use do not look like human beings. However, many are designed to do what human beings have long done, only more efficiently and effectively. In the auto industry, robots are used to weld, paint, and screw nuts. Much of the automotive and other manufacturing work done manually until the early 1980s is now done by robots. In many industries, only the research and development phase of making products is performed by human beings; the actual production is done by robots. For instance, the manufacture of microprocessors is almost completely automated with robots, which is the main reason that computer prices have dropped so sharply over the years. At **Lexmark**, an IBM subsidiary that manufactures printers, the use of smart robots reduced cycle time by 90 percent. A printer that once took four hours to assemble now takes only 24 minutes. Consequently, a Lexmark printer that used to cost $200 not long ago now costs only $50.

Robots are also extremely useful in environments where people can be easily and seriously injured. For example, police forces use remote control units and television monitors to guide robots to defuse bombs. Some sophisticated robots are even capable of detecting explosives by "smelling" objects suspected to be bombs (that is, sensing the molecular structure of certain elements in the air). Similar robots are used in nuclear power plants to perform duties that pose health hazards.

Some companies have developed robots that carry out household chores such as vacuuming, sweeping, and even removing dishes from tables and turning on appliances. Some companies have developed commercial lawn-mowing robots.

All robots either contain a computer or are connected to one. In general, they need to sense their position and their surroundings, execute the functions they are programmed to perform, and provide feedback as needed. With the advancement of voice recognition, some robots are programmed to recognize and execute vocal commands.

Engineers who specialize in robotics are working on improving robot operation and mode of interaction. They program specially built machines with mechanical limbs to move, recognize their position in space, grab objects, lay them down, and so on.

Artificial Vision

Another important feature needed for robots to function successfully in their environments is artificial vision. **Artificial vision** is the ability of a machine to "see" its environment, to make choices about its actions based on what it sees, and to recognize visual input (such as handwriting) according to general patterns. For instance, robots must recognize their position in space so they do not bump into obstacles, and they must recognize their position relative to an object that they must act on, pick up, or push. Currently, trial devices are being used in the U.S. Postal Service to recognize handwriting, parse it correctly, and digitize the information so it can be used for sorting.

Exhibit 800.23 *The Various Research Efforts in Artificial Intelligence*

Subfields of Artificial Intelligence			
Robotics	Artificial Vision	Natural Language Processing	Expert Systems
Neural Networks	Fuzzy Logic	Genetic Algorithms	Intelligent Agents

Natural Language Processing

Natural language processors (**NLPs**) are programs that are designed to take human language as input and translate it into a standard set of statements that a computer can execute. The programs work by parsing sentences and trying to eliminate ambiguity in a given context. The purpose of these sophisticated programs is to allow human beings to use their own natural language when interacting with programs such as database management systems (DBMSs) or decision-support systems (DSSs).

The goal of natural language processors is to eventually eliminate the need for people to learn programming languages or customized commands for computers to understand them. Their great advantage is in the way they can be combined with voice-recognition devices to allow the user to command computers to perform tasks without touching a keyboard or any other input device.

One of the greatest challenges in natural language processing is the completely different meanings the same combination of words may take on in different contexts. The challenge is to teach the machine to interpret the words correctly, according to their context.

In recent years, NLP applications have been developed for use in Web search engines and as the front end of data-mining software. AI-based search engines enable users to enter simple English questions or sentences from which they can understand which information to fetch from pages throughout the Web. The challenge is to make the applications understand what the user needs within a context, so that the engine does not fetch millions of irrelevant pages along with the few that are relevant. In data mining, the challenge is similar: to have the application understand what relationships among business variables exist within a context. Companies use data mining in data warehouses to find relationships that help in target marketing, fraud detection, and other areas.

Expert Systems

The purpose of *expert systems (ESs)* is to replicate the unstructured and undocumented knowledge of the few (the experts), and put it at the disposal of others. Because of the way ESs are formulated (based on the experience of experts), ESs cannot help users deal with events that are not considered by the experts during development. However, more advanced programs that include what are called "neural networks" can learn from new situations and formulate new rules in their knowledge bases to address events not originally considered in their development.

To build an ES, a specialist called a **knowledge engineer** questions experts and translates their knowledge into code. In most systems, the knowledge is represented in one of several forms. The most popular form is IF-THEN rules. For example: "If the patient is female, and if the patient's temperature is over 100°F, and if the patient has a rash (and so on), then the patient has disease X."

Two other methods used to represent knowledge in a computer program are semantic frames, which are tables that list entities and their attributes, and semantic networks, which are maps of entities and their related attributes, both of which are discussed later.

ES shells—programs designed to facilitate development of ESs with minimal programming—have facilitated the building of ESs. ES researchers continue to look for ways to better capture knowledge and represent it. They test the results of such efforts in highly unstructured problem-solving domains, including games. One such game, which has intrigued both researchers and laypeople, is chess. The game is a highly unstructured environment in which the number of possible moves is enormous, and hence, the player must be an expert to select the best move for every board configuration.

Some companies that specialize in building the systems stopped calling them expert systems and now prefer to call them *knowledge management systems* and *data miners,* especially when the systems are used to "mine" for unknown relationships in data warehouses.

Neural Networks

Rather than containing a set of IF-THEN rules (as explained later), more sophisticated ESs use programs called **neural networks,** which are designed to mimic the way a human brain operates—the way it links facts, draws conclusions, and uses experience to learn and to understand how new facts relate to each other. Neural networks enable machine learning, the ability of a system to update its knowledge dynamically from its own experiences and apply them to future sessions.

Neural networks are software applications programmed to simulate the "wiring" style of a human brain, whose software "cells," or nodes, are connected to other software "cells," or nodes, to form a network. The network consists of several layers of nodes and each layer is represented by a different color. The network of software nodes is programmed to mimic the physical network of neurons in our own, human brains. The software nodes are linked logically rather than physically and simulate brain activity by having different processes take place in different locations and assimilating them to create the output.

Unlike expert systems, a neural net system learns through trial and error. After an action, which is based on advice from the system, produces results, the knowledge engineer provides the results as feedback, which the system records. The system then changes the code to refine its decision rules. As the number of trials and amount of feedback increase, the system becomes more and more accurate in its evaluation and output. Many systems let the user view a graphical representation of the logical connections among the nodes on the computer monitor; these connections are sometimes called "wires." As the system learns, it starts to see the favored path to a solution, which the graphical representation indicates by color-coding.

The uncanny ability of neural networks to learn by themselves, without benefit of explicit software instructions, has been enticing scientists for several years. But implementation of the technology in the business world is progressing slowly, mainly because businesspeople find the technology difficult to understand. Many systems that are now marketed as ESs have neural net technology integrated into them. Sometimes they are called *neural net ESs*.

Business applications have increasingly used combined neural networks and ES technologies in software that monitors business processes and supply chain management.

Fuzzy Logic

Fuzzy logic is based on rules that do not have discrete boundaries but lie along a continuum, enabling a system to better deal with ambiguity. This reasoning process mirrors the way people tend to think, which is in relative, not absolute, terms. As a result, fuzzy logic allows computer applications to solve problems in a more humanlike manner. When fuzzy logic is incorporated into an ES, the result is a system that more closely mimics the natural manner in which a human expert would solve a problem.

Because fuzzy logic can support decisions in highly unstructured environments, it also has applicability in more information-oriented industries such as finance, insurance, and pharmaceuticals. A good example in the finance field is a system that combines neural networks and fuzzy logic to forecast convertible bond ratings.

Genetic Algorithms

Sometimes, scientists or engineers understand what occurs in a natural process, recognize that it would be helpful to adapt the process to occur in a program, and figure out how to artificially replicate the process in a program that is designed to solve problems. **Genetic algorithms** are mathematical functions that use Darwinian principles to improve an application. The functions are designed to simulate in the software environment, in minutes or seconds, what happens in natural environments over millions of years. In nature, living organisms improve through mutation and natural selection based on their success or failure surviving in the physical environment; with genetic algorithms, software mimics this process, within a very short time, to produce the "fittest," that is the optimal, computer program that can solve a problem.

The process starts with a large collection of functions, which are relatively small and well-defined computer programs designed to solve part of an overall problem. Each function is equivalent to a chromosome in nature. They are randomly combined into programs. The programs are run, and the results are tested to determine which programs give the best results in solving a problem. The best programs are kept (this is the "natural" selection), the others are mutated (broken up into functions that are recombined), and the new generation of programs is tested. The process is repeated until a clear best program emerges.

Unlike neural nets, which start work with a clean slate and learn patterns through analysis of feedback, genetic algorithms start their work with a large number of building blocks. Through an enormous number of trials and errors, they produce viable solutions that could take human beings years to reach.

Intelligent Agents

The latest development in AI is **intelligent agents,** computer programs that automatically wade through massive amounts of data and select and deliver the most suitable information for the user, according to contextual or specific requirements that automatically perform tasks for organizations or individuals based on certain conditions. Intelligent agents have been used most often on the Web. In addition to bringing useful information to the desktops of their "masters," advanced intelligent agents are also expected to execute some operations such as retrieving price lists of specified consumer goods, copying articles related to certain subjects, paying outstanding debts electronically, and purchasing goods and services. Note that intelligent agents are not expert systems, which are programmed to provide expert advice in a narrow field of expertise. The main purpose of intelligent agents is to carry out their assignments significantly faster, more frequently, and more effectively than human beings. Experts say that soon intelligent agents will automatically link your computer to your favorite sites, alert you when these sites have been updated, and tailor specific pages to suit your preferences.

As in the case of expert systems, one of the most difficult problems that researchers must overcome is how to install common sense in intelligent agent programs. In the future, the research is expected to address not only the technical challenges of developing agents but the social and ethical issues as well, such as who should have control (the human owner or the program) in which situations.

Contribution of Expert Systems

Expert Systems can make valuable contributions to organizations. Although the cost of developing some systems can reach seven figures or more, the benefits can outweigh the expense. The greatest benefit of ESs is their contribution to productivity—they perform some time-consuming tasks, freeing employees to focus on work only human beings can do. ESs have been applied to several areas.

1. *Planning.* ESs can use information from previous projects to improve subsequent plans, by cautioning the planner against pitfalls that may cause budget and time overruns, for example.
2. *Decision Making.* ESs can support decision making by bringing input from several experts, rather than from a single expert, thereby providing the organization with a true strategic weapon.
3. *Monitoring.* ESs can be used to monitor industrial processes, cash management, and employee activities, easily providing security against fraud by identifying aberrations in cash disbursement.
4. *Diagnosis.* ESs can provide valuable support in diagnosing different conditions: human diseases in medicine; malfunctioning equipment, products, or processes in industry; or hardware problems and their solutions in business. Major Swedish corporations such as **Volvo, Saab, Asea Brown Boveri**, and **Televerket** have developed ESs to solve control and processing problems in their plants. The British steel industry developed ESs that help in the production of stainless steel slabs.
5. *Training.* Many ESs contain an explanation facility that describes the logic being used to address the problem at hand. This feature makes AI techniques handy in producing ESs that are devoted to training. Training ESs teach users decision rules, which the user can then bring to his or her own work.
6. *Incidental Learning.* Studies have shown that while using an ES in the regular course of their work, people internalize how the system reaches decisions. This unplanned learning increases their own expertise and makes them better decision makers, even in times when an ES is not available.
7. *Replication of Expertise.* Once the expertise is captured in the system, it can easily and inexpensively be replicated and disseminated. Thus, many employees in various divisions and sites can enjoy the knowledge of the same experts.
8. *Timely Response.* Unlike human expert consultants, ESs are on call at all times to provide immediate support and to perform processes, in moments, that would be prohibitively time-consuming for human beings.
9. *Consistent Solutions.* Many organizations want their managers and employees to be consistent in their decision making. For example, a bank would not like its credit officers to evaluate creditworthiness following different guidelines. Since ESs are programmed to solve a certain problem in the same way every time they are queried, they provide the desired consistency.

Development of Expert Systems

Expert systems have caught the attention of knowledge workers in a wide variety of industries. Because they are designed for use in highly unstructured settings such as investment in securities, tax planning, and financial analysis, accountants and other professionals have recognized the potential of ESs to provide expert advice without the need for a human expert. However, development of ESs is usually a major undertaking. Thus, you should be familiar with the concept of expertise and the way it is translated into an ES.

What Is Expertise?

Consider what happens when your car malfunctions and emits a strange sound. You realize you do not have a clue how to diagnose the problem. When you take it to a repair shop, the mechanic listens to the noise, looks at something under the hood, and decides that the water pump is broken. Solving the problem seemed simple for this expert mechanic. However, gaining the expertise might have taken many years of work. Through years of dealing with this problem and this noise, the expert mechanic knows what is *not* the right diagnosis, and through many trials and errors, the mechanic has formulated rules that lead him or her to the diagnosis. These rules make up a mechanic's expertise in solving car problems.

Expertise is the skill and knowledge, primarily gained from experience, whose input into a process results in performance that is far above the norm. Expertise often consists of massive amounts of factual information, coupled with rules of thumb, simplifications, rare facts, and wise procedures, all compiled in a way that allows an expert to analyze specific problems efficiently. Some expertise can be acquired through formal education, but to a large extent, expertise is gained through trial and error. Such experience allows experts to skip options they know will not be fruitful and choose those that will. Most of the rules that experts accumulate over time are **heuristics** (from the Greek word *Heuristikein,* "to find"): rules that cannot be formulated as a result of ordinary, proven knowledge but only through experience. Heuristics are compiled hindsight, and they draw their power from the regularity and continuity in the world. They arise through specialization, generalization, and analogy.

Components of Expert Systems

An expert system consists of three components (see Exhibit 800.24): (1) The "interface," or **dialog,** program facilitates interaction between the user and the system. It is similar to the dialog program in a DSS. The dialog module prompts the user to enter parameters required to make a decision in an orderly manner. (2) The **knowledge base** is a set of facts and the relationships among the facts provided as input to the system. (3) The **inference engine** is a program that associates the user-supplied data with a set of rules to deduce solutions and explain how they were reached. The inference engine takes the input the user supplies through the dialog component and combines it with knowledge in the knowledge base to produce a solution to a problem: a decision or a diagnosis.

Construction of Expert Systems

While decision-support systems use databases and data warehouses as their information sources, ESs use knowledge bases. A knowledge base contains, in a computer-readable form, the facts, associations, relationships, and beliefs supplied by an expert. There are several methods used to organize knowledge in a knowledge base, such as IF-THEN rules, frames, and semantic nets. We then discuss details of expert system development, functioning, and rationale: knowledge engineering, chaining, and factors justifying acquisition of ESs.

Exhibit 800.24 *Components of an Expert System; Numbers Indicate the Order of the Processes*

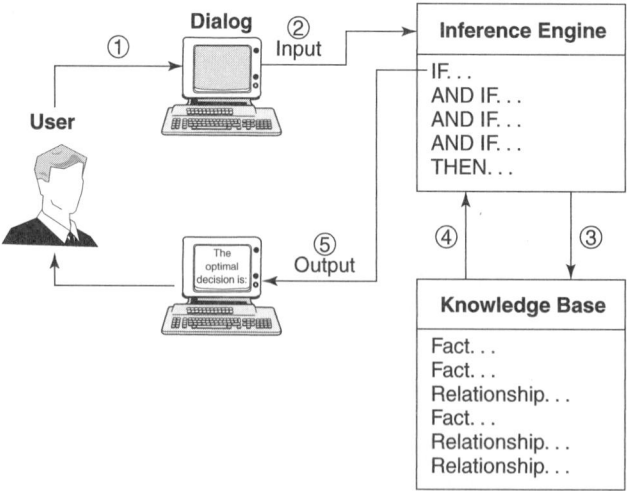

Exhibit 800.25 *A Frame Describing a Dog*

Attribute	Value
Mammal	Yes
Fur	Yes
Sound	Barks
Legs	Four
Tail	Yes

IF-THEN Rules

IF-THEN rules, also called **production rules,** are by far the most popular method of knowledge representation, found in over 70 percent of all ESs. As a simple example, consider a knowledge base for classifying animals. The system holds the facts in the form of IF-THEN statements such as: "If it has *four legs,* and if it has *a tail,* and if it *barks,* then it is *a dog.*" The knowledge base may contain hundreds or thousands of such rules.

Frames

Knowledge can also be organized as facts in tables, referred to as **frames,** where each table is devoted to one entity or occurrence and its attributes (see Exhibit 800.25). For instance, the frame for the entity *dog* would include the facts that it is a mammal, has fur, has four legs, barks, and so on. When queried, the inference engine searches the tables. Conditions are satisfied if the information is found in the frame relating to the event or entity.

Semantic Nets

When knowledge is stored in the form of objects and the relationships among them, it is said to be stored in **semantic nets** because, when graphed, the knowledge base looks like a network where the boxes contain objects, and the lines represent attributes and relationships. To reach a solution to a problem, the system navigates along the network according to the parameters supplied by the user until it finds a unique object that satisfies the parameters.

Knowledge Engineering

It takes more than a good programmer to construct an ES. A *knowledge engineer* is a programmer who specializes in developing ESs. He or she is skilled in asking experts the appropriate questions and translating the answers into a knowledge base that follows one of the preceding approaches. Interestingly, but not surprisingly, many successful knowledge engineers have a formal education in psychology. This background enables knowledge engineers to help people work cooperatively to provide all the information they can, which can be a process requiring excellent communications skills and great patience. For instance, imagine trying to get the mechanic described earlier to explain how she knows what is wrong with a car by listening to the motor. She may tell you she knows "from experience." But what does that mean? Is there a certain irregular sound coming from the motor? Is it always associated with the same malfunction? Is there a combination of factors that lead her to her diagnosis? Clearly, it is not easy to obtain a step-by-step explanation of facts and link them.

Expert System Shells

Early ESs were developed using programming languages that were invented especially for AI applications: LISP (LISt Processing), KEE (Knowledge Engineering Environment), Prolog, and others. While some ESs are still constructed using these languages, most knowledge engineers now use **expert system shells,** which are programs that provide an interface to assist the developer in creating an ES. The shell queries the developer for facts and the links among them, and enters the information into a knowledge base. Vendors now offer expert system shells that enable novice programmers to develop their own ESs.

Forward Chaining and Backward Chaining

An ES that takes certain values of parameters as input, runs them through an inference engine, and outputs the solution to the problem is said to be carrying out **forward chaining** (forward reasoning). That is, the system starts the process with facts and works its way to a result. Therefore, forward chaining is also referred to as a *result-driven* process. If the system is given a goal and asked to state the conditions that would bring about the desired outcome, then the process is **backward chaining** (backward reasoning), or a *goal-driven* process. For example, if an investor decides to invest $100,000 for one year in municipal bonds, forward chaining will predict an annual return of 3 percent. If the investor wants to earn at least a 20 percent annual return, backward chaining will lead to recommending an investment in technology stocks for more than two years.

While it may sound as if the system must be developed to do either forward chaining or backward chaining, this is not the case. Think of decision making as traversing a decision tree, where at each junction you must find the best path. The same decision tree can serve you to move from a set of givens to a result (forward chaining) or from a goal to the givens (backward chaining). Indeed, many ES shell programs accommodate the usage of the ES they help to build both in forward and backward chaining modes.

While a person can use an ES blindly, providing information as asked and letting the ES do the work, most people want to understand how the system is approaching a problem. So, if an ES requests certain data in the process of considering a problem, a user may ask to see the reasoning behind the request. In backward chaining, the system simply goes one step back, fetches the previous step's set of conditions, and presents them as an explanation. In many ESs the menu item or icon for this feature is "Why?" or "Explain."

Factors Justifying the Acquisition of Expert Systems

There are certain factors that should be considered before deciding to develop an ES, (see Exhibit 800.26). First, the problem to be solved should not be trivial. Trivial problems can be solved by novices without any aid. Second, the problem must be in a highly unstructured domain that requires the wisdom of an expert. Third, the problem should occur frequently. Fourth, an expert must be available for building the expert system. The development of an ES requires that an expert contribute much of his or her time in long sessions with a knowledge engineer. This time is expensive and not always available.

Expert Systems in Action

Expert Systems have been implemented to help professionals in many different industries, such as telecommunications, credit, tax, securities, mining, agriculture, and manufacturing. The following is a small sample.

Telephone Network Maintenance

Pacific Bell uses an ES to diagnose network failures and fix them. The system consists of three parts: Monitor, Consultant, and Forecaster. Monitor constantly monitors Pacific Bell's telephone network, checking for errors. When a problem is detected, the system uses a synthesized voice to warn network specialists, who can then use Consultant to walk them through recommended troubleshooting and repair procedures to correct the problem. Before the company

Exhibit 800.26 *Justification Factors for the Acquisition of an Expert System*

- The problem must be nontrivial.
- The problem must occur in a highly unstructured setting.
- The problem must occur frequently.
- An expert must be available to develop the system.

started using the ES, a small number of highly trained specialists did the troubleshooting, which is now done by employees with less training. Forecaster, the third part of the ES, checks system files and notifies personnel of problems likely to occur, based on previous experience, allowing the staff to prevent problems from occurring.

Credit Evaluation

Holders of **American Express (AmEx)** charge cards can potentially charge the card for hundreds of thousands of dollars per purchase. Obviously, most retailers and restauranteurs will not process a charge before they contact AmEx for approval. The AmEx clerk who considers the request uses an ES. The system requests data such as account number, location of the establishment, and amount of the purchase. Coupled with information from a database that contains previous data on the account, and a knowledge base with criteria for approving or denying credit, the ES provides a response.

Another expert system called FAST (Financial Analysis Support Techniques) helps with credit analysis. The system is used by over 30 of the top 100 U.S. and Canadian banks as well as some of the largest industrial and financial companies in the world. It gives a credit analyst access to the expertise of more experienced advisors, accelerating the training process and increasing productivity.

The system provides complex analysis of the data contained in applicants' financial reports. The expert system not only provides English language interpretation of the historical financial output but also prepares the assumptions for annual projections and produces text output linkable to word processing software. It eliminates much of the tedious writing of analytical reports, producing standard financial statement reviews.

Loan officers periodically update the knowledge base to customize it for a bank's current loan policy, as well as national and local economic forecasts and interest rate projections. The system consistently and reliably interprets the relationship of these variable factors and the levels of sensitivity that the loan officers associate with a particular financial statement.

Tax Planning

Because federal and state tax laws are so complex, choosing business strategies to minimize tax payments requires expertise. Several tax ESs have been developed for this purpose. For instance, TaxAdvisor solves problems dealing with income and transfer tax planning for individuals. The system makes recommendations, based on projected events, for tax-related actions to maximize the wealth that an individual transfers at death.

Financial Advisor is used by tax consultants to get advice on projects, products, mergers, and acquisitions. A consultant provides information about a company, and the system evaluates how proposed transactions, changes in the tax law, or other factors affect the tax owed.

Detection of Insider Securities Trading

Like other similar institutions, the American Stock Exchange (AMEX) has a special department to prevent insider trading of the securities under its supervision. Insider trading is the trading of stocks based on information available only to those affiliated with a company, not to the general public. This practice is a serious breach of U.S. federal law. To detect insider trading, the department receives information, from several sources, on unusual trading activity and uses this information to identify a stock it may want to investigate. Using an ES, the department's analysts access a large database of the stock's history and choose a time period of interest. The system provides questions that the analysts can answer with the information they received from the database. The questions are formulated to reflect the experience of expert investigators. After the analysts finish answering all the questions, the system provides two numbers: the probability that a further investigation is warranted, and the probability that it is not.

Detection of Common Metals

Metallurgists are experts, and their time is expensive. Also, they usually work in laboratories, which are expensive, too. **General Electric Corp.** developed an expert system that helps nonexperts to identify common metals and alloys outside laboratories. The user provides information on density, color, and hardness of the metal and results of simple chemical tests that can be performed by novices outside the laboratory setting. If the user provides sufficient information, the system will positively identify the metal or alloy. If there is not sufficient information, the system will provide a list of possible metals in order of likelihood. Even such a list can be helpful in some situations, saving much time, labor cost, and the need to wait for lab testing.

Mineral Exploration

Another common application of ESs is in identifying whether drilling should continue during a mineral exploration. For instance, when prospecting for molybdenum, the composition of mud samples helps determine whether the likelihood of finding deposits is high enough to warrant continued drilling. Assessing the chances of hitting deposits requires the input of a highly experienced and expensive engineer. PROSPECTOR takes mud composition as input and provides the likelihood of finding deposits based on the knowledge base of experts. Using the program, less experienced and less expensive engineers can analyze the mud samples, and the ES does the expensive work.

Irrigation and Pest Management

Knowing the quantities of water and pesticides to use at different stages of peanut growing can save farmers millions of dollars. After much research, the U.S. Department of Agriculture developed an ES called EXNUT to help peanut growers make these decisions. Scientists produced a large knowledge base on plants, weather, soil, and other factors that affect the yield of peanut fields. Farmers feed EXNUT with data about the field throughout the growing season, and the program provides recommendations on irrigation, the application of fungicide, and the likelihood of pest conditions. It recommends that farmers withhold water during certain stages and that they use the highest and lowest soil temperatures as indicators of soil moisture and plant health.

By 1997, the system had been used by more than 50 farms in Georgia that cultivate about 10,000 acres. Farmers who are not considered experts were able to increase their yield to quantities greater than those harvested by expert farmers, while using less water and fungicide. Versions of EXNUT have been developed for many other states.

Predicting Failure of Diesel Engines

A reliable way to predict the failure of diesel locomotive engines is to examine the oil from the engine. Experienced technicians at **Canadian Pacific Railroad** took many years to develop this expertise, which involves a technician analyzing a sample of lubrication oil for metal impurities, and a mechanic analyzing the data. The process not only takes years to learn but is difficult to teach to novices, so Canadian Pacific decided to develop an ES for this purpose.

Limitations of Expert Systems

While the use of expert systems can save resources, the systems have their limitations. Time and research efforts will be needed to overcome the limitations that ESs still have, including the following:

- **ESs can handle only narrow domains.** Early attempts to create general problem solvers failed miserably. Current ESs perform well if the domain they handle is narrowly defined.
- **ESs do not possess common sense.** With all their sophistication, ESs cannot recognize problems that require common sense. The system will be able to solve only those problems it was specifically programmed to solve.
- **ESs have a limited ability to learn.** While neural network technology made great strides in the area of machine learning, the ability of computer-based programs to learn remains limited. Knowledge engineers must coach the systems and provide continual feedback for the systems to learn. It may take many years for scientists to produce an ES that can quickly learn and apply self-learned knowledge.

Systems Development and Acquisition

Systems Development

Why Develop an Information System?

As we have discussed, while some organizations develop their enterprisewide information systems (ISs) by combining many different smaller divisional or departmental systems, others create their ISs from the ground up. The process of developing ISs within a planned framework, which is the topic of this section, often creates the best systems and helps organizations avoid patching together a collection of incompatible ISs. Companies usually embark on a systematic development of ISs when they find they are losing competitive ground because they have either inefficient ISs or no ISs to support a business process. Developing an IS is not a trivial matter. It requires a thorough understanding of existing processes, a vision of how an organization should operate, discipline, knowledge, and excellent communication skills.

Three phenomena can trigger the development of a new IS: an opportunity, a problem, or a directive. In this context, an **opportunity** means a potential increase in revenue, reduction of costs, or gain in competitive advantage that can be achieved using an IS. A **problem** is any undesired situation. Many problems can be resolved by using an IS. For instance, an organization may realize that certain processes are too slow, cost too much, or produce products or services of inferior quality and that a new IS could solve the problem. Seeking an opportunity is considered proactive, while solving a problem is considered reactive. A **directive** is an order to take a certain action. In this context, an organization may need an IS to comply with a law or regulation. For example, a law may require that patient or financial records be recorded and maintained in a certain manner that can only be implemented with an IS.

The phase of planning an IS should always precede systems development. The IS plan provides a framework within which new ISs are acquired, either by purchasing them or by developing them.

Note that nowadays most organizations do not develop their ISs themselves unless they want the system to be proprietary, the system will be mission-critical, or they cannot find a commercial application that satisfies requirements. The great majority purchase ready-made applications or contract with firms that specialize in application development. Often, organizations adopt ready-made software and have IT professionals change elements of the software to tailor it to their business processes. Yet, many organizations use some phases of the systems development life cycle when considering and implementing a new IS. These phases include analysis of the current and proposed system and the method of conversion from an existing system to a new one, whether developed especially for the organization or purchased. This section discusses what happens when the decision is made to develop, rather than purchase, a new system. Once the decision is made, the systems development life cycle begins.

The Systems Development Life Cycle

Large ISs that address structured problems, such as accounting and payroll systems, are usually conceived, planned, developed, and maintained within a framework called the **systems development life cycle** (**SDLC**). The SDLC consists of several distinct phases that are followed methodically. While the SDLC is a powerful methodology for systems development, organizations are sometimes forced to take shortcuts, skipping a step here or there. Sometimes, time pressures, funding constraints, or other factors lead developers to use other types of systems development, such as outsourcing, purchased software, or end-user systems.

The SDLC approach assumes that the life of an IS starts with a need, followed by an assessment of the functions that a system must have to fulfill that need, and ends when the benefits of the system no longer outweigh its maintenance

Exhibit 800.27 *The Systems Development Life Cycle*

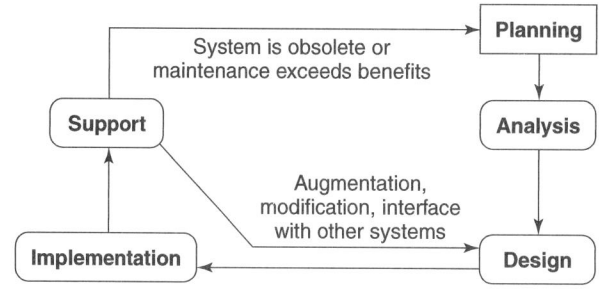

Exhibit 800.28 *Phases in Systems Analysis*

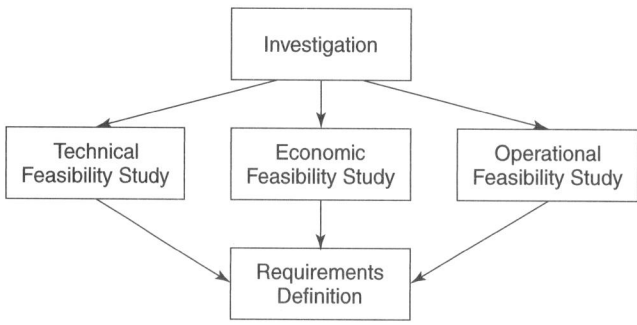

costs, at which point the life of a new system begins. Hence, the process is called a *life cycle*. After the planning phase, the SDLC includes four major phases: analysis, design, implementation, and support. Exhibit 800.27 depicts the cycle and the conditions that may trigger the return to a previous phase. The analysis and design phases are broken down into several steps, as described in the following discussion.

Analysis

The *systems analysis* phase is a five-step process (summarized in Exhibit 800.28) that is designed to answer these questions.

Investigation:

- How does the existing system work?
- What business opportunity do we want the system to seize, or what problems do we want it to solve, or what directive must we fulfill?

Technical Feasibility Study:

- Is there technology to create the system we want?

Economic Feasibility Study:

- What resources do we need to implement the system?
- Will the system's benefits outweigh its costs?

Operational Feasibility Study:

- Will the system be used appropriately by its intended users?
- Will the system be used to its full capacity?

Requirements Definition:

- What features do we want the system to have?
- What interfaces will the system have with other systems?

INVESTIGATION The first step in systems analysis is investigation, which determines whether there is a real need for a system and whether the system as conceived is feasible. Usually, a small ad hoc team—consisting of a representative of the sponsoring executive, one or two systems analysts, and representatives of business units that would use the new system or be affected by it—is put together to perform a quick preliminary investigation. The team may also be hired from a consulting firm.

The team interviews staff, spends time with employees at their workstations to learn first-hand about the way they currently carry out their duties, and interviews the workers about problems with the current system. This direct contact with users gives workers the opportunity to express their ideas about the way they would like a new IS to function to improve their work. The investigative team prepares a written report summarizing the information gathered. The team members also forward their own opinions on the need for a new system. They may or may not agree with the requesting managers that a new system is justified.

If the preliminary report concludes that the business situation warrants investment in a new IS, a more comprehensive investigation may be authorized. The sponsoring executive selects members for a larger analysis team. Usually, members of the original team are included in this augmented group. The objective of the larger investigation team is to determine whether the proposed system is feasible technically, economically, and operationally.

THE TECHNICAL FEASIBILITY STUDY In a **technical feasibility study**, a new IS is technically feasible if its components exist or can be developed with available tools. As we know by now, ISs consist of hardware, software, and, often, telecommunications equipment. The investigators use their own knowledge and information from trade journals and from hardware and software vendors to determine whether the proposed system can be built. Prospective users occasionally ask for technical features that cannot be developed.

The team must also consider the organization's existing commitments to hardware, software, and telecommunications equipment. For example, if the company recently purchased hundreds of units of a certain computer, it is unlikely that management will approve the purchase of computers of another model for a single new application. Thus, the investigators must find out whether the proposed system can run on existing hardware.

THE ECONOMIC FEASIBILITY STUDY Like any project, the development of a new IS must be economically justified, so organizations conduct an **economic feasibility study.** That is, over the life of the system, the benefits must outweigh the costs. To this end, the analysts prepare a **cost/benefit analysis,** which can be a spreadsheet showing all the costs incurred by the system and all the benefits that are expected from its operation (such as shown in Exhibit 800.29).

The most accurate method of economic analysis is **internal rate of return** (**IRR**), which is a calculation of the difference between the stream of benefits and the stream of costs over the life of the system, discounted by the applicable interest rate. To find the IRR, the net present value of the system is calculated by combining the net present value of the costs of the system with the net present value of the benefits of the system, using calculations based on annual costs and benefits and using the appropriate interest rate. If the IRR is positive, the system is economically feasible, or cost-justified.

Exhibit 800.29 *Estimated Benefits and Costs of an IS ($000).*

Year	2002	2003	2004	2005	2006	2007
Benefits						
Increase in sales			56,000	45,000	30,000	10,000
Reduction in clerical staff			20,000	20,000	20,000	20,000
Total benefits	0	0	76,000	65,000	50,000	30,000
Costs						
Analysis	15,000					
Design	37,500					
Implementation	0	56,000				
Hardware	0	20,000				
Operation and maintenance	0	0	5,000	5,000	5,000	5,000
Total costs	52,000	76,000	5,000	5,000	5,000	5,000
Difference	(−52,000)	(−76,000)	71,000	60,000	45,000	25,000
Discounted at 5%	(−49,524)	(−68,934)	61,332	49,362	32,259	18,657
Net present value for six years	43,152					

Remember that during the time the system is developed, which may be several years, there are no benefits, only development costs. Operational costs during the system's life include maintenance personnel, telecommunications, computer-related supplies (such as replacement of hardware during breakdowns, upgrading of software, and purchase of paper and toner), and power. If the system involves a Web site, the cost of revising and enhancing the site by Webmasters and other professionals must also be included. Usually, if the net present value is positive, the IRR will be positive too.

Exhibit 800.29 presents a simplified example of a cost/benefit spreadsheet and analysis for a small system. Because the net present value of the system is positive ($43,152), and therefore the benefits exceed the investment, the development effort is economically justified. In the figure, in the year 2005, the net present value starts to diminish. As this value continues to diminish, the organization should consider creating a new system. If the system is not replaced or significantly upgraded, the existing system will become a drain on the organization over time.

Often, it is difficult to justify the cost of a new IS because too many of the benefits are **intangible,** that is, they cannot be quantified in dollar terms. Improved customer service, better decision making, and the creation of a more enjoyable workplace are all benefits that might eventually increase profit but are very difficult to estimate in dollar amounts. This inability to measure benefits is especially true when the new IS is intended not merely to automate a manual process but to support a new business initiative or improve intellectual activities such as decision making. In addition, other benefits, although tangible, can sometimes be overlooked. Furthermore, often the mere fact that a company does not install the latest ISs that competitors have installed may make it less competitive and push it out of business. Savings from staff reductions are probably the most common tangible benefit of new information systems such as client/server applications or sales force automation. But other tangible benefits from new technologies often go unrecognized in the standard IRR analyses used in most corporations, such as those listed in Exhibit 800.29, including the following:

- A new IS may help to turn over accounts receivable faster. If a new system can send invoices out just one day sooner, then annual cash flow may increase by 1/365. For a company with $365 million in sales, that translates into $1 million in increased cash flow per year. If the interest cost on $1 million is 5 percent, that translates into savings of $50,000 per year.
- A new IS may help shorten the monthly general ledger closing cycles, allowing managers to make better decisions based on analysis of more timely financial information.
- A new IS may allow managers to perform "what if" analyses in real time during the financial planning cycle, testing ideas that may improve business.
- A new client/server accounting IS may reduce system support costs for an existing mainframe-based IS.
- A new IS may improve efficiencies by reducing errors in billings.
- A new IS may reduce the time (and cost) of preparing budgets, business plans, and proposals by making business data increasingly available in real time.
- A new IS may make it possible to track, and therefore control, costs more closely.

These benefits are extremely important in business and must be considered, even if they are not quantifiable. To convince management that a new IS is needed, the system's champion and systems analysts must consider all the benefits and present them in a compelling manner. Yet, calculating IRR is extremely difficult, and many executives now understand that even the most experienced IS professionals cannot always quantify the benefits of new ISs. Perhaps the question that decision makers should ask themselves is not "What is the return on investment of this proposed IS?" but "Can we continue to be competitive without this proposed IS?"

THE OPERATIONAL FEASIBILITY STUDY The purpose of the **operational feasibility study** is to determine whether the new system will be used as intended. More specifically, this analysis answers the following questions:

- Will the system fit into the culture of this organization?
- Will all the intended users use the system to its full capacity?
- Will the system interfere with company policies or statutory laws?

Organizational culture is an umbrella term referring to the general tone of the corporate environment. It includes issues such as the nature of relationships between supervisors and subordinates (casual or formal); the existence or lack of dress code; the use of or ban on flex time, which allows employees to start and stop work anytime within a range of hours as long as they work the required total; and acceptance or rejection of telecommuting, which allows employees to work at home. The development team must consider culture to ensure that the new system will fit the organization. For example, if the system will be used by telecommuters, it must be open to telecommunications from external telephone lines. The analysts must find out whether this need would compromise information security and confidentiality.

Another point the team considers is compliance with statutory regulations and company policy. For example, the record-keeping system the staff wants to use may violate customer privacy or risk the confidentiality of government contracts with the company. If these issues cannot be overcome at the outset, then the proposed system is not operationally feasible.

REQUIREMENTS DEFINITION When the analysts determine that the proposed system is feasible, the project team is installed. Management or the consulting firm nominates a project leader who puts together a project team that will develop the system until it is ready for delivery. The team includes systems analysts, programmers, and, often, representatives from the prospective group of users.

One of the first pieces of information the analysts need to know is the system requirements. **System requirements** are the functions that the system is expected to fulfill and the features through which it will perform its tasks. In other words, system requirements are what the system should be able to do and the means by which it will fulfill its stated goal. For example, the prospective users may want to be able to capture orders via a Web-based transaction system and have the system route some of the data into a file that can later be used for marketing. This need would be a system requirement. Definition of requirements is often also called *fact finding*. There are several ways to collect information for system requirements:

- *Interviews.* The analysts meet with prospective users and ask questions. The users are given an opportunity to discuss problems with the existing system and ways they would like these problems solved.
- *Questionnaires.* Employees involved in the business processes for which the system is to be developed fill out questionnaires. The analysts glean the information they need from the answers.
- *Examination of documents.* The employees give the analysts forms and other documents containing input data and output information involved in their work.
- *On-the-job observation.* The analysts spend time with employees while they carry out their normal work. The analysts follow the business process firsthand.

Once facts are gathered, they are organized into a document detailing the system requirements. The analysts then present the list to the users and their managers to confirm that they are the features they need. In many organizations, the project leader requests that the prospective owners of the system sign a requirements report indicating their agreement with its content. This formal sign-off is a crucial milestone in the analysis process; if the requirements are not well defined, resources will be wasted or underbudgeted, and the completion of the project will be delayed.

It is important to understand that the requirements report does not include any details of the hardware and software that will ultimately be used. For example, there is no mention at this point of the specific computer models that will be used or of the programming languages in which the software will be written. In fact, at this early stage, the analysts have not yet decided whether to develop the application in-house or purchase a ready-made software package.

For instance, the requirements report may say that the accounting department needs a new client/server IS that is capable of accepting bar-coded information entered by shipping personnel at shipping docks, automatically generating invoices, and allowing authorized users to generate financial reports from their PCs. The document would not say what type of computer or software the system would use to accomplish these goals.

Design

With a comprehensive list of requirements, the project team can begin the next step in systems development, designing the new system. **Systems design** is the evaluation of alternative solutions to a business problem and the specification of hardware, software, and communications technology for the selected solution. The purpose of this phase is to devise the means to meet all the business requirements detailed in the requirements report. As indicated in Exhibit 800.30, systems design comprises four steps, one that describes how the system will work logically, one that describes the physical layout, and others that deal with the construction and testing of the system.

LOGICAL DESIGN The **logical design,** which immediately precedes the physical design of the system, is a translation of the user requirements into detailed functions of the system. During the logical design phase, the designers determine the following components:

- *Input files:* the files that will be used to capture the input data.
- *Procedures:* the logical algorithms used to process the input. The procedures will later be transformed into code written in a programming language.
- *Output files:* the files that will be used to capture information that is the result of processing data, and the files that will record input by customers, employees, suppliers, job applicants, or other parties.

- *User dialog:* the manner in which the users will interact with the system—windows, menus, icons, or provisions for query by example. Usually, creating an intuitive, easy-to-use graphical user interface (GUI) is emphasized.
- *Interfaces:* how the system will interact with other systems. Interface decisions include provisions for input of data and information from the files of other systems, lookups in other systems for decision making, retrieval of data from other systems, and output of data to other systems.

Neither the logical nor the physical design steps include any construction of real code. At this point, the analysts have not yet chosen the tools with which the application will be built, the programming languages that will be used, the DBMS that will be used to construct the databases, the Web page authoring tools to construct the Web site, or any similar tools.

Designing and constructing a new IS can be very complex and even complicated. The approach used most often by managers to simplify the task is "divide and conquer;" that is, break the assignment down into small, hierarchical modules and assign one or several modules to each team. Dividing the system into modules isolates problems and delays to avoid hampering the progress of other modules.

Let us consider how the development of a payroll system might be managed in modules, as shown in Exhibit 800.31. One module would be the database of hourly employees, which includes the processes of collecting data about the number of hours worked and maintaining the correct hourly rates. Another module maintains the database of salaried staff. The third module, the tax table database, would be accessed by the first two modules for tax calculation. It includes tax rate tables and procedures for calculating tax amounts. The check production module receives the gross and net amounts to be paid from either of the first two modules for an employee, and the total tax from the tax table module, and then prints out the paycheck or activates an electronic funds transfer. The first three modules are further broken

Exhibit 800.30 *Phases in Systems Design*

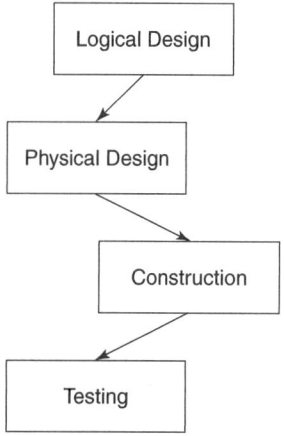

Exhibit 800.31 *Payroll System Development*

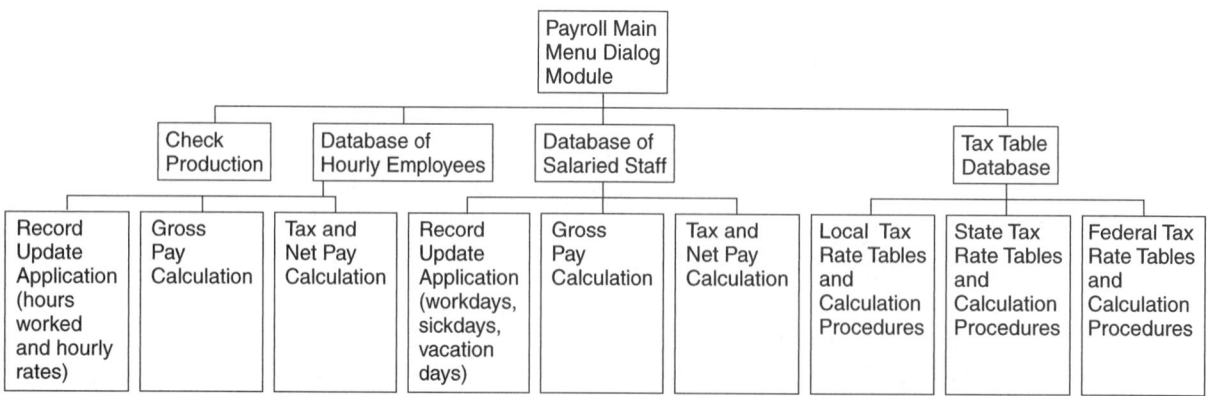

(Using the divide-and-conquer approach, the planned system is broken into hierarchical modules.)

into smaller modules. The four major modules are linked to a dialog module, the payroll main menu, which provides the main menu for selection of the desired operation.

Although potential users may not bring up security issues, the project leader should raise them and propose alternative methods of addressing these potential problems. For instance, the system should be designed to minimize unauthorized access to procedures and files. This protection is especially important if the system will be connected to the Internet and be part of an intranet or an extranet or if the system will serve consumers.

Flowcharts **Flowcharts** use graphical symbols to illustrate a system's logical operations as well as the physical parts involved. For instance, there are symbols that represent different pieces of hardware, such as terminals, disks, and communications lines, and also logical operations such as the beginning and ending points of a process and points of decision making. Flowcharts used to be one of the most important tools in systems development, but they have largely been replaced with other tools, which are discussed later.

Exhibit 800.32 shows an example of a flowchart representing the following logic for giving salespeople bonuses: A salesperson with sales over $1 million will get a bonus of $1,000 plus 0.5 percent of sales; a salesperson with less than $1 million in sales will receive a bonus of 0.4 percent of the sales volume.

For over 50 years, systems analysts and programmers have used flowcharts as a language-independent means of describing a system's logical sequence. After detailing the logic of a process in a flowchart, programmers translate the logic into a computer program. There are more than 30 different symbols, each representing an event, a process, a hardware device, or a report type. While some symbols have been standardized by the American National Standards Institute (ANSI), others remain nonstandard. Occasionally, analysts may use the same symbol to represent different things. The multitude of symbols, the use of nonstandard symbols, and the use of symbols to represent too many things in the same chart (processes, hardware, and so on) have rendered flowcharting less and less popular in recent years. A simpler alternative to graphically representing ISs has been developed. This method is called *data flow diagrams*.

Software programs are used to create flowcharts, data flow diagrams, and other graphical renditions of ISs.

Data Flow Diagrams **Data flow diagrams** (**DFDs**) are used to describe the flow of data in a business operation, using only four symbols for these elements: external entities, processes, data stores, and the direction in which data flows (see Exhibit 800.33). **Entities** include individuals and groups of people that are external to the system, such as customers, employees, other departments in the organization, or other organizations. A **process** is any event or sequence of events in which data are either changed or acted on, such as the processing of data into information or the application of data to decision making. A **data store** is any form of data at rest, such as a filing cabinet or a database. Data flow from an entity to a process, from a process to a data store, from a data store to a process, and so on. Thus, a carefully drawn DFD can provide a useful representation of a system, whether existing or planned.

Exhibit 800.32 *A Flowchart Describing a Sales Bonus System*

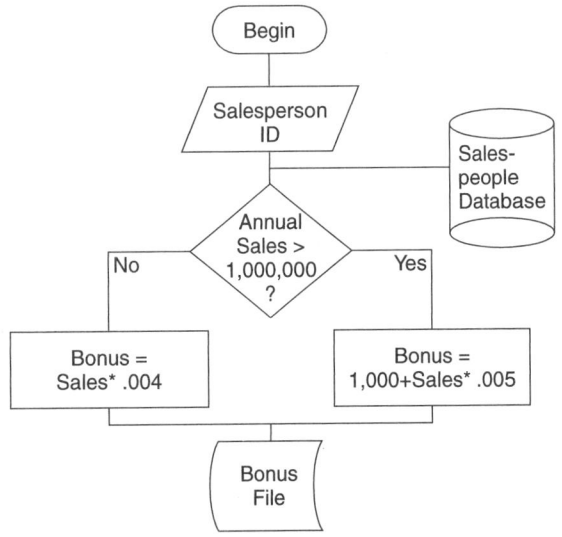

850. SYSTEMS DEVELOPMENT AND ACQUISITION

Exhibit 800.33 *Data Flow Diagram Symbols*

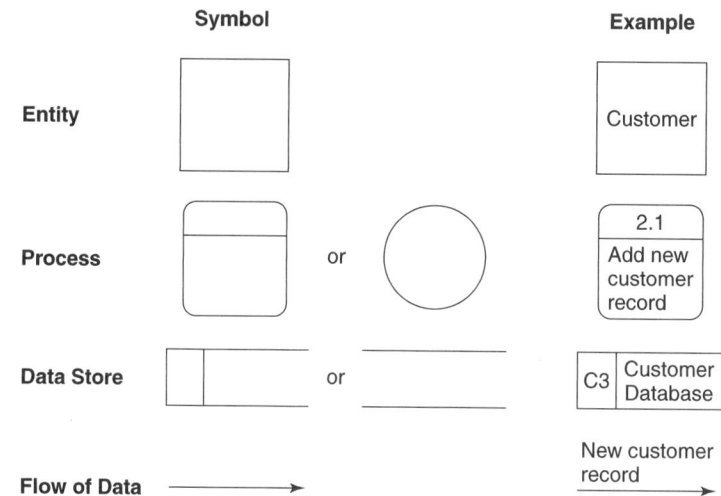

Exhibit 800.34 *A Data Flow Diagram Describing a Sales Bonus System*

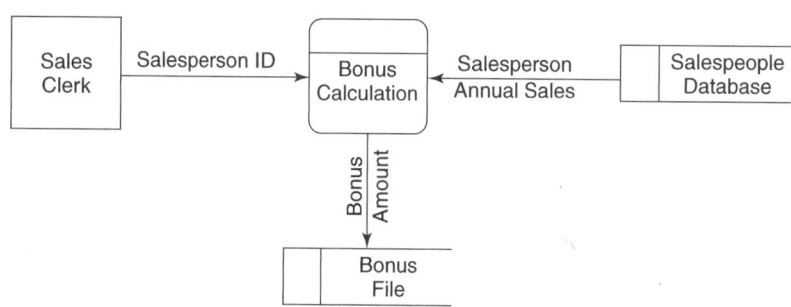

It is important to understand that DFDs describe only entities, processes, data stores, and data flows—nothing else. They are not meant to represent hardware devices or types of reports, nor are they meant to detail the logic of processes. The use of only four symbols and the simplicity of DFDs are their great advantage. They are easy to learn and use. Often, systems analysts produce three levels of a system's DFD. The first level contains the least number of symbols and is the least detailed. The second level is more detailed; what may be represented only as a general process in the first level is exploded into several subprocesses and several databases. The third level diagram explodes some processes further and is the most detailed; it shows every possible process, data store, and entity involved. Usually, the first and second level diagrams are presented to non-IS executives, and the third level DFD is considered by the IS professionals while they analyze or develop the system.

The DFD in Exhibit 800.34 shows the same process of calculating a sales bonus that Exhibit 800.32 showed using a flowchart. A sales clerk is an entity entering data (in this case, salespeople's ID numbers), which flow into a process, namely, the bonus calculation, which also receives data from the salespeople database (in this case, the dollar amount each salesperson sold over the past year). The result of the process is the bonus amount for each salesperson, information that flows into a bonus file. Later, the company's controller will use the information to generate bonus checks.

DFDs are used in both the analysis and design phases of systems development. In the analysis phase, they are used to describe and illustrate how the existing system operates. DFD symbols are suitable for describing any IS, even if it is not computer based. A DFD of the existing system helps pinpoint its weaknesses by describing data flow graphically and allowing analysts to pinpoint which processes and databases can be automated, shared by different processes, or otherwise changed to strengthen the IS. If a new IS is needed, a DFD of the conceptualized new system is drawn to provide the logical blueprint for its construction.

PHYSICAL DESIGN Once the logical blueprint for the new system is ready, the **physical design** begins. A system's physical design process includes specifying the necessary software and hardware needed to support it. Many organizations have hardware that is not being used to full capacity, in which case the project team designs software to fit the existing hardware. Of course, organizations usually look first for packaged software, and only if the appropriate system cannot be purchased off the shelf do companies develop systems from scratch.

If a program has to be developed in-house, the project leader will choose development tools (which the organization may already have) such as programming languages, database management systems for building databases, and special software tools to facilitate the development effort. As with hardware, if certain software development tools are the standard at the organization, only these tools will be used.

To ease maintenance of the new code, the programmers practice structured programming, in which the logical process is divided into small functional units, such as the modules described in the payroll system previously, which are programmed independently. Then each program unit is designed to be triggered from a controlling module. Such programs are often referred to as "GOTO-less" programs because they do not use GOTO statements. It is best to avoid too many GOTO commands because they create code that logically resembles spaghetti, which is difficult to follow. In structured programs in general, each logical unit starts with a comment, or nonexecutable remark in plain English, explaining each part of the code to any person who needs to debug or modify it.

CONSTRUCTION Once the software development tools are chosen, the construction of the system begins. System construction is predominantly programming. Professional programmers translate input, output, and processes, as described in flowcharts and data flow diagrams, into programs. When a program module is completed, it is tested. Testing is performed by way of walk-through and simulation.

In a walk-through, the systems analysts and programmers follow the logic of the program, conduct processes that the system is programmed to execute when running, produce output, and compare output with what they know the results should be. In simulation, the team actually runs the program with these data. When all the modules of the application are completed and successfully tested, the modules are integrated into one coherent program.

TESTING Although simulation with each module provides some testing, it is important to test the entire integrated system. The system is checked against the system requirements originally defined in the analysis phase by running typical data through the system. The quality of the output is examined, and processing times are measured to ensure that the original requirements are met.

Testing should include attempts to get the system to fail, by violating processing and security controls. The testers should try to "outsmart" the system, entering unreasonable data and trying to access files that should not be accessed directly by some users or, under certain circumstances, by any user. This violation of typical operating rules is a crucial step in the development effort, because many unforeseen snags can be discovered and fixed before the system is introduced for daily use. If the new system passes the tests, it is ready for introduction in the business units that will use it.

Testing tends to be the least respected phase in systems development. Too often project managers who are under time pressure to deliver a new IS either hasten testing or forego it altogether. Since it is the last phase before delivery of the new system, it is the natural "victim" when time and budget have run out. This rush has caused many failures and, eventually, longer delays than if the system had undergone comprehensive testing. A thorough testing phase may delay delivery, but it drastically reduces the probability that flaws will be discovered only after the new system is delivered.

Implementation

The **implementation** of a new IS, also called *delivery*, consists of two steps: training and conversion. Although training usually precedes conversion, if training is done on the job it may occur after conversion.

TRAINING To operate the new IS, the staff must be trained. People can be trained in several ways. The most common methods are in classes or on the job. The main advantage of classes is the economical use of instructors, and the main disadvantage is that large classes are generally only suitable for general information and presentation of the major features of a new system. They are ineffective in teaching the detailed features and modes of operation. Because people learn by doing, on-the-job training, in which a trainer coaches a new user or a small group of users as they perform their jobs with the new system, is much more effective in teaching the day-to-day uses of a new system. Multimedia technology and other training software can also be used. This approach frees systems analysts to attend to other business while employees train themselves and also allows each trainee to learn the system at his or her own pace.

Several vendors of widely sold packaged programs such as word processors and spreadsheets now offer training software that employees can use individually for self-training. Large companies often develop their own multimedia programs to train employees to use tailor-made ISs.

Exhibit 800.35 *Strategies Used to Convert from One Information System to Another*

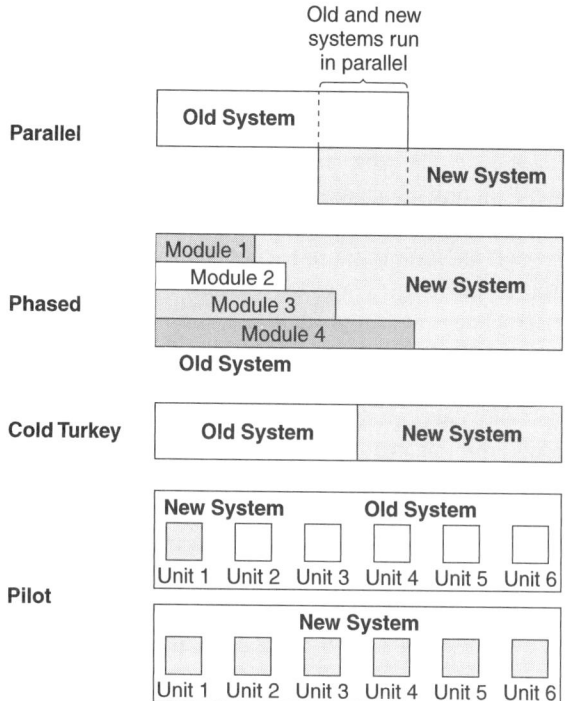

CONVERSION Conversion takes place when an operation switches from using an old system to using a new system. Conversion can be a difficult time for an organization. Operators need time to get used to new systems, and although every effort may be made to thoroughly test systems, conversion can hold some unpleasant surprises if certain bugs or problems have not been discovered earlier. Services to other departments and to customers may be delayed, and data may be lost. There are four basic conversion strategies designed to manage the transition (see Exhibit 800.35). They include parallel, phased, cold turkey (cut over), and pilot conversions.

Parallel Conversion In **parallel conversion,** the old system is used along with the new system for a predetermined period of time. This duplication minimizes risk because if the new system fails, operations are not stopped and no damage is caused to the organization. However, parallel conversion is costly because of the expenses, especially labor costs, associated with running two systems.

Phased Conversion ISs, especially large ones, can often be broken into functional modules and phased into operation one at a time, a process called **phased conversion.** For example, conversion of an accounting IS can be phased, with the accounts receivable module converted first, then the accounts payable, then the general ledger, and so on. A supply chain management system may be implemented one module at a time: first, the customer order module, then the shipment module, then the inventory control module, and so on, up to the collection module. This phased approach also reduces risk, although the benefits of using the entire integrated system are delayed. Also, users can learn how to use one module at a time, which is easier than learning the entire system at once.

Cold Turkey Conversion In a "**cold turkey,**" or "**cut over**," **conversion,** the old system is discarded, and the new one takes over the entire business operation for which it was developed. This strategy is highly risky, but it can be inexpensive, if successful, because no resources are spent on running two systems in parallel, and the benefits of the entire new system are immediately realized.

Pilot Conversion If the new system is to be used in more than one business unit, it may first be introduced for a period of time in a single unit, where problems can be addressed and the system can be polished before implementing it in the other business units. This trial conversion is also possible for systems shared by many departments and disparate sites, as is increasingly the case due to the growing popularity of intranets and extranets. Obviously, **piloting** reduces risks because it confines any problems to fewer business units. It is especially useful for determining how comfortable

Exhibit 800.36 *Activities in Information Systems Support*

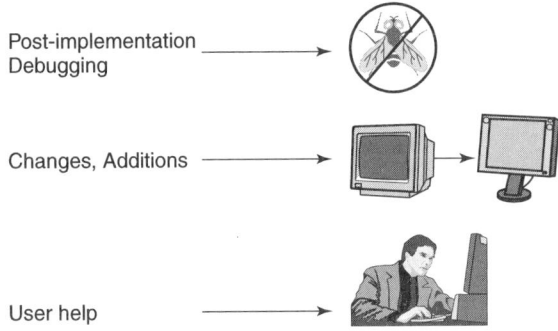

staff members are with a new system, a lesson that can be applied to the later business units. As with the parallel strategy, the pilot strategy means that benefits of the full implementation of the system are delayed.

Support

The role of IS professionals does not end with the delivery of the new system. They must support it and ensure that it can be operated satisfactorily by users. **Support** includes two main responsibilities: maintenance and user help (see Exhibit 800.36). Maintenance consists of post-implementation debugging and updating (making changes and additions). Usually, updating is the greater effort.

Debugging is the correction in programs of bugs or problems that were not discovered during tests. Updating is revising the system to comply with changing business needs that occur after the implementation phase. For example, if a company collects personal data for market analysis, managers may want to use the new IS to collect more data, which may require new fields in the databases. Over the past few years, companies that use Web sites for e-commerce have updated both the sites' pages and the databases connected to them continually, as more sophisticated software became available. It is expected that once XML (Extensible Markup Language) standards are agreed on, many companies will move from traditional EDI (electronic data interchange) to Web-based EDI, requiring a major update effort.

Although maintenance is viewed by IS professionals as glamorless, it should not be taken lightly or left to less-experienced professionals. Although maintenance costs vary widely from system to system, company surveys show that up to 80 percent of IS budgets is spent on maintenance. The major reason for this huge sum is that support is the longest phase in a system's life cycle. While development takes several months to about three years, the system is expected to yield benefits over many years. Efficient and effective system maintenance is possible only if good documentation is written while the system is being developed, and if the code is written in a structured, easy-to-follow manner.

Documentation consists of three main types: paper books, electronic documents, and in-program documentation. The latter are nonexecutable comments in the code, seen only when reviewing the application's source code. You can see this type of documentation when you retrieve the source code of many Web pages. In-program documentation briefly describes what each module of the program does, and sometimes who developed it. Printed and electronic documentation is prepared both for programmers, who can better understand how to revise code, and for users who want to learn about the various features of the application.

Support also includes user help. The people who work at an organization's help desk must be familiar with the new system so that they can provide advice and guidance to users.

Prototyping

While the traditional SDLC has its advantages for new-system development, it is a lengthy process and requires a rather inflexible and formal series of steps. To overcome these drawbacks, an increasing number of ISs are being developed under a looser approach called *prototyping*. In manufacturing, a prototype is an original machine or system that serves as a model for production of more machines or systems. So, in that context it is an actual physical product that is later mass-produced for marketing. IS **prototyping,** however, has a slightly different meaning, whereby

In prototyping, prospective users of an IS are involved in many steps of the development process.

Exhibit 800.37 *The Meaning of IS Prototyping*

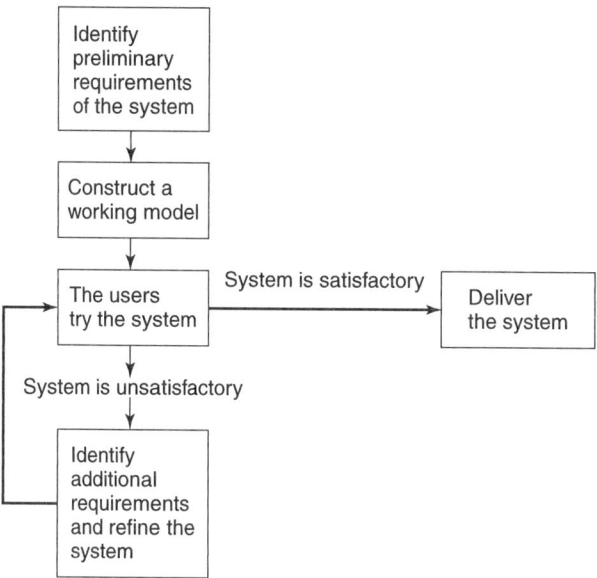

(In prototyping, refinement of the system continues until users are satisfied.)

Exhibit 800.38 *When to Prototype and When Not to Prototype*

When to Prototype	When Not to Prototype
Small-scale systems	Large-scale systems
Systems solving unstructured problems	Complex systems
When it is difficult for user to specify system requirements	Systems with interfaces to other systems

systems are developed through an iterative rather than a systematic process: the developers and users are constantly interacting, revising, and testing the prototype system until it evolves into an acceptable application (see Exhibit 800.37). This process is unlike the traditional step-by-step analysis and development process used in the SDLC.

The purpose of prototyping is to develop a working model as quickly as possible, which can then be revised and tweaked as developers and users work together. Developers construct a "quick and dirty" model; the model is tested by the prospective users, who provide feedback; using the feedback, developers add some features, delete others, enhance input, output, and processes, and then submit the revised system for the users to test again. This iterative process goes on until the users are satisfied with the product. Then, the productive life of the system starts. While a prototype IS can be duplicated and introduced in many business units, the process is still called "prototyping" even if only one copy of the system will be used. A developer once described this process as a "two steps forward, one step back" procedure. Prototyping is commonly used to develop Web sites.

Several studies have shown that prototyping has become a popular approach to systems development, mainly because it requires fewer staff hours and usually leads to a new system more quickly than the SDLC. These studies have shown that the greatest cost component of systems development is personnel time and that prototyping can translate into cost savings of up to 85 percent, compared with full SDLC. Prototyping also significantly shortens systems development backlog, the time users have to wait for a response to their system requests because IS departments cannot respond to them in a timely fashion.

The benefits of prototyping do not come without risks, however. First, the analysis phase is reduced to a minimum or is sometimes eliminated completely. Reducing or skipping analysis increases the risk of incompatibilities and other unforeseen mishaps. Also, the developers devote most of their time to construction and hardly any time to documentation, so modification at a later date can be extremely time-consuming, if not impossible. Because of the inherent risks, there are times when prototyping is appropriate and others when it is not (see Exhibit 800.38).

When to Prototype

Prototyping is an efficient approach to development when a system is small, when it deals with unstructured problems, and when the users cannot specify all the requirements at the start of the project.

When a system to be developed is small in scale, the risk involved in the lack of thorough analysis is minimal, partly because the investment of resources is small. (A small system is one that serves one person or a small group of employees. A large system is one that serves many employees, who may be accessing the system via a network from different sites.) If the small-system development takes longer than planned, the overall cost is still likely to be smaller than if a full SDLC were performed.

Even if the IS is large, it is impractical to carry out a formal SDLC when the system is to function in an unstructured environment. With many decision support systems (DSSs) and expert systems (ESs), for example, developers must hold frequent sessions with the experts who provide the sequences of problem solving. This ongoing refinement leads to *de facto* prototyping. The developer interviews the experts, builds a crude system or part thereof, lets the experts try it, improves it, and so on until the system performs satisfactorily. Then it is delivered to its intended users.

When users cannot communicate their requirements, either because they are not familiar with technological developments or because they find it hard to conceptualize the system's input and output files, processes, and user interface, developers have no choice but to prototype. In this case the users are often able to communicate their requirements as the development proceeds. For example, it is easier for marketing personnel to evaluate Web pages designed for a new electronic catalog and promotion site than to describe in detail what they want before seeing anything. Without being shown actual examples, users often can offer little guidance beyond "I will know it when I see it." Similarly, a witness who remembers the face of a suspected criminal but cannot describe it may be able to recognize it when police show photos or illustrations. It is easier for future users to respond to screens, menus, procedures, and other features developed by IS professionals than to provide a list of requirements for them.

When Not to Prototype

Prototyping is not appropriate for all systems development. If a system is large or complex, or if it is designed to interface with other systems, prototyping may pose too great a risk because it skips some major phases of systems development, including the feasibility studies.

Prototyping is not recommended for large systems because they require a significant investment of resources; therefore, system failure could entail great financial loss. The systematic approach of the SDLC is also recommended if the system is complex and consists of many modules, because extra care must be applied in documenting requirements and the manner in which components will be integrated, to ensure smooth and successful development.

For the same reasons, prototyping should be avoided when a system is to be interfaced with other systems. The system requirements and integration must be analyzed carefully, documented, and carried out according to a plan agreed on by the users and developers before the design and construction phases start. This early consensus reduces the risk of incompatibility and damage to other, existing systems. Therefore, accounting ISs, large order-entry systems, and payroll systems as whole systems are rarely prototyped. However, prototyping is almost always used nowadays in the construction phase. Programmers use visual programming languages such as Visual Basic and object-oriented languages such as C++ and Java to quickly develop elements of the application and test them.

Computer-Aided Software Engineering

Computer-aided software engineering (**CASE**) **tools** ease and speed the analysis, design, and programming of new ISs. Systems analysts can use CASE tools to build data flow diagrams of a new IS and flowcharts for the different program modules. They can use CASE tools to plan data dictionaries and database schemas for ISs, which, once found to satisfy users' needs, become the basis of a DBMS.

CASE tools draw their users' attention to flaws in some logic processes and to violations of data flow rules. They also automate the documentation of all phases of systems analysis, design, and programming. Developers of such tools constantly add sophisticated features to shorten the time between conceptualization of an application and its programming and documentation. The ultimate CASE tool will be one that takes requirements as input and then generates the necessary software and documents it.

Project Management

Like any other organizational effort, **project management** is a critical part of systems development. When management decides to develop a system, it places the responsibility for the effort with a senior executive, often a vice-president. The executive nominates a project manager, sometimes referred to as the project leader, who is responsible for the timely execution of the project within the budget's limits.

To maximize the success of IS projects, organizations need not only good project managers but also involved top management. A 2001 study of 159 CIOs and their immediate subordinates revealed that the major reasons for failure are lack of communication between top management and project leaders. It also found that lack of clear goals and deliverables were a major factor in project failures.[1]

Systems Development Led by End Users

Before 1980, the users' role in systems development ended in the formulation of system requirements. At that point, the end users were practically disconnected from the development effort, which was carried out by IS professionals until the system was complete. In the 1980s, prototyping promised more user involvement because users were polled for their input throughout the project. But they still did not lead IS development projects.

In the 1990s, a new phenomenon started to take root: users assuming a greater role in *leading* organizational IS development projects. The projects they lead are not small systems developed by the users for their own work but large organizational systems for use across business units. **Systems development led by users** (**SDLU**) reflects the view that users, not systems analysts, programmers, or information service organizations, are responsible for their ISs. The concept reinforces the users' ownership of their new systems. SDLU's benefits are (1) better design, (2) an increased willingness by business units to use the system, and (3) a more favorable attitude toward computer-based systems in general. But SDLU requires that business leaders have at the very least a basic understanding of ISs.

A survey of IS managers and executives of 77 companies was conducted at Drake and Auburn Universities and reported in the August 1994 *Journal of Systems Management*. The results indicated that 59 percent of the companies studied granted users voting or leadership responsibilities during program development; 1 company in 7 placed users in positions of leadership on the requirement team; and 1 in 11 placed users in positions of leadership on the program development team. The researchers were surprised by the high rate of SDLU.[2] It is doubtful that users will be leaders of many large-scale systems development projects, because they lack the technical expertise and because a smaller and smaller number of applications are developed in-house. But we may see a greater number of users on the leadership team.

JAD: An Example of User-Led Systems Development

In the 1980s, IBM developed **joint application development** (**JAD**), a method to be used in SDLU. The method is an alternative to the SDLC, but it doesn't skip thorough analysis, as prototyping often does. While the traditional SDLC is sequential and lengthy, JAD facilitates analysis and design by involving representatives of the prospective users in all of the phases (not only in the requirements definition step, as does the SDLC) and by using prototyping wherever possible. It is, however, more systematic than applying prototyping alone.

As shown in Exhibit 800.39 JAD uses a six-step process to take the team through the project's two phases: plan and design. Each of the two phases consists of three steps: customize, workshop, and wrap-up. In the first phase of JAD, management appoints a team to determine what the new system must do, what business processes to use in managing the new system, how big the new system should be, and what the overall time frame for the project is. The customer-led team creates specifications in a workshop setting with a facilitator. The team includes an executive sponsor who is often not an IS professional, a team leader, IS team members, customer team members who are usually cross-functional, experts who are part-time members as needed, a facilitator who is not necessarily an IS person, and a recording secretary, referred to as a *scribe*. Usually, this phase involves members of senior management who do not participate in subsequent phases.

The second phase, JAD design, determines how the system will work. These team sessions produce business flow diagrams, data elements in databases, data dictionaries, screens and reports, edit and validation criteria, interfaces, and processing routines. Since many members of the team are people who will actually use the new system, a strong emphasis is placed on developing a design that satisfies the specific requirements of the users. Prototyping is heavily used in designing the system, especially screens, forms, files, and the like, to provide the customer with an idea of how the system will "feel."

Exhibit 800.39 *The Six Steps of Joint Application Development (JAD)*

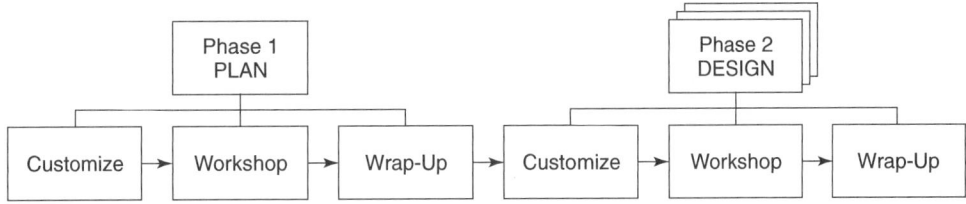

The following factors have been identified as critical to successful use of JAD:

- All participants must be committed to the JAD process.
- The customers and IS people must agree on the project's scope.
- The sponsor must be supportive and involved.
- JAD team members must be empowered decision makers.
- Business objectives must be clearly defined.
- Business processes must be understood.
- Team members must be able to meet two or more days per week.
- Members must be committed to the team.

Proponents of the JAD method cite the following benefits:

- JAD speeds up the development process by shortening the time required to gather requirements and resolve business issues.
- JAD increases customer commitment, confidence, and involvement, while improving communication and design quality.
- There is increased commitment to the process because the IS unit and the customers are partners, each with a vested interest in the project.
- The resulting system costs less than one developed in a traditional SDLC.

While the method has few disadvantages, it does require participants to dedicate significant amounts of time, which are often difficult to schedule.

Systems Integration

Firms often must wrestle with highly distributed, heterogeneous environments populated with applications for special tasks, which cannot be accessed by systems used for other tasks. Often, the disparate systems cannot "talk to each other" because they run on different operating systems (or, as IS professionals say, on "different platforms").

Much of what systems analysts do is systems integration, rather than the more traditional analysis and development of a stand-alone IS. **Systems integration** takes a look at the information needs of an entire organization, or at least of a major division of it. The analysts consider the existing, but often disparate, ISs and then produce a plan to integrate them so that (1) data can flow more easily among different units of the organization, and (2) users can access different types of data via a single interface. Consequently, many IS service companies call themselves "systems integrators."

Systems integration is far more difficult than systems development. In fact, systems development is regarded as a subspecialty of systems integration because the integrator must develop systems with an understanding of how data maintained in disparate systems can be efficiently retrieved and used for effective business processes.

For example, marketing managers can have richer information for decision making if they have easy access to accounting and financial data through their own marketing IS. The better the integration, the better they can incorporate this information into their marketing information.

Systems integrators must also be well versed in hardware and software issues, because different ISs often use incompatible hardware and software. Often, overcoming incompatibility issues is one of the most difficult aspects of integration.

Systems integration has become increasingly complex because it now involves the ISs not only of a single organization but of several organizations. In the era of extranets, the challenge is many times more difficult because IT professionals must integrate systems of several different companies so that they can communicate and work well using

Exhibit 800.40 *Alternatives to In-House Development of Information Systems*

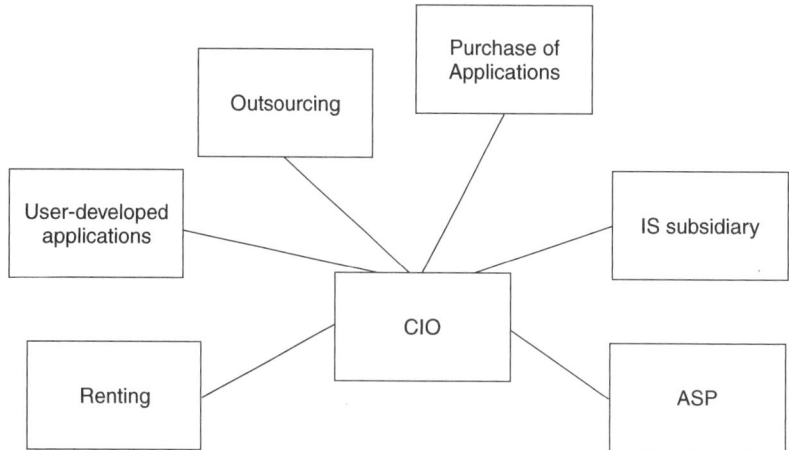

telecommunications. Imagine how difficult it is to integrate existing, disparate, legacy systems of several companies. (*Legacy* in this context means "old.") For this reason, companies often contract with highly experienced experts or consultants for such projects.

Systems Acquisition

Sources of Information Systems

The past decade has seen the increasing use of several alternatives to traditional in-house development of information systems (see Exhibit 800.40). **Outsourcing**—trusting all or part of an organization's IS operation to an outside company—has become a popular way to manage IT. In addition, the proliferation of **prepackaged software** that satisfies increasingly specific business needs has resulted in suitable applications for many situations, and they are immediately available. A more recent alternative to IS acquisition is the ability to **rent applications.** One option is to rent software from a third party and install it on your hardware. Another option is to contract with an **application service provider, (ASP)** who lets your organization use applications via an Internet link. At some corporations, the IS units have grown so much that top management has turned them into **IS subsidiaries,** independent corporations that offer services not only to the parent company but also to other companies. And in many organizations the ever-more sophisticated and easy-to-use development tools allow many computer-literate **users to develop their own applications.**

How do IS managers learn about these alternatives, find out who offers them, and determine which is best suited to their particular needs? The best initial source is paper and on-line trade journals.

If your company has decided to acquire a new IS, how should it choose which course to take: develop in-house or outsource the development? Purchase a packaged application or contract with an application service provider for its use? Or should it outsource the management of its ISs, including their acquisition, to another company? First, it is important to understand the pluses and minuses of each approach and then to analyze the needs specific to your company.

Managers' input into the process of deciding whether to develop a system in-house, purchase it off the shelf, outsource the development of part or all of IS services and products, or use the services of an ASP may have a tremendous effect on how managers and their subordinates will work for many years. Issues such as incompatibility of purchased software with existing applications, disclosure of strategic positioning when outsourcing, and possible poor performance of user-developed applications are the business not only of IS professionals but of every manager.

Outsourcing

A multitude of companies specializing in IS services provide expertise and economies of scale that no single organization can achieve. "Outsourcing" used to refer only to contracting with an IT company for the development of a system. However, in the 1990s the term has come to mean more than that. Currently, outsourcing often means that an organization

Exhibit 800.41 *Outsourced Information Systems (IS) Services*

- Application development and software maintenance
- Hardware purchasing and hardware maintenance
- Telecommunications installation and maintenance
- Help-desk services
- Web site design and maintenance
- Staff training

trusts all the activities associated with its ISs, including development of new systems, to another company. A growing number of businesses turn to IS companies not just for specific hardware or software purchases, but for long-term IS services: purchasing and maintenance of hardware; development, purchasing, and maintenance of software; installation and maintenance of communications networks; development, maintenance, and operation of Web sites; help desks, running of the IS daily operation, managing customer and supplier relations, and so on. An organization may use a combination of in-house and outsourced services. It may outsource the development of an IS but then put its own employees in charge of its operation, or it may outsource both the development and operation of the system to another company.

In considering whether to develop systems in-house or to outsource their development, top managers should ask the following questions:

1. What are our core business competencies? Of the business we conduct, what specialties should we continue to practice ourselves?
2. What do we do outside our specialties that could be done better for us by organizations that specialize in that area?
3. Which of our activities could be improved if we created an alliance with IS organizations?
4. Which of our activities should we work to improve internally?

Many companies have come to realize that IT is not their core competency and should not be a focus of their efforts. In addition, the fast pace of developments in IT require more and more expertise that is unavailable within many organizations.

Outsourcing has come to mean two different things: (1) a short-term contractual relationship with a service firm to develop a specific application for an organization and (2) a long-term contractual relationship with a service firm to take over all or some of an organization's IS functions (see Exhibit 800.41). We will use the term to mean the latter—that is, subcontracting all, or major segments of, IT services. Sometimes an organization hires the services of a consulting firm to satisfy its needs in only one specialized segment of IT, such as telecommunications. In other cases, a company outsources distinct segments of its IS needs to different providers, each specializing in its own segment. It is not uncommon for an organization to outsource help-desk services to one company and its hardware support to another.

Thus, when an organization decides to outsource IS services to another party, it does not have to outsource all of the services to a single company. Clients often outsource each type of service to an organization they consider best in the service.

There is a peculiar—and paradoxical—aspect to IT outsourcing. While contracts are signed for long periods of time, they typically involve rapidly changing technologies. As a result, clients sometimes find themselves bound by contracts that no longer satisfy their needs. They then try to renegotiate the contract.

Advantages of Outsourcing

Clients contract for IT services to offload in-house responsibility and to better manage risks. When a client outsources, management knows how much the outsourced services will cost; thus, the risk of miscalculation is eliminated. But there are additional advantages that make the option attractive.

- *Improved financial planning.* Outsourcing allows a client to know exactly what the cost of its IS functions will be over the period of the contract, which is usually several years. This certainty allows for better financial planning.
- *Reduced license and maintenance fees.* Professional IS firms often pay discounted prices for CASE tools and other resources, based on volume purchases; they can pass these savings on to their clients.

- *Increased attention to core business.* Letting outside experts manage IT frees executives from managing an IS business. They can thus concentrate on the company's core business—including developing and marketing new products.
- *Shorter implementation cycles.* IS vendors can usually complete a new application project in less time than an in-house development team can, thanks to their experience with development projects of similar systems for other clients.
- *Reduction of personnel and fixed costs.* In-house IS salaries and benefits and expensive capital expenditures for items such as CASE tools are paid whether or not the IS staff is productive. IS firms, on the other hand, spread their fixed and overhead costs (office space, furnishings, systems development software, and the like) over many projects and many clients, thereby decreasing the expense absorbed by any single client.
- *Increased access to highly qualified know-how.* Outsourcing allows clients to tap into one of the greatest assets of an IS vendor: experience gained through work with many clients in different environments.
- *Availability of ongoing consulting as part of standard support.* Most outsourcing contracts allow client companies to consult the vendor for all types of IT advice, which would otherwise be unavailable (or only available from a highly paid consultant). Such advice may include guidance on how to use a feature of a recently purchased application or on how to move data from one application to another.
- *Increased security.* An experienced IS vendor is more qualified to implement control and security measures than a client company.

As you can see, cost savings is only one reason to outsource IS functions. In fact, studies show that saving money is not the most common reason for seeking other companies' services. Other benefits, such as access to technological skills and industry expertise, are more important to IS executives than cost savings. The benefits that managers expect from outsourcing have not changed over the past decade.

Increasingly, companies purchase enterprise applications such as enterprise resource planning (ERP) and supply-chain management (SCM) systems, whose installation is very complex. Few companies have staffs that are qualified to install—and sometimes maintain—such systems. Often, the systems must be modified ("tweaked," in professional lingo) to fit idiosyncratic business needs, a process that requires highly experienced professionals. For these reasons, the vast majority of businesses outsource the selection, modification, installation, testing, and, often, maintenance of such systems to the vendors who sell the systems or to firms that can provide the necessary experienced staff. Often, these professionals are people who took courses and exams with the software vendors (such as SAP AG, Oracle, and PeopleSoft) and are certified by the companies. Even if management decides to have its own staff maintain the systems after installation and testing, the implementation project itself takes a long time, typically 6 to 24 months.

Risks of Outsourcing

Despite its popularity, outsourcing is not a panacea and should be considered carefully before it is adopted. There are conditions under which organizations should avoid outsourcing. The major risks are as follows:

Outsourcing strategic or core business ISs incurs more risk than outsourcing the routine tasks of operational ISs such as payroll.

- Loss of control
- Loss of experienced employees
- Risks of losing a competitive advantage
- High price

The most important element of an outsourcing agreement for both parties, but mostly for the client, is what professionals call **service level agreement.** The negotiators for the client must carefully list all the types of services expected of the vendor as well as the metrics that will be used to measure the degree to which the vendor has met the level of promised services. Clients should not expect vendors to list the service level and metrics; *the clients* must do it. It is in the client's interest to have as specific a contract as possible, because any service that is not included in the contract, or is mentioned only in general terms, leaves the door open for the vendor not to render it, or not to render it to a level expected by the client.

Purchased Applications (Prepackaged Software)

The last decade has seen a huge growth in high-quality packaged software, from office applications that fit on a CD to large enterprise applications. Therefore, purchasing prepackaged software should be the first alternative considered when a company needs to acquire a new system. Unless an IS must be tailored to uncommon needs in an organization, purchasing a prepackaged system may well be the best option. Software vendors now offer a huge variety of applications in business, often even those for highly specialized businesses.

Why Purchase?

When purchasing a software package, the buyer gains several benefits: immediate system availability, high quality, low price, and available support. Immediate availability helps shorten the software development backlog, the long list of applications waiting to be developed for a company's various business units. Purchasing software frees the company's IS professionals to develop the systems that must be specifically tailored to its business needs.

High-quality software is guaranteed through purchase partly because the software company specializes in developing its products and partly because its products would not survive on the market if they weren't strong. Often, large developers distribute prerelease versions, called beta versions, or simply betas, of software to be tested by companies (called beta sites) that agree to use the application with actual data for several months. The beta sites then report problems and propose improvements in return for receiving the fully developed software free. By the time the software is released to the general market, it has been well tested.

Because software companies spread product development costs over many units, the price to a single customer is a fraction of what it would cost to develop a similar application in-house or to hire an outside company to develop it. Also, instead of tying up its own personnel to maintain the software, the buyer can usually contract for long-term service and be notified of new, advanced versions of the application. Most software development companies provide a telephone number that users can call when they encounter a problem. Often, buyers enjoy a period of 3 to 12 months of free service.

There are many sources for packaged software, which is available for almost any imaginable application. Organizations cannot simply purchase the software and install it; they must employ professionals who specialize in the installation of the software, which may take months. Within limits, the providers of these large applications agree to customize part of the applications to the specific needs of a client. However, such customization is very expensive and is often risky; in some cases customization takes significantly longer than planned and cannot be done to the full satisfaction of the client.

Steps in Purchasing Prepackaged Software

Most people tend to think of ready-made or prepackaged software in terms of $200 word-processing or spreadsheet applications, but enterprise applications cost hundreds of thousands of dollars. Usually, the software's price is only a fraction of the price tag for acquiring the systems, because of the expense involved in hiring the specialists to install it. Thus, purchasing and installation often cost several million dollars.

When selecting a particular software package, companies invest a lot of money and make a long-term commitment to conducting their business in a particular manner. Factors such as the complexity of installation, cost of training, and quality and cost of after-sale service must be considered in addition to the demonstrable quality of the software. Once a company decides that it will purchase a ready-made application, a project management team is formed to oversee system implementation and handle all vendor contact. The project management team has the following responsibilities (see Exhibit 800.42):

- *Identifying the problem.* This step is similar to the initial inquiry and fact-finding step in the systems development life cycle (SDLC). The inquiry results in the identification of gross functional requirements and key integration points with other systems. The report generated often serves as a basis for a request for information from potential vendors.

Exhibit 800.42 *The Process of Choosing Prepackaged Software*

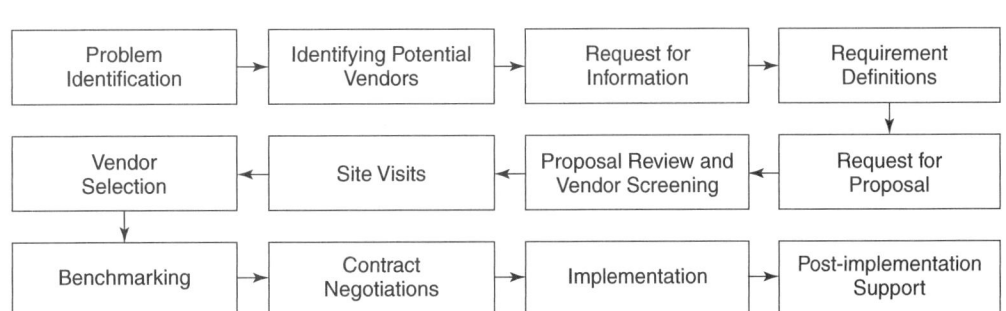

- *Identifying potential vendors.* On the basis of information in trade journals (printed and on the Web) and previously received promotional material, as well as client references, vendors are identified who offer applications in the domain at hand. In addition to these sources, IS people may gather information at trade shows, from other organizations that have used similar technology, and from colleagues.
- *Soliciting vendor information.* The project manager sends a **request for information (RFI)** to the vendors identified, requesting general, somewhat informal, information about the product.
- *Defining system requirements.* The project manager lists a set of functional and technical requirements and identifies the functional and technical capabilities of all vendors, highlighting the items that are common to both lists, as well as those that are not. The project management team involves the users in defining system requirements to ensure that the chosen application will integrate with existing and planned systems.
- *Requesting vendor proposals.* The team prepares a **request for proposal (RFP),** a document specifying all the system requirements and soliciting a proposal from each vendor contacted. The response should include not only technical requirements but also a detailed description of the implementation process as well as a timetable and budget that can be easily transformed into a contractual agreement. The team should strive to provide enough detail and vision to limit the amount of precontract clarification and negotiation.
- *Reviewing proposals and screening vendors.* The team reviews the proposals and identifies the most qualified vendors. Vendor-selection criteria include functionality, architectural fit, price, services, and support.
- *Visiting sites.* The complexity of the RFP responses may make evaluation impossible without a visit to a client site where a copy of the application is in use. The team should discuss with other clients the pros and cons of the application.

A system should be purchased only if all or most needs are met.

- *Selecting the vendor.* The team ranks the remaining vendors. The selection factors are weighted, and the vendor with the highest total points is chosen for contract negotiation. Sometimes make-or-break factors are identified early in the process, to eliminate vendors that cannot provide the essential service. By now, the team has gathered enough information on the functionality of the various systems.
- *Benchmarking.* Before finalizing the purchasing decision, the system should be tested using **benchmarking,** which is a codified system for comparing actual performance against specific quantifiable criteria. If all other conditions are the same for all the bidders, the vendor whose application meets or exceeds the benchmarks best is selected.
- *Negotiating a contract.* The contract should clearly define performance expectations and include penalties if requirements are not met. Special attention should be given to schedule, budget, responsibility for system support, and support response times. Some clients include a clause on keeping the source code in escrow. If the vendor goes out of business, the client will receive the source code, without which the system cannot be maintained. The client should tie all payments to completion of milestones by the vendor and acceptance of deliverables.
- *Implementing the new system.* The new system is introduced in the business units it will serve. Training and conversion take place.
- *Managing post-implementation support.* Vendors expect buyers of their large applications to request extensive on-site post-implementation support. Unexpected lapses or unfamiliarity with the system may require fine-tuning, additional training, and modification of the software. It is best to develop an ongoing relationship with the vendor because a solid relationship will foster timely service and support.

When choosing a vendor, organizations look for the quality and reliability of the product, but there are additional factors, such as quality of service and support, vendor's support for industry standards, and vendor financial soundness, that are extremely important. In surveys, IS managers have almost invariably revealed the importance of factors considered in selecting a vendor as shown in Exhibit 800.43 (in descending order). Product quality and reliability stood well ahead of the price/performance ratio.

Benchmarking—An Evaluation and Testing Tool

In addition to being used in the evaluation process, benchmarking is a powerful testing tool when used as an ongoing check after a new system is implemented. This codified system of comparing one system's performance with another's uses general performance measurements, which are not specific to a particular system. For instance, one benchmark might be the average time required to train someone; another might be a more technical performance measurement,

Exhibit 800.43 *How IS Managers Rank the Importance of Product Purchase Factors (in Descending Order)*

Factor
Product quality and reliability
Product performance
Quality of after-sale service and support
Trustworthiness of vendor
Price/performance ratio
Ease of doing business with vendor
Vendor's support for industry standards
Openness of future strategies and plans
Vendor financial stability

such as the rate of transactions per second, the speed of locating a record in a database, the speed of transferring a file from one computer to another, and the like.

When choosing which vendor to use, professionals in the client organization set certain minimum measurable levels for each performance criterion that the software must meet. The software should be temporarily installed in the organization's computers to be tested against the benchmark in a demonstration before finalizing the purchase, then retested continually after the purchase.

The key to meaningful benchmarking is to measure the identified criteria during typical daily operations, under a wide range of circumstances. This spectrum of testing will demonstrate how the system runs in extreme cases of work load and time pressure. For example, a new client/server system should be tested with the maximum number of users on the system to determine whether response time decreases to an unacceptable degree as more and more users log on.

There are many methods of benchmarking. But since applications are different, and organizations may even use the same application differently, the best benchmark is one that is tailored by the client organization.

Learning from Experience in Purchased Software

Learning from others' experience can save you time and headaches. After one large company purchased software that had been successfully implemented, its evaluation leader was asked what improvements he would make the next time. His answer could serve as a good checklist for all IS managers.

- Double the number of users on the evaluation team.
- Obtain more raw information from suppliers early in the process and force the vendors to give more details about their products, training, consulting services, financing options, and discounts.
- Hold all vendor demonstrations on the same day, at specific sites, for better comparison.
- Insist that vendors use scenarios and data supplied by the purchasing company, not by the vendors.
- Use consultants to help narrow the field to a list of finalist vendors in less time.
- Don't divulge to users which product has been selected before the contract is signed; the information may leak out and undermine the negotiations for better price and terms.
- Use more multiple-choice questions in the original customer survey to get more user responses and to make evaluating the responses easier.
- Ascertain that vendors know that their representatives will meet with real end users.
- Leverage existing relationships with vendors.

Risks in Purchased Software

Although purchasing a ready-made application is attractive, it has its risks.

- *Loose fit between needs and features.* Ready-made software is developed for the widest common denominator of potential user organizations. It may be useful to many, but it will be optimal for few. Companies must take extra

care to ensure that ready-made software truly complies with company needs, including organizational culture. Obtaining input from many potential users in the selection process reduces this risk.
- *Bankruptcy of the vendor.* If the vendor goes out of business, the purchaser is left without support, maintenance service, and the opportunity to purchase upgrades to an application to which it is committed. Arranging for software escrow can reduce this risk.
- *High turnover of vendor personnel.* Turnover among IS professionals is significantly higher than in other occupations. If a substantial number of employees involved in application development and upgrading leave a vendor, support is likely to deteriorate, and upgrades will be of poor quality. Developing an in-house support staff as backup personnel can reduce this risk.

Renting Software

The life expectancy of software, especially purchased software, has become shorter and shorter over the years. While in the past an organization could be on the cutting edge of technology for five or six years with the software it had, now some applications become obsolete within two or three years. If you want to use the most current applications, such as word processors and spreadsheets, you must pay several tens or hundreds of dollars to upgrade your version every two or three years. Now imagine how much money organizations have to pay for the same privilege for hundreds or thousands of employees. Worse, unlike households and small firms, many organizations spend millions of dollars on enterprisewide applications, such as SCM, ERP, and Web-based transaction systems only to find that two or three years later their version is old and lags behind the newer versions that their competitors use. Also, for small companies, the cost of even a single module of an enterprise-wide system may be too high to purchase. They often cannot afford to pay a large sum for a new application. One solution to these challenges is renting.

Many IS executives would rather rent software for a limited period and pay less than own it for a much higher cost. To satisfy this need, many software vendors now offer rental programs. For example, many organizations rent antivirus software. **Network Associates**, the company that owns the popular McAfee antivirus software, offers rental contracts for limited periods as short as one year. The company realized that since thousands of new computer viruses are launched every year, its customers prefer to rent a version for only one year and, when the next version is available, to rent the newer version to provide updated protection.

When a company rents software, the rental rate is determined by the number of users and the length of time. At the end of the rental period, the company must delete all copies of the software from its computers or renew the rental agreement. Thus, the only difference between owning and renting software is the period of use: in the former, it is unlimited; in the latter, it is limited.

The major advantage of renting is the flexibility of choice and the lower sums that need to be committed up front. At the end of the rental period, the company can either rent an advanced version of the application from the same vendor or opt to rent (or purchase) a different application from another vendor. There are no apparent risks in this approach.

Application Service Providers

The ability to rent and use software through the Web was introduced in 1999. An organization that offers the use of software through communication lines is called an *application service provider* (ASP).

An ASP does not install any software on a client's computers. Rather, the application is installed at the ASP's location, along with the databases and other files that the application processes for the client. However, clients can choose to save all the files produced by the application on their own local storage devices. The clients' employees access the application through the Web. They invoke the application, enter data, process the data, produce reports on line and on paper, and in general use the application the same way they would had it been installed at their location.

ASPs do not necessarily rent their own software packages. They often rent software developed by other companies. For some small companies, renting enterprise applications through the Web is their only option, because they cannot afford to build their own, or even pay for the installation of a packaged application.

As Exhibit 800.44 shows, there are several benefits to renting and using software through the Web. As in any time-limited rental, the client does not have to commit large sums of money up front. No employees have to devote time to learning how to maintain the software, nor to maintaining it once it is installed. No storage hardware is required for the

Exhibit 800.44 *Benefits and Risks of Application Service Provider (ASP) Services*

> **Benefits**
> - No need to learn to maintain the application
> - No need to maintain the application
> - No need to allocate hardware for the installation
> - No need to hire experts for installation and maintenance
> - Timely availability
>
> **Risks**
> - Possible long transaction response time on the Internet
> - Security risks, such as interception by competitors

applications and associated data, because the vendor uses its own hardware. And the software is usually available significantly sooner than if installed at the client's location; while it may take years to install and test enterprise applications on-site, an on-line renter can use the same application three to six weeks after signing a contract. And even if an organization is willing to pay for the software, it may not find skilled personnel to install and maintain the software.

The obvious risk is that the client cedes control of the systems, the application—and its related data—to another party. Although some vendors are willing to make minor changes to suit the client's needs, they will not make all that are requested. Some experts argue that by renting, clients have less control over their systems and that it is better to retain the ability to modify applications in-house. Response time may become a problem as well, because neither the ASP nor the client have full control over traffic on the Internet. Also, as with all activities through a public network, there are security risks, such as interception of information by a competitor.

For this reason, some clients prefer to use a leased line rather than the Internet to connect to the ASP. Organizations should also consider the type of application and data their company is about to use. The application should not reveal any vital information to competitors.

The Application Service Provider (ASP) Industry

The ASP industry has been infamous for its instability. Many ASPs had short life spans. Others made promises to clients that they could not keep. Even with reputable providers, some clients were disappointed because the scope of services and level of reliability were not what they had expected when they signed the contract. Managers in organizations considering ASPs should heed the following commandments:

1. *Check the ASP's history.* Ask the provider for a list of references, and contact these customers to ask about their experience. Ask how soon the provider switched to a new version of the application they rented.
2. *Check the financial strength.* Request copies of the ASP's financial reports. Ensure that it has enough funds or secured funding to stay in business for the duration of your planned contract.
3. *Ensure you understand the price scheme.* Ask whether the price changes when you decide to switch to using another application. Ask whether the price includes help-desk services.
4. *Get a list of the provider's infrastructure.* Ask to see a list of the ASP's hardware, software, and telecommunication facilities. Ask who the ASP's business partners are that provide hardware, software, and telecommunication services.
5. *Craft the service contract carefully.* Ensure that the contract includes penalties the ASP will pay if services are not rendered fully. Ensure that your organization will not have to pay penalties for early termination.

One important point to check when examining the list of ASP facilities is up time. **Up time** is the proportion of time that the ASP's systems and communication links are up. Since no provider can guarantee 100 percent up time, ASPs often promise 99.9 percent ("three nines," in professional lingo) up time, which sounds satisfactory, but it may not be. Three nines mean that down time may reach 500 minutes per year. This is usually acceptable for customer relationship management systems. Human resource managers or sales representatives, who typically use ISs less than 50 hours per week, may settle even for two nines (99 percent guaranteed up time). However, experts recommend that organizations look for ASPs that can guarantee five nines—99.999 percent up time. This high up-time ratio will ensure down time of no more than five minutes per year.

Who hires the services of ASPs? Although you will find a variety of companies among ASP clients, the majority of the clients fall into four categories.

1. Companies that are growing fast and rely on software for deployment of their operations
2. Small companies that do not have the cash to pay up front but must use office, telecommunications, and basic business operations applications
3. Midsize companies that need expensive software, such as enterprise applications for their operations, but cannot afford the immediate payment of large sums (examples are ERP applications from companies such as **SAP** and **PeopleSoft**)
4. Organizational units at geographical sites where it is difficult to obtain desired software or personnel to install and maintain the software. These sites are typically located far away from a regional headquarters in a less-developed country. The office at that site can then use applications from a more developed country.

A new type of service provider, similar to an ASP, has started to catch the attention of businesses in need of IT services: the **storage service provider** (**SSP**). An SSP does not sell the use of software but of storage space. Instead of spending money on the purchase of magnetic disks, a company can contract with an SSP and have all or some of its files stored remotely on the SSP's storage devices. The storage and retrieval are executed through communication lines, in most cases the Internet.

The Information Systems Subsidiary

Some large companies—such as **Boeing**, **Dun & Bradstreet**, **Bell Atlantic**, and **Chevron**—own IS subsidiaries, so they have IS services at their disposal while avoiding the direct burden of maintaining an in-house IS organization. IS subsidiaries are IS vendors like any other IT consulting firm, except that they almost always have a primary client—the company that owns them. The main advantage of a parent company's having an IS subsidiary is that the parent company has priority over other clients, without having to carry all the overhead costs during its times of low IS demand. The other advantage is the subsidiary's potential to generate additional revenue for the parent. The creation of an IS subsidiary occurs in one of two ways.

Corporations that use a lot of IT often see their in-house IS organizations grow to levels where they can render services not only to the corporation but to outside parties as well. To optimize this overcapacity, management then incorporates the IS organization as an independent subsidiary authorized to render services to any organization.

User Application Development

If an adequate application is not available on the market, or if an organization does not wish to take the risks we discussed earlier with purchasing or renting, and if the application is not too complex, there is another alternative to software development: **user application development,** in which nonprogrammer users write their own business applications. Typically, user-developed software is fairly simple and limited in scope; it is unlikely that users could develop complex applications such as SCM and ERP systems. If end users do have the necessary skills, they should be allowed to develop small applications for immediate needs, and when they do, such applications can be maintained by the end users (see Exhibit 800.45). They should be encouraged to develop applications that will be used for a brief time and then discarded. End users should not develop large or complex applications, applications that interface with other systems, or applications

Exhibit 800.45 *Guidelines for End-User Development of Applications*

End User Should Develop if . . .	End User Should Not Develop if . . .
End users have the necessary skills.	The application is large or complex.
The application is small.	The application interfaces with other systems.
The application is needed immediately.	The application is vital for the organization's survival.
The application can be maintained by the users.	The application will survive the user's tenure.
The application will be used briefly and discarded.	

that are vital for the survival of the organization. They should also be discouraged from developing applications that may survive their own tenure in the organization.

Until the early 1980s, computer programs were always developed by professional systems analysts and programmers, but now an increasing number of applications in organizations are developed by their own users. Usually, these are small-scale programs that fit the immediate needs of the individual user, or those of small groups of users.

Factors Encouraging User Application Development

Several factors led to the shift of development efforts from specialized programmers to end-users themselves.

The Programming Backlog

Until the early 1980s, virtually all scientific and business applications were created by professional programmers. The increasing need for ISs caused a great backlog of programming assignments. In some companies, systems that had been approved for development had to wait two or more years before the professional programming staff started writing code. This lag put increasing pressure on business units to develop their own applications.

As higher-level programming languages (for example, 4GLs) emerged, business units in many organizations decided to allow their own staff to develop applications. With high-level visual programming languages, organizations find that they no longer have to employ professional programmers to develop every single application; they can quickly have nonprogrammers learn how to develop simple applications.

The Widespread Use of PCs

Highly centralized mainframe architectures did not offer business units easy access to computing resources. At best, procedures dictated a rigid schedule of use by business units other than the IS department. The IS staff did not encourage direct access to computing resources.

This situation changed with the proliferation of PCs in businesses. Users were no longer dependent on a mainframe but owned their own computing resource. This widespread access to PCs, coupled with friendlier software development tools, encouraged many lay users to experiment with application development.

The Emergence of 4GLs

The availability of PCs alone could not solve the programming backlog problem. Easy-to-use programs, such as electronic spreadsheets, encouraged users to do a little programming through the use of macros. User-friendly versions of third-generation languages, such as BASIC, also contributed to self-reliance. But the greatest encouragement came from fourth-generation languages (4GLs). These tools are easy to learn, and programming skills can be put to use within days.

Graphical 4GLs, such as Focus or Magic, may further augment the circle of end users who develop their own applications. With a graphical 4GL, the programmer uses icons rather than commands to create code. The program contains prebuilt modules and forms. It offers comprehensive data-modeling capabilities helping the developer to construct a database.

Increasing Popularity of Prototyping

The increasing use of prototyping (with software tools that support the approach), as well as the availability of graphical development tools and support from information centers, creates a convenient environment for the lay developer to become more self-sufficient. The new software eliminates much of the need to master any code-writing skills, and the end user requires less of IS professionals' time, leaving information center staff free to assist more users in their systems development efforts.

Increasing Popularity of Client/Server Architecture

A major purpose of the adoption of client/server architecture is to empower end users in their daily data processing. Therefore, most client/server environments make additional tools available to users for the development of applications on their own desktop computers.

Managing User-Developed Applications

The proliferation of user-developed applications poses challenges to managers, both in IS units and other business units. In addition to the guidelines outlined in Exhibit 800.45, management must cope with the following challenges:

- *Managing the reaction of IS professionals.* IS professionals often react negatively to user development because they perceive it as undermining their own duties and authority. To solve this problem, management must set clear guidelines delineating what types of applications end users may and may not develop.
- *Providing support.* To encourage users to develop applications, IS managers must designate a single technical contact for users. Usually, this resource is a function of the help desk in the information center.

    It is difficult to provide IS support for user-developed applications, because the IS staff members are usually unfamiliar with an application developed without their involvement. Yet, IS staff should help solve problems or enhance such applications when end users think their own skills are not adequate.
- *Compatibility.* To ensure compatibility with other applications within an organization, the organization's IS professionals should adopt and supply standard development tools to interested users. Users should not be allowed to use nonstandard tools. Note that compatibility in this context is for the purpose of transferring data among end users; interfacing user-developed applications with other organizational systems should be discouraged.
- *Managing access.* Sometimes, users need to copy data from organizational databases to their own developed spreadsheets or databases. If access to organizational databases is granted at all for such a purpose, access should be tightly controlled by the IS staff to maintain data integrity and security. Users should be forewarned not to rely on such access when developing their own applications if this is against the organization's policy.

Advantages and Risks in User-Developed Applications

There are several important advantages to user development of applications:

- *Shortened lead times.* Users almost always develop applications more quickly than IS personnel, because they are highly motivated (they will benefit from the new system); their systems are usually simpler in design; and they have a head start by being totally familiar with the business function for which they are developing the application.
- *Good fit to needs.* Nobody knows the users' specific business needs better than the users themselves. Thus, they are apt to develop an application that will satisfy all their needs.
- *Compliance with culture.* User-developed software closely conforms to an individual unit's subculture, which makes the transition to a new system easier for employees.
- *Efficient utilization of resources.* Developing software on computers that are already being used for many other purposes is an efficient use of IT resources.
- *Acquisition of skills.* The more employees who know how to develop applications, the greater an organization's skills inventory.
- *Free IS staff time.* User-developers free IS staff to develop and maintain an organization's more complex and sophisticated systems.

However, with all the pros, there are also cons to application development by users. They must be considered seriously. The risks are as follows:

- *Poorly developed applications.* User-developers are not as skilled as IS personnel. On average, the applications they develop are of lower quality than systems developed by professionals. Users are often tempted to develop applications that are too complex for their skills and tools, resulting in systems that are difficult to use and maintain.
- *Islands of information.* An organization that relies on user development runs the risk of creating islands of information and "private" databases not under the control of the organization's IS managers. This lack of control may make it difficult to achieve the benefits of integrated ISs.
- *Duplication.* User-developers often waste resources developing applications that are identical or similar to systems that already exist elsewhere within the organization.
- *Security problems.* Giving end users access to organizational databases for the purpose of creating systems may result in violations of security policies. This risk is especially true in client/server environments. The creation of

"private databases" known only to the individual user is risky. The user may not be aware that the information he or she produces from the data is "classified" under an organization's policy.

- *Poor documentation.* Practically speaking, "poor documentation" may be a misnomer. Usually, users do not create any documentation at all because (1) they do not know how to write documentation and (2) they develop the application on their own to have it ready as soon as possible, and they don't want to take the time to document it. Lack of documentation makes system maintenance difficult at best, and impossible at worst. Often, applications are patched together by new users, and pretty soon nobody knows how to correct errors or modify programs.

Managing Information Technology Resources

Information Systems Architecture and Management

Organizations have their own distinct managerial styles, most of which fall somewhere between two extremes on a spectrum. One extreme is centralized management, which designates staff positions and departments in a strict vertical hierarchy and places control of the organization in a few hands. The other is decentralized management, which delegates authority to lower-level managers. In most organizations, the management and structure of information systems follow the same pattern as the organization's overall management: centralized management tends to want centralized control over ISs; decentralized management is more likely to be comfortable with decentralized ISs.

If you pick up an IS trade journal, you are likely to come across two terms: *IS infrastructure* and *IS architecture.* **IS infrastructure** refers to the IS resources that an organization owns: hardware, software, telecommunications devices and lines, and other IS assets. **IS architecture** refers to the manner in which these assets are deployed and connected and the ways they interact with each other. Also, be aware that the term *enterprise* in IS lingo refers to any organization that uses ISs. (Thus, the term *enterprise applications* is used for organizationwide shared ISs.)

Because of the influence of an organization's overall management style on other systems, companies with centralized IS management tend to have centralized IS architecture, and companies with decentralized IS management tend to have decentralized IS architecture, although exceptions may be found. Remember that architecture does not strictly dictate how systems are managed (a decentralized architecture can be managed centrally, and a centralized architecture can be decentrally managed), but architecture always has an impact on the way access to data is controlled.

With the recent e-commerce boom, organizations have faced new challenges of managing their Web sites, including linking internal applications and databases to those sites. Large organizations especially have more than one server linked to the Internet. So, they must question whether individual organizational units should manage their own Web sites or whether the company should manage all Web activities through a single home page—essentially a central Web site. Different business functions can use the Web for different purposes. For instance, marketing and sales can promote products and services. Human resources can recruit employees, and finance can make electronic payments. Should the design and implementation of these various functions be the responsibilities of individual departments, or should they be cleared through a central department or manager? The challenge becomes even more complex for multinational organizations with regional headquarters in different countries. Because many workers today can easily design and create Web pages for their departments, managers are often tempted to establish their own unit's Web site, independent of the central IS organization's priorities. Also, senior executives of some organizations have actually left the IS unit out of the loop when deciding on Web design and operational issues, not realizing that problems can arise later—when the Web site evolves from a mere presence to an important e-commerce vehicle involving many internal resources such as transactional databases and data warehouses. Thus, in many companies the issue of management of IS resources has become more complicated as technology advances.

Exhibit 800.46 *Centralized IS Architecture*

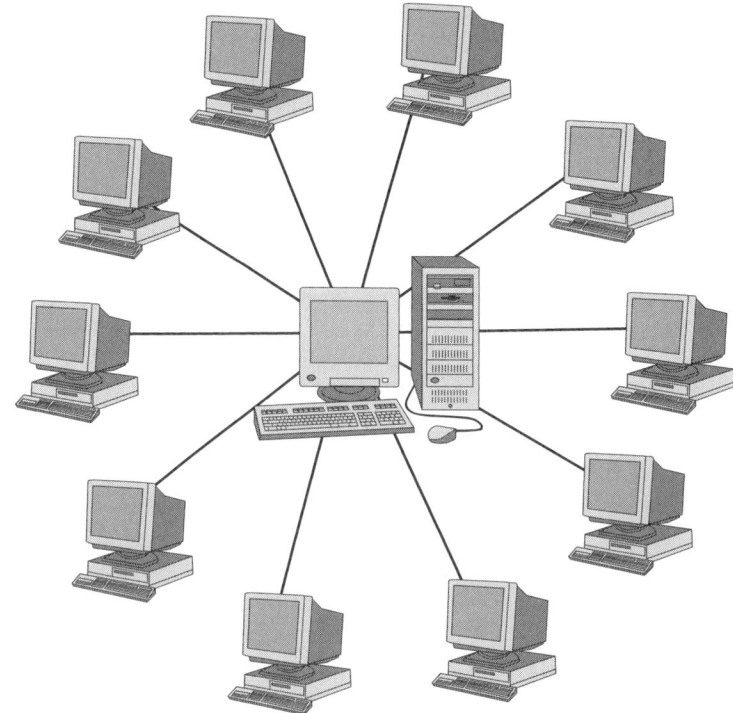

(In centralized IS architecture, information resources are maintained on one or several large computers that are centrally controlled.)

Centralized Information Systems Architecture

For a long time, mainframes were the only computers available for business. By their nature, they dictated a **centralized architecture** because all applications and data were usually stored on a company's single mainframe. As an example, Exhibit 800.46 shows a typical physical layout of the centralized IS of a single-site company whose general management philosophy advocates upper management's tight control of operations. A centralized IS is still favored in some organizations. However, with the introduction of inexpensive desktop computers and reliable data communications technology, many organizations moved to a decentralized or distributed architecture, which we discuss next.

The great advantage of a centralized architecture is that it allows top management and the IS department a high degree of control, making it easy to (1) maintain standards of hardware, software, procedures, and operations and (2) control access to information. The main disadvantage of a centralized system is its inflexibility. A centralized system is run so that it can be used by everyone, but that does not mean the system is optimal for everyone. Different departments and remote sites have different information needs; usually with a centralized system, everyone is served, but few are completely satisfied. These disadvantages are especially problematic when an organization consists of multiple remote sites.

Decentralized Information Systems Architecture

A **decentralized architecture** allows departments and remote sites a large degree of independence in organizing and utilizing their information systems (see Exhibit 800.47). In a decentralized model, each unit within an organization has its own local IS department to establish an infrastructure and to select hardware and software to satisfy the specific information needs of that unit, without necessarily considering other units. In fully decentralized architectures the systems of the independent units are not linked to each other or to the organization's headquar-

Exhibit 800.47 *Decentralized IS Architecture*

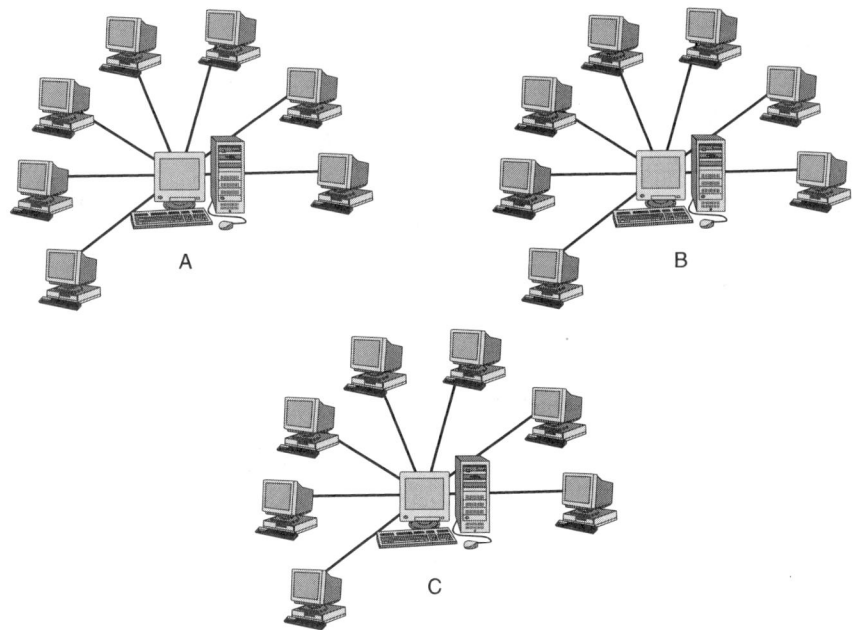

(In decentralized IS architecture, workers at different sites and departments (A, B, C) use information resources that are dedicated to their site or department.)

ters. Nowadays, however, this situation is rare; even remote units that used to be decentralized are now linked, at least by the Internet.

The major disadvantage of decentralized ISs is that the variety of independent systems makes it difficult to share applications and data. It is also more expensive for an organization to establish maintenance and service contracts with many vendors than with just one or a few.

Distributed Information Systems

Organizations that wish to give their employees independence without losing centralized control of their ISs prefer to rely on what is called **distributed architecture.** With distributed architecture, an organization can enjoy the benefits of both decentralized and centralized architectures. Each unit enjoys sufficient independence in selecting and implementing its own system to optimize its operation, but it can also share resources remotely with other units through communications lines (see Exhibit 800.48).

The increasing reliability and affordability of data communications and PC technology have encouraged organizations to change from centralized and decentralized architectures to distributed architecture. Now, when IS professionals say "decentralized systems" they usually mean "distributed systems."

Centralized versus Decentralized Information Systems: Advantages and Disadvantages

Thanks to telecommunications technology and the growing use of intranets, organizations can choose to manage any type of architecture centrally or locally. However, the different architectures make some operations easier to manage and others harder. In this discussion we use the terms *centralized* and *decentralized IS* to mean centralized and decentralized management of IS resources. As summarized in Exhibit 800.49, when choosing between more or less centralized IS management, organizations trade off different advantages and disadvantages in IS efficiency, ease of training, level of control, and other factors.

Exhibit 800.48 *Distributed IS Architecture*

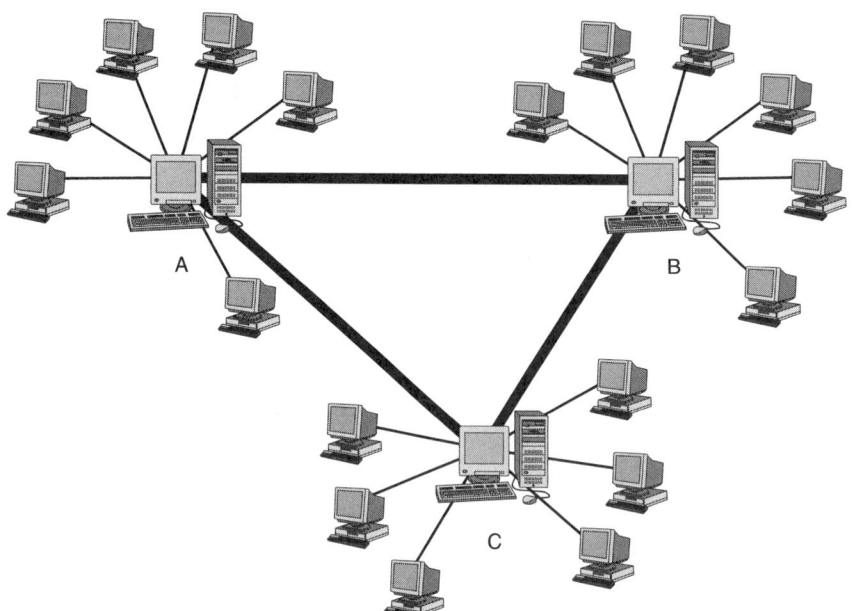

(In distributed IS architecture, workers use the information resources of their own site or department but can also use the resources of other sites or departments through communications lines.)

Exhibit 800.49 *Centralized versus Decentralized IS Trade-offs*

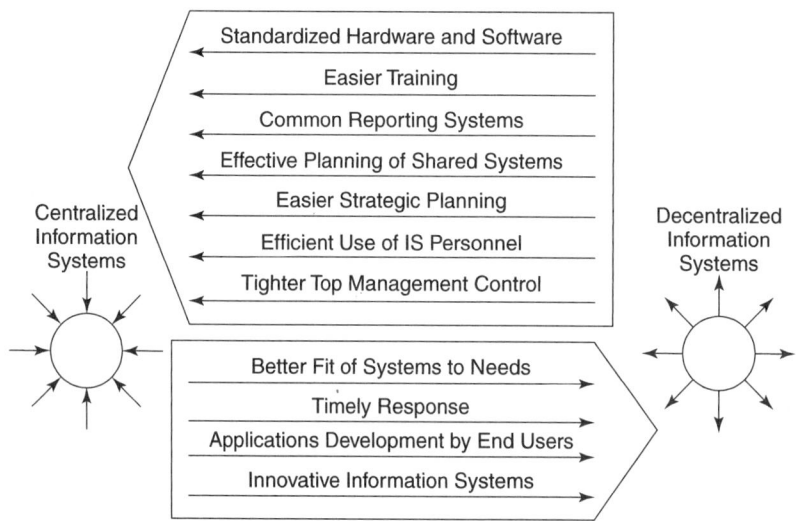

Exhibit 800.50 *Centralized Management of ISs*

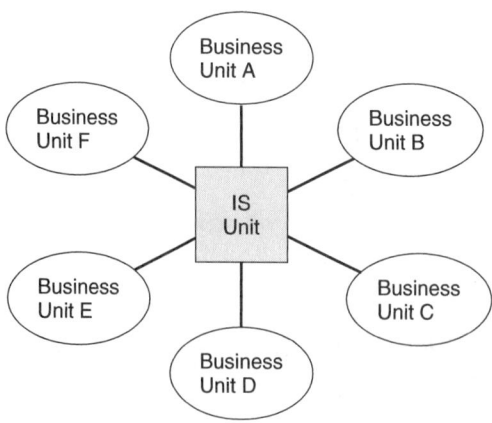

Advantages of Centralized IS Management

Centralized IS management, as illustrated in Exhibit 800.50, has several major advantages.

- *Standardized hardware and software.* Centralized ISs can establish corporate software and hardware standards, which saves time and money in purchasing and installation and simplifies interdepartmental sharing of data and information. Standardizing software is particularly important for facilitating data exchange and the sharing of applications.
- *Easier training.* Training, often a major expense in a company's budget, is much more efficient and less expensive when an organization uses standardized hardware and software. The training staff can do a better job when they can specialize in a small variety of hardware and software.
- *Common reporting systems.* Central IS management can easily standardize reporting systems and formats across departments, which many companies and some laws and regulations require for accounting or tax reporting. With standardized reporting, managers do not have to "re-map" the information they receive from one unit to a report with a different format used by another unit. This uniformity saves time and increases clarity. When reports need to be merged, it is easier to merge them (using spreadsheets, for instance) when they share the same format.
- *Effective planning of shared systems.* Large and complex systems that are shared by several organizational units can best be developed by a central IS department that knows the "big picture."
- *Easier strategic planning.* Strategic IS planning considers an organization's entire IS resources. It is easier to link an IS strategic plan to an organization's overall strategic plan when IS management is centralized.
- *Efficient use of IS personnel.* With a centralized IS department, an organization is more likely to employ highly specialized IS professionals who are better qualified to develop information systems, especially the larger and more complex ones, than are IS professionals who are dispersed in non-IS organizational units.
- *Tighter control by top management.* A centralized IS management allows top management to maintain control over the often vast resources spent on ISs.

Advantages of Decentralized IS Management

Historically, most organizations have moved from a centralized IS management to a decentralized management. Decentralized IS management, illustrated in Exhibit 800.51, has several advantages.

- *Better fit of ISs to business needs.* The individual IS units can use their familiarity with their departments' information needs to develop systems that fit those needs more closely.
- *Timely response of IS units to business demands.* Individual IS units can arrange IS development and maintenance to fit their business units' priorities. They can be more responsive because their responsibility is more focused.
- *End user development of applications.* In a decentralized setting, end users are usually encouraged to develop their own small applications to increase their productivity.
- *Innovative use of ISs.* Since a business IS unit knows its clients better than a centralized one, it has a better chance of devising innovative ISs.

Exhibit 800.51 *Decentralized Management of ISs*

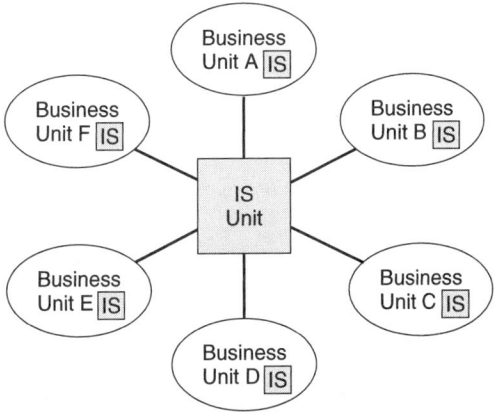

- *Support for delegation of authority.* Decentralized IS management works best if top management wishes to delegate more authority to lower-level managers.

Although you will find many companies with centralized IS management, fully decentralized IS management is rare. Because telecommunications technology is so pervasive and there are so many advantages of sharing information, systems that may have started as separate ISs years ago are usually networked now. Relatively speaking, decentralized management is more advantageous if an organization has divisions that produce completely different products and services. That way, each unit's information needs can be more closely served. Then, the decentralized units can share resources through networking. Some types of systems must be managed centrally even if they span many different business units, however. With enterprise applications, such as ERP systems, the one large integrated system must be managed by a single team.

Organizing the IS Staff

Now that we have addressed the advantages and disadvantages of centralized and decentralized IS management, we turn to the organization of the IS unit itself. There are various ways to deploy IS staff, even if an organization operates from a single site. In this section we discuss the two extremes of organizing IS professionals in an organization: central IS organization and functional IS organization. Not surprisingly, decentralized IS management often calls for functional organization of the IS staff.

In **central IS organization** there is a corporate IS team to whom all units turn with their IS needs. In **functional IS organization** there is a separate IS team for each business unit. Some arrangements combine elements of both. The approach selected has a direct effect on how IS professionals are positioned in the organizational structure of the business. But regardless of the structure, the goal of any IS organization is to optimize IS services to fit the organization's goals and culture.

Central IS Organization

A centrally organized IS department has what we will call an IS director, who may in fact be a member of top management or a high-level executive who reports to a vice president (usually of finance or operations). The highest-ranking IS officer in an organization is often given the title of chief information officer (CIO) or chief technology officer (CTO) and in many organizations that person is also a vice president.

As seen in Exhibit 800.52, the most common central IS unit organization has the IS director overseeing several departments. One department implements and maintains current systems. Another department runs the information center, whose function is to provide ad hoc advice about hardware and software to business units. The communications department develops and manages local-area and wide-area networks. And the data administration department develops and maintains corporate databases, data warehouses, and data management and analysis applications. In large organizations there may also be a research and development department, which keeps the IS unit abreast of technological advances and develops ideas for the strategic uses of ISs.

Exhibit 800.52 *An Example of an IS Unit's Organization with Centrally Managed ISs*

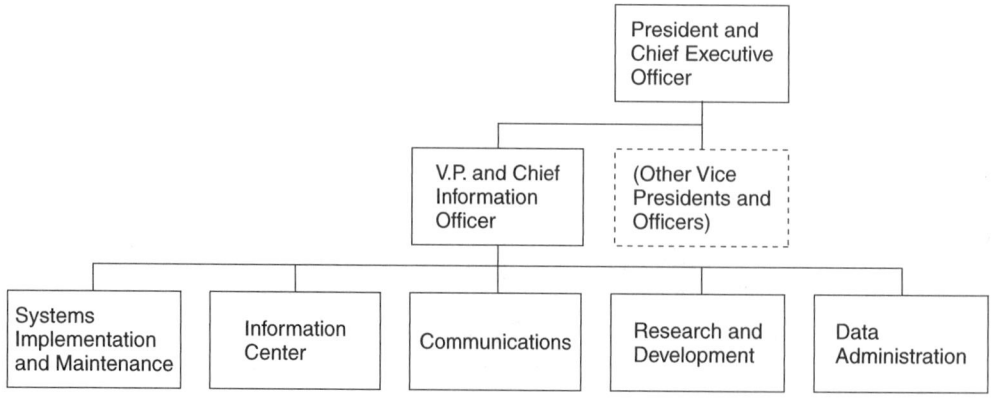

A central IS unit is usually involved in virtually every aspect of IT in an organization. It determines which computers and peripheral equipment are approved for purchasing; in some cases it is the only unit that is authorized to purchase hardware. It approves or rejects software purchases, is in charge of training new users, and (except for small and simple programs) is the only body that is authorized to develop ISs for business units.

The advantages and disadvantages of a centrally organized IS unit are essentially the same as those for centralized IS management. When centrally managed, the IS unit ensures compatibility of hardware and software and provides the interface between different systems that must work together, such as purchasing and cost accounting; payroll, accounts payable, and cost accounting; and sales and accounts receivable. This approach helps all top managers share an organizational vision of how information technology will serve the corporation in the future.

Regardless of architecture, central IS management usually includes a **steering committee** with representatives from a variety of key business units. It establishes priorities for systems development and implementation of communications networks; it considers and prioritizes requests for new systems; and it commits funds to projects. It is the organizational institution in charge of the budgets for all or most of the IS services.

In recent years the great majority of organizations have adopted ready-made software such as ERP systems. Others have outsourced some or all of their IS functions. Some now use the services of application service providers. But, the central IS unit still oversees the implementation of ready-made software, outsourcing, and relationships with ASPs.

It is often easier to integrate an IS plan into an organization's overall strategic plan with centralized IS management rather than decentralized IS services. On the other hand, when only a central department is available, business units often find themselves overly dependent on—and at times resentful of—the department. The resentment often springs from the lack of control over the services the IS department renders as other units depend on it for their success. Under a centralized IS organization, business units must receive approval for almost anything they do with computers, software, and telecommunications—a situation that can discourage the development of applications by end users, even if they are technologically knowledgeable enough to do so.

Functional IS Organization

At the other end of the IS staffing spectrum is the approach whereby each unit fulfills its IS needs independently, deciding for itself which systems it needs and how to develop them (see Exhibit 800.53). There is usually still an IS unit at corporate headquarters, but it is relatively small and serves to coordinate IS needs for departments that cannot handle their own needs. Only large and complex systems, especially those that affect several departments, are implemented under the auspices of this unit.

Each business unit has one or several IS professionals who report to the unit's manager. These workers know their non-IS colleagues' daily operations well and understand their information needs better than central IS personnel do.

In a functional IS organization, funds for the development and maintenance of the unit's ISs always come from the unit's own budget, which is intended to optimize the use of resources. While the unit's IS professionals may seek input from their central IS colleagues, decisions are made by the units fairly independently. In this environment, IS

Exhibit 800.53 *An Example of IS Personnel Locations in an Organization with Functionally Managed ISs*

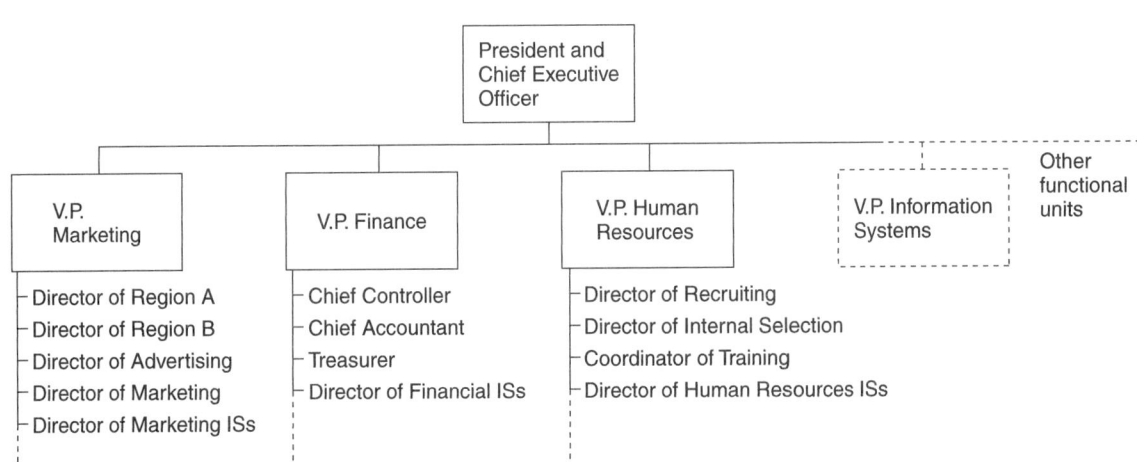

professionals are often involved in many aspects of operations that do not necessarily involve IT, and they may be promoted from an IT position into another type of position within the business. Such a system enhances their chances of advancing up the organizational ladder to general managerial positions.

As Exhibit 800.53 indicates, an organization that chooses the functional IS staffing approach may still have a corporate IS director, possibly a vice president, who oversees a small central IS unit, consults with functional IS units, and concentrates on larger, more complex enterprise-wide IS projects. However, the IS personnel of the various units do not report to the central IS unit.

The Best of Both Approaches

Small companies typically use the central approach to IS personnel because their IT staffs are small. Among mid-size and large companies, a purely central or functional IS organization is rare. Most of them use elements of both central and functional organization of IS personnel. For instance, a large corporate IS unit may have liaisons in the functional units who report to the corporate IS unit. **Gillette**, the world's largest supplier of shaving blades and other toiletry products, has established such an arrangement and found it very beneficial. A relatively large corporate IS unit coordinates intraorganizational systems, while the different sites (including international divisions) develop and maintain their own local systems. This approach helped the company remain on the leading edge of IT while maintaining a strong sense of ownership at the local sites.

In addition to their own personnel, in many organizations you will also find employees of other companies serving alongside the IS personnel. These professionals handle services that were outsourced by the company to an IS service firm. These people may work in a central IS unit or anywhere else in the organization, depending on the contract signed with the service firm. Many organizations also hire consultants for several weeks or months to help find and implement IT solutions to ad hoc problems or to seize opportunities. Again, these consultants work alongside the organization's employees as if they, too, were its employees. Senior consultants often take part in top management conferences.

Regardless of the approach to managing IS personnel and other resources, surveys show that IS implementation is handled differently according to the position of the highest IS officer in the organizational structure. If this person reports to the vice president of finance or another vice president, it is a sign that top management decided that IT can help automate processes but cannot change the company's strategic position significantly; the IS personnel then tend to provide mere technical solutions to business problems. However, if the highest-ranking IS executive reports to the CEO, it is a sign that top management considers IT as holding the potential to significantly change the organization's future; the IS professionals are then significantly more involved in strategic planning, and they also search for opportunities rather than just solve problems. The trend has been to upgrade the position from reporting to a vice president to reporting to the chief executive officer because of the importance of ISs to companies' survival.

Challenges for IS Managers and Line Managers

For ISs to be developed and maintained successfully, IS managers and line managers must understand what each party expects from the other and must find the best ways to respond to those expectations. By "line managers," we mean all managers in charge of areas other than ISs. What are the expectations?

Line Managers' Expectations of IS Managers

The first thing that line managers must remember is that they should have a continual dialogue with the company's IS managers, to explore new ways to help their operations. Although line managers are not expected to be well versed in IT's cutting edge, they should collaborate with the IS manager to explore new technologies to support the work of their subordinates. Line managers need the following from the IS unit:

- *A broad understanding of the business activities.* IS professionals are expected to understand the nature of the activities of the business unit they support. Whom does the business unit serve? Where do its raw data come from? What information does it use? What systems do the business unit's systems interface with? Understand-

ing the business helps IS professionals put themselves in the users' shoes and develop systems from the users' point of view.
- *Prompt response to the information needs of the business unit.* Line managers are often disappointed with the long time it takes IS units to react to business needs. A business unit that cannot elicit a prompt response from the IS staff may resort to finding haphazard—and ultimately problematic—solutions to its information needs.
- *A clear, jargon-free explanation of what the technology can and cannot do for the business unit.* To show off their expertise, IS professionals sometimes use technical jargon to communicate ideas. While use of technical terms facilitates communication among professionals, it may cause problems for lay users. Line managers and their employees may be reluctant to admit that they do not understand certain terms, so communication can break down, resulting in costly misunderstandings. If technical terms must be used, IS professionals should explain them.
- *Candid explanations of what information systems can and cannot do.* Line managers and their employees count on IS professionals to tell them not only what marvels a planned information system will accomplish but also what the system's limitations are. Outlining the limitations of a system will eliminate disappointment and ensure proper usage of the system.
- *Honest budgeting.* Line managers depend on IS managers for an honest, detailed assessment of the resources needed to develop a new IS and maintain an existing one. Time and budget overruns often occur in systems development projects. IS managers must detail the work that will be done, how much it will cost in terms of person hours and other resources, and how much time each project phase will take.
- *Single point of contact.* To serve the business units after an IS is installed or modified, IS managers should assign one contact person to respond to the business units' questions and problems.

In general, IS managers should treat line managers as clients, although they all work for the same organization. This approach has been adopted in an increasing number of companies. Some have taken the client/vendor model to such an extreme that line managers are allowed to use outside IS vendors if the internal IS unit cannot offer comparable service at comparable prices.

The dialogue between IS managers and general managers must be ongoing for an organization to take full advantage of IT to improve business operations.

IS Managers' Expectations of Line Managers

IS managers are expected to keep themselves abreast of developments in the IT field, suggest adoption of new technologies, and make recommendations to improve business operations. To do this job well, IS managers also need clear communication from line managers in three basic areas: basic business planning, general systems planning, and specific systems development.

- *Basic business planning.* To plan ahead, IS managers need to know their own business, but they also need to know their clients' (the business units') plans and needs. For instance, if a business department is planning to hire 10 new people to introduce a new product, the IS manager must be informed to budget for purchasing and installing new equipment, installing new software, and training the new employees to use it. Business plans for, say, three years into the future will become a part of the organization's overall IS plan, which in turn is a part of the organization's overall strategic plan.
- *General systems planning.* Once an IS unit is called on to develop a new system, it needs a clear explanation of business processes that need support. An IS manager can only develop an effective IS if line managers and their employees clearly communicate the exact processes they want automated.
- *Specific systems selection or development.* Once the general automation plan is agreed on, the IS manager needs to know what features the business manager wants in the new system. Although IS professionals are more familiar with IT than many users, they still need to know how a new system will be used in daily operations to design or install it correctly. The business manager is responsible for communicating what features are needed in a new system.

This information helps IS professionals include all input, processing, and output mechanisms, as well as user interfaces that are intuitive, easy to learn, and easy to use.

855. MANAGING INFORMATION TECHNOLOGY RESOURCES

The Information Center

Users of IT in all organizations need professional help with hardware, software, and telecommunications in their daily work. To satisfy this need, organizations often establish a separate organizational unit for support. The unit may have many names, but we refer to it by the most common one: the **information center.** The need for such a unit is especially high if the company maintains a decentralized IS organization and, in particular, when management encourages the development of applications by non-IS employees (sometimes called *local systems development*). Local systems development can create problems, including incompatibility of data files and databases throughout the company, isolation of useful data in "private" databases that are not accessible to the rest of the company, and inability to control sensitive information. Also, individual users, even in organizations with functional IS management, find they need advice on new software and the compatibility of files and documents created with different software packages. Thus, a typical information center has two functions: coordination and control, and support.

Coordination and Control

One way to allow sufficient local independence in IS acquisition and use, while controlling the problems it can create, is to coordinate and control hardware and software purchases by end users through an information center. A user who needs a tailored application would contact the center to determine whether anyone else has already developed a similar application that could be replicated or adapted. The information center also notifies departments of new hardware or software that could be useful and may also determine which hardware or software to purchase for a department so that its system remains compatible with other departments.

The same approach applies to coordinating data collection among departments. A department that needs access to certain data can check with the information center to see whether someone else in the business has already organized a database that can satisfy its needs. Information center personnel may also determine which data may or may not be gathered and kept by individual departments.

Central coordination and control is especially a challenge when an organization is involved in mergers and acquisitions. When a company acquires other companies, top management must implement standards that mesh with corporate strategy.

Support Through Help Desk

Another important function of the information center is providing hardware and software support through both training and responding to ongoing requests for help. The latter is usually accomplished through a help desk. The **help desk** usually consists of small teams specializing in troubleshooting problems in different areas: hardware, software, communications, and so on. The success of the help desk depends largely on its ability to provide a single point of contact that can connect the user to the appropriate expert, on demand (see Exhibit 800.54).

Exhibit 800.54 *The Help Desk Is an Essential Resource for Information Systems (IS) Users*

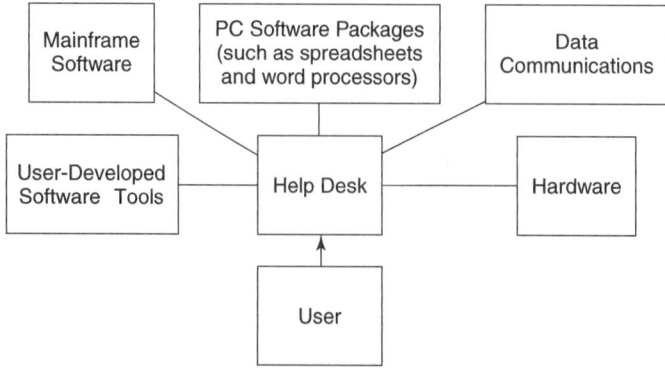

Charge-Back Methods

Some companies treat the cost of the IS function as a part of **overhead cost,** a general expense carried by all departments that is considered essential to running the company—like the lights or phone service. In companies such as these, business units don't purchase services from the IS departments, they simply call on IS services at will and receive them seemingly "free," that is, without a direct impact on their budgets. But this arrangement has a downside—IS services can be easily, if not intentionally, abused, mostly because departments are tempted to order many additional services because no cost is directly associated with them.

To mitigate this problem, many organizations have established charge-back systems. A **charge-back system** is a method by which organizational units pay for the services they receive, often referred to as *service charges.* Charge-back systems may reduce tension between providers and receivers of IS services, because the receivers know exactly what they are being charged for. It also makes the allocation of the services more efficient, because it encourages individual departments to use only those services that they really need for their operations.

Service Charges

Without a charge-back system, politics often prevail as the controlling factor in deciding who receives IS services. Even if top management limits IS services, business units with strong political clout tend to receive more service than other units that may, objectively, need it more. Politics becomes less of a problem as units start paying for their service, but other problems may appear.

For instance, although many users now know how to develop their own simple applications, they still count on a central IS unit to satisfy most of their information needs. When a functional unit depends on a central IS unit to provide a service, tensions may grow. The functional IS staff has only its department and commitments as a priority, but the central IS personnel must prioritize many requests from a corporate perspective. When a service is eventually delivered and charged, tension may build if the users do not understand what their department is being charged for, and by what criteria.

What Is Chargeable?

The items for which a functional unit may be charged fall into the following categories:

- *Personnel hours.* Usually, IS staff time is the largest part of the charge for systems development or systems maintenance. The IS unit charges either a fixed hourly rate or hourly rates that differ according to the level of expertise being provided.
- *Computer time.* This charge is normally billed to departments for the use of mainframe computers or computers on loan.
- *External storage space.* IS departments charge for storing data according to the amount stored. The charge is so many dollars per megabyte per month.
- *Number of input and output operations.* Some IS departments charge business departments for each log-on involving a shared computer.
- *Paper output.* Some IS departments charge business departments per page of paper printout.

Costs that cannot be definitely attributed to specific business units are generally not charged back. For example, the purchase price of any hardware or software that is to be shared by many departments cannot be charged directly to any one department.

Desirable Charge-Back Features

Charge-back methods are successful when they have the following features:

- *Accountability.* Every element of the IS service—including personnel time, computer time, and paper—must be accounted for and attributed to the manager who ordered it. If the cost of some services, such as intraorganizational communication time, cannot be accurately allocated to individual units, they are not charged to individual units. Such costs are considered overhead and are absorbed by divisional or corporate headquarters.

- *Controllability.* Managers who order services should be able to control what they purchase. The charge-back system should be designed so that business managers can determine the type and amount of service to purchase to best fit their specific information needs.
- *Timeliness.* The IS unit must bill managers periodically, with reasonable intervals between billings, so that the managers can track the IS costs they incur and change their request if they so wish.
- *Congruence with organizational goals.* Charge-back rates should be established to encourage business units to use resources that are in the interests of the corporation and to discourage business units from using services that are not in the corporation's overall interest. For example, a low hourly rate may be charged for the time IS personnel spend on training employees to use their PC software to develop applications, if management wishes to encourage application development by users. A high per-page rate may be charged for the generation of paper reports if management wants to encourage on-line ad hoc reports and paperless operations.

Charge-Back Criticism

The charge-back approach is not without its critics. The major argument against charge-back systems is that the expense may discourage managers from exploring new IT opportunities for business activities. Because IS technology is adopted for current and future needs, there is an element of long-term investment. Managers who are focused on quick profitability may opt to spend their budgets on other resources that they believe will generate immediate benefits. Also, in many organizations managers and other employees are frustrated at the high rates their departments must pay for what they perceive as simple services. Disagreement over how much a job should cost may create friction rather than cooperation. The goal of charge-back systems is to increase efficiency in the allocation of IS services, but if IS charge backs are unreasonably priced, the system may create the opposite of its goal: managers may try to do by themselves what only professionals can do well, creating inefficiencies.

Overhead Expenditures

Some IS department expenses—such as research and development, and corporate-wide data communications installation and maintenance—cannot be directly attributed to the services the IS department performs for business units. These costs are often treated as overhead expenses shared by the entire organization and are therefore excluded from the charge-back scheme. In many corporations, the cost of implementing systems that are used by a large number of organizational units, such as ERP systems, is treated as overhead expense. It is practically impossible to determine how much each unit will use the new system and therefore how much to charge. Another reason these systems are not charged back to business units is that their managers may elect not to have them installed. Since it is in corporate management's interest to install such systems, management takes away both the decision and the financial burden from the individual units.

Telecommunications and Networks

Telecommunications in Business

Telecommunications, which is essential to today's smooth business operations, is the transmittal of data and information from one point to another. Thus, telecommunications is communications over a distance. Telephone, fax, e-mail, the World Wide Web—none of these essential business services would be available without fast, reliable telecommunications. In fact, electronic commerce, popularly called *e-commerce*, would be impossible. This section will help you understand the technical foundations of telecommunications, an essential ingredient to managing its role in business. We will discuss the hardware and software needed for telecommunications, the cost/benefit trade-offs of different systems, and the technical trade-offs a successful manager needs to understand to participate in critical business decisions. It is equally, if not more, important to understand how telecommunications affects the way businesses run and how managers can use technology to do a better job. Telecommunications has brought four basic improvements to business processes.

- *Better business communication.* When no physical objects need to be transferred from one place to another, telecommunications technology can make geographical distance irrelevant. E-mail, voice mail, faxing, file transfer, cellular telephony, and teleconferencing enable detailed and instant communication, whether among managers, between managers and their staffs, or among different organizations. Telecommunications can also be used by one person to monitor another person's performance in real time. Telecommunications is used to communicate directions and receive feedback without requiring people to coordinate their schedules to hold a meeting. And the use of e-mail has brought some secondary benefits to business communications by establishing a permanent written record of, and accountability for, ideas. The result is more accurate business communications.
- *Higher efficiency.* Telecommunications has made business processes more efficient. Many business processes are serial in nature: one department must have the input of another department before acting and must then produce its own information, which in turn serves as input for a third department, and so on. For example, when the sales department receives a purchase order from a customer, it must communicate the order to the warehouse, which needs the information to prepare the package. The warehouse workers must then forward shipping documents to the accounts receivable department for billing. With telecommunications, all documents can be accessed electronically by many different departments at the same time. Furthermore, processes that used to take a long time for action and counteraction by two or more parties can now be carried out in one session attended by all parties involved, through telecommunication lines.
- *Better distribution of data.* Organizations that can quickly transmit vital data from one computer to another no longer need centralized databases. Business units that need certain data frequently may store it locally, while others can access it remotely. Only fast, reliable transfer of data makes this efficient arrangement possible.
- *Instant transactions.* The availability of the Internet to millions of businesses and consumers has shifted a significant volume of business transactions to the Web. Both businesses and consumers can shop, purchase, and pay instantly on line. In addition to commercial activities, people can use telecommunications for on-line education and entertainment.

As a manager, you will be responsible for ensuring that your organization maximizes its benefits from fast and reliable telecommunications. To do so, you may be involved in selecting a telecommunications system or in exploring the demands on your organization's system. To be a creative and productive contributor to these key decisions, it is essential that you grasp the basic technology behind telecommunications.

At the same time we enjoy the great opportunities created by telecommunications technology, we must recognize that it poses great risks as well. Once an organization connects its ISs to a public network, security issues become extremely important. Unauthorized access and data destruction are constant threats. Thus, organizations must establish proper security controls as preventive measures. Security issues have become especially important due to the popularity of the Internet and its growing accessibility.

Data Communications

Data communications is any transfer of data within a computer, between a computer and another device, or between two computers. For a computer to function, binary data in the form of electrical impulses must flow from one component to another, such as from the CPU to the primary memory, from the CPU to the monitor, or from the primary memory to the hard disk. This type of communication is done through the computer's bus. The bus is a system of wires, or strings of conductive material, soldered on the surface of a computer board. It is a communications channel that allows the transmission of a whole byte or more in one pass.

Telecommunications is communication of data and information between two devices over a distance. In our discussion, we will refer to telecommunication among computers or between computers and other digital devices. The data may represent any number of media, including voice, video, animation, or text. Once communications are transmitted *between* computer systems rather than *within* a single system, the rules of the communications game become more complex. A number of questions about how to manage communications arise, such as the following:

- What physical channels should be used to transmit and receive signals?
- How can we maximize communication speed per dollar spent on communication links?
- What is the best layout of the nodes in an internal network for our business?

Other issues must be taken into account when considering a telecommunications system. For instance, communications devices must be compatible. As always, the benefits of the telecommunications devices and software have to be weighed against their costs.

Types of Data Communications

Data can be transmitted in two basic modes: a whole byte at a time, which is feasible only over very short distances, or a single bit at a time, currently the only practical mode for communicating over long distances. Within the computer, and between the computer and its peripheral equipment (such as its printer and external hard disk), the transmission can take the form of parallel transmission. In **parallel transmission,** each byte is transmitted in its entirety. The electrical impulses representing the bits of a byte are transmitted along a bundle of parallel lines, one bit through each line. These lines are often called a "bus" (although the word *bus* is not reserved only for parallel transmission). In **serial transmission,** on the other hand, data are transmitted one bit at a time through a single line.

Parallel and serial data transmission require different types of wiring. In the back of a computer are several outlets for connecting different cables. An outlet that can accept multiwire cord to transmit in parallel is a **parallel port.** An outlet that accepts a cord for serial transmission is a **serial port.**

Rules must be set so that both the transmitting and the receiving devices can "understand" each other. For instance, in serial transmission, rules determine when each byte begins and ends. The transmitting and receiving ends must agree on details such as whether each byte is transmitted with bits indicating the start and stop of the byte, the number of bits to be transmitted per second, and other features. Without rules, the transmission may result in a long stream of meaningless bits. Sets of such rules are called **protocols.** We discuss protocols later in this section.

Why not transmit only in parallel? Because the public infrastructure that can accommodate parallel transmission is limited. The communications networks available to most people are the telephone network and the Internet, and these networks can accommodate only serial transmission of data.

Communication Direction

The three modes of communication between devices—simplex, half-duplex, and full-duplex—are distinguished by whether communication is one-way in one direction, one-way at a time in two directions, or two-way (see Exhibit 800.55).

Exhibit 800.55 *Simplex, Half-Duplex, and Full-Duplex Communication*

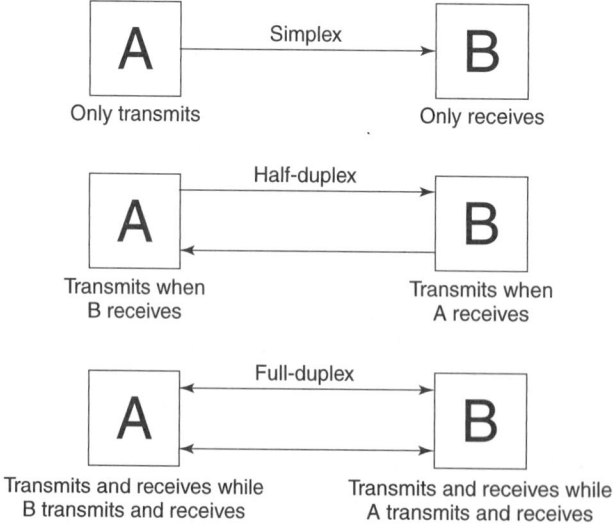

MODULE 800. INFORMATION TECHNOLOGY

Simplex

In **simplex** communication, device A can transmit to device B, but device B cannot transmit to device A. An example of simplex communication is commercial radio transmission. Your car radio can receive signals from a radio station but cannot transmit back to it.

Half-Duplex

In **half-duplex** mode, device A can transmit to device B while device B receives the signal. Device B can transmit to device A while device A receives the signal. However, the two devices cannot transmit to each other simultaneously, and one device can transmit to the other only when the other device is in reception mode. One example of half-duplex is CB (citizens band) communication. Half-duplex may also take place when you use a computer terminal to communicate with a mainframe computer.

Full-Duplex

In **full-duplex** communication, either device can transmit to the other device while simultaneously receiving signals from the other device. That is, device A can transmit to B and receive from B at the same time, and vice versa. Telephony is an example of full-duplex: both parties can talk and listen at once (although this method is neither a practical nor a polite way to use the telephone). Full-duplex data communication is often used between computers.

Synchronization

Telecommunications can work only if the transmitting and receiving devices are synchronized, or "time-coordinated." Otherwise, the receiving device cannot correctly interpret the message encoded in the stream of bits it receives. There are two ways to synchronize communication: one is called *synchronous* and, despite the seeming contradiction in terminology, the other is called *asynchronous*.

Asynchronous Communication

In asynchronous transmission, the devices are not synchronized by timing aids as they are in synchronous communication. Rather, each character (that is, each byte) is transmitted along with additional special bits that tell the receiving device how to interpret the transmission. A start bit indicates the beginning of the byte, a stop bit indicates its end, and an additional bit may be added for error detection.

Regardless of transmission type, synchronous or asynchronous, to ensure accurate reception of a stream of bytes, the receiving end has to "sample the line" at the same rate the transmitting end is sending. Sampling means detecting the signal at preset time intervals. For example, if the transmitter sends at a rate of 56,000 bits per second, the receiver must sample the transmission once every 1/56,000 of a second. If the receiver samples at a different rate, after several thousand bits the reception will be out of sequence with the transmission; the receiver will misinterpret the location and meaning of bits.

The timing of communications devices—that is, the sampling rate—can vary slightly from one machine to another, throwing off the coordination between the transmitting and receiving devices. To overcome timing differences that may arise, a start bit (a 1) is added to the beginning of the transmittal of each byte, and a stop bit (a 0) is added at the end of each byte. The start-bit signal tells the receiver to realign with the transmitter. At worst, sampling rate differences between the parties will be very small, too small to disrupt smooth communication. Realigning at the beginning of each byte ensures that the sampling gap never becomes so large that the receiving device misses an entire bit. Still, we call this type of data communication **asynchronous,** because transmission and reception are synchronized only at the byte level, not for every single bit.

Sometimes, power brownouts or other mishaps may disrupt a connection, resulting in unintended addition or loss of bits. **Parity check** is an error-detection method used to assure that no bits are added or deleted during transmission. Parity checks eliminate a lot of errors in telecommunication but not all.

The advantage of asynchronous transmission is that it does not require sophisticated and expensive timing hardware. The disadvantage of asynchronous transmission is its high *overhead,* or time spent transmitting bits that are not a part of the primary data (the "start," "stop," and "parity check" bits).

Synchronous Communication

The use of timing devices in **synchronous** transmission allows several bytes to be transmitted without the great overhead of start, stop, and parity check bits for each byte. The basic unit transmitted is called a *packet*, rather than a single byte (see Exhibit 800.56). A **packet** is a group of bytes transmitted together with no overhead bits added between them, although some precede and follow the packet. As indicated in Exhibit 800.56, a single message consists of several streams of bits that make up synchronization bytes ("sync bytes," to announce the beginning and end of an entire packet), a packet, and error check bits. Each of the message's packets is passed from the source computer to the destination computer, often through intermediate nodes. (A node is a computer or a communications device in a communications network.) At each node, the entire packet is received, stored, and then passed on to the next node, until all packets, either kept together or reassembled, reach the destination. Because overhead bits only precede and trail each packet, the overall overhead in synchronous communication is significantly smaller than in asynchronous communication.

Channels and Media

A communications **channel** is the physical medium, such as telephone lines or television cables, through which data can be communicated. In our context, the term is synonymous with communications links and communications paths. The **capacity** of the channel is the speed at which data are communicated, which is also called the **transmission rate.** Capacity is measured in **bits per second** (**bps**); the greater the capacity, the faster the transmission. As is often the case, communications speed, also called *channel capacity* and *bandwidth*, is a limited resource. The greater the speed, the higher the cost of the communications line. Thus, determining the type of communications lines to install or subscribe to is an important business decision.

Channel Capacity

When the channel is of small capacity, it is said to be **narrow band.** (Media with the lowest capacity—such as copper telephone wires—are considered to have **baseband** capacity.) When a channel has great capacity and can carry several streams of data simultaneously, it is said to be **broadband.** For example, copper wire telephone lines are a baseband medium that cannot transmit effectively at speeds of more than 56,000 bps and, even at this speed, only for short distances, unless special software is used. Other specially treated, or "conditioned," telephone lines can handle greater capacities. Of course, you can force your computer to deliver signals into the line at a higher rate, but the destination will receive a garbled message.

Exhibit 800.56 *Synchronous Transmission*

| Sync Byte | Sync Byte | Error Check Bits | Packet | Sync Byte | Sync Byte | → |

Media

A channel is also called a **medium,** but not every medium requires a physical line. A medium is anything through which data are transmitted. In the examples of channel capacity, a *guided medium* carried the first transmission. An *unguided medium,* air (which has no physical channel), carried the second transmission. Another example of unguided media is outer space. Unguided media allow wireless telecommunications, which is so important for businesspeople outside the office; however, as you will see later, it is also useful in computer networks inside offices.

Transmission Speeds

A medium's capacity is determined by the maximum number of bits per second that it can carry. You should remember, though, that the number of signals per second is not always equal to the number of bits per second. Sometimes one signal can represent two or more bits. The number of signals per second is called **baud.** If the baud rate is 28,800 and each signal represents two bits, then the bps rate is 57,600.

The bit rate of any communication should be chosen on the basis of the distance over which it must be carried because the greater the distance, the less clear the signal. Therefore, the farther a signal must travel, the more slowly it must be transmitted in order to be received correctly. To illustrate, consider a flashlight as an example. If your friend is standing nearby, she can easily detect the flashes of light. But if she is standing at a great distance, she cannot detect the bursts of light; the signals will blur. Even sending the bursts more slowly (at greater intervals) will not help. Signals become weaker as the distance they travel gets longer. The signals will be too weak to be perceived unless you use a repeater—such as a reflector—to capture the signal and retransmit it at its original strength. A **repeater** receives and strengthens signals and then sends them on the next leg of their journey.

The many different media—including twisted pair, coaxial cable, microwaves, and optical fibers—vary in a number of ways: how much information they can carry, what their vulnerability to corrupting interference is, what they cost, whether they guide the data, and how readily available they are (see Exhibit 800.57).

Twisted Pair

The most pervasive and commonly available communications network is the telephone network. Telephones are connected either directly to a local telephone company office or to a local **private branch exchange** (**PBX**), which is connected to a telephone company office. A traditional telephone line is made of a pair of twisted copper wires that acts as a single communications link. The wires are twisted to reduce electromagnetic interference (EMI), which can alter voice and data and make them unclear.

In much of the telephone network in the United States and many other countries, copper has been replaced with higher-capacity media such as optical fibers; only the line from the telephone company's office to the home or office telephone jack is still made of copper. Although the line's length varies, we often refer to that distance as "the last mile," because this is the last part of the telephone network that is still made of copper wires, and probably will stay so for many years.

Exhibit 800.57 *Characteristics of Channel Media*

Medium	Capacity	Vulnerability to Electromagnetic Interference	Cost	Guided/ Unguided	Availability
Twisted Pair	Lower	High	Lower	Guided	Everywhere
Coaxial Cable	↑	Low	↑	Guided	Low
Microwave	↓	Low	↓	Unguided	High
Optical Fiber	Higher	Nonexistent	Higher	Guided	Most of United States and parts of other countries

The rate at which digital data completes its transmittal depends on the distance it travels. When twisted pair is used for local area networks supporting personal computers, the transmission rate may reach 100 Mbps (megabits per second, or one million bits per second). The "last mile" of copper wires can be enabled to transmit digital signals at speeds up to 8 Mbps with special equipment and software both at the telephone exchange (often called "central office") and at the subscriber's end. The service is called **digital subscriber line** (**DSL**) and is provided by telecommunication companies both to businesses and households in a growing number of regions in the United States and other countries. DSL enables high-speed connection to the Internet.

Coaxial Cable

- *Twisted pairs, previously the most common telecommunications medium, are being replaced by optical fibers.*
- *Coaxial cables are used primarily for television transmission but are also used for data communications.*

Coaxial cable is sometimes called *TV cable* because of its common use for cable television transmission. Like telephone lines, it is made of two conductors but is constructed differently to permit operation over a wider range of frequencies. It consists of a hollow outer conductor and an inner wire conductor, with an insulator between them, usually of wax or plastic. The outer conductor is covered with PVC, a special plastic.

Coaxial cable is significantly more expensive than twisted pair, but its transmission rate is greater. Thanks to its shielded concentric construction, coaxial cable is much less susceptible to EMI. In voice communication, it is less prone to cross talk (the intrusion of a third party's conversation on your line) than twisted pair.

In recent years the use of coaxial cable for Internet connection has been popular among households. Companies that provide cable television service use their networks to link subscribers to the Internet.

Microwaves

- *Microwave transceivers are used by many businesses to communicate data.*
- *Low earth orbit (LEO) satellites blanket the earth to provide uninterrupted communication.*
- *Large companies lease frequencies of telecommunications satellites to transmit data coast to coast and across national borders.*

Microwaves are high-frequency, short radio-frequency (RF) waves. Short radio-frequency waves can carry signals over long distances with high accuracy. RF uses different waves to represent bits. You have probably noticed the ubiquitous parabolic antennas on the roofs of buildings. They are so numerous because microwave communication is effective only if the line of sight between the transmitter and receiver is unobstructed. Microwave antennas are also often installed on high buildings and the tops of mountains to obtain a clear line of sight.

Terrestrial Microwave

Microwave communication requires far fewer repeaters and amplifiers than coaxial cable and optical fibers, for the same distance. Terrestrial microwave communication—so-called because signals are sent from and received by stations on the ground—is good for long-distance telecommunications but can also be used in local-area networks in and among buildings. It is commonly used for voice and television communications.

Satellite Microwave

Signals can also be transmitted using microwaves via satellite technology. There are two major types of satellites: geostationary, also called GEO, and low earth orbit, also called LEO. Both types serve as radio relay stations in orbit above the earth that receive, amplify, and redirect signals. Microwave **transceiver** (transmitter-receiver) dishes are aimed at the satellite, which has antennas, amplifiers, and transmitters. The satellite receives a signal, amplifies it, and retransmits it to the destination.

Communications satellites are launched not only by private enterprises but also by national governments. The satellites are used for television broadcasts, long-distance telephone transmissions, and private business networks. A satellite owner can divide the frequency (that is, the band) into several channels and lease different channels to different users. Large companies, such as **Kmart** and **Wal-Mart**, have leased satellite channels. They use the links to quickly transmit business data among stores and distribution centers.

Optical Fiber

Fiber-optic technology uses light instead of electricity to represent bits. Fiber-optic lines are made of thin fiberglass filaments. A transmitter sends bursts of light using a laser or a light-emitting diode device. The receiver detects the light and samples the line to receive the data bits. Optical-fiber systems operate in the infrared and visible light frequencies. Because light is not susceptible to EMI (electromagnetic interference) and RFI (radio-frequency interference), fiber-optic communication is much less error-prone than twisted pair and radio transmission.

Optical fibers compare favorably with coaxial cable networks in providing a fast, reliable medium for telecommunications. As a result, they are rapidly replacing both twisted-pair and coaxial cable telephone lines. **Sprint Communications**, a major telephone carrier, implemented its entire network using trunk lines of optical fibers, and other carriers have followed suit. In 1991, optical fibers surpassed satellites as the dominant means for global digital network communications. Expanding fiber-optic networks and their declining prices offer great opportunities for businesses.

Modulation

Until several years ago, the most widespread communications network was a huge web of twisted-pair telephone lines designed to carry voice communication. The majority of homes and many offices still have telephone hookups suitable only for voice communication. More recently, however, business demands and technological progress have required that the same lines be used to transmit data. Unfortunately, the type of signal used to transmit voice messages—called **analog,** or continuous, signals—is not well suited to the communication of digital signals, such as data communications.

Analog Versus Digital

Exhibit 800.58 graphically represents an analog signal as a continuous series of waves and a digital signal as a series of short lines of two different heights. Analog signals transmit voice communications well: these signals are not limited to one high pitch and one low pitch but can reproduce all variations of voice, with an infinite number of pitches and sound levels over a wide continuous range. Computer data, on the other hand, is **digital** because it consists of a series of discrete bits represented by only two different states and nothing in between. Ideally, we want to transmit data communications over a line that can carry a digital signal. If the line can carry only analog signals, we must translate digital signals into equivalent analog signals as they pass from the computer to the analog line and then translate them back to the original digital signals just before they are transferred to the receiving computer. This modification

Exhibit 800.58 *Signal Modulation*

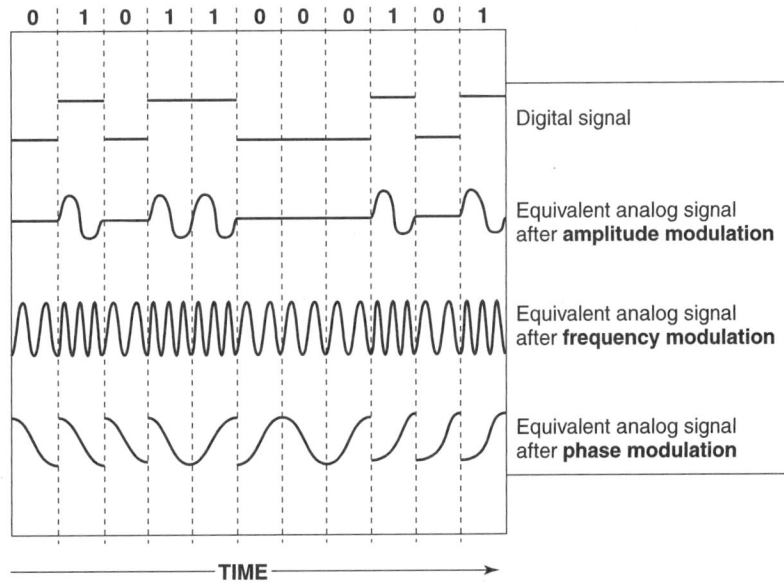

860. TELECOMMUNICATIONS AND NETWORKS

of a digital signal (from the computer) into an analog signal (for the phone line to transmit) is called **modulation**. The transformation of an analog signal (from the phone line) into a digital signal (so the computer can understand it) is called **demodulation**. There are three different types of modulation: amplitude modulation, frequency modulation, and phase modulation.

Amplitude Modulation

An analog signal can be graphically represented as a continuous series of waves of different heights. The height of the wave is its amplitude. Amplitude modulation uses differences in amplitude to express digital signals. The 0 bits are transformed into an analog signal whose amplitude is either zero (flat) or very low. The 1 bits are transformed into a higher wave of a fixed amplitude. The two amplitudes represent the 0s and 1s of digital transmission.

Frequency Modulation

In frequency modulation, the amplitude of the wave remains constant, but variations in frequency are used to represent digital signals. Frequency is the number of waves per second. Whenever a 0 bit is transmitted, the frequency is low. Whenever a 1 bit is transmitted, the frequency is higher. The two frequencies represent the 0s and 1s.

Phase Modulation

In phase modulation, transmission always starts with a certain bit, 0 or 1. When the wave abruptly stops and immediately continues at another phase, it indicates a shift from the previously transmitted bit to the other bit, such as from 0 to 1 or from 1 to 0.

Modems

Because the telephone company's signaling is already set up for analog wave transmission, it is easier for the company to use analog rather than digital signals to send information back and forth between your telephone and the telephone company.

Much of the telephone networking in North America, Western Europe, and Japan is technically ready for digital transmission. However, modulation/demodulation devices are still needed, because the "last mile" between the telephone company's switching office and the home or office of the telephone user are made of copper wires (twisted pairs) set up for analog signals only, unless the household or business subscribes to DSL service.

A **modem**—a word contracted from *modulator-demodulator*—is a device whose purpose is to modulate and demodulate communications signals. A modem can be internal (plugged into the computer's motherboard) or external (outside the computer, plugged into a serial port or a universal serial bus port). To use a modem, the user needs to attach it to a computer and use communications software, which is part of today's operating systems.

Modems are rated by their transmission for different speeds. Practically all new PCs come with an internal modem installed. If you want to use coaxial cable for telecommunications, you must use a cable modem (and subscribe to a cable service). Cable modems cost significantly more than standard modems because of their more sophisticated circuitry and the significantly smaller number of units sold. Subscription to DSL service requires a DSL modem, which is actually not a modem but a bridge. A **bridge** is a device that connects dissimilar networks into a seamless network. A DSL bridge enables the smooth flow of the digital signals between the computer and the "last mile" wires.

Set-Up

To set up a modem for transmission and reception, you must select the communication protocol, that is, the number of data bits in each byte, the number of start and stop bits, whether there is a parity check bit, and if so, whether it is odd or even. Operating systems contain help software, or "wizards," to help users set up their connections.

Fax/Voice

Nowadays, all PC modems are also fax-capable, that is, they allow the computer to be used as a fax machine. First the modem "digitizes" any page that needs to be faxed. Digitization is a way of "taking a picture" of a page and relaying it as an array of dots. Special software divides the page into many tiny areas. Each area is assigned a binary code that represents its location on the page and its color, or hue. This digital code is then transmitted as a stream of bits. The receiving device transforms the digitized stream and reconstructs the picture.

To receive a fax through a fax-modem, the receiving computer must be on. The received digitized page is saved in a file. Note that the fax is an *image* of the page. If a letter or other text is faxed, the digital file is *not* the ASCII code representing the characters; it is just a picture of the characters. As such, the file cannot be manipulated and edited with a word processor. Many modems also allow callers to leave voice messages, which are digitized and stored for later retrieval.

A fax-modem can transmit to a fax machine or another fax-modem only from a computer file. For example, you cannot transmit your picture via a fax-modem unless the picture is in digital form on the computer. However, you can use a scanner to scan the picture, store the scanned version in a file, and fax the file via the fax-modem.

Most modems are connected to telephone lines. More recently, cable modems have started to take advantage of the high transmission rates of coaxial cable. Cable modems are becoming increasingly popular as the use of coaxial cable for digital communication becomes more widespread, especially due to the popularity of the Web and the growing amount of data retrieved and transmitted through the Internet.

Multiplexers

Multiplexers are communications devices that allow several telephones or computers to transmit voice or digital data through a single line. Multiplexers sometimes incorporate modem technology, so the telephone line can be used to transmit data as well. The great advantage of multiplexers is cost savings. Instead of installing a line between a central computer and each terminal with which it communicates, terminals can be connected to one channel through a multiplexer (see Exhibit 800.59). Another multiplexer serves the host computer. There are two types of multiplexing: frequency division and time division.

Exhibit 800.59 *Multiplexing*

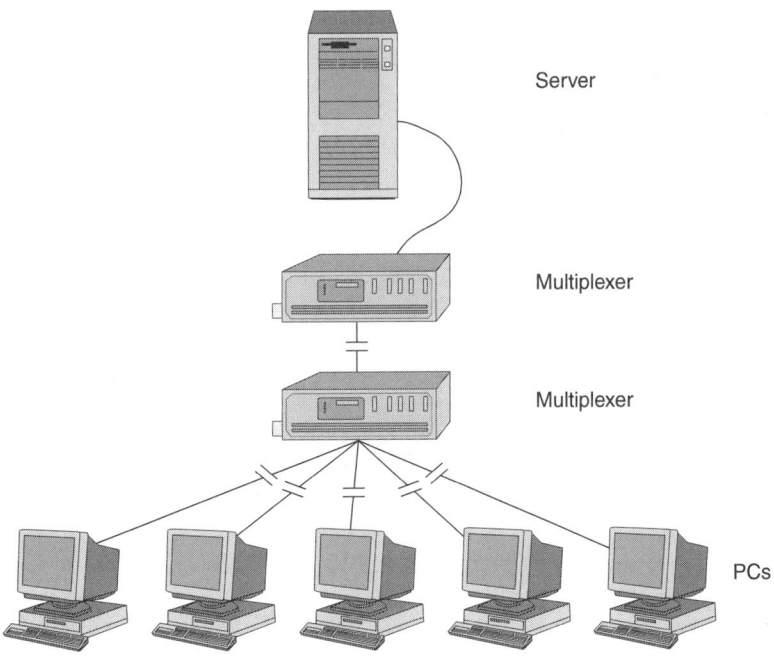

Frequency-Division Multiplexing

If the bandwidth of a carrier channel—that is, the range of frequencies it can carry—is large enough, it can be divided into several narrower bandwidths. This allows for *frequency-division multiplexing,* whereby several computers transmit data, each at its own assigned frequency, to the host computer. The multiplexer can literally transmit data from several computers at the same time. The multiplexer attached to the host computer identifies the source of the data according to its unique frequency.

Time-Division Multiplexing

Some multiplexers allocate specified equal amounts of time to each connected terminal, receiving a part of each terminal's signal at a time, in a round-robin fashion, and piecing the signals together again. This is called *time-division multiplexing* and is most commonly used by terminals interacting with a host computer.

In time-division multiplexing, each terminal is allotted its time slots whether it uses the time to communicate or not. Often, some terminals use their time slots less than others, which causes inefficient use of communication resources. A statistical multiplexer dynamically allocates time slots to those devices that need to transmit more frequently. This way, terminals that need the line more frequently can use time that would otherwise be automatically allocated to other terminals that don't need it.

Networks in Business

The key to fast and efficient telecommunications is networks. In the context of data communications, a **network** is a combination of devices (at least two computers) connected to each other through one of the communication channels just discussed. Networks in which a single host computer serves only dumb terminals (computers with no processing capability of their own) are becoming obsolete as prices of microcomputers are plummeting.

We usually refer to two types of networks: LANs (local-area networks), which serve an office or several adjacent offices; and WANs (wide-area networks), which are larger, national and global networks. Often, both types of networks use the same type of layout, also called **topology,** and the same types of protocols for signal transmission and reception. In such cases, the only difference between LANs and WANs is the distance between the networked computers.

Local-Area Networks (LANs)

A computer network within a building, or among adjacent buildings, is called a **local-area network,** or **LAN.** No specific distance classifies a network as local, but usually as long as it is confined to a radius of three to four miles, it is called a LAN. LANs, which can be hardwired or wireless, are the most common way to let users share software and hardware resources and to enhance communication among workers.

In LANs one computer is often used as a central repository of programs and files that all connected computers can use; this computer is called a server. Connected computers can store documents on their own disks or on the server, can share hardware such as printers, and can exchange e-mail.

When a LAN has a server, the server usually has centralized control of communications among the connected computers and between the computers and the server itself. Another computer or special communications device can also exercise this control. A **peer-to-peer LAN** is one in which no central device controls communications.

Although wireless LANs are still expensive, they offer significant benefits: installation is much easier because companies don't have to drill through walls to install wires, and they can move equipment wherever it is needed. Wireless networks offer significant savings in some environments. Wireless LANs are less costly to maintain when the network spans two or more buildings. They are also more scalable. **Scalability** is the ease of augmenting a system. It is relatively easy to add more nodes, or clients, to a wireless LAN. The installation of wireless LANs is expected to continue to grow significantly.

Wide-Area Networks (WANs)

A network that crosses organizational boundaries or, in the case of a multisite organization, reaches outside the immediate environment of local offices and factory facilities is called a **wide-area network** (**WAN**). WANs can be public or private. The Internet is an example of a public WAN. A private WAN may use either dedicated lines or very-small-aperture-terminal satellites (VSATs), which provide narrow bandwidths and are less expensive.

Many organizations cannot afford to maintain a private WAN. They pay to use existing networks, which are provided in two basic formats: common carriers or value-added networks.

A **common carrier** provides public telephone lines that anyone can access or dial up and leased lines, which are dedicated to the leasing organization's exclusive use. The user pays for public lines based on time used and distance called. **AT&T**, **WorldCom**, and **Sprint** are common carriers. Leased lines are dedicated to the lease-holder and have a lower error rate than dial-up lines, because they are not switched among many different subscribers.

Value-added networks (**VANs**) such as Tymnet and Sprintnet provide enhanced network services such as protocol conversion and error detection and correction. VANs fulfill organizational needs for reliable data communications while relieving the organization of providing its own network management and maintenance. Many businesses use VANs for their electronic data interchange (EDI) with other businesses, suppliers, and buyers. However, due to cost considerations, an increasing number of organizations prefer to conduct e-commerce via the Internet rather than through VANs. VAN services cost much more than those offered by Internet service providers.

As with LANs, **wireless communication** is being used more and more in WANs. Outfitted with a radio modem, which is a regular modem with an antenna for communicating radio signals, a user can send data on a radio frequency to a selected recipient or for Internet connection. There are no wires to connect and no telephone jacks to look for. The most visible use of wireless WANs may be with hand-held PDAs (personal digital assistants) such as Palm VII and several models of cellular phones that serve the dual purpose of a phone and an Internet-enabled PDA. Note, however, that the small screens of such units do not allow the same reception of Web pages as your PC does. The pages displayed on these devices are limited. The units are capable of sending and receiving e-mail, stock quotes, and other information, but graphic content is limited.

Network Topology

Network topology is the physical layout of nodes in a network, which often dictates the type of communications protocol used by the network. (For the sake of simplicity, we use the term *node* to denote any computer or communications device in a network.) In reality, only small LANs use a single topology. Larger networks are usually a combination of two or more different topologies. Exhibit 800.60 illustrates the main network topologies; we describe these topologies with their advantages and disadvantages.

Star

As illustrated in Exhibit 800.60, in a **star topology** all nodes connect to one central device. That device may be a file sever, a private branch exchange (PBX), or a network "hub." When the user of a node wants to transmit to another node, the communication is managed by, and transmitted through, the central device, which contains the communications software.

Star topology is the most popular network topology at present. The advantage of star topology is that it is easy to determine the source of a network problem, such as a cable failure. The main disadvantage of star topology is that if the central device is not working, the entire network is down. Another disadvantage is that adding computers can be costly, because each connected computer needs a cable to the central device. Star networks are considered more difficult to implement and maintain than the ring and bus topologies.

Ring

Exhibit 800.60 shows the **ring topology** employed in LANs. Every node connects to two other nodes through a single line: a twisted pair, coaxial cable, or optical fiber. No central computer manages communication. Usually one computer with a large storage capacity is used as a server; however, it does not control the network. Signals flow in the ring in one direction. Each node filters signals that are addressed to it from all signals. If a token ring protocol is employed, a token, which is a special byte, travels around the ring until a node wishing to send a message seizes it, launches the message to the token, and then releases the token back into the ring.

The major advantage of ring topology is its simplicity. Adding a new computer to the existing network is easy. Also, because each computer regenerates the messages that pass through it, ring networks can be deployed over larger areas than other topologies such as bus. The failure of a single node or a node connector does not affect the network. However, a failure (such as a break) of the ring cable affects the entire network.

Exhibit 800.60 *Network Topologies*

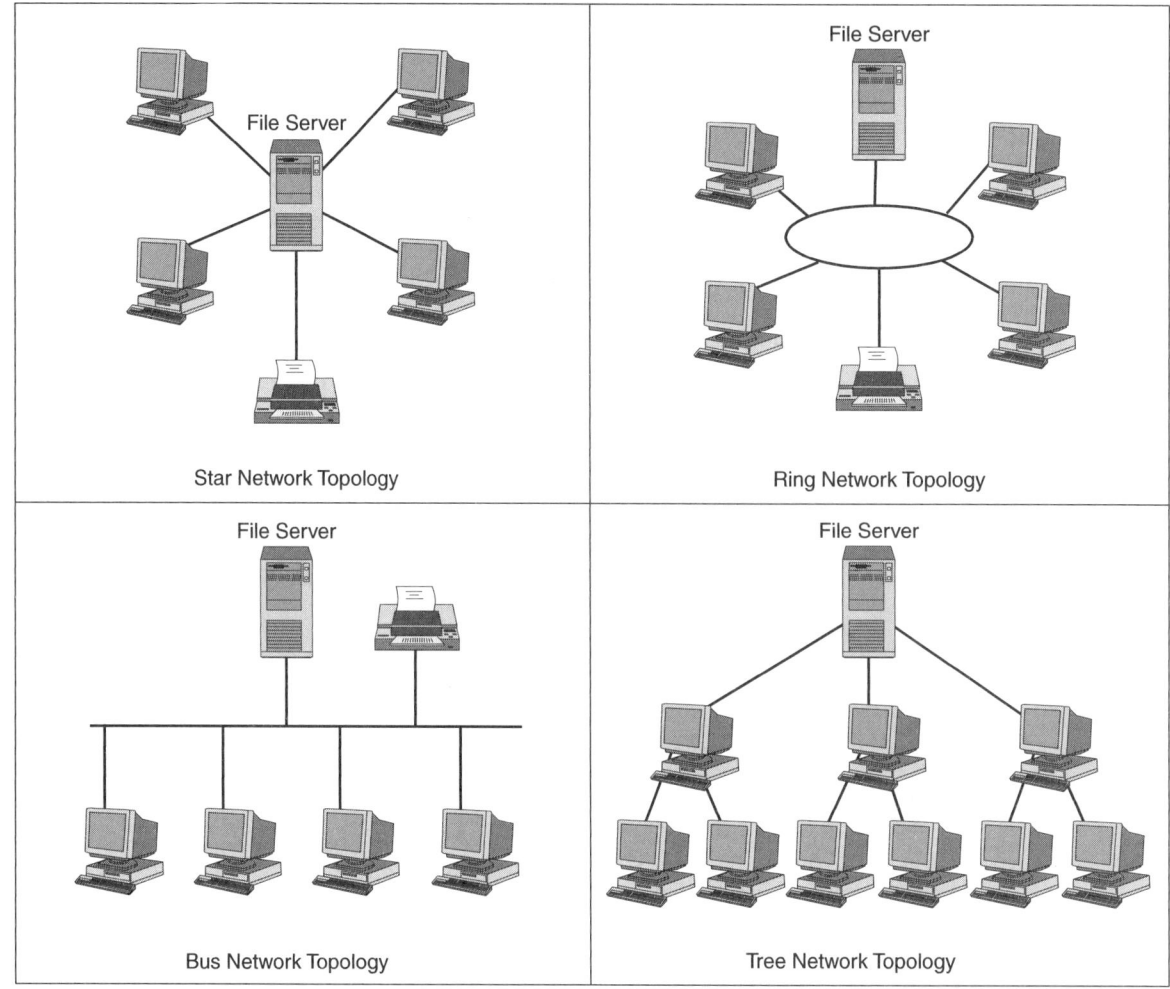

Bus

Bus topology is an open-ended ring. As Exhibit 800.60 shows, all devices connect to an open-ended line. A bus network is the simplest to design and easiest to wire. Individual nodes (such as PCs and printers) connect to a single cable using a network interface connector with a terminator at each end to prevent signal echo (signals bouncing back). When a computer transmits a signal, it is broadcast to every other node. A receiving node filters signals addressed to it from other signals. A file server is typically treated just as any other node. Individual nodes can be added. Also, branches, which are essentially also buses, can be connected to the single cable bus as long as each cable has a terminator at the end. Failure of a single node does not affect the network, but failure of the cable does affect the entire network. Bus networks do not handle high traffic as well as ring networks.

Tree

Tree topology—or hierarchical topology—consists of several stars connected to form a treelike structure. Exhibit 800.60 shows this configuration, which is typical of large computer networks. A tree lends itself to broadcasting messages in organizations because once the "root" computer launches a message, the message can be transmitted in parallel by the next layer of computers, each sending the message to several other computers. Parallel transmission is its main advantage. Its main disadvantage is that if the link of one star is disabled, all computers on that branch of the tree are disconnected from the rest of the network. The tree topology is more difficult to wire and configure than other topologies.

Virtual Private Networks (VPNs)

A LAN is a private network because it only provides access to members of an organization. When a firm leases lines, although it does not own them, the network of leased lines may be considered a private network because only members authorized by the organization can use it. In the Internet age, many companies that cannot afford a private network may create a virtual private network (VPN).

A VPN is a combination of public and private lines. To allow employees, customers, and suppliers access to its network, an organization can connect it to the largest of all public networks, the Internet. The Internet is accessible to any party. Thus, the organization need only create a link between its private network and the Internet to allow anyone it wishes to access its private network. The link between the Internet and the organization's network is often called a "tunnel," as if this is a tunnel through which travelers access the organization's territory. "Virtual" in VPN refers to the illusion that the user is accessing a private network directly, rather than through public lines. VPNs allow the use of intranets and extranets, which are discussed in the next chapter. An intranet is a network that uses Web technologies to serve an organization's employees who are located in several sites that are many miles apart from each other; an extranet also uses Web technologies but serves both the employees and other enterprises that do business with the organization. It is important to understand that once a LAN is linked to a public network, such as the Internet, technically anyone with access to the public network can obtain access to the LAN. Therefore, organizations that link their LANs to the Internet implement sophisticated security measures to control or totally deny such access.

Protocols

As discussed earlier, a communications protocol is a set of rules that govern communication between computers or between computers and other computer-related devices that exchange data. When these rules govern a network of devices, the rule set is often referred to as **network protocol**. If a device does not know what the network's agreed-upon protocol is, or cannot comply with it, that device cannot communicate on that network.

In a way, a protocol is like human language and basic understanding. Human beings make certain gestures when they start a conversation, and certain words signal its end. Each element of the language, be it English, French, or German, means the same thing to all parties who speak that language. Computers, too, need an agreed-upon set of rules to communicate.

A network protocol determines a number of factors, such as whether transmission is synchronous or asynchronous. If asynchronous, the protocol determines how many data bits and how many control bits (start bit, stop bit, and parity check bit) are transmitted at a time. Both transmitter and receiver must "understand" which stream of bits signals the beginning of the transmission and which signals the end. And, of course, both parties must transmit and receive at an agreed-upon speed. If the transmission is synchronous, a specified protocol determines for all parties features such as the number of bytes per packet and the specific header and trailer bytes.

Some communications software allows a user to establish protocols: bit rate, parity, number of data bits, stop bits, and a handshake procedure.

Before you log on to a network from your PC, you must ascertain that your communication software is set to conform with the corresponding elements of the network's protocol. If your computer is not instructed to follow the protocol, you cannot communicate on the network.

LAN Protocols

Before sending a message, a node must announce its intention and determine that the receiving node is ready. There are several methods for establishing this understanding before the actual transmission of data. The most popular methods are polling, contention, and token passing.

In **polling**, a communications processor—a special device or a host computer—conducts a continuous roll-call of the nodes. It sends an electrical pulse to each node in the network in a sequence. A node that has a message to send responds to the call. The communications processor then instructs the node to send the message. When the communication is over, polling resumes. This protocol is used in star networks.

860. TELECOMMUNICATIONS AND NETWORKS

1229

In **contention,** each node has to contend for the line. When a node has a message to send, it checks the line. If the line is not in use, the message will be sent. Obviously, two or more nodes may start sending messages at the same time, and the messages could be garbled. To prevent this problem, a protocol called CSMA/CD (carrier sense multiple access with collision detection) is used. When a collision occurs, the communications processor stops both transmissions and forces the colliding nodes to wait for varying lengths of time. Then, the first node to seize the line transmits first.

The contention approach was first introduced by **Xerox** and subsequently adopted by **Digital Equipment Corporation** (now part of **Compaq**) and **Novell**. The design is usually referred to as **Ethernet,** the name given it by Xerox. It is typically used in bus networks.

Another popular access method is token passing. In **token passing,** a special signal is transmitted on the line by the communications processor. Usually, the signal—or token—is a byte that is not used for any other purpose. Token passing is used in both bus and ring LANs. The token may be "empty," or it may contain a message. If an empty token is received and the node wishes to transmit data, it holds the token and adds to it the destination address, its own address, and the message itself. The token is then passed on to the next node. Because the token is no longer marked as "empty," other computers cannot transmit messages at the same time. When the token is finally passed to the computer that has an address corresponding to the token's destination address, that station reads the message and then marks the token as having been read. The token is then passed on to the next node. In a ring, it continues to be passed until it completes a full circuit and reaches the originating node. At this point the message is erased, and the token is again marked as being "empty." The token then continues to travel until captured by another computer that wishes to send a message. In a bus, the procedure is similar, but the token is sent back and forth between the two farthest nodes.

WAN Protocols

Wide-area network protocols are significantly more complex than LAN networks. WANs are often made up of incompatible lines, communications processors, and nodes. Also, because of the long distances between nodes, signals may deteriorate and become garbled. There are several WAN protocols. After many years of international negotiations, **Open Systems Interconnection** (**OSI**), developed by the International Standards Organization (ISO), has emerged as the dominant standard. Note that although OSI is often called a protocol, it is actually a general model for protocols.

As illustrated in Exhibit 800.61, OSI consists of seven layers. Conceptually, they operate in the following way: each computer need only concern itself with the message and identifying the receiver. The OSI views the telecommunication

Exhibit 800.61   *The Seven Layers of the OSI Model*

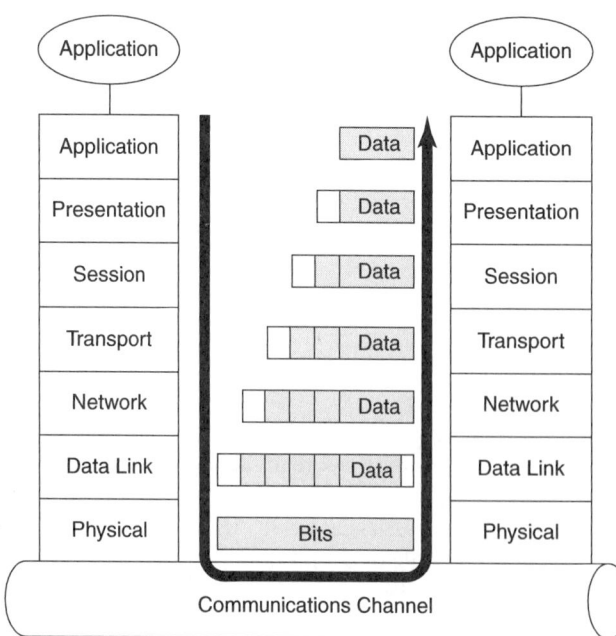

process as a layered activity, where each layer deals with another aspect of the process, and each must have a protocol in order for communication to take place. OSI establishes a protocol for each layer.

The *physical layer* protocols are concerned with the physical medium, or the channel, such as wires, radio waves, and optical fibers. This layer deals with the transmission of an unstructured stream of bits over the physical channel and the properties of the transmission. Included at this level is information about (1) the voltages used to represent a 1 and a 0, respectively, (2) the duration of bit transmission, and (3) the procedures used to maintain the channel.

The next OSI layer, the *data link layer*, takes a raw stream of bits and organizes it into frames by adding special header and trailer bits to indicate the boundaries of each frame. The data link layer transmits the message frames to the physical layer for actual transmittal over the line and provides error detection and control.

In the third layer, the *network layer,* the computer interacts with the network to specify the destination address and to request network facilities and priorities. The network layer is where switching and routing take place.

The *transport layer* provides a transparent transport of data from one computer to another, free of error or duplication. "Transparent" means that neither the user nor other layers need to be aware of error detection. This layer may also be concerned with optimizing the use of network services. At this layer, security measures are taken.

The *session layer* provides the mechanism for controlling the dialogue between the communicating systems. For example, in this layer the communication direction dialogue type is coordinated: half-duplex or full-duplex.

The *presentation layer* defines the format of the communicated data. For example, data encryption and data compression take place at this layer. Data **encryption** is the scrambling of data at the transmitting end to minimize the risk that an unauthorized party will understand it. The receiving end has the appropriate descrambling device or software. Data compression procedures allow the transmission of significantly fewer bits to convey a message. For example, instead of using five bytes for five spaces, the transmitter can send one byte for the number "five" and one byte for a "space."

The *application layer* contains management functions and useful mechanisms to support distributed applications such as file transfer, electronic mail, and node access to remote computers.

The sending and receiving ends transmit and receive data only. Senders do not have to concern themselves with anything except the message itself and the address to which they wish to send it. At each layer, special software adds a header to the message frame in the form of several special bytes. The next level adds its own header, while regarding the previous headers as part of the stream of bits. At the data link layer, in addition to a header, a trailer is added as a rear boundary of the frame. The physical layer regards the data bits, headers, and trailers as one long stream of bits. At the receiving end, each layer strips the frame off the corresponding header and trailer until the user receives a data-only message at the application layer. The other layers are transparent to users.

Switching Techniques

Imagine that your telephone could connect to only one other telephone. Of course, this limitation would render the telephone impractical. The same is true of communications when using computers. You want to be able to link your computer to every other computer on a network. Or, imagine that you can link to any other computer but you have to wait for a specific communications path to open to conduct a conversation; no other path is available to you. So you may wait a long time until no one is using any segment of that path to make your call. Obviously, this wait would be very inconvenient. To avoid such inconveniences, data communications must have mechanisms to allow your messages to be routed through any number of paths: if one is busy, then another can be used. These mechanisms, called **switching techniques,** provide answers to questions such as: Will the transmitter send its messages all at once, break them into a few large pieces, or divide them into many small pieces before sending them? Will the entire message travel the same path, or will different parts travel different paths? We examine the two major switching techniques—circuit switching and packet switching—next.

Circuit Switching

In **circuit switching,** a dedicated channel (a circuit) is established for the duration of the transmission. The sending node signals the receiving node that it is going to send a message. The receiver must acknowledge the signal. The receiving node then receives the entire message. Telephone communication is the most common type of circuit switching communication. The advantages of circuit switching are that data and voice can use the same line and that no special training or protocols are needed to handle data traffic. One disadvantage is the requirement that the communications devices be compatible at both ends.

Packet Switching

In **packet switching,** a message is divided into packets, each of which is a fixed number of bytes or a frame of a variable number of bytes. On their way to their final destination, the packets are transmitted separately to intermediate nodes. Different packets of the same message may be routed through different paths to minimize delay. This type of switching offers some advantages. Sending and receiving devices do not have to be data-rate compatible because buffers in the network may receive data at one rate and retransmit it at another. The lines are used on demand rather than being dedicated to a particular call. Packet switching lends the lines to multiplexing: a host computer can have simultaneous exchanges with several nodes over a single line. The main disadvantage of packet switching is its requirement for complex routing and control software. When the load is high, there are delays. When the network is used for voice communication, a conversation with long delays may sound unnatural, so voice communication in telephone systems uses circuit switching. The Internet is based on a packet-switching protocol called **TCP/IP** (**Transmission Control Protocol/Internet Protocol**), which is actually a set of related protocols.

Circuit switching is ideal for real-time communications, when the destination must receive the message without delay. Packet switching is more efficient, but it is suitable only if some delay in reception is acceptable. A high-level TCP/IP protocol, TCP, supports packet switching, but in a manner suitable for real-time communication: the protocol guarantees that the packets are delivered in the order they were sent and also handles differences in transmission and reception rates so that the destination receives a stream of packets without delay. This protocol, along with growing additions of high-speed media to the Internet, enables growing use of the Internet for packet-switching telephoning.

A Variety of Services

Both organizations and individuals can now choose from a variety of different options when subscribing to networking services. Technological improvements and new standards have enabled networking companies to provide high-speed lines. The proliferation of high-speed connection services, also called *broadband services*, is mainly the result of businesses' and individuals' rush to the Internet. Some of the services, such as ISDN, cable, DSL, and satellite links, are offered both to businesses and residences. Others, such as T1 and T3 lines, are offered only to businesses, largely because of their high cost. All the services except ISDN connect subscribers directly to the Internet.

Integrated Services Data Networks (ISDNs)

ISDN lines transmit data at speeds up to 128 Kbps. They are available to millions of people in North America and other regions of the world. Years ago they were expected to support all the data, voice, and television communication we could possibly desire. However, as the richness and sophistication of data, voice, and television content increased, it became clear that such speeds cannot accommodate fast communication. The signals traveling in ISDN lines are digital, but the connection is circuit-switched. When using an ISDN line from home for data communications, you still need to use a modem because the "last mile" link is analog. Because of its relative slow speed now, most experts do not refer to ISDN as broadband.

Cable

Cable links are provided by television cable firms. The medium is the same as for television reception, but the firms connect the cable to an Internet server. At the subscriber's residence, the cable is split—one end is connected to the television set, and the other is connected to the computer via a bridge that is often called a cable modem. Both television transmission and data are transmitted through the same line. The cable link is always on, so the computer is constantly connected to the Internet. The subscriber does not have to dial up any telephone number. More than 90 percent of cable operators in the Unites States offer Internet access.

The major downside of cable is that cable nodes are shared by all the subscribers connected to the node. Therefore, at peak time, such as evening television prime time, communication speed slows down. The speed also slows down as more subscribers join the service in a given territory.

Digital Subscriber Line (DSL)

With normal telephone service, the telephone company filters information that arrives in digital form and then transforms it to analog form; thus, it requires a modem to transform the signal back to digital form. This conversion constrains the capacity of the link between your telephone (or computer) and the telephone company's switching center to a low speed of 56 Kbps (or 128 Kbps with ISDN service).

With DSL, digital data remain digital throughout their entire transmission; they are never transformed into analog signals. So, the telephone company can transmit to subscribers' computers at significantly higher speeds: up to 8 Mbps. To provide DSL service, the telecommunications company connects your telephone line to a DSL bridge (often called a DSL modem). At the telephone company's regional central office, DSL traffic is aggregated in a unit called the DSL Access Multiplexer (DSLAM) and forwarded to the Internet service provider (ISP) or data network provider with which the subscriber has a contract. As with cable connection, DSL connection is always on.

There are several types of DSL, but they can be generally placed in one of two categories: symmetric and asymmetric. *Asymmetric DSL (ADSL)* allows reception at a much faster rate than transmission, or in professional lingo they are faster "downstream" than "upstream." (Often, the respective terms *download* and *upload* are used.) The reason for the faster download is that home users and small businesses usually receive significantly more information (from the Web, for example) than they transmit. *Symmetric DSL (SDSL)* is designed for short distance connections that require high speed in both directions. Many ADSL technologies are actually RADSL (Rate Adjusted DSL) technologies; the speed is adjusted based on signal quality. Some ADSL technologies let subscribers use the same telephone lines for both Internet connection and analog voice telephone service. Symmetric DSL lines cannot share lines with telephones.

The bit rates of DSL lines are closely related to the distance of the subscriber's computer from the regional central office of the telephone company. Telecommunications companies may offer the service to subscribers as far as 20,000 feet from the central office, but the speed then is usually not faster than 144 Kbps. Some companies do not offer the service if the subscriber's address is not within 15,000 feet of the central office.

T1 and T3 Lines

A T1 line is a point-to-point dedicated digital circuit provided by telephone companies. It is made up of 24 channels (groups of wires) of 64 Kbps each. T3 lines are similar to T1 lines but are made up of 672 channels of 64 Kbps. T1 and T3 lines are expensive. Therefore, only businesses that must rely on high speeds are willing to accept the high cost of subscribing to the service. Most universities use T1 lines for Internet connection.

Satellite

Households in rural areas and other regions that cannot obtain the preceding services may be able to obtain satellite services. In fact, satellite service providers target these households. The service provider installs a dish antenna that is tuned to a communications satellite. Satellite connection may reach a speed of 45 Mbps.

Fixed Wireless

Another alternative for households and small businesses that cannot obtain cable or DSL connections to the Internet is fixed wireless. Fixed wireless is point-to-point transmission between two stationary devices, as opposed to mobile wireless, in which people carry a mobile device. Companies such as **WorldCom**, **Sprint**, and **AT&T** offer the service. They install microwave transceivers on rooftops instead of laying physical wires and cables. Subscribers connect their computers to the rooftop transceiver. They can communicate at speeds up to 2 Mbps. Repeaters are installed close to each other to enhance the signal, which can deteriorate in the presence of buildings, trees, and foul weather. Transmission rates depend on the distance between the receiver and the base station. Up to 9 miles from the base station, the speed is 100 Mbps; speeds drop to about 2 Mbps at 35 miles from the base.

Fixed wireless is highly modular—the telecommunications company can add as many transceivers as it needs to serve a growing number of subscribers. Unlike cable service, the company does not need franchise licenses. Only 3 percent of U.S. commercial buildings have a fiber-optic connection, but almost anybody in an area served by fixed wireless can install a transceiver on the roof. This potential attracts telecommunications companies to the fixed wireless market.

Gigabit Ethernet

The latest development in high-speed Internet access for businesses is gigabit Ethernet, a communications standard that until recently was used only for the backbones of networks, including the Internet and LANs. With this technology, the telecommunications company connects an existing office network directly to a fiber-optic line outside the office at a high speed of 1 Gbps. Because Ethernet technology has been around for many years, the hardware (such as routers and switches) is relatively inexpensive, and network administrators know how to maintain it. It may take several years, though, until gigabit Ethernet becomes a viable option.

The Changing Business Environment

In addition to understanding the technical foundations of telecommunications, you need to understand its continuing impact on business operations. The same technologies that have served us so well for voice and television communications also serve us for data communications. In fact, we no longer refer to telephone numbers for telephony only, nor do we use Internet links for data communications only. The lines of *uses* are blurred, and now we simply speak of telecommunications, regardless of form. But to get a comprehensive grasp of the effect of telecommunications on day-to-day business operations, we must include in our "portfolio" all technologies that facilitate telecommunications. Therefore, we now turn to a discussion of some of the technologies most commonly used in business today.

Cellular Phones

Cellular phones derive their name from the territories of service providers, which are divided into areas known as cells. Each cell has at its center a computerized *transceiver,* because it both transmits signals to another receiver and receives signals from another transmitter. When a call is placed on a cellular phone, the signal is first transmitted to the closest transceiver, which sends a signal that dials the desired phone number. If the receiving telephone is not in the same cell as the sending phone, a series of transceivers receive and retransmit the message until it reaches the destination phone. Communication takes place between the cellular phone and the receiving party through the transceivers. As the user moves from one area, or cell, to another, other transceivers pick up the transmission and receiving tasks.

Millions of people use cellular phones: as long as a cellular service is available, people can transmit and receive calls anywhere, freeing them from a fixed office location. Cellular phones can also be used for e-mail and faxing, and some are designed to enable use of the Web. "My car is my office" is a reality for many managers who spend much of their time traveling. As technology advances, we will soon be able to say "My pocket is my office."

Videoconferencing

Until recently, when managers from two remote sites wanted to confer in person, they had to travel to a meeting place. Now, people sitting in conference rooms thousands of miles apart are brought together by their transmitted images and speech in what is called videoconferencing.

Videoconferencing saves travel costs and the time of highly salaried employees, whether they work in different organizations or in different sites of the same organization. From national and global perspectives, videoconferencing also reduces traffic congestion and air pollution.

Voice Mail

Virtually every personal computer can be equipped with hardware and software that allows its user to transmit and receive voice mail. Many PCs are sold with the appropriate software already installed. Everyone is familiar with the basic idea of voice mail. With PC-based voice mail, a telephone line is connected to a modem, which in turn is connected to a PC. When a person calls the line and leaves a voice message, the message is translated into bytes and stored on the PC. Then, the voice-mail file can be retrieved and played through the PC's speakers. Alternatively, the voice-mail file can be accessed by calling the PC again and listening to the stored message over the phone. Voice mail has largely replaced answering machines in the business environment. Digitized messages are significantly clearer than those recorded on tape.

Facsimile

Facsimile (from the Latin word for duplicate), or fax, is the transmission and reception of images over telephone lines. As we discussed with fax/modems earlier, a fax machine digitizes an image and transmits the representative bits to a receiving fax machine. The receiving machine converts the digitized codes back into an image. The great advantage of using fax machines is their ability to transmit original documents, both text and images, without first converting them into a computer file. Fax machines also provide an easy means of communicating graphical images. Virtually every modem offered on the market now is a fax/modem.

Web-Based Electronic Commerce

Fast digital communication enables millions of organizations to conduct business using the Web. Whole industries, such as on-line exchanges and auctions, have been created thanks to the Web. Some technologies, such as electronic data interchange, are migrating to the Web.

Business Information Systems

Information Systems in Business Functions

Effectiveness and Efficiency

The telephones at the offices of **Capital One Financial Corp.**, a leading credit-card issuer, ring more than a million times per week. Cardholders call to ask about their balance or to ensure that the company received their recent payment. While callers almost immediately hear a human voice at the other end, computers actually do the initial work. The computers use the caller's telephone number to search the company's huge databases. Inferring from previous calls and numerous recorded credit-card transactions of the caller, the computers predict the reason for calling. Based on the assumed reason, the computers channel the call to one of 50 employees who can best handle the situation. On the computer monitor of that employee, the computers bring up important information about the caller. Although callers usually do not contact the company to make purchases, the computer also brings up information about what the caller may want to purchase. As soon as the customer service representative provides the caller with satisfactory answers, he or she also offers the cardholder special sales. Many callers do indeed purchase the offered merchandise. All of these steps—accepting the call, reviewing and analyzing the data, routing the call, and recommending merchandise—take the computers a mere one tenth of a second.

It is often said that the use of information technology makes our work more effective, more efficient, or both. What do these terms mean? **Effectiveness** defines the degree to which a goal is achieved. Thus, a system is more or less effective depending upon (1) how much of its goal it achieves and (2) the degree to which it achieves better outcomes than other systems do.

Efficiency is determined by the relationship between resources expended and the benefits gained in achieving a goal. Expressed mathematically,

$$\text{Efficiency} = \frac{\text{Benefits}}{\text{Costs}}$$

Thus, one system is more efficient than another if its operating costs are lower for the same or better quality product, or if its product's quality is greater for the same or lower costs. The term productivity is commonly used as a synonym for efficiency. However, **productivity** specifically refers to the efficiency of *human* resources. Productivity improves when fewer workers are required to produce the same amount of output, or, alternately, when the same number of workers produces a larger output. This is why IS professionals often speak of "productivity tools," which are software applications that help workers produce more in less time. The closer the result of an effort is to the ultimate goal, the more effective the effort. The fewer the resources spent on achieving a goal, the more efficient the effort.

Suppose your goal is to design a new car that reaches a speed of 60 miles per hour in 10 seconds. If you manage to build it, then you produce the product effectively. If the car does not meet the requirement, your effort is ineffective. If your competitor makes a car with the same features and performance but uses fewer people and fewer other resources, then your competitor is as effective but more efficient than you.

ISs contribute to both the effectiveness and efficiency of businesses, especially when positioned in specific business functions, such as accounting, finance, and engineering, and when used to help companies achieve their goals more quickly by facilitating collaborative work (see Exhibit 800.62). ISs can be used in a wide variety of applications. They can automate manual processes, such as painting cars; they can make innovative products and services accessible, such as Web-based customer service available 24 hours per day, 365 days per year; they can shorten routine processes, such as issuing purchase orders; and they can improve an organization's strategic position, such as establishing a Web site for selling products directly to consumers before the competition does.

Exhibit 800.62 *Information Technology Supports a Variety of Business Functions*

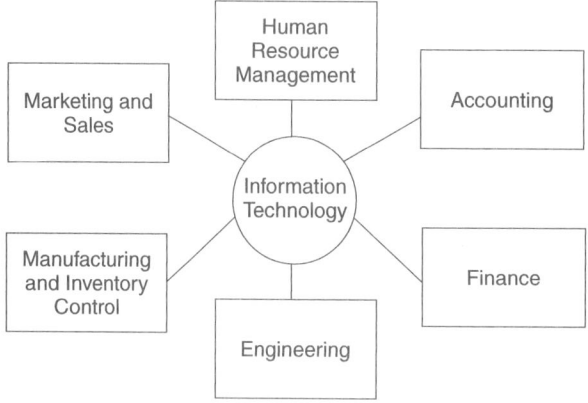

Exhibit 800.63 *Information Systems in Different Business Functions Are Interdependent*

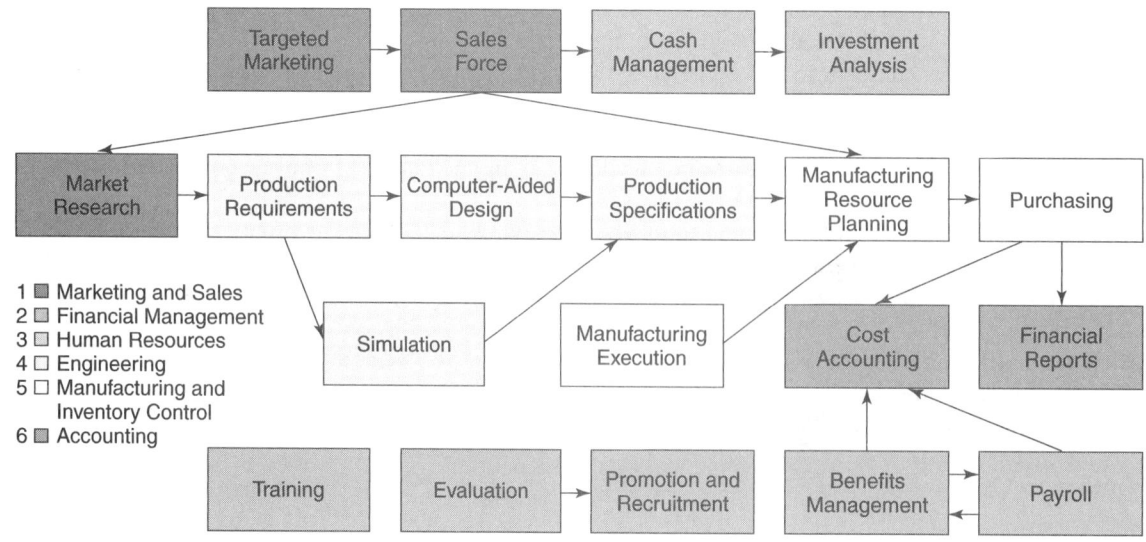

Organizing the information systems department one business function at a time does not take full advantage of IT, but most businesses do operate many ISs separately: one for engineering, one for marketing, one for finance, and so on. Usually, they do this because systems developed at different times for different business functions are often incompatible in hardware, software, data sharing, and the like. However, business functions do, in fact, have substantial information interdependencies. Systems thinking tells us that, ideally, ISs supporting different functions would connect so that information from one system flows into another accurately and without delay. For example, a business can develop information from market research to define design requirements for products, and the sales force can then use the information to sell the products.

Exhibit 800.63 illustrates how information systems commonly used in various business functions can be interdependent. Organizations that have the opportunity to create systems from the ground up try to implement this model. However, ISs have typically evolved independently for each business function in organizations. Companies whose systems have operated separately for years often opt to replace them with an integrated enterprise-wide IS.

Information Technology Security and Controls

Goals of Information Security

As you have already seen, the development, implementation, and maintenance of ISs constitute a large and growing part of the cost of doing business; protecting these resources is a primary concern. The increasing reliance on ISs, combined with their connection to the outside world in the form of the Internet, makes securing corporate ISs increasingly challenging. What would happen if an enterprise-wide system were infected with a virus and ceased operating? What would happen if an errant employee accessed confidential data and sold them? How would illicit interception of information affect an organization that takes orders through the Internet? Needless to say, these questions highlight the potential for catastrophe if a system is not secure. The role of computer controls and security is to protect systems against these and many other mishaps, as well as to help organizations ensure that their IS operations comply with the law and with expectations of employees and customers for privacy. The major goals of information security are as follows:

- To reduce the risk of systems and organizations ceasing operations
- To maintain information confidentiality
- To ensure the integrity and reliability of data resources
- To ensure the uninterrupted availability of data resources and on-line operations
- To ensure compliance with national security laws and privacy policies and laws

These goals can be jeopardized in the ways indicated previously, perhaps most of all by the explosion of on-line activity over the Internet and the increasing use of intranets and extranets. To plan measures to support these goals, organizations first must be aware of the possible risks to their information resources, which include hardware, applications, data, and networks; then they must execute security measures (controls) to defend against those risks.

Controls

Controls are constraints and other restrictions imposed on a user or a system, and they can be used to secure systems against the risks just discussed or to reduce damage caused to systems, applications, and data. Exhibit 800.64 lists the most common controls.

Exhibit 800.64 *Common Controls to Protect Computer Systems from Risk*

- Program robustness and data entry controls
- Backup
- Access controls
- Atomic transactions
- Audit trail

Program Robustness and Data Entry Controls

A computer program is said to be *robust* if it is free of bugs and can handle unforeseen situations well. While programmers debate whether any software can be fully bug-free, they can develop it so that it does not lock up the computer, cause damage to files, or display dialog boxes that do not help the users fix the problem. Robust applications can resist inappropriate usage, such as incorrect data entry or processing. An application can be written with different levels of robustness, depending on the developers' expectations about the way the program will be used. The least robust program assumes that the user is experienced and will enter only parameters that are expected of him or her. The most robust program considers every possible misuse or abuse. A highly robust program includes code that promptly produces a clear message if a user either errs or tries to circumvent a process.

For example, a system programmed to accept telephone numbers may have a number of controls built into it. Let's say the phone numbers should be input only in a certain format, such as 10 digits (3-digit area code followed by 3-digit exchange and 4-digit phone number). If a user enters a 7- or 11-digit number, a system with data entry controls might display an error message, such as "You must enter a 10-digit number." The system might also be programmed to accept a record into a file only if the telephone number is included, rejecting any record that doesn't include a phone number or displaying a message if the user leaves a field empty or enters invalid data into a field.

Controls also translate business policies into system features. For example, **Blockbuster Video** used its IS to implement a policy limiting debt for each customer to a certain level. When a renter reaches the debt limit and tries to rent another tape, a message appears on the cash register screen: "Do not rent!" Thus, the policy is implemented by using a control at the point of sale.

Menus are useful control tools. Systems can be programmed so that different menu options are displayed, depending on a user's access authorization. By providing limited menus, a system forcibly restricts what users can do with the system.

Clear error messages are an important data entry control.

Another effective way to control system use, especially when dealing with a transaction-processing system (TPS), is to program limits on the numerical values that can be either entered into quantitative fields or output through processing. Upper limits are often set on quantities such as payments, salaries, number of units ordered, and lengths of time (such as the number of hours spent on a task). Systems often establish both a minimum and maximum that are reasonable in a particular type of transaction. For example, an organization may set a minimum for the sum paid for a purchase at zero and a maximum at $50,000, if that is the most expensive item the organization purchases. Another example: upper and lower limits for a field recording the daily number of hours worked by an individual would be 24 and 0, respectively.

Backup

Probably the easiest way to protect against loss of data caused by natural disasters, computer viruses, or human errors is to automatically duplicate all data periodically, a process referred to as data **backup**. Many systems have built-in automatic backup programs. The data may be duplicated on inexpensive storage devices such as magnetic tapes. Manufacturers of storage devices also offer redundant arrays of independent disks (RAID) for this purpose. A **RAID** is a set of disks that is programmed to redundantly store data to provide a higher degree of reliability.

Redundant arrays of independent disks (RAID) automatically backup transactions onto disks that can be removed and stored in a safe place.

Of course, backing up data is not enough. The disks or tapes with backed-up data must be routinely transported off-site, so that if a business site is damaged by a disaster, the remote storage can be used since it is likely to be spared. In the past, many companies had a truck haul backup disks and tapes to the storage location at the end of every business day, and some may still do so. However, due to the great developments in telecommunications in recent years, most corporations prefer to back up data at a remote site through communications lines. Often, the backup disks or tapes reside thousands of miles away from the organization's business offices. For additional protection, the disks or tapes are locked in safes that can withstand fire and floods.

Companies can also use the services of firms that specialize in providing backup facilities. The vendor maintains a site with huge amounts of disk space linked to the Internet. The company typically provides the client organizations with an application that copies designated files from the client's systems to the remote disks. For obvious reasons, some professionals call this type of service *e-vaulting*.

Access Controls

Unauthorized access to information systems, usually via public networks such as the Internet, does not always damage IT resources. However, it is regarded as one of the most serious threats to security because it is often the prelude to the destruction of Web sites, databases, and other resources.

Access controls are measures taken to ensure that only those who are authorized have access to a computer or network or to certain applications or data. One way to block access to a computer is by physically locking it in a facility to which only authorized users have a key or by locking the computer itself with a physical key. However, in the age of networked computers, this solution is often impractical. Organizations rightfully need to protect their systems from harm, but access controls are also being used by some governments to limit their citizens' access to information.

The most common way to control access is through the combination of an access code (also called a *user ID*) and a password. While access codes usually are not secret, passwords are. IS managers encourage users to change their passwords frequently, which most systems easily allow, so that others do not have time to figure them out. Some organizations have systems that force users to change their passwords at preset time intervals, such as once a month, once every three months, and the like. Some systems also prevent users from selecting a password that they have used in the past, to minimize the chance that someone else might guess it.

> Passwords are by far the most widely used type of access control.

Access codes and their related passwords are maintained either in a special list that becomes part of the operating system or in a database that the system searches before allowing access, to determine whether a user is authorized to access the desired resource. In many business situations, employees or customers have "read" access (whereby they can view data) but not "write" or "update" access (which would allow them to change data). Apparently, many companies do a poor job maintaining their password lists, especially in times of high employee turnover. Research indicates that as many as 30 percent of a company's approved passwords are for employees who have left. In some cases, laid-off employees accessed their former employer's system to cause damage.

In recent years, some companies have adopted physical access controls called biometrics. A **biometric** is a unique physical, measurable characteristic of a human being that is used to identify a person. Characteristics such as fingerprints, retinal pictures, or voiceprints can be used as *biometrics*. When a fingerprint is used, the user presses a finger on a scanner or puts it before a digital camera. The fingerprint is compared against a database of digitized fingerprints of people with authorized access. The procedure is similar when the image of a person's retina is scanned. With voice, the user is instructed to utter a word or several words. The intonation and accent are digitized and compared with a list of digitized voice samples.

> Fingerprint readers have been adopted by an increasing number of organizations as biometric access controls.

For instance, **Compaq**, the giant PC maker, introduced a device called *Fingerprint Identification Technology* (FIT), which is the size of a deck of cards and is used to access personal computers. Instead of keying in a password, employees hold one of their fingers up to a camera that allows the system to compare the image to a database of fingerprints. Using biometric access devices is the best way not only to prevent unauthorized access to computers but also to reduce the workload of help-desk personnel. Up to 50 percent of the calls help-desk personnel receive come from employees who have forgotten their passwords.

Atomic Transactions

As you know, in an efficient IS, a user enters data only once, and the data are recorded in different files for different purposes, according to the system's programmed instructions. For instance, in a typical order system, a sale is recorded in several files: the shipping file (so that the warehouse knows what to pack and ship), the invoice file (to produce an

Atomic transactions ensure updating of all appropriate files. Either all files are updated, or none is updated and the control produces an error message.

invoice and keep a copy in the system), the accounts receivable file (for accounting purposes), and the commission file (so that the salesperson can be compensated with the appropriate commission fee at the end of the month). A system supports atomic transactions when its code will only allow the recording of data if they successfully reach all their many destinations. Using **atomic transactions** ensures that only full entry occurs in all the appropriate files.

For instance, suppose the different files just mentioned reside on more than one disk, one of which is malfunctioning. When the clerk enters the sales transaction, the system tries to automatically record the appropriate data from the entry into each of the files. The shipping, accounts receivable, and invoice files are updated, but the malfunctioning commission file cannot accept the data. Without controls, the sale would be recorded, but unknown to anyone, the commission would not be updated, and the salesperson would be deprived of the commission on this deal. However, an atomic transactions control mechanism detects that not all four files have been updated with the transaction, and it doesn't update any of the files. The system may try to update again later, but if the update does not go through, the application will produce an appropriate error message for the clerk, and remedial action can be taken.

Note that this is a control not only against a malfunction but also against fraud. Suppose the salesperson collaborates with the clerk to enter the sale only in the commission file, so she can be rewarded for a sale that has never taken place—and then plans to split the fee with the clerk. The atomic transactions control would not let this happen.

Audit Trail

In spite of the many steps taken to prevent system abuse, it nonetheless occurs. Consequently, further steps are needed to track transactions so that (1) when abuses are found, they can be traced and (2) fear of detection will indirectly discourage abuse. One popular tracking tool is the **audit trail:** a series of documented facts that help detect who recorded which transactions, at what time, and under whose approval. Whenever an employee records a transaction, such a system prompts the employee to provide certain information: an invoice number, account number, salesperson ID number, and the like. Sometimes an audit trail is automatically created using data, such as the date and time of a transaction or the name or password of the user updating the file. These data are recorded directly from the computer—often unbeknownst to the user—and attached to the record of the transaction.

Audit trail information helps uncover undesirable acts, from innocent mistakes to premeditated fraud. The information helps determine who authorized and/or made the entries, the date and time of the transactions, and other identifying data that are essential in correcting mistakes or recovering losses. The audit trail is the most important tool of the **information systems auditor,** the professional whose job it is to find erroneous or fraudulent cases and investigate them.

Encryption

When communicating sensitive information via a public network such as the Internet, the parties must authenticate each other and keep the message secret. **Authentication** is the process of ensuring that the person who sends a message to or receives a message from you is indeed that person. Authentication can be accomplished by senders and receivers exchanging codes known only to them. Once authentication is established, keeping a message secret, too, can be accomplished by transforming it into a form that cannot be read by anyone who intercepts it. Coding a message into a form unreadable to an interceptor is called *encryption.*

Both authentication and secrecy are important when communicating confidential information such as financial and medical records. Authentication and secrecy are also essential when transacting business through a public network. For example, millions of people now buy and sell shares and other financial products on the Web, businesses and individuals make purchases through the Web and use credit-card account numbers for payment, and medical clinics use the Web to transmit patient records to insurance companies and prescriptions to pharmacies. All must authenticate the recipient and keep the entire communication confidential.

Encrypting communications increases security.

To authenticate the users and maintain secrecy, the parties can use encryption programs. Encryption programs scramble information transmitted over the network so that an interceptor will receive unintelligible data. The original message is called **plaintext**; the coded message is called **ciphertext.** Encryption uses a mathematical algorithm, which is a formula, and a key. The key is a combination of bits that must be used to figure out the formula. The receiving computer uses the key to activate the algorithm that translates the ciphertext back into plaintext.

```
                    Encryption                    Decryption
     Plain Text ───────────────▶ Encrypted Message ───────────────▶ Decrypted Message
```

Digital Signatures and Digital Certificates

With the increasing use of e-commerce for all types of business transactions came the pressure to allow legally binding transactions on line as well. Some countries have now broken that barrier and recognized the legal validity of electronic signatures.

Electronic Signatures

In the information age, it was only a matter of time until electronic signatures would become legally binding in commercial transactions. As of October 2000, U.S. law recognizes such signatures. The Electronic Signatures in Global and National Commerce Act states that electronic contracts with electronic signatures have the same legal validity as paper contracts. The law defines the term *electronic signature* as "an electronic sound, symbol, or process attached to or logically associated with a contract or other record and executed or adopted by a person with the intent to sign the record." Other countries, including Ireland, Mexico, and Bermuda, have enacted similar laws.

Electronic signatures can take several forms. In one form, instead of signing on paper, the user signs with a stylus on a special clear plastic pad. The signature is recorded as a graphic. Along with it, some systems also record how quickly the signature is written and how much force the signer uses against the pad so that subsequent signatures can be compared with these characteristics for authentication. You may have already used this system when you signed an authorization to charge your credit card at **OfficeMax** or when you received a package delivered by **UPS**.

Another electronic signature method records a biometric of the signer. Remember that a biometric is a physical characteristic of a person, such as a fingerprint, retina pattern, or voice signature. A person's biometric is recorded once and then compared with subsequent signatures for authentication. For example, **Sony**, the electronics giant, offers a product that digitally records a user's fingerprints. The users can then access their electronic signature only after placing a finger or thumb on a scanner for comparison.

Electronic signatures alone do not provide any security when transmitted in a communication network. On the contrary, they raise the necessity to authenticate the signer. To ensure authenticity that the sender of a message is indeed who he or she claims to be, digital signatures can be used. Note that the term *digital certificate* has a special technical meaning in the context of the following discussion. A digital signature in the context of public key encryption is *not* simply any electronic signature.

Digital Signatures

Every electronic signature is digitized, or it could not be stored and processed by a computer. However, in the great majority of electronic signatures, no physical characteristics will be involved. Rather, people will use *digital signatures* instead. A **digital signature,** to differentiate it from an electronic signature, is an encrypted digest of the text that is sent along with a message, usually a text message, but possibly one that contains other types of information, such as pictures. A digital signature authenticates the identity of the sender of a message and also guarantees that no one has altered the sent document; it is as if the message were carried in an electronically sealed envelope.

When you send an encrypted message, two phases are involved in creating a digital signature. First, the encryption software uses a hashing algorithm (a mathematical formula) to create a message digest from the file you wish to transmit. A message digest is akin to the unique fingerprint of a file. Then, the software uses your private (secret) key to encrypt the message digest. The result is a digital signature for that specific file.

Digital Certificates

To authenticate a digital signature, both buyers and sellers must use digital certificates (also known as digital IDs). **Digital certificates** are computer files that serve as the equivalent of ID cards. Issuers of digital certificates are called certificate authorities, and therefore many of them have the letters CA as part of their names. Some are subsidiaries of banks and credit-card companies and others are independent. **American Express CA**, **Digital Signature Trust Co.**, **VeriSign Inc.**, and **GlobalSign Toot CA** are just a few of the numerous companies that sell digital certificates. (Certificate authorities also issue public and private keys, and they have arranged with financial corporations, such as credit-card issuers, to verify information that applicants provide for the certificates.)

A digital certificate contains its holder's name, a serial number, expiration dates, and a copy of the certificate holder's public key (used to encrypt messages and digital signatures). It also contains the digital signature of the certificate authority so that a recipient can verify that the certificate is real. To view the digital certificate of a secure online business, click on the lock icon at the bottom right corner of your browser. Click the Details tab to view the version, serial number, signature encryption method, issuer name, and other details of the certificate (right).

Digital certificates are the equivalent of tamper-proof photo identification cards. They are based on public key encryption techniques that verify the identities of the buyer and seller in electronic transactions and prevent documents from being altered after the transaction is completed. Consumers have their own digital certificates stored on their home computers' hard disks. In a transaction, a consumer uses one digital key attached to the certificate that he or she sends to the seller. The seller sends the certificate and his own digital key to a certificate authority, which then can determine the authenticity of the digital signature. Completed transaction documents are stored on a secure hard disk maintained by a trusted third party.

The recipient of an encrypted message uses the certificate authority's public key to decode the digital certificate attached to the message, verifies it as issued by the certificate authority, and then obtains the sender's public key and identification information held within the certificate. With this information, the recipient can send an encrypted reply.

When using the Web, encryption and authentication take place automatically and are transparent to the users. However, there is an indication in the browser's window if the communication is secure. In **Microsoft's** Internet Explorer, a small padlock appears in the lower-right corner. In **Netscape's** Communicator, an open padlock appears in the lower-left corner if the site you reached is not secure, and a closed padlock appears if it is secure. You may see these signs as soon as the page requiring your password appears in your browser. If you double-click on the padlock, a window will open with details on the digital certificate that the site uses, such as the certificate issuer's name, the date it was issued, and the date it will expire.

Firewalls

As we discussed earlier, the great increase in the number of people and organizations using the Internet, and especially Web sites, has provided fertile ground for unauthorized and destructive activity. The best defense against unauthorized access to systems over the Internet is a **firewall,** which is software whose purpose is to block access to computing resources. (Early firewalls used combinations of hardware and software.) Firewall software screens the activities of a person who logs on to a Web site; it allows retrieval and viewing of certain material but blocks attempts to change the information or to access other resources that reside on the same computer or computers connected to it.

It is important to note that while firewalls are used to keep unauthorized users out, they are also used to keep unauthorized software or instructions away such as computer viruses and other rogue software. When an employee uses a company computer to access external Web sites, the firewall screens for viruses and active attempts to invade company resources through the open communications line. It may also be programmed to block employee access to sites that are suspected of launching rogue programs, or to sites that provide no useful resources. The firewall then prohibits the user from logging on to those sites.

As Exhibit 800.65 illustrates, a firewall controls communication between a trusted network and the "untrusted" Internet. The firewall is installed between the organization's internal network and a router. A router is a communication device that forwards communications data from one network to another, in this case from the organization's network to the Internet and vice versa. Network professionals use the firewall software to check which applications can access the Internet and which servers may be accessed from the organization's network.

Exhibit 800.65 *A Firewall for Security*

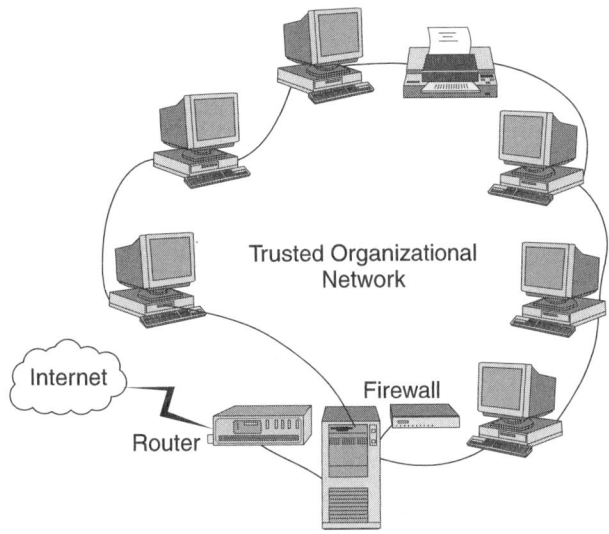

To increase security, some companies implement the DMZ (De-Militarized Zone) approach. The DMZ is a link between two servers, one of which is a proxy server. A proxy server "represents" another server for all information requests and acts as a buffer between internal and external networks. When a business hires the services of an ISP, the proxy server is often the one operated by an Internet Service Provider (ISP). The DMZ provides a barrier between the Internet and a company's organizational network, which is usually an intranet. Both the organizational network server and proxy server employ firewalls. In Exhibit 800.65, the firewalls would be installed on the gray server of the organizational network and the router. The router is often called a *boundary router*. The double firewall architecture adds an extra measure of security for the intranet.

Information Security Standards

Developers of ISs can use one of several sets of standards when integrating security measures into new systems. Some companies that specialize in development of enterprise applications have their own standards, but others usually follow well-established national or international standards, especially if the systems they develop are to be used by government agencies or contractors. There are two prominent standards, one developed by the U.S. government (The Orange Book) and the other developed by the International Standard Organization.

The Orange Book

Perhaps the best-known security standards are those detailed in *Trusted Computer System Evaluation Criteria (TC-SEC)*, a book published by the National Computer Security Center (NCSC), an arm of the U.S. Department of Defense (DOD) and popularly known as "The Orange Book" because of the color of its cover. (The document is DOD Standard 5200.28.) The book was originally written for military ISs, but it is now used by the IT industry as a guide. In it, NCSC defines four security levels, ranging from minimal protection, called Division D, to ultrasecurity called Division A.

1. Division A: Verified Protection (has only one class—A1)
2. Division B: Mandatory Protection (has three classes — B1, B2, and B3)
3. Division C: Discretionary Protection (has two classes—C1 and C2)
4. Division D: Minimal Protection (has only one class)

870. INFORMATION TECHNOLOGY SECURITY AND CONTROLS

The four categories are further broken down into subclasses (seven in all) that represent, as the book itself puts it, "increasing desirability from a computer security point of view." These subclasses are numbered, with 1 indicating the lowest security within a class, and subsequent numerals indicating increasingly rigorous security.

Essentially, a level D classification means that a system is unrated, or that it has no inherent security. An example would be an out-of-the-box plain PC. Systems that merit a level B3 or A1 rating—the top two levels defined by the NCSC—are assumed to be "bulletproof" since they are designed from scratch to protect classified military information and government secrets.

Most commercial-grade systems, both hardware and software, fall into either the C1 or C2 rating. At this level, the owner of data can determine who has access to it. C1 indicates that a system employs user IDs; C2 indicates that a system employs a user ID and a password. The Orange Book says that a C1 system "satisfies discretionary security requirements" by providing separation of users and data. Essentially, C1 systems let users protect their data from the roaming hands of other users.

The more robust C2 rating "makes users individually accountable for their actions through log-in procedures, auditing of security-relevant events, and resources isolations," The Orange Book states. Practically speaking, a C2 rating means that the system automatically creates an audit trail, as explained before. Many commercial operating systems, such as **Microsoft Corporation's** Windows NT and Windows 2000, **Apple Computer Inc.'s** A/UX, and **IBM's** OS/2, meet the C2 requirement.

Levels B and A include mandatory access control, whereby access is based on standard Department of Defense (DOD) clearances. In A and B levels, each data structure contains a sensitivity level, such as top-secret, secret, or unclassified, and is available only to users with that level of clearance. B1 is DOD clearance levels. B2 provides that the system can be tested and that these clearances cannot be downgraded. A1, the highest security level, requires access methods that rely on a mathematical model whose robustness can be proven. This is the level used by U.S. military computers.

The European Information Technology Security Evaluation Criteria (ITSEC) issued by a European Community organization called SOG-IS (Senior Officials Groups—Information Systems Security) is similar to The Orange Book.

Critics of The Orange Book claim that it is fine for protection of secrecy but not for protection from other damage, such as monetary fraud. Because the emphasis is on secrecy, the only aspect considered is access. Critics also claim that The Orange Book does not address networking issues. All these concerns are addressed by the new ISO/IEC Standard.

The ISO Standard

In 1999, the ISO (International Organization for Standardization) and the IEC (International Electrotechnical Commission), which are international bodies, published ISO/IEC Standard 15408 titled *Information Technology-Security Techniques-Evaluation Criteria for IT Security*. The purpose of the document is to provide "a common set of requirements for the security functions of IT products and systems and for assurance measures applied to them during a security evaluation."

The organizations say that the standard permits comparability between the results of independent security evaluations and that it does so by providing common requirements for the security functions of IT products and systems and for assurance measures applied to them during a security evaluation. The evaluation may help consumers determine whether the IT product or system is secure enough for their intended application and whether the security risks implicit in its use are tolerable.

Experience shows that once a set of standards is established, it becomes a reference for many players in the industry, and manufacturers start incorporating the standards into their products. Makers of hardware and developers of software will no doubt take notice and soon adhere to the ISO/IEC standard.

The Downside of Security Controls

Security controls, especially passwords, encryption applications, and firewalls, have a price that relates to more than money: they slow down data communications, and they require user discipline, which is not always easy to maintain. Employees tend to forget their passwords, especially if they must replace them every 30 or 90 days. To remember their passwords, many employees write them on a piece of paper and keep them where they are most likely to need them: taped to their computers. Any office visitor can see many of these little notes on computers in cubicles.

Employees are especially annoyed when they have to use a different password for every system they use; in some companies, there may be four or five different systems, each with its own access control. A simpler solution is an approach called SSO (single sign-on). With SSO, users are required to identify themselves only once before accessing several different systems. However, SSO requires special software that interacts with all the systems in an organization, and the systems must be linked through a network. Not many organizations have installed such software.

Encryption slows down communication because the software must encrypt and decrypt every message. Remember that when you use a secure Web site, much of the information you view on your screen was encrypted by the software installed on the site's server and then decrypted by your browser. All this activity takes time, and the delay only exacerbates the Internet's low download speed during periods of heavy traffic. (Low download speed is also caused by the use of regular modems; high-speed links such as cable and DSL are still not widespread.)

Firewalls have the same slowing effect; screening every download takes time, which affects anyone trying to access information, including employees, business partners, and individual consumers. Customers may become frustrated if they have to wait too long for response from a Web site. They may turn away and decide to shop and buy at a competitor's site. Business partners may complain about inconvenience.

IT specialists must clearly explain to managers the implications of applying security measures, especially on systems connected to the Internet. The IT specialists and other managers must first determine which resource should be accessed only with passwords and which also require other screening methods, such as firewalls. They must tell employees what impact a new security measure will have on their daily work, and if the measure will adversely affect their work, the specialists must convince the employees that the inconvenience is the price for protecting data.

The Economic Aspect of Security Measures

A study by research firm GartnerGroup revealed that most companies spend less than 1 percent of their budgets on computer security; the firm says that the figure should be closer to 5 to 8 percent in light of the great risks resulting from the growing business activity on the Internet. Apparently, consulting firms spend the largest sums of money on IT security, followed by financial institutions and high-tech companies. In recent years, the largest portions of IT security budgets have been dedicated to firewalls. Budgets for encryption technologies have also been increasing. Both facts are a reflection of the growing use of the Internet in business and the commensurate concern for security.

From a pure cost point of view, how much should an organization spend on data security measures? There are two types of costs that must be considered to answer this question: the cost of the potential damage, and the cost of implementing a preventive measure. The cost of potential damage is the aggregate of all the cost of disruptions multiplied by their respective probabilities, as follows:

$$\text{Cost of Potential Damage} = \sum_{i=1}^{n} \text{Cost-of-disruption}_i \times \text{Probability-of-disruption}_i$$

Where i is a probable event, and n is the number of events.

Experts are usually employed to estimate the cost and probabilities of damages, as well as the cost of security measures. Obviously, the more extensive the preventive measures, the smaller the damage potential. So, as the cost of security measures goes up, the cost of potential damage goes down. Ideally, the enterprise will place itself at the optimum point, which is the point at which the total of the two costs is minimized, as Exhibit 800.66 illustrates.

When budgeting for IT security, managers need to define what they want to protect. They should focus on the assets they must protect, which in most cases is information, not applications. Copies of applications are usually kept in a safe place to replace those that get damaged. They should also estimate the loss of revenue from downtime. Then, they should budget sums that do not exceed the value of what the measures protect—information and potential revenues. Even the most ardent IT security advocates agree that there is no point spending $100,000 to protect information that is worth $10,000.

Exhibit 800.66 *Cost of Security Measures*

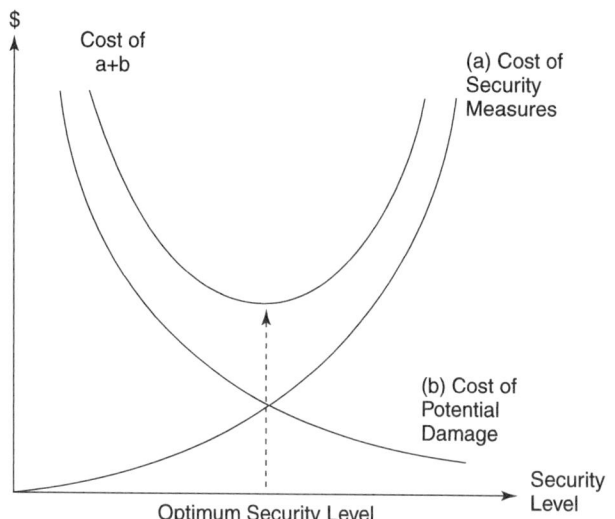

(The total cost to the enterprise is lowest at "optimum." No less, and no more, should be spent on information security measures.)

Electronic Commerce and Information Technology

What Are the Internet, Intranet, and Extranet?

Internet

The Development of the Internet

Today, the Internet is a network of networks, with millions of servers. Tens of millions of people take for granted that with a simple phone connection via their modems or permanent cable link, they can access a huge number of files from Internet servers, do research, participate in electronic discussions, shop, make purchases, and make payments. Just a few years ago, the picture was completely different.

What's on the Internet?

The Internet is a vast resource—much more than the multimedia world of the Web. One way to categorize the massive amount of information available via the Internet is to segment it by the manner in which it is organized, searched, and transmitted. Information is posted, retrieved, transmitted, and received differently, depending on the standards to which the different segments adhere. Accordingly, the applications that are used to post, retrieve, transmit, and receive it vary also. The most popular segment of the Internet is e-mail, consisting mainly of text. Other uses of the Internet include file transfer, news groups, Internet relay chat, and Internet telephoning.

Exhibit 800.67 *Internet, Intranet, and Extranet Potential for Productivity Enhancement*

An Internet Web site can enhance productivity through . . .
- Providing product information
- Sending and receiving external e-mail
- Accepting orders
- Processing orders and payment
- Conducting research

An Intranet can enhance productivity through . . .
- Sending and receiving internal e-mail
- Collaborative processing
- Allowing access to "organizational memory" residing in databases
- Order processing
- Providing personal Web pages
- Providing departmental Web pages
- Permitting group communications
- Permitting organizationwide communications
- Providing product and company information

An extranet can enhance productivity through . . .
- Implementing electronic data interchange (EDI) with suppliers and clients
- Collaborating with other organizations in development of new products and services
- Sharing product catalogs exclusively with wholesalers
- Sharing news and other information of shared interest exclusively with business partners

---

Intranets and Extranets

Soon after the Web caught the interest of the corporate world, IS managers conceived a simple idea: if HTML can be used to communicate information effectively on the Internet, why not use the same technology for communications *within* an organization?

So a new concept was created: the **intranet.** An intranet is a computer network within an organization that uses Internet technologies, such as hypertext markup language (HTML) and extensible markup language (XML), to communicate. The designers use the same tools to build sites and pages, and the users can use the same browsers on their intranet sites as they use to access external sites. In fact, many of today's intranets did not require any additional hardware; the existing LANs and other intraorganizational networks already used for telecommunications were sufficient. Web applications, such as server programs and browsers, were simply added to these networks to allow access to all the advanced features that are available on the Web.

An intranet is a private network in the sense that its content is shared only by members of one organization. Intranets are often used in multisite organizations. They offer employees information, enable them to change benefits programs on line, and help them access organizational databases for their daily work. This is accomplished through virtual private networks (VPNs). In order to give remote sites or traveling managers access, a "tunnel" is created between the Internet and intranet, which allows those outside an organization to use the Internet to access the intranet.

VPN technology is also used to establish extranets. An **extranet** is similar to an intranet, but its purpose is to facilitate communication and trade between an organization and its business partners, such as suppliers. It is not meant to serve consumers. Unlike an intranet, an extranet is not limited to employee use. It may be thought of as the part of an intranet that is extended to business partners. Exhibit 800.67 lists the potential of the Internet, intranets, and extranets to enhance productivity for a business. Doing business via the Internet, intranets, and extranets lowers the average cost of typical transactions compared to traditional systems.

Establishing an E-Commerce Web Site

To establish a Web business, an organization must have access to an Internet server. Recall that an Internet server is a computer that is connected to the Internet backbone. Businesses have several options when establishing a Web site.

1. Installing their own server (i.e., a dedicated server)
2. Contracting with an ISP site
3. Contracting with a Web portal
4. Establishing an electronic storefront
5. Contracting with a Web-hosting service
6. Using a virtual Web server
7. Setting up a subdomain

In the following sections, we discuss the benefits and disadvantages of each option for different types of businesses.

Dedicated Server

Installing and maintaining the business's own server is the most expensive option, but it gives the business the greatest degree of control. Setting up a server requires expertise, which may or may not be available within the business. The business must also employ specialists to maintain the server. In large organizations they may be employees of the company; in smaller ones, they may be consultants whose services the company hires. The specialists purchase a server (or several servers) for the company, connect it to the Internet through a dedicated line (such as a T1 line), and install the proper software for managing the server and creating Web pages. They "scale up" the server system when the business grows and handle issues such as load balancing to ensure quick response and to minimize the probability of site crashing. A site crashes when too many people try to log on and the software stops responding to anyone. **Load balancing** transfers visitor inquiries from a busy server to a less busy server.

ISP Site

Internet service providers (ISPs) offer low-fee or free space for individual or business Web sites. If the hosting ISP is named Oz and the business name is Great Stuff, a typical URL for a business of this sort would be *members.oz.com/greatstuff*. Some small businesses have chosen this option, but many others avoid it because it can give the appearance that such on-line businesses are ephemeral. Using an ISP's Web site service is probably more appropriate for individual Web sites than for business sites.

Web Portal

Large portals are another option. A **portal** is a site that enjoys heavy traffic and often offers a search engine and general information such as weather, news, and stock market quotations. Examples include *www.yahoo.com, www.lycos.com,* and *www.msn.com*. Most large portals offer free hosting of personal Web pages. Some allow small businesses to maintain their pages on the portal's servers. As with ISPs, this option is suitable only for small businesses. The space provided is usually limited, and the businesses must comply by using templates for their sites. Templates are set formats for Web pages.

Electronic Storefront

Some companies provide a **cybermall,** which is a virtual shopping mall on the Web. A cybermall hosts all the Web pages of a business that make up the business's site. The company offering the service develops the pages for the hosted businesses. This variation of Web hosting, also called an **electronic storefront,** can be quite expensive, and service quality varies widely. Yahoo! and Lycos are two of the major portals that offer storefront services. The service typically costs several hundred dollars per month. One of the benefits of posting a storefront with a large portal is the heavy traffic the business may enjoy. Portals are visited by millions of people daily.

Many local newspapers that maintain Web sites also offer electronic storefronts. On the Web home page of the newspaper, a list of participating local businesses appears, often with clickable logos. The target audience of newspaper cybermalls are residents of the newspaper's city and suburbs. The main purpose of the client business's site is to attract customers to the brick-and-mortar business. A client pays a fee of several thousand dollars to have the newspaper staff build its business's pages.

Web-Hosting Service

Some companies specialize in offering Web-hosting services for businesses. Most of them specifically target small businesses. The hosting companies offer space on their servers for hosting of Web sites. All provide templates for pages, and some provide software tools for more flexible page development. For an additional monthly fee, several of them offer transaction and payment software for use by the subscribing businesses' clients. For example, a company named Bigstep provides "wizards" that walk you through the otherwise time-consuming process of setting up catalogs and reports. Monthly fees are usually small amounts. Due to the space and trading limits that these companies offer, hosting is appropriate for individuals and small businesses only.

Virtual Web Server

A virtual Web server creates the impression that it is owned by the business, but it is actually owned and operated by another business. To establish a virtual Web server, a business must have its own registered domain name. Shoppers may assume that the business maintains its own server; in reality the domain name points to the server of another company. To arrange a virtual Web server, the business must ask the domain name registrar to associate the domain name with the other company's server. This arrangement is popular and usually more cost-effective for many companies than maintaining their own Web server or using a cybermall. The company owning the server provides all the maintenance services, such as running the server management software, adding servers when the business grows, and keeping and updating security measures. If the client business wishes to leave a service company and move to another, it can move the Web pages to a server of another company and ask the registrar to reassociate the domain name with the new server.

Subdomain

A business can also use a subdomain instead of registering its own domain name and use the services of a hosting company for hosting the Web pages. For example, if the business name is SmallBiz, and if Oz is the host company that owns the name ozhosting, it may host the site with the subdomain *smallbiz.ozhosting.net*. There are two disadvantages to this option: the business's domain name contains the name of another entity, and unlike with virtual Web servers, the business's on-line address (the URL) is associated with a single Web server. If the client business moves the Web pages to another server, it can no longer use this URL.

Considerations in Selection of a Web Service Provider

The majority of businesses do not maintain their own Web server; they use host services. When doing so, managers must consider several factors. Exhibit 800.68 lists the factors and provides a template where points can be logged for comparison. A simple evaluation method is for managers to compare each factor for the prospective companies, compare the total scores, and then make a decision. The evaluators may wish to assign different weights to the various items based on how important each item is to the business.

Technical support involves the quality of the equipment that the hosting company provides, security measures it maintains, the sophistication of server and load management, and the technical skill of its personnel. Companies should inquire about past down times and recovery time frames for the hosting company because they are such an important part of technical support.

In addition, if the client needs help in developing and updating Web pages, the evaluators should explore the appearance and functionality of current clients of the hosting company. They should also examine the credentials and experience of the Web page designers.

Exhibit 800.68 *Factors to Consider in Web Service Providers*

Factor	Points	Hosting Company A	Hosting Company B
Quality of technical support			
Quality of content support			
Setup fee			
Monthly fee			
Amount of disk space			
Traffic limits and fees			
Availability of e-mail accounts and services			
Availability of FTP service			
CGI scripts			
Scalability			
Support of page design standards			

Setup and monthly fees are self-explanatory. Monthly fees can range from several dollars to several hundred dollars. Some hosting companies offer large discounts to clients that sign annual contracts.

As the business grows and more information and services are provided, the number and complexity of Web pages also grows. So the business will need more disk space on the host's server. Therefore, it is advisable to contract with a host that is responsive to requests for additional disk space. Large hosting companies often provide only a limited amount of disk space, and any additional space may incur high costs. Smaller companies are usually more flexible and responsive to the individual needs of clients.

Some Web-hosting companies charge extra fees if the site experiences activity above a predetermined amount of data that is downloaded from the site or number of visits from Web surfers. These visits are called *hits*. Usually, the first 5,000 hits per month are free, and there is a per-hit charge above this level. Web hosting companies price this way because the greater the number of hits, the more bandwidth they must allocate.

Most hosting companies provide e-mail services. The most popular type is a Post Office Protocol 3 (POP3) account. There is usually no extra charge for such accounts. Clients may want to inquire about additional services, such as mail forwarding (channeling e-mail messages to another e-mail address), auto-responding (automating e-mail reply), and access to mailing lists, and find out which e-mail services are free and which carry a charge.

For many on-line businesses it is important to have file transfer protocol (FTP) capabilities. FTP allows the site's owner to upload pages to the site and post downloadable files, as explained earlier. Uploading enables the site personnel to update the Web pages whenever they need to, which makes them independent of other companies, including the hosting firm. The ability to post uploadable files lets the business serve its customers better.

The availability of common gateway interface (CGI) scripts lets visitors interact with the site. CGI allows site visitors to use a local "find" mechanism to find products by name, manufacturer, or style within the client business pages; fill out forms and submit them; or change the appearance of pages they often access. Most Web-hosting companies provide CGI scripts and data access applications. A good hosting company should have a large library of such scripts and allow you to add your own CGI scripts.

Scalability is the ability for a Web site to grow—an important factor for most businesses. It is best to select a hosting company that has the hardware, software, and expertise to accommodate varying traffic levels and that can demonstrate its site's ability to develop from a simple, static one to a heavily trafficked, interactive one.

The better hosting companies maintain software that supports a large variety of standards, so the client business can rest assured that all the features it develops for its pages can be supported by the hosting company's servers. For example, if there are ActiveX features in the business's Web pages, the host's server must support ActiveX. The same principle applies to features developed with the FrontPage design application. Some attractive features may not run properly unless the proper software is installed on the server to support FrontPage.

E-Commerce Practices on the Internet

The Internet offers not only a means for conducting existing day-to-day business but also opportunities for companies to generate revenue purely by establishing a whole new business on the Web. Web pages provide different types of interactivity. The simplest is publication of static company information on a home page, similar to a billboard advertisement. An increasing number of businesses do not settle for that, however; they have established Web sites that enable customers to search for specific items offered for sale, dropping items into a virtual shopping cart and paying for the purchases.

Although electronic business, popularly called e-business, had been conducted before the advent of the Web, most of it is now conducted using Web technologies and the Internet. E-commerce is usually classified by the parties involved in the interaction: business-to-business (B2B) and business-to-consumer (B2C). Some people also add government-to-consumer, government-to-government, and government-to-business.

Examples of applications in B2B include electronic data interchange (EDI), exchanges and auctions, on-line business alliances, and application service providers (ASPs).

Examples of applications in B2C include advertising, e-retailing, auctions and reverse auctions, software sales, and stock trading.

Rules for Successful On-line Business Transactions

Once an organization has a solid business plan for e-commerce, it should consider the manner in which it will conduct on-line business and try to exploit its site's potential. There are several elements to consider.

Target the Right Customers

Targeting the people who are most likely to need the products and services you offer has always been the most important effort in marketing, with or without the Web. On the Web targeting includes identifying the sites your audience frequently visits. For instance, a business that sells sporting goods should create clickable links at sites that cover sporting events and provide sports statistics. Banks that offer mortgage loans should create links at realtors' sites. And any business that targets its products to young people should do so at music sites.

Own the Customer's Total Experience

By using cookies and recording shoppers' movements, sophisticated customer relationship management (CRM) software can create electronic consumer profiles for each shopper and buyer. The shopper's experience with the site then becomes an asset of the business. Such marketing research fine-tunes the portfolio of products that the business offers and tailors Web pages for individual customers. It also can be used to "market to one" by e-mailing the shopper about special deals on items in which he or she showed interest.

Personalize the Service

A combination of CRM software and Web page customization software can be combined to enable *customers* to personalize the pages and the service they receive when they log on to the site. On-line businesses should not force customization and promotions. They should allow customers the option to receive certain information through pop-up browser windows and e-mail messages. Most importantly, they must respect customers' privacy by letting customers opt in rather than opt out. Opting in means that the customer can actively check options to receive e-mail and other promotions, while opting out requires the customer to select *not* to receive such information—an annoyance to some customers. Some companies have created sites that enable customers to customize the products they purchase.

Shorten the Business Cycle

One of the reasons people like to do business on the Net is that it saves them time. Businesses should keep looking for opportunities to shorten the business cycle for their customers, from shopping to paying to receiving the items they ordered. **Fulfillment**, the activities taking place after customers place orders on line, is one of the greatest challenges for on-line businesses. The **Boston Consulting Group** found that pure-play Internet retailers do poorly in comparison with traditional catalog-based retailers. The reason for this disappointing performance is that most on-line retailers underestimate the challenges of fulfillment.

Those who can ship the ordered products fastest are likely to sustain or increase their market shares. Some have decided to outsource the entire fulfillment task to organizations that specialize in fulfillment, such as **UPS's e-Logistics**, **FedEx's** Supply Chain Services, and **SubmitOrder.com**. E-Logistics, for example, offers to receive and store the business's merchandise in its warehouses, receive orders on line, and then pick, pack, and ship them to the on-line business's customers. It also offers a product return service.

Let Customers Help Themselves

Customers often need information from an e-commerce organization. Such information includes the status of an order, the status of a shipped item, and after-the-sale information such as installation of add-on components and troubleshooting. Much of this information is still provided over the telephone, but customers prefer to have access to the information any time—not only on weekdays and during normal work hours—and they prefer not to wait for it.

Practically every on-line business now sends e-mail messages with the status of the order, a tracking number, and a link to the shipping company for checks on the shipping status. Hardware companies can post on-line assembly instructions for their "assembly required" products. In addition to including frequently asked questions (FAQs) information, some companies have experimented with artificial intelligence software that can answer open-ended questions. Some sites provide a link to internet relay chat (IRC) or to Internet voice, software to enable shoppers to communicate with a salesperson rather than hear only inanimate textual information.

Be Proactive

Expecting customers to visit your Web site every time they need your service may not be enough in today's competitive marketplace. Customers now demand not only prompt replies via the Net but also proactive alerts. For example, Travelocity, a travel Web site, e-mails customers information on gate and time information if a customer's flight is delayed. Similarly, businesses should use customers' profiles (assembled through previous transactions and cookies) to e-mail them information on special sales and availability of new or previously unavailable items.

Successful Business Models

Although there are many successful on-line business models, among the most successful of them we find the following types:

1. *Niche retailing.* Niche retailers do not sell a large array of items. They specialize in a narrow selection of the best and most expensive items, which have a wide profit margin. All the items offered on line are tightly related. For example, **Waggin' Tails** sells high-margin pet supplies and is profitable, unlike **Pets.com,** the large pet supplier that went bankrupt in 2000. Many small on-line suppliers of exotic dry and canned foods have been profitable as well, for the same reason: they specialize in a narrow range of high-margin products, many of which are not easy to find off line.
2. *Selling hard-to-obtain information.* The main reason organizations and individuals come to the Internet is to find information. Companies that sell useful information that is available only to them can make a profit from its sale. For example, Monster.com, a leading job-posting site, charges employers (but not job seekers) for the service and is profitable.
3. *Click-and-mortar retailing.* Traditional, brick-and-mortar retailers that extended their operations to the Web managed to generate new business and increase profits. **Staples**, **Sears**, and **Kmart** have all capitalized on their existing reputations as they moved on line. Kmart has an on-line arm called BlueLight.com. The existing stores provide a means for consumers to return products with which they are not satisfied. The fact that the chain has been around for some time and has an established brand name helps attract consumers.

While entrepreneurs are looking for new business models, a developing technology may add an interesting twist to e-commerce: mobile commerce (m-commerce).

M-Commerce

As mobile devices proliferate, some people can already do what Internet prophets say will be the wave of the future: mobile commerce, popularly called **m-commerce.** Mobile devices already let users log on to the Internet, but they can also provide an additional benefit to businesses: The device can be located within several feet of a business, much like locating a cellular phone. As soon as you come within a few blocks of a store, your hand-held computer may beep and display a promotional message on its monitor.

Mobile devices need to use a special protocol to enable conversion of HTML (and XML and other Web standards) into formats that can be displayed on mobile devices. The most common protocol is Wireless Access Protocol (WAP).

Smart mobile devices may be helpful in sales force automation. Instead of connecting laptop computers to telephone jacks and modems or to cellular phones, traveling salespeople will be able to access data through the mobile device anywhere. They will be able to access corporate databases through their company's intranet.

Although the United States has usually been the leader in Internet technologies, mobile communication in general and m-commerce in particular seem to be developing faster in Europe and Japan. Mobile connections are still too slow to attract a large number of users, especially consumers. However, when mobile technologies mature, m-commerce may pick up speed. Experts opine that the most attractive mobile application may not be buying, but the delivery of highly relevant information, custom-tailored to the user's current location and activity. Location services include downloading coupons at the store in which the consumer has just entered, finding out about nearby restaurants, or reading product reviews while shopping at an appliance store. Because location services need technology that locates the hand-held device more accurately than networks can currently, and because of privacy fears, such services may not emerge for several years.

Privacy proponents have already voiced concerns about m-commerce. Apparently, not many people are happy to find out that commercial organizations can track them down anytime as long as their mobile device is on. These devices will not only allow consumer profiling as is already practiced by many on-line retailers but also tell retailers and other organizations your exact location at any given time.

Sharing Information Systems: The Rise of E-Commerce

The future of many organizations depends on their ability to adopt an IS perspective that considers the organizations with which they interact. Large organizations have discovered the benefits of sharing their ISs with other organizations. Small organizations are slowly realizing that they must collaborate with their more powerful clients when flow of information is involved. One example is the numerous manufacturers of auto parts who must share ISs with **General Motors**, **Ford**, and **DaimlerChrysler** to survive, because the alternative would be being cut from these big companies' supplier lists. And in the global arena, the future of the world economy depends, to a large extent, on the flow of information across national borders. Many organizations now acknowledge that they are just links in a series of activities performed by a chain of players, as in a relay race. They do not just exchange goods and services for money; they also interchange information to facilitate their interactions.

From an interactive perspective, commercial organizations can be roughly classified into two categories: vertical markets and horizontal markets. A **vertical market** is one in which the goods of one business are used as raw materials or components in the production or sale process of another business: one business sells to another business until the final product is sold either to consumers or to a business that uses the product as a means of production, such as a machine. In a **horizontal market,** all players buy or sell the same products, so they are competitors. Nevertheless, they can share ISs to cooperate on certain elements of their activities or to exchange products through a bidding process. Obviously, a single business is in a vertical market with some businesses and in a horizontal market with others. Both vertical and horizontal markets have benefited greatly from Internet technologies. E-commerce has turned markets into electronic markets, in which significantly larger numbers of businesses can participate.

E-commerce has also brought many markets closer to perfect markets. In a perfect market, anyone can join or leave the market at any time; no seller or buyer is so powerful that it can influence prices; and all participants have access to the same information simultaneously. The latter condition has been chiefly aided by the growing accessibility to the Web and the advancement of its technologies.

Electronic Data Interchange

A significant portion of the cost of products and services can be attributed to the creation, handling, and storage of paper documents: requests for proposals, purchase orders, shipping documents, invoices, payment approvals, and checks, not to mention the equipment such as file cabinets and shelves to store the documents and the time spent preparing, processing, and shipping documents. The cost of handling a single paper transaction is estimated between tens and hundreds of dollars, depending on the industry. An increasing number of organizations

Suppliers, manufacturers, and retailers cooperate in some of the most successful applications of EDI.

Exhibit 800.69 *Benefits of Electronic Data Interchange (EDI)*

Cost savings	• Reduction of employee hours involved in creation and handling of paper documents • Reduction in the cost of funds transfer • Reduction in the cost of storage space • No mailing cost
Speed	• Faster forwarding of documents through a computer network than mail
Accuracy	• Rekeying of information minimized • Direct and easily verifiable communication • No loss of mail
Security	• Less susceptibility to interception and falsification of information
System integration	• Increasing interface of EDI software with internal systems so that incoming data trigger applications and further automation of data processing
Just-in-time support	• Increased communication speed enhances intercompany just-in-time operations, which significantly reduces inventory costs—vendor ships only the necessary items to arrive directly at the manufacturing or assembly line

that share information for their mutual benefit have replaced their paper-based transactions. Instead, they use interorganizational information systems that utilize telecommunications to exchange electronic data. This concept, called **electronic data interchange** (**EDI**), has been used in some industries since the early 1970s, but the popularity of EDI grew tremendously in the late 1980s and the 1990s. While technically EDI can be executed on any wide-area network, its popularity has grown in the late 1990s and early 2000s, thanks to the ability to implement the concept on the Internet.

As enumerated in Exhibit 800.69, tremendous benefits are being realized by companies that have adopted the EDI concept—especially manufacturing companies. By linking its vendors, customers, and subcontractors, a manufacturing firm can use EDI to quickly query raw or interim goods suppliers, who in turn can provide on-time delivery of the exact amount of resources needed. EDI technology also allows changes in production schedules to be communicated quickly both to suppliers and customers, minimizing the disruption in the plans of either the buying or supplying firm. Therefore, EDI is the underlying concept for interorganizational supply chain management, which we discuss later in the section.

An example of how EDI may work between two organizations is as follows:

- First, the supplier's proposal is sent electronically to the purchasing organization.
- Next, an electronic contract is approved over the network, with both organizations maintaining a digital copy.
- The supplier manufactures and packages the goods, attaching to each box shipping data recorded on a bar code (including quantities packaged, date of shipment, means of shipment, and so on).
- Quantities shipped and their prices are entered into the system and flow automatically to an invoicing program; the shipping data documents and invoices are transmitted to the purchasing organization, so the receiving workers know what items they will receive.
- The manufacturer ships the order.
- When the packages are received at the purchasing organization, the bar codes are scanned, and the data are compared with both the data transmitted with the invoices and the actual items received.
- If there are no discrepancies, an approval for payment is transferred electronically by the purchaser to its accounts payable department, which instructs the bank to pay the supplier.
- Using EFT (electronic funds transfer), the bank reduces the purchasing organization's balance by the proper amount, and electronically transfers the sum to the supplier's account at its bank.

None of the documents involved in the process is on paper.

Most EDI users are in the health-care, insurance, and retailing industries. In health care, hospitals and private clinics use networks to transmit claim forms and disbursement approvals. Similarly, insurance companies accept electronic claims. Retailers accept paperless invoices and approve payment on line. Other major industries that have implemented EDI include finance and banking, automotive, petroleum and chemical, and transportation companies.

Consider the case of **Toys R Us**, the world's largest toy retailer. Annually, the company processes over half a million invoices electronically, dramatically reducing costs and improving the integrity and management of related information. Some of its most important suppliers even have direct access to point-of-sale information to determine sales trends and generate purchase orders on behalf of Toys R Us.

Making electronic signatures legally binding fosters the proper legal environment for e-commerce in general and EDI in particular. An *electronic signature* is any signature made and kept digitally, such as a digitized written signature or a special code that uniquely identifies the signer. By 2001, the United States, Ireland, Mexico, and Bermuda had enacted electronic signature laws.

EDI is conducted in two major forms: value-added networks and the Web. We discuss both of these forms next.

Value-Added Network EDI

The earliest form of EDI business partners used was subscription to the service with a **value-added network (VAN)** operator, also referred to simply as a VAN. We use the term VAN EDI for this service.

To use VAN EDI, business partners subscribe to the service and use the VAN's private communication lines, mailboxes, and special software. The VAN mediates all EDI communication between the companies with special software that translates business documents into EDI documents. It batches electronic documents several times per day and transmits them to the destination company. The software that translates business documents to and from EDI convention strictly conforms to EDI standards, the most prevalent of which are the United Nations–supported EDIFACT (EDI for Administration Commerce and Transport) and the American National Standards Institute's (ANSI) X12. Standards determine such conventions as codes for address lines and product prices and the length of text comments in an invoice. If the subscribers use two different standards, the VAN must use special software to transform the EDI document from one standard's conventions to the other's.

VAN EDI provides several advantages.

- *Transaction integrity.* The entire transaction must be communicated without interference. VAN EDI software is designed to ensure transaction integrity. If the software senses that there might be interference or that only a part of an electronic document reached the VAN's mailbox, it requests retransmission.
- *Privacy and security.* Business partners expect and need privacy for their transactions. Private networks are fully controlled by the VANs and are accessible only to subscribers of the EDI service, so their security is a plus. The VANs implement strict security measures that practically prevent any interception of electronic documents.
- *Nonrepudiation.* The parties involved in EDI need to be certain that transactions are verified. For example, if a purchasing officer launched a purchase order to a supplier, she should not be able to deny the fact later—the supplier must be certain transactions will proceed once initiated. A VAN's mailbox system ensures that the sender cannot repudiate sent documents, so both parties can feel secure that transactions requested will be fulfilled.
- *Solid standards.* EDI standards such as EDIFACT are solid and universally accepted for numerous industries, such as manufacturing, trucking, hospitals, and many others.

Web EDI

In 1997, about 95 percent of all EDI transactions took place through VAN lines. Because of the increasing popularity of the Web, the rate was expected to decrease to about 50 percent. Practically all new EDI implementations use Web technologies. The Internet is a natural vehicle for EDI because of its ease of access and inexpensive implementation. A huge global network has become available to even the smallest and poorest businesses. Recall that many trading partners now use extranets for transactions that have been executed on traditional EDI systems for decades. Many organizations that would balk at the cost of implementing EDI can now do it quite comfortably by using the Internet.

The success of Web EDI can largely be attributed to XML standards. Recall that XML (extensible markup language) is a programming language for the Web, which is complementary to hypertext markup language (HTML). The important difference between HTML and XML is this: HTML tags around text, pictures, and other elements instruct a Web browser how to display the elements; XML tags around an element tell the browser the data content. As long as there is a universal agreement on such tags, they can be devised to communicate any business data, from company addresses to product specifications and prices to shipping dates. The universal agreement is what makes such tags a standard.

Extranet EDI offers several advantages over VAN EDI, including these:

- *Lower cost.* Compared with implementing VAN EDI, a business has to invest only modest amounts of money to implement extranet EDI. The network already exists, so there is no need to lease the services of VAN providers, which are quite expensive. A business just needs to pay the monthly ISP's fee, which is a small amount per month per server. The cost of the software is modest as well. The most common interface used with extranet EDI is a standard Web browser, which is free.

- *More familiar software.* Users are already familiar with Web browsers, which they have used for other purposes, such as surfing the Web at home. So, adding Web EDI functions includes very little training.
- *Worldwide connectivity.* In VAN EDI, partners have to coordinate connectivity and ensure compatibility of their telecommunications equipment and software. In contrast, access to the Web is available to almost every business in the world, which makes it relatively easy for any two businesses located thousands of miles apart to immediately implement EDI.
- *Fast communication.* By and large, the Internet backbone is made of communication lines capable of greater speeds than most VAN lines, which are generally older. Also, electronic documents on the Internet are not batched, as they are by the VAN, before they are launched from the mailbox to the recipient. Thus, transactions can be communicated faster on the Internet. However, VAN speeds are guaranteed, but Internet communication speed is not guaranteed because the network is shared by many parties, and communication can slow down when traffic is heavy.

With such cost and efficiency advantages, it is not surprising that Web EDI has grown so rapidly.

Supply Chain Management

The activities of commercial organizations, especially those that produce physical goods, fall into a general pattern. Each takes in input in the form of raw materials and parts, adds value to the parts by assembling or processing them, then delivers the output to another unit for further processing or to a customer. Eventually, one of the organizations in the sequence sells a final product to a customer, which may be a consumer or another business. This chain of purchase, process, and delivery is called a *supply chain*. Monitoring and controlling the supply chain is called *supply chain management (SCM)*, and ISs that support such management are called *supply chain management systems.*

Several enterprise applications, such as ERP systems, also serve as SCM systems. Many such systems enable managers not only to monitor what goes on at their own units or organization but also to follow what goes on at the facilities of their suppliers and contractors. For example, at any given point in time managers can know the status of the following: an order now being handled by a contractor, by order number; the phase of manufacturing the produced units have reached; and the date of delivery, including any delays and their length. When purchasing parts, managers use the systems for issuing electronic purchase orders, and they can follow the fulfillment process at the supplier's facilities, such as when the parts were packed, when they were loaded on trucks, and when they are estimated to arrive at the managers' floor or the floor of another business partner who needed the parts.

SCM applications streamline operations throughout the chain, from suppliers to customers, lowering inventories, decreasing production costs, and improving responsiveness to suppliers and clients. Now most such systems are designed to use the Internet. Harnessing the global network, managers can supervise an entire supply chain regardless of the location of the activity—at their own facilities or another organization's, at the same location or thousands of miles away. Older SCM systems connected two organizations. New ones connect several. For example, a distributor can reorder products from Organization A and simultaneously alert Organization B, the supplier of Organization A. The systems let all parties—suppliers, manufacturers, distributors, and customers—see the same information. A change made by any organization that affects an order can effect a corresponding change in scheduling and operations in the other organization's activities.

Companies that have adopted SCM systems have seen improvement in three major areas: reduction in inventory, reduction in cycle time, and, as a result, reduction in production cost. (Cycle time is the time it takes to complete a business process, such as purchasing or production. Every hour that a plant can gain from reducing its production cycle saves labor and allows the company to deliver and collect payment earlier.) Companies can reduce their inventory by communicating to their suppliers through a shared SCM system the exact number of units of each item they need and the exact time they need them. In ideal situations, they do not need to stockpile any inventory, saving warehouse costs.

Similar to ready-made ERP applications, SCM applications can also be purchased packaged. Experts usually praise the software for its benefits and ease of use, but there are some implementation challenges. The greatest obstacle to successful implementation is planning and training. The move to the systems must be well planned, and the systems must be fully tested before they are put into use. Employees must also be educated about the changes that come with such systems and be well trained to use the system's features.

Information Technology Contingency Plans

Crisis Management Planning

A special type of contingency planning is crisis management planning. Sometimes, events are so sudden and devastating that they require immediate response. For managers to respond appropriately, they need carefully thought-out and coordinated plans. Although crises may vary, a good crisis management plan can be used to respond to any disaster at any time of the day or night.

The three stages of crisis management include prevention, preparation, and containment. The prevention stage involves activities managers undertake to try to prevent crises from occurring and to detect warning signs of potential crises. The preparation stage includes all the detailed planning to handle a crises when it occurs. Containment focuses on the organization's response to an actual crisis and any follow-up concerns.

Prevention

Although unexpected events and disasters will happen, managers should do everything they can to prevent crises. One critical part of the prevention stage is building relationships with key stakeholders such as employees, customers, suppliers, governments, unions, and the community. By developing favorable relationships, managers can often prevent crises from happening. Similarly, organizations that build a reputation as a solid, reputable company are able to avert many crises and respond more effectively to those that cannot be avoided.

Open communication with employees, customers, and all stakeholders enables the organization and stakeholder groups to better understand one another and develop mutual respect. For example, organizations that have open, trusting relationships with employees and unions may avoid crippling labor strikes. Open communication also helps managers identify problems early so they do not turn into major issues.

Preparation

Three steps in the preparation stage are designating a crisis management team and spokesperson, creating a detailed crisis management plan, and setting up an effective communications system. The crisis management team is a cross-functional group of people who are designated to swing into action if a crisis occurs. They are closely involved in creating the crisis management plan, and they will be called upon to implement the plan if a disaster hits.

The organization should also designate a spokesperson who will be the voice of the company during the crisis. The spokesperson in many cases is the top leader of the organization. However, organizations typically assign more than one spokesperson so that someone else will be prepared if the top leader is not available.

The crisis management plan (CMP) should be a detailed, written plan that specifies the steps to be taken, and by whom, if a crisis occurs. The CMP should list complete contact information for members of the crisis management team, as well as for outside agencies such as emergency personnel, insurance companies, and so forth. It should include plans for ensuring the safety of employees and customers, procedures for back-up and recovery of computer systems and protecting proprietary information, details on where people should go if they need to be evacuated, plans for alternative work sites if needed, and guidelines for handling media and other outside communications. Some firms hand out wallet-sized cards that inform employees about evacuation procedures and what to do following an evacuation.[3] A key point is that a crisis management plan should be a living, changing document that is regularly reviewed, practiced, and updated as needed.

A major part of the CMP is a communications plan that designates a crisis command center and sets up a complete communications and messaging system. The command center serves as a place for the crisis management team to meet, gather data and monitor incoming information, and disseminate information to the media and the public. The plan should designate alternate communication centers in case the main center is disrupted and should include plans for varied communication methods, such as toll-free call centers, Internet and intranet communications, and plans for rerouting data traffic if necessary. All employees should have multiple ways to get in touch with the organization and report their whereabouts and status after a disaster. The organization should also have varied ways to contact employees and notify them of changing circumstances and plans.

Containment

Some crises are inevitable no matter how well prepared an organization is. When a crisis hits, a rapid response is crucial. The team should be able to immediately implement the crisis management plan, so training and practice are important. In addition, the organization should "get the awful truth out" to employees and the public as soon as possible.[4] This is the stage where it becomes critical for the organization to speak with one voice so that employees, customers, and the public do not get conflicting stories about what happened and what the organization is doing about it. The crisis team gathers as much information as possible and the designated spokesperson presents the facts as they are known. Failing to get the truth out quickly lowers an organization's chances of recovering from the crisis.

After ensuring the physical safety of people (and in some cases, animal life), the next focus should be on responding to the emotional needs of employees, customers, and the public. Giving facts and statistics to try to downplay the disaster always backfires because it does not meet people's emotional need to feel that someone cares about them and what the disaster has meant to their lives. After a crisis as devastating as the World Trade Center attacks or the Columbine school shootings, companies may provide counseling and other services to help people cope.

Organizations also strive to give people a sense of security and belonging. Getting back to business quickly is essential because it helps people believe that things can return to normal. Companies that cannot get up and running within 10 days after any major crisis are not likely to stay in business.[5] People want to feel that they are going to have a job and be able to take care of their families. Taking steps to protect people from danger during future disasters is important at this stage also. In this sense, crisis management planning comes full circle, because managers use the crisis to strengthen their prevention abilities and be better prepared in the future. A crisis is an important time for companies to strengthen their stakeholder relationships. By being open and honest about the crisis and putting people first, organizations build stronger bonds with employees, customers and other stakeholders, and gain a reputation as a trustworthy company. Although layoffs might be necessary in some situations, experts on crisis management suggest they should be a last resort following a major crisis because they damage trust, morale, and the company's reputation.

Recovery Measures

In 1998, although the company had not experienced any server overload, **Schwab's** chief information officer decided to play it safe and double the number of servers that route and process customer inquiries and transactions. The extra servers turned out to be a good investment. Despite occasional attacks by hackers and viruses, the firm has never experienced any downtime, and clients have never complained about slow response. On the other hand, the world's largest auction site, **eBay**, and many other on-line merchants have had to apologize to clients several times for long hours of no response—from unforeseen load or because of denial of service (DoS) attacks.

Security measures may reduce undesirable mishaps, but nobody can control all disasters. To be prepared for disasters when they do occur, organizations must have recovery measures in place. Organizations that depend heavily on ISs for their daily business often use redundancy; that is, they run all systems and transactions on two computers in parallel to protect against loss of data and business. If one computer is down, the work can continue on the other computer. Redundancy makes the system fault-tolerant. However, in distributed systems, doubling every computing resource is extremely expensive, so other measures must be taken.

To prepare for mishaps, either natural or malicious, many organizations have well-thought-out programs in place, called **business recovery plans** or **business continuity plans.** The plans detail what should be done and by whom if critical ISs go down or if IS operations become untrustworthy. Business recovery plans deal mostly with steps to take when ISs are incapacitated.

The Business Recovery Plan

Concern about disaster recovery has spread beyond banks, insurance companies, and data centers, the traditional disaster recovery fanatics. Many customer service and retail firms realize that they can easily lose customers if they don't deliver services and products in a timely manner, which is why the term *business recovery* or *business resumption* has caught on in some circles. In interactive-computing environments, when business systems are idle, so are the people who bring in revenue. In addition, companies' reputations can be harmed, and competitive advantage and market share lost.

Experts propose nine steps for the development of a business recovery plan.

1. **Obtain management's commitment to the plan.** Development of a recovery plan requires substantial resources. Top management must be convinced of the potential damages that paralysis of information systems may cause. Once management is committed, it should appoint a business recovery coordinator who will develop the plan and execute it if disaster occurs.
2. **Establish a planning committee.** The coordinator establishes a planning committee comprising representatives from all business units that are dependent on computer-based ISs. The members serve as liaisons between the coordinator and their unit managers. The managers are authorized to establish emergency procedures for their own departments.
3. **Perform risk-assessment and impact analysis.** The committee assesses which operations would be hurt by disasters, and how long the organization could continue to operate without the damaged resources. This analysis is carried out through interviews with managers of functional business areas. The committee compiles information regarding maximum allowable down time, required backup information, and the financial, operational, and legal consequences of extended down time.
4. **Prioritize recovery needs.** The disaster recovery coordinator ranks each IS application according to its effect on an organization's ability to achieve its mission. **Mission-critical applications,** those without which the business cannot conduct its operations, are given the highest priority. The largest or most widely used system may not be the most critical. Applications may be categorized into several classes, such as:
    - 4.1 *Critical.* Applications that cannot be replaced with manual systems under any circumstances
    - 4.2 *Vital.* Applications that can be replaced with manual systems for a brief period, such as several days
    - 4.3 *Sensitive.* Applications that can be replaced with acceptable manual systems for an extended period of time, though at great cost
    - 4.4 *Noncritical.* Applications that can be interrupted for an extended period of time at little or no cost to the organization
5. **Select a recovery plan.** Recovery plan alternatives are evaluated by considering advantages and disadvantages in terms of risk reduction, cost, and the speed at which employees can adjust to the alternative system.
6. **Select vendors.** If it is determined that an external vendor can better respond to a disaster than in-house staff and provide a better alternate system, then the external vendor that will be most cost-effective is selected. Factors considered should include the vendor's ability to provide telecommunications alternatives, experience, and capacity to support current applications.
7. **Develop and implement the plan.** The plan includes organizational and vendor responsibilities and the sequence of events that will take place. Each business unit is informed of its responsibilities, key contacts in each department, and training programs for personnel.
8. **Test the plan.** Testing includes a walk-through with each business unit, simulations as if a real disaster had occurred, and (if no damage will be caused) a deliberate interruption of the system and implementation of the plan. In mock disasters, the coordinator measures the time it takes to implement the plan and its effectiveness.
9. **Continually test and evaluate.** The staff must be aware of the plan at all times. Therefore, the plan must be tested periodically. It should be evaluated in light of new business practices and the addition of new applications. If necessary, the plan should be modified to accommodate these changes.

The plan should include the key personnel and their responsibilities, as well as a procedure to reinstitute interactions with outside business partners and suppliers. Because an organization's priorities and environment change over time, the plan must be examined periodically and updated if necessary. There will be new business processes or changes in the relative importance of existing processes or tasks, new or different application software, changes in hardware, and new or different IS and end-user personnel. The plan must be modified to reflect the new environment, and the changes must be thoroughly tested. A copy of the plan should be kept off-site, because if a disaster occurs, an on-site copy may not be available.

Consider the effort **Kodak Corporation** exerted to protect its ISs. With $14 billion in annual sales, the company has a detailed business recovery plan. Executives from every division agreed on a nine-step restoration sequence: First priority goes to order-entry systems, second priority is attached to inventory control, then come systems that support manufacturing processes, purchasing systems, warehouse control systems, payroll and accounting, and then quality assurance and master data. Not only does the list help the IS professionals to prioritize their response in case of a natural disaster or another mishap, but the sequence allows members of each business unit to understand their importance in the company. The firm's CIO said that the existence of the plan helps managers in every facility of this multisite international company know what they are to do when ISs go down; there are no questions about where to start, what to do, whom to call, and how to be involved. To shorten the restoration time of its ERP system, the company can use an ERP system at a standby site. Moving operations to that system now takes fewer than eight hours.

CIOs often find the tasks of earmarking funds for disaster recovery programs difficult because they cannot show the return on investment (ROI) of such "investment." Most companies institute recovery programs only after a disaster or near disaster occurs. Usually, the larger companies have such programs. **Gratner Group** found that 85 percent of Fortune 1000 companies have such programs. However, of these companies, 80 percent have only programs to rescue corporate centers, 50 percent of the plans cover networks, and fewer than 35 percent protect data that reside on networked PCs.

Selecting a Recovery Plan

Strategies for alternate computer processing capability are normally grouped into several categories: hot site, cold site, warm site, mobile site, redundant site, reciprocal/mutual agreements, and hybrids. These terms originated with recovery strategies for data centers but can be applied to other platforms. When comparing alternate computer processing facilities, the objective should be to select the alternative with the smallest annualized cost. Initial costs, recurring operating costs, and activation costs are three types of costs associated with alternate computer processing support. Disaster notification fees are part of activation costs.

HOT-SITE   A building already equipped with processing capability and other services. It is the most expensive alternative.

WARM-SITE   It has telecommunications ready to be utilized and is recommended for users of sophisticated telecommunications and network needs. It is partially equipped.

COLD-SITE   A building for housing processors that can be easily adapted for use. It does not present a problem of hardware compatibility since it is an empty shell without hardware. It is the least expensive choice but it is the most difficult and expensive method to test.

MOBILE-SITE   Specific equipment is available on a trailer.

REDUNDANT SITE   A site equipped and configured exactly like the primary site. Some organizations plan on having partial redundancy for a disaster and partial processing for normal operations. The stocking of spare personal computers and their parts or LAN servers also provides some redundancy.

The need for computer security does not go away when an organization is processing in a contingency mode. In some cases, the need may increase due to sharing of processing facilities, concentrating resources in fewer sites, or using additional contractors and consultants. Security should be an important consideration when selecting contingency strategies.

RECIPROCAL/MUTUAL AGREEMENT   An informal agreement that allows two organizations to back each other up. While this approach often sounds desirable, it is important to note that this alternative has the greatest chance of failure due to problems keeping agreements and plans up-to-date as systems and personnel change. This alternative is inexpensive and unreliable because there are no written agreements.

HYBRIDS   Any combination of the above such as having a hot site as a backup in case a redundant or reciprocal agreement site is damaged by a separate contingency.

Recovery may include several stages, perhaps marked by increasing availability of processing capability. Resumption planning may include contracts or the ability to place contracts to replace equipment.

Testing the Recovery Plan

A contingency plan or recovery plan should be tested periodically because there will undoubtedly be flaws in the plan and in its implementation. The plan will become dated as time passes and as the resources used to support critical functions change. Responsibility for keeping the contingency plan current should be specially assigned. The extent and frequency of testing will vary between organizations and among systems. *There are several types of testing, including reviews and walkthroughs, analyses or desk checking, disaster simulations, and end-to-end testing.*

1. **Reviews and Walkthroughs.** A review can be a simple test to check the accuracy of contingency plan documentation. For instance, a reviewer could check if individuals listed are still in the organization and still have the responsibilities that caused them to be included in the plan. This test can check home and work telephone numbers, organizational codes, and building and room numbers. The review can determine if files can be restored from backup tapes or if employees know emergency procedures. *A checklist is used during reviews to ensure that all items are addressed.*

   > The results of a "test" often imply a grade assigned for a specific level of performance or simply pass/fail. However, in the case of contingency planning, a test should be used to improve the plan. If organizations do not use this approach, flaws in the plan may remain hidden and uncorrected.

2. **Analyses or Desk-Checking.** An analysis or **desk checking** may be performed on the entire plan or portions of it, such as emergency response procedures. It is beneficial if the analysis is performed by someone who did not help develop the contingency plan but has a good working knowledge of the critical function and supporting resources. The analyst(s) may mentally follow the strategies in the contingency plan, looking for flaws in the logic or processes used by the plan's developers. The analyst also may interview functional managers, resource managers, and their staff to uncover missing or unworkable pieces of the plan.

3. **Disaster Simulations.** Organizations may also arrange disaster simulations. These tests provide valuable information about flaws in the contingency plan and provide practice for a real emergency. While they can be expensive, these tests can also provide critical information that can be used to ensure the continuity of important functions. In general, the more critical the functions and the resources addressed in the contingency plan, the more cost-beneficial it is to perform a disaster simulation.

4. **End-to-End Testing.** The purpose of end-to-end testing is to verify that a defined set of interrelated systems, which collectively support an organizational core business area or function, interoperate as intended in an operational environment (either actual or simulated). These interrelated systems include not only those owned and managed by the organization but also the external systems with which they interface.

Generally, end-to-end testing is conducted when one major system in the end-to-end chain is modified or replaced, and attention is rightfully focused on the changed or new system. The boundaries on end-to-end tests are not fixed or predetermined but vary depending on a given business area's system dependencies (internal and external) and criticality to the mission of the organization. Therefore, in planning end-to-end tests, it is critical to analyze the organization's core business functions, the interrelationships among systems supporting these functions, and potential risk exposure due to system failures in the chain of support. It is also important to work early and continuously with the organization's data exchange partners so that end-to-end tests can be effectively planned and executed.

Outsourcing the Recovery Plan

Companies that choose not to develop their own recovery plan can outsource it to companies that specialize in recovery. The major companies in this industry include **IBM**, **SunGard**, and **Strohl Systems**. Another industry leader, **Comdisco**, sold its business continuity services division to **Hewlett-Packard** in 2001. These services include an all-encompassing system called GroundZero, which addresses every aspect of disaster preparedness. Small companies that cannot afford an expensive recovery plan can opt for Web-based services such as EmergencyPlan.com and Evergreen Data Continuity, Inc. In case of a natural disaster or another mishap, employees can access business data remotely.

Usually, a company that outsources its recovery plan uses a remote link to storage devices at the vendor's site to periodically store all its essential data files. It may also save a copy of unique applications there. If the client cannot use its own system for any reason—a natural disaster or a crippling hacker attack—the client's employees can either physically move to the vendor's facility or move to an office that provides Internet links. The latter option is becoming highly popular because it does not require relocation of employees during the recovery period. Employees simply move to an office located close to the organization's office and use the applications and data files remotely. Vendors usually have widely used applications (such as the MS Office suite) and proper use licenses available to clients.

Ethics and Information Technology

Codes of Ethics for IT Professionals

IS/IT professionals have a huge impact on planning, building, and maintaining ISs. Their decisions commit organizations to large investments and may radically change the way in which the organizations operate. Yet, unlike doctors, lawyers, public accountants, and other professionals, they do not have obligatory codes of ethics and professional standards.

Like other professionals, IS professionals must protect the interests of different constituencies: society at large, their employers, the employers' clients, and their own colleagues. Often, IT professionals find themselves in situations where the interests of two, or even three, of these constituencies collide. While some organizations have professional codes of conduct addressing many aspects of the IS profession, most do not provide guidelines for resolving conflicts-of-interest situations.

Consider this conflict. A programmer working for a consulting firm is involved in a large project for a client. The programmer comes to realize that the software has security holes. When she approaches her supervisor at the consulting firm, her boss demands that she ignore these holes and not alert the client because, "we are doing everything according to the contract." Her obligation to her employer is to follow his instructions. However, her obligation to the client is to inform him about the incompatibility. The programmer is faced with an ethical dilemma.

As another example, what would you do in the following situation? You are an independent database expert involved in the upgrading of a database for a large bank. Your contact at the bank is one of its senior vice presidents, who hired you and approved the payment for your consulting fees. While analyzing the database, you discover that the vice president has been involved in embezzlement. The victims are some bank clients (that is, the public) and, of course, the bank. What should you do? Is it your obligation to inform the bank's management? Should you inform the public by contacting a reporter? Or should you simply go on with the work for which you were hired, and for which you are being paid?

Although ethical conflicts are not less frequent in other professions, the ethical codes of other professions provide clearer decision rules than those of IT professionals. For example, a lawyer's first obligation is always to his client. The same principle applies to physicians. The ethical code of journalism is to strictly obey the rule of not exposing a source without the source's consent. Journalists have protected their sources to the point of obstructing justice; that is, they have honored the source's interests over the public's interests. An architect who learns that a building may not meet safety standards is expected to halt his work to protect the public, even though this may conflict with his obligations to an employer or client. Unlike physicians, attorneys, certified public accountants, and many other professionals, IT professionals must resolve their ethical dilemmas by themselves.

Information Ethical Standards

The information technology (IT) manager needs to understand what motivates people to behave in an unethical manner in the information age and in an environment conducive to computer crime, misuse, and fraud. A good manager can create an environment that will discourage computer abuse and promote ethical behavior.

Computer hardware and software vendors, service contractors, systems developers and maintainers, system managers, and system users all have an **equal role** in sharing ethical responsibilities. The key issues involved in information ethics are:

1. Software piracy
2. Data security and individual privacy
3. Data integrity
4. Human/product safety
5. Fairness, honesty, and loyalty

Each issue is discussed here briefly.

Software Piracy

Software piracy conveys that the creative and intellectual work of the author has been used or duplicated without permission, compensation, or payment of royalty to the author. Software piracy is an act of infringement on ownership rights, and the person who violates it could be sued civilly for damages, criminally prosecuted, or both. Software piracy is the most difficult act to control and enforce. Self-monitoring and honesty are the best controls.

The vast majority of the software involved in software piracy legal cases is off-the-shelf, PC software, such as word processing, spreadsheets, graphics, and databases. The issue is illegal use, copying, and distribution of software both inside and outside the organization. Here, *illegal* means a user has not paid for the software.

What Can Go Wrong in Software Use?
- User organizations can be sued by software vendors or copyrighted owners for using their software illegally.
- Disgruntled employees are the major source of reporting illegal use of software to owners, followed by consultants.
- Most often, employees inherit their computers and are not aware of illegal software on the hard disk their predecessors left behind.
- In addition to actual users, software dealers and hard-disk loaders are equally guilty of pirated software. They are also subject to legal suits.

Software piracy policies are needed to protect the organization from legal suits by owners. The policy should do the following:

- Prohibit illegal copying and use of software.
- Develop a software inventory management system that includes a list of popular application programs. This list can be compared to the organization's purchase orders, original software diskettes, or original documentation manual.
- Periodically check the hard disks for illegally copied software.
- Make illegal copying of software grounds for employee dismissal.
- Require all employees to sign a statement pledging not to use illegal software at work and not to use software taken illegally from work to home.
- Prohibit copying of internally developed software.
- Prohibit pirated, externally developed software from being brought into the organization.
- Monitor all sensitive programs to prevent illegal copying.

Data Security and Individual Privacy

Data security and individual privacy includes all the controls and procedures developed to protect against unauthorized individuals accessing the computer system, disclosing confidential data, and denying essential computer services to those who need them the most. Specifically, it requires the careful protection of personal records such as medical reports and credit reports. Privacy issues raise questions such as (1) Who is collecting the data? (2) For what use is the data being collected? and (3) For what purpose will the data be disseminated? Education and training programs should help the employee treat data as resources and respect their confidentiality.

The objective is to eliminate or minimize emotional, financial, or other damage to the owners of the data due to disclosure and misuse of inaccurate and/or incomplete data.

Data Integrity

Data integrity requires that personal data contained in certain documents such as credit reports, medical reports, police reports, debt default notices, and insurance reports be absolutely accurate, complete, up-to-date, relevant, and timely. Because these reports are automated, it puts more responsibility on information systems professionals and auditors to ensure data integrity.

Human/Product Safety

Software developers and maintainers and hardware manufacturers could be liable if their products and devices cause physical, financial, or other damage to the users. It could even cost human loss due to erroneous system design or incorrect data in the system. Other considerations include exposure to radiation and eye strain resulting from computer terminals, personal computers, workstations, or workbenches.

A risk is that people can die or become seriously ill based on output results from computer software or hardware. For example, a medical doctor could prescribe a medicine based on diagnostic results from an erroneously designed or incompletely tested expert-knowledge-based computer system.

Fairness, Honesty, and Loyalty

Fairness depends on the relationship between parties such as computer vendors and customers, their relative power structure, and the size and nature of the business transaction. Unfair practices toward employees can encourage fraudulent activities. Honesty deals with truthful representations between sellers and buyers of information technology products, devices, and services. Product advertising and labeling and contract negotiations are some areas where honesty is important. Loyalty is supposed to be a two-way street between employees and employers, between buyers and sellers, and between manufacturers and suppliers of information technology products, devices, and services. The relationship between the affected parties should be based on mutual trust, confidence, and faith instead of solely on paycheck, price, commission, and profits.

Legal Issues in Information Ethics

- Entrapment is useful for making computers more secure. Entrapment of hackers is permitted because they have no right to attack an organization. It is best to try preventive controls first and detective controls next. When these controls do not work, entrapment should begin. Entrapment is a controversial issue.
- Prelogging questionnaires are legally appropriate. Prelogging questionnaires include ascertaining whether users are authorized to use the computer and making sure that they access only the data and system to which they are entitled. Post-logging questionnaires are used after the fact and are not of much use.
- Both welcome and unwelcome screens make the computer installation and the organization name known to the public. Legal issues may arise from these screens.
- A "no trespassing" notice at a computer system's initial logon screen is an all-inclusive warning to confront potential system intruders. It is a deterrent tactic to scare system intruders. Placing this notice is legal.
- Use of pirated (bootleg) software can lead to legal problems because it allows users to obtain software from unauthorized sources (e.g., the Internet). It can also introduce some risks such as computer viruses and infringement of freeware copyrights. Freeware is software that is made available to the public at no cost. The author retains copyrights and can place restrictions on how the program is used and distributed.
- An effective way to prevent software piracy is to use a dongle device. A dongle is a small hardware device that is shipped with some software packages. The dongle is hard-coded with a unique serial number that corresponds to the software. When the program runs, it checks for the presence of the device. If the device is not plugged in, the program will not run.

Module 800 Endnotes

1. E. Oz and J.J. Sosik, "Why Information Systems Projects are Abandoned: A Leadership and Communication Theory and Exploratory Study," *Journal of Computer Information Systems,* Vol. 41, No. 1, (Fall 2000), 66–78.
2. J.L. Dodd and H.C. Houston, "Systems Development Led by End-Users: An Assessment of End-User Involvement in Information Systems Development," *Journal of Systems Management* (August 1994), 34.
3. "Diaster Planning," *Ioma's Report on Controlling Law Firm Costs* (October 2001), 9.
4. Ian Mitroff, "Crisis Leadership," *Executive Excellence.* (August 2001), 19.
5. Kirsten Downey Grimsey, "Girding Against New Risks:" Global Executives Are Working to Better Protect Their Employees and Businesses from Calamity," *Time,* October 8, 2001, B8.

MODULE 900

Corporate Control and Governance

901
Corporate Control Strategies, 1268

910
Internal Control Framework and Control Models, 1270

930
Corporate Fraud, 1277

940
Corporate Risk Management, 1293

950
Corporate Citizenship, Accountability, and Public Policy, 1311

970
Issues Management and Crisis Management, 1326

980
Corporate Ethics and Management Assurance, 1336

990
Corporate Governance, 1347

Module 900 Endnotes, 1358

Corporate Control Strategies

Control strategies should be linked to business strategies in that controls and the control environment in an organization should facilitate the achievement of business objectives. Here, controls are labeled into three categories such as management control, operational control, and internal control.

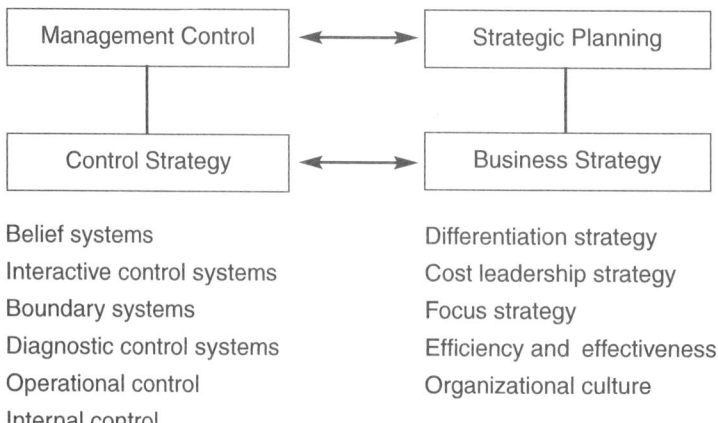

Belief systems
Interactive control systems
Boundary systems
Diagnostic control systems
Operational control
Internal control

Differentiation strategy
Cost leadership strategy
Focus strategy
Efficiency and effectiveness
Organizational culture

Management Control

Management control is the process by which managers assure that resources are obtained and used effectively and efficiently in the accomplishment of the organization's objectives.[1] Management control is a process carried on within the framework established by strategic planning. Decisions about next year's budget, for example, are constrained within policies and guidelines prescribed by top management. The management control process is intended to make possible the achievement of planned objectives as effectively and efficiently as possible within these givens.

The purpose of a management control system is to encourage managers to take actions that are in the best interests of the company. Technically, this purpose can be described as *goal congruence*. Ordinarily, a management control system is a total system in the sense that it embraces all aspects of the company's operations.

The management control process tends to be rhythmic; it follows a definite pattern and timetable, month after month and year after year. The management control system is a single system consisting of interlocking subsystems that are highly coordinated and integrated. Above all, line managers, not the staff, are the focal points in management control.

Examples of activities for which management control is necessary are the total operations in manufacturing activities consisting of plant inputs such as materials, direct and indirect labor, employee safety and training programs; marketing activities dealing with advertising, sales promotions, pricing, and selling decisions; human resource activities to select and recruit employees; financing activities to raise money; research and development activities to bring out new products; and the activities of top management such as strategic planning, implementation, and control.

Strategic Planning

Strategic planning is the process of deciding on the objectives of the organization, on changes in these objectives, on the resources used to attain these objectives, and on the policies that are to govern the acquisition, use, and disposition of these resources.

Business Strategy

Business strategy is derived from the strategic planning process. We defined how one model (Section 101), Porter's competitive strategy, can be used to affect organization design. Porter's strategy emphasizes three items: (1) product or service differentiation, (2) low-cost leadership, and (3) focus on a specific market or customer group. Porter's strategic model should be combined with organizational culture to achieve effectiveness and efficiency of operations.

Control Strategy

Robert Simons, of Harvard Business School, in his book *Levers of Control*, describes four control levers for an effective implementation of business strategy.[2] The first two levers include belief systems and interactive control systems, which create positive and inspirational forces. The last two levers include boundary systems and diagnostic control systems, which create negative forces such as constraints for compliance with policies and rules. More specifically, the four levers of control include the following:

1. **Belief systems** are used to inspire, empower, and direct the search for new opportunities.
2. **Interactive control systems** are used to stimulate and expand organizational learning and to guide the emergence of new ideas and strategies.
3. **Boundary systems** are used to set limits or rules on opportunity-seeking behavior.
4. **Diagnostic control systems** are used to motivate, monitor, and reward achievement of specified goals and objectives. These systems focus attention on the implementation of intended strategies.

These four levers of control, working together, can help in the achievement of intended strategies. They provide the motivation, measurement, learning, and control that allow efficient goal achievement, creative adaptation, and profitable growth.

Operational Control

Operational control is the process of assuring that specific tasks are carried out effectively and efficiently. The focus of operational control is on individual tasks or transactions, scheduling and controlling individual jobs through a production shop, procuring specific items for inventory, and specific personnel actions and rules.

Examples of activities that are susceptible to operational control are automated plants for power and cement production, production scheduling operations, inventory control systems, order processing systems, billing systems, payroll accounting, human resource administration tasks, and other routine functions.

Comparison of Management Control With Operational Control

Management control covers the whole of an organization. Each operational control procedure is restricted to a subunit, often a narrow activity. Just as management control occurs within a set of policies derived from strategic planning, so operational control occurs within a set of well-defined procedures and rules derived from management control.

Control is more difficult in management control than in operational control because of the absence of a scientific standard with which actual performance can be compared. A good operational control system can provide a much higher degree of assurance that actions are proceeding as desired than can a management control system.

An operational control system is a rational system; that is, the action to be taken is decided by a set of logical rules programmed into a computer. In management control, psychological considerations are dominant in that it requires management's action or intervention.

The management control system is ordinarily built around a financial structure, whereas operational control data are often nonfinancial in nature. Data in an operational control system are often in real time and relate to individual events, whereas data in a management control system are often retrospective and summarize many separate events.

Similarly, operational control uses exact data, whereas management control needs only approximations. Material is ordered and scheduled in specific quantities and employees are paid the exact amount due them in operational control systems. An operational control system requires a mathematical model of the operation. Models are not so important in management control.

The success or failure of the management control system depends on the personal characteristics of the manager—his or her judgment, knowledge, and ability to influence others. An operational control system states what action should be taken; it makes the decisions.

In general, the degree of management involvement in operational control is small, whereas in management control it is large. As new techniques are developed, there is a tendency for more and more business activities to become susceptible to operational control. This includes manufacturing, marketing, human resources, finance, and other functions.

Internal Control

The scope of internal controls is broad in nature in that it consists of organizational structure that creates a division of responsibilities among employees, management authorization of business transactions, communication programs explaining the company's policies and standards to all employees, and selection and training of qualified and competent managers. The scope also includes procedural checks and balances that safeguard assets and assure integrity of data. Without basic internal controls, the risks of significant control failure become unacceptably high. Internal control is fully discussed in Section 910.

Internal Control Framework and Control Models

Internal Control Framework

The Committee of Sponsoring Organizations (COSO) of the Treadway Commission in the United States published an internal control-integrated framework to guide management in 1992.[3] Senior executives have long sought ways to better control the enterprises they run. Internal controls are put in place to keep the company on course toward profitability goals and achievement of its mission, and to minimize surprises along the way. They enable management to deal with rapidly changing economic and competitive environments, shifting customer demands and priorities, and restructuring for future growth. Internal controls promote efficiency, reduce risk of asset loss, and help ensure the reliability of financial statements and compliance with laws and regulations.

Internal Control Definition and Objectives

Internal control is broadly defined as a process, effected by an entity's board of directors, management, and other personnel, designed to provide reasonable assurance regarding the achievement of objectives in the following three categories:

1. Effectiveness and efficiency of operations
2. Reliability of financial reporting
3. Compliance with applicable laws and regulations

The first category addresses an entity's basic business objectives, including performance and profitability goals and safeguarding of resources. The second category relates to the preparation of reliable published financial statements, including interim and condensed financial statements and selected financial data derived from such statements, such as earnings releases, reported publicly. The third category deals with complying with those laws and regulations to which the entity is subject. These distinct but overlapping categories address different needs and allow a directed focus to meet the separate needs.

Internal control systems operate at different levels of effectiveness. Internal control can be judged effective in each of the three categories, respectively, if the board of directors and management have reasonable assurance that:

- They understand the extent to which the entity's operations objectives are being achieved.
- Published financial statements are being prepared reliably.
- Applicable laws and regulations are being complied with.

While internal control is a process, its effectiveness is a state or condition of the process at one or more points in time.

Components of Internal Control

According to the COSO report, internal control consists of five interrelated components. These are derived from the way management runs a business, and are integrated with the management process.

1. **Control Environment.** The core of any business is its people—their individual attributes, including integrity, ethical values, and competence—and the environment in which they operate. They are the engine that drives the entity and the foundation on which everything rests. An entity's objectives and the way they are achieved are based on preferences, value judgments, and management styles. There often is a trade-off between competence and cost and between the extent of supervision and the requisite competence level of the individual. Companies can operate in a formal or informal mode. Formal documentation is not always necessary for a policy to be in place and operating effectively. A more formally managed company may rely more on written policies, performance indicators, and exception reports.

2. **Risk Assessment.** The entity must be aware of and deal with the risks it faces. It must set objectives that are integrated with the sales, production, marketing, financial, and other activities so that the organization is operating in concert. It also must establish mechanisms to identify, analyze, and manage the related risks.

    Objective setting is a precondition to risk assessment. There must first be objectives before management can identify risks to their achievement and take necessary actions to manage the risks. Objective setting, then, is a key part of the management process. While not an internal control component, it is a prerequisite to and an enabler of internal control.

3. **Control Activities.** Control policies and procedures must be established and executed to help ensure that the actions identified by management as necessary to address risks to achievement of the entity's objectives are effectively carried out. Examples of control activities include approvals, authorizations, verifications, reconciliations, reviews of operating performance, security of assets, and segregation of duties. Types of control activities can include preventive controls, detective controls, manual controls, computer controls, and management controls. Regardless of whether a policy is written, it must be implemented thoughtfully, conscientiously, and consistently. Controls are also classified into two categories: hard controls and soft controls. Hard controls are formal, tangible, and easier to measure and evaluate. Examples of hard controls include budgets, dual controls, written approvals, reconciliations, authorization levels, verifications, and segregation of duties. On the other hand, soft controls are informal, intangible, and difficult to measure and evaluate. Examples of soft controls include ethics, integrity, values, culture, vision, commitment to competence, management philosophy, level of understanding and commitment, and communication. Tools to evaluate hard controls include flowcharts, system narratives, testing, and counting. Tools to evaluate soft controls include self-assessments, questionnaires, interviews, and workshops. Generally speaking, senior managers most often use soft skills and soft controls to achieve their objectives while other managers most often use hard skills and hard controls. Soft skills include people skills such as interpersonal skills, motivation, leadership, and communications skills. Hard skills include technical skills such as functional skills, problem identification and solving skills, and decision-making skills.

4. **Information and Communication.** Surrounding these activities are information and communication systems. These enable the entity's people to capture and exchange the information needed to conduct, manage, and control its operations. Reliable internal financial measurements are also essential to planning, budgeting, pricing, evaluating vendor performance, and evaluating joint ventures and other alliances. Information can be obtained through questionnaires, interviews, broad-based market demand studies, or targeted focus groups. Information systems must provide the right information on time and at the right place. Because of these requirements, information systems must be controlled due to their influence on control.

5. **Monitoring.** The entire process must be monitored, and modifications must be made as necessary. In this way, the system can react dynamically, changing as conditions warrant. Monitoring is not a precondition to internal control because it is a part of internal control. Monitoring activities include management or supervisory

Exhibit 900.1 *Relationship of Internal Control Objectives and Components*

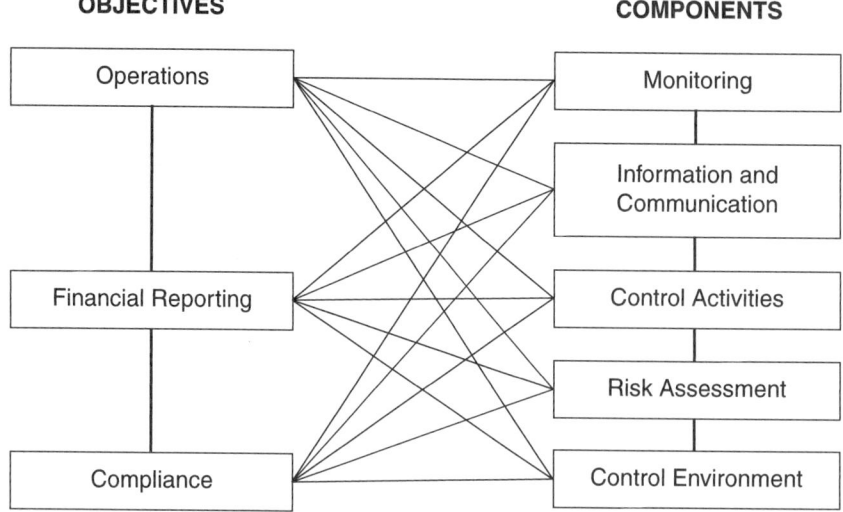

reviews, comparisons, and reconciliations. Emphasis should be put on "building in" rather than "adding on" controls. Monitoring can be done in two ways: through ongoing activities or through separate evaluations. Usually, some combination of ongoing monitoring and separate evaluations will ensure that the internal control system maintains its effectiveness over time.

The internal control definition—with its underlying fundamental concepts of a process, effected by people, providing reasonable assurance—together with the categorization of objectives and the components and criteria for effectiveness, and the associated discussions, constitute this internal control framework.

There is a direct relationship between the three categories of objectives, which are what an entity strives to achieve, and components, which represent what is needed to achieve the objectives. All components are relevant to each objectives category. When looking at any one category—the effectiveness and efficiency of operations, for instance—all five components must be present and functioning effectively to conclude that internal control over operations is effective. See Exhibit 900.1 for the relationship between internal control objectives and components.

What an Internal Control Can and Cannot Do

Internal control can help an entity achieve its performance and profitability targets and prevent loss of resources. It can help ensure reliable financial reporting. And it can help ensure that the enterprise complies with laws and regulations, avoiding damage to its reputation and other consequences. In sum, internal control can help an entity get to where it wants to go, while avoiding pitfalls and surprises along the way.

Internal controls promote efficiency, reduce risk of asset loss, and help ensure the reliability of financial statements and compliance with laws and regulations.

What internal control cannot do is (1) ensure an entity's success or survival or (2) ensure the reliability of financial reporting and compliance with laws and regulations.

Internal Control Is a Process

Internal control is not one event or circumstance, but a series of actions that permeate an entity's activities. These actions are pervasive and are inherent in the way management runs the business. Internal controls are most effective when they are built into the entity's infrastructure and are part of the essence of the enterprise. Controls should be "built in" rather than "built on." "Building in" controls can directly affect an entity's ability to reach its goals, and supports a business's quality initiatives. In fact, internal control not only is integrated with quality programs, it is usually critical to their success.

Internal Control Is People

Internal control is effected by a board of directors, management, and other personnel in an entity. It is accomplished by the people of an organization, by what they do and say. People establish the entity's objectives and put control mechanisms in place.

Similarly, internal control affects people's actions. Internal control recognizes that people do not always understand, communicate, or perform consistently. Each individual brings to the workplace a unique background and technical ability, and each has different needs and priorities.

The Limitations of Internal Control

No two entities will or should have the same internal control system. Companies and their internal control needs differ dramatically by industry and size and by culture and management philosophy. Internal control has been viewed by some observers as ensuring that an entity will not fail—that is, the entity will always achieve its operations, financial reporting, and compliance objectives. In this sense, internal control sometimes is looked upon as a cure-all for all real and potential business ills. This view is misguided. Internal control is not a panacea.

Even effective internal control operates at different levels with respect to different objectives. Also, internal control sometimes cannot provide reasonable assurance, due to differences in judgment, breakdowns in controls, management overrides, collusion, and problems in cost/benefit measurements.

Roles and Responsibilities in Internal Control

Everyone in an organization has responsibility for internal control. We will discuss briefly the responsibility of management, board of directors, auditors, and employees.

Management

The chief executive officer is ultimately responsible and should assume "ownership" of the internal control system. More than any other individual, the chief executive sets the "tone at the top" that affects integrity and ethics and other factors of a positive control environment. In a large company, the chief executive fulfills this duty by providing leadership and direction to senior managers and reviewing the way they are controlling the business. Senior managers, in turn, assign responsibility for establishment of more specific internal control policies and procedures to personnel responsible for the business unit's functions. In a smaller entity, the influence of the chief executive, often an owner-manager, is usually more direct. In any event, in a cascading responsibility, a manager is effectively a chief executive of his or her sphere of responsibility. Of particular significance are financial officers and their staffs, whose control activities cut across, as well as up and down, the operating and other units of an enterprise.

Board of Directors

Management is accountable to the board of directors, which provides corporate governance, guidance, and oversight. Effective board members are objective, capable, and inquisitive. They also have a knowledge of the entity's activities and environment, and commit the time necessary to fulfill their broad responsibilities. Management may be in a position to override controls and ignore or stifle communications from subordinates, enabling a dishonest management which intentionally misrepresents results to cover its tracks. A strong, active board, particularly when coupled with effective upward communication channels and capable financial, legal, and internal audit functions, is often best able to identify and correct such a problem.

In 1978, the Securities and Exchange Commission (SEC) proposed a list of eight "customary functions" of audit committees. The audit committee consists of board members and is similar to other committees such as compensation, standing, or legal committees. The "customary functions" of the audit committees include the following:

1. Recommend engagement or discharge of the independent auditors
2. Direct and supervise investigations into matters within the scope of their duties
3. Review with the independent auditors the plan and results of the auditing engagement

4. Review the scope and results of internal auditing activities
5. Approve each professional service provided by the independent auditor prior to its performance
6. Review the independence of the independent auditors
7. Consider the range of audit and non-audit fees
8. Review the adequacy of the systems of internal controls

Auditors

Both internal and external auditors are committed to improving internal controls. Internal auditors play an important role in evaluating the effectiveness of the control system and contribute to ongoing effectiveness. Because of organizational position and authority in an entity, an internal audit function often plays a significant monitoring role. External auditors, bringing an independent and objective view, contribute directly through the financial statement audit and indirectly by providing information useful to management and the board in carrying out their responsibilities.

Employees

Virtually all employees produce information used in the internal control system or take other actions needed to effect control. Also, all employees should be responsible for communicating upward problems in operations, noncompliance with the code of conduct, or other policy violations or illegal actions.

Control Models

In this section, we will discuss several control models for effective functioning of internal control systems. These include the COSO model, the CoCo model, the Control Self-Assessment model, the Turnbull model, the King model, the KonTraG model, the COBIT model, and the CONCT model.

The COSO Model in the United States

The COSO model was discussed earlier in this section.

The CoCo Model in Canada

The Canadian Institute of Chartered Accountants (CICA) has issued 20 "criteria of control" (CoCo) as a framework for making judgments about control. The term *control* has a broader meaning than internal control over financial reporting. CoCo defines control as "those elements of an organization (including its resources, systems, processes, culture, structure, and tasks) that, taken together, support people in the achievement of the organization's objectives." It defines three categories of objectives:

- Effectiveness and efficiency of operations
- Reliability of internal/external reporting
- Compliance with applicable laws, regulations, and internal policies

The criteria of control are the basis for understanding control in an organization and for making judgments about the effectiveness of control. The criteria are formulated to be broadly applicable. The effectiveness of control in any organization, regardless of the objective it serves, can be assessed using these criteria. The criteria are phrased as goals to be worked toward over time; they are not minimum requirements to be passed or failed.

CoCo defines four types of criteria: purpose, commitment, capability, and monitoring and learning. The *purpose* type groups criteria that provide a sense of the organization's direction and address objectives (including mission, vision, and strategy); risks (and opportunities); policies; planning; and performance targets and indicators. The *commitment* type groups criteria that provide a sense of the organization's identity and values and address ethical values, including integrity, human resource policies, authority, responsibility, accountability, and mutual trust. The *capability* type groups criteria that provide a sense of the organization's competence and address knowledge, skills, and tools; communication processes; information; coordination; and control activities. The *monitoring and learning* type groups criteria that provide a sense of the organization's evolution and address monitoring internal and external environment, monitoring performance, challenging assumptions, reassessing information needs and information systems, follow-up procedures, and assessing the effectiveness of control.

The Control Self-Assessment Model

Overview

The Control Self-Assessment Model (CSA) deals with evaluating the system of internal control in any organization. CSA is a shared responsibility among all employees in the organization, not just internal auditing or senior management. The examination of the internal control environment is conducted within a structured, documented, and repetitive process. The formal assessment approach takes place in workshop sessions with business users as participants (process owners) and internal auditors as facilitators (subject-matter experts) and as nonfacilitators (note takers). The purpose of the sessions is conversation and mutual discovery and information sharing.

Definition of CSA

CSA has five elements: (1) up-front planning and preliminary audit work, (2) the gathering of process owners with a meeting facilitator, (3) a structured agenda to examine the process's risks and controls, (4) a note taker and electronic voting technology to input comments and opinions, and (5) reporting the results and the development of corrective action plans.

Scope of CSA

CSA can be done either as a stand-alone project or as a supplement to traditional audit work. CSA is not suitable to situations such as (1) finding fraud, (2) compliance reviews (for example, regulatory audits), or (3) when participants have conflicting objectives, as in third-party contracts. CSA can be applied to numerous situations, business issues, and industries, regardless of size. It is a management tool that has equal application to horizontal (organization-wide), vertical (single department), or diagonal (process inquiries) issues.

Effect on Auditors

CSA can be used to assess business and financial statement risks, control activities, ethical values, and control effectiveness; the controls that mitigate those risks; and overall compliance with policies and procedures.

During the assessment process, there is a constant interactive dialogue between the auditor and the auditee, as well as between the auditees. This interaction increases communication and builds trust and confidence between each party. At the same time, it is educational to both parties because there is a knowledge transfer between the auditor and the auditee. The auditors will have a greater knowledge of business functions, while the auditees will have a better understanding of and appreciation for controls and the business process of which they are a part.

The increased communication and the knowledge transfer adds value to the organization in the following ways:

- Auditors accomplish control assessment.
- Auditees understand the purpose of controls.
- Management takes responsibility for the development and maintenance of the control environment.
- Process improvement issues are identified and resolved (that is, implemented or deferred).

Interrelationships Between CSA, CoCo, and COSO

CSA can be an effective tool for accomplishing the objectives of both CoCo and COSO. CSA acts as a link to the CoCo and COSO.

The CSA audit can address the four elements of the CoCo framework (that is, purpose, commitment, capability, and monitoring and learning). Both commitment and capability are examples of soft controls (for example, risk assessment, the achievement of business objectives and goals, and the attitude of people toward controls).

Conclusions for CSA

CSA is a dynamic business process improvement and control-enhancing technique. The CSA in relation to internal auditing is like total quality management and continuous process improvement techniques in relation to other parts of the organization. The only difference is how the CSA program is implemented in each organization, but the benefits are real and long-lasting.

The Turnbull Model in the United Kingdom

In 1998, the London Stock Exchange developed a Combined Code for corporate governance. The Code requires that company directors should, at least annually, conduct a review of the effectiveness of the system of internal control and should report to shareholders that they have reviewed the effectiveness of all three types of controls, including financial, operational, and compliance control.

The King Model in South Africa

The Institute of Directors in Southern Africa has established the King Committee on Corporate Governance that produced the King Report in 1994. The Committee has developed a Code of Corporate Practices and Conduct, and compliance with the Code is a requirement to be listed in the JSE Securities Exchange in South Africa.

The KonTraG Model in Germany

In 1998, the German government proposed changes for the reform of corporate governance. The model affects control and transparency in business. Specifically, it impacts the board of directors, supervisory board, corporate capitalization principles, authorization of no-par-value shares, small nonlisted stock corporations, banks investing in industrial companies, and the acceptance of internationally recognized accounting standards.

The COBIT Model

Control objectives for information and related technology (COBIT), issued by the Information Systems Audit and Control Foundation (ISACF), are aimed at addressing business objectives. The control objectives make a clear and distinct link to business objectives in order to support significant use outside the audit community. Control objectives are defined in a process-oriented manner following the principle of business reengineering [ISACF].

The COBIT framework includes (1) the classification of domains where high-level control objectives apply (domains and processes), (2) an indication of the business requirements for information in that domain, and (3) the IT resources primarily impacted by control objectives. The framework is based on research activities that have identified 34 high-level control objectives and 318 detailed control objectives. In establishing the list of business requirements, COBIT combines the principles embedded in existing and known reference models.

1. Quality requirements cover quality, cost, and delivery.
2. Fiduciary requirements (COSO report) cover effectiveness and efficiency of operations, reliability of information, and compliance with laws and regulations.
3. Security requirements cover confidentiality, integrity, and availability.

The COBIT framework consists of high-level control objectives and an overall structure for their classification. The underlying theory of the classification is that there are, in essence, three levels of IT efforts when considering the management of IT resources. Starting at the bottom, there are activities and tasks needed to achieve a measurable result. Activities have a life-cycle concept while tasks are more discrete. The life-cycle concept has typical control requirements that are different from discrete activities. Processes are then defined one layer up as a series of joined activities or tasks with natural (control) breaks. At the highest level, processes are naturally grouped together into domains.

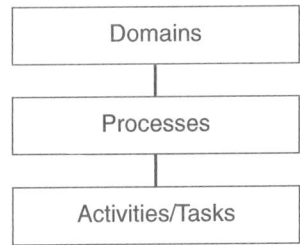

The conceptual framework can be approached from three vantage points: (1) information criteria, (2) IT resources, and (3) IT processes. Four domains were identified: planning and organization, acquisition and implementation, delivery and support, and monitoring.

In summary, in order to provide the information that the organization needs to achieve its objectives, IT governance must be exercised by the organization to ensure that IT resources are managed by a set of naturally grouped IT processes.

The CONCT Model

Control Objectives for Net Centric Technology (CONCT), issued by the ISACF, focus on the following activities: intranet, extranet, Internet; data warehouses; and on-line transaction processing systems. CONCT provides well-structured ways of understanding and assessing the very complex centric technology environment that exists.

The IT governance model for the centric technology has three dimensions. They are: IT control objectives for information services, IT activities, and the IT resources required for the accomplishment of these activities.

Corporate Fraud

The Nature of Fraud

Seriousness of the Fraud Problem

Although most people and even researchers believe that fraud is increasing both in size and frequency, it is very difficult to know for sure. First, it is impossible to know what percentage of fraud *perpetrators* are caught. Are there perfect frauds that are never discovered, or are all frauds eventually discovered? In addition, many frauds that are discovered are handled quietly within the victim organization and never made public. In many cases, companies merely hide the frauds and quietly terminate or transfer perpetrators rather than make them public.

Statistics on how much fraud is occurring, whether it is increasing or decreasing, and how much the average fraud costs come from four basic sources.

1. **Government agencies.** Agencies such as the FBI or various health agencies publish fraud statistics from time to time, but only those statistics related to their *jurisdiction*. Generally, their statistics are not complete, are not collected randomly, and do not provide a total picture even of all the fraud in the areas for which they have responsibility.
2. **Researchers.** Researchers often conduct studies about particular types of fraud in particular industrial sectors. Unfortunately, data on actual frauds is difficult to get and, as a result, most research studies only provide small

insights into the magnitude of the problem, even in the specific area being studied. Comprehensive research on the occurrence of fraud is rare and is not always based on sound scientific approaches.

3. **Insurance companies.** Insurance companies often provide fidelity bonding or other types of coverage against employee and other fraud. When fraud occurs, they undertake investigations and, as a result, have collected some fraud statistics. Generally, however, their statistics relate only to actual cases where they provided employee bonding or other insurance. At best, their look at the problem is incomplete.
4. **Victims of fraud.** Sometimes we learn about fraud from those who have been *victims*. In almost all industries, there is no organized way for victims to report fraud and, even if there were, many companies would choose not to make their fraud losses public.

Even with the difficulties in measuring fraud, most people believe that fraud is a growing problem. Both the numbers of frauds committed and the total dollar amounts lost from fraud seem to be increasing. Because fraud affects how much we pay for goods and services, each of us pays not only a portion of the fraud bill but also for the detection and investigation of fraud. It is almost impossible to read a newspaper or business magazine without coming across multiple incidents of fraud.

Even more alarming than the increased number of fraud cases is the size of discovered frauds. In earlier times, if a thief wanted to steal from his or her employer, the perpetrator had to physically remove the assets from the business premises. Because of fear of being caught with the goods, frauds tended to be small. With the advent of computers, the Internet, and complex accounting systems, employees now need only make a telephone call, misdirect purchase invoices, bribe a supplier, manipulate a computer program, or simply push a key on the keyboard to misplace company assets. Because physical possession of stolen property is no longer required and because it is just as easy to program a computer to misdirect $100,000 as it is $1,000, the size and number of frauds have increased tremendously.

To understand how costly fraud is to organizations, consider what happens when fraud is committed against a company. Losses incurred from fraud reduce a firm's income on a dollar-for-dollar basis. This means that for every $1 of fraud, *net income* is reduced by $1. Because fraud reduces net income, it takes significantly more *revenue* to recover the effect of the fraud on net income. To illustrate, consider the $436 million fraud loss that a U.S. automobile manufacturer experienced a few years ago.[4] If the automobile manufacturer's *profit margin* (net income divided by revenues) at the time was 10 percent, the company would have to generate up to $4.36 billion in additional revenue (or 10 times the amount of the fraud) to recover the effect on net income. If we assume an average selling price of $20,000 per car, the company must make and sell an additional 218,000 cars. Considered this way, fighting fraud is a serious business. The automobile company can spend its efforts manufacturing and marketing additional new cars, or trying to reduce fraud, or a combination of both.

As another example, a large bank was the victim of a fraud that totaled $100 million in one year. With a profit margin of 5 percent, and assuming that the bank made $100 per year per checking account, how many new checking accounts must the bank generate to compensate for the fraud losses? The answer, of course, is up to 20 million new checking accounts ($100 million fraud loss ÷ 0.05 = $2 billion in additional revenues; $2 billion ÷ $100 per account = 20 million new accounts).

Because of different cost/revenue structures, the amount of additional revenues a firm must generate to recover fraud losses varies from firm to firm. It is easy to see that in order to maximize profits eliminating fraud should be a key goal of every business. The best way to minimize fraud is to prevent it from occurring.

What Is Fraud?

There are two principal methods of getting something from others illegally. Either you physically force someone to give you what you want, or you trick them out of their assets. The first type of theft we call robbery, and the second type we call *fraud*. Robbery is generally more violent and more traumatic than fraud and attracts much more media attention, but losses from fraud far exceed losses from robbery. Fraud always involves deception, confidence, and trickery.

Although there are many definitions of fraud, probably the most common is the following:

> Fraud is a generic term, and embraces all the multifarious means which human ingenuity can devise, which are resorted to by one individual, to get an advantage over another by false representations. No definite and invariable rule can be laid down as a general proposition in defining fraud, as it includes surprise, trickery, cunning and unfair ways by which another is cheated. The only boundaries defining it are those which limit human knavery.[5]

Fraud is deception that includes the following elements.

1. A *representation*
2. About a *material* point
3. Which is *false*
4. And *intentionally or recklessly* so
5. Which is *believed*
6. And *acted upon* by the victim
7. To the victim's *damage*

Fraud is different from unintentional error. If, for example, someone mistakenly enters incorrect numbers on a *financial statement*, is this fraud? No, it is not fraud because it was not done with intent or for the purpose of gaining advantage over another through false pretense. But, if in the same situation, someone purposely enters incorrect numbers on a financial statement to trick investors, then it *is* fraud!

Types of Fraud

The most common way to classify fraud is to divide frauds into those committed *against* an organization and those committed *on behalf* of an organization.

In occupational fraud—fraud committed against an organization—the victim of the fraud is the employee's organization. The Association of Certified Fraud Examiners (ACFE) defines this type of fraud as, *"The use of one's occupation for personal enrichment through the deliberate misuse or misapplication of the employing organization's resources or assets."*[6] Occupational fraud results from the misconduct of employees, managers, or executives. Occupational fraud can be anything from lunch break abuses to high-tech schemes. *The Report to the Nation on Occupation Fraud and Abuse* by the ACFE states that, "The key to occupational fraud is that the activity (1) is clandestine, (2) violates the employee's fiduciary duties to the organization, (3) is committed for the purpose of direct or indirect financial benefit to the employee, and (4) costs the employing organization assets, revenues, or reserves."[7]

The most common fraud committed on behalf of an organization—usually through actions of the top management—is fraudulent financial reporting. These frauds are committed to make reported earnings look better or to increase a company's stock price. Sometimes, executives misstate earnings in order to ensure a larger year-end bonus. Financial statement fraud often occurs in companies that are experiencing net losses or have profits much less than expectations. See Exhibit 900.2 for types of fraud.

In June, 2001, a "Big 5" CPA firm and three of its partners were fined by the Securities and Exchange Commission for allowing a client to engage in a series of improper accounting practices that inflated its earnings for several years. The fine against the CPA firm and its partners totaled $7 million. The firm agreed to pay the fine and settle the case, although it would not admit to or deny the allegations. The fines against specific partners were the first since the mid-1980s and were imposed by the SEC because it is trying to curb what it sees as a growing problem of accounting fraud.[8]

Exhibit 900.2 *Types of Fraud*

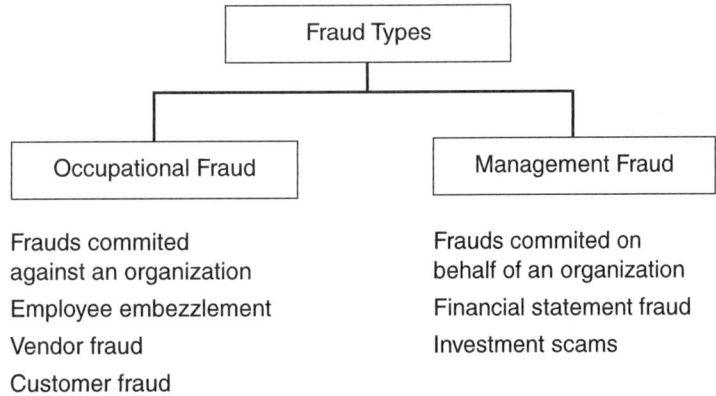

Exhibit 900.3 *Summary of Fraud Types*

Type of Fraud	Victim	Perpetrator	Explanation
1. Employee embezzlement or occupational fraud	Employers	Employees	Employees directly or indirectly steal from their employers.
2. Management fraud	Stockholders, lenders, and others who rely on financial statements	Top management	Top management provides misrepresentation, usually in financial information.
3. Investment scams	Investors	Individuals	Individuals trick investors into putting money into fraudulent investments.
4. Vendor fraud	Organizations that buy goods or services	Organizations or individuals that sell goods or services	Organizations overcharge for goods or services or nonshipment of goods, even though payment is made.
5. Customer fraud	Organizations that sell goods or services	Customers	Customers deceive sellers into giving customers something they should not have or charging them less than they should.

A more inclusive classification scheme divides fraud into the following six types:

1. employee embezzlement
2. management fraud
3. investment scams
4. vendor fraud
5. customer fraud
6. miscellaneous fraud

Fraud that does not fall into one of the first five types and that may have been committed for reasons other than financial gain is simply labeled *miscellaneous fraud*. The other five types of fraud are summarized in Exhibit 900.3.

Criminal and Civil Prosecution of Fraud

When people commit fraud, they can be prosecuted criminally and/or civilly. To succeed in a criminal or civil prosecution, it is usually necessary to show that the perpetrator acted with *intent* to defraud the victim. This is best accomplished by gathering evidential matter. *Evidential matter* consists of the underlying data and all corroborating information available. More is said later.

Who Commits Fraud and Why

Who Commits Fraud

Past research has shown that anyone can commit fraud.[9] Fraud perpetrators usually cannot be distinguished from other people by demographic or psychological characteristics. Most fraud perpetrators have profiles that look like those of other honest people.

It is important to understand the characteristics of fraud perpetrators because they appear to be very much like people who have traits that organizations look for in hiring employees, seeking out customers and clients, and selecting vendors. This knowledge helps us to understand that (1) most employees, customers, vendors, and business associates and partners fit the profile of fraud perpetrators and are probably capable of committing fraud, and (2) it is impossible to predict in advance which employees, vendors, clients, and customers will become dishonest. In fact, when fraud does occur, the most common reaction by those around the fraud is denial. Victims cannot believe that individuals who look and behave much like them and who are usually well trusted can behave dishonestly.

Why People Commit Fraud

Although there are thousands of ways to perpetrate fraud, three key elements are common to all of them. Fraud includes: (1) a perceived pressure, (2) a perceived opportunity, and (3) some way to rationalize the fraud as acceptable. These three elements make up what we call the *fraud triangle*.

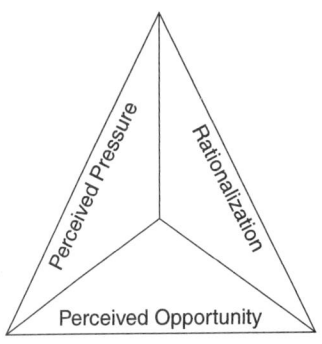

Perceived pressure, perceived opportunity, and rationalization are common to every fraud. Whether the fraud is one that benefits the perpetrators directly, such as employee fraud, or one that benefits the perpetrator's organization, such as management fraud, the three elements are always present. In the case of management fraud, for example, the pressure may be the need to make earnings look better to meet debt covenants, the opportunity may be a weak audit committee, and the rationalization may be that "we'll only cook the books until we can get over this temporary hump."

Fraud resembles fire in many ways. For a fire to occur, three elements are necessary: (1) oxygen, (2) fuel, and (3) heat. These three elements make up the "fire triangle." When all three elements come together, there is fire.

Firefighters know that a fire can be extinguished by eliminating any one of the three elements. Oxygen is often eliminated by smothering, by using chemicals, or by causing explosions, as is the case in oil well fires. Heat is most commonly eliminated by pouring water on fires. Fuel is removed by building fire lines or fire breaks or by shutting off the source of the fuel.

As with the elements in the fire triangle, the three elements in the fraud triangle are also interactive. With fire, the more flammable the fuel, the less oxygen and heat it takes to ignite. Similarly, the purer the oxygen, the less flammable the fuel needs to be to ignite. With fraud, the greater the perceived opportunity or the more intense the pressure, the less rationalization it takes to motivate someone to commit fraud. Likewise, the more dishonest a perpetrator is, the less opportunity and/or pressure it takes to motivate fraud.

People who try to prevent fraud usually work on only one of the three elements of the fraud triangle: opportunity. Because fraud-fighters generally believe that opportunities can be eliminated by having good internal controls, they focus all or most of their preventive efforts on implementing controls and ensuring adherence to them. Rarely do they focus on the pressures motivating fraud or on the rationalizations of perpetrators.

It is interesting to note that almost every study of honesty reveals that levels of honesty are decreasing.[10] Given the interactive nature of the elements in the fraud triangle, society's retreat from this value presents a scary future for companies combatting fraud. Less honesty makes it easier to rationalize, thus requiring less perceived opportunity and/or pressure for fraud to occur.

The First Element of Fraud: Perceived Pressure

Fraud is perpetrated to benefit oneself or to benefit an organization, or both. Employee fraud, in which individuals embezzle from their employers, usually benefits the perpetrator. Management fraud, in which an organization's officers deceive investors and creditors (usually by manipulating financial statements), is most often perpetrated to benefit an organization and its officers. In this section we will discuss the different pressures that motivate individuals to perpetrate fraud on their own behalf. Most experts on fraud believe these pressures can be divided into four types: (1) financial pressures, (2) vices, (3) work-related pressures, and (4) other pressures.

Financial Pressures

Studies conducted by Steven Albrecht show that approximately 95 percent of all frauds involve either financial or vice-related pressures.[11] Here are the common financial pressures associated with fraud that benefits perpetrators directly:

1. Greed
2. Living beyond one's means
3. High bills or personal debt

4. Poor credit
5. Personal financial losses
6. Unexpected financial needs

This list is not exhaustive, and these pressures are not mutually exclusive. However, each pressure in this list has been associated with numerous frauds. We know of individuals who committed fraud because they were destitute. We know of perpetrators who were living lifestyles far beyond that of their peers.

Financial pressures can occur suddenly or can be long term. Unfortunately, very few fraud perpetrators inform others when they are having financial problems.

Financial pressure is the most common pressure that drives people to commit fraud. Usually when management fraud occurs, companies overstate assets on the balance sheet and net income on the income statement. They usually feel pressured to do so because of a poor cash position, receivables that aren't collectible, a loss of customers, obsolete inventory, a declining market, or restrictive loan covenants that the company is violating. **Regina Vacuum's** management committed massive financial statement fraud. The main pressure that drove them to fraud was that their vacuum cleaners were defective—parts melted—and thousands were being returned. The large number of returns reduced revenues significantly and created such income pressures that management intentionally understated sales returns and overstated sales.[12]

Vices

Closely related to financial pressures are *vices*—addictions such as gambling, drugs, and alcohol—and expensive extramarital relationships.

Vices are the worst kind of pressure—out-of-control lifestyles are frequently cited as the trigger that drives previously honest people to commit fraud. We know of female employees who embezzled because their children were on drugs and they could not stand to see them go through withdrawal pains. We also know of "successful" managers who, in addition to embezzling from their companies, burglarized homes and engaged in other types of theft to support their drug habits.

Work-Related Pressures

Whereas financial pressures and vices motivate most frauds, some people commit fraud to get even with their employer. Factors such as not enough recognition for job performance, dissatisfaction with the job, fear of losing one's job, being overlooked for a promotion, and feeling underpaid motivate many frauds.

Other Pressures

Once in a while, fraud is motivated by other pressures, such as a spouse who insists on an improved lifestyle or a desire to beat the system.

All of us face pressures in our lives. We have legitimate financial needs, we make foolish or speculative investments, we are possessed by addictive vices, we feel overworked and/or underpaid, or we simply want more than we have. We sometimes have a difficult time distinguishing between wants and needs. Indeed, the objective of most people in capitalistic societies is to obtain wealth. We often measure success by how much money or wealth a person has. If you say you have a very successful relative, you probably mean that he or she lives in a big house, has a cabin or a condominium, drives expensive automobiles, and has money to do whatever he wants. But most of us don't put our success ahead of our honesty and integrity.

To some people, however, being successful is more important than being honest. If they were to rank the personal characteristics they value most in their lives, success would rank higher than integrity. Psychologists tell us that most people have a price at which they will be dishonest. Individuals with high integrity and low opportunity need high pressure to be dishonest.

Most of us can think of scenarios in which we, too, might commit fraud. If for example, we were starving, and we worked in an environment where cash was abundant and not accounted for, and we really believed that we would repay the money taken to feed ourselves, we might commit fraud. The U.S. president most famous for his honesty, Abraham Lincoln, once threw a man out of his office, angrily turning down a substantial bribe. When someone asked why he was so angry, he said, "Every man has his price, and he was getting close to mine."[13] One thing is for certain—eliminating pressures in the fraud triangle has an effect similar to removing heat from the fire triangle. Without some kind of pressure, fraud rarely occurs.

The Second Element of Fraud: Perceived Opportunity

A perceived opportunity to commit fraud, to conceal it, or to avoid being punished is the second element in the fraud triangle. At least six major factors increase opportunities for individuals to commit fraud in organizations. The following list is not exhaustive, but it does show system weaknesses that create opportunity.

1. Lack of or circumvention of controls that prevent and/or detect fraudulent behavior
2. Inability to judge quality of performance
3. Failure to discipline fraud perpetrators
4. Lack of access to information
5. Ignorance, apathy, and incapacity
6. Lack of an audit trail

The Third Element of Fraud: Rationalization

Nearly every fraud involves rationalization. Most perpetrators are first-time offenders who would not commit other crimes. Rationalizing helps them hide from the dishonesty of their acts. Here are some common rationalizations used by fraudsters:

- The organization owes it to me.
- I am only borrowing the money—I will pay it back.
- Nobody will get hurt.
- I deserve more.
- It's for a good purpose.
- We'll fix the books as soon as we get over this financial difficulty.
- Something has to be sacrificed—my integrity or my reputation. (If I don't embezzle to cover my inability to pay, people will know I can't meet my obligations and that will be embarrassing because I'm a professional.)

Certainly, there are countless other rationalizations. These, however, are representative and serve as an adequate basis to discuss the role rationalization plays in fraud.

It is important to recognize that there are very few, if any, people who do not rationalize. We rationalize being overweight. We rationalize not exercising enough. We rationalize spending more than we should. Most of us rationalize being dishonest.

We rationalize dishonesty by our desire to make other people feel good. The same sort of rationalization often enables fraud to be perpetrated. Sometimes, one lies to oneself; sometimes one lies to others.

Control Factors: Controls That Prevent and Detect Fraud

Having an effective control structure is probably the single most important step organizations can take to prevent and detect employee fraud. There are three components in a company's control structure: (1) the control environment, (2) the accounting system, and (3) control activities or procedures. The accounting profession and the Committee of Sponsoring Organizations (COSO) have defined these components; here we discuss only those components that are most effective in deterring fraud.

The Control Environment

Taken together, the five elements—(1) proper management modeling, (2) good communication or labeling, (3) effective hiring procedures, (4) clear organizational structure and assigned responsibilities, and (5) an effective internal audit department and security function—create an atmosphere in which fraud opportunities are decreased because employees see that fraud is neither acceptable nor tolerated. Relaxing any one of these elements increases opportunities for committing fraud.

930. CORPORATE FRAUD

The Accounting System

The second component of the control structure is a good *accounting system*. Every fraud is comprised of three elements: (1) the theft, in which assets are taken; (2) concealment, which is the attempt to hide the fraud from others; and (3) conversion, in which the perpetrator spends the money or converts the stolen assets to cash and then spends the money. An effective accounting system provides an *audit trail* that allows frauds to be discovered and makes concealment difficult. Unlike bank robbery, in which there is usually no effort to conceal the theft, concealment is a distinguishing element of fraud.

Frauds are often concealed in the accounting records. Accounting records are based on transaction documents, either paper or electronic. To cover up a fraud, paper or electronic documentation must be altered or misplaced. Frauds can be discovered in the accounting records by examining transaction entries that have no support or by probing financial statement amounts that are not reasonable. Without a good accounting system, distinguishing between actual fraud and unintentional errors is often difficult. A good accounting system ensures that recorded transactions are (1) valid, (2) properly authorized, (3) complete, (4) properly classified, (5) reported in the proper period, (6) properly valued, and (7) summarized correctly.

Control Activities (Procedures)

The third component of the control structure is good *control activities (or procedures)*. Individuals who own their own businesses and are the sole "employee" probably do not need many control procedures. Although these people may have ample opportunity to defraud their own business, they have no incentive to do so. They would not steal from themselves, and they would never want to treat customers poorly. However, organizations that involve many employees must have control procedures so that the actions of employees are congruent with the goals of management or the owners. In addition, with control procedures, opportunities to commit and/or conceal frauds are eliminated or minimized. No matter what the business is, whether it is the business of operating a financial institution, a grocery store, or a Fortune 500 company, or the business of investing personal assets, there are five primary control procedures or activities.

1. Segregation of duties or dual custody
2. System of authorizations
3. Independent checks
4. Physical safeguards
5. Documents and records

Although there are thousands of control activities used by businesses, they are basically all variations of these five basic procedures. Good fraud detection and prevention efforts involve matching the most effective control procedures with the various risks of fraud.

SEGREGATION OF DUTIES OR DUAL CUSTODY Activities can usually be better controlled by invoking either *segregation of duties* or dual-custody control. Segregation of duties involves dividing a task into two parts, so that one person does not have complete control of the task. Dual custody requires two individuals to work together at the same task. Either way, it takes two people to do one job. This control, like most preventive controls, is most often used when cash is involved. For example, the opening of incoming cash in a business is usually done by two people or by segregating duties. The accounting for, and the handling of, cash are separated so that one person does not have access to both.

There are at least three critical functions that even small business owners should either set up as segregated duties or always do themselves: (1) writing checks, (2) making bank deposits, and (3) reconciling bank statements.

Because two individuals are involved, dual custody or segregation of duties is usually the most expensive of all controls. Labor costs are high, and hiring two people to complete one job is a luxury that most businesses do not believe they can afford. This control always involves a trade-off between higher labor cost and less opportunity for error and fraud. Besides being expensive, good dual custody is often difficult to enforce. When two individuals are working on the same task, they shouldn't take their eyes or their minds off the task to answer telephones, use the restroom, respond to a question, or even sneeze.

SYSTEM OF AUTHORIZATIONS The second internal control procedure is a proper system of authorizations. Authorization control procedures take many forms. Passwords authorize individuals to use computers and to access certain databases. Signature cards authorize individuals to enter safe deposit boxes, to cash checks, and to perform other functions at financial institutions. Spending limits authorize individuals to spend only what is in their budget or approved level.

When people are not authorized to perform an activity, the opportunity to commit fraud is reduced. For example, when individuals are not authorized to enter safe deposit boxes, they cannot enter and steal the contents of someone else's box. When individuals are not authorized to approve purchases, they cannot order items for personal use and have their companies pay for the goods.

INDEPENDENT CHECKS   The theory behind *independent checks* is that if people know their work or activities are monitored by others, the opportunity to commit and conceal a fraud is reduced. There are many varieties of independent checks. The Office of the Controller of the Currency (OCC) requires that every bank employee in the United States take one week's vacation (five consecutive days) each year. While employees are gone, others are supposed to perform their work. If an employee's work piles up while he or she is out for the week, this "mandatory vacation" control is not working as it should and the opportunity to commit fraud is not eliminated.

Periodic job rotations, cash counts or certifications, supervisor reviews, employee hotlines, and the use of auditors are other forms of independent checks. One large department store in Europe has a complete extra staff of employees for its chain of department stores. This staff goes to a store and works while everyone who is employed there goes on vacation for a month. While they are gone, the transient staff operates the store. One purpose of this program is to provide complete, independent checks on the activities of store employees. If someone who is committing fraud is forced to leave for a month, the illegal activity is often discovered.

PHYSICAL SAFEGUARDS   Physical safeguards protect assets from theft by fraud or other means. *Physical safeguards,* such as vaults, safes, fences, locks, and keys, take away opportunities to commit fraud by making it difficult for people to access assets. Money locked in a vault, for example, cannot be stolen unless someone gains unauthorized access or unless someone who has access violates the trust. Physical controls also protect inventory by storing it in locked cages or warehouses; small assets such as tools or supplies by locking them in cabinets; and cash by locking it in vaults or safes.

DOCUMENTS AND RECORDS   The fifth control procedure involves using *documents or records* to create a record of transactions and an audit trail. Documents rarely serve as preventive controls, but they do provide excellent detective tools. Banks, for example, prepare kiting-suspect reports as well as reports of employee bank account activity to detect abuse by employees or customers. Most companies require a customer order to initiate a sales transaction. In a sense, the entire accounting system serves as a documentary control. Without documents, no accountability exists. Without accountability, it is much easier to perpetrate fraud and not get caught.

Summary of the Controls That Prevent or Detect Fraud

The control environment, the accounting system, and the many variations of the five control activities work together to eliminate or reduce the opportunity for employees and others to commit fraud. A good control environment establishes an atmosphere in which proper behavior is modeled and labeled, honest employees are hired, and all employees understand their job responsibilities. The accounting system provides records that make it difficult for perpetrators to gain access to assets, to conceal frauds, and to convert stolen assets without being discovered. Together, these three components make up the control structure of an organization. Exhibit 900.4 summarizes these components and their elements.

Exhibit 900.4   *Summary of Internal Control Structure*

Control Environment	Accounting System	Control Activities
1. Management philosophy and operating style, modeling	1. Valid transactions	1. Segregation of duties
2. Effective hiring procedures	2. Properly authorized	2. Proper procedures for authorization
3. Clear organizational structure of proper modeling and labeling	3. Completeness	3. Independent checks on performance
4. Effective internal audit department	4. Proper classification	4. Physical control over assets and records
	5. Proper timing	5. Adequate documents and records
	6. Proper valuation	
	7. Correct summarization	

Unfortunately, many frauds are perpetrated in environments in which controls that are supposed to be in place are not being followed. Indeed, it is the overriding and ignoring of existing controls, not the lack of controls, that allow most frauds to be perpetrated. Next, we will discuss noncontrol factors influencing fraud.

Noncontrol Factors Influencing Fraud

Noncontrol Factor: Inability to Judge the Quality of Performance

If you pay someone to construct a fence, you can examine the completed job and determine whether or not the quality of work meets your specifications and is consistent with the agreed contract. If, however, you hire a lawyer, a doctor, a dentist, an accountant, an engineer, or an auto mechanic, it is often difficult to know whether you are paying an excessive amount or receiving inferior service or products. With these kinds of contracts, it is easy to overcharge, perform work not needed, provide inferior service, or charge for work not performed.

Noncontrol Factor: Failure to Discipline Fraud Perpetrators

Fraudsters are repeat offenders who are neither prosecuted nor disciplined. An individual who commits fraud and is not punished or is merely terminated suffers no significant penalty and often resumes the fraudulent behavior.

Fraud perpetrators often command respect in their jobs, communities, churches, and families. If they are marginally sanctioned or terminated, they rarely inform their families and others of the real reason for their termination or punishment. On the other hand, if they are prosecuted, they usually suffer significant embarrassment when family, friends, and business associates find out about their offenses. Indeed, humiliation is often the strongest factor in deterring future fraud activity.

Because of the expense and time involved in prosecuting, many organizations simply dismiss dishonest employees, hoping to rid themselves of the problem. What these organizations fail to realize is that such action is shortsighted. They may rid themselves of one fraudster, but they have also sent a message to others in the organization that perpetrators will not suffer significant consequences for their actions. Indeed, lack of prosecution gives others "perceived opportunity" that, when combined with pressure and rationalization, can result in additional frauds in the organization. Perceived opportunity is removed when employees understand that perpetrators will be punished according to the law, not merely terminated.

In a society in which workers are mobile and often move from job to job, termination often helps perpetrators build an attractive resume, but it does not deter future fraud.

Noncontrol Factor: Lack of Access to Information

Many frauds occur because victims don't have access to information possessed by the perpetrators. This is especially prevalent in large management frauds that are perpetrated against stockholders, investors, and debt holders.

Most investment scams and management frauds depend on their ability to withhold information from victims. Individuals can attempt to protect themselves against such scams by insisting on full disclosure, including audited financial statements, a business history, and other information that could reveal the fraudulent nature of such organizations.

Noncontrol Factor: Ignorance, Apathy, and Incapacity

Older people, individuals with language difficulties, and other vulnerable citizens are often victims of fraud because perpetrators know that such individuals may not have the capacity or the knowledge to detect their illegal acts. Vulnerable people are, unfortunately, easier to deceive.

Noncontrol Factor: Lack of an Audit Trail

Organizations go to great lengths to create documents that provide an audit trail so that transactions can be reconstructed and understood at a later time. Many frauds, however, involve cash payments or manipulation of records that cannot be followed. Smart perpetrators understand that their frauds must be concealed. They also know that such concealment usually involves manipulation of financial records. When faced with a decision about which financial record to manipulate, perpetrators almost always manipulate the income statement, because they understand that the audit trail will quickly be erased. This is because income statement accounts start with zero every year.

Fighting Fraud: An Overview

The four activities of fighting fraud include (1) fraud prevention, (2) fraud detection, (3) fraud investigation, and (4) fraud resolution (follow-up legal action). Comprehensive fraud programs focus on all four. Investigation and resolution are the least effective and most expensive fraud-fighting efforts.

Fraud Prevention

Preventing fraud is the most cost-effective way to reduce losses from fraud. Once a fraud has been committed, there are no winners. Perpetrators lose—they suffer humiliation and legal consequences. They must make tax and restitution payments, and they also face financial penalties and other consequences. Victims lose—assets have been stolen and they must now incur legal fees, lost time, negative publicity, and other adverse consequences. Organizations and individuals that install proactive fraud-prevention measures find that the measures pay big dividends. Because investigating fraud can be very expensive, *preventing* it is crucial.

As we noted earlier, people commit fraud because of three factors: (1) perceived pressure, (2) perceived opportunity, and (3) some way to rationalize the fraud as acceptable. When perceived pressures and opportunities are high, a person needs less rationalization to commit fraud. When perceived pressures and opportunities are low, a person needs more rationalization. Unfortunately, sometimes pressures and/or the ability to rationalize are so high that, no matter how hard an organization tries to prevent fraud, theft still occurs. Indeed, fraud is often impossible to prevent, especially in a cost-effective way. The best an organization can hope for is to minimize the costs of fraud.

Certain organizations have significantly higher levels of employee fraud and are more susceptible to fraudulent financial reporting. Research consistently shows that almost all organizations have fraud of one type or another.[14] Only those organizations that carefully examine their risk for fraud and take proactive steps to create the right kind of environment succeed in preventing fraud.

Fraud prevention involves two fundamental activities: (1) creating and maintaining a culture of honesty and integrity and (2) assessing and mitigating the risk of fraud and developing concrete responses to minimize risk and eliminate opportunity.

Creating and Maintaining a Culture of Honesty and Integrity

There are several ways to create such a culture: (1) insist that top management model appropriate behavior, (2) hire the right kind of employees, (3) communicate expectations throughout the organization and require periodic written confirmation of acceptance of those expectations, (4) create a positive work environment, and (5) develop and maintain effective policies for punishing perpetrators once fraud occurs.

Research in moral development strongly suggests that honesty is reinforced when proper examples are set—sometimes referred to as "the tone at the top."[15] Management cannot act one way and expect others in the organization to behave differently. Management must reinforce through its own actions that dishonest, questionable, or unethical behavior will not be tolerated.

The second element is hiring the right employees. People are not equally honest, nor do they embrace equally well-developed personal codes of ethics. In fact, research indicates that many people, when faced with significant pressure and opportunity, will behave dishonestly rather than face the "negative consequences" of honest behavior (for example, loss of reputation or esteem, failure to meet quotas or expectations, exposure of inadequate performance, inability to pay debts, and so on). If an organization is to be successful in preventing fraud, it must have effective hiring policies that distinguish between marginal and highly ethical individuals, especially when they recruit for high-risk positions. Proactive hiring procedures include such things as conducting background investigations on prospective employees, thoroughly checking references and learning how to interpret responses to inquiries about candidates, and testing for honesty and other attributes.

The third critical element—communicating expectations—includes (1) identifying appropriate values and ethics, (2) fraud-awareness training that helps employees understand potential problems they may encounter and how to resolve or report them, and (3) communicating consistent punishment of violators. For codes of conduct to be effective, they must be written and communicated to employees, vendors, and customers. They must also be developed in such a manner that management and employees "own" them. Requiring employees to confirm in writing that they understand the organization's expectations goes a long way toward creating a culture of honesty. In fact, many organizations have found that annual written confirmations are very effective in both preventing frauds and detecting them before they become large. The punishment for fraud must be clearly communicated by top management throughout the organization. For example, a strong statement from management that dishonest actions will not be tolerated and that violators will be terminated and prosecuted to the fullest extent of the law does help prevent fraud.

The fourth element in creating an honesty-driven culture involves developing a positive work environment. Research indicates that fraud occurs less frequently when employees have feelings of ownership toward their organization than when they feel abused, threatened, or ignored by it.[16] Factors associated with high levels of fraud that detract from a positive work environment include the following:

1. Top management does not care about or pay attention to appropriate behavior.
2. Negative feedback and lack of recognition of job performance are present.
3. Perceived inequities exist in the organization.
4. Autocratic rather than participative management is present.
5. There is low organizational loyalty.
6. Budget expectations are perceived as unreasonable.
7. Pay is unrealistically low.
8. Poor training and promotion opportunities are present.
9. There is high turnover and/or absenteeism.
10. Organizational responsibilities are unclear.
11. There are poor communication practices within the organization.

The last critical element is the organization's policy for handling fraud once it occurs. No matter how well developed the culture of honesty and integrity in an organization, it is still likely to experience some fraud. How the organization reacts to incidents of fraud sends a strong signal that affects the rate at which future incidents occur. An effective policy for handling fraud assures that the facts are investigated thoroughly, firm and consistent actions are taken against perpetrators, risks and controls are assessed and improved, and communication and training are ongoing.

Assessing and Mitigating the Risk of Fraud

Neither fraud committed by top management on behalf of an organization nor fraud committed against an organization can occur without opportunity. Organizations can eliminate opportunity by (1) accurately identifying sources and measuring risks; (2) implementing appropriate preventative and detective controls; (3) creating widespread monitoring by employees; and (4) installing independent checks, including an effective audit function.

Identifying sources and measuring risk means that an organization needs a process in place that both defines areas of greatest risk and evaluates and tests controls that minimize those risks. In identifying risk, organizations should consider organizational, industry, and country-specific characteristics that encourage and discourage fraud.

Risks that are inherent in the environment of an organization can be addressed with an appropriate system of control. Once risks have been assessed, the organization can identify processes, controls, and other procedures that can minimize risks. Appropriate internal systems include well-developed control environments, effective accounting systems, and appropriate control procedures.

Research has shown that employees and managers—not auditors—detect most frauds.[17] Therefore, employees and managers must be taught how to watch for and recognize fraud. To involve employees in the all-important monitoring process, provide a protocol for communication. Such protocol details to whom employees should report suspected fraud and what form their communication should take. The protocol should assure confidentiality and stress that retribution will not be tolerated. Organizations that are serious about fraud prevention must make it easy for employees and managers to come forward and must reward (not punish) them for doing so.

Fraud Detection

Most frauds start small and, if not detected, continue to get larger and larger. Events that scare or threaten the perpetrator result in discontinuance of the theft, which is then resumed when the threats pass. Because those that commit fraud increase the amounts they steal, in most cases, amounts taken just before discovery far exceed those taken earlier. In one case, the amounts taken *quadrupled* every month during the period of the fraud! Indeed, small frauds are just large frauds that got caught early. And, in cases where top management or owners are perpetrating the fraud, prevention is difficult, so early detection is critical.

When fraud is committed by owners of small organizations, who perform the accounting tasks themselves, fraud is not preventable. If owners commit fraud, there is nothing anyone can do to stop them. Rather, the emphasis in these situations must be on detecting the fraud.

Because most frauds increase dramatically over time, it is extremely important that frauds, when they occur, be detected early. Detection, of course, involves steps and actions taken to uncover a fraud. It does not include investigations taken to determine motives, extent, method of embezzlement, or other elements of the theft. Fraud is unlike other crimes in which the occurrence of the crime is easily recognized. Because fraud is rarely obvious, one of the most difficult tasks is determining whether one has actually occurred.

Detection usually begins when employees, managers, or victims notice "red flags," symptoms such as disturbing trends in numbers or missing assets that indicate something is awry. Unfortunately, red flags don't always mean that fraud is occurring. There are two primary ways to detect fraud: (1) by chance and (2) by proactively searching for and encouraging early recognition of symptoms. In the past, most frauds were detected by accident. Unfortunately, by the time detection occurred, the frauds had been going on for some time and the losses were large. In most cases, individuals in the victim organizations suspected that fraud was occurring but did not come forward because they weren't sure, didn't want to wrongly accuse someone, didn't know how to report the fraud, or were fearful of being branded a whistle-blower.

In recent years, organizations have implemented a number of initiatives to better detect fraud. Probably the most common detection initiative has been hotlines whereby employees, coworkers, and others can phone in anonymous tips. Some hotlines are maintained within the company, and others are outsourced to independent organizations. Organizations that have installed hotlines now detect many frauds that would previously have gone undetected, but they also pay a price for doing so. Not surprisingly, many calls do not involve fraud at all. Some are hoaxes; some are motivated by grudges, anger, or a desire to do harm to an organization or individual; and some are about reasonable red flags that are caused by factors other than fraud.

Except for hotlines, organizations have only recently undertaken other serious proactive detection efforts. Advances in technology now allow organizations to analyze and mine databases to search for red flags. Banks, for example, use software that identifies suspected kiting. These programs draw the bank's attention to customers who have high volumes of bank transactions in short periods of time. Insurance companies use programs that examine claims within a short time after purchasing insurance. Some programs systematically identify the kinds of frauds that may be occurring by cataloging the various symptoms those frauds generate, and then building real-time queries into their computer systems to search for these symptoms.

Fraud Investigation

Investigation should be based on a "predication of fraud." *Predication* refers to circumstances that, taken as a whole, would lead a reasonable, prudent professional to believe a fraud has occurred, is occurring, or will occur. Fraud investigations should not be conducted without predication. A specific allegation of fraud against another party is not necessary, but there must be some reasonable basis for concern that fraud may be occurring. Once predication is present, an investigation is usually undertaken to determine whether or not fraud is occurring, as well as the who, why, how, when, and where elements of the fraud. The purpose of an investigation is to find the truth—to determine whether the symptoms actually represent fraud or whether they represent unintentional errors or other factors. Fraud investigation is a complex and sensitive matter. If investigations are not properly conducted, the reputations of innocent individuals can be irreparably injured, guilty parties can go undetected and be free to repeat the act, and the offended entity may not have information to use in preventing and detecting similar incidents or in recovering damages.

Approaches to Fraud Investigation

Investigations must have management's approval. Because they can be quite expensive, investigations should be pursued only when there is reason to believe that fraud has occurred (when predication is present). Investigative approaches vary, although most investigators rely heavily on interviews.

Fraud investigations can be classified by the types of evidence produced or by the elements of fraud. Using the first approach, the *evidence square* below shows the four classifications of evidence.

The four types of evidence that can be collected in fraud investigations are as follows:

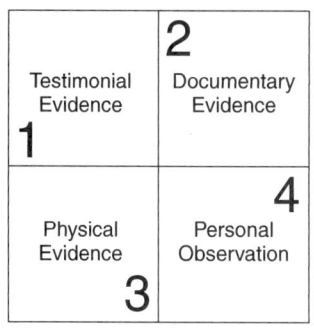

1. *Testimonial evidence,* which is gathered from individuals. Specific investigative techniques used to gather testimonial evidence include interviewing, interrogation, and honesty tests.
2. *Documentary evidence,* which is gathered from paper, computers, and other written or printed sources. Some of the most common techniques for gathering this evidence include document examination, public records searches, audits, computer searches, net worth calculations, and financial statement analysis.
3. *Physical evidence* includes fingerprints, tire marks, weapons, stolen property, identification numbers or marks on stolen objects, and other tangible evidence that can be associated with the act. The gathering of physical evidence often involves forensic analysis by experts.
4. *Personal observation* involves evidence that is collected by the investigators themselves, including *invigilation,* surveillance, and covert operations, among others.

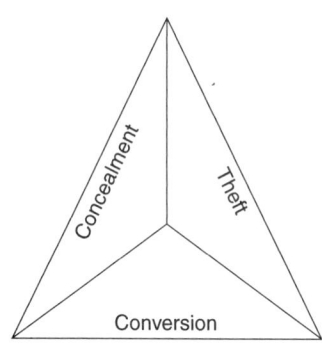

Many professionals prefer to classify investigative approaches according to the three elements of fraud, as shown in the triangle.

Investigation of the theft involves efforts to catch the perpetrator(s) in the act itself and information-gathering efforts. Investigation of the concealment focuses on records, documents, computer programs and servers, and other places where perpetrators might try to conceal or hide their deceit. Investigation of the conversion involves searching out the ways in which perpetrators have spent the stolen assets. A fourth set of investigative techniques, *inquiry methods,* has to do with the overall approach as it applies to all these elements. Thus, this approach to classifying investigative techniques is called the *fraud triangle plus inquiry approach.*

Conducting a Fraud Investigation

It is important to know that fraud investigators need some way to coordinate the investigation. Some investigations are very large and conducting investigative steps in the wrong order or doing them inappropriately can lead to a failed investigation and other problems. In fact, it is extremely important that you understand the significant risks that investigators face.

You must also remember that investigating a fraud is a traumatic experience for everyone involved, including the perpetrators. As we stated previously, most fraud perpetrators are first-time offenders who have pristine reputations at work, and in their community, family, and church. Sometimes, admitting that they are being investigated for fraud or have committed fraud is more than they can take.

Maintaining high ethics in conducting investigations is also important. As a minimum, investigations of fraud must proceed as follows:

1. They must be undertaken only to "establish the truth of a matter under question."
2. The individuals who conduct the investigation must be experienced and objective. If such individuals do not exercise care in choosing words to describe the incident or do not maintain a neutral perspective, their objectivity immediately becomes suspect in the eyes of management and employees. Investigators should never jump to conclusions.
3. Any hypothesis investigators have about whether or not someone committed fraud should be closely guarded when discussing the progress of an investigation with others. Even though good investigators often form preliminary opinions or impressions, they must objectively weigh every bit of information against known facts and evidence and must always protect the confidentiality of the investigation.
4. Investigators must ensure that those who have a need to know (for example, management) are kept apprised of investigation activities and agree to the investigation and techniques employed.
5. Good investigators must ensure that all information collected during an inquiry is independently corroborated and determined to be factually correct. Failure to corroborate evidence is a common mistake of inexperienced investigators.

6. Investigators must exercise care to avoid questionable investigative techniques. Experienced investigators make sure that the techniques used are scientifically and legally sound and fair. Thoroughness and dogged tenacity, not questionable techniques, lead to successful conclusions.

7. Investigators must report all facts fairly and objectively. Communications throughout the term of an investigation, from preliminary stage to final report, should be carefully controlled to avoid obscuring facts and opinions. Communications, including investigative reports, must not only include information obtained that points to guilt, but must also include facts and information that may exonerate someone. Ignoring and failing to document information is a serious investigative flaw, with potential for serious consequences.

Fraud Resolution

One of the major decisions a company, stockholders, and others must make when fraud is committed is what kind of follow-up action should be taken. Why the fraud occurred should always be determined, and controls or other measures to prevent or deter its reoccurrence should be implemented. The bigger and often troubling question that must then be addressed is what legal action should be taken with respect to the perpetrators.

Most organizations and other victims of fraud usually make one of three choices: (1) take no legal action; (2) pursue civil remedies; and/or (3) pursue criminal action against the perpetrators, which is sometimes done for them by law enforcement agencies.

Take No Legal Action

Research shows that legal action is taken against perpetrators in less than half of all fraud cases.[18] Management often wants only to get the fraud behind it as quickly as possible. They understand that pursuing legal action is expensive, time-consuming, sometimes embarrassing, and is often *considered* an unproductive use of time. Thus, management most often terminates perpetrators, but sometimes it doesn't even go that far. Unfortunately, when organizations do not pursue legal action, the word spreads quickly that "nothing serious will happen if you steal from the company." Employees who receive this message are more likely to steal than are employees who understand that punishment "to the letter of the law" will follow for all dishonest acts. When one Fortune 500 company changed its stance on fraud from "the CEO is to be informed when someone is prosecuted for fraud" to "the CEO is to be informed when someone who commits fraud is not prosecuted," the number of frauds in the company decreased significantly.

Pursue Civil Action

The purpose of a civil action is to recover money or other assets from the perpetrators and others associated with the fraud. Civil actions are quite rare in cases of employee fraud (because perpetrators have usually spent the money), but are much more common when frauds involve other organizations. Vendors who pay kickbacks to company employees often find themselves the target of civil actions by victim companies, especially if losses are high. Likewise, stockholders and creditors who suffer losses from management fraud almost always sue not only the perpetrators, but usually the auditors and others associated with the company as well. The plaintiff's lawyers are usually more than willing to represent shareholders in a class-action, contingent-fee lawsuit.[19]

Pursue Criminal Action

Criminal action can only be brought by law enforcement or statutory agencies. Organizations that decide to pursue criminal action against perpetrators must work with local, state, or federal agencies to get their employees or other perpetrators prosecuted. Criminal penalties involve fines, prison terms, or both. Perpetrators may be required to enter into restitution agreements to pay back stolen funds over a period of time. Pursuing criminal penalties for fraud is becoming more and more common. Corporate executives who commit fraud are often given 10-year jail sentences and are ordered to pay fines equal to the amounts they embezzled. However, it is much more difficult to get a criminal conviction than it is to get a judgment in a civil case. Whereas only a preponderance of the evidence (more than 50 percent) is necessary to win a civil case, convictions are only successful if there is proof "beyond a reasonable doubt" that the perpetrator "intentionally" stole money or other assets.

Financial Shenanigans

What Are Financial Shenanigans?

Financial fraud causes great harm to individuals, to companies, and to society at large. Financial shenanigans (a form of financial fraud) are actions or omissions intended to hide or distort the real financial performance or financial condition of a business entity. They range from minor deceptions (such as failing to segregate operating gains and losses from nonoperating gains and losses) to more serious misapplication of accounting principles (such as failing to write off worthless assets), and outright fraudulent behavior (such as the recording of fictitious revenue to overstate an entity's real financial performance).[20]

Why Do Shenanigans Exist?

There are three general reasons for shenanigans: (1) it pays to do it, (2) it is easy to do it, and (3) it is unlikely that perpetrators will get caught (at least in the short term).

1. *It pays to do it.* When a bonus plan encourages managers to post higher sales and profits (with no questions asked about how those gains were achieved), it may create an incentive for using shenanigans. Misguided incentive plans should be revisited.
2. *It is easy to do it.* Honest managers select accounting methods from a variety of acceptable choices to portray fairly the company's financial performance. Unscrupulous managers use the flexibility offered in generally accepted accounting principles (GAAP) to distort financial reports.
3. *It is unlikely that perpetrators will get caught.* Companies may use accounting tricks because they believe that they will not get caught by auditors or regulators. Consider that only the annual financial statements of publicly held companies are audited by an independent, certified public accountant. Privately held companies are not required to be audited.

The Seven Shenanigans

Companies with a weak "control environment"—those that lack independent members of the board, a competent independent auditor, or an adequate internal audit function—have a greater tendency toward committing shenanigans than others.

Financial shenanigans, which permit companies to manipulate net income, may be separated into seven broad categories. The first five boost current-year profits; the last two shift current-year profits to the future.

1. Recording revenue too soon to show more sales
2. Recording bogus revenue to show more income
3. Boosting income with one-time gains to show more income
4. Shifting current expenses to a later period to show more income
5. Failing to record or disclose all liabilities to show more assets
6. Shifting current income to a later period to minimize taxes
7. Shifting future expenses to the current period to show less income

Shenanigan Prevention Techniques

The primary shenanigan prevention strategies available to the board of directors are to improve the company's incentive structure (to motivate) and to strengthen its control environment (to monitor). Specific prevention techniques include the following:

1. Structure managers' incentives to reward honest financial reporting and to punish any activities that might constitute or contribute to financial shenanigans.
2. Establish and encourage managers to adopt conservative accounting principles and policies.
3. Appoint outside board members as watchdogs over senior management and corporate officers, with wide-ranging and early access to corporate financial data.
4. Appoint both internal auditors and independent auditors and assign them the mission of preventing and detecting shenanigans. Grant internal auditors both the power and the security to communicate directly with outside board members about their findings.
5. Establish a senior-level audit committee with the same mission of preventing and detecting shenanigans.

Shenanigan Detection Techniques

Sometimes, even the best intentions and the most comprehensive preventive measures fail, and gimmicks begin to spread. Shenanigan detection approaches include both general attention to certain "red flags" and detailed review of particular data from the company's financial statements.

At a general level, warning signs of a financially troubled business that might be resorting to financial shenanigans or prone to committing them include the following:

1. Weak internal control environment
2. Inadequate outside checks and balances
3. Vulnerability to external influences
4. Poor organizational culture
5. Convoluted financial, legal, and organizational structure
6. Shortage of "free" cash flows from operations
7. Unusually low or high operating revenues
8. Profits out of line with current sales and with previous quarters and years
9. Inventories and receivables out of balance with sales
10. Too many "irregular" events

Role of Directors in Controlling Corporate Fraud

Corporate directors have a direct liability in fraudulent activities perpetrated against a corporation. They have the power to control fraud with their position in the company. They should look for early warning signs from financial statements such as uncollectibility of receivables, inadequate salability of inventory, improper valuation of investments, obsolescence of fixed assets, overstatement of intangibles, and unreported or underreported liabilities. By taking proper steps to prevent and detect shenanigans, the board of directors can not only shield itself from undue liability but also contribute toward a more ethical corporate world.

Corporate Risk Management

Introduction to Risk

Risk, which is often used to mean "uncertainty," creates both problems and opportunities for businesses and individuals in nearly every walk of life. Executives, employees, investors, students, householders, travelers, and farmers all confront risk and deal with it in various ways. Sometimes a particular risk is consciously analyzed and managed; other times risk is simply ignored, perhaps out of lack of knowledge of its consequences.

Risk regarding the possibility of loss can be especially problematical. If a loss is certain to occur, it may be planned for in advance and treated as a definite, known expense. It is when there is uncertainty about the occurrence of a loss that risk becomes an important problem. Thus, if a store owner knows for sure that a certain amount of shoplifting will occur, this loss may be recovered by marking up all goods by the necessary percentage. There is little or no risk involved unless actual shoplifting is greater than normal. The store is more concerned about the risk of abnormal shoplifting losses than about those viewed as normal or expected.

The Burden of Risk

The idea of risk bearing can be tantalizing. After all, it is a well-known investment principle that the largest potential returns are associated with the riskiest ventures. There are some risks, however, that involve only the possibility of loss. For example, businesses located near the Mississippi River confront the possibility of periodic flooding. When a flood occurs, loss caused by property damage and lost revenues is likely. On the other hand, no gain is expected merely because in some years a flood does not occur.

The risk surrounding potential losses creates significant economic burdens for businesses, government, and individuals. Billions of dollars are spent each year on strategies for financing potential losses. But when losses are not planned for in advance, they may cost even more. For example, a multimillion-dollar adverse liability judgment may reduce a business's profitability, lower its credit ratings, cause a loss of customers, and perhaps result in bankruptcy if the firm has not made adequate plans to pay for the loss.

Risk of loss may also deprive society of services judged to be too risky, such as medicine and law. Similarly, businesses of all types may be reluctant to engage in projects that are otherwise strategically attractive if the potential losses appear to be unmanageable.

Businesses, as well as individuals, may try either to avoid risk of loss as much as possible or to reduce its negative consequences. Overall, an entity's **cost of risk** is the sum of: (1) expenses of strategies to finance potential losses, (2) the cost of unreimbursed losses, (3) outlays to reduce risks, and (4) the opportunity cost of activities forgone due to risk considerations. For a particular firm, the first two components of the cost of risk are often the easiest to measure. To minimize the cost of risk efficiently, one must study the subject of risk, learn more about the different types of risk, and find ways to deal with risk more effectively.

Definitions of Risk

Thus far, the terms *risk* and *uncertainty* have been used interchangeably. However, many forms of uncertainty exist and, in a comprehensive study of risk, it is helpful to define the concept more precisely. Three common groups to classify risk are described in this section. As illustrated in Exhibit 900.5, these groupings are not mutually exclusive. Rather, risks can be categorized simultaneously according to all three types of classifications.

Pure Versus Speculative Risk

An important classification of risk involves the concepts of pure risk and speculative risk. **Pure risk** exists when there is uncertainty as to whether loss will occur. No possibility of gain is presented by pure risk—only the potential for

Exhibit 900.5 *Types of Risk*

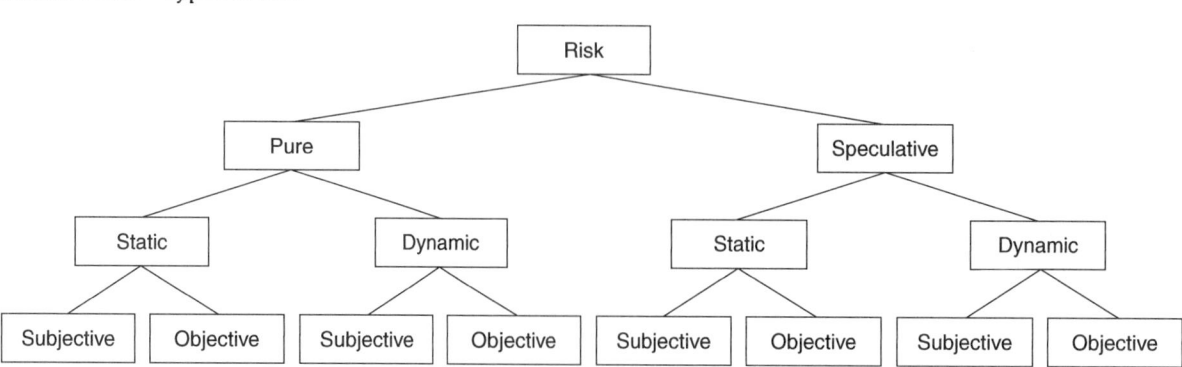

loss. Examples of pure risk include the uncertainty of damage to property by fire or flood or the prospect of premature death caused by accident or illness. In contrast to pure risk, **speculative risk** exists when there is uncertainty about an event that could produce either a profit or a loss. Business ventures and investment decisions are examples of situations involving speculative risk. Gains as well as losses may occur, changing the nature of the uncertainty that is present.

Both pure and speculative risks may be present in some situations. It is important to recognize that many profit-motivated, speculative-risk decisions made by individuals and firms can have an impact on pure risk exposures. For example, a firm purchasing land for development is making a decision that entails speculative risk. However, if after the purchase it discovers that the land contains a latent pollution problem, the firm would then face a new pure risk. Another example is the decision that a firm makes to introduce a new product. This decision may represent primarily a speculative risk. But as has been seen for products like asbestos and silicon breast implants, this decision also is accompanied by the pure risk associated with potential product liability. Failure to consider the overlapping effects of these two types of risk can lead to decisions that overstate the potential benefits to the firm.

Static Versus Dynamic Risk

Another way of classifying risk involves the extent to which uncertainty changes over time. **Static risks,** which can be either pure or speculative, stem from an unchanging society that is in stable equilibrium. Examples of pure static risks include the uncertainties due to such random events as lightning, windstorms, and death. Business undertakings in a stable economy illustrate the concept of speculative static risk. In contrast, **dynamic risks** are produced because of changes in society. Dynamic risks also can be either pure or speculative. Examples of sources of dynamic risk include urban unrest, increasingly complex technology, and changing attitudes of legislatures and courts about a variety of issues.

Static and dynamic risks are not independent; greater dynamic risks may increase some types of static risks. An example involves uncertainty due to weather-related losses. This risk is usually considered to be static. However, recent evidence suggests that environmental pollution caused by increased industrialization may be affecting global weather patterns and thereby increasing this source of static risk.

Subjective Versus Objective Risk

A third way to classify risk is by whether it is objective or subjective. **Subjective risk** refers to the mental state of an individual who experiences doubt or worry as to the outcome of a given event. In addition to being subjective, a particular risk may also be either pure or speculative and either static or dynamic. Subjective risk is essentially the psychological uncertainty that arises from an individual's mental attitude or state of mind. **Objective risk** differs from subjective risk primarily in the sense that it is more precisely observable and therefore measurable. In general, objective risk is the probable variation of the actual experience from the expected experience. This term is most often used in connection with pure static risks, although it can also be applied to the other types of uncertainties. Details regarding measurement of objective risk are included later in this section.

The concept of subjective risk is especially important because it provides a way to interpret the behavior of individuals faced with seemingly identical situations yet arriving at different decisions. For example, one person may be ultraconservative and tend always to take the "safe way" out, even in cases that may seem quite risk-free to other decision makers. Objective risk may actually be the same in two cases but may be viewed very differently by those examining this risk from their own perspectives. Thus, it is not enough to know only the degree of objective risk; the attitude toward risk of the person who will act on the basis of this knowledge must also be known.

Sources of Risk

The emphasis of this section is on pure risks. The array of pure risks encountered is vast. Some of these risks are static, while many others are extremely dynamic. This section briefly describes the common sources of pure risks, which include **property risks; liability risks;** and **life, health, and loss of income risks,** with some consideration also given to financial risks of a speculative nature.

Property Risks

All businesses and individuals that own, rent, or use property are exposed to the risk that the property may be damaged, destroyed, or stolen. For example, lightning may strike a building, causing a fire that destroys the structure and the inventory, supplies, and equipment inside. Property owned or used outside of the building may also be susceptible to loss. Typical examples include trucks, automobiles, and mobile equipment. To fully analyze property risk exposures, businesses must consider both the types of property susceptible to loss and the potential sources of such risk. Sources include not only fire and lightning but also theft, tornadoes, hurricanes, explosions, riots, collisions, falling objects, floods, earthquakes, and freezing, to name only a few.

If property damage is extensive, a business may be forced to shut down temporarily, thereby incurring a loss of income in addition to the expense of replacing the damaged property. But in some instances involving severe property damage, management may decide that temporarily closing the business is not a viable option. For example, Rocky Mountain Bank likely would never regain its customers if it were to close for several months following a fire and not allow its customers to transact necessary banking business. In this situation, the bank would probably incur the extra expenses necessary to continue operations from a different location while repairs were made to its own premises.

In addition to risks arising out of property they own and/or use, businesses also are exposed to risks associated with property owned or used by other firms. Another illustration of losses to one business affecting another business involves companies selling primarily over the Internet. Such firms typically utilize others to make deliveries to their customers and could suffer significant losses if the delivery firms were unable to perform.

Liability Risks

A second major category of risks is liability exposure. U.S. society has become increasingly litigious in recent years, with businesses and individuals often held financially liable for damages resulting from a vast and expanding array of situations. Liability judgments may result in payments made to compensate injured parties as well as to punish those responsible for the injuries, with multimillion-dollar awards no longer rare. Even when an individual is eventually absolved of liability, the expenses involved in defending a case often prove to be substantial. Consequently, both individuals and businesses must be careful to identify all sources of liability risk that may affect them and then make suitable arrangements for dealing with such exposures to loss.

Life, Health, and Loss of Income Risks

Potential losses associated with the health and well-being of individuals make up the third and final category of sources of risk. The possibility of the untimely death of a star salesperson exposes the person's employer to potential loss if a replacement with the same skills and experience is not readily available. Even if the salesperson could be easily replaced, in many cases employee deaths are disruptive for other workers and may result in temporarily reduced productivity. This phenomenon is especially true if the death is due to job-related conditions.

Businesses and individuals also face risks associated with health problems. Persons who become ill or who are injured in accidents will incur expenses for medical treatment, and the cost of such treatment is becoming increasingly expensive. Sometimes businesses arrange to pay some or all of such expenses for their employees, regardless of whether a sickness or injury is job related. As medical costs increase, however, more and more individuals (whether employed or not) must pay substantial sums each year for medical care for themselves and their families. In addition to these expenses, there is another potential loss associated with sickness and accidents. If a previously employed individual is severely injured or gravely ill, that person may be unable to work for several months or even years. The resultant loss of income can have serious repercussions on the financial stability of the person and family involved.

Other risks that confront an employed individual are those associated with unemployment and retirement. Both events result in the loss of an income source that previously existed. A significant difference, however, relates to timing. Retirement usually is not a surprise and therefore presents many options for advance planning. In contrast, abrupt layoffs often are not expected and are therefore harder to plan for ahead of time. Through pension and other retirement benefits, as well as unemployment insurance provided in each state, businesses are also affected by these risks that their employees face.

Financial Risk

Although the major emphasis of this section is on pure risks, it is increasingly important that risks from other sources be considered as well. A variety of **financial risks,** which often are speculative in nature, can impact on a firm's earnings. Examples of these financial risks include credit risk, foreign exchange risk, commodity risk, and interest rate risk. Although most of these financial risks tend to have the characteristics of speculative risks, they still present the firm with some of the same problems associated with pure risks. Although the techniques used to manage these risks may be very different from those used to manage pure risks, it remains critical that these risks be identified and assessed in order for the firm to achieve its business goals.

Measurement of Risk

Once risk sources have been identified, it is often helpful to measure the extent of the risk that exists. As noted earlier, risks that are classified as subjective cannot be precisely measured. In contrast, the amount of objective risk is often more readily observable. Several important concepts related to the measurement of objective risk are discussed in this section.

Chance of Loss

The long-term chance of occurrence, or relative frequency of loss, is defined to be the **chance of loss.** The concept has little meaning if applied to the chance of occurrence of a single event. Rather, it is meaningful primarily when applied to the chance of a loss occurring among a large number of possible events. Thus, chance of loss is expressed as the ratio of the number of losses that are likely to occur compared to the larger number of possible losses in a given group. For example, suppose 1,000 buildings in a particular city are considered to be susceptible to the risk of loss due to a tornado. If past experience indicates that 20 of these buildings are likely to be damaged by a tornado during a given time period, then the chance of loss due to a tornado is 2 percent. This number is determined by dividing the probable number of losses (20) by the number of buildings exposed to loss (1,000).

In making chance of loss calculations, it is common practice to perform separate computations for different causes of loss. In this sense, the term **peril** is used to describe a specific contingency that may cause a loss. For example, one of the perils that can cause loss to an automobile is collision. Other perils are illustrated by considering ways in which a building can be damaged; examples include fires, tornadoes, and explosions. Sometimes conditions exist that either increase the chance of loss from particular perils or tend to make the loss more severe once the peril has occurred. Such conditions are known as **hazards** and can be classified in the following three ways.

PHYSICAL HAZARD A **physical hazard** is a condition stemming from the material characteristics of an object. Consider the peril of collision, which may cause loss to an automobile. A physical condition that makes the occurrence of collision more likely is an icy street. The icy street is the hazard, and the collision is the peril. The chance of loss due to collision may be higher in winter than at other times of the year because of the greater incidence of the physical hazard of icy streets.

Physical hazards include such phenomena as the existence of dry forests (a hazard affecting the peril of fire), earth faults (a hazard for earthquakes), and the existence of oily rags in a firm's storage closet (a hazard for fire). Such hazards may or may not be within human control. For example, the oily rag hazard can easily be eliminated. Other physical hazards, such as weather conditions, usually cannot be controlled, although their existence often may be observed.

MORALE HAZARD The mental attitude of a careless or accident-prone person is known as **morale hazard.** Sometimes a subconscious desire for a loss may exist, even though the individual is not fully aware of this desire. In other cases, circumstances may cause someone to be indifferent to the possibility of a loss, thus causing that person to behave in a careless manner. For example, suppose the managers of ABC Company believe the federal government will provide disaster assistance that will fully compensate ABC for all earthquake losses it may incur. In making plans for a new building near a major fault line, ABC's management may be tempted to ignore more expensive construction designs and procedures that can lessen damage from earthquakes. In essence, ABC's assumption regarding the potential for federal disaster aid makes its management indifferent to the prospect of loss and, therefore, more prone to make unmindful decisions.

MORAL HAZARD The condition known as **moral hazard** also stems from an individual's mental attitude. It is associated with intentional actions designed either to cause a loss or to increase its severity. Moral hazards often are typified by individuals with known records of dishonesty. In addition, the existence of insurance may sometimes exacerbate the existence of moral hazard. For example, managers who purchase fire insurance on a factory full of unprofitable, out-of-date equipment may feel an incentive to "sell the building to the insurance company" by arranging for a fire to destroy the property. Moral hazard also describes the change in attitude that can occur when insurance is available to pay for loss, such as the tendency for individuals to consume more health care if the costs are covered by insurance.

Other examples of moral hazards involve accidents and sicknesses, especially where an employer provides generous income replacement during the time an employee is unable to work. In these situations, workers who are not pleased with their jobs or who fear being laid off in the future may be inclined to suffer an "accident" or contract an "illness." Closely related to this are cases where the original accident or illness is indeed legitimate but the recovery period is intentionally extended by the injured or sick person. Reasons for such behavior include the lack of a sufficient financial incentive to return to work and the psychological satisfaction some sick persons experience from the attention and concern given to them by their family and friends.

Degree of Risk

The amount of objective risk present in a situation, sometimes referred to as the **degree of risk,** is the relative variation of actual from expected losses. More precisely, the degree of risk is the range of variability around the expected losses, which are calculated using the chance of loss concept by means of the following formula:

$$\text{Objective risk} = \frac{\text{Probable variation of actual from expected losses}}{\text{Expected losses}}$$

Consider the possibility of fire losses to buildings in Acworth and Branson. There are 100,000 buildings in each city and, on average, each city has 100 fire losses per year. By looking at historical data, statisticians are able to estimate that the actual number of fire losses in Acworth during the next year will very likely range from 95 to 105. In Branson, however, the range probably will be greater, with at least 80 fire losses expected and possibly as many as 120. The degree of risk for each city is computed as follows.

$$\text{Risk}_{Acworth} = (105 - 95) / 100 = 10\%$$
$$\text{Risk}_{Branson} = (120 - 80) / 100 = 40\%$$

As shown, the degree of risk for Branson is four times that for Acworth, even though the chances of loss are the same.

A few other observations are important regarding degree of risk and chance of loss. If a loss has already occurred, the probable variation of actual from expected losses in that particular situation is zero and, therefore, the degree of risk is zero. At the opposite extreme, if it is impossible for a loss to occur, the probable variation also is zero and the degree of risk is zero as well. Finally, in measuring the degree of risk, results are meaningful only in terms of a group large enough to analyze statistically. If the numbers involved are very small, then the range of probable variation may be so large as to seem virtually infinite when viewed in a relative sense.

To illustrate this latter point, consider the Online Action Corporation, which is concerned about the possible death of Barbara Thomas, a valuable, highly paid 24-year-old worker in its product development department. Online Action has been informed that Barbara's probability of dying during the next year is 0.3 percent. Or, using the terminology introduced in this section, the chance of loss due to the peril of death is 0.003. The degree of risk is not particularly meaningful, however, when applied only to Barbara's life. Either Barbara will die or she will not, making the relative variation of actual from expected losses extremely large.

$$\frac{(1 - 0)}{0.003} = 333.33 = 33{,}333\%$$

Management of Risk

In the previous sections, several types of risk that affect individuals and businesses were introduced, together with ways to measure the amount of objective risk present. After sources of risk are identified and measured, a decision can be made as to how the risk should be handled. A pure risk that is not identified does not disappear; the business or individual merely loses the opportunity to consciously decide on the best technique for dealing with that risk. The process used to systematically manage risk exposures is known as **risk management.**

Some persons use the term *risk management* only in connection with businesses, and often the term refers only to the management of pure risks. In this sense, the traditional risk-management goal has been to minimize the cost of pure risk to the company. But as firms broaden the ways that they view and manage many different types of risk, the need for new terminology has become apparent. The terms **integrated risk management** and **enterprise risk management** reflect the intent to manage all forms of risk, regardless of type.

Many businesses have a special department charged with overseeing the firm's risk-management activities; the head of such a department often has the title of **risk manager.** The traditional type of risk manager may be charged with minimizing the adverse impact of losses on the achievement of the company's goals. In implementing the more integrated approach to risk management, however, some firms have formed risk-management committees. Others have created a new position of **chief risk officer** (CRO) to coordinate the firm's risk-management activities, regardless of the source of the risk. As part of his or her duties, the risk manager and/or CRO is likely to be involved in many aspects of a firm's activities. Examples may include developing employee safety programs, examining planned mergers and acquisitions, analyzing investment opportunities, purchasing insurance to protect against some types of risk, and setting up pension and health plans for employees. The evolution of integrated risk management reflects a realization of the importance of coordinating the many risk-management activities of the firm in order to meet its strategic goals.

Whether the concern is with a business or an individual situation, the same general steps can be used to systematically analyze and deal with risk. Known as the **risk-management process,** these steps form the basis for the remainder of discussion. At this point they can be summarized as follows.

1. *Identify risks.* There are many potential risks that confront individuals and businesses. Therefore, the first step in the risk-management process is to identify relevant exposures to risks. This step is important not only for traditional risk management, which focuses on pure risks, but also for enterprise risk management, where much of the focus is on identifying the firm's exposures from a variety of sources, including operational, financial, and strategic activities. Objectives should be determined prior to identifying risks.

2. *Evaluate risks.* For each source of risk that is identified, an evaluation should be performed. At this stage, pure risks can be categorized as to how often associated losses are likely to occur. In addition to this evaluation of loss **frequency,** an analysis of the size, or **severity,** of the loss is helpful. Consideration should be given both to the most probable size of any losses that may occur and to the maximum possible losses that might happen. As part of the overall risk evaluation, in some situations it may be possible to measure the degree of risk in a meaningful way. In other cases, especially those involving individuals, computation of the degree of risk may not yield helpful information.

3. *Select risk-management techniques.* The results of the analyses in step 2 are used as the basis for decisions regarding ways to handle existing risks. In some situations, the best plan may be to do nothing. In other cases, sophisticated ways to finance potential losses may be arranged. The available techniques for managing risks are discussed later, together with consideration of when each technique is appropriate.

4. *Implement and review decisions.* Following a decision about the optimal methods for handling identified risks, the business or individual must implement the techniques selected. However, risk management should be an ongoing process in which prior decisions are reviewed regularly. Sometimes new risk exposures arise or significant changes in expected loss frequency or severity occur. As noted in this section, even pure risks are not necessarily static; the dynamic nature of many risks requires a continual scrutiny of past analyses and decisions.

Risk Identification and Evaluation

Risk Identification

The identification of risks and exposures to loss is perhaps the most important element of the risk-management process. Unless the sources of possible losses are recognized, it is impossible to consciously choose appropriate, efficient methods for dealing with those losses, should they occur.

A **loss exposure** is a potential loss that may be associated with a specific type of risk. Loss exposures are typically classified as to whether they result from property, liability, life, health, and loss of income or financial risks.

Approaches used by many risk managers involve loss exposure checklists, financial statement analysis, flowcharts, contract analysis, on-site inspections, and statistical analysis of past losses.

Loss-Exposure Checklists

One risk-identification tool that can be used both by businesses and by individuals is a **loss-exposure checklist,** which specifies numerous potential sources of loss from the destruction of assets and from legal liability. For each item on the checklist, the user asks the question, "Is this a potential source of loss to me or my firm?" In this way, the systematic use of loss-exposure checklists reduces the likelihood of overlooking important sources of risk. Also, checklists can be helpful not only in risk identification but also in compiling information necessary for an in-depth evaluation of risks that are identified.

Financial Statement Analysis

Another approach that can be used by businesses to identify risks is **financial statement analysis.** Using this method, all items on a firm's balance sheet and income statement are analyzed in regard to risks that may be present. By including budgets, long-range forecasts, and written strategic plans in the analysis, this method can also help identify possible future risks that may not currently exist.

To illustrate this method of risk identification, consider the asset categories included on the balance sheets of business entities. Buildings owned by a firm are usually noted on its balance sheet, and leased buildings may be noted in footnotes to the financial statements. Future building acquisitions may be noted in budgets and strategic plans. Once such present and future buildings are identified, potential losses associated with them can then be considered. The loss exposures associated with building damage may include repair costs, the value of inventories and equipment inside, loss of income while the building cannot be used, and injuries to employees and customers inside the building. If a building is leased, relevant concerns would also include the disposition of the lease if the building is destroyed, including cost estimates of alternative facilities. This example does not begin to exhaust the range of possible losses that might result from damage to a building. It does, however, illustrate the thought process that is essential to the financial statement analysis method of risk identification.

Flowcharts

A third tool—the **flowchart**—is especially useful for businesses in identifying sources of risk in their production processes. The simplified flowchart in Exhibit 900.6 illustrates how they can pinpoint areas of potential losses. The question may be asked, "What events could disrupt the even and uninterrupted flow of parts to the final assembly floor, on which the whole production process depends?" For example, where are paints and solvents kept for the activities undertaken at Stage 3 in the exhibit? Are appropriate steps being taken to safeguard these materials from fire? Are floors kept clean and free of grease that might cause spills? Are any particular dangers threatening the storage of finished products that may require special protection? If the finished products are fragile, are appropriate protective measures being taken in loading and unloading?

Only through careful inspection of the entire production process can the full range of loss exposures be identified. And for some firms, even that may not be sufficient. It may be important, for example, to expand the flowchart to include the suppliers of parts and materials, particularly if a firm's production process is dependent on only a few suppliers. Thus, if there is only one possible supplier of a crucial part, a complete risk analysis will include identification of potential losses to that supplier as well as to the firm itself. Similar situations may arise if a firm manufactures products that are purchased by only a few customers. In this case, expansion of the flowchart to include customers will help identify risks that might otherwise be overlooked.

Contract Analysis

The analysis of contracts into which the firm enters is another method for identifying potential exposures to risk. It is not unusual for contracts to state that some losses, if they occur, are to be borne by specific parties. For example, a company may require building contractors that it hires to bear the cost of any liability suits arising out of the builder's construction operations. In this way, suits that might otherwise be directed against the hiring firm will be directed against the builder.

This type of **contractual liability** may be found not only in construction contracts but also in sales contracts and lease agreements. For example, a property owner with a superior bargaining position may require her tenants to be responsible for all injuries that occur on the leased premises, even if caused by the property owner's own negligence. In other situations, she might agree to bear the liability arising out of a tenant's negligence. Ideally, the specification of who is to pay for various losses should be a conscious decision that is made as part of the overall contract negotiation process. But even when that ideal is not possible, it is important to examine all contracts so that important sources of risk are identified prior to the occurrence of any losses.

Exhibit 900.6 *Flowchart for a Production Process*

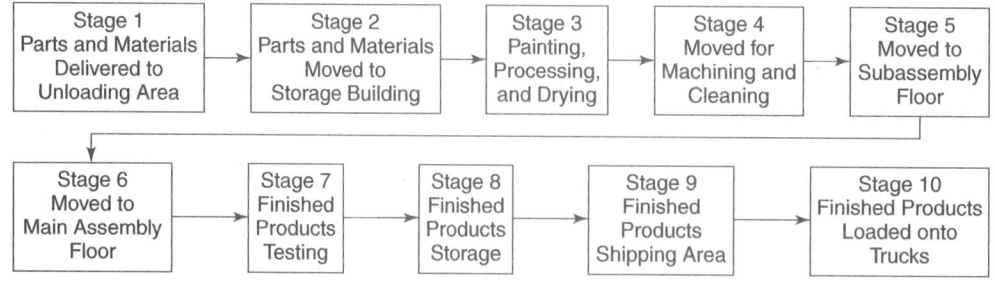

On-Site Inspections

Because some risks may exist that are not readily identifiable with the tools discussed thus far, it is important for business risk managers to visit periodically the various locations and departments within the firm. During these visits, it can be especially helpful to talk with department managers and other employees regarding their activities. Through this type of personal interaction, the risk manager can become better informed about current exposures to risk as well as potential future exposures that may arise.

Statistical Analysis of Past Losses

A final risk-identification tool that may be helpful for very large firms is that of statistical analysis of past losses. A **risk-management information system (RMIS)** is a computer software program that assists in performing this task. Some characteristics of past losses that may prove to be important in this regard include the cause of loss, the particular employees (if any) involved, where the loss occurred, and the total dollar amount of the loss.

To illustrate how these factors can prove important, suppose a trucking company experiences several vehicle accidents involving the same driver. Upon further investigation, the firm may discover that it has several problem drivers because it is not adequately checking the driving records of its employment applicants. Similarly, a restaurant chain that experiences a large number of employee injuries at its Dallas location may have safety hazards present that warrant additional investigation. As risk-management information systems become increasingly sophisticated and user-friendly, it is anticipated that more businesses will be able to effectively use statistical analysis in their risk-management activities.

Risk Evaluation

Once a risk is identified, the next step in the risk-management process is to estimate both the frequency and severity of potential losses. In this way, the risk manager obtains information that is helpful in determining the relative importance of identified risks and in selecting particular techniques for managing those risks.

In some cases, no particular problem would arise even if losses were incurred regularly, because the potential size of each loss is small. Thus, the daily occurrence of some inventory breakage may be an expected part of some businesses and would warrant only minimal attention from the risk manager. But other losses that occur infrequently yet are relatively large when they do occur (such as accidental deaths or destruction by a large fire) may be treated entirely differently. Such losses might cause bankruptcy if they were to happen with no means in place to counteract the resulting adverse financial effects for the firm.

One complicating factor in evaluating exposures is that many losses do not result in complete destruction of the asset involved. For example, if David Sommer's business is struck by lightning, the building will not necessarily burn to the ground. In evaluating the risk of loss from this peril, David should consider three things: (1) the frequency with which lightning may strike his building, (2) the **maximum probable loss** that would likely result if lightning did strike, and (3) the **maximum possible loss** if the building were completely destroyed. The difference between these last two factors is that the maximum probable loss is an estimate of the likely severity of losses that occur, whereas the maximum possible loss is an estimate of the catastrophe potential associated with a particular exposure to risk. In other words, what is the worst possible loss that might result from a given occurrence? To assess that potential, David needs to consider not only the loss of the building itself but also the destruction of inventory and equipment located inside. Furthermore, if David would seek to operate his business from another location in the event of loss, then his estimate of maximum possible loss should also include the cost of such temporary facilities.

The actual estimation of the frequency and severity of losses may be done in various ways. Some risk managers consider these concepts informally in evaluating identified risks. They may broadly classify the frequency of various losses into categories such as "slight," "moderate," and "certain," and may have similarly broad estimates for loss severity. Even this type of informal evaluation is better than none at all. But as risk management becomes increasingly sophisticated, most large firms attempt to be more precise in evaluating risks. It is now common to use probability distributions and statistical techniques in estimating both loss frequency and severity.

Risk Mapping or Profiling

With the evolution of integrated or enterprise risk management, alternative methods of risk identification and assessment have emerged. One such method is **risk mapping,** sometimes referred to as **risk profiling.** Because integrated risk management is based on identifying all the risks facing the firm, it is not unusual for a firm to identify in excess of 100 risks when using this approach. Cataloguing and making sense of so many risks requires a structured process. Risk mapping or profiling involves arraying these risks in a matrix, with one dimension being the frequency of events and the other being the severity. Each risk is then marked to indicate whether it is covered by insurance or not. By considering the likelihood and severity of each of the risks in this matrix, as well as the extent to which insurance protection is already available, it becomes possible for the firm to identify the risks that are most likely to seriously affect the firm's ability to achieve its goals.

Risk-Management Techniques

After identifying and evaluating exposures to risk, systematic consideration can be given to alternative techniques for managing each exposure. Techniques for managing exposures include (1) risk avoidance, (2) loss control, (3) risk retention, and (4) risk transfer. Broadly speaking, techniques 1 and 2 can be classified as risk-control methods, while techniques 3 and 4 can be classified as risk-financing methods.

Risk Avoidance

Risk avoidance is a conscious decision not to expose oneself or one's firm to a particular risk of loss. In this way, risk avoidance can be said to decrease one's chance of loss to zero. For example, the eccentric chief executive of a multi-billion-dollar firm may decide not to fly to avoid the risk of dying in an airplane crash. Dr. Gary Luke may decide to leave the practice of medicine rather than contend with the risk of malpractice liability losses. Similarly, firms may decide not to enter the pharmaceutical line of business to avoid costly product liability suits. Yet another example of risk avoidance is to delay taking responsibility for goods during transportation. A customer presented with a choice of terms of sale may have the seller assume all risks of loss until the goods arrive at the buyer's warehouse. In this way the buyer avoids the risk of loss to the property until delivery has actually occurred.

Risk avoidance is common, particularly among those with a strong aversion to risk. However, avoidance is not always feasible and may not be desirable even when it is possible. Risk managers must always weigh the relative costs and benefits associated with activities that give rise to risks. When a risk is avoided, the potential benefits, as well as costs, are given up. For example, the doctor who quits practicing medicine avoids future liability risks but also forfeits the income and other forms of satisfaction that may be associated with a career in medicine. The firm that avoids manufacturing pharmaceuticals relinquishes potential profits as well as liability risks. And if a business is to operate at all, certain risks are nearly impossible to avoid. An example is the liability risk of owning or leasing premises from which the business is conducted.

Loss Control (Risk Reduction or Mitigation)

When particular risks cannot be avoided, actions may often be taken to reduce the losses associated with them. This method of dealing with risk is known as **loss control.** It is different than risk avoidance, because the firm or individual is still engaging in operations that give rise to particular risks. Rather than abandoning specific activities, loss control involves making conscious decisions regarding the manner in which those activities will be conducted. Common goals are either to reduce the probability of losses or to decrease the cost of losses that do occur.

Risk Retention

A third technique for managing risk, known as **risk retention,** involves the assumption of risk. That is, if a loss occurs, an individual or firm will pay for it out of whatever funds are available at the time. Retention can be planned or unplanned, and losses that occur can either be funded or unfunded in advance.

Planned Versus Unplanned Retention

Planned retention involves a conscious and deliberate assumption of recognized risk. Sometimes planned retention occurs because it is the most convenient risk-treatment technique or because there are simply no alternatives available short of ceasing operations. At other times, a risk manager has thoroughly analyzed all of the alternative methods of treating an existing risk and has decided that retention is the most appropriate technique.

When a firm or individual does not recognize that a risk exists and unwittingly believes that no loss could occur, risk retention also is under way—albeit **unplanned retention.** Sometimes unplanned retention occurs even when the existence of a risk is acknowledged. This result can ensue if the maximum possible loss associated with a recognized risk is significantly underestimated. For example, a manufacturer of kitchen appliances may recognize the potential for product liability suits. But the potential size of adverse liability judgments may be much greater than the manufacturer anticipates. Thus, even though the exposure is recognized, the firm is engaging in unplanned retention of losses that exceed its estimate of the maximum possible loss.

Funded Versus Unfunded Retention

Many risk-retention strategies involve the intention to pay for losses as they occur, without making any funding arrangements in advance of a loss. If a loss happens, it is paid for from the firm's current revenues. For example, a convenience food store may decide to absorb the expense of shoplifting losses as they occur, rather than making any special advance arrangements to pay for them. This **unfunded retention** makes sense in this situation because some level of shoplifting loss is often viewed as part of the overall cost of doing business. Glass breakage is another exposure that many firms manage using unfunded retention. In general, unfunded retention should be used with caution, because financial difficulties may arise if the actual total losses are considerably greater than what was expected. In contrast to unfunded retention, a firm or individual may decide to practice **funded retention** by making various preloss arrangements to ensure that money is readily available to pay for losses that occur.

CREDIT The use of credit may provide some limited opportunities to fund losses that result from retained risks. It is usually not a viable source of funds for the payment of large losses, however. Further, unless the risk manager has already established a line of credit prior to the loss, the very fact that the loss has occurred may make it impossible to obtain credit when needed. For example, creditors may be unwilling to loan money to replace destroyed assets if those are the very assets that normally would have been used as collateral for the loan. For these reasons, credit tends not to be a major source of financial resources for most firms' funded retention programs.

RESERVE FUNDS Sometimes a reserve fund is established to pay for losses arising out of risks a firm has decided to retain. If the maximum possible loss due to a particular risk is relatively small, the existence of a reserve fund may be an efficient means of managing risk. For example, a firm may set aside $5,000 in liquid assets to pay for periodic repair or replacement of office equipment. Thus, when a fax machine or computer breaks down, the firm has funds readily available for the repair bill, which likely will be considerably less than the total reserve fund.

When the maximum possible loss is quite large, however, a reserve fund may not be appropriate. If a small employer plans for a $50,000 reserve fund to pay for any hospital costs its employees incur, it has no way of knowing whether or not this fund is adequate. A single period of hospitalization could easily exhaust the savings, and a second period of hospitalization might occur before the fund could be restored. For this type of exposure, alternative risk-management techniques probably would be more appropriate than risk retention, especially for a small firm.

SELF-INSURANCE If a firm has a group of exposure units large enough to reduce risk and thereby predict losses, the establishment of a fund to pay for those losses is a special form of planned, funded retention known as **self-insurance.** Some people object to this particular term, because the word *insurance* usually implies that a risk is transferred to another party. Obviously, self-insurance will not involve a transfer of risk in this sense. In spite of such objections, the term *self-insurance* continues to be used to describe some special situations in which risk retention has been consciously selected as an appropriate risk-management technique. The mere establishment of a reserve fund is not self-insurance. There are two necessary elements of self-insurance: (1) existence of a group of exposure units that is sufficiently large to enable accurate loss prediction and (2) prefunding of expected losses through a fund specifically designed for that purpose.

CAPTIVE INSURERS One final form of funded risk retention is the establishment of a **captive insurer,** which combines the techniques of risk retention and risk transfer.

Decisions Regarding Retention

In any given situation, there are several factors to consider in assessing retention as a potential risk-management technique. These factors include financial resources, ability to predict losses, and feasibility of establishing retention programs.

FINANCIAL RESOURCES A large business can often use risk retention to a greater extent than can a small firm or an individual, in part because of the large firm's greater financial resources. Thus, losses due to many risks may merely be absorbed by such a firm as the losses occur, without much advance planning. Some risks are recognized and their retention is planned, but in many cases no attempt is made to prefund those losses because their potential size would not cause undue financial hardship. Examples for some businesses might include pilferage of office supplies, breakage of windows, and burglary of vending machines.

In the case of funded retention, large firms also are often better able to utilize the retention technique than are small firms. For a given size, firms that are financially healthy will be better able to retain risk than those that are not. The following elements from a firm's financial statements should be considered when choosing possible retention levels:

1. Total assets
2. Total revenues
3. Asset liquidity
4. Ratio of revenues to net worth
5. Retained earnings
6. Ratio of total debt to net worth

For all of these items except the last one, the greater the number, the greater is the firm's ability to retain risk. In the case of the ratio of total debt to net worth, firms with lower ratios are in a better position to fund risk retention than are those with higher ratios.

ABILITY TO PREDICT LOSSES Another important consideration in evaluating the desirability of risk retention is the degree to which losses may or may not be predictable. Although a firm may be able to retain the maximum probable loss associated with a particular risk, problems may result if there is considerable variability in the range of possible losses. The ability to predict losses is enhanced when a firm has a large enough group of items exposed to the same risk to enable it to accurately predict loss experience.

Thus, if **RWT Company** employs 30,000 workers nationwide, it should be able to accurately predict its likely costs associated with work-related injuries. It can then make careful estimates of the funds needed to meet these losses and decide if it wants to pay for them as they are incurred or set aside money ahead of time. In the latter case, RWT probably can set up a fund with relative certainty that, within some margin for error, the fund will actually equal the losses incurred.

FEASIBILITY OF ESTABLISHING THE RETENTION PROGRAM If the decision to retain losses involves advance funding, administrative issues may need to be considered. Similarly, if the risk is likely to result in several losses over time, there will be administrative expenses associated with investigating and paying for those losses. An example is a decision by **MWT Corporation** to retain expenses arising from injuries to its employees. Because many relatively small losses can be expected over time, MWT must prepare for the administrative issues that will arise in its retention program. Administrative issues are of particular concern when a firm decides to set up a self-insurance or captive-insurer arrangement.

Risk Transfer

The final risk-management tool is **risk transfer,** which involves payment by one party (the **transferor**) to another (the **transferee,** or risk bearer). The transferee agrees to assume a risk that the transferor desires to escape. Sometimes the degree of risk is reduced through the transfer process, because the transferee may be in a better position to use the law of large numbers to predict losses. In other cases the degree of risk remains the same and is merely shifted from the transferor to the transferee for a price. Risk sharing can be viewed as a special case of risk transfer. Note that risk retention is mutually exclusive with risk transfer. Five forms of risk transfer are hold-harmless agreements, incorporation, diversification, hedging, and insurance.

Hold-Harmless Agreements

Provisions inserted into many different kinds of contracts can transfer responsibility for some types of losses to a party different than the one that would otherwise bear it. Such provisions are called **hold-harmless agreements,** or sometimes **indemnity agreements.** The intent of these contractual clauses is to specify the party that will be responsible for paying for various losses. Usually, no dollar limit is stated. Thus, the transferee must pay for all losses covered by the agreement, regardless of size.

An example of a hold-harmless agreement is that of a landlord who includes a clause in his apartment leases making tenants responsible for all injuries that guests may suffer while on the leased premises. This transfer entails a shift in responsibility for paying for losses, but there is no actual reduction in the original risk because the tenants' ability to predict losses is no greater than that of the landlord.

FORMS OF HOLD-HARMLESS AGREEMENTS   Hold-harmless agreements differ in the extent to which risk is transferred. The **limited form** merely clarifies that all parties are responsible for liabilities arising from their own actions. A second type of hold-harmless agreement is the **intermediate form,** in which the transferee agrees to pay for any losses in which both the transferee and transferor are jointly liable. The **broad form** is the third type of hold-harmless agreement. It requires the transferee to be responsible for all losses arising out of particular situations, regardless of fault.

ENFORCEMENT OF HOLD-HARMLESS AGREEMENTS   Hold-harmless agreements are not always legally enforceable. If the transferor is in a superior position to the transferee with respect to either bargaining power or knowledge of the factual situation, an attempt to transfer risk through a hold-harmless agreement may not be upheld by the courts. This result is particularly true of broad-form hold-harmless agreements.

Incorporation

Another way for a business to transfer risk is to incorporate. In this way, the most that an incorporated firm can ever lose is the total amount of its assets. Personal assets of the owners cannot be attached to help pay for business losses, as can be the case with sole proprietorships and partnerships. Through this act of incorporation, a firm transfers to its creditors the risk that it might not have sufficient assets to pay for losses and other debts.

Diversification

While risk management might not be the primary motivation, many of the production decisions that a firm makes can serve to transfer risk. **Diversification** across various businesses or geographic locations, while frequently justified by business synergies or economies of scale, also results in the transfer of risk across business units. Additionally, this combining of businesses or geographic locations in one firm can even result in a reduction in total risk through the portfolio effect of pooling individual risks that have different correlations. For example, a firm with two production facilities may sustain windstorm damages to its facility in Nebraska resulting from a tornado. However, it is unlikely that the same storm would cause damage to its facility in Georgia.

Hedging

Hedging involves the transfer of a speculative risk. It is a business transaction in which the risk of price fluctuations is transferred to a third party, which can be either a **speculator** or another **hedger.** In addition to futures contracts, forwards, swaps, and options are other commonly used tools for hedging speculative risk.

Insurance

The most widely used form of risk transfer is insurance.

The Value of Risk Management

Some elements of risk management, such as loss-control decisions, can be viewed as positive net present value projects. If the expected gains from an investment in loss control exceed the expected costs associated with that investment, the project should increase the value of the firm.

However, shareholders in a publicly traded corporation can eliminate firm-specific risk by holding a diversified portfolio of different company stocks. As a result, the shareholder would appear to care little about the management of nonsystematic or firm-specific risk, risk that the shareholder can eliminate through portfolio diversification. This would appear to make many risk-management activities, such as various forms of risk transfer, negative net present value projects. Nevertheless, corporations do engage in a number of activities directed at managing firm-specific risk, including the use of risk transfer. Why is this economically justified?

When evaluating risk management from the perspective of its impact on the value of the corporation, the source of the risk is less important than its effect on volatility. Regardless of whether the reduction in earnings comes from fire damage to the corporation's property, or from an increase in commodity prices, the financial impact on the shareholders is the same. This broader view of risk underpins the movement toward **enterprise-wide risk management.** Additionally, this holistic view reflects the realization that appropriate risk management must consider the fact that the corporation faces a portfolio of risks. And just as investment theory suggests that diversification can reduce the risk associated with a portfolio of securities, diversification within the portfolio of risks facing the corporation can alter the firm's risk profile. Ignoring these diversification effects by managing the firm's many risks independently can lead to inefficient use of the corporation's resources.

Selecting and Implementing Risk-Management Techniques

The selection of appropriate risk-management techniques is a dynamic problem. The best method for handling a particular exposure today may not be the best method a year from now because so many relevant factors change regularly. For example, the nature of an exposure may shift over time. Or the expected frequency and severity of losses may vary, causing estimates for the maximum possible loss and maximum probable loss to fluctuate. Finally, the cost and availability of different risk-management tools cannot be assumed to remain constant. Thus a risk-management plan that seems to be both effective and efficient one year may not make as much sense in the next.

All of these factors make it clear that the risk-management process should be an ongoing one rather than an exercise that is performed once and then forgotten. As exposures to risk are identified and analyzed, available risk-management tools and techniques must be considered. The steps for selecting among available risk-management techniques for a given situation may be summarized as follows:

1. Avoid risks if possible.
2. Implement appropriate loss control measures.
3. Select the optimal mix of risk retention and risk transfer.

Avoid Risks If Possible

Risks that can be eliminated without an adverse effect on the goals of an individual or business probably should be avoided. Without a systematic identification of pure risk exposures, however, some risks that easily could be avoided may inadvertently be retained.

Implement Appropriate Loss-Control Measures

For risks that a business or individual cannot or does not wish to avoid, consideration should be given to available loss-control measures. In analyzing the likely costs and benefits of loss-control alternatives, it should be recognized that loss control will always be used in conjunction with either risk retention or risk transfer. That is, even if substantial funds are spent to reduce loss frequency and severity, some risk will still be present. In fact, objective risk may actually increase when actions are taken that decrease the chance of loss. Thus, either the remaining risk will be retained or it will be transferred to another party. This phenomenon is true whether it is specifically planned or happens by default.

Therefore, part of the cost/benefit analysis regarding potential loss control is recognition of the likely effects on the transfer or retention of the risk existing after loss-control measures are implemented.

The selection between risk retention and risk transfer as the optimal risk-management technique may change after loss-control expenditures are made. It may involve purchasing less insurance and engaging in relatively more risk retention following the loss-control measures.

Analyzing Loss-Control Decisions

Fortunately, the techniques used in making capital budgeting decisions in finance and accounting can be applied to risk-management decisions regarding loss control. Consider Cole Department Store, which has been experiencing both substantial shoplifting losses as well as occasional vandalism to its building. Cole is considering hiring 24-hour security guards in an attempt to decrease both the frequency and severity of these losses. The estimated annual cost of this 24-hour protection is $60,000, which will cover salaries and employee benefits for the guards. By analyzing the pattern of past losses, Cole estimates that the presence of security guards will decrease shoplifting losses by $30,000 and vandalism losses by $20,000. In addition, Cole's property insurance premiums are expected to decrease by $5,000. Should the guards be hired?

An answer based only on these financial considerations can be obtained by comparing the size of the savings with the amount of cash outlay required to hire the guards. The estimated savings are:

$30,000	Decreased shoplifting losses
20,000	Decreased vandalism losses
5,000	Lower insurance premium
$55,000	Estimated savings from hiring guards

Because the $55,000 in savings is less than the $60,000 cost of hiring the guards, Cole may conclude that the potential savings do not justify the loss control expense. Before making a final decision, however, Cole should review both the estimated costs and savings. Cole should also consider whether there are any additional relevant factors that may have been overlooked. For example, would the presence of a security guard make employees feel safer? Would this intangible consideration make it possible to hire better employees? What about customer relations? Would they be enhanced by the presence of a guard? The financial calculations provide a good starting point for decision making, but the final decision often will be made in light of additional, less quantifiable, nonfinancial considerations.

Select the Optimal Mix of Risk Retention and Risk Transfer

As previously stated, loss-control decisions should be made as part of an overall risk-management plan that also considers the techniques of risk retention and risk transfer. To further complicate the decision-making process, risk retention and risk transfer often will both be used, with the relevant question being, "What is the appropriate mix between these two techniques?" Usually a loss-control or loss-prevention decision makes sense for losses that have a low expected frequency and low expected severity.

General Guidelines

As a rule, risk retention is optimal for losses that have a low expected severity, with the rule becoming especially appropriate when expected frequency is high. Physical damage losses to the cars within a large fleet driven by thousands of salespersons working for the same firm may fall into this category. Thus, no attempt may be made to transfer this risk to a third party; rather, the risk is retained, and an extra amount is added to the price of the product being sold to pay for expected losses due to collision and other damages to the cars. Of course, loss-control measures such as safety instruction may be implemented as well. But due to the nature of the risk, retention likely will make sense. At some point, however, the company may also want insurance to protect against the possibility that the total of the losses could be greater than expected. Management must decide how to distinguish between losses that are to be retained and those that are to be transferred to a third party.

Another general guideline applies to risks that have a low expected frequency but a high potential severity. In this situation, risk transfer often is the optimal choice. Small business owner Michael is concerned about possible tornado losses. He knows that it is quite possible his firm will never be damaged by a tornado. If he does have such a loss, though, Michael also knows that his building and all its contents could be completely destroyed. Because his firm would not be

Exhibit 900.7 *Guidelines for Using Different Risk-Management Techniques*

Expected Frequency	Expected Severity	Technique*
Low	Low	Retention
High	Low	Retention
Low	High	Transfer
High	High	Avoidance

*Loss control also should be considered in conjunction with each technique.

able to pay for such a large loss from either current income or accumulated savings, the appropriate decision for Michael is to transfer this risk to a third party, probably an insurance company. As part of this decision, Michael may decide to retain part of the exposure and only buy insurance for losses that exceed a specified level.

Finally, when losses have both high expected severity and high expected frequency, it is likely that risk transfer, risk retention, and loss control all will need to be used in varying degrees. Such a situation is, of course, not a desirable one to be in and should probably be accompanied by a reexamination of overall goals and priorities. Thus, some doctors in medical specialties that are frequent targets of large malpractice suits have decided either to change specialties or to leave the practice of medicine altogether. In the latter case, risk avoidance is seen as a rational response to potential losses that have high frequency as well as high potential severity.

What constitutes "high" and "low" loss frequency and severity in applying the preceding guidelines must be established on an individual basis. What is low loss severity for a multimillion-dollar company may be quite high for a small firm or an individual. In this regard, concepts such as total assets, net worth, and expected future income all are relevant. Subjective risk considerations also are important, as persons with a different tolerance for risk will often classify situations differently. A summary of the guidelines discussed in this section is provided in Exhibit 900.7.

Selecting Retention Amounts

Because in many situations both risk retention and risk transfer will be used in varying degrees, it is important to determine the appropriate mix of these two risk-management techniques. Both capital budgeting methods and statistical procedures may be used in selecting an appropriate retention level, with insurance purchased for losses in excess of that level.

But because the price of insurance does not necessarily vary proportionately with different levels of retention, the appropriate mix between retention and transfer is not an exact science. In general, decision makers try to minimize their total costs, considering not only the losses that are retained but also the premiums that must be paid for insurance that is purchased. Only at the end of the year (or other relevant time period) will it be known what the optimal decision at the beginning of the year would have been.

THE DEDUCTIBLE DECISION Selecting a particular deductible level is one way of mixing risk retention and risk transfer. Deductibles help lower the cost of insurance as well as increase its availability. They may also make management more loss conscious, because a firm must absorb losses within the deductible level. However, as a general rule, risk managers do not accept a deductible unless (1) the firm can afford the associated losses and (2) sufficient premium savings will result.

For example, the risk manager of Alliance Corporation is faced with the following choices in purchasing automobile insurance for the company-owned cars used by the Alliance sales force. As the deductible increases, the premium decreases. But the amount of premium savings is not in direct proportion to the size of the deductible. Thus, $300 in premium savings results by increasing the deductible from $100 to $250. But only $100 in savings results from increasing the deductible from $500 to $1,000. The risk manager may decide that the additional premium savings from a $1,000 deductible does not sufficiently justify the associated increase in risk retention.

THE SELF-INSURANCE DECISION The possibility of self-insurance is another way of mixing risk retention and risk transfer. For example, suppose past loss data for a large fleet of automobiles owned by BNM Corporation indicate a 95 percent probability that total annual collision losses for BNM will be less than $50,000. BNM may then decide to self-insure losses up to this level and purchase insurance that will pay only if total losses for the year exceed $50,000. In this way, BNM realizes some of the advantages of self-insurance while still maintaining adequate protection if losses are greater than expected. The most important element in the previous example, of course, is the specific dollar amount of losses that should be retained. The same statistical techniques used to select deductibles can be used in choosing a retention level for a self-insurance program.

The cash flow advantage of funds set aside in a reserve fund is an additional factor that must be considered in assessing the value of self-insurance as a way of handling risk. Because losses are not always paid out in the year in which the event producing them occurs, a company has the use of self-insurance funds for varying periods and may earn interest on them until such time as the losses are actually paid. The concept of present value methods can be helpful in analyzing self-insurance funding decisions.

Even though it may be clear that a firm can save money in the long run with self-insurance, management may prefer stable, predictable insurance premiums each year. Further, some companies prefer to avoid the details of managing self-insurance programs and instead to concentrate on their main operations. The following conditions are suggestive of the types of situations where self-insurance by a business is both possible and feasible:

1. The firm should have a sufficient number of objects so situated that they are not subject to simultaneous destruction. The objects also should be reasonably similar in nature and value so that calculations of probable losses will be accurate within a narrow range.
2. The firm must have accurate records or have access to satisfactory statistics to enable it to make good estimates of expected losses. To increase the accuracy of the calculations, it may be wise to use data that cover a long period of time. If outside data are used, caution must be employed to assure that the data are applicable to the firm's own experience.
3. The firm must make arrangements for administering the plan and managing the self-insurance fund. Someone must pay claims, inspect exposures, implement appropriate loss-control measures, keep necessary records, and take care of the many administrative details. If the necessary specialized executive talent is not available within the firm, it may be possible to contract for these services to be done by an independent **third-party administrator.** However, if management does not appreciate the necessity of paying continuing attention to numerous details in some manner, then the self-insurance arrangement will not be a satisfactory risk-management solution.
4. The general financial condition of the firm should be satisfactory, and the firm's management must be willing and able to deal with large and unusual losses. If management is unwilling to set up adequate reserves for funding the optimal retention level, then insurance may be used to a greater extent than might be indicated by mathematical analyses.

Enterprise Risk Management and Alternative Risk Transfer

Firms increasingly are broadening their perspective of risk. Enterprise risk management, rather than focusing solely on pure or hazard risks, seeks to consider all exposures that could negatively affect the firm's ability to achieve its strategic goals. Russ Banham, in the April 1999 issue of *CFO Magazine,* states that the goal of enterprise risk management is to identify, analyze, quantify, and compare all of a firm's exposures stemming from operational, financial, and strategic activities. The exposures in this enterprisewide view of risk include traditional insurable risks such as liability, as well as financial, commodity, legal, environmental, and other less-tangible exposures such as reputational effects and reduction in brand image.

Traditionally, the risk-management tools—avoidance, loss control, retention, and transfer—have been applied primarily to the pure or hazard risks facing a firm. Further, even when similar risk-management techniques have been applied to other categories of risk, the risk-management activities of the firm have remained compartmentalized and relatively uncoordinated. Evan R. Busman, in the January 1998 issue of *Risk-Management,* observes that risk management for many firms has been performed by different individuals with narrowly defined specialties. The traditional risk manager handles pure or hazard risk; the treasurer focuses on credit and financial risk; strategic business units develop controls for operational and commodity risk; and marketing and public relations staff focus on reputational risk.

In addition to the organizational segmentation of risk management within the firm, risk-management tools that are used to manage risks in these separate categories often differ. The techniques of insurance and self-insurance are commonly limited to the treatment of pure risks, such as fire, product liability, and workers' compensation. However, futures, options, swaps, and other derivatives contracts are typically applied to the management of financial risks, such as foreign exchange, commodity price, and interest rate risk.

The traditional method of assigning the risk-management process to different functional areas, using what has been called a "silo" approach, can lead to a less efficient management of risk for the firm as a whole. Many types of risks may be relatively uncorrelated with each other. As a result, combining these risks produces a form of "natural" hedging. As an example, earthquake damage to a multinational firm's property in one part of the world would be unlikely to have any correlation with its exposure to foreign exchange risk in another part of the world. The combination of these risks within the same firm reduces the level of risk. The traditional silo approach could actually reduce the overall efficiency of the firm's risk-management activities by destroying the natural hedging that exists at the enterprisewide level.

As the enterprisewide view of risk management has progressed, the role of the traditional risk manager and risk-management tools also have been evolving. Indicative of their changing role, traditional risk managers are increasingly being called on to become involved in the management of various nonhazard or financial risks facing their firms.

Alternative Risk-Transfer Tools

A growing array of alternative risk-transfer tools have been introduced since the mid-1990s (*alternative* here means an option to traditional insurance). Although the market shares of some of the alternative risk-transfer tools are relatively small, the pace of innovation and new product development has been very brisk. A sampling of alternative risk-transfer tools includes the following:

- **Captives.** An insurer owned by a noninsurance firm or organization for the purpose of accepting the risks of the parent firm. Although captives were originally conceived as an alternative to traditional insurance, they provide firms with a potentially effective vehicle for assuming the broader risks involved in enterprise risk management.
- **Finite risk or financial insurance.** Risk transfer contracts which are based on the concept of spreading risk over time, as opposed to across a pool of similar exposures. Generally, these contracts involve a limit on the extent of risk ultimately transferred by the insured. The primary focus is on smoothing losses during the period of the contract, usually 5 to 10 years. Further, these contracts usually involve a sharing of the investment returns between the insurer and the insured.
- **Multiline/multiyear insurance.** Insurance contracts that combine a broad array of risks (multiline) into a contract with a policy period that extends over multiple years (multiyear). The combination of risks might be limited to pure risks, such as a blending of liability, workers' compensation, auto, and property risks into one policy with common limits and deductibles. Alternatively, the contract might involve a blending of insurance risks with financial risks such as commodity, credit, or currency risks.
- **Multiple-trigger policies.** These contracts reflect the notion that to the shareholders of the firm, the source of the risk is not as important as the impact of the risk on the earnings of the firm. These contracts pool risks that in combination could have a very serious impact on the value of the firm. Most of the multiple-trigger policies issued thus far have combined a pure risk with a financial risk. The policy is "triggered," and payment is made, only upon the occurrence of an adverse event in each risk category. For example, a power company might buy a policy that is triggered if it experiences an unscheduled outage at one of its power plants, the first risk, during a period of extreme price volatility for electricity, the second risk.
- **Securitization.** The creation of securities, such as bonds or derivatives contracts, options, swaps, and futures, that have a payout or price movement that is linked to an insurance risk. Examples include catastrophe options, earthquake bonds, catastrophe bonds, and catastrophe equity puts. The driving motivation behind many of the securitized contracts is the interest in tapping the extensive risk transfer potential available in the capital markets. **USAA** and **Tokyo Fire and Marine** are two insurers that have used such tools to transfer hurricane and earthquake risks, respectively. Additionally, **Tokyo Disneyland** was purported to be the first noninsurer to use earthquake bonds to transfer risk to the capital markets, without the involvement of any insurer.

The risk managers forecast an almost fourfold increase in their use of the vehicles that involve the highest degree of risk integration, pure and financial risk integrated contracts, and securitization.

Corporate Citizenship, Accountability, and Public Policy

The Scope of Corporate Citizenship

The scope of corporate citizenship includes corporate social responsibility, corporate social responsiveness, and corporate social performance. Each one is described next.

Corporate Social Responsibility

Raymond Bauer presented an early view of corporate social responsibility (CSR) as follows: "Corporate social responsibility is seriously considering the impact of the company's actions on society."[21] Another definition that may be helpful is "The idea of social responsibility ... requires the individual to consider his [or her] acts in terms of a whole social system, and holds him [or her] responsible for the effects of his [or her] acts anywhere in that system."[22]

Both of these definitions provide preliminary insights into the idea of social responsibility. Exhibit 900.8 illustrates the business criticism/social response cycle, depicting how the concept of CSR grew out of business criticism and the increased concern for the social environment and the changed social contract. We see also in Exhibit 900.8 that the commitment to social responsibility by businesses has led to increased corporate responsiveness to stakeholders and improved social (stakeholder) performance.

Exhibit 900.8 *Business Criticism/Social Response Cycle*

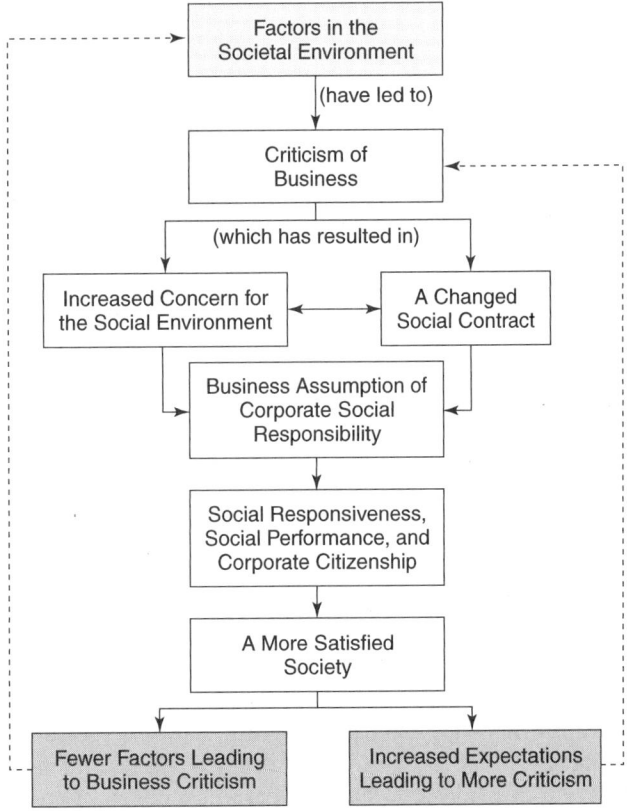

As we will discuss later, some observers today prefer the language of "corporate citizenship" to collectively embrace the host of concepts related to CSR.

CORPORATE CITIZENSHIP CONCEPTS

Corporate social *responsibility*—emphasizes obligation, accountability.
↓
Corporate social *responsiveness*—emphasizes action, activity.
↓
Corporate social *performance*—emphasizes outcomes, results.

The growth of these ideas has brought about a society more satisfied with business. However, this satisfaction, although it has reduced the number of factors leading to business criticism, has at the same time led to increased expectations that may result in more criticism; this double effect is indicated in Exhibit 900.8. The net result is that the overall levels of business performance and societal satisfaction should increase with time in spite of this interplay of positive and negative factors. Should business not be responsive to societal expectations, it could conceivably enter a downward spiral, resulting in significant changes in the business/society relationship.

Carroll's Four-Part Definition of Corporate Social Responsibility (CSR)

We would like to present Archie Carroll's four-part definition of corporate social responsibility (CSR) that focuses on the types of social responsibilities it might be argued that business has. Carroll's definition helps us to understand the component parts that make up CSR:

> The social responsibility of business encompasses the economic, legal, ethical, and discretionary (philanthropic) expectations that society has of organizations at a given point in time.[23]

Carroll's four-part definition attempts to place economic and legal expectations of business in context by relating them to more socially-oriented concerns. These social concerns include ethical responsibilities and philanthropic (voluntary/discretionary) responsibilities. This definition, which includes four kinds of responsibilities, elaborates and builds upon the definition proposed by McGuire.

ECONOMIC RESPONSIBILITIES   First, there are business's **economic responsibilities**. It may seem odd to call an economic responsibility a social responsibility, but, in effect, this is what it is. First and foremost, the American social system calls for business to be an economic institution. That is, it should be an institution whose orientation is to produce goods and services that society wants and to sell them at fair prices—prices that society thinks represent the true values of the goods and services delivered and that provide business with profits adequate to ensure its perpetuation and growth and to reward its investors. While thinking about its economic responsibilities, business employs many management concepts that are directed toward financial effectiveness—attention to revenues, costs, strategic decision making, and the host of business concepts focused on maximizing the long-term financial performance of the organization.

LEGAL RESPONSIBILITIES   Second, there are business's **legal responsibilities.** Just as society has sanctioned our economic system by permitting business to assume the productive role mentioned earlier, as a partial fulfillment of the social contract, it has also laid down the ground rules—the laws—under which business is expected to operate. Legal responsibilities reflect society's view of "codified ethics" in the sense that they embody basic notions of fair practices as established by our lawmakers. It is business's responsibility to society to comply with these laws. If business does not agree with laws that have been passed or are about to be passed, our society has provided a mechanism by which dissenters can be heard through the political process. In the past 30 years, our society has witnessed a proliferation of laws and regulations striving to control business behavior.

As important as legal responsibilities are, legal responsibilities do not cover the full range of behaviors expected of business by society. The law is inadequate for at least three reasons. First, the law cannot possibly address all the topics, areas, or issues that business may face. New topics continually emerge such as Internet-based business (e-commerce) and genetically engineered foods. Second, the law often lags behind more recent concepts of what is considered appropriate behavior. For example, as technology permits more exact measurements of environmental contamination, laws based on measures made by obsolete equipment become outdated but not frequently changed. Third, laws are made by lawmakers and may reflect the personal interests and political motivations of legislators rather than appropriate ethical justifications. A wise sage once said: "Never go to see how sausages or laws are made." It may not be a pretty picture.

ETHICAL RESPONSIBILITIES Because laws are important but not adequate, **ethical responsibilities** embrace those activities and practices that are expected or prohibited by societal members even though they are not codified into law. Ethical responsibilities embody the full scope of norms, standards, and expectations that reflect a belief of what consumers, employees, shareholders, and the community regard as fair, just, and in keeping with the respect for or protection of stakeholders' moral rights.[24]

In one sense, changes in ethics or values precede the establishment of laws because they become the driving forces behind the initial creation of laws and regulations. For example, the civil rights, environmental, and consumer movements reflected basic alterations in societal values and thus may be seen as ethical bellwethers foreshadowing and leading to later legislation. In another sense, ethical responsibilities may be seen as embracing and reflecting newly emerging values and norms that society expects business to meet, even though they may reflect a higher standard of performance than that currently required by law. Ethical responsibilities in this sense are often ill defined or continually under public scrutiny and debate as to their legitimacy and thus are frequently difficult for business to agree upon. Regardless, business is expected to be responsive to newly emerging concepts of what constitutes ethical practices.

Superimposed on these ethical expectations emanating from societal and stakeholder groups are the implied levels of ethical performance suggested by a consideration of the great ethical principles of moral philosophy, such as justice, rights, and utilitarianism.[25]

For the moment, let us think of ethical responsibilities as encompassing those areas in which society expects certain levels of moral or principled performance but for which it has not yet articulated or codified into law.

PHILANTHROPIC RESPONSIBILITIES Fourth, there are business's voluntary/discretionary or **philanthropic responsibilities**. These are viewed as responsibilities because they reflect current expectations of business by the public. These activities are voluntary, guided only by business's desire to engage in social activities that are not mandated, not required by law, and not generally expected of business in an ethical sense. Nevertheless, the public has an expectation that business will engage in philanthropy and thus this category has become a part of the social contract between business and society. Such activities might include corporate giving, product and service donations, volunteerism, partnerships with local government and other organizations, and any other kind of voluntary involvement of the organization and its employees with the community or other stakeholders.

The distinction between ethical responsibilities and philanthropic responsibilities is that the latter typically are not expected in a moral or an ethical sense. Communities desire and expect business to contribute its money, facilities, and employee time to humanitarian programs or purposes, but they do not regard firms as unethical if they do not provide these services at the desired levels. Therefore, these responsibilities are more discretionary, or voluntary, on business's part, although the societal expectation that they be provided is always present. This category of responsibilities is often referred to as good "corporate citizenship."

In essence, then, our definition forms a four-part conceptualization of corporate social responsibility that encompasses the economic, legal, ethical, and philanthropic expectations placed on organizations by society at a given point in time. Exhibit 900.9 summarizes the four components, society's expectation regarding each component, and examples. The implication is that business has accountability for these areas of responsibility and performance. This four-part definition provides us with categories within which to place the various expectations that society has of business. With each of these categories considered as indispensable facets of the total social responsibility of business, we have a conceptual model that more completely describes the kinds of expectations that society expects of business. One advantage of this model is that it can accommodate those who have argued against CSR by characterizing an economic emphasis as separate from a social emphasis. This model offers these two facets along with others that collectively make up corporate social responsibility.

THE PYRAMID OF CORPORATE SOCIAL RESPONSIBILITY A helpful way of graphically depicting the four-part definition is envisioning a pyramid composed of four layers. The pyramid portrays the four components of CSR, beginning with the basic building block of economic performance (making a profit), at the base. At the same time, business is expected to obey the law, because the law is society's codification of acceptable and unacceptable behavior. Next is business's responsibility to be ethical. At its most basic level, this is the obligation to do what is right, just, and fair and to avoid or minimize harm to stakeholders (employees, consumers, the environment, and

A socially responsible firm should strive to:

- Make a profit.
- Obey the law.
- Be ethical.
- Be a good corporate citizen.

Exhibit 900.9 *Understanding the Four Components of Corporate Social Responsibility*

Type of Responsibility	Societal Expectation	Examples
Economic	REQUIRED of business by society	Be profitable. Maximize sales, minimize costs. Make sound strategic decisions. Be attentive to dividend policy.
Legal	REQUIRED of business by society	Obey all laws, adhere to all regulations. Environmental and consumer laws. Laws protecting employees. Obey Foreign Corrupt Practices Act. Fulfill all contractual obligations. Honor warranties and guarantees.
Ethical	EXPECTED of business by society	Avoid questionable practices. Respond to spirit as well as letter of law. Assume law is a floor on behavior, operate above minimum required. Do what is right, fair, and just. Assert ethical leadership.
Philanthropic	DESIRED of business by society	Be a good corporate citizen. Make corporate contributions. Provide programs supporting community—education, health/human services, culture and arts, civic. Provide for community betterment. Engage in volunteerism.

others). Finally, business is expected to be a good corporate citizen—to fulfill its voluntary/discretionary or philanthropic responsibility to contribute financial and human resources to the community and to improve the quality of life.

The most critical tensions, of course, are those between economic and legal, economic and ethical, and economic and philanthropic. The traditionalist might see this as a conflict between a firm's "concern for profits" and its "concern for society," but it is suggested here that this is an oversimplification. A CSR or stakeholder perspective would recognize these tensions as organizational realities but would focus on the total pyramid as a unified whole and on how the firm might engage in decisions, actions, policies, and practices that simultaneously fulfill all its component parts. This pyramid should not be interpreted to mean that business is expected to fulfill its social responsibilities in some sequential fashion, starting at the base. Rather, business is expected to fulfill all its responsibilities simultaneously.

In summary, the total social responsibility of business entails the concurrent fulfillment of the firm's economic, legal, ethical, and philanthropic responsibilities. In equation form, this might be expressed as follows:

$$\text{Economic Responsibilities} + \text{Legal Responsibilities} + \text{Ethical Responsibilities}$$
$$+ \text{Philanthropic Responsibilities}$$
$$= \text{Total Corporate Social Responsibility}$$

Arguments Against and for Corporate Social Responsibility

In an effort to provide a balanced view of CSR, we will consider the arguments that traditionally have been raised against and for it. We should state clearly at the outset, however, that those who argue against corporate social responsibility are not using in their considerations the comprehensive CSR definition and model presented in Exhibit 900.9.

Rather, it appears that the critics are viewing CSR more narrowly—as only the efforts of the organization to pursue social, noneconomic/nonlegal goals (our ethical and philanthropic categories). Some critics equate CSR with only the philanthropic category. We should also state that only a very few businesspeople and academics continue to argue against the fundamental notion of CSR today. The debate among businesspeople more often centers on the kinds and degrees of CSR and on subtle ethical questions, rather than on the basic question of whether or not business should be socially responsible. Among academics, economists and finance professors are probably the easiest groups to single out as being against the pursuit of corporate social goals. But even some of them no longer resist CSR on the grounds of economic theory.

Arguments Against Corporate Social Responsibility

Let us first look at the arguments that have surfaced over the years from the anti-CSR school of thought. Most notable has been the classical economic argument. This traditional view holds that management has one responsibility: to maximize the profits of its owners or shareholders. This classical economic school, led by economist Milton Friedman, argues that social issues are not the concern of businesspeople and that these problems should be resolved by the unfettered workings of the free market system.[26] Further, this view holds that if the free market cannot solve the social problem, then it falls upon government and legislation to do the job. Friedman softens his argument somewhat by his assertion that management is "to make as much money as possible while conforming to the basic rules of society, both those embodied in the law and those embodied in ethical customs."[27] When Friedman's entire statement is considered, it appears that he accepts three of the four categories of the four-part model—economic, legal, and ethical. The only item not specifically embraced in his quote is the voluntary or philanthropic category. In any event, it is clear that the economic argument views corporate social responsibility more narrowly than we have in our conceptual model.

A second major objection to CSR has been that business is not equipped to handle social activities. This position holds that managers are oriented toward finance and operations and do not have the necessary expertise (social skills) to make social decisions.[28] Although this may have been true at one point in time, it is less true today. Closely related to this argument is a third: If managers were to pursue corporate social responsibility vigorously, it would tend to dilute the business's primary purpose.[29] The objection here is that CSR would put business into fields not related, as F. A. Hayek has stated, to their "proper aim."[30]

A fourth argument against CSR is that business already has enough power—economic, environmental, and technological—and so why should we place in its hands the opportunity to wield additional power?[31] In reality, today, business has this social power regardless of the argument. Further, this view tends to ignore the potential use of business's social power for the public good.

One other argument that merits mention is that by encouraging business to assume social responsibilities we might be placing it in a deleterious position in terms of the international balance of payments. One consequence of being socially responsible is that business must internalize costs that it formerly passed on to society in the form of dirty air, unsafe products, consequences of discrimination, and so on. The increase in the costs of products caused by including social considerations in the price structure would necessitate raising the prices of products, making them less competitive in international markets. The net effect might be to dissipate the country's advantages gained previously through technological advances. This argument weakens somewhat when we consider the reality that social responsibility is quickly becoming a global concern, not one restricted to U.S. firms and operations.

The arguments presented here constitute the principal claims made by those who oppose the CSR concept, as it once was narrowly conceived. Many of the reasons given appear quite rational. Value choices as to the type of society the citizenry would like to have, at some point, become part of the total social responsibility question. Whereas some of these objections might have had validity at one point in time, it is doubtful that they carry much weight today.

Arguments for Corporate Social Responsibility

Thomas Petit's perspective is useful as our point of departure in discussing support of the CSR doctrine. He says that authorities have agreed upon two fundamental points: "(1) Industrial society faces serious human and social problems brought on largely by the rise of the large corporations, and (2) managers must conduct the affairs of the corporation in ways to solve or at least ameliorate these problems."[32]

This generalized justification of corporate social responsibility is appealing. It actually comes close to what we might suggest as a first argument for CSR—namely, that it is in business's long-range self-interest to be socially responsible. Petit's argument provides an additional dimension by suggesting that it was partially business's fault that many of today's social problems arose in the first place and, consequently, that business should assume a role in remedying these problems. It may be inferred from this that deterioration of the social condition must be halted if business is to survive and prosper in the future.

The long-range self-interest view holds that if business is to have a healthy climate in which to exist in the future, it must take actions now that will ensure its long-term viability. Perhaps the reasoning behind this view is that society's expectations are such that if business does not respond on its own, its role in society may be altered by the public—for example, through government regulation or, more dramatically, through alternative economic systems for the production and distribution of goods and services.

It is sometimes difficult for managers who have a short-term orientation to appreciate that their rights and roles in the economic system are determined by society. Business must be responsive to society's expectations over the long term if it is to survive in its current form or in a less restrained form.

One of the most practical reasons for business to be socially responsible is to ward off future government intervention and regulation. Today there are numerous areas in which government intrudes with an expensive, elaborate regulatory apparatus to fill a void left by business's inaction. To the extent that business polices itself with self-disciplined standards and guidelines, future government intervention can be somewhat forestalled. Later, we will discuss some areas in which business could have prevented intervention and simultaneously ensured greater freedom in decision making had it imposed higher standards of behavior on itself.

Keith Davis has presented two additional supporting arguments that deserve mention together: "Business has the resources" and "Let business try."[33] These two views maintain that because business has a reservoir of management talent, functional expertise, and capital, and because so many others have tried and failed to solve general social problems, business should be given a chance. These arguments have some merit, because there are some social problems that can be handled, in the final analysis, only by business. Examples include a fair workplace, providing safe products, and engaging in fair advertising. Admittedly, government can and does assume a role in these areas, but business must make the final decisions.

Another argument is that "proacting is better than reacting." This position holds that proacting (anticipating and initiating) is more practical and less costly than simply reacting to problems once they have developed. Environmental pollution is a good example, particularly business's experience with attempting to clean up rivers, lakes, and other waterways that were neglected for years. In the long run, it would have been wiser to have prevented the environmental deterioration from occurring in the first place. A final argument in favor of CSR is that the public strongly supports it. A 2000 *Business Week*/Harris poll revealed that, with a stunning 95 percent majority, the public believes that companies should not only focus on profits for shareholders but that companies should be responsible to their workers and communities, even if making things better for workers and communities requires companies to sacrifice some profits.[34]

Millennium Poll on Corporate Social Responsibility

The Conference Board Survey in 1999 suggests that CSR is fast becoming a global expectation that requires a comprehensive strategic response. Ethics and CSR need to be made a core business value integrated into all aspects of the firm.

In the twenty-first century, major companies will be expected to do all the following:

- Demonstrate their commitment to society's values and their contribution to society's social, environmental, and economic goals through actions.
- Fully insulate society from the negative impacts of company operations and its products and services.
- Share the benefits of company activities with key stakeholders as well as with shareholders.
- Demonstrate that the company can make more money by doing the right thing, in some cases reinventing its business strategy. This "doing well by doing good" will reassure stakeholders that the new behavior will outlast good intentions.

Corporate Social Responsiveness

We have discussed the evolution of corporate social responsibility, a model for viewing social responsibility, and the arguments for and against it. It is now important to address a concept that has arisen over the use of the terms *responsibility* and *responsiveness*. We will consider the views of several writers to develop the idea of **corporate social responsiveness**—the action-oriented variant of corporate social responsibility (CSR).

Ackerman and Bauer's Action View

A general argument that has generated much discussion over the past several decades holds that the term *responsibility* is too suggestive of efforts to pinpoint accountability or obligation. Therefore, it is not dynamic enough to fully describe business's willingness and activity—apart from obligation—to respond to social demands. For example, Robert Ackerman and Raymond Bauer criticized the CSR term by stating, "The connotation of 'responsibility' is that of the process of assuming an obligation. It places an emphasis on motivation rather than on performance." They go on to say, "Responding to social demands is much more than deciding what to do. There remains the management task of doing what one has decided to do, and this task is far from trivial."[35] They argue that "social responsiveness" is a more apt description of what is essential in the social arena.

Their point was well made, especially when it was first set forth. *Responsibility*, taken quite literally, does imply more of a state or condition of having assumed an obligation, whereas *responsiveness* connotes a dynamic, action-oriented condition. We should not overlook, however, that much of what business has done and is doing has resulted from a particular motivation—an assumption of obligation—whether assigned by government, forced by special-interest groups, or voluntarily assumed. Perhaps business, in some instances, has failed to accept and internalize the obligation, and thus it may seem odd to refer to it as a responsibility. Nevertheless, some motivation that led to social responsiveness had to be there, even though in some cases it was not articulated to be a responsibility or an obligation.

Sethi's Three-Stage Schema

S. Prakash Sethi takes a slightly different, but related, path in getting from social responsibility to social responsiveness. He proposes a three-stage schema for classifying corporate behavior in responding to social or societal needs: social obligation, social responsibility, and social responsiveness.

Social obligation, Sethi argues, is corporate behavior in response to market forces or legal constraints. Corporate legitimacy is very narrow here and is based on legal and economic criteria only. *Social responsibility,* Sethi suggests, "implies bringing corporate behavior up to a level where it is congruent with the prevailing social norms, values, and expectations."[36] He argues that whereas the concept of social obligation is proscriptive in nature, social responsibility is prescriptive in nature. *Social responsiveness,* the third stage in his schema, suggests that what is important is "not how corporations should respond to social pressure but what should be their long-run role in a dynamic social system."[37] He suggests that here business is expected to be "anticipatory" and "preventive." Note that his obligation and responsibility categories embody essentially the same message we were attempting to convey with our four-part conceptual definition of CSR.

Frederick's CSR_1, CSR_2, and CSR_3

William Frederick has distinguished between corporate social responsibility, which he calls CSR_1, and corporate social responsiveness, which he terms CSR_2, in the following way:

> Corporate social responsiveness refers to the capacity of a corporation to respond to social pressures. The literal act of responding, or of achieving a generally responsive posture, to society is the focus.... One searches the organization for mechanisms, procedures, arrangements, and behavioral patterns that, taken collectively, would mark the organization as more or less capable of responding to social pressures.[38]

Frederick further argued that advocates of social responsiveness (CSR_2) "have urged corporations to eschew philosophic questions of social responsibility and to concentrate on the more pragmatic matter of responding effectively to environmental pressures." He later articulated an idea known as CSR_3—corporate social rectitude—which addressed the moral correctness of actions taken and policies formulated.[39] However, we would argue that the moral dimension is implicit in CSR, as we included it in our basic four-part definition.

Epstein's Process View of Social Responsiveness

Edwin Epstein discusses corporate social responsiveness within the context of a broader concept that he calls the corporate social policy process. In this context, Epstein emphasizes the *process* aspect of social responsiveness. He asserts that corporate social responsiveness focuses on the individual and organizational processes "for determining, implementing, and evaluating the firm's capacity to anticipate, respond to, and manage the issues and problems arising from the diverse claims and expectations of internal and external stakeholders."[40]

Other Views of Social Responsiveness

Several other writers have provided conceptual schemes that describe the responsiveness facet. Ian Wilson, for example, asserts that there are four possible business strategies: reaction, defense, accommodation, and proaction.[41] Terry McAdam has likewise described four social responsibility philosophies that mesh well with Wilson's and describe the managerial approach that would characterize the range of the responsiveness dimension: "Fight all the way," "Do only what is required," "Be progressive," and "Lead the industry."[42] Davis and Blomstrom describe alternative responses to societal pressures as follows: withdrawal, public relations approach, legal approach, bargaining, and problem solving.[43] Finally, James Post has articulated three major social-responsiveness categories: adaptive, proactive, and interactive.[44]

Thus, the corporate social-responsiveness dimension that has been discussed by some as an alternative focus to that of social responsibility is, in actuality, an action phase of management's response in the social sphere. In a sense, the responsiveness orientation enables organizations to rationalize and operationalize their social responsibilities without getting bogged down in the quagmire of definition problems, which can so easily occur if organizations try to get an exact determination of what their true responsibilities are before they take any action.

In an interesting study of social responsiveness among Canadian and Finnish forestry firms, researchers concluded that the social responsiveness of a corporation will proceed through a predictable series of phases and that managers will tend to respond to the most powerful stakeholders.[45] This study demonstrates that social responsiveness is a process and that stakeholder power, in addition to a sense of responsibility, may sometimes drive the process.

Corporate Social Performance

For the past few decades, there has been a trend toward making the concern for social and ethical issues more and more pragmatic. The responsiveness thrust that we just discussed was a part of this trend. It is possible to integrate some of the concerns into a model of corporate social performance (CSP). The performance focus is intended to suggest that what really matters is what companies are able to accomplish—the results of their acceptance of social responsibility and adoption of a responsiveness philosophy. In developing a conceptual framework for CSP, we not only have to specify the nature (economic, legal, ethical, philanthropic) of the responsibility, but we also need to identify a particular philosophy, pattern, or mode of responsiveness. Finally, we need to identify the stakeholder issues or topical areas to which these responsibilities are manifested. One need not ponder the stakeholder issues that have evolved under the rubric of social responsibility to recognize how they have changed over time. The issues, and especially the degree of organizational interest in the issues, are always in a state of flux. As the times change, so does the emphasis on the range of social issues that business must address.

Also of interest is the fact that particular issues are of varying concern to businesses, depending on the industry in which they exist as well as other factors. A bank, for example, is not as pressed on environmental issues as a manufacturer. Likewise, a manufacturer is considerably more absorbed with the issue of environmental protection than is an insurance company.

Carroll's Corporate Social Performance (CSP) Model

Carroll's **corporate social performance (CSP) model** brings together the three major dimensions we have discussed.

1. Social responsibility categories—economic, legal, ethical, and (philanthropic) discretionary
2. Philosophy (or mode) of social responsiveness—for example, reaction, defense, accommodation, and proaction
3. Social (or stakeholder) issues involved—consumerism, environment, discrimination, and so on[46]

The first dimension of this model pertains to all that is included in our definition of social responsibility—the economic, legal, ethical, and (philanthropic) discretionary components. Second, there is a social responsiveness continuum. Although some writers have suggested that this is the preferable focus when one considers social responsibility, Carroll's model suggests that responsiveness is but one additional aspect to be addressed if CSP is to be achieved. The third dimension concerns the scope of social or stakeholder issues (for example, consumerism, environment, and discrimination) that management must address.

Usefulness of the CSP Model to Academics and Managers

The corporate social performance model is intended to be useful to both academics and managers. For academics, the model is primarily a conceptual aid to perceiving the distinction among the concepts of corporate social responsibility that have appeared in the literature. What previously have been regarded as separate definitions of CSR are treated here as three separate aspects pertaining to CSP. The model's major use to the academic, therefore, is in helping to systematize the important concepts that must be taught and understood in an effort to clarify the CSR concept. The model is not the ultimate conceptualization. It is, rather, a modest but necessary step toward understanding the major facets of CSP.

The conceptual model can assist managers in understanding that social responsibility is not separate and distinct from economic performance. The model integrates economic concerns into a social performance framework. In addition, it places ethical and philanthropic expectations into a rational economic and legal framework. The model can help the manager systematically think through major stakeholder issues. Although it does not provide the answer to how far the organization should go, it does provide a conceptualization that could lead to better-managed social performance. Moreover, the model could be used as a planning tool and as a diagnostic problem-solving tool. The model can assist the manager by identifying categories within which the organization can be situated.

Corporate Citizenship

Corporate citizenship has been described by some as a broad, encompassing term that basically embraces all that is implied in the concepts of social responsibility, responsiveness, and performance. Graves, Waddock, and Kelly, for example, define good corporate citizenship as "serving a variety of stakeholders well."[47] Fombrun also proposes a broad conception. He holds that corporate citizenship is composed of a three-part view that encompasses (1) a reflection of shared moral and ethical principles, (2) a vehicle for integrating individuals into the communities in which they work, and (3) a form of enlightened self-interest that balances all stakeholders' claims and enhances a company's long-term value.[48]

Davenport's research also resulted in a broad definition of corporate citizenship that includes a commitment to ethical business behavior, and balancing the needs of stakeholders, while working to protect the environment.[49] Finally, Carroll has recast his four categories of corporate social responsibility as embracing the "four faces of corporate citizenship,"—economic, legal, ethical, and philanthropic. Each face, aspect, or responsibility reveals an important facet that contributes to the whole. He poses that "just as private citizens are expected to fulfill these responsibilities, companies are as well."[50]

At the narrow end of the spectrum, Altman speaks of corporate citizenship in terms of corporate community relations. In this view, it embraces the functions through which business intentionally interacts with nonprofit organizations, citizen groups, and other stakeholders at the community level.[51] Other definitions of corporate citizenship fall in between these broad and narrow perspectives, and some refer to global corporate citizenship as well, as increasingly companies are expected to conduct themselves appropriately wherever they are doing business.

The benefits of good corporate citizenship to stakeholders is fairly apparent. But, what are the benefits of good corporate citizenship to business itself? A literature review of studies attempting to discern the benefits to companies of corporate citizenship, defined broadly, revealed empirical and anecdotal evidence supporting the following:[52]

- Improved employee relations (for example, improves employee recruitment, retention, morale, loyalty, motivation, and productivity)
- Improved customer relationships (for example, increased customer loyalty, acts as a tiebreaker for consumer purchasing, enhances brand image)
- Improved business performance (for example, positively impacts bottom-line returns, increases competitive advantage, encourages cross-functional integration)
- Enhanced company's marketing efforts (for example, helps create a positive company image, helps a company manage its reputation, supports higher prestige pricing, and enhances government affairs activities)

The terminology of corporate citizenship is especially attractive because it resonates so well with the business community's attempts to describe its own socially responsive activities and practices. Therefore, we can expect that this concept will be around for some years to come. Generally speaking, as we refer to CSR, social responsiveness, and social performance, we are also embracing activities that would typically fall under the purview of a firm's corporate citizenship.[53]

Social Performance and Financial Performance

One issue that comes up frequently in considerations of corporate social performance is whether or not there is a demonstrable relationship between a firm's social responsibility or performance and its financial performance. Unfortunately, attempts to measure this relationship are typically hampered by measurement problems. The appropriate performance criteria for measuring financial performance and social responsibility are subject to debate. Furthermore, the measurement of social responsibility is fraught with definitional problems. Even if a definition of CSR could be agreed on, there still would remain the complex task of operationalizing the definition. Exhibit 900.10 presents three perspectives.

A Multiple Bottom-Line Perspective

A basic premise of all these perspectives is that there is only one "bottom line"—a corporate bottom line that addresses primarily the stockholders', or owners', investments in the firm. An alternative view is that the firm has "multiple bottom

Exhibit 900.10 *Relationships Among Corporate Social Performance (CSP), Corporate Financial Performance (CFP), and Corporate Reputation (CR)*

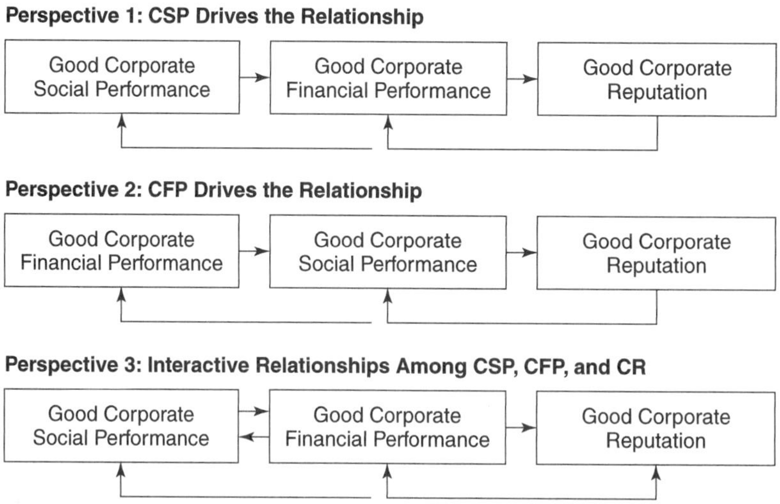

Perspective 1: CSP Drives the Relationship

Good Corporate Social Performance → Good Corporate Financial Performance → Good Corporate Reputation

Perspective 2: CFP Drives the Relationship

Good Corporate Financial Performance → Good Corporate Social Performance → Good Corporate Reputation

Perspective 3: Interactive Relationships Among CSP, CFP, and CR

Good Corporate Social Performance ↔ Good Corporate Financial Performance → Good Corporate Reputation

Exhibit 900.11 *Relationship Between Corporate Social Performance (CSP) and Stakeholders' "Multiple Bottom Lines"*

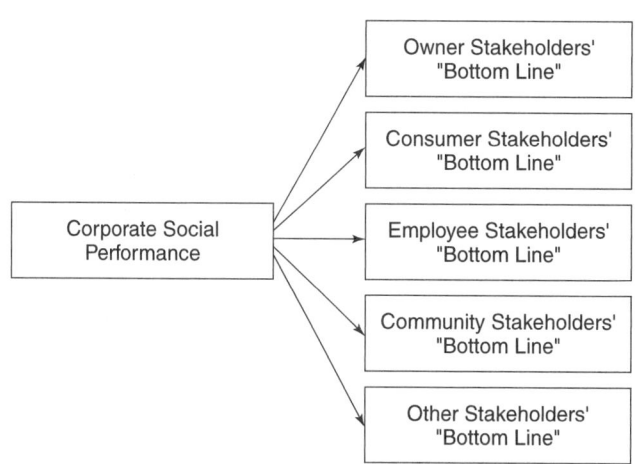

lines" that benefit from corporate social performance. This stakeholder-bottom-line perspective argues that the impacts or benefits of CSP cannot be fully measured or appreciated by considering only the impact of the firm's financial bottom line.

To truly operate with a stakeholder perspective, companies need to accept the multiple-bottom-line view. Thus, CSP cannot be fully comprehended unless we also consider that its impacts on stakeholders, such as consumers, employees, the community, and other stakeholder groups, are noted, measured, and considered. Research may never conclusively demonstrate a relationship between CSP and financial performance. If a stakeholder perspective is taken, however, it may be more straightforward to assess the impact of CSP on multiple stakeholders' bottom lines. This model of CSP and stakeholders' bottom lines might be depicted as shown in Exhibit 900.11.

Socially Conscious or Ethical Investing

Special-interest groups, the media, and academics are not alone in their interest in business's social performance. Investors are also interested. The **socially conscious** or **ethical investing** movement arrived on the scene in the 1970s and has continued to grow and prosper. By the early 2000s, social investing had matured into a comprehensive investing approach complete with social and environmental screens, shareholder activism, and community investment, accounting for over $2 trillion of investments in the United States, according to the Social Investment Forum.[54]

The concept of *social screening* is the backbone of the socially conscious investing movement. Investors seeking to put their money into socially responsible firms want to screen out those firms they consider to be socially irresponsible or to actively invest in those firms they think of as being socially responsible. Thus, there are negative social screens and positive social screens. Some of the negative social screens that have been used in recent years include the avoidance of investing in tobacco manufacturers, gambling casino operators, and defense or weapons contractors.

It is more difficult, and thus more challenging, to implement positive social screens, because they require the potential investor to make judgment calls as to what constitutes an acceptable or a good level of social performance on social investment criteria. Criteria that may be used as either positive or negative screens, depending on the firm's performance, might include the firm's record on issues such as equal employment opportunity and affirmative action, environmental protection, treatment of employees, corporate citizenship (broadly defined), and treatment of animals.

The financial performance of socially conscious funds shows that investors do not have to sacrifice profitability for principles. Recent evidence suggests that investors expect and receive competitive returns from social investments.[55]

It should be added, however, that there is no clear and consistent evidence that returns from socially conscious funds will equal or exceed the returns from funds that are not so carefully screened. Therefore, socially conscious funds are valued most highly by those investors who really care about the social performance of companies in their portfolios and are willing to put their money at some risk. A recent study concluded that there is no penalty for improved CSP in terms of institutional ownership and that high CSP tends, in fact, to lead to an increase in the number of institutional investors holding a given stock.[56]

The Council on Economic Priorities has suggested that there are at least three reasons why there has been an upsurge in socially conscious or ethical investing:[57]

1. There is more reliable and sophisticated research on corporate social performance than in the past.
2. Investment firms using social criteria have established a solid track record, and investors do not have to sacrifice gains for principles.
3. The socially conscious 1960s generation is now making investment decisions.

In recent years, as more and more citizen employees are in charge of their own IRAs and 401(k)s, people have become much more sophisticated about making investment decisions than in the past. Further, more people are seeing social investments as a way in which they can exert their priorities concerning the balance of financial and social concerns.

Corporate Public Policy

The impact of the social-ethical-public-stakeholder environment on business organizations is becoming more pronounced each year. It is an understatement to suggest that this multifaceted environment has become tumultuous, and brief reminders of a few actual cases point out the validity of this claim quite dramatically. **Procter & Gamble** and its Rely tampon recall, **Firestone** and its radial tire debacle, **Ford Motor Company** and its disastrous Pinto gas tank problem, and **Johnson & Johnson** and its tainted Tylenol capsules are *classic* reminders of how social issues can directly affect a firm's product offerings. In addition, there are many examples in which social issues have had major impacts on firms at the general-management level. **Exxon's** catastrophic *Valdez* oil spill, **Dow Corning's** ill-fated silicone breast implants, and the tobacco industry's battles with the federal and state government over the dangers of its product are all examples of the impacts of top-level decisions that entail ethical ramifications. More recently, **Coca-Cola's** disastrous and massive recall of soft drinks in Belgium and France and **Bridgestone-Firestone's** tire-tread separations in a number of countries of the world and the United States provide examples of ethical issues that have dramatic implications for top executive decision makers.

What started as an awareness of social issues and social responsibility matured into a focus on the management of social responsiveness and performance. Today, the trend reflects a preoccupation with ethics, stakeholders, and corporate citizenship as we navigate the first decade of the new millennium. The term *corporate public policy* is an outgrowth of an earlier term, *corporate social policy,* which had been in general usage for over 20 years. The two concepts have essentially the same meaning, but we will use "corporate public policy" because it is more in keeping with terminology more recently used in business. Much of what takes place under the banner of corporate public policy is also referred to as corporate citizenship by businesses today.

What is meant by corporate public policy? **Corporate public policy** is a firm's posture, stance, strategy, or position regarding the public, social, and ethical aspects of stakeholders and corporate functioning. We will discuss how businesses formalize this concern under the rubric of corporate public affairs, or public affairs management. Businesses encounter many situations in their daily operations that involve highly visible public and ethical issues. Some of these issues are subject to intensive public debate for specific periods of time before they become institutionalized. Examples of such issues include sexual harassment, AIDS in the workplace, affirmative action, product safety, and employee privacy. Other issues are more basic, more enduring, and more philosophical. These issues might include the broad role of business in society, the corporate governance question, and the relative balance of business versus government direction that is best for our society.

The idea behind corporate public policy is that a firm must give specific attention to issues in which basic questions of right, wrong, justice, fairness, or public policy reside. The dynamic stakeholder environment of the past 40 years has necessitated that management apply a policy perspective to these issues. At one time, the social environment was thought to be a relatively constant backdrop against which the real work of business took place. Today these issues are center stage, and managers at all levels must address them. Corporate public policy is the process by which management addresses these significant concerns.

Public Policy as a Part of Strategic Management

Where does corporate public policy fit into strategic management? First, let us briefly discuss strategic management. **Strategic management** refers to the overall management process that focuses on positioning a firm relative to its environment. A basic way in which the firm relates to its environment is through the products and services it produces and the markets it chooses to address. Strategic management is also thought of as a kind of overall or comprehensive organizational management by the firm's top-level executives. In this sense, it represents the overall executive leadership function in which the sense of direction of the organization is decided upon and implemented.

Top management teams must address many issues as a firm is positioning itself relative to its environment. The more traditional issues involve product/market decisions—the principal decision thrust of most organizations. Other decisions relate to marketing, finance, accounting, information systems, human resources, operations, research and development, competition, and so on. Corporate public policy is that part of the overall strategic management of the organization that focuses specifically on the public, ethical, and stakeholder issues that are embedded in the functioning and decision processes of the firm. Therefore, just as a firm needs to develop policy on human resources, operations, marketing, or finance, it also must develop corporate public policy to proactively address the host of issues it is facing.

Relationship of Public Policy to Strategic Management

Although a consideration of ethics is implicit in corporate public policy discussions, it is useful to make this relationship more explicit. The concept of corporate public policy and the linkage between ethics and strategy are better understood when we think about (1) the four key levels at which strategy decisions arise and (2) the steps in the strategic management process.

Four Key Strategy Levels

Because organizations are hierarchical, it is not surprising to find that strategic management is hierarchical, too. That is, there are several different levels in the firm at which strategic decisions are made or the strategy process occurs. These levels range from the broadest or highest levels (where missions, visions, goals, decisions, and policies entail higher risks and are characterized by longer time horizons, more subjective values, and greater uncertainty) to the lowest levels (where planning is done for specific functional areas, where time horizons are shorter, where information needs are less complex, and where there is less uncertainty). Four key strategy levels have been recognized and are important to consider: enterprise-level strategy, corporate-level strategy, business-level strategy, and functional-level strategy.

The broadest level of strategic management is known as *societal-level strategy* or *enterprise-level strategy*, as it has come to be known. **Enterprise-level strategy** is the overarching strategy level that poses the basic questions, "What is the role

Exhibit 900.12 *The Hierarchy of Strategy Levels*

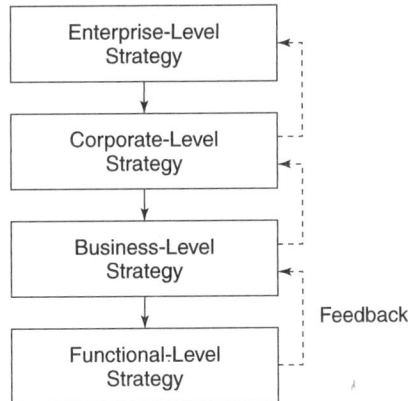

of the organization in society?" and "What do we stand for?" Enterprise-level strategy encompasses the development and articulation of corporate public policy. It may be considered the first and most important level at which ethics and strategy are linked. Until fairly recently, corporate-level strategy was thought to be the broadest strategy level. In a limited, traditional sense, this is true, because **corporate-level strategy** addresses what is often posed as the most defining question for a firm, "What business(es) are we in or should we be in?" It is easy to see how **business-level strategy** is a natural follow-on because this strategy level is concerned with the question, "How should we compete in a given business or industry?" Thus, a company whose products or services take it into many different businesses or industries might need a business-level strategy to define its competitive posture in each of them. A competitive strategy might be based on low cost or a differentiated product. Finally, **functional-level strategy** addresses the question, "How should a firm integrate its various subfunctional activities and how should these activities be related to changes taking place in the various functional areas (finance, marketing, operations)?"[58]

The purpose of identifying the four strategy levels is to clarify that corporate public policy is primarily a part of enterprise-level strategy, which, in turn, is but one level of strategic decision making that occurs in organizations. Exhibit 900.12 illustrates that enterprise-level strategy is the broadest level and that the other levels are narrower concepts that cascade from it.

Another major indicator of enterprise-level strategic thinking is the extent to which the firm attempts to identify social or public issues, analyze them, and integrate them into its strategic management processes. We will now discuss how corporate public policy is integrated into the strategic management process.

The Steps in the Strategic Management Process

To understand how corporate public policy is but one part of the larger system of management decision making, it is useful to provide an overview of the major steps that make up the strategic management process. There are several acceptable ways to conceptualize this process, but we will use the six-step process identified by Hofer and Schendel. These six steps are (1) goal formulation, (2) strategy formulation, (3) strategy evaluation, (4) strategy implementation, (5) strategic control, and (6) environmental analysis.[59] Exhibit 900.13 graphically portrays an expanded view of this process.

Narayanan and Fahey's conceptualization of the environmental analysis stage in the strategic management process is useful. They suggest that the process consists of four analytical stages.

1. *Scanning* the environment to detect warning signals
2. *Monitoring* specific environmental trends
3. *Forecasting* the future directions of environmental changes
4. *Assessing* current and future environmental changes for their organizational implications[60]

Note that the environmental analysis component collects information on trends, events, and issues that are occurring in the stakeholder environment and that this information is then fed into the other steps of the process. Note that these six steps are interactive and nonlinear.

Exhibit 900.13 *The Strategic Management Process and Corporate Public Policy*

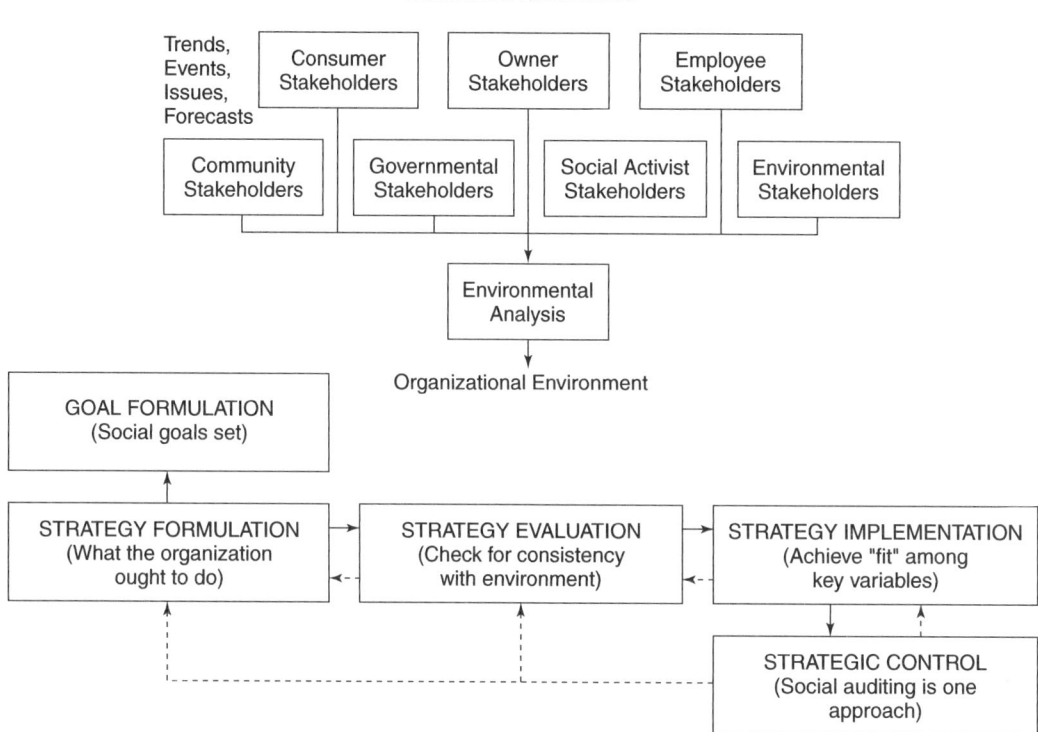

Corporate Public Affairs

Corporate public affairs and **public affairs management** are umbrella terms used by companies to describe the management processes that focus on the formalization and institutionalization of corporate public policy. The public affairs function is a logical and increasingly prevalent component of the overall strategic management process. As an overall concept, public affairs management embraces corporate public policy, along with **issues management** and **crisis management**. Indeed, many issues management and crisis management programs are housed in public affairs departments or intimately involve public affairs professionals. Corporate public affairs also embraces the broad areas of governmental relations and corporate communications.

Public Affairs as a Part of Strategic Management

In a comprehensive management system, the overall flow of activity would be as follows. A firm engages in strategic management, part of which includes the development of enterprise-level strategy, which poses the question, "What do we stand for?" The answers to this question should help the organization to form a corporate public policy, which is a more specific posture on the public, social, or stakeholder environment or specific issues within this environment. Some firms call this a public affairs strategy. Two important planning approaches in corporate public policy are issues management and, often, crisis management. These two planning aspects frequently derive from or are related to environmental analysis, which we discussed earlier. Some companies embrace these processes as part of the corporate public affairs function. These processes are typically housed, from a departmental perspective, in a **public affairs department**. *Public affairs management* is a term that often describes all these components. Exhibit 900.14 helps illustrate likely relationships among these processes.

We will now consider how the public affairs function has evolved in business firms, what issues public affairs departments currently face, and how public affairs thinking might be incorporated into the operating manager's job. This last issue is crucial, because public affairs management, to be most effective, is best thought of as an indispensable part of every manager's job, not as an isolated function or department that alone is responsible for the public issues and stakeholder environment of the firm.

Exhibit 900.14 *Relationships Among Key Corporate Public Affairs Concepts*

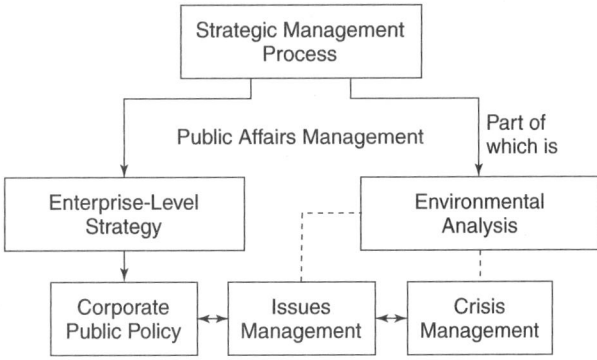

Public Affairs Strategy

We will not discuss the issue of public affairs strategy extensively, but we want to report the findings of a major research project that was undertaken by Robert H. Miles and resulted in a book entitled *Managing the Corporate Social Environment: A Grounded Theory*. Because very little work has been done on public affairs strategy, Miles's work deserves reference even though we cannot do it complete justice here. Miles's study focused on the insurance industry, but many of his findings may be applicable to other businesses.[61]

Design of the Corporate External Affairs Function and Corporate Social Performance

Miles studied the external affairs strategies (also called public affairs strategies) of major insurance firms in an effort to see what relationships existed between the strategy and design of the corporate external affairs function and corporate social performance. He found that the companies that ranked best in corporate social performance had top management philosophies that were *institution oriented*. That is, top management saw the corporation as a social institution that had a duty to adapt to a changing society and thus needed a collaborative/problem-solving external affairs strategy. The **collaborative/problem-solving strategy** was one in which firms emphasized long-term relationships with a variety of external constituencies and broad problem-solving perspectives on the resolution of social issues affecting their businesses and industries.[62]

Miles also found that the companies with the worst social performance records employed top management philosophies based on operation of the company as an independent economic franchise. Such philosophies were in sharp contrast with the institution-oriented perspectives of the best social performers. In addition, Miles found that these worst social performers employed an **individual/adversarial external affairs strategy**. In this posture, the executives denied the legitimacy of social claims on their businesses and minimized the significance of challenges they received from external critics. Therefore, they tended to be adversarial and legalistic.[63]

Business Exposure and External Affairs Design

On the subject of the external affairs units within firms, Miles found that a contingency relationship existed between what he called business exposure to the social environment and the four dimensions of the external affairs design: breadth, depth, influence, and integration. High business exposure to the social environment means that the firm produces products that move them into the public arena because of such issues as their availability, affordability, reliability, and safety. In general, consumer products tend to be more exposed to the social environment than do commercial or industrial products.[64]

Breadth, depth, influence, and integration refer to dimensions of the external affairs unit that provide a measure of sophistication versus simplicity. Units that are high on these dimensions are sophisticated, whereas units low on these dimensions are simple. Miles found that firms with high business exposure to the social environment require more sophisticated units, whereas firms with low business exposure to the social environment could manage reasonably well with simple units.[65]

It is tempting to overgeneralize Miles's study, but we must note it as a significant advance in the realm of public affairs strategy and organizational design research. The important conclusion seems to be that a firm's corporate social performance (as well as its industry legitimacy and viability and economic performance) is a function of business exposure, top management philosophy, external affairs strategy, and external affairs design.

Other initiatives in public relations strategy include integrating public affairs into corporate strategic planning, using strategic management audits for public affairs, building a balanced performance scorecard for public affairs, managing the corporation's reputation, and using core competencies to manage performance.[66]

Incorporate Public Affairs Thinking Into Managers' Jobs

In today's highly specialized business world, it is easy for operating managers to let public affairs (PA) departments worry about government affairs, community relations, issues management, or any of the numerous other PA functions. David H. Blake has taken the position that organizations ought to incorporate public affairs, or what we would call *public affairs thinking*, into every operating manager's job. He argues that operating managers are vital to a successful PA function, especially if they can identify the public affairs consequences of their actions, be sensitive to the concerns of external groups, act to defuse or avoid crisis situations, and know well in advance when to seek the help of the PA experts. There are no simple ways to achieve these goals, but Blake proposes four specific strategies that may be helpful: (1) make public affairs truly relevant, (2) develop a sense of ownership of success, (3) make it easy for operating managers, and (4) show how public affairs makes a difference.[67]

Issues Management and Crisis Management

Managerial decision-making processes known as issues management and crisis management are two major ways by which business has responded to these situations. These two approaches symbolize the extent to which the environment has become turbulent and the public has become sensitized to business's responses to the issues that have emerged from this turbulence. In the ideal situation, issues management and crisis management might be seen as the natural and logical by-products of a firm's development of enterprise-level strategy and overall corporate public policy, but this has not always been the case. Some firms have not thought seriously about public and ethical issues; for them, these approaches represent first attempts to come to grips with the practical reality of a threatening social environment.

Examples of issues include employee rights, sexual harassment, product safety, workplace safety, sweatshops, bribery and corruption, smoking in the workplace, affirmative action, and deceptive advertising.

Like all planning processes, issues management and crisis management have many characteristics in common. They also have differences, and we have chosen to treat them separately for discussion purposes. One common thread that should be mentioned at the outset is that both processes are focused on improving stakeholder management and enabling the organization to be more ethically responsive to stakeholders' expectations. Issues and crisis management, to be effective, must have as their ultimate objective an increase in the organization's social responsiveness to its stakeholders. They are also related to the extent that effective issues management may enable managements to engage in more effective crisis management. That is, some crises may be anticipated and avoided through a carefully implemented issues management initiative.

Issues Management

Issues management is a process by which organizations identify issues in the stakeholder environment, analyze and prioritize those issues in terms of their relevance to the organization, plan responses to the issues, and then evaluate and monitor the results. It is helpful to think of issues management in connection with concepts such as the strategic management process, enterprise-level strategy, corporate public policy, and environmental analysis. The process of strategic management and environmental analysis requires an overall way of managerial thinking that includes economic, technological, social, and political issues. Enterprise-level strategy and corporate public policy, on the other hand, focus on public or ethical issues. Issues management, then, devolves from these broader concepts.

Two Approaches to Issues Management

Thinking about the concepts mentioned here requires us to make some distinctions. A central consideration seems to be that issues management has been thought of in two major ways: (1) narrowly, in which public, or social, issues are the primary focus; and (2) broadly, in which strategic issues and the strategic management process are the focus of attention. Liam Fahey provides a useful distinction between these two approaches. He refers to (1) the conventional approach and (2) the strategic management approach.[68] The **conventional approach** (narrowly focused) **to issues management** has the following characteristics:[69]

- Issues fall within the domain of public policy or public affairs management.
- Issues typically have a public policy/public affairs orientation or flavor.
- An issue is any trend, event, controversy, or public policy development that might affect the corporation.
- Issues originate in social/political/regulatory/judicial environments.

The **strategic management approach** (broadly inclusive) **to issues management** has evolved in a small number of companies and is typified by the following:[70]

- Issues management is typically the responsibility of senior line management or strategic planning staff.
- Issues identification is more important than it is in the conventional approach.
- Issues management is seen as an approach to the anticipation and management of external and internal challenges to the company's strategies, plans, and assumptions.

At the risk of oversimplification, we will consider the principal distinction between the two perspectives on issues management to be that the conventional approach focuses on public/social issues, whereas the strategic approach is broadly inclusive of all issues. In addition, the conventional approach can be used as a "stand alone" decision-making process, whereas the strategic approach is intimately interconnected with the strategic management process as a whole. Another difference may be whether operating managers/strategic planners or public affairs staff members are implementing the system. Beyond these distinctions, the two approaches have much in common.

The Changing Issue Mix

The emergence in the past two decades of new "company issues management groups" and "issues managers" has been a direct outgrowth of the changing mix of issues that managers have had to handle. Economic and financial issues have always been an inherent part of the business process, although their complexity seems to have increased as international markets have broadened and competitiveness has become such an important issue. The growth of technology, especially the Internet, has presented business with other issues that need to be addressed. The most dramatic growth has been in social, ethical, and political issues—all public issues that have high visibility, media appeal, and interest among special-interest stakeholder groups. We should further observe that these issues become more interrelated over time.

For most firms, social, ethical, political, and technological issues are at the same time economic issues, because firms' success in handling them frequently has a direct bearing on their financial statuses and well-being. Over time, there is a changing mix of issues and an escalating challenge that management groups face as these issues create a cumulative effect.

Issue Definition and the Issues Management Process

Before describing the issues management process, we should briefly discuss what constitutes an issue and what assumptions we are making about issues management. An issue may be thought of as a matter that is in dispute between two or more parties. The dispute typically evokes debate, controversy, or differences of opinion that need to be resolved. At some point, the organization needs to make a decision on the unresolved matter, but such a decision does not mean that the issue is resolved. Once an issue becomes public and subject to public debate and high-profile media exposure,

Exhibit 900.15 *A Model of the Issues Management Process*

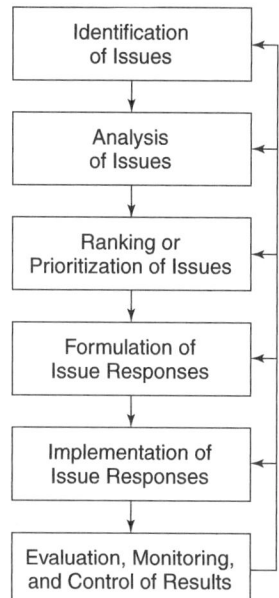

its resolution becomes increasingly difficult. One of the features of issues, particularly those arising in the social or ethical realm, is that they are ongoing and therefore require ongoing responses.

Model of the Issues Management Process

Exhibit 900.15 presents a model of the issues management process. It contains planning aspects (identification, analysis, ranking/prioritization of issues, and formulation of responses) and implementation aspects (implementation of responses and evaluation, monitoring, and control of results). Although we will discuss the stages in the issues management process as though they were discrete, we should recognize that in reality they may be interrelated and overlap one another.

Identification of Issues

Many names have been given to the process of issue identification. At various times, the terms *social forecasting, futures research, environmental scanning,* and *public issues scanning* have been used. Similarly, many techniques have been employed. All of these approaches/techniques are similar, but each has its own unique characteristics. Common to all of them, however, is the need to scan the environment and to identify emerging issues or trends that might later be determined to have some relevance to or impact on the organization.

Issue identification, in its most rudimentary form, involves the assignment to some individual in the organization the tasks of continuously scanning a variety of publications—newspapers, magazines, specialty publications, the World Wide Web—and developing a comprehensive list of issues. Often this same person, or group, is instructed to review public documents, records of congressional hearings, and other such sources of information. One result of this scanning is an internal report or a newsletter that is circulated throughout the organization. The next step in this evolution may be for the company to subscribe to a trend-information service or newsletter that is prepared and published by a private individual or consulting firm that specializes in environmental or issue scanning.[71]

Analysis of Issues

The next two steps (analysis and ranking of issues) are closely related. To analyze an issue means to carefully study, dissect, break down, group, or engage in any specific process that helps you better understand the nature or characteristics of the issue. An analysis requires that you look beyond the obvious manifestations of the issue and strive to learn more of its history, development, current nature, and potential for future relevance to the organization. William King proposed a series of key questions that focus on stakeholder groups in attempting to analyze issues.[72]

- Who (which stakeholders) are affected by the issue?
- Who has an interest in the issue?

- Who is in a position to exert influence on the issue?
- Who has expressed opinions on the issue?
- Who ought to care about the issue?

In addition to these questions, a consulting firm—Human Resources Network—proposed the following key questions to help with issue analysis:[73]

- Who started the ball rolling? (Historical view)
- Who is now involved? (Contemporary view)
- Who will get involved? (Future view)

Answers to these questions place management in a better position to rank or prioritize the issues so that it will have a better sense of the urgency with which the issues need to be addressed.

Ranking or Prioritization of Issues

Once issues have been carefully analyzed and are well understood, it is necessary to rank them in some form of a hierarchy of importance or relevance to the organization. We should note that some issues management systems place this step before analysis. This is done especially when it is desired to screen out those issues that are obviously not relevant and deserving of further analysis.

The prioritization stage may range from a simple grouping of issues into categories of urgency to a more elaborate or sophisticated scoring system. Two examples will serve to illustrate the grouping technique. **Xerox** has used a process of categorizing issues into three classifications: (1) *high priority* (issues on which management must be well informed), (2) *nice to know* (issues that are interesting but not critical or urgent), and (3) *questionable* (issues that may not be issues at all unless something else happens). **PPG Industries** has grouped issues into three priorities: *Priority A* (critical issues that warrant executive action and review), *Priority B* (issues that warrant surveillance by the division general manager or staff), and *Priority C* (issues that have only potential impact and warrant monitoring by the public affairs department).[74]

A somewhat more sophisticated approach uses a **probability-impact matrix** requiring management to assess the *probability of occurrence of an issue* (high, medium, or low) on one dimension and its *impact on the company* (high, medium, or low) on the other dimension. In using such an approach, management would place each issue in the appropriate cell of the matrix, and the completed matrix would then serve as an aid to prioritization. As a variation on this theme, management could rank issues by considering the mathematical product of each issue's impact (for example, on a scale from 1 to 10) and probability of occurrence (on a scale from 0 to 10).

William R. King has provided a somewhat more elaborate issues-ranking scheme. He recommends that issues be screened on five filter criteria: strategy, relevance, actionability, criticality, and urgency.[75] Once each issue has been scored on a 10-point scale on each criterion, issues are then ranked according to their resulting point totals. In addition to this filtering/ranking process, other techniques that have been used in issues identification, analysis, and prioritization include polls/surveys, expert panels, content analysis, the Delphi technique, trend extrapolation, scenario building, and the use of precursor events or bellwethers.[76]

Earlier we described a simple issues-identification process as involving an individual in the organization or a subscription to a newsletter or trend-spotting service. The analysis and ranking stages could be done by an individual, but more often the company has moved up to a next stage of formalization. This next stage involves assignment of the issues management function to a team, often as part of a public affairs department, which begins to specialize in the issues management function. This group of specialists can provide a wide range of issues management activities, depending on the commitment of the company to the process.

Formulation and Implementation of Responses to Issues

We should observe that the formulation and implementation stages in the issues management process are quite similar to the corresponding stages pertained to the strategic management process as a whole.

Formulation in this case refers to the response design process. Based on the analysis conducted, companies can then identify options that might be pursued in dealing with the issues, in making decisions, and in implementing those decisions. Strategy formulation refers not only to the formulation of the actions that the firm intends to take but also to the creation of the overall strategy, or degree of aggressiveness, employed in carrying out those actions. Options might include aggressive pursuit, gradual pursuit, or selective pursuit of goals, plans, processes, or programs.[77] All of these more detailed plans are part of the strategy-formulation process.

Once plans for dealing with issues have been formulated, implementation becomes the focus. There are many organizational aspects that need to be addressed in the implementation process. Some of these include the clarity of the plan itself, resources needed to implement the plan, top management support, organizational structure, technical competence, and timing.[78]

Evaluation, Monitoring, and Control of Issues

These recognizable steps in the issues management process were also treated as steps in the strategic management process. In the present context, they mean that companies should continually evaluate the results of their responses to the issues and ensure that these actions are kept on track. In particular, this stage requires careful monitoring of stakeholders' opinions. A form of stakeholder audit—something derivative of the social audit—might be used. The information that is gathered during this final stage in the issues management process is then fed back to the earlier stages in the process so that changes or adjustments might be made as needed. Evaluation information may be useful at each stage in the process.

Social Audit Versus Stakeholder Audit

- The social audit is a systematic attempt to identify, measure, monitor, and evaluate an organization's performance with respect to its social efforts, goals, and programs.

- The stakeholder audit is a systematic attempt to identify and measure an organization's stakeholder's issues and measure and evaluate their opinions with respect to its effective resolution.

We have presented the issues management process as a complete system. In actual practice, companies apply the stages in various degrees of formality or informality as needed or desired. For example, because issues management is more important in some situations than in others, some stages of the process may be truncated to meet the needs of different firms in different industries. In addition, some firms are more committed to issues management than others.

Issues Development Process

A vital attribute of issues management is that issues tend to develop according to an evolutionary pattern. This pattern might be thought of as a developmental or growth process or, as some have called it, a life cycle. It is important for managers to have some appreciation of this **issues development process** so that they can recognize when an event or trend is becoming an issue and also because it might affect the strategy that the firm employs in dealing with the issue. Com-

Exhibit 900.16 *Issue Development Life-Cycle Process*

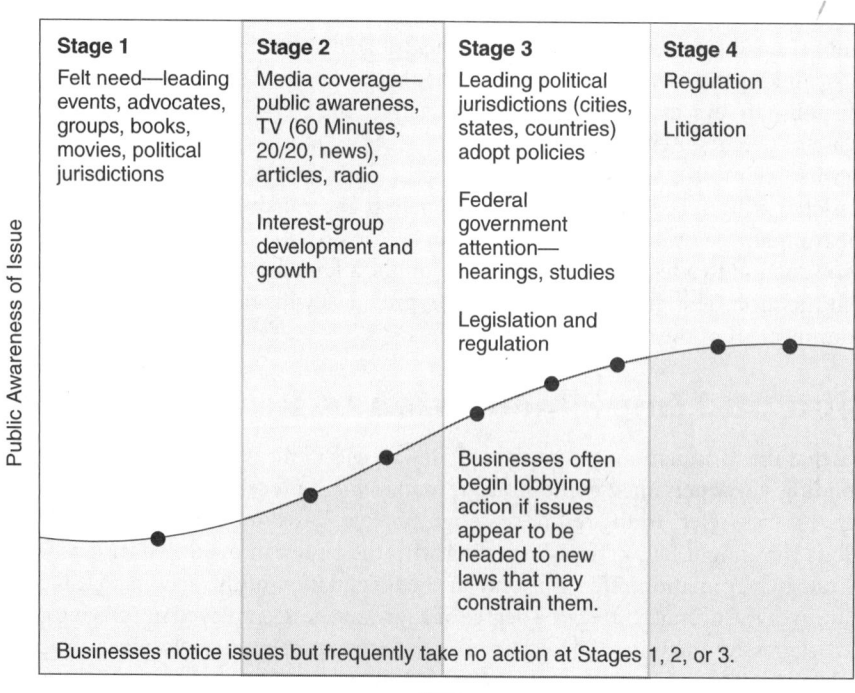

panies may take a variety of courses of action depending on the stage of the issue in the process. Exhibit 900.16 presents a simplified view of the issue development life-cycle process.

We should note that the stages in the process, especially the early stages, might occur in a different sequence or in an iterative pattern. Further, not all issues complete the process; some are resolved before they reach the stage of legislation or regulation.

Finally, we are reminded by Bigelow, Fahey, and Mahon that "issues do not necessarily follow a linear, sequential path, but instead follow paths that reflect the intensity and diversity of the values and interests stakeholders bring to an issue and the complexity of the interaction among . . ." all the variables.[79] This should serve as a warning not to oversimplify the issues development process.

Issues Management in Practice

Issues management in practice today has very much become a subset of activities performed by the public affairs departments of major corporations. A late 1990s survey of corporate public affairs officers of major corporations revealed that 67 percent engage in issues management functions. Furthermore, the survey revealed that there is now greater use of interdepartmental issues teams, with the public affairs department serving as coordinator and strategist but with appropriate line and staff executives charged with ultimate accountability for implementation. In practice, therefore, it can be seen that issues management does not function as a stand-alone activity but has been subsumed into a host of functions for which modern public affairs departments take responsibility.[80]

Issues management faces a serious challenge in business today. From the standpoint of the turbulence in the stakeholder environment, issues management may be needed. To become a permanent part of the organization, however, issues management will have to continuously prove itself. We can talk conceptually about the process with ease, but the field still remains somewhat nebulous even though it is struggling to become more scientific and legitimate. Managers in the real world want results, and if issues management cannot deliver those results, it will be destined for failure as a management process.

Issues Management Is a Bridge to Crisis Management

Ideally, firms use issues management to assist them in planning for and preventing crises that then require crisis management. Issues management represents careful planning that may head off impending crises. This is because many crises are embedded in issues or erupt from issues that could have been anticipated and studied in carefully designed issues management processes. Issues management can be seen as a form of precrisis planning. It is intended to help organizations anticipate and plan for possible crisis eruptions. Not all crises can be planned for, of course, but many can be anticipated through effective issues management programs. It has been suggested by Kate Miller that one of the most effective ways for keeping a crisis plan "living" is issues management.[81] Thus, we can see how issues and crisis management are different, but related.

Crisis Management

Issues typically evolve gradually over a period of time. Issues management is a process of identifying and preparing to respond to potential issues. Crises, on the other hand, occur abruptly. They cannot always be anticipated or forecast. Some crises occur within an issue category considered; many do not. Issues and crisis management are related, however, in that they both are concerned about organizations becoming prepared for uncertainty in the stakeholder environment.

The Nature of Crises

There are many kinds of crises. Hurt or killed customers, hurt employees, injured stockholders, and unfair practices are the concerns of modern crisis management. Not all crises involve such public or ethical issues, but these kinds of crises almost always ensure front-page status. Major companies can be seriously damaged by such episodes, especially if the episodes are poorly handled. Very quickly, they achieve a high-visibility status.

What is a crisis? Dictionaries state that a crisis is a "turning point for better or worse," an "emotionally significant event," or a "decisive moment." We all think of crises as being emotionally charged, but we do not always think of them as turning points for better or for worse. The implication here is that a crisis is a decisive moment that, if managed one way, could make things worse but, if managed another way, could make things better. Choice is present, and how the crisis is managed can make a difference.

From a managerial point of view, a line needs to be drawn between a problem and a crisis. Problems, of course, are common in business. A crisis, however, is not as common. A useful way to think about a **crisis** is with a definition set forth by Laurence Barton:

> A crisis is a major, unpredictable event that has potentially negative results. The event and its aftermath may significantly damage an organization and its employees, products, services, financial condition, and reputation.[82]

Another definition set forth by Pearson and Clair is also helpful in understanding the critical aspects of a crisis:

> An organizational crisis is a low-probability, high-impact event that threatens the viability of the organization and is characterized by ambiguity of cause, effect, and means of resolution, as well as by a belief that decisions must be made swiftly.[83]

Types of Crises

Situations in which the executives surveyed by Steven Fink felt they were vulnerable to crises included industrial accidents, environmental problems, union problems/strikes, product recalls, investor relations, hostile takeovers, proxy fights, rumors/media leaks, government regulatory problems, acts of terrorism, and embezzlement.[84] Other common crises include product tampering, executive kidnapping, work-related homicides, malicious rumors, terrorism, and natural disasters that destroy corporate offices or information bases.[85]

Mitroff and Anagnos have suggested that crises may be categorized according to the following types of crises.[86]

Economic. Labor strikes, market crashes, major declines in earnings

Informational. Loss of proprietary information, false information, tampering with computer records

Human resource. Loss of key executives, personnel, or workplace violence

Reputational. Slander, tampering with corporate logos

Psychopathic. Product tampering, kidnapping, hostage taking

Natural. Earthquakes, fire, tornadoes

Of the major crises that have recently occurred, the majority of the companies reported the following outcomes: The crises escalated in intensity, were subjected to media and government scrutiny, interfered with normal business operations, and damaged the company's bottom line.

Four Crisis Stages

There are a number of ways we could categorize the stages through which a crisis may progress. According to Steven Fink, a crisis may consist of as many as four distinct stages: (1) a **prodromal crisis stage,** (2) an **acute crisis stage,** (3) a **chronic crisis stage,** and (4) a **crisis resolution stage.**[87]

Prodromal Crisis Stage. This is the warning stage. ("Prodromal" is a medical term that refers to a previous notice or warning.) This warning stage could also be thought of as a symptom stage. Although it could be called a "precrisis" stage, this presupposes that one knows that a crisis is coming. According to Mitroff and Anagnos, crises "send out a repeated trail of early warning signals" that managers can learn to recognize.[88] Perhaps management should adopt this perspective: Watch each situation with the thought that it could be a crisis in the making. Early symptoms may be quite obvious, such as in the case where a social activist group tells management it will boycott the company if a certain problem is not addressed. On the other hand, symptoms may be more subtle, as in the case where defect rates for a particular product a company makes start edging up over time.

Acute Crisis Stage. This is the stage at which the crisis actually occurs. There is no turning back; the incident has occurred. Damage has been done at this point, and it is now up to management to handle or contain the damage. If the prodromal stage is the precrisis stage, the acute stage is the actual crisis stage. The crucial decision point at which things may get worse or better has been reached.

Chronic Crisis Stage. This is the lingering period. It may be the period of investigations, audits, or in-depth news stories. Management may see it as a period of recovery, self-analysis, or self-doubt. In Fink's survey of major companies, he found that crises tended to linger as much as two and a half times longer in firms without crisis management plans than in firms with such plans.

Exhibit 900.17 *Fink's Four Stages in a Management Crisis*

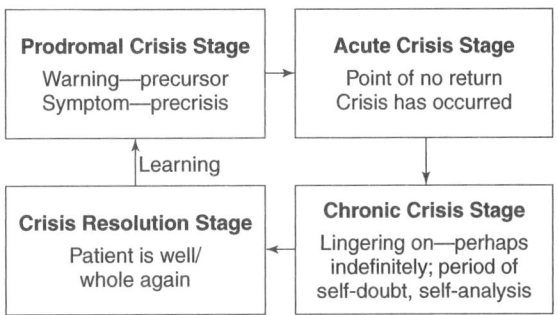

Crisis Resolution Stage. This is the final stage—the goal of all crisis management efforts. Fink argues that when an early warning sign of a crisis is noted, the manager should seize control swiftly and determine the most direct and expedient route to resolution. If the warning signs are missed in the first stage, the goal is to speed up all phases and reach the final stage as soon as possible.

Exhibit 900.17 presents one way in which these four stages might be depicted. It should be noted that the phases may overlap and that each phase varies in intensity and duration. It is hoped that management will learn from the crisis and thus will be better prepared for, and better able to handle, any future crisis.

Other views of crises and crisis management may be taken. Gerald C. Meyers, former chairman of **American Motors Corporation** and a consultant on crisis management, and others lay out the scenario for a *poorly managed crisis,* which typically follows a predictable pattern.[89] The pattern is as follows:

- Early indications that trouble is brewing occur.
- Warnings are ignored/played down.
- Warnings build to a climax.
- Pressure mounts.
- Executives are often overwhelmed or can't cope effectively.
- Quick-fix alternatives look appealing. Hasty moves create trouble.
- Clamming-up versus opening-up options present themselves.
- Most firms choose the former.
- A siege mentality prevails.

Visualizing the attributes or pattern of a poorly managed crisis is valuable because it illustrates how not to do it—a lesson that many managers may find quite valuable.

Managing Business Crises

Business Week's Five Practical Steps in Managing Crises

A more complete view of crisis management holds that a series of five steps must be taken. These five steps, synthesized by *Business Week* magazine from the actual experiences of companies experiencing crises, are discussed next and are summarized in Exhibit 900.18.[90]

FIRST: IDENTIFYING AREAS OF VULNERABILITY   In this first step, some areas of vulnerability are obvious, such as potential chemical spills, whereas others are more subtle. The key seems to be in developing a greater consciousness of how things can go wrong and get out of hand. At **Heinz**, after the "Tunagate" incident, a vice president set up brainstorming sessions. He said, "We're brainstorming about how we would be affected by everything from a competitor who had a serious quality problem to a scandal involving a Heinz executive."[91]

SECOND: DEVELOPING A PLAN FOR DEALING WITH THREATS   A plan for dealing with the most serious crisis threats is a logical next step. One of the most crucial issues is communications planning. After a **Dow Chemical** railroad car derailed near Toronto, forcing the evacuation of 250,000 people, Dow Canada prepared information kits on the hazards of its products so that executives would be knowledgeable enough to respond properly if a similar crisis

Exhibit 900.18 *Business Week's Five Steps in Crisis Management*

> 1. Identifying areas of vulnerability
>   A. Obvious areas
>   B. Subtle areas
> 2. Developing a plan for dealing with threats
>   A. Communications planning is vital
>   B. Training executives in product dangers and dealing with media
> 3. Forming crisis teams
>   A. Vital to successful crisis management
>   B. Identifying executives who can work well under stress
> 4. Simulating crisis drills
>   A. Experience/practice is helpful
>   B. "War rooms" serve as gathering places for team members
> 5. Learning from experience
>   A. Assess effectiveness of crisis strategies
>   B. Move from reaction to proaction

were to arise in the future. Dow Canada also trained executives in interviewing techniques. This effort paid off several years later when an accident caused a chemical spill into a river that supplied drinking water for several nearby towns. The company's emergency response team arrived at the site almost immediately and established a press center that distributed information about the chemicals. In addition, the company recruited a neutral expert to speak on the hazards and how to deal with them. Officials praised Dow for its handling of this crisis.[92]

Richard J. Mahoney, former CEO of **Monsanto Company**, has offered the following *10 "Rs" for the effective handling of public policy crises.* He recommends these steps as part of an overall crisis plan.[93]

- Respond early.
- Recruit a credible spokesperson.
- Reply truthfully.
- Respect the opposition's concerns.
- Revisit the issue with follow-up.
- Retreat early if it's a loser.
- Redouble efforts early if it's a critical company issue.
- Reply with visible top management.
- Refuse to press for what is not good public policy.
- Repeat the prior statement regularly.

Some of these steps may not apply to every crisis situation, but many may be useful as part of a crisis management plan. Mahoney notes that getting an entire organization trained to deal with crises is difficult and expensive, but he paraphrases what a car repairman said in a TV commercial: "You can pay now or pay a lot more later." Mahoney thinks that now is infinitely better for everyone.[94]

THIRD: FORMING CRISIS TEAMS Another step that can be taken as part of an overall planning effort is the formation of **crisis teams**. Such teams have played key roles in many well-managed disasters. A good example is the team formed at **Procter & Gamble** when its Rely tampon products were linked with the dreaded disease toxic shock syndrome. The team was quickly assembled, a vice president was appointed to head it, and after one week the decision was made to remove Rely from marketplace shelves. The quick action earned the firm praise, and it paid off for P&G in the long run.

Another task in assembling crisis teams is identifying managers who can cope effectively with stress. Not every executive can handle the fast-moving, high-pressured, ambiguous decision environment that is created by a crisis, and early identification of executives who can is important. We should also note that it is not always the CEO who can best perform in such a crisis atmosphere.

Despite the careful use of crisis teams, crises can often overwhelm a carefully constructed plan. When **ValuJet's** Flight 592 crashed in the Florida Everglades in 1996, for example, ValuJet flawlessly executed a three-pronged, team-based crisis management plan calling for the company to (1) show compassion, (2) take responsibility, and (3) demonstrate that the airline learned from the crisis. Experts have said that the company handled the crisis well. However, a close look at the tragedy revealed that a series of complicating factors turned the crisis into something even more difficult than a well-scripted, perfectly executed crisis management plan could handle.[95]

FOURTH: SIMULATING CRISIS DRILLS Some companies have gone so far as to run crisis drills in which highly stressful situations are simulated so that managers can "practice" what they might do in a real crisis. As a basis for conducting crisis drills and experiential exercises, a number of companies have adopted a software package known as Crisis Plan wRiter. This software allows companies to centralize and maintain up-to-date crisis management information and allows company leaders to assign responsibilities to their crisis team, target key audiences, identify and monitor potential issues, and create crisis-response processes.[96]

FIFTH: LEARNING FROM EXPERIENCE The final stage in crisis management is learning from experience. At this point, managers need to ask themselves exactly what they have learned from past crises and how that knowledge can be used to advantage in the future. Part of this stage entails an assessment of the effectiveness of the firm's crisis-handling strategies and identification of areas where improvements in capabilities need to be made. Without a crisis management system of some kind in place, the organization will find itself reacting to crises after they have occurred. If learning and preparation for the future are occurring, however, the firm may engage in more proactive behavior.[97]

Augustine's Six Stages of Crisis Management

As an alternative to the previous steps in crisis management, Norman Augustine, former president of **Lockheed Martin** Corporation, distinguished among six stages of crisis management. To some extent, these overlap and embrace the steps, but it is useful to see an alternative conceptualization of the steps that should be taken in crisis management. Augustine's list begins with the idea that the crisis should be avoided.[98]

- Stage 1: Avoiding the Crisis
- Stage 2: Preparing to Manage the Crisis
- Stage 3: Recognizing the Crisis
- Stage 4: Containing the Crisis
- Stage 5: Resolving the Crisis
- Stage 6: Profiting from the Crisis

We should note that Pearson and Mitroff have accurately observed that effective crisis management requires a program that is tailored to a firm's specific industry, business environment, and crisis management experience. Effective crisis managers will understand that there are major crisis management factors that may vary from situation to situation, such as the type of crisis (for example, natural disaster or human induced), the phase of the crisis, the systems affected (for example, humans, technology, culture), and the stakeholders affected. Managers cannot eliminate crises. However, they can become keenly aware of their vulnerabilities and make concerted efforts to understand and reduce these vulnerabilities through continuous crisis management programs.[99]

Crisis Communications

An illustration of crisis management without effective communications occurred during the **Jack in the Box** hamburger disaster of 1993. There was an outbreak of E. coli bacteria in the Pacific Northwest area, resulting in the deaths of four children. Following this crisis, the parent company, San Diego-based **Foodmaker**, entered a downward spiral after lawsuits by the families of victims enraged the public and franchises. Foodmaker did most of the right things and did them quickly. The company immediately suspended hamburger sales, recalled suspect meat from its distribution system, increased cooking time for all foods, pledged to pay for all the medical costs related to the disaster, and hired a food safety expert to design a new food-handling system. But, it forgot to do one thing: communicate with the public, including its own employees.[100]

The company's **crisis communications** efforts were inept. It waited a week before accepting any responsibility for the tragedy, preferring to point fingers at its meat supplier and even the Washington state health officials for not explaining the state's new guidelines for cooking hamburgers at higher temperatures. The media pounced on the company. The company was blasted for years even though within the company it was taking the proper steps to correct the problem. The company suffered severe financial losses, and it took at least six years before the company really felt it was on the road to recovery. "The crisis," as it is still called around company headquarters, taught the firm an important lesson. CEO Robert Nugent was quoted as saying in 1999, "Nobody wants to deal with their worst nightmare, but we should have recognized you've got to communicate."[101]

Virtually all crisis management plans call for effective crisis communications. There are a number of different stakeholder groups with whom effective communications are critical, especially the media and those immediately affected by the crisis. Many companies have failed to successfully manage their crises because of inadequate or failed communications with key stakeholder groups. Successful communications efforts are crucial to effective crisis management. It is axiomatic that *prepared* communications will be more helpful than *reactive* communications. Jonathan L. Bernstein has offered **10 steps of crisis communication** that are worth summarizing.[102]

1. Identify your crisis communications team.
2. Identify key spokespersons who will be authorized to speak for the organization.
3. Train your spokespersons.
4. Establish communications protocols.
5. Identify and know your audience.
6. Anticipate crises.
7. Assess the crisis situation.
8. Identify key messages you will communicate to key groups.
9. Decide on communications methods.
10. Be prepared to ride out the storm.

A brief elaboration on the importance of identifying key messages that will be communicated to key groups is useful (point 8). It is important that you communicate with your *internal stakeholders* first because rumors are often started there, and uninformed employees can do great damage to a successful crisis management effort. Internal stakeholders are your best advocates and can be supportive during a crisis. Prepare news releases that contain as much information as possible and get this information out to all *media outlets* at the same time. Communicate with *others in the community* who have a need to know, such as public officials, disaster coordinators, stakeholders and others. *Uniformity of response* is of vital importance during a crisis. Finally, have a designated "release authority" for information (point 2). The first 24 hours of a crisis can make or break the organization, and how these key spokespersons work is of vital importance to handling the crisis.[103]

Mitroff and Anagnos have stressed the importance of "telling the truth" in effective crisis communications. They argue that there are no secrets in today's society and that eventually the truth will get out. Therefore, from a practical point of view, the question is not whether the truth will be revealed but rather when that truth will become public and under what circumstances.[104] From both an ethical and a practical perspective, truth-telling is an important facet of crisis communications.

980 Corporate Ethics and Management Assurance

The scope of corporate ethics includes business ethics and management ethics.

Business Ethics

To understand business ethics, it is useful to comment on the relationship between ethics and morality. **Ethics** is the discipline that deals with what is good and bad and with moral duty and obligation. Ethics can also be regarded as a set of moral principles or values. **Morality** is a doctrine or system of moral conduct. Moral conduct refers to that which relates to principles of right and wrong in behavior. For the most part, then, we can think of ethics and morality as being so similar to one another that we may use the terms interchangeably to refer to the study of fairness, justice, and right and wrong behavior in business.

Business ethics, therefore, is concerned with good and bad or right and wrong behavior and practices that take place within a business context. Concepts of right and wrong are increasingly being interpreted today to include the more difficult and subtle questions of fairness, justice, and equity.

Two key branches of moral philosophy, or ethics, are descriptive ethics and normative ethics. It is important to distinguish between the two because they each take a different perspective. **Descriptive ethics** is concerned with describing, characterizing, and studying the morality of a people, a culture, or a society. It also compares and contrasts different moral codes, systems, practices, beliefs, and values.[105] In descriptive business ethics, therefore, our focus is on learning what is occurring in the realm of behavior, actions, decisions, policies, and practices of business firms, managers, or, perhaps, specific industries. The public opinion polls give us glimpses of descriptive ethics—what people believe to be going on based on their perceptions and understandings. Descriptive ethics focuses on "what is" the prevailing set of ethical standards in the business community, specific organizations, or on the part of specific managers. A real danger in limiting our attention to descriptive ethics is that some people may adopt the view that "if everyone is doing it," it must be acceptable. For example, if a survey reveals that 70 percent of employees are padding their expense accounts, this describes what is taking place but it does not describe what *should* be taking place. Just because many are participating in this questionable activity doesn't make it an appropriate practice. This is why normative ethics is important.

Normative ethics, by contrast, is concerned with supplying and justifying a coherent moral system of thinking and judging. Normative ethics seeks to uncover, develop, and justify basic moral principles that are intended to guide behavior, actions, and decisions.[106] Normative business ethics, therefore, seeks to propose some principle or principles for distinguishing ethical from unethical in the business context. It deals more with "what ought to be" or "what ought not to be" in terms of business practices. Normative ethics is concerned with establishing norms or standards by which business practices might be guided or judged.

In our study of business ethics, we need to be ever mindful of this distinction between descriptive and normative perspectives. It is tempting to observe the prevalence of a particular practice in business (for example, discrimination or deceptive advertising) and conclude that because so many are doing it (descriptive ethics), it must be acceptable behavior. Normative ethics would insist that a practice be justified on the basis of some ethical principle, argument, or rationale before being considered acceptable. Normative ethics demands a more meaningful moral anchor than just "everyone is doing it." Normative ethics is our primary frame of reference in this discussion, though we will frequently compare "what ought to be" with "what is (going on in the real world)."

We will introduce three major approaches to thinking about business ethics.

1. Conventional approach
2. Principles approach
3. Ethical tests approach

We will focus on the conventional approach to business ethics in this section and the other two approaches are briefly mentioned here.

The principles approach to ethics or ethical decision making is based on the idea that managers may desire to anchor their decisions on a more solid foundation than the conventional approach to ethics. A principle of business ethics is a concept, guideline, or rule that, if applied when faced with an ethical dilemma, will assist an individual in making an ethical decision. The principles approach augments the conventional approach. Examples of major principles include utilitarianism, rights, justice, caring, virtue ethics, servant leadership, and the golden rule.

The ethical tests approach is based on practice while the principles approach is based on philosophy. No single test is recommended as a universal answer; instead a combination will be useful. Examples of tests include common sense, one's best self, making something public, ventilation, purified idea, and gag test.

The Conventional Approach to Business Ethics

The **conventional approach to business ethics** is essentially an approach whereby we compare a decision or practice with prevailing norms of acceptability. We call it the conventional approach because it is believed that this is the way that general society thinks. The major challenge of this approach is answering the questions "Whose norms do we use?" in making the judgment, and "What norms are prevailing?" This approach may be depicted by highlighting the major variables to be compared with one another:

Decision or Practice ↔ Prevailing Norms of Acceptability

There is considerable room for variability on both of these issues. With respect to whose norms are used as the basis for ethical judgments, the conventional approach would consider as legitimate those norms emanating from family, friends, religious beliefs, the local community, one's employer, law, the profession, and so on. In addition, one's conscience, or the individual, would be seen by many as a legitimate source of ethical norms.

Exhibit 900.19 *Sources of Ethical Norms Communicated to Individuals*

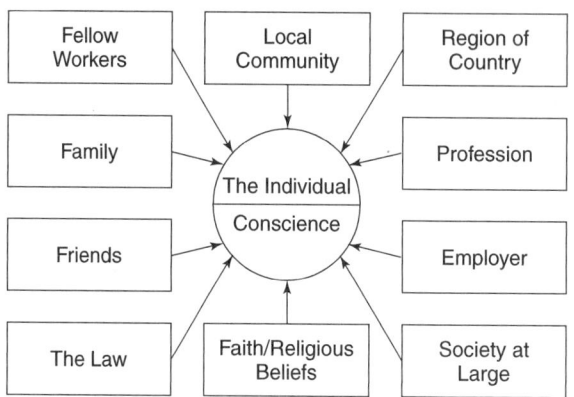

Exhibit 900.19 illustrates some of the sources of norms that come to bear on the individual and that might be used in various circumstances, and over time, under the conventional approach. These sources compete in their influence on what constitutes the "prevailing norms of acceptability" for today.

In many circumstances, the conventional approach to ethics may be useful and applicable. What does a person do, however, if norms from one source conflict with norms from another source? Also, how can we be sure that societal norms are really appropriate or defensible? Our society's culture sends us many and often conflicting messages about what is appropriate behavior. We get these messages from television, movies, music, and other sources in the culture.

Ethics and the Law

We have made various references to ethics and the law. We said that ethical behavior is typically thought to reside above behavior required by the law. This is the generally accepted view of ethics. We should make it clear, however, that in many respects the law and ethics overlap. To appreciate this, you need to recognize that the law embodies notions of ethics. That is, the law may be seen as a reflection of what society thinks are minimal standards of conduct and behavior. Both law and ethics have to do with what is deemed appropriate or acceptable, but law reflects society's *codified* ethics. Therefore, if a person breaks a law or violates a regulation, she or he is also behaving unethically. In spite of this overlap, we continue to talk about desirable ethical behavior as behavior that extends beyond what is required by law. Viewed from the standpoint of minimums, we would certainly say that obedience to the law is generally regarded to be a minimum standard of behavior.

In addition, we should make note of the fact that the law does not address all realms in which ethical questions might be raised. Thus, there are clear roles for both law and ethics to play. It should be noted that research on illegal corporate behavior has been conducted for some time. Illegal corporate behavior, of course, comprises business practices that are in direct defiance of law or public policy. Research has focused on two dominant questions: (1) Why do firms behave illegally or what leads them to engage in illegal activities, and (2) what are the consequences of behaving illegally?[107]

Making Ethical Judgments

When a decision is made about what is ethical (right, just, fair) using the conventional approach, there is room for variability on several counts (see Exhibit 900.20). Three key elements compose such a decision. First, we observe the *decision, action,* or *practice* that has been committed. Second, we *compare the practice with prevailing norms of acceptability*—that is, society's or some other standard of what is acceptable or unacceptable. Third, *we must recognize that value judgments are being made* by someone as to what really occurred (the actual behavior) and what the prevailing norms of acceptability really are. This means that two different people could look at the same behavior, compare it with their concepts of what the prevailing norms are, and reach different conclusions as to whether the behavior was ethical or not. This becomes quite complex as perceptions of what is ethical inevitably lead to the difficult task of ranking different values against one another.

If we can put aside for a moment the fact that perceptual differences about an incident do exist, and the fact that we differ among ourselves because of our personal values and philosophies of right and wrong, we are still left with the problematic task of determining society's prevailing norms of acceptability of business behavior. As a whole,

Exhibit 900.20 *Making Ethical Judgments*

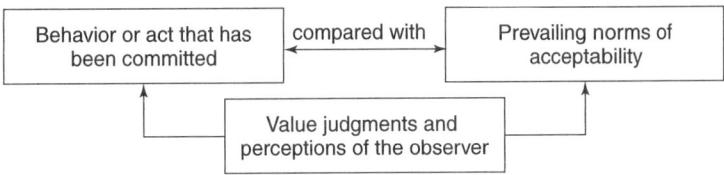

members of society generally agree at a very high level of abstraction that certain behaviors are wrong. However, the consensus tends to disintegrate as we move from the general to specific situations.

The conventional approach to business ethics can be valuable, because we all need to be aware of and sensitive to the total environment in which we exist. We need to be aware of how society regards ethical issues. It has limitations, however, and we need to be cognizant of these as well. The most serious danger is that of falling into an **ethical relativism** where we pick and choose which source of norms we wish to use based on what will justify our current actions or maximize our freedom.

Ethics, Economics, and Law: A Venn Diagram Model

When we focus on ethics and ethical decision making, it is useful to consider the primary forces that come into tension while making ethical judgments. When we are discussing a firm's corporate social responsibility (CSR), philanthropy definitely enters the discussion. This is because philanthropic initiatives are the primary way many companies display their CSR in the community—through good and charitable works. In ethical decision making, however, we tend to set aside philanthropic expectations and focus on ethical expectations and, especially, those forces that primarily come into tension with ethics—economics (the quest for profits) and law. Thus, in most decision-making situations, ethics, economics, and law become the central expectations that must be considered and balanced against each other in the quest to make wise decisions.

A firm's economic, legal, and ethical responsibilities can be depicted in a Venn diagram model illustrating how certain actions, decisions, or policies fulfill one, two, or three of these responsibility categories. Exhibit 900.21 presents this Venn diagram model, illustrating the overlapping potential of these responsibility categories.

In Area 1, where the decision, action, or practice fulfills all three responsibilities, the management prescription is to "go for it." That is, the action is profitable, in compliance with the law, and represents ethical behavior. In Area 2a, the action under consideration is profitable and legal, but its ethical status may be uncertain. The guideline here is to "proceed cautiously." In these kinds of situations, the ethics of the action needs to be carefully considered. In Area 2b, the action is profitable and ethical, but perhaps the law does not clearly address the issue or is ambiguous. If it is ethical, there is a good chance it is also legal, but the guideline again is to proceed cautiously. In Area 3, the action is legal and ethical but not profitable. Therefore, the strategy here would be to avoid this action or find ways to make it profitable. However, there may be a compelling case to take the action if it is legal and ethical and, thus, represents the right thing to do. Mark Schwartz has agreed that the four-part CSR model can appropriately be recast into a Venn model, especially for ethical analysis.[108]

Exhibit 900.21 *A Venn Diagram Model for Ethical Decision Making*

By taking philanthropy out of the picture, the ethics Venn model serves as a useful template for thinking about the more immediate expectations that society has on business in a situation in which the ethical dimension plays an important role.

Four Important Ethics Questions

It is also useful to provide some additional "big picture" perspectives that could legitimately be asked of ethics, in general, or of business ethics, in particular. Philosophers have concepts and terminology that are more academic, but let us approach this broad perspective, as Otto Bremer has done,[109] by starting with four apparently simple but really different kinds of questions:

1. What really is?
2. What ought to be?
3. How do we get from what is to what ought to be?
4. What is our motivation in all this?

These four questions capture the core of what ethics is all about. They force an examination of *what really is* (descriptive ethics) going on in a business situation, *what ought to be* (normative ethics), how we *close the gap* between what is and what ought to be (practical question), and what our *motivation* is for doing all this.

Before we discuss each question briefly, let us suggest that these four questions may be asked at five different levels: the level of the individual (the personal level), the level of the organization, the level of the industry or profession, the societal level, and the global or international level. By asking and then answering these questions, a greater understanding of a business ethics dilemma may be achieved.

What Really Is?

The "what really is?" question forces us to face the reality of what is actually going on in an ethical sense in business or in a specific decision or practice. Ideally it is a factual, scientific, or descriptive question. Its purpose is to help us understand the reality of the ethical behavior we find before us in the business environment. As we discussed earlier when we were describing the nature of making ethical judgments, it is not always simple to state exactly what the "real" situation is. This is because we are humans and thus make mistakes when we "sense" what is happening. Also, we are conditioned by our personal beliefs, values, and biases, and these factors affect what we see or sense. Or, we may perceive real conditions for what they are but fail to think in terms of alternatives or in terms of "what ought to be." Think of the difficulty you might have in attempting to describe "what really is" with respect to business ethics at the personal, organizational, industry/professional, societal, or global levels. The questions then become:

- What are your personal ethics?
- What are your organization's ethics?
- What are the ethics of your industry or profession?
- What are society's ethics?
- What are global ethics?

What Ought to Be?

This second question is quite different from the first question. It is normative rather than descriptive. It is certainly not a scientific question. The "what ought to be?" question seldom gets answered directly, particularly in a managerial setting. Managers are used to identifying alternatives and choosing the best one, but seldom is this done with questions that entail moral content or the "rightness, fairness, or justice" of a decision. The "ought to be" question is often viewed in terms of what management *should* do (in an ethical sense) in a given situation. Examples of this question in a business setting might be the following:

- How *ought* we treat our aging employees whose productivity is declining?
- How safe *ought* we make this product, knowing full well we cannot pass all the costs on to the consumer?

- How clean an environment *should* we aim for?
- How *should* we treat long-time employees when the company is downsizing or moving the plant to a foreign country?

How Do We Get From What Is to What Ought to Be?

This third question represents the challenge of bridging the gap between where we are and where we ought to be with respect to ethical practices. Therefore, it represents an action dimension. We may discuss endlessly where we "ought" to be in terms of our own personal ethics or the ethics of our firm, of our industry, or of society. As we move further away from the individual level, we have less control or influence over the "ought to be" question.

When faced with these ideas as depicted by our "ought to be" questions, we may find that from a practical point of view we cannot achieve our ideals. This does not mean we should not have asked the question in the first place. Our "ought to be" questions become goals or objectives for our ethical practices. They form the normative core of business ethics. They become moral benchmarks that help us to measure progress.

This is also the stage at which managerial decision making and strategy come into play. The first step in managerial problem solving is identifying the problem (what "is"). Next comes identifying where we want to be (the "ought" question). Then comes the managerial challenge of closing the gap. "Gap analysis" sets the stage for concrete business action.

What Is Our Motivation in All This?

Pragmatic businesspeople do not like to dwell on this fourth question, which addresses the motivation for being ethical, because sometimes it reveals some manipulative or self-centered motive. At one level, is it perhaps not desirable to discuss motivation, because isn't it really actions that count?

Although we would like to believe that managers are appropriately motivated in their quest for ethical business behavior and that motivations are important, we must continue to understand and accept Andrew Stark's observation that we live in a "messy world of mixed motives." Therefore, managers do not typically have the luxury of making abstract distinctions between altruism and self-interest but must get on with the task of designing structures, systems, incentives, and processes that accommodate the "whole" employee, regardless of motivations.[110]

Management Ethics

Three Models of Management Ethics

In attempting to understand the basic concepts of business ethics, it is useful to think in terms of key ethical models that might describe different types of management ethics found in the organizational world.[111] These models should provide some useful base points for discussion and comparison. The media have focused so much on immoral or unethical business behavior that it is easy to forget or not think about the possibility of other ethical styles or types. For example, scant attention has been given to the distinction that may be made between those activities that are *immoral* and those that are *amoral*; similarly, little attention has been given to contrasting these two forms of behavior with ethical or *moral* management.

Believing that there is value in developing descriptive models for purposes of clearer understanding, here we will describe, compare, and contrast three models or types of ethical management.

1. Immoral management
2. Moral management
3. Amoral management

Let us consider the two extremes first—immoral and moral management—and then amoral management, as depicted below.

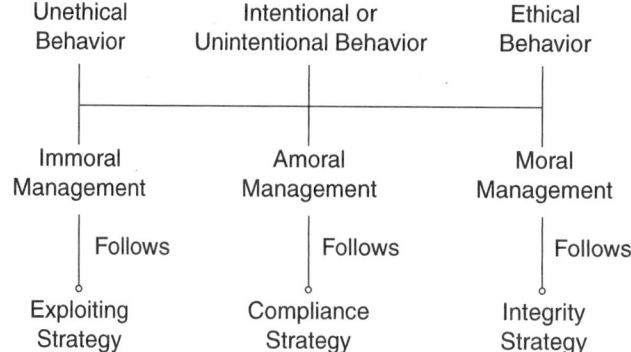

Immoral Management

Using *immoral* and *unethical* as synonyms, **immoral management** is defined as a posture that not only is devoid of ethical principles or precepts but also implies a positive and active opposition to what is ethical. Immoral management decisions, behaviors, actions, and practices are discordant with ethical principles. This model holds that management's motives are selfish and that it cares only or principally about its own or its company's gains. If management's activity is actively opposed to what is regarded as ethical, this suggests that management knows right from wrong and yet chooses to do wrong. Thus, its motives are deemed greedy or selfish. According to this model, management's goals are profitability and organizational success at virtually any price. Management does not care about others' claims to be treated fairly or justly.

What about management's orientation toward the law, considering that law is often regarded as an embodiment of minimal ethics? Immoral management regards legal standards as barriers that management must avoid or overcome in order to accomplish what it wants. Immoral management would just as soon engage in illegal activity as in immoral or unethical activity.

OPERATING STRATEGY OF IMMORAL MANAGEMENT The operating strategy of immoral management is focused on exploiting opportunities for corporate or personal gain. An active opposition to what is moral would suggest that managers cut corners anywhere and everywhere it appears useful. Thus, the key operating question guiding immoral management is, "Can we make money with this action, decision, or behavior, *regardless of what it takes?*" Implicit in this question is that nothing else matters, at least not very much. We can call this "exploiting strategy."

Moral Management

At the opposite extreme from immoral management is **moral management.** Moral management conforms to the highest standards of ethical behavior or professional standards of conduct. Although it is not always crystal clear what level of ethical standards prevail, moral management strives to be ethical in terms of its focus on high ethical norms and professional standards of conduct, motives, goals, orientation toward the law, and general operating strategy.

In contrast to the selfish motives in immoral management, moral management aspires to succeed, but only within the confines of sound ethical precepts—that is, standards predicated on such norms as fairness, justice, respect for rights, and due process. Moral management's motives, therefore, likely would be termed fair, balanced, or unselfish. Organizational goals continue to stress profitability, but only within the confines of legal obedience and sensitivity to and responsiveness to ethical standards. Moral management pursues its objectives of profitability, legality, and ethics as both required and desirable. Moral management would not pursue profits at the expense of the law and sound ethics. Indeed, the focus here would be not only on the letter of the law but on the spirit of the law as well. The law would be viewed as a minimal standard of ethical behavior, because moral management strives to operate at a level above what the law mandates.

OPERATING STRATEGY OF MORAL MANAGEMENT The operating strategy of moral management is to live by sound ethical standards, seeking out only those economic opportunities that the organization or management can pursue within the confines of ethical behavior. The organization assumes a leadership position when ethical dilemmas arise. The central question guiding moral management's actions, decisions, and behaviors is, "Will this action, decision, behavior, or practice be fair to all stakeholders involved as well as to the organization?"

Lynn Sharp Paine has set forth what she calls an "integrity strategy" that closely resembles the moral management model.[112] The **integrity strategy** is characterized by a conception of ethics as the driving force of an organization. Ethical values shape management's search for opportunities, the design of organizational systems, and the decision-making process. Ethical values in the integrity strategy provide a common frame of reference and serve to unify different functions, lines of business, and employee groups. Organizational ethics, in this view, helps to define what an organization is and what it stands for. Some common features of an integrity strategy include the following,[113] which are all consistent with the moral management model:

- Guiding values and commitments make sense and are clearly communicated.
- Company leaders are personally committed, credible, and willing to take action on the values they espouse.
- Espoused values are integrated into the normal channels of management decision making.
- The organization's systems and structures support and reinforce its values.
- All managers have the skills, knowledge, and competencies to make ethically sound decisions on a daily basis.

Amoral Management

Amoral management is not just a middle position on a continuum between immoral and moral management. Conceptually it has been positioned between the other two, but it is different in kind from both. There are two kinds of **amoral management.** First, there is **intentional amoral management.** Amoral managers of this type do not factor ethical considerations into their decisions, actions, and behaviors because they believe business activity resides outside the sphere to which moral judgments apply. These managers are neither moral nor immoral. They simply think that different rules apply in business than in other realms of life. Intentionally amoral managers are in a distinct minority today. At one time, however, as managers first began to think about reconciling business practices with sound ethics, some managers adopted this stance. A few intentionally amoral managers are still around, but they are a vanishing breed in today's ethically conscious world.

Second, there is **unintentional amoral management.** Like intentionally amoral managers, unintentionally amoral managers do not think about business activity in ethical terms. These managers are simply casual about, careless about, or inattentive to the fact that their decisions and actions may have negative or deleterious effects on others. These managers lack ethical perception and moral awareness; that is, they blithely go through their organizational lives not thinking that what they are doing has an ethical dimension or facet. These managers are well intentioned but are either too insensitive or too self-absorbed to consider the effects of their behavior on others.

Amoral management pursues profitability as its goal but does not cognitively attend to moral issues that may be intertwined with that pursuit. If there is an ethical guide to amoral management, it would be the marketplace as constrained by law—the letter of the law, not the spirit. The amoral manager sees the law as the parameters within which business pursuits take place.

OPERATING STRATEGY OF AMORAL MANAGEMENT The operating strategy of amoral management is not to bridle managers with excessive ethical structure but to permit free rein within the unspoken but understood tenets of the free enterprise system. Personal ethics may periodically or unintentionally enter into managerial decisions, but it does not preoccupy management. Furthermore, the impact of decisions on others is an afterthought, if it ever gets considered at all. Amoral management represents a model of decision making in which the managers' ethical mental gears, to the extent that they are present, are stuck in neutral. The key management question guiding decision making is, "Can we make money with this action, decision, or behavior?" Note that the question does not imply an active or implicit intent to be either moral or immoral.

Paine has articulated a "compliance strategy" that is consistent with amoral management. The **compliance strategy,** as contrasted with her integrity strategy, is more focused on obedience to the law as its driving force. The compliance strategy is legally driven and is oriented not toward ethics or integrity but more toward compliance with existing regulatory and criminal law. The compliance approach uses deterrence as its underlying assumption. This approach envisions managers as rational maximizers of self-interest, responsive to the personal costs and benefits of their choices, yet indifferent to the moral legitimacy of those choices.[114]

Making Moral Management Actionable

The characteristics of immoral, moral, and amoral management discussed should provide some useful benchmarks for managerial self-analysis, because self-analysis and introspection will ultimately be the way in which managers will recognize the need to move from the immoral or amoral ethic to the moral ethic. Numerous others have suggested management training for business ethics; therefore, this prescription will not be further developed here, although it has great potential. However, until senior management fully embraces the concepts of moral management, the transformation in organizational culture that is so essential for moral management to blossom, thrive, and flourish will not take place. Ultimately, senior management has the leadership responsibility to show the way to an ethical organizational climate by leading the transition from amoral to moral management, whether this is done by business ethics training and workshops, codes of conduct, mission/vision statements, ethics officers, tighter financial controls, more ethically sensitive decision-making processes, or leadership by example.

Underlying all these efforts, however, needs to be the fundamental recognition that amoral management exists and that it is an undesirable condition that can be certainly, if not easily, remedied. Most notably, organizational leaders must acknowledge that amoral management is a morally vacuous condition that can be quite easily disguised as just an innocent, practical, bottom-line philosophy—something to take pride in. Amoral management is, however, and will continue to be, the bane of American management until it is recognized for what it really is and until managers take steps to overcome it. American managers are not all "bad guys," as they so frequently are portrayed, but the idea that managerial decision making can be ethically neutral is bankrupt and no longer tenable in the society of the new millennium.[115]

Elements of Moral Judgment

For growth in moral judgment to take place, it is useful to appreciate the key elements involved in making moral judgments. This is a notion central to the transition from the amoral management state to the moral management state. Charles Powers and David Vogel suggest that there are six major elements or capacities that are essential to making moral judgments: (1) moral imagination, (2) moral identification and ordering, (3) moral evaluation, (4) tolerance of moral disagreement and ambiguity, (5) integration of managerial and moral competence, and (6) a sense of moral obligation and integrity.[116] Each reveals an essential ingredient in developing moral judgment.

Moral Imagination

Moral imagination refers to the ability to perceive that a web of competing economic relationships is, at the same time, a web of moral or ethical relationships. Developing moral imagination means not only becoming sensitive to ethical issues in business decision making but also developing the perspective of searching out subtle places where people are likely to be detrimentally affected by decision making or behaviors of managers. This is a necessary first step but is extremely challenging because of prevailing methods of evaluating managers on bottom-line results. It is essential before anything else can happen, however.

Moral Identification and Ordering

Moral identification and ordering refers to the ability to discern the relevance or nonrelevance of moral factors that are introduced into a decision-making situation. Are the moral issues real or just rhetorical? The ability to see moral issues as issues that can be dealt with is at stake here. Once moral issues have been identified, they must be ranked, or ordered, just as economic or technological issues are prioritized during the decision-making process. A manager must not only develop this skill through experience but also finely hone it through repetition. It is only through repetition that this skill can be developed.

Moral Evaluation

Once issues have been identified and ordered, evaluations must be made. *Moral evaluation* is the practical phase of moral judgment and entails essential skills, such as coherence and consistency, that have proved to be effective principles in other contexts. What managers need to do here is to understand the importance of clear principles, develop processes for weighing ethical factors, and develop the ability to identify what the likely moral as well as economic outcomes of a decision will be.

The real challenge in moral evaluation is to integrate the concern for others into organizational goals, purposes, and legitimacy. In the final analysis, though, the manager may not know the "right" answer or solution, although moral sensitivity has been introduced into the process. The important point is that amorality has not prevailed or driven the decision process.

Tolerance of Moral Disagreement and Ambiguity

An objection managers often have to ethics discussions is the amount of disagreement generated and the volume of ambiguity that must be tolerated in thinking ethically. This must be accepted, however, because it is a natural part of ethics discussions. To be sure, managers need closure and precision in their decisions. But the situation is seldom clear in moral discussions, just as it is in many traditional and more familiar decision contexts of managers, such as introducing a new product based on limited test marketing, choosing a new executive for a key position, deciding which of a number of excellent computer systems to install, or making a strategic decision based on instincts. All of these are precarious decisions, but managers have become accustomed to making them in spite of the disagreements and ambiguity that prevail among those involved in the decision or within the individual.

In a real sense, the *tolerance of moral disagreement and ambiguity* is simply an extension of a managerial talent or facility that is present in practically all decision-making situations managers face. But managers are more unfamiliar with this special kind of decision making because of a lack of practice.

Integration of Managerial and Moral Competence

The *integration of managerial and moral competence* underlies all that we have been discussing. Moral issues in management do not arise in isolation from traditional business decision making but right smack in the middle of it. The scandals that major corporations face today did not occur independently of the companies' economic activities but were embedded in a series of decisions that were made at various points in time and culminated from those earlier decisions. Therefore, moral competence is an integral part of managerial competence. Managers are learning—some the hard way—that there is a significant corporate, and in many instances personal, price to pay for their amorality. The amoral manager sees ethical decisions as isolated and independent of managerial decisions and competence, but the moral manager sees every evolving decision as one in which an ethical perspective must be integrated. This kind of future-looking view is an essential executive skill.

A Sense of Moral Obligation and Integrity

The foundation for all the capacities we have discussed is a *sense of moral obligation* and integrity. This sense is the key to the process but is the most difficult to acquire. This sense requires the intuitive or learned understanding that moral fibers—a concern for fairness, justice, and due process to people, groups, and communities—are woven into the fabric of managerial decision making and are the integral components that hold systems together.

These qualities are perfectly consistent with, and indeed are essential prerequisites to, the free enterprise system as we know it today. One can go back in history to Adam Smith and the foundation tenets of the free enterprise system and not find references to immoral or unethical practices as being elements that are needed for the system to work. Milton Friedman, our modern-day Adam Smith, even alluded to the importance of ethics when he stated that the purpose of business is "to make as much money as possible while conforming to the basic rules of society, both those embodied in the law and those embodied in ethical custom."[117] The moral manager, then, has a sense of moral obligation and integrity that is the glue that holds together the decision-making process in which human welfare is inevitably at stake. Exhibit 900.22 presents a brief sketch of some ethical principles for a business manager.

Management Assurance

Management Discussion and Analysis

Management of an organization is responsible for preparing the financial statements and the external auditor is responsible for expressing an opinion on them. The fact that the auditor assists the management in the preparation of financial statements does not relieve management from its responsibility. Ultimately, management is responsible for all decisions concerning the form and content of the financial statements.

Many companies include a management responsibility report titled "Management Discussion and Analysis" in their annual reports to stockholders. In this report, management assures stockholders of the following:

- The company maintains a system of internal controls that are continuously reviewed by both internal and external auditors for their adequacy and effectiveness.
- The company's financial statements are prepared in accordance with generally accepted accounting principles (GAAP).
- The company's assets (for example, inventory, equipment, and machinery) are properly accounted for and safeguarded against loss from unauthorized use.

Exhibit 900.22 *A Brief Sketch of Some Ethical Principles*

- **THE CATEGORICAL IMPERATIVE:** Act only according to that maxim by which you can at the same time "will" that it should become a universal law. In other words, one should not adopt principles of action unless they can, without inconsistency, be adopted by everyone else.
- **THE CONVENTIONALIST ETHIC:** Individuals should act to further their self-interests so long as they do not violate the law. It is allowed, under this principle, to bluff (lie) and to take advantage of all legal opportunities and widespread practices and customs.
- **THE DISCLOSURE RULE:** If the full glare of examination by associates, friends, family, newspapers, television, and so on, were to focus on your decision, would you remain comfortable with it? If you think you would, it probably is the right decision.
- **THE GOLDEN RULE:** Do unto others as you would have them do unto you. It includes not knowingly doing harm to others.
- **THE HEDONISTIC ETHIC:** Virtue is embodied in what each individual finds meaningful. There are no universal or absolute moral principles. If it feels good, do it.
- **THE INTUITION ETHIC:** People are endowed with a kind of moral sense with which they can apprehend right and wrong. The solution to moral problems lies simply in what you feel or understand to be right in a given situation. You have a "gut feeling" and "fly by the seat of your pants."
- **THE MARKET ETHIC:** Selfish actions in the marketplace are virtuous because they contribute to efficient operation of the economy. Decision makers may take selfish actions and be motivated by personal gain in their business dealings. They should ask whether their actions in the market further financial self-interest. If so, the actions are ethical.
- **THE MEANS-ENDS ETHIC:** Worthwhile ends justify efficient means—that is, when ends are of overriding importance or virtue, unscrupulous means may be employed to reach them.
- **THE MIGHT-EQUALS-RIGHT ETHIC:** Justice is defined as the interest of the stronger. What is ethical is what an individual has the strength and power to accomplish. Seize what advantage you are strong enough to take without respect to ordinary social conventions and laws.
- **THE ORGANIZATION ETHIC:** The wills and needs of individuals should be subordinated to the greater good of the organization (be it church, state, business, military, or university). An individual should ask whether actions are consistent with organizational goals and what is good for the organization.
- **THE PROFESSIONAL ETHIC:** You should do only that which can be explained before a committee of your peers.
- **THE PROPORTIONALITY PRINCIPLE:** I am responsible for whatever I "will" as a means or an end. If both the means and the end are good in and of themselves, I may ethically permit or risk the foreseen but unwilled side effects if, and only if, I have a proportionate reason for doing so.
- **THE REVELATION ETHIC:** Through prayer or other appeal to transcendent beings and forces, answers are given to individual minds. The decision makers pray, meditate, or otherwise commune with a superior force or being. They are then apprised of which actions are just and unjust.
- **THE UTILITARIAN ETHIC:** The greatest good for the greatest number. Determine whether the harm in an action is outweighed by the good. If the action maximizes benefit, it is the optimum course to take among alternatives that provide less benefit.

Source: T. K. Das, "Ethical Preferences Among Business Students: A Comparative Study of Fourteen Ethical Principles," *Southern Management Association* (November 13–16, 1985), 11–12. For further discussion, see T. K. Das, "Ethical Principles in Business: An Empirical Study of Preferential Rankings," *International Journal of Management* (Vol. 9, No. 4, December, 1992), 462–472. With permission from Blackwell Publishing. www.blackwellpublishing.com

- Both the internal and external auditors have unrestricted and unlimited access to the board of directors and the audit committee.
- The board of directors fulfills their responsibility in financial statements through its audit committee, which consists solely of directors who are neither officers nor employees of the company. The audit committee meets periodically with independent public accountants, internal auditors, and representatives of company management to discuss internal control, auditing, and financial reporting matters.

The auditor should maintain professional skepticism toward management's assertions. This means that the auditor should neither disbelieve management's assertions nor blindly accept them without concern for their truthfulness. Rather, the auditor recognizes the need to objectively verify data, evaluate conditions observed, and evaluate evidence gathered during the audit.

Accounting Reform Legislation

As a result of recent corporate scandals resulting from management's "lack of integrity," management fraud, accounting firms' negligence, and use of earnings management techniques, both investors and creditors have lost confidence in corporate America. In light of this financial crisis, the U.S. Congress passed new legislation entitled Sarbanes-Oxley Act of 2002 to reform the accounting profession and corporate management.

Essentially, the Act creates a five-member Public Company Accounting Oversight Board, which has the authority to set and enforce auditing, attestation, quality control, and ethics (including independence) standards for auditors of public companies. It also is empowered to inspect the auditing operations of public accounting firms that audit public companies as well as impose disciplinary and remedial sanctions for violations of the board's rules, securities laws, and professional auditing and accounting standards.

Other provisions affecting the accounting profession include requiring the rotation of the lead audit partner and reviewing audit partner every five years, and extending the statute of limitations for the discovery of fraud to two years from the date of discovery and five years after the act. The law restricts the consulting work public company auditors can perform for their publicly traded audit clients and establishes harsh penalties for securities-law violations, corporate fraud, and document shredding. Regarding sanctions, fines range from $100,000 for individual negligent conduct to $15 million to a firm for knowing or intentional conduct, including recklessness and repeated acts of negligence.

The Act also requires CEOs and CFOs to certify their company's financial statements as part of the annual report to stockholders. They also have a greater duty to communicate and coordinate with corporate audit committees who are now responsible for hiring, compensating, and overseeing the independent auditors. There are new requirements regarding enhanced financial disclosures as well.

Corporate Governance

Owner Stakeholders and Corporate Governance

Throughout the 1980s and 1990s, there was rampant shareholder unrest. Shareholder groups became increasingly critical of how management groups and boards of directors ran their firms. They complained about management's lack of accountability, ineffective and complacent boards, excessive managerial compensation, and a general lack of focus on the importance of shareholders relative to management. Today the evidence suggests that their complaints were heard. Although problems certainly remain, the state of corporate governance in the United States has never been stronger.

In this section, we will explore corporate governance and the ways in which it has evolved. First, we will examine the concept of legitimacy and the part that corporate governance plays in establishing the legitimacy of the firm. We will explore how good corporate governance can mitigate the problems created by the separation of ownership and control and examine some of the specific challenges facing board members today.

Legitimacy and Corporate Governance

To understand corporate governance, it is useful to understand the idea of **legitimacy**. Legitimacy is a somewhat abstract concept, but it is vital in that it helps explain the importance of the relative roles of a corporation's charter, shareholders, board of directors, management, and employees—all of which are components of the modern corporate governance system.

Let us start with a slightly modified version of Talcott Parsons's definition of legitimacy. He argued that "organizations are legitimate to the extent that their activities are congruent with the goals and values of the social system within which they function."[118] From this definition, we may see legitimacy as a condition that prevails when there is a congruence between the organization's activities and society's expectations. Thus, whereas legitimacy is a condition, **legitimation** is a dynamic process by which business seeks to perpetuate its acceptance. The dynamic process aspect should be emphasized, because society's norms and values change, and business must change if its legitimacy is to continue. It is also useful to consider legitimacy at both the micro, or company, level and the macro, or business institution, level.

At the *micro level of legitimacy*, we refer to individual business firms achieving and maintaining legitimacy by conforming with societal expectations. According to Epstein and Votaw, companies seek legitimacy in several ways. First, a company may adapt its methods of operating to conform to what it perceives to be the prevailing standard. For example, a company may discontinue door-to-door selling if that marketing approach comes to be viewed in the public mind as a shoddy sales technique,[119] or a pharmaceutical company may discontinue offering free drug samples to medical students if this practice begins to take on the aura of a bribe. Second, a company may try to change the public's values and norms to conform to its own practices by advertising and other techniques.[120] **Amazon.com** was successful at this when it began marketing through the Internet.

Finally, an organization may seek to enhance its legitimacy by identifying itself with other organizations, people, values, or symbols that have a powerful legitimate base in society.[121] This occurs at several levels. At the national level, companies proudly announce appointments of celebrities, former politicians, or other famous people to managerial positions or board directorships. At the community level, the winning local football coach may be asked to endorse a company by sitting on its board or promoting its products.[122]

The *macro level of legitimacy* is the level with which we are most concerned in this section. The macro level refers to the corporate system—the totality of business enterprises. It is difficult to talk about the legitimacy of business in pragmatic terms at this level. American business is such a potpourri of institutions of different shapes, sizes, and industries that saying anything conclusive about it is difficult. Yet this is an important level at which business needs to be concerned about its legitimacy. What is at stake is the existence, acceptance, and form of business as an institution in our society. William Dill has suggested that business's social (or societal) legitimacy is a fragile thing.

> Business has evolved by initiative and experiment. It never had an overwhelmingly clear endorsement as a social institution [emphasis added]. The idea of allowing individuals to joust with one another in pursuit of personal profit was an exciting and romantic one when it was first proposed as a way of correcting other problems in society; but over time, its ugly side and potential for abuse became apparent.[123]

Quite a bit of the excitement and romanticism has long since worn off; business must accept that it has a fragile mandate.[124] It must realize that its legitimacy is constantly subject to ratification. And it must realize that it has no inherent right to exist—it exists solely because society has given it that right.[125]

In comparing the micro view of legitimacy with the macro view, one may observe that, although specific business organizations try to perpetuate their own legitimacy, the corporate or business system as a whole rarely addresses the issue at all. This is unfortunate because the spectrum of powerful issues regarding business conduct clearly indicates that such institutional introspection is needed if business is to survive and prosper. If business is to continue to justify its right to exist, the question of legitimacy and its operational ramifications must be remembered.

The Issue of Corporate Governance

The issue of corporate governance is a direct outgrowth of the question of legitimacy. For business to be legitimate and to maintain its legitimacy in the eyes of the public, its governance must correspond to the will of the people.

Corporate governance refers to the method by which a firm is being governed, directed, administered, or controlled and to the goals for which it is being governed. Corporate governance is concerned with the relative roles, rights, and accountability of such stakeholder groups as owners, boards of directors, managers, employees, and others who assert to be stakeholders.

Components of Corporate Governance

To appreciate fully the legitimacy and corporate governance issues, it is important that we understand the major groups that make up the corporate form of business organization, because it is only by so doing that we can appreciate how the system has failed to work according to its intended design.

Roles of Four Major Groups

The four major groups we need to mention in setting the stage are the shareholders (owners/stakeholders), the board of directors, the managers, and the employees. Overarching these groups is the **charter** issued by the state, giving the corporation the right to exist and stipulating the basic terms of its existence. Exhibit 900.23 presents these four groups, along with the state charter, in a hierarchy of corporate governance authority.

Exhibit 900.23 *The Corporation's Hierarchy of Authority*

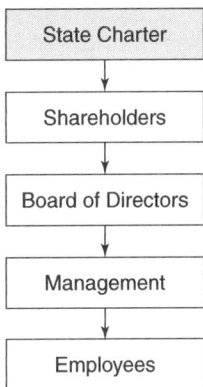

Under American corporate law, **shareholders** are the owners of a corporation. As owners, they should have ultimate control over the corporation. This control is manifested primarily in the right to select the board of directors of the company. Generally, the degree of each shareholder's right is determined by the number of shares of stock owned. The individual who owns 100 shares of **Apple Computer**, for example, has 100 "votes" when electing the board of directors. By contrast, the large public pension fund that owns 10 million shares has 10 million "votes."

Because large organizations may have hundreds of thousands of shareholders, they elect a smaller group, known as the **board of directors,** to govern and oversee the management of the business. The board is responsible for ascertaining that the manager puts the interests of the owners (that is, shareholders) first. The third major group in the authority hierarchy is **management**—the group of individuals hired by the board to run the company and manage it on a daily basis. Along with the board, top management establishes overall policy. Middle- and lower-level managers carry out this policy and conduct the daily supervision of the operative employees. **Employees** are those hired by the company to perform the actual operational work. Managers are employees, too, but in this discussion we use the term *employees* to refer to nonmanagerial employees.

Separation of Ownership From Control

The social and ethical issues that have evolved in recent years focus on the *intended* versus *actual* roles, rights, responsibilities, and accountability of these four major groups. The major condition embedded in the structure of modern corporations that has contributed to the corporate governance problem has been the **separation of ownership from control.** In the precorporate period, owners were typically the managers themselves. Thus, the system worked the way it was intended; the owners also controlled the business. Even when firms grew larger and managers were hired, the owners often were on the scene to hold the management group accountable.

As the public corporation grew and stock ownership became widely dispersed, a separation of ownership from control became the prevalent condition. Exhibit 900.24 illustrates the precorporate and corporate periods. The dispersion of ownership into hundreds of thousands or millions of shares meant that essentially no one or no one group owned enough shares to exercise control. This being the case, the most effective control that owners could exercise was the election of the board of directors to serve as their representative and watch over management.

The problem with this evolution was that authority, power, and control rested with the group that had the most concentrated interest at stake—management. The corporation did not function according to its designed plan with effective authority, power, and control flowing downward from the owners. The shareholders were owners in a technical sense, but most of them perceived themselves as investors rather than owners. If you owned 100 shares of **Walt Disney Co.** and there were 10 million shares outstanding, you likely would see yourself as an investor rather than an owner. With just a telephone call issuing a sell order to your stockbroker, your "ownership" stake could be gone. Furthermore, with stock ownership so dispersed, no conscious, intended supervision of corporate boards would be possible.

The other factors that added to management's power were the corporate laws and traditions that gave the management group control over the **proxy process**—the method by which the shareholders elected boards of directors. Over time, it was not difficult for management groups to create boards of directors of like-minded executives who would simply collect their fees and defer to management on whatever it wanted. The result of this process was that power, authority, and control began to flow upward from management rather than downward from the shareholders

Exhibit 900.24 *Precorporate Versus Corporate Ownership and Control*

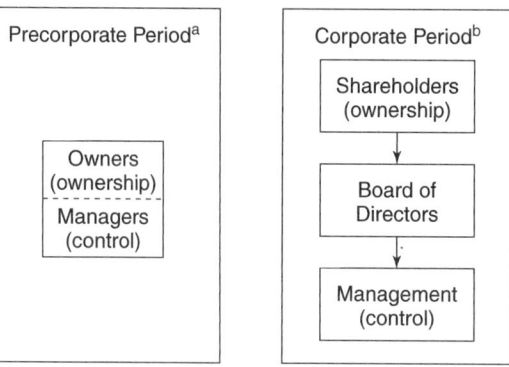

^a In the precorporate period, the owners were also the managers, and therefore ownership and control were combined. Later, large companies hired managers, but the owners were always there to exercise control.

^b In the corporate period, ownership was separated from control by the intervention of a board of directors. Theoretically, the board should have kept control on behalf of owners, but it did not always turn out that way.

(owners). **Agency problems** developed when the interests of the shareholders were not aligned with the interests of the manager, and the manager (who is simply a hired *agent* with the responsibility of representing the owner's best interest) began to pursue self-interest instead.

The Role of the Board of Directors

It is clear from the preceding discussion that a potential governance problem is built into the corporate system because of the separation of ownership from control. It is equally clear that the board of directors is intended to oversee management on behalf of the shareholders. However, this is where the system had once broken down. For corporate governance to function as it was originally intended, the board of directors must be an effective, potent body carrying out its roles and responsibilities in ascertaining that management pursue the shareholders' best interests.

Are boards doing what they are supposed to be doing? Problems in some corporations remain. In March 2001, *Business Week* characterized the board of **Xerox** as being "asleep at the wheel" with a "host of governance problems."[126] The board had too many members with ties to the firm, board members sat on too many other boards, and the directors owned little equity in the firm.[127]

In spite of the problems that remain, most of the corporate governance news is decidedly good. In its annual report on the "Best and Worst Corporate Boards in America," *Business Week* offered the following assessment of the trend in corporate governance:

> The governance revolution that swept through Corporate America's boardrooms in the 1990s has led to far more active oversight. Composed largely of independent directors, boards are more accountable than ever. Directors who rarely if ever bought a single share of their company's stock in the past are often significantly invested today. And in the face of shareholder dissatisfaction they are more likely to demand change. "All of the rhetorical battles are over," comments James E. Heard, chairman of Proxy Monitor and a longtime player in governance circles. "With the exception of a few rogues, most boards are doing the job they are supposed to do."[128]

Credit for the turnaround in corporate governance goes to several sources. Robert Lear and Boris Yavitz credit Arthur Levitt and the SEC for the changes in proxy statements. Information on executive and director compensation is much more clearly presented than it was in the 1980s and early 1990s. They also credit "enlightened CEOs and directors" who didn't wait for regulatory reforms but put changes through voluntarily.[129]

Although the governance battle has been won at large U.S. companies, the war is not over. Midsize and smaller companies, and overseas boards, still do not often follow the guidelines for good governance. Dotcoms in particular have tended to have boards dominated by insiders, a combination of current management and others with connections to the company.[130] Europe too is just entering the corporate governance battle. Mass stock ownership is a new phenomenon but investors who feel stung by steep price drops are taking action. European shareholders are going to court and showing up en masse at annual meetings.[131]

The Need for Board Independence

Board independence from management is a crucial aspect of good governance. It is here that the difference between **inside directors** and **outside directors** becomes most pronounced. Outside directors are independent from the firm and its top managers. In contrast, inside directors have some sort of ties to the firm. Sometimes they are top managers in the firm; other times, insiders are family members or others with close ties to the CEO. To varying degrees, each of these parties is "beholden" to the CEO and, therefore, might be hesitant to speak out when necessary. Courtney Brown, an experienced director who served on many boards, said that he never saw a subordinate officer serving on a board dissent from the position taken by the CEO.[132] Insiders might also be professionals such as lawyers under contract to the firm or bankers whose bank does business with the firm: This can create conflict-of-interest situations.[133] For example, a commercial banker/director may expect the company on whose board she or he is serving to restrict itself to using the services of her or his own firm and be willing to support the CEO in return for the business provided.

Another problem is managerial control of the board processes. CEOs often can control board perks such as director compensation and committee assignments. Board members who rock the boat may find they are left out in the cold. As one corporate board member told *Fortune*, under conditions of anonymity, "This stuff is wrong.... What people understand they have to do is go along with management, because if they don't they won't be part of the club.... What it comes down to is that directors aren't really independent. CEOs don't want independent directors."[134]

Issues Surrounding Compensation

CEO Compensation

The issue of executive pay was a lightning rod for the concern that managers place their own interests over those of their shareholders. Two issues are at the heart of the CEO pay controversy: (1) the extent to which CEO pay is tied to firm performance and (2) the overall level of CEO pay.

The move to tie CEO pay more closely to firm performance grew in momentum when shareholders observed CEO pay rising as firm performance fell. Many executives had gotten staggering salaries, even while profits were falling, workers were being laid off, and shareholder return was dropping. Shareholders were assisted in their effort to monitor CEO pay by stricter disclosure requirements from the Securities and Exchange Commission (SEC). The revised compensation disclosure rule, adopted by the SEC in 1992, was designed to provide shareholders with more information about the relationship between firm performance and CEO compensation.[135] According to the results of one study, it seems to have worked. Since the rule's implementation, compensation committees have met more frequently, lessened the number of insiders as members, and become more moderate in size. More importantly, largely through the use of stock options, CEO pay has become more closely aligned with accounting and market performance measures than it was before the rule's implementation.[136] There is some evidence that boards of directors are becoming the watchdogs they are always supposed to be.[137]

Outside Director Compensation

It was suggested earlier that there may be some link between CEO and executive compensation and board members. Therefore, it should not be surprising that directors' pay is becoming an issue, too. According to a survey by *Executive Compensation Reports*, the average annual compensation for a 1996 nonexecutive board member was $73,473, with an additional fee of $1,284 for each meeting attended. In addition, 94 percent of the companies surveyed gave their directors stock.[138] Paying board members is a relatively recent idea. Eighty years ago, it was illegal to pay nonexecutive board members. The logic was that because board members represented the shareholders, paying them out of the company's (that is, shareholders') funds would be self-dealing.[139] A 1992 Korn/Ferry survey showed that board members typically spent 95 hours a year on the board. By 2000, that figure had increased to 173 hours. The average director received a 23 percent increase in pay for the 82 percent increase in time spent on the job.[140]

Consequences of the Merger, Acquisition, and Takeover Wave

Mergers and acquisitions are another form of corporate governance, one that comes from outside the corporation. The expectation is that the threat of a possible takeover will motivate top managers to pursue shareholder interest rather than self-interest. The merger, acquisition, and hostile takeover wave of the 1980s brought out many new issues related to corporate governance. The economic prosperity of the 1980s, coupled with the rise of junk bonds and other creative methods of financing, made it possible for small firms and individuals to buy large corporations. Many corporate CEOs and boards went to great lengths to protect themselves from these takeovers. A major criticism of CEOs and boards during this period was that they were overly obsessed with self-preservation rather than making optimal decisions on behalf of their owners/stakeholders. Three of the most questionable top management practices to emerge from the hostile takeover wave were greenmail, poison pills, and golden parachutes. We will briefly consider each of these and see how they fit into the corporate governance problem we have been discussing. Then, we will examine the issue of insider trading.

Greenmail

Named after blackmail, **greenmail** is the repurchase of stock from an unwanted suitor at a higher-than-market price. Companies pay the greenmail to end the threat of a takeover.[141] For example, assume that Corporate Raider A quietly purchases a 5 percent stake in the ABC Corporation. It threatens to launch an all-out hostile takeover of ABC. ABC's management sees this as a threat to their jobs and agrees to pay greenmail for (buy back) the shares from Corporate Raider A at a premium price. This example is somewhat simplified, but it basically describes the process. With greenmail, the potential acquirer wins big, and management gets to keep its jobs and perks. The losers are the shareholders of the target company who are left sitting with shares whose underlying value has been eroded.[142] Some companies have passed corporate bylaws that prohibit greenmail. In addition, the courts now limit the tax deductibility of greenmail payments.[143]

Poison Pill

A **poison pill** is a shareholder-rights plan aimed at discouraging or preventing a hostile takeover. Typically, the poison pill provides that when a hostile suitor acquires more than a certain percentage of a company's stock, other shareholders receive share purchase rights designed to dilute the suitor's holdings and make the acquisition prohibitively expensive. Some poison pills adopted by companies have been ruled illegal by the courts.[144] However, efforts to adopt poison pills continue. In 2001, **Yahoo!'s** board of directors adopted a poison pill that would make a hostile takeover prohibitively expensive. The plan gives Yahoo! shareholders the right to buy one unit of a share of preferred stock for $250 if a person or group acquires at least 15 percent of Yahoo!'s stock. According to the company, the poison pill was not instituted in response to any specific acquisition threat but instead to "deter coercive takeover tactics."[145]

Golden Parachutes

A **golden parachute** is a contract in which a corporation agrees to make payments to key officers in the event of a change in the control of the corporation.[146] The original intent of golden parachutes was to prevent top executives involved in takeover battles from putting themselves before their shareholders. However, in a study of over 400 tender offers (that is, takeover attempts in which the acquirers offered shareholders premiums to sell their shares), golden parachutes showed no effect on takeover resistance. Neither the existence of the parachute, nor the magnitude of the potential parachute payout, influenced CEO reactions to takeover attempts.[147]

Cochran and Wartick offer several arguments against golden parachutes. They argue that executives are already being paid well to represent their companies and that their getting additional rewards constitutes "double dipping." They also argue that these executives are, in essence, being rewarded for failure. The logic here is that if the executives have managed their companies in such a way that the companies' stock prices are low enough to make the firms attractive to takeover specialists, the executives are being rewarded for failure. Another argument is that executives, to the extent that they control their own boards, are giving themselves the golden parachutes. This represents a conflict of interest.[148]

Insider Trading Scandals

Insider trading is the practice of obtaining critical information from inside a company and then using that information for one's own personal financial gain. A scandal began in 1986 when the Securities and Exchange Commission (SEC) filed a civil complaint against Dennis B. Levine, a former managing partner of the **Drexel Burnham Lambert** investment banking firm, and charged him with illegally trading in 54 stocks. Levine then pleaded guilty to four criminal charges and gave up $10.6 million in illegal profits—the biggest insider trading penalty up to that point.[149] He also spent 17 months in prison.

Levine's downfall set off a chain reaction on Wall Street. His testimony led directly to the SEC's $100 million judgment against Ivan Boesky, one of Wall Street's most frenetically active individual speculators. In a consent decree, Boesky agreed to pay $100 million, which was then described as by far the largest settlement ever obtained by the

SEC in an insider trading case. Boesky, it turns out, had made a career of the high-rolling financial game known as **risk arbitrage**—the opportunistic buying and selling of companies that appear on the verge of being taken over by other firms.[150] The Boesky settlement set off a flurry of litigation as dozens of private and corporate lawsuits were filed in response to these disclosures.[151]

Ivan Boesky then fingered Martin Siegel, one of America's most respected investment bankers, at **Kidder Peabody**. Apparently Siegel and Boesky began conspiring in 1982, and over the next 2 years Siegel leaked information about upcoming takeovers to Boesky in exchange for $700,000 cash. Siegel pleaded guilty and began cooperating with investigators, and then he himself proceeded to finger two former executives at Kidder Peabody and one at **Goldman Sachs**.[152]

The insider trading scandals rocked Wall Street as accusations reached the upper levels of the financial industry's power and salary structure. New arrests seemed to occur weekly, and one of the most frequently asked questions was "Who's next?"[153] In 1987, Ivan Boesky was sentenced to 3 years in prison. However, Boesky helped prosecutors reel in the biggest fish of all—junk bond king Michael Milkin. The Securities and Exchange Commission accused Milkin and his employer, Drexel Burnham, of insider trading, stock manipulation, and other violations of federal securities laws. Drexel Burnham agreed in 1988 to plead guilty to six felonies, settle SEC charges, and pay a record fine of $650 million. A year later, the junk bond market crashed and Drexel Burnham filed for bankruptcy. In 1990, Milkin agreed to plead guilty to six felony counts of securities fraud, market manipulation, and tax fraud. He agreed to pay a personal fine of $600 million and later was sentenced to 10 years in prison.[154] He served only 2 years in prison before being released.

Although insider trading scandals of this magnitude have not recurred, the revelations and repercussions of the Wall Street scandal will be with us for years. Unfortunately, the scandal gave the financial industry on Wall Street the biggest "black eye" it has had in over 50 years. Not only are shareholders suspicious of what has been going on unbeknownst to them, but small investors and the general public have lost faith in what they thought was the stable and secure financial industry. In 2001, the SEC instituted new disclosure rules designed to aid the small investor who historically has not had access to the information large investors hold. Regulation FD (fair disclosure) set limits on the common company practice of selective disclosure. When companies disclose meaningful information to shareholders and securities professionals, they must now do so publicly so that small investors can enjoy a more level playing field.[155]

Board Member Liability

In the mid to late 1980s, not many individuals wanted board director positions. Concerned about increasing legal hassles emanating from stockholder, customer, and employee lawsuits, directors were quitting such positions or refusing to accept them in the first place. Although courts rarely hold directors personally liable in the hundreds of shareholder suits filed every year, over the past several years there have been a few cases in which directors have been held personally and financially liable for their decisions. The **Trans Union Corporation** case involved an agreement among the directors to sell the company for a price the owners later decided was too low. A suit was filed, and the court ordered that the board members be held personally responsible for the difference between the price the company was sold for and a later-determined "fair value" for the deal.[156] In addition to the Trans Union case, **Cincinnati Gas and Electric** reached a $14 million settlement in a shareholder suit that charged directors and officers with improper disclosure concerning a nuclear power plant.[157]

The **Caremark** case further heightened directors' concerns about **personal liability.** Caremark, a home health care company, paid substantial civil and criminal fines for submitting false claims and making illegal payments to doctors and other health-care providers. The Caremark board of directors was then sued for breach of fiduciary duties because the board members had failed in their responsibility to monitor effectively the Caremark employees who violated various state and federal laws. In late 1996, the Delaware Chancery Court ruled that it is the duty of the board of directors to ensure that a company has an effective reporting and monitoring system in place. If the board fails to do this, individual directors can be held personally liable for losses that are caused by their failure to meet appropriate standards.[158]

Improving Corporate Governance

Efforts to improve corporate governance may be classified into two major categories for discussion purposes. First, changes could be made in the composition, structure, and functioning of boards of directors. Second, shareholders—on their own initiative or on the initiative of management or the board—could assume a more active role in governance. Each of these possibilities deserves closer examination.

Changes in Boards of Directors

In the past decade or so, changes have begun to be made in boards of directors. These changes have occurred because of the growing belief that CEOs and executive teams need to be made more accountable to shareholders and other stakeholders. Here we will discuss several of these changes and some other recommendations that have been set forth for improving board functioning.

COMPOSITION OF THE BOARD Prior to the 1960s, boards were composed primarily of white, male inside directors. It was not until the 1960s that pressure from Washington, Wall Street, and various stakeholder groups began to emphasize the concept of board diversity. By 2000, their efforts were beginning to pay off: 78 percent of U.S. board members were outsiders.[159] Of the S&P 500 companies, 93 percent had at least one woman director in 2000. Although most firms still only have one token woman director, the tide seems to be shifting. In 2000, 21 percent of new board members were women, and 25 percent of the nation's largest companies had more than one female director.[160] Ethnic minorities are making inroads, too. Sixty percent of U.S. corporate boards now have ethnic minority directors, with African-Americans comprising 39 percent, Latinos comprising 12 percent, and Asians comprising 9 percent of the positions. The world seems to be awakening to the importance of diverse and independent boards. The problem is that good candidates are increasingly hard to find.[161]

Part of the problem is an increase in demand for good independent directors. Institutional investors value good corporate governance so highly that they are willing to pay a premium for firms with outside directors. A 2000 study by the McKinsey Company found that the premium was as high as 28 percent in Venezuela. Although it varied, each country's premium was well above 15 percent.[162] South Korea passed a law requiring that outside directors occupy at least one-fourth of the positions on large company boards.[163] This increase in demand for outside directors is part of the reason they are in increasingly short supply.

Another factor limiting the supply of directors is the greater level of expectations placed on board members. Board committees and subcommittees are now given more to do than ever before. Furthermore, the globalization of business has placed new demands on board members for travel. Last, firms realize the time demands placed on outside directors and so they limit the number of outside boards on which their own executives may sit. For example, former **GE** CEO Jack Welch would not allow his senior managers to sit on the boards of other companies.[164]

The difficulty in finding outside board members is exacerbated when searching for members of minority groups or women to bring diversity to the board. In the past, many candidates were excluded because they never had the title of CEO. A new trend in board recruitment, focusing more on experience than title, is helping to bring more independence and diversity to the boardroom. This broadens the pool of candidates available.[165]

Today, advocates of strong, independent, and diverse boards have largely succeeded in convincing corporations of the importance of board composition. The difficulty now is in putting those recommendations into effect.

USE OF BOARD COMMITTEES The **audit committee** is typically responsible for assessing the adequacy of internal control systems and the integrity of financial statements. Scandals such as the revelation that **Cendant Corporation** booked almost $300 million in fake revenues, underscore the importance of a strong audit committee. Commenting on the Cendant Corporation situation, *The Wall Street Journal* opined, "Too many audit committees are turning out to be toothless tigers."[166] To lessen the occurrence of such scandals, the Securities and Exchange Commission has placed much emphasis on audit committees, and the New York Stock Exchange mandates such committees, composed of independent outside directors, for the firms listed with it. Charles Anderson and Robert Anthony, authors of *The New Corporate Directors: Insights for Board Members and Executives*,[167] argue that the principal responsibilities of an audit committee are as follows:

1. To ensure that published financial statements are not misleading
2. To ensure that internal controls are adequate
3. To follow up on allegations of material, financial, ethical, and legal irregularities
4. To ratify the selection of the external auditor

According to Arjay Miller, a board member and former president of **Ford Motor Company**, there should be at least one meeting per year between the audit committee and the firm's internal auditor.[168] The internal auditor should be scheduled to meet alone with the committee and always be instructed to speak out whenever she or he believes something should be brought to the committee's attention. The committee should also meet with the outside auditor in a setting in which members of management are not present. Three major questions should be asked of the outside auditor by the audit committee.

1. Is there anything more that you think we should know?
2. What is your biggest area of concern?
3. In what area did you have the largest difference of opinion with company accounting personnel?

The **nominating committee,** which should be composed of outside directors, or at least a majority of outside directors, has the responsibility of ensuring that competent, objective board members are selected. The American Assembly recommended that this committee be composed entirely of independent outside directors. The function of the nominating committee is to nominate candidates for the board and for senior management positions. In spite of the suggested role and responsibility of this committee, in most companies the CEO continues to exercise a powerful role in the selection of board members.

The **compensation committee** has the responsibility of evaluating executive performance and recommending terms and conditions of employment. This committee should be composed of outside directors. Although most large companies have compensation committees, one might ask how objective these board members are when the CEO has played a significant role in their being elected to the board.

Finally, each board has a **public issues committee,** or **public policy committee.** Although it is recognized that most management structures have some sort of formal mechanism for responding to public or social issues, this area is important enough to warrant a board committee that would become sensitive to these issues, provide policy leadership, and monitor management's performance on these issues. Most major companies today have public issues committees that typically deal with such issues as affirmative action, equal employment opportunity, environmental affairs, employee health and safety, consumer affairs, political action, and other areas in which public or ethical issues are present. Debate continues over the extent to which large firms really use such committees, but the fact that they have institutionalized such concerns by way of formal corporate committees is encouraging. The American Assembly recommends that firms develop evaluation systems to help them monitor the social performance of their corporate executives, but the evidence does not show that companies are doing this.[169]

Recently, the National Association of Corporate Directors (NACD) issued a director's handbook titled *The Governance Committee*. Its purpose is to raise the bar of board performance through effective oversight of the board's governance practices, use of ethics, and the process for director recruitment and retention. It is hoped that this handbook will improve the corporate governance process through the **governance committee.**

GETTING TOUGH WITH CEOS It has always been a major responsibility of board directors to monitor CEO performance and to get tough if the situation dictates. Historically, chief executives were protected from the axe that hit other employees when times got rough. Changes are now occurring that are resulting in CEOs being taken to task, or even fired, for reasons that heretofore did not create a stir in the boardroom. These changes include the tough, competitive economic times, the rising vigilance of outside directors, and the increasing power of large institutional investors.

Other suggestions have been proposed for creating effective boards of directors and for improving board members' abilities to monitor executive teams to ensure that crises do not occur undetected. Exhibit 900.25 summarizes some of these recommendations.

Increased Role of Shareholders

Prior to the 1980s, civil rights activists, consumer groups, and other social activist pressure groups insisted that companies join their causes. Today, companies are increasingly understanding the stakeholder perspective. However, it has created a new dilemma for companies as they deal with two broad types of shareholders. First, there are the traditional shareholder groups that are primarily interested in the firm's financial performance. Examples of such groups include the large institutional investors, such as pension funds. Second, there are growing numbers of social activist shareholders. These groups are typically pressuring firms to adopt their desired postures on social causes, such as third world employment practices, animal testing, affirmative action, and environmental protection.

A major problem seems to be that both groups of shareholders feel like neglected constituencies. They are attempting to rectify this condition through a variety of means. They are demanding effective power. They want to hold management groups accountable. They want to make changes, including changes in management if necessary. Like companies' earlier responses to other stakeholder activist groups, many managements are resisting. The result is a battle between managers and shareholders for corporate control.[170]

Our discussion of an increased role for shareholders centers around two perspectives: (1) the perspective of shareholders themselves asserting their rights on their own initiative and (2) initiatives being taken by companies to make shareholders a true constituency. The shareholder initiatives will dominate our discussion, because they clearly constitute the bulk of the activity underway.

Exhibit 900.25 *Recommendations for Improving Boards and Board Members*

BUILDING A BETTER BOARD[a]
- Don't overload it with too many members.
- Don't meet too often.
- Don't think you need high-profile CEOs or famous academics.
- Keep directors on for at least 5 years.
- Encourage directors to buy large quantities of stock.
- Pay directors with stock options, not with restricted stock.

SHARPENING THE BOARD'S SENSORS[b]
- Insist that board members become educated about their company.
- Insist that information-gathering systems deliver quickly the right information from the bottom to the top.
- Insist that board members understand board decision-making processes and do not operate by consensus.
- Insist that the company undergo periodic audits of corporate activities and results.

BOARD ACTIONS[c]
- Directors should evaluate regularly the CEO's performance against established goals and strategies.
- Evaluations of the CEO should be done by "outside directors."
- Outside directors should meet alone at least once a year.
- Directors should set qualifications for board members and communicate these expectations to shareholders.
- Outside directors should screen and recommend board candidates who meet the established qualifications.

KEEP DIRECTORS' EYES ON CEO[d]
- CEOs need written job descriptions and annual report cards.
- Boards should measure their own performance as well as assess individual members.
- Board nominating committees should exclude the company's major suppliers, officials of nonprofit organizations that receive substantial donations from the corporation, and the CEO's close friends.
- A chief executive should hold only one outside board seat.

Sources: [a]Graef S. Crystal, "Do Directors Earn Their Keep?" *Fortune* (May 6, 1991), 79. [b]Richard O. Jacobs, "Why Boards Miss Black Holes," *Across the Board* (June 1991), 54. [c]The Working Group on Corporate Governance, "A New Compact for Owners and Directors," *Harvard Business Review* (July–August 1991), 142–143. [d]Joann S. Lublin, "How to Keep Directors' Eyes on the CEO," *The Wall Street Journal,* July 20, 1994, B1.

SHAREHOLDER INITIATIVES These initiatives may be classified into three major, overlapping areas: (1) the rise of shareholder activist groups, (2) the filing of shareholder resolutions and activism at annual meetings, and (3) the filing of shareholder lawsuits.

Rise of Shareholder Activist Groups One major reason that relations between management groups and shareholders have heated up is that shareholders have discovered the benefits of organizing and wielding power. **Shareholder activism** is not a new phenomenon. It goes back over 60 years to 1932, when Lewis Gilbert, then a young owner of 10 shares, was appalled by the absence of communication between New York-based **Consolidated Gas Company's** management and its owners. Supported by a family inheritance, Gilbert decided to quit his job as a newspaper reporter and "fight this silent dictatorship over other people's money." He resolved to devote himself "to the cause of the public shareholder."[171]

Filing of Shareholder Resolutions and Activism at Annual Meetings One of the major vehicles by which shareholder activists communicate their concerns to management groups is through the filing of **shareholder resolutions,** or shareholder proposals. An example of such a resolution is, "The company should name women and minorities to the board of directors." To file a resolution, a shareholder or a shareholder group must obtain a stated number of signatures to require management to place the resolution on the proxy statement so that it can be voted on by all the shareholders. Resolutions that are defeated (fail to get majority votes) may be resubmitted provided that they meet certain SEC requirements for such resubmission.

Because most shareholder resolutions never pass, one might ask why groups pursue them. The main reason is that they gain national publicity, which is part of what protesting groups are out to achieve. Increasingly, companies are negotiating with groups to settle issues before resolutions ever come up for a vote.

Closely related to the surge in shareholder resolutions has been the increased activism at corporate annual meetings in the past decade. Professional "corporate gadflies" purchase small numbers of shares of a company's stock and then attend its annual meetings to put pressure on managers to explain themselves. An example of the kind of social activism that can occur during an annual meeting was the case in which **GM** shareholders sought explanations for a series of embarrassing controversies surrounding the automaker. Some shareholders wanted to know why the company substituted Chevrolet engines in cars sold by some of its other divisions, a move that infuriated many consumers who were not notified of the changes.[172] More recently, corporate executives have been asked to explain high executive compensation packages, positions on hostile takeover attempts, plant closings, greenmail, golden parachutes, and environmental issues.

The motives for bringing up these issues at annual meetings are similar to those for filing shareholder resolutions: to put management on the spot and publicly demand some explanation or corrective action. Activism at annual meetings is one of the few methods shareholders have of demanding explanations and obtaining accountability from top management.

Defending a company at annual meetings has become such an important task of top management that several consulting firms now publish annual booklets of shareholder questions that are likely to be asked. These booklets are intended to help management and directors anticipate and plan for what they might be quizzed on at annual meetings.

Filing of Shareholder Lawsuits   We earlier made reference to the **Trans Union** case wherein shareholders sued the board of directors for approving a buyout offer that the shareholders argued should have had a higher price tag. Their suit charged that the directors had been negligent in failing to secure a third-party opinion from experienced investment bankers. The case went to trial and resulted in a $23.5 million judgment against the directors.[173] The Trans Union case may be one of the largest successful shareholder suits, but it does not stand alone. One estimate was that the number of **shareholder lawsuits** quadrupled over the decade from 1977 to 1987.[174] The large number of shareholder suits being filed today makes one think that almost every decision a company makes is subject to a shareholder suit. As these suits proliferate, many wonder whose interests are really being served. Quite often, the shareholders' attorneys walk away with more money than the protesting shareholders receive.

Shareholder suits are easy to file but difficult to defend. One study estimated that 70 percent of the suits are settled out of court. Therefore, charges of corporate wrongdoing are seldom resolved. Quite often, these lawsuits are seen as legitimate protests by shareholders against management actions, and the threat of litigation does deter corporate misbehavior. From the company's viewpoint, however, such lawsuits are an expensive nuisance. Some experts argue that management's quick willingness to settle before going to trial invites more suits. In spite of this, companies give in because the downside risks of trials and adverse publicity are too great.[175]

In 1995, Congress sought to stem the growing tide of shareholder lawsuits by passing the **Private Securities Litigation Reform Act of 1995.** The law made it more difficult for companies to bring class-action lawsuits to federal court.[176] However, rather than stemming the tide of lawsuits, the act simply prompted shareholders to change their venue. Suits filed in federal court decreased, while suits filed in state courts increased. The Securities Litigation Uniform Standards Act of 1998 was designed to plug that loophole. It says that "Any covered class action brought into any state courts shall be removable to the federal district courts for the district in which the action is pending."[177]

COMPANY INITIATIVES   The need for companies to reestablish a relationship with their owners/stakeholders is somewhat akin to parents having to reestablish relations with their children once the children have grown up. Over the years, the evidence suggests that corporate managements have neglected their owners rather than making them a genuine part of the family. As share ownership has dispersed, there are several legitimate reasons why this separation has taken place. But there is also evidence that management groups have been too preoccupied with their own self-interests. In either case, corporations are beginning to realize that they have a responsibility to their shareholders that cannot be further neglected. Owners are demanding accountability, and it appears that they will be tenacious until they get it.

Public corporations have obligations to their shareholders and to potential shareholders. **Full disclosure** is one of these responsibilities. Disclosure should be made at regular and frequent intervals and should contain information that might affect the investment decisions of shareholders. This information might include the nature and activities of the business, financial and policy matters, tender offers, and special problems and opportunities in the near future and in the longer term.[178] Of paramount importance are the interests of the investing public, not the interests of the incumbent management team. Board members should avoid conflicts between personal interests and the interests of shareholders. Company executives and directors have an obligation to avoid taking personal advantage of information that is not disclosed to the investing public and to avoid any personal use of corporation assets and influence.

With regard to corporate takeovers, fair treatment of shareholders necessitates special safeguards, including (1) candor in public statements on the offer made, (2) full disclosure of all information, (3) absence of undue pressure, and (4) sufficient time for shareholders to make considered decisions. A constructive purpose, not a predatory one, should be served by takeovers. The firm's major stakeholders are its owners. They are interdependent with other stakeholders, and, therefore, management should carry out its obligations to other constituency groups within the context of shareholder concern.[179]

Shareholder programs are not a substitute for keeping shareholders foremost in the minds of managements and boards when economic decisions are being made. However, they do demonstrate an attempt by managements to give serious consideration to corporate/shareholder relations. These types of programs help the corporate governance problem because they show the shareholders that they matter and that they are important to the firm.

Module 900 Endnotes

1. William E. Thomas, Jr., *Readings in Cost Accounting, Budgeting, and Control*, 4th ed. (Cincinnati, OH: Southwestern Publishing, 1973).
2. Robert Simons, *Levers of Control: How Managers Use Innovative Control Systems to Drive Strategic Renewal* (Boston, MA: President and Fellows of Harvard College, 1995).
3. Committee of Sponsoring Organizations of the Treadway Commission, *Internal Control-Integrated Framework* (Jersey City, New Jersey: American Institute of Certified Public Accountants, 1994).
4. "McNamara's Money Game," *Newsday: The Long Island Newspaper,* April 16, 1992, pp. 4–5.
5. *Webster's New World Dictionary, College Edition* (Cleveland and New York: World, 1964), p. 380.
6. The Association of Certified Fraud Examiners, *The Report to the Nation on Occupation Fraud and Abuse,* Austin TX: ACFE), p. 4.
7. Ibid., p. 9.
8. U.S. Securities and Exchange Commission, *Litigation Release No. 17039,* June 19, 2001, http://www.sec.gov.
9. See, for example, W. S. Albrecht, D. Cherrington, R. Payne, A. Roe, and M. Romney, *How to Detect and Prevent Business Fraud,* (Prentice-Hall, 1981).
10. For example, several studies on retail theft over time by Richard C. Hollinger (University of Florida) and others have shown that a higher percentage of employees were dishonest in later years than in earlier years. Other studies have found similar results.
11. See *How to Detect and Prevent Business Fraud,* op. cit.
12. http://www.better-investing.org.
13. From speech by Lynn Turner, former chief accountant of U.S. Securities and Exchange Commission, given at the 39th Annual Corporate Counsel Institute, Northwestern University School of Law, October 12, 2000.
14. Almost every year, KPMG Forensic and Investigative Services conducts a fraud survey. These surveys show that almost all companies surveyed have major frauds. For more information about the surveys, contact Michael D. Carey, NY (212-872-6825).
15. For example, read the research of the Social and Moral Research Group, University of Maryland (http://www.education.umd.edu/Depts/EDHD/faculty/killen/SMDRG).
16. See, for example, *Theory O: Creating an Ownership Style of Management*, discussed at http://www.nceo.org/pubs/theoryo.html.
17. See, for example, *2002 Report to the Nation: Occupational Fraud and Abuse* (Austin, TX: Association of Certified Fraud Examiners, 2002).
18. See, for example, W. Steve Albrecht, K. Howe, and M. Romney, *Deterring Fraud: The Internal Auditor's Perspective* (Altamonte Spring, FL: The Institute of Internal Auditors, 1984).
19. Class-action lawsuits are permitted under federal law and some state rules of court procedure in the United States. In a class-action suit, a relatively small number of aggrieved plaintiffs with small individual claims can bring suit for large damages in the name of an extended class. After a fraud, for example, 40 bondholders who lost $40,000 might decide to sue, and they can sue on behalf of the entire class of bondholders for all their alleged losses (say $50 million). Lawyers are more than happy to take such suits on a contingency fee basis (a percentage of the judgment, if any).
20. Howard M. Schilit, *What Directors Can Do to Prevent and Detect Financial Shenanigans* (Washington DC: National Association of Corporate Directors [NACD], 1994).
21. Quoted in John L. Paluszek, *Business and Society: 1976–2000* (New York: AMACOM, 1976), 1.
22. Keith Davis, "Understanding the Social Responsibility Puzzle," *Business Horizon* (Winter 1967), 45–50.
23. Archie B. Carroll, "A Three-Dimensional Conceptual Model of Corporate Social Performance," *Academy of Management Review,* Vol. 4, No. 4 (1979), 497–505.

24. Archie B. Carroll, "The Pyramid of Corporate Social Responsibility: Toward the Moral Management of Organizational Stakeholders," *Business Horizons* (July–August 1991), 39–48. Also see Archie B. Carroll, "The Four Faces of Corporate Citizenship," *Business and Society Review* (Vol. 100–101, 1998), 1–7.

25. Ibid.

26. Milton Friedman, "The Social Responsibility of Business Is to Increase Its Profits," *New York Times* (September 1962), 126.

27. Ibid., 33 (emphasis added).

28. Christopher D. Stone, *Where the Law Ends* (New York: Harper Colophon Books, 1975), 77.

29. Keith Davis, "The Case For and Against Business Assumption of Social Responsibilities," *Academy of Management Journal* (June 1973), 312–322.

30. F. A. Hayek, "The Corporation in a Democratic Society: In Whose Interest Ought It and Will It Be Run?" in H. Ansoff (ed.), *Business Strategy* (Middlesex: Penguin, 1969), 225.

31. Davis, 320.

32. Thomas A. Petit, *The Moral Crisis in Management* (New York: McGraw-Hill, 1967), 58.

33. Davis, 316.

34. Cited in Aaron Bernstein, "Too Much Corporate Power," *Business Week,* September 11, 2000, 149.

35. Robert Ackerman and Raymond Bauer, *Corporate Social Responsiveness: The Modern Dilemma* (Reston, VA: Reston Publishing Company, 1976), 6.

36. S. Prakash Sethi, "Dimensions of Corporate Social Performance: An Analytical Framework," *California Management Review* (Spring 1975), 58–64.

37. Ibid., 62–63.

38. William C. Frederick, "From CSR_1 to CSR_2: The Maturing of Business-and-Society Thought," Working Paper No. 279 (Graduate School of Business, University of Pittsburgh, 1978), 6. See also *Business and Society*, Vol. 33, No. 2 (August 1994), 150–164.

39. William C. Frederick, "Toward CSR_3: Why Ethical Analysis Is Indispensable and Unavoidable in Corporate Affairs," *California Management Review* (Winter 1986), 131.

40. Edwin M. Epstein, "The Corporate Social Policy Process: Beyond Business Ethics, Corporate Social Responsibility and Corporate Social Responsiveness," *California Management Review,* (Vol. XXIX, No. 3, 1987), 107.

41. Ian Wilson, "What One Company Is Doing About Today's Demands on Business," in G.A. Steiner (ed.), *Changing Business-Society Interrelationships* (UCLA, 1975).

42. T. W. McAdam, "How to Put Corporate Responsibility into Practice," *Business and Society Review/Innovation* (Summer 1973), 8–16.

43. Keith Davis and Robert L. Blomstrom, *Business and Society: Environment and Responsibility,* 3rd ed. (New York: McGraw-Hill, 1975), 85–86.

44. James E. Post, *Corporate Behavior and Social Change* (Reston, VA: Reston Publishing Co., 1978), 39.

45. Juha Näsi, Salme Näsi, Nelson Phillips, and Stelios Zyglidopoulos, "The Evolution of Corporate Responsiveness," *Business and Society,* Vol. 36, No. 3 (September 1997), 296–321.

46. Carroll, 1979, 502–504.

47. Samuel P. Graves, Sandra Waddock, and Marjorie Kelly, "How Do You Measure Corporate Citizenship?" *Business Ethics,* March/April 2001, 17.

48. Charles J. Fombrum, "Three Pillars of Corporate Citizenship," in Noel Tichy, Andrew McGill, and Lynda St. Clair (eds.), *Corporate Global Citizenship* (San Francisco: The New Lexington Press), 27–61.

49. Kimberly S. Davenport, "Corporate Citizenship: A Stakeholder Approach for Defining Corporate Social Performance and Identifying Measures for Assessing It," doctoral dissertation, The Fielding Institute, Santa Barbara, CA.

50. Archie B. Carroll, "The Four Faces of Corporate Citizenship," *Business and Society Review,* 100/101, 1998, 1–7.

51. Barbara W. Altman, *Corporate Community Relations in the 1990s: A Study in Transformation,* unpublished doctoral dissertation, Boston University.

52. Archie B. Carroll, Kim Davenport, and Doug Grisaffe, "Appraising the Business Value of Corporate Citizenship: What Does the Literature Say?" Proceedings of the International Association for Business and Society, Essex Junction, VT, 2000.

53. For more on corporate citizenship, see the special issue "Corporate Citizenship," *Business and Society Review,* 105:1, Spring 2000, edited by Barbara W. Altman and Deborah Vidaver-Cohen; also see Jorg Andriof and Malcolm McIntosh (eds.) *Perspectives on Corporate Citizenship* (London: Greenleaf Publishing, 2001). Also see, Isabelle Maignan, O. C. Ferrell, and G. Tomas M. Hult, "Corporate Citizenship: Cultural Antecedents and Business Benefits," *Journal of the Academy of Marketing Science,* Vol. 27, No. 4, Fall 1999, 455–469. Also see Malcolm McIntosh, Deborah Leipziger, Keith Jones, and Gill Coleman, *Corporate Citizenship: Successful Strategies for Responsible Companies* (London: Financial Times/ Pitman Publishing), 1998.

54. Philip Johansson, "Social Investing Turns 30," *Business Ethics* (January–February 2001), 12–16.

55. "Good Works and Great Profits," *Business Week,* February 16, 1998, 8.

56. Samuel B. Graves and Sandra A. Waddock, "Institutional Owners and Corporate Social Performance," *Academy of Management Journal,* Vol. 37, No. 4, August 1994, 1034–1046.
57. *Ibid.*
58. Charles W. Hofer, Edwin A. Murray, Jr., Ram Charan, and Robert A. Pitts, *Strategic Management: A Casebook in Policy and Planning,* 2nd ed. (St. Paul, MN: West Publishing Co., 1984), 27–29. Also see Gary Hamel and C. K. Prahalad, *Competing for the Future* (Boston: Harvard Business School Press, 1994).
59. C. W. Hofer and D. E. Schendel, *Strategy Formulation: Analytial Concepts* (St. Paul: West, 1978), 52–55. Also see J. David Hunger and Thomas L. Wheelen, *Essentials of Strategic Management* (Reading, MA: Addison-Wesley, 2000).
60. V. K. Narayanan and Liam Fahey, "Environmental Analysis for Strategy Formulation," in William R. King and David I. Cleland (eds.), *Strategic Planning and Management Handbook* (New York: Van Nostrand Reinhold, 1987), 156.
61. Robert H. Miles, *Managing the Corporate Social Environment: A Grounded Theory* (Englewood Cliffs, NJ: Prentice-Hall, Inc., 1987).
62. *Ibid.,* 8.
63. *Ibid.,* 9–10, 111.
64. *Ibid.,* 2–3.
65. *Ibid.,* 11, 113.
66. Fleisher (ed.), 1997, 139–196.
67. David H. Blake, "How to Incorporate Public Affairs into the Operating Manager's Job," *Public Affairs Review* (1984), 35.
68. Liam Fahey, "Issues Management: Two Approaches," *Strategic Planning Management* (November 1986), 81, 85–96.
69. *Ibid.,* 81.
70. *Ibid.,* 86.
71. *Ibid.,* 32.
72. William R. King, "Strategic Issue Management," in William R. King and David I. Cleland (eds.), *Strategic Planning and Management Handbook* (New York: Van Nostrand Reinhold, 1987), 257.
73. James K. Brown, *This Business of Issues: Coping with the Company's Environment* (New York: The Conference Board, 1979), 45.
74. *Ibid.,* 33.
75. King, 257.
76. Joseph F. Coates, Vary T. Coates, Jennifer Jarratt, and Lisa Heinz, *Issues Management* (Mt. Airy, MD: Lomond Publications, 1986), p. 46.
77. I. C. MacMillan and P. E. Jones, "Designing Organizations to Compete," *Journal of Business Strategy,* Vol. 4, No. 4, Spring 1984, 13.
78. Roy Wernham, "Implementation: The Things That Matter," in King and Cleland, 453.
79. Barbara Bigelow, Liam Fahey, and John Mahon, "A Typology of Issue Evolution," *Business and Society* (Spring 1993), 28. For another useful perspective, see John F. Mahon and Sandra A. Waddock, "Strategic Issues Management: An Integration of Issue Life Cycle Perspectives," *Business and Society* (Spring 1992), 19–32. Also see Steven L. Wartick and Robert E. Rude, "Issues Management: Fad or Function?" *California Management Review* (Fall 1986), 134–140.
80. Public Affairs Council, "Public Affairs: Its Origins, Its Present, and Its Trends," 2001, http://www.pac.org/whatis/index.htm.
81. Kate Miller, "Issues Management: The Link Between Organization Reality and Public Perception," *Public Relations Quarterly,* Vol. 44, No. 2 (Summer 1999), 5–11.
82. Laurence Barton, *Crisis in Organizations: Managing and Communicating in the Heat of Chaos* (Cincinnati: South-Western Publishing Co., 1993), 2.
83. Christine M. Pearson and Judith Clair, "Reframing Crisis Management," *Academy of Management Review,* Vol. 23, No. 1, (1998), 60.
84. Steven Fink, *Crisis Management: Planning for the Inevitable* (New York: Amacom, 1986), p. 68. For further discussion of types of crises, see Ian Mitroff, "Crisis Management and Environmentalism: A Natural Fit," *California Management Review* (Winter 1994), 101–113.
85. Pearson and Clair, 60.
86. Ian Mitroff, with Gus Anagnos, *Managing Crises Before They Happen: What Every Executive and Manager Needs to Know About Crisis Management* (New York: AMACOM, 2001), Chapter 3.
87. Fink, 20.
88. Mitroff and Anagnos, 2001.
89. "How Companies Are Learning to Prepare for the Worst," *Business Week,* December 23, 1985, 74–75.
90. "How Companies Are Learning to Prepare for the Worst," *Business Week,* December 23, 1985, 76.
91. *Ibid.*
92. *Ibid.*

93. Richard J. Mahoney, "The Anatomy of a Public Policy Crisis," *The CEO Series,* Center for the Study of American Business (May 1996), 7.
94. *Ibid.*
95. Greg Jaffe, "How Florida Crash Overwhelmed ValuJet's Skillful Crisis Control," *Wall Street Journal* (June 5, 1996), S1.
96. Melissa Master, "Keyword: Crisis," *Across the Board* (September 1998), 62.
97. Ian Mitroff, Paul Shrivastava, and Firdaus Udwadia, "Effective Crisis Management," *Academy of Management Executive* (November 1987), 285.
98. Norman R. Augustine, "Managing the Crisis You Tried to Prevent," *Harvard Business Review* (November–December 1995), 147–158.
99. Christine M. Pearson and Ian I. Mitroff, "From Crisis Prone to Crisis Prepared: A Framework for Crisis Management," *Academy of Management Executive* (Vol. VII, No. 1, February 1993), 58–59. Also see Ian Mitroff, Christine M. Pearson, and L. Katherine Harrington, *The Essential Guide to Managing Corporate Crises* (New York: Oxford University Press, 1996).
100. Robert Goff, "Coming Clean," *Forbes,* May 17, 1999, 156–160.
101. *Ibid.*
102. Johnathan L. Bernstein, "The Ten Steps of Crisis Communications," June 4, 2001, http://www.crisisnavigator.org.
103. Richard Wm. Brundage, "Crisis Management—An Outline for Survival." June 4, 2001, http://www.crisisnavigator.org.
104. Mitroff and Anagnos, 2001.
105. Richard T. DeGeorge, *Business Ethics,* 4th ed. (New York: Prentice Hall, 1995), 20–21; See also Rogene A. Buchholz and Sandra B. Rosenthal, *Business Ethics* (Upper Saddle River, NJ: Prentice Hall, 1998), 3.
106. DeGeorge, op. cit.15.
107. See, for example, Melissa Baucus and Janet Near, "Can Illegal Corporate Behavior Be Predicted? An Event History Analysis," *Academy of Management Journal,* Vol. 34, No. 1, 1991, 9–36; and P. L. Cochran and D. Nigh, "Illegal Corporate Behavior and the Question of Moral Agency," in William C. Frederick (ed.), *Research in Corporate Social Performance and Policy,* Vol. 9 (Greenwich, CT: JAI Press, 1987), 73–91.
108. For examples that may fit in the various portions of the model, see Mark Schwartz, "Developing Portraits of Corporate Social Responsibility," 1995, unpublished manuscript; See also Mark Schwartz, "Carroll's Pyramid of Corporate Social Responsibility: A New Approach," IABS Proceedings, 1997, 236–241.
109. Otto A. Bremer, "An Approach to Questions of Ethics in Business," *Audenshaw Document No. 116* (North Hinksey, Oxford: The Hinksey Centre, Westminster College, 1983), 1–12.
110. Andrew Stark, "What's the Matter with Business Ethics?" *Harvard Business Review* (May–June, 1993), 7.
111. Most of the material in this section comes from Archie B. Carroll, "In Search of the Moral Manager," *Business Horizons* (March/April 1987), 7–15; See also Archie B. Carroll, "Models of Management Morality for the New Millennium," *Business Ethics Quarterly,* Vol. 11, Issue 2 (April 2001), 365–371.
112. Lynn Sharp Paine, "Managing for Organizational Integrity," *Harvard Business Review* (March–April, 1994), 106–117.
113. *Ibid.,* 111–112.
114. Paine, 109–113.
115. Carroll, 1987, 7–15.
116. Charles W. Powers and David Vogel, *Ethics in the Education of Business Managers* (Hastings-on-Hudson, NY: The Hastings Center, 1980), 40–45. Also see Patricia H. Werhane, *Moral Imagination and Management Decision Making,* (New York: Oxford University Press, 1999).
117. Milton Friedman, "The Social Responsibility of Business Is to Increase Its Profits," *The New York Times* (September 1962), 126 (italics added).
118. Cited in Edwin M. Epstein and Dow Votaw (eds.), *Rationality, Legitimacy, Responsibility: Search for New Directions in Business and Society* (Santa Monica, CA: Goodyear Publishing Co., 1978), 72.
119. *Ibid.,* 73.
120. *Ibid.*
121. *Ibid.*
122. *Ibid.*
123. William R. Dill (ed.) *Running the American Corporation* (Englewood Cliffs, NJ: Prentice-Hall, 1978), 11.
124. *Ibid.*
125. *Ibid.*
126. Louis Lavelle, "Shhh, You'll Wake the Board," *Business Week,* March 5, 2001, 92.
127. *Ibid.*
128. John A. Byrne, "The Best and Worst Boards," *Business Week,* January 24, 2000 142.

129. Robert W. Lear and Boris Yavitz, "Boards on Trial," *Chief Executive* (October 2000), 40–48.
130. "The Fading Appeal of the Boardroom," *The Economist*, February 10, 2001, 67–69.
131. "Europe's Shareholders to the Barricades," *Business Week*, March 19, 2001.
132. Murray L. Weidenbaum, *Strengthening the Corporate Board: A Constructive Response to Hostile Takeovers* (St. Louis: Washington University, Center for the Study of American Business, September 1985), 4–5.
133. Linda Himelstein, "Boardrooms: The Ties That Blind," *Business Week*, May 2, 1994, 112–114.
134. Carol J. Loomis, "This Stuff Is Wrong," *Fortune*, June 25, 2001, 72–84.
135. John A. Byrne, "Executive Pay: Deliver—Or Else," *Business Week*, March 27, 1995, 36–38.
136. Nikos Vafeas and Zaharoulla Afxentiou, "The Association Between the SEC's 1992 Compensation Disclosure Rule and Executive Compensation Policy Changes," *Journal of Accounting and Public Policy* (Spring 1998), 27–54.
137. Ann Buchholtz, Michael Young, and Gary Powell, "Are Board Members Pawns or Watchdogs? The Link Between CEO Pay and Firm Performance," *Group and Organization Management* (March 1998), 6–26.
138. Tracey Grant, "Big Bucks on Board," *The Washington Post*, September 29, 1997, F3.
139. Geoffrey Colvin, "Is the Board Too Cushy?" *Director* (February 1997), 64–65.
140. "The Fading Appeal of the Boardroom," *The Economist*, February 10, 2001, 67.
141. Ed Leefeldt, "Greenmail, Far from Disappearing, Is Doing Quite Well in Disguised Forms," *Wall Street Journal*, December 4, 1984, 15.
142. Ruth Simon, "Needed: A Generic Remedy," *Forbes*, November 5, 1984, 40.
143. Craig W. Friedrich, "Recent Developments," *Journal of Corporate Taxation* (Winter 1998), 422–425.
144. *Ibid.*
145. Verne Kopytoff, "Yahoo's Not an Attractive Target for a Takeover, Analysts Say," *San Francisco Chronicle*, March 3, 2001, D1.
146. Philip L. Cochran and Steven L. Wartick, "Golden Parachutes: Good for Management and Society?" in S. Prakash Sethi and Cecilia M. Falbe (eds.), *Business and Society: Dimensions of Conflict and Cooperation* (Lexington, MA: Lexington Books, 1987), 321.
147. Ann K. Buchholtz and Barbara A. Ribbens, "Role of Chief Executive Officers in Takeover Resistance: Effects of CEO Incentives and Individual Characteristics," *Academy of Management Journal* (June 1994), 554–579.
148. Cochran and Wartick, 325–326.
149. George Russell, "The Fall of a Wall Street Superstar," *Time*, November 24, 1986, 71.
150. *Ibid.*
151. Donald Baer, "Getting Even with Ivan and Company," *U.S. News and World Report*, March 2, 1987, 46.
152. Anthony Bianco and Gary Weiss, "Suddenly the Fish Get Bigger," *Business Week*, March 2, 1987, 29–30.
153. "New Arrests on Wall Street: Who's Next in the Insider Trading Scandal?" *Newsweek*, February 23, 1987, 48–50.
154. James B. Stewart, "Scenes from a Scandal: The Secret World of Michael Milkin and Ivan Boesky," *The Wall Street Journal*, October 2, 1991, B1.
155. Christopher H. Schmitt, "The SEC Lifts the Curtain on Company Info," *Business Week*, August 11, 2000.
156. "A Landmark Ruling That Puts Board Members in Peril," *Business Week*, March 18, 1985, 56–57.
157. Laurie Baum and John A. Byrne, "The Job Nobody Wants: Outside Directors Find That the Risks and Hassles Just Aren't Worth It," *Business Week*, September 8, 1986, 57.
158. Paul E. Fiorella, "Why Comply? Directors Face Heightened Personal Liability After Caremark," *Business Horizons* (July/August 1998), 49–52.
159. "The Fading Appeal of the Boardroom," *The Economist*, February 10, 2001, 67.
160. Toddi Gutner, "Wanted: More Diverse Directors," *Business Week*, April 30, 2001, 134.
161. "Board Diversity Increases," *Association Management* (January 2000), 25.
162. Paul Coombes and Mark Watson, "Three Surveys on Corporate Governance," *McKinsey Quarterly* (2000, No. 4), cited in "The Fading Appeal of the Boardroom," *The Economist*, February 10, 2001, 67–69.
163. "The Fading Appeal of the Boardroom," *The Economist*, February 10, 2001, 67.
164. *Ibid.*
165. Gutner, 134.
166. Joann S. Lublin and Elizabeth MacDonald, "Scandals Signal Laxity of Audit Panels," *Wall Street Journal*, July 17, 1998, B1.
167. Charles A. Anderson and Robert N. Anthony, *The New Corporate Directors: Insights for Board Members and Executives* (New York: John Wiley & Sons, 1986), 141.
168. Arjay Miller, "A Director's Questions," *The Wall Street Journal*, August 18, 1980, 10.

169. Donald E. Schwartz, "Corporate Governance," in Thorton Bradshaw and David Vogel (eds.), *Corporations and Their Critics* (New York: McGraw-Hill, 1981), 227–228.
170. Bruce Nussbaum and Judith Dobrzynski, "The Battle for Corporate Control," *Business Week,* May 18, 1987, 102–109.
171. Lauren Tainer, *The Origins of Shareholder Activism* (Washington, DC: Investor Responsibility Research Center, July 1983), 2.
172. Leonard Apcar and Terry Brown, "GM Reputation Is Defended by Chairman Under Barrage of Shareholder Questions," *The Wall Street Journal,* May 23, 1977, 17.
173. Thomas J. Neff, "Liability Panic in the Board Room," *The Wall Street Journal,* November 10, 1986, 22.
174. Julie Amparano, "A Lawyer Flourishes by Suing Corporations for Their Shareholders," *The Wall Street Journal,* April 28, 1987, 1.
175. Richard B. Schmitt, "Attorneys Are Often Big Winners When Shareholders Sue Companies," *The Wall Street Journal,* June 12, 1986, 31.
176. Steven M. Schatz and Douglas J. Clark, "Securities Litigation," *International Financial Law Review* (June 1998), 27.
177. "Securities Litigation Reform Revisited," *Journal of Accountancy* (January 1999), 20–21.
178. "The Responsibility of a Corporation to Its Shareholders," *Criteria for Decision Making* (C.W. Post Center, Long Island University, 1979), 14.
179. *Ibid.,* 14–15.

MODULE 1000

International Business

1001 Global Business Strategies, 1366

1010 Forms of International Business and Marketing Strategies, 1371

1020 International Risks, 1383

1030 Global Organization Structure and Control, 1386

1040 International Trade and Investment, 1403

1050 International Payments, 1414

1060 International Cultures and Protocols, 1419

1070 International Economics, 1428

1075 International Banking, 1449

1080 International Law, 1456

1090 Ethics and International Business, 1467

Module 1000 Endnotes, 1472

Global Business Strategies

Why Firms Internationalize Their Operations

Historically, domestic enterprises have **internationalized their business operations** either to seize **opportunities** or to deal with **threats,** or both.[1] For example, the European Union's (EU) current efforts to become more unified are expected to present both opportunities and threats for non-EU business enterprises. The advent of the Internet as a means of conducting international business also presents opportunities and threats. The ensuing sections discuss the opportunities and threats that cause domestic enterprises to internationalize their operations.

Opportunity Reasons

The opportunity reasons for internationalizing operations include greater profits, appearance of new markets, faster growth in new markets, obtaining new products for the domestic market, and globalization of financial markets.

Greater Profits

Many domestic firms have internationalized their operations because their managers saw the opportunity to earn greater profits by charging higher prices in a higher per capita income foreign country where a high demand for the product or service existed or where there was less competition. Enterprises have also internationalized their operations because their managers determined that they could earn higher profits by attaining greater *economies of scale* with foreign expansion. Additionally, many enterprises have been able to earn greater profits by producing in a country where labor was cheaper and/or where materials cost less than at home.

Appearance of New Markets

Population expansion, income growth, and technological advancements around the globe have created **new markets** and demands and thus new business opportunities. Many domestic firms have internationalized their operations to meet those new demands.

Faster Growth in New Markets

Many domestic organizations have a strong growth orientation. These firms often enter foreign markets because they can grow at a faster rate there than they can in the established domestic market.

Obtaining New Products for the Domestic Market

Many individuals from the home market travel abroad and develop a desire for a product that they would like to have available in their home market. For example, English ales, German beers, and French wines sell well in the U.S. market. Domestic enterprises therefore internationalize their operations to obtain products for domestic consumers. If they do not, their competitors will.

Globalization of Financial Markets

In recent decades, there has been an expansion in the ways in which international business can be financed. This growth in **financial options** has been the catalyst for the expansion of international business. These tools include the International Monetary Fund, created in 1945 by the United Nations to encourage and aid world trade, and the World Bank, created by the United Nations for the purpose of encouraging the extension of loans to less-developed countries. Banks such as **Citicorp, Dai-ichiKangyo Bank,** and **Bank Nationale de Paris** have grown into international organizations that draw on a variety of investors from many parts of the world.[2]

Threat Reasons

The threat reasons for internationalizing operations include protection from declining demand in the home market, acquisition of raw materials, acquisition of managerial know-how and capital, protection of the home market, and protection from imports.

Protection from Declining Demand in Home Market

Demand for a firm's product or service may be low in the home market due to recessionary conditions, a saturated market, or a declining product life cycle. Many firms have been able to hedge against recessions at home and maintain their growth by expanding into foreign markets.

Acquisition of Raw Materials

Many domestic manufacturers depend on and import raw materials available in foreign countries. To be assured of the necessary raw materials, numerous enterprises have set up operations overseas. For example, rubber, which is required by numerous U.S. manufacturers, is not available in the continental United States. Tire-producing firms must acquire rubber from other countries—those in Southeast Asia, for instance. Likewise, oil companies search the world for new petroleum reserves.

Acquisition of Managerial Know-How and Capital

Enterprises sometimes must go abroad to obtain the managerial know-how and capital that they lack but need to improve their operations. For example, in recent years, there has been a booming demand for travel in Russia. The Russian airline, **Aeroflot,** was one of the least efficient airlines in the world. To deal with this problem, the Russian carrier's management shopped around for Western partners who could bring the managerial know-how and capital it needed to meet its expansion demands.[3]

Protection of Home Market

Many firms have internationalized their operations to protect their home market. For example, a firm services a domestic manufacturer which, for its own reasons, decides to set up subsidiary operations abroad. The service enterprise would be wise to follow and provide the services required by the manufacturer's foreign subsidiaries. Otherwise, an aggressive competitor that gets its "foot in the door" through the manufacturer's foreign subsidiary may soon take over the service activities in the domestic market as well.

Protection from Imports

Foreign competitors often hold an advantage over domestic firms because they have access to cheaper labor and/or materials in a foreign country. To remain competitive, domestic firms must often transfer their production activities to a foreign country to obtain the same cost advantages the foreign competitors enjoy. For example, many of the parts used to manufacture U.S.-produced automobiles are actually manufactured abroad.

The Internal Review

Environmental changes, which are detected through an **external review** of the global environment, often require that firms develop international strategies. To help them develop effective international strategies, along with total familiarity with the external environment, managers must examine their enterprises' internal conditions; they must conduct an internal review to become familiar with the company's internal situation. Knowledge of their firm's internal factors will help its managers develop wise strategies for penetrating a foreign market or for coping with environmental changes. Basically, managers need to determine how much money the firm has access to, including cash on hand, borrowing power, and ability to sell stock, which can be used to finance the strategy; the nature of its physical assets; its personnel capabilities; and its strengths.

Foreign Sources of Finance

Even if an enterprise has access to the funds required to finance the expansion, managers should inquire about the availability of **financial assistance in the foreign market.** The governments of many foreign countries make special concessions to foreign firms that bring them the technologies they believe will aid their nations' development efforts. For example, the government of Morocco was actively seeking foreign investment in its tourism sector. To attract investment, it offered several incentives, such as the possibility of 100 percent foreign ownership; tax exemptions of up to 10 years, depending on the location of investment; and the availability of long-term, low-interest financing.[4]

Nature of the Firm's Physical Assets and Personnel Competencies

Managers also need to obtain information about the enterprise's physical assets and their current state. Is their manufacturing capacity capable of producing for the foreign market? Or are new manufacturing means needed? Furthermore, managers must obtain information about their firm's **personnel competencies** in relation to the company's international strategy. Does the enterprise have the personnel capable of producing for the foreign market(s)? Does it have personnel with the ability to manage the international operations? Again, the governments of many foreign countries will help foreign firms finance machinery and factories and will provide trained personnel, or assist in training personnel, as a means of attracting technologies to aid in accomplishing the nation's developmental objectives.

The firm's internal conditions also affect how it enters a foreign market. Two fundamental approaches to conducting business abroad are by exporting to it or by manufacturing in it. Exporting involves manufacturing at home and shipping the goods to the foreign market. Exporting generally requires less investment than manufacturing abroad. If the firm is cash-short, has idle equipment, and its personnel is not highly competent in international business, the firm may prefer to export. However, by producing abroad, the company can often save on transportation, labor, and materials costs, as well as on tariffs. Therefore, if an enterprise has adequate cash to invest, has international managerial know-how, the foreign demand justifies the investment, and the foreign environment is conducive to the investment, it may want to produce abroad.

Lead from Strength

The internal review should also include an assessment of the enterprise's strengths. A business should always "**lead from strength**"; that is, it should focus on doing what it can do better than its competitors. For example, a firm's strength may be engineering and design. Instead of manufacturing, it may be more efficient for the firm to farm it out to a company whose strength is manufacturing.

Furthermore, a firm may be strong in production, but weak in conducting foreign business. This firm may therefore have to form a joint venture or enter into a strategic alliance with an enterprise that is strong in conducting foreign business. Basically, organizations enter into joint ventures or strategic alliances to share costs and risks, to gain additional technical and market knowledge, to complement each other, to serve an international market, to strengthen themselves against other competitors, and to develop industry standards together.[5] Managers should be aware, however, that joint ventures and strategic alliances can backfire, especially when one of the partners becomes stronger by learning more than the other(s). The stronger partner may break up the alliance and go on its own, which may harm the weaker partner.

It should be noted that foreign countries' environments generally have an effect on a firm's strengths and weaknesses. For example, an organization may possess a strong ability to distribute a product in one nation because it is capable of dealing with that country's distribution laws and practices. At the same time it may possess a weak capability to distribute in another country because it lacks the ability to deal with that nation's distribution laws and practices. For instance, international business transactions are either in cash or in barter trade. Many enterprises have experience in cash transactions but not in barter trade transactions. In the latter case, if the enterprise wishes to penetrate a foreign market where barter trade is required, it may have to form a partnership with a firm that has experience in barter trade.

Also, an enterprise may possess the ability to differentiate a product to fit the needs of a specific country's culture, and at the same time lack the ability to differentiate to fit another country's cultural needs. U.S. car manufacturers, for example, have historically possessed the capability of differentiating their automobiles to fit the needs of many countries, but not the needs of some countries, such as England, where the steering wheel is located on the right-hand side of the automobile. In this case, if a U.S. car manufacturer wanted to penetrate the British car market, it might have to form a partnership with a car manufacturer that has the capability of producing cars with the steering wheel on the right-hand side.

Types of International Strategies

International firms typically develop their core strategy for the home country first. Subsequently, they internationalize their core strategy through international expansion of activities and through adaptation. Eventually, they globalize their strategy by integrating operations across nations.[6] These steps translate into four distinct types of strategies applied by international enterprises: ethnocentric, multidomestic, global, and transnational.

Ethnocentric Strategy

Following World War II, U.S. enterprises operated mainly from an **ethnocentric** perspective. These companies produced unique goods and services, which they offered primarily to the domestic market. The lack of international competition offset their need to be sensitive to cultural differences. When these firms exported goods, they did not alter them for foreign consumption—the costs of alterations for cultural differences were assumed by the foreign buyers. In effect, this type of company has one strategy for all markets.

Multidomestic Strategy

The multidomestic firm has a different strategy for each of its foreign markets. In this type of strategy, "a company's management tries to operate effectively across a series of worldwide positions with diverse product requirements, growth rates, competitive environments, and political risks. The company prefers that local managers do what is necessary to succeed in R&D, production, marketing, and distribution, but holds them responsible for results."[7] In essence, this type of corporation competes with local competitors on a market-by-market basis. A multitude of American corporations use this strategy, for example, **Procter & Gamble** in household products, **Honeywell** in controls, **Alcoa** in aluminum, and **General Foods** in consumer goods. Japanese car manufacturer **Toyota** also follows this strategy.

Global Strategy

The **global corporation** uses all of its resources against its competition in a very integrated fashion. All of its foreign subsidiaries and divisions are highly interdependent in both operations and strategy. As Thomas Hout et al., said:

> In a global business, management competes worldwide against a small number of other multinationals in the world market. Strategy is centralized, and various aspects of operations are decentralized or centralized as economics and effectiveness dictate. The company seeks to respond to particular local market needs, while avoiding a compromise of efficiency of the overall global system.[8]

Therefore, whereas in a multidomestic strategy the managers in each country react to competition without considering what is taking place in other countries, in a global strategy, competitive moves are integrated across nations. The same kind of move is made in different countries at the same time or in a systematic fashion. For example, a competitor is attacked in one nation in order to exhaust its resources for another country, or a competitive attack in one nation is countered in a different country—for instance, the counterattack in a competitor's home market as a parry to an attack on one's home market.[9]

Advantages and Disadvantages of the Global Strategy

Outlined next are the advantages and disadvantages of the global strategy.[10] The advantages of the global strategy would negate the disadvantages of the multidomestic strategy, and the disadvantages of the global strategy would be negated by the advantages of the multidomestic strategy.

Advantages of the Global Strategy (Multidomestic strategy does not provide these advantages.)
- By pooling production or other activities for two or more nations, a firm can increase the benefits derived from economies of scale.
- A company can cut costs by moving manufacturing or other activities to low-cost countries.
- A firm that is able to switch production among different nations can reduce costs by increasing its bargaining power over suppliers, workers, and host governments.
- By focusing on a smaller number of products and programs than under a multidomestic strategy, a corporation is able to improve both product and program quality.

- Worldwide availability, serviceability, and recognition can increase preference through reinforcement.
- The company is provided with more points from which to attack and counterattack competition.

Disadvantages of the Global Strategy (Multidomestic strategy can reduce these disadvantages.)
- Through increased coordination, reporting requirements, and added staff, substantial management costs can be incurred.
- Overcentralization can harm local motivation and morale, therefore reducing the firm's effectiveness.
- Standardization can result in a product that does not totally satisfy any customers.
- Incurring costs and revenues in multiple countries increases currency risk.
- Integrated competitive moves can lead to the sacrificing of revenues, profits, or competitive positions in individual countries—especially when the subsidiary in one country is told to attack a global competitor in order to convey a signal or divert that competitor's resources from another nation.

Transnational Strategy

The **transnational strategy** provides for global coordination (like the global strategy) and at the same time it allows local autonomy (like the multidomestic strategy). **Nestlé**, the world's largest food company, headquartered in Switzerland, follows this strategy.[11] The challenges managers of transnational corporations face are to identify and exploit cross-border synergies and to balance local demands with the global vision for the corporation. Building an effective transnational organization requires a corporate culture that values global dissimilarities across cultures and markets.[12]

International Strategic and Tactical Objectives

Organizations generally establish two kinds of measurable objectives: strategic and tactical. **Strategic objectives,** which are guided by the enterprise's mission or purpose and deal with long-term issues, associate the enterprise to its external environment and provide management with a basis for comparing performance with that of its competitors and in relation to environmental demands. Examples of strategic objectives include to increase sales, to increase market share, to increase profits, and to lower prices by becoming an international firm. **Tactical objectives,** which are guided by the enterprise's strategic objectives and deal with shorter term issues, identify the key result areas in which specific performance is essential for the success of the enterprise and aim to attain internal efficiency. They identify specifically how, for example, to lower costs, to lower prices, to increase output, to capture a larger portion of the market, and to penetrate an international market.

Technology and Global Strategy

Technology has been the root of the most dramatic changes occurring in commerce today. It now enables organizations to integrate their systems, where changes in one part ripple throughout the system, causing shifts in the other parts. Therefore, no strategy has been left untouched. It has leveled the playing field for small firms, allowing them to compete successfully with large corporations in the same markets. With e-mail, teleconferencing, multimedia CD-ROMs, and networked databases, small businesses can emulate the marketing tactics of much larger companies—they can set up a home page on the World Wide Web right next door to **Wal-Mart.** And electronic networks and the Internet have enabled organizations to decentralize business activities and to outsource activities to other organizations.

From a strategic viewpoint, technology impacted international strategy in several ways.[13]

- Emphasis has moved from products to information and solutions.
- Products can be launched from commercialization tactics based on identifying specific customer needs.
- Relationships with customers have been made easier, which enhances product acceptance and minimizes costs due to redesign.
- Firms can now target specific products and services to specific customers.
- Technology supports the integration of engineering and commercialization to get the product to the customer in the least amount of time.
- Technology helps prevent midcourse corrections in product design, which usually result in higher costs and longer time to commercialize.

From a tactical viewpoint, current technology aids businesses in the commercialization of their products and services in numerous ways.

- E-mail enables firms to communicate rapidly and easily with customers, strategic partners, suppliers, distributors, and others around the globe. This lowers the costs of travel and speeds up response time.
- Teleconferencing allows enterprises to hold international strategic meetings without getting on an airplane.
- Networked databases provide organizations with on-line access to research and development information existing around the globe.
- Modems and laptop computers let employees work from virtually anywhere in the world, increasing efficiency and bringing the organization closer to the customer.
- Voice mail lets organizations record telephone messages when no one is available to receive them.
- Satellite systems, which a firm can lease from a provider, allow organizations to receive broadcast messages from chain manufacturers that help move the product.
- Laser color printers let enterprises quickly produce signs, banners, cards, price tags, and so on, that look as good as those printed by a professional.
- Some industries have CD-ROM services that businesses can tie into on a regular basis to receive updated information of things such as equipment and supplies. This also makes it easier for a firm to quickly locate customer items that it normally does not carry in stock.
- The World Wide Web as a commercial tool is enabling smaller businesses to be on the same playing field as larger businesses.
- On-line databases have put information at the hands of anyone who chooses to access them.

One must bear in mind that **technology is a tool used by strategists to improve business activities.** It is not intended to replace personal contact with the customer, nor is it intended to replace a manager's unique ability to take vast amounts of information and make sense of it in terms of strategy for the organization. It does make it easier for the manager to integrate all activities of the firm, to automate routine tasks, and generally free up more time to focus on the firm's strategy.

Forms of International Business and Marketing Strategies

Forms of International Business

We classify international business into three categories: (1) trade, (2) intellectual property rights (trademarks, patents, and copyrights) and international licensing agreements, and (3) foreign direct investment. To the marketer, these broad categories describe three important methods for entering a foreign market. To the lawyer, they also represent the form of doing business in a foreign country and the legal relationship between parties to a business transaction. Each method brings a different set of problems to the firm because the level of **foreign penetration** and entanglement in that country is different. Trade usually represents the least entanglement, and thus, the least political, economic, and legal risk, especially if the exporting firm is not soliciting business overseas or maintaining sales agents or inventories there. An investment in a plant and operations overseas usually represents the greatest market penetration and thus, the greatest risk to the firm.

Considerable overlap occurs among these different forms of doing business. A business plan for the production and marketing of a single product may contain elements of each form. To illustrate, a U.S. firm might purchase the rights to a trademark for use on an article of high-fashion clothing made from fabric exported from China and assembled in offshore plants in the Caribbean for shipment to the United States and Europe. Here, a business strategy encompasses elements of trade, licensing, and investment. For firms just entering a new foreign market, the method of entry might depend on a host of considerations, including the sophistication of the firm, its overseas experience, the nature of its product or services, its commitment of capital resources, and the amount of risk it is willing to bear.

Trade

Trade consists of the import and export of goods and services. *Exporting* is the term generally used to refer to the process of sending goods out of a country, and *importing* is used to denote when goods are brought into a country. However, a more accurate definition is that *exporting is the shipment of goods or the rendering of services to a foreign buyer located in a foreign country. Importing* is then defined as *the process of buying goods from a foreign supplier and entering them into the customs territory of a different country.* Every export entails an import, and vice versa.

Exporting

Trade is often a firm's first step into international business. Compared to the other forms of international business (licensing and investment), trade is relatively uncomplicated. It provides the inexperienced or smaller firm with an opportunity to penetrate a new market, or at least to explore foreign market potential, without significant capital investment and the risks of becoming a full-fledged player (that is, citizen) in the foreign country. For many larger firms, including multinational corporations, exporting may be an important portion of their business operations. The U.S. aircraft industry, for example, relies heavily on exports for significant revenues.

Firms that have not done business overseas before should first prepare an export plan, which may mean assembling an export team, composed possibly of management and outside advisors and trade specialists. Their plan should include the assessment of the firm's readiness for exporting, the export potential of its products or services, the firm's willingness to allocate resources (including financial, production output, and human resources), and the selection of its channels of distribution. The firm may need to modify products, design new packaging and foreign language labeling, and meet foreign standards for product performance or quality assurance. The firm must also gauge the extent to which it can perform export functions in-house or whether these functions should best be handled indirectly through an independent export company. Export functions include foreign marketing, sales and distribution, shipping, and handling international transfers of money.

Firms accept varying levels of responsibility for moving goods and money and for other export functions. The more experienced exporters can take greater responsibility for themselves and are more likely to export directly to their foreign customers. Firms that choose to accept less responsibility in dealing with foreign customers, or in making arrangements for shipping, for example, must delegate many export functions to someone else. As such, exporting is generally divided into two types: direct and indirect.

DIRECT EXPORTING At first glance, **direct exporting** seems similar to selling goods to a domestic buyer. A prospective foreign customer may have seen a firm's products at a trade show, located a particular company in an industrial directory, or been recommended by another customer. A firm that receives a request for product and pricing information from a foreign customer may be able to handle it routinely and export directly to the buyer. With some assistance, a firm can overcome most hurdles, get the goods properly packaged and shipped, and receive payment as anticipated. Although many of these one-time sales are turned into long-term business success stories, many more are not. A firm hopes to develop a regular business relationship with its new foreign customer. However, the problems that can be encountered even in direct exporting are considerable.

Many firms engaged in direct exporting on a regular basis reach the point at which they must hire their own full-time export managers and international sales specialists. These people participate in making export marketing decisions, including product development, pricing, packaging, and labeling for export. They should take primary responsibility for dealing with foreign buyers, for attending foreign trade shows, for complying with government export and import regulations, for shipping, and for handling the movement of goods and money in the transaction. Direct exporting is often done through **foreign sales agents** who work on commission. It also can be done by selling directly to **foreign distributors.** Foreign distributors are independent firms, usually located in the country to which a firm is exporting, that purchase goods for resale to their customers. They assume the risks of buying and warehousing goods in their market and provide additional product-support services. The distributor usually services the products they sell, thus relieving the exporter of that responsibility. They often train end users to use the product, extend credit to their customers, and bear responsibility for local advertising and promotion.

INDIRECT EXPORTING **Indirect exporting** is used by companies seeking to minimize their involvement abroad. Lacking experience, personnel, or capital, they may be unable to locate foreign buyers or are not yet ready to be handling the mechanics of a transaction on their own. There are several different types of indirect exporting. **Export trading companies,** commonly called ETCs, are companies that market the products of several manufacturers in foreign markets. They have extensive sales contacts overseas and experience in air and sea shipping. They often operate with the assistance and financial backing of large banks, thus making the resources and international contacts of the bank's foreign branches available to the manufacturers whose products they market. ETCs are licensed to operate under the U.S. antitrust laws.

Export management companies (EMC)s, on the other hand, are really consultants that advise manufacturers and other exporters. They are used by firms that cannot justify their own in-house export managers. They engage in foreign market research, identify overseas sales agents, exhibit goods at foreign trade shows, prepare documentation for export, and handle language translations and shipping arrangements. As in direct exporting, all forms of indirect exporting can involve sales through agents or to distributors.

Importing and Global Sourcing

Here, importing is presented from the perspective of the global firm for which importing is a regular and necessary part of their business. **Global sourcing** is the term commonly used to describe the process by which a firm attempts to locate and purchase goods or services on a worldwide basis. These goods may include, for example, raw materials for manufacturing, component parts for assembly operations, commodities such as agricultural products or minerals, or merchandise for resale.

Government Controls over Trade: Tariffs and Nontariff Barriers

Both importing and exporting are governed by the laws and regulations of the countries through which goods or services pass. Nations regulate trade in many ways. The most common methods are **tariffs** and **nontariff barriers.** Tariffs are import duties or taxes imposed on goods entering the customs territory of a nation. Tariffs are imposed for many reasons, including (1) the collection of revenue, (2) the protection of domestic industries from foreign competition, and (3) political control (for example, to provide incentives to import products from politically friendly countries and to discourage importing products from unfriendly countries).

NONTARIFF BARRIERS TO TRADE   Nontariff barriers are *all barriers to importing or exporting other than tariffs.* Nontariff barriers are generally a greater barrier to trade than are tariffs because they are more insidious. Unlike tariffs, which are published and easily understood, nontariff barriers are often disguised in the form of government rules or industry regulations and are often not understood by foreign companies. Countries impose nontariff barriers to protect their national economic, social, and political interests. Imports might be banned for health and safety reasons. Imported goods usually have to be marked with the country-of-origin and labeled in the local language so that consumers know what they are buying. One form of nontariff barrier is the **technical barrier to trade,** or **product standard.** Examples of product standards include safety standards, electrical standards, and environmental standards (for example, German cars meeting U.S. emission standards not mandated in Europe). A **quota** is a restriction imposed by law on the numbers or quantities of goods, or of a particular type of good, allowed to be imported. Unlike tariffs, quotas are not internationally accepted as a lawful means of regulating trade except in some special cases. An **embargo** is a total or near-total ban on trade with a particular country, sometimes enforced by military action and usually imposed for political purposes. An internationally orchestrated embargo was used against Iraq after its invasion of Kuwait in 1990. A **boycott** is a refusal to trade or do business with certain firms, usually from a particular country, on political or other grounds.

Tariffs and nontariff barriers have a tremendous influence on how firms make their trade and investment decisions. These decisions, in turn, are reflected in the patterns of world trade and the flows of investment capital.

TRADE LIBERALIZATION AND THE WORLD TRADE ORGANIZATION   **Trade liberalization** refers to the efforts of governments to reduce tariffs and nontariff barriers to trade. In the 20th century, the most important effort to liberalize trade came with the international acceptance of the **General Agreement on Tariffs and Trade (GATT).** This is an agreement between nations, first signed in 1947, and continually expanded since that time, that sets the rules for how nations will regulate international trade in goods and services. In 1995, the Geneva-based **World Trade Organization (WTO)** was created to administer the rules and to assist in settling trade disputes between its member nations. All WTO nations are entitled to **normal trade relations** with one another. This is referred to as **Most Favored Nation (MFN)** trading status. This means that a member country must charge the same tariff on imported goods, and not a higher one, as that charged on the same goods coming from other WTO member countries. Trade liberalization has led to increased economic development and an improved quality of life around the world.

EXPORT CONTROLS Another type of restriction over trade is export control. An **export control** limits the type of product that may be shipped to any particular country. They are usually imposed for economic or political purposes and are used by all nations of the world. For instance, high-tech computers might not be allowed to be shipped from the United States or Canada to another country without a license from the U.S. or Canadian government. Before signing a contract for the sale of certain products or technical know-how to a foreign customer, U.S. exporters must consider whether they will be able to obtain U.S. licensing for the shipment.

Intellectual Property Rights and International Licensing Agreements

Intellectual property rights are a grant from a government to an individual or firm of the exclusive legal right to use a copyright, patent, or trademark for a specified time. **Copyrights** are legal rights to artistic or written works, including books, software, films, music, or to such works as the layout design of a computer chip. **Trademarks** include the legal right to use a name or symbol that identifies a firm or its product. **Patents** are governmental grants to inventors assuring them of the exclusive legal right to produce and sell their inventions for a period of years. Copyrights, trademarks, and patents compose substantial assets of many domestic and international firms. As valuable assets, intellectual property can be sold or licensed for use to others through a licensing agreement.

International licensing agreements are contracts by which the holder of intellectual property will grant certain rights in that property to a foreign firm under specified conditions and for a specified time. Licensing agreements represent an important foreign market entry method for firms with marketable intellectual property. For example, a firm might license the right to manufacture and distribute a certain type of computer chip or the right to use a trademark on apparel such as bluejeans or designer clothing. It might license the right to distribute Hollywood movies or to reproduce and market word-processing software in a foreign market, or it might license its patent rights to produce and sell a high-tech product or pharmaceutical. United States firms have extensively licensed their property around the world, and in recent years have purchased the technology rights of Japanese and other foreign firms.

A firm may choose licensing as its market-entry method because licensing can provide a greater entrée to the foreign market than is possible through exporting. A firm may realize many advantages in having a foreign company produce and sell products based on its intellectual property instead of simply shipping finished goods to that market. When exporting to a foreign market, the firm must overcome obstacles such as long-distance shipping and the resulting delay in filling orders. Exporting requires a familiarity with the local culture. Redesign of products or technology for the foreign market may be necessary. Importantly, an exporter may have to overcome trade restrictions, such as quotas or tariffs, set by the foreign government. Licensing to a foreign firm allows the licensor to circumvent trade restrictions by having the products produced locally, and it allows entrance to the foreign market with minimal initial start-up costs. In return, the licensor might choose to receive a guaranteed return based on a percentage of gross revenues. This arrangement ensures payment to the licensor whether or not the licensee earns a profit. Even though licensing agreements give the licensor some control over how the licensee utilizes its intellectual property, problems can arise. For instance, the licensor may find that it cannot police the licensee's manufacturing or quality control process. Protecting itself from the unauthorized use or "piracy" of its copyrights, patents, or trademarks by unscrupulous persons not party to the licensing agreement is also a serious concern for the licensor.

Protecting Intellectual Property Rights

Rights in property can be rendered worthless if those rights cannot be protected by law. The protection of intellectual property is a matter of national law (as in the United States where it is protected primarily under federal statutes). However, intellectual property rights granted in one nation are not legally recognized and enforceable in another, unless the owner takes certain legal steps to protect those rights under the laws of that foreign country. Most developed countries, such as Canada, Western Europe, and Japan, have laws that protect the owners of intellectual property, and they enforce those laws. However, copyrights, patents, and trademarks are widely pirated in the developing countries of Asia, Latin America, Africa, Russia, Eastern Europe, and the Middle East, whose protection laws are either nonexistent or not enforced. Indeed, some developing countries encourage piracy because of the perceived financial gains to their economies. Some products deemed indispensable to the public, such as pharmaceuticals and chemicals, are often not covered by patent laws at all in these countries.

Lost profits and lost royalties to U.S. firms now amount to billions of dollars each year in counterfeited goods sold overseas. But international efforts are being made to rectify the problem. At the behest of U.S. movie and record producers, pharmaceutical manufacturers, software makers, and publishers, the United States has encouraged these countries to pass legislation protecting intellectual property and to ensure the enforcement of these laws. For instance, in 1991, the People's Republic of China acted to avert a trade war with the United States by agreeing to bring its intellectual property laws in line with those in other developing countries. The United States had been losing an estimated $700 million per year in China due to piracy. The United States threatened to impose punitive tariffs on Chinese goods (toys, games, footwear, clothing, and textiles). China announced stricter enforcement efforts and a new copyright law, and a major trade war was averted. Today, the protection of property rights abroad is a principal objective of U.S. trade policy.

Technology Transfer

The exchange of technology and manufacturing know-how between firms in different countries through arrangements such as licensing agreements is known as **technology transfer.** Transfers of technology and know-how are regulated by government control in some countries. This control is common when the licensor is from a highly industrialized country such as the United States and the licensee is located in a developing country such as those in Latin America, the Middle East, or Asia. In their efforts to industrialize, modernize, and develop a self-sufficiency in technology and production methods, these countries often restrict the terms of licensing agreements in a manner benefiting their own country. For instance, government regulation might require that the licensor introduce its most modern technology to the developing countries or train workers in its use.

International Franchising

Franchising is a form of licensing that is gaining in popularity worldwide. The most common form of franchising is known as a **business operations franchise,** usually used in retailing. Under a typical franchising agreement, the franchisee is allowed to use a trade name or trademark in offering goods or services to the public in return for a royalty based on a percentage of sales or other fee structure. The franchisee will usually obtain the franchiser's know-how in operating and managing a profitable business and its other "secrets of success" (ranging from a "secret recipe" to store design to accounting methods). Franchising in the United States accounts for a large proportion of total retail sales. In foreign markets as well, franchising has been successful in fast-food retailing, hotels, video rentals, convenience stores, photocopying services, and real estate services, to name but a few. U.S. firms have excelled in franchising overseas, making up the majority of new franchise operations worldwide. The prospects for future growth in foreign markets are enormous, especially in developing countries such as in Latin America. For instance, American fast-food and retail franchises are common throughout Mexico City, Brazil, Eastern Europe, and the former Soviet Union.

Some Legal Aspects of Franchising

Franchising is a good vehicle for entering a foreign market because the local franchisee provides capital investment, entrepreneurial commitment, and on-site management to deal with local customs and labor problems. However, many legal requirements affect franchising. Franchising in the United States is regulated primarily by the Federal Trade Commission at the federal level. The agency requires the filing of extensive disclosure statements to protect prospective investors. Other countries have also enacted new franchise disclosure laws. Some developing countries have restrictions on the amount of money that can be removed from the country by the franchiser. Moreover, some countries, such as China, also require government approval for franchise operations. Other countries might have restrictions on importing supplies (ketchup, bed linens, paper products, or whatever) for the operation of the business to protect local companies. However, more progressive developing countries are now abandoning these strict regulations because they want to welcome franchisers, their high-quality consumer products, and their managerial talent to their markets. Because of this more receptive attitude toward foreign firms, Mexico and Brazil have become home to many profitable new franchise operations.

Foreign Direct Investment

The term **foreign investment,** or **foreign direct investment,** refers to the ownership and active control of ongoing business concerns, including investment in manufacturing, mining, farming, assembly operations, and other facilities of production. A distinction is made between the home and host countries of the firms involved. The **home country** refers to that country under whose laws the investing corporation was created or is headquartered. For example, the United States is home to multinational corporations such as **Ford, Exxon,** and **IBM,** to name a few, but they operate in **host countries** throughout every region of the world. Of the three forms of international business, foreign investment provides the firm with the most involvement, and perhaps the greatest risk, abroad. Investment in a foreign plant is often a result of having had successful experiences in exporting or licensing, and of the search for ways to overcome the disadvantages of those other entry methods. For example, by producing its product in a foreign country, instead of exporting, a firm can avoid quotas and tariffs on imported goods, avoid currency fluctuations on the traded goods, provide better product service and spare parts, and more quickly adapt products to local tastes and market trends. Manufacturing overseas for foreign markets can mean taking advantage of local natural resources, labor, and manufacturing economies of scale. Foreign investment in the United States is often called reverse investment. Most of the foreign investment in the United States has come from the United Kingdom.

Multinational Corporations

Multinational corporations (MNCs) are firms with significant foreign direct investment assets. They are characterized by their ability to derive and transfer capital resources worldwide and to operate facilities of production and penetrate markets in more than one country, usually on a global scale. Over the past 20 years, many writers have argued over the best name to use in referring to these companies. **Multinational enterprise** (MNE) has been a popular term because it reflects the fact that many global firms are not, technically speaking, "corporations." The terms **transnational corporation** and **supranational corporation** are often used within the United Nations system, in which many internationalists argue that the operations and interests of the modern corporation "transcend" national boundaries.

One significant trend in business during the last half of the 20th century has been the globalization of multinational corporations. At one time, multinational corporations were simply large domestic companies with foreign operations. Today, they are global companies. They typically make decisions and enter strategic alliances with each other without regard to national boundaries. They move factories, technology, and capital to those countries with the most hospitable laws, the lowest tax rates, the most qualified workforce, or abundant natural resources. They see market share and company performance in global terms. Foreign sales and operations are extremely profitable for many multinationals. As an example, **Gillette, Colgate, IBM, Coca-Cola,** and many of the 500 largest U.S. corporations collected over 50 percent of their revenues from products sold outside the United States. Switzerland's **Nestlé Corporation** garnered over 95 percent of its revenues from outside Switzerland.

Subsidiaries, Joint Ventures, Mergers, and Acquisitions

Multinational corporations wishing to enter a foreign market through direct investment can structure their business arrangements in many different ways. Their options and eventual course of action may depend on many factors, including industry and market conditions, capitalization of the firm and financing, and legal considerations. Some of these options include the start-up of a new foreign subsidiary company, the formation of a joint venture with an existing foreign company, or the acquisition of an existing foreign company by stock purchase. For now, keep in mind that multinational corporations are usually not a single legal entity. They are global enterprises that consist of any number of interrelated corporate entities, connected through extremely complex chains of stock ownership. Stock ownership gives the investing corporation tremendous flexibility when investing abroad.

The **wholly owned foreign subsidiary** is a "foreign" corporation organized under the laws of a foreign host country, but owned and controlled by the parent corporation in the home country. Because the parent company controls all of the stock in the subsidiary, it can control management and financial decision making.

The **joint venture** is a cooperative business arrangement between two or more companies for profit. A joint venture may take the form of a partnership or corporation. Typically, one party will contribute expertise and another the capital, each bringing its own special resources to the venture. Joint ventures exist in all regions of the world and in all types of industries. Where the laws of a host country require local ownership or that investing foreign firms have a local partner, the joint venture is an appropriate investment vehicle. **Local participation** refers to the requirement that a share of the business be owned by nationals of the host country. These requirements are gradually being reduced in most countries that, in an effort to attract more investment, are permitting wholly owned subsidiaries. Many American companies do not favor the joint venture as an investment vehicle because they do not want to share technology, expertise, and profits with another company.

Another method of investing abroad is for two companies to **merge** or for one company to acquire another ongoing firm. This option has appeal because it requires less know-how than does a new start-up and can be concluded without disruption of business activity.

International Marketing Strategies

To remain competitive and to increase their opportunities, domestic enterprises will need to develop strategies for entering the international business arena. Effective internationalization of business operations marketing relies on managers' ability to develop international product/service, place/entry, price, and promotion strategies. We discuss each of these in turn.

International Product/Service Strategy

In developing **product/service strategy,** managers are typically concerned with what the product or service should look like and what it should be able to do. In conducting this assessment for foreign markets, managers must overcome the *self-reference criterion* (SRC). They must determine whether their product or service can be sold in standard form or whether it must be customized to fit differing foreign market needs. They must understand that many products or services do not immediately sell well in foreign markets but that they must undergo a diffusion process.

The Self-Reference Criterion (SRC)

The **self-reference criterion (SRC)** is the unconscious reference to one's own cultural values. This unconscious reference is the root of many international business problems.[14] Huge problems can occur when the SRC leads a manager to assume that a product or service that sells well in the home market will sell well in foreign markets. In many cases it does not because the needs for products and services differ among societies. Managers can eliminate the SRC by first defining the problem in terms of the home society's cultural traits, values, habits, and norms, and then redefining the problem, without value judgments, in terms of the foreign market's cultural traits, values, habits, and norms. The difference represents the cultural influence on the problem. The manager subsequently restates and solves the problem in the context of both cultures.

It should be noted that the assessment may sometimes reveal that the firm's product or service, because of cultural or other factors, cannot be customized for a foreign market. Therefore, international strategists should seek answers to four basic questions.[15]

1. *Who in the foreign market uses the product?* In what way(s) are the targeted foreign buyers similar to or different from domestic buyers? How can this product be incorporated into the foreign market's lifestyle?
2. *What are the values of the people in the foreign market?* Is their value based on timeliness, quality, service, or price? What changes in the products/services need to be made to meet the foreign customers' needs?
3. *What are the signals that indicate change in the market?* Does the market accept foreign ideas? Are there cross-cultural trends?
4. *How can the firm increase market share?* Who are the local competitors? Who are the foreign competitors? How much disposable income do consumers have?

Next, we present separate strategies for products and services.

Product Strategy

CUSTOMIZATION VERSUS STANDARDIZATION Fundamentally, there are three viable alternatives when entering a foreign market: (1) market the same product everywhere (**standardization**), (2) adapt the product for foreign markets (**customization**), and (3) develop a totally new product. By combining these three alternatives with promotional efforts, five different product strategies can be developed.[16]

1. **Standardize product/standardize message.** Using this strategy, a firm sells the same product and uses the same promotional appeals in all markets. In other words, product and promotional appeals are globally standardized. **Coca-Cola, Pepsi-Cola, Avon, McDonald's, Sony Walkman, Levi's,** and **Maidenform** follow this strategy.
2. **Standardize product/customize message.** Enterprises using this approach customize only the promotional message. For example, a bicycle may be sold in the U.S. market as a pleasure vehicle. In an economically poor country, however, the promotional message may have to be customized to stress economy; that is, the bicycle would be promoted as a means of relatively inexpensive basic transportation.
3. **Customize product/standardize message.** Using this strategy, the company customizes the product to meet the needs of the specific foreign market, but promotes the same use as it does in the domestic market. For example, electric sewing machines manufactured for the U.S. market would not sell well in a market where few

residents have access to electricity. The manufacturer could, however, customize the machine to sell in that market by producing hand- or foot-cranked sewing machines. The hand- or foot-cranked machine would be promoted in the foreign market in the same way it is in the U.S. market—to sew clothes.

4. **Customize product/customize message.** Manufacturers applying this strategy customize the product to meet different use patterns in the foreign market and customize the promotional message attached to it as well. For example, bicycles in the United States are usually lightweight and are generally promoted for use in leisure activities. In many less-developed countries, however, because of rough roads, the need may be for a stronger bicycle, and the bicycle is often used as a major form of transportation. China is one example of a country where bicycles are heavyweight and are used as a major means of transportation.

5. **Different product.** Using this approach, rather than adapting an existing product, the manufacturer invests in the development of a totally new one to fit the needs of specific foreign markets. For example, Coca-Cola's and Pepsi's diet sodas do not sell well in Asia and Europe because consumers there prefer the creamy sweetness of regular Coke or Pepsi and consider sugar-free sodas as drinks of diabetics and the obese, not of the young and vital. To deal with this problem, Pepsi designed a new diet cola, called Pepsi Max, specifically for these and other markets. Pepsi Max uses a sweetener that makes it close to the regular colas in taste.[17]

American marketing professor Theodore Levitt contends that in an era of global competition, the product strategy of successful firms is evolving from offering customized products (a multidomestic strategy) to offering globally standardized ones (a global strategy). Such a product strategy requires the development of universal products or products that require no more than a cosmetic change for adaptation to different local needs and use conditions.[18] Japanese automobile manufacturer **Honda** has a strategy to build a global car. The strategy entails using a new standardized manufacturing system with flexibility to build cars customized to fit specific market needs. Using this new manufacturing system, the costs of customization are far lower than when using the older systems.

Service Strategy

As indicated, a dilemma in global strategy for manufacturing businesses is the need to balance standardization with local customization. In contrast, in service delivery, in many cases, standardization and customization is equally feasible. There are three broad service categories: people-processing, possession-processing, and information-based services.[19]

PEOPLE-PROCESSING SERVICES In these services, customers become part of the production process. Such services include passenger transportation, health care, food services, and lodging services. The customer is present during the service. For example, **Disney** provides entertainment services in theme parks in Paris, France, and in Tokyo, Japan. (Of course, Disney also provides these services for foreign customers in California and Florida.) London hospitals maintain a lucrative business caring for wealthy Middle Eastern patients, as do Miami, Florida, hospitals caring for patients from Latin America.

POSSESSION-PROCESSING SERVICES Services of this nature involve tangible actions to tangible objects to enhance their value to customers. The customer need not be present. These services include transporting freight, installing equipment, and maintenance. For example, an American living near the Canadian border could go into Canada to have his or her car serviced because of lower costs resulting from favorable exchanges rates. For instance, if it costs $300 in both countries to have a car tuned-up, and the exchange rate is U.S. $1 equals Canadian $1.50, the American who goes into Canada for the service would save U.S. $100, less the expense of driving across the border. An international corporation might provide such services as bridge repair services or elevator repair services throughout the world.

INFORMATION-BASED SERVICES The provision of these services involves collecting, manipulating, interpreting, and transmitting data to create value. Examples include such services as accounting, banking, consulting, education, insurance, legal services, and news. For instance, **CNN** provides news service in most countries. **Prudential** provides insurance services in many countries. **Citicorp** provides banking services in many parts of the world. Many American colleges and universities service a multitude of students from foreign countries around the globe in the United States, and a number of them (American University in Cairo, Egypt, for example) have established satellites in foreign countries to service students abroad. Many American students are now pursuing college degrees in Canadian universities because the cost of tuition there is much lower than at home.[20]

INFORMATION TECHNOLOGY AND SERVICE STRATEGY For all three types of services described above, use of current information technology, such as the Internet, may enable businesses to benefit from favorable labor costs or exchange rates by consolidating operations of supplementary services (such as reservations) or certain office functions (such as accounting) in just one or a few countries.

International Place/Entry Strategy

Managers of business enterprises must determine how their products or services will reach the consumer—the **place/entry strategy.** Distribution methods generally require variations from country to country as well as within each country. Generally, the methods are shaped by the size of the market, by the scope and quality of the competition, by the available distribution channels, and by the firm's resources. Distribution methods are also shaped by the laws of the country (the laws of some countries require foreign companies to use local distribution systems) and by the firm's entry strategy.

Basically, manufacturing enterprises can enter a foreign country by:

1. Manufacturing the product at home and exporting it to the foreign country for distribution in the local market.
2. Manufacturing parts at home and exporting them to the foreign country for assembly, for distribution in the local market, and/or for export to other markets (including back to the home market).
3. Manufacturing the product in the foreign country for distribution in the local market and/or for export to other markets (including back to the home market).

With respect to service enterprises,

1. Some, such as consulting companies, can provide the services from their home country or they can set up subsidiaries in the foreign country.
2. Others, such as insurance and banking companies, generally must establish subsidiaries in the foreign country.

The above suggests that firms enter a foreign market either by **exporting to it or setting up manufacturing facilities in it.**

International Pricing Strategy

Operating in foreign markets brings new price-strategy challenges as there are new market variables to consider. For example, the attitudes of foreign governments are an important and serious problem that differs from one country to another. Sometimes foreign governments act as price arbiters. Therefore, effective price setting consists of much more than mechanically adding a standard markup to cost. International pricing strategy is much more complex than domestic pricing strategy.

International pricing strategy is made complex by monetary exchange factors as well as by firms often being required to countertrade, that is, to trade by barter or a similar system. Pricing policy is also affected by the commercial practices of the country in which the firm is doing business, by the type of product being merchandised, and by existing competitive conditions. In establishing pricing policy, some firms are influenced by the view that pricing is an **active tool** by which to accomplish their marketing objectives, and some are influenced by the belief that price is a **static element** in business decisions. Furthermore, some firms emphasize control over final prices and some over the net price received by the enterprise.

Pricing as an Active Tool

Utilizing the view that pricing is an active tool, the firm uses pricing to accomplish its objective relative to a target return from its overseas operations or to accomplish a target volume of market share.

Pricing as a Static Element

If a firm follows the view that **pricing is a static element,** it will most likely be content to sell what it can overseas and consider it to be a bonus value. Pricing as an active tool is more closely allied with firms that make direct investment in the foreign country, whereas pricing as a static element is more closely allied with firms that export.

Control over Final Prices

To achieve a desired level of foreign-market penetration, a firm must have the ability to control the end price. Enterprises with the desire to attain a high level of market penetration therefore attempt to obtain all possible **control over the final price.** These firms are more likely to view pricing as an active tool than as a static element.

Net Price Received

Firms using this approach do not attempt to control the price at which the product is finally sold. The enterprise's main concern is with the **net price it receives.** This type of firm most likely shares the view of pricing as a static element more than as an active tool.

Foreign National Pricing and International Pricing

Pricing for foreign markets is further complicated by managers' having to be concerned with two types of pricing: foreign national pricing and international pricing. Basically, the former is pricing for selling in another country and the latter is pricing in another country for export.

Foreign National Pricing

A firm's **foreign national pricing** is influenced by its international pricing strategy as well as by foreign governments. A government can influence its nation's prices by taking various actions. It can institute **national price controls.** These controls may encompass all products sold within the nation's borders or impose them on only specific products. Some governments influence prices on foreign imports by levying higher import duties or subsidizing local industries. Governments can also affect prices by applying legislation relative to labor costs.

The product life cycle in a specific market also influences the price. If it is a new product and there is a demand for it, a higher price can often be charged. On the other hand, to achieve market penetration where the product is in a late life-cycle stage, a firm may have to charge a lower price.

International Pricing

International pricing basically relates to the managerial decision of what to charge for goods produced in one nation and sold in another. A common practice of global corporations to establish a strong position in global markets is intracorporate sales. In applying this practice, a global corporation attempts to rationalize production by requiring subsidiaries to specialize in the manufacture of some items while importing others. The subsidiaries' imports may consist of components assembled into the end product, or they may be finished products imported to complement their product mix. This import-export practice among subsidiaries located in different countries enables the global corporation to control and transfer prices and to control the profits and losses of its subsidiaries. These corporations will realize no profits in a country where, for reasons discussed next, it is not beneficial to do so, and will realize them in a country where it is beneficial.

REASON 1. AVOIDING A COUNTRY'S HIGH TAX RATE   Both foreign and domestic governments are interested in profits and the role of transfer prices in their attainment. This is because of the consequences profits have on the amount of taxes paid. Because of the differences in tax structures among nations, global corporations can often obtain significant profits by instructing a subsidiary in a country that has a **high corporate tax rate** to sell the product at cost to another subsidiary in a country where taxes are lower. The profit is thereby earned in the country where taxes are lower.

REASON 2. AVOIDING A COUNTRY'S CURRENCY RESTRICTIONS   Transfer pricing may also be used to get around **currency restrictions.** For example, a nation suffering from a lack of foreign exchange may impose controls that limit the amount of profit that can be repatriated, that is, profits that can be transferred back to the corporation's home base. For instance, suppose nation X imposes controls on the amount of profits that can be repatriated and that there is trade with country Y, which does not have such controls. The corporation at home could instruct the subsidiary in country X to sell its product to a subsidiary in country Y at cost. This would transfer X's profit to Y, from where the global corporation can repatriate profits.

REASON 3. AVOIDING CURRENCY DEVALUATIONS, HAVING TO REDUCE PRICES, AND HAVING TO INCREASE WAGES The international pricing approach could also be employed by global corporations when a foreign nation's **currency is devalued,** when there is government pressure in the foreign country to **reduce prices** because of excessive profits, and when labor in the foreign country demands **higher wages** because of high profits earned.

REASON 4. ARMS-LENGTH PRICING Because of these manipulative practices, many governments insist on **arms-length pricing;** that is, the price charged to company affiliates must be the same as that paid by unrelated customers. For example, under section 482 of the U.S. Internal Revenue Code, U.S. tax authorities have the authority to reconstruct an intracorporate transfer price. When they suspect that low prices were set to avoid taxes, the tax authorities may recalculate the tax. It should be noted that many U.S. executives prefer the arms-length approach because it enables them to properly monitor and evaluate foreign managements.[21] They also tend to prefer it because the transfers can demoralize the management of the foreign subsidiaries that do not show positive results—they were transferred to another subsidiary.

Fluctuating Exchange Rates and Costs

Fluctuating exchange rates force periodic adjustments in price. The same principle applies to fluctuating costs, including costs of raw materials and supplies, inflation, and interest rates. When a firm enters into a long-term contract at a fixed rate, shifts can prove disastrous if the firm cannot adjust its prices in some way. The lesson is that in international pricing, a firm must develop strong international money management skills.

Countertrade

Pricing strategies are further complicated by the fact that not all foreign transactions can be in cash. For example, sales to communist countries and to third world countries with "soft currency," currency that is not readily accepted in international transactions, often take place in the form of countertrade, which fundamentally means the buyer of a product pays the seller with another product that has the equivalent monetary value. The pricing problem derives from the difficulty of assessing the value of the product received in exchange. A miscalculation could lead to financial disaster. There are four basic types of countertrade transactions: barter, compensation, switch, and counterpurchase.[22]

BARTER **Barter** is an arrangement in which the exporter sells goods to a foreign importer without the exchange of cash. That is, specified goods are sold to the importer for other specified goods.

COMPENSATION Using the **compensation** procedure, the exporter sells technology and equipment to an importer in the foreign market. The importer pays the exporter with goods produced with the imported technology or equipment.

SWITCH In the **switch** procedure, the exporter transfers the commitment to a third party who may be an end user of the product received by the exporter or to a trading house employed to dispose of the product. An advantage here is that the third party can be highly effective in selling the product. A disadvantage is that the third party often seeks to obtain the product at a bargain price, therefore lessening profit and complicating negotiations.

COUNTERPURCHASE Under a **counterpurchase** agreement, two parties agree to sell each other products or services with some balancing of values. The exporter sells goods, technology, or services to the foreign importer for cash, but agrees to purchase goods with the cash equivalent from the importer within a specified period—the goods are selected from a list that usually excludes those items produced by the technology being imported. An advantage of this approach is that the exporter has use of the cash for the specified period.

Exporters entering into countertrade agreements must often use a trading firm to market the goods they purchase. However, the goods purchased can often be distributed or used by a subsidiary of the exporter. For example, **PepsiCo** has been selling to Russia the concentrate for a drink to be bottled and sold in Russia. In return, PepsiCo has been paid with vodka, which it has distributed through a subsidiary. Often, exporters receive raw materials or parts that can be used in their production process.

In general, the major problem in countertrade is determining the value and the potential demand of the goods offered by the other firm, and it is time consuming. Firms, however, are motivated to participate in countertrade for various reasons, including to make sales in nonmarket nations and in many less-developed countries and to adjust their accounting records to enable them to pay lower taxes and tariffs. This occurs when both parties underestimate the value of the goods.

International Promotion Strategy

In general, problems related to international promotion strategy include the legal aspects of the country, tax considerations, language complexities, cultural diversity, media limitations, credibility of advertising, and degree of illiteracy. Some governments regulate advertising more closely than others. Laws in some nations restrict the amount of money that may be spent on advertising, the media utilized, the type of product advertised, the methods used in advertising, and the way in which the price is advertised. Some nations have special taxes on advertisements. Language translation presents many barriers. For example, translation of semantic and idiomatic meanings across cultures are difficult to make, which presents huge impediments to communication.

Why International Promotional Strategies Fail

There are numerous reasons international promotional strategies fail. The reasons include insufficient research, overstandardization, poor follow-up, narrow vision, and rigid implementation.[23]

INSUFFICIENT RESEARCH **Insufficient research** prior to making international strategic decisions generally leads to failure. For example, **Lego A/S,** the Danish toy company, had improved its penetration in the American market by offering "bonus" packs and gift promotion. Encouraged by its success in the United States, Lego decided to apply the same approaches, unaltered, to other markets, including Japan, where penetration had been lagging. The Japanese customers were not attracted to those tactics. A later investigation revealed that Japanese consumers viewed the promotions as wasteful, expensive, and not too appealing. The results were similar in other countries as well.

OVERSTANDARDIZATION Some commodities, such as Coca-Cola, have a global appeal. In this situation, the message to be communicated can be much the same throughout the world. Many products, however, do not have universal appeal.[24] The message to be communicated must therefore be tied to individual motivation; the promotional campaign, instead of being **overstandardized,** must reflect local tastes. The foreign environment thus has a significant effect on promotional strategy. Failure to adapt promotional strategy to the foreign environment inevitably creates difficulties. Managers therefore need to determine whether or not a promotional message is appropriate for the foreign culture, and if not, what adoptions must be made.

POOR FOLLOW-UP Failure to monitor the promotional campaign for problems and solve them as they arise will contribute to failure. For instance, a U.S.-based computer company implemented a software house cooperation program in Europe to help penetrate the small- and medium-sized accounts market segment, where it was weak. The program needed a large change in sales force operation. The sales force, no longer in control of the hardware and software package, had to determine its content together with a software house that had access to the smaller accounts. The success of the new program depended on how effectively the sales force carried out its new assignments as well as on central coordination and attention, which it never got. Lacking central coordination and **follow-up,** there was no communication channel for sharing and building on the experiences of subsidiaries.

NARROW VISION An enterprise may centralize promotional strategic decision making or it may decentralize it to its local managers. Both approaches have pros and cons. The centralized approach can be effective by providing an overall global perspective, but it can be ineffective because decision making is not close to the market. The decentralized approach may be effective since decision making is close to the market; however, it may be ineffective because it does not provide a global perspective.

RIGID IMPLEMENTATION High-level managers sometimes ignore local managers' reservations about **rigidly implementing** a standardized promotional program and force compliance, which usually leads to failure. This is so because local managers' reservations are often based on a solid understanding of local conditions. Top management may also become inflexible to changing market conditions.

Developing an Effective International Promotional Strategy

To develop an effective international promotional strategy, strategists must determine (a) the promotional mix—the blend of advertising, personal selling, and sales promotions—needed for each market; (b) the extent of worldwide promotional standardization; (c) the most effective message; (d) the most effective medium; and (e) the necessary controls to aid in assessing whether or not the potential objectives are being met.[25]

Factors to Consider When Doing Business Abroad

This section presents some questions that the strategist should answer, or factors that should be considered, to be successful doing business abroad.

- Does your firm have a mission statement? That is, do you know why the company exists and what it plans to do? If you don't, you won't have a sense of direction.
- Why do you want to go international? Is it for opportunity or threat reasons, or both? Or is it because it is currently fashionable to internationalize? If it is the latter, you might not apply the intensity needed to be successful abroad.
- Are you ready to go abroad? Will going abroad really solve your problems? How long has the company been in business? Is it stable enough (financially and psychologically) to endure the initial hardship of internationalization? Does it have a national reputation? Being successful at home will help mitigate the internationalization hardship.
- Have you done your homework? That is, have you ascertained where there may be a demand for your product/service? Are you totally familiar with domestic and international environments? Have you thoroughly familiarized yourself with the potential market's cultural, economic, legal, political, competitive, trade and monetary barriers, and labor relations factors? That is, are you thoroughly familiar with the challenge you will be facing in internationalizing?
- Are you thoroughly familiar with your strengths and weaknesses? That is, do you have a thorough understanding of your international management capabilities? Do you have a clear understanding of the nature of your product/service? Do you know how to capitalize on your product's/service's strengths, how to minimize its weaknesses, how to correct its shortcomings, and how to customize it to fit the needs of the foreign market? How strong or weak is your firm with respect to e-commerce?
- Have you developed viable product/service, place/entry, pricing, and promotion strategies that are based on the answers to the questions posed above?

In essence, the above means that, to be successful in internationalizing a business, the strategist must do his or her homework. Those who do their homework will have a far greater chance of succeeding abroad than those who do not.

International Risks

Two types of risks related to international business are discussed in this section: political risk and economic risk.

Political Risk

Politics and laws of a host country affect international business operations in a variety of ways. The good manager will understand these dimensions of the countries in which the firm operates so that he or she can work within existing parameters and can anticipate and plan for changes that may occur.

Firms usually prefer to conduct business in a country with a stable and friendly government, but such governments are not always easy to find. Managers must therefore continually monitor the government, its policies, and its stability to determine the potential for political change that could adversely affect corporate operations.

There is **political risk** in every nation, but the range of risks varies widely from country to country. In general, political risk is lowest in countries that have a history of stability and consistency. Political risk tends to be highest in nations that do not have this sort of history. In a number of countries, however, consistency and stability that were apparent on the surface have been quickly swept away by major popular movements that drew on the bottled-up frustrations of the population. Three major types of political risk can be encountered: **ownership risk,** which exposes property and life; **operating risk,** which refers to interference with the ongoing operations of a firm; and **transfer risk,** which is mainly encountered when attempts are made to shift funds between countries. Firms can be exposed to political risk due to government actions or even actions outside the control of governments.

Transfer Risks versus Operating Risks versus Ownership Risks

- *Political risks can be broken down into transfer risks, operating risks, and ownership risks. Transfer risks stem from government policies that limit the transfer of capital, payments, production, people, and technology in or out of a country. Examples of transfer risks include tariffs on exports and imports, restrictions on exports, dividend remittance, and capital repatriation.*

- *Operating risks stem from government policies and procedures that directly constrain the international management and performance of local business activities. Examples of operating risks include price controls, financing restrictions, export commitments, taxes, and local-sourcing requirements.*

- *Ownership risks are brought about by govenment policies or actions that inhibit ownership or control of local operations. Pressure for local participation, confiscation, expropriation, and abrogation of property rights are examples of ownership risks.*

A major political risk in many countries is that of conflict and violent change. A manager will want to think twice before conducting business in a country in which the likelihood of such change is high. To begin with, if conflict breaks out, violence directed toward the firm's property and employees is a strong possibility. Guerrilla warfare, civil disturbances, and terrorism often take an anti-industry bent, making companies and their employees potential targets. International corporations are often subject to major threats, even in countries that boast great political stability. Sometimes the sole fact that a firm is market oriented is sufficient to attract the wrath of terrorists.

Less drastic, but still worrisome, are changes in government policies that are not caused by changes in the government itself. These occur when, for one reason or another, a government feels pressured to change its policies toward foreign businesses. The pressure may be the result of nationalist or religious factions or widespread anti-Western feeling.

A broad range of policy changes is possible as a result of political unrest. All of the changes can affect the company's international operations, but not all of them are equal in weight. Except for extreme cases, companies do not usually have to fear violence against their employees, although violence against company property is quite common. Also common are changes in policy that result from a new government or a strong new stance that is nationalist and opposed to foreign investment. The most drastic public steps resulting from such policy changes are usually expropriation and confiscation.

Expropriation is the transfer of ownership by the host government to a domestic entity with payment of compensation. Expropriation was an appealing action to many countries because it demonstrated their nationalism and transferred a certain amount of wealth and resources from foreign companies to the host country immediately. It did have costs to the host country, however, to the extent that it made other firms more hesitant to invest there. Expropriation does not relieve the host government of providing compensation to the former owners. However, these compensation negotiations are often protracted and frequently result in settlements that are unsatisfactory to the owners. For example, governments may offer compensation in the form of local, nontransferable currency or may base compensation on the book value of the firm. Even though firms that are expropriated may deplore the low levels of payment obtained, they frequently accept them in the absence of better alternatives.

The use of expropriation as a policy tool has sharply decreased over time. In the mid-1970s, more than 83 expropriations took place in a single year. By the turn of the century, the annual average had declined to fewer than 3. Apparently, governments have come to recognize that the damage they inflict on themselves through expropriation exceeds the benefits they receive.

Confiscation is similar to expropriation in that it results in a transfer of ownership from the firm to the host country. It differs in that it does not involve compensation for the firm. Some industries are more vulnerable than others to confiscation and expropriation because of their importance to the host country's economy and their lack of ability to shift operations. For this reason, such sectors as mining, energy, public utilities, and banking have frequently been targets of such government actions.

Confiscation and expropriation constitute major political risk for foreign investors. Other government actions, however, are equally detrimental to foreign firms. Many countries are turning from confiscation and expropriation to more subtle forms of control, such as **domestication.** The goal of domestication is the same—that is, to gain control over foreign investment—but the method is different. Through domestication, the government demands transfer of ownership and management responsibility. It can impose **local content** regulations to ensure that a large share of the product is locally produced or demand that a larger share of the profit is retained in the country. Changes in labor laws, patent protection, and tax regulations are also used for purposes of domestication.

Domestication can have profound effects on an international business operation for a number of reasons. If a firm is forced to hire nationals as managers, poor cooperation and communication can result. If domestication is imposed within a very short time span, corporate operations overseas may have to be headed by poorly trained and inexperienced local managers. Domestic content requirements may force a firm to purchase its supplies and parts locally. This can result in increased costs, less efficiency, and lower-quality products. Export requirements imposed on companies may create havoc for their international distribution plans and force them to change or even shut down operations in other countries.

Finally, domestication usually will shield an industry within one country from foreign competition. As a result, inefficiencies will be allowed to thrive due to a lack of market discipline. This will affect the long-run international competitiveness of an operation abroad and may turn into a major problem when, years later, domestication is discontinued by the government.

If government action consists of weakening or not enforcing **intellectual property rights** protection, companies run the risk of losing their core competitive edge. Such steps may temporarily permit domestic firms to become quick imitators. Yet, in the longer term, they will not only discourage the ongoing transfer of technology and knowledge by multinational firms, but also reduce the incentive for local firms to invest in innovation and progress.

One might ask why companies would choose to do business in risky markets. However, as with anything international (or any business for that matter), the issue is not whether there is any risk but rather the degree of risk that exists. Key links to risk are the dimensions of reward. With appropriate rewards, many risks become more tolerable.

Economic Risk

Most businesses operating abroad face a number of other risks that are less dangerous, but probably more common, than the drastic ones already described. A host government's political situation or desires may lead it to impose economic regulations or laws to restrict or control the international activities of firms.

Nations that face a shortage of foreign currency will sometimes impose controls on the movement of capital into and out of the country. Such controls may make it difficult for a firm to remove its profits or investments from the host country. Sometimes **exchange controls** are also levied selectively against certain products or companies in an effort to reduce the importation of goods that are considered to be luxuries or to be sufficiently available through domestic production. Such regulations often affect the importation of parts, components, or supplies that are vital to production operations in the country. They may force a firm either to alter its production program or, worse yet, to shut down its entire plant. Prolonged negotiations with government officials may be necessary to reach a compromise on what constitutes a "valid" expenditure of foreign currency resources. Because the goals of government officials and corporate managers are often quite different, such compromises, even when they can be reached, may result in substantial damage to the international operations of the firm.

Countries may also use **tax policy** toward foreign investors in an effort to control multinational corporations and their capital. Tax increases may raise much-needed revenue for the host country, but they can severely damage the operations of foreign investors. This damage, in turn, will frequently result in decreased income for the host country in the long run. The raising of tax rates needs to be carefully differentiated from increased tax scrutiny of foreign investors. Many governments believe that multinational firms may be tempted to shift tax burdens to lower-tax countries by using artificial pricing schemes between subsidiaries. In such instances, governments are likely to take measures to obtain their fair contribution from multinational operations. In the United States, for example, increased focus on the taxation of multinational firms has resulted in various back-tax payments by foreign firms and the development of corporate pricing policies in collaboration with the Internal Revenue Service.[26]

The international executive also has to worry about **price controls.** In many countries, domestic political pressures can force governments to control the prices of imported products or services, particularly in sectors considered highly sensitive from a political perspective, such as food or health care. A foreign firm involved in these areas is vulnerable to price controls because the government can play on citizens' nationalistic tendencies to enforce the controls. Particularly in countries that suffer from high inflation, frequent devaluations, or sharply rising costs, the international executive may be forced to choose between shutting down the operation or continuing production at a loss in the hope of recouping profits when the government loosens or removes its price restrictions. Price controls can also be administered to prevent prices from being too low. Governments have enacted antidumping laws, which prevent foreign competitors from pricing their imports unfairly low in order to drive domestic competitors out of the market. Since dumping charges depend heavily on the definition of "fair" price, a firm can sometimes become the target of such accusations quite unexpectedly. Proving that no dumping took place can become quite onerous in terms of time, money, and information disclosure.

Managing the International Risk

Managers face the risk of confiscation, expropriation, domestication, or other government interference whenever they conduct business overseas, but ways exist to lessen the risk. Obviously, if a new government comes into power and is dedicated to the removal of all foreign influences, there is little a firm can do. In less extreme cases, however, managers can take actions that will reduce the risk, provided they understand the root causes of the host country's policies.

Adverse governmental actions are usually the result of nationalism, the deterioration of political relations between home and host country, the desire for independence, or opposition to colonial remnants. If a host country's citizens feel exploited by foreign investors, government officials are more likely to take antiforeign action. To reduce the risk of government intervention, the international firm needs to demonstrate that it is concerned with the host country's society and that it considers itself an integral part of the host country, rather than simply an exploitative foreign corporation. Ways of doing this include intensive local hiring and training practices, better pay, contributions to charity, and societally useful investments. In addition, the company can form joint ventures with local partners to demonstrate that it is willing to share its gains with nationals. Although such actions will not guarantee freedom from political risk, they will certainly lessen the exposure.

Another action that can be taken by corporations to protect against political risk is the close monitoring of political developments. Increasingly, private sector firms offer such monitoring assistance, permitting the overseas corporation to discover potential trouble spots as early as possible and to react quickly to prevent major losses.

Firms can also take out insurance to cover losses due to political and economic risk. Most industrialized countries offer insurance programs for their firms doing business abroad. In Germany, for example, Hermes Kreditanstalt (www.hermes.de) provides exporters with insurance. In the United States, the Overseas Private Investment Corporation (OPIC) (www.opic.gov) can cover three types of risk insurance: currency inconvertibility insurance, which covers the inability to convert profits, debt service, and other remittances from local currency into U.S. dollars; expropriation insurance, which covers the loss of an investment due to expropriation, nationalization, or confiscation by a foreign government; and political violence insurance, which covers the loss of assets or income due to war, revolution, insurrection, or politically motivated civil strife, terrorism, and sabotage. The cost of coverage varies by country and type of activity, but for manufacturers it averages $0.30 for $100 of coverage per year to protect against inconvertibility, $0.60 to protect against expropriation, and $1.05 to compensate for damage to business income and assets from political violence.[27] Usually the policies do not cover commercial risks and, in the event of a claim, cover only the actual loss—not lost profits. In the event of a major political upheaval, however, risk insurance can be critical to a firm's survival.

The discussion to this point has focused primarily on the political and economic environment. Laws have been mentioned only as they appear to be the direct result of political change. However, the laws of host countries need to be considered on their own to some extent, for the basic system of law is important to the conduct of international business.

1030

Global Organization Structure and Control

As companies evolve from purely domestic to multinational, their organizational structure and control systems must change to reflect new strategies. With growth comes diversity in terms of products and services, geographic markets, and people in the company itself, bringing along a set of challenges for the company. Two critical issues are basic to all of these challenges: (1) the type of organization that provides the best framework for developing worldwide strategies while at the same time maintaining flexibility in implementation with respect to individual markets and operations and (2) the type and degree of control to be exercised from headquarters to maximize total effort. Organizational structures, organizations' abilities to implement strategies, and control systems have to be adjusted as market conditions change.

This section will focus on the advantages and disadvantages of various organizational structures, as well as their appropriateness at different stages of internationalization. A determining factor is where decision-making authority within the organizational structure will be placed. The roles of the different entities that make up the organization need to be defined, including how to achieve collaboration among the units for the benefit of the entire network. The section will also outline the need for devising a control system to oversee the international operations of the company, emphasizing the additional control instruments needed beyond those used in domestic business and the control strategies of multinational corporations. The appropriateness and eventual cost of the various control approaches will vary as the firm expands its international operations. The overall objective of the section is to study the intraorganizational relationships critical to the firm's attempt to optimize its competitiveness.

Organizational Structure

The basic functions of an organization are to provide: (1) a route and locus of decision making and coordination and (2) a system for reporting and communications. Authority and communication networks are typically depicted in the organizational chart.

Organizational Designs

The basic configurations of international organizations correspond to those of purely domestic ones; the greater the degree of internalization, the more complex the structures can become. The types of structures that companies use to manage foreign activities can be divided into three categories, based on the degree of internationalization.

1. *Little or no formal organizational recognition of international activities of the firm.* This category ranges from domestic operations handling an occasional international transaction on an ad hoc basis to firms with separate export departments.
2. *International division.* Firms in this category recognize the ever-growing importance of the international involvement.
3. *Global organizations.* These can be structured by product, area, function, process, or customer, but ignore the traditional domestic-international split.

Hybrid structures may exist as well, in which one market may be structured by product, another by areas. Matrix organizations have merged in large multinational corporations to combine product-specific, regional, and functional expertise. As worldwide competition has increased dramatically in many industries, the latest organizational response is networked global organizations in which heavy flows of hardware, software, and personnel take place between strategically interdependent units to establish greater global integration. The ability to identify and disseminate best practices throughout the organization is an important competitive advantage for global companies. For example, a U.S. automaker found that in the face of distinctive challenges presented by the local environment, Brazilian engineers developed superior seals, which the company then incorporated in all its models worldwide.[28]

Little or No Formal Organization

In the very early stages of international involvement, domestic operations assume responsibility for international activities. The role of international activities in the sales and profits of the corporation is initially so minor that no organizational adjustment takes place. No consolidation of information or authority over international sales is undertaken or is necessary. Transactions are conducted on a case-by-case basis, either by the resident expert or quite often with the help of facilitating agents, such as freight forwarders.

As demand from the international marketplace grows and interest within the firm expands, the organizational structure will reflect it. As shown in Exhibit 1000.1, an export department appears as a separate entity. This may be an outside export management company—that is, an independent company that becomes the de facto export department

Exhibit 1000.1 *The Export Department Structure*

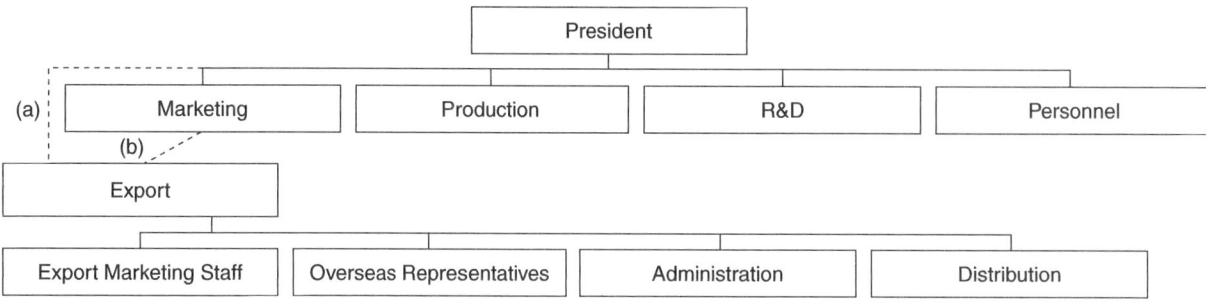

of the firm. This is an indirect approach to international involvement in that very little experience is accumulated within the firm itself. Alternatively, a firm may establish its own export department, hiring a few seasoned individuals to take responsibility for international activities. Organizationally, the department may be a subdepartment of marketing (alternative b in Exhibit 1000.1) or may have equal ranking with the various functional departments (alternative a). The choice will depend on the importance assigned to overseas activities by the firm. The export department is the first real step toward internationalizing the organizational structures. It should be a full-fledged marketing organization and not merely a sales organization; that is, it should have the resources for market research and market-development activities (such as trade show participation).

Licensing as an international entry mode may be assigned to the R&D function despite its importance to the overall international strategy of the firm. A formal liaison among the export, marketing, production, and R&D functions has to be formed for the maximum utilization of licensing.[29] If licensing indeed becomes a major activity for the firm, a separate manager should be appointed.

The more the firm becomes involved in foreign markets, the more quickly the export department structure will become obsolete. For example, the firm may undertake joint ventures or direct foreign investment, which require those involved to have functional experience. The firm therefore typically establishes an international division.

Some firms that acquire foreign production facilities pass through an additional stage in which foreign subsidiaries report directly to the president or to a manager specifically assigned the duty.[30] However, the amount of coordination and control that are required quickly establish the need for a more formal international organization in the firm.

The International Division

The international division centralizes in one entity, with or without separate incorporation, all of the responsibility for international activities, as illustrated in Exhibit 1000.2. The approach aims to eliminate a possible bias against international operations that may exist if domestic divisions are allowed to serve international customers independently. In some cases, international markets have been treated as secondary to domestic markets. The international division concentrates international expertise, information flows concerning foreign market opportunities, and authority over international activities. However, manufacturing and other related functions remain with the domestic divisions to take advantage of economies of scale.

To avoid putting the international division at a disadvantage in competing for products, personnel, and corporate services, coordination between domestic and international operations is necessary. Coordination can be achieved through a joint staff or by requiring domestic and international divisions to interact in strategic planning and to submit the plans to headquarters. Further, many corporations require and encourage frequent interaction between domestic and international personnel to discuss common problems in areas such as product planning. Coordination is also important because domestic operations are typically organized along product or functional lines, whereas international divisions are geographically oriented.

International divisions best serve firms with few products that do not vary significantly in terms of their environmental sensitivity and with international sales and profits that are still quite insignificant compared with those of the domestic divisions.[31] Companies may outgrow their international divisions as their sales outside of the domestic market grow in significance, diversity, and complexity. European companies have traditionally used international divisions far less than their U.S. counterparts due to the relatively small size of their domestic markets. **Philips, Nestlé,** or **Nokia,** for example, would have never grown to their current prominence by relying on their home markets alone. While international divisions were popular among U.S. companies in the 1970s and 1980s, globalization of markets

Exhibit 1000.2 *The International Division Structure*

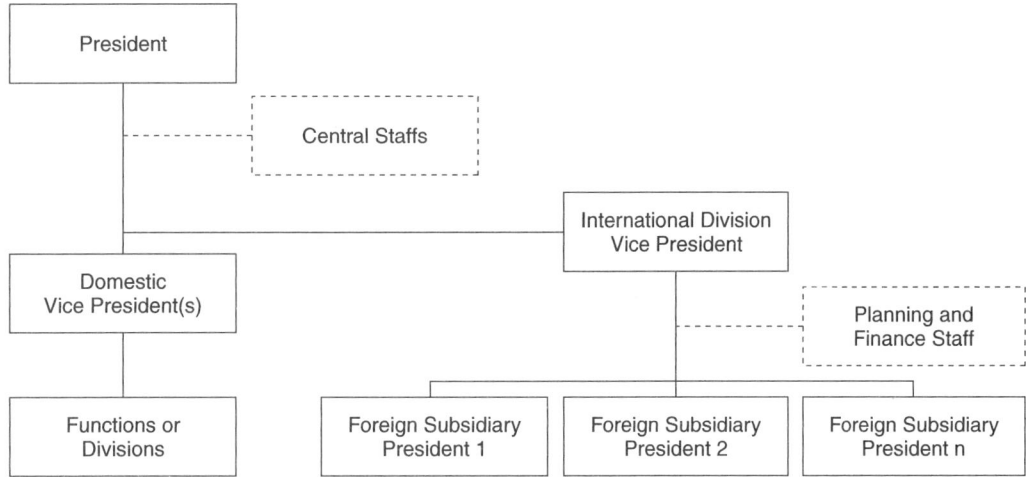

and the increased share of overseas sales have made international divisions less suitable, in favor of global structures.[32] For example, **Loctite,** a leading marketer of sealants, adhesives, and coatings, moved from an international division to a global structure by which the company is managed by market channel (for example, industrial automotive and electronics industry) to enable **Loctite** employees to synergize efforts and expertise worldwide.[33]

Global Organizational Structures

Global structures have grown out of competitive necessity. In many industries, competition is on a global basis, with a result that companies must have a high degree of reactive capability.

Six basic types of global structures are available.

1. Global product structure, in which product divisions are responsible for all manufacture and marketing worldwide
2. Global area structure, in which geographic divisions are responsible for all manufacture and marketing in their respective areas
3. Global functional structures, in which functional areas (such as production, marketing, finance, and personnel) are responsible for the worldwide operations of their own functional area
4. Global customer structures, in which operations are structured based on distinct, worldwide customer groups
5. Mixed—or hybrid—structures, which may combine the other alternatives
6. Matrix structures, in which operations have reporting responsibility to more than one group (typically, product, functions, or area)

PRODUCT STRUCTURE The **product structure** is the form most often used by multinational corporations.[34] The approach gives worldwide responsibility to strategic business units for the marketing of their product lines, as shown in Exhibit 1000.3. Most consumer-product firms use some form of this approach, mainly because of the diversity of their products. One of the major benefits of the approach is improved cost efficiency through centralization of manufacturing facilities. This is crucial in industries in which competitive position is determined by world market share, which in turn is often determined by the degree to which manufacturing is rationalized.[35] Adaptation to this approach may cause problems because it is usually accompanied by consolidation of operations and plant closings. A good example is **Black & Decker,** which rationalized many of its operations in its worldwide competitive effort against **Makita,** the Japanese power-tool manufacturer. Similarly, **Goodyear** reorganized itself into a single global organization with a complete business-team approach for tires and general products. The move was largely prompted by tightening worldwide competition.[36] In a similar move, **Ford** merged its large and culturally distinct European and North American auto operations by vehicle platform type to make more efficient use of its engineering and product-development resources against rapidly globalizing rivals.[37] The Ford Focus, Ford's compact car introduced in 1999, was designed by one team of engineers for worldwide markets.

Exhibit 1000.3 *The Global Product Structure*

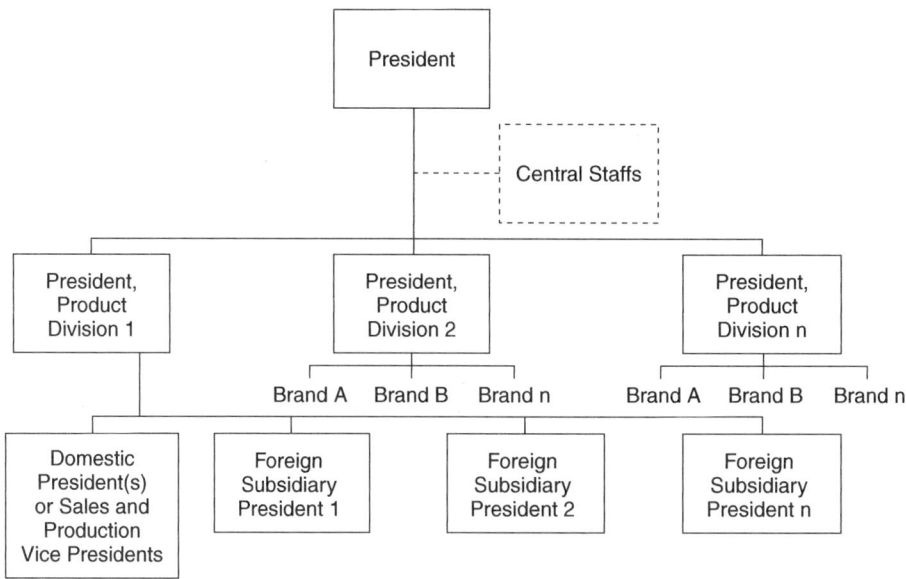

Other benefits of the product structure are the ability to balance the functional inputs needed for a product and the ability to react quickly to product-specific problems in the marketplace. Even smaller brands receive individual attention. Product-specific attention is important because products vary in terms of the adaptation they need for different foreign markets. All in all, the product approach is ideally suited to the development of a global strategic focus in response to global competition.

At the same time, the product structure fragments international expertise within the firm because a central pool of international experience no longer exists. The structure assumes that managers will have adequate regional experience or advice to allow them to make balanced decisions. Coordination of activities among the various product groups operating in the same markets is crucial to avoid unnecessary duplication of basic tasks. For some of these tasks, such as market research, special staff functions may be created and then filled by the product divisions when needed. If they lack an appreciation for the international dimension, product managers may focus their attention only on the larger markets or only on the domestic, and fail to take the long-term view.

AREA STRUCTURE The second most used approach is the **area structure**, illustrated in Exhibit 1000.4. Such firms are organized on the basis of geographical areas; for example, operations may be divided into those dealing with North America, the Far East, Latin America, and Europe. Ideally, no special preference is given to the region in which the headquarters is located—for example, North America or Europe. Central staffs are responsible for providing coordination support for worldwide planning and control activities performed at headquarters.

Regional integration is playing a major role in area structuring; for example, many multinational corporations have located their European headquarters in Brussels, where the EU has its headquarters. In some U.S. companies, North American integration led to the development of a North American division, which replaced the U.S. operation as the power center of the company. The driver of structural choices may also be cultural similarity, such as in the case of Asia, or historic connections between countries, such as in the case of combining Europe with the Middle East and Africa.

The area approach follows the marketing concept most closely because individual areas and markets are given concentrated attention. If market conditions with respect to product acceptance and operating conditions vary dramatically, the area approach is the one to choose. Companies opting for this alternative typically have relatively narrow product lines with similar end uses and end users. However, expertise is needed in adapting the product and its marketing to local market conditions. Once again, to avoid duplication of effort in product management and in functional areas, staff specialists—for product categories, for example—may be used.

Without appropriate coordination from the staff, essential information and experience may not be transferred from one regional entity to another. Also, if the company expands its product lines and if end markets begin to diversify, the area structure may become inappropriate.

Some managers may feel that going into a global product structure may be too much, too quickly, and opt, therefore, to have a regional organization for planning and reporting purposes. The objective may also be to keep profit or sales cen-

Exhibit 1000.4 *The Global Area Structure*

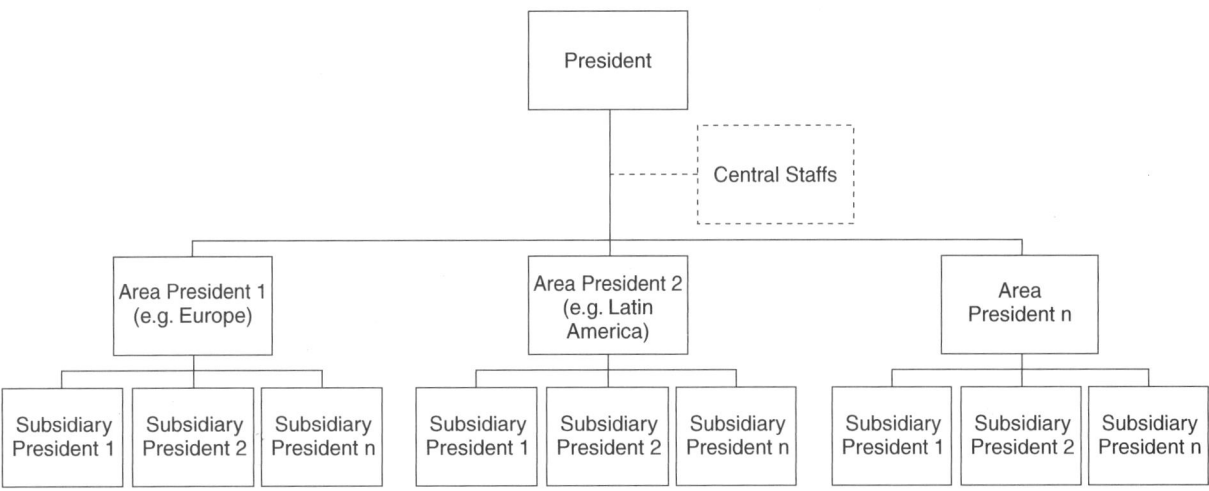

ters of similar size at similar levels in the corporate hierarchy. If a group of countries has small sales as compared with other country operations, they may be consolidated into a region. The benefit of a regional operation and regional headquarters would be the more efficient coordination of programs across the region (as opposed to globally), a more sensitized management to country-market operations in the region, and the ability to have the region's voice heard more clearly at global headquarters (as compared to what an individual, especially smaller, country operation could achieve).[38]

FUNCTIONAL STRUCTURE Of all the approaches, the **functional structure** is the simplest from the administrative viewpoint because it emphasizes the basic tasks of the firm—for example, manufacturing, sales, and research and development. The approach, illustrated in Exhibit 1000.5, works best when both products and customers are relatively few and similar in nature. Coordination is typically the key problem; therefore, staff functions have been created to interact between the functional areas. Otherwise, the company's marketing and regional expertise may not be exploited to the fullest extent possible.

A variation of the functional approach is one that uses processes as a basis for structure. The **process structure** is common in the energy and mining industries, where one corporate entity may be in charge of exploration worldwide and another may be responsible for the actual mining operations.

CUSTOMER STRUCTURE Firms may also organize their operations using the **customer structure**, especially if the customer groups they serve are dramatically different—for example, consumers and businesses and governments. Catering to such diverse groups may require concentrating specialists in particular divisions. The product may be the same, but the buying processes of the various customer groups may differ. Governmental buying is characterized by bidding, in which price plays a larger role than when businesses are the buyers.

MIXED STRUCTURE In some cases, mixed, or hybrid, organizations exist. A **mixed structure** combines two or more organizational dimensions simultaneously. It permits adequate attention to product, area, or functional needs as is needed by the company. The approach may only be a result of a transitional period after a merger or an acquisition, or it may come about due to unique market characteristics or product line. It may also provide a useful structure before the implementation of a worldwide matrix structure.[39]

Naturally, organizational structures are never as clear-cut and simple as presented here. Whatever the basic format, product, functional, and area inputs are needed. Alternatives could include an initial product structure that would subsequently have regional groupings or an initial regional structure with subsequent product groupings. However, in the long term, coordination and control across such structures become tedious.

MATRIX STRUCTURE Many multinational corporations, in an attempt to facilitate planning for, organizing, and controlling interdependent businesses, critical resources, strategies, and geographic regions, have adopted the **matrix structure**.[40] **Eastman Kodak** shifted from a functional organization to a matrix system based on business units. Business is driven by a worldwide business unit (for example, photographic products or commercial and information systems)

Exhibit 1000.5 *The Global Functional Structure*

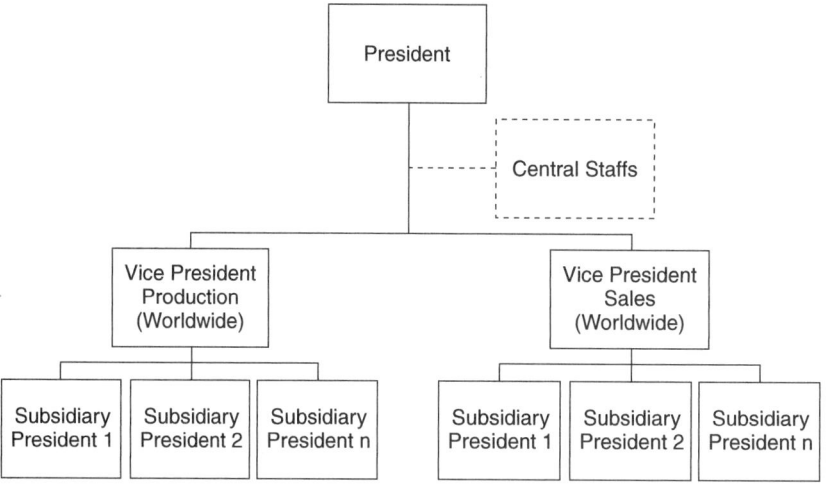

Exhibit 1000.6 *The Global Matrix Structure at Philips*

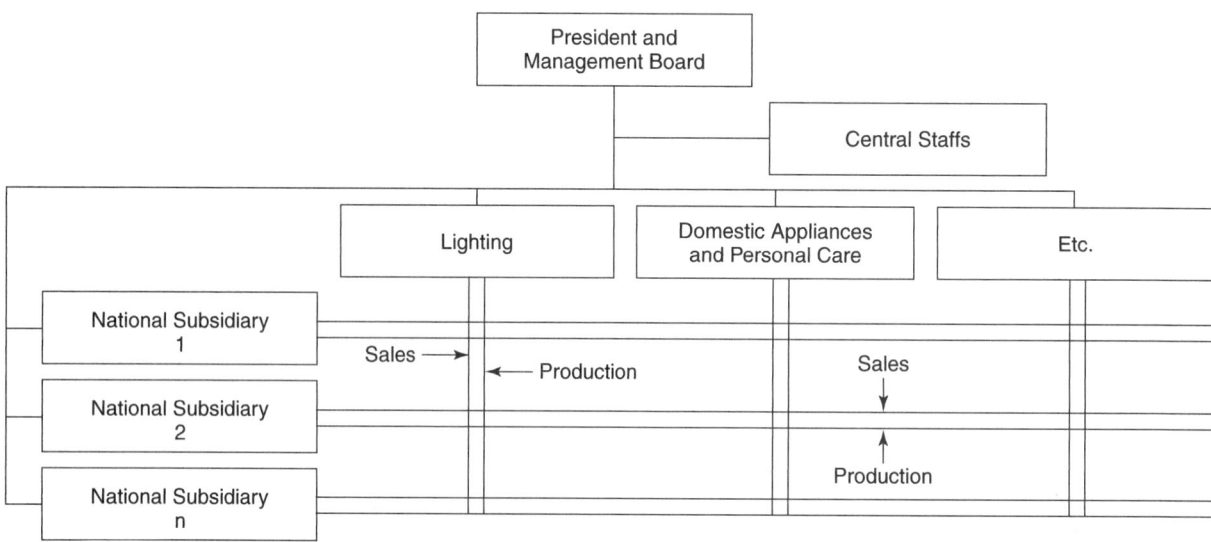

and implemented by a geographic unit (for example, Europe or Latin America). The geographical units, as well as their country subsidiaries, serve as the "glue" between autonomous product operations.[41]

Organizational matrices integrate the various approaches already discussed, as the **Philips** example in Exhibit 1000.6 illustrates. The seven product divisions (which are then divided into 60 product groups) have rationalized manufacturing to provide products for continentwide markets rather than lines of products for individual markets.[42] Philips has three general types of country organizations. In "key" markets, such as the United States, France, and Japan, product divisions manage their own marketing as well as manufacturing. In "local business" countries, such as Nigeria and Peru, the organizations function as importers from product divisions, and if manufacturing occurs, it is purely for the local market. In "large" markets, such as Brazil, Spain, and Taiwan, a hybrid arrangement is used, depending on the size and situation. The product divisions and the national subsidiaries interact in a matrixlike configuration, with the product divisions responsible for the globalization dimension and the national subsidiaries responsible for local representation and coordination of common areas of interest, such as recruiting.

Matrices vary in terms of their number of dimensions. For example, **Dow Chemical's** three-dimensional matrix consists of five geographic areas, three major functions (marketing, manufacturing, and research), and more than 70 products. The matrix approach helps cut through enormous organizational complexities in making business managers, functional managers, and strategy managers cooperate. However, the matrix requires sensitive, well-trained middle managers who can cope with problems that arise from reporting to two bosses—for example, a product-line manager and an area manager. For example, every management unit may have a multidimensional reporting relationship, which may cross functional, regional, or operational lines. On a regional basis, group managers in Europe for example, report administratively to a vice president of operations for Europe, but report functionally to group vice presidents at global headquarters.

Most companies have found the matrix arrangement problematic.[43] The dual reporting channel easily causes conflict, complex issues are forced into a two-dimensional decision framework, and even minor issues may have to be solved through committee discussion. Ideally, managers should solve the problems themselves through formal and informal communication; however, physical and psychic distance often make that impossible. The matrix structure, with its inherent complexity, may actually increase the reaction time of a company, a potentially serious problem when competitive conditions require quick responses. As a result, the authority has started to shift in many organizations from area to product, although the matrix still may officially be used.

Evolution of Organizational Structures

Companies have been shown to develop new structures in a pattern of stages as their products diversify and share of foreign sales increases.[44] At the first stage of autonomous subsidiaries reporting directly to top management, the establishment of an international division follows. As product diversity and the importance of the foreign marketplace increase, companies develop global structures to coordinate subsidiary operations and to rationalize worldwide production. As multinational corporations have been faced with simultaneous pressures to adapt to local market conditions and to rationalize production and globalize competitive reactions, many have opted for the matrix structure.[45] The matrix structure probably allows a corporation to best meet the challenges of global markets (to be global and local, big and small, decentralized with centralized reporting) by allowing the optimizing of businesses globally and maximizing performance in every country of operation.[46]

Implementation

Organizational structures provide the frameworks for carrying out decision-making processes. However, for that decision making to be effective, a series of organizational initiatives are needed to develop the strategy to its full potential, that is, to secure implementation both at the national level and across markets.[47]

Locus of Decision Making

Organizational structures themselves do not indicate where the authority for decision making and control rests within the organization, nor will they it reveal the level of coordination between the units. Once a suitable structure is found, it has to be made to work.

If subsidiaries are granted a high degree of autonomy, the system is called **decentralization.** In decentralized systems, controls are relatively loose and simple, and the flows between headquarters and subsidiaries are mainly financial; that is, each subsidiary operates as a profit center. On the other hand, if controls are tight and the strategic decision making is concentrated at headquarters, the system is described as **centralization.** Firms are typically neither completely centralized nor decentralized; for example, some functions of the firm—such as finance—lend themselves to more centralized decision making; others—such as promotional decisions—do so far less. Research and development in organizations is typically centralized, especially in cases of basic research work. Some companies have, partly due to governmental pressures, added R&D functions on a regional or local basis. In many cases, however, variations are product and market based; for example, **Corning Incorporated's** TV tube marketing strategy requires global decision making for pricing and local decision making for service and delivery.

The basic advantage of allowing maximum flexibility at the country-market level is that subsidiary management knows its market and can react to changes more quickly. Problems of motivation and acceptance are avoided when decision makers are also the implementors of the strategy. On the other hand, many multinationals faced with global competitive threats and opportunities have adopted global strategy formulation, which by definition requires a higher degree of centralization. What has emerged as a result can be called **coordinated decentralization.** This means that overall corporate strategy is provided from headquarters, while subsidiaries are free to implement it within the range agreed on in consultation between headquarters and the subsidiaries.

However, companies moving into this new mode may face significant challenges. Among these systemic difficulties are a lack of widespread commitment to dismantling traditional national structures, driven by an inadequate understanding of the larger, global forces at work. Power barriers from perceived threats to the personal roles of national managers, especially if their tasks are under the threat of being consolidated into regional organizations, can lead to proposals being challenged without valid reason. Finally, some organizational initiatives (such as multicultural teams or corporate chat rooms) may be jeopardized by the fact the people do not have the necessary skills (for example, language ability) or that an infrastructure (for example, intranet) may not exist in an appropriate format.[48]

One particular case is of special interest. Organizationally, the forces of globalization are changing the country manager's role significantly. With profit-and-loss responsibility, oversight of multiple functions, and the benefit of distance from headquarters, country managers enjoyed considerable decision-making autonomy as well as entrepreneurial initiative when country operations were largely stand-alone. Today, however, many companies have to emphasize global and regional priorities, which means that the power has to shift at least to some extent from the country manager to worldwide strategic business unit and product-line managers. Many of the local decisions are now subordinated to global strategic moves. Therefore, the future country manager will have to wear many hats in balancing the needs of the operation for which the manager is directly responsible with those of the entire region or strategic business unit.[49] To emphasize the importance of the global/regional dimension in the country manager's portfolio, many companies have tied the country manager's compensation to how the company performs globally or regionally, not just in the market for which the manager is responsible.

Factors Affecting Structure and Decision Making

The organizational structure and locus of decision making in a multinational corporation are determined by a number of factors, such as: (1) its degree of involvement in international operations, (2) the products the firm markets, (3) the size and importance of the firm's markets, and (4) the human resource capability of the firm.[50]

The effect of the degree of involvement on structure and decision making was discussed earlier. With low degrees of involvement, subsidiaries can enjoy high degrees of autonomy as long as they meet their profit targets. The same situation can occur even with the most globally oriented companies, but within a different framework. Consider, for example, **Philips USA,** which generates 20 percent of the company's worldwide sales. Even more important it serves as a market that is on the leading edge of digital media development. Therefore, it enjoys independent status in terms of local policy setting and managerial practices but is still, nevertheless, within the parent company's planning and control system.

The firm's country of origin and the political history of the area can also affect organizational structure and decision making. For example, Swiss-based **Nestlé,** with only 3 to 4 percent of its sales from its small domestic market, has traditionally had a highly decentralized organization. Moreover, European history for the past 80 years—particularly the two world wars—has often forced subsidiaries of European-based companies to act independently to survive.

The type and variety of products marketed will affect organizational decisions. Companies that market consumer products typically have product organizations with high degrees of decentralization, allowing for maximum local flexibility. On the other hand, companies that market technologically sophisticated products—such as **GE,** which markets turbines—display centralized organizations with worldwide product responsibilities. Even within matrix organizations, one of the dimensions may be granted more say in decisions; for example, at **Dow Chemical,** geographical managers have been granted more authority than other managers.

Going global has recently meant transferring world headquarters of important business units abroad. For example, Philips has moved headquarters of several of its global business units to the United States, including its Digital Video Group, Optimal Storage, and Flat Panel Display activities to Silicon Valley.

The human factor in any organization is critical. Managers at both headquarters and the country organizations must bridge the physical and cultural distances separating them. If country organizations have competent managers who rarely need to consult headquarters about their challenges, they may be granted high degrees of autonomy. In the case of global organizations, local management must understand overall corporate goals in that decisions that meet the long-term objectives may not be optimal for the individual local market.

The Networked Global Organization

No international structure is ideal and some have challenged the wisdom of even looking for one. They have recommended attention to new processes that would, in a given structure, help to develop new perspectives and attitudes that reflect and respond to the complex, opposing demands of global integration and local responsiveness.[51] The question thus changes from which structural alternative is best to how the different perspectives of various corporate entities can better be taken into account when making decisions. In structural terms, nothing may change. As a matter of fact, Philips has not changed its basic matrix structure, yet major changes have occurred in internal relations. The basic change was from a decentralized federation model to a networked global organization. The term **glocal** has been coined to describe this approach.[52]

Companies that have adopted the approach have incorporated the following three dimensions into their organizations: (1) the development and communication of a clear corporate vision, (2) the effective management of human resource tools to broaden individual perspectives and develop identification with corporate goals, and (3) the integration of individual thinking and activities into the broad corporate agenda.[53] The first dimension relates to a clear and consistent long-term corporate mission that guides individuals wherever they work in the organization. Examples of this are **Johnson & Johnson's** corporate credo of customer focus and NEC's C&C (computers and communications). The second relates both to the development of global managers who can find opportunities in spite of environmental challenges as well as creating a global perspective among country managers. The last dimension relates to the development of a cooperative mind-set among country organizations to ensure effective implementation of global strategies. Managers may believe that global strategies are intrusions on their operations if they do not have an understanding of the corporate vision, if they have not contributed to the global corporate agenda, or if they are not given direct responsibility for its implementation. Defensive, territorial attitudes can lead to the emergence of the "not-invented-here" syndrome, that is, country organizations objecting to or rejecting an otherwise sound strategy.

The network avoids the problems of effort duplication, inefficiency and resistance to ideas developed elsewhere by giving subsidiaries the latitude, encouragement, and tools to pursue local business development within the framework of the global strategy. Headquarters considers each unit a source of ideas, skills, capabilities, and knowledge that can be utilized for the benefit of the entire organization. This means that subsidiaries must be upgraded from mere implementors and adaptors to contributors and partners in the development and execution of worldwide strategies. Efficient plants may be converted into international production centers, innovative R&D units converted into centers of excellence (and thus role models), and leading subsidiary groups given the leadership role in developing new strategies for the entire corporation.

Promoting Internal Cooperation

The global business entity in today's environment can only be successful if is able to move intellectual capital within the organization; that is, take ideas and move them around faster and faster.[54] One of the tools is teaching.

Another method to promote internal cooperation for global strategy implementation is the use of international teams or councils. In the case of a new product or program an international team of managers may be assembled to develop strategy. While final direction may come from headquarters, it has been informed of local conditions, and implementation of the strategy is enhanced since local-country managers were involved in its development. The approach has worked even in cases involving seemingly impossible market differences.

The term *network* also implies two-way communications between headquarters and subsidiaries and between subsidiaries themselves. While this communication can take the form of newsletters or regular and periodic meetings of appropriate personnel, new technologies are allowing businesses to link far-flung entities and eliminate the traditional barriers of time and distance. **Intranets** integrate a company's information assets into a single accessible system using Internet-based technologies such as e-mail, news groups, and the World Wide Web. In effect, the formation of **virtual teams** becomes a reality.

The benefits of intranet are: (1) increased productivity in that there is no longer a time lag between an idea and the information needed to assess and implement it; (2) enhanced knowledge capital, which is constantly updated and upgraded; (3) facilitated teamwork enabling on-line communication at insignificant expense; and (4) incorporation of best practice at a moment's notice by allowing managers and functional-area personnel to make to-the-minute decisions anywhere in the world.

As can be seen from the discussion, the networked approach is not a structural adaptation but a procedural one, calling for a change in management mentality. It requires adjustment mainly in the coordination and control functions of the firm. Of the many initiatives developed to enhance the workings of a networked global organization, such as cross-border task forces and establishment of centers of excellence, the most significant was the use of electronic networking capabilities.[55]

Further adjustment in organizational approaches is required as businesses face new challenges such as emerging markets, global accounts, and the digitization of business.[56] Emerging markets present the company with unique challenges such as product counterfeiters and informal competitors who ignore local labor and tax laws. How these issues are addressed may require organizational rethinking. **Colgate-Palmolive,** for example, grouped its geographies under two different organizations: one responsible for mature, developed economies and the other for high-growth, emerging markets.[57] Global account managers need to have skills and the empowerment to work across functional areas and borders to deliver quality service to the company's largest clients. Finally, digital business, such as business-to-business and business-to-consumer Internet-based activities, need to be brought into the mainstay of the businesses activities and structures and not seen as a separate activity.

The Role of Country Organizations

Country organizations should be treated as a source of supply as much as a source of demand. Quite often, however, headquarters managers see their role as the coordinators of key decisions and controllers of resources and perceive subsidiaries as implementors and adaptors of global strategy in their respective local markets. Furthermore, they may see all country organizations as the same. This view severely limits utilization of the firm's resources and deprives country managers of the opportunity to exercise their creativity.[58]

The role that a particular country organization can play naturally depends on that market's overall strategic importance as well as its organizational competence. Using these criteria, four different roles emerge: strategic leader, contributor, implementor, and black hole.

The role of a **strategic leader** can be played by a highly competent national subsidiary located in a strategically critical market. Such a country organization serves as a partner of headquarters in developing and implementing strategy.

A **contributor** is a country organization with a distinctive competence, such as product development. Increasingly, country organizations are the source of new products.

Implementors provide the critical mass for the global effort. These country organizations may exist in smaller, less-developed countries in which there is less corporate commitment for market development. Although most entities are given this role, it should not be slighted, since the implementors provide the opportunity to capture economies of scale and scope that are the basis of a global strategy.

The **black hole** situation is one in which the international company has a low-competence country organization—or no organization at all—in a highly strategic market. In strategically important markets such as the European Union, a local presence is necessary to maintain the company's global position and, in some cases, to protect others. One of the major ways of remedying the black hole situation is to enter into strategic alliances. In some cases, firms may use their presence in a major market as an observation post to keep up with developments before a major thrust for entry is executed.

Depending on the role of the country organization, its relationship with headquarters will vary from loose control based mostly on support to tighter control to ensure that strategies get implemented appropriately. Yet, in each of these cases, it is imperative that country organizations have enough operating independence to cater to local needs and to provide motivation to country managers. For example, an implementor's ideas concerning the development of a regional or global strategy or program should be heard. Country organization initiative is the principal means by which global companies can tap into new opportunities in markets around the world.[59] For example, customers' unmet demands in a given market may result not only in the launch of a local product but subsequently in its roll-out regionally or even globally. Furthermore, in executing global strategies, country-specific buy-in is best secured through involvement of these organizations at the critical points in strategy development. Strategy formulators should make sure that appropriate implementation can be achieved at the country level.

Organizational Controls

The function of the organizational structure is to provide a framework in which objectives can be met. A set of instruments and processes is needed, however, to influence the performance of organizational members so as to meet the goals. Controls focus on means to verify and correct actions that differ from established plans. Compliance needs to be secured from subordinates through different means of coordinating specialized and interdependent parts of the organization.[60] Within an organization, control serves as an integrating mechanism. Controls are designed to reduce uncertainty, increase predictability, and ensure that behaviors originating in separate parts of the organization are compatible and in support of common organizational goals despite physical, psychic, and temporal distances.[61]

The critical issue here is the same as with organizational structure: What is the ideal amount of control? On the one hand, headquarters needs controls to ensure that international activities contribute the greatest benefit to the overall organization. On the other hand, they should not be construed as a code of laws and subsequently allowed to stifle local initiative.

This section will focus on the design and functions of control instruments available for international business operations, along with an assessment of their appropriateness. Emphasis will be placed on the degree of formality of controls used by firms.

Types of Controls

Most organizations display some administrative flexibility, as demonstrated by variations in how they apply management directives, corporate objectives, or measurement systems. A distinction should be made, however, between variations that have emerged by design and those that are the result of autonomy. The first are the result of a management decision, whereas the second typically have grown without central direction and are based on emerging practices. In both instances, some type of control will be exercised. Controls that result from a headquarters initiative rather than those that are the consequences of tolerated practices will be discussed here. Firms that wait for self-emerging controls often experience rapid international growth but subsequent problems in product-line performance, program coordination, and strategic planning.[62]

Whatever the system, it is important in today's competitive environment to have internal benchmarking. This relates to organizational learning and sharing of best practices throughout the corporate system to avoid the costs of reinventing solutions that have already been discovered. Three critical features are necessary in sharing best practice. First, there needs to be a device for organizational memory. For example, at **Xerox,** contributors to solutions can send their ideas to an electronic library where they are indexed and provided to potential adopters in the corporate family. Second, best practice must be updated and adjusted to new situations. For example, best practice adopted by a company's China office will be modified and customized, and this learning should then become part of the database. Finally, best practice must be legitimized. This calls for a shared understanding that exchanging knowledge across units is organizationally valued and that these systems are important mechanisms for knowledge exchange. Use can be encouraged by including an assessment in employee performance evaluations of how effectively employees share information with colleagues and utilize the databases.

In the design of the control systems, a major decision concerns the object of control. Two major objects are typically identified: output and behavior.[63] Output controls include balance sheets, sales data, production data, product-line growth, and performance reviews of personnel. Measures of output are accumulated at regular intervals and forwarded from the foreign locale to headquarters, where they are evaluated and critiqued based on comparisons to the plan or budget. Behavioral controls require the exertion of influence over behavior after—or, ideally, before—it leads to action. Behavioral controls can be achieved through the preparation of manuals on such topics as sales techniques to be made available to subsidiary personnel or through efforts to fit new employees into the corporate culture.

To institute either of these measures, instruments of control have to be decided upon. The general alternatives are either bureaucratic/formalized control or cultural control.[64] Bureaucratic controls consist of a limited and explicit set of regulations and rules that outline the desired levels of performance. Cultural controls, on the other hand, are much less formal and are the result of shared beliefs and expectations among the members of an organization. Exhibit 1000.7 provides a schematic explanation of the types of controls and their objectives.

Exhibit 1000.7 *Comparison of Bureaucratic and Cultural Control Mechanisms*

	Type of Control	
Object of Control	Pure Bureaucratic/Formalized Control	Pure Cultural Control
Output	Formal performance reports	Shared norms of performance
Behavior	Company policies, manuals	Shared philosophy of management

Source: B. R. Baliga and Alfred M. Jaeger, "Multinational Corporations: Control Systems and Delegation Issues," *Journal of International Business Studies* 15 (Fall 1984): 25–40.

Bureaucratic/Formalized Control

The elements of a bureaucratic/formalized control system are: (1) an international budget and planning system, (2) the functional reporting system, and (3) policy manuals used to direct functional performance.

Budgets refers to shorter term guidelines regarding investment, cash, and personnel policies, while *plans* refers to formalized plans with more than a one-year horizon. The budget and planning process is the major control instrument in headquarters-subsidiary relationships. Although systems and their execution vary, the objective is to achieve as good a fit as possible with the objectives and characteristics of the firm and its environment.

The budgetary period is typically one year, since it is tied to the accounting systems of the multinational. The budget system is used for four main purposes: (1) allocation of funds among subsidiaries; (2) planning and coordination of global production capacity and supplies; (3) evaluation of subsidiary performance; and (4) communication and information exchange among subsidiaries, product organizations, and corporate headquarters.[65] Long-range plans vary dramatically, ranging from 2 years to 10 years in length, and are more qualitative and judgmental in nature. However, shorter periods such as two years are the norm, considering the added uncertainty of diverse foreign environments.

Although firms strive for uniformity, achieving it may be as difficult as trying to design a suit to fit the average person. The processes themselves are very formalized in terms of the schedules to be followed.

Functional reports are another control instrument used by headquarters in managing subsidiary relations. Examples of functional reports include balance sheet, income statement, production output, market share, and sales per product. These vary in number, complexity, and frequency. The structure and elements of the reports are typically highly standardized to allow for consolidation in the headquarters level.

Since the frequency of reports required from subsidiaries is likely to increase due to globalization, it is essential that subsidiaries see the rationale for the often time-consuming exercise. Two approaches, used in tandem, can facilitate the process: participation and feedback. The first refers to avoiding the perception at subsidiary levels that reports are "art for art's sake" by involving the preparers in the actual use of the reports. When this is not possible, feedback about their consequences is warranted. Through this process, communication is enhanced as well.

On the behavioral front, headquarters may want to guide the way in which subsidiaries make decisions and implement agreed-upon strategies. U.S.-based multinationals tend to be far more formalized than their Japanese and European counterparts, with a heavy reliance on manuals for all major functions.[66] The manuals discuss such items as recruitment, training, motivation, and dismissal policies. The use of manuals is in direct correlation with the required level of reports from subsidiaries.

Cultural Control

As seen from the country comparisons, less emphasis is placed outside the United States on formal controls, as they are viewed as too rigid and too quantitatively oriented. Rather, MNCs in other countries emphasize corporate values and culture, and evaluations are based on the extent to which an individual or entity fits in with the norms. Cultural controls require an extensive socialization process to which informal, personal interaction is central. Substantial resources have to be spent to train the individual to share the corporate cultures, or "the way things are done at the company."[67] To build common vision and values, managers spend a substantial share of their first months at **Matsushita** in what the company calls "cultural and spiritual training." They study the company credo, the "Seven Spirits of Matsushita," and the philosophy of the founder, Konosuke Matsushita and learn how to translate the internalized lessons into daily behavior and operational decisions. Although more prevalent in Japanese organizations, many Western entities have similar programs, such as **Philips's** "organization cohesion training" and **Unilever's** "indoctrination."[68] This corporate acculturation will be critical to achieve the acceptance of possible transfers of best practice within the organization.[69]

The primary instruments of cultural control are the careful selection and training of corporate personnel and the institution of self-control. The choice of cultural controls can be justified if the company enjoys a low turnover rate; they are thus applied when companies can offer and expect lifetime or long-term employment, as many firms do in Japan.

In selecting home-country nationals and, to some extent, third-country nationals, MNCs are exercising cultural control. The assumption is that the managers have already internalized the norms and values of the company and they tend to run a country organization with a more global view. In some cases, the use of headquarters personnel to ensure uniformity in decision making may be advisable; for example, **Volvo** uses a home-country national for the position of chief financial officer. Expatriates are used in subsidiaries not only for control purposes but also to effect change processes. Companies control the efforts of management specifically through compensation and promotion policies, as well as through policies concerning replacement.

When the expatriate corps is small, headquarters can still exercise its control through other means. Management training programs for overseas managers as well as time at headquarters will indoctrinate individuals to the company's ways of doing things. Similarly, formal visits by headquarters teams (for example, for a strategy audit) or informal visits (perhaps to launch a new product) will enhance the feeling of belonging to the same corporate family. Some of the innovative global companies assemble temporary teams of their best talent to build local skills. **IBM,** for example, drafted 50 engineers from its facilities in Italy, Japan, New York, and North Carolina to run three-week to six-month training courses on all operations carried on at its Shenzhen facility in China. After the trainers left the country, they stayed in touch by e-mail, so whenever the Chinese managers have a problem, they know they can reach someone for help. The continuation of the support has been as important as the training itself.[70]

Corporations rarely use one pure control mechanism. Rather, most use both quantitative and qualitative measures. Corporations are likely, however, to place different levels of emphasis on different types of performance measures and on how they are derived.

Exercising Controls

Within most corporations, different functional areas are subject to different guidelines because they are subject to different constraints. For example, the marketing function has traditionally been seen as incorporating many more behavioral dimensions than manufacturing or finance. As a result, many multinational corporations employ control systems that are responsive to the needs of the function. Yet such differentiation is sometimes based less on appropriateness than on personalities. It has been hypothesized that manufacturing subsidiaries are controlled more intensively than sales subsidiaries because production more readily lends itself to centralized direction, and technicians and engineers adhere more firmly to standards and regulations than do salespeople.[71]

In their international operations, U.S.-based multinationals place major emphasis on obtaining quantitative data. Although this allows for good centralized comparisons against standards and benchmarks or cross-comparisons among different corporate units, it entails several drawbacks. In the international environment, new dimensions—such as inflation, differing rates of taxation, and exchange-rate fluctuations—may distort the performance evaluation of any given individual or organizational unit. For the global corporation, measurement of whether a business unit in a particular country is earning a superior return on investment relative to risk may be irrelevant to the contribution an investment may make worldwide or to the long-term results of the firm. In the short term, the return may even be negative.[72] Therefore, the control mechanism may quite inappropriately indicate reward or punishment. Standardizing the information received may be difficult if the various environments involved fluctuate and require frequent and major adaptations. Further complicating the issue is the fact that although quantitative information may be collected monthly, or at least quarterly, environmental data may be acquired annually or "now and then," especially when a crisis seems to loom on the horizon. To design a control system that is acceptable not only to headquarters but also to the organization and individuals abroad, great care must be taken to use only relevant data. Major concerns, therefore, are the data collection process and the analysis and utilization of data. Evaluators need management information systems that provide for greater comparability and equity in administering controls. The more behaviorally based and culture-oriented controls are, the more care needs to be taken.[73]

In designing a control system, management must consider the costs of establishing and maintaining it versus the benefits to be gained. Any control system will require investment in a management structure and in systems design. Consider, for example, costs associated with cultural controls: personal interaction, use of expatriates, and training programs are all quite expensive. Yet these expenses may be justified by cost savings through lower employee turnover, an extensive worldwide information system, and an improved control system.[74] Moreover, the impact goes beyond the administrative component. If controls are misguided or too time-consuming, they can slow or undermine the strategy implementation process and thus the overall capability of the firm. The result will be lost opportunities or, worse yet, increased threats. In addition, time spent on reporting takes time from everything else, and if the exercise is seen as mundane, it results in lowered motivation. A parsimonious design is therefore imperative. The control system should collect all the information required and trigger all the intervention necessary; however, it should not lead to the pulling of strings by a puppeteer.

The impact of the environment has to be taken into account, as well, in two ways. First, the control system must measure only those dimensions over which the organization has actual control. Rewards or sanctions make little sense if they are based on dimensions that may be relevant to overall corporate performance but over which no influence can be exerted, such as price controls. Neglecting the factor of individual performance capability would send wrong signals and severely harm motivation. Second, control systems have to be in harmony with local regulations and customs. In some cases, however, corporate behavioral controls have to be exercised against local customs even though overall operations may be affected negatively. This type of situation occurs, for example, when a subsidiary operates in markets in which unauthorized facilitating payments are a common business practice.

Corporations are faced with major challenges in appropriate and adequate control systems in today's business environment. Given increased local government demands for a share in companies established, controls can become tedious, especially if the MNC is a minority partner. Even if the new entity is a result of two companies' joining forces through a merger—such as the one between **Ciba** and **Sandoz** to create **Novartis**—or two companies joining forces to form a new entity—such as **Siecor** established by **Siemens AG** and **Corning Incorporated**—the backgrounds of the partners may be different enough to cause problems in devising the required controls.

Export Controls

Many nations have **export-control systems,** which are designed to deny or at least delay the acquisition of strategically important goods by adversaries. The legal basis for export controls varies in different nations. For example, in Germany, armament exports are covered in the so-called War Weapons list which is a part of the War Weapons Control Law. The exports of other goods are covered by the German Export List. **Dual-use items,** which are goods useful for both military and civilian purposes, are then controlled by the Joint List of the European Union.[75] In the United States, the export control system is based on the Export Administration Act and the Munitions Control Act. These laws control all export of goods, services, and ideas from the United States. The determinants for controls are national security, foreign policy, short supply, and nuclear nonproliferation.

Export licenses are issued by the Department of Commerce, which administers the Export Administration Act.[76] In consultation with other government agencies—particularly the Departments of State, Defense, and Energy—the Commerce Department has drawn up a list of commodities whose export is considered particularly sensitive. In addition, a list of countries differentiates nations according to their political relationship with the United States. Finally, a list of individual firms that are considered to be unreliable trading partners because of past trade-diversion activities exists for each country.

After an export license application has been filed, specialists in the Department of Commerce match the commodity to be exported with the **critical commodities list,** a file containing information about products that are either particularly sensitive to national security or controlled for other purposes. The product is then matched with the country of destination and the recipient company. If no concerns regarding any of the three exist, an export license is issued. Control determinants and the steps in the decision process are summarized in Exhibit 1000.8

The international business repercussions of export controls are important. It is one thing to design an export-control system that is effective and that restricts those international business activities subject to important national concerns. It is, however, quite another when controls lose their effectiveness and when one country's firms are placed at a competitive disadvantage with firms in other countries whose control systems are less extensive or even nonexistent.

Exhibit 1000.8 *U.S. Export-Control System*

Determinants of Export Controls
- National Security
- Foreign Policy
- Short Supply
- Nuclear Nonproliferation

Decision Steps in the Export Licensing Process

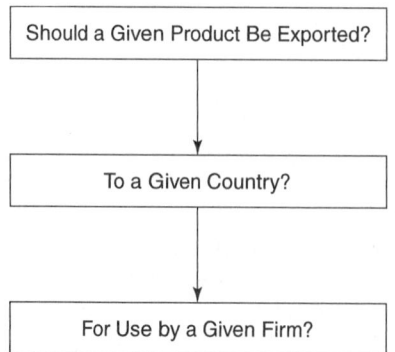

Export Control Problems and Conflicts

There are several key export-control problem areas for firms and policymakers. First is the continuing debate about what constitutes military-use products, civilian-use products, and **dual-use items.** Increasingly, goods are of a dual-use nature, typically commercial products that have potential military applications. The classic example is a pesticide factory that, some years later, is revealed to be a poison gas factory.[77] It is difficult enough to clearly define weapons. It is even more problematic to achieve consensus among nations regarding dual-use goods. For example, what about quite harmless screws if they are to be installed in rockets or telecommunications equipment used by the military? The problem becomes even greater with attempts to classify and list subcomponents and regulate their exportation. Individual country lists will lead to a distortion of competition if they deviate markedly from each other. The very task of drawing up any list is itself fraught with difficulty when it comes to components that are assembled. For example, the Patriot missile, which was deployed in the Persian Gulf War, consists, according to German law, only of simple parts whose individual export is permissible.

Even if governments were to agree on lists and continuously update them, the resulting control aspects would be difficult to implement. Controlling the transfer of components within and among companies across economic areas such as NAFTA or the European Union (EU) would significantly slow down business. Even more importantly, to subject only the export of physical goods to surveillance is insufficient. The transfer of knowledge and technology is of equal or greater importance. Weapons-relevant information easily can be exported via books, periodicals, and disks, therefore their content also would have to be controlled. Foreigners would need to be prevented from gaining access to such sources during visits or from making use of data networks across borders. Attendance at conferences and symposia would have to be regulated, the flow of data across national borders would have to be controlled, and today's communication systems and highways such as the Internet would have to be scrutinized. All these concerns have led to the emergence of controls of **deemed exports.** These controls address people rather than products in those instances where knowledge transfer could lead to a breach of export restrictions.

Conflicts also result from the desire of nations to safeguard their own economic interests. Due to different industrial structures, these interests vary between nations. For example, Germany, with a strong world-market position in machine tools, motors, and chemical raw materials, will think differently about manufacturing equipment controls than a country such as the United States, which sees computers as an area of its competitive advantage.

These problems and conflicts seem to ensure that dissent and disagreement in the export control field are unlikely to decrease, but rather will multiply in the future. As long as regulations are not harmonized internationally, firms will need to be highly sensitive to different and perhaps rapidly changing export control regimens.

Regulating International Business Behavior

Home countries may implement special laws and regulations to ensure that the international business behavior of firms headquartered in them is conducted within moral and ethical boundaries considered appropriate. The definition of appropriateness may vary from country to country and from government to government. Therefore, the content, enforcement, and impact of such regulations on firms may vary substantially among nations. As a result, the international manager must walk a careful line, balancing the expectations held in different countries.

One major area in which nations attempt to govern international business activities involves **boycotts.** Caught in a web of governmental activity, firms may be forced either to lose business or to pay substantial fines. This is especially true if the firm's products are competitive yet not unique, so that the supplier can opt to purchase them elsewhere. The heightening of such conflict can sometimes force companies to search for new, and possibly risky ways to circumvent the law or to totally withdraw operations from a country.

Another area of regulatory activity affecting the international business efforts of firms is **antitrust laws.** These laws often apply to international operations as well as to domestic business. In many countries, antitrust agencies watch closely when a firm buys a company, engages in a joint venture with a foreign firm, or makes an agreement abroad with a competing firm in order to ensure that the action does not result in restraint of competition.

Given the increase in worldwide cooperation among companies, however, the wisdom of extending antitrust legislation to international activities is being questioned. Some limitations to these tough antitrust provisions were already implemented decades ago. For example, in the United States the **Webb-Pomerene Act** of 1918 excludes from antitrust prosecution firms cooperating to develop foreign markets. This law was passed as part of an effort to aid export efforts in the face of strong foreign competition by oligopolies and monopolies. The exclusion of international activities from antitrust regulation was further enhanced by the Export Trading Company Act of 1982, which ensures that cooperating firms are not exposed to the threat of treble damages. Further steps to loosen the application of antitrust laws to international business are under consideration because of increased competition from strategic alliances and global megacorporations.

Firms operating abroad are also affected by laws against **bribery** and **corruption.** In many countries, payments or favors are a way of life, and "a greasing of the wheels" is expected in return for government services. As a result, many companies doing business internationally routinely are forced to pay bribes or do favors for foreign officials in order to gain contracts. Even in the late 1990s, the British Chamber of Commerce reported that bribery and corruption was a problem for 14 percent of exporters.[78] In the 1970s, a major national debate erupted in the United States about these business practices, led by arguments that U.S. firms have an ethical and moral leadership obligation and that contracts won through bribes do not reflect competitive market activity. As a result, the **Foreign Corrupt Practices Act** was passed in 1977, making it a crime for U.S. executives of publicly traded firms to bribe a foreign official in order to obtain business.

A number of U.S. firms have complained about the act, arguing that it hinders their efforts to compete internationally against companies whose home countries have no such antibribery laws. The problem is one of ethics versus practical needs and, to some extent, of the amounts involved. For example, it may be hard to draw the line between providing a generous tip and paying a bribe in order to speed up a business transaction. Many business executives believe that the United States should not apply its moral principles to other societies and cultures in which bribery and corruption are endemic. To compete internationally, executives argue, they must be free to use the most common methods of competition in the host country.

On the other hand, applying different standards to executives and firms based on whether they do business abroad or domestically is difficult to do. Also, bribes may open the way for shoddy performance and loose moral standards among executives and employees and may result in a spreading of general unethical business practices. Unrestricted bribery could result in firms concentrating on how to bribe best rather than on how to best produce and market their products. Typically, international businesses that use bribery fall into three categories: those who bribe to counterbalance the poor quality of their products or their high price; those who bribe to create a market for their unneeded goods; and, in the bulk of cases, those who bribe to stay competitive with other firms that bribe.[79] In all three of these instances, the customer is served poorly, the prices increase, and the transaction does not reflect economic competitiveness.

The international business manager must carefully distinguish between reasonable ways of doing business internationally—that is, complying with foreign expectations—and outright bribery and corruption. To assist the manager in this task, the 1988 Trade Act clarifies the applicability of the Foreign Corrupt Practices legislation. The revisions outline when a manager is expected to know about violation of the act, and they draw a distinction between the facilitation of routine governmental actions and governmental policy decisions. Routine actions concern issues such as the obtaining of permits and licenses, the processing of governmental papers (such as visas and work orders), the providing of mail and phone service, and the loading and unloading of cargo. Policy decisions refer mainly to situations in which the obtaining or retaining of a contract is at stake. While the facilitation of routine actions is not prohibited, the illegal influencing of policy decisions can result in the imposition of severe fines and penalties. The risks inherent in bribery have grown since 1999, when the Organization for Economic Cooperation and Development (OECD) adopted a treaty criminalizing the bribery of foreign public officials, moving well beyond its previous discussions, which only sought to outlaw the tax deductibility of improper payments. The Organization of American States (OAS) has also officially condemned bribery. Similarly, the World Trade Organization (WTO) has decided to consider placing bribery rules on its agenda. In addition, nongovernmental organizations such as Transparency International are conducting widely publicized efforts to highlight corruption and bribery and even to rank countries on a Corruption Perceptions Index.

These issues place managers in the position of having to choose between home-country regulations and foreign business practices. This choice is made even more difficult because diverging standards of behavior are applied to businesses in different countries. However, the gradually emerging consensus among international organizations may eventually level the playing field.

A final, major issue that is critical for international business managers is that of general standards of behavior and ethics. Increasingly, public concerns are raised about such issues as environmental protection, global warming, pollution, and moral behavior. However, these issues are not of the same importance in every country. What may be frowned upon or even illegal in one nation may be customary or at least acceptable in others. For example, the cutting down of the Brazilian rainforest may be acceptable to the government of Brazil, but scientists and concerned consumers may object vehemently because of the effect on global warming and other climatic changes. The export of U.S. tobacco products may be legal but results in accusations of exporting death to developing nations. China may use prison labor in producing products for export, but U.S. law prohibits the importation of such products. Mexico may permit the use of low safety standards for workers, but the buyers of Mexican products may object to the resulting dangers.

International firms must understand the conflicts in standards and should assert leadership in implementing change. Not everything that is legally possible should be exploited for profit. By acting on existing, leading-edge knowledge and standards, firms will be able to benefit in the long term through consumer goodwill and the avoidance of later recriminations.

International Trade and Investment

The Theory of International Trade

Topics include classical trade theory, factor proportions trade theory, product ranges theory, product cycle theory, and the new trade theory.

Classical Trade Theory

International trade is expected to improve the productivity of industry and the welfare of consumers. The question of why countries trade has proven difficult to answer. Since the second half of the 18th century, academicians have tried to understand not only the motivations and benefits of international trade, but also why some countries grow faster and wealthier than others through trade. Exhibit 1000.9 provides an overview of the evolutionary path of trade theory since the fall of mercantilism. Although somewhat simplified, it shows the line of development of the major theories put forward over the past two centuries. It also serves as an early indication of the path of modern theory: the shifting focus from the country to the firm, from cost of production to the market as a whole, and from the perfect to the imperfect market.

The Theory of Absolute Advantage

Generally considered the father of economics, Adam Smith published *The Wealth of Nations* in 1776 in London. In this book, Smith attempted to explain the process by which markets and production actually operate in society. Smith's two main areas of contribution, *absolute advantage* and the *division of labor* were fundamental to trade theory.

Production, the creation of a product for exchange, always requires the use of society's primary element of value, human labor. Smith noted that some countries, owing to the skills of their workers or the quality of their natural resources, could produce the same products as others with fewer labor-hours. He termed this efficiency **absolute advantage.**

Adam Smith observed the production processes of the early stages of the Industrial Revolution in England and recognized the fundamental changes that were occurring in production. In previous states of society, a worker performed all stages of a production process, with resulting output that was little more than sufficient for the worker's own needs. The factories of the industrializing world were, however, separating the production process into distinct stages, in which each stage would be performed exclusively by one individual, the **division of labor.** This specialization increased the production of workers and industries.

Adam Smith then extended his division of labor in the production process to a division of labor and specialized product across countries. Each country would specialize in a product for which it was uniquely suited. More would be produced for less. Thus, by each country specializing in products for which it possessed absolute advantage, countries could produce more in total and exchange products—trade—for goods that were cheaper in price than those produced at home.

The Theory of Comparative Advantage

Although Smith's work was instrumental in the development of economic theories about trade and production, it did not answer some fundamental questions about trade. First, Smith's trade relied on a country possessing absolute advantage in production, but did not explain what gave rise to the production advantages. Second, if a country did not possess absolute advantage in any product, could it (or would it) trade?

Exhibit 1000.9 *The Evolution of Trade Theory*

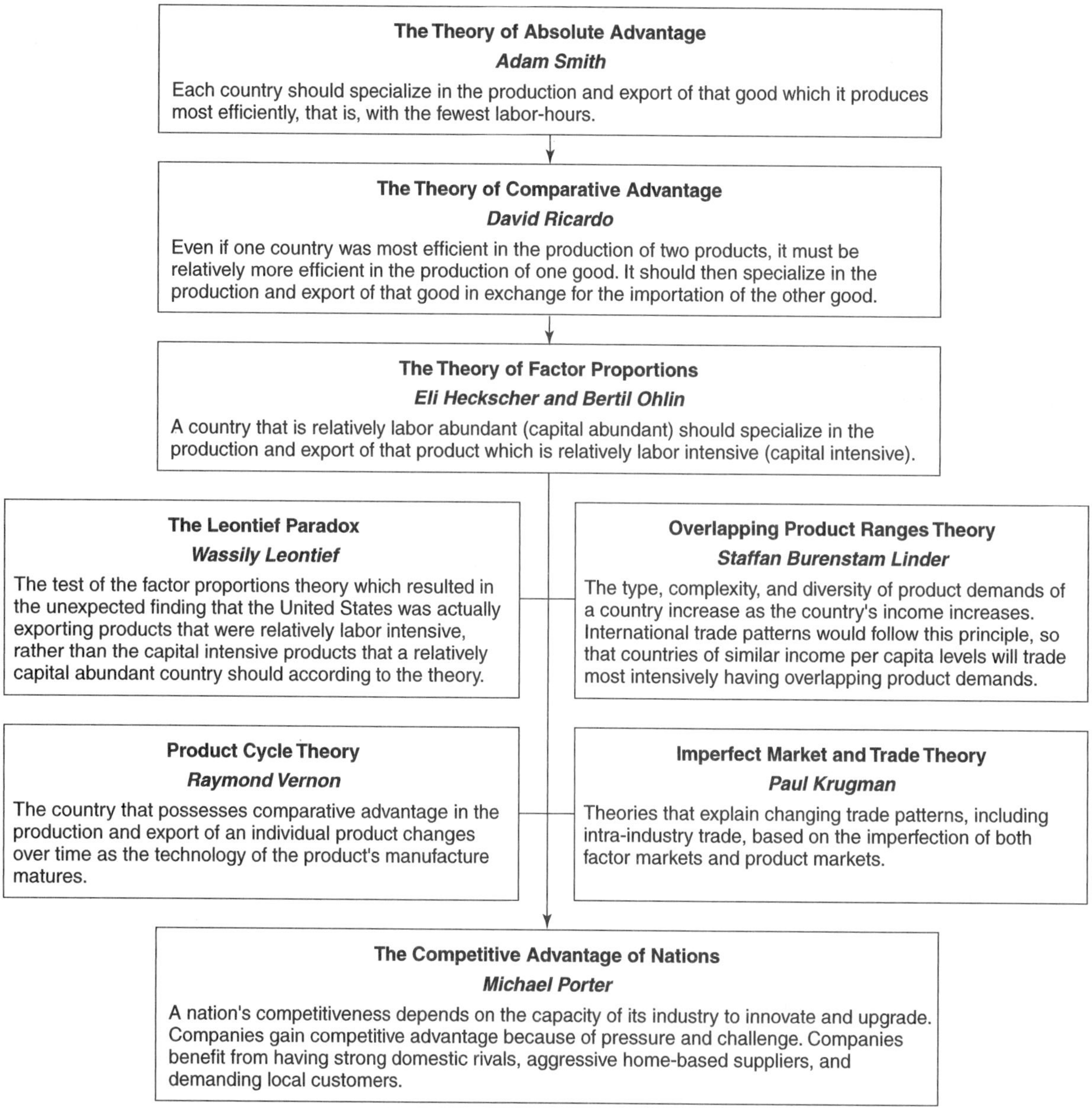

The Theory of Absolute Advantage
Adam Smith
Each country should specialize in the production and export of that good which it produces most efficiently, that is, with the fewest labor-hours.

The Theory of Comparative Advantage
David Ricardo
Even if one country was most efficient in the production of two products, it must be relatively more efficient in the production of one good. It should then specialize in the production and export of that good in exchange for the importation of the other good.

The Theory of Factor Proportions
Eli Heckscher and Bertil Ohlin
A country that is relatively labor abundant (capital abundant) should specialize in the production and export of that product which is relatively labor intensive (capital intensive).

The Leontief Paradox
Wassily Leontief
The test of the factor proportions theory which resulted in the unexpected finding that the United States was actually exporting products that were relatively labor intensive, rather than the capital intensive products that a relatively capital abundant country should according to the theory.

Overlapping Product Ranges Theory
Staffan Burenstam Linder
The type, complexity, and diversity of product demands of a country increase as the country's income increases. International trade patterns would follow this principle, so that countries of similar income per capita levels will trade most intensively having overlapping product demands.

Product Cycle Theory
Raymond Vernon
The country that possesses comparative advantage in the production and export of an individual product changes over time as the technology of the product's manufacture matures.

Imperfect Market and Trade Theory
Paul Krugman
Theories that explain changing trade patterns, including intra-industry trade, based on the imperfection of both factor markets and product markets.

The Competitive Advantage of Nations
Michael Porter
A nation's competitiveness depends on the capacity of its industry to innovate and upgrade. Companies gain competitive advantage because of pressure and challenge. Companies benefit from having strong domestic rivals, aggressive home-based suppliers, and demanding local customers.

David Ricardo, in his 1819 work entitled *On the Principles of Political Economy and Taxation,* sought to take the basic ideas set down by Smith a few steps further. Ricardo noted that even if a country possessed absolute advantage in the production of two products, it still must be relatively more efficient than the other country in one good's production than the other. Ricardo termed this the **comparative advantage.** Each country would then possess comparative advantage in the production of one of the two products, and both countries would then benefit by specializing completely in one product and trading for the other.

A Numerical Example of Classical Trade Theory

To fully understand the theories of absolute advantage and comparative advantage, consider the following example. Two countries, France and England, produce only two products, wheat and cloth (or beer and pizza, guns and butter, and so forth). The relative efficiency of each country in the production of the two products is measured by comparing the number of labor-hours needed to produce one unit of each product. Exhibit 1000.10 provides an efficiency comparison of the two countries.

Exhibit 1000.10 *Absolute Advantage and Comparative Advantage**

Country	Wheat	Cloth
England	2	4
France	4	2

- England has absolute advantage in the production of wheat. It requires fewer labor-hours (2 being less than 4) for England to produce one unit of wheat.
- France has absolute advantage in the production of cloth. It requires fewer labor-hours (2 being less than 4) for France to produce one unit of cloth.
- England has comparative advantage in the production of wheat. If England produces one unit of wheat, it is forgoing the production of 2/4 (0.50) of a unit of cloth. If France produces one unit of wheat, it is forgoing the production of 4/2 (2.00) of a unit of cloth. England therefore has the lower opportunity cost of producing wheat.
- France has comparative advantage in the production of cloth. If England produces one unit of cloth, it is forgoing the production of 4/2 (2.00) of a unit of wheat. If France produces one unit of cloth, it is forgoing the production of 2/4 (0.50) of a unit of wheat. France therefore has the lower opportunity cost of producing cloth.

*Labor-hours per unit of output.

England is obviously more efficient in the production of wheat. Whereas it takes France four labor-hours to produce one unit of wheat, it takes England only two hours to produce the same unit of wheat. France takes twice as many labor-hours to produce the same output. England has absolute advantage in the production of wheat. France needs two labor-hours to produce a unit of cloth that it takes England four labor-hours to produce. England therefore requires two more labor-hours than France to produce the same unit of cloth. France has absolute advantage in the production of cloth. The two countries are exactly opposite in relative efficiency of production.

David Ricardo took the logic of absolute advantages in production one step further to explain how countries could exploit their own advantages and gain from international trade. Comparative advantage, according to Ricardo, was based on what was given up or traded off in producing one product instead of the other. In this numerical example, England needs only two-fourths as many labor-hours to produce a unit of wheat as France, while France needs only two-fourths as many labor-hours to produce a unit of cloth. England therefore has comparative advantage in the production of wheat, while France has comparative advantage in the production of cloth. A country cannot possess comparative advantage in the production of both products, so each country has an economic role to play in international trade.

Concluding Points about Classical Trade Theory

Classical trade theory contributed much to the understanding of how production and trade operates in the world economy. Although like all economic theories they are often criticized for being unrealistic or out of date, the purpose of a theory is to simplify reality so that the basic elements of the logic can be seen. Several of these simplifications have continued to provide insight in understanding international business.

- **Division of labor.** Adam Smith's explanation of how industrial societies can increase output using the same labor-hours as in preindustrial society is fundamental to our thinking even today. Smith extended this specialization of the efforts of a worker to the specialization of a nation.
- **Comparative advantage.** David Ricardo's extension of Smith's work explained for the first time how countries that seemingly had no obvious reason for trade could individually specialize in producing what they did best and trade for products they did not produce.
- **Gains from trade.** The theory of comparative advantage argued that nations could improve the welfare of their populations through international trade. A nation could actually achieve consumption levels beyond what it could produce by itself. To this day this is one of the fundamental principles underlying the arguments for all countries to strive to expand and "free" world trade.

Factor Proportions Trade Theory

Trade theory changed drastically in the first half of the 20th century. The theory developed by the Swedish economist Eli Heckscher and later expanded by his former student Bertil Ohlin formed the theory of international trade that is still widely accepted today, **factor proportions theory.**

Exhibit 1000.11 *Factor Proportions in Production*

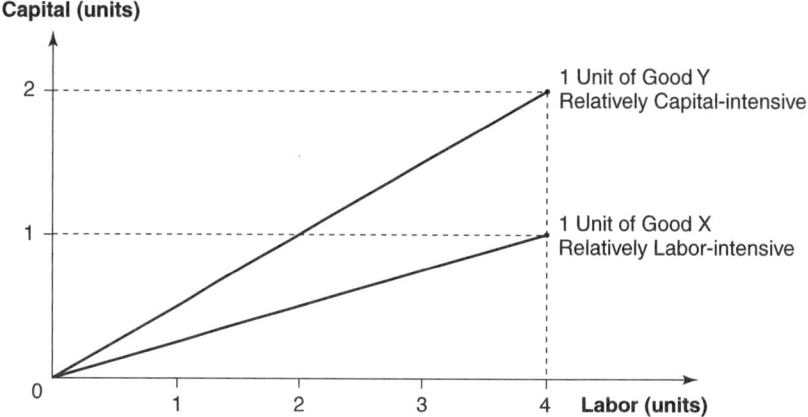

Factor Intensity in Production

The Heckscher-Ohlin theory considered two **factors of production,** labor and capital. Technology determines the way they combine to form a good. Different goods required different proportions of the two factors of production.

Exhibit 1000.11 illustrates what it means to describe a good by its factor proportions. The production of one unit of good X requires 4 units of labor and 1 unit of capital. At the same time, to produce 1 unit of good Y requires 4 units of labor and 2 units of capital. Good X therefore requires more units of labor per unit of capital (4 to 1) relative to Y (4 to 2). X is therefore classified as a relatively labor-intensive product, and Y is relatively capital intensive. These **factor intensities,** or **proportions,** are truly relative and are determined only on the basis of what product X requires relative to product Y and not to the specific numbers of labor to capital.

It is easy to see how the factor proportions of production differ substantially across goods. For example, the manufacturing of leather footwear is still a relatively labor-intensive process, even with the most sophisticated leather treatment and patterning machinery. Other goods, such as computer memory chips, however, although requiring some highly skilled labor, require massive quantities of capital for production. These large capital requirements include the enormous sums needed for research and development and the manufacturing facilities needed for clean production to ensure the extremely high quality demanded in the industry.

According to factor proportions theory, factor intensities depend on the state of technology—the current method of manufacturing a good. The theory assumes that the same technology of production would be used for the same goods in all countries. It is not, therefore, differences in the efficiency of production that will determine trade between countries as it did in classical theory. Classical theory implicitly assumes that technology or the productivity of labor is different across countries. Otherwise, there would be no logical explanation why one country requires more units of labor to produce a unit of output than another country. Factor proportions theory assumes no such productivity differences.

Factor Endowments, Factor Prices, and Comparative Advantage

If there is no difference in technology or productivity of factors across countries, what, then, determines comparative advantage in production and export? The answer is that factor prices determine cost differences. And these prices are determined by the endowments of labor and capital the country possesses. The theory assumes that labor and capital are immobile; factors cannot move across borders. Therefore, the country's endowment determines the relative costs of labor and capital as compared with other countries.

Using these assumptions, factor proportions theory states that a country should specialize in the production and export of those products that use intensively its relatively abundant factor.

- A country that is relatively labor abundant should specialize in the production of relatively labor-intensive goods. It should then export those labor-intensive goods in exchange for capital-intensive goods.
- A country that is relatively capital abundant should specialize in the production of relatively capital-intensive goods. It should then export those capital-intensive goods in exchange for labor-intensive goods.

The Leontief Paradox

One of the most famous tests of any economic or business theory occurred in 1950, when economist Wassily Leontief tested whether the factor proportions theory could be used to explain the types of goods the United States imported and exported. Leontief's premise was the following:

> A widely shared view on the nature of the trade between the United States and the rest of the world is derived from what appears to be a common sense assumption that this country has a comparative advantage in the production of commodities which require for their manufacture large quantities of capital and relatively small amounts of labor. Our economic relationships with other countries are supposed to be based mainly on the export of such "capital intensive" goods in exchange for forgoing products which—if we were to make them at home—would require little capital but large quantities of American labor. Since the United States possesses a relatively large amount of capital—so goes this oft-repeated argument—and a comparatively small amount of labor, direct domestic production of such "labor intensive" products would be uneconomical; we can much more advantageously obtain them from abroad in exchange for our capital intensive products.[80]

Leontief first had to devise a method to determine the relative amounts of labor and capital in a good. His solution, known as **input-output analysis,** was an accomplishment on its own. Input-output analysis is a technique of decomposing a good into the values and quantities of the labor, capital, and other potential factors employed in the good's manufacture. Leontief then used this methodology to analyze the labor and capital content of all U.S. merchandise imports and exports. The hypothesis was relatively straightforward: U.S. exports should be relatively capital intensive (use more units of capital relative to labor) than U.S. imports. Leontief's results were, however, a bit of a shock.

Leontief found that the products that U.S. firms exported were relatively more labor intensive than the products the United States imported.[81] It seemed that if the factor proportions theory was true, the United States is a relatively labor-abundant country! Alternatively, the theory could be wrong. Neither interpretation of the results was acceptable to many in the field of international trade.

A variety of explanations and continuing studies have attempted to solve what has become known as the **Leontief Paradox.** At first, it was thought to have been simply a result of the specific year (1947) of the data. However, the same results were found with different years and data sets. Second, it was noted that Leontief did not really analyze the labor and capital contents of imports but rather the labor and capital contents of the domestic equivalents of these imports. It was possible that the United States was actually producing the products in a more capital-intensive fashion than were the countries from which it also imported the manufactured goods.[82] Finally, the debate turned to the need to distinguish different types of labor and capital. For example, several studies attempted to separate labor factors into skilled labor and unskilled labor. These studies have continued to show results more consistent with what the factor proportions theory would predict for country trade patterns.

Linder's Overlapping Product Ranges Theory

The difficulties in empirically validating the factor proportions theory led many in the 1960s and 1970s to search for new explanations of the determinants of trade between countries. The work of Staffan Burenstam Linder focused not on the production or supply side, but instead on the preferences of consumers—the demand side. Linder acknowledged that in the natural-resource–based industries, trade was indeed determined by relative costs of production and factor endowments.

However, Linder argued, trade in manufactured goods was dictated not by cost concerns but rather by the similarity in product demands across countries. Linder's was a significant departure from previous theory and was based on two principles.

1. As income, or more precisely per-capita income, rises, the complexity and quality level of the products demanded by the country's residents also rises. The total range of product sophistication demanded by a country's residents is largely determined by its level of income.
2. The entrepreneurs directing the firms that produce society's needs are more knowledgeable about their own domestic market than about foreign markets. An entrepreneur could not be expected to effectively serve a foreign market that is significantly different from the domestic market because competitiveness comes from experience. A logical pattern would be for an entrepreneur to gain success and market share at home first then expand to foreign markets that are similar in their demands or tastes.

International trade in manufactured goods would then be influenced by similarity of demands. The countries that would see the most intensive trade are those with similar per-capita income levels, for they would possess a greater likelihood of overlapping product demands.

So where does trade come in? According to Linder, the overlapping ranges of product sophistication represent the products that entrepreneurs would know well from their home markets and could therefore potentially export and compete with in foreign markets. For example, the United States and Canada have almost parallel sophistication ranges, implying they would have a lot of common ground, overlapping product ranges, for intensive international trade and competition. They are quite similar in their per-capita income levels. But Mexico and the United States, or Mexico and Canada, would not. Mexico has a significantly different product-sophistication range as a result of a different per-capita income level.

The overlapping product ranges described by Linder would today be termed **market segments.** Not only was Linder's work instrumental in extending trade theory beyond cost considerations, but it also found a place in the field of international marketing.

International Investment and Product Cycle Theory

A very different path was taken by Raymond Vernon in 1966 concerning what is now termed **product cycle theory.** Diverging significantly from traditional approaches, Vernon focused on the product (rather than the country and the technology of its manufacture), not its factor proportions. Most striking was the appreciation of the role of information, knowledge, and the costs and power that go hand in hand with knowledge.

> ... we abandon the powerful simplifying notion that knowledge is a universal free good, and introduce it as an independent variable in the decision to trade or to invest.

Using many of the same basic tools and assumptions of factor proportions theory, Vernon added two technology-based premises to the factor-cost emphasis of existing theory.

1. Technical innovations leading to new and profitable products require large quantities of capital and highly skilled labor. These factors of production are predominantly available in highly industrialized capital-intensive countries.

2. These same technical innovations, both the product itself and more importantly the methods for its manufacture, go through three stages of maturation as the product becomes increasingly commercialized. As the manufacturing process becomes more standardized and low-skill labor-intensive, the comparative advantage in its production and export shifts across countries.

The Stages of the Product Cycle

Product cycle theory is both supply-side (cost of production) and demand-side (income levels of consumers) in its orientation. Each of these three stages that Vernon described combines differing elements of each.

STAGE I: THE NEW PRODUCT Innovation requires highly skilled labor and large quantities of capital for research and development. The product will normally be most effectively designed and initially manufactured near the parent firm and therefore in a highly industrialized market due to the need for proximity to information and the need for communication among the many different skilled-labor components required.

In this development stage, the product is nonstandardized. The production process requires a high degree of flexibility (meaning continued use of highly skilled labor). Costs of production are therefore quite high. The innovator at this stage is a monopolist and therefore enjoys all of the benefits of monopoly power, including the high profit margins required to repay the high development costs and expensive production process. Price elasticity of demand at this stage is low; high-income consumers buy it regardless of cost.

STAGE II: THE MATURING PRODUCT As production expands, its process becomes increasingly standardized. The need for flexibility in design and manufacturing declines, and therefore the demand for highly skilled labor declines. The innovating country increases its sales to other countries. Competitors with slight variations develop, putting downward pressure on prices and profit margins. Production costs are an increasing concern.

As competitors increase, as well as their pressures on price, the innovating firm faces critical decisions on how to maintain market share. Vernon argues that the firm faces a critical decision at this stage, either to lose market share to foreign-based manufacturers using lower-cost labor or to invest abroad to maintain its market share by exploiting the comparative advantages of factor costs in other countries. This is one of the first theoretical explanations of how trade and investment become increasingly intertwined.

STAGE III: THE STANDARDIZED PRODUCT In this final stage, the product is completely standardized in its manufacture. Thus, with access to capital on world capital markets, the country of production is simply the one with the cheapest unskilled labor. Profit margins are thin, and competition is fierce. The product has largely run its course in terms of profitability for the innovating firm.

The country of comparative advantage has therefore shifted as the technology of the product's manufacture has matured. The same product shifts in its location of production. The country possessing the product during that stage enjoys the benefits of net trade surpluses. But such advantages are fleeting, according to Vernon. As knowledge and technology continually change, so does the country of that product's comparative advantage.

Trade Implications of the Product Cycle

Product cycle theory shows how specific products were first produced and exported from one country but, through product and competitive evolution, shifted their location of production and export to other countries over time. As the product and the market for the product mature and change, the countries of its production and export shift.

The Contributions of Product Cycle Theory

Although interesting in its own right for increasing emphasis on technology's impact on product costs, product cycle theory was most important because it explained international investment. Not only did the theory recognize the mobility of capital across countries (breaking the traditional assumption of factor immobility), it shifted the focus from the country to the product. This made it important to match the product by its maturity stage with its production location to examine competitiveness.

Product cycle theory has many limitations. It is obviously most appropriate for technology-based products. These are the products that are most likely to experience the changes in production process as they grow and mature. Other products, either resource-based (such as minerals and other commodities) or services (which employ capital but mostly in the form of human capital), are not so easily characterized by stages of maturity. And product cycle theory is most relevant to products that eventually fall victim to mass production and therefore cheap labor forces. But, all things considered, product cycle theory served to breach a wide gap between the trade theories of old and the intellectual challenges of a new, more globally competitive market in which capital, technology, information, and firms themselves were more mobile.

Imperfect Markets and the New Trade Theory

Global trade developments in the 1980s and 1990s led to much criticism of the existing theories of trade. First, although there was rapid growth in trade, much of it was not explained by current theory. Secondly, the massive size of the merchandise trade deficit of the United States—and the associated decline of many U.S. firms in terms of international competitiveness—served as something of a country-sized lab experiment demonstrating what some critics termed the "bankruptcy of trade theory." Academics and policymakers alike looked for new explanations.

Two new contributions to trade theory were met with great interest. Paul Krugman, along with several colleagues, developed a theory of how trade is altered when markets are not perfectly competitive, or when production of specific products possess economies of scale. A second and very influential development was the growing work of Michael Porter, who examined the competitiveness of industries on a global basis, rather than relying on country-specific factors to determine competitiveness.

Economies of Scale and Imperfect Competition

Paul Krugman's theoretical developments once again focused on cost of production and how cost and price drive international trade. Using theoretical developments from microeconomics and market structure analysis, Krugman focused on two types of economics of scale, *internal economies of scale* and *external economies of scale*.[83]

INTERNAL ECONOMIES OF SCALE When the cost per unit of output depends on the size of an individual firm, the larger the firm the greater the scale benefits, and the lower the cost per unit. A firm possessing internal economies of scale could potentially monopolize an industry (creating an *imperfect market*), both domestically and internationally. If it produces more, lowering the cost per unit, it can lower the market price and sell more products, because it *sets* market prices.

The link between dominating a domestic industry and influencing international trade comes from taking this assumption of imperfect markets back to the original concept of comparative advantage. For this firm to expand sufficiently to enjoy its economies of scale, it must take resources away from other domestic industries in order to expand. A country then sees its own range of products in which it specializes narrowing, providing an opportunity for other countries to specialize in these so-called **abandoned product ranges.** Countries again search out and exploit comparative advantage.

A particularly powerful implication of internal economies of scale is that it provides an explanation of intra-industry trade, one area in which traditional trade theory had indeed seemed bankrupt. **Intra-industry trade (IIT)** is when a country seemingly imports and exports the same product, an idea that is obviously inconsistent with any of the trade theories put forward in the past three centuries. According to Krugman, internal economies of scale may lead a firm to specialize in a narrow product line (to produce the volume necessary for economies of scale cost benefits); other firms in other countries may produce products that are similarly narrow, yet extremely similar: product differentiation. If consumers in either country wish to buy both products, they will be importing and exporting products that are, for all intents and purposes, the same.[84]

Intra-industry trade has been studied in detail in the past decade. Intra-industry trade is measured with the Grubel-Lloyd Index, the ratio of imports and exports of the same product occurring between two trading nations. It is calculated as follows:

$$\text{Intra-Industry Trade Index}_i = \frac{|X_i - M_i|}{(X_i + M_i)}$$

where i is the product category and $|X - M|$ is the absolute value of net exports of that product (exports − imports). For example, if Sweden imports 100 heavy machines for its forest products industry from Finland, and at the same time exports to Finland 80 of the same type of equipment, IIT index would be:

$$\text{IIT Index} = \frac{|80 - 100|}{(80 + 100)} = 1 - 0.1111 = .89$$

The closer the index value to 1, the higher the level of intra-industry trade in that product category. The closer the index is to 0, the more one-way the trade between the countries exists, as traditional trade theory would predict.

Intra-industry trade is now thought to compose roughly 25 percent of global trade. And to its credit, intra-industry trade is increasingly viewed as having additive benefits to the fundamental benefits of comparative advantage. Intra-industry trade does allow some industrial segments in some countries to deepen their specialization while simultaneously allowing greater breadth of choices and commensurate benefits to consumers. Of course, one potentially disturbing characteristic of the growth in intra-industry trade is the potential for trade of all kinds to continue to expand in breadth and depth between the most industrialized countries (those producing the majority of the more complex manufactured goods) while those less industrialized nations do not see this added boost to trade growth.

EXTERNAL ECONOMIES OF SCALE When the cost per unit of output depends on the size of an industry, not the size of the individual firm, the industry of that country may produce at lower costs than the same industry that is smaller in size in other countries. A country can potentially dominate world markets in a particular product, not because it has one massive firm producing enormous quantities (for example, **Boeing**), but rather because it has many small firms that interact to create a large, competitive, critical mass (for example, semiconductors in Penang, Malaysia). No one firm need be all that large, but several small firms in total may create such a competitive industry that firms in other countries cannot ever break into the industry on a competitive basis.[85]

Unlike internal economies of scale, external economies of scale may not necessarily lead to imperfect markets, but they may result in an industry maintaining its dominance in its field in world markets. This provides an explanation as to why all industries do not necessarily always move to the country with the lowest-cost energy, resources, or labor. What gives rise to this critical mass of small firms and their interrelationships is a much more complex question. The work of Michael Porter provides a partial explanation of how these critical masses are sustained.

The Competitive Advantage of Nations

The focus of early trade theory was on the country or nation and its inherent, natural, or endowment characteristics that might give rise to increasing competitiveness. As trade theory evolved, it shifted its focus to the industry and product level, leaving the national-level competitiveness question somewhat behind. Recently, many have turned their attention to the question of how countries, governments, and even private industry can alter the conditions within a country to aid the competitiveness of its firms.

The leader in this area of research has been Michael Porter of Harvard. Porter argued that innovation is what drives and sustains competitiveness. A firm must avail itself of all dimensions of competition, which he categorized into four major components of "the diamond of national advantage."

1. *Factor conditions.* The appropriateness of the nation's factors of production to compete successfully in a specific industry. Porter notes that although these factor conditions are very important in the determination of trade, they are not the only source of competitiveness as suggested by the classical, or factor proportions, theories of trade. Most importantly for Porter, it is the ability of a nation to continually create, upgrade, and deploy its factors (such as skilled labor) that is important, not the initial endowment.

2. *Demand conditions.* The degree of health and competition the firm must face in its original home market. Firms that can survive and flourish in highly competitive and demanding local markets are much more likely to gain the competitive edge. Porter notes that it is the character of the market, not its size, that is paramount in promoting the continual competitiveness of the firm. And Porter translates *character* as demanding customers.

3. *Related and supporting industries.* The competitiveness of all related industries and suppliers to the firm. A firm that is operating within a mass of related firms and industries gains and maintains advantages through close working relationships, proximity to suppliers, and timeliness of product and information flows. The constant and close interaction is successful if it occurs not only in terms of physical proximity but also through the willingness of firms to work at it.

4. *Firm strategy, structure, and rivalry.* The conditions in the home-nation that either hinder or aid in the firm's creation and sustaining of international competitiveness. Porter notes that no single managerial, ownership, or operational strategy is universally appropriate. It depends on the fit and flexibility of what works for that industry in that country at that time.

These four points, as illustrated in Exhibit 1000.12 constitute what nations and firms must strive to "create and sustain through a highly localized process" to ensure their success.

Porter's emphasis on innovation as the source of competitiveness reflects an increased focus on the industry and products that we have seen in the past three decades. The acknowledgment that the nation is "more, not less, important" is to many eyes a welcome return to a positive role for government and even national-level private industry in encouraging international competitiveness. Including factor conditions as a cost component, demand conditions as a

Exhibit 1000.12 *Determinants of National Competitive Advantage: Porter's Diamond*

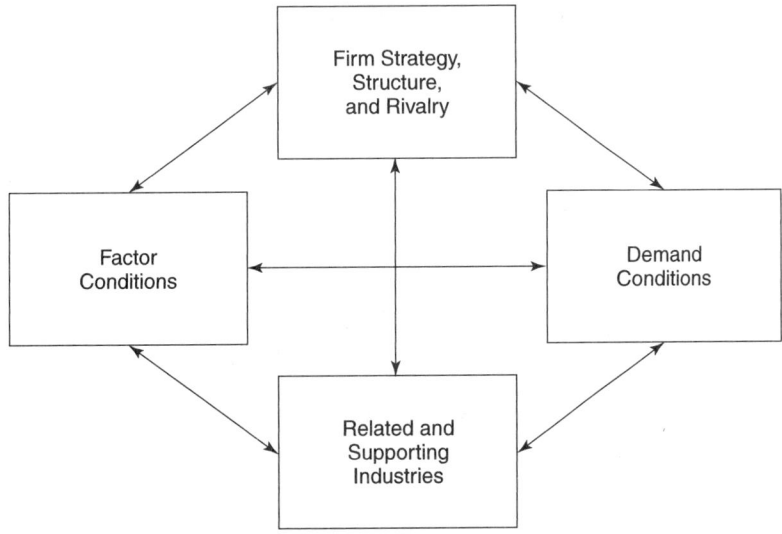

motivator of firm actions, and competitiveness all combine to include the elements of classical, factor proportions, product cycle, and imperfect competition theories in a pragmatic approach to the challenges that the global markets of the 21st century present to the firms of today.

The Theory of International Investment

Trade is the production of a good or service in one country and its sale to a buyer in another country. In fact, it is a firm (not a country) and a buyer (not a country) that are the subjects of trade, domestically or internationally. A firm is therefore attempting to access a market and its buyers. The producing firm wants to utilize its competitive advantage for growth and profit and can also reach this goal by international investment.[86]

Although this sounds easy enough, consider any of the following potholes on the road to investment success. Any of the following potholes may be avoided by producing within another country:

- Sales to some countries are difficult because of tariffs imposed on your good when it is entering. If you were producing within the country, your good would no longer be an import.
- Your good requires natural resources that are available only in certain areas of the world. It is therefore imperative that you have access to the natural resources. You can buy them from that country and bring them to your production process (import) or simply take the production to them.
- Competition is constantly pushing you to improve efficiency and decrease the costs of producing your good. You therefore may want to produce where it will be cheaper—cheaper capital, cheaper energy, cheaper natural resources, or cheaper labor. Many of these factors are still not mobile, and therefore you will go to them instead of bringing them to you.

There are thousands of reasons why a firm may want to produce in another country, and not necessarily in the country that is cheapest for production or the country where the final good is sold.

The subject of international investment arises from one basic idea: the mobility of capital. Although many of the traditional trade theories assumed the immobility of the factors of production, it is the movement of capital that has allowed **foreign direct investments** across the globe. If there is a competitive advantage to be gained, capital can and will get there.

The Theory of Foreign Direct Investment

What motivates a firm to go beyond exporting or licensing? What benefits does the multinational firm expect to achieve by establishing a physical presence in other countries? These are the questions that the theory of foreign direct investment has sought to answer. As with trade theory, the questions have remained largely the same over time, while the answers have continued to change. With hundreds of countries, thousands of firms, and millions of products and services, there is no question that the answer to such an enormous question will likely get messy.

The following overview of investment theory has many similarities to the preceding discussion of international trade. The theme is a global business environment that attempts to satisfy increasingly sophisticated consumer demands, while the means of production, resources, skills, and technology needed become more complex and competitive.

Firms as Seekers

A firm that expands across borders may be seeking any of a number of specific sources of profit or opportunity.

1. *Seeking resources.* There is no question that much of the initial foreign direct investment of the 18th and 19th centuries was the result of firms seeking unique and valuable natural resources for their products. Whether it be the copper resources of Chile, the linseed oils of Indonesia, or the petroleum resources spanning the Middle East, firms establishing permanent presences around the world are seeking access to the resources at the core of their businesses.

2. *Seeking factor advantages.* The resources needed for production are often combined with other advantages that are inherent in the country of production. The same low-cost labor at the heart of classical trade theory provides incentives for firms to move production to countries possessing these factor advantages. As noted by Vernon's product cycle theory, the same firms may move their own production to locations of factor advantages as the products and markets mature.
3. *Seeking knowledge.* Firms may attempt to acquire other firms in other countries for the technical or competitive skills they possess. Alternatively, companies may locate in and around centers of industrial enterprise unique to their specific industry, such as the footwear industry of Milan or the semiconductor industry of the Silicon Valley of California.
4. *Seeking security.* Firms continue to move internationally as they seek political stability or security. For example, Mexico has experienced a significant increase in foreign direct investment as a result of the tacit support of the United States, Canada, and Mexico itself as reflected by the North American Free Trade Agreement.
5. *Seeking markets.* Not the least of the motivations, the ability to gain and maintain access to markets is of paramount importance to multinational firms. Whether following the principles of Linder, in which firms learn from their domestic market and use that information to go international, or the principles of Porter, which emphasize the character of the domestic market as dictating international competitiveness, foreign-market access is necessary.

Firms as Exploiters of Imperfections

Much of the investment theory developed in the past three decades has focused on the efforts of multinational firms to exploit the imperfections in factor and product markets created by governments. The work of Hymer, Kindleberger, and Caves noted that many of the policies of governments create imperfections. These market imperfections cover the entire range of supply and demand of the market: trade policy (tariffs and quotas), tax policies and incentives, preferential purchasing arrangements established by governments themselves, and financial restrictions on the access of foreign firms to domestic capital markets.

1. *Imperfections in access.* Many of the world's developing countries have long sought to create domestic industry by restricting imports of competitive products in order to allow smaller, less competitive domestic firms to grow and prosper—so-called **import substitution** policies. Multinational firms have sought to maintain their access to these markets by establishing their own productive presence within the country, effectively bypassing the tariff restriction.
2. *Imperfections in factor mobility.* Other multinational firms have exploited the same sources of comparative advantage identified throughout this chapter—the low-cost resources or factors often located in less-developed countries or countries with restrictions on the mobility of labor and capital. However, combining the mobility of capital with the immobility of low-cost labor has characterized much of the foreign direct investment seen throughout the developing world over the past 50 years.
3. *Imperfections in management.* The ability of multinational firms to successfully exploit or at least manage these imperfections still relies on their ability to gain an "advantage." Market advantages or powers are seen in international markets as in domestic markets: cost advantages, economies of scale and scope, product differentiation, managerial or marketing technique and knowledge, and financial resources and strength.

All these imperfections are the things of which competitive dreams are made. The multinational firm needs to find these in some form or another to justify the added complexities and costs of international investments.

Firms as Internalizers

Questions still plague the field of foreign direct investment: Why can't all of the advantages and imperfections mentioned be achieved through management contracts or licensing agreements? Why is it necessary for *the firm itself* to establish a physical presence in the country? What pushes the multinational firm further down the investment decision tree?

The research of Buckley and Casson and Dunning has attempted to answer these questions by focusing on nontransferable sources of competitive advantage—proprietary information possessed by the firm and its people. Many advantages firms possess center around their hands-on knowledge of producing a good or providing a service. By establishing their own multinational operations they can internalize the production, thus keeping confidential the information that is at the core of the firm's competitiveness. **Internalization** is preferable to the use of arms-length arrangements such as management contracts or licensing agreements. They either do not allow the effective transmission of the knowledge or represent too serious a threat to the loss of the knowledge to allow the firm to successfully achieve the hoped-for benefits of international investment.

International Payments

Balance of Payments

International business transactions occur in many different forms over the course of a year. The measurement of all international economic transactions between the residents of a country and foreign residents is called the **balance of payments (BOP)**.[87] Government policymakers need such measures of economic activity to evaluate the general competitiveness of domestic industry, to set exchange-rate or interest-rate policies or goals, and for many other purposes. Individuals and businesses use various BOP measures to gauge the growth and health of specific types of trade or financial transactions by country and regions of the world against the home country.

International transactions take many forms. Each of the following examples is an international economic transaction that is counted and captured in the U.S. balance of payments.

- U.S. imports of **Honda** automobiles, which are manufactured in Japan.
- A U.S.-based firm, **Bechtel,** is hired to manage the construction of a major water-treatment facility in the Middle East.
- The U.S. subsidiary of a French firm, **Saint Gobain,** pays profits (dividends) back to the parent firm in Paris.
- **Daimler-Benz,** the well-known German automobile manufacturer, purchases a small automotive parts manufacturer outside Chicago, Illinois.
- An American tourist purchases a hand-blown glass figurine in Venice, Italy.
- The U.S. government provides grant financing of military equipment for its NATO (North Atlantic Treaty Organization) military ally, Turkey.
- A Canadian dentist purchases a U.S. Treasury bill through an investment broker in Cleveland, Ohio.

These are just a small sample of the hundreds of thousands of international transactions that occur each year. The balance of payments provides a systematic method for the classification of all of these transactions. There is one rule of thumb that will always aid in the understanding of BOP accounting: watch the direction of the movement of money.

The balance of payments is composed of a number of subaccounts that are watched quite closely by groups as diverse as investors on Wall Street, farmers in Iowa, politicians on Capitol Hill, and in board members across America. These groups track and analyze the two major subaccounts, the **current account** and the **capital/financial account,** on a continuing basis. Before describing these two subaccounts and the balance of payments as a whole, it is necessary to understand the rather unusual features of how balance of payments accounting is conducted.

Fundamentals of Balance of Payments Accounting

The balance of payments must balance. If it does not, something has either not been counted or has not been counted properly. It is therefore improper to state that the BOP is in disequilibrium. It cannot be. The supply and demand for a country's currency may be imbalanced, but that is not the same thing. Subaccounts of the BOP, such as the merchandise trade balance, may be imbalanced, but the entire BOP of a single country is always balanced.

There are three main elements to the process of measuring international economic activity: (1) identifying what is and is not an international economic transaction; (2) understanding how the flow of goods, services, assets, and money creates debits and credits to the overall BOP; and (3) understanding the bookkeeping procedures for BOP accounting, called double entry.

Defining International Economic Transactions

Identifying international transactions is ordinarily not difficult. The export of merchandise, goods such as trucks, machinery, computers, telecommunications equipment, and so forth, is obviously an international transaction. Imports such as French wine, Japanese cameras, and German automobiles are also clearly international transactions. But this merchandise trade is only a portion of the thousands of different international transactions that occur in the United States or any other country each year.

Many other international transactions are not so obvious. The purchase of a glass figure in Venice, Italy, by an American tourist is classified as a U.S. merchandise import. In fact, all expenditures made by American tourists around the globe that are for goods or services (meals, hotel accommodations, and so forth) are recorded in the U.S. balance of payments as imports of travel services in the current account. The purchase of a U.S. Treasury bill by a foreign resident is an international financial transaction and is dutifully recorded in the capital account of the U.S. balance of payments.

The BOP as a Flow Statement

The BOP is often misunderstood because many people believe it to be a balance sheet, rather than a cash flow statement. By recording all international transactions over a period of time, it is tracking the continuing flow of purchases and payments between a country and all other countries. It does not add up the value of all assets and liabilities of a country like a balance sheet does for an individual firm.

Two types of business transactions dominate the balance of payments.

1. *Real Assets.* The exchange of goods (for example, automobiles, computers, watches, textiles) and services (for example, banking services, consulting services, travel services) for other goods and services (barter) or for the more common type of payment, money.

2. *Financial Assets.* The exchange of financial claims (for example, stocks, bonds, loans, purchases or sales of companies) in exchange for other financial claims or money.

Although assets can be separated as to whether they are real or financial, it is often easier to simply think of all assets as being goods that can be bought and sold. An American tourist's purchase of a handwoven area rug in a shop in Bangkok is not all that different from a Wall Street banker buying a British government bond for investment purposes.

BOP Accounting: Double-Entry Bookkeeping

The balance of payments employs an accounting technique called **double-entry bookkeeping.** Double-entry bookkeeping is the age-old method of accounting in which every transaction produces a debit and a credit of the same amount simultaneously. It has to. A debit is created whenever an asset is increased, a liability is decreased, or an expense is increased. Similarly, a credit is created whenever an asset is decreased, a liability is increased, or an expense is decreased.

An example clarifies this process. A U.S. retail store imports from Japan $2 million worth of consumer electronics. A negative entry is made in the merchandise-import subcategory of the current account in the amount of $2 million. Simultaneously, a positive entry of the same $2 million is made in the capital account for the transfer of a $2 million bank account to the Japanese manufacturer. Obviously, the result of hundreds of thousands of such transactions and entries should theoretically result in a perfect balance.

The Accounts of the Balance of Payments

The balance of payments is composed of two primary subaccounts, the *Current Account* and the *Capital/Financial Account*. In addition, the *Official Reserves Account* tracks government currency transactions, and a fourth statistical subaccount, the *Net Errors and Omissions Account*, is produced to preserve the balance in the BOP.

The Current Account

The Current Account includes all international economic transactions with income or payment flows occurring within the year, the current period. The Current Account consists of four subcategories.

1. *Goods trade.* This is the export and import of goods. Merchandise trade is the oldest and most traditional form of international economic activity. Although many countries depend on imports of many goods (as they should according to the theory of comparative advantage), they also normally work to preserve either a balance of goods trade or even a surplus.
2. *Services Trade.* This is the export and import of services. Some common international services are financial services provided by banks to foreign importers and exporters, travel services of airlines, and construction services of domestic firms in other countries. For the major industrial countries, this subaccount has shown the fastest growth in the past decade.
3. *Income.* This category is predominantly *current income* associated with investments that were made in previous periods. If a U.S. firm created a subsidiary in South Korea to produce metal parts in a previous year, the proportion of net income that is paid back to the parent company in the current year (the dividend) constitutes current investment income. Additionally, wages and salaries paid to nonresident workers is also included in this category.
4. *Current Transfers.* Transfers are the financial settlements associated with the change in ownership of real resources or financial items. Any transfer between countries that is one-way, a gift, or a grant, is termed a *current transfer*. A common example of a current transfer would be funds provided by the United States government to aid in the development of a less-developed nation. Transfers associated with the transfer of fixed assets are included in a new separate account, the Capital Account, which now follows the Current Account. The contents of what previously had been called the capital account are now included within the Financial Account.

All countries possess some amount of trade, most of which is merchandise. Many smaller and less-developed countries have little in the way of service trade, or items that fall under the income or transfers subaccounts.

The Current Account is typically dominated by the first component described—the export and import of merchandise. For this reason, the *Balance on Trade* (BOT), which is so widely quoted in the business press in most countries, refers specifically to the balance of exports and imports of goods trade only. For a larger industrialized country, however, the BOT is somewhat misleading because service trade is not included; it may be opposite in sign on net, and it may actually be fairly large as well.

Exhibit 1000.13 summarizes the Current Account and its components for the United States for the 1996–1999 period. As illustrated, the U.S. goods trade balance has consistently been negative, but has been partially offset by the continuing surplus in services trade.

The Capital and Financial Account

The *Capital and Financial Account* of the balance of payments measures all international economic transactions of financial assets. It is divided into two major components, the Capital Account and the Financial Account.

- **The Capital Account.** The Capital Account is made up of transfers of financial assets and the acquisition and disposal of nonproduced/nonfinancial assets. The magnitude of capital transactions covered is of relatively minor amount, and will be included in principle in all of the following discussions of the Financial Account.
- **The Financial Account.** The Financial Account consists of three components: *direct investment, portfolio investment,* and *other asset investment*. Financial assets can be classified in a number of different ways including the length of the life of the asset (its maturity) and by the nature of the ownership (public or private). The Financial Account, however, uses a third way. It is classified by the degree of control over the assets or operations the claim represents: *portfolio investment,* where the investor has no control, or *direct investment,* where the investor exerts

Exhibit 1000.13 *The U.S. Current Account, 1996–1999 (billions of U.S. dollars)*

	1996	1997	1998	1999
Goods exports	614	682	672	687
Goods imports	−803	−876	−917	−1030
Goods trade balance (BOT)	−189	−195	−245	−343
Services trade credits	238	255	261	270
Services trade debits	−151	−167	−183	−191
Services trade balance	87	89	78	78
Income receipts	224	257	258	276
Income payments	−205	−251	−265	−295
Income balance	19	6	−6	−18
Current transfers, credits	9	8	9	9
Current transfers, debits	−49	−49	−53	−57
Net transfers	−40	−41	−44	−48
Current Account Balance	−123	−141	−217	−331

Source: Derived from International Monetary Fund's *Balance of Payments Statistics Yearbook 2000.*

Exhibit 1000.14 *The U.S. Financial Account and Components, 1996–1999 (billions of U.S. dollars)*

	1996	1997	1998	1999
Direct Investment				
Direct investment abroad	−92	−105	−146	−151
Direct investment in the United States	87	106	186	276
Net direct investment	−5	1	40	125
Portfolio Investment				
Assets, net	−150	−119	−136	−129
Liabilities, net	368	386	269	342
Net portfolio investment	218	267	133	214
Other Investment				
Other investment assets	−179	−264	−47	−159
Other investment liabilities	117	265	27	136
Net other investment	−61	1	−20	−24
Net Financial Account Balance	151	269	154	315

Source: Derived from International Monetary Fund's *Balance of Payments Statistics Yearbook 2000.*

some explicit degree of control over the assets. (The contents of the Financial Account are for all intents and purposes the same as those of the Capital Account under the IMF's BOP accounting framework used prior to 1996.)

Exhibit 1000.14 shows the major subcategories of the U.S. Financial Account balance from 1996–1999, *direct investment, portfolio investment,* and *other investments.*

1. *Direct investment.* This is the net balance of capital dispersed out of and into the United States for the purpose of exerting control over assets. For example, if a U.S. firm either builds a new automotive parts facility in another country or actually purchases a company in another country, this would fall under *direct investment* in the U.S. balance of payments accounts. When the capital flows out of the United States, it enters the balance of payments as a negative cash flow. If, however, foreign firms purchase firms in the United States (for example, **Sony** of Japan purchased **Columbia Pictures** in 1989) it is a capital inflow and enters the balance of payments positively. Whenever 10 percent or more of the voting shares in a U.S. company is held by foreign investors, the company is classified as the U.S. affiliate of a foreign company, and a *foreign direct investment.* Similarly, if U.S. investors hold 10 percent or more of the control in a company outside the United States, that company is considered the foreign affiliate of a U.S. company.

2. *Portfolio investment.* This is net balance of capital that flows in and out of the United States, but does not reach the 10 percent ownership threshold of direct investment. If a U.S. resident purchases shares in a Japanese firm, but does not attain the 10 percent threshold, it is considered a *portfolio investment* (and in this case an outflow of capital). The purchase or sale of debt securities (like U.S. Treasury bills) across borders is also classified as *portfolio investment* because debt securities by definition do not provide the buyer with ownership or control.
3. *Other investment assets/liabilities.* This final category consists of various short-term and long-term trade credits, cross-border loans from all types of financial institutions, currency deposits and bank deposits, and other accounts receivable and payable related to cross-border trade.

Current and Financial Account Balance Relationships

One of the basic economic and accounting relationships of the balance of payments is *the inverse relationship between the Current and Financial Accounts.* This inverse relationship is not accidental. The methodology of the balance of payments, double-entry bookkeeping, requires that the Current and Financial Accounts be offsetting. Countries experiencing large current account deficits "finance" these purchases through equally large surpluses in the Financial Account and vice versa.

Official Reserves Account

The **Official Reserves Account** is the total currency and metallic reserves held by official monetary authorities within the country. These reserves are normally composed of the major currencies used in international trade and financial transactions (so-called "hard currencies" like the U.S. dollar, German mark, and Japanese yen) and gold. Note that the official reserve account should offset the total of current account, capital account, financial account, and net errors and omissions account. If the total of these four accounts is negative (deficit), the reserve account should be positive (surplus), and vice versa.

The significance of official reserves depends generally on whether the country is operating under a **fixed exchange rate** regime or a **floating exchange rate** system. If a country's currency is fixed, this means that the government of the country officially declares that the currency is convertible into a fixed amount of some other currency. For example, for many years the South Korean won was fixed to the U.S. dollar at 484 won equal to 1 U.S. dollar. It is the government's responsibility to maintain this fixed rate (also called *parity rate*). If for some reason there is an excess supply of Korean won on the currency market, to prevent the value of the won from falling, the South Korean government must support the won's value by purchasing won on the open market (by spending its hard currency reserves, its *official reserves*) until the excess supply is eliminated. Under a floating rate system, the government possesses no such responsibility and the role of official reserves is diminished.

Net Errors and Omissions Account

As noted before, because Current Account and Financial Account entries are collected and recorded separately, errors or statistical discrepancies will occur. The **Net Errors and Omissions Account** (this is the title used by the International Monetary Fund) makes sure that the BOP actually balances.

The Balance of Payments and Economic Crises

The sum of cross-border international economic activity—the balance of payments—can be used by international managers to forecast economic conditions and, in some cases, the likelihood of economic crises. The mechanics of international economic crisis often follow a similar path of development.

1. A country that experiences rapidly expanding current account deficits will simultaneously build financial account surpluses (note the inverse relationship).
2. The capital that flows into a country, giving rise to the financial account surplus, acts as the "financing" for the growing merchandise/services deficits—the constituent components of the current account deficit.

3. Some event, whether it be a report, a speech, or an action by a government or business inside or outside the country, raises the question of the country's economic stability. Investors of many kinds, portfolio and direct investors in the country, fearing economic problems in the near future, withdraw capital from the country rapidly to avoid any exposure to this risk. This is prudent for the individual, but catastrophic for the whole if all individuals move similarly.
4. The rapid withdrawal of capital from the country, so-called "capital flight," results in the loss of the financial account surplus, creating a severe deficit in the country's overall balance of payments. This is typically accompanied by rapid currency depreciation (if a floating-rate currency) or currency devaluation (if a fixed-rate currency).

International debt and economic crises have occurred for as long as there have been international trade and commerce. And they will occur again. Each crisis has its own unique characteristics, but all follow the economic fundamentals described earlier (the one additional factor which differentiates many of the crises is whether inflation is a component). The recent Asian economic crisis was a devastating reminder of the tenuousness of international economic relationships.

International Cultures and Protocols

The Cross-Cultural Communication Process

Effective communication across nations/cultures can take place only when the sender encodes the message using language, idioms, norms and values, and so on that are familiar to the receiver or when the receiver (or receivers) is familiar with the language, idioms, and so on used by the sender. Attaining familiarity with language, slang, norms and values, and so on across nations/cultures is by no means an easy task because words and concepts are often not easily translatable (and sometimes not translatable at all) from one culture to another. For example, the concept of "self-fulfillment" is well understood in the American culture, but such a concept is not translatable to many cultures throughout the world, who understand better the concept of "group-fulfillment." Furthermore, words often have different meanings when translated into another language. For instance, U.S. manufacturer **General Motors Corporation** advertised on many of the automobiles it produced that the body was made by Fisher ("Body by Fisher"). The Flemish interpreted it to mean "Corpse by Fisher." The above suggests that communication is bound to create many problems for people conducting international/cross-cultural business. And international managers cannot generally be effective if they do not possess strong cross-cultural communication skills.

Expressions and Nonverbal Communication

Expressions and nonverbal communication play an important role in cross-cultural encoding. For example, U.S. movie-making firms export movies and television programs made for American audiences. Usually, these must be modified by dubbing in the local language. Accurate language translation is therefore essential. But what is also important is the nonverbal communication contained in the films. For example, the ways of depicting affection in American-made movies and television programs are viewed by some cultures as being offensive. Gestures are widely used as a means of communication in films and television programs, and the same sign has different meanings across different cultures. Some gestures may offend many foreign viewers and must therefore be edited out or somehow isolated before the film is distributed in the foreign culture. For example, Americans form a circle with their index finger and thumb to communicate that something is "OK." Imagine the embarrassment of a former U.S. president who visited Brazil, stepped out of the airplane, and made that gesture to a waiting crowd of Brazilians. The same sign in Brazil means that one is interested in having sex. The same OK sign means zero in France and is a symbol for money in Japan. In many cultures, including those of the United States and China, pointing one's thumb up is a gesture meaning "good" or "great," but in Australia it is a crude gesture.

The Role of Formality and Informality in Communication

Cultures vary in their **requirements for formality and informality,** and these variations also affect cross-cultural communication encoding. Some cultures, especially American and Australian, value informality in communication, but most cultures throughout the world value formality.[88] Individuals in cultures that value informality place low importance on the use of rank, status, and position in communication and often use first names when communicating with each other, even in business settings. On the other hand, individuals in cultures that value formality place high importance on the use of last names, titles, and other indications of rank and status in communication.

In many cultures rank and status are shown by seating arrangements, by the way individuals enter a room, and by who speaks first. In Japan, for instance, the oldest male is normally the most senior, and he must not be the first to enter a room; he is preceded by his assistants, and followed by other assistants, and he sits in the middle. Correspondence to people of higher status must be written individually, and mass mailings are often disliked because they emphasize efficiency over the honoring of individuals' rank and position. People in cultures that value informality, such as Americans, often become frustrated when forced to pay deference to someone simply because of his or her status (family ties, schooling, age, and so on), and not because of the person's accomplishments.

How Much Information Is Needed?

Individuals in some cultures, such as Japan, France, and Germany, can be generally categorized as risk-avoidant. These individuals make decisions slowly, avoid risks, and dislike ambiguity. (Conditions of uncertainty and ambiguity make them feel uncomfortable.) They therefore have a strong need for much detail and information. On the other hand, people in some cultures, such as Singapore, the United States, and Australia, feel relatively more comfortable with risk and ambiguity, make decisions more quickly, and require less detail and information.[89]

Language Translation

The discussion this far suggests that cross-cultural, cross-national communicators, to communicate effectively, must make certain that the language used, including the words, symbols, slang, formal and informal behaviors, as well as nonverbal behaviors, is the one that will be understood by the receiver(s). In conducting global business, businesspeople often do not the possess the command of the language necessary to communicate effectively with foreign associates. These senders therefore have to find a way to convert the language they understand into the language understood by the foreign associates (the receivers).

Translating one language into another is a huge problem confronting cross-cultural, cross-national communicators. To overcome translation problems of written communications, international businesspeople often use the **dual-translation** approach. This involves having a translator in the home country interpret and convert the message into the foreign language, and before the message is communicated, having another translator in the foreign country interpret and convert the message back into the home country's language. For example, a communicator transmitting a message from the United States to Angola, where Portuguese is spoken, first has a translator of English to Portuguese in the United States interpret the message from English to Portuguese. The translated message is then sent to a translator of Portuguese to English in Angola to be interpreted back to English. The sender will transmit the message after he or she has been assured that the translated message will be understood by the receiver(s) as intended.

The Effective Translator

It is obvious that the lack of an effective translator will lead to problems. Several factors help define the **effective translator.**[90] These factors include characteristics of the message itself (both implicit and explicit content), characteristics of the language involved (job titles, first-name basis), the interpreter's relationship with the client, the interpreter's skills (listening skills), context, characteristics of the parties, and cultural norms and values. The last three factors are discussed next.

Context

The time, place, and purpose of the meeting affect a translator's ability. High-stakes negotiations that take place in a hostile environment and that must be accomplished in a short period of time create stress for the translator and for the communicator, reducing their effectiveness. Negotiations should therefore be arranged to cause minimum stress for the translator and the communicator.

Characteristics of the Parties

The translator is familiar with the personal styles, idiosyncrasies, and communication strengths, including encoding and decoding abilities, of the parties for whom he or she is interpreting.

Cultural Norms and Values

The effective translator is familiar with the cultural norms and values of both cultures. For example, some cultures are high context and some are low context. When conducting business, people in **high-context cultures,** including the Chinese, Korean, Japanese, Vietnamese, Arab, Greek, and Spanish cultures, (1) establish social trust first, (2) value personal relations and goodwill, (3) make agreements on the basis of general trust, and (4) like to conduct slow and ritualistic negotiations.[91] People in these cultures prefer that messages not be structured directly, that they do not get right to the point and state conclusions or bottom lines first. Instead, they prefer that a message be indirect, building up to the point and stating conclusions or bottom lines last.[92] On the other hand, individuals in **low-context cultures,** including the Italian, English, North American, Scandinavian, Swiss, and German cultures, (1) get down to business first; (2) value expertise and performance; (3) like agreement by specific, legalistic contract; and (4) like to conduct negotiations as efficiently as possible.[93] Individuals in these cultures prefer that messages be structured directly, that they get immediately to the point and state conclusions or bottom lines first.[94]

The translator can guide the communication flow accordingly, and when the parties for whom he or she is acting as intermediary are opposites (one is high context and the other low context), the translator educates his or her clients accordingly and applies the most viable communication customs. For instance, if a Japanese businessperson is competing with other companies to obtain a contract from a German company, the German customs are likely to be the most applicable. If, however, a German businessperson is competing with other companies to obtain a contract from a Japanese company, the Japanese customs are likely to be the most applicable.

Identifying the Right Transmission Channel Stage

A message is typically transmitted in writing, orally, and nonverbally (body/facial expressions). Ongoing advancements in communications technologies present new means of transmitting messages. Written messages can now be transmitted via mail, computer, fax, and e-mail. Oral messages can be transmitted via meetings, telephone, and videoconferencing. Nonverbal messages can be sent via videoconferencing. Some of these communication channels are not available in many countries, especially in the less-developed countries.

Written or Spoken Message?

Regardless of the channels available, the sender must decide whether to transmit the message orally or in writing. Cultural norms affect the decision. Some cultures prefer written messages and others prefer spoken messages. Individuals in high-context cultures, which value trust, tend to prefer spoken communication and agreements; confirming an idea in writing may be taken as an indication that you think their word is no good. On the other hand, people in low-context cultures, which value efficiency, tend to prefer written communication and agreements.[95] Also many people who understand English as a second or third language learned it by reading and listening, and have not developed a strong command of the language. These receivers may therefore feel more comfortable with written communication than with oral communication, because written communication gives them more time to understand the message. The literacy level of the audience also affects the decision. If the illiteracy rate is high, oral messages would be more effective than written messages.

Body Language

Body language, including eye contact, physical distance and touching, hand movements, pointing, and facial expressions, which vary across cultures,[96] also affects the transmission of a message.

EYE CONTACT **Eye contact** between superiors and subordinates is avoided in many Southeast Asian cultures because it is a sign of disrespect. On the other hand, in Western cultures avoiding eye contact is a sign of disrespect. Therefore, an American and a Malaysian subordinate may very well view each other as being disrespectful when the American attempts to make eye contact and the Malaysian avoids it. Both are correct in their own cultures.

PHYSICAL DISTANCE AND TOUCHING In Asia, once a relationship is established between individuals, **physical distance** is placed between them, and touching or display of emotions are substantially reduced. On the other hand, in Latin America, once a relationship is established between individuals, physical distance between them is reduced, and touching and display of emotions are increased.

HAND MOVEMENTS Some cultures make greater use of **hand movements** when communicating than others. For example, Italians tend to use their hands extensively, while Americans make limited use of hand movements—they believe that too much hand movement while communicating orally distracts the receiver(s).

POINTING **Pointing** with the index finger is rude in some cultures, including those of Sudan, Venezuela, and Sri Lanka. Pointing your index finger toward yourself is insulting in Germany, the Netherlands, and Switzerland.

FACIAL EXPRESSIONS Russians do not use **facial expressions** very much and Scandinavians do not use many gestures. This does not mean that they are not enthusiastic.[97]

Transmission of Messages Through Mediators

Messages (written, spoken, and nonverbal) are typically sent directly to the receiver(s). In some situations in some cultures, it is not wise to send messages directly to the receiver(s); it is wise to use a **mediator**—the encoder sends the message to a mediator (a third party), who in turn conveys it to the receiver(s). For example, sincere Americans are often factually blunt and frank, even if it upsets the listeners.[98] The Japanese, however, culturally neither practice nor accept overt criticism and bluntness well. In Japan, to be sincere means having concern for the emotional, not the factual. In fact, to avoid being offensive (a concern for the emotional), a Japanese receiver may not even say "no" to a request from a sender with which he or she does not want to comply; instead, he or she would respond "maybe" (which really means "no" in Japan). Therefore, when a message being transmitted to a Japanese receiver must contain critical and blunt facts, it is better to submit it through a mediator. The bluntness is mitigated because the message was only indirectly passed from the sender to the receiver.

In Japan, when use of a mediator or message is too impractical, the Japanese use **informal get-togethers** to discuss formal matters. At the informal meeting's setting (often after work hours in bars, nightclubs, and restaurants), serious matters can be obscured as entertainment. Discussions in such settings can be semi-serious and hint of disagreements (the message can be blunt, but not too blunt) that would be unwelcome in formal settings.

To communicate effectively across cultures also requires good listening skills. One must be able to listen to spoken messages as well as respond to nonverbal (such as facial expressions) messages. An impatient American who constantly looks at his or her watch is not likely to communicate effectively across cultures.

Developing Cross-Cultural Communication Competence

Professor Linda Beamer of California State University, Los Angeles, has developed a model for the purpose of describing the process of **developing cross-cultural communication competence.**[99] The model proposes five levels of learning: acknowledgment of diversity, organizing information according to stereotypes, posing questions to challenge the stereotypes, analyzing communication episodes, and generating "other culture" messages. The intent of the learning process, according to Beamer, "is to develop the ability to decode effectively signs that come from members of other cultures, within a business context, and to encode messages using signs that carry the encoder's intended meaning to members of other cultures."[100] The five levels do not cease to exist once attained; they are continually revisited in the process of learning. This means that newer differences in a culture are constantly being discovered.

Cross-Cultural Business Practices

As corporations become increasingly international and competition for global markets increases, business managers who are not attentive to cultural differences will not be able to function in foreign markets effectively—they will make their companies less competitive. Effective international managers have learned how varying cultural practices across societies affect business and management practices and how to adapt to the differences. Learning something about the culture of a country before transacting business there shows respect, and those who understand the culture are more likely to develop successful, long-term business relationships than those who do not.[101]

Approaches to conducting business vary from culture to culture, making the practice of business at the international level much more complex than in the home market. Some factors that affect **cross-cultural business** include time, thought patterns, personal space, material possessions, family roles and relationships, competitiveness and individuality, and social behavior[102] as well as whether a culture is high-context or low-context.

People transacting business across cultures must be sensitive to these dynamics, as well as to varying business customs. Culture affects business behavior and customs. Business customs from around the world that differ from country to country are presented in Exhibit 1000.15. Note that the descriptions in Exhibit 1000.15 are generalizations. Not all residents of a country necessarily adhere to those customs—especially the immigrants in a country. For example, many people in Australia are from other countries, such as China and Italy. These people may adhere to the customs of their country of birth.

Cross-Cultural Negotiations

Negotiating across cultures is far more complex than negotiating within a culture because foreign negotiators have to deal with differing negotiating styles and cultural variables simultaneously. In other words, the negotiating styles that work at home generally do not work in other cultures. As a result, cross-cultural business negotiators have one of the most complicated business roles to play in organizations. They are often thrust into a foreign society consisting of what appears to be "hostile" strangers. They are put in the position of negotiating profitable business relationships with these people or suffering the negative consequences of failure. And quite often they find themselves at a loss as to why their best efforts and intentions have failed them.

How to Avoid Failure in International Negotiations

Negotiators in a foreign country often fail because the local counterparts have taken more time to learn how to overcome the obstacles normally associated with international/cross-cultural negotiations. Failure may occur because of time and/or cost constraints. For example, a negotiator may be given too a short period of time to obtain better contract terms than were originally agreed to in a country where negotiations typically take a long time. A negotiator may think that "what works in the home country is good enough for the rest of the world," which is far from the truth. In fact, strategies that fail to take into account cultural factors are usually naive or misconceived. Typically, the obstacles to overcome include

- **Learning the local language,** or at least being able to select and use an effective language translator.
- **Learning the local culture,** including how the culture handles conflict, its business practices, and its business ethics, or at least being able to select and use an effective cultural translator.
- **Becoming well-prepared for the negotiations,** that is, along with the above, the negotiator must have a thorough knowledge of the subject matter being negotiated.

Effective cross-cultural negotiators understand the cultural differences existing between all parties involved; and they know that failure to understand the differences serves only to destroy potential business success.[103]

How Much Must One Know About the Foreign Culture?

Realistically, it is nearly impossible to learn everything about another culture, although it may be possible if one lives in the culture for several years. The reason for this is that each culture has developed, over time, multifaceted structures that are much too complex for any foreigner to understand totally. Therefore, foreign negotiators need not have total awareness of the foreign culture; they do not need to know as much about the foreign culture as the locals, whose frames of reference

Exhibit 1000.15 *Business Customs around the World*

Australia	Business is almost always conducted over drinks, and it is considered rude to buy out of turn. Australians like to be addressed by their titles.
Austria	Austrians prefer to be addressed by their titles and consider it rude if a business associate tries to pick up the tab for a lunch or dinner they have initiated. They enjoy discussing art and music as well as skiing.
Belgium	Belgians like to get down to business immediately and are very conservative and efficient in their approach to business meetings. One must address French-speaking Belgians as "monsieur" or "madame," while Dutch-speaking Belgians must be addressed as "Mr." or "Mrs."
Egypt	Egypt is dominated by the Muslim faith, and its business customs reflect this. Business is slow-paced and the red tape is limitless. Egyptians take offense at refusals and at the use of direct negatives.
France	Conducting business in France in August is difficult because most people are on vacation. The French use titles until use of first names is proposed. In negotiations, they like to debate issues; they like to show their intellect and to challenge your intellect. To successfully sell the French requires convincing them of the merits of the product/service through intellectual debate, not through flashy, high-powered presentations. They use sophisticated table manners.
Germany	One should expect much handshaking, but in order of the person's importance in the enterprise. Germans insist on using titles, seldom use first names, use surname preceded by title, dislike small talk, and are very punctual. Germans are competitive negotiators who get straight to the point and leave little room for debate. German executives tend to have an engineering and science background, and one must therefore appeal to their technical tastes—glitzy presentations are likely to fail. They do not strongly emphasize the development of personal relationships with business associates—they value their privacy and keep business and private matters separate.
Greece	The Greeks are famous for their extensive bargaining and for never discussing business without a cup of coffee. Building a personal rapport with Greeks is important. Business entertaining normally takes place in the evening at a local tavern, and spouses are often included. It is important that a business relationship be built on trust. Government plays an important role in business, which means that one must work through bureaucracy. Business is highly personalized—family connections, political connections, and business connections. How one connects is often more important than the quality of the product/service. In Greece, negotiations are not finished even after the contract has been awarded—a contract is viewed as an evolving document of agreement.
Guatemala	A luncheon set for a specific time means that some guests may arrive 10 minutes early, while others may be 45 minutes late.
India	Business is conducted at an extremely leisurely pace; therefore, Indians are very patient, unlike their American counterparts. When invited to dinner, one should accept and pass the food with the right hand only and expect to be asked many personal questions—which Indians see as a sign of politeness. Indians avoid discussing political issues with their business contacts.
Ireland, Republic of	Do not confuse it with Northern Ireland or the United Kingdom—it is politically and culturally distinct from both.
Italy	Italians use a handshake for greetings and goodbyes. Unlike in the United States, men do not stand when a woman enters or leaves a room, and they do not kiss a woman's hand—this is reserved for royalty. Appearance and style are very important to Italian businesspeople. The appeal and polish of a presentation reflect the quality of the product/service or the firm itself. Italian businesspeople are confident, shrewd, and competent negotiators, and they tend to rely mainly on their instincts and not as much on the advice of specialists.
Malaysia	Most Malaysians are Muslims, so they do not eat pork, drink alcohol, or party on Friday night, the eve of the Muslim sabbath. They are very status- and role-conscious, and therefore do not readily mingle at social gatherings, particularly if men and women are together at the same gathering.
Mexico	Local contacts (connections) are required prior to arrival in Mexico. It is impolite to make extended eye contact with Mexicans. Timeliness is not important—it is OK for your host to keep you waiting. Don't say "America" to mean the U.S.A. because Mexicans are Americans too, and don't say "the United States" to mean the U.S.A. because Mexico is a "United States" too—the United States of Mexico. Don't get down to business right away. First get to know your prospective Mexican clients and their families by socializing.
Netherlands	The Dutch are competitive negotiators who get straight to the point and normally have little conflict or debate.
Nigeria	Business is slow-paced and never conducted over the telephone.

Exhibit 1000.15 *(continued)*

Pakistan	The Islamic faith is a dominant factor in Pakistani life and in business as well. It is a male-dominated country where women are largely confined to the domestic sphere; hence Pakistani men are uncomfortable or may even refuse to transact business with a woman. They refuse alcohol, cigarettes, and pork. One should never try to take a picture of a Pakistani without his or her permission.
Portugal	One must take the time to establish a rapport with Portuguese business associates.
Saudi Arabia	Business is informal, slow paced, and male-dominated. The Saudies are insulted if forced to deal with a representative rather than with the main person. When invited to a Saudi home, never bring flowers or gifts to the lady of the house, never eat or drink with the left hand, and never praise the house furnishings unless you would like to receive them as a gift the following day.
South Africa	Businesspeople like to discuss politics with their peers, and they are generally ultraconservative.
Spain	The Spanish work long days and break appointments often. The business lunch is an important part of conducting business in Spain, and great ceremony is applied in lunch meetings. Lunches stretch from 2:30 P.M. to 5:00 P.M.; then work goes on until 8:30 P.M. or 9:00 P.M. These lunches are used to develop the relationship required before business can be conducted.
Thailand	Thailand's traditional greeting is the *wai,* which is made by the placement of both hands together in a prayer-like position at the chin and bowing slightly. The gesture means "thank you" and "I am sorry" as well as "hello." The higher the hands, the more respect is symbolized. The fingertips, however, should never be raised above the eye level. Failure to return a *wai* is equivalent to refusing to shake hands in the West. In Thailand it is considered offensive to place one's arm over the back of the chair in which another person is sitting, and men and women should not show affection in public. First names are used, and last names are reserved for very formal occasions or in writing.
United Kingdom	In the United Kingdom, never sit with the ankle resting on the knee; one should instead cross his or her legs with one knee on top of the other. Avoid backslapping and putting an arm around a new acquaintance. Use titles until use of first names is suggested. Gift-giving is not a normal custom in the United Kingdom. The British are very civil and reserved, they do not admire overt ambition and aggressiveness, and are offended by hard-sell tactics. They do not brag about their finances or positions. And they are good negotiators, but do not have a high regard for bargaining in general.
United States	Americans often feel that the European practice of meticulously cultivating personal relationships with business associates slows the expedient conduct of business; they agree that time is money, and the Europeans waste time. Business comes first, and friendship or pleasure comes later, if at all.

Source: Excerpted from David Altany, "It Takes Cultural Savvy," *Industry Week,* October 2, 1989; M. Katherine Glover, "Do's and Taboos: Cultural Aspects of International Business," *Business America* (August 13, 1990): 3; Dean Foster, "Business Across Borders: International Etiquette for the Effective Secretary," *The Secretary* (October 1992): 23, and excerpted from Valeria Frazee, "Getting Started in Mexico," *Workforce* 2, no. 1 (January 1997), 16, 17.

were shaped by that culture. However, they will need to know enough about the culture and about the locals' negotiating styles to avoid being uncomfortable during (and after) negotiations.[104] Besides knowing enough to not fail, they also need to know enough to win. For example, in negotiations between Japanese and American businesspeople, Japanese negotiators have sometimes used their knowledge that Americans have a low tolerance for silence to their advantage.

In other words, for negotiation to take place, the foreigner must at least recognize those ideas and behaviors that the locals intentionally put forward as part of the negotiation process—and the locals must do the same for the foreigners. Both sides must be capable of interpreting these behaviors sufficiently to distinguish common from conflicting positions, to spot movement from positions, and to respond in ways that sustain communication. Ultimately, cross-cultural negotiators must determine their counterparts' personal motivations and agendas and adapt the negotiation style to them.

The purpose of the previous discussion is to help the reader develop a cross-cultural negotiations process. The process includes both strategy and tactics. **Strategy** refers to a long-term plan, and **tactics** refers to the actual means used to implement the strategy.[105]

Strategic Planning for International Negotiations

Strategic planning for international negotiations involves several stages: preparation for face-to-face negotiations, determining settlement range, determining where the negotiations should take place, deciding whether to use an individual or a group of individuals in the negotiations, and learning about the country's views on agreements/contracts.

Preparation for Face-to-Face Negotiations

Generally, at the preparation stage, the issues to be identified are common interests, desired outcomes, possible conflicts (and tactics for handling them), participants' abilities and limitations, business markets, financial status, participants' reputation, and similar products/services.[106] Typically, the negotiating strategy that is effective in the home market will have to be modified for negotiating with foreign businesses; as indicated earlier, cultural factors, business customs, and ethical standards of the foreign country must be considered.[107] For instance, in negotiating with the Chinese, Americans want to agree on specific terms first while the Chinese want to determine general principles (the "spirit of the contract") and then discuss specifics. In other words, Americans tend to be concerned with short-term goals, such as profits, while the Chinese are more concerned with long-term interests, such as the procurement of American technology and business techniques.[108]

Determining a Settlement Range

At this phase, a negotiation or **settlement range** (all possible settlements a negotiator would be willing to make) must be established. The "least acceptable result" and a "maximum supportable position" must be identified. In this respect, the Japanese have a saying, "*Banana no tataki uri,*" which means "ask outrageous prices and lower them when faced with buyer objections."[109] Establishing a range provides negotiators the ability to make concessions and therefore more flexibility in the negotiations. Some cultures, Russia, for example, view concessions as a sign of weakness, not gestures of goodwill or flexibility. To be able to establish a reasonable negotiating range, an accurate analysis of the nature of all relevant markets must be conducted.[110] If there are other options, that is, if either the seller or the buyer has other forms of leverage or enticement, he or she may not need to make as many concessions or may not need to make any concessions at all.

Where Should Negotiations Take Place?

Negotiations can take place in the home country, in the counterpart's home country, or at a neutral site. Most negotiators would prefer that negotiations take place on their home turf. Familiar surroundings and easy access to information provide more leverage; fatigue and stress associated with foreign travel are not experienced; and, of course, lower travel costs are incurred.[111] On the other hand, negotiating in the foreign country does have its advantages, such as sometimes receiving certain concessions because you have endured the burdens of traveling. And quite often it is a good idea to base decisions on site observations—for example, it is a good idea to see the plant where your product is going to be manufactured. A neutral site that is equally advantageous to both parties is often ideal. For example, an American executive from Park Avenue in New York City may not adapt well in a Brazilian village in the Amazon, and an executive from this village may not adapt well in New York City. A negotiating site that falls between the two extremes may be the most viable.

Individual or Team Negotiations?

An organization can assign one individual or a group of individuals to conduct the negotiations. The obvious advantages of using **one person** are that it is cheaper and a decision can be made quickly. An obvious disadvantage is that one person may not have sufficient ability to deal with the other side, which typically consists of a group of experts and negotiating specialists—an advantage of the group approach. Furthermore, in Japan, for instance, not using a group may be interpreted to mean that you are not very serious about the negotiation or the business deal. Also, the individual negotiator often finds himself or herself pressed to make a decision when it is not the right time to do so. In a group, the members can always take a break to confer, therefore "buying time" to assess the situation and develop new strategies and tactics. (The Japanese typically use this method because their decisions usually require group consensus.) Thus, in negotiating situations where the cost and speed of a decision are more important than the other factors, use one negotiator; otherwise, use a group of experts and negotiating specialists.

To speed up decision making a bit and still have access to expert input, a **team of negotiators** can be used, but one member is given full negotiating authority (Americans generally use this approach). Of course, the other side may know this. And in the negotiations game, for tactical reasons, both parties try to learn who the decision maker is. In this respect, American decision makers usually reveal themselves quickly because they tend to be very active in the negotiations. On the other hand, Japanese decision makers are usually not very active in the negotiations—they simply remain silent and listen. It should also be noted that the Japanese tend to include several young executives in the negotiations team simply for exposure and on-site development purposes.[112]

What Are the Country's Views on Agreements/Contracts?

Countries existing on a high commercial level have generally developed a working base on which agreements can rest. The base may be on one or a combination of these three types:[113]

1. Rules that are spelled out technically as laws or regulations
2. Moral practices mutually agreed upon and taught to the young as a set of principles
3. Information customs to which everyone conforms without being able to state the exact rules

Some cultures favor one type, and some another. Americans, for example, rely heavily on written contracts, and they tend to consider the negotiations ended when the contract is signed. Many societies, however, do not place much importance on written contracts; they rely more on the development of a social relationship. And in many countries, Greece, for instance, a signed contract is simply a starting point for negotiations, which end only when the project is completed—the clauses in the contract are subject to renegotiation. Thus, the international negotiator must understand the nature of the other country's views and practices relating to agreements and contracts.

Tactical Planning for International Negotiations

Tactical planning for international negotiations involves determining how to obtain leverage, use delay tactics, and deal with emotions.

Leverage

In negotiations, it is generally accepted that the more options you have, the more leverage you have, and the more concessions your opponents may be willing to make. For example, if you are negotiating with the Argentinean government to establish a manufacturing subsidiary in Argentina, and the Argentinean negotiators know that their site is the only viable one you have, they will not make any concessions, and are likely to ask you for some concessions. But if the Argentinean negotiators believe that you can just as easily set up the subsidiary in Peru or Brazil, and they need the technology—as most less-developed nations do—they are likely to be willing to make concessions.

Less-developed countries appear to have leverage over multinational corporations because they control access to their own territory, including markets, local labor supplies, investment opportunities, sources of raw materials, and other resources that multinational corporations need or desire. China, for instance, is developing economically rather quickly these days. Its more than one billion prospective customers, along with its relatively inexpensive cost of labor, make China an attractive place for many foreign companies to establish operations. This, it seems, would give Chinese negotiators considerable leverage, and concessions would often have to be made by foreign negotiators. This may be true in some cases, but in many instances, multinational corporations have negotiating advantages because they possess the capital, technology, managerial skills, access to global markets, and other resources that governments in less-developed countries need for economic development.[114]

Delay

Applying **delay tactics** is another form of leverage. If you walk away from the negotiations and your opponents become overly anxious, they may be willing to make some concessions. On the other hand, if you become anxious before your opponent does, you may have to make some concessions. Furthermore, the pause in the negotiations enables you to rest and recuperate, assess progress, obtain other information, and reformulate strategy.[115] In this context, patience is generally recognized as being a key personal attribute in negotiators. Americans tend to be low on patience, while the Japanese tend to be high.

Emotions

Even though behavior in negotiations is mainly intuitive, it should never be judgmental. To be able to listen to other negotiators, one should exclude his or her subjective opinions, preconceptions, and emotional filters. By becoming aware of your **emotions,** you can learn to change your reactions and avoid being manipulated by others or by the emotions themselves—you prevent emotion from controlling a negotiation. On the other hand, if you negotiate solely on the basis of logic, you will miss emotional signals sent out by the other negotiator. Thus, the key to negotiations is to be perceptive of feelings (your and theirs) without being reactive.[116]

Ethical Constraints

Business ethics and corporate social responsibility place constraints on negotiators. For example, a negotiator's ethical concerns for honesty and fair dealings, regardless of the power status of negotiating parties, will affect the outcome. There is no global standard or view of what is ethical or unethical behavior in business transactions—what is viewed as unethical behavior in one culture may be viewed as ethical in another culture, and vice versa. For instance, if a negotiator on one side "pays off" an influential decision maker on the other side to obtain a favorable decision, it would be an unethical business practice in some cultures (and illegal in the United States), but it would be quite acceptable in other cultures.

International Economics

Macroeconomic Policy in an Open Economy

A nation with a closed economy can select its economic policies in view of its own goals. In an open world economy, however, consequences of a nation's activities are felt by its trading partners. The result has been efforts among nations to coordinate their economic policies.

Economic Policy in an Open Economy

International economic policy refers to activities of national governments that affect the movement of trade and factor inputs among nations. Included are not only the obvious measures such as import tariffs and quotas, but also domestic measures such as monetary policy and fiscal policy. Policies that are undertaken to improve the conditions of one sector in a nation tend to have repercussions that spill over into other sectors. Because an economy's *internal* (domestic) sector is tied to its *external* (foreign) sector, one cannot designate economic policies as purely domestic or purely foreign. Rather, the effects of economic policy should be viewed as being located on a continuum between two poles—an internal-effects pole and an external-effects pole. Although the primary impact of an import restriction is on a nation's trade balance, for example, there are secondary effects on national output, employment, and income. Most economic policies are located between the external and internal poles rather than falling directly on either one.

Economic Objectives of Nations

What are the basic objectives of economic policies? Since the Great Depression of the 1930s, governments have actively pursued the goal of economic stability at full employment. Known as **internal balance,** this objective has two dimensions: (1) a fully employed economy, and (2) no inflation—or, more realistically, a reasonable amount of inflation. Nations traditionally have considered internal balance to be of primary importance and have formulated economic policies to attain this goal.

Policy makers are also aware of a nation's balance-of-payments (BOP) position. A nation is said to be in **external balance** when it realizes neither BOP deficits nor BOP surpluses. In practice, policy makers usually express external balance in terms of a BOP subaccount, such as the current account. In this context, external balance occurs when the current account is neither so deeply in deficit that the home nation is incapable of repaying its foreign debts in the future nor so strongly in surplus that foreign nations cannot repay their debts to it. Although nations usually consider internal balance to be the highest priority, they are sometimes forced to modify priorities when confronted with large and persistent external imbalances.

Nations have economic targets other than internal balance and external balance, such as long-run economic development and a reasonably equitable distribution of national income. Although these and other commitments may influence international economic policies, the discussion in this section is confined to the pursuit of internal balance and external balance.

Policy Instruments

To attain the objectives of external balance and internal balance, policy makers enact expenditure-changing policies, expenditure-switching policies, and direct controls. **Expenditure-changing policies** alter the level of aggregate demand for goods and services, including those produced domestically and those imported. They include **fiscal policy,** which refers to changes in government spending and taxes, and **monetary policy,** which refers to changes in the money supply by a nation's central bank (such as the Federal Reserve). Depending on the direction of change, expenditure-changing policies are either expenditure increasing or expenditure reducing.

If *inflation* is a problem, it is likely to be because the level of aggregate demand (total spending) is too high for the level of output that can be sustained by the nation's resources at constant prices. The standard recommendation in this case is for policy makers to reduce aggregate demand by implementing *expenditure-decreasing policies* such as reductions in government expenditures, tax increases, or decreases in the money supply; these policies offset the upward pressure on prices resulting from excess aggregate demand. If *unemployment* is excessive, the standard recommendation is for policy makers to increase aggregate demand for goods and services by initiating *expenditure-increasing policies.*

Expenditure-switching policies modify the direction of demand, shifting it between domestic output and imports. Under a system of fixed exchange rates, a trade-deficit nation could devalue its currency to increase the international competitiveness of its industries, thus diverting spending from foreign goods to domestic goods. To increase its competitiveness under a managed floating exchange-rate system, the nation could purchase other currencies with its currency, thereby causing the exchange value of its currency to depreciate. The success of these policies in promoting trade balance largely depends on switching demand in the proper direction and amount, as well as on the capacity of the home economy to meet the additional demand by supplying more goods. Exchange-rate adjustments are general switching policies that influence the balance of payments indirectly, through their effects on the price mechanism and national income.

Direct controls consist of government restrictions on the market economy. They are selective expenditure-switching policies whose objective is to control particular items in the balance of payments. Direct controls, such as automobile tariffs and dairy quotas, are levied on imports in an attempt to switch domestic spending away from foreign goods to domestic goods. Similarly, the object of an export subsidy is to enhance exports by switching foreign spending to domestic output. When a government wishes to limit the volume of its overseas sales, it may impose an export quota (such as Japan's automobile export quotas of the 1980s). Direct controls may also be levied on capital flows so as to either restrain excessive capital outflows or stimulate capital inflows.

Economic policy formation is subject to **institutional constraints** that involve considerations of fairness and equity.[117] Policy makers are aware of the needs of groups they represent, such as labor and business, especially when pursuing conflicting economic objectives. For example, to what extent are policy makers willing to permit reductions in national income, output, and employment at the cost of restoring BOP equilibrium? The outcry of adversely affected groups within the nation may be more than sufficient to convince policy makers not to pursue external balance as a goal. During election years, government officials tend to be especially sensitive to domestic economic problems. Reflecting perceptions of fairness and equity, policy formation tends to be characterized by negotiation and compromise.

Inflation with Unemployment

The analysis so far has looked at internal balance under special circumstances. It has been assumed that as the economy advances to full employment, domestic prices remain unchanged until full employment is reached. Once the nation's capacity to produce has been achieved, further increases in aggregate demand pull prices upward. This type of inflation is known as **demand-pull inflation.** Under these conditions, internal balance (full employment with stable prices) can be viewed as a single target that requires but one policy instrument: reductions in aggregate demand via monetary policy or fiscal policy.

A more troublesome problem is the appropriate policy to implement when a nation experiences *inflation with unemployment.* Here the problem is that internal balance cannot be achieved just by manipulating aggregate demand. To decrease inflation, a reduction in aggregate demand is required; to decrease unemployment, an expansion in aggregate demand is required. Thus, the objectives of full employment and stable prices cannot be considered as one and the same target; rather, they are two independent targets, requiring two distinct policy instruments.

Achieving overall balance thus involves three separate targets: (1) BOP equilibrium, (2) full employment, and (3) price stability. To ensure that all three objectives can be achieved simultaneously, monetary/fiscal policies and exchange-rate adjustments may not be enough; direct controls may also be needed.

Inflation with unemployment has been a problem for the United States. In 1971, for example, the U.S. economy experienced *inflation with recession and BOP deficit.* Increasing aggregate demand to achieve full employment would presumably intensify inflationary pressures. The President therefore implemented a comprehensive system of **wage and price controls** to remove the inflationary constraint. Later the same year, the United States entered into exchange-rate realignments that resulted in a depreciation of the dollar's exchange value by 12 percent against the trade-weighted value of other major currencies. The dollar depreciation was intended to help the United States reverse its BOP deficit. In short, it was the President's view that the internal and external problems of the United States could not be eliminated through expenditure-changing policies alone.

International Economic-Policy Coordination

Policy makers have long been aware that the welfare of their economies is linked to that of the world economy. Because of the international mobility of goods, services, capital, and labor, economic policies of one nation have spillover effects on others. This spillover is especially true for the larger industrial economies, but even here, the linkages are stronger among some nations, such as those within Western Europe, than for others. Recognizing these spillover effects, governments have often made attempts to coordinate their economic policies.

International Equilibrium

We have emphasized the role of international differences in the cost of producing tradable goods as the main determinant of international trade patterns. By considering only supply-side factors, however, we could not determine (1) the equilibrium point on each nation's production possibilities schedule, (2) the equilibrium value of the international terms of trade, or (3) the equilibrium consumption point of each nation under free trade. Let us now include the role of demand conditions in our trade model so that we can determine the magnitude of these items.

Indifference Curves

Modern trade theory contends that the pattern of world trade is governed by international differences in *supply conditions* and *demand conditions.* Therefore, the role of demand must be developed and introduced into the trade model. Economic theory reasons that an individual's demand curve is based on several underlying determinants, among them (1) the level of disposable income and (2) personal tastes and preferences. Here we consider the role of personal tastes and preferences in demand analysis.

The role of tastes and preferences can be illustrated graphically by a consumer's indifference curve. An **indifference curve** depicts the various combinations of two commodities that are equally preferred in the eyes of the consumer—that is, yield the same level of satisfaction. The term *indifference curve* stems from the idea that the consumer is indifferent about the many possible commodity combinations that provide identical amounts of satisfaction. Exhibit 1000.16 illustrates a consumer's **indifference map,** which consists of a set of indifference curves. Referring to indifference curve I, a consumer is just as happy consuming, say, 6 bushels of wheat and 1 auto at point *A* as consuming 3 bushels of wheat and 2 autos at point *B*. All combination points along an indifference curve are equally desirable because they yield the same level of satisfaction. Besides this fundamental characteristic, indifference curves have several other features.

Inspection of Exhibit 1000.16 reveals that an indifference curve tends to be negatively sloped—that is, sloped downward to the right. This is assured by the assumption that a consumer always desires more of a commodity than less of it. Because each combination of goods along an indifference curve provides the same level of satisfaction, it follows that a consumer who increases auto holdings must decrease wheat intake by some amount if the initial level of satisfaction is to be maintained. If the wheat holdings are not decreased, the new market basket would include more of the combined amount of both commodities, resulting in a higher level of satisfaction. Because changes in the consumption of one commodity are inversely related to changes in the amount consumed of another for a given level of satisfaction to be maintained, it follows that an indifference curve slopes downward to the right.

Indifference curves are also generally convex (bowed in) to the diagram's origin. The negative slope of an indifference curve indicates that, for any given level of satisfaction, some amount of one good must be sacrificed if more of another is to be acquired. The rate at which the substitution occurs is called the **marginal rate of substitution (MRS).** In terms of Exhibit 1000.16, the marginal rate of substitution indicates the extent to which a consumer is will-

Exhibit 1000.16 *A Consumer's Indifference Map*

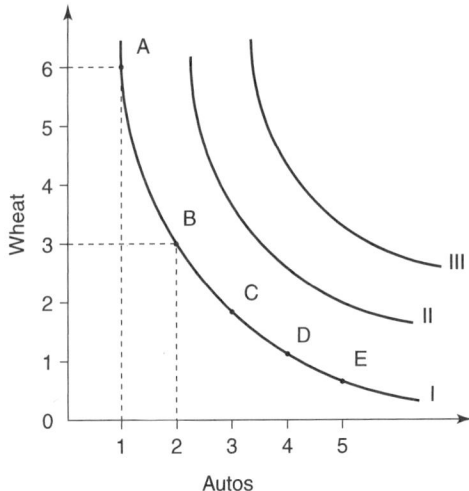

An indifference map is a graph that illustrates an entire set of indifference curves. Each higher indifference curve represents a greater level of satisfaction for the consumer. A community indifference curve denotes various combinations of two goods that yield equal amounts of satisfaction to the nation as a whole.

ing to substitute autos for wheat (or vice versa) while maintaining a given level of satisfaction. The marginal rate of substitution of autos for wheat is expressed algebraically as

$$MRS = \frac{\Delta Wheat}{\Delta Autos}$$

The marginal rate of substitution is equal to an indifference curve's absolute slope. As we move downward along the indifference curve, autos become relatively plentiful while wheat becomes relatively scarce. With less wheat and more autos, each additional auto becomes less valuable to the consumer. For each additional auto consumed, the consumer is willing to sacrifice smaller amounts of wheat. This means that the marginal rate of substitution of autos for wheat decreases as more autos are consumed—hence, the convex nature of an indifference curve.

The indifference map in Exhibit 1000.16 shows several of the consumer's indifference curves. Those indifference curves lying farther from the origin (the "higher" curves) represent greater levels of satisfaction. This is because any point on a higher indifference curve suggests at least the same amount of one commodity plus more of another commodity. Although the figure contains only three indifference curves, an infinite number can be drawn.

Having developed an indifference curve for one individual, can we assume that the preferences of all consumers in the entire nation could be added up and summarized by a **community indifference curve**? Strictly speaking, the answer is no, because it is impossible to make interpersonal comparisons of satisfaction. For example, person A may prefer a lot of coffee and little sugar, whereas person B prefers the opposite. The dissimilar nature of individuals' indifference curves results in their being noncomparable. Despite these theoretical problems, a community indifference curve can be used as a pedagogical device that depicts the role of consumer preferences in international trade.

Equilibrium in the Absence of Trade

Beginning once again with the assumption of isolation, what is the optimal level of production and consumption for a nation? In other words, *at what point on its production possibilities schedule will a nation choose to locate in the absence of trade?*

Assuming that a nation wishes to maximize satisfaction, it will attempt to consume some combination of goods on the highest indifference curve that it can reach. But an indifference curve only tells what a nation would like to do. Given the availability and quality of resources and the level of technology, there is a constraint on how many goods will actually be available to consume. For a nation, this production constraint is represented by its production possibilities schedule. A nation in the absence of trade will maximize satisfaction if it can reach the highest attainable indifference curve, given the production constraint of its production possibilities schedule. This will occur when the production possibilities schedule is *tangent* to an indifference curve.

Exhibit 1000.17 *Indifference Map and Production Possibilities Schedule*

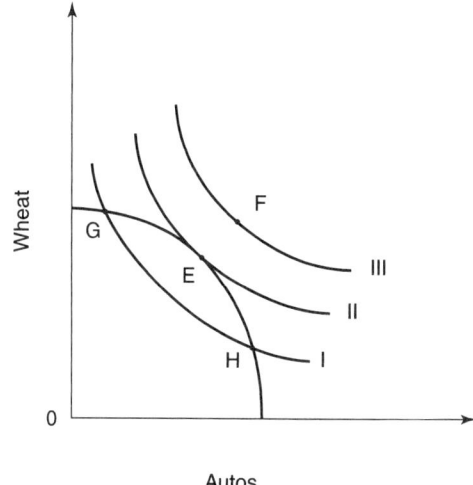

In the absence of trade, a nation achieves equilibrium at the point where its community indifference curve is tangent to its production possibilities schedule. At this point, the nation experiences the highest attainable level of satisfaction given the constraint of its production possibilities schedule, which limits the amount of goods available for consumption.

Exhibit 1000.17 illustrates the production possibilities schedule and indifference map for a single nation. In the absence of trade, the nation will maximize satisfaction if it produces and consumes at point E, where indifference curve II is tangent to its production possibilities schedule. Any point on a higher indifference curve—say, F—is unattainable because it is beyond the economy's capacity to produce. Any point on a lower indifference curve, such as G or H, does not represent maximum satisfaction. This is because a higher indifference curve can be reached with the existing production possibilities schedule. Point E, then, represents the equilibrium of production and consumption in the absence of trade.

A Restatement: Basis for Trade, Gains from Trade

Using indifference curves, let us now develop a trade example to restate the basis-for-trade and the gains-from-trade issues. Exhibit 1000.18 depicts the trading position of the United States. Assuming that the United States attempts to maximize satisfaction, its location of production and consumption will be at point A, where the U.S. production possibilities schedule is just tangent to indifference curve I. At point A, the U.S. relative price ratio is denoted by line $t_{U.S.}$, which equals the absolute slope of the production possibilities curve at that point.

Suppose that the United States has a comparative advantage vis-à-vis Canada in the production of autos. The United States will find it advantageous to specialize in auto production until the two countries' relative prices of autos equalize. Suppose this occurs at production point B (24 autos and 240 bushels of wheat), where the U.S. price rises to Canada's price, depicted by line tt. Also suppose that tt becomes the international terms-of-trade line. Starting at production point B, the United States will export autos and import wheat, trading along line tt. The immediate problem the United States faces is to determine the *level of trade that will maximize its welfare*.

Suppose that the United States exchanges 6 (24 − 6 = 18) autos for 50 (240 + 50 = 290) bushels of wheat at terms-of-trade tt. This would shift the United States from production point B to posttrade consumption point D. But the United States would be no better off with trade than it was in the absence of trade. This is because in both cases the consumption points are located along indifference curve I. Trade volume of 6 autos and 50 bushels of wheat thus represents the *minimum* acceptable volume of trade for the United States. Any smaller volume would force the United States to locate on a lower indifference curve.

Suppose instead that the United States decides to trade 22 (24 − 22 = 2) autos for 183 (240 + 183 = 423) bushels of wheat. The United States would move from production point B to post-trade consumption point E. With trade, the United States would again locate on indifference curve I, resulting in no gains from trade. From the U.S. viewpoint, trade volume of 22 autos and 183 bushels of wheat therefore represents the *maximum* acceptable volume of trade. Any greater volume would find the United States moving to a lower indifference curve.

Exhibit 1000.18 *Basis for Trade, Gains from Trade*

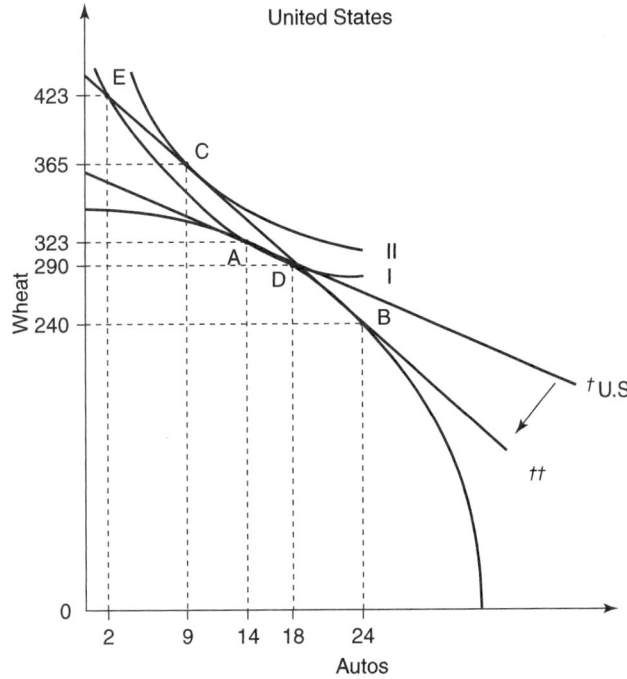

A nation benefits from international trade if it can achieve a higher level of satisfaction (indifference curve) than it can attain in the absence of trade. Maximum gains from trade occur at the point where the international terms-of-trade line is tangent to a community indifference curve.

Trading along terms-of-trade line *tt*, the United States can achieve *maximum welfare* if it exports 15 (24 − 15 = 9) autos and imports 125 (240 + 125 = 365) bushels of wheat. The U.S. post-trade consumption location would be at point *C* along indifference curve II, the highest attainable level of satisfaction. Comparing point *A* and point *C* reveals that with trade the United States consumes more wheat, but fewer autos, than it does in the absence of trade. Yet point *C* is clearly a preferable consumption location. This is because under indifference-curve analysis, the gains from trade are measured in terms of total satisfaction rather than in terms of number of goods consumed.

Terms-of-Trade Estimates

The gains a nation enjoys from its foreign trade consist of a larger income owing to a wider range of goods available to consumers and the favorable influence trade has on productivity levels. Estimating these gains at a particular time would be extremely difficult, for it would require knowledge of what a nation's imports would cost if it produced them itself instead of purchasing them from a less expensive foreign source. Instead, economists have attempted to measure the direction of these gains over time. This is accomplished by calculating changes in the terms of trade.

The **commodity terms of trade** (also referred to as the *barter terms of trade*) is the most frequently used measure of the direction of trade gains. It measures the relationship between the prices a nation gets for its exports and the prices it pays for its imports. This is calculated by dividing a nation's export price index by its import price index, multiplied by 100 to express the terms of trade in percentages.

$$\text{Terms of Trade} = \frac{\text{Export Price Index}}{\text{Import Price Index}} \times 100$$

An *improvement* in a nation's terms of trade requires that the prices of its exports rise relative to the prices of its imports over the given time period. A smaller quantity of export goods sold abroad is required to obtain a given quantity of imports. Conversely, a *deterioration* in a nation's terms of trade is due to a rise in its import prices relative to its export prices over a time period. The purchase of a given quantity of imports would require the sacrifice of a greater quantity of exports.

Tariffs

The conclusion of the trade models presented so far is that free trade leads to the most efficient use of world resources. When nations specialize according to the comparative-advantage principle, the level of world output is maximized. Not only does free trade enhance world welfare, but it can also benefit each participating nation. Every nation can overcome the limitations of its own productive capacity to consume a combination of goods that exceeds the best it can produce in isolation.

Despite the power of the free-trade argument, however, free-trade policies meet major resistance among those companies and workers who face losses in income and jobs because of import competition. Policy makers are torn between the appeal of greater global efficiency made possible by free trade and the needs of the voting public whose main desire is to preserve short-run interests such as employment and income. The benefits of free trade may take years to achieve and are spread out over wide segments of society, whereas the costs of free trade are immediate and fall on specific groups (for example, workers in the import-competing industry).

In today's world, restrictions on the flow of goods and services in international trade are widespread. This section considers one type of restriction, tariffs, and their impact on trade.

The Tariff Concept

A **tariff** is simply a tax (duty) levied on a product when it crosses national boundaries. The most widespread tariff is the *import tariff*, which is a tax levied on an imported product. A less common tariff is an *export tariff*, which is a tax imposed on an exported product. Export tariffs have often been used by developing nations. For example, cocoa exports have been taxed by Ghana, and oil exports have been taxed by the Organization of Petroleum Exporting Countries (OPEC) in order to raise revenue or promote scarcity in global markets and hence increase the world price.

Did you know that the United States cannot levy export tariffs? When the U.S. Constitution was written, southern cotton-producing states feared that northern textile-manufacturing states would pressure the federal government into levying export tariffs to depress the price of cotton. An export duty would lead to decreased exports and thus a fall in the price of cotton within the United States. As the result of negotiations, the Constitution was worded so as to prevent export taxes: "No tax or duty shall be laid on articles exported from any state."

Tariffs may be imposed for protection or revenue purposes. A **protective tariff** is designed to insulate import-competing producers from foreign competition. Although a protective tariff generally is not intended to totally prohibit imports from entering the country, it does place foreign producers at a competitive disadvantage when selling in the domestic market. A **revenue tariff** is imposed for the purpose of generating tax revenues and may be placed on either exports or imports.

Over time, tariff revenues have decreased as a source of government revenue for industrial nations, including the United States. In 1900, tariff revenues constituted more than 41 percent of U.S. government receipts; by 1998, the figure stood at 1 percent. However, many developing nations currently rely on tariffs as a major source of government revenue.

Types of Tariffs

Tariffs can be specific, ad valorem, or compound. A **specific tariff** is expressed in terms of a fixed amount of money per physical unit of the imported product. For example, a U.S. importer of a German computer may be required to pay a duty to the U.S. government of $100 per computer, regardless of the computer's price. An **ad valorem tariff,** much like a sales tax, is expressed as a fixed percentage of the value of the imported product. Suppose that an ad valorem duty of 15 percent is levied on imported trucks. A U.S. importer of a Japanese truck valued at $20,000 would be required to pay a duty of $3,000 to the government ($20,000 × 15% = $3,000). A **compound tariff** is a combination of specific and ad valorem tariffs. For example, a U.S. importer of a television might be required to pay a duty of $20 plus 5 percent of the value of the television.

Effective Rate of Protection

A main objective of an import tariff is to protect domestic producers from foreign competition. By increasing the domestic price of an import, a tariff serves to make home-produced goods more attractive to resident consumers. Output in the import-competing industry can thus expand beyond what would exist in the absence of a tariff. The degree of protection afforded by a tariff reflects the extent to which domestic prices can rise above foreign prices before the home producers are priced out of the market.

The **nominal tariff rate** published in a country's tariff schedule gives us a general idea of the level of protection afforded the home industry. But it may not always truly indicate the actual, or effective, protection given. For example, it is not necessarily true that a 25 percent import tariff on an automobile provides the domestic auto industry a protective margin of 25 percent against foreign producers. This is because the nominal tariff rates apply only to the total value of the final import product. But in the production process, the home import-competing industry may use imported material inputs or intermediate products that are subject to a different tariff than that on the final product; in this case, the **effective tariff rate** will differ from the nominal tariff rate. The effective tariff is a measure that applies to a single nation. In a world of floating exchange rates, if all nominal or effective tariff rates rose, the effect would be offset by a change in the exchange rate.

The effective tariff rate is an indicator of the actual level of protection that a nominal tariff rate provides the domestic import-competing producers. It signifies *the total increase in domestic productive activities (value added) that an existing tariff structure makes possible,* compared with what would occur under free-trade conditions. The effective rate tells us how much more expensive domestic production can be relative to foreign production and still compete in the market.

Assume that the domestic radio industry adds value to imported inputs by assembling component radio parts imported from abroad. Suppose the imported components can enter the home country on a duty-free basis. Suppose also that 20 percent of a radio's final value can be attributed to domestic assembly activities (value added), the remaining 80 percent reflecting the value of the imported components. Furthermore, let the cost of the radio components be the same for both the domestic country and the foreign country. Finally, assume that the foreign country can produce a radio for $100.

Suppose the home country imposes a nominal tariff of 10 percent on finished radios, so that the domestic import price rises from $100 to $110 per unit (see Exhibit 1000.19). Does this mean that home producers are afforded an effective rate of protection equal to 10 percent? Certainly not! The imported component parts enter the country duty-free (at a nominal tariff rate less than that on the finished import product), so the effective rate of protection is 50 percent. Compared with what would exist under free trade, domestic radio producers can be 50 percent more costly in their assembly activities and still be competitive!

Exhibit 1000.19 shows the figures in detail. Under free trade (zero tariff), a foreign radio could be imported for $100. To meet this price, domestic producers would have to hold their assembly costs down to $20. But under the protective umbrella of the tariff, domestic producers can afford to pay up to $30 for assembly and still meet the $110 domestic price of imported radios. The result is that domestic assembly costs could rise to a level of 50 percent above what would exist under free-trade conditions: ($30 − $20) / $20 = 0.5.

In general, the effective tariff rate is given by the following formula.

$$e = \frac{(n - ab)}{(1 - a)}$$

where

$e =$ the effective rate of protection
$n =$ the nominal tariff rate on the final product
$a =$ the ratio of the value of the imported input to the value of the final product
$b =$ the nominal tariff rate on the imported input

When the values from the radio example are plugged into this formula, we obtain

$$e = \frac{0.1 - 0.8\,(0)}{1 - 0.8}$$

$$e = 0.5$$

Exhibit 1000.19 *The Effective Rate of Protection*

Foreign Radio Import	Cost	Domestic Competing Radio	Cost
Component parts	$ 80	Component parts	$ 80
Assembly activity (value added)	20	Assembly activity (value added)	30 (?)
Nominal tariff	10	Domestic price	$110
Import price	$110		

The nominal tariff rate of 10 percent levied on the final import product thus affords domestic production activities an effective degree of protection equal to 50 percent—five times the nominal rate.

Two consequences of the effective-rate calculation are worthy of mention. First, the degree of effective protection increases as the value added by domestic producers declines (the ratio of the value of the imported input to the value of the final product increases). In the formula, the higher the value of a, the greater the effective-protection rate for any given nominal tariff rate on the final product. Second, a tariff on imports used in the production process reduces the level of effective protection. The higher the value of b, the lower the effective-protection rate for any given nominal tariff on the final product. In the formula, as b rises, the numerator of the formula decreases and hence e decreases. Note that is possible for the effective-tariff rate to assume a negative value, depending on the values of the components in the formula for the calculation of the effective-tariff rate.

Generalizing from this analysis, *when material inputs or intermediate products enter a country at a very low duty while the final imported commodity is protected by a high duty, the result tends to be a high protection rate for the domestic producers.* The nominal-tariff rate on finished goods thus understates the effective rate of protection. But should a tariff be imposed on imported inputs that exceeds that on the finished good, the nominal-tariff rate on the finished product would tend to overstate its protective effect. Such a situation might occur if the home government desired to protect suppliers of raw materials more than domestic manufacturers.

Tariff Escalation

In many industrialized nations the effective rate of protection is more than twice the nominal rate. An apparently low nominal tariff on a final import product may thus understate the effective rate of protection, which takes into account the effects of tariffs levied on raw materials and intermediate goods. In addition, the tariff structures of industrialized nations have generally been characterized by rising rates that give greater protection to intermediate and finished products than to primary commodities. This is commonly referred to as **tariff escalation.** Although raw materials are often imported at zero- or low-tariff rates, the nominal and effective protection increases at each stage of production. Many industrialized nations afford a relatively high degree of protection to their manufacturing sector.

The tariff structures of the industrialized nations may indeed discourage the growth of processing and manufacturing industries in the less-developed nations. The industrialized nations' low tariffs on primary commodities encourage the developing nations to expand operations in these sectors, while the high protective rates levied on manufactured goods pose a significant entry barrier for any developing nation wishing to compete in this area. From the point of view of the less-developed nations, it may be in their best interest to discourage disproportionate tariff reductions on raw materials. The effect of these tariff reductions is to magnify the discrepancy between the nominal and effective tariffs of the industrialized nations, worsening the potential competitive position of the less-developed nations in the manufacturing and processing sectors.

Who Pays for Import Restrictions?

Empirical studies often maintain that the total cost of trade restrictions can be high. Trade restrictions also affect the distribution of income within a society. A legitimate concern of government officials is whether the welfare costs of protectionism are shared uniformly by all people in a country, or whether some income groups absorb a disproportionate share of the costs.

How a Tariff Burdens Exporters

The benefits and costs of protecting domestic producers from foreign competition are based on the direct effects of an import tariff. Import-competing businesses and workers can benefit from tariffs through increases in output, profits, jobs, and compensation. A tariff imposes costs on domestic consumers in the form of higher prices of protected products and reductions in consumer surplus. There is also a net welfare loss for the economy because not all of the loss of consumer surplus is transferred as gains to domestic producers and the government (the protective effect and consumption effect).

A tariff carries additional burdens. In protecting import-competing producers, a tariff leads indirectly to a reduction in domestic exports. The net result of protectionism is to move the economy toward greater self-sufficiency, with lower imports and exports. For domestic workers, the protection of jobs in import-competing industries comes at the expense of jobs in other sectors of the economy, including exports. Although a tariff is intended to help domestic producers, the economy-wide implications of a tariff are adverse for the export sector. The welfare losses due to restrictions in output and employment in the economy's export industry may offset the welfare gains enjoyed by import-competing producers.

Because a tariff is a tax on imports, the burden of a tariff falls initially on importers, who must pay duties to the domestic government. However, importers generally try to shift increased costs to buyers through price increases. There are at least three ways in which the resulting higher prices of imports injure domestic exporters.

First, exporters often purchase imported inputs subject to tariffs that *increase the cost of inputs*. Because exporters tend to sell in competitive markets where they have little ability to dictate the prices they receive, they generally cannot pass on a tariff-induced increase in cost to their buyers. Higher export costs thus lead to higher prices and reduced overseas sales.

Tariffs also *raise the cost of living* by increasing the price of imports. Workers thus have the incentive to demand correspondingly higher wages, resulting in higher production costs. Tariffs lead to expanding output for import-competing companies that in turn bid for workers, causing money wages to rise. As these higher wages pass through the economy, export industries ultimately face higher wages and production costs, which lessen their competitive position in international markets.

Finally, import tariffs have *international repercussions* that lead to reductions in domestic exports. Tariffs cause the quantity of imports to decrease, which in turn decreases other nations' export revenues and ability to import. The decline in foreign export revenues results in a smaller demand for a nation's exports and leads to falling output and employment in its export industries.

If domestic export companies are damaged by import tariffs, why don't they protest such policies more vigorously? One problem is that tariff-induced increases in costs for export companies are subtle and invisible. Many exporters may not be aware of their existence. Also, the tariff-induced cost increases may be of such magnitude that some potential export companies are incapable of developing and have no tangible basis for political resistance.

Arguments for Trade Restrictions

The **free-trade argument** is, in principle, persuasive. It states that if each nation produces what it does best and permits trade, over the long run all will enjoy lower prices and higher levels of output, income, and consumption than could be achieved in isolation. In a dynamic world, comparative advantage is constantly changing, owing to shifts in technologies, input productivities, and wages, as well as tastes and preferences. A free market compels adjustment to take place. Either the efficiency of an industry must improve, or else resources will flow from low-productivity uses to those with high productivity. Tariffs and other trade barriers are viewed as tools that prevent the economy from undergoing adjustment, resulting in economic stagnation.

Virtually all nations have imposed restrictions on the international flow of goods, services, and capital. Often, proponents of protectionism say that free trade is fine in theory, but that it does not apply in the real world. Modern trade theory assumes perfectly competitive markets whose characteristics do not reflect real-world market conditions. Moreover, even though protectionists may concede that economic losses occur with tariffs and other restrictions, they often argue that noneconomic benefits such as national security more than offset the economic losses. In seeking protection from imports, domestic industries and labor unions attempt to secure their economic welfare. Over the years, a number of arguments have been advanced to pressure the U.S. president and Congress to enact restrictive measures.

These arguments include job protection, protection against cheap foreign labor, fairness in trade (a level playing field), maintenance of the domestic standard of living, equalization of production costs, infant-industry argument, and noneconomic arguments such as national security and cultural and sociological considerations.

Nontariff Trade Barriers

This section considers policies other than tariffs that restrict international trade. Referred to as **nontariff trade barriers (NTBs),** such measures have been on the rise since the 1960s and have become the most widely discussed topics at recent rounds of international trade negotiations. Indeed, the post–World War II success in international negotiations for the reduction of tariffs has made remaining NTBs even more visible.

NTBs encompass a variety of measures. Some have unimportant trade consequences; for example, labeling and packaging requirements can restrict trade, but generally only marginally. Other NTBs significantly affect trade patterns;

examples include import quotas, domestic content requirements, and subsidies. These NTBs are intended to reduce imports and thus benefit domestic producers.

Import Quotas

An **import quota** is a physical restriction on the quantity of goods that may be imported during a specific time period; the quota generally limits imports to a level below that which would occur under free-trade conditions.

Quotas versus Tariffs

Besides differing in their revenue effects and restrictive impacts on the volume of trade, tariffs and quotas have several other notable differences. Quotas are administratively easier to manage than tariffs, but they normally do not provide government tax revenues. Quotas are relatively easy to enact for emergency purposes, whereas enactment of tariffs is a time-consuming process requiring Congress to enact legislation.

Tariff-Rate Quota: A Two-Tier Tariff

Another restriction used to insulate a domestic industry from foreign competition is the **tariff-rate quota.** The U.S. government has imposed tariff-rate quotas on imports such as stainless steel flatware, brooms, cattle, fish, sugar, and milk.

As its name suggests, a tariff-rate quota displays both tariff-like and quota-like characteristics. This device allows a specified number of goods to be imported at one tariff rate (the *within-quota rate*), whereas any imports above this level face a higher tariff rate (the *over-quota rate*). A tariff-rate quota is thus a *two-tier tariff.*

Domestic Content Requirements

Today, many products, such as autos and aircraft, embody worldwide production. Domestic manufacturers of these products purchase resources or perform assembly functions outside the home country, a practice known as **foreign sourcing** (outsourcing) or production sharing. For example, **General Motors** has obtained engines from its subsidiaries in Mexico, **DaimlerChrysler** has purchased ball joints from Japanese producers, and **Ford** has acquired cylinder heads from European companies. Firms have used foreign sourcing to take advantage of lower production costs overseas, including lower wage rates. Domestic workers often challenge this practice, maintaining that foreign sourcing means that cheap foreign labor takes away their jobs and imposes downward pressure on the wages of those workers who are able to keep their jobs.

To limit the practice of foreign sourcing, organized labor has lobbied for the use of **domestic content requirements.** These requirements stipulate the minimum percentage of a product's total value that must be produced domestically. The effect of content requirements is to force both domestic and foreign firms who sell products in the home country to use domestic inputs (workers) in the production of those products. The demand for domestic inputs thus increases, contributing to higher input prices. Manufacturers generally lobby against domestic content requirements because they prevent manufacturers from obtaining inputs at the lowest cost, thus contributing to higher product prices and loss of competitiveness.

Worldwide, local content requirements have received most attention in the automobile industry. Developing countries have often used content requirements to foster domestic automobile production.

Subsidies

National governments sometimes grant **subsidies** to domestic producers to help improve their trade position. Such devices are an indirect form of protection provided to home businesses, whether they be import-competing producers or exporters. By providing domestic firms a cost advantage, a subsidy allows them to market their products at prices lower than warranted by their actual cost or profit considerations. Governments wanting to see certain domestic industries expand may provide subsidies to encourage their development. Governmental subsidies assume a variety of forms, including outright cash disbursements, tax concessions, insurance arrangements, and loans at below-market interest rates. Exhibit 1000.20 provides examples of governmental subsidies for several nations.

For purposes of our discussion, two types of subsidies can be distinguished: a **domestic subsidy,** which is sometimes granted to producers of import-competing goods, and an **export subsidy,** which goes to producers of goods

Exhibit 1000.20 *Examples of Governmental Subsidies*

Country	Subsidy Policy
Australia	Export market development grants extended to Australian exporters to seek out and develop overseas markets.
Canada	Rail transportation subsidies granted to Canadian exporters of wheat, barley, oats, and alfalfa.
European Union	Export subsidies provided to many agricultural products such as wheat, beef, poultry, fruits, and dairy products. Financial assistance extended to Airbus.
Japan	Financial assistance extended to Japanese aerospace producers, including loans at low interest rates and assistance with R&D costs.
United States	Export subsidies provided to U.S. producers of agricultural and manufactured goods through the Commodity Credit Corporation and the Export Import Bank

Source: Office of the U.S. Trade Representative, *Foreign Trade Barriers,* Washington, DC, U.S. Government Printing Office, various issues.

that are to be sold overseas. In both cases, the recipient producer views the subsidy as tantamount to a negative tax: the government adds an amount to the price the purchaser pays rather than subtracting from it. The net price actually received by the producer equals the price paid by the purchaser plus the subsidy. The subsidized producer is thus able to supply a greater quantity at each consumer's price.

Dumping

The case for protecting import-competing producers from foreign competition is bolstered by the antidumping argument. **Dumping** is recognized as a form of international price discrimination. It occurs when foreign buyers are charged lower prices than domestic buyers for an identical product, after allowing for transportation costs and tariff duties. Selling in foreign markets at a price below the cost of production is also considered dumping.

Forms of Dumping

Commercial dumping is generally viewed as sporadic, predatory, or persistent in nature. Each type is practiced under different circumstances.

Sporadic dumping (distress dumping) occurs when a firm disposes of excess inventories on foreign markets by selling abroad at lower prices than at home. This form of dumping may be the result of misfortune or poor planning by foreign producers. Unforeseen changes in supply and demand conditions can result in excess inventories and thus in dumping. Although sporadic dumping may be beneficial to importing consumers, it can be quite disruptive to import-competing producers, who face falling sales and short-run losses. Temporary tariff duties can be levied to protect home producers, but because sporadic dumping has minor effects on international trade, governments are reluctant to grant tariff protection under these circumstances.

Predatory dumping occurs when a producer temporarily reduces the prices charged abroad to drive foreign competitors out of business. When the producer succeeds in acquiring a monopoly position, prices are then raised commensurate with its market power. The new price level must be sufficiently high to offset any losses that occurred during the period of cutthroat pricing. The firm would presumably be confident in its ability to prevent the entry of potential competitors long enough for it to enjoy economic profits. To be successful, predatory dumping would have to be practiced on a massive basis to provide consumers with sufficient opportunity for bargain shopping. Home governments are generally concerned about predatory pricing for monopolizing purposes and may retaliate with antidumping duties that eliminate the price differential. Although predatory dumping is a theoretical possibility, economists have not found empirical evidence that supports its existence.

Persistent dumping, as its name suggests, goes on indefinitely. In an effort to maximize economic profits, a producer may consistently sell abroad at lower prices than at home. The rationale underlying persistent dumping is excess capacity.

International Price Discrimination

Consider the case of a domestic seller that enjoys market power as a result of barriers that restrict competition at home. Suppose this firm sells in foreign markets that are highly competitive. This means that the domestic consumer response to a change in price is less than that abroad; the home demand is less elastic than the foreign demand. A profit-maximizing firm would benefit from international price discrimination, charging a higher price at home, where competition is weak and demand is less elastic, and a lower price for the same product in foreign markets to meet competition. The practice of identifying separate groups of buyers of a product and charging different prices to these groups results in increased revenues and profits for the firm as compared to what would occur in the absence of price discrimination.

Excess Capacity

Another reason for sporadic or distress dumping is that producers sometimes face reductions in demand that leave them with idle productive capacity. This *excess capacity* is of particular concern to a nation such as Japan, which has guaranteed lifetime employment to much of its industrial labor force. For many Japanese companies, therefore, labor comes close to being a fixed cost because wages must be paid regardless of the company's production, sales, or profitability. Management thus has the incentive to compete vigorously for sales and to keep output high to generate revenues.

Should a firm find that its productive capacity exceeds the requirements of the domestic market, it may consider it more profitable to use the capacity to fulfill export orders at low prices rather than to allow the capacity to go idle. If necessary to keep exports high, a firm may be willing to sell abroad at a loss. Any profits generated by higher-priced domestic sales can help subsidize the goods that are dumped in foreign markets.

Antidumping Regulations

Despite the benefits that dumping may offer to importing consumers, governments have often levied stiff penalty duties against commodities they believe are being dumped into their markets from abroad. U.S. antidumping law is designed to prevent price discrimination and below-cost sales that injure U.S. industries. Under U.S. law, an **antidumping duty** is levied when the U.S. Department of Commerce determines a class or kind of foreign merchandise is being sold at *less than fair value* (LTFV) and the U.S. International Trade Commission (ITC) determines that LTFV imports are causing or threatening material injury (such as unemployment and lost sales and profits) to a U.S. industry. Such antidumping duties are imposed in addition to the normal tariff in order to neutralize the effects of price discrimination or below-cost sales.

The **margin of dumping** is calculated as the amount by which the foreign market value exceeds the U.S. price. Foreign market value is defined in one of two ways. According to the **priced-based definition,** dumping occurs whenever a foreign company sells a product in the U.S. market at a price below that for which the same product sells in the home market. When a home-nation price of the good is not available (for example, if the good is produced only for export and is not sold domestically), an effort is made to determine the price of the good in a third market.

In cases where the price-based definition cannot be applied, a **cost-based definition** of foreign market value is permitted. Under this approach, the Commerce Department "constructs" a foreign market value equal to the sum of (1) the cost of manufacturing the merchandise, (2) general expenses, (3) profit on home-market sales, and (4) the cost of packaging the merchandise for shipment to the United States. The amount for general expenses must equal at least 10 percent of the cost of manufacturing, and the amount for profit must equal at least 8 percent of the manufacturing cost plus general expenses.

Other Nontariff Trade Barriers

Other NTBs consist of governmental codes of conduct applied to imports. Even though such provisions are often well disguised, they remain important sources of commercial policy. Let's consider three such barriers: government procurement policies, social regulations, and sea transport and freight restrictions.

Government Procurement Policies

Because government agencies are large buyers of goods and services, they are attractive customers for foreign suppliers. If governments purchased goods and services only from the lowest-cost suppliers, the pattern of trade would not differ significantly from that which occurs in a competitive market. Most governments, however, favor domestic suppliers over foreign ones in the procurement of materials and products. This is evidenced by the fact that the ratio of imports to total purchases in the public sector is much smaller than in the private sector.

Governments often extend preferences to domestic suppliers in the form of **buy-national policies.** The U.S. government, through explicit laws, openly discriminates against foreign suppliers in its purchasing decisions. Although most other governments do not have formally legislated preferences for domestic suppliers, they often discriminate against foreign suppliers through hidden administrative rules and practices. Such governments utilize closed bidding systems that restrict the number of companies allowed to bid on sales, or they may publicize government contracts in such a way as to make it difficult for foreign suppliers to make a bid.

Social Regulations

Since the 1950s, nations have assumed an ever-increasing role in regulating the quality of life for society. **Social regulation** attempts to correct a variety of undesirable side effects in an economy that relate to health, safety, and the environment—effects that markets, left to themselves, often ignore. Social regulation applies to a particular issue, say environmental quality, and affects the behavior of firms in many industries such as automobiles, steel, and chemicals.

Sea Transport and Freight Restrictions

During the 1990s, U.S. shipping companies serving Japanese ports complained of a highly restrictive system of port services. They contended that Japan's association of stevedore companies (companies that unload cargo from ships) used a system of prior consultations to control competition, allocate harbor work among themselves, and frustrate the implementation of any cost-cutting by shipping companies.

In particular, shipping companies contended that they were forced to negotiate with the Japanese stevedore-company association on everything from arrival times to choice of stevedores and warehouses. Because port services were controlled by the stevedore-company association, foreign shippers could not negotiate with individual stevedore companies about prices and schedules. Moreover, U.S. shippers maintained that the Japanese government approved these restrictive practices by refusing to license new entrants into the port service business and by supporting the requirement that foreign shippers negotiate with Japan's stevedore-company association.

Exchange-Rate Systems

In choosing an exchange-rate system, a nation must decide whether to allow its currency to be determined by free-market forces (floating rate) or to be fixed (pegged) against some standard of value. If a nation adopts floating rates, it must decide whether to float independently, to float in unison with a group of other currencies, or to crawl according to a predetermined formula such as relative inflation rates. The decision to peg a currency includes the options of pegging to a single currency, to a basket of currencies, or to gold. Since 1971, however, the technique of expressing official exchange rates in terms of gold has not been used; gold has been phased out of the international monetary system.

Members of the International Monetary Fund (IMF) have been free to follow any exchange-rate policy that conforms to three principles: (1) exchange rates should not be manipulated to prevent effective balance-of-payments adjustments or to gain unfair competitive advantage over other members, (2) members should act to counter short-term disorderly conditions in exchange markets, and (3) when members intervene in exchange markets, they should take into account the interests of other members. Exhibit 1000.21 summarizes the exchange-rate practices of IMF member countries as of 1999; Exhibit 1000.22 highlights some of the factors that affect the choice of an exchange-rate system.

Fixed (pegged) **exchange rates** are used primarily by small, developing nations that maintain pegs to a **key currency,** such as the U.S. dollar or the French franc. A key currency is widely traded on world money markets, has demonstrated relatively stable values over time, and has been widely accepted as a means of international settlement.

One reason why developing nations choose to tie their currencies to a key currency is that it is used as a means of international settlement. Consider a Norwegian importer who wants to purchase Argentinean beef over the next year. If the Argentine exporter is unsure of what the Norwegian krone will purchase in one year, he might reject the krone in settlement. Similarly, the Norwegian importer might doubt the value of Argentina's peso. One solution is for the contract to be written in terms of a key currency such as the U.S. dollar. Generally speaking, smaller nations with relatively undiversified economies and large foreign-trade sectors have been inclined to peg their currencies to one of the key currencies.

Maintaining pegs to a key currency provides several benefits for developing nations. First, the prices of the traded products of many developing nations are determined primarily in the markets of industrialized nations such as the United States; by pegging, say, to the dollar, these nations can stabilize the domestic-currency prices of their imports and exports. Second, many nations with high inflation have pegged to the dollar (the United States has relatively low inflation) in order to exert restraint on domestic policies and reduce inflation. By making the commitment to stabilize their exchange rates against the dollar, governments hope to convince their citizens that they are

Exhibit 1000.21 *Exchange-Rate Arrangements of IMF Members, 1999*

Exchange Rate Arrangement	Number of Countries
Exchange arrangements with no separate legal tender*	37
Currency board arrangements	8
Conventional pegged (fixed) exchange rates	44
Pegged exchange rates within horizontal bands	8
Crawling pegged exchange rates	6
Exchange rates within crawling bands	9
Managed floating exchange rates	25
Independently floating exchange rates	48
	185

*The currency of another country circulates as the sole legal tender, or the member belongs to a monetary or currency union in which the same legal tender is shared by the members of the union.

Source: *International Financial Statistics,* June 2000, p. 2.

Exhibit 1000.22 *Factors for Choosing an Exchange-Rate System*

Characteristics of Economy	Implication for the Desired Degree of Exchange-Rate Flexibility
Size and openness of the economy	If trade is a large share of national output, then the costs of currency fluctuations can be high. This suggests that small, open economies may best be served by fixed exchange rates.
Inflation rate	If a country has much higher inflation than its trading partners, its exchange rate needs to be flexible to prevent its goods from becoming uncompetitive in world markets. If inflation differentials are more modest, a fixed rate is less troublesome.
Labor-market flexibility	The more rigid wages are, the greater the need for a flexible exchange rate to help the economy respond to an external shock.
Degree of financial development	In developing countries with immature financial markets, a freely floating exchange rate may not be sensible because a small number of foreign-exchange trades can cause big swings in currencies.
Credibility of policy makers	The weaker the reputation of the central bank, the stronger the case for pegging the exchange rate to build confidence that inflation will be controlled.
Capital mobility	The more open an economy to international capital, the harder it is to sustain a fixed rate.

Source: International Monetary Fund, *World Economic Outlook,* October 1997, p. 83.

willing to adopt the responsible monetary policies necessary to achieve low inflation. Pegging the exchange rate may thus lessen inflationary expectations, leading to lower interest rates, a lessening of the loss of output due to disinflation, and a moderation of price pressures.

In maintaining fixed exchange rates, nations must decide whether to peg their currencies to another currency or to a currency basket. Pegging to a *single currency* is generally done by developing nations whose trade and financial relationships are mainly with a single industrial-country partner. For example, Ivory Coast, which trades primarily with France, pegs its currency to the French franc.

Developing nations with more than one major trading partner often peg their currencies to a group or *basket of currencies*. The basket is composed of prescribed quantities of foreign currencies in proportion to the amount of trade done with the nation pegging its currency. Once the basket has been selected, the currency value of the nation is computed using the exchange rates of the foreign currencies in the basket. Pegging the domestic-currency value of the basket enables a nation to average out fluctuations in export or import prices caused by exchange-rate movements. The effects of exchange-rate changes on the domestic economy are thus reduced.

Rather than constructing their own currency basket, many nations peg the value of their currencies to the **special drawing right (SDR)**, a basket of five currencies established by the IMF. The IMF requires that the valuation of the SDR basket be reviewed every five years; the basket is to include, in proportional amounts, the currencies of the members having the largest exports of goods and services during the previous five years. The currencies comprising the basket as of 1999, along with their amounts and percentage weights, are listed in Exhibit 1000.23.

Exhibit 1000.23 *Special Drawing Right (SDR) Basket of Currencies*

Currency	Amount
U.S. dollar	0.5821
Euro (Germany)	0.2280
Japanese yen	27.2000
Euro (France)	0.1239
Pound sterling	0.1050

Source: International Monetary Fund, *Annual Report*, 1999, p. 109.

The idea behind the SDR basket valuation is to make the SDR's value more stable than the foreign-currency value of any single national currency. The SDR is valued according to an index based on the moving average of those currencies in the basket. Should the values of the basket currencies either depreciate or appreciate against one another, the SDR's value would remain in the center. The SDR would depreciate against those currencies that are rising in value and appreciate against currencies whose values are falling. Nations desiring exchange-rate stability are attracted to the SDR as a currency basket against which to peg their currency values.

Fixed Exchange-Rate System

Few nations have allowed their currencies' exchange values to be determined solely by the forces of supply and demand in a free market. Until the industrialized nations adopted managed floating exchange rates in the 1970s, the practice generally was to maintain a pattern of relatively fixed (pegged) exchange rates among national currencies. Changes in national exchange rates presumably were to be initiated by domestic monetary authorities when long-term market forces warranted it.

Par Value and Official Exchange Rate

Under a fixed exchange-rate system, governments assign their currencies a **par value** in terms of gold or other key currencies. By comparing the par values of two currencies, we can determine their **official exchange rate.** For example, the official exchange rate between the U.S. dollar and the British pound was $2.80 = £1 as long as the United States bought and sold gold at a fixed price of $35 per ounce and Britain bought and sold gold at £12.50 per ounce (35.00 / 12.50 = 2.80). The major industrial nations set their currencies' par values in terms of gold until gold was phased out of the international monetary system in the early 1970s.

Today, many developing nations choose to define their par values in terms of certain key currencies, such as the U.S. dollar. Under this arrangement, the monetary authority first defines its official exchange rate in terms of the key currency. It then defends the fixed parity by purchasing and selling its currency for the key currency at that rate. Assume, for example, that Bolivian central bankers fix their peso at 20 pesos = US$1, whereas Ecuador's sucre is set at 10 sucres = US$1. The official exchange rate between the peso and sucre becomes 1 peso = 0.5 sucre.

Exchange-Rate Stabilization

A first requirement for a nation participating in a fixed exchange-rate system is to determine an official exchange rate for its currency. The next step is to set up an **exchange-stabilization fund** to defend the official rate. Through purchases and sales of foreign currencies, the exchange-stabilization fund attempts to ensure that the market exchange rate does not move above or below the official exchange rate.

Devaluation and Revaluation

Under a fixed exchange-rate system, a nation's monetary authority may decide to pursue balance-of-payments equilibrium by devaluing or revaluing its currency. The purpose of **devaluation** is to cause the home currency's exchange value to *depreciate*, thus counteracting a payments *deficit*. The purpose of currency **revaluation** is to cause the home currency's exchange value to *appreciate*, thus counteracting a payments *surplus*.

The terms *devaluation* and *revaluation* refer to a legal redefinition of a currency's par value under a system of fixed exchange rates. The terms *depreciation* and *appreciation* refer to the actual impact on the market exchange rate caused by a redefinition of a par value or to changes in an exchange rate stemming from changes in the supply of or demand for foreign exchange.

Devaluation and revaluation policies are considered to be *expenditure-switching* instruments because they work on relative prices to divert domestic and foreign expenditures between domestic and foreign goods. By raising the home price of the foreign currency, a devaluation makes the home country's exports cheaper to foreigners in terms of the foreign currency, while making the home country's imports more expensive in terms of the home currency. Expenditures are diverted from foreign to home goods as home exports rise and imports fall. In like manner, a revaluation discourages the home country's exports and encourages its imports, diverting expenditures from home goods to foreign goods.

Before implementing a devaluation or revaluation, the monetary authority must decide (1) if an adjustment in the official exchange rate is necessary to correct a payments disequilibrium, (2) when the adjustment will occur, and (3) how large the adjustment should be. Exchange-rate decisions of government officials may be incorrect—that is, ill timed and of improper magnitude.

In making the decision to undergo a devaluation or revaluation, monetary authorities generally attempt to hide behind a veil of secrecy. Just hours before the decision is to become effective, public denials of any such policies by official government representatives are common. This is to discourage currency speculators, who try to profit by shifting funds from a currency falling in value to one rising in value. Given the destabilizing impact that massive speculation can exert on financial markets, it is hard to criticize monetary authorities for being secretive in their actions. However, the need for devaluation tends to be obvious to outsiders as well as to government officials and in the past has nearly always resulted in heavy speculative pressures.

Legal versus Economic Implications

Currency devaluations and revaluations are used in conjunction with a *fixed* exchange-rate system. The monetary authority changes a currency's exchange rate by decree, usually by a sizable amount at one time. How is such a policy implemented?

Recall that under a fixed exchange-rate system, the home currency is assigned a par value by the nation's monetary authorities. The par value is the amount of a nation's currency that is required to purchase a fixed amount of gold, a key currency, or the special drawing right. These assets represent the legal *numeraire*, or the unit of contractual obligations. By comparing various national currency prices of the numeraire, monetary authorities determine the official rate of exchange for the currencies.

In the *legal* sense, a devaluation or revaluation occurs when the home country redefines its currency price of the official numeraire, changing the par value. The *economic* effect of the par value's redefinition is the impact on the market rate of exchange. Assuming that other trading nations retain their existing par values, one would expect (1) a devaluation to result in a depreciation in the currency's exchange value, or (2) a revaluation to result in an appreciation in the currency's exchange value.

Stabilizing Currencies of Developing Countries: Currency Boards versus Dollarization

In recent years, stabilization of the beleaguered currencies of the developing countries has been a hotly debated topic. Rather than relying on a central bank's exchange-stabilization fund, developing countries have increasingly resorted to currency boards and dollarization as stabilization devices. Let us examine these techniques.

Currency Board

A **currency board** is a monetary authority that issues notes and coins convertible into a foreign anchor currency at a *fixed exchange rate*. The anchor currency is a currency chosen for its expected stability and international acceptability. For most currency boards, the U.S. dollar or British pound has been the anchor currency. Also, a few currency boards have used gold as the anchor. Usually, the fixed exchange rate is set by law, making changes to the exchange rate very costly for governments. Put simply, currency boards offer the strongest form of a fixed exchange rate that is possible short of full currency union.

Dollarization

Instead of using a currency board to promote a stable currency, why not "dollarize" an economy? This is what several Latin American countries, such as Argentina and Mexico, were considering at the turn of the millennium.

Dollarization occurs when residents of, say, Argentina, use the U.S. dollar alongside or instead of the peso. *Unofficial dollarization* (partial dollarization) occurs when Argentines hold dollar-denominated bank deposits or Federal Reserve notes to protect against high inflation in the peso. Unofficial dollarization has existed for years in many Latin American and Caribbean countries, where the United States is a major trading partner and a major source of foreign investment.

Official dollarization (full dollarization) means the elimination of the Argentine peso, and its complete replacement with the U.S. dollar. The monetary base of Argentina, which initially consists entirely of peso-denominated currency, would be converted into U.S. Federal Reserve notes. To replace its currency, Argentina would sell foreign reserves (mostly U.S. Treasury securities) to buy dollars and exchange all outstanding peso notes for dollar notes. The U.S. dollar would be the sole legal tender and sole unit of account in Argentina. As of 2000, there were 13 officially dollarized countries in Latin America and the Caribbean.

Floating Exchange Rates

Instead of utilizing fixed exchange rates, some nations allow their currencies to float in the foreign-exchange market. By **floating** (or flexible) **exchange rates**, we mean currency prices that are established daily in the foreign-exchange market, without restrictions imposed by government policy on the extent to which the prices can move. With floating rates, there is an equilibrium exchange rate that equates the demand for and supply of the home currency. Any other rate can create either a surplus or shortage of currency. Changes in the exchange rate will ideally correct a payments imbalance by bringing about shifts in imports and exports of goods, services, and short-term capital movements. The exchange rate depends on relative money supplies, income levels, interest rates, prices, and other factors.

Unlike fixed exchange rates, floating exchange rates are not characterized by par values and official exchange rates; they are determined by market supply and demand conditions rather than central bankers. Although floating rates do not have an exchange-stabilization fund to maintain existing rates, it does not necessarily follow that floating rates must fluctuate erratically. They will do so if the underlying market forces become unstable. Because there is no exchange-stabilization fund under floating rates, any holdings of international reserves serve as working balances rather than to maintain a given exchange rate for any currency.

Arguments for and against Floating Rates

One advantage claimed for floating rates is their simplicity. Floating rates allegedly respond quickly to changing supply and demand conditions, clearing the market of shortages or surpluses of a given currency. Instead of having formal rules of conduct among central bankers governing exchange-rate movements, floating rates are market determined. They operate under simplified institutional arrangements that are relatively easy to enact.

Because floating rates fluctuate throughout the day, they permit continuous adjustment in the balance of payments. The adverse effects of prolonged disequilibriums that tend to occur under fixed exchange rates are minimized under floating rates. It is also argued that floating rates partially insulate the home economy from external forces. This means that governments will not have to restore payments equilibrium through painful inflationary or deflationary adjustment policies. Switching to floating rates frees a nation from having to adopt policies that perpetuate domestic disequilibrium as the price of maintaining a satisfactory balance-of-payments position. Nations thus have greater freedom to pursue policies that promote domestic balance than they do under fixed exchange rates.

Although there are strong arguments in favor of floating exchange rates, this system is often considered to be of limited usefulness for bankers and businesspeople. Critics of floating rates maintain that an unregulated market may lead to wide fluctuations in currency values, discouraging foreign trade and investment. Although traders and investors may be able to hedge exchange-rate risk by dealing in the forward market, the cost of hedging may become prohibitively high.

Floating rates in theory are supposed to allow governments to set independent monetary and fiscal policies. But this flexibility may cause a problem of another sort: *inflationary bias*. Under a system of floating rates, monetary authorities may lack the financial discipline required by a fixed exchange-rate system. Suppose a nation faces relatively high rates of inflation compared with the rest of the world. This domestic inflation will have no negative impact on the nation's trade balance under floating rates because its currency will automatically depreciate in the exchange market. However, a protracted depreciation of the currency would result in persistently increasing import prices and a rising price level, making inflation self-perpetuating and the depreciation continuous. Because there is greater freedom for domestic financial management under floating rates, there may be less resistance to overspending and to its subsequent pressure on wages and prices.

Adjustable Pegged Rates

Rather than maintaining completely fixed exchange rates or allowing the exchange rate to be determined by the free-market forces of supply and demand, nations have often pursued limited exchange-rate flexibility. Such is the case of the adjustable pegged-rate system.

In 1944, delegates from 44 member nations of the United Nations met at Bretton Woods, New Hampshire, to create a new international monetary system. They were aware of the unsatisfactory monetary experience of the 1930s, during which the international gold standard collapsed as the result of the economic and financial crises of the Great Depression and nations experimented unsuccessfully with floating exchange rates and exchange controls. The delegates wanted to establish international monetary order and avoid the instability and nationalistic practices that had been in effect until 1944.

The international monetary system that was created became known as the **Bretton Woods system.** The founders felt that neither completely fixed exchange rates nor floating rates were optimal; instead, they adopted a kind of managed exchange-rate system known as **adjustable pegged exchange rates.** The Bretton Woods system lasted from 1946 until 1973.

The main feature of the adjustable peg system is that currencies are tied to each other to provide stable exchange rates for commercial and financial transactions. When the balance of payments moves away from its long-run equilibrium position, however, a nation can repeg its exchange rate via devaluation or revaluation policies. Member nations agreed in principle to defend existing par values as long as possible in times of balance-of-payments disequilibrium. They were expected to use fiscal and monetary policies first to correct payments imbalances. But if reversing a persistent payments imbalance would mean severe disruption to the domestic economy in terms of inflation or unemployment, member nations could correct this *fundamental disequilibrium* by repegging their currencies up to 10 percent without permission from the International Monetary Fund and by greater than 10 percent with the Fund's permission.

Although adjustable pegged rates are intended to promote a viable balance-of-payments adjustment mechanism, they have been plagued with operational problems. In the Bretton Woods system, adjustments in prices and incomes often conflicted with domestic-stabilization objectives. Also, currency devaluation was considered undesirable because it seemed to indicate a failure of domestic policies and a loss of international prestige. Conversely, revaluations were unacceptable to exporters, whose livelihoods were vulnerable to such policies. Repegging exchange rates only as a last resort often meant that when adjustments did occur, they were sizable. Moreover, adjustable pegged rates posed difficulties in estimating the equilibrium rate to which a currency should be repegged. Finally, once the market exchange rate reached the margin of the permissible band around parity, it in effect became a rigid fixed rate that presented speculators with a one-way bet. Given persistent weakening pressure, for example, at the band's outer limit, speculators had the incentive to move out of a weakening currency that was expected to depreciate further in value as the result of official devaluation.

Managed Floating Rates

In 1973, a **managed floating system** was adopted, under which informal guidelines were established by the IMF for coordination of national exchange-rate policies.

The motivation for the formulation of guidelines for floating arose from two concerns. The first was that nations might intervene in the exchange markets to avoid exchange-rate alterations that would weaken their competitive position. When the United States suspended its gold-convertibility pledge and allowed its overvalued dollar to float in the exchange markets, it hoped that a free-market adjustment would result in a depreciation of the dollar against other, undervalued currencies. Rather than permitting a **clean float** (a free-market solution) to occur, foreign central banks refused to permit the dollar depreciation by intervening in the exchange market. The United States considered this a **dirty float,** because the free-market forces of supply and demand were not allowed to achieve their equilibrating role. A second motivation for floating guidelines was the concern that free floats over time might lead to disorderly markets with erratic fluctuations in exchange rates. Such destabilizing activity could create an uncertain business climate and reduce the level of world trade.

Under managed floating, a nation can alter the degree to which it intervenes on the foreign-exchange market. Heavier intervention moves the nation nearer the fixed exchange-rate case, whereas less intervention moves the nation nearer the floating exchange-rate case. Concerning day-to-day and week-to-week exchange-rate movements, a main objective of the floating guidelines has been to prevent the emergence of erratic fluctuations. Member nations should intervene on the foreign-exchange market as necessary to prevent sharp and disruptive exchange-rate fluctuations from day to day and week to week. Such a policy is known as **leaning against the wind**—intervening to reduce short-term fluctuations in exchange rates without attempting to adhere to any particular rate over the long run. Members should also not act aggressively with respect to their currency exchange rates; that is, they should not enhance the value when it is appreciating or depress the value when it is depreciating.

Under the managed float, some nations choose target exchange rates and intervene to support them. Target exchange rates are intended to reflect long-term economic forces that underlie exchange-rate movements. One way for managed floaters to estimate a target exchange rate is to follow statistical indicators that respond to the same economic forces as the exchange-rate trend. Then, when the values of indicators change, the exchange-rate target can be adjusted accordingly. Among these indicators are rates of inflation in different nations, levels of official foreign reserves, and persistent imbalances in international payments accounts. In practice, defining a target exchange rate can be difficult in a market based on volatile economic conditions.

Managed Floating Rates in the Short Run and Long Run

Managed floating exchange rates attempt to combine market-determined exchange rates with foreign-exchange market intervention in order to take advantage of the best features of floating exchange rates and fixed exchange rates. Under a managed float, market intervention is used to stabilize exchange rates in the short run; in the long run, a managed float allows market forces to determine exchange rates.

The Crawling Peg

Since 1968, the Brazilian government has announced a change in the par value of the cruzeiro several times a year. The frequent adjustments in Brazil's exchange rate occur in response to the following indicators: (1) the movement in prices in Brazil relative to those of its main trading partners, (2) the level of foreign-exchange reserves, (3) export performance, and (4) the position of the current account of the balance of payments. These exchange-rate adjustments are an application of a mechanism dubbed the **crawling peg.** Not only has Brazil adopted this system, but it also has been used by Argentina, Chile, Israel, and Peru.

The crawling-peg system, a compromise between fixed and floating rates, means that a nation makes small, frequent changes in the par value of its currency to correct balance-of-payments disequilibriums. Deficit and surplus nations both keep adjusting until the desired exchange-rate level is attained. The term *crawling peg* implies that par-value changes are implemented in a large number of small steps, making the process of exchange-rate adjustment continuous for all practical purposes. The peg thus crawls from one par value to another.

The crawling-peg mechanism has been used primarily by nations with high inflation rates. Some developing nations, mostly South American, have recognized that a pegging system can operate in an inflationary environment only if there is provision for frequent changes in the par values. Associating national inflation rates with international competitiveness, these nations have generally used price indicators as a basis for adjusting crawling pegged rates. In these nations, the primary concern is the criterion that governs exchange-rate movements, rather than the currency or basket of currencies against which the peg is defined.

The crawling peg differs from the system of adjustable pegged rates. Under the adjustable peg, currencies are tied to a par value that changes infrequently (perhaps once every several years) but suddenly, usually in large jumps. The idea behind the crawling peg is that a nation can make small, frequent changes in par values, perhaps several times a year, so that they creep along slowly in response to evolving market conditions.

Supporters of the crawling peg argue that the system combines the flexibility of floating rates with the stability usually associated with fixed rates. They contend that a system providing continuous, steady adjustments is more responsive to changing competitive conditions and avoids a main problem of adjustable pegged rates—that changes in par values are frequently wide of the mark. Moreover, small, frequent changes in par values made at random intervals frustrate speculators with their irregularity.

In recent years, the crawling-peg formula has been used by developing nations facing rapid and persistent inflation. But the IMF has generally contended that such a system would not be in the best interests of nations such as the United States or Germany, which bear the responsibility for international currency levels. The IMF has felt that it would be hard to apply such a system to the industrialized nations, whose currencies serve as a source of international liquidity. Although even the most ardent proponents of the crawling peg admit that the time for its widespread adoption has not yet come, the debate over its potential merits is bound to continue.

Exchange Controls

The exchange-rate mechanisms discussed so far all have one important characteristic in common: all are based on the principle of a free exchange market and automatic market forces. It is true that monetary authorities may modify the exchange-rate outcome by purchasing and selling national currencies, but the foreign-exchange transactions conducted among private exporters and importers are free from government regulation. A private foreign-exchange market thus exists.

A government that does not wish to permit a free foreign-exchange market can set up a system of exchange measures to keep its balance of payments under control when the exchange rate moves away from its equilibrium level. Among the devices that have been used to achieve this objective are direct control over balance-of-payments transactions and multiple exchange rates.

Exchange controls achieved prominence during the economic crises of the late 1930s and immediately after World War II. It was not until the late 1950s that the industrialized nations of Western Europe considered themselves financially stable enough so that most controls could be dismantled and a high degree of freedom provided for many international transactions. Exchange controls are still widespread today in the less developed nations of Africa, South America, and the Far East.

At one extreme, a government may seek to gain control over its payments position by directly circumventing market forces through the imposition of direct controls on international transactions. For example, a government that has a virtual monopoly over foreign-exchange dealings may require that all foreign-exchange earnings be turned over to authorized dealers. The government then allocates foreign exchange among domestic traders and investors at government-set prices.

The advantage of such a system is that the government can influence its payments position by regulating the amount of foreign exchange allocated to imports or capital outflows, limiting the extent of these transactions. Exchange controls also permit the government to encourage or discourage certain transactions by offering different rates for foreign currency for different purposes. Furthermore, exchange controls can give domestic monetary and fiscal policies greater freedom in their stabilization roles. By controlling the balance of payments through exchange controls, a government can pursue its domestic economic policies without fear of balance-of-payments repercussions.

A related method of gaining control of the balance of payments is the practice of **multiple exchange rates.** Used primarily by the developing nations, multiple exchange rates attempt to ensure that necessary goods are imported and less essential goods are discouraged. Essential imports, such as raw materials or capital goods, are subsidized when the government sets a low exchange rate for these commodities, resulting in lower prices to domestic buyers. For less desirable imports, such as luxury products, a higher price will be set when the government makes foreign exchange available only at a high rate. Multiple exchange rates can thus be used to subsidize or tax import purchases so that a nation's scarce supply of foreign exchange will be rationed among only the most essential commodities. Obviously, the implementation of such a mechanism requires an elaborate classification system, as well as strict penalties against smuggling.

Nations have also used **dual** *(two-tier)* **exchange rates** to cope with destabilizing international capital flows. Short-term capital tends to move across national borders in response to anticipated changes in exchange rates and interest-rate differentials. Such movements may prevent monetary authorities from pursuing policies insulated from balance-of-payments considerations or even from defending official exchange rates.

Dual exchange rates attempt to insulate a nation from the balance-of-payments effects of capital flows while providing a stable business climate for commercial (current account) transactions involving merchandise trade and services. This is accomplished by having separate exchange rates for commercial and capital transactions. *Commercial* transactions must be conducted in a market where exchange rates are officially *pegged* by national monetary authorities, whereas *capital* transactions occur in a financial market in which exchange rates are *floating*. Although history gives no example of a dual exchange-rate system in which complete segregation of commercial and capital transactions has been achieved, the experiences of Belgium, France, and Italy have approximated such a mechanism.

International Banking

International Banking: Reserves, Debt, and Risk

The world's banking system plays a vital role in facilitating international transactions and maintaining economic prosperity. Commercial banks, such as **Citicorp,** help finance trade and investment and provide loans to international borrowers. Central banks, such as the Federal Reserve, serve as a lender of last resort to commercial banks and sometimes intervene in foreign-currency markets to stabilize currency values. Finally, the International Monetary Fund (IMF) serves as a lender to nations having long-term deficits in their balance of payments. This section concentrates on the role that banks play in world financial markets, the risks associated with international banking, and strategies employed to deal with these risks.

We'll begin with an investigation of the nature of international reserves and their importance for the world financial system. This is followed by a discussion of banks as international lenders and the problems associated with international debt.

Nature of International Reserves

The need of a central bank, such as the Bank of England, for international reserves is similar to an individual's desire to hold cash balances (currency and checkable deposits). At both levels, monetary reserves are intended to bridge the gap between monetary receipts and monetary payments.

Suppose that an individual receives income in equal installments every minute of the day and that expenditures for goods and services are likewise evenly spaced over time. The individual will require only a minimum cash reserve to finance purchases, because no significant imbalances between cash receipts and cash disbursements will arise. In reality, however, individuals purchase goods and services on a fairly regular basis from day to day, but receive paychecks only at weekly or longer intervals. A certain amount of cash is therefore required to finance the discrepancy that arises between monetary receipts and payments.

When an individual initially receives a paycheck, cash balances are high. But as time progresses, these holdings of cash may fall to virtually zero just before the next paycheck is received. Individuals are thus concerned with the amount of cash balances that, on average, are necessary to keep them going until the next paycheck arrives.

Although individuals desire cash balances primarily to fill the gap between monetary receipts and payments, this desire is influenced by a number of other factors. The need for cash balances may become more acute if the absolute dollar volume of transactions increases, because larger imbalances may result between receipts and payments. Conversely, to the extent that individuals can finance their transactions on credit, they require less cash in hand.

Just as an individual desires to hold cash balances, national governments have a need for **international reserves.** The chief purpose of international reserves is to enable nations to finance disequilibriums in their balance-of-payments positions. When a nation finds its monetary receipts falling short of its monetary payments, the deficit is settled with international reserves. Eventually, the deficit must be eliminated, because central banks tend to have limited stocks of reserves.

From a policy perspective, the advantage of international reserves is that they enable nations to sustain temporary balance-of-payments deficits until acceptable adjustment measures can operate to correct the disequilibrium. Holdings of international reserves facilitate effective policy formation because corrective adjustment measures need not be implemented prematurely. Should a deficit nation possess abundant stocks of reserve balances, however, it may be able to resist unpopular adjustment measures, making eventual adjustments even more troublesome.

Demand for International Reserves

When a nation's international monetary payments exceed its international monetary receipts, some means of settlement is required to finance its payments deficit. Settlement ultimately consists of transfers of international reserves among nations. Both the magnitude and the longevity of a balance-of-payments deficit that can be sustained in the absence of equilibrating adjustments are limited by a nation's stock of international reserves.

On a global basis, the **demand for international reserves** depends on two related factors: (1) the monetary value of international transactions and (2) the disequilibrium that can arise in balance-of-payments positions. The demand for international reserves is also contingent on such things as the speed and strength of the balance-of-payments adjustment mechanism and the overall institutional framework of the world economy.

Exchange-Rate Flexibility

One determinant of the demand for international reserves is the *degree of exchange-rate flexibility* of the international monetary system. This is because exchange-rate flexibility in part underlies the efficiency of the balance-of-payments adjustment process.

If exchange rates are fixed or pegged by the monetary authorities, international reserves play a crucial role in the exchange-rate stabilization process. If the U.S. dollar is not to depreciate beyond the pegged rate, the monetary authorities—that is, the Federal Reserve—must enter the market to supply pounds, in exchange for dollars, in the amount necessary to eliminate the disequilibrium.

Rather than operating under a rigidly pegged system, suppose a nation makes an agreement to foster some automatic adjustments by allowing market rates to float within a narrow band around the official exchange rate. This limited exchange-rate flexibility would be aimed at correcting minor payments imbalances, whereas large and persistent disequilibriums would require other adjustment measures.

A fundamental purpose of international reserves is to facilitate government intervention in exchange markets to stabilize currency values. The more active a government's stabilization activities, the greater is the need for reserves. Most exchange-rate standards today involve some stabilization operations and require international reserves. However, if exchange rates were allowed to float freely without government interference, theoretically there would be no need for reserves. This is because a floating rate would serve to eliminate an incipient payments imbalance, negating the need for stabilization operations.

Other Determinants

Changes in the degree of exchange-rate flexibility are inversely related to changes in the quantity of international reserves demanded. In other words, a monetary system characterized by more rapid and flexible exchange-rate adjustments requires smaller reserves, and vice versa.

In addition to the degree of exchange-rate flexibility, several other factors underlie the demand for international reserves, including (1) automatic adjustment mechanisms that respond to payments disequilibriums, (2) economic policies used to bring about payments equilibrium, and (3) the international coordination of economic policies.

Analysis has shown that adjustment mechanisms involving prices, interest rates, incomes, and monetary flows automatically tend to correct balance-of-payments disequilibriums. A payments deficit or surplus initiates changes in each of these variables. The more efficient each of these adjustment mechanisms is, the smaller and more short-lived market imbalances will be and the fewer reserves will be needed. The demand for international reserves therefore tends to be smaller with speedier and more complete automatic adjustment mechanisms.

The demand for international reserves is also influenced by the choice and effectiveness of government policies adopted to correct payments imbalances. Unlike automatic adjustment mechanisms, which rely on the free market to identify industries and labor groups that must bear the adjustment burden, the use of government policies involves political decisions. All else being equal, the greater a nation's propensity to apply commercial policies (including tariffs, quotas, and subsidies) to key sectors, the less will be its need for international reserves. This assumes, of course, that the policies are effective in reducing payments disequilibriums. Because of uncertainties about the nature and timing of payments disturbances, however, nations are often slow to initiate such trade policies and find themselves requiring international reserves to weather periods of payments disequilibriums.

The international coordination of economic policies is another determinant of the demand for international reserves. A primary goal of economic cooperation among finance ministers is to reduce the frequency and extent of payments imbalances and hence the demand for international reserves. Since the end of World War II, nations have moved toward the harmonization of national economic objectives by establishing programs through such organizations as the International Monetary Fund and the Organization of Economic Cooperation and Development. Another example of international economic organization has been the European Union, whose goal is to achieve a common macroeconomic policy and full monetary union. By reducing the intensity of disturbances to payments balance, such policy coordination reduces the need for international reserves.

Other factors influence the demand for international reserves. The quantity demanded is positively related to the level of world prices and income. One would expect rising price levels to inflate the market value of international transactions and, therefore, to increase the potential demand for reserves. The need for reserves would also tend to rise with the level of global income and trade activity.

In summary, central banks need international reserves to cover possible or expected excess payments to other nations at some future time. The quantity of international reserves demanded is directly related to the size and duration of these payment gaps. If a nation with a payments deficit is willing and able to initiate quick actions to increase receipts or decrease payments, the amount of reserves needed will be relatively small. Conversely, the demand for reserves will be relatively large if nations initiate no actions to correct payments imbalances or adopt policies that prolong such disequilibriums.

Supply of International Reserves

The analysis so far has emphasized the demand for international reserves. But what about the **supply of international reserves?** The total supply of international reserves consists of two distinct categories: *owned reserves* and *borrowed reserves*. Reserve assets such as acceptable nationals (foreign) currencies, gold, and special drawing rights (SDRs) are generally considered to be directly owned by the holding nations. But if nations with payments deficits find their stocks of owned reserves falling to unacceptably low levels, they may be able to borrow international reserves as a cushioning device. Lenders may be foreign nations with excess reserves, foreign financial institutions, or international agencies such as the IMF.

Owned Reserves: National (Foreign) Currencies

International reserves are a means of payment used in financing foreign transactions. One such asset is holdings of *national currencies* (foreign currencies) such as pounds and dollars. Using the dollar as a reserve currency meant that the supply of international reserves varied with the payments position of the United States. During the 1960s, this situation gave rise to the so-called **liquidity problem.** To preserve confidence in the dollar as a reserve currency, the United States had to strengthen its payments position by eliminating its deficits. But correction of the U.S. deficits would mean elimination of additional dollars as a source of reserves for the international monetary system. The creation in 1970 of SDRs as reserve assets and their subsequent allocations have been intended as a solution for this problem.

Owned Reserves: Gold

The historical importance of gold as an international reserve asset should not be underemphasized. At one time, gold served as the key monetary asset of the international payments mechanism; it also constituted the basis of the money supplies of many nations.

As an international money, gold fulfilled several important functions. Under the historic **gold standard,** gold served directly as an international means of payment. It also provided a unit of account against which commodity prices as well as the parities of national currencies were quoted. Although gold holdings do not yield interest income, gold has generally served as a viable store of value despite inflation, wars, and revolutions. Perhaps the greatest advantage of gold as a monetary asset is its overall acceptability, especially when compared with other forms of international monies.

Today, the role of gold as an international reserve asset has declined. Over the past 30 years, gold has fallen from nearly 70 percent to less than 3 percent of world reserves. Private individuals rarely use gold as a medium of payment and virtually never as a unit of account. Nor do central banks currently use gold as an official unit of account for stating the parities of national currencies. The monetary role of gold is currently recognized by only a few nations, mostly in the Middle East. In most nations outside the United States, private residents have long been able to buy and sell gold as they would any other commodity.

Owned Reserves: Special Drawing Rights

The liquidity and confidence problems of the gold exchange standard that resulted from reliance on the dollar and gold as international monies led in 1970 to the creation by the IMF of a new reserve asset, termed **special drawing rights (SDRs).** The objective was to introduce into the payment mechanism a new reserve asset, in addition to the dollar and gold, that could be transferred among participating nations in settlement of payments deficits. With the IMF managing the stock of SDRs, world reserves would presumably grow in line with world commerce.

SDRs are unconditional rights to draw currencies of other nations. When the fund creates a certain number of SDRs, they are allocated to the member nations in proportion to the relative size of their fund quotas. Nations can then draw on their SDR balances in financing their payments deficits. The key point is that certain surplus nations are designated by the fund to trade their currencies for an equivalent amount in SDRs to deficit nations in need of foreign-exchange reserves. Nations whose currencies are acquired as foreign exchange are not required to accept more than three times their initial SDR allotments.

SDRs pay interest to surplus nations on their net holdings (the amount by which a nation's SDR balance exceeds its allocation as determined by its fund quota). Interest payments come from deficit nations that draw their SDR balances below their original allotments. The SDR interest rate is adjusted periodically in line with the short-term interest rates in world money markets. It is reviewed quarterly and adjusted on the basis of a formula that takes into account the short-term interest rates of the United States, the United Kingdom, Germany, France, and Japan.

When the SDR was initially adopted, it was agreed that its value should be maintained at a fixed tie to the U.S. dollar's par value, which was then expressed in terms of gold. The value of the SDR was originally set at US $1. After several monetary developments, this linkage became unacceptable. With the suspension of U.S. gold convertibility in 1971, it was doubted whether the gold value of the dollar should serve as the official unit of account for international transactions. The United States was making it known that it wished to phase out gold as an international monetary instrument. Furthermore, the dollar's exchange rate against gold fell twice as the result of U.S. devaluations in 1971 and 1973. Finally, under the system of managed floating exchange rates, adopted by the industrialized nations in 1973, it became possible for the SDR's value to fluctuate against other currencies while still bearing a fixed tie to the dollar's value. In view of these problems, in 1974, a new method of SDR valuation was initiated—the **basket valuation.**

Basket valuation is intended to provide stability for the SDR's value under a system of fluctuating exchange rates, making the SDR more attractive as an international reserve asset. The SDR is called a basket currency because it is based on the value of five currencies: the U.S. dollar, German mark, Japanese yen, French franc, and British pound. An appreciation, or increase in value, of any one currency in the basket in terms of all other currencies will raise the value of the SDR in terms of each of the other currencies. Conversely, a depreciation, or decline in value, of any one currency will lower the value of the SDR in terms of each other currency. Because the movements of some currencies can be offset or moderated by the movements of other currencies, the value of the SDR in terms of a group of currencies is likely to be relatively stable.

Besides helping nations finance balance-of-payments deficits, SDRs have a number of other uses. Some of the fund's member nations peg their currency values to the SDR. The SDR is the unit of account for IMF transactions and is used as a unit of account for individuals (such as exporters, importers, or investors) who desire protection against the risk of fluctuating exchange rates.

For example, several major banks in London offer certificates of deposit (CDs) denominated in SDRs. The major attraction of SDR-denominated CDs is that they offer investors a financial instrument that is less susceptible to exchange-rate fluctuations than financial assets denominated in any single currency. Although the SDR-denominated CDs are sold for and repaid in dollars, their dollar value at, or any time before, maturity depends on the dollar/SDR exchange rate. Because the dollar/SDR rate is a weighted average of the dollar exchange rates relative to other currencies in the SDR basket, the exchange-rate gains or losses over the term of the deposit will be less than those for any one of the currencies making up the SDR. Therefore, by purchasing SDR-indexed CDs, investors can reduce their overall exchange-rate risk, because losses on one currency may be offset by gains on another in the SDR basket.

Facilities for Borrowing Reserves

The discussion so far has considered the different types of *owned reserves*—national currencies, gold, and SDRs. Various facilities for *borrowing reserves* have also been implemented for nations with weak balance-of-payments positions. Borrowed reserves do not eliminate the need for owned reserves, but they do add to the flexibility of the international monetary system by increasing the time available for nations to correct payments disequilibriums. Let's examine the major forms of international credit for borrowing reserves.

IMF Drawings

One of the original purposes of the IMF was to help member nations finance balance-of-payments deficits. The fund has furnished a pool of revolving credit for nations in need of reserves. Temporary loans of foreign currency are made to deficit nations, which are expected to repay them within a stipulated time. The transactions by which the fund makes foreign-currency loans available are called **IMF drawings.**

Deficit nations do not borrow from the fund. Instead they purchase with their own currency the foreign currency required to help finance deficits. When the nation's balance-of-payments position improves, it is expected to reverse the transaction and make repayment by repurchasing its currency from the fund. The fund currently allows members to purchase other currencies at their own option up to the first 50 percent of their fund quotas, which are based on the nation's economic size. Special permission must be granted by the fund if a nation is to purchase foreign currencies in excess of this figure. The fund extends such permission once it is convinced that the deficit nation has enacted reasonable measures to restore payments equilibrium.

Since the early 1950s, the fund has also fostered liberal exchange-rate policies by entering into *standby arrangements* with interested member nations. These agreements guarantee that a member nation may draw specified amounts of foreign currencies from the fund over given time periods. The advantage is that participating nations can count on credit from the fund should it be needed. It also saves the drawing nation from administrative time delays when the loans are actually made.

General Arrangements to Borrow

The General Arrangements to Borrow do not provide a permanent increase in the supply of world reserves once the loans are repaid and world reserves revert back to their original levels. However, these arrangements have made world reserves more flexible and adaptable to the needs of deficit nations.

Swap Arrangements

During the early 1960s, there occurred a wave of speculative attacks against the U.S. dollar, based on expectations that it would be devalued in terms of other currencies. To help offset the flow of short-term capital out of the dollar into stronger foreign currencies, the U.S. Federal Reserve agreed with several central banks in 1962 to initiate reciprocal currency arrangements, commonly referred to as **swap arrangements.** Today, the swap network on which the United States depends to finance its interventions in the foreign-exchange market includes the central banks of Canada and Mexico.

Swap arrangements are bilateral agreements between central banks. Each government provides for an exchange, or swap, of currencies to help finance temporary payments disequilibriums. If Mexico, for example, is short of dollars, it can ask the Federal Reserve to supply them in exchange for pesos. A drawing on the swap network is usually initiated by telephone, followed by an exchange of wire messages specifying terms and conditions. The actual swap is in the form of a foreign-exchange contract calling for the sale of dollars by the Federal Reserve for the currency of a foreign central bank. The nation requesting the swap is expected to use the funds to help ease its payments deficits and discourage speculative capital outflows. Swaps are to be repaid (reversed) within a stipulated period of time, normally within 3 to 12 months.

International Lending Risk

In many respects, the principles that apply to international lending are similar to those of domestic lending: the lender needs to determine the credit risk that the borrower will default. When making international loans, however, bankers face two additional risks: country risk and currency risk.

Credit risk is financial and refers to the probability that part or all of the interest or principal of a loan will not be repaid. The larger the potential for default on a loan, the higher the interest rate that the bank must charge the borrower.

Assessing credit risk on international loans tends to be more difficult than on domestic loans. U.S. banks are often less familiar with foreign business practices and economic conditions than those in the United States. Obtaining reliable information to evaluate foreign credit risk can be time-consuming and costly. Many U.S. banks, therefore, confine their international lending to major multinational corporations and financial institutions. To attract lending by U.S. banks, a foreign government may provide assurances against default by a local private borrower, thus reducing the credit risk of the loan.

Country risk is political and is closely related to political developments in a country, especially the government's views concerning international investments and loans. Some governments encourage the inflow of foreign funds to foster domestic economic development. Fearing loss of national sovereignty, other governments may discourage such inflows by enacting additional taxes, profit restrictions, and wage/price controls that can hinder the ability of local borrowers to repay loans. In the extreme, foreign governments can expropriate the assets of foreign investors or make foreign loan repayments illegal.

Currency risk is economic and is associated with currency depreciations and appreciations as well as exchange controls. Some loans of U.S. banks are denominated in foreign currency instead of dollars. If the currency in which the loan is made depreciates against the dollar during the period of the loan, the repayment will be worth fewer dollars. If the foreign currency has a well-developed forward market, the loan may be hedged. But many foreign currencies, especially of the developing nations, do not have such markets, and loans denominated in these currencies cannot always be hedged to decrease this type of currency risk. Another type of currency risk arises from exchange controls, which are common in developing nations. Exchange controls restrict the movement of funds across national borders or limit a currency's convertibility into dollars for repayment, thus adding to the risk of international lenders.

When lending overseas, bankers must evaluate credit risk, country risk, and currency risk. Evaluating risks in foreign lending often results in detailed analyses, compiled by a bank's research department, that are based on a nation's financial, economic, and political conditions. When international lenders consider detailed analyses too expensive, they often use reports and statistical indicators to help them determine the risk of lending.

The Problem of International Debt

Much concern has been voiced over the volume of international lending in recent years. At times, the concern has been that international lending was insufficient. Such was the case after the oil shocks in 1974–1975 and 1979–1980, when it was feared that some oil-importing developing nations might not be able to obtain loans to finance trade deficits resulting from the huge increases in the price of oil. It so happened that many oil-importing nations were able to borrow dollars from commercial banks. They paid the dollars to OPEC nations, who redeposited the money in commercial banks, which then re-lent the money to oil importers, and so on. In the 1970s, the banks were part of the solution; if they had not lent large sums to the developing nations, the oil shocks would have done far more damage to the world economy.

Reducing Bank Exposure to Developing-Nation Debt

When developing nations cannot meet their debt obligations to foreign banks, the stability of the international financial system is threatened. Banks may react to this threat by increasing their capital base, setting aside reserves to cover losses, and reducing new loans to debtor nations.

Banks have additional means to improve their financial position. One method is to liquidate developing-nation debt by engaging in outright *loan sales* to other banks in the secondary market. But if there occurs an unexpected increase in the default risk of such loans, their market value will be less than their face value. The selling bank thus absorbs costs because its loans must be sold at a discount. Following the sale, the bank must adjust its balance sheet to take account of any previously unrecorded difference between the face value of the loans and their market value. Many small and medium-sized U.S. banks eager to dump their bad loans in the 1980s were willing to sell them in the secondary market at discounts as high as 70 percent, or 30 cents on the dollar. But many banks could not afford such huge discounts. Even worse, if the banks all rushed to sell bad loans at once, prices would fall further. Sales of loans in the secondary market were often viewed as a last-resort measure.

Another debt-reduction technique is the *debt buyback,* in which the government of the debtor nation buys the loans from the commercial bank at a discount. Banks have also engaged in *debt-for-debt swaps,* in which a bank exchanges its loans for securities issued by the debtor nation's government at a lower interest rate or discount.

Cutting losses on developing-nation loans has sometimes involved banks in **debt/equity swaps.** Under this approach, a commercial bank sells its loans at a discount to the developing-nation government for local currency, which it then uses to finance an equity investment in the debtor nation. In the late 1980s, **Citicorp** converted some of its Chilean loans into pesos, which were used to purchase ownership shares in Chilean gold mines and pulp mills. Citicorp maintained that it could get better value by selling and swapping the loans without using the secondary market. In Chile, Citicorp typically converted debt at about 87 cents worth of local currency for each $1 of debt. Although debt/equity swaps enhance a bank's chances of selling developing-nation debt, they do not necessarily decrease its risk. Some equity investments in developing nations may be just as risky as the loans that were swapped for local factories or land. Moreover, banks that acquire an equity interest in developing-nation assets may not have the knowledge to manage those assets. Debtor nations also worry that debt/equity swaps will allow major companies to fall into foreign hands.

Debt Reduction and Debt Forgiveness

Another method of coping with developing-nation debt involves programs enacted for debt reduction and debt forgiveness. **Debt reduction** refers to any voluntary scheme that lessens the burden on the debtor nation to service its external debt. Debt reduction is accomplished through two main approaches. The first is the use of negotiated modifications in the terms and conditions of the contracted debt, such as debt reschedulings, retiming of interest payments, and improved borrowing terms. Debt reduction may also be achieved through measures such as debt/equity swaps and debt buybacks. The purpose of debt reduction is to foster comprehensive policies for economic growth by easing the ability of the debtor nation to service its debt, thus freeing resources that will be used for investment.

Some proponents of debt relief maintain that the lending nations should permit **debt forgiveness.** Debt forgiveness refers to any arrangement that reduces the value of contractual obligations of the debtor nation; it includes schemes such as markdowns or write-offs of developing-nation debt or the abrogation of existing obligations to pay interest.

Debt-forgiveness advocates maintain that the most heavily indebted developing nations are unable to service their external debt and maintain an acceptable rate of per-capita income growth because their debt burden is overwhelming. They contend that if some of this debt were forgiven, a debtor nation could use the freed-up foreign-exchange resources to increase its imports and invest domestically, thus increasing domestic economic growth rates. The release of the limitation on foreign exchange would provide the debtor nation additional incentive to invest because it would not have to share as much of the benefits of its increased growth and investment with its creditors in the form of interest payments. Moreover, debt forgiveness would allow the debtor nation to service its debt more easily; this would reduce the debt-load burden of a debtor nation and could potentially lead to greater inflows of foreign investment.

Debt-forgiveness critics question whether the amount of debt is a major limitation on developing-nation growth and whether that growth would in fact resume if a large portion of that debt were forgiven. They contend that nations such as Indonesia and South Korea have experienced large amounts of external debt relative to national output but have not faced debt-servicing problems. Also, debt forgiveness does not guarantee that the freed-up foreign-exchange resources will be used productively—that is, invested in sectors that will ultimately generate additional foreign exchange.

The Eurocurrency Market

One of the most widely misunderstood topics in international banking is the nature and operation of the **Eurocurrency market.** This market operates as a financial intermediary, bringing together lenders and borrowers. It serves as one of the most important tools for moving short-term funds across national borders. When the Eurocurrency market first came into existence in the 1950s, its volume was estimated to be approximately $1 billion. The size of the Eurocurrency market in the mid-1990s was estimated to be more than $5 trillion.

Eurocurrencies are deposits, denominated and payable in dollars and other foreign currencies—such as the Swiss franc—in banks outside the United States, primarily in London, the market's center. The term *Eurocurrency market* is something of a misnomer because much Eurocurrency trading occurs in non-European centers, such as Hong Kong and Singapore. Dollar deposits located in banks outside the United States are known as *Eurodollars,* and banks that conduct trading in the markets for Eurocurrencies (including the dollar) are designated *Eurobanks.*

Eurocurrency depositors may be foreign exporters who have sold products in the United States and have received dollars in payment. They may also be U.S. residents who have withdrawn funds from their accounts in the United States and put them in a bank overseas. Foreign-currency deposits in overseas banks are generally for a specified time period and bear a stated yield, because most Eurocurrency deposits are held for investment rather than as transaction balances.

Borrowers go to Eurocurrency banks for a variety of purposes. When the market was first developed, borrowers were primarily corporations that required financing for international trade. But other lending opportunities have evolved with the market's development. Borrowers currently include the British government and U.S. banks.

Development of the Eurocurrency Market

Although several hundred banks currently issue Eurocurrency deposits on investor demand, it was not until the late 1950s and early 1960s that the market began to gain prominence as a major source of short-term capital. Several factors contributed to the Eurocurrency market's growth.

One factor was fear that deposits held in the United States would be frozen by the government in the event of an international conflict. The Eastern European countries, notably Russia, were among the first depositors of dollars in

European banks, because during World War II the United States had impounded Russian dollar holdings located in U.S. banks. Russia was thus motivated to maintain dollar holdings free from U.S. regulation.

Ceilings on interest rates that U.S. banks could pay on savings deposits provided another reason for the Eurocurrency market's growth. These ceilings limited the U.S. banks in competing with foreign banks for deposits. During the 1930s, the Federal Reserve system under Regulation Q established ceiling rates to prevent banks from paying excessive interest rates on savings accounts and thus being forced to make risky loans to generate high earnings. By the late 1950s, when London was paying interest rates on dollar deposits that exceeded the levels set by Regulation Q, it was profitable for U.S. residents and foreigners to transfer their dollar balances to London. Large U.S. banks directed their foreign branches to bid for dollars by offering higher interest rates than those allowed in the United States. The parent offices then borrowed the money from their overseas branches. To limit such activity, the Federal Reserve in 1969 established high reserve requirements on head-office borrowings from abroad. In 1973, the Federal Reserve system made large-denomination certificates of deposit exempt from Regulation Q ceilings, further reducing the incentive to borrow funds from overseas branches.

Throughout the 1970s, 1980s, and 1990s, the Eurocurrency market has continued to grow. A major factor behind the sustained high growth of the market has been the risk-adjusted interest-rate advantage of Eurocurrency deposits relative to domestic deposits, reflecting increases in the level of dollar interest rates and reductions in the perceived riskiness of Euromarket deposits.

Financial Implications

Eurocurrencies have significant implications for international finance. By increasing the financial interdependence of nations involved in the market, Eurocurrencies facilitate the financing of international trade and investment. They may also reduce the need for official reserve financing, because a given quantity of dollars can support a large volume of international transactions. On the other hand, it is argued that Eurocurrencies may undermine a nation's efforts to implement its monetary policy. Volatile movements of these balances into and out of a nation's banking system complicate a central bank's attempt to hit a monetary target.

Another concern is that the Eurocurrency market does not face the same financial regulations as do the domestic banking systems of most industrialized nations. Should the Eurocurrency banks not maintain sound reserve requirements or enact responsible policies, the pyramid of Eurocurrency credit might collapse. Such fears became widespread in 1974 with the failure of the Franklin National Bank in the United States and the Bankus Herstatt of Germany, both of which lost huge sums speculating in the foreign-exchange market.

International Law

International Laws and Politics

Legal Differences and Restraints

Countries differ in their laws as well as in their use of the law. For example, over the past decade the United States has become an increasingly litigious society in which institutions and individuals are quick to initiate lawsuits. Court battles are often protracted and costly, and even the threat of a court case can reduce business opportunities. In contrast, Japan's tradition tends to minimize the role of the law and of lawyers. On a per-capita basis, Japan has only about 5 percent of the number of lawyers that the United States has.[118] Whether the number of lawyers is cause or effect, the Japanese tend not to litigate. Litigation in Japan means that the parties have failed to compromise, which is contrary to Japanese tradition and results in loss of face. A cultural predisposition therefore exists to settle conflicts outside the court system.

While legal systems are important to society, from an international business perspective, the two major legal systems worldwide can be categorized into common law and code law. **Common law** is based on tradition and depends less on written statutes and codes than on precedent and custom. Common law originated in England and is the system of law in the United States. **Code law** on the other hand, is based on a comprehensive set of written statutes. Countries with code law try to spell out all possible legal rules explicitly. Code law is based on Roman law and is found in the majority of the nations of the world.

In general, countries with the code law system have much more rigid laws than those with the common-law system. In the latter, courts adopt precedents and customs to fit cases, allowing a better idea of basic judgment likely to be rendered in new situations. The differences between code law and common law and their impact on international business, while wide in theory, are not as broad in practice. One reason is that many common-law countries, including the United States, have adopted commercial codes to govern the conduct of business.

Host countries may adopt a number of laws that affect the firm's ability to do business. Tariffs and quotas, for example, can affect the entry of goods. Special licenses for foreign goods may be required.

Other laws may restrict entrepreneurial activities. In Argentina, for example, pharmacies must be owned by the pharmacist. This legislation prevents an ambitious businessperson from hiring druggists and starting a pharmacy chain. Similarly, the law prevents the addition of a drug counter to an existing business such as a supermarket and thus the broadening of the product offering to consumers.

Specific legislation may also exist, regulating what does and does not constitute deceptive advertising. Many countries prohibit specific claims that compare products to the competition, or they restrict the use of promotional devices. Even when no laws exist, regulations may hamper business operations. For example, in some countries, firms are required to join the local chamber of commerce or become a member of the national trade association. These institutions in turn may have internal sets of rules that specify standards for the conduct of business that may be quite confining.

Seemingly innocuous local regulations that may easily be overlooked can have a major impact on the international firm's success. For example, Japan had an intricate process regulating the building of new department stores or supermarkets. The government's desire to protect smaller merchants brought the opening of new, large stores to a virtual standstill. Since department stores and supermarkets serve as the major conduit for the sale of imported consumer products, the lack of new stores severely affected opportunities for market penetration of imported merchandise.[119] Only after intense pressure from the outside did the Japanese government decide to reconsider the regulations. Another example concerns the growing global controversy that surrounds the use of genetic technology. Governments increasingly devise new rules that affect trade in genetically modified products. Australia introduced a mandatory standard for foods produced using biotechnology, which prohibits the sale of such products unless the food has been assessed by the Australia New Zealand Food Authority.

Other laws may be designed to protect domestic industries and reduce imports. For example, Russia charges a 20 percent value-added tax (VAT) on most imported goods, assesses high excise taxes on goods such as cigarettes, automobiles, and alcoholic beverages, and provides a burdensome import licensing regime for alcohol to depress Russian demand for imports.[120]

Finally, the interpretation and enforcement of laws and regulations may have a major effect on international business activities. For example, in deciding what product can be called a "Swiss" Army knife or "French" wine, the interpretation given by courts to the meaning of a name can affect consumer perceptions and sales of products.

The Influencing of Politics and Laws

To succeed in a market, the international business manager needs much more than business know-how. He or she must also deal with the intricacies of national politics and laws. Although to fully understand another country's legal political system will rarely be possible, the good manager will be aware of its importance and will work with people who do understand how to operate within the system.

Many areas of politics and law are not immutable. Viewpoints can be modified or even reversed, and new laws can supersede old ones. Therefore, existing political and legal restraints do not always need to be accepted. To achieve change, however, some impetus for it—such as the clamors of a constituency—must occur. Otherwise, systemic inertia is likely to allow the status quo to prevail.

The international business manager has various options. One is to simply ignore prevailing rules and expect to get away with it. Pursuing this option is a high-risk strategy because the possibility of objection and even prosecution exists. A second, traditional, option is to provide input to trade negotiators and expect any problem areas to be resolved in multilateral negotiations. The drawbacks to this option are, of course, the quite time-consuming process involved and the lack of control by the firm.

A third option involves the development of coalitions and constituencies that can motivate legislators and politicians to consider and ultimately implement change. This option can be pursued in various ways. One direction can be the recasting or redefinition of issues. Often, specific terminology leads to conditioned, though inappropriate responses. For example, in the United States, the trade status accorded to the People's Republic of China has been controversial for many years. The U.S. Congress had to decide annually whether or not to grant "Most Favored Nation" (MFN) status to China. The debate on this decision was always very contentious and acerbic, and often framed around the question as to why China deserved to be treated the "most favored way." Lost in the debate was often the fact that the term "most favored" was simply taken from WTO terminology, and only indicated that trade with China would be treated like that with any other country. Only in late 1999 was the terminology changed from MFN to NTR or "normal trade relations." Even though there was still considerable debate regarding China, at least the controversy about special treatment had been avoided.[121]

Beyond terminology, firms can also highlight the direct links and their costs and benefits to legislators and politicians. For example, a manager can explain the employment and economic effects of certain laws and regulations and demonstrate the benefits of change. The picture can be enlarged by including indirect links. For example, suppliers, customers, and distributors can be asked to help explain to decision makers the benefit of change. In addition, the public at large can be involved through public statements or advertisements.

Developing such coalitions is not an easy task. Companies often seek assistance in effectively influencing the government decision-making process. Such assistance is particularly beneficial when narrow economic objectives or single-issue campaigns are involved. Typically, **lobbyists** provide this assistance. Usually, there are well-connected individuals and firms that can provide access to policymakers and legislators in order to communicate new and pertinent information.

Many U.S. firms have representatives in Washington, DC, as well as in state capitals, and are quite successful at influencing domestic policies. Often, however, they are less adept at ensuring proper representation abroad even though, for example, the European Commission in Brussels wields far-reaching economic power. For example, a survey of U.S. international marketing executives found that knowledge and information about foreign trade and government officials was ranked lowest among critical international business information needs. This low ranking appears to reflect the fact that many U.S. firms are far less successful in their interactions with governments abroad and far less intensive in their lobbying efforts than are foreign entities in the United States.[122]

Many countries and companies have been effective in their lobbying in the United States. As an example, Brazil has retained nearly a dozen U.S. firms to cover and influence trade issues. Brazilian citrus exporters and computer manufacturers have hired U.S. legal and public relations firms to provide them with information on relevant U.S. legislative activity. The Banco do Brasil also successfully lobbied for the restructuring of Brazilian debt and favorable U.S. banking regulations.

Although representation of the firm's interests to government decision makers and legislators is entirely appropriate, the international business manager must also consider any potential side effects. Major questions can be raised if such representation becomes very overt. Short-term gains may be far outweighed by long-term negative repercussions if the international firm is perceived as exerting too much political influence.

International Relations and Laws

In addition to understanding the politics and laws of both home and host countries, the international business manager must also consider the overall international political and legal environment. This is important because policies and events occurring among countries can have a profound impact on firms trying to do business internationally.

International Politics

The effect of politics on international business is determined by both the bilateral political relations between home and host countries and by multilateral agreements governing the relations among groups of countries.

The government-to-government relationship can have a profound influence in a number of ways, particularly if it becomes hostile. President Bush's characterization in February 2002 of Iran, Iraq, and North Korea as an "axis of evil" aggravated already unstable political relationships and threatened to set back negotiations by U.S. companies to secure lucrative oil deals.[123] In another example, although the internal political changes in the aftermath of the Iranian revolution certainly would have affected any foreign firm doing business in Iran, the deterioration in U.S.–Iranian political relations that resulted had a significant additional impact on U.S. firms, which were injured not only by the physical damage caused by the violence, but also by the anti-American feelings of the Iranian people and their government. The resulting clashes between the two governments subsequently destroyed business relationships, regardless of corporate feelings or agreements on either side.

International political relations do not always have harmful effects. If bilateral political relations between countries improve, business can benefit. One example is the improvement in Western relations with Central Europe following the official end of the Cold War. The political warming opened the potentially lucrative former Eastern bloc markets to Western firms.

The overall international political environment has effects, whether good or bad, on international business. For this reason, the good manager will strive to remain aware of political currents and relations worldwide and will attempt to anticipate changes in the international political environment so that his or her firm can plan for them.

International Law

International law plays an important role in the conduct of international business. Although no enforceable body of international law exists, certain treaties and agreements are respected by a number of countries and profoundly influence international business operations. For example, the World Trade Organization (WTO) defines internationally acceptable economic practices for its member nations. Although it does not directly deal with individual firms, it does affect them indirectly by providing some predictability in the international environment.

The **Patent Cooperation Treaty (PCT)** provides procedures for filing one international application designating countries in which a patent is sought, which has the same effect as filing national applications in each of those countries. Similarly, the European Patent Office examines applications and issues national patents in any of its member countries. Other regional offices include the African Industrial Property Office (ARIPO), the French-speaking African Intellectual Property Organization (OAPI), and one in Saudi Arabia for six countries in the Gulf region.

International organizations such as the United Nations and the Organization for Economic Cooperation and Development (OECD) have also undertaken efforts to develop codes and guidelines that affect international business. These include the Code on International Marketing of Breast-milk Substitutes, which was developed by the World Health Organization (WHO), and the UN Code of Conduct for Transnational Corporations. Even though there are 34 such codes in existence, the lack of enforcement ability hampers their full implementation.

In addition to multilateral agreements, firms are affected by bilateral treaties and conventions between the countries in which they do business. For example, a number of countries have signed bilateral Treaties of Friendship, Commerce, and Navigation (FCN). The agreements generally define the rights of firms doing business in the host country. They normally guarantee that firms will be treated by the host country in the same manner in which domestic firms are treated. While these treaties provide for some sort of stability, they can also be canceled when relations worsen.

The international legal environment also affects the manager to the extent that firms must concern themselves with jurisdictional disputes. Because no single body of international law exists, firms usually are restricted by both home and host country laws. If a conflict occurs between contracting parties in two different countries, a question arises concerning which country's laws are to be used and in which court the dispute is to be settled. Sometimes the contract will contain a jurisdictional clause, which settles the matter with little problem. If the contract does not contain such a clause, however, the parties to the dispute have a few choices. They can settle the dispute by following the laws of the country in which the agreement was made, or they can resolve it by obeying the laws of the country in which the contract will have to be fulfilled. Which laws to use and in which location to settle the dispute are two different decisions. As a result, a dispute between a U.S. exporter and a French importer could be resolved in Paris but be based on New York State law. The importance of such provisions was highlighted by the lengthy jurisdictional disputes surrounding the Bhopal incident in India.

In cases of disagreement, the parties can choose either arbitration or litigation. **Litigation** is usually avoided for several reasons. It often involves extensive delays and is very costly. In addition, firms may fear discrimination in foreign countries. Therefore, companies tend to prefer conciliation and **arbitration,** because they result in much quicker decisions. Arbitration procedures are often spelled out in the original contract and usually provide for an intermediary who is judged to be impartial by both parties. Intermediaries can be representatives of chambers of commerce, trade associations, or third-country institutions. One key nongovernmental organization handling international commercial disputes is the International Court of Arbitration, founded in 1923 by the International Chamber of Commerce (ICC). Each year it handles arbitrations in some 48 different countries with arbitrators of some 57 different nationalities. Arbitration usually is faster and less expensive than litigation in the courts. In addition, the limited judicial recourse available against arbitral awards, as compared with court judgments, offers a clear advantage. Parties that use arbitration rather than litigation know that they will not have to face a prolonged and costly series of appeals. Finally, arbitration offers the parties the flexibility to set up a proceeding that can be conducted as quickly and economically as the circumstances allow. For example, a multimillion dollar ICC arbitration was completed in just over two months.[124]

International Business Law

Today every aspect of business, including business law, requires some understanding of international business practices. Since World War II, the global economy has become increasingly interconnected. Many U.S. corporations now have investments or manufacturing facilities in other countries; simultaneously, the number of foreign corporations with business operations in the United States has increased dramatically. Furthermore, whether a domestic corporation exports goods or not, it competes with imports from many other countries. For example, U.S. firms face competition from Japanese electronics and automobiles, French wines and fashions, German machinery, and Taiwanese textiles. In order to compete effectively, U.S. firms need to be aware of international business practices and developments.

Laws vary greatly from country to country: what one nation requires by law, another may forbid. To complicate matters, there is no single authority in international law that can compel countries to act. When the laws of two or more nations conflict, or when one party has violated an agreement and the other party wishes to enforce it or to recover damages, establishing who will adjudicate the matter, which laws will be applied, what remedies will be available, or where the matter should be decided often is very confusing. Nonetheless, given the growing impact of the global economy, a basic understanding of international business law is essential.

The International Environment

International law deals with the conduct and relations between nation-states and international organizations, as well as some of their relations with persons. Unlike domestic law, international law generally cannot be enforced. Consequently, international courts do not have compulsory jurisdiction, though they do have authority to resolve an international dispute if the parties to the dispute accept the court's jurisdiction over the matter. Furthermore, a sovereign nation that has adopted an international law will enforce that law to the same extent as all of its domestic laws. In this section, we will examine some of the sources and institutions of international law.

International Court of Justice

The United Nations, which is probably the most famous international organization, has a judiciary branch called the **International Court of Justice (ICJ).** The ICJ consists of 15 judges, no two of whom may be from the same sovereign state, elected for nine-year terms by a majority of both the U.N. General Assembly and the U.N. Security Council. The usefulness of the ICJ is limited, however, because only nations (not private individuals or corporations) may be parties to an action before the court. Furthermore, the ICJ has contentious jurisdiction only over nation-parties who agree both to allow the ICJ to decide the case and to be bound by its decision. Moreover, because the ICJ cannot enforce its rulings, countries displeased with an ICJ decision may simply ignore it. Consequently, few nations submit their disputes to the ICJ.

The ICJ also has advisory jurisdiction if requested by a U.N. organ or specialized U.N. agency. Neither sovereign states nor individuals may request an advisory opinion. These opinions are nonbinding, and the U.N. agency requesting the opinion usually votes to decide whether to follow it.

International law Includes law that deals with the conduct and relations of nation-states and international organizations as well as some of their relations with persons; such law is enforceable by the courts of a nation that has adopted the international law as domestic law.

International Court of Justice Judicial branch of the United Nations having voluntary jurisdiction over nations.

Regional trade communities International organizations, conferences, and treaties focusing on business and trade regulations; the EU (European Union) is the most prominent of these.

Regional Trade Communities

Of much greater significance are international organizations, conferences, and treaties that focus on business and trade regulation. **Regional trade communities,** such as the European Union (EU), promote common trade policies among member nations. Other important regional trade communities include the Central American Common Market (CACM), the Caribbean Community Market (CARICOM), the Association of South East Asian Nations (ASEAN), the Andean Common Market (ANCOM), the Common Market for Eastern and Southern Africa (COMESA), the Asian Pacific Economic Cooperation (APEC), Mercado Comun del Cono Sur (Latin American Trading Group, MERCO-SUR), and the Economic Community of West African States (ECOWAS).

EUROPEAN UNION (EU) The European Community (EC), the predecessor to the European Union, was formed in 1967 through a merger between the European Economic Community (better known as the Common Market), the European Coal and Steel Community, and the European Atomic Energy Community (Euratom). The EC worked to remove trade barriers between its member nations and to unify their economic policies. The EC had the power to make rules that bound member nations and that preempted its members' domestic laws.

In 1993 the Treaty on European Union (popularly called the Maastricht Treaty) took effect. It changed the name of the EC to the European Union and stated the Union's objectives to include (1) promoting economic and social progress by creating an area without internal borders and by establishing an economic and monetary union, (2) asserting its identity on the international scene by implementing a common foreign and security policy, (3) strengthening the protection of the rights and interests of citizens of its member states, and (4) developing close cooperation on justice and home affairs. The EU currently has 15 full members: Austria, Belgium, Denmark, Finland, France, Germany, Greece, Ireland, Italy, Luxembourg, the Netherlands, Portugal, Spain, Sweden, and the United Kingdom.

NAFTA The North American Free Trade Agreement, which took effect in 1994, established a free trade area among the United States, Canada, and Mexico. Its objectives are to (1) eliminate trade barriers to the movement of goods and services across the borders, (2) promote conditions of fair competition in the free trade area, (3) increase investment opportunities in the area, and (4) provide adequate and effective enforcement of intellectual property rights. Over 15 years, the treaty will gradually eliminate all tariffs between the three countries.

International Treaties

A treaty is an agreement between or among independent nations. The U.S. Constitution authorizes the president to enter into treaties with the advice and consent of the Senate "providing two-thirds of the Senators present concur." The U.S. Constitution provides that all valid treaties are "the law of the land," having the legal force of a federal statute.

Nations have entered into bilateral and multilateral treaties in order to facilitate and regulate trade and to protect their national interests. In addition, treaties have been used to serve as constitutions of international organizations, to establish general international law, to transfer territory, to settle disputes, to secure human rights, and to protect investments. The Treaty Section of the Office of Legal Affairs within the United Nations Secretariat is responsible for registering and publishing treaties and agreements among member nations. Since its inception in 1946, the U.N. Secretariat has registered and published more than 30,000 treaties that expressly or indirectly concern international business.

> *International treaties*
> Agreements between or among independent nations, such as the General Agreement on Tariffs and Trade (GATT), now called the World Trade Organization (WTO).

Probably the most important multilateral trade treaty is the General Agreement on Tariffs and Trade (GATT). The basic purpose of GATT (now called the World Trade Organization, with more than 130 members) is to facilitate the flow of trade by establishing agreements on potential trade barriers such as import quotas, customs, export regulations, antidumping restrictions (the prohibition against selling goods for less than their fair market value), subsidies, and import fees. Such agreements arise under GATT's ***most favored nation provision,*** which states that all signatories must treat each other as favorably as they treat any other country. Thus, any privilege, immunity, or favor given to one country must be given to all. Nevertheless, nations may give preferential treatment to developing nations and may enter into free trade areas with one or more other nations. A free trade area permits countries to discriminate in favor of their free trade partners, provided that the agreement covers substantially all trade among the partners. A second important principle adopted by GATT is that the protection offered domestic industries should take the form of customs tariffs, rather than other, more trade-inhibiting measures.

The most recent set of accords, adopted in 1994, included agreements on such matters as agricultural products, textiles and clothing, technical barriers to trade, trade-related investment measures, customs valuation, subsidies and countervailing measures, trade in services, antidumping measures, and protection of intellectual property rights. It also created the Dispute Settlement Body and increased the scope of GATT's dispute resolution process.

Jurisdiction over Actions of Foreign Governments

In this section, we will focus on a sovereign nation's power—and the factors limiting that nation's power—to exercise jurisdiction over a foreign nation or to take over property owned by foreign citizens. More specifically, we will examine state immunities (the principle of sovereign immunity and the act of state doctrine) and the power of a state to take foreign investment property.

Sovereign Immunity

One of the oldest concepts in international law is that each nation has absolute and total authority over the events occurring within its territory. It has also been long recognized, however, that in order to maintain international relations and trade, a host country must refrain from imposing its laws on a foreign sovereign nation present within its borders. This absolute immunity from the courts of a host country is known as **sovereign immunity.** Originally, all acts of a foreign sovereign nation within a host country were considered immune from the host country's laws.

Sovereign immunity *Foreign country's freedom from a host country's laws.*

In modern times, however, international law distinguishes between a foreign nation's public acts and its commercial ones. Only public acts, such as those concerning diplomatic activity, internal administration, or armed forces, will be granted sovereign immunity. By engaging in trade or commercial activities, a foreign nation subjects itself to the jurisdiction of its host country's courts with respect to any disputes that arise out of those commercial activities.

In 1976, Congress enacted the Foreign Sovereign Immunities Act in order to establish exactly the circumstances under which the United States would extend immunity to foreign nations. The act specifically provides that a foreign state shall be immune from neither federal nor state court jurisdiction if the suit is based upon (1) a commercial activity conducted in the United States by the foreign state, (2) an act that the foreign state performed in the United States in connection with a commercial activity it conducted elsewhere, or (3) a commercial activity performed outside the United States that nonetheless directly affects the United States. If an activity is one that a private party could normally carry on, it is commercial and a foreign government engaging in that activity is not immune. On the other hand, if the activity is one that only governments can undertake, it is noncommercial under the act. Examples of commercial activities include a contract by a foreign government to buy provisions or equipment for its armed forces; a foreign government's contract to construct or repair a government building; and a foreign government's sale of a service or a product or its leasing of property, borrowing of money, or investing in a security of a U.S. corporation. Examples of public (noncommercial) activities to which sovereign immunity would extend include nationalizing a corporation, determining limitations upon the use of the foreign state's natural resources, and the granting of licenses to export a natural resource.

Act of State Doctrine

Act of state doctrine *Rule that a court should not question the validity of actions taken by a foreign government in its own country.*

Expropriation *Governmental taking of foreign-owned property for a public purpose and with payment of just compensation.*

Confiscation *Governmental taking of foreign-owned property without payment (or for a highly inadequate payment) or for a nonpublic purpose.*

The **act of state doctrine** provides that a nation's judicial branch should not question the validity of the actions a foreign government takes within that foreign sovereign's own borders. In 1897, the U.S. Supreme Court described the act of state doctrine in terms that remain valid today: "Every sovereign State is bound to respect the independence of every other sovereign State, and the courts of one country will not sit in judgment on the acts of the government of another done within its own territory."

In the United States, there are several possible exceptions to the act of state doctrine. Some courts hold (1) that a sovereign may waive its right to raise the act of state defense and (2) that the doctrine may be inapplicable to commercial activities of a foreign sovereign. In addition, by federal statute, courts will not apply the act of state doctrine to a claim to specific property located in the United States when such a claim is based on the assertion that a foreign state confiscated the property in violation of international law, unless the president of the United States determines that the doctrine should be applied to that particular case.

Taking of Foreign Investment Property

Investing in foreign states involves the risk that the host nation's government may take the investment property. An **expropriation** or nationalization occurs when a government seizes foreign-owned property or assets for a public purpose and pays the owner just compensation for what is taken. In contrast, **confiscation** occurs when a government offers no payment (or a highly inadequate payment) in exchange for seized property, or seizes it for a nonpublic purpose. Confiscations violate generally observed principles of international law, whereas expropriations do not. In either case, few remedies are available to injured parties.

The World Bank established the Multilateral Investment Guarantee Agency (MIGA) to encourage increased investment in developing nations. The MIGA Convention has been signed by more than 150 nations. It offers foreign investment risk insurance for noncommercial risks including deprivation of ownership or control by governmental actions, breach of contract by a government when there is no judicial recourse, and loss from military action or civil disturbance.

If you invest in foreign states, consider obtaining expropriation insurance from a private insurer or from the Overseas Private Investment Corporation (OPIC), an agency of the U.S. government.

Transacting Business Abroad

Transacting business abroad may involve activities such as selling goods, information, or services; investing capital; or arranging for the movement of labor. Because these transactions may affect the national security, economy, foreign policy, and interests of both the exporting and importing countries, nations have imposed measures to restrict or encourage such transactions. In this section, we will examine the legal controls imposed upon the flow of trade, labor, and capital across national borders. International contracts, antitrust laws, securities regulation, and intellectual property are also discussed.

Flow of Trade

Advances in modern technology, communication, transportation, and production methods have swelled the flow of goods across national boundaries. The governments within each country thereby face a dilemma. On the one hand, they wish to protect and stimulate domestic industry. On the other hand, they want to provide their citizens with the best quality goods at the lowest possible prices and to encourage exports from their own countries.

Governments have used a variety of trade barriers to protect domestic businesses. A frequently applied device is the **tariff**, which is a duty or tax imposed on goods moving into or out of a country. Tariffs raise the price of imported goods, prompting some consumers to purchase less expensive, domestically produced items. Governments can also use **nontariff barriers** to give local industries a competitive advantage. Examples of nontariff barriers include unilateral or bilateral import quotas, import bans, overly restrictive safety, health, or manufacturing standards, environmental laws, complicated and time-consuming customs procedures, and subsidies to local industry.

Dumping is the sale of exported goods from one country to another country at less than normal value. Under the WTO's Antidumping Code, "normal value" is the price that would be charged for the same or a similar product in the ordinary course of trade for domestic consumption in the exporting country. Dumping violates the GATT "if it causes or threatens material injury to an established industry in the territory of a contracting party or materially retards the establishment of a domestic industry."

Governments also control the flow of goods out of their countries by imposing quotas, tariffs, or total prohibitions. **Export controls** or restrictions usually result from important policy considerations, such as national defense, foreign policy, or the protection of scarce national resources. For example, the United States passed the Export Administration Act of 1979, which, as amended in 1985 and 1988, restricts the flow of technologically advanced goods and data from the United States to other countries. Nonetheless, in order to assist domestic businesses, countries generally encourage exports through the use of *export incentives* and *export subsidies*.

Flow of trade Controlled by trade barriers on imports and exports.

Tariff Duty or tax imposed on goods moving into or out of a country.

Nontariff barriers Include quotas, bans, safety standards, and subsidies.

If you export goods, be sure to determine whether you must obtain an export license from the U.S. government and what import barriers, such as tariffs, you must satisfy in the countries to which you are sending the goods.

Flow of Labor

The **flow of labor** across national borders generates policy questions concerning the employment needs of local workers. Each country has its own immigration policies and regulations. Almost all countries require that foreigners obtain valid passports before entering their borders; citizens, in turn, often must have passports in order to leave or reenter the country. In addition, a country may issue foreign citizens visas that permit them to enter the country for identified purposes or for specific periods of time. For example, the U.S. Immigration and Naturalization Service issues various types of visas to persons who are temporarily visiting the

Flow of labor Controlled through passport, visa, and immigration regulations.

United States for pleasure or business, to persons who enter the United States to perform services that the unemployed in this country cannot perform, and to persons who are transferred to the United States by their employers.

Flow of Capital

Multinational businesses frequently need to transfer funds to, and receive money from, operations in other countries. Because there is no international currency, nations have sought to ease the **flow of capital** among themselves. In 1945, the International Monetary Fund (IMF) was established to facilitate the expansion and balanced growth of international trade, to assist in the elimination of foreign exchange restrictions that hamper such growth, and to shorten the duration and ease the disequilibrium in the international balance of payments between the members of the fund. Currently, more than 150 countries are members of the IMF.

> *Flow of capital* International Monetary Fund facilitates the expansion and balanced growth of international trade, assists in eliminating foreign exchange restrictions, and smooths the international balance of payments.

Many nations have laws regulating foreign investment. Restrictions on the establishment of foreign investment tend to limit the amount of equity and the amount of control allowed to foreign investors. They may also restrict the way in which the investment is created, such as limiting or prohibiting investment by acquiring an existing locally owned business. Approximately 100 nations have become parties to the Convention on the Settlement of Investment Disputes Between States and Nationals of Other States. The Convention created the International Centre for the Settlement of Investment Disputes, which offers a form of arbitration for investment disputes.

Nations also have cooperated in forming international and regional banks to facilitate the flow of capital and trade. Such banks include the International Bank for Reconstruction and Development (part of the World Bank), the African Development Bank, the Asian Development Bank, the European Investment Bank, and the Inter-American Development Bank.

International Contracts

The legal issues inherent in domestic commercial contracts also arise in international contracts. Moreover, additional issues, such as differences in language, customs, legal systems, and currency, are peculiar to international contracts. Such a contract should specify its official language and include definitions for all the significant legal terms used in it. In addition, it should specify the acceptable currency (or currencies) and payment method. The contract should include a choice of law clause designating what law will govern any breach or dispute regarding the contract, and a choice of forum clause designating whether the parties will resolve disputes through one nation's court system or through third-party arbitration. Finally, the contract should include a *force majeure* (unavoidable superior force) clause apportioning the parties' liabilities and responsibilities in the event of an unforeseeable occurrence, such as a typhoon, tornado, flood, earthquake, war, or nuclear disaster.

> *International contracts* Involve additional issues beyond those in domestic contracts, such as differences in language, legal systems, and currency.

> When you enter into international contracts, be sure that your contracts include provisions for payment, including acceptable currencies, choice of law, choice of forum, and force majeure (acts of God).

> *CISG* (United Nations Convention on Contracts for the International Sales of Goods) governs all contracts for international sales of goods between parties located in different nations that have ratified the CISG.

CISG The United Nations Convention on Contracts for the International Sales of Goods (**CISG**), which has been ratified by the United States and more than 40 other countries, governs all contracts for the international sales of goods between parties located in different nations that have ratified the CISG. Because treaties are federal law, the CISG supersedes the Uniform Commercial Code in any situation to which either could apply. The CISG includes provisions dealing with interpretation, trade usage, contract formation, obligations and remedies of sellers and buyers, and risk of loss. Parties to an international sales contract may, however, expressly exclude CISG governance from their contract. The CISG specifically excludes sales of (1) goods bought for personal, family, or household use; (2) ships or aircraft; and (3) electricity. In addition, it does not apply to contracts in which the primary obligation of the party furnishing the goods consists of supplying labor or services.

LETTERS OF CREDIT International trade involves a number of risks not usually encountered in domestic trade, most notably governmental controls over the export or import of goods and currency. The most effective means of managing these risks—as well as the ordinary trade risks of nonperformance by seller and buyer—is the irrevocable documentary letter of credit. Most international letters of credit are governed by the Uniform Customs and Practices for Documentary Credits, a document drafted by commercial law experts from many countries and adopted by the International Chamber of Commerce. A **letter of credit** is a promise by a buyer's bank to pay the seller, provided certain conditions are met. The letter of credit transaction involves three or four different parties and three underlying contracts. To illustrate: a U.S. business wishes to sell computers to a Belgian company. The U.S. and Belgian firms enter into a sales agreement that includes details such as the number of computers, the features they will have, and the date they will be shipped. The buyer then enters into a second contract with a local bank, called an *issuer,* committing the bank to pay the agreed price upon receiving specified documents. These documents normally include a bill of lading (proving that the seller has delivered the goods for shipment), a commercial invoice listing the purchase terms, proof of insurance, and a customs certificate indicating that customs officials have cleared the goods for export. The buyer's bank's commitment to pay is the irrevocable letter of credit. Typically, a *correspondent* or *paying bank* located in the seller's country makes payment to the seller. Here, the Belgian issuing bank arranges to pay the U.S. correspondent bank the agreed sum of money in exchange for the documents. The issuer then sends the U.S. computer firm the letter of credit. When the U.S. firm obtains all the necessary documents, it presents them to the U.S. correspondent bank, which verifies the documents, pays the computer company in U.S. dollars, and sends the documents to the Belgian issuing bank. Upon receiving the required documents, the issuing bank pays the correspondent bank and then presents the documents to the buyer. In our example, the Belgian buyer pays the issuing bank in Belgian francs for the letter of credit when the buyer receives the specified documents from the bank.

> **Letter of credit** Bank's promise to pay the seller, provided certain conditions are met; used to manage the payment risks in international trade.

Antitrust Laws

Section 1 of the Sherman Act provides that U.S. **antitrust laws** shall have a broad, extraterritorial reach. Contracts, combinations, or conspiracies that restrain trade with foreign nations, as well as among the domestic states, are deemed illegal. Therefore, agreements among competitors to increase the cost of imports, as well as arrangements to exclude imports from U.S. domestic markets in exchange for agreements not to compete in other countries, clearly violate U.S. antitrust laws. The antitrust provisions are also designed to protect U.S. exports when privately imposed restrictions seek to exclude U.S. competitors from foreign markets. Amendments to the Sherman Act and the Federal Trade Commission Act limit their application to unfair methods of competition that have a direct, substantial, and reasonably foreseeable effect on U.S. domestic commerce, U.S. import commerce, or U.S. export commerce.

> **Antitrust laws** Apply to unfair methods of competition that have a direct, substantial, and reasonably foreseeable effect on the domestic, import, or export commerce of the United States.

Securities Regulation

The securities markets have become increasingly internationalized, thereby raising questions regarding which country's law governs a particular transaction in securities. Foreign issuers who issue securities in the United States must register them under the 1933 Act unless an exemption is available. Foreign issuers whose securities are sold in the secondary market in the United States must register under the 1934 Act unless the issuer is exempt. Some nonexempt foreign issuers may avoid registration under the 1934 Act by providing the SEC with copies of all information material to investors that they have made public in their home country. Regulation S provides a **safe harbor** from the 1933 Act registration requirements for offshore sales of equity securities of U.S. issuers. The antifraud provisions of the U.S. securities laws apply to securities sold by the use of any means or instrumentality of interstate commerce. In determining the extraterritorial application

> **Securities regulation** Foreign issuers who issue securities, or whose securities are sold in the secondary market in the United States, must register them unless an exemption is available; the antifraud provisions apply where there is either conduct or effects in the United States relating to a violation of the federal securities laws.

of these provisions, the courts have generally found jurisdiction where there is either *conduct* or *effects* in the United States relating to a violation of the federal securities laws.

Protection of Intellectual Property

Protection of intellectual property *The owner of an intellectual property right must comply with each country's requirements to obtain from that country whatever protection is available.*

The U.S. laws protecting intellectual property do not apply to transactions in other countries. Generally, the owner of an intellectual property right must comply with each country's requirements to obtain from that country whatever protection is available. The requirements vary substantially from country to country, as does the degree of protection. The United States belongs to multinational treaties that try to coordinate the application of member nations' intellectual property laws. The principal treaties for patent protection are the Paris Convention for the Protection of Industrial Property and the Patent Cooperation Treaty. International treaties protecting trademarks are the Paris Convention, the Arrangement of Nice Concerning the International Classification of Goods and Services, and the Vienna Trademark Registration Treaty. Copyrights are covered by the Universal Copyright Convention and the Berne Convention for the Protection of Literary and Artistic Works. The Trade-Related Aspects of Intellectual Property Rights portion of the World Trade Organization Agreement covers the range of intellectual property.

Foreign Corrupt Practices Act

In 1977, Congress enacted the **Foreign Corrupt Practices Act (FCPA)** prohibiting all domestic concerns from bribing foreign governmental or political officials. The FCPA makes it unlawful for any domestic concern or any of its officers, directors, employees, or agents to offer or give anything of value directly or indirectly to any foreign official, political party, or political official for the purpose of (1) influencing any act or decision of that person or party in his or its official capacity, (2) inducing an act or omission in violation of his or its lawful duty, or (3) inducing such person or party to use his or its influence to affect a decision of a foreign government in order to assist the domestic concern in obtaining or retaining business. An offer or promise to make a prohibited payment is a violation even if the offer is not accepted or the promise is not performed. The 1988 amendments to the FCPA explicitly excluded routine governmental actions not involving the discretion of the official, such as obtaining permits or processing applications. This exclusion does *not* cover any decision by a foreign official whether, or on what terms, to award new business or to continue business with a particular party. The amendments also added an affirmative defense for payments that are lawful under the written laws or regulations of the foreign official's country.

Foreign Corrupt Practices Act *Prohibits all U.S. companies from bribing foreign governmental or political officials.*

Violations can result in fines of up to $2 million for companies; individuals may be fined a maximum of $100,000 or imprisoned up to five years, or both. Fines imposed upon individuals may not be paid directly or indirectly by the domestic concern on whose behalf they acted. In addition, the courts may impose civil penalties of up to $11,000.

In 1997 the United States and 33 other nations signed the Organization for Economic Cooperation and Development Convention on Combating Bribery of Foreign Public Officials in International Business Transactions (OECD Convention). In 1998 Congress enacted the International Anti-Bribery and Fair Competition Act of 1998 to conform the FCPA to the Convention. The 1998 Act expands the FCPA to include (1) payments made to "secure any improper advantage" from foreign officials, (2) all foreign persons who commit an act in furtherance of a foreign bribe while in the United States, and (3) officials of public international organizations within the definition of a "foreign official." A public international organization is defined as either an organization designated by executive order pursuant to the International Organizations Immunities Act or any other international organization designated by executive order of the president.

Employment Discrimination

Title VII of the Civil Rights Act of 1964, the Americans with Disabilities Act, and the Age Discrimination in Employment Act apply to U.S. citizens employed abroad by U.S. employers or by foreign companies controlled by U.S. employers. Employers, however, are not required to comply with these employment discrimination laws if compliance would violate the law of the foreign country in which the workplace is located.

> *Take care to instruct your employees and agents not to bribe foreign officials, political parties, or political officials. Moreover, train them to distinguish between bribes, which are prohibited, and nondiscretionary facilitating (grease) payments, which are permitted.*

Ethics and International Business

Cross-National Ethics

Some businesspeople believe that what is **ethical** or **unethical** is governed by the legality of the situation and by the social aspects of the situation (what members of the society generally accept as being "right" or "wrong"). For example, if it is illegal to practice the act of bribery in a country and a firm's manager bribes someone there to obtain a favor, it would be unethical, and the violator could be prosecuted under the law. And if **bribery** is not illegal in a country, but it is known to be generally **socially unacceptable,** it would be unethical to practice it; the violator would be punished not by formal law but by informal means, such as by negative publicity and/or by customers boycotting the firm's product or service.

Regarding the social aspects of the situation, many cultures establish informal ethical principles or moral standards that define "right" and "wrong" conduct. However, what is right or wrong is difficult to define conclusively and agree upon in any culture. For example, in the United States, some Americans believe legal abortion is right; others think it is wrong. And what is right or wrong is far more difficult to define conclusively and agree upon among the different cultural environments around the globe. This is because different societies are confronted with different opportunities and constraints, and to cope, each society develops a unique culture and standard of ethics. As a result, what is right and wrong may differ dramatically from one culture to another. This means that managers of MNCs will often find themselves with **conflicting ethical responsibilities;** that is, one's own nation's standard of ethics often collides with those of other nations. For example, the practice of bribery in business transactions is acceptable in Thailand but not in the United States. An American executive transacting business in Thailand would thus be confronted with conflicting ethical responsibilities.

In part because of these conflicting ethical responsibilities, the actions of many U.S. MNCs have been subjected to considerable criticism, which in turn has led to a wide range of negative consequences, such as bad publicity, consumer boycotts, lawsuits, and government intervention, such as the passage of the Foreign Corrupt Practices Act.

Bribery and Payoffs Abroad

Forms of Bribery

Basically, a **bribe** can be defined as *a payment in any form (cash or gift) for the purpose of influencing action by a government official in order to obtain or retain business.* Bribes can be classified as "whitemail bribes" or as "lubrication bribes."

WHITEMAIL BRIBES   Whitemail bribery refers to payments made to induce an official in a position of power to give favorable treatment where such treatment is either illegal or not warranted on an efficiency, economic benefit scale. Fundamentally, a key point in this type of bribery is that the payment be intended to induce the official "to do or omit doing something in violation of his lawful duty, or to exercise his [or her] discretion in favor of the payor's request for a contract, concession, or privilege on some basis other than merit."[125] These payments, when exposed, can lead to scandals, fines, and so on. Payments of this nature have historically been "buried" in the books of MNCs or concealed in some other way.

LUBRICATION BRIBES This type of bribe is typically described as payment to facilitate, expedite, or speed up routine government approvals or other actions to which the firm would legally be entitled. Such payments are generally made to minor officials like custom agents or licensing clerks. Another trait of **lubrication bribes** is that the amounts are generally smaller than whitemail bribes although there have been cases where large lubrication-type payments were made. The number and acceptability of the practice of lubrication bribes is much greater than that of whitemail bribes. Officials in many Third World countries are especially noted for requiring "grease" to make their political and administrative wheels turn. Somewhat similar to waiters or waitresses in the United States who receive a low salary and rely on customers' tips to supplement their income, in many countries, numerous officials receive a low salary and rely on "grease" payments to supplement their income.

Extortion

A distinction can be made between bribery and extortion. Bribery is offered by an individual or a corporation seeking an unlawful advantage, while extortion is force exerted in the other direction—an official seeking payment from an individual or corporation for an action to which the individual or corporation may lawfully be entitled. **Gulf Oil's** dilemma in South Korea is an example of extortion.

To Bribe or Not to Bribe?

Bribery and corruption top the list of global ethics issues. Thus, when a manager crosses a nation's borders to conduct or negotiate business, he or she will sometimes be confronted with the need to decide whether or not to practice the act of bribery.

The U.S. Foreign Corrupt Practices Act of 1977

The revelations by the SEC and Senate Foreign Relations subcommittee investigations of U.S. MNCs' "whitemail bribery" practices abroad, and the concern for the negative image such practices generated for the United States, helped plant the seed that eventually produced U.S. Senate Bill 305, the **Foreign Corrupt Practices Act (FCPA)**. The FCPA was passed and signed into law in 1977. Its purpose was twofold:

1. To establish a worldwide code of conduct for any kind of payment by United States businesses to foreign government officials, political parties, and political candidates
2. To require appropriate accounting controls for full disclosure of firms' transactions

The law applies even if such payments are common practice (viewed as an ethical practice) in the country where they are made. Some of the basic provisions of the FCPA are as follows:

- It is a criminal offense for a firm to make payments to a foreign government official, political party, party official, or candidate for political office in order to secure or retain business in another nation.
- Sales commissions to independent agents are illegal if the business has knowledge that any part of the commission is being passed to foreign officials.
- Government employees whose duties are essentially ministerial or clerical are excluded, so expediting payments to persons such as customs agents and bureaucrats are permitted. (Thus, the FCPA does not apply to small "lubrication" bribes.)
- In addition to the antibribery provisions that apply to all businesses, all publicly held corporations that are subject to the SEC are required to establish internal accounting controls to ensure that all payments abroad are authorized and properly recorded.[126]

The penalty levied on the business enterprise for not complying with the FCPA was set at $1 million for each count. The penalty levied on individual members of the corporation found guilty of making the illegal payments is a fine of up to a $10,000 and/or five years imprisonment, with the added provision that the firm may not pay or reimburse the employees for the fines levied on them. Thus, the FCPA calls for both civil and criminal penalties.

Enforcement of the FCPA was assigned to two federal agencies: the SEC and the Department of Justice. The SEC's responsibility included enforcement of the record keeping and accounting control provisions of the FCPA and civil authority to enforce the prohibitions against foreign bribery by U.S. publicly held corporations. The Department of Justice was given the responsibility to enforce the criminal penalties for corporate bribery of foreign officials and the authority to bring civil actions against domestic concerns whose securities are not registered with the SEC.

COMPLAINTS FROM MNCs OVER THE FCPA The major areas of concern communicated by U.S. multinational corporations over the FCPA were as follows:

- The FCPA placed them at a competitive disadvantage because companies from other countries, as well as from the host country, were not bound by the FCPA laws and could continue making whitemail payments to secure business, thus putting them at a competitive advantage.
- The accounting burden of internal controls, along with the vagueness of this section of the law, makes the MNCs' duty and liability difficult to assess.
- MNCs complain that the FCPA forces them to become political tools of the U.S. government because they have to exert its will in the world through their economic power.

1988 AMENDMENTS TO THE FCPA In early 1981 and again in early 1983, the U.S. Senate attempted to repair some of the uncertainties associated with the FCPA. The Senate's proposed amendments were rejected by the House of Representatives. The amendment finally passed as a section of the Omnibus Trade and Competitiveness Act of 1988. The amendment clarifies various provisions of the FCPA, consolidates most of the enforcement responsibilities for bribery violations into the U.S. Department of Justice, and increases the civil and criminal penalties for violating the FCPA. Relative to the accounting aspects of the FCPA, the amendment limits future criminal liability to intentional actions to circumvent the internal accounting control system or falsify the corporation's books. With respect to payments made through third parties, the amendment eliminates the "reason to know" standard and modified the "knowing" standard. Under the act, "knowing" is defined to entail the substantial certainty or conscious disregard of a high probability that the third-party payment will become a bribe.[127]

Relative to enforcement of the FCPA, the amendment increased the civil and criminal penalties for violations. Criminal penalties were increased from $1 million to $2 million for corporations and from $10,000 to $100,000 for individuals. The maximum imprisonment remained five years. A civil penalty of $10,000 for individuals was established and may not be paid by the corporation. All jurisdictions for enforcing the antibribery provisions of the FCPA were consolidated within the Department of Justice. The SEC remained responsible for civil enforcement of the records and internal accounting control provisions of the FCPA.[128]

An Alternative Payoff Approach

Many international executives do not view the FCPA as hindering their competitiveness in the global marketplace. These executives enhance their competitiveness by improving their enterprises' technical expertise, their customer service, and their responsibility to the customer through quality. Furthermore, there are indications that the practice of bribery is not as widespread as it once was; it seems to be waning. And when these executives must make some sort of payment to obtain a favor, they do not pay "private individuals"; instead, they make payments to institutions, such as contributions to build schools, hospitals, medical clinics, or agricultural projects.[129] Payments of this nature obtain favors and goodwill for the MNC; they also improve the local situation, such as by increasing local employment. This payment approach, thus, does not improve only one person's bank account; instead, the payment is shared with the community.

Cross-National Social Responsibility

Social responsibility has been defined as "the notion that corporations have an obligation to constituent groups in society other than stockholders and beyond that prescribed by law or union contract."[130] Corporate social responsibility therefore means that a firm's actions must take into account not only the well-being of the stockholders but also the well-being of the community, the employees, and the customers. With respect to MNCs' **cross-national social responsibility,** many international business executives condone the concept of cultural relativism, while others condone the concept of universalism.

The Concept of Cultural Relativism

Cultural relativism holds that "no culture's ethics are any better than any other's."[131] Under this standard there are no international "rights" or "wrongs." Thus, if Thailand tolerates the bribery of public officials, then Thai tolerance is no worse than American or German intolerance. If Switzerland is liberal with respect to insider trading, then Swiss liberalism is no worse than American restrictiveness.[132] These executives would therefore not support the FCPA.

But the concept of cultural relativism can backfire. For example, suppose a U.S. corporation invents a product and patents it. Patent piracy is wrong (and illegal) in the United States, but it is not wrong in some nations (and if it is illegal, culturally, it is not enforced). What if a company in one of these countries pirated the patent? Would the executives in the company from which the patent was pirated simply write the loss off as, "Oh well, that's culture"? As illustration, some enterprises in China readily pirate U.S. firms' copyrighted computer software, movies, and music and put phony American labels on consumer products. If the American pirated firms' executives adhered to the cultural relativism concept, they would not complain about the Chinese firms' pirating practices because they are not viewed as being unethical in China. However, U.S. trade representatives are currently applying strong pressure on Chinese government officials to implement and enforce policies that preclude Chinese enterprises from undertaking such activities.[133] Suppose also that a U.S. MNC is manufacturing in Bangladesh using cheap child labor. Use of child labor in such a way is not tolerable in the United States, but it is tolerable in Bangladesh. What happens to the MNC when the U.S. press gets hold of the information and promulgates it among the U.S. public? Will it result in a boycott? It therefore seems that the concept of cultural relativism is often not very practical.

The Concept of Universalism

On the other hand, the concept of **universalism,** a rigid global yardstick by which to measure all moral issues (for example, the FCPA), is often not very practical either. This is because its application would show disrespect for valid cultural differences and different economic needs. For example, people in the United States do not tolerate manufacturing facilities that disperse health-damaging smog. Under the concept of universalism, it would be unethical to transfer such manufacturing facilities to another country. But in countries where people are starving, economic development may be more important than health, and such manufacturing facilities would thus be welcome. A manager guided by the cultural relativism view would export such manufacturing facilities to the starving country. But, as mentioned above, it is likely to backfire.

Thus, developing, implementing, and controlling cross-cultural business ethics and social responsibility programs is an enormous challenge confronting the managers of MNCs. The problem is enlarged by the press sometimes persuading MNCs to impose their social responsibility on their manufacturing subcontractors. For example, **Starbucks Coffee** has agreed to adopt a "code of conduct" that must be adhered to by its coffee suppliers and may help workers in Guatemala and other Third World nations. Starbucks' management made the decision after stores in British Columbia, Canada, and the U.S. were targeted in a February 1995 leafletting blitz. The protesters were concerned about "harsh working conditions, paltry pay, and human rights violations on Guatemalan coffee plantations."[134] The press therefore often asks MNCs to reject the concept of cultural relativism and apply the concept of universalism.

Toward the Globalization of Business Ethics

The U.S. approach to business ethics is unique. In comparison with other capitalistic societies, it is more individualistic, legalistic, and universalistic.[135] In other words, issues of business ethics are far more visible in the United States than they are in other capitalistic societies. This may be because there are far more laws regulating business in the United States than there are in other capitalistic countries. Therefore, the American public reads and hears far more about business misconduct than do people in other countries. Hence, the "**ethics gap**" between the United States and the rest of the developed world is considerably large.[136]

The Impact of Culture on the Business Ethics Visibility Gap

The United States is one of the most individualistic cultures in the world. People's decisions in individualistic cultures tend to be guided by self-interests, as opposed to group interests. On the other hand, managers in group-oriented cultures tend to reflect less their personal moral guidance and more their shared understanding of the nature and scope of the corporation's responsibilities—and the enterprise's moral expectations are shaped by the norms of the community, not the personal values and reflections of the individual.[137] This helps explain why there are far more laws regulating business in the United States than there are in other advanced nations, and it helps explain why there is such a large business ethics gap between the United States and other nations.

This suggests that globalization of business ethics (application of the concept of universalism) is distant and that the concept of cultural relativism still prevails. Thus, as the integration of the global economy increases, effective international managers develop a "better appreciation of the differences in the legal and cultural context of business ethics between the United States and other capitalist nations and between Western and Asian economies as well."[138]

Business Ethics and the Internet

The **World Wide Web,** an area of the Internet, is a virtual, global, open-ended organization of interconnected information sources. It is now a quick way for companies, large or small, to market products or services globally to people who access the Internet. However, managers of such a global network are faced with the challenge of addressing the concerns of its constituents with respect to confidentiality, authenticity, and integrity, balancing security against responsiveness and performance. The system needs to be secure against malicious use, misuse, and data corruption while protecting the privacy of its users and the intellectual property of the vendors. For example, providing copyright protection for knowledge providers on the Internet is quite different from providing it to their counterparts in hardcopy publication. However, hardcopy publications do not have much protection in numerous countries. The Internet may thus be a great challenge in this respect.[139]

Ethical Issues in International Business

Just as laws differ from country to country, so does the definition of ethical behavior. In international business, *"the law is a floor for our behavior, but ethical codes and personal values call on us to exceed that which is required by law."* When called on to evaluate a course of action according to a code of ethics or personal value system, one must consider the decision in the cultural context. In other words, what is considered appropriate behavior in one culture may not be so in another. Managers often must evaluate their actions according to ethical codes or personal values that may or may not be commonly accepted in the country in which they are operating. The following examples serve as preparation for the consideration of ethical issues:

Example 1 You have been negotiating with a representative of the Portuguese government to sell products to them for a new state building project. He arrives at your company's offices with a blank purchase order in hand. After negotiating a fixed price and delivery, he "suggests" that you prepare a price quotation on a "pro forma invoice"—at double the negotiated price. His government will pay the full amount shown on the invoice through a Portuguese bank, and your firm will pay him the difference as a "commission" in U.S. dollars deposited to his bank account in New York. He convincingly argues that this practice is customary in his country. The temptation for you might be great; the deal would be a profitable one. But would it be legal or ethical? Certainly, laws and ethical standards vary from country to country. In this example, you would have to consider the laws and ethical codes of both Portugal and the United States. Even though bribery is more common in certain other countries, this transaction would clearly be illegal under U.S. law, and you would be subject to criminal prosecution, fines, and possible imprisonment.

Example 2 Imagine that your firm enters into a contract to sell drilling equipment to a Korean company. The contract is closed while the Korean company president is visiting the U.S. plant. After closing, the Korean executive points out that all imports to Korea must be channeled through a registered "local agent." He quickly suggests that a wholly owned trading company *that he owns* could handle all of the paperwork—for a fee. Compare this with the first example. Should you comply with his request? Is it legal? If it is, is it ethical? The prudent manager will avoid potential legal liability and will also attempt to conform to what he or she deems to be ethical.

Example 3 Your company intends to locate a plant in Mexico for the assembly of automobile engines. If the plant were in the United States, the laws require considerable expenditures for environmental controls such as antipollution equipment. United States law also mandates expensive safeguards to protect the health and safety of U.S. workers, as well as the added cost of minimum wage rules, social security contributions, health care, and other employee benefits. Assume that Mexican law is not so strict and that operating costs there are less as a result. To what extent should you conform to the legal standards applicable in the United States? Is it ethical not to? Indeed, should any firm operating in a host country carry with it the ethical codes of its home country? How does the international manager justify decisions in cross-cultural situations?

Example 4 You are an international manager for a U.S. apparel designer that sells to major U.S. department stores and retailers. Several years ago your firm decided to have clothing sewn in India and Pakistan, which resulted in tremendous cost savings as opposed to having the work done in the United States. In making the decision, the firm considered its impact on U.S. families who depend on the income from these jobs. It opted for the cost savings, seeing its responsibility to produce a profit for shareholders as more important than providing jobs in the United States. Now, however, it finds that its contractor in India is overworking and abusing child labor in violation of internationally accepted standards for the treatment of children in the workplace. The Indian government shows little interest in policing its own labor practices. The sad story of the Indian children is run on national television and appears in the national press. If you decide to discontinue working with sewing contractors in India, would you do so to protect Indian children or because of the adverse publicity in the United States, or both? Consider the company's course of action and how you should react now.

Module 1000 Endnotes

1. Part of this discussion draws from S. Rose, "Why the Multinational Is Ebbing," *Fortune* (August 1977), 111–120. Rose uses the labels "aggressive" and "defensive" reasons.
2. D. C. Shanks, "Strategic Planning for Global Competition," *Journal of Business Strategy 5*, no. 3 (Winter 1985), 80.
3. R. Brady, M. Maremont, and P. Galuszka, "Aeroflot Takes Off for Joint-Ventureland," *Business Week*, October 30, 1989, 48–49.
4. Frank E. Bair, (Ed.), *International Marketing Handbook*, 2nd Edition (Detroit: Michigan: Gale Research Company, 1985), 1582.
5. J. G. Wissema and L. Euser, "Successful Innovation Through Inter-Company Networks," *Long-Range Planning 24* (December 1991), 33–39.
6. Thomas Hout, Michael E. Porter, and Eileen Rudden, "How Global Companies Win Out," *Harvard Business Review* (September–October 1982), 103.
7. *Ibid.*
8. *Ibid.*
9. George S. Yip, "Global Strategy . . . in a World of Nations?" *Sloan Management Review* (Fall 1989), 29.
10. *Ibid.*
11. Nestlé Home Page, February 8, 1998 (http://www.nestle.com).
12. M. A. Hitt, B. W. Keats, and S. M. DeMario, "Navigating in the New Competitive Landscape: Building Strategic Flexibility and Competitive Advantage in the 21st Century," *Academy of Management Executive 12*, no. 4 (November 1998), 23.
13. Charles K. Kao, *A Choice Fulfilled: The Business of High Technology* (New York: St. Martin's Press, 1991).
14. James E. Lee, "Cultural Analysis in Overseas Operations," *Harvard Business Review* (March–April 1966), 106–114.
15. Adapted from Allison Lucas, "Market Researchers Study Abroad," *Sales and Marketing Management* (February 1996), 13.
16. Warren J. Keegan, "Multinational Product Planning: Strategic Alternatives," *Journal of Marketing* (January 1969), 58–62.
17. Laurie M. Grossman, "PepsiCo Plans Big Overseas Expansion in Diet Cola Wars with Its Pepsi Max," *Wall Street Journal*, April 4, 1994, p. B6.
18. Theodore Levitt, "The Globalization of Markets," *Harvard Business Review 61* (May–June 1983), 92–102.
19. This discussion draws from C.H. Lovelock and G.S. Yip, "Developing Global Strategies for Service Businesses," *California Management Review* 38, no. 2 (Winter 1996), 64–86.
20. William M. Bulkeley, "Having High-Tuition Blues? Look North," *Wall Street Journal*, November 26, 1997, pp. C1, C19.
21. J. Greene and M. Duerr, *International Transactions in the Multinational Firm* (New York: The Conference Board, 1970), p. 8.
22. This discussion draws from P. Maher, "The Countertrade Boom," *Business Marketing* (January 1984), 50–52; and "Countertrade Without Cash?" *Finance and Development* (December 1983), 14.
23. The following discussion is adopted from Kamran Kashiani, "Beware the Pitfalls of Global Marketing," *Harvard Business Review* (September–October 1989), 91–98.
24. "Global Messages for the Global Village Are Here," *Business World* (Autumn 1983), 51.
25. Adapted from Cateora and Hess, *International Marketing*, p. 417.
26. Paul Blustein, "Kawasaki to Pay Additional Taxes to U.S.," *The Washington Post*, December 11, 1992, D1.
27. www.opic.gov, Washington, DC: Overseas Private Investment Corporation, May 2, 2001.
28. Robert J. Flanagan, "Knowledge Management in the Global Organization in the 21st Century," *HR Magazine* 44, 11 (1999): 54–55.
29. Michael Z. Brooke, *International Management: A Review of Strategies and Operations* (London: Hutchinson, 1986), 173–174.
30. Stefan Robock and Kenneth Simmonds, *International Business and Multinational Enterprises* (Homewood, IL: Richard D. Irwin, 1973), 429.
31. Richard D. Robinson, *Internationalization of Business: An Introduction* (Hinsdale, IL: The Dryden Press, 1984).
32. William H. Davidson and Philippe Haspeslagh, "Shaping a Global Product Organization," *Harvard Business Review* 59 (March/April 1982), 69–76.
33. See http://www.loctite.com/about/global_reach.html, and "How Loctite Prospers with 3-Man Global HQ, Strong Country Managers," *Business International*, May 2, 1988, 129–130.
34. See Joan P. Curhan, William H. Davidson, and Suri Rajan, *Tracing the Multinationals* (Cambridge, MA: Ballinger, 1977); M. E. Wicks, *A Comparative Analysis of the Foreign Investment Evaluation Practices of U.S.-Based Multinational Corporations* (New

York: McKinsey & Co., 1980); and Lawrence G. Franko, "Organizational Structures and Multinational Strategies of Continental European Enterprises," in Michel Ghertman and James Leontiades, eds., *European Research in International Business.* (Amsterdam, Holland: North Holland Publishing Co., 1977).

35. Davidson and Haspeslagh, "Shaping a Global Product Organization."
36. "How Goodyear Sharpened Organization and Production for a Tough World Market," *Business International* (January 16, 1989): 11–14.
37. "Red Alert at Ford," *Business Week,* December 2, 1996, 38–39.
38. John D. Daniels, "Bridging National and Global Marketing Strategies Through Regional Operations," *International Marketing Review* 4 (Autumn 1987), 29–44; and Philippe Lasserre, "Regional Headquarters: The Spearhead for Asia Pacific Markets," *Long Range Planning* 29 (February, 1996), 30–37.
39. Daniel Robey, *Designing Organizations: A Macro Perspective* (Homewood, IL: Richard D. Irwin, 1982), 327.
40. Thomas H. Naylor, "International Strategy Matrix," *Columbia Journal of World Business* 20 (Summer 1985), 11–19.
41. "Kodak's Matrix System Focuses on Product Business Units," *Business International* (July 18, 1988), 221–223.
42. See http://www.philips.com/finance/investor/divstruc.html.
43. Thomas J. Peters, "Beyond the Matrix Organization," *Business Horizons* 22 (October 1979), 15–27.
44. See John M. Stopford and Louis T. Wells, *Managing the Multinational Enterprise* (New York: Basic Books, 1972); also A. D. Chandler, *Strategy and Structure* (Cambridge, MA: MIT Press, 1962); and B. R. Scott, *Stages of Corporate Development* (Boston: ICCH, 1971).
45. Stanley M. Davis, "Trends in the Organization of Multinational Corporations," *Columbia Journal of World Business* 11 (Summer 1976), 59–71.
46. William Taylor, "The Logic of Global Business," *Harvard Business Review* 68 (March–April 1990), 91–105.
47. Ilkka A. Ronkainen, "Thinking Globally, Implementing Successfully," *International Marketing Review* 13, 3 (1996), 4–6.
48. Norman Blackwell, Jean-Pierre Bizet, Peter Child, and David Hensley, "Creating European Organizations That Work," *The McKinsey Quarterly* 27, 2 (1991), 376–385.
49. John A. Quelch and Helen Bloom, "The Return of the Country Manager," *International Marketing Review* 13, 3 (1996), 31–43.
50. Rodman Drake and Lee M. Caudill, "Management of the Large Multinational: Trends and Future Challenges," *Business Horizons* 24 (May–June 1981), 83–91.
51. Christopher Bartlett, "MNCs: Get off the Reorganization Merry-Go-Round," *Harvard Business Review* 60 (March–April 1983), 138–146.
52. Thomas Gross, Ernie Turner, and Lars Cederholm, "Building Teams for Global Operations" *Management Review* (June 1987), 32–36.
53. Christopher A. Bartlett and Sumantra Ghoshal, "Matrix Management: Not a Structure, a Frame of Mind," *Harvard Business Review* 68 (July–August 1990), 138–145.
54. "See Jack. See Jack Run Europe," *Fortune,* September 27, 1999, 127–136.
55. Ingo Theuerkauf, David Ernst, and Amir Mahini, "Think Local, Organize...." *International Marketing Review* 13, 3 (1996), 7–12.
56. C.K. Prahalad, "Globalization, Digitization, and the Multinational Enterprise," paper presented at the Annual Meetings of the Academy of International Business, November, 1999.
57. James A. Gingrich, "Five Rules for Winning Emerging Market Consumers," *Strategy and Business* (Second Quarter, 1999), 19–33.
58. Christopher A. Bartlett and Sumantra Ghoshal, "Tap Your Subsidiaries for Global Reach," *Harvard Business Review* 64 (November–December 1986), 87–94.
59. Julian Birkinshaw and Nick Fry, "Subsidiary Initiatives to Develop New Markets," *Sloan Management Review* 19 (Spring 1998), 51–61.
60. Amitai Etzioni, *A Comparative Analysis of Complex Organizations* (Glencoe, England: Free Press, 1961).
61. William G. Egelhoff, "Patterns of Control in U.S., U.K., and European Multinational Corporations," *Journal of International Business Studies* 15 (Fall 1984), 73–83.
62. William H. Davidson, "Administrative Orientation and International Performance," *Journal of International Business Studies* 15 (Fall 1984), 11–23.
63. William G. Ouchi, "The Relationship Between Organizational Structure and Organizational Control," *Administrative Science Quarterly* 22 (March 1977), 95–112.
64. B. R. Baliga and Alfred M. Jaeger, "Multinational Corporations: Control Systems and Delegation Issues," *Journal of International Business Studies* 15 (Fall 1984), 25–40.
65. Laurent Leksell, *Headquarters-Subsidiary Relationships in Multinational Corporations* (Stockholm, Sweden: Stockholm School of Economics, 1981), Chapter 5.
66. Anant R. Negandhi and Martin Welge, *Beyond Theory Z* (Greenwich, CT: JAI Press, 1984), 16.
67. Richard Pascale, "Fitting New Employees into the Company Culture," *Fortune* (May 28, 1984), 28–40.

68. Bartlett and Ghoshal, "Matrix Management: Not a Structure, a Frame of Mind."
69. Michael R. Czinkota and Ilkka A. Ronkainen, "International Business and Trade in the Next Decade: Report from a Delphi Study," *Journal of International Business Studies* 28, 4 (1997), 676–694.
70. Tsun-Yuan Hsieh, Johanne La Voie, and Robert A. P. Samek, "Think Global, Hire Local," *The McKinsey Quarterly* 35, 4 (1999), 92–101.
71. R. J. Alsegg, *Control Relationships Between American Corporations and Their European Subsidiaries,* AMA Research Study No. 107 (New York: American Management Association, 1971), 7.
72. John J. Dyment, "Strategies and Management Controls for Global Corporations," *Journal of Business Strategy* 7 (Spring 1987), 20–26.
73. Hans Schoellhammer, "Decision-Making and Intra-organizational Conflicts in Multinational Companies," presentation at the Symposium on Management of Headquarter-Subsidiary Relationships in Transnational Corporations, Stockholm School of Economics, June 2–4, 1980.
74. Alfred M. Jaeger, "The Transfer of Organizational Culture Overseas: An Approach to Control in the Multinational Corporation," *Journal of International Business Studies* 14 (Fall 1983), 91–106.
75. Michael R. Czinkota and Erwin Dichtl, "Export Controls and Global Changes," *der markt,* 35, 3 (1996), 148–155.
76. Robert M. Springer, Jr., "New Export Law an Aid to International Marketers," *Marketing News,* January 3, 1986, pp. 10, 67.
77. E. M. Hucko, *Aussenwirtschaftsrecht-Kriegswaffenkontrollrecht, Textsammlung mit Einführung,* 4th ed. (Cologne, 1993).
78. "Bribery a Problem with Overseas Customers," *Management Accounting* 75, 6 (June 1997), 61.
79. George Moody, *Grand Corruption: How Business Bribes Damage Developing Countries* (Oxford: World View Publishing, 1997), 23.
80. Wassily Leontief, "Domestic Production and Foreign Trade: the American Capital Position Re-Examined," *Proceedings of the American Philosophical Society,* 97, no. 4 (September 1953), as reprinted in Wassily Leontief, *Input-Output Economics* (New York: Oxford University Press, 1966), 69–70.
81. In Leontief's own words: "These figures show that an average million dollars' worth of our exports embodies considerably less capital and somewhat more labor than would be required to replace from domestic production an equivalent amount of our competitive imports.... The widely held opinion that—as compared with the rest of the world—the United States' economy is characterized by a relative surplus of capital and a relative shortage of labor proves to be wrong. As a matter of fact, the opposite is true" (Leontief, 1953, p. 86).
82. If this were true, if would defy one of the basic assumptions of the factor proportions theory, that all products are manufactured with the same technology (and therefore same proportions of labor and capital) across countries. However, continuing studies have found this to be quite possible in our imperfect world.
83. For a detailed description of these theories see Elhanan Helpman and Paul Krugman, *Market Structure and Foreign Trade* (Cambridge: MIT Press, 1985).
84. This leads to the obvious debate as to what constitutes a "different product" and what is simply a cosmetic difference. The most obvious answer is found in the field of marketing: If the consumer believes the products are different, then they are different.
85. There are a variety of potential outcomes from external economies of scale. For additional details see Paul R. Krugman and Maurice Obstfeld, *International Economics: Theory and Policy,* 3rd ed. (HarperCollins, 1994).
86. The term *international investment* will be used in this chapter to refer to all nonfinancial investment. International financial investment includes a number of forms beyond the concerns of this chapter, such as the purchase of bonds, stocks, or other securities issued outside the domestic economy.
87. The official terminology used throughout this chapter, unless otherwise noted, is that of the International Monetary Fund (IMF). Since the IMF is the primary source of similar statistics for balance of payments and economic performance worldwide, it is more general than other terminology forms, such as that employed by the U.S. Department of Commerce.
88. This discussion draws from Dean Foster, "Business Across Borders: International Etiquette for the Effective Global Secretary," *The Secretary* (October 1992), 20–24.
89. *Ibid.,* p. 24.
90. Lyle Sussman and Denise M. Johnson, "The Interpreted Executive: Theory, Models, and Implications," *The Journal of Business Communication, 30,* no. 4 (1993), 419–420.
91. Edward T. Hall, "How Cultures Collide," *Psychology Today* (July 1976), 67–74.
92. Mary Munter, "Cross-Cultural Communication for Managers," *Business Horizons* (May–June 1993), p. 74.
93. Hall, "How Cultures Collide," pp. 67–74.
94. *Ibid.,* p. 74.
95. Munter, "Cross-Cultural Communication for Managers," p. 74.
96. *Ibid.,* p. 75.
97. *Ibid.,* p. 76.
98. This discussion draws from Jon P. Alston, "Wa, Guanxi, and Inhwa: Managerial Principles in Japan, China, and Korea," *Business Horizons* 32, no. 2 (March–April 1989), 27–28.

99. Linda Beamer, "Learning Intercultural Communication Competence," *The Journal of Business Communication 29,* no. 3 (1992), 291–301.
100. Ibid., p. 291.
101. M. Katherine Glover, "Do's and Taboos: Cultural Aspects of International Business," *Business America,* August 13, 1990, 3.
102. Adapted from R. Knotts, "Cross-Cultural Management: Transformations and Adaptations," *Business Horizons* (January–February 1989), 29–33.
103. Dean Allan Foster, *Bargaining Across Borders* (New York: McGraw-Hill, 1992), 5.
104. *Ibid.*
105. Hokey Min and William Galle, "International Negotiation Strategies of U.S. Purchasing Professionals," *International Journal of Purchasing and Materials Management* (Summer 1993), 43.
106. Trenholme J. Griffin and W. Russell Daggatt, *The Global Negotiator* (New York: Harper Business Publishers, 1990), p. 74.
107. Min and Galle, "International Negotiation Strategies," p. 42.
108. Robert O. Joy, "Cultural and Procedural Differences That Influence Business Strategies and Operations in the People's Republic of China," *SAM Advanced Management Journal* (Summer 1989), 31.
109. Griffin and Daggatt, *The Global Negotiator,* p. 77.
110. Min and Galle, "International Negotiation Strategies," p. 43.
111. *Ibid.,* pp. 43–44.
112. *Ibid.,* p. 44.
113. Edward T. Hall, "The Silent Language in Overseas Business," *Harvard Business Review* (May–June 1960), 93.
114. Shah M. Tarzi, "Third World Governments and Multinational Corporations: Dynamics of Host's Bargaining Power" (n.d., n.p.), p. 237.
115. Griffin and Daggatt, *The Global Negotiator,* p. 120.
116. *Ibid.,* p. 106.
117. See A. C. Day, "Institutional Constraints and the International Monetary System," in R. Mundell and A. Swoboda, eds., *Monetary Problems of the International Economy* (Chicago: University of Chicago Press, 1969), 333–342.
118. Federal News Service, *Hearing of the House Judiciary Committee,* April 23, 1997.
119. Michael R. Czinkota and Jon Woronoff, *Unlocking Japan's Market* (Chicago: Probus Publishing, 1991).
120. *National Trade Estimate Report on Foreign Trade Barriers,* Washington, DC: Office of the United States Trade Representative, 2000, www.ustr.gov.
121. Michael R. Czinkota, "The Policy Gap in International Marketing," *Journal of International Marketing,* 8, 1, 2000, 99–111.
122. Michael R. Czinkota, "International Information Needs for U.S. Competitiveness," *Business Horizons* 34, 6 (November/December 1991), 86-91.
123. Najmeh Bozorgmehr and Stefan Wagstyl, "European Business Sees New Area of Potential," *Financial Times,* February 6, 2002, www.ft.com.
124. *International Court of Arbitration: 1999 Statistical Report* (Paris: International Chamber of Commerce, 2001).
125. W. A. Label and J. Kaikati, "Foreign Antibribery Law: Friend or Foe?" *Columbia Journal of World Business* (Spring 1980), 46.
126. O. Ronald Gray, "The Foreign Corrupt Practices Act: Revisited and Amended," *Business and Society* (Spring 1990), 14.
127. Andrew W. Singer, "Ethics: Are Standards Lower Overseas?" *Across the Board* (September 1991), 15–16.
128. *Ibid.,* p. 16.
129. Kent Hodgson, "Adapting Ethical Decisions to a Marketplace," *Management Review* (May 1992), 56–57.
130. Donna J. Wood, "Corporate Social Performance Revisited," *Academy of Management Review* 16 (October 1991), 691–718.
131. Thomas Donaldson, "Values in Tension: Ethics Away from Home," *Harvard Business Review* (September–October 1996), 48–62.
132. Donaldson, "Global Business Must Mind Its Morals."
133. David E. Rosenbaum, "China Trade Rift with U.S. Deepens," *The New York Times,* January 29, 1995, p. 1.
134. Sarah Cox, "Starbucks Pours One for Coffee Workers," *Monday Magazine* (Victoria, B.C.) (March 16–22, 1995), 6
135. David Vogel, "The Globalization of Business Ethics: Why America Remains Distinctive," *California Management Review 35,* no. 1 (Fall 1992), 30.
136. *Ibid.,* pp. 35–37.
137. *Ibid.,* pp. 46–47.
138. *Ibid.,* p. 49.
139. N. A. Adam, B. Slonim, J. Wagner, P. Yesha, Yelena, "Globalizing Business, Education, Culture, Through the Internet," *Communications of the ACM 40,* no. 2 (February 1997), 115–121.

Glossary*

Numbers

4/5ths Rule Rule stating that discrimination generally is considered to occur if the selection rate for a protected group is less than 80 percent (4/5ths) of the selection rate for the majority group or less than 80 percent of the group's representation in the relevant labor market.

8-K Monthly report to the SEC when significant events occur.

10-K Annual report filed by publicly traded companies to the SEC.

10-Q Quarterly report filed by publicly traded companies to the SEC.

40/30/30 rule A rule that identifies the sources of scrap, rework, and waste as 40 percent product design, 30 percent manufacturing processing, and 30 percent from suppliers.

100 percent location Occurs when there is no better use for a site than the retail store that is being planned for that site.

360-degree feedback A process that uses multiple raters, including self-rating, to appraise employee performance and guide development.

401(k) plan An agreement in which a percentage of an employee's pay is withheld and invested in a tax-deferred account.

A

Abandoned product ranges The outcome of a firm narrowing its range of products to obtain economies of scale, which provides opportunities for other firms to enter the markets for the abandoned products.

ABC classification The classification of a group of items in decreasing order of annual dollar volume (price multiplied by projected volume) or other criteria. This array is then split into three classes, called A, B, and C. The A group usually represents 10 percent to 20 percent by number of items and 50 percent to 70 percent by projected dollar volume. The next grouping, B, usually represents about 20 percent of the items and about 20 percent of the dollar volume. The C class contains 60 percent to 70 percent of the items and represents about 10 percent to 30 percent of the dollar volume. The ABC principle states that effort and money can be saved through applying looser controls to the low-dollar-volume class items than will be applied to high-dollar-volume class items. The ABC principle is applicable to inventories, purchasing, sales, and so on. *Syn:* ABC analysis, distribution by value, Pareto analysis.

Ability test An assessment device that measures a person's capability to learn or acquire skills. Also referred to as an aptitude test.

Abnormal demand Demand in any period that is outside the limits established by management policy. This demand may come from a new customer or from existing customers whose own demand is increasing or decreasing. Care must be taken in evaluating the nature of the demand: Is it a volume change, is it a change in product mix, or is it related to the timing of the order?

Above-market pricing policy A policy where retailers establish high prices because nonprice factors are more important to their target market than price.

Absolute advantage The ability to produce a good or service more cheaply than it can be produced elsewhere.

Absolute form of purchasing power parity Also called the "law of one price," this theory suggests that prices of two products of different countries should be equal when measured by a common currency.

Absorption costing A product costing approach that assigns all fixed and variable manufacturing costs to the units produced.

Accelerated depreciation method A depreciation method that provides for a high depreciation expense in the first year of use of an asset and a gradually declining expense thereafter.

Acceptable Quality Level (AQL) When a continuing series of lots is considered, a quality level that, for the purposes of sampling inspection, is the limit of a satisfactory process average.

Acceptance sampling Inspection of a sample from a lot to decide whether to accept or not accept that lot. There are two types: attributes sampling and variables sampling. In attributes sampling, the presence or absence of a characteristic is noted in each of the units inspected. In variables sampling, the numerical magnitude of a characteristic is measured and recorded for each inspected unit; this involves reference to a continuous scale of some kind.

Acceptance sampling plan A specific plan that indicates the sampling sizes and the associated acceptance or nonacceptance criteria to be used. In attributes sampling, for example, there are single, double, multiple, sequential, chain, and skip-lot sampling plans. In variables sampling, there are single, double, and sequential sampling plans.

Access control Hardware and software measures, such as user IDs and passwords, used to control access to information systems.

Account The form used to record additions and deductions for each individual asset, liability, owner's equity, revenue, and expense.

---

*Selected terms in Glossary are from *APICS Dictionary,* 10th edition, © 2002 by APICS—The Educational Society for Resource Management, Alexandria, Virginia, USA. Reprinted with permission.

Selected terms in Glossary are from the *Certified Quality Manager Handbook,* 2nd ed., by Duke Okes and Russell T. Westcott (eds), © 2001 by ASQ Quality Press, Milwaukee, Wisconsin, USA. Reprinted with permission.

Account form The form of balance sheet with the assets section presented on the left-hand side and the liabilities and owner's equity sections presented on the right-hand side.

Account parameters and records Credit customer identifiers such as name, address, and the customer's bank transit routing number. These items are included in the customer's credit file.

Account receivable A claim against a customer for services rendered or goods sold on credit.

Account reconciliation A disbursement-related service in which the bank develops a detailed report of checks paid as well as miscellaneous debits and stopped payments. In a full account reconciliation, the company also provides the bank with a record of checks drawn, and the bank informs the company of which checks remain outstanding.

Accountability 1: The fact that the people with authority and responsibility are subject to reporting and justifying task outcomes to those above them in the chain of command. **2:** A corporation is subject to less accountability than public bodies.

Accounting The process of identifying, measuring, and communicating economic information to permit informed judgments and decisions by users of the information.

Accounting and Auditing Enforcement Release (AAER) Public document released by the SEC when a company commits financial statement fraud or other inappropriate activities.

Accounting anomalies Inaccuracies in source documents, journal entries, ledgers, or financial statements.

Accounting cycle 1: Procedures for analyzing, recording, classifying, summarizing, and reporting the transactions of a business. **2:** The sequence of basic accounting procedures during a fiscal period.

Accounting diversity The range of differences in national accounting practices.

Accounting equation The expression of the relationship between assets, liabilities, and owner's equity; it is most commonly stated as Assets = Liabilities + Owner's Equity.

Accounting exposures The transaction and translation risk exposures.

Accounting period concept An accounting principle that requires accounting reports be prepared at periodic intervals.

Accounting principles See: Accounting standards.

Accounting Principles Board (APB) Opinion No. 15 A standard issued by the Accounting Principles Board in the United States that outlines all the factors pertinent to the computation of earnings per common share.

Accounting profit A firm's net income as reported on its income statement.

Accounting standards The rules that govern the measuring and recording of economic activities and the reporting of accounting information to external users.

Accounting system 1: The methods and procedures used by a business to record and report financial data for use by management and external users. **2:** Policies and procedures for recording economic transactions in an organized manner.

Accounts and/or notes receivable Amounts of money that customers owe the retailer for goods and services.

Accounts payable 1: A liability that is generated by purchasing a good or service on credit. **2:** A financial obligation that is created when goods or services are purchased on credit. **3:** Amounts of money owed vendors for goods and services.

Accounts receivable financing Indirect financing provided by an exporter for an importer by exporting goods and allowing for payment to be made at a later date.

Accounts receivable turnover 1: Computed by dividing days' sales outstanding into the number of days in the calculation period, which is usually 365. Indicates how many times per year the seller's investment in accounts receivable "turns over" into sales, which is an efficiency measure giving the same signal as days' sales outstanding. **2:** A measure used to determine a company's average collection period for receivables; computed by dividing net sales (or net credit sales) by average accounts receivable. **3:** Sales divided by average accounts receivable; a measure of the efficiency with which receivables are being collected.

Accreditation Certification by a duly recognized body of the facilities, capability, objectivity, competence, and integrity of an agency, service, or operational group or individual to provide the specific service or operation needed. For example, the Registrar Accreditation Board (U.S.) accredits those organizations that register companies to the ISO 9000 series standards.

Accrual 1: A liability account that results from expenses incurred during the operating process that are not yet paid. **2:** Continually recurring short-term liabilities; liabilities such as wages and taxes that increase spontaneously with operations.

Accrued expenses Expenses that have been incurred but not paid. Sometimes called *accrued liabilities*.

Accrued liability Liabilities arising from end-of-period adjustments, not from specific transactions.

Accrued revenues Revenues that have been earned but not collected. Sometimes called accrued assets.

Acculturation The process of adjusting and adapting to a specific culture other than one's own.

Accumulated depreciation account The contra-asset account used to accumulate the depreciation recognized to date on plant assets.

Accuracy A characteristic of measurement which addresses how close an observed value is to the true value. It answers the question, "Is it right?"

ACH credit Payment order transmitted through the automated clearing house system and originated by the payor. The routing bank (originating institution) in this case is the payor's disbursement bank.

ACH debit Payment order for payment through the automated clearing house system and originated by the payee, based on the prior authorization by the payor. This order is routed through the payee's bank (originating financial depository institution, or OFDI). Another name for an *electronic depository transfer*.

Acid rain Standards are established to protect against acid rain (precipitation that contains high levels of sulfuric or nitric acid).

Acid-test ratio A ratio that measures the "instant" debt-paying ability of a company. Also known as *quick ratio*.

Acquisition The purchase of something, such as the purchase of one company by another company.

Acquisition of shares A corporation's repurchase of its own shares.

ACSI The American Customer Satisfaction Index, released for the first time in October 1994, is a new economic indicator, a cross-industry measure of the satisfaction of U.S. household customers with the quality of the goods and services available to them—both those goods and services produced within the United States and those provided as imports from foreign firms that have substantial market shares or dollar sales. The ACSI is cosponsored by the University of Michigan Business School and ASQ.

Act of state doctrine Rule that a court should not question the validity of actions taken by a foreign government in its own country.

Act utilitarianism Concept that each separate act must be assessed according to whether it maximizes pleasure over pain.

Action plan The detailed plan to implement the actions needed to achieve strategic goals and objectives (similar to but not as comprehensive as a *project plan*).

Action taken without a meeting Permitted if a consent in writing is signed by all of the directors.

Active information gathering Occurs when consumers proactively gather information.

Active investment strategy An approach to investing that involves relatively more trading and active monitoring of the portfolio, and many times is motivated by a philosophy that the investor can "beat the market." Active strategy managers would rarely buy a security with the intention of holding it to maturity. For example, when an analyst forecasts a change in interest rates, trading strategies can be devised to enhance investment profits.

Active listening Paying attention solely to what others are saying (for example, rather than what you think of what they're saying or what you want to say back to them).

Active practice The performance of job-related tasks and duties by trainees during training.

ActiveX A Microsoft scripting language for small applications for specific tasks.

Activity A defined piece of work that consumes time; task.

Activity analysis The study of employee effort and other business records to determine the cost of activities.

Activity base The measure used to allocate factory overhead. Also known as allocation base, or activity driver.

Activity base usage The amount of activity base used by a particular product.

Activity-Based Costing (ABC) An accounting framework based on determining the cost of activities and allocating these costs to products, using activity rates. An approach to costing that focuses on activities as the fundamental cost objects. It uses the cost of these activities as the basis for assigning costs to other cost objects such as products, services, or customers. It provides more accurate allocation of indirect costs than traditional methods.

Activity-Based Management (ABM) 1: A discipline that focuses on the management of activities for improving the value received by the customer and the profit achieved by providing this value. **2:** Managing with an accounting system that allocates costs to products based on resources employed to produce the product.

Activity cost pools Cost accumulations that are associated with a given activity, such as machine usage, inspections, moving, and production setups.

Activity in the Box (AIB) A form of network diagramming in which activities are represented by boxes.

Activity Network Diagram (AND) *See:* Arrow diagram.

Activity on the Arrow (AOA) A form of network diagramming in which activities are represented by arrows.

Activity rates The cost of an activity per unit of activity base, determined by dividing the activity cost pool by the activity base.

Activity ratios *See:* Efficiency ratios.

Actual cost The amount that has actually been expended.

Actual demand Actual demand is composed of customer orders (and often allocations of items, ingredients, or raw materials to production or distribution). Actual demand nets against or "consumes" the forecast, depending upon the rules chosen over a time horizon. For example, actual demand will totally replace forecast inside the sold-out customer order backlog horizon (often called the demand time fence), but will net against the forecast outside this horizon based on the chosen forecast consumption rule.

Actual express authority Authority set forth in the partnership agreement, in additional agreements among the partners, or in decisions made by a majority of the partners regarding the ordinary business of the partnership. Arises from the incorporation statute, the charter, the bylaws, and resolutions of the directors.

Actual implied authority 1: Authority that is reasonably deduced from the nature of the partnership, the terms of the partnership agreement, or the relations of the partners. **2:** Authority to do what is reasonably necessary to perform actual authority.

Actual notice Knowledge actually and expressly communicated.

Actual (realized) rate of return, $\bar{k}_s$ The rate of return on a common stock actually received by stockholders. $\bar{k}_s$ may be greater than or less than $\hat{k}_s$ and/or k_s.

Actual volume Actual output expressed as a volume of capacity. It is used in the calculation of variances when compared with demonstrated capacity (practical capacity) or budgeted capacity.

Acute crisis stage The stage at which a crisis actually occurs.

Ad hoc groups Problem-specific teams or groups consisting of individuals who possess the relevant knowledge to address a particular organizational problem.

Ad hoc reports Unplanned, special reports designed to help solve specific problems. Also called *on-demand reports*.

Adaptability/entreprenuerial culture A culture characterized by strategic focus on the external environment through flexibility and change to meet customer needs.

Adaptability screening A selection procedure that usually involves interviewing both the candidate for an overseas assignment and his or her family members to determine how well they are likely to adapt to another culture.

Adaptable management A firm's management is able to adapt managerial techniques to the unique needs of specific countries.

Adaptation Refers to the stage in the expatriation process in which the expatriate must learn to cope with cultures, laws, political systems, legal processes, and other subtleties that are different from his or her own.

Adaptation problems Difficulties that arise for expatriates during the adaptation process. They are especially common when the physical and sociocultural environments are at odds with the expatriate's own value system and living habits.

Adaptive transformative innovations Modify and adjust existing modern technologies (for example, in farming, a modern, more efficient tractor replaces an older, less efficient model).

Additional Funds Needed (AFN) Funds that a firm must raise externally through borrowing or by selling new stock.

Additional paid-in capital Funds received in excess of par value when a firm issues new stock.

Add-on interest Interest that is calculated and then added to the amount borrowed to obtain the total dollar amount to be paid back in equal installments.

Adjourning The stage of team development in which members prepare for the team's disbandment.

Adjustable-Rate Preferred Stock (ARPS) Preferred stock on which the dividend is reset quarterly.

Adjusted r^2 A measure for a statistical model's goodness of fit that compensates for the upward bias in goodness-of-fit resulting from the inclusion of additional predictor variables.

Adjusted trial balance The trial balance that is prepared after all the adjusting entries have been posted. Used to verify the equality of the total debit balances and total credit balances before preparing the financial statements.

Adjusting entries Entries required at the end of an accounting period to bring the ledger up to date.

Adjusting process The process of updating the accounts at the end of a period.

Administered vertical marketing channels Channels that exist when one of the channel members takes the initiative to lead the channel by applying the principles of effective interorganizational management.

Administrative expenses (general expenses) Expenses incurred in the administration or general operations of a business.

Administrative model A decision-making model that describes how managers actually make decisions in situations characterized by nonprogrammed decisions, uncertainty, and ambiguity.

Administrative principles 1: A subfield of the classical management perspective that focuses on the total organization rather than the individual worker, delineating the management functions of planning, organizing, commanding, coordinating, and controlling. **2:** A closed systems management perspective that focuses on the total organization and grows from the insights of practitioners.

Admissions An admission by one partner within the scope of his authority may be used as evidence against the partnership.

ADSL (Asymmetric DSL) DSL technology in which the downstream communication (to the subscriber) is several times greater than the upstream communication (from the subscriber). *See:* DSL.

Adult learning principles Key issues about how adults learn, which impact how education and training of adults should be designed.

Advance pricing agreement An agreement between a company and tax authorities that gives the company approval for using certain transfer pricing methods and the procedures for its application.

Advanced Determination Ruling (ADR) A transfer pricing guideline in the United States that allows a company to get approval for a parent-subsidiary specific product pricing.

Adverse selection Situation in which only higher-risk employees select and use certain benefits.

Advertising 1: Nonpersonal communication that is paid for by an identified sponsor, and involves either mass communication via newspapers, magazines, radio, television, and other media (for example, billboards, bus stop signage) or direct-to-consumer communication via direct mail. **2:** Paid, nonpersonal communication through various media by business firms, nonprofit organizations, and individuals who are in some way identified in the advertising message and who hope to inform or persuade members of a particular audience; includes communication of products, services, institutions, and ideas.

Advertising effectiveness The extent to which the advertising has produced the result desired.

Advertising efficiency is concerned with whether the advertising result was achieved with the minimum financial expenditure.

Advised line A standard lending service used abroad, which is very similar to credit lines in the United States. The advised line involves unsecured lending of up to one year maturity, available on short notice to the borrower.

Advising bank Corresponding bank in the beneficiary's country to which the issuing bank sends the letter of credit.

Affidavit Written statement or declaration given under oath.

Affiliate One who controls, is controlled by, or is under common control with the issuer.

Affiliate programs Advertisers pay for each person who enters their Web site via a link on the host site or pays for each sale generated.

Affinity diagram A management and planning tool used to organize ideas into natural groupings in a way that stimulates new, creative ideas. Also known as the "KJ" method.

Affirmative action 1: A policy requiring employers to take positive steps to guarantee equal employment opportunities for people within protected groups. **2:** Process in which employers identify problem areas, set goals, and take positive steps to enhance opportunities for protected-class members. **3:** Active recruitment of a designated group of applicants.

Affirmative Action Plan (AAP) Formal document that an employer compiles annually for submission to enforcement agencies.

Affordable method A technique for budgeting advertising in which all the money a retailer can afford to spend on advertising in a given time period becomes the advertising budget.

After-tax cost of debt, k_{dT} The relevant cost of new debt, taking into account the tax deductibility of interest; used to calculate the WACC.

Age Discrimination in Employment Act (ADEA) Act that prohibits discrimination on the basis of age in hiring, firing, or compensating.

Agencies Securities issued by governmental agencies and several private financing institutions that have governmental backing.

Agency problem 1: A potential conflict of interest between 1) the principals (outside shareholders) and the agent (manager) or 2) stockholders and creditors (debtholders). **2:** May develop when the interests of the shareholders are not aligned with the interests of the manager.

Agent 1: A representative or intermediary for the firm that works to develop business and sales strategies and that develops contacts. **2:** Marketing intermediary who does not take title to the products but develops marketing strategy and establishes contacts abroad.

Agent of change Any person (such as an employee, a consultant, or a board member) whose work results in significant changes in the way workers perform their jobs. Often, systems analysts are agents of change because they drive companies to take fuller advantage of information technology.

Agents/brokers Independent middlemen who bring buyers and sellers together, provide market information to one or the other parties, but never take title to the merchandise. While most agents/brokers work for the seller, some do work for buyers.

Aggregate forecast An estimate of sales, often time phased, for a grouping of products or product families produced by a facility or firm. Stated in terms of units, dollars, or both, the aggregate forecast is used for sales and production planning (or for sales and operations planning) purposes.

Aggregate plan 1: *n:* A plan that includes budgeted levels of finished goods, inventory, production backlogs, and changes in the workforce to support the production strategy. Aggregated information (for example, product line, family) rather than product information is used, hence the name aggregate plan. **2: Aggregate planning** *v:* A process to develop tactical plans to support the organization's business plan. Aggregate planning usually includes the development, analysis, and maintenance of plans for total sales, total production, targeted inventory, and targeted customer backlog for families of products. The production plan is the result of the aggregate planning process. Two approaches to aggregate planning exist—production planning and sales and operations planning.

Aggressive approach A policy where all of the fixed assets of a firm are financed with long-term capital, but *some* of the firm's permanent current assets are financed with short-term nonspontaneous sources of funds.

Aggressive strategy A strategy that minimizes the amount of long-term financing used. This strategy generally results in a lower current ratio and higher but more volatile profitability during periods of normal yield curves.

Agile approach or agility *See:* Lean approach.

Agility The ability to successfully manufacture and market a broad range of low-cost, high-quality products and services with short lead times and varying volumes that provide enhanced value to customers through customization. Agility merges the four distinctive competencies of cost, quality, dependability, and flexibility.

Aging schedule A report showing how long accounts receivable have been outstanding; the report divides receivables into specified periods, which provides information about the proportion of receivables that is current and the proportion that is past due for given lengths of time. Shows a percent breakdown of present receivables, with the categories shown typically as follows: current, 0–30 days past due, 31–60 days past due, and over 90 days past due.

Airfreight Transport of goods by air; accounts for less than 1 percent of the total volume of international shipments, but more than 20 percent of value.

Airway bill Receipt for a shipment by air, which includes freight charges and title to the merchandise.

Algorithm A sequence of steps one takes to solve a problem. Often, these steps are expressed as mathematical formulas.

Alliances Firms with unique strengths that join to be more effective and efficient than their competitors. *See:* partnership/alliances.

All-in-rate Rate used in charging customers for accepting banker's acceptances, consisting of the discount interest rate plus the commission.

Allocated item In an MRP system, an item for which a picking order has been released to the stockroom but not yet sent from the stockroom.

Allocation mentality The tradition of acquiring resources based not on what is needed but on what is available.

Allowance for doubtful accounts A contra-asset (receivable) account representing the amount of receivables that are estimated to be uncollectible.

Allowance for uncollectible assets as a percentage of receivables Allowance for doubtful accounts divided by accounts receivable; a measure of the percentage of receivables estimated to be uncollectible.

Allowance method A method of accounting for uncollectible receivables, whereby advance provision for the uncollectibles is made.

Allowances for deferred income tax assets A contra account to the deferred income tax assets account.

Alpha risk *See:* Producer's risk for sampling plan.

Alternative evaluation Stage in the consumer decision process when consumers select one of the several alternatives (brands, dealers, and so on) available to them.

Ambiance The overall feeling or mood projected by a store through its aesthetic appeal to human senses.

Ambidextrous approach A characteristic of an organization that can behave both in an organic and a mechanistic way.

Ambiguity The goal to be achieved or the problem to be solved is unclear, alternatives are difficult to define, and information about outcomes is unavailable.

American-based leadership and motivation theories Traditionally, these theories advance the notion that participative leadership behavior is more effective than authoritative leadership behavior. Popular theories include McGregor's *Theory X and Theory Y Managers* and Likert's *System 4 Management*.

American Depository Receipts (ADRs) Certificates representing ownership in stocks of foreign companies, which are held in trust by a bank located in the country in which the stock is traded. ADRs are traded on stock exchanges in the United States.

American Institute of Certified Public Accountants (AICPA) An organization that issues the generally accepted auditing standards in the form of Statements on Auditing Standards in the United States.

American terms Quoting a currency rate as the U.S. dollar against a country's currency (for example, U.S. dollars/yen).

Amortization The periodic expense attributed to the decline in usefulness of an intangible asset.

Amortized loan A loan that is repaid in equal payments over its life.

Amount of consideration for shares Shares are deemed fully paid and nonassessable when a corporation receives the consideration for which the board of directors authorized the issuance of the shares, which in the case of par value stock must be at least par.

Analog model While physical in form, an analog model does not have a physical appearance similar to the real object or situation it represents.

Analog signal A continuous signal, for example a human voice or the movement of the hands in an analog watch, that represents different degrees of mechanical or electrical power.

Analogy 1: A method for estimating market potential when data for the particular market do not exist. **2:** A technique used to generate new ideas by translating concepts from one application to another.

GLOSSARY

Analysis of Means (ANOM) A statistical procedure for troubleshooting industrial processes and analyzing the results of experimental designs with factors at fixed levels. It provides a graphical display of data. Ellis R. Ott developed the procedure in 1967 because he observed that nonstatisticians had difficulty understanding analysis of variance. Analysis of means is easier for quality practitioners to use because it is an extension of the control chart. In 1973, Edward G. Schilling further extended the concept, enabling analysis of means to be used with nonnormal distributions and attributes data where the normal approximation to the binomial distribution does not apply. This is referred to as analysis of means for treatment effects.

Analysis of Variance (ANOVA) A basic statistical technique for analyzing experimental data. It subdivides the total variation of a data set into meaningful component parts associated with specific sources of variation in order to test a hypothesis on the parameters of the model or to estimate variance components. There are three models: fixed, random, and mixed.

Analytical anomalies Relationships, procedures, or events that do not make sense.

Analytical thinking Breaking down a problem or situation into discrete parts to understand how each part contributes to the whole.

Analyzability A dimension of technology in which work activities can be reduced to mechanical steps and participants can follow an objective, computational procedure to solve problems.

Anchor stores Dominant, large-scale stores that are expected to draw customers to a shopping center.

Andon board A visual device (usually lights) displaying status alerts that can easily be seen by those who should respond.

Angel financing Financing provided by a wealthy individual who believes in the idea for a start-up and provides personal funds and advice to help the business get started.

Annual compounding The arithmetic process of determining the final value of a cash flow or series of cash flows when interest is added once a year.

Annual Percentage Rate (APR) The rate reported to borrowers—it is the periodic rate times the number of periods in the year; thus, interest compounding is not considered. The periodic rate × the number of periods per year.

Annual report A report issued annually by a corporation to its stockholders. It contains basic financial statements, as well as management's opinion of the past year's operations, and the firm's future prospects.

Annuity A series of payments of an equal amount at fixed intervals for a specified number of periods.

Annuity due An annuity whose payments occur at the beginning of each period.

ANOVA *See:* analysis of variance.

ANSI American National Standards Institute.

Antecedent The *if* component of an *if-then* rule knowledge representation.

Antecedent debts The liability of an incoming partner for antecedent debts of the partnership is limited to his capital contribution.

Antibribery provision of FCPA Prohibited bribery can result in fines and imprisonment.

Anticipation 1: This transfer rule initiates a cash transfer before the related deposit is made. **2:** Situation that allows the retailer to pay the invoice in advance of the end of the cash discount period and earn an extra discount.

Antidumping laws Laws that many countries use to impose tariffs on foreign imports. They are designed to help domestic industries that are injured by unfair competition from abroad due to imported products being sold at less than fair market value.

Antiplanning Belief that any attempt to lay out specific and "rational" plans is either foolish or dangerous and downright evil. Correct approach is to live in existing systems, react in terms of one's own experience, and not try to change them by means of some grandiose scheme or mathematical model.

Antifraud provision Rule 10b–5 makes it unlawful to **1:** employ any device, scheme, or artifice to defraud; **2:** make any untrue statement of a material fact; **3:** omit to state a material fact; or **4:** engage in any act that operates as a fraud.

Antitrust laws Laws that prohibit monopolies, restraint of trade, and conspiracies to inhibit competition. Apply to unfair methods of competition that have a direct, substantial, and reasonably foreseeable effect on the domestic, import, or export commerce of the United States.

Antivirus software Software designed to detect and intercept computer viruses.

AOQ Average outgoing quality.

AOQL Average outgoing quality limit.

Apparent authority 1: Acts of the corporation that lead a third party to believe reasonably and in good faith that an officer has the required authority. **2:** Authority that a third person may reasonably assume to exist in light of the conduct of the partners, so long as that third person has no knowledge or notice of the lack of actual authority.

Appellate Court Review court to which participants in lower court cases can have their cases reviewed or retried if they are unhappy with the outcome.

Applet A small software application, usually written in Java or another programming language for the Web.

Applicant pool All persons who are actually evaluated for selection.

Applicant population A subset of the labor force population that is available for selection using a particular recruiting approach.

Application A computer program that addresses a general or specific business or scientific need. General applications include electronic spreadsheets and word processors. Specific applications are written especially for a business unit to accommodate special activities.

Application controls Programmed procedures in application software and related manual procedures, designed to help ensure the completeness and accuracy of information processing. Examples include computerized edit checks of input data, and numerical sequence checks and manual procedures to follow up on items listed in exception reports.

Application/Data independence A situation in which an application can be developed to manipulate data without regard to the physical organization of the data in the files. This is achieved in the database approach to data management.

Application form A device for collecting information about an applicant's education, previous job experience, and other background characteristics.

Application generator A software tool that expedites the application development process. Often, the term is synonymous with fourth-generation language. Modern application generators include graphical user interfaces.

Application Program Interface (API) An interface that allows applications to make use of the operating system.

Application Service Provider (ASP) A firm that rents the use of software applications through an Internet link.

Application-specific software A collective term for all computer programs that are designed specifically to address certain business problems, such as a program specifically written to deal with a company's market research effort.

Appraisal costs Costs to detect, measure, evaluate, and audit products and processes to ensure that they conform to customer requirements and performance standards.

Appraisal remedy The right of a dissenter to receive the fair value of his shares (the value of shares immediately before the corporate action to which the dissenter objects takes place, excluding any appreciation or depreciation in anticipation of such corporate action unless such exclusion would be inequitable).

Appreciation Increase in the value of a currency.

Appropriation The amount of a corporation's retained earnings that has been restricted and therefore is not available for distribution to shareholders as dividends.

Approval of fundamental changes Shareholder approval is required for charter amendments, most acquisitions, and dissolution.

AQL Acceptable quality level.

Arbitrage 1: An activity done to take advantage of rate discrepancies by buying the currency in the low-cost markets and selling in the high-cost markets. **2:** Action to capitalize on a discrepancy in quoted prices; in many cases, there is no investment of funds tied up for any length of time.

Arbitration The procedure for settling a dispute in which an objective third party hears both sides and makes a decision; a procedure for resolving conflict in the international business arena through the use of intermediaries such as representatives of chambers of commerce, trade associations, or third-country institutions.

Arc elasticity Average elasticity over a given range of a function.

Area expertise A knowledge of the basic systems in a particular region or market.

Area structure An organizational structure in which geographic divisions are responsible for all manufacturing and marketing in their respective areas.

Area studies Training programs that provide factual preparation prior to an overseas assignment.

Arithmetic Logic Unit (ALU) The electronic circuitry in the central processing unit of a computer responsible for arithmetic and logic operations.

Arm's-length price A price that unrelated parties would have reached.

Arraignment Court hearing where charges against the defendant are read. At the arraignment, the defendants may plead guilty, not guilty, or nolo contendere.

Arrow diagram A management and planning tool used to develop the best possible schedule and appropriate controls to accomplish the schedule; the critical path method (CPM) and the program evaluation review technique (PERT) make use of arrow diagrams.

Articles of incorporation The charter or basic organizational document of a corporation.

Articles of partnership Written partnership agreement; it is preferable, although not usually required, that the partners enter into a written partnership agreement.

Artificial Intelligence (AI) The study and creation of computer programs that mimic human behavior. This discipline combines the interests of computer science, cognitive science, linguistics, and management information systems. The main subfields of AI are: robotics, artificial vision, natural language processors, and expert systems.

Artificial vision A subfield of artificial intelligence devoted to the development of hardware and software that can mimic human vision.

As a citizen A corporation is considered a citizen for some but not all purposes.

As a person A corporation is considered a person for some but not all purposes.

AS-9100 A standard for the aeronautics industry embracing the ISO 9001 standard.

ASCII (pronounced: AS-kee) American Standard Code for Information Interchange, a computer encoding scheme whereby each group of eight bits (a byte) uniquely represents a character.

Asian dollar market Market in Asia in which banks collect deposits and make loans denominated in U.S. dollars.

Asia-Pacific Economic Cooperation (APEC) An organization committed to the trade and investment concept of open regionalism. Its 20 member countries include Australia, Brunei, Canada, Chile, China (including Hong Kong), Indonesia, Japan, Korea, Malaysia, Mexico, New Zealand, Papua New Guinea, Peru, Philippines, Russia, Singapore, Chinese Taipei, Thailand, the United States, and Vietnam.

Ask price Price at which a trader of foreign exchange (typically a bank) is willing to sell a particular currency.

ASP *See:* Application Service Provider.

ASQ American Society for Quality, a society of individual and organizational members dedicated to the ongoing development, advancement, and promotion of quality concepts, principles, and technologies.

Assembler A compiler for an assembly language.

Assemble-to-order A production environment where a good or service can be assembled after receipt of a customer's order. The key components (bulk, semifinished, intermediate, subassembly, fabricated, purchased, packing, and so on) used in the assembly or finishing process are planned and usually stocked in anticipation of a customer order. Receipt of an order initiates assembly of the customized product. This strategy is useful where a large number of end products (based on the selection of options and accessories) can be assembled from common components. *Syn:* finish-to-order. *See:* make-to-order, make-to-stock.

Assembly languages Second-generation programming languages that assemble several bytes into groups of characters that are human-readable, to expedite programming tasks.

Assessment An estimate or determination of the significance, importance, or value of something.

Assessment center A technique for selecting individuals with high managerial potential based on their performance on a series of simulated managerial tasks.

Asset Anything of value that is owned by the retail firm.

Asset-and-liability approach The recognition of deferred tax liabilities or deferred tax assets for the income tax that will be levied or recovered on temporary timing differences between the taxable income amount and the pretax financial income amount.

Asset-based lending A form of collateralized lending which has a claim on an asset or group of assets, ordinarily receivables or inventory, which could be easily sold if the borrower defaults on the loan.

Asset fraud Financial statement fraud in which assets are recorded at higher amounts than they should be.

Asset management ratios A set of ratios that measures how effectively a firm is managing its assets.

Asset misappropriations Theft that is committed by stealing receipts, stealing assets on hand, or by committing some type of disbursement fraud.

Asset securitization Has become prevalent in the United States because of the need for banks to increase their capital-to-assets ratio.

Asset swap A swap created to hedge cash flows related to assets or investments.

Asset turnover Total sales divided by average total assets; a measure of the amount of sales revenue generated with each dollar of assets.

Assets Physical items (tangible) or rights (intangible) that have value and that are owned by the business entity.

Assignability A partner may sell or assign his interest in the partnership; the new owner becomes entitled to the assigning partner's share of profits and surplus but does not become a partner.

Assignable cause *See:* special causes.

Assignment of LLC interest Unless otherwise provided in the LLC's operating agreement, a member may assign his financial interest in the LLC; an assignee of a financial interest in an LLC may acquire the other rights by being admitted as a member of the company by all the remaining members.

Assignment of partnership interest Unless otherwise provided in the partnership agreement, a partner may assign his partnership interest; an assignee may become a limited partner if all other partners consent.

Assignment of proceeds Arrangement which allows the original beneficiary of a letter of credit to pledge or assign proceeds to an end supplier.

Associated firms *See:* Representative firms.

Association of Certified Fraud Examiners (ACFE) An international organization, based in Austin, Texas, dedicated to fighting fraud and white-collar crime.

Association of Southeast Asian Nations (ASEAN) The most important trading bloc in Southeast Asia. The member countries include Brunei, Cambodia, Indonesia, Laos, Malaysia, Myanmar, the Philippines, Singapore, Thailand, and Vietnam. The member countries established a free-trade area.

Asymmetric information The situation in which managers have different (better) information about their firm's prospects than do outside investors.

Asymmetric key encryption Encryption technology in which a message is encrypted with one key and decrypted with another.

Asynchronous communications Data communications whereby the communications devices must synchronize the transmission and reception after the transmission of each byte. Each byte is accompanied by synchronization bits, such as start and stop bits.

Atomic transaction A transaction whose entry is not complete until all entries into the appropriate files have been successfully completed. A data entry control.

Attempts to monopolize Specific intent to monopolize, plus a dangerous probability of success.

Attitude 1: A cognitive and affective evaluation that predisposes a person to act in a certain way. **2:** Learned predispositions to respond to an object or class of objects in a consistently favorable or unfavorable way.

Attitude survey One that focuses on employees' feelings and beliefs about their jobs and the organization.

Attribute data Go/no-go information. The control charts based on attribute data include fraction defective chart, number of affected units chart, count chart, count per-unit chart, quality score chart, and demerit chart.

Attributes Refers to the characteristics of the store and its products and services.

Attributions Judgments about what caused a person's behavior—either characteristics of the person or of the situation.

Auction Preferred Stock (APS) Preferred stock on which the dividend is reset every 49 days through an auction bidding process.

Audit A planned, independent, and documented assessment to determine whether agreed-upon requirements are being met.

Audit Command Language (ACL) Popular commercial data-mining software; helps investigators detect fraud.

Audit committee Responsible for assessing the adequacy of internal control systems and the integrity of financial statements.

Audit program The organizational structure, commitment, and documented methods used to plan and perform audits.

Audit team The group of individuals conducting an audit under the direction of a team leader, relevant to a particular product, process, service, contract, or project.

Audit trail 1: Documents and records that can be used to trace transactions. **2:** Names, dates, and other references in computer files that can help an auditor track down the person who used an IS for a transaction, legal or illegal.

Auditee The individual or organization being audited.

Auditor An individual or organization carrying out an audit.

Auditor's report A report that communicates the results of the external audit, and the format of the report is necessarily mandated by the nature of the audit. Because there are no worldwide uniform accounting and auditing standards, there is no worldwide uniform format of an auditor's report.

Autarky Self-sufficiency: a country that is not participating in international trade.

Authentication The process of ensuring that the person who sends a message to or receives a message from another party is indeed that person.

Authoritarianism The belief that power and status differences *should* exist within the organization.

Authoritative decision making Refers to a style of decision making in which the leader simply makes a decision and instructs followers what to do without consulting or involving them in the decision-making process.

Authority 1: A force for achieving desired outcomes that is prescribed by the formal hierarchy and reporting relationships. **2:** A partner's actual authority to act for the partnership terminates, except so far as may be necessary to wind up partnership affairs; apparent authority continues unless notice of the dissolution is given to a third party. **3:** The formal and legitimate right of a manager to make decisions, issue orders, and allocate resources to achieve organizationally desired outcomes.

Authority to amend Statutes permit charters to be amended.

Authority to bind partnership A partner who has actual authority (express or implied) or apparent authority may bind the partnership.

Authority to issue Only those share authorized in the articles of incorporation may be issued.

Authority to issue debt securities Each corporation has the power to issue debt securities as determined by the board of directors.

Autocratic leader A leader who tends to centralize authority and rely on legitimate, reward, and coercive power to manage subordinates.

Autocratic management 1: Autocratic managers are concerned with developing an efficient workplace and have little concern for people (theory X assumptions about people). They typically make decisions without input from subordinates, relying on their positional power. **2:** Management conducted by a few key people who do not accept advice or participation from other employees.

Automated Clearing House (ACH) A quick and relatively inexpensive means of electronically processing large numbers of routine transactions. This system is comprised of a loosely tied network of associations spread across the country. The electronic equivalent of the paper check-clearing system.

Automated Storage/Retrieval System (AS/RS) A high-density rack inventory storage system with vehicles automatically loading and unloading the racks.

Autonomation 1: Automated shutdown of a line, process, or machine upon detection of an abnormality or defect. **2:** (Jidoka) Use of specially equipped automated machines capable of detecting a defect in a single part, stopping the process, and signaling for assistance.

Autonomy The extent of individual freedom and discretion in the work and its scheduling.

Autoregressive model A time series model that uses a regression relationship based on historical time series values to predict the future time series values.

Availability The ability of a product to be in a state to perform its designated function under stated conditions at a given time. Availability can be expressed by the ratio:

$$\frac{\text{uptime}}{\text{uptime + downtime}}$$

Availability analysis An analysis that identifies the number of protected-class members available to work in the appropriate labor markets in given jobs.

Availability float The delay from the time a check is deposited and the time when funds are available to be spent. This time lag may not always coincide with the amount of time it takes the check to actually clear, but generally the two are closely linked. Delays in collecting checks caused by delays in the check-clearing process after the check has been deposited.

Availability schedule Listing of how long after deposit checks will become "good funds" for spending by the depositor. Prior to recording available funds, the bank will credit the depositor's ledger balance, but the portion of the total deposit available as "good funds" ready to be spent varies according to the bank's schedule.

Available-for-sale security A debt or equity security that is not classified as either a held-to-maturity or a trading security.

Available inventory The on-hand inventory balance minus allocations, reservations, backorders, and (usually) quantities held for quality problems. Often called beginning available balance. *Syn:* beginning available balance, net inventory.

Available-to-Promise (ATP) The uncommitted portion of a company's inventory and planned production maintained in the master schedule to support customer-order promising. The ATP quantity is the uncommitted inventory balance in the first period and is normally calculated for each period in which an MPS receipt is scheduled. In the first period, ATP includes on-hand inventory less customer orders that are due and overdue. Three methods of calculation are used: discrete ATP, cumulative ATP with lookahead, and cumulative ATP without lookahead. *See:* Discrete available-to-promise, Cumulative available-to-promise.

Average *See:* Mean

Average chart A control chart in which the subgroup average, $\overline{X}$, is used to evaluate the stability of the process level.

Average collection period How long the typical customer is taking to pay its bills. Alternately, how long, on average, the seller is taking to collect its receivables. It is computed by dividing accounts receivable by daily sales. Also known as *days sales outstanding*.

Average cost method 1: The method of inventory costing that is based on the assumption that costs should be charged against revenue in accordance with the weighted average unit costs of the items sold. **2:** An accounting principle by which the value of inventory is estimated as the average cost of the items in inventory.

Average cost minimization Activity level that generates the lowest average cost, MC = AC.

Average inventory One-half the average lot size plus the safety stock, when demand and lot sizes are expected to be relatively uniform over time. The average can be calculated as an average of several inventory observations taken over several historical time periods; for example, 12-month ending inventories may be averaged. When demand and lot sizes are not uniform, the stock level versus time can be graphed to determine the average.

Average Outgoing Quality (AOQ) The expected average quality level of outgoing product for a given value of incoming product quality.

Average Outgoing Quality Limit (AOQL) The maximum average outgoing quality over all possible levels of incoming quality for a given acceptance sampling plan and disposal specification.

Average rate of return A method of evaluating capital investment proposals that focuses on the expected profitability of the investment.

Average tax rate Taxes paid divided by taxable income.

Avoidance The pricing of invoices in the seller's currency.

B

B2B marketplace An electronic marketplace set up by an intermediary where buyers and sellers meet.

Back scheduling A technique for calculating operation start dates and due dates. The schedule is computed starting with the due date for the order and working backward to determine the required start date and/or due dates for each operation. *Syn:* backward scheduling. *Ant:* forward scheduling.

Back value date The date that cleared checks are assigned and may cause funds to be drawn from an account before the check actually arrives at the drawee bank.

Backbone The network of copper lines, optical fibers, and radio satellites that supports the Internet.

Backflush A method of inventory bookkeeping where the book (computer) inventory of components is automatically reduced by the computer after completion of activity on the component's upper-level parent item based on what should have been used as specified on the bill of material and allocation records. This approach has the disadvantage of a built-in differential between the book record and what is physically in stock. *Syn:* explode-to-deduct, post-deduct inventory transaction processing.

Backflush costing The application of costs based on the output of a process. Backflush costing is usually associated with repetitive manufacturing environments.

Backtranslation The retranslation of text to the original language by a different person than the one who made the first translation. Useful to find translation errors.

Backup Periodic duplication of data in order to guard against loss.

Backward chaining (backward reasoning) The processes in which an expert system searches the conditions that would bring about the achievement of a specified goal. For example, an ES uses backward chaining to determine how long to invest how much money in which stocks to achieve a specified yield.

Backward innovation The development of a drastically simplified version of a product.

Bad debt expense An expense representing receivables and/or revenues that are presumed not to be collectible.

Badwill What international corporations create when they exploit foreign markets without sharing benefits with locals.

Bait-and-switch Advertising or promoting a product at an unrealistically low price to serve as "bait" and then trying to "switch" the customer to a higher-priced product.

Balance fractions, inventory The percent of an inventory purchase order that remains as inventory over succeeding months.

Balance fractions, payables The dollar amount remaining to be paid in succeeding months as a percent of the original accounts payable balance.

Balance of payments 1: Statement of inflow and outflow payments for a particular country. **2:** A statement of all transactions between one country and the rest of the world during a given period; a record of flows of goods, services, and investments across borders.

Balance of payments deficit When a country's cumulative imports exceed its cumulative exports.

Balance of payments surplus When a country's cumulative exports exceed its cumulative imports.

Balance of the account The amount of difference between the debits and the credits that have been entered into an account.

Balance of trade Difference between the value of merchandise exports and merchandise imports.

Balance on goods and services Balance of trade, plus the net amount of payments of interest and dividends to foreign investors and from investment, as well as receipts and payments resulting from international tourism and other transactions.

Balance reporting services Means by which the treasurer may inquire by phone or PC hook-up about the balance positions in many different accounts and about transactions affecting the accounts.

Balance sheet 1: A financial statement that shows the firm's financial position with respect to assets and liabilities at a specific point in time. **2:** A financial statement listing the assets, liabilities, and owner's equity of a business entity as of a specific date.

Balance-sheet approach Compensation package that equalizes cost differences between international assignments and those in the home country.

Balance sheet recognition Information presented within the balance sheet.

Balance sheet test Varies among the states and includes the earned surplus test (available in all states), the surplus test, and the net assets test (used by the Model and Revised Acts).

Balanced scorecard 1: Translates an organization's mission and strategy into a comprehensive set of performance measures to provide a basis for strategic measurement and management, utilizing four balanced views: financial, customers, internal business processes, and learning and growth. **2:** A comprehensive management control system that balances traditional financial measures with measures of customer service, internal business processes, and the organization's capacity for learning and growth. **3:** A set of financial and nonfinancial measures that reflect multiple performance dimensions of a business.

Balanced tenancy Occurs where the stores complement each other in merchandise offerings.

Balancing operations In repetitive just-in-time production, matching actual output cycle times of all operations to the demand or use for parts as required by final assembly and, eventually, as required by the market.

Balassa-Samuelson Theory A theory that states inflation is difficult to get rid of in a fast-growing economy.

Bandwidth The capacity of the communications channel; the number of signal streams the channel can support. A greater bandwidth also supports a greater bit rate, that is, transmission speed.

Bank deposit notes Short-term debt securities issued by banks, which range from nine months to 30 years in maturity, and have an active secondary market.

Bank draft A financial withdrawal document drawn against a bank.

Banker's Acceptance (BA) A corporate time draft drawn on the buyer, whose bank agrees to pay ("accepts") the amount if the buyer does not. Related to this, a short-term acceptance facility allows the selling firm to initiate drafts (called *bills of exchange*) against the buyer's bank instead of against the buyer, which can be discounted at the bank. A time draft drawn against a deposit in a commercial bank but with payment at maturity guaranteed by the bank.

Bank for International Settlements (BIS) Institution that facilitates cooperation among countries involved in international transactions and provides assistance to countries experiencing international payment problems.

Bank Holding Company Act of 1956 Prohibited further acquisitions by bank holding companies unless specifically allowed by state law in the state of the proposed acquisition.

Bank Letter of Credit Policy Policy that enables banks to confirm letters of credit by foreign banks supporting the purchase of U.S. exports.

Bank notes Technically not deposits, these bank debt obligations thereby avoid FDIC insurance premiums, which also forfeits deposit insurance coverage.

Bank reconciliation The analysis that details the items responsible for the difference between the cash balance reported in the bank statement and the balance of the cash account in the ledger.

Bank relationship policy Document that establishes the company's objectives, compensations, and review process for the banks with which it has a relationship.

Bank selection process Involves assembling a system of banks to serve all of a company's cash management and related needs.

Banking Act, 1991 Prohibited the FDIC from voluntarily covering a bank's uninsured depositors except when the Department of Treasury, the Federal Reserve Board, the FDIC, and the president all agree that the financial system would be endangered by the bank's closure.

Bankruptcy A legal process that either allows a debtor to work out an orderly plan to settle debts or to liquidate a debtor's assets and distribute them to creditors.

Bankruptcy Code Title 11 of the U.S. Code—the federal statute that governs the bankruptcy process.

Bankruptcy Courts Federal courts that hear only bankruptcy cases.

Banner ad Animated GIF graphic placed on a host site and hyperlinked to the URL of the advertiser.

Banners Advertisements that appear on a Web page.

Bar chart *See:* Gantt chart.

Bar code A series of wide and narrow lines that represents data. Usually printed on product tags for ease of data entry and the recording of shipment and sales by a specific machine used to read the code.

Barometric price leadership A situation in which one firm in an industry announces a price change in response to what it perceives as a change in industry supply and demand conditions and other firms respond by following the price change.

Barriers Elements that inhibit the implementation and maintenance of various business programs and strategies.

Barriers to entrants Any and all of the measures that a business can take to prevent potential competitors from entering the market.

Barrier to entry Any advantage for industry incumbents over new arrivals.

Barrier to exit Any limit on asset redeployment from one line of business or industry to another.

Barrier to mobility Any advantage for large, leading firms over small, nonleading rivals.

Barter Exchange of goods between two parties without the use of any currency as a medium of exchange.

Base case An analysis in which all of the input variables are set at their most likely values.

Base-case scenario Determining the output given the most likely values for the probabilistic inputs of a model.

Base demand The percentage of a company's demand that derives from continuing contracts and/or existing customers. Because this demand is well known and recurring, it becomes the basis of management's plans. *Syn:* baseload demand.

Base inventory level The inventory level made up of aggregate lot-size inventory plus the aggregate safety stock inventory. It does not take into account the anticipation inventory that will result from the production plan. The base inventory level should be known before the production plan is made. *Syn:* basic stock.

Base pay The basic compensation an employee receives, usually as a wage or salary.

Base salary Salary not including special payments such as allowances paid during overseas assignments.

Base stock system A method of inventory control that includes as special cases most of the systems in practice. In this system, when an order is received for any item, it is used as a picking ticket, and duplicate copies, called replenishment orders, are sent back to all stages of production to initiate replenishment of stocks. Positive or negative orders, called base stock orders, are also used from time to time to adjust the level of the base stock of each item. In actual practice, replenishment orders are usually accumulated when they are issued and are released at regular intervals.

Baseband link A communications channel that allows only a very low bit rate in telecommunications, such as unconditioned telephone twisted pair cables.

Basel Accord Agreement among country representatives in 1988 to establish standardized risk-based capital requirements for banks across countries.

Baseline plan The original plan, or roadmap, laying out the way in which the project scope will be accomplished on time and within budget.

Basic Stock Method (BSM) A technique for planning dollar inventory investments that allows for a base stock level plus a variable amount of inventory that will increase or decrease at the beginning of each sales period in the same dollar amount as the period's expected sales.

Basis of the bargain Part of the buyer's assumption underlying the sale.

BAT Best available technology economically achievable.

Batch processing 1: A mode of transaction processing in which all the transactions of the same type for a given period of time are collected, and then entered into a computer system together and processed. **2:** Running large batches of a single product through the process at one time, resulting in queues awaiting next steps in the process.

Bathtub curve Also called "life-history curve." A graphic demonstration of the relationship of life of a product versus the probable failure rate. Includes three portions: early or infant failure (break-in), a stable rate during normal use, and wearout.

Battle of the brands Occurs when retailers have their own products competing with the manufacturer's products for shelf space and control over display location.

Baud After J. M. Emile Baudot, a French scientist; the number of signals per second that a communications channel can support.

Bayes theorem A probability expression that enables the use of sample information to revise prior probabilities.

BCG matrix A concept developed by the Boston Consulting Group (BCG) that evaluates SBUs with respect to the dimensions of business growth rate and market share.

BCT Best conventional pollution control technology.

Beachhead merger A business merger which is used to enter a new industry to exploit perceived opportunities.

Bearer bond A bond owned officially by whoever is holding it.

Behavior modeling Copying someone else's behavior.

Behavior modification The set of techniques by which reinforcement theory is used to modify human behavior.

Behavioral equations Economic relations that are hypothesized to be true.

Behavioral interview Interview in which applicants give specific examples of how they have performed a certain task or handled a problem in the past.

Behavioral rating approach Assesses an employee's behaviors instead of other characteristics.

Behavioral sciences approach A subfield of the humanistic management perspective that applies social science in an organizational context, drawing from economics, psychology, sociology, and other disciplines.

Behaviorally Anchored Rating Scale (BARS) A rating technique that relates an employee's performance to specific job-related incidents.

Below-market pricing policy A policy that regularly discounts merchandise from the established market price in order to build store traffic and generate high sales and gross margin dollars per square foot of selling space.

Benchmark job Job found in many organizations and performed by several individuals who have similar duties that are relatively stable and require similar KSAs.

Benchmarking 1: An improvement process in which a company measures its performance against that of best-in-class companies (or others who are good performers), determines how those companies achieved their performance levels, and uses the information to improve its own performance. The areas that can be benchmarked include strategies, operations, processes, and procedures. **2:** Comparing specific measures of performance against data on those measures in other "best practice" organizations. **3:** The measurement of time intervals and other important characteristics of hardware and software, usually when testing them before a decision to purchase or reject. **4:** An ongoing, systematic approach by which a public affairs unit measures and compares itself with higher performing and world-class units in order to generate knowledge and action about public affairs roles, practices, processes, products, services, and strategic issues that will lead to improvement in performance. Originated in the total quality management (TQM) movement.

Benefit Indirect compensation given to an employee or group of employees as a part of organizational membership.

Benefit concept Encapsulation of the benefits of a product in the customer's mind.

Benefit-cost analysis Collection of the dollar value of benefits derived from an initiative and the associated costs incurred and computing the ratio of benefits to cost.

Benefits needs analysis A comprehensive look at all aspects of benefits.

Best and Final Offer (BAFO) A final price for a project, submitted by a contractor at the request of a customer who is considering proposals from several contractors for the same project.

Best-case scenario An analysis in which all of the input variables are set at their best reasonably forecasted values.

Best efforts arrangement Agreement for the sale of securities in which the investment bank handling the transaction gives no guarantee that the securities will be sold.

Best practices Refer to approaches that produce exceptional results.

Beta coefficient, β A measure of the extent to which the returns on a given stock move with the stock market.

Beta (market) risk That part of a project's risk that cannot be eliminated by diversification; it is measured by the project's beta coefficient.

Beta probability distribution A distribution that is frequently used to calculate the expected duration and variance for an activity based on the activity's optimistic, most likely, and pessimistic time estimates.

Beta risk *See:* Consumer's risk.

Beta site An organization that agrees to use a new application for a specific period and report errors and unsatisfactory features to the developer in return for free use and support.

Betterment An expenditure that increases operating efficiency or capacity for the remaining useful life of a plant asset.

Bias A characteristic of measurement that refers to a systematic difference.

Biased expectations hypothesis A theory of the term structure of interest rates in which market expectations are modified by some degree of liquidity preference.

Biculturalism The sociocultural skills and attitudes used by racial minorities to move back and forth between the dominant culture and their own ethnic or racial culture.

Bid/ask spread Difference between the price at which a bank is willing to buy a currency and the price at which it will sell that currency.

Bid/no-bid decision An evaluation by a contractor of whether to go ahead with the preparation of a proposal in response to a customer's request for proposal.

Bid price Price that a trader of foreign exchange (typically a bank) is willing to pay for a particular currency.

Bid-rigging scheme Collusive fraud wherein an employee helps a vendor illegally obtain a contract that was supposed to involve competitive bidding.

Big Five Public accounting firms that have the capability to perform external audits in different parts of the world. The Big Five accounting firms include Andersen, KPMG Peat Marwick, Deloitte Touche Tohmatsu, Ernst & Young, and PricewaterhouseCoopers.

Big Five personality factors Dimensions that describe an individual's extroversion, agreeableness, conscientiousness, emotional stability, and openness to experience.

Big Q, little q A term used to contrast the difference between managing for quality in all business processes and products (big Q) and managing for quality in a limited capacity, traditionally in only factory products and processes (little q).

Bilan Social (social report) A required report in France. It contains mainly employee-related information covering topics such as pay structure, hiring policies, health and safety conditions, training, and industrial relations.

Bilateral advance pricing agreement When the multinational company receives the approval of proposed transfer pricing approaches from tax authorities of two countries.

Bilateral and multilateral netting systems Are centralized bookkeeping entries made to eliminate ("net out") offsetting amounts owed by divisions or subsidiaries within a company.

Bilateral contract Contract in which both parties exchange promises.

Bilateral negotiations Negotiations carried out between two nations focusing only on their interests.

Bill of batches A method of tracking the specific multilevel batch composition of a manufactured item. The bill of batches provides the necessary where-used and where-from relationships required for lot traceability.

Bill of exchange (draft) Promise drawn by one party (usually an exporter) to pay a specified amount to another party at a specified future date, or upon presentation of the draft.

Bill of labor A structured listing of all labor requirements for the fabrication, assembly, and testing of a parent item. *See:* bill of resources, capacity bill procedure, routing.

Bill of lading 1: Document serving as a receipt for shipment and a summary of freight charges and conveying title to the merchandise. **2:** A contract between an exporter and a carrier indicating that the carrier has accepted responsibility for the goods and will provide transportation in return for payment. **3:** In case of loss, damage, or delay, the bill of lading is the basis for filing freight claims.

Bill of Material (BOM) 1: A listing of all the subassemblies, intermediates, parts, components, and raw materials that go into a parent assembly showing the quantity of each required to make an assembly. It is used in conjunction with the master production schedule to determine the items for which purchase requisitions and production orders must be released. A variety of display formats exist for bills of material, including the single-level bill of material, indented bill of material, modular (planning) bill of material, transient bill of material, matrix bill of material, summarized bill of material, and costed bill of material. **2:** A list of all the materials needed to make one production run of a product, by a contract manufacturer, of piece parts/components for its customers. The bill of material may also be called the formula, recipe, or ingredients list in certain process industries. **3:** A list showing an explosion of the materials that go into the production of an item. Used in planning the purchase of raw materials.

Bill of resources A listing of the required capacity and key resources needed to manufacture one unit of a selected item or family. Rough-cut capacity planning uses these bills to calculate the approximate capacity requirements of the master production schedule. Resource planning may use a form of this bill. *Syn:* bill of capacity. *See:* Bill of labor, Capacity planning using overall factors, Product load profile, Resource profile, Rough-cut capacity planning, Routing.

Bill presentation Sending a bill (especially for telephone use, electricity, and similar services) via e-mail; usually with an option to pay on-line by credit card or bank transfer.

Billing scheme Submission of a false or altered invoice that causes an employer to willingly issue a check.

Binary number system A number system in which 2 is the base (rather than 10, which is the normal base human beings use in everyday counting). Used in computers.

Biometric A unique, measurable characteristic or trait of a human being used for automatically authenticating a person's identity. Biometrics include digitized fingerprints, retinal pictures, and voice. Used with special hardware to uniquely identify a person who tries to access a facility or an IS, instead of a password.

Bit Binary digit; either a zero or a one. The smallest unit of information used in computing.

Bit map The arrangement of bits representing an image for display on a computer monitor or a paper printout.

Bits Per Second (bps) The measurement of the capacity (or transmission rate) of a communications channel.

Black hole The situation that arises when an international marketer has a low-competence subsidiary—or none at all—in a highly strategic market.

Blackouts and brownouts Periods of power loss or a significant fall in power. Such events may cause computers to stop working, or even damage them. Computers can be protected against these events by using proper equipment, such as UPS (uninterruptible power supply) systems.

Bleeding edge The situation in which a business fails because it tries to be on the technological leading edge.

Blemish An imperfection that is severe enough to be noticed but should not cause any real impairment with respect to intended normal or reasonably foreseeable use. *See:* Defect, Imperfection, and Nonconformity.

Block diagram A diagram that shows the operation, interrelationships, and interdependencies of components in a system. Boxes, or blocks (hence the name) represent the components; connecting lines between the blocks represent interfaces. There are two types of block diagrams: a functional block diagram, which shows a system's subsystems and lower-level products, their interrelationships, and interfaces with other systems; and a reliability block diagram, which is similar to the functional block diagram except that it is modified to emphasize those aspects influencing reliability.

Blocked operation An upstream work center that is not permitted to produce because of a full queue at a downstream work center or because no kanban authorizes production.

Blue sky laws State laws that prevent the sale of securities that have little or no asset backing.

Board of Governors The main Federal Reserve System's policy-making body, which is comprised of seven members. Governors are appointed by the president and confirmed by the U.S. Senate. The Board of Governors supervises the district Federal Reserve banks, limiting to some extent the powers and privileges of their stockholders.

Body language Includes eye contact, physical distance and touching, hand movements, pointing, and facial expressions.

Bona Fide Occupational Qualification (BFOQ) Characteristic providing a legitimate reason why an employer can exclude persons on otherwise illegal bases of consideration.

Bond 1: A form of interest-bearing note employed by corporations to borrow on a long-term basis. **2:** A debt security.

Bond anticipation notes Short-term debt instrument which provides working capital financing for states and localities as they await anticipated revenues from upcoming bond issuance.

Bond indenture The contract between a corporation issuing bonds and the bondholders.

Bonus A one-time payment that does not become part of the employee's base pay.

Book value The amount at which an asset or liability is reported on the balance sheet. Also called basis or carrying value.

Book value of the asset The difference between the balance of a fixed asset account and its related accumulated depreciation account.

Book value per share The accounting value of a share of common stock; equal to common equity (common stock plus additional paid-in capital plus retained earnings) divided by the number of shares outstanding.

Boomerang effect Occurs when grown children return home to live with their parents.

Boot The cash balance owed the seller when an old asset is traded for a new asset.

Bottleneck A facility, function, department, or resource whose capacity is less than the demand placed upon it. For example, a bottleneck machine or work center exists where jobs are processed at a slower rate than they are demanded.

Bottom-up budgeting A budgeting process in which lower-level managers budget their departments' resource needs and pass them up to top management for approval.

Bottom-up planning An approach to planning based on satisfying the needs of individual business units. Reactive in nature.

Bottom-up replanning In MRP, the process of using pegging data to solve material availability or other problems. This process is accomplished by the planner (not the computer system), who evaluates the effects of possible solutions. Potential solutions include compressing lead time, cutting order quantity, substituting material, and changing the master schedule.

Boundary-spanning roles Roles assumed by people and/or departments that link and coordinate the organization with key elements in the external environment.

Boundaryless organization An organization without the internal or external boundaries limiting the traditional structures. Also known as a network organization, a modular corporation, or a virtual corporation.

Bounded rationality perspective 1: The concept that people have the time and cognitive ability to process only a limited amount of information on which to base decisions. **2:** How decisions are made when time is limited, a large number of internal and external factors affect a decision, and the problem is ill-defined.

Box-Jenkins model A type of time-series forecasting technique. Named after two pioneers in the field of time series modeling, this approach lets the data specify the best model.

Boycott 1: An organized effort to refrain from conducting business with a particular seller of goods or services; used in the international arena for political or economic reasons. **2:** Agreement among parties not to deal with a third party.

BPR (Business Process Reengineering) *See:* Reengineering.

BPT Best practicable control technology currently available.

Brain drain A migration of professional people from one country to another, usually for the purpose of improving their incomes or living conditions.

Brainstorming A problem-solving tool that teams use to generate as many ideas as possible related to a particular subject. Team members begin by offering all their ideas; the ideas are not discussed or reviewed until after the brainstorming session.

Branch Lines showing the alternatives from decision nodes and the outcomes from chance nodes.

Brand equity Marketplace value of a brand based on reputation and goodwill.

Brands Name, representative symbol or design, or any other feature that identifies one firm's product as distinct from another firm's. Trademark is the legal term for a brand. Brands may be associated with one product, a family of products, or with all of the products sold by a firm.

Breach Failure properly to perform a contractual obligation.

Breadth (or assessment) 1: Refers to the number and size of parties that are potential buyers of the instruments in a market. **2:** The number of merchandise brands that are found in a merchandise line.

Break-even point 1: Literally, "to have zero profit." It is that point at which total cost and total revenue are equal. **2:** The level of business operations at which revenues and expired costs are equal. **3:** Point at which total revenues equal total expenses and the retailer is making neither a profit nor a loss.

Break Point (BP) The dollar value of new capital that can be raised before an increase in the firm's weighted average cost of capital occurs.

Breakthrough A method of solving chronic problems that results from the effective execution of a strategy designed to reach the next level of quality. Such change often requires a paradigm shift within the organization.

Bretton Woods Agreement 1: An agreement signed by the major trading countries following World War II which returned the world economy to a type of gold standard. The U.S. dollar was pegged to the dollar at $35 per ounce. Currencies of all other countries were then fixed in price to the dollar and the countries agreed to maintain the established exchange rate within 1 percent. **2:** An agreement reached in 1944 among finance ministers of 45 Western nations to establish a system of fixed exchange rates.

Bribery 1: The offering, giving, receiving, or soliciting anything of value to influence an official act. **2:** The use of payments or favors to obtain some right or benefit to which the briber has no legal right; a criminal offense in the United States but a way of life in many countries.

Bridge A device connecting two communications networks that use similar hardware.

Broadband link A communications channel that supports high-speed communication.

Broadbanding Practice of using fewer pay grades having broader ranges than in traditional compensation systems.

Brokers Middlemen who do not inventory the securities they arrange transactions for.

Browsers Special software designed to search the Web for specific sites and retrieve information in the form of text, pictures, sound, and animation.

Browsing Using a special application called a Web browser to move from one Web site to another.

Bubble concept Views an entire plant as one source of pollution.

Bucketed system An MRP, DRP, or other time-phased system in which all time-phased data are accumulated into time periods, or buckets. If the period of accumulation is one week, then the system is said to have weekly buckets.

Bucketless system An MRP, DRP, or other time-phased system in which all time-phased data are processed, stored, and usually displayed using dated records rather than defined time periods, or buckets.

Budget An outline of a business's future plans, stated in financial terms. A budget is used to plan and control operational departments and divisions.

Budget performance report A report comparing actual results with budget figures.

Buffer 1: A quantity of materials awaiting further processing. It can refer to raw materials, semifinished stores or hold points, or a work backlog that is purposely maintained behind a work center. *Syn:* bank. **2:** In the theory of constraints, buffers can be time or material and support throughput and/or due date performance. Buffers can be maintained at the constraint, convergent points (with a constraint part), divergent points, and shipping points.

Buffer management In the theory of constraints, a process in which all expediting in a shop is driven by what is scheduled to be in the buffers (constraint, shipping, and assembly buffers). By expediting this material into the buffers, the system helps avoid idleness at the constraint and missed customer due dates. In addition, the causes of items missing from the buffer are identified, and the frequency of occurrence is used to prioritize improvement activities.

Buffer stock Stock of a commodity kept on hand to prevent a shortage in times of unexpectedly great demand; under international commodity and price agreements, the stock controlled by an elected or appointed manager for the purpose of managing the price of the commodity.

Buffering roles Activities that absorb uncertainty from the environment.

Bug An error in a computer program. Despite a famous story about a real insect that interrupted the work of a 1940s computer, the word "bug" had been used for "error" a long time before the advent of computers, and has nothing to do with that event.

Build cycle The time period between a major setup and a cleanup. It recognizes cyclical scheduling of similar products with minor changes from one product/model to another.

Bulk or capacity fixture A display fixture that is intended to hold the bulk of merchandise without looking as heavy as a long straight rack of merchandise.

Bulk service Ocean shipping provided on contract either for individual voyages or for prolonged periods of time.

Bullwhip effect An extreme change in the supply position upstream in a supply chain generated by a small change in demand downstream in the supply chain. Inventory can quickly move from being backordered to being excess. This is caused by the serial nature of communicating orders up the chain with the inherent transportation delays of moving product down the chain. The bullwhip effect can be eliminated by synchronizing the supply chain.

Bundling Occurs when distinct multiple items, generally from different merchandise lines, are offered at a special price.

Bureaucracy An organizational framework marked by rules and procedures, specialization and division of labor, hierarchy of authority, technically qualified personnel, separate position and incumbent, and written communications and records.

Bureaucratic control The use of rules, policies, hierarchy of authority, reward systems, and other formal devices to influence employee behavior and assess performance.

Bureaucratic culture A culture that has an internal focus and a consistency orientation for a stable environment.

Bureaucratic organizations A subfield of the classical management perspective that emphasized management on an impersonal, rational basis through such elements as clearly defined authority and responsibility, formal record-keeping, and separation of management and ownership.

Bus The set of wires or soldered conductors in the computer through which the different components (such as the CPU and RAM) communicate. It also refers to a data communications topology whereby communicating devices are connected to a single, open-ended medium.

Business An organization in which basic resources (inputs), such as materials and labor, are assembled and processed to provide goods or services (outputs) to customers.

Business continuity plan Organizational plan that prepares for disruption in information systems, detailing what should be done and by whom, if critical information systems fail or become untrustworthy; also called *business recovery plan* and *disaster recovery plan*.

Business cycle Rhythmic pattern of contraction and expansion in the overall economy.

Business entity concept The concept that accounting applies to individual economic units and that each unit is separate from the persons who supply its assets.

Business ethics 1: Concerned with good and bad or right and wrong behavior and practices that take place within a business context. **2:** The study of what is right and good in a business setting; includes the moral issues that arise from business practices, institutions, and decision making.

Business ethics gap Compared with other capitalistic societies, the approach to ethics is more individualistic, legalistic, and universalistic in the United States.

Business ethics visibility gap The people of the United States read and hear far more about business misconduct than people in other countries.

Business incubator An innovation that provides shared office space, management support services, and management advice to entrepreneurs.

Business judgment rule Precludes imposing liability on directors and officers for honest mistakes in judgment if they act with due care, in good faith, and in a manner reasonably believed to be in the best interests of the corporation.

Business-level strategy The level of strategy concerned with the question "How do we compete?" Pertains to each business unit or product line within the organization.

Business market All organizations that buy goods and services for use in the production of other goods and services or for resale.

Business model The manner in which businesses generate income.

Business necessity A practice necessary for safe and efficient organizational operations.

Business partnering The creation of cooperative business alliances between constituencies within an organization or between an organization and its customers or suppliers. Partnering occurs through a pooling of resources in a trusting atmosphere focused on continuous, mutual improvement. *See:* Customer–supplier partnership.

Business plan A document specifying the business details prepared by an entrepreneur in preparation for opening a new business.

Business planning The general idea or explicit statement of where an organization wishes to be at some time in the future.

Business processes Processes that focus on what the organization does as a business and how it goes about doing it. A business has functional processes (generating output within a single department) and cross-functional processes (generating output across several functions or departments).

Business Recovery Plan (BRP) *See:* Business continuity plan.

Business report A report that covers many of the matters typically found in the Management Discussion and Analysis part of companies' annual reports in North America.

Business risk The possibility that a company will not be able to meet ongoing operating expenditures. The risk associated with projections of a firm's future returns on assets (ROA) or returns on equity (ROE) if the firm uses no debt.

Business stakeholder A person or entity that has an interest in the economic performance of the business.

Business-to-business (B2B) model A form of e-commerce model in which the participants are organizations (profit or non-profit).

Business-to-consumer (B2C) model A form of e-commerce model in which customers deal directly with the organization, avoiding any intermediaries.

Business transaction The occurrence of an economic event or a condition that must be recorded in the accounting records.

Business trust A trust (managed by a trustee for the benefit of a beneficiary) established to conduct a business for a profit.

Bustarella Italian term for bribery/payoffs.

Bustout A planned bankruptcy.

Buy-and-hold strategy An approach to investing that involves holding until maturity securities purchased. Quite often, this is part of a "maturity matching" approach to investing that prescribes investing in a security that will mature at the end of the investment horizon.

Buy-back A refinement of simple barter with one party supplying technology or equipment that enables the other party to produce goods, which are then used to pay for the technology or equipment that was supplied.

Buy hedge A hedge created by purchasing a futures contract.

Buyers Consumers who actually purchase the product.

Buying center Those individuals who participate in the purchasing decision and who share the goals and risks arising from the decision.

Buying Power Index (BPI) An indicator of a market's overall retail potential and is composed of weighted measures of effective buying income (personal income, including all nontax payments such as Social Security, minus all taxes), retail sales, and population size.

Buzzword A new or existing word that takes on a very specific meaning when used in a particular context. Buzzwords are usually used to impress someone with new jargon or to promote a product, service, or idea.

Bylaws 1: A set of rules drawn up by the founders of the corporation that indicate how the company is to be governed; includes procedures for electing directors, whether the common stock has a preemptive right, and how to change the bylaws when necessary. **2:** Rules governing a corporation's internal management.

Byte A standard group of bits. In ASCII, a byte comprises seven bits. In ASCII-8 and EBCDIC, a byte comprises eight bits.

C

C chart Count chart. *See:* Attribute data.

Cache From French, pronounced "cash." A part of RAM devoted to the most frequently used instructions and data of a program for faster retrieval.

CAD A production technology in which computers perform new-product design.

Calibration The comparison of a measurement instrument or system of unverified accuracy to a measurement instrument or system of a known accuracy to detect any variation from the true value.

Call *See:* Currency call option.

Call option A contract that allows the owner to purchase the underlying asset at a specific price over a specific span of time. An option to buy, or "call," a share of stock at a certain price within a specified period.

Call option on real assets Project that contains an option of pursuing an additional venture.

Call premium The amount in excess of par value that a company must pay when it calls a security.

Call provision A provision in a bond contract that gives the issuer the right to redeem ("recall") the bonds under specified terms prior to the normal maturity date.

Callable bond Bond that is subject to redemption (reacquisition) by the corporation.

Callback A telecommunications security measure whereby the communications device at the destination end disconnects and calls the user back at the user-provided telephone number, to ensure the authenticity of the caller.

CAM A production technology in which computers help guide and control the manufacturing system.

Canonical analysis Considers possible interrelationships among independent variables and dependent variables.

Can-order point An ordering system used when multiple items are ordered from one vendor. The can-order point is a point higher than the original order point. When any one of the items triggers an order by reaching the must-order point, all items below their can-order point are also ordered. The can-order point is set by considering the additional holding cost that would be incurred should the item be ordered early.

Capability ratio (Cp) Is equal to the specification tolerance width divided by the process capability.

Capable-to-Promise (CTP) The process of committing orders against available capacity as well as inventory. This process may involve multiple manufacturing or distribution sites. Capable-to-promise is used to determine when a new or unscheduled customer order can be delivered. Capable-to-promise employs a finite-scheduling model of the manufacturing system to determine when an item can be delivered. It includes any constraints that might restrict the production, such as availability of resources, lead times for raw materials or purchased parts, and requirements for lower-level components or subassemblies. The resulting delivery date takes into consideration production capacity, the current manufacturing environment, and future order commitments. The objective is to reduce the time spent by production planners in expediting orders and adjusting plans because of inaccurate delivery-date promises.

Capacity 1: The capability of a system to perform its expected function. **2:** The capability of a worker, machine, work center, plant, or organization to produce output per time period. Capacity required represents the system capability needed to make a given product mix (assuming technology, product specification, and so on). As a planning function, both capacity available and capacity required can be measured in the short term (capacity requirements plan), intermediate term (rough-cut capacity plan), and long term (resource requirements plan). Capacity control is the execution through the I/O control report of the short-term plan. Capacity can be classified as budgeted, dedicated, demonstrated, productive, protective, rated, safety, standing, or theoretical. *See:* Capacity available, Capacity required. **3:** Required mental ability to enter into a contract.

Capacity control The process of measuring production output and comparing it with the capacity requirements plan, determining if the variance exceeds preestablished limits, and taking corrective action to get back on plan if the limits are exceeded.

Capacity management The function of establishing, measuring, monitoring, and adjusting limits or levels of capacity in order to execute all manufacturing schedules, that is, the production plan, master production schedule, material requirements plan, and dispatch list. Capacity management is executed at four levels: resource requirements planning, rough-cut capacity planning, capacity requirements planning, and input/output control.

Capacity planning The process of determining the amount of capacity required to produce in the future. This process may be performed at an aggregate or product-line level (resource requirements planning), at the master-scheduling level (rough-cut capacity planning), and at the material requirements planning level (capacity requirements planning). *See:* Capacity requirements planning, Resource planning, Rough-cut capacity planning.

Capacity Requirements Planning (CRP) The function of establishing, measuring, and adjusting limits or levels of capacity. The term *capacity requirements planning* in this context refers to the process of determining in detail the amount of labor and machine resources required to accomplish the tasks of production. Open shop orders and planned orders in the MRP system are input to CRP, which through the use of parts routings and time standards translates these orders into hours of work by work center by time period. Even though rough-cut capacity planning may indicate that sufficient capacity exists to execute the MPS, CRP may show that capacity is insufficient during specific time periods. *See:* Capacity planning.

Capacity strategy One of the strategic choices that a firm must make as part of its manufacturing strategy. There are three commonly recognized capacity strategies: lead, lag, and tracking. A lead capacity strategy adds capacity in anticipation of increasing demand. A lag strategy does not add capacity until the firm is operating at or beyond full capacity. A tracking strategy adds capacity in small amounts to attempt to respond to changing demand in the marketplace.

Capital account 1: Account reflecting changes in country ownership of long-term and short-term financial assets. **2:** An account in the BOP statement that records transactions involving borrowing, lending, and investing across borders. It is also called financial account.

Capital Asset Pricing Model (CAPM) A model used to determine the required return on an asset, which is based on the proposition that any asset's return should be equal to the risk-free rate of return plus a risk premium that reflects the asset's nondiversifiable risk.

Capital budget 1: The financial evaluation of a proposed investment to determine whether the expected returns are sufficient to justify the investment expenses. **2:** A budget that plans and reports investments in major assets to be depreciated over several years.

Capital budgeting 1: The process of identifying, evaluating, and planning long-term investment decisions. **2:** The process of planning and evaluating expenditures on assets whose cash flows are expected to extend beyond one year.

Capital component One of the types of capital used by firms to raise money.

Capital expenditures Costs that add to the usefulness of assets for more than one accounting period.

Capital expenditures budget The budget summarizing future plans for acquiring fixed assets.

Capital flight The flow of private funds abroad because investors believe that the return on investment or the safety of capital is not sufficiently ensured in their own countries.

Capital gain (loss) The profit (loss) from the sale of a capital asset for more (less) than its purchase price.

Capital gains yield The change in price (capital gain) during a given year divided by the price at the beginning of the year.

Capital investment analysis The process by which management plans, evaluates, and controls long-term capital investments involving property, plant, and equipment.

Capital lease A lease treated as a purchase of property by the lessee. Leases that treat the leased assets as purchased assets in the accounts.

Capital markets The financial markets for stocks and long-term debt (generally longer than one year).

Capital rationing 1: The process by which management allocates available investment funds among competing capital investment proposals. **2:** A situation in which a constraint is placed on the total size of the firm's capital investment.

Capital stock The portion of a corporation's owner's equity contributed by investors (owners) in exchange for shares of stock.

Capital structure The combination of debt and equity used to finance a firm.

Capital structure ratios *See:* Coverage ratios.

Capital surplus Surplus other than earned surplus.

Capitalization Recording expenditures as assets rather than as expenses. (For example, start-up costs that are "capitalized" are recorded as assets and amortized.)

Captive finance companies A financing subsidiary of a corporation that facilitates arranging financing for customers of the firm's products.

Captive finance subsidiary Separate entity within a company that provides financing for parent company or its customers, and which is thought to provide a marketing advantage or debt capacity advantage.

Captive insurer A type of insurer that is generally formed and owned by potential insureds to meet their own distinctive needs.

Capture theory Economic hypothesis suggesting that regulation is sometimes sought to limit competition and obtain government subsidies.

Career The series of work-related positions a person occupies throughout life.

Caribbean Basin Initiative (CBI) Extended trade preferences to Caribbean countries and granted them special access to the markets of the United States.

Carnegie model Organizational decision making involving many managers and a final choice based on a coalition among those managers.

Carriage and Insurance Paid to (CIP) The price quoted by an exporter for shipments not involving waterway transport, including insurance.

Carriage Paid To (CPT) The price quoted by an exporter for shipments not involving waterway transport, not including insurance.

Carryforwards Tax losses that are applied in a future year to offset income in the future year.

Carrying amount The amount at which a long-term investment or a long-term liability is reported on the balance sheet.

Cartel 1: Organization of firms in an industry where the central organization makes certain management decisions and functions (often regarding pricing, outputs, sales, advertising, and distribution) that would otherwise be performed within the individual firms. **2:** Groups of private businesses that agree to set prices, share markets, and control production. An association of producers of a particular good, consisting either of private firms or of nations, formed for the purpose of suppressing the market forces affecting prices. **3:** Firms operating with a formal agreement to fix prices and output.

Cascading training Training implemented in an organization from the top down, where each level acts as trainers to those below.

CASE (Computer-Aided Software Engineering) Software tools that expedite systems development. The tools provide a 4GL or application generator for fast code writing, facilities for flowcharting or data-flow diagramming, data-dictionary facility, word-processing capability, and other features required to develop and document the new software. Modern CASE is often called I-CASE (integrated CASE).

Case study A prepared scenario (story) which when studied and discussed serves to illuminate the learning points of a course of study.

Cash Coins, currency (paper money), checks, money orders, and money on deposit that is available for unrestricted withdrawal from banks or other financial institutions.

Cash and securities mix decision The proportional breakdown of cash and securities held by a company as part of its current asset holdings.

Cash application Crediting the account upon payment for a credit sale, this process frees up that amount of the credit limit for additional orders from this customer.

Cash basis A basis of accounting in which revenue is recognized in the period cash is received, and expenses are recognized in the period cash is paid.

Cash budget 1: One of the most important elements of the budgeted balance sheet. It presents the expected receipts (inflows) and payments (outflows) of cash for a period of time. **2:** A budget that estimates and reports cash flows on a daily or weekly basis to ensure that the company has sufficient cash to meet its obligations. **3:** Forecast showing cash receipts and disbursements on a monthly basis for a minimum horizon of one year, typically assembled before the beginning of a new fiscal year.

Cash collection system A management-designed system that converts checks to cash and considers mail float, processing float, and availability float.

Cash concentration The process of moving dollar balances from deposit banks to concentration banks.

Cash conversion cycle The length of time from the payment for the purchase of raw materials to manufacture a product until the collection of accounts receivable associated with the sale of the product.

Cash conversion period A liquidity measure that takes a going-concern approach. It measures the difference in time from when cash is received from credit customers and when cash is paid to suppliers. The length of time from when cash is paid out for purchases and when cash is received from collections on credit sales.

Cash cycle The time that elapses from the purchase of raw materials until cash is received from the sale of the final product.

Cash discount 1: The percentage amount that can be subtracted from the invoice if the customer pays within a stated period of time. **2:** A discount offered to the retailer for the prompt payment of bills.

Cash dividend A cash distribution of earnings by a corporation to its shareholders.

Cash equivalents Highly liquid investments that are usually reported on the balance sheet with cash.

Cash flow The actual cash, as opposed to accounting net income, that a firm receives or pays during some specified period.

Cash flow cycle The way in which actual net cash, as opposed to accounting net income, flows into or out of the firm during some specified period.

Cash flow from operations One of the most direct measures of liquidity found by subtracting operating cash disbursements from operating cash receipts.

Cash flow test A corporation must not be or become insolvent (unable to pay its debts as they become due in the usual course of business).

Cash flow timeline An important tool used in time value of money analysis; it is a graphical representation used to show the timing of cash flows.

Cash flows from financing activities The section of the statement of cash flows that reports cash flows from transactions affecting the equity and debt of the entity.

Cash flows from investing activities The section of the statement of cash flows that reports cash flows from transactions affecting investments in noncurrent assets.

Cash flows from operating activities The section of the statement of cash flows that reports the cash transactions affecting the determination of net income.

Cash inflows The cash benefits arising from sources of cash increases.

Cash items Deposited checks given immediate, provisional credit by the bank.

Cash letter The accompanying listing of checks that are bundled by the deposit bank for routing through the check-clearing process.

Cash management Optimization of cash flows and investment of excess cash.

Cash management systems Information systems that help reduce the interest and fees that organizations have to pay when borrowing money, and increase the yield that organizations can receive on unused funds.

Cash outflows Cash being disbursed.

Cash payback period The expected period of time that will elapse between the date of a capital expenditure and the complete recovery in cash (or equivalent) of the amount invested.

Cash pooling Used by multinational firms to centralize individual units' cash flows, resulting in less spending or foregone interest unnecessary cash balances.

Cash short and over account An account which has recorded errors in cash sales or errors in making change causing the amount of actual cash on hand to differ from the beginning amount of cash plus the cash sales for the day.

Catchball A term used to describe the interactive process of developing and deploying policies and plans with hoshin planning.

Category killers A name that comes from a marketing strategy in which a company carries such a large amount of merchandise in a single category at such good prices that they make it impossible for customers to walk out without purchasing what they needed, thus "killing" the competition.

Category Management (CM) 1: Process of managing and planning all SKUs within a product category as a distinct business. **2:** A process of managing all SKUs within a product category that involves the simultaneous management of price, shelf space, merchandising strategy, promotional efforts, and other elements of the retail mix within the category based on the firm's goals, the changing environment, and consumer behavior; refers to the management of merchandise categories, or lines, rather than individual products, as a strategic business unit.

Category manager An employee designated by a retailer for each category sold in their store. The category manager leverages detailed knowledge of the consumer and consumer trends, detailed point-of-sales information, and specific analysis provided by each supplier to tailor a store's offerings to the specific needs of each market. The category manager works with the suppliers to plan promotions throughout the year.

Category signage The use of signs that are smaller than directional and departmental signage and are intended to be seen from a shorter distance; they are located on or close to the fixture itself where the merchandise is displayed.

Cathode-ray tube A display (for a computer or television set) that uses an electronic gun to draw and paint on the screen by bombarding pixels on the internal side of the screen.

Causal analysis A method for analyzing the possible causal associations among a set of variables.

Causal distributions A set of outcomes characterized by situations where a predictor variable has changed from what was expected, causing the forecast variable to deviate from what was expected.

Causal forecasting methods Forecasting methods that relate a time series to other variables that are believed to explain or cause its behavior.

Causal techniques Forecasting methods linking the forecast values of an effect variable to one or more hypothesized causes.

Cause-and-effect diagram A tool for analyzing process variables. It is also referred to as the Ishikawa diagram, because Kaoru Ishikawa developed it and the fishbone diagram, because the complete diagram resembles a fish skeleton. The diagram illustrates the main causes and sub-causes leading to an effect (symptom). The cause-and-effect diagram is one of the seven tools of quality.

Cause-related marketing Form of corporate philanthropy that links a company's contributions (usually monetary) to a predesignated worthy cause with the purchasing behavior of consumers.

Causes of dissolution The limited partners have neither the right nor the power to dissolve the partnership, except by decree of the court. The following events trigger a dissolution: 1) the expiration of the time period; 2) the withdrawal of a general partner, unless all partners agree to continue the business; or 3) a decree of judicial dissolution.

CBT Computer-based training is training delivered via computer software.

CD-ROM (Compact Disc Read-Only Memory) A compact disc whose data were recorded by the manufacturer and cannot be changed.

Cell A layout of workstations and/or various machines for different operations (usually in a U-shape) in which multi-tasking operators proceed, with a part, from machine to machine, to perform a series of sequential steps to produce a whole product or major subassembly.

Cellular layout A facility's layout in which machines dedicated to sequences of production are grouped into cells in accordance with group-technology principles.

Cellular manufacturing A manufacturing process that produces families of parts within a single line or cell of machines controlled by operators who work only within the line or cell.

Central Business District (CBD) Usually consists of an unplanned shopping area around the geographic point at which all public transportation systems converge; it is usually in the center of the city and often where the city originated historically.

Center of excellence The location of product development outside the home country because of an advantage of skills.

Central exchange rate Exchange rate established between two European currencies through the European Monetary System arrangement; the exchange rate between the two currencies is allowed to move within bands around that central exchange rate.

Central IS organization Organizational structure that includes a corporate information systems team to whom all units turn with their information systems needs.

Central plan The economic plan for the nation devised by the government of a socialist state; often a five-year plan that stipulated the quantities of industrial goods to be produced.

Central planning department A group of planning specialists who develop plans for the organization as a whole and its major divisions and departments and typically report to the president or CEO.

Central Processing Unit (CPU) The circuitry of a computer microprocessor that fetches instructions and data from the primary memory and executes the instructions. The CPU is the most important electronic unit of the computer.

Central tendency The propensity of data collected on a process to concentrate around a value situated somewhere midway between the lowest and highest value.

Central tendency error Rating all employees in a narrow range in the middle of the rating scale.

Centrality A trait of a department whose role is in the primary activity of an organization.

Centralization The concentrating of control and strategic decision making at headquarters. Most of the important decisions relative to local matters are made by headquarters management rather than by managers in the local subsidiary.

Centralized architecture Information systems architecture in which all applications and data are stored in a single mainframe.

Centralized cash flow management Policy that consolidates cash management decisions for all MNC units, usually at the parent's location.

Centralized disbursing An organizational structure that disburses corporate cash from a central area, allowing the corporate headquarters' staff to check each disbursement and possibly initiate each payment as well.

Centralized internal audit model In this type of organization, there is only one central internal audit organization that is located at the headquarters of the parent company. The internal auditors travel to various parts of the world where operations are located to perform internal audits, and to perform other functions such as quality control, audit research, liaison with external auditors, training, and technical support.

Centralized management Shareholders of a corporation elect the board of directors to manage its business affairs; the board appoints officers to run the day-to-day operations of the business.

Centralized multinational organizations Organizations that retain to a great extent the authority to make decisions at parent company headquarters.

Centralized network A team communication structure in which team members communicate through a single individual to solve problems or make decisions.

Centralized processing system A cash collection system where corporate headquarters receives all customer remittances.

Centralized transfer initiation The timing and amount of the transfer is centered either at the concentration bank or corporate headquarters.

Certainty All the information the decision maker needs is fully available.

Certificate of Deposit (CD) An interest-bearing account that evidences (certifies) that a certain amount of money has been deposited at the bank for a prespecified period of time, and that will be redeemed with interest at the end of that time (maturity).

Certified Internal Auditor (CIA) A certification program sponsored by the Institute of Internal Auditors consisting of an examination and a mandatory two years of practical experience in internal auditing before certification.

Certified Public Accountant (CPA) The professional designation for public accountants and independent (external) auditors in the United States and some other countries.

Chain of command An unbroken line of authority that links all individuals in the organization and specifies who reports to whom.

Chain of custody Maintaining detailed records about documents from the time they are received in the investigation process until the trial is completed. Helps to substantiate that documents have not been altered or manipulated since coming into the investigator's hands.

Chain stores Normally refers to operations having 11 or more units.

Chaku-chaku (Japanese) Meaning "load-load" in a cell layout where a part is taken from one machine and loaded into the next.

Champion 1: An individual who has accountability and responsibility for many processes or who is involved in making strategic-level decisions for the organization. The champion ensures ongoing dedication of project resources and monitors strategic alignment (also referred to as a *sponsor*). **2:** An executive with much clout who supports a project and endeavors to muster support from top management. A champion is important for the success of a project, such as developing a new information system.

Chance event An uncertain future event affecting the consequence, or payoff, associated with a decision.

Chance nodes Nodes indicating points where an uncertain event will occur.

Change agent 1: A person or institution that facilitates change in a firm or in a host country. **2:** An organizational development specialist who contracts with an organization to facilitate change. **3:** The person who takes the lead in transforming a company into a quality organization by providing guidance during the planning phase, facilitating implementation, and supporting those who pioneer the changes.

Change in the quantity demanded Movement along a given demand curve reflecting a change in price and quantity.

Change in the quantity supplied Movement along a given supply curve reflecting a change in price and quantity.

Change process The way in which changes occur in an organization.

Changeover Changing a machine or process from one type of product or service to another.

Changing An intervention stage of organizational development in which individuals experiment with new workplace behavior.

Channel (link, path) 1: The guiding or nonguiding environment in which communications signals are transmitted. **2:** Term used interchangeably with supply chain.

Channel captain The institution (manufacturer, wholesaler, broker, or retailer) in the marketing channel who is able to plan for and get other channel institutions to engage in activities they might not otherwise engage in. Large store retailers are often able to perform the role of channel captain.

Channel design The length and width of the distribution channel.

Channel intensity The number of intermediaries at each level of the marketing channel.

Channel length Number of levels in a marketing channel.

Channel richness The amount of information that can be transmitted during a communication episode.

Channel strategy Broad set of principles by which a firm seeks to achieve its distribution objectives to satisfy its customers.

Channel structure All of the businesses and institutions (including producers or manufacturers and final customers) who are involved in performing the functions of buying, selling, or transferring title.

Chapter 7 bankruptcy Complete liquidation or "shutting down of a business" and distribution of any proceeds to creditors.

Chapter 11 bankruptcy Bankruptcy that allows the bankrupt entity time to reorganize its operational and financial affairs, settle its debts, and continue to operate in a reorganized fashion.

Character The smallest piece of data in the data hierarchy.

Characteristic A property that helps to identify or to differentiate between entities and that can be described or measured to determine conformance or nonconformance to requirements.

Chargeback A method used to manage the expenses involved in rendering information system services. The greater part of the expense is charged to the budget of the business unit that ordered it.

Charging order Judicial lien against a partner's interest in the partnership.

Charismatic authority Authority based in devotion to the exemplary character or heroism of an individual and the order defined by him or her.

Charismatic leader A leader who has the ability to motivate subordinates to transcend their expected performance.

Chart of accounts The system of accounts that make up the ledger for a business.

Charter A documented statement officially initiating the formation of a committee, team, project, or other effort in which a clearly stated purpose and approval is conferred.

Chase production method A production planning method that maintains a stable inventory level while varying production to meet demand. Companies may combine chase and level production schedule methods. *Syn:* chase strategy.

Chat room A facility that enables two or more people to engage in interactive "conversations" over the Internet.

Check processing float Delays in collecting cash caused by delays between the time a check is received and when it is deposited in the banking system.

Check sheet A simple data-recording device. The check sheet is custom-designed for the particular use, allowing ease in interpreting the results. The check sheet is one of the seven tools of quality. Check sheets are often confused with data sheets and checklists. *See:* checklist.

Check tampering Scheme in which dishonest employees 1) prepare fraudulent checks for their own benefit or 2) intercept checks intended for a third party and convert the checks for their own benefit.

Check truncation Involves expediting clearing by scanning the data on the check's MICR line, and then processing only that data back to the payee's bank.

Checklist 1: A tool used to ensure that all important steps or actions in an operation have been taken. Checklists contain items that are important or relevant to an issue or situation. Checklists are often confused with check sheets and data sheets. *See:* Check sheet. **2:** Performance appraisal tool that uses a list of statements or words that are checked by raters.

Chief Executive Officer (CEO) The top leader in an organization, to whom a small group of executives reports.

Chief learning officer Responsible for developing on a worldwide scale the organization's human talent and for using the human knowledge present in the organization. *See:* CKO.

Children The data records linked to a parent record.

Chip A flat piece of silicon in which electronic circuitry is integrated.

CHIPS Short for Clearing House Interbank Payment System, the institution which was established in 1970 to handle interbank transactions needed to settle international transactions. CHIPS is a private association of banks that operates through the New York Clearinghouse Association.

Choice of associates No person may be added as a general partner or a limited partner without the consent of all partners.

Chronic crisis stage The lingering period of a crisis; may involve investigations, audits, or in-depth news stories.

Chronic problem A long-standing adverse situation that can be remedied by changing the status quo. For example, actions such as revising an unrealistic manufacturing process or addressing customer defections can change the status quo and remedy the situation.

CISG United Nations Convention on Contracts for the International Sales of Goods governs all contracts for international sales of goods between parties located in different nations that have ratified the CISG.

CIO (Chief Information Officer) The highest-ranking IS officer in the organization, usually a vice president, who oversees the planning, development, and implementation of IS and serves as leader to all IS professionals in the organization.

Ciphertext A coded message designed to authenticate users and maintain secrecy.

Circuit switching A communication process in which a dedicated channel (circuit) is established for the duration of a transmission; the sending node signals the receiving node; the receiver acknowledges the signal and then receives the entire message.

Circular cultures Belief that since individuals can see what has happened in the past, their past is ahead of them, and since they cannot see into the future, their future is behind them.

CISG United Nations Convention on Contracts for the International Sales of Goods governs all contracts for international sales of goods between parties located in different nations that have ratified the CISG.

Civil law Body of law that provides remedies for violation of private rights deals with rights and duties between individuals.

Civil penalties for inside trading Penalties that are imposed on inside traders in an amount up to three times the gains they made or losses they avoided.

Civil Rights Act of 1964 Law that prohibits employment discrimination on the basis of race, color, gender, religion, or national origin.

CKO (Chief Knowledge Officer) A relatively new position in some large organizations. The CKO is responsible for garnering knowledge and making it available for future operations in which employees can learn from previous experience. The CKO works closely with the CIO, who is in charge of the technical means for garnering the necessary information. In some firms, the position is called *chief learning officer*.

Clan control The use of social characteristics, such as corporate culture, shared values, commitments, traditions, and beliefs, to control behavior.

Clan culture A culture that focuses primarily on the involvement and participation of the organization's members and on rapidly changing expectations from the external environment.

Class A vendors Those vendors from whom the retailer purchases large and profitable amounts of merchandise.

Class B vendors Vendors that generate satisfactory sales and profits for the retailer.

Class C vendors Vendors that carry outstanding merchandise lines but do not currently sell to the retailer.

Class D vendors Vendors from whom the retailer purchases small quantities of goods on an irregular basis.

Class E vendors Vendors with whom the retailer has had an unfavorable experience.

Classic system A national tax system that subjects income to taxes when income is received by the taxable entity.

Classical model A decision-making model based on the assumption that managers should make logical decisions that will be in the organization's best economic interests.

Classical perspective A management perspective that emerged during the 19th and early 20th centuries that emphasized a rational, scientific approach to the study of management and sought to make organizations efficient operating machines.

Classified stock Common stock that is given a special designation, such as Class A, Class B, and so forth, to meet special needs of the company.

Clean Air Act Law enacted to control and reduce air pollution.

Clean Water Act Law enacted to protect against water pollution.

Cleansing phase The stage at which database builders modify data into a form that allows insertion into the data warehouse.

Clearing agent Often a Federal Reserve bank, branch or RCPC, an entity that uses the information printed at the bottom of the check to process the check.

Clearing bank(s) When checks are deposited, the bank(s) used for processing those checks into the clearing system. Sometimes called *deposit bank(s)*.

Clearing float Sometimes called "availability float," the delay in availability incurred after deposit. The length of this component of float is linked to the bank's availability schedule in connection with the location of the payor's bank.

Clearing house A central location where representatives of area banks meet, and each bank settles its balances with one institution (the clearing house) instead of with each bank individually.

Click through Term that describes the act of clicking on an advertising banner located at a host site and being transported electronically to the advertiser's site.

Clientele effect The tendency of a firm to attract the type of investor who likes its dividend policy.

Client/server An information system arrangement in which one large computer holds large databases that are tapped by the users of smaller local microcomputers, but much discretion and the creation of the applications that manipulate the data are in the hands of the users. The larger computer is the server, while the local computers are the clients.

Clock rate The rate of repetitive machine cycles that a computer can perform. Also called *frequency*.

Closed-loop MRP A system built around material requirements planning that includes the additional planning processes of production planning (sales and operations planning), master production scheduling, and capacity requirements planning. Once this planning phase is complete and the plans have been accepted as realistic and attainable, the execution processes come into play. These processes include the manufacturing control processes of input-output (capacity) measurement, detailed scheduling and dispatching, as well as anticipated delay reports from both the plant and suppliers, supplier scheduling, and so on. The term closed loop implies not only that each of these processes is included in the overall system, but also that feedback is provided by the execution processes so that the planning can be kept valid at all times.

Closed shop Business in which the employer can only hire union members.

Closed system 1: A system that stands alone, with no connection to another system. **2:** A system that does not interact with the external environment.

Closely held corporation A corporation that is owned by a few individuals who are typically associated with the firm's management.

Closing entries Entries necessary to eliminate the balances of temporary accounts in preparation for the following accounting period.

Closing the sale The action the salesperson takes to bring a potential sale to its natural conclusion.

Cluster analysis 1: Geographical grouping and labeling of individuals based on their buying behavior, demographics, and lifestyles. **2:** Used to create a classification by using single or multiple dimensions.

Clusters Geographic concentrations of interconnected companies and institutions in a particular field.

Coaching A continuous improvement technique by which people receive one-to-one learning through demonstration and practice and that is characterized by immediate feedback and correction.

Coalition An informal alliance among managers who support a specific goal.

Coaxial cable A transmission medium consisting of thick copper wire insulated and shielded by a special sheath of meshed wires to prevent electromagnetic interference. Supports high-speed telecommunication.

Code law Law based on a comprehensive set of written statutes.

Code of ethics A formal statement of the organization's values regarding ethics and social issues.

Codetermination A management approach in which employees are represented on supervisory boards to facilitate communication and collaboration between management and labor.

Coding Categorizing customers based on how profitable their past business has been.

Coefficient of determination Measure of the percentage variation in the dependent variable that can be explained by the independent variables when using regression analysis.

Coefficient of Variation (CV) Standardized measure of the risk per unit of return; calculated as the standard deviation divided by the expected return.

Coercive power 1: Power that stems from the authority to punish or recommend punishment. **2:** Situation based on B's belief that A has the capability to punish or harm B if B doesn't do what A wants.

Cofinancing agreements Arrangement in which the World Bank participates along with other agencies or lenders in providing funds to developing countries.

Cognitive ability tests Tests that measure an individual's thinking, memory, reasoning, and verbal and mathematical abilities.

Cognitive dissonance A condition in which two attitudes or a behavior and an attitude conflict.

Coin and currency services Procedures provided by banks that include receiving of bulk cash deposits sent by armed courier, sorting of deposit items, same day verification of the total deposit if received by the bank's cutoff time, and supply of coins and currency for the company's cash payment needs.

Cold calling Contacting prospective customers without a prior appointment.

Cold turkey conversion A swift switch from an old information system to the new; also called cut-over conversion.

Collaborative problem-solving strategy Firms emphasize long-term relationships with a variety of external constituencies and broad problem-solving perspectives on the resolution of social issues affecting their businesses and industries.

Collected balance Sometimes called the *available balance*, this amount represents how much of a deposit balance is immediately spendable. It may be somewhat less than the ledger balance because of availability delays applied to the checks by the bank.

Collection bank The bank of deposit that encodes the dollar amount of the check in magnetic ink on the bottom right side of the check and then routes the check through the clearing process.

Collection float The sum of the delays in collecting cash from customers caused by mail, process, and availability delays.

Collection policy The procedures followed by a firm to collect its accounts receivables.

Collection procedures Detailed statements regarding when and how the company will carry out collection of past due accounts. These policies specify how long the company will wait past the due date to initiate collection efforts, the method(s) of contact with delinquent customers and whether and at what point accounts will be referred to an outside collection agency.

Collective In stage six of the social interaction paradigm, leaders look for opportunities that benefit the group as a whole.

Collective bargaining The negotiation of an agreement between management and workers.

Collectivism 1: A preference for a tightly knit social framework in which individuals look after one another and organizations protect their members' interests. **2:** The belief that interests of the organization should have top priority.

Collectivity stage The life cycle phase in which an organization has strong leadership and begins to develop clear goals and direction.

Collusion 1: Fraud perpetrated by two or more employees or others, each of whose job responsibilities is necessary to complete the fraud. **2:** A covert, informal agreement among firms in an industry to fix prices and output levels.

Comarketing agreement Two or more companies who share the risks and rewards of long-term marketing programs.

Comment cards Printed cards or slips of paper used to solicit and collect comments from users of a service or product.

Commercial data-mining software Commercial software packages that use query techniques to detect patterns and anomalies in data that may suggest fraud.

Commercial enterprises Sector of the business market represented by manufacturers, construction companies, service firms, transportation companies, professional groups, and resellers that purchase goods and services.

Commercial/industrial market Refers to business market customers who are described by variables such as location, SIC code, buyer industry, technological sophistication, purchasing process, size, ownership, and financial strength.

Commercial invoice A bill for transported goods that describes the merchandise and its total cost and lists the addresses of the shipper and seller and delivery and payment terms.

Commercial letter of credit A guarantee of payment by an importer, made by its bank, that becomes binding when the shipping and other documents related to the goods sold are presented to the bank.

Commercial paper An unsecured IOU issued mainly by financial companies such as banks, their parent holding companies, and consumer or commercial finance companies. A short-term promissory note issued by a corporation for a fixed maturity generally in the 30-day range but can be as much as 270 days. Unsecured, short-term promissory notes issued by large, financially sound firms to raise funds.

Commercial Service A department of the U.S. Department of Commerce that gathers information and assists business executives in business abroad.

Commission Compensation computed as a percentage of sales in units or dollars.

Commitment An important reciprocal relationship in which the employee is committed to the organization and its goals and is matched by the employer's commitment to the employee's welfare.

Commitment fee A fee charged on the *unused* balance of a revolving credit agreement to compensate the bank for guaranteeing that the funds will be available when needed by the borrower; the fee normally is about 1/4 percent of the unused balance.

Committed cost The funds that are unavailable to be spent elsewhere because they will be needed at some later time to pay for an item, such as material, that has been ordered; commitment; encumbered cost.

Committed facility Lending arrangement in which the bank charges a fee to compensate it for agreeing to lend upon request for a period of five to seven years.

Committed line A line of credit where the firm pays a commitment fee that obligates the bank to provide funding for the credit line with a formal written agreement.

Committee A long-lasting, sometimes permanent team in the organization structure created to deal with tasks that recur regularly.

Committee of Sponsoring Organizations (COSO) Organization made up of representatives from major accounting firms that focus on internal controls and financial statement fraud.

Committee on Foreign Investments in the United States (CFIUS) A federal committee, chaired by the U.S. Treasury, with the responsibility to review major foreign investments to determine whether national security or related concerns are at stake.

Commodity analysis Researching the requirements for a commodity purchase. Some of the elements of a thorough commodity analysis include the buyer's/supplier's needs and objectives, importance of the item cost/quality/delivery/packaging requirements, manufacturing process, cost structure and pricing trends, substitutions, major suppliers and customers, and other relevant information that can facilitate a sound sourcing decision.

Commodity price agreement An agreement involving both buyers and sellers to manage the price of a particular commodity, but often only when the price moves outside a predetermined range.

Common Agricultural Policy (CAP) An integrated system of subsidies and rebates applied to agricultural interests in the European Union.

Common causes Are factors internal to a process.

Common causes of variation Causes that are inherent in any process all the time. A process that has only common causes of variation is said to be stable or predictable or in-control. Also called "chance causes."

Common equity The sum of the firm's common stock, paid-in capital, and retained earnings, which equals the common stockholders' total investment in the firm stated at book value.

Common Gateway Interface (CGI) Special software used in Internet servers that allows the capture of data from a form displayed on a page and the storage of the data in a database.

Common law 1: Law based on tradition and depending less on written statutes and codes than on precedent and custom—used in the United States. **2:** Most contracts are primarily governed by state common law, including contracts involving employment, services, insurance, real property, patents, and copyrights.

Common market A group of countries that agree to remove all barriers to trade among members, to establish a common trade policy with respect to nonmembers, and also to allow mobility for factors of production—labor, capital, and technology.

Common-size financial statements 1: Financial statements that have been converted to percentages. **2:** A financial statement in which all items are expressed only in relative terms.

Common stock The basic ownership class of corporate stock.

Common stockholders' equity (net worth) The capital supplied by common stockholders—capital stock, paid-in capital, retained earnings, and, occasionally, certain reserves.

Communication The process by which information is exchanged and understood by two or more people, usually with the intent to motivate or influence behavior.

Communication services Services that are provided in the areas of videotext, home banking, and home shopping, among others.

Communications channel Any medium that supports the transmission and reception of data and information. May be a guided channel, such as wires, or an unguided channel, such as the atmosphere or space. Also called communications link and communications path.

Communications protocol The set of rules that govern data communications. When more than two parties participate in the communication, it is also called *network protocol.*

Compact Disc (CD) A plastic disk in which pits and flat areas represent bits. A laser beam "reads" the data. Also called "optical disc" and "laser disc." CDs have a storage capacity 100–150 times that of regular magnetic disks. Used as the predominant medium for storing musical works and archival data.

Company/brand sites Web sites that provide information about a company, such as history, mission, financial statements, and so on.

Company processing center An administrative office or area within the corporation that processes payments received from customers.

Company-Wide Quality Control (CWQC) Similar to Total Quality Management.

Compa-ratio Current pay level divided by the midpoint of the pay range.

Comparable worth Equal pay for jobs of equal value to the employer.

Comparative advantage 1: Results when a strategic advantage is held relative to the competition. **2:** Theory suggesting that specialization by countries can increase worldwide production. **3:** The ability to produce a good or service more cheaply, relative to other goods and services, than is possible in other countries. **4:** When one nation or region of the country is better suited to the production of one product than to the production of some other product.

Comparative negligence Most states have applied the rule of comparative negligence to strict liability in tort.

Comparative statics analysis Study of changing demand and supply conditions.

Comparative ratio analysis An analysis based on a comparison of a firm's ratios with those of other firms in the same industry.

Compensable factor Identifies a job value commonly present throughout a group of jobs.

Compensating Balance (CB) A minimum checking account balance that a firm must maintain with a bank to borrow funds—generally 10 to 20 percent of the amount of loans outstanding.

Compensation 1: Monetary payments (wages, salaries) and nonmonetary goods/commodities (benefits, vacations) used to reward employees. **2:** Arrangement in which the delivery of goods to a party is compensated for by buying back a certain amount of the product from that same party. **3:** Includes direct dollar payments (wages, commission, bonuses) and indirect payments (insurance, vacation time, retirement plans).

Compensation committee 1: Has the responsibility of evaluating executive performance and recommending terms and conditions of employment. **2:** A subgroup of the board of directors composed of directors who are not officers of the firm.

Compensatory Financing Facility (CFF) Facility that attempts to reduce the impact of export instability on country economies.

Compensatory justice The concept that individuals should be compensated for the cost of their injuries by the party responsible and also that individuals should not be held responsible for matters over which they have no control.

Compensatory time off Hours given in lieu of payment for extra time worked.

Competence Refers to a person's ability to learn and perform a particular activity. Competence generally consists of skill, knowledge, experience, and attitude components.

Competencies Basic characteristics that can be linked to enhanced performance by individuals or teams.

Competency-based training A training methodology that focuses on building mastery of a redetermined segment or module before moving on to the next.

Competition Rivalry between groups in the pursuit of a common prize.

Competitive advantage 1: A position in which one dominates a market; also called *strategic advantage.* **2:** The ability to produce a good or service more cheaply than other countries due to favorable factor conditions and demand conditions, strong related and supporting industries, and favorable firm strategy, structure, and rivalry conditions. **3:** A unique or rare ability to create, distribute, or service products valued by customers.

Competitive analysis The gathering of intelligence relative to competitors in order to identify opportunities or potential threats to current and future strategy.

Competitive assessment A research process that consists of matching markets to corporate strengths and providing an analysis of the best potential for specific offerings.

Competitive bids Offers to buy securities at a given price or yield. In the Treasury auctions, these are mainly entered by financial institutions, including dealers.

Competitive environment This environment is affected by bribery and the existence of cartels.

Competitive Equality Banking Act of 1987 Allows existing nonbank banks to continue to operate, but prohibits the establishment of new nonbank banks.

Competitive strategy The search for a favorable competitive position in an industry or line of business.

Competitively advantaged product Product that solves a set of customer problems better than any competitor's product. This product is made possible due to this firm's unique technical, manufacturing, managerial, or marketing capabilities, which are not easily copied by others.

Compiler A program whose purpose is to translate code written in a high-level programming language into the equivalent code in machine language for execution by the computer.

Complaint 1: Request filed by a plaintiff to request civil proceedings against someone—usually to seek damages. **2:** Indication of employee dissatisfaction.

Complementary marketing Contractual arrangement where participating parties carry out different but complementary activities.

Complements Related products for which a price increase for one leads to a reduction in demand for the other.

Complete enumeration A lockbox model that analyzes all possible lockbox sites to determine the optimal combination that maximizes shareholder wealth.

Compliance An affirmative indication or judgment that the supplier of a product or service has met the requirements of the relevant specifications, contract, or regulation; also the state of meeting the requirements.

Compliance strategy Focuses on obedience to the law as its driving force.

Components of internal control The internal control components are the control environment, risk assessment, control activities, information and communication, and monitoring.

Composite index Weighted average of leading, coincident, or lagging economic indicators.

Composite key In a data file, a combination of two fields that can serve as a unique key to locate specific records.

Composition of trade The ratio of primary commodities to manufactured goods in a country's trade.

Compounded interest Interest earned on interest.

Compounding The process of determining the value of a cash flow or series of cash flows some time in the future when compound interest is applied.

Comprehensive income All changes in stockholders' equity during a period, except those resulting from dividends and stockholders' investments.

Comprehensive payables Is the outsourcing of part or all of the accounts payable and/or disbursement functions.

Compressed workweek One in which a full week's work is accomplished in fewer than five days.

Compression (data compression) The restorage or communication of data, using special software techniques, so that the new file takes up significantly less space on the storage medium, or takes less time to communicate over a channel.

Compulsory share exchange A transaction by which a corporation becomes the owner of all of the outstanding shares of one or more classes of stock of another corporation by an exchange that is compulsory on all owners of the acquired shares; the board of directors of each corporation and the shareholders of the corporation whose shares are being acquired must approve.

Computer-Aided Design (CAD) Special software used by engineers and designers that facilitates engineering and design work.

Computer-Based Information System (CBIS) A single set of hardware, software, databases, telecommunications, people, and procedures that are configured to collect, manipulate, store, and process data into information.

Computer controls 1: Controls performed by a computer, that is, controls programmed into computer software (contrast with manual controls). **2:** Controls over computer processing of information, consisting of general controls and application controls (both programmed and manual).

Computer-Integrated Manufacturing (CIM) Computer systems that link together manufacturing components, such as robots, machines, product design, and engineering analysis.

Computer Virus (virus) Destructive software that propagates and is activated by unwary users; a virus usually damages applications and data files or disrupts communications.

Computerized Numeric Control (CNC) Control by computers that take data and create instructions that tell robots how to manufacture and assemble parts and products.

Concealment investigative methods Investigating a fraud by focusing on the cover-up efforts, such as the manipulation of source documents.

Concentration account Deposit account into which funds are pooled at the endpoint(s) of a company's collection system.

Concentration bank A bank that receives balance transfers from several deposit or gathering banks.

Concentration banking A technique used to move funds from many bank accounts to a more central cash pool in order to more effectively manage cash.

Concentration ratios Data that show the percentage market share held by a group of leading firms.

Concentration services Closely linked to collection services, these services mobilize and pool collected cash in order to increase interest income and reduce interest expense.

Concentration strategy Market development strategy that involves focusing on a smaller number of markets.

Concept Written description or visual depiction of a new product idea. A concept includes the product's primary features and benefits.

Conceptual skill The cognitive ability to see the organization as a whole and the relationship among its parts.

Conclusion The *then* component of an *if-then* rule in knowledge representation.

Concurrency control A method of dealing with a situation in which two or more people need to access the same record in a database at the same time.

Concurrent control Control that consists of monitoring ongoing activities to ensure their consistency with standards.

Concurrent engineering A process in which an organization designs a product or service using input and evaluations from business units and functions early in the process, anticipating problems, and balancing the needs of all parties. The emphasis is on upstream prevention versus downstream correction.

Concurrent validity Measured when an employer tests current employees and correlates the scores with their performance ratings.

Conditional probabilities The probability of one event given the known outcome of a (possibly) related event.

Confidential vendor analysis Identical to the vendor profitability analysis but also provides a three-year financial summary as well as the names, titles, and negotiating points of all the vendor's sales staff.

Confiscation Governmental taking of foreign-owned property without payment (or for a highly inadequate payment) or for a nonpublic purpose.

Conflict Antagonistic interaction in which one party attempts to thwart the intentions or goals of another.

Conflict in marketing channels Occurs when one channel member believes that another channel member is impeding the attainment of its goals.

Conflict resolution A process for resolving disagreements in a manner acceptable to all parties.

Conformance An affirmative indication or judgment that a product or service has met the requirements of a relevant specification, contract, or regulation.

Confrontation A situation in which parties in conflict directly engage one another and try to work out their differences.

Confucianism A system of practical ethics based on a set of pragmatic rules for daily life derived from experience.

Congeneric merger A merger of firms in the same general industry, but for which no customer or supplier relationship exists.

Conglomerate merger 1: A merger of companies in totally different industries. **2:** An acquisition by one company of another that is not a competitor, customer, or supplier.

Conquest marketing Strategy for constantly seeking new customers by offering discounts and markdowns and developing promotions that encourage new business.

Conscious parallelism Similar patterns of conduct among competitors.

Consensus 1: Finding a proposal acceptable enough that all team members can support the decision and no member opposes it. **2:** Employed in choice and implementation tactics within collectivist cultures to maintain harmony and unity.

Consequence The result obtained when a decision alternative is chosen and a chance event occurs. A measure of the consequence is often called a payoff.

Conservative approach 1: An approach to choosing a decision alternative without using probabilities. For a maximization problem, it leads to choosing the decision alternative that maximizes the minimum payoff; for a minimization problem, it leads to choosing the decision alternative that minimizes the maximum payoff. **2:** A policy where all of the fixed assets, all of the permanent current assets, and some of the temporary current assets of a firm are financed with long-term capital.

Conservative strategy A strategy that uses a majority of long-term sources to fulfill its financing needs. This strategy results in a higher current ratio but a lower level but more stable level of profitability during periods of normal yield curves.

Consideration A type of leader behavior that describes the extent to which a leader is sensitive to subordinates, respects their ideas and feelings, and establishes mutual trust.

Consigned stocks Inventories, generally of finished goods, that are in the possession of customers, dealers, agents, and so on, but remain the property of the manufacturer by agreement with those in possession. *Syn:* consignment inventory.

Consignment An arrangement whereby a retailer obtains an inventory item without obligation. If not sold, the inventory can be returned.

Consistency principle A requirement that accounting methods be used consistently from one period to the next unless conditions have changed that make it appropriate to switch to another method to provide more useful information.

Consistent norms Values that are more culturally specific, but that are consistent with hypernorms and other legitimate norms.

Consol A perpetual bond issued by the British government to consolidate past debts; in general, any perpetual bond.

Consolidated financial statements Financial statements resulting from combining parent and subsidiary company statements. The statements prepared by the parent company that essentially portray the financial position and results of operations of the parent and its subsidiaries as though they were one economic unit.

Consolidation The creation of a new corporation by the transfer of assets and liabilities from two or more existing corporations.

Constancy of purpose Occurs when goals and objectives are properly aligned to the organizational vision and mission.

Constant dollar accounting *See:* Constant monetary unit restatement.

Constant growth model Also called the Gordon Model, it is used to find the value of a stock that is expected to experience constant growth.

Constant monetary unit restatement A general term for restating historical cost basis financial statements for changes in general purchasing power of the monetary unit.

Constant payout ratio Payment of a constant *percentage* of earnings as dividends each year.

Constraint 1: Restriction or limitation imposed on a problem **2:** A constraint may range from the intangible (for example, beliefs, culture) to the tangible (for example, posted rule prohibiting smoking, buildup of work-in-process awaiting the availability of a machine or operator).

Constraint management Pertains to identifying a constraint and working to remove or diminish the constraint, while dealing with resistance to change.

Construct A formally proposed concept representing relationships between empirically verifiable events and based on observed facts.

Construct validity Validity showing a relationship between an abstract characteristic and job performance.

Constructive notice Knowledge imputed by law.

Consultative Decision-making approach in which a person talks to others and considers their input before making a decision.

Consultative selling Process of helping customers reach their strategic goals by using the products and expertise of the sales organization.

Consulting services Services that are provided in the areas of management expertise on such issues as transportation and logistics.

Consumer behavior Process by which individuals or groups select, use, or dispose of goods, services, ideas, or experiences to satisfy needs and wants.

Consumer decision making Process that typically involves whether to purchase, what to purchase, when to purchase, from whom to purchase, and how to pay for a purchase.

Consumer goods Goods normally used for personal, family, or household purposes.

Consumer market customers End users of a product or service.

Consumer profiling The collection of information about individual shoppers in order to know and serve consumers better.

Consumer sovereignty Buyer supremacy in the marketplace.

Consumer-to-Consumer (C2C) model A form of e-commerce model in which consumers deal directly with consumers, avoiding any intermediaries. eBay is an example of a C2C model

Consumer's risk For a sampling plan, refers to the probability of acceptance of a lot, the quality of which has a designated numerical value representing a level that is seldom desirable. Usually the designated value will be the lot tolerance percent defective (LTPD). Also called *beta risk* or *type 2 error*.

Consumers' surplus The value to customers of goods and services above and beyond the amount they pay sellers.

Consumption satiation Occurs when the more units of a product that are consumed in a short period of time, the less the added value of consuming another unit of the same product and the greater the variety-seeking behavior.

Container ships Ships designed to carry standardized containers, which greatly facilitate loading and unloading as well as intermodal transfers.

Content The Environmental Impact Statement (EIS) must contain, among other items, a detailed statement of the environmental impact of the proposed action, any adverse environmental effects that cannot be avoided, and alternative proposals. *See* Environmental inpact statement.

Content analysis A set of procedures for transforming unstructured written material into a format for analysis.

Content theories 1: A group of theories that emphasize the needs that motivate people. **2:** refer to theories on motivation that ask, "What motivates an individual to behave?"

Content validity Validity measured by use of a logical, nonstatistical method to identify the KSAs and other characteristics necessary to perform a job.

Contests and sweepstakes Sales promotion techniques in which customers have a chance of winning a special prize based on entering a contest in which the entrant competes with others, or a sweepstakes in which all entrants have an equal chance of winning a prize.

Contextual dimensions Traits that characterize the whole organization, including its size, technology, environment, and goals.

Contingency 1: An amount a contractor may include in a proposal to cover unexpected costs that may arise during a project; management reserve. **2:** A theory meaning one thing depends on other things; the organization's situation dictates the correct management approach.

Contingency approach A model of leadership that describes the relationship between leadership styles and specific organizational situations.

Contingency decision making A style of decision making committed to recognizing the uniqueness of different situations and therefore using different approaches when confronting varying situations, cultures, and so on.

Contingency graph Graph showing the net profit to a speculator in currency options under various exchange rate scenarios.

Contingency plans Plans that define company responses to specific situations, such as emergencies, setbacks, or unexpected conditions.

Contingency view An extension of the humanistic perspective in which the successful resolution of organizational problems is thought to depend on managers' identification of key variables in the situation at hand.

Contingent liability A possible liability. If the likelihood of payment is "probable," the contingent liability must be reported as a liability on the financial statements; if likelihood of payment is reasonably possible, it must be disclosed in the footnotes to the financial statements; if likelihood of payment is remote, no mention of the possible liability needs to be made.

Contingent workers People who work for an organization, but not on a permanent or full-time basis, including temporary placements, contracted professionals, or leased employees.

Continuation after expulsion The expelled partner is entitled to be discharged from partnership liabilities and to receive cash in the net amount due him from the partnership.

Continuation after wrongful dissolution The aggrieved partners can continue the firm by paying the withdrawing partner the value of his interest less the amount of damages they sustained as a result of the breach.

Continuation agreement of the partners Agreement that permits the remaining partners to keep partnership property and to carry on its business; provides a specified settlement to the departing partner.

Continuous budgeting A method of budgeting that provides for maintaining a 12 month projection into the future.

Continuous compounding A situation in which interest is added continuously rather than at discrete points in time.

Continuous improvement A management philosophy embraced by companies who constantly improve the quality and productivity of their operations in order to survive. A wide range of approaches to continuous improvement exist, including total quality management (TQM), and statistical process control (SPC).

Continuous probability distribution 1: A graph or formula representing the probability of a particular numeric value of continuous (variable) data, based on a particular type of process that produces the data. **2:** The number of possible outcomes is unlimited or infinite.

Continuous process improvement Includes the actions taken throughout an organization to increase the effectiveness and efficiency of activities and processes in order to provide added benefits to the customer and organization. It is considered a subset of total quality management and operates according to the premise that organizations can always make improvements. Continuous improvement can also be equated with reducing process variation.

Continuous process production A completely mechanized manufacturing process in which there is no starting or stopping.

Continuous reinforcement schedule A schedule in which every occurrence of the desired behavior is reinforced.

Continuously compounding When compounding is done every moment.

Contra accounts Accounts that are offset against other accounts.

Contra asset An account that affects an asset account, such as the allowance for uncollectible accounts receivable or accumulated depreciation.

Contract 1: An agreement between two or more parties that can be legally enforced. A contractual relationship between two or more commercial entities allows the shifting of risk between the entities in order to obtain the stated purpose of the contract. **2:** An agreement between a contractor, who agrees to provide a product or service (deliverables), and a customer, who agrees to pay the contractor a certain amount of money in return.

Contract enforcement Usually, a contract entered into by firms from different nations that stipulates whose law is applied in the event of default. However, some countries' legal

GLOSSARY

systems mandate that the laws of the nation where the contract was signed shall be applied. Other legal systems mandate that the laws of the country where the contract was executed shall be applied.

Contract manufacturing Using another firm for the manufacture of goods so that the marketer may concentrate on the research and development as well as marketing aspects of the operation.

Contract rate The interest rate specified on a bond; sometimes called the *coupon interest rate.*

Contract review Systematic activities carried out by an organization before agreeing to a contract to ensure that requirements for quality are adequately defined, free from ambiguity, documented, and can be realized by the supplier.

Contracting cost motive Theoretical motive for trade credit extension in which the buyers' sales contracting costs are reduced in that they can inspect the quantity and quality of the goods prior to payment due to the delayed payment offered.

Contractual alliances Many enterprises enter foreign markets via non–equity-based joint ventures, often referred to as contractual alliances or strategic alliances.

Contractual hedging A multinational firm's use of contracts to minimize its transaction exposure.

Contractual vertical marketing systems Systems that use a contract to govern the working relationship between channel members and include wholesaler-sponsored voluntary groups, retailer-owned cooperatives, and franchised retail programs.

Contrast error Tendency to rate people relative to others rather than against performance standards.

Contribution The contribution of a member to a limited liability company may be cash, property, services rendered, a promissory note, or other obligation to contribute cash, property, or to perform services.

Contribution margin Sales less variable costs and variable selling and administrative expenses.

Contribution margin analysis The systematic examination of the differences between planned and actual contribution margins.

Contribution margin ratio The percentage of each sales dollar that is available to cover the fixed costs and provide an operating income.

Contributions May be cash, property, services, or a promise to contribute cash, property, or services.

Contributor A national subsidiary with a distinctive competence, such as product development.

Contributory negligence Not a defense in the majority of states.

Contributory plan Pension plan in which the money for pension benefits is paid in by both employees and employers.

Control 1: A policy or procedure that is part of internal control. **2:** Refers to restrictions on what a foreign investor may own or control in another country. **3:** The direct or indirect possession of the power to direct the management and policies of a person through ownership of securities, by contract, or otherwise. **4:** The general partners have almost exclusive control and management of the limited partnership; a limited partner who participates in the control of the limited partnership may lose limited liability.

Control activities or procedures Specific error-checking routines performed by company personnel.

Control chart Basic tool that consists of a chart with upper and lower control limits on which values of some statistical measure for a series of samples or subgroups are plotted. It frequently shows a central line to help detect a trend of plotted values toward either control limit. It is used to monitor and analyze variation from a process to see whether the process is in statistical control.

Control environment The actions, policies, and procedures that reflect the overall attitudes of top management, the directors, and the owners about control and its importance to the entity.

Control limits Trigger points that signal a purchase or sale of securities, and are part of the decision-making apparatus in the Miller-Orr cash management model.

Control plan Document that may include the characteristics for quality of a product or service, measurements, and methods of control.

Control sample That part of a sample group that is left unchanged and receives no special treatment, and serves as a basis of comparison to allow analysis of the results of an experiment.

Control system A system that compares the actual performance (results) with planned performance (goals) so that management may take appropriate action as necessary.

Control unit The circuitry in the CPU that fetches instructions and data from the primary memory, decodes the instructions, passes them to the ALU for execution, and stores the results in the primary memory.

Controllable costs Cost that can be influenced (increased, decreased, or eliminated) by someone such as a manager or factory worker.

Controllable expenses Costs that can be influenced by the decisions of a manager.

Controllable input The decision alternatives or inputs to a simulation model that can be specified by the decision maker.

Controllable variance The difference between the actual amount of variable factory overhead cost incurred and the amount of variable factory overhead budgeted for the standard product.

Controlled Disbursement Accounts (CDA) Checking accounts in which funds are not deposited until checks are presented for payment, usually on a daily basis.

Controller The chief management accountant of a business.

Controlling account The account in the general ledger that summarizes the balances of the accounts in a subsidiary ledger.

Controls Constraints applied to a system to ensure proper use and security standards.

Convenience quota sample Sample of consumers that is not randomly sampled from a population (for example, users of the product) but is obtained through approaching people in a mall to participate. Quotas are placed on how many men and women should be interviewed (for example, 200 of each) or some other demographic categorization such as age, education, or income.

Convenience translation Translation of currency using the year-end exchange rates.

Conventional marketing channel Channel in which each channel member is loosely aligned with the others and takes a short-term orientation.

Conversation analysis A study of talk-in-interaction with people (that is, analyzing spoken words).

Conversational principles Those principles governing verbal and nonverbal communication applicable in all aspects of cross-cultural communication.

Conversion The process of abandoning an old information system and implementing a new one.

Conversion costs The combination of direct labor and factory overhead costs.

Conversion rate The percentage of shoppers that enter the store that are converted into purchasers.

Conversion Ratio (CR) The number of shares of common stock that can be obtained by converting a convertible bond or a share of convertible preferred stock.

Conversion value The equivalent amount of another currency at a given exchange rate.

Convertible bond A bond that is exchangeable, at the option of the holder, for common stock of the issuing firm.

Convertible security A security, usually a bond or preferred stock, that is exchangeable at the option of the holder for the common stock of the issuing firm.

Cookie A small file that a Web site places on a visitor's hard disk so that the Web site can remember something about the visitor later, such as an ID number or user name.

Cooptation Situation that occurs when leaders from important sectors in the environment are made part of an organization.

Coordinated decentralization The providing of overall corporate strategy by headquarters while granting subsidiaries the freedom to implement it within established ranges.

Coordinated intervention A currency value management method whereby the central banks of the major nations simultaneously intervene in the currency markets, hoping to change a currency's value.

Coordination The quality of collaboration across departments.

Coordination costs The time and energy needed to coordinate the activities of a team to enable it to perform its task.

Co-payment Employee's payment of a portion of the cost of both insurance premiums and medical care.

Coping with uncertainty A source of power for a department that reduces uncertainty for other departments by obtaining prior information, prevention, and absorption.

Copromotion agreement A product that is promoted jointly by two companies under the same brand name and marketing plan. Generally the manufacturing company handles receivables, inventory, and so on, and pays a commission to the copromotor. Compensation is almost always based on the product sales level.

Copyright The exclusive right to publish and sell a literary, artistic, or musical composition.

Core Benefit Proposition (CBP) Primary benefit or purpose for which a customer buys a product. The CBP may reside in the physical good or service performance, or it may come from augmented dimensions of the product.

Core competence 1: A business activity that an organization does particularly well in comparison to competitors. **2:** A unique capability that creates high value and that differentiates the organization from its competition.

Core processes Have a major impact on the strategic goals of an organization.

Corporate agency services Security-related services, some of which are related to short-term borrowing and investing, offered by financial institutions to publicly held corporations.

Corporate charter A document filed with the secretary of the state in which the firm is incorporated that provides information about the company, including its name, address, directors, and amount of capital stock.

Corporate citizenship Includes corporate social responsiveness and corporate social performance.

Corporate culture 1: (While the word "corporate" typically appears, the culture referred to may be that of any type of organization, large or small.) Relates to the collective beliefs, values, attitudes, manners, customs, behaviors, and artifacts unique to an organization. **2:** Refers to an organization's practice, such as its symbols, heroes, and rituals, and its values, such as its employees' perception of good/evil, beautiful/ugly, normal/abnormal, and rational/irrational. The practice aspects differ from corporation to corporation within a national culture, and the value aspects vary from country to country.

Corporate governance 1: The method by which a firm is being governed, directed, administered, or controlled and to the goals for which it is being governed. Corporate governance is concerned with the relative roles, rights, and accountability of such stakeholder groups as owners, boards of directors, managers, employees, and others who assert to be stakeholders. **2:** Belief that because vast amounts of wealth and power have become concentrated in a small number of corporations, which are in turn controlled by a small group of people, that they therefore have a responsibility to undertake projects to benefit society.

Corporate income tax A tax applied to all residual earnings, regardless of what is retained or what is distributed as dividends.

Corporate-level strategy The level of strategy concerned with the question "What business are we in?" Pertains to the organization as a whole and the combination of business units and product lines that make it up.

Corporate public affairs and public affairs management The management processes that focus on the formalization and institutionalization of corporate public policy. The public affairs function is a logical and increasingly prevalent component of the overall strategic management process.

Corporate public policy A firm's posture, stance, strategy, or position regarding the public, social, and ethical aspects of stakeholders and corporate functioning.

Corporate social performance model Includes social responsibility categories, philosophy (or mode) of social responsiveness, and social (or stakeholder) issues involved.

Corporate social responsibility An objective to respond appropriately everywhere possible to societal expectations and environmental needs.

Corporate social responsiveness The action-oriented variant of corporate social responsibility.

Corporate sponsorships Involve investments in events or causes for the purpose of achieving various corporate objectives, such as increasing sales volume, enhancing a company's reputation or a brand's image, and increasing brand awareness.

Corporate university An in-house training and education facility that offers broad-based learning opportunities for employees.

Corporate (within-firm) risk Risk that does not take into consideration the effects of stockholders' diversification; it is measured by a project's effect on the firm's earnings variability.

Corporate vertical marketing systems Systems that exist where one channel institution owns multiple levels of distribution and typically consists of either a manufacturer that has integrated vertically forward to reach the consumer or a retailer that has integrated vertically backward to create a self-supply network.

Corporation 1: A legal entity created by a state, separate and distinct from its owners and managers, having unlimited life, easy transferability of ownership, and limited liability. **2:** An artificial entity created by the state and existing apart from its owners. **3:** A separate legal entity that is organized in accordance with state or federal statutes and in which ownership is divided into shares of stock.

Corporation by estoppel Prevents a person from raising the question of a corporation's existence.

Corporation *de facto* A corporation not formed in compliance with the statute but recognized for most purposes as a corporation.

Corporation *de jure* A corporation formed in substantial compliance with the incorporation statute and having all corporate attributes.

Corporations as moral agents Situation that exists because a corporation is a statutory entity, making it difficult to resolve whether it should be morally accountable.

Corrective action Action taken to eliminate the root cause(s) and symptom(s) of an existing deviation or nonconformity to prevent recurrence.

Corrective control An action or procedure that will ensure the correction of an error or omission.

Correlation Refers to the measure of the relationship between two sets of numbers or variables.

Correlation coefficient 1: Describes the magnitude and direction of the relationship between two variables. **2:** Index number giving the relationship between a predictor and a criterion variable.

Correlation coefficient, r A measure of the degree of relationship between two variables.

Correspondent banks Banks located in different countries and unrelated by ownership that have a reciprocal agreement to provide services to each other's customers.

Correspondent firms *See:* Representative firms.

Corruption Dishonesty that involves the following schemes: 1) bribery, 2) conflicts of interest, 3) economic extortion, and 4) illegal gratuities.

Cost 1: The amount the customer has agreed to pay for acceptable project deliverables. **2:** A disbursement of cash (or a commitment to pay cash in the future) for the purpose of generating revenues.

Cost accounting system A system used to accumulate manufacturing costs for financial reporting and decision-making purposes.

Cost allocation The process of assigning indirect cost to a cost object, such as a job.

Cost and Freight (CFR) Seller quotes a price for the goods, including the cost of transportation to the named port of debarkation. Cost and choice of insurance are left to the buyer.

Cost-based transfer pricing The price one segment of a company charges another segment of the same company for the transfer of a good or a service based on some type of cost. Examples include variable manufacturing costs, full manufacturing (absorption) costs, and full product costs.

Cost-benefit analysis An evaluation of the costs incurred by a system or project and the benefits gained by the system or the project.

Cost behavior The manner in which a cost changes in relation to its activity base (driver).

Cost center A responsibility center in which a manager is accountable for costs only. A decentralized unit in which the department or division manager has responsibility for the control of costs incurred and the authority to make decisions that affect these costs.

Cost concept The basis for entering the exchange price, or cost, into the accounting records.

Cost distortion Inaccurate product costs that are the result of applying a cost allocation method that is inappropriate for the situation.

Cost driver Any factor that causes a change in the cost of an activity.

Cost driver analysis In activity-based cost accounting, the examination of the impact of cost drivers. The results of this analysis are useful in the continuous improvement of cost, quality, and delivery times.

Cost estimate Estimate of total cost of an activity based on the types and quantities of resources required for that activity.

Cost, Insurance, and Freight (CIF) Seller quotes a price including insurance, all transportation, and miscellaneous charges to the point of debarkation from the vessel or aircraft.

Cost leadership 1: A pricing tactic where a company offers an identical product or service at a lower cost than the competition. **2:** A type of competitive strategy with which the organization aggressively seeks efficient facilities, cuts costs, and employs tight cost controls to be more efficient than competitors.

Cost method 1: A method of accounting for an investment in common stock, by which the investor recognizes as income its share of cash dividends of the investee. **2:** An inventory valuation technique that provides a book valuation of inventory based solely on the retailer's cost of merchandise including freight.

Cost object Any customer, product, service, project, or other work unit for which a separate cost measurement is desired.

Cost of communication The cost of communicating electronically or by telephone with other locations. These costs have been drastically reduced through the use of fiber-optic cables.

Cost of goods sold The cost of goods sold to customers; calculated by subtracting ending inventory from the sum of beginning inventory plus purchases.

Cost of goods sold budget A budget in which the desired ending inventory and the estimated beginning inventory data are combined with data from direct materials budget, direct labor budget, and factory overhead cost budget.

Cost of Living Allowance (COLA) An allowance paid during assignment overseas to enable the employee to maintain the same standard of living as at home.

Cost of merchandise sold The cost of merchandise purchased by a merchandise business and sold.

Cost of new common equity, k^e The cost of external equity; based on the cost of retained earnings, but increased for flotation costs.

Cost of Poor Quality (COPQ) Costs associated with providing poor-quality products or services.

Cost of preferred stock, k_{ps} The rate of return investors require on the firm's preferred stock. k_{ps} is calculated as the preferred dividend, D_{ps}, divided by the net issuing price, NP.

Cost of production report A report prepared periodically by a processing department, summarizing 1) the units for which the department is accountable and the disposition of those units and 2) the costs incurred by the department and the allocation of those costs between completed and incomplete production.

Cost of Quality (COQ) Costs incurred in assuring quality of a product or service. There are four categories of poor quality costs: internal failure costs (costs associated with defects found before delivery of the product or service); external failure costs (costs associated with defects found during or after product or service delivery); appraisal costs (costs incurred to determine the degree of conformance to quality requirements); and prevention costs (costs incurred to keep failure and appraisal costs to a minimum).

Cost of quality report A report summarizing the costs, percent of total, and percent of sales by appraisal, prevention, internal failure, and external failure cost of quality categories.

Cost of retained earnings, k_s The rate of return required by stockholders on a firm's existing common stock.

Cost of risk The sum of 1) outlays to reduce risks, 2) the opportunity cost of activities forgone due to risk considerations, 3) expenses of strategies to finance potential losses, and 4) the cost of reimbursed losses.

Cost per equivalent unit The rate used to allocate costs between completed and partially completed production in a process costing system.

Cost per thousand 1: Calculated by dividing the cost of an ad placed in a particular ad vehicle (for example, certain magazine) by the number of people (expressed in thousands) who are exposed to that vehicle. **2:** A technique used to evaluate advertisements in different media based on cost. The cost per thousand is the cost of the advertisement divided by the number of people viewing it, which is then multiplied by 1,000.

Cost Per Thousand—Target Market (CPM-TM) A technique used to evaluate advertisements in different media based on cost. The cost per thousand per target market is the cost of the advertisement divided by the number of people in the target market viewing it, which is then multiplied by 1,000.

Cost Performance Index (CPI) A measure of the cost efficiency with which the project is being performed; the cumulative earned value divided by the cumulative actual cost.

Cost price approach An approach to transfer pricing that uses cost as the basis for setting the transfer price.

Cost-plus method A pricing policy in which there is a full allocation of foreign and domestic costs to the product.

Cost-reimbursement contract A contract in which a customer agrees to pay a contractor for all actual costs incurred during a project, plus some agreed-upon profit.

Cost Variance (CV) 1: An indicator of cost performance; the cumulative earned value minus the cumulative actual cost. **2:** The difference between actual cost and the flexible budget at actual volumes.

Cost-benefit analysis Analysis that quantifies in monetary terms the benefits and costs of alternatives.

Cost-volume-profit analysis The systematic examination of the relationships among selling prices, volume of sales and production, costs, expenses, and profits.

Cost-volume-profit chart A chart used to assist management in understanding the relationships among costs, expenses, sales, and operating profit or loss.

Costly trade credit Credit taken in excess of "free" trade credit, whose cost is equal to the discount lost.

Council on Environmental Quality (CEQ) Three-member advisory group in the Executive Office of the president that makes recommendations to the president on environmental matters.

Count chart Control chart for evaluating the stability of a process in terms of the count of events of a given classification occurring in a sample.

Countercyclical Inferior goods whose demand falls with rising income, and rises with falling income.

Counterpurchase 1: A refinement of simple barter that unlinks the timing of the two transactions. **2:** Exchange of goods between two parties under two distinct contracts expressed in monetary terms.

Countertrade 1: A buyer of a product pays the seller with another product of the equivalent monetary value. **2:** Sale of goods to one country which is linked to the purchase or exchange of goods from that same country.

Countervailing power Buyer market power that offsets seller market power, and vice versa.

Count-per-unit chart Control chart for evaluating the stability of a process in terms of the average count of events of a given classification per unit occurring in a sample.

Country-related cultural factors framework Identifies certain national cultural dimensions and their impact on decision-making behavior.

Country risk Characteristics of the host country, including political and financial conditions, that can affect the MNC's cash flows. The possibility of loss of assets due to political, economic, or regulatory instability in a nation in which business is being conducted.

Coupon-equivalent yield Interest return figure calculated based on a 365-day year instead of 360 days. For a discount security maturing within one year, it is also adjusted to account for the fact that the price paid is less than the face value, which increases the true yield.

Coupon interest rate The stated annual rate of interest paid on a bond.

Coupon payment The specified number of dollars of interest paid each period, generally each six months, on a bond.

Coupon security One which pays interest periodically prior to maturity.

Coupons Sales promotion tool in which the shopper is offered a price discount on a specific item if the retailer is presented with the appropriate coupon at time of purchase.

Coups d'état A forced change in a country's government, often resulting in attacks of foreign firms and policy changes by the new government.

Coverage The theoretical maximum number of consumers in the retailer's target market that can be reached by a medium and not the number actually reached.

Coverage ratios Ratios that measure the degree of protection for long-term creditors and investors.

Covered interest arbitrage Investment in a foreign money market security with a simultaneous forward sale of the currency denominating that security.

Covert operations Placing an agent in an undercover role in order to observe the suspect.

Cp Widely used process capability index. It is expressed as:

$$\frac{\text{upper spec limit} - \text{lower spec limit}}{6\sigma}$$

Cpk Widely used process capability index. It is expressed as: (ratio with smallest answer)

$$\frac{\text{upper specification limit} - \overline{X}}{3\sigma}$$

or

$$\frac{\overline{X} - \text{lower specification limit}}{3\sigma}$$

CQI Continuous quality improvement.

Craft technology Technology characterized by a fairly stable stream of activities but in which the conversion process is not analyzable or well-understood.

Crash cost The estimated cost of completing an activity in the shortest possible time (the crash time).

Crash time The shortest estimated length of time in which an activity can be completed.

Crawford Slip Method Method of gathering and presenting anonymous data from a group.

Creative departments Organizational departments that initiate change, such as research and development, engineering, design, and systems analysis.

Creativity The generation of novel ideas that may meet perceived needs or offer opportunities for the organization.

Creature of the state A corporation may be formed only by substantial compliance with a state incorporation statute.

Credence attributes Cannot be evaluated confidently even immediately after consumption.

Credit The right side of an account; the amount entered on the right side of an account; to enter an amount on the right side of an account.

Credit administration The establishment of credit policy and planning, organizing, directing, and controlling all aspects of the credit function.

Credit decision process Sequence beginning with the marketing contact with potential customers and ending with the credit extension decision. Includes credit investigation, customer information contacts, written document preparation, credit file establishment, and financial analysis.

Credit extension The decision to sell on credit to a customer.

Credit-granting decision Determination of whether and how much credit to give customers, a process which involves four distinct steps: development of credit standards, getting necessary information about customers, application of credit standards, and setting credit limits.

Credit interchange bureaus Departments of local credit associations that provide information on the credit history of local businesses and individuals.

Credit limit Where credit is extended, the maximum dollar amount that cumulative credit purchases can reach for a given customer. Also known as the credit line.

Credit memorandum The form issued by a seller to inform a buyer that a credit has been posted to the buyer's account receivable.

Credit period The length of time for which credit is granted; after that time, the credit account is considered delinquent.

Credit policy A set of decisions that includes a firm's credit standards, credit terms, methods used to collect credit accounts, and credit monitoring procedures.

Credit reporting agencies Sources of business credit information, such as Dun & Bradstreet.

Credit scoring models Evaluation approach that weights variables depending on their helpfulness in discriminating between "good" and "bad" applicants, based on past payment histories. These models are developed with the assistance of computerized statistical techniques such as multiple discriminant analysis.

Credit standards Standards that indicate the minimum financial strength a customer must have to be granted credit.

Credit terms Specification of when invoiced amounts are due and whether a cash discount can be taken for earlier payment.

Creditor A person or entity owed money by a debtor.

Creditor's rights A partner's interest is subject to the claims of creditors, who may obtain a charging order against the partner's interest.

Crime A corporation may be criminally liable for violations of statutes imposing liability without fault or for an offense perpetrated by a high corporate officer or its board of directors.

Criminal law Branch of law that deals with offenses of a public nature or against society.

Criminal sanctions 1: Individuals who willfully violate the 1934 Act are subject to a fine of not more than $1 million and/or imprisonment of not more than 10 years. **2:** Willful violations are subject to a fine of not more than $10,000 and/or imprisonment of not more than five years.

Crisis A major, unpredictable event that has potentially negative results. The event and its aftermath may significantly damage an organization and its employees, products, services, financial condition, and reputation.

Crisis resolution stage The final stage of a crisis and the goal of all crisis management efforts.

Criteria A set of standards against which an internal control system can be measured in determining its effectiveness.

Criteria for successful segmentation Includes target markets that are heterogeneous, measurable, substantial, actionable, and accessible.

Criterion Standard, rule, or test upon which a judgment or decision can be based.

Criterion-related validity Validity measured by a procedure that uses a test as the predictor of how well an individual will perform on the job.

Critical commodities list A U.S. Department of Commerce file containing information about products that are either particularly sensitive to national security or controlled for other purposes.

Critical incident Event that has greater than normal significance, often used as a learning or feedback opportunity.

Critical path 1: The sequence of tasks that takes the longest time and determines a project's completion date. **2:** In a network diagram, any path of activities with zero or negative total slack. *See:* Most critical path.

Critical Path Method (CPM) 1: Activity-oriented project management technique that uses arrow-diagramming techniques to demonstrate both the time and cost required to complete a project. It provides one time estimate—normal time. **2:** A network planning technique.

Critical ratio A dispatching rule that calculates a priority index number by dividing the time to due date remaining by the expected elapsed time to finish the job. For example,

$$\text{critical ratio} = \frac{\text{time remaining}}{\text{work remaining}} = \frac{30}{40} = .75$$

A ratio less than 1.0 indicates the job is behind schedule, a ratio greater than 1.0 indicates the job is ahead of schedule, and a ratio of 1.0 indicates the job is on schedule.

Critical success factors Processes and their results that are critical to the success of business units. One approach to defining requirements for information systems is the outlining of CSFs by managers.

Cross-border factoring Factoring by a network of factors across borders. The exporter's factor can contact correspondent factors in other countries to handle the collections of accounts receivable.

Cross-cultural communication Effective communication across nations/cultures can only take place when the sender encodes the message using language, idioms, norms and values, and so on, that are familiar to the receiver or when the receiver is familiar with the language, idioms, and so on, used by the sender. Also, the sender and receiver must be aware of both his or her own and the other's environmental, cultural, sociocultural, and psychocultural contexts.

Cross-cultural message adjustment The process of adjusting and adapting incoming signifiers to the existing repository of signs, and of adapting and adjusting the repository of signifieds to create new signs.

Cross-cultural research Conducted by researchers from one culture to ascertain how people in one or more other cultures behave—usually to identify the similarities and differences existing among the cultures.

Cross-cultural social responsibility A firm's actions must take into account not only the well-being of stockholders, but also the well-being of the community, the employees, and the customers.

Cross-currency swap An agreement by two parties to exchange their liabilities or assets in different currencies.

Cross exchange rate Exchange rate between currency A and currency B, given the values of currencies A and B with respect to a third currency.

Cross-functional team A group of employees from various functional departments that meet as a team to resolve mutual problems.

Cross hedge A hedge that uses a futures contract that has a different underlying instrument from the cash market instrument being hedged.

Cross hedging Hedging an open position in one currency with a hedge on another currency that is highly correlated with the first currency. This occurs when for some reason the common hedging techniques cannot be applied to the first currency. A cross hedge is not a perfect hedge, but can substantially reduce the exposure.

Cross-marketing activities A reciprocal arrangement whereby each partner provides the other access to its markets for a product.

Cross-price elasticity Responsiveness of demand for one product to changes in the price of another.

Cross rates Exchange rate quotations which do not include the U.S. dollar as one of the two currencies quoted.

Crossover rate The discount rate at which the NPV profiles of two projects cross and, thus, at which the projects' NPVs are equal.

Cross-sectional analysis Analysis of relationships among a cross-section of firms, countries, or some other variable at a given point in time.

Cross-subsidization The use of resources accumulated in one part of the world to fight a competitive battle in another.

Crown jewels Firms either sell or threaten to sell their major assets (crown jewels) when faced with a takeover threat. This tactic often involves a lockup and is sometimes called "scorched earth" strategy.

Cue Refers to any object or phenomenon in the environment that is capable of eliciting a response.

Cultural assimilator A program in which trainees for overseas assignments must respond to scenarios of specific situations in a particular country.

Cultural barriers Business behavior in one culture does not transfer well to another culture due to cultural differences. For example, Americans' "spirit of competitiveness" culture does not transfer well to "spirit of cooperation" cultures, such as Japan.

Cultural briefing Predeparture education and orientation of the expatriate and his or her family about the foreign country. The briefing includes the country's cultural traditions, history, government, economy, living conditions, and so on.

Cultural contexts *See:* Cross-cultural communication.

Cultural convergence Increasing similarity among cultures accelerated by technological advances.

Cultural differences The many ways in which people from different countries vary in their tastes, gestures, treatment of others, attitudes, and opinions.

Cultural environment To develop an effective international business strategy, the critical aspects of culture must be identified.

Cultural fluency A strong command of not only the language of a foreign country, but also its culture. This is required for effective cross-cultural communication.

Cultural imperialism Criticism by some that the United States is forcing its products and culture on other cultures through technological advances and the globalization of business.

Cultural leader A manager who uses signals and symbols to influence corporate culture.

Cultural relativism The belief that no culture's ethics are any better than any other's.

Cultural risk The risk of business blunders, poor customer relations, and wasted negotiations that results when firms fail to understand and adapt to the differences between their own and host countries' cultures.

Cultural-toughness dimension Through a battery of tests, an assessor determines if an applicant for an expatriate assignment has the ability to adapt to the "toughness" of a specific culture.

Cultural universals Manifestations of the total way of life of any group of people.

Culture 1: Comprises an entire set of social norms and responses that condition people's behavior; it is acquired and inculcated, a set of rules and behavior patterns that an individual learns but does not inherit at birth. **2:** System of values, beliefs, and behaviors inherent in an organization or society. *See:* Corporate culture. **3:** The buffer that people have created between themselves and the raw physical environment and includes the characteristics of the population, humanly created objects, and mobile physical structures. **4:** The set of norms, values, beliefs, understandings, and ways of thinking that is shared by members of an organization and is taught to new members as correct.

Culture changes Changes in the values, attitudes, expectations, beliefs, abilities, and behavior of employees.

Culture-free A theory proposing that managerial behavior is affected by specific situations in all cultures.

Culture/people change A change in employees' values, norms, attitudes, beliefs, and behavior.

Culture gap The difference between an organization's desired cultural norms and values and actual norms and values.

Culture shock The more pronounced reactions to the psychological disorientation that most people feel when they move for an extended period of time into a markedly different culture. What expatriates experience after the novelty of living in a new culture wears out.

Culture shock phase The third phase in the expatriation process usually begins two months into the disillusionment phase. After two months of day-to-day confusion, the expatriate faces culture shock and wishes to go back to his or her old, familiar environment.

Culture-specific A theory proposing that managerial behavior is affected by a nation's culture.

Culture strength The degree of agreement among members of an organization about the importance of specific values.

Cumulative Actual Cost (CAC) The amount that has actually been expended to accomplish all the work performed up to a specific point in time.

Cumulative Available-to-Promise (ATP) A calculation based on the available-to-promise (ATP) figure in the master schedule. Two methods of computing the cumulative available-to-promise are used, with and without lookahead calculation. The cumulative with lookahead ATP equals the ATP from the previous period plus the MPS of the period minus the backlog of the period minus the sum of the differences between the backlogs and MPSs of all future periods until, but not to include, the period where point production exceeds the backlogs. The cumulative without lookahead procedure equals the ATP in the previous period plus the MPS, minus the backlog in the period being considered. *See:* Available-to-promise.

Cumulative Budgeted Cost (CBC) The amount budgeted to accomplish all the work scheduled to be performed up to a specific point in time.

Cumulative dividends A protective feature on preferred stock that requires preferred dividends previously not paid to be paid before any common dividends can be paid.

Cumulative Earned Value (CEV) The value of the work actually performed up to a specific point in time; total budgeted cost multiplied by the percent of the work estimated to be complete.

Cumulative lead time The longest planned length of time to accomplish the activity in question. For any item planned through MRP, it is found by reviewing the lead time for each bill of material path below the item; whichever path adds up to the greatest number defines cumulative lead time. *Syn:* aggregate lead time, combined lead time, composite lead time, critical path lead time, stacked lead time. *See:* Planning time fence.

Cumulative manufacturing lead time The cumulative planned lead time when all purchased items are assumed to be in stock. *Syn:* composite manufacturing lead time.

Cumulative MRP The planning of parts and subassemblies by exploding a master schedule, as in MRP, except that the master-scheduled items and therefore the exploded requirements are time phased in cumulative form. Usually these cumulative figures cover a planning year.

Cumulative preferred stock Preferred stock that is entitled to current and past dividends before dividends may be paid on common stock.

Cumulative quantity discount A discount based on the total amount purchased over a period of time.

Cumulative reach The reach that is achieved over a period of time.

Cumulative receipts A cumulative number, or running total, as a count of parts received in a series or sequence of shipments. The cumulative receipts provide a number that can be compared with the cumulative figures from a plan developed by cumulative MRP.

Cumulative sum control chart Control chart on which the plotted value is the cumulative sum of deviations of successive samples from a target value. The ordinate of each plotted point represents the algebraic sum of the previous ordinate and the most recent deviations from the target.

Cumulative Transaction Adjustment (CTA) A balance sheet account created to maintain a balanced translation for the purchase of a subsidiary; the CTA has no effect on the firm until the subsidiary is either sold or liquidated.

Cumulative Trauma Disorders (CTDs) Muscle and skeletal injuries that occur when workers repetitively use the same muscles to perform tasks.

Cumulative voting Voting arrangement that entitles shareholders to multiply the number of votes they are entitled to cast by the number of directors for whom they are entitled to vote and to cast the product for a single candidate or to distribute the product among two or more candidates.

Currency Board System for maintaining the value of the local currency with respect to some other specified currency.

Currency call option Contract that grants the right to purchase a specific currency at a specific price (exchange rate) within a specific period of time.

Currency cocktail bond Bond denominated in a mixture (or cocktail) of currencies.

Currency diversification Process of using more than one currency as an investing or financing strategy. Exposure to a diversified currency portfolio typically results in less exchange rate risk than if all of the exposure was in a single foreign currency.

Currency exchange rate 1: The rates at which currency in another country can be exchanged for U.S. dollars. **2:** Countries' currency exchange rates fluctuate. Fluctuations can be dirty or clean. Dirty fluctuations result when a government adjusts the exchange rate up or down. Clean fluctuations are the result of supply and demand.

Currency flows The movement of currency from nation to nation, which in turn determines exchange rates.

Currency futures contract Contract specifying a standard volume of a particular currency to be exchanged on a specific settlement date.

Currency options contract A contract giving one of the parties the right to decide in the future whether an exchange will actually take place at a certain price.

Currency put option Contract granting the right to sell a particular currency at a specified price (exchange rate) within a specified period of time.

Currency swap 1: Agreement to exchange one currency for another at a specified exchange rate and date. Banks commonly serve as intermediaries between two parties who wish to engage in a currency swap. **2:** An agreement by which a firm exchanges or swaps its debt service payments in one currency for debt service payments in a different currency. The equivalent of the interest rate swap, only the currency of denomination of the debt is different.

Current account An account in the BOP statement that records the results of transactions involving merchandise, services, and unilateral transfers between countries.

Current assets 1: Cash or other assets that are expected to be converted to cash or sold or used up, usually within a year or less, through the normal operations of a business. **2:** Assets that can be easily converted into cash within a relatively short period of time (usually a year or less).

Current cost accounting *See:* Current value accounting.

Current exchange rate The exchange rate on the balance sheet date.

Current liabilities Liabilities that will be due within a short time (usually one year or less) and that are to be paid out of current assets.

Current liquidity index A cash coverage ratio found by adding beginning of period balance of cash assets and the cash flow from operations during the period and then dividing this sum by the sum of beginning of period notes payable and current maturing debt.

Current maturity The length of time remaining until a security matures. When first issued a five-year Treasury note has an original maturity of five years; one year later it has a current maturity of four years.

Current-noncurrent method A translation method in which balance sheet items classified as "current" are translated at the current exchange rate on the balance sheet date, and items classified as "noncurrent" are translated at appropriate historical rates.

Current purchasing power accounting *See:* Constant monetary unit restatement.

Current rate method A translation method that translates all assets and all liabilities at the current exchange rate—the rate on the balance sheet date. Paid-in capital accounts are translated at the applicable historical rates, dividends at the exchange rate on the date of declaration and on the income statement, and all revenue and expense items at the weighted average exchange rate for the period.

Current ratio Measure of the liquidity of a business; equal to current assets divided by current liabilities. It indicates the extent to which current liabilities are covered by assets expected to be converted into cash in the near future.

Current reality tree Technique used in applying Goldratt's Theory of Constraints.

Current transfer A current account on the Balance of Payments statement that records gifts from the residents of one country to the residents of another.

Current value accounting Valuation systems designed to show the effects of changes in prices of individual items on financial statements.

Current yield The annual interest payment on a bond divided by its current market value.

Currently attainable standards Standards that represent levels of operation that can be attained with reasonable effort.

Custody account Specialized account in which financial institution holds securities, automatically reinvests interest and other investment-related cash receipts, transfers funds per corporate instructions, monitors issuers actions such as calls and refundings, and provides a monthly statement on all account transactions.

Custom-designed software Software designed to meet the specific needs of a particular organization or department; also called tailored software.

Customary pricing A policy in which the retailer sets prices for goods and services and seeks to maintain those prices over an extended period of time.

Customer 1: The entity that provides the funds necessary to accomplish a project. A customer may be a person, an organization, or a group of people or organizations. **2:** Recipient of a product or service provided by a supplier. *See:* external customer and internal customer.

Customer-centric companies Companies that set explicit targets for retaining customers and make extraordinary efforts to exceed their customer loyalty goals.

Customer council Group usually composed of representatives from an organization's largest customers who meet to discuss common issues.

Customer delight Result achieved when customer requirements are exceeded in ways the customer finds valuable.

Customer fraud Customers not paying for goods purchased, getting something for nothing, or deceiving organizations into giving them something they should not have.

Customer involvement The active participation of customers; a characteristic of services in that customers often are actively involved in the provision of services they consume.

Customer loyalty/retention Result of an organization's plans, processes, practices, and efforts designed to deliver their services or products in ways which create retained and committed customers.

Customer-oriented The salesperson seeks to elicit customer needs/problems and then takes the necessary steps to meet those needs or solve the problem in a manner that is in the best interest of the customer.

Customer prototypes Detailed pictures and descriptions of individuals or firms in the target market for a product. Creating these descriptions helps firms envision how products and the marketing mix might best be combined to maximize profits.

Customer Relationship Management (CRM) 1: The process of identifying, attracting, differentiating, and retaining customers; relies on systematized processes to profile key segments so that marketing and retention strategies can be customized for these customers. **2:** Refers to an organization's knowledge of their customers' unique requirements and expectations, and using the information to develop a closer and more profitable link to business processes and strategies. **3:** Is comprised of an integrated information system where the fundamental unit of data collection is the customer, supplemented by relevent information about the customer.

Customer Relationship Management (CRM) systems Systems that help companies track customers' interaction with the firm and allow employees to call up information on past transactions.

Customer requirements Specifications for a project and/or attributes of a deliverable specified by a customer in a request for proposal. Requirements may include size, quantity, color, speed, and other physical or operational parameters that a contractor's proposed solution must satisfy.

Customer retention Focusing a firm's marketing efforts toward the existing customer base.

Customer satisfaction 1: Short-term, transaction-specific measure of whether customer perceptions meet or exceed customer expectations. Result of delivering a product or service that meets customer requirements, needs, and expectations. An important measure of quality. **2:** Occurs when the total shopping experience of the customer has been met or exceeded.

Customer segmentation Process of differentiating customers based on one or more dimensions for the purpose of developing a marketing strategy to address specific segments.

Customer service 1: A total corporate effort aimed at customer satisfaction; customer service levels in terms of responsiveness that inventory policies permit for a given situation. **2:** Activities of dealing with customer questions; also sometimes the department that takes customer orders or provides post-delivery services. **3:** The function within an organization responsible for taking orders from customers and ensuring that the finished goods or services are delivered at the right time and in the right condition and quantity, and are billed correctly. This function may be located in the marketing, logistics, or operations part of an organization.

Customer service and sales enhancement audit Provides management with a detailed analysis of current sales activity by location and by selling area.

Customer structure An organizational structure in which divisions are formed on the basis of customer groups.

Customer–supplier partnership Long-term relationship between a buyer and supplier characterized by teamwork and mutual confidence. The supplier is considered an extension of the buyer's organization. The partnership is based on several commitments. The buyer provides long-term contracts and uses fewer suppliers. The supplier implements quality assurance processes so that incoming inspection can be minimized. The supplier also helps the buyer reduce costs and improve product and process designs.

Customer theft Also known as shoplifting and occurs when customers or individuals disguised as customers steal merchandise from the retailer's store.

Customer value Market-perceived quality adjusted for the relative price of a product.

Customization Products are modified to fit the needs of specific markets.

Customized application A computer program designed especially for an organization to satisfy particular business needs.

Customs union Collaboration among trading countries in which members dismantle barriers to trade in goods and services and also establish a common trade policy with respect to nonmembers.

Cutoff time Deposit deadline for receiving a given day's stated availability.

Cybermall A virtual shopping mall on the Web.

Cybernetic system A system that enables corporations to monitor and coordinate the activities of its subsidiaries around the globe.

Cycle counting An inventory accuracy audit technique where inventory is counted on a cyclic schedule rather than once a year. A cycle inventory count is usually taken on a regular, defined basis (often more frequently for high-value or fast-moving items and less frequently for low-value or slow-moving items). Most effective cycle counting systems require the counting of a certain number of items every workday with each item counted at a prescribed frequency. The key purpose of cycle counting is to identify items in error, thus triggering research, identification, and elimination of the cause of the errors.

Cycle stock One of the two main conceptual components of any item inventory, the cycle stock is the most active component, that is, that which depletes gradually as customer orders are received and is replenished cyclically when supplier orders are received. The other conceptual component of the item inventory is the safety stock, which is a cushion of protection against uncertainty in the demand or in the replenishment lead time. *Syn:* cycle inventory.

Cycle-time 1: In industrial engineering, the time between completion of two discrete units of production. For example, the cycle time of motors assembled at a rate of 120 per hour would be 30 seconds. **2:** In materials management, it refers to the length of time from when material enters a production facility until it exits. *Syn:* throughput time.

Cycle-time reduction To reduce the time that it takes, from start to finish, to complete a particular process.

Cyclical component The component of the time series model that results in periodic above-trend and below-trend behavior of the time series lasting more than one year.

Cyclical fluctuation Rhythmic fluctuation in an economic series due to expansion or contraction in the overall economy.

Cyclical normal goods Products for which demand is strongly affected by changing income.

D

Daily NPV Is the difference between the present value of a project's daily inflows and the present value of its daily outflows.

Daily transfer rule The simplest and most common transfer rule that initiates a daily transfer from the deposit bank to the concentration bank in the amount of the daily deposit.

DASD (Direct Access Storage Device) An external storage medium that allows direct storage and retrieval of records from stored files. Example: magnetic disks and optical discs.

Data 1: Facts about people, other subjects, and events. May be manipulated and processed to produce information. **2:** Raw, unsummarized, and unanalyzed facts and figures. **3:** Facts presented in descriptive, numeric, or graphic form.

Data communication The transmission and reception of digitized data in the computer, between the computer and its peripheral devices, and between computers. Data communication over a distance is called *telecommunication*.

Data Definition Language (DDL) The part of the database management system that allows the builder of a database to define the characteristics of fields and records, and the relationships among records.

Data dictionary The part of the database that contains information about the different sets of records and fields.

Data entry control Software controls whose purpose is to minimize errors in data entry, such as rejecting a Social Security number with more or fewer than nine digits.

Data Flow Diagram (DFD) A convention of four symbols used to describe external entities, data stores, processes, and direction of data flow in an information system.

Data management module In a decision support system, a database or data warehouse that allows a decision maker to conduct the intelligence phase of decision making.

Data Manipulation Language (DML) The part of a database management system that allows the user to enter commands to retrieve, update, and manipulate data in a database.

Data mart A subset of a data warehouse.

Data mining Using a special application that scours large databases for relationships among business events, such as items typically purchased together on a certain day of the week, or machinery failures that occur along with a specific use mode of a machine. Instead of the user querying the databases, the application dynamically looks for such relationships.

Data model A diagram of data entities and their relationships.

Data privacy Electronic information security that restricts secondary use of data according to laws and preferences of the subjects.

Data processing The operation of changing and manipulating data.

Data range The amount of data from which information is extracted, in terms of the number of organizational units supplying data or the length of time the data cover.

Data redundancy The existence of the same data in more than one place in a computer system. Although some data redundancy is unavoidable, efforts should be made to minimize it.

Data store Any form of data at rest, such as a filing cabinet or a database.

Data theft Theft of data or personal information through such means as sniffing, spoofing, and customer impersonation.

Data warehouse 1: A huge collection of data that supports management decision making. **2:** The use of a huge database that combines all of a company's data and allows users to access the data directly, create reports, and obtain answers to what-if questions.

Database 1: Set of interrelated, centrally controlled data files that are stored with as little redundancy as possible. A database consolidates many records previously stored in separate files into a common pool of data and serves a variety of users and data processing applications. **2:** A collection of shared, interrelated records, usually in more than one file. An approach to data management that facilitates data entry, update, and manipulation.

Database Administrator (DBA) The individual in charge of organizational databases.

Database approach An approach to maintaining data that contains a mechanism for tagging, retrieving, and manipulating data.

Database marketing Collecting and electronically storing (in a database) information about present, past, and prospective customers.

Database model The general logical structure in which records are stored within a database.

Daylight overdrafts Bookkeeping negative account balances which occur when a bank's Federal Reserve account book balance is negative during the day or it sends more funds via Fedwire than it receives, prior to final end-of-day settlements. Many of the overdrafts occur because of international funds transfers of government securities transactions.

Days of cost of goods sold invested in inventory An inventory activity measure which indicates the average number of days it takes to sell inventory.

Days inventory held The average number of days a firm holds inventory found by dividing average daily cost of goods sold into the balance sheet inventory account.

Days payables outstanding The average number of days the firm takes to pay for its purchases found by dividing average daily purchases into the balance sheet accounts payable balance.

Days purchases outstanding The average number of days a firm takes to pay its payables.

Days Sales Outstanding (DSO) Measure of how long a company is taking to collect receivables. Also known as average collection period. It is computed by taking the latest period's accounts receivables and dividing it by daily credit sales. Daily credit sales, in turn, are computed by taking the period's sales and dividing by the number of days in the period—365 when computing DSO over a yearly period. The average number of days credit customers take to pay for their purchases found by dividing average daily sales into the accounts receivable balance.

DBA (Database Administrator) The IS professional in charge of building and maintaining the organization's databases.

DBMS (Database Management System) A computer program that allows the user to construct a database, populate it with data, and manipulate the data.

Dealers Market participants which typically "take a position" in the security instrument(s) they trade, meaning they hold an inventory of securities.

Debenture A long-term bond that is not secured by a mortgage on specific property that has only the obligation of the corporation behind it.

Debit 1: The left side of an account. **2:** The amount entered on the left side of an account. **3:** To enter an amount on the left side of an account.

Debit cards Similar to credit cards except the transaction amount is immediately (or within two business days) charged against the user's checking account balance. These cards allow consumers to pay grocery and other bills through an electronic charge to their bank accounts.

Debit memorandum The form issued by a buyer to inform a seller that a debit has been posted to the seller's account payable.

Debt capital Capital that is financed by borrowing.

Debt financing Borrowing money that has to be repaid at a later date in order to start a business.

Debt ratio The ratio of total debt to total assets. It is a measure of the percentage of funds provided by creditors.

Debt security Source of capital creating no ownership interest and involving the corporation's promise to repay funds lent to it.

Debt-to-equity ratio The number of dollars of borrowed funds for every dollar invested by owners; computed as total liabilities divided by total equity.

Debtor A person or entity declaring bankruptcy.

GLOSSARY

Debugging The process of finding and correcting errors in software programs.

Decentralization 1: The separation of a business into more manageable operating units. **2:** Managers at the subsidiary are given the autonomy to make most of the important decisions relative to local matters.

Decentralized control The use of organization culture, group norms, and a focus on goals, rather than rules and procedures, to foster compliance with organizational goals.

Decentralized disbursing Corporate arrangement which allows payments to be made by divisional offices or individual stores, usually from accounts held at nearby banks.

Decentralized internal audit model In this type of organization, the internal auditors are on locations throughout the world, wherever international operations are located. Each international operation has its own internal audit organization.

Decentralized multinational organizations Organizations that give managements of the subsidiaries considerable independence of action.

Decentralized network A team communication structure in which team members freely communicate with one another and arrive at decisions together.

Decentralized planning Managers work with planning experts to develop their own goals and plans.

Decentralized processing system A collection system that has the company's various field offices or stores receive payments from the company's customers.

Decentralized transfer initiation The cash transfer decision initiated by the field office manager.

Deceptive advertising Occurs when a retailer makes false or misleading advertising claims about the physical makeup of a product, the benefits to be gained by its use, or the appropriate uses for the product.

Deceptive pricing Occurs when a misleading price is used to lure customers into the store; usually there are hidden charges or the item advertised may be unavailable.

Decision A choice that must be made from between two or more alternatives.

Decision learning A process of recognizing and admitting mistakes that allows managers and organizations to acquire the experience and knowledge to perform more effectively in the future.

Decision making The process of defining the problem, identifying the alternatives, determining the criteria, evaluating the alternatives, and choosing an alternative.

Decision matrix Matrix used by teams to evaluate problems or possible solutions. For example, after a matrix is drawn to evaluate possible solutions, the team lists them in the far-left vertical column. Next, the team selects criteria to rate the possible solutions, writing them across the top row. Then, each possible solution is rated on a scale of one to five for each criterion and the rating recorded in the corresponding grid. Finally, the ratings of all the criteria for each possible solution are added to determine its total score. The total score is then used to help decide which solution deserves the most attention.

Decision nodes Nodes indicating points where a decision is made.

Decision premises Constraining frames of reference and guidelines placed by top managers on decisions made at lower levels.

Decision strategy A strategy involving a sequence of decisions and chance outcomes to provide the optimal solution to a decision problem.

Decision style Differences among people with respect to how they perceive problems and make decisions.

Decision Support System (DSS) 1: An interactive, computer-based system that uses decision models and specialized databases to support an organization's decision makers. **2:** Information systems that aid managers in making decisions based on built-in models. DSSs comprise three modules: data management, model management, and dialog management.

Decision tree A graphical representation of the decision problem that shows the sequential nature of the decision-making process.

Decision variable Another term for controllable input.

Declining-balance depreciation method A method of depreciation that provides declining periodic depreciation expense over the estimated life of an asset.

Decode To translate the symbols used in a message for the purpose of interpreting its meaning.

Decomposition method Analysis of collection experience which involves segregating the period-to-period changes in receivables into three effects: the collection effect, the sales effect, and the interaction effect.

Decoupling inventory An amount of inventory kept between entities in a manufacturing or distribution network to create independence between processes or entities. The objective of decoupling inventory is to disconnect the rate of use from the rate of supply of the item. *See:* Buffer.

Dedicated capacity A work center that is designated to produce a single item or a limited number of similar items. Equipment that is dedicated may be special equipment or may be grouped general-purpose equipment committed to a composite part.

Deductive fraud detection Determining the types of frauds that can occur and then using query techniques and other methods to determine if those frauds may actually exist.

Deemed exports Addresses people rather than products where knowledge transfer could lead to a breach of export restrictions.

Default risk The possibility that the issuer will not meet contractual obligations to pay interest or repay principal or will violate a covenant in a debt agreement.

Default Risk Premium (DRP) The difference between the interest rate on a U.S. Treasury bond and a corporate bond of equal maturity and marketability.

Defect A product's or service's nonfulfillment of an intended requirement or reasonable expectation for use, including safety considerations. They are often classified, such as:

- Class 1, Critical, leads directly to severe injury or catastrophic economic loss
- Class 2, Serious, leads directly to significant injury or significant economic loss
- Class 3, Major, is related to major problems with respect to intended normal or reasonably foreseeable use
- Class 4, Minor, is related to minor problems with respect to intended normal or reasonably foreseeable use. *See:* Blemish, Imperfection, and Nonconformity.

Defective corporation The associates are denied the benefits of incorporation.

Defective formation If no certificate is filed or if the one filed does not substantially meet the statutory requirements, the formation is defective and the limited liability of the limited partners is jeopardized.

Defensive merger A merger designed to make a company less vulnerable to a takeover.

Deferred asset Expenditure that has been capitalized to be expensed in the future.

Deferred expenses Items that are initially recorded as assets but are expected to become expenses over time or through the normal operations of the business. Sometimes called *prepaid expenses.*

Deferred income tax asset The future tax benefits from earnings that have already been taxed but have not been reported in the income statement yet.

Deferred income tax liability The future tax liability that results from current or past periods' earnings that have already been reported in the financial statements but have not been taxed yet.

Deferred revenues Items that are initially recorded as liabilities but are expected to become revenues over time or through the normal operations of the business. Sometimes called unearned revenues.

Deficiency A perceived, potential, or real internal control shortcoming, or an opportunity to strengthen the internal control system to provide a greater likelihood that the entity's objectives will be achieved.

Defined-benefit plan One in which an employee is promised a pension amount based on age and service.

Defined-contribution plan One in which the employer makes an annual payment to an employee's pension account.

Degree of Financial Leverage (DFL) The percentage change in earnings available to common stockholders associated with a given percentage change in earnings before interest and taxes.

Degree of individualism Extent to which individual interests prevail over group interests.

Degree of Operating Leverage (DOL) The percentage change in operating income (EBIT) associated with a given percentage change in sales.

Degree of Total Leverage (DTL) The percentage change in EPS that results from a given percentage change in sales; DTL shows the effects of both operating leverage and financial leverage.

Delay tactics Another form of leverage. A pause, or delay, by one party during a negotiation may make the other party overly anxious, causing them to make concessions. A delay tactic also allows a negotiator time to rest, recuperate, assess progress, obtain other information, and reformulate strategy.

Delegation The process managers use to transfer authority and responsibility to positions below them in the hierarchy.

Delegation of board powers Committees may be appointed to perform some but not all of the board's functions.

Deliverables The tangible items or products that the customer expects the contractor to provide during performance of the project.

Delivery Duty Paid (DDP) Seller delivers the goods, with import duties paid, including inland transportation from import point to the buyer's premises.

Delivery Duty Unpaid (DDU) Only the destination customs duty and taxes are paid by the consignee.

Delphi approach A decision-making approach in which group decision makers are geographically dispersed; this approach encourages diversity among group members and fosters creativity and original thinking in decision making.

Delphi method A qualitative forecasting method that obtains forecasts through group consensus.

Delphi studies A research tool using a group of participants with expertise in the area of concern to state and rank major future developments.

Delphi technique Collection of independent opinions without group discussion by the assessors who provide the opinions; used for various types of assessments (such as country risk assessment).

Demand 1: A need for a particular product or component. The demand could come from any number of sources, for example, customer order or forecast, an interplant requirement, or a request from a branch warehouse for a service part or for manufacturing another product. At the finished goods level, demand data are usually different from sales data because demand does not necessarily result in sales (that is, if there is no stock, there will be no sale). There are generally up to four components of demand: cyclical component, random component, seasonal component, and trend component. A demand on one partner is a demand on the partnership. **2:** Total quantity customers are willing and able to purchase.

Demand curve Relation between price and the quantity demanded, holding all else constant.

Demand density The extent to which the potential demand for the retailer's goods and services is concentrated in certain census tracts, ZIP code areas, or parts of the community.

Demand Deposit Account (DDA) Noninterest-bearing checking accounts. This account is the foundation for all other cash management services the bank might offer to the corporate client.

Demand flow An inventory system similar to the just-in-time system, but more encompassing.

Demand function Relation between demand and factors influencing its level.

Demand management 1: The function of recognizing all demands for goods and services to support the market place. It involves prioritizing demand when supply is lacking. Proper demand management facilitates the planning and use of resources for profitable business results. **2:** In marketing, the process of planning, executing, controlling, and monitoring the design, pricing, promotion, and distribution of products and services to bring about transactions that meet organizational and individual needs. *Syn:* marketing management.

Demand pull The triggering of material movement to a work center only when that work center is ready to begin the next job. It in effect eliminates the queue from in front of a work center, but it can cause a queue at the end of a previous work center.

Demand schedules Provide a systematic look at the relationship between price and quantity sold.

Demand-side market failure Cumulative effect of the marketing practice of many thousands of advertising campaigns that has a residual negative impact on the values of buyers and the demand for various products (for example, voting).

Demerit chart A control chart for evaluating a process in terms of a demerit (or quality score), such as a weighted sum of counts of various classified nonconformities.

Deming Cycle *See:* Plan-do-check-act cycle.

Deming Prize Award given annually to organizations that, according to the award guidelines, have successfully applied company-wide quality control based on statistical quality control and will keep up with it in the future. Although the award is named in honor of W. Edwards Deming, its criteria are not specifically related to Deming's teachings. There are three separate divisions for the award: the Deming Application Prize, the Deming Prize for Individuals, and the Deming Prize for Overseas Companies. The award process is overseen by the Deming Prize Committee of the Union of Japanese Scientists and Engineers in Tokyo.

Democratic leader A leader who delegates authority to others, encourages participation, and relies on expert and referent power to manage subordinates.

Demodulation The transformation of an analog signal (from a phone line) into a digital signal (so a computer can understand it).

Demographics Variables among buyers in the consumer market, which include geographic location, age, sex, marital status, family size, social class, education, nationality, occupation, and income.

Demonstrated capacity Proven capacity calculated from actual performance data, usually expressed as the average number of items produced multiplied by the standard hours per item.

Demonstrations and sampling In-store presentations with the intent of reducing the consumer's perceived risk of purchasing a product.

Denial of Service (DoS) The inability of legitimate visitors to log on to a Web site when too many malicious requests are launched by an attacker.

Denomination Refers to a security's dollar amount or face value.

Density Weight-to-volume ratio; often used to determine shipping rates.

Deontology Belief that actions must be judged by their motives and means as well as their results.

Departmental grouping A structure in which employees share a common supervisor and resources, are jointly responsible for performance, and tend to identify and collaborate with each other.

Departmentalization The basis on which individuals are grouped into departments and departments into total organizations.

Dependability Degree to which a product is operable and capable of performing its required function at any randomly chosen time during its specified operating time, provided that the product is available at the start of that period. (Nonoperation-related influences are not included.) Dependability can be expressed by the ratio:

$$\frac{\text{time available}}{\text{time available} + \text{time required}}$$

Dependent demand Demand that is directly related to or derived from the bill of material structure for other items or end products. Such demands are therefore calculated and need not and should not be forecast. A given inventory item may have both dependent and independent demand at any given time. For example, a part may simultaneously be the component of an assembly and sold as a service part. *See:* Independent demand.

Dependent demand inventory Inventory in which item demand is related to the demand for other inventory items.

Dependent variables 1: Term used in regression analysis to represent the variable that is dependent on one or more other variables. **2:** Y variable determined by X values.

Depletion The cost of metal ores and other minerals removed from the earth.

Deployment (to spread around) Used in strategic planning to describe the process of cascading plans throughout an organization.

Deposit reconciliation One type of account reconciliation, this service minimizes the number of depository accounts a company must have while offering the added advantage of convenience.

Deposit reporting service Information on account balances offered by a bank or third-party vendor, which enables the treasury staff to know when and where the company's operations have deposited money into bank accounts.

Deposition Sworn testimony taken before a trial begins. At depositions, the opposing side's attorneys ask questions of witnesses.

Depository Institution Deregulation and Monetary Control Act of 1980 Landmark legislation which enabled savings and loans, mutual savings banks, and credit unions to operate more like commercial banks. Also established reserve requirement ranges for various deposit accounts.

Depository Transfer Checks (DTC) Nonnegotiable, unsigned checks used by firms to move funds from one account to another. They are often used to move (concentrate) monies collected in many different locations into a pooled account in a "concentration bank," where the money can be invested as a single large amount.

Depreciation 1: Decrease in the value of a currency. **2:** In a general sense, the decrease in usefulness of plant assets other than land. In accounting, refers to the systematic allocation of a fixed asset's cost to expense.

Depreciation expense The portion of the cost of a fixed asset that is recorded as an expense each year of its useful life.

Depths 1: A characteristic of a market in which a very large dollar amount of securities can be easily absorbed without large changes in the market price. **2:** The average number of stock-keeping units within each brand of the merchandise line.

Deregulation Removal of government regulation.

Derivative A contract whose market value fluctuates in direct proportion to fluctuations in the market value of a commodity or a financial instrument or a foreign currency.

Derivative actions A member has the right to bring an action on behalf of a limited liability company to recover a judgment in its favor if the managers or members with authority to bring the action have refused to do so.

Derivative suit Suit brought by a shareholder on behalf of the corporation to enforce a right belonging to the corporation.

Derived demand Demand for component products that arises from the demand for final design products. For example, the demand for steel is derived from the demand for automobiles.

Descriptive An approach that describes how managers actually make decisions rather than how they should.

Descriptive ethics Concerned with describing, characterizing, and studying the morality of a people, a culture, or a society.

Deseasonalized time series A time series that has had the effect of season removed by dividing each original time series observation by the corresponding seasonal index.

Design defect Plans or specifications inadequate to ensure the product's safety.

Design engineering The discipline consisting of process engineering and product engineering.

Design For Manufacturability (DFM) Simplification of parts, products, and processes to improve quality and reduce manufacturing costs.

Design for manufacture and assembly A product development approach that involves the manufacturing function in the initial stages of product design to ensure ease of manufacturing and assembly. *See:* Early manufacturing involvement.

Design for quality A product design approach that uses quality measures to capture the extent to which the design meets the needs of the target market (customer attributes), as well as its actual performance, aesthetics, and cost. *See:* Total quality engineering.

Design of Experiments (DOE) Branch of applied statistics dealing with planning, conducting, analyzing, and interpreting controlled tests to evaluate the factors that control the value of a parameter or group of parameters.

Design review Documented, comprehensive, and systematic examination of a design to evaluate its capability to fulfill the requirements for quality.

Designation The name of the LLP must include the words "limited liability partnership" or "registered limited liability partnership," or the abbreviation "LLP."

Designing in quality vs. inspecting in quality *See:* Prevention vs. detection.

Desired quality Additional features and benefits a customer discovers when using a product or service which lead to increased customer satisfaction. If missing, a customer may become dissatisfied.

Desktop publishing Using word-processing programs and high-quality printers to prepare books and pamphlets for publication.

Detachable warrant A warrant that can be detached from a bond and traded independently of it.

Detective control A control designed to discover an unintended event or undesirable result that has been detected.

Deterministic model 1: Data input for deterministic models are single point estimates. **2:** A model in which all uncontrollable inputs are known and cannot vary.

Development Efforts to improve employees' ability to handle a variety of assignments.

Deviation Nonconformance or departure of a characteristic from specified product, process, or system requirements.

Devil's advocate A decision-making technique in which an individual is assigned the role of challenging the assumptions and assertions made by the group to prevent premature consensus.

DFD (Data Flow Diagram) A graphical method to communicate the data flow in a business unit. Usually serves as a blueprint for a new information system in the development process. The DFD uses four symbols, for entity, process, data store, and data flow.

Diagnosis The step in the decision-making process in which managers analyze underlying causal factors associated with the decision situation.

Diagnostic journey and remedial journey A two-phase investigation used by teams to solve chronic quality problems. In the first phase, the diagnostic journey, the team moves from the symptom of a problem to its cause. In the second phase, the remedial journey, the team moves from the cause to a remedy.

Dialog module The part of a decision-support system, or any other system, that allows the user to interact with it.

Dialogue A group communication process aimed at creating a culture based on collaboration, fluidity, trust, and commitment to shared goals.

Differential analysis The area of accounting concerned with the effect of alternative courses of action on revenues and costs.

Differential cost The amount of increase or decrease in cost expected from a particular course of action as compared with an alternative.

Differential piece-rate system A system in which employees are paid one piece-rate wage for units produced up to a standard output and a higher piece-rate wage for units produced over the standard.

Differential revenue The amount of increase or decrease in revenue expected from a particular course of action as compared with an alternative.

Differentiation 1: A type of competitive strategy with which the organization seeks to distinguish its products or services from competitors. **2:** Takes advantage of the company's real or perceived uniqueness on elements such as design or after-sales service. **3:** Process of creating and sustaining a strong, consistent, and unique image about one product in comparison to others. **4:** The cognitive and emotional differences among managers in various functional departments of an organization and formal structure differences among these departments.

Diffusion of innovation The process by which innovation is communicated through certain channels over time among members of a social system.

Digital certificates Computer files that serve as the equivalent of ID cards.

Digital signal An expression of discrete, noncontinuous signals produced by electrical or electromagnetic bursts of different power levels. Only a digital signal can represent bits, and therefore be processed by a computer.

Digital signature An encrypted digest of the text that is sent along with a message that authenticates the identity of the sender and guarantees that no one has altered the sent document.

Digital signatures and certificates A signature sent over the Internet.

Digital Subscriber Line (DSL) Technology that relieves individual subscribers of the need for the conversion of digital signals into analog signals between the telephone exchange and the subscriber jack. DSL lines are linked to the Internet on a permanent basis and support bit rates significantly greater than a normal telephone line between the subscriber's jack and the telephone exchange. The service is not offered everywhere.

Digital technology Technology characterized by use of the Internet and other digital processes to conduct or support business operations.

Dimensions of quality Different ways in which quality may be viewed, for example, meaning of quality, characteristics of quality, drivers of quality, and so on.

Direct access The manner in which a record is retrieved from a storage device, without the need to seek it sequentially. The record's address is calculated from the value in its logical key field.

Direct demand Demand for consumption products.

Direct deposit Service in which the employer's bank automatically deposits employees' wages and salaries. The bank sorts out the on-us checks for employees having checking accounts at that bank, and credits their accounts. Employees banking elsewhere are paid through the local clearing house or ACH-initiated transactions. Direct deposit of payroll is easily the most popular electronic payment application.

Direct export sales Seller contracts directly with the buyer in the other country.

Direct exporting The firm produces at home and creates a division to export to foreign markets.

Direct-financing lease A lease where the lessor provides financing only, and assumes financial risks but does not assume inventory risk.

Direct Foreign Investment (DFI) Investment in real assets (such as land, buildings, or even existing plants) in foreign countries.

Direct format One possible format allowed for presenting the Statement of Cash Flows that computes cash inflows and cash outflows directly, showing the major components of operating cash receipts and operating cash disbursements.

Direct hedge A hedge using a futures contract that is of the same type as the cash market instrument being hedged.

Direct interlock A situation that occurs when a member of the board of directors of one company sits on the board of another.

Direct intervention The process governments used in the 1970s if they wished to alter the current value of their currency. It was done by simply buying or selling their own currency in the market using their reserves of other major currencies.

Direct investing 1: An entry strategy in which the organization is involved in managing its production facilities in a foreign country. **2:** Established operations in a country.

Direct investment account An account in the BOP statement that records investments with an expected maturity of more than one year and an investor's ownership position of at least 10 percent.

Direct involvement Participation by a firm in international business in which the firm works with foreign customers or markets to establish a relationship.

Direct labor cost Wages of factory workers who are directly involved in converting materials into a finished product.

Direct labor rate variance The cost associated with the difference between the standard rate and the actual rate paid for direct labor used in producing a commodity.

Direct labor time variance The cost associated with the difference between the standard hours and the actual hours of direct labor spent producing a commodity.

Direct loan program Program in which Ex-Im Bank offers fixed-rate loans directly to the foreign buyer to purchase U.S. capital equipment and services.

Direct materials cost The cost of materials that are an integral part of the finished product.

Direct materials price variance The cost associated with the difference between the standard price and the actual price of direct materials used in producing a commodity.

Direct materials quantity variance The cost associated with the difference between the standard quantity and the actual quantity of direct materials used in producing a commodity.

Direct method A method of reporting the cash flows from operating activities as the net income from operations adjusted for all deferrals of past cash receipts and payments and all accruals of expected future cash receipts and payments.

Direct presenting Situation in which checks are sent to the drawee bank or its local clearinghouse via courier. Direct presenting is mainly used for large checks.

Direct quotation 1: A foreign exchange quotation that specifies the amount of home country currency needed to purchase one unit of foreign currency. **2:** Exchange rate quotations representing the value measured by number of dollars per unit.

Direct suit Suit brought by a shareholder or a class of shareholders against the corporation based upon the ownership of shares.

Direct supply chain The channel that results when a manufacturer sells its goods directly to the final consumer or end user.

Direct taxes Taxes applied directly to income.

Direct write-off method A method of accounting for uncollectible receivables, whereby an expense is recognized only when specific accounts are judged to be uncollectible.

Directional and departmental signage Large signs that are usually placed fairly high, so they can be seen throughout the store.

Directive An order to take a certain action.

Directors' inspection rights Directors have the right to inspect corporate books and records.

Directors' liability The directors who assent to an improper dividend are liable for the unlawful amount of the dividend.

Disability law Several federal acts, including the Americans with Disabilities Act, provide assistance to the disabled in obtaining rehabilitation training, access to public facilities, and employment.

Disabled person Someone who has a physical or mental impairment that substantially limits life activities, who has a record of such an impairment, or who is regarded as having such an impairment.

Disassembly bill of material In remanufacturing, a bill of material used as a guide for the inspection in the teardown and inspection process. On the basis of inspection, this bill is modified to a bill of repair defining the actual repair materials and work required. *Syn:* teardown bill of material.

Disaster recovery plan *See:* Business continuity plan.

Disbursement float The delay between the time when the company writes the check and the time when its bank charges the checking account for the amount of the check.

Disbursement fraud Having an organization pay for something it shouldn't pay for or pay too much for something it purchases.

Disbursement policy Whether an informal strategy or a formal written document, specifies which payment mechanism to utilize for a given disbursement, when to pay a given invoice, and the setup of guidelines regarding the disbursement system (including which bank[s] might be involved).

Disbursement system A company's payment methods, disbursement banks, and disbursing locations.

Disbursements and receipts method (scheduling) The net cash flow is determined by estimating the cash disbursements and the cash receipts expected to be generated each period.

Disbursing bank Bank used to pay from.

Disclaimer Negation of a warranty.

Disclosure Financial statements.

Disclosure fraud The issuance of fraudulent or misleading statements or press releases without financial statement line-item effect or the lack of appropriate disclosures that should have been, but were not, made by management.

Disclosure requirements A statement disclosing specified information must be filed with the SEC and furnished to each offeree.

Discontinued operations The operations of a business segment that has been disposed of.

Discount 1: The interest deducted from the maturity value of a note. The excess of the face amount of bonds over their issue price. The excess of par value of stock over its sales price. **2:** As related to forward rates, represents the percentage amount by which the forward rate is less than the spot rate.

Discount basis When the selling price of a financial instrument is less than its face value or value at maturity.

Discount bond A bond that sells below its par value; occurs whenever the going rate of interest rises above the coupon rate.

Discount interest loan A loan in which the interest, which is calculated on the amount borrowed, is paid at the beginning of the loan period; interest is paid in advance.

Discount rate 1: In a capital project evaluation it is the opportunity cost of the use of funds, which is used to determine the present value of cash flows. **2:** The rate used in computing the interest to be deducted from the maturity value of a note.

Discount rate (Fed) The rate charged depository institutions when they borrow reserves from the Fed in order to meet their reserve requirements or meet unusual loan demand.

Discount security One which does not pay regular interest payments, but compensates the investor for implied interest by returning at maturity a principal amount greater than the purchase price.

Discount yield The difference between the maturity cash flow and the purchase price on a discount (noninterest bearing) security, expressed as a percentage of the purchase price.

Discounted Cash Flow (DCF) techniques Methods of evaluating investment proposals that employ time value of money concepts; two of these are the net present value and the internal rate of return.

Discounted payback The length of time it takes for a project's *discounted* cash flows to repay the cost of the investment.

Discounting The process of finding the present value of a cash flow or a series of cash flows; the reverse of compounding.

Discovery Legal process by which each party's attorneys try to find all information about the other side's case before a trial begins.

Discovery sampling Sampling used in fraud detection that assumes a zero expected error rate. The methodology allows an auditor to determine confidence levels and make inferences from the sample to the population.

Discrepancies between production and consumption Differences in quantity, assortment, time, and place that must be overcome to make goods available to final customers.

Discrete Available-to-Promise (ATP) calculation based on the available-to-promise figure in the master schedule. For the first period, the ATP is the sum of the beginning inventory plus the MPS quantity minus backlog for all periods until the item is master scheduled again. For all other periods, if a quantity has been scheduled for that time period then the ATP is this quantity minus all customer commitments for this and other periods until another quantity is scheduled in the MPS. For those periods where the quantity scheduled is zero, the ATP is zero (even if deliveries have been promised). The promised customer commitments are accumulated and shown in the period where the item was most recently scheduled. *Syn:* incremental available-to-promise. *See:* Available-to-promise.

Discrete-event simulation model A simulation model that describes how a system evolves over time by using events that occur at discrete points in time.

Discrete probability distribution The measured process variable takes on a finite or limited number of values; no other possible values exist.

Discretionary income Disposable income minus the money needed for necessities to sustain life.

Discriminant analysis An identification procedure to interpret and classify data.

Discrimination 1: The hiring or promoting of applicants based on criteria that are not job relevant. **2:** Discrimination prohibited by the Civil Rights Act; includes 1) using proscribed criteria to produce disparate treatment, 2) engaging in nondiscriminatory conduct that perpetuates past discrimination, and 3) adopting neutral rules that have a disparate impact.

Discriminatory regulations Regulations that impose larger operating costs on foreign service providers than on local competitors, that provide subsidies to local firms only, or that deny competitive opportunities to foreign suppliers.

Disequilibrium losses Below-normal returns that can be suffered in the time interval that often exists between when an unfavorable influence on industry demand or cost conditions first transpires and the time when exit or downsizing finally occurs.

Disequilibrium profits Above-normal returns that can be earned in the time interval between when a favorable influence on industry demand or cost conditions first transpires and the time when competitor entry or growth finally develops.

Dishonored note receivable A note that the maker fails to pay on its due date.

Disillusionment phase Beginning two months into the expatriation process, the novelty of the new culture wears out, and day-to-day inconveniences caused by different practices in the local culture along with the inability to communicate effectively create disillusionment for the expatriate.

Disparate impact Occurs when substantial underrepresentation of protected-class members results from employment decisions that work to their disadvantage.

Disparate treatment Situation that exists when protected-class members are treated differently from others.

Displacement Act of moving employment opportunities from the country of origin to host countries.

Disposable income Personal income less personal taxes.

Disposition Activities that involve the management of excess or waste packaging and materials. In the past, organizations frequently used landfills for disposition. Today, more organizations are increasingly exploring alternative environmentally friendly forms of disposition, including recycling, reuse, remanufacturing, and other similar options. This approach is sometimes referred to as reverse logistics.

Disposition of nonconformity Action taken to deal with an existing nonconformity; action may include: correction (repair), rework, regrade, scrap, obtain a concession, or amendment of a requirement.

Dissatisfiers Those features or functions which the customer or employee has come to expect and which, if they were no longer present, would result in dissatisfaction.

Dissenting shareholder A shareholder who opposes a fundamental change and has the right to receive the fair value of her shares.

Dissociation A member has ceased to be associated with the company and includes voluntary withdrawal, death, incompetence, expulsion, or bankruptcy.

Dissolution 1: An LLC will automatically dissolve upon 1) the dissociation of a member, 2) the expiration of the LLC's agreed duration or the happening of any of the events specified in the articles, 3) the unanimous written consent of all the members, or 4) a decree of judicial dissolution. **2:** Change in the relation of partners caused by any partner's ceasing to be associated with the carrying on of the business.

Dissolution by act of the partners A partner always has the power to dissolve a partnership, but the partnership agreement determines whether he has the right to do so.

Dissolution by court order A court will order dissolution of a partnership under certain conditions.

Dissolution by operation of law A partnership is dissolved by operation of law upon **1:** the death of a partner, **2:** the bankruptcy of a partner or of the partnership, or **3:** the subsequent illegality of the partnership.

Distance learning Learning where student(s) and instructor(s) are not co-located, often carried out through electronic means.

Distributed Denial of Service (DDoS) Multiple log-in requests from many computers to the same Web site, so that the Web site is jammed with requests and cannot accept inquiries of legitimate visitors.

Distributed earnings The proportion of a firm's net income after taxes which is paid out or distributed to the stockholders of the firm.

Distribution 1: Amount of potential variation in outputs of a process; it is usually described in terms of its shape, average, and standard deviation. **2:** Moving finished products to customers; also called *order fulfillment*. **3:** Transfer of partnership property from the partnership to a partner. **4:** The members share distributions of cash or other assets of a limited liability company as provided in the operating agreement; if the LLC's operating agreement does not allocate distributions, they are typically made on the basis of the contributions each member made. **5:** The partners share distributions of cash or other assets of a limited partnership as provided in the partnership agreement.

Distribution of assets The liabilities of a partnership are to be paid out of partnership assets in the following order: 1) amounts owing to nonpartner creditors, 2) amounts owing to partners other than for capital and profits, 3) amounts owing to partners for capital contributions, and 4) amounts owing to partners for profits.

Distribution method A regression-based cash forecasting approach which spreads, or "distributes," a monthly total across the weeks or days within that month. This method has also been used to model payroll-related cash disbursements by relating cash outflows to how many business days have elapsed since payroll checks have been issued.

Distribution Requirements Planning (DRP) 1: The function of determining the need to replenish inventory at branch warehouses. A time-phased order point approach is used where the planned orders at the branch warehouse level are "exploded" via MRP logic to become gross requirements on the supplying source. In the case of multilevel distribution networks, this explosion process can continue down through the various levels of regional warehouses (master warehouse, factory warehouse, and so on.) and become input to the master production schedule. Demand on the supplying sources is recognized as dependent, and standard MRP logic applies. **2:** More generally, replenishment inventory calculations, which may be based on other planning approaches such as period order quantities or "replace exactly what was used," rather than being limited to the time-phased order point approach.

Distributive justice 1: Focuses on the specific outcome of a firm's recovery efforts. **2:** The concept that different treatment of people should not be based on arbitrary characteristics. In the case of substantive differences, people should be treated differently in proportion to the differences among them. **3:** Perceived fairness in the distribution of outcomes.

Distributor Marketing intermediary that purchases products from the domestic firm and assumes the trading risk.

Distributorship MNE sells to a foreign distributor who takes title to the merchandise.

Diversification 1: A market expansion policy characterized by growth in a relatively large number of markets or market segments. **2:** Process of spreading risk through a firm's involvement in various businesses or through the location of its operations in different geographic areas.

Diversification strategy Market development strategy that involves expansion to a relatively large number of markets.

Diversity The differences among people.

Diversity awareness training Special training designed to make people aware of their own prejudices and stereotypes.

Diverter An unauthorized member of a channel who buys and sells excess merchandise to and from authorized channel members.

Diverting Occurs when a manufacturer restricts an off-invoice allowance to a limited geographical area, resulting in some wholesalers and retailers buying abnormally large quantities at the deal price and then transshipping the excess quantities to other geographical areas.

Divertive competition Occurs when retailers intercept or divert customers from competing retailers.

Dividend capture strategy Corporate investment strategy involving buying a common or preferred stock shortly before it pays its dividend, or buying a preferred stock having an adjustable dividend payment. Because intercorporate dividends have been largely excludable for income tax purposes (presently there is a 70 percent exclusion), corporate investors buy stocks with high dividend yields, hold them at least 49 days (until the record date for payment), and then sell.

Dividend irrelevance theory The theory that a firm's dividend policy has no effect on either its value or its cost of capital.

Dividend policy decision The decision as to how much of current earnings to pay out as dividends rather than to retain for reinvestment in the firm.

Dividend preference Preference that must receive full dividends before any dividend may be paid on common stock.

Dividend relevance theory The value of a firm is affected by its dividend policy—the optimal dividend policy is the one that maximizes the firm's value.

Dividend Reinvestment Plan (DRIP) A plan that enables a stockholder to automatically reinvest dividends received back into the stock of the paying firm.

Dividend roll An investment approach that involves buying stocks with high dividend yields, holding them at least 49 days to collect the dividend, and then selling the stocks.

Dividend yield 1: The expected dividend divided by the current price of a share of stock. **2:** The rate of return to stockholders in terms of cash dividend distributions.

Dividends 1: Distributions made to stockholders from the firm's earnings, whether those earnings were generated in the current period or in previous periods. **2:** Directors declare the amount and type of dividends.

Dividends per share The cash dividends per common shares commonly used by investors in assessing alternative stock investments, computed by dividing dividends by the number of shares of stock outstanding.

Division A decentralized organizational unit that is structured around a common function, product, customer, or geographical territory. Divisions can be cost, profit, or investment centers.

Division of labor The premise of modern industrial production where each stage in the production of a good is performed by one individual separately, rather than one individual being responsible for the entire production of the good.

Divisional grouping A grouping in which people are organized according to what the organization produces.

Divisional structure 1: An organization structure in which departments are grouped based on similar organizational outputs. **2:** The structuring of the organization according to individual products, services, product groups, major projects, or profit centers; also called *product structure* or *strategic business units*.

DMAIC Methodology used in the six-sigma approach: define, measure, analyze, improve, control.

Document examiner Specialized investigator who applies forensic chemistry, microscopy, photography, and other scientific methods to determine whether documents or other evidence are genuine, forged, counterfeit, or fraudulent.

Documentary collections Trade transactions handled on a draft basis.

Documentary evidence Evidence gathered from paper, documents, computer records, and other written, printed, or electronic sources.

Documents against acceptance Situation in which the buyer's bank does not release shipping documents to the buyer until the buyer has accepted (signed) the draft.

Documents against payment Shipping documents that are released to the buyer once the buyer has paid for the draft.

Documents and records Documentation of all transactions in order to create an audit trail.

Dodge–Romig sampling plans Plans for acceptance sampling developed by Harold F. Dodge and Harry G. Romig. Four sets of tables were published in 1940: single-sampling lot tolerance tables, double-sampling lot tolerance tables, single-sampling average outgoing quality limit tables, and double-sampling average outgoing quality limit tables.

Dollar-day float A measure of delay that considers both the dollar amount and the time lag.

Domain An organization's chosen environmental field of activity.

Domain disagreements Occur when there is disagreement about which member of the marketing channel should make decisions.

Domain name The name assigned to an Internet server.

Domains of political activity Areas in which politics plays a role. Three domains in organizations are structural change, management succession, and resource allocation.

Domestic corporation A corporation created under the laws of a given state.

Domestic enterprises Companies that derive all of their revenues from their home market.

Domestic environment Home country factors, including the political, competitive, economic, and legal and governmental climates, affect the enterprise.

Domestication Government demand for partial transfer of ownership and management responsibility from a foreign company to local entities, with or without compensation.

Dominant Securities which provide a higher expected return for a given amount of risk than other securities.

Dominant strategy Decision that gives the best result for either party regardless of the action taken by the other.

Doomsday ratio The ratio of cash and cash equivalents to current liabilities.

Dot-matrix printer A printer on which the print head consists of a matrix of little pins; thus, each printed character is made up of tiny dots.

Double counting This can either occur when a bank counts the same balances as compensation for a loan and as compensation for cash management services, or if the company has written a depository check for which it has been granted availability at the concentration bank, but has not had its checking account debited.

Double-entry accounting A system for recording transactions, based on recording increases and decreases in accounts so that debits always equal credits.

Double-entry bookkeeping Accounting methodology where each transaction gives rise to both a debit and a credit of the same currency amount. It is used in the construction of the Balance of Payments.

Double taxation The situation in which an expatriate is taxed by both the home-country and host-country governments. In some cases the firm will pay for the over-taxation.

Downloading The copying of data or applications from a computer to your computer, for example from a mainframe computer to a notebook computer. The term has come to mean the copying from another computer to your own computer, regardless of computer size.

Downsizing Planned reduction in workforce due to economics, competition, merger, sale, restructuring, or reengineering.

Downstream Used as a relative reference within a firm or supply chain to indicate moving in the direction of the end customer.

Downward communication Messages sent from top management down to subordinates.

Draft A written order to make payment to a third party, where the entity ordered to pay the draft is usually a bank. Any party holding a credit balance for the person writing the draft may have a draft drawn on it.

Draft (bill of exchange) Unconditional promise drawn by one party (usually the exporter) instructing the buyer to pay the face amount of the draft upon presentation.

Draw An amount advanced from and repaid to future commissions earned by the employee.

Drawee bank The bank on which a check or draft was written ("drawn").

Drill down The process of finding the most relevant information for executive decision making within a database or data warehouse.

Drive Refers to a motivating force that directs behavior.

Driver The software that enables an operating system to control a device, such as an optical disc drive or joystick.

Drivers of quality Include customers, products/services, employee satisfaction, total organizational focus.

Driving variable A key variable in most financial planning models to which most relationships are tied. Sales is generally such a variable in many financial planning models.

Drug and alcohol tests Some states either prohibit such tests or prescribe certain scientific and procedural safeguards.

Drum-buffer-rope In the theory of constraints, the generalized process used to manage resources to maximize throughput. The drum is the rate or pace of production set by the system's constraint. The buffers establish the protection against uncertainty so that the system can maximize throughput. The rope is a communication process from the constraint to the gating operation that checks or limits material released into the system to support the constraint. *See:* finite scheduling, synchronized production.

Dual balance The same dollar balance that is temporarily on deposit at two different banks.

Dual distribution Occurs when a manufacturer sells to independent retailers and also through its own retail outlets.

Dual pricing Price-setting strategy in which the export price may be based on marginal cost pricing, resulting in a lower export price than domestic price; may open the company to dumping charges.

Dual role A role in which the individual both contributes to the team's task and supports members' emotional needs.

Dual translation Using an interpreter in a country to translate a sender's message into a foreign language and then using an interpreter in the foreign country to translate the message back into the sender's language.

Dual-use items Goods and services that are useful for both military and civilian purposes.

Dual-core approach An organizational change perspective that identifies the unique processes associated with administrative change compared to those associated with technical change.

Due date The date, specified in a request for proposal, by which a customer expects potential contractors to submit proposals.

Due diligence defense Defense to liability for false registration statements available to defendants who had a reasonable (non-negligent) belief that there were no untrue statements and no material omissions.

Dummy activity A special type of activity, used in the activity-on-the-arrow form of network diagramming, that consumes no time. A dummy activity is represented by a dashed arrow.

Dummy or shell company Fictitious entity created for the sole purpose of committing fraud; usually involves an employee making fraudulent payments to the dummy company.

Dummy variables Variables included in the regression equation when modeling seasonal or monthly effects. The number included is one less than the number of seasons. Each dummy variable that is included as an independent variable takes on a value of one only when the season it represents is the season for which the forecast is being made, and zero at all other times.

Dumping 1: Selling products overseas at unfairly low prices (a practice perceived to result from subsidies provided to the firm by its government). **2:** The practice by an MNC of selling a product in a foreign market at a price lower than the price for which it sells the product in its own market and/or below production cost with the intent to eliminate its competition.

Dumpster diving Searching through the garbage for important pieces of information that can help crack an organization's computers or be used to persuade someone at the company to give criminals access to the computers.

DuPont chart A chart designed to show the relationships among return on investment, asset turnover, the profit margin, and leverage.

DuPont equation A formula that gives the rate of return on assets by multiplying the profit margin by the total assets turnover.

Duration A tool for evaluating the interest rate risk of interest-bearing notes and bonds. It is defined as the weighted average time until the investor receives an investment's discounted cash flows.

Duration estimate The estimated total time an activity will take from start to finish, including associated waiting time; time estimate.

Duty A larger work segment composed of several tasks that are performed by an individual.

Duties General partners owe a duty of care and loyalty (fiduciary duty) to the general partners, the limited partners, and the limited partnership; limited partners do not.

Duty of care Duty owed by partners to manage the partnership affairs without culpable negligence, which is greater than ordinary negligence but less than gross negligence.

Duty of diligence Must exercise ordinary care and prudence.

Duty of loyalty Requires undeviating loyalty to the corporation.

Duty of obedience Duty to act in accordance with the partnership agreement and any business decisions properly made by the partners. Must act within respective authority.

DVD (Digital Video Disc) A collective term for several types of high-capacity storage optical discs, used for data storage and motion pictures.

Dwell time Refers to the amount of time a consumer must spend waiting to complete a purchase.

Dynamic hedging Strategy of hedging in those periods when existing currency positions are expected to be adversely affected, and remaining unhedged in other periods when currency positions are expected to be favorably affected.

Dynamic IP number The IP number assigned to a computer that is connected to the Internet intermittently for the duration of the computer's connection.

Dynamic risks Uncertainties, either pure or speculative, that are produced because of societal changes.

Dynamic simulation model A simulation model used in situations where the state of the system affects how the system changes or evolves over time.

E

Earliest Finish time (EF) The earliest time by which a particular activity can be completed; the activity's earliest start time plus the activity's estimated duration.

Earliest Start time (ES) The earliest time at which a particular activity can begin; the project's estimated start time plus the estimated duration of preceding activities.

Early manufacturing involvement The process of involving manufacturing personnel early in the product design activity and drawing on their expertise, insights, and knowledge to generate better designs in less time and to generate designs that are easier to manufacture. Early involvement of manufacturing, field service, suppliers, customers, and so on means drawing on their expertise, knowledge, and insight to improve the design. Benefits include increased functionality, increased quality, ease of manufacture and assembly, ease of testing, better testing procedures, ease of service, decreased cost, and improved aesthetics. *See:* Design for manufacture and assembly, Participative design/engineering.

Early Supplier Involvement (ESI) The process of involving suppliers early in the product design activity and drawing on their expertise, insights, and knowledge to generate better designs in less time and designs that are easier to manufacture with high quality. *See:* Participative design/engineering.

Earned surplus Undistributed net profits, income, gains, and losses.

Earned Value (EV) The value of the work actually performed.

Earnings Credit Rate (ECR) A rate that banks credit collected balances with as compensation for leaving the balances in the account.

Earnings flexibility *See:* Income smoothing.

Earnings Per Share (EPS) Net income divided by the number of shares of common stock outstanding. A measure of profitability.

Ease of access Refers to the consumer's ability to easily and quickly find a retailer's Web site in cyberspace.

EBCDIC (Extended Binary Coded Decimal Interchange Code) A binary computer encoding scheme devised by IBM. Consists of eight bits per byte, each byte uniquely representing a character.

E-Business 1: The use of information technology and electronic communication networks to exchange business information and conduct transactions in electronic, paperless form. **2:** Work an organization does using electronic linkages; any business that takes place by digital processes over a computer network rather than in a physical space.

E-commerce 1: Business activity that is electronically executed between parties, such as between two businesses or between a business and a consumer. **2:** The ability to offer goods and services over the Web.

Econometric methods Use of economic theory and mathematical and statistical tools to forecast economic relations.

Economic and Monetary Union (EMU) The ideal among European leaders that economic integration should move beyond the four freedoms; specifically, it entails 1) closer coordination of economic policies to promote exchange rate stability and convergence of inflation rates and growth rates, 2) creation of a European central bank, and 3) replacement of national monetary authorities by the European Central Bank and adoption of the euro as the European currency.

Economic census A comprehensive statistical profile of the economy, from the national, to the state, to the local level.

Economic environment The way in which people of a society manage their material wealth and the results of their management.

Economic expansion A period of rising economic activity.

Economic exposure Refers to the possibility that the long-term net present value of a firm's expected cash flows will change due to unexpected changes in exchange rates.

Economic extortion scheme Involves an employee demanding payment from a vendor in order to make or influence a decision in that vendor's favor.

Economic feasibility study An evaluation of whether the benefits outweigh the costs of a proposed information system over the life of the system.

Economic forces Forces that affect the availability, production, and distribution of a society's resources among competing users.

Economic indicators Data that describe projected, current, or past economic activity.

Economic infrastructure The transportation, energy, and communication systems in a country.

Economic luck Temporary good fortune due to unexpected changes in industry demand or cost conditions.

Economic Order Quantity (EOQ) 1: The optimal quantity of a specific raw material that allows a business to minimize overstocking and save cost without risking understocking and missing production deadlines. **2:** A type of fixed order quantity model that determines the amount of an item to be purchased or manufactured at one time. The intent is to minimize the combined costs of acquiring and carrying inventory. The basic formula is

$$\text{Quantity} = \sqrt{\frac{2(d)(c)}{(i)(u)}}$$

where d = annual demand, c = average cost of order preparation, i = annual inventory carrying cost percentage, and u = unit cost. *Syn:* economic lot size, minimum cost order quantity.

Economic recession A decline in economic activity that lasts more than a few months.

Economic rents Profits due to uniquely productive inputs.

Economic risk The uncertainty surrounding key elements of the investment process.

Economic security Perception of a business activity as having an effect on a country's financial resources, often used to restrict competition from firms outside the country.

Economic union A union among trading countries that has the characteristics of a common market and also harmonizes monetary policies, taxation, and government spending and uses a common currency.

Economic Value Added (EVA) 1: A firm's net operating profit after the cost of capital is deducted. **2:** A control system that measures performance in terms of after-tax profits minus the cost of capital invested in tangible assets.

Economies of scale 1: Achievement of lower average cost per unit by means of increased production. **2:** Production economies made possible by the output of larger quantities.

Economies of scale and economies of scope Obtained by spreading the costs of distribution over a large quantity of products (scale) or over a wide variety of products (scope).

ECU The outgrowth of the European Monetary System is a new currency, referred to as the ECU, which represents a basket of currencies of the members of the EEC.

EDLP (Everyday Low Prices) Occurs when a retailer charges the same low price every day throughout the year and seldom runs the product on sale.

Education Process undertaken to learn required additional knowledge. *See:* Training.

Education allowance Reimbursement by company for dependent educational expenses incurred while a parent is assigned overseas.

EEC The European Economic Community.

Effect The surviving corporation receives title to all of the assets of the merged corporation and assumes all of its liabilities; the merged corporation ceases to exist.

Effect of declaration Once properly declared, a cash dividend is considered a debt the corporation owes to the shareholders.

Effect of *ultra vires* acts Under RMBCA, *ultra vires* acts and conveyances are not invalid.

Effective Annual Rate (EAR) The annual rate earned or paid considering interest compounding during the year (that is, the annual rate that equates to a given periodic rate compounded for *m* periods during the year).

Effective interest rate The rate of interest that is equal to or greater than the stated interest rate because of out-of-pocket expenses and usable funds that are less than the face value of the loan.

Effective interest rate method One method of amortizing a bond discount. Also known as the interest method.

Effective internal control This reflects a state or condition of internal control. While internal control is a process, its effectiveness is a state or condition of the process at a point in time.

Effective rate of interest The market rate of interest when bonds are issued.

Effective tax rate Actual total tax burden after including all applicable tax liabilities and credits.

Effective yield Yield or return to an MNC on a short-term investment after adjustment for the change in exchange rates over the period of concern.

Effectiveness 1: The degree to which the organization achieves a stated goal. **2:** The measure of how well a job is performed.

Effects of dissolution Upon dissolution a partnership is not terminated but continues until the winding up is completed.

Efficiency A measurement (usually expressed as a percentage) of the actual output to the standard output expected. Efficiency measures how well something is performing relative to existing standards; in contrast, productivity measures output relative to a specific input, for example, tons/labor hour. Efficiency is the ratio of 1) actual units produced to the standard rate of production expected in a time period or 2) standard hours produced to actual hours worked (taking longer means less efficiency) or 3) actual dollar volume of output to a standard dollar volume in a time period. Illustrations of these calculations follow. 1) There is a standard of 100 pieces per hour and 780 units are produced in one eight-hour shift; the efficiency is 780/800 converted to a percentage, or 97.5 percent. 2) The work is measured in hours and took 8.21 hours to produce eight standard hours; the efficiency is 8/8.21 converted to a percentage or 97.5 percent. 3) The work is measured in dollars and produces $780 with a standard of $800; the efficiency is $780/$800 converted to a percentage, or 97.5 percent.

Efficiency ratios Ratios that measure how effectively the enterprise is using the assets employed.

Efficient markets Where prices change freely and instantly in response to supply and demand and are not significantly affected by poor information or tax code barriers.

Efficient Markets Hypothesis (EMH) The hypothesis that securities are typically in equilibrium—that they are fairly priced in the sense that the price reflects all publicly available information on each security.

Effluent limitation Technology-based standard that limits the amount of pollutant that a point source may discharge.

Eighth Directive, The The EU Eighth Directive deals with auditing of financial statements of companies in EU countries, and specifies that they be consistent with EU law. It also sets qualifications for auditors and the firms conducting audits, including education and experience requirements. In addition, the Directive deals with ethical matters such as independence, and includes sanctions for cases in which audits are not conducted as prescribed by statute. *See:* Fourth Directive, Seventh Directive.

Eighty–twenty (80–20) rule Term referring to the Pareto principle, which suggests that most effects come from relatively few causes; that is, 80 percent of the effects come from 20 percent of the possible causes.

Elaboration stage The organizational life cycle phase in which the red tape crisis is resolved through the development of a new sense of teamwork and collaboration.

Elastic demand Situation in which a price change leads to a more than proportionate change in quantity demanded.

Elasticity Percentage change in a dependent variable resulting from a 1 percent change in an independent variable.

Elasticity of demand Relationship between changes in price and quantity sold.

e-learning The use of the Internet or an organizational intranet to conduct training on line.

Election of directors The shareholder elect the board at the annual meeting of the corporation.

Electronic agent A computer program that searches Internet sites and other resources in a telecommunications network to respond to a request made by its user.

Electronic brochures Digital versions of a company's brochures.

Electronic Business Data Interchange (EBDI) The electronic movement of information such as invoices between corporate trading partners.

Electronic check presentment An arrangement in which the image of the MICR line of a check is presented to the paying back, instead of presenting the physical check, shortening clearance float.

Electronic commerce Information systems that allow transactions between parties in a supply chain to be automatically completed via electronic data interchange (EDI), electronic funds transfer (EFT), bar codes, and a variety of other electronic mediums. The "paper" transactions of the past are becoming increasingly obsolete. At the same time, the proliferation of new telecommunications and computer technology has also made instantaneous communications a reality. Such information systems—like Wal-Mart's satellite network—can link together suppliers, manufacturers, distributors, retail outlets, and ultimately, customers, regardless of location.

Electronic corporate trade payment An arrangement between two corporations (a buyer and a seller) and the banks of the two parties so that payment is effected without a paper check being issued.

Electronic Data Interchange (EDI) 1: A network that links the computer systems of buyers and sellers to allow the transmission of structured data primarily for ordering, distribution, and payables and receivables. **2:** Computer-to-computer exchange of invoices, orders, and other business documents; a computer-to-computer communications protocol that allows basic information on purchases and invoices to be transferred.

Electronic Depository Transfer (EDT) Payment process in which a local or regional account is debited electronically and the amount sent through an automated clearing house to the concentration bank account. Also known as an ACH debit, is an electronic equivalent to the paper DTC. The electronic transaction provides quicker availability in the concentration account for the company.

Electronic Funds Transfer (EFT) A payment system that uses computerized information rather than paper (money, checks, and so on.) to effect a cash transaction between trading partners.

Electronic intermediary Profit model based on commissions received by bringing buyers and sellers together.

Electronic lockbox Collection system offered by banks for companies to receive payments, via wire transfers or ACH, from customers.

Electronic retailing (e-tailing) The direct sales from business to consumer through electronic storefronts, typically designed around an electronic catalog and shopping cart model.

Electronic superhighway The Internet. Often called *the information superhighway.*

Electronic surveillance Using video, e-mail, wiretapping, and so on to watch fraud suspects.

Elements of fraud The theft act, concealment, and conversion that are present in every fraud.

Elements of internal control The control environment, risk assessment, control activities, information and communication, and monitoring.

E-mail (electronic mail) The exchange of messages between computers either in the same building or over great distances.

E-marketing The set of activities that bring customers and companies together using electronic means such as the Internet.

Embargo A governmental action, usually prohibiting trade entirely, for a decidedly adversarial or political rather than economic purpose.

Embezzlement Theft or fraudulent appropriation of money through deception; often used interchangeably with the term *fraud.*

Emotions 1: Even though behavior in business and negotiations is mainly intuitive, it should never be judgmental. To be able to listen to other negotiators, one should exclude his or her subjective opinions, preconceptions, or emotional filters. It is important to prevent emotions from controlling negotiations. **2:** Strong, relatively uncontrolled feelings that affect our behavior.

Employee assistance program One program that provides counseling and other help to employees having emotional, physical, or other personal problems.

Employee discrimination Hiring, firing, compensating, promoting, or training of employees based on race, color, gender, religion, or national origin.

Employee embezzlement Employees deceiving their employers by taking company assets.

Employee fraud The intentional act of deceiving an employer for personal gain.

Employee involvement Practice within an organization whereby employees regularly participate in making decisions on how their work areas operate, including making suggestions for improvement, planning, objectives setting, and monitoring performance.

Employee network groups Groups based on social identity, such as gender or race, and organized by employees to focus on concerns of employees from that group.

Employee Stock Ownership Plan (ESOP) A plan whereby employees gain stock ownership in the organization for which they work.

Employee termination at will Under the common law, a contract of employment for other than a definite term is terminable at will by either party.

Employee theft Occurs when employees of the retailer steal merchandise where they work.

Employee's earnings record A detailed record of each employee's earnings.

Employment test 1: Any employment procedure used as the basis for making an employment-related decision. **2:** A written or computer-based test designed to measure a particular attribute such as intelligence or aptitude.

Empowerment 1: Condition whereby employees have the authority to make decisions and take action in their work areas, within stated bounds, without prior approval. For example, an operator can stop a production process upon detecting a problem, or a customer service representative can send out a replacement product if a customer calls with a problem. **2:** Occurs when employees are given the power in their jobs to do the things necessary to satisfy and make things right for customers.

Encapsulated development Situation in which an individual learns new methods and ideas in a development course and returns to a work unit that is still bound by old attitudes and methods.

Encode To select symbols with which to compose a message.

Encoding scheme A convention of representing characters with another, small, set of characters or special marks. Morse code, EBCDIC, and ASCII are encoding schemes.

Encryption The conversion of plaintext to an unreadable stream of characters, especially to prevent a party that intercepts telecommunicated messages from reading them. Special encryption software is used by the sending party to encrypt messages, and by the receiving party to decipher them.

End-of-month (EOM) dating System that allows the retailer to take a cash discount and the full payment period to begin on the first day of the following month instead of on the invoice date.

End users External customers who purchase products/services for their own use.

Endogenous variables Factors controlled by the firm.

Engineering change order A document that initiates a change in the specification of a product or process.

Engineering services Services that are provided in the areas of construction, design, and engineering.

Engineering technology Technology in which there is substantial variety in the tasks performed, but the activities are usually handled on the basis of established formulas, procedures, and techniques.

Engineer-to-order Products whose customer specifications require unique engineering design, significant customization, or new purchased materials. Each customer order results in a unique set of part numbers, bills of material, and routings. *Syn:* design-to-order.

Enterprise Application Systems Information systems that fulfill a number of functions together, such as inventory planning, purchasing, payment, and billing.

Enterprise-level strategy The overarching strategy level that poses the basic questions, "What is the role of the organization in society?" and "What do we stand for?"

Enterprise Resource Planning (ERP) system 1: An information system that supports different activities for different departments, assisting executives with planning and running different functions. **2:** Systems that unite a company's major business functions—order processing, product design, purchasing, inventory, and so on; a networked information system that collects, processes, and provides information about an organization's entire enterprise, from identification of customer needs and receipt of orders to distribution of products and receipt of payments. **3:** Accounting-oriented information systems used for identifying and planning the enterprise-wide resources needed to take, make, ship, and account for customer orders. **4:** An ERP system differs from the typical MRP II system in technical requirements such as graphical user interface, relational database, use of fourth-generation language, and computer-assisted software engineering tools in development, client/server architecture, and open-system portability. **5:** More generally, a method for the effective planning and control of all resources needed to take, make, ship, and account for customer orders in a manufacturing, distribution, or service company.

Enterprise risk management Approach for managing both pure and speculative risks together. Another name for *integrated risk-management*.

Entity Any object about which an organization chooses to collect data.

Entity relationship diagram One of several conventions for graphical rendition of the data elements involved in business processes and the logical relationships among the elements.

Entrepreneur Someone who recognizes a viable idea for a business product or service and carries it out.

Entrepreneurial stage The life cycle phase in which an organization is born and its emphasis is on creating a product and surviving in the marketplace.

Entrepreneurship The process of initiating a business venture, organizing the necessary resources, and assuming the associated risks and rewards.

Entropy The tendency for a system to run down and die.

Environmental analysis/scanning Relates to monitoring factors from both inside and outside the organization that may impact the long-term viability of the organization.

Environmental contexts *See:* Cross-cultural communication.

Environmental Impact Statement (EIS) Detailed statement concerning the environmental impact of a proposed federal action. *See* Content.

Environmental monitoring stage Focuses on the tracking of specific trends and events with an eye toward confirming or disconfirming trends or patterns.

Environmental protection Actions taken by governments to protect the environment and resources of a country.

Environmental scanning 1: Obtaining ongoing data about a country. **2:** Process of studying the environment of the organization to pinpoint opportunities and threats. **3:** Identifies important trends in the microand macroenvironments, then considers the potential impact of these changes on a firm's existing marketing strategy.

Environmental scanning stage Focuses on identification of precursors or indicators of potential environmental changes and issues.

Environment-specific An accounting system designed to provide information for making decisions in a given environment. Five major environmental influences on accounting consist of the economic system, political system, legal system, educational system, and religion.

E $\to$ P expectancy Expectancy that putting effort into a given task will lead to high performance.

EPA Environmental Protection Agency.

EPS indifference point The level of sales at which EPS will be the same whether the firm uses debt or common stock financing.

Equal Employment Opportunity (EEO) 1: Individuals should have equal treatment in all employment-related actions. **2:** Enforcement agency for the Civil Rights Act.

Equal Pay Act Law that prohibits an employer from discriminating between employees on the basis of gender by paying unequal wages for the same work.

Equation Analytical expression of functional relationships.

Equilibrium The condition under which the expected return on a security is just equal to its required return, $\hat{k} = k$, and the price is stable.

Equilibrium exchange rate Exchange rate at which demand for a currency is equal to the supply of the currency for sale.

Equity 1: A situation that exists when the ratio of one person's outcomes to inputs equals that of another. **2:** The perceived fairness of what the person does compared with what the person receives. **3:** Concern for a just distribution of wealth.

Equity capital Capital that is financed by shares (stocks).

Equity financing Financing that consists of funds that are invested in exchange for ownership in the company.

Equity method A method of accounting for investments in common stock, by which the investment account is adjusted for the investor's share of periodic net income and dividends of the investee. A method in which income of a subsidiary is recognized by the parent company according to ownership percentage. The investment in the subsidiary account balance is adjusted accordingly.

Equity multiplier Assets divided by equity.

Equity reserves A general term to describe many different types of reserves that serve different purposes.

Equity security A security that represents ownership in a business, such as stock in a corporation.

Equity theory 1: A process theory that focuses on individuals' perceptions of how fairly they are treated relative to others. **2:** Theory that states that job motivation depends upon how equitable the individual believes the rewards or punishment to be.

Equivalent Annual Annuity (EAA) method A method that calculates the annual payments a project would provide if it were an annuity. When comparing projects of unequal lives, the one with the higher equivalent annual annuity should be chosen.

Equivalent units of production The number of units that could have been completed within a given accounting period with respect to direct materials and conversion costs. Equivalent units are used to allocate departmental costs incurred during the period between completed units and in-process units at the end of the period.

ERG theory A modification of the needs hierarchy theory that proposes three categories of needs: existence, relatedness, and growth.

Ergonomics 1: The study and design of the work environment to address physiological and physical demands on individuals. **2:** The science of designing and modifying machines to better suit people's health and comfort.

Error distribution The shape or pattern of the array of forecast errors.

Escalating commitment 1: Continuing to invest time and resources into a failing decision. **2:** Persisting in a course of action when it is failing; occurs because managers block or distort negative information and because consistency and persistence are valued in contemporary society.

Essential job functions Fundamental duties of a job.

Estimated start time The time or date when a project is expected to begin.

Ethernet The design, introduced and named by Xerox, for the contention data communications protocol.

Ethical What members of a given society generally accept as being "right."

Ethical dilemma A situation that arises when all alternative choices or behaviors have been deemed undesirable because of potentially negative ethical consequence, making it difficult to distinguish right from wrong.

Ethical fundamentalism Situation in which individuals look to a central authority or set of rules to guide them in ethical decision making.

Ethical impact statement An attempt to assess the underlying moral justifications for corporate actions and the consequent results of those actions.

Ethical relativism 1: Picking and choosing which source of norms to use based on what will justify current actions or maximize freedom. **2:** Belief that actions must be judged by what individuals subjectively feel is right or wrong for themselves.

Ethical responsibilities Those activities and practices that are expected or prohibited by societal members even though they are not codified into law.

Ethical values Moral values that enable a decision maker to determine an appropriate course of behavior; these values should be based on what is "right," which may go beyond what is "legal."

Ethical vigilance Paying constant attention to whether one's actions are "right" or "wrong," and if ethically "wrong," asking why one is behaving in that manner.

Ethics 1: Code of conduct that is based on moral principles, and which tries to balance what is fair for individuals with what is right for society. **2:** The code of moral principles and values that govern the behaviors of a person or group with respect to what is right or wrong. **3:** The discipline that deals with what is good and bad and with moral duty and obligation.

Ethics committee A group of executives appointed to oversee company ethics.

Ethics ombudsperson A single manager who serves as the corporate conscience.

Ethnocentric Tending to regard one's own culture as superior; tending to be home-market oriented.

Ethnocentric staffing outlook The belief that key positions in foreign subsidiaries should be staffed by citizens from the parent company's home country.

Ethnocentric strategy Companies produce unique goods and services that they offer primarily to their domestic market, and when they export, they do not modify the product or service for foreign consumption.

Ethnocentrism A cultural attitude marked by the tendency to regard one's own culture as superior to others; the belief that one's own group or subculture is inherently superior to other groups or cultures.

Ethnorelativism The belief that groups and subcultures are inherently equal.

Euro A single currency proposed for use by the European Union that will eventually replace all the individual currencies of the participating member states.

Euro cp Similar in concept to domestic commercial paper except issued in the Euromarket which has fewer restrictions, is unrated, and generally has a longer maturity averaging from 60 to 90 days.

Eurobanks Commercial banks that participate as financial intermediaries in the Eurocurrency market.

Eurobond A bond that is denominated in a currency other than the currency of the country in which the bond is sold.

Euro-clear Telecommunications network that informs all traders about outstanding issues of Eurobonds for sale.

Euro-commercial paper Debt securities issued by MNCs for short-term financing.

Eurocredit loans Loans of one year or longer extended by Eurobanks.

Eurocredit market Collection of banks that accept deposits and provide loans in large denominations and in a variety of currencies. The banks that comprise this market are the same banks that comprise the Eurocurrency market; the difference is that the Eurocredit loans are longer term than so-called Eurocurrency loans.

Eurocurrency A bank deposit in a currency other than the currency of the country where the bank is located; not confined to banks in Europe.

Eurocurrency market Collection of banks that accept deposits and provide loans in large denominations and in a variety of currencies.

Eurodebt Debt sold in a country other than the one in whose currency the debt is denominated.

Eurodollar Term used to describe United States dollar deposits placed in banks located in Europe.

Eurodollar CDs Dollar-denominated deposits held in banks or bank branches outside the U.S. or in International Banking Facilities (IBFs, which can offer Eurodollar deposits only to non-U.S. residents) located within the United States.

Eurodollars United States dollars deposited in banks outside the United States; not confined to banks in Europe.

Euromarkets Money and capital markets in which transactions are denominated in a currency other than that of the place of the transaction; not confined to Europe.

Euronotes Unsecured debt securities issued by MNCs for short-term financing.

European Article Numbering (EAN) system European version of the Universal Product Code located on a product's package that provides information read by optical scanners.

European Central Bank (ECB) Central bank created to conduct the monetary policy for the countries participating in the single European currency, the euro.

European Confederation of Institutes of Internal Auditing This organization, comprised of 17 internal audit organizations representing 18 European nations plus Israel, helps in the development of internal auditing standards.

European Currency Unit (ECU) Unit of account representing a weighted average of exchange rates of member countries within the European Monetary System.

European Monetary System (EMS) An organization formed in 1979 by eight EC members committed to maintaining the values of their currencies within 2 1/4 percent of each other's.

European terms Quoting a currency rate as a country's currency against the U.S. dollar (for example, yen/U.S. dollars).

European Union (EU) The January 1, 1994, organization created by the 12 member countries of the European Community (now 15 members). A single trading block currently linking 15 European nations into a single market in order to eliminate tariff and custom restrictions. The 15 nations include Austria, Belgium, Denmark, Finland, France, Germany, Great Britain, Greece, Ireland, Italy, Luxembourg, Netherlands, Portugal, Spain, and Sweden.

European Union directives Rules issued by the European Union. These are binding on member countries.

Evaluated receipt settlement An electronic payment process in which receipt of shipment (not receipt of invoice) triggers payment by the purchasing company.

Evaluation criteria The standards, specified in a request for proposal, that a customer will use to evaluate proposals from competing contractors.

Evaluative criteria Specifications that organizational buyers use to compare alternative goods and services.

Event 1: An instantaneous occurrence that changes the state of the system in a simulation model. **2:** Starting or ending point for a task or group of tasks. **3:** Interconnecting points that link activities in the activity-on-the-arrow form of network diagramming. An event is represented by a circle.

Event risk Includes any security feature or possible event that subjects the investor to a disruption to or reduction in the expected yield.

Event-Related Marketing (ERM) Form of brand promotion that ties a brand to a meaningful cultural, social, athletic, or other type of high-interest public activity.

Every Day Low Pricing (EDLP) Pricing strategy in which a firm charges the same low price every day.

Evidence square A categorization of fraud investigative procedures that includes testimonial evidence, documentary evidence, physical evidence, and personal observation.

Evidential matter The underlying data and all corroborating information available about a fraud.

EVOP Process of adjusting variables in a process in small increments in a search for a more optimum point on the response surface.

Exception reports Periodic or ad hoc reports that flag facts or numbers that deviate from preset standards.

Excess capacity A situation where the output capabilities at a nonconstraint resource exceed the amount of productive and protective capacity required to achieve a given level of throughput at the constraint.

Excess inventory Any inventory in the system that exceeds the minimum amount necessary to achieve the desired throughput rate at the constraint or that exceeds the minimum amount necessary to achieve the desired due date performance. Total inventory = productive inventory + protective inventory + excess inventory.

Exchange controls Controls on the movement of capital in and out of a country, sometimes imposed when the country faces a shortage of foreign currency.

Exchange principle Maintains that when an exchange benefits both trading partners, the exchange adds value. This principle is derived from the raw material scarcity, labor specialization, and consumption satiation principles.

Exchange rate The amount of one currency needed to obtain one unit of another currency.

Exchange Rate Mechanism (ERM) The acceptance of responsibility by a European Monetary System member to actively maintain its own currency within agreed-upon limits versus other member currencies established by the European Monetary System.

Exchange rate risk The uncertainty associated with the price at which the currency from one country can be converted into the currency of another country. The risk that a firm faces when buying or selling in one or more currencies different from its domestic currency.

Excited quality Additional benefit a customer receives when a product or service goes beyond basic expectations. Excited quality "wows" the customer and distinguishes the provider from the competition. If missing, the customer will still be satisfied.

Exclusive dealing arrangement Seller or lessor conditions agreement upon the buyer's or lessee's promise not to deal in competing goods.

Exclusive distribution Only one intermediary is used at a particular level in the marketing channel.

Ex-dividend date The date on which the right to the next dividend no longer accompanies a stock; it usually is two working days prior to the holder-of-record date.

Executed contract Contract fully performed by all of the parties.

Execution error A program error in which a certain operation cannot be carried out, such as division by zero.

Executive education Education (and training) provided to top management.

Executive Information System (EIS) 1: A management information system designed to facilitate strategic decision making at the highest levels of management by providing executives with easy access to timely and relevant information. **2:** An information system that extracts high-level organization-wide information from large amounts of data stored in the business' databases. Typically, an EIS presents information graphically as charts and diagrams, allowing for a quick grasp of patterns and trends. Also called executive support system.

Executive order Prohibits discrimination by federal contractors on the basis of race, color, gender, religion, or national origin on any work the contractors perform during the period of the federal contract.

Executory contract Contract not fully performed.

Executive stock option A type of incentive plan that allows managers to purchase stock at some future time at a given price.

Exempt employees Employees to whom employers are not required to pay overtime under the Fair Labor Standards Act.

Exempt securities Securities not subject to the registration requirements of the 1933 Act.

Exempt transactions for issuers Issuance of securities not subject to the registration requirements of the 1933 Act.

Exempt transactions for non-issuers Resales by persons other than the issuer that are exempted from the registration requirements of the 1933 Act.

Exercise of directors' functions Directors have the power to bind the corporation only when acting as a board.

Exercise price (strike price) Price (exchange rate) at which the owner of a currency call option is allowed to buy a specified currency; or the price (exchange rate) at which the owner of a currency put option is allowed to sell a specified currency.

Existing liability Dissolution does not in itself discharge the existing liability of any partner.

Exit interview An interview in which individuals are asked to identify reasons for leaving the organization.

Exit measurement *See:* Output price measurement.

Exogenous variables Factors outside the control of the firm.

Expansion decisions Whether to purchase capital projects and add them to existing assets to *increase* existing operations.

Expansion project A project that is intended to increase sales.

Expatriate 1: An employee, working in an operation, who is not a citizen of the country in which the operation is located, but is a citizen of the country of the headquarters organization. **2:** Employees who live and work in a country other than their own.

Expatriation Preparing and sending global employees to their foreign assignments.

Expatriation program Takes place while the expatriate is working in the foreign operations; certain delivery and communications programs are required.

Expectancy theory 1: A process theory that proposes that motivation depends on individuals' expectations about their ability to perform tasks and receive desired rewards. **2:** Suggests that an employee will expend effort on some task because the employee expects that the effort will lead to a performance outcome that will lead in turn to a reward or bonus that the employee finds desirable or valued.

Expectations theory The theory that the shape of the yield curve depends on investors' expectations about future inflation rates.

Expected duration (t_e) Also called the mean or average duration. The expected duration for an activity, calculated from the activity's optimistic, most likely, and pessimistic time estimates, as follows:

$$t_e = \frac{t_o + 4(t_m) + t_p}{6}$$

Expected quality Also known as *basic quality,* the minimum benefit a customer expects to receive from a product or service.

Expected rate of return, $\hat{k}_s$ The rate of return on a common stock that an individual stockholder expects to receive; equal to the expected dividend yield plus the expected capital gains yield.

Expected return on a portfolio, $\hat{k}_p$ The weighted average expected return on the stocks held in the portfolio.

Expected Utility (EU) The weighted average of the utilities associated with a decision alternative. The weights are the state-of-nature probabilities.

Expected Value (EV) For a chance node, it is the weighted average of the payoffs. The weights are the state-of-nature probabilities.

Expected value approach An approach to choosing a decision alternative that is based on the expected value of each decision alternative. The recommended decision alternative is the one that provides the best expected value.

Expected Value of Perfect Information (EVPI) The expected value of information that would tell the decision maker exactly which state of nature is going to occur (that is, perfect information).

Expected Value of Sample Information (EVSI) The difference between the expected value of an optimal strategy based on sample information and the "best" expected value without any sample information.

Expedited check processing Speedier check clearing provided by the clearing bank if the depositor is willing to perform extra tasks or pay the bank the extra charge involved.

Expedited Funds Availability Act of 1987 Required that shorter availability schedules be put in place to reduce arbitrarily long holds on deposited checks.

Expense budget A budget that outlines the anticipated and actual expenses for each responsibility center.

Expense liability reserves An equity reserve used to achieve income smoothing or to show a steady growth in income from year to year.

Expense scheme Scheme in which perpetrators produce false documents to claim false expenses.

Expenses Assets used up or services consumed in the process of generating revenues.

Experience attributes Can be evaluated only during and after consumption.

Experiential knowledge Knowledge acquired through involvement (as opposed to information, which is obtained through communication, research, and education).

Experimental design Formal plan that details the specifics for conducting an experiment, such as which responses, factors, levels, blocks, treatments, and tools are to be used.

Experimentation A research tool to determine the effects of a variable on an operation.

Expert power Power that stems from special knowledge of or skill in the tasks performed by subordinates.

Expert System (ES) A computer program that mimics the decision process of a human expert in providing a solution to a problem. Current expert systems deal with problems and diagnostics in narrow domains. An ES consists of a knowledge base, an inference engine, and a dialog management module.

Expert system shell An expert system without a knowledge base. A tool that eases the building of an expert system by prompting the designer for facts and relationships among the facts that are built into the shell as a knowledge base.

Expert witness Trial witness who can offer opinions about a matter, based on unique experience, education, or training.

Expertise 1: The skill and knowledge, primarily gained from experience, whose input into a process results in performance that is far above the norm. **2:** Although a corporation may have a high level of expertise in selling its goods and services, there is absolutely no guarantee that any promotion of social activities will be carried on with the same degree of competence.

Expertise power Power based on B's perception that A has some special knowledge.

Explicit code of ethics Consists of a written policy that states what is ethical and unethical behavior.

Explicit knowledge Represented by the captured and recorded tools of the day, for example, procedures, processes, standards, and other like documents.

Exponential distribution Continuous distribution where data are more likely to occur below the average than above it. Typically used to describe the break-in portion of the "bathtub" curve.

Exponential smoothing 1: A forecasting technique that uses a weighted average of past time series values to arrive at smoothed time series values that can be used as forecasts. **2:** Statistical forecasting technique similar to a moving average, but overcoming the slowness of adaptation to changing patterns inherent in the moving average by allowing a greater weighting for more recent data.

Export complaint systems Allow customers to contact the original supplier of a product in order to inquire about products, make suggestions, or present complaints.

Export-control system A system designed to deny or at least delay the acquisition of strategically important goods to adversaries; in the United States, based on the Export Administration Act and the Munitions Control Act.

Export-Import Bank (Ex-Im Bank) Bank that attempts to strengthen the competitiveness of U.S. industries involved in foreign trade.

Export license A license obtainable from the U.S. Department of Commerce Bureau of Export Administration, which is responsible for administering the Export Administration Act.

Export Management Companies (EMCs) Domestic firms that specialize in performing international business services as commissioned representatives or as distributors.

Export Trading Company (ETC) The result of 1982 legislation to improve the export performance of small and medium-sized firms, the export trading company allows businesses to band together to export or offer export services. Additionally, the law permits bank participation in trading companies and relaxes antitrust provisions.

Exporting An entry strategy in which the organization maintains its production facilities within its home country and transfers its products for sale in foreign markets.

Express charter powers Those stated in the articles of incorporation.

Express contract Agreement of parties that is stated in words either in writing or orally.

Express insider trading liability Liability imposed on any person who sells or buys a security while in possession of inside information.

Express warranty 1: Affirmation of fact or promise about the goods, which may consist of a description or a sample, which becomes part of the basis of the bargain. **2:** Not usually possible to disclaim.

Expressed warranties Are either written or verbalized agreements about the performance of a product and can cover all attributes of the merchandise or only one attribute.

Expropriation Government takeover of a company's operations frequently at a level lower than the value of the assets.

Extended enterprise An organizing principle that views multiple tiers of suppliers and multiple tiers of customers as part of the integrated supply chain.

Extended problem solving Occurs when the consumer recognizes a problem but has decided on neither the brand nor the store.

Extensible Markup Language (XML) A programming language that tags data elements in order to indicate what the data mean.

External adaptation The manner in which an organization meets goals and deals with outsiders.

External collaboration *See:* External cooperation.

External cooperation To be more effective and efficient, a firm focuses on what it can do best, and forms an alliance with other firms to obtain the additional organizational capabilities needed to be more effective and efficient than their competitors.

External customer Person or organization who receives a product, a service, or information but is not part of the organization supplying it. *See:* Internal customer.

External data Data that are collected from a wide array of sources outside the organization, including mass communications media, specialized newsletters, government agencies, and the Web.

External economies of scale Lower production costs resulting from the free mobility of factors of production in a common market.

External failure costs Costs associated with defects found during or after delivery of the product or service.

External locus of control The belief by individuals that their future is not within their control but rather is influenced by external forces.

External review A company's management becoming familiar with the domestic, international, and foreign factors that affect its business activities.

Externalities 1: The effect accepting a project will have on the cash flows in other parts (areas) of the firm. **2:** Differences between private and social costs or benefits.

Extortion An official in a foreign country in a position of power seeking payment from an individual or corporation for an action to which the individual or corporation may be lawfully entitled.

Extra dating Occurs when the vendor allows the retailer extra or interest-free days before the period of payment begins.

Extra dividend A supplemental dividend paid in years when the firm does well and excess funds are available for distribution.

Extraction phase The stage of data warehouse building in which the builders create the files from transactional databases and save them on the server that will hold the data warehouse.

Extranet A company communications system that gives access to suppliers, partners, and others outside the company; an external communications system that uses the Internet and is shared by two or more organizations.

Extraordinary items Events or transactions that are unusual and infrequent.

Extraordinary repair An expenditure that increases the useful life of an asset beyond the original estimate.

Extraterritoriality An exemption from rules and regulations of one country that may challenge the national sovereignty of another. The application of one country's rules and regulations abroad.

Extrinsic forecast A forecast based on a correlated leading indicator, such as estimating furniture sales based on housing starts. Extrinsic forecasts tend to be more useful for large aggregations, such as total company sales, than for individual product sales. *Ant:* intrinsic forecast method.

Extrinsic reward A reward given by another person.

Ex-Works (EXW) Price quotes that apply only at the point of origin; the seller agrees to place the goods at the disposal of the buyer at the specified place on a date or within a fixed period.

F

Face value Investors holding an investment to maturity will receive this amount back from the issuer. Also called the *investment's principal.* The amount of the loan, or the amount borrowed; also called the principal amount of the loan.

Facilitating marketing institutions Those institutions that do not actually take title but assist in the marketing process by specializing in the performance of certain marketing functions.

Facilitating payments Payments made to influence an official to take an action that the official must take anyway.

Facilitator Individual who is responsible for creating favorable conditions that will enable a team to reach its purpose or achieve its goals by bringing together the necessary tools, information, and resources to get the job done.

Factor Firm specializing in collection on accounts receivable; exporters sometimes sell their accounts receivable to a factor at a discount.

Factor analysis 1: Used in the exploratory or confirmatory of "interdependence" among the variables. **2:** Statistical technique that examines the relationships between a single dependent variable and multiple independent variables. For example, it is used to determine which questions on a questionnaire are related to a specific question such as "Would you buy this product again?"

Factor intensities The proportion of capital input to labor input used in the production of a good.

Factor mobility The ability to freely move factors of production across borders, as among common market countries.

Factor proportions theory Systematic explanation of the source of comparative advantage.

Factoring Purchase of receivables of an exporter by a factor without recourse to the exporter. The outright sale of receivables.

Factors of production All inputs into the production process, including capital, labor, land, materials, machines, buildings, and technology, that are necessary for bringing the good to the market.

Factory overhead cost All of the costs of operating the factory except for direct materials and direct labor.

Factual cultural knowledge Knowledge obtainable from specific country studies published by governments, private companies, and universities and also available in the form of background information from facilitating agencies such as banks, advertising agencies, and transportation companies.

Failsafe work methods Methods of performing operations so that actions that are incorrect cannot be completed. For example, a part without holes in the proper place cannot be removed from a jig, or a computer system will reject invalid numbers or require double entry of transaction quantities outside the normal range. Called *poka-yoke* by the Japanese. *Syn:* failsafe techniques, mistake-proofing, poka-yoke.

Failure by incentive Breakdown of the pricing mechanism as a reflection of all costs and benefits of production and consumption.

Failure by market structure Insufficient market participants for active competition.

Failure Mode Analysis (FMA) Procedure to determine which malfunction symptoms appear immediately before or after a failure of a critical parameter in a system. After all the possible causes are listed for each symptom, the product is designed to eliminate the problems.

Failure Mode Effects Analysis (FMEA) Procedure in which each potential failure mode in every subitem of an item is analyzed to determine its effect on other subitems and on the required function of the item.

Failure Mode Effects and Criticality Analysis (FMECA) Procedure that is performed after a failure mode effects analysis to classify each potential failure effect according to its severity and probability of occurrence.

Failure to warn Failure to provide adequate warning of possible danger or to provide appropriate directions for use of a product.

Fair Labor Standards Act Law that regulates the employment of child labor outside of agriculture.

False registration statements Section 11 imposes liability on the issuer, all persons who signed the statement, every director or partner, experts who prepared or certified any part of the statement, and all underwriters; defendants other than issuer may assert the defense of due diligence.

Falsified identity (customer impersonation) Pretending to be someone you're not—a major problem in e-business transactions.

Family and Medical Leave Act of 1993 Law that requires some employers to grant employees leave for serious health conditions or certain other events.

FASB Statement 95 The accounting standard that created the Statement of Cash Flows.

Fatalism A view that individuals cannot control their destiny, that God has predetermined the course of their life.

Fault tree analysis A logical approach to identify the probabilities and frequencies of events in a system that are most critical to uninterrupted and safe operation. This analysis may include failure mode effects analysis (determining the result of component failure interactions toward system safety) and techniques for human error prediction.

Fault-tolerant computer system A computer system that has extra hardware, software, and power lines that guarantee that the system will continue running even when a mishap occurs.

Feasibility studies A series of studies conducted to determine if a proposed information system can be built, and whether or not it will benefit the business; the series includes technical, economic, and operational feasibility studies.

Feasible solution A decision alternative or solution that satisfies all constraints.

Feature fixture A display that draws special attention to selected features (e.g., color, shape, or style) of merchandise.

Features The way that benefits are delivered to customers. Features provide the solution to customer problems.

Fed float Part of the clearing float for a mailed check, it arises because the Fed may grant availability to the clearing bank before it presents the check (and debits the account of) the payee's bank. Fed float has been greatly reduced since 1980, because the 1980 Monetary Control Act mandated that the Fed eliminate or charge for Fed float.

Fed funds rate The rate charged on reserve borrowings, mostly overnight, transacted between banks.

Federal Advisory Council A group of prominent commercial bankers which gives input into Fed decision making.

Federal bankruptcy Marshaling of assets is not followed if the partnership is a debtor.

Federal Courts Courts established by the federal government to enforce federal laws and statutes.

Federal Deposit Insurance Corp. Improvement Act of 1991 Requires the FDIC to give acquiring banks the choice of whether to bid for all of a failed bank's deposits or just the insured deposits, signaling a reduction in coverage for uninsured deposits.

Federal legislation relating to warranties of consumer goods The Magnuson-Moss Warranty Act protects purchasers of consumer goods by providing that warranty information be clear and useful and that a seller who makes a written warranty cannot disclaim any implied warranty.

Federal Open Market Committee (FOMC) The seven members of the Board of Governors are also members of this group, which makes most of the monetary policy for the United States in its eight regularly scheduled meetings per year. The FOMC effects changes in the money supply by buying and selling Treasury securities (open market operations), which affects the reserve position of banks, and ultimately the money supply.

Federal Reserve Act (1913) Established the Federal Reserve System to oversee and regulate the national money and credit system.

Federal Reserve member banks *See:* Member banks.

Federal Reserve System (Fed) The nation's central bank, this organization oversees the national money and credit system by acting as lender of last resort, lending money to banks through the "discount window," and facilitating the payments mechanism, and is one of several national bodies that supervises and regulates banks.

Federal Trade Commission Act Entity created to prevent unfair methods of competition and unfair or deceptive practices. Actions may be brought by the FTC, not by private individuals.

Fedwire A linked network of the 12 Fed district banks which transfers funds for banks (and by extension their customers) by debiting or crediting the banks' reserve accounts. It is a major part of the Federal Reserve System's payment system involvement.

Feedback 1: Return of information in interpersonal communication; it may be based on fact or feeling and helps the party who is receiving the information judge how well he or she is being understood by the other party. More generally, information about a process that is used to make decisions about its performance and to adjust the process when necessary. **2:** The amount of information received about how well or how poorly one has performed.

Feedback control Control that focuses on the organization's outputs; also called postaction or output control.

Feedback loops Open-loop and closed-loop feedback.

Feedforward control Control that focuses on human, material, and financial resources flowing into the organization; also called preliminary or preventive quality control.

Femininity 1: A cultural preference for cooperation, group decision making, and quality of life. **2:** The quality of life, nurturing, and relationships.

FICA tax Federal Insurance Contributions Act tax used to finance federal programs for old-age and disability benefits (Social Security) and health insurance for the aged (Medicare).

Fiduciary duty Duty of utmost loyalty, fairness, and good faith owed by partners to each other and to the partnership.

Field A data element in a record, describing one aspect of an entity or event.

Field experience Experience acquired in actual rather than laboratory settings; training that exposes a corporate manager to a different cultural environment for a limited amount of time.

Field selling Involves calling on prospective customers in either their business or home locations.

Field warehouse agreement Inventories pledged as collateral and physically segregated from other inventory generally on the borrower's premises.

FIFO 1: Method of valuation of inventories for accounting purposes, meaning First-In First-Out. The principle rests on the assumption that costs should be charged against revenue in the order in which they occur. **2:** Stands for First In, First Out and values inventory based on the assumption that the oldest merchandise is sold before the more recently purchased merchandise.

FIFRA The Federal Insecticide, Fungicide, and Rodenticide Act regulates the sale and distribution of pesticides.

File A collection of records of the same type, for different entities or events.

File Transfer Protocol (FTP) Software that allows the transfer of files over communications lines.

Filing of certificate Two or more persons must file a signed certificate of limited partnership.

Filters Relative to human to human communication, those perceptions (based on culture, language, demographics, experience, and so on) that affect how a message is transmitted by the sender and how a message is interpreted by the receiver.

Final Assembly Schedule (FAS) A schedule of end items to finish the product for specific customers' orders in a make-to-order or assemble-to-order environment. It is also referred to as the finishing schedule because it may involve operations other than just the final assembly; also, it may not involve assembly, but simply final mixing, cutting, packaging, and so on. The FAS is prepared after receipt of a customer order as constrained by the availability of material and capacity, and it schedules the operations required to complete the product from the level where it is stocked (or master scheduled) to the end-item level.

Finance lease *See:* Capital lease.

Financial accounting A component of an organization's internal accounting system that provides information primarily for users outside the organization. The branch of accounting that is concerned with the recording of transactions using generally accepted accounting principles (GAAP) for a business or other economic unit and with a periodic preparation of various statements from such records.

Financial Accounting Standards Board (FASB) The main body responsible for promulgating accounting standards in the United States.

Financial Accounting Standards Board (FASB) Statement 95 Provides a set of guidelines to help classify cash r receipts and disbursement according to type of activity.

Financial break-even analysis Determining the operating income (EBIT) the firm needs to just cover all of its fixed financing costs and produce earnings per share equal to zero.

Financial break-even point The level of EBIT at which EPS equals zero.

Financial control The phase in which financial plans are implemented; control deals with the feedback and adjustment process required to ensure adherence to plans and modification of plans because of unforeseen changes.

Financial EDI (FEDI) The exchange of electronic business information such as lockbox information reports, daily balance reports, and monthly account analysis reports between a firm and its bank. In the context of payments, financial EDI refers to electronic data interchange combined with payment instructions. This allows customers to include invoice data and payment instructions in the same payment order.

Financial engineering A unique model is developed for a specific real currency option. Used when the results of a decision tree analysis are not adequate and cannot find a standard option that corresponds to the real option.

Financial flexibility The ability of the firm to augment its future cash flows to cover any unforeseen needs or to take advantage of any unforeseen opportunities.

Financial incentives Monetary offers intended to motivate; special funding designed to attract foreign direct investors that may take the form of land or building, loans, or loan guarantees.

Financial infrastructure Facilitating financial agencies in a country; for example, banks.

Financial Institution Buyer Credit Policy Policy that provides insurance coverage for loans by banks to foreign buyers of exports.

Financial Institutions Reform, Recovery and Enforcement Act (1989) Allowed bank holding companies to buy healthy savings and loan associations.

Financial intermediaries Specialized financial firms that facilitate the transfer of funds from savers to borrowers.

Financial lease A lease that does not provide for maintenance services, is not cancelable, and is fully amortized over its life. Also called a *capital lease*.

Financial leverage 1: The extent to which fixed-income securities (debt and preferred stock) are used in a firm's capital structure. The use of debt financing. **2:** Total assets divided by net worth or owners' equity that shows how aggressive the retailer is in its use of debt.

Financial markets "Mechanisms" by which borrowers and lenders get together.

Financial motive One of the theoretical motives for trade credit extension, applies where the seller has a lower cost of capital than the buyer and is able to pass along some of the difference.

Financial performance objectives Objectives that represent the profit and economic performance a retailer desires.

Financial planning The projection of sales, income, and assets based on alternative production and marketing strategies, as well as the determination of the resources needed to achieve these projections.

Financial ratio analysis An evaluation of financial performance and financial position between two or more firms.

Financial reporting disclosures The information presented in financial statements. Such disclosures may be either within the statements or in the accompanying notes.

Financial restructuring Situation in which the company changes its product lines or its relative use of assets with heavy fixed operating costs, altering the company's business risk.

Financial risk 1: The portion of stockholders' risk, over and above basic business risk, resulting from the manner in which the firm is financed. The possibility that a company will not be able to cover financing-related expenditures such as lease payments, interest, principal repayment, and referred stock dividends. **2:** Risk involving credit, foreign exchange, commodity trading, and interest rate; may involve chance for gain as well as loss.

Financial Services Modernization Act of 1999 Also known as the Gramm-Leach-Bliley Act, this law repealed the 1933 Glass-Steagall Act's prohibition on bank-investment company affiliations.

Financial shenanigans Actions or omissions intended to hide or distort the real financial performance or financial condition of a business entity.

Financial statement analysis The conversion of the data in financial statements into useful information.

Financial statement fraud Intentional misstatement of financial statements by omitting critical facts or disclosures, misstating amounts, or misapplying GAAP.

Financial statements Financial reports such as the balance sheet, income statement, and statement of cash flows that summarize the profitability and cash flows of an entity for a specific period and the financial position of the entity as of a specific date.

Financing activities Defined as cash flows resulting from proceeds of issuance of securities, retirement of debt, and payments of dividends or other distributions to shareholders.

Financing cash flows The cash flows arising from the firm's funding activities.

Financing feedbacks The effects on the income statement and balance sheet of actions taken to finance forecasted increases in assets.

Finding Conclusion of importance based on observation(s).

Finished-goods inventory 1: Inventory consisting of items that have passed through the complete production process but have yet to be sold. **2:** The cost of finished products on hand that have not been sold.

Finished goods ledger The subsidiary ledger that contains the individual accounts for each kind of commodity or product produced.

Finite forward scheduling An equipment scheduling technique that builds a schedule by proceeding sequentially from the initial period to the final period while observing capacity limits. A Gantt chart may be used with this technique. *See:* Finite scheduling.

Finite loading Assigning no more work to a work center than the work center can be expected to execute in a given time period. The specific term usually refers to a computer technique that involves calculating shop priority revisions in order to level load operation by operation.

Finite scheduling A scheduling methodology where work is loaded into work centers such that no work center capacity requirement exceeds the capacity available for that work center. *See:* Drum-buffer-rope, Finite forward scheduling.

Firewall Hardware and software designed to control access by Internet surfers to an information system, and access to Internet sites by organizational users.

Firm Planned Order (FPO) A planned order that can be frozen in quantity and time. The computer is not allowed to change it automatically; this is the responsibility of the planner in charge of the item that is being planned. This technique can aid planners working with MRP systems to respond to material and capacity problems by firming up selected planned orders. In addition, firm planned orders are the normal method of stating the master production schedule. *See:* Planning time fence.

Firm-specific, or diversifiable, risk That part of a security's risk associated with random outcomes generated by events, or behaviors, specific to the firm; it can be eliminated by proper diversification.

First differencing A means of correcting a data series for autocorrelation, which is accomplished by subtracting the previous value for the dependent variable from the current value, and then using the differences as the dependent variable (in lieu of the original values of the dependent variable).

First-Generation Languages (1GL) Machine languages.

First-In, First-Out (FIFO) method A method of inventory costing based on the assumption that the costs of merchandise sold should be charged against revenue in the order in which the costs were incurred.

First-line manager A manager who is at the first or second management level and is directly responsible for the production of goods and services.

Fiscal incentives Incentives used to attract foreign direct investment that provide specific tax measures to attract the investor.

Fiscal year The annual accounting period adopted by a business.

Fishbone diagram *See:* Cause-and-effect diagram.

Fisher effect Theory that nominal interest rates are composed of a real interest rate and anticipated inflation.

Fitness for a particular purpose Warranty that goods are fit for a stated purpose, provided the seller selects the product knowing the buyer's intended use and that the buyer is relying on the seller's judgment.

Fitness for use Term used to indicate that a product or service fits the customer's defined purpose for that product or service.

Five-Ss (5-Ss) Five practices for maintaining a clean and efficient workplace (Japanese). These include sort, set in order, shine, standardize, and sustain.

Five C's of credit Traditional means of evaluating a corporate credit applicant by investigating character, collateral, capacity, conditions, and capital. Character is thought to be the single most important aspect in this approach.

Five focusing steps In the theory of constraints, a process to continuously improve organizational profit by evaluating the production system and market mix to determine how to make the most profit using the system constraint. The steps consist of 1) identifying the constraint to the system, 2) deciding how to exploit the constraint to the system, 3) subordinating all nonconstraints to the constraint, 4) elevating the constraint to the system, 5) returning to step 1 if the constraint is broken in any previous step, while not allowing inertia to set in.

Five stages of national economic development A theory proposing that nations advance from an agricultural economy to an advanced industrial economy in five stages.

Five whys Persistent questioning technique to probe deeper to surface the root cause of a problem.

Fixed assets 1: Physical resources that are owned and used by a business and are permanent or have a long life. **2:** Property, plant, and equipment assets of an organization; also called *long-term* and *noncurrent assets.*

Fixed assets turnover ratio The ratio of sales to net fixed assets.

Fixed charge coverage ratio This ratio expands the TIE ratio to include the firm's annual long-term lease payments and sinking fund payments.

Fixed component Typically is composed of some base wage per hour, week, month, or year.

Fixed costs The portion of the total costs that do not depend on the volume; these costs remains the same no matter how much is produced.

Fixed exchange rate The government of a country officially declares that its currency is convertible into a fixed amount of some other currency.

Fixed exchange rate system Monetary system in which exchange rates are either held constant or allowed to fluctuate only within very narrow boundaries.

Fixed-for-floating rate swap In this type of swap, Party A, with floating rate debt, agrees to pay Party B, who has fixed rate debt, a fixed-rate interest payment based on the intended dollar amount stated in the agreement, in exchange for receipt of a floating-rate interest payment.

Fixed-interval review system A hybrid inventory system in which the inventory analyst reviews the inventory position at fixed time periods. If the inventory level is found to be above a preset reorder point, no action is taken. If the inventory level is at or below the reorder point, the analyst orders a variable quantity equal to $M - x$, where M is a maximum stock level and x is the current quantity on hand and on order (if any). This hybrid system does not reorder every review interval. It therefore differs from the fixed-interval order system, which automatically places an order whenever inventory is reviewed.

Fixed order quantity A lot-sizing technique in MRP or inventory management that will always cause planned or actual orders to be generated for a predetermined fixed quantity, or multiples thereof, if net requirements for the period exceed the fixed order quantity.

Fixed point surveillance Watching a fraud suspect from a fixed point, such as a restaurant, office, or other set location.

Fixed-position layout A facility's layout in which the product remains in one location and the required tasks and equipment are brought to it.

Fixed-price contract A contract in which a customer and a contractor agree on a price that will not change no matter how much the project actually costs the contractor.

Fixed rate currency Currency with a fixed rate of exchange within narrow limits against a major currency, such as the U.S. dollar or the British pound.

Fixed reorder cycle inventory model A form of independent demand management model in which an order is placed every *n* time units. The order quantity is variable and essentially replaces the items consumed during the current time period. Let *M* be the maximum inventory desired at any time, and let *x* be the quantity on hand at the time the order is placed. Then, in the simplest model, the order quantity will be $M - x$. The quantity *M* must be large enough to cover the maximum expected demand during the lead time plus a review interval. The order quantity model becomes more complicated whenever the replenishment lead time exceeds the review interval, because outstanding orders then have to be factored into the equation. These reorder systems are sometimes called fixed-interval order systems, order level systems, or periodic review systems. *Syn:* fixed-interval order system, fixed-order quantity system, order level system, periodic review system, time-based order system. *See:* Fixed reorder quantity inventory model, Independent demand item management models.

Fixed reorder quantity inventory model A form of independent demand item management model in which an order for a fixed quantity, Q, is placed whenever stock on hand plus on order reaches a predetermined reorder level, R. The fixed order quantity Q may be determined by the economic order quantity, by a fixed order quantity (such as a carton or a truckload), or by another model yielding a fixed result. The reorder point, R, may be deterministic or stochastic, and in either instance is large enough to cover the maximum expected demand during the replenishment lead time. Fixed reorder quantity models assume the existence of some form of a perpetual inventory record or some form of physical tracking, for example, a two-bin system that is able to determine when the reorder point is reached. These reorder systems are sometimes called fixed order quantity systems, lot-size systems, or order point-order quantity systems. *Syn:* fixed order quantity system, lot size system, order point-order quantity system, quantity-based order system. *See:* Fixed reorder cycle inventory model, Independent demand item management models, Order point, Order point system.

Flash memory A memory chip that can be rewritten and hold its content without electric power.

Flat structure A management structure characterized by an overall broad span of control and relatively few hierarchical levels.

Flat yield curve Horizontally shaped graph of the yields to maturity of securities with various maturities, implying a "no change" forecast of future interest rates.

Flexible benefits plan One that allows employees to select the benefits they prefer from groups of benefits established by the employer.

Flexible budget A budget that adjusts for varying rates of activity.

Flexible capacity The ability to operate manufacturing equipment at different production rates by varying staffing levels and operating hours or starting and stopping at will.

Flexible Manufacturing System (FMS) A group of numerically controlled machine tools interconnected by a central control system. The various machining cells are interconnected via loading and unloading stations by an automated transport system. Operational flexibility is enhanced by the ability to execute all manufacturing tasks on numerous product designs in small quantities and with faster delivery.

Flexible pricing A policy that encourages offering the same products and quantities to different customers at different prices.

Flexible spending account Account that allows employees to contribute pretax dollars to buy additional benefits.

Flexible staffing Use of recruiting sources and workers who are not traditional employees.

Flextime A modification of work scheduling that allows workers to determine their own starting and ending times within a broad range of available hours.

Float The delay between the time a payment is initiated and the time when the payment is debited to the payor (disbursement float) or credited to the payee (collection float). Within ethical limits companies try to maximize it on payments or minimize it on collections, and float continues to be an important fact of life that must be coped with. The difference between the balance shown in a firm's (or individual's) checkbook and the balance on the bank's records. *See:* Total slack.

Floating exchange rate Under this system, the government possesses no responsibility to declare that its currency is convertible into a fixed amount of some other currency; this diminishes the role of official reserves.

Floating lien A financing arrangement where a borrower's inventory in general is pledged as collateral for a loan.

Floating rate bond A bond whose interest rate fluctuates with shifts in the general level of interest rates.

Floating rate currency Currency whose exchange rate is determined by market forces.

Floating Rate Notes (FRNs) 1: Provision of some Eurobonds, in which the coupon rate is adjusted over time according to prevailing market rates. **2:** Type of loan in which the interest rate is reset either daily, weekly, monthly, quarterly, or semi-annually.

Floor plan A schematic that shows where merchandise and customer service departments are located, how customers circulate through the store, and how much space is dedicated to each department.

Floor planning The common name used for trust receipt loans made to automobile dealerships.

Flotation costs The costs associated with issuing new stocks or bonds.

Flow of capital International Monetary Fund facilitates the expansion and balanced growth of international trade, assists in eliminating foreign exchange restrictions, and smoothes the international balance of payments.

Flow of labor Controlled through passport, visa, and immigration regulations.

Flow of trade Controlled by trade barriers on imports and exports.

Flowchart 1: A graphical method used to describe an information system, including hardware pieces and logical processes. Over 30 symbols represent various types of operations, processes, input and output devices, and communication. **2:** Graphical representation of the steps in a process. Flowcharts are drawn to better understand processes. The flowchart is one of the seven tools of quality. **3:** Movement of products, negotiation, ownership, information, and promotion through each participant in the marketing channel.

FOB (free on board) destination Terms of agreement between buyer and seller whereby ownership passes when merchandise is received by the buyer and the seller pays the transportation costs.

FOB (free on board) shipping point Terms of agreement between buyer and seller whereby ownership passes when merchandise is delivered to the freight carrier and the buyer pays the transportation costs.

Focus A type of competitive strategy that emphasizes concentration on a specific regional market or buyer group.

Focus group Qualitative discussion group consisting of 8 to 10 participants, invited from a segment of the customer base to discuss an existing or planned product or service, led by a facilitator working from predetermined questions (focus groups may also be used to gather information in a context other than customers).

Focus strategy A strategy in which an organization concentrates on a specific regional market or buyer group.

Focused factory A plant established to focus the entire manufacturing system on a limited, concise, manageable set of products, technologies, volumes, and markets precisely defined by the company's competitive strategy, technology, and economics. *See:* Cellular manufacturing.

Footnote disclosure Information contained in a note accompanying the financial statements.

Footnotes Information that accompanies a company's financial statements and that provides interpretive guidance to the financial statements or includes related information that must be disclosed.

Forecast group Subsample of data used to test a forecast model.

Forecast reliability Predictive consistency.

Forced distribution Performance appraisal method in which ratings of employees' performance are distributed along a bell-shaped curve.

Force-field analysis Technique for analyzing the forces that aid or hinder an organization in reaching an objective.

Forecast A projection or prediction of future values of a time series.

Forecast bias Tendency for a forecasting model to systematically over- or under-predict the variable of interest. It can often be detected on a graph of forecast errors over time or across values of an important predictor variable.

Forecast horizon How far ahead the cash balance is being projected.

Forecast interval The units the horizon is segmented into, such as months in a year-ahead forecast.

Forecasted Cost at Completion (FCAC) The projected total cost of all the work required to complete a project.

Forecasting 1: An important activity that provides operations and supply chain managers with the numbers needed to make both long-term capacity decisions and short-term planning decisions. For example: What will the total demand for a new product be over the next five years? How many customers will we serve next week? **2:** Use of information from the past and present to identify expected future conditions.

Foreign agents A local agent in the host country is used to provide limited involvement for an MNE.

Foreign availability The ability of a firm's products to be obtained in markets outside the firm's home country.

Foreign bond Bonds that are issued by a country's borrowers in other countries, subject to the same restrictions as bonds issued by domestic borrowers.

Foreign corporation A corporation created under the laws of any other state, government, or country; it must obtain a certificate of authority from each state in which it does intrastate business.

Foreign Corrupt Practices Act (FCPA), An established U.S. code of conduct making it illegal for U.S. businesses to bribe foreign government officials, political parties, and political candidates, even if it is an acceptable practice in the foreign country; requires appropriate accounting controls for full disclosure of firms' foreign transactions.

Foreign currency transactions Transactions denominated in a currency other than the reporting currency of the entity.

Foreign currency translation A conversion of amounts in accounts of international subsidiaries (recorded in a foreign currency) to the currency used for consolidated financial statements.

Foreign debt A debt instrument sold by a foreign borrower but denominated in the currency of the country in which it is sold.

Foreign direct investment 1: International entry strategy that is achieved through the acquisition of foreign firms. **2:** The establishment or expansion of operations of a firm in a foreign country. Like all investments, it assumes a transfer of capital.

Foreign environment Refers to factors in a country that affect international business, including the country's cultural, legal, political, competitive, economic, and technological systems.

Foreign exchange market Market composed primarily of banks, serving firms, and consumers who wish to buy or sell various currencies.

Foreign exchange rate The price of one currency stated in relation to the price of another currency.

Foreign exchange risk The possibility that exchange rates will move adversely, causing results of foreign business activities to have a reduced value when converted into the company's home currency.

Foreign exchange risk management The management of the risk of loss from currency exchange rate movements on transactions, translation, or remeasurement involving foreign currency.

Foreign investment Many countries' laws dictate that foreign investments in their nation must be in the form of a joint venture with local partners and that the local partners must be majority owners.

Foreign Investment Risk Matrix (FIRM) Graph that displays financial and political risk by intervals, so that each country can be positioned according to its risk ratings.

Foreign key In a relational database, a field in a file that is a primary key in another file. Foreign keys allow association of data between the two files.

Foreign limited liability companies A limited liability company is considered "foreign" in any state other than that in which it was formed.

Foreign limited partnerships A limited partnership is considered "foreign" in any state other than that in which it was formed.

Foreign market opportunity analysis Broad-based research to obtain information about the general variables of a target market outside a firm's home country.

Foreign policy The area of public policy concerned with relationships with other countries.

Foreign service premium A financial incentive to accept an assignment overseas, usually paid as a percentage of the base salary.

Foreign subsidiary An international firm's operating unit established in foreign countries. It typically has its own management structure.

Foreign tax credit Credit applied to home-country tax payments due for taxes paid abroad.

Foreign trade zones Special areas where foreign goods may be held or processed without incurring duties and taxes.

Forfaiting Method of financing international trade of capital goods.

Form utility Achieved by the conversion of raw and component materials into finished products that are desired by the marketplace.

Formal account Complete review of all financial transactions of a partnership.

Formal accounting Equitable proceeding for a complete settlement of all partnership affairs.

Formal communication Officially sanctioned data within an organization, which includes publications, memoranda, training materials/events, public relations information, and company meetings.

Formal communication channel A communication channel that flows within the chain of command or task responsibility defined by the organization.

Formal team A team created by the organization as part of the formal organization structure.

Formalities Most statutes require only a majority of the partners to authorize registration as an LLP; others require unanimous approval.

Formalization 1: Represents decision making through bureaucratic mechanisms such as formal systems, established rules, and prescribed procedures. **2:** The written documentation used to direct and control employees. **3:** The degree to which an organization has rules, procedures, and written documentation.

Formalization stage The phase in an organization's life cycle involving the installation and use of rules, procedures, and control systems.

Formation The formation of a limited liability company requires substantial compliance with a state's limited liability company statute.

Fortress Europe Suspicion raised by trading partners of Western Europe, claiming that the integration of the European Union may result in increased restrictions on trade and investment by outsiders.

Forward buying (bridge buying) Retailers purchase enough product during a manufacturer's off-invoice allowance period to carry the retailers over until the manufacturer's next regularly scheduled deal.

Forward chaining (forward reasoning) The process in which an expert system looks for an outcome under the constraints of given conditions. Example: A medical ES accepts the conditions (age, temperature, and so on) of a patient and provides a diagnosis of the patient's disease.

Forward contract Agreement between a commercial bank and a client about an exchange of two currencies to be made at a future point in time at a specified exchange rate.

Forward discount Percentage by which the forward rate is less than the spot rate; typically quoted on an annualized basis.

Forward exchange contract An agreement to buy (or sell) a foreign currency in the future at a fixed rate called a *forward rate*.

Forward premium Percentage by which the forward rate exceeds the spot rate; typically quoted on an annualized basis.

Forward pricing Setting the price of a product based on its anticipated demand before it has been introduced to the market.

Forward rate(s) 1: The fixed future rate used in a forward exchange contract. **2:** Contracts that provide for two parties to exchange currencies on a future date at an agreed-upon exchange rate. **3:** Prices or yields which the market collectively forecasts today for future periods. In foreign exchange markets, forward rates refer to exchange rates between currencies which is contracted to exist at a future value date.

Forward scheduling A scheduling technique where the scheduler proceeds from a known start date and computes the completion date for an order, usually proceeding from the first operation to the last. Dates generated by this technique are generally the earliest start dates for operations. *Syn:* forward pass. *Ant:* back scheduling.

Forward value date The date that good funds will be credited to the account (similar to availability schedules in the United States).

Founders' shares Stock owned by the firm's founders who have sole voting rights; this type of stock generally has restricted dividends for a specified number of years.

Fourteen (14) points Both W. Edwards Deming and Philip B. Crosby have advocated 14 management practices to help organizations increase their quality and productivity.

Fourth Directive, The The EU Fourth Directive contains comprehensive accounting rules relevant to corporate accounting. It covers financial statements, their contents, methods of presentation, valuation methods, and disclosure of information. *See:* Eighth Directive, Seventh Directive.

Fourth-generation languages (4GLs) High-level programming languages that allow the programmer to concentrate on what the program should do, rather than on how it should do it. 4GLs contain many preprogrammed functions to expedite code writing. Sometimes called *application generators*.

Fraction defective chart (p chart) Attribute control chart used to track the proportion of defective units.

Franchise A form of licensing by which the owner of a product, service, or business method (the franchisor) obtains distribution through affiliated dealers (franchisees).

Franchise holding/loading Includes manufacturers' efforts to hold on to their franchise of current users by rewarding them for continuing to purchase the promoted brand, or to load them so they have no need to switch to another brand.

Franchising 1: A form of licensing in which an organization provides its foreign franchisees with a complete assortment of materials and services; an arrangement by which the owner of a product or service allows others to purchase the right to distribute the product or service with help from the owner. **2:** A form of licensing that allows a distributor or retailer exclusive rights to sell a product or service in a specified area. **3:** Agreement by which a firm provides a specialized sales or service strategy, support assistance, and possibly an initial investment in the franchise in exchange for periodic fees. **4:** Form of licensing that grants a wholesaler or a retailer exclusive rights to sell a product or a service in a specified area.

Fraud A generic term that embraces all the multifarious means which human ingenuity can devise, which are resorted to by one individual, to get an advantage over another by false representations. No definite and invariable rule can be laid down as a general proposition in defining fraud, as it includes surprise, trickery, cunning, and unfair ways by which another is cheated. The only boundaries defining it are those that limit human knavery.

Fraudulent tender offers Section 14(e) imposes civil liability for false and material statements or omissions or fraudulent, deceptive, or manipulative practices in connection with any tender offer.

Free Alongside Ship (FAS) Exporter quotes a price for the goods, including charges for delivery of the goods alongside a vessel at a port. Seller handles cost of unloading and wharfage; loading, ocean transportation, and insurance are left to the buyer.

Free Carrier (FCA) Applies only at a designated inland shipping point. Seller is responsible for loading goods into the means of transportation; buyer is responsible for all subsequent expenses.

Free cash flow The amount of operating cash flow remaining after replacing current productive capacity and maintaining current dividends.

Free cash flow hypothesis All else equal, firms that pay dividends from cash flows that cannot be reinvested in positive net present value projects, which are termed *free cash flows*, have higher values than firms that retain free cash flows.

Free market economic system An economic concept used to denote the economic system of a country unimpeded by government restrictions, and ideally subject to the laws of supply and demand of the market.

Free merchandise A discount whereby merchandise is offered in lieu of price concessions.

Free on Board (FOB) 1: Applies only to vessel shipments. Seller quotes a price covering all expenses up to and including delivery of goods on an overseas vessel provided by or for the buyer. **2:** A method of charging for transportation in which the vendor pays for all transportation costs and the buyer takes title on delivery.

Free on Board (FOB) factory A method of charging for transportation where the buyer assumes title to the goods at the factory and pays all transportation costs from the vendor's factory.

Free on Board (FOB) shipping point A method of charging for transportation in which the vendor pays for transportation to a local shipping point where the buyer assumes title and then pays all further transportation costs.

Free on Board (FOB) pricing Leaves the cost and responsibility of transportation to the customer.

Free rider A person who benefits from team membership but does not make a proportionate contribution to the team's work.

Free riding When a consumer seeks product information, usage instructions, and some times even warranty work from a full-service store but then, armed with the brand's model number, purchases the product from a limited-service discounter or over the Internet.

Free Slack (FS) The amount of time that a particular activity can be delayed without delaying the earliest start time of its immediately succeeding activities; the relative difference between the amounts of total slack for activities entering into that same activity. It's always a positive value.

Free trade area An area in which all barriers to trade among member countries are removed, although sometimes only for certain goods or services.

Free Trade Area of the Americas (FTAA) A hemispheric trade zone covering all of the Americas. Organizers hope for it to be operational by 2005.

"Free" trade credit Credit received during the discount period.

Free transferability of corporate shares Unless otherwise specified in the charter, corporate shares are freely transferable.

Free-flow layout A type of store layout in which fixtures and merchandise are grouped into free-flowing patterns on the sales floor.

Freely floating exchange rate system Monetary system in which exchange rates are allowed to move due to market forces without intervention by country governments.

Freestanding retailer Retailer that generally locates along major traffic arteries and does not have any adjacent retailers to share traffic.

Freight forwarders Specialists in handling international transportation by contracting with carriers on behalf of shippers.

Frequency The average number of times each person who is reached is exposed to an advertisement during a given time period.

Fringe benefits A variety of employee benefits that may take many forms, including vacations, pension plans, and health, life, and disability insurance.

Frustration-regression principle The idea that failure to meet a high-order need may cause a regression to an already satisfied lower-order need.

Fulfillment Picking, packing, and shipping after a customer places an order on line.

Full compensation An arrangement in which the delivery of goods to one party is fully compensated for by buying back more than 100 percent of the value that was originally sold.

Full disclosure One of the responsibilities of a public corporation to its shareholders and potential shareholders.

Full reconciliation Service which provides detailed checks outstanding information along with the checks paid data from company-supplied check issue detail.

Full-duplex Telecommunications whereby a party can transmit and receive data at the same time while the other party also transmits and receives.

Full-service merchant wholesalers Provide a wide range of services for retailers and business purchasers.

Functional currency The currency of the primary environment in which the international subsidiary operates.

Functional grouping The placing together of employees who perform similar functions or work processes or who bring similar knowledge and skills to bear.

Functional manager A manager who is responsible for a department that performs a single functional task and has employees with similar training and skills.

Functional matrix A structure in which functional bosses have primary authority and product or project managers simply coordinate product activities.

Functional organization Organization organized by discrete functions, for example, marketing/sales, engineering, production, finance, human resources.

Functional organization structure An organizational structure in which groups are made up of individuals who perform the same function, such as engineering or manufacturing, or have the same expertise or skills, such as electronics engineering or testing.

Functional structure An organization structure in which positions are grouped into departments based on similar skills, expertise, and resource use.

Functional-level strategy Addresses the question, "How should a firm integrate its various subfunctional activities and how should these activities be related to changes taking place in the various functional areas?" Pertains to all of the organization's major departments.

Fundamental attribution error The tendency to underestimate the influence of external factors on another's behavior and to overestimate the influence of internal factors.

Fundamental changes The directors have the power to make, amend, or repeal the bylaws, unless this power is exclusively reserved to the shareholders.

Fundamental forecasting Forecasting based on fundamental relationships between economic variables and exchange rates.

Funded debt Long-term debt; "funding" means replacing short-term debt with securities of longer maturity.

Funnel experiment Experiment that demonstrates the effects of tampering. Marbles are dropped through a funnel in an attempt to hit a flat-surfaced target below. The experiment shows that adjusting a stable process to compensate for an undesirable result or an extraordinarily good result will produce output that is worse than if the process had been left alone.

Future reality tree Technique used in the application of Goldratt's Theory of Constraints.

Future Value (FV) The amount to which a cash flow or series of cash flows will grow over a given period of time when compounded at a given interest rate.

Future Value Interest Factor for an Annuity (FVIFA$_{i,n}$) The future value interest factor for an annuity of n periods compounded at i percent.

Future Value Interest Factor for i and n (FVIF$_{i,n}$) The future value of $1 left on deposit for n periods at a rate of i percent per period—the multiple by which an initial investment grows because of the interest earned.

Futures contract A standardized contract that obligates the buyer (issuer) to purchase (sell) a specified amount of the item represented by the contract at a set price at the expiration of the contract.

Futures option An option contract that gives the buyer (issuer) the right to purchase (sell) the futures contract underlying the options contract.

Futures rates An exchange rate at which currencies can be traded at a future date. Futures differ from forwards in that the futures contract is standardized and traded on a national exchange.

Fuzzy logic A rule-based method used in artificial intelligence to solve problems with imprecise conditions. The method uses membership functions to characterize a situation.

FVA$_n$ The future value of an ordinary annuity over n periods.

FVIFA(DUE)$_{i,n}$ The future value interest factor for an annuity due—FVIFA(DUE)$_{i,n}$ = FVIFA$_{i,n}$ × (1 + i).

G

Gainsharing Type of program that rewards individuals financially on the basis of organizational performance.

Game theory General framework to help decision making when a firm payoff depends on actions taken by other firms.

Gantt chart Type of bar chart used in process/project planning and control to display planned work and finished work in relation to time. Also called a *milestone chart*.

Gap analysis Technique that compares a company's existing state to its desired state (as expressed by its long-term plans) to help determine what needs to be done to remove or minimize the gap.

Garbage can model Model that describes the pattern or flow of multiple decision within an organizaion.

Garnishment A court action in which a portion of an employee's wages is set aside to pay a debt owed a creditor.

Garn-St. Germain Depository Institutions Act (1982) Enacted alterations allowing: 1) depository institutions to pay interest on money market deposit accounts in order to compete with money market mutual funds and 2) savings and loans associations to lend to businesses.

Gatekeeping Role of an individual (often a facilitator) in a group meeting in helping ensure effective interpersonal interactions (for example, someone's ideas are not ignored due to the team moving on to the next topic too quickly).

Gateway A device that connects two communications networks, each consisting of different hardware devices, for example an IBM- and a Macintosh-based network.

Gauge Repeatability and Reproducibility (GR&R) Evaluation of a gauging instrument's accuracy by determining whether the measurements taken with it are repeatable (that is, there is close agreement among a number of consecutive measurements of the output for the same value of the input under the same operating conditions) and reproducible (that is, there is close agreement among repeated measurements of the output for the same value of input made under the same operating conditions over a period of time).

Gearing adjustment A gearing adjustment equals the average borrowing divided by average operating assets multiplied by total current value adjustments for cost of goods sold, depreciation, and so on. It shows the benefit (or disadvantage) to shareholders from debt financing during a period of changing prices. The amount of gearing adjustment is added (deducted) to current cost income.

General Adaptation Syndrome (GAS) The physiological response to a stressor, beginning with an alarm response, continuing to resistance, and sometimes ending in exhaustion if the stressor continues beyond the person's ability to cope.

General Agreement on Tariffs and Trade (GATT), now called World Trade Organization (WTO) A 124-nation organization that provides the conditions under which a nation can impose trade barriers such as tariffs. The new World Trade Organization was created to settle trade disputes.

General Agreement on Trade in Services (GATS) A legally enforceable pact among GATT participants that covers trade and investments in the services sector.

General controls Policies and procedures that help ensure the continued, proper operation of computer information systems. They include controls over data center operations, system software acquisition and maintenance, access security, and application system development and maintenance. General controls support the functioning of programmed application controls. Other terms sometimes used to describe general controls are general computer controls and information technology controls.

General environment Includes those sectors that may not directly affect the daily operations of a firm but will indirectly influence it.

General ledger The primary ledger, when used in conjunction with subsidiary ledgers, that contains all of the balance sheet and income statement accounts.

General manager A manager who is responsible for several departments that perform different functions.

General obligation The banking for the interest principal payments of these securities is simply future general revenues and the issuer's capacity to raise taxes.

General partner Member of either a general or limited partnership with unlimited liability for its debts, full management powers, and a right to share in the profits.

General partnership An unincorporated business association of two or more persons to carry on as co-owners of a business for profit.

General price index An index used to estimate the amount of inflation or deflation in an economy.

General price-level accounting *See:* Constant monetary unit restatement.

General purpose application software Programs that serve varied purposes, such as developing decision-making tools or creating documents; examples include spreadsheets and word processors.

General reserve An equity reserve that normally serves the same purpose as an appropriation of retained earnings; that is, it temporarily restricts the maximum amount that can be declared for dividends.

Generally Accepted Accounting Principles (GAAP) Accounting principles in the United States that are recognized by a standard-setting body or by authoritative support for the preparation of financial statements.

Generally Accepted Manufacturing Practices (GAMP) A group of practices and principles, independent of any one set of techniques, that defines how a manufacturing company should be managed. Included are such elements as the need for data accuracy, frequent communication between marketing and manufacturing, top management control of the production planning process (sales and operations planning process), systems capable of validly translating high-level plans into detailed schedules, and so on. Today GAMP includes such paradigms as just-in-time, theory of constraints, total quality management, business process reengineering, and supply chain management.

Genetic algorithms Sets of algorithms used in artificial intelligence to solve complex problems for which the number of models for a solution is huge. The algorithms are either eliminated or combined with other algorithms to eventually produce the one that can solve the problem optimally. Called *genetic algorithms* because the method mimics the evolution of species over millions of years through changes in their genetic codes.

Geocentric staffing outlook Holds that nationality should not make any difference in the assignment of key positions anywhere (local subsidiary, regional headquarters, or central headquarters); that competence should be the prime criterion for selecting managerial staff.

Geodemographic information Allows identification of customer segments based on geographical location and demographic information.

Geographic Information Systems (GIS) 1: Information systems that exhibit information visually on a computer monitor with local, regional, national, or international maps, so that the information can easily be related to locations or routes on the map. GISs are used, for example, in the planning of transportation and product distribution, or the examination of government resources distributed over an area. **2:** A computerized system that combines physical geography with cultural geography.

Geographic organization Organization structured by geography, territory, region, and so on.

Geometric Dimensioning and Tolerancing (GDT) Method to minimize production costs by considering the functions or relationships of part features in order to define dimensions and tolerances.

Giro acceptance Foreign payment method in which computer-processable stub card is signed by the customer, who then takes it to the post office. The bill mailed to the customer has a stub attached to it that includes the seller's bank and account number.

GIRO systems A collection system for consumer payments that is commonplace in Europe. Sellers send customers an invoice with a payment stub encoded with the seller's bank account number. The customer signs the stub and then takes it to a GIRO processor. The processor delivers the stubs to the nearest GIRO bank which then debits the customer's account and credits the seller's account.

Glasnost The Soviet policy of encouraging the free exchange of ideas and discussion of problems, pluralistic participation in decision making, and increased availability of information.

Glass ceiling 1: Discriminatory practices that have prevented women and other protected-class members from advancing to executive-level jobs. **2:** Invisible barrier that separates women and minorities from top management positions.

Global Worldwide interdependencies of financial markets, technology, and living standards.

Global account management Global customers of a company may be provided with special services including a single point of contact for domestic and international operations and consistent worldwide service.

Global capital markets Capital markets in a global economy that attract investors and investees from throughout the world.

Global corporate culture Corporate core values that cut across all of a firm's subsidiaries located around the globe.

Global corporations International businesses that view the world as their marketplace.

Global manager An international executive with the ability to manage enterprises in diverse cultures.

Global mind-set In today's global environment, even for employees who may not go abroad, it is necessary to constantly sensitize everyone to the notion that the company is in a global business.

Global organization One having corporate units in a number of countries integrated to operate worldwide.

Global outsourcing Engaging in the international division of labor so as to obtain the cheapest sources of labor and supplies regardless of country; also called global sourcing.

Global reporting initiative An international, multistakeholder effort to create a common framework for voluntary reporting of the economic, environmental, and social impact of organization-level activity.

Global strategy A corporation using this strategy uses all of its resources against its competition in a very integrated fashion—all of its foreign subsidiaries and divisions are highly interdependent in both operations and strategy.

Global team A work team made up of members of different nationalities whose activities span multiple countries; may operate as a virtual team or meet face to face.

Global village A term used to refer to our world in the age of information and telecommunications because people are highly accessible to each other.

Globalization 1: Refers to the global economic integration of many formerly national economies into one global economy. **2:** The notion that in the future more and more companies will have to conduct their business activities in a highly interconnected world, thus presenting their managements with the challenge of reengineering their systems to cope with this new environment. Awareness, understanding, and response to global developments as they affect a company. **3:** The standardization of product design and advertising strategies throughout the world.

Globalization approach Approach to international marketing in which differences are incorporated into a regional or global strategy that will allow for differences in implementation.

Glocalization 1: A term coined to describe the networked global organization approach to an organizational structure. **2:** The planning and designing of global Web sites so that they also cater to local needs and preferences.

Go/no-go State of a unit or product. Two parameters are possible: go conforms to specifications, and no-go does not conform to specifications.

Goal 1: A desired future state that the organization attempts to realize. **2:** Statement of general intent, aim, or desire; it is the point toward which management directs its efforts and resources; goals are often nonquantitative.

Goal approach An approach to organizational effectiveness that is concerned with output and whether the organization achieves its output goals.

Goal conflict Occurs when an employee's self-interest differs from business objectives.

Goal incompatibility Occurs when achieving the goals of either the supplier or the retailer would hamper the performance of the other.

Goal setting The process in which management and employees establish goals that become the basis for performance appraisal and review.

Goals and objectives Are the performance results intended to be brought about through the execution of a strategy.

Going concern concept The accounting concept that an economic entity will continue in operation for the foreseeable future.

Going private transactions A combination that makes a publicly held corporation a private one; includes cash-out combinations and management buyouts.

Going public The act of selling stock to the public at large by a closely held corporation or its principal stockholders.

Gold standard 1: A standard for international currencies in which currency values were stated in terms of gold. **2:** Era in which each currency was convertible into gold at a specified rate, allowing the exchange rate between two currencies to be determined by their relative convertibility rates per ounce of gold.

Golden parachute 1: A contract in which a corporation agrees to make payments to key officers in control of the corporation. **2:** A payment to senior management to make it less concerned for its own welfare and more interested in stockholders when considering a takeover bid.

Good person philosophy Philosophy that holds that individuals seek out and emulate good role models.

Goods 1: Objects, devices, or things. **2:** Tangible personal property.

Goods trade An account of the BOP statement that records funds used for merchandise imports and funds obtained from merchandise exports.

Goodwill 1: The amount paid by the buyer of a business for above-normal profits. An intangible asset of a business due to such favorable factors as location, product superiority, reputation, and managerial skill. **2:** What international corporations create when they share with locals the benefits derived from the markets they exploit. **3:** An intangible asset, usually based on customer loyalty, that a retailer pays for when buying an existing business.

Government policies Extreme social and economic conditions may sometimes force a political party into radical policy changes. Generally, however, governments change their policies gradually; they implement new policies to attract the foreign investments needed by the nation to attain its economic development objectives.

Government regulation Interference in the marketplace by governments.

Government warrant Essentially a payable-through-draft issued by a government agency.

Governmental units Comprise the sector of the business market represented by federal, state, and local governmental units that purchase goods and services.

Grade Planned or recognized difference in requirements for quality.

Gramm-Leach Bliley Act Passed in 1999, this law prohibits the use of false pretenses to access the personal information of others. It does allow banks and other financial institutions to share or sell customer information, unless customers proactively "opt out" and asks that their information not be shared.

Grand jury Body of 4 to 23 individuals who deliberate in secret to decide whether there is sufficient evidence to charge someone in a preliminary hearing.

Grand strategy The general plan of major action by which an organization intends to achieve its long-term goals.

Grapevine Informal communication channels over which information flows within an organization, usually without a known origin of the information and without any confirmation of its accuracy or completeness (sometimes referred to as the rumor mill).

Graph Visual representation of data.

Graphic rating scale A scale that allows the rater to mark an employee's performance on a continuum.

Graphical Evaluation and Review Technique (GERT) A type of network planning technique.

Graphical User Interface (GUI) Icons, frames, scroll bars, and other graphical means that make software easy and intuitive to learn and use.

Gray market A market entered in a way not intended by the manufacturer of the goods.

Gray marketing Marketing of authentic, legally trademarked goods through unauthorized channels.

Grease payments Minor, facilitating payments to officials for the primary purpose getting them to do whatever they are supposed to do anyway.

Green-circled employee An incumbent who is paid below the range set for the job.

Greenfield venture The most risky type of direct investment, whereby a company builds a subsidiary from scratch in a foreign country.

Greenmail A situation in which a firm, trying to avoid a takeover, buys back stock at a price above the existing market price from the person(s) trying to gain control of the firm.

GLOSSARY

Grid layout A type of store layout in which counters and fixtures are placed in long rows or "runs," usually at right angles, throughout the store.

Gross margin 1: Net sales minus the cost of goods sold. **2:** The difference between net sales and cost of goods sold.

Gross margin percentage 1: Shows how much gross margin a retailer makes as a percentage of sales. **2:** The gross margin divided by net sales or what percent of each sales dollar is gross margin.

Gross margin return on inventory Gross margin divided by average inventory at cost; alternatively it is the gross margin percent multiplied by net sales divided by average inventory investment.

Gross pay The total earnings of an employee for a payroll period.

Gross profit The excess of net sales over the cost of merchandise sold.

Gross profit margin Gross profit margin divided by net sales; a measure of markup.

Gross profit method A means of estimating inventory based on the relationship of gross profit to sales.

Gross Rating Points (GRPs) Accumulation of rating points including all vehicles in a media purchase over the span of a particular campaign.

Gross requirement The total of independent and dependent demand for a component before the netting of on-hand inventory and scheduled receipts.

Gross sales The retailer's total sales including sales for cash or for credit.

Group consensus approach A decision-making approach that forces members in the group to reach a unanimous decision.

Group decision support system A set of personal computers and one large screen with special software that facilitates brainstorming, the examination of ideas, voting, and reaching a decision by a group of decision makers.

Group Technology (GT) An engineering and manufacturing philosophy that identifies the physical similarity of parts (common routing) and establishes their effective production. It provides for rapid retrieval of existing designs and facilitates a cellular layout.

Groupware Any of several types of software that enable users of computers in remote locations to work together on the same project. The users can create and change documents and graphic designs on the same monitor.

Growth rate, g The expected rate of change in dividends per share.

Growth trend analysis Assumes constant percentage change over time.

H

Habitual problem solving Occurs when the consumer relies on past experiences and learning to convert the problem into a situation requiring less thought. The consumer has a strong preference for the brand to buy and the retailer from which to purchase it.

Hacker A person who accesses a computer system without permission.

Half-duplex Telecommunications whereby the receiving party must wait until the transmitting party finishes, before transmitting to the party. A party cannot receive while transmitting or transmit while receiving.

Halo effect An overall impression of a person or situation based on one characteristic, either favorable or unfavorable; a type of rating error that occurs when an employee receives the same rating on all dimensions regardless of his or her performance on individual ones.

Hand-held computers Computers that are small enough to fit in the palm of a person's hand. Also called *palm computers* or *personal digital assistants (PDAs)*.

Handling costs Costs to a firm associated with the act of transferring inventory to customers.

Hands-on consumer research Conducted by direct observation by managers of the way current customers use specific products and brands. The opposite is arm's-length research, which is undertaken by external suppliers.

Hard controls Based on objective evidence, hard controls are formal and tangible, and easier to measure and evaluate. An example is budget.

Hard currencies Money that is readily acceptable as payment in international business transactions—usually the currencies of industrially advanced countries (for example, dollars and pounds).

Hard disk A stack of several rigid aluminum platters usually installed in the same box that holds the CPU and other computer components; may be portable.

Hard sell Trying every means to get the prospective customer to buy, regardless of whether it is in the prospect's best interest.

Hard skills Include technical skills such as functional skills, problem-solving skills, and decision-making skills. In a way, hard skills are acquired.

Hardship allowance An allowance paid during an assignment to an overseas area that requires major adaptation.

Harmonization Keeping the differences among national accounting standards to a minimum. Alternative accounting rules or practices may exist in different countries as long as they are "in harmony" with one another and can be reconciled.

Hawthorne studies A series of experiments on worker productivity begun in 1924 at the Hawthorne plant of Western Electric Company in Illinois; attributed employees' increased output to managers' better treatment of them during the study.

Hazardous air pollutants To protect the public health, the EPA administrator must establish hazardous air pollutants standards that provide ample safety margins.

Health A general state of physical, mental, and emotional well-being.

Health Maintenance Organization (HMO) Managed care plan that provides services for a fixed period on a prepaid basis.

Health promotion A supportive approach to facilitate and encourage employees to enhance healthy actions and lifestyles.

Hedge inventory A form of inventory buildup to buffer against some event that may not happen. Hedge inventory planning involves speculation related to potential labor strikes, price increases, unsettled governments, and events that could severely impair a company's strategic initiatives. Risk and consequences are unusually high, and top management approval is often required.

Hedge To counterbalance a present sale or purchase with a sale or purchase for future delivery as a way to minimize loss due to price fluctuations; to make counterbalancing sales or purchases in the international market as protection against adverse movements in the exchange rate.

Hedger A person who has a cash position or an anticipated cash position that he or she is trying to protect from adverse interest rate movements.

Hedging 1: A transfer of risk from one party to another; similar to speculation and may be used to handle risks not subject to insurance, such as price fluctuations. **2:** Measures taken to protect against risks associated with foreign exchange fluctuations.

Held-to-maturity securities Investments in bonds or other debt securities that management intends to hold to their maturity.

Help desk The group of small teams who specialize in troubleshooting problems in different areas of an information system—hardware, software, communications, and so forth.

Herfindahl Hirschmann Index (HHI) The sum of squared market shares for all *n* industry competitors.

Heroes Organizational members who serve as models or ideals for serving cultural norms and values.

Heterogeneity Distinguishing characteristic of services that reflects the variation in consistency from one service transaction to the next.

Heuristics Rules that cannot be formulated as a result of ordinary, proven knowledge but only through experience.

Hierarchical database A database model that generally follows an upside-down tree structure, in which each record can have only one parent record.

Hierarchy of needs model Model that theorizes that individuals have lower-level physiological and safety and security needs, which are first satisfied before higher-level needs of belongingness or social esteem and self-actualization are pursued.

Hierarchy of needs theory A content theory that proposes that people are motivated by five categories of needs—physiological, safety, belongingness, esteem, and self-actualization—that exist in a hierarchical order.

Hierarchy structure Organization that is organized around functional departments/product lines or around customers/customer segments and is characterized by top-down management. Also referred to as a *bureaucratic model* or *pyramid structure*.

High-context culture A culture in which behavioral and environmental nuances are an important means of conveying information. In the course of business, participants establish social trust first, value personal relations and goodwill, make agreements on the basis of general trust, and like to conduct slow and ritualistic business negotiations.

High dollar group sort A special expediting of large dollar amounts through the clearing system, with the Fed granting the depositing bank immediate credit if it deposits the check early in the morning.

High liquidity strategy Current asset allocation strategy which prescribes a high proportion of assets to be held in cash and securities in order to reduce the chance of running out of cash.

High-low method A technique that uses the highest and lowest total costs as a basis for estimating the variable cost per unit and the fixed cost component of a mixed cost.

High-low pricing System that involves the use of high everyday prices and low leader "specials" on items typically featured in weekly ads.

High-margin/high-turnover retailer Retailer that operates on a high gross margin percentage and a high rate of inventory turnover.

High-margin/low-turnover retailer Retailer that operates on a high gross margin percentage and a low rate of inventory turnover.

High-performance retailers Retailers that produce financial results substantially superior to the industry average.

High performance work Defined by the MBNQA criteria as work approaches systematically directed toward achieving ever higher levels of overall performance, including quality and productivity.

High power distance culture A state in which a person at a higher position in the organizational hierarchy makes the decision and the employees at the lower levels simply follow the instructions.

High-quality service The type of service that meets or exceeds customers' expectations.

High-velocity environments Industries in which competitive and technological change is so extreme that market data is either unavailable or obsolete, strategic windows open and shut quickly, and the cost of a decision error is company failure.

Higher trial courts State courts that try felony (larger crimes) and civil cases above a predetermined amount.

Histogram Graphic summary of variation in a set of data. The pictorial nature of the histogram lets people see patterns that are difficult to see in a simple table of numbers. The histogram is one of the seven tools of quality.

Historical cost convention A method of accounting using data in terms of the units of currency in which a transaction originally took place.

Historical yield spread analysis Study of risk-related and maturity-related interest rate differences, motivated by a desire to detect profitable trading strategies.

Hold point Point, defined in an appropriate document, beyond which an activity must not proceed without the approval of a designated organization or authority.

Holder-of-record date (date of record) The date the company opens the ownership books to determine who will receive the dividend; the stockholders of record on this date receive the dividend.

Holding costs The costs associated with the storage of inventory.

Holistic planning Organizational planning that focuses on the big picture, including objectives and goals; also called *top-down planning*.

Home page 1: The opening page of a Web site. **2:** The introductory or first material viewers see when they access a retailer's Internet site. It is the equivalent to a retailer's store front in the physical world.

Horizontal analysis Financial analysis that compares an item in a current statement with the same item in prior statements.

Horizontal communication The lateral or diagonal exchange of messages among peers or coworkers.

Horizontal cooperative advertising Occurs when two or more retailers band together to share the cost of advertising usually in the form of a joint promotion of an event or sale that would benefit both parties.

Horizontal dependency The relationship between the components at the same level in the bill of material, in which all must be available at the same time and in sufficient quantity to manufacture the parent assembly.

Horizontal information interchange The sharing of information by organizations in a horizontal market.

GLOSSARY

Horizontal linkage The amount of communication and coordination that occurs horizontally across organizational departments.

Horizontal linkage model A model of the three components of organizational design needed to achieve new product innovation: departmental specialization, boundary spanning, and horizontal linkages.

Horizontal market A market in which all players buy or sell the same type of product, making them competitors.

Horizontal merger 1: A combination of two firms that produce the same type of good or service. **2:** Acquisition by one company of a competing company.

Horizontal merger guidelines Government approval standards for combinations among competitors.

Horizontal price fixing Occurs when a group of competing retailers (or other channel members operating at a given level of distribution) establishes a fixed price at which to sell certain brands of products.

Horizontal privity Determines who benefits from a warranty and therefore may bring a cause of action.

Horizontal promotions Instead of slowly climbing the organizational ladder, workers and managers make lateral movements, acquiring expertise in different functions such as marketing or manufacturing.

Horizontal restraints Agreements among competitors.

Horizontal structure Organization that is organized along a process or value-added chain, eliminating hierarchy and functional boundaries (also referred to as a *systems structure*).

Horizontal team A formal team composed of employees from about the same hierarchical level but from different areas of expertise.

Hoshin kanri, hoshin planning Japanese-based strategic planning/policy deployment process which involves consensus at all levels as plans are cascaded throughout the organization, resulting in actionable plans and continual monitoring and measurement.

Host-country national An employee working for a firm in an operation who is a citizen of the country where the operation is located, but where the headquarters for the firm are in another country.

Hostile environment Sexual harassment where an individual's work performance or psychological well-being is unreasonably affected by intimidating or offensive working conditions.

Hostile takeover The acquisition of a company over the opposition of its management.

House of Quality Diagram (named for its house-shaped appearance) that clarifies the relationship between customer needs and product features. It helps correlate market or customer requirements and analysis of competitive products with higher level technical and product characteristics and makes it possible to bring several factors into a single figure. Also known as *Quality Function Deployment* (QFD).

Household decision making Occurs when significant decisions are made by individuals jointly with other members of their household, and for joint use by the members of the household.

Housing allowance An allowance paid during assignment overseas to provide living quarters.

HR audit A formal research effort that evaluates the current state of HR management in an organization.

HR research The analysis of data from HR records to determine the effectiveness of past and present HR practices.

HR strategies Means used to anticipate and manage the supply of and demand for human resources.

Human capital The economic value of the knowledge, experience, skills, and capabilities of employees.

Human relations movement A movement in management thinking and practice that emphasized satisfaction of employees' basic needs as the key to increased worker productivity.

Human relations theory Theory focusing on the importance of human factors in motivating employees.

Human Resource Information System (HRIS) An integrated computer system designed to provide data and information used in HR planning and decision making.

Human Resource Management (HRM) 1: Activities undertaken to attract, develop, and maintain an effective workforce within an organization. **2:** The design of formal systems in an organization to ensure effective and efficient use of human talent to accomplish organizational goals.

Human Resource (HR) planning Process of analyzing and identifying the need for and availability of human resources so that the organization can meet its objectives.

Human resources perspective A management perspective that suggests jobs should be designed to meet higher-level needs by allowing workers to use their full potential.

Human skill The ability to work with and through other people and to work effectively as a group member.

Hybrid production method A production planning method that combines the aspects of both the chase and level production planning methods. *Syn:* hybrid strategy. *See:* chase production method, level production method, production planning method.

Hygiene factors 1: Factors that involve the presence or absence of job dissatisfiers, including working conditions, pay, company policies, and interpersonal relationships. **2:** Term used by Frederick Herzberg to label "dissatisfiers." *See:* Dissatisfiers.

Hypergeometric distribution Discrete distribution defining the probability of *r* occurrences in *n* trials of an event, when there are a total of *d* occurrences in a population of *N*.

Hypermedia Perhaps the Web's most essential ingredient, this feature enables a computer user to access additional information by clicking on selected text or graphics displayed on-screen.

Hypernorms Transcultural values, including fundamental human rights.

Hypertext Computer-generated text that allows the reader to click designated words (typically colored or boldfaced) to open a linked file that elaborates on the topic, or to invoke images or sound associated with the topic.

Hypertext Markup Language (HTML) A programming language for Web pages and Web browsers.

Hypertext Transfer Protocol (HTTP) Software that allows browsers to log on to Web sites.

I

Iconic model A physical replica, or representation, of a real object.

Idea champion 1: A person who sees the need for and champions productive change within the organization. **2:** Organizational members who provide the time and energy to make things happen; sometimes called "advocates," "intrapreneurs," and "change agents."

Idea incubator An in-house program that provides a safe harbor where ideas from employees throughout the organization can be developed without interference from company bureaucracy or politics.

Identities Economic relations that are true by definition.

Idle capacity The unused capacity of a selling segment that is not needed for producing products or services to meet demand from the external market.

If-then rules A method of knowledge representation that holds the facts in the form of if-then statements; also called *production rules*.

Illegal gratuities Similar to bribery, except that there is no intent to influence a particular business decision, but rather to reward someone for making a favorable decision.

Illegal per se Conclusively presumed unreasonable and therefore illegal.

Illegitimate norms Norms that are incompatible with hypernorms (for example, exposing employees to unacceptable levels of carcinogens.

Image reinforcement Careful selection of the right premium object, or appropriate sweepstakes prize, to reinforce a brand's desired image.

Imaging The transformation of text and graphical documents into digitized files. The document can be electronically retrieved and printed to reconstruct a copy of the original. Imaging has saved much space and expense in paper-intensive business areas.

Immoral management A posture that is devoid of ethical principles or precepts and that implies a positive and active opposition to what is ethical.

Impact Refers to how strong an impression an advertisement makes and how well it ultimately leads to a purchase.

Impact printer A printer that reproduces an image on a page using mechanical impact.

Imperfect market 1: A market where factors of production are somewhat immobile. **2:** The condition where, due to the costs to transfer labor and other resources used for production, firms may attempt to use foreign factors of production when they are less costly than local factors.

Imperfect market theory A firm engages in international trade to gain access to factors of production.

Imperfection Quality characteristic's departure from its intended level or state without any association to conformance to specification requirements or to the usability of a product or service. *See also:* blemish, defect, and nonconformity.

Implementation 1: The step in the decision-making process that involves using managerial, administrative, and persuasive abilities to translate the chosen alternative into action. **2:** The phase of implementing a new information system that includes training and conversion. Also called *delivery*.

Implementor A type of leader who takes a newly initiated vision and systematically puts into operation the desired changes. The typical subsidiary role, which involves implementing strategy that originates with headquarters.

Implicit code of ethics An unwritten but well understood set of rules or standards of moral responsibility.

Implied in fact contract Contract where agreement of the parties is inferred from their conduct.

Implied powers Those necessary or convenient to and consistent with the express powers.

Implied warranty Contractual obligation arising out of certain circumstances of the sale.

Implied warranty of fitness A warranty that implies that the merchandise is fit for a particular purpose and arises when the customer relies on the retailer to assist or make the selection of goods to serve a particular purpose.

Implied warranty of merchantability Warranty made by every retailer when the retailer sells goods and implies that the merchandise sold is fit for the ordinary purpose for which such goods are typically used. The disclaimer must mention "merchantability" and, in the case of a writing, must be conspicuous (in a lease the disclaimer must be in writing and conspicuous).

Implosion The process of determining the where-used relationship for a given component. Implosion can be single-level (showing only the parents on the next higher level) or multilevel (showing the ultimate top-level parent). *See:* Where-used list. *Ant:* explosion.

Import/export letters of credit Trade-related letters of credit.

Import substitution A policy for economic growth adopted by many developing countries that involves the systematic encouragement of domestic production of goods formerly imported.

Importing and exporting Selling and buying goods and services with organizations in other countries.

Improper accumulation Retention of earnings by a business for the purpose of enabling stockholders to avoid personal income taxes.

Incentive-based regulation Rules that benefit consumers through enhanced efficiency.

Incentives Bonuses or rewards (sweepstakes, coupons, premiums, display allowances, and so on) for purchasing one brand rather than another.

Income bond 1: A bond that pays interest to the holder only if the interest is earned by the firm. **2:** Bond that conditions payment of interest on corporate earnings

Income elasticity Responsiveness of demand to changes in income, holding constant the effect of all other variables.

Income elasticity of demand A means of describing change in demand in relative response to a change in income.

Income from operations (operating income) The excess of gross profit over total operating expenses.

Income leveling *See:* Income smoothing.

Income smoothing Use of reserves to transfer income between periods.

Income statement 1: A financial statement that summarizes the firm's financial performance for a given time interval; sometimes called a profit-and-loss statement. **2:** A summary of the revenues and expenses of a business entity for a specific period of time. **3:** A statement summarizing the firm's revenues and expenses over an accounting period, generally a quarter or a year. **4:** Financial statement that reports the amount of net income earned by a company during a specified period.

Income summary The account used in the closing process for transferring the revenue and expense account balances to the retained earnings account at the end of the period.

In-control process Process in which the statistical measure being evaluated is in a state of statistical control; that is, the variations among the observed sampling results can be attributed to a constant system of chance/common causes. *See:* out-of-control process.

Incorporators The persons who sign the articles of incorporation.

GLOSSARY 1545

Incoterms International Commerce Terms. Widely accepted terms used in quoting export prices.

Incremental cash flow The change in a firm's net cash flow attributable to an investment project.

Incremental change Total difference resulting from a decision.

Incremental decision process model A model that describes the structured sequence of activities undertaken from the discovery of a problem to its solution.

Incremental operating cash flows The changes in day-to-day cash flows that result from the purchase of a capital project and continue until the firm disposes of the asset.

Incremental profit Gain or loss associated with a given managerial decision.

Indemnification A corporation may indemnify a director or officer for liability incurred if he acted in good faith and was not adjudged negligent or liable for misconduct.

Indented bill of material A form of multilevel bill of material. It exhibits the highest level parents closest to the left margin, and all the components going into these parents are shown indented toward the right. All subsequent levels of components are indented farther to the right. If a component is used in more than one parent within a given product structure, it will appear more than once, under every subassembly in which it is used.

Indented where-used A listing of every parent item, and the respective quantities required, as well as each of their respective parent items, continuing until the ultimate end item or level-0 item is referenced. Each of these parent items calls for a given component item in a bill-of-material file. The component item is shown closest to the left margin of the listing, with each parent indented to the right, and each of their respective parents indented even further to the right.

Indenture 1: A formal agreement (contract) between the issuer of a bond and the bondholders. **2:** Debt agreement specifying loan terms.

Independent checks Procedures for verifying and monitoring other controls.

Independent contractors Workers who perform specific services on a contract basis.

Independent demand The demand for an item that is unrelated to the demand for other items. Demand for finished goods, parts required for destructive testing, and service parts requirements are examples of independent demand. *See:* Dependent demand.

Independent demand item management models Models for the management of items whose demand is not strongly influenced by other items managed by the same company. These models can be characterized as follows: 1) stochastic or deterministic, depending on the variability of demand and other factors; 2) fixed quantity, fixed cycle, or hybrid (optional replenishment). *See:* Fixed reorder cycle inventory model, fixed reorder quantity inventory model.

Independent projects Projects whose cash flows are not affected by decisions made about other projects.

Independent variable 1: Term used in regression analysis to represent the variable that is expected to influence another (so-called "dependent") variable. **2:** X variable determined separately from the Y variable.

Index fund A managed portfolio assembled to mirror a particular financial market composite.

Index of Retail Saturation (IRS) The ratio of demand for a product (households in the geographic area multiplied by annual retail expenditures for a particular line of trade per household) divided by available supply (the square footage of retail facilities of a particular line of trade in the geographic area).

Indexed (purchasing power) bond A bond that has interest payments based on an inflation index to protect the holder from inflation.

Indexed file A data file that contains an index, a directory-like table that indicates where each record physically resides on the storage medium by the value of its key field. The records are usually organized sequentially, so that retrieval can be carried out either sequentially, without using the index, or through the index. To retrieve a record, a lookup is performed to find the record's location.

Indexed sequential organization A method of file organization that allows direct access to specific records in a sequential file by using an index of key fields.

Indirect costs *See:* Overhead.

Indirect exporting The firm manufactures at home and employs a middle person to export its product(s) to foreign markets.

Indirect format One possible format allowed for presenting the Statement of Cash Flows that begins with net profit and then presents adjustments for items that do not results in current-period cash transactions including depreciation and changes in the various working capital accounts.

Indirect interlock A situation that occurs when a director of one company and a director of another are both directors of a third company.

Indirect investment Buying equity or debt securities originating from a country as investments.

Indirect involvement Participation by a firm in international business through an intermediary, in which the firm does not deal with foreign customers or firms.

Indirect method A method of reporting the cash flows from operating activities as the net income from operations adjusted for all deferrals of past cash receipts and payments and all accruals of expected future cash receipts and payments.

Indirect quotation 1: Foreign exchange quotation that specifies the units of foreign currency that could be purchased with one unit of the home currency. **2:** Exchange rate quotations representing the value measured by number of units per dollar.

Indirect supply chain The channel that results once independent channel members are added between the manufacturer and the consumer.

Indirect taxes Taxes applied to nonincome items, such as value-added taxes, excise taxes, tariffs, and so on.

Individual/adversarial external affairs strategy Executives deny the legitimacy of social claims on their businesses and minimize the significance of challenges they receive from external critics.

Individual-centered career planning Career planning that focuses on individuals' careers rather than on organizational needs.

Individual development Process that may include education and training, but also includes many additional interventions and experiences to enable an individual to grow and mature both intellectually as well as emotionally.

Individual Retirement Account (IRA) A special account in which an employee can set aside funds that will not be taxed until the employee retires.

Individualism 1: A preference for a loosely knit social framework in which individuals are expected to take care of themselves. **2:** Dimension of culture that refers to the extent to which people in a country prefer to act as individuals instead of members of groups. **3:** The trait in which the employee attaches higher importance to personal and family interests than to the organization. **4:** Refers to the degree to which people in a society look after primarily their own interests or belong to and depend on "in-groups."

Individualism approach The ethical concept that acts are moral when they promote the individual's best long-term interests, which ultimately leads to the greater good.

Inductive fraud detection Proactively searching for fraud by identifying anomalies or unusual or unexpected patterns and/or relationships, without determining in advance the kinds of fraud for which you are looking.

Inefficient targeting Results when advertising and distribution reach too broad an audience, most of whom are not interested in the product.

Inelastic demand Situation in which a price change leads to a less than proportionate change in quantity demanded.

Infeasible solution A decision alternative or solution that violates one or more constraints.

Inference engine The part of an expert system that links facts and relationships in the knowledge base to reach a solution to a problem.

Inferior goods Products for which consumer demand declines as income rises.

Inflation A period when prices in general are rising and the purchasing power of money is declining.

Inflation accounting Accounting to cope with changing price levels.

Inflation premium A premium for expected inflation that investors add to the real risk-free rate of return.

Inflection point Point of maximum or minimum slope.

Inflow A receipt of cash from an investment, an employer, or other sources.

Influence diagram A graphical device that shows the relationship among decisions, chance events, and consequences for a decision problem.

Influence peddling Providing monetary or nonmonetary benefits to a person in a position of authority in exchange for an action by that person that benefits the company—normally an action that would not have been taken without the monetary or nonmonetary benefit.

Informal communication Unofficial communication that takes place in an organization as people talk freely and easily; examples include impromptu meetings and personal conversations (verbal or e-mail).

Informal communication channel A communication channel that exists outside formally authorized channels without regard for the organization's hierarchy of authority.

Informal integration Allowing a foreign subsidiary to adopt the corporation's global vision, core values, and cultural principles in its own way. That is, the corporation's central management does not formally force these on the foreign subsidiaries; rather it listens to people at the local level and communicates with them.

Informal training Training that occurs through interactions and feedback among employees.

Information 1: Data transferred into an ordered format that makes it usable and allows one to draw conclusions. **2:** The product of processing data so that they can be used in a context by human beings. **3:** Each partner may demand full information about all partnership matters, and each partner has a duty to supply other partners with full and accurate information.

Information-based services The provision of these services involves collecting, manipulating, interpreting, and transmitting data to create value. Examples include such services as accounting, banking, consulting, education, insurance, legal services, and news.

Information center The unit within an organization that provides coordination, control, and support for all aspects of the organization's information systems and its users.

Information content (signaling) hypothesis The theory that investors regard dividend changes as signals of management's earnings forecasts.

Information map The description of data and information flow within an organization set out in a visual chart or map.

Information overload A situation in which people have too much information from which to choose for their problem solving and decision making.

Information reporting system A system that organizes information in the form of prespecified reports that managers use in day-to-day decision making.

Information search Stage in the consumer decision process when consumers collect information on only a select subset of brands.

Information sites Web sites that generate revenue through advertising or the subscription rates that are charged to members.

Information System (IS) 1: A computer-based set of hardware, software, and telecommunications components, supported by people and procedures, to process data and turn them into useful information. **2:** Technology-based systems used to support operations, aid day-to-day decision making, and support strategic analysis (other names often used include: management information system, decision system, information technology [IT], data processing). **3:** Can provide the decision maker with basic data for most ongoing decisions.

Information systems auditor The information systems professional whose job is to find erroneous or fraudulent transactions and investigate them; auditing.

Information Technology (IT) 1: Refers to all technologies that collectively facilitate construction and maintenance of information systems. **2:** The hardware, software, telecommunications, database management, and other technologies used to store, process, and distribute information.

Informational power Is based on A's ability to provide B with factual data.

Infrastructure A country's physical facilities that support economic activities.

Infrastructure shortages Problems in a country's underlying physical structure, such as transportation, utilities, and so on.

Infringement Occurs when a person without authorization uses a substantially indistinguishable mark that is likely to cause confusion, mistake, or deception.

Inherent limitations The limitations that apply to all internal control systems. The limitations relate to the limits of human judgment, resource constraints and the need to consider the cost of controls in relation to expected benefits, the reality that breakdowns can occur, and the possibility of management override and collusion.

Inherent risks A business's susceptibility to fraud, assuming that appropriate controls are not in place.

Inhwa Influences South Korean business behavior; stresses harmony; links people who are unequal in rank, prestige, and power; and stresses loyalty to hierarchical rankings and superiors' concern for the well-being of subordinates.

Initial investment Expenses necessary to implement a capital budgeting proposal must be determined. This may include set-up costs, physical asset acquisition or disposition costs, permanent increases in the company's investment in cash, receivables, and inventories, and other cash outflows incurred at the time the project is initiated.

Initial investment outlay Includes the incremental cash flows associated with a project that will occur only at the start of a project's life, $\hat{C}F_0$.

Initial phase The first phase in the expatriation process. When the expatriate transfers to the foreign assignment, the newness of the culture creates a great deal of excitement for him or her.

Initial pleading Complaint filed by a plaintiff to request legal proceedings against someone.

Initial Public Offering (IPO) market The market consisting of stocks of companies that have just gone public.

Initiating structure A type of leader behavior that describes the extent to which a leader is task oriented and directs subordinates' work activities toward goal achievement.

Ink-jet printer Inexpensive type of printer that sprays ink to create the printed text or pictures of a computer-generated document.

Innovator A type of leader who identifies new ideas and visions and "sells" them to the institution.

Input Raw data entered into a computer for processing.

Input device A tool, such as a keyboard or voice recognition system, used to enter data into an information system.

Input-output analysis A method for estimating market activities and potential that measures the factor inflows into production and the resultant outflow of products.

Input price measurement A current value is assigned to an item on the basis of its replacement cost.

In-sample validation Involves gauging forecast errors by using the data set on which the model is fitted. This gives an upward bias to forecast accuracy.

Inseparability Distinguishing characteristic of services that reflects the interconnection among the service provider, the customer receiving the service, and other customers sharing the service experience.

Inside directors Persons with some sort of ties to the firm.

Insider trading 1: The practice of obtaining critical information inside a company and then using that information for one's own personal financial gain. **2:** "Insiders" are liable under Rule 10b–5 for failing to disclose material, nonpublic information before trading on the information.

Insiders 1: Officers, directors, major stockholders, or others who might have inside, or privileged, information on a company's operations. **2:** Directors, officers, employees, and agents of the issuer, as well as those with whom the issuer has entrusted information solely for corporate purposes.

Insolvency (equity) Situation that exists when a business is unable to pay debts as they become due in the usual course of business.

Insourcing Assigning an IS service function to the organization's own IS unit. The term was invented to emphasize a decision not to outsource.

Inspection Measuring, examining, testing, and gauging one or more characteristics of a product or service and comparing the results with specified requirements to determine whether conformity is achieved for each characteristic.

Instant messaging 1: Technology that provides a way to send quick notes from PC to PC over the Internet so two people who are online at the same time can communicate instantly. **2:** The capability for several online computer users to share messages in real time; also called chatting online.

Institute of Internal Auditors (IIA) The most influential international organization in the development of internal auditing standards. It was established in 1941.

Institutional advertising A type of advertising in which the retailer attempts to gain long-term benefits by promoting and selling the store itself rather than the merchandise in the store.

Institutional customers Comprise the sector of the business market represented by health care organizations, colleges and universities, libraries, foundations, art galleries, and clinics that purchase goods and services.

In-store displays Promotional fixtures of displays that seek to generate traffic, highlight individual items, and encourage impulse buying.

Instrument A class of similar investments. Examples are agency notes, commercial paper, Treasury bills, certificates of deposit (CDs), banker's acceptances, and repurchase agreements.

Insurance services Services that are provided in underwriting, risk evaluation, and operations.

Intangibility The inability to be seen, tasted, or touched in a conventional sense; the characteristic of services that most strongly differentiates them from products.

Intangible assets 1. Long-lived assets that are useful in the operations of a business, are not held for sale, and are without physical qualities. **2:** Assets that have no tangible existence (for example, goodwill).

Integrated circuits Electronic semiconductors within computers that integrate a large number of circuits into one silicon chip.

Integrated disability management programs A benefit that combines disability insurance programs and efforts to reduce workers' compensation claims.

Integrated international operation A foreign operation whose economic activities have a direct impact on the reporting (parent) entity.

Integrated Marketing Communications (IMC) System of management and integration of marketing communication elements—advertising, publicity, sales promotion, sponsorship marketing, and point-of-purchase communications—with the result that all elements adhere to the same message.

Integrated risk management Approach for managing both pure and speculative risks together; another name for *enterprise risk management.*

Integrated system A national tax system that attempts to eliminate double taxation by taxing corporate income differently depending on whether it is distributed to shareholders.

Integration The quality of collaboration between departments of an organization.

Integrator A position or department created solely to coordinate several departments.

Integrity The quality or state of being of sound moral principle; uprightness, honesty, and sincerity; the desire to do the right thing and to profess and live up to a set of values and expectations.

Integrity strategy Is driven by ethical values that provide a common frame of reference and that serve to unify different functions, lines of business, and employee groups.

Intellectual property rights 1: Legal rights resulting from industrial, scientific, literary, or artistic activity. **2:** Protection provided by patents, copyrights, and trademarks.

Intelligence 1: The ability to learn, think, and deduce; **2:** The first phase in the decision-making process: gathering relevant data.

Intelligent agent A sophisticated program that can be instructed to perform services for human beings, especially on the Internet.

Intensive distribution 1: Occurs when all possible intermediaries at a particular level of the channel are used. **2:** All possible retailers are used in a trade area.

Intensive technologies A variety of products or services provided in combination to a client.

Intentional amoral management Does not factor ethical considerations into decisions, actions, and behaviors because of the belief that business activity resides outside the sphere to which moral judgments apply.

Interactional justice Human interaction during service recovery efforts.

Interactive leadership A leadership style characterized by values such as inclusion, collaboration, relationship building, and caring.

Interactive multimedia Term encompassing technology that allows the presentation of facts and images with interaction by the viewer.

Interbank interest rates The interest rate charged by banks to banks in the major international financial centers.

Interbank market Market that facilitates the exchange of currencies between banks.

Interdependence The extent to which departments depend on each other for resources or materials to accomplish their tasks.

Interdistrict Transportation System Redesign of the Federal Reserve's routing modes and techniques to shorten delays and minimize system-wide float.

Interest-bearing When the interest paid is based on a quoted rate based on the face value of the financial instrument.

Interest Equalization Tax (IET) Tax imposed by the U.S. government in 1963 to discourage U.S. investors from investing in foreign securities.

Interest in partnership Partner's share in the partnership's profits and surplus.

Interest rate cap A financial contract which limits the rise in a selected interest rate.

Interest rate collar A financial contract which restricts the movement of a selected interest rate within a narrow band referred to as a collar. It is essentially a combination of an interest rate floor and cap.

Interest rate floor A financial contract which limits the decline in a selected interest rate.

Interest rate parity 1: Holds that investors should expect to earn the same return on their money in all countries after adjusting for risk. **2:** Theory specifying that the forward premium (or discount) is equal to the interest rate differential between the two currencies of concern.

Interest Rate Parity (IRP) line Diagonal line depicting all points on a four-quadrant graph that represent a state of interest rate parity.

Interest rate parity theory Theory suggesting that the forward rate differs from the spot rate by an amount that reflects the interest differential between two currencies.

Interest rate price risk The risk of changes in bond prices to which investors are exposed due to changing interest rates.

Interest rate reinvestment risk The risk that income from a bond portfolio will vary because cash flows have to be reinvested at current market rates.

Interest rate risk The possibility that interest rates will increase, causing the prices of existing fixed-income securities to drop.

Interest rate swap 1: Agreement to swap interest payments, whereby interest payments based on a fixed interest rate are exchanged for interest payments based on a floating interest rate. **2:** A firm uses its credit standing to borrow capital at low fixed rates and exchange its interest payments with a slightly lower credit-rated borrower who has debt service payments at floating rates.

Interface The connection of two systems to establish interaction.

Intergroup conflict Behavior that occurs between organizational groups when participants identify with one group and perceive that other groups may block their group's goal achievement or expectations.

Interlocking directorate A formal linkage that occurs when a member of the board of directors of one company sits on the board of another company.

Intermediate customers Distributors, dealers, or brokers who make products and services available to the end user by repairing, repackaging, reselling, or creating finished goods from components or subassemblies.

Intermodal movements The transfer of freight from one mode or type of transportation to another.

Internal audit 1: Audit conducted within an organization by members of the organization to measure its strengths or weaknesses against its own procedures and/or external standards—a "first-party audit." **2:** An objective evaluation of operations and control systems of an organization to determine whether its policies and procedures are being followed, and also whether its resources are safeguarded and used efficiently to achieve organizational objectives.

Internal bank A multinational firm's financial management tool that actually acts as a bank to coordinate finances among its units.

Internal capability analysis Detailed view of the internal workings of the organization (for example, determine how well the capabilities of the organization match to strategic needs).

Internal collaboration *See:* Internal cooperation.

Internal control A process effected by an entity's board of directors, management, and other personnel that is designed to provide reasonable assurance regarding the achievement of objectives such as 1) effectiveness and efficiency of operations, 2) reliability of financial reporting, and 3) compliance with applicable laws and regulations.

Internal control structure Specific policies and procedures designed to provide management with reasonable assurance that the goals and objectives it believes important to the entity will be met.

Internal control weakness Weakness in the control environment, accounting system, or the control activities or procedures.

GLOSSARY

Internal cooperation The organization develops an internal environment where there is downward, upward, and horizontal communication, as well as a focal point to coordinate the communication, for the purpose of making effective and efficient decisions.

Internal customer Recipient, person, or department of another person's or department's output (product, service, or information) within an organization. *See:* External customer.

Internal data Data that are collected within the organization, usually by transaction processing systems but also through employee and customer surveys.

Internal economies of scale Lower production costs resulting from greater production for an enlarged market.

Internal failure costs The costs associated with defects that are discovered by the organization before the product or service is delivered to the consumer.

Internal integration A state in which organization members develop a collective identity and know how to work together effectively.

Internal locus of control The belief by individuals that their future is within their control and that external forces will have little influence.

Internal memory The memory circuitry inside the computer, communicating directly with the CPU. Consists of RAM and ROM.

Internal process approach An approach that looks at internal activities and assesses effectiveness by indicators of internal health and efficiency.

Internal Rate of Return (IRR) The discount rate that forces the PV of a project's expected cash flows to equal its initial cost. IRR is similar to the YTM on a bond.

Internal rate of return method A method of analysis of proposed capital investments that focuses on using present value concepts to compute the rate of return from the net cash flows expected from the investment.

Internal review A company's management becoming familiar with the firm's ability to implement a strategy aimed at coping with external demands.

Internalization Occurs when a firm establishes its own multinational operation, keeping information that is at the core of its competitiveness within the firm.

International *See:* Global.

International accounting Accounting for international transactions, comparisons of accounting principles in different countries, harmonization of diverse accounting standards worldwide, and accounting information for the management and control of global operations.

International Accounting Standard (IAS) Rule developed by the International Accounting Standards Committee in order to harmonize accounting standards worldwide.

International Bank for Reconstruction and Development (IBRD) Bank established in 1944 to enhance economic development by providing loans to countries. Also referred to as the World Bank.

International bond Bond issued in domestic capital markets by foreign borrowers (foreign bonds) or issued in the Eurocurrency markets in currency different from that of the home currency of the borrower (Eurobonds).

International competitiveness The ability of a firm, an industry, or a country to compete in the international marketplace at a stable or rising standard of living.

International contracts Involve additional issues beyond those in domestic contracts, such as differences in language, legal systems, and currency.

International corporation International business that produces products in its home country and exports to other countries.

International Court of Justice Judicial branch of the United Nations having voluntary jurisdiction over nations.

International debt load Total accumulated negative net investment of a nation.

International Development Association (IDA) Association established to stimulate country development; it was especially suited for less prosperous nations, since it provided loans at low interest rates.

International division A unit established to supervise a firm's exports, foreign distribution agreements, foreign sales forces, foreign sales branches, and foreign subsidiaries.

International environment Refers to groupings of nations (such as the European Union), worldwide bodies (such as the World Bank), and organizations of nations by industry (such as the Organization of Petroleum Exporting Countries).

International Federation of Accountants (IFAC) An organization engaged in efforts to harmonize auditing standards worldwide.

International Financial Corporation (IFC) Firm established to promote private enterprise within countries; it can provide loans to and purchase stock of corporations.

International Fisher Effect (IFE) line Diagonal line on a graph that reflects points at which the interest rate differential between two countries is equal to the percentage change in the exchange rate between their two respective currencies.

International human resource management function Consists of interplay among three dimensions: the broad function, country categories, and types of employees.

International intermediaries Marketing institutions that facilitate the movement of goods and services between the originator and customer.

International labor relations The management of an MNC interacting with organized labor units in each country.

International law Includes law that deals with the conduct and relations of nation-states and international organizations as well as some of their relations with persons; such law is enforceable by the courts of a nation that has adopted the international law as domestic law.

International management The management of business operations conducted in more than one country.

International marketing Process of planning and conducting transactions across national borders to create exchanges that satisfy the objectives of individuals and organizations.

International Monetary Fund (IMF) A specialized agency of the United Nations established in 1944. An international financial institution for dealing with Balance of Payment problems; the first international monetary authority with at least some degree of power over national authorities.

International mutual funds Mutual funds containing securities of foreign firms.

International Organization of Securities Commission (IOSCO) A private organization of securities market regulators that promotes the integration of securities markets worldwide.

International Organization for Standardization (ISO) Nongovernmental organization that promotes the development of standardization to facilitate the international exchange of goods and services.

International organizational structures The firm's organizational structure is its "skeleton"; it provides support and ties together disparate functions.

International pricing A managerial decision about what to charge for goods produced in one nation and sold in another.

International Product Life Cycle (IPLC) A theory that many products that are exported to foreign countries are eventually produced abroad, and that foreign producers subsequently obtain a competitive edge over the original producers, forcing them to either create a new product or go out of business.

International relocation and orientation The making of arrangements for predeparture training, immigration and travel details, and finalizing compensation details between the expatriate and the home country.

International Standards on Auditing (ISA) A comprehensive set of auditing standards issued by the International Federation of Accountants. Audits conducted in accordance with these standards can be relied on by securities regulatory authorities for multinational reporting purposes.

International Trade Organization (ITO) A forwardlooking approach to international trade and investment embodied in the 1948 Havana Charter; due to disagreements among sponsoring nations, its provisions were never ratified.

International treaties Agreements between or among independent nations, such as the General Agreement on Tariffs and Trade (GATT), now called the World Trade Organization.

Internationalization A process by which firms increase their awareness of the influence of international activities on their future and establish and conduct transactions with firms from other countries.

Internet 1: A global collection of computer networks linked together for the exchange of data and information. **2:** Worldwide network of interconnected computer networks originally built by the U.S. government. **3:** An international network of networks providing millions of people with access to rich information resources.

Internet domain The part of an Internet address, such as .com, .edu, or .gov, that is shared by many users and indicates the particular community of their owners.

Internet hosts Provide high-speed connections to the Web.

Internet Protocol (IP) A telecommunication standard that enables traffic on the Internet to be routed from one network to another as needed.

Internet Protocol (IP) number A unique number assigned to a server or another device that is connected to the Internet, for identification purposes consists of 32 bits.

Internet Relay Chat (IRC) Internet software that allows remote users to correspond in real time.

Internet servers The computers that are linked directly to the Internet backbone and carry the files accessed over the Internet.

Internet Service Provider (ISP) An individual or organization that provides Internet connection, and sometimes other related services, to subscribers.

Interoperability The ability of two or more systems or components to exchange information and to use the information that has been exchanged. It is the capability of systems to communicate with one another and to exchange and use information, including content, format, and semantics.

Interorganizational context Channel management that extends beyond a firm's own organization into independent businesses.

Interorganizational information systems Systems that are shared by two or more organizations to transfer data electronically.

Interpreter A programming language translator that translates the source code, one statement at a time, and executes it. If the instruction is erroneous, the interpreter produces an appropriate error message.

Interpretive knowledge An acquired ability to understand and appreciate the nuances of foreign cultural traits and patterns.

Interrelationship digraph Management and planning tool that displays the relationship between factors in a complex situation. It identifies meaningful categories from a mass of ideas and is useful when relationships are difficult to determine.

Interrogatory A series of written questions that specifically identify information needed from the opposing party.

Interstate Banking and Branching Efficiency Act (1994) Permitted interstate bank acquisitions, mergers, and branching.

Intertype competition Occurs when two or more retailers of a different type, as defined by NAICS codes in the Census of Retail Trade, compete directly by attempting to sell the same merchandise lines to the same households.

Interval scale Intervals of measure that stay constant along the scale. For example, the interval between the measures of one and three on the scale is the same as the interval between five and seven.

Intervention 1: Action taken by a leader or a facilitator to support the effective functioning of a team or work group. **2:** An action taken by the central bank of a country to influence the exchange rate of its currency in the market.

Intervention intensity Strength of the intervention by the intervening person; intensity is affected by words, voice inflection, and nonverbal behaviors.

Interviews A face-to-face research tool to obtain in-depth information.

In-the-money option When it is beneficial financially for the option holder to exercise the option.

Intracompany trade International trade between subsidiaries that are under the same ownership.

Intra-industry trade The simultaneous export and import of the same good by a country. It is of interest due to the traditional theory that a country will either export or import a good, but not do both at the same time.

Intranet 1: An internal communication system that uses the technology and standards of the Internet but is accessible only to people within the organization. **2:** A process that integrates a company's information assets into a single accessible system using Internet-based technologies such as e-mail, news groups, and the World Wide Web.

Intransit lead time The time between the date of shipment (at the shipping point) and the date of receipt (at the receiver's dock). Orders normally specify the date by which goods should be at the dock. Consequently, this date should be offset by intransit lead time for establishing a ship date for the supplier.

Intratype competition Occurs when two or more retailers of the same type, as defined by NAICS codes in the Census of Retail Trade, compete directly with each other for the same households.

Intrinsic forecast method A forecast based on internal factors, such as an average of past sales. *Ant:* extrinsic forecast.

Intrinsic reward The satisfaction received in the process of performing an action.

Intrinsic value, $\hat{P}_0$ The value of an asset that in the mind of a particular investor is justified by the facts; $\hat{P}_0$ may be different from the asset's current market price, its book value, or both.

Intuition The immediate comprehension of a decision situation based on past experience but without conscious thought.

Intuitionism A rational person possesses inherent powers to assess the correctness of actions.

Intuitive decision making The use of experience and judgment rather than sequential logic or explicit reasoning to solve a problem.

Inventory 1: The goods that the organization keeps on hand for use in the production process up to the point of selling the final products to customers. **2:** Materials used in producing a final product. Raw materials inventory includes items purchased from suppliers to directly support production requirements. Work in process inventory is the total inventory that exists within and among all processing centers located throughout the operations system. Finished goods inventory includes completed items or products that are available for shipment or future customer orders. Maintenance, repair, and operating (MRO) inventory includes all the items used to support operations but which are not directly in the finished product. Pipeline or in-transit inventory includes items on their way to customers or located throughout a firm's distribution channels.

Inventory carrying costs The expense of maintaining inventories.

Inventory control systems An information system employed to help control inventory.

Inventory financing A very important component of the total financial plan of most corporations because inventory makes up a significant portion of total working capital.

Inventory management Activities involved in ensuring that the right materials and goods are in the right place at the right time at the lowest cost possible. Inventory management (also called materials management in some organizations) may involve automated and/or manual systems for tracking inventory, as well the physical facilities for storing the materials.

Inventory ordering system Inventory models for the replenishment of inventory. Independent demand inventory ordering models include but are not limited to fixed reorder cycle, fixed reorder quantity, optional replenishment, and hybrid models. Dependent demand inventory ordering models include material requirements planning, kanban, and drum-buffer-rope.

Inventory shrinkage Loss of inventory due to shoplifting, employee theft, or errors in recording or counting inventory.

Inventory turnover ratio 1: The number of times that an inventory cycles, or "turns over" during the year. A frequently used method to compute inventory turnover is to divide the average inventory level into the annual cost of sales. For example, an average inventory of $3 million divided into an annual cost of sales of $21 million means that inventory turned over seven times. *Syn:* inventory turns, inventory velocity, turnover. **2:** A ratio that measures the relationship between the volume of goods (merchandise) sold and the amount of inventory carried during the period. **3:** Refers to the number of times per year, on average, that a retailer sells its inventory. **4:** Measure of the efficiency with which inventory is managed; computed by dividing cost of goods sold by average inventory for a period. **5:** A measure of inventory usage that is found by dividing cost of goods sold by either the year-end inventory balance or by the average inventory balance.

Inverted "abnormal" yield curve Downward-sloping graph of yields to maturity of securities with different maturities. Given the possibility to engage in arbitrage (simultaneously buy and sell otherwise identical securities having different maturities), this slope implies that the market collectively anticipates future shorter-term interest rates to decline.

Investing activities On the statement of cash flows items that are defined as receipts of cash from loans, sale of property, and cash disbursed for loans to other business entities and payments for property, plant, and equipment.

Investment banker An organization that underwrites and distributes new issues of securities; helps businesses and other entities obtain needed financing.

Investment center A responsibility center where the manager is responsible for costs, revenues, profits, and investment in assets. A decentralized unit in which the manager has the responsibility and authority to make decisions that affect not only costs and revenues but also the plant assets available to the center.

Investment contract Any investment of money or property made in expectation of receiving a financial return solely from the efforts of others.

Investment grade bonds Bonds rated A or triple-B; many banks and other institutional investors are permitted by law to hold only investment-grade or better bonds.

Investment income The proportion of net income that is paid back to a parent company.

Investment Opportunity Schedule (IOS) A graph of the firm's investment opportunities ranked in order of the projects' internal rates of return.

Investment policy Defines the company's posture toward risk and return and specifies how that posture is to be implemented.

Investment scams The selling of fraudulent and worthless investments to unsuspecting investors.

Investment turnover A component of the rate of return on investment, computed as the ratio of sales to invested assets.

Investments The balance sheet caption used to report long-term investments in stocks or bonds not intended as a source of cash in the normal operations of the business.

Invigilation Imposing strict temporary controls on an activity so that, during the observation period, fraud is virtually impossible. Involves keeping detailed records before, during, and after the invigilation period and comparing suspicious activity during the three periods to obtain evidence about whether fraud is occurring.

Invoice The bill provided by the seller (who refers to it as a sales invoice) to a buyer (who refers to it as a purchase invoice) for items purchased.

Involvement Degree of personal relevance of a product to a consumer.

Involuntary dissolution Dissolution that occurs by administrative or judicial action taken 1) by the attorney general, 2) by shareholders under certain circumstances, and 3) by a creditor on a showing that the corporation has become unable to pay its debts and obligations as they mature in the regular course of its business.

IRR (internal rate of return) Discount rate that causes net present value to equal zero.

Irregular component The component of the time series model that reflects the random variation of the actual time series values beyond what can be explained by the trend, cyclical, and seasonal components.

Irregular or random influences Unpredictable shocks to the economic system.

Irrevocable letter of credit Letter of credit issued by a bank that cannot be cancelled or amended without the beneficiary's approval.

Ishikawa diagram See: Cause-and-effect diagram.

IS architecture The manner in which an organization's IS assets are deployed and connected.

IS infrastructure The IS resources that an organization owns, including hardware, software, and telecommunications devices and lines.

IS planning Planning for the deployment and for the resources needed to develop and maintain information systems.

IS subsidiaries Independent corporations that offer services not only to the parent company but also to other companies.

ISDN (Integrated Services Digital Network) A set of hardware and software standards that support the transmission of text, images, and sounds through the same communications channel. ISDN will result in the combination of the telephone, fax, computer, and television into one device.

ISO "equal" (Greek). A prefix for a series of standards published by the International Organization for Standardization.

ISO 9000 A set of international standards for quality management, setting uniform guidelines for processes to ensure that products conform to customer requirements. Requires each enterprise to define and document its own quality process and provide evidence of their implementation. ISO stands for International Organization for Standardization.

ISO 9000-series standards Set of individual but related international standards and guidelines on quality management and quality assurance developed to help companies effectively document the quality system elements to be implemented to maintain an efficient quality system. The standards, initially published in 1987, revised in 1994 and 2000, are not specific to any particular industry, product, or service. The standards were developed by the International Organization for Standardization, a specialized international agency for standardization composed of the national standards bodies of nearly 100 countries.

ISO 14000-series Set of standards and guidelines relevant to developing and sustaining an environmental management system.

Issues management and crisis management Two major ways by which business has responded to critical situations.

Issuing bank Bank that issues a letter of credit.

J

J-curve effect Effect of a weaker dollar on the U.S. trade balance, in which the trade balance initially deteriorates; it only improves once U.S. and non-U.S. importers respond to the change in purchasing power that is caused by the weaker dollar.

Jamaica Agreement As a result of the inflation and balance of payment problems after World War II, causing many countries great difficulty in maintaining their appropriate exchange rate, the major trading nations signed the Jamaica Agreement in 1976 to demonetize gold and create a system of floating exchange rates.

Java Object-oriented programming language that allows Web browsers to download applets that can run on any computer with any operating system.

Jidoka Japanese method of autonomous control involving the adding of intelligent features to machines to start or stop operations as control parameters are reached, and to signal operators when necessary.

Job Grouping of tasks, duties, and responsibilities that constitutes the total work assignment for employees.

Job aid Any device, document, or other media which can be provided a worker to aid in correctly performing their tasks (for example, laminated setup instruction card hanging on machine, photos of product at different stages of assembly, metric conversion table).

Job analysis Systematic way to gather and analyze information about the content, context, and the human requirements of jobs.

Job anxiety Tension caused by the pressures of the job.

Job characteristics model A model of job design that comprises core job dimensions, critical psychological states, and employee growth-need strength.

Job cost sheet An account in the work in process subsidiary ledger in which the costs charged to a particular job order are recorded.

Job criteria Important elements in a given job.

Job description Narrative explanation of the work, responsibilities, and basic requirements of the job.

Job design 1: The application of motivational theories to the structure of work for improving productivity and satisfaction. **2:** Organizing tasks, duties, and responsibilities into a productive unit of work. **3:** The assignment of goals and tasks to be accomplished by employees.

Job enlargement 1: A job design that combines a series of tasks into one new, broader job to give employees variety and challenge. **2:** The designing of jobs to expand the number of different tasks performed by an employee.

Job enrichment 1: A job design that incorporates achievement, recognition, and other high-level motivators into the work. **2:** Increasing the depth of a job by adding the responsibility for planning, organizing, controlling, and evaluating the job. **3:** The designing of jobs to increase responsibility, recognition, and opportunities for growth and achievement.

Job evaluation The process of determining the value of jobs within an organization through an examination of job content.

Job order cost system A type of cost accounting system that provides for a separate record of the cost of each particular quantity of product that passes through the factory.

Job posting A system in which the employer provides notices of job openings and employees respond to apply.

Job rotation A job design that systematically moves employees from one job to another to provide them with variety and stimulation.

Job satisfaction A positive emotional state resulting from evaluating one's job experience.

Job simplification 1: A job design whose purpose is to improve task efficiency by reducing the number of tasks a single person must do. **2:** The reduction of the number and difficulty of tasks performed by a single person.

Job specifications The knowledge, skills, and abilities (KSAs) an individual needs to perform a job satisfactorily.

Join The joining of data from multiple tables.

Joint and several liability The partners are jointly and severally liable for a tort or breach of trust committed by any partner or by an employee of the firm in the course of partnership business; under such liability, the creditors may sue the partners jointly as a group or separately as individuals.

Joint Application Development (JAD) A method of systems development that facilitates analysis and design by involving representatives of the prospective users in all of the phases and by using prototyping wherever possible.

Joint liability Liability where creditor must sue all of the partners as a group.

Joint occurrence Occurrence of a phenomenon affecting the business environment in several locations simultaneously.

Joint optimization The goal of the sociotechnical systems approach, which states that an organization will function best only if its social and technical systems are designed to fit the needs of one another.

Joint planning meetings Meeting involving representatives of a key customer and the sales and service team for that account to determine how better to meet the customer's requirements and expectations.

Joint probabilities The probabilities of both sample information and a particular state of nature occurring simultaneously.

Joint Research and Development Act A 1984 act that allows both domestic and foreign firms to participate in joint basic-research efforts without fear of U.S. antitrust action.

Joint ventures 1: Two or more firms that band together to establish operations in foreign markets in order to capitalize on each other's resources and reduce risk. They share profits, liabilities, and duties. **2:** Result from the participation of two or more companies in an enterprise in which each party contributes assets, owns the new entity to some degree, and shares risk. **3:** An unincorporated business association of two or more persons to carry out a particular business enterprise for profit. **4:** A separate entity for sharing development and production costs and penetrating new markets that is created with two or more active firms as sponsors.

Journal The initial record in which the effects of a transaction on accounts are recorded.

Journal entry The form of recording a transaction in a journal.

Journalizing The process of recording a transaction in a journal.

Judgmental approach Relies heavily on intuition to adjust what is known about upcoming cash flows to arrive at the cash forecast.

Judicial limitations Based on contract law, tort law, or public policy.

Junk bond A high-risk, high-yield bond used to finance mergers, leveraged buyouts, and troubled companies.

Juran's Trilogy *See:* Quality trilogy.

Jurisdiction The limit or territory over which an organization has authority.

JUSE Union of Japanese Scientists and Engineers.

Justice approach The ethical concept that moral decisions must be based in standards of equity, fairness, and impartiality.

Just-in-Time (JIT) A philosophy of manufacturing based on planned elimination of all waste and on continuous improvement of productivity. It encompasses the successful execution of all manufacturing activities required to produce a final product, from design engineering to delivery, and includes all stages of conversion from raw material onward. The primary elements of just-in-time are to have only the required inventory when needed; to improve quality to zero defects; to reduce lead times by reducing setup times, queue lengths, and lot sizes; to incrementally revise the operations themselves; and to accomplish these activities at minimum cost. In the broad sense, it applies to all forms of manufacturing—job shop, process, and repetitive—and to many service industries as well. *Syn:* short-cycle manufacturing, stockless production, zero inventories.

Just-in-Time (JIT) inventory Materials scheduled to arrive precisely when they are needed on a production line.

Just-in-time inventory system An inventory system designed to reduce the levels of inventory kept at the manufacturing site increasing quality in the production process and by shifting the inventory burden to the supplier.

Just-in-time manufacturing 1: A business philosophy that focuses on eliminating time, cost, and poor quality within manufacturing processes. **2:** Optimal material requirement planning system for a manufacturing process in which there is little or no manufacturing material inventory on hand at the manufacturing site and little or no incoming inspection.

Just-in-time processing A processing approach that focuses on eliminating time, cost, and poor quality within manufacturing and nonmanufacturing processes.

Just-in-time training Providing job training coincidental with, or immediately prior to its need for the job.

K

Kaikaku (Japanese) Breakthrough improvement in eliminating waste.

Kaizen Japanese term that means gradual unending improvement by doing little things better and setting and achieving increasingly higher standards. The term was made famous by Masaaki Imai in his book *Kaizen: The Key to Japan's Competitive Success. See:* continuous process improvement.

Kaizen **blitz/event** Intense, short time-frame, team approach to employ the concepts and techniques of continuous improvement (for example, to reduce cycle time, increase throughput).

Kanban 1: A method of just-in-time production that uses standard containers or lot sizes with a single card attached to each. It is a pull system in which work centers signal with a card that they wish to withdraw parts from feeding operations or suppliers. The Japanese word kanban, loosely translated, means card, billboard, or sign. The term is often used synonymously for the specific scheduling system developed and used by the Toyota Corporation in Japan. *See:* Move card, Production card, Synchronized production. **2:** System inspired by Tauchi Ohno's (Toyota) visit to a U.S. supermarket. The system signals the need to replenish stock or materials or to produce more of an item. Also called a "pull" approach.

Kano model Representation of the three levels of customer satisfaction defined as dissatisfaction, neutrality, and delight.

Keiretsu A form of cooperative relationship among companies in Japan where the companies largely remain legally and economically independent, even though they work closely in various ways such as sole sourcing and financial backing. A member of a keiretsu generally owns a limited amount of stock in other member companies. A keiretsu generally forms around a bank and a trading company but "distribution" (supply chain) keiretsus exist linking companies from raw material suppliers to retailers.

Keogh plan A type of individualized pension plan for self-employed individuals.

Key A field in a database table whose values identify records either for display or for processing. Typical keys are part number (in an inventory file) and Social Security number (in a human resources file).

Key buying influentials Individuals in the buying organization who have the power to influence the buying decision.

Kickback fraud Fraud perpetrated by an employee and the employee's vendor or customer. Usually involves the employee buying goods or services from the vendor at an overstated price or giving the customer a lower-than-normal price, and in return the vendor or customer pays the employee a "kickback."

Kinked demand curve A theory assuming that rival firms follow any decrease in price in order to maintain their respective market shares but refrain from following increases, allowing their market share to increase at the expense of the firm making the initial price increase.

Kiting Fraud that conceals cash shortages by 1) transferring funds from one bank to another and 2) recording the receipt on or before the balance sheet date and the disbursement after the balance sheet date.

KJ method *See:* Affinity diagram.

Knowledge base The collection of facts and the relationships among them that mimic the decision-making process in an expert's mind and constitute a major component of an expert system.

Knowledge engineer A programmer whose expertise is the extraction of knowledge from a domain expert and the transformation of the knowledge into code, that is, into the knowledge base of an expert system. Knowledge engineers construct expert systems.

Knowledge management 1: The efforts to systematically find, organize, and make available a company's intellectual capital and to foster a culture of continuous learning and knowledge sharing; the process of systematically gathering knowledge, making it widely available throughout the organization, and fostering a culture of learning. **2:** Transforming data into information, the acquisition or creation of knowledge, as well as the processes and technology employed in identifying, categorizing, storing, retrieving, disseminating, and using information and knowledge for the purposes of improving decisions and plans.

Knowledge management portal A single point of access for employees to multiple sources of information that provides personalized access on the corporate intranet.

Knowledge worker Any worker who produces information. The term roughly overlaps with "professional."

Kohlberg's stages of moral development Theory that moral development consists of preconventional (childhood), conventional (adolescence), and postconventional (adulthood) levels, with corresponding perspectives and justifications.

Kyoto Protocol Resolution on greenhouse gases.

L

Labeling Teaching and training.

Labor dispute Any controversy concerning terms or conditions of employment or union representation.

Labor force population All individuals who are available for selection if all possible recruitment strategies are used.

Labor laws 1: Laws in many countries provide extensive security for workers and make it extremely expensive to terminate an employee. **2:** Provide the general framework in which management and labor negotiate terms of employment.

Labor-Management Relations Act Law that 1) prohibits unfair labor practices by a union; 2) prohibits closed shops; and 1) allows union shops.

Labor-Management Reporting and Disclosure Act Law aimed at eliminating corruption in labor unions.

Labor markets The external supply pool from which organizations attract employees.

Labor productivity A measure of the relationship between workers' hours and the actual output produced.

Labor specialization Occurs when labor and management undertake specific activities and processes, the repetition and focus increase the effectiveness, efficiency, and learning of labor and management.

Laddering A method of showing the logical precedential relationship of a set of activities that is repeated several times consecutively.

Lagged regression analysis A quick and relatively inexpensive way of determining a company's collection experience by determining a mathematical equation relating cash collections to the sales that gave rise to them.

Lagging Strategy used by a firm to stall payments, normally in response to exchange rate projections. The practice of delaying collections or payments.

Lags Paying a debt late to take advantage of exchange rates.

Lambda A liquidity measure from a function of the likelihood that a firm will exhaust its liquid reserve. The measure's numerator is the sum of the firm's initial liquid reserve and total anticipated net cash flow during the analysis horizon and denominator is the standard deviation of the net cash flow during the analysis horizon.

LAN (Local Area Network) A computer network confined to a building or a group of adjacent buildings, as opposed to a wide-area network.

Land bridge Transfer of ocean freight on land among various modes of transportation.

Language Slogans, sayings, metaphors, or other expressions that convey a special meaning to employees.

Language translator Fluent in both languages being used in a cross-cultural communication, translators help eliminate the verbal and nonverbal communication barriers.

Lapping Fraud that involves stealing one customer's payment and then crediting that customer's account when a subsequent customer pays.

Larceny Intentionally taking an employer's cash or other assets without the consent and against the will of the employer, after it has been recorded in the company's accounting system.

Large-batch production A manufacturing process characterized by long production runs of standardized parts.

Large power distance culture The culture where a person at a higher position in the organizational hierarchy makes the decisions, and the employees at the lower levels simply follow the instructions.

Large-group intervention An approach that brings together participants from all parts of the organization (and may include key outside stakeholders as well) to discuss problems or opportunities and plan for major change.

Laser printer A nonimpact printer that uses laser beams to produce high-quality printouts.

Last-In, First-Out (LIFO) method A method of inventory costing based on the assumption that the most recent merchandise costs incurred should be charged against revenue.

Latest Finish time (LF) The latest time by which a particular activity must be completed in order for the entire project to be finished by its required completion time.

Latest Start time (LS) The latest time by which a particular activity must be started in order for the entire project to be finished by its required completion time; the activity's latest finish time minus the activity's estimated duration.

Law of effect The assumption that positively reinforced behavior tends to be repeated and unreinforced or negatively reinforced behavior tends to be inhibited.

Law of one price The theory that the relative prices of any single good between countries, expressed in each country's currency, is representative of the proper or appropriate exchange rate value.

Lead, or managing, underwriter The member of an underwriting syndicate that actually *manages* the distribution and sale of a new security offering.

Lead time The elapsed time between starting a unit of product into the beginning of a process and its completion.

Leader Individual, recognized by others, as the person to lead an effort. One cannot be a "leader" without one or more "followers." The term is often used interchangeably with "manager" (*see:* Manager). A "leader" may or may not hold an officially designated management-type position.

Leader pricing A technique whereby a high-demand item is priced low and is heavily advertised in order to attract customers into the store.

Leadership Essential part of a quality improvement effort. Organization leaders must establish a vision, communicate that vision to those in the organization, and provide the tools, knowledge, and motivation necessary to accomplish the vision.

Leadership grid A two-dimensional leadership theory that measures a leader's concern for people and concern for production.

Leading 1: The management function that involves the use of influence to motivate employees to achieve the organization's goals. **2:** Strategy used by a firm to accelerate payments, normally in response to exchange rate expectations. The practice of accelerating collections or payments.

Leads Paying a debt early to take advantage of exchange rates.

Leaky bucket theory Traditionally associated with conquest marketing where new customers replace disloyal customers at the same rate; hence, the firm never grows.

Lean approach/lean thinking ("lean" and "agile" may be used interchangeably) Focus on reducing cycle time and waste using a number of different techniques and tools, for example, value stream mapping, and identifying and eliminating "monuments" and nonvalue-added steps.

Lean manufacturing Applying the lean approach to improving manufacturing operations.

Lean production A philosophy of production that emphasizes the minimization of the amount of all the resources (including time) used in the various activities of the enterprise. It involves identifying and eliminating nonvalue-adding activities in design, production, supply chain management, and dealing with the customers. Lean producers employ teams of multiskilled workers at all levels of the organization and use highly flexible, increasingly automated machines to produce volumes of products in potentially enormous variety. It contains a set of principles and practices to reduce cost through the relentless removal of waste and through the simplification of all manufacturing and support processes. *Syn:* lean, lean manufacturing.

Learner-controlled instruction (also called *self-directed learning*) The learner working without an instructor, at their own pace, building mastery of a task (computer-based training is a form of LCI).

Learning 1: Change in the content of long-term memory. As consumers, we learn to adapt better to our environment. **2:** A change in behavior or performance as the result of experience.

Learning curve 1: A curve reflecting the rate of improvement in time per piece as more units of an item are made. A planning technique, the learning curve is particularly useful in project-oriented industries in which new products are frequently phased in. The basis for the learning curve calculation is that workers will be able to produce the product more quickly after they get used to making it. *Syn:* experience curve, manufacturing progress curve. **2:** Time it takes to achieve mastery of a task or body of knowledge.

Learning objectives (also called *terminal objectives*) The objectives to be met upon completion of a course of study or the learning of a skill.

Learning organization 1: An organization in which everyone is engaged in identifying and solving problems, enabling the organization to continuously experiment, improve, and increase its capability. **2:** Organization that has as a policy to continue to learn and improve its products, services, processes and outcomes; "an organization that is continually expanding its capacity to create its future" (Senge). **3:** The concept of an organization that accumulates knowledge through the experiences of its employees. Information systems facilitate learning by organizations.

Lease A contract between a lessor and a lessee that gives the lessee the right to use specific property owned by the lessor, for a given time period, in exchange for cash or other consideration—typically a commitment to make future cash payments.

Leaves The lowest-level records in a hierarchical database.

Ledger The group of accounts used by a business.

Ledger balance Reflects all credits and debits posted to an account as of a certain time, but this balance may not be entirely spendable.

Legacy system An old information system still in use. Usually, the term is used when contrasting such a system with a new information system, or a new type of information system.

Legal aggregate A group of individuals not having a legal existence separate from that of its members; the UPA considers a partnership a legal aggregate for some purposes.

Legal entity 1: A corporation is an entity apart from its shareholders, with entirely distinct rights and liabilities. **2:** An organization having a legal existence separate from that of its members; the UPA considers a partnership a legal entity for some purposes.

Legal environment Includes rules of competition, packaging laws, patents, trademarks, copyright laws and practices, labor laws, and contract enforcement.

Legal restrictions on acquisition of shares Restrictions similar to those on cash dividends usually apply.

Legal restrictions on distributions Dividends may be paid only if the cash flow and applicable balance-sheet tests are satisfied.

Legal restrictions on liquidating distributions States usually permit distribution in partial liquidation from capital surplus unless the company is insolvent.

Legal restrictions on redemptions of shares In most states, a corporation may not redeem shares when insolvent or when such redemption would render it insolvent.

Legends Stories of events based in history that may have been embellished with fictional details.

Legitimacy The general perspective that an organization's actions are desirable, proper, and appropriate within the environment's system of norms, values, and beliefs.

Legitimate power 1: Power that stems from a formal management position in an organization and the authority granted to it. **2:** Power based on A's right to influence B, or B's belief that B should accept A's influence.

Legitimation Dynamic process by which a business seeks to perpetuate its acceptance.

Leontief Paradox Wassily Leontief's studies of U.S. trade indicated that the United States was a labor-abundant country, exporting labor-intensive products. This was a paradox because of the general belief that the United States was a capital-abundant country which should be exporting capital-intensive products.

Less-Developed Country (LDC) 1: An emerging or developing nation. **2:** A country with a less diversified economy, a lower than average gross national product, and a lower than average per capita income.

Less government regulation By taking a proactive role in addressing society's problems, corporations create a climate of trust and respect that has the effect of reducing government regulation.

Lessee The party that uses, rather than the one who owns, the leased property.

Lessor The owner of the leased property.

Letter of Credit (L/C) 1: A promise by a bank to make payment to a party upon presentation of a draft provided that the party complies with certain documentary requirements. This guarantees the investor of principal repayment, and the use of backup bank financing allows the bank's credit rating to be substituted for the issuer's. **2:** Bank's promise to pay the seller, provided certain conditions are met; used to manage the payment risks in international trade.

Level of analysis In systems theory, this is the subsystem on which the primary focus is placed; four levels of analysis normally characterize organizations.

Level of detail The degree to which the information generated is specific.

Level of equality Extent to which less powerful members accept that power is distributed unequally.

Level of service A measure (usually expressed as a percentage) of satisfying demand through inventory or by the current production schedule in time to satisfy the customers' requested delivery dates and quantities. In a make-to-stock environment, level of service is sometimes calculated as the percentage of orders picked complete from stock upon receipt of the customer order, the percentage of line items picked complete, or the percentage of total dollar demand picked complete. In make-to-order and design-to-order environments, level of service is the percentage of times the customer-requested or acknowledged date was met by shipping complete product quantities. *Syn:* measure of service, service level.

Level production method A production planning method that maintains a stable production rate while varying inventory levels to meet demand. *Syn:* level strategy, production leveling. *See:* Level schedule.

Level schedule 1: In traditional management, a production schedule or master production schedule that generates material and labor requirements that are as evenly spread over time as possible. Finished goods inventories buffer the production system against seasonal demand. *See:* Level production method. **2:** In JIT, a level schedule (usually constructed monthly) in which each day's customer demand is scheduled to be built on the day it will be shipped. A level schedule is the output of the load-leveling process. *Syn:* JIT master schedule, level production schedule. *See:* Load leveling.

Leverage 1: Generally refers to the power you have in a negotiation. In negotiations, the more leverage (options) you have, the more concessions your opponent will have to make. **2:** The tendency of the rate earned on stockholders' equity to vary from the rate earned on total assets because the amount earned on assets acquired through the use of funds provided by creditors varies from the interest paid to these creditors. **3:** The ratio of the book value of assets divided by stockholders' equity.

Leverage ratios *See:* Coverage ratios.

Leveraged Buyout (LBO) A transaction in which a firm's publicly owned stock is bought up in a mostly debt-financed tender offer, and a privately owned, highly leveraged firm results.

Liabilities 1: Debts owed to outsiders (creditors). **2:** Any legitimate financial claims against the retailer's assets.

Liability frauds Financial statement fraud in which liabilities (amounts owed to others) are understated.

Liability limitation Some statutes limit liability only for negligent acts; others limit liability to any partnership tort or contract obligation that arose from negligence, malpractice, wrongful acts, or misconduct committed by any partner, employee, or agent of the partnership; some provide limited liability for all debts and obligations of the partnership.

Liability limitation statutes Many states now authorize corporations—with shareholder approval—to limit or eliminate the liability of directors for some breaches of duty.

Liability of general partners The general partners have unlimited liability.

Liability swap A swap created to hedge cash flows related to liabilities.

Liaison role The function of a person located in one department who is responsible for communicating and achieving coordination with another department.

Libertarians People who stress market outcomes as the basis for distributing society's rewards.

LIBOR The London InterBank Offer Rate. The rate of interest charged by top-quality international banks on loans to similar quality banks in London. This interest rate is often used in both domestic and international markets as the rate of interest on loans and other financial agreements.

Licensing 1: Arrangement in which a local firm in the host country produces goods in accordance with another firm's (the licensing firm's) specifications; as the goods are sold, the local firm can retain part of the earnings. **2:** MNE sells a foreign company the right to use technology or information. A firm gives a license to another firm to produce or package its product.

Licensing agreement Arrangement in which one firm permits another to use its intellectual property in exchange for compensation, typically a royalty.

Licensing program Proprietary information, such as patent rights or expertise, that is licensed by the owner (licenser) to another party (licensee). Compensation paid to the licenser usually includes license issuance fees, milestone payments, and/or royalties.

Lie detector tests Federal statute prohibits private employers from requiring employees or prospective employees to take such tests.

Lien Claim on property for the satisfaction of just debt.

Life cycle 1: Product life cycle is the total time frame from product concept to the end of its intended use; a project life cycle is typically divided into five stages: concept, planning, design, implementation, evaluation and close-out. **2:** A perspective on organizational growth and change that suggests organizations are born, grow older, and eventually die.

LIFO 1: Method of valuation of inventories for accounting purposes, meaning Last-In, First-Out. The principle rests on the practice of recording inventory by "layer" of the cost at which it was incurred. **2:** Stands for last in, first out and values inventory based on the assumption that the most recently purchased merchandise is sold first and the oldest merchandise is sold last.

Limit concentration Social goal of regulation is to restrict undue influence.

Limitation or modification of warranties Permitted as long as it is not unconscionable.

Limited liability 1: A shareholder's liability is limited to the amount invested in the business enterprise. **2:** The limited partners have limited liability (liability for partnership obligations only to the extent of the capital that the limited partner contributed or agreed to contribute).

Limited Liability Company (LLC) An unincorporated business association that provides limited liability to all of its owners (members) and permits all of its members to participate in management of the business.

Limited Liability Limited Partnership (LLLP) A limited partnership in which the liability of the general partners has been limited to the same extent as in an LLP.

Limited Liability Partnership (LLP) A general partnership that, by making the statutorily required filing, limits the liability of its partners for some or all of the partnership's obligations.

Limited partner Member of a limited partnership with liability for its debts only to the extent of her capital contribution.

Limited partnership A partnership formed by two or more persons under the laws of a state and having one or more general partners and one or more limited partners.

Limited problem solving Occurs when the consumer has a strong preference for either the brand or the store, but not both.

Limited-service merchant wholesalers Perform only a few services for manufacturers or other customers, or they perform all of them on a more restricted basis than do full-service wholesalers.

Limiting operation The operation with the least capacity in a series of operations with no alternative routings. The capacity of the total system can be no greater than the limiting operation, and as long as this limiting condition exists, the total system can be effectively scheduled by scheduling the limiting operation and providing this operation with proper buffers.

Line 1: A specific physical space for the manufacture of a product that in a flow shop layout is represented by a straight line. In actuality, this may be a series of pieces of equipment connected by piping or conveyor systems. **2:** A type of manufacturing process used to produce a narrow range of standard items with identical or highly similar designs. Production volumes are high, production and material handling equipment is specialized, and all products typically pass through the same sequence of operations.

Line authority A form of authority in which individuals in management positions have the formal power to direct and control immediate subordinates.

Line balancing 1: The balancing of the assignment of the tasks to workstations in a manner that minimizes the number of workstations and minimizes the total amount of idle time at all stations for a given output level. In balancing these tasks, the specified time requirement per unit of product for each task and its sequential relationship with the other tasks must be considered. **2:** A technique for determining the product mix that can be run down an assembly line to provide a fairly consistent flow of work through that assembly line at the planned line rate.

Line efficiency A measure of actual work content versus cycle time of the limiting operation in a production line. Line efficiency (percentage) is equal to the sum of all station task times divided by the longest task time multiplied by the number of stations. In an assembly line layout, the line efficiency is 100 percent minus the balance delay percentage.

Line extensions New products that are developed as variations of existing products.

Line loading The loading of a production line by multiplying the total pieces by the rate per piece for each item to come up with a finished schedule for the line.

Line of credit An arrangement in which a bank agrees to lend up to a specified maximum amount of funds during a designated period. Short-term lending arrangement which allows the company to borrow up to a prearranged dollar amount during the one-year term.

Linear cultures View the past as being behind them and the future in front of them; they view change as good and attempt to take advantage of business opportunities that they foresee.

Linear regression Mathematical application of the concept of a scatter diagram where the correlation is actually a cause-and-effect relationship.

Linear responsibility matrix Matrix providing a three-dimensional view of project tasks, responsible person, and level of relationship.

Linear trend analysis Assumes constant unit change over time.

Liner service Ocean shipping characterized by regularly scheduled passage on established routes.

Lingua franca The language habitually used among people of diverse speech to facilitate communication.

Link analysis Connects relevant data segments with each other, forming categories, clusters, or networks of information.

Liquid asset An asset that can be easily converted into cash without significant loss of its original value.

Liquid Crystal Display (LCD) A flat-panel computer monitor in which a conductive-film-covered screen is filled with a liquid crystal whose molecules can align in different planes when charged with certain electrical voltage, which either blocks light or allows it to pass through the liquid. The combination of light and dark produces images of characters and pictures.

Liquidating dividend A distribution of capital assets to shareholders.

Liquidation When a corporation is dissolved, its assets are liquidated and used first to pay its liquidation expenses and its creditors according to their respective contract or lien rights; any remainder is proportionately distributed to shareholders according to their respective contract rights.

Liquidation preference Priority over common stock in corporate assets upon liquidation.

Liquidity The ability to sell an asset quickly, at or very close to the present market price. For a company the ability of the firm to pay its bills on time.

Liquidity preference hypothesis Theoretical explanation for the term structure of interest rates that hypothesizes that higher yields will be necessary to induce investors to tie their funds up for long time periods (in other words, to be illiquid) in light of the increasing interest rate risk. Preference for liquidity is thought to characterize enough investors that the yield curve (in the absence of expectations or other influences on other than the shortest-term securities) should slope upward from left to right. The longer the maturity, the larger the liquidity premium must be to attract investors.

Liquidity preference theory The theory that, all else equal, lenders prefer to make short-term loans rather than long-term loans; hence, they will lend short-term funds at lower rates than long-term funds.

Liquidity Premium (LP) A premium added to the rate on a security if the security cannot be converted to cash on short notice and at close to the original cost.

Liquidity ratios Ratios that show the relationship of a firm's cash and other current assets to its current liabilities.

Liquidity risk The inability to sell quickly at or very near the current market price, which is tied to the marketability of a security.

Listening The skill of receiving messages to accurately grasp facts and feelings to interpret the genuine meaning.

Listening post data Customer data and information gathered from designated "listening posts."

Little's law Relates three performance measures of a business process: average flow rate (R, throughput), average flow time (T), and average inventory (I). $I = R \times T$

Load The amount of planned work scheduled for and actual work released to a facility, work center, or operation for a specific span of time. Usually expressed in terms of standard hours of work or, when items consume similar resources at the same rate, units of production. *Syn:* workload.

Load balancing The transfer of visitor inquiries from a busy server to a less busy server.

Load leveling Spreading orders out in time or rescheduling operations so that the amount of work or similar considerations make it more economical to purchase or produce in larger lots than are needed for immediate purposes.

Loan participation After a bank or syndicate of banks arranges a large loan, part or all of the loan may be sold off to corporate or other institutional investors, as well as to other banks.

Loans Both general and limited partners may be secured or unsecured creditors of the partnership.

Lobbyist Typically, a well-connected person or firm that is hired by a business to influence the decision making of policymakers and legislators.

Local content Regulations to gain control over foreign investment by ensuring that a large share of the product is locally produced or a larger share of the profit is retained in the country.

Location The geographic space or cyberspace where the retailer conducts business.

Location decision A decision concerning the number of facilities to establish and where they should be situated.

Locational arbitrage Action to capitalize on a discrepancy in quoted exchange rates between banks.

Lock out/tag out regulations Requirements that locks and tags be used to make equipment inoperative for repair or adjustment.

Lockbox A special post office box where customers are instructed to mail their remittances.

Lockbox arrangement A technique used to reduce float by having payments sent to post office boxes located near the customers.

Lockbox collection system A cash collection system that intercepts customer remittances close to the sending location and deposits the checks in the banking system prior to the company receiving notification.

Lockbox consortium A system composed of several independent banks operating under a contractual agreement to provide lockbox services for each other's customers.

Lockbox optimization model A set of variables, relationships, and rules that determine the optimal number of lockboxes, their locations, and the customer allocations to the selected lockbox sites.

Lockbox services A collection service offered by banks, with the emphasis being to reduce collection float. Banks receiving one million or more pieces of mail per year can have a unique zip code set up for them, saving one or more sorts by post office personnel.

Lockbox study A study usually conducted by a bank consulting group to help a corporation decide the structure of its collection system.

Lockups A lockup is an option granted to a friendly suitor (e.g., a white knight) giving them the right to purchase stock or some of the major assets (e.g., crown jewels) of a target firm at a fixed price in the event of an unfriendly takeover.

Locus of control The tendency to place the primary responsibility for one's success or failure either within oneself (internally) or on outside forces (externally).

Log-linear regression An approach to estimating a variable's growth rate, which takes into account all of the variable's observed values.

Logic bomb A destructive computer program that is inactive until it is triggered by an event taking place in the computer, such as the deletion of a certain record from a file. When the event is the occurrence of a particular time, the logic bomb is referred to as a *time bomb*.

Logic error A program error that occurs when the logic of the program does not achieve its goals.

Logical design A translation of user requirements into detailed functions of a proposed information system.

Logistical service standards Kinds of quantifiable distribution services performed by a logistical system to meet the needs of customers.

Logistics Also called *physical distribution,* logistics focuses on the physical movement and storage of goods and materials. Managers in this area must evaluate various transportation options, develop and manage networks of warehouses when needed, and manage the physical flow of materials into and out of the organization, what are often called *inbound* and *out-bound logistics.* In some cases, logistics managers help decide on the appropriate type of packaging for the product. Logistics must also work closely with marketing to determine the appropriate channels (for example, wholesalers, retailers, mail order) by which to market the firm's products and services.

Logistics platform Vital to a firm's competitive position, it is determined by a location's ease and convenience of market reach under favorable cost circumstances.

London Interbank Offer Rate (LIBOR) The short-term interest rate at which banks offer Eurodollar loans to each other.

Longitudinal analysis A method of estimating market demand by factoring in the time lag of demand patterns.

Long-linked technology The combination within one organization of successive stages of production, with each stage using as its inputs the production of the preceding stage.

Long-run profits Corporate involvement in social causes creates goodwill, which simply makes good business sense.

Long-term forward contracts Contracts that state any exchange rate at which a specified amount of a specified currency can be exchanged at a future date (more than one year from today). Also called long forwards.

Long-term goals Goals that an organization hopes to achieve in the future, usually in three to five years. They are commonly referred to as strategic goals.

Long-term liabilities Liabilities that are not due for a long time (usually more than one year).

Long-term orientation 1: A greater concern for the future and high value on thrift and perseverance. **2:** Dimension of culture that refers to values people hold that emphasize the future, as opposed to short-term values focusing on the present and the past. **3:** The adaptation of traditions to meet current needs.

Loop layout A type of store layout in which a major customer aisle begins at the entrance, loops through the store—usually in the shape of a circle, square, or rectangle—and then returns the customer to the front of the store.

Loss control Actions taken to reduce the frequency and/or severity of losses (risk reduction or mitigation).

Loss exposure A potential loss that may be associated with a specific type of risk.

Loss exposure checklist A risk identification tool used by businesses and individuals that lists many different potential losses. The user can determine which of the potential losses is relevant.

Loss from operations The excess of operating expenses over gross profit.

Loss leader An extreme form of leader pricing where an item is sold below a retailer's cost.

Lot Defined quantity of product accumulated under conditions that are considered uniform for sampling purposes.

Lot tolerance percent defective (LTPD) *See:* Consumer's risk.

Lottery A hypothetical investment alternative with a probability p of obtaining the best payoff and a probability of $(1-p)$ of obtaining the worst payoff.

Louvre Accord 1987 agreement between countries to attempt to stabilize the value of the U.S. dollar.

Low-context culture A culture in which communication is used to exchange facts and information.

Low-cost leadership A strategy that tries to increase market share by emphasizing low cost compared to competitors.

Low liquidity strategy Aggressive current asset allocation strategy which entails driving the company's investment in cash and securities to a minimum.

Low-margin/high-turnover retailer A retailer that operates on a low gross margin percentage and a high rate of inventory turnover.

Low-margin/low-turnover retailer A retailer that operates on a low gross margin percentage and a low rate of inventory turnover.

Low power distance culture A state in which employees perceive few power differences and follow a superior's instructions only when either they agree or feel threatened.

Lower Control Limit (LCL) Control limit for points below the central line in a control chart.

Lower-of-Cost-or-Market (LCM) method A method of valuing inventory that reports the inventory at the lower of its cost or current market value (replacement cost).

Lower trial courts State courts that try misdemeanors (small crimes) and pretrial issues.

Loyalty programs A form of sales promotion program in which buyers are rewarded with special rewards, which other shoppers are not offered, for purchasing often from the retailer.

Lubrication bribes A payment made to an official to facilitate, expedite, and speed up routine government approvals or other actions to which the firm would be legally entitled. They are also called *grease payments.*

Lump-Sum Increase (LSI) A one-time payment of all or part of a yearly pay increase.

Lumpy assets Assets that cannot be acquired in small increments; instead, they must be obtained in large, discrete amounts.

M

Maastricht Treaty The agreement signed in December 1991 in Maastricht, the Netherlands, in which European Community members agreed to a specific timetable and set of necessary conditions to create a single currency for the EU countries.

Machiavellianism The tendency to direct much of one's behavior toward the acquisition of power and the manipulation of others for personal gain.

Machine center A production area consisting of one or more machines (and, if appropriate for capacity planning, the necessary support personnel) that can be considered as one unit for capacity requirements planning and detailed scheduling.

Machine cycle The four steps that the CPU follows repeatedly: fetch an instruction, decode the instruction, execute the instruction, and store the result.

Machine language Binary programming language that is specific to a computer. A computer can execute a program only after the program's source code is translated to object code expressed in the computer's machine language.

Machine loading The accumulation by workstation, machine, or machine group of the hours generated from the scheduling of operations for released orders by time period.

Machine loading differs from capacity requirements planning in that it does not use the planned orders from MRP but operates solely from released orders. It may be of limited value because of its limited visibility of resources.

Machine productivity A partial productivity measure. The rate of output of a machine per unit of time compared with an established standard or rate of output. Machine productivity can be expressed as output per unit of time or output per machine hour.

Machine utilization A measure of how intensively a machine is being used. Machine utilization compares the actual machine time (setup and run time) to available time.

MacOS The family of Macintosh operating systems.

Macro processes Broad, far-ranging processes that often cross functional boundaries.

Macroassessment Overall risk assessment of a country without considering the MNC's business.

Macroeconomic forecasting Prediction of aggregate economic activity.

Macroeconomic level Level at which trading relationships affect individual markets.

Magnetic disk A disk, or set of disks sharing a spindle, coated with an easily magnetized substance to record data in the form of tiny magnetic fields.

Magnetic-Ink Character Recognition (MICR) A technology that allows a special electronic device to read data printed with special magnetic ink. The data are later processed by a computer. MICR is widely used in banking. The bank code, account number, and the amount of a check are printed on the bottom of checks.

Magnetic Ink Character Recognition (MICR) line The clearing agent, often a Federal Reserve bank, branch, or RCPC, uses the information printed at the bottom of the check to process the check. This information can be read by scanning machines and indicates several items about the drawee bank.

Magnetic tape Coated polyester tape used to store computer data; similar to tape recorder or VCR tape.

Mail float The time that elapses from the point when the check is written until it is received by the payee. It may range from a day for local checks immediately mailed out to ten days for a check sent to New York from Rome, Italy.

Mainframe A computer larger than a midrange computer, but smaller than a supercomputer.

Maintainability The probability that a given maintenance action for an item under given usage conditions can be performed within a stated time interval when the maintenance is performed under stated conditions using stated procedures and resources. Maintainability has two categories: serviceability, the ease of conducting scheduled inspections and servicing, and repairability, the ease of restoring service after a failure.

Maintenance Ironing out bugs that went undetected in the final testing of a program and modifying a program to meet new business needs.

Maintenance margin The level that the margin account returns to after a margin call.

Make-to-order A production environment where a good or service can be made after receipt of a customer's order. The final product is usually a combination of standard items and items custom-designed to meet the special needs of the customer. Where options or accessories are stocked before customer orders arrive, the term assemble-to-order is frequently used. *See:* Assemble-to-order, Make-to-stock.

Make-to-stock A production environment where products can be and usually are finished before receipt of a customer order. Customer orders are typically filled from existing stocks, and production orders are used to replenish those stocks. *See:* Assemble-to-order, Make-to-order.

Malcolm Baldrige National Quality Award (MBNQA) An award established by Congress in 1987 to raise awareness of quality management and to recognize U.S. companies that have implemented successful quality management systems. A *Criteria for Performance Excellence* is published each year. Three awards may be given annually in each of five categories: manufacturing businesses, service businesses, small businesses, education institutions, and health care organizations. The award is named after the late Secretary of Commerce Malcolm Baldrige, a proponent of quality management. The U.S. Commerce Department's National Institute of Standards and Technology (NIST) manages the award, and ASQ administers it. The major emphasis in determining success is achieving results.

Managed care Approaches that monitor and reduce medical costs using restrictions and market system alternatives.

Managed earnings *See:* Income smoothing.

Managed float Exchange rate system in which currencies have no explicit boundaries, but central banks may intervene to influence exchange rate movements.

Management The attainment of organizational goals in an effective and efficient manner through planning, organizing, leading, and controlling organizational resources.

Management accounting A component of an organization's internal accounting system that provides financial and nonfinancial information used by managers and others within the organization for use in planning, controlling, and decision making.

Management by Exception (MBE) An approach for reducing the amount of information that managers must consume that allows managers to review only exceptions from expected results that are of a certain size or type.

Management by fact Business philosophy that decisions should be based on data.

Management by Objectives (MBO) 1: A method of management whereby managers and employees define goals for every department, project, and person and use them to monitor subsequent performance. **2:** Specifies the perfor-mance goals that an individual and her or his manager agree to try to attain within an appropriate length of time.

Management by policy Organizational infrastructure that ensures that the right things are done at the right time.

Management by walking around A manager's planned, but usually unannounced, walk-through of their organization to gather information from employees and make observations; may be viewed in a positive light by virtue of giving employees opportunity to interact with top management; has the potential of being viewed negatively if punitive action is taken as a result of information gathered.

Management by wandering around A communication technique in which managers interact directly with workers to exchange information.

Management champion A manager who acts as a supporter and sponsor of a technical champion to shield and promote an idea within the organization.

Management contract An international business alternative in which the firm sells its expertise in running a company while avoiding the risk or benefit of ownership.

Management control systems The formalized routines, reports, and procedures that use information to maintain or alter patterns in organizational activity.

Management controls Controls performed by one or more managers at any level in an organization.

Management Discussion and Analysis (MDA) A required disclosure in the annual report filed with the Securities and Exchange Commission; it provides critical information in interpreting financial statements.

Management fraud Deception perpetrated by an organization's top management through the manipulation of financial statement amounts or disclosures.

Management In the absence of a contrary agreement, each member has equal rights in the management of the LLC; but LLCs may be managed by one or more managers who may be members.

Management Information System (MIS) A computer-based system that provides information and support for effective managerial decision making.

Management intervention Management's actions to overrule prescribed policies or procedures for legitimate purposes; management intervention is usually necessary to deal with nonrecurring and nonstandard transactions or events that otherwise might be handled inappropriately by the system.

Management override Management's overruling of prescribed policies or procedures for illegitimate purposes with the intent of personal gain or an enhanced presentation of an entity's financial condition or compliance status.

Management process The series of actions taken by management to run an entity. An internal control system is a part of and integrated with the management process.

Management reserve *See:* Contingency.

Management review Formal evaluation by top management of the status and adequacy of the quality system in relation to the quality policy and objectives.

Management science approach Organizational decision making that is the analog to the rational approach by individual managers.

Management science perspective A management perspective that emerged after World War II and applied mathematics, statistics, and other quantitative techniques to managerial problems.

Management styles Predominant personal styles used by managers; styles may be based on prevalent management theories or assumptions about people.

Management training Training and/or education provided to any management or professional level person from front-line supervision up to, but not including executives.

Manager Individual who manages and is responsible for resources (people, material, money, time). A person officially designated with a management-type position title. A "manager" is granted authority from above, whereas a "leader's" role is derived by virtue of having followers. However, the terms "manager" and "leader" are often used interchangeably.

Managerial accounting The branch of accounting that uses both historical and estimated data in providing information that management uses in conducting daily operations, in planning future operations, and in developing overall business strategies.

Managerial commitment Desire and drive on the part of management to act on an idea and support it in the long run.

Managerial ethics Principles that guide the decisions and behaviors of managers with regard to whether they are morally right or wrong.

Managerial grid Management theory developed by Robert Blake and Jane Mouton, that maintains that a manager's management style is based on his or her mind-set toward people; it focuses on attitudes rather than behavior. The theory uses a grid to measure concern with production and concern with people.

Manager-managed LLCs The managers of manager-managed LLCs have a duty of care and loyalty; usually, members of a manager-managed LLC have no duties to the LLC or its members by reason of being a member.

Managing about a target rule Rather than make daily transfers, this transfer rule makes only one transfer for several days of deposits and the amount transferred takes into consideration a desired target balance that is to be left at the deposit bank.

Mandated benefits Benefits that employers in the United States must provide to employees by law.

Manufacturability A measure of the design of a product or process in terms of its ability to be produced easily, consistently, and with high quality.

Manufacturer's agents Independent middlemen who handle a manufacturer's marketing functions by selling part or all of a manufacturer's product line in an assigned geographic area.

Manufacturer's sales branches Sales outlets owned by the manufacturer.

Manufacturing businesses A type of business that changes basic inputs into products that are sold to individual customers.

Manufacturing cells A grouping of production processes where employees are cross-trained to perform more than one function.

Manufacturing cycle efficiency The ratio of value-added time to manufacturing lead time or cycle time. Manufacturing cycle time can be improved by the reduction of manufacturing lead time by eliminating non-value-added activities such as inspecting, moving, and queuing.

Manufacturing defect Not produced according to specifications.

Manufacturing environment The framework in which manufacturing strategy is developed and implemented. Elements of the manufacturing environment include external environmental forces, corporate strategy, business unit strategy, other functional strategies (marketing, engineering, finance, and so on), product selection, product/process design, product/process technology, and management competencies. Often refers to whether a company, plant, product, or service is make-to-stock, make-to-order, or assemble-to-order. *Syn:* production environment.

Manufacturing execution system An information system that helps pinpoint bottlenecks in production lines.

Manufacturing lead time The total time required to manufacture an item, exclusive of lower level purchasing lead time. For make-to-order products, it is the length of time between the release of an order to the production process and shipment to the final customer. For make-to-stock products, it is the length of time between the release of an order to the production process and receipt into finished goods inventory. Included here are order preparation time, queue time, setup time, run time, move time, inspection time, and put-away time. *Syn:* manufacturing cycle, production cycle, production lead time.

Manufacturing margin The variable cost of goods sold deducted from sales.

Manufacturing organization An organization that produces physical goods.

Manufacturing process The series of operations performed upon material to convert it from the raw material or a semifinished state to a state of further completion. Manufacturing processes can be arranged in a process layout, product layout, cellular layout, or fixed-position layout. Manufacturing processes can be planned to support make-to-stock, make-to-order, assemble-to-order, and so on, based on the strategic use and placement of inventories.

Manufacturing Resource Planning (MRP II) 1: The combination of MRP with other manufacturing-related activities to plan the entire manufacturing process, not just inventory. **2:** A method for the effective planning of all resources of a manufacturing company. Ideally, it addresses operational planning in units, financial planning in dollars, and has a simulation capability to answer what-if questions. It is made up of a variety of processes, each linked together: business planning, production planning (sales and operations planning), master production scheduling, material requirements planning, capacity requirements planning, and the execution support systems for capacity and material. Output from these systems is integrated with financial reports such as the business plan, purchase commitment report, shipping budget, and inventory projections in dollars. Manufacturing resource planning is a direct outgrowth and extension of closed-loop MRP.

Manufacturing strategy A collective pattern of decisions that acts upon the formulation and deployment of manufacturing resources. To be most effective, the manufacturing strategy should act in support of the overall strategic direction of the business and provide for competitive advantages (edges).

Manufacturing volume strategy An element of manufacturing strategy that includes a series of assumptions and predictions about long-term market, technology, and competitive behavior in the following areas: 1) the predicted growth and variability of demand, 2) the costs of building and operating different sized plants, 3) the rate and direction of technological improvement, 4) the likely behavior of competitors, and 5) the anticipated impact of international competitors, markets, and sources of supply. It is the sequence of specific volume decisions over time that determines an organization's long-term manufacturing volume strategy.

Maquiladoras Mexican border plants that make goods and parts or process food for export back to the United States. They benefit from lower labor costs.

Margin A small percentage of the contract price that is put up rather than paying the full price of the contract.

Margin call A call from a broker asking for more money to support a stock purchase loan.

Margin requirement Deposit placed on a contract (such as a currency futures contract) to cover the fluctuations in the value of that contract; this minimizes the risk of the contract to the counterparty.

Margin of safety The difference between current sales revenue and the sales at the break-even point.

Marginal Change in the dependent variable caused by a one-unit change in an independent variable.

Marginal cost 1: Change in total cost following a one-unit change in output. **2:** The rate of change of the total cost with respect to volume. **3:** Change in a firm's total costs-per-unit change in its output level.

Marginal cost method This method considers the direct costs of producing and selling goods for export as the floor beneath which prices cannot be set.

Marginal Cost of Capital (MCC) The cost of obtaining another dollar of new capital; the weighted average cost of the last dollar of new capital raised.

Marginal functions Duties that are part of a job but are incidental or ancillary to the purpose and nature of a job.

Marginal profit Change in total profit due to a one-unit change in output.

Marginal revenue 1: Change in a firm's total revenue-per-unit change in its sales level. **2:** Change in total revenue associated with a one-unit change in output.

Marginal tax rate The tax applicable to the last unit of income.

Markdown Any reduction in the price of an item from its initially established price.

Marked-to-market When changes in the market price of the futures contract impact the margin account on a daily basis.

Market Firms and individuals willing and able to buy or sell a given product.

Market allocation Division of markets by customers, geographic location, or products.

Market audit A method of estimating market size by adding together local production and imports, with exports subtracted from the total.

Market-based forecasting Use of a market-determined exchange rate (such as the spot rate or forward rate) to forecast the spot rate in the future.

Market-based transfer pricing The price one segment of a company charges another segment of the same company for the transfer of a good or a service based on its current market price.

Market/Book (M/B) ratio The ratio of a stock's market price to its book value.

Market control A situation that occurs when price competition is used to evaluate the output and productivity of an organization.

Market-differentiated pricing Price-setting strategy based on demand rather than cost.

Market entry strategy An organizational strategy for entering a foreign market.

Market equilibrium price Market clearing price.

Market failure The inability of market institutions to sustain desirable activity or eliminate undesirable activity.

Market line The line on a graph showing the relationship between job value, as determined by job evaluation points and pay survey rates.

Market microstructure Consists of the participants and mechanics involved in making transactions.

Market niche A segment of a market that can be successfully exploited through the special capabilities of a given firm or individual.

Market, or nondiversifiable, risk That part of a security's risk that *cannot* be eliminated by diversification because it is associated with economic, or market, factors that systematically affect most firms.

GLOSSARY

Market-perceived quality The customer's opinion of your products or services as compared to those of your competitors.

Market performance objectives Objectives that represent how a retailer desires to be compared to its competitors.

Market potential Level of sales that might be available to all marketers in an industry in a given market.

Market price approach An approach to transfer pricing that uses the price at which the product or service transferred could be sold to outside buyers as the transfer price.

Market price, P_0 The price at which a stock sells in the market.

Market risk premium, RP_M The additional return over the risk-free rate needed to compensate investors for assuming an average amount of risk.

Market (price) skimming Strategy of pricing the new product at a relatively high level and then gradually reducing it over time.

Market segment 1: Overlapping ranges of trade targets with common ground and levels of sophistication. **2:** A portion of business that can be assigned to a manager for profit responsibility. **3:** Those segments of the market or submarkets that seek similar benefits from product usage, and that shop and buy in similar ways that are different from other market segments and submarkets; consist of groups of consumers who are alike based on some characteristic(s). **4:** A division or fragment of the overall market with essentially unique characteristics.

Market segmentation The dividing of a heterogeneous consumer population into smaller, more homogeneous groups based on their characteristics.

Market segmentation hypothesis A theoretical explanation of the term structure of interest rates which contends that instead of being close substitutes, securities with short, medium, and long maturities are seen by investors (fund suppliers) and issuers (funds demanders) as quite different. Thus interest rates for securities with different maturities are set by diverse supply and demand conditions.

Market segmentation theory The theory that each borrower and lender has a preferred maturity and that the slope of the yield curve depends on the supply of and demand for funds in the long-term market relative to the short-term market.

Market share The retailer's total sales divided by total market sales.

Market structure The competitive environment.

Market transparency Availability of full disclosure and information about key market factors such as supply, demand, quality, service, and prices.

Market Value-Added (MVA) system A control system that measures the stock market's estimate of the value of a company's past and expected capital investment projects.

Market value ratios A set of ratios that relate the firm's stock price to its earnings and book value per share.

Marketable securities 1: Securities that can be sold on short notice without loss of principal or original investment. **2:** Stocks, bonds, and other noncash assets; sometimes called *short-term investments*.

Marketing Process of planning and executing the conception, pricing, promotion, and distribution of ideas, goods, and services to create exchanges that satisfy individual and organizational goals.

Marketing channel Network of organizations that creates time, place, and possession utilities.

Marketing channel management Analysis, planning, organizing, and controlling of a firm's marketing channels.

Marketing channel power Capacity of one channel member to influence the behavior of another channel member.

Marketing concept How organizational goals are achieved by identifying the needs and wants of customers and delivering products that satisfy customers more effectively than competitors could.

Marketing environment Involves the micro- and macroenvironmental influences, including the company's own objectives and resources, the sociocultural environment, the competitive environment, the economic environment, the technological environment, and the political and legal environment.

Marketing infrastructure Facilitating marketing agencies in a country; for example, market research firms, channel members.

Marketing mix Composed of product, price, place (distribution), and promotion decisions and programs that the company decides to pursue in implementing its marketing strategy.

Marketing myopia Too narrowly defining one's business.

Marketing strategy Using vision and planning to create and deploy a company's assets and capabilities most profitably.

Marking the evidence Placing unique identification tags or descriptions on documents when they are received, so that they can be identified during the investigation and trial process.

Markup 1: An amount that is added to a "cost" amount to determine product price. **2:** The selling price of the merchandise less its cost, which is equivalent to gross margin.

Markup laws Require a specified markup above cost in particular industries.

Markup on cost The difference between price and cost, measured relative to cost, expressed as a percentage.

Markup on price The difference between price and cost, measured relative to price, expressed as a percentage.

Markup pricing Setting prices to cover direct costs plus a percentage profit contribution.

Marshaling of assets Only applies when a state court of equity administers the assets of a partnership and of its members; the process of segregating and considering separately the assets and liabilities of the partnership and the respective assets and liabilities of the individual partners.

Masculinity 1: A cultural preference for achievement, heroism, assertiveness, work centrality, and material success. **2:** The relative importance of the qualities associated with men, such as assertiveness and materialism. **3:** Refers to the degree to which people in a society stress material success and assertiveness and assign different roles to males and females.

Masculinity/femininity Dimension of cultures that refers to the degree to which "masculine" values prevail over "feminine" values.

Maslow's hierarchy of needs Classification scheme of needs satisfaction where higher level needs are dormant until lower level needs are satisfied.

Mass customization 1: The creation of a high-volume product with large variety so that a customer may specify his or her exact model out of a large volume of possible end items while manufacturing cost is low because of the large volume. An example is a personal computer order in which the customer may specify processor speed, memory size, hard disk size and speed, removable storage device characteristics, and many other options when PCs are assembled on one line and at low cost. **2:** The use of computer-integrated systems and flexible work processes to enable companies to mass produce a variety of products or services designed to exact customer specification.

Massed practice The performance of all of the practice at once.

Master budget The comprehensive budget plan encompassing all the individual budgets related to sales, cost of goods sold, operating expenses, capital expenditures, and cash.

Master note Open-ended commercial paper that allows the investor to add or withdraw monies on a daily basis, up to a specified maximum amount.

Master of destiny A view that individuals can substantially influence their future, that they control their destiny, and through hard work they can make things happen.

Master operating budget A plan for achieving the corporate goals for a period of time (normally one year).

Master planning A group of business processes that includes the following activities: demand management (which includes forecasting and order servicing); production and resource planning; and master scheduling (which includes the master schedule and the rough-cut capacity plan).

Master planning of resources A grouping of business processes that includes the following activities: demand management, which includes the forecasting of sales, the planning of distribution, and the servicing of customer orders; sales and operations planning, which includes sales planning, production planning, inventory planning, backlog planning, and resource planning; master scheduling, which includes the preparation of the master production schedule and the rough-cut capacity plan.

Master Production Schedule (MPS) 1: The component of an MRP II system that specifies production capacity to meet customer demands and maintain inventories. **2:** The master production schedule is a line on the master schedule grid that reflects the anticipated build schedule for those items assigned to the master scheduler. The master scheduler maintains this schedule, and in turn, it becomes a set of planning numbers that drives material requirements planning. It represents what the company plans to produce expressed in specific configurations, quantities, and dates. The master production schedule is not a sales item forecast that represents a statement of demand. The master production schedule must take into account the forecast, the production plan, and other important considerations such as backlog, availability of material, availability of capacity, and management policies and goals. *Syn:* master schedule.

Matching concept The concept that expenses incurred in generating revenue should be matched against the revenue in determining the net income or net loss for the period.

Matching model An employee selection approach in which the organization and the applicant attempt to match each other's needs, interests, and values.

Material Matters to which a reasonable investor would attach importance in deciding whether to purchase a security.

Material achievement Extent to which the dominant values in society are success, money, and things.

Material possessions Individuals in some cultures equate success with material wealth. However, individuals in many cultures place relatively little importance on material possessions and view the flaunting of wealth as disrespectful.

Material Requirements Planning (MRP) 1: An inventory planning system that focuses on the amount and timing of finished goods demanded and translates this into the derived demand for raw materials and subassemblies at various stages of production. **2:** A set of techniques that uses bill of material data, inventory data, and the master production schedule to calculate requirements for materials. It makes recommendations to release replenishment orders for material. Further, because it is time-phased, it makes recommendations to reschedule open orders when due dates and need dates are not in phase. Time-phased MRP begins with the items listed on the MPS and determines 1) the quantity of all components and materials required to fabricate those items and 2) the date that the components and material are required. Time-phased MRP is accomplished by exploding the bill of material, adjusting for inventory quantities on hand or on order, and offsetting the net requirements by the appropriate lead times. **3:** A dependent demand inventory planning and control system that schedules the precise amount of all materials required to support the production of desired end products. **4:** Inventory control system that includes a calculation of future need.

Materiality concept A concept of accounting that accounts for items that are deemed significant for a given size of operations. This concept, requiring use of professional judgment, describes information that must be included or disclosed to prevent financial statements from misleading their users.

Materials inventory The cost of materials that have not yet entered into the manufacturing process.

Materials ledger The subsidiary ledger that contains the individual accounts for each type of material.

Materials management 1: An approach to management that seeks to organize and coordinate the activities responsible for managing the inbound flow of materials and information from suppliers through to the point of finished goods. The various functions that often fall under the materials umbrella include material planning and control, materials and procurement research, purchasing, incoming traffic, receiving, incoming quality control, stores, materials movement, and scrap and surplus disposal. **2:** The timely movement of raw materials, parts, and supplies into and through the firm.

Materials requisitions The form or electronic transmission used by a manufacturing department to authorize materials issuances from the storeroom.

Materials Review Board (MRB) Quality control committee or team, usually employed in manufacturing or other materials-processing installations, that has the responsibility and authority to deal with items or materials that do not conform to fitness-for-use specifications. An equivalent, error review board, is sometimes used in software development.

Mathematical model Mathematical symbols and expressions used to represent a real situation.

Matrix approach An organization structure that utilizes functional and divisional chains of command simultaneously in the same part of the organization.

Matrix chart/diagram Management and planning tool that shows the relationships among various groups of data; it yields information about the relationships and the importance of task/method elements of the subjects.

Matrix organization An organization in which managers report to both a divisional executive and a functional executive.

For instance, the marketing manager of the Manufacturing Division reports both to the division's president and to the corporate vice president of marketing.

Matrix organization structure A hybrid of the functional and project organizational structures, in which resources from appropriate functional components of a company are temporarily assigned to particular projects.

Matrix structure 1: Describes an organization that is organized into a combination of functional and product departments; it brings together teams of people to work on projects and is driven by product scope. **2:** An organizational structure that uses functional and divisional structures simultaneously. This structure is strongly decentralized: it allows local subsidiaries to develop products that fit into local markets. And yet at its core, it is very centralized; it allows companies to coordinate activities across the globe and capitalize on synergies and economies of scale. **3:** A strong form of horizontal linkage in which both product and functional structures (horizontal and vertical) are implemented simultaneously.

Maturity curve Curve that depicts the relationship between experience and pay rates.

Maturity date A specified date on which the par value of a bond must be repaid.

Maturity extension swap Situation where a security is sold and replaced or exchanged with another security which will increase the yield or dollar return, while affecting credit risk minimally. The swap is executed when the manager wishes to ride the yield curve, but to make the investment he must liquidate another security.

Maturity matching, or "self-liquidating," approach A financing policy that matches asset and liability maturities. This would be considered a moderate current asset financing policy.

Maturity Risk Premium (MRP) A premium that reflects interest rate risk; bonds with longer maturities have greater interest rate risk.

Maturity value The amount due (face value plus interest) at the maturity or due date of a note.

Maximization of shareholder value The ultimate goal of the management of a multinational firm is to increase the value of the shareholder's investment as much as possible.

MBCA Unlimited personal liability is imposed on all persons who act on behalf of a defectively formed corporation.

MBO In this approach, the manager and subordinate meet, and together set objectives for the subordinate.

McFadden Act (1927) Limited branch banking by national banks to the same areas in which state-chartered banks in that state were permitted to branch, effectively prohibiting interstate branching.

M-commerce Mobile commerce, spawned by advances in technology for mobile communications devices.

Mean Measure of central tendency and is the arithmetic average of all measurements in a data set.

Mean Absolute Deviation (MAD) A measure of forecast accuracy. The average of the absolute values of the forecast errors.

Mean Absolute Error (MAE) Measure of forecast error calculated by adding up the absolute values of the difference between forecasted and actual values, and then dividing by the number of forecasts.

Mean square error Weights large errors more than small ones, and thus favors forecasting models that rarely if ever miss by a large amount.

Mean Squared Error (MSE) An approach to measuring the accuracy of a forecasting model. This measure is the average of the sum of the squared differences between the actual time series values and the forecasted values.

Mean Time Between Failures (MTBF) Average time interval between failures for repairable product for a defined unit of measure (for example, operating hours, cycles, or miles).

Means (in the hoshin planning usage) The step of identifying the ways by which multi-year objectives will be met, leading to the development of action plans.

Measurement 1: Reference standard or sample used for the comparison of properties. **2:** Recording economic transactions in the accounting system.

Mechanistic An organization system marked by rules, procedures, a clear hierarchy of authority, and centralized decision making.

Mechanistic organization Roles and objectives are clearly and rigidly outlined for employees—managers and subordinates are allowed little or no discretion. Historically, large organizations have tended to adopt the mechanistic form.

Media strategy 1: Strategy applied to the selection of media vehicles and the development of a media schedule. **2:** Four sets of interrelated activities: 1) selecting the target audience, 2) specifying media objectives, 3) selecting media categories and vehicles, and 4) buying media.

Median Middle number or center value of a set of data when all the data are arranged in an increasing sequence.

Mediating technology The provision of products or services that mediate or link clients from the external environment and allow each department to work independently.

Mediation Process by which a third party assists negotiators in reaching a settlement.

Mediators In some situations within cultures, it is not wise to send messages directly to the receiver(s); it is wise to use a mediator. The encoder sends the message to a mediator (a third party), who in turn conveys it to the receiver(s).

Medium Anything through which data are transmitted; may be guided or unguided.

Medium-Term Guarantee Program Program conducted by Ex-Im Bank in which commercial lenders are encouraged to finance the sale of U.S. capital equipment and services to approved foreign buyers; Ex-Im Bank guarantees the loan's principal and interest on these loans.

Member banks Commercial banks which belong to the Federal Reserve System. Being a member of the Federal Reserve System has historically been a requirement of all national banks, and many state-chartered banks joined voluntarily. Subsequent to the 1980 Monetary Control Act membership has been much less important, in that all depository institutions must adhere to reserve requirements and can now borrow from the Fed.

Member-managed LLCs Members of member-managed LLCs have the same duties of care and loyalty that managers have in manager.

Mentor A higher-ranking, senior organizational member who is committed to providing upward mobility and support to a protégé's professional career.

Mentoring A relationship in which experienced managers aid individuals in the earlier stages of their careers.

Mercantilism Political and economic policy in the 17th and early 18th centuries aimed at increasing a nation's wealth and power by encouraging the export of goods in return for gold.

Merchandise budget A plan of projected sales for an upcoming season, when and how much merchandise is to be purchased, and what markups and reductions will likely occur.

Merchandise inventory Merchandise on hand and available for sale to customers.

Merchandise line A group of products that are closely related because they are intended for the same end use (all televisions); are sold to the same customer group (junior miss clothing); or fall within a given price range (budget women's wear).

Merchandise management The analysis, planning, acquisition, handling, and control of the merchandise investments of a retail operation.

Merchandising The planning and control of the buying and selling of goods and services to help the retailer realize its objectives.

Merchandising businesses A type of business that purchases products from other businesses and sells them to customers.

Merchant wholesalers Independent firms that purchase a product from a manufacturer and resell it to other manufacturers, wholesalers, or retailers, but not to the final consumer.

Merchantability Warranty by a merchant seller that the goods are fit for their ordinary purpose.

Merger 1: The combining of two corporations by the acquisition of the properties of one corporation by another, with the dissolution of one of the corporations. **2:** The combination of the assets of two or more corporations into one of the corporations. Prohibited if it tends to create a monopoly or may substantially lessen competition.

Message The tangible formulation of an idea to be sent to a receiver.

Meso theory A new approach to organization studies that integrates both micro- and macro-levels of analysis.

Metadata It is the data that describes the contents of a database.

Methods analysis That part of methods engineering normally involving an examination and analysis of an operation or a work cycle broken down into its constituent parts to improve the operation, eliminate unnecessary steps, and/or establish and record in detail a proposed method of performance.

Metric A standard of measurement.

Metrology Science and practice of measurements.

Metropolitan statistical areas Areas that are freestanding urban areas with populations in excess of 50,000.

Micro managing Managing every little detail (for example, approving requisition for paper clips).

Micro processes Narrow processes made up of detailed steps and activities that could be accomplished by a single person.

Microassessment The risk assessment of a country as related to the MNC's type of business.

Microcomputer The smallest type of computer; includes desktop, laptop, and hand-held computers. The term is used less and less. Trade journals now use the terms *PC* and *PDA*.

Microeconomic forecasting Prediction of partial economic data.

Microeconomic level Level of business concerns that affect an individual firm or industry.

Micromarketing merchandising The tailoring of merchandise in each store to the preferences of its neighborhood.

Micromarkets Very small market segments, such as zip code areas or even neighborhoods.

Microprocessor An electronic chip that contains the circuitry of either a CPU or a processor with a dedicated and limited purpose, for example a communications processor.

Middle manager A manager who works at the middle levels of the organization and is responsible for major departments.

Middle-of-Month (MOM) dating Technique that allows the retailer to take a cash discount and the full payment period to begin on the middle of the month.

Midrange computer A computer larger than a microcomputer but smaller than a mainframe.

Migration The move from old hardware or software to new hardware or software.

Milestone Point in time when a critical event is to occur; a symbol placed on a milestone chart to locate the point when a critical event is to occur.

Milestone chart Another name for a *Gantt chart.*

MIL-STD Military standard.

Mind mapping Technique for creating a visual representation of a multitude of issues or concerns by forming a map of the interrelated ideas.

Minimax regret approach An approach to choosing a decision alternative without using probabilities. For each alternative, the maximum regret is computed, which leads to choosing the decision alternative that minimizes the maximum regret.

Mininationals Newer companies with sales between $200 million and $1 billion that are able to serve the world from a handful of manufacturing bases.

Minority interest The portion of a subsidiary corporation's stock that is not owned by the parent corporation.

Minority participation Participation by a group having less than the number of votes necessary for control.

MIPS Millions of instructions per second.

Mirror An Internet server that holds the same software and data as another server, which may be located thousands of miles away.

Miscellaneous fraud Deception that doesn't fall into any of the other five categories of fraud.

Misleading proxy statement Any person who distributes a false or misleading proxy statement is liable to injured investors.

Misleading statements in reports Section 18 imposes civil liability for any false or misleading statement made in a registration or report filed with the SEC.

Mission The organization's reason for existence.

Mission-critical applications Applications without which a business cannot conduct its operations.

Mission-critical hardware or software Hardware or software without which the business cannot operate and survive.

Mission culture A culture that places emphasis on a clear vision of the organization's purpose and on the achievement of specific goals.

Mission statement 1: A broadly stated definition of the organization's basic business scope and operations that distinguishes it from similar types of organizations. **2:** A basic description of the fundamental nature, rationale, and direction of the firm.

Misuse or abuse of the product A defense.

Mixed aid credits Credits at rates composed partially of commercial interest rates and partially of highly subsidized developmental aid interest rates.

Mixed approach When applied to forecasting, involves the use of both quantitative and judgmental approaches.

Mixed cost A cost with both variable and fixed characteristics, sometimes called a semivariable or semifixed cost.

Mixed forecasting Development of forecasts based on a mixture of forecasting techniques.

Mixed instruments Specialized investment instruments which offer tailoring to the specific desires of the investor.

Mixed-model production Making several different parts or products in varying lot sizes so that a factory produces close to the same mix of products that will be sold that day. The mixed-model schedule governs the making and the delivery of component parts, including those provided by outside suppliers. The goal is to build every model every day, according to daily demand.

Mixed structure An organizational structure that combines two or more organizational dimensions; for example, products, areas, or functions.

Mobile observation Another term for *tailing*.

Mode Value that occurs most frequently in a data set.

Model A representation of a real object or situation.

Model audit The monitoring of an existing model to ensure its continued validity.

Model estimation Includes the selection of an appropriate forecasting technique and model calibration.

Model management module A collection of models that a decision-support system draws on to assist in decision making.

Modeling 1: The process of establishing a relationship between a set of independent variables in order to produce an estimate of a dependent variable. **2:** Setting an example.

Modem (modulator/demodulator) A communications device that transforms digital signals to analog telephone signals, and vice versa, for data communications over voice telephone lines. Almost all of the commercial modems currently offered on the market also serve as fax devices, and are, therefore, called fax/modems. ("Fax" comes from the Latin words *fac simile*, "make alike" or "copy.")

Moderate current asset investment policy A policy that is between the relaxed and restrictive policies.

Moderate liquidity strategy An approach to liquidity management which implies an intermediate concentration of current assets in the form of cash and securities, with corresponding intermediate levels of risk. This strategy falls between and should be contrasted with conservative and aggressive liquidity strategies.

Moderate strategy In short-term financing, a strategy that is a blend of the aggressive and conservative financing strategies.

Modified accrual technique Sometimes called the "accrual addback technique" or "adjusted net income technique," this cash forecasting approach begins with accounting reports or the operating budget and then adjusts these number to reflect the timing of cash flows related to these transactions.

Modified buy-and-hold strategy An approach to investing in which the investor plans to hold the security to maturity, but will selectively sell securities on which capital gains might be realized. This strategy might be utilized when the investor wishes to take advantage of anticipated favorable interest rate movements.

Modified IRR (MIRR) The discount rate at which the present value of a project's cost is equal to the present value of its terminal value, in which the terminal value is found as the sum of the future values of the cash inflows, compounded at the firm's required rate of return (cost of capital).

Modified rebuy Purchase where the buyers have experience in satisfying the need but feel the situation warrants reevaluation of a limited set of alternatives before making a decision.

Modular approach A manufacturing company uses outside suppliers to provide the large components of the product, which are then assembled into a final product by a few workers.

Modular bill of material A type of planning bill that is arranged in product modules or options. It is often used in companies where the product has many optional features, for example, assemble-to-order companies such as automobile manufacturers.

Modulation The modification of a digital signal (from a computer) into an analog signal (for a phone line to transmit).

Moment-of-truth (MOT) A *MOT* is described by Jan Carlzon, former CEO of Scandinavian Air Services, in the 1980s as: "Any episode where a customer comes into contact with any aspect of your company, no matter how distant, and by this contact, has an opportunity to form an opinion about your company."

Monetary barriers Sometimes employed by governments to restrict trade, reduce competition, or encourage certain imports. Monetary barriers occur when governments sell foreign currencies needed to pay for undesired imports at a higher rate than the one charged for currencies needed to pay for desired imports.

Monetary items All assets and liabilities expressed in fixed amounts of currency.

Monetary-nonmonetary method A translation method that restates monetary items on the balance sheet at the current exchange rate on the balance sheet date and nonmonetary items at their historical exchange rates.

Money market A financial market in which funds are borrowed or loaned for short periods (generally one year or less).

Money market deposit accounts Savings accounts offered by depository institutions which pay interest. These were introduced to give depository institutions an account to compete with money market mutual funds.

Money market hedge Use of international money markets to match future cash inflows and outflows in a given currency.

Money market mutual fund A mutual fund that invests in short-term, low-risk securities and allows investors to write checks against their accounts.

Monoculture A culture that accepts only one way of doing things and one set of values and beliefs.

Monopolistic competition 1: A market structure characterized by a large number of sellers of differentiated products. **2:** Occurs when the products offered are different, yet viewed as substitutable for each other and the sellers recognize that they compete with sellers of these different products.

Monopolization Situation that requires market power (ability to control or exclude others from the marketplace) plus either the unfair attainment of the power or the abuse of such power.

Monopoly A market structure characterized by a single seller of a highly differentiated product. Section 2 prohibits monopolization, attempts to monopolize, and conspiracies to monopolize.

Monopoly power Ability to control price or exclude others from the marketplace.

Monopsony A market with one buyer.

Montreal Protocol Treaty by which countries agreed to cut production of chlorofluorocarbons (CFSs) by 50 percent.

Monte Carlo simulation A risk analysis technique in which probable future events are simulated on a computer, generating a probability distribution that indicates the most likely outcomes.

Monument The point in a process which necessitates a product must wait in a queue before processing further; a barrier to continuous flow.

Moods Emotions that are less intense and transitory.

Moral free space Norms that are inconsistent with at least some legitimate norms existing in other economic cultures.

Moral management Conforms to the highest standards of ethical behavior or professional standards of conduct; strives to be ethical in terms of its focus on high ethical norms and professional standards of conduct, motives, goals, orientation toward the law, and general operating strategy.

Moral-rights approach The ethical concept that moral decisions are those that maintain the rights of those people affected by them.

Mortgage Long-term loan secured by property, such as a home mortgage.

Mortgage bond A bond backed by fixed assets. First mortgage bonds are senior in priority to claims of second mortgage bonds.

Most critical path In a network diagram, the most time-consuming (longest) path of activities; the path of activities that has the lowest value—either least positive or most negative—for total slack.

Most-Favored Nation (MFN) A term describing a GATT/WTO clause that calls for member countries to grant other member countries the same most favorable treatment they accord any country concerning imports and exports.

Most likely time estimate (t_m) The time in which an activity can most frequently be completed under normal conditions.

Motion Response to a complaint or pleading by the defendant. Sometimes "motion" refers to any request made to the judge for a ruling in a case by either party.

Motion for dismissal Request to the judge to dismiss a claim because there is no genuine issue of a material fact.

Motivating channel members Action taken by a manufacturer or franchiser to get channel members to implement its channel strategies.

Motivation 1: The arousal, direction, and persistence of behavior. **2:** The desire within a person causing that person to act. **3:** State of drive or arousal that moves us toward a goal-object. **4:** The drive that a person has to excel at activities, such as a job, that he or she undertakes.

Motivational research Research method directed at discovering the conscious or subconscious reasons that motivate a person's behavior.

Motivators Factors that influence job satisfaction based on fulfillment of high-level needs such as achievement, recognition, responsibility, and opportunity for growth.

Moving average 1: Statistical forecasting technique which evens out temporary ups and downs by taking the mean of the most recent observations. **2:** A method of forecasting or smoothing a time series by averaging each successive group of data points.

Moving surveillance Another term for tailing; involves following suspects wherever they go (within limits) and observing or recording their activities.

Muda (Japanese) Activity that consumes resources but creates no value; seven categories are correction, processing, inventory, waiting, over-production, internal transport, and motion.

Multiattribute evaluation Simpler than QFD, this process rank orders and weights customer requirements relative to the competition. In addition it estimates the cost of each requirement in order to prioritize improvement actions.

Multibuyer policy Policy administered by Ex-Im Bank that provides credit risk insurance on export sales to many different buyers.

Multicollinearity Presence of moderate or high correlation between predictor variables in a regression equation. This condition is a violation of one of the assumptions of ordinary least squares regression modeling, the most common form of regression analysis.

Multicriteria decision problem A problem that involves more than one criterion; the objective is to find the "best" solution, taking into account all the criteria.

Multicultural centers Some countries, such as the United States, are multicultural centers. These countries' residents came from many parts of the world and maintain much of their former country's culture.

Multicultural team Team whose members represent diverse views and come from varied cultures.

Multidimensional development The ninth stage in the social interaction paradigm is characterized by "stepping aside," that is, leaving an important position and distributing political and economic power across private and public sectors.

Multidomestic approach Approach to international marketing in which local conditions are adapted to in each and every target market.

Multidomestic strategy 1: The modification of product design and advertising strategies to suit the specific needs of individual countries. **2:** A business strategy where each individual country organization is operated as a profit center.

Multifocused grouping A structure in which an organization embraces structural grouping alternatives simultaneously.

Multilateral Investment Guarantee Agency (MIGA) Agency established by the World Bank that offers various forms of political risk insurance to corporations.

Multilateral negotiations Trade negotiations among more than two parties; the intricate relationships among trading countries.

Multilateral netting system Complex interchange for netting between a parent and several subsidiaries.

Multilevel bill of material A display of all the components directly or indirectly used in a parent, together with the quantity required of each component. If a component is a subassembly, blend, intermediate, and so on, all its components and all their components also will be exhibited, down to purchased parts and raw materials.

Multilevel master schedule A master scheduling technique that allows any level in an end item's bill of material to be master scheduled. To accomplish this, MPS items must receive requirements from independent and dependent demand sources.

GLOSSARY

Multilevel where-used A display for a component listing all the parents in which that component is directly used and the next higher level parents into which each of those parents is used, until ultimately all top-level (level 0) parents are listed.

Multimedia Computer-based technology that provides information comprising text, images, motion pictures, and sound from the same source.

Multinational Corporation (MNC) 1: An organization that receives more than 25 percent of its total sales revenues from operations outside the parent company's home country; also called global corporation or transnational corporation. **2:** Company that has production operations in at least one country in addition to its domestic base. **3:** A company that considers the globe as a single marketplace. **4:** Companies that invest in countries around the globe. International businesses that establish subsidiaries in foreign markets.

Multinational Enterprise (MNE) 1: Any business that engages in transactions involving the movement of goods, information, money, people, or services across national borders. **2:** An organization with operating units located in foreign countries. *See:* Multinational corporation.

Multinational restructuring Restructuring of the composition of an MNC's assets or liabilities.

Multiple-drawee checks Negotiable payment order having more than one bank listed on the face of the check, with one of the banks being a bank located near the disbursing location, for which the check is an "on us" item.

Multiple IRRs The situation in which a project has two or more IRRs.

Multiple processing centers Processing centers established around the country to pick up lockbox mail and do the processing while the processed checks are deposited in accounts at correspondent banks in the company's name. Cash is then concentrated in the company's account at the lockbox bank's headquarters.

Multiple production department factory overhead rate method A method that allocates factory overhead to products by using factory overhead rates for each production department.

Multiple regression Statistical model incorporating two or more predictor variables to explain the movement in the variable of interest. The form of a multiple regression model having two predictor variables is generally of the form: $Y = a + b_1 X_1 + b_2 X_2$.

Multiple-step income statement An income statement with several sections, subsections, and subtotals.

Multiple-unit pricing Occurs when the price of each unit in a multiple-unit package is less than the price of each unit if it were sold individually.

Multiplexer A device that allows a single channel to communicate data from multiple sources simultaneously.

Multiplicative time series model A model that assumes that the separate components of the time series can be multiplied together to identify the actual time series value. When the four components of trend, cyclical, seasonal, and irregular are assumed present, we obtain $Y^t \times T^t \times C^t \times S^t \times I^t$. When cyclical effects are not modeled, we obtain $Y^t = T^t \times S^t \times I^t$.

Multiprocessing The mode in which a computer uses more than one processing unit simultaneously to process data.

Multiprogramming The capacity to allow several people to use the same computer simultaneously via different terminals.

Multitasking The ability of a computer to run more than one program seemingly at the same time; it enables the notion of windows in which different programs are represented.

Multivariate control chart Control chart for evaluating the stability of a process in terms of the levels of two or more variables or characteristics.

Multivariate models Description of the relationship between three or more variables, typically with one of the variables being explained as the influence of two or more predictor variables.

Multivoting Decision-making tool that enables a group to sort through a long list of ideas to identify priorities.

Municipal obligations Securities issued by governmental authorities, governments, or government-authorized entities at other than the federal level. These securities, sometimes called "munis," pay interest that is not taxable for federal income tax purposes and usually not taxable for state income tax purposes in the state in which the issuer is located. Examples of issuers would be states, counties, localities, and school districts.

Mutual trust Occurs when both the retailer and its supplier have faith that each will be truthful and fair in their dealings with the other.

Mutually exclusive projects A set of projects in which the acceptance of one project means the others cannot be accepted.

Mystery shopper Person who pretends to be a regular shopper in order to get an unencumbered view of how a company's service process works.

Myths Stories that are consistent with the values and beliefs of the organization but are not supported by facts.

N

n sample size The number of units in a sample.

NACHA The National Automated Clearing House Association. NACHA has been involved in developing five format options that allow the movement of funds electronically, each with varying amounts of data.

Name Inclusion of a limited partner's surname in the partnership name in most instances will result in the loss of the limited partner's limited liability. LLC statutes generally require the name of the LLC to include the words "limited liability company" or the abbreviation "LLC".

Name-your-price auction An on-line auction in which participants post the prices they are willing to pay for certain goods or services and sellers are given the opportunity to meet the terms; also called a *reverse auction*.

Narrow band A small-capacity communications channel.

Nash bargaining Where two competitors haggle over some item of value.

Nash equilibrium Set of decision strategies where no player can improve through a unilateral change in strategy.

National Ambient Air Quality Standards (NAAQS) Allowable limits for air pollutants that endanger the public health and welfare.

National Crime Information Center (NCIC) The major criminal database maintained by the FBI. This database contains information on stolen vehicles, securities, boats, missing persons, and other information helpful in fraud investigations.

National-culture scheme Proposes that HSRs are affected by national cultural dimensions.

National Environmental Policy Act (NEPA) Law that establishes environmental protection as a goal of federal policy.

National Labor Relations Act Law that **1:** declares it a federally protected right of employees to unionize and to bargain collectively; **2:** identifies five unfair labor practices by an employer; and **3:** was created to administer these rights.

Natural monopoly 1: An industry in which the market-clearing price occurs at a point at which the monopolist's long-run average costs are still declining. **2:** The preeminence of a single efficient supplier.

National security The ability of a nation to protect its internal values from external threats.

National sovereignty The supreme right of nations to determine national policies; freedom from external control.

Nationalization Occurs when a government takes over private property—reasonable compensation is usually paid by the government.

Native application A computer program originally written for the specific type of computer that is running it. As opposed to a native application, a cross-system application is one that was originally written for one type of machine, but then adapted for a newer computer. Usually, a cross-system application exhibits slow or poor performance.

Natural business year A year that ends when a business's activities have reached the lowest point in its annual operating cycle.

Natural hedging The structuring of a firm's operations so that cash flows by currency, inflows against outflows, are matched.

Natural Language Processors (NLPs) Programs that are designed to take human language input and translate it into a standard set of statements that a computer can execute.

Natural team Work group having responsibility for a particular process.

NDE Nondestructive evaluation. *See:* Nondestructive testing and evaluation.

Nearby contract The futures contract with a maturity date that occurs nearest to, but after, the date of the cash market transaction that is to be hedged.

Need to achieve A human quality linked to entrepreneurship in which people are motivated to excel and pick situations in which success is likely.

Needs Unsatisfactory conditions of the consumer that prompt him or her to an action that will make the condition better.

Negative exposure A condition that exists when a foreign subsidiary has more current liabilities than current assets.

Negotiable bill of lading Contract that grants title of merchandise to the holder, which allows banks to use the merchandise as collateral.

Negotiable certificate of deposit Bank deposits that come in $100,000 and larger denominations. Negotiability means the security can be legally sold and exchanged between investors, circumventing the early withdrawal penalty charged by the issuing bank. Only the first $100,000 is insured by the Federal Deposit Insurance Corporation, however.

Negotiated price approach An approach to transfer pricing that allows managers of decentralized units to agree (negotiate) among themselves as to the transfer price.

Negotiated transfer pricing A system that requires managers of selling and buying divisions to negotiate a mutually acceptable transfer price.

Negotiation 1: A process of formal communication, either face to face or electronic, where two or more people come together to seek mutual agreement about an issue or issues. **2:** The bargaining process that often occurs during confrontation and enables the parties to systematically reach a solution.

Neighborhood business district (NBD) A shopping area that evolves to satisfy the convenience-oriented shopping needs of a neighborhood, generally contains several small stores (with the major retailer being a super market or a variety store), and is located on a major artery of a residential area.

Nemawashi A Japanese term borrowed from gardening. In business terms, it means many private or semiprivate meetings in which true opinions are shared before a major decision-making meeting takes place.

Nepotism 1: Practice of allowing relatives to work for the same employer. **2:** Relatives of those in power tend to easily obtain business licenses, lucrative government contracts, real estate deals, and so on.

Net assets Total assets minus total debts.

Net change MRP An approach in which the material requirements plan is continually retained in the computer. Whenever a change is needed in requirements, open order inventory status, or bill of material, a partial explosion and netting is made for only those parts affected by the change. *Ant:* regeneration MRP.

Net profit Operating profit plus or minus other income or expenses.

Net profit margin The ratio of net profit (after taxes) to total sales and shows how much profit a retailer makes on each dollar of sales after all expenses and taxes have been met.

Net errors and omissions account Makes sure the balance of payments (BOP) actually balances.

Net float The difference between disbursement float and collections float; the difference between the balance shown in the checkbook and the balance shown on the bank's books.

Net income An overall measure of the performance of a company; equal to revenues minus expenses for the period.

Net liquid balance Cash and marketable securities less notes payable and current maturities of long-term debt.

Net loss The amount by which expenses exceed revenues.

Net operating loss carrybacks Practice of applying losses to offset earnings in previous years.

Net operating loss carryforwards Practice of applying losses to offset earnings in future years.

Net pay Gross pay less payroll deductions; the amount the employer is obligated to pay the employee.

Net Present Value (NPV) Method 1: A measure of the present dollar equivalent of all cash inflows and outflows flowing from a capital investment proposal. To compute net present value each cash inflow and outflow must be converted to its dollar value at a standard point in time. Calculation of NPV involves discounting all cash flows to the beginning of the cash flow timeline, then subtracting the present value of the outflows from the present value of the inflows. **2:** The sum of the present values of all cash inflows and outflows from an investment project discounted at the cost of capital. **3:** A method of evaluating capital investment proposals by finding the present value of future net cash flows, discounted at the rate of return required by the firm.

GLOSSARY

Net Present Value (NPV) profile A curve showing the relationship between a project's NPV and various discount rates (required rates of return).

Net profit margin on sales This ratio measures net income per dollar of sales; it is calculated by dividing net income by sales.

Net realizable value The valuation of an asset at an amount equal to the estimated selling price less any direct cost of disposal.

Net requirements In MRP, the net requirements for a part or an assembly are derived as a result of applying gross requirements and allocations against inventory on hand, scheduled receipts, and safety stock. Net requirements, lot-sized and offset for lead time, become planned orders.

Net sales Gross sales less returns and allowances.

Net transaction exposure Consideration of inflows and outflows in a given currency to determine the exposure after offsetting inflows against outflows.

Net working capital Current assets minus current liabilities—the amount of current assets financed by long-term liabilities.

Net worth (owner's equity) Total assets less total liabilities.

Net worth method Analytical method that estimates a suspect's unexplained income. Liabilities are subtracted from assets to give net worth, then the previous year's net worth is subtracted to find the increase in net worth. Living expenses are then added to the change in net worth to determine a person's total income, and finally known income is subtracted from total income to determine the unknown income.

Netting 1: Combining of future cash receipts and payments to determine the net amount to be owed by one subsidiary to another. **2:** Cash flow coordination between a corporation's global units so that only one smaller cash transfer must be made.

Network 1: A combination of a communications device and a computer, or several computers, or two or more computers and terminals, so that the various devices can send and receive text or audiovisual information. **2:** A system in which everyone is linked and interconnected and where there is a free exchange of ideas and data.

Network centrality Top managers increase their power by locating themselves centrally in an organization and surrounding themselves with loyal subordinates.

Network diagram A graphic display of the activities to be performed to achieve the overall project work scope, showing their sequence and interdependencies.

Network externality Added value that new users add to network goods and services.

Network model A type of database that has the ability to store a record only once in the entire database, while creating links that establish relationships with several records of another type of entity.

Network protocol The set of rules that governs a network of communications devices.

Network structure An organization structure that disaggregates major functions to separate companies that are brokered by a small headquarters organization.

Networks Similar to the contractual alliance arrangement, a corporation subcontracts its manufacturing functions to other companies.

Neural net An artificial intelligence computer program that emulates the way in which the human brain operates, especially its ability to learn.

Neutralizer A situational variable that counteracts a leadership style and prevents the leader from displaying certain behaviors.

New economy High productivity and low inflation.

Newsgroup A group of people who share questions, opinions, and information about a specific subject at a specific site.

New stationary sources Owners/operators must employ the best technological system of continuous emission reduction that has been adequately demonstrated.

New-task buying situation Purchase situation that results in an extensive search for information and a lengthy decision process.

New vehicles Extensive emission standards are established.

New-venture fund A fund providing resources from which individuals and groups can draw to develop new ideas, products, or businesses.

New-venture team A unit separate from the mainstream of the organization that is responsible for developing and initiating innovations.

Next operation as customer Concept that the organization is comprised of service/product providers and service/product receivers or "internal customers."

Niche marketing Process of targeting a relatively small market segment with a specific, specialized marketing mix.

Node An intersection or junction point of an influence diagram or a decision tree.

Nolo contendere Plea by a defendant that does not contest the charges but does not admit guilt.

Nominal group technique Technique similar to brainstorming, used by teams to generate ideas on a particular subject. Team members are asked to silently come up with as many ideas as possible, writing them down. Each member is then asked to share one idea, which is recorded. After all the ideas are recorded, they are discussed and prioritized by the group.

Nominal interest rate The stated interest rate for an investment or borrowing opportunity, ignoring the effect of the frequency of compounding. In order to compare various investments, the nominal rate is usually converted to an effective annual rate.

Nominal (quoted) risk-free rate, k_{RF} The rate of interest on a security that is free of all risk; k_{RF} is proxied by the T-bill rate or the T-bond rate. k_{RF} includes an inflation premium.

Nominating committee Has the responsibility of ensuring that competent, objective board members are selected; usually composed of outside directors.

Nonattainment areas Areas that do not meet NAAQSs.

Nonbank banks Make loans or accept deposits, but not both.

Noncallable A feature of a security which stipulates that the investor need not worry about a forced buyback of the security if interest rates fall subsequent to issuance. The absence of a call feature allows the issuer to pay a slightly lower interest rate due to the lower risk to the investor.

Noncompetitive bid Bids that are entered directly through a tender offer to the nearest Federal Reserve district bank, or through a broker or commercial bank. Investors willing to accept the average yield of all accepted competitive bids enter a noncompetitive bid.

Nonconformity Nonfulfillment of a specified requirement. *See:* Blemish, Defect, and Imperfection.

Nonconstant growth The part of the life cycle of a firm in which growth either is much faster or much slower than that of the economy as a whole.

Noncontributory plan Pension plan in which all the funds for pension benefits are provided by the employer.

Noncontrollable costs Costs that cannot be influenced (increased, decreased, or eliminated) by someone such as a manager or factory worker.

Noncumulative quantity discount A discount based on a single purchase.

Noncurrent assets Those assets that cannot be converted to cash in a short period of time (usually 12 months) in the normal course of business.

Noncyclical normal goods Products for which demand is relatively unaffected by changing income.

Nondeliverable Forward Contracts (NDFs) Like a forward contract, represents an agreement regarding a position in a specified currency, a specified exchange rate, and a specified future settlement date, but does not result in delivery of currencies. Instead, a payment is made by one party in the agreement to the other party based on the exchange rate at the future date.

Nondestructive Testing and Evaluation (NDT) Testing and evaluation methods that do not damage or destroy the product being tested.

Nondirective interview Interview that uses questions that are developed from the answers to previous questions.

Nonexempt employees Employees who must be paid overtime under the Fair Labor Standards Act.

Nonfinancial incentives Nonmonetary offers intended to motivate; special offers designed to attract foreign direct investors that may take the form of guaranteed government purchases, special protection from competition, or improved infrastructure facilities.

Nonfinancial measure A performance measure that has not been stated in dollar terms.

Nonimpact printer A printer that creates an image on a page without pressing any mechanism against the paper; includes laser, ink-jet, electrostatic, and electrothermal printers.

Nonmonetary item An item that does not represent a claim to, or for, a specified number of monetary units.

Nonparticipating preferred stock Preferred stock with a limited dividend preference.

Nonparticipator role A role in which the individual contributes little to either the task or members' socioemotional needs.

Nonpartnership creditors Have first claim to the individually owned assets of their respective debtor-partners.

Nonpoint source Land use that causes pollution.

Nonprofit corporation A corporation whose profits must be used exclusively for the charitable, educational, or scientific purpose for which it was formed.

Nonprogrammed decision making 1: A decision made in response to a situation that is unique, is poorly defined and largely unstructured, and has important consequences for the organization. **2:** Novel and poorly defined, these are used when no procedure exists for solving the problem. **3:** Entails analyzing current data and information, which was obtained through a systematic investigation of the current environment, for the purpose of identifying and solving a problem.

Nonrecourse or without recourse When a factor buys receivables and the selling firm is not ultimately responsible for final payment.

Nonresponse or participation bias Created by underrepresentation and overrepresentation in a sample of different groups. For example, most studies have an overrepresentation of consumers who are interested in the product and a nonresponse underrepresentation of consumers not interested in the product.

Nonroutine reports Reports prepared for the purpose of providing information to managers to assist them in formulating policies, preparing strategic plans, and preparing tactical (operational) plans.

Nonroutine technology Technology in which there is high task variety and the conversion process is not analyzable or well understood.

Nonsampling risk Risk that a sample will be examined and the characteristics of the sample will be misinterpreted.

Nonsterilized intervention Intervention in the foreign exchange market without adjusting for the change in money supply.

Nonstore-based retailers Intercept customers at home, at work, or at a place other than a store where they might be susceptible to purchasing.

Nonsubstitutability A trait of a department whose function cannot be performed by other readily available resources.

Nontariff barriers Include quotas, bans, safety standards, and subsidies. Sometimes employed by governments to restrict trade or reduce competition. Nontariff barriers occur when governments impose restrictive and costly administrative and legal requirements on imports.

Nonvalue-added activities 1: Tasks that can be eliminated with no deterioration in product or service functionality, performance, or quality in the eyes of the customer. **2:** The cost of activities that are perceived as unnecessary from the customer's perspective and are thus candidates for elimination.

Nonvalue-added lead time The time that units wait in inventories, move unnecessarily, and wait during machine breakdowns.

Nonverbal communication A communication transmitted through actions and behaviors rather than through words.

Nonvolatile memory Storage media that keep data and programs unchanged because they do not need electric power to maintain the stored material. Examples: ROM chips and magnetic disks.

Norm A standard of conduct that is shared by team members and guides their behavior.

Normal cost The estimated cost of completing an activity under normal conditions, according to the plan.

Normal goods Products for which demand is positively related to income.

Normal (constant) growth Growth that is expected to continue into the foreseeable future at about the same rate as that of the economy as a whole; g is a constant.

Normal distribution Bell-shaped distribution for continuous data where most of the data are concentrated around the average, and it is equally likely that an observation will occur above or below the average.

Normal probability distribution A bell-shaped distribution of values that is symmetrical around its mean value.

Normal profits/rates of return Those profits and rates of return that are close to the average for all firms and are just sufficient to attract capital.

Normal time The estimated length of time required to perform an activity under normal conditions, according to the plan.

Normal yield curve Upward-sloping graph of yields to maturity for securities with various maturities, with longer-term maturities yielding more than shorter-term maturities.

Normative An approach that defines how a decision maker should make decisions and provides guidelines for reaching an ideal outcome for the organization.

Normative ethics Concerned with supplying and justifying a coherent moral system of thinking and judging.

Normative integration The headquarters-foreign subsidiary control relationship relies neither on direct headquarters involvement nor on impersonal rules but on the socialization of managers into a set of shared goals, values, and beliefs that then shape their perspectives and behavior.

Norming The stage of team development in which conflicts developed during the storming stage are resolved and team harmony and unity emerge.

Norms Behavioral expectations, mutually agreed-upon rules of conduct, protocols to be followed, social practice.

Norris–La Guardia Act Law established as U.S. policy the full freedom of labor to form labor unions without employer interference and withdrew from the federal courts the power to issue injunctions in nonviolent labor disputes.

North American Free Trade Agreement (NAFTA) A trade agreement among Canada, Mexico, and the United States with the objective of creating a single market with no trade barriers.

North American Industry Classification System (NAICS) A method for categorizing establishments by the principal economic activity in which they are engaged.

Notebook computer A computer as small as a book, yet with computing power similar to that of a desktop microcomputer.

Notes receivable A written promise to pay by the maker, representing an amount to be received by the payee.

Notice A partnership is bound by notice to and knowledge of a partner.

Notice of breach of warranty If the buyer fails to notify the seller of any breach within a reasonable time, she is barred from any remedy against the seller.

Not-invented-here syndrome A defensive, territorial attitude that, if held by managers, can frustrate effective implementation of global strategies.

Notional amount The agreed upon face amount of the swap contract which exchange rates or interest rates are to be applied to calculate the cash flows which are to be swapped.

NPV (net present value) Discounted cash flow technique for finding the present value of each future year's cash flow.

Number of affected units chart (np chart) Control chart for evaluating the stability of a process in terms of the total number of units in a sample in which frequency of an event of a given classification occurs.

Number of days in receivables 365 (number of days in a year) divided by accounts receivable turnover; a measure of how long it takes to collect receivables.

Number of Days of Payables Outstanding (DPO) A payables activity measure found by dividing the payables balance by average daily purchases (alternatively, average daily cost of goods sold can be used in the denominator).

Number of days' sales in inventory A measure of the length of time it takes to acquire, sell, and replace the inventory.

Number of days' sales in receivables An estimate of the length of time the accounts receivable have been outstanding.

Number of times the interest charges are earned A ratio that measures the risk that interest payments to debtholders will continue to be made if earnings decrease.

O

Object code Program code in machine language, immediately processable by the computer.

Object Linking and Embedding (OLE) The linking of different applications to the same software so that it can be addressed and used by any of these applications. The object may be text, graphic, or audiovisual material.

Object-Oriented Programming (OOP) A programming method that combines data and the procedures that process the data into a single unit called an "object," which can be invoked from different programs.

Objective 1: The expected result or product of a project, usually defined in terms of scope, schedule, and cost. **2:** Quantitative statement of future expectations and an indication of when the expectations should be achieved; it flows from goals and clarifies what people must accomplish.

Objective evidence Verifiable qualitative or quantitative observations, information, records, or statements of fact pertaining to the quality of an item or service or to the existence and implementation of a quality system element.

Objective function A mathematical expression that describes the problem's objective.

Objective risk The probable variation of actual from expected experience.

Objectivity concept Requires that the accounting records and reports be based upon objective evidence.

Observation 1: Item of objective evidence found during an audit. **2:** A research tool where the subjects' activity and behavior are observed.

Obsolescence costs Costs to a firm associated with holding inventory that is not selling due to a loss in demand for the product.

OC (Operating Characteristic) curve For a sampling plan, the OC curve indicates the probability of accepting a lot based on the sample size to be taken and the fraction defective in the batch.

Occupational Safety and Health Act Law enacted to ensure workers a safe and healthful work environment.

Ocean bill of lading Receipt for a shipment by boat, which includes freight charges and title to the merchandise.

Ocean shipping The forwarding of freight by ocean carrier.

Odd pricing The practice of setting retail prices that end in the digits 5, 8, 9—such as $29.95, $49.98, or $9.99.

Off-balance-sheet financing Financing in which the assets and liabilities involved do not appear on the firm's balance sheet.

Off-invoice allowance Deals offered periodically to the trade that allow wholesalers and retailers to simply deduct a fixed amount, say 15 percent, from the full price at the time the order is placed.

Off-peak Period of excess capacity.

Off-price retailers Retailers that sell products at a discount but do not carry certain brands on a continuous basis. They carry those brands they can buy from manufacturers at closeout or deep one-time discount prices.

Off-the-job training Training that takes place away from the actual work site.

Off-target The output of a process deviates from the established target.

Offering price The price at which common stock is sold to the public.

Official goals The formally stated definition of business scope and outcomes the organization is trying to achieve; another term for mission.

Office automation systems Systems that combine modern hardware and software to handle the tasks of publishing and distributing information.

Official reserves account An account in the BOP statement that shows 1) the change in the amount of funds immediately available to a country for making international payments and 2) the borrowing and lending that has taken place between the monetary authorities of different countries either directly or through the International Monetary Fund.

Offshore banking The use of banks or bank branches located in low-tax countries, often Caribbean islands, to raise and hold capital for multinational operations.

OLAP (online analytical processing) A type of application that operates on data stored in databases and data warehouses to produce summary tables with multiple combinations of dimensions. An OLAP server is connected to the database or data warehouse server at one end, and to the user's computer at the other.

Oligopolistic competition Occurs when relatively few sellers, or many small firms who follow the lead of a few larger firms, offer essentially homogeneous products and any action by one seller is expected to be noticed and reacted to by the other sellers.

Oligopoly A market structure characterized by few sellers and interdependent price/output decisions.

Omitted variables Independent variables which should have been included in a regression model, and that could have helped the analyst predict the variable of interest. If important, omission may give rise to a violation of ordinary least squares assumption, a condition known as serial correlation.

Omnibus surveys Survey research service offered by a number of large marketing research companies where several companies' research studies and sets of questions are included in a single questionnaire sent to representative panels of households.

One-parameter (simple) exponential smoothing Method for forecasting slowly changing levels.

One-price policy A policy that establishes that the retailer will charge all customers the same price for an item.

One-shot game A one-time interaction.

One-stop logistics Allows shippers to buy all the transportation modes and functional services from a single carrier.

One-to-one marketing Concept of knowing customers' unique requirements and expectations and marketing to these. *See:* Customer relationship management.

One-transaction approach An approach used to translate foreign currency where the transaction is not considered to be completed until the final settlement. Any transaction gain or loss will be reflected on the settlement date in an adjustment to the value of the resource acquired.

One-way exclusive dealing Occurs when the supplier agrees to give the retailer the exclusive right to merchandise the supplier's product in a particular trade area.

Ongoing validation Involves continually checking a model's forecast accuracy by monitoring each period's forecast error and comparing it to past forecast errors.

On-Line Transaction Processing (OLTP) A computerized processing in which each transaction is processed immediately, without the delay of accumulating transactions into a batch.

On-shelf merchandising The display of merchandise on counters, racks, shelves, and fixtures throughout the store.

On-the-Job Training (OJT) A type of training in which an experienced employee "adopts" a new employee to teach him or her how to perform job duties.

On-us When the payee deposits the check in the bank on which it is drawn.

Online processing Using a computer while in current interaction with the CPU, so that the data are processed as they are entered, as opposed to batch processing.

Open account (or open book account) Once approved for credit, a customer can make repeated purchases as long as the total amount owed at any one time is less than some predetermined ceiling.

Open account transaction Sale in which the exporter ships the merchandise and expects the buyer to remit payment according to agreed-upon terms.

Open-book management Approach to managing that exposes employees to the organization's financial information, provides instruction in business literacy, and enables employees to better understand their role and contribution and its impact on the organization.

Open communication Sharing all types of information throughout the company, across functional and hierarchical levels.

Open criticism A style of Chinese management in which the practice of public scolding (*ma ren*) is used frequently. Represents the Chinese view that the practice of quiet, subtle criticism is sneaky and therefore all communication, including criticism, should take place in the open.

Open Database Connectivity (ODBC) Standards that ensure that software written to comply with these standards can be used with any ODBC-compliant database.

Open-ended questions Allow respondents to determine the direction of the answer without being led by the question. They also prevent "yes" or "no" answers.

Open regionalism The use of declarations instead of treaties to combine an informal regional trading strategy with a commitment to global openness.

Open source software Software whose source code can be accessed by the general public.

Open system 1: A system that interfaces and interacts with other systems. **2:** A system that must interact with the environment to survive.

Open Systems Interconnection (OSI) The dominant standard that works as a general model for wide area network protocols.

Open-to-buy Refers to the dollar amount that a buyer can currently spend on merchandise without exceeding the planned dollar stocks.

Operating activities Those cash flows that are not classified as either investing or financing activities. Generally operating cash flows are related to cash collected from sales and cash disbursed to supplies, workers, management, and taxes.

Operating break-even analysis An analytical technique for studying the relationship between sales revenues, operating costs, and profits.

Operating break-even point Represents the level of production and sales at which operating income is zero; it is the

GLOSSARY

point at which revenues from sales just equal total operating costs.

Operating cash flows Those cash flows that arise from normal operations; the difference between cash collections and cash expenses.

Operating Characteristic curve *See:* OC curve.

Operating controls Regulation by government directive.

Operating cycle The process of funds flowing from inventory to receivables to payables.

Operating expenses Costs a retailer incurs in running a business, other than the cost of merchandise.

Operating lease A lease where the lessor retains most of the risks and rewards of ownership; commonly referred to as rentals. Leases that do not meet the criteria for capital leases and thus are accounted for as operating expenses. Also called a service lease.

Operating leverage 1: A measure of the relative mix of a business's variable costs and fixed costs, computed as contribution margin divided by operating income. **2:** The existence of fixed operating costs, such that a change in sales will produce a larger change in operating income (EBIT).

Operating motive Theoretical motive for trade credit extension in which the seller responds to variable and uncertain demand by altering its trade credit availability.

Operating performance ratio Net income divided by total sales; a measure of the percentage of revenues that become profits.

Operating profit Gross margin less operating expenses.

Operating or service lease A lease that transfers most but not all benefits and costs inherent in the ownership of the property to the lessee. Payments do not fully cover the cost of purchasing the asset or incurring the liability.

Operating risk The danger of interference by governments or other groups in one's corporate operations abroad.

Operating system System software that supports the running of applications developed to utilize its features and controls peripheral equipment.

Operation start date The date when an operation should be started so that its order due date can be met. It can be calculated based on scheduled quantities and lead times or on the work remaining and the time remaining to complete the job.

Operational feasibility study An evaluation made to determine whether a new information system will be used as intended.

Operational goals Specific, measurable results expected from departments, work groups, and individuals within the organization.

Operational managers Individuals who are in charge of small groups of workers.

Operational plans Plans developed at the organization's lower levels that specify action steps toward achieving operational goals and that support tactical planning activities.

Operational restructuring When a company changes its product lines or use of assets with heavy fixed operating costs and alters the company's business risk.

Operations 1: The collection of people, technology, and systems within a company that has primary responsibility for providing the organization's products or services. **2:** Used with "objectives" or "controls" and having to do with the effectiveness and efficiency of an entity's operations, including performance and profitability goals, and safeguarding resources.

Operations information system A computer-based information system that supports a company's day-to-day operations.

Operations management 1: The design, implementation, and improvement of a firm's operations. All organizations have an operations function. But not all organizations manage their operations. A firm must constantly ask itself, "How can we use our operations to create the greatest value for our customers and to meet our business strategy?" **2:** Management model that deals with activities directed at maximizing the efficiency of the retailer's use of resources. It is frequently referred to as day-to-day management.

Operations scheduling The actual assignment of starting or completion dates to operations or groups of operations to show when these operations must be done if the manufacturing order is to be completed on time. These dates are used in the dispatching function. *Syn:* detailed scheduling, order scheduling, shop scheduling.

Operations sequence The sequential steps for an item to follow in its flow through the plant. For instance, operation 1) cut bar stock; operation 2) grind bar stock; operation 3) shape; operation 4) polish; operation 5) inspect and send to stock. This information is normally maintained in the routing file.

Operations sequencing A technique for short-term planning of actual jobs to be run in each work center based upon capacity (that is, existing workforce and machine availability) and priorities. The result is a set of projected completion times for the operations and simulated queue levels for facilities.

Operations strategy The recognition of the importance of operations to the firm's success and the involvement of operations managers in the organization's strategic planning.

Operative goals Descriptions of the ends sought through the actual operating procedures of the organization; these explain what the organization is trying to accomplish.

Opportunity 1: A situation in which managers see potential organizational accomplishments that exceed current goals. **2:** A potential increase in revenue, reduction of costs, or gain in competitive advantage that can be achieved using an information system.

Opportunity cost 1: The return on the best alternative use of an asset; the highest return that will not be earned if funds are invested in a particular project. **2:** Cost incurred by a firm as the result of foreclosure of other sources of profit; for example, for the licenser in a licensing agreement, the cost of forgoing alternatives such as exports or direct investment.

Opportunity cost rate The rate of return on the best available alternative investment of equal risk.

Opportunity costs per unit The contribution margin per unit sacrificed by the selling segment due to the internal transfer of one unit of the good or service, rather than selling it in the external market.

Opportunity loss, or regret The amount of loss (lower profit or higher cost) from not making the best decision for each state of nature.

Optical Character Recognition (OCR) A way of capturing data from source documents, in which scanning devices read characters and transform them into digital data processable by the computer.

Optical disc A disc on which data are recorded by treating the disc surface so it reflects light in different ways; also called a *compact disc* (CD).

Optical fiber A thin fiberglass filament used as a medium for transmitting bursts of light that represent bits. The most advanced physical communications channel, now in use for data, voice, and image telecommunication.

Optical tape A storage device that uses the same principles as a compact disc.

Optimal decision Choice alternative that produces a result most consistent with managerial objectives.

Optimal dividend policy The dividend policy that strikes a balance between current dividends and future growth and maximizes the firm's stock price.

Optimal markup on cost The profit-maximizing cost markup, equal to –1 divided by the quantity 1 plus the price elasticity of demand.

Optimal markup on price The profit-maximizing price markup, equal to –1 times the inverse of the price elasticity of demand.

Optimal solution The specific decision variable value or values that provide the "best" output for the model.

Optimistic approach An approach to choosing a decision alternative without using probabilities. For a maximization problem, it leads to choosing the decision alternative corresponding to the largest payoff; for a minimization problem, it leads to choosing the decision alternative corresponding to the smallest payoff.

Optimistic time estimate (t^o) The time in which an activity can be completed if everything goes perfectly well and there are no complications.

Optimization Achieving planned process results that meet the needs of the customer and supplier alike and minimize their combined costs.

Opting-out right Right of customers to give written notice to financial institutions that prohibits the institution from sharing or selling customer's personal information.

Option A contract that gives the option holder the right to buy or sell an asset at some predetermined price within a specified period of time.

Option overplanning Typically, scheduling extra quantities of a master schedule option greater than the expected sales for that option to protect against unanticipated demand. This schedule quantity may only be planned in the period where new customer orders are currently being accepted, typically just after the demand time fence. This technique is usually used on the second level of a two-level master scheduling approach to create a situation where more of the individual options are available than of the overall family. The historical average of demand for an item is quantified in a planning bill of material. Option overplanning is accomplished by increasing this percentage to allow for demands greater than forecast. *See:* Hedge, Planning bill of material.

Optional stock list A merchandising method in which each store in a retail chain is given the flexibility to adjust its merchandise mix to local tastes and demands.

Order control Control of manufacturing activities by individual manufacturing, job, or shop orders, released by planning personnel and authorizing production personnel to complete a given batch or lot size of a particular manufactured item. Information needed to complete the order (components required, work centers and operations required, tooling required, and so on.) may be printed on paper or tickets, often called shop orders or work orders, which are distributed to production personnel. This use of order control sometimes implies an environment where all the components for a given order are picked and issued from a stocking location, all at one time, and then moved as a kit to manufacturing before any activity begins. It is most frequently seen in job shop manufacturing.

Order cycle time The total time that passes between the placement of an order and the receipt of the merchandise.

Order getter Salesperson who seeks to actively provide information to prospects, persuade prospective customers, and close sales.

Order handling Disposition of orders that are within credit limits and handling of orders which violate limits.

Order losers Capabilities of an organization in which poor performance can cause loss of business. Failure to meet customer expectations with delivery of the product is an order loser. *See:* Order qualifiers, Order winners.

Order management The planning, directing, monitoring, and controlling of the processes related to customer orders, manufacturing orders, and purchase orders. Regarding customer orders, order management includes order promising, order entry, order pick, pack and ship, billing, and reconciliation of the customer account. Regarding manufacturing orders, order management includes order release, routing manufacture, monitoring, and receipt into stores or finished goods inventories. Regarding purchasing orders, order management includes order placement, monitoring, receiving, acceptance, and payment of supplier.

Order point A set inventory level where, if the total stock on hand plus on order falls to or below that point, action is taken to replenish the stock. The order point is normally calculated as forecasted usage during the replenishment lead time plus safety stock. *Syn:* reorder point, statistical order point, trigger level. *See:* Fixed reorder quantity inventory model.

Order point system The inventory method that places an order for a lot whenever the quantity on hand is reduced to a predetermined level known as the order point. *Syn:* statistical order point system. *See:* Fixed reorder quantity inventory model.

Order promising The process of making a delivery commitment, that is, answering the question, When can you ship? For make-to-order products, this usually involves a check of uncommitted material and availability of capacity, often as represented by the master schedule available-to-promise. *Syn:* customer order promising, order dating.

Order qualifiers Those competitive characteristics that a firm must exhibit to be a viable competitor in the marketplace. For example, a firm may seek to compete on characteristics other than price, but in order to "qualify" to compete, its costs and the related price must be within a certain range to be considered by its customers. *Syn:* qualifiers. *See:* order losers, order winners.

Order taker Salesperson who only processes the purchase that the customer has already selected.

Order winners Those competitive characteristics that cause a firm's customers to choose that firm's goods and services over those of its competitors. Order winners can be considered to be competitive advantages for the firm. Order winners usually focus on one (rarely more than two) of the following strategic initiatives: price/cost, quality, delivery speed, delivery reliability, product design, flexibility, after-market service, and image. *See:* Order losers, Order qualifiers.

Ordering costs Costs associated with the inventory ordering process.

Ordinary (deferred) annuity An annuity whose payments occur at the end of each period.

GLOSSARY

Organic An organization system marked by free-flowing, adaptive processes, an unclear hierarchy of authority, and decentralized decision making.

Organic organization Allows employees considerable discretion in defining their roles and the organization's objectives. Historically, small organizations have tended to adopt the organic form.

Organization A social entity that is goal directed and deliberately structured.

Organization-centered career planning Career planning that focuses on jobs and on identifying career paths that provide for the logical progression of people between jobs in an organization.

Organization chart The visual representation of an organization's structure.

Organization for Economic Cooperation and Development (OECD) An organization that promotes worldwide economic development in general, and economic growth and stability of its member countries in particular. Its work focuses primarily on providing financial accounting and reporting guidelines to multinational corporations for disclosures to host countries.

Organization structure The framework in which the organization defines how tasks are divided, resources are deployed, and departments are coordinated.

Organization theory A macro approach to organizations that analyzes the whole organization as a unit.

Organizational behavior 1: An interdisciplinary field dedicated to the study of how individuals and groups tend to act in organizations. **2:** A micro approach to organizations that focuses on the individuals within organizations as the relevant units for analysis.

Organizational change The adoption of a new idea or behavior by an organization.

Organizational citizenship Work behavior that goes beyond job requirements and contributes as needed to the organization's success.

Organizational commitment 1: Loyalty to and heavy involvement in one's organization. **2:** The degree to which employees believe in and accept organizational goals and desire to remain with the organization.

Organizational control The systematic process through which managers regulate organizational activities to make them consistent with expectations established in plans, targets, and standards of performance.

Organizational culture 1: The pattern of basic assumptions that a given group has invented, discovered, or developed in learning to cope with its problems of external adaptation and internal integration; having worked well enough to be considered valid, the pattern may therefore be taught to new members as the correct way to perceive, think, and feel in relation to those problems. **2:** An umbrella term referring to the general tone of a corporate environment.

Organizational decision making The organizational process of identifying and solving problems.

Organizational Development (OD) 1: The application of behavioral science techniques to improve an organization's health and effectiveness through its ability to cope with environmental changes, improve internal relationships, and increase problem-solving capabilities. **2:** A behavioral science field devoted to improving performance through trust, open confrontation of problems, employee empowerment and participation, the design of meaningful work, cooperation between groups, and the full use of human potential.

3: Organization-wide (usually) planned effort, managed from the top, to increase organization effectiveness and health through interventions in the organization's processes, using behavioral science knowledge.

Organizational environment All elements that exist outside the boundary of the organization and have the potential to affect all or part of the organization.

Organizational goal A desired state of affairs that the organization attempts to reach.

Organizational innovation The adoption of an idea or behavior that is new to an organization's industry, market, or general environment.

Organizational meeting The first meeting, held to adopt the bylaws and appoint officers.

Organizational politics Activities to acquire, develop, and use power and other resources to obtain one's preferred outcome when there is uncertainty or disagreement about choices.

Organizations Social entities that are goal-directed, deliberately structured activity systems linked to the external environment.

Organized anarchy Extremely organic organization characterized by highly uncertain conditions.

Organizational socialization Process by which an individual adapts to and comes to appreciate the values, norms, and required behavior patterns of an organization.

Organized security exchange A formal organization, having a tangible physical location, that facilitates trading in designated ("listed") securities. The two major national security exchanges in the United States are the New York Stock Exchange (NYSE) and the American Stock Exchange (AMEX).

Organizing The management function concerned with assigning tasks, grouping tasks into departments, and allocating resources to departments; the deployment of organizational resources to achieve strategic goals.

Orientation The planned introduction of new employees to their jobs, co-workers, and the organization.

Orientation program A program that familiarizes new workers with their roles; the preparation of employees for assignment overseas.

Original maturity Length of time until principal is repaid, measured at the time the security is first sold.

Originating ACH The automated clearing house contacted by the bank initiating the transaction. The originating ACH must then transmit the payment order to the receiving institution's ACH (termed the receiving ACH).

Originating Depository Financial Institution (ODFI) Bank that is contacted by the payment initiator.

Other disclaimers of implied warranties The implied warranties of merchantability and fitness for a particular purpose may also be disclaimed 1) by expressions like "as is," "with all faults," or other similar lang-uage; 2) by course of dealing, course of performance, or usage of trade; or 3) as to defects an examination ought to have revealed where the buyer has examined the goods or where the buyer has refused to examine the goods.

Other expense An expense that cannot be traced directly to operations.

Other income Revenue from sources other than the primary operating activity of a business.

Other income or expenses Income or expense items that the firm incurs which are not in the course of its normal retail operations.

Other than in regular course of business Approval by the board of directors and shareholders of the selling corporation is required.

Out-of-control process Process in which the statistical measure being evaluated is not in a state of statistical control (that is, the variations among the observed sampling results cannot all be attributed to a constant system of chance causes); special or assignable causes exist. *See:* In-control process.

Out-of-the-money option When it is *not* beneficial financially for the option holder to exercise the option—a loss would be incurred if the option is exercised.

Out-of-pocket expenses Financing expenses that include interest and bank commitment fees.

Out-of-sample validation Using a new data set to assess a forecasting model's forecast accuracy.

Out of spec Term used to indicate that a unit does not meet a given specification.

Outflow A payment, or disbursement, of cash for expenses, investments, and so on.

Outpartnering The process of involving the supplier in a close partnership with the firm and its operations management system. Outpartnering is characterized by close working relationships between buyers and suppliers, high levels of trust, mutual respect, and emphasis on joint problem solving and cooperation. With outpartnering, the supplier is viewed not as an alternative source of goods and services (as observed under outsourcing) but rather as a source of knowledge, expertise, and complementary core competencies. Outpartnering is typically found during the early stages of the product life cycle when dealing with products that are viewed as critical to the strategic survival of the firm. *See:* Customer-supplier partnership, Supplier partnership.

Output The result of processing data by the computer; usually, information.

Output device A device, usually a monitor or printer, that delivers information from a computer to a person.

Output price measurement The current value of an item equals its net realizable value.

Outshopping Occurs when individuals in one community travel regularly to a larger community to shop.

Outside directors Persons who are independent of the firm and its top managers.

Outsourcing 1: Using another firm for the manufacture of needed components or products or delivery of a service. **2:** Buying the services of an information service firm that undertakes some or all of the organization's IS operations. **3:** Strategy to relieve an organization of processes and tasks in order to reduce costs, improve quality, reduce cycle time (for example, by parallel processing), reduce the need for specialized skills, and increase efficiency.

Outstanding stock The stock that is in the hands of stockholders.

Overapplied factory overhead The amount of factory overhead applied in excess of the actual factory overhead costs incurred for production during a period.

Overcentralization Expatriates are unable to establish and maintain an effective relationship with local associates because their authority is constrained by headquarters management overcentralizing decision making.

Overdraft credit lines Whether uncommitted or committed, have the added feature of being automatically drawn down whenever the company writes a check for which it does not have the sufficient funds to cover when it clears. Used extensively in foreign countries.

Overdraft facility A banking service that allows a firm to overdraw its account. The overdraft is then charged interest as if it were a loan.

Overhead A percentage of the direct costs of a particular project, added to a contractor's proposal to cover costs of doing business, such as insurance, depreciation, general management, and human resources; indirect costs.

Overhead cost A general expense carried by all departments that is considered essential to running a company.

Overhedging Hedging an amount in a currency larger than the actual transaction amount.

Overstored A condition in a community where the number of stores in relation to households is so large that engaging in retailing is usually unprofitable or marginally profitable.

Over-the-Counter (OTC) market A large collection of brokers and dealers, connected electronically by telephones and computers, that provides for trading in securities not listed on the organized exchanges.

Owner's equity The owner's right to the assets of the business after the total liabilities are deducted.

Ownership The author of the copyrighted work is usually the owner of the copyright, which may be transferred in whole or in part.

Ownership risk The risk inherent in maintaining ownership of property abroad. The exposure of foreign owned assets to governmental intervention.

P

P chart Fraction defective chart. Also called a proportion chart.

Pacifier-oriented leader The type of leader needed in an organization that has achieved a certain level of stability and in which daily operations are running smoothly.

Packaged software General purpose applications that come ready to install from a magnetic disk, CD, or file downloaded from a vendor's Web site.

Packet Several bytes that make up a part of a telecommunicated message.

Packet switching A telecommunications method whereby messages are broken into groups of fixed amounts of bytes, and each group (packet) is transmitted through the shortest route available. The packets are assembled at the destination into the original message.

Paid-only reconciliation Bank-provided demand deposit report which indicates all paid checks by check number, with check number, dollar amount, and date paid.

Paid time-off plan Plan that combines all sick leave, vacation time, and holidays into a total number of hours or days that employees can take off with pay.

Palm computer A computer that is small enough to be held in a person's palm; also called a *hand-held computer* or *personal digital assistant* (PDA).

Palming off Occurs when a retailer represents that merchandise is made by a firm other than the true manufacturer.

Panel consensus Forecast method based on the informed opinion of several individuals.

Panel interview Interview in which several interviewers interview the candidate at the same time.

Panels Groups of customers recruited by an organization to provide ad hoc feedback on performance or product development ideas.

Panels of households Groups of households (for example, 5,000) recruited by market research firms and rewarded for participating in market research surveys. The firm creates a panel by carefully selecting the composition of the group so that it is representative of the general population in terms of demographics such as geographical location, income, education, and age of the heads of households.

Par The monetary amount printed on a stock certificate.

Par value The nominal or face value of a stock or bond.

Parallel bonds Bonds placed in different countries and denominated in the respective currencies of the countries where they are placed.

Parallel conversion Using an old information system along with a new system for a predetermined period of time before relying only on the new one.

Parallel loan Loan involving an exchange of currencies between two parties, with a promise to reexchange the currencies at a specified exchange rate and future date.

Parallel processing The capacity for several CPUs in one computer to process different data at the same time.

Parallel structure Describes an organizational module in which groups, such as quality circles or a quality council, exist in the organization in addition to and simultaneously with the line organization (also referred to as collateral structure).

Parallel transmission Transmission of more than one bit at a time; usually the transmission of one byte at a time via parallel channels. Such transmission can take place only inside the computer or between the computer and its physically close peripheral equipment, such as a printer.

Parameter design (Taguchi) Use of design of experiments for identifying the major contributors to variation.

Parameters 1: The categories that are considered when following a sequence of steps in problem solving. **2:** Numerical values that appear in the mathematical relationships of a model. Parameters are considered known and remain constant over all trials of a simulation.

Parent 1: The company acquiring the stock of a subsidiary. **2:** In a hierarchical database, the data record to which several records of a lower level are linked.

Parent company The company owning a majority of the voting stock of another corporation.

Parent corporation Corporation that controls another corporation.

Parent/subsidiary relationship A combination of companies where control of other companies, known as subsidiaries, is achieved by a company, known as the parent, through acquisition of voting stock.

Pareto chart Basic tool used to graphically rank causes from most significant to least significant. It utilizes a vertical bar graph in which the bar height reflects the frequency or impact of causes.

Parity check A method to reduce errors in data communication both inside the computer and among remote communications devices. An extra bit is added to each transmitted byte to ascertain that the number of 1s is odd (in an odd parity check) or even (if an even parity check).

Partial compensation An arrangement in which the delivery of goods to one party is partially compensated for by buying back a certain amount of product from the same party.

Partial productivity The ratio of total outputs to the inputs from a single major input category.

Partial reinforcement schedule A schedule in which only some occurrences of the desired behavior are reinforced.

Participating bond Bond that calls for a stated percentage of return regardless of earnings, with additional payments dependent upon earnings.

Participation Involving employees in the decision-making process.

Participative decision making Refers to making decisions after consulting others. This style of decision making is perceived negatively in many cultures and causes the decision maker to lose credibility in the eyes of subordinates.

Participative design/engineering A concept that refers to the participation of all the functional areas of the firm in the product design activity. Suppliers and customers are often also included. The intent is to enhance the design with the inputs of all the key stakeholders. Such a process should ensure that the final design meets all the needs of the stakeholders and should ensure a product that can be quickly brought to the marketplace while maximizing quality and minimizing costs. *Syn:* co-design, concurrent design, concurrent engineering, neural network, parallel engineering, simultaneous design/engineering, simultaneous engineering, team design/engineering. *See:* Early manufacturing involvement.

Participative management Management style that expects everyone in the organization to take ownership and responsibility for their conduct and responsibilities and that allows input into decisions.

Participatory design approach The design of the information system where all users must be actively involved.

Partnership 1: An unincorporated business owned by two or more individuals. **2:** An unincorporated business association of two or more persons to carry on as co-owners a business for profit.

Partnership/alliance Strategy leading to a relationship with suppliers or customers aimed at reducing costs of ownership, maintenance of minimum stocks, just-in-time deliveries, joint participation in design, exchange of information on materials and technologies, new production methods, quality improvement strategies, and the exploitation of market synergy.

Partnership at will A partnership with no definite term or specific undertaking.

Partnership by estoppel Partnership that imposes partnership duties and liabilities on a nonpartner who has either represented himself or consented to be represented as a partner.

Partnership creditors Are entitled to be first satisfied out of partnership assets.

Partnership property Sum of all of the partnership's assets, including all property brought into the partnership or subsequently acquired by it.

Passive information gathering The receiving and processing of information regarding the existence and quality of merchandise, services, stores, shopping, convenience, pricing, advertising, and any other factors that a consumer might consider in making a purchase.

Passive investment strategy Involves a minimal amount of oversight and very few transactions once the portfolio has been selected.

Passwords Secret codes or names that allow users to access networks and other computer systems.

Patent The exclusive right to an invention for 20 years from the date of application for utility and plant patents; 14 years from grant for design patents.

Patent Cooperations Treaty (PCT) An agreement that outlines procedures for filing one international patent application rather than individual national applications.

Patentability To be patentable as a utility patent, the invention must be 1) novel, 2) useful, and 3) not obvious.

Patents Exclusive rights to produce and sell goods with one or more unique features.

Path-goal theory A contingency approach to leadership specifying that the leader's responsibility is to increase subordinates' motivation by clarifying the behaviors necessary for task accomplishment and rewards.

Pax Americana An American peace between 1945 through 1990 that led to increased international business transactions.

Pay compression Situation in which pay differences among individuals with different levels of experience and performance in the organization becomes small.

Pay equity Similarity in pay for all jobs requiring comparable levels of knowledge, skill, and ability, even if actual duties and market rates differ significantly.

Pay-for-performance Incentive pay that ties at least part of compensation to employee effort and performance.

Pay grade A grouping of individual jobs having approximately the same job worth.

Pay survey A collection of data on compensation rates for workers performing similar jobs in other organizations.

Payable Through Draft (PTD) Gives the payor 24 hours to decide whether to honor or refuse payment after it has been presented to the payor's bank. They are used for claim reimbursement by insurance companies, which use the 24 hour period to verify the signature and endorsements.

Payables turnover ratio Found by dividing purchases over a given time period by the year-end or average payables balance. Indicates the firm's payment behavior.

Payback period Number of years it will take the results of a project or capital investment to recover the investment from net cash flows.

Payback Period (PBP) method A capital budgeting method that measures the time it will take to recoup, in the form of net cash inflows, the net dollars invested in a project.

Payers Consumers who actually pay for the product.

Paying agent The bank performing this function makes interest and dividend payments to bondholders and shareholders, respectively, and repays the bond principal at maturity.

Payment (PMT) This term designates constant cash flows.

Payment date The date on which a firm actually mails dividend checks.

Payment for shares Payment that may be cash, property, and services actually rendered, as determined by the board of directors; under the Revised Act, promises to contribute cash, property, or services are also permitted.

Payoff 1: A measure of the consequence of a decision such as profit, cost, or time. Each combination of a decision alternative and a state of nature has an associated payoff (consequence). **2:** Illegal payment made abroad by MNCs to foreign government officials and politicians in the course of conducting business.

Payoff table A tabular representation of the payoffs for a decision problem.

Payroll The total amount paid to employees for a certain period.

Payroll fraud scheme Using the payroll function to commit fraud, such as creating ghost employees or overpaying wages.

Payroll register A multicolumn form used to assemble and summarize payroll data at the end of each payroll period.

PDSA cycle Plan-do-study-act cycle (a variation of PDCA developed by Deming).

Peak Period of full capacity usage.

Peer-to-Peer (P2P) file sharing File sharing that allows PCs to communicate directly with one another over the Internet, bypassing central databases, servers, control points, and Web pages.

Peer-to-peer LAN A local-area network (LAN) in which no central device controls communications.

Pegged exchange rate Exchange rate whose value is pegged to another currency's value or to a unit of account.

Pegging In MRP and MPS, the capability to identify for a given item the sources of its gross requirements and/or allocations. Pegging can be thought of as active where-used information.

Penetration A pricing objective in which price is set at a low level in order to penetrate the market and establish a loyal customer base.

Penetration strategy Requires that the firm enter the market at a relatively low price in an attempt to obtain market share and expand demand for its product.

Pension Postretirement cash benefits paid to former employees.

Pension liabilities The accumulating obligations of employers to fund the retirement or pension plans of employees.

Pension plans Retirement benefits established and funded by employers and employees.

People-processing services In these services, customers become part of the production process. Such services include passenger transportation, health care, food services, and lodging services.

Perceived opportunity A situation where people believe they have a favorable or promising combination of circumstances to commit fraud and not be detected.

Perceived pressure A situation where people perceive they have a need to commit fraud; a constraining influence on the will or mind, as a moral force.

Percent complete An estimate in percentage form of the proportion of the work involved in a particular work package that has been completed.

Percentage-of-sales method 1: Forecasting model in which an expense or balance sheet amount is expressed as some fraction of sales. **2:** A technique for budgeting in which the retailer targets a specific percentage of forecasted sales as the advertising budget.

Percentage Variation Method (PVM) A technique for planning dollar inventory investments that assumes that the percentage fluctuations in monthly stock from average stock should be half as great as the percentage fluctuations in monthly sales from average sales.

Perception The cognitive process people use to make sense out of the environment by selecting, organizing, and interpreting information.

Perceptual defense The tendency of perceivers to protect themselves by disregarding ideas, objects, or people that are threatening to them.

GLOSSARY

Perceptual distortions Errors in perceptual judgment that arise from inaccuracies in any part of the perceptual process.

Perceptual incongruity Occurs when the retailer and supplier have different perceptions of reality.

Perceptual mapping Commonly used, multidimensional scaling method of graphically depicting a product's performance on selected attributes or the "position" of a product against its competitors on selected product traits.

Perceptual selectivity The process by which individuals screen and select the various stimuli that vie for their attention.

Perfect competition A market structure characterized by a large number of buyers and sellers of an identical product.

Perfect forecast line A 45-degree line on a graph that matches the forecast of an exchange rate with the actual exchange rate.

Performance 1: The organization's ability to attain its goals by using resources in an efficient and effective manner. **2:** What an employee does or does not do.

Performance appraisal and review 1: The process of evaluating how well employees perform their jobs when compared to a set of standards, and then communicating that information to employees. **2:** The formal, systematic assessment of how well employees are performing their jobs in relation to established standards and the communication of that assessment to employees.

Performance-based pay Pay related to and directly derived from performance.

Performance consulting A process in which a trainer and the organizational client work together to boost workplace performance in support of business goals.

Performance gap A disparity between existing and desired performance levels.

Performance management system 1: System that supports and contributes to the creation of high-performance work and work systems by translating behavioral principles into procedures. **2:** Processes used to identify, encourage, measure, evaluate, improve, and reward employee performance.

Performance plan Performance management tool that describes desired performance and provides a way to assess the performance objectively.

Performance report A routine report that compares actual performance against budgetary goals.

Performance shares A type of incentive plan in which managers are awarded shares of stock on the basis of the firm's performance over given intervals with respect to earnings per share or other measures.

Performance standards Expected levels of performance.

Performance test Assessment device that requires candidates to complete an actual work task in a controlled situation.

Performing The stage of team development in which members focus on problem solving and accomplishing the team's assigned task.

Period costs Those costs that are used up in generating revenue during the current period and that are not involved in the manufacturing process These costs are recognized as expenses on the current period's income statement.

Period order quantity A lot-sizing technique under which the lot size is equal to the net requirements for a given number of periods, for example, weeks into the future. The number of periods to order is variable, each order size equalizing the holding costs and the ordering costs for the interval.

Periodic inventory system A system of inventory accounting in which only the revenue from sales is recorded each time a sale is made. The cost of merchandise on hand at the end of a period is determined by a detailed listing (physical inventory) of the merchandise on hand.

Periodic rate The rate charged by a lender or paid by a borrower each interest period (for example, monthly, quarterly, annually, and so on).

Periodic replenishment A method of aggregating requirements to place deliveries of varying quantities at evenly spaced time intervals, rather than variably spaced deliveries of equal quantities.

Peripheral equipment The additional equipment, such as a printer and keyboard, connected to a computer.

Perishability Distinguishing characteristic of services in that they cannot be saved, their unused capacity cannot be reserved, and they cannot be inventoried.

Permanent current assets Current assets' balances that do not change due to seasonal or economic conditions; these balances exist even at the trough of a firm's business cycle. The minimum amount of funds that are invested in current assets over the firm's operating cycle.

Permanent differences Differences that are caused by certain types of revenues that are exempted from taxation and certain types of expenses that are not deductible for tax purposes.

Permanent teams A group of participants from several functions who are permanently assigned to solve ongoing problems of common interest.

Permissive issues Collective bargaining issues that are not mandatory but relate to certain jobs.

Perpetrator A person who has committed a fraud.

Perpetual existence Unless the charter provides otherwise, a corporation has perpetual existence.

Perpetual inventory system A system of inventory accounting in which both the revenue from sales and the cost of merchandise sold are recorded each time a sale is made, so that the records continually disclose the amount of the inventory on hand.

Perpetuity A cash flow stream of equal dollar amounts that will last indefinitely into the future.

Perquisites (perks) Special benefits—usually noncash items—for executives.

Person-job fit 1: Matching the KSAs of people with the characteristics of jobs. **2:** The extent to which a person's ability and personality match the requirements of a job.

Person-organization fit The congruence between individuals and organizational factors.

Personal decision-support system A decision-support system that is built for the individual knowledge worker to use in his or her daily work.

Personal Digital Assistant (PDA) A small handheld computer. Many PDAs require the use of a special stylus to enter handwritten information that is recognized by the computer.

Personal insight Forecast method based on personal or organizational experience.

Personal liability If the partnership is contractually bound, each partner has joint, unlimited personal liability.

Personal objectives Objectives that reflect the retailers' desire to help individuals employed in retailing fulfill some of their needs.

Personal property Property other than an interest in land.

Personal observation evidence Evidence that is sensed (seen, heard, felt, and so on) by investigators.

Personal selling 1: Person-to-person communication in which a seller informs and educates prospective customers and attempts to influence their purchase choices; direct oral communication designed to explain how an individual's or firm's goods, services, or ideas fit the needs of one or more prospective customers. **2:** Technique that involves a face-to-face interaction with the consumer with the goal of selling the consumer merchandise or services.

Personal shopping Occurs when an individual who is a professional shopper performs the shopping role for another; very upscale department and specialty stores offer personal shoppers to their clients.

Personality The set of characteristics that underlie a relatively stable pattern of behavior in response to ideas, objects, or people in the environment.

Personality test Assessment device that measures a person's interaction skills and patterns of behavior.

Personnel competencies The ability of a firm's personnel to implement its strategy to internationalize its operations.

Personnel ratios The proportions of administrative, clerical and professional support staff.

PERT chart A chart showing events, the activities required to reach the events, and the interdependencies among activities. The events are usually completion milestones.

Pessimistic time estimate (t_p) The time in which an activity can be completed under adverse conditions, such as in the presence of unusual or unforeseen complications.

Petrodollars Deposits of dollars by countries which receive dollar revenues due to the sale of petroleum to other countries; the term commonly refers to OPEC deposits of dollars in the Eurocurrency market.

Petty cash fund A special cash fund used to pay relatively small amounts.

Phantom bill of material A bill-of-material coding and structuring technique used primarily for transient (non-stocked) subassemblies. For the transient item, lead time is set to zero and the order quantity to lot-for-lot. A phantom bill of material represents an item that is physically built, but rarely stocked, before being used in the next step or level of manufacturing. This permits MRP logic to drive requirements straight through the phantom item to its components, but the MRP system usually retains its ability to net against any occasional inventories of the item. This technique also facilitates the use of common bills of material for engineering and manufacturing. *Syn:* blowthrough, transient bill of material.

Phased conversion Implementing a new information system one module at a time.

Phased retirement Approach in which employees reduce their workloads and pay.

Philanthropic responsibilities Responsibilities viewed as such because they reflect current expectations of business by the public.

Philanthropy Contributions to charity and other worthy causes.

Physical ability tests Tests that measure individual abilities such as strength, endurance, and muscular movement.

Physical design The process of information system design that includes specifying the necessary software and hardware needed to support it.

Physical distribution 1: Planning, implementing, and controlling of the physical flows of materials and final products from points of origin to points of use to meet customers' needs at a profit. **2:** The movement of finished products from suppliers to customers.

Physical distribution management An approach to management that seeks to organize and coordinate the activities responsible for managing the outbound flow of materials and information from finished goods operations through to end customers. The various functions that often fall under the physical distribution umbrella include distribution planning and control, forecasting, outbound transportation, material handling, inventory planning and control, and warehousing.

Physical evidence Evidence of a tangible nature—includes fingerprints, tire marks, weapons, stolen property, identification numbers or marks on stolen objects, and so on—that can be used in an investigation to provide information about a fraud or other crime.

Physical inventory The detailed listing of merchandise on hand.

Physical safeguards Vaults, fences, locks, and so on that protect assets from theft.

Piercing the corporate veil The courts will disregard the corporate entity when it is used to defeat public convenience, commit a wrongdoing, protect fraud, or circumvent the law.

Piggyback Situation in which a bank is permitted to add a check or checks it is clearing and an accompanying listing to whatever checks the local Fed district bank is sending to the distant Fed office. This way the clearing bank can miss the local Fed's cutoff time but still meet the distant Fed's cutoff.

Piloting A trial conversion in which a new information system is introduced in one business unit before introducing it in others.

Pipeline stock Inventory in the transportation network and the distribution system, including the flow through intermediate stocking points. The flow time through the pipeline has a major effect on the amount of inventory required in the pipeline. Time factors involve order transmission, order processing, scheduling, shipping, transportation, receiving, stocking, review time, and so on. *Syn:* pipeline inventory.

Pipelining A technique in which one part of a CPU can do its job while others do theirs, allowing faster processing.

Pixel (picture element) A phosphor dot on the inside of a cathode-ray tube monitor. In a color monitor a triad of red, green, and blue dots is used. When the pixels are bombarded by electrons shot from the tube's electron gun, they emit light, thereby creating an image on the screen. The larger the number of pixels on the screen, the better the resolution.

Place/entry strategy Managers of business enterprises must determine how their products or services will reach the consumer. Distribution methods generally require variations from country to country as well as within each country.

Placement Fitting a person to the right job.

Plaintext An original message, before encryption.

Plan A blueprint specifying the resource allocations, schedules, and other actions necessary for attaining goals.

Plan-Do-Check-Act Cycle (PDCA) Four-step process for quality improvement. In the first step (plan), a plan to effect improvement is developed. In the second step (do), the plan is carried out, preferably on a small scale. In the third step (check), the effects of the plan are observed. In the last step (act), the results are studied to determine what was learned and what can be predicted. The plan-do-check-act cycle is sometimes referred to as the Shewhart cycle because Walter A. Shewhart discussed the concept in his book *Statistical Method from the Viewpoint of Quality Control* and as the Deming cycle because W. Edwards Deming introduced the concept in Japan. The Japanese subsequently called it the *Deming cycle*.

Planned issue receipt A transaction that updates the on-hand balance and the related allocation or open order.

Planned obsolescence Design of a product with features that the company knows will soon be superseded, thus making the model obsolete.

Planned order A suggested order quantity, release date, and due date created by the planning system's logic when it encounters net requirements in processing MRP. In some cases, it can also be created by a master scheduling module. Planned orders are created by the computer, exist only within the computer, and may be changed or deleted by the computer during subsequent processing if conditions change. Planned orders at one level will be exploded into gross requirements for components at the next level. Planned orders, along with released orders, serve as input to capacity requirements planning to show the total capacity requirements by work center in future time periods. *See:* Planning time fence.

Planned order receipt The quantity planned to be received at a future date as a result of a planned order release. Planned order receipts differ from scheduled receipts in that they have not been released. *Syn:* planned receipt.

Planned order release A row on an MRP table that is derived from planned order receipts by taking the planned receipt quantity and offsetting to the left by the appropriate lead time.

Planning 1: The management function concerned with defining goals for future organizational performance and deciding on the tasks and resource use needed to attain them; the act of determining the organization's goals and the means for achieving them. The systematic arrangement of tasks to accomplish an objective; determining what needs to be done, who will do it, how long it will take, and how much it will cost. **2:** The anticipation and organization of what needs to be done to reach an objective.

Planning bill of material An artificial grouping of items or events in bill-of-material format used to facilitate master scheduling and material planning. It may include the historical average of demand expressed as a percentage of total demand for all options within a feature or for a specific end item within a product family and is used as the quantity per in the planning bill of material. *Syn:* planning bill.

Planning task force A group of managers and employees who develop a strategic plan.

Planning time fence A point in time denoted in the planning horizon of the master scheduling process that marks a boundary inside of which changes to the schedule may adversely affect component schedules, capacity plans, customer deliveries, and cost. Outside the planning time fence, customer orders may be booked and changes to the master schedule can be made within the constraints of the production plan. Changes inside the planning time fence must be made manually by the master scheduler. *Syn:* planning fence. *See:* Cumulative lead time, Firm planned order, Planned order.

Platform Either the standard hardware or the standard operating system that the organization uses. The term has been used differently in different contexts by IS professionals and trade journals.

Plaza Accord Agreement among country representatives in 1985 to implement a coordinated program to weaken the dollar.

Plaza Agreement An accord reached in 1985 by the Group of Five that held that the major nations should join in a coordinated effort to bring down the value of the U.S. dollar.

Pledging receivables A lender makes a loan protected by a lien placed on a certain portion of the firm's receivables. Using accounts receivable as collateral for a loan.

Plug-and-play The ability of an operating system to recognize a new attachment and its function without a user's intervention.

Pluralism The organization accommodates several subcultures, including employees who would otherwise feel isolated and ignored.

PM theory of leadership A Japanese leadership theory; the P stands for showing a concern for subordinates and leadership that is oriented toward forming and reaching group goals; the M stands for leadership that is oriented toward preserving group stability.

P→O expectancy Expectancy that successful performance of a task will lead to the desired outcome.

Point-counterpoint A decision-making technique in which people are assigned to express competing points of view.

Point elasticity Elasticity at a given point on a function.

Point estimate Single value used to estimate a population parameter. Point estimates are commonly referred to as the points at which the interval estimates are centered; these estimates give information about how much uncertainty is associated with the estimate.

Point of indifference The extremity of a city's trading area where households would be indifferent between shopping in that city or in an alternative city in a different geographical direction.

Point of Presence (POP) A telephone number that a user can dial to log on to a server even if the server is many miles away, to save the user long-distance call charges.

Point-of-purchase communications Signage—displays, posters, signs, shelf cards, and a variety of other visual materials—designed to influence buying decisions at the point of sale.

Point-of-Sale Signage (POS) A relatively small signage that is placed very close to the merchandise and is intended to give details about specific items.

Point-to-Point Protocol (PPP) A protocol for communication between two computers (as opposed to a network).

Point source Any discernible, confined, and discrete conveyance from which pollutants are or may be discharged.

Poison pill 1: An action taken by management to make a firm unattractive to potential buyers and thus to avoid a hostile takeover. **2:** A shareholder rights plan aimed at discouraging or preventing a hostile takeover.

Poison puts A poison put is a variation on the poison pill as it forces a firm to buy its securities back at some set price.

Poisson distribution Distribution used for discrete data, applicable when there are many opportunities for occurrence of an event but a low probability (less than 0.10) on each trial.

Poka-yoke Term that means to mistake-proof a process by building safeguards into the system that avoid or immediately find errors. It comes from poka, which means "error," and yokeru, which means "to avoid."

Policy Management's dictate of what should be done to effect control. A policy serves as the basis for procedures for its implementation.

Political environment A nation's political system, government policies, attitude toward the product, and management of scarce foreign exchange.

Political forces The influence of political and legal institutions on people and organizations.

Political instability Events such as riots, revolutions, or government upheavals that affect the operations of an international company.

Political model A definition of an organization as being made up of groups that have separate interests, goals, and values in which power and influence are needed to reach decisions.

Political risk 1: The risk of loss by an international corporation of assets, earning power, or managerial control as a result of political actions by the host country. **2:** Political actions taken by the host government or the public that affect the MNC's cash flows. The risk of expropriation (seizure) of a foreign subsidiary's assets by the host country or of unanticipated restrictions on cash flows to the parent company.

Political systems The types of political system—one-party, two-party, or multiparty—affects the level of stability and consistency in governmental policies as it relates to business.

Political tactics for using power Tactics that include build coalitions, expand networks, control decision premises, enhance legitimacy and expertise, and make preferences explicit while keeping power implicit.

Political union A group of countries that have common foreign policy and security policy and that share judicial cooperation.

Polling A protocol in which a communications processor conducts a continuous roll-call of the nodes.

Polycentric staffing outlook The belief that key positions in foreign subsidiaries should be staffed by host-country nationals (locals).

Polygamous loyalty Reflects the notion that customer loyalty tends to be divided among a number of providing firms.

PONC Price of nonconformance: the cost of not doing things right the first time.

Pooled interdependence The lowest form of interdependence among departments, in which work does not flow between units.

Pooling A banking service offered by many banking systems outside the United States which allows a firm's excess balances spread across its bank branches to offset corporate deficit balances in other branches of the same bank.

Pooling-of-interests method An accounting method used for a business combination where the acquired entity's assets and equities are combined at book value. No goodwill is created in a pooling of interests. A method of accounting for an affiliation of two corporations resulting from an exchange of voting stock of one corporation for substantially all the voting stock of the other corporation.

Population Group of people, objects, observations, or measurements about which one wishes to draw conclusions.

Population increase The effect of changes in countries' populations on economic matters.

Population stabilization An attempt to control rapid increases in population and ensure that economic development exceeds population growth.

Population variables Indicators that include population growth trends, age distributions, and geographic trends.

Port A socket on a computer to which external devices, such as printers, keyboards, and scanners, can be connected.

Portability A pension plan feature that allows employees to move their pension benefits from one employer to another.

Portal A site that offers a search engine and general information such as weather, news, and stock market quotations; Yahoo! is one example.

Portfolio analysis Process of comparing the value of proposed projects or acquisitions relative to the financial impacts on current projects as well as the potential impact on resources of the proposed project or acquisitions.

Portfolio approach A method used to manage economic exposure of a company by offsetting negative exposure in one country with positive exposure in another.

Portfolio investment account An account in the BOP statement that records investments in assets with an original maturity of more than one year and where an investor's ownership position is less than 10 percent.

Portfolio models Tools that have been proposed for use in market and competitive analysis. They typically involve two measures—internal strength and external attractiveness.

Portfolio risk The risk associated with an investment when it is held in combination with other assets, not by itself.

Portfolio strategy A type of corporate-level strategy that pertains to the organization's mix of SBUs and product lines that fit together in such a way as to provide the corporation with synergy and competitive advantage.

Ports Harbor towns or cities where ships may take on or discharge cargo; the lack of ports and port services is the greatest constraint in ocean shipping.

Positioning Image that customers have about a product, especially in relation to the product's competitors.

Positive adjustment phase Beginning at about month four of the expatriation phase, the expatriate begins to adapt, and by about month six of the assignment, the expatriate feels more positive about the foreign environment; in this phase, he or she will attain neither the "high" of the first phase nor the "low" of the second or third phases.

Positive exposure A condition that exists when a foreign subsidiary has more current assets than current liabilities.

Positive float The time period between receipt of the goods or services and the date on which cash payment is made.

Positive pay A company sends its daily check issue file to its disbursing bank. Before the bank honors incoming checks, it refers to the issue file to see if the payee and check amounts match up.

Possession-processing services Services of this nature involve tangible actions to tangible objects to enhance their value to customers. The customer may not be present. These services include transporting freight and installing and maintaining equipment.

Postal inspectors Inspectors or investigators hired by the U.S. Postal Service to handle major fraud cases that are perpetrated through the U.S. mail system.

Post-audit A comparison of the actual and expected results for a given capital project.

Post-closing trial balance A trial balance prepared after all of the temporary accounts have been closed.

Posterior (revised) probabilities The probabilities of the states of nature after revising the prior probabilities based on sample information.

Post-incorporation subscription A subscription agreement entered into after incorporation.

Posting The process of transferring debits and credits from a journal to the accounts.

Post-purchase behavior Last stage in the consumer decision process, when the consumer experiences an intense need to confirm the wisdom of that decision.

Post-purchase resentment Feeling that arises after the purchase when the consumer becomes dissatisfied with the product, service, or retailer and thus begins to regret that the purchase was made.

Post-retirement benefits Rights to benefits that employees earn during their term of employment for themselves and their dependents after they retire.

Post-transaction services Services provided to customers after they have purchased merchandise or services.

Potential entrants Firms and individuals with the economic resources to enter a particular market, given sufficient economic incentives.

Power 1: The potential ability to influence others' behavior. **2:** The ability of one person or department in an organization to influence others to bring about desired outcomes.

Power distance 1: The degree to which people accept inequality in power among institutions, organizations, and people. **2:** Dimension of culture that refers to the inequality among the people of a nation. **3:** Refers to the degree to which people in a society accept centralized power and depend on superiors for structure and direction.

Power sources There are five sources of horizontal power in organizations: dependency, financial resources, centrality, nonsubstitutability, and the ability to cope with uncertainty.

Ppk Potential process capability used in the validation stage of a new product launch (uses the same formula as Cpk, but a higher value is expected due to the smaller time span of the samples).

PPM Parts per million.

Practices Cultural foundations of organizational behavior, including symbols, heroes, rituals, and values.

Preauthorized debit system A system that allows a customer's bank to periodically transfer funds from its account to a selling firm's bank account for the payment of bills.

Preauthorized debits Arrangement in which a customer agrees to allow his bank to automatically charge his checking account balance to make a fixed or variable payment each month.

Preauthorized draft Payment order initiated by the payee, who has been authorized to draw against the payor's account. Banks sometimes collect mortgage payments this way, and most automobile dealerships now make payments to Ford, GM, and Chrysler by these drafts.

Preauthorized payment The seller and buyer agree to a payment date and the seller initiates a request to the buyer's bank for payment of the predetermined amount.

Precautionary balances A cash balance held in reserve for unforeseen fluctuations in cash flows.

Precautionary motive Additional inventory held as a cushion for an unexpected increase in demand.

Precedence Diagramming Method (PDM) A type of network planning technique.

Precedential relationship The order in which activities must be finished before other activities can start.

Precision Characteristic of measurement that addresses the consistency or repeatability of a measurement system when the identical item is measured a number of times.

Pre-control Control process, with simple rules, based on tolerances. It is effective for any process where a worker can measure a quality characteristic (dimension, color, strength, and so on) and can adjust the process to change that characteristic, and where there is either continuous output or discrete output totaling three or more pieces.

Predatory pricing 1: Practice where one firm attempts to drive out rivals (usually smaller ones) by pricing at such a low level that the rival cannot make money. **2:** System that exists when a retail chain charges different prices in different geographic areas to eliminate competition in selected geographic areas.

Predecessor event The event at the beginning of an activity (tail of the arrow) in the activity-on-the-arrow form of network diagramming; start event.

Predetermined factory overhead rate The rate used to apply factory overhead costs to the goods manufactured. It is determined by dividing the budgeted overhead cost by the estimated activity usage at the beginning of the fiscal period.

Predication Circumstances that, taken as a whole, would lead a reasonable, prudent professional to believe that a fraud has occurred, is occurring, or will occur.

Predictive validity Measured when test results of applicants are compared with subsequent job performance.

Preemptive right 1: A provision in the corporate charter or bylaws that gives common stockholders the right to purchase on a *pro rata* basis new issues of common stock (or convertible securities). **2:** Shareholder's right to purchase a *pro rata* share of new stock offerings.

Pre-expatriation program Once the expatriate has been selected for the foreign assignment, but before leaving the home country, he or she is involved in certain training to prepare for what will be encountered in the foreign country.

Preferential policies Government policies that favor certain (usually domestic) firms; for example, the use of national carriers for the transport of government freight even when more economical alternatives exist.

Preferred Provider Organization (PPO) A health-care provider that contracts with an employer group to provide health-care services to employees at a competitive rate.

Preferred stock A class of stock with preferential rights over common stock.

Preincorporation subscription Offer to purchase capital stock in a corporation yet to be formed.

Preliminary hearing Pretrial hearing to determine whether there is "probable cause" to charge the defendant with a crime.

Preloss activities Loss control methods implemented before any losses occur. All measures with a frequency-reduction focus, as well as some based on severity reduction, are of this type.

Premium As related to forward rates, represents the percentage amount by which the forward rate exceeds the spot rate. As related to currency options, represents the price of a currency option.

Premium bond A bond that sells above its par value; occurs whenever the going rate of interest falls below the coupon rate.

Premiums Extra items offered to the customer when purchasing promoted products.

Prepaid expenses 1: Purchased commodities or services that have not been used up at the end of an accounting period. **2:** Those items for which the retailer has already paid, but the service has not been completed.

Prepayment Method which exporter uses to receive payment before shipping goods.

Prerequisite tree Technique used in the application of Goldratt's Theory of Constraints.

Present Value (PV) The value today of a future cash flow or series of cash flows.

Present value concept A concept in which cash to be received (or paid) in the future is worth less than the same amount of money held today.

Present value index An index computed by dividing the total present value of the net cash flow to be received from a proposed capital investment by the amount to be invested.

Present Value Interest Factor for an Annuity (PVIFA$_{i,n}$) The present value interest factor for an annuity of n periods discounted at i percent.

Present Value Interest Factor for i and n (PVIF$_{i,n}$) The present value of $1 due n periods in the future discounted at i percent per period.

Present value of an annuity The sum of the present values of a series of equal cash flows to be received at fixed intervals.

Presentation principles Those principles governing verbal and nonverbal communication that are applicable when making a presentation to a foreign audience.

Presentment Step seven in the check-clearing process, when the check is returned to the drawee bank for payment.

Pretest Undertaken before the major study to test the validity and reliability of measures and other components of the study's research methodology.

Pretransaction services Services provided to the customer prior to entering the store.

Prevention costs 1: Costs incurred to prevent defects from occurring during the design and delivery of products or services. **2:** Costs incurred to keep internal and external failure costs and appraisal costs to a minimum.

Prevention of significant deterioration areas Areas where air quality is higher than required.

Prevention vs. detection Term used to contrast two types of quality activities. Prevention refers to those activities designed to prevent nonconformances in products and services. Detection refers to those activities designed to detect nonconformances already in products and services. Another term used to describe this distinction is "designing in quality vs. inspecting in quality."

Preventive action Action taken to eliminate the causes of a potential nonconformity, defect, or other undesirable situation in order to prevent occurrence.

Preventive control A control designed to avoid an unintended event or result.

Price Some unit of value given up by one party in return for something from another party.

Price controls Government regulation of the prices of goods and services; control of the prices of imported goods or services as a result of domestic political pressures.

Price/cost analysis The ongoing evaluation of price and cost trends. Price analysis is the process of comparing supplier prices against external price benchmarks, without direct knowledge of the supplier's actual costs. Cost analysis is the process of analyzing each individual cost element that together add up to the final price.

Price discrimination 1: A seller offers a lower price to some buyers than to other buyers. **2:** A pricing practice that sets prices in different markets that are not related to differences in costs. **3:** Occurs when two retailers buy an identical amount of "like grade and quality" merchandise from the same supplier but pay different prices.

Price/Earnings (P/E) ratio The ratio of the price per share to earnings per share; it shows the dollar amount investors will pay for $1 of current earnings; computed by dividing the market price per share of common stock at a specific date by the company's earnings per share on common stock.

Price-elastic Sensitive to price changes.

Price elasticity of demand Responsiveness of the quantity demanded to changes in the price of the product, holding constant the values of all other variables in the demand function.

Price escalation The establishing of export prices far in excess of domestic prices—often due to a long distribution channel and frequent markups.

Price factor The effect of a difference in unit sales price or unit cost on the number of units sold.

Price-fixing 1: Conspiracy to fix competitive prices. **2:** An agreement with the purpose or effect of inhibiting price competition.

Price leadership A situation in which one firm establishes itself as the industry leader and all other firms in the industry accept its pricing policy.

Price lining A pricing policy that is established to help customers make merchandise comparisons and involves establishing a specified number of price points for each merchandise classification.

Price makers Buyers and sellers whose large transactions affect market prices.

Price promotions Short-term price reductions designed to create an incentive for consumers to buy now rather than later and/or stock up on the specially priced product.

Price strategy Some firms are influenced by the view that pricing is an active tool by which to accomplish their marketing objectives, while some are influenced by the belief that price is a static element in business decisions.

Price takers Buyers and sellers whose individual transactions are so small that they do not affect market prices.

Price zone A range of prices for a particular merchandise line that appeals to customers in a certain market segment.

Pricing market Also called the original issue market, is centered in money centers such as New York City, London, Frankfurt, Singapore, and Hong Kong. Investors can access this "over-the-counter" market from anywhere, as the market consists of phone and computer hook-ups among all participating dealers and brokers.

Pricing motive Theoretical motive for trade credit extension in which sellers unable to change prices, perhaps due to market conditions or regulation, alter trade credit instead in order to charge varying amounts to buyers.

Primacy effect Information received first gets the most weight.

Primary Process that refers to the basic steps or activities that will produce the output without the "nice-to-haves."

Primary audience In the communication process, those who receive a message directly.

Primary data Data obtained directly for a specific research purpose through interviews, focus groups, surveys, observation, or experimentation.

Primary key In a file, a field that holds values that are unique to each record. Only a primary key can be used to uniquely identify and retrieve a record.

Primary-line injury Injury to a seller's competitors.

Primary market The market in which firms issue new securities to raise corporate capital.

Primary marketing institutions Those channel members that take title to the goods as they move through the marketing channel. They include manufacturers, wholesalers, and retailers.

Primary memory (primary storage, main memory, main storage) The built-in memory chips in the computer, made of transistors. The majority of the memory is of the RAM type, and the rest is of the ROM type.

Primary research Research method in which data are gathered firsthand for the specific project being conducted.

Primary trading area The geographic area where the retailer can serve customers, in terms of convenience and accessibility, better than the competition.

Prime rate A published rate of interest charged by banks to short-term borrowers (usually large, financially secure corporations) with the best credit; rates on short-term loans generally are "pegged" to the prime rate.

Principal The original amount invested or borrowed.

Principal amount, face value, maturity value, par value The amount of money the firm borrows and promises to repay at some future date, often at maturity.

Prior-period adjustments Corrections of material errors related to a prior period or periods, excluded from the determination of net income.

Prior probabilities The probabilities of the states of nature prior to obtaining sample information.

Priorities matrix Tool used to choose between several options that have many useful benefits, but where not all of them are of equal value.

Prisoner's Dilemma A classic conflict-of-interest situation.

Privacy The ability to control information about ourselves. In a larger sense, "the right to be left alone." Information technology has made invasion of privacy a major issue in our society, due to its ability to collect, maintain, store, and manipulate huge amounts of personal information.

Private Branch Exchange (PBX) A computer-based digital switching device that simultaneously handles communications of internal voice telephones, computers, and the external telephone network.

Private corporation One founded by and composed of private persons for private purposes and having no governmental duties.

Private label branding Also often called store branding, occurs when a retailer develops its own brand name and contracts with a manufacturer to produce the merchandise with the retailer's brand on it instead of the manufacturer's name.

Private nuisance Interference with use and enjoyment of a person's land.

Private placement 1: Security issuance transaction in which a large institution such as a retirement fund or insurance company buys the entire issue. **2:** The sale of debt securities to private or institutional investors without going through a public issuance like that of a bond issue or equity issue.

Private Securities Litigation Reform Act of 1995 Law that made it more difficult for companies to bring class-action lawsuits to federal court.

Privatization A policy of shifting government operations to privately owned enterprises to cut budget costs and ensure more efficient services.

Privity Contractual relationship.

Pro forma **balance sheet approach** Method of generating a cash forecast which involves determination of the amount of cash and marketable securities by computing the difference between projected assets (excluding cash and marketable securities) and the sum of projected liabilities and owner's equity.

Proactive Marketing Public Relations (proactive MPR) Offensively rather than defensively oriented, and opportunity-seeking rather than problem-solving. The major role of proactive MPR is in the area of product introductions or product revisions.

Probabilistic input Input to a simulation model that is subject to uncertainty. A probabilistic input is described by a probability distribution.

Probability Likelihood of occurrence.

Probability distribution Mathematical formula that relates the values of characteristics to their probability of occurrence in a population.

Probability-impact matrix Assesses the probability of occurrence of an issue on one dimension and its impact on the company on the other dimension.

Problem 1: A situation in which organizational accomplishments have failed to meet established goals. **2:** Any undesirable situation.

Problem identification The decision-making stage in which information about environmental and organizational conditions is monitored to determine if performance is satisfactory and to diagnose the cause of shortcomings.

Problem recognition 1: Consumer's realization that he or she needs to buy something to get back to a normal state of comfort. **2:** Occurs when the consumer's desired state of affairs departs sufficiently from the actual state of affairs, placing the consumer in a state of unrest.

Problem solution The decision-making stage in which alternative courses of action are considered and one alternative is selected and implemented.

Problem solving Rational process for identifying, describing, analyzing, and resolving situations in which something has gone wrong without explanation.

Problem-solving team Typically 5 to 12 hourly employees from the same department who meet to discuss ways of improving quality, efficiency, and the work environment.

Problemistic search Occurs when managers look around in the immediate environment for a solution to resolve a problem quickly.

Procedural justice 1: The concept that rules should be clearly stated and consistently and impartially enforced. **2:** Examines the process a customer is required to travel in order to arrive at a final outcome. **3:** Perceived fairness of the process used to make decisions about employees.

Procedure Document that answers the questions: What has to be done? Where is it to be done? When is it to be done? Who is to do it? Why do it? (contrasted with a work instruction which answers: How is it to be done? With what materials and tools is it to be done?); in the absence of a work instruction, the instructions may be embedded in the procedure. Examples include 1) The board of directors adopts a resolution, which must be approved by a majority vote of the shareholders. 2) Patents are issued upon application to and after examination by the U.S. Patent and Trademark Office. Registration is not required but provides additional remedies for infringement.

Proceeds The net amount available from discounting a note.

Process 1: Activity or group of activities that takes an input, adds value to it, and provides an output to an internal or external customer; a planned and repetitive sequence of steps by which a defined product or service is delivered. **2:** Any manipulation of data, usually with the goal of producing information. *See:* Management process.

Process capability Statistical measure of the inherent process variability for a given characteristic. *See:* Cp, Cpk, and Ppk.

Process capability index Value of the tolerance specified for the characteristic divided by the process capability. There are several types of process capability indexes, including the widely used Cp and Cpk.

Process control system A computer system that monitors and controls ongoing physical processes, such as temperature or pressure changes.

Process cost system A type of cost accounting system that accumulates costs for each of the various departments or processes within a manufacturing facility.

Process Decision Program Chart (PDPC) Management and planning tool that identifies all events that can go wrong and the appropriate countermeasures for these events. It graphically represents all sequences that lead to a desirable effect.

Process improvement Act of changing a process to reduce variability and cycle time and make the process more effective, efficient, and productive.

Process Improvement Team (PIT) Natural work group or cross-functional team whose responsibility is to achieve needed improvements in existing processes. The life span of the team is based on the completion of the team purpose and specific goals.

Process layout A facilities layout in which machines that perform the same function are grouped together in one location.

Process management Collection of practices used to implement and improve process effectiveness; it focuses on holding the gains achieved through process improvement and assuring process integrity.

Process manufacturers Manufacturers that use machines to process a continuous flow of raw materials through various stages of completion into a finished state.

Process mapping Flowcharting of a work process in detail, including key measurements.

Process organization Form of departmentalization where each department specializes in one phase of the process.

Process-oriented layout Organizing work in a plant or administrative function around processes (tasks).

Process owner Manager or leader who is responsible for ensuring that the total process is effective and efficient.

Process quality audit Analysis of elements of a process and appraisal of completeness, correctness of conditions, and probable effectiveness.

Process structure A variation of the functional structure in which departments are formed on the basis of production processes.

Process theories 1: A group of theories that explain how employees select behaviors with which to meet their needs and determine whether their choices were successful. **2:** Refer to theories on motivation that ask, "How can I motivate an individual?"

Process village Machines grouped by type of operation (contrast with a cell layout).

Processing float The amount of time that transpires from the point of receipt of the check at a post office box or company mail room and the time when the check is deposited at the bank is termed processing float.

Procurement Purchasing supplies, services, and raw materials for use in the production process.

Procurement costs Costs to a firm associated with the process of receiving customers' orders.

Prodromal crisis stage Warning or symptom stage of a crisis.

Producer's risk for a sampling plan The probability of not accepting a lot, the quality of which has a designated numerical value representing a level that is generally desirable. Usually the designated value will be the acceptable quality level (also called *alpha risk* and *type 1 error*).

Product and service changes Changes in an organization's product or service outputs.

Product cost concept A concept used in applying the cost-plus approach to product pricing in which only the costs of manufacturing the product, termed the product cost, are included in the cost amount to which the markup is added.

Product costing Determining the cost of a product.

Product costs The three components of manufacturing cost: direct materials, direct labor, and factory overhead costs.

Product cycle theory 1: Theory suggesting that a firm initially establish itself locally and expand into foreign markets in response to foreign demand for its product; over time, the MNC will grow in foreign markets; after some point, its foreign business may decline unless it can differentiate its product from competitors. **2:** A theory that views products as passing through four stages: introduction, growth, maturity, decline; during which the location of production moves from industrialized to lower-cost developing nations.

Product development process Clearly defined set of tasks and steps that describes the normal means by which product development proceeds. The process outlines the order and sequence of the tasks and indicates who is responsible for each.

Product differentiation The effort to build unique differences or improvements into products.

Product division structure Each of the enterprise's product divisions is responsible for the sale and profits of its product.

Product liability laws Deal with the seller's responsibility to market safe products. These laws invoke the "foreseeability" doctrine, which states that a seller of a product must attempt to foresee how a product may be misused and warn the consumer against the hazards of misuse.

Product layout A facilities layout in which machines and tasks are arranged according to the sequence of steps in the production of a single product.

Product life cycle Cycle of stages that a product goes through from birth to death: introduction, growth, maturity, and decline.

Product line Set of products a firm targets to one general market. These products are likely to share some common features and technology characteristics or be complementary products. They also are likely to share several elements of the marketing mix, such as distribution channels.

Product load profile A listing of the required capacity and key resources needed to manufacture one unit of a selected item or family. The resource requirements are further defined by a lead-time offset to predict the impact of the product on the load of the key resources by specific time period. The product load profile can be used for rough-cut capacity planning to calculate the approximate capacity requirements of the master production schedule. *See:* Bill of resources, Rough-cut capacity planning.

Product matrix A variation of the matrix structure in which project or product managers have primary authority and functional managers simply assign technical personnel to projects and provide advisory expertise.

Product mix Full set of a firm's products across all markets served.

Product organization Departmentalization where each department focuses on a specific product type or family.

Product-oriented layout Organizing work in a plant or administrative function around products; sometimes referred to as product cells.

Product orientation Tendency to see customers' needs in terms of a product they want to buy, not in terms of the services, value, or benefits the product will produce.

Product positioning Refers to how customers perceive a product's position in the marketplace relative to the competition.

Product quality audit Quantitative assessment of conformance to required product characteristics.

Product/service liability Obligation of a company to make restitution for loss related to personal injury, property damage, or other harm caused by its product or service.

Product/service strategy Managers are typically concerned with what the product or service should look like and what it should be able to do. In foreign markets, they must determine whether their product or service can be sold in standard form or be customized to fit differing foreign market needs.

Product structure The sequence of operations that components follow during their manufacture into a product. A typical product structure would show raw material converted into fabricated components, components put together to make subassemblies, subassemblies going into assemblies, and so on.

Product tree A graphical (or tree) representation of the bill of material such as is shown below:

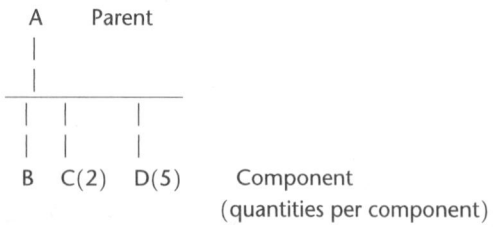

Production bottleneck A condition that occurs when product demand exceeds production capacity The bottleneck resource is a portion of the production process that is operating at 100 percent of capacity and is unable to meet product demand.

Production budget A budget of estimated production.

Production capability 1: The highest sustainable output rate that could be achieved for a given product mix, raw materials, worker effort, plant, and equipment. **2:** The collection of personnel, equipment, material, and process segment capabilities. **3:** The total of the current committed, available, and unattainable capability of the production facility. The capability includes the capacity of the resource.

Production forecast A projected level of customer demand for a feature (option, accessory, and so on.) of a make-to-order or an assemble-to-order product. Used in two-level master scheduling, it is calculated by netting customer backlog against an overall family or product line master production schedule and then factoring this product's available-to-promise by the option percentage in a planning bill of material. *See:* assemble-to-order, Planning bill of material.

Production management 1: The planning, scheduling, execution, and control of the process of converting inputs into finished goods. **2:** A field of study that focuses on the effective planning, scheduling, use, and control of a manufacturing organization through the study of concepts from design engineering, industrial engineering, management information systems, quality management, inventory management, accounting, and other functions as they affect the transformation process.

Production opportunities The returns available within an economy from investment in productive (cash-generating) assets.

Production plan The agreed-upon plan that comes from the production planning (sales and operations planning) process, specifically the overall level of manufacturing output planned to be produced, usually stated as a monthly rate for each product family (group of products, items, options, features, and so on). Various units of measurement can be used to express the plan: units, tonnage, standard hours, number of workers, and so on. The production plan is management's authorization for the master scheduler to convert it into a more detailed plan, that is, the master production schedule.

Production planning A process to develop tactical plans based on setting the overall level of manufacturing output (production plan) and other activities to best satisfy the current planned levels of sales (sales plan or forecasts), while meeting general business objectives of profitability, productivity, competitive customer lead times, and so on, as expressed in the overall business plan. The sales and production capabilities are compared, and a business strategy that includes a sales plan, a production plan, budgets, pro-forma financial statements, and supporting plans for materials and workforce requirements, and so on, is developed. One of its primary purposes is to establish production rates that will achieve management's objective of satisfying customer demand by maintaining, raising, or lowering inventories or backlogs, while usually attempting to keep the workforce relatively stable. Because this plan affects many company functions, it is normally prepared with information from marketing and coordinated with the functions of manufacturing, sales, engineering, finance, materials, and so on. *See:* Aggregate planning.

Production planning and control strategies An element of manufacturing strategy that includes the design and development of manufacturing planning and control systems in relation to the following considerations: 1) market-related criteria—the required level of delivery speed and reliability in a given market segment, 2) process requirement criteria—consistency between process type (job shop, repetitive, continuous, and so on) and the production planning and control system, 3) organization control levels—systems capable of providing long-term planning and short-term control capabilities for strategic and operational considerations by management. Production planning and control strategies help firms develop systems that enable them to exploit market opportunities while satisfying manufacturing process requirements.

Production possibilities frontier A theoretical method of representing the total productive capabilities of a nation used in the formulation of classical and modern trade theory.

Production rules A method of knowledge representation that holds the facts in the form of *if-then* statements; also called *if-then rules*.

Production scheduling The systems and activities involved with coordinating materials, manpower, and machines to produce a given amount of finished product or service and meet customer requirements.

Productivity 1: An overall measure of the ability to produce a good or a service. It is the actual output of production compared to the actual input of resources. Productivity is a relative measure across time or against common entities (labor, capital, and so on). In the production literature, attempts have been made to define total productivity where the effects of labor and capital are combined and divided into the output. One example is a ratio that is calculated by adding the dollar value of labor, capital equipment, energy, and material, and so on, and dividing it into the dollar value of output in a given time period. This is one measure of total factor productivity. *See:* Efficiency, Labor productivity, Machine productivity, Utilization. **2:** In economics, the ratio of output in terms of dollars of sales to an input such as direct labor in terms of the total wages. This is called single factor productivity or partial factor productivity.

Productivity objectives Objectives that state the sales objectives that the retailer desires for each unit of resource input: floor space, labor, and inventory investment.

Products Set of features, functions, and benefits that customers purchase. Products may consist primarily of tangible (physical) attributes or intangibles, such as those associated with services, or some combination of tangible and intangible.

Professional corporation Corporate form under which duly licensed individuals may practice their professions.

Professional development plan Individual development tool for an employee. Working together, the employee and his/her supervisor create a plan that matches the individual's career needs and aspirations with organizational demands.

Profit and loss sharing Profits and losses are allocated among the partners as provided in the partnership agreement; if the partnership agreement has no such provision, then profits and losses are allocated on the basis of the contributions each partner actually made.

Profit center A responsibility center where the manager is responsible for both revenues and costs. A decentralized unit in which the manager has the responsibility and the authority to make decisions that affect both costs and revenues (and thus profits).

Profit corporation A corporation founded for the purpose of operating a business for profit.

Profit margin 1: Measure of the profit generated from each dollar of revenue; calculated by dividing net income by revenue. Also known as return on sales, profit margin percentage, profit margin ratio, or operating performance ratio. **2:** Net income expressed as a percentage of sales revenue. The difference between the price and cost of a product.

Profit maximization 1: The maximization of the firm's net income. **2:** A pricing objective that seeks to obtain as much profit as possible. Activity level that generates the highest profit, MR = MC and Mπ = 0.

Profit repatriation limitations Restrictions set up by host governments in terms of a company's ability to pay dividends from its operations back to its home base.

Profit sharing A system to distribute a portion of the profits of the organization to employees.

Profit-volume chart A chart used to assist management in understanding the relationship between profit and volume.

Profitability 1: The ability of a firm to earn income. **2:** The belief that the business of doing business should be to return as much money as possible to shareholders.

Profitability ratios 1: Ratios that measure the degree of success or failure of an enterprise or division for a given period of time. **2:** A group of ratios showing the effect of liquidity, asset management, and debt management on operating results.

Profound knowledge, system of As defined by W. Edwards Deming, states that learning cannot be based on experience only; it requires comparisons of results to a prediction, plan, or an expression of theory. Predicting why something happens is essential to understand results and to continually improve. The four components of the system of profound knowledge are: appreciation for a system, knowledge of variation, theory of knowledge, and understanding of psychology.

Program A set of instructions to a computer.

Program Evaluation and Review Technique (PERT) Event-oriented project management planning and measurement technique that utilizes an arrow diagram or road map to identify all major project events and demonstrates the amount of time (critical path) needed to complete a project. It provides three time estimates: optimistic, most likely, and pessimistic.

Programmable problem A problem that can be solved by a computer program.

Programmed decision making 1: A decision made in response to a situation that has occurred often enough to enable decision rules to be developed and applied in the future. **2:** Repetitive and well-defined procedures that exist for resolving problems. **3:** Making decisions based on precedent, custom, policies and procedures, and on training and development.

Programming The process of writing software.

Programming languages Sets of syntax for abbreviated forms of instructions that special programs can translate into machine language so a computer can understand the instructions.

Project 1 (*n*): An endeavor to accomplish a specific objective through a unique set of interrelated tasks and the effective utilization of resources. **2 (*v*):** The selection of certain columns from a table.

Project control Regularly gathering data on actual project performance, comparing actual performance to planned performance, and taking corrective measures if actual performance is behind planned performance.

Project life cycle 1: The four phases through which a project moves: identification of a need, problem, or opportunity; development of a proposed solution; implementation of the proposed solution; and termination of the project. **2:** Five sequential phases of project management: concept, planning, design, implementation, and evaluation.

Project Finance Loan Program Program that allows banks, Ex-Im Bank, or a combination of both to extend long-term financing for capital equipment and related services for major projects.

Project management The set of activities that is performed to ensure the timely and successful completion of a project within the budget. Project management includes planning activities, hiring and managing personnel, budgeting, conducting meetings, and tracking technical and financial performance. Project management software applications facilitate these activities.

Project manager A manager responsible for a temporary work project that involves the participation of other people from various functions and levels of the organization; a person responsible for coordinating the activities of several departments on a full-time basis for the completion of a specific project.

Project manufacturing A type of manufacturing process used for large, often unique, items or structures that require a custom design capability (engineer-to-order). This type of process is highly flexible and can cope with a broad range of product designs and design changes. Product manufacturing usually uses a fixed-position type layout. *See:* Batch (fourth definition), Continuous production, Process manufacturing, Project, Repetitive manufacturing.

Project organization structure An organization structure in which each project has its own project manager and project team and all the resources needed to accomplish an individual project are assigned full time to the project.

Project plan All the documents that comprise the details of why the project is to be initiated, what the project is to accomplish, when and where it is to be implemented, who will have responsibility, how the implementation will be carried out, how much it will cost, what resources are required, and how the project's progress and results will be measured.

Project required rate of return, k_{proj} The risk-adjusted required rate of return for an individual project.

Project scope All the work that must be done to accomplish the project's objective to the customer's satisfaction; scope of the project; work scope.

Project selection Evaluating various needs or opportunities and then deciding which of these should move forward as a project to be implemented.

Project strategy (protocol) Statement of the attributes the project is expected to have, the market at which it is targeted, and the purpose behind commercializing the product.

Projected (pro forma) balance sheet method A method of forecasting financial requirements based on forecasted financial statements.

Projection The tendency to see one's own personal traits in other people.

Promisee Person to whom a promise is made.

Promisor Person making a promise.

Promissory estoppel Doctrine enforcing noncontractual promises where there has been justifiable reliance on the promise and justice requires enforcement.

Promissory note A document specifying the terms and conditions of a loan, including the amount, interest rate, and repayment schedule.

Promoter Person who takes the preliminary steps to organize a corporation

Promoters' contracts Promoters remain liable on preincorporation contracts made in the name of the corporation unless the contract provides otherwise or unless a novation is effected.

Promoters' fiduciary duty Promoters owe a fiduciary duty among themselves and to the corporation, its subscribers, and its initial shareholders.

Promotion A means that retailers use to bring traffic into their stores, and it includes advertising, sales promotion, publicity, and personal selling.

Promotional advertising A type of advertising in which the retailer attempts to increase short-term performance by using product availability or price as a selling point.

Promotional discount A discount provided for the retailer performing an advertising or promotional service for the manufacturer.

Promotion strategy Problems related to international promotion strategy include the legal aspects of the country, tax considerations, language complexities, cultural diversity, media limitations, credibility of advertising, and degree of illiteracy.

Promotional message The content of an advertisement or a publicity release.

Property dividend A distribution in form of property.

Property rights The license to limit use by others.

Proposal A document, usually prepared by a contractor, that outlines an approach to meeting a need or solving a problem for a potential customer.

Proposal for appropriation of retained earnings A report prepared for approval at the stockholders' meeting for dividend payments and bonus payments to members of the board of directors and statutory auditors.

Proprietorship An unincorporated business owned by one individual.

Prospecting The process of locating or identifying potential customers that have the ability and willingness to purchase your product.

Prospectus A document describing a new security issue and the issuing company.

Protected class Individuals within a group identified for protection under equal employment laws and regulations.

Protection of intellectual property The owner of an intellectual property right must comply with each country's requirements to obtain from that country whatever protection is available.

Protectionistic legislation A trade policy that restricts trade to or from one country to another country.

Protocol A standard set of rules that governs telecommunication between two communications devices or in a network.

Prototype Product concept in physical form. A prototype may be a full working model that has been produced by hand or a nonworking physical representation of the final product. It is used to gather customer reaction to the physical form (aesthetics and ergonomics) or to initial operating capability. It is also used in internal performance tests to ensure that performance goals have been met.

Prototyping An approach to the development of information systems in which several analysis steps are skipped, to accelerate the development process. A "quick and dirty" model is developed and continually improved until the prospective users are satisfied.

Prox Payment due on a specific day in the following month.

Proxies Authorization to vote another's shares at a shareholder meeting.

Proxy A document giving one person the authority to act for another, typically the power to vote shares of common stock.

Proxy fight An attempt by a person or group of people to gain control of a firm by getting its stockholders to grant that person or group the authority to vote their shares in order to elect a new management team.

Proxy information Data used as a substitute for more desirable data that are unobtainable.

Proxy process The method by which shareholders elect boards of directors.

Proxy statements Proxy disclosure statements are required when proxies are solicited or an issuer submits a matter to a shareholder vote.

Prudence concept The concept that provision be made for all known liabilities and losses whether the amount is known with certainty or not.

Psychocultural contexts *See:* Cross-cultural communication.

Psychographic customer characteristics Variables among buyers in the consumer market that address lifestyle issues and include consumer interests, activities, and opinions.

Psychographics Characteristics of individuals that describe them in terms of their psychological and behavioral makeup.

Psychological contract The unwritten expectations employees and employers have about the nature of their work relationships.

Psychomotor tests Tests that measure dexterity, hand-eye coordination, arm-hand steadiness, and other factors.

Psychopath A person with a personality disorder, especially one manifested in aggressively antisocial behavior.

Public corporation A corporation created to administer a unit of local civil government or one created by the United States to conduct public business.

Public interest theory A view of regulation as a government-imposed means of private-market control.

Public issues committee (public policy committee) A firm's mechanism for responding to public or social issues.

Public nuisance Interference with health, safety, or comfort of the public.

Public Relations (PR)/Public affairs (PA) Principal distinctions are that, whereas PR deals with government as one of many publics, PA professionals are experts on government, and that whereas PR has many communication responsibilities, PA deals with issues management and serves as a corporate conscience.

Public warehouse A facility that stores goods for safekeeping for any owner in return for a fee, usually based on space occupied.

Publicity 1: Like advertising, is nonpersonal communication to a mass audience, but unlike advertising, publicity is not directly paid for by the company that enjoys the publicity. **2:** Is non-paid-for communications of information about the company or product, generally in some media form.

Publicly held (owned) corporation 1: Corporation whose shares are owned by a large number of people and are widely traded. **2:** A corporation that is owned by a relatively large number of individuals who are not actively involved in its management.

Public-key encryption Encryption technology in which a public key is used to encrypt and a private key is used to decrypt.

Pull manufacturing A just-in-time method wherein customer orders trigger the release of finished goods, which triggers production, which triggers release of materials from suppliers.

Pull strategy Heavy emphasis on consumer-oriented advertising to encourage consumer demand for a new brand and thereby obtain retail distribution. The brand is "pulled" through the channel system in the sense that there is a backward tug from the consumer to the retailer.

Pull system 1: In production, the production of items only as demanded for use or to replace those taken for use. *See:* Pull signal. **2:** In material control, the withdrawal of inventory as demanded by the using operations. Material is not issued until a signal comes from the user. **3:** In distribution, a system for replenishing field warehouse inventories where replenishment decisions are made at the field warehouse itself, not at the central warehouse or plant. *See:* Kanban

Punitive tariff A tax on an imported good or service intended to punish a trading partner.

Purchase Stage in the consumer decision process when transaction terms are arranged, title of ownership is transferred, the product is paid for, and the consumer takes possession of the product from the seller.

Purchase method An accounting method used for a business combination where the acquired entity's assets and equities are combined at fair market value. Goodwill is created to the extent that cost exceeds the fair market value of the identifiable assets of the unit acquired. The accounting method employed when a parent company acquires a controlling share of the voting stock of a subsidiary other than by the exchange of voting common stock.

Purchase of shares A transaction by which one corporation acquires all of, or a controlling interest in, the stock of another corporation; no change occurs in the legal existence of either corporation and no formal shareholder approval of either corporation is required.

Purchase or lease of all or substantially all of the assets Results in no change in the legal personality of either corporation.

Purchase order with payment voucher attached A draft coupled with a purchase order, which eliminates the need for a supplier to issue an invoice and for a customer to process the invoice and issue a check.

Purchase terms Terms of credit offered by suppliers.

Purchases discounts An available discount taken by a buyer for early payment of an invoice.

Purchases returns and allowances Reductions in purchases resulting from merchandise being returned to the seller or from the seller's reduction in the original purchase price.

Purchasing (or procurement) A functional activity carried out in just about every organization, most often referring to the day-to-day tactical management of material flows and information. It begins with the determination of needs and specifications for internal customers, matching market and commodity information to customer needs, developing a purchase order (a paper or electronic form that specifies that type and quantity of material or service required), tracking and follow-up on the order, and issuing a payment to the supplier.

Purchasing cards Credit cards used by businesses to make small dollar purchases of maintenance, repair, and operating supplies. Use of purchasing, or procurement, cards greatly reduces the number of purchase orders and invoices processed and payments made.

Purchasing power gain A gain that arises from holding monetary items during times when the general purchasing power of the monetary unit changes.

GLOSSARY

Purchasing power loss A loss that arises from holding monetary items during times when the general purchasing power of the monetary unit changes.

Purchasing Power Parity (PPP) line Diagonal line on a graph that reflects points at which the inflation differential between two countries is equal to the percentage change in the exchange rate between the two respective currencies.

Purchasing Power Parity (PPP) theory Theory suggesting that exchange rates will adjust over time to reflect the differential in inflation rates in the two countries; in this way, the purchasing power of consumers when purchasing domestic goods will be the same as that when they purchase foreign goods.

Purchasing power risk The possibility that an investment's proceeds will not be worth as much as anticipated due to general price level increases in the economy. Anticipated inflation is built into the risk-free interest rate, but investors are still vulnerable to losses in purchasing power from unanticipated inflation and will require a higher yield when price levels are volatile.

Pure competition Occurs when a market has homogeneous products and many buyers and sellers, all having perfect knowledge of the market, and ease of entry for both buyers and sellers. It is rare in retailing.

Pure monopoly Occurs when there is only one seller for a product or service. It is very rare in retailing.

Pure play method An approach used for estimating the beta of a project in which a firm identifies companies whose only business is the product in question, determines the beta for each firm, and then averages the betas to find an approximation of its own project's beta.

Pure risk Uncertainty as to whether a loss will occur.

Push manufacturing Materials are released into production and work in process is released into finished goods in anticipation of future sales.

Push strategy Aggressive trade allowances and personal selling efforts to obtain distribution for a new brand through wholesalers and retailers. The brand is "pushed" through the channel system in the sense that there is a forward thrust from the manufacturer to the trade.

Push system 1: In production, the production of items at times required by a given schedule planned in advance. **2:** In material control, the issuing of material according to a given schedule or issuing material to a job order at its start time. **3:** In distribution, a system for replenishing field warehouse inventories where replenishment decision making is centralized, usually at the manufacturing site or central supply facility.

Put *See:* Currency put option.

Putable bond A bond that can be redeemed at the bondholder's option.

Put option A contract that allows the owners to sell the underlying asset at a specific price over a specific span of time. The option to sell a specified number of shares of stock at a prespecified price during a particular period.

Put option on real assets Project that contains an option of divesting part or all of the project.

PVA$_n$ The present value of an ordinary annuity with n payments.

PVIFA(DUE)$_{i,n}$ The present value interest factor for an annuity due—PVIFA(DUE)$_{i,n}$ = PVIFA$_{i,n}$ × (1 + i).

Pyramid forecasting A forecasting technique that enables management to review and adjust forecasts made at an aggregate level and to keep lower level forecasts in balance. The procedure begins with the roll up (aggregation) of item forecasts into forecasts by product group. The management team establishes a (new) forecast for the product group. The value is then forced down (disaggregation) to individual item forecasts so that they are consistent with the aggregate plan. The approach combines the stability of aggregate forecasts and the application of management judgment with the need to forecast many end items within the constraints of an aggregate forecast or sales plan.

Pyramid model A management structure in which the CEO is at the top, a small group of senior managers are one level down, a larger number of middle managers are the next level down, and so forth.

Q

Qualified sales leads Potential customers who have a need for the salesperson's product, and are able to buy; that is, they have the financial means to purchase the product and the authority to make the buying decision.

Qualitative analysis An intuitive judgmental approach to forecasting based on opinion.

Qualitative information Data that have been analyzed to provide a better understanding, description, or prediction of given situations, behavioral patterns, or underlying dimensions.

Quality 1: Refers to products/services that meet or exceed consumers' expectations at the lowest cost possible. **2:** Subjective term for which each person has his or her own definition. In technical usage, quality can have two meanings: 1) the characteristics of a product or service that bear on its ability to satisfy stated or implied needs and 2) a product or service free of deficiencies.

Quality adviser Person (facilitator) who helps team members work together in quality processes and is a consultant to the team. The adviser is concerned about the process and how decisions are made rather than about which decisions are made.

Quality assessment Process of identifying business practices, attitudes, and activities that are enhancing or inhibiting the achievement of quality improvement in an organization.

Quality Assurance/Quality Control (QA/QC) Two terms that have many interpretations because of the multiple definitions for the words *assurance* and *control*. For example, *assurance* can mean the act of giving confidence, the state of being certain, or the act of making certain; *control* can mean an evaluation to indicate needed corrective responses, the act of guiding, or the state of a process in which the variability is attributable to a constant system of chance causes. One definition of quality assurance is: all the planned and systematic activities implemented within the quality system that can be demonstrated to provide confidence that a product or service will fulfill requirements for quality. One definition for quality control is: the operational techniques and activities used to fulfill requirements for quality. Often, however, *quality assurance* and *quality control* are used interchangeably, referring to the actions performed to ensure the quality of a product, service, or process.

Quality audit Systematic, independent examination and review to determine whether quality activities and related results comply with planned arrangements and whether these arrangements are implemented effectively and are suitable to achieve the objectives.

Quality characteristics Unique characteristics of products and of services by which customers evaluate their perception of quality.

Quality circle 1: Small group of employees who monitor productivity and quality and suggest solutions to problems. **2:** Groups of 6 to 12 volunteer workers who meet to analyze and solve problems.

Quality cost reports System of collecting quality costs that uses a spreadsheet to list the elements of quality costs against a spread of the departments, areas, or projects in which the costs occur and summarizes the data to enable trend analysis and decision making. The reports help organizations review prevention costs, appraisal costs, and internal and external failure costs.

Quality costs *See:* Cost of quality. Same as poor quality cost.

Quality council (sometimes called "quality steering committee") Group driving the quality improvement effort and usually having oversight responsibility for the implementation and maintenance of the quality management system; operates in parallel with the normal operation of the business.

Quality culture Employee opinions, beliefs, traditions, and practices concerning quality.

Quality engineering Analysis of a manufacturing system at all stages to maximize the quality of the process itself and the products it produces.

Quality function Entire collection of activities through which an organization achieves fitness for use, no matter where these activities are performed.

Quality Function Deployment (QFD) Structured method in which customer requirements are translated into appropriate technical requirements for each stage of product development and production. The QFD process is often referred to as listening to the voice of the customer. *See:* House of quality.

Quality improvement Actions taken throughout the organization to increase the effectiveness and efficiency of activities and processes in order to provide added benefits to both the organization and its customers.

Quality Level Agreement (QLA) Internal service/product providers assist their internal customers in clearly delineating the level of service/product required in quantitatively measurable terms. A QLA may contain specifications for accuracy, timeliness, quality/usability, product life, service availability, responsiveness to needs, and so on.

Quality loop Conceptual model of interacting activities that influence quality at the various stages ranging from the identification of needs to the assessment of whether those needs are satisfied.

Quality loss function Parabolic approximation of the quality loss that occurs when a quality characteristic deviates from its target value. The quality loss function is expressed in monetary units: The cost of deviating from the target increases as a quadratic function the farther the quality characteristic moves from the target. The formula used to compute the quality loss function depends on the type of quality characteristic being used. The quality loss function was first introduced in this form by Genichi Taguchi.

Quality management All activities of the overall management function that determine the quality policy, objectives, and responsibilities, and implement them by means such as quality planning, quality control, quality assurance, and quality improvement within the quality system.

Quality manual Document stating the quality policy and describing the quality system of an organization.

Quality metrics Numerical measurements that give an organization the ability to set goals and evaluate actual performance versus plan.

Quality of life The standard of living combined with environmental factors, it determines the level of well-being of individuals.

Quality of work life Various corporate efforts in the areas of personal and professional development undertaken with the objectives of increasing employee satisfaction and increasing productivity.

Quality plan Document setting out the specific quality practices, resources, and sequence of activities relevant to a particular product, project, or contract.

Quality planning Activity of establishing quality objectives and quality requirements.

Quality policy Top management's formally stated intentions and direction for the organization pertaining to quality.

Quality principles Rules or concepts that an organization believes in collectively. The principles are formulated by senior management with input from others and are communicated and understood at every level of the organization.

Quality score chart (Q chart) Control chart for evaluating the stability of a process in terms of a quality score. The quality score is the weighted sum of the count of events of various classifications in which each classification is assigned a weight.

Quality system Organizational structure, procedures, processes, and resources needed to implement quality management.

Quality system audit Documented activity performed to verify, by examination and evaluation of objective evidence, that applicable elements of the quality system are suitable and have been developed, documented, and effectively implemented in accordance with specified requirements.

Quality trilogy Three-pronged approach to managing for quality. The three legs are quality planning (developing the products and processes required to meet customer needs), quality control (meeting product and process goals), and quality improvement (achieving unprecedented levels of performance). Attributed to Joseph M. Juran.

Quantitative approach Any forecasting technique which involves the use of a numerical model to forecast; the technique is usually implemented on a computer.

Quantity discounts 1: A reduction in the cost per order based on the quantity ordered. **2:** A price reduction offered as an inducement to purchase large quantities of merchandise.

Quantity factor The effect of a difference in the number of units sold, assuming no change in unit sales price or unit cost.

Quasi contract Obligation *not* based upon contract that is imposed to avoid injustice.

Query An instruction to a database management system to retrieve records that meet certain conditions.

Questionnaires *See:* Surveys.

Queue processing Processing in batches (contrast with continuous flow processing).

Queue time Wait time of product awaiting next step in process.

Quick (acid-test) ratio This ratio is calculated by deducting inventories from current assets and dividing the remainder by current liabilities. The quick ratio is a variation of the current ratio.

Quick assets The sum of cash, receivables, and marketable securities.

Quick ratio A financial ratio that measures the ability to pay current liabilities within a short period of time.

GLOSSARY

Quick Response (QR) systems Systems that are also known as efficient consumer response (ECR) systems, are integrated information, production, and logistical systems that obtain real-time information on consumer actions by capturing sales data at point-of-purchase terminals and then transmitting this information back through the entire channel to enable efficient production and distribution scheduling.

Quid pro quo Sexual harassment in which employment outcomes are linked to the individual's granting sexual favors.

Quincunx Tool that creates frequency distributions. Beads tumble over numerous horizontal rows of pins, which force the beads to the right or left. After a random journey, the beads are dropped into vertical slots. After many beads are dropped, a frequency distribution results. In the classroom, quincunxes are often used to simulate a manufacturing process. The quincunx was invented by English scientist Francis Galton in the 1890s.

Quorum Minimum number necessary to be present at a meeting to transact business.

Quotas Legal restrictions on the import quantity of particular goods, imposed by governments as barriers to trade.

R

Radar chart Visual method to show in graphic form the size of gaps among a number of both current organization performance areas and ideal performance areas; resulting chart resembles a radar screen.

RAID (Redundant Array of Independent Disks) A set of magnetic disk packs maintained for backup purposes. Sometimes RAIDs are used for storing large databases.

Random Access Memory (RAM) The major part of a computer's internal memory. RAM is volatile; that is, software is held in it temporarily and disappears when the machine is unplugged or turned off, or it may disappear when operations are interrupted or new software is installed or activated. RAM is made of microchips containing transistors. Many computers have free sockets that allow the expansion of RAM.

Random number generator Used to select a stated quantity of random numbers from a table of random numbers, the resulting selection is then used to pull specific items or records corresponding to the selected numbers to comprise a "random sample."

Random sample Set of items that have been drawn from a population in such a way that each time an item was selected, every item in the population had an equal opportunity to appear in the sample.

Random sampling Sampling method in which every element in the population has an equal chance of being included.

Range chart (R chart) Control chart in which the subgroup range, R, is used to evaluate the stability of the variability within a process.

Range Measure of dispersion; highest value minus lowest value.

Range reconciliation Provides subtotals of all checks within a range of check serial numbers. This is especially useful for identifying disbursements from the same account but from several locations.

Ranking Listing of all employees from highest to lowest in performance.

Rapid Application Development (RAD) Methods using I-CASE tools and 4GLs to quickly prototype an information system. Often, software is reused in RAD.

Rapid prototyping Using software and special output devices to create prototypes to test design in three dimensions.

Rate earned on common stockholders' equity A measure of profitability computed by dividing net income, reduced by preferred dividend requirements, by common stockholders' equity.

Rate earned on stockholders' equity A measure of profitability computed by dividing net income by total stockholders' equity.

Rate earned on total assets A measure of the profitability of assets, computed as net income plus interest expense divided by total average assets.

Rate of Return on Investment (ROI) A measure of managerial efficiency in the use of investments in assets, computed as income from operations divided by invested assets.

Rate-based scheduling A method for scheduling and producing based on a periodic rate, for example, daily, weekly, or monthly. This method has traditionally been applied to high-volume and process industries. The concept has recently been applied within job shops using cellular layouts and mixed-model level schedules where the production rate is matched to the selling rate.

Rated capacity The expected output capability of a resource or system. Capacity is traditionally calculated from such data as planned hours, efficiency, and utilization. The rated capacity is equal to hours available × efficiency × utilization. *Syn:* calculated capacity, effective capacity, nominal capacity, standing capacity.

Rater bias Error that occurs when a rater's values or prejudices distort the rating.

Ratification A corporation may ratify the unauthorized acts of its officers.

Ratio analysis Process of relating isolated business numbers, such as sales, margins, expenses, debt, and profits, to make them meaningful.

Ratio of fixed assets to long-term liabilities A financial ratio that provides a measure indicating the margin of safety to creditors.

Ratio of liabilities to stockholders' equity The relationship between the total claims of the creditors and owners.

Ratio of net sales to assets A profitability measure that shows how effectively a firm utilizes its assets.

Ratio scale Scale that measures length, weight, or income.

Rational approach A process of decision making that stresses the need for systematic analysis of a problem followed by choice and implementation in a logical sequence.

Rational model A description of an organization characterized by a rational approach to decision making, extensive and reliable information systems, central power, a norm of optimization, uniform values across groups, little conflict, and an efficiency orientation.

Rational-legal authority Authority based on employees' belief in the legality of rules and the right of those in authority to issue commands.

Rational subgroup Subgroup which is expected to be as free as possible from assignable causes (usually consecutive items).

Rationalization Self-satisfying but incorrect reasons for one's behavior.

Raw and in process inventory The capitalized cost of direct materials purchases, labor, and overhead charged to the production cell.

Raw material scarcity Occurs when valuable raw material resources are geographically concentrated in some locations and not in others, resulting in resource scarcity in some locations.

Raw materials inventory Inventory consisting of the basic inputs to the organization's production process.

RCRA The Resource Conservation and Recovery Act provides a comprehensive scheme for treatment of solid waste, particularly hazardous waste.

Reach The actual total number of target customers who come into contact with an advertising message.

Reach percentage The percentage of Web users who have visited a site in the past month, or the ratio of visitors to the total Web population.

Reactive MPR Form of defensively oriented public relations that deals with developments (such as product defects or flaws) having negative consequences for the organization. Reactive MPR attempts to repair a company's reputation, prevent market erosion, and regain lost sales.

Read-Only Memory (ROM) The minor part of a computer's internal memory. ROM is loaded by the manufacturer with software that cannot be changed. Usually, ROM holds very basic system software, but sometimes also applications. Like RAM, ROM consists of microchips containing transistors.

Real accounts Balance sheet accounts.

Real cost of hedging The additional cost of hedging when compared to not hedging (a negative real cost would imply that hedging was more favorable than not hedging).

Real interest rate Nominal (or quoted) interest rate minus the inflation rate.

Real options Implicit options on real assets.

Real risk-free rate of interest, k^* The rate of interest that would exist on default-free U.S. Treasury securities if no inflation were expected.

Real property Land and anything attached to it.

Realistic Job Preview (RJP) A recruiting approach that gives applicants all pertinent and realistic information about the job and the organization.

Realized gains Gains that are actually incurred.

Realized losses Losses that are actually incurred.

Realized rate of return, $\bar{k}$ The return that is actually earned. The actual return $(\bar{k})$ is usually different from the expected return $(\hat{k})$.

Reasonable accommodation A modification or adjustment to a job or work environment for a qualified individual with a disability.

Reasonable assurance The concept that internal control, no matter how well designed and operated, cannot guarantee that an entity's objectives will be met. This is because of inherent limitations in all internal control systems.

Reasons organizations grow Growth occurs because it is an organizational goal; it is necessary to attract and keep quality managers; or it is necessary to maintain economic health.

Receipt of Goods (ROG) dating Situation that allows the retailer to take a cash discount and the full payment period to begin when the goods are received by the retailer.

Receipts and disbursements method A commonly used cash forecasting approach which involves determining upcoming sources of cash inflows and outflows, then laying these out on a schedule to see the aggregate effect.

Receivables All money claims against other entities, including people, business firms, and other organizations.

Receivables control Procedures and methods for following up credit extensions, including monitoring and corrective actions.

Receivables monitoring The process of evaluating the credit policy to determine if a shift in the customers' payment patterns occurs.

Receiving Depository Financial Institution (RDFI) ACH payee's bank in an ACH credit transaction.

Receiving report The form or electronic transmission used by the receiving personnel to indicate that materials have been received and inspected.

Recency effect Error in which the rater gives greater weight to recent events when appraising an individual's performance.

Reciprocal interdependence The highest level of interdependence, in which the output of one operation is the input of a second, and the output of the second operation is the input of the first (for example, a hospital).

Record 1: A set of standard field types. All the fields of a record contain data about a certain entity or event. **2:** Document or electronic medium which furnishes objective evidence of activities performed or results achieved.

Recourse The lender can seek payment from the borrowing firm when receivables' accounts used to secure a loan are uncollectible. When a factor buys receivables with recourse, the selling firm is ultimately responsible for payment if the customer defaults.

Recruiting 1: The activities or practices that define the desired characteristics of applicants for specific jobs. **2:** The process of generating a pool of qualified applicants for organizational jobs.

Recursive Least Squares (RLS) In the context of receivables monitoring, a regression model which allows the estimated receivables collection fractions (the regression coefficients) to change over time.

Recycled merchandise retailers Establishments that sell used and reconditioned products.

Red bead experiment Experiment developed by W. Edwards Deming to illustrate that it is impossible to put employees in rank order of performance for the coming year based on their performance during the past year because performance differences must be attributed to the system, not to employees. Four thousand red and white beads, 20 percent red, in a jar and six people are needed for the experiment. The participants' goal is to produce white beads because the customer will not accept red beads. One person begins by stirring the beads and then, blindfolded, selects a sample of 50 beads. That person hands the jar to the next person, who repeats the process, and so on. When everyone has his or her sample, the number of red beads for each is counted. The limits of variation between employees that can be attributed to the system are calculated. Everyone will fall within the calculated limits of variation that could arise from the system. The calculations will show that there is no evidence one person will be a better performer than another in the future. The experiment shows that it would be a waste of management's time to try to find out why, say, John produced four red beads and Jane produced 15; instead, management should improve the system, making it possible for everyone to produce more white beads.

Red-circled employee An incumbent who is paid above the range set for the job.

Red herring A preliminary prospectus distributed to potential investors in a new issue of financial securities.

GLOSSARY

Red-lining Practice of identifying and avoiding unprofitable types of neighborhoods or people.

Redemption of shares A corporation's exercise of the right to repurchase its own shares.

Redundant Array of Independent/Inexpensive Disks (RAID) A method of storing data that allows the system to create a "reconstruction map" so that if a hard drive fails, it can rebuild lost data.

Reengineering (also: business process engineering) 1: Completely redesigning or restructuring a whole organization, an organizational component, or a complete process. It's a "start all over again from the beginning" approach, sometimes called a "breakthrough." In terms of improvement approaches, reengineering is contrasted with incremental improvement (*kaizen*). **2:** A cross-functional initiative involving the radical redesign of business processes to bring about simultaneous changes in organization structure, culture, and information technology and produce dramatic performance improvements.

Reference groups Groups such as the family, coworkers, and professional and trade associations that provide the values and attitudes that influence and shape behavior, including consumer behavior.

Referent power 1: Power that results from characteristics that command subordinates' identification with, respect and admiration for, and desire to emulate the leader. **2:** Power based on the identification of B with A.

Referrals Usually obtained by the salesperson asking current customers if they know of someone else, or another company, who might need the salesperson's product.

Refreezing The reinforcement stage of organizational development in which individuals acquire a desired new skill or attitude and are rewarded for it by the organization.

Refunding Retiring an existing bond issue with the proceeds of a newly issued bond.

Regiocentric staffing outlook The belief that key positions at the regional headquarters should be staffed by individuals from one of the region's countries.

Regional audit staff internal audit model In this type of organization, the regional staff is responsible for performing audits in all of the operations in the region. This model has recently been gaining popularity among many multinationals.

Regional Check Processing Centers (RCPCs) 11 Fed offices set up to help clear checks. Together the 12 district banks plus the 25 regional branches and eleven RCPCs gives the Fed a network of 48 offices to clear checks.

Regional structure An international corporate structure wherein regional heads are made responsible for specific territories, usually consisting of multiple countries, such as Europe, East Asia, and South America.

Regional trade communities International organizations, conferences, and treaties focusing on business and trade regulations; the EU (European Union) is the most prominent of these.

Register A fast memory location in the CPU, made of special semiconductors and circuitry.

Register disbursement scheme Scheme that involves false refunds or false voids.

Registrar Bank which keeps records of the number of shares of stock authorized, issued, and redeemed, and ensures that the number of share issued does not exceed those authorized.

Registration of securities Disclosure of accurate material information required in all public offerings of nonexempt securities unless offering is an exempt transaction.

Registration statement A statement of facts filed with the SEC about a company that plans to issue securities.

Registration to standards Process in which an accredited, independent third-party organization conducts an on-site audit of a company's operations against the requirements of the standard to which the company wants to be registered. Upon successful completion of the audit, the company receives a certificate indicating that it has met the standard requirements.

Regression analysis Study used to understand the relationship between two or more variables. Regression analysis makes it possible to predict one variable from knowledge about another. The relationship can be determined and expressed as a mathematical equation.

Regression coefficient Term measured by regression analysis to estimate the sensitivity of the dependent variable to a particular independent variable.

Regular course of business Approval by the selling corporation's board of directors is required, but shareholder authorization is not.

Regular reports Reports that assist managers in planning activities and controlling operations.

Regulation Government order having the force of law.

Regulation CC Effective September 1990, this ruling stipulates that from the day of deposit local checks must be given availability within two business days, and nonlocal checks within five days.

Regulation Q A Federal Reserve regulation that restricts banks from paying interest on demand deposit accounts.

Regulation of business Governmental regulation that's necessary because all the conditions for perfect competition have not been satisfied and free competition cannot by itself achieve other social goals.

Regulatory lag The delay between when a change in regulation is appropriate and the date it becomes effective.

Regulatory reform Improvement in government control to enhance efficiency and fairness.

Reilly's law of retail gravitation Based on Newtonian gravitational principles, this rule explains how large urbanized areas attract customers from smaller rural communities.

Reinforcement Process of providing positive consequences when an individual is applying the correct knowledge and skills to the job. It has been described as "catching people doing things right and recognizing their behavior." Caution: less-than-desired behavior can also be reinforced unintentionally.

Reinforcement theory A motivation theory based on the relationship between a given behavior and its consequences.

Reinvestment rate assumption The assumption that cash flows from a project can be reinvested 1) at the cost of capital, if using the NPV method, or 2) at the internal rate of return, if using the IRR method.

Reinvestment rate risk The possibility that the investor will have to invest cash proceeds at a lower interest rate for the remainder of a predetermined investment horizon.

Reinvoicing The policy of buying goods from one unit and selling them to a second unit and reinvoicing the sale to the next unit, to take advantage of favorable exchange rates.

Reinvoicing center Facility that centralizes payments and charges subsidiaries fees for its function; this can effectively shift profits to subsidiaries where tax rates are low.

Relational database A database in which the records are organized in individual tables (called "relations"). In order for data from different tables to be related, tables must contain foreign keys, which are primary keys in other tables in the database. The ease of building and maintaining a relational database has made it more popular than the hierarchical and network models.

Relational operation An operation that creates a temporary table that is a subset of the original table or tables in a relational database.

Relationship approach One view of the corporation's link to its banks, in which the corporation chooses its bank services primarily based on preexisting business dealings. Loyalty to prior arrangements is considered to be more important than price when selecting banks for cash management or lending services. Usually implies that credit and cash management services will both be handled by the same bank or network of banks.

Relationship retailing System that comprises all the activities designed to attract, retain, and enhance long-term relationships with customers.

Relationship selling Requires the development of a trusting partnership in which the salesperson seeks to provide long-term customer satisfaction by listening, gathering information, educating, and adding value for the customer.

Relative form of purchasing power parity Theory stating that the rate of change in the prices of products should be somewhat similar when measured in a common currency, as long as transportation costs and trade barriers are unchanged.

Relaxed current asset investment policy A policy under which relatively large amounts of cash and marketable securities and inventories are carried and under which sales are stimulated by a liberal credit policy that results in a high level of receivables.

Relevant cash flows The specific cash flows that should be considered in a capital budgeting decision.

Relevant range The range of activity over which changes in cost are of interest to management.

Relevant risk The risk of a security that cannot be diversified away, or its market risk. This reflects a security's contribution to the risk of a portfolio.

Reliability 1: Dependability; the predictability of the outcome of an action. For example, the reliability of arrival time for ocean freight or airfreight. **2:** In measurement system analysis, refers to the ability of an instrument to produce the same results over repeated administration—to measure consistently. In reliability engineering it is the probability of a product performing its intended function under stated conditions for a given period of time. *See:* Mean time between failures.

Religion Different societies develop different religious systems, which are major causes of cultural differences in many societies. Religious systems provide motivation and meaning beyond the material aspects of life.

Remanufacturing 1: An industrial process in which worn-out products are restored to like-new condition. In contrast, a repaired product normally retains its identity, and only those parts that have failed or are badly worn are replaced or serviced. **2:** The manufacturing environment where worn-out products are restored to like-new condition.

Remedy 1: Judgments asked for in civil cases (what it would take to right a private wrong). **2:** Something that eliminates or counteracts a problem cause; a solution.

Remedies Damages and injunctions are available if infringement of a trade name occurs. Remedies for infringement of a patent are 1) injunctive relief; 2) damages; 3) treble damages, when appropriate; 4) attorneys' fees; and 5) costs.

Remedies for *ultra vires* acts The RMBCA provides three possible remedies.

Remittance advice A document that usually accompanies payment, indicating customer, account number, date, and invoice(s) being paid.

Removal of directors The shareholders may by majority vote remove directors with or without cause, subject to cumulative voting rights.

Rental A type of lease in which the lessor retains not only legal title, but most of the risks and rewards of ownership.

Reorder point The inventory level at which an order should be placed.

Repair Action taken on a nonconforming product so that it will fulfill the intended usage requirements although it may not conform to the originally specified requirements.

Repatriation Planning, training, and reassignment of global employees to their home countries.

Repatriation of earnings The process of sending cash flows from a foreign subsidiary back to the parent company.

Repatriation program Programs that assist the returning expatriate in readjusting to the home country's environment. Attempts to alleviate the effects of reverse culture shock.

Repeat game A comprehensive statistical profile of the economy, from the national, to the state, to the local level. Ongoing interaction.

Repeatability and Reproducibility (R&R) Measurement validation process to determine how much variation exists in the measurement system (including the variation in product, the gage used to measure, and the individuals using the gage).

Repeater A device that strengthens signals and then sends them on their next leg toward their next destination.

Repetitive manufacturing The repeated production of the same discrete products or families of products. Repetitive methodology minimizes setups, inventory, and manufacturing lead times by using production lines, assembly lines, or cells. Work orders are no longer necessary; production scheduling and control are based on production rates. Products may be standard or assembled from modules. Repetitive is not a function of speed or volume. *Syn:* repetitive process, repetitive production.

Replacement chain (common life) approach A method of comparing projects of unequal lives that assumes each project can be replicated as many times as necessary to reach a common life span; the NPVs over this life span are then compared, and the project with the higher common life NPV is chosen.

Replacement cost The total cost to acquire another item that would perform the functions identical to those performed by an existing item.

Replacement decisions Whether to purchase capital assets to take the place of existing assets to maintain or improve existing operations.

Replication A process in which a full copy of an entire database is stored at all the sites that need access to it.

Report form The form of balance sheet with the liabilities and owner's equity sections presented below the assets section.

Reportable condition An internal control deficiency related to financial reporting; it is a significant deficiency in the design or operation of the internal control system that could adversely affect the entity's ability to record, process, summarize, and report financial data consistent with the assertions of management in the financial statements.

Reporting period The time interval at which actual project performance will be compared to planned performance.

Representative firms Locally owned accounting firms that have agreements with a Big Five or some other accounting firm. The agreement covers areas such as standards of performance and standards of conduct.

Representative office An office of an international bank established in a foreign country to serve the bank's customers in the area in an advisory capacity; does not take deposits or make loans.

Repurchase Agreement (RP) 1: The sale of a portfolio of securities with a prearranged buyback one or several days later. A repurchase agreement, or "repo" as it is often called, involves the bank "selling" the investor a portfolio of securities, then agreeing to buy the securities back (repurchase) at an agreed-upon future date. **2:** Agreement to buy back something previously sold.

Request for admission Request that the opposing party admit designated facts relevant to litigation.

Request for Information (RFI) A request to vendors for general, somewhat informal, information about their products.

Request for Proposal (RFP) A document specifying all the system requirements and soliciting a proposal from vendors who might want to bid on a project or service.

Required completion time The time or date by which a project must be completed.

Required rate of return, k_s The minimum rate of return on a stock that stockholders consider acceptable.

Required rate of return, or hurdle rate The discount rate (cost of funds) that the IRR must exceed for a project to be considered acceptable.

Requirements explosion The process of calculating the demand for the components of a parent item by multiplying the parent item requirements by the component usage quantity specified in the bill of material. *Syn:* explosion.

Requisites of Rule 10b–5 Recovery requires 1) a misstatement or omission, 2) materiality, 3) scienter (intentional and knowing conduct), 4) reliance, and 5) connection with the purchase or sale of a security.

Research and development costs The direct and indirect outlays for exploring potential new products and developing new products.

Research collaboration Two or more companies that participate in a defined research program and benefit from the results. Research costs can be funded entirely by one of the parties, shared equally by the parties, or shared according to some other agreed-upon proportion.

Reserve borrowing capacity The ability to borrow money at a reasonable cost when good investment opportunities arise; firms often use less debt than specified by the MM optimal capital structure to ensure that they can obtain debt capital later if they need to.

Resident staff and central reviewers internal audit model In this type of organization, the resident internal auditors located on site perform the audit work. Their work is periodically reviewed by the traveling members of the parent company's central internal audit staff.

Resident staff and regional and central reviewers internal auditing model In this type of organization, the resident staff conducts the internal audits. Regional reviewers, responsible for certain geographical areas, oversee their work to ensure compliance with the parent company policies. The central staff from headquarters makes periodic reviews to ensure reporting uniformity throughout all the regions.

Resident staff and regional reviewers internal audit model In this type of organization, the work of the resident internal auditors is reviewed by the regional reviewers to ensure uniformity. Independent review from regional staff also enhances the degree of reliability of the reports.

Residual dividend policy A policy in which the dividend paid is set equal to the actual earnings minus the amount of retained earnings necessary to finance the firm's optimal capital budget.

Residual Income (RI) RI expresses performance in the form of a profit amount that is left after the cost of invested capital has been subtracted. The excess of income from operations over a "minimum" amount of desired income from operations.

Residual value 1: The estimated recoverable cost of a depreciable asset as of the time of its removal from service. **2:** The value of leased property at the end of the lease term.

Resiliency Condition of a market in which new orders enter when a temporary imbalance of buy or sell orders push the price away from its equilibrium level.

Resistance to change Unwillingness to change beliefs, habits, and ways of doing things.

Resolution The degree to which the image on a computer monitor is sharp. Higher resolution means a sharper image. Resolution depends on the number of pixels on the screen and the dot pitch.

Resource-based approach An organizational perspective that assesses effectiveness by observing how successfully the organization obtains, integrates, and manages valued resources.

Resource dependence A situation in which organizations depend on the environment but strive to acquire control over resources to minimize their dependence.

Resource leveling A method for developing a schedule that attempts to minimize the fluctuations in requirements for resources without extending the project schedule beyond the required completion time; resource smoothing. *Syn:* leveling.

Resource-limited scheduling The scheduling of activities so that predetermined resource availability pools are not exceeded. Activities are started as soon as resources are available (with respect to logical constraints), as required by the activity. When not enough of a resource exists to do all tasks on a given day, a priority decision is made. Project finish may be delayed, if necessary, to alter schedules constrained by resource usage.

Resource requirements matrix Tool to relate the resources required to the project tasks requiring them (used to indicate types of individuals needed, material needed, subcontractors, and so on).

Respect-oriented leadership Prevalent in China, Japan, Korea, Singapore, and Turkey; characterized by avoiding confrontation, displaying patience, listening to others, and avoiding losing face.

Responsibility Obligation to perform certain tasks and duties.

Responsibility accounting The process of measuring and reporting operating data by areas of responsibility.

Responsibility center An organizational unit for which a manager is assigned responsibility for the unit's performance.

Responsibility matrix A table that lists the individuals or organizational units responsible for accomplishing each work item in a work breakdown structure.

Restraint of trade Section 1 prohibits contracts, combinations, and conspiracies that restrain trade.

Restricted current asset investment policy A policy under which holdings of cash and marketable securities, inventories, and receivables are minimized.

Restricted securities Securities issued under an exempt transaction and subject to resale restrictions.

Restrictive covenant A provision in a debt contract that constrains the actions of the borrower.

Restructuring Reevaluation of a company's assets because of impairment of value or for other reasons. Restructured companies usually have lower amounts of assets and look quite different than before the restructuring.

Retail accordion Term that describes how retail institutions evolve from outlets that offer wide assortments to specialized stores and continue repeatedly through the pattern.

Retail gravity theory Theory that suggest that there are underlying consistencies in shopping behavior that yield to mathematical analysis and prediction based on the notion or concept of gravity.

Retail inventories Inventories that comprise merchandise that the retailer has in the store or in storage and is available for sale.

Retail inventory method A means of estimating inventory based on the relationship of the cost and the retail price of merchandise.

Retail life cycle 1: Description of competitive development in retailing that assumes that retail institutions pass through an identifiable cycle that includes four distinct stages: 1) introduction, 2) growth, 3) maturity, and 4) decline. **2:** Term that describes four distinct stages that a retail institution progresses through: introduction, growth, maturity, and decline.

Retail lockbox system 1: A lockbox system structured to handle a large volume of standardized invoice materials where the remittance checks have a relatively low average dollar face value. **2:** A system set up for a business receiving a large volume of relatively small dollar checks. Processing costs must be considered here along with collection float, and optically scannable invoices are read by machine to minimize human processing.

Retail market An exchange situation where the buyers and/or sellers are primarily small entities, especially individuals.

Retail method An inventory valuation technique that values merchandise at current retail prices, which is then converted to cost based on a formula.

Retail mix Retailer's combination of merchandise, prices, advertising, location, customer services, selling, and store layout and design that is used to attract customers.

Retail store saturation A condition where there are just enough store facilities for a given type of store to efficiently and satisfactorily serve the population and yield a fair profit to the owners.

Retailer-owned cooperatives Wholesale institutions, organized and owned by member retailers, that offer scale economies and services to member retailers, which allows them to compete with larger chain buying organizations.

Retailing The final activity and steps needed to place merchandise made elsewhere into the hands of the consumer or to provide services to the consumer.

Retained earnings Net income retained in a corporation.

Retained earnings statement A summary of the changes in the earnings retained in the corporation for a specific period of time.

Retained earnings The balance sheet account that indicates the total amount of earnings the firm has not paid out as dividends throughout its history; these earnings have been reinvested in the firm.

Retaliation Punitive actions taken by employers against individuals who exercise their legal rights.

Return items Checks that bounce, leading to their return to the bank of first deposit through each bank involved in the forward presentment.

Return of advances If a partner makes an advance (loan) to the firm, he is entitled to repayment of the advance plus interest; but his repayment is subordinate to that of non-partner creditors.

Return of capital After all partnership creditors have been paid, each partner is entitled to be repaid his capital contribution when the firm is terminated.

Return on Assets (ROA) ROA equals net income divided by total assets.

Return on Common Equity (ROCE) The ratio of net income to common equity; it measures the rate of return on common stockholders' investment.

Return on Equity (ROE) Net profit after taxes, divided by last year's tangible stockholders' equity, and then multiplied by 100 to provide a percentage (also referred to as return on net worth).

Return on Investment (ROI) 1: Calculation showing the value of expenditures for HR activities. **2:** ROI incorporates the investment base and profits to assess performance. **3:** Umbrella term for a variety of ratios measuring an organization's business performance and calculated by dividing some measure of return by a measure of investment and then multiplying by 100 to provide a percentage. In its most basic form, ROI indicates what remains from all money taken in after all expenses are paid.

Return on Net Assets (RONA) Measurement of the earning power of the firm's investment in assets, calculated by dividing net profit after taxes by last year's tangible total assets and then multiplying by 100 to provide a percentage.

Return on Net Worth (RONW) Net profit (after taxes) divided by owners' equity.

Return on quality Measurement of the expected revenue against the expected costs associated with quality efforts.

Return on Stockholders' Equity (ROE) Business profits expressed as a percentage of owner-supplied capital.

Return on total assets The ratio of net income to total assets; it provides an idea of the overall return on investment earned by the firm.

Returns and allowances Refunds of the purchase price or downward adjustments in selling prices due to customers returning purchases, or adjustments made in the selling price due to customer dissatisfaction with product or service performance.

Revaluation reserve An equity reserve used to value fixed assets at an appraised value or a replacement value. This is done by upward adjustment of the asset and correspondingly recording an equal amount in a revaluation reserve.

Revenue 1: Increases in a company's resources from the sale of goods or services. **2:** The gross increase in owner's equity as a result of business and professional activities that earn income.

Revenue anticipation notes Short-term debt instruments that provide working capital financing for states and localities as they await anticipated revenues from other sources of revenue.

Revenue budget A budget that identifies the forecasted and actual revenues of the organization.

Revenue center A responsibility center in which a manager is accountable for revenues only.

Revenue expenditures Expenditures that benefit only the current period.

Revenue maximization Activity level that generates the highest revenue, MR = 0.

Revenue recognition Determining that revenues have been earned and are collectible and thus should be reported on the income statement.

Revenue recognition concept The principle by which revenues are recognized in the period in which they are earned.

Revenue securities Issues which tie cash flows to pledged revenue from the facility(ies) being financed: rental revenue from a convention center, or tolls from a bridge or toll road.

Reverse auction An on-line auction in which participants post the price they want to pay for a good or service, and retailers compete to make the sale; also called a *name-your-price auction*.

Reverse culture shock What expatriates experience upon returning home after a long assignment in a foreign country.

Reverse discrimination 1: When a person is denied an opportunity because of preferences given to protected-class individuals who may be less qualified. **2:** Employment decisions taking into account race or gender in order to remedy past discrimination.

Reverse distribution A system responding to environmental concerns that ensures a firm can retrieve a product from the market for subsequent use, recycling, or disposal.

Reverse engineering Learning to reproduce technology by taking it apart to determine how it works and then copying it.

Reversion to the mean Over time, the tendency for business profit rates to revert toward a risk-adjusted normal rate of return.

Reverse positive pay The disbursing bank sends the check presentment file to the company to see if all the items should be honored.

Reverse repo The other side of a repurchase agreement. In this case a firm needing a temporary source of cash for a few days can negotiate with its bank to temporarily sell securities with an agreement to repurchase them at the end of the specified period.

Revocable letter of credit Letter of credit issued by a bank that can be cancelled at any time without prior notification to the beneficiary.

Revolving (guaranteed) line of credit A formal, committed line of credit extended by a bank or other lending institution.

Revolving credit agreement Allows the borrower to continually borrow and repay amounts up to an agreed-upon limit. The agreement is annually renewable at a variable interest rate during an interim period of anywhere from one to five years.

Reward power 1: Power that results from the authority to bestow rewards on other people. **2:** Power based on B's perception that A has the ability to provide rewards for B.

Rework Action taken on a nonconforming product so that it will fulfill the specified requirements (may also pertain to a service).

Riding the yield curve Investing strategy that involves buying securities with maturities longer than the investment horizon, fully intending to liquidate the position early.

Right the first time Term used to convey the concept that it is beneficial and more cost effective to take the necessary steps up front to ensure a product or service meets its requirements than to provide a product or service that will need rework or not meet customers' needs. In other words, an organization should engage in defect prevention rather than defect detection.

Rightsizing *See:* Downsizing.

Right to choose associates Under the doctrine of *delectus personae,* no person can become a member of a partnership without the consent of all of the partners.

Right to compensation Unless otherwise agreed, no partner is entitled to payment for acting in the partnership business.

Right to continue partnership The remaining partners have the right to continue the partnership in the following situations: 1) wrongful dissolution, 2) expulsion, or 3) agreement of the partners.

Right to inspect books and records If the demand is made in good faith and for a proper purpose.

Right-to-sue letter A letter issued by the EEOC that notifies a complainant that he or she has ninety days in which to file a personal suit in federal court.

Right to wind up On dissolution, any partner has the right to insist on the winding up of the partnership unless the partnership agreement provides otherwise; however, a partner who has wrongfully dissolved the partnership or who has been properly expelled cannot force the liquidation of the partnership.

Right-to-work law State statute that prohibits union shop contracts.

Rights 1: A general partner in a limited partnership has all the rights and powers of a partner in a general partnership. **2:** Copyright protection provides the exclusive right to 1) reproduce the copyrighted work, 2) prepare derivative works based on the work, 3) distribute copies of the work, and 4) perform or display the work publicly.

Rights of creditors The creditors of the old partnership have claims against the continuing (new) partnership and may also proceed against all the members of the dissolved partnership.

Rights of members A member's interest in the LLC includes the financial interest (the right to distributions) and the management interest (which consists of all other rights granted to a member by the LLC operating agreement and the LLC statute).

Ring A communications network topology in which each computer (or other communications device) is connected to two other computers.

Ringi A group-oriented participative decision-making technique used in many Japanese organizations.

RISC (Reduced Instruction Set Computer) A computer whose CPU includes only the most commonly used functions. A reduced instruction set makes the computer significantly faster than the same computer with a full instruction set in its CPU.

Risk 1: A decision has clear-cut goals, and good information is available, but the future outcomes associated with each alternative are subject to chance. **2:** Uncertainty as to economic loss. **3:** In a financial market context, the chance that a financial asset will not earn the return promised.

Risk-adjusted discount rate Higher (lower) interest rate used in present value calculations when the project is of greater (lesser) risk than the average capital budgeting project invested in by the company.

Risk-Adjusted Return on Capital (RAROC) Assesses how much capital would be required by the organization's various activities (such as products, projects, loans, and so on) to keep the probability of bankruptcy below a specified probability level.

Risk analysis The process of predicting the outcome of a decision in the face of uncertainty. The study of the possible payoffs and probabilities associated with a decision alternative or a decision strategy.

Risk arbitrage The opportunistic buying and selling of companies that appear on the verge of being taken over by other firms.

Risk assessment The identification, analysis, and management of risk, such as the risk associated with the possibility of fraud.

Risk assessment/management Process of determining what risks are present in a situation (for example, project plan) and what actions might be taken to eliminate or mediate them.

Risk aversion Risk-averse investors require higher rates of return to invest in higher-risk securities.

Risk avoidance A conscious decision not to expose oneself or one's firm to a particular risk of loss.

Risk avoider A decision maker who tends to avoid decisions that have the risk of an extremely bad (low) payoff.

Risk classes An approach to risk adjusting potential capital projects by developing discount rates based on anticipated variability in the projects' cash flows. Proposals with longer time horizons, permanent effects on the firm's cash flows, or those with a short time horizon that might result in a very large range or standard deviation of outcomes would be assigned a higher discount rate.

Risk exposure Possible terrorism in a foreign country, especially in countries where some groups hold hostile feelings toward "capitalists," or where there is a high possibility of the expatriate being kidnapped for ransom.

Risk-free rate Determined primarily by investors' collective time preferences, the rate of inflation expected over the maturity period, and demand-side influences such as economic productivity.

Risk management 1: The identification of threats and the design of an approach to their containment. **2:** The process used to systematically manage pure risk exposures.

Risk-management policy A plan, procedure, or rule of action followed for the purpose of securing consistent action over a period of time.

Risk-management process 1) Identify risks, 2) evaluate risks as to frequency and severity, 3) select risk-management techniques, and 4) implement and review decisions.

Risk-Management Information System (RMIS) A computer software program that assists in tracking and statistical analysis of past losses.

Risk manager An individual charged with minimizing the adverse impact of losses on the achievement of a company's goals.

Risk mapping (risk profiling) Method of risk identification and assessment by arranging all risks in a matrix reflecting frequency, severity, and existing insurance coverage.

Risk neutral A decision maker who is indifferent to risk where an alternative with the best expected monetary value is identical to an alternative with the highest expected utility.

Risk Premium (RP) The portion of the expected return that can be attributed to the additional risk of an investment; it is the difference between the expected rate of return on a given risky asset and that on a less risky asset.

Risk profile The probability distribution of the possible payoffs associated with a decision alternative or decision strategy.

Risk propensity The willingness to undertake risk with the opportunity of gaining an increased payoff.

Risk reduction A decrease in the total amount of uncertainty present in a particular situation.

Risk retention Handling risk by bearing the results of risk, rather than employing other methods of handling it, such as transfer or avoidance.

Risk spread The added yield necessary to compensate for risk factors other than maturity differences, such as default risk and liquidity risk.

Risk structure of interest rate Set of interest rate differences between various securities which arise due to any factor other than a different maturity. The main risk factors giving rise to this structure are default risk, reinvestment rate risk, and purchasing power risk.

Risk taker A decision maker that tends to prefer decisions that, although risky, have a possibility for an extremely good (high) payoff.

Risk transfer A risk-management technique whereby one party (transferor) pays another (transferee) to assume a risk that the transferor desires to escape.

Rites and ceremonies The elaborate, planned activities that make up a special event and often are conducted for the benefit of an audience.

RMBCA Liability is imposed only on persons who act on behalf of a defectively formed corporation knowing that there was no incorporation.

Robotics The science and specialty of developing machines that can mimic human movement. Robots are highly automated machines controlled by computers.

Robustness Condition of a product or process design that remains relatively stable with a minimum of variation even though factors that influence operations or usage, such as environment and wear, are constantly changing.

ROI *See:* Return on investment.

Role A set of expectations for one's behavior.

Role ambiguity 1: Uncertainty about what behaviors are expected of a person in a particular role. **2:** Anxiety caused by inadequate information about job responsibilities and performance-related goals.

Role conflict 1: Incompatible demands of different roles. **2:** Anxiety caused by conflicting job demands.

Role of officers Officers are agents of the corporation.

Role-playing Training technique whereby participants spontaneously perform in an assigned scenario.

Roll-On-Roll-Off (RORO) Transportation vessels built to accommodate trucks, which can drive on in one port and drive off at their destinations.

Root cause analysis Quality tool used to distinguish the source of defects or problems. It is a structured approach that focuses on the decisive or original cause of a problem or condition.

Root mean square error Has become increasingly popular in business and economic applications. It simply involves taking the square root of the mean square error (MSE).

Rough-Cut Capacity Planning (RCCP) The process of converting the master production schedule into requirements for key resources, often including labor, machinery, warehouse space, suppliers' capabilities, and, in some cases, money. Comparison to available or demonstrated capacity is usually done for each key resource. This comparison assists the master scheduler in establishing a feasible master production schedule. Three approaches to performing RCCP are the bill of labor (resources, capacity) approach, the capacity planning using overall factors approach, and the resource profile approach. *See:* Bill of resources, Capacity planning, Product load profile.

Routine reporting Reports that enable managers to plan activities and control operations.

Routine technology Technology characterized by little task variety and the use of objective, computational procedures.

Routing Process of directing incoming calls to customer service representatives in which more profitable customers are more likely to receive faster and better customer service.

Royalty Compensation paid by one firm to another under licensing and franchising agreements.

Rule of law That which arises from a set of codified principles and regulations that describe how people are required to act, are generally accepted in society, and are enforceable in the courts.

Rule of reason Standard that balances the restraint's anticompetitive effects against its procompetitive effects.

Rule utilitarianism Concept that supports rules that on balance produce the greatest good.

Rules of Professional Conduct A section in the American Institute of Certified Public Accountants' Code of Professional Conduct that contains rules that govern the performance of professional services and identify both acceptable and unacceptable behavior.

Run Consecutive points on one side of the centerline.

Run chart Line graph showing data collected during a run or an uninterrupted sequence of events. A trend is indicated when the series of collected data points head up or down.

S

S corporation A small corporation which, under Subchapter S of the Internal Revenue Code, elects to be taxed as a proprietorship or a partnership yet retains limited liability and other benefits of the corporate form of organization.

Safety Condition in which the physical well-being of people is protected.

Safety capacity The planned amount by which the available capacity exceeds current productive capacity. This capacity provides protection from planned activities, such as resource contention, and preventive maintenance and unplanned activities, such as resource breakdown, poor quality, rework, or lateness. Safety capacity plus productive capacity plus excess capacity is equal to 100 percent of capacity.

Safety lead time An element of time added to normal lead time to protect against fluctuations in lead time so that an order can be completed before its real need date. When used, the MRP system, in offsetting for lead time, will plan both order release and order completion for earlier dates than it would otherwise. *Syn:* protection time, safety time.

Safety stock 1: In general, a quantity of stock planned to be in inventory to protect against fluctuations in demand or supply. **2:** In the context of master production scheduling, the additional inventory and capacity planned as protection against forecast errors and short-term changes in the backlog. Overplanning can be used to create safety stock. *Syn:* buffer stock, reserve stock.

Salaries Consistent payments made each period regardless of number of hours worked.

Sale The transfer of title from seller to buyer.

Sale and leaseback An operation whereby a firm sells land, buildings, or equipment and simultaneously leases the property back for a specified period under specific terms.

Sales agents Dealers sometimes function as brokers in their role as for banks and other issuers of short-term securities. For a commission the agent will locate buyers for the institution's securities, again without risk because the agent does not have to buy and resell the securities.

Sales budget One of the major elements of the income statement budget that indicates the quantity of estimated sales and the expected unit selling price.

Sales call anxiety Fear of negative evaluation and rejection by customers.

Sales discounts An available discount granted by a seller for early payment of an invoice; a contra account to sales.

Sales force automation Equipping traveling salespeople with notebook computers, PDAs, telecommunications devices, and other devices that allow them to communicate with the home office, retrieve and store information from and to other computers remotely, and fax information.

Sales forecast A forecast of a firm's unit and dollar sales for some future period; generally based on recent sales trends plus forecasts of the economic prospects for the nation, region, industry, and so forth.

Sales leveling Strategy of establishing a long-term relationship with customers to lead to contracts for fixed amounts and scheduled deliveries in order to smooth the flow and eliminate surges.

Sales mix The relative distribution of sales among the various products available for sale.

Sales potential Share of the market potential that a particular marketer may hope to gain over the long term.

Sales promotion 1: All marketing activities that attempt to stimulate quick buyer action or, in other words, attempt to promote immediate sales of a product (thereby yielding the name *sales promotion*). **2:** Technique that involves the use of media and nonmedia marketing pressure applied for a predetermined, limited period of time at the level of consumer, retailer, or wholesaler in order to stimulate trial, increase consumer demand, or improve product availability.

Sales return percentage (ratio) Sales returns divided by total sales; a measure of the percentage of sales being returned by customers.

Sales returns (sales returns and allowances) 1: Sold merchandise that is returned by customers and/or damaged, or other sold merchandise for which credit is given. **2:** Reductions in sales resulting from merchandise being returned by customers or from the seller's reduction in the original sales price; a contra account to sales.

Sales-type lease In the United States, a type of capital lease where a dealer's or manufacturer's profit or loss is a basic part of the transaction for the lessor.

Same-day settlement Presentment of a check to the paying bank by 8:00 A.M. local time, with payment of the check required by Fedwire by the close of business day. This Fed initiative was enacted to reduce arbitrary holds or fees used by disbursing banks to slow check clearing.

Same-store sales Tally that compares an individual store's sales to its sales for the same month in the previous year.

Sample Finite number of items of a similar type taken from a population for the purpose of examination to determine whether all members of the population would conform to quality requirements or specifications.

Sample information New information obtained through research or experimentation that enables an updating or revision of the state-of-nature probabilities.

Sample mean forecast error Estimate of average forecast error.

Sample size Number of units in a sample chosen from the population.

Sample standard deviation chart (s chart) Control chart in which the subgroup standard deviation, s, is used to evaluate the stability of the variability within a process.

Sampling risk Risk that a sample is not representative of the population.

Sanction A governmental action, usually consisting of a specific coercive trade measure, that distorts the free flow of trade for an adversarial or political purpose rather than an economic one.

Satisficing 1: To choose the first solution alternative that satisfies minimal decision criteria regardless of whether better solutions are presumed to exist. **2:** The acceptance by organizations of a satisfactory rather than a maximum level of performance.

Scalability The ability to adapt applications as business needs grow.

Scale of market entities Displays a range of products along a continuum based on their tangibility.

Scanner A device that scans pictures and text and transforms them into digitized files.

Scanning system A system that enables corporations to monitor the activities taking place in markets around the globe for the purpose of responding to changing market needs.

Scatter diagram Graphical technique to analyze the relationship between two variables. Two sets of data are plotted on a graph, with the y-axis being used for the variable to be predicted and the x-axis being used for the variable to make the prediction. The graph will show possible relationships (although two variables might appear to be related, they might not be: Those who know most about the variables must make that evaluation). The scatter diagram is one of the seven tools of quality.

Scenario analysis A risk analysis technique in which "bad" and "good" sets of financial circumstances are compared with a most likely, or base case, situation.

Scenario building The identification of crucial variables and determining their effects on different cases or approaches.

Scenario planning Strategic planning process that generates multiple stories about possible future conditions, allowing an organization to look at the potential impact on them and different ways they could respond.

Scenario writing A qualitative forecasting method that consists of developing a conceptual scenario of the future based on a well-defined set of assumptions.

Schedule A timetable for a project plan.

Schedule of reinforcement The frequency with which and intervals over which reinforcement occurs.

Schema The structure of a database, detailing the names and types of fields in each set of records, and the relationships among sets of records.

Scienter Intentional and knowing conduct.

Scientific management 1: A subfield of the classical management perspective that emphasized scientifically determined changes in management practices as the solution to improving labor productivity. **2:** A classical approach that claims decisions about organization and job design should be based on precise, scientific procedures.

Scope NEPA applies to a broad range of activities, including direct action by an federal agency as well as any action by a federal agency that permits action by other parties that will affect the quality of the environment.

Scrambled merchandising Handling of merchandise lines based solely on the profitability criterion and without regard to the consistency of the product or merchandise mix.

Scrap factor A factor that expresses the quantity of a particular component that is expected to be scrapped upon receipt from a vendor, completion of production, or while that component is being built into a given assembly. It is usually expressed as a decimal value. For a given operation or process, the scrap factor plus the yield factor is equal to one. If the scrap factor is 30 percent (or .3) then the yield is 70 percent (or .7). In manufacturing planning and control systems, the scrap factor is usually related to a specific item in the item master, but may be related to a specific component in the product structure. For example, if 50 units of a product are required by a customer and a scrap factor of 30 percent (a yield of 70 percent) is expected then 72 units (computed as 50 units divided by .7) should be started in the manufacturing process. *Syn:* scrap rate. *See:* Yield.

Sea bridge The transfer of freight among various modes of transportation at sea.

Search The process of learning about current developments inside or outside the organization that can be used to meet a perceived need for change.

Search attributes Physical properties that customers can evaluate prior to their purchase decision.

Search warrant Order issued by a judge that gives the investigator consent to search a suspect's personal information, such as bank records, tax returns, or their premises.

Seasonal component The component of the time series model that shows a periodic pattern over one year or less.

Seasonal dating Allows customers to purchase inventory before the peak buying season and defer payment until after the peak season.

Seasonal discount A discount provided to retailers if they purchase and take delivery of merchandise in the off season.

Seasonal index A measure of the seasonal effect on a time series. A seasonal index above one indicates a positive effect, a seasonal index of one indicates no seasonal effect, and a seasonal index less than one indicates a negative effect.

Seasonality Rhythmic annual patterns in sales or profits.

Second-generation languages (2GL) Assembly languages.

Secondary audience In the communication process, those who do not receive a message directly, but who will hear about the message, need to participate in the decision making, or are affected by the message.

Secondary Business District (SBD) A shopping area that is smaller than the CBD and that revolves around at least one department or variety store at a major street intersection.

Secondary data Data originally collected to serve another purpose than the one in which the researcher is currently interested.

Secondary market The market in which "used" stocks are traded after they have been issued by corporations.

Secondary research Research method using data already gathered by others and reported in books, articles in professional journals, or other sources.

Secondary statement approach A complete set of financial statements including accompanying notes prepared according to the accounting standards of another country. Independent auditors express an opinion on secondary statements using the auditing standards of that country.

Secondary trading area The geographic area where the retailer can still be competitive despite a competitor having some locational advantage.

Secondary-line injury Injury to competitors of the buyers.

Section 12(a)2 Imposes liability upon the seller to the immediate purchaser, provided the purchaser did not know of the untruth or omission; but the seller is not liable if he did not know, and in the exercise of reasonable care could not have known, of the untrue statement or omission.

Section 17(a) Broadly prohibits fraud in the sale of securities.

Section 402A Imposes strict liability in tort.

Sectors Subdivisions of the external environment that contain similar elements.

Secular trend Long-run pattern of increase or decrease.

Secure strategy Decision that guarantees the best possible outcome given the worst possible scenario.

Secured bonds Claims against a corporation's general assets and also a lien on specific property.

Secured loan A loan backed by collateral; for short-term loans, the collateral often is inventory, receivables, or both.

Securities and Exchange Commission (SEC) The U.S. government agency that regulates the issuance and trading of stocks and bonds.

Securities regulation Foreign issuers who issue securities, or whose securities are sold in the secondary market in the United States, must register them unless an exemption is available; the antifraud provisions apply where there is either *conduct* or *effects* in the United States relating to a violation of the federal securities laws.

Securitization Involves issuing debt securities collateralized by a pool of selected financial assets such a mortgages, auto loans or credit card receivables.

Security 1: A specific investment offered by a given issuer. **2:** Protection of employees and organizational facilities. **3:** Includes any note, stock, bond, preorganization subscription, and investment contract.

Security audit A comprehensive review of organizational security.

Security Market Line (SML) The line that shows the relationship between risk as measured by beta and the required rate of return for individual securities.

Security measures Systems or application programs that provide such services as tracking account numbers and passwords, and controlling access to files and programs.

Segregation of duties Division of tasks into two parts, so one person does not have complete control of the task.

Select In a relational database, the selection of records that meet certain conditions.

Selection Process of choosing individuals who have needed qualifications to fill jobs in an organization.

Selection criterion 1: Characteristic that a person must have to do a job successfully. **2:** Factor that a firm uses to choose which intermediaries will become members of its marketing channel.

Selection of name The name must clearly designate the entity as a corporation.

Selection rate The percentage hired from a given group of candidates.

Selective distribution 1: A carefully chosen group of intermediaries is used at a particular level in the marketing channel. **2:** A moderate number of retailers are used in a trade area.

Selective listening One hears what he or she is predispositioned to hear.

Selective restatements Partial restatements of companies' reports used to help resolve the problems created by diversity in accounting standards throughout the world.

Self-concept A person's self-image.

Self-directed learning *See:* learner-controlled instruction.

Self-directed team A team consisting of 5 to 20 multi-skilled workers who rotate jobs to produce an entire product or service, often supervised by an elected member.

Self-efficacy A person's belief that he/she can successfully learn the training program content.

Self-inspection Process by which employees inspect their own work according to specified rules.

Self-managed team Team that requires little supervision and manages itself and the day-to-day work it does; self-directed teams are responsible for whole work processes with each individual performing multiple tasks.

Self-management Independent decision making; a high degree of worker involvement in corporate decision making.

Self-Reference Criterion (SRC) The unconscious reference to one's own cultural values.

Self-serving bias The tendency to overestimate the contribution of internal factors to one's successes and the contribution of external factors to one's failures.

Self-sustaining international operation A foreign operation whose activities generally have no direct impact on the reporting entity's operations.

Sell hedge A hedge created by selling a futures contract.

Selling expenses Expenses incurred directly in the sale of merchandise.

Selling forward A market transaction in which the seller promises to sell currency at a certain future date at a pre-specified price.

Selling group A group (network) of brokerage firms formed for the purpose of distributing a new issue of securities.

Selling sites Web sites that provide products for purchase over the Internet.

Semantic nets A method of representing knowledge where-by facts are linked by relationships. The links create a "net."

Semantics The meaning of words and the way they are used.

Semiannual compounding The arithmetic process of determining the final value of a cash flow or series of cash flows when interest is added twice a year.

Semistrong-form efficient Description of foreign exchange markets, implying that all relevant public information is already reflected in prevailing spot exchange rates.

Semistructured problem An unstructured problem with which the decision maker may have had some experience. Requires expertise to resolve.

Seniority Time spent in the organization or on a particular job.

Sensitivity analysis 1: The study of how changes in the probability assessments for the states of nature and/or changes in the payoffs affect the recommended decision alternative. **2:** Using a model to determine the extent to which a change in a factor affects an outcome. The analysis is done by repeating *if-then* calculations. **3:** Means of incorporating risk in financial outcomes which involves varying key inputs, one at a time, and observing the effect on the decision variable(s). For example, the analyst might vary the sales level, and observe the effect on the company's cash forecast.

Sensitivity training Training in human relations that focuses on personal and interpersonal interactions; training that focuses on enhancing an expatriate's flexibility in situations quite different from those at home.

Sequential access A file organization for sequential record entry and retrieval. The records are organized as a list that follows a logical order, such as ascending order of ID numbers, or descending order of part numbers. To retrieve a record, the application must start the search at the first record and retrieve every record, sequentially, until the desired record is encountered.

Sequential interdependence A serial form of interdependence in which the output of one operation becomes the input to another operation.

Sequential-move game Choices are made after observing competitor moves.

Sequential oral interpreters Used by clients involved in cross-language business negotiations and social functions. Unlike simultaneous oral interpreters, they translate both language and culture.

Serial correlation The existence of correlated errors in a regression model of a time series of data points.

Serial port An outlet that accepts a cord for serial transmission.

Serial transmission Transmission of streams of bits one after another. This is the only kind of transmission possible in telecommunications.

Serious health condition A health condition requiring inpatient, hospital, hospice, or residential medical care or continuing physician care.

Servant leader A leader who works to fulfill subordinates' needs and goals as well as to achieve the organization's larger mission.

Servant leadership An employee's recognition that their primary responsibility is to be of service to others.

Server A computer connected to several less powerful computers that can utilize its databases and applications.

Service blueprint A service analysis method that allows service designers to identify processes involved in the service delivery system, isolate potential failure points in the system, establish time frames for the service delivery, and set standards for each step that can be quantified for measurement.

Service capacity The maximum level at which a service provider is able to provide services to customers.

Service consistency Uniform quality of service.

Service department charges The costs of services provided by an internal service department and transferred to a responsibility center.

Service gap The gap between customers' expectations of service and their perception of the service actually delivered, which is a function of the knowledge gap, the standards gap, the delivery gap, and the communications gap.

Service heterogeneity The difference from one delivery of a product to another delivery of the same product as a result of the inability to control the production and quality of the process.

Service Level Agreement (SLA) A document that lists all the types of services expected of an outsourcing vendor as well as the metrics that will be used to measure the degree to which the vendor has met the level of promised services. Usually, the client makes the list.

Service organization An organization that produces non-physical outputs that require customer involvement and cannot be stored in inventory.

Service quality Attitude formed by a long-term, overall evaluation of performance.

Service recovery A firm's reaction to a complaint that results in customer satisfaction and goodwill.

Service sites Web sites that provide a customer service interface for a company.

Service technology 1: Technology characterized by intangible outputs and direct contact between employees and customers. **2:** Technology characterized by simultaneous production and consumption, customized output, customer participation, intangible output, and being labor intensive.

Serviceability 1: Design characteristic that facilitates the easy and efficient performance of service activities. Service activities include those activities required to keep equipment in operating condition, such as lubrication, fueling, oiling, and cleaning. **2:** A measurement of the degree to which servicing of an item will be accomplished within a given time under specified conditions. *See:* Maintainability. **3:** The competitive advantage gained when an organization focuses on aspects such as the speed and courtesy in which customer complaints and questions are answered, following up with customers after the sale to ensure satisfaction, and offering on-site service for product repairs.

Services Deeds, efforts, or performances.

Services businesses A business providing services rather than products to customers.

Services trade The international exchange of personal or professional services, such as financial and banking services, construction, and tourism.

Servicescapes Use of physical evidence to design service environments.

Settlement Negotiated pretrial agreement between the parties to resolve a legal dispute.

Settlement date The date when payment of funds is made on the maturity of a foreign exchange contract.

Settlement range A phase of strategic planning in which a negotiation range (all possible settlements that a negotiator would be willing to take) must be established. During this phase, the LAR (least acceptable result) and MSP (most supportable position) must be identified.

Setup Changing the characteristics of a machine to produce a different product.

Setup time Time taken to change over a process to run a different product or service.

Seven basic tools of quality Help organizations understand their processes in order to improve them. The tools are the cause-and-effect diagram, check sheet, control chart, flowchart, histogram, Pareto chart, and scatter diagram. *See:* individual tool entries.

Seven management tools of quality Tools used primarily for planning and managing are activity network diagram (AND) or arrow diagram, affinity diagram (KJ method), interrelationship digraph, matrix diagram, priorities matrix, process decision program chart (PDPC), and tree diagram.

Seventh Directive, The The EU Seventh Directive addresses consolidated financial statement issues. *See:* Eighth Directive, Fourth Directive.

Severance pay A security benefit voluntarily offered by employers to employees who lose their jobs.

Sexual harassment 1: Actions that are sexually directed, are unwanted, and subject the worker to adverse employment conditions or create a hostile work environment. **2:** An illegal form of sexual discrimination that includes unwelcome sexual advances, requests for sexual favors, and other verbal or physical conduct of a sexual nature.

Shamrock team One composed of a core of members, resource experts who join the team as appropriate, and part-time/temporary members as needed.

Shape Pattern or outline formed by the relative position of a large number of individual values obtained from a process.

Share A proportionate ownership interest in a corporation.

Share in profits Each partner is entitled to an equal share of the profits unless otherwise agreed.

Shareholder meetings Shareholders may exercise their voting rights at both annual and special shareholder meetings.

Shareholder value maximization Presumed goal of publicly held companies, in which decisions are made which will lead to the greatest anticipated increase in the value of the financial claims on the company. In practice, the company's stock price is utilized as a measure of the value of all financial claims.

Shareholder voting agreement Used to provide shareholders with greater control over the election and removal of directors and other matters.

Shareholder's right to dissent A shareholder has the right to dissent from certain corporate actions that require shareholder approval.

Shareholders' liability A shareholder must return illegal dividends if he knew of the illegality, if the dividend resulted from his fraud, or if the corporation is insolvent.

Shareholders' right to compel a dividend The declaration of dividends is within the discretion of the board of directors and only rarely will a court substitute its business judgment for that of the board.

Sharing Making key customer information accessible to all parts of the organization and in some cases selling that information to other firms.

Shark repellent A shark repellent is any tactic (e.g., a poison pill) designed to discourage unwanted merger offers.

Shelf registration Securities are registered with the SEC for sale at a later date; the securities are held "on the shelf" until the sale.

Sherman Antitrust Act Prohibits any contract, combination, or conspiracy that restrains trade. It was passed by Congress in 1890 in an effort to prevent companies from controlling (monopolizing) an industry.

Shewhart cycle *See:* Plan-do-check-act cycle.

Shift in demand Switch from one demand curve to another following a change in a nonprice determinant of demand.

Shift in supply Movement from one supply curve to another following a change in a nonprice determinant of supply.

Shingo's seven wastes Shigeo Shingo, a pioneer in the Japanese just-in-time philosophy, identified seven barriers to improving manufacturing. They are the waste of overproduction, waste of waiting, waste of transportation, waste of stocks, waste of motion, waste of making defects, and waste of the processing itself.

Shipper's order A negotiable bill of lading that can be bought, sold, or traded while the subject goods are still in transit and that is used for letter of credit transactions.

Ship-to-stock program Arrangement with a qualified supplier whereby the supplier ships material directly to the buyer without the buyer's incoming inspection; often a result of evaluating and approving the supplier for certification.

Shop floor control A system for using data from the shop floor to maintain and communicate status information on shop orders (manufacturing orders) and on work centers. The major subfunctions of shop floor control are 1) assigning priority of each shop order; 2) maintaining work-in-process quantity information; 3) conveying shop order status information to the office; 4) providing actual output data for capacity control purposes; 5) providing quantity by location by shop order for work-in-process inventory and accounting purposes; and 6) providing measurement of efficiency, utilization, and productivity of the workforce and machines. Shop floor control can use order control or flow control to monitor material movement through the facility. *Syn:* production activity control.

Shopping center (or mall) A centrally owned or managed shopping district that is planned, has balanced tenancy (the stores complement each other in merchandise offerings), and is surrounded by parking facilities.

Shortage Excess demand.

Short-form merger A corporation that owns at least 90 percent of the outstanding shares of a subsidiary may merge the subsidiary into itself without approval by the shareholders of either corporation.

Short-swing profits Section 16(b) imposes liability on certain insiders (directors, officers, and shareholders owning more than 10 percent of the stock of a corporation) for all profits made on sales and purchases within six months of each other, with any recovery going to the issuer.

Short-term credit Any liability originally scheduled for repayment within one year.

Short-term orientation A concern with the past and present and a high value on meeting social obligations.

Short-term orientation Values that respect tradition, personal stability, quick results from the efforts made, and concern with appearances.

Shrinkage Reduction of merchandise through theft, loss, and damage.

Sight draft A formal, written agreement whereby an importer (drawee) contracts to pay a certain amount on demand ("at sight") to the exporter. The bank is not extending credit, but simply helping in the payment process by receiving the draft and presenting it to the drawee. Sight drafts often must have documentation attached to verify that conditions for payment (receipt, or "sight" of goods) have been met.

Sigma Greek letter that stands for the standard deviation of a process.

Sign A signal that is recognized, structured into a category, and assigned meaning.

Signal 1: An action taken by a firm's management that provides clues to investors about how management views the firm's prospects. **2:** Transmitted by a sender to a receiver; the receiver must decode and try to understand the signal.

Signal-to-Noise Ratio (S/N ratio) Mathematical equation that indicates the magnitude of an experimental effect above the effect of experimental error due to chance fluctuations.

Signified The meaning attached to the signifier.

Signifier The sound or shape of the signal that is sensorially perceived without meaning yet attached to it.

Silo (as in *functional silo*) Organization where cross-functional collaboration and cooperation is minimal and where the functional "silos" tend to work toward their own goals to the detriment of the organization as a whole.

Simple (quoted) interest rate The contracted, or quoted, interest rate that is used to compute the interest paid per period.

Simple interest Arrangement in which interest is only added to the account at maturity. Because no compounding occurs, the nominal interest rate is also the annual effective rate.

Simple interest approximation formula Simple interest formula to approximate the present value effect of a financial decision. The simplicity of this approach makes its use desirable where the effect of ignoring cash flow compounding would not have a significant effect on the valuation of those flows.

Simple interest loan Both the amount borrowed and the interest charged on that amount are paid at the maturity of the loan; there are no payments made before maturity.

Simple, or quoted, rate, i_{SIMPLE} The rate quoted by borrowers and lenders that is used to determine the rate earned per compounding period (periodic rate).

Simple regression A statistical model in which the equation used to predict the value of the variable of interest (dependent variable) involves just one predictor (independent) variable.

Simple-complex dimension The number and dissimilarity of external elements relevant to an organization's operation.

Simplex Transmission from a device that can only transmit, to devices that can only receive. Example: radio and television broadcasts.

Simulation Technique for assessing the degree of uncertainty. Probability distributions are developed for the input variables; simulation uses this information to generate possible outcomes.

Simulation experiment The generation of a sample of values for the probabilistic inputs of a simulation model and computing the resulting values of the model outputs.

Simultaneous oral interpreters Used by speakers in formal situations such as conferences, where the audience and the speaker communicate using different languages.

Simultaneous-move game Choices are made without specific knowledge of competitor counter moves.

Single European Act Act intended to remove numerous barriers imposed on trade and capital flows between European countries.

Single plantwide factory overhead rate method A method that allocates all factory overhead to products by using a single factory overhead rate.

Single-buyer policy Policy administered by Ex-Im Bank which allows the exporter to selectively insure certain transactions.

Single-criterion decision problem A problem in which the objective is to find the "best" solution with respect to just one criterion.

Single-Mminute Exchange of Dies (SMED) Goal to be achieved in reducing the setup time required for a changeover to a new process; the methodologies employed in devising and implementing ways to reduce setup.

Single-piece flow Method whereby the product proceeds through the process one piece at a time, rather than in large batches, eliminating queues and costly waste.

Single-source systems Measurement of the effectiveness of advertising (whether it leads to increased sales activity). They are unique in that all the relevant data is collected by a single source, processed, and then made available in a readily usable format to retailers and manufacturers.

Single-step income statement An income statement in which the total of all expenses is deducted in one step from the total of all revenues.

Single-use plans Plans that are developed to achieve a set of goals that are unlikely to be repeated in the future.

Sinking fund 1: A required annual payment designed to amortize a bond or preferred stock issue. **2:** Assets set aside in a special fund to be used for a specific purpose.

SIPOC Macro-level analysis of the suppliers, inputs, processes, outputs, and customers.

Site analysis An evaluation of the density of demand and supply within each market with the goal of identifying the best retail site(s).

Situation analysis Analysis of the strengths, weaknesses, opportunities, and threats (SWOT) that affect organizational performance.

Situational ethics 1: Societal condition where "right" and "wrong" are determined by the specific situation, rather than by universal moral principles. **2:** Judging a person's actions by first putting oneself in the actor's situation.

Situational interview A structured interview composed of questions about how applicants might handle specific job situations.

Situational leadership Leadership theory that maintains that leadership style should change based on the person and the situation, with the leader displaying varying degrees of directive and supportive behavior.

Situational scheme Proposes that certain situational factors influence the HSR in all countries.

Situational theory A contingency approach to leadership that links the leader's behavioral style with the task readiness of subordinates.

Six-sigma quality 1: Term used generally to indicate that a process is well controlled, that is, process limits 63 sigma from the centerline in a control chart, and requirements/tolerance limits 66 sigma from the centerline. The term was initiated by Motorola. **2:** 3.4 defects per million units processed.

Six-sigma approach Quality philosophy; a collection of techniques and tools for use in reducing variation; a program of improvement.

Skill variety The extent to which the work requires several different activities for successful completion.

Skimming 1: Removal of cash from a victim organization prior to its entry in an accounting system. **2:** A pricing objective in which price is initially set high on merchandise to skim the cream of demand before selling at more competitive prices.

Skip-level meeting Evaluation technique which occurs when a member of senior management meets with persons two or more organizational levels below, without the intervening management present, to allow open expression about the effectiveness of the organization.

SKU Stock Keeping Unit; refers to a distinct merchandise item in the retailer's merchandise assortment.

Skunkworks A separate small, informal, highly autonomous, and often secretive group that focuses on breakthrough ideas for the business.

Slack time Time an activity can be delayed without delaying the entire project; it is determined by calculating the difference between the latest allowable date and the earliest expected date. *See:* Project evaluation and review technique.

Slide The erroneous movement of all digits in a number, one or more spaces to the right or the left, such as writing $542 as $5,420.

Slope Measure of the steepness of a line.

Slotting fees (slotting allowances) Fees paid by a vendor for space or a slot on a retailer's shelves, as well as having its UPC number given a slot in the retailer's computer system.

Small-batch production A manufacturing process, often custom work, that is not highly mechanized and relies heavily on the human operator.

Small business policy Policy providing enhanced coverage to new exporters and small businesses.

Small power distance culture A culture where employees perceive few power differences and follow a superior's instructions only when they either agree or feel threatened.

Smithsonian Agreement Conference between nations in 1971 that resulted in a devaluation of the dollar against major currencies and a widening of boundaries (2 percent in either direction) around the newly established exchange rates.

Smoot-Hawley Act A 1930 act that raised import duties to the highest rates ever imposed by the United States; designed to promote domestic production, it resulted in the downfall of the world trading system.

Smoothing *See:* Resource leveling.

Smoothing constant A parameter of the exponential smoothing model that provides the weight given to the most recent time series value in the calculation of the forecast.

Snail mail Regular mail handled by the Postal Service (as opposed to e-mail).

Snake Arrangement established in 1972, whereby European currencies were tied to each other within specified limits.

Social altruism An individual's major concern is the functioning of society. He or she acts to generate vital long-term benefits for others without the want or need to acquire rewards for him or herself.

Social audit A systematic attempt to identify, measure, monitor, and evaluate an organization's performance with respect to its social efforts, goals, and programs.

Social awareness Understanding human/societal needs outside one's own individual-based ends furnishes a base for interorganizational cooperative behavior and for molding effective strategies to merge human endeavors to solve difficult problems.

Social contract Because society allows for the creation of corporations and gives them special rights, including a grand of unlimited liability, corporations owe a responsibility to society.

Social egalitarians People who believe that society should provide all members with equal amounts of goods and services irrespective of their relative contributions.

Social ethical theories The focus on a person's obligations to other members in society and on the individuals rights and obligations.

Social contribution Refers to the mixture of striving to fulfill other people's needs while simultaneously pursuing one's own growth and social power.

Social facilitation The tendency for the presence of others to influence an individual's motivation and performance.

Social forces The aspects of a culture that guide and influence relationships among people—their values, needs, and standards of behavior.

Social infrastructure The housing, health, educational, and other social systems in a country.

Social interaction paradigm Used to explain the inherent cooperative culture behind the economic success of the Pacific Rim economies; extends the hierarchy of needs beyond the self-actualization model.

Social responsibility 1: The notion that corporations have an obligation to constituent groups in society other than stockholders and beyond that prescribed by law or union contract. **2:** Collection of marketing philosophies, policies, procedures, and actions intended primarily to enhance society's welfare. **3:** Management's obligation to make choices and take action so that the organization contributes to the welfare and interest of society as well as itself.

Social Security Measures by which the government provides economic assistance to disabled or retired employees and their dependents.

Social stratification The division of a particular population into classes.

Socially conscious (or ethical investing) movement A comprehensive investing approach complete with social and environmental screens, shareholder activism, and community investment.

Socially acceptable and unacceptable Standards or practices determined by each individual culture such that what is acceptable in one culture might be unacceptable in another.

Societal objectives Objectives that reflect the retailers' desire to help society fulfill some of its needs.

Sociocultural contexts *See:* Cross-cultural communication.

Socioemotional role A role in which the individual provides support for team members' emotional needs and social unity.

Sociotechnical systems approach An approach that combines the needs of people with the needs of technical efficiency.

Soft controls Based on subjective evidence, soft controls are informal and intangible, and difficult to measure and evaluate. An example is ethical behavior.

Soft currencies Refers to money that is not readily acceptable in international business transactions—usually the currencies of industrially less-advanced countries and of communist countries.

Soft skills Include interpersonal skills, motivation, leadership, and communication skills. Also known as people skills. In a way, soft skills are innate.

Software Sets of instructions that control the operations of a computer.

Software piracy The act of copying software illegally.

Sogoshosha Trading companies of Japan, including firms such as Sumitomo, Mitsubishi, and Mitsui.

SOHO (Small Office/Home Office) The fastest growing type of business, thanks to the availability of inexpensive microcomputers and fax/modems. Also called TOHO (Tiny Office/Home Office).

Sole proprietorship An unincorporated business owned by an individual for profit.

Solidarity Situation that exisits when a high value is placed on the relationship between a supplier and retailer.

Solvency The ability of a business to pay its debts. A firm is solvent when the dollar level of its assets exceed the dollar level of its liabilities.

Solvency ratios *See:* Liquidity ratios.

Source code An application's code written in the original high-level programming language.

Sources of intergroup conflict Factors that generate conflict, including goal incompatibility, differentiation, task interdependence, and limited resources.

Southeast Asian management The basis of an opposing theory to Theory X and Y known as Theory T and T+, representing two styles and attitudes found to be prevalent in Southeast Asian countries.

Sovereign immunity Foreign country's freedom from a host country's laws.

Space productivity Condition that represents how effectively the retailer utilizes its space and is usually measured by sales per square foot of selling space or gross margin dollars per square foot of selling space.

Space productivity index A ratio that compares the percentage of the store's total gross margin that a particular merchandise category generates to its percentage of total store selling space used.

Spaced practice Several practice sessions spaced over a period of hours or days.

Spaghetti chart Before improvement chart of existing steps in a process and the many back and forth interrelationships (can resemble a bowl of spaghetti); used to see the redundancies and other wasted movements of people and material.

Spamming Posting identical messages to multiple unrelated newsgroups. Often used as cheap advertising to promote pyramid schemes or simply to annoy other people.

Span of control How many subordinates a manager can effectively and efficiently manage.

Span of management The number of employees reporting to a supervisor; also called *span of control.*

Special causes Causes of variation that arise because of special circumstances. They are not an inherent part of a process. Special causes are also referred to as assignable causes. *See:* Common causes.

Special Drawing Rights (SDRs) Reserves established by the International Monetary Fund; they are used only for intergovernment transactions; the SDR also serves as a unit of account (determined by the values of five major currencies) that is used to denominate some internationally traded goods and services, as well as some foreign bank deposits and loans.

Special economic zones Areas created by a country to attract foreign investors, in which there are no tariffs, substantial tax incentives, and low prices for land and labor.

Special reports Reports that help managers formulate policies, prepare strategic plans, and prepare operational plans.

Specialization or division of labor Each participant in the marketing channel focuses on performing those activities at which it is most efficient.

Special-purpose team Organizational team formed to address specific problems, improve work processes, and enhance product and service quality.

Specie Gold and silver.

Specific price index An index that shows the price changes for a specific good or service over time.

Specification Engineering requirement, used for judging the acceptability of a particular product/service based on product characteristics, such as appearance, performance, and size. In statistical analysis, specifications refer to the document that prescribes the requirements with which the product or service has to perform.

Speculative balance A cash balance that is held to enable the firm to take advantage of any bargain purchases that might arise.

Speculative motive Additional inventory held to take advantage of unique business opportunities such as future shortages.

Speculative risk The uncertainty of an event that could produce either a profit or a loss, such as a business venture or a gambling transaction.

Speculator A person who has no operating cash flow position to protect and is trying to profit solely from interest rate movements.

Speech recognition The process of translating human speech into computer-readable data and instructions.

Speech synthesizing Technology that allows machines to create sounds emulating a human voice.

Spine layout A type of store layout in which a single main aisle runs from the front to the back of the store, transporting customers in both directions, and where on either side of this spine, merchandise departments using either a free-flow or grid pattern branch off toward the back side walls.

Sponsorship marketing Practice of promoting the interests of a company and its brands by associating the company with a specific event (for example, a golf tournament) or a charitable cause (for example, the Leukemia Society).

Spontaneous financing Those financing sources such as accounts payables and accruals that are generated as a part of the operations of the firm.

Spontaneously generated funds Funds that are obtained from routine business transactions.

Spoofing 1: Changing the information in an e-mail header or an IP address used to hide identities. **2:** Deception for the purpose of gaining access to a Web site, or deception of users to make them think they are logged on to a certain Web site when they are actually logged on to another. **3:** The deliberate inducement of a user or a computer resource to take an incorrect action. Assuming the characteristics of another computer system or user for purposes of deception. Using various techniques to subvert IP-based access control mechanism by masquerading as another system by using its IP address.

Sporadic problem Sudden adverse change in the status quo that can be remedied by restoring the status quo. For example, actions such as changing a worn part or proper handling of an irate customer's complaint can restore the status quo.

Spot market Market in which exchange transactions occur for immediate exchange.

Spot rates 1: Contracts that provide for two parties to exchange currencies with delivery in two business days. **2:** Existing prices or interest rates in today's markets. In foreign exchange, the spot rate is an exchange rate quote based on immediate delivery of the currency being traded.

Spreadsheet Table of electronically stored data.

Spurious correlation Chance association between two variables, which the analyst should watch for because it might account for a high coefficient of determination.

SQL (Structured Query Language) A data manipulation language for relational database management systems that has become a de facto business standard.

Square root law States that total safety stock inventories in a future number of facilities can be approximated by multiplying the total amount of inventory at existing facilities by the square root of the number of future facilities divided by the number of existing facilities. Used to consolidate inventories at multiple distribution centers.

Stable distribution Pattern of outcomes which characterizes a variable with a well-defined, consistent trend or seasonal component.

Stable-unstable dimension The state of an organization's environmental elements.

Stable, predictable dividends Payment of a specific dollar dividend each year, or periodically increasing the dividend at a constant rate—the annual dollar dividend is relatively predictable by investors.

Stack-outs Pallets of merchandise set out on the floor in front of the main shelves.

Staff authority A form of authority granted to staff specialists in their areas of expertise.

Stage of subsidiary development Traditionally, MNCs have staffed foreign subsidiaries with expatriates in the early stages of establishing operations in the foreign country. In the later stages, at least at the lower levels, host-country nationals are employed.

Stage-Gate process Common new product development process that divides the repeatable portion of product development into a time-sequenced series of stages, each of which is separated by a management decision gate. In each stage, a team completes a set of tasks that span the functions involved in product development. At the end of each stage, management reviews the results obtained and, based on the team's ability to meet the objectives in that stage, provides the resources to continue to the next stage ("go"), requests additional work ("recycle"), or stops the project ("kill").

Stages of creativity One model gives the following stages: generate, percolate, illuminate, and verify.

Stages of team growth Four development stages through which groups typically progress: forming, storming, norming, and performing. Knowledge of the stages help team members accept the normal problems that occur on the path from forming a group to becoming a team.

Stakeholder approach Also called the constituency approach, this perspective assesses the satisfaction of stakeholders as an indicator of the organization's performance.

Stakeholder 1: People, departments, and organizations that have an investment or interest in the success or actions taken by the organization. **2:** The users of financial reports. **3:** Any group within or outside an organization that has a stake in the organization's performance.

Stakeholder audit A systematic attempt to identify and measure an organization's stakeholders' issues and measure and evaluate their opinions with respect to its effective resolution.

Stakeholder environment Composed of trends, events, issues, expectations, and forecasts that may have a bearing on the strategic management process and the development of corporate public policy.

Stakeholder model Corporations have fiduciary duty to all of their stakeholders, not just their stockholders.

Stakeholders Individuals or entities that have an interest in the well-being of a firm—stockholders, creditors, employees, customers, suppliers, and so on.

Stand-alone risk The risk an asset would have if it were a firm's only asset; it is measured by the variability of the asset's expected returns.

Standard Statement, specification, or quantity of material against which measured outputs from a process may be judged as acceptable or unacceptable.

Standard check processing When the deposit bank verifies the depositor's cash letter—which lists the checks and their amounts—and then encodes the dollar amount on the MICR line and sends the checks to a correspondent bank or the nearest Federal Reserve facility to be cleared back to the disbursing bank on which the check was written.

Standard cost A detailed estimate of what a product should cost.

Standard cost systems Accounting systems that use standards for each element of manufacturing cost entering into the finished product.

Standard deviation (σ) 1. A measure of the dispersion, or spread, of a distribution from its expected value; the square root of the variance. **2:** Calculated measure of variability that shows how much the data are spread around the mean. **3:** A measure of the tightness, or variability, of a set of outcomes.

Standard of living The level of material affluence of a group or nation, measured as a composite of quantities and qualities of goods.

Standard worldwide pricing Price-setting strategy based on average unit costs of fixed, variable, and export-related costs.

Standard stock list A merchandising method in which all stores in a retail chain stock the same merchandise.

Standardization 1: The process of designing and altering products, parts, processes, and procedures to establish and use standard specifications for them and their components.

2: Reduction of the total numbers of parts and materials used and products, models, or grades produced. **3:** The function of bringing a raw ingredient into standard (acceptable) range per the specification before introduction to the main process. **4:** Products sold unchanged or only slightly changed in all markets. **5:** Full comparability of accounting information.

Standardized approach Approach to international marketing in which products are marketed with little or no modification.

Standby letter of credit Document used to guarantee invoice payments to a supplier; it promises to pay the beneficiary if the buyer fails to pay.

Standing plans Ongoing plans used to provide guidance for tasks performed repeatedly within the organization.

Star A network topology in which many computers are linked to a single computer through which all messages must be passed.

Stated value A value approved by the board of directors of a corporation for no-par stock. Similar to par value.

State Implementation Plan (SIP) Plan detailing how a state will implement and maintain an NAAQS within its borders.

State of the art The state of technology current at the time the product is made.

Stated capital Consideration, other than that allocated to capital surplus, received for issued stock.

Statement of cash flows Financial statement that reports an entity's cash inflows (receipts) and outflows (payments) during an accounting period.

Statement of Financial Accounting Standards No. 52 A U.S. foreign currency standard issued by the Financial Accounting Standards Board (FASB) acknowledging that the functional currency of an entity is the currency of the primary environment in which the entity operates.

Statement of retained earnings A statement reporting the change in the firm's retained earnings as a result of the income generated and retained during the year. The balance sheet figure for retained earnings is the sum of the earnings retained for each year the firm has been in business.

Statement of stockholders' equity A summary of the changes in the stockholders' equity of a corporation that have occurred during a specific period of time.

Statement of Work (SOW) Description of the actual work to be accomplished. It is derived from the work breakdown structure and, when combined with the project specifications, becomes the basis for the contractual agreement on the project (also referred to as scope of work).

Statements on Auditing Standards (SAS) Standards issued by the American Institute of Certified Public Accountants in the United States concerning generally accepted auditing standards.

State-owned enterprise A corporate form that has emerged in non-Communist countries, primarily for reasons of national security and economic security.

States of nature The possible outcomes for chance events that affect the payoff associated with a decision alternative.

Static budget A budget that does not adjust to changes in activity levels.

Static IP number An Internet Protocol number permanently associated with a device.

Static simulation model A simulation model used in situations where the state of the system at one point in time does not affect the state of the system at future points in time. Each trial of the simulation is independent.

Static surveillance Another term for fixed-point surveillance.

Stationary surveillance Locating a scene to be observed, anticipating the actions that are most likely to occur at the scene, and keeping detailed notes on tape or film on all activities involving the suspect.

Statistical analysis The use of statistics and number patterns to discover relationships in certain data, such as Benford's law.

Statistical confidence The level of accuracy expected of an analysis of data. Most frequently it is expressed as either a "95 percent level of significance," or "5 percent confidence level." Also called *statistical significance*.

Statistical decomposition A complex forecasting technique which uses the past observations of a variable to forecast future values. Sometimes called Census X-11 decomposition (after the computer software developed by the Census Bureau), this approach is especially useful for forecasting variables which have trend, seasonal, and cyclical variations.

Statistical Process Control (SPC) Application of statistical techniques to control a process.

Statistical Quality Control (SQC) Application of statistical techniques to control quality. Often the term "statistical process control" is used interchangeably with "statistical quality control" although statistical quality control includes acceptance sampling as well as statistical process control.

Statistical thinking Philosophy of learning and action based on fundamental principles:

- all work occurs in a system of interconnected processes
- understanding and reducing variation are vital to improvement
- variation exists in all processes

Statute A law or regulation; a law enacted by the legislative branch of a government.

Statute of repose Limits the time period for which a manufacturer is liable for injury caused by its product.

Statutory limitations Limitations that have been enacted by the federal government and some states.

Statutory powers Typically include perpetual existence, right to hold property in the corporate name, and all powers necessary or convenient to effect the corporation's purposes.

Statutory (legal) reserve An equity reserve required by several countries to provide additional protection to creditors.

Statutory merger One company acquires the net assets of another company or companies.

Steering committee A group of representatives from a variety of key business units that establishes priorities for systems development and implementation of communications networks, prioritizes requests for new systems, and commits funds to projects.

Stepped-up exercise price An exercise price that is specified to be higher if a warrant is exercised after a designated date.

Stereotypes Generalizations about a particular culture and its members. Normally simple or brief, these are statements that characterize an entire group, culture, or its members. For example, "Americans are efficiency-oriented" or "The French are rude to non–French-speaking visitors."

Stereotyping Placing an employee into a class category based on one or a few traits or characteristics.

Sterilized intervention Intervention by the Federal Reserve in the foreign exchange market, with simultaneous intervention in the Treasury securities markets to offset any effects on the dollar money supply; thus, the intervention in the foreign exchange market is achieved without affecting the existing dollar money supply.

Stimulus Refers to a cue that is external to the individual or a drive that is internal to the individual.

Stochastic model A model in which at least one uncontrollable input is uncertain and subject to variation; stochastic models are also referred to as probabilistic models.

Stock Shares of ownership of a corporation.

Stock dividend A dividend paid in the form of additional shares of stock rather than cash.

Stock option A plan that gives an individual the right to buy stock in a company, usually at a fixed price for a period of time.

Stock split 1: A reduction in the par or stated value of a share of common stock and the issuance of a proportionate number of additional shares. **2:** An action taken by a firm to increase the number of shares outstanding, such as doubling the number of shares outstanding by giving each stockholder two new shares for each one formerly held.

Stock-keeping units The lowest level of identification of merchandise.

Stock-to-Sales Method (SSM) A technique for planning dollar inventory investments where the amount of inventory planned for the beginning of the month is a ratio (obtained from trade associations or the retailer's historical records) of stock-to-sales.

Stock-to-sales ratio Ratio that depicts the amount of stock to have at the beginning of each month to support the forecasted sales for that month.

Stockholder wealth maximization The appropriate goal for management decisions; considers the risk and timing associated with expected earnings per share in order to maximize the price of the firm's common stock.

Stockholders The owners of a corporation.

Stone model Optimization process similar to Miller-Orr but allows the cash manager's knowledge of imminent cash flows to permit him to selectively override model directives.

Storage The operation of storing data and information in an information system.

Storage Area Network (SAN) A technology that uses computer servers, distributed storage devices, and networks to tie the storage systems together.

Storage costs Costs to a firm associated with the act of storing inventory.

Storage Service Provider (SSP) A firm that rents storage space for software through an Internet link.

Store-based retailers Retailers that operate from a fixed store location that requires customers to travel to the store to view and select merchandise or services.

Store compatibility Condition that exists when two similar retail businesses locate next to or nearby each other and they realize a sales volume greater than what they would have achieved if they were located apart from each other.

Store image The overall perception the consumer has of the store's environment.

Store positioning A retailer identifies a well-defined market segment using demographic or lifestyle variables and appeals to this segment with a clearly differentiated approach.

Stories Narratives based on true events that are frequently shared among organizational employees and told to new employees to inform them about an organization.

Storming The stage of team development in which individual personalities and roles, and resulting conflicts, emerge.

Storyboarding Technique that visually displays thoughts and ideas and groups them into categories, making all aspects of a process visible at once. Often used to communicate to others the activities performed by a team as they improved a process.

Straddle Combination of a put option and a call option.

Straight bill of lading A nonnegotiable bill of lading usually used in prepaid transactions in which the transported goods involved are delivered to a specific individual or company.

Straight piece-rate system A pay system in which wages are determined by multiplying the number of units produced by the piece rate for one unit.

Straight rebuy Routine reordering from the same supplier of a product that has been purchased in the past.

Straight voting Directors are elected by a plurality of votes.

Straight-line depreciation method A method of depreciation that provides for equal periodic depreciation expense over the estimated life of an asset.

Strategic activities Refers to activities that support the "long-term" objectives of an organization. Examples include strategic planning, strategic sourcing, and so on.

Strategic advantage A position in which one dominates a market; also called competitive advantage.

Strategic alliance 1: A firm's collaboration with companies in other countries to share rights and responsibilities as well as revenues and expenses as defined in a written agreement. Some common types of strategic alliances include research collaboration, a licensing program, and a copromotion deal. **2:** Two or more companies band together to attain efficiency. *See:* Joint ventures.

Strategic Business Unit (SBU) A division of the organization that has a unique business mission, product line, competitors, and markets relative to other SBUs in the same corporation.

Strategic contingencies Events and activities inside and outside an organization that are essential for attaining organizational goals.

Strategic fit review Process by which senior managers assess the future of each project to a particular organization in terms of its ability to advance the mission and goals of that organization.

Strategic goals Broad statements of where the organization wants to be in the future; pertain to the organization as a whole rather than to specific divisions or departments.

Strategic human resource management Organizational use of employees to gain or keep a competitive advantage against competitors.

Strategic information system Any information system that gives its owner a competitive advantage.

Strategic leader A highly competent firm located in a strategically critical market.

Strategic management The set of decisions and actions used to formulate and implement strategies that will provide a competitively superior fit between the organization and its environment so as to achieve organizational goals.

Strategic managers Individuals who make decisions that affect an entire organization, or large parts of it, and leave an impact in the long run.

Strategic marketing concept Company's mission to identify, generate, and sustain competitive advantage through superior positioning and vision.

Strategic objectives Guided by the enterprise's mission or purpose, they associate the enterprise with its external environment and provide management with a basis for comparing performance with that of its competitors, in relation to environmental demands.

Strategic plan A plan that integrates an organization's major goals, policies, and action sequences into a cohesive whole.

Strategic planning 1: Process to set an organization's long-range goals and identify the actions needed to reach the goals. **2:** Strategy that involves adapting the resources of the firm to the opportunities and threats of an ever-changing retail environment.

Strategic plans The action steps by which an organization intends to attain its strategic goals.

Strategic sourcing A cross-functional process that involves members of the firm other than those who work in the purchasing department. A strategic sourcing team may include members from engineering, quality, design, manufacturing, marketing, accounting, strategic planning and other departments. The focus of strategic sourcing management involves integrating supplier capabilities into organizational processes to achieve a competitive advantage through cost reduction, technology development, quality improvement, cycle time, and delivery capabilities to meet customer requirements.

Strategy 1: The plan of action that prescribes resource allocation and other activities for dealing with the environment and helping the organization attain its goals. **2:** A carefully designed plan for achieving the retailer's goals and objectives.

Strategy and structure changes Changes in the administrative domain of an organization, including structure, policies, reward systems, labor relations, coordination devices, management information control systems, and accounting and budgeting.

Strategy formulation The stage of strategic management that involves the planning and decision making that lead to the establishment of the organization's goals and of a specific strategic plan.

Strategy implementation The stage of strategic management that involves the use of managerial and organizational tools to direct resources toward achieving strategic outcomes.

Stratified random sampling Technique to segment (stratify) a population prior to drawing a random sample from each strata, the purpose being to increase precision when members of different strata would, if not stratified, cause an unrealistic distortion.

Stress A physiological and emotional response to stimuli that place physical or psychological demands on an individual.

Stress interview Interview designed to create anxiety and put pressure on an applicant to see how the person responds.

Stretch goals Force an organization to think in a radically different way for major and incremental improvements.

Stretching accounts payable The practice of deliberately paying accounts payable late.

Strict liability Liability without fault for an individual who engages in an unduly dangerous activity in an inappropriate location.

Strict liability in tort Merchant seller is liable for selling a product in a defective condition, unreasonably dangerous to the user.

Strike price *See:* Exercise price.

Striking (exercise) price The price that must be paid (buying or selling) for a share of common stock when an option is exercised.

Strong-form efficient Description of foreign exchange markets, implying that all relevant public information and private information is already reflected in prevailing spot exchange rates.

Structural Adjustment Loan Facility (SAL) Facility established in 1980 by the World Bank to enhance a country's long-term economic growth through financing projects.

Structural causes Are factors both internal and external to a process.

Structural variation Variation caused by regular, systematic changes in output, such as seasonal patterns and long-term trends.

Structure The formal reporting relationships, groupings, and systems of an organization.

Structured data Numbers and facts that can be conveniently stored and retrieved in an orderly manner for operations and decision making.

Structured interview Interview that uses a set of standardized questions asked of all job applicants.

Structured problem A problem for whose solution there is a known set of steps to follow. Also called a *programmable problem*.

Structured Query Language (SQL) The data definition and manipulation language of choice for many developers of relational database management systems.

Stylus A penlike marking device used to enter commands and data on a computer screen.

Subchapter S corporation Eligible corporation electing to be taxed as a partnership under the Internal Revenue Code.

Subcultures Cultures that develop within an organization to reflect the common problems, goals, and experiences that members of a team, department, or other unit share.

Subjective risk The risk based on the mental state of an individual who experiences uncertainty or doubt as to the outcome of a given event.

Suboptimization Need for each business function to consider overall organizational objectives, resulting in higher efficiency and effectiveness of the entire system, although performance of a function may be suboptimal.

Subordinated debenture A bond having a claim on assets only after the senior debt has been paid off in the event of liquidation.

Subscriber A person who agrees to purchase stock in a corporation.

Subscription Fee paid by users to be granted access to certain online information or services.

Subsequent alteration Liability exists only if the product reaches the user or consumer without substantial change in the condition in which it is sold.

Subsequent debts The liability of an incoming partner for subsequent debts of the partnership is unlimited.

Subsidiary 1: A subunit of a business entity established in a foreign country for the purpose of serving that market or other markets, including the business entity's home-country market. **2:** The company whose voting stock is acquired by a parent company to exercise control over it.

Subsidiary company The corporation that is controlled by a parent company.

Subsidiary corporation Corporation controlled by another corporation.

Subsidiary ledger A ledger containing individual accounts with a common characteristic.

Subsidy policy Government grants that benefit firms and individuals.

Substance abuse The use of illicit substances or the misuse of controlled substances, alcohol, or other drugs.

Substitute A situational variable that makes a leadership style redundant or unnecessary.

Substitutes Related products for which a price increase for one leads to an increase in demand for the other.

Subsystem 1: A component of a larger system. **2:** Parts of a system that depend on one another for their functioning. **3:** Divisions of an organization that perform specific functions for the organization's survival; organizational subsystems perform the essential functions of boundary spanning, production, maintenance, adaptation, and management.

Succession planning Process of identifying a longer-term plan for the orderly replacement of key employees.

Successor event The event at the end of an activity (head of the arrow) in the activity-on-the-arrow form of network diagramming; finish event.

Suggestion selling Occurs when the salesperson points out available complementary items in line with the selected item(s), in order to encourage an additional purchase.

Sugging Illegal survey conducted under the guise of research but with the intent of selling.

Suite A group of general software applications that are often used in the same environment. The strengths of the different applications can be used to build a single powerful document. Current suites are usually a combination of a spreadsheet, a word processor, and a database management system.

Sum-of-the-years-digits depreciation method A method of depreciation that provides for declining periodic depreciation expense over the estimated life of an asset.

Sunk cost 1: A cash outlay that already has been incurred and that cannot be recovered regardless of whether the project is accepted or rejected. **2:** A cost that is not affected by subsequent decisions.

Supercenters Retailers that combine a discount store and grocery store and carry 80,000 to 100,000 products in order to offer one-stop shopping.

Supercomputer The most powerful class of computers, used by large organizations, research institutions, and universities for complex scientific computations and the manipulation of very large databases.

Superfund, The The Comprehensive Environmental Response, Compensation, and Liability Act (CERCLA) establishes 1) a National Contingency plan for responding to releases of hazardous substances and 2) a trust fund to pay for removal and cleanup of hazardous waste.

Super-NOW accounts While banks continue to set higher minimum balance requirements for NOW accounts, in 1986 regulators removed interest rate distinctions between the accounts by eliminating the maximum NOW rate of 5 1/4 percent.

Superordinate goal A goal that cannot be reached by a single party.

Supplier Any provider whose goods and services may be used at any stage in the production, design, delivery, and use of another company's products and services. Suppliers include businesses, such as distributors, dealers, warranty repair services, transportation contractors, and franchises, and service suppliers, such as health care, training, and education. Internal suppliers provide materials or services to internal customers.

Supplier audits Reviews that are planned and carried out to verify the adequacy and effectiveness of a supplier's quality program, drive improvement, and increase value.

Supplier certification Process of evaluating the performance of a supplier with the intent of authorizing the supplier to self-certify shipments if such authorization is justified.

Supplier credit Credit provided by the supplier to itself to fund its operations.

Supplier development The process providing on-site help, training, or other improvement measures to suppliers.

Supplier evaluation and selection The process of determining if a given supplier is capable of meeting a purchasing organization's needs. This is typically carried out by an on-site visit to the supplier's facility.

Supplier identification The process of searching multiple sources (Internet, catalogs, interviews, trade shows, and so on) to find potential suppliers to meet a need.

Supplier integration The process of involving suppliers in new product development and ongoing production processes.

Supplier management The ongoing coordination of all suppliers being used. This is a broad term that often includes supplier identification, evaluation, performance measurement, and development.

Supplier network A group of organizations that provide inputs, either directly or indirectly, to the focal firm.

Supplier partnering A just-in-time method that views suppliers as a valuable contributor to the overall success of the business.

Supplier performance measurement The ongoing process of tracking cost, quality, delivery, and service performance of suppliers, as well as updating a database of all supplier's performance over time.

Supplier quality assurance Confidence that a supplier's product or service will fulfill its customers' needs. This confidence is achieved by creating a relationship between the customer and supplier that ensures the product will be fit for use with minimal corrective action and inspection. According to J. M. Juran, there are nine primary activities needed: 1) define product and program quality requirements, 2) evaluate alternative suppliers, 3) select suppliers, 4) conduct joint quality planning, 5) cooperate with the supplier during the execution of the contract, 6) obtain proof of conformance to requirements, 7) certify qualified suppliers, 8) conduct quality improvement programs as required, and 9) create and use supplier quality ratings.

Supplier selection strategy and criteria Selection of new suppliers is based on the type and uniqueness of the product or service to be purchased, and the total cost. Suppliers of commodity-type items and basic supplies may be selected from directories and catalogs. For more sophisticated products and services stringent evaluation criteria may be established.

Supply Total quantity offered for sale.

Supply chain 1: The activities associated with the flow and transformation of goods from the raw materials stage (extraction), through to the end user, as well as the associated information flows. Material and information flows both up and down the supply chain. The supply chain includes systems management, manufacturing and assembly, sourcing and procurement, production scheduling, order processing, inventory management, warehousing, and customer service. **2:** Series of processes and/or organizations that are involved in producing and delivering a product to the final user. **3:** A set of institutions that moves goods from the point of production to the point of consumption.

Supply Chain Management (SCM) 1: The coordination of purchasing, manufacturing, shipping, and billing operations, often supported by an enterprise resource planning system. **2:** The integration of the activities in the supply chain through improved supply chain relationships, information systems, and other means to achieve a sustainable competitive advantage. The supply chain includes the management of information systems, sourcing and procurement, production scheduling, order processing, inventory management, warehousing, customer service, and aftermarket disposition of packaging and materials. **3:** Results where a series of value-adding activities connect a company's supply side with its demand side. **4:** Technique for linking a manufacturer's operations with those of all of its strategic suppliers and its key intermediaries and customers to enhance efficiency and effectiveness; managing logistical systems to achieve close cooperation and comprehensive interorganizational management so as to integrate the logistical operations of different firms in the marketing channel.

Supply curve Relation between price and the quantity supplied, holding all else constant.

Supply function Relation between supply and all factors influencing its level.

Supply side market failure Results when the individual activities of a supplier inadvertently lead to destructive effects on the overall supply.

Support processes Will provide infrastructure for core processes.

Support systems Starting with top-management commitment and visible involvement, support systems are a cascading series of interrelated practices or actions aimed at building and sustaining support for continuous quality improvement. Such practices/actions may include: mission statement, transformation of company culture, policies, employment practices, compensation, recognition and rewards, employee involvement, rules and procedures, quality-level agreements, training, empowerment, methods and tools for improving quality, tracking-measuring-evaluating-reporting systems, and so on.

Support The maintenance and provision for user help on an information system.

Surfers Computer users who have dial-up or faster access to the Internet and who visit Web sites.

Surplus Ecess of net assets over stated capital.

Surplus Excess supply.

Surveillance 1: Continual monitoring of a process. **2:** Investigation technique that relies on the senses, especially hearing and seeing.

Surveillance audit Regular audits conducted by registrars to confirm that a company registered to the ISO 9001 standard still complies; usually conducted on a six-month or one-year basis.

Survey Examination for some specific purpose; to inspect or consider carefully; to review in detail (survey implies the inclusion of matters not covered by agreed-upon criteria). Also, a structured series of questions designed to elicit a predetermined range of responses covering a preselected area of interest. May be administered orally by a survey-taker, by paper and pencil, or by computer. Responses are tabulated and analyzed to surface significant areas for change.

Survey feedback A type of OD intervention in which questionnaires on organizational climate and other factors are distributed among employees and the results reported back to them by a change agent.

Survey techniques Interview or mailed questionnaire approach to forecasting.

Sustainable competitive advantage Competitive edge that cannot be easily or quickly copied by competitors in the short run.

Sustainable growth The rate of sales growth that is compatible with a firm's established financial policies including asset turnover, net profit margin, dividend payout, and debt to equity ratio and assumes that new equity is derived only through retained earnings, not new common stock.

Swap Exchange of securities between two parties, often with the assistance of an intermediary known as a swap dealer. In its simplest form, a company engaging in a swap exchanges a fixed interest rate obligation for one that has a variable, or floating interest rate.

Swap strategies *See for example:* Maturity extension swap and Yield spread swap.

Sweatshops Businesses characterized by child labor, low pay, poor working conditions, worker abuse, and health and safety violations.

Sweep accounts Special accounts whereby excess funds are automatically or at the cash manager's request transferred ("swept") from the demand deposit account into an interest-bearing overnight investment.

SWIFT The Society of Worldwide Interbank Financial Telecommunications, a communication network for relaying payment instructions for international transactions. It boasts roughly 1,500 member banks in 68 counties, and almost 3,000 banks are connected to the network.

Switching costs Expenses that are incurred when a customer stops buying a product or service from one business and starts buying it from another.

Switching structures An organization creates an organic structure when such a structure is needed for the initiation of new ideas.

Switching techniques Data communications mechanisms that allow messages to be routed through a variety of paths; if one is busy, another can be used.

SWOT analysis Assessment of an organization's key strengths, weaknesses, opportunities, and threats. It considers factors such as the organization's industry, the competitive position, functional areas, and management.

Symbol Something that represents another thing.

Symmetric encryption Encryption technology in which both the sender and recipient of a message use the same key for encryption and decryption.

Symmetric information The situation in which investors and managers have identical information about the firm's prospects.

Symptom Indication of a problem or opportunity.

Symptoms of structural deficiency Signs of the organizational structure being out of alignment, including delayed or poor-quality decision making, failure to respond innovatively to environmental changes, and too much conflict.

Synchronized cash flows A situation in which cash inflows coincide with cash outflows, thereby permitting a firm to hold low transactions balances.

Synchronized production A manufacturing management philosophy that includes a consistent set of principles, procedures, and techniques where every action is evaluated in terms of the global goal of the system. Both kanban, which is a part of the JIT philosophy, and drum-buffer-rope, which is a part of the theory of constraints philosophy, represent synchronized production control approaches. *Syn:* synchronous manufacturing. *See:* Drum-buffer-rope, Kanban, Synchronous scheduling.

Syndicate Sometimes a group of investment banks works together on the marketing and shares the risk involved with bringing a new issue to market, which may or may not be acceptable at the predetermined price. This grouping is called a *syndicate*.

Syndicated Eurocredit loans Loans provided by a group (or syndicate) of banks in the Eurocredit market.

Synergy From Greek "to work together." The attainment of output, when two factors work together, that is greater or better than the sum of their products when they work separately.

Syntax error A program error that is equivalent to a typo in regular written language.

Synthetic composite An artificial security which is devised to mirror the portfolio's average coupon interest rate, maturity, and risk rating.

System 1: A set of interrelated parts that function as a whole to achieve a common purpose. **2:** Network of connecting processes that work together to accomplish the aim of the system. **3:** A set of interacting elements that acquires inputs from the environment, transforms them, and discharges outputs to the external environment.

System clock Special circuitry within the computer control unit that synchronizes all tasks.

System of authorizations A system of limits on who can and cannot perform certain functions.

System of Profound Knowledge (SoPK) *See:* Profound knowledge.

System requirements The functions that an information system is expected to fulfill and the features through which it will perform its tasks.

System software Software that executes routine tasks. System software includes operating systems, language translators, and communications software. Also called support software.

Systematic risk The degree of sensitivity of the company's stock returns to market-wide returns.

Systems analysis The early steps in the systems development process, to define the requirements of the proposed system and determine its feasibility.

Systems approach to management Management theory that views the organization as a unified, purposeful combination of interrelated parts; managers must look at the organization as a whole and understand that activity in one part of the organization affects all parts of the organization. Also known as *systems thinking*.

Systems concept of logistics 1: A concept of logistics based on the notion that materials-flow activities are so complex that they can be considered only in the context of their interaction. **2:** Viewing all components of a logistical system together and understanding the relationships among them.

Systems design The evaluation of alternative solutions to a business problem and the specification of hardware, software, and communications technology for the selection solution.

Systems Development Led by Users (SDLU) An approach to systems development that reflects the view that users, not information systems professionals, are responsible for their information systems.

Systems Development Life Cycle (SDLC) The oldest method of developing an information system, consisting of several phases of analysis and design, which must be followed sequentially.

Systems integration Interfacing several information systems.

Systems integrator An individual or an organization that specializes in integrating several different hardware items and software applications for business operations. Often, the system integrator integrates one new information system into the existing information resources of the business.

Systems theory An extension of the humanistic perspective that describes organizations as open systems that are characterized by entropy, synergy, and subsystem interdependence.

Systems thinking The approach of thinking of an organization in terms of its suborganizations or systems; a framework for problem solving and decision making.

T

T account A form of account resembling the letter T, showing debits on the left and credits on the right.

T test Method for testing hypotheses about the population mean; the t statistic measures the deviation between the sample and population means, in terms of the number of standard errors.

Table List of economic data.

Tablet computer A full-power personal computer in the form of a thick writing tablet.

Tacit knowledge 1: Knowledge that is implied by or inferred from actions or statements. **2:** Unarticulated heuristics and assumptions used by any individual or organization.

Tactical activities The short-term activities associated with the day-to-day management. Over time, tactical activities serve to eventually support the organization's long-term strategic goals.

Tactical goals Goals that define the outcomes that major divisions and departments must achieve in order for the organization to reach its overall goals.

Tactical managers Individuals who receive general directions and goals from their superiors and, within those guidelines, make decisions for their subordinates; also called middle managers.

Tactical objectives Guided by the enterprise's strategic objectives, they identify the key result areas in which specific performance is essential for the success of the enterprise, and aim to attain internal efficiency.

Tactical plans Short-term plans, usually of one- to two-year duration, that describe actions the organization will take to meet its strategic business plan.

Tactics Strategies and processes that help an organization meet its objectives.

Tactics for enhancing collaboration Techniques such as integration devices, confrontation and negotiation, intergroup consultation, member rotation, and shared mission and superordinate goals that enable groups to overcome differences and work together.

Tactics for increasing power Tactics that include entering areas of high uncertainty, creating dependencies, providing resources, and satisfying strategic contingencies.

Taguchi loss function Product characteristics deviate from the normal aim and losses increase according to a parabolic function; merely attempting to produce a product within specifications doesn't prevent loss (loss is that inflicted on society after shipment of a product).

Taguchi methods The American Supplier Institute's trademarked term for the quality engineering methodology developed by Genichi Taguchi. In this engineering approach to quality control, Taguchi calls for off-line quality control, on-line quality control, and a system of experimental design to improve quality and reduce costs.

Tailing Secretly following a fraud suspect in an attempt to gain additional information; another name for moving surveillance.

Takeover An action whereby a person or group succeeds in ousting a firm's management and taking control of the company.

Takt time Available production time divided by the rate of customer demand. Operating to takt time sets the production pace to customer demand.

Tall structure A management structure characterized by an overall narrow span of management and a relatively large number of hierarchical levels.

Tally sheet Another term for *checksheet*.

Tampering Action taken to compensate for variation within the control limits of a stable system. Tampering increases rather than decreases variation, as evidenced in the funnel experiment.

Tangent A straight line that touches a curve at only one point.

Target (optimal) capital structure The combination (percentages) of debt, preferred stock, and common equity that will maximize the price of the firm's stock.

Target (minimum) cash balance The minimum cash balance a firm desires to maintain in order to conduct business.

Target cost concept A concept used to design and manufacture a product at a cost that will deliver a target profit for a given market-determined price.

Target costing A costing method that sets cost targets for new products based on market price.

Target market The group or groups of customers that the retailer is seeking to serve.

Target marketing Promoting products and services to the people who are most likely to purchase them.

Target markets Market segments whose needs and demands a company seeks to serve and satisfy.

Target return objective A pricing objective that states a specific level of profit, such as percentage of sales or return on capital invested, as an objective.

Target zones Implicit boundaries established by central banks on exchange rates.

Targeting Offering the firm's most profitable customers special deals and incentives.

Tariffs Duties or taxes on imported goods and services, instituted by governments as a means to raise revenue and as barriers to trade.

Tariffs and quotas Often employed by governments to restrict trade or reduce competition. Tariffs are a form of tax imposed on incoming goods, and quotas specify the number of foreign units that can be imported.

Task 1: A distinct, identifiable work activity composed of motions. **2:** A narrowly defined piece of work assigned to a person.

Task and objective method A technique for budgeting in which the retailer establishes its advertising objectives and then determines the advertising tasks that need to be performed to achieve those objectives.

Task environment Sectors with which the organization interacts directly and that have a direct effect on the organization's ability to achieve its goals.

Task force A temporary team or committee formed to solve a specific short-term problem involving several departments.

Task identity The extent to which the job includes a "whole" identifiable unit of work that is carried out from start to finish and that results in a visible outcome.

Task significance The impact the job has on other people.

Task specialist role A role in which the individual devotes personal time and energy to helping the team accomplish its task.

Tax-advantaged instruments Those on which part or all of the income is exempted from taxation, or where the tax is deferred.

Tax anticipation notes Short-term debt instruments which provide working capital financing for states and localities as they await anticipated revenues from tax collections.

Tax burden Economic cost of tax.

Tax courts Federal courts that hear only tax cases.

Tax credit The reduction of a tax liability by an amount equal to the amount of the tax credit.

Tax equalization Reimbursement by the company when an employee in an overseas assignment pays taxes at a higher rate than if he or she were at home.

Tax equalization plan Compensation plan used to protect expatriates from negative tax consequences.

Tax-exempt commercial paper States and localities also issue some of these items. The risks are very similar to those of anticipation notes.

Tax holiday The period of time during which a foreign investor is exempted from taxes.

Tax incidence Point of tax collection.

Tax loss carryback and carryover Losses that can be carried backward or forward in time to offset taxable income in a given year.

Tax policy 1: A means by which countries may control foreign investors. **2:** Fines and penalties that limit undesirable performance.

Taxable-equivalent yield The yield of a tax-exempt security on an after-tax basis, which facilitates comparison with the yield of taxable securities. The taxable-equivalent yield is the nominal (stated) yield divided by (1 − corporation's marginal tax rate).

Taxable income **1:** Gross income minus exemptions and allowable deductions as set forth in the tax code. **2:** The base on which the amount of income tax is determined.

Taxable instruments Security types that are not given preferential tax treatment, including commercial paper, domestic and Eurodollar certificates of deposit, banker's acceptances, repurchase agreements, and money market mutual funds invested in these instruments.

TCP/IP (Transmission Control Protocol/Internet Protocol) A packet-switching protocol that is actually a set of related protocols that can guarantee packets are delivered in the correct order and can handle differences in transmission and reception rates.

Teaching services Services that are provided in the areas of training and motivating as well as in teaching of operational, managerial, and theoretical issues.

Team **1:** Set of two or more people who are equally accountable for the accomplishment of a purpose and specific performance goals; it is also defined as a small number of people with complimentary skills who are committed to a common purpose. **2:** Many organizations manage themselves through empowered self-managed teams.

Team-based structure **1:** Describes an organizational structure in which team members are organized around performing a specific function of the business, such as handling customer complaints or assembling an engine. **2:** Structure in which the entire organization is made up of teams that coordinate their work and work directly with customers to accomplish the organization's goals.

Team building **1:** A process that enhances the cohesiveness of a department or group by helping members learn how to organize their work and assume responsibility for it. **2:** A type of OD intervention that enhances the cohesiveness of departments by helping members learn to function as a team. **3:** Activities that promote the idea that people who work together can work together as a team.

Team building/development Process of transforming a group of people into a team and developing the team to achieve its purpose.

Team cohesiveness The extent to which team members are attracted to the team and motivated to remain in it.

Team dynamics Interactions which occur among team members under different conditions.

Team facilitation Deals with both the role of the facilitator on the team and the techniques and tools for facilitating the team.

Team interview Interview in which applicants are interviewed by the team members with whom they will work.

Team performance evaluation, rewards, and recognition Special metrics are needed to evaluate the work of a team (to avoid focus on any individual on the team) and as a basis for rewards and recognition for team achievements.

Team structure Type of organization based on teams.

Teams Permanent task forces often used in conjunction with a full-time integrator.

Technical champion A person who generates or adopts and develops an idea for a technological innovation and is devoted to it, even to the extent of risking position or prestige; also called product champion.

Technical complexity The extent of mechanization in the manufacturing process.

Technical core The heart of the organization's production of its product or service.

Technical feasibility study An evaluation of whether the components of a proposed information system exist or can be developed with available tools.

Technical forecasting Development of forecasts using historical prices or trends.

Technical skill The understanding of and proficiency in the performance of specific tasks.

Technology The knowledge, tools, techniques, and activities used to transform the organization's inputs into outputs.

Technology changes Changes in an organization's production process, including its knowledge and skills base, that enable distinctive competence.

Technology transfer The transfer of systematic knowledge for the manufacture of a product, the application of a process, or the rendering of a service.

Telecommunications Communications over a long distance, as opposed to communication within a computer, or between adjacent hardware pieces.

Telecommunications manager The individual who is responsible for the acquisition, implementation, management, maintenance, and troubleshooting of computer networks throughout the organization.

Telecommuting The phenomenon of working from home or another remote location with the help of information technology, rather than performing the same tasks in the office.

Teleconferencing The ability to hold conferences with a number of other people who are all geographically remote from one another, via telecommunications devices.

Temporal method A currency translation method in which translation is viewed as a restatement of the financial statements. The foreign currency amounts are translated at the exchange rates in effect at the dates when those items were measured in the foreign currency.

Temporary accounts Revenue, expense, or income summary accounts that are periodically closed; nominal accounts.

Temporary current assets Current assets that fluctuate with seasonal or cyclical variations in a firm's business. The accumulation of inventory in anticipation of the peak selling season and the resulting receivables generated by the increased sales. This bulge then subsides as the firm passes through its peak selling season.

Temporary differences Differences between income before income tax and taxable income created by items that are recognized in one period for income statement purposes and in another period for tax purposes. Such differences reverse, or turn around, in later years.

Temporary investments Investments in securities that can be readily sold when cash is needed.

Tenancy in partnership Type of joint ownership that determines partners' rights in specific partnership property.

Tender offer General invitation to all of the shareholders of a target company to tender their shares for sale at a specified price.

Tenor Time period of drafts.

"Tentative U.S. tax" The calculation of U.S. taxes on foreign source incomes to estimate U.S. tax payments.

Term loan A loan made with an initial maturity of more than one year.

Term repos Repurchase agreement that is arranged with a maturity of several days to several weeks, making them well-suited for the investor having an investment horizon longer than one day.

Term spread The component of a security's return that is necessary to induce investors to bear risks linked to maturity.

Term structure of interest rates The relationship between yields and maturities of securities.

Terminal cash flow The *net* cash flow that occurs at the end of the life of a project, including the cash flows associated with 1) the final disposal of the project and 2) returning the firm's operations to where they were before the project was accepted.

Terminal value The future value of a cash flow stream.

Terminal warehouse agreement Inventories pledged as collateral are moved to a public warehouse that is physically separated from the borrower's premises.

Terms of credit The payment conditions offered to credit customers; the terms include the length of the credit period and any cash discounts offered.

Territorial approach A national tax system that only taxes domestic income.

Territorial restrictions Attempts by the supplier, usually a manufacturer, to limit the geographic area in which a retailer may resell its merchandise.

Terrorism Illegal and violent acts toward property and people.

Tertiary-line injury Injury to purchasers from other secondary-line sellers.

Test group Subsample of data used to generate a forecast model.

Tests of partnership existence The formation of a partnership requires all of the following: 1) association, 2) business for profit, and 3) co-ownership.

Testimonial evidence Evidence based on querying techniques, such as interviewing, interrogation, and honesty testing.

Theft investigation methods Investigation methods that focus on the actual transfer of assets from the victim to the perpetrator; helps determine how the theft was committed and often includes methods such as surveillance and covert operations, invigilation, and the obtaining of physical evidence.

Thematic maps Maps that visual techniques such as colors, shading, and lines to display cultural characteristics of the physical space.

Theocracy A legal perspective based on religious practices and interpretations.

Theoretical capacity The maximum output capability, allowing no adjustments for preventive maintenance, unplanned downtime, shutdown, and so on.

Theoretical standards Standards that represent levels of performance that can be achieved only under perfect operating conditions.

Theory of comparative advantage Each country should produce only those goods and services that it can produce with relative efficiency.

Theory of Constraints (TOC) 1: A management philosophy developed by Dr. Eliyahu M. Goldratt that can be viewed as three separate but interrelated areas—logistics, performance measurement, and logical thinking. Logistics include drum-buffer-rope scheduling, buffer management, and VAT analysis. Performance measurement includes throughput, inventory and operating expense, and the five focusing steps. Thinking process tools are important in identifying the root problem (current reality tree), identifying and expanding win-win solutions (evaporating cloud and future reality tree), and developing implementation plans (prerequisite tree and transition tree). *Syn:* constraint theory. **2:** A manufacturing strategy that attempts to remove the influence of bottlenecks (constraints) on a process.

Theory of dual entitlement Consumers believe there are terms in a transaction to which both consumers and sellers are "entitled" over time. Cost-driven price increases are believed to be fair because they allow sellers to maintain their profit entitlement. Demand-driven price increases are not believed to be fair, however, since they allow sellers to increase per-unit profit, while buyers receive nothing in return.

Theory of knowledge Belief that management is about prediction, and people learn not only from experience but also from theory. When people study a process and develop a theory, they can compare their predictions with their observations; profound learning results.

Theory T and Theory T+ Complementary theories based on Southeast Asian assumptions that work is a necessity but not a goal itself, people should find their rightful place in peace and harmony with their environment; absolute objectives exist only with God; in the world, persons in authority positions represent God, so their objectives should be followed; and people behave as members of a family and/or group, and those who do not are rejected by society.

Theory X and theory Y Theory developed by Douglas McGregor that maintains that there are two contrasting assumptions about people, each of which is based on the manager's view of human nature. Theory X managers take a negative view and assume that most employees do not like work and try to avoid it. Theory Y managers take a positive view and believe that employees want to work, will seek and accept responsibility, and can offer creative solutions to organizational problems.

Theory Z Coined by William G. Ouchi, refers to a Japanese style of management that is characterized by long-term employment, slow promotions, considerable job rotation, consensus-style decision making, and concern for the employee as a whole.

Thin capitalization The set of taxation issues from a host government's perspective, arising from the perceived imbalance between debt capital and equity capital when a foreign investor is financing a business operation in the country.

Thin client A computer without an external storage device.

Thin market One with little participation by buyers and/or sellers.

Third-country national 1: A citizen of one country, working in a second country, and employed by an organization headquartered in a third country. **2:** A resident of a country other than the home-country or host-country assigned to manage a firm's foreign subsidiary.

Third-Generation Languages (3GLs) Higher-level programming languages that let the programmer focus on a problem without being concerned with how the hardware will execute the program; but they require the programmer to detail a logical procedure to solve the problem.

Three-parameter (Winters) exponential smoothing Method for forecasting seasonally adjusted growth.

Third-party information vendor An information service that receives deposit information from field offices and transmits that information to the appropriate concentration banks and to corporate headquarters.

Three-sixty-degree (360°) feedback process Evaluation method that provides feedback from the perspectives of self, peers, direct reports, superior, customers, and suppliers.

GLOSSARY

Throughput 1: The total volume of production through a facility (machine, work center, department, plant, or network of plants). **2:** In the theory of constraints, the rate at which the system (firm) generates money through sales. Throughput is a separate concept from output.

Throughput time Total time required (processing + queue) from concept to launch or from order received to delivery, or raw materials received to delivery to customer.

Tiered pricing The Fed has proposed this method where it reduces its charges to banks submitting large volumes of checks. This move to preserve its market share is seen as contradictory to the privatization initiative that the Fed officially espouses.

Time-based competition A strategy of competition based on the ability to deliver products and services faster than competitors.

Time bomb Rogue code that is installed in a computer system and starts destroying data files and applications at a preset time.

Time draft Involves a credit element, because the payment obligation agreed to by the drawee is designated as due at a specified future date. Time drafts are usually dated after verification of a shipment of goods.

Time equals money The perception of people in some cultures that time is a commodity and an asset and high importance is placed on it.

Time estimate *See:* Duration estimate.

Times-Interest-Earned (TIE) ratio A ratio that measures the firm's ability to meet its annual interest obligations; calculated by dividing earnings before interest and taxes by interest charges.

Time preferences for consumption The preferences of consumers for current consumption as opposed to saving for future consumption.

Time series A set of observations measured at successive points in time or over successive periods of time.

Time series models Models that examine series of historical data; sometimes used as a means of technical forecasting, by examining moving averages.

Time series regression A naive modeling approach in the sense that the mere passage of time generally does not cause the variable to change in value.

Time span The period of time that a set of data covers.

Time tickets The form on which the amount of time spent by each employee and the labor cost incurred for each individual job, or for factory overhead, are recorded.

Time to market The time between generating an idea for a product and completing a prototype that can be mass-manufactured. Also called *engineering lead time*.

Time value of money concept The concept that money invested today will earn income.

Time, place, and possession utilities Conditions that enable consumers and business users to have products available for use when and where they want them and to actually take possession of them.

Time-series analysis Analysis of relationships between two or more variables over periods of time.

Time-series techniques Forecasting methods which predict future movements in the forecast variable based on patterns revealed in historical movements of that same variable.

TL 9000 Series of standards pertaining to the telecommunications industry; ISO 9001 is embedded in the standard.

Tobin's q ratio A ratio calculated as the market value of the firm divided by the replacement cost of tangible assets.

Token passing A telecommunications method whereby a computer that needs to send a message captures a "token," consisting of a small group of bytes, and releases the token with the message.

Tolerance design (Taguchi) Provides a rational grade limit for components of a system; determines which parts and processes need to be modified and to what degree it is necessary to increase their control capacity; a method for rationally determining tolerances.

Tolerance for ambiguity The psychological characteristic that allows a person to be untroubled by disorder and uncertainty.

Tolerance Variability of a parameter permitted and tolerated above or below a nominal value.

Top-down budgeting A budgeting process in which middle and lower-level managers set departmental budget targets in accordance with overall company revenues and expenditures specified by top management.

Top-down planning Planning that begins at the top level of an organization and focuses on clear objectives for the entire organization; also called *holistic planning*.

Top-management commitment Participation of the highest-level officials in their organization's quality improvement efforts. Their participation includes establishing and serving on a quality committee, establishing quality policies and goals, deploying those goals to lower levels of the organization, providing the resources and training that the lower levels need to achieve the goals, participating in quality improvement teams, reviewing progress organization-wide, recognizing those who have performed well, and revising the current reward system to reflect the importance of achieving the quality goals. Commitment is top management's visible, personal involvement as seen by others in the organization.

Top manager A manager who is at the top of the organizational hierarchy and is responsible for the entire organization.

Topology The physical layout of a network.

Tort system A body of law that provides a means for victims of accidents and injury to receive just compensation for their loss.

Torts Under the doctrine of *respondeat superior,* a corporation is liable for torts committed by its employees within the course of their employment.

Total asset turnover Sales revenue divided by the book value of total assets.

Total assets Current assets plus noncurrent assets plus goodwill.

Total liabilities Current liabilities plus long-term liabilities.

Total assets turnover ratio The ratio calculated by dividing sales by total assets.

Total Budgeted Cost (TBC) The portion of the entire project budget that is allocated to complete all of the activities and work associated with a particular work package.

Total cost approach Calculating the cost of a logistical system by addressing all of the costs of logistics together rather than individual costs taken separately, so as to minimize the total cost of logistics.

Total cost concept 1: A concept used in applying the cost-plus approach to product pricing in which all the costs of manufacturing the product plus the selling and administrative expenses are included in the cost amount to which the markup is added. **2:** A decision concept that uses cost as a basis for measurement in order to evaluate and optimize logistical activities.

Total cost of ownership Considers not only the purchase price but also an array of other factors such as complete life cycle.

Total factor productivity A measure of the productivity of a department, plant, strategic business unit, firm, and so on, that combines the individual productivities of all its resources including labor, capital, energy, material, and equipment. These individual factor productivities are often combined by weighting each according to its monetary value and then adding them. For example, if material accounts for 40 percent of the total cost of sales and labor 10 percent of the total cost of sales, and so on, total factor productivity = .4 (material productivity) + .1 (labor productivity) + and so on.

Total Productive Maintenance (TPM) Aimed at reducing and eventually eliminating equipment failure, setup and adjustment, minor stops, reduced speed, product rework, and scrap. The five Ss are relevant here. It is operator-oriented maintenance with the involvement of all qualified employees in all maintenance activities.

Total Quality Management (TQM) 1: Term initially coined by the Naval Air Systems Command to describe its management approach to quality improvement. Total quality management (TQM) has taken on many meanings. Simply put, TQM is a management approach to long-term success through customer satisfaction. TQM is based on the participation of all members of an organization in improving processes, products, services, and the culture they work in. TQM benefits all organization members and society. The methods for implementing this approach are found in the teachings of such quality leaders as Philip B. Crosby, W. Edwards Deming, Armand V. Feigenbaum, Kaoru Ishikawa, J. M. Juran, and others. Four significant elements of TQM are employee involvement, focus on the customer, benchmarking, and continuous improvement. **2:** An organizational approach in which workers, not managers, are handed the responsibility for achieving standards of quality.

Total Slack (TS) Float. If it's a positive value, it's the amount of time that the activities on a particular path can be delayed without jeopardizing completion of the project by its required completion time. If it's a negative value, it's the amount of time that the activities on a particular path must be accelerated in order to complete the project by its required completion time.

Touch screen A computer monitor that serves both as input and output device. The user touches the areas of a certain menu item to select options, and the screen senses the selection at the point of the touch.

Tourism The economic benefit of money spent in a country or region by travelers from outside the area.

Traceability Ability to trace the history, application, or location of an item or activity and like items or activities by means of recorded identification.

Track pad A device used for clicking, logging, and dragging displayed information; the cursor is controlled by moving one's finger along a touch-sensitive pad.

Trackball A device similar to a mouse, used for clicking, locking, and dragging displayed information; in this case, the ball moves within the device rather than over a surface.

Tracking The capability of a shipper to track goods at any point during the shipment.

Tradable emissions permits Permits that give firms the property right to pollute and then sell that right to others.

Trade acceptance Draft that allows the buyer to obtain merchandise prior to paying for it.

Trade allowances (trade deals) Offered to retailers simply for purchasing the manufacturer's brand or for performing activities in support of the manufacturer's brand.

Trade barriers Imposed by nations to limit or restrict competition.

Trade creation A benefit of economic integration; the benefit to a particular country when a group of countries trade a product freely among themselves but maintain common barriers to trade with nonmembers.

Trade credit Permission to delay payment which arises when goods are sold under delayed payment terms.

Trade discount 1: Percent reduction to quoted price offered to all customers, and not linked to early payment. This discount is typically offered to all customers, and the seller expects all customers to pay at the discounted price within the agreed-upon period. One example is a quantity discount, a price break given for a large purchase. **2:** Special discounts from published list prices offered by sellers to certain classes of buyers. **3:** Also referred to as a functional discount and is a form of compensation that the buyer may receive for performing certain wholesaling or retailing services for the manufacturer.

Trade diversion A cost of economic integration; the cost to a particular country when a group of countries trade a product freely among themselves but maintain common barriers to trade with nonmembers.

Trade draft A withdrawal document drawn against a company.

Trade name Any name used to identify a business, vocation, or occupation.

Trade-in allowance The amount a seller grants a buyer for a fixed asset that is traded in for a similar asset.

Tradeoff analysis Trading one variable against another variable such as time versus cost. Used in problem-solving and decision-making situations.

Trade-off concept A decision concept that recognizes linkages within the decision system.

Trade policy measures Mechanisms used to influence and alter trade relationships.

Trade promotion authority The right to negotiate, accept, or reject trade treaties and agreements with minimal amendments by other parties.

Trademark A name, term, or symbol used to identify a business and its products.

Traders Market participants which try to profit on anticipated interest rate or currency movements. They hold securities not as intermediaries, but as investors attempting to gain profits for their company's own account.

Trading area The geographic area from which a retailer, or group of retailers, or community draws its customers.

Trading blocs 1: Formed by agreements among countries to establish links through movement of goods, services, capital, and labor across borders. **2:** Free trade zones created by member countries through mutual agreements.

Trading company Marketing intermediary that undertakes exporting, importing, countertrading, investing, and manufacturing.

Trading down Occurs when a retailer uses price lining, and a customer initially exposed to higher-priced lines expresses the desire to purchase a lower-priced line.

Trading security A debt or equity security that management intends to actively trade for profit.

Trading up Occurs when a retailer uses price lining and a salesperson moves a customer from a lower-priced line to a higher one.

Traditional authority Authority based in the belief in traditions and the legitimacy of the status of people exercising authority through those traditions.

Traditional organizations Those organizations not driven by customers and quality policies. Also refers to organizations managed primarily through functional units.

Tragedy of the commons Name given to the process in which individuals, pursuing their own self interest, overuse a common good to such an extent that the common good is destroyed.

Training Skills that employees need to learn in order to perform or improve the performances of their current job or tasks, or the process of providing those skills.

Training evaluation Techniques and tools used and the process of evaluating the effectiveness of training.

Training needs assessment Techniques and tools used and the process of determining an organization's training needs.

Traits Distinguishing personal characteristics, such as intelligence, values, and appearance.

Tramp service Ocean shipping via irregular routes, scheduled only on demand.

Transaction A business event. In an IS context, the record of a business event.

Transaction approach An approach to bank selecting in which there is a decoupling or "unbundling" of services, meaning the company will not necessarily borrow from the bank(s) it utilizes for cash management services. Increasingly prevalent, in this approach the treasurer selects the bank(s) that can best provide a specific service or can provide it at the best price.

Transaction-Based Information System (TBIS) Captures and analyzes all of the transactions between a company and its customers.

Transaction efficiency Designing marketing channels to minimize the number of contacts between producers and consumers.

Transaction exposure 1: Degree to which the value of future cash transactions can be affected by exchange rate fluctuations. **2:** The potential for losses or gains when a firm is engaged in a transaction denominated in a foreign currency.

Transaction motive Inventory held in relation to the level of operating activity expected by the firm.

Transaction Processing System (TPS) A type of operations information system that records and processes data resulting from routine business transactions such as sales, purchases, and payroll.

Transaction risk exposure A condition that is caused by the changes in the exchange rate between the transaction date and the settlement date.

Transaction services Services provided to customers when they are in the store shopping and transacting business.

Transaction sets A set of standards for EDI information flows developed by the ANSI X12 committee to facilitate the electronic communication between trading patterns.

Transactional leader A leader who clarifies subordinates' role and task requirements, initiates structure, provides rewards, and displays consideration for subordinates.

Transactional leadership Style of leading whereby the leader sees the work as being done through clear definitions of tasks and responsibilities and the provision of resources as needed.

Transactions balance A cash balance necessary for day-to-day operations; the balance associated with routine payments and collections.

Transceiver A communications device that can receive messages, amplify them, and retransmit them to their destination. Transceivers are used when the distance is long, and the signal may weaken on its way to the destination.

Transfer agent The financial institution that takes care of updating the records for the corporation's stock and registered bonds.

Transfer items Checks drawn on banks that do not participate in a bank's local clearing house or exchange; these are sometimes called "out-of-town" checks.

Transfer price The price one segment of a company charges another segment of the same company for the transfer of a good or a service.

Transfer pricing Policy for pricing goods sent by either the parent or a subsidiary to a subsidiary of an MNC.

Transfer risk The danger of having one's ability to transfer profits or products in and out of a country inhibited by governmental rules and regulations.

Transferable letter of credit Document that allows the first beneficiary on a standby letter of credit to transfer all or part of the original letter of credit to a third party.

Transformational leader A leader distinguished by a special ability to bring about innovation and change.

Transformational leadership Style of leading whereby the leader articulates the vision and values necessary for the organization to succeed.

Transformative technological innovations Replace traditional technologies (in farming, a tractor replaces the plow).

Transient customer An individual who is dissatisfied with the level of customer service offered at a store or stores and is seeking an alternative store with the level of customer service that he or she thinks is appropriate.

Transit items Checks drawn on banks that do not participate in a deposit bank's local clearinghouse or exchange.

Transit routing number Also called the FRD/ABA (Federal Reserve District/American Banker's Association) bank ID number, a number imprinted on checks which identifies the payee's bank. This number is used by the deposit bank to determine how best to clear the check.

Transit time The period between departure and arrival of a carrier.

Transition stay bonus Extra payment for employees whose jobs are being eliminated, thereby motivating them to remain with the organization for a period of time.

Transition tree Technique used in applying Goldratt's Theory of Constraints.

Translation exposure Degree to which a firm's consolidated financial statements are exposed to fluctuations in exchange rates.

Transmission rate The speed at which data are communicated over a channel.

Transnational Corporation (TNC) The term favored by the United Nations as an alternative to the term multinational corporation.

Transnational strategy A strategy that combines global coordination to attain efficiency with flexibility to meet specific needs in various countries. *See:* Global strategy.

Transparency A desired environment for the use of applications and telecommunication whereby the user is not exposed to the inner workings of the software or to the fact that information may actually come from different sources.

Transport Control Procedure (TCP) A protocol that includes rules that computers on a network use to establish and break connections.

Transposition The erroneous arrangement of digits in a number, such as writing $542 as $524.

Trash investigation Searching through a person's trash for possible evidence in an investigation.

Treadway Commission National Commission on Fraudulent Financial Reporting that made recommendations on financial statement fraud and other matters in 1987.

Treasury management workstation A computer system that provides a means for the treasury manager to efficiently manage cash concentration, account balances at banks, cash transfers, and the short-term investment and borrowing portfolio. These are sold by banks and some specialized vendors.

Treasury stock A corporation's issued stock that has been reacquired.

Treble damages Three times actual loss.

Tree A network topology in which each computer (or other communications device) is connected to several other computers in a shape that resembles the breaches of a tree.

Tree diagram Management and planning tool that shows the complete range of subtasks required to achieve an objective. A problem-solving method can be identified from this analysis.

Trend 1: Consecutive points that show a nonrandom pattern. **2:** The long-run shift or movement in the time series observable over several periods of data.

Trend analysis 1: A financial analysis that provides intrafirm as well as interfirm comparisons for two or more periods or dates. **2:** An analysis of a firm's financial ratios over time, used to determine the improvement or deterioration in its financial situation. **3:** Charting of data over time to identify a tendency or direction. **4:** Forecasting the future path of economic variables based on historical patterns.

Trespass to land Interference with the right of exclusive possession of the property.

Trial balance A summary listing of the titles and balances of the accounts in the ledger.

Trial impact Inducing nonusers to try a brand for the first time, or encouraging retrial by consumers who have not purchased the brand for an extended period.

Triangular arbitrage 1: Action to capitalize on a discrepancy where the quoted cross exchange rate is not equal to the rate that should exist at equilibrium. **2:** The exchange of one currency for a second currency, the second for a third, and the third for the first in order to make a profit.

Trigger mechanisms Specific acts or stimuli that set off reactions.

True and fair view A British concept of what financial statements ought to convey and an important feature of the Fourth Directive. The implementation of this concept means that companies may be required to disclose additional or different information. Each country determines, based on its own circumstances, how its corporations should comply with the true and fair view concept.

Trust receipt loans A financing arrangement where the collateralized inventory items are noted by serial number or some other readily identifiable mark.

Trust services Safekeeping, record keeping, and perhaps investing of corporate or individual pension or profit-sharing plans. For a corporate pension, the trustee institution receives the payments, invests them, maintains record for each of the employees, and pays the pensioners after they retire.

Trustee 1: An official who ensures that the bondholders' interests are protected and that the terms of the indenture are carried out. **2:** Individual or firm who collects a debtor's assets and distributes them to creditors.

Trustee under indenture The third-party financial institution charged by investors with the responsibility of monitoring the issuing corporation to ensure that it abides by all provisions of the bond agreement, called *indenture*.

TSCA The Toxic Substances Control Act provides a comprehensive scheme for regulation of toxic substances.

Tunneling The process by which virtual private networks (VPNs) transfer information by encapsulating traffic in IP packets over the Internet.

Turnkey operation A specialized form of management contract between a customer and an organization to provide a complete operational system together with the skills needed for unassisted maintenance and operation.

Turnover Process in which employees leave the organization and have to be replaced.

Turnover ratios *See:* Efficiency ratios.

Twisted-pair-cable Traditional telephone wires, twisted in pairs to reduce electromagnetic interference.

Two-bin inventory system A type of fixed-order system in which inventory is carried in two bins. A replenishment quantity is ordered when the first bin (working) is empty. During the replenishment lead time, material is used from the second bin. When the material is received, the second bin (which contains a quantity to cover demand during lead time plus some safety stock) is refilled and the excess is put into the working bin. At this time, stock is drawn from the first bin until it is again exhausted. This term is also used loosely to describe any fixed-order system even when physical "bins" do not exist. *Syn:* bin reserve system.

Two-card kanban system A kanban system where a move card and production card are employed. The move card authorizes the movement of a specific number of parts from a source to a point of use. The move card is attached to the standard container of parts during movement to the point of use of the parts. The production card authorizes the production of a given number of parts for use or replenishment. *Syn:* dual-card kanban system.

Two-column journal An all-purpose journal.

Two-parameter (Holt) exponential smoothing Method for forecasting stable growth.

Two-transaction approach An approach used to translate foreign currency where any gains or losses are separately recorded as gains or losses from exchange rate exchanges.

Two-way communication Occurs when both retailer and supplier communicate openly their ideas, concerns, and plans.

Two-way exclusive dealing Occurs when the supplier offers the retailer the exclusive distribution of a merchandise line or product in a particular trade area if in return the retailer will agree to do something for the manufacturer such as heavily promote the supplier's products or not handle competing brands.

Type A behavior Behavior pattern characterized by extreme competitiveness, impatience, aggressiveness, and devotion to work.

Type B behavior Behavior pattern that lacks Type A characteristics and includes a more balanced, relaxed lifestyle.

Type I error An incorrect decision to reject something (such as a statistical hypothesis or a lot of products) when it is acceptable. Also known as "producer's risk" and "alpha risk."

Type II error An incorrect decision to accept something when it is unacceptable. Also known as "consumer's risk" and "beta risk."

Tying agreement Agreement that exists when a seller with a strong product or service requires a buyer (the retailer) to purchase a weak product or service as a condition for buying the strong product or service.

Tying arrangement Conditioning a sale of a desired product (tying product) on the buyer's purchasing a second product (tied product). Prohibited if it tends to create a monopoly or may substantially lessen competition.

U

U chart Count per unit chart.

Ubuntu An African thought system that stresses a high degree of harmony and emphasizes unity of the whole, rather than its distinct parts.

Ultra vires Any action or contract that goes beyond a corporation's express and implied powers.

Umbrella policy Policy issued to a bank or trading company to insure exports of an exporter and handle all administrative requirements.

Unattainable capability The portion of the production capability that cannot be attained. This is typically caused by factors such as equipment unavailability, suboptimal scheduling, or resource limitations.

Unbiased expectations hypothesis A theory of interest rate determination which posits that the prevailing yield curve is mathematically derived from the present short-term rate and expectations for rates that will exist at various points in time in the future.

Uncertainty 1: Managers know what goal they wish to achieve, but information about alternatives and future events is incomplete. **2:** Situation that occurs when decision makers do not have sufficient information about environmental factors and have a difficult time predicting external changes.

Uncertainty acceptance The extent to which uncertainty is considered a normal part of life; feeling comfortable with ambiguity and unfamiliar risks.

Uncertainty avoidance 1: A value characterized by people's intolerance for uncertainty and ambiguity and resulting support for beliefs that promise certainty and conformity. **2:** Dimension of culture that refers to the preference of people in a country for structured rather than unstructured situations.

Uncollected balance percentages A proportional breakdown of the present accounts receivable balance, with the proportions based on the month the credit sales originated. The pitfalls of DSO, accounts receivable turnover, and the aging schedule have led to the development of this improved measure, in which the receivables balance is broken down, and the monthly components are divided by the credit sales in the month in which the receivables originated. Sometimes called the "payments pattern approach," the uncollected balance percentages accurately depict a company's collection experience, even when sales are changing.

Uncollectible accounts expense The operating expense incurred because of the failure to collect receivables.

Uncommitted lines of credit Short-term lending agreements which are not technically binding on the bank, although they are almost always honored. Uncommitted lines are usually renewable annually if both parties are agreeable. A less formal agreement than a committed line and the availability of funds may be in question if the general economic or bank internal liquidity position slips.

Unconditional guarantee Organizational policy of providing customers unquestioned remedy for any product or service deficiency.

Uncontrollable input The environmental factors or inputs that cannot be controlled by the decision maker.

Underapplied factory overhead The amount of actual factory overhead in excess of the factory overhead applied to production during a period.

Underproduction A situation that occurs when a monopolist curtails production to a level at which marginal cost is less than price.

Understored A condition in a community where the number of stores in relation to households is relatively low so that engaging in retailing is an attractive economic endeavor.

Underwriter's spread The difference between the price at which the investment banking firm buys an issue from a company and the price at which the securities are sold in the primary market; it represents the investment banker's gross profit on the issue.

Underwriting syndicate A syndicate of investment firms formed to spread the risk associated with the purchase and distribution of a new issue of securities.

Underwritten arrangement Agreement for the sale of securities in which the investment bank guarantees the sale by purchasing the securities from the issuer, thus agreeing to bear any risks involved in the transaction.

Undistributed earnings The proportion of a firm's net income after taxes which is retained within the firm for internal purposes.

Undue hardship Significant difficulty or expense imposed on an employer when making an accommodation for individuals with disabilities.

Unearned revenues 1: Amounts that have been received from customers but for which performance of a service or sale of a product has not yet been made. **2:** The liability created by receiving cash in advance of providing goods or services.

Unemployment compensation Compensation awarded to workers who have lost their jobs and cannot find other employment.

Unenforceable contract Contract for the breach of which the law does not provide a remedy.

Unethical What members of the society generally accept as being "wrong."

Uneven cash flow stream A series of cash flows in which the amount varies from one period to the next.

Unfair employer practice Conduct in which an employer is prohibited from engaging.

Unfair labor practice Conduct in which an employer or union is prohibited from engaging.

Unfair union practice Conduct in which a union is prohibited from engaging.

Unfairness Whenever corporations engage in social activities, they divert funds rightfully belonging to shareholders and/or employees.

Unfreezing A stage of organizational development in which participants are made aware of problems in order to increase their willingness to change their behavior.

Uniform commercial code 1: A system of standards that simplifies procedures for establishing loan security. **2:** Article 2 of the UCC governs the sales of goods.

Uniform delivered pricing The seller charges all customers the same transportation cost regardless of their location.

Uniform Resource Locator (URL) The address of a Web site. Always starts with *http://*

Unilateral contract Contract in which only one party makes a promise.

Unilateral transfers Accounting for government and private gifts and grants.

Unintentional amoral management Results when managers are casual about, careless about, or inattentive to the fact that their decisions and actions may have negative or deleterious effects on others.

Uninterruptible Power Supply (UPS) A system that provides an alternative power supply as soon as a power network fails.

Union shop An employer can hire nonunion members, but the employee must join the union.

Unique visitor pages The number of different pages at a Web site that a single visitor accesses.

Unique visitors per month The number of people who visit a Web site each month; each person is counted only once, even if that person visits the site more than once during the month.

Unique ZIP code Used by banks to increase the efficiency of their lockbox operations.

Unit contribution margin The dollars available from each unit of sales to cover fixed costs and provide operating profits.

Unit labor cost Computed by dividing the average cost of workers by their average levels of output.

Unit of measure concept A concept of accounting that requires that economic data be recorded in dollars.

Unitary elasticity Situation in which price and quantity changes exactly offset each other.

United Nations (UN) An organization representing governments of all countries in the world.

United States Foreign Corrupt Practices Act (FCPA) Makes it illegal for U.S. citizens and businesses to practice bribery in the conduct of business not only in the United States but in other countries as well, even when it is an acceptable or expected business practice there.

Units-of-production depreciation method A method of depreciation that provides for depreciation expense based on the expected productive capacity of an asset.

Unity of command Concept that a subordinate should be responsible to only one superior.

Universal *See:* Global.

Universal factors framework Identifies various universal situations and their impact on decision-making behavior.

Universal Product Code (UPC) Bar code on a product's package that provides information read by optical scanners.

Universalism A rigid global yardstick by which to measure all moral issues.

UNIX A popular operating system, versions of which run on machines from different manufacturers, and therefore make the software almost machine-independent.

Unrealized (holding) gains Gains that are not yet actually incurred, for example, as a result of a foreign currency translation.

Unrealized holding gain or loss The difference between the fair market values of the securities and their cost.

Unrealized (holding) losses Losses that are not yet actually incurred, for example, as a result of a foreign currency translation.

Unreasonably dangerous Situation that contains a danger beyond that which would be contemplated by the ordinary consumer.

Unregistered sales Section 12(a) imposes absolute civil liability; there are no defenses.

Unsecured Lending arrangement in which there is no collateral backing up the loan in the event of a default.

Unsolicited order An unplanned business opportunity that arises as a result of other activities.

Unstructured data Information collected for analysis with open-ended questions.

Unstructured problem A problem for whose solution there is no pretested set of steps, and with which the solver is not familiar—or is only slightly familiar—from previous experience.

Uploading Copying from one computer onto another computer.

Upper Control Limit (UCL) 1: Cash balance that triggers a purchase of securities large enough to reduce excess cash balances to a predetermined return point. **2:** Control limit for points above the central line in a control chart.

Upstream Used as a relative reference within a firm or supply chain to indicate moving in the direction of the raw material supplier.

Upward communication Messages transmitted from the lower to the higher level in the organization's hierarchy.

Usable funds The net proceeds the firm receives from the financing sources. This represents the amount borrowed less compensating balances, in the case of credit lines, and the bid-ask spread in the case of commercial paper.

Usage rate The daily rate of drawing down the inventory balance. Calculated by dividing the total inventory needs by the number of days in the production planning period.

Users Consumers who actually use the product.

Utilitarian approach The ethical concept that moral behaviors produce the greatest good for the greatest number.

Utilitarianism Concept that moral actions are those that produce the greatest net pleasure compared to net pain.

Utilities Computer programs that provide help in routine user operations.

Utility 1: A measure of the total worth of a consequence reflecting a decision maker's attitude toward considerations such as profit, loss, and risk. **2:** Value.

GLOSSARY

Utility analysis Analysis in which economic or other statistical models are built to identify the costs and benefits associated with specific HR activities.

Utilization 1: A measure (usually expressed as a percentage) of how intensively a resource is being used to produce a good or service. Utilization compares actual time used to available time. Traditionally, utilization is the ratio of direct time charged (run time plus setup time) to the clock time available. Utilization is a percentage between 0 percent and 100 percent that is equal to 100 percent minus the percentage of time lost due to machine, tool, worker, and so on, unavailability. *See:* Efficiency, Productivity. **2:** In the theory of constraints, utilization is the ratio of the time the resource is needed to support the constraint to the time available for the resource, expressed as a percentage.

Utilization analysis An analysis that identifies the number of protected-class members employed and the types of jobs they hold in an organization.

Utilization review An audit and review of the services and costs billed by health-care providers.

V

Valence The value or attraction an individual has for an outcome.

Valid contract Contract that meets all of the requirements of a binding contract.

Validation 1: Confirmation by examination of objective evidence that specific requirements and/or a specified intended use are met. **2:** The process of determining that a simulation model provides an accurate representation of a real system.

Validity 1: Ability of a feedback instrument to measure what it was intended to measure. **2:** The relationship between an applicant's score on a selection device and his or her future job performance.

Valuation approach Method of financial decision-making in which the anticipated shareholder value effect determines which alternative is chosen. The present values of cash inflows and outflows are compared for each alternative.

Valuation The determination of the present dollar value of a series of cash flows.

Value Refers to the usefulness, desirability, and worth of a product, object, or thing.

Value added 1: Value added equals total revenue minus the cost of goods, materials, and services purchased externally. **2:** Tasks or activities that convert resources into products or services consistent with customer requirements. The customer can be internal or external to the organization.

Value-added activities 1: The cost of activities that are needed to meet customer requirements. **2:** Activities that customers perceive as increasing the utility (usefulness) of the products or services they purchase.

Value-added lead time The time required to manufacture a unit of product or other output.

Value-Added Network (VAN) A computer system that receives EDI information from one firm in one format and transmits to another firm or bank in a different format. The system transmits messages and data from point of origination to prespecified endpoints, and which may offer one or more auxiliary services.

Value-Added Tax (VAT) A tax on the value added at each stage of the production and distribution process; a tax assessed in most European countries and also common among Latin American countries.

Value analysis Method of weighing the comparative value of materials, components, and manufacturing processes from the standpoint of their purpose, relative merit, and cost in order to uncover ways of improving products, lowering costs, or both.

Value analysis, value engineering, and value research Value analysis assumes that a process, procedure, product, or service is of no value unless proven otherwise. It assigns a price to every step of a process and then computes the worth-to-cost ratio of that step. VE points the way to elimination and reengineering. Value research, related to value engineering, for given features of the service/product, helps determine the customers' strongest "likes" and "dislikes" and those for which customers are neutral. Focuses attention on strong dislikes and enables identified "neutrals" to be considered for cost reductions.

Value at Risk (VAR) Estimate of the risk of loss at various probability levels.

Value chain Activities in an organization are related to what is sometimes referred to as the *value chain:* inbound (receiving), operations (production or service), outbound (shipping), marketing, sales, and service. *See:* Supply chain.

Value dating Involves forward movement of the amount of a deposited check and back dating of a presented check. This is a common practice by some European banks.

Value engineering and/or analysis A disciplined approach to the elimination of waste from products or processes through an investigative process that focuses on the functions to be performed and whether such functions add value to the good or service.

Value proposition 1: Program of goods, services, ideas, and solutions that a business marketer offers to advance the performance goals of the customer organization. **2:** The promised benefits a retailer offers in relation to the cost the customer incurs.

Value stream The processes of creating, producing, and delivering a good or service to the market. For a good, the value stream encompasses the raw material supplier, the manufacture and assembly of the good, and the distribution network. For a service, the value stream consists of suppliers, support personnel and technology, the service "producer," and the distribution channel. The value stream may be controlled by a single business or a network of several businesses.

Value stream mapping Technique of mapping the value stream.

Values 1: A company's vision, objective, and philosophy as communicated to employees and the public worldwide. National values include good/evil, beautiful/ugly, normal/abnormal, and rational/irrational. Values vary from corporation to corporation, and national values vary from country to country. **2:** End-states or goals one lives for. **3:** Statements that clarify the behaviors that the organization expects in order to move toward its vision and mission. Values reflect an organization's personality and culture.

Variable component Situation that is often composed of some bonus that is received if performance warrants.

Variable cost 1: Expenses that increase or decrease with the level of production or sales, such as direct labor or raw materials. **2:** The portion of the total cost that is dependent on and varies with the volume.

Variable cost concept A concept used in applying the cost-plus approach to product pricing in which only the variable costs are included in the cost amount to which the markup is added.

Variable costing The concept that considers the cost of products manufactured to be composed only of those manufacturing costs that increase or decrease as the volume of production rises or falls (direct materials, direct labor, and variable factory overhead).

Variable data Data resulting from the measurement of a parameter or a variable. Control charts based on variables data include average ($\bar{X}$) chart, individuals (X) chart, range (R) chart, sample standard deviation (s) chart, and CUSUM chart.

Variable identification Involves determining what items need to be forecasted and how best to measure those items.

Variable pay Type of compensation linked to individual, team, or organizational performance.

Variable pricing A policy that recognizes that differences in demand and cost necessitate that the retailer change prices in a fairly predictable manner.

Variable rate demand notes Medium-term debt instruments issued by municipalities, which are found in some corporate short-term investments portfolios because their interest rates are periodically reset.

Variable sampling plan Plan in which a sample is taken and a measurement of a specified quality characteristic is made on each unit. The measurements are summarized into a simple statistic, and the observed value is compared with an allowable value defined in the plan.

Variance 1: A measure of the dispersion, or spread, of a distribution from its expected value. **2:** The difference between actual performance and planned performance. **3:** The standard deviation squared. The amount by which the actual amount is over or under the forecasted or budgeted amount.

Variance analysis model Receivables control technique that builds on the decomposition model, and compares actual receivables performance to the budgeted amounts. If the budget captures the unique conditions and sales levels a company is experiencing, or is so adjusted after the period is over ("flexible budgeting") then one can discern the true reason(s) for changes in receivables levels.

Variation Change in data, a characteristic, or a function that is caused by one of four factors: special causes, common causes, tampering, or structural variation. *See:* individual entries.

Variety 1: Refers to the number of different merchandise lines that the retailer stocks in the store. **2:** In terms of tasks, the frequency of unexpected and novel events that occur in the conversion process.

VAT analysis In the theory of constraints, a procedure for determining the general flow of parts and products from raw materials to finished products (logical product structure). A V logical structure starts with one or a few raw materials, and the product expands into a number of different products as it flows through divergent points in its routings. The shape of an A logical structure is dominated by converging points. Many raw materials are fabricated and assembled into a few finished products. A T logical structure consists of numerous similar finished products assembled from common assemblies, subassemblies, and parts. Once the general parts flow is determined, the system control points (gating operations, convergent points, divergent points, constraints, and shipping points) can be identified and managed.

VAT concept A concept based on taxing each production activity or business activity that adds value to materials or goods purchased from other businesses.

Vendor collusion Occurs when an employee of one of the retailer's vendors steals merchandise as it is delivered to the retailer.

Vendor fraud An overcharge for purchased goods, the shipment of inferior goods, or the nonshipment of goods even though payment is made.

Vendor profitability analysis statement A tool used to evaluate vendors and shows all purchases made the prior year, the discount granted, the transportation charges paid, the original markup, markdowns, and finally the season-ending gross margin on that vendor's merchandise.

Venture capital firm A group of companies or individuals that invests money in new or expanding businesses for ownership and potential profits.

Venture teams A technique to foster creativity within organizations in which a small team is set up as its own company to pursue innovations.

Verification 1: Act of reviewing, inspecting, testing, checking, auditing, or otherwise establishing and documenting whether items, processes, services, or documents conform to specified requirements. **2:** The process of determining that a computer program implements a simulation model as it is intended.

Vertical analysis 1: An analysis that compares each item in a current statement with a total amount within the same statements. **2:** Tool that converts financial statement numbers to percentages so that they are easy to understand and analyze.

Vertical cooperative advertising Occurs when the retailer and other channel members (usually manufacturers) share the advertising budget. Usually the manufacturer subsidizes some of the retailer's advertising that features the manufacturer's brands.

Vertical linkages Communication and coordination activities connecting the top and bottom of an organization.

Vertical market A market in which the goods of one business are used as raw materials or components in the production or sale process of another business.

Vertical marketing channels Capital-intensive networks of several levels that are professionally managed and centrally programmed to realize the technological, managerial, and promotional economies of a long-term relationship orientation.

Vertical price fixing Occurs when a retailer collaborates with the manufacturer or wholesaler to resell an item at an agreed-on price.

Vertical privity Determines who is liable for breach of warranty.

Vertical restraints Agreements among parties at different levels in the chain of distribution.

Vertical merger A merger between a firm and one of its suppliers or customers.

Vertical team A formal team composed of a manager and his or her subordinates in the organization's formal chain of command.

Vertically integrate To bring together more of the steps involved in producing a product in order to form a continuous chain owned by the same firm; typically involves taking on activities that were previously in the external portion of the supply chain.

Vesting The right of employees to receive benefits from their pension plans.

Victim The person or organization deceived by the perpetrator.

Videoconferencing A telecommunication system that allows people who are in different locations to meet via transmitted images and speech.

Virtual memory Storage space on a disk that is treated by the operating system as if it were part of the computer's RAM.

Virtual organization 1: An organization that has few full-time employees and temporarily hires outside specialists who form teams to work on specific opportunities, then disband when objectives are met. **2:** An organization that requires very little office space. Its employees telecommute, and services to customers are provided through telecommunications lines.

Virtual Private Network (VPN) A network that transfers information by encapsulating traffic in IP packets and sending the packets over the Internet.

Virtual reality A set of hardware and software that creates images, sounds, and possibly the sensation of touch that give the user the feeling of a real environment and experience. In advanced VR systems, the user wears special goggles and gloves.

Virtual Reality Modeling Language (VRML) A standard programming language that supports three-dimensional presentation on the Web.

Virtual store The total collection of all the pages of information on the retailer's Internet site.

Virtual team A team that uses advanced information and telecommunications technologies so that geographically distant members can collaborate on projects and reach common goals.

Virus (computer virus) A rogue computer program that infects any computers it is entered into. It spreads in computers like a biological virus.

Visible pay inequity Visible pay inequity between the expatriates and their local peers could demoralize the foreign subsidiary's staff.

Vision 1: An attractive, ideal future that is credible yet not readily attainable. **2:** Statement that explains what the company wants to become and what it hopes to achieve.

Visual control Technique of positioning all tools, parts, production activities, and performance indicators so that the status of a process can be understood at a glance by everyone; provide visual clues to aid the performer in correctly processing a step or series of steps, to reduce cycle time, to cut costs, to smooth flow of work, to improve quality.

Visual merchandising The artistic display of merchandise and theatrical props used as scene-setting decoration in the store.

Vital few, useful many Term used by J. M. Juran to describe his use of the Pareto principle, which he first defined in 1950. (The principle was used much earlier in economics and inventory control methodologies.) The principle suggests that most effects come from relatively few causes; that is, 80 percent of the effects come from 20 percent of the possible causes. The 20 percent of the possible causes are referred to as the "vital few"; the remaining causes are referred to as the "useful many." When Juran first defined this principle, he referred to the remaining causes as the "trivial many," but realizing that no problems are trivial in quality assurance, he changed it to "useful many."

Voice of the Customer (VOC) Expression of the preferences, opinions, and motivations of the customer that need to be listened to by managers; a one-on-one interviewing process to elicit an in-depth set of customer needs.

Voice recognition Technology that enables computers to recognize human voice, translate it into program code, and act upon the voiced commands.

Voice-Over-Internet Protocol (VOIP) VOIP technology enables network managers to route phone calls and fax transmissions over the same network they use for data.

Void contract An agreement without legal effect.

Voidable contract Contract capable of being made void.

Voir dire Legal process of qualifying an expert witness.

Volatile memory Computer memory that cannot hold the original data when the machine is unplugged. Example: RAM.

Volume variance The difference between the budgeted fixed overhead at 100 percent of normal capacity and the standard fixed overhead for the actual production achieved during the period.

Voluntary assumption of the risk A defense.

Voluntary dissolution Dissolution that may be brought about by a resolution of the board of directors that is approved by the shareholders.

Voluntary restraint agreements Trade-restraint agreements resulting in self-imposed restrictions not covered by the GATT rules; used to manage or distort trade flows. For example, Japanese restraints on the export of cars to the United States.

Voting LLC statutes often specify the voting rights of members, subject to a contrary provision in an LLC's operating agreement.

Voting trust Transfer of corporate shares' voting rights to a trustee.

Voucher A document that serves as evidence of authority to pay cash.

Voucher system Records, methods, and procedures used in verifying and recording liabilities and paying and recording cash payments.

Vroom-Jago model A model designed to help managers gauge the amount of subordinate participation in decision making.

Vulnerability chart Tool that coordinates the various elements of a fraud investigation to help identify possible suspects.

W

Wa A Japanese concept that necessitates that members of a group, be it in a work team, or a company, or a nation, cooperate with and trust each other.

Wage and salary surveys Surveys that show what other organizations pay incumbents in jobs that match a sample of "key" jobs selected by the organization.

Wages Payments directly calculated on the amount of time worked.

Wait states The clock-beat intervals during which a CPU sits idle.

Walk the talk Means not only talking about what one believes in but also being observed acting out those beliefs. Employees' buy-in of the TQM concept is more likely when management is seen involved in the process, every day.

Walkabout Visual, group technique used in resolving resource planning conflicts among organizational components.

WAN (Wide Area Network) A network of computers and other communications devices that extends over a large area, possibly comprising national territories. Example: the Internet.

Wants Desires to obtain more satisfaction than is absolutely necessary to improve an unsatisfactory condition.

Warehousing The management of distribution of products to a market by storing a product in a facility. Warehouses often include the following activities: consolidation (combining a large number of small shipments into a smaller number of large shipments, in order to gain transportation economies, by getting truckload rates); mixing (providing a mix of different items in a single shipment, using a "cross-dock" operation); service (making items available when needed, and reducing lead time for delivery); contingencies uncertainties (holding inventory in a warehouse as safety stock, in order to accommodate unpredictably high demand for a product); and smoothing (decoupling one entity from another in the supply chain—for example, decoupling the manufacturer from his supplier, or decoupling the manufacturer from his market).

Warrant 1: A long-term option issued by a corporation to buy a stated number of shares of common stock at a specified price. **2:** Order issued by a judge to arrest someone.

Warranty Obligation of the seller concerning title, quality, characteristics, or condition of goods.

Warranty liabilities Obligation to perform service and repair items sold within a specific period of time and/or use after sale.

Warranty of title Obligation to convey the right of ownership without any lien. May be excluded or modified by specific language or by certain circumstances, including judicial sale or a sale by a sheriff, executor, or foreclosing lienor.

Waste Activities that consume resources but add no value; visible waste (for example, scrap, rework, downtime) and invisible waste (for example, inefficient setups, wait times of people and machines, inventory).

WCR/S Working capital requirements divided by sales.

Weak-form efficient Description of foreign exchange markets, implying that all historical and current exchange rate information is already reflected in prevailing spot exchange rates.

Web page A screen of text, pictures, sounds, and animation that the user encounters when using a Web browser.

Web page authoring tools Software tools that make Web page composition easier and faster than writing code by providing icons and menus.

Web site The electronic presence of an organization or individual on the World Wide Web. The site is composed of Web pages and either shares a server with other sites or has a dedicated server.

Web-visit hijacking Mimicking another, similarly named Web site in order to trick or confuse e-mail and e-business users into sending information to a business other than the intended one.

Webb-Pomerene Act A 1918 statute that excludes from antitrust prosecution U.S. firms cooperating to develop foreign markets.

Webmaster The person who is in charge of constructing and maintaining the organization's Web site.

Weekend effect A concern in making cash transfers that takes into account weekend balances, since deposit accounts in the United States do not earn interest, and also considers weekend deposits that will be credited to the deposit account on Monday.

Weeks' Supply Method (WSM) A technique for planning dollar inventory investments that states that the inventory level should be set equal to a predetermined number of weeks' supply, which is directly related to the desired rate of stock turnover.

Weibull distribution Distribution of continuous data that can take on many different shapes and is used to describe a variety of patterns; used to define when the "infant mortality rate" has ended and a steady state has been reached (decreasing failure rate); relates to the "bathtub" curve.

Weighted moving averages A method of forecasting or smoothing a time series by computing a weighted average of past time series values. The sum of the weights must equal 1.

Weighted-Average Cost of Capital (WACC) The summed product of the proportion of each type of capital used and the cost of that capital source, this "hurdle rate" for capital investments is usually based on a company's long-term financing sources.

Wellness programs Programs designed to maintain or improve employee health before problems arise.

Well-pay Extra pay for not taking sick leave.

What-if analysis 1: A trial-and-error approach to learning about the range of possible outputs for a model. Trial values are chosen for the model inputs (these are the what-ifs) and the value of the output(s) is computed. **2:** An analysis that is conducted to test the degree to which one variable affects another. Also called *sensitivity analysis*.

Wheel of retailing theory Pattern of competitive development in retailing which states that new types of retailers enter the market as low-status, low-margin, low-price operators. However, as they meet with success, these new retailers gradually acquire more sophisticated and elaborate facilities, thereby becoming less efficient and vulnerable to new types of low-margin retail competitors who progress through the same pattern.

Whistle-blowing The disclosure by an employee of illegal, immoral, or illegitimate practices by the organization.

White knight A firm facing an unfriendly merger offer might arrange to be acquired by a different, friendly firm. The friendly firm is the white knight.

Whitemail When white knights or others are granted exceptional merger terms or otherwise compensated well, it is referred to as whitemail.

Whitemail bribery Payments made to induce an official in a foreign country who is in a position of power to give favorable treatment where such treatment is either illegal or not warranted on an efficiency or economic benefit scale.

Wholesale lockbox system Special arrangement for collecting mailed payments, established for collecting relatively few large dollar remittances. Because the dollar amounts per check are larger (perhaps $1 million or more), the received checks are processed more often and checks are processed for deposit more rapidly by bank than by company personnel.

Wholesale market Investment supply and demand interaction for large dollar transactions between large investors (such as the money market).

Wholesaler-sponsored voluntary groups Groups that involve a wholesaler that brings together a group of independently owned retailers and offers them a coordinated merchandising and buying program that will provide them with economies like those their chain-store rivals are able to obtain.

Wholesalers Persons or establishments that sell to retailers and/or other organizational buyers for industrial, institutional, and commercial use, but do not sell in significant amounts to ultimate consumers.

Wholesaling Activities of persons or establishments that sell to retailers and/or other organizational buyers for industrial, institutional, and commercial use, but do not sell in significant amounts to final consumers.

Wholly owned foreign affiliate A foreign subsidiary over which an organization has complete control.

Wholly-owned subsidiary Enables an MNE to retain control and authority over all phases of operation. The firm establishes a subsidiary in a foreign country maintaining 100 percent ownership; unlike joint ventures, risks are not shared.

Winding up 1: Completing unfinished business, collecting debts, and distributing assets to creditors and partners; also called liquidation. **2:** Unless otherwise provided in the partnership agreement, the general partners who have not wrongfully dissolved the partnership may wind up its affairs.

"Window dressing" techniques Techniques employed by firms to make their financial statements look better than they actually are.

Wire drawdowns Wire transfers that are initiated by the receiving party, instead of the sender or payor.

Wire transfers Are bookkeeping entries that simultaneously debit the payor's account and credit the payee's account. The best way to quickly move money from one place to another is with a wire transfer. A real-time transfer of account balances between banks.

Wireless Access Protocol (WAP) A protocol used in mobile communication (M-commerce).

Wireless communication Transmission of data as radio signals without wires or telephone jacks.

Wireless LAN A local-area network that uses electromagnetic waves (radio or infrared light) as the medium of communication.

Wisdom Culmination of the continuum from data to information to knowledge to wisdom.

With recourse When the factor can demand funds returned for uncollected receivables.

Withdrawal A general partner may withdraw from a limited partnership at any time by giving written notice to the other partners; a limited partner may withdraw as provided in the limited partnership certificate.

Withholding taxes Taxes applied to the payment of dividends, interest, or royalties by firms.

Without recourse The seller is not liable for uncollected receivables.

Word (data word) The number of bits that the control unit of a computer fetches from the primary memory in one machine cycle. The larger the word, the faster the computer.

Work Effort directed toward producing or accomplishing results.

Work analysis Analysis, classification and study of the way work is done. Work may be categorized as value-added work (necessary work), non-value-added (rework, unnecessary work, idle). Collected data may be summarized on a Pareto chart, showing how people within the studied population work. The need for and value of all work is then questioned and opportunities for improvement identified. A time use analysis may also be included in the study.

Work Breakdown Structure (WBS) 1: A hierarchical tree of work elements or items that will be accomplished or produced by the project team during the project. **2:** Project management technique by which a project is divided into tasks, subtasks, and units of work to be performed.

Work cycle A series of sequentially repeated activities involved in providing a service or creating a product.

Work group Group composed of people from one functional area who work together on a daily basis and whose goal is to improve the processes of their function.

Work-in-Process (WIP) inventory 1: The direct materials costs, the direct labor costs, and the factory overhead costs that have entered into the manufacturing process, but are associated with products that have not been finished. **2:** Inventory composed of the materials that still are moving through the stages of the production process.

Work instruction Document which answers the question: How is the work to be done? *See:* Procedure.

Work package The lowest-level item of any branch of a work breakdown structure.

Work redesign The altering of jobs to increase both the quality of employees' work experience and their productivity.

Work redesign programs Programs that alter jobs to both the quality of the work experience and productivity.

Work sample tests Tests that require an applicant to perform a simulated job task.

Work scheduling Preparing schedules of when and how long workers are at the workplace.

Work scope *See:* Project scope.

Work sheet A working paper used to summarize adjusting entries and assist in the preparation of financial statements.

Work specialization The degree to which organizational tasks are subdivided into individual jobs. Also called division of labor.

Workbook Collection of exercises, questions, or problems to be solved during training; a participant's repository for documents used in training (for example, handouts).

Worker Adjustment and Retraining Notification (WARN) Act Federal statute that requires an employer to provide 60 days' advance notice of a plant closing or mass layoff.

Worker efficiency A measure (usually computed as a percentage) of worker performance that compares the standard time allowed to complete a task to the actual worker time to complete it. *Syn:* labor efficiency.

Workers' compensation Benefits provided to persons injured on the job.

Workflow analysis A study of the way work (inputs, activities, and outputs) moves through an organization.

Workforce diversity Hiring people with different human qualities or who belong to various cultural groups.

Working capital 1: A firm's investment in short-term assets—cash, marketable securities, inventory, and accounts receivable. **2:** The excess of the current assets of a business over its current liabilities.

Working capital cycle The continual flow of resources through the various working capital accounts such as cash, accounts receivables, inventory, and payables.

Working Capital Guarantee Program Program conducted by Ex-Im Bank which encourages commercial banks to extend short-term export financing to eligible exporters; Ex-Im Bank provides a guarantee in the loan's principal and interest.

Working capital investment decision The proportion of total assets held in current asset accounts, with the outcome usually linked closely to the company's risk posture.

Working capital management The management of a firm's current assets (cash, accounts receivable, inventories) and current liabilities (accounts payable, short-term debt).

Working capital policy Decisions regarding 1) the target levels for each current asset account and 2) how current assets will be financed.

Working capital requirements The difference between current operating assets (receivables, inventory, and prepaids) and current operating liabilities (accounts payable and accruals).

Working capital turnover ratio Sales divided by average working capital; a measure of the amount of working capital used to generate revenues.

Works council Councils that provide labor a say in corporate decision making through a representative body that may consist entirely of workers or of a combination of managers and workers.

Workstation A powerful microcomputer providing high-speed processing and high-resolution graphics. Used primarily for scientific and engineering assignments.

World Bank Bank established in 1944 to enhance economic development by providing loans to countries.

World-class competitors Multinational firms that can compete globally with domestic products.

World-class quality Term used to indicate a standard of excellence: best of the best.

World Trade Organization (WTO) Institution that administers international trade and investment accords. It supplanted the General Agreement on Tariffs and Trade (GATT) in 1995.

World Wide Web (Web, WWW) 1: The application of the Internet that allows the posting and retrieval of text, pictures, sounds, and motion pictures. "Surfing" the Web is done by way of clicking on marked text and pictures to move to other pages at the same site or to a different site. **2:** A collection of central servers for accessing information on the Internet.

Worldwide approach A national tax system that subjects both domestic source and foreign source income to taxes.

Worm A rogue code that spreads in a computer network.

Worst-case scenario An analysis in which all of the input variables are set at their worst reasonably forecasted values.

Write Once, Read Many (WORM) A storage medium that is loaded with software by the manufacturer, and can never be overwritten. *Example:* CD-ROM.

Writer Seller of an option.

Written principles Those principles governing language and behavior that must be transmitted when sending a written message across cultures.

X

X-bar ($\bar{X}$) chart Average chart.

Y

Yankee stock offerings Offerings of stock by non–U.S. firms in the U.S. markets.

Yield 1: A measure of materials usage efficiency; it measures the ratio of the materials output quantity to the materials input quantity. Yields less than 1.0 are the result of materials losses in the process. **2:** Ratio between salable goods produced and the quantity of raw materials and/or components put in at the beginning of the process. **3:** The amount of good or acceptable material available after the completion of a process. Usually computed as the final amount divided by the initial amount converted to a decimal or percentage. In manufacturing planning and control systems, yield is usually related to specific routing steps or to the parent item to determine how many units should be scheduled to produce a specific number of finished goods. For example, if 50 units of a product are required by a customer and a yield of 70 percent is expected then 72 units (computed as 50 units divided by .7) should be started in the manufacturing process.

Yield curve A graph showing the relationship between yields and maturities of securities.

Yield ratios A comparison of the number of applicants at one stage of the recruiting process to the number at the next stage.

Yield spread The difference between two interest rates, expressed as a percentage difference.

Yield spread swap Exchange of one debt security for another, usually with the motivation of taking advantage of a mispriced security, based on the investor's study of historical interest rate differences.

Yield to Maturity (YTM) The average rate of return earned on a bond if it is held to maturity.

Z

Zero coupon bond A bond that pays no annual interest but is sold at a discount below par, thus providing compensation to investors in the form of capital appreciation.

Zero defects Performance standard popularized by Philip B. Crosby to address a dual attitude in the workplace: People are willing to accept imperfection in some areas, while in other areas, they expect the number of defects to be zero. This dual attitude developed because of the conditioning that people are human and humans make mistakes. However, the zero-defects methodology states that if people commit themselves to watching details and avoiding errors, they can move closer to the goal of zero.

Zero-Balance Account (ZBA) A special checking account used for disbursements that has a balance equal to zero when there is no disbursement activity.

Zero-based budgeting A concept of budgeting that requires all levels of management to start from zero and estimate budget data as if there had been no previous activities in their unit.

Zero-growth stock A common stock whose future dividends are not expected to grow at all; that is, $g = 0$, and $\hat{D}_1 = \hat{D}_2 = \cdots = \hat{D}_\infty$.

Zero investment improvement Another term for a *kaizen blitz*.

GLOSSARY

Subject Index

A

Abandoned product ranges, 1410
ABC analysis, 393–396
ABI/Inform, 1165
Ability tests, 748
Absenteeism, 717–718
Absolut, 501
Absolute advantage, 1403, 1405
Absorption, 263
Absorption costing
  income analysis under, 930–931
  income statements under, 929–930
  management's use of, 931–937
Abuse, of products, 153
Academics, CSP model and, 1318–1319
Acceptable products, 977
Acceptance, 127
Acceptance rate, 742
Acceptance theory of authority, 26–27, 37
Access controls, 1239
Access imperfections, 1413
Accessories, as business-to-business products, 477–478
Accountability, 37, 1215
Accountants, ethics for, 941
Account form, 835
Accounting
  balance of payments, 1414–1418
  balance sheet budgets, 896–900
  control and, 937–940
  cost behavior, 861–866
  cost-volume-profit relationships, 866–875
  decision models in, 915–928
  ethics and, 940–941
  financial, 825
  fraud and, 1284
  general partnerships and, 15
  income models and decision making, 929–937
  information, 63
  managerial, 825
  operating budgets, 885–896
  performance evaluation, 900–902
  product and service costs, 875–885
  responsibility accounting, 902–912
  transfer pricing, 912–914
  See also Financial statement analysis; Financial statements
Accounting cycle, 826
Accounting equation, 827–831
Accounting function, 822–823
Accounting income, 1074–1075
Accounting inventory system, 428–431
AccountingNet, 229

Accounting process, accounting cycle, 826–827
Accounting rate of return (ARR), 1072
Accounting reform legislation, 1347
Accounting strategies
  accounting function, 822–823
  generally accepted accounting principles, 824–825
  managerial and financial accounting, 825
  role of, 823–824
Accounts payable, 829, 970–971
Accounts receivable, 829
Accounts receivable analysis, 852–853
Accounts receivable financing, 974–976
Accounts receivable turnover, 852–853
Accruals, 970
Accrue Software, 1153
Ace, 588
Achievement-oriented leadership, 43
Achievement tests, 748
Acid-test ratio, 851–852
Ackerman, Robert, 1316–1317
Ackerman, Val, 6
Acquisition of shares, 21
Acquisitions, 228. *See also* Mergers and acquisitions
Action plans, 33, 34
Action taken without a meeting, 22
Active investment strategy, 968
Active listening, 66
Active practice, 761
Active selling, 449
Active tool, 1379
Activities
  control, 1271, 1284–1285
  managers, 53
  workforce diversity, 786–787
Activity base, 862, 878, 905
Activity drivers, 862, 878
Activity-based costing (ABC), 49, 387, 879, 927
Act of state doctrine, 1462
Actual authority, 129
Actual cost, in project management, 277–278
Actual express authority, 15, 22
Actual implied authority, 15, 22
Actual rate of return, 1009
Actual self, 522
Acute crisis stage, 1332, 1333
Adaptability/entrepreneurial culture, 84
Adaptive selling, 621
Additional funds needed (AFN), 1016, 1018–1019
Additional paid-in capital, 982
Adidas, 555
Adjourning stage, in team development, 283

Adjustable capacity, 414
Adjustable pegged exchange rates, 1446
Adjustable rate mortgages. *See* ARMs
Administered vertical marketing channels, 589
Administrative expenses, 880
Administrative law, 130
Administrative principles, 26–27
Administrative support, 220
Administrative uses, of performance appraisals, 776–777
Admissions, 16
Adobe, 1131
Adoption, 248
Adoption process, 494–495
Ad substantiation, 139
Ad valorem tariffs, 1434
Advances, 15
Adverse selection, 798
Advertising, 498, 499–504
  corrective, 139
  demand management and, 368
  environmental resources and, 229
  optimal level of, 184–185
Advertising budgeting, 499–500
Advertising effectiveness, 502
Advertising media, 501–502, 503
Advertising messages, 500–501
Advertising objectives, 499
Advertising strategy, 499
Aeroflot, 1367
Affinity diagrams, 643–644
Affirmation of fact, 147
Affirmative action, 104, 788
Affirmative disclosure, 139
After-tax cash flows, 1042, 1074
After-tax cost of debt, 1046
Age Discrimination in Employment Act of 1967 (ADEA), 105, 106, 792
Age distribution, 572–573
Age issues, 792, 799
Agency, 128, 129
Agency problem, 946, 987, 1350
Agency relationships, 946–948
Agenda setting, 771
Agents, 1089
Aggregate decision techniques, 372
Aggregate inventory costs, 371
Aggregate investment, in cash and securities, 969
Aggregate planning, 363, 366–373
Aggregate planning models, 372
Aggregate planning problem, 356, 366–373
Aggressive accounting, 941
Aggressive approach, 956
Aggressive financing strategy, 978–979

Agility, 680
Aging schedule, 963–964
Agreeableness, 749
Agreements, country goals on, 1427
Airline overbooking, 293
Albany Ladder Company, 235
Albertson's, 576
Alcoa, 1369
Alcohol testing, 108
Allocation base, 878
Alta Distributing, 811
Alteration, subsequent, 153
Alternative evaluation, 524–525
Alternative payoff approach, 1469
Alternative risk transfer, 1309–1310
Alternative sources of capital, 1062
Amazon.com, 418, 495–496, 544, 576, 840, 911, 1128, 1144, 1348
Ambiance, 456
Ambidextrous approach, 249
Ambiguity, moral, 1344–1345
American Airlines, 241, 562, 869, 888, 1135
American Automobile Labeling Act (1992), 551
American Bar Association (ABA), 1141
American Depository Receipts (ADRs), 1091–1092
American Express, 1130, 1177
American Express CA, 1242
American Marketing Association (AMA), 548, 549
American Motors Corporation, 1333
American Productivity and Quality Center (APQC), 689
American Society for Quality, 649
American Stock Exchange (AMEX), 1088, 1089, 1177
Americans with Disabilities Act (1990)
Americans with Disabilities Act (ADA), 102, 106, 551, 729–730, 748, 792
Amiable social style, 618
Amoral management, 1341, 1343
Amortization methods, 297–298
Amortized loans, 306–307
Amplitude modulation, 1223, 1224
Analog, 1223–1224
Analogies, 69
Analysis, systems, 1180–1183
Analytical social style, 618
Analytic hierarchy process, 287
Analytic modeling, 513
Analyzability, 350
Anchor stores, 602
Anglia Water, 247
Anheuser-Busch, 240
Ann Taylor, 600, 602
Annual percentage rate (APR), 143, 308
Annuity
  future value of, 302–304
  present value of, 304–306
Annuity due, 302, 303–304, 305–306
Antecedent debts, 16
Anthropological excursions, 483
Anti-boycott legislation, 137
Anticipation, 443
Anticipatory breach, 133
Antidumping duty, 1440

Antidumping regulations, 1440
Antitrust policy, 110
  Clayton Act, 114–115
  Federal Trade Commission Act, 116–117
  international business and, 1401, 1465
  market economy regulation and, 92
  purchasing law and, 137
  Robinson-Patman Act, 115–116
  Sherman Antitrust Act, 110–114
Antivirus software, 1142
AOL, 211
AOL-Time Warner, Inc., 211
Apathy, 1286
Apparent authority, 15, 22, 129
Apple Computer Inc., 115, 229, 237, 241–242, 495, 1082, 1244, 1349
Applebaum, William, 609
Applicant pools, 733
Applicant population, 733
Application forms, 747–748
Application layer, 1231
Applications, risks to, 1140–1143
Application service provider (ASP), 1194, 1200–1202
Application time limit, 748
Appraisal costs, 655
Appraisal remedy, 23
Appreciation, 1443–1444
Approval of fundamental changes, 22
Arbitrage, 507
Arbitration, 1459
Arby's, 207
Arc elasticity, 195–196
Archer Farms, 583
Area structure, 1390–1391
Argyris, Chris, 7
ARM (adjustable rate mortgage), 143
ARM disclosure rules, 143
Arms-length approach, 334
Arms-length pricing, 1381
Arrow diagrams, 647
Arthur Andersen, 547
Articles of incorporation, 19
Articles of partnership, 13
Artificial intelligence (AI), 1169–1173
Artificial vision, 1170
Asea Brown Boveri (ABB), 245, 1173
"As is" clauses, 149
Asked price, 1089
Assemble-to-order, 375, 376, 381
Assessment
  fraud risks, 1288
  human resources effectiveness, 709–711
  organizational workforce, 705
Assessment, retention, 719–721
Asset-based financing, 974
Asset investments, 1416, 1417, 1418
Assets
  accounting equation and, 827
  balance sheets and, 835
  control procedures and, 938–939
  financial, 1415
  lumpy, 1021
  marketing strategy and, 473
  marshaling of, 14
  misuse of, 598
  physical, 1368

portfolio risk and, 1097–1098
preferred stock and, 996
purchase or lease of, 23
quick, 852
real, 1415
  See also Distribution of assets; Short-term asset management
Asset valuation, 309
  bonds, 1004–1007
  capital budgeting and, 1066
  equity (stock), 1007–1014
  real (tangible) assets, 1014–1015
Assignability, 14
Assignable causes, 672
Associates
  general partnerships, 15
  limited partnerships, 16
Association, 14
Association of Certified Fraud Examiners (ACFE), 1279
Assortment, 436, 534–535
Assumption of the risk, 153
Assurance, 684
Asymmetric DSL (ADSL), 1233
Asymmetric information, 1057
Asynchronous communication, 1219–1220
AT&T, 90, 181, 183, 229, 659, 675, 689, 1002, 1069, 1093, 1227, 1233
A. T. Kearney, 235
Atomic transactions, 1239–1240
Attempts to monopolize, 114
Attitudes, 523
Attitude survey, 721
Attribute control charts, 673–675
Attribute listing, 71
Auction markets, 1089
Audit committee, 1354
Auditors, 1274, 1275
Audits
  current competitors, 528–530
  customer service and sales enhancement, 449–450
  human resources, 705, 709–710
  social versus stakeholder, 1330
Audit trail, 1240, 1286
Augustine, Norman, 1335
Australian business customs, 1424
Australian Business Excellence Awards, 671
Australian Business Excellence Prize, 671
Australian Quality Awards Foundation, 671
Austrian business customs, 1424
Authentication, 1240
Authority, 14, 15
  acceptance theory of, 26–27
  chain of command and, 36–37
  charismatic, 244
  hierarchy of, 221
  legal, 128–133
  officers, 22
  power versus, 259–260
  rational-legal, 244
  traditional, 244
Authority-compliance management, 41
Authority to amend, 23
Authority to bind partnership, 15
Authority to issue, 20
Authorization, 78, 1284–1285

SUBJECT INDEX 1635

Auto-By-Tel, 518
Autocratic leaders, 40–41
Automated inventory-tracking systems, 399
Automation, 336–337
Autonomy, 724, 725
AutoVantage, 518
Availability, 23
Availability delay, 960
Average expected rate of inflation, 215
Average relations, 160–161
Average revenue, price elasticity and, 200
Average total cost, 512
Avon Products Inc., 576, 580, 1377
Award Gold Level, 671
Award Level, 671
Awards, as incentives, 807
Awareness set, 525

B

Baan, 1131
Baby Bells, 230
Baby boomers, 416, 572
Baby busters. *See* Generation X
Background investigation, 756
Backlogs, 368–369
Backup, 1238–1239
Backward chaining, 1176
Bailments, 151
Balanced scorecard, 50, 911–912
Balance of payments (BOP), 1414–1419
Balance of payments (BOP) deficit, 1430
Balance of power transfer, 504
Balance on trade (BOT), 1416
Balances, 828
Balance sheet, 832, 835–836, 837, 1017–1018, 1063
Balance sheet accounts and definitions, 981–982
Balance sheet budgets, 896–900
Balance sheet test, 21
Baldridge National Quality Award. *See* Malcolm Baldridge National Quality Award
Banana Republic, 421
Bandwidth, 1220
Bangor Hydro-Electric Company, 996–997
Bank, John, 668
BankAmerica Corporation, 1088
Banker's acceptance, 973
Bankers' ratio, 851
Bank loans
    cost of, 973–974
    short-term, 971–972
Bank Nationale de Paris, 1366
Bank of America, 1088, 1168
Bank One, 83
Bankruptcy, 14, 154
Bankruptcy Act, 154
Banks/banking
    commercial, 1086–1087
    developing-nation debt and, 1454
    international, 1449–1456
    investment, 1085, 1086, 1092–1095
Bargaining, 78
Barnard, Chester I., 26–27

Barnes & Noble, 223, 228, 516, 576, 1129
BarnesandNoble.com, 1128
Barrier to entry, 174, 1128
Barrier to exit, 174
Barrier to mobility, 174
Barter, 1381
Barter terms of trade, 1433
Barton, Laurence, 1332
Baseband, 1220
Base case, 1080
Baseline plan, 275
Base pay, 800
Base price, 511–514
Base price adjustments, 517–519
Basic stock method (BSM), 432–433
Basis of the bargain, 148
Basket of currencies, 1442
Basket valuation, 1452
Bass Pro, 419
Bath & Body Works, 457
Battle Creek Cereal Co., 917
Battle of the brands, 436
Baud, 1221
Bauer, Raymond, 1316–1317
Beall's, 48
Bechtel, 1414
Beckhard, Richard, 7
Beginning-of-the-month (BOM) inventories, planned, 426
Behavior
    budgeting and, 887
    competitor, 420
    consumer, 420
    decision making and, 77
    ethical, 460, 462–463, 625, 814, 1342
    intentional, 1342
    international business, 1401–1403
    job analysis and, 729
    leader, 43–44
    motivation and, 57
    organizational, 222
    supply chain, 405–406, 420
    training and, 764
    unethical, 459, 460–461, 463, 625, 1342
    unintentional, 1342
    See also Consumer behavior; Cost behavior
Behavioral approaches, 41
Behavioral event interviews, 732
Behavioral interview, 752
Behavioral/objective methods, 779, 780
Behavioral rating approaches, 780
Behavioral sciences approach, 28
Behavior-based performance information, 774
Belgian business customs, 1424
Bell Atlantic, 1202
Bell Canada, 994
Bell Laboratories, 181, 651, 1069
Belonging and needs, 713
Benchmarking, 530, 681, 688–689, 691
    human resources, 711–712
    prepackaged software, 1197, 1198–1199
    training, 764
Benchmarking analysis, 711–712
Benefits, 560, 619. *See also* Employee benefits management
Benefits needs analysis, 794

Benetton, 604
Bennis, Warren G., 7
Bernstein, Jonathan L., 1336
Bertelsmann AG, 228
Best Buy, 339, 576, 603
Best-case scenario, 1080
Best efforts arrangement, 1093
Best operating level, 191
Best practices, 411, 688
Beta coefficient, 1099
Beta risk, 1078, 1081–1082
Bethlehem Steel, 410
Bethune, Gordon M., 73
Biases, 755
Bid price, 1089
Bilateral contract, 123–124
Billing errors, 143
Bill of lading, 131
Bill of material (BOM), 375, 376–380
Biometric, 1239
Bits per second (bps), 1220
Black & Decker, 34, 250, 1389
Black hole, 1396
Blackouts, 1140
Blake, Robert, 267
Blanchard, Kenneth H., 42–43
Blanket liens, 976
Blasting, 71
Blevins, Randy, 250
Blockbuster Entertainment, 1106
Blockbuster Video, 456, 1238
Blue Cross and Blue Shield, 557
Blue sky laws, 94, 155, 1091
Board committees, 1354–1355
Board of directors
    changes in, 1354–1355
    composition of, 1354
    corporate governance and, 1349, 1351
    executive compensation and, 814
    financial shenanigans and, 1293
    function of, 22
    internal control and, 1273–1274
    liability of, 1353
Board of Governors of the Federal Reserve System, 1091
Body language, 1422
Body Shop, 602
Boeing, 234, 241, 1202, 1410
Boesky, Ivan, 1352–1353
BoiseCascade Corporation, 354
Bollinger Shipyards, 1147
Bolshoi Ballet, 410
BOM files, 377
Bond indentures, 987
Bond ratings, 989–990
Bond refunding, 987, 993–994
Bonds
    foreign, 994
    innovations, 988–989
    types of, 20, 985–986
Bond valuation, 1004–1007
Bond-yield-plus-risk-premium approach, 1044
Bonuses, 806–807, 808
Bookkeeping, double-entry, 1415
Books, right to inspect, 22
Book value model, 1108–1109

Book value per share, 982
Borden, 80–81
Borders, 516, 521
Borrowing, country risk and, 1103. *See also* Loans
Borrowing reserves, 1452–1453
Boston Consulting Group, 1251
Bottlenecks. *See* Production bottlenecks
Boundary-spanning, 220, 251
Boundary-spanning roles, 226–227
Bounded reality perspective, 73, 74–75
Boycotts, 112, 113, 137, 1373, 1401
Brady Law (1993), 551
Brainstorming, 68–69
Brand equity, 491–492, 546
Branding, 418
Branding decisions, 491–492
Branding strategies, 492
Brand loyalty, 505
Brand parity, 505
Brand positioning, 500
Brands, 477
Braniff Airlines, 957
Breach of contract, 122, 133–135
Breach of warranty, notice of, 150
Breadth, 436
Breakeven analysis, 289–290
    financial, 1028–1030
    operating, 1022, 1025
Breakeven chart, 1023
Breakeven computation, 1023–1024, 1030
Breakeven graph, 1029
Breakeven point, 289, 577, 868–871, 1027–1028, 1029
Breaking the glass, 790
Break point (BP), 1048
Breakthrough improvement, 680–681
Breakthrough objectives, 681
Bretton Woods system, 1446
Brevity, 53
Bribery, 598, 1402, 1467–1469
Bridge, 1224
Bridge buying, 507
Bridgestone-Firestone, 1321
British Airways, 234, 562
British business customs, 1425
Broadband, 1220
Broad form, 1305
Brochures, electronic, 545
Brokerage departments, 1088
Brokers, 1089
Brookings Institution, 515
Brown, Courtney, 1350
Brown, Mark, 406
Brownouts, 1140
Budgetary slack, 887
Budget deficits, federal, 216
Budgeted balance sheet, 900
Budgeted income statement, 896
Budgeting/budgets, 885
    advertising, 499–500
    cash, 959
    projects, 277
    See also Capital budgeting; Operating budgets
Budgeting systems, 887–890
Buffering roles, 226–227

Build-a-Bear Workshops, 558
Building management, 446
Bulldog bonds, 994
Bundle pricing, 210
Bureau of National Affairs, 711
Bureaucracy, 26, 243
Bureaucratic control, 244–246
Bureaucratic control process, 48
Bureaucratic culture, 84, 85
Bureaucratic/formalized control, 1398
Bureaucratic organizations, 26
Burger King, 207, 478, 555
Business
    artificial intelligence in, 1169–1173
    decision making in, 1148
    government influence on, 89–90
    differential analysis and, 921–922
Business activity, interest rate levels and, 216–217
Business combinations, 23
Business continuity plans, 1258–1262
Business crises, managing, 1333–1335
Business customers
    price flexing and, 517–518
    researching, 530–531
    See also Customers
Business cycle, forecasting and, 171–172
Business decisions, interest rate levels and, 217
Business districts, 601–602
Business entity concept, 824
Business environment, networks and, 1234–1235
Business ethics, 85–86
    accounting and, 940–941
    corporations and, 1336–1339
    finance and, 1114–1115
    human resources management and, 814–815
    information technology and, 1262–1264
    international business and, 1467–1472
    international negotiations and, 1428
    managerial ethics, 85–86
    marketing and, 547–553
    purchasing ethics, 459–463
    quality and, 693
    retail marketing and, 597–599
    sales and, 624–625
    sources of, 86–89
Business ethics visibility gap, 1470
Business exposure, 1325–1326
Business for profit, 14
Business Improvement Level, 671
Business information systems, 1235–1237
Business judgment rule, 23
Business law
    contract law, 121–127
    finance and, 154–156
    information technology and, 156
    international, 1460–1467
    marketing and, 138–146
    product liability, 146–154
    purchasing and, 128–137
    quality and, 157
Business-level strategy, 1323. *See also* Strategy
Business models, for e-commerce, 1252

Business operations franchise, 1375
Business organizations, 8
    business trusts, 13
    corporate powers, 20
    corporateness, recognition or disregard of, 19
    corporation attributes, 18
    corporation classifications, 18–19
    corporation formation, 19
    corporations, 11–12
    debt securities, 20
    directors and officers, role of, 22–24
    dividends and other distributions, 21
    equity securities, 20–21
    general partnership, 9–10
    general partnership dissolution, 14–15
    general partnership formation, 13–14
    joint ventures, 11
    limited liability company, 12–13
    limited liability limited partnership, 10
    limited liability partnership, 10
    limited partnership, 10
    partner/partner relationships, 15
    partner/third party relationships, 15–18
    shareholders, role of, 21–22
    sole proprietorship, 8–9
Business plan, manufacturing, 359–360
Business policy, 81
Business practices, cross-cultural, 1423, 1424–1425
Business process, 50
Business process analysis
    benchmarking, 688–689, 691
    business process improvement, 690
    change management, 692–693
    continuous process improvement, 691
    process improvement types, 691
    redesign, 691–692
    reengineering, 689–690
Business process improvement (BPI), 690
Business process reengineering (BPR), 689–690
Business recovery plans, 1258–1262
Business risk, 1050, 1099, 1100. *See also* Risks
Business strategy, 759, 1268–1269. *See also* Strategy
Business-to-business markets, 543
Business-to-business products, 477–478
Business-to-consumer markets, 543
Business-to-government markets, 543
Business transactions. *See* Transactions
Business trusts, 13
Business valuations, 1107–1114
Business Week, 1333–1335
Bus topology, 1228
Buy-and-hold investment strategy, 968
Buy.com, 84
Buyer power, 177
Buyers
    competition and, 175
    consumers as, 520
    information systems and, 1131
    JIT purchasing and, 390
    rights of, 133
Buyer-seller relationships, 463
Buyer's examination, 149
Buying. *See* Purchasing

Buying power index (BPI), 606–607
Buy-national policies, 1440
Buy orders, 1089
Bylaws, 19

C

Cable links, 1232
Cable modems, 1225
CAD (computer-aided design), 337, 346, 354
Cafeteria plan, 798
Caliber Systems Inc., 342
Callable bonds, 20
Call option, 1000
Call premium, 987, 996
Call protection, 987
Call provision, 987, 996–997, 1004
CAM (computer-aided manufacturing), 337, 346, 354
Campbell, Kenneth L., 396
Canada Awards for Excellence, 670
Canadian Awards for Business Excellence, 670–671
Canadian Institute of Chartered Accountants (CICA), 1274–1275
Canadian Pacific Railroad, 1178
Cancellation by mutual consent, 133
Cancellation clause, 998
Cancellation for default, 133
Cancellation for the convenience of the purchaser, 133
Canned presentation, 619
Capacity, 123, 1220. *See also* Service capacity management
Capacity planning, 338, 366–373
Capacity requirements planning (CRP), 373
Capital
    contributed, 155
    general partnerships and, 15
    international business strategies and, 1367
    legal (stated), 155
    partnership, 14
    raising, 1092–1093
    See also Cost of capital; Working capital; Working capital management
Capital Asset Pricing Model (CAPM), 1012–1014, 1043–1044, 1081, 1082, 1099
Capital budgeting
    capital rationing, 1083–1084
    cash flow estimations and risks, 1074–1077
    country risk and, 1102–1103
    evaluation techniques, 1066–1074
    importance of, 1064–1066
    project risk and, 1082–1083
    risk and, 1078–1082
Capital components, 1042
Capital expenditures budget, 900
Capital/financial account, 1414, 1416–1418
Capital gains yield, 1008
Capitalizing the lease, 999
Capital leases, 998
Capital markets, 1085
Capital One Financial Corp., 1235
Capital projects, 1065–1066

Capital rationing, 1083–1084
Capital sources, alternative, 1062
Capital stock, 828
Capital structure, 22, 1050
    degree of leverage, 1052, 1054–1056
    liquidity and, 1056
    optimal, 1051–1052, 1053
    target, 1050–1051
Capital structure theory, 1056–1057
Captive insurers, 1303
Captives, 1310
Capture theory, 92–93
Care, duty of, 15
Career development and planning, 721
Career planning, 766
Career progression, 767–768
Careers, 765–773
Caremark, 1353
Carleton Corporation, 947
Carnegie-Mellon University, 76
Carnegie model of organizational decision making, 76–77
Carolina Power & Light (CP&L), 1084, 1085
Carriers
    reducing number of, 391
    selecting, 403–405
Carroll, Archie, 1312–1314, 1318, 1319
Carrying cost, 386–387
Carrying cost rate changes, 373
Cartels, 183, 552
Carter, Larry, 232
Case view, 29
Cash
    aggregate securities in, 969
    sources and uses of, 842–844
Cash before delivery (CBD), 963
Cash budget, 896–900, 949, 959
Cash conversion cycle, 951–953
Cash discount, 443, 518, 963
Cash dividends, 21
Cash flow per share, 840
Cash flows
    country risk and, 1102–1103
    estimations and risks, 1074–1077
    forecasting, 1035
Cash flows after taxes, 1074
Cash flows from financing activities, 836, 839–840
Cash flows from investing activities, 836, 839
Cash flows from operating activities, 836, 838–839
Cash flows statement, 832, 836, 838–844, 1036
Cash flow synchronization, 959
Cash flow test, 21
Cash flow timeline, 977–978
    amortized loans, 307
    future value, 299
    future value of an annuity, 302, 303
    present value, 301
    present value of an annuity, 304, 305
Cash forecasting, 1035–1041
Cash management
    multinational working capital management, 966–967
    working capital management, 958–959
Cash management model, 296–297
Cash management techniques, 959–961

Cash on delivery (COD), 963
Catalogs, 1165
Catalog sales, 580
Categorical imperative, 1346
Category killer, 416
Category management (CM), 436, 594–595
Category manager, 594
Category rating methods, 779, 780
Category signage, 458
Caterpillar, 242
Cause-and-effect diagrams, 72, 652, 653, 667
Cause-related marketing, 509, 551
CBS, 989
CDNow, 1164
Cease and desist order, 138
Celler-Kefauver Antimerger Act (1950), 551, 1105
Cellular layout, 336
Cellular phones, 1234
Cendant Corporation, 1354
Census of Retail Trade, 418, 576
Center for Business Ethics, 88
Central business district (CBD), 601
Central information systems organization, 1210–1211, 1212
Centrality, 262
Centralization, 38, 221, 243–244, 351–352, 901–902, 1393
Centralized information systems architecture, 1206, 1207–1210
Centralized management, 18
Centralized network, 64
Central tendency error, 782
Centrobe, 235
Ceremonies, 83
Certification mark, 96
Chaconas, Peter, 250
Chain of command, 36–37, 235
Chain reaction theory, 663
Champions, 490, 1137–1138
Chance causes, 672
Chance of loss, 1297
Change, in new workplace, 56. *See also* Innovation goals; Organizational change
Change agents, 1138–1139
Change initiatives, 63
Change leadership, 45
Change management, 692–693
Change process, 248
Change teams, 256
Changing expectations, forecasting and, 164–165
Channel capacity, 1220
Channel flows, 536–538
Channel functions, 534
Channel intensity, 533
Channel length, 532–533
Channel of distribution. *See* Marketing channels
Channel research, 530–531
Channels, 61, 62, 1220–1223. *See also* Communication channels
Chapter 11 (bookseller), 516
Character, 1158
Charge-back methods, 1215–1216
Charismatic authority, 244
Charismatic leaders, 45

Charles Schwab, 1130, 1170, 1258
Charming Shoppes, 600
Charter amendments, 23
Charters, 1348, 1349
Chase Manhattan Bank, 660, 1168
Chase strategy, 369
Check-clearing process, 959–960
Checklists, 72
Check sheets, 651
Chevron, 1105, 1202
Chicago Board Options Exchange (CBOE), 999–1000
Chief executive officers (CEOs), 1350, 1355
Chief information officers (CIOs), 1157
Chief risk officer (CRO), 1298
Child Protection Act (1966), 551
Choice models, 524
Choice of associates. *See* Associates
Chronic crisis stage, 1332, 1333
Chrysler Corporation, 233, 1050, 1106. *See also* DaimlerChrysler
CHS Electronics, 223
Ciba, 1400
Cincinnati Gas and Electric, 1353
Cincinnati Milacron, 247
Ciphertext, 1241
Circle K, 419
Circuit City, 576, 1138
Circuit switching, 1231
Circulation, 453–454
Cisco Systems, 232
Citicorp, 1088, 1138, 1366, 1378, 1449, 1454
Citigroup, 1088, 1138
Citizenship, corporate, 18, 1311–1321
Civil prosecution, of fraud, 1280, 1291
Civil Rights Act (1964), 103–105, 106, 792
Civil Rights Act (1991), 102, 104, 789
Clan control, 246
Clan culture, 84
Class A vendors, 439
Class B vendors, 439
Class C vendors, 439
Class D vendors, 439
Class E vendors, 439
Classical perspective, 24–27
Classical trade theory, 1403–1405
Classified stock, 983
Clayton Antitrust Act (1914), 114–115, 137, 551, 552, 1105
Clean Air Act, 119, 120
Clean float, 1446
Cleansing phase, 1167
Clean Water Act, 119–120
Clearing delay, 960
Click-and-mortar retailing, 1252
Clientele effect, 1058–1059
Client lists and profiles, 1165
Client needs, identifying, 618
Clients
    approaching, 617–618
    outsourcing and, 1196
Client/server systems, 1164, 1203
Closed-ended credit, 143
Closed loop, 390, 391
Closed shop, 102
Closed systems, 29, 218–219
Closely held corporations, 19, 1089

Closely held stock, 1089
Closure, 72
CNN, 1144, 1378
Coach, 419
Coalition, 76, 77
Coalition building, 266
Coaxial cable, 1222
Coca-Cola Bottling Company, 186, 187–188, 224, 240, 356, 823, 887, 933, 1321, 1376, 1377
CoCo model, 1274–1276
Code law, 1457
Code of conduct, 625
Code of ethics, 88–89, 941
Coding, 564
Coefficient of variation (CV), 1097
Coercive power, 39, 256, 259, 590
Cognitive ability tests, 748
Cognitive dissonance, 525
Cognitive responses, 521
Cohen, Michael, 78
Cold-calling, 617
Cold-site, 1260
Cold turkey conversion, 1188
Coldwell Banker & Company, 1106
Colgate, 1376
Colgate-Palmolive, 1396
Collaboration
    organizational, 267–268
    retail marketing and, 592–595
    See also Organizational collaboration
Collaborative/problem-solving strategy, 1325
Collateral, availability of, 993
Collection policy, 963
Collections float, 960
Collective bargaining, 267
Collective mark, 96
Collectivity stage, 241, 242
College recruiting, 738
Collusion, 183, 444
Columbia Pictures, 1417
Combination approach, 717–718
Comdisco, 1261
Comiskey, Eugene E., 941
Command, unity of, 26, 36. *See also* Chain of command
Commercial banks, 1086–1087
Commercialization, new product development and, 490
Commercial paper, 972–973, 980–981
Commission, 808
Commitment, 33
    escalating, 80–81
    gaining, 620
    organizational, 716–718
    referent power and, 40
Commitment fee, 972
Committed cost, 278
Committee of Sponsoring Organizations (COSO), 1270, 1274, 1275–1276, 1283
Commodity terms of trade, 1433
Common carrier, 404, 1227
Common causes, 672
Common law, 1456–1457
    contracts and, 121, 122
    environmental damage and, 117–118
    purchasing and, 130

Common law approach, 19
Common-size statement analysis, 848–849
Common stock, 21, 1007
    dividends per share, 859
    dividend yield, 859–860
    long-term financing and, 981–984
    newly issued, 1045
Common stockholders, legal rights and privileges of, 982–983
Common stock market, 1089–1091
Communication
    asynchronous, 1219–1220
    control procedures and, 939–940
    crisis, 1335–1336
    cross-cultural, 1419–1422
    data, 1217–1218
    department design and, 352
    employee benefits, 797–798
    internal control and, 1271
    managers and, 61
    networks and, 1217
    new workplace and, 64–65
    nonverbal, 1419
    open, 64–65
    organizational, 62–64, 65–67
    organizational change and, 256
    point-of-purchase, 499, 509–510
    project management and, 272
    synchronous, 1220
    two-way, 593
    visual, 457–458
    Web EDI and, 1256
    wireless, 1227
    See also Marketing communications
Communication barriers
    individual, 65–66
    organizational, 66
    overcoming, 66–67
Communication channels, 61, 62
    communication barriers and, 65, 66
    formal, 62–64, 66
    informal, 64
    team, 64
Communication direction, 1218–1219
Communication flow, 66
Communication needs, 67
Communication process, 61, 62
Communications gap, 566, 567
Communication skills, individual, 66–67
Communications Satellite Corporation (Comsat), 1094
Community indifference curve, 1431
Company. *See* Limited liability company
Company/brand sites, 543
Compaq Computer Corporation, 181, 240, 478, 1230, 1239
Comparable worth, 105
Comparative advantage, 189, 471, 1403–1404, 1405, 1406
Comparative methods, 779, 780
Comparative negligence, 153
Comparative price advertising, exaggerated, 552
Compatibility, 1136
Compelling experiences, 563
Compensating balance (CB), 958, 972

SUBJECT INDEX 1639

Compensation, 15
  CEO, 1350
  countertrade and, 1381
  ethics and, 461
  executive, 813–814
  management, 22
  motivational programs for, 60
  nature of, 799–801
  outside director, 1350
  retention interventions and, 721
  sales, 807–809
  sales force, 622–623
Compensation committee, 1355
Compensation levels, decisions about, 801–802
Compensation philosophies, 801
Compensation responsibilities, 800–801
Compensation strategies and practices, 799–804
Compensation system design issues, 801–804
Compensatory approach, 746
Compensatory model, 524
Competencies, 731
Competency analysis methodology, 732
Competency approach, to job analysis, 731–732
Competency-based pay, 803
Competent parties, 127
Competition
  Clayton Act and, 116
  dynamic nature of, 181
  factors determining, 173–175
  government regulation and, 89–91
  imperfect, 1409–1410
  intergroup conflict and, 257
  nonprice, 183–185
  potential, 190
  pricing and, 516
  retail, 576–583
  See also Monopolistic competition; Perfect competition
Competitive advantage, 189
  human resources and, 701–702
  information systems and, 1126–1131
  of nations, 1404, 1411–1412
  quality and, 660–661
Competitive analysis, 488
Competitive benchmarking, 688–689
Competitive bids, 1092–1093
Competitive environment, 474, 476
Competitively advantaged products, 485
Competitiveness, 476
Competitive price moves, 517
Competitive quotations, 461
Competitive recruiting sources, 739
Competitive strategy, 3–4
  monopolistic competition and oligopoly markets, 188–190
  perfectly competitive and monopoly markets, 178–180
Competitor behavior, 420
Competitor research, 526–530
Competitors, auditing, 528–530
Complaints, discrimination-related, 786
Complementary products, 368
Complementary services, 414
Complements, 203
Compliance, 39

Compliance strategy, 1342, 1343
Component cost, 1042
Component life cycles, 397
Component parts and materials, as business-to-business products, 478
Composite index, 171
Composite keys, 1161
Compounding, 299, 308–309
Compound tariffs, 1434
Comprehensive Environmental Response, Compensation and Liability Act (CERCLA), 120
Compulsory share exchange, 23
Computer-aided craftsmanship, 347
Computer-aided software engineering (CASE), 1191
Computer-aided software engineering (CASE) tools, 1191
Computer implementation, 294
Computer-integrated manufacturing (CIM), 346–347
Computerized budgeting systems, 890
Computers
  cost-volume-profit analysis, 872
  user application development and, 1203
Computer viruses, 1141–1143
Concentration, 534
Concentration banking, 960
Concentration of power, limiting, 91
Concept, 483
Concept test, 488
Conceptual skills, 51
Concerted action, 111–112
Concerted refusal to deal, 112, 113
Concurrent control, 47, 48
Conditional offers, 127
Conduct codes, 625
Conference Board, 711
Conference Board Survey, 1316
Confidential information, 136
Confidential vendor analysis, 439
Confiscation, 1384–1385, 1462–1463
Conflict, 77
  exporting, 1401
  project teams and, 285
  retail marketing and, 591–592
  structural deficiencies and, 240
  See also Organizational conflict
Conflicting ethical responsibilities, 1467
Conflicts of interest, financial, 461
Confrontation, 267
Congeneric merger, 1106
Conglomerate merger, 115, 1106
Conjunctive models, 524
Connectivity, 1136, 1256
Conquest marketing, 568
Conscientiousness, 749
Conscious parallelism, 112
Consensual relationships, 790
Conservative approach, 956
Conservative financing strategy, 979–980
Consideration, 41, 122, 127
Consideration set, 525
Consignment, 437
Consolidated Gas Company, 1356
Consolidated Omnibus Budget Reconciliation Act (COBRA), 795

Consolidation, 23
Conspiracies to monopolize, 114
Constant growth model, 1011, 1044–1045
Constant growth stock, 1010–1012
Constant payout ratio, 1060
Construction, systems design and, 1187
Construction industry, 105
Consultation, intergroup, 267–268
Consultative selling, 613
Consulting, 1196
Consumer behavior, 420
  household decision making, 525
  individual consumer decision making, 523–525
  psychographics, 522–523
  psychological bases of, 520–521
  scope of, 520
Consumer credit card fraud, 144
Consumer credit contract, 144
Consumer Credit Protection Act (1968), 551
Consumer credit transactions, 142–145
Consumer decision making, individual, 523–525
Consumer emotions, 521
Consumer moods, 521
Consumer needs and wants, 520, 521
Consumer-oriented sales promotion, 499
Consumer products, 141, 477, 478
Consumer Product Safety Act (CPSA), 139–140, 551
Consumer Product Safety Commission (CPSC), 139–140, 157, 551
Consumer protection, 138
Consumer protection agencies, 138
Consumer purchases, 140–142
Consumer research, 526
Consumer responsiveness, 505
Consumer right of rescission, 142
Consumers
  e-marketing and, 546
  point-of-purchase communications and, 510
  price flexing to, 518–519
Consumer sales promotions, 507–508
Consumer sovereignty, 91
Consumers' surplus, 208–209
Consumer-to-consumer markets, 543
Consumption discrepancies, 534
Consumption satiation, 470
Containment, 1258
Contemporary motivation approach, 58
Contention, 1230
Content theories, 58
Context, translators and, 1421
Contextual dimensions, 220, 221
Continental Airlines, 73, 718
Continental Divide Robotics (CDR), 1170
Contingencies, situational, 44
Contingency approaches, 41–42
Contingency effectiveness approaches, 5–8
Contingency plans, 32, 35, 1257–1262
Contingency theory (Fiedler's), 42
Contingency view, 29–30
Continuance commitment, 716
Continuation after dissolution, 14–15
Continuation after expulsion, 15
Continuation after wrongful dissolution, 14

Continuation agreement of the partners, 15
Continuity, 11, 501
Continuous budgeting, 888
Continuous improvement, 641, 691
Continuous process improvement, 691
Continuous process production, 345
Contract analysis, 1300
Contract carriers, 404
Contract implied in law, 125
Contract law, 121–122, 126–127
Contract negotiations, 1197, 1198
Contracts, 15
    classification of, 123–124
    consumer credit, 144
    country goals on, 1427
    definition of, 122
    essential elements of, 126–127
    international, 1464–1465
    introduction to, 121
    JIT transportation and, 391
    privity of, 150
    project management and, 274
    promissory estoppel, 125
    promoters, 19
    psychological contract, 715–716
    quasi contracts, 125–126
    requirements of, 122–123
    See also Breach of contract; Debt contracts
Contract terms, 144
Contractual liability, 1300
Contractual vertical marketing channels, 588
Contrast error, 782
Contributed capital, 155
Contribution margin, 866–868, 929–930, 1024
Contribution margin analysis, 935–937
Contribution margin ration, 867
Contributions, 16, 17
Contributors, 1396
Contributory infringer, 100
Contributory negligence, 150, 153
Control, 11
    accounting and, 937–940
    aggregate plan, 373
    budgeting and, 886–887
    charge-back services, 1216
    corporate fraud and, 1283–1286
    corporate governance and, 1349–1350
    cost, 280–281
    decision premises, 266
    dollar merchandise, 434–435
    dynamic systems of, 244–246
    environmental resources, 228–230
    export, 1463
    import, 1463
    information center, 1214
    information technology, 1237–1240, 1244–1245
    internal, 1270–1274
    international pricing strategy, 1380
    international trade, 1373–1374
    interviews, 754
    inventory investment, 393
    issues, 1330
    limited partnerships, 16
    loss, 1302, 1306–1307
    management, 31, 47–50, 1268, 1269–1270
    mergers and acquisitions, 1105
    operational, 1269–1270
    project managers and, 282
    supply chain, 586–589
    supply chain inventory management, 398–399
    wage and price, 1430
    See also Corporate control; Financial control; Inventory control; Organizational control
Control activities, 1271, 1284–1285
Control charts, 650–651, 672–673
Control environment, 1271, 1283
Control groups, training evaluation and, 765
Controllable costs, 931
Controllable expenses, 904
Controllable inputs, 293
Controllable revenues, 904
Controllable turnover, 718
Controlled disbursement accounts (CDAs), 961
Control limits, 651
Controlling costs, 931–932
Control models, 1274–1277
Control objectives for information and related technology (COBIT) model, 1276–1277
Control Objectives for Net Centric Technology (CONCT) model, 1277
Control over final price, 1380
Control Self-Assessment Model (CSA), 1275–1276
Control strategy, 1269
Control threats, 938
Convenience products, 477
Conventional approach to business ethics, 1337–1338
Conventional approach to issues management, 1327
Conventionalist ethic, 1346
Conventional marketing channels, 587
Conversion, 1188–1189
Conversion costs, 877
Conversion price, 1002–1003
Conversion ratio, 1002–1003
Convertibility, 996
Convertible bonds, 20, 986
Convertibles, 1002–1004
Conway, William E., 665–666
Conway quality model, 665–666
Cooper, Martha C., 538
Cooper, Robert G., 495
Cooperation, 255
Cooperative agreements, 372
Cooptation, 228–229
Coordinated decentralization, 1393
Coordination
    department design and, 352
    information center, 1214
    organizational change and, 255
    poor, 66
Coors Brewing Company, 536, 537, 1090
Co-ownership, 14
Coping with uncertainty, 262, 263
Copyrights, 98–99, 100, 136, 1374
Core benefit proposition (CBP), 480, 485
Core business, increased attention to, 1196
Core competency, human resources as, 699–702
Core job dimensions, 59
Corning Incorporated, 1393, 1400
Corporate citizenship, 1311–1321
Corporate control
    control models, 1274–1277
    internal control framework, 1270–1274
    strategies, 1268–1270
Corporate culture, 621. *See also* Organizational culture
Corporate ethics
    business ethics, 1336–1339
    ethics questions, 1340–1341
    management assurance, 1345–1347
    management ethics, 1341–1345
    Venn diagram model for ethical decision making, 1339–1340
    See also Business ethics
Corporate external affairs strategy, 1325
Corporate financial performance, 1319–1320
Corporate fraud
    fighting, 1287–1291
    financial shenanigans, 1292–1293
    nature of, 1277–1280
    reasons for, 1280–1286
Corporate governance, 1347–1358
Corporate mission statements, 1134
Corporateness, recognition or disregard of, 19
Corporate period, 1350
Corporate powers, 20
Corporate public affairs, 1324–1326
Corporate public policy, 1321–1324
Corporate reward structures, 505
Corporate risk management, 1293–1294, 1298–1299
    risk burdens, 1294
    risk definitions, 1294–1295
    risk evaluation, 1301–1302
    risk identification, 1299–1301
    risk measurement, 1297–1298
    risk sources, 1295–1296
    techniques, 1302–1310
Corporate risk, 1078, 1081
Corporate social performance (CSP), 1312, 1318–1320, 1325
Corporate social policy, 1321
Corporate social responsibility (CSR), 1311–1316, 1428
Corporate social responsiveness, 1312, 1316–1318
Corporate sponsorships, 509
Corporate strategies, 2, 1323
    contingency effectiveness approaches, 5–8
    organizational purpose, 2–3
    organizational strategies and design, 3–5
Corporate vertical marketing channels, 587–588
Corporation by estoppel, 19
Corporation de facto, 19
Corporation de jure, 19
Corporations, 11–12
    attributes, 18
    classifications, 18–19
    closely held, 1089

common stock and, 983–984
crisis management, 1324, 1326, 1331–1336
debt securities, 20
directors and officers, role of, 22–24
dividends and other distributions, 21
equity securities, 20–21
formation of, 19
goals of, 944–945
issues management, 1324, 1326–1331
multinational, 1100–1104, 1376, 1469
publicly held, 1089, 1090
shareholders, role of, 21–22
supranational, 1376
transnational, 1376
Corrective action costs, 655
Corrective advertising, 139
Correlation, 653
Correlation analysis, 169
Correspondent bank, 1465
Corruption, 1402
COSO model, 1274, 1275–1276
Cost accounting system overview, 877
Cost allocation, 878
Cost and volume models, 288–289
Cost-based definition, 1440
Cost-based index, 657
Cost-based pricing, 512–513
Cost behavior, 861–866
Cost/benefit analysis, 712, 764, 765, 1181
Cost centers, responsibility accounting for, 902–903
Costco, 585, 603
Cost concept, 824–825
Cost control, 280–281
Cost estimates, for projects, 275, 276–277
Cost flows, 883
Cost forecasting, 279–280
Cost justification, 116
Cost-leadership, 701–702
Cost method of inventory valuation, 428
Cost of capital, 1041
  capital components, 1042
  cost of debt, 1042
  cost of newly issued common stock, 1045
  cost of preferred stock, 1042–1043
  cost of retained earnings, 1043–1045
  marginal cost of capital, 1046–1050
  weighted average cost of capital, 1041, 1046
Cost of debt, 1042
Cost of goods sold, 878, 879
Cost of goods sold budget, 895
Cost of merchandise sold, 878
Cost of new common equity, 1045
Cost of preferred stock, 1042–1043
Cost of production report, 884–885
Cost of quality (COQ), 654–659
Cost of retained earnings, 1043–1045
Cost of risk, 1294
Cost per thousand (CPM), 502
Cost performance analysis, 278–279
Cost performance index (CPI), 278
Cost planning and performance, in project management, 276–281
Cost-plus, 206
Cost-plus approach cost concept, 926–927

Cost-plus pricing, 511–514
Cost price approach, 914
Costs
  advertising, 501
  aggregate planning and, 370–372
  bank loans, 973–974
  commercial paper, 973
  definition of, 875
  discrimination-related, 786
  e-marketing, 545–546
  exchange, 824
  exchange rates and, 1381
  financing, 1028
  flotation, 1042, 1045, 1093
  hiring, 720
  information systems and, 1127–1129
  information technology security controls, 1245–1246
  inventory financing, 977
  inventory-related, 386–387
  issuance, 1093
  logistics and, 539
  long-term versus short-term debt, 957
  marginal, 160
  market economy regulation, 91, 92
  markup pricing and, 207
  money, 213
  opportunity, 920
  organizational change and, 255
  product and service, 335, 875–885
  productivity, 721
  project management and, 271, 272
  receivables financing, 975
  recruiting, 740
  separation, 721
  service quality, 685–686
  shipping and installation, 1076
  sunk, 915, 1075–1076
  switching, 1128–1129
  training, 721
  turnover, 720–721
  Web EDI, 1255–1256
  See also Absorption costing; Effective cost; Fixed costs; Job order cost systems; Process cost systems; Variable costing
Cost variance (CV), 279
Cost-volume profit analysis, 866
Cost-volume-profit relationships, 866–875
Council on Environmental Quality (CEQ), 119
Countercyclical demand, 204
Counterfeit mark, 97
Counterpurchase, 1381–1382
Countertrade, 1381–1382
Countervailing power, 177–178
Country club management, 41
Country organizations, 1396
Country risk, 1099, 1100–1104, 1453
County Seat Jeans, 604
Couponing, 519
Coupon interest rate, 1004
Coupon payment, 1004
Covenant, 48
Covered options, 1000
Craft technologies, 350, 351
Crate & Barrel, 602
Crawling peg, 1447–1448

Creating, 71
Creating standards, 1131
Creative accounting practices, 941
Creative departments, 249
Creative recruiting methods, 740
Creature of the state, 18
Credence attributes, 558
Credit
  risk retention and, 1303
  short-term, 970
  trade, 970
Credit accounts, 143
Credit card fraud, 144
Credit card holder, 144
Credit evaluations, 1177
Credit management, 447, 962–966, 967
Creditors
  general partnership dissolution and, 14, 15
  stockholders versus, 947–948
Creditors' remedies, 145–146
Creditor's rights, 14
Credit policy, 962–963, 964–966, 970
Credit risk, 1453
Credit standards, 962–963
Credit terms, 963, 970
Credit transactions, consumer, 142–145
Credit unions, 1087
Crimes, liability for, 20
Criminal penalties, for trade secret violations, 95–96
Criminal prosecution, of fraud, 1280, 1291
Crises
  balance of payments and, 1418–1419
  nature of, 1331–1332
  types of, 1332
Crisis communications, 1335–1336
Crisis drills, simulating, 1335
Crisis management, 1324, 1326, 1331–1336
Crisis management planning (CMP), 1257–1258
Crisis resolution stage, 1332, 1333
Crisis stages, 1332–1333
Crisis teams, 1334
Critical commodities list, 1400
Crosby, Philip B., 664–665, 681
Crosby quality model, 664–665
Cross-cultural business practices, 1423, 1424–1425
Cross-cultural communication competence, 1422
Cross-cultural communication process, 1419–1422
Cross-cultural negotiations, 1423, 1425–1428
Cross-docking, 540
Cross-national ethics, 1467–1469
Cross-national social responsibility, 1469–1471
Cross-price elasticity of demand, 203
Cubic efficiency, 493
Cues, inconsistent, 66
Cultural awareness, 787
Cultural control, 1398–1399
Cultural environment, purchasing ethics and, 460
Cultural noise, 756
Cultural norms and values, 1421

Cultural relativism, 1469–1470
Culture
   business ethics and, 1470
   high-context, 1421
   See also International cultures and protocols; Organizational culture
Culture change, 247, 253–254
Culture strength, 85
Cumulative actual cost (CAC), 278
Cumulative budgeted cost (CBC), 277, 278
Cumulative dividends, 996
Cumulative earned value (CEV), 278
Cumulative quantity discount, 441
Cumulative voting, 22
Currencies, national, 1451
Currency board, 1444
Currency devaluations, 1381
Currency restrictions, 1380
Currency risk, 1454
Currency stabilization, 1444–1445
Current account, 1414, 1416, 1417
Current asset financing policies, 954–956
Current asset investment policies, 953–954
Current assets, 835, 978
Current competitors, auditing, 528–530
Current income, 1416
Current liabilities, 835–836
Current position analysis, 851–852
Current ratio, 851, 949
Current transfers, 1416
Custom design, 376
Customer acknowledgment, 449
Customer-based quality, 683
Customer complaints and returns, costs due to, costs, 656
Customer contact, 449
Customer Contact Model, 410
Customer-driven quality, 639
Customer errors at the resolution stage, 654
Customer errors during an encounter, 654
Customer errors in preparation, 654
Customer fraud, 1280
Customer holding/loading, 508
Customer management, 445–446
Customer needs, new product development and, 482–485
Customer orders, 408
Customer-oriented salespeople, 614
Customer participation, 414
Customer profiles, 493, 495
Customer prototypes, 485
Customer relationship management (CRM), 564–565, 613, 1147–1148, 1251
Customer retention, 567–570
Customers
   downstream, 384, 385
   e-commerce, 1251, 1252
   new product development and, 482
   new workplace and, 56
   price flexing and, 517–519
   project management and, 272, 273
   proximity to, 410
   quality management and, 640
   retail, 570–572
   service quality and, 683
   services marketing and, 559, 562–563
   transient, 446
Customer satisfaction
   new product development and, 480
   project management and, 271, 272, 276
   retail marketing and, 570
   service quality and, 685
   services marketing and, 563–565
Customer service, 50
   e-marketing and, 546
   logistics and, 542–543
   retail marketing and, 570
   retail selling and, 445–450
Customer service and sales enhancement audit, 449–450
Customer service levels, 447–448
Customer service skills, 780
Customer structure, 1391
Customer surveys, 513
Customer theft, 444
Customization, 1377–1378
Customized output, 348
Custom Research, Inc., 638
Custom Shirt Shop, 369
Customs laws, 137
Cut over conversion, 1188
Cybermall, 1248
Cycle time, 671
Cycle-time reduction, 399, 680
Cyclical normal goods, 205
Cyert, Richard, 76

D

Dai-ichiKangyo Bank, 1366
Daimler-Benz, 1414
Daimler-Benz AG, 1106
DaimlerChrysler, 181, 188, 233, 885, 911, 1253, 1438
Damages, 134
Das, T. K., 1346
Data
   information versus, 1156–1157
   risks to, 1140–1143
Data alteration, 1141
Database administrator (DBA), 1163
Database approach, 1158–1159
Database architecture, 1163–1164
Database management systems (DBMS), 1158–1160
Database marketing, 502
Database models, 1160–1162
Databases
   data warehousing and, 1166–1167
   distributed, 1163
   fragmented, 1163
   organizational, 735–736
   Web, 1164–1165
Data communications, 1217–1218
Data definition language (DDL), 1163
Data destruction, 1141
Data dictionary, 1162
Data distribution, 1217
Data entry controls, 1238
Data flow diagrams (DFDs), 1185–1186
Data integrity, 1264
Data items, 1158
Data link layer, 1231
Data management
   components of, 1162–1163
   data mining, 1167–1169
   data warehousing, 1166–1167
   database architecture, 1163–1164
   database models, 1160–1162
   digital data, 1157–1160
   Web databases, 1164–1165
Data management module, 1149
Data manipulation language (DML), 1163
Data marts, 1166
Data mining, 1167–1169
Data processing departments, 1132
Data requirements, for forecasting, 170
Data security, 1263
Data sheets, 651
Data store, 1185
Data warehousing, 1166–1167
Days sales outstanding (DSO), 951, 963
Dealers, 1089
Dean Witter Reynolds Organization Inc., 1106
Debentures, 986
Debt
   antecedent, 16
   cost of, 1042
   developing-nation, 1454
   international, 1454
   long-term, 957, 984–991
   short-term, 957
   subsequent, 16
Debt buyback, 1454
Debt collection practices, 145–146
Debt contracts, 987, 993
Debt/equity swaps, 1454
Debt-for-debt swaps, 1454
Debt forgiveness, 1455
Debt instruments, traditional, 985–986
Debt markets, 1084
Debt reduction, 1455
Debt securities, 20, 154–155
Decentralization, 38, 901–902, 1393
Decentralized control, 48–49
Decentralized information systems architecture, 1206–1210
Decentralized network, 64
Deception, 139, 461
Decisional roles, of managers, 54
Decision analysis, 287, 290, 292
Decision interrupts, 77
Decision learning, 80
Decision makers, 67
Decision making, 67, 287–288
   business and, 1148
   cost of production report and, 884–885
   definitions, 73
   ethical, 1339–1340
   expert systems, 1173
   household, 525
   income models and, 929–937
   individual, 73–75
   individual consumer, 523–525
   information technology and, 1144–1156
   interest rate levels and, 217
   international organizational structures and, 1393–1394
   intuitive, 75

SUBJECT INDEX   1643

job order costs systems for, 880–881
long-term financing and, 991–993
marginal analysis in, 161
organizational, 75–79
planning and, 33
special circumstances, 80–81
structural deficiencies and, 240
supply chain performance and, 405
transportation strategy and, 401–405
utility and, 292–293
variable and fixed costs, 866
Decision making processes, 73–81
Decision mistakes, 80
Decision models, 915
　differential analysis, 915–922
　product profitability and pricing under production bottlenecks, 927–928
　product-selling prices, 922–927
Decision premises, controlling, 266
Decisions, 288
　compensation-related, 801–802
　expansion, 1065
　manufacturing planning, 359
　marketing mix and, 473, 474
　optimal, 158
　price change, 517
　product mix, 496–497
　replacement, 1065, 1077
　strategic recruiting, 734–735
　See also Product decisions
Decision-support systems (DSSs), 1146
　components, 1148–1153
　developing, 1154–1155
　electronic spreadsheets, 1155
Decision techniques, aggregate, 372
Declaration, effect of, 21
Declaration date, 1061
Decline phase, 414
Decline stage, 578–579
Decline strategies, 496
Decoding, 61, 62
Decomposition, 167
Dedicated carriers, 404
Dedicated servers, 1248
Deductibles, 1308
Deemed exports, 1401
Deere & Company, 337
Defacement, 1141
Default risk premium (DRP), 214
Defective condition, 151–152
Defective corporation, 19
Defective formation, 16
Defective incorporation, 19
Defective products, 389
Defects, 681
Defects per million opportunities (dpmo), 647
Defects per unit (DPU), 647, 681
Defensive mergers, 1105
Deferred annuity, 302–303
Deferred call, 987
Deficits. See Federal budget deficits
Defined work activities, 235
Degree of financial leverage (DFL), 1030, 1054–1055
Degree of leverage, 1052, 1054–1056
Degree of operating leverage (DOL), 1025, 1054

Degree of risk, 1298
Degree of total leverage (DTL), 1031–1032, 1055–1056
Delay, 1427
Delayed rewards, 507–508
Delectus personae, 15
Delegating leadership style, 42
Delegation, 36–37
Deliberately structured, 50–51
Deliverables, 272
Delivery gap, 566, 567
Delivery terms, 131–132, 443
Delivery-to-customer response times, 381
Dell Computer Corporation, 10, 181, 341, 410, 532, 699, 1127
Delphi Automotive Systems, 915
Delphi technique, 72
Delta Air Lines, 901
Demand, 16
　basis for, 192–193
　heterogeneous, 553
　human resources, 705–708
　international business strategies and, 1366
　international reserves, 1449–1451
　markup pricing and, 207
　off-peak, 414
　partitioning, 414
　retail location and, 607–608
　supply and, 192
　See also Cross-price elasticity of demand; Income elasticity of demand; Price elasticity of demand
Demand analysis, 195–205
Demand curve
　kinked, 183
　price elasticity and, 198–199
Demand density, 610
Demand management, 368–369
Demand-pull inflation, 1429
Demand sensitivity analysis, 195–196
Deming, W. Edwards, 661–663, 681, 686, 701
Deming Prize, 670
Deming quality model, 661–663
Democratic leaders, 40–41
Demodulation, 1224
Demographics, 416
Demographic segments, 519
Denial of service (DoS), 1143–1144
Denny's, 498
Department design, 351–352
Departmental differences, as communication barrier, 66
Departmental grouping options, 235
Departmental specialization, 251
Departmental technology, 349–351
Departments
　environmental uncertainty and, 226
　workflow interdependence among, 352–354
Dependency, 261–262, 265, 590
Dependent data marts, 1166
Dependent demand inventory, 340
Dependent variables, 159
Depletion methods, 297–298
Depository receipts, 1091–1092
Depreciation, 1443–1444
Depreciation methods, 297–298

Depth, 437
Deregulation movement, 93
Derivative actions
　limited liability company, 17
　limited partnerships, 16
Derivative securities, 1000
Derivative suits, 22
Derived demand, 192–193, 202
Description, 147
Descriptive ethics, 1337
Design
　compensation systems, 801–804
　custom, 376
　decision making and, 78
　department, 351–352
　external affairs, 1325–1326
　master scheduling and, 382
　operations management systems, 334–338
　product, 676, 677–678
　service organizations, 348–349
　service quality, 684
　store, 456–457
　suppliers and, 329
　systems development life cycle, 1183–1187
　training, 760–761
　Web, 545
　See also Job design; Organizational design
Design defects, 152
Design for manufacturability and assembly (DFMA), 334–335
Designation, 18
Design patent, 100
Desk checking, 1261
Detachable warrants, 1002
Detailed financial analysis, 488
Detailed investigation, 488
Detection
　financial shenanigans, 1293
　fraud, 1288–1289
Devaluation, 1443–1444
Developing cross-cultural communication competence, 1422
Developing-nation debt, 1454
Development, 768. *See also* Human resources development
Development needs analyses, 769
Development phase, in decision making, 78
Development uses, of performance appraisals, 777
Devil's horns, 755, 782
Diagnosis, 78, 1173
Dialog, 1174
Dialog module, 1149, 1151
Dialogue, 65
Diesel engine failures, predicting, 1178
Difference chart, 675
Differential analysis, 915–922
Differential income or loss, 915
Differential management efficiency, 1105
Differential piece-rate system, 806
Differential revenue, 915
Differentiation, 3
　environmental uncertainty and, 227
　human resources and, 701–702
　information systems and, 1129–1130
　intergroup conflict and, 258

1644　　SUBJECT INDEX

service marketing and, 562
  See also Product differentiation
Differentiation business strategy, 759
Diffusion process, 495–496
Digate, Charles, 7
Digital, 1223–1224
Digital certificate, 1241, 1242
Digital data management, 1157–1160
Digital Equipment Corporation, 1230
Digital Millennium Copyright Act (1998), 99
Digital networking, 55
Digital signatures, 1241
Digital Signature Trust Co., 1242
Digital subscriber line (DSL), 1222, 1233
Diligence, duty of, 23
Dillards, 608
Direct advertising, 502–504
Direct contact, 233
Direct controls, 1429
Direct costing, 866, 929
Direct demand, 192–193
Direct exporting, 1372
Direct infringer, 100
Directing, 886
Direct interaction, 348
Direct interlock, 229
Direct investment, 1416–1417
Direction, unity of, 26
Directional and departmental signage, 458
Directive leadership, 43
Directives, 1179
Direct labor cost, 876
Direct labor cost budget, 893–894
Direct marketing, 502
Direct materials cost, 876
Direct materials purchases budget, 892–893
Direct method, 838, 839
Directories, 1165
Directors, 21
  election of, 22
  financial shenanigans and, 1293
  inside and outside, 1351
  removal of, 22
  role of, 22–24
  See also Board of directors
Direct selling, 580
Direct suits, 22
Direct transfer, 1085
Dirty float, 1446
Disabilities. *See* also Individuals with disabilities
Disability laws, 105–6. *See also* Americans with Disabilities Act
Disagreement, moral, 1344–1345
Disaster simulations, 1261
Disbursement control, 961
Disbursement float, 960
Disciplinary approach, 717
Discipline failures, 1286
Disclaimer of warranties, 149, 152
Disclaimers, limitation of, 141
Disclosure, 139
  ARMs, 143
  consumer credit transactions and, 142–144
  full, 1357
  presale, 141
Disclosure rule, 1346

Discount rate, 1102
Discounted cash flow (DCF), 1043, 1044–1045, 1068, 1069, 1075, 1113–1114
Discounted payback, 1069
Discounting abnormal earnings model, 1109
Discounts/discounting, 301, 309
  price flexing and, 518
  retail, 441–443
  techniques, 1066
Discrepancies between production and consumption, 534
Discrepancies in assortment, 534–535
Discrepancies in place, 535
Discrepancies in quantity, 534
Discrepancies in time, 535
Discretionary income, 575
Discrimination
  Civil Rights Act of 1964, 103
  employment, 1466–1467
  Equal Pay Act, 103
  reverse, 104, 788
  sex, 789–790
  workforce diversity management and, 786
  See also Employment discrimination law; Price discrimination; Workforce diversity management
Diseconomies of scale, 191
Disequilibrium losses, 179
Disequilibrium profits, 179
Disjunctive models, 524
Disney Enterprises, 479, 562, 591, 946, 947, 1378
Disney Stores, 453–454
Disparate impact, 103
Disparate treatment, 103
Dispersed supply base, 390
Dispersion, 534
Disposable income, 575
Disputes, 63
Dissatisfiers, 669
Disseminator roles, of managers, 54
Dissenting shareholders, 22, 23
Dissociation, 18
Dissolution
  corporations, 24
  general partnerships, 14–15
  involuntary, 24
  limited liability company, 18
  limited partnerships, 17
  voluntary, 24
Dissolution by act of the partners, 14
Dissolution by court order, 14
Dissolution by operation of law, 14
Distributed databases, 1163
Distributed denial of service (DDoS), 1143–1144
Distributed information systems, 1207, 1208
Distribution, 342
  corporations, 21
  dual, 595–596
  exclusive, 533
  flow-through, 540
  general partnerships and, 14, 15
  intensive, 533
  limited liability company, 17

  limited partnerships, 16
  management and, 536
  selective, 533
Distribution channels. *See* Marketing channels
Distribution decisions, 473, 474
Distribution management, 342
Distribution of assets
  general partnerships, 14
  limited liability company, 18
  limited partnerships, 17
Distribution requirements planning (DRP), 373
Distribution resource planning (DRP) systems, 398
Distribution tasks, 534–535
Distributive justice, 87, 569
Distributors, foreign, 1372
Disturbance handler roles, of managers, 54
Diverse thinking, 786
Diversifiable risk, 1098–1099
Diversification, 1105, 1305
Diversity, 55–56. *See also* Workforce diversity management
Diversity training, 787–788
Diverter, 591
Diverting, 507
Divertive competition, 576–577
Dividend irrelevance theory, 1058
Dividend payment, 1059–1060
Dividend payment constraints, 1061
Dividend payment procedures, 1061
Dividend payout ratio (dpo), 1033
Dividend policy, 1057–1064
Dividend policy decision, 946
Dividend preferences, 21
Dividend relevance theory, 1058
Dividends, 21
  accounting equation and, 830
  board of directors and, 22
  cumulative, 996
  finance law and, 156
  stock values and, 1009–1010
Dividends per share (DPS), 859, 1062
Dividend yield, 859–860
Divisional grouping, 235
Divisional structure, 236–237, 352
Division of labor, 36, 221, 535, 1403, 1405
Division of work, 26
Divisions, 901, 1388–1389
Divorce, retail marketing and, 575
DMAIC approach, 648–649
Documentary evidence, of fraud, 1290
Documents
  examination of, 1183
  fraud control and, 1285, 1290
Dole, 342
Dollar General, 575, 576, 579, 604
Dollarization, 1445
Dollar merchandise constraints, 437
Dollar merchandise control, 434–435
Dollar merchandise planning, 431–434
Domain disagreements, 591
Domain name system (DNS) software, 1144
Domains of political activity, 264
Domestication, 1385
Domestic content requirements, 1438

SUBJECT INDEX 1645

Domestic corporations, 19
Domestic market, international business strategies and, 1366, 1367
Domestic subsidy, 1438
Dominant strategy, 185
Domino Pizza, 686
Dormant partners, 13
Double-entry bookkeeping, 1415
Double taxation, 12
Dow Chemical, 1333, 1392, 1393
Dow Corning, 1321
Downgrading costs, 655
Downsizing, 253, 708
Downstream customers, 384, 385
Downtime, costs of, 1139
Downward communication, 62–63
Draw, 808
Drexel Burnham Lambert, 989, 1114, 1352–1353
Drill down, 1154
Drivers, 618
Drop off, 63
Drug and alcohol testing, 108
Drugstore.com, 84
Dual-authority structure, 238
Dual-core approach, 252–253
Dual custody, 1284
Dual distribution, 591, 595–596
Dual entitlement, 515
Dual exchange rates, 1448
Dual-translation, 1420
Dual-use items, 1400, 1401
Dumping, 455, 1439–1440, 1463
Dun & Bradstreet, 1202
Dunkin' Donuts, 603
DuPont, 34
Dutch business customs, 1424
Duties
  control procedures and, 937–938
  directors and officers, 23
  general partnerships, 15
  job analysis, 727
  limited liability company, 17–18
  limited partnerships, 16
  segregation of, 1284
Duty of care, 15
Duty of diligence, 23
Duty of loyalty, 23
Duty of obedience, 15, 23
Dynamic control systems, 244–246
Dynamic risks, 1295
Dynamic thought, 527
Dysfunctional turnover, 718

E

Early adopters, 493, 495
Early majority, 493, 495
Earned value (EV), 278
Earnings, preferred stock and, 996. *See also* Retained earnings
Earnings before interest and taxes (EBIT), 1022, 1025, 1030, 1051–1052, 1055
Earnings management, 941
Earnings per share (EPS), 945–946, 1004, 1011, 1029, 1030, 1051–1052, 1062

Earnings per share on common stock, 858
Ease of access, 600
Eastman Kodak, 1060, 1061, 1391. *See also* Kodak Corporation
eBay, 84, 1144, 1258
E-business, 30, 55
Echo boomers. *See* Generation Y
Eckerd, 416
E-commerce, 30, 1216
  electronic data interchange, 1253–1256
  information systems and, 1253
  Internet and, 1250–1253
  supply chain management, 1256
  Web-based, 1235
  Web sites, 1248–1250
  See E-marketing
Econometric methods, 165, 169
Economic analysis, 191
Economic conditions sector, 224
Economic crises, 1332, 1418–1419
Economic environment, 474, 476
Economic Espionage Act (1996), 95–96
Economic expansion, 172
Economic feasibility study, 1180, 1181–1182
Economic forces, 24
Economic indicators, 171, 172
Economic luck, 178
Economic man, 58
Economic markets, measuring, 188
Economic objectives, of nations, 1428
Economic order quantity (EOQ), 339–340, 541
Economic profit model, 1111–1112
Economic recessions, 171–172
Economic relations, basic, 159–161
Economic rents, 178
Economic responsibilities, 1312, 1314, 1339
Economic risks, 1385–1386
Economics
  ethics and, 1339–1340
  government regulations and, 90–91
  See also International economics; Managerial economics
Economic transactions, international, 1415
Economic trends, 575–576
Economic value added (EVA), 49, 711–712, 1110–1111
Economies of scale, 191, 535, 1021, 1409–1410
Economies of scope, 191, 535
Eddie Bauer, 458
EDGAR (Electronic Data Gathering, Analysis, and Retrieval), 94
EDIFACT, 1255
Edison, Thomas, 72
Edisonian problem solving, 72
EDS, 235
Education
  executive, 773
  retail marketing and, 574
Effect, 23
Effective annual rate (EAR), 308
Effective cost
  commercial paper, 980–981
  short-term financing, 980
Effective interest rate, 980, 981

Effective interviewing, 754
Effectiveness, 5, 66
  advertising, 502
  business information systems, 1235–1237
  human resources, 709–711
  international promotion strategy, 1383
  marketing, 547
  marketing environment and, 476
  performance appraisals, 784–785
  recruiting, 742
  supply chain performance, 405
  See also Contingency effectiveness approaches; Organizational effectiveness
Effective rate of protection, 1434–1436
Effective tariff rate, 1435
Effective translators, 1420–1421
Effect of declaration, 21
Efficiency, 5
  business information systems, 1235–1237
  government regulation and, 90
  marketing, 547
  marketing environment and, 476
  networks and, 1217
  organizational, 51
  supply chain performance, 405
  transaction, 535–536
Efficient consumer response (ECR) systems, 587
Efficient Markets Hypothesis (EMH), 1014
Effort-performance expectations, 714, 715
E. F. Hutton, 1114
Egyptian business customs, 1424
Eisenhower, Dwight D., 771
Elaboration stage, 242
Elastic demand, 196, 197
Elasticity, point and arc, 195–196. *See also* Price elasticity of demand
Elasticity concept, 195
E-learning, 763
Election of directors, 22
Electronic brochures, 545
Electronic data interchange (EDI), 399, 408, 1253–1256
Electronic media, 94
Electronic networks, 1089
Electronic signatures, 1241, 1255
Electronic spreadsheets, 1155
Electronic storefront, 1248–1249
Elimination by aspects model, 525
Ellram, Lisa M., 538
E-Logistics, 1251
E-marketing, 543
  costs and benefits of, 545–546
  marketing mix and, 543–545
Embargos, 1373
Embezzlement, 1280
Emery Global Logistics, 342
Emotional responses, 521
Emotional stability, 749
Emotions, 521, 1427
Empathy, 684
Employee benefits
  compensation and, 800
  nature and types of, 795–797
Employee benefits administration, 797–799
Employee benefits communication, 797–798

Employee benefits management, 793–799
  benefits administration, 797–799
  strategic perspectives on, 793–794
Employee benefits statements, 798
Employee-centered leaders, 41
Employee development, 3
Employee embezzlement, 1280
Employee-focused recruiting, 736–737
Employee growth-need strength, 60
Employee performance and retention management, 712
  individual employee performance, 712–715
  individual/organizational relationships, 715–716
  job satisfaction and organizational commitment, 716–718
  retention, 719
  retention determinants, 719
  retention management process, 719–722
  See also Performance; Performance appraisals
Employee Polygraph Protection Act, 750
Employee privacy, 108–9
Employee protection, 107–110
Employee referrals, 737
Employee relations, 721
Employee-retailer relationship, ethical behavior in, 598–599
Employees
  appraised, 784
  corporate governance and, 1349
  empowered, 54–55
  hiring and releasing, 371
  internal control, 1274
  new workplace and, 56
Employee stock options, 812
Employee stock ownership plan (ESOP), 60, 811, 812–813
Employee stock ownership trust (ESOT), 812
Employee surveys, 721
Employee termination at will, 107
Employee theft, 444, 599
Employment, part-time and temporary, 371–372
Employment agencies, 738–739
Employment-at-will, 747
Employment discrimination, 102–106, 1466–1467
Employment law, 101
  employee protection, 107–110
  employment discrimination law, 102–106
  labor law, 101–102
Employment testing, 747
Emporio Armani, 500
Empowered employees, 54–55
Empowerment, 40, 60–61, 637
Encapsulated development, 773
Encoding, 61, 62
Encryption, 1231, 1240–1241
Encumbered costs, 278
End-of-month (EOM) cash balances, 1037
End-of-month (EOM) dating, 443
End-of-month (EOM) inventories, 426–427
Endogenous variables, 195
End-to-end testing, 1261

Enduring involvement, 521
End-user systems development. *See* Systems development led by end users
Enforcement rights, 15, 22
Engineering
  knowledge, 1175
  software, 1191
Engineering technologies, 350, 351
Enron, 547, 1105
Enterprise (car rental franchise), 559
Enterprise applications, 1205
Enterprise-level strategy, 1322–1323
Enterprise resource planning (ERP), 30, 341, 387, 890, 1147
Enterprise risk management, 1298, 1309–1310
Enterprise-wide risk management, 1306
Entities, 1158
Entitlement-oriented compensation philosophies, 801
Entity-relationship (ER) diagrams, 1162
Entity theory, 13
Entrepreneurial stage, 241, 242, 414
Entrepreneur roles, of managers, 54
Entropy, 29
Entry barriers, 174
Environmental damage, common law actions for, 117–118
Environmental domain, 223–225, 229–230
Environmental impact statement (EIS), 119
Environmental law, 117–121
Environmental Protection Agency (EPA), 92, 118, 119, 120, 551
Environmental resources, controlling, 228–230
Environmental scanning, 474, 704, 1328
Environmental sustainability, 87
Environmental uncertainty, 225–228
EPS indifference point, 1052
Epstein, Edwin, 1317
Equal Credit Opportunity Act (1974), 142
Equal employment, sex/gender issues in, 789–790. *See also* Workforce diversity management
Equal Employment Opportunity Commission (EEOC), 103, 104, 784, 792
Equal employment opportunity regulations, 746, 751, 784
Equalization, 534
Equal Pay Act, 103, 105, 106
Equal Protection Clause, 104
Equal role, 1263
Equal work, 103
Equations, 159–160, 296
Equilibrium
  international, 1430–1433
  under monopoly, 177
  stock market, 1012–1014
  See also Market equilibrium
Equipment
  leasing or selling, 916–917
  replacing, 919–920
Equipment costs, 371
Equipment setup reductions, 392
Equity
  external, 1045

  government regulation and, 90
  as motivator, 714
Equity insolvency test, 156
Equity instruments, foreign, 1092
Equity markets, 1084
Equity securities, 20–21, 155
Equity valuation, 1007–1014
Escalating commitment, 80–81
Essential job functions, 729
Esteem needs, 713
Estimated cash flows, 1102–1103
Estimated cash payments, 897–898
Estimated cash receipts, 897
Estimation, 195–205, 1074–1077
Estoppel
  corporation by, 19
  partnership by, 15
  promissory, 125, 126
E-tailing, 415–416, 580–581
Ethernet, 1230, 1234
Ethical behavior, 460, 462–463, 625, 814, 1342
Ethical decision making, Venn diagram model for, 1339–1340
Ethical dilemma, 86
Ethical environment, 420
Ethical framework, 87
Ethical investing, 1320–1321
Ethical issues
  pricing-related, 552–553
  recognizing, 549–550
  See also Business ethics
Ethical judgments, 1338–1339
Ethical relativism, 1339
Ethical responsibilities, 1313, 1314, 1339
Ethical tests approach to business ethics, 1337
Ethical training, 463
Ethical vigilance, 550
Ethics, 85, 597
  cross-national, 1467–1469
  descriptive, 1337
  normative, 1337
  personal, 86, 87
  See also Business ethics; Corporate ethics; Social responsibility
Ethics committee, 88
Ethics gap, 1470
Ethics ombudsperson, 88
Ethics questions, 1340–1341
Ethics statements, 463
Ethnocentric strategy, 1369
E*Trade, 419
Eurobanks, 1455
Eurobonds, 994
Euro-commercial paper (Euro-CP), 995
Eurocredits, 995
Eurocurrency market, 1455–1456
Eurodebt, 998
Eurodollar bond, 992
Eurodollars, 1455
Euronotes, 995
European Information technology Security Evaluation Criteria (ITSEC), 1244
European Quality Award, 670
European Quality Prize, 670
European Union (EU), 1461

Euro stock, 1092
Evaluation
  capital budgeting, 1066–1074
  credit, 1177
  inventory financing, 977
  issue management and, 1330
  moral, 1344
  receivables financing, 976
  recruiting, 740–742
  retention management and, 722
  risk, 1299, 1301–1302
  training, 763–765
  See also Performance appraisal
Event-related marketing (ERM), 509
Every day low pricing (EDLP), 519
Evidence, of fraud, 1290
Evidence square, 1290
Evidential matter, 1280
Evoked set, 525
Exaggerated comparative price advertising, 552
Exaggeration, 461
Examination, 149
Excellence, striving for, 388
Excess capacity, 1019, 1021, 1440
Excess inventory, continuous review of, 396–397
Exchange controls, 1385, 1448
Exchange price or cost, 824
Exchange principle, 471
Exchange rates, 1101
  fixed, 1418, 1441, 1443–1444
  floating, 1418, 1445–1446
  fluctuating, 1381
Exchange-rate flexibility, 1450
Exchange-rate stabilization, 1443
Exchange-rate systems, 1441–1448
Exciters/delighters, 669
Exclusive dealing, 114–115, 596
Exclusive distribution, 533
Ex-convicts, 733
Excursions, 69
Ex-dividend, 1061
Executed contracts, 124
Executive compensation, 813–814
Executive education, 773
Executive information systems (EISs), 1146–1147, 1154
Executive leadership, 636
Executive order, 105
Executive recruitment, 229
Executive stock options, 947
Executory contracts, 124
Exempt carriers, 404
Exercise price, 999
Existence, tests of, 14
Existing customers, 482
Existing liability, 14
Exit barriers, 174
Exit interview, 721
Exogenous variables, 195
Expansion decisions, 1065
Expectancy, 134
Expectancy theory, 714, 715
Expectations theory, 215
Expected dividends, 1009–1010

Expected rate of return, 1009, 1010, 1011–1012, 1013
Expected return on a portfolio, 1097–1098
Expenditure-changing policies, 1429
Expenditure-decreasing policy, 1429
Expenditure-increasing policies, 1429
Expenditure-switching policies, 1429
Expenses
  accounting equation and, 829
  administrative, 880
  controllable, 904
  operating, 418
  out-of-pocket, 980
  overhead, 1216
  prepaid, 829
  selling, 880
  See also Costs
Experience, 771
  learning from, 1335
  openness to, 749
Experience attributes, 558
Experienced meaningfulness of work, 59
Experienced responsibility, 59
Experiments, 513
Expertise, 266, 1174
Expertise power, 590
Expertise replication, 1173
Expert power, 40, 259
Expert systems (ESs), 1146
  applications of, 1176–1178
  artificial intelligence and, 1171
  construction of, 1174–1176
  contribution of, 1173
  development of, 1173–1174
  limitations of, 1178
Expert system shells, 1175
Explicit code of ethics, 597
Exploiting strategy, 1342
Exponential smoothing techniques, 168–169
Export Administration Act, 137
Export controls, 1374, 1400–1401, 1463
Exporters, tariffs and, 1436–1437
Export incentives, 1463
Exporting, 1372–1373
Export licenses, 1400
Export management companies (EMCs), 1373
Export subsidy, 1438–1439, 1463
Export tariffs, 1434
Export trading companies (ETCs), 1372–1373
Export Trading Company Act (1982), 1402
Express charter powers, 20
Express contracts, 123
Express warranties, 131, 147–148, 149
Expressions, nonverbal, 1419, 1422
Expressive social style, 618
Expropriation, 1384, 1462
Exterior design, 456
External adaptation, 82
External affairs design, 1325–1326
External affairs strategy, 1325
External balance, 1428
External economies of scale, 1410
External environment, 948–949
External equity costs, 1045
External failure costs, 656
External human resources supply, 707

Externalities, 90–91, 1076
External marketing environment, 475–476
External markets, 211–212
External messages, 32
External recruiting, 735, 738–740
External review, 1367
Externals, 522
External stakeholders, business ethics and, 86, 87–88
External stimuli, 524
External training, 762–763
External working capital financing, 950
Extortion, 1468
Extraction phase, 1167
Extra dating, 437, 443
Extra dividend, 1060
Extranets, 30, 55, 1247
Extrinsic rewards, 57, 799–800
Extroversion, 749
Exxon, 190, 992, 1093, 1321, 1376
ExxonMobil, 1130
Eye contact, 1422
Eziba, 580

F

Face-to-face negotiations, 1426
Face value, 1004
Facial expressions, 1422
Facilitating agencies, 532
Facilitating channel, 532
Facilitating goods, 409
Facilitating marketing institutions, 585–586
Facilitating service, 409
Facility costs, 371
Facility layout, 335–336, 392–393
Facility layout decisions, 359
Facility location, 337–338, 359
Facility size, 359
Facsimile, 1235
Fact finding, 1183
Factor advantages, 1413
Factor endowments, 1406
Factoring, 974, 975
Factor intensities/proportions, 1406
Factor mobility imperfections, 1413
Factor prices, 1406
Factor proportions trade theory, 1404, 1405–1406
Factors of production, 1406
Factory burden, 877
Factory labor, 876–877
Factory overhead allocations, 878
Factory overhead applications, 879
Factory overhead balance, disposal of, 879
Factory overhead cost, 877
Factory overhead cost budget, 895
Fail-safe service quality, 686
Failure, defining, 479–481
Failure by incentives, 90
Failure by market structure, 90
Failure costs, 656
Failure to warn, 152
Fair Credit and Charge Card Disclosure Act (1988), 143

Fair Credit Billing Act, 143, 144
Fair Credit Reporting Act, 145
Fair Debt Collection Practices Act (1977), 145–146
Fair Labor Standards Act (FLSA), 109–110, 730
Fairness, 1264
Fair Packaging and Labeling Act (1967), 551
Fair reportage, 144–145
Family and Medical Leave Act (FMLA), 110, 789, 795
Family bill, 380
Family branding, 492
Family Dollar, 576
Family-oriented benefits, 795, 797
Famolare, 587
Fantasies, 69
Favors, supplier, 461
Fax-modem, 1225
Fayol, Henri, 26
Features, 477, 619
Federal bankruptcy, 14
Federal budget deficits, 216
Federal Communications Commission (FCC), 89–90, 93
Federal Consumer Credit Protection Act (FCCPA), 142, 144
Federal consumer protection agencies, 138
Federal Copyright Act, 98, 99, 135
Federal Employee Polygraph Protection Act (1988), 108
Federal environmental regulations, 118–121
Federal Express. *See* FedEx
Federal Insecticide, Fungicide and Rodenticide Act (FIFRA), 120
Federal Reserve policy, 216
Federal Trade Commission (FTC), 92, 116–117, 138–139, 461, 551, 1105
Federal Trade Commission Act (1914), 116–117, 137, 551, 596
Federal Trademark Act, 96
Federal Trademark Dilution Act (1995), 97
Federal Unemployment Tax Act, 109
Federal warranty protection, 140–141
Federal Water Pollution Control Act. *See* Clean Water Act
FedEx, 260, 344, 403, 404, 412, 532, 544, 586, 686, 699, 1129, 1131, 1251
Feedback, 29, 724, 725, 886
 communication and, 61, 62, 63, 65
 communication barriers and, 67
 motivation and, 57
 performance, 63
 performance appraisals, 782–784
 supply chain performance, 405
Feedback control, 47, 48
Feedforward control, 47, 48
Fees earned, 829
Fees on account, 829
Feigenbaum, A. V., 666
Feigenbaum quality model, 666
Ferris, Richard, 37
Fiduciary duty, 15, 19
Fiedler, Fred E., 42–43
Fields, 1158
Field selling, 615–616

FIFO (first in, first out), 431, 879, 883–884
Figurehead roles, of managers, 54
Files, 1158
Filing
 limited liability company, 17
 limited partnerships, 16
Final assembly scheduling (FAS), 373, 375, 382–384
Final consumer, 474
Final price, control over, 1380
Finance
 business valuations, 1107–1114
 capital structure, 1050–1057
 cost of capital, 1041–1050
 dividend policy, 1057–1064
 economics and, 212–217
 ethics and, 1114–1115
 foreign sources of, 1368
 mergers and acquisitions, 1104–1107
 quantitative techniques and, 296
 working capital policy, 949–958
 See also Capital budgeting; Short-term asset management
Finance law, 154–156
Finance management, retail, 422–431
Finance strategies
 agency relationships, 946–948
 corporation goals, 944–945
 external environment, 948–949
 managerial actions to maximize shareholder wealth, 945–946
Financial account, 1414, 1416–1418
Financial accounting, 825
Financial Accounting Standards Board (FASB), 813, 824, 999
Financial analysis, detailed, 488
Financial analysis model, 1110
Financial asset markets, 1084
Financial assets, 1415. *See also* Assets; Asset valuation
Financial benefits, 795, 796–797
Financial break-even analysis, 1028–1030
Financial break-even point, 1029
Financial conflicts of interest, 461
Financial control, 49, 1016, 1022
 break-even chart, 1023
 break-even computation, 1023–1024
 financial break-even analysis, 1028–1030
 financial leverage, 1030–1032
 leverage and forecasting, 1032–1033
 operating break-even analysis, 1022, 1025
 operating break-even point, 1027–1028
 operating leverage, 1025–1028, 1031–1032
 See also Control
Financial economies, 1104
Financial environment, 1084
 common stock market, 1089–1091
 financial institutions, 1085–1088
 financial instruments in international markets, 1091–1092
 financial markets, 1084–1085
 stock market, 1088–1089
Financial flexibility, 1050
Financial forecasting. *See* Forecasting
Financial information, 63
Financial institutions, 1085–1088

Financial instruments, in international markets, 1091–1092
Financial insurance, 1310
Financial intermediary, 1085–1086
Financial leases, 998
Financial leverage, 1030–1032, 1051–1052, 1100
Financial management, short-term, 949, 956–957
Financial markets, 1084–1085, 1366
Financial Numbers Game, The (Mulford and Comiskey), 941
Financial options, 1366
Financial performance, corporate, 1319–1320
Financial perspective, 50
Financial planning, 1015–1016
 forecasting and, 1016–1021
 outsourcing and, 1195
 short-term, 1033–1035
Financial pressures, 1281–1282
Financial reporting, fraudulent, 941
Financial resources
 power sources and, 262
 resource requirements planning, 365–366
 risk retention and, 1304
Financial resources sector, 224
Financial risk, 1099, 1100, 1101, 1296
Financial risk management
 host government takeovers, 1103–1104
 investment risk, 1095–1099
 risk types, 1099–1103
Financial shenanigans, 1292–1293
Financial statement analysis, 845, 1299–1300
 basic procedures, 845–850
 profitability analysis, 855–860
 solvency analysis, 850–855
 summary, 860–861
Financial statements, 831–832
 balance sheet, 835–836, 837
 income statement, 832
 leases and, 998–999
 projected, 1016–1019
 retained earnings statement, 832–835
 statement of cash flows, 836, 838–844
Financial success, 480
Financing, 471. *See also* Long-term financing; Short-term financing
Financing activities
 cash flows from, 836, 839–840
 noncash, 840
Financing costs, 1028
Financing feedbacks, 1019, 1020
Financing policies
 external working capital, 950
 working capital, 953–956
Financing section, 1029
Fingerprint Identification Technology (FIT), 1239
Finished-goods inventory, 338, 386, 878
Finish-to-order, 376, 381
Finite risk, 1310
Firestone, 1321
Firewalls, 30, 1165, 1242–1243
Firing, threat of, 946
Firm demand, 193

SUBJECT INDEX 1649

Firm financial conditions, 992–993
Firm price/output decision. *See* Price/output decisions
Firm supply, 194
Firm supply curve. *See* Supply curve
Firm-specific risk, 1098–1099
First-degree price discrimination, 209
First-line managers, 52
First mortgage bonds, 986
First-stage leverage, 1030
Fiscal policy, 1429
Fiscal year, 826–827
Fishbone diagram, 652
Fitness for a particular purpose, 148
Fitness for use, 131
Fixed assets, 835
Fixed costs, 288, 512, 863–864, 869, 1100, 1196
Fixed exchange rate, 1418, 1441, 1443–1444
Fixed-position layout, 336
Fixed wireless, 1233
Fixture management, 446
Fixtures, selecting, 455
Flat structure, 38
Flexibility, 54, 84
   exchange-rate, 1450
   financial, 1050
   information systems planning, 1135
   process improvement and, 680
   short-term financing and, 957
Flexible benefits plan, 798
Flexible budget, 889–890
Flexible manufacturing systems, 337
Flexible presentation, 619
Flexible spending accounts, 798
Flextime, 60
Float, 960
Floating exchange rate, 1418, 1445–1446
Floating lien, 976
Floating rate bond, 989
Floating rate debt, 989
Floor plan, 453
Florida Power and Light (FP&L), 886
Flotation costs, 1042, 1045, 1093
Flowcharts, 650, 1185, 1300
Flow of capital, 1464
Flow of labor, 1463–1464
Flow of trade, 1463
Flows, 388, 536–538. *See also* Cash flows; Cost flows; Physical flows
Flows in marketing channels, 537
Flow statements, BOP as, 1415
Flow-through distribution, 540
F.O.B. destination, 401, 443, 444
F.O.B. factory, 443
F.O.B. origin, 132
F.O.B. pricing, 518
F.O.B. shipping point, 132, 401, 443, 444
Focus decisions, for manufacturing, 359
Focused differentiation, 3
Focused low cost, 3
Focus strategy, 4
Folding, 455
Follett, Mary Parker, 26, 27
Follow-ups, 620, 722, 1382
Food and Drug Administration (FDA), 140, 911

Food, Drug and Cosmetic Act (1938), 140
Foodmaker, 1335
Foot Joy, 555
Foot Locker, 420, 591
Force-field analysis, 68, 70
Forcing, organizational change and, 256
Ford Motor Company, 181, 224, 233, 253, 340, 479, 888, 994, 934, 1253, 1321, 1354, 1376, 1389, 1438
Forecasted cost at completion (FCAC), 279, 280
Forecast group, 169
Forecasting, 287
   business cycle and, 171–172
   cost, 279–280
   defining, 163
   environmental uncertainty and, 227–228
   financial control and, 1032–1033
   financial planning and, 1016–1021
   firm financial conditions, 992–993
   human resources supply and demand, 705–708
   operations, 295
   percent-of-sales, 1033–1034
   post-audits and, 1073
   social, 1328
   supply chain inventory management and, 397
Forecasting periods, 706
Forecasting problems, 164–165
Forecasting techniques
   choosing, 170–171
   types of, 165–169
Forecast reliability, 169–170
Foreign bonds, 994
Foreign corporations, 19
Foreign Corrupt Practices Act (FCPA), 137, 598, 1402, 1466, 1468–1469
Foreign currencies, 1451
Foreign debt instruments, 994–995
Foreign direct investment, 1375–1376, 1412–1414, 1417
Foreign distributors, 1372
Foreign equity instruments, 1092
Foreign finance sources, 1368
Foreign key, 1161
Foreign limited liability companies, 17
Foreign limited partnerships, 16
Foreign national pricing, 1380
Foreign penetration, 1371
Foreign purchasing laws, 137
Foreign sales agents, 1372
Foreign sourcing, 1438
Foreign trade balance, 216
Formal account, 15
Formal communication channels, 62–64, 66
Formal information channels, 67
Formalities, 18
Formality, requirements for, 1420
Formalization, 38, 220–221, 243–244, 351
Formalization stage, 241–242
Formal position, 260
Formal strategic alliances, 228
Forming stage, in team development, 282–283
For-profit services, 557
Forward buying, 507

Forward chaining, 1176
Forward mergers, 115
Fotomart, 96
Founders' shares, 983
Four fitnesses, 669
4GLs (fourth-generation languages), 1203
Four Seasons Hotels, 687
14 Points for Management, 662
Fourteenth Amendment, 104
Fourth-generation languages (4GLs), 1203
Fragmentation, 53
Fragmented databases, 1163
Frames, 1175
Framework, 350–351
Franchise holding/loading, 507
Franchises/franchising, 588–589, 1375
Fraud
   consumer credit card, 144
   corporate, 1277–1293
Fraud detection, 1288–1289
Fraud investigation, 1289–1291
Fraud perpetrators, 1277, 1280–1281, 1286
Fraud prevention, 1285–1286, 1287–1288
Fraud resolution, 1291
Fraud triangle, 1281
Fraud triangle plus inquiry approach, 1290
Fraudulent financial reporting, 941
Frederick, William, 1317
Free agents, 55
Free cash flow, 840–841
Free cash flow hypothesis, 1059
Free exchange rate, 1444
Free merchandise, 441
Free riding, 592
Freestanding inserts (FSIs), 519
Freestanding location, 603
Free-trade argument, 1437
Freewheeling, 68
Freight bill, 131–132
Freight restrictions, 1441
French business customs, 1424
Frequency, 501, 1299
Frequency-division multiplexing, 1226
Frequency modulation, 1223, 1224
Freudenberg–NOK, 249
Fujitsu, 890
Full disclosure, 1357
Full-duplex communication, 1218, 1219
Full-line policy, 596
Full-time integrator, 233–234
Fully diluted EPS, 1004
Functional capacity testing, 748
Functional discount, 441
Functional grouping, 235
Functional IS organization, 1210, 1211–1212
Functional-level strategy, 1323
Functional managers, 53
Functional matrix, 239
Functional relations, 159–160
Functional structure, 235–236, 1391, 1392
Functional turnover, 718
Functional-type organizations, 268–269, 271
Funded debt, 985
Funded retention, 1303
Funding
   country risk and, 1103
   employee benefits, 794

Future interest rates, expectations about, 992
Future value (FV), 299–301, 308
Future value interest factor for an annuity of *n* payments at *i* interest, 303
Future value interest factor for i and n, 300
Future value of an annuity, 302–304
Future value tables, 1120–1123
Futures markets, 1085
Futures research, 1328

G

Gain sharing, 60, 811
Galaxy Foods, 1062
Game theory, 185–188
Gantt, Henry, 25
Gantt Chart, 25
GAP, 421
Gap analysis, 760
GAP for Kids, 421
Gap model, 566–567, 683, 684
Garbage can model, 78–79
Garnishment, 145
GartnerGroup, 1245, 1260
Gateway, 181
Gender
    Equal Pay Act and, 103
    leadership and, 46
    management development and, 772
    workforce diversity management and, 789–790
General Agreement on Tariffs and Trade (GATT), 1373, 1461
General and Industrial management (Fayol), 26
General Aptitude Test Battery (GATB), 748
General Electric (GE), 48, 65, 237, 344, 492, 589, 648–649, 1072, 1085, 1099, 1177, 1354, 1394
General environment, 223
General Foods, 491, 1369
Generally accepted accounting principles (GAAP), 824–825, 941, 1115
General managers, 53
General Mills, 183, 342, 492, 689
General Motors Corporation, 181, 190, 233, 338, 349, 557, 869, 886, 915, 1026, 1057, 1072, 1078, 1095, 1253, 1357, 1419, 1438
General partners, 10, 13
General partnerships, 9–10, 11
    dissolution of, 14–15
    formation of, 13–14
Generational issues, 416, 572, 574, 799
Generation X, 416, 572, 574, 799
Generation Y, 416, 572, 799
Generic designation, 97
Genetic algorithms, 1172
Genetic Concepts, 983
Geographical organization, 623–624
Geographical structure, 237
Geographic centers, shifting, 573
Geographic grouping, 235
Geographic information systems (GISs), 1156
Geographic market, 114
Geographic pricing, 518

Geographic segments, 519
Geographic trends, 573–574
German business customs, 1424
Get-togethers, informal, 1422
Giant Food, Inc., 582
Gigabit Ethernet, 1234
Gilbert, Lewis, 1356
Gilbreth, Frank B., 25
Gilbreth, Lillian M., 25
Gillette, 1212, 1376
Glass ceiling, 789
Glass Ceiling Commission, 789
Glass elevator, 789–790
Glass-Steagall Act (1933), 1087
Glass walls, 789–790
Global business strategies, 1366–1371
Global competition, retail marketing and, 581–582
Globalization, 55
Global Maintech, 996
Global purchasing, laws affecting, 136–137
GlobalSign Toot CA, 1242
Global sourcing, 329, 1373
Global Sports and Entertainment, Ltd., 1066
Global strategy, 1369–1371
Globe Metallurgical, 247
Glocal, 1395
Goal approach, 5, 6
Goal conflict, 887
Goal directed, 50
Goal incompatibility, 258, 591
Goal programming, 287
Goals
    affirmative action, 788
    agreements/contracts, 1427
    budget, 887
    charge-back services and, 1216
    communication and, 63
    communication barriers and, 66
    employee benefits, 794
    information security, 1237
    management and, 32–33
    organizational, 2, 221, 1216
    organizational change and, 256
    shared, 268
    stretch, 681
Goal setting, 33, 34, 515
Going private transactions, 23
Going public, 1090
Golden parachutes, 947, 1352
Golden Rule, 1346
Goldman Sachs, 1086, 1092, 1353
Gold standard, 1451
Golf Channel, 870
Gomes, Roger, 542
Goods, 122, 557–558
    acceptance and rejection of, 134–135
    inferior, 204
    normal, 204–205
    services and, 558–560
Goods trade, 1416
Goodyear Tire & Rubber Company, 807, 1389
Gordon, Myron J., 1011
Gordon Model, 1011
Gouging laws, 553
Governance, corporate, 1347–1358

Governance committee, 1355
Government agencies, 1277
Government-mandated benefits, 795–796
Government procurement policies, 1440–1441
Government regulation, 89
    accounting, 1347
    employment law, 101–110
    environmental law, 117–121
    intellectual property, 94–100
    international business behavior, 1401–1403
    international law and, 1465–1466
    international trade, 1373–1374
    market economy regulation, 89–93
    mergers and acquisitions, 1105
    organizational environment and, 229–230
    securities markets, 1090–1091
    securities regulation, 94
    wage/hour, 730
    See also Equal employment opportunity regulations
Government sector, 224
Government services, 557
Government-supported job training, 762–763
Government takeovers, 1103–1104
Government-to-consumer markets, 543
Grading, 472
Grapevines, 64
Graphics, lifestyle, 458
Graphology, 750
Graphs, 159
Gray marketing, 592
Great Indoors, 576, 580
Great man approach, 40
Greek business customs, 1424
Greenleaf, Robert, 46
Greenmail, 947, 1352
Grievances, 63
Gross margin, 418, 422, 427–428
Gross margin percentage, 418
Gross margin return on inventory (GMROI), 432, 436
Gross profit, 1026
Gross profit margin, 1024
Gross rating points (GRPs), 501
Gross working capital, 949
Group-based variable pay, 804, 805, 809–811
Group decision-support systems (GDSSs), 1153
Groupware, 1146
Growth
    international business strategies and, 1366
    pressures for, 240
Growth opportunities, 12
Growth phase, 414, 415
Growth potential, 50
Growth rate, 1008
Growth stage, 578
Growth strategies, 496
Guatemalan business customs, 1424
Gucci, 578
Guided medium, 1221
Gulf Oil, 1105, 1468

H

Häagen Dazs, 252
Hackman, Richard, 59
Half-duplex communication, 1218, 1219
Halo effect, 755, 782
Handicapped person, 106
Handling. *See* Material handling; Merchandise management
Hand movements, 1422
Handy Hardware, 588
Hanging, 454
Hard sell, 613
Hardware
　data warehousing and, 1167
　risks to, 1139–1140
Hardware planning, 1136
Harrod's, 581
Hart, Christopher, 687
Hart Schaffner Marx, 587
Hawthorne studies, 27
Hazardous substances, 120
Hazards, 1297
Health, job design and, 723
Health-care benefits, 795, 796
Health Insurance Portability and Accountability Act (HIPAA), 795
Health risks. *See* Life, health, and loss of income risks
Heard, James E., 1350
Heckscher, Eli, 1404, 1405–1406
Hedging, 1305
Hedonistic ethic, 1346
Heinz, 492, 1333
Help desk, 1214
Heroes, 83
Hersey, Paul, 42–43
Hershey Foods, 1147
Hertz, 1130
Herzberg, Frederick, 714
Heterogeneity, 559
Heterogeneous demand, 553
Heuristics, 500, 1174
Hewlett-Packard, 181, 237, 243–244, 407, 556, 1131, 1261
Hidden factory, 666
Hierarchical referral, 232
Hierarchy of authority, 221
High corporate tax rate, 1380
Higher wages, 1381
High-liquidity strategy, 969
High-low method, 864
High-margin/high-turnover retailers, 419
High-margin/low-turnover retailers, 419
High-performance retailers, 418
High-profit retailing, 421–422
High-quality service, 445
High readiness level, 43
High-velocity environments, 80
Hilton, 1130
Hiring costs, 371, 721
Histograms, 651
Historical yield spread analysis, 968
Hitchhiking, 68
Hits, 1250
Holder-of-record date, 1061

Hold-harmless agreements, 1304–1305
Holding costs, 339
Holiday Inn, 205, 447, 500, 587
Holloway, Kevin, 233
Home country, 1375–1376
Home Depot, 339, 416, 457, 535, 598, 604, 606, 611, 851
Home Equity Loan Consumer Protection Act (HELCPA), 143
Home equity loans, 143
Home pages, 600
HomeRuns, 241
Honda, 38, 181, 555, 1378, 1414
Honesty, 1264, 1287–1288
Honesty/integrity testing, 749–750
Honeywell, 947, 1369
Honkworm International, 229
Horizontal analysis, 845–847
Horizontal communication, 63–64
Horizontal information systems, 233
Horizontal linkages, 233–234, 251–252
Horizontal markets, 1253
Horizontal mergers, 115, 1106
Horizontal power sources, 261–263
Horizontal price fixing, 112
Horizontal privity, 150
Horizontal restraint, 111
Horizontal structures/hierarchy, management types in, 53
Host countries, 1376
Host government takeovers, 1103–1104
Hostile environments, 790–791
Hostile takeovers, 947, 1105
Hot-site, 1260
Household decision making, 525
Houston Natural Gas Company, 1105
Howard Johnson's, 96
Human relations approach, 58
Human relations movement, 27
Human resource crises, 1332
Human resource information system (HRIS), 703, 705, 712, 798
Human resources, as core competency, 699–702
Human resources activities, 698
Human resources approach, 58
Human resources audit, 705, 709–710
Human resources development, 765–773
Human resources management
　background investigation, 756
　compensation strategies and practices, 799–804
　effectiveness, assessment of, 709–711
　employee benefits management, 793–799
　environmental scanning, 704
　ethics and, 814–815
　forecasting supply and demand, 705–708
　human resource information system, 712
　internal assessment of organizational workforce, 705
　jobs and, 722
　nature of, 698
　performance and benchmarking, 711–712
　placement, 742–746
　planning, 702–704
　selection, 742–746

　selection interviewing, 751–756
　selection process, 746–748
　selection testing, 748–751
　strategic, 698–699
　surpluses and shortages, 708–709
　variable pay and executive compensation, 804–814
　See also Employee performance and retention management; Job analysis; Job design; Performance appraisals; Recruiting; Training; Workforce diversity management
Human resources planning, 701, 702–704
Human resources research, 710–711
Human resources sector, 224
Human resources viewpoint, 27–28
Humanistic perspective, 27–28
Human safety, 1264
Human skills, 51
Humor, 72
Hurdle rates, 1070, 1112
Hybrids, 1260
Hygiene factors, 714

I

Iacocca, Lee, 233
IBM, 4, 115, 181, 190, 219, 222, 229, 253, 442, 496, 519, 562, 946, 986, 988, 998, 999, 1000, 1009, 1057, 1072, 1082, 1085, 1089, 1093, 1164–1165, 1169, 1244, 1261, 1376, 1399
IBM Credit Corporation, 690
Idea champions, 250, 256
Idea evaluation, 68
Idea generation and screening, 68, 486–487
Ideal expectation, 682
Ideal self, 522
IEC standards, 1244
IF-THEN rules, 1174, 1175
IGA, 418
Ignorance, 1286
IKEA, 582
Illegal *per se*, 111
Illegitimate activities, 230
Illnesses, life-threatening, 792
Image reinforcement, 507–508
Imagination, moral, 1344
Imagineering, 71
Imai, Masaaki, 668
Imai quality model, 668
IMF drawings, 1452–1453
Immediate rewards, 507–508
Immoral management, 1341, 1342
Impairment of capital rule, 1061
Imperfect competition, 1409–1410
Imperfectly competitive external markets, transfer pricing with, 212
Imperfectly competitive markets, competitive strategy in, 188–189
Imperfect markets, 1404, 1409–1410
Implementation cycles, 1196
Implementation strategies, for organizational change, 248, 255–256

Implementation
  international organizational structures, 1393
  prepackaged software, 1197, 1198
  systems development life cycle, 1187–1189
Implementors, 1396
Implicit code of ethics, 597
Implied in fact contract, 123
Implied powers, 20
Implied warranties, 131, 148, 149
Implied warranty of fitness for the particular purpose, 149
Implied warranty of merchantability, 149
Import controls, 1463
Import quotas, 1438
Import restrictions, 1436
Imports/importing, 1367, 1373
Import substitution, 1413
Import tariffs, 1434
Impoverished management, 41
Improvements, 63
Impulse purchasing, 449
Inbound telemarketers, 615
Incapacity, 1286
Incentive failures, 90, 91
Incentive-based regulation, 93
Incentives, 504
  executive compensation, 813–814
  individual, 804, 805–807
  organizational, 804, 805, 811–813
  sales, 807–809
  types of, 804–805
Incidental learning, 1173
Income
  accounting, 1074–1075
  differential, 915
  operating, 1026
  residual, 910–911
Income analysis, under variable costing and absorption costing, 930–931
Income bonds, 986
Income elasticity of demand, 204–205
Income form operations, 906
Income growth, 575
Income models, decision making and, 929–937
Income smoothing, 941
Income statement budgets, 890–896
Income statements, 832, 929–930, 1016–1017
Incoming partners, liability of, 16
Inconsistent cues, 66
Incorporation, 1305
Incorporators, 19
Incremental cash flows, 1074, 1075–1077
Incremental change, 161
Incremental concept, 161–163
Incremental decision process model, 77–78
Incremental operating cash flows, 1077
Incremental profit, 161–162
Indemnification, 23
Indemnity agreements, 1304–1305
Indented BOM, 377, 378
Indentures, 987
Independent checks, 1285
Independent projects, 1065, 1071
Independent retailers, 588
Independent variables, 159

Indexed bonds, 986
Indexes, quality cost, 657–658
Index of retail saturation (IRS), 606
Indian business customs, 1424
Indifference curves, 1430–1432
Indifference map, 1432
Indirect expenses, 904
Indirect exporting, 1372–1373
Indirect infringer, 100
Indirect interlock, 229
Indirect labor, 877
Indirect materials, 876
Indirect method, 838, 839
Individual adoption process, 494–495
Individual/adversarial external affairs strategy, 1325
Individual brand name strategy, 492
Individual communication barriers, 65–66
Individual communication skills, 66–67
Individual consumer decision making, 523–525
Individual decision making, 73–75
Individual employee performance, 712–715
Individual incentives, 804, 805–807
Individual motivation, 713–715
Individual negotiations, 1426
Individual/organizational relationships, 715–716
Individual performance factors, 713
Individual piracy, 1263
Individual power, 259
Individual rewards, 803–804
Individuals
  career planning and, 766
  job design and, 722–725
Individuals with disabilities, 792. See also Americans with Disabilities Act
Individual trade customers, researching, 530–531
Indoctrination, 63
Industry demand, 193
Industry environment, purchasing ethics and, 460
Industry sector, 224
Industry supply, 194
Inelastic demand, 196, 197
Inference engine, 1174
Inferior goods, 204
Inflation, 213, 1076, 1101, 1429
Inflation premium (IP), 214
Inflation with recession and BOP deficit, 1430
Inflation with unemployment, 1429–1430
Inflow, 299
Influence, 39
Informal appraisal, 777–778
Informal communication channels, 64
Informal get-togethers, 1422
Informality, requirements for, 1420
Informal organizations, 26
Informal training, 762
Information, 15
  characteristics of, 1157
  control procedures and, 939–940
  cross-cultural communication and, 1420
  data versus, 1156–1157
  ethical standards for, 1262–1263

  financial and accounting, 63
  fraud and, 1286
  incomplete and incorrect, 389
  internal control and, 1271
  limited partnerships, 16
  market, 472
  new workplace and, 54
  prior, 263
  selling, 1252
Informational crises, 1332
Informational power, 590
Informational roles, of managers, 53–54
Information-based services, 1378
Information center, 1214
Information channels, 67
Information content hypothesis, 1058
Information controls, 1237–1240
Information falsification, 748
Information flow, 537
Information overload, 1154
Information-processing perspective, on organization structure, 231–234
Information reporting systems, 1146
Information requests, 1197, 1198
Information search, 524
Information security
  downside of, 1244–1245
  goals of, 1237
  standards, 1243–1244
Information sites, 543
Information systems (IS)
  architecture and management, 1205–1210
  business, 1235–1237
  charge-back methods, 1215–1216
  decision-support systems, 1146, 1148–1153, 1154–1155
  e-commerce and, 1253
  executive, 1146–1147, 1154
  geographic, 1156
  horizontal, 233
  information center, 1214
  infrastructure, 1205
  management, 1145, 1146–1147
  managers and, 1144–1148, 1212–1213
  mission statements, 1134
  MPS, 384
  operations, 1145–1146
  planning, 1132–1139
  risk-management, 1301
  risks to, 1139–1143
  sources of, 1194
  staff organization, 1210–1212
  strategic, 1126–1131
  vertical, 232
  vision, 1134
  See also Human resource information system
Information systems auditor, 1240
Information systems costs, 655
Information systems subsidiary, 1194, 1202
Information technology (IT), 28, 355
  application service providers, 1200–1202
  business information systems, 1235–1237
  business law and, 156
  computer-aided software engineering, 1191
  contingency plans, 1257–1262

SUBJECT INDEX 1653

data and knowledge management, 1156–1178
decision making and, 1144–1156
e-commerce and, 1246–1256
ethics and, 1262–1264
information systems planning, 1132–1139
information systems strategies, 1126–1131
information systems subsidiary, 1202
international service strategy, 1378–1379
management implications of, 1148
networks, 1226–1235
outsourcing, 1194–1196
project management, 1192
prototyping, 1189–1191
purchased applications (prepackaged software), 1196–1200
risk management, 1139–1144
security and controls, 1237–1246
software rentals, 1200
systems acquisition, 1194
systems development, 1179–1189, 1192–1193
systems integration, 1193–1194
telecommunications, 1216–1226
user application development, 1202–1205
Information technology resource management
charge-back methods, 1215–1216
information center, 1214
information systems architecture and management, 1205–1210
information systems manager and line managers, 1212–1213
staff organization, 1210–1212
Information theft, 1140–1141
Information transfer, 546
Infrastructure, quality management and, 641–642
Infringement, 94–95
copyrights, 99
patents, 100
trade symbols, 97
Ingram Micro, Inc., 6
Inheritance, 1161
Initial investment outlay, 1077
Initial public offering (IPO) market, 1090, 1115
Initiating structure, 41
Innovation, 240. *See also* Organizational innovation
Innovation goals, 3
Innovators, 493, 495
Input files, 1183
Input-output analysis, 1407
Input price variability, 1100
Inputs, 29, 640, 714
Inquiry methods, 1290
In Search of Excellence (Peters and Waterman, Jr.), 64
Inseparability, 558–559
Inside directors, 1350
Insiders, 1091
Insider securities trading, detection of, 1177
Insider trading scandals, 1352–1353
Inspection rights, of board of directors, 22
Inspections, on-site, 1301
Installation costs, 1076

Installations, as business-to-business products, 478
Institute for Supply Management (ISM), 462
Institutional constraints, 1429
Institutional signage, 458
In-store merchandise handling, 444
Instrumental values, 522
Instrument maintenance costs, 655
Insufficient research, 1382
Insurance
country risk and, 1103–1104
risk transfer and, 1305, 1310
Insurance benefits, 795, 796–797
Insurance companies, 1278
Intangibility, 557, 558
Intangible benefits, 1182
Intangible-dominant goods, 558
Intangible output, 348
Integer linear programming, 286
Integrated enterprise, 333–334
Integrated information network, 346
Integrated risk management, 1298
Integrated Services Data Networks (ISDNs), 1232
Integration, 227
Integration devices, 267
Integrity, 1287–1288, 1345
Integrity strategy, 1342, 1343
Integrity testing. *See* Honesty/integrity testing
Intel, 34, 501, 702
Intellectual property, 94–95
copyrights, 98–99
international protections, 1466
patents, 99–100
purchasing law and, 135–136
trade names, 98
trade secrets, 95–96
trade symbols, 96–98
Intellectual property rights, 1374–1375, 1385
Intelligent agents, 1172–1173
Intensive distribution, 533
Intensive technologies, 353
Intentional amoral management, 1343
Intentional behavior, 1342
Interactional justice, 569, 570
Interactive leadership, 46
Interdepartmental activities, 254
Interdepartmental coordination, 63
Interdependence, workflow, 352–354
Interdependent tasks, 271
Interest, LLC, 17
Interest in partnership. *See* Partnership interest
Interest rate levels, 213
business decisions and, 217
factors influencing, 216–217
long-term financing and, 992
stock prices and, 217
Interest rate risk, 214
Interest rates
bonds and, 1006–1007
comparisons of, 307–309
financial risk and, 1101
future, 992
market, 213–215
term structure of, 213, 215–216

Interest revenue, 829
Interest tables. *See* Tabular solution
Interfaces, 374–375, 1174, 1184
Intergroup conflict, 257–258
Intergroup consultation, 267–268
Interior design, 456
Interlocking directorates, 228–229
Intermediate form, 1305
Intermediate planning, 706
Internal assessment, of organizational workforce, 705
Internal balance, 1428
Internal benchmarking, 689
Internal control, 1270–1274
Internal cooperation, 1395–1396
Internal economies of scale, 1410
Internal failure costs, 655–656
Internal functions, 384
Internal human resources supply, 707–708
Internal integration, 82
Internalization, 1413–1414
Internal marketing environment, 474–475
Internal messages, 32
Internal process approach, 5, 7
Internal rate of return (IRR), 1066, 1069–1070, 1071–1072, 1181
Internal recruiting, 735–737
Internal reporting, of unethical behavior, 463
Internal Revenue Service (IRS), 814, 1061, 1105
Internal review, 1367–1368
Internals, 522
Internal stimuli, 524
Internal training, 761–762
International banking, 1449–1456
International business
forms of, 1371–1376
organizational control, 1386–1387, 1396–1403
organizational structure, 1386–1396
regulating, 1401–1403
International business ethics, 1467–1472
International business law, 1460–1467
International business strategies, 1366–1371
International contracts, 1464–1465
International Court of Justice (ICJ), 1460
International cultures and protocols
cross-cultural business practices, 1423, 1424–1425
cross-cultural communication competence, 1422
cross-cultural communication process, 1419–1422
cross-cultural negotiations, 1423, 1425–1428
International debt, problem of, 1454
International division, 1388–1389
International economics
exchange-rate systems, 1441–1448
international equilibrium, 1430–1433
macroeconomic policy in open economy, 1428–1430
nontariff trade barriers, 1437–1441
tariffs, 1434–1437
International Electrotechnical Commission (IEC), 1244

International environment, 223–225, 1460–1461
International equilibrium, 1430–1433
International franchising, 1375
International investment, 1408–1409, 1412–1414
International law, 1456–1467
International lending risk, 1453–1454
International licensing agreements, 1374
International marketing strategies, 1377–1383
International markets, 1085, 1091–1092
International Monetary Fund (IMF), 1452–1453, 1464
International Organization for Standardization (ISO), 49, 1244
International payments, 1414–1419
International place/entry strategy, 1379
International politics, 1458–1459
International price discrimination, 1439–1440
International pricing, 1380–1381
International pricing strategy, 1379–1382
International product/service strategy, 1377–1379
International promotion strategy, 1382–1383
International purchasing laws, 137
International relations, 1458–1459
International reserves, 1449–1453
International risks, 1383–1386
International sector, 224
International trade, 1403–1412
International treaties, 1461
Internet recruiting, 737–738
Internet service providers (ISPs), 1248
Internet sites, types of, 543
Internet, 55, 543, 763, 1246–1247, 1250–1253, 1471
Interorganizational context, 538
Interorganizational linkages, 228–229
Interpersonal communication barriers, 65
Interpersonal roles, of managers, 54
Interpersonals, 522
Interrelationship diagram, 644–645
Interstate Land Sales Full Disclosure Act, 142
Intertype competition, 576
Interviews/interviewing
  exit, 721
  performance appraisal, 783
  selection, 751–756
  systems design and, 1183
In-the-money option, 1000
Intradepartmental problem solving, 63
Intra-industry trade (IIT), 1410
Intranets, 30, 55, 1247, 1395
In-transit inventory. See Pipeline/in-transit inventory
Intratype competition, 576
Intrinsic rewards, 57, 799
Intrinsic value, 1008
Introduction stage, 578
Introduction strategies, 493–496
Intuition, 637
Intuition ethic, 1346
Intuitive decision making, 75
Intuitive problem-solving approach, 72

Inventory, 338
  benefits of, 387–388
  disadvantages of, 388
  excess and obsolete, 396–397
  on-site supplier-managed, 397–398
  planned BOM and EOM, 426–427
  services and, 410
  supply chain performance measurement and, 407
  types of, 385–386
Inventory analysis, 853–854
Inventory control, 540–541
Inventory conversion period, 951
Inventory costs, 370, 371
Inventory financing, 976–977
Inventory investment, 371, 387
Inventory investment control, 393
Inventory management, 338–342, 967–968. See also Supply chain inventory management
Inventory models, 286
Inventory planning, retail, 435–438
Inventory policy, 293
Inventory pricing method, 431
Inventory pull systems, 392
Inventory-related costs, 386–387
Inventory-tracking systems, automated, 399
Inventory turnover, 418–419, 853–854
Inventory valuation, 428–431
Investigation, 1180, 1181
  detailed, 488
  fraud, 1289–1291
  preliminary, 487–488
Investigative questions, 72
Investing activities
  cash flows from, 836, 839
  noncash, 840
Investment bankers, 1086, 1092, 1093
Investment banking house, 1085
Investment banking process, 1092–1095
Investment centers, responsibility accounting for, 907–912
Investment grade bonds, 990
Investment opportunities, 1061
Investment policies, 953–956
Investment risk, 1095–1099
Investments
  capital/financial accounts, 1416–1417
  international, 1408–1409, 1412–1414
  socially conscious or ethical, 1320–1321
Investment scams, 1280
Investment strategies, short-term, 968–969
Investment turnover, 908
Invigilation, 1290
Involuntary absenteeism, 717
Involuntary dissolution, 24
Involuntary turnover, 718
Involvement, 256, 521
IPS sites, 1248
Irish business customs, 1424
Irrigation, 1178
Ishikawa, Kaoru, 652, 667
Ishikawa quality model, 667
ISO 9000, 49
ISO standards, 1244
Issuance costs, 1093
Issue analysis, 1328–1329

Issue identification, 1328
Issue mix, 1327
Issuer, 1465
Issue ranking/prioritization, 1329
Issues development process, 1330–1331
Issues management, 1324, 1326–1331
Issues management process, 1327–1330
Italian business customs, 1424

J

Jack in the Box, 1335
Japanese quality awards. *See* Deming Prize
JCPenney Co., 229, 576, 583, 900, 988
J. Crew, 458
J.D. Edwards, 1131
Jiro, Kawakita, 643, 691
Job analysis
  behavioral aspects of, 729
  competency approach to, 731–732
  legal aspects of, 729–730
  methods, 727, 728
  nature of, 726–727
  process, 727, 728
Job anxiety, 614
Job assignments, sex discrimination and, 789
Job-centered leaders, 41
Job characteristics model, 59–60, 724–725
Job criteria, 774, 775
Job descriptions, 730, 731
Job design
  individuals and teams, 722–725
  motivation, 58–60
  technology and, 354–355
  work schedules and locations, 725
Job enlargement, 58, 355, 724
Job enrichment, 58, 355, 724
Job fairs, 739–740
Job instruction and rationale, 63
Job instruction training, 762
Job offers, 756
Job order cost system, 877
  decision making, 880–881
  manufacturing businesses, 878–880
  process costing and, 882–883
  professional service businesses, 881–882
Job performance, 745–746
Job performance standards, 730
Job posting, 736
Job rotation, 354, 724
Jobs, 58, 722
  auditing, 705
  human resources management and, 722
  nontraditional, 789
Job satisfaction, 716–718, 723
Job shops, 877
Job simplification, 58, 59, 355
Job specifications, 730
Job switching, 599
Job transfers, 736
Job transitions, 771
Johnson, Lyndon B., 105
Johnson & Johnson, 38, 81, 237, 241, 497, 594, 934, 1321, 1395
Joint and several liability, 16

SUBJECT INDEX 1655

Joint application development (JAD), 1192–1193
Joint liability, 15
Joint optimization, 355
Joint ventures, 11, 228, 1376
Jones, Daniel, 388
Judgment, 78, 170–171
Judgment-driven quality, 638
Judicial limitations, 107
Junior mortgages, 986
Junk bonds, 989
Juran, Joseph M., 640, 651, 663–664, 681
Juran quality model, 663–664
Jurisdiction, 1277, 1461–1463
Justice, distributive, 87
Just-in-time (JIT), 679
Just-in-time (JIT) inventory systems, 341
Just-in-time (JIT) production, 391–393
Just-in-time (JIT) purchasing, 389–390
Just-in-time (JIT) transportation, 390–391

K

Kahle, Lynn, 522
Kaizen, 668, 679–680, 690
Kamprad, Ingar, 582
Kanban systems, 341
Kano, Noriaki, 669
Kano quality model, 669
Kawamoto, Nobuhiko, 38
Keepsake, 589
Kelleher, Herb, 244
Kellogg, 81, 183, 251, 492
Key currency, 1441
Keys, 1160–1161
KFC, 901
Kidder Peabody, 1353
Kidder-Stacy Company, 372
Kimberly-Clark, 224
King model, 1276
King Report, 1276
Kinked demand curve, 183
Kinko's, 1130
Kirkpatrick, Donald L., 763
KJ method, 643
Kmart, 442, 576, 583, 604, 849, 1222, 1252
Kmart's BlueLight.com, 342
Knapfel, Robert E., 542
Knowledge, 30, 1157
  foreign cultures, 1423, 1425
  foreign direct investment and, 1413
  pay for, 60
  skills, and abilities (KSAs), 705, 730, 732, 736, 744
Knowledge base, 1174
Knowledge engineering/engineers, 1171, 1175
Knowledge gap, 566
Knowledge management, 31, 1157, 1169. See also Artificial intelligence; Expert systems
Knowledge of actual results, 59
Knowledge work, 30–31, 768
Kodak Corporation, 81, 253, 492, 1260. See also Eastman Kodak
Kohlberg Kravis Roberts (KKR), 491, 1107

Kohl's, 602
KonTraG model, 1276
Korn, Lester B., 903
Korn/Ferry International, 903
KPMG, 1169
Kraft Foods, 183, 491, 616
Kroc, Ray, 248
Kroger, 337, 576, 604
Krugman, Paul, 1404, 1409–1410
Kurt Salmon Associates, 580
KWorld, 1169

L

Labeling decisions, 493
Labeling requirements, 141
Labor
  country risk and, 1103
  factory, 876–877
Labor-based index, 657
Labor disputes, 101
Labor force population, 733
Labor law, 101–102
Labor-Management Relations Act (LMRA), 101–102
Labor-Management Reporting and Disclosure Act, 102
Labor markets, recruiting and, 733
Labor specialization, 470
Labor unions, 738
Laggards, 493, 495
Landrum-Griffin Act. See Labor-Management Reporting and Disclosure Act
Lands' End, 458, 576
Language, 83
Language learning, 1423
Language translation, 1420
Lanham Act, 96
La Porta, Rafael, 1064
Large-batch production, 345
Large-group intervention, 254
Late majority, 493, 495
Laventhol and Horwath, 9–10
Law, ethics and, 1338, 1339–1340. See also Business law; Government regulations; International law
Lawler, E. E., 714
Laws of agency, 128, 129
Lawsuits, shareholder, 22, 1357
Layout management, for retail stores, 450–458
Lea & Perrins, 342
Leader behavior, 43–44
Leaders
  autocratic versus democratic, 40–41
  charismatic, 45
  employee-centered, 41
  job-centered, 41
  relationship-oriented, 42, 44
  servant, 46–47
  task-oriented, 42, 44
  transactional, 45
  transformational, 46
  visionary, 45
Leadership
  management and, 31, 38–47

  new workplace and, 46–47, 56
  quality and, 636–638
  substitutes for, 44–45
  See also Low-cost leadership
Leadership grid, 41
Leadership roles, of managers, 54
Leadership situations, 42
Leadership style, 42
Leadership traits, 40
Lead from strength, 1368
Lead-time offsets, 364
Lead underwriter, 1094
Leaky bucket theory, 568
Leaning against the wind, 1447
Lean supply chains, 388–393
Lean Thinking (Womack and Jones), 388
Leapfrogging, 71
Lear, Robert, 1350
Learning
  communication and, 65
  communication barriers and, 67
  consumer behavior and, 520–521
  decision, 80
  e-learning, 763
  incidental, 1173
  quality management and, 641
  training and, 763
Learning curve, 191
Learning organization, 30, 56
Learning potential, 50
Leases, 151, 997–999
Leasing
  equipment, 916–917
  retail sites, 612
Legacy, 1194
Legal aggregate, 13
Legal authority, 128–133
Legal awareness, 787
Legal capital, 155
Legal entity, 13, 18
Legal environment, 420
Legal issues
  exchange rates, 1444
  information ethics, 1264
  international franchising, 1375
  job analysis, 729–730, 732
  pricing-related, 552–553
  selection process, 746–747, 751
  sexual harassment, 791–792
Legality of object, 122
Legal performance appraisals, 784–785
Legal/political environment, 474, 476
Legal responsibilities, 624–625, 1312–1313, 1314, 1339
Legal rights and privileges, of common stockholders, 982–983
Legal subject matter, 127
Legends, 83
Legislation, accounting reform, 1347
Legitimacy, 33, 266, 1347–1348
Legitimate power, 39, 259, 590
Legitimation, 1347
Lego A/S, 1382
Lemon laws, 141
Lending risk, international, 1453–1454
Leniency errors, 782
Leontief, Wassily, 1404, 1407

Leontief paradox, 1404, 1407
Less structured selection interviews, 752–753
Lessee, 997
Lessor, 997
Letter of credit (LOC), 973
Letters of credit, 1465
Level 5 leadership, 46
Level of analysis, 222–223
Level production strategy, 369
Level scheduling, 393
Leverage, 1427
   degree of, 1052, 1054–1056
   financial control and, 1032–1033
   financial, 1030–1032, 1051–1052, 1100
   operating, 1025–1028, 1031–1032, 1100
Leveraged buyouts (LBOs), 948, 989, 1106–1107
Levi Strauss, 252, 511, 877, 1377
Levine, Dennis B., 1352
Levitt, Arthur, 1350
Lexicographic models, 524
Lexmark, 1170
Liability, 11
   accounting equation and, 827
   balance sheets and, 835–836
   board of directors, 1353
   contractual, 1300
   corporations, 18, 20, 21
   dividends and distributions, 21
   existing, 14
   incoming partners, 16
   investment, 1418
   joint, 15
   joint and several, 16
   limited, 12
   limited liability company, 18
   limited liability partnerships, 18
   limited partnerships, 16–17
   personal, 15, 128–133, 1353
   short-term, 969–974
   strict, 118
   torts and crimes, 20
   unlimited, 9
   See also Strict liability in tort
Liability limitation, 18
Liability limitation statutes, 23
Liability risks, 1295, 1296
Liaison role, 54, 233
Liberty, personal, 87
Libraries, 1165
License arrangements, 228
License fees, 1195
Licenses, export, 1400
Licensing agreements, international, 1374
Lie detector tests, 108–9
Liens, blanket, 976
Life cycle. *See* Organizational life cycle
Life, health, and loss of income risks, 1295, 1296
Life insurance companies, 1088
Lifestyle graphics, 458
Lifestyles, 522, 793
Life-threatening illnesses, 792
LIFO (last in, first out), 431, 879
Lighting design, 456–457
Likert, Rensis, 7
Limitation, of warranties, 149

Limited form, 1305
Limited liability, 12, 18
Limited liability company (LLC), 11, 12–13, 17–18
Limited liability limited partnerships (LLLPs), 10, 18
Limited liability partnerships (LLPs), 10, 18
Limited partners, 10, 13
Limited partnerships, 10, 11, 16–17
LimitedToo, 342
Linder, Staffan Burenstam, 1404, 1407–1408
Lindgren, John H., Jr., 475
Linear programming, 286, 295, 296
Linear regression model, 1150
Line authority, 37
Line departments, 37
Line extensions, 479
Line managers, 1212–1213
Line of credit, 972
Linking, 1161
Liquidating dividend, 21, 156
Liquidation, 24, 154
Liquidation preferences, 21
Liquidation value model, 1109
Liquidity, 850, 962, 1056
Liquidity preference theory, 215
Liquidity premium (LP), 214
Liquidity problem, 1451
Listening, active, 66
Listening responses, 754
Litigation, 1459
L.L. Bean, 458, 580, 685, 686, 689
Load balancing, 1248
Loading phase, 1167
Loans
   amortized, 306–307
   country risk and, 1103
   limited partnerships, 16
   secured, 974
   term, 985
   See also Bank loans
Lobbyists, 1458
Loblaw, 419
Local area networks (LANs), 1226
Local area networks (LANs) protocols, 1229–1230
Local content, 1385
Local cultures, 1423
Local languages, 1423
Local markets, 1085
Local participation, 1376
Local systems development, 1214
Location
   facility, 337–338
   international negotiations, 1426
   job design and, 725
   retailer, 419
   See also Retail location analysis
Lockbox arrangement, 960
Lockheed Martin Corporation, 1335
Loctite, 1389
Logical design, 1183–1186
Logic bombs, 1141–1143
Logistical service standards, 542
Logistics, 342, 400, 538–543
London InterBank Offer Rate (LIBOR), 985, 995

London Stock Exchange, 1276
Long-linked technology, 353
Long-range planning, 356–359, 706
Long-run production processes, 675
Long-term assets, 835
Long-term debt, 957, 984–991
Long-term financing
   bond refunding operations, 993–994
   bond valuation, 1004–1007
   common stock, 981–984
   convertibles, 1002–1004
   decision-making factors, 991–993
   equity (stock) valuation, 1007–1014
   foreign debt instruments, 994–995
   leases, 997–999
   long-term debt, 984–991
   options, 999–1001
   preferred stock, 995–997
   real (tangible) asset valuation, 1014–1015
   warrants, 1001–1002
Long-term liabilities, 836
Lopez-de-Silanes, Florencio, 1064
Loss control, 1302, 1306–1307
Losses
   chance of, 1297
   differential, 915
   disequilibrium, 179
   predicting, 1304
   risk of, 131–132
   statistical analysis of, 1301
Loss exposure, 1299
Loss-exposure checklist, 1299
Loss of income risks. *See* Life, health, and loss of income risks
Loss sharing, 16, 17
Lotus Development Corporation, 1129, 1169
Low-context cultures, 1421
Low-cost leader business strategy, 759
Low-cost leadership, 4
Lowe's, 416, 611
Lower control limit (LCL), 296, 651
Low-liquidity strategy, 969
Low-margin/high-turnover retailers, 419
Low-margin/low-turnover retailers, 419
Low readiness level, 43
Loyalty, 23, 716, 1264
LTV Corp., 224, 1105
Lubrication bribes, 1468
Lucent Technologies, Inc., 518
Lump-sum bonuses, 60
Lumpy assets, 1021
Lying, 461

M

MacQuaire Test for Mechanical Ability, 748
Macroassessment, 1101–1102
Macroeconomic forecast problems, 164
Macroeconomic policy, in open economy, 1428–1430
Macroenvironment, 474
Macrofinancial risk, 1102
Macro level of legitimacy, 1348
Macropolitical risk, 1102
Macy's, 575

SUBJECT INDEX   1657

Magnuson-Moss Warranty Act, (1974), 140–141, 149, 157
Mahoney, Richard J., 1334
Maidenform, 1377
Mail delay, 960
Maintenance, repair and operating (MRO) supplies inventory, 386
Maintenance fees, 1195
Make-to-order, 375, 376, 381
Make-to-stock, 375, 381
Makita, 1389
Malaysian business customs, 1424
Malcolm Baldridge National Quality Award, 670
Malls, 602–603
Managed floating exchange rate system, 1446–1447
Management
 centralized, 18
 corporate governance and, 1349
 corporations, 18
 definition of, 31
 distribution and, 536
 ethics for, 941
 general partnerships and, 15
 internal control and, 1273
 international business strategies and, 1367
 limited liability company, 17
 marketing channels, 538
 new product development and, 490–491
 new workplace and, 54–56
 open-book, 50
 organizational configuration and, 220
 organizational performance, 50–51
 purchasing ethics and, 463
 shareholder wealth and, 944, 945–946
 types of, 52–53
 variable costing and absorption costing, 931–937
 See also Supply chain inventory management; Working capital management
Management assurance, 1345–1347
Management by objectives (MBO), 29, 33–35
Management by wandering around (MBWA), 64, 67
Management champion, 250
Management coaching, 772
Management compensation, 22
Management competencies, in new workplace, 56
Management control, 1268, 1269–1270
Management control systems, 245
Management development, 771–773
Management discussion and analysis, 1345–1346
Management ethics, 1341–1345
Management fraud, 1279, 1280
Management functions
 controlling, 47–50
 leading, 38–47
 organizing, 36–38
 planning, 31–35
Management imperfections, 1413
Management information systems (MISs), 1145, 1146–1147

Management perspectives
 classical perspective, 24–27
 current directions in management thinking, 30–31
 humanistic perspective, 27–28
 management science perspective, 28
 recent historical trends, 29–30
Management Principle of Materiality, 393
Management processes, organic versus mechanistic, 227
Management science model, decision making and, 75–76
Management science perspective, 28
Management skills, 51–52
Management structure, of corporations, 21
Management thinking, current directions in, 30–31
Management values, 771
Managerial accounting, 825
Managerial attitude, 1051
Managerial compensation plans, 947
Managerial competence, 1345
Managerial economics
 demand analysis and estimation, 195–205
 finance and, 212–217
 forecasting, 163–172
 marketing and, 192–195
 monopolistic competition and oligopoly, 180–190
 operations and, 190–191
 perfect competition and monopoly, 172–180
 pricing practices, 205–212
 value maximization, 158–163
Managerial ethics, 85–86
Managerial judgment, 513
Managerial modeling, 771
Managerial productivity, 343
Managerial tests, 749
Manager-managed LLCs, 17
Managers
 activities, 53
 communication and, 61
 CSP model and, 1318–1319
 first-line, 52
 functional, 53
 general, 53
 information systems and, 1144–1148, 1212–1213
 line, 1212–1213
 middle, 52
 performance appraisal and, 783
 project, 52, 270, 281–282
 public affairs and, 1326
 risk, 1298
 roles of, 53–54
 stockholders versus, 946–947
 top, 52
 See also Purchasing managers
Managing underwriter, 1094
Mandated benefits, 795–796
Mandatory safety standards, 140
Mandatory vacations, 937–938
Manufacturers
 marketing mix and, 474

 point-of-purchase communications and, 510
 process, 882, 883
Manufacturing-based quality, 683
Manufacturing businesses, 875, 878–880
Manufacturing cost terms, 875–877
Manufacturing defect, 151
Manufacturing-driven quality, 639
Manufacturing focus, 359
Manufacturing management philosophy decisions, 359
Manufacturing margin, 929
Manufacturing operations
 departmental technology, 349–351
 department design, 351–352
 inventory management, 338–342
 job design and technology, 354–355
 manufacturing and service technologies, 344
 master scheduling, 373–384
 operations management systems, designing, 334–338
 organization-level manufacturing technology, 344–347
 organization-level service technology, 347–349
 organizations as production systems, 330–334
 planning and scheduling, 355–356
 productivity management, 342–344
 workflow interdependence among departments, 352–354
 See also Manufacturing resource planning
Manufacturing organizations, 331–332
Manufacturing overhead, 877
Manufacturing plan integration, 366
Manufacturing planning, 355–356, 358–359
Manufacturing resource planning
 aggregate planning problem and capacity planning, 366–373
 business plan, 359–360
 long-range planning, 356–359
 plan integration, 366
 production planning, 360–363
 resource requirements planning, 363–366
Manufacturing scheduling, 355–356
Manufacturing strategy, 328
Manufacturing technologies, 344–347
Mapping, risk, 1301–1302
March, James, 76, 78
Marcus, Bernie, 598
Margin, 418–419
Margin calls, 1091
Margin of dumping, 1440
Margin of safety, 873
Margin requirements, 1091
Margin stabilization, 515
Marginal analysis, 161
Marginal cost, 160, 288
Marginal cost of capital (MCC), 1046–1050
Marginal cost of capital schedule, 1046–1050
Marginal functions, 729
Marginal profit, 160
Marginal rate of substitution (MRS), 1430–1431
Marginal relations, 160–161
Marginal revenue, 160, 198–201, 289

Marion Laboratories, Inc., 370
Marketable securities, 961–962
Market access, 142
Market allocations, 112, 113
Market analysis, 488
Market constraints, 437–438
Market control, 245–246
Market demand potential, 607–608
Market development, 496, 497
Market economy regulation
 antitrust policy, 92
 competition and government, 89–91
 costs of, 91
 deregulation movement, 93
 incentive failures, 91
 problems with, 92–93
 structural failures, 91
Market entrant barriers, 1128
Market equilibrium, 194–195
Market ethic, 1346
Market failure, 90
Market goals, 3
Market information, 472
Marketing, 612–613
 business ethics and, 547–553
 cause-related, 551
 economics and, 192–195
 evolution of, 470–472
 as organizational process, 472–474
 quantitative techniques and, 296
 sponsorship, 499, 509
 total sensory, 457
 as trading relationship exchange process, 471–472
 See also Niche marketing; Retail marketing; Services marketing; Target marketing
Marketing channel research, 530–531
Marketing channels, 474
 defining, 531–532
 flows in, 536–538
 logistics in, 538–543
 management, 538
 structure, 532–536
 supply chain management and, 586–589
Marketing communications, 498–499
 advertising, 498, 499–504
 personal selling, 498
 point-of-purchase communications, 499, 509–510
 public relations, 498, 508–509
 sales promotion, 498–499, 504–508
 sponsorship marketing, 499, 509
Marketing concept, 472
Marketing environment, 474–476
Marketing era, 470
Marketing functions, 534
Marketing institutions, 585–586
Marketing law
 consumer credit transactions, 142–145
 Consumer Product Safety Commission, 139–140
 consumer protection, 138
 consumer purchases, 140–142
 creditors' remedies, 145–146

 Federal Trade Commission, 138–139
 state and federal consumer protection agencies, 138
Marketing mix, 472, 473, 478, 543–545
Marketing myopia, 558
Marketing PR (MPR), 508, 509
Marketing strategies, 470–476, 1377–1383
Market interest rates, determinants of, 213–215
Market makers, 1089
Market penetration, 496, 497
Market power, 1105
Market price, 1008
Market price approach, 913
Market price determination, 176
Market research
 competitive importance of, 526
 competitor research, 526–530
 consumer research, 526
 marketing channel research, 530–531
Market risk, 1078, 1081–1082, 1098–1099
Markets, 173
 common stock, 1089–1091
 defining, 526–527
 e-marketing and, 543
 financial, 1084–1085
 foreign direct investment and, 1413
 horizontal, 1253
 international, 1091–1092
 international business strategies and, 1366, 1367
 labor, 733
 options, 999–1000
 spontaneous economic combustion and, 470
 stock, 1088–1089
 target marketing and, 553–555
 vertical, 1253
 See also External markets
Market sector, 224
Market segmentation
 retail marketing and, 571, 600
 target marketing and, 553–555
Market segmentation theory, 216
Market segments, 208, 472, 554, 933–935, 1408
Market selection, 599–612
Market share, 113–114, 416, 480, 526
Market share target, 515–516
Market skimming, 516
Market structure
 defining, 173
 measurement of, 188
 product characteristics and, 174
 profit rates and, 178
Market supply factors, in retail location, 608–609
Market-to-book ratio, 1110
Market value, 1108
Market value-added (MVA), 49, 1111
Markov chain analysis, 296
Markov matrix, 707
Markov-process models, 287
Marks, 96
Markup, 512, 922
Markup laws, 552
Markup on cost, 206, 512

Markup on price, 206–207
Markup on retail price, 512
Markup pricing, 205–207
Marriage, retail marketing and, 574
Marriott, 248, 567, 915
Marshaling of assets, 14
Martinez, Alfred C., 88
Mary Kay Cosmetics, 576, 689
Maslow, Abraham, 27, 521, 713–714
Mass customization, 347, 678
Massed practice, 761
Mass markets, 505, 554–555
Mass services, 411
Master budget, 890
Master production schedule (MPS), 360, 374, 375, 383, 384, 398
Master schedule planning horizon, 381–382
Master scheduler, 383
Master scheduling (MS), 373
 bill of material, 376–380
 designing, creating, and managing, 382
 final assembly schedule, 382–384
 interfaces, 374–375
 master schedule planning horizon, 381–382
 MPS and, 374
 production environment, 375–376
MasterCard, 596, 975, 976
Matching concept, 825, 832
Material handling
 excessive, 389
 JIT transportation and, 391
Material requirements planning (MRP), 340–341, 398
Materials
 as business-to-business products, 478
 cost of, 876
Materials handling, logistics and, 540
Materials inventory, 878
Mathematical tables, 1116–1123
Mathsoft, Inc., 7
Matrix data analysis, 646–647
Matrix diagrams, 646
Matrix structure, 237–239, 1391–1393
Matrix-type organizations, 270, 271
Matsushita, 1398
Maturing products, 1408–1409
Maturity
 commercial paper, 973
 marketable securities, 962
 preferred stock, 997
 short-term bank loans, 972
Maturity date, 1004
Maturity matching, 991–992
Maturity matching approach, 954–956
Maturity phase, 414, 415
Maturity risk premium (MRP), 214–215, 989
Maturity stage, 578
Maturity strategies, 496
Maturity value, 1004
Maximum possible loss, 1301
Maximum probable loss, 1301
May Department Stores, 576
MBNA, 557
McAdam, Terry, 1317
McCormick & Company, Inc., 396

SUBJECT INDEX 1659

McDonald's, 207, 237, 248, 338, 352, 410, 411, 419, 478, 491, 500, 555, 591, 601, 654, 1377
McDonnell, John, 67
McDonnell Douglas Corporation, 67, 356
McGill University, 77
McGregor, Douglas, 27, 58
MCI WorldCom, 181, 183
M-commerce, 1252–1253
Means-ends ethic, 1346
Mechanistic management processes, 227
Mechanistic structure, 351
Medco Containment, 1106
Media, 1220–1223
Media effectiveness, reduced, 505
Media recruiting sources, 739
Mediating technology, 352
Mediators, message transmission through, 1422
Medical examinations and inquiries, 756
Meetings
  board of directors and, 22
  organizational, 19
  shareholder, 21
Meijer's, 577
Member-managed LLCs, 18
Member rights, in limited liability companies, 17
Member rotation, 268
Memorized presentation, 619
Mental budgeting, 523
Mental health job design and, 723
Mentoring, 772
Mentzer, John T., 542
Merchandise, free, 441
Merchandise budget, 422–428
Merchandise knowledge, 449
Merchandise line, 435
Merchandise management, 432, 446
  dollar merchandise control, 434–435
  dollar merchandise planning, 431–434
  in-store merchandise handling, 444
  merchandising sources, 438–440
  retail inventory planning, 435–438
  vendor negotiations, 440–443
Merchandise presentation planning, 454–455
Merchandise turnover constraints, 437
Merchandising, 422
  retail store, 454–456
  scrambled, 416, 534
  visual, 455–456
Merchandising sources, 438–440
Merchant seller, 148, 151
Merchantability, 131, 148, 149
Merck & Co., 911, 1106
Mergers and acquisitions, 23, 115, 228, 1104–1107, 1350–1352, 1376
Merrill Lynch, 1086, 1089, 1092, 1130
Meso theory, 222
Messages
  communication process and, 61
  external and internal, 32
  mediators and, 1422
  written or spoken, 1421
Metadata, 1162
Mexican business customs, 1424
Meyers, Gerald C., 1333

Micro level of legitimacy, 1348
Microassessment, 1101–1102
Microeconomic forecast problems, 164
Microenvironment, 474
Microfinancial risk, 1102
Micromarketing, 554, 574
Micromarkets, 554
Micropolitical risk, 1102
Microsoft, 10, 230, 237, 518, 702, 969, 1012, 1050, 1128–1129, 1242, 1244
Microwaves, 1222
Midas Muffler, 590
Middle managers, 52
Middle-of-month (MOM) dating, 443
Middle-of-the-road management, 41
Midwest Contract Furnishings, 248
Might-equals-right ethic, 1346
Milken, Michael, 989, 1114, 1353
Millennium Chemicals Inc., 910
Millennium generation. *See* Generation Y
Miller, Merton, 1056
Miller Fluid Power, 370
Miller-Orr model, 296–297
Miller-Tydings Resale Price Maintenance Act (1937), 551
Mind share, 528
Mineral exploration, 1178
Minimally acceptable level, 682
Minnesota Multiple Personality Inventory (MMPI), 749
Mintzberg, Henry, 53, 77, 78
Misappropriation, 95
Miscellaneous fraud, 1280
Misinformation, 461
Misleading, 461
Mission, 2, 1133
Missionary salespeople, 616
Mission-critical applications, 1259
Mission culture, 84
Mission goals, 268
Mission statement, 32, 1134
Mistake-proofing, 653–654
Mistakes, 80, 135
Misuse, of products, 153
MIT Commission on Industrial Productivity, 679
Mitsukoshi Ltd., 581
Mixed costs, 864–865
Mixed structure, 1391
Mobile commerce. *See* M-commerce
Mobile-site, 1260
Mobility barriers, 174
Model Business Corporation Act (MBCA), 19
Model management module, 1149, 1150–1151
Modems, 1224–1225
Moderate current asset investment policy, 953
Moderate financing strategy, 980
Moderate-liquidity strategy, 969
Moderate readiness level, 43
Modification, of warranties, 149
Modified accrual method, 1038–1039
Modified buy-and-hold investment strategy, 968
Modigliani, Franco, 1056

Modulation, 1223–1226
Monetary policy, 1429
Money, cost of, 213. *See also* Time value of money
Money market funds, 1088
Money markets, 1085
Monitoring, 939
  by expert systems, 1173
  internal control, 1271–1272
  issues, 1330
  by managers, 53–54
Monopolies, 113–114
Monopolistically competitive markets, characteristics of, 181–182
Monopolistic competition, 180–190
Monopolization, 113–114
Monopoly
  defining, 180
  equilibrium under, 177
  monopsony versus, 177–178
  perfect competition and, 172–180
  price/output decision under, 176–177
Monopoly markets, 176, 179–180
Monopoly power, 113
Monopsony, 175, 177–178
Monsanto Co., 233, 1334
Monsanto Co. v. Spray-Rite Service Corporation, 111
Monte Carlo simulation, 1080–1081
Monthly cash flows, forecasting, 1035
Montreal Protocol, 121
Moods, consumer, 521
Moody's Investors Service, 989–990
Moral competence, 1345
Moral disagreement and ambiguity, 1344–1345
Morale hazard, 1297
Moral evaluation, 1344
Moral hazard, 1297
Moral identification and ordering, 1344
Moral imagination, 1344
Morality, 1336
Moral judgment, 1344–1345
Moral management, 1341, 1342–1343
Moral obligation and integrity, 1345
Morgan Guaranty Trust, 1057
Morgan Stanley Dean Witter, 1085, 1086, 1089, 1092
Morphological analysis, 72
Mortgage bonds, 986
Mortgage markets, 1085
Morton, Thomas, 669
Morton Salt, 557
Most Favored Nation (MFN), 1373, 1461
Motivation
  business ethics and, 1340, 1341
  concept of, 57
  consumer behavior and, 521
  foundations of, 57–58
  individual, 713–715
  job design for, 58–60
  model of, 57
  new workplace and, 60–61
  planning and, 33
  sales force, 621–622
  supply chain performance and, 405–406
Motivational compensation programs, 60

Motivators, 714
Motorola, 229, 242, 678, 681
Mouton, Jane, 267
Moving averages techniques, 167–168
Mrs. Fields Cookies, 1152
Mulford, Charles W., 941
Multicriteria decision problems, 287
Multidomestic strategy, 1369
Multifocused grouping, 235
Multifunctional project team, 269
Multilateral Investment Guarantee Agency (MIGA), 1104, 1462–1463
Multilevel tree structure and levels, 377–380
Multiline insurance, 1310
Multinational corporations (MNCs), 1100–1104, 1376, 1469
Multinational enterprise (MNEs), 1376
Multinational working capital management, 957–958, 966–968
Multiple bottom-line perspective, 1319–1320
Multiple channels, 67
Multiple exchange rates, 1448
Multiple hurdles, 746
Multiple IRRs, 1072
Multiple product orders, 139
Multiple-product pricing, 210
Multiple-trigger policies, 1310
Multiple-unit pricing strategies, 210
Multiplexers, 1225–1226
Multisite rationalization stage, 414–415
Multisite services life cycle, 414–415
Multiyear, 1310
MuseumCompany.com, 342
Mutual agreement, 1260
Mutual assent, 122, 127
Mutual funds, 1088
Mutually exclusive projects, 1065–1066, 1071–1072
Mutual trust, 592–593
MWT Corporation, 1304
Myers-Briggs test, 749
Myths, 83

N

Nabisco, 183, 342, 491
Naked options, 1000
Names
  corporations, 19
  limited liability company, 17
  limited partnerships, 16
Narrative methods, 779, 780
Narrow band, 1220
NASDAQ, 1089
Nasdaq-Amex Market Group, 1089
Nash bargaining, 186–187
Nash equilibrium, 186
National Academy of Engineering, 92
National account managers, 615–616
National Association of Attorneys General (NAAG), 138
National Association of Corporate Directors (NACD), 1355
National Association of Purchasing Managers (NAPM), 462
National Association of Security Dealers (NASD), 1089, 1091
National Bureau of Economic Research (NBER), 171–172
National Center for Employee Ownership, 812
National Cooperative Research Act, 112
National currencies, 1451
National Discount Brokers Group, 1143
National Environmental Policy Act (1970), 551
National Environmental Policy Act (NEPA), 118–119, 120
National Highway Traffic Safety Administration (NHTSA), 140
National Labor Relations Act (NLRA), 101, 102
National Labor Relations Board (NLRB), 101–102
National markets, 1085
National price controls, 1380
National Quality Institute (NQI), 670
National Securities Market Improvements Act (1996), 94
NationsBank Corporation, 343, 1088
Natural business year, 826
Natural crises, 1332
Natural disasters, 1139–1140
Natural language processing (NLP), 1171
Natural monopoly, 177
NBC, 1065
Near-cash assets, 961
Needed external funds (NEF), 1033
Needs, 57
  communication, 67
  communication barriers and, 66
  consumer, 520, 521
  new product development and, 482–485
  organizational change and, 248, 256
Needs assessment, training, 760
Need-satisfaction presentation, 619
Needs clarification, 449
Needs hierarchy, 713–714
Negative emphasis, 755
Negotiated deals, 1092–1093
Negotiated price approach, 913–914
Negotiation, 267
  contract, 1197, 1198
  cross-cultural, 1423, 1425–1428
  vendor, 440–443
  transportation rates and service levels, 404–405
Negotiation flow, 537
Negotiator roles, of managers, 54
Neighborhood business district (NBD), 602
Neighbors, of retail sites, 611–612
Neiman Marcus, 575, 576
Nepotism, 789
Nestlé, 237, 1370, 1376, 1388, 1394
Net assets, 1108
Net cash flow, 1067
Net cash flow provided by financing activities, 839
Net cash flow provided by investing activities, 839
Net cash flow used for financing activities, 839
Net cash flow used for investing activities, 839
Net Errors and Omissions Account, 1416, 1418
Net float, 960
Netherlands, business customs of, 1424
Net income, 832
Net loss, 832
Net operating income (NOI), 1022, 1024
Net present value (NPV), 660, 1066, 1068–1069
  country risk and, 1102
  IRR and, 1071–1072
  rationale for, 1069
  risk and, 1079–1081
Net present value (NPV) model, 1112
Net present value (NPV) profile, 1071
Net price received, 1380
Net profit, 832
Net working capital, 949
Net worth, 1108
Netscape Corporation, 230, 1129, 1242
Network Associates, 1200
Network centrality, 260–261
Network diagram, 275
Networked global organization, 1394–1395
Network layer, 1231
Networks, 1226
  business environment and, 1234–1235
  expanding, 266
  local area networks, 1226
  protocols, 1229–1231
  service variety, 1232–1234
  switching techniques, 1231–1232
  virtual private networks, 1229
  wide area networks, 1226–1227
Network topology, 1226, 1227–1228
Neural networks, 1171–1172
  fuzzy logic, 1172
Neutralizers, 44
New issues, 20, 1005, 1045, 1090
Newness, defining, 479–481
New product development (NPD), 293, 478
  competitively advantaged products, 485
  defining, 479–481
  requirements, 481–482
  shepherding, 490–491
  strategy, 485–490
  unmet needs and problems, 482–485
New product development teams (NPT), 481
New product pricing, 516
New products, 250, 1408
New-to-the-world products, 479
New trade theory, 1404, 1409–1410
New-venture fund, 250
New workplace
  communication and, 64–65
  control in, 49
  leadership and, 46–47, 56
  management and, 54–56
  motivation and, 60–61
New York Stock Exchange (NYSE), 1085, 1088, 1089, 1092
Niche marketing, 502–503, 554
Niche retailing, 1252
Nigerian business customs, 1424
Nike, 227, 591, 597, 1144

Nissan, 181
No Electronic Theft Act (1997), 99
No fault absenteeism, 718
Noise, 62
Nokia, 1388
Nominal chart, 675
Nominal group technique (NGT), 68, 69–70
Nominal risk-free rate of interest, 213, 214
Nominal specification, 667
Nominal tariff rate, 1435
Nominating committee, 1355
Noncash investing and financing activities, 840
Noncompensatory models, 524–525
Nonconstant growth stocks, 1012
Nonconstruction contractors, 105
Noncontrol fraud factors, 1286
Noncontrollable costs, 931
Noncumulative quantity discount, 441
Noncurrent assets, 835
Noncyclical normal goods, 204–205
Nondirective interview, 753
Nondisclosure agreement, 136
Nondiscounting technique, 1066, 1068
Nondiversifiable risk, 1098–1099
Nonpartnership creditors, 14
Nonpoint source, 120
Nonprice competition, 183–185
Nonprofit corporations, 18
Nonprofit services, 557
Nonprogrammed decision, 73
Nonrepudiation, 1255
Nonroutine technologies, 350–351
Nonstore retailing, 580–581
Nonstore-based retailers, 601, 603–604
Nonsubstitutability, 262–263
Nontariff trade barriers, 1373, 1437–1441, 1463
Nontraditional jobs, sex discrimination and, 789
Nontraditional retail locations, 603
Nonverbal communication, 1419
No-par stock, 981
Norbom, Rolf, 396
Nordstrom, 575, 600, 608, 687, 699, 904
Normal goods, types of, 204–205
Normal growth, 1010–1012
Normal trade relations, 1373
Normative ethics, 1337
Norming stage, in team development, 283
Norms, cultural, 1421
Norris-La Guardia Act (1932), 101
North American Free Trade Agreement (NAFTA), 551, 1461
North American Industry Classification System (NAICS), 416, 417
North Star Steel, 224
Northwest, 552
Norwalk, 589
Notes receivable, 835
Notice, 16, 152
Notice of breach of warranty, 150
Novartis, 1400
Novell, 1230
NPD project success, 480
Nucor, 224
Nugent, Robert, 1335

Nuisance, 117
Number of days' sales in inventory, 854
Number of days' sales in receivables, 853
Number of times interest charges are earned, 855
Number of times preferred dividends are earned, 855
Numerical solution, 300
  amortized loans, 307
  bond valuation, 1006
  future value, 300
  future value of an annuity, 302, 303–304
  internal rate of return, 1070
  net present value, 1068–1069
  present value of an annuity, 305–306
  real asset valuation, 1015
Nutritional Labeling and Education Act (1990), 551

O

Oakland, John S., 668
Oakland quality model, 668
Obedience, duty of, 15, 23
Objections, handling, 619–620
Objective-and-task method, 500
Objective performance criteria measures, 775
Objective risks, 1295
Objectives
  advertising, 499
  breakthrough, 681
  budgeting, 886–887
  consumer sales promotions, 507–508
  economic, 1428
  internal control, 1270–1271
  marketing mix and, 474
  pricing, 517
  pricing strategy, 515–516
  project management and, 271
  sales promotion, 505–506
  trade promotions, 506–507
  See also Goals; Management by objectives; Strategic objectives; Tactical objectives
Objective-setting, 515
Objectivity concept, 824
Object-oriented structure, 1161
Obligation
  moral, 1345
  social, 1317
Observation
  fraud, 1290
  on-the-job, 1183
Obsolete inventory, continuous review of, 396–397
Obstacles, 663, 771
Occidental Petroleum, 946
Occupational fraud, 1279, 1280
Occupational Safety and Health Act, 107–8
Occupational Safety and Health Administration (OSHA), 92, 107–8
O'Connor, Michael, 581–582
Off-balance-sheet financing, 998
Offering price, 1093
Offers, 126–127
Office automation systems (OASs), 1146

Office Depot, 339, 436
OfficeMax, 1241
Office of Federal Contract Compliance Programs (OFCCP), 105
Officers
  authority of, 22
  role of, 22–24
  selection and removal of, 22
Official dollarization, 1445
Official exchange rates, 1443
Official goals, 2
Official Reserves Account, 1416, 1418
Off-invoice allowance, 507
Off-line quality control, 668
Off-peak, 207
Off-peak demand, 414
Off-target, 672
Ohio State University, 41
Ohlin, Bertil, 1404, 1405–1406
Old Navy, 421, 458
Oldham, Greg, 59
Oligopoly
  defining, 181
  monopolistic competition and, 180–190
Oligopoly markets
  characteristics of, 182–183
  competitive strategy in, 188–190
Olsen, Johan, 78
On account, 829
100 percent location, 611
One-shot game, 185
One-way exclusive dealing, 596
On-line analytical processing (OLAP), 1148, 1168
On-line operations, risks to, 1143–1144
On-line quality control, 668
On-line training, 763
On-line transaction processing (OLTP), 1148
On-shelf merchandising, 454
On-site inspections, 1301
On-site supplier-managed inventory, 397–398
On-the-job observation, 1183
On-the-job training (OJT), 762
On the Principles of Political Economy and Taxation, 1404
Open communication, 64–65
Open economy, macroeconomic policy in, 1428–1430
Open systems, 29, 71, 218–219
Open Systems Interconnection (OSI), 1230
Open-book management, 50
Open-ended credit, 143
Openness, climate of, 67
Open-to-buy (OTB), 434
Operating activities, cash flows from, 836, 838–839
Operating agreement, 17
Operating break-even analysis, 1022, 1025
Operating break-even point, 1027–1028
Operating budgets, 885
  income statement budgets, 890–896
  master budget, 890
  nature and objectives of, 885–887
  systems, 887–890
Operating cash flows, 1077
Operating economies of scale, 1104

Operating expenses, 418
Operating income, 1026
Operating leases, 998
Operating leverage, 874–875, 1025–1028, 1031–1032, 1100
Operating risk, 1384
Operating section, 1022
Operating strategy, 412
   amoral management, 1343
   immoral management, 1342
   moral management, 1342–1343
Operational control, 1269–1270
Operational feasibility study, 1180, 1182–1183
Operational plans, 32
Operations
   control procedures and, 938–939
   economics and, 190–191
   post-audits and, 1073
   purchasing ethics and, 459–463
   quantitative techniques and, 295
   See also Manufacturing operations; Retail operations; Service operations
Operations forecasting, 295
Operations information systems (OISs), 1145–1146
Operations management, 28, 331, 420–422
Operations management systems, designing, 334–338
Operations research, 28, 72
Operations strategies, 332–333
   manufacturing strategy, 328
   purchasing/supply chain strategy, 328–330
   retail strategy, 328
   service strategy, 328
Operative goals, 2–3
Opinion, 147
Opportunity, 1179, 1281, 1283, 1366
Opportunity cost, 920, 1059, 1076
Opportunity cost principle, 1043
Opportunity cost rate, 301
Optical fiber, 1223
Optimal capital structure, 1046, 1051–1052, 1053
Optimal decision, 158
Optimal dividend policy, 1057
Optimal merchandise mix, 435–437
Optimal price formula, 201
Optimal price range, 1062
Optimal pricing policy, price elasticity and, 201–202
Option overplanning, 380
Options, 999–1001
Option values, 1000–1001
Oracle, 1131
Orange Book, 1243–1244
Order-cycle time, 399, 540
Order entry and promise, 373
Order fulfillment, 342
Order getters, 615
Ordering costs, 339, 386
Order processing, 540
Order takers, 615
Ordinary, 148
Ordinary annuity, 302–303
Organic management processes, 227

Organic structure, 351
Organizational behavior, 222
Organizational bureaucracy and control, 242–246
Organizational change, 246
   culture change, 253–254
   elements for, 247–249
   implementation strategies, 255–256
   products and services change, 250–252
   strategic role of, 246
   strategic types of, 247
   strategy and structure change, 252–253
   technology change, 249–250
Organizational collaboration, 267–268
Organizational commitment, 716–718
Organizational communication, 62
   formal communication channels, 62–64
   informal communication channels, 64
   managing, 65–67
   team communication channels, 64
Organizational communication barriers, 66
Organizational configuration, 219–220
Organizational conflict, 256–257
   intergroup conflict, 257
   sources of, 257–259
   structural deficiencies and, 240
Organizational control, 47
   environmental resources, 228–230
   international, 1386–1387, 1396–1403
   size and, 243–244
Organizational control focus, 47
Organizational culture, 81, 221
   business ethics and, 86, 87
   business process change management and, 692–693
   defining, 81–82
   design and, 83–85
   emergence and purpose of, 82
   human resources and, 699
   interpreting, 83
   operational feasibility study and, 1182
   perceived hostile, 785
   strength of, 85
Organizational databases, 735–736
Organizational decision making, 73, 75–79
Organizational design
   alternatives, 235
   culture and, 83–85
   dimensions of, 220–221
   international, 1387–1393
   role of, 222–223
Organizational effectiveness, 4–5, 51
Organizational efficiency, 51
Organizational environment, 221
   domain of, 223–225
   environmental resources, 228–230
   environmental uncertainty, 225–228
   purchasing ethics and, 460
Organizational goals, 2, 221, 1216
Organizational incentives, 804, 805, 811–813
Organizational/individual relationships, 715–716
Organizational innovation, 246, 247
Organizational-level quality, 642–643
Organizational life cycle, 241–242
Organizational meeting, 19

Organizational performance, 50–51, 785–786
Organizational politics, 256–257
   environmental domain and, 229–230
   processes, 263–264
   using, 264–268
Organizational power, 256–257
   authority versus, 259–260
   horizontal sources of, 261–263
   individual power versus, 259
   politics and, 264–268
   vertical sources of, 260–261
Organizational process, marketing as, 472–474
Organizational purpose, 2–3
Organizational recruiting activities, 734
Organizational socialization, 561–562
Organizational strategies and design, 3–5, 699–700, 773
Organizational structure
   business ethics and corporate culture, 88
   computer-integrated manufacturing, 347
   department design and, 351
   international, 1386–1396
   JIT transportation, 391
   management types, 52–53
   workflow interdependence and, 354
Organizational subcultures, 85
Organizational systems, business ethics and, 86, 87, 88
Organizational technology, 221
Organizational workforce, internal assessment of, 705
Organization chart, 36
Organization development (OD), 28, 254
Organization-environment integrative framework, 230
Organization ethic, 1346
Organization for Economic Cooperation and Development (OECD), 1402, 1466
Organization-level manufacturing technology, 344–347
Organization-level service technology, 344, 347–349
Organization of American States (OAS), 1402
Organizations
   bureaucratic, 26
   business ethics in, 86–89
   career planning and, 766
   country, 1396
   definition of, 24, 50, 217–218
   importance of, 218
   informal, 26
   information systems, 1210–1212
   learning, 30, 56
   manufacturing, 331–332
   as production systems, 330–334
   productivity and, 700
   project, 268–271
   service, 331–332, 348–349
   service marketing and, 563
   as systems, 218–220
   See also Business organizations; Service organizations
Organization size, 221, 240–241, 243–244

Organization structure, 36, 230–231
   divisional structure, 236–237
   functional structure, 235–236
   geographical structure, 237
   information-processing perspective on, 231–234
   matrix structure, 237–239
   organization design alternatives, 235
   structural design applications, 239–240
Organization theory
   role of, 222–223
   value of, 222
Organized anarchy, 78–79
Organized exchanges, 1088
Organized investment network, 1089
Organized security exchanges, 1088–1089
Organizing, 31, 36–38
   project managers and, 281
   sales territories, 623–624
Orientation, 721
Original expression, 98
Original issue discount bonds (OIDs), 988
Original maturities, 1004
Other than regular course of business, 23
Ouchi, William, 27, 28
Outback Steakhouse, 557
Outbound telemarketers, 615
Outcomes, 714, 773
Outflow, 299
Outlets, number of, 418
Out-of-pocket costs, 980
Out-of-pocket expenses, 980
Out-of-the-money option, 1000
Outplacement services, 708–709
Output control, 48
Output files, 1183
Output price flexibility, 1100
Outputs, 29, 640
Outshopping, 605
Outside directors, 1351
Outsourcing, 762, 1194–1196, 1261–1262
Outstanding bonds, 1005
Overabsorbed factory overhead, 879
Overall performance, 2
Overapplied factory overhead, 879
Overhead expenditures, 1216
Overlapping product ranges theory, 1404, 1407–1408
Overplanning, option, 380
Overproduction, 389
Over-quota rate, 1438
Overseas Private Investment Corporation (OPIC), 1103–1104
Overstandardization, 1382
Overstored, 605
Over-the-counter (OTC) market, 1088, 1089
Over-the-counter (OTC) selling, 615
Overt integrity, 750
Overtime, 371
Owned reserves, 1451–1452
Owner's equity, 827
Ownership
   copyrights, 98–99
   corporate governance and, 1349–1350
   interorganizational linkages and, 228
   total cost of, 330
Ownership flow, 537

Ownership risk, 1384
Owner stakeholders. *See* Stakeholders
Ozone layer, international protection of, 121

P

Pac-Atlantic Air (PAA), 1001, 1002
Pace, 53
Pacific Bell, 1176
Pacific Gas & Electric Company (PG&E), 985
Package-to-order, 376
Packaging
   logistics and, 541
   services, 561
Packaging decisions, 492–493
Packet switching, 1232
Paid time-off (PTO) programs, 718
Pakistani business customs, 1425
Palm Pilot, 482, 495
Pampered Chef Ltd., 580
Panel consensus technique, 72
Panel interview, 753
Parallel conversion, 1188
Parallel ports, 1218
Parallel transmission, 1218
Paramount Communications, 1106
Parent-subsidiary corporations, 19
Pareto, Vilfredo, 393
Pareto charts, 72
Pareto diagrams, 651–652
Pareto distribution, 652
Pareto principle, 651
Parity check, 1220
Parity rate, 1418
Part simplification and redesign, 397
Participating bonds, 20
Participating leadership style, 42
Participating preferred stocks, 996
Participation
   organizational change and, 256
   quality management and, 640
Participative leadership, 43
Partnering processes. *See* Supplier and partnering processes
Partners
   dormant, 13
   general, 10, 13
   incoming, 16
   liability, 15
   limited, 10, 13
   relationships between, 15
   secret, 13
   silent, 13
   third parties and, 15–18
Partnership approach, 334
Partnership by estoppel, 15
Partnership capital, 14
Partnership creditors, 14
Partnership interest, 14, 15, 16
Partnership property, 14
Partnerships. *See* General partnerships; Limited liability limited partnerships; Limited liability partnerships; Limited partnerships

Parts
   as business-to-business products, 478
   making or buying, 918–919
Part-time employee benefits, 799
Part-time personnel, 371–372
Party characteristics, translators and, 1421
Par value, 996, 1004, 1443
Passion for Excellence, A (Peters and Austin), 64
Passive investment strategy, 968
Patentability, 99–100
Patent Act, 100, 135
Patent Cooperation Treaty (PCT), 1459
Patent indemnification clause, 131
Patents, 99–100, 135–136, 1374
Path-goal theory, 43–44
Payables concentration, 961
Payables deferral period, 952
Payback, 1066, 1069
Payback period, 1067–1068
Pay discussions, performance appraisals and, 778
Payers, consumers as, 520
Pay for knowledge, 60
Pay for performance, 60
Paying bank, 1465
Payment date, 1061
Payment discounts, 518
Payments, balance of, 1414–1419
Payoffs, 1467–1469
Payroll system development, 1184
p chart, 674
Peak, 207
Peapod, 241
Peer-to-peer LAN, 1226
Pegging, 454
Peltzman, Sam, 92
Penetration strategy, 516
Pension funds, 1087
Penske Logistics, 342
People-processing services, 1378
PeopleSoft, 1131, 1202
Pep Boys, 1132
PepsiCo, 80, 237, 690, 1377
Pepsi-Cola, 186, 187–188
Perceived hostile organizational cultures, 785
Perceived opportunity, 1281, 1283
Perceived pressure, 1281–1282
Percent complete, 278
Percentage-of-sales method, 500
Percentage variation method (PVM), 433
Percent-of-sales forecasting model, 1033–1034
Perception, 520
Perceptual incongruity, 591
Per credit period, 971
Perfect competition, monopoly and, 172–180
Perfectly competitive external markets, transfer pricing with, 211–212
Perfectly competitive markets
   characteristics of, 175–176
   competitive strategy in, 178–179, 180
Performance, 774
   appraising, 34
   computer-integrated manufacturing, 347
   corporate financial, 1319–1320

corporate social, 1312, 1318–1320, 1325
human resources, 711–712
job design and, 723
organizational, 50–51
overall, 2
pay for, 60
planning and, 33, 34
project management and, 276–281
salespeople, 623
supplier quality, 390
traditional manufacturing, 346
See also Employee performance and retention management; Job performance
Performance appraisals, 773–776
conducting, 778–779
feedback, 782–784
informal versus systematic, 777–778
legal and effective, 784–785
methods for, 779–781
rater errors, 781–782
uses of, 776–777
Performance consulting, 757–758
Performance criteria
potential problems, 775
relevance of, 774
Performance evaluation
accounting, 900–902
salespeople, 623
Performance feedback, 63, 405
Performance incentive, variable pay as, 804–805
Performance information, types of, 774
Performance management outcomes, 773
Performance management practices, 773
Performance management system, 773
Performance measurement, 405–408, 807–808
Performance-oriented compensation philosophies, 801
Performance quality judgments, 1286
Performance reports, 63
Performance-reward linkage, 714, 715
Performance shares, 947
Performance standards, 33, 730, 775–776
Performance variables, transportation, 402, 403
Performer/job-level quality, 642–643
Performing stage, in team development, 283
Peril, 1297
Period costs, 880
Periodic rate, 307–308
Perishability, 559–560
Perlak, Frederick, 233
Permanent current assets, 954, 978
Perpetrators, 1277, 1280–1281, 1286
Perpetual existence, 18
Perpetuity, 1010
Perrier, 498
Perrow, Charles, 261
Persistent dumping, 1439
Person, corporation as, 18
Personal buying, 461
Personal competencies, 1368
Personal computers (PCs), 1203
Personal decision-support systems, 1152–1153

Personal ethics, 86, 87
Personal experiences, purchasing ethics and, 460
Personality, 771
Personality-oriented integrity tests, 750
Personality tests, 749
Personalization, 1251
Personal liability, 9, 15, 128–133, 1353
Personal liberty, 87
Personal observation, of fraud, 1290
Personal outcomes, 60
Personal power, 40
Personal property, 122
Personal savings, 575–576
Personal selling, 498, 612–613
e-marketing and, 545
evolution of, 613
strategic importance of, 613
Personal time management, 286
Person-job fit, 744
Personnel
control procedures and, 937–938
outsourcing and, 1196
part-time and temporary, 372
Personnel ratios, 221, 244
Person-organization fit, 744–745
Peruvian Connection, 580
Pest management, 1178
Pets.com, 1252
Phantom bill, 380
Phantom parts, 380
Phase modulation, 1223, 1224
Phased conversion, 1188
Philadelphia Stock Exchange, 1089
Philanthropic responsibilities, 1313, 1314
Philco-Ford Corporation, 396
Philip Morris, 491
Philips, 1388, 1392, 1398
Philips USA, 1394
Physical ability tests, 748
Physical asset markets, 1084
Physical assets, 1368
Physical design, 1186–1187
Physical distance, 1422
Physical distribution (PD), 538–543
Physical evidence, of fraud, 1290
Physical flows, 883
Physical hazard, 1297
Physical health, job design and, 723
Physical layer, 1231
Physical safeguards, 1285
Physiological needs, 713
Piece-rate systems, 806
Piercing the corporate veil, 19
Pilot conversion, 1188–1189
Piloting, 1188–1189
PIMS Associates, Inc., 660
Pipeline/in-transit inventory, 386
Pitney Bowes Management Services (PBMS), 88, 343
Pizza Hut, 419, 901
Place
discrepancies in, 535
e-marketing and, 544
Place/entry strategy, international, 1379
Placement, 744–745
Place utility, 474

Plaintext, 1241
Plaintiff's conduct, warranties and, 150, 153
Planned BOM and EOM inventories, 426–427
Planned gross margin, 427–428
Planned purchasing, 427
Planned retail reductions, 427
Planned retention, 1302–1303
Planned sales, determining, 423, 425–426
Planning
aggregate, 363, 366–373
budgeting and, 886
capacity, 366–373
career, 766
cost, 276–281
crisis management, 1257–1258
dollar merchandise, 431–434
environmental uncertainty and, 227–228
expert systems and, 1173
human resources, 701, 702–704, 706
information systems, 1132–1139
interviews, 754
management and, 31–35
manufacturing, 355–356, 358–359. *See also* Manufacturing resource planning
merchandise presentation, 454–455
production, 932–933
project management and, 272, 275
project managers and, 281
retail inventory, 435–438
retail store, 452–454
sales and, 617
stock, 438
succession, 769–770
supply chain inventory management, 398–399
tax, 1177
See also Financial planning; Seven management and planning tools; Strategic planning; Tactical planning
Planning bill, 380
Plans
baseline, 275
contingency, 32, 35
overview of, 32
purpose of, 32
single-use, 35
standing, 35
vertical linkages and, 232
Plant assets, 835
Planters Peanuts, 233
Plant loading, uniform, 393
Plant patent, 100
Pledging, 974, 975
Point elasticity, 195–196
Pointing, 1422
Point of indifference, 605
Point of Purchase Advertising International (POPAI), 510
Point-of-purchase communications, 499, 509–510
Point-of-sale (POS) signage, 458
Point source, 120
Poison pill, 947, 982, 1352
Poka-yoke, 653–654, 684–685
Policy instruments, 1429
Political activity, domains of, 264

SUBJECT INDEX 1665

Political forces, 24
Political model, 257, 258–259
Political risks, 1101, 1383–1385
Political tactics for increasing power, 265, 266–267
Politics
   definition of, 263
   international law and, 1456–1459
Polling, 1229
Polygamous loyalty, 568
Polygraphs, 750
Pooled interdependence, 352, 353
Poorly managed crisis, 1333
Popcorn Factory, 580
Population growth, 572
Population trends, 572–574
Population variables, 572
Portals, 1248
Porter, Lyman, 714
Porter, Michael E., 3–4, 328, 411–412, 1404, 1411–1412
Porter's competitive strategies, 3–4
Portfolio investment, 1416, 1417, 1418
Portfolio returns, 1097–1098
Portfolio risk, 1096, 1097–1098, 1099
Portuguese business customs, 1425
Positioning strategy, 515
Positioning
   brand, 500
   product, 472
   See also Strategic positioning
Position power, 39
Positions, 226, 259
Positive reinforcement, 717
Possession-processing services, 1378
Possession utility, 474
Postaction control, 48
Post-audit, 1073–1074
Posterior probabilities, 292
Postincorporation subscription, 19
Postpurchase behavior, 525
Postpurchase evaluations, 525
Postransaction services, 447
Potential competition, threat of, 190
Potential customers, 482
Potential entrant, 173
Potential for learning and growth, 50
Pottery Barn, 602
Power, 39
   authority versus, 259–260
   concentration of, 91
   countervailing, 177–178
   empowerment and, 40
   personal, 40
   position, 39
   retail marketing and, 590–591
   See also Organizational power
Power base, increasing, 265
Power differences, as communication barrier, 66
Powers, Charles, 1344
Power sources, 261–263
PPG Industries, 1329
Practices, quality management, 642
Preapproach, 617
Preauthorized debit system, 960
Precautionary balances, 958

Precedence, 130
Precorporate period, 1350
Predatory dumping, 1439
Predatory pricing, 552
Predetermined factory overhead rate, 878–879
Predication, 1289
Predictive capability, tests of, 169
Predictors, 746
Pre-employment screening, 747
Preemptive right, 20, 983
Preferences, problematic, 79
Preferential selection, 788
Preferred stock, 21, 995–997, 1007, 1042–1043
Pregnancy Discrimination Act, 103
Preincorporation subscription, 19
Preliminary control, 47
Preliminary investigation, 487–488
Prepackaged software, 1194, 1196–1200
Prepaid expenses, 829
Preparation, in crisis management planning, 1257–1258
Prepurchase information, 558
Presale disclosure, 141
Presentation layer, 1231
Presentation styles, 619
Present value (PV), 301, 309
Present value interest factor for an annuity of n payments at i interest, 305, 306
Present value interest factor for i and n, 301
Present value of an annuity, 304–306
Present value tables, 1116–1119
Pressure, perceived, 1281–1282
Pretransaction services, 447
Prevention, 263
   crisis management planning and, 1257
   financial shenanigans, 1292–1293
   fraud, 1285–1286, 1287–1288
Prevention costs, 655
Preventive control, 47
Price
   definition of, 510–511
   e-marketing and, 544
   exchange, 824
   stock splits and stock dividends, 1064
   striking, 999
   See also Base price; Pricing
Priced-based definition, 1440
Price changes, 199–201, 517
Price controls, 1385
Price customization, 518, 519
Price discrimination, 115, 207–210, 552, 1439–1440
Price drivers, 514–517
Price-earnings (P/E) ratio, 859
Price elasticity of demand, 196–202
Price fixing, 112, 113, 552
Price flexing, 517–519
Price incentives, 368, 414
Price leadership, 183
Priceline.com, 419, 585, 915, 1128
Price makers, 173
Price management, 446
Price multiples model, 1109–1110
Price/output decisions
   monopolistic competition and, 182

   monopoly and, 176–177
   oligopoly and, 183
   perfect competition and, 176
Price penetration, 516
Price promotion, 519
Price-quality inferences, 516–517
Price reductions, 1381
Prices
   factor, 1406
   stepped-up exercise, 1002
   stock, 217
Price sensitivity, 505
Price shading, 517–518
Price skimming, 516
Price stabilization, 515
Price takers, 173
Price-to-book ratio, 1110
Price-to-cash-flow ratio, 1110
Price-to-earning (P/E) ratio, 1109–1110
Price-to-sales ratio, 1110
Pricing
   cost-plus, 511–514
   inventory, 431
   legal and ethical issues in, 552–553
   predatory, 552
   product, 927–928, 932
   transfer, 912–914
Pricing decisions, 473, 474
Pricing practices, 205
   markup pricing, 205–207
   multiple-product pricing, 210
   multiple-unit pricing strategies, 210
   price discrimination, 207–210
   riddles in, 212
   transfer pricing, 210–212
Pricing strategies
   base price adjustments, 517–519
   international, 1379–1382
   price drivers, 514–517
Primacy effect, 781
Primary duties, 730
Primary EPS, 1004
Primary key, 1161
Primary-line injury, 115–116
Primary market, 1085, 1090
Primary marketing institutions, 585
Primary research, 710–711
Prime rate, 973
Principal amount, 1004
Principles approach to business ethics, 1337
Prior information, 263
Prior probability, 292
Prisoner's dilemma, 185–186, 519
Privacy
   employee, 108–9
   VAN EDI and, 1255
Private branch exchange (PBX), 1221
Private carriers, 404
Private causes of action, 118
Private corporations, 18
Private label branding, 418
Private labels, 583
Privately owned corporations, 1089
Private nuisance, 117
Private Securities Litigation Reform Act of 1995 (Reform Act), 94, 1357
Privity of contract, 150, 152–153

Proactive MPR, 508
Probabilistic inputs, 293
Probability-impact matrix, 1329
Probing questions, 618
Problematic preferences, 79
Problem identification, 1197
Problem identification stage, 73, 77–78
Problemistic search, 76–77
Problem recognition, 524
Problems, defining, 1179
Problem solution stage, 73
Problem solving, 67–68, 287–288
    brainstorming, 68–69
    diversity and, 786
    expert systems and, 1173
    force-field analysis, 70
    intradepartmental, 63
    nominal group technique, 69–70
    synectics, 69
    systems analysis, 70–71
    tools and techniques for, 68, 71–72
Procedural justice, 569–570
Procedures, 23, 1183, 1284–1285
Process benchmarking, 689
Process control costs, 655
Process control systems (PCSs), 1146
Process cost systems, 877, 882–885
Process decision program chart (PDPC), 647
Processes, 1185
    defining, 692
    internal control, 1272
    stable and unstable, 673
Process failures, 655
Process flow decisions, 359
Process focus, 640–641
Process improvement, 679–681, 691
Processing delay, 960
Process layout, 335–336
Process management
    definition of, 675–676
    process improvement, 679–681
    product design processes, 677–678
    production/delivery and support processes, 678
    scope of, 676–677
    supplier and partnering processes, 678–679
Process-level quality, 642–643
Process manufacturers, 882, 883
Process mapping, 650
Process measurement and control costs, 655
Process owners, 490, 676
Process structure, 1391
Process theories, 58
Proclaiming, 61
Procter & Gamble, 115, 224, 439, 492, 569, 583, 594, 901, 1321, 1334, 1369
Procurement, 335
Prodromal crisis stage, 1332, 1333
Producibility, 335
Product and service changes, 247
Product-based quality, 682–683
Product category, 493
Product champion, 250
Product cost concept, 924–925
Product costs, 875–885
Product cycle theory, 1404, 1408–1409

Product decisions, 473, 474, 491–493
Product design, 334–335
Product design processes, 676, 677–678
Product development, 496, 1129. See also New product development
Product development process, 485
Product development strategy, 497
Product differentiation, 175
Product diversification, 497
Product-driven quality, 639
Product enhancement, 1130
Product features, 477
Product flow, 537
Product growth opportunities, 497
Production
    competition and, 174
    factor intensity in, 1406
    just-in-time, 391–393
    planning, 932–933
    See Simultaneous production and consumption
Production Activity Control (PAC), 373
Production bottlenecks, product profitability and pricing under, 927–928
Production budget, 891–892
Production/delivery and support processes, 676, 678
Production discrepancies, 534
Production environment, 375–376
Production era, 470
Production opportunities, 213
Production planning, 360–363, 367, 373
Production process, 675, 920–921
Production rate change costs, 370–372
Production rules, 1175
Production schedule. See Master production schedule
Production systems, organizations as, 330–334
Productivity, 342, 700–701, 1236
Productivity costs, 721
Productivity goals, 3
Productivity improvement, 343–344
Productivity management, 342–344
Productivity measurement, 342–343
Product knowledge, 621
Product launch, 490
Product layout, 336
Product liability, 146
    strict liability in tort, 150–154
    warranties, 146–150
Product liability chain, 157
Product liability costs, 656
Product life cycle, 357–358, 517
Product life cycle management, 493–496
Product line, 496
Product line organization, 623–624
Product management, 493–497
    duct management, product portfolio, 496–497
Product market, 113
Product matrix, 239
Product misuse and abuse, 153
Product mix, 480. See also Sales mix
Product mix decisions, 496–497
Product mix depth, 496
Product mix width, 496

Product planning, 356–358
Product portfolio, 496–497
Product positioning, 472
Product presentation, 619
Product profitability analysis, 934–935
Product profitability and pricing, under production bottlenecks, 927–928
Product quality, 597, 638–639
Product recall costs, 656
Products
    acceptable, 977
    business-to-business, 477–478
    complementary, 368
    consumer, 141, 477, 478
    defective, 389
    differential analysis and, 920–921
    discontinuing, 917–918
    e-marketing and, 544
    international business strategies and, 1366
    market structure and, 174
    pricing, 932
    service marketing and, 569
    transfer pricing and, 211
    See also New products
Product safety, 1264
Product standard, 1373
Products and services change, 250–252
Product-selling prices, 922–927
Product strategies, 357–358, 1377–1378
Product structure, 1389–1390. See also Divisional structure
Professional corporations, 19
Professional ethic, 1346
Professionalism, 221
Professional salespeople, 615
Professional selling method, 616
Professional service businesses, job order costs systems for, 881–882
Professional services, 411, 557
Profiling, risk, 1301–1302
Profitability, 612, 850, 927–928
Profitability analysis, 855–860
    product, 934–935
    sales territory, 933–934
    salesperson, 935
Profitability index (PI), 1072
Profitable price discrimination, 208
Profit and volume models, 289
Profit-center approach, 622–623
Profit center reporting, 906–907
Profit centers, responsibility accounting for, 903–907
Profit corporations, 18
Profit margin, 206, 908
Profit maximization, 516, 945
Profit rates, 178
Profits
    disequilibrium, 179
    general partnerships and, 15
    incremental, 161–162
    international business strategies and, 1366
    marginal, 160
    quality and, 686
    social responsibility and, 944
    target, 871–872
    See also Cost-volume-profit relationships
Profit sharing, 16, 17, 811–812

SUBJECT INDEX   1667

Profit-volume ratio, 867
Pro forma balance sheet method, 1016, 1040–1041
Pro forma financial statements, 1016–1019
Programmed decision, 73
Programming backlog, 1203
Program robustness, 1238
Programs, 786–787, 807
Progress, reviewing, 34
Projected balance sheet method, 1016
Projected financial statements, 1016–1019
Project leaders, 490
Project life cycle, 273–274
Project management, 1192
    benefits of, 276
    cost planning and performance, 276–281
    process, 275–276
    project attributes, 271–273
    project life cycle, 273–274
    project manager, 281–282
    project organizations, 268–271
    project team, 282–286
Project managers, 52, 270, 281–282
Project mortality, 481
Project organizations, 268–271
Project required rate of return, 1082
Project risk, 1078–1083
Projects
    attributes of, 271–273
    budgeting, 277
    conflicts on, 285
    cost estimates, 276–277
    See Capital projects
Project scheduling, 286
Project scope, 271, 272
Project strategy, 481, 485
Project teams, 269, 282
    conflicts and, 285
    development and effectiveness, 282–285
    multifunctional, 269
    personal time management, 286
Project-type organizations, 269–270, 271
Promise, 147
Promisee, 123
Promises, keeping, 620
Promisor, 123
Promissory estoppel, 125, 126
Promissory notes, 972
Promoters, 19
Promotion
    demand management and, 368
    e-marketing and, 544–545
    price, 519
    See also Sales promotion
Promotional discount, 442–443
Promotion decisions, 473, 474
Promotion flow, 537
Promotion management, 446
Promotions (job), 736
Promotion strategy, international, 1382–1383
Proofs, 939
Property
    partnership, 14
    personal, 122
    real, 122
Property dividends, 21

Property risks, 1295–1296
Proportionality principle, 1346
Proportionality rule, 1346
Proposal requests, 1197, 1198
Proposal review, 1197, 1198
Proposals, 274
Proprietorships. *See* Sole proprietorships
Prosecution, of fraud, 1280
Prospecting, 617
Prospectus, 1090–1091
Protection, 492
Protective tariffs, 1434
Protocols, network, 1218, 1229–1231. *See also* International cultures and protocols
Prototyping, 483, 1189–1191, 1203
Proxy, 22, 982
Proxy fight, 982
Proxy process, 1349
Prudent claims, 625
Prudential, 491, 1378
Pseudo bill, 380
Psychics, 750
Psychodramatic problem solving approaches, 72
Psychographics, 522–523
Psychological contract, 715–716
Psychological price range, 1062
Psychological states, motivation and, 59
Psychology, of consumer behavior, 520–521
Psychopathic crises, 1332
Public affairs, corporate, 1324–1326
Public affairs department, 1324
Public affairs management, 1324–1326
Public affairs strategy, 1325–1326
Public corporations, 18
Public interest theory, 93
Public issues committee, 1355
Public issues scanning, 1328
Publicly held corporations, 19
Publicly held stock, 1089, 1090
Publicly owned corporations, 1089, 1090
Public nuisance, 117
Public policy committee, 1355
Public policy, corporate, 1321–1324
Public relations, 229, 498, 508–509
Public Service of New Hampshire, 989
Public warehouse, 586
Pull, 388
Pull systems, 392
Purchased applications, 1194, 1196–1200
Purchase order cancellations, 133–135
Purchasing ethics, 459–463
Purchasing law, 128
    antitrust laws and unfair trade practices, 137
    global, 136–137
    legal authority and personal liability, 128–133
    patents and intellectual property, 135–136
    purchase order cancellations and breach of contract, 133–135
Purchasing managers, legal authority and personal liability of, 128–133
Purchasing, 471
    consumer, 140–142
    consumer behavior and, 525

    ethical behavior and, 597–598
    just-in-time, 389–390
    planned, 427
    retail sites, 612
    supply chain performance measurement and evaluation and, 405–408
    transportation services, 399–405
    See also Merchandise management
Purchasing power bonds, 986
Purchasing/supply chain strategy, 328–330
Pure play firms, 1082
Pure play method, 1082
Pure risk, 1294–1295
Putable bonds, 986
Put option, 1000
Pyramid of corporate social responsibility, 1313–1314
Pythons, 56

Q

Quaker Oats, 183, 252
Qualitative forecasting techniques, 165
Qualitative performance evaluation, of salespeople, 623
Quality awards, 669–670
Quality control, 49, 671–675
Quality control practices, 671–675
Quality control tools, 650–654
Quality cost indexes, 657–658
Quality costs, 387
Quality management practices
    competitive advantage and quality, 660–661
    cost of quality, 654–659
    infrastructure, practices, and tools, 641–642
    quality awards, 669–670
    quality levels, 642–643
    quality models, 661–669
    return on quality, 659–660
    seven management and planning tools, 643–647
    Seven QC Tools, 650–654
    Six-Sigma, 647–650
    total quality principles, 639–641
Quality models, 661–669
Quality philosophers, 661–669
Quality planning costs, 655
Quality returns. *See* Return on quality
Quality strategies, 636–638
Quality trilogy, 664
Quality
    business law and, 157
    competitive advantage and, 660–661
    ethics and, 693
    human resources and, 701
    levels of, 642–643
    product, 638–639
    product and service design, 335
    service, 565–567
    See also Service quality; Total quality
Quantitative forecasting techniques, 165, 166–167
Quantitative performance evaluation, of salespeople, 623

Quantitative techniques, 286–287
  amortization methods, 297–298
  asset valuation, 309
  breakeven analysis, 289–290
  cash management model, 296–297
  cost and volume models, 288–289
  decision analysis, 290
  decision analysis with sample information, 292
  depletion methods, 297–298
  depreciation methods, 297–298
  finance and, 296
  marketing and, 296
  operations and, 295
  problem solving and decision making, 287–288
  profit and volume models, 289
  revenue and volume models, 289
  risk analysis, 290–291
  sensitivity analysis, 290, 291
  simulation, 293–295
  time value of money, 299–309
  utility and decision making, 292–293
Quantity, discrepancies in, 534
Quantity discount, 441–442
Quantity factor, 936
Quartile strategy, 802
Quasi contract, 125–126
Queries, 1159
Questioning techniques, 754
Questionnaires, 1183
Questions
  investigative, 72
  selection interviews, 754, 755
Queuing models, 286
Quick assets, 852
Quick Mart, 419
Quick ratio, 852
Quick response (QR) systems, 587
Quid pro quo sexual harassment, 790–791
Quorum, 21
Quotas, 622, 1373, 1438
Quoted rate, 307
Quoted risk-free rate of interest, 213, 214

R

RAID (redundant arrays of independent disks), 1238
Ralph Lauren, 533, 595–596
Random causes, 672
Rapid prototyping (RP), 337
Rate earned on common stockholders' equity, 857–858
Rate earned on total assets, 856–857
Rate earned on total stockholders' equity, 857
Rate of income from operations to total assets, 857
Rate of return on investment, 907–910, 944
Rater bias, 782
Rater errors, 781–782
Ratification, 22
Rating patterns, 782
Rational decision making approach, 73–74
Rationalization, 1281, 1283

Rational-legal authority, 244
Rational model, 257, 258–259
Rationing, capital, 1083–1084
Ratio of fixed assets to long-term liabilities, 854
Ratio of liabilities to stockholders' equity, 854–855
Ratio of net sales to assets, 856
Raw material inventory, 385
Raw materials, as business-to-business products, 477
Raw material scarcity, 470
Raw materials inventory, 339, 878
Raw materials sector, 224
Rayovac, 590
R chart, 673, 674, 675
Reach, 501
Reaction, 763
Reactive MPR, 509
Readiness levels, 43
Real asset markets, 1084
Real assets, 1415
Real asset valuation, 1014–1015
Real Estate Settlement Procedures Act (RESPA), 144
Realistic job preview (RJP), 721, 747
Realized rate of return, 1009, 1098
Real property, 122
Real risk-free rate of interest, 213, 214
Receipt of goods (ROG) dating, 443
Receipts
  acceleration of, 960
  trust, 976
  warehouse, 977
Receipts and disbursements method, 1035–1038
Receivables collection period, 951–952
Receivables financing. *See* Accounts receivable financing
Receivables monitoring, 963–964
Receivers, 61, 62
Recency effect, 781
Recession, 171–172, 1430
Reciprocal agreement, 1260
Reciprocal interdependence, 353
Reciprocity, 461
Recognition, 77
Recognition awards, 807
Record structure, 1162
Records, 22, 709, 1158, 1285
Recourse, 974
Recovery, obstacles to, 152–154
Recovery measures, 1258–1262
Recreational benefits, 795, 797
Recruiting, 732
  diversity and, 786
  evaluation, 740–742
  external, 738–740
  internal, 735–737
  Internet, 737–738
  labor markets and, 733
  sales force, 620–621
  strategic, 734–735
Recruiting process, 721
Recruitment costs, 371
Redemption of shares, 21
Redesign, 397, 691–692

Red-lining, 565
Reduction in force (RIF), 708
Redundant arrays of independent disks (RAID), 1238
Redundant site, 1260
Reengineering, 681, 689–690
Reference contacts, 747
Referent power, 40, 259, 590
Referrals, 617, 737
Refining, 71
Reform Act. *See* Private Securities Litigation Reform Act of 1995
Refunds, 686–687
Refusal to examine, 149
Regeneration phase, 414, 415
Regina Vacuum, 1282
Regional markets, 1085
Regional trade communities, 1460–1461
Registration, of trade symbols, 96–97
Registration statement, 1090
Regular course of business, 23
Regulation. *See* Government regulation
Regulation Z, 143
Rehabilitation Act (1973), 105–6
Reilly, William, 605
Reilly's law of retail gravitation, 605
Reinforcement theories, 58
Reinvestment rate assumption, 1072
Reinvestment rate risk, 215
Relationship marketing era, 470
Relationship-oriented leaders, 42, 44
Relationship retailing, 445
Relationships
  handling, 771
  in new workplace, 56
  workplace, 790–792
Relationship selling, 613
Relaxed current asset investment policy, 953
Relevant cash flows, 1074–1076
Relevant range, 862
Relevant revenues and costs, 915
Relevant risk, 1099
Reliability, 335, 683, 746, 756
Reliance, 134
Reliance Group, 947
Reliant Energy, 1084
Religion, 792
Remedies
  Civil Rights Act of 1964 violations, 104
  copyright infringement, 99
  creditors', 145–146
  Federal Trade Commission, 139
  patent infringement, 100
  trade secret infringement, 95
  trade symbol infringement, 97–98
Renaissance Hotels, 248
Rent applications, 1194, 1200
Rent revenue, 829
Reorder point (ROP), 340
Reorganization, 154, 253
Repeater, 1221
Repeat games, 185, 187–188
Replacement charts, 707
Replacement cost model, 1109
Replacement decision, 1065, 1077
Replication, 1163
Report form, 835

Reporting, of unethical behavior, 463
Reporting relationships, 235
Reports, performance, 63
Report to the Nation on Occupation Fraud and Abuse, The, 1279
Repose, statute of, 153–154
Republic of Ireland, business customs of, 1424
Republic Steel, 1105
Reputational crises, 1332
Request for information (RFI), 1197, 1198
Request for proposal (RFP), 273–274, 1197, 1198
Required rate of return, 1008, 1041, 1070, 1081–1082
Required return, 1005
Requirements definition, 1180, 1183, 1197, 1198
Requirements for formality and informality, 1420
Re-recruiting, 737
Resale price maintenance, 552
Rescission, 142
Research
   human resources, 710–711
   insufficient, 1382
   See also Market research
Research and development share, 528
Researchers, 1277–1278
Reservations, 368–369
Reserve borrowing capacity, 1057
Reserve funds, 1303
Residual dividend policy, 1059–1060
Residual income, 910–911
Resistance, 39
Resistance to change, 255
Resolution, fraud, 1291
Resource-advantage theory, 579–580
Resource allocator roles, of managers, 54
Resource-based approach, 5, 6–7
Resource Conservation and Recovery Act (RCRA), 120
Resource goals, 2–3
Resource management. *See* Human resource management; Information technology resource management
Resource profile, 363–364
Resource requirements, 364–365
Resource requirements planning (RRP), 363–366, 373
Resources
   environmental, 228–230
   foreign direct investment and, 1412
   intergroup conflict and, 258
   marketing mix and, 474
   organizational change and, 248
   organizational power and, 260, 265
   project management and, 271
Respondeat superior, 16
Response times
   delivery-to-customer, 381
   by expert systems, 1173
Responsibility, 36–37
   appraisal, 777–778
   compensation, 800–801
   control procedures and, 938
   economic, 1312, 1314, 1339

   ethical, 1313, 1314, 1339
   experienced, 59
   internal control, 1273–1274
   job analysis, 727
   legal, 1312–1313, 1314, 1339
   philanthropic, 1313, 1314
   selection, 743
   See also Social responsibility
Responsibility accounting, 902–912
   cost centers, 902–903
   investment centers, 907–912
   profit centers, 903–907
Responsibility centers, 886, 902
Responsiveness, 683
Restitution, 134
Restraint of trade, 111–113
Restricted current asset investment policy, 953
Restrictive covenants, 987
Restructuring, 253
Results, training evaluation and, 764
Results-based performance information, 774
Retail accordion, 578
Retail competition, 576–583
Retail customers, 570–572
Retail format, 581
Retail gravity theory, 605
Retail identity, 457–458
Retail inventory planning, 435–438
Retail life cycle, 578–579
Retail location analysis, 599–612
Retail location theories, 604–607
Retail marketing
   economic trends, 575–576
   ethics, 597–599
   market selection and retail location analysis, 599–612
   population trends, 572–574
   retail competition, 576–583
   retail customers, 570–572
   social trends, 574–575
   supply chain management and, 584–596
Retail method of inventory valuation, 428–431
Retail operations, 415
   customer services and retail selling, 445–450
   finance management, 422–431
   merchandise buying and handling, 431–444
   retailer categories, 417–419
   retailing changes, 415–417
   store layout management, 450–458
   strategic planning and operations management model, 420–422
Retail price maintenance, 112
Retail reductions, planned, 427
Retail selling, 445–450
Retail site analysis, 609–610
Retail site availability, 610
Retail site selection, 610–612
Retail store saturation, 605
Retail strategic planning and operations management model, 420–422
Retail strategy, 328
Retailer-employee relationship, ethical behavior in, 598–599

Retailer location, 419
Retailer-owned cooperatives, 588
Retailers
   categorizing, 417–419
   independent, 588
   marketing mix and, 474
   point-of-purchase communications and, 510
Retailer size, 419
Retailer-supplier relations, 589–592
Retailing
   changes in, 415–417
   click-and-mortar, 1252
   niche, 1252
Retailing formats, 581
Retained earnings, 155, 829, 981, 1043–1045
Retained earnings break point, 1048
Retained earnings statement, 832–835
Retention, 719, 786, 1302–1304, 1307–1309
Retention amounts, 1308–1309
Retention determinants, 719, 720
Retention interventions, 721–722
Retention management. *See* Employee performance and retention management
Retention management process, 719–722
Retirement security benefits, 795, 796
Return on investment (ROI), 515, 711–712, 764. *See also* Rate of return on investment
Return on quality (ROQ), 659–660, 681, 685
Returns
   marketable securities and, 962
   portfolio, 1097–1098
   See also Return on quality
Revaluation, 1443–1444
Revco Discount Drug Stores, 115
Revelation ethic, 1346
Revenue and volume models, 289
Revenue potential, 624
Revenues
   accounting equation and, 829
   controllable, 904
   differential, 915
   marginal, 160
   See also Average revenue; Marginal revenue; Total revenue
Revenue tariffs, 1434
Reverse discrimination, 104, 788
Reverse repurchase agreement, 973
Reverse splits, 1062
Reviewing, progress, 34
Review of turnover data, 722
Reviews, recovery plan, 1261
Revised Model Business Corporation Act (RMBCA), 19, 20
Revolving credit agreement, 972
RevPASH, 623
Reward power, 39, 259, 590
Rewards
   compensation strategies and, 799–800, 803–804
   consumer sales promotions, 507–508
   extrinsic, 57
   intrinsic, 57
   leadership and, 44
Ricardo, David, 1404

Riding the yield curve, 968
Rights
　buyers, 133
　copyrights, 98
　creditors, 15
　enforcement, 15, 22
　inspection, 22
　intellectual property, 100, 1374–1375, 1385
　limited liability company, 17
　limited partnerships, 16
　partners, 15
　preemptive, 20
　sellers, 132–133
　stock, 21
Right-sizing, 328
Right Start, 580
Right to continue partnership, 14–15
Right to wind up, 14
Right-to-work law, 102
Rigid implementation, 1382–1383
Ring topology, 1227, 1228
Risk-adjusted discount rate, 1083
Risk analysis, 290–291
Risk arbitrage, 1353
Risk assessment, 1271
Risk avoidance, 1302, 1306
Risk evaluation, 1299, 1301–1302
Risk identification, 1299–1301
Risk management
　corporate, 1293–1310
　　financial, 1095–1104
　　information technology, 1139–1144
Risk-management information systems (RMIS), 1301
Risk-management process, 1299
Risk managers, 1298
Risk mapping, 1301–1302
Risk mitigation, 1302
Risk profile, 290
Risk profiling, 1301–1302
Risk reduction, 1302
Risk retention, 1302–1304, 1307–1309
Risk taking, 471
Risk transfer, 1304–1305, 1307–1310
Risks, 1293–1294
　burden of, 1294
　business, 1050, 1099, 1100
　capital budgeting and, 1078–1083
　cash flow, 1074–1077
　corporate fraud, 1288
　corporations and, 12
　cost of money and, 213
　country, 1099, 1100–1104
　defining, 1095–1096, 1294–1295
　degree of, 1298
　economic, 1385–1386
　financial, 1099, 1100, 1101
　firm-specific, 1098–1099
　international, 1383–1386
　international lending, 1453–1454
　investment, 1095–1099
　long-term versus short-term debt, 957
　market, 1098–1099
　marketable securities, 962
　measurement of, 1297–1298
　outsourcing, 1196

　political, 1101, 1383–1385
　portfolio, 1096, 1097–1098, 1099
　purchased software, 1199–1200
　relevant, 1099
　sources, 1295–1296
　stand-alone, 1096–1097
　types of, 1099–1103
Rites, 83
Rites of enhancement, 83
Rites of integration, 83
Rites of passage, 83
Rites of renewal, 83
Ritz Carlton, 348, 562, 687
RJR Nabisco, 948, 987, 989, 1107
Roadway, 404
Robinson-Patman Act (1936), 115–116, 137, 440, 441, 517, 551, 552
Robotics, 1170
Rodney Hunt Company, 234
Role, 53
Role ambiguity, 614
Role conflict, 614
Romance, workplace, 790
Ross Dress for Less, 600
Ross-Simon, 580
Rough-cut capacity planning (RCCP), 373, 376
Routine technologies, 350–351
Routing, 564, 565
Ruggieri & Sons, 343
Rule of law, 85
Rule of reason test, 111
Rules, vertical linkages and, 232
RWT Company, 1304
Ryder Systems, 342

S

Saab, 1173
Sabre Inc., 1135
Safe harbor, 1466
Safety, human/product, 1264
Safety and security needs, 713
Safety stock levels, 397
Safety stocks, 953, 958
Safeway Stores, 576, 987
Saint Gobain, 1414
St. Luke's Communications Ltd., 246
Saks Fifth Avenue, 48, 576, 608
Salaries, 800, 808
Salary plus commission, 622, 623
Salary plus commission or bonuses, 808
Sale and leaseback, 997–998
Sales, 122, 612–613
　accounting equation and, 829
　changing face of, 613
　ethics and, 624–625
　planned, 423, 425–426
　same-store, 416
Sales administration and management, 612–624
Sales agents, foreign, 1372
Sales-based index, 657
Sales bonus system data flow diagram, 1186
Sales bonus system flowchart, 1185
Sales budget, 891

Sales call anxiety (SCA), 622
Sales channel, 532
Sales coaching, 622
Sales compensation and incentives, 807–809
Sales enhancement, 449
Sales enhancement audit. *See* Customer service and sales enhancement audit
Sales era, 470
Sales force, building and managing, 620–624
Sales force compensation, 622–623
Sales force quotas, 622
Sales force technology, 621
Sales forecasts, 1016
Sales management, ethics and, 624–625
Salesmanship, 449
Sales mix, 872–873, 934
Sales on account, 829
Salespeople, types of, 614–616
Salesperson-initiated contact, 449
Salesperson profitability analysis, 935
Sales performance, measuring, 807–808
Sales planning, 356–358
Sales process, 616–620
Sales professions, rewards and drawbacks, 613–614
Sales promotion, 498–499, 504–508
Sales promotion allowances, 518
Sales representatives, legal responsibilities of, 624
Sales skills, 621
Sales territories, organizing and managing, 623–624
Sales territory profitability analysis, 933–934
Sales variability, 1100
Salomon Brothers Inc., 988, 1088, 1114
Salomon Smith Barney, 988
Same-store sales, 416
Sample, 147–148
Sample information, 292
Sample mean forecast error analysis, 170
Sampling error, 782
Sam's, 585
Samurai bonds, 998
Sandoz, 1400
SAP, 1131
Sarbanes-Oxley Act (2002), 1347
Satellite microwave, 1222
Satellite services, 1233
Satisficing, 76
Satisfiers, 669
Saturation theory, 605–606
Saturn, 190, 518
Saudi Arabian business customs, 1425
Savannah Electric Company, 986
Savings, personal, 575–576
Savings and loan associations (S&Ls), 1087
Scalability, 1136, 1226
Scalar chain, 26
Scalar principle, 36
Scale of market entities, 557–558
Scatter diagrams, 653
Scenario analysis, 1079–1080
Scenarios, 35
Schedules/scheduling
　JIT production and, 393
　job design and, 725
　manufacturing, 355–356

project management and, 271, 272
project, 286
worksh!ft, 414
See also Master scheduling
Schema, 1162
Schmenner, R., 411
Schmidt, W. H., 41
Schneider National, 48, 404
School recruiting, 738
Scientific management, 25
Scobes Corporation, 986
Scope, project, 271, 272
S corporations, 19
Scott Industries, 947
Scrambled merchandising, 416, 534
Scrap and rework costs, 655
Sealy, 589
Search attributes, 557
Search firms, 738–739
Sears, Roebuck & Company, 4, 88, 175, 492, 574, 576, 580, 900, 1106, 1252
Seasonal discount, 443
Seasoned issue, 1005
Sea transport restrictions, 1441
Second mortgage bonds, 986
Secondary business district (SBD), 602
Secondary-line injury, 116
Secondary market, 1085, 1090, 1095
Secondary meaning, 97
Second-degree price discrimination, 209
Second-stage leverage, 1030
Secret partners, 13
Section 402A, 150–151, 152
Sectors, 223, 224
Secure strategy, 186
Secured bonds, 20
Secured loans, 974
Securities
  aggregate securities in, 969
  convertible, 1002–1004
  marketable, 961–962
  short-term financing and, 974–977
  See also Common stock; Debt securities; Equity securities; Preferred stock
Securities Act (1933), 94
Securities and Exchange Commission (SEC), 92, 94, 814, 987, 998, 1000, 1090–1091, 1094, 1273, 1352–1353
Securities Enforcement Remedies and Penny Stock Reform Act (1990), 94
Securities Exchange Act (1934), 94
Securities Litigation Uniform Standards Act (1998), 94
Securities regulation, 94, 1465–1466
Securities trading, insider, 1177
Securitization, 1310
Security
  data, 1263
  database management systems, 1159
  foreign direct investment and, 1413
  information technology, 1237, 1243–1246
  outsourcing and, 1196
  VAN EDI and, 1255
  See also Information security
Security benefits, 795, 796
Security breaches, 1142
Security interest, 145

Security Market Line (SML), 1012
Security measures, 939
Segments, discontinuing, 917–918
Segregation of duties, 1284
Selection, 742–743
Selection criterion, 745
Selection interviewing, 751–756
Selection phase, in decision making, 78
Selection process, 721, 746–748
Selection rate, recruiting and, 741–742
Selection responsibilities, 743
Selection testing, 748–751
Selective distribution, 533
Self-actualization needs, 713
Self-awareness, 771
Self-concept, 522
Self-control, 246
Self-efficacy, 61
Self-insurance, 1303, 1308–1309
Self-liquidating approach, 954–956
Self-reference criterion (SRC), 1377
Self-understanding, 637
Sellers
  JIT purchasing and, 390
  purchasing law and, 132
  rights of, 132–133
Seller-buyer relationships, 463
Seller power, 177
Selling, 471
  adaptive, 621
  equipment, 916–917
  ethical behavior and, 598
  ethics and, 624–625
  investment banking process and, 1094
  retail, 445–450
  See also Direct selling; Personal selling
Selling accounts receivable, 974
Selling and administrative expenses budget, 896
Selling environments, 614–616
Selling expenses, 880
Selling group, 1094
Selling leadership style, 42
Selling sites, 543
Sell orders, 1089
Semantic nets, 1175
Semantics, 66, 72
Semifinished item inventory, 385
Semifixed costs, 864
Semistrong form, 1014
Semivariable costs, 864
Senders, 61, 62
Senior mortgages, 986
Senior Officials Groups—Information Systems Security (SOG-IS), 1244
Sensitivity analysis, 290, 291, 372–373, 872, 1079, 1153
Sensitivity training, 787
Sensory marketing, 457
Separation costs, 721
Separation of ownership from control, 1349
Sequential interdependence, 353
Sequential-move game, 185
Serial ports, 1218
Serial transmission, 1218
Servant leadership, 46–47
Service awards, 807

Service capacity management, 413–414
Service charges, 1215–1216
Service concept, 412
Service costs, 875–885
Service delivery process, 569
Service delivery system, 412
Service department charge rates, 905
Service department charges, 904–906
Service departments, 904
Service design, 334–335
Service development, 1129
Service elastic, 446
Service enhancement, 1130
Service experience, 560–563
Service factory, 411
Service firm classification frameworks, 410–411
Service firms, 347–348
Service gap, 566–567
Service growth management, 414–415
Service guarantees, 569
Service guarantees, 686–687
Service leases, 998
Service level agreement, 1196
Service mark, 96
Service operations, 331–332, 409
  service capacity management, 413–414
  service characteristics, 409–410
  service firm classification frameworks, 410–411
  service growth management, 414–415
  strategic positioning, 411–412
  strategic service vision, 412
Service organizations, 331–332, 348–349, 658–659
Service process facilitation, 561
Service Process Matrix, 411
Service providers
  application, 1200–1202
  Internet, 1248
  services marketing and, 558–559, 562
  storage, 1202
  Web, 1249–1250
Service quality, 565–567
  achieving, 685–686
  concepts, 681
  customer satisfaction measures, 685
  customers and, 683
  defining, 682–683
  design, 684
  gaps in, 684
  implementing, 686–687
  measuring, 683–684
  poka-yoke, 684–685
  service recovery and, 687–688
Service quality costs, 685–686
Service recovery, 569–570, 687–688
Services
  complementary, 414
  customer service and sales enhancement audit and, 449
  defining, 557
  denial of, 1143–1144
  goods versus, 558–560
  high-quality, 445
  human resources and, 701
  intangibility of, 409

network, 1232–1234
personalizing, 1251
transportation, 399–405
Servicescape, 560, 561
Service shops, 411
Service sites, 543
Services marketing, 556–557
compelling experiences and, 563
customer retention, 567–570
customer satisfaction and, 563–565
scale of market entities, 557–558
service experience and, 560–563
service quality, 565–567
services versus goods, 558–560
Service strategy, 328, 1377, 1378–1379
Service technology, 336–337, 344, 347–349
Services trade, 1416
SERVQUAL, 683, 684
Session layer, 1231
Sethi, S. Prakash, 1317
Settlement charges, 144
Settlement range, 1426
7-Eleven, 419, 576
Seven management and planning tools, 643–647
Seven QC Tools, 650–654
Severity, 1299
Sex discrimination, 789–790
Sex/gender issues, in equal employment, 789–790
Sexual harassment, 104–105, 625, 790–792
Sexual orientation, 793
Shared resource systems, 1164
Shareholder activist groups, 1356
Shareholder lawsuits, 1357
Shareholder meetings, 21
Shareholder resolutions, 1356–1357
Shareholder rights, 22
Shareholders, 21–22, 23. *See also* Stakeholders
Shareholders' equity, 1108
Shareholders' right to compel a dividend, 21
Shareholder suits, 22
Shareholder voting agreement, 22
Shareholder wealth maximization, 944, 945–946
Shares, 20–21
acquisition of, 21
purchase of, 23
redemption of, 21
transfer restrictions, 22
Sharing, 61, 564, 565
Sharper Image, 419
Sharp practices, 461
Shelf registrations, 1094
Shelving, 454
Shenandoah Life Insurance Company, 247
Shenanigans, financial, 1292–1293
Sherman Antitrust Act, 110–114, 137, 550, 551, 552, 595, 596, 1105
Sherwin Williams, 587
Shewhart, Walter, 651
Shiba, S., 669
Shiba quality model, 669
Shimp, Terence A., 475
Shingo, Shigeo, 654, 669, 684
Shingo quality model, 669
Shipping costs, 1076

Shleifer, Andrei, 1064
Shoenfeld, David, 260
Shook, John, 388
ShopLink, 241
Shopping centers/malls, 602–603
Shopping products, 477
Shortages, human resources, 708–709
Short-form merger, 23
Short-run production processes, 675
Short-term asset management
credit management, 962–966
multinational working capital management, 966–968
short-term investment strategies, 968–969
working capital management policies, 958–962
Short-term bank loans, 971–972
Short-term credit, 970
Short-term debt, 957
Short-term financial management, 949, 956–957
Short-term financial planning, 1033–1035
Short-term financing
commercial paper and, 980–981
effective cost of, 980
security in, 974–977
short-term liabilities, 969–974
strategies, 977–980
Short-term horizons, 1103
Short-term investment strategies, 968–969
Short-term liabilities, 969–974
Short-term planning, human resources, 706
Should expectation, 682
Shrinkage, 444, 452
Shrinkage prevention, 454
Siegel, Martin, 1353
Siemens AG, 1400
Signage, 458
Signal, 1057
Signaling hypothesis, 1058
Signaling theory, 1057
Signal modulation, 1223–1226
Signatures
digital, 1241
electronic, 1241, 1255
Silent partners, 13
Silver bullet, 480
Similar to/different from me (rater error), 782
Simon, Herbert, 76
Simple–complex dimension, 225
Simple EPS, 1004
Simple rate, 307
Simplex communication, 1218, 1219
Simplification, part, 397
Simplified product-structure diagram, 380
Simulation experiment, 293
Simulations, 286, 293–295
crisis drills, 1335
disaster, 1261
Monte Carlo, 1080–1081
Simultaneous equations, 296
Simultaneous-move game, 185
Simultaneous production and consumption, 348, 409–410
Singapore Airlines, 562
Single-criterion decision problems, 287

Single level BOM, 377
Single Minute Exchange of Die (SMED), 669
Single-product companies, 1082
Single-source systems, 502
Single-use plans, 35
Sinking fund requirements, 155
Sinking funds, 988, 996
Site analysis, 609–610
Site selection, 348
Site visits, 1197, 1198
Situational contingencies, 44
Situational interview, 752
Situational involvement, 521
Situational theory, 42–43
Situations, leadership, 42
Six-Sigma, 647–650
Six-Sigma metrics, 647
Size-efficiency problem, 92
SKI Ltd., 886
Skills, auditing, 705
Skill variety, 724, 725
Slotting fees, 598
Small-batch production, 345
Smells, 457
Smith, Adam, 547, 1403
Snap judgments, 754
Social audit, 1330
Social benefits, 795, 797
Social considerations, in government regulation, 91
Social contract, 24
Social entity, 50
Social forces, 24
Social forecasting, 1328
Social issues, common stock and, 984
Socialization, organizational, 561–562
Socially conscious investing, 1320–1321
Social man, 58
Social obligation, 1317
Social performance, corporate, 1312, 1318–1320, 1325
Social regulations, 1441
Social responsibility, 86, 944–945
corporate, 1311–1316, 1428
cross-national, 1469–1471
marketing and, 547–551
Social responsiveness, corporate, 1312, 1316–1318
Social Security, 109, 795
Social Security Act (1935), 109
Social styles, 618
Social trends, 574–575
Social welfare, 945
Societal-level strategy, 1322
Society for Human Resource Management (SHRM), 815
Sociocultural environment, 474, 475–476
Sociocultural sector, 224
Socioeconomic environment, 420
Sociotechnical systems, 355
Software
antivirus, 1142
data warehousing and, 1167
domain name system, 1144
prepackaged, 1194, 1196–1200
renting, 1194, 1200

unintentional damage to, 1143
    Web EDI, 1256
Software engineering, computer-aided, 1191
Software piracy, 1263
Sole proprietorships, 8–9
Solidarity, 593
Solvency, 850
Solvency analysis, 850–855
Sonny Bono Copyright Extension Act (1998), 98
Sony, 1241, 1377, 1417
Sounds, 457
Sourcing, ethics of, 597–598
South African business customs, 1425
Southwest Airlines, 81, 82
Sovereign immunity, 1462
Space allocation, 453
Space constraints, 437
Spaced practice, 761
Space productivity, 450, 451, 452
Spanish business customs, 1425
Span of control, 37, 221, 352
Span of management, 37–38
Special causes, 672
Special drawing right (SDR), 1442, 1451–1452
Special events, for recruiting, 739–740
Special incentive programs, 807
Specialization, 221
Specialty products, 477
Specific tariffs, 1434
Specifications, 639, 730
Speculative balances, 958–959
Speculative risk, 1294–1295
Speculator, 1305
Speed
    new workplace, 56
    short-term financing and, 956
Spending accounts, flexible, 798
Spirituality, 792
Spoken messages, 1421
Spokesperson roles, of managers, 54
Sponsorship marketing, 499, 509
Spontaneous economic combustion, 470
Spontaneously generated funds, 1017
Spoofing, 1144
Sporadic dumping, 1439
Sports Illustrated, 502
Sportsmart, 436
Spot markets, 1085
Spreadsheets, 159, 1155
Sprint Communications, 181, 183, 1223, 1227, 1233
Stability, 84
Stable, predictable dividends, 1060
Stable process, 673
Stable—unstable dimension, 225
Stacking, 455
Stack-outs, 453
Staff, 389, 1210–1212
Staff authority, 37
Staff departments, 37
Staff qualifications, 352
Stage-Gate process, 485–490
Stakeholder approach, 5, 7–8
Stakeholder audit, 1330

Stakeholders, 7–8, 948
    accounting and, 823
    business ethics and, 86, 87–88
    corporate governance and, 1347–1348, 1355–1358
    quality management and, 640
    See also Shareholders
Stand-alone risk, 1078, 1096–1097
Standard & Poor's Corporation (S&P), 989–990
Standard deviation, 1096
Standardization, 472, 1136, 1377–1378
Standardized products, 1409
Standard markup, 512
Standards gap, 566, 567
Standby arrangements, 1453
Standing plans, 35
Stanley, 589, 594
Staples, 1252
Starbucks Coffee, 602, 603, 1470
Stark, Andrew, 1341
Star topology, 1227, 1228
State charters, 1349
State consumer protection agencies, 138
Stated capital, 155
Stated risk-free rate of interest, 213, 214
State Farm Insurance, 557
State lemon laws, 141
Statement of cash flows, 832, 836, 838–844, 1036
Statement of ethics, 463
State of the art, 152
State Street Corporation, 1128
Static budget, 888–889
Static element, 1379
Static risks, 1295
Static thought, 527
Statistical analysis, of losses, 1301
Statistics, quality control and, 671–675
Status differences, as communication barrier, 66
Statute of repose, 153–154
Statutes, liability limitation, 23
Statutory approach, 19
Statutory limitations, 107
Statutory powers, 20
Stead, Jerre, 6
Steering committee, 1211
Steinberg, Saul, 947
Steinway & Sons, 350
Stepped-up exercise prices, 1002
Stereotyping, 755, 785
Stigler, George, 92
Stock dividends, 21, 1062–1064
Stock exchanges, 1088–1089
Stockholders, 946–948. *See also* Stakeholders
Stockholders' equity, 155, 836
Stockholder wealth maximization, 944, 945–946
Stock-keeping units (SKUs), 437, 438, 498, 583, 587
Stockless systems, 341
Stock market, 1088–1089
Stock market equilibrium, 1012–1014
Stock market transactions, 1090
Stock options, 812

Stock ownership plans. *See* Employee stock ownership plans
Stock planning, conflicts in, 438
Stock prices, interest rate levels and, 217
Stock rights, 21
Stocks
    closely held, 1089
    common, 21
    preferred, 21
    publicly held, 1089, 1090
    treasury, 20, 155
    See also Common stock; Preferred stock
Stock splits, 21, 1062–1064
Stock-to-sales method (SSM), 434
Stock-to-sales ratio, 426
Stock valuation, 1007–1014, 1058
Storage, 471
Storage service provider (SSP), 1202
Store-based retailers, location of, 601–603
Store branding, 418
Store compatibility, 611
Store design, 456–457
Store environment, 450–452
Store image, 450, 451
Store layout management, 450–458
Store merchandising, retail, 454–456
Store planning, retail, 452–454
Store size, 416
Storefront design, 456
Stories, 83
Storming stage, in team development, 283
Storyboards, 72
Straight commission, 622, 623, 808
Straight piece-rate system, 806
Straight salary, 622, 623
Straight voting, 22
Strategic advantage, 1126
Strategic alliances, 228, 1130–1131
Strategic benchmarking, 689
Strategic business units. *See* Divisional structure
Strategic contingencies, 261, 265
Strategic employee benefits management, 793–794
Strategic goals, 32
Strategic human resources management, 698–699
Strategic information systems (SISs), 1126, 1134–1135
Strategic leader, 1396
Strategic management, 1322–1325
Strategic management approach to issues management, 1327
Strategic moves, in information technology, 1126
Strategic objectives, international business and, 1370
Strategic performance measures, for supply chain, 408
Strategic planning, 1268
    international negotiations, 1425–1427
    quality and, 636
    retail, 420–422
Strategic Planning Institute, 660
Strategic positioning, 411–412
Strategic recruiting, 734–735
Strategic service vision, 412

Strategic thinking, 51
Strategic training, 758–760
Strategic training plan, 759
Strategy, 3
    advertising, 499
    branding, 492
    business, 759, 1268–1269
    chase, 369
    communication and, 63
    control, 1269
    corporate control, 1268–1270
    corporate culture and, 84
    cross-cultural negotiations, 1425
    decline, 496
    dominant, 185
    financing, 978–980
    growth, 496
    human resources, 701, 703
    information technology, 1126–1131
    international business, 1366–1371
    international marketing, 1377–1383
    introduction, 493–496
    investment, 968
    level production, 369
    liquidity, 969
    manufacturing, 328
    maturity, 496
    new product development, 485–490
    operating, 412
    operations, 332–333
    organizational, 3–5, 221, 773
    penetration, 516
    positioning, 515
    pricing, 515–516
    product, 357–358
    product development, 497
    public affairs, 1325–1326
    purchasing/supply chain, 328–330
    quality, 636–638
    quartile, 802
    retail, 328
    secure, 186
    service, 328
    short-term financing, 977–980
    traditional manufacturing, 346
    transportation, 401–405
    See also Competitive strategy; Marketing strategies; Operating strategy; Pricing strategies
Strategy and structure change, 247, 252–253
Stream of events, 79
Stress interview, 753
Stretch goals, 681
Stretching accounts payable, 971
Strict liability, 118
Strict liability in tort, 150–154
Strictness errors, 782
Striking price, 999
Striving for excellence, 388
Strohl Systems, 1261
Strong form, 1014
Structural barriers, JIT purchasing, 390
Structural causes, 672
Structural contingencies, 239
Structural control, organizational size and, 243–244
Structural deficiency, symptoms of, 240

Structural design applications, 239–240
Structural dimensions, 220–221
Structural failures, government regulation and, 91
Structural framework, 231
Structural implications, of workflow interdependence, 354
Structural priority, 354
Structure. *See* Organizational structure
Structured selection interviews, 752
Subchapter S corporations, 19
Subcontracting, 372
Subcultures, organizational, 85
Subdomain, 1249
Subjective performance criteria measures, 775
Subjective risks, 1295
SubmitOrder.com, 342, 1251
Subordinated debentures, 986
Subordinates
    authority and, 37, 259
    supervisory rating of, 778–779
Subscribers, 19
Subsequent debts, 16
Subsidiaries, 1376
Subsidies, 1438–1439, 1463
Substitute for cash balances, 961
Substitutes, 44–45, 203
Subsystems, 29, 219
Success, defining, 479–481
Success base rate, 742
Succession analysis, 707
Succession planning, 769–770
Suggestion selling, 449, 615
Sundance, 580
SunGard, 1261
Sunglass Hut, 48
Sunk costs, 915, 1075–1076
Sun Microsystems, 3, 230, 1129
Sunnen Products Company, 371
Super bill, 380
Superfund. *See* Comprehensive Environmental Response, Compensation and Liability Act
Superfund Amendments and Reauthorization Act (SARA), 120
Super Market Institute, 581
Superordinate goals, 268
SuperTarget, 419
Supervisory rating, of subordinates, 778–779
Supplier and partnering processes, 676, 678–679
Supplier arrangements, 228
Supplier-buyer cycle-time reduction, 399
Supplier certification, 679
Supplier development, 329–330
Supplier development support, 399
Supplier favors, 461
Supplier-managed inventory, on-site, 397–398
Supplier performance measures, 407
Supplier quality performance, 390
Supplier relationships, longer-term, 329
Supplier-retailer relations, 589–592
Suppliers
    design involvement of, 329
    information systems and, 1131

    number of, 390
    purchasing ethics and, 461
    second-tier and third-tier, 399
    TQM of, 329
    upstream, 384, 385
Supplies
    as business-to-business products, 477
    country risk and, 1103
Supply
    basis for, 193–194
    demand and, 192
    human resources, 705–708
    international reserves, 1451
    retail location and, 607, 608–609
Supply base, dispersed, 390
Supply-base optimization, 328
Supply chain, 384, 584–586, 1147
Supply chain behavior, 420
Supply chain constraints, 595–596
Supply chain control, 586–589
Supply chain inventory management
    ABC analysis, 393–396
    automated inventory-tracking systems, 399
    distribution resource planning systems, 398
    excess and obsolete inventory, continuous review of, 396–397
    inventory benefits, 387–388
    inventory disadvantages, 388
    inventory investment, 387
    inventory investment control, 393
    inventory-related costs, 386–387
    inventory types, 385–386
    lean supply chains, 388–393
    material requirement planning systems, 398
    on-site supplier-managed inventory, 397–398
    part simplification and redesign, 397
    planning and control, 398–399
    safety stock levels and forecasting techniques, 397
    supplier-buyer cycle-time reduction, 399
Supply chain management, 333–334, 384–385, 538
    e-commerce and, 1256
    performance measurement and evaluation, 405–408
    retail marketing and, 584–596
    supply chain inventory management, 385–399
    transportation services purchasing, 399–405
Supply chain management strategies, evolving, 330
Supply chain performance measurement and evaluation, 405–408
Supply chain strategy, 328–330
Supply chain waste, 389
Supply curve, 176
Supply density, 610
Supply management, 369–370
Support
    information center, 1214
    outsourcing and, 1196
    prepackaged software, 1197, 1198
    systems development life cycle, 1189

SUBJECT INDEX

Supporting evidence, 619–620
Supportive leadership, 43
Support processes. *See* Production/delivery and support processes
Support salespeople, 616
Supranational corporations, 1376
Surge capacity, 414
Surplus, 156, 708–709
Surveys, employee, 721
Survival, pricing for, 516
Sustainable development, 87
Swap arrangements, 1453
Switch, 1381
Switching costs, 1128–1129
Switching structures, 249
Switching techniques, 1231–1232
Swofford, Inc., 292
Symantec, 1142
Symbols, 83, 1186
Symmetric DSL (SDSL), 1233
Symmetric information, 1057
Symptoms of structural deficiency, 240
Synchronization, 1219–1220
Synchronized cash flows, 959
Synchronous communication, 1220
Synectics, 68, 69
Synergy, 29, 1104–1105, 1130
System, 29
Systematic appraisal, 777–778
Systematic risk, 1098–1099
System of authorizations, 1284–1285
Systems, 219, 563
Systems acquisition, 1194
Systems analysis, 68, 70–71, 1180–1183
Systems analysts, 1138–1139
Systems concept of logistics, 539–541
Systems development, 1179
Systems development led by end users (SDLU), 1192–1193
Systems development life cycle (SDLC), 1179–1189
Systems integration, 1193–1194
Systems theory, 29

T

T1 lines, 1233
T3 lines, 1233
Tables, 159
Tabular solution
 amortized loans, 307
 bond valuation, 1006
 future value, 300–301
 future value of an annuity, 303, 304
 internal rate of return, 1070
 net present value, 1069
 present value, 301
 present value of an annuity, 305, 306
 real asset valuation, 1015
Tacit knowledge, 483
Taco Bell, 54, 349, 560, 603
Tactical goals, 32
Tactical information systems planning, 1134–1137
Tactical objectives, international business and, 1370

Tactical planning, 420, 1427
Tactics, 1425
Tactics for enhancing collaboration, 265, 267–268
Tactics for increasing power, 265
Tactics for using power, 265
Taft-Hartley Act. *See* Labor-Management Relations Act
Taguchi, Genichi, 667–668
Takeovers
 corporate governance and, 1350–1352
 host government, 1103–1104
 threat of, 947
 See also Hostile takeovers
Talbots, 582
Tall structure, 38
T-analysis, 72
Tangible asset valuation, 1014–1015
Tangible-dominant goods, 557
Tangible errors, 654
Tangibles, 684
Tannenbaum, R., 41
Target audience, e-marketing, 546
Target capital structure, 991, 1046, 1050–1051
Target cash balance (TCB), 296
Target chart, 675
Target cost concept, 927
Targeting, 564, 565
Target marketing
 markets and, 553–555
 market segmentation and, 555–556
Target markets, 472
 definition of, 600
 reaching, 601–604
 selection of, 599–601
 strategic service vision and, 412
Target profit, 871–872
Target return pricing, 512–513
Target ROI, 515
Targets, 175, 416, 583, 788
Tariff escalation, 1436
Tariff-rate quota, 1438
Tariffs, 1373–1374, 1434–1437, 1463
Task-based job analysis, 727
Task environment, 223
Task errors, 654
Task Force on Computer Crime, 1141
Task forces, 233, 269
Task identity, 724, 725
Task interdependence, 258
Task-oriented leaders, 42, 44
Tasks
 interdependent, 271
 job analysis, 727
Task significance, 724, 725
Taxation, 11
 corporations and, 12
 double, 12
Tax benefit/bankruptcy cost trade-off theory, 1066–1067
Tax considerations, in mergers and acquisitions, 1105
Tax planning, 1177
Tax policy, 1385
Tax position, 1050
Tax rate, 1380

Taylor, Frederick W., 25, 58
TCP/IP (Transmission Control Protocol/Internet Protocol), 1232
Team-based compensation, 60
Team-based variable pay, 804, 805, 809–811
Team building, 254, 285
Team-building skills, 56
Team communication channels, 64
Team interviews, 753
Team management, 41
Team members, effective, 284–285
Team negotiations, 1426
Team rewards, 803–804
Teams, 234
 change, 256
 crisis, 1334
 job design and, 722–725
 new product development, 481
 project, 282–286
 venture, 250
 virtual, 1395
Teamwork, quality management and, 640
Technical assessment, 488
Technical Assistance Research Programs (TARP), 688
Technical barriers to trade, 1373
Technical champion, 250
Technical complexity, 345
Technical core, 220, 330, 331
Technical feasibility study, 1180, 1181
Technical performance success, 480
Technical skills, 52
Technical support, 220
Technological environment, 420, 474, 476
Technological productivity, 343
Technology, 344
 categories of, 350
 country risk and, 1103
 decision making and, 79
 global strategy and, 1370–1371
 intensive, 353
 job design and, 354–355
 long-linked, 353
 manufacturing, 344–347
 markup pricing, 205–206
 mediating, 352
 new workplace and, 55
 organizational, 221
 retail marketing and, 582–583
 sales force, 621
 service, 344, 347–349
 See also Information technology
Technology automation, 336–337
Technology changes, 247, 249–250
Technology-driven workplace, managing, 30–31
Technology sector, 224
Technology transfer, 1375
TechWave, 229
Telecommunications, 1216–1217
 channels and media, 1220–1223
 communication direction, 1218–1219
 data communications, 1217–1218
 modulation, 1223–1226
 synchronization, 1219–1220
Telemarketing, 615
Telephone network maintenance, 1176–1177

Televerket, 1173
Telling leadership style, 42
Temporary current assets, 954, 978
Temporary employee benefits, 799
Temporary investment, 961
Temporary personnel, 371–372
Tenancy in partnership, 14, 15
Tenneco, 34
10 steps of crisis communication, 1336
Terminal cash flow, 1077
Terminal values, 522
Term loans, 985
Terms-of-trade estimates, 1433
Term structure of interest rates, 213, 215–216
Terrestrial microwave, 1222
Territorial restrictions, 595
Territory allocation, for sales, 624
Territory potential, for sales, 624
Tertiary-line injury, 116
Test and inspection costs, 655
Test group, 169
Testimonial evidence, of fraud, 1290
Testing
   employment, 747
   new product development and, 489
   recovery plan, 1261
   selection, 748–751
   systems design and, 1187
Tests of existence, 14
Texas Instruments, 689
Thai business customs, 1425
Theft, 444, 599
The Limited, 600
Theoretical value, 1008
Theory of constraints (TOC), 927
Theory of dual entitlement, 515
Theory T, 28
Theory T+, 28
Theory X, 27–28, 58
Theory Y, 27–28, 58
Theory Z, 28
Third-degree price discrimination, 209–210
Third-party administrator, 1309
Third-party relationships, 15–18
Threats, 1333–1334, 1367
3M, 80, 81, 516
Time
   discrepancies in, 535
   information and, 1157
   project management and, 271
   recruiting and, 740
Time and motion study, 25
Time-division multiplexing, 1226
Time estimates, for projects, 275
Time fences, 381
Time horizon considerations, for forecasting, 170
Timeliness, of charge-back services, 1216
Time management, personal, 286
Time-off benefits, 795, 797
Time preferences for consumption, 213
Time segments, 519
Time series analysis, 165, 167–169
Time-series patterns, 166
Times-interest-earned (TIE) ratio, 1056
Time tables, for affirmative action, 788

Time utility, 474
Time value of money (TVM), 299
   amortized loans, 306–307
   cash flow timelines, 299
   future value, 299–301
   future value of an annuity, 302–304
   interest rate comparisons, 307–309
   present value, 301
   present value of an annuity, 304–306
Timing, of performance appraisals, 778
Title VII of Civil Rights Act of 1964. *See* Civil Rights Act (1964)
TNT UK, 245
Toguchi quality model, 667–668
Token passing, 1230
Tokyo Disneyland, 1310
Tokyo Fire and Marine, 1310
Tolerance range, 667
Tools, quality management, 642
Top managers, 52
Topology, network, 1226, 1227–1228
Torts, 16, 20. *See also* Strict liability in tort
Total budgeted cost (TBC), 277, 278
Total cost approach, 539
Total cost concept, 922–924
Total cost of ownership, 330, 1136–1137
Total factor productivity, 343
Total leverage. *See* Degree of total leverage
Total new capital, 1047
Total operating costs, 1023
Total quality, principles of, 639–641
Total quality control, 666
Total quality management (TQM), 49, 329, 681
Total relations, 160–161
Total revenue, price elasticity and, 196–198, 200
Total sensory marketing, 457
Touching, 1422
Toxic Substances Control Act (TSCA), 120
Toyota, 181, 555, 679, 1369
Toyota production system (TPS), 654, 669
Toys 'R' Us, 339, 457, 604, 1254–1255
Tracking intervention, 722
Trade
   international economics and, 1431–1433
   international, 1372–1374, 1403–1412
   restraint of, 111–113
Trade allowances, 504
Trade associations, 230
Trade barriers. *See* Nontariff trade barriers; Tariffs
Trade credit, 970
Trade customers, researching, 530–531
Trade discount, 441
Trade diversion laws, 461
Trade liberalization, 1373
Trademarks, 96, 1374
Trade names, 98
Trade-oriented sales promotion, 498–499
Trade promotions, 506–507
Trade responsiveness, 505
Trade restrictions, arguments for, 1437
Trader Joe's, 598
Trade secrets, 95–96, 100, 136
Trade symbols, 96–98, 100
Trading area, 604

Trading areas, size and description, 609
Trading partners, trust and, 472
Trading relationship exchange process, marketing as, 470–472
Traditional authority, 244
Traditional debt instruments, 985–986
Traditional file approach, 1158, 1160
Traditional manufacturing, 344–346
Traditional marketing view, 470–471
Traditional motivation approach, 58
Traditional selling method, 616
Traffic, 611
Traffic flow, 294
Training, 756–757
   delivery, 761–763
   design, 760–761
   diversity, 787–788
   ethical, 463
   evaluation of, 763–765
   expert systems and, 1173
   human resources development and, 768
   nature of, 757–760
   organizational change and, 256
   retention interventions and, 721
   sales force, 621
   systems implementation and, 1187
Training and general management costs, 655
Training costs, 371, 721
Training needs assessment, 760
Training process, 759–760
Training programs, business ethics and, 89
Traits, leadership, 40
Transactional leaders, 45
Transaction balances, 958
Transaction efficiency, 535–536
Transaction integrity, 1255
Transaction Processing Systems (TPSs), 1145
Transactions
   accounting equation and, 827–831
   atomic, 1239–1240
   consumer credit, 142–145
   going private, 23
   international, 1415
   networks and, 1217
   stock market, 1090
Transaction services, 447
Transceiver, 1222
Transcendent quality, 682
Transfer pricing, 210–212, 912–914
Transfer pricing problem, 211
Transfer risk, 1304–1305, 1307–1310, 1384
Transferability, 11, 12, 18, 22
Transferee, 1304
Transferor, 1304
Transformation, 29
Transformational leaders, 46
Transient customer, 446
Transition matrix, 707
Translation, language, 1420
Translators, effective, 1420–1421
Transmission, synchronous, 1220
Transmission channel stage, 1421–1422
Transmission rate, 1220
Transmission speeds, 1221
Transnational corporations, 1376
Transnational strategy, 1370
Transparency International, 598

Transportation, 471
  excessive, 389
  just-in-time, 390–391
  logistics and, 539–540
  supply chain performance measurement and, 407
Transportation mode, 402, 403
Transportation performance variables, 402, 403
Transportation rates, negotiating, 404–405
Transportation restrictions, international, 1441
Transportation service levels, negotiating, 404–405
Transportation services, purchasing, 399–405
Transportation strategy, 401–405
Transportation terms, 131–132
Transport layer, 1231
TransUnion Corporation, 1353, 1357
Travelers Group, 1088
Treasury shares, 155
Treasury stock, 20, 155
Treaties, 1461
Treatment errors, 654
Treble damages, 111
Tree diagrams, 645
Tree topology, 1228
Trespass to land, 118
Trial impact, 507–508
Tricon Global Restaurants, 901
Trigger limits, 396
TRU*SERV, 588
Trust, 67, 472
Trusted Computer System Evaluation Criteria (TC-SEC), 1243–1244
Trustees, 987
Trusting relationships, 568
Trust receipts, 976
Trusts. *See* Business trusts
Truth-in-Lending Act, 142, 143
Turbulence, 56
Turnbull model, 1276
Turner, Ted, 989
Turnover, 79, 418–419, 718
TV cable, 1222
TWA, 915
Twisted pair, 1221–1222
Two in the box, 233
Two-part pricing, 210
Two-tier tariff, 1438
Two-way communication, 593
Two-way exclusive dealing, 596
Tying agreements, 596
Tying arrangements, 113, 114

U

Ultra vires acts, 20
UMI, 1165
Uncertainty, 77
  coping with, 262, 263
  environmental, 225–228
  organizational change and, 255
  organizational power and, 265
  project management and, 272

Uncontrollable turnover, 718
Underlying stock, 1000
Underproduction, 177
Understored, 605
Undertime, 371
Underwriter's spread, 1093
Underwriting syndicate, 1094
Underwritten arrangement, 1093
Unemployment, 1429–1430
Unemployment compensation, 109
Unemployment insurance, 109
Unenforceable contracts, 124
Unethical behavior, 459, 460–461, 463, 625, 1342
Unfair conduct, 114
Unfair employer practices, 101, 102
Unfair labor practices, 101
Unfairness, 139
Unfair trade practices, purchasing law and, 137
Unfair union practices, 101, 102
Unfunded retention, 1303
Unguided medium, 1221
Uniform Commercial Code (UCC), 122, 974
  finance law and, 155
  purchasing law and, 130, 132–135
  security interest and, 145
  transportation strategy and, 402
Uniform Consumer Credit Code (UCCC), 142
Uniform delivered pricing, 518
Uniform Selection Guidelines, 729, 748
Uniform Trade Secrets Act, 95
Unilateral conduct, 111
Unilateral contracts, 123–124
Unilever, 594, 1398
Unintentional amoral management, 1343
Unintentional behavior, 1342
Uninterruptable power supply (UPS) systems, 1140
Union shop, 102
Unitary changes, 161
Unitary elasticity, 196
Unit-based index, 657
Unit contribution margin, 867–868
Unit contribution ratio, 867
Unit cost factor, 936
Unit costs, 386
United Airlines, 37, 234, 562, 946
United Kingdom, business customs of, 1425
United Nations Convention on Contracts for the International Sales of Goods (CISG), 1464
United States, business customs of, 1425
U.S. Census Bureau, 418, 609
U.S. Department of Agriculture (USDA), 92, 1178
U.S. Department of Defense, 1243
U.S. Department of Justice, 111, 1105, 1106
U.S. Department of Labor, 92, 597, 717, 719
U.S. Patent and Trademark Office, 100
U.S. Postal Service, 1129
U.S. quality awards. *See* Malcolm Baldrige National Quality Award
U.S. Tax code, 1064
Unit labor cost, 700
Unit of measure concept, 825

Unit price factor, 936
Unit selling price, 870–871
Unity of command, 26, 36
Unity of direction, 26
Universalism, 1470
Universalist view, 29
Universal principles of management, 344–345
Universal product code (UPC), 502
University of Chicago, 92
University of Michigan, 41
University of North Carolina, 598
University of Texas, 41
University recruiting, 738
Unlimited life, 11
Unlimited personal liability, 9
Unocal, 227
Unofficial dollarization, 1445
Unplanned retention, 1302–1303
Unpredictability, 56
Unrealized customers, 482
Unreasonably dangerous, 152
Unsecured bonds, 20
Unsought products, 477
Unstable processes, 673
Unstructured selection interviews, 752–753
Unsystematic risk, 1098–1099
Up time, 1201
Upper control limit (UCL), 296, 651
UPS, 260, 403, 404, 412, 532, 544, 586, 700, 1129, 1241, 1251
Upstream suppliers, 384, 385
Upward communication, 63
USAA, 348, 1310
Usable funds, 980, 981
Usage segments, 519
US Airways, 568
User application development, 1194, 1202–1205
User-based quality, 683
User dialog, 1184
User-driven quality, 639
User ID, 1239
Users, consumers as, 520
USR Industries, 1057
USX, 478
Utilitarian ethic, 1346
Utilitarian theory, 87
UtiliTech Inc., 227
Utility, 192, 292–293, 474
Utility analysis, 712
Utility patents, 99

V

Vacancies, on board of directors, 22
Vacation benefits, 795, 797
Vacations, mandatory, 937–938
Validation, 294–295, 489
Valid contracts, 124
Validity, 745, 756
Valuation of financial assets. *See* Asset valuation
Value, 147
Value-added decisions, 359
Value-added networks (VANs), 1227

Value-added-network (VAN) EDI, 1255–1256
Value analysis, 71
Value-based quality, 683
Value congruence, 637
Value-driven quality, 639
Value maximization, 158–163
Value of rewards, 714, 715
Value pricing, 519
Values, 522, 1421
ValuJet, 1334
ValuPage, 1165
Vandalism, 1140
Variable control charts, 673
Variable cost concept, 925–926
Variable costing, 866
   income analysis under, 930–931
   income statements under, 929–930
   management's use of, 931–937
Variable costs, 288, 512, 862–863, 869–870
Variable pay, 800
   executive compensation, 813–814
   group/team-based, 804, 805, 809–811
   individual, 804, 805–807
   organizational, 804, 805, 811–813
   sales, 807–809
   types of, 804–805
Variables, 673
Variation, 672
Variety, 53, 349, 350, 436
Vendor collusion, 444
Vendor fraud, 1280
Vendor identification, 1197, 1198
Vendor negotiations, 440–443
Vendor profitability analysis statement, 439
Vendor screening, 1197, 1198
Vendor selection, 1197, 1198
Venn diagram model, for ethical decision making, 1339–1340
Venture teams, 250
Verification, 294–295
VeriSign Inc., 1242
Vernon, Raymond, 1404, 1408–1409
Vertical analysis, 847–848
Vertical hierarchy
   authority and, 259
   power and, 260–261
Vertical information systems, 232
Vertical integration, 211
Vertical linkages, 232
Vertical marketing channels, 587–589
Vertical markets, 1253
Vertical mergers, 115, 1106
Vertical price fixing, 112
Vertical privity, 150
Vertical relation, 211
Vertical restraint, 111
Vertical structure/hierarchy
   authority and, 37
   organizing, 36
   management types in, 52
Very high readiness level, 43
Viacom, 1106
Vices, 1282
Victims, of fraud, 1278
Videoconferencing, 1234
Video interviewing, 753–754

Vietnam Veterans Readjustment Act (1974), 106
Villager, 589
Virtual leadership, 46
Virtual private networks (VPNs), 1229
Virtual stores, 600
Virtual teams, 1395
Virtual Web server, 1249
Virtual work, 55
Viruses, computer, 1141–1143
Visa, 596, 975, 976
Vishny, Robert W., 1064
Vision, 45, 637
   artificial, 1170
   information systems, 1133, 1134
   international promotion strategy and, 1382
Visionary leadership, 45
Visual communications, 457–458
Visual merchandising, 455–456
Vogel, David, 1344
Voice mail, 1234–1235
Voice modems, 1225
Voice of the customer (VOC), 484
Voice share, 528
Voidable contracts, 124
Void contracts, 124
Volkswagen, 531, 532
Volume. *See* Cost-volume-profit relationships
Volume discounting, 518
Voluntary absenteeism, 717
Voluntary assumption, 150
Voluntary assumption of the risk, 153
Voluntary benefits, 796
Voluntary dissolution, 24
Voluntary safety standards, 140
Voluntary turnover, 718
Volvo, 1173, 1398
Voting
   cumulative, 22
   limited liability company, 17
   straight, 22
Voting power, concentrations of, 22
Voting rights, 21–22, 996
Voting trust, 22
Vulnerability identification, 1333

W

Wage and price controls, 1430
Wage assignments, 145
Wage/hour regulations, 730
Wages, 800, 1381
Waggin'Tails, 1252
Wagner Act. *See* National Labor Relations Act
Waiting, 389
Waiting line, 294
Waiting-line models, 286
Walgreens, 416
Walkouts, 449
Walkthroughs, 1261
Wall Street Journal, The, 1089
Wal-Mart, 175, 188, 339, 342, 399, 416, 421, 454, 457, 458, 552, 576, 577, 578, 579, 581, 583, 589, 590, 594, 595, 598, 599, 602, 603, 604, 608, 701–702, 849, 975, 1131, 1222, 1370
Walt Disney Co., 1349
Walton, Richard, 267
Walton, Sam, 457
Wang Laboratory, 513
Wants, consumer, 520
Warehouse receipts, 977
Warehousing, 541
Warm-site, 1260
Warner Bros., 211
Warrants, 986, 1001–1002, 1004
Warranty, 131, 146–148
Warranty actions, obstacles to, 149–150
Warranty claims, costs due to, 656
Warranty of infringement, 131
Warranty of title, 131, 147, 149
Warranty protection, federal, 140–141
Warren Buffett's Nebraska Furniture Mart, 456
WavePhone, 227
Weak form, 1014
Wealth of Nations, The, 1403
Web-based electronic commerce, 1235
Webb-Pomerene Act, 1401
Web databases, 1164–1165
Web design, 545
Web EDI, 1255–1256
Weber, Max, 26, 242–243
Web-hosting service, 1249
Web portals, 1248
Web service provider, 1249–1250
Weeks' supply method (WSM), 434
Weighted average cost of capital (WACC), 1041, 1042, 1046, 1047
Weighted moving averages techniques, 168
Welch, Jack, 244, 1354
Welfare-to-work programs, 733
Wells Fargo Bank, 348, 603
Wendover Financial Services, 235
Wendy's, 337
Werner, 404
Wet Seal, 578
What if analysis, 872, 1153
Wheeler-Lea Act (1938), 551
Wheel of retailing theory, 577–578
Wheelwright, S. C., 660
Whirlpool, 37
Whistle-blowing, 88
Whitemail bribery, 1467
Whole person, 58
Wholesalers, 474
Wholesaler-sponsored voluntary groups, 588
Wholly owned foreign subsidiary, 1376
Wide area networks (WANs), 1226–1227
Will expectation, 682
Williams-Sonoma, 580, 600, 602
Wilson, Ian, 1317
Winding up, 14, 17
Winn-Dixie, 263
Wireless, fixed, 1233
Wireless communication, 1227
Wireless technology, 55
Withdrawal, 16
Within-firm risk, 1078, 1081
Within-quota rate, 1438

Wm. Wrigley Company, 852
Womack, James, 388
Women
    Equal Pay Act and, 103
    leadership and, 46
    management development and, 772
    workforce diversity management and, 789–790
Women's National Basketball Association (WNBA), 6
Wonderlic Personality Test, 748
Woodward, Joan, 344–346
Work
    division of, 26
    experienced meaningfulness of, 59
Work breakdown structure (WBS), 275
Worker Adjustment and Retraining Notification Act (WARN), 110, 708
Worker productivity, 343
Workers' compensation, 109
Workflow interdependence, among departments, 352–354
Workforce, internal assessment of, 705
Workforce diversity management, 785
    age issues, 792
    approaches to, 785–786
    diversity training, 787–788
    individuals with disabilities, 792
    lifestyles and sexual orientation issues, 793
    programs and activities, 786–787
    religion and spirituality, 792
    sex/gender issues in equal employment, 789–790
    sexual harassment and workplace relationships, 790–792
Workforce Investment Partnership Act (WIPA), 763
Workforce realignment, 708
Workforce reductions, 708
Working capital, 851, 949

Working capital management, 949–950
    cash budget, 959
    cash management, 958–959
    cash management techniques, 959–961
    investment and financing policies, 953–956
    marketable securities, 961–962
    multinational, 957–958, 966–968
    short-term financial management, 949, 956–957
Working capital policy, 949–958
Working capital ratio, 851
Working capital terminology, 949
Work-in-process (WIP) inventory, 338–339, 386, 389, 878
Work locations, job design and, 725
Work measurement, 72
Work outcomes, 60
Work pace, 53
Work packages, 275
Workplace. *See* New workplace
Workplace mediation, 267
Workplace relationships, 790–792
Workplace romances, 790
Work redesign, 58
Work-related pressures, 1282
Work sample tests, 748
Work schedules, 60, 725
Work scope, 272
Works for hire, 98
Workshift scheduling, 414
Work specialization, 36, 535
Work teams, 811
WorldCom, 1227, 1233
World markets. *See* International markets
World Trade Organization (WTO), 1373, 1402
World Wide Web (WWW), 543
    databases, 1164–1165
    e-commerce on, 1235
    EDI, 1255–1256

Worst-case scenario, 1080
Worst possible level, 682
Written law, 130
Written messages, 1421
Written warranties, 141

X

X bar chart, 673, 674, 675
Xerox, 113, 237, 689, 945, 1230, 1329, 1350, 1397

Y

Yankee bonds, 994
Yankee stock, 1092
Yavitz, Boris, 1350
Yellow dog contracts, 101
Yield, 885, 962
Yield curve, 215
Yield management, 414
Yield ratios, 741
Yield to maturity (YTM), 1007, 1069

Z

Zero-balance account (ZBA), 961
Zero-based budgeting, 888
Zero coupon bonds, 988–989
Zero defections, 566
Zero defects, 566
Zero-growth stock, 1010
Zero inventory systems, 341
Zero quality control (ZQC), 669
Zimmerman, Gary, 396
Zombies, 1143